THE
Family Tree
Resource Book
for Genealogists

Edited by Sharon DeBartolo Carmack and Erin Nevius

FAMILY TREE BOOKS
CINCINNATI, OH
www.familytreemagazine.com/store

Other fine Family Tree Books are available from your local bookstore or on our Web site at www.familytreemagazine.com/store.

08   07   06   05   04   5   4   3   2   1

Library of Congress Cataloging-in-Publication Data

Carmack, Sharon DeBartolo and Erin Nevius
   The family tree resource book for genealogist's : the essential guide to American county and
   town sources / edited by Sharon DeBartolo Carmack and Erin Nevius—1st ed.

   Cataloging-in-Publication Data is available online at http://catalog.loc.gov.

Editors: Sharon DeBartolo Carmack, CG and Erin Nevius
Production coordinator: Robin Richie
Assistant production coordinator: Logan Cummins
Interior design by Clare Finney
Cover design by Jeremy Loyd, Real Art Design Group

F+W PUBLICATIONS, INC.

Contents

By Sharon DeBartolo Carmack, CG Executive Editor of Family Tree Books

Introduction

The county courthouse. It's *the* place to find your ancestors. Today's genealogist is so accustomed to heading straight to the computer to uncover information about their ancestors on Web sites they often forget the wealth of information available in the files at the local courthouse. Waiting to be discovered in hundreds of brick-and-mortar sites across the nation are historical records galore! Just look at the variety of records you might find on your ancestors in the county courthouse or town hall:

adoptions
affidavits
appeals
apprenticeships and indentures
bastardy cases
bills of sale
birth and death records
bonds
burial permits and corpse transfers
business and professional licenses
civil court proceedings
coroner's files and inquests
county hospital records
criminal court records
divorce petitions, cases, and decrees
dockets
estate inventories
executions and stays of executions
fornication and adultery cases
guardianship papers
homestead files
injunctions
insanity and commitment hearings
judgments
jury lists
justice of the peace records
land deeds
land surveys and plat maps
licenses and permits
livestock brands and marks
manumissions
marriage bonds, licenses, and certificates
military service discharges
mining records
minute books
mortgages and leases
name changes
naturalization records
oaths of allegiance
orders and judgments
orphan's records
petitions
poor house/county farm records
powers of attorney
prenuptial agreements
promissory notes
property foreclosures
releases of dower
relief, welfare, and public assistance records
sheriff's sales
subpoenas
summons
tax rolls
verdicts
voter registrations
warrants
wills, administrations, and probate documents
wolf-scalp bounties

And the best part is that most of these records are available to you without making a trip to the courthouse in the county where your ancestor lived. While you probably won't find many of these actual courthouse records online, you can write to the county clerk to obtain copies of many documents, or you can find microfilmed copies of many courthouse and town records as close as your neighborhood Family History Center. The Church of Jesus Christ of Latter-day Saint's Family History Library in Salt Lake City, Utah, has thousands of Family History Centers across the nation, where you can order rolls of microfilm that contain these county and town records. Visit <www.familysearch.org> for a Family History Center near you, or pick up a copy of *Your Guide to the Family History Library* by Paula Stuart Warren and James W. Warren (Cincinnati: Betterway Books, 2001).

You can also find microfilmed county courthouse records at state libraries and archives and some large public libraries. In fact, if you have ancestors from several counties in a state, it might be more beneficial to you, both time and money-wise, to go to the state library or archives, where many of the courthouses and towns deposit the original records they no longer have room to store. For more details on state resources, see *The Family Tree Guide Book* (Cincinnati: Betterway Books, 2002).

MICROFILM AND MICROFICHE

Many records are transferred to some sort of microform and then destroyed. There just isn't enough space to store all that paper. *Microfilm* comes on a roll, usually in 16 mm or 35 mm format. Indexes are usually on 16 mm rolls—skinny reels—whereas the records are usually on 35 mm film. Many microfilm readers have different zoom lenses and magnifications. Most readers have instructions permanently affixed to them on how to thread the film, but typically the full reel is on the left and an empty take-up reel is on the right. If you've never used a microfilm reader before, have a staff person or volunteer show you how.

Microfiche (pronounced either micro-fish or micro-feesh, depending on what part of the country you come from) is a flat piece of film that is viewed, appropriately, on a microfiche reader. The film is placed between two pieces of flat glass and is magnified for viewing.

There are also microfilm and microfiche printers so you can make photocopies of what you find. Once again, ask the attendant for help. At the Family History Library in Salt Lake City, Utah, you can also burn images from microfilm onto a CD-ROM.

The National Archives, the independent federal agency that manages all federal records, is the source of much of the microfilm genealogists use. You can view the subject catalogs, with the roll listings, in several ways.

- National Archives Microfilm Catalogs online at <www.archives.gov/publications/genealogy_microfilm_catalogs.html>.
- National Archives Microfilm Publications added from 2000 forward, described mostly without roll lists, online at <www.archives.gov/research_room/genealogy/>. Scroll down to "New Microfilm Publications," currently listed under "Now Featuring."
- Hard copies of the catalogs at many libraries.

- Hard copies for sale from genealogy booksellers and from the National Archives. Learn about these catalogs online at <www.archives.gov/publications/genealogy_microfilm_catalogs.html#subject>. Scroll down to the catalog that interests you. Then go to <www.archives.gov/publications/how_to_obtain_publications.html> for ordering information.

You can use National Archives microfilm at many libraries and National Archives regional branches. To learn which National Archives branches hold microfilm publications of interest to you, go to <www.archives.gov/research_room/alic/research_tools/search_microfilm_catalog.html> and click "Search the Microfilm Catalog" or "Search the Microfilm Publications Catalog." Under "Enter Keywords," enter a state name to learn of state-specific microfilm, or enter a microfilm ID (M or T number) under "Enter the Microfilm ID." Click "Submit Search," then click "Display Search Results." From the results screen, click "Full Record" and scroll down the page to learn which regional branches have the microfilm.

As mentioned, the Family History Library (FHL) in Salt Lake City, Utah, is also a valuable source of microfilm for genealogical research. You can rent microfilm of records from many locations around the world through a Family History Center near you. To find a Family History Center, visit <www.familysearch.org/Eng/Library/FHC/frameset_fhc.asp>. Before placing an order, you need to review what is available from your ancestral location and get the microfilm roll number(s) of the records you want to see.

Go to <www.familysearch.org/Eng/Library/FHLC/frameset_fhlc.asp> and click "Place Search." Enter the name of the county or state, but don't use the word "county." Using only the state name helps you narrow the search. On the "Place Search Results" page, click the state name to find the list of subjects for which the FHL holds state-specific materials. Or narrow your search to your specific county by clicking on "View Related Places" at the top of the state screen and clicking your county's name.

From either the state or county subject list, choose a subject heading for a list of specific titles, and click on the title of interest. On the "Title Details" page, if you see "There are no film notes available for this title," you know that the work is available at the FHL or other genealogy libraries, but not on microfilm through the FHL. If you see "View Film Notes," click the tab to get the microfilm number you need for ordering.

If you want to learn more about a specific film number that you found elsewhere, do a "Film/Fiche Search" instead of a "Place Search." Enter the film or fiche number and click on the link(s) on the "Film/Fiche Search Results" page, then on "View Film Notes."

WRITING TO THE COUNTY CLERK

Writing an old-fashioned letter to the county clerk to request records of your ancestors has worked for genealogists for decades, and it's still a good way to obtain records when you can't go to the courthouse yourself or the records you need haven't been microfilmed. When writing for records, however, you need to be specific in your request, as the county clerk is a busy person and responding to letters from genealogists usually isn't high on her list of things to do.

Let's say you want to see if great-great Grandpa William Shough, who died in 1878, left a will in Orange County, Virginia. First, turn to page 731 in this book and find the listing for that county. It will give you the year probate records begin for that county, what court holds the records, and the address for the clerk's office. From there you'll write your letter with enough information so the clerk can help you, but not so much that she ignores your request. You might word your letter like this:

> Central Virginia Genealogical Association
> 109-A W. Main St.
> Orange, VA 22960
>
> To Whom it May Concern (always safer than Dear Sir or Madam),
>
> I am seeking the will of William Shough, who died in your county in 1878. Could you please check your index for this (as well as under the spelling "Show"), and let me know if you have a will recorded for him and what the cost would be to obtain a copy of the full record?
>
> Thank you for your assistance. I am enclosing a self-addressed, stamped envelope for your reply.
>
> Sincerely,
>
> Your Name Here

Some people prefer to include a check for, say, $5 with the self-addressed, stamped envelope, and then mention in the letter that you will send any additional fee. (Even if you include a check, it's always a good idea to include that self-addressed, stamped envelope.) Keep in mind that most clerks will search only for what you specifically ask. Although William Shough may have died in 1878, his will might not have been recorded until several years later, so you might want to include a five- to ten-year search span. Likewise, the clerk probably won't check under different spellings, so you should include a couple of those variations. If you get a negative response, however, you have to wonder how thorough a search the clerk provided, so

this might be an item to recheck should you ever be able to visit the courthouse in person.

If you've borrowed a microfilm of courthouse record indexes from a Family History Center, or you've found a book of abstracted records but don't have access to the actual records, you'll be making the clerk's job easier if you include the volume and page number from the index in your letter.

VISITING THE COURTHOUSE OR TOWN HALL

Sooner or later, you may find that a trip to your ancestor's courthouse is necessary to uncover additional documents. Unfortunately, county and town clerks usually don't share your interest and enthusiasm for family history research. Assisting genealogists is not their primary duty. When asking for help, it's best not to go into detail about your research. Give them only enough information so that they can help you find what you're looking for. Be as pleasant and friendly as possible, even though the person behind the counter may not be. Remember, the clerk has what you want—the records.

Some researchers go the extra mile when they have a particularly helpful clerk and send a thank you note, candy, and even flowers. They reference their visit in some way so that the clerk will remember them; then the next time they need help, the clerk is likely to be even more helpful.

In some courthouses you will be allowed to search the indexes and records yourself; in others, a clerk will do it for you. Some will only let you view the records on microfilm, as the originals have been transferred to the state archives or an off-site storage facility. If the courthouse or town hall has off-site storage, you may have to wait a day or two for the records to be brought to the courthouse or town hall for research.

It's always a good idea to write or call the courthouse prior to your visit to see what hours they're open, or if it will be closed for any special reason, like a state holiday. (The listings in this book may refer you to a Web site where you can find out information for your visit.) Here are some other questions to ask:

- Is there a photocopy machine for public use?
- How much does it cost?
- Can I make change there, or should I bring dimes, quarters, and nickels?
- How much does it cost to obtain a certified and non-certified copy of a record?
- Where is the nearest place to eat? Park?
- Is handicap access available?
- Can researchers take in briefcases or must these be locked up?
- Are laptop computers allowed?

- Is there a particular person I need to see about looking at a particular record?
- Does the office close for lunch?
- Are there any records stored elsewhere, and how can I get access to them?
- Is there a pamphlet that outlines the repository's holdings?

Ethics for the Genealogist

Genealogists, whether by vocation or avocation, must abide by certain ethics. One of the most important is the care and handling of historical documents and published records. It is *not* acceptable under *any* circumstance to tear, erase, mark, or remove any document, book, or microfilm. Under no circumstance may you mutilate, deface, or destroy a document or book. We are a community of researchers who must respect each other, the people who assist us in our search, and the historical records that help us learn about our heritage.

USING THE *RESOURCE BOOK*

For each state, you'll find an introduction with the following information:

- A map of the state showing each county
- The year it became a territory and the year it became a state
- Listing of state repositories
- Historical Overview, giving a brief history of the state including when people began settling the area and from where, territorial status, and so on
- Record Highlights, discussing unusual records or those unique to that state
- Research Tips, offering helpful tips for researching records in that state or visiting the state or county courthouses and repositories.

Following the introduction are the listings of county, parish, or town hall contacts. Here you'll find the date the county was formed, from which county it was created (the parent county), and when specific records began being recorded in that county.

A crucial part of your research is knowing when a county was formed and from which counties it was created, and this is why this book is so helpful to your search. Suppose you have an ancestor who was married in Teller County, Colorado, in 1895. Turning to page 79, you'll find that this county wasn't created until 1899, and marriage records there didn't begin until that year. You'll need to look in the parent county of El Paso. Turning to that listing, you'll learn that El Paso marriage records began in 1861, and this is likely where you'll find your ancestor's marriage recorded.

HOW THE *RESOURCE BOOK* WAS COMPILED

This book was made possible by the talents and efforts of a number of contributors, fact checkers, editors, and proofreaders. Most obvious to the reader are the authors of the state chapters. While they wrote the introductions, they were not responsible for compiling the bulk of this volume. Behind the scenes was a team of dedicated fact checkers who worked diligently to verify county courthouse addresses, county formation dates, dates when records began, and the bibliographic information. We extend our appreciation to Jim Cappo, Brad Crawford, Jason Cutler, Karrie Jackson, Nicolas Krupar, Barbara Poe, Matthew Wagner, and everyone who helped with the inputting and fact checking along the way. Another critical member of the backstage crew was Erin Nevius, associate editor of Family Tree Books. She coordinated and managed the fact checkers, copy editors, proofreaders, design, and production of this book. It wouldn't have happened without her, or without the efforts of our spectacular production team, Clare Finney, Kim Kane, Joan Kuritar, Belinda McCann, Carol O'Connor, Jill Pressler, and Robin Richie.

It seems that all works of this nature relied on the initial compilation of Everton's *Handy Book for Genealogists*. First published in 1947, no doubt the Evertons queried every courthouse for information, and theoretically, the dates records began and counties were formed should not have changed. Hence, similar works, such as the Family History Library catalogers, relied on this information. When our team of fact checkers tried to verify all the dates and data, however, they ran into discrepancies even on the county's own Web sites! Telephone calls to county clerks typically resulted in less-than-helpful responses, and one had to wonder if they hadn't pulled the *Handy Book* off their shelf to answer the questions. So, by consulting a multitude of sources, we have done our best to ensure that the information in this book is as accurate as possible. Naturally, with a work of this type and magnitude there will always be discrepancies and errors, despite everyone's best efforts. We hope that the reader will take this into consideration and not be overly critical or frustrated when an error is discovered.

While the *Handy Book* has become a classic in the genealogy field, other publishers have tried to improve on it, as we are doing with our *Resource Book*, and we feel we have succeeded. We strove to make our guide not only more affordable, but also easier to use. If you have suggestions on how we can make this guide better, or if you find errors, we welcome your comments and input. Please e-mail them to resourcebook@fwpubs.com.

Alabama

By Emily Anne Croom

HISTORICAL OVERVIEW

Alabama's history is entwined with the histories of many cultures. Although Indians long inhabited the region and the Spanish explored there in the sixteenth century, France established the first permanent white settlement near Mobile Bay in 1702 as part of its Louisiana colony. At the end of the French and Indian War (1763), France ceded to Britain lands east of the Mississippi River, including Alabama, as part of West Florida. However, Spain occupied Alabama's coastal area in 1780. At the end of the American Revolution, the 1783 Treaty of Paris gave the United States the territory north of the present Alabama-Florida boundary, the thirty-first parallel of latitude; Spain retained the Mobile Bay area as part of what was now Spanish West Florida.

The U.S. portion became part of Mississippi Territory in 1798, with most non-Indian residents living in Washington County, northwest of Mobile Bay. Although claimed by Georgia until 1802, the northern portion of the present state remained Indian lands. The Mobile Bay area was disputed territory after the Louisiana Purchase (1803), and U.S. troops took the Spanish garrison at Mobile during the War of 1812. When Mississippi attained statehood in 1817, Alabama became a separate territory and two years later (1819) became the twenty-second state.

Between 1805 and 1838, the U.S. government forced most Indians westward and opened former Indian lands to white settlement. The newly opened land lured thousands of settlers, largely from neighboring Tennessee and Georgia, the Carolinas, and Virginia. Numerous immigrants into central and southern Alabama used the Federal Road that stretched from Athens, Georgia, to New Orleans.

Settlers found grasslands, forests, and abundant wildlife, hills and plateaus in north and central counties, and

Courtesy of Birmingham Convention and Visitors Bureau

ALABAMA AT A GLANCE

Motto: We Dare Defend Our Rights

Population: 4.4 million

Prevalent Religions: Christianity, particularly Southern Baptist, Methodist, Pentecostal, and Roman Catholic

Major Industries: Steel, iron, piping, poultry, eggs, cattle, nursery stock, peanuts, cotton, vegetables, milk, soybeans, lumber, paper, mining, rubber and plastic products, transportation equipment, apparel

Ethnic Makeup (in percent): Caucasian 71.1%, African American 26%, Hispanic 1.7%, Asian 0.7%, Native American 0.5%, Other 0.7%

Famous Alabamians: Hank Aaron, Nat King Cole, Zelda Fitzgerald, Lionel Hampton, W.C. Handy, Emmylou Harris, Helen Keller, Coretta Scott King, Harper Lee, Carl Lewis, Joe Louis, Willie Mays, Jim Nabors, Jesse Owens, Rosa Parks, George Wallace, Hank Williams Sr.

Above: Birmingham skyline

coastal plains in the south. Agriculture, especially the cultivation of cotton and corn, dominated the economy until the twentieth century.

Most of Alabama's navigable rivers eventually empty into Mobile Bay or the Gulf of Mexico. However, the Tennessee River dips across northern Alabama before heading north again to the Ohio River. Early planters in the state's northern counties shipped cotton to New Orleans via the Tennessee, Ohio, and Mississippi rivers; those in central and southern counties, accessing the southerly flow of the other rivers, used the port of Mobile for exporting crops and importing supplies. These geographic factors and the long-time lack of north-south roads kept the northern part of the state fairly isolated from central and southern Alabama and helped create regional and political differences.

Many, but not the majority, of Alabama farmers, planters, and townspeople were slaveholders. By 1860, of Alabama's nearly one million people, 55 percent were white and 45 percent were black, of whom less than 1 percent were free. The foreign-born population was about 1 percent of the total. Ninety-five percent of the state's population was rural. Not until 1960 did the urban population surpass the rural population of the state.

After Alabama seceded from the Union in January 1861, Montgomery briefly became the capital of the Confederate States of America. Confederate troops held the important port of Mobile almost until the end of the Civil War in April 1865, but the state saw about two hundred engagements on its soil and waters. Although most Alabamians supported the Confederate cause, a considerable number did not and served in the Union forces.

Left with widespread poverty after the war, Alabama did not experience significant recovery until the early 1900s. By the mid-twentieth century, the state's economy had diversified to include livestock, mining and steel industries, commercial forestry and related manufacturing, and production of numerous consumer goods.

RECORD HIGHLIGHTS

The state health department maintains birth and death records from 1908, marriage records from August 1936, and divorce records from 1950. The health department Web site <http://ph.state.al.us/chs/VitalRecords/VRECO RDS.HTMl> also provides information for adoptees. Some county probate courts hold pre-1908 birth and death records. Before 1865, the state legislature had jurisdiction over most divorces.

A significant number of Alabama counties have lost records in courthouse fires or other disasters. Contrary to common opinion, few of the fires occurred during the Civil War. Since not all fires or storms destroy everything, check for surviving records. Consult records of parent

RESEARCH TIPS

for more info

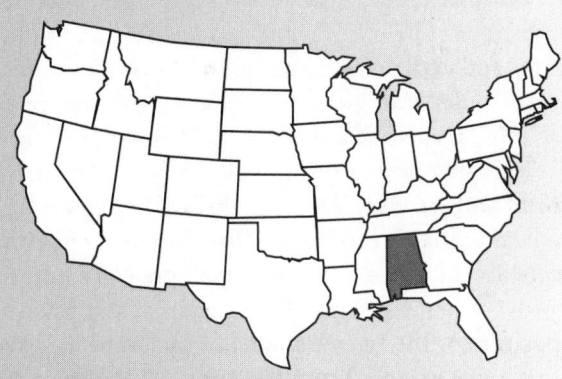

- Until 1850, probate courts were called Orphans Courts.
- Some probate courts maintain packets of "loose papers" related to individual probate cases; older probate records often have been microfilmed.
- Ancestors reportedly born in Mississippi before 1817 or West Florida before 1813 may have been born in what is now Alabama.
- Alabama's federal censuses date from 1830.
- Much of Perry County's 1890 census survives.
- Research materials are found in many places, especially the Alabama Department of Archives and History (<www.archives.state.al.us/index.html>), Birmingham Public Library, Samford University, and the University of Alabama.
- www.segenealogy.com/index.htm

Census Records

- Federal Census population schedules: 1830, 1840, 1850, 1860, 1870, 1880, 1900, 1910, 1920, 1930
- Federal Census Soundex: 1880, 1900, 1910, 1920, 1930
- Alabama State Census: 1820, 1855, 1866
- Early Alabama settlers Mississippi Territorial Census: 1810, 1816
- Federal Mortality Schedules for counties in existence: 1850, 1860, 1870, 1880
- Federal Slave Schedules: 1850, 1860. Schedules name slaveholders but rarely name slaves.

and neighboring counties and records created in colonial, local, state, and federal jurisdictions. Also consider archival materials in libraries, local historical societies, and the state archives.

Alabama is a federal land state. Its federal land patents are searchable at the Bureau of Land Management Web

Alabama

site <www.glorecords.blm.gov>. Subsequent land transactions between individuals were recorded at county courthouses.

Alabama-specific resources include territorial censuses; state censuses (1820, 1855, 1866); censuses of Confederate veterans (1907, 1921) and widows (1927); territorial militia and civil service appointments; state militia records; Confederate pensions; 1862 salt allotment lists; 1867 voter registrations; Mobile Municipal Archives; state legislative acts involving individuals and families; territorial and state tax records; *Territorial Papers of the United States* and *Territorial Papers of the United States Senate*, for Alabama and Mississippi; pre-1817 territorial records at the Mississippi State Archives; and records of depositors of the two Alabama branches of the Freedman's Savings and Trust Company (FHL microfilm 928571-72).

STATE RESOURCES

■ ARCHIVES, LIBRARIES, AND SOCIETIES

Alabama Department of Archives & History (AHAH)
624 Washington Ave., Montgomery, AL 36130-0100
Tel: (334) 242-4435
E-mail: MarkPalmer@archives.al abama.gov
Web site: <www.archives.state.a l.us>

Alabama Department of Public Health
Center for Health Statistics
P.O. Box 5625, Montgomery, AL 36103-5625
Web site: <http://ph.state.al .us/chs/Index.htm>

Alabama Genealogical Society, Inc.
Samford University Library, AGS Depository and Headquarters,
P.O. Box 2296, Birmingham, AL 35229-0001
Web site: <www.archives.state.a l.us/ags/>

Alabama Historical Association (AHA)
% Alabama Department of Archives and History
624 Washington Ave.
Montgomery, AL 36130
Web site: <www.archives.state.a l.us/aha/aha.html/>

Andalusia Public Library
212 S. Three Notch St., Andalusia, AL 36420
Tel/Fax: (334) 222-6612

E-mail: andylib@alaweb.com
Web site: <www.andylibrary .com>

Anniston Liles Memorial Library
P.O. Box 308, Anniston, AL 36202
Web site: <www.rootsweb.com/ ~alabgs>

Archdiocese of Mobile Archives
(Roman Catholic Church Records) Chancery Office
P.O. Box 1966, Mobile, AL 36633
Tel: (334) 434-1583
Fax: (334) 434-1588

Auburn University Library
Ralph Brown Draughton Library, 231 Mell St., Auburn University, Auburn, AL 36849-5606
Tel: (334) 844-1738 or (800) 446-0387
Web site: <www.lib.auburn.edu>

Autauga Genealogical Society
P.O. Box 680668, Prattville, AL 36068-0668
Web site: <www.rootsweb.com/ ~alags/>

Baldwin County Genealogical Society
P.O. Box 108, Foley, AL 36536-0108

Barbour County Genealogy Group
% Eufala Carnegie Library, 217 N. Eufala Ave., Eufala, AL 36027

Birmingham Genealogical Society, Inc.
P.O. Box 2432, Birmingham, AL 35201

Web site: <www.birminghamgene alogy.org>

Birmingham Public Library
Tutwiler Collection of Southern History and Literature, 2100 Park Place, Birmingham, AL 35203
Tel: (205) 226-3610
Web site: <www.bplonline.org>

Birmingham Southern College
Charles Andrew Rush Library (Methodist Church Records) 900 Arkadelphia Rd., Birmingham, AL 35254
Tel: (205) 226-4740
Web site: <www.bsc.edu/libr ary/info.htm>

Bullock County Historical Society
P.O. Box 563, Union Springs, AL 36089

Butler County Historical & Genealogical Society
P.O. Box 561, Greenville, AL 36037
Tel: (334) 383-9564
E-mail: historyroom@alaweb .com

Central Alabama Genealogical Society
P.O. Box 125, Selma, AL 36702

Chambers County Valley Library
Chattahoochee Valley Historical Society
3419 Twentieth Ave., Valley, AL 36854

Choctaw County Genealogical Society
620 County Rd. 43, Butler, AL 36904
Web site: <www.rootsweb.com/ ~alccgs/>

Coosa County Historical Society
P.O. Box 388, Rockford, AL 35136

Cullman County Public Library
200 Clark Street, NE, Cullman, AL 35055-2997

Dale County Genealogical and Historical Society
% Ozark-Dale County Public Library, 416 James St., Ozark, AL 36360
Tel: (334) 774-5480
Fax: (334) 774-9156
Web site: <www.graceba.net/~li brary/a.society.genealogical.hi storical.html>

Dekalb County Genealogical Society, Inc.
P.O. Box 681087, Fort Payne, AL 35968-1612
E-mail: w4ctk@farmerstel.com
Web site: <www.webspawner. com/users/dekalbsociety/>

Evergreen-Conecuh Public Library
201 Park St., Evergreen, AL 36401
Web site: <www.evergreenal. com/html/library/index.html>

Family History Library
35 North West Temple St., Salt Lake City, UT 84150-3400
Tel: (801) 240-2331 or (800) 453-3860 x22331
Fax: (801) 240-5551
Web site: <www.familysearch .org>
To find a Family History Center near you: <www.familysearch. org/Eng/Library/FHC/ frameset_fhc.asp>

Florence-Lauderdale Public Library
350 N. Wood Avenue, Florence, AL 35630
Tel: (256) 764-6564
Fax: (256) 764-6629
E-mail: information@flpl.lib.al.us
Web site: <www.flpl.lib.al.us>

Genealogical Society of East Alabama, Inc.
P.O. Box 2892, Opelika, AL 36803

Genealogy Society of Washington County
P.O. Box 399, Chatom, AL 36518
Web site: <www.members.aol. com/JORDANJM2/WCGS.html>

Hueytown Historical Society
P.O. Box 3313, Hueytown, AL 35023-3313
Web site: <www.hueytown.com/ historical/index.html>

Huntingdon College
Houghton Memorial Library, 1500 E. Fairview Ave., Montgomery, AL 36106
Tel: (334) 833-4421
Web site: <http://library.hunting don.edu>

Huntsville Public Library
The Heritage Room, 915 Monroe St., Huntsville, AL 35801
Tel: (256) 532-5969
Web site: <www.hpl.lib.al.us/dep artments/hhr/>

Jackson County Historical Association
P.O. Box 1494, Scottsboro, AL 35768

Lamar County Genealogical Society
P.O. Box 357, Vernon, AL 35592
Web site: <www.fayette.net/carr uth/genealogysociety.htm>

Lawrence County Historical Commission, Inc.
Lawrence County Archives, P.O. Box 728, Moulton, AL 35650
Web site: <http://home.hiwaay. net/~lcc/arch1.htm>

Limestone County Historical Society
P.O. Box 82, Athens, AL 35611

Lowndes County Historical & Genealogical Society
5935 County Rd., Minter, AL 36761
E-mail: cgolowka@prodigy.net

Marion County Genealogical Society
P.O. Box 360, Winfield, AL 35594
Web site: <www.rootsweb.com/ ~almarion/mcgs.htm>

Mobile Genealogical Society, Inc.
P.O. Box 6224, Mobile, AL 36606-6224
Tel: (251) 432-6474
Web site: <www.siteone.com/cl ubs/mgs/index.html>

Montgomery County Historical Society
P.O. Box 1829, Montgomery, AL 36102
Tel: (334) 264-1837
Fax: (334) 834-9292
Web site: <www.mindspring. com/~mchs>

Montgomery Genealogical Society, Inc.
P.O. Box 230194, Montgomery, AL 36123-0194
Web site: <www.rootsweb.com/ ~almgs>

Natchez Trace Genealogical Society
P.O. Box 420, Florence, AL 35631
Web site: <www.rootsweb.com/ ~alntgs>

National Archives-Southeast Region (Georgia)
1557 St. Joseph Ave., East Point, GA 30344-2593

Tel: (404) 763-7474
Fax: (404) 763-7059
Web site: <www.archives.gov/fa cilities/ga/atlanta.html>

North Central Alabama Genealogical Society
P.O. Box 13, Cullman, AL 35056-0013
Web site: <http://home.hiwaay. net/~lthurman/society.htm>

Northeast Alabama Genealogical Society
P.O. Box 8268, Gadsden, AL 35902

Ozark-Dale County Public Library
416 James St., Ozark, AL 36360
Tel: (334) 774-5480
Fax: (334) 774-9156
E-mail: library@odcpl.com
Web site: <www.snowhill.com/~l ibrary>

Pea River Historical and Genealogical Society
P.O. Box 310628, Enterprise, AL 36331
Tel: (334) 393-2901
Web site: <www.rootsweb.com/ ~alprhgs/>

Piedmont Historical and Genealogical Society
P.O. Box 47, Spring Garden, AL 36275

Pike County Historical and Genealogical Society
% Mrs. Clara Miller, 6754 Elba Hwy., Troy, AL 36079
Web site: <www.intersurf.com/ ~johnjanr/hsp.htm>

Samford University
Harwell Goodwin Davis Library (Baptist Church Records)
800 Lakeshore Dr., Birmingham, AL 35229
Tel: (205) 726-2748
Web site: <www.library.samford .edu>

Shelby County Historical Society, Inc.
P.O. Box 457, Columbiana, AL 35051-0457
Tel: (205) 669-3912
Web site: <www.rootsweb.com/ ~alshelby/schs.html>

Southeast Alabama Genealogical Society (SEAGS)
P.O. Box 246, Dothan, AL 36302-0245

Southern Society of Genealogists, Inc.
Stewart University, P.O. Box 295, Centre, AL 35960
Tel: (205) 447-2939

St. Clair Historical Society
11068 Greensport Rd., Ashville, AL 35953
Web site: <www.stclairhistorical society.org>

Steward University System Library
RFD 5, Box 109, Piedmont, AL 36272

Tennessee Valley Genealogical Society
P.O. Box 1568, Huntsville, AL 35807
Web site: <www.tvgs.org/genera l.htm>

Tennessee Valley Historical Society
P.O. Box 149, Sheffield, AL 35660-0149
Web site: <http://home.hiwaay. net/~krjohn/>

Tuscaloosa Genealogical Society
P.O. Box 020802, Tuscaloosa, AL 35402-0802

Vernon, Mary Wallace Cobb Memorial Library
110 First Ave. NW, Vernon, AL 35592
Tel: (205) 695-6123
Web site: <www.rootsweb.com/ ~allamar2/resources.htm>

University of Alabama, William Stanley Hoole Special Collections Library
University Libraries, Box 870266, Tuscaloosa, AL 35487-0266
Tel: (205) 348-0266
Fax: (205) 348-1699
E-mail: archives@bama.ua.edu
Web site: <www.lib.ua.edu/librar ies/hoole>

Walker County Genealogical Society
P.O. Box 3408, Jasper, AL 35502-3408

Wallace State College Library
Family & Regional History Program, Wallace State College, P.O. Box 2000, 801 Main St., Hanceville, AL 35077-2000
Tel: (256) 352-8000
E-mail: library@wallacestate.edu
Web site: <www.wallacestate. edu/library.html>

Washington County Historical Society
P.O. Box 456, Chatom, AL 36518
Web site: <www.members.aol. com/JORDANJM2/WCHS.htm>

Wilcox Historical Society
P.O. Box 464, Camden, AL 36726
Tel: (334) 682-9825
Fax: (334) 682-9387
E-mail: grsouth@frontiernet.com
Web site: <www.wilcoxwebworks .com/history>

Winston County Genealogical Society
P.O. Box 112, Double Springs, AL 35553
E-mail: winstoncounty@hotmail .com
Web site: <http://wcgs.ala.nu/ wcgs.htm>

BIBLIOGRAPHY

■ GENERAL RESOURCES

African-American Genealogy: A Bibliography and Guide to Sources
by Curt Bryan Witcher (Fort Wayne, IN: Round Tower Books, 2000)

"Alabama"
chapter by Elizabeth Shown Mills, edited by Kenn Stryker-Rodda (in *Genealogical Research: Methods and Sources*, vol. 2. Washington, D.C.: the American Society of Genealogists, 1983)

Alabama Bible Records
by Jeannette Holland Austin (Riverdale, GA: J.H. Austin, 1987)

Alabama: The History of a Deep South State.
William Warren Rogers, et al. (Tuscaloosa, AL: University of Alabama Press, 1994)

Alabama, Her History, Resources, War Record, and Public Men, from 1540 to 1872
by Willis Brewer (Baltimore, MD: Clearfield Co., 1995)

Alabama Research Outline
from the Church of Jesus Christ of Latter-day Saints (Salt Lake City: Corp. of the President of the Church of Jesus Christ of L.D.S., 1988)

The Federal Road Through Georgia, the Creek Nation, and Alabama, 1806–1836
by Henry deLeon Southerland Jr. and Jerry Elijah Brown; maps by Charles Jefferson Hiers (Tuscaloosa, AL: University of Alabama Press, 1989)

The Formative Period in Alabama, 1815–1828
by Thomas Perkins Abernethy (Tuscaloosa, AL: University of Alabama Press, 1990)

The Genealogist's Companion and Sourcebook, 2d ed.
by Emily Anne Croom (Cincinnati: Betterway Books, 2003)

A Genealogist's Guide to Discovering Your African-American Ancestors
by Franklin Carter Smith and Emily Anne Croom (Cincinnati: Betterway Books, 2003)

Guide to Genealogical Research in the National Archives of the United States
edited by Anne Bruner Eales and Robert M. Kvasnicka (Washington, D.C.: National Archives and Records Administration, 2000

History of Alabama and Dictionary of Alabama Biography, 4 vols.
Thomas McAdory Owen (Spartanburg, SC: Reprint Co., 1978)

Index to Colonel James Edmons Saunders' Early Settlers of Alabama: With Notes and Genealogies by Elizabeth Saunders Blair Stubbs
by Lloyd F. Oliver (Tomball, TX: Genealogical Publications, 1978)

Indian Place Names in Alabama, rev. ed.
by William A. Read (University, AL: University of Alabama Press, 1984)

National Archives Microfilm Catalogs online:
<www.archives.gov/publica tions/genealogy_microfilm_ catalogs.html>

Notable Men of Alabama: Personal and Genealogical, with Portraits
edited by Joel Campbell DuBose (Spartanburg, SC: Reprint Co., 1976)

Place Names in Alabama
by Virginia O. Foscue (Tuscaloosa, AL: University of Alabama Press, 1989)

Researching in Alabama: A Genealogical Guide, rev. ed.
edited by Marilyn Davis Barefield and Yvonne Shelton Crumpler (Birmingham, AL: Birmingham Public Library, 1998)

Some Early Alabama Churches (Established Before 1870)
compiled by Mabel Ponder Wilson, Dorothy Youngblood Woodyerd, and Rosa Lee Busby (Birmingham, AL: Alabama Society, Daughters of the American Revolution)

Tracing Your Alabama Past
by Robert Scott Davis (Jackson: University Press of Mississippi, 2003)

■ CENSUS RECORDS

1907 Alabama Census of Confederate Soldiers, 5 vols.
from the Department of Archives and History in Montgomery, AL (Cullman, AL: Gregath, 1982)

Alabama Census Returns, 1820, and an Abstract of Federal Census of Alabama, 1830
edited by the Department of Archives and History and Marie Bankhead Owen (Baltimore, MD: Genealogical Pub. Co., 1967)

Alabama Mortality Schedule 1850
by Marilyn Davis Hahn (Easley, SC: Southern Historical Press, 1983)

Alabama Mortality Schedule 1860
by Marilyn Davis Hahn (Easley, SC: Southern Historical Press, 1987)

The American Census Handbook
by Thomas Jay Kemp (Wilmington, DE: Scholarly Resources, 2001)

The Census Book: A Genealogist's Guide to Federal Census Facts, Schedules, and Indexes
by William Dollarhide (Bountiful, UT: Heritage Quest, 2000)

Census of Confederate Veterans Residing in Southeast Alabama in 1907
compiled by Homer T. Jones (Carollton, MI: Pioneer Pub., 1998)

Finding Answers in U.S. Census Records
by Loretto Dennis Szucs and Matthew Wright (Orem, UT: Ancestry Publishing, 2002)

Map Guide to the U.S. Federal Censuses, 1790–1920
by William Thorndale and William Dollarhide (Baltimore, MD: Genealogical Pub. Co., 1987)

State Census Records
by Ann S. Lainhart (Baltimore, MD: Genealogical Publishing, 1992)

Your Guide to the Federal Census
by Kathleen W. Hinckley (Cincinnati: Betterway Books, 2002)

■ IMMIGRATION RECORDS

American Naturalization Records, 1790–1990: What They Are and How to Use Them
by John J. Newman (North Salt Lake, UT: HeritageQuest, 1998)

American Passenger Arrival Records
by Michael Tepper (Baltimore: Genealogical Publishing Co., 1993)

Declarations of Intention, Naturalizations, and Petitions, 1855–1960
from the United States District Court, Southern District of Alabama (Salt Lake City: Family History Library) Microfilm nos. 1,481,392-398 and 2,080,628

Lists of Ships' Passengers, Mobile, Alabama, 2 vols.
compiled by Lucille Mallon Connick (Mobile, AL: L.M. Connick, 1988)

Mobile Ship News
transcribed by Lois Dumas Mitchell (Mobile, AL: 1964)

Naturalization Records, Mobile, Alabama, 1833–1906
by Clinton P. King and Meriem A. Barlow (Baltimore: Gateway Press, 1986)

They Became Americans: Finding Naturalization Records and Ethnic Origins
by Loretto Dennis Szucs (Salt Lake City: Ancestry, Inc., 1998)

They Came in Ships: A Guide to Finding Your Immigrant Ancestor's Arrival Records, 2d ed.
by John P. Colletta (Salt Lake City: Ancestry, Inc., 1993)

■ LAND RECORDS

English Land Grants in West Florida: A Register for the States of Alabama, Mississippi, and Parts of Florida and Louisiana, 1766–1776
by Winston DeVille (Ville Platte, LA: W. De Ville, 1986)

Locating Your Roots: Discover Your Ancestors Using Land Records
by Patricia Law Hatcher (Cincinnati: Betterway Books, 2003)

Old Cahaba Land Office Records and Military Warrants, 1817–1853
by Marilyn Davis Hahn (Mobile, AL: Old South Print & Publishing Co., 1981)

Old Huntsville Land Office Records and Military Warrants, 1810–1854
compiled by Marilyn Davis Barefield (Easley, SC: Southern Historical Press, 1985)

Old Land Records of Colbert County, Alabama
by Margaret Matthews Cowart (Huntsville, AL: M.M. Cowart, 1985)

Old Land Records of Franklin County, Alabama
by Margaret Matthews Cowart (Huntsville, AL: M.M. Cowart, 1986)

Old Land Records of Jackson County, Alabama: Government Land Tract Book
by Margaret Matthews Cowart (Huntsville, AL: Cowart, 1980)

Old Land Records of Lauderdale County, Alabama: A Comparison of Three Copies of the Government Tract Book for Lauderdale County, Alabama.
by Margaret Matthews Cowart (Huntsville, AL: M.M. Cowart, 1996)

Old Land Records of Lawrence County, Alabama
by Margaret Matthews Cowart (Huntsville, AL: M.M. Cowart, 1991)

Old Land Records of Limestone County, Alabama
by Margaret Matthews Cowart (Huntsville, AL: M.M. Cowart, 1984)

Old Land Records of Madison County, Alabama
by Margaret Matthews Cowart (Huntsville, AL: Cowart, 1979)

Old Land Records of Marshall County, Alabama: A Comparison of Three Copies of the Government Tract Book for Marshall County, Alabama
by Margaret Matthews Cowart (Huntsville, AL: M.M. Cowart, 1988)

Old Land Records of Morgan County, Alabama
by Margaret Matthews Cowart (Huntsville, AL: M.M. Cowart, 1981)

Old Sparta & Elba Land Office Records & Military Warrants, 1822–1860
by Marilyn Davis Hahn (Easley, SC: Southern Historical Press, 1983)

Old St. Stephen's Land Office Records & American State Papers, Public Lands, Vol. I, 1768–1888
by Marilyn Davis Hahn (Easley, SC: Southern Historical Press, 1983)

Old Tuscaloosa Land Office Records & Military Warrants, 1821–1855
compiled by Marilyn Davis Barefield (Easley, SC: Southern Historical Press, 1984)

Private Land Claims, Alabama, Arkansas, Florida
by Fern C. Ainsworth (Natchitoches, LA: F. Ainsworth, 1978)

Robert Armstrong's Survey Book of Cherokee Lands: Lands Granted from the Treaty of 27 February 1819
by James L. Douthat and Robert Armstrong (Signal Mountain, TN:

Institute of Historical Research, 1993)

■ MAPS

Atlas of Historical County Boundaries, Alabama
edited by John H. Long, and compiled by Peggy Sinko (New York: Charles Scribner's Sons, 1996)

Dead Towns of Alabama
by W. Stuart Harris (University, AL: University of Alabama Press, 1977)

Handbook of Alabama: A Complete Index to the State, with map, 2d ed.
Saffold Berney (Spartanburg, SC: Reprint Co., 1975)

Historical Atlas of Alabama
by Donald B. Dodd; cartography by Borden D. Dent (University, AL: University of Alabama Press, 1974)

A List of Nineteenth Century Maps of the State of Alabama
by Sara Elizabeth Mason (Birmingham, AL: Birmingham Public Library, 1973)

Yesterday's Faces of Alabama: A Collection of Maps, 1822–1909
edited by Society of Pioneers of Montgomery and John H. Napier III (Montgomery, AL: Brown Print Co., 1978)

■ MILITARY RECORDS

Compendium of the Confederate Armies, 11 vols.
by Stewart Sifakis (New York: Facts on File, 1992–1995)

First Tennessee and Alabama Independent Cavalry, 1863–1864, Roster: Companies A, B, C, D, E, F, G, H
compiled by John L.T.N. Potter and the United States Army Alabama and Tennessee Cavalry, 1st, Vidette Cavalry (Chatanooga, TN: Mountain Press, 1995)

An Index to Alabama Society Sons of the American Revolution, Members and their Ancestors, 1903–1996
compiled by Clifford D. Black and the Sons of the American Revolution, Alabama Society (Rainsville, AL: C.D. Black, 1996)

Law's Alabama Brigade in the War Between the Union and the Confederacy
by J. Gary Laine and Morris M. Penny (Shippensburg, PA: White Mane Pub. Co., 1996)

Revolutionary Soldiers in Alabama: Being a List of Names, Compiled from Authentic Sources, of Soldiers of the American Revolution who Resided in the State of Alabama
compiled by Thomas McAdory Owen and the Alabama Department of Archives and History in Montgomery, AL (Baltimore, MD: Genealogical Pub. Co., 1975)

Uncle, We Are Ready! Registering America's Men, 1917–1918: A Guide to Researching World War I Draft Registration Cards
by John J. Newman (North Salt Lake, UT: HeritageQuest, 2001)

U.S. Military Records: A Guide to Federal & State Sources, Colonial America to the Present
by James C. Neagles (Salt Lake City: Ancestry, Inc., 1994)

World War II: A Family Historian's Guide
by Debra Johnson Knox (Spartanburg, SC: MIE Publishing, 2003)

Volunteer Soldiers in the Cherokee War, 1836–1839
by James L. Douthat (Signal Mountain, TN: Mountain Press, 1995)

■ PROBATE RECORDS

Index to Alabama Wills, 1808–1870
compiled by the Daughters of the American Revolution, Alabama Society (Baltimore, MD: Genealogical Pub. Co., 1977)

■ VITAL RECORDS

Alabama Marriages Early to 1825: A Research Tool
compiled and transcribed by Liahona Research, Inc., edited by Jordan R. Dodd and Norman L. Moyes (Bountiful, UT: Precision Indexing, 1991, ca. 1990)

Alabama Notes, 4 vols.
compiled by Flora Dainwood England (Baltimore, MD: Genealogical Pub. Co., 1977–1989)

Bible and Cemetery Records, 2 vols.
from the Birmingham Genealogical Society (Birmingham, AL, 1962–1966)

Divorces Copied from Printed Acts of Alabama, 1818–1864
by Donald F. Watson (Montgomery: Alabama Department of Archives and History, 1971)

Marriage Certificates, 1936–1992; Index, 1936–1959
from the Alabama Department of Health in Montgomery, AL (Salt Lake City, UT: filmed by the Genealogical Society of Utah, 1993)

Marriage & Death Notices from Alabama Newspapers and Family Records, 1819–1890
compiled by Helen S. Foley (Easley, SC: Southern Historical Press, 1981)

Marriage, Death, and Legal Notices from Early Alabama Newspapers, 1819–1893
compiled by Pauline Jones Gandrud (Easley, SC: Southern Historical Press, 1981)

Your Guide to Cemetery Research
by Sharon DeBartolo Carmack (Cincinnati: Betterway Books, 2002)

■ Autauga 21 Nov. 1818
134 N. Court St. Suite 106, Prattville, AL 36067
Phone: (334)361-3725
Web site: www.rootsweb.com/~alautaug
Parent County: Montgomery
Comments/research tips: Marriage records from 1829–1898, Birth from 1871–1928 (delayed birth cert. rec.), and Death from March 1908–February 1916.

Record Type	Year Begun	Jurisdiction
Land	ca. 1809	Probate Judge
Probate	1810	Probate Judge
Court	1831	Clerk/Circuit Ct.

■ Baine 7 Dec. 1866
Parent County: Blount, Calhoun, Cherokee, DeKalb, Marshall, St. Clair
Comments/research tips: Abolished 3 December 1867. Established as Etowah County 1 December 1868.

■ Baker 30 Dec. 1868
Parent County: Autauga, Bibb, Perry, Shelby
Comments/research tips: (See Chilton) Name changed to Chilton 17 December 1874.

■ Baldwin 21 Dec. 1809
1 Court Sq., P.O. Box 459, Bay Minette, AL 36507
Phone: (251)937-0399
Web site: www.co.baldwin.al.us/
Parent County: Washington, West Florida

Record Type	Year Begun	Jurisdiction
Birth	1908	Dept./Health
Marriage	1819	Probate Court
Death	1908	Dept./Health
Land	1809	Probate Court
Probate	1810	Probate Court
Court	1811	Clerk/Circuit Ct.

■ Barbour 18 Dec. 1832
1800 Fifth Ave. N., P.O. Box 398, Clayton, AL 36016-0398
Phone: (334)775-8371
Web site: www.rootsweb.com/~albarbou/barbour.html
Parent County: Pike County and Original Territory
Comments/research tips: Birth records from 1891–1899 and 1906–1923 and Death records from 1906–1923.

Record Type	Year Begun	Jurisdiction
Marriage	1838	Probate Judge
Land	1832	Probate Judge
Probate	1833	Probate Judge
Court	1832	Clerk/Circuit Ct.

■ Benton 18 Dec. 1832
Parent County: Creek Cession of 1832
Comments/research tips: (See Calhoun) Name changed to Calhoun 29 January 1858.

■ Bibb 7 Feb. 1818
Centreville, AL 35042
Phone: (205)926-4747
Web site: www.dbtech.net/bibbco/
Parent County: Monroe, Montgomery
Comments/research tips: Formerly Cahawba County. Name changed to Bibb 2 December 1820.

Record Type	Year Begun	Jurisdiction
Marriage	1820	County Clerk
Land	1818	County Clerk
Probate	1830	County Clerk
Court	1830	Clerk/Circuit Ct.

■ Blount 6 Feb. 1818
220 Second Ave., E., Room 208, Oneonta, AL 35121
Phone: (256)625-4153
Web site: www.rootsweb.com/~alblount/
Parent County: Montgomery County and land acquired from the Creek Cession of 1814.
Comments/research tips: Clerk of Circuit Court has court records 1829–1852/1872.

Record Type	Year Begun	Jurisdiction
Marriage	1820	County Archivist
Land	1818	County Archivist
Probate	1829	County Archivist
Burial	1820	County Archivist

■ Bullock 5 Dec. 1866
P.O. Box 71, Union Springs, AL 36089
Phone: (334)738-2250
Web site: www.rootsweb.com/~albulloc/
Parent County: Barbour, Macon, Montgomery, Pike counties

Record Type	Year Begun	Jurisdiction
Marriage	1819	Probate Judge
Land	1809	County Commissioner
Probate	1810	Probate Judge
Court	1811	Clerk/Circuit Ct.

■ Butler 13 Dec. 1819
700 Court Sq., P.O. Box 756, Greenville, AL 36037
Phone: (334)382-3512
Web site: www.rootsweb.com/~albutler/
Parent County: Conecuh, Montgomery
Comments/research tips: Courthouse burned 1853. County Health Department–has Birth records from 1886–May 1891, March 1894–November 1919, delayed birth cert. records 1870–1930, and Death records 1894–1919.

Record Type	Year Begun	Jurisdiction
Marriage	1853	Probate Judge
Land	1853	Probate Judge
Probate	1853	Probate Judge
Court	1853	Clerk/Circuit Ct.

■ Cahawba 7 Feb. 1818
Parent County: Monroe, Montgomery
Comments/research tips: (See Bibb) Name changed to Bibb 4 December 1820.

■ Calhoun 18 Dec. 1832
1702 Noble St., Suite 103, Anniston, AL 36202
Phone: (256)236-8231
Web site: www.rootsweb.com/~alcalhou/
Parent County: Creek Cession of 1832

Comments/research tips: Formerly Benton County. Name changed to Calhoun 29 January 1858.

Record Type	Year Begun	Jurisdiction
Marriage	1834	Probate Judge
Land	1832	Probate Judge
Probate	1850	Probate Judge
Court	1891	Clerk/Circuit Ct.

■ **Chambers** 18 Dec. 1832

Court Square, Lafayette, AL 36862

Phone: (334)664-1224

Web site: www.rootsweb.com/~alchambe/

Parent County: Creek Cession of 1832

Record Type	Year Begun	Jurisdiction
Birth	1833	Dept./Health
Marriage	1833	Probate Office
Land	1833	Probate Office
Probate	1833	Probate Office
Court	1833	Clerk/Circuit Ct.

■ **Cherokee** 9 Jan. 1836

102 W. Main St., Centre, AL 35960

Phone: (256)927-3363

Web site: www.rootsweb.com/~alcherok/

Parent County: Cherokee Cession 1835

Comments/research tips: Records burned in 1882.

Record Type	Year Begun	Jurisdiction
Marriage	1882	Probate Judge
Land	1882	Probate Judge
Probate	1882	Probate Judge
Court	1882	Clerk/Circuit Ct.
Military	1882	Probate Judge

■ **Chilton** 30 Dec. 1868

P.O. Box 557, Clanton, AL 35045

Phone: (205)755-1555

Web site: www.rootsweb.com/~alchilto

Parent County: Autauga, Bibb, Perry, Shelby

Comments/research tips: Formerly Baker County. Name changed to Chilton 17 December 1874.

Record Type	Year Begun	Jurisdiction
Marriage	1870	Probate Judge
Land	1868	Probate Judge
Probate	1887	Clerk/Circuit Ct.
Court	1843	Clerk/Circuit Ct.

■ **Choctaw** 29 Dec. 1847

117 S. Mulberry Ave., Butler, AL 36904

Phone: (205)459-2417

Web site: www.rootsweb.com/~alchocta

Parent County: Sumter, Washington

Comments/research tips: County Health Department has Birth records 1870–1900 (delayed birth cert. rec.) and Death records 1881–1893.

Record Type	Year Begun	Jurisdiction
Marriage	1871	County Clerk
Land	1873	County Clerk
Probate	1873	County Clerk
Court	1871	Clerk/Circuit Ct.

■ **Clarke** 10 Dec. 1812

117 Court St., P.O. Box 548, Grove Hill, AL 36451

Phone: (334)275-3251

Web site: www.rootsweb.com/~alclarke/clarke.html

Parent County: Washington

Record Type	Year Begun	Jurisdiction
Birth	1908	Health Clinic
Marriage	1814	Probate Judge
Death	1908	Health Clinic
Land	1812	Probate Judge
Probate	1810	Probate Judge
Court	1813	Clerk/Circuit Ct.

■ **Clay** 7 Dec. 1866

P.O. Box 187, Ashland, AL 36251

Phone: (256)354-2198

Web site: www.rootsweb.com/~alclay

Parent County: Randolph, Talladega

Comments/research tips: County Court has Death records 1920–1940 and County Health Department has Birth records from 1920 and Death records from 1920, and Voting Registry 1906–1936.

Record Type	Year Begun	Jurisdiction
Marriage	1872	Probate Court
Land	1875	Probate Court
Probate	1876	Probate Court
Court	1875	Clerk/Circuit Ct.

■ **Cleburne** 6 Dec. 1866

406 Vickery St., Heflin, AL 36264

Phone: (256)463-5655

Web site: www.rootsweb.com/~alclebur/

Parent County: Calhoun, Raldolph, Talladega

Comments/research tips: Probate Judge has Birth and Death records 1911–1921, and County Health Department has Birth/Death records from 1908.

Record Type	Year Begun	Jurisdiction
Marriage	1819	Probate Judge
Land	1809	Probate Judge
Probate	1810	Probate Judge
Court	1811	Clerk/Circuit Ct.

■ **Coffee** 29 Dec. 1841

230 Court St., Elba, AL 36323

Phone: (334)897-2211

Web site: www.rootsweb.com/~alcoffee/

Parent County: Dale

Record Type	Year Begun	Jurisdiction
Marriage	1866	Probate Judge
Land	1887	Probate Judge
Court	1811	Clerk/Circuit Ct.

■ **Colbert** 6 Feb. 1867

201 N. Main St., Tuscumbia, AL 35674

Phone: (256)386-8500

Web site: www.colbertcounty.org/

Parent County: Franklin

Comments/research tips: Abolished same year created, re-established 1869.

Alabama

Record Type	Year Begun	Jurisdiction
Birth	1881	Dept./Health
Marriage	1867	Probate Judge
Death	1881	Dept./Health
Land	1867	Probate Judge
Probate	1867	Probate Judge
Court	1867	Clerk/Circuit Ct.

■ Conecuh 13 Feb. 1818

P.O. Box 347, Evergreen, AL 36401
Phone: (334)578-2095
Web site: www.rootsweb.com/~alconecu/
Parent County: Monroe

Record Type	Year Begun	Jurisdiction
Birth	1881	Dept./Health
Marriage	1866	Probate Judge
Death	1881	Dept./Health
Land	1866	Probate Judge
Probate	1870	Probate Judge
Court	1881	Clerk/Circuit Ct.

■ Coosa 18 Dec. 1832

P.O. Box 218, Rockford, AL 35136
Phone: (256)362-5721
Web site: www.rootsweb.com/~alcoosa/
Parent County: Creek Indian Treaty of Cusseta
Comments/research tips: Probate Records has a few Birth and Death records 1920–1945.

Record Type	Year Begun	Jurisdiction
Birth	1878	Dept./Health
Marriage	1834	Probate Records
Death	1920	Dept./Health
Divorce	1834	Probate Records
Land	1832	Probate Records
Probate	1834	Probate Records
Court	1834	Circuit Court Office
Military	1834	Probate Records

■ Cotaco 6 Feb. 1818

Parent County: Cherokee Turkeytown Cession
Comments/research tips: (See Morgan) Name changed to Morgan 14 June 1821.

■ Covington 7 Dec. 1821

Court Square, Andalusia, AL 36420
Phone: (334)428-2520
Web site: www.rootsweb.com/~alcoving/
Parent County: Henry
Comments/research tips: Records burned 1895. Some prior records may still exist. Probate Judge has Marriage, Land, and Probate records 1895–1896. Clerk of Circuit Court has Divorce records 1895–1896.

Record Type	Year Begun	Jurisdiction
Court	na	Clerk/Circuit Ct.

■ Crenshaw 24 Nov. 1866

P.O. Box 227, Luvern, AL 36049
Phone: (334)335-6568
Web site: www.rootsweb.com/~alcrensh/
Parent County: Butler, Coffee, Covington, Lowndes, Pike

Record Type	Year Begun	Jurisdiction
Birth	1889	Dept./Health
Marriage	1895	Probate Judge
Death	1909	Dept./Health
Land	1896	Probate Judge
Probate	1896	Probate Judge

■ Cullman 24 Jan. 1877

500 Second Ave. SW, Cullman, AL 35055
Phone: (256)739-3530
Web site: www.co.cullman.al.us/
Parent County: Blount, Morgan, Winston

Record Type	Year Begun	Jurisdiction
Birth	1877	Dept./Health
Marriage	1877	Probate Judge
Death	1877	Dept./Health
Divorce	1877	Probate Judge
Land	1877	Probate Judge
Probate	1877	Probate Judge
Court	1877	Probate Judge

■ Dale 22 Dec. 1824

1702 Hwy. 123 S., P.O. Box 246, Ozark, AL 36361
Phone: (334)774-6025
Web site: www.rootsweb.com/~aldale
Parent County: Covington and Henry
Comments/research tips: In 1885 the court house was destroyed by fire and all the records were destroyed.

Record Type	Year Begun	Jurisdiction
Birth	1919	Dept./Health
Marriage	1884	Probate Judge
Death	1920	Dept./Health
Divorce	1885	Clerk/Circuit Ct.
Land	1884	Probate Judge
Probate	1895	Probate Judge
Court	1884	Clerk/Circuit Ct.

■ Dallas 9 Feb. 1818

P.O. Box 987, Selma, AL 36702
Phone: (334)874-4401
Web site: www.prairiebluff.com/algenweb/dallas/
Parent County: Montgomery and Monroe
Comments/research tips: County Health Department has Birth records from 1880–1930 (delayed birth cert. rec.) and Death records from 1882–1888.

Record Type	Year Begun	Jurisdiction
Marriage	1818	Probate Judge
Divorce	1917	Probate Judge
Land	1818	Probate Judge
Probate	1821	Probate Judge
Court	1821	Clerk/Circuit Ct.

■ DeKalb 9 Jan. 1836

111 Grand Ave. SW, Fort Payne, AL 35967
Phone: (256)845-8525
Web site: www.segenealogy.com/alabama/al_county.htm
Parent County: Cherokee Cession of 1835

Record Type	Year Begun	Jurisdiction
Birth	1885	Dept./Health
Marriage	1836	Probate Judge

Death .... 1885 ....Dept./Health
Land .... 1836 ....Probate Judge
Probate .... 1836 ....Probate Judge
Court .... 1836 ....Clerk/Circuit Ct.

■ Elmore 15 Feb. 1866

P.O. Box 280, Wetumpka, AL 36092
Phone: (334)567-1138
Web site: www.rootsweb.com/~alelmore/
Parent County: Autauga, Coosa, Montgomery, Tallapoosa
Comments/research tips: Probate Judge has Birth and Death records 1909–1913 and County Health Department has Birth records from 1884 and Death records 1927.

Record Type	Year Begun	Jurisdiction
Marriage	1867	Probate Judge
Land	1867	Probate Judge
Probate	1867	Probate Judge
Court	1876	Clerk/Circuit Ct.
Military	1919	Probate Judge

■ Escambia 10 Dec. 1868

P.O. Box 848, Brewton, AL 36427
Phone: (334)867-3252
Web site: www.rootsweb.com/~alescamb/
Parent County: Baldwin, Conecuh
Comments/research tips: There was a record loss in 1868.

Record Type	Year Begun	Jurisdiction
Marriage	1879	Probate Court
Land	1868	Probate Court
Probate	1868	Probate Court
Court	1882	Clerk/Circuit Ct.

■ Etowah 7 Dec. 1866

800 Forrest Ave., Gadsden, AL 35901
Phone: (256)546-2821
Web site: www.etowahcounty.org/
Parent County: Blount, Calhoun, Cherokee, DeKalb, Marshall, St. Clair
Comments/research tips: Formerly Baine County, abolished 3 December 1867. Reestablished as Etowah County 1 December 1868.

Record Type	Year Begun	Jurisdiction
Birth	1894	Dept./Health
Marriage	1867	Probate Judge
Death	1898	Dept./Health
Land	1867	Probate Judge
Probate	1867	Probate Judge
Court	1867	Clerk/Circuit Ct.

■ Fayette 20 Dec. 1824

P.O. Box 509, Fayette, AL 35555
Phone: (205)932-4519
Web site: www.rootsweb.com/~alfayett/
Parent County: Marion, Pickens, Tuscaloosa
Comments/research tips: Probate Judge has Birth records 1884–1941 and Death records 1899–1941. There was a record loss in 1866 and in 1916.

Record Type	Year Begun	Jurisdiction
Marriage	1850	Probate Judge
Land	1824	Probate Judge

Probate .... 1851 ....Probate Judge
Military .... 1919 ....Probate Judge

■ Franklin 6 Feb. 1818

410 N. Jackson St., Russellville, AL 35653
Phone: (256)332-1210
Web site: www.rootsweb.com/~alfrankl/
Parent County: Cherokee & Chickasaw Cession of 1816
Comments/research tips: Records burned 1890.

Record Type	Year Begun	Jurisdiction
Marriage	1890	Probate Judge
Land	1818	Probate Judge
Probate	1890	Probate Judge
Court	1890	Clerk/Circuit Ct.

■ Geneva 26 Dec. 1868

P.O. Box 430, Geneva, AL 36340-0430
Phone: (334)684-9300
Web site: www.rootsweb.com/~algeneva
Parent County: Dale, Henry, Coffee
Comments/research tips: Probate Judge has Birth records 1909–1918 and Death records 1909–1941. There was a record loss in 1898.

Record Type	Year Begun	Jurisdiction
Marriage	1898	Probate Judge
Land	1868	Probate Judge
Probate	1888	Probate Judge
Court	1898	Clerk/Circuit Ct.
Military	1930	Probate Judge

■ Greene 13 Dec. 1819

P.O. Box 656, Eutaw, AL 35462
Phone: (205)372-3349
Web site: home.earthlink.net/~rodbush/GreeneHP.htm
Parent County: Marengo, Tuscaloosa
Comments/research tips: County Health Department has Birth records from June 1881–1896.

Record Type	Year Begun	Jurisdiction
Marriage	1823	Probate Judge
Death	1881	Dept./Health
Land	1821	Probate Judge
Probate	1820	Probate Judge
Court	1821	Clerk/Circuit Ct.

■ Hale 30 Jan. 1867

1001 Main St., P.O. Box 396, Greensboro, AL 36744
Phone: (334)624-8740
Web site: www.halecoal.org/
Parent County: Greene, Marengo, Perry, Tuscaloosa

Record Type	Year Begun	Jurisdiction
Marriage	1867	Probate Judge
Divorce	1868	Probate Judge
Land	1867	Probate Judge
Probate	1867	Probate Judge
Court	1867	Probate Judge

■ Hancock 12 Feb. 1850

Parent County: Walker
Comments/research tips: (See Winston) Name changed to Winston 22 January 1858.

■ Henry 13 Dec. 1819
101 W. Court Sq., Suite A, Abbeville, AL 36310
Phone: (334)585-3257
Web site: www.rootsweb.com/~alhenry/
Parent County: Conecuh
Comments/research tips: Probate Judge has Birth records 1895–1922 and Death records 1895–1906. County Health Department has Birth and Death records from 1931.

Record Type	Year Begun	Jurisdiction
Marriage	1823	Probate Judge
Land	1819	Probate Judge
Probate	1822	Probate Judge
Court	1822	Clerk/Circuit Ct.

■ Houston 9 Feb. 1903
P.O. Box 6406, Dothan, AL 36302
Phone: (334)677-4700
Web site: www.houstoncounty.org/
Parent County: Dale, Geneva, Henry

Record Type	Year Begun	Jurisdiction
Birth	1908	Dept./Health
Marriage	1903	Probate Office
Death	1908	Dept./Health
Divorce	1903	Reg. in Chancery
Land	1903	Probate Office
Probate	1903	Probate Office
Court	1903	Clerk/Circuit Ct.

■ Jackson 13 Dec. 1819
P.O. Box 397, Scottsboro, AL 35768
Phone: (256)574-9320
Web site: fly.hiwaay.net/~prm/jcalgenweb.html
Parent County: Cherokee Cession of 1816
Comments/research tips: Record loss in 1860 and 1920.

Record Type	Year Begun	Jurisdiction
Marriage	1851	Probate Judge
Divorce	1895	Clerk/Circuit Ct.
Land	1819	Probate Judge
Probate	1866	Probate Judge

■ Jefferson 13 Dec. 1819
716 N. Twenty-first St., Birmingham, AL 35263
Phone: (205)325-5300
Web site: www.rootsweb.com/~aljeffer/
Parent County: Blount
Comments/research tips: Birth and Death records are from 1871 and 1882 (partial).

Record Type	Year Begun	Jurisdiction
Marriage	1818	Probate Judge
Land	1819	Probate Judge
Probate	1819	Probate Judge
Court	1826	Clerk/Circuit Ct.

■ Jones 4 Feb. 1867
Parent County: Marion, Fayette
Comments/research tips: Abolished 13 November 1867. Reestablished as Sanford County 8 October 1868. Name changed to Lamar 8 February 1877.

■ Lamar 4 Feb. 1867
P.O. Box 338, Vernon, AL 35592
Phone: (205)695-9119
Web site: www.rootsweb.com/~allamar2/
Parent County: Marion, Fayette
Comments/research tips: Formerly Jones County. Abolished 13 November 1867 and reestablished as Sanford County 8 October 1868. Name changed to Lamar 8 February 1877.

Record Type	Year Begun	Jurisdiction
Land	1967	Probate Office
Probate	1967	Probate Office
Court	1967	Circuit Clerk

■ Lauderdale 6 Feb. 1818
P.O. Box 1059, Florence, AL 35631
Phone: (256)760-5800
Web site: www.rootsweb.com/~allauder/
Parent County: Cherokee & Chickasaw Cession in 1816

Record Type	Year Begun	Jurisdiction
Marriage	1818	Probate Judge
Land	1818	Probate Judge
Probate	1818	Probate Judge
Court	1821	Clerk/Circuit Ct.

■ Lawrence 6 Feb. 1818
Courthouse, Moulton, AL 35650
Phone: (256)974-0663
Web site: www.rootsweb.com/~allawren/
Parent County: Cherokee & Chickasaw in 1816

Record Type	Year Begun	Jurisdiction
Marriage	1828	Probate Judge
Divorce	1810	Probate Judge
Land	1810	Probate Judge
Probate	1818	Probate Judge
Court	1828	Clerk/Circuit Ct.

■ Lee 5 Dec. 1866
215 S. Ninth St., P.O. Box 666, Opelika, AL 36801
Phone: (334)749-7141
Web site: www.rootsweb.com/~allee/
Parent County: Chambers, Macon, Russell, Tallapoosa

Record Type	Year Begun	Jurisdiction
Marriage	1867	Probate Judge
Land	1867	Probate Judge
Probate	1867	Probate Judge
Court	1867	Clerk/Circuit Ct.
Military	1919	Probate Judge

■ Limestone 6 Feb. 1818
310 W. Washington St., Athens, AL 35611
Phone: (256)233-6404
Web site: www.co.limestone.al.us/
Parent County: Cherokee & Chickasaw Cession in 1806 and 1816
Comments/research tips: County Archivist has Birth and Death records 1881–1913 and County Health Department has Birth and Death records from 1881, Land, Probate and Court records 1818–1900, Divorce records 1896–1947, Marriage records 1832–1900, Tax records 1861–1900 and Newspapers 1868–1985. There was a record loss in 1862.

■ **Lowndes** 20 Jan. 1830
P.O. Box 65, Hayneville, AL 36040
Phone: (334)548-2331
Web site: www.rootsweb.com/~allownde/
Parent County: Butler, Dallas, Montgomery
Comments/research tips: Birth records from 1881–1904, delayed birth cert. records 1879–1911 are held by County Health Deparment.

Record Type	Year Begun	Jurisdiction
Marriage	1830	Probate Judge
Death	1832	Probate Judge
Land	1830	Probate Judge
Probate	1830	Probate Judge
Court	1830	Clerk/Circuit Ct.
Military	1919	Probate Judge

■ **Macon** 18 Dec. 1832
101 E. Northside St., Tuskegee, AL 36083
Phone: (334)727-1800
Web site: www.rootsweb.com/~almacon
Parent County: Creek Cession of 1832

Record Type	Year Begun	Jurisdiction
Marriage	1832	Probate Judge
Land	1832	Probate Judge
Probate	1834	Probate Judge
Court	1828	Clerk/Circuit Ct.

■ **Madison** 13 Dec. 1808
100 North Side Sq., Huntsville, AL 35801
Phone: (256)532-3330
Web site: www.co.madison.al.us
Parent County: Cherokee & Chickasaw Cession of 1806

Record Type	Year Begun	Jurisdiction
Birth	1881	Dept./Health
Marriage	1809	Probate Judge
Death	1881	Dept./Health
Land	1810	Probate Judge
Probate	1818	Probate Judge
Court	1808	Clerk/Circuit Ct.

■ **Marengo** 6 Feb. 1818
101 E. Coats Ave., Linden, AL 36748
Phone: (334)295-2210
Web site: www.rootsweb.com/~almareng/
Parent County: Choctaw Cession of 1816
Comments/research tips: Record loss in 1848 and 1965.

Record Type	Year Begun	Jurisdiction
Birth	1881	Dept./Health
Marriage	1818	Probate Judge
Death	1906	Dept./Health
Land	1820	Probate Judge
Probate	1818	Probate Judge
Court	1819	Clerk/Circuit Ct.

■ **Marion** 13 Feb. 1818
P.O. Box 460, Hamilton, AL 35570
Phone: (205)921-3172
Web site: www.rootsweb.com/~almarion/marion1.htm
Parent County: Tuscaloosa

Comments/research tips: Courthouse destroyed by fire in 1883, all records wre destroyed.

Record Type	Year Begun	Jurisdiction
Birth	1902	Dept./Health
Marriage	1887	Probate Judge
Death	1902	Dept./Health
Land	1887	Probate Judge
Probate	1887	Probate Judge
Court	1887	Clerk/Circuit Ct.
Military	1920	Probate Judge

■ **Marshall** 9 Jan. 1836
424 Blount Ave., Guntersville, AL 35976
Phone: (256)571-7701
Web site: www.marshallco.org/www/
Parent County: Blount, Cherokee Cession of 1836, Jackson

Record Type	Year Begun	Jurisdiction
Birth	1920	Probate Judge
Marriage	1836	Probate Judge
Death	1920	Probate Judge
Land	1836	Probate Judge
Probate	1843	Probate Judge
Court	1836	Probate Court

■ **Mobile** 18 Dec. 1812
109 Government St., Mobile, AL 36602
Phone: (334)690-8502
Web site: www.mobilecounty.org/
Parent County: West Florida, Baldwin

Record Type	Year Begun	Jurisdiction
Birth	1820	Dept./Health
Marriage	1814	Probate Judge
Land	1812	Probate Judge
Probate	1814	Probate Judge
Court	1814	Clerk/Circuit Ct.

■ **Monroe** 29 June 1815
County Courthouse, P.O. Box 8, Monroeville, AL 36461
Phone: (334)575-3778
Web site: www.rootsweb.com/~almonroe
Parent County: Creek Cession 1814
Comments/research tips: Courthouse fire destroyed all records prior to 1833. 1816 Census of Monroe County published by Monroe Journal, Monroeville, Alabama.

Record Type	Year Begun	Jurisdiction
Birth	1881	Dept./Health
Marriage	1833	Probate Judge
Death	1908	Dept./Health
Land	1833	Probate Judge
Probate	1833	Probate Judge
Court	1833	Clerk/Circuit Ct.

■ **Montgomery** 6 Dec. 1816
P.O. Box 223, Montgomery, AL 36101
Phone: (334)832-4950
Web site: www.mc-ala.org/
Parent County: Monroe
Comments/research tips: Alabama Department of Archivists & Historians has Marriage records 1817–1928.

Alabama

Record Type	Year Begun	Jurisdiction
Marriage	1917	Probate Judge
Divorce	1852	Clerk/Board/Revenue
Land	1819	Probate Judge
Probate	1819	Probate Judge
Court	1811	Clerk/Circuit Ct.

■ Morgan 6 Feb. 1818
302 Lee St. NE, Decatur, AL 35601
Phone: (256)351-4600
Web site: www.co.morgan.al.us/
Parent County: Cherokee Turkeytown Cession of 1818
Comments/research tips: Formerly Cotaco County. Name changed to Morgan 14 June 1821.

Record Type	Year Begun	Jurisdiction
Birth	1893	Dept./Health
Marriage	1818	Probate Judge
Death	1893	Dept./Health
Land	1818	Probate Judge
Probate	1818	Probate Judge
Court	1817	Clerk/Circuit Ct.

■ Perry 13 Dec. 1819
P.O. Box 478, Marion, AL 36756
Phone: (334)683-2210
Web site: www.rootsweb.com/~alperry/index.htm
Parent County: Montgomery, Creek Cession of 1814

Record Type	Year Begun	Jurisdiction
Birth	1908	Dept./Health
Marriage	1820	Probate Judge
Death	1908	Dept./Health
Land	1819	Probate Judge
Probate	1823	Probate Judge
Court	1821	Clerk/Circuit Ct.

■ Pickens 20 Dec. 1820
P.O. Box 370, Carrollton, AL 35447
Phone: (205)367-2010
Web site: www.rootsweb.com/~alpicken/pcpage.htm
Parent County: Tuscaloosa
Comments/research tips: Record loss in 1864 and 1876, all records destroyed.

Record Type	Year Begun	Jurisdiction
Birth	1903	Dept./Health
Marriage	1876	Probate Judge
Death	1903	Dept./Health
Land	1876	Probate Judge
Probate	1876	Probate Judge
Court	1876	Clerk/Circuit Ct.

■ Pike 17 Dec. 1821
P.O. Box 1008, Troy, AL 36081
Phone: (334)566-1246
Web site: www.rootsweb.com/~alpike
Parent County: Henry, Montgomery
Comments/research tips: County Health Department has Birth records from 1886 (with broken year). Courthouse destroyed by fire in 1830, all records were destroyed.

Record Type	Year Begun	Jurisdiction
Marriage	1830	Probate Judge

Record Type	Year Begun	Jurisdiction
Death	1881	Dept./Health
Land	1830	Probate Judge
Probate	1830	Probate Judge
Court	1830	Clerk/Circuit Ct.

■ Randolph 18 Dec. 1832
P.O. Box 249, Wedowee, AL 36278
Phone: (256)357-4933
Web site: www.rootsweb.com/~alrandol/
Parent County: Creek Cession 1832
Comments/research tips: Courthouse burned 1897, all Probate records destroyed. Probate Judge has Military Pensions 1904–1909.

Record Type	Year Begun	Jurisdiction
Birth	1886	Dept./Health
Marriage	1897	Probate Judge
Death	1886	Dept./Health
Land	1897	Probate Judge
Probate	1897	Probate Judge

■ Russell 18 Dec. 1832
P.O. Box 969, Phenix City, AL 36868
Phone: (334)298-7979
Web site: www.rootsweb.com/~alrussel/
Parent County: Creek Cession 1832

Record Type	Year Begun	Jurisdiction
Birth	1893	Dept./Health
Marriage	1928	Probate Judge
Death	1893	Dept./Health
Land	1832	Probate Judge
Probate	1832	Probate Judge
Court	1832	Clerk/Circuit Ct.

■ Sanford 8 Oct. 1867
Parent County: Jones
Comments/research tips: (See Lamar) Formed from abolished Jones County. Name changed to Lamar 8 February 1877.

■ Shelby 7 Feb. 1818
P.O. Box 1810, Columbiana, AL 35051
Phone: (205)669-3760
Web site: www.shelbycountyalabama.com/index.shtm
Parent County: Montgomery

Record Type	Year Begun	Jurisdiction
Marriage	1819	Probate Judge
Land	1819	Probate Judge
Probate	1819	Probate Judge
Court	1819	Clerk/Circuit Ct.

■ St. Clair 20 Nov. 1818
P.O. Box 397, Ashville, AL 35953
Phone: (205)594-5114
Web site: www.rootsweb.com/~alstclai/
Parent County: Shelby

Record Type	Year Begun	Jurisdiction
Birth	1893	Dept./Health
Marriage	1819	Probate Judge
Death	1908	Dept./Health

Alabama

Record Type	Year Begun	Jurisdiction
Land	1818	Probate Judge
Probate	1818	Probate Judge
Court	1818	Clerk/Circuit Ct.

■ Sumter 18 Dec. 1832
Franklin St., P.O. Box 70, Livingston, AL 35470
Phone: (205)652-2731
Web site: www.rootsweb.com/~alsumter/index.htm
Parent County: Choctaw Cession of 1832
Comments/research tips: Probate Judge has a few Birth records 1888–1918.

Record Type	Year Begun	Jurisdiction
Birth	1888	Dept./Health
Marriage	1833	Probate Judge
Death	1881	Dept./Health
Land	1825	Probate Judge
Probate	1828	Probate Judge
Court	1876	Clerk/Circuit Ct.

■ Talladega 18 Dec. 1832
P.O. Box 755, Talladega, AL 35160
Phone: (256)362-4175
Web site: www.rootsweb.com/~altallad/
Parent County: Creek Cession of 1832
Comments/research tips: Chancery Court has Divorce records 1888–1892.

Record Type	Year Begun	Jurisdiction
Birth	1897	Dept./Health
Marriage	1834	Probate Court
Death	1897	Dept./Health
Land	1833	Probate Court
Probate	1833	Probate Court
Court	1833	Clerk/Circuit Ct.
Military	1930	Probate Court

■ Tallapoosa 18 Dec. 1832
125 N. Broadnax St., Dadeville, AL 36853
Phone: (256)825-4266
Web site: www.rootsweb.com/~altallap/
Parent County: Creek Cession of 1832
Comments/research tips: 90 acres were swapped between Tallapoosa and Coosa Counties in 1963. Probate Judge has a few Birth and Death records 1881–1991.

Record Type	Year Begun	Jurisdiction
Marriage	1834	Probate Judge
Land	1832	Probate Judge
Probate	1838	Probate Judge
Court	1835	Clerk/Circuit Ct.

■ Tuscaloosa 6 Feb. 1818
714 Greensboro Ave., Tuscaloosa, AL 35401
Phone: (205)349-3870
Web site: www.tuscco.com/
Parent County: Cherokee & Choctaw Cession 1816

Record Type	Year Begun	Jurisdiction
Birth	1880	Dept./Health

Record Type	Year Begun	Jurisdiction
Marriage	1823	Probate Judge
Death	1880	Dept./Health
Land	1823	Probate Judge
Probate	1821	Probate Judge

■ Walker 26 Dec. 1823
P.O. Box 1447, Jasper, AL 35502
Phone: (205)384-3404
Web site: www.walkercounty.com/
Parent County: Tuscaloosa, Blount, Jefferson
Comments/research tips: All court records burned in 1877.

Record Type	Year Begun	Jurisdiction
Marriage	1877	Probate Judge
Death	1890	Dept./Health
Land	1877	Probate Judge
Probate	1877	Probate Judge
Court	1877	Clerk/Circuit Ct.

■ Washington 4 June 1800
P.O. Box 549, Chatom, AL 36518
Phone: (334)847-2208
Web site: members.aol.com/JORDANJM2/washingtn.html
Parent County: Mississippi Territory

Record Type	Year Begun	Jurisdiction
Birth	1908	Probate Judge
Marriage	1802	Probate Judge
Death	1908	Probate Judge
Land	1786	Probate Judge
Probate	1820	Probate Judge
Military	1919	Probate Judge

■ Wilcox 13 Dec. 1819
12 Water St., P.O. Box 488, Camden, AL 36726
Phone: (334)682-4883
Web site: www.prairiebluff.com/algenweb/wilcox
Parent County: Monroe, Dallas

Record Type	Year Begun	Jurisdiction
Birth	1905	Dept./Health
Marriage	1820	Probate Judge
Death	1905	Dept./Health
Land	1820	Probate Judge
Probate	1820	Probate Judge

■ Winston 12 Feb. 1850
P.O. Box 27, Double Springs, AL 35553
Phone: (205)489-5219
Web site: www.rootsweb.com/~alwinsto/
Parent County: Walker
Comments/research tips: Formerly Hancock County. Name changed to Winston 22 January 1858. Probate records lost in 1891 courthouse fire.

Record Type	Year Begun	Jurisdiction
Marriage	1891	Probate Judge
Divorce	na	Clerk/Circuit Ct.
Land	1891	Probate Judge
Probate	1891	Probate Judge
Court	1892	Clerk/Circuit Ct.

Alaska

By David A. Fryxell

HISTORICAL OVERVIEW

Although Alaska didn't become part of the United States until 1959, joining as the forty-ninth state, it was home to the very first Americans. Asians from Siberia crossed a land bridge spanning the Bering Strait between 21,000 and 42,000 years ago. Those who stayed rather than fanning out across the continent became the precursors of Alaska's native peoples—the Athabascans, Haida, Tlingit, and Inuit (often called "Eskimos"). If you have Native American roots in Alaska, records of these tribes from modern times include a collection of *Genealogical Records of Barrow Eskimo Families* and Juneau Area Agency records (1905–1964), both on microfilm at the Family History Library (FHL), and the Oregon Province Archives of the Society of Jesus Alaska Mission Collection (1853–1960) at Gonzaga University in Spokane, WA, also on FHL microfilm.

The first Europeans came to Alaska from Russia when Vitus Bering's expedition discovered it in 1741, and sea-otter hunters arrived soon after. The Russian Orthodox church came to Kodiak, Alaska, in 1795, and remained dominant until the twentieth century. Archives for the Diocese of Alaska were given to the Library of Congress in 1927; translated and microfilmed, these are available through the FHL.

Although the U.S. purchase of Alaska from Russia for $7.2 million in 1867 became known as "Seward's Folly," the Russians—strapped for cash after the Crimean War—knew the area was rich not only in furs but in gold, already found in 1861 near Telegraph Creek. A series of subsequent gold strikes sparked the Alaska Gold Rush, which brought 50,000 fortune-seekers between 1897 and 1920. Gold miners founded Nome in 1899 and Fairbanks in 1902. After a period under the jurisdiction of the War Department (1867–1877) and the Treasury Department

ALASKA AT A GLANCE

Motto: North to the Future
Population: 626,932
Prevalent Religions: Christianity, particularly Baptist and Episcopalian, Roman Catholic, Methodist, Lutheran, Presbyterian, and nondenominational, also Buddhism and Bahá'í
Major Industries: Petroleum and natural gas, gold and other mining, food processing, lumber and wood products, tourism, seafood, nursery stock, dairy products, vegetables, livestock
Ethnic Makeup (in percent): Caucasian 69.3%, African American 3.5%, Hispanic 4.1%, Asian 4.0%, Native Alaskan 15.6 %, Other 1.6%
Famous Alaskans: Clarence L. Andrews, Aleksandr Baranov, Margaret Elizabeth Bell, Benny Benson, Vitus Bering, Susan Butcher, William A. Egan, Carl Ben Eielson, Henry E. Gruennig, B. Frank Heintzleman, Walter J. Hickel, Sheldon Jackson, Joe Juneau, Sydney Lawrence, Ray Mala, Tommy Moe, Virgil F. Partch

Above: Anchorage amidst snow-capped peaks

(1877–1884), Alaska was made a U.S. District in 1884 and finally a territory in 1912.

World War II brought a fresh wave of "immigration" to Alaska with the 140,000 U.S. military stationed there, some of whom stayed after the war. Not long after statehood, Alaska's "black gold" rush began with oil at Prudhoe Bay in 1968. Even so, the largest state geographically remains the least densely populated.

RECORD HIGHLIGHTS

Unlike most states, Alaska has no counties; fourteen "municipalities" and "boroughs" and thirteen native corporations were formed post-statehood. Census takers from 1880 to 1900 created enumeration districts, and enumerators in 1910 used the four federal judicial districts. The 1870 census skipped newly acquired Alaska, and the 1880 and 1890 censuses have been lost. Various pre-territory local censuses are indexed in *Alaskan Census Records, 1870–1907*, edited by Ronald Vern Jackson and Gary Ronald Teeples (Bountiful, Utah: Accelerated Indexing Systems, ca. 1976). There are also 1870 and 1880 territorial censuses for Sitka. Federal census coverage begins with 1900.

Although Alaska didn't begin the official recording of births, marriages, and deaths until 1913, churches previously kept such records. The Bureau of Vital Statistics has microfilmed these church records and created delayed birth certificates. Note that in the absence of counties, vital records are kept almost entirely on the state level.

Until statehood created the superior court, probate records were kept at the district courts in Juneau and Ketchikan (First District), Nome (Second District), Anchorage (Third District), and Fairbanks (Fourth District). These records are now at the state archives, as are many territorial court records.

Land records can offer clues to your Alaska ancestors. These are mostly kept by the Bureau of Land Management in Washington, D.C., and the National Archives/Pacific-Alaska Region in Anchorage. Mining claims can be found at the Department of Natural Resources in Fairbanks. You can also search for Gold Rush ancestors in the state archives' collection of records from the Pioneers' Homes, state institutions established in Sitka, Anchorage, Juneau, Fairbanks, Ketchikan, and Palmer.

Cemetery records can be hard to find for Alaska, given the remoteness of many of their locations. The Sitka National Cemetery has been indexed, however, as has the Clay Street and Birch Hill Cemetery in Fairbanks, which is online at Ancestry.com. The FHL has microfilm on remote Alaska cemeteries and those on the Kenai Peninsula.

Professional researcher Connie Malcolm Bradbury, coauthor with David Albert Hales of *Alaska Sources: A Guide to Historical Records and Information Resources* (North Salt Lake, Utah: HeritageQuest, 2001), emphasizes the importance of first understanding the state's history and vast geography. Second, if you're seeking a lost relative from the gold rush period, she says, know the dates of the various strikes—and remember that the Klondike is in Canada, not Alaska. "The Klondike Stampede started in Alaska only because that is where the people disembarked from the ships bringing them north. Their destination was the Dawson, Yukon Territory, Canada area. As gold was prospected for on the creeks, some of the creeks extended to and from Alaska and the miners followed the creeks."

Whatever you're after in Alaska records, Bradbury says, you need to know exactly what you're looking for and determine where the record or material is located. The National Archives branch in Anchorage has a large collection of records generated by the federal government since statehood. Prior to statehood, the collections are divided between it and the state library and archives. "The Alaska State Library History Department has a wonderful collection," Bradbury adds. "They have good coverage of southeast Alaska but also have collections that are statewide or cover other areas. They have a Web site <www.library.state.ak.us/hist/hist.html> that will be helpful to researchers. The Alaska State Archives is a marvelous repository of records generated by the state government. The University of Alaska in both Anchorage and Fairbanks has archives. The Alaska and Polar Regions Department, Elmer E. Rasmusun Library, University of Alaska Fairbanks has the largest manuscript collection in the state, an excellent rare book collection, and a large Alaskana Collection of books. They also have an excellent Web site <www.uaf.edu/library> that researchers should visit before they plan to travel for research purposes. At that Web site they will find a link to the Alaska and Polar Periodical Index, which is an index to periodicals containing articles about Alaska and Alaskans. This would be a good place to start *before* doing anything else."

STATE RESOURCES

■ ARCHIVES, LIBRARIES, AND SOCIETIES

Alaska Historical Society
P.O. Box 100299, Anchorage, AK 99510-0299
Tel: (907) 276-1596
E-mail: ahs@alaska.net
Web site: <www.alaskahistorical society.org>

Alaska Moravian Church; Anchorage Morvian Church
8008 Bearberry St., Anchorage, AK 99502
Tel: (907) 243-3837

Alaska State Library and Historical Collections
P.O. Box 110571 or 333 Willoughby Ave., 8th Floor, Juneau, AK 99811-0571
Tel: (907) 465-2910
E-mail: asl@eed.state.ak.us
Web site: <wwww.library.state .ak.us>

Anchorage Genealogical Society
P.O. Box 242294, Anchorage, AK 99524-2294
E-mail: ags@ak.net

Web site: <www.rootsweb.com/ ~akags/>

Anchorage Museum of History and Art
121 W. Seventh Ave., Anchorage, AK 99501
Tel: (907) 343-4326
Web site: <www.anchoragemuse um.org>

Anchorage Superior Courts
825 W. Fourth Ave., Anchorage, AK 99501-2004
Web site: <www.state.ak.us/cou rts/home.htm>

Archdiocese of Fairbanks, Catholic Bishop of Northern Alaska
1316 Peger Rd., Fairbanks, AK 99709-5199
Tel: (907) 374-9500
E-mail: info@cbna.org
Web site: <www.cbna.info>

Bethel Moravian Church
P.O. Box 312, Bethel, AK 99559
Tel: (907) 543-3174
Web site: <www.alaskamoravian .org>

Department of Health and Social Services
Bureau of Vital Statistics, 5441 Commercial Blvd., Juneau, AK 99801
Web site: <http://health.hss.sta te.ak.us/dph/bvs/default.htm>

Eagle Historical Society and Museum
P.O. Box 23, Eagle, AK 99738
Tel/Fax: (907) 547-2325
E-mail: ehsmus@aptalaska.net
Web site: <www.eagleak.org>

Elmer E. Rasmuson Library
310 Tanana Dr., University of Alaska Fairbanks, USA 99775-6800
Tel: (907) 474-7481
Web site: <www.uaf.edu/library/>

Fairbanks Genealogical Society
P.O. Box 60534, Fairbanks, AK 99706-0534
E-mail: bradbury@ptialaska.net
Web site: <www.ptialaska.net/ ~fgs/index.htm>

Gastineau Genealogical Society
3270 Nowell Ave., Juneau, AK 99801-1934
Tel: (907) 586-3695
E-mail: ggs@alaska.com
Web site: <http://home.gci.net/

~westjuneau/ggs/ggshome .htm>

Genealogical Society of Southeastern Alaska
P.O. Box 6313, Ketchikan, AK 99901

Kenai Totem Tracers
% Kenai Community Library, 163 Main St. Loop, Kenai, AK 99611
E-mail: totemtracers@hotmail .com
Web site: <www.kenailibrary. org/totem_tracers.htm>

National Archives, Alaska Facility
654 W. Third Ave., Anchorage, AK 99501-2145
Tel: (907) 271-2441
E-mail: alaska.archives@nara .gov
Web site: <www.archives.gov/fa cilities/ak/anchorage.html>

Palmer Historical Society
P.O. Box 1925, Palmer, AK 99645
Tel: (907) 745-3703
Web site: <www.customcpu. com/ait/david/psociety.htm>

Roman Catholic Archdiocese of Anchorage
225 Cordova St., Anchorage, AK 99501
Tel: (907) 297-7700
E-mail: archdiocesegeneraldelive ry@caa-ak.org
Web site: <www.archdioceseofan chorage.org>

Roman Catholic Diocese of Juneau
415 Sixth St., Suite 300, Juneau, AK 99801-1091
Tel: (907) 586-2227
E-mail: junodio@gci.net
Web site: <www.dioceseofjuneau .org>

St. Herman's Theological Seminary, Russian Orthodox Church
414 Mission Rd., Kodiak, AK 99615-6329
Tel: (907) 486-3524
E-mail: stherman@gci.net
Web site: <http://alaskanchurch .org/shs/html/home/html>

Sisters of Providence Archives
4800 Thirty-seventh Ave. SW, Seattle, WA 98126-2793
Tel: (206) 937-4600
E-mail: archives@providence.org
Web site: <www.providence.org/ phs/archives/default.htm>

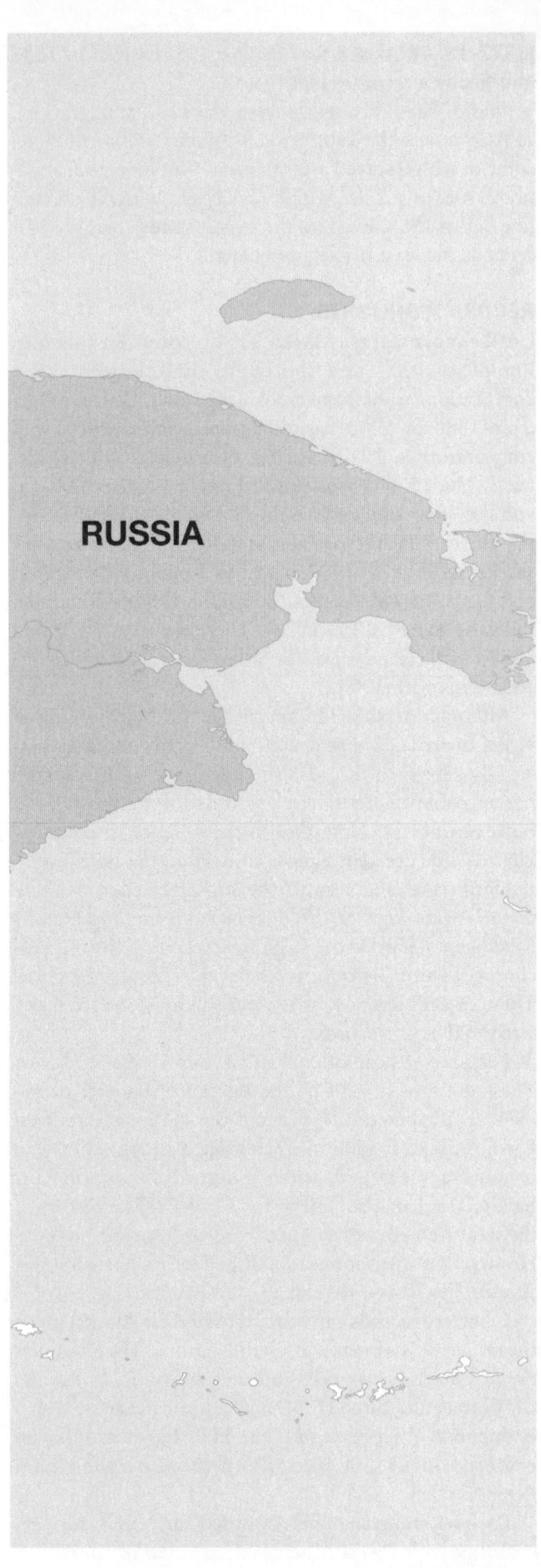

RUSSIA

Barrow

NORTH SLOPE   NORTH SLOPE

KOBUK

KOBUK

YUKON-KOYUKUK

USA

NORTH STAR
Fairbanks
FAIRBANKS

NOME

Nome

ALASKA

SOUTHEAST
FAIRBANKS

WADE
HAMPTON

MATANUSKA
SUSITNA

VALDEZ
CORDOVA

BETHEL

Anchorage
ANCHORAGE

Palmer

Valdez

Bethel

KENAI
Seward

BETHEL

Homer

DILLINGHAM

BRISTOL BAY
KODIAK

Kodiak

KODIAK

ALEUTIAN ISLANDS

Unalaska

Whitehorse

HAINES
SKAGAWAY-YAKUTAT-ANGOON
JUNEAU
Juneau

BRI
COL

Sitka
SITKA

Petersburg

WRANGELL-PETERSBURG

KETCHIKAN GATEWAY

PRINCE OF WALES-
OUTER KETCHIKAN

Alaska

Sitka National Cemetery
803 Sawmill Creek Rd., Sitka, AK 99835
For information, contact Fort Richardson National Cemetery at (907) 384-7075.

State of Alaska Archives and Records Management
141 Willoughby Ave., Juneau, AK 99801
Tel: (907) 465-2270
Email: archives@eed.state.ak.us
Web site: <www.archives.state .ak.us>

U.S. District Court, Anchorage Office
222 W. Seventh Ave., Rm. 229, Anchorage, AK 99513
Tel: (866) 243-3814
Web site: <www.akd.uscourts .gov/default.htm>

U.S. District Court, Fairbanks Office
101 Twelfth Ave., Rm. 332, Fairbanks, AK 99701
Tel: (866) 243-3813
Web site: <www.akd.uscourts .gov/default.htm>

U.S. District Court, Juneau Office
P.O. Box 020349, Juneau, AK 99802
Tel: (866) 243-3812
Web site: <www.akd.uscourts .gov/default.htm>

U.S. District Court, Nome Office
P.O. Box 130, Nome, AK 99762
Tel: (907) 443-5216
Web site: <www.akd.uscourts. gov/default.htm>

Wrangell Genealogical Society
P.O. Box 928EP, Wrangell, AK 99929

BIBLIOGRAPHY

■ GENERAL RESOURCES

Alaska, 1741–1953
by Clarence Charles Hulley (Portland, OR: Binfords & Mort, 1953)

Alaska, a Bicentennial History
by William R. Hunt (New York: Norton, 1976)

The Alaska Gold Rush
by David Wharton (Bloomington, IN: Indiana University Press, 1972)

The Alaska Handbook
by R.K. Woerner (Jefferson, NC: McFarland, 1986)

Alaska, a History of the 49th State, 2d ed.
by Claus-M. Naske and Herman E. Slotnick (Norman, OK: University of Oklahoma Press, 1987)

Alaska and Its History
compiled and edited by Morgan B. Sherwood (Seattle, WA: University of Washington Press, 1967)

The Alaska Newspaper Tree
by William R. Galbraith (Fairbanks: Elmer Rasmuson Library, 1975)

Alaska: Research Outline.
compiled by the Church of Jesus Christ of Latter-day Saints, Family History Library (Salt Lake City, UT: Corp. of the President of the Church of Jesus Christ of L.D.S., 1988)

Alaska Sources: A Guide to Historical Records and Information Sources
by Connie Malcolm Bradbury and David Albert Hales (North Salt Lake, UT: Heritage Quest, 2001)

Alaska Women's Oral History Collection: Catalogue with Subject Index
compiled by Maria Brooks (Anchorage, AK: Learning Resources Center at Anchorage Community College, 1983)

The Alaska-Yukon Gold Book; A Roster of the Progressive Men and Women who were the Argonauts of the Klondike Gold Stampede and those who are Identified with the Pioneer Days and Subsequent Development of Alaska and the Yukon Territory
(Seattle, WA: Sourdough Stampede Association, Inc., 1930)

Alaskan Census Records, 1870–1907
edited by Roland Vern Jackson and Gary Roland Teeples (Bountiful, UT: Accelerated Indexing Systems, 1976)

Alaskan Maps: A Cartobibliography of Alaska to 1900
by Marvin W. Falk (New York: Garland Pub., 1983)

The Alaskan Russian Church Archives: Records of the Russian Orthodox Greek Catholic Church of North America—Diocese of Alaska.
by Antoinette Shalkop (Washington, District of Columbia: Manuscript Division, Library of Congress, 1984)

RESEARCH TIPS

for more info

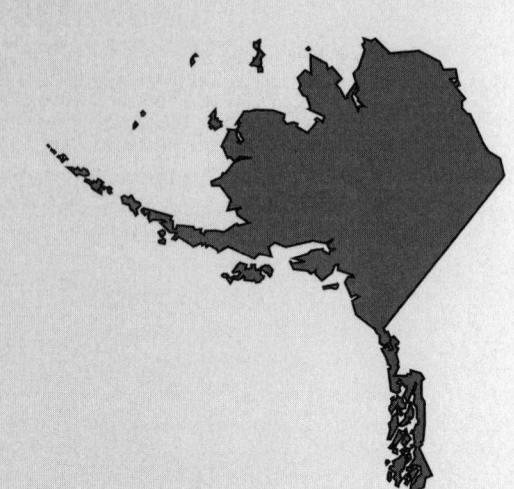

- It's crucial to understand the state's history and vast geography.
- Know the dates of the various gold rushes.
- The National Archives branch in Anchorage has a large collection of records generated by the federal government since statehood (1959). Prior to statehood, the collections are divided between it and the state library and archives.
- Visit The Alaska and Polar Regions Department, Elmer E. Rasmusun Library, University of Fairbanks, Alaska, <www.uaf.edu/library> when beginning your research. The site links to the Alaska and Polar Periodical Index, which is an index to periodicals containing articles about Alaska and Alaskans.
- www.kindredtrails.com/alaska.html

Census Records
- Federal Census 1900, 1910, 1920, 1930
- Territorial Census: Sitka, AK, 1870, 1880, 1881

Bibliography of Books on Alaska Published Before 1868
by Valerian Lada-Mocarski (New Haven, CT: Yale University Press, 1969)

Biographies of Alaska-Yukon Pioneers, 1850–1950
compiled and edited by Ed Ferrell (Bowie, MD: Heritage Books, 1994–2000)

The Dictionary Catalog of the Pacific Northwest Collection of the University of Washington Libraries, Seattle
from the University of Washington Libraries (Boston: G.K. Hall, 1972)

Documenting Alaskan History: Guide to Federal Archives Relating to Alaska
by George S. Ulibarri (Fairbanks, AK: University of Alaska Press, 1982)

The Founding of Juneau
by R.N. DeArmound (Juneau, AK: Gastineau Channel Centennial Association, 1967)

The Genealogist's Companion and Sourcebook, 2d ed.
by Emily Anne Croom (Cincinnati: Betterway Books, 2003)

A Genealogist's Guide to Discovering Your African-American Ancestors
by Franklin Carter Smith and Emily Anne Croom (Cincinnati: Betterway Books, 2003)

Guide to Genealogical Research in the National Archives of the United States
edited by Anne Bruner Eales and Robert M. Kvasnicka (Washington, D.C.: National Archives and Records Administration, 2000

History of Alaska, 1730–1885
by Hubert Howe Bancroft (San Francisco: A.L. Bancroft & Company, 1886)

How to Find Your Gold Rush Relative: Sources on the Klondike and Alaska Gold Rushes (1896–1914)
compiled by R. Bruce Parham and the Alaska Gold Rush Centennial Task Force (Anchorage, AK: National Archives and Records Administration, Pacific Alaska Region, 1997)

An Index of Alaska Oral History Collections
compiled by the Program for the Preservation of Oral History and Traditions, Alaska and Polar Regions Department, University of Alaska, Fairbanks (Fairbanks, AK: The Program, 1986)

Melvin Ricks' Alaska Bibliography: An Introductory Guide to Alaskan Historical Literature
by Melvin Byron Ricks, edited by Stephen W. Haycox and Betty J. Haycox (Portland, OR: Published by Binford & Mort for the Alaska Historial Commission, 1977)

National Archives Microfilm Catalogs online:
<www.archives.gov/publica tions/genealogy_microfilm_ catalogs.html>

Russian America: A Biographical Dictionary
by Richard A. Pierce (Kingston, Ontario; Fairbanks, AK: Limestone Press, 1990)

■ **CENSUS RECORDS**

The American Census Handbook
by Thomas Jay Kemp (Wilmington, DE: Scholarly Resources, 2001)

The Census Book: A Genealogist's Guide to Federal Census Facts, Schedules, and Indexes
by William Dollarhide (Bountiful, UT: Heritage Quest, 2000)

Finding Answers in U.S. Census Records
by Loretto Dennis Szucs and Matthew Wright (Orem, UT: Ancestry Publishing, 2002)

Map Guide to the U.S. Federal Censuses, 1790–1920
William Thorndale and William Dollarhide (Baltimore, MD: Genealogical Publishing Co., 1987)

State Census Records
by Ann S. Lainhart (Baltimore, MD: Genealogical Publishing, 1992)

Your Guide to the Federal Census
by Kathleen W. Hinckley (Cincinnati: Betterway Books, 2002)

■ **IMMIGRATION RECORDS**

American Naturalization Records, 1790–1990: What They Are and How to Use Them
by John J. Newman (North Salt Lake, UT: HeritageQuest, 1998)

American Passenger Arrival Records
by Michael Tepper (Baltimore: Genealogical Publishing Co., 1993)

New Land, New Lives: Scandinavian Immigrants to the Pacific Northwest
by Janet Elaine Rasmussen (Northfield, MN: Norwegian-American Historical Association; Seattle, WA: University of Washington Press, 1993)

They Became Americans: Finding Naturalization Records and Ethnic Origins
by Loretto Dennis Szucs (Salt Lake City: Ancestry, Inc., 1998)

They Came in Ships: A Guide to Finding Your Immigrant Ancestor's Arrival Records, 2d ed.
by John P. Colletta (Salt Lake City: Ancestry, Inc., 1993)

■ **LAND RECORDS**

Alaska: Message from the President of the United States in Relation to the Transfer of Territory from Russia to the United States
From the Department of States (Washington, D.C.: G.P.O., 1868)

Land & Property Research in the United States
by Wade E. Hone (Salt Lake City: Ancestry, 1997)

Locating Your Roots: Discover Your Ancestors Using Land Records
by Patricia Law Hatcher (Cincinnati: Betterway Books, 2003)

Records of the Russian-American Company, 1802, 1817–1867
by Raymond H. Fisher and the United States National Archives and Records Service, General Services Administration (Washington, D.C.: The National Archives, 1971)

■ **MAPS**

Alaska Atlas and Gazetteer
DeLorme Mapping Company (Freeport, ME: DeLorme Mapping, 1992)

Alaska Place Names, 4th ed.
Alan Edward Schorr (Juneau, AK: Denali Press, 1991)

Alaska-Yukon Place Names
by James Wendell Phillips (Seattle, WA: University of Washington Press, 1973)

Dictionary of Alaska Place Names
by Donald J. Orth (Washington, D.C.: U.S. Government Printing Office, 1967)

Geographic Dictionary of Alaska, 2d ed.
by Marcus Baker, prepared by James McCormick (Washington, D.C.: Government Printing Office, 1906)

■ **MILITARY RECORDS**

American Forts, Yesterday and Today
by Bruce Grant, illustrated by Lorence F. Björklund (New York: Dutton, 1965)

Uncle, We Are Ready! Registering America's Men, 1917–1918: A Guide to Researching World War I Draft Registration Cards
by John J. Newman (North Salt Lake, UT: HeritageQuest, 2001)

U.S. Military Records: A Guide to Federal & State Sources, Colonial America to the Present
by James C. Neagles (Salt Lake City: Ancestry, Inc., 1994)

World War II: A Family Historian's Guide
by Debra Johnson Knox (Spartanburg, SC: MIE Publishing, 2003)

■ **PROBATE RECORDS**

District and Territorial Court System: Record Group Inventory
Alaska State Archives (Juneau, AK: State Archives, 1987)

■ **VITAL RECORDS**

Your Guide to Cemetery Research
by Sharon DeBartolo Carmack (Cincinnati: Betterway Books, 2002)

Alaska

Alaska

■ Aleutians East Borough 1987
P.O. Box 349, Sand Point, AK 99501
Phone: (907)383-5334
Web site: www.aleutianseast.org/
Comments/research tips: For Vital records write to the Department of Health and Social Services, Bureau of Vital Statistics, P.O. Box 110675, Juneau, AK 99811-0675.

■ Aleutians West Census Area N/A
Comments/research tips: This area has no form of county government. For Vital records, write to the Department of Health and Social Services, Bureau of Vital Statistics, P.O. Box 110675, Juneau, AK 99811-0675.

■ Bethel Census Area
P.O. Box 388, AK
Comments/research tips: This area has no form of county government. For Vital records, write to the Deptartment of Health and Social Services, Bureau of Vital Statistics, P.O. Box 110675, Juneau, AK 99811-0675.

■ Bristol Bay Borough 1962
P.O. Box 189, Naknek, AK 99633-0189
Phone: (907)246-4224
Web site: www.theborough.com/

■ Denali Borough 1990
P.O. Box 480, Healy, AK 99743-0480
Phone: (907)683-1330
E-mail: dbgovt@mtaonline.net
Web site: www.denaliborough.com

■ Dillingham Census Area
Phone: (907)842-5211
Comments/research tips: This area has no form of county government. For Vital records, write to the Department of Health and Social Services, Bureau of Vital Statistics, P.O. Box 110675, Juneau, AK 99811-0675.

■ Fairbanks North Star Borough 1964
809 Pioneer Rd., P.O. Box 71267, Fairbanks, AK 99707-1267
Phone: (907)459-1000
Web site: www.co.fairbanks.ak.us/

■ Haines Borough 1968
P.O. Box 1209, Haines, AK 99827
Phone: (907)766-2231
Web site: www.haines.ak.us/

■ Juneau, City and Borough 1963
155 S. Seward St., Juneau, AK 99801
Phone: (907)586-5278
Web site: www.juneau.org/

■ Kenai Peninsula Borough 1964
144 N. Binkley, Soldotna, AK 99669
Phone: (907)262-4441
Web site: www.borough.kenai.ak.us/

■ Ketchikan Gateway Borough 1963
344 Front St., Ketchikan, AK 99901
Phone: (907)228-6625
Web site: www.borough.ketchikan.ak.us/

■ Kodiak Island Borough 1963
710 Mill Bay Rd., Kodiak, AK 99615-6340
Phone: (907)486-9300
Web site: www.kib.co.kodiak.ak.us/

■ Lake and Peninsula Borough 1989
P.O. Box 495, King Salmon, AK 99613
Phone: (907)246-3421
Web site: www.lakeandpen.com

■ Matanuska-Susitna Borough 1964
350 E. Dahlia Ave, Palmer, AK 99645-1608
Phone: (907)745-4801
Web site: www.co.mat-su.ak.us/

■ Municipality of Anchorage 1975
3601 C St., Anchorage, AK 99501
Phone: (907)264-0514
Web site: www.ci.anchorage.ak.us./
Comments/research tips: City of Anchorage and Greater Anchorage Area Bureau unified into the Municipality of Anchorage in 1975.

■ Nome Census Area
Comments/research tips: This area has no form of county government. For Vital records, write to the Department of Health and Social Services, Bureau of Vital Statistics, P.O. Box 110675, Juneau, AK 99811-0675.

■ North Slope Borough 1972
P.O. Box 69, Barrow, AK 99723
Phone: (907)852-2611
Web site: www.co.north-slope.ak.us/

■ Northwest Arctic Borough 1986
P.O. Box 1110, Kotzebue, AK 99752-1110
Phone: (907)442-2500
Web site: www.nwabor.org

■ Prince of Wales-Outer Ketchika N/A
Comments/research tips: This area has no form of county government. For Vital records, write to the Department of Health and Social Services, Bureau of Vital Statistics, P.O. Box 110675, Juneau, AK 99811-0675.

■ Sitka Borough 1971
100 Lincoln St., Sitka, AK 99835
Phone: (907)747-3294
Web site: www.sitka.org

■ Skagway-Hoonah-Angoon Census Area
Comments/research tips: This area has no form of county government. For Vital records, write to the Department of Health and Social Services, Bureau of Vital Statistics, P.O. Box 110675, Juneau, AK 99811-0675.

■ Southeast Fairbanks Census Area N/A

Comments/research tips: This area has no form of county government. For Vital records, write to the Department of Health and Social Services, Bureau of Vital Statistics, P.O. Box 110675, Juneau, AK 99811-0675.

■ Valdez Cordova Census Area N/A

Comments/research tips: This area has no form of county government. For Vital records, write the Department of Health and Social Services, Bureau of Vital Statistics, P.O. Box 110675, Juneau, AK 99811-0675.

■ Wade Hampton Census Area N/A

Comments/research tips: This area has no form of county government. For Vital records, write to the Department of Health and Social Services, Bureau of Vital Statistics, P.O. Box 110675, Juneau, AK 99811-0675.

■ Wrangell-Petersburg Census Area N/A

Comments/research tips: This area has no form of county government. For Vital records, write to the Department of Health and Social Services, Bureau of Vital Statistics, P.O. Box 110675, Juneau, AK 99811-0675.

■ Yakutat Borough 1992

P.O. Box 160, Yukutat, AK 99689
Phone: (907)784-3323

■ Yukon-Koyukuk Census Area N/A

Comments/research tips: This area has no form of county government. For Vital records, write to the Department of Health and Social Services, Bureau of Vital Statistics, P.O. Box 110675, Juneau, AK 99811-0675.

Alaska

Arizona

By David A. Fryxell

HISTORICAL OVERVIEW

Francisco Vasquera de Coronado came to Arizona in 1540 in search of the "seven cities of gold." The Zuni Indians pointed him west, hoping to get the Spanish to leave their area that, after all, had already been inhabited by native people for some 12,000 years. Other tribes that called Arizona home over the centuries included the Cochise, Anasazi, Mogollon, Apache, Navajo, and Hopi. The Hopi village of Old Oraibi is the oldest continuously inhabited place in the United States, dating back more than a thousand years.

Though the Zuni didn't entirely detour the Spanish, Arizona was slower to be colonized than neighboring New Mexico. Tucson wasn't founded until 1775, and the settlements were concentrated in the southern part of the state when Arizona became part of Mexico (as a part of the state of Sonora) with independence in 1821. The Treaty of Guadalupe Hidalgo in 1848 ended the Mexican-American War and closed the long chapter of Spanish-Mexican rule north of the Gila River in Arizona. The rest of present-day Arizona was added to the U.S. with the Gadsden Purchase in 1853. The Arizona Territory was split off from the New Mexico Territory in 1863, but statehood didn't follow until 1912—the last of the contiguous United States.

Today's Arizona largely sprang up after World War II, as Americans flocked to the sun. Between 1950 and 1990 the population of Phoenix increased from 100,000 to 980,000. In 1960, the Del Webb Corporation. created Sun City, launching Arizona as a retirement haven.

RECORD HIGHLIGHTS

Because settlement was later and thinner, Arizona's records from the Spanish and Mexican periods aren't as rich as those of neighboring New Mexico. The state archives in Phoenix and the Arizona Historical Society in Tucson

ARIZONA AT A GLANCE

Motto: *Ditat Deus* (God enriches)
Population: 5 million
Prevalent Religions: Roman Catholic, Baptist, Methodist, and Church of Jesus Christ of Latter-day Saints
Major Industries: Manufacturing (electronic and aerospace machinery, electrical and transportation equipment), mining (predominately copper), tourism, agriculture (cotton, citrus fruits, vegetables), cattle ranching
Ethnic Makeup (in percent): Caucasian 75.5%, African American 3.1%, Hispanic 25.3%, Asian 1.8%, Native American 5.0%, Other 11.6%
Famous Arizonans: Linda Carter, César Chávez, Cochise, Alice Cooper, Barbara Eden, Geronimo, Barry Goldwater, Charlie Mingus, Stevie Nicks, Linda Ronstadt, Kerri Strug, Mare Winningham

Above: Rock formations in Monument Valley

do hold some documents from this era, such as the 1832 census of Santa Cruz County.

Territorial records begin with the 1860 census, in which Arizona was a county in the New Mexico Territory. A special census was taken in 1864 after the establishment of a separate Arizona Territory, with others in 1866, 1867, 1869, 1871, 1872, and 1882. (Note that what was called Pah-Ute County was included in the Arizona Territory until 1866; thereafter it was part of the new state of Nevada.) The new territory was included in the regular federal headcount beginning in 1870. Various "great registers" of voters, housed in the state archives, may also be used as census substitutes, generally covering 1882–1911.

Statewide birth and death records didn't begin until 1909, just before statehood. Because state law protects the privacy of birth records for seventy-five years and death records for fifty years, many of these records can be accessed only by family members with proof of relationship. Recently, however, Arizona unveiled a state-of-the-art Web site <genealogy.az.gov> that lets you search for birth certificates (1887–1928) and death certificates (1878–1953) and then view images of your results in PDF format.

The Office of Vital Records also maintains a sampling of delayed birth records (from 1855) and death records (from 1877) from other sources. Marriage and divorce records, as well as probate records and any surviving information on pre-1909 births and deaths, are maintained by the clerk of the superior court in the county where the event occurred.

Obituaries and cemetery records can help fill in blanks when there's no available death certificate. The state archives has a collection of cemetery records gathered by the Arizona Genealogical Society, as well as microfiche drawn from an index of obituaries covering 1865–1986.

Daniela Moneta, MLS, genealogy librarian for the Arizona State Archives, cautions researchers to remember that although Arizona is a large state, it's divided into just fifteen counties. (Originally, only *four* counties were created: Yavapai, Mohave, Yuma and Puma.) Several Rhode Islands would fit into one of Arizona's counties. This makes travel from one county to the next time-consuming, especially if you want to visit historical societies and county courthouses.

You'll find a wealth of records post-1863, Moneta adds, but not much for the pre-territory years when Arizona was on the frontier and not as heavily populated as its neighbors. There are, however, several published indexes to Mexican censuses for the area that is now Arizona: 1801 for Pimeria Alta; 1831 for Tucson, Tubac, and Santa Cruz; and 1852 for Pimeria Alta. Remember

RESEARCH TIPS

for more info

- Although Arizona is a large state, it's divided into just 15 counties.
- There are several published indexes to Mexican censuses for the area that is now Arizona: 1801 for Pimeria Alta; 1831 for Tucson, Tubac, and Santa Cruz; and 1852 for Pimeria Alta.
- Remember to check repositories for Arizona, New Mexico, and Mexico for those early years.
- A good place to begin is the Arizona State Library, Archives, and Public Record's Web site <www.lib .az.us>.
- An upcoming book will make things easier for researchers in southern Arizona: The Arizona State Genealogical Society is publishing *Arizona Genealogical and Historical Research Guide: Early to Present Sources for Pima County* in 2005.

Census Records
- Federal Census: 1860, 1870, 1880, 1900, 1910, 1920
- Federal Mortality Schedules: 1870, 1880
- Territorial Census: 1864, 1866, 1867, 1869, 1871, 1872, 1882

to check repositories for Arizona, New Mexico, and Mexico for those early years.

For statewide information post-1863, Barbara B. Sayler, a professional genealogist and past president of the Arizona State Genealogical Society, says the state archives is the place to start. The collection includes records of marriage, civil and criminal cases, probates, insanity, inquests, wills and estates, naturalization, census, assessor rolls, the Great Register (voters), and real-estate deeds. You'll find an obituary index, a cemetery index, city directories, school yearbooks, maps and a 15,000-volume genealogy collection. The state library has the best collection of Arizona newspapers on microfilm, going back to 1864.

To see holdings, go to <www.lib.az.us> and look under "Collections" for the Arizona Newspaper Project.

You can also try some unusual sources for clues to your Arizona ancestors. Moneta mentions the archives' collection of more than two hundred pioneer certificate applications, containing histories of families in Arizona before statehood. If your ancestors were ranchers, try the archives' library of cattle-brand books, in which families registered their unique marks.

Arizona researchers are also fortunate in having access to the second-largest Family History Library outside Salt Lake City, the Mesa Regional Family History Library at 41 S. Hobson in Mesa, (480) 964-1200, <www.mesarfhc .org/resources.htm>.

And a new book will make things easier for researchers in southern Arizona: The Arizona State Genealogical Society is publishing *Arizona Genealogical and Historical Research Guide: Early to Present Sources for Pima County* in 2005.

Besides the state genealogical society, Sayler advises researchers to contact the genealogical or historical societies for the specific area you're investigating. The Arizona Genealogical Advisory Board lists societies and professional researchers on its Web site, <www.azgab.org>. For specific county information, Sayler adds, contact the societies and courthouses in that county, along with the libraries and special collections at the three state universities. Northern Arizona University in particular also holds a wealth of visual history of the state and region; its online Image Database <www.nau.edu/cline/speccoll/image db.html> features 700,000-plus images.

STATE RESOURCES

■ ARCHIVES, LIBRARIES, AND SOCIETIES

Arizona Chapter of the Association of Professional Genealogists
14623 N. Forty-ninth Pl., Scottsdale, AZ 85254-2207
Web site: <www.rootsweb.com/ ~azapg/>

Arizona Historical Foundation
Hayden Library, Arizona State University, Box 871006, Tempe, AZ 85287-1006
Tel: (480) 966-8331
E-mail: azhistoryinfo@arizonahist oricalfoundation.org
Web site: <www.users.qwest. net/~azhistoricalfdn/>

Arizona Historical Society
949 E. Second St., Tuscon, AZ 85719
Tel: (520) 628-5774

Web site: <www.arizonahistorical society.org>

Arizona Jewish Historical Society
4710 N. Sixteenth St., Suite 201, Phoenix, AZ 85016
Tel: (602) 241-7870
E-mail: azjhs@aol.com
Web site: <www.azjhs.org>

Arizona State Library, Archives, and Public Records
1700 W. Washington, Suite 200, Phoenix, AZ 85007
Tel: (602) 542-4035
E-mail: services@lib.az.us
Web site: <www.dlapr.lib.az.us/>

Arizona Sun Chapter, American Historical Society of Germans from Russia (AHSGR)
2002 W. Sunnyside Drive #3105, Phoenix, AZ 85029
Tel: (602) 944-1684
E-mail: hildewas@msn.com
Web site: <www.ahsgr.org/arizo na_sun_chapter.htm>

Black Family Historical Society
P.O. Box 1515, Gilbert, AZ 85299-1515

Central Arizona Division, Arizona Historical Society
1300 N. College Ave., Tempe, AZ 85281-1211
Web site: <www.azcama.com/ museums/az_hist_society.htm>

Cochise Genealogical Society, Douglas-Williams House
1001 Ave. D, Douglas, AZ 85608
Tel: (520) 364-7370
Web site: <www.mycochise. com/gene.php>

Czech and Slovak Genealogical Society of Arizona
4921 E. Exeter Blvd., Phoenix, AZ 85018-2942
E-mail: djanca@worldnet.att.net
Web site: <www.rootsweb.com/ ~azcsgsa/>

Family History Society of Arizona
P.O. Box 63094, Phoenix, AZ 85082-3094
Web site: <www.fhsa.org>

Genealogical Workshop of Mesa
P.O. Box 6052, Mesa, AZ 85216
Web site: <http://members.cox .net/gwom>

Genealogy Society of Pinal County, Arizona, Inc.
1107 E. Tenth St., Casa Grande, AZ 85222

Green Valley Genealogical Society
P.O. Box 1009, Green Valley, AZ 85622
Web site: <www.rootsweb.com/ ~azgvgs/>

Jerome Historical Society
Tel: (928) 634-7349
E-mail: jeromearchives@earthlink .net
Web site: <www.jeromehistorical society.org>

Jewish Historical Society of Southern Arizona
P.O. Box 57482, Tuscon, AZ 85732-7482
Tel: (520) 882-6648
E-mail: ajfmaz@mindspring.com

Lake Havasu Genealogical Society, Inc./LHGS Library
P.O. Box 953 or 2126 N. McCulloch Blvd., Lake Havasu City, AZ 86405-0953

Tel: (928) 854-5447
E-mail: gloharr@rraz.net
Web site: <www.rootsweb.com/ ~azlhgs/>

M.H.E. Heritage Library
Circle-M Farm-Ranch, Rt. 1, Box 60-H, McNeal, AZ 85617

Mesa Genealogical Society
P.O. Box 6052, Mesa, AZ 85216

Mohave Genealogical Society/ Mohave Museum of History and Arts
400 West Beale St., Kingman, AZ 86401
Tel: (928) 753-3195
E-mail: mocohist@citilink.net
Web site: <www.ctaz.com/~moc ohist/museum/geneal.htm>

Mohave Valley Genealogical Society
P.O. Box 6045, Mohave Valley, AZ 86440

National Archives and Record Administration, Pacific Region (California)
24000 Avila Rd., 1st Fl., East Entrance, Laguna Niguel, CA 92677-3497
Tel: (949) 360-2641
E-mail: randy.thompson@nara .gov
Web site: <www.archives.gov/fa cilities/ca/laguna_niguel.html>

Navajo County Genealogical Society
P.O. Box 1403, Winslow, AZ 86047

Northern Arizona Genealogical Society
P.O. Box 695, Prescott, AZ 86302
Web site: <www.rootsweb.com/ ~aznags/>

Northern Gila County Genealogical Society/Library
302 E. Bonita, Payson, AZ 85541-5012
Tel: (928) 474-2139
Web site: <http://user.rootsweb .com/~azngcgs/index.html>

Oracle Historical Society/ Arcadia Ranch Museum
P.O. Box 10/Museum or 825 Mt. Lemmon Rd., Oracle, AZ 85623
Web site: <www.oraclehistorical society.org>

Phoenix Genealogical Society
P.O. Box 38703, Phoenix, AZ 85069-8703

Arizona

Tel: (602) 943-1408
E-mail: cactusBL2@cox.net
Web site: <http://phxgensoc
.org>

**Prescott Historical Museum/
Sharlot Hall Museum**
415 W. Gurley St., Prescott, AZ
86301
Tel: (928) 445-3122
Web site: <www.sharlot.org/
index.shtml>

**Rio Colorado Division, Arizona
Historical Society**
240 Madison Ave., Yuma, AZ
85364
Tel: (928) 782-1841
E-mail: azhistyuma@cybertrails
.com
Web site:
**Roman Catholic Diocese of
Phoenix**
400 E. Monroe St., Phoenix, AZ
85004-2336
Tel: (602) 257-0030
E-mail: communications@diocese
phoenix
.org
Web site: <www.diocesephoenix.
org>

**Roman Catholic Diocese of
Tucson, Bishop Moreno
Pastoral Center**
111 S. Church Ave., P.O. Box 31,
Tuscon, AZ 85702
Tel: (520) 792-3410
E-mail: diocese@diocesetucson
.org
Web site: <www.diocesetucson
.org>

Sedona Genealogy Club
P.O. Box 4258, Sedona, AZ
86340
Web site: <http://fp.sedona.
net/genealogy/>

**Sierra Vista Genealogical
Society**
P.O. Box 1084, Sierra Vista, AZ
85636-1084
Web site: <www.rootsweb.com/
~azsvgs/>

Tempe Historical Society
809 E. Southern Ave., Tempe, AZ
85282
Tel: (480) 350-5141
Web site: <www.tempe.gov/mus
eum/ahistsoc.htm>

Tri-State Genealogical Society
% Mohave Community College,
3400 Hwy. 95, Bullhead City, AZ
86442

Web site: <www.rootsweb.com/
~azcanvtsgs>

**University Library, University of
Arizona**
1510 E. University, Tuscon, AZ
85721-0055
Tel: (520) 621-2101
Web site: <www.library.arizona
.edu>

**West Valley Genealogical
Society**
First Presbyterian Church, Swain
Hall, 12225 N. 103rd Ave., Sun
City, AZ 85723
Mailing address: WVGS, 12222
N. 111th Ave.,
Youngstown, AZ 85363
Web site: <www.rootsweb.com/
~azwvgs/>

BIBLIOGRAPHY

■ GENERAL RESOURCES

*Arizona Gathering II,
1950–1969; an Annotated
Bibliography*
by Donald M. Powell (Tucson, AZ:
University of Arizona Press,
1973)

*Arizona, the History of the
Frontier State*
by Rufus Kay Wyllys (Phoenix,
AZ: Hobson & Herr, 1950)

Arizona: Research Outline
from the Church of Jesus Christ of
Latter-day Saints Family History
Library (Salt Lake City, UT: Corp.
of the President of the Church of
Jesus Christ of L.D.S., 1988)

*Directory of Churches and
Religious Organizations in
Arizona*
from the United States Works
Progress Administration (Phoenix, AZ: Arizona Statewide Archival and Records Project, 1940)

*Genealogical Guide to Arizona
and Nevada*
by Joyce V. Hawley Spiros (Gallup, NM: Verlene Pub., 1983)

*The Genealogist's Companion
and Sourcebook, 2d ed.*
by Emily Anne Croom (Cincinnati:
Betterway Books, 2003)

*A Genealogist's Guide to
Discovering Your African-
American Ancestors*
by Franklin Carter Smith and
Emily Anne Croom (Cincinnati:
Betterway Books, 2003)

*Guide to Genealogical
Research in the National
Archives of the United States*
edited by Anne Bruner Eales and
Robert M. Kvasnicka (Washing-
ton, D.C.: National Archives and
Records Administration, 2000

*History of Arizona, by Thomas
Edwin Farish, Arizona Historian,
8 vols.*
by Thomas Edwin Farish (San
Francisco: The Filmer Brothers
Electrotype Company,
1915–1918)

*Mormons and Their Neighbors:
An Index to Over 75,000
Biographical Sketches from
1820 to the Present, 2 vols.*
compiled by Marvin E. Wiggins
(Provo, UT: Harold B. Lee Library,
Brigham Young University, 1984)

*National Archives Microfilm
Catalogs online:*
<www.archives.gov/publica
tions/genealogy_microfilm_
catalogs.html>

*Newspapers and Periodicals of
Arizona, 1859–1911*
by Estelle Lutrell (Tucson, AZ:
University of Arizona, 1950)

*Official Directory Arizona
Historical Museums and
Related Support Organizations*
from the Arizona Historical Society (Tucson, AZ: Arizona Historical Society, 1994)

*Spanish & Mexican Records of
the American Southwest: A
Bibliographical Guide to
Archive and Manuscript
Sources*
by Henry Putney Beers (Tucson,
AZ: University of Arizona Press,
1979)

*Surname Index for the Arizona
Sentinel, 1875–1905*
from the Genealogial Society of
Yuma, Arizona, and Arizona Sentinel (Yuma, AZ: Genealogical. Society of Yuma, Arizona, 1997)

■ CENSUS RECORDS

*The American Census
Handbook*
by Thomas Jay Kemp (Wilmington, DE: Scholarly Resources,
2001)

*The Census Book: A
Genealogist's Guide to Federal
Census Facts, Schedules, and
Indexes*
by William Dollarhide (Bountiful,
UT: Heritage Quest, 2000)

*Finding Answers in U.S. Census
Records*
by Loretto Dennis Szucs and Matthew Wright (Orem, UT: Ancestry
Publishing, 2002)

*Map Guide to the U.S. Federal
Censuses, 1790–1920*
by William Thorndale and William
Dollarhide (Baltimore, MD: Genealogical Pub. Co., 1987)

State Census Records
by Ann S. Lainhart (Baltimore,
MD: Genealogical Publishing,
1992)

*Your Guide to the Federal
Census*
by Kathleen W. Hinckley (Cincinnati: Betterway Books, 2002)

■ IMMIGRATION
RECORDS

*American Naturalization
Records, 1790–1990: What
They Are and How to Use Them*
by John J. Newman (North Salt
Lake, UT: HeritageQuest, 1998)

*American Passenger Arrival
Records*
by Michael Tepper (Baltimore:
Genealogical Publishing Co.,
1993)

*They Became Americans:
Finding Naturalization Records
and Ethnic Origins*
by Loretto Dennis Szucs (Salt
Lake City: Ancestry, Inc., 1998)

*They Came in Ships: A Guide to
Finding Your Immigrant
Ancestor's Arrival Records, 2d
ed.*
by John P. Colletta (Salt Lake
City: Ancestry, Inc., 1993)

■ LAND RECORDS

*Locating Your Roots: Discover
Your Ancestors Using Land
Records*
by Patricia Law Hatcher (Cincinnati: Betterway Books, 2003)

*Miscellaneous Archives
Relating to New Mexico Land
Grants, 1695–1842*
from the United States Bureau of
Land Management (Albuquerque,

NM: University of New Mexico Library, 1955–1957)

Record of Private Land Claims Adjudicated by the U.S. Surveyor General, 1855–1890
from the New Mexico (Territory) Surveyor-General's Office (Albuquerque, NM: University of New Mexico Library, 1955–1957)

Records of Land Titles, 1847–1852
from the New Mexico (Territory) Secretary's Office (Albuquerque, NM: University of New Mexico Library, 1955–1957)

Spanish & Mexican Land Grants in New Mexico and Colorado
edited by John R. Van Ness and Christine M. Van Ness (Manhattan, KS: Sunflower University Press, 1980)

Vigil's Index, 1681–1846
by Donaciano Vigil (Albuquerque, NM: University of New Mexico Library, 1955–1957)

■ MAPS

Arizona Place Names
by Will Croft Barnes (Tucson, AZ: University of Arizona Press, 1988)

Arizona Territory: Post Offices and Postmasters
by John Theobald and Lillian Theobald (Phoenix, AZ: Arizona Historical Foundation, 1961)

Arizona's Names: X Marks the Place
by Byrd Howell Granger, illustrated by Connie Asch (Tucson, AZ: Falconer Pub., 1983)

Ghost Towns of Arizona
by James E. Sherman and Barbara H. Sherman, Don Percious, maps (Norman, OK: University of Oklahoma Press, 1969)

Historical Atlas of Arizona, 2d ed.
by Henry P. Walker and Don Bufkin (Norman, OK: University of Oklahoma Press, 1986)

A History of Arizona's Counties and Courthouses
edited by John J. Dreyfuss (Tuscon, AZ: National Society of the

Colonial Dames of America in the State of Arizona, 1972)

■ MILITARY RECORDS

Arizona Frontier Military Place Names, 1846–1912, rev. ed.
by David V. Alexander and Daniel C.B. Rathbun (Las Cruces, NM: Yucca Tree Press, 2002)

Arizona's Memorial to Vietnam Veterans
by Frances Arthur Hortsch (Phoenix, AZ: Phoenix Genealogical Society, 1987)

The Army in the West, A Guide to Microfilmed Records in the Library of the Arizona Pioneers' Historical Society
from the Arizona Pioneers' Historical Society (Tucson, AZ: W.C. Cox, 1974)

Chains of Command: Arizona and the Army, 1856–1875
by Constance Wynn Altschuler, Don Bufkin, maps (Tucson, AZ: Arizona Historical Society, 1981)

Frontier Military Posts of Arizona
by Ray Brandes (Globe, AZ: Dale Stuart King, 1960)

The Rough Riders: A Brief Study and Indexed Roster of the 1st Regiment, U.S. Volunteer Cavalry, 1898
by Howard Markland Gabbart with the United States Army Volunteer Cavalry Regiment, 1st (Tucson, AZ: Arizona State Genealogical Society, 1992)

The Transformation of Arizona into a Modern State: The Contribution of War to the Modernization Process
by Charles Ynfante (Lewiston, NY: Edwin Mellen Press, 2002)

Uncle, We Are Ready! Registering America's Men, 1917–1918: A Guide to Researching World War I Draft Registration Cards
by John J. Newman (North Salt Lake, UT: HeritageQuest, 2001)

U.S. Military Records: A Guide to Federal & State Sources, Colonial America to the Present
by James C. Neagles (Salt Lake City: Ancestry, Inc., 1994)

World War II: A Family Historian's Guide
by Debra Johnson Knox (Spartanburg, SC: MIE Publishing, 2003)

■ PROBATE RECORDS

A Guide to Arizona Courts
(Phoenix, AZ: Arizona Supreme Court, 1997)

■ VITAL RECORDS

Arizona Death Records: An Index Compiled from Mortuary, Cemetery, and Church Records, 3 vols.
(Tucson, AZ: Arizona State Genealogical Society, 1976–1982)

Northern Arizona Territorial Death and Burial Records, 1870–1910
by Dora M. Whiteside (Prescott, AZ: D.M. Whiteside)

Your Guide to Cemetery Research
by Sharon DeBartolo Carmack (Cincinnati: Betterway Books, 2002)

■ Apache 24 Feb. 1879
P.O. Box 365, St. Johns, AZ 85936
Phone: (928)337-4364
Web site: www.kindredtrails.com/AZ_Apache.html
Parent County: Yavapai

Record Type	Year Begun	Jurisdiction
Birth	1909	Dept./Health
Marriage	1879	Clerk/Superior Ct.
Death	1909	Dept./Health
Divorce	1879	Clerk/Superior Ct.
Land	1879	Clerk of Courts
Probate	1879	Clerk/Superior Ct.

■ Castle Dome 1860
Parent County: Original county
Comments/research tips: (See Yuma) Name changed to Yuma 8 November 1864.

■ Cochise 1 Feb. 1881
P.O. Box CK, Bisbee, AZ 85603
Phone: (520)432-9364
Web site: www.co.cochise.az.us/
Parent County: Pima

Record Type	Year Begun	Jurisdiction
Birth	1909	Dept./Health
Marriage	1881	Clerk/Superior Ct.
Death	1909	Dept./Health
Divorce	na	Clerk/Superior Ct.
Land	na	County Recorder
Probate	na	Clerk/Superior Ct.
Nat.	na	Clerk/Superior Ct.

■ Coconino 19 Feb. 1891
100 E. Birch Ave., Flagstaff, AZ 86001-4625
Phone: (928)779-6536
Web site: co.coconino.az.us/
Parent County: Yavapai

Record Type	Year Begun	Jurisdiction
Birth	1909	Dept./Health

Record Type	Year Begun	Jurisdiction
Marriage	1891	Clerk/Superior Ct.
Death	1909	Dept./Health
Divorce	1891	Clerk/Superior Ct.
Land	na	County Recorder
Probate	1891	Clerk/Superior Ct.
Court	1891	Clerk/Superior Ct.
Nat.	1891	Clerk/Superior Ct.

■ Ewell   1860
Parent County: Original county
Comments/research tips: (See Pima) Name changed to Pima 8 November 1864.

■ Gila   8 Feb. 1881
1400 E. Ash St., Globe, AZ 85501
Phone: (520)425-3231
Web site: www.rootsweb.com/~azgila/index.htm
Parent County: Maricopa, Pinal
Comments/research tips: District Court has Naturalization records 1894–1912. Clerk of the Superior Court has Probate records 1880–1953.

Record Type	Year Begun	Jurisdiction
Marriage	1881	Clerk/Superior Ct.
Divorce	1914	Clerk/Superior Ct.
Land	na	County Recorder
Birth	1909	Dept./Health
Death	1909	Dept./Health

■ Graham   10 Mar. 1881
800 Main St., Safford, AZ 85546
Phone: (529)428-3250
Web site: www.rootsweb.com/azgrahamcounty.htm
Parent County: Apache, Pima
Comments/research tips: Clerk of the Superior Court has Naturalization records 1903–1973.

Record Type	Year Begun	Jurisdiction
Birth	1909	Dept./Health
Marriage	1909	Dept./Health
Death	1909	Dept./Health
Divorce	1881	Clerk/Superior Ct.
Land	na	County Recorder
Probate	1881	Clerk/Superior Ct.
Nat.	1881	Clerk/Superior Ct.

■ Greenlee   10 Mar. 1909
Webster St., Clifton, AZ 85533
Phone: (928)865-3872
Web site: www.rootsweb.com/~azgreenl
Parent County: Graham

Record Type	Year Begun	Jurisdiction
Birth	1909	Dept./Health
Marriage	1911	Clerk/Superior Ct.
Death	1909	Dept./Health
Divorce	1911	Clerk/Superior Ct.
Land	1911	County Recorder
Probate	1911	Clerk/Superior Ct.

■ La Paz   1 Jan. 1983
1108 Joshua Ave., Parker, AZ 85344
Phone: (928)669-6115

Web site: www.co.la-paz.az.us/
Parent County: Yuma

Record Type	Year Begun	Jurisdiction
Birth	1909	Dept./Health
Marriage	na	Clerk/Superior Ct.
Death	1909	Dept./Health
Divorce	na	Clerk/Superior Ct.
Land	na	County Recorder
Probate	na	Clerk/Superior Ct.
Nat.	na	Clerk/Superior Ct.

■ Maricopa   14 Feb. 1871
201 W. Jefferson, Phoenix, AZ 85003
Phone: (602)506-3204
Web site: www.maricopa.gov/
Parent County: Pima, Yavapai, Yuma

Record Type	Year Begun	Jurisdiction
Birth	1909	Dept./Health
Marriage	1871	Clerk/Superior Ct.
Death	1909	Dept./Health
Divorce	1871	Clerk/Superior Ct.
Land	na	County Recorder
Probate	1916	Clerk/Superior Ct.
Nat.	1912	Clerk/Superior Ct.

■ Mohave   8 Nov. 1864
401 E. Spring St., Kingman, AZ 86401
Phone: (928)753-9141
Web site: www.co.mohave.az.us/
Parent County: Original county
Comments/research tips: Clerk of Superior Court has Marriage records 1919–1943 and Probate records that include an Estate Register 1913–1922, Minutes 1865–1915, Letters of Administration 1877–1921, and files of Guardianships 1885–1951.

Record Type	Year Begun	Jurisdiction
Birth	1909	Dept./Health
Death	1909	Dept./Health
Divorce	na	Clerk/Superior Ct.
Land	na	County Recorder
Nat.	na	Clerk/Superior Ct.

■ Navajo   21 Mar. 1895
P.O. Box 668, Holbrook, AZ 86025
Phone: (928)524-6161
Web site: www.co.navajo.az.us/
Parent County: Apache
Comments/research tips: Clerk of Superior Court has Marriage records 1895–1970.

Record Type	Year Begun	Jurisdiction
Birth	1909	Dept./Health
Death	1909	Dept./Health
Divorce	na	Clerk/Superior Ct.
Land	na	County Recorder
Probate	na	Clerk/Superior Ct.
Nat.	na	Clerk/Superior Ct.

■ Pima   8 Nov. 1864
130 W. Congress St., Tucson, AZ 85701
Phone: (520)740-8552

Arizona

Web site: www.co.pima.az.us/
Parent County: Original county
Comments/research tips: Clerk of Superior Court has Marriage records 1908–1921 and Probate records 1866–1909.

Record Type	Year Begun	Jurisdiction
Birth	1909	Dept./Health
Death	1909	Dept./Health
Divorce	na	Clerk/Superior Ct.
Land	1864	County Recorder
Nat.	1864	Clerk/Superior Ct.

■ **Pinal** 1 Feb. 1875
P.O. Box 2730, Florence, AZ 85232
Phone: (520)866-5300
Web site: www.co.pinal.az.us/
Parent County: Pima, Yavapai
Comments/research tips: Clerk of Superior Court has Marriage records 1874–1910 and Probate records 1875–1949.

Record Type	Year Begun	Jurisdiction
Birth	1909	Dept./Health
Death	1909	Dept./Health
Divorce	1883	Clerk/Superior Ct.
Land	na	County Recorder
Nat.	1875	Clerk/Superior Ct.

■ **Santa Cruz** 15 Mar. 1899
P.O. Box 1929, Nogales, AZ 85628
Phone: (520)375-7730
Web site: www.co.santa-cruz.az.us
Parent County: Cochise, Pima
Comments/research tips: Clerk of Superior Court has Military records 1907–1922 and Naturalization records 1888–1985.

Record Type	Year Begun	Jurisdiction
Birth	1909	Dept./Health
Marriage	1899	Clerk/Superior Ct.
Divorce	na	Clerk/Superior Ct.
Land	1899	County Recorder
Death	1909	Dept./Health
Adoption	1940	Clerk/Superior Ct.

■ **Yavapai** 8 Nov. 1864
120 S. Cortez, Prescott, AZ 86301
Phone: (928)771-3312
Web site: www.co.yavapai.az.us/
Parent County: Original county

Record Type	Year Begun	Jurisdiction
Birth	1909	Dept./Health
Marriage	1870	Clerk/Superior Ct.
Death	1909	Dept./Health
Divorce	na	Clerk/Superior Ct.
Land	1864	County Recorder
Probate	1865	Clerk/Superior Ct.
Nat.	na	Clerk/Superior Ct.

■ **Yuma** 8 Nov. 1864
168 S. Second Ave., Yuma, AZ 85364
Phone: (928)329-2164
Web site: www.co.yuma.az.us/
Parent County: Original county
Comments/research tips: Clerk of Superior Court has Marriage records 1864–1927.

Record Type	Year Begun	Jurisdiction
Birth	1909	Dept./Health
Death	1909	Dept./Health
Divorce	1863	Clerk/Superior Ct.
Land	1863	County Recorder
Probate	1876	Clerk/Superior Ct.
Nat.	1863	Clerk/Superior Ct.

Arizona

Arkansas

Emily Anne Croom

HISTORICAL OVERVIEW

In what is now Arkansas, sixteenth-century Spanish explorers found a considerable Indian population living in permanent agricultural settlements. Between 1673 and 1740, French explorers, trappers, and traders traversed the area; for many years after 1686, the French also maintained a settlement at Arkansas Post on the Arkansas River. By the end of the Seven Years' War (1763), France ceded to Spain all of Louisiana, the vast territory west of the Mississippi that included Arkansas. Later, as Napoleon prepared for retrocession of Louisiana to France, the Louisiana Purchase (1803) made Arkansas U.S. territory. By that time, Osage, Caddo, and Quapaw Indians were feeling the push of both Cherokee and white settlers moving into Arkansas.

Present Missouri and Arkansas were part of an undefined district called Upper Louisiana, and in 1805 became Louisiana Territory. For several decades Arkansas was not only a destination of white explorers and settlers, but also a travel route for thousands of Indians being forced from the Southeast to Indian Territory. The Caddo signed the last Indian land cession in Arkansas in 1835.

When Orleans Territory became the state of Louisiana in 1812, Arkansas and Missouri became part of Missouri Territory. Originally part of New Madrid County, Arkansas County was established in 1813. "Arkansaw" Territory, created in 1819, included most of present Oklahoma as Indian lands; the present western boundary was established when Arkansas became the twenty-fifth state in 1836.

The numerous rivers running through the state drain into the Mississippi and were significant transportation routes in the nineteenth century, especially after the arrival of steamboats in the 1820s. Many settlers came to the state via the Mississippi and its tributaries, but the swampy and flood-prone plains along the rivers in the

Courtesy of Little Rock Convention and Visitors Bureau

ARKANSAS AT A GLANCE

Motto: The People Rule

Population: 2.7 million

Prevalent Religions: Christianity, particularly Southern Baptist and Pentecostal

Major Industries: Food processing, poultry and eggs, soybeans, sorghum, cattle, cotton, rice, hogs, milk, electric equipment, fabricated metal products, machinery, paper products

Ethnic Makeup (in percent): Caucasian 80.0%, African American 15.7%, Hispanic 3.2%, Asian 0.8%, Native American 0.7%, Other 1.5%

Famous Arkansasans: Maya Angelou, Helen Gurley Brown, Glen Campbell, Johnny Cash, Eldridge Cleaver, Dizzy Dean, John Gould Fletcher, Al Green, John H. Johnson, Scott Joplin, Alan Ladd, Douglas MacArthur, Mary Steenburgen, CK Williams, Miller Williams

Above: The Old State House in Little Rock

eastern part of the state limited the growth of towns there. The major towns developed farther upriver. During the early nineteenth century, roads traversing the state were primitive at best. One that invited settlement along its route was the Southwest Trail that crossed Arkansas from northeast to southwest, leading into Texas.

Despite mountainous terrain in the north and west and numerous forests statewide, settlers saw agricultural opportunity combined with the availability of cheap federal land or, for some, bounty land due them for military service. Before the Civil War, settlers streamed into Arkansas from neighboring states—especially Tennessee—and from Alabama, other southern states, and the Ohio Valley. In 1860, less than 1 percent of the state's residents were foreign-born.

Cotton, often cultivated with slave labor, became the dominant crop on farms and plantations in the east and south. By 1860, slaves were a quarter of the state's population. Wheat production was important in the north and west. Corn was a principal staple for people and livestock throughout the state, as it was throughout the South.

Due largely to geography, settlement patterns, and the state's regional economies, antebellum political power rested generally in the south and east. By 1861, a large number of Arkansans were Unionists, and secession was hotly debated. Only after war began at Fort Sumter, South Carolina, did Arkansas secede and join the Confederacy. The Union army occupied northwest Arkansas during much of the Civil War and took the capital, Little Rock, in September 1863. From that time, the Union occupied most of the state except the southwest, but both pro Union and Confederate state governments operated during the last year of the war. Hostilities in Arkansas included both formal military operations and guerrilla warfare.

Although the state rejoined the Union in 1868, reconstruction was a difficult, sometimes violent period, with widespread poverty and discontent. However, economic development in the late nineteenth century included the coming of railroads and extensive logging, with related timber manufacturing. Post-Civil War decades also saw expansion of cotton farming, the sharecropper labor force, and European immigration to the state. In the early twentieth century, Arkansas experienced growth in the textile, petroleum, and mining industries. However, the state remained generally a rural, cotton-dominated economy until after World War II. Since then, the economy and population have diversified; by 1980, the rural population was slightly less than half the state total.

RECORD HIGHLIGHTS

Statewide vital records include birth and death records from 1914, evidence of marriage records from 1917, and evidence of divorce records from 1923. Check in the city or county for any vital records created prior to statewide registration. Request copies of divorce decrees or marriage licenses from the county court that issued the original documents; consult the *Acts of Arkansas* for legislature-granted divorces. For more information, see the Arkansas Department of Health Web site <www.healthyarkansas.com/certificates/certificates.html>.

A number of Arkansas counties have lost some records to floods or fires, few of which occurred during the Civil War. Nevertheless, investigate surviving county records, resources in parent and neighboring counties, and records of territorial, local, state, and federal jurisdictions.

The following are some of the Arkansas-specific sources available through the Family History Library (Salt Lake City) and/or at the Arkansas History Commission in Little Rock:

- Territorial sheriffs' censuses, 1823 (Arkansas County), 1829 (various counties)
- Territorial and state tax lists—various counties, various years
- *Territorial Papers of the United States* (National Archives microfilm M721) and *Territorial Papers of the United States Senate* (M200) for Orleans, Louisiana, Missouri, and Arkansas Territories; *State Department Territorial Papers, Missouri* (M1134)
- Records of depositors, Little Rock branch of the Freedman's Savings and Trust Company (FHL microfilm 928573)
- 1911 census of Confederate veterans in Arkansas
- Confederate pension applications
- Records of the Arkansas Confederate Home, 1890–1963, searchable at <http://arkansashistory.arkansas.com/resource_types/military_records/>

STATE RESOURCES

■ ARCHIVES, LIBRARIES, AND SOCIETIES

Arkansas Genealogical Society
P.O. Box 17653, Little Rock, AR 72212
E-mail: AskAGS@comcast.net
Web site: <www.rootsweb.com/~args/>

Arkansas Historical Association
416 Old Main, University of Arkansas, Fayetteville, AR 72701
Tel: (479) 575-5884
E-mail: dludlow@uark.edu
Web site: <www.uark.edu/depts/arkhist/home/>

Arkansas History Commission and State Archives
One Capitol Mall, Little Rock, AR 72201

Tel: (501) 682-6900
Web site: <www.ark-ives.com>

Ashley County Genealogical Society
P.O. Drawer R, Crossett, AR 71635

Ashley County Library
211 East Lincoln, Hamburg, AR 71646
Tel: (870) 853-8781
E-mail: ashlib@cei.net

Batesville Genealogical Society
P.O. Box 3883, Batesville, AR 72503-3883
Web site: http://fly.hiwaay.net/~dmglenn/bitsbark.htm

Baxter County Historical and Genealogical Society
P.O. Box 1611, Mountain Home, AR 72654
E-mail: calamity@mymtnhome.com
Web site: <www.baxtercountyonline.com/bchgs/>

Benton County Historical Society
P.O. Box 1034, Bentonville, AR 72712
Tel: (479) 273-3890
E-mail: BCHSArk@juno.com
Web site: <www.uark.edu/depts/globmark/bchsark/>

Bradley County Genealogical Society
P.O. Box 837, Warren, AR 71671
Web site: <www.rootsweb.com/~arbradle/bradcogensoc.shtml>

Butler Center for Arkansas Studies, Central Arkansas Library
100 Rock St., Little Rock, AR 72201
Tel: (501) 918-3056
Web site: <www.cals.lib.ar.us/butlercenter/index.html>

Carroll County Historical and Genealogical Society, Inc.
P.O. Box 249, Berryville, AR 72616-0249
Tel: (870) 423-6312
Web site: <www.rootsweb.com/~arcchs/>

Clark County Historical Association/Library
P.O. Box 516, Arkadelphia, AR 71923

Clark County Library
609 Caddo St., Arkadelphia, AR 71923

Clay County Genealogical Club
% Piggott Public Library, 361 West Main, Piggott, AR 72454-2099

Cleburne County Historical Society
P.O. Box 794, Heber Springs, AR 72543
Tel: (501) 362-5225
E-mail: cchist@ipa.net
Web site: <www.rootsweb.com/~arclebur/clebhist.htm>

Craighead County Historical Society
P.O. Box 1011, Jonesboro, AR 72403-1011

Crawford County Genealogical Society
P.O. Box 276, Alma, AR 72921
Web site: <www.rootsweb.com/~arcrawfo/>

Crawford County Historical Society
929 E. Main St., Van Buren, AR 72956
Web site: <www.rootsweb.com/~arcrawfo/>

Craighead County Jonesboro Public Library, Headquarters for the Crowley Ridge Regional Library System
315 W. Oak, Jonesboro, AR 72401
Tel: (870) 935-5133
Web site: <www.libraryinjonesboro.org>

Crowley Ridge Genealogical Society
P.O. Box 2091, State University, AR 72467

Dallas County Arkansas Genealogical and Historical Society
% Dallas County Library, Fordyce, AR 71742

Department of Arkansas Heritage
1500 Tower Bldg., 323 Center St., Little Rock, AR 72201
Tel: (501) 324-9150
E-mail: info@arkansasheritage.com
Web site: <www.arkansasheritage.com>

Desha County Historical Society
506 Henry Dr., Dumas, AR 76139
Web site: <http://home.earthlink.net/~reitzamm/>

Arkansas

Faulkner County Historical Society
1501 College Ave., Conway, AR 72032
Web site: <www.faulknerhistory .com>

Fayetteville Public Library
217 E. Dickson St., Fayetteville, AR 72701
Tel: (479) 571-2222
E-mail: fpl@faylib.org
Web site: <www.faylib.org>

Fort Smith Historical Society
61 S. Eighth St., Fort Smith, AR 72901-2480

Fort Smith Public Library
3201 Rogers Ave., Fort Smith, AR 72903
Tel: (479) 783-0229
Web site: <www.fspl.lib.ar.us/>

Frontier Researchers Genealogical Society
P.O. Box 2123, Fort Smith, AR 72902

Garland County Historical Society
222 McMahan Dr., Hot Springs, AR 71913
Archives: 328 Quapaw Ave., Hot Springs, AR 71901
Tel: (501) 321-2159
E-mail: bjmclane@cablelynx.com
Web site: <www.obu.edu/libr ary/gchs.htm>

Garland-Montgomery Regional Library
200 Woodbine St., Hot Springs, AR 71901

Grand Prairie Genealogical Society
% Stuttgart Public Library, 2002 S. Buerkle St., Stuttgart, AR 72160
Tel: (870) 673-1966
Web site: <www.rootsweb.com/ ~ararkans/grandpra.htm>

Grand Prairie Historical Society
P.O. Box 122, Gillett, AR 72055-0122

Greene County Historical and Genealogical Society
% The Paragould Library, 120 N. Twelfth St., Paragould, AR 72450
Web site: <www.couchgenweb .com/arkansas/greene/gchgs/ htm>

Hempstead County Genealogical Society
P.O. Box 1158, Hope, AR 71801-1158

Heritage Club
218 Howard, Nashville, AR 71852

Heritage Seekers Genealogical Club
P.O. Box 532, North Little Rock, AR 72115-0532

The Historic Genealogical Society of Marion County, Arkansas (HGSMCA)
P.O. Box 761, Yellville, AR 72687
Web site: <www.rootsweb.com/~a rmarion/historicalsociety.html>

Hot Springs County Historical Society
P.O. Box 674, Malvern, AR 72104

Independence County Historical Society
P.O. Box 2722, Batesville, AR 72503
Web site: <http://fly.hiwaay .net/~dmglenn/ichs.htm>

Izard County Historical Society
P.O. Box 110, Dolph, AR 72528
Web site: <www.couchgenweb .com/arkansas/izard/>

Jefferson County Genealogical Society
P.O. Box 2215, Pine Bluff, AR 71613
Web site: <www.rootsweb.com/ ~arjcgs>

Johnson County Historical Society
P.O. Box 505, Clarksville, AR 72830
Web site: <www.oklahoma.net/ ~pvtspark/society.html>

Johnson County Public Library
Taylor Circle #2, Clarksville, AR 72830
Tel: (479) 754-3135

Lafayette County Historical Society
P.O. Box 758, Lewisville, AR 71845
Tel: (870) 921-5252
E-mail: knight@magnolia-net .com
Web site: <www.rootsweb.com/ ~arlafaye/society.html>

Logan County Historical Society
P.O. Box 40, Magazine, AR 72943-0040

RESEARCH TIPS

for more info

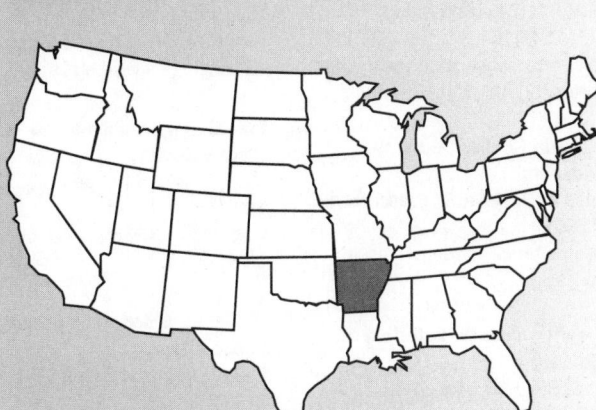

- Someone reportedly born in Missouri or Louisiana during either territorial period could have been born in what is now Arkansas.
- Arkansas is a federal land state, whose land patents are searchable at <www.glorecords.blm .gov>.
- Arkansas federal censuses date from 1830.
- Learn more about Arkansas History Commission (archives) records at <www.ark-ives.com/resour ce_types/index.php>.
- www.segenealogy.com/index

Census Records
- Federal Census Population Schedules: 1830, 1840, 1850, 1860, 1870, 1880, 1900, 1910, 1920, 1930
- Federal Census Soundex or Miracode: 1880, 1900, 1910, 1920, 1930
- Federal Mortality Schedules: 1850, 1860, 1870, 1880
- Federal Slave Schedules: 1850, 1860 (schedules name slaveholders but rarely name slaves)
- Territorial Sheriffs' Censuses: 1823 (Arkansas County), 1829 (various counties)

Madison County Genealogical & Historical Society
P.O. Box 427, Huntsville, AR 72740
Tel: (501) 738-6408
Web site: <www.members.aol .com/madcounty/ mcindex.htm>

Marion County Public Library
308 W. Old Main St., Yellville, AR 72687-7991
Tel: (870) 449-6015

Melting Pot Genealogical Society
P.O. Box 936, Hot Springs, AR 71902-0936
Tel: (501) 624-0229
E-mail: meltingpot@cablelynx .com
Web site: <www.rootsweb.com/ ~armpgs/index1.htm>

Montgomery County Historical Society
P.O. Box 520, Mount Ida, AR 71957-0520

Arkansas

National Archives and Record Administration, Southwest Region (Texas)
501 W. Felix St., Bldg. 1, Fort Worth, TX 76115-3405 or P.O. Box 6216, Fort Worth, TX 76115-0216
Web site: <www.archives.giv/fac ilities/tx/fort_worth.html>

Nevada County Depot and Museum
403 W. First St. S., Prescott, AR 71857
Web site: <www.depotmuseum .org>

Newton County Historical Society
P.O. Box 360, Jasper, AR 72641
Web site: <http://newtoncounty ar.com>

North Little Rock, William F. Laman Public Library
2801 Orange St., North Little Rock, AR 72114-2296
Tel: (501) 758-1720
Web site: <www.laman.net>

Northwest Arkansas Genealogical Society
P.O. Box 796, Rogers, AR 72756-0796
Tel: (479) 273-3890
E-mail: nags2@juno.com
Web site: <www.rootsweb.com/ ~arnwags/>

Orphan Train Heritage Society of America, Inc.
P.O. Box 322, Concordia, KS 66901
Tel: (785) 243-4471
E-mail: othsa@msn.com
Web site: <www.orphantrainrider s.com>

Ouachita Baptist University, Riley-Hickingbotham Library
410 Ouachita St., Arkadelphia, AR 71998
Web site: <www.obu.edu/libr ary/>

Ouachita-Calhoun Genealogical Society
P.O. Box 2092, Camden, AR 71711
Web site: <www.rootsweb.com/ ~arouachi/societie.htm>

Ouachita-Calhoun Genealogical Society Archives
% Public Library of Camden & Ouachita County, 120 Harrison St., NW, Camden, AR 71701
Tel: (870) 836-5083

Ouachita County Historical Society & McCollum-Chidester House Museum
926 Washington St., Camden, AR 71701
Tel: (870) 836-9243
Web site: <www.rootsweb.com/ ~arouachi/societie.htm>

Pike County Archives and History Society
P.O. Box 875, Murfreesboro, AR 71958
Web site: <www.rootsweb.com/ ~arpcahs/>

Pine Bluff & Jefferson County Public Library
200 E. Eighth Ave., Pine Bluff, AR 71601
Tel: (870) 534-4802
E-mail: pbjc-lib@pbjc-lib.state.ar .us
Web site: <http://pbjc-lib.state.ar .us>

Polk County Genealogical Society
P.O. Box 1525, Mean, AR 71953-1525
E-mail: arkgenealogy@polk.org
Web site: <www.arkgenealogy.po lk.org>

Polk County Library
410 Eighth St., Mena, AR 71953
Tel: (479) 394-2314

Pope County Historical Association
214 E. Tucker Rd., Pottsville, AR 72858-9998
Web site: <www.rootsweb.com/ ~arpope2/assoc.htm>

Pope County Library System
116 E. Third St., Russellville, AR 72801
Tel: (479) 968-4368
Web site: <www.ohwy.com/ar/ p/plar0021.htm>

Pulaski County Historical Society
P.O. Box 251903, Little Rock, AR 72225
E-mail: pchs@swbell.net
Web site: <http://users.aristotle .net/~davisvh/>

Randolph County Historical Society
111 W. Everett St., Pocahontas, AR 72455
Web site: <www.geocities.com/ Heartland/Orchard/8659/>

Saline County Historical Commission
% Gunn Museum Saline County, 218 S. Market St., Benton, AR 72015

Saline County History and Heritage Society
P.O. Box 1712, Benton, AR 72018-1712
Tel: (501) 778-3335
Web site: <www.rootsweb.com/ ~arsaline/schhs.html>

Scott County Historical & Genealogical Society
P.O. Box 1560, Waldron, AR 72958-1560
Tel: (479) 637-2466
Web site: <www.rootsweb.com/ ~arscott/schs.htm>

Sevier County Historical Society
717 Maple Ave., De Queen, AR 71832
Web site: <www.genealogyshopp e.com/arsevier/>

Southwest Arkansas Genealogical Society
1022 Lawton Circle, Magnolia, AR 71753

Southwest Arkansas Regional Archives
201 Hwy. 195 S., P.O. Box 134, Washington, AR 71862
Tel: (870) 983-2633
E-mail: online@southwestarchive s.com
Web site: <www.southwestarchiv es.com>

Stone County Historical Society
P.O. Box 210, Mountain View, AR 72560
E-mail: stonecoargen@email .com
Web site: <http://rootsweb .com/~arscgs/>

Stuttgart Public Library
2002 S. Buerkle St., Stuttgart, AR 72160-6508
Tel: (870) 673-1966
Web site: <www.ar-net.com/ sttg/library/library.htm>

Tri-County Genealogical Society
Tri-County Genealogy Bldg., 602 Remley St., Marvell, AR 72366-0580
E-mail: cndavison@centurytel .net
Web site: <www.couchgenweb .com/arkansas/tricou/society .htm>

Union County Genealogical Society
% Barton Library, 200 E. Fifth St., El Dorado, AR 71730

University of Arkansas Libraries
365 Ozark Ave., Fayetteville, AR 72701-4002
Tel: (479) 575-4101
E-mail: refer@uark.edu
Web site: <http://libinfo.uark .edu>

Van Buren County Library
110 Page St., Clinton, AR 72031-6896
Tel: (501) 745-2100

Van Buren Historical Society/ Museum
P.O. Box 1023, Clinton, AR 72031
Tel: (501) 745-4066
Web site: <www.gozarks.com/pr ide/vbcmuseum/>

Washington County Arkansas Genealogical Society (WCAGS)
P.O. Box 41, Fayetteville, AR 72702-0041
E-mail: wcags@hotmail.com
Web site: <www.rootsweb.com/ ~arwcags/>

Washington County Historical Society
118 E. Dickson St., Fayetteville, AR 72701
Tel: (479) 521-2970
E-mail: info@washcohistoricalsoc iety.org
Web site: <www.washcohistorica lsociety.org/>

Yell County Historical and Genealogical Society
P.O. Box 622, Dardanelle, AR 72834
Web site: <www.rootsweb.com/ ~aryell/yhs.htm>

BIBLIOGRAPHY

■ GENERAL RESOURCES

Abstracts of Arkansas Reports, January 1837 through January 1861
compiled by Joan Thurman Taunton (Hot Springs, AR: Arkansas Genealogical Society, 1988)

"Arkansas" (In Genealogical Research: Methods and Sources), rev. ed.
by James R. Johnson, edited by Kenn Stryker-Rodda (Washington, D.C.: The American Society of Genealogists, 1983)

Arkansas Families: Glimpses of Yesterday Columns from the Arkansas Gazette
by Lucy Marion Reaves, edited by Desmond Walls Allen (Conway, AR: Arkansas Research, 1995)

Arkansas and Its People, a History, 1541–1930
edited by David Yancey Thomas (New York: The American Historical Society, Inc., 1930)

Arkansas Links: A Comprehensive Guide to Genealogical Research in the Natural State
by Rhonda S. Norris (Kearney, NE: Morris Pub., 1999)

Arkansas Pensioners, 1818–1900: Records of Some Arkansas Residents Who Applied to the Federal Government for Benefits Arising from Service in Federal Military Organizations (Revolutionary War, War of 1812, Indian and Mexican Wars)
compiled by Dorothy E. Payne (Easley, SC: Southern Historical Press, 1985)

Arkansas: Research Outline
from the Church of Jesus Christ of Latter-day Saints, Family History Library (Salt Lake City, UT: Corp. of the President of the Church of Jesus Christ of L.D.S., 1988)

Arkansas Researchers' Handbook
by Claudia Wagoner (Fayetteville, AR: Research Plus, 1986)

Biographical and Historical Memoirs of Eastern Arkansas, Comprising a Condensed History of the State, a Number of Biographies and Distinguished Citizens of the Same, a Brief Descriptive History of Each of the Counties
(Chicago, St. Louis: The Goodspeed Publishing Co., 1890)

The By-Name Index to the Centennial History of Arkansas
compiled and edited by Lewis E. Roberts (Kirkland, WA: L.E. Roberts, 1991)

Early Days in Arkansas
by William F. Pope (Little Rock, AR: F.W. Allsopp, 1895)

From Slavery to Uncertain Freedom: The Freedmen's Bureau in Arkansas, 1865–1869
by Randy Finley (Fayetteville, AR: University of Arkansas Press, 1996)

The Genealogist's Companion and Sourcebook, 2d ed.
by Emily Anne Croom (Cincinnati: Betterway Books, 2003)

Genealogist's Guide to Arkansas Courthouse Research
by Jack Damon Ruple, Sr. (Little Rock, AR: J.D. Ruple, 1989)

A Genealogist's Guide to Discovering Your African-American Ancestors
by Franklin Carter Smith and Emily Anne Croom (Cincinnati: Betterway Books, 2003)

Guide to Genealogical Research in the National Archives of the United States
edited by Anne Bruner Eales and Robert M. Kvasnicka (Washington, D.C.: National Archives and Records Administration, 2000)

History of the Arkansas Press for a Hundred Years and More
by Frederick William Allsopp (Little Rock, AR: Parke-Harper Publishing, 1922)

Lest We Forget, or, Character Gems Gleaned from South Arkansas
by J.H. Riggin and W.F. Evans (Easley, SC: Southern Historical Press, 1978)

National Archives Microfilm Catalogs online:
<www.archives.gov/publications/genealogy_microfilm_catalogs.html>

Pioneers and Makers of Arkansas
by Josiah Hazen Shinn (Baltimore, MD: Genealogical Pub. Co., 1967)

They Sought a Land: A Settlement in the Arkansas River Valley, 1840–1870
by William Oates Ragsdale (Fayetteville, AR: University of Arkansas Press, 1997)

Union List of Arkansas Newspapers, 1819–1942 A Partial Inventory of Arkansas Newspaper Files Available in Offices of Publishers, Libraries, and Private Collections in Arkansas. Prepared by Historical Records Survey, Division of Community Service Programs, Works Projects Administration
from the Historical Records Survey (Little Rock, AR: 1942)

■ CENSUS RECORDS

1820 Census of the Territory of Arkansas (Reconstructed)
by James Logan Morgan (Conway, AR: Arkansas Research, 1992)

The American Census Handbook
by Thomas Jay Kemp (Wilmington, DE: Scholarly Resources, 2001)

Arkansas 1850 Census Every-Name Index
by Bobbie Jones McLane and Desmond Walls Allen (Conway, AR: Arkansas Research, 1995)

The Census Book: A Genealogist's Guide to Federal Census Facts, Schedules, and Indexes
by William Dollarhide (Bountiful, UT: Heritage Quest, 2000)

Finding Answers in U.S. Census Records
by Loretto Dennis Szucs and Matthew Wright (Orem, UT: Ancestry Publishing, 2002)

Your Guide to the Federal Census
by Kathleen W. Hinckley (Cincinnati: Betterway Books, 2002)

■ IMMIGRATION RECORDS

American Naturalization Records, 1790–1990: What They Are and How to Use Them
by John J. Newman (North Salt Lake, UT: HeritageQuest, 1998)

American Passenger Arrival Records
by Michael Tepper (Baltimore: Genealogical Publishing Co., 1993)

Cherokee Emigration Rolls, 1817–1835
transcribed by Jack D. Baker (Oklahoma City, OK: Baker Pub. Co., 1977)

They Became Americans: Finding Naturalization Records and Ethnic Origins
by Loretto Dennis Szucs (Salt Lake City: Ancestry, Inc., 1998)

They Came in Ships: A Guide to Finding Your Immigrant Ancestor's Arrival Records, 2d ed.
by John P. Colletta (Salt Lake City: Ancestry, Inc., 1993)

■ LAND RECORDS

Arkansas Land Patents, Eastern Arkansas (Clay, Craighead, Crittenden, Cross, Greene, Lee, Mississippi, Monroe, Phillips, Poinsett, and St. Francis counties): Granted through 30 June 1908
by Desmond Walls Allen and Bobbie Jones McLane (Conway, AR: Ark. Research, 1991)

Arkansas Military Bounty Grants (War of 1812)
compiled by Katheren Christensen (Hot Springs, AR: Arkansas Ancestors, 1971)

Locating Your Roots: Discover Your Ancestors Using Land Records
by Patricia Law Hatcher (Cincinnati: Betterway Books, 2003)

■ MAPS

Arkansas Atlas & Gazetteer: GPS Grid, Topo Maps of the Entire State, Back Roads, Outdoor Recreation
from the DeLorme Publishing Company (Yarmouth, ME: DeLorme, 1997)

Arkansas Township Atlas: A History of the Minor Civil Divisions in Each Arkansas County
by Russell Pierce Baker (Hot Springs, AR: Arkansas Genealogical Society, 1984)

Arkansas Township Digest: Minor Civil Divisions, 1820–1990
by Desmond Walls Allen (Conway, AR: Arkansas Research, 1994)

Arkansas

The Atlas of Arkansas
edited by Richard M. Smith (Fayetteville, AR: University of Arkansas Press, 1989)

Historical Atlas of Arkansas
by Gerald T. Hanson and Carl H. Moneyhon (Norman, OK: University of Oklahoma Press, 1989)

■ MILITARY RECORDS

Arkansas 1911 Census of Confederate Veterans
transcribed and edited by Bobbie J. McLane and Capitola Glazner (Hot Springs National Park, AR: B.J. McLane: C. Glazner, 1977–1981)

Arkansas Confederate Veterans and Widows Pension Applications
compiled by Frances Terry Ingmire (St. Louis, MO: F.T. Ingmire, 1985)

Arkansas' Damned Yankees: An Index to Union Soldiers in Arkansas Regiments
by Desmond Walls Allen (Conway, AR: D.W. Allen, 1987)

Arkansas' Mexican War Soldiers
by Desmond Walls Allen (Conway, AR: Arkansas Research, 1988)

Arkansas' Spanish American War Soldiers
by Desmond Walls Allen (Conway, AR: Arkansas Research, 1988)

Arkansas Union Soldiers Pension Application Index
compiled by Desmond Walls Allen (Conway, AR: D.W. Allen, 1987)

Compendium of the Confederate Armies, 11 vols.
by Stewart Sifakis (New York: Facts on File, 1992–1995)

Confederate Arkansas: The People and Policies of a Frontier State in Wartime
by Michael B. Dougan (University, AL: University of Alabama Press, 1976)

First Arkansas Confederate Mounted Rifles
by Desmond Walls Allen (Conway, AR: Arkansas Research, 1988)

Forty-Fifth Arkansas Confederate Cavalry
by Desmond Walls Allen (Conway, AR: Arkansas Research, 1988)

The Fourteenth Arkansas Confederate Infantry
by Desmond Walls Allen (Conway, AR: Arkansas Research, 1988)

History of the Twenty-Seventh Arkansas Confederate Infantry
by Silas Claiborn Turnbo, edited by Desmond Walls Allen (Conway, AR: Arkansas Research, 1988)

Index to Arkansas Confederate Pension Applications
compiled by Desmond Walls Allen (Conway, AR: Arkansas Research, 1991)

Index to Arkansas Confederate Soldiers, 3 vols.
by Desmond Walls Allen (Conway, AR: Arkansas Research, 1990)

Rugged and Sublime: The Civil War in Arkansas
edited by Mark K. Christ (Fayetteville, AR: University of Arkansas Press, 1994)

The Seventh Arkansas Confederate Infantry
by Desmond Walls Allen (Conway, AR: Arkansas Research, 1988)

Thirty-Eighth Arkansas Confederate Infantry
by Desmond Walls Allen (Conway, AR: Arkansas Research, 1988)

The Twenty-Seventh Arkansas Confederate Infantry
by Desmond Walls Allen (Conway, AR: D.W. Allen, 1987)

Uncle, We Are Ready! Registering America's Men, 1917–1918: A Guide to Researching World War I Draft Registration Cards
by John J. Newman (North Salt Lake, UT: HeritageQuest, 2001)

U.S. Military Records: A Guide to Federal & State Sources, Colonial America to the Present
by James C. Neagles (Salt Lake City: Ancestry, Inc., 1994)

World War II: A Family Historian's Guide
by Debra Johnson Knox (Spartanburg, SC: MIE Publishing, 2003)

■ PROBATE RECORDS

Index to Wills and Administrations of Arkansas from the Earliest to 1900
edited by Mrs. James Harold and Mrs. Edward Lynn Westbrooke

(Jonesboro, AR: Vowels Print Co., 1986)

■ VITAL RECORDS

Arkansas Death Record Index, 4 vols.
by Desmond Walls Allen with the Arkansas State Department of Health (Conway, AR: Arkansas Research, 1996–1999)

The Arkansas Gazette Obituaries Index, 1819–1879
by Stephen J. Chism (Greenville, SC: Southern Historical Press, 1990)

Arkansas Marriage Notices, 1819–1845
by James Logan Morgan (Conway, AR: Arkansas Research, 1992)

Arkansas Marriage Records
by James Logan Morgan (Conway, AR: Arkansas Research, 1994)

Arkansas Newspaper Abstracts, 1819–1845
by James Logan Morgan (Conway, AR: Arkansas Research, 1992)

Arkansas Newspaper Index, 1819–1845: Index to Obituaries, Biographical Notes and Probate and Chancery Notices from Arkansas Newspapers, 1819–1845
by James Logan Morgan (Newport, AR: Morgan Books, 1981)

Guide to Vital Statistic Records in Arkansas: Volume II, Church Archives
from the Arkansas Historical Survey Project, Division of Community Service Programs, Work Projects Administration (Little Rock, AR: Historical Records Survey)

Index to Sources for Arkansas Cemetery Inscriptions
compiled by the Daughters of the American Revolution, Prudence Hall (North Little Rock, AR: D.A.R., 1976)

Your Guide to Cemetery Research
by Sharon DeBartolo Carmack (Cincinnati: Betterway Books, 2002)

■ Arkansas   31 Dec. 1813
101 Court Sq., DeWitt, AR 72042
Phone: (870)946-4349
Parent County: Original County
Web site: www.rootsweb.com/~ararkans/

Record Type	Year Begun	Jurisdiction
Birth	1914	Dept./Health
Death	1914	Dept./Health
Marriage	1838	County Clerk
Divorce	1803	Clerk/Circuit Ct.
Land	na	Clerk/Circuit Ct.
Probate	1809	County Clerk
Court	1803	Clerk/Circuit Ct.

■ Ashley   30 Nov. 1848
215 E. Jefferson St., Hamburg, AR 71646
Phone: (870)853-5243
Web site: www.rootsweb.com/~arashley/
Parent County: Chicot, Union, Drew

Record Type	Year Begun	Jurisdiction
Birth	1914	Dept./Health
Death	1914	Dept./Health
Marriage	1848	County Clerk
Divorce	na	Clerk/Circuit Ct.
Land	na	County Clerk
Probate	na	County Clerk

■ **Baxter** 24 Mar. 1873
Courthouse Sq., 1 E. Seventh St., Mountain Home, AR 72653
Phone: (870)425-3475
Web site: www.baxtercounty.org
Parent County: Fulton, Izard, Marion, Searcy

Record Type	Year Begun	Jurisdiction
Birth	1914	Dept./Health
Death	1914	Dept./Health
Marriage	na	County Clerk
Divorce	na	County Clerk
Land	na	County Clerk
Probate	na	County Clerk
Court	na	County Clerk

■ **Benton** 30 Sep. 1836
P.O. Box 699, Bentonville, AR 72712
Phone: (479)271-1013
Web site: www.co.benton.ar.us/
Parent County: Washington

Record Type	Year Begun	Jurisdiction
Birth	1914	Dept./Health
Death	1914	Dept./Health
Marriage	1861	County Clerk
Divorce	na	Clerk/Circuit Ct.
Land	na	Clerk/Circuit Ct.
Probate	1859	County Clerk
Court	na	Clerk/Circuit Ct.

■ **Boone** 9 Apr. 1869
100 N. Main St., Harrison, AR 72601
Phone: (870)741-8428
Web site: www.rootsweb.com/~arboone/
Parent County: Carrol, Madison

Record Type	Year Begun	Jurisdiction
Birth	1914	Dept./Health
Death	1914	Dept./Health
Marriage	1869	County Clerk
Divorce	na	Clerk/Circuit Ct.
Land	na	Clerk/Circuit Ct.
Probate	1869	County Clerk
Court	na	Clerk/Circuit Ct.

■ **Bradley** 18 Dec. 1840
101 E. Cedar St., Warren, AR 71671-0000
Phone: (870)226-3853
Web site: www.rootsweb.com/~arbradle/
Parent County: Union

Record Type	Year Begun	Jurisdiction
Birth	1914	Dept./Health
Death	1914	Dept./Health
Marriage	1846	County Clerk
Divorce	na	Clerk/Circuit Ct.
Land	na	Clerk/Circuit Ct.
Probate	1850	County Clerk
Court	na	Clerk/Circuit Ct.

■ **Calhoun** 6 Dec. 1850
P.O. Box 626, Hampton, AR 71744
Phone: (870)798-2517

Web site: www.rootsweb.com/~arcalhou/
Parent County: Bradley, Dallas, Ouachita

Record Type	Year Begun	Jurisdiction
Birth	1914	Dept./Health
Death	1914	Dept./Health
Marriage	1851	County Clerk
Divorce	1880	County Clerk
Land	1851	County Clerk
Probate	1880	County Clerk
Court	1880	County Clerk

■ **Carroll** 1 Nov. 1833
210 W. Church St., Berryville, AR 72616-4233
Phone: (870)423-2967
Web site: www.rootsweb.com/~arcarrol/
Parent County: Izard

Record Type	Year Begun	Jurisdiction
Birth	1914	Dept./Health
Death	1914	Dept./Health
Marriage	1870	County Clerk
Divorce	1870	Clerk/Circuit Ct.
Land	1870	Clerk/Circuit Ct.
Probate	1870	County Clerk
Court	1870	Clerk/Circuit Ct.

■ **Chicot** 25 Oct. 1823
108 Main St., Lake Village, AR 71653
Phone: (870)265-8000
Web site: www.seark.net/~sabra/chicotco.html
Parent County: Arkansas

Record Type	Year Begun	Jurisdiction
Birth	1914	Dept./Health
Death	1914	Dept./Health
Marriage	1839	County Clerk
Divorce	na	Clerk/Circuit Ct.
Land	na	Clerk/Circuit Ct.
Probate	1839	County Clerk
Court	1824	Clerk/Circuit Ct.

■ **Clark** 15 Dec. 1818
Courthouse Sq., 401 Clay St., Arkadelphia, AR 71923
Phone: (870)246-4491
Web site: www.pastracks.com/states/arkansas/clark/
Parent County: Arkansas

Record Type	Year Begun	Jurisdiction
Birth	1914	Dept./Health
Death	1914	Dept./Health
Marriage	1821	County Clerk
Divorce	na	Clerk/Circuit Ct.
Land	na	Clerk/Circuit Ct.
Probate	1800	County Clerk
Court	na	Clerk/Circuit Ct.

■ **Clay** 24 Mar. 1873
P.O. Box 306, Piggott, AR 72454
Phone: (870)598-2813
Web site: www.rootsweb.com/~arclay/
Parent County: Randolph, Greene
Comments/research tips: Formerly Clayton County. Name

Arkansas

changed to Clay 6 December 1875. Records were burned in 1893.

Record Type	Year Begun	Jurisdiction
Birth	1914	Dept./Health
Death	1914	Dept./Health
Marriage	1893	County Clerk
Divorce	1893	Clerk/Circuit Ct.
Land	1893	Clerk/Circuit Ct.
Probate	1893	County Clerk
Court	1893	Clerk/Circuit Ct.

■ Clayton   24 Mar. 1873
Parent County: Randolph, Greene
Comments/research tips: (See Clay) Named changed to Clay 6 December 1875.

■ Cleburne   20 Feb. 1883
301 W. Main St., Heber Springs, AR 725443
Phone: (501)362-4620
Web site: www.rootsweb.com/~arclebur/
Parent County: White, Van Buren, Independence

Record Type	Year Begun	Jurisdiction
Birth	1914	Dept./Health
Death	1914	Dept./Health
Marriage	1883	County Clerk
Divorce	1883	County Clerk
Land	1883	County Clerk
Probate	1883	County Clerk
Court	1883	County Clerk

■ Cleveland   17 Apr. 1873
Main & Magnolia Sts., P.O. Box 348, Rison, AR 71665
Phone: (870)325-6521
Web site: www.rootsweb.com/~arclevel/
Parent County: Dallas, Bradley, Jefferson, Lincoln
Comments/research tips: Formerly Dorsey County. Name changed to Cleveland 5 March 1885.

Record Type	Year Begun	Jurisdiction
Birth	1914	Dept./Health
Death	1914	Dept./Health
Marriage	1880	County Clerk
Divorce	na	County Clerk
Probate	na	County Clerk
Court	na	County Clerk

■ Columbia   17 Dec. 1852
1 Court Sq. #1, Magnolia, AR 71753
Phone: (870)235-3774
Web site: www.rootsweb.com/~arcolumb/
Parent County: Lafayette, Hempstead, Ouachita

Record Type	Year Begun	Jurisdiction
Birth	1914	Dept./Health
Death	1914	Dept./Health
Marriage	1853	County Clerk
Divorce	1860	County Clerk
Land	1853	County Clerk
Probate	na	County Clerk
Court	1860	County Clerk
Cemetery	na	County Librarian

■ Conway   20 Oct. 1825
117 S. Moose St., Morrilton, AR 72110
Phone: (501)354-9621
Web site: www.rootsweb.com/~arconway/
Parent County: Pulaski

Record Type	Year Begun	Jurisdiction
Birth	1914	Dept./Health
Death	1914	Dept./Health
Marriage	1858	County Clerk
Divorce	na	Clerk/Circuit Ct.
Land	na	Clerk/Circuit Ct.
Probate	na	County Clerk
Court	na	Clerk/Circuit Ct.

■ Craighead   19 Feb. 1859
511 S. Main St., Jonesboro, AR 72401
Phone: (501)354-9621
Web site: www.craigheadcounty.org/
Parent County: Mississippi, Greene, Poinsett

Record Type	Year Begun	Jurisdiction
Birth	1914	Dept./Health
Death	1914	Dept./Health
Divorce	1878	Clerk/Circuit Ct.
Land	1900	Clerk/Circuit Ct.
Probate	1878	County Clerk
Court	1878	Clerk/Circuit Ct.
Marriage	1878	County Clerk

■ Crawford   18 Oct. 1820
300 Main St., Van Buren, AR 72956
Phone: (501)474-1312
Web site: www.rootsweb.com/~arcrawfo/
Parent County: Pulaski

Record Type	Year Begun	Jurisdiction
Birth	1914	Dept./Health
Death	1914	Dept./Health
Marriage	1877	County Clerk
Divorce	na	Clerk/Circuit Ct.
Land	1877	Clerk/Circuit Ct.
Probate	1877	County Clerk
Court	1877	Clerk/Circuit Ct.

■ Crittenden   22 Oct. 1825
100 Court St., Marion, AR 72364
Phone: (870)739-4434
Web site: www.rootsweb.com/~arcritte/
Parent County: Phillips

Record Type	Year Begun	Jurisdiction
Birth	1914	Dept./Health
Death	1914	Dept./Health
Marriage	na	County Clerk
Divorce	na	Clerk/Circuit Ct.
Land	na	County Assessor
Probate	na	County Clerk
Court	na	Clerk/Circuit Ct.
Military	na	Clerk/Circuit Ct.

■ Cross   15 Nov. 1862
705 Union Ave. E. #8, Wynne, AR 72364
Phone: (870)238-5735

Web site: www.rootsweb.com/~arcross/
Parent County: Crittenden, Poinsett, St. Francis

Record Type	Year Begun	Jurisdiction
Birth	1914	Dept./Health
Death	1914	Dept./Health
Marriage	1863	County Clerk
Divorce	1866	Chancery Circuit Clerk
Land	1865	Clerk/Circuit Ct.
Probate	1863	County Clerk
Tax	1865	County Clerk
County Court	1865	County Clerk
Newspapers	1935	County Historical Society
Cemetery	na	County Historical Society
Court	1865	Clerk/Circuit Ct.

■ **Dallas** 1 Jan. 1845
206 W. Third St., Fordyce, AR 71742
Phone: (870)238-5735
Web site: www.rootsweb.com/~ardallas/
Parent County: Clark, Bradley

Record Type	Year Begun	Jurisdiction
Birth	1914	Dept./Health
Death	1914	Dept./Health
Marriage	1855	County Clerk
Divorce	na	County Clerk
Land	1845	County Clerk
Probate	na	County Clerk
Court	na	County Clerk

■ **Desha** 12 Dec. 1838
Robert Moore Ave., P.O. Box 188, Arkansas City, AR 71630
Phone: (870)877-2323
Web site: home.earthlink.net/~reitzamm/
Parent County: Arkansas, Chicot

Record Type	Year Begun	Jurisdiction
Birth	1914	Dept./Health
Death	1914	Dept./Health
Marriage	1865	County Clerk
Divorce	na	Clerk/Circuit Ct.
Land	na	Clerk/Circuit Ct.
Probate	na	County Clerk
Court	na	Clerk/Circuit Ct.

■ **Dorsey** 17 Apr. 1873
Parent County: Dallas, Bradley, Jefferson, Lincoln
Comments/research tips: (See Cleveland) Name changed to Cleveland 5 March 1885.

■ **Drew** 26 Nov. 1846
210 S. Main St., Monticello, AR 71655
Phone: (870)460-6260
Web site: www.rootsweb.com/ardrew
Parent County: Arkansas, Bradley

Record Type	Year Begun	Jurisdiction
Birth	1914	Dept./Health
Death	1914	Dept./Health
Marriage	na	County Clerk
Divorce	na	Clerk/Circuit Ct.

Land	na	County Assessor
Probate	na	County Clerk
Court	na	Clerk/Circuit Ct.
Military	na	Clerk/Circuit Ct.

■ **Faulkner** 12 Apr. 1873
801 Locust St., Conway, AR 72032
Phone: (501)450-4910
Parent County: Pulaski, Conway

Record Type	Year Begun	Jurisdiction
Birth	1914	Dept./Health
Death	1914	Dept./Health
Marriage	1873	County Clerk
Probate	1873	County Clerk
Court	1873	County Clerk

■ **Franklin** 19 Dec. 1837
211 W. Commercial St., Ozark, AR 72949-0000
Phone: (501)667-3607
Web site: www.rootsweb.com/~arfrankl/
Parent County: Crawford

Record Type	Year Begun	Jurisdiction
Birth	1914	Dept./Health
Death	1914	Dept./Health
Marriage	1850	County Clerk
Land	1899	County Clerk
Probate	1838	County Clerk

■ **Fulton** 21 Dec. 1842
P.O. Box 278, Salem, AR 72576-0278
Phone: (870)895-3310
Web site: www.rootsweb.com/~arfulton/
Parent County: Izard

Record Type	Year Begun	Jurisdiction
Birth	1914	Dept./Health
Death	1914	Dept./Health
Marriage	1887	County Clerk
Divorce	1891	County Clerk
Probate	1891	County Clerk
Land	1891	County Clerk
Court	1891	County Clerk

■ **Garland** 5 Apr. 1873
501 Ouachita Ave., Hot Springs, AR 71901
Phone: (501) 622-3610
Web site: www.garlandcounty.org/
Parent County: Saline

Record Type	Year Begun	Jurisdiction
Birth	1914	Dept./Health
Death	1914	Dept./Health
Marriage	na	County Clerk
Divorce	na	Clerk/Circuit Ct.
Land	na	Clerk/Circuit Ct.
Probate	na	County Clerk
Court	na	Clerk/Circuit Ct.

■ **Grant** 4 Feb. 1869
101 W. Center St. #106, P.O. Box 364, Sheridan, AR 72150
Phone: (870)942-2551

Arkansas

Parent County: Jefferson, Hot Springs, Saline

Record Type	Year Begun	Jurisdiction
Birth	1914	Dept./Health
Death	1914	Dept./Health
Marriage	1877	County Clerk
Divorce	1877	County Clerk
Land	1877	County Clerk
Probate	1877	County Clerk
Court	1877	County Clerk

■ Greene 5 Nov. 1833
P.O. Box 62, Paragould, AR 72451-0364
Phone: (870)239-6311
Web site: www.rootsweb.com/~argreene/
Parent County: Lawrence

Record Type	Year Begun	Jurisdiction
Birth	1914	Dept./Health
Death	1914	Dept./Health
Marriage	1876	County Clerk
Divorce	na	Clerk/Circuit Ct.
Land	1876	County Clerk
Probate	1876	County Clerk
Court	1876	County Clerk

■ Hempstead 15 Dec. 1818
P.O. Box 1420, Hope, AR 71801-1420
Phone: (870)777-2241
Web site: www.rootsweb.com/~arhempst/
Parent County: Arkansas

Record Type	Year Begun	Jurisdiction
Birth	1914	Dept./Health
Death	1914	Dept./Health
Marriage	1823	County Clerk
Land	1900	County Clerk
Probate	1823	County Clerk

■ Hot Spring 2 Nov. 1829
210 Locust St., Malvern, AR 72104
Phone: (501)332-2291
Web site: www.rootsweb.com/~arhotspr/
Parent County: Clark

Record Type	Year Begun	Jurisdiction
Birth	1914	Dept./Health
Death	1914	Dept./Health
Marriage	1825	County Clerk
Divorce	na	Clerk/Circuit Ct.
Probate	1834	County Clerk
Court	na	Clerk/Circuit Ct.

■ Howard 17 Apr. 1873
421 N. Main St., Nashville, AR 71852
Phone: (870)845-7502
Web site: www.genealogyshoppe.com/arhoward/
Parent County: Pike, Hempstead, Polk, Sevier

Record Type	Year Begun	Jurisdiction
Birth	1914	Dept./Health
Death	1914	Dept./Health
Marriage	1873	County Clerk
Divorce	1873	Clerk/Circuit Ct.

Land	1873	Clerk/Circuit Ct.
Probate	1873	County Clerk
Court	1873	Clerk/Circuit Ct.
Cemetery	na	County Clerk

■ Independence 23 Oct. 1820
192 E. Main St., Batesville, AR 72501
Phone: (870)793-8828
Parent County: Lawrence, Arkansas

Record Type	Year Begun	Jurisdiction
Birth	1914	Dept./Health
Death	1914	Dept./Health
Marriage	1826	County Clerk
Divorce	na	Clerk/Circuit Ct.
Land	na	Clerk/Circuit Ct.
Probate	1839	County Clerk
Court	na	Clerk/Circuit Ct.
Burial	na	County Librarian

■ Izard 27 Oct. 1825
P.O. Box 327, Melbourne, AR 72556
Phone: (870)368-4328
Web site: www.pastracks.com/states/arkansas/izard/
Parent County: Independence
Comments/research tips: Line between Izard and Sharp Counties changed 9 March 1877.

Record Type	Year Begun	Jurisdiction
Birth	1914	Dept./Health
Death	1914	Dept./Health
Marriage	1889	County Clerk
Divorce	1889	County Clerk
Land	1889	County Clerk
Probate	1889	County Clerk
Court	1889	County Clerk

■ Jackson 5 Nov. 1829
208 Main St., Newport, AR 72112
Phone: (870)523-7420
Web site: www.rootsweb.com/~arjackso/
Parent County: Independence

Record Type	Year Begun	Jurisdiction
Birth	1914	Dept./Health
Death	1914	Dept./Health
Marriage	1843	County Clerk
Divorce	1845	Clerk/Circuit Ct.
Land	na	Clerk/Circuit Ct.
Probate	1845	County Clerk
Court	1845	Clerk/Circuit Ct.

■ Jefferson 2 Nov. 1829
101 W. Barraque St., Pine Bluff, AR 71601
Phone: (870)541-5360
Web site: www.rootsweb.com/~arjeffer/
Parent County: Arkansas, Pulaski

Record Type	Year Begun	Jurisdiction
Birth	1914	Dept./Health
Death	1914	Dept./Health
Marriage	1830	County Clerk
Divorce	na	Clerk/Circuit Ct.

Record Type	Year Begun	Jurisdiction
Land	na	Clerk/Circuit Ct.
Probate	1845	County Clerk
Court	na	Clerk/Circuit Ct.

■ Johnson 16 Nov. 1833
215 W. Main St., P.O. Box 57, Clarksville, AR 72830
Phone: (501)754-3967
Web site: www.oklahoma.net/~pvtspark/johnson.html
Parent County: Pope

Record Type	Year Begun	Jurisdiction
Birth	1914	Dept./Health
Death	1914	Dept./Health
Marriage	1855	County Clerk
Divorce	na	Clerk/Circuit Ct.
Land	na	Clerk/Circuit Ct.
Probate	1844	County Clerk
Court	na	Clerk/Circuit Ct.
Burial	na	Extension Office

■ Lafayette 15 Oct. 1827
2 Courthouse Sq., Lewisville, AR 71845
Phone: (870)921-4633
Web site: www.rootsweb.com/~arlafaye/
Parent County: Hempstead

Record Type	Year Begun	Jurisdiction
Birth	1914	Dept./Health
Death	1914	Dept./Health
Marriage	1848	County Clerk
Divorce	na	Clerk/Circuit Ct.
Land	na	Clerk/Circuit Ct.
Probate	na	County Clerk

■ Lawrence 15 Jan. 1815
P.O. Box 553, 315 W. Main, Walnut Ridge, AR 72476
Phone: (870)886-1111
Web site: www.arkansasgenealogy.com/lawrence
Parent County: New Madrid, MO

Record Type	Year Begun	Jurisdiction
Birth	1914	Dept./Health
Death	1914	Dept./Health
Marriage	na	County Clerk
Probate	na	County Clerk

■ Lee 17 Apr. 1873
15 E. Chestnut St., Marianna, AR 72360
Phone: (870)295-7715
Web site: www.rootsweb.com/~arlee2/lee.htm
Parent County: Phillips, Monroe, Crittenden, St. Francis

Record Type	Year Begun	Jurisdiction
Birth	1914	Dept./Health
Death	1914	Dept./Health
Marriage	1873	County Clerk
Divorce	1873	Clerk/Circuit Ct.
Probate	1873	County Clerk
Tax	1873	County Clerk
Court	1873	Clerk/Circuit Ct.
Military	1873	Clerk/Circuit Ct.

■ Lincoln 28 Mar. 1871
300 S. Drew St., Star City, AR 71667
Phone: (870)628-7208
Web site: www.rootsweb.com/~arlee2/lee.htm
Parent County: Arkansas, Bradley, Desha, Drew, Jefferson

Record Type	Year Begun	Jurisdiction
Birth	1914	Dept./Health
Death	1914	Dept./Health
Marriage	1871	County Clerk
Land	1871	County Clerk
Probate	1871	County Clerk
Tax	na	County Clerk

■ Little River 5 Mar. 1867
351 N. Second St., Ashdown, AR 71822
Phone: (870)898-7208
Web site: www.rootsweb.com/~arlittle/
Parent County: Hempstead

Record Type	Year Begun	Jurisdiction
Birth	1914	Dept./Health
Death	1914	Dept./Health
Marriage	1880	County Clerk
Divorce	na	Clerk/Circuit Ct.
Land	na	Clerk/Circuit Ct.
Probate	1880	County Clerk

■ Logan 22 Mar. 1871
Courthouse Sq., Paris, AR 72855
Phone: (501)963-2618
Web site: www.rootsweb.com/~arlogan/index.htm
Parent County: Pope, Franklin, Johnson, Scott, Yell
Comments/research tips: Formerly Sarber County. Name changed to Logan 14 December 1875.

Record Type	Year Begun	Jurisdiction
Birth	1914	Dept./Health
Death	1914	Dept./Health
Marriage	na	County Clerk
Divorce	na	Clerk/Circuit Ct.
Land	na	Clerk/Circuit Ct.
Probate	na	County Clerk
Court	na	Clerk/Circuit Ct.

■ Lonoke 16 Apr. 1873
3rd & N. Center St., P.O. Box 431, Lonoke, AR 72086-0431
Phone: (501)676-2368
Web site: www.rootsweb.com/~arlonoke/
Parent County: Pulaski, Prairie
Comments/research tips: Some records of Lonoke County are in Des Arc, Prairie County, AR.

Record Type	Year Begun	Jurisdiction
Birth	1914	Dept./Health
Death	1914	Dept./Health
Marriage	na	County Clerk
Probate	na	County Clerk

■ Lovely 1827
Parent County: Northwest Arkansas & Northeast Oklahoma
Comments/research tips: Lost to Oklahoma and abolished 1828.

■ Madison 30 Sep. 1836
1 Main St., P.O. Box 37, Huntsville, AR 72740-0037
Phone: (501)738-6721

Web site: members.aol.com/madcounty/mcindex.htm
Parent County: Washington

Record Type	Year Begun	Jurisdiction
Birth	1914	Dept./Health
Death	1914	Dept./Health
Marriage	1901	County Clerk
Probate	1901	County Clerk

■ Marion 3 Nov. 1835

Hwy. 62, P.O. Box 545, Yellville, AR 72687
Phone: (870)449-6226
Web site: www.rootsweb.com/~armarion/
Parent County: Izard
Comments/research tips: Formerly Searcy County. Name changed to Marion 29 September 1836.

Record Type	Year Begun	Jurisdiction
Birth	1914	Dept./Health
Death	1914	Dept./Health
Marriage	1888	County Clerk
Divorce	1888	County Clerk
Land	1888	County Clerk
Probate	1888	County Clerk
Court	1888	County Clerk

■ Miller Dec. 1874

400 Laurel St., Texarkana, AR 71854
Phone: (870)744-1501
Web site: www.rootsweb.com/~armiller/
Parent County: Lafayette

Record Type	Year Begun	Jurisdiction
Birth	1914	Dept./Health
Death	1914	Dept./Health
Marriage	1875	County Clerk
Divorce	na	Clerk/Circuit Ct.
Land	1875	County Clerk
Probate	1875	County Clerk
Court	na	Clerk/Circuit Ct.

■ Miller, old 1 Apr. 1820

Parent County: Hempstead
Comments/research tips: Abolished 1836. Re-established December 1874 from Lafayette County.

■ Mississippi 1 Nov. 1833

200 W. Walnut, Blytheville, AR 72315
Phone: (870)763-3212
Web site: www.rootsweb.com/~armissi2/
Parent County: Crittenden

Record Type	Year Begun	Jurisdiction
Birth	1914	Dept./Health
Death	1914	Dept./Health
Marriage	1850	County Clerk
Divorce	1866	Clerk/Circuit Ct.
Land	1865	Clerk/Circuit Ct.
Probate	1865	County Clerk
Court	1866	Clerk/Circuit Ct.

■ Monroe 2 Nov. 1829

123 Madison St., Clarendon, AR 72029-2794
Phone: (870)747-3921

Web site: www.rootsweb.com/~armonro2/
Parent County: Phillips, Arkansas

Record Type	Year Begun	Jurisdiction
Birth	1914	Dept./Health
Death	1914	Dept./Health
Marriage	1850	County Clerk
Divorce	1839	Clerk/Circuit Ct.
Land	1829	Clerk/Circuit Ct.
Probate	1839	County Clerk
Court	1830	Clerk/Circuit Ct.

■ Montgomery 9 Dec. 1842

1 George St., Mount Ida, AR 71957
Phone: (870)887-3521
Web site: www.rootsweb.com/~armontgo/
Parent County: Hot Spring

Record Type	Year Begun	Jurisdiction
Birth	1914	Dept./Health
Death	1914	Dept./Health
Marriage	1845	County Clerk
Divorce	1845	County Clerk
Land	1845	County Clerk
Probate	1845	County Clerk
Court	1845	County Clerk
Burial	na	County Agent

■ Nevada 20 Mar. 1871

215 E. Second St. S., Prescott, AR 71857
Phone: (870)887-3115
Web site: www.rootsweb.com/~arnevada/
Parent County: Hempstead, Columbia, Ouachita

Record Type	Year Begun	Jurisdiction
Birth	1914	Dept./Health
Death	1914	Dept./Health
Marriage	1871	County Clerk
Divorce	1871	Clerk/Circuit Ct.
Land	1871	Clerk/Circuit Ct.
Probate	1871	County Clerk
Court	1871	Clerk/Circuit Ct.
Cemetery	na	County Clerk

■ Newton 14 Dec. 1842

Court St., Jasper, AR 82641-0435
Phone: (870)446-5125
Web site: www.rootsweb.com/~arnewton/
Parent County: Carroll

Record Type	Year Begun	Jurisdiction
Birth	1914	Dept./Health
Death	1914	Dept./Health
Marriage	1866	County Clerk
Land	1866	County Clerk
Probate	1880	County Clerk
Court	1880	County Clerk

■ Ouachita 29 Nov. 1842

145 Jackson St., Camden, AR 71701
Phone: (870)837-2220
Web site: www.rootsweb.com/~arouachi/index.html
Parent County: Union

Record Type	Year Begun	Jurisdiction
Birth	1914	Dept./Health
Death	1914	Dept./Health
Court	na	Clerk/Circuit Ct.
Marriage	1875	County Clerk
Divorce	na	Clerk/Circuit Ct.
Land	na	Clerk/Circuit Ct.
Probate	1875	County Clerk

■ Perry 18 Dec. 1840
P.O. Box 358, Perryville, AR 72126-0358
Phone: (501)889-5126
Web site: www.rootsweb.com/~arperry/
Parent County: Conway

Record Type	Year Begun	Jurisdiction
Birth	1914	Dept./Health
Death	1914	Dept./Health
Marriage	1882	County Clerk
Divorce	1882	County Clerk
Land	1882	County Clerk
Probate	1882	County Clerk
Court	1882	County Clerk

■ Phillips 1 May. 1820
600 Cherry St., Helena, AR 72342
Phone: (870)338-5505
Web site: www.rootsweb.com/~arpphill2/phillips.htm
Parent County: Arkansas, Hempstead

Record Type	Year Begun	Jurisdiction
Birth	1914	Dept./Health
Death	1914	Dept./Health
Marriage	1831	County Clerk
Divorce	1820	Clerk/Circuit Ct.
Land	1820	Clerk/Circuit Ct.
Probate	1850	County Clerk
Court	1820	Clerk/Circuit Ct.

■ Pike 1 Nov. 1833
P.O. Box 219, Murfreesboro, AR 71958
Phone: (870)285-2231
Web site: www.rootsweb.com/~arpike/
Parent County: Clark, Hempstead

Record Type	Year Begun	Jurisdiction
Birth	1914	Dept./Health
Death	1914	Dept./Health
Marriage	1895	County Clerk
Divorce	1895	County Clerk
Land	1895	County Clerk
Probate	1895	County Clerk
Court	1895	County Clerk
Military	1895	County Clerk

■ Poinsett 28 Feb. 1838
401 Market St., Harrisburg, AR 72432
Phone: (870)578-4410
Web site: www.rootsweb.com/~arpoinse/
Parent County: Greene, St. Francis

Record Type	Year Begun	Jurisdiction
Birth	1914	Dept./Health

Record Type	Year Begun	Jurisdiction
Death	1914	Dept./Health
Marriage	1873	County Clerk
Divorce	na	Clerk/Circuit Ct.
Land	na	Clerk/Circuit Ct.
Probate	na	County Clerk
Court	na	Clerk/Circuit Ct.

■ Polk 30 Nov. 1844
507 Church Ave., Mena, AR 71953
Phone: (501)394-8123
Web site: www.rootsweb.com/~arpolk/
Parent County: Sevier

Record Type	Year Begun	Jurisdiction
Birth	1914	Dept./Health
Death	1914	Dept./Health
Marriage	1885	County Clerk
Divorce	na	Clerk/Circuit Ct.
Land	1885	Clerk/Circuit Ct.
Probate	1900	County Clerk
Court	1885	Clerk/Circuit Ct.
Cemetery	na	County Clerk
Military	na	Clerk/Circuit Ct.

■ Pope 2 Nov. 1829
100 W. Main St., Russellville, AR 72801
Phone: (501)968-6064
Web site: www.rootsweb.com/~arpope2/
Parent County: Crawford

Record Type	Year Begun	Jurisdiction
Birth	1914	Dept./Health
Death	1914	Dept./Health
County Court	1857	County Clerk
Military	na	Clerk/Circuit Ct.
Death	1965	County Clerk
Marriage	1831	County Clerk
Voter	1965	County Clerk
Divorce	na	Clerk/Circuit Ct.
Land	na	Clerk/Circuit Ct.
Probate	1831	County Clerk

■ Prairie 25 Nov. 1846
P.O. Box 278, Des Arc, AR 72040-0278
Phone: (870)256-3741
Web site: www.rootsweb.com/~arprairi/
Parent County: Pulaski, Monroe
Comments/research tips: Part of the county was taken from Monroe in 1869. Check Monroe County for records prior to this date. County Clerk in DeValls Bluff, AR has Naturalization records 1907–1912, as well as the records listed below.

Record Type	Year Begun	Jurisdiction
Birth	1914	Dept./Health
Death	1914	Dept./Health
Marriage	1885	see Comments, above
Divorce	1885	see Comments, above
Land	1885	see Comments, above
Probate	1885	see Comments, above
Court	1885	see Comments, above
Military	1917	see Comments, above

■ Pulaski 15 Dec. 1818
401 W. Markham St., Little Rock, AR 72201
Phone: (501)340-8500
Web site: www.co.pulaski.ar.us/index.htm
Parent County: Arkansas
Comments/research tips: History Commission has Probate records before 1920. Real estate, personal property, and poll tax records from the mid-1800s are with the county clerk.

Record Type	Year Begun	Jurisdiction
Birth	1914	Dept./Health
Death	1914	Dept./Health
Marriage	1838	County Clerk
Divorce	na	Clerk/Chancery Ct.
Land	na	Clerk/Circuit Ct.
Probate	1820	County Clerk
Probate	na	Clerk/Circuit Ct.
Vote Reg.	1952	County Clerk
Court	na	Clerk/Circuit Ct.

■ Randolph 18 Dec. 1832
107 W. Broadway, Pocahontas, AR 72455
Phone: (870)892-5822
Web site: www.randolphchamber.com/
Parent County: Creek Cession of 1832

Record Type	Year Begun	Jurisdiction
Birth	1914	Dept./Health
Death	1914	Dept./Health
Marriage	1837	County Clerk
Divorce	1836	County Clerk
Land	1836	County Clerk
Probate	1837	County Clerk
Court	1836	County Clerk
Military	1836	County Clerk

■ Saline 2 Nov. 1835
215 N. Main, Suite 9, Benton, AR 72015
Phone: (501)303-5630
Web site: www.salinecounty.org/
Parent County: Pulaski, Hempstead

Record Type	Year Begun	Jurisdiction
Birth	1914	Dept./Health
Death	1914	Dept./Health
Marriage	1836	County Clerk
Land	1871	County Clerk
Probate	1836	County Clerk

■ Sarber 22 Mar. 1871
Parent County: Pope, Franklin, Johnson, Scott, Yell
Comments/research tips: (See Logan) Name changed to Logan 14 December 1875.

■ Scott 5 Nov. 1833
100 W. 1 St., Suite 1, Waldron, AR 72958
Phone: (501)637-2155
Web site: www.rootsweb.com/~arscott/scott.htm
Parent County: Pulaski, Crawford, Pope

Record Type	Year Begun	Jurisdiction
Birth	1914	Dept./Health
Death	1914	Dept./Health

Marriage	1882	County/Circuit Clerk
Divorce	1882	County/Circuit Clerk
Probate	1882	County/Circuit Clerk
Land	1882	County/Circuit Clerk
Court	1882	County/Circuit Clerk

■ Searcy 13 Dec. 1838
Courthouse Sq., P.O. Box 297, Marshall, AR 72650
Phone: (870)448-3807
Parent County: Marion

Record Type	Year Begun	Jurisdiction
Birth	1914	Dept./Health
Death	1914	Dept./Health
Marriage	1881	County Clerk
Divorce	1881	County Clerk
Land	1866	County Clerk
Court	1881	County Clerk
Nat.	1881	County Clerk

■ Sebastian 6 Jan. 1851
35 S. Sixth, Fort Smith, AR 72901
Phone: (501)782-5065
Web site: www.sebastiancountyonline.com
Parent County: Scott, Polk, Crawford, Van Buren

Record Type	Year Begun	Jurisdiction
Birth	1914	Dept./Health
Death	1914	Dept./Health
Marriage	1865	County Clerk
Divorce	na	Clerk/Circuit Ct.
Land	na	Clerk/Circuit Ct.
Probate	1866	County Clerk
Court	na	Clerk/Circuit Ct.

■ Sevier 17 Oct. 1828
115 N. Third, De Queen, AR 71832
Phone: (870)642-2425
Web site: www.genealogyshoppe.com/arsevier/
Parent County: Hempstead, Miller

Record Type	Year Begun	Jurisdiction
Birth	1914	Dept./Health
Death	1914	Dept./Health
Marriage	1829	County Clerk
Divorce	na	Clerk/Circuit Ct.
Land	na	Clerk/Circuit Ct.
Probate	1829	County Clerk
Court	na	Clerk/Circuit Ct.

■ Sharp 18 July 1868
P.O. Box 307, Ash Flat, AR 72513
Phone: (870)994-7338
Web site: www.sharpcounty.org/
Parent County: Lawrence
Comments/research tips: Line between Sharp and Izard changed 1877.

Record Type	Year Begun	Jurisdiction
Birth	1914	Dept./Health
Death	1914	Dept./Health
Marriage	1880	County Clerk
Divorce	1880	County Clerk

Land	1880	County Clerk
Probate	1880	County Clerk
Court	1880	County Clerk

■ St. Francis 13 Oct. 1827
313 S. Izard St., Forrest City, AR 72335-3856
Phone: (870)261-1725
Parent County: Phillips

Record Type	Year Begun	Jurisdiction
Birth	1914	Dept./Health
Death	1914	Dept./Health
Marriage	1875	County Clerk
Divorce	na	Clerk/Circuit Ct.
Land	na	Clerk/Circuit Ct.
Probate	1910	County Clerk
Tax	1910	County Clerk
Court	na	Clerk/Circuit Ct.

■ Stone 21 Apr. 1873
P.O. Box 120, Mountain View, AR 72560
Phone: (870)269-5550
Web site: www.arkansasfamilies.net/afcostone.html
Parent County: Izard, Independence, Searcy, Van Buren

Record Type	Year Begun	Jurisdiction
Birth	1914	Dept./Health
Death	1914	Dept./Health
Marriage	1873	County Clerk
Divorce	1873	County Clerk
Land	1873	Clerk/Circuit Ct.
Probate	1873	Clerk/Circuit Ct.
Court	1873	Clerk/Circuit Ct.
Military	1873	Clerk/Circuit Ct.

■ Union 2 Nov. 1829
101 N. Washington, El Dorado, AR 71730
Phone: (870)864-1910
Web site: www.rootsweb.com/~arunion/
Parent County: Hempstead, Clark

Record Type	Year Begun	Jurisdiction
Birth	1914	Dept./Health
Death	1914	Dept./Health
Marriage	1846	County Clerk
Divorce	na	Clerk/Circuit Ct.
Land	na	Clerk/Circuit Ct.
Probate	1846	County Clerk
Court	na	Clerk/Circuit Ct.

■ Van Buren 11 Nov. 1833
P.O. Box 180, Clinton, AR 72031
Phone: (501)745-4140
Web site: www.rootsweb.com/~arvanbur/
Parent County: Independence, Conway, Izard

Record Type	Year Begun	Jurisdiction
Birth	1914	Dept./Health
Death	1914	Dept./Health
Marriage	1859	County Clerk
Divorce	1874	County Clerk
Land	1859	County Clerk
Probate	1860	County Clerk
Court	1859	County Clerk

■ Washington 17 Oct. 1828
280 N. College Ave. #300, Fayetteville, AR 72701
Phone: (501)444-1711
Web site: www.co.washington.ar.us/
Parent County: Crawford

Record Type	Year Begun	Jurisdiction
Birth	1914	Dept./Health
Death	1914	Dept./Health
Marriage	1845	County Clerk
Divorce	na	Clerk/Circuit Ct.
Land	na	Clerk/Circuit Ct.
Probate	1828	County Clerk
Court	na	Clerk/Circuit Ct.

■ White 23 Oct. 1835
300 N. Spruce St., Searcy, AR 72143
Phone: (501)279-6200
Web site: www.cswnet.com/~wccomp/
Parent County: Pulaski, Jackson, Independence

Record Type	Year Begun	Jurisdiction
Birth	1914	Dept./Health
Death	1914	Dept./Health
Marriage	na	County Clerk
Divorce	na	County Clerk
Land	na	County Clerk
Probate	na	County Clerk
Tax	na	County Clerk
Court	na	County Clerk

■ Woodruff 26 Nov. 1862
500 N. Third St., Augusta, AR 72006-0356
Phone: (870)347-5206
Web site: www.rootsweb.com/~arwoodru/
Parent County: Jackson, St. Francis

Record Type	Year Begun	Jurisdiction
Birth	1914	Dept./Health
Death	1914	Dept./Health
Marriage	1865	County Clerk
Divorce	na	Clerk/Circuit Ct.
Land	na	Clerk/Circuit Ct.
Probate	1865	County Clerk
Court	na	Clerk/Circuit Ct.

■ Yell 5 Dec. 1840
Web site: www.rootsweb.com/~aryell/
Parent County: Pope, Scott
Comments/research tips: Yell County has two county courthouses: P.O. Box 219, Danville, AR 72833, Tel: (504)495-2414 or P.O. Box 457, Dardanelle, AR 72834, Tel: (504)229-4404.

Record Type	Year Begun	Jurisdiction
Birth	1914	Dept./Health
Death	1914	Dept./Health
Marriage	1865	County Clerk
Divorce	1865	County Clerk
Land	1865	County Clerk
Probate	1865	County Clerk
Court	1865	County Clerk

California

By David A. Fryxell

HISTORICAL OVERVIEW

California's vast territory and varied cultures make it seem more like a nation—which it was briefly in 1846—than a state. Eyed by England and Russia, California was first settled by the Spanish: Father Junipero Serra arrived at the future site of San Diego in 1769 and began a string of missions along El Camino Real (The Royal Highway). Missions would be crucial to the state's history under Spain and, after 1821, Mexico. The Spanish divided California into four districts—San Diego, Monterey, San Francisco, and Santa Barbara—each with a *presidio* (prison) and at least one mission.

Americans had begun crossing the continent to California in 1841, forming a small population that launched the "Bear-Flag Republic" in 1846. The breakaway republic was swiftly swept into the U.S. war with Mexico, becoming an American protectorate. California was ceded to the U.S. in 1848 and became a state just two years later.

The fast track to statehood was paved with gold, famously discovered at Sutter's Mill in 1848. More than 300,000 people—the greatest numbers from New England, Pennsylvania, and New York—would follow the Gold Rush to California by 1854.

Also among the early arrivals were Irish, Italians, and Chinese, whose numbers swelled from seven in 1848 to 20,000 in 1852. The Chinese also came to work on the transcontinental railroad, which linked California to the East in 1869. An 1880s real-estate boom attracted English, Germans, and transplants from the Midwest. After 1885, when Japanese could legally leave their native country, many came to California.

The Great Depression brought the "Okies," immortalized by John Steinbeck in *The Grapes of Wrath*. After the industrial boom of World War II, California's population surged, including influxes of African Americans, Mexicans, and Southeast Asians. Today the "Golden State"

CALIFORNIA AT A GLANCE

Motto: Eureka!

Population: 33.9 million

Prevalent Religions: They're all here, of course, but Roman Catholics have the greatest numbers, followed by Lutherans and Baptists.

Major Industries: Electronic components and equipment, aerospace, film production, food processing, petroleum, computers and computer software, tourism, vegetables, fruits and nuts, dairy products, cattle, nursery stock, grapes, wine

Ethnic Makeup (in percent): Caucasian 59.5%, African American 6.7%, Hispanic 32.4%, Asian 10.9%, Native American 1.0%, Other 16.8%

Famous Californians: Julia Child, Leonardo DiCaprio, Joe DiMaggio, Isadora Duncan, John Charles Frémont, Jerry Garcia, William Randolph Hearst, Sidney Howard, Jack London, George Lucas, Richard Nixon, Isamu Noguchi, George Patton, Robert Redford, Sally Ride, John Steinbeck, Shirley Temple, Earl Warren, Tiger Woods

Above: A typical California surfer

of Hollywood and Silicon Valley, wineries and freeways, redwoods and the Rose Bowl is America's most populous.

RECORD HIGHLIGHTS

Pre-statehood censuses, called *padrons*, were taken for places including Los Angeles (1790, 1836, 1840), San Carlos (1769), San Luis Obispo (1797, 1798), San Antonio (1798), and Soledad (1798). A state census in 1852 covered the entire household and listed each person's previous residence. Several cities also took censuses from 1897 to 1938, including Los Angeles (1897), San Jose (1897), San Diego (1899), and Oakland (1902).

The first federal census to cover California was in 1850. The state library has mortality schedules for the 1850, 1860, 1870, and 1880 censuses.

You can supplement the censuses with the "Great Registers," detailed county voting registers compiled roughly every two years. Early registers included naturalization data for foreign-born voters and even physical descriptions. The state library has registers from 1866–1944.

Churches kept the first vital records, then counties, with statewide registration of births, deaths, and marriages beginning in 1905. Counties began delayed registration of births in 1943.

Land records can provide clues to early California ancestors. For example, the Spanish Archive Record Group, at the state archives and on FHL microfilm, covers 1833 to 1845. The National Archives has Mexican land records from 1822 to 1846, as well as the papers of the U.S. commission set up in 1852 to process claims based on Spanish and Mexican land grants. Later federal land records are at the National Archives regional offices in San Bruno and Laguna Niguel, and in the state archives. The FHL also has microfilm of many county deeds and mortgage filings.

If your ancestors arrived in California by sea, you can find San Francisco ship passenger lists in the state library and the National Archives. Angel Island in San Francisco harbor became known as the "Ellis Island of the West," and was the gateway to America for many Chinese immigrants.

The biggest challenge facing California researchers, according to Nancy Hendrickson, a San Diego genealogist and author of *Finding Your Roots Online* (Cincinnati: Betterway Books, 2003), is getting official vital records from the state. The wait for marriage certificates, for example, can stretch to three years. A new law combating identify theft will complicate obtaining birth and death certificates. Frederick Sherman, director of research for the California Genealogical Society, recommends contacting the county recorder's office instead of the state. "It's much faster," he says, "and the cost is the same."

Hendrickson suggests turning to published and online

RESEARCH TIPS

for more info

- The biggest challenge facing California researchers can be getting official vital records from the state. Try contacting the county recorder's office where the document was recorded instead.
- The state library's death index, 1905 to 1997, and its marriage index, 1949 to 1986, are online from 1940 at <http://userdb.rootsweb.com/ca/death/search.cgi>.
- An often-overlooked resource is the collection of the Daughters of the American Revolution transcripts of records, which includes cemeteries (18 volumes), Los Angeles baptisms, pioneer obituaries, Bibles, early wills, and veteran grave registrations.
- Since California is such a large and populous state some of its counties are enormous, so you should always try to pin down the exact locality of your ancestors before contacting an office or society for records.
- Unorthodox resources, such as newspapers, family letters, county records, cemetery inscriptions, etc., can sometimes assist you more in California research than traditional genealogical records.

Census Records
- Federal Census: 1850, 1860, 1870, 1880, 1900, 1910, 1920, 1930
- Federal Mortality Schedules: 1850, 1860, 1870, 1880
- State Census: 1852
- Los Angeles Census: 1790, 1816, 1836, 1844
- Early mission censuses: 1790s

California

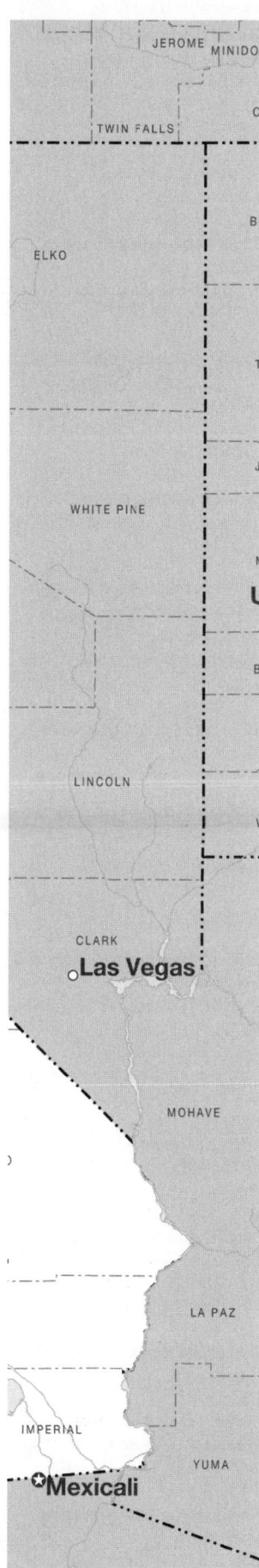

transcripts, often from local genealogy societies. Or try the state library's death index, 1905 to 1997, (searchable online from 1940 at <http://userdb.rootsweb.com/ca/death/search.cgi>) and its marriage index, 1949 to 1986. For marriages, Hendrickson notes that many Californians went to Nevada to get hitched (or un-hitched); the state library also has Nevada marriage and divorce indexes on microfiche.

An often-overlooked resource, Hendrickson adds, is the collection of Daughters of the American Revolution (DAR) transcripts of records, which includes cemeteries (18 volumes), Los Angeles baptisms, pioneer obituaries, Bibles, early wills, and veteran grave registrations. You can access these at the state library or borrow many through the FHL.

Sherman cautions, "California is a large and populous state. Some of its counties, e.g. Los Angeles, are huge, so it pays off to make every effort to pin down the town or small locality in which your target persons lived or live, before you ask for help from a countywide or statewide office or society. This is especially true if you are searching for an obituary."

"Almost everybody in California arrived fairly recently, since 1850, from somewhere else," Sherman goes on. "The population grew explosively before record-keeping systems had become well-established and efficient. Many of the early arrivals came in through San Francisco, which lost almost all its civil records and many of its church records in the 1906 earthquake and fire. Reconstructing a picture of the early days depends more on scattered resources, such as newspapers, family letters, county records, cemetery inscriptions, etc., than traditional genealogical records."

The Internet can help, too: The Federation of East European Family History Societies' site <http://feefhs.org> includes an ambitious reconstruction of records from when San Francisco was home to so many European immigrants. The San Francisco GenWeb page <www.sfgenealogy.com/sf/sfranvit.htm> has an extensive list of links to pre-1906 information.

STATE RESOURCES

■ ARCHIVES, LIBRARIES, AND SOCIETIES

African-American Genealogical Society of Northern California (AAGSNC)
P.O. Box 27485, Oakland, CA 94602-0985
Tel: (877) 884-2843
E-mail: baobabtree@aagsnc.org
Web site: <www.aagsnc.org>

Alameda County Library
2400 Stevenson Blvd., Fremont, CA 94538

Tel: (510) 745-1400
Web site: <www.aclibrary.org>

Alhambra Historical Society
P.O. Box 6687
Alhambra, CA 91802

Alhambra Historical Society Museum
1550 W. Alhambra Rd., Alhambra, CA 91802
Tel: (626) 284-6692
Web site: <www.cityofalhambra.org/government/Parks_Recreation/Parks/historical_society.html>

Altadena Heritage
P.O. Box 218, Altadena, CA 91003
Tel: (626) 683-1785

Altadena Historical Society
730 E. Altadena Dr., Altadena, CA 91001
Tel: (626) 794-4967
Web site: <www.mtlowe.net/altadenahistoricalsociety.htm>

Amador County Archives
E-mail: archives@amadorarchives.org
Web site: <www.amadorarchives.org>

American Historical Society of Germans from Russia (AHSGR), Central California Chapter
3233 N. West Ave., Fresno, CA 93705-3402
Tel: (559) 229-8287
E-mail: ahsgrfr@mindspring.com
Web site: <www.ahsgr.org/fresno/cacentra.html>

Angel Island Association
P.O. Box 866, Tiburon, CA 94920
Tel: (415) 435-3522
Web site: <www.angelisland.org>

Antelope Valley Genealogical Society
P.O. Box 1049, Lancaster, CA 93584-1049

Augustan Society and Museum
P.O. Box 75, Daggett, CA 92327-0075
Tel: (760) 254-9223
Web site: <www.augustansociety.org>

Azusa Historical Society
City Hall Complex, 213 E. Foothill Blvd., Azusa, CA 91702

Baldwin Park Historical Society
P.O. Box 1, Baldwin Park, CA 91706
Tel: (818) 338-7130

The Bancroft Library
University of California, Berkeley, Berkeley, CA 94720-6000
Tel: (510) 642-3781
E-mail: bancref@library.berkeley.edu
Web site: <http://bancroft.berkeley.edu>

Bay Area Library and Information Systems (BALIS)
2471 Flores St., San Mateo, CA 94403-2273

Tel: (650) 349-5538
Web site: <http://baylibraries
.org>

Berkeley Historical Society
1931 Center St.
Mailing address: P.O. Box 1190,
Berkeley, CA 94701-1190
E-mail: berkhist@sbcglobal.net
Web site: <www.ci.berkeley.ca
.us/histsoc/>

**British Family Historical
Society of Los Angeles**
22941 Felbar Ave., Torrance, CA
90505

**British Isles Family History
Society**
2531 Sawtelle Blvd., PMB 134,
Los Angeles, CA 90064-3124
Web site: <www.rootsweb.com/
~bifhsusa/>

Burbank Historical Society
1015 W. Olive Ave., Burbank, CA
91506
Tel: (818) 841-6333
E-mail: ghowardmuseum@earthli
nk.net
Web site: <www.burbankhistsoc
.com>

Calabasas Historical Society
P.O. Box 8067, Calabasas, CA
91372
Web site: <http://digital-library.
csun.edu/heritage_network/
calhs.html>

**Calaveras County Library, San
Ansreas Central**
P.O. Box 338, 891 Mountain
Ranch Rd., San Andreas, CA
95249
Tel: (209) 754-6510
Web site: <www.co.calaveras.ca
.us/libraryinfo.html>

Calaveras Genealogical Society
P.O. Box 184, Angels Camp, CA
95222-184

**California African-American
Genealogical Society**
P.O. Box 8442, Los Angeles, CA
90008-0442
Web site: <www.nhm.org/africa/
america/caags>

**California Department of Health
Services, Office of Vital
Records**
1501 Capitol Ave., Sacramento,
CA 95814
Mailing address: M.S. 5103, P.O.
Box 997410, Sacramento, CA
95899-7410

Web site: <www.dhs.ca.gov/
hisp/chs/>

**California Genealogical Society
and Library**
1611 Telegraph Ave., Ste. 100,
Oakland, CA 94612-2154
Tel: (510) 663-1358
Web site: <www.calgensoc
.org/>

**California Mennonite Historical
Society**
4824 E. Butler, Fresno, CA
93727-5097
Web site: <www.fresno.edu/affili
ation/cmhs>

**California Mission Studies
Association**
P.O. Box 3357, Bakersfield, CA
93385-3357
Web site: <www.ca-missions
.org>

The California Pioneer Society
300 Fourth St., San Francisco, CA
94107-1272
Tel: (415) 957-1849
E-mail: info@californiapioneers
.org
Web site: <www.californiapionee
rs.org/>

California State Archives
1020 O St., Sacramento, CA
95814
Tel: (916) 653-7715
Web site: <www.ss.ca.gov/archi
ves/archives/htm>

**California State Genealogical
Alliance**
P.O. Box 311, Danville, CA
94526-0311
Web site: <http://feefhs.org/
csga/frg-csga.html>

California State Library
900 N St., Sacramento, CA
95814
Tel: (916) 654-0176
E-mail: cslcal@library.ca.gov
Web site: <www.library.ca.gov>

**California State Library, Sutro
Library Branch**
480 Winston Dr., San Francisco,
CA 94132
Tel: (415) 731-4477
E-mail: sutro@library.ca.gov
Web site: <www.library.ca.gov>

Carlsbad Historical Society
P.O. Box 252, Carlsbad, CA
92018-0252
Tel: (760) 434-9189
Web site: <www.carlsbad.ca.us/
chs.html>

**Clayton Historical Society and
Museum**
6101 Main St., Clayton, CA
94517
Tel: (925) 672-0240
Web site: <http://claytonhs
.com>

**Colorado River
Blythe-Quartzsite Genealogical
Society**
411 S. Fifth St., Blythe, CA
92225-2816

**Conejo Valley Genealogical
Society**
P.O. Box 1228, Thousand Oaks,
CA 91358-0228
E-mail: cvgsweb@prodigy.net
Web site: <www.rootsweb.com/
~cacvgs/>

**Contra Costa County
Genealogical Society**
P.O. Box 910, Concord, CA
94522-0910
E-mail: cccgs_ca@hotmail.com
Web site: <www.rootsweb.com/
~cacccgs/>

**Contra Costa County Historical
Society**
610 Main St., Martinez, CA
94553
Tel: (925) 229-1042
E-mail: cchistry@ix.netcom.com
Web site: <www.cocohistory
.com>

Covina Valley Historical Society
125 E. College St., Covina, CA
91723
Tel: (626) 966-9871
E-mail: cvhs@earthlink.net
Web site: <http://firehousejailm
useum.tripod.com/covinamus
eum/>

Dalton Genealogical Club
880 Ames Ct., Palo Alto, CA
94303
E-mail: millicenty@aol.com
Web site: <http://members.aol.
com/DaltonGene/>

**The Davis Genealogical Club
and Library**
% The Davis Senior Center, 646
A St., Davis, CA 95616-3602
Tel: (916) 757-5696
Web site: <http://cefha.org/
usa/ca/yolo/dgcl/dgcl-fp.html>

**Delta Genealogical Interest
Group**
P.O. Box 157, Knightsen, CA
94548

**Clayton Historical Society and
Museum**

**Downey Historical Society/
Downey History Center**
P.O. Box 554, 12540 Rives Ave.,
Downy, CA 90241
Tel: (562) 862-2777

Duarte Historical Society
P.O. Box 263, Duarte, CA 91010

**Eagle Rock Valley Historical
Society**
2035 Colorado Blvd., Eagle Rock,
CA 90041

East Bay Genealogical Society
P.O. Box 20417, Oakland, CA
94620-0417
Web site: <www.katpher.com/
EBGS/EBGS.html>

East Kern Genealogical Society
P.O. Box 961, North Edwards, CA
93523-0961

Echo Park Historical Society
P.O. Box 261022, Los Angeles,
CA 90026
Web site: <www.historicechopar
k.org>

**El Dorado County Historical
Museum**
104 Placerville Dr., Placerville,
CA 95667
E-mail: mcory@co.el-dorado
.ca.us
Web site: www.co.el-dorado.ca
.us/generalservices/
museum.html>

**El Monte Historical Society and
Museum**
3150 N. Tyler Ave., El Monte, CA
91731
Tel: (626) 580-2232
Web site: <www.caohwy.com/e/
elmohiso.htm>

Encino Historical Society
16756 Moorpark St., Encino, CA
91436

**Escondido Genealogical
Society**
P.O. 2190, Escondido, CA
92025-0380

Forestville Historical Society
P.O. Box 195, Forestville, CA
95436
E-mail: history@sonic.net
Web site: <www.sonic.net/forest
ville/>

**Fresno County Genealogical
Society**
P.O. Box 1429, Fresno, CA
93716-1429

California

Web site: <www.rootsweb.com/ ~cafcgs/>

Fresno Historical Society
7160 W. Kearney Blvd., Fresno, CA 93706
Tel: (559) 441-0862
E-mail: FrHistSoc@aol.com
Web site: <www.valleyhistory .org>

Genealogical Association of Sacramento (GAS)
P.O. Box 292145, Sacramento, CA 95829-2145
Web site: <www.quiknet.com/~b betts/gas.htm>

Genealogical and Historical Council of the Sacramento Valley
P.O. Box 214749, Sacramento, CA 95821-0749
E-mail: pbdallas@earthlink.net
Web site: <www.sacvalleygenes .org>

Genealogical Society of Coachella Valley
P.O. Box 124, Indio, CA 92202

Genealogical Society of the Morongo Basin
P.O. Box 234, Yucca Valley, CA 92284
Web site: <www.yuccavalley. com/genealogy>

Genealogical Society of North Orange County California (GSNOCC)
P.O. Box 706, Yorba Linda, CA 92885-0706
E-mail: wynn@finders-binders .com
Web site: <www.rootsweb.com/ ~cagsnocc/>

Genealogical Society of Riverside (GSOR)
P.O. Box 2557, Riverside, CA 92516
Web site: <www.goecities.com/ Heartland/Woods/6250/>

Genealogical Society of Santa Cruz County (GSSCC)
P.O. Box 7, Santa Cruz, CA 95063-0072
Web site: <www.cagenweb.com/ santacruz/scruzgs/htm>

Genealogical Society of Stanislaus County, CA, Inc.
P.O. Box A, Modesto, CA 95352-3660
Tel: (209) 571-3227
E-mail: gssc@worldnet.att.net

Web site: <www.cagenweb.com/ lr/stanislaus/gssc.html>

Genealogy Club of Sun City
P.O. Box 175, Sun City, CA 92586
Tel: (909) 244-0229

Genealogy Society of Hispanic Americans of Southern California
P.O. Box 2472, Santa Fe Springs, CA 90670
Tel: (310) 202-1122
E-mail: DonieGSJA@earthlink.net
Web site: <www.gsha.net>

Genealogy Society of Vallejo-Benicia
734 Marin St., Vallejo, CA 94590-5913
Web site: <www.rootsweb.com/ ~cagsv/>

German Genealogical Society of America
% Southern California Genealogical Society and Family Research Library, 417 Irving Dr., Burbank, CA 91504
Tel: (818) 843-7247
E-mail: scgs@earthlink.net
Web site: <http://feefhs.org/ ggsa/frg-ggsa.html>

German Research Association, Inc.
P.O. Box 711600, San Diego, CA 92171-1600
E-mail: donaritchi@aol.com
Web site: <http://feefhs.org/ gra/frg-gra.html>

The Glendale Historical Society (TGHS)
P.O. Box 4173, Glendale, CA 91202
Tel: (818) 242-7447
E-mail: glendalehistorical@yahoo .com
Web site: <www.glendalehistoric al.org>

Glendora Genealogical Group
P.O. Box 1141, Glendora, CA 91741
Tel: (909) 592-4030

Glendora Historical Society and Museum
314 N. Glendora Ave., Glendora, CA 91740
Tel: (626) 963-0419

Golden Gate Chapter, American Historical Society of Germans from Russia (AHSGR)
1225 Vienna Dr. #917, Sunnyvale, CA 94089

Tel: (408) 734-2261
Web site: <www.ahsgr.org/golde n_gate_chapter.htm>

Hayward Area Genealogical Society
P.O. Box 754, Hayward, CA 94543
Web site: <www.hagsociety.tripo d.com/>

Hemet-San Jacinto Genealogical Society
P.O. Box 2516, Hemet, CA 92343

Hi Desert Genealogical Society
P.O. Box 1271, Victorville, CA 92392

Historical Society of Centinela Valley
7634 Midfield Ave., Los Angeles, CA 90045
Tel: (213) 649-6272

Historical Society of Long Beach
P.O. Box 1869, Long Beach, CA 90802
Tel: (562) 495-1210
E-mail: hslb@historicalsocietylb .org
Web site: <www.historicalsociety lb.org>

Historical Society of Monterey Park
781 S. Orange Ave., P.O. Box 172, Monterey Park, CA 91754

Historical Society of Pomona Valley
1460 E. Holt Blvd., Suite 78, Pomona, CA 91767
E-mail: ogallivan@earthlink.net
Web site: <www.osb.net/Pom ona/default.htm>

Historical Society of Southern California
200 E. Ave. 43, Los Angeles, CA 90031
Tel: (323) 222-0546
E-mail: HSSC@socalhistory.org
Web site: <www.socalhistory .org>

Historical Society of the Upper Mojave Desert
P.O. Box 2001, Ridgecrest, CA 93556-2001
Tel: (760) 375-8456
E-mail: hsumd@ridgenet.net
Web site: <www.maturango.org/ Hist.html>

Holt-Atherton Church Archives
University of the Pacific, 3601 Pacific Ave., Stockton, CA 95211
Tel: (209) 946-2404

Hungarian/American Friendship Society
1035 Starbrook Dr., Galt, CA 95632
Tel: (209) 744-8099
E-mail: holmes@dholmes.com
Web site: <www.dholmes.com/ hafs.html>

Humboldt County Genealogical Society
2336 G St., Eureka, CA 95501

Humboldt County Historical Society
703 Eighth St., P.O. Box 8000, Eureka, CA 95502
Tel: (707) 445-4342
E-mail: hchs@reninet.com
Web site: <www.humboldthistory .org>

Immigrant Genealogical Society (IGS)
P.O. Box 7369, Burbank, CA 91510-7369
Web site: <http://feefhs.org/ igs/frg-igs.html>

Jewish Genealogical Society of Los Angeles (JGSLA)
P.O. Box 55443, Sherman Oaks, CA 91413
Tel: (818) 771-5554
Web site: <www.jewishgen.org/ jgsla/>

Jewish Genealogical Society of Orange County
11751 Cherry St., Los Alamitos, CA 90720

Jewish Genealogical Society of Sacramento
2351 Wyda Way, Sacramento, CA 95825
Web site: <www.jewishgen.org/ jgs-sacramento/>

Jewish Historical Society of Southern California
6505 Wilshire Blvd., Los Angeles, CA 90048
Tel: (323) 761-9961
E-mail: jhsociety@aol.com
Web site: <www.jhsociety.igetne t.com/>

Kern County Genealogical Society
P.O. Box 2214, Bakersfield, CA 93303-2214
Web site: <www.kerncountylibrar y.org/about_genesoc.html>

La Puente Valley Historical Society
P.O. Box 522, La Puente, CA 91744
Tel: (626) 336-7644

Lake County Genealogical Society
Tel: (707) 263-5588
Web site: <www.cagenweb.com/lake/lakehistornetwork.htm>

Lake Elsinore Genealogical Society (LEGS)
P.O. Box 807, Lake Elsinore, CA 92531
Web site: <www.bakerfamily.org/legs/>

Leisure World Genealogical Workshop
Leisure World Library, P.O. Box 2069, Club House 5, Seal Beach, CA 90740-2069

Livermore-Amador Genealogical Society
P.O. Box 901, Livermore, CA 94551
E-mail: president@l-ags.org
Web site: <www.l-ags.org>

Lomita Historical Society
24016 Benhill Ave., Lomita, CA 90717

Los Angeles City Historical Society
P.O. Box 41046, Los Angeles, CA 90041
Tel: (213) 891-4600

Los Banos Genealogical Society
P.O. Box 2525, Los Banos, CA 93635

Lucerne Valley Genealogy Association
Web site: <www.lucernevalley.net/orgs/roots/>

Madera County Genealogical Society
P.O. Box 495, Madera, CA 93639
Tel: (559) 675-7871
Web site: <www.cagenweb.com/madera/MadGenSoc.html>

Maidu Genealogical Society
Maidu Community Center, 1550 Maidu Dr., Roseville, CA 95661
Tel: (916) 786-0186

Marin County Genealogical Society
P.O. Box 1511, Novato, CA 94948
Web site: <www.maringensoc.org>

Martinez Historical Society
E-mail: webmaster@martinezhistory.org

Web site: <www.martinezhistory.org>

Mendocino Coast Genealogical Society
P.O. Box 762, Fort Bragg, CA 95437

Mendocino County Historical Society
603 W. Perkins St., Ukiah, CA 95482
E-mail: mchs@pacific.net
Web site: <www.pacificsites.com/%7Emchs/>

Merced County Genealogical Society
P.O. Box 3061, Merced, CA 95344
E-mail: family_ties@sbcglobal.net
Web site: <www.rootsweb.com/~camcgs/>

Monterey County Genealogical Society, Inc.
P.O. Box 8144, Salinas, CA 93912-8144
Web site: <www.mocogenso.org>

Monterey County Historical Society
P.O. Box 3576, Salinas, CA 93912
Tel: (831) 757-8085
E-mail: mchs@dedot.com
Web site: <http://users.dedot.com/mchs/>

Moraga Historical Society
1500 St. Mary's Rd., Moraga, CA 94556
Mailing address: P.O. Box 103, Moraga, CA 94556
Tel: (925) 377-8734
E-mail: mhistory@silcon.com
Web site: <www.moragahistory.org>

Moravian Heritage Society
17907 Kuykendahl, Suite 202, Spring, TX 77379
Tel: (281) 251-7690
Web site: <http://feefhs.org/czs/frg-mohs.html>

Mt. Diablo Chapter, American Historical Society of Germans from Russia (AHSGR)
Wandel Dr., Moraga, CA 94556-1829
Tel: (925) 376-3002
Web site: <www.ahsgr.org/mtdiablo_chapter.htm>

Mt. Diablo Genealogical Society
P.O. Box 4654, Walnut Creek, CA 94596

Napa Valley Genealogical and Biographical Society
1701 Menlo Ave., Napa, CA 94558
Tel: (707) 252-2252
E-mail: nvgbs@napanet.net
Web site: <www.napanet.net/~nvgbs/index.shtml>

National Archives and Record Administration (NARA), Pacific Region
24000 Avila Rd., Laguna Niguel, CA 92677-3497
Tel: (949) 360-2641
E-mail: randy.thompson@nara.gov
Web site: <www.archives.gov/facilities/ca/laguna_niguel.html>

National Archives and Record Administration (NARA), Pacific Region
1000 Commodore Dr., San Bruno, CA 94066-2350
Tel: (650) 238-3501
E-mail: sanbruno.archives@nara.gov
Web site: <www.archives.gov/facilities/ca/san_francisco.html>

Nevada County Genealogical Society
P.O. 176, Cedar Ridge, CA 95924
Web site: <www.rootsweb.com/~cancgs/>

North San Diego County Genealogical Society (NSDCGS)
P.O. Box 581, Carlsbad, CA 92018-0581
Web site: <www.cagenweb.com/nsdcgs/>

Orange County California Genealogical Society (OCCGS)
P.O. Box 1587, Orange, CA 92856-1587
Web site: <www.occgs.com>

Pacific Palisades Historical Society
P.O. Box 1299, Pacific Palisades, CA 90272
Tel: (310) 454-5037

Palm Springs Genealogical Society
P.O. Box 2093, Palm Springs, CA 92263-2093

Paradise Genealogical Society, Inc.
P.O. Box 460, Paradise, CA 95967-0460
E-mail: pargenso@PacBell.net
Web site: <www.pargenso.org>

Pasadena Genealogical Society
P.O. Box 94774, Pasadena, CA 91109-4774

Pasadena Heritage
651 S. St. John Ave., Pasadena, CA 91105
Tel: (626) 441-6333
E-mail: preservation@pasadenaheritage.org
Web site: <www.pasadenaheritage.org>

Pasadena Historical Society
470 W. Walnut St., Pasadena, CA 91103
Tel: (626) 577-1660

Patterson Genies
525 Clover Ave., Patterson, CA 95363

Pico Rivera History and Heritage Society
P.O. Box 313, Pico Rivera, CA 90666
Tel: (213) 948-2408

Placer County Genealogical Society
P.O. Box 7385, Auburn, CA 95604
Web site: <www.pcgenes.com/pcgs.html>

Plumas County Historical Society
P.O. Box 695, Quincy, CA 95971

Pocahontas Trails Genealogical Society
3628 Cherokee Lane, Modesto, CA 95356

Polish Genealogical Society of California (PGSCA)
P.O. Box 713, Midway City, CA 92655-0713
E-mail: Information@pgsca.org
Web site: <http://feefhs.org/pol/pgsca/frgpgsca.html>

Pomona Valley Genealogical Society (PVGS)
P.O. Box 286, Pomona, CA 91769-0286
Web site: <http://home.earthlink.net/~hazefam/PVGS.html>

Questing Heirs Genealogical Society, Inc.
P.O. Box 15102, Long Beach, CA 90815-0102

Web site: <www.cagenweb.com/questing>

Redondo Beach Historical Society
P.O. Box 978, Redondo Beach, CA 90277
Tel: (310) 372-0197
E-mail: RBHistSoc@aol.com
Web site: <http://members.aol.com/RBHistSoc/index.htm>

Redwood Genealogical Society, Inc.
P.O. 645, Fortuna, CA 95540
Tel: (707) 725-3791

Renegade Root Diggers
9171 Fargo Ave., Hanford, CA 93230

Roman Catholic Diocese of Los Angeles—The Cathedral Center of St. Paul
840 Echo Park Ave., Los Angeles, CA 90026
Tel: (213) 482-2040
Web site: <www.ladiocese.org/cathedral>

Roman Catholic Diocese of San Diego—Diocesan Pastoral Center
3888 Paducah Dr., San Diego, CA 92117 or P.O. Box 85728, San Diego, CA 92186-5728
Tel: (858) 490-8200
Web site: <www.diocese-sdiego.org/>

Root Cellar—Sacramento Genealogical Society
P.O. Box 265, Citrus Heights, CA 95611-0265
Web site: <www.rootcellar.org>

Roseville Genealogical Society
P.O. Box 459, Roseville, CA 95678
Web site: <www.rootsweb.com/~carvgs/rgs.htm>

Sacramento German Genealogy Society
Web site: <www.sacgergensoc.org>

Sacramento Valley Chapter, American Historical Society of Germans from Russia (AHSGR)
Web site: <http://ahsgr_sac.tripod.com/>

San Bernardino Valley Genealogical Society
P.O. Box 2128, San Bernardino, CA 92406
E-mail: sbvgs@sbpl.org

Web site: <www.sbpl.org/genealogy.html>

San Diego Genealogical Society
1050 Pioneer Way, Suite E, El Cajon, CA 92020-1943
Tel: (619) 588-0065
E-mail: sdgs2000@yahoo.com
Web site: <www.rootsweb.com/~casdgs/>

San Diego Historical Society
P.O. Box 81825, San Diego, CA 92138
Web site: <www.sandiegohistory.org>

San Fernando Valley Genealogical Society
P.O. Box 3486, Winnetka, CA 91396-3486
Web site: <www.rootsweb.com/~casfvgs/>

San Fernando Valley Historical Society
Andrew Pico Adobe, Box 7039, 10940 Sepulvade Blvd., Mission Hills, CA 91346
Tel: (818) 365-7810
Web site: <www.sfvhs.com>

San Francisco Bay Area Jewish Genealogical Society (SFBAJGS)
P.O. Box 471616, San Francisco, CA 94147
E-mail: sfbajgs@ix.netcom.com
Web site: <www.jewishgen.org/sfbajgs/>

San Gorginio Genealogical Society
1050 Brinton Ave., Banning, CA 92220

San Joaquin Genealogical Society
P.O. Box 4817, Stockton, CA 95204-0817
Web site: <www.rootsweb.com/~sjgs/>

San Luis Obispo County Genealogical Society, Inc.
P.O. Box 4, Atascadero, CA 93423-0004
Web site: <http://kcbx.net/~slogen/>

San Luis Obispo County Genealogical Society Library—North County Branch
1288 Morro St., San Luis Obispo, CA 93401
Tel: (805) 785-0383
Web site: <http://kcbx.net/~slogen/>

San Luis Obispo County Genealogical Society Library—South County Branch
% Arroyo Grande Public Library, South County Regional Center, 800 W. Branch St., Arroya Grande, CA 93420-1901
Web site: <http://kcbx.net/~slogen/>

San Marino Historical Society
P.O. Box 80222, San Marino, CA 91118-8222
Web site: <www.smnet.org/comm_group/historical/>

San Mateo County Genealogical Society
P.O. Box 5083, San Mateo, CA 94402-0083
Tel: (650) 572-2929

San Ramon Valley Genealogical Society
P.O. Box 521, Danville, CA 94526
Tel: (501) 820-9171

Santa Barbara County Genealogical Society
P.O. Box 1303, Goleta, CA 93116-1303
Tel: (805) 884-9909
E-mail: sbcgs@msn.com
Web site: <www.cagenweb.com/santabarbara/sbcgs/>

Santa Clara County Public Libraries
1095 N. Seventh St., San Jose, CA 95112-4446
Tel: (408) 293-2326
Web site: <www.santaclaracountylib.org>

The Santa Clara County Historical and Genealogical Society
2635 Homestead Rd., Santa Clara, CA 95051-5387
Web site: <www.rootsweb.com/~cascchgs/>

Santa Clarita Valley Historical Society
P.O. Box 221925, Newhall, CA 91322-1925
Tel: (661) 254-1275
E-mail: scvhistory@yahoo.com or info@scvhistory.com
Web site: <www.scvhs.org>

Santa Cruz Public Libraries, System Headquarters
1543 Pacific Ave., Santa Cruz, CA 95060
Tel: (831) 420-5600
Web site: <www.santacruzpl.org>

Santa Maria Public Library
420 S. Broadway, Santa Maria, CA 93454
Tel: (805) 925-0994
E-mail: smref@blackgold.org
Web site: <www.ci.santa-maria.ca.us/210.html>

Santa Maria Valley Genealogical Society and Library
P.O. Box 1215, Santa Maria, CA 93456-1215
Tel: (805) 922-3202

Santa Monica Historical Society Museum
P.O. Box 3059, Santa Monica, CA 90408
Tel: (310) 395-2290
Web site: <www.santamonicahistory.org>

Sequoia Genealogical Society
% Tulare City Library Genealogical Room, 113 N. F St., Tulare, CA 93274
Tel: (559) 685-2342
Web site: <www.cagenweb.com/cpl/tulare/>

Shasta Genealogical Society
P.O. Box 493431, Redding, CA 96049-3431
E-mail: sgs106@hotmail.com
Web site: <www.rootsweb.com/~cascogs/>

Peter J. Shields Library, University of California, Davis
100 NW Quad, Davis, CA 95616-5292
Tel: (530) 752-6561
E-mail: libinfo@ucdavis.edu
Web site: <www.lib.ucdavis.edu/info/Shields.html>

Siskiyou County Genealogy Society
P.O. Box 225, Yreka, CA 96097

Siskiyou County Library
719 Fourth St., Yreka, CA 96097
Tel: (530) 841-4175
E-mail: siskiyoulibrary@snowcrest.net
Web site: <www.snowcrest.net/siskiyoulibrary/>

Slovak Genealogical Research Center (SGRC)
6862 Palmer Ct., Chino, CA 91710-7343
Tel: (909) 627-2897
E-mail: rplutko@aol.com
Web site: <http://feefhs.org/slovak/frg-sgrc.html>

California

Solano County Genealogical Society and Library
620 Main St., Vacaville, CA
Mailing address: P.O. Box 2494, Fairfield, CA 94533-0249
Tel: (707) 446-6869
E-mail: scgs@cwnet.com
Web site: <www.rootsweb.com/~cascgsi/>

Sonoma County Library—Santa Rosa Central Library
Third & E Sts., Santa Rosa, CA 95404
Tel: (707) 545-0831
Web site: <www.sonoma.lib.ca.us/>

Sonoma Genealogical Society, Inc.
P.O. Box 2273, Santa Rosa, CA 95405-0273
Web site: <www.scgs.org/scgs.html>

South Bay Cities Genealogical Society
P.O. Box 11069, Torrance, CA 90510-1069
E-mail: sbcgs@hotmail.com
Web site: <www.rootsweb.com/~cabcgs/>

South Orange County California Genealogical Society (SOCCGS)
P.O. Box 4513, Mission Viejo, CA 92690-4513
Web site: <www.rootsweb.com/~casoccgs/>

Southern California Chapter, American Historical Society of Germans from Russia (AHSGR)
16371 Silver Lane, Huntington Beach, CA 92647
E-mail: AHHart@aol.com
Web site: <www.ehrman.net/ahsgr/casocal.html>

Southern California Genealogical Society and Family Research Library
417 Irving Dr., Burbank, CA 91504
Tel: (818) 843-7247
E-mail: scgs@earthlink.net
Web site: <www.scgsgenealogy.com/>

Spanishtown Historical Society
P.O. Box 62, Half Moon Bay, CA 94019
Tel: (650) 726-7084
Web site: <www.spanishtownhs.org>

St. Ives Historical Society
8648 Lupine Loop Dr. #5, California City, CA 93505
Web site: <www.saintives.com>

Stanislaus County Free Library
1500 I St., Modesto, CA 95354
Tel: (209) 558-7800
Web site: <www.stanislauslibrary.org>

Sutro Branch, California State Library
480 Winston Dr., San Francisco, CA 94132
Tel: (415) 731-4477
E-mail: sutro@library.ca.gov
Web site: <www.library.ca.gov>

Taft Genealogical Society
P.O. Box 7411, Taft, CA 93268

Tehama County Genealogical and Historical Society
P.O. Box 415, Red Bluff, CA 96080
E-mail: tcmuse@tco.net
Web site: <www.tco.net/tehama/museum/tcmgene/html>

Temple City Historical Society
P.O. Box 1379, Temple City, CA 91780
Tel: (626) 279-1784

Topanga Historical Society
P.O. Box 1214, Topanga, CA 90290
Tel: (310) 455-1111
Web site: <www.topangaonline.com/hsociety.html>

Tracy Area Genealogical Society (TAGS)
1141 Adam St., Tracy, CA 95376
Tel: (209) 832-1106
E-mail: TAGSCA@sbcglobal.net
Web site: <www.rootsweb.com/~catags/>

Triadoption Library
P.O. Box 5218, Huntington Beach, CA 92615-5218

TRW Genealogical Society
One Space Park S-1420, Redondo Beach, CA 90278

Tulare County Public Library
113 N. F St., Tulare, CA 93274
Tel: (559) 685-2341
Web site: <www.sjvls.org/tularepub/>

Tuolumne County Genealogical Society
P.O. Box 3956, Sonora, CA 95370-3956

Tel: (209) 532-1317
E-mail: info@tcgsonline.org
Web site: <www.tcgsonline.org>

Vandenberg Genealogical Society
P.O. Box 814, Lompoc, CA 93438-0814
Tel: (805) 736-9637

Ventura County Genealogical Society
P.O. Box 24608, Ventura, CA 93002
Web site: <www.rootsweb.com/~cavcgs/>

Ventura County Genealogical Society Library
% E.P. Foster Library, 651 Main St., Ventura, CA 93001
Tel: (805) 648-2716
Web sites: <www.vencolibrary.org/libraries/foster.html> or <www.rootsweb.com/%7Ecavcgs/Library.htm>

West Covina Historical Society
3510 E. Cameron Ave.
Mailing address: P.O. Box 4597, West Covina, CA 91793
Tel: (626) 339-4419

Whittier Area Genealogical Society (WAGS)
P.O. Box 4367, Whittier, CA 90607-4367
Web site: <www.cagenweb.com/kr/wags>

Whittier Historical Society and Museum
6755 Newlin Ave., Whittier, CA 90601
Tel: (562) 945-3871
E-mail: info@whittiermuseum.org
Web site: <www.whittiermuseum.org>

Workman and Temple Family Homestead Museum
15415 E. Don Julian Rd., City of Industry, CA 91745-1029
Tel: (626) 968-8492
E-mail: info@homesteadmuseum.org
Web site: <www.homesteadmuseum.org>

Yolo County Archives
226 Buckeye St., Woodland, CA 95695
Tel: (530) 666-8010

Yolo County Historical Society
P.O. Box 1447, Woodland, CA 95776
Tel: (530) 661-2212

E-mail: bjford@pacbell.net
Web site: <www.yolo.net/ychs/>

Yorba Linda Heritage Museum and Historical Society
5700 Susanna Bryant Dr., Yorba Linda, CA 92887-5646
Tel: (714) 694-0235
Web site: <www.ylpl.lib.ca.us/sbb.php>

Yucaipa Valley Genealogical Society
P.O. Box 32, Yucaipa, CA 92399

BIBLIOGRAPHY

■ GENERAL RESOURCES

California Local History: A Bibliography and Union List of Library Holdings: Supplement to the 2nd Edition Covering Works Published 1961 through 1970
edited by Margaret Miller Rocq for the California Library Association (Stanford, CA: Standford University Press, 1976)

The California Locator: A Directory of Public Records for Locating People Dead or Alive in California
by Laurie Nicklas (Modesto, CA: Nicklas Publishing Co., 1996)

California Pioneer Register and Index, 1542–1848. Including Inhabitants of Calfornia, 1769–1800, and List of Pioneers
by Hubert Howe Bancroft (Baltimore, MD: Regional Pub. Co., 1964)

California Research Outline
from the Church of Jesus Christ of Latter-day Saints, Family History Library (Salt Lake City, UT: Corp. of the President of the Church of L.D.S., 1988)

Contemporary Biography of California's Representative Men, 2 vols.
by Alonzo Phelps (Woodbridge, CT: Research Publications, Inc., 1968)

The Foreign-Born Voters of 1872: Including Naturalization Dates, Places, and Courts of Record
compiled by Jim W. Faulkinbury (Sacramento, CA: J.W. Faulkinbury, 1994)

The Genealogist's Companion and Sourcebook, 2d ed.
by Emily Anne Croom (Cincinnati: Betterway Books, 2003)

A Genealogist's Guide to Discovering Your African-American Ancestors
by Franklin Carter Smith and Emily Anne Croom (Cincinnati: Betterway Books, 2003)

Genealogical Records of California
by Sherman Lee Pompey (Fresno, CA: 1968)

Gold! German Transcontinental Travelers to California, 1849–1851
by Clifford Neal Smith (McNeal, AZ: Westland Publications, 1988)

Guide to Genealogical Research in the National Archives of the United States
edited by Anne Bruner Eales and Robert M. Kvasnicka (Washington, D.C.: National Archives and Records Administration, 2000

An Index to the Biographies in 19th Century California County Histories
by J. Carlyle Parker (Detroit: Gale Research Co., 1979)

Index to the D.A.R. Records of the Families of the California Pioneers
by the Solano County Genealogical Society, Inc. (Fairfield, CA: The Society, 1988–1990)

National Archives Microfilm Catalogs online:
<www.archives.gov/publica tions/genealogy_microfilm_ catalogs.html>

Sources of Genealogical Help in California Libraries
by the Southern California Genealogical Society (Burbank, CA: The Society, 1990)

The Spanish Borderlands; a Chronicle of Old Florida and the Southwest
by Herbert Eugene Bolton (New Haven: Yale University Press, 1921)

■ CENSUS RECORDS

The American Census Handbook
by Thomas Jay Kemp (Wilmington, DE: Scholarly Resources, 2001)

The California 1890 Great Register of Voters Index, 3 vols.
compiled by the California State Genealogical Alliance, edited by Janice G. Cloud; Margaret Goodwin, database manager (North Salt Lake, UT: Heritage Quest, 2001)

The Census Book: A Genealogist's Guide to Federal Census Facts, Schedules and Indexes
by William Dollarhide (Bountiful, UT: Heritage Quest, 2000)

Finding Answers in U.S. Census Records
by Loretto Dennis Szucs and Matthew Wright (Orem, UT: Ancestry Publishing, 2002)

Map Guide to the U.S. Federal Censuses, 1790–1920
by William Thorndale and William Dollarhide (Baltimore, MD: Genealogical Pub. Co., 1987)

Your Guide to the Federal Census
by Kathleen W. Hinckley (Cincinnati: Betterway Books, 2002)

■ IMMIGRATION RECORDS

American Naturalization Records, 1790–1990: What They Are and How to Use Them
by John J. Newman (North Salt Lake, UT: HeritageQuest, 1998)

American Passenger Arrival Records
by Michael Tepper (Baltimore: Genealogical Publishing Co., 1993)

Manifests of Alien Arrivals at San Ysidro (Tia Juana) California, April 21, 1908–December 1952
by the United States Immigration and Naturalization Service and Claire Prechtel-Kluskens (College Park, MD: National Archives and Records Administration, 1999)

San Francisco Passenger Departure Lists, 3 vols.
by Peter E. Carr (San Bernardino, CA: Cuban Index, 1991–1993)

Sea Routes to the Gold Fields; the Migration by Water to California in 1849–1852
by Oscar Lewis (New York: A.A. Knopf, 1949)

They Became Americans: Finding Naturalization Records and Ethnic Origins
by Loretto Dennis Szucs (Salt Lake City: Ancestry, Inc., 1998)

They Came in Ships: A Guide to Finding Your Immigrant Ancestor's Arrival Records, 2d ed.
by John P. Colletta (Salt Lake City: Ancestry, Inc., 1993)

■ LAND RECORDS

California Ranchos: Patented Private Land Grants, Listed by County
by Burgess McK. Shumway and edited by Michael and Mary Burgess (San Bernardino, CA: Borgo Press; Glendale, CA: Sidewinder Press, 1988)

Index to the Spanish-Mexican Private Land Grant Records and Cases of California
by J.N. Bowman (Berkeley, CA: J.N. Bowman, 1958)

Locating Your Roots: Discover Your Ancestors Using Land Records
by Patricia Law Hatcher (Cincinnati: Betterway Books, 2003)

Ranchos of California: A List of Spanish Concessions, 1775–1822 and Mexican Land Grants, 1822–1846
by Robert G. Cowan (San Bernardino, CA: Borgo Press, 1985, ca. 1956)

Spanish and Mexican Land Grants in California
by Rose Hollenbaugh Aviña (New York: Arno Press, 1976)

Veterans Who Applied for Land in Southern California, 1851–1911
compiled by Judy A. Deeter (Baltimore, MD: Gateway Press, 1993)

■ MAPS

California City and Unincorporated Place Names
by the California Division of Highways (Sacramento: 1971)

California County Boundaries: A Study of the Division of the State Into Counties and the Subsequent Changes in their Boundaries
by Owen C. Coy (Berkeley, CA: California Historical Survey Commission, 1923)

California, Index to Topographic and Other Map Coverage
by the United States Geological Survey (Reston, VA: United States Geological Survey, National Mapping Program, 1983)

California Place Names; the Origin and Etymology of Current Geographical Names, 3d ed.
by Erwin Gustav Gudde (Berkeley, CA: University of California Press, 1969)

The Dictionary of California Land Names
compiled by Phil Townsend Hanna (Los Angeles: Automobile Club of Southern California, 1951)

Early California; early forts, old mines, old town sites
northern edition prepared by Ralph N. Preston (Corvallis, OR: Western Guide Publishers, 1974)

Historical Atlas of California
by Warren A. Beck and Ynez D. Haase (Norman, OK: University of Oklahoma Press, 1974)

History of California Post Offices, 1849–1976: Includes Branches and Stations, Navy Numbered Branches, Highway and Railway Post Offices
research by Harold E. Salley (La Mesa, CA: Postal History Associates, 1977)

History of California Post Offices, 1849–1990, 2d ed.
by Harold E. Salley, edited by Edward L. Patera; research by H.E. Salley and E.L. Patera (Lake Grove, OR: The Depot, 1991)

Patterns on the Land; Geographical, Historical, and Political Maps of California, 4th ed.
by Robert W. Durrenberger (Palo Alto, CA: National Press Books, 1972)

Southern and Central California Atlas & Gazeteer, 2d ed.
by the DeLorme Mapping Company (Freeport, ME: DeLorme Mapping Company, 1990)

Spanish and Indian Place Names of California: Their Meaning and Their Romance
by Nellie Van de Grift Sanchez (New York: Arno Press, 1976, ca. 1930)

■ MILITARY RECORDS

California Conquered: War and Peace on the Pacific, 1846–1850
by Neal Harlow (Berkeley, CA: University of California Press, 1982)

Honorable Remembrance: the San Diego Master List of the Mormon Battalion
edited by Elmer J. Carr and compiled by the Mormon Battalion Visitors Center (S.I.: s.n., 1978?)

Records of California Men in the War of the Rebellion, 1861 to 1867
by the California Adjutant General's Office and Richard H. Orton (Detriot, MI: Gale Research, 1979)

Sons of the Revolution in the State of California, Centennial Register, 1893–1993
by Richard Hoag Breithaupt Jr., and the Sons of the Revolution in the State of California (University City, CA: Walika, 1994)

Spanish Bluecoats: the Catalonian Volunteers in Northwestern New Spain, 1767–1810
by Joseph P. Sánchez (Albuquerque, NM: University of New Mexico Press, 1990)

Uncle, We Are Ready! Registering America's Men, 1917–1918: A Guide to Researching World War I Draft Registration Cards
by John J. Newman (North Salt Lake, UT: HeritageQuest, 2001)

U.S. Military Records: A Guide to Federal & State Sources, Colonial America to the Present
by James C. Neagles (Salt Lake City: Ancestry, Inc., 1994)

World War II: A Family Historian's Guide
by Debra Johnson Knox (Spartanburg, SC: MIE Publishing, 2003)

■ PROBATE RECORDS

1860 California Census Index: Heads of Households and Other Surnames in Households Index, 2d ed.
compiled by Bryan Lee Dilts (Salt Lake City, UT: Index Pub., 1984)

California County Courthouse Records: A Directory of Vital Records Found in Each County Office in California
by Laurie Nicklas (Modesto, CA: L. Nicklas, 1998)

■ VITAL RECORDS

California County Courthouse Records: a Directory of Vital Records Found in Each County Office in California
by Laurie Nicklas (Modesto, CA: L. Nicklas, 1998)

California Marriage Records Indexes, 1960–1985
by the California State Registrar (Sacramento, CA: Office of the State Registrar, 1983)

California's Old Burying Grounds
by Helen Marcia Bruner, prepared for the National Society of Colonial Dames of America resident in the state of California (San Francisco: Portal Press, 1945)

Graves and Sites on the Oregon and California Trails: a Chapter in OCTA's Efforts to Preserve the Trails
by the Oregon-California Trails Association (Independence, MO: Oregon-California Trails Association, 1991)

Guide to Public Vital Statistics Records in California
by the Historical Records Survey (San Francisco, CA: Northern California Historical Records Survey, 1941)

Northern California Marriage Index, 1850–1860: Marriages from Twenty-Two Northern California Counties
by Nancy Justus Morebeck (Vacaville, CA: N.J. Morebeck, 1993)

Permanant Californians: an Illustrated Guide to the Cemetaries of California
by Judi Culbertson and Tom Randall (Chelsea, VT: Chelsea Green Pub. Co., 1989)

A Personal Name Index to Orton's Records of California Men in the War of the Rebellion, 1861 to 1867: index
compiled by J. Carlyle Parker (Detroit, MI: Gale Research Co., 1978)

Your Guide to Cemetery Research
by Sharon DeBartolo Carmack (Cincinnati: Betterway Books, 2002)

■ Alameda   25 Mar. 1853
1106 Madison St., Room 101, Oakland, CA 94607
Phone: (510)272-6362
Web site: www.katpher.com/alamecty/alamecty.htm
Parent County: Contra Costa, Santa Clara
Comments/research tips: County Clerk has Birth records 1919–1988 [some from 1873]. County Clerk has Death records 1905–1988 [some from 1876].

Record Type	Year Begun	Jurisdiction
Marriage	1854	County Clerk
Divorce	1853	County Clerk
Land	1853	County Clerk
Court	1853	County Clerk
Probate	1853	County Clerk

■ Alpine   16 Mar. 1864
99 Water St., P.O. Box 158, Markleeville, CA 96120
Phone: (530)694-2287
Web site: www.cagenweb.com/alpine
Parent County: El Dorado, Amador, Calaveras, Mono, Tuolumne

Record Type	Year Begun	Jurisdiction
Birth	1900	County Clerk
Marriage	1900	County Clerk
Death	1900	County Clerk
Divorce	1900	County Clerk
Land	1900	County Clerk
Court	1900	County Clerk
Probate	1900	County Clerk

■ Amador   11 May 1854
500 Argonaut Ln., Jackson, CA 95642
Phone: (209)223-6468
Web site: www.cagenweb.com/amador
Parent County: Calaveras, El Dorado

Record Type	Year Begun	Jurisdiction
Birth	1872	County Clerk
Death	1872	County Clerk

■ Branciforte   18 Feb. 1850
Parent County: Original county
Comments/research tips: (See Santa Cruz) Name changed to Santa Cruz 5 April 1850.

■ Butte   18 Feb. 1850
25 County Center Dr., Oroville, CA 95965
Phone: (530)538-7691
Web site: www.kindredtrails.com/CA_butte.html

Parent County: Original county
Comments/research tips: Meriam Library, California State University Chico has Divorce, Probate, and Court records 1850–1879 and Naturalization records 1850–1960. You can find Probate and Court records with the County Clerk 1850 along with Divorce records 1850.

Record Type	Year Begun	Jurisdiction
Birth	1859	County Recorder
Marriage	1851	County Recorder
Death	1859	County Recorder
Land	na	County Recorder

■ Calaveras 18 Feb. 1850
891 Mountain Ranch Rd., San Andreas, CA 95249
Phone: (209)754-6376
Web site: www.cagenweb.com/lr/calavaras
Parent County: Original county

Record Type	Year Begun	Jurisdiction
Birth	1860	County Recorder
Marriage	1882	County Recorder
Death	1882	County Recorder
Divorce	1882	County Recorder
Land	1852	County Recorder
Probate	1866	County Recorder
Court	1866	County Recorder
Mining Claims	1850	County Recorder

■ Colusa 18 Feb. 1850
546 Jay St., Colusa, CA 95932-2443
Phone: (530)458-0500
Web site: www.cagenweb.com/colusa.
Parent County: Original county
Comments/research tips: Colusa County was created in 1850 but attached to Butte County for administration until it was organized in January 1851.

Record Type	Year Begun	Jurisdiction
Birth	1873	County Clerk
Marriage	1853	County Clerk
Death	1889	County Clerk
Land	1851	County Clerk
Probate	1851	County Clerk
Court	1851	County Clerk
Great Registers	1866	County Clerk
Military Rolls	1879	County Clerk
Assess. Rolls	1851	County Clerk

■ Contra Costa 18 Feb. 1850
730 Las Juntas St., P.O. Box 350, Martinez, CA 94553
Phone: (925)646-2360
Web site: www.kindredtrails.com/CA_Contra_Costa.html
Parent County: Original county

Record Type	Year Begun	Jurisdiction
Birth	na	County Recorder
Marriage	na	County Clerk
Death	na	County Recorder
Divorce	na	County Clerk
Probate	na	County Clerk
Court	na	County Clerk

■ Del Norte 2 Mar. 1857
981 H St., Crescent City, CA 95531
Phone: (707)464-7204
Web site: www.cagenweb.com/delnorte
Parent County: Klamath
Comments/research tips: County Recorder has Leases and Agreements records 1857–1954.

Record Type	Year Begun	Jurisdiction
Birth	1873	County Recorder
Marriage	1873	County Recorder
Death	1873	County Recorder
Divorce	1848	County Clerk
Land	1853	County Recorder
Probate	1848	County Clerk
Court	1848	County Clerk

■ El Dorado 18 Feb. 1850
360 Fair Ln., Placerville, CA 95667
Phone: (530)621-5490
Web site: www.cagenweb.com/eldorado
Parent County: Original county

Record Type	Year Begun	Jurisdiction
Birth	na	County Recorder
Marriage	na	County Recorder
Death	na	County Recorder
Divorce	na	County Clerk
Land	na	County Recorder
Probate	na	County Clerk
Court	na	County Clerk
Burial	na	County Recorder
Military	na	County Recorder

■ Fresno 19 Apr. 1856
2221 Kern St., Fresno, CA 93721
Phone: (559)488-3003
Web site: www.cagenweb.com/re/fresno
Parent County: Merced, Mariposa, Tulare

Record Type	Year Begun	Jurisdiction
Birth	1855	County Clerk
Marriage	1855	County Clerk
Death	1855	County Clerk

■ Glenn 11 Mar. 1891
526 W. Sycamore St., P.O. Box 391, Willows , CA 95988
Phone: (530)934-6419
Web site: www.cagenweb.com/glenn
Parent County: Colusa

Record Type	Year Begun	Jurisdiction
Birth	1887	County Recorder
Marriage	1891	County Recorder
Death	1905	County Recorder
Land	1891	County Recorder
Probate	na	Superior Ct.
Court	na	Superior Ct.
Military	1919	County Recorder

■ Humboldt 12 May 1853
825 Fifth St., Eureka, CA 95501
Phone: (707)476-2384

California

Web site: www.cagenweb.com/humboldt
Parent County: Trinity, Klamath

Record Type	Year Begun	Jurisdiction
Birth	na	County Recorder
Marriage	na	County Recorder
Death	na	County Recorder
Divorce	1853	County Clerk
Land	na	County Recorder
Probate	1853	County Clerk
Court	1853	County Clerk
Burial	na	County Recorder

■ Imperial 6 Aug. 1907
940 W. Main St., El Centro, CA 92243
Phone: (760)482-4220
Web site: www.cagenweb.com/eb/imperial
Parent County: San Diego

Record Type	Year Begun	Jurisdiction
Birth	1907	County Recorder
Marriage	1907	County Recorder
Marriage	1907	County Clerk
Death	1907	County Recorder
Divorce	1907	County Clerk
Probate	1907	County Clerk
Court	1907	County Clerk

■ Inyo 22 Mar. 1866
168 N. Edwards St., P.O. Box F, Independence, CA 93526
Phone: (760)878-0218
Web site: www.cagenweb.com/inyo
Parent County: Tulare, Mono

Record Type	Year Begun	Jurisdiction
Birth	1904	County Clerk
Marriage	1866	County Clerk
Death	1904	County Clerk
Land	1866	County Clerk
Mining	1872	County Clerk

■ Kern 2 Apr. 1866
1655 Chester Ave., Bakersfield, CA 93301
Phone: (661)868-6449
Web site: www.cagenweb.com/eb/kern
Parent County: Tulare, Los Angeles
Comments/research tips: An exchange of territory with San Bernardino County took place in 1963.

Record Type	Year Begun	Jurisdiction
Birth	1850	County Recorder
Marriage	1850	County Recorder
Death	1850	County Recorder
Divorce	1866	County Recorder
Land	1850	County Recorder
Probate	1866	County Recorder
Court	1866	County Recorder
Vote Reg.	1866	County Recorder

■ Kings 22 Mar. 1893
1400 W. Lacey Blvd., Hanford, CA 93230
Phone: (559)582-3211
Web site: www.cagenweb.com/re/kings

Parent County: Tulare

Record Type	Year Begun	Jurisdiction
Birth	1893	County Clerk
Marriage	1893	County Clerk
Death	1893	County Clerk
Divorce	1893	County Clerk
Land	1893	County Clerk
Probate	1893	County Clerk
Nat.	1893	County Clerk
Court	1893	County Clerk

■ Klamath 25 Apr. 1851
Parent County: Original county
Comments/research tips: Dissolved 28 March 1874.

■ Lake 20 May 1861
255 N. Forbes St., Lakeport, CA 95453
Phone: (707)263-2368
Web site: www.cagenweb.com/lake
Parent County: Napa

Record Type	Year Begun	Jurisdiction
Birth	1867	County Clerk
Marriage	1867	County Clerk
Death	1867	County Clerk
Divorce	na	Clerk/Superior Ct.
Land	1867	County Clerk
Probate	na	Clerk/Superior Ct.
Court	na	Clerk/Superior Ct.
Mining	na	County Clerk

■ Lassen 1 Apr. 1864
220 S. Lassen St., Susanville, CA 96130
Phone: (530)251-8216
Web site: www.cagenweb.com/tp/lassen
Parent County: Plumas, Shasta
Comments/research tips: County Recorder has Birth and Death records, some prior to 1907 but incomplete before 1929.

Record Type	Year Begun	Jurisdiction
Marriage	1864	County Recorder
Divorce	1864	County Clerk
Land	1857	County Recorder
Probate	1864	County Clerk
Court	1864	County Clerk
Nat.	1864	County Clerk

■ Los Angeles 18 Feb. 1850
12400 E. Imperial Hwy., P.O. Box 1024, Norwalk, CA 90650
Phone: (562)462-2137
Web site: www.ca.genweb.com/re/losangeles
Parent County: Original county

Record Type	Year Begun	Jurisdiction
Birth	na	County Recorder
Marriage	na	County Recorder
Death	na	County Recorder
Divorce	1880	County Clerk
Land	na	County Recorder
Probate	1850	County Clerk
Court	1850	County Clerk

California

■ Madera 11 Mar. 1893
209 W. Yosemite Ave., Madera, CA 93637
Phone: (559)675-7700
Web site: www.cagenweb.com/madera
Parent County: Fresno
Comments/research tips: County Clerk has some Voting records.

Record Type	Year Begun	Jurisdiction
Birth	1893	County Clerk
Marriage	1893	County Clerk
Death	1893	County Clerk
Divorce	1893	County Clerk
Land	1893	County Clerk
Probate	1893	County Clerk
Court	1893	County Clerk

■ Marin 18 Feb. 1850
3501 Civic Center Dr., San Rafael, CA 94903
Phone: (415)499-6094
Web site: www.cagenweb.com/marin
Parent County: Original county

Record Type	Year Begun	Jurisdiction
Birth	1863	County Recorder
Marriage	1856	County Recorder
Death	1863	County Recorder
Divorce	1900	County Clerk
Land	1852	County Recorder
Probate	1880	County Clerk
Court	1900	County Clerk

■ Mariposa 18 Feb. 1850
5100 Bullion St., P.O. Box 35, Mariposa, CA 95338
Phone: (209)966-5719
Web site: www.mariposaresearch.net
Parent County: Original county

Record Type	Year Begun	Jurisdiction
Birth	na	County Recorder
Marriage	na	County Recorder
Death	na	County Recorder
Divorce	na	County Clerk
Probate	na	County Clerk
Court	na	County Clerk
Burial	na	County Recorder

■ Mendocino 18 Feb. 1850
501 Low Gap Rd., Room 1090, Ukiah, CA 95482
Phone: (707)463-4221
Web site: www.cagenweb.com/lr/mendocino/mendolok.hym
Parent County: Original county
Comments/research tips: Some old records are in Sonoma County.

Record Type	Year Begun	Jurisdiction
Birth	na	County Recorder
Marriage	na	County Recorder
Death	na	County Recorder
Divorce	1858	Superior Ct.
Land	na	County Recorder
Probate	1872	Superior Ct.
Court	1858	Superior Ct.

■ Merced 19 Apr. 1855
2222 M St., Merced, CA 95340
Phone: (209)385-7627
Web site: www.cagenweb.com/merced
Parent County: Mariposa

Record Type	Year Begun	Jurisdiction
Birth	na	County Recorder
Marriage	na	County Recorder
Death	na	County Recorder
Divorce	1855	County Clerk
Probate	1855	County Clerk
Court	1855	County Clerk
Burial	na	County Recorder

■ Modoc 17 Feb. 1874
204 Court St., P.O. Box 131, Alturas, CA 96101-0131
Phone: (530)233-6205
Web site: www.rh20.com/modoc/
Parent County: Siskiyou

Record Type	Year Begun	Jurisdiction
Birth	na	County Recorder
Marriage	na	County Recorder
Death	na	County Recorder
Divorce	1874	County Clerk
Probate	1874	County Clerk
Court	1874	County Clerk
Vote Reg.	1874	County Clerk

■ Mono 24 Apr. 1861
Bryant Annex 2, P.O. Box 537, Bridgeport, CA 93517
Phone: (760)932-5241
Web site: www.cagenweb.com/mono
Parent County: Calaveras, Fresno

Record Type	Year Begun	Jurisdiction
Birth	1861	County Clerk
Marriage	1861	County Clerk
Death	1900	County Clerk
Divorce	1900	County Clerk
Land	1900	County Clerk
Probate	1900	County Clerk
Court	1900	County Clerk
Burial	1900	County Clerk

■ Monterey 18 Feb. 1850
240 Church St., P.O. Box 29, Salinas, CA 93902
Phone: (831)755-5041
Web site: www.rootsweb.com/~camonter
Parent County: Original county

Record Type	Year Begun	Jurisdiction
Birth	1893	County Recorder
Marriage	1893	County Recorder
Death	1893	County Recorder
Divorce	na	County Court
Land	na	Clerk/Superior Ct.
Probate	na	Clerk/Superior Ct.
Court	na	County Court

■ Napa 18 Feb. 1850
900 Coombs, P.O. Box 298, Napa, CA 94559-0298
Phone: (707)253-4246

Web site: www.cagenweb.com/napa
Parent County: Original county

Record Type	Year Begun	Jurisdiction
Birth	1873	County Recorder
Marriage	1850	County Recorder
Death	1873	County Recorder
Divorce	1850	Court Executive Officer
Land	1850	County Recorder
Probate	1850	Court Executive Officer
Court	1850	Court Executive Officer

■ Nevada 25 Apr. 1851
950 Maidu Ave., Nevada City, CA 95959
Phone: (530)265-1221
Web site: www.cagenweb.com/nevada
Parent County: Yuba

Record Type	Year Begun	Jurisdiction
Birth	1873	County Clerk
Marriage	1856	County Clerk
Death	1873	County Clerk
Divorce	1880	County Clerk
Land	1856	County Clerk
Probate	1880	County Clerk
Court	1880	County Clerk

■ Orange 11 Mar. 1889
12 Civic Center Pl., Santa Ana, CA 92701
Phone: (714)834-2500
Web site: www.rootsweb.com/~caorange
Parent County: Los Angeles

Record Type	Year Begun	Jurisdiction
Birth	na	County Recorder
Marriage	na	County Recorder
Death	na	County Recorder
Divorce	1964	County Clerk
Land	na	County Recorder
Probate	1964	County Clerk
Court	1964	County Clerk

■ Placer 25 Apr. 1851
2954 Richardson Dr., Auburn, CA 95603
Phone: (530)886-5600
Web site: www.rootsweb.com/~placer
Parent County: Yuba, Sutter

Record Type	Year Begun	Jurisdiction
Birth	1873	County Recorder
Marriage	1873	County Recorder
Death	1873	County Recorder
Land	1850	County Recorder
Probate	1851	County Clerk
Court	1880	County Clerk

■ Plumas 18 Mar. 1854
520 Main St., Quincy, CA 95971
Phone: (530)283-6218
Web site: www.cagenweb.com/tp/plumas
Parent County: Butte
Comments/research tips: County Museum Archives has biographies and photographs.

Record Type	Year Begun	Jurisdiction
Birth	1860	County Recorder
Marriage	1860	County Recorder
Death	1860	County Recorder
Divorce	1860	County Clerk
Land	1860	County Recorder
Probate	1860	County Recorder
Court	1860	County Recorder

■ Riverside 11 Mar. 1893
4080 Lemon St., First Floor, P.O. Box 12004, Riverside, CA 92502
Phone: (909)486-7000
Web site: www.cagenweb.com/sl/riverside
Parent County: San Diego, San Bernardino

Record Type	Year Begun	Jurisdiction
Birth	1893	County Recorder
Marriage	1893	County Recorder
Death	1893	County Recorder
Divorce	1893	Superior Ct.
Land	1893	County Recorder
Probate	1893	Superior Ct.
Court	1893	Superior Ct.

■ Sacramento 18 Feb. 1850
600 Eighth St., P.O. Box 839, Sacramento, CA 95812-0893
Phone: (916)874-6334
Web site: www.kindredtrails.com/CA_Sacramento.html
Parent County: Original county

Record Type	Year Begun	Jurisdiction
Birth	na	County Recorder
Marriage	na	County Recorder
Death	na	County Recorder
Divorce	1880	County Clerk
Land	na	County Recorder
Probate	1880	County Clerk
Court	1880	County Clerk

■ San Benito 12 Feb. 1874
440 Fifth St., Second Floor, Hollister, CA 95023
Phone: (831)636-4029
Web site: www.cagenweb.com/Sanbenito
Parent County: Monterey

Record Type	Year Begun	Jurisdiction
Birth	1894	County Clerk
Marriage	1894	County Clerk
Death	1894	County Clerk
Divorce	na	Superior Ct.
Land	1894	County Clerk
Probate	na	Superior Ct.
Court	na	Superior Ct.
Burial	1894	County Clerk
Nat.	1894	County Clerk

■ San Bernardino 26 Apr. 1853
22 W. Hospitality Ln., San Bernardino, CA 92415
Phone: (909)387-8306
Web site: www.kindredtrails.com/CA_San_Bernadino.html
Parent County: Los Angeles, San Diego

Record Type	Year Begun	Jurisdiction
Birth	1853	County Recorder
Marriage	1857	County Recorder
Death	1853	County Recorder
Divorce	1856	County Clerk
Land	1854	County Clerk
Probate	1856	County Clerk
Court	1853	County Clerk

■ San Diego 18 Feb. 1850

1600 Pacific Hwy., San Diego, CA 92101
Phone: (619)238-8158
Web site: www.cagenweb.com/sandiego
Parent County: Original county

Record Type	Year Begun	Jurisdiction
Birth	1857	County Recorder
Marriage	1856	County Recorder
Death	1873	County Recorder
Divorce	na	Superior Ct.
Land	ca. 1850	County Recorder
Probate	na	Superior Ct.
Court	na	Superior Ct.

■ San Francisco 18 Feb. 1850

1 Dr. Carlton B. Goodlett Pl., San Francisco, CA 94102
Phone: (415)554-4950
Web site: www.sfgenealogy.com/sf
Parent County: Original county

Record Type	Year Begun	Jurisdiction
Birth	na	Department of Public Health
Marriage	na	County Recorder
Divorce	na	Clerk/Superior Ct.
Probate	na	Clerk/Superior Ct.
Court	na	Clerk/Superior Ct.

■ San Joaquin 18 Feb. 1850

24 S. Hunter St. #304, P.O. Box 1968, Stockton, CA 95201
Phone: (209)468-8075
Web site: www.cagenweb.com/sanjoaquin
Parent County: Original county

Record Type	Year Begun	Jurisdiction
Birth	na	County Recorder
Marriage	na	County Recorder
Death	na	County Recorder
Divorce	1851	County Clerk
Land	na	County Recorder
Probate	1851	County Clerk
Court	1851	County Clerk

■ San Luis Obispo 18 Feb. 1850

1144 Monterey St., Suite C, San Luis Obispo, CA 93408
Phone: (805)781-5080
Web site: www.cagenweb.com/slo
Parent County: Original county

Record Type	Year Begun	Jurisdiction
Birth	1873	County Recorder
Marriage	1850	County Recorder
Death	1850	County Recorder
Divorce	na	County Clerk

Record Type	Year Begun	Jurisdiction
Land	1842	County Recorder
Probate	na	County Clerk
Court	na	County Clerk

■ San Mateo 19 Apr. 1856

400 County Center, Redwood City, CA 94063
Phone: (650)363-4712
Web site: http://resources.rootsweb.com/USA/CA/SanMateo/
Parent County: San Francisco

Record Type	Year Begun	Jurisdiction
Birth	1866	County Recorder
Marriage	1866	County Recorder
Death	1866	County Recorder
Divorce	1880	County Recorder
Land	1880	County Recorder
Probate	1856	County Recorder
Court	1880	County Recorder

■ Santa Barbara 18 Feb. 1850

105 E. Anapamu, Room #204, Santa Barbara, CA 93101
Phone: (805)568-2550
Web site: www.cagenweb.com/santabarbara
Parent County: Original county

Record Type	Year Begun	Jurisdiction
Birth	1850	County Recorder
Marriage	1850	County Recorder
Death	1850	County Recorder
Divorce	na	Superior Ct.
Land	1850	County Recorder
Probate	na	Superior Ct.
Court	na	Superior Ct.
Nat.	na	Superior Ct.

■ Santa Clara 18 Feb. 1850

70 W. Hedding St., First Floor, San Jose, CA 95110-1768
Phone: (408)299-2481
Web site: www.cagenweb.com/santaclara
Parent County: Original county

Record Type	Year Begun	Jurisdiction
Birth	1873	County Recorder
Marriage	1850	County Recorder
Death	1873	County Recorder
Divorce	na	County Clerk
Land	1846	County Recorder
Probate	na	County Clerk
Nat.	na	County Clerk
Military	1920	County Recorder

■ Santa Cruz 18 Feb. 1850

701 Ocean St., Santa Cruz, CA 95060
Phone: (831)454-2800
Web site: www.cagenweb.com/santacruz
Parent County: Original county
Comments/research tips: Formerly Branciforte County. Name changed to Santa Cruz 5 April 1850.

Record Type	Year Begun	Jurisdiction
Birth	1905	County Recorder
Marriage	1850	County Recorder

Record Type	Year Begun	Jurisdiction
Death	1905	County Recorder
Divorce	na	Clerk/Superior Ct.
Land	1850	County Recorder
Probate	na	Clerk/Superior Ct.
Court	na	Clerk/Superior Ct.
Military	1930	County Recorder

■ **Shasta** 18 Feb. 1850
1643 Market St., P.O. Box 990880, Redding, CA 96099
Phone: (530)225-5730
Web site: www.cagenweb.com/shasta
Parent County: Original county

Record Type	Year Begun	Jurisdiction
Birth	na	County Recorder
Marriage	na	County Recorder
Death	na	County Recorder
Divorce	1880	County Clerk
Probate	1880	County Clerk
Court	1880	County Clerk

■ **Sierra** 16 Apr. 1852
100 Courthouse Sq., Suite 11, P.O. Box D, Downieville, CA 95936
Phone: (530)289-6295
Web site: www.cagenweb.com/sierra
Parent County: Yuba

Record Type	Year Begun	Jurisdiction
Birth	1857	County Recorder
Marriage	1852	County Recorder
Death	1862	County Recorder
Divorce	1852	Superior Ct.
Land	1852	County Recorder
Probate	1852	Superior Ct.
Court	1852	Superior Ct.
Nat.	1852	Superior Ct.

■ **Siskiyou** 22 Mar. 1852
311 Fourth St., P.O. Box 338, Yreka, CA 96097
Phone: (530)842-8084
Web site: www.kindredtrails.com/CA_Siskiyou.html
Parent County: Shasta, Klamath
Comments/research tips: County Clerk has Board of Supervisors minutes from 1860.

Record Type	Year Begun	Jurisdiction
Birth	na	County Recorder
Marriage	na	County Recorder
Death	na	County Recorder
Divorce	1853	Court Services
Probate	1853	Court Services
Court	1853	Court Services
Burial	na	County Recorder
Election	na	County Clerk

■ **Solano** 18 Feb. 1850
701 Texas St., Fairfield, CA 94533
Phone: (707)421-6265
Web site: www.cagenweb.com/solano
Parent County: Original county

Record Type	Year Begun	Jurisdiction
Birth	na	County Recorder

Record Type	Year Begun	Jurisdiction
Marriage	na	County Recorder
Death	na	County Recorder
Divorce	1850	County Clerk
Land	na	County Recorder
Probate	1850	County Clerk
Court	1850	County Clerk

■ **Sonoma** 18 Feb. 1850
2300 County Center Dr., LaPlaza Building B177, Santa Rosa, CA 95403
Phone: (707)565-3800
Web site: http://users.ap.net/~chenae/sonoma.html
Parent County: Original county

Record Type	Year Begun	Jurisdiction
Birth	na	County Recorder
Marriage	na	County Recorder
Death	na	County Recorder
Divorce	1850	County Clerk
Land	na	County Recorder
Probate	1850	County Clerk
Court	1850	County Clerk
Burial	na	County Recorder

■ **Stanislaus** 1 Apr. 1854
1021 I St., Modesto, CA 95354
Phone: (209)525-5250
Web site: www.cagenweb.com/lr/stanislaus
Parent County: Tuolumne

Record Type	Year Begun	Jurisdiction
Birth	1900	County Clerk Recorder
Marriage	1870	County Clerk Recorder
Death	1900	County Clerk Recorder
Divorce	1854	Clerk/Superior Ct.
Land	1854	County Recorder
Probate	1854	Clerk/Superior Ct.
Court	1854	Clerk/Superior Ct.

■ **Sutter** 18 Feb. 1850
433 Second St., Yuba City, CA 95992
Phone: (530)822-7120
Web site: www.rootsweb.com/~casutter
Parent County: Original county

Record Type	Year Begun	Jurisdiction
Birth	1873	County Recorder
Marriage	1850	County Recorder
Death	1873	County Recorder
Divorce	na	Civil Div./Courts
Land	1850	County Recorder
Probate	na	Civil Div./Courts
Court	na	Civil Div./Courts
Military	1850	County Recorder

■ **Tehama** 9 Apr. 1856
633 Washington St., Red Bluff, CA 96080
Phone: (530)527-3350
Web site: www.cagenweb.com/eb/tehama
Parent County: Colusa, Butte, Shasta

Record Type	Year Begun	Jurisdiction
Birth	1889	County Clerk

Marriage .... 1856 .... County Clerk
Death .... 1889 .... County Clerk
Military .... 1944 .... County Clerk

■ Trinity 18 Feb. 1850
101 Court St., P.O. Box 1258, Weaverville, CA 96093
Phone: (530)623-1215
Web site: www.cagenweb.com/lr/trinity
Parent County: Original county
Comments/research tips: County Recorder has Birth and Death record indexes 1873–1905, Marriage record indexes 1857–1905, and Naturalization records 1850–1940.

Record Type	Year Begun	Jurisdiction
Birth	1905	County Recorder
Marriage	1905	County Recorder
Death	1905	County Recorder
Divorce	1881	Court Services
Land	na	Court Services
Probate	1887	Court Services
Court	1881	Court Services

■ Tulare 20 Apr. 1852
221 S. Mooney Blvd., Visalia, CA 93291
Phone: (559)733-6418
Web site: www.cagenweb.com/cpi/tulare
Parent County: Mariposa

Record Type	Year Begun	Jurisdiction
Birth	1852	County Clerk Recorder
Marriage	1852	County Clerk Recorder
Death	1873	County Clerk Recorder
Divorce	na	Clerk/Superior Ct.
Land	na	County Assessor
Probate	na	Clerk/Superior Ct.
Nat.	na	Clerk/Superior Ct.
Court	na	Clerk/Superior Ct.
Military	1919	County Clerk Recorder

■ Tuolumne 18 Feb. 1850
2 S. Green St., Sonora, CA 95370-4679
Phone: (209)533-5570
Web site: www.cagenweb.com/tuolumne
Parent County: Original county
Comments/research tips: County Clerk/Recorder has old newspapers 1862–1948.

Record Type	Year Begun	Jurisdiction
Birth	1858	County Recorder
Marriage	1850	County Recorder
Death	1859	County Recorder

Divorce	1850	County Recorder
Land	1850	County Recorder
Probate	1850	County Recorder
Court	1850	County Recorder
Burial	1916	County Recorder

■ Ventura 22 Mar. 1872
800 S. Victoria Ave., Ventura, CA 93009
Phone: (805)654-2267
Web site: www.cagenweb.com/ventura
Parent County: Santa Barbara
Comments/research tips: Some land went to Kern and Los Angeles Counties in boundary change.

Record Type	Year Begun	Jurisdiction
Birth	1873	County Recorder
Marriage	1873	County Recorder
Death	1873	County Recorder
Divorce	1873	Clerk/Superior Ct.
Land	1850	County Recorder
Probate	1873	Clerk/Superior Ct.
Court	1873	Clerk/Superior Ct.

■ Yolo 18 Feb. 1850
625 Court St., Woodland, CA 95695; P.O. Box 1130, Woodland, CA 95776
Phone: (530)666-8130
Web site: www.cagenweb.com/yolo
Parent County: Original county

Record Type	Year Begun	Jurisdiction
Birth	1850	County Clerk
Marriage	1850	County Clerk
Death	1850	County Clerk
Divorce	1850	County Clerk
Land	1850	County Clerk
Probate	1850	County Clerk
Court	1850	County Clerk

■ Yuba 18 Feb. 1850
935 Fourteenth St., Marysville, CA 95901
Phone: (530)741-6547
Web site: www.cagenweb.com/yuba
Parent County: Original county

Record Type	Year Begun	Jurisdiction
Marriage	1865	County Clerk
Divorce	1850	County Clerk
Probate	1850	County Clerk
Court	1850	County Clerk
Voter	1866	County Clerk

Colorado

By James W. Warren

HISTORICAL OVERVIEW

Zebulon Pike arrived to explore the area that would become Colorado in 1806. Half a century later, the promise of gold brought early settlers to the mountains of Colorado. Living with those mountains later inspired Molly Brown to be Unsinkable, Kathy Lee Bates to write "America the Beautiful," John Elway to throw a football a mile high, and Alfred Packer to work up a big appetite. Today, genealogists are still mining the records to learn the stories of their Colorado ancestors.

In 1803, the Louisiana Purchase brought the part of Colorado north and east of the Arkansas River under U.S. control. Beginning in 1806, government expeditions began to map the area. By the 1820s, fur trappers and traders had begun to seek work there.

In the 1840s, Mexican land grants issued in Southwestern Colorado brought Hispanic settlers to the area. In 1848, the United States acquired the rest of present-day Colorado from Mexico and agreed to honor claims to the earlier Spanish and Mexican land grants. Settlers from Spanish New Mexico settled in the San Luis Valley beginning in 1851. In 1852 Fort Massachusetts was built, and later abandoned. Fort Garland was the second military outpost in Colorado built to protect the area's settlers.

Gold was discovered in 1858. Denver and many other mining towns were formed as the Pikes Peak Gold Rush brought a flood of settlers. They came primarily from midwestern and northeastern states but there were some from almost every part of the U.S., as well as many foreign immigrants.

In 1861 Colorado Territory was organized, two years after congress failed to recognize Jefferson Territory, which Colorado pioneers had created without Congressional blessings. By the time of the 1870 census, the transcontinental railroad had been completed. Denver was linked with Cheyenne and Kansas City, providing direct

COLORADO AT A GLANCE

Motto: Nothing Without Providence

Population: 4.3 million

Prevalent Religions: Roman Catholic, Baptist, Methodist, Lutheran, and Church of Jesus Christ of Latter-day Saints

Major Industries: Mining, agriculture, tourism, federal military

Ethnic Makeup (in percent): Caucasian 82.8%, African American 3.8%, Hispanic 17.2%, Asian 2.2%, Native American 1.0%, Other 7.2%

Famous Coloradoans: Tim Allen, Roseanne Barr, Scott Carpenter, Lon Chaney, Don Cheadle, Jack Dempsey, Douglas Fairbanks, John Fante, Hattie McDaniel, Barbara Rush, Lowell Thomas, Hunter S. Thompson

Above: A skier on the Colorado slopes

© PhotoDisc/Getty Images

connections to the East and West coasts. At that point, the original Plains Indian inhabitants, primarily Arapaho, Cheyenne, Kiowa, and Comanche, had been forced off their lands to Indian Territory in Oklahoma, leaving only the Ute Indians behind.

In 1876 Colorado achieved statehood, the thirty-eighth state. The Utes were permanently relocated to Utah reservation lands, and in 1881 western Colorado was opened for settlement.

The gold rush era began to wane after the last major gold strike at Cripple Creek in 1890. By 1910, the midwestern states were the primary feeders for migration to Colorado, but there were also immigrants from Germany, Russia, Italy, Austria, Sweden, and England. Mining, ranching, and, later, oil and industry continued to be prominent in the development of Colorado throughout the twentieth century. Denver grew to be a major western city, and Colorado Springs became the home of the U.S. Air Force Academy.

RECORD HIGHLIGHTS

On the 1860 federal population census, what would eventually become Colorado is split among four territories: Kansas, Nebraska, New Mexico, and Utah. The 1870 and 1880 decennial censuses and a special 1885 federal census, all of Colorado Territory, are available. They include population, agricultural, manufacturing, and mortality schedules. The Social Statistics Schedules survived for 1870, and the seven supplemental schedules (*Defective, Dependent, and Delinquent* classes) are available for 1880. After Colorado's statehood, the available federal censuses are 1900, 1910, 1920, and 1930 (state). The 1890 census, including the Union Veterans' and Widows schedule, was destroyed. Unlike many states, Colorado did not take separate state censuses.

Local registration of vital records was mandated in 1876. Those early records may be available at the county courthouse or the Colorado Department of Health, Vital Records Section. Statewide registration began in 1907

Colorado

and was generally complied with by the 1920s, and those records are available from the Vital Records Section at the Department of Health.

Marriage records are available from county courthouses, and many of the early marriage records have been turned over to the State Archives. The Colorado Department of Health (CDH) does have two statewide marriage indexes, 1900–1939 and 1975 to the present, which they will check. CDH also has copies of marriage records for twenty of Colorado's sixty-three counties. Divorce records are available only from the county clerk where the divorce took place. CDH does have statewide divorce indexes for the years 1900–1939 and 1968 to the present, but has no copies of divorce records.

Court records in Colorado are held by the county and district courts. Probate records and wills are with the county clerk in each county except Denver, which has a separate probate court. Land records are in the office of the county recorder. The Family History Library has a few microfilmed Colorado vital, probate, land, and court records. Naturalization records for most counties are at the State Archives.

Many local cemetery and church records or abstracts have been published or uploaded to GenWeb or other Web sites. However, in most cases you will need to contact the church or cemetery to obtain information. Published abstracts of or indexes to other records and sources, as well as church or business histories, may be found in county and local libraries, museums, and historical societies. One helpful guide is Kay R. Merrill's *Colorado Cemetery Directory* (Denver, CO: Colorado Council of Genealogical Societies, 1985).

Colorado has been a hotbed of genealogical activity for many years. Effective genealogical societies and excellent reference collections provide lots of resources for anyone tracking their ancestors. University and college collections as well as major libraries and historical societies have significant collections of historical materials, including manuscripts, published books, newspapers, periodicals, and maps. And at any of these locations, staff or other patrons may be the real treasure to find, offering knowledge and help.

The Colorado Historical Society's collection of microfilmed newspapers is the most complete available. The Society also has valuable newspaper indexes and clipping files. And that's just the newspaper resources. The Society offers extensive historical and genealogical materials in its collections.

The Western History/Genealogy Department at the Denver Public Library is a major national genealogical repository. The Genealogy Collection, begun in 1910, includes more than 60,000 published volumes, 75,000 microforms, a massive photograph collection, and much

RESEARCH TIPS

for more info

- The Western History/Genealogy Department at the Denver Public Library is a major national genealogical repository, and for those doing Colorado research, it's an indispensable resource <http://denver.lib.co.us/whg/>.
- The Colorado State Archives has court records from most counties, and their Web site has several helpful databases <www.colorado.gov/dpa/doit/archives>.
- The Colorado Department of Health (CDH) has two statewide marriage indexes, 1900–1939 and 1975 to the present, and two divorce indexes, 1900–1939 and 1968 to the present. The state archives or county courthouses have copies of the actual records.
- Vital records can be obtained from the Vital Records Section at the Colorado Department of Health.
- <www.searchsystems.net/list.php?nid=11> (click state; click county)

Census Records
- Federal Census: 1880, 1885, 1900, 1910, 1920, 1930
- Federal Mortality Schedules: 1860 (with Kansas), 1870, 1880
- 1860 Territorial Census and Mortality Schedules: Nebraska 1860 (schedules designated "unorganized territory" which became northeastern Colorado), Arapahoe County, Kansas Territory 1860 (central eastern Colorado), Toas and Mora Counties of New Mexica Territory 1860 (southeastern Colorado)
- 1870 Colorado Territory Census and Mortality Schedules

more. Among the many special resources for those re-searching Colorado ancestors are several obituary indexes, Denver Naturalization Records 1877–1952, and the Colorado Index to Marriages and Divorces, 1900–1939 and 1975 to the present. The Library offers online access to several indexes, including the Colorado State Reformatory Records 1887–1939, Colorado Mining Fatalities 1884–1963, Civil War Grand Army of the Republic listings, and *Denver Post* Obituaries <http://denver.lib.co.us/whg/>.

The Colorado State Archives houses court records from most counties. That includes naturalization records, probate cases, and civil and criminal cases. Often the indexes for civil and criminal case files will still be at the county courthouse, even though the case files themselves have been transferred to the Archives. The Archives has extensive collections of school records, and their Web site <www.colorado.gov/dpa/doit/archives/> also has a number of online Colorado databases. Examples of just a few are the 1870 Federal Census Index; Civilian Conservation Corps (CCC) Enrollment Index (For Colorado Only); county divorce records (indexes to the records of seven counties); school censuses for three counties; Gilpin County Marriages, 1864–1944; Colorado State Penitentiary Indexes, 1871–1973; probate and will indexes for eleven counties; Mother's Compensation, Boulder County, 1914–1934; and Old Age Pension Records for thirteen counties (Depression years assistance programs, ca. 1933–1937.)

The Western Historical Collection in the Norlin Library at the University of Colorado at Boulder has extensive map collections. The Colorado Genealogical Society has published many early Colorado county records in its journal, *The Colorado Genealogist*. Membership in CGS is one of the best ways to stay current with developments in Colorado genealogy <www.rootsweb.com/~cogs/>. The Colorado GenWeb Project has an extensive array of volunteer projects that provide information, indexes, transcriptions, and actual record copies for Colorado research <www.rootsweb.com/~cogenweb/comain.htm>.

Finally, no matter what the online indexes show you, it's always important to work back to other original records that aren't available online or on microfilm. For example, you can find the Denver Public Library's *Reformatory Prisoner's Record Index (1887–1939)* online. But to find out if the story had a happy ending for your ancestor, you'll have to use the original records collection at the State Archives: *Parole Record With Index (1898–1951)*. Here's hoping any of your ancestors who needed reforming were paroled!

STATE RESOURCES

■ ARCHIVES, LIBRARIES, AND SOCIETIES

Archdiocese of Denver, Catholic Pastoral Center
1300 S. Steele St., Denver, CO 80210
Tel: (303) 722-4687
E-mail: rossana.goni@archden.org
Web site: <www.archden.org/parishes/>

Archuleta County Genealogical Society (ACGS)
P.O. Box 1611, Pagosa Springs, CO 81147
E-mail: <oldham@centurytel.net>
Web site: <www.rootsweb.com/~cosjhs/acgs.htm>

Aspen Historical Society
620 W. Bleeker, Aspen, CO 81611
Tel: (970) 925-3721 or (800) 925-3721
E-mail: info@aspenhistory.org
Web site: <www.aspenhistory.org>

Association of Professional Genealogists
P.O. Box 350998; Westminster, CO 80035-0998
Tel: (303) 422-9371
E-mail: admin@apgen.org
Web site: <www.apgen.org>

Aurora Genealogical Society of Colorado
P.O. Box 31439, Aurora, CO 80041-0439

The Black Genealogy Search Group of Denver, Colorado
P.O. Box 40674, Denver, CO 80204-0674
Web site: <www.coax.net/people/lwf/bgsg_den.htm>

Boulder Genealogical Society
P.O. Box 3246, Boulder, CO 80307-3246
Web site: <www.rootsweb.com/~bgs>

Boulder Public Library
1000 Canyon Blvd., Boulder, CO 80302
Tel: (303) 441-3100
E-mail: feedback@boulder.lib.co.us
Web site: <www.boulder.lib.co.us>

Brighton Genealogical Society
343 S. Twenty-first Ave., Brighton, CO 80601-2525

Bureau of Land Management, Colorado State Office
2850 Youngfield St., Lakewood, CO 80215
Tel: (303) 239-3600
Web site: <www.co.blm.gov>

Carnegie Branch Library
1125 Pine St., Boulder, CO 80302
Tel: (303) 441-3110
Web site: <www.boulder.lib.co.us/branch/carnegie.html>

Colorado College, Tutt Library
1021 N. Cascade Ave., Colorado Springs, CO 80903
Tel: (719) 389-6668
E-mail: tuttspec@ColoradoCollege.edu
Web site: <www.cc.colorado.edu/Library/SpecialCollections/Special.html>

Colorado Coalition for Women's History
P.O. Box 673, Denver, CO 80206
Tel: (303) 377-6315

Colorado Council of Genealogical Societies
P.O. Box 40270, Denver, CO 80204-0270
Web site: <www.rootsweb.com/~coccgs/>

Colorado Department of Personnel and Administration, Division of Information Technologies, Colorado State Archives
1313 Sherman, Rm. 1B20, Denver, CO 80203
Tel: (303) 866-2358
Web site: <www.colorado.gov/dpa/doit/archives>

Colorado Department of Public Health and Environment
4300 Cherry Creek Dr. S., Denver, CO 80246-1530
Tel: (303) 692-2000
Web site: <www.cdphe.state.co.us/cdphehom.asp>

Colorado Genealogical Society
P.O. Box 9218, Denver, CO 80209-0218
E-mail: info@cogensoc.us
Web site: <www.rootsweb.com/~cocgs>

Colorado Historical Society
1300 Broadway, Denver, CO 80203

Tel: (303) 866-3682
Web site: <www.coloradohistory.org>

Colorado Springs Chapter, American Historical Society of Germans from Russia (AHSGR),
70 Watch Hill Dr., Apt. A, Colorado Springs, CO 80906-7935
Tel: (719) 282-9364
Web site: <www.ahsgr.org/colorado_springs_chapter.htm>

Columbine Genealogical and Historical Society
P.O. Box 2074, Little, CO 80161-2074
Web site: <www.rootsweb.com/~cocghs/>

Denver Metro Chapter of the American Historical Society of Germans from Russia
401 Ivanhoe St., Denver, CO 80220
Web site: <www.ahsgr.org/denver/codenver.htm>

Denver Public Library, Main Branch
10 W. Fourteenth Ave., Denver, CO 80204
Tel: (720) 865-1111
Web site: <www.denver.lib.co.us>

Eagle County Historical Society
P.O. Box 192, Eagle, CO 81631

The Episcopal Diocese of Colorado
1300 Washington St., Denver, CO 80203-2008
Tel: (303) 837-1173 or (800) 446-3081
Web site: <www.coloradodiocese.org>

Estes Park Genealogical Society
1281 High Dr. MR, Estes Park, CO 80517

Foothills Genealogical Society, Inc.
P.O. Box 150382, Lakewood, CO 80215-0382
Tel: (303) 232-1483 ext. 2306
E-mail: foothills@jefferson.lib.co.us
Web site: <www.foothillsgenealogy.org>

Fore-Kin Trails Genealogical Society
P.O. Box 802, Montrose, CO 81402-0802

Web site: <www.rootsweb.com/~comontro/forekin.htm>

Four Corners Genealogy Society
P.O. Box 2636, Durango, CO 81302

Fremont County Genealogical Society
1836 Flora Ct., Cañon City, CO 81212

Frontier Historical Society
1001 Colorado Ave., Glenwood Springs, CO 81601-3319
Tel: (970) 945-4448
E-mail: history@rof.net
Web site: <www.glenwoodhistory.com>

Genealogical Research Society of Durango
2720 Delwood, Durango, CO 81301

Genealogical Society of Hispanic America
P.O. Box 9606, Denver, CO 80209-0606
Web site: <www.gsha.net>

Stephen H. Hart Library, Colorado Historical Society
1300 Broadway, Denver, CO 80203
Tel: (303) 866-5739
E-mail: research@chs.state.co.us
Web site: <www.coloradohistory.org/chs_library/lib_contact.htm>

Jewish Genealogical Society of Colorado
6965 E. Girard Ave., Denver, CO 80224
Tel: (303) 756-6028
Web site: <www.jewishgen.org/jgs-colorado/>

Lafayette & Louisville Genealogy Society
1248 Illium, Lafayette, CO 80026
Web site: <www.rootsweb.com/~collgs/index.html>

Larimer County Genealogical Society
P.O. Box 9502, Fort Collins, CO 80525-9502
Web site: <http://jymis.com/~lcgs/>

Logan County Genealogical Society
723 Taylor St., Sterling, CO 80751-3733

Longmont Genealogical Society
P.O. Box 6081, Longmont, CO 80501-2077
Web site: <www.rootsweb.com/~colgs/>

Mesa County Genealogical Society
P.O. Box 1506, Grand Junction, CO 81502-1506
Tel: (970) 242-0971
Web site: <www.gjmesa.com/mcgs/>

National Archives and Record Administration, Rocky Mountain Region
P.O. Box 25307, Denver, CO 80225-0307
E-mail: denver.archives@nara.gov
Web site: <www.archives.gov/facilities/co/denver.html>

Norlin Library, University of Colorado
184 UCB, Boulder, CO 80309-0184
Tel: (303) 492-8705
E-mail: libweb@colorado.edu
Web site: <www.libraries.colorado.edu/ps/nor/frontpage.htm>

Northern Colorado Chapter, American Historical Society of Germans from Russia (AHSGR)
Tel: (970) 284-5301
Web site: <www.ahsgr.org/conorthe.htm>

Old Colorado City Historical Society
One S. Twenty-fourth St., Colorado Springs, CO 80904-3319
Tel: (719) 636-1225
Web site: <http://history.oldcolo.com>

Palatines to America, Colorado Chapter
2880 S. Locust #208, South Denver, CO 80222-7130
Tel: (303) 756-7330

Penrose Public Library
P.O. Box 1579, Colorado Springs, CO 80901
Tel: (719) 389-8968
Web site: <http://library.ppld.org/AboutYourLibrary/HoursLocations/penrose.asp>

Pikes Peak Genealogical Society, Inc.
P.O. Box 1262, Colorado Springs, CO 80901
Web site: <www.rootsweb.com/~coelpaso/ppgspubs.htm>

Prowers County Genealogical Society
P.O. Box 929, Lamar, CO 81052

Pueblo City-County Library District
100 E. Abriendo Ave., Pueblo, CO 81004-4290
Tel: (719) 562-5600
Web site: <www.pueblolibrary.org/>

Rio Blanco County Historical Society
Web site: <www.meekercolorado.com/HSociety.htm>

Rocky Mountain Jewish Historical Society; Center for Judaic Studies
2000 E. Asbury, Denver, CO 80208
Tel: (303) 871-3020
E-mail: dshneer@du.edu
Web site: <www.du.edu/cjs/rmjhs/>

San Juan Historical Society
P.O. Box 1711, Pagosa Springs, CO 81147
Web site: <www.rootsweb.com/~cosjhs/museum.htm>

Sedgwick County Genealogy Society
P.O. Box 86, Julesburg, CO 80737
Web site: <www.rootsweb.com/~cosedgwi/society.htm>

Sheridan Historical Society
4101 S. Federal Blvd., Sheridan, CO 80110-5399
Web site: <www.rootsweb.com/~coshs/>

Southern Peaks Public Library
423 4th St., Alamosa, CO 81101
Tel: (719) 589-6592
Web site: <www.alamosalibrary.org/>

Summit Historical Society
P.O. Box 745, Breckenridge, CO 80424
Tel: (970) 453-9022
E-mail: mail@summithistorical.org
Web site: <www.summithistorical.org>

Ira J. Taylor Library, Iliff School of Theology
2201 S. University Blvd., Denver, CO 80210
Tel: (303) 744-1287
Web site: <http://discuss.iliff.edu/taylor/>

Ute Pass Historical Society
P.O. Box 6875, Woodland Park,
CO 80866
Tel: (719) 686-7512
E-mail: Info@UtePassHistoricalS
ociety.org
Web site: <www.utepasshistoric
alsociety.org>

**Weld County Genealogical
Society**
P.O. Box 278, Greeley, CO 80632
E-mail: gen@weld.lib.co.us
Web site: <www.rootsweb.com/
~cowcgs>

**Weld County Public Library,
Centennial Park Branch**
2227 Twenty-third Ave., Greeley,
CO 80634
Tel: (970) 506-8600
Web site: <www.weld.lib.co.us>

Ann Zugelder Library
307 N. Wisconsin Ave., Gunnison,
CO 81230
Tel: (970) 641-3485
Web site: <www.co.gunnison.co
.us/Library/library.html>

BIBLIOGRAPHY

■ GENERAL RESOURCES

*Colorado Area Key: A
Comprehensive Study of
Genealogical Records Sources
of Colorado, Including Maps
and Brief General History*
compiled by Florence Runyan
Clint (Denver, CO: Eden Press,
1968)

Colorado Bibliography
edited by Bohdan S. Wynar and
Roberta J. Depp, assistant editor
(Littleton, CO: Published by Li-
braries Unlimited for the National
Society of Colonial Dames of
America in the State of Colorado,
1980)

*Colorado Families, a Territorial
Heritage*
compiled and published by the
Colorado Genealogical Society,
Inc. (Denver, CO: The Colorado
Genealogical Society, 1981)

*Colorado Postal History: The
Post Offices*
by William H. Bauer, James L. Oz-
ment, and John H. Willard (Crete,
Nebraska: J-B Pub. Co., 1971)

Colorado Research Outline
by the Church of Jesus Christ of
Latter-day Saints, Family History

Library (Salt Lake City, UT: Corp.
of the President of the Church of
Jesus Christ of L.D.S., 1988)

*Genealogical Index to the
Records of the Society of
Colorado Pioneers*
by the Society of Colorado Pio-
neers, the Colorado Genealogical
Society, and Bette D. Peters
(Denver, CO: Colorado Genealogi-
cal Society, 1990)

*The Genealogist's Companion
and Sourcebook, 2d ed.*
by Emily Anne Croom (Cincinnati:
Betterway Books, 2003)

*A Genealogist's Guide to
Discovering Your African-
American Ancestors*
by Franklin Carter Smith and
Emily Anne Croom (Cincinnati:
Betterway Books, 2003)

*Guide to Colorado Newspapers,
1859–1963*
compiled by Donald E. Oehlerts
(Denver: Bibliographical Center
for Research, Rocky Mountain
Region, 1964)

*Guide to Genealogical
Research in the National
Archives of the United States*
edited by Anne Bruner Eales and
Robert M. Kvasnicka (Washing-
ton, D.C.: National Archives and
Records Administration, 2000)

*National Archives Microfilm
Catalogs online:*
<www.archives.gov/publica
tions/genealogy_microfilm_
catalogs.html>

*Pioneers of the Territory of
Southern Colorado*
by the Territorial Daughters of
Colorado, Southern Colorado Aux-
iliary ([S.l.: s.n.], 1980)

*Subject Index to the Colorado
Genealogist*
by Kay R. Merrill (Denver, CO: Colorado Genealogical Society,
1982)

■ CENSUS RECORDS

*The American Census
Handbook*
by Thomas Jay Kemp (Wilmington, DE: Scholarly Resources,
2001)

*The Census Book: A
Genealogist's Guide to Federal
Census Facts, Schedules and
Indexes*
by William Dollarhide (Bountiful,
UT: Heritage Quest, 2000)

*Finding Answers in U.S. Census
Records*
by Loretto Dennis Szucs and Matthew Wright (Orem, UT: Ancestry
Publishing, 2002)

State Census Records
by Ann S. Lainhart (Baltimore,
MD: Genealogical Publishing,
1992)

*Your Guide to the Federal
Census*
by Kathleen W. Hinckley (Cincinnati: Betterway Books, 2002)

■ IMMIGRATION
RECORDS

*American Naturalization
Records, 1790–1990: What
They Are and How to Use Them*
by John J. Newman (North Salt
Lake, UT: HeritageQuest, 1998)

*American Passenger Arrival
Records*
by Michael Tepper (Baltimore:
Genealogical Publishing Co.,
1993)

*Colorado and its People: A
Narrative and Topical History of
the Centennial State*
compiled by LeRoy R. Hafen (New
York: Lewis Historical Pub. Co.,
1948)

*Naturalization Records: Index
to U.S. District Court—Denver,
Colorado*
compiled by Patricia Crayne-Tru-
dell, Joan Thomas and the United
States District Court (Lakewood,
CO: Foothills Genealogical Society of Colorado, 1997)

*They Became Americans:
Finding Naturalization Records
and Ethnic Origins*
by Loretto Dennis Szucs (Salt
Lake City: Ancestry, Inc., 1998)

*They Came in Ships: A Guide to
Finding Your Immigrant
Ancestor's Arrival Records, 2d
ed.*
by John P. Colletta (Salt Lake
City: Ancestry, Inc., 1993)

■ LAND RECORDS

*Locating Your Roots: Discover
Your Ancestors Using Land
Records*
by Patricia Law Hatcher (Cincinnati: Betterway Books, 2003)

*Mercedes Reales: Hispanic
Land Grants of the Upper Rio
Grande Region*
by Victor Westphall (Albuquerque, NM: University of New Mexico Press, 1983)

*Record of Private Land Claims
Adjudicated by the U.S.
Surveyor General, 1855–1890*
by the New Mexico (Territory)
Surveyor General's Office (Albu-
querque, NM: University of New
Mexico Library, 1955–1957)

*Spanish and Mexican Land
Grants in New Mexico and
Colorado*
edited by John R. Van Ness and
Christine M. Van Ness (Manhat-
tan, KS: Sunflower University
Press, 1980)

*Spanish & Mexican Records of
the American Southwest: A
Bibliographical Guide to
Archive and Manuscript
Sources*
by Henry Putney Beers (Tuscon,
AZ: University of Arizona Press,
1979)

Vigil's Index, 1681–1846
by Donaciano Vigil (Albuquerque,
NM: University of New Mexico Library, 1955–1957)

■ MAPS

*Colorado Ghost Towns and
Mining Camps*
by Sandra Dallas; photographs by
Kendal Atchison (Norman, OK:
University of Oklahoma Press,
1985)

*Colorado Place Names:
Communities, Counties, Parks,
Passes with Historical Lore and
Fact Plus a Pronunciation
Guide*
by George R. Eichler (Boulder,
CO: Johnson Pub., 1980)

*Crofutt's Grip-Sack Guide of
Colorado*
by George A. Crofutt (Golden, CO:
Cubar Associates, 1966)

A Gazetteer of Colorado
by Henry Gannett (Washington,
D.C.: Government Print Office,
1906)

Colorado

Map Guide to the U.S. Federal Censuses, 1790–1920
by William Thorndale and William Dollarhide (Baltimore, MD: Genealogical Pub. Co., 1987)

■ MILITARY RECORDS

Colorado Volunteers in New Mexico, 1862
edited by Richard Harwell (Chicago: R.R. Donnelley, 1962)

Confederate Soldiers Buried in Colorado
by Sherman Lee Pompey (Independence, CA: Historical and Genealogical Pub., 1995)

Just Outside of Manila: Letters from Members of the First Colorado Regiment in the Spanish-American and Philippine-American Wars
compiled and edited by Frank Harper (Denver, CO: Colorado Historical Society, 1991)

Uncle, We Are Ready! Registering America's Men, 1917–1918: A Guide to Researching World War I Draft Registration Cards
by John J. Newman (North Salt Lake, UT: HeritageQuest, 2001)

U.S. Military Records: A Guide to Federal & State Sources, Colonial America to the Present
by James C. Neagles (Salt Lake City: Ancestry, Inc., 1994)

World War II: A Family Historian's Guide
by Debra Johnson Knox (Spartanburg, SC: MIE Publishing, 2003)

■ PROBATE RECORDS

Abstract of Early Probate Records
by Ella Ruland MacDougall (19-?)

■ VITAL RECORDS

Colorado Cemetery Directory
edited by Kay R. Merrill (Denver, CO: Colorado Council of Genealogical Societies, 1985)

Colorado Cemetery Inscriptions
compiled by Lela O. McQueary (Englewood, CO: K.R. Merrill, 1985)

From the Grave: A Roadside Guide to Colorado's Pioneer Cemeteries
by Linda Wommack (Caldwell, Idaho: Caxton Press, 1998)

Guide to Vital Statistics Records in Colorado
by the Historical Records Survey and the United States Works Progress Administration (Denver, CO: The Survey, 1942)

Marriages of Arapahoe County, Colorado, 1859–1901: Including Territory that Became Adams, Denver and Other Counties
compiled by the Arapahoe County Marriage Committee (Denver, CO: Colorado Genealogical Society, 1986)

Statewide Marriage Index, 1900–1939, 1975–1992
by the Colorado Department of Health (Denver, CO: Colorado Department of Health, 1975–1992)

Your Guide to Cemetery Research
by Sharon DeBartolo Carmack (Cincinnati: Betterway Books, 2002)

■ Adams 15 Apr. 1901
450 S. Fourth Ave., Brighton, CO 80601
Phone: (303)654-6026
Web site: www.rootsweb.com/~coadams
Parent County: Arapahoe
Comments/research tips: County Clerk has some Burial records, some Land records from Arapahoe County prior to 1901, and School census 1902–1964. State Archives has Naturalization records 1906–1954.

Record Type	Year Begun	Jurisdiction
Birth	1876	Clerk/Recorder
Marriage	1902	Clerk/Recorder
Death	1907	Clerk/Recorder
Divorce	1905	County Court Clerk
Land	1902	Clerk/Recorder
Probate	1905	County Court Clerk
Court	1905	County Court Clerk

■ Alamosa 8 Mar. 1913
402 Edison Ave., P.O. Box 178, Alamosa, CO 81101-2560
Phone: (719)589-6681
Web site: www.rootsweb.com/~coalamos/
Parent County: Costilla, Conejos
Comments/research tips: County Clerk has Marriage records for Costilla and Conejos Counties for late 1800s. State Archives has Naturalization records 1915–1991.

Record Type	Year Begun	Jurisdiction
Birth	1870	County Clerk
Marriage	1914	County Clerk
Death	1902	County Clerk
Divorce	1914	Clerk/District Ct.
Land	1914	County Clerk
Probate	1914	Clerk/District Ct.
Court	1914	Clerk/District Ct.

■ Arapahoe 1 Nov. 1861
5334 S. Prince St., Littleton, CO 80166-0060
Phone: (303)795-4200
Web site: www.co.arapahoe.co.us/
Parent County: Original county
Comments/research tips: First formed in 1855 as Territorial County. Clerk/Recorder has some incomplete Land records from late 1800s. See Kansas 1860 for census records.

Record Type	Year Begun	Jurisdiction
Birth	1876	Clerk/Recorder
Marriage	1902	Clerk/Recorder
Death	1907	Clerk/Recorder
Divorce	1903	Clerk/District Ct.
Land	1902	Clerk/Recorder
Probate	1903	Clerk/District Ct.
Court	1903	Clerk/District Ct.

■ Archuleta 14 Apr. 1885
P.O. Box 2589, Pagosa Springs, CO 81147-1507
Phone: (970)264-8350
Web site: www.archuletacounty.org.
Parent County: Conejos

Record Type	Year Begun	Jurisdiction
Birth	1880	County Clerk
Marriage	1886	County Clerk
Death	1907	County Clerk
Divorce	1885	Clerk/Combined Courts
Land	1886	County Clerk
Probate	1885	Clerk/Combined Courts
Court	1885	Clerk/Combined Courts

■ Baca 16 Apr. 1889
741 Main St., Springfield, CO 81073
Phone: (719)523-4372
Web site: www.rootsweb.com/~cobaca/

Parent County: Las Animas

Record Type	Year Begun	Jurisdiction
Marriage	1889	County Clerk
Divorce	ca. 1918	Clerk/Combined Courts
Land	1889	County Clerk
Probate	ca. 1918	Clerk/Combined Courts
Court	ca. 1918	Clerk/Combined Courts
Birth	1910	County Clerk
Death	1911	County Clerk
Nat.	na	Clerk/District Ct.

■ Bent   11 Feb. 1870

P.O. Box 350, Las Animas, CO 81054
Phone: (719)456-2009
Web site: www.rootsweb.com/~cobent/
Parent County: Huerfano, Indian Reserve Lands
Comments/research tips: Clerk of Combined Courts has Divorce records 1907–1919.

Record Type	Year Begun	Jurisdiction
Birth	1905	Nursing Service
Marriage	1888	County Recorder
Death	1908	Nursing Service
Land	1888	County Recorder
Probate	1888	Clerk/Combined Courts
Court	1888	Clerk/Combined Courts

■ Boulder   1 Nov. 1861

1750 Thirty-Third St., Boulder, CO 80301-2549
Phone: (303)413-7770
Web site: www.co.boulder.co.us/
Parent County: Original county
Comments/research tips: Clerk of District Court has Divorce records 1904–1912. State Archives has Naturalization records 1872–1958.

Record Type	Year Begun	Jurisdiction
Birth	1866	Dept./Health
Marriage	1864	County Recorder
Death	1866	Dept./Health
Land	1865	County Recorder
Probate	1862	Probate Register
Court	1862	Clerk/District Ct.

■ Broomfield   15 Nov. 2001

One DesCombes Dr., Broomfield, CO 80020
Phone: (303)438-6252
Web site: www.ci.broomfield.co.us/
Parent County: Adams, Boulder, Jefferson, Weld
Comments/research tips: Colorado's newest county.

Record Type	Year Begun	Jurisdiction
Land	2001	Central Records Office
Marriage	2001	Central Records Office
Death	2001	Dept./Health
Birth	2001	Dept./Health
Court	2001	Clerk of County Court
Divorce	2001	Clerk of County Court
Probate	2001	Clerk of County Court

■ Carbonate   8 Feb. 1879

Parent County: Lake
Comments/research tips: (See Lake County) Name changed to Lake 10 February 1879.

■ Chaffee   10 Feb. 1879

132 Crestone Ave., P.O. Box 699, Salida, CO 81201-1566
Phone: (719)539-6913
Web site: www.chaffeecounty.org
Parent County: Lake
Comments/research tips: Clerk/Recorder has very few Birth and Death records from early 1900s. State Archives has Naturalization records 1881–1906.

Record Type	Year Begun	Jurisdiction
Marriage	ca. 1890	Clerk/Recorder
Land	ca. 1890	Clerk/Recorder
Court	ca. 1880	Clerk/Combined Courts
Divorce	ca. 1880	Clerk/Combined Courts
Probate	ca. 1880	Clerk/Combined Courts

■ Cheyenne   25 Mar. 1889

51 S. First St., P.O. Box 567, Cheyenne Wells, CO 80810
Phone: (719)767-5685
Web site: www.rootsweb.com/~cocheyen/
Parent County: Bent, Elbert

Record Type	Year Begun	Jurisdiction
Birth	1910	County Vital Records Office
Marriage	1906	Clerk/Recorder
Death	1911	County Vital Records Office
Divorce	ca. 1920	Clerk/Combined Courts
Land	1906	Clerk/Recorder
Probate	ca. 1920	Clerk/Combined Courts
Court	ca. 1920	Clerk/Combined Courts

■ Clear Creek   1 Nov. 1861

405 Argentine St., Georgetown, CO 80444
Phone: (303)679-2357
Web site: www.co.clear-creek.co.us/
Parent County: Mountain

Record Type	Year Begun	Jurisdiction
Marriage	1882	County Archives
Land	1862	County Clerk
Court	1862	Clerk/Combined Courts
Divorce	1862	Clerk/Combined Courts
Probate	1862	Clerk/Combined Courts

■ Conejos   9 Sep. 1861

P.O. Box 157, Conejos, CO 81129-0157
Phone: (719)376-5422
Web site: www.rootsweb.com/~coconejo/
Parent County: Original county
Comments/research tips: Formerly Guadalupe County. Name changed to Conejos 7 November 1861. Courthouse burned in 1980, destroying many county clerk records. County Clerk has Birth records 1877–1910. Clerk of Combined Courts has Court and Probate records from early 1900s and Divorce records 1899–1915. State Archives has Naturalization records 1882–1948.

Record Type	Year Begun	Jurisdiction
Marriage	ca. 1940	County Clerk
Death	1918	County Clerk
Land	1900	County Clerk

■ Costilla   1 Nov. 1861

P.O. Box 100, San Luis, CO 81152
Phone: (719)672-3681

Colorado

Web site: www.rootsweb.com/~cocostil/main.htm
Parent County: Original county
Comments/research tips: State Archives has Naturalization records 1877–1931.

Record Type	Year Begun	Jurisdiction
Marriage	1853	County Clerk
Divorce	na	Clerk/Combined Courts
Land	1853	County Clerk
Court	1874	Clerk/Combined Courts
Probate	1874	Clerk/Combined Courts

■ **Crowley** 6 May 1911
110 E. Sixth St., Ordway, CO 81063
Phone: (719)267-4643
Web site: www.rootsweb.com/~cocrowle/
Parent County: Otero

Record Type	Year Begun	Jurisdiction
Court	1911	Clerk/Combined Courts
Marriage	1911	County Clerk
Land	1911	County Clerk
Divorce	1911	Clerk/Combined Courts
Probate	1911	Clerk/Combined Courts
Birth	1909	County Registrar
Death	1909	County Registrar

■ **Custer** 9 Mar. 1877
205 S. Sixth St, Westcliffe, CO 81252
Phone: (719)783-0441
Web site: http://home.ix.netcom.com/~gsdownr/usgw/custer1.html
Parent County: Fremont
Comments/research tips: State Archives has Naturalization records 1881–1927.

Record Type	Year Begun	Jurisdiction
Marriage	1876	County Clerk
Land	1876	County Clerk
Court	ca. 1900	Clerk/Combined Courts
Divorce	ca. 1900	Clerk/Combined Courts
Probate	ca. 1900	Clerk/Combined Courts

■ **Delta** 11 Feb. 1883
501 Palmer St., Suite 211, Delta, CO 81416-1764
Phone: (970)874-2150
Web site: www.deltacounty.com
Parent County: Gunnison
Comments/research tips: County Clerk has School census 1891–1964.

Record Type	Year Begun	Jurisdiction
Birth	1897	County Recorder
Marriage	1883	County Recorder
Death	1883	County Recorder
Divorce	1883	Clerk/Combined Courts
Land	1883	County Recorder
Probate	1883	Clerk/Combined Courts
Court	1883	Clerk/Combined Courts

■ **Denver** 18 Mar. 1901
Municipal Office Bldg., Dept. 101, 201 W. Colfax Ave., Denver, CO 80202
Phone: (720)865-8400
Web site: www.denvergov.org/
Parent County: Arapahoe
Comments/research tips: Has annexed territory from Arapahoe, Adams, and Jefferson Counties on several occasions. State Archives has Naturalization records 1862–1915.

Record Type	Year Begun	Jurisdiction
Marriage	1897	County Recorder
Divorce	1901	Clerk/District Ct.
Land	1901	County Assessor
Probate	1901	Probate Administrator
Court	1901	Clerk/District Ct.
Birth	1906	County Vital Records Office

■ **Dolores** 19 Feb. 1881
P.O. Box 608, Dove Creek, CO 81324-0608
Phone: (970)677-2381
Web site: www.rootsweb.com/~codolore/
Parent County: San Juan
Comments/research tips: State Archives has Naturalization records 1881–1906.

Record Type	Year Begun	Jurisdiction
Birth	1887	County Clerk
Marriage	1887	County Clerk
Death	1887	County Clerk
Land	1887	County Clerk
Probate	1881	Clerk/Combined Courts
Court	1881	Clerk/Combined Courts
Divorce	1881	Clerk/Combined Courts

■ **Douglas** 1 Nov. 1861
301 Wilcox St., Castle Rock, CO 80104
Phone: (303)660-7469
Web site: www.douglas.co.us/
Parent County: Original county
Comments/research tips: County Clerk/Recorder has Marriage records 1864–1925. State Archives has Naturalization records 1903–1920.

Record Type	Year Begun	Jurisdiction
Court	na	Clerk/Combined Courts
Land	1864	County Recorder
Divorce	na	Clerk/Combined Courts
Probate	na	Clerk/Combined Courts

■ **Eagle** 11 Feb. 1883
500 Broadway, Eagle, CO 81631-0850
Phone: (970)328-8723
Web site: www.eagle-county.com/
Parent County: Summit
Comments/research tips: Clerk of Combined Courts has Naturalization records 1883–1928. County Clerk/Recorder has Marriage records 1883–1940.

Record Type	Year Begun	Jurisdiction
Birth	1894	Dept./Health
Death	1894	Dept./Health
Divorce	1883	Clerk/District Ct.
Land	1883	County Recorder
Probate	1883	Clerk/Combined Courts
Court	1883	Clerk/Combined Courts

■ **El Paso** 1 Nov. 1861
200 S. Cascade Ave., Colorado Springs, CO 80903
Phone: (719)520-6200
Web site: www.elpasoco.com
Parent County: Original county
Comments/research tips: Clerk of Combined Courts has Divorce records 1903–1941. State Archives has Naturalization records 1869–1970.

Record Type	Year Begun	Jurisdiction
Marriage	1861	County Recorder
Death	1893	Dept./Health & Environment
Land	1861	County Clerk
Probate	1876	Clerk/Combined Courts
Birth	1890	Dept./Health & Environment
Court	1876	Clerk/Combined Courts

■ **Elbert** 13 Feb. 1874
215 Comanche St., P.O. Box 37, Kiowa, CO 80117
Phone: (303)621-3128
Web site: www.elbertcounty-co.gov
Parent County: Douglas, Greenwood
Comments/research tips: State Archives has Naturalization records 1886–1931.

Record Type	Year Begun	Jurisdiction
Court	1876	Clerk/Combined Courts
Marriage	1816	County Recorder
Divorce	na	Clerk/Combined Courts
Land	1816	County Recorder
Probate	1876	Clerk/Combined Courts

■ **Fremont** 1 Nov. 1861
615 Macon, Room 100, Canon City, CO 81212
Phone: (719)276-7330
Web site: www.rootsweb.com/~cofremon/
Parent County: Original county
Comments/research tips: Clerk of Combined Courts has Court, Divorce, and Probate records from early 1900s. State Archives has Naturalization records 1882–1966.

Record Type	Year Begun	Jurisdiction
Marriage	1861	County Clerk
Land	1861	County Clerk

■ **Garfield** 10 Feb. 1883
109 Eighth St., Suite 200, Glenwood Springs, CO 81601
Phone: (970)945-2377
Web site: www.garfield-county.com/home/index.asp
Parent County: Summit
Comments/research tips: Clerk of Combined Courts has Divorce records 1906–1916.

Record Type	Year Begun	Jurisdiction
Birth	1883	County Recorder
Marriage	1883	County Recorder
Death	1883	County Recorder
Land	1883	County Recorder
Probate	1892	Clerk/Combined Courts
Court	1892	Clerk/Combined Courts

■ **Gilpin** 1 Nov. 1861
203 Eureka St., P.O. Box 429, Central City, CO 80427
Phone: (303)582-5321
Web site: http://co.gilpin.co.us
Parent County: Original county
Comments/research tips: State Archives has Naturalization records 1869–1917.

Record Type	Year Begun	Jurisdiction
Marriage	1850	County Recorder
Divorce	na	Clerk/Combined Courts
Land	1850	County Recorder
Probate	na	Clerk/Combined Courts

■ **Grand** 2 Feb. 1874
308 Byers Ave., P.O. Box 120, Hot Sulphur Springs, CO 80451-120
Phone: (970)725-3347
Web site: www.co.grand.co.us/
Parent County: Summit

Record Type	Year Begun	Jurisdiction
Birth	1907	Clerk/Recorder
Marriage	1874	County Recorder
Divorce	ca. 1880	Clerk/Combined Courts
Land	1874	Clerk/Recorder
Probate	ca. 1880	Clerk/Combined Courts
Court	ca. 1880	Clerk/Combined Courts

■ **Greenwood** 11 Feb. 1870
Parent County: Indian Lands
Comments/research tips: Abolished 6 February 1874. Bent and Elbert Counties formed from Greenwood.

■ **Guadalupe** 1 Nov. 1861
Parent County: Original county
Comments/research tips: (See Conejos) Name changed to Conejos 7 November 1861.

■ **Gunnison** 9 Mar. 1877
221 N. Wisconsin Ave., Suite C, Gunnison, CO 81230-2297
Phone: (970)641-1516
Web site: www.co.gunnison.co.us/
Parent County: Lake

Record Type	Year Begun	Jurisdiction
Birth	ca. 1880	Dept./Social Services
Marriage	1877	County Recorder
Death	ca. 1880	Dept./Social Services
Divorce	1877	Clerk/Combined Courts
Land	1877	County Recorder
Probate	1877	Clerk/Combined Courts
Court	1877	Clerk/Combined Courts

■ **Hinsdale** 10 Feb. 1874
P.O. Box 277, Lake City, CO 81235
Phone: (970)944-2228
Web site: www.hinsdalecountycolorado.us/home.html
Parent County: Conejos, Lake, Costilla

Record Type	Year Begun	Jurisdiction
Marriage	1880	County Recorder
Divorce	1874	Clerk/Combined Courts
Land	1874	County Recorder
Probate	1874	County Court
Court	1874	County Court
Birth	1900	Clerk/Recorder

■ Huerfano 1 Nov. 1861
401 Main St., Walsenburg, CO 81089-2045
Phone: (719)738-2380
Parent County: Original county
Comments/research tips: State Archives has Naturalization records 1882–1958.

Record Type	Year Begun	Jurisdiction
Marriage	1870	County Clerk
Divorce	1872	Clerk/Combined Courts
Land	1874	County Clerk
Probate	1872	Clerk/Combined Courts
Court	1872	Clerk/Common Pleas Ct.

■ Jackson 5 May 1909
P.O. Box 337, Walden, CO 80480
Phone: (970)723-4334
Web site: www.rootsweb.com/~cojackso/
Parent County: Larimer
Comments/research tips: State Archives has Naturalization records 1910–1940.

Record Type	Year Begun	Jurisdiction
Marriage	1909	County Clerk
Death	1909	County Clerk
Divorce	1909	Clerk/Combined Courts
Land	1909	County Clerk
Probate	1909	Clerk/Combined Courts
Court	1909	Clerk/Combined Courts
Birth	1909	County Clerk

■ Jefferson 1 Nov. 1861
100 Jefferson City Pkwy., Suite 2530, Golden, CO 80419-2530
Phone: (303)271-8168
Web site: co.jefferson.co.us
Parent County: Original county
Comments/research tips: State Archives has Naturalization records 1862–1955.

Record Type	Year Begun	Jurisdiction
Birth	1907	Dept./Health
Marriage	1868	County Recorder
Death	1868	Dept./Health
Divorce	1863	Clerk/Combined Courts
Land	1867	County Recorder
Probate	1863	Clerk/Combined Courts
Court	1863	Clerk/Combined Courts

■ Kiowa 11 Apr. 1889
1305 Goff, Eads, CO 81036-0037
Phone: (719)438-5421
Web site: www.kiowacountycolo.com/
Parent County: Bent

Record Type	Year Begun	Jurisdiction
Marriage	1889	County Clerk
Divorce	1889	Clerk/District Ct.
Land	1908	County Clerk
Probate	1889	Clerk/District Ct.
Court	1889	Clerk/District Ct.

■ Kit Carson 11 Apr. 1889
251 Sixteenth St., Suite 201, P.O. Box 160, Burlington, CO 80807
Phone: (719)346-8638
Web site: www.kitcarsoncounty.org
Parent County: Elbert

Record Type	Year Begun	Jurisdiction
Birth	na	County Commissioner
Marriage	1908	County Clerk
Death	na	County Commissioner
Divorce	1910	Clerk/Combined Courts
Land	1908	County Clerk
Probate	1910	Clerk/Combined Courts
Court	1910	Clerk/Combined Courts

■ La Plata 10 Feb. 1874
1060 E. Second Ave., Room 134, Durango, CO 81301
Phone: (970)382-6280
Web site: co.laplata.co.us/
Parent County: Conejos, Lake
Comments/research tips: Clerk of Combined Courts has Court, Divorce, and Probate records from early 1900s. State Archives has Naturalization records 1873–1908.

Record Type	Year Begun	Jurisdiction
Birth	na	San Juan Basin Dept./Hlth.
Marriage	1878	County Clerk/Registrar
Death	na	San Juan Basin Dept./Hlth.
Land	1876	County Recorder

■ Lake 1 Nov. 1861
505 Harrison Ave., Leadville, CO 80461
Phone: (719)486-1410
Web site: www.rootsweb.com/~colake/lake.html
Parent County: Original county
Comments/research tips: Known as Carbonate County for two days 8 February 1879–10 February 1879. County Clerk has some burial records 1885–1903.

Record Type	Year Begun	Jurisdiction
Marriage	1869	County Recorder
Divorce	na	Clerk/Combined Courts
Land	1876	County Recorder
Probate	1879	Clerk/Combined Courts
Court	1879	Clerk/Combined Courts

■ Larimer 1 Nov. 1861
200 W. Oak St., Fort Collins, CO 80521
Phone: (970)498-7860
Web site: www.larimer.org
Parent County: Original county
Comments/research tips: State Archives has Naturalization records 1872–1958.

Record Type	Year Begun	Jurisdiction
Birth	1902	Dept./Health
Marriage	1862	County Clerk/Registrar
Death	1902	Dept./Health
Land	1862	County Recorder
Court	1862	Clerk/Combined Courts
Divorce	1862	Clerk/Combined Courts
Probate	1862	Clerk/Combined Courts

■ Las Animas 9 Feb. 1866
200 E. First St., P.O. Box 115, Trinidad, CO 81082
Phone: (719)846-3314

Web site: www.tlac.net/county
Parent County: Huerfano
Comments/research tips: County Health Department has Birth and Death records from late 1800s. State Archives has Naturalization records 1881–1958.

Record Type	Year Begun	Jurisdiction
Marriage	1887	County Recorder
Divorce	1881	Clerk/Common Pleas Ct.
Land	1883	County Recorder
Probate	1881	Clerk/Combined Courts
Court	1881	Clerk/Combined Courts

■ Lincoln 11 Apr. 1889
103 Third Ave., P.O. Box 67, Hugo, CO 80821-0067
Phone: (719)743-2444
Web site: www.rootsweb.com/~colincol/
Parent County: Elbert, Bent
Comments/research tips: State Archives has Naturalization records 1889–1947.

Record Type	Year Begun	Jurisdiction
Marriage	1889	County Recorder
Divorce	1889	Clerk of Court
Land	1889	County Recorder
Probate	1889	Clerk of County Court
Court	1889	Clerk of County Court

■ Logan 25 Feb. 1887
315 Main St., Sterling, CO 80751-4357
Phone: (970)522-1544
Web site: www.loganco.gov
Parent County: Weld

Record Type	Year Begun	Jurisdiction
Birth	1894	Dept./Health
Marriage	1887	County Recorder
Death	1894	Dept./Health
Divorce	1887	Clerk/District Ct.
Land	1887	Clerk/Recorder
Probate	1887	Clerk/District Ct.
Court	1887	Clerk/District Ct.

■ Mesa 14 Feb. 1883
544 Rood Ave., Grand Junction, CO 81502-5007
Phone: (970)244-1607
Web site: www.co.mesa.co.us/
Parent County: Gunnison
Comments/research tips: State Archives has Naturalization records 1884–1994.

Record Type	Year Begun	Jurisdiction
Birth	1890	Dept./Health
Marriage	1883	County Recorder
Death	1890	Dept./Health
Divorce	1884	Clerk/District Ct.
Land	1883	County Recorder
Probate	1884	Clerk/District Ct.
Court	1884	Clerk/District Ct.

■ Mineral 27 Mar. 1893
P.O. Box 70, Creede, CO 81130-0070
Phone: (719)658-2440

Web site: www.rootsweb.com/~cominera/
Parent County: Hinsdale, Rio Grande, Saguache
Comments/research tips: State Archives has Naturalization records 1893–1905.

Record Type	Year Begun	Jurisdiction
Marriage	1893	County Clerk
Divorce	1893	Clerk/Combined Courts
Land	1893	County Clerk
Probate	1893	Clerk/Combined Courts
Court	1893	Clerk/Combined Courts

■ Moffat 27 Feb. 1911
221 W. Victory Way, Suite 200, Craig, CO 81625
Phone: (970)824-9119
Web site: www.co.moffat.co.us/
Parent County: Routt
Comments/research tips: State Archives has Naturalization records 1902–1959.

Record Type	Year Begun	Jurisdiction
Birth	1900	Reg./Vital Records
Marriage	1911	County Recorder
Death	1900	Reg./Vital Records
Divorce	1911	Clerk/Combined Courts
Land	1911	County Clerk/Registrar
Probate	1911	Clerk/Combined Courts
Court	1911	Clerk/Combined Courts

■ Montezuma 16 Apr. 1889
109 W. Main St., Cortez, CO 81321
Phone: (970)565-3728
Web site: www.co.montezuma.co.us
Parent County: La Plata
Comments/research tips: State Archives has Naturalization records 1889–1906.

Record Type	Year Begun	Jurisdiction
Birth	1879	County Recorder
Marriage	1889	County Recorder
Death	1892	County Recorder
Divorce	1889	Clerk/District Ct.
Land	1879	County Recorder
Probate	1889	Clerk/District Ct.
Court	1889	Clerk/District Ct.

■ Montrose 11 Feb. 1883
320 S. First St., Montrose, CO 81402
Phone: (970)249-3362
Web site: www.co.montrose.co.us
Parent County: Gunnison

Record Type	Year Begun	Jurisdiction
Birth	1910	County Recorder
Marriage	1883	County Recorder
Death	1907	County Recorder
Land	1883	County Recorder
Court	1883	Clerk/Combined Courts
Divorce	1883	Clerk/Combined Courts
Probate	1883	Clerk/Combined Courts

■ Morgan 19 Feb. 1889
P.O. Box 596, Fort Morgan, CO 80701
Phone: (970)542-3521

Colorado

Web site: www.rootsweb.com/~comorgan/
Parent County: Weld

Record Type	Year Begun	Jurisdiction
Birth	1906	NE Colorado Health Dept.
Marriage	1898	County Clerk
Death	1900	NE Colorado Health Dept.
Divorce	1889	Clerk/District Ct.
Land	1898	County Clerk
Probate	1889	Probate Clerk
Court	1889	Clerk/District Ct.

■ Otero 25 Mar. 1889
13 W. Third St., Room 210, La Junta, CO 81050
Phone: (719)383-3020
Web site: www.rootsweb.com/~cootero/
Parent County: Bent
Comments/research tips: County Health Department has Birth and Death records from the late 1800s.

Record Type	Year Begun	Jurisdiction
Marriage	1889	County Recorder
Divorce	1889	Clerk/Combined Courts
Land	1889	County Recorder
Probate	1889	Clerk/Combined Courts
Court	1889	Clerk/Combined Courts

■ Ouray 18 Jan. 1877
P.O. Box C, 541 Fourth St., Ouray, CO 81427
Phone: (970)325-4961
Web site: www.co.ouray.co.us/
Parent County: Hinsdale, Lake
Comments/research tips: State Archives has Naturalization records 1878–1918. Name changed to Uncompahgre County 27 February 1883, renamed Ouray County 2 March 1883.

Record Type	Year Begun	Jurisdiction
Birth	1880	County Treasurer
Marriage	1881	County Recorder
Death	1894	County Treasurer
Divorce	1878	Clerk/Combined Courts
Land	1881	County Recorder
Probate	1878	Clerk/Combined Courts
Court	1878	Clerk/Combined Courts

■ Park 1 Nov. 1861
501 Main St., Fairplay, CO 80440
Phone: (719)836-4222
Web site: www.parkco.us
Parent County: Original county
Comments/research tips: State Archives has Naturalization records 1909–1930.

Record Type	Year Begun	Jurisdiction
Birth	1875	Clerk/Recorder
Marriage	1881	County Recorder
Divorce	1861	Clerk/Combined Courts
Land	1861	County Recorder
Probate	1861	Clerk/Combined Courts
Court	1861	Clerk/Common Pleas Ct.
Death	1903	Clerk/Recorder

■ Phillips 27 Mar. 1889
221 S. Interocean Ave., Holyoke, CO 80734
Phone: (970)854-3131
Web site: www.rootsweb.com/~cophilli/
Parent County: Logan
Comments/research tips: State Archives has Naturalization records 1889–1930.

Record Type	Year Begun	Jurisdiction
Birth	na	City Registrar
Marriage	1892	County Clerk
Death	na	City Registrar
Divorce	1889	Clerk/Combined Courts
Land	1892	County Clerk
Probate	1889	Clerk/Combined Courts
Court	1889	Clerk/Combined Courts

■ Pitkin 23 Feb. 1881
530 E. Main St. #101, Aspen, CO 81611
Phone: (970)920-5180
Web site: www.aspenpitkin.com
Parent County: Gunnison

Record Type	Year Begun	Jurisdiction
Court	na	Clerk/Combined Courts
Marriage	1890	County Recorder
Land	1890	County Recorder
Probate	na	Clerk/Combined Courts
Divorce	na	Clerk/Combined Courts

■ Prowers 11 Apr. 1889
300 S. Main St., Lamar, CO 81052
Phone: (719)336-8011
Web site: www.prowerscounty.net
Parent County: Bent

Record Type	Year Begun	Jurisdiction
Marriage	1889	County Recorder
Divorce	1889	Clerk/Combined Courts
Land	1889	County Recorder
Probate	1889	Clerk/Combined Courts
Court	1889	Clerk/Combined Courts
Birth	1908	County Recorder
Death	1908	County Recorder

■ Pueblo 1 Nov. 1861
215 W. Tenth St., Pueblo, CO 81003
Phone: (719)583-6507
Web site: www.co.pueblo.co.us/
Parent County: Original county
Comments/research tips: State Archives has Naturalization records 1878–1913, 1949–1983.

Record Type	Year Begun	Jurisdiction
Birth	1887	Dept./Health
Marriage	1865	County Recorder
Death	1887	Dept./Health
Divorce	1876	Clerk/Combined Courts
Land	1865	County Recorder
Probate	1876	Clerk/Combined Courts
Court	1876	Clerk/Combined Courts

■ Rio Blanco 25 Mar. 1889
555 Main St., P.O. Box 1067, Meeker, CO 81641
Phone: (970)878-5068

Colorado

Web site: www.co.rio-blanco.co.us
Parent County: Summit

Record Type	Year Begun	Jurisdiction
Birth	1902	County Recorder
Marriage	1889	County Recorder
Death	1902	County Recorder
Divorce	1889	Clerk/Combined Courts
Land	1889	County Recorder
Probate	1889	Clerk/Combined Courts
Court	1889	Clerk/Combined Courts

■ Rio Grande   10 Feb. 1874
925 Sixth St., P.O. Box 160, Del Norte, CO 81132
Phone: (719)657-3334
Web site: www.riograndecounty.org
Parent County: Conejos, Costilla
Comments/research tips: State Archives has Naturalization records 1874–1906.

Record Type	Year Begun	Jurisdiction
Marriage	1876	County Recorder
Divorce	1876	Clerk/Combined Courts
Land	1874	County Recorder
Probate	1876	Clerk/Combined Courts
Court	1876	Clerk/Combined Courts

■ Routt   29 Jan. 1877
522 Lincoln Ave., P.O. Box 773598, Steamboat Springs, CO 80487-3598
Phone: (970)870-5556
Web site: www.co.routt.co.us/
Parent County: Grand
Comments/research tips: State Archives has Naturalization records 1885–1966.

Record Type	Year Begun	Jurisdiction
Marriage	1877	County Recorder
Divorce	1877	Clerk/Combined Courts
Land	1877	County Recorder
Probate	1877	Clerk/Combined Courts
Court	1877	Clerk/Combined Courts

■ Saguache   29 Dec. 1866
501 Fourth St., P.O. Box 176, Saguache, CO 81149
Phone: (719)655-2512
Web site: www.slv.org/saguachecounty/
Parent County: Costilla, Lake
Comments/research tips: Clerk of Combined Courts has Court, Divorce, and Probate records from the late 1800s. State Archives has Naturalization records 1878–1940.

Record Type	Year Begun	Jurisdiction
Marriage	1885	County Recorder
Land	1885	County Recorder

■ San Juan   31 Jan. 1876
P.O. Box 466, Silverton, CO 81433-0466
Phone: (970)387-5671
Web site: www.rootsweb.com/~cosanjua/
Parent County: Lake
Comments/research tips: State Archives has Naturalization records 1877–1926.

Record Type	Year Begun	Jurisdiction
Birth	1880	County Treasurer
Marriage	1880	County Clerk
Death	1901	County Treasurer
Divorce	1876	Clerk/Combined Courts
Land	1880	County Clerk
Probate	1876	Clerk/Combined Courts
Court	1876	Clerk/Combined Courts

■ San Miguel   2 Mar. 1883
305 W. Colorado Ave., P.O. Box 548, Telluride, CO 81435
Phone: (970)728-3954
Web site: www.sanmiguelcounty.org
Parent County: San Juan
Comments/research tips: County Clerk/Recorder has Marriage records from the early 1800s.

Record Type	Year Begun	Jurisdiction
Divorce	1883	Clerk/Combined Courts
Land	1890	County Recorder
Probate	1883	Clerk/Combined Courts
Court	1883	Clerk/Combined Courts
Birth	1897	County Treasurer
Death	1906	County Treasurer

■ Sedgwick   9 Apr. 1889
315 Cedar St., Julesburg, CO 80737
Phone: (970)474-3346
Web site: www.rootsweb.com/~cosedgwi/
Parent County: Logan

Record Type	Year Begun	Jurisdiction
Marriage	1889	County Clerk
Divorce	1889	Clerk/Combined Courts
Land	1889	County Clerk
Probate	1888	Clerk/Combined Courts
Court	1888	Clerk/Combined Courts

■ Summit   1 Nov. 1861
208 E. Lincoln Ave., P.O. Box 1538, Breckenridge, CO 80424
Phone: (970)453-3470
Web site: www.co.summit.co.us/
Parent County: Original county
Comments/research tips: Clerk of Combined Courts has Court, Divorce, and Probate records form the late 1800s.

Record Type	Year Begun	Jurisdiction
Marriage	1900	County Recorder
Land	1861	County Recorder

■ Teller   23 Mar. 1899
101 W. Bennett Ave., P.O. Box 1010, Cripple Creek, CO 80813
Phone: (719)689-2951
Web site: www.co.teller.co.us/
Parent County: El Paso
Comments/research tips: State Archives has Naturalization records 1899–1941.

Record Type	Year Begun	Jurisdiction
Marriage	1899	County Recorder
Divorce	1899	Clerk/Combined Courts

Colorado

Land .... 1899 ....County Recorder
Probate .... 1899 ....Clerk/Combined Courts
Court .... 1899 ....Clerk/Combined Courts
Birth .... 1876 ....County Recorder
Death..................... 1902 ....County Recorder

■ Uncompahgre 27 Feb. 1883

Parent County: Ouray
Comments/research tips: Name changed to Ouray 2 March 1883.

■ Washington 9 Feb. 1887

150 Ash Ave., Akron, CO 80720-1510
Phone: (970)345-6565
Web site: www.rootsweb.com/~cowashin/
Parent County: Weld

Record Type	Year Begun	Jurisdiction
Marriage	1887	County Clerk
Divorce	1887	Clerk/District Ct.
Land	1887	County Clerk
Probate	1887	Clerk/District Ct.
Court	1887	Clerk/District Ct.

■ Weld 1 Nov. 1861

1402 N. Seventeenth Ave., Greeley, CO 80631
Phone: (970)304-6530

Web site: www.co.weld.co.us/
Parent County: Original county
Comments/research tips: State Archives has Naturalization records 1871–1961.

Record Type	Year Begun	Jurisdiction
Marriage	1861	County Recorder
Divorce	1876	Clerk/Combined Courts
Land	1861	County Recorder
Probate	1876	Clerk/Combined Courts
Court	1876	Clerk/Combined Courts
Birth	1908	Dept./Health
Death	1900	Dept./Health

■ Yuma 15 Mar. 1889

310 Ash St., P.O. Box 467, Wray, CO 80758
Phone: (970)332-5809
Web site: www.rootsweb.com/~coyuma/yuma.htm
Parent County: Washington

Record Type	Year Begun	Jurisdiction
Marriage	1889	County Recorder
Land	1887	County Recorder
Court	1889	Clerk/Combined Courts
Divorce	1889	Clerk/Combined Courts
Probate	1889	Clerk/Combined Courts

Colorado

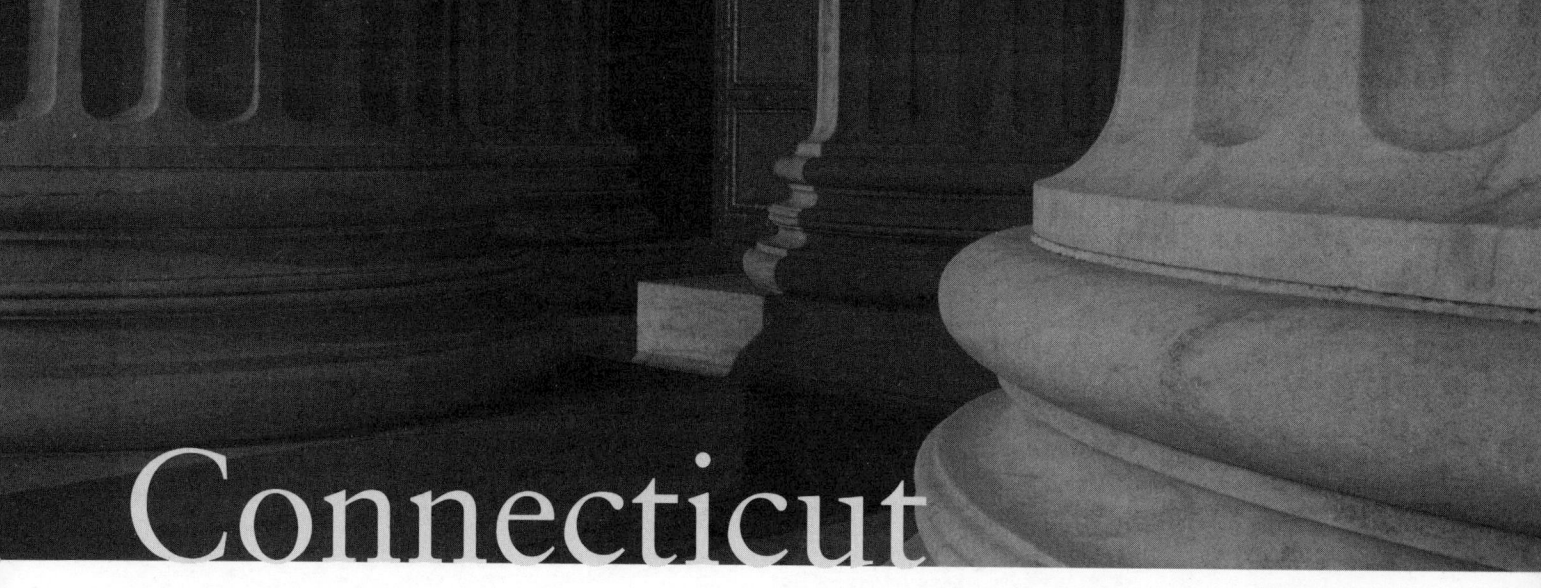

Connecticut

By Maureen Taylor

HISTORICAL OVERVIEW

Prior to European settlement, Native American tribes including the Mohegan, Nipmuc, and Pequot resided in the area that would become present-day Connecticut. Connecticut towns founded in the early seventeenth century by European settlers include Windsor (1633), Wethersfield (1634), and Saybrook (1635). Congregational minister Reverend Thomas Hooker and his followers from Massachusetts, seeking greater political and religious freedoms, established Hartford in 1636, becoming part of Connecticut Colony. Hooker's beliefs formed the foundation of *The Fundamental Orders of Connecticut* (1639), the first written constitution in the colonies that codified laws and allowed residents to elect public officials.

In 1662, King Charles granted Connecticut Colony a new charter that gave settlers land and control over their governance. Connecticut Colony merged with New Haven Colony, which included only six towns along the Long Island Sound, in 1665. Colonial conflicts between native populations and Europeans erupted in the seventeenth century, such as the Pequot War of 1636 and King Philip's War of 1675–76.

During the American Revolution, British troops captured Fort Griswold in New London and raided towns along the coastline. After the successful revolution against England's rule, Connecticut delegates objected to the strong central government proposed for the new country. They lobbied for The Connecticut Compromise, the two-house legislature with equal representation in the Senate and population-based leadership in the House—still used today. Connecticut became the fifth state after ratifying the Constitution in 1788.

In 1818, a new state constitution allowed most men age twenty-one and over to vote and disestablished the Congregational Church. Connecticut outlawed buying

CONNECTICUT AT A GLANCE

Motto: He Who Transplanted Still Sustains

Population: 3.4 million

Prevalent Religions: Christianity, particularly Roman Catholic, as well as some Baptist, Methodist, Lutheran, Episcopalian, and Church of Jesus Christ of Latter-day Saints; also Judaism and Muslim

Major Industries: Transportation equipment, machinery, electric equipment, fabricated metal products, chemical products, scientific endeavors, eggs, dairy products, cattle instruments

Ethnic Makeup (in percent): Caucasian 81.6%, African American 9.1%, Hispanic 3.4%, Asian 2.4%, Native American 0.3%, Other 4.3%

Famous Nutmeggers: Ethan Allen, Benedict Arnold, P.T. Barnum, Henry Ward Beecher, John Brown, Samuel Colt, Oliver Ellsworth, Nathan Hale, Robert N. Hall, Katharine Hepburn, Collis Potter Huntington, Charles E. Ives, Edwin H. Land, Annie Leibovitz, John Pierpont Morgan, Frederick Law Olmsted, Kenneth H. Olsen, Rosa Ponselle, Adam Clayton Powell Jr., Benjamin Spock, Harriet Beecher Stowe, Noah Webster

Above: A replica of the Amistad at Mystic

© PhotoDisc/Getty Images

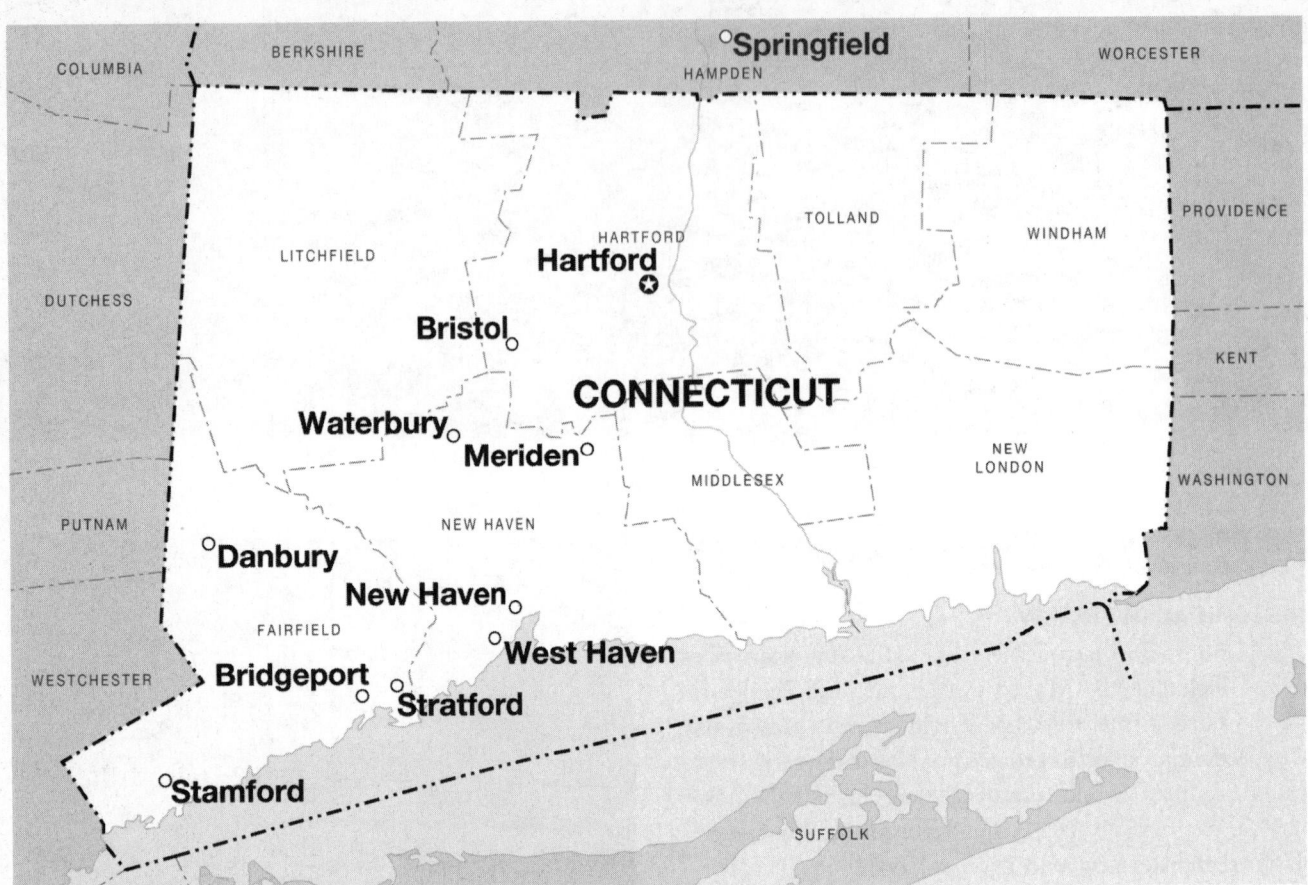

and selling slaves in the state in 1784, completely abolishing slavery in 1848.

Until the early eighteenth century the majority of the population farmed the rocky soil, but in the 1720s they began migrating to the cities to find work in the mills, mines, and small factories of the colony. "Yankee Peddlers" traded the manufactured goods to other areas of the country. During the nineteenth century, immigrants from Italy, Germany, Canada, Ireland, and Poland sought employment in Connecticut's growing industrial economy.

Transportation innovations improved the exportation of produced goods via the Farmington Canal (1828–1847) and rail lines that initially ran between Providence and Stonington (1837) and between New Haven and New York City (1848), just two of the many that operated in the state in the nineteenth century. Several towns along the southern coast built ships and participated in the whaling industry. Many of the United States early insurance companies formed in Hartford to insure the goods being transported overseas.

Nearly sixty thousand Connecticut soldiers fought in the Civil War, and its factories produced uniforms, weapons, and ships. Connecticut men and women participated in all the major military conflicts of the twentieth century and manufactured many of the weapons.

RECORD HIGHLIGHTS

"Connecticut's historic records are among the most complete and best kept in the nation," according to Certified Genealogist Joyce Pendery. Many Connecticut records are either microfilmed or published, with most indexes available at the Connecticut State Library. The University of Connecticut digitized the multivolume *Public Records of Colonial Connecticut* <www.colonialct.uconn.edu/>.

Like other states in New England, Connecticut town clerks began recording vital records by 1650. In addition to the extensive Barbour Collection of Connecticut Vital Records to 1850, over a million tombstone inscriptions up to 1933 are included in the Hale Collection of Connecticut Cemetery Inscriptions at the Connecticut State Library.

Tracking your colonial ancestors is easier due to the *Connecticut Census of 1670* by Jay Holbrook (Oxford, Mass.: Holbrook Research Institute, 1977), a census substitute based on information from tax, land, church, probate, and freeman records that counts the heads of households by name from 1667–1673. With the exception of the federal census of 1890, a full set of census records exists for Connecticut.

Look for tax lists and vital, probate, and land records on the town level. Land records contain deeds, attachments, mortgages, tax liens, and other materials.

Grantor-grantee indexes, maps, surveys, and zoning records are also with town clerks. While the probate indexes and the bound volumes with copies of the records are available in probate clerk offices in town halls, there are more towns than probate district offices. You may have to look in a town different than the one in which your ancestor lived to find the relevant records. Local tax lists exist for many cities and towns. The 1798 U.S. Direct Tax, along with several early nineteenth century tax rosters, are on microfilm, and the originals are housed at the Connecticut Historical Society.

Congregationalists helped settle Connecticut and established their churches in most cities and towns, so their records can be quite extensive. Many churches sent their records to the Connecticut State Library, where they have been partially indexed.

Find your ancestors in the pages of historic newspapers at both the Connecticut State Library and Connecticut Historical Society. Some are indexed. Also available at the Connecticut Historical Society is a large collection of genealogical manuscripts.

Records of military service for the colonial period from the Pequot War are published. The Connecticut Historical Society maintains a collection of original and published military documents. A military census for 1917 exists that was intended to count men between twenty and thirty years of age, but many towns included names for those between sixteen and sixty. A card index of deceased veterans and their places of burial is at the Connecticut State Library.

Connecticut researchers visiting Hartford can access a wide variety of records at two repositories—the Connecticut Historical Society and the Connecticut State Library. Start research with resources in these two facilities, and then move to the towns to visit town halls, libraries, and historical societies once you have determined the location of records based on the date the town was established. Probate, court, cemetery, and some church records, as well as state papers, are centrally located at the Connecticut State Library. The Connecticut Historical Society maintains a general genealogical and historical library, loans books to members, and has an outstanding manuscript collection. Good documentation exists for the Native American population of the state.

Some town clerks offices are open limited hours, so call beforehand for information. Proof of membership in a genealogical society registered with the state is required to access birth records since 1900. Connecticut vital record information is available online at <www.vitalrec.com/ct .html>.

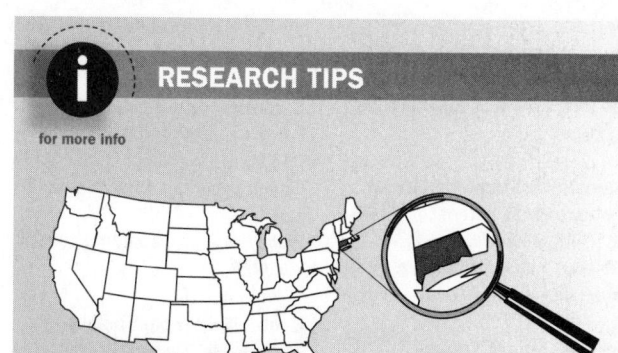

RESEARCH TIPS

for more info

- Many Connecticut vital records from 1650 are either microfilmed or published, and most have indexes that are available at the Connecticut State Library <www.cslib.org>.
- If tracking colonial ancestors, check out *Connecticut Census of 1670* by Jay Holbrook (Oxford, Mass.: Holbrook Research Institute, 1977). It's a census substitute based on information from tax, land, church, probate, and freeman records that lists heads of households by name from 1667–1673.
- Land records contain deeds, attachments, mortgages, tax liens, and other useful materials, and can be found in the town in which they were recorded.
- Records of military service for the colonial period from the Pequot War are published and can be found at the Connecticut Historical Society.

Census Records
- Federal Census: 1790, 1800, 1810, 1820, 1830, 1840, 1850, 1860, 1870, 1880, 1900, 1910, 1920
- Federal Mortality Schedules: 1850, 1860, 1870, 1880
- Connecticut State Library: Special Military Census 1917

STATE RESOURCES

■ ARCHIVES, LIBRARIES, AND SOCIETIES

Abington Social Library
536 Hampton Rd., Pomfret, CT 06230-0118
Tel: (860) 974-0415

Amity & Woodbridge Historical Society, Inc.
1907 Litchfield Turnpike, Woodbridge, CT 06525
Web site: <www.woodbridgehistory.org>

Aspinock Historical Society of Putnam
P.O. Box 465, Putnam, CT 06260
Tel: (860) 963-0092
Web site: <http://aspinockhs-putnam.org>

The Avon Historical Society, Inc.
P.O. Box 448, Avon, CT 06001
Tel: (860) 678-1043
E-mail: oakeshoward@aol.com
Web site: <www.vintageaviation.net/ahs/ahshomepage/htm>

Barkhamsted Historical Society
P.O. Box 94, Pleasant Valley, CT 06063

Tel: (860) 738-2456
E-mail: bhs@barkhamstedhistory
.org
Web site: <www.barkhamstedhis
tory.org>

Beardsley & Memorial Library
40 Munro Pl., Winsted, CT 06098
Tel: (860) 379-6043
Web site: <www.beardsleyandme
morial.org>

Berlin Historical Society
305 Main St., Berlin, CT
06037-2636
Web site: <http://berlincthistori
cal.org>

Cyrenius H. Booth Library
25 Main St., Newtown, CT 06470
Web site: <www.biblio.org/chbo
oth/>

**The Branford Historical
Society, Harrison House**
124 Main St., Branford, CT
06405
Tel: (202) 488-4828
Web site: <http://members.aol
.com/dtrofatter/histsoc.htm>

Bridgeport Public Library
925 Broad St., Bridgeport, CT
06604-4871
Tel: (203) 576-7403
Web site: <www.bridgeportpublic
library.org>

Bristol Public Library
5 High St., Bristol, CT 06010
Tel: (860) 584-7787
Web site: <www.ci.bristol.ct.us/
data/dynamic_content_104645
002299.php>

**Brookfield Museum and
Historical Society**
165 Whisconier Rd.
Mailing address:
P.O. Box 5231, Brookfield, CT
06804
Tel: (203) 740-8140
Web site: <www.brookfieldcthist
ory.org>

Brooklyn Historical Society
25 Canterbury Rd., P.O. Box 90,
Brooklyn, CT 06234-0090
Tel: (860) 774-7728

Burlington Historical Society
781 George Washington Turnpike
Mailing address:
P.O. Box 1215, Burlington, CT
06013
Tel: (860) 404-0152
E-mail: info@burlington-history
.org

Web site: <www.burlington-histor
y.org>

Canterbury Historical Society
P.O. Box 2, Canterbury, CT
06331
E-mail: info@canterburyhistorical
.org
Web site: <www.canterburyhistor
ical.org>

Canton Historical Society
11 Front St., Collinsville, CT
06019
Tel: (860) 693-2793
Web site: <www.cantonmuseum
.org>

Cheshire Historical Society
P.O. Box 281, Cheshire, CT
06410
Tel: (203) 272-2574
Web site: <http://users.rcn.
com/ansdersonel/chs.htm>

Chester Historical Society
P.O. Box 204, Chester, CT 06412
E-mail: info@chesterhistoricalsoc
iety.org
Web site: <www.chesterhistorica
lsociety.org>

**Colebrook Historical Society,
Inc.**
558 Colebrook Rd.
Mailing address:
P.O. Box 85, Colebrook, CT
06021

Columbia Historical Society
486 Rt. 66, Columbia, CT 06237
Tel: (203) 228-9385

**Congregational Library and
Archives**
14 Beacon St., Boston, MA
02108
Tel: (617) 523-0470
Web site: <www.14beacon.org>

Connecticut College Library
% Connecticut College, 270
Mohegan Ave., New London, CT
06320-4196
Tel: (860) 447-1911
Web site: <www.conncoll.edu/
is/info-resources/>

**Connecticut Commission on
Art, Tourism, Culture, History
and Film**
59 S. Prospect St., Hartford, CT
06106
Tel: (860) 566-3005
E-mail: chc@po.state.ct.us
Web site: <www.chc.state
.ct.us>

Connecticut Historical Society
One Elizabeth St. at Asylum Ave.,
Hartford, CT 06105
Tel: (860) 236-5621
E-mail: ask_us@chs.org
Web site: <www.chs.org>

**Connecticut League of History
Organizations**
940 Whitney Ave., Hamden, CT
06517-4002
Tel: (203) 624-9186
E-mail: information@clho.org
Web site: <www.clho.org>

**Connecticut Professional
Genealogists Council**
P.O. Box 4273, Hartford, CT
06147-4273
Web site: <www.rootsweb.com/
~ctpgc>

**Connecticut State Archives at
the Connecticut State Library**
231 Capitol Ave., Hartford, CT
06106
Tel: (860) 757-6595
Web site: <www.cslib.org/archiv
es.htm>

**Connecticut State Library—
History & Genealogy**
231 Capitol Ave., Hartford, CT
06106
Tel: (860) 757-6580
Web site: <www.cslib.org/ha
ndg/htm>

**Connecticut Trust for Historic
Preservation**
940 Whitney Ave., Hamden, CT
06517-4002
Tel: (203) 562-6312
E-mail: contact@cttrust.org
Web site: <www.cttrust.org>

**The Connecticut Valley
Tobacco Historical Society,
Inc.**
P.O. Box 241, Windsor, CT 06095
Tel: (860) 285-1888
Web site: <www.tobaccohistsoc.
org/connecti.htm>

Cornwall Historical Society
P.O. Box 115, Cornwall, CT
06753

Coventry Historical Society
P.O. Box 534, Coventry, CT
06238
Tel: (860) 742-9025
E-mail: WriteToUs@coventrythis
toricalsociety.org
Web site: <www.coventrycthistor
icalsociety.org>

Cromwell Historical Society
395 Main St., Cromwell, CT
06416-2308

E-mail: cromwellhistory@aol.com
Web site: <http://hometown.aol.
com/cromwellhistory/>

**Danbury Museum and
Historical Society**
43 Main St., Danbury, CT 06810
Tel: (203) 743-5200
E-mail: dmhs@danburyhistorical
.org
Web site: <www.danburyhistoric
al.org>

Danbury Public Library
170 Main St., Danbury, CT 06810
Tel: (203) 797-4505
Web site: <http://danburylibrary
.org>

**The Darien Historical Society,
Inc.**
45 Old Kings Hwy. N., Darien, CT
06820
Tel: (203) 655-9233
Web site: <http://historical.dari
en.org/>

Deep River Historical Society
245 Main St., Deep River, CT
06417-2055
Tel: (860) 526-1449

Derby Historical Society
37 Elm St., Ansonia, CT 06401
Tel: (203) 735-1908
E-mail: Derbyhistoricalsoc@juno
.com
Web site: <www.elctronicvalley.
org/derby/history/derbyhist
.htm>

East Granby Historical Society
P.O. Box 188, East Granby, CT
06026
E-mail: zshook@cox.net
Web site: <www.eastgranby.
com/HistoricalSociety/>

**East Haddam Historical Society
and Museum**
264 Town St., East Haddam, CT
06423-1426
Tel: (860) 873-3944

East Hartford Public Library
840 Main St., East Hartford, CT
06108
Tel: 1-860-289-6429
Web site: <www.easthartford.lib.
ct.us/>

East Haven Historical Society
200 Tyler St.
Mailing address:
P.O. Box 120052, East Haven, CT
06512

East Lyme Historical Society
P.O. Box 112, East Lyme, CT
06333

Web site: <www.eltownhall.com/
Town%20Dpmnts%20Comm%20
Cmtes%20Bds/HistoricalSoci
ety/historicalsociety.htm>

East Windsor Historical Society
P.O. Box 363, E. Windsor Hill, CT
06028
Web site: <http://eastwindsorhi
story.home.att.net/>

Easton Historical Society
P.O. Box 121, Easton, CT 06612
Tel: (203) 261-4622

Ellington Historical Society
70 Main St.
Mailing address:
P.O. Box 73, Ellington, CT 06029
Web site: <www.ellingtonhistsoc
.org>

Enfield Historical Society
1294 Enfield St.
Mailing address:
P.O. Box 586, Enfield, CT 06083
Tel: (860) 745-1729
Web site: <http://home.att.net/
~mkm-of-enfct/EHS/EHSabout
Us.html>

**Episcopal Diocese of
Connecticut**
1335 Asylum Ave., Hartford, CT
06105-2295
Tel: (860) 233-4481
E-mail: diocese@ctdiocese.org
Web site: <www.ctdiocese.org>

Essex Historical Society
P.O. Box 123, Essex, CT 06426
Web site: <www.essexhistory
.org>

Fairfield Historical Society
636 Old Post Rd., Fairfield, CT
06430
Tel: (203) 259-1598
E-mail: info@fairfieldhs.org
Web site: <www.fairfieldhs.org>

Fairfield Public Library
1080 Old Post Rd., Fairfield, CT
06824
Tel: (203) 256-3155
Web site: <www.fairfieldpubliclib
rary.org>

**The Falls Village—Canaan
Historical Society**
P.O. Box 206, Falls Village, CT
06031
Tel: (860) 824-7893
Web site: <www.betweenthelake
s.com/canaan/falls_village_
depot.htm>

Farmington Historical Society
P.O. Box 1645, Farmington, CT
06034

Ferguson Library
One Public Library Plaza (corner
of Broad & Bedford Sts.), Stamford, CT 06904
Tel: (203) 964-1000
Web site: <www.futuris.net/
ferg>

**Finnish-American Heritage
Society**
P.O. Box 252, Canterbury, CT
06331
E-mail: info@fahs-ct.org
Web site: <www.fahs-ct.org>

Franklin Historical Society
P.O. Box 73, North Franklin, CT
06254-0073

**French-Canadian Genealogical
Society of Connecticut**
P.O. Box 928, Tolland, CT 06084
Tel: (860) 872-2597
Web site: <www.fcgsc.org>

**The Gaylordsville Historical
Society**
P.O. Box 25, Gaylordsville, CT
06755
Tel: (860) 350-0300
Web site: <www.gaylordsville
.org>

Glastonbury Historical Society
976 Main St., South Glastonbury,
CT 06073
Tel: (860) 633-4572

Godfrey Memorial Library
134 Newfield St., Middletown, CT
06457
Tel: (860) 346-4375
E-mail: library@godfrey.org
Web site: <www.godfrey.org>

Goshen Historical Society
21 Old Middle Rd., P.O. Box 457,
Goshen, CT 06756-0457
Tel: (860) 491-9610
Web site: <www.goshenhistorical
society.org>

The Greenwich Library
101 W. Putnam Ave., Greenwich,
CT 06830-5387
Tel: (203) 622-7900
Web site: <www.greenwich.lib.ct
.us/>

Groton Public Library
52 Newtown Rd., Groton, CT
06340
Tel: (860) 441-6750
Web site: <www.town.groton.ct
.us/library/index.asp>

Haddam Historical Society
14 Hayden Hill Rd.
Mailing address:
P.O. Box 97, Haddam, CT 06438

Hamden Historical Society
Miller Memorial Cultural Center,
2901 Dixwell Ave., Hamden, CT
06518
E-mail: hhs@hamdenlibrary.org
Web site: <www.hamdenlibrary.
org/Historical%20Society/
historicalsociety.html>

Hampton Historical Society
P.O. Box 12, Hampton, CT 06247

Hartford Public Library
500 Main St., Hartford, CT 06103
Tel: (860) 695-6300
Web site: <www.hartfordpl.lib.ct
.us/>

Hartland Historical Society
P.O. Box 221, East Hartland, CT
06027
Web site: <http://vvv.munic.state
.ct.us/hartland/Historical.htm>

**Harwinton Historical Society,
Inc.**
P.O. Box 84, Harwinton, CT
06791
Tel: (860) 485-1202

Hebron Historical Society
P.O. Box 43, Hebron, CT 06248

**Historical Society of East
Hartford, Inc.**
P.O. Box 380166, East Hartford,
CT 06138-0166
Tel: (860) 568-7645
E-mail: hseh@hseh.org
Web site: <www.hseh.org>

**The Historical Society of the
Town of Greenwich**
39 Strickland Rd., Cos Cob, CT
06807
Tel: (203) 896-6899
Web site: <www.hstg.org>

**Indian & Colonial Research
Center**
P.O. Box 525, Old Mystic, CT
06372
Tel: (860) 536-9771
E-mail: icrc06372@yahoo.com
Web site: <www.theicrc.org>

**Jewish Genealogical Society of
Connecticut**
22 Marilyn Rd., South Windsor,
CT 06074
Web site: <www.geocities.com/
jgsct/>

**The Jewish Historical Society of
Greater New Haven**
P.O. Box 3251, New Haven, CT
06515-0351
Tel: (203) 392-6125

Web site: <http://pages.cthome
.net/hirsch/>

**The Jewish Historical Society of
Lower Fairfield County**
P.O. Box 16918, Stamford, CT
06905-8901
Tel: (203) 359-2196
E-mail: IMVM@aol.com
Web site: <www.stamfordhistory
.org/jhsgs.htm>

Kent Memorial Library
50 N. Main St., Suffield, CT
06078
Tel: (860) 668-3896
Web site: <www.suffield-library
.org>

**The Killingly Historical and
Genealogical Society**
196 Main St.
Mailing address:
P.O. Box 6000, Danielson, CT
06239
Tel: (860) 779-7250
E-mail: information@killinglyhisto
ry.org
Web site: <www.killinglyhistory
.org>

**Lebanon Historical Society
Museum and Visitor's Center**
856 Trumbull Hwy., Lebanon, CT
06249-1546
Tel: (860) 642-6579
Web site: <www.lebanoncthistso
c.org>

**The Litchfield Historical
Society**
P.O. Box 385, 7 South St., Litch-
field, CT 06759
Tel: (860) 567-4501
Web site: <www.litchfieldhistoric
alsociety.org>

Lyme Historical Society
96 Lyme St., Old Lyme, CT 06371

Madison Historical Society
Allis-Bushnell House, 853 Boston
Post Rd., Madison, CT 06443
Tel: (203) 245-4567
E-mail: achard@cshore.com
Web site: <www.cttourism.org/
detail.cfm?ID=84>

Manchester Historical Society
106 Hartford Rd., Manchester,
CT 06040
Tel: (860) 647-9983
E-mail: manchesterhistory@juno.
com
Web site: <www.manchesterhist
ory.org>

Mansfield Historical Society/ Museum
954 Storrs Rd. (Route 195), Storrs, CT 06268
Tel: (860) 429-6575

Meriden Public Library
105 Miller St., Meriden, CT 06450-4213
Tel: (203) 238-2344
E-mail: mtrotta@ci.meriden.ct.us
Web site: <www.cityofmeriden. org/services/library/default .asp>

The Middlebury Historical Society
P.O. Box 104, Middlebury, CT 06762
Web site: <www.middlebury-ct. org/historical.shtml>

Middlefield Historical Society
405 Main St., Middlefield, CT 06455
Tel: (860) 349-0665

Middlesex County Historical Society
151 Main St., Middletown, CT 06457
Tel: (860) 346-0746

The Middlesex Genealogical Society
P.O. Box 1111, Darien, CT 06820-1111
E-mail: mgs2@optonline.net
Web site: <http://mgs.darien .org>

The Milford Historical Society
34 High St., Milford, CT 06460-4732
Tel: (203) 874-2664
E-mail: mhsoc@hotmail.com
Web site: <www.geocities.com/ SiliconValley/Park/3831/>

Monroe Historical Society
P.O. Box 212, Monroe, CT 06468
Tel: (203) 261-1383
E-mail: geodesign1@aol.com
Web site: <www.monroehistorics ociety.org>

Montville Historical Society
P.O. Box 1786, Montville, CT 06353

Morris Historical Society
P.O. Box 234, Morris, CT 06763

Mystic River Historical Society
74 High St.
Mailing address:
P.O. Box 245, Mystic, CT 06355

Web site: <www.mystichistory .org>

Mystic Seaport (Museum)
Web site: <www.mysticseaport .org>

National Archives and Record Administration (NARA), Northeast Region (Boston)
Frederick C. Murphy Federal Center, 380 Trapelo Rd., Waltham, MA 02452-6399
Tel: (781) 663-0127
Web site: <www.archives.gov/fa cilities/ma/boston.html>

Naugatuck Historical Society
P.O. Box 317, 195 Water St., Naugatuck, CT 06770
Tel: (203) 729-9039
Web site: <http://naugatuckhist ory.com>

New Britain Public Library
20 High St., New Britain, CT 06051
Tel: (860) 224-3155
Web site: <www.nbpl.lib.ct.us>

New Canaan Historical Society
13 Oenoke Ridge, New Canaan, CT 06840
Tel: (203) 966-1776
E-mail: newcanaan.historical@sn et.net
Web site: <www.nchistory.org>

New England Historic Genealogical Society
101 Newbury St., Boston, MA 02116-3007
Tel: (617) 536-5740
Web site: <www.nehgs.org>

New Fairfield Historical Society
P.O. Box 8156, New Fairfield, CT 06812
Tel: (203) 746-3289

New Hartford Historical Society
P.O. Box 41, New Hartford, CT 06057
Tel: (860) 379-6894
Web site: <www.newhartfordhist ory.org>

New Haven Colony Historical Society
114 Whitney Ave., New Haven, CT 06510
Tel: (203) 562-4183

New Haven Free Public Library
133 Elm St., New Haven, CT 06510
Tel: (203) 946-8130

Web site: <www.cityofnewhaven. com/library/>

New London County Historical Society (NLCHS)
11 Blinman St., New London, CT 06320
Tel: (860) 443-1209
E-mail: nlchsinc@aol.com
Web site: <www.newlondonhistor y.org>

New London Public Library
63 Huntington St., New London, CT 06320-6110
Tel: (860) 447-1411
Web site: <www.lioninc.org/newl ondon/>

New Milford Historical Society & Museum
P.O. Box 359, New Milford, CT 06776-0359
Web site: <www.nmhistorical .org>

Newtown Historical Society
P.O. Box 189, Newtown, CT 06470
Web site: <http://members.tripo d.com/newtown_historical>

Norfolk Historical Society
13 Village Green
Mailing address:
P.O. Box 288, Norfolk, CT 06058
E-mail: norfolkhistorical@snet .net

North Haven Historical Society
27 Broadway, North Haven, CT 06473-2302
Tel: (203) 239-7722
Web site: <www.geocities.com/ northhavenhistoricalsociety/ho me.htm>

North Stonington Historical Society
1 Wyassup Rd., North Stonington, CT 06359-1322
Web site: <www.nostoningtonhis tsoc.homestead.com/>

Norwalk Historical Society, Inc.
P.O. Box 335, 2 E. Wall St., Norwalk, CT 06852
Tel: (203) 846-0525
Web site: <www.geocities.com/ Heartland/Trail/8030/>

Old Saybrook Historical Society
P.O. Box 4, Old Saybrook, CT 06475
Tel: (860) 388-2622
Web site: <www.oldsaybrook. com/History/>

Old Woodbury Historical Society, Inc.
P.O. Box 705, Woodbury, CT 06798

The Orange Historical Society
P.O. Box 784, Orange, CT 06477
E-mail: questions@orangehistory .org
Web site: <www.orangehistory .org>

Otis Library
261 Main St., Norwich, CT 06360
Tel: (860) 889-2365
Web site: <www.otislibrarynorwic h.org/otis_home.htm>

Phoebe Griffin Noyes Library
2 Library Lane, Old Lyme, CT 06371
Tel: (860) 434-1684
Web site: <www.oldlyme.lioninc .org/>

Polish Genealogical Society of Connecticut and the Northeast Inc.
8 Lyle Rd., New Britain, CT 06053-2104
E-mail: pgsctne@yahoo.com
Web site: <www.pgsctne.org>

Portland Historical Society
492 Main St.
Mailing address:
P.O. Box 98, Portland, CT 06480-0098
Web site: <www.geocities.com/ portlandhistsoc/>

Preston Historical Society
Town Hall, 389 Rt. 2, Preston, CT 06365
Tel: (860) 887-0662

Ridgefield Historical Society
4 Sunset Lane, Ridgefield, CT 06877
Tel: (203) 438-5821
E-mail: ridgefieldhistory@sbcglo bal.net
Web site: <www.ridgefieldhistori calsociety.org/>

Rocky Hill Historical Society
785 Old Main St.
Mailing address:
P.O. Box 185, Rocky Hill, CT 06067
Tel: (860) 563-6704
E-mail: info@rockyhillhistory.org
Web site: <www.rockyhillhistory .org>

Roman Catholic Archdiocese of Hartford
134 Farmington Ave., Hartford, CT 06105

Tel: (860) 541-6491
E-mail: info@archdioceseofhartford.org
Web site: <www.archdioceseofhartford.org>

Seymour Public Library
46 Church St., Seymour, CT 06483
Tel: (203) 888-3903
E-mail: webmaster@seymourpubliclibrary.org
Web site: <www.seymourpubliclibrary.org/>

Sharon Historical Society
The Gay-Hoyt House, 18 Main St., Sharon, CT 06069
Tel: (860) 364-5688
E-mail: director@sharonhist.org
Web site: <www.sharonhist.org>

Shelton Historical Society
70 Ripton Rd., Shelton, CT 06484-2668
Tel: (203) 929-7963
Web site: <www.electronicvalley.org/shelton/history.html>

Simsbury Public Library
725 Hopmeadow St., Simsbury, CT 06070
Tel: (860) 658-7663
Web site: <www.simsbury.lib.ct.us/>

Somers Historical Society, Inc.
P.O. Box 652, Somers, CT 06071
Web site: <www.somershistoricalsociety.org>

South Windsor Historical Society
P.O. Box 216, South Windsor, CT 06074
Web site: <http://southwindsorhistory.home.att.net/>

Southington Genealogical Society, Inc.
P.O. Box 698, Plantsville, CT 06479
Tel: (860) 628-7831

Southington Historical Society
Tel: (860) 621-4811
E-mail: SouthingtonHeritage@yahoo.com
Web site: <http://southington.com/History/>

Southington Public Library
255 Main St., Southington, CT 06489
Tel: (860) 628-0947
Web site: <www.southingtonlibrary.org>

Stamford Historical Society
1508 High Ridge Rd., Stamford, CT 06903
Tel: (203) 329-1183
E-mail: history@stamfordhistory.org
Web site: <www.stamfordhistory.org>

State of Connecticut Department of Public Health
410 Capitol Ave.
Mailing address:
P.O. Box 340308, Hartford, CT 06134-0308
Tel: (860) 509-7897
Web site: <www.dph.state.ct.us/OPPE/hpvital.htm>

Sterling Memorial Library, Yale University
130 Wall St.
Mailing address:
P.O. Box 208240, New Haven, CT 06520-8240
Tel: (203) 432-1810
Web site: <www.library.yale.edu>

Stonington Historical Society
P.O. Box 103, Stonington, CT 06378
Web site: <www.stoningtonhistory.org/>

Stratford Historical Society
967 Academy Hill, Stratford, CT 06615

Thompson Historical Society
P.O. Box 47, Thompson, CT 06277
Tel: (860) 923-3200
Web site: <www.thompsonhistorical.org>

Trinity College, Watkinson Library
Tel: (860) 297-2268
Web site: <www.trincoll.edu/depts/library/watkinson/>

Trumbull Historical Society
P.O. Box 312, Trumbull, CT 06611
Web site: <www.trumbullhistory.org/>

United Methodist Archives Center, Drew University Library
Tel: (973) 408-3486
E-mail: drewlib@drew.edu
Web site: <www.depts.drew.edu/lib/uma.html>

Vernon Historical Society
P.O. Box 2055, Vernon, CT 06066

Tel: (860) 875-4326
E-mail: VernonHistSoc@juno.com
Web site: <http://vhsvernonct.tripod.com/>

The Wadsworth Atheneum
Museum of Art, 600 Main St., Hartford, CT 06103
Tel: (860) 278-2670
E-mail: info@wadworthatheneum.org
Web site: <www.wadsworthatheneum.org>

Wallingford Historical Society
P.O. Box 73, Wallingford, CT 06492-0073
Tel: (203) 294-1996

Waterbury Public Library
267 Grand St., Waterbury, CT 06702-1981
Tel: (203) 574-8222
Web site: <www.bronsonlibrary.org>

West Hartford Historical Society/Noah Webster House
227 S. Main St., West Hartford, CT 06107
Tel: (860) 521-5362
Web site: <http://noahwebsterhouse.org>

West Hartford Public Library
20 S. Main St., West Hartford, CT 06107
Tel: (860) 523-3275
E-mail: whpl@westhartford.org
Web site: <www.west-hartford.com/library/>

West Haven Historical Society
219 Court St., West Haven, CT 06516

Westbrook Historical Society
1196 Boston Post Rd., Westbrook, CT 06498
Tel: (860) 399-7473

Weston Historical Society
P.O. Box 1092, Weston, CT 06883
Tel: (203) 226-1804
E-mail: westonhistoricalsociety@msn.com
Web site: <www.wvfd.com/whs.htm>

Westport Historical Society
25 Avery Pl., Westport, CT 06880
Tel: (203) 222-1424
E-mail: info@westporthistory.org
Web site: <www.westporthistory.org>

Wethersfield Historical Society
150 Main St., Wethersfield, CT 06109
Tel: (860) 529-7656
E-mail: weth.hist.society@snet.net
Web site: <www.wethhist.org>

Willington Historical Society
48 Red Oak Hill, Willington, CT 06279
Web site: <www.willingtonct.org/Public_Documents/WillingtonCT_Historical/historical>

Wilton Historical Society
224 Danbury Rd., Wilton, CT 06897
Tel: (203) 762-7257
Web site: <www.wiltonhistorical.org>

Winchester Historical Society
225 Prospect St., Winsted, CT 06098
Tel: (860) 379-8433

Windham Historical Society
627 Main St., Willimantic, CT 06226
E-mail: jillson@windhamhistory.org
Web site: <www.windhamhistory.org>

Windsor Historical Society
96 Palisado Ave. (Rte. 159), Windsor, CT 06095-2526

Wintonbury Historical Society, Inc.
P.O. Box 7454, Bloomfield, CT 06002
Web site: <www.bloomfieldcthistory.org>

Wolcott Historical Society
P.O. Box 6410, Wolcott, CT 06716
Tel: (203) 879-3013
Web site: <www.wolcotthistory.org>

Woodstock Historical Society
523 Route 169, Woodstock, CT 06281
Tel: (860) 928-1035

BIBLIOGRAPHY

■ GENERAL RESOURCES

The American Genealogical and Biographical Index to American Genealogical, Biographical, and Local History Materials edited by Fremont Rider (Middletown, CT: Godfrey Memorial Library, 1952–2000)

Connecticut

Connecticut

Black Roots in Southeastern Connnecticut, 1650–1900
by Barbara W. Brown and James M. Rose (New London, CT: New London County Historical Society, 2001)

Burpee's The Story of Connecticut, 4 vols.
by Charles W. Burpee (New York: The American Historical Company, Inc., 1939)

A Catalogue of the Names of the Puritan Settlers of the Colony of Connecticut; With the Time of Their Arrival in the Colony, and their Standing in Society, Together with their Place of Residence, as far as can be Discovered by the Records
by Royal Ralph Hinman (Hartford, CT: Printed by E. Gleason, 1846)

A Complete History of Connecticut
by Benjamin Trumbull (New York: Arno Press, 1972)

Connecticut, a Bibliography of its History
prepared by the committee for a New England Bibliography, edited by Roger Parks (Hanover, NH: University Press of New England, 1986)

Connecticut Genealogical Resources: Including Selected Bibliographies
compiled by Barbar S. Giles, for Fiske Genealogical Foundation (Seattle: Fiske Genealogical Foundation, 1991)

Connecticut Research Outline
by the Church of Jesus Christ of Latter-day Saints (Salt Lake City, UT: Corp. of the President of the Church of Jesus Christ of L.D.S., 1988, 1997)

Connecticut Researcher's Handbook
by Thomas Jay Kemp (Gale Research, 1981)

Connecticut Sources for Family Historians and Genealogists
by Kip Sperry (Logan, UT: Everton Publishers, 1980)

Connecting to Connecticut
by Betty Jean Morrison (East Hartford: CT Society of Genealogists, 1995)

Early Connecticut Marriages as Found on Ancient Church Records Prior to 1800, 7 vols.
by Frederic William Bailey (New Haven, CT: Bureau of Ancestry 1896–1906)

Encyclopedia of Connecticut Biography, Genealogical-Memorial; Representative Citizens, 10 vols.
compiled with the assistance of the following advisory committee: Samuel Hart, Thomas Snell Weaver, Joseph Anderson, Walter Ralph Steiner, Hadlai Austin Hull, Storrs Ozias Seymour, John Gaylord Davenport, George Curtis Waldo, Frederick Bostwick, Guildford Smith, Lewis Eliot Stanton (Boston, New York [etc.]: The American Historical Society, Incorporated, 1917–1923)

Families of Ancient New Haven
compiled by Donald Lines Jacobus and Helen D. Love Scranton (Baltimore, MD: Genealogical Pub. Co., 1974)

Founders and Leaders of Connecticut, 1633–1783
by Charles E. Perry (Freeport, NY: Books for Libraries Press, 1971)

A Genealogical Dictionary of the First Settlers of New England, Showing Three Generations of Those who Came Before May, 1962, on the Basis of the Farmer's Register, 4 vols.
by James Savage (Baltimore, MD: Genealogical Pub. Co., 1965)

Genealogical and Family History of the State of Connecticut: A Record of the Achievements of Her People in the Making of a Commonwealth and the Founding of a Nation
editorial staff, William Richard Cutter, et al. (Baltimore, MD: Clairfield Co., 1994)

Genealogical Research in New England
edited by Ralph J. Crandall (Baltimore, MD: Genealogical Pub. Co., 1984)

The Genealogist's Companion and Sourcebook, 2d ed.
by Emily Anne Croom (Cincinnati: Betterway Books, 2003)

A Genealogist's Guide to Discovering Your African-American Ancestors
by Franklin Carter Smith and Emily Anne Croom (Cincinnati: Betterway Books, 2003)

Genealogist's Handbook for New England Research
by Marcia Melnyk (Boston: NEHGS, 1999)

The Greenlaw Index of the New England Historic Genealogical Society, 2 vols.
by William Prescott Greenlaw and the New England Historic Genealogical Society

Guide to Archives in the Connecticut State Library
by the Connecticut State Library (Hartford, CT: Connecticut State Library, 1981)

Guide to Genealogical Research in the National Archives of the United States
edited by Anne Bruner Eales and Robert M. Kvasnicka (Washington, D.C.: National Archives and Records Administration, 2000

Guide to Vital Statistics in the Church Records of Connecticut
by the Historical Records Survey (New Haven, CT: The Survey, 1942)

The History of the Episcopal Church in Connecticut
by Eben Edwards Beardsley (Boston: 1893)

Illustrated Popular Biography of Connecticut
compiled and published by J.A. Spalding (Hartford, CT: Press of the Case, Lockwood & Brainard Company, 1891)

Inventory of the Church Archives of Connecticut, Lutheran
by the Historical Records Survey (New Haven, CT: The Survey, 1941)

Inventory of the Church Archives of Connecticut, Protestant Episcopal
by the Historical Records Survey (New Haven, CT: The Survey, 1940)

Lists of Officials, Civil, Military and Ecclesiastical of Connecticut Colony: From March 1636 through 11 October 1677, and of New Haven Colony Throughout Its Seperate Existence, Also Soldiers in the Pequot War who then or Subsequently Resided within the Present Bounds of Connecticut
compiled by Donald Lines Jacobus (New Haven, CT: R.M. Hooker, 1935)

Men of Mark in Connecticut; Ideals of American Life Told in Biographies and Autobiographies of Eminent Living Americans
edited by Colonel N.G. Osborn (Hartford, CT: W.R. Goodspeed, 1906–1910)

National Archives Microfilm Catalogs online:
<www.archives.gov/publications/genealogy_microfilm_catalogs.html>

New England Family Histories. State of Connecticut.
by Lu Verne V. Hall and Donald O. Virdin (Bowie, MD: Heritage Books, 1999)

Nutmegger Index: An Index to Non-Alphabetical Articles and a Subject Index to the Connecticut Nutmegger, Volumes 1-28, 1968–1996
by Helen S. Ullmann (Camden, ME: Picton Press, 1996)

The Public Records of the State of Connecticut, 7 vols.
by Charles J. Hoadly, Forrest Morgan, Leonard W. Labaree, the Connecticut General Assembly, and the Connecticut Council of Safety (Hartford, CT: Case, Lockwood & Brainard Company, 1894–1948)

The Refugees of 1776 from Long Island to Connecticut
by Frederic Gregory Mather (Baltimore, MD: Genealogical Publishing Co., 1972)

Report of the Temporary Examiner of Public Records, 1906
by the Connecticut Temporary Examiner of Public Records (Hartford, CT: Hartford Press, 1907)

The Rogerenes; Some Hithero Unpublished Annals Belonging to the Colonial History of Connecticut
by John Rogers Bolles (Boston: Stanhope Press, F.H. Gilson Company, 1904)

Sketches of Church Life in Colonial Connecticut; Being the Story of the Transplanting of the Church of England into Forty Two Parishes on Connecticut, with the Assistance of the Society for the Propagation of the Gospel; Written by Members of the Parishes in Celebration of the 200th Anniversary of the Society
edited by Lucy Cushing Jarvis (New Haven, CT: The Tuttle, Morehouse & Taylor Company, 1902)

Who's Who in Connecticut
by Ward E. Duffy (Tucson, AZ: W.C. Cox Co., 1975)

Women Before the Bar: Gender, Law, and Society in Connecticut, 1639–1789
by Cornelia Hughes Dayton (Chapel Hill, NC: University of North Carolina Press, 1995)

■ CENSUS RECORDS

The American Census Handbook
by Thomas Jay Kemp (Wilmington, DE: Scholarly Resources, 2001)

The Census Book: A Genealogist's Guide to Federal Census Facts, Schedules and Indexes
by William Dollarhide (Bountiful, UT: Heritage Quest, 2000)

Connecticut 1670 Census
by Jay Mack Holbrook (Oxford, MA: Holbrook Research Institute, 1977)

Finding Answers in U.S. Census Records
by Loretto Dennis Szucs and Matthew Wright (Orem, UT: Ancestry Publishing, 2002)

Map Guide to the U.S. Federal Censuses, 1790–1920
by William Thorndale and William Dollarhide (Baltimore, MD: Genealogical Pub. Co., 1987)

Your Guide to the Federal Census
by Kathleen W. Hinckley (Cincinnati: Betterway Books, 2002)

■ IMMIGRATION RECORDS

American Naturalization Records, 1790–1990: What They Are and How to Use Them
by John J. Newman (North Salt Lake, UT: HeritageQuest, 1998)

American Passenger Arrival Records
by Michael Tepper (Baltimore: Genealogical Publishing Co., 1993)

Copies of Lists of Passengers Arriving at Miscellaneous Ports on the Atlantic and Gulf Coasts and at Ports on the Great Lakes, 1820–1873
by the United States Bureau of Customs (Washington, District of Columbia: The National Archives, 1964)

Passenger and Immigration Lists Index: A Guide to Published Arrival Records of About 500,000 Passengers who Came to the United States and Canada in the Seventeenth, Eighteenth and Nineteenth Centuries
edited by P. William Filby, with Mary K. Meyer (Detroit, MI: Gale Research Co., 1981)

They Became Americans: Finding Naturalization Records and Ethnic Origins
by Loretto Dennis Szucs (Salt Lake City: Ancestry, Inc., 1998)

They Came in Ships: A Guide to Finding Your Immigrant Ancestor's Arrival Records, 2d ed.
by John P. Colletta (Salt Lake City: Ancestry, Inc., 1993)

■ LAND RECORDS

Locating Your Roots: Discover Your Ancestors Using Land Records
by Patricia Law Hatcher (Cincinnati: Betterway Books, 2003)

Lyme Records, 1667–1730: A Literal Transription of the Minutes of the Town Meeting with Marginal Notations, to which Hath Been Appended Land Grants and Ear Marks
compiled and edited by Jean Chandler Burr (Stonington, CT: Pequot Press, 1968)

■ MAPS

Connecticut Place Names
by Arthur H. Hughes and Morse S. Allen (Hartford, CT: Connecticut Historical Society, 1976)

Connecticut Town Origins
by Helen Earle Sellers (Stonington, CT: Pequot Press, ca. 1964)

Connecticut Towns and Counties: What was What, Where and When
by Michael J. Denis (Oakland, ME: Danbury House Books, 1985)

A Gazetteer of the States of Connecticut and Rhode-Island
by John Chauncey Pease (Hartford, CT: Printed and Published by William S. Marsh, 1819)

A Geographic Dictionary of Connecticut and Rhode Island
by Henry Gannett (Baltimore, MD: Genealogical Pub. Co., 1978)

Town and City Atlas of the State of Connecticut
by D.H. Hurd and company (Boston: 1893)

■ MILITARY RECORDS

Catalogue of Connecticut Volunteer Organizations (Infantry, Cavalry and Artillery) in the Service of the United States, 1861–1865: with Additional Enlistments, Casualties, and Brief Summaries Showing the Operations and Service of the Several Regiments and Batteries
by the Connecticut Adjutant General's Office (Bethesda, MD: University Publications of America, 1991)

Collections of the Connecticut Historical Society
by the Connecticut Historical Society (Hartford, CT: The Society, 1860–1895)

Connecticut Soldiers of the Pequot War of 1637: With Proof of Service, a Brief Record for Identification, and References to Various Publications in which Further Data May be Found
by James Shepard (Meriden, CT: Journal Pub. Co., 1913)

Connecticut's Black Soldiers, 1775–1783
by David O. White (Chester, CT: Pequot Press, 1973)

The Military and Civil History of Connecticut During the War of 1861–65: Comprising a Detailed Account of the Various Regiments and Batteries, Through March, Encampment, Bivouac, and Battle; Also Instances of Distinguished Personal Gallantry, and Biographical Sketches of Many Heroic Soldiers: Together with a Record of the Patriotic Action of Citizens at Home, and of the Liberal Support Furnished by the State in its Executive and Legislative Departments
by W.A. Croffut and John M. Morris (New York: Ledyard Bill, 1869)

Pension Records of the Revolutionary Soldiers from Connecticut
by the United States Pension Bureau (Washington, District of Columbia: 1919)

Record of Service of Connecticut Men in the Army and Navy of the United States During the War of the Rebellion
compiled by the authority of the General Assembly under the direction of the Adjutants-General (Hartford, CT: Case, Lockwood & Brainard Company, 1889)

Record of Service of Connecticut Men in the I. War of the Revolution, II. War of 1812, III. Mexican War
by the Connecticut Adjutant General's Office and Henry P. Johnston (Hartford, CT: Case, Lockwood & Brainard, 1889)

Register of Pedigrees and Services of Ancestors
by the Society of the Colonial Wars in the State of Connecticut (Hartford, CT: The Society of Colonial Wars in the State of Connecticut, 1941)

Revolutionary War Pension and Bounty-Land-Warrant Application Files
by the United States Veterans Administration (Washington, D.C.: The National Archives, 1969)

Roll and Journal of Connecticut Service in Queen Anne's War, 1710–1711
by Thomas Buckingham (New Haven, CT: The Tuttle, Morehouse & Taylor Press, 1916)

Rolls of Connecticut Men in the French and Indian War, 1755–1762
by the Connecticut Historical Society (Hartford: Connecticut Historical Society, 1903–1905)

Connecticut

Rolls and Lists of Connecticut Men in the Revolution, 1775–1783
by the Connecticut Historical Society (Hartford, CT: Connecticut Historical Society, 1901)

Uncle, We Are Ready! Registering America's Men, 1917–1918: A Guide to Researching World War I Draft Registration Cards
by John J. Newman (North Salt Lake, UT: HeritageQuest, 2001)

U.S. Military Records: A Guide to Federal & State Sources, Colonial America to the Present
by James C. Neagles (Salt Lake City: Ancestry, Inc., 1994)

World War II: A Family Historian's Guide
by Debra Johnson Knox (Spartanburg, SC: MIE Publishing, 2003)

■ PROBATE RECORDS

A Digest of the Early Connecticut Probate Records
compiled by Charles William Manwaring (Baltimore, MD: Genealogical Pub. Co., 1995)

Guide to the Archives in the Connecticut State Library
by the Connecticut State Library (Hartford: Connecticut Library, 1981)

Property and Kinship: Inheritance in Early Connecticut, 1750–1820
by Toby L. Ditz (Princeton, NJ: Princeton University Press, 1986)

Records of the Particular Court of Connecticut, 1639–1663
by the Connecticut Particular Court (Bowie, MD: Heritage Books, 1987)

■ VITAL RECORDS

Early Connecticut Marriages as Found on Ancient Church Records Prior to 1800
by Frederic William Bailey (New Haven, CT: Bureau of American Ancestry, 1896–1906)

New England Marriages Prior to 1700
by Clarence Almon Torrey and the New England Historic Genealogical Society (Andover, MA: Northeast Document Conversion Center, ca. 1983)

Your Guide to Cemetery Research
by Sharon DeBartolo Carmack (Cincinnati: Betterway Books, 2002)

■ Fairfield 10 May 1666
1061 Main St., Bridgeport, CT 06604
Phone: (203)579-6527
Web site: www.rootsweb.com/~ctfairfi/
Parent County: Original county
Comments/research tips: Towns Organized Before 1800: Brookfield 1788, Danbury 1687, Fairfield settled in 1639 incorporated in 1947, Greenwich settled in 1640 incorporated in 1665, Huntington (Shelton) 1789, New Fairfield 1740, Newtown 1711, Norwalk 1651, Redding 1767, Ridgefield 1709, Stamford 1641, Stratford 1639, Trumbull 1797, Weston 1787, Westport 1735.

Record Type	Year Begun	Jurisdiction
Vital	1640	Town/City Clerks
Birth	1700	Town Clerk
Marriage	1700	Town Clerk
Death	1700	Town Clerk
Land	1649	Town/City Clerks
Probate	1648	Town Probate Clerks

■ Hartford 10 May 1666
95 Washington St., Hartford, CT 06106
Phone: (860)548-2700

Web site: www.rootsweb.com/~cthartfo/
Parent County: Original county
Comments/research tips: Towns Organized Before 1800: Berlin 1785, Bristol 1785, Canton 1737 incorporated 1806, East Hartford 1783, East Windsor 1768, Enfield 1683, Farmington 1685, Glastonbury 1690, Granby 1664 incorporated 1786, Hartford 1635, Hartland 1761, Simsbury 1670, Southington 1779, Suffield 1674, Wethersfield 1634, Windsor 1633.

Record Type	Year Begun	Jurisdiction
Birth	na	Town/City Clerks
Marriage	na	Town/City Clerks
Death	na	Town/City Clerks
Land	1635	Town/City Clerks
Probate	1641	Town Probate Clerks
Burial	na	Town/City Clerks
Vital	1621	Town/City Clerks

■ Litchfield 14 Oct. 1751
P.O. Box 247, Litchfield, CT 06759
Phone: (860)567-0885
Web site: www.geocities.com/TheTropics/1926/litchfield.html
Parent County: Hartford, Fairfield
Comments/research tips: Towns Organized Before 1800: Barkhamstead 1779, Bethlehem 1787, Canaan 1739, Colebrook 1779, Cornwall 1740, Goshen 1739, Harwinton 1737, Kent 1739, Litchfield 1719, New Hartford 1738, New Milford 1712, Norfolk 1758, Plymouth 1795, Roxbury 1796, Salisbury 1741, Sharon 1739, Torrington 1740, Washington 1779, Warren 1786, Watertown 1780, Winchester 1771, Woodbury 1674.

Record Type	Year Begun	Jurisdiction
Birth	na	Town Clerk
Marriage	na	Town Clerk
Death	na	Town Clerk
Divorce	1752	Clerk/Superior Ct.
Land	1659	Town/City Clerks
Probate	1719	Probate Judge
Court	ca.1800	Clerk/Superior Ct.
Vital	1683	Town/City Clerks

■ Middlesex 2 May 1785
1 Court St., 2nd Floor, Middletown, CT 06457-3374
Phone: (860)343-6400
Web site: www.rootsweb.com/~ctmiddle/midlsxco.htm
Parent County: Hartford, New London, New Haven
Comments/research tips: Towns Organized Before 1800: Chatham 1767, Durham 1708, East Haddam 1734, Haddam 1668, Killingsworth 1667, Middletown 1651, Saybrook 1635.

Record Type	Year Begun	Jurisdiction
Birth	na	Town Clerk
Marriage	na	Town Clerk
Death	na	Town Clerk
Divorce	1800	Clerk/Superior Ct.
Land	1647	Town/City Clerks
Probate	1741	Town Probate Clerks
Court	1639	Clerk/Superior Ct.
Vital	1640	Town/City Clerks

■ **New Haven**   10 May 1666
235 Church St., New Haven, CT 06510
Phone: (203)503-6800
Web site: www.geocities.com/TheTropics/1926/
newhaven.html
Parent County: Original county
Comments/research tips: Towns Organized Before 1800:
Branford settled 1644 incorporated 1685, Cheshire 1780,
East Haven 1785, Guilford 1639, Hamden 1786, Meriden
incorporated 1806, Milford 1639, New Haven 1784, North
Haven 1786, Oxford 1798, Seymour settled 1678
incorporated 1850, Southbury 1787, South Derby 1675,
Wallingford 1670, Waterbury 1686, Wolcott 1796,
Woodbridge 1784.

Record Type	Year Begun	Jurisdiction
Birth	na	Town Clerk
Marriage	na	Town Clerk
Death	na	Town Clerk
Divorce	na	Clerk/Superior Ct.
Land	1639	Town/City Clerks
Probate	1647	Town Probate Clerks
Court	na	Clerk/Superior Ct.
Vital	1639	Town/City Clerks

■ **New London**   10 May 1666
70 Huntington St., New London, CT 06320
Phone: (860)443-5363
Web site: www.rootsweb.com/~ctnewlon/index.htm
Parent County: Original county
Comments/research tips: Towns Organized Before 1800:
Bozrah 1786, Colchester 1699, Franklin 1786, Groton
1705, Lebanon 1700, Lisbon 1786, Lyme 1667, Montville
1786, New London 1648, Norwich 1662, Preston 1687,
Stonington settled 1649 incorporated 1662, Voluntown
1721.

Record Type	Year Begun	Jurisdiction
Birth	1659	Town Clerk
Marriage	1659	Town Clerk
Death	1659	Town Clerk
Divorce	na	Clerk/Superior Ct.
Land	1646	Town/City Clerks

Probate	1675	Town Probate Clerks
Burial	1893	Town/City Clerks
Vital	1640	Town/City Clerks

■ **Tolland**   13 Oct. 1785
69 Brooklyn St., Rockville, CT 06066-3643
Phone: (860)896-4920
Web site: http://users.rcn.com/lmerrell/tolland.html
Parent County: Windham
Comments/research tips: Towns Organized Before 1800:
Bolton 1720, Coventry 1711, Ellington 1786, Hebron 1708,
Mansfield 1702, Somers 1749, Stafford 1719, Tolland
1715, Union 1734, Vernon settled 1726 incorporated 1808,
Willington 1727.

Record Type	Year Begun	Jurisdiction
Birth	na	Town Clerk
Marriage	na	Town Clerk
Death	na	Town Clerk
Land	1702	Town/City Clerks
Probate	1759	Town Probate Clerks
Court	na	Clerk/Superior Ct.
Vital	1665	Town/City Clerks

■ **Windham**   12 May 1726
155 Church St., Putnam, CT 06260
Phone: (860)928-7749
Web site: http://users.rcn.com/lmerrell/windham.html
Parent County: Hartford, New London
Comments/research tips: Towns Organized Before 1800:
Ashford 1714, Brooklyn 1786, Canterbury 1703, Hampton
1786, Killingly 1708, Plainfield 1699, Ponfret 1713, Sterling
1794, Thompson 1785, Windham 1692, Woodstock (New
Roxbury) 1690.

Record Type	Year Begun	Jurisdiction
Birth	1692	Town Clerk
Marriage	1692	Town Clerk
Death	1692	Town Clerk
Divorce	na	Clerk/Superior Ct.
Land	1686	Town/City Clerks
Probate	1719	Town Probate Clerks
Burial	1900	Town/City Clerks
Vital	1665	Town/City Clerks

Connecticut

District of Columbia

By James W. Warren

HISTORICAL OVERVIEW

In late 1800, President John Adams and Congress moved from Philadelphia to the almost uninhabited town of Washington, built from swampland to be the new seat of the U.S. government. The staff of federal employees who accompanied them consisted of about one hundred forty people. Today, over 350,000 people staff the federal offices in Washington alone. (And on any given day, about that many lobbyists presumably add to the excitement.)

The Federal District was formed over three years (1788–1791) from land ceded by Maryland and Virginia to the United States. George Washington oversaw the surveying of the District. Originally a diamond-shaped area ten miles on each side, the District's land was modified after the federal government relocated to Washington. In 1801 the District was divided into two counties: Washington County on the east (Maryland) side of the Potomac, and Alexandria County on the west (Virginia) side. The City of Washington was officially established in 1802.

During the war of 1812 the British captured Washington, and in 1814 much of the city and its records were burned. In 1846, the portion of the District west of the Potomac was returned to the State of Virginia. D.C. grew slowly until the Civil War era, when the population more than doubled in just a few years. In 1871 Congress changed Washington City's status to that of a federal territory.

In 1895 Congress merged Georgetown into the city of Washington, making the city's boundaries identical to the District's, which they still are today.

D.C. developed through the twentieth century from a sleepy southern town into one of the most cosmopolitan and frequently-visited metropolitan areas in the country. Today, the District is home to several of the nation's most

Photo Courtesy of the Washington, DC Convention and Tourism Corporation

WASHINGTON, DC AT A GLANCE

Population: 573,000 in the city; 5.5 million in the Greater Metro area

Prevalent Religions: Roman Catholicism, Baptist, Judaism, Muslim, Buddhist, and small pockets of about any other type of worship—this is a melting pot of a town.

Top Employers: Lockheed Martin Corporation, General Dynamics Corporation, Marriott International Inc., US Airways Group Inc., Gannett Company Inc., America Online, Sodexho, Crestline Capital Corporation, Nextel Communications, AES Corporation, *The Washington Post*

Per Capita Income: $38,403

Average Daily Temperature: January, 35° F; July, 78° F

Ethnic Makeup (in percent): Caucasian 30.8%, African American 60.0%, Hispanic 7.9%, Asian 2.7%, Native American 0.3%, Other 3.8%

Newspapers and Magazines: *The Washington Post, The Washington Times, The Washingtonian, Capital Style*

Free Weekly Alternative Paper: *Washington City Paper*

Famous DCers: Edward Albee, Billie Burke, Ina Claire, John Foster Dulles, Duke Ellington, Jane Greer, Goldie Hawn, Helen Hayes, J. Edgar Hoover, William Hurt, Roger Mudd, John Philip Sousa, Frances Sternhagen

Above: The National Capitol Columns

significant genealogical collections. The National Archives, the Daughters of the American Revolution Library, and the Library of Congress are three whose collections offer much about ancestors from any state. For those with D.C. ancestors, these repositories and others offer specific records and resources to help build your family history.

RECORD HIGHLIGHTS

The federal census population records for the District of Columbia begin with 1800. The 1810 census and almost all of 1890 were destroyed. The 1890 veteran's census for D.C. has survived. Slave Schedules for 1850 and 1860 are also available, as are Mortality Schedules for 1850, 1860, 1870, and 1880. Police censuses were taken in twelve various years between 1885 and 1925, but contain only basic information similar to the 1820 census data. District censuses taken in 1803, 1807, and 1818 are also skimpy on details. Two other District censuses, 1867 and 1878, offer far more information, including marital status, length of residence, occupation, and parents' birthplace.

The D.C. local courts have been identified by various names over time: Circuit Court from 1801–1863, Supreme Court from 1863–1928, and Superior Court from 1928 to the present. The federal court that serves the area has been identified as District Court since 1813. All the pre-1863 records and most of the later records of these courts are in the custody of the National Archives, and are inventoried as part of Record Group 21, Records of the District Courts.

For local court naturalization records, check with the Superior Court (500 Indiana Avenue NW). Federal District Court naturalizations (1802–1906) are held by the National Archives. Wills (1801–present) are with the Register of Wills and Clerk of Probate Court at the U.S. Courthouse (500 Indiana Avenue NW). Other probate records are with the National Archives. Land records are available at the Recorder of Deeds (515 "D" Street NW). However, the D.C. land records for 1792–1886 and a grantee/grantor index from 1792–1919 are microfilmed and available through the Family History Library. Land records for the surrounding counties (Alexandria County, Virginia, and Montgomery and Prince George counties in Maryland) are also available on FHL film up to the 1860s or later.)

Registration of births and deaths was required in the District starting in 1874. Compliance with registration was generally upheld for births by 1915 and for deaths by 1880. One glaring gap is the Civil War era, when death records were not kept. Copies of the records are available from the Vital Records Section (4265 "I" Street NW). The Family History Library has microfilmed births from 1874–1897 and deaths from 1855–1949. Registration of

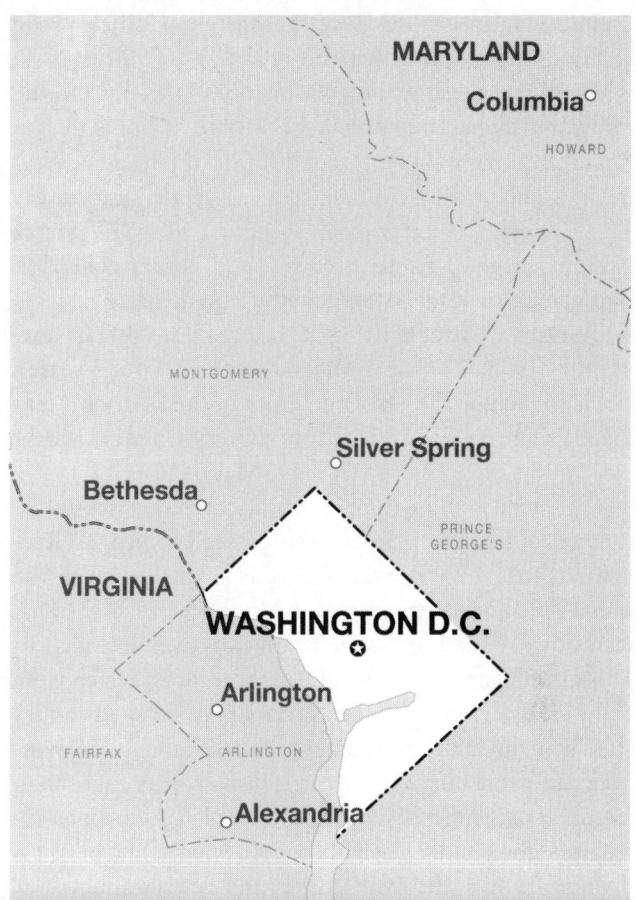

marriages began in 1811, and those records are available from the Marriage License Bureau (500 Indiana Avenue NW). Most pre-1956 divorce records are with the Clerk of the U.S. District Court (Constitution Ave. and John Marshall Place NW), though some have been turned over to the National Archives.

The nature of federal government employment meant that many people came to the area but did not remain. Church and cemetery records can be helpful in tracking such nonpermanent residents and families, and can also provide clues for searches in court and vital records.

Federal records cannot be overlooked in dealing with D.C. research. This applies not only to District residents, but also the many people who lived in Virginia or Maryland and worked for the federal government in the District. Federal records and government publications are rich with detail about federal employees. *Preliminary Inventory of the Records of the Government of the District of Columbia, Record Group 351*, by Dorothy S. Provine, is a starting point. Many other federal record groups held by the National Archives give extensive information on government employees. For example, most agencies prepared annual reports to Congress that often listed all agency employees and included more details than just their names. Information about records at the National Archives is available at <www.archives.gov>.

The Martin Luther King Jr. Memorial Library, the District's main downtown library at 901 "G" Street NW, is a significant resource for the history of the city and the individuals who lived and worked here. It holds microfilmed D.C. newspapers from 1800 to the present, with indexes and subject clipping files <www.dclibrary.org>. The Historical Society of Washington, 801 "K" Street NW, has a photograph, archives, and library collection that can be of value <www.citymuseumdc.org>

To research people living in the area pre-1800 or during the first half of the nineteenth century, your research needs to include the parent counties of the District: Alexandria County, Virginia, Montgomery County, Maryland, and Prince George County, Maryland.

One facility whose valuable historical records are unfortunately difficult to access are those stored at the D.C. Records Center, 1300 Naylor Court NW. It opened in the mid-1980s under former mayor Marion Berry as the District's own (local) archives. The facility was intended to house the District's historical federal records, which were to be transferred from the National Archives. It would showcase the D.C. residents' move to "Home Rule," symbolically reclaiming the District's history after more than a century of "Congressional rule." The plan never materialized, and the building, neighborhood, budget, and priceless documents all suffer from neglect and deterioration.

While there have been many changes since it was written, the best available guide for researchers remains Erma Miller Angevine's *Research in the District of Columbia*, first published in March 1990 as an article in the *National Genealogical Society Quarterly*.

STATE RESOURCES

■ ARCHIVES, LIBRARIES, AND SOCIETIES

Afro-American Historical and Genealogical Society, Inc.
P.O. Box 73067, Washington, DC 20056-3067
E-mail: info@aahgs.org
Web site: <www.aahgs.org>

Arlington National Cemetery
Administrative Bldg., Arlington, VA 22211
Tel: (703) 607-8000
Web site: <www.arlingtoncemetery.net/>

District of Columbia Public Library
901 "G" St. NW, Washington, DC 20001
Tel: (202) 727-0321
Web site: <http://dclibrary.org>

District of Columbia Superior Court, Family Court, H. Carl Moultrie Courthouse
500 Indiana Ave. NW, Fourth Fl., East Wing, Washington, DC 20001
Tel: (202) 879-1633

Episcopal Diocese of Washington Archives
Massachusetts and Wisconsin Avenues NW, Washington, DC 20016
Tel: (202) 537-8981
E-mail: rhewlett@cathedral.org

Historic Congressional Cemetery
1801 "E" St., SE, Washington, DC 20003
Tel: (202) 543-0539
E-mail: CongressionalCemetery@mail.org
Web site: <www.congressionalcemetery.org/>

Historiographer, Archdiocese of Washington
5001 Eastern Ave., Hyattsville, MD 20782
Tel: (301) 853-4500

Library of Congress
101 Independence Ave., SE, Washington, DC 20540
Tel: (202) 707-5000
Web site: <www.loc.gov>

The Library of Virginia
800 E. Broad St., Richmond, VA 23219-8000
Tel: (804) 692-3500
Web site: <www.lva.lib.va.us>

Maryland State Archives, Reference Department
350 Rowe Blvd., Annapolis, MD 21401
E-mail: ref@mdarchives.state.md.us
Web site: <www.mdarchives.state.md.us>

Mt. Olivet Cemetery
1300 Bladensburg Rd. NE, Washington, DC 20002
Tel: (202) 399-3000
Web site: <www.ccaw.org/cemeteries/mtolivet.htm>

The National Archives and Records Administration
8601 Adelphi Rd., College Park, MD 20740-6001
Tel: 1-866-272-6272 or 1-86-NARA-NARA
Web site: <www.archives.gov>

National Society, Daughters of the American Revolution Library
1776 "D" Street NW, Washington, DC 20006-5303
Tel: (202) 628-1776
Web site: <www.dar.org/library/default.cfm>

Nation's Capital Area Chapter of the American Historical Society of Germans from Russia (AHSGR)
6431 Sleepy Ridge Rd., Falls Church, VA 22042
Tel: (703) 536-3878
Web site: <www.ahsgr.org/nation_capital_area.htm>

Oak Hill Cemetery
3001 "R" St. NW, Washington, DC 20007
Tel: (202) 337-2835

Prospect Hill Cemetery
2201 N. Capitol St., NE, Washington, DC 20002
Tel: (202) 667-0676

St. Alban's Episcopal Church
3001 Wisconsin Ave. NW, Washington, DC 20016
Tel: (202) 363-8286
Web site: <www.st-albans-parish.org>

Society of the Cincinnati Anderson House Museum
2118 Massachusetts Ave., NW, Washington, DC 20008-2810
Tel: (202) 785-2040
Web site: <www.hereditary.us/cin_anderson.htm>

State Center for Health Statistics Administration, Vital Records Division
825 N. Capitol St. NE, 2nd floor, Washington, DC 20002
Tel: (202) 442-5865
Web site: <http://dchealth.dc.gov/about/index_schs.shtm#vrd>

United Methodist Archives Center, Drew University Library
Tel: (973) 408-3486
E-mail: drewlib@drew.edu
Web site: <www.depts.drew.edu/lib/uma.html>

United States Court of Appeals for the District of Columbia Circuit
333 Constitution Ave. NW, Washington, DC 20001
Tel: (202) 216-7000

The White House Historical Association
P.O. Box 27624, Washington, DC 20038-7624
Tel: (202) 789-0440
Web site: <www.whitehousehistory.org>

BIBLIOGRAPHY

■ GENERAL RESOURCES

A Biographical Congressional Directory With an Outline History of the National Congress, 1774–1911: the Continental Congress, September 5, 1774–October 21, 1788 [and] the United States Congress from the First to Sixty-Second Congress, March 4, 1789–March 3, 1911
by the United States Congress (61st, 2nd Session: 1909–1911) (Washington, D.C.: Government Printing Office, 1913)

Capital Collections: Resources for Jewish Genealogical Research in the Washington, DC Area
edited by Sharlene Kranz (Vienna, VA: Jewish Genealogical Society of Greater Washington, 1995)

Centennial History of the City of Washington, D.C.
by Harvey W. Crew (Dayton, OH: pub. by the United Brethren Publishing House, 1892)

The Center: A Guide to Genealogical Research in the National Capital Area
by Christina K. Schaefer (Baltimore, MD: Genealogical Pub., 1996)

The City of Washington, its Origin and Administration
by John Addison Porter (New York: Johnson Reprint Corp., 1973)

A Directory of Churches and Religious Organizations in the District of Columbia, 1939
by the Historical Records Survey (Washington, D.C.: District of Columbia Historical Records Survey, 1939)

District of Columbia Ancestors
by Wesley E. Pippenger (Westminster, MD: Family Line Publications, 1997)

District of Columbia: A Bicentennial History
by David L. Lewis (New York: Norton, 1976)

District of Columbia Free Negro Registers, 1821–1861
compiled and edited by Dorothy S. Provine (Bowie, MD: Heritage Books, 1996)

District of Columbia Indentures of Apprenticeship, 1801–1893
compiled by Dorothy S. Provine (Lovettsville, VA: Willow Bend Books, 1998)

Early Days of Washington
by Sally Somervell Mackall (Washington, D.C.: The Neale Company, 1899)

Federal Assessment, 1790–1805, Maryland, District of Columbia
by the United States Congress (Baltimore, MD: Maryland, Hall of Records Commission, 1965)

The Genealogist's Companion and Sourcebook, 2d ed.
by Emily Anne Croom (Cincinnati: Betterway Books, 2003)

A Genealogist's Guide to Discovering Your African-American Ancestors
by Franklin Carter Smith and Emily Anne Croom (Cincinnati: Betterway Books, 2003)

Guide to Genealogical Research in the National Archives
by the United States National Archives and Records Service (Washington, D.C.: National Archives and Records Service, 1983)

Guide to Genealogical Research in the National Archives of the United States
edited by Anne Bruner Eales and Robert M. Kvasnicka (Washington, D.C.: National Archives and Records Administration, 2000

Guide to the Records of Your District of Columbia Ancestors
by Eleanor Mildred Vaughan Cook (Silver Spring, MD: Family Line Publications, 1987)

Guide to Washington National Records Center Services
by the National Archives and Records Administration (Washington, D.C.: National Archives and Records Administration)

Historical Collections of Virginia; Containing a Collection of the Most Interesting Facts, Traditions, Biographical Sketches, Anecdotes, etc., Relating to its History and Antiquities, Together With Geographical and Statistical Descriptions. To Which is Appended an Historical and Descriptive Sketch of the District of Columbia
by Henry Howe (Baltimore, MD: Regional Pub. Co., 1969)

Inventory of Church Archives in the District of Columbia: The Protestant Episcopal Church, Diocese of Washington
by the Historical Records Survey (Washington, D.C.: Historical Records Survey, 1940)

Lest we Forget: A Guide to Genealogical Research in the Nation's Capital
by H. Byron Hall (Annandale, VA: Annandale Stake of the Church of

RESEARCH TIPS

for more info

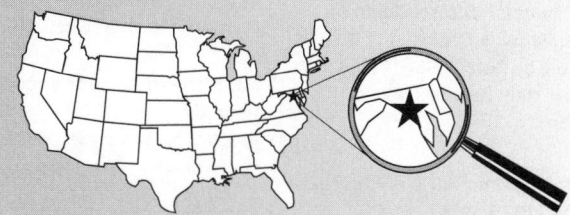

- The best available guide for researchers in D.C. is Erma Miller Angevine's *Research in the District of Columbia,* which is available from the National Genealogical Society <www.ngsgenealogy.org>.
- The Martin Luther King Jr. Memorial Library is an invaluable source for the history of the city and its people <www.dclibrary.org>.
- All the pre-1863 records and most of the later records of D.C. courts are in the custody of the National Archives <www.archives.gov>.
- To research people living in D.C. before 1800 or during the first half of the nineteenth century, your research needs to include the parent counties of the District: Alexandria County, Virginia, and Montgomery and Prince George Counties, Maryland.

Census Records

- Federal Census: 1790 (with Maryland), 1800, 1820, 1830, 1840, 1850, 1860, 1870, 1880, 1890 (only a small part of the 1890 census still survives), 1900, 1910, 1920, 1930
- Federal Mortality Schedules: 1850, 1860, 1870, 1880
- District Census: 1867, 1878
- Police Census: 1885, 1894, 1905, 1906, 1907, 1908, 1909, 1912, 1915, 1917, 1919

Jesus Christ of Latter-day Saints, 1992)

National Archives Microfilm Catalogs online:
<www.archives.gov/publications/genealogy_microfilm_catalogs.html>

Official Congressional Directory
by the United States Congress (Washington, D.C.: U.S. Government Printing Office, 1865)

Official Register of the United States: Containing a List of Officers and Employees in the Civil, Military, and Naval Service
(Washington, D.C.: US Government Printing Office, 1863)

The Postal History of Maryland, the Delmarva Peninsula, and the District of Columbia: The Post Offices and First Postmasters from 1775 to 1984
by Chester M. Smith Jr. and John L. Kay (Burtonsville, MD: The Depot, 1984)

Research in the District of Columbia
by Erma Miller Angevine (Arlington, VA: National Genealogical Society, 1992)

Standard History of the City of Washington from a Study of the Original Sources
by William Tindall (Knoxville, TN: H.W. Crew & co., 1914)

District of Columbia

Washington: A History of the Capital, 1800–1950
by Constance McLaughlin Green (Princeton: Princeton University Press, 1964)

Washington D.C.; a Guide to the Nation's Capital
edited by Randall Bond Truett (New York: Hastings House, 1986, ca. 1942)

Washington, Past and Present; a History, 4 vols.
by John Proctor Clagett (New York: Lewis Historical Company, Inc., 1930)

Washington; or, The Revolution. A Drama. (In Blank Verse.) Founded Upon the Historic Events of the War for American Independence.
by Ethan Allen and illustrated by Henry Kratzner (London, Chicago, etc.: F.T. Neely, 1899)

CENSUS RECORDS

The American Census Handbook
by Thomas Jay Kemp (Wilmington, DE: Scholarly Resources, 2001)

The Census Book: A Genealogist's Guide to Federal Census Facts, Schedules and Indexes
by William Dollarhide (Bountiful, UT: Heritage Quest, 2000)

Finding Answers in U.S. Census Records
by Loretto Dennis Szucs and Matthew Wright (Orem, UT: Ancestry Publishing, 2002)

An Illustrated Genealogy of the Counties of Maryland and the District of Columbia as a Guide to Locating Records
by Mary Ross Brown (Baltimore, MD: French-Bray Print Co., 1967)

Map Guide to the U.S. Federal Censuses, 1790–1920
by William Thorndale and William Dollarhide (Baltimore, MD: Genealogical Pub. Co., 1987)

Your Guide to the Federal Census
by Kathleen W. Hinckley (Cincinnati: Betterway Books, 2002)

IMMIGRATION RECORDS

American Naturalization Records, 1790–1990: What They Are and How to Use Them
by John J. Newman (North Salt Lake, UT: HeritageQuest, 1998)

American Passenger Arrival Records
by Michael Tepper (Baltimore: Genealogical Publishing Co., 1993)

Copies of Lists of Passengers Arriving at Miscellaneous Ports on the Atlantic and Gulf Coasts and at Ports on the Great Lakes, 1820–1873
by the United States Bureau of Customs (Washington, D.C.: The National Archives, 1964)

They Became Americans: Finding Naturalization Records and Ethnic Origins
by Loretto Dennis Szucs (Salt Lake City: Ancestry, Inc., 1998)

They Came in Ships: A Guide to Finding Your Immigrant Ancestor's Arrival Records, 2d ed.
by John P. Colletta (Salt Lake City: Ancestry, Inc., 1993)

LAND RECORDS

District of Columbia Original Land Owners, 1791–1800
by Wesley E. Pippenger (Westminster, MD: Willow Bend Books, 1999)

Locating Your Roots: Discover Your Ancestors Using Land Records
by Patricia Law Hatcher (Cincinnati: Betterway Books, 2003)

Original Patentees of Land at Washington Prior to 1700
by Bessie Wilmarth Gahn (Baltimore, MD: Genealogical Pub. Co., 1969)

MAPS

Atlas of Historical County Boundaries. Delaware, Maryland, and the District of Columbia
edited and compiled by John H. Long (New York: Charles Scribner's Sons, Simon & Schuster Macmillan, 1995)

District of Columbia Geographic Names
by the United States Office of Geographic Research, Branch of Geographic Names (Reston, VA: United States Branch of Geographic Names, 1981)

A New and Comprehensive Gazetteer of Virginia and the District of Columbia . . .
by Joseph Martin (Charlottesville: J. Martin, 1836)

Round About the Nation's Capital with Descriptive Notes
by the National Geographic Society Cartographic Division (Washington, D.C.: The Society, 1956)

Washington D.C.; a Guide to the Nation's Capital
edited by Randall Bond Truett (New York: Hastings House, 1968, ca. 1942)

MILITARY RECORDS

Civil War Cemeteries of the District of Columbia Metropolitan Area
compiled by Paul E. Sluby, Sr., edited by Stanton L. Wormley (Washington, D.C.: Columbian Harmony Society, 1982)

Maryland and the District of Columbia Volunteers in the Mexican War
by Charles J. Wells (Westminster, MD: Family Line Publications, 1991)

Roll of Honor: Names of Soldiers who Died in Defense of the American Union, Interred in the National Cemeteries
by the United States Quartermaster's Department (Baltimore, MD: Genealogical Pub. Co., 1994)

Selected Final Pension Payment Vouchers, 1818–1864. District of Columbia
abstracted by Alycon Trubey Pierce (Leesburg, VA: Willow Bend Books, 1998)

Uncle, We Are Ready! Registering America's Men, 1917–1918: A Guide to Researching World War I Draft Registration Cards
by John J. Newman (North Salt Lake, UT: HeritageQuest, 2001)

U.S. Military Records: A Guide to Federal & State Sources, Colonial America to the Present
by James C. Neagles (Salt Lake City: Ancestry, Inc., 1994)

World War II: A Family Historian's Guide
by Debra Johnson Knox (Spartanburg, SC: MIE Publishing, 2003)

PROBATE RECORDS

Abstracts of Wills in the District of Columbia, 1776–1815: Compiled From Records in the Office of the Register of Wills
compiled by Mrs. Alexander H. Bell (Washington, D.C.: s.n., 1945–1946)

District of Columbia, D.C. Department of Corrections Runaway Slave Book, 1848–1863; U.S. District Court for the District of Columbia Fugitive Slave Cases, 1862–1863
by Jerry M. Hynson (Westminster, MD: Willow Bend Books, 1999)

District of Columbia Probate Records: Will Books 1 Through 6, 1801–1852 and Estate Files, 1801–1852
compiled by Wesley E. Pippenger (Westminster, MD: Family Line Publications, 1996)

Indentures of Apprenticeship Recorded in the Orphans Court, Washington County, District of Columbia, 1802–1811
by the District of Columbia Orphans Court (Washington, D.C.: National Archives and Records Service, 2000)

Index to District of Columbia Wills, 1801–1920
prepared by Dorothy S. Province (Baltimore, MD: Genealogical Pub. Co., 1992)

Index to District of Columbia Wills, 1921–1950
prepared by Dorothy S. Province (Leesburg, VA: Willow Bend Books, 1998)

VITAL RECORDS

Blacks in the Marriage Records of the District of Columbia, Dec. 23, 1811–Jun. 16, 1870
by Paul E. Sluby and Stanton L. Wormley (Washington, D.C.: Columbian Harmony Society, 1988)

District of Columbia Marriage Licenses: Register 1, 1811–1858
compiled by Wesley E. Pippenger (Westminster, MD: Family Line Publications, 1994)

District of Columbia Marriage Licenses: Register 2, 1858–1870
compiled by Wesley E. Pippenger (Leesburg, VA: Willow Bend Books, 1996)

Historical Court Records of Washington, District of Columbia
by Homer A. Walker (Washington: 1956)

Historical Graves of Maryland and the District of Columbia, With the Inscriptions on the Tombstones in Most of the Counties of the State and in Washington and Georgetown
by Helen W. Ridgely (Baltimore, MD: Genealogical Pub. Co., 1967)

Marriage Licenses of Washington, D.C., 1811–1830
by F. Edward Wright (Silver Spring, MD: Family Line Publications, 1988)

Your Guide to Cemetery Research
by Sharon DeBartolo Carmack (Cincinnati: Betterway Books, 2002)

■ **District of Columbia** 1790
500 Indiana Ave. NW, Washington, DC 20001-2131
Phone: (202)879-1010

District of Columbia

Delaware

By Maureen Taylor

HISTORICAL OVERVIEW

In 1638, two ships—the *Kalmar Nyckel* and the *Fogel Grip*—brought thirty people from Sweden to settle near present-day Wilmington, Delaware. They gave the area the name "New Sweden." Ownership of the area changed several times during the seventeenth century. The Dutch took over the Colony from the Swedish settlers, then the British captured the renamed New Netherland in 1664. The Dutch reasserted their rights of ownership in 1673, but ended up returning the area to the British a year later. The three lower counties of the Colony—New Castle, Kent, and Sussex—became part of William Penn's Pennsylvania, while Maryland also claimed part of the region.

The residents declared their independence from both Great Britain and Pennsylvania 15 June 1776, renaming the area Delaware. On 7 December 1787, Delaware became the first state to ratify the Constitution.

A central location, harbors, and waterways made the state ideal for transportation systems. Steamboats carried passengers along the Delaware River, while the Chesapeake and Delaware Canal connected the two bays of the same names. In 1831, the New Castle and Frenchtown Railroad connected the eastern and western parts of the state.

Early in the nineteenth century, the du Pont family arrived and began manufacturing gunpowder. Their success made them the wealthiest family in Delaware and their chemical research firm one of the largest in the world. Irish and German immigrants arrived in the area to work in chemical manufacturing, shipbuilding, and agriculture. Jews, Poles, Italians, and Scandinavians immigrated later in the nineteenth century. Major industries in the twentieth century included shipbuilding, chemicals (nylon for parachutes), textile mills, and gunpowder factories in the northern part of the state, with agriculture and poultry farming in the southern half.

DELAWARE AT A GLANCE

Motto: Liberty and Independence

Population: 784,000

Prevalent Religions: Methodist, Roman Catholic, and Jewish

Major Industries: Chemicals products, rubber, plastic and synthetic products, fishing (mostly crabs, clams, and oysters), agriculture (predominantly broiler chickens and eggs)

Ethnic Makeup (in percent): Caucasian 74.6%, African American 19.2%, Hispanic 4.8%, Asian 2.1%, Native American 0.3%, Other 2.0%

Famous Delawareans: Valerie Bertinelli, du Pont family, Henry Heimlich, George Thorogood

Above: "The Greens" in Dover

RECORD HIGHLIGHTS

According to the Historical Society of Delaware's Web site, "Delaware's rich and complex colonial history offers genealogists a special challenge. Early colonial documents might be found in many places, including the archives of New York State and Pennsylvania, as well as those of Sweden, the Netherlands, and Great Britain."

Records for colonial Delaware are plentiful and varied.

The Delaware Public Archives has documents from the Swedish colonial period, 1638–55; the Dutch settlement, 1655–64; the Duke of York regime, 1664–82; and the Penn Proprietorship, 1682–1776, with the majority of their holdings dating from statehood in 1776.

Use the Archives online guide to the collections <www.archives.state.de.us> and search the database, which is just a portion of their holdings, for types of records—not individual names. For example, type in "birth records, 1864" to find out where your ancestor's birth certificate may be located. The Archives is constantly adding new information to their Web site.

The Archives has an index to marriages, births, and deaths from marriage bonds, church and Bible records, and newspapers from 1680 to the present. According to Russ McCabe, Outreach Services Administrator of the Delaware Public Archives, "Official state vital records didn't formally begin until the nineteenth century." There are marriage records from ca. 1790 on, but births and deaths weren't kept until the late nineteenth century. The Archives encourages people to deposit Bible records, which are transcribed by staff and added to the vital records index. Contemporary researchers can access birth records older than seventy-two years and marriages and deaths older than forty years.

The Federal Census of 1790 is not totally extant. A reconstruction from tax and assessment records exists. Tax records can also substitute for the colonial censuses. There are no state censuses.

During the colonial period Presbyterians settled in the area first, followed by English Quakers, Baptists, Catholics, and Methodists. Many church records are in print, with originals and some card indexes at various repositories including the Delaware Public Archives and the Historical Society of Delaware.

The Delaware Public Archives is the primary facility for noncurrent state and local government records, such as probate records, court documents (civil, criminal, naturalization, indenture), and municipal papers (minutes, accounts, reports). The collection inventory is online at <www.state.de.us/sos/dpa/collections/guideintro.shtml>. Original deeds and mortgages from 1680 are also there, as are miscellaneous genealogical manuscripts and a large collection of grave records known as the Tatnell Tombstone collection. McCabe emphasizes that the Archives has a "fairly large and growing library of printed and unpublished genealogies, and they solicit gifts of genealogical materials."

"Visit both the Historical Society of Delaware and the Delaware Public Archives to thoroughly research Delaware Families," says Constance Cooper, Manuscript Librarian of the Historical Society of Delaware. The Historical Society of Delaware is a private, nonprofit

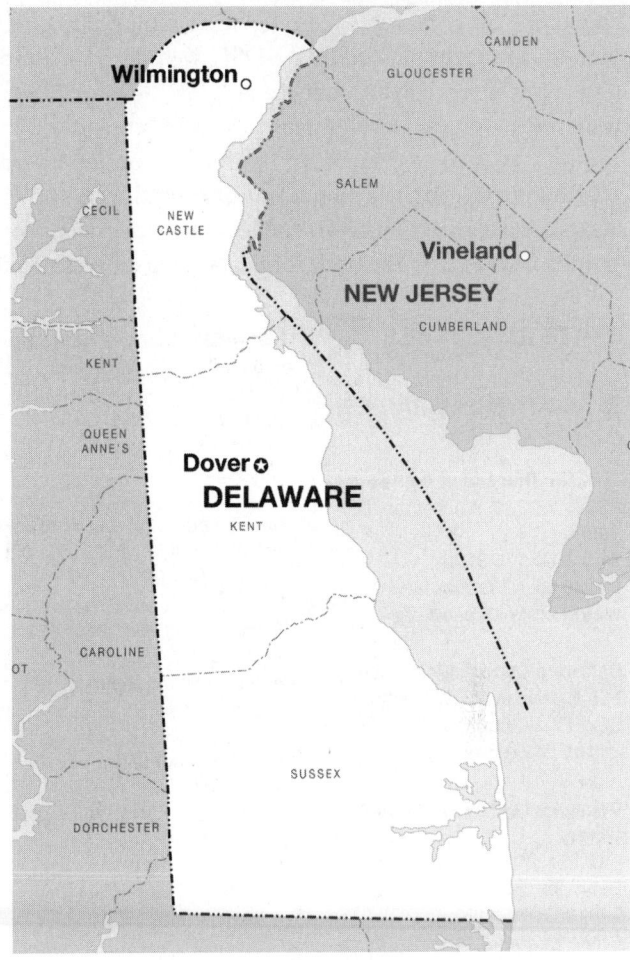

organization that collects nongovernmental records such as genealogies, manuscripts, and church records, while the Public Archives maintains the governmental records. The Historical Society of Delaware's Web site <www.hsd.org> features *A Guide to Research in the Delaware Historical Society Library*, an online instruction manual for research at their library. Cooper says "a personal visit is the best way to research your Delaware families, because staff provides an orientation to the collection as well as assistance." One helpful on-site resource is the Genealogical Surname File, a card catalog of names and references arranged alphabetically by surname. According to the HSD Web site "These cards were compiled over the years from newspapers printed before 1850, books, journals, church records, and other sources."

The Delaware Genealogical Society compiles information and guides on Delaware research, including the *Delaware Genealogical Research Guide*, 3d ed., by Thomas P. Doherty (Wilmington, Delaware: Delaware Genealogical Society, 2002). Search their Web site <delgensoc.org> for names entered into their Delaware Families Project.

There are only three counties in Delaware—New Castle, Kent, and Sussex—so research in the state initially appears simple. However, William Penn decided to divide

Delaware

the colony into "hundreds" for taxation. This old English land division is explained by the DSG Web site as a "land division which is smaller than a county or shire and larger than a tithing. It comprises ten tithings of ten freeholder families each or one hundred families." Cooper stated that hundreds "are the equivalent of townships in other states." Once used as judicial and legislative districts, they remain now only as the basis for property tax assessment.

STATE RESOURCES

■ ARCHIVES, LIBRARIES, AND SOCIETIES

Catholic Diocese of Delaware
P.O. Box 2030, Wilmington, DE 19899
Tel: (302) 573-3100
E-mail: pbossi@cdow.org
Web site: <www.cdow.org>

Delaware Genealogical Society
505 N. Market St., Wilmington, DE 19801–3091
<http://delgensoc.org/>

Delaware Legislative Council Library
P.O. Box 1401, Legislative Hall, Dover, DE 19903
Tel: (302) 744-4308
E-mail: rmelson@legis.state.de.us
Web site: <www.delaware.gov>

Delware Public Archives, Vital Statistics Records
121 Duke of York St., Dover, DE 19901
Web site: <www.state.de.us/sos/dpa/collections/vital.shtml>

Fort Delaware Society
P.O. Box 553, Delaware City, DE 19706
Tel: (302) 834-1630
E-mail: FtDSociety@del.net
Web site: <www.del.net/org/fort/>

Friends Historical Library of Swarthmore College
500 College Ave., Swarthmore, PA 19081–1905
Tel: (610) 328-8497
E-mail: friends@swarthmore.edu
Web site: <www.swarthmore.edu/Library/friends>

Hagley Museum and Library
P.O. Box 3630, Wilmington, DE 19807-0630
Tel: (302) 658-2400
Web site:

Historical Society of Delaware
505 Market St., Wilmington, DE 19801
Tel: (302) 655-7161
E-mail: hsd@hsd.org
Web site: <www.hsd.org>

Jewish Federation of Delaware
100 W. Tenth St., Suite 301, Wilmington, DE 19801
Tel: (302) 427-2100
E-mail: todd.polikoff@shalomdel.org
Web site: <www.shalomdelaware.org>

Jewish Historical Society of Delaware
505 Market St. Mall, Wilmington, DE 19801
Tel: (302) 655-6232
Web site: <www.hsd.org/jhsd.htm>

National Archives and Record Administration, Mid-Atlantic Region
900 Market St., Philadelphia, PA 19107–4292
Tel: (215) 606-0100
E-mail: philadelphia.archives@nara.gov
Web site: <www.archives.gov/midatlantic/index.html>

Presbyterian Church (USA), Department of History
425 Lombard St., Philadelphia, PA 19147
Tel: (215) 627-1852

United Methodist Archives Center, Drew University Library
P.O. Box 127, Madison, NJ 07940
Tel: (973) 408-3486
Web site: <www.depts.drew.edu/lib/uma.html>

University of Delaware Library
181 S. College Ave., Newark, DE 19717–5267
Tel: (302) 831–2965
Web site:

Wilmington Institute Library
Tenth & Market Sts., Wilmington, DE 19899

RESEARCH TIPS

for more info

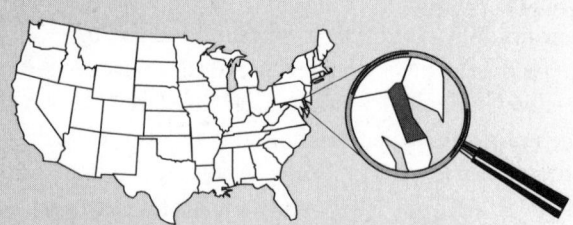

- The Historical Society of Delaware collects non-governmental records such as genealogies, manuscripts, and church records, while the Public Archives maintains governmental records.
- The Delaware Public Archives is the primary facility for non-current state and local government records, including deeds, mortgages, probate records, court documents, and municipal papers <www.state.de.us/sos/dpa/collections/guideintro.shtml>.
- Be on the lookout for the land division "hundreds." While there are only three counties in Delaware, there are many hundreds—akin to townships in other states—that were created for taxation purposes.

Census Records

- Federal Census: 1800, 1810, 1820, 1830, 1840, 1850, 1860, 1870, 1880, 1900, 1910, 1920, 1930
- Federal Mortality Schedules: 1850, 1860, 1870, 1880
- Reconstructed State Census: 1790
- Slave Schedules: 1850, 1860. NOTE: The Slave Schedules generally do not list the names of slaves, only the names of slave owners. The number of slaves, their gender, and age ranges are given, however.
- Tax Lists: 1700s–1915 (preserved in the Delaware Public Archives)
- Militia Records: 1765–1841 (preserved in the Delaware Public Archives)

Tel: (302) 571–7400

BIBLIOGRAPHY

■ GENERAL RESOURCES

Abstracts from the Pennsylvania Gazette, 1748–1755
by Kenneth Scott and Janet R. Clarke (Baltimore, MD: Genealogical Pub. Co., 1977)

The American Genealogical-Biographical Index to American Genealogical, Biographical and Local History Materials, 206 vols.
edited by Fremont Rider (Middletown, CT: The Godfrey Memorial Library, 1952)

A Bibliography of Delaware Through 1960
compiled by Henry Clay Reed and Marion Björnson Reed (Newark,

DE: Published for the Institute of Delaware History and Culture by the University of Delaware Press, 1966)

Chronology and Documentary Handbook of the State of Delaware
by Mary L. Frech (Dobbs Ferry, NY: Oceana Publications, 1973)

The Colonial Clergy of Maryland, Delaware, and Georgia
by Frederick Lewis Weis (Baltimore, MD: Genealogical Pub. Co., 1978, ca. 1950)

Colonial Delaware Assemblymen, 1682–1776
by Bruce A. Bendler (Westminster, MD: Family Line Publications, 1989)

Colonial Delaware Records, 1681–1713
by Bruce A. Bendler (Westminster, MD: Family Line Publications, 1992)

Colonial Families of Delaware, 4 vols.
by F. Edward Wright (Westminster, MD: Willow Bend Books, 1999)

Delaware Archives . . . , 4 vols.
by the Delaware Public Archives Commission (Wilmington, DE: 1911)

Delaware Church Records: A Collection of Baptisms, Marriages, Deaths, and Other Records and Tombstone Inscriptions, from 1686–1880, Five Important Religious Groups: Baptist, Episcopal, Methodist, Presbyterian, and Quaker, with Historical Sketches of the Churches or Groups, and with Illustrations of the Churches
compiled and indexed by Raymond B. Clark Jr. (St. Michaels, MD: R.B. Clark, 1986)

Delaware Family Histories and Genealogies
compiled by Donald Ordell Virdin; edited and published by Raymond B. Clark Jr. (St. Michaels, MD: R.B. Clark Jr., 1984)

Delaware Genealogical Research Guide
edited by Thomas P. Doherty (Wilmington, DE: Delaware Genealogical Society, 1997)

Delaware Genealogical Society Surname Index, 1995
compiled by Robert Joseph Redden, Barbara Fooks Redden, and the Delaware Genealogical Society (Wilmington, DE: The Delaware Genealogical Society, 1995)

Delaware Genealogy
by Jean Foight Trumbore and the Hugh M. Morriss Library (Newark, Delaware) (S.l.:s.n., 1979)

The Delaware Historical and Genealogical Recall of Matilda Spicer Hart
by Matilda Spicer Hart (Wilmington, DE: Delaware Genealogical Society, 1984)

Delaware, a History of the First State
edited by Henry Clay Reed with Marion Björnson Reed (New York: Lewis Historical Pub. Co., 1947)

Delaware 1782 Tax Assessment and Census
by Ralph D. Nelson, et al. (Wilmington, DE: Delaware Genealogical Society, 1994)

Delaware Trails: Some Tribal Records, 1842–1907
transcribed by Fay Louise Smith Arellano (Baltimore, MD: Clearfield, 1996)

Directory of Churches and Religious Organizations in Delaware
by the Delaware Historical Records Survey (Dover, DE: Public Archives Commission, 1942)

Directory of Libraries and Information Sources in the Philadelphia Area (Eastern Pennsylvania, Southern New Jersey and Delaware)
edited by Barbara Ann Holley for the Philadelphia Chapter Special Libraries Association (Philadelphia, PA: [s.n.], 1977)

The Genealogist's Companion and Sourcebook, 2d ed.
by Emily Anne Croom (Cincinnati: Betterway Books, 2003)

A Genealogist's Guide to Discovering Your African-American Ancestors
by Franklin Carter Smith and Emily Anne Croom (Cincinnati: Betterway Books, 2003)

Guide to Genealogical Research in the National Archives of the United States
edited by Anne Bruner Eales and Robert M. Kvasnicka (Washington, D.C.: National Archives and Records Administration, 2000)

A Guide to Manuscripts in the Eleutherain Mills Historical Library: Supplement Containing Accessions for the Years 1966 Through 1975
by John Beverley Riggs (Greenville, DE: The Library, 1978)

History of Delaware, 1609–1888
by John Thomas Scharf (Tucson, AZ: W.C. Cox Co., 1974)

History of Delaware, Past and Present
edited by Wilson Lloyd Bevan, associate editor, E. Melvin Williams (New York: Lewis Historical Pub., 1929)

A History of the Original Settlements on the Delaware— & a History of Wilmington
by Benjamin Ferris (Baltimore, MD: Gateway Press, 1987)

Index to the History of Delaware, 1609–1888
by J. Thomas Scharf, edited by Gladys M. Coghlan and Dale Fields (Wilmington, DE: Historical Society of Delaware, 1976)

Inventory of the County Archives of Delaware, no. 1, New Castle County
prepared by the Delaware Historical Records Survey and the United States Works Progress Administration (Dover, DE: Public Archives Commission, state of Delaware, 1941)

Key Title Index to the American Genealogical-Biographical Index: Register of the Family History Library Call Numbers
edited by Patricia L. Clark and Dorothy Huntsman (Salt Lake City, UT: Family History Library, 1990)

National Archives Microfilm Catalogs online:
<www.archives.gov/publications/genealogy_microfilm_catalogs.html>

Old Bible Records
by the Daughters of the American Revolution (Newark, DE: Daughters of the American Revolution, Delaware, 1950–1973)

A Preliminary Inventory of the Older Records in the Delaware Archives
compiled by Joanne Mattern, Harold B. Hancock and the Delaware Bureau of Archives and Records (Dover, DE: Bureau of Archives and Records, 1978)

The Records of Holy Trinity (Old Swedes) Church, Wilmington, Del., from 1697 to 1773
translated from the original Swedish by Horace Burr, with an abstract of English records from 1773 to 1810 (Wilmington, DE: Historical Society of Delaware, 1890)

The Rise and Fall of New Sweden: Governor Johan Risingh's Journal 1654–1655 in its Historical Context
by John Claesson Rising, Hans Norman, Marie Clark Nelson, and Stellan Dahlgren (Stockholm, Sweden: Almqvist & Wiskell International, 1988)

Selected Delaware Bibliography and Resources
compiled by Barbara S. Giles (Seattle, WA: B.S. Giles, 1990)

The Swedish Settlements on the Delaware, 1638–1664, 2 vols.
by Amandus Johnson (Baltimore, MD: Genealogical Pub. Co., 1969)

This is Good Country: A History of Amish Delaware, 1915–1988
by Rev. Allen B. Clark (Gordonville, PA: Gordonville Print Shop, 1988)

■ CENSUS RECORDS

The 1693 Census of the Swedes on the Delaware
by Peter Stebbins Craig (Winter Park, FL: SAG Publications, 1993)

The American Census Handbook
by Thomas Jay Kemp (Wilmington, DE: Scholarly Resources, 2001)

The Census Book: A Genealogist's Guide to Federal Census Facts, Schedules and Indexes
by William Dollarhide (Bountiful, UT: Heritage Quest, 2000)

Delaware

Delaware 1782 Tax Assessment and Census
by Ralph D. Nelson (Wilmington, DE: Delaware Genealogical Society, 1994)

Finding Answers in U.S. Census Records
by Loretto Dennis Szucs and Matthew Wright (Orem, UT: Ancestry Publishing, 2002)

The First Tax List for the Province of Pennsylvania and the Three Lower Counties, 1693
by Adams Apple Press (Bedminster, PA: The Press, 1994)

Index to the 1850 Census of Delaware
by Virginia L. Olmstead (Baltimore, MD: Genealogical Publishing, 1977)

Map Guide to the U.S. Federal Censuses, 1790–1920
by William Thorndale and William Dollarhide (Baltimore, MD: Genealogical Pub. Co., 1987)

Reconstructed 1790 Census of Delaware
by Leon Devalinger Jr. (Washington, DC: National Genealogical Society, 1962)

The Reconstructed Delaware Census of 1782
by Harold B. Hancock (Wilmington, DE: Delaware Genealogical Society, 1973)

State Census Records
by Ann S. Lainhart (Baltimore, MD: Genealogical Publishing, 1992)

U.S. 1910 Federal Census: Unindexed States: A Guide to Finding Census Enumeration Districts for Unindexed Cities, Towns, and Villages
by G. Eileen Buckway (Salt Lake City, UT: Family History Library, 1992)

Your Guide to the Federal Census
by Kathleen W. Hinckley (Cincinnati: Betterway Books, 2002)

■ IMMIGRATION RECORDS

American Naturalization Records, 1790–1990: What They Are and How to Use Them
by John J. Newman (North Salt Lake, UT: HeritageQuest, 1998)

American Passenger Arrival Records
by Michael Tepper (Baltimore: Genealogical Publishing Co., 1993)

The Complete Book of Emigrants: 1607–1776 and Emigrants in Bondage, 1614–1775
by Peter Wilson Coldham (S.l.: Brøderbund, 1996. CD-ROM)

Copies of Lists of Passengers Arriving at Miscellaneous Ports on the Atlantic and Gulf Coasts and at Ports on the Great Lakes, 1820–1873
by the United States Bureau of Customs (Washington, DC: The National Archives, 1964)

Philadelphia Naturalization Records: An Index to Records of Aliens' Declarations of Intention and/or Oaths of Allegiance, 1789–1880, in United States Circuit Court, United States District Court, Supreme Court of Pennsylvania, Quarter Sessions Court, Court of Common Pleas, Philadelphia
edited by P. William Filby (Detroit: Gale Research Company, 1982)

Ship Passenger Lists: Pennsylvania and Delaware (1641–1825)
edited and indexed by Carl Boyer (Newhall, CA: Boyer, 1980)

They Became Americans: Finding Naturalization Records and Ethnic Origins
by Loretto Dennis Szucs (Salt Lake City: Ancestry, Inc., 1998)

They Came in Ships: A Guide to Finding Your Immigrant Ancestor's Arrival Records, 2d ed.
by John P. Colletta (Salt Lake City: Ancestry, Inc., 1993)

■ LAND RECORDS

Colonial Delaware Records, 1681–1713
by Bruce A. Bendler (Westminster, MD: Family Line Publications, 1992)

Delaware's Fugitive Records: An Inventory of the Official Land Grant Records Relating to the Present State of Delaware
by the Delaware Bureau of Archives and Records (Dover, DE:

Department of State, Division of Historical and Cultural Affairs, 1980)

Land & Property Research in the United States
by Wade E. Hone (Salt Lake City, UT: Ancestry, 1997)

Locating Your Roots: Discover Your Ancestors Using Land Records
by Patricia Law Hatcher (Cincinnati: Betterway Books, 2003)

Original Land Titles in Delaware, Commonly Known as the Duke of York Record: Being an Authorized Transcript From the Official Archives of the State of Delaware, and Comprising the Letters Patent, Permits, Commissions, Surveys, Plats and Confirmations by the Duke of York and Other High Officials, From 1646 to 1679, With Revised Index
(Westminster, MD: Family Line Publications, 1988)

Warrants and Surveys of the Province of Pennsylvania Including the Three Lower Counties, 1759
compiled by Allen Weinberg and Thomas E. Slattery, under the direction of Charles E. Hughes Jr. (Philadelphia: Dept. of Records, 1965)

■ MAPS

Atlas of Historical County Boundaries. Delaware, Maryland, and the District of Columbia
edited and compiled by John H. Long (New York: Charles Scribner and Sons, Simon & Schuster Macmillan, 1995)

Atlas of the State of Delaware
by Daniel G. Beers (Philadelphia: Pomery & Beers, 1868)

Delaware Geographic Names: Alphabetical Finding List
by the United States Geological Survey (Reston, VA: U.S.G.S. Topographic Division, 1981)

Delaware Place Names
by L.W. Heck (Washington, District of Columbia: U.S. Govt. Print. Off., 1966)

A Gazetteer of Maryland and Delaware
by Henry Gannett and the United States Geological Survey (Baltimore, MD: Genealogical Pub. Co., 1976)

Maryland, Delaware Atlas & Gazetteer
by the DeLorme Mapping Company (Freeport, ME: DeLorme Mapping, 1993)

The National Gazetteer of the United States of America: Delaware, 1983
by the United States Geological Survey and the United States Board on Geographic Names (Washington, D.C.: United States Government Printing Office, 1984)

A Postal History of Delaware
by Harvey Cochran Bounds (Newark, DE: Printed by Press of Kells, 1938)

The Postal History of Maryland, the Delmarva Peninsula, and the District of Columbia: The Post Offices and First Postmasters From 1775 to 1984
by Chester M. Smith Jr., and John L. Kay (Burtonsville, MD: The Depot, 1984)

■ MILITARY RECORDS

Colonial Delaware Soldiers and Sailors, 1638–1776
by Henry C. Peden Jr. (Westminster, MD: Family Line Publications, 1995)

Delaware Archives, 5 vols.
by the Delaware Public Archives Commission (Wilmington, DE: s.n., 1911–)

Delaware, World War I Selective Service System Draft Registration Cards, 1917–1918
United States Selective Service System (Washington, DC: The National Archives, 1987–1988)

Delaware's Role in World War II
by William H. Conner and Leon de-Valinger Jr. (Wilmington, DE: Delaware Heritage Press, 2003)

Index to Revolutionary War Service Records, 4 vols.
transcribed by Virgil D. White (Waynesboro, TN: The National Historical Publishing Company, 1995)

Revolutionary Patriots of Delaware, 1775–1783: A Genealogical and Historical Information on the Men and Women of Delaware who Served the American Cause During the War Against Great Britain, 1775–1783
by Henry C. Peden Jr. (Westminster, MD: Family Line Publications, 1996)

Uncle, We Are Ready! Registering America's Men, 1917–1918: A Guide to Researching World War I Draft Registration Cards
by John J. Newman (North Salt Lake, UT: HeritageQuest, 2001)

U.S. Military Records: A Guide to Federal & State Sources, Colonial America to the Present
by James C. Neagles (Salt Lake City: Ancestry, Inc., 1994)

World War II: A Family Historian's Guide
by Debra Johnson Knox (Spartanburg, SC: MIE Publishing, 2003)

■ PROBATE RECORDS

A Calender of Delaware Wills, New Castle County, 1682–1800
abstracted and compiled by the Historical Research Committee of the Colonial Dames of Delaware (Baltimore, MD: Genealogical Pub. Co., 1969)

Calender of Sussex County, Delaware, Probate Records, 1680–1800
by the Delaware Public Archives Commission (Dover, DE: 1964)

Colonial Delaware Wills and Estates to 1800: An Index
by Donald O. Virdin (Bowie, MD: Heritage Books, 1994)

Court Records of Kent County, Delaware, 1680–1705
edited by Leon deValinger Jr. (Washington, DC: American Historical Association, 1959)

Delaware Papers, 2 vols.
edited and translated by Charles T. Gehring, Edmund Bailey Callaghan, and the Holland Society of New York (Baltimore, MD: Genealogical Pub. Co., 1977–1981)

Documents Relative to the Colonial History of the State of New York
procured in Holland, England, and France by John Romeyn Brodhead; edited by E.B. O'Callaghan (Albany, NY: Weed, Parsons, Printers, 1853–87)

The First Laws of the State of Delaware
by John D. Cushing (Wilmington, DE: Michael Glazier, Inc., 1981)

■ VITAL RECORDS

Delaware Marriages and Deaths From the Delaware Gazette, 1875–1879
edited by Mary Fallon Richards and John C. Richards (Westminster, MD: Published for the Delaware Genealogical Society by Willow Bend Books, 2000)

Delaware Tombstone Inscriptions: 700 Revolutionary Soldiers in Three Counties; 600 in Small Church & Family Cemeteries, Chiefly in Sussex County
compiled and edited by Raymond B. Clark Jr. (St. Michaels, MD: R.B. Clark, 1989)

Souls in Heaven, Names in Stone: Kent County, Delaware, Cemetery Records, 2 vols.
by Raymond Walter Dill, William Martin Dill, and Elizabeth Ann Bostick Dill (Baltimore, MD: Gateway Press, 1989)

Your Guide to Cemetery Research
by Sharon DeBartolo Carmack (Cincinnati: Betterway Books, 2002)

■ Deale 1680
Parent County: Whorekill
Comments/research tips: (See Sussex) Formerly Whorekill County. Name changed to Deale 30 June 1680. Name changed to Sussex 4 December 1682.

■ Kent 1682
414 Federal St., Dover, DE 19901
Phone: (302)736-2040
Web site: www.negenealogy.com/de/de_records.htm
Parent County: St. Jones
Comments/research tips: Formerly St. Jones County. Name changed to Kent 1682. County Courthouse has Land records 1680–1800 and State Archives has Probate and Court records 1680–1800.

Record Type	Year Begun	Jurisdiction
Marriage	na	Clerk of Peace
Divorce	na	County Courthouse

■ New Castle 1664
310 Kiamensi Rd., Wilmington, DE 19804
Phone: (302)995-8588
Web site: www.negenealogy.com/de/de_records.htm
Parent County: Original County
Comments/research tips: Once named New Amstel. State Archives has Wills 1682–1800.

Record Type	Year Begun	Jurisdiction
Marriage	1911	Clerk of Peace
Divorce	na	County Court
Land	na	Recorder/Deeds
Court	na	State Archives

■ St. Jones 1680
Parent County: Whorekill County
Comments/research tips: (See Kent) Name changed to Kent 1682.

■ Sussex 1670
2 The Circle, P.O. Box 589, Georgetown, DE 19947
Phone: (302)855-7785
Web site: www.negenealogy.com/de/de_records.htm
Parent County: Deale
Comments/research tips: Formerly Whorekill formed in 1670. Renamed in 1680 as Deale County. Name changed to Sussex 1682. State Archives has Probate records 1680–1800.

Record Type	Year Begun	Jurisdiction
Land	1693	Recorder/Deeds

■ Whorekill 1670
Parent County: Original county
Comments/research tips: (See Deale) Whorekill was divided into Deale and Saint Jones Counties in 1680.

Florida

By Rhonda R. McClure

HISTORICAL OVERVIEW

Though Massachusetts and Virginia continue to duke it out over which of them founded the "new country," in actuality the history of Florida predates both of them—St. Augustine was founded in 1565. However, it is perhaps the fact that settlement of Florida did not begin in earnest until the late eighteenth century that causes researchers to think of the state as a late bloomer.

Florida was long used as a pawn, traded back and forth between England and Spain until well after the American Revolution. In 1763, at the end of the French and Indian War, Britain had control of Florida, and it was at this time that the provinces of East Florida (which consisted of the land from the Atlantic Ocean to the Apalachicola River) and West Florida (from the Apalachicola River to the Mississippi River) were formed.

England didn't have Florida for very long—in 1783 Spain again regained both provinces, and most of the British settlers moved out. In 1812, parts of West Florida were annexed to Louisiana and the Mississippi Territory. Seven years later, Spain ceded the remaining land that was West Florida and all of East Florida to the United States. By 1822 Florida was a territory, and it finally gained statehood on 3 March 1845.

All of this back and forth between Spain and England has resulted in the history of Florida being broken up into different periods: first Spanish colonial period (1565–1763), British colonial period (1763–1783), second Spanish period (1784–1821), and territorial status (1821–1845). With each period came different records, and in the case of the Spanish periods, records in a different language.

RECORD HIGHLIGHTS

Before traditional land records in the state, you will find the Spanish Land Grants. These records were created

FLORIDA AT A GLANCE

Motto: In God We Trust

Population: 15.9 million

Prevalent Religions: Christianity, including Southern Baptist, Roman Catholic, Santería (Cuban Catholicism), Pentecostal, Episcopalian, Judaism

Major Industries: Tourism and related services, agriculture (citrus, sugarcane, fishing and fisheries), small-scale manufacturing, paper and pulp, aerospace, real estate, international banking

Ethnic Makeup (in percent): Caucasian 65.4%, African American 14.6%, Hispanic 16.8%, Asian 1.7%, Native American 0.3%, Other 3.0%

Famous Floridians: Julian "Cannonball" Adderley, Dave Barry, Faye Dunaway, Zora Neale Hurston, James Weldon Johnson, Butterfly McQueen, Jim Morrison, Tom Petty, Sidney Poitier, Janet Reno, Ben Vereen

Above: One of the state's Alligator Crossing road signs

© PhotoDisc/Getty Images

from 1820–22 and were used by the federal government to establish land ownership from early Spanish land grants. While these records are available they are also fragile, and it's recommended that you use the published five-volume transcript *Spanish Land Grants in Florida* (Tallahassee, Florida: Florida State Library Board, 1940).

In addition to the federal census records that begin in 1830 and continue decennially until the most recently released, 1930, there are a few fragments of colonial, territorial, and state censuses that have survived for Florida. Most of what has survived can be found at the Florida Department of State, Division of Library & Information Services, Bureau of Archives & Records Management, 500 South Bronough Street, Tallahassee, Florida 32399-0250, (850) 245-6700, <http://dlis.dos.state.fl.us/barm/index.html>. Ten of the Spanish colonial censuses are reproduced in William S. Coker and G. Douglas Inglis's *The Spanish Censuses of Pensacola, 1784–1820: A Genealogical Guide to Spanish Pensacola* (Pensacola, Florida: Perdido Bay Press, 1980). Some of these land grants are also available online through the Florida State Archives Web site <http://dlis.dos.state.fl.us/barm/fsa.html>. One census that is often misidentified as a state census is the one taken in 1885. This was actually a census conducted by the federal government, but it is an excellent resource for filling the void left by the 1890 burned census.

Other useful land records include the homestead applications from 1881–1905 that are housed at the Florida State Archives. These records, along with the Homestead Contest Dockets (1887–1891), Homestead Occupying Claimant Files (1881–1904), and Homestead Swampland Claim Files (1846–1918) are all available on microfilm through the Family History Library.

Birth and death records at the state level are primarily available beginning in January 1917 and can be requested from the Bureau of Vital Statistics of the State Department of Health and Rehabilitative Services, P.O. Box 210, Jacksonville, Florida 32231-0042, <www.doh.state.fl.us/planning_eval/vital_statistics/index.html>. Vital records before this time are incomplete, though you will certainly want to investigate to see if your ancestor's records were filed. In addition, you may want to check with the health department in your ancestor's county, as some of the early records may be found there. When it comes to marriages, the state vital statistics office has marriages, divorces, and annulments from 6 June 1927. The marital events that took place before then will be found in the county courts. If you want a copy of the marriage license application, then you will also want to contact the county clerk where the marriage took place.

The Florida State Genealogical Society has a program

RESEARCH TIPS

for more info

- Birth and death records at the state level are primarily available beginning in January 1917 and can be requested from the Bureau of Vital Statistics of the State Department of Health and Rehabilitative Services.
- The state vital statistics office has marriages, divorces, and annulments from 6 June 1927.
- A few fragments of colonial, territorial, and state censuses have survived in addition to the federal censuses beginning in 1830, and can be found at the Florida Department of State, Division of Library & Information Services, Bureau of Archives & Records Management.
- A proven list of people who lived in the state before 3 March 1845 can be found on the Florida State Genealogical Society Web site <www.rootsweb.com/~flsgs/pioneers/2003index.html>
- www.segenealogy.com/

Census Records
- Federal Census: 1830, 1840, 1850, 1860, 1870, 1880, 1900, 1910, 1920, 1930
- State Census: 1825 (Leon County), 1855 (Marion County), 1867 (Hernando, Madison, Orange, Santa Rosa Counties), 1875 (Alachua County), 1885 (all counties except Alachua, Clay, Nassau, and Columbia), 1935, 1945
- Mortality Schedules: 1850, 1860, 1870, 1880

set up to honor those descendants who can prove relationship to a resident who was living in Florida before 3 March 1845. A list of established pioneers can be found on their Web site <www.rootsweb.com/~flsgs/pioneers/2003index.html>. The packets for those descendants who applied before 1995 can be found on fifty-four rolls of microfilm through the Family History Library. These packets contain copies of original records to prove the

applicant's descent from a Florida pioneer.

An often overlooked alternative to vital records is the WPA compiled *Register of Deceased Veterans Buried in Florida* (St. Augustine, Florida: Veterans' Graves Registration Project, 1940–41). These volumes cover fifty-one of the sixty-seven counties in Florida. Among other repositories, the Orlando Public Library has a complete set in their Genealogy Department. They can't do look ups for you, so you will have to either visit in person or hire a professional genealogist if you cannot get access to these volumes elsewhere.

STATE RESOURCES

■ ARCHIVES, LIBRARIES, AND SOCIETIES

Afro-American Historical and Genealogical Society, Central Florida Chapter
P.O. Box 1347, Orlando, FL 32802-1347
E-mail: cf_aahgs@yahoo.com
Web site: <www.rootsweb.com/~flcfaahg/member.html>

Alachua County Genealogical Society
P.O. Box 12078, Gainesville, FL 32604
Web site: <www.afn.org/~acgs/>

Amelia Island Genealogical Society
P.O. Box 6005, Fernandina Beach, FL 32035-6005
Tel: (904) 261-2139
Web site: <www.net-magic.net/biz-directory/genelogy.htm>

Apalachicola Historical Society, Inc.
P.O. Box 75, Apalachicola, FL 32329

Web site: <http://mailer.fsu.edu/~rthompso/fchs_adr.html>

The Archer Historical Society
P.O. Box 1850, Archer, FL 32618
Web site: <www.afn.org/~archer/>

Baker County Historical Society
P.O. Box 856, MacClenny, FL 32063
Web site: <www.rootsweb.com/~flbaker/books.html>

Big Lake Family History Society
P.O. Box 592, Okeechobee, FL 34973-0592

Bonita Springs Genealogy Club
P.O. Box 366471, Bonita Springs, FL 34136

Bonita Springs Public Library
26876 Pine Ave., Bonita Springs, FL 33923

Bowling Green Historical Council
P.O. Box 478, Bowling Green, FL 33834

Boynton Beach Historical Society
P.O. Box 12, Boynton Beach, FL 33425-0012
Tel: (561) 965-9860

Brevard Community College Library
1519 Clearlake Rd., Cocoa, FL 32922-6597
Tel: (888) 747-2802

Brevard County Genealogical Society
P.O. Box 1123, Cocoa, FL 32923-1123
Web site: <www.rootsweb.com/~flbgs/>

Broward County Historical Commission
151 SW Second St., Fort Lauderdale, FL 33301
Tel: (954) 765-4670
Web site: <www.co.broward.fl.us/history.htm>

Burdick International Ancestry Library
2317 Riverbluff Pkwy. #249, Sarasota, FL 34231-5032
Tel: (941) 922-7931
Web site: <www.burdickfamily.org/library.html>

Cape Coral-Lee County Public Library
921 SW Thirty-ninth Terrace, Cape Coral, FL 33914
Tel: (239) 542-3953
Web site: <www.lee-county.com/library/library/branches/cc.htm>

Central Florida Genealogical Society, Inc.
P.O. Box 536309, Orlando, FL 32853-6309

E-mail: cfgs@cfgs.org
Web site:

Charlotte County Genealogical Society
P.O. Box 494707, Port Charlotte, FL 33949-4707
E-mail: <charleyslady@yahoo.com>

Citrus County Genealogical Society
P.O. Box 2211, Inverness, FL 34451-2211

Citrus Springs Genealogical Society
1826 W. Country Club Blvd., Citrus Springs, FL 34434

Clay County Genealogical Society
P.O. Box 1071, Green Cove Springs, FL 32043

Cocoa Public Library
430 Delannoy Ave., Cocoa, FL 32922

Collier County Public Library
Library Headquarters
2385 Orange Blossom Dr., Naples, FL 34109

Cooper Memorial Library
620 Montrose St., Clermont, FL 34711-2166
Tel: (352) 394-4265
Web site: <www.lakeline.lib.fl.us/cmlintro.htm>

DeLand Public Library
130 E. Howry Ave., DeLand, FL 32724
Tel: (386) 822-6430

Department of Military Affairs
Office of the Adjutant General
P.O. Box 1008, St. Augustine, FL
32085-1008

DeSoto Correctional Institution Library
P.O. Box 1072, Arcadia, FL
33821

DeSoto County Historical Society
P.O. Box 1824, Arcadia, FL
34265

Dixie County Historical Society
P.O. Box 928, Cross City, FL
32628
Tel: (352) 542-3128
E-mail: hland@DIXIEHISTORY
.ORG
Web site:
East Hillsborough Historical Society
605 N. Collins St., Plant City, FL
33563
Tel: (813) 757-9226
Web site: <www.rootsweb.com/
~flqgbac/ehhs.html>

Elmer's Genealogy Library
203 S. Range St., Madison, FL
32340-2437
Tel: (850) 973-3282
E-mail: research@elmerslibrary
.com
Web site:
Englewood Genealogical Society
P.O. Box 795, Englewood, FL
34295-0795
Web site: <www.rootsweb.com/
~flegsf/>

The Alma Clyde Field Library of Florida History
435 Brevard Ave., Historic Cocoa
Village, 32922
Tel: (321) 690-1971
Web site:
Florida Baptist Historical Society, Stetson University
P.O. Box 8353, DeLand, FL
32720

Florida Department of State
Division of Library & Information
Services, Bureau of Archives &
Records Management, 500 S.
Bronough St., Tallahassee, FL
32399-0250
Tel: (850) 245-6700

E-mail: BARM@dos.state.fl.us
Web site: <http://dlis.dos.state.
fl.us/barm/index.html>

Florida Genealogical Society
P.O. Box 18624, Tampa, FL
33679-8624

The Florida Historical Society
1320 Highland Ave, Melbourne,
FL 32935
Tel: (321) 254-9855
E-mail: Flahistoricalsoc@aol
.com
Web site:
**Florida State Genealogical
Society**
P.O. Box 10249, Tallahassee, FL
32302-2249
Web site: <www.rootsweb.com/
~flsgs/>

Florida Suncoast Chapter
3748 Russian Olive Lane, Zephyr-
hills, FL 33541
Tel: (813) 788-1077
Web site: <www.ahsgr.org/florid
a_suncoast_chapter.htm>

**Fort Lauderdale Historical
Society**
219 SW Second Ave., Fort Lauderdale, FL 33301
Tel: (954) 463-4431

**Fort Myers-Lee County Public
Library**
2050 Central Ave., Fort Myers, FL
33901
Tel: (239) 479-4635
Web site: <www.lee-county.com/
library/library/branches/
fm.htm>

**Genealogical Group of
Seminole County, FL**
P.O. Box 180993, Casselberry,
FL 32718-0993

**Genealogical Society of
Broward County Inc.**
P.O. Box 485, Fort Lauderdale,
FL, 33302
Web site: <www.rootsweb.com/
~flgsbc/>

**Genealogical Society of Collier
County**
P.O. Box 7933, Naples, FL 34101
Web site: <www.naples.net/pres
ents/gscc/>

**Genealogical Society of Flagler
County**
P.O. Box 35-4671, Palm Coast,
FL 32135-4671

Web site: <www.flaglerlibrary.
org/genealogy/genealogy.htm>

**The Genealogical Society of
Greater Miami, Inc.**
P.O. Box 162905, Miami, FL
33116-2905
Web site: <www.rootsweb.com/
~flgsgm/>

**Genealogical Society of North
Brevard, Inc.**
P.O. Box 897, Titusville, FL
32781-0897
Website: <www.nbbd.com/npr/
gsnb/index.html>

**The Genealogical Society of
Okaloosa County**
P.O. Box 1175, Fort Walton
Beach, FL 32549
Web site: <www.rootsweb.com/
~flwalton/gsoc.txt>

**Genealogical Society of
Okeechobee, Florida**
P.O. Box 371, Okeechobee, FL
34973-0371
Tel: (863) 467-2674
Web site: <www.rootsweb.com/
~flgso/>

**The Genealogical Society of
Santa Rosa County**
Milton Public Library Branch,
805 Alabama St., Milton, FL
32570
Web site: <www.db229.com/abo
utus.htm>

**Genealogical Society of
Sarasota, Inc.**
P.O. Box 1917, Sarasota, FL
34230-1917
Web site: <www.rootsweb.com/
~flgss/>

**Genealogical Society of South
Brevard**
P.O. Box 786, Melbourne, FL
32902-0786
E-mail: gssbinfo@gssb.net
Web site: <www.rootsweb.com/
~flgssb/>

**Genealogical Society of
Southeast Volusia County**
% New Smyrna Beach Public Li-
brary, 105 S. Riverside Dr., New
Smyrna Beach, FL 32168
Tel: (386) 424-2910

**Genealogy Club of Osceola
County**
P.O. Box 701295, St. Cloud, FL
34770-1295
Web site: <www.rootsweb.com/
~flosceol/osceola.htm>

**Genealogy Society of Hernando
County**
P.O. Box 1793, Brooksville, FL
34605-1793
Web site: <www.rootsweb.com/
~flhernan/>

**Geneva Historical and
Genealogical Society, Inc.**
P.O. Box 91, Geneva, FL 32732
E-mail: GenevaHGS@aol.com
Web site: <www.usgennet.org/
usa/fl/county/seminole/
Geneva/society.htm>

**Gulf County Genealogical
Society**
P.O. Box 541, Port St. Joe, FL
32457
Web site: <www.geocities.com/
Heartland/Meadows/5551/
gcgsfl.html>

Halifax Historical Society
252 S. Beach St., Daytona
Beach, FL 32114
Tel: (904) 255-6976
E-mail: mail@halifaxhistorical
.org

**Hamilton County Historical
Museum, Inc.**
P.O. Box 929, Jasper, FL 32052
Tel: (386) 792-3850
Web site: www.rootsweb.com/~f
lhchms/index.htm

Haydon Burns Library
122 N. Ocean St., Jacksonville,
FL 32202
Tel: (904) 630-2665

**Highlands County Genealogical
Society**
% the Sebring Public Library
319 W. Center Ave., Sebring, FL
33870
Web site:
**Hillsborough County Historical
Commission, Museum,
Historical & Genealogical
Library**
County Courthouse, Tampa, FL
33602

**Historic Ocala/Marion County
Genealogical Society**
P.O. Box 1206, Ocala, FL
34478-1206

**Imperial Polk Genealogical
Society**
P.O. Box 10, Kathleen, FL 33849
Web site: <www.ipgs.org>

**Indian River County Main
Library**
1600 Twenty-first St., Vero
Beach, FL 32960
Tel: (772) 770-5060
Web site:
**Indian River Genealogical
Society, Inc.**
P.O. Box 1850, Vero Beach, FL
32961-1850
Web site: <www.rootsweb.com/
~flindigs/>

Jackson County Florida Library
413 N. Green St., Marianna, FL
32446
Tel: (850) 482-9631

**Jacksonville Genealogical
Society, Inc.**
P.O. Box 60756, Jacksonville,
Duval Co., FL 32236-0756
E-mail: jaxgen@comcast.net
Web site: <http://jaxgen.home.c
omcast.net/>

Jacksonville Public Library
122 N. Ocean St., Jacksonville,
FL 32202
Tel: (904) 630-2410

**Jewish Genealogical Society of
Broward County, Inc.**
P.O. Box 17251, Fort Lauderdale,
FL 33318
E-mail: info@jgsbroward.org
Web site:
**Jewish Genealogical Society of
Central Florida**
P.O. Box 520583, Longwood, FL
32752

**Jewish Genealogical Society of
Greater Orlando**
P.O. Box 941332, Maitland, FL
32794-1332
Tel: (407) 682-7799
Web site: <www.rootsweb.com/
~fljgscf/>

**Jewish Genealogical Society of
Palm Beach County, Inc.**
P.O. Box 7796, Delray Beach, FL
33482-7796
Tel: (561) 734-7946
Web site:
**Jewish Genealogical Society of
Tampa Bay**
P.O. Box 3252, Holiday, FL
34690-0252
Tel: (727) 539-4521
E-mail: JGSTampaBay@yahoo
.com

Keystone Genealogical Society
P.O. Box 50, Monticello, FL 32344

Keystone Genealogy Library
695 E. Washington St., Monticello, FL 32345

Kinseekers Genealogical Society of Lake County
P.O. Box 492711, Leesburg, FL 34749-2711
E-mail: gfahs@aol.com
Web site: <http://members.aol.com/LakeCo1887/>

Largo Library
351 E. Bay Dr., Largo, FL 33770
Tel: (727) 587-6715
Web site: <www.largo.com/index.cfm?action=dept&drill=library>

Lee County Genealogical Society
P.O. Box 150153, Cape Coral, FL 33915-0153
Web site: <www.rootsweb.com/~fllcgs/>

Lehigh Acres Genealogical Society
P.O. Box 965, Lehigh Acres, FL 33970-0965

Lemon Bay Historical and Genealogical Society
P.O. Box 236, Englewood, FL 33533

Levy County Genealogy Society
% Levy County Journal, P.O. Box 159, Bronson, FL 32631

Madison County, Florida Genealogical Society
P.O. Box 136, Madison, FL 32341-0136
Web site: <www.rootsweb.com/~flmadcgs/>

Manasota Genealogical Society
6023 Twenty-sixth St. W., PMB 269, Bradenton, FL 34207
Web site: <www.rootsweb.com/~flmgs/>

Manatee County Central Library
1301 Barcarrota Blvd. W., Bradenton, FL 34205-7522
Tel: (941) 748-5555
Web site: <www.co.manatee.fl.us/service/library/library_locations.html>

Marco Island Historical Society
P.O. Box 2282, Marco Island, FL 34146

Tel: (941) 394-6917
Web site: <www.marco-island-florida.com/history/>

Martin County Genealogical Society, Inc.
P.O. Box 275, Stuart, FL 34995
Web site: <www.rootsweb.com/~flmcgs/>

Melbourne Public Library
540 E. Fee Ave., Melbourne, FL 32901
Tel: (321) 952-4514
Web site: <www.brev.org/locations/melbourne/>

Micanopy Historical Society Museum
P.O. Box 462, Micanopy, FL 32667
Tel: (352) 466-3200
Web site: <www.afn.org/~micanopy/>

Monroe County Genealogical Society
21 Ventana Ln., Big Coppitt Key, FL 33040

National Archives—Southeast Region (Atlanta)
1557 St. Joseph Ave., East Point, GA 30344-2593
Tel: (404) 763-7477
E-mail: atlanta.center@nara.gov
Web site: <www.archives.gov/facilities/ga/atlanta.html>

Northwest Regional Library System, Hdq. Bay County Public Library
25 W. Government St., Panama City, FL 32402
Tel: (850) 872-7500
E-mail: gvickery@nwrls.lib.fl.us
Web site: <www.nwrls.lib.fl.us/contact_bcpl.htm>

Office of Vital Statistics
P.O. Box 210, Jacksonville, FL 32231-0042
Tel: (904) 359-6900

Orlando County Library System
101 E. Central Blvd., Orlando, FL 32801
Tel: (407) 835-7323
Web site: <www.ocls.lib.fl.us/Locations/locations_main_downtown.asp>

Ormond Beach Public Library
30 S. Beach St., Ormond Beach FL 32174
Tel: (386) 676-4191

Osceola County Department
326 Eastern Ave., St. Cloud, FL 32769

Osceola County Historical Society
750 N. Bass Rd., Kissimmee, FL 34746-6307
Tel: (407) 396-8644
Web site: <www.flamuseums.org/fam/flamuseums/pages/241.htm>

Palatka Public Library
216 Reid St., Palatka, FL 32077

Palm Beach County Genealogical Society
100 Clematis St., West Palm Beach, FL 33402
Web site:

Palm Harbor Library
2330 Nebraska Ave., Palm Harbor, FL 34683
Tel: (727) 784-3332
E-mail: coppolg@tblc.org
Web site:

Pasco County Genealogical Society
P.O. Box 2072, Dade City, FL 33526-2072
E-mail: pcgslibrary@yahoo.com>
Web site: <www.rootsweb.com/~flpcgs/>

The Pastfinders of South Lake County
620 Montrose St., Clermont, FL 34711
Web site: <www.rootsweb.com/~flpslc/>

Pinellas Genealogical Society
% Largo Library, 351 E. Bay Dr., Largo, FL 33770-3715
Web site: <www.rootsweb.com/~flpgs/index.htm>

Polk County Historical Association
P.O. Box 2749, Bartow, FL 33830-2749

Polk County Historical & Genealogical Library
100 E. Main St., Bartow, FL 33830
Tel: (863) 534-4380
Web site: <www.polk-county.net/county_offices/leisure_svcs/hist_library/index.aspx>

Putnam County Genealogical Society
P.O. Box 2354, Palatka, FL 32178-2354
Web site: <www.afn.org/~pcgs/>

Putnam County Historical Society
P.O. Box 35, Palatka, FL 32178-0035
Web site: <www.rootsweb.com/~flpchs/>

Quintilla Geer Bruton Archives Center
605 N. Collins St., Plant City, FL 33563-3321
Tel: (813) 754-7031
E-mail: qcenter@tampabay.rr.com
Web site: <www.rootsweb.com/~flqgbac/>

Ridge Genealogical Society
P.O. Box 477, Babson Park, FL 33827

Roman Catholic Archdiocese of Miami Pastoral Center/ Chancery
9401 Biscayne Blvd., Miami, FL 33138
Tel: (954) 525-5157

Roots and Branches Genealogical Society
P.O. Box 612, DeLand, FL 32721-0612

Sebring Historical Society
P.O. Box 3313, Sebring, FL 33871-3313
Tel: (863) 471-2522
Web site: <www.heartlineweb.org/shs/>

Seminole County Historical Society Incorporated
P.O. Box 409, Sanford, FL 32771-0409
Web site: <http://members.tripod.com/~UNX3/seminolecounty.html>

Slovenian Genealogical Society
7605 Harvey St., Pensacola, FL 32506-5022
Web site: <www.sloveniangenealogy.org/chapters/Florida.htm>

South Hillsborough Genealogists
Rte. 1, Box 400, Palmetto, FL 33561

The Southern Baptist Convention Building
901 Commerce St. #400, Nashville, TN 37203-3630

Tel: (615) 244-0344
Web site: <www.sbhla.org/info
.htm>

**Southern Genealogist's
Exchange Society, Inc.**
P.O. Box 2801, Jacksonville, FL
32203-2801
Web site: <http://sgesjax.tripod
.com/>

**St. Augustine Genealogical
Society**
% Southeast Branch, St Johns
County Public Library, 6670 US1
South St., Augustine FL 32086
Web site: <www.drbronsontours.
com/Stauggen.html>

**St. Johns County Public Library
System**
1920 N. Ponce De Leon Blvd.,
Saint Augustine, FL 32084
Tel: (904) 823-2650

**St. Lucie Historical Society,
Inc.**
P.O. Box 578, Fort Pierce, FL
34954-0578
E-mail: SLCHistoricalSoc@aol
.com
Web site: <www.rootsweb.com/
~flslchs/>

State Library of Florida
500 S. Bronough St., Tallahassee, FL 32399
Tel: (850) 245-6600
E-mail: info@dlis.state.fl.us
Web site: <http://dlis.dos.state.
fl.us/stlib/>

**Suwannee Valley Genealogical
Society, Inc.**
P.O. Box 967, Live Oak, FL 32064
Tel: (386) 330-0110
Web site: <www.rootsweb.com/
~flsvgs/svgs.htm>

**Tallahassee Genealogical
Society**
P.O. Box 4371, Tallahassee, FL
32315
Web site: <www.rootsweb.com/
~fltgs/>

Tarpon Springs Public Library
138 E. Lemon St., Tarpon Springs,
FL 34689
Tel: (727) 943-4922
Web site: <www.tblc.org/tar
pon/>

**Taylor County Historical
Society**
118 E. Main St., Perry, FL 32347
Web site: <www.rootsweb.com/~f
ltaylor/historical_society.html>

**Treasure Coast Genealogical
Society**
P.O. Box 12582, Fort Pierce, FL
34979-2582
Web site: <www.rootsweb.com/
~fltcgs/>

**University of Florida George A.
Smathers Libraries**
Department of Special Collec-
tions, P.O. Box 117007, Gaines-
ville, FL 32611-7007
Tel: (352) 392-9075

**University of Miami, Otto G.
Richter Library**
P.O. Box 248214, Coral Gables,
FL 33124-0320
Tel: (305) 284-3551
Web site: <www.library.miami.
edu/Richterlibrary.html>

**University of West Florida, John
Chandler Pace Library**
11000 University Pkwy., Pensacola, FL 32514-5750
Tel: (850) 474-2424

Villages Genealogical Society
<www.angelfire.com/fl3/
genie3/new_index.html>

Volusia County Library Center
City Island, Daytona Beach, FL
32114
Tel: (386) 257-6036

**Volusia Genealogical &
Historical Society**
P.O. Box 2039, Daytona Beach,
FL 32015

**Wakulla County Historical
Society**
P.O. Box 151, Crawfordville, FL
32326-0151
Tel: (850) 926-7405
Web site: <www.psy.fsu.edu/~tho
mpson/wchs/wchs_page.html>

**Washington County
Genealogical Society**
205 Wells Ave., Chipley, FL
32428

**West Florida Genealogical
Society**
Web site: <www.rootsweb.com/
~flwfgs/index.htm>

**West Pasco County
Genealogical Society**
P.O. Box 1142, Port Richey, FL
34673
Web site: <homepages.rootsweb.
com/~wpcgs/wpsgmember.htm>

**West Volusia Historical
Society, Inc.**
137 W. Michigan Ave., DeLand,
FL 32720
Tel: (386) 740-6813
Web site: <volusia.com/delandh
ouse/>

**P.K. Yonge Library of Florida
History**
P.O. Box 117007, Gainesville, FL
32611
Web site: <http://web.uflib.ufl.
edu/spec/pkyonge/>

BIBLIOGRAPHY

■ GENERAL RESOURCES

*1830 Private Land Claims in
East Florida*
(Signal Mountain, TN: Institute of
Historic Research, ca. 1990)

*The Black Experience: A Guide
to Afro-American Resources in
the Florida State Archives*
by Debra D. McGriff (Tallahassee,
FL: Florida Department of State
Division of Library and Information
Services, 1991)

*Catalog of the Florida State
Archives*
(Tallahassee, FL: Dept. of State,
1975)

*Church and State in the
Spanish Floridas, 1783–1822*
by Michael Joseph Curley (New
York: AMS Press, 1974)

*The Cross in the Sand: The Early
Catholic Church in Florida,
1513–1870*
by Michael V. Gannon (Gainesville, FL: University of Florida
Press, 1965)

*The Episcopal Diocese of
Florida, 1892–1975*
by George R. Bentley (Gainesville, FL: University of Florida
Press, ca. 1989)

*Florida Connections Through
Bible Records*
by Anne Wood Taylor (Tallahassee, FL: Florida State Genealogical Society, ca. 1993)

*Florida: Historic-Dramatic-
Contemporary, 4 vols.*
by Junius E. Dovell (New York:
Lewis Historical Publishing Co.,
1952)

*Florida Pioneers and Their
Descendants*
by Anne Wood Taylor (Tallahassee, FL: Florida State Genealogical Society, ca. 1992)

*Florida Prison Records,
1875–1900*
by Carol Cox Bouknecht (Tallahassee, FL: C.C. Bouknecht, ca.
1993)

*The Florida State Genealogical
Society, Inc. Surname
Directory, 1995*
by Linda Pazics Kleback (Tallahassee, FL: The Society, ca.
1995)

*Florida's Indians from Ancient
Times to the Present*
by Jerald T. Milanich (Gainesville,
FL: University Press of Florida, ca.
1998)

*The Genealogist's Companion
and Sourcebook, 2d ed.*
by Emily Anne Croom (Cincinnati:
Betterway Books, 2003)

*A Genealogist's Guide to
Discovering Your African-
American Ancestors*
by Franklin Carter Smith and
Emily Anne Croom (Cincinnati:
Betterway Books, 2003)

*Genealogy and Local History: A
Bibliography, rev. ed.*
by Gill T. Bodziony (Tallahassee,
FL: State Library of Florida, 1978)

*Genealogy and Local History: A
Bibliography (supplement)*
by Beverly Pittman Byrd (Tallahassee, FL: Department of State,
Division of Library Services,
1983)

*Guide to Depositories of
Manuscript Collections in the
United States: Florida*
by the Historical Records Survey
(Jacksonville, FL: Florida Historical Records Survey Project,
1940)

*Guide to Genealogical
Research in the National
Archives of the United States*
edited by Anne Bruner Eales and
Robert M. Kvasnicka (Washing-
ton, D.C.: National Archives and
Records Administration, 2000

A Guide to the History of Florida
by Paul S. George and Samuel
Proctor (New York: Greenwood
Press, ca. 1989)

Guide to the Microfilm Edition of the Records of the Diocese of Louisiana and the Floridas, 1576–1803
by Thomas Timothy McAvoy (Notre Dame, IN: University of Notre Dame Archives, 1967)

Guide to Public Vital Statistics Records in Florida
by Historical Records Survey (Jacksonville, FL: Florida Historical Records Survey, 1941)

History of Florida, Past and Present, Historical and Biographical
by Harry Gardner Cutler (Chicago: Lewis Publishing Co., ca. 1923)

The History of Methodism in Georgia and Florida: from 1785 to 1865
by Geo. G. Smith Jr. (Macon, GA: Jno. W. Burke & Co., 1877)

A History of the Timucua Indians and Missions
by John H. Hann (Gainesville, FL: University Press of Florida, ca. 1996)

Index to the Archives of Spanish West Florida, 1782–1810
by Stanley Clisby Arthur (New Orleans: Polyanthos, Inc., 1975)

Index to Florida Jewish History in the American Israelite, 1854–1900
by Yael Herbsman (Gainesville, FL: University of Florida, George A. Smathers Libraries, ca. 1992)

Inventory of the Church Archives of Florida Baptist Bodies
by the Historical Records Survey (Jacksonville, FL: Historical Records Survey, 1939–1940)

Missions of Spanish Florida
by David Hurst Thomas (New York: Garland, ca. 1991)

Names and Abstracts from the Acts of the Legislative Council of the Territory of Florida, 1822–1845
by William A. Wolfe and Janet B. Wolfe (Tallahassee, FL: Florida State Genealogical Society, ca. 1991, 1985)

National Archives Microfilm Catalogs online:
<www.archives.gov/publications/genealogy_microfilm_catalogs.html>

Pioneers of Florida's First Coast
by the Southern Genealogist's Exchange Society (Cullman, AL: Gregath, 1991)

A Preliminary List of Religious Bodies in Florida
by Historical Records Survey (Jacksonville, FL: Historical Records Survey, 1939)

Searching in Florida: A Reference Guide to Public and Private Records
by Diane C. Robie (Costa Mesa, CA: Independent Search Consultants, Inc., 1982)

Seminole Indians of Florida
by Raymond C. Lantz (Bowie, MD: Heritage Books, ca. 1994)

The Seminole and Miccosukee Tribes: A Critical Bibliography
by Harry A. Kersey (Bloomington, IN: Indiana University Press, ca. 1987)

The Spanish Borderlands: A Chronicle of Old Florida and the Southwest
by Herbert Eugene Bolton (New Haven: Yale University Press, 1921)

A Story of the Southern Synod of the Evangelical and Reformed Church, 1740–1968
by Banks J. Peeler (Salisbury, NC: Southern Synod of the Evangelical and Reformed Church, ca. 1968)

The Story of Southwestern Florida
by James Warren Covington (New York: Lewis Historical Pub. Co., 1957)

The Trail of the Florida Circuit Rider: An Introduction to the Rise of Methodism in Middle and East Florida
by Charles Tinsley Thrift Jr. (Lakeland, FL: The Florida Southern College Press, ca. 1944)

■ CENSUS RECORDS

The American Census Handbook
by Thomas Jay Kemp (Wilmington, DE: Scholarly Resources Inc., ca. 2001)

The Census Book: A Genealogist's Guide to Federal Census Facts, Schedules and Indexes; With Master Extraction Forms for Federal Census Schedules, 1790–1930
by William Dollarhide (Bountiful, UT: Heritage Quest, ca. 1999)

Finding Answers in U.S. Census Records
by Loretto Dennis Szucs & Matthew Wright (Orem, UT: Ancestry Pub., ca. 2001)

Florida voter registration lists, 1867–68
by the Tallahassee Genealogical Society (Tallahassee, FL: Tallahassee Genealogical Society, ca. 1992)

Florida Voters in Their First Statewide Election, May 26, 1845
by Brian E. Michaels (Tallahassee, FL: Florida State Genealogical Society, ca. 1987)

Florida's First Families: Translated Abstracts of Pre-1821 Spanish Censuses
by Donna Rachal Mills (Tuscaloosa, AL: Mills Historical Press, ca. 1992)

Map Guide to the U.S. Federal Censuses, 1790–1920
by William Thorndale and William Dollarhide (Baltimore, MD: Genealogical Pub. Co., ca. 1987)

State Census Records
by Ann S. Lainhart (Baltimore, MD: Genealogical Pub. Co., ca. 1992)

Your Guide to the Federal Census
by Kathleen W. Hinckley (Cincinnati: Betterway Books, 2002)

■ IMMIGRATION RECORDS

American Naturalization Records, 1790–1990: What They Are and How to Use Them
by John J. Newman (North Salt Lake, UT: HeritageQuest, 1998)

American Passenger Arrival Records
by Michael Tepper (Baltimore: Genealogical Publishing Co., 1993)

Havana, USA; Cuban Exiles and Cuban Americans in South Florida, 1959–1994
by María Cristina García (Berkeley, CA: University of California Press, ca. 1996)

Index to passenger lists of vessels arriving at miscellaneous ports in Alabama, Florida, Georgia, and South Carolina, 1890–1924
by the United States Immigration and Naturalization Service (Washington, DC: Immigration and Naturalization Service, 1957)

Passenger lists of vessels arriving at Key West, 1898–1920
by the United States Immigration and Naturalization Service (Washington, DC: Immigration and Naturalization Service, 1946)

They Became Americans: Finding Naturalization Records and Ethnic Origins
by Loretto Dennis Szucs (Salt Lake City: Ancestry, Inc., 1998)

They Came in Ships: A Guide to Finding Your Immigrant Ancestor's Arrival Records, 2d ed.
by John P. Colletta (Salt Lake City: Ancestry, Inc., 1993)

■ LAND RECORDS

English Land Grants in West Florida: A Register for the States of Alabama, Mississippi, and Parts of Florida and Louisiana, 1766–1776
by Winston De Ville (Ville Platte, LA: W. De Ville, ca. 1986)

Florida Land: Records of the Tallahassee and Newnansville General Land Office, 1825–1892
by Alvie L. Davidson (Bowie, MD: Heritage Books, ca. 1989)

Land & Property Research in the United States
by E. Wade Hone (Salt Lake City, UT: Ancestry, ca. 1997)

Locating Your Roots: Discover Your Ancestors Using Land Records
by Patricia Law Hatcher (Cincinnati: Betterway Books, 2003)

Private Land Claims, Alabama, Arkansas, Florida
by Fern Ainsworth (Natchitoches, LA: F. Ainsworth, 1978)

Spanish Land Grants in Florida: Brief Translations from the Archives of the Board of Commissioners for Ascertaining Claims and Titles to Land in the Territory of Florida
by the Historical Records Survey (Tallahassee, FL: State Library Board, 1940–1941)

Spanish Plat Book of Land Records of the District of Pensacola, Province of West Florida, British and Spanish Land Grants, 1763–1821
by Billie Ford Snider (Pensacola, FL: Antique Compiling, ca. 1994)

■ MAPS

A Chronology of Florida Post Offices
by Alford G. Bradbury and E. Story Hallock (Sewall's Point, FL: Florida Classics Library, 1993)

Florida Atlas and Gazetteer
(Freeport, ME: DeLorme Mapping, ca. 1987)

Florida, Atlas of Historical County Boundaries
by Peggy Tuck Sinko (New York, NY: Charles Scribner, ca. 1997)

Florida Place Names
by Allen Covington Morris (Coral Gables, FL: University of Miami Press, ca. 1974)

Florida State Gazetteer and Business Directory
by R.L. Polk and Company (Jacksonville, FL: R.L. Polk, 1907–08)

■ MILITARY RECORDS

Compendium of the Confederate Armies
by Stewart Sifakis (New York, NY: Facts on File, ca. 1992–1995)

The Defenses of Spanish Florida, 1565 to 1763
by Verne E. Chatelain (Baltimore, MD: Baltimore Press, 1941)

General index to pension files, 1861–1934
by the United States Veterans Administration (Washington, DC: Veterans Administration, Publications Service, 1953)

Index to compiled service records of volunteer soldiers who served during Indian wars and disturbances, 1815–1858
by the United States Adjutant General's Office (Washington, DC: The National Archives, 1966)

Index to compiled service records of volunteer Union soldiers who served in organizations from the state of Florida
by the United States Adjutant General's Office (Washington, DC: The National Archives, 1958)

Pension index files, Indian wars, 1892–1926
by the United States Veterans Administration (Washington, DC: Veterans' Administration, 1959)

Register of Florida CSA Pension Applications
by Virgil D. White (Waynesboro, TN: National Historical Pub. Co., ca. 1989)

Uncle, We Are Ready! Registering America's Men, 1917–1918: A Guide to Researching World War I Draft Registration Cards
by John J. Newman (North Salt Lake, UT: HeritageQuest, 2001)

U.S. Military Records: A Guide to Federal & State Sources, Colonial America to the Present
by James C. Neagles (Salt Lake City: Ancestry, Inc., 1994)

World War II: A Family Historian's Guide
by Debra Johnson Knox (Spartanburg, SC: MIE Publishing, 2003)

■ VITAL RECORDS

Cemetery Records of Florida
by E.H. Hayes (Salt Lake City, UT: Genealogical Society of Utah, 1946)

Guide to Public Vital Statistics Records in Florida
by the Historical Records Survey (Jacksonville, FL: Florida Historical Records Survey, 1941)

Guide to Supplementary Vital Statistics from Church Records in Florida (preliminary)
by the Historical Records Survey (Jacksonville, FL: Florida Historical Records Survey, 1942)

Your Guide to Cemetery Research
by Sharon DeBartolo Carmack (Cincinnati: Betterway Books, 2002)

■ Alachua   29 Dec. 1824
201 E. University Ave., P.O. Box 600, Gainesville, FL 32602
Phone: (352)374-3636
Web site: www.clerk-alachua-fl.org/Archive/
Parent County: Duval, St. Johns
Comments/research tips: County Clerk has incomplete Marriage records from 1837.

Record Type	Year Begun	Jurisdiction
Probate	1840	County Clerk
Court	na	County Clerk
Land	1848	County Clerk

■ Baker   8 Feb. 1861
339 E. Macclenny Ave., Macclenny, FL 32063
Phone: (904)259-8113
Web site: bakercountyfl.org
Parent County: New River

Record Type	Year Begun	Jurisdiction
Marriage	1877	County Clerk
Court	1880	Clerk/Circuit Ct.
Divorce	1880	Clerk/Circuit Ct.
Probate	1877	County Clerk

■ Bay   1 July 1913
300 E. Fourth St., P.O. Box 2269, Panama City, FL 32402
Phone: (850)763-9061
Web site: www.bocc.co.bay.fl.us/
Parent County: Calhoun

Record Type	Year Begun	Jurisdiction
Birth	na	Dept./Health
Death	na	Dept./Health
Marriage	1913	Clerk/Circuit Ct.
Probate	1913	Clerk/Circuit Ct.
Divorce	1913	Clerk/Circuit Ct.
Court	1913	Clerk/Circuit Ct.
Land	1913	Clerk/Circuit Ct.

■ Benton   6 Mar. 1844
Parent County: Alachua
Comments/research tips: (See Hernando) Formerly Hernando County. Name changed to Benton 6 March 1844. Name changed back to Hernando 24 December 1850.

■ Bradford   21 Dec. 1858
P.O. Box B, Starke, FL 32091
Phone: (904)964-6280
Web site: www.rootsweb.com/~flbradfo/
Parent County: Columbia
Comments/research tips: Formerly New River County. Name changed to Bradford 6 December 1861.

Record Type	Year Begun	Jurisdiction
Marriage	1875	County Clerk
Probate	1892	County Clerk
Court	1892	County Clerk
Land	1876	County Clerk

■ Brevard   14 Mar. 1844
400 South St., Titusville, FL 32780
Phone: (321)633-1924

Web site: www.brev.org
Parent County: Mosquito
Comments/research tips: Formerly St. Lucie County. Name changed to Brevard 6 January 1855. Some records prior to 1885 were destroyed.

Record Type	Year Begun	Jurisdiction
Marriage	1868	Clerk/Circuit Ct.
Land	1871	Clerk/Circuit Ct.
Court	1879	Clerk/Circuit Ct.
Divorce	1879	Clerk/Circuit Ct.
Probate	1917	Clerk/Circuit Ct.
Military	1919	Clerk/Circuit Ct.
Death	1985	Dept./Health
Birth	na	Dept./Health

■ Broward 30 Apr. 1915
201 SE Sixth St., Ft. Lauderdale, FL 33301
Phone: (954)765-4578
Web site: www.co.broward.fl.us/
Parent County: Dade, Palm Beach

Record Type	Year Begun	Jurisdiction
Court	1915	Clerk/Circuit Ct.
Probate	1915	Clerk/Circuit Ct.
Land	1915	Clerk/Circuit Ct.
Marriage	1915	Clerk/Circuit Ct.
Divorce	1915	Clerk/Circuit Ct.

■ Calhoun 26 Jan. 1838
425 E. Central Ave., Blountstown, FL 32424
Phone: (850)674-4545
Web site: www.rootsweb.com/~flcalhou/index.htm
Parent County: Franklin

Record Type	Year Begun	Jurisdiction
Court	na	County Clerk
Land	na	County Clerk
Divorce	na	County Clerk
Marriage	na	County Judge
Probate	na	County Judge

■ Charlotte 23 Apr. 1921
350 E. Marion Ave., P.O. Box 511687, Punta Gorda, FL 33950
Phone: (941)637-2199
Web site: www.co.charlotte.fl.us/
Parent County: DeSoto

Record Type	Year Begun	Jurisdiction
Marriage	1921	Clerk/Circuit Ct.
Divorce	1921	Clerk/Circuit Ct.
Probate	1921	Clerk/Circuit Ct.
Court	1921	Clerk/Circuit Ct.
Land	1921	Clerk/Circuit Ct.

■ Citrus 2 June 1887
111 W. Main St., Inverness, FL 34450
Phone: (352)637-9470
Web site: www.bocc.citrus.fl.us/
Parent County: Hernando
Comments/research tips: Office of Historical Resources has Marriage records 1887-1945 and Military Discharge records 1919-1969.

Record Type	Year Begun	Jurisdiction
Cemetery	1887	Office of Hist. Resources
Probate	1887	Office of Hist. Resources
Land	1887	Office of Hist. Resources
Court	1887	Office of Hist. Resources
Birth	na	Dept./Health
Death	na	Dept./Health

■ Clay 31 Dec. 1858
P.O. Box 698, Green Cove Springs, FL 32043
Phone: (904)284-6317
Web site: www.claycountygov.com/
Parent County: Duval

Record Type	Year Begun	Jurisdiction
Marriage	1872	Clerk/Circuit Ct.
Probate	1872	Clerk/Circuit Ct.
Court	1872	Clerk/Circuit Ct.
Land	1872	Clerk/Circuit Ct.
Divorce	1859	Clerk/Circuit Ct.
Birth	1973	Dept./Health
Death	1973	Dept./Health

■ Collier 8 May 1923
3301 Tamiami Trail E., Naples, FL 33962
Phone: (941)732-2646
Web site: www.co.collier.fl.us/
Parent County: Lee

Record Type	Year Begun	Jurisdiction
Divorce	1923	Clerk/Circuit Ct.
Court	1923	Clerk/Circuit Ct.
Land	1923	Clerk/Circuit Ct.
Marriage	na	County Judge
Probate	na	County Judge

■ Columbia 4 Feb. 1832
145 N. Hernando St., P.O. Box 2069, Lake City, FL 32055
Phone: (386)758-1041
Web site: www.columbiacountyfla.com/
Parent County: Alachua

Record Type	Year Begun	Jurisdiction
Marriage	1875	Clerk/Circuit Ct.
Land	1875	Clerk/Circuit Ct.
Divorce	1892	Clerk/Circuit Ct.
Court	1892	Clerk/Circuit Ct.
Probate	1895	Clerk/Circuit Ct.
Birth	na	Public Health Unit
Death	na	Public Health Unit
Burial	na	Public Health Unit

■ Dade 4 Feb. 1836
Parent County: Monroe
Comments/research tips: (See Miami-Dade) Name changed to Miami-Dade 2 December 1997.

■ De Soto 19 June 1887
115 Oak St., Arcadia, FL 33821
Phone: (863)993-4876
Web site: co.desoto.fl.us/
Parent County: Manatee

Record Type	Year Begun	Jurisdiction
Court	1887	Clerk/Circuit Ct.
Divorce	1887	Clerk/Circuit Ct.
Land	1887	Clerk/Circuit Ct.
Probate	1887	County Judge

■ Dixie 25 Apr. 1921
P.O. Box 1206, Cross City, FL 32628
Phone: (352)498-1200
Web site: www.dixie-county.com/
Parent County: Lafayette

Record Type	Year Begun	Jurisdiction
Marriage	1973	Clerk/Circuit Ct.
Divorce	na	Clerk/Circuit Ct.
Probate	na	Clerk/Circuit Ct.
Court	na	Clerk/Circuit Ct.
Land	na	Clerk/Circuit Ct.

■ Duval 12 Aug. 1822
330 E. Bay St., Jacksonville, FL 32202
Phone: (904)630-2028
Web site: www.coj.net/
Parent County: St. Johns

Record Type	Year Begun	Jurisdiction
Divorce	1921	Clerk/Circuit Ct.
Court	1921	Clerk/Circuit Ct.
Land	1921	Clerk/Circuit Ct.
Marriage	na	County Judge
Probate	na	County Judge

■ Escambia 21 July 1821
223 S. Palafox Pl., Pensacola, FL 32501
Phone: (850)595-4310
Web site: www.co.escambia.fl.us/
Parent County: Original county. Only other original is St. Johns.

Record Type	Year Begun	Jurisdiction
Marriage	1821	Clerk/County Ct
Probate	1821	Clerk/County Ct.
Court	1821	Clerk/County Ct.
Birth	na	Dept./Health
Death	na	Dept./Health
Land	1821	Comptroller

■ Flagler 28 Apr. 1917
200 E. Moody Blvd., Bunnell, FL 32110
Phone: (386)437-7414
Web site: www.flaglercounty.org
Parent County: St. Johns

Record Type	Year Begun	Jurisdiction
Marriage	1917	Clerk/Circuit Ct.
Divorce	1917	Clerk/Circuit Ct.
Probate	1917	Clerk/Circuit Ct.
Court	1917	Clerk/Circuit Ct.
Land	1917	Clerk/Circuit Ct.

■ Franklin 8 Feb. 1832
33 Market St., Apalachicola, FL 32320
Phone: (850)653-8861

Web site: www.franklincountyflorida.com/
Parent County: Jackson

Record Type	Year Begun	Jurisdiction
Divorce	na	Clerk/Circuit Ct.
Court	na	Clerk/Circuit Ct.
Land	na	Clerk/Circuit Ct.
Marriage	na	County Judge
Probate	na	County Judge

■ Gadsden 24 June 1823
10 E. Jefferson St., P.O. Box 1799, Quincy, FL 32351
Phone: (850)875-8622
Web site: www.rootsweb.com/~flgadsde/
Parent County: Jackson

Record Type	Year Begun	Jurisdiction
Marriage	na	County Judge
Probate	na	County Judge
Divorce	na	Clerk/Circuit Ct.
Court	na	Clerk/Circuit Ct.
Land	na	Clerk/Circuit Ct.

■ Gilchrist 4 Dec. 1925
112 S. Main St., Trenton, FL 32693
Phone: (352)463-3170
Web site: www.co.gilchrist.fl.us/
Parent County: Alachua

Record Type	Year Begun	Jurisdiction
Marriage	1926	Clerk/Circuit Ct.
Divorce	1926	Clerk/Circuit Ct.
Probate	1926	Clerk/Circuit Ct.
Court	1926	Clerk/Circuit Ct.

■ Glades 23 Apr. 1921
P.O. Box 10, Moore Haven, FL 33471
Phone: (863)946-0361
Web site: www.gladescofl.us
Parent County: DeSoto

Record Type	Year Begun	Jurisdiction
Marriage	1921	Clerk of Courts
Divorce	1921	Clerk of Courts
Land	1921	Clerk of Courts
Probate	1921	Clerk of Courts
Court	1921	Clerk of Courts
Burial	1925	Clerk of Courts
Birth	1921	Dept./Health
Death	1921	Dept./Health

■ Gulf 6 June 1925
1000 Cecil G. Costin Sr. Blvd., Port St. Joe, FL 32456
Phone: (850)229-6112
Web site: www.gulfcountybusiness.com/
Parent County: Calhoun

Record Type	Year Begun	Jurisdiction
Marriage	1925	Clerk/Circuit Ct.
Probate	1925	Clerk/Circuit Ct.
Divorce	1925	Clerk/Circuit Ct.
Court	1925	Clerk/Circuit Ct.
Land	1925	Clerk/Circuit Ct.
Military	1925	Clerk/Circuit Ct.

Florida

■ Hamilton   26 Dec. 1827
207 NE First St., Jasper, FL 32052
Phone: (904)792-1288
Web site: www.rootsweb.com/~flhamilt/hamilton.html
Parent County: Jefferson

Record Type	Year Begun	Jurisdiction
Divorce	1881	Clerk/Circuit Ct.
Court	1881	Clerk/Circuit Ct.
Land	1837	Clerk/Circuit Ct.
Marriage	na	County Judge
Probate	na	County Judge

■ Hardee   23 Apr. 1921
412 W. Orange St., Wauchula, FL 33873
Phone: (863)773-4174
Web site: www.hardeecounty.net/start.html
Parent County: DeSoto

Record Type	Year Begun	Jurisdiction
Marriage	1921	Clerk/Circuit Ct.
Death	1921	Clerk/Circuit Ct.
Divorce	1921	Clerk/Circuit Ct.
Probate	1921	Clerk/Circuit Ct.
Court	1921	Clerk/Circuit Ct.
Land	1921	Clerk/Circuit Ct.

■ Hendry   11 May 1923
25 E. Hickpochee Ave., P.O. Box 1760, LaBelle, FL 33975
Phone: (863)675-5217
Web site: www.hendryfla.net/
Parent County: Lee

Record Type	Year Begun	Jurisdiction
Marriage	1923	Clerk/Circuit Ct.
Divorce	1923	Clerk/Circuit Ct.
Land	1923	Clerk/Circuit Ct.
Probate	1923	Clerk/Circuit Ct.
Court	1923	Clerk/Circuit Ct.
Burial	1953	Clerk/Circuit Ct.
Birth	na	Dept./Health
Death	na	Dept./Health

■ Hernando   24 Feb. 1843
20 N. Main St., Brooksville, FL 34601
Phone: (352)754-4201
Web site: www.co.hernando.fl.us/
Parent County: Alachua
Comments/research tips: Name changed to Benton 6 March 1844. Name changed back to Hernando 24 December 1850.

Record Type	Year Begun	Jurisdiction
Marriage	na	Clerk of County Court
Divorce	1877	Clerk/Circuit Ct.
Probate	1877	Clerk/Circuit Ct.
Court	1877	Clerk/Circuit Ct.
Land	1877	Clerk/Circuit Ct.

■ Highlands   23 Apr. 1921
590 S. Commerce Ave., Sebring, FL 33870
Phone: (863)402-6565
Web site: www.heartlineweb.org/highlandsbcc/
Parent County: DeSoto

Record Type	Year Begun	Jurisdiction
Marriage	1921	Clerk/Circuit Ct.
Divorce	1921	Clerk/Circuit Ct.
Probate	1921	Clerk/Circuit Ct.
Court	1921	Clerk/Circuit Ct.
Land	1921	Clerk/Circuit Ct.

■ Hillsborough   25 Jan. 1834
419 N. Pierce St., Tampa, FL 33602
Phone: (813)276-8100
Web site: www.hillsboroughcounty.org/
Parent County: Alachua

Record Type	Year Begun	Jurisdiction
Marriage	na	County Judge
Probate	na	County Judge
Divorce	ca. 1800	Clerk/Circuit Ct.
Land	ca. 1800	Clerk/Circuit Ct.

■ Holmes   8 Jan. 1848
201 N. Oklahoma St., Bonifay, FL 32425
Phone: (850)547-1100
Web site: www.rootsweb.com/~flholmes/holmes.htm
Parent County: Jackson

Record Type	Year Begun	Jurisdiction
Marriage	na	Clerk/Circuit Ct.
Probate	na	Clerk/Circuit Ct.
Divorce	na	Clerk/Circuit Ct.
Court	na	Clerk/Circuit Ct.
Land	na	Clerk/Circuit Ct.

■ Indian River   30 May 1925
1840 Twenty-fifth St., Vero Beach, FL 32960
Phone: (561)567-8000
Web site: http://indian-river.fl.us
Parent County: St. Lucie

Record Type	Year Begun	Jurisdiction
Marriage	1925	Clerk/Circuit Ct.
Divorce	1925	Clerk/Circuit Ct.
Probate	1925	Clerk/Circuit Ct.
Court	1925	Clerk/Circuit Ct.
Land	1925	Clerk/Circuit Ct.
Birth	na	Dept./Health
Death	na	Dept./Health

■ Jackson   12 Aug. 1822
2864 Madison St., P.O. Box 510, Marianna, FL 32447
Phone: (850)482-9552
Web site: www.jacksoncounty-fl.com
Parent County: Escambia

Record Type	Year Begun	Jurisdiction
Marriage	1845	Clerk/Circuit Ct.
Land	1824	Clerk/Circuit Ct.
Divorce	1900	Clerk/Circuit Ct.
Probate	1900	Clerk/Circuit Ct.
Military	1900	Clerk/Circuit Ct.
Court	1900	Clerk/Circuit Ct.

■ Jefferson   6 Jan. 1827
Courthouse #10, P.O. Box 547, Monticello, FL 32344
Phone: (850)342-0218

Web site: www.co.jefferson.fl.us/
Parent County: Leon

Record Type	Year Begun	Jurisdiction
Marriage	1840	Clerk/Circuit Ct.
Divorce	1900	Clerk/Circuit Ct.
Probate	1850	Clerk/Circuit Ct.
Court	1850	Clerk/Circuit Ct.
Land	1827	Clerk/Circuit Ct.

■ **Lafayette** 23 Dec. 1826
Main St., P.O. Box 88, Mayo, FL 32066
Phone: (904)294-1600
Web site: www.rootsweb.com/~fllafaye/lafayette.html
Parent County: Madison

Record Type	Year Begun	Jurisdiction
Divorce	1902	Clerk/Circuit Ct.
Court	1907	Clerk/Circuit Ct.
Land	1893	Clerk/Circuit Ct.
Marriage	na	County Judge
Probate	na	County Judge

■ **Lake** 27 May 1887
315 W. Main St., P.O. 7800, Tavares, FL 32778
Phone: (352)742-4100
Web site: www.lakegovernment.com/
Parent County: Orange

Record Type	Year Begun	Jurisdiction
Marriage	1887	Clerk/Circuit Ct.
Divorce	1887	Clerk/Circuit Ct.
Court	1887	Clerk/Circuit Ct.
Land	1887	Clerk/Circuit Ct.
Probate	1893	Clerk/Circuit Ct.
Death	na	Dept./Health

■ **Lee** 13 May 1887
2115 Second St., Fort Myers, FL 33901
Phone: (941)335-2283
Web site: www.lee-county.com/
Parent County: Monroe

Record Type	Year Begun	Jurisdiction
Marriage	na	Clerk/Circuit Ct.
Divorce	na	Clerk/Circuit Ct.
Probate	na	Clerk/Circuit Ct.
Court	na	Clerk/Circuit Ct.
Land	na	Clerk/Circuit Ct.

■ **Leon** 29 Dec. 1824
301 S. Monroe St., P.O. Box 726, Tallahassee, FL 32302
Phone: (850)577-4000
Web site: www.co.leon.fl.us/leon.htm
Parent County: Gadsden

Record Type	Year Begun	Jurisdiction
Marriage	1825	Clerk/Circuit Ct.
Divorce	1825	Clerk/Circuit Ct.
Probate	1825	Clerk/Circuit Ct.
Court	1825	Clerk/Circuit Ct.
Land	1825	Clerk/Circuit Ct.
Military	1914	Clerk/Circuit Ct.
Birth	na	Dept./Health

Death	na	Dept./Health
Burial	na	Dept./Health

■ **Levy** 10 Mar. 1845
355 Court St., Bronson, FL 32621
Phone: (352)486-5229
Web site: www.rootsweb.com/~fllevy/
Parent County: Alachua

Record Type	Year Begun	Jurisdiction
Marriage	1850	Clerk/Circuit Ct.
Divorce	1850	Clerk/Circuit Ct.
Probate	1850	Clerk/Circuit Ct.
Court	1850	Clerk/Circuit Ct.
Land	1850	Clerk/Circuit Ct.

■ **Liberty** 15 Dec. 1855
Hwy. 20, P.O. Box 399, Bristol, FL 32321
Phone: (850)643-2237
Web site: www.libertycountyflorida.com
Parent County: Gadsden

Record Type	Year Begun	Jurisdiction
Divorce	na	Clerk/Circuit Ct.
Court	na	Clerk/Circuit Ct.
Land	na	Clerk/Circuit Ct.
Marriage	na	County Judge
Probate	na	County Judge

■ **Madison** 26 Dec. 1827
P.O. Box 237, Madison, FL 32341
Phone: (850)973-1500
Web site: www.madisonfl.org/
Parent County: Jefferson

Record Type	Year Begun	Jurisdiction
Marriage	1838	Clerk/Circuit Ct.
Probate	1838	Clerk/Circuit Ct.
Court	1838	Clerk/Circuit Ct.
Land	1831	Clerk/Circuit Ct.
Divorce	na	Clerk/Circuit Ct.

■ **Manatee** 9 Jan. 1855
1115 Manatee Ave. W., P.O. Box 25400, Bradenton, FL 34206
Phone: (941)749-1800
Web site: www.co.manatee.fl.us/
Parent County: Hillsborough

Record Type	Year Begun	Jurisdiction
Marriage	1857	Clerk/Circuit Ct.
Divorce	1857	Clerk/Circuit Ct.
Probate	1857	Clerk/Circuit Ct.
Court	1857	Clerk/Circuit Ct.
Land	1857	Clerk/Circuit Ct.

■ **Marion** 14 Mar. 1844
P.O. Box 1030, Ocala, FL 34478
Phone: (352)620-3904
Web site: www.rootsweb.com/~flmarion/index.html
Parent County: Alachua

Record Type	Year Begun	Jurisdiction
Land	na	Recording Office

Divorce .... na ....Recording Office
Probate .... na ....Recording Office
Court .... na ....Recording Office
Birth .... na ....Dept./Health
Marriage .... na ....Clerk of Courts
Death .... na ....Dept./Health

■ Martin 30 May 1925
2401 SE Monterey Rd., Stuart, FL 34995
Phone: (561)288-5576
Web site: www.martin.fl.us/
Parent County: Palm Beach

Record Type	Year Begun	Jurisdiction
Marriage	1925	Clerk/Circuit Ct.
Divorce	1925	Clerk/Circuit Ct.
Probate	1925	Clerk/Circuit Ct.
Court	1925	Clerk/Circuit Ct.
Land	1925	Clerk/Circuit Ct.
Birth	na	Dept./Health
Death	na	Dept./Health
Burial	na	Dept./Health

■ Miami-Dade 13 Nov. 1997
111 NW First St., Suite 200, Miami, FL 33128
Phone: (305)375-5124
Web site: http://miamidade.gov/
Parent County: Monroe, Dade
Comments/research tips: Formerly Dade County. Name changed to Miami-Dade 2 December 1997.

Record Type	Year Begun	Jurisdiction
Divorce	1890	Clerk/Circuit Ct.
Land	1890	Clerk/Circuit Ct.
Marriage	na	County Judge
Probate	na	County Judge

■ Monroe 3 July 1823
500 Whitehead St., Key West, FL 33040
Phone: (305)292-3540
Web site: www.co.monroe.fl.us/
Parent County: St. Johns

Record Type	Year Begun	Jurisdiction
Marriage	1853	Clerk/Circuit Ct.
Divorce	1853	Clerk/Circuit Ct.
Probate	1853	Clerk/Circuit Ct.
Court	1853	Clerk/Circuit Ct.
Land	1853	Clerk/Circuit Ct.

■ Mosquito 29 Dec. 1824
Parent County: St. Johns
Comments/research tips: (See Orange) Name changed to Orange 30 January 1845.

■ Nassau 29 Dec. 1824
P.O. Box 456, Fernandina Beach, FL 32034
Phone: (904)321-5700
Web site: www.nassauclerk.org/
Parent County: Duval

Record Type	Year Begun	Jurisdiction
Marriage	ca. 1800	Clerk/Circuit Ct.

Divorce	ca. 1800	Clerk/Circuit Ct.
Probate	ca. 1800	Clerk/Circuit Ct.
Court	ca. 1800	Clerk/Circuit Ct.
Land	ca. 1800	Clerk/Circuit Ct.

■ New River 21 Dec. 1858
Parent County: Columbia
Comments/research tips: (See Bradford) Name changed to Bradford 6 December 1861.

■ Okaloosa 3 June 1915
101 E. James Lee Blvd., Crestview, FL 32536
Phone: (850)689-5800
Web site: www.co.okaloosa.fl.us/
Parent County: Santa Rosa

Record Type	Year Begun	Jurisdiction
Divorce	1915	Clerk/Circuit Ct.
Court	1915	Clerk/Circuit Ct.
Land	1915	Clerk/Circuit Ct.
Marriage	na	County Judge
Probate	na	County Judge

■ Okeechobee 8 May 1917
304 NW Second St., Okeechobee, FL 34972
Phone: (863)763-6441
Web site: www.rootsweb.com/~flokeech/index.html
Parent County: Brevard

Record Type	Year Begun	Jurisdiction
Marriage	1917	Clerk/Circuit Ct.
Divorce	1917	Clerk/Circuit Ct.
Probate	1917	Clerk/Circuit Ct.
Court	1917	Clerk/Circuit Ct.
Land	ca.1880	Clerk/Circuit Ct.
Birth	ca. 1900	Dept./Health
Death	ca. 1880	Dept./Health

■ Orange 29 Dec. 1824
425 N. Orange Ave., Orlando, FL 32801
Phone: (407)863-6321
Web site: www.orangecountyfl.net/Default.asp
Parent County: St. Johns
Comments/research tips: Formerly Mosquito County. Name changed to Orange 30 January 1845.

Record Type	Year Begun	Jurisdiction
Marriage	1890	Clerk/Circuit Ct.
Court	1869	Clerk/Circuit Ct.
Probate	1869	Clerk/Circuit Ct.

■ Osceola 12 May 1887
2 Courthouse Sq., Suite 2000, Kissimmee, FL 34741
Phone: (407)343-3500
Web site: www.osceola.org/
Parent County: Brevard

Record Type	Year Begun	Jurisdiction
Marriage	1887	Clerk/Circuit Ct.
Divorce	1887	Clerk/Circuit Ct.
Probate	1887	Clerk/Circuit Ct.
Court	1887	Clerk/Circuit Ct.
Land	1887	Clerk/Circuit Ct.

Florida

■ **Palm Beach** 30 Apr. 1909
301 N. Olive Ave., West Palm Beach, FL 33401
Phone: (561)355-2754
Web site: www.co.palm-beach.fl.us/
Parent County: Dade

Record Type	Year Begun	Jurisdiction
Divorce	na	Clerk/Circuit Ct.
Court	na	Clerk/Circuit Ct.
Land	na	Clerk/Circuit Ct.
Marriage	na	County Judge
Probate	na	County Judge

■ **Pasco** 2 June 1887
38053 Live Oak Ave., New Port Richey, FL 33523
Phone: (352)521-4545
Web site: www.pascocounty.com/
Parent County: Hernando

Record Type	Year Begun	Jurisdiction
Divorce	1887	Clerk/Circuit Ct.
Court	1887	Clerk/Circuit Ct.
Land	1887	Clerk/Circuit Ct.
Marriage	ca. 1890	Clerk/Circuit Ct.
Probate	ca. 1890	Clerk/Circuit Ct.

■ **Pinellas** 23 May 1911
315 Court St., Clearwater, FL 34616
Phone: (727)464-3377
Web site: www.co.pinellas.fl.us/bcc/
Parent County: Hillsborough

Record Type	Year Begun	Jurisdiction
Marriage	1912	Clerk/Circuit Ct.
Divorce	1912	Clerk/Circuit Ct.
Probate	1912	Clerk/Circuit Ct.
Court	1912	Clerk/Circuit Ct.
Land	1912	Clerk/Circuit Ct.

■ **Polk** 8 Feb. 1861
255 N. Broadway Ave., Bartow, FL 33830
Phone: (863)534-4540
Web site: www.polk-county.net/
Parent County: Brevard
Comments/research tips: Boundaries changed 1871.

Record Type	Year Begun	Jurisdiction
Marriage	1861	Clerk/Circuit Ct.
Divorce	1861	Clerk/Circuit Ct.
Probate	1861	Clerk/Circuit Ct.
Court	1861	Clerk/Circuit Ct.
Land	1861	Clerk/Circuit Ct.

■ **Putnam** 13 Jan. 1849
410 St. Johns Ave., P.O. Box 758, Palatka, FL 32178
Phone: (386)329-0361
Web site: www.co.putnam.fl.us/
Parent County: Alachua
Comments/research tips: Clerk of Circuit Court has Naturalization records 1849–1914.

Record Type	Year Begun	Jurisdiction
Marriage	1849	Clerk/Circuit Ct.
Divorce	1849	Clerk/Circuit Ct.
Probate	1849	Clerk/Circuit Ct.
Court	1849	Clerk/Circuit Ct.
Land	1849	Clerk/Circuit Ct.
Cemetery	na	Clerk/Circuit Ct.

■ **Santa Rosa** 18 Feb. 1842
6865 Caroline St., Milton, FL 32570
Phone: (850)623-0135
Web site: www.co.santa-rosa.fl.us/
Parent County: Escambia
Comments/research tips: Courthouse burned in 1869.

Record Type	Year Begun	Jurisdiction
Marriage	1869	County Archives
Divorce	1869	County Archives
Probate	1869	County Archives
Court	1869	County Archives
Land	1869	Main Courthouse

■ **Sarasota** 14 May 1921
2000 Main St., Sarasota, FL 34237
Phone: (941)362-4066
Web site: www.co.sarasota.fl.us/
Parent County: Manatee

Record Type	Year Begun	Jurisdiction
Marriage	1921	Clerk/Circuit Ct.
Probate	1921	Clerk/Circuit Ct.
Court	1921	Clerk/Circuit Ct.
Land	1921	Clerk/Circuit Ct.
Divorce	1945	Clerk/Circuit Ct.
Birth	ca. 1920	Dept./Health
Death	ca. 1920	Dept./Health

■ **Seminole** 25 Apr. 1913
301 N. Park Ave., Sanford, FL 32771
Phone: (407)665-4330
Web site: www.co.seminole.fl.us/
Parent County: Orange

Record Type	Year Begun	Jurisdiction
Divorce	1915	Clerk/Circuit Ct.
Court	1915	Clerk/Circuit Ct.
Land	1915	Clerk/Circuit Ct.
Marriage	na	County Judge
Probate	na	County Judge

■ **St. Johns** 21 July 1821
4010 Lewis Speedway Blvd., P.O. Box 300, Saint Augustine, FL 32085
Phone: (904)823-2333
Web site: www.co.st-johns.fl.us/
Parent County: Original county. Only other original is Escambia.

Record Type	Year Begun	Jurisdiction
Divorce	1900	Clerk/Circuit Ct.
Court	1821	Clerk/Circuit Ct.
Land	1821	Clerk/Circuit Ct.
Marriage	na	Clerk/Circuit Ct.
Probate	na	Clerk/Circuit Ct.

■ **St. Lucie** 24 May 1905
2300 Virginia Ave., Fort Pierce, FL 34982
Phone: (561)462-1400

Web site: www.stlucieco.gov/
Parent County: Brevard

Record Type	Year Begun	Jurisdiction
Marriage	1905	Clerk/Circuit Ct.
Probate	1905	Clerk/Circuit Ct.
Divorce	1905	Clerk/Circuit Ct.
Court	1905	Clerk/Circuit Ct.
Land	1905	Clerk/Circuit Ct.
Death	na	Dept./Health
Burial	na	Dept./Health

■ Sumter 8 Jan. 1853

209 N. Florida St., Bushnell, FL 33513
Phone: (352)793-0200
Web site: http://bocc.co.sumter.fl.us/
Parent County: Marion
Comments/research tips: Clerk of Circuit Courts has delayed Birth records 1943–1972.

Record Type	Year Begun	Jurisdiction
Land	1853	Clerk/Circuit Ct.
Divorce	1900	Clerk/Circuit Ct.
Court	1913	Clerk/Circuit Ct.
Marriage	1853	Clerk/Circuit Ct.
Probate	1856	Clerk/Circuit Ct.

■ Suwannee 21 Dec. 1858

224 Pine Ave., Live Oak, FL 32060
Phone: (940)364-3450
Web site: www.rootsweb.com/~flsuwann/suwannee.htm
Parent County: Columbia

Record Type	Year Begun	Jurisdiction
Marriage	1859	Clerk/Circuit Ct.
Divorce	1859	Clerk/Circuit Ct.
Land	1859	Clerk/Circuit Ct.
Probate	1859	Clerk/Circuit Ct.
Military	1859	Clerk/Circuit Ct.
Court	1859	Clerk/Circuit Ct.
Death	ca. 1900	Dept./Health

■ Taylor 23 Dec. 1856

P.O. Box 620, Perry, FL 32347
Phone: (850)838-3500
Web site: http://perry.gulfnet.com/new_perry/taylor.htm
Parent County: Madison

Record Type	Year Begun	Jurisdiction
Marriage	1908	Clerk/Circuit Ct.
Divorce	1898	Clerk/Circuit Ct.
Land	1857	Clerk/Circuit Ct.
Probate	1941	Clerk/Circuit Ct.
Court	1946	Clerk/Circuit Ct.
Military	1914	Clerk/Circuit Ct.

■ Union 20 May 1921

15 NE First St., Lake Butler, FL 32054
Phone: (904)496-4241
Web site: www.rootsweb.com/~flunion/index.htm
Parent County: Bradford

Record Type	Year Begun	Jurisdiction
Divorce	ca. 1920	Clerk/Circuit Ct.
Court	ca. 1920	Clerk/Circuit Ct.

■ Volusia 29 Dec. 1854

123 W. Indiana, DeLand, FL 32720
Phone: (904)736-5920
Web site: www.volusia.org/
Parent County: Orange

Record Type	Year Begun	Jurisdiction
Marriage	na	Clerk/Circuit Ct.
Divorce	na	Clerk/Circuit Ct.
Court	na	Clerk/Circuit Ct.
Probate	na	Clerk/Circuit Ct.
Land	na	Clerk/Circuit Ct.

■ Wakulla 11 Mar. 1843

Hwy. 319, Crawfordville, FL 32327
Phone: (850)926-0905
Web site: http://mailer.fsu.edu/~rthompso/wakulla.html
Parent County: Leon
Comments/research tips: Courthouse burned in 1896. County Health Deparment has some Birth records.

Record Type	Year Begun	Jurisdiction
Marriage	1896	Clerk/Circuit Ct.
Divorce	1896	Clerk/Circuit Ct.
Probate	1896	Clerk/Circuit Ct.
Court	1896	Clerk/Circuit Ct.
Land	1896	Clerk/Circuit Ct.

■ Walton 29 Dec. 1824

571 E. Nelson Ave., P.O. Box 1260, DeFuniak Springs, FL 32433
Phone: (850)892-8118
Web site: www.rootsweb.com/~flwalton/walton.htm
Parent County: Escambia

Record Type	Year Begun	Jurisdiction
Marriage	1885	Clerk/Circuit Ct.
Probate	1882	Clerk/Circuit Ct.
Divorce	1905	Clerk/Circuit Ct.
Court	1905	Clerk/Circuit Ct.
Land	1905	Clerk/Circuit Ct.
Newspaper	1905	Clerk/Circuit Ct.
Birth	na	Dept./Health
Death	na	Dept./Health

■ Washington 9 Dec. 1825

711 Third St., Chipley, FL 32428
Phone: (850)638-6200
Web site: www.rootsweb.com/~flwashin/
Parent County: Jackson

Record Type	Year Begun	Jurisdiction
Marriage	1890	Clerk/Circuit Ct.
Divorce	1890	Clerk/Circuit Ct.
Probate	1890	Clerk/Circuit Ct.
Land	1890	Clerk/Circuit Ct.
Court	1890	Clerk/Circuit Ct.

Florida

Georgia

By Emily Anne Croom

HISTORICAL OVERVIEW

After the era of French and Spanish exploration in the sixteenth century, Spain claimed the Georgia-Florida area, established missions among coastal Indians, and in 1565 founded the town of St. Augustine in present-day Florida. A century later, Britain chartered the Carolina colony. By the early 1700s, with Spanish settlements to the south and the French to the west in greater Louisiana, Britain wanted to strengthen its presence in the region and provide a buffer against possible attack on Carolina. Thus, in 1732 Britain chartered the Georgia colony to twenty trustees for twenty-one years, and the first settlers founded Savannah in 1733. Early immigrants included English, Welsh, Scottish, and Irish, with some Italian, Portuguese, Swiss, and German settlers. Protestants and Jews were welcome, but not Catholics. Slavery was prohibited until 1749.

When the Georgia trustees relinquished their charter in 1752, Georgia became a royal colony. Thereafter, more settlers arrived from other British colonies, especially Virginia and the Carolinas. In southern Georgia, they found flat-to-rolling coastal plains ripe for plantation agriculture. The northern portion of the state, with highlands and mountains, remained largely Indian lands until the 1830s.

As the thirteen colonies moved toward independence, loyalist feelings were strong in Georgia, and it was the last colony to send representatives to the Continental Congress. The Georgia delegation joined the other twelve colonies in voting for independence in July 1776. During the Revolution, the British occupied both Savannah and Augusta and controlled most of the state. In 1787 Georgia ratified the U.S. Constitution.

As the new nation expanded into its frontiers, Georgians pushed into Indian lands in the state's northeastern region to pursue agriculture and gold. Although gold had

GEORGIA AT A GLANCE

Motto: Wisdom, Justice, and Moderation

Population: 8.18 million

Prevalent Religions: Christianity, particularly Southern Baptist, Lutheran, Pentecostal, and Roman Catholic

Major Industries: Paper products, chemical products, electric equipment, tourism, poultry and eggs, peanuts, cattle, hogs, dairy products, vegetables, textiles and apparel, transportation equipment, food processing

Ethnic Makeup (in percent): Caucasian 65.1%, African American 28.7%, Hispanic 5.3%, Asian 2.1%, Native American 0.3%, Other 2.4%

Famous Georgians: B-52s, Black Crowes, Jim Brown, Erskine Caldwell, Jimmy Carter, Ray Charles, Ty Cobb, Charles Coburn, James Dickey, Lawrence Fishburne, Newt Gingrich, Amy Grant, Joel Chandler Harris, Larry Holmes, Holly Hunter, Indigo Girls, Little Richard, Martin Luther King Jr., Carson McCullers, Johnny Mercer, Margaret Mitchell, Flannery O'Connor, Otis Redding, Burt Reynolds, REM, Julia Roberts, Jackie Robinson, RuPaul, Dean Rusk, Janelle Taylor, Clarence Thomas, Travis Tritt, Alice Walker, Trisha Yearwood

Above: Atlanta's skyline at sunset

© PhotoDisc/Getty Images

been found and reported periodically in Cherokee territory since the sixteenth century, a gold rush began with new discoveries about 1828. The forced removal of thousands of Cherokees from northern Georgia in 1838, during which some four thousand died, became one of several Trails of Tears.

Railroads came to Georgia in the 1830s and gave impetus to some industries, especially textiles. Before the Civil War the core of the state's economy was agriculture, especially cotton cultivation using slave labor. By 1860, 44 percent of Georgia's million people were slaves; 1 percent, foreign-born immigrants.

In January 1861, Georgia joined the Lower South in seceding from the Union, despite a sizeable antisecession minority. Deprivation and destruction characterized the Civil War years, and in September 1864, General Sherman's army destroyed Atlanta as it burned its way toward the coast.

Reconstruction was a period of continued hardship and poverty. By the turn of the twentieth century, Georgia's economy was gradually industrializing, with the growth of logging, mining, and related industries stemming from the state's numerous natural resources. Cotton still fed Georgia's textile industry as it had before the war, but crop diversification encouraged food-processing industries. By the mid-twentieth century, the population and economy were no longer predominantly agricultural; by the 1960 census, the urban population surpassed the rural population of the state.

RECORD HIGHLIGHTS

Statewide birth and death records date from 1919. Check major cities and the state archives for earlier records. Most counties kept marriage records from the county's inception; statewide records date from 1952. For more information, see the Division of Public Health Web site <www.ph.dhr.state.ga.us/programs/vitalrecords/index.html>.

Georgia had a unique system of distributing newly-opened state land by lottery. Eligible state citizens registered in their home county, and drawings in the state capital matched winners with specific newly-surveyed lots. Winners paid a registration fee to claim the land, but many sold their claims. Lotteries were held in 1805, 1807, 1820, 1821, 1827, and 1832 (two drawings). Qualifications and land locations are on the Georgia archives Web site, <www.sos.state.ga.us/archives/rs/lotteries.htm>. Most lottery results have been published; indexes to the state's lottery records are available through the Family History Library.

Although the 1790–1810 federal censuses for Georgia are lost (except for Oglethorpe County, 1800), partial substitutes have been compiled from land, tax, and other

RESEARCH TIPS

for more info

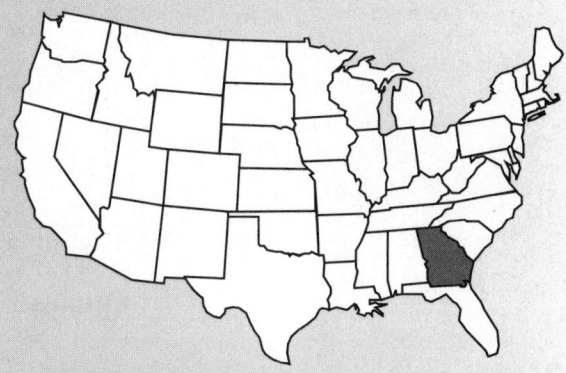

Georgia-specific sources for various counties in various years are available on microfilm at the state archives and often from the Family History Library. They include

- State tax digests, by county, from the 1780s— very important Georgia source
- Poor school and academy lists, fragmentary from the late 1820s to the 1860s
- Civil War salt allotments
- Men subject to military duty, March 1862; men from sixteen to sixty who had not enlisted by the beginning of 1864
- Reconstruction registration oath books and returns of qualified voters, 1867–1868
- Register of "inmates," 1901–1941, and applications of Confederate widows for the Confederate Soldiers' Home of Georgia
- Confederate pension records from 1870
- 1890 federal census for Washington County
- www.segenealogy.com

Census Records

- Federal Census Schedules: 1820 (except Franklin, Rabun and Twiggs Counties), 1830, 1840, 1850, 1860, 1870, 1880, 1900, 1910, 1920, 1930
- Federal Census Soundex: 1880, 1900, 1910, 1920, 1930
- Federal Mortality Schedules for all GA counties available at the Georgia Archives for the years: 1850, 1860, 1870, 1880
- Federal Slave Schedules: 1850, 1860. Schedules name slaveholders but rarely name slaves.
- State Census: 1798–about 1879, various years, various counties

records. Because citizens eligible for the 1805 lottery had to have been in Georgia before mid-1802, those lottery records act as one substitute for the 1800 census. From 1798 to about 1879 Georgia also took septennial censuses, naming heads of household. Surviving records vary by year and county; some are published.

Special African-American resources include numerous slave narratives, microfilmed records of antebellum plantations and industries, and records of Georgia's three branches of the Freedman's Savings and Trust Company (see FHL microfilm 928576-80).

Georgia was originally divided into districts and towns, then into parishes as a royal colony. In 1777 the parishes became the seven original counties. Before 1777 and during British occupation in the American Revolution, the districts and parishes were not governmental entities and did not create books of record. Deed, estate, and other books of record were kept centrally in Savannah. Surviving colonial records have been microfilmed; some abstracts have been published.

Of Georgia's 159 counties, more than a third have suffered varying degrees of record losses due to fires and storms. Nevertheless, check for surviving county records along with family, colonial, local, state, federal, parent county, and neighboring county sources.

STATE RESOURCES

■ ARCHIVES, LIBRARIES, AND SOCIETIES

African-American Family Historical Association, Inc.
P.O. Box 115268, Atlanta, GA 30310

Alma-Bacon Count Historical Society
201 N. Pierce St., Alma, GA 31510
Tel: (912) 632-8450
Fax: (912) 632-4512

Alpharetta Historical Society
P.O. Box 1386, 1835 Old Milton Pkwy., Alpharetta, GA 30004
Tel: (770) 475-4663
E-mail: info@ahsga.org
Web site: <www.ahsga.org>

Andrew College Archives, Pitts Library
413 College St., Cuthbert, GA 39840-1395
Tel: (229) 732-5944
Web site: <www.andrewcollege. edu/NewFiles/academic/ academic1.html>

Appling County Heritage Center, Inc.
209 Thomas St., Baxley, GA 31513
Tel: (912) 367-8133

Aragan Historical Society
P.O. Box 333, Aragon GA, 30104
Tel: (770) 684-3771

Ashantilly Center
P.O. Box 1449, Darien, GA 31305
Tel: (912) 634-0303
E-mail: info@ashantilly.org
Web site: <www.ashantilly.org/ index.htm>

Athens-Clarke County Library
2025 Baxter St., Athens, GA 30606
Tel: (706) 613-3650
Web site: <www.clarke.public.lib .ga.us>

Athens Historical Society
P.O. Box 7745, Athens, GA 30604-7745
Tel: (706) 548-6325

Atlanta-Fulton Public Library
1 Margaret Mitchell Square, Atlanta, GA 30303
Tel: (404) 730-1700
E-mail: Referenceline@co.fulton .ga.us

Web site: <www.af.public.lib.ga
.us>

Atlanta History Center
130 W. Paces Ferry Rd. NW, Atlanta, GA 30305-1366
Fax: (404) 814-2041
Tel: (404) 814-4000
E-mail: Information@AtlantaHistoryCenter.com
Web site: <www.atlantahistorycenter.com>

Augusta Genealogical Society, Inc.
P.O. Box 3743, Augusta, GA
30614-3743
Tel: (706) 722-4073
Web site: <www.augustagensociety.org>

Augusta Museum of History
560 Reynolds St., Augusta, GA
30901
Tel: (706) 722-8454
Fax: (706) 724-5192
E-mail: amh@csra.net
Web site: <www.augustamuseum.org>

Augusta-Richmond County Public Library
902 Greene St., Augusta, GA
30901
Tel: (706) 821-2600
Web site: <www.ecgrl.public.lib.ga.us/rco.htm>

Banks County Historical Society
P.O. Box 473, Homer, GA
30547-0473
Tel: (706) 335-3786
Web site: <www.rootsweb.com/~gabchs/html/>

Barnesville-Lamar County Historical Society
P.O. Box 805, Barnesville, GA
30204
Tel: (770) 358-0150
Fax: (770) 358-5149
Web site: <www.rootsweb.com/~galamar/society.html>

Bartow County Genealogical Society
P.O. Box 993, 425 W. Main St., Cartersville, GA 30512-0993
Tel: (770) 606-0706 or (770) 382-6676
Web site: <www.geocities.com/Heartland/Park/9465/bartowcoga.html/>

Bethesda-Union Society
P.O. Box 13039, Savannah, GA
31416-0039
Tel: (912) 351-2061

Bonaventure Historical Society
1317 E. Fifty-fifth St., Savannah, GA 31404-4615

Brantley County Historical and Preservation Society, Inc.
P.O. Box 1096, Nahunta, GA
31553
Web site: <www.rootsweb.com/~gabrant/branco-home.html>

Bulloch County Historical Society
P.O. Box 42, Statesboro, GA
30459
Tel: (912) 681-1956

Burke County Genealogical Society
536 Liberty St., Waynesboro, GA
30830
Web site: <members.aol.com/J2525/gen.htm>

Byron Area Historical Society
P.O. Box 755, Byron, GA 31008
Tel: (478) 956-3600 or (478)
956-5299

Candler County Historical Society
P.O. Box 325, Metter, GA 30439

Carroll County Genealogical Society
P.O. Box 576, Carrollton, GA
30112
Tel: (770) 832-7746
Web site: <ccgs.westgeorgia.org>

Carroll County Historical Society
P.O. Box 1308, Carrollton, GA
30117
Tel: (765) 564-3152
Fax: (765) 564-6161
E-mail: cchs@dcwi.com
Web site: <dcwi.com/~cchs/cchs.html>

Catoosa County Historical Society
P.O. Box 113, Ringgold, GA
30736
Tel: (706) 935-4875

Catoosa County Library
108 Catoosa Circle, Ringgold, GA
30736
Tel: (706) 965-3600
Web site: <www.whitfield.public.lib.ga.us/catoosa.html>

Central Georgia Genealogical Society
1600 Elberta Rd., P.O. Box 2024, Warner Robins, GA 31099-2024
Web site: <www.ccgs.org>

Chattahoochee Valley Historical Society
1213 Fifth Ave., West Point, GA
31833

Chattooga County Historical Society
P.O. Box 626, Summerville, GA
30747

Cherokee County Historical Society
P.O. Box 1287, Canton, GA
30114
E-mail: info@rockbarn.org
Web site: <www.rockbarn.org>

Cherokee Regional Library, LaFayette-Walker County Library
305 S. Duke St., LaFayette, GA
30728
Tel: (706) 638-2992
Fax: (706) 638-4028
Web site: <www.walker.public.lib.ga.us>

Clark Oconee Genealogical Society
P.O. Box 6403, Athens, GA
30604
Web site: <www.rootsweb.com/~gacogs/>

Clay County Library
208 S. Hancock St., Fort Gaines, GA 39851-0275
Tel: (229) 768-2248

Clayton County Library System, Headquarters Library
865 Battlecreek Rd., Jonesboro, GA 30236
Tel: (770) 473-3850
Web site: <www.clayton.public.lib.ga.us>

Coastal Georgia Historical Society
101 Twelfth St., P.O. Box 21136, St. Simons Island, GA 31522
Tel: (912) 638-4666
Fax: (912) 638-6609
Web site: <www.saintsimonslighthouse.org>

Cobb County Genealogical Society, Inc.
P.O. Box 1413, Marietta, GA
30061-1413
Web site: <www.rootsweb.com/~gaccgs/>

Cobb County Public Library
266 Roswell St., Marietta, GA
30060
Tel: (770) 528-2320
E-mail: 1cobbcat@cobbcat.org

Web site: <http://library.cobbcat.org>

Cobb Landmarks and Historical Society, Inc.
145 Denmead St., Marietta, GA
30060
Tel: (770) 426-4982
Fax: (770) 499-9540
E-mail: clhs2@bellsouth.net
Web site: <www.cobblandmarks.com>

Colquitt County Historical Society
214 Sixteenth Ave. SE, Moultrie, GA 31778
Tel: (229) 985-3413

Coweta County Genealogical Society, Inc.
P.O. Box 1014, Newman, GA
30264
Web site: <members.tripod.com/~CowetaGS/>

Decatur County Historical Society
P.O. Box 682, Bainbridge, GA
31717

Decatur-DeKalb Library
215 Sycamore St., Decatur, GA
30030
Tel: (404) 370-3070
Web site: <www.dekalb.public.lib.ga.us/branches/deca.htm>

DeKalb Historical Society
101 E. Court Square, Decatur, GA
30030
Tel: (404) 373-1088

Delta Genealogical Society
504 McFarland Ave., Rossville, GA 30741-1255
Web site: <www.rootsweb.com/~gadgs/>

Dodge Historical Society, Inc.
5315 Eastman St., Eastman, GA
31023
Tel: (478) 374-4533

Douglas County Genealogical Society
P.O. Box 5667, Douglasville, GA
30154
Tel: (770) 920-1917

Douglas County Historical Society
8562 Campbellton St., P.O. Box 2018, Douglasville, GA 30133

Early County Historical Society
P.O. Box 564, Blakely, GA 31723
Tel: (912) 723-4977

East Georgia Genealogical Society
P.O. Box 117, Winder, GA 30680
E-mail: gaeggs@yahoo.com
Web site: <www.rootsweb.com/~gaeggs/>

Eatonton-Putnam County Historical Society
104 Church St., Eatonton, GA 31024
Tel: (706) 485-6442

Echols County Historical Society
814 Bethel Church Rd., Lake Park, GA 31636
Tel: (229) 559-5230 or (229) 559-7052

Elbert County Historical Society
1 Deadwyler St., P.O. Box 1033, Elberton, GA 30635

Emanuel County Historic Preservation Society
P.O. Box 353, Swainsboro, GA 30401
Tel: (478) 237-7317

Etowah Valley Historical Society
115 W. Cherokee Ave., P.O. Box 1886, Cartersville, GA 30120
Tel: (770) 606-8862
E-mail: evhs@evhsonline.org
Web site: <www.evhsonline.org>

Evans County Historical Society, Inc.
P.O. Box 6, Claxton, GA 30417

Fannin County Ancestral Hunters, GA
Web site: <homepages.rootsweb.com/~fcgs/>

Fayette County Historical Society
P.O. Box 421, Fayetteville, GA 30214
Tel: (770) 716-6020
E-mail: info@historyfayettecoga.org
Web site: <historyfayettecoga.org/index.html>

Flowery Branch Chapter of the Hall County Historical Society
P.O. Box 1994, Flowery Branch, GA 30542
Tel: (770) 641-2308

Foxfire Fund, Inc.
P.O. Box 541, Mountain City, GA 30562-0541
Tel: (706) 746-5828

Fax: (706) 746-5829
E-mail: foxfire@foxfire.org
Web site: <www.foxfire.org>

Franklin County Historical Society
P.O. Box 482, 310 McFarlin Bridge Rd., Carnesville, GA 30521
Tel: (706) 384-4361

Genealogical Center Library
P.O. Box 71343, Marietta, GA 30007-1343
E-mail: gencenlib@aol.com
Web site: <homepages.rootsweb.com/~gencenlb/>

Genealogy Unlimited Society, Lowndes County
P.O. Box 3013, Valdosta, GA 31604-3013
Web site: <www.rootsweb.com/~gagus/>

Georgia Genealogical Society
P.O. Box 54575, Atlanta, GA 30308-0575
Web site: <www.gagensociety.org>

Georgia Historical Society
501 Whitaker St., Savannah, GA 31401
Tel: (912) 651-2125 or
Library Tel: (912) 651-2128
Fax: (912) 651-2831
E-mail: ghslib@georgiahistory.com
Web site: <www.georgiahistory.com>

Georgia Salzburger Society
2980 Ebenezer Rd., Rincon, GA 31326
Tel: (912) 754-7001
E-mail: Info@GeorgiaSalzburgers.com
Web site: <www.georgiasalzburgers.com>

Georgia State Archives
5800 Jonesboro Rd., Morrow, GA 30260
Tel: (678) 364-3700
Web site: <www.georgiaarchives.org>

Georgia State University Library
100 Decatur St. SE, Atlanta, GA 30303-3202
Tel: (404) 651-2422
Web site: <www.library.gsu.edu>

The Georgia Trust
1516 Peachtree St. NW, Atlanta, GA 30309
Tel: (404) 881-9980

Fax: (404) 875-2205
E-mail: info@georgiatrust.org
Web site: <www.georgiatrust.org>

Gordon County Historical Society
335 S. Wall St., Calhoun, GA 30703
Tel: (706) 629-1515

Grady County Historical Society
P.O. Box 586, Cairo, GA 31728

Gilbert H. Gragg Decatur County Library
301 S. Monroe St., Bainbridge, GA 39819
Tel: (229) 248-2665
Fax: (229) 248-2670

Greene County Historical Society
201 Green St., P.O. Box 238, Greensboro, GA 30642
Tel: (706) 453-2588
Fax: (706) 453-4970

Griffin Spalding Historical Society
P.O. Box 196, Griffin, GA 30224
Tel: (770) 229-2432
E-mail: ghisto@bellsouth.net

Guale Historical Society
P.O. Box 398, St. Marys, GA 31558

Gwinnett-Forsyth Regional Library
1001 Lawrenceville Hwy., Lawrenceville, GA 30045-45707
Tel: (770) 822-4522

Gwinnett Historical Society
P.O. Box 261, Lawrenceville, GA 30046
Tel: (770) 822-5174
Fax: (770) 237-5616
E-mail: ghs@gwinnetths.org
Web site: <www.gwinnetths.org>

Hall County Historical Society
380 Green St., Historic District, P.O. Box 2999, Gainesville, GA 30503
Tel: (770) 503-1319
Fax: (770) 536-7072
E-mail: hchsgeorgia@aol.com
Web site: <www.hallcountyhistoricalsociety.org>

Hart County Historical Society
31 E. Howell St., P.O. Box 96, Hartwell, GA 30643
Tel: (706) 376-6330
Fax: (706) 376-1456

Sara Hightower Regional Library
205 Riverside Pkwy. NE, Rome, GA 30161
Tel: (706) 236-4611
Web site: <www.floyd.public.lib.ga.us>

Historic Oglethorpe County, Inc.
P.O. Box 1793, Lexington, GA 30648

Historical Society of Forsyth County, Inc.
P.O. Box 1334, Cumming GA 3028
Web site: <www.rootsweb.com/~gafchs>

Historical Society of the Georgia National Guard, Inc.
P.O. Box 17965, Atlanta, GA 30316-0965
Tel: (404) 624-6061
Web site: <www.hsgng.org>

Huxford Genealogical Society, Inc.
P.O. Box 595, Homerville, GA 31634
Tel: (912) 487-2310
Fax: (912) 487-3881
E-mail: huxford@planttel.net
Web site: <www.huxford.com>

Jefferson County Historical Society, Inc.
P.O. Box 491, Louisville, GA 30434-0491

Jewish Genealogical Society of Georgia, Inc.
2492 Madison Commons, Atlanta, GA 30360
Tel: (404) 822-62803
Web site: <www.jewishgen.org/jgsg/index.htm>

Johnson County Historical Society
Rte. 1, Box 795, Wrightsville, GA 31096

Kennesaw Historical Society, Inc.
% Southern Museum of Civil War and Locomotive History
2829 Cherokee St., Kennesaw, GA 30144
E-mail: khsociety@earthlink.net
Web site: <www.mindspring.com/~robertcjones/khs/khs.htm>

Kennesaw Mountain Historical Association
900 Kennesaw Mountain Dr., Kennesaw, GA 30152

Tel: (770) 422-3696
Fax: (770) 423-1890
E-mail: info@kmha.org
Web site: <www.kmha.org>

Ladson Genealogical Library
% Vidalia-Toombs County Library
610 Jackson St., Vidalia, GA
30474
Tel: (912) 537-8186
Fax: (912) 537-3735
E-mail: ladsonl@mail.toombs.pub
lic.lib.ga.us
Web site: <www.toombs.lib.ga
.us/ladson.htm>

**Lake Blackshear Regional
Library**
307 E. Lamar St., Americus, GA
31709
Tel: (229) 924-8091
Web site: <www.lbrl.org>

**Lake Park Area Historical
Society**
P.O. Box 803, Lake Park, GA
31636-0803
Tel: (229) 559-5771

**Laurens County Historical
Society, Inc.**
P.O. Box 1461, Dublin, GA 31040
Tel: (478) 272-9242
E-mail: history@nlamerica.com
Web site: <http://organizations.
nlamerica.com/historical>

Lee County Historical Society
P.O. Box 393, Leesburg, GA
31763

**Liberty County Historical
Society**
P.O. Box 982, Hinesville, GA
31310

Lincoln County Library
181 N. Peachtree St., Lincolnton,
GA 30817
Tel: (706) 359-4014
Fax: (706) 359-1105
Web site: <www.duesouth.net/
~ecgrl/lincoln/lco.htm>

**Lincoln County Historical
Society, Inc.**
Rte. 4, P.O. Box 222, Lincolnton,
GA 30817

**Lower Altamaha Historical
Society**
P.O. Box 1405, Darien, GA 31305
Tel: (912) 485-2251
Fax: (912) 485-2141

**Lowndes County Historical
Society and Museum**
305 W. Central Ave., P.O. Box
434, Valdosta, GA 31603-0434

Tel: (229) 247-4780
Fax: (229) 247-2840
E-mail: history@valdostamuseum
.org
Web site: <www.valdostamuseu
m.org>

**Lumpkin County Historical
Society**
P.O. Box 894, Dahlonega, GA
30533
Tel: (706) 864-3668

**Macon County Historical
Society**
N. Dooly St., P.O. Box 571, Mon-
tezuma, GA 31063

**Macon, Washington Memorial
Library, Middle Georgia
Archives**
1180 Washington Ave., Macon,
GA 31201
Tel: (478) 744-0851
Web site: <www.co.bibb.ga.us/li
brary/mgarchives.htm>

**Madison County Heritage
Association**
P.O. Box 74, Danielsville, GA
30633
Tel: (706) 795-2017

**Marble Valley Historical
Society**
P.O. Box 815, Jasper, GA 30143
E-mail: mvhs@marblevalley.org
Web site: <www.marblevalley
.org>

**McDonough, The Genealogical
Society of Henry and Clayton
Counties, Inc.**
P.O. Box 1296, McDonough, GA
30253-1296
Tel: (770) 954-1456
E-mail: gensociety@att.net
Web site: <www.rootsweb.com/
~gagshcc/>

**McDuffie County Historical
Society**
635 Hemlock Dr., P.O. Box 1816,
Thomson, GA 30824
Tel: (706) 595-5584
Fax: (706) 595-4710

Meriwether Historical Society
P.O. Box 741, Greenville, GA
30222

**Middle Georgia Historical
Society**
935 High St., P.O. Box 13358,
Macon, GA 31208-3358
Tel: (912) 743-3851

**Monroe County Historical
Society**
E. Johnston St., P.O. Box 401,
Forsyth, GA 31029
Tel: (478) 994-5070

**Morgan County Historical
Society**
277 S. Main St., Madison, GA
30650
Tel: (706) 342-9627

**Moultrie-Colquitt County
Library**
The Odom Library, 204 Fifth St.
SE, Moultrie, GA 31768, P.O. Box
2828, Moultrie, GA 31776
Tel: (229) 985-6540
Fax: (229) 985-0936

Murrell Memorial Library
P.O. Box 606, 531 Second Ave.,
Eastman, GA 31203-6107
Tel: (478) 374-4711
Fax: (478) 374-5716

**Muscogee Genealogical
Society**
P.O. Box 761, Columbus, GA
31902
Web site: <www.muscogeegenea
logy.com>

**National Archives and Records
Administration, Southeast
Region**
1557 St. Joseph Ave., East Point
GA 30344-2593
Tel: (404) 763-7477
Fax: (404) 763-7234
Web site: <www.archives.gov/fa
cilities/ga/atlanta.html>

**Newnan-Coweta Historical
Society**
% Male Academy Museum,
30 Temple Ave., P.O. Box 1001,
Newnan, GA 30263
Tel: (770) 251-0207
Fax: (770) 683-0208
E-mail: nchs@newnanbiz.net
Web site: <www.nchistoricalsoci
ety.org>

**Newton County Historical
Society**
Chamber of Commerce Building
2100 Washington St., P.O. Box
2415, Covington, GA 30210
Tel: (770) 786-7310
Fax: (770) 786-1294

**Northeast Georgia Historical
and Genealogical Society**
P.O. Box 907643 NLS, Gainesville, GA 30501
Tel: (770) 967-3808

**Northwest Georgia Historical
and Genealogical Society**
P.O. Box 5063, Rome, GA 30162
Tel: (706) 236-4607
Fax: (706) 236-4605
Web site: <www.rootsweb.com/
~ganwhags/>

Oconee County Library
1080 Experiment Station Rd.,
Watkinsville, GA 30677
Tel: (706) 769-3950
E-mail: watkinsville@athenslibrar
y.org
Web site: <www.clarke.public.lib
.ga.us/oconee.html>

Okefenokee Heritage Center
1460 N. Augusta Ave., Waycross,
GA 31503
Tel: (912) 285-4260
Fax (912) 283-2858
E-mail: ohc@accessetc.net

Old Capital Historical Society
P.O. Box 4, Milledgeville, GA
31061
Tel: (478) 453-9040 or (478)
452-4637

Old Clinton Historical Society
154 Randolph St., Gray, GA
31032
Tel: (478) 986-3384

**Orphans Cemetery Association,
Inc.**
P.O. Box 4411, Eastman, GA
31023
Tel: (478) 374-2180

**Paulding County Historical
Society**
P.O. Box 333, Dallas, GA 30132

**Peach County Historical
Society**
P.O. Box 889, Fort Valley, GA
31030
Web site: <www.rootsweb.com/
~gapchs/>

Piedmont Regional Library
189 Bell View St., Winder, GA
30680
Tel: (770) 867-2762
Fax: (770) 867-7483
Web site: <library.barrow.public.li
b.ga.us>

**Pierce County Historical and
Genealogical Society**
P.O. Box 443, Blackshear, GA
31516
E-mail: piercecounty@postmark
.net
Web site: <http://piercecounty.
www.50megs.com>

Pine Mountain Regional Library
218 Perry St., P.O. Box 709, Manchester, GA 31816
Tel: (706) 846-2186
Fax: (706) 846-8455
Web site: <www.meriwether.public.lib.ga.us>

Polk County Historical Society
P.O. Box 203, 205 N. College St., Cedartown, GA 30125
Tel: (770) 749-0073
E-mail: polkhist@mindspring.com
Web site: <polkhist.home.mindspring.com/home.htm>

Quitman/Brooks County Historical Museum and Cultural Center
121 North Culpepper St., Quitman, GA 31643
Tel: (229) 263-7080

Rabun County Historical Society
P.O. Box 921, Clayton, GA 30525
Web site: <www.rootsweb.com/~garchs>

Randolph Historical Society
P.O. Box 456, Cuthbert, GA 31740
Tel: (229) 679-5165

Richmond County Historical Society
% Reese Library, Augusta State University
2500 Walton Way, Augusta, GA 30904-2200
Tel: (706) 737-1532
Fax: (706) 667-4415

Richmond Hill Historical Society, Inc.
P.O. Box 381, Richmond Hill, GA 31324
Web site: <www.richmondhillga.com/museum/>

Rockdale County Genealogical Society
954 Green St., Conyers, GA 30012
E-mail: heloisesmith@msn.com

Rockdale County Historical Society
967 Milstead Ave., P.O. Box 351, Conyers, GA 30207
Tel: (770) 483-4398

Rome Area History Museum Archives
305 Broad St., Rome, GA 30161
Tel: (706) 235-8051
Fax: (706) 235-6631

E-mail: info@romehistorymuseum.com
Web site: <www.romehistorymuseum.com>

Roopville Historical Society and Archives
P.O. Box 285, Roopville, GA 30170
Tel: (770) 854-4170 or (770) 854-4460

Roswell Historical Society
617 Atlanta St., Roswell, GA 30075
Tel: (770) 992-1665

Satilla Regional Library
201 S. Coffee Ave., Douglas, GA 31533
Tel: (912) 384-4667

Savannah Area Genealogical Society
P.O. Box 15385, Savannah, GA 31416
Tel: (912) 631-2201
E-mail: admin@savannahgenealogy.org
Web site: <www.savannahgenealogy.org>

Savannah, Live Oak Public Libraries Bull Street Library
2002 Bull St., Savannah, GA 31401
Tel: (912) 652-3600
Fax: (912) 652-3649

Schley County Historical Society
P.O. Box 326, Ellaville, GA 31806

Screven County Library
Sylvania, GA 30467
Tel: (912) 564-7526
Fax: (912) 564-7580
Web site: <www.sjrls.public.lib.ga.us/index.htm>

Seminole County Historical Society
P.O. Box 713, Donalsonville, GA 31759

Smyrna Historical and Genealogical Society
2861 Atlanta St., Smyrna, GA 30082
Web site: <www.rootsweb.com/~gashgs/>

South Georgia Genealogical Society
P.O. Box 246, Ochlocknee, GA 31773

Southwest Georgia Genealogical Society
P.O. Box 4672, Albany, GA 31706
E-mail: swggs@swggs.org
Web site: <www.swgs.org>

Sparta-Hancock County Historical Society
526 Court St., Sparta, GA 31087
Web site: <www.shchs.org>

Statesboro-Bulloch County Library
124 S. Main St., Statesboro, GA 30458
Tel: (912) 764-1340
Web site: <www.srls.public.lib.ga.us>

Stephens County Historical Society
P.O. Box 125, Toccoa, GA 30577
Tel: (706) 282-5055

Taliaferro County Historical Society
P.O. Box 32, Crawfordville, GA 30631
Tel: (706) 456-2776

Tattnall County Historical Society
P.O. Box 2012, Reidsville, GA 30453
Tel: (912) 557-4402

Taylor County Historical-Genealogical Society
P.O. Box 1925, Butler, GA 31006
Tel: (478) 862-3410

Terrell County Restoration Society
P.O. Box 63, Dawson, GA 31742
Tel: (229) 995-2125
Fax: (229) 995-4000

Thomas County Historical Society
725 N. Dawson St., P.O. Box 1922, Thomasville, GA 31799
Tel: (229) 226-7664
Fax: (229) 226-7466
Web site: <home.rose.net/~history/>

Thomaston-Upson Archives
P.O. Box 1137, Thomaston, GA 30286-0015
Tel: (706) 646-2437
E-mail: tuarch@alltell.net
Web site: <home.alltell.net/tuarch/index.htm>

Thomasville Genealogical, History, and Fine Arts Library
135 N. Broad St., Thomasville, GA 31792

Tel: (229) 226-9640
Fax: (229) 226-3199
E-mail: glibrary@rose.net
Web site: <home.rose.net/~glibrary/>

Thronateeska Heritage Center
100 W. Roosevelt Ave., Albany, GA 31701
Tel: (229) 432-6955
Fax: (229) 435-1572
E-mail: info@heritagecenter.org
Web site: <www.heritagecenter.org>

Toombs County Historical Society
P.O. Box 2825, Vidalia, GA 30474
Tel: (912) 537-3477

Towns County Historical and Genealogical Society
P.O. Box 101, Young Harris, GA 30582-0101
Tel: (706) 379-3150

Treutlen County Historical Society
206 Second St. S., Soperton, GA 30457
Tel: (912) 529-6711
Fax: (912) 529-6062

Troup County Historical Society and Archives
136 Main St., P.O. Box 1051, LaGrange, GA 30241
Tel: (706) 884-1828
Fax: (706) 884-1840
E-mail: info@trouparchives.org
Web site: <www.trouparchives.org>

Turner County Historical Society
233 E. College Ave., P.O. Box 766, Ashburn, GA 31714
Tel: (229) 567-3431
Fax: (229) 567-9284

Tybee Island Historical Society
30 Meddin Ave., Tybee Island, GA 31328
Tel: (912) 786-5801

Union County Historical Society
P.O. Box 35, Blairsville, GA 30514-0035
Tel: (706) 745-5493
E-mail: history1@Alltel.net
Web site: <www.ngeorgia.com/uchs.html>

Upson Historical Society
P.O. Box 363, Thomaston, GA 30286
Web site: <www.rootsweb.com/~gauhs>

Georgia

Vienna Historic Preservation Society
% The Walter F. George Law Office Museum
Fourth St., Vienna, GA 31092
Tel: (229) 268-3663
E-mail: vhps@sowega.net
Web site: <www.historicvienna .org>

Walker County Historical Society
305 S. Duke St., P.O. Box 707, LaFayette, GA 30728-2936
Web site: <www.geocities.com/ Heartland/Prairie/6370/walker/ wchs.html>

Walton County Historical Society
P.O. Box 1733, Monroe, GA 30655
Tel: (770) 207-1229

Washington County Historical Society
129 Jones St., P.O. Box 6088, Sandersville, GA 31082
Tel: (478) 552-6965
Fax: (478) 552-1449

Wayne County Historical Society
125 NE Broad St., Jesup, GA 31545-5516
Tel: (912) 427-3233

West Georgia Genealogical Society
% Troup County Archives, P.O. Box 1051, LaGrange, GA 30241

White County Historical Society
P.O. Box 1139, Cleveland, GA 30528
Tel: (706) 865-3225
Web site:

Whitfield-Murray Historical Society, Crown Garden and Archives
715 Chattanooga Ave., Dalton, GA 30720
Tel: (706) 278-0217

Wilkinson County Historical Society
P.O. Box 159, Gordon, GA 31031
Tel: (478) 528-5102 or (478) 946-2723

Wiregrass Genealogical Society
Rte. 3, P.O. Box 2520, Cochran, GA 31014

Web site: <www.rootsweb.com/ ~gawgs/>

Worth County Historical Society
P.O. Box 5040, Sylvester, GA 31791
Tel: (229) 776-3364

BIBLIOGRAPHY

■ GENERAL RESOURCES

African-American Genealogy: A Bibliography and Guide to Sources
by Curt Bryan Witcher (Fort Wayne, IN: Round Tower Books, 2000. Includes white families' papers.)

Ambiguous Lives: Free Women of Color in Rural Georgia, 1789–1879
by Adele Logan Alexander (Fayetteville, AR: University of Arkansas Press, 1991)

A Bibliography of the Writings on Georgia History, 1900–1970 rev. and enl. ed.
by Arthur Ray Rowland and James E. Dorsey (Spartanburg, SC: Reprint Co., 1978)

Biographical Souvenir of the States of Georgia and Florida
(Chicago, IL: F.A. Battey and Company, 1889)

Checklist of Eighteenth Century Manuscripts in the Georgia Historical Society
compiled by Lilla Mills Hawes and Karen Elizabeth Osvald (Savannah, GA: Georgia Historical Society, 1976)

Colonial Georgia Genealogical Data, 1748–1783
by William H. Dumont (Washington: National Genealogical Society, 1971)

The Colonial Records of the State of Georgia
compiled by Allen D. Candler, et al. (Atlanta, GA: state printer, 1904)

Confederate Imprints at the Georgia Historical Society
by Richard Barksdale Harwell (Savannah, GA: Georgia Historical Society, 1975)

Dictionary of Georgia Biography
edited by Kenneth Coleman and Charles Stephen Gurr (Athens,

GA: University of Georgia Press, 1983)

The Federal Road Through Georgia, the Creek Nation, and Alabama, 1806–1836
by Henry deLeon Southerland Jr. and Jerry Elijah Brown; maps by Charles Jefferson Hiers (Tuscaloosa, AL: University of Alabama Press, 1989)

The Fledgling Province: Social and Cultural Life in Colonial Georgia, 1733–1776
by Harold E. Davis (NC: University of North Carolina Press, 1976)

The Genealogist's Companion and Sourcebook, 2d ed.
by Emily Anne Croom (Cincinnati: Betterway Books, 2003)

A Genealogist's Guide to Discovering Your African-American Ancestors
by Franklin Carter Smith and Emily Anne Croom (Cincinnati: Betterway Books, 2003)

Genealogical Encyclopedia of the Colonial Americas
by Christina K. Schaefer (Baltimore: Genealogical Publishing Co., 1998. Pages 549-556, Georgia)

Genealogical Material From Legal Notices in Early Georgia Newspapers
abstracted by Folks Huxford (Easley, SC: Southern Historical Press, 1989)

Georgia Baptists: Historical and Biographical
by Jesse H. Campbell (Macon, GA: J.W. Burke and Co., 1874)

Georgia Bible Records
compiled by Jeannette Holland Austin (Baltimore, MD: Genealogical Pub. Co., 1985)

Georgia Biographical Dictionary: People of all Times and Places Who Have Been Important to the History and Life of the State
(New York: Somerset Publishers, 1994)

The Georgia Black Book: Morbid, Macabre & Sometimes Disgusting Records of Genealogical Value
by Robert Scott Davis Jr. (Easley, SC: Southern Historical Press, 1982–1987)

Georgia Genealogical Gems: A Gathering of Articles Previously Published in the NGSQ
(Washington, DC: National Genealogical Society, 1981)

Georgia Genealogical Research
by George K. Schweitzer (Knoxville, TN: G.K. Schweitzer, 1987)

Georgia Genealogical Research: a Practical Guide
by David H. Robertson (Stone Mountain, GA: D.H. Robertson, 1989)

Georgia Genealogy and Local History: a Bibliography
compiled by James E. Dorsey (Spartanburg, SC: Reprint Co., 1983)

The Georgia Gold Rush: Twenty-Niners, Cherokees, and Gold Fever
by David Williams (Columbia, SC: University of South Carolina Press 1993)

Georgia Governor and Council Journal, 1761–1767
abstracted by Mary Bondurant Warren and Jack Moreland Jones (Athens, GA: Heritage Press, 1992)

Georgia: a Guide to its Towns and Countryside
compiled and written by the Work Projects Administration (Athens, GA: University of Georgia Press, 1940)

Georgia History: a Bibliography
compiled by John Eddins Simpson (Metuchen, NJ: Scarecrow Press, 1976)

Georgia Indian Depredation Claims
edited, arranged, and indexed by Donna B. Thaxton, associate editor: C. Stanton Thaxton, special consultant: Carlton J. Thaxton (Americus, GA: Thaxton Co., ca. 1988)

Georgia Local and Family History Sources in Print,
compiled by Marilyn Adams (Clarkston, GA: Heritage Research, 1982)

Georgia Pioneers Genealogical Magazine, 24 vols.
(Albany, GA: Georgia Pioneers Publications, 1964–1987)

Georgia Sources for Family History
compiled by Robert Holcomb Warnock (Atlanta, GA: Georgia Genealogical Society, 1995)

Georgia Through Two Centuries
edited by E. Merton Coulter (New York: Lewis Historical Pub. Co., ca. 1966)

The Georgians: Genealogies of Pioneer Settlers
compiled by Jeannette Holland Austin (Baltimore, MD: Genealogical Pub. Co., 1984)

Georgians Past: Special Files of Georgia Settlers and Citizens, Subjects and Counties, 1722–1970s
edited by Robert Scott Davis Jr. (Milledgeville, GA: Boyd Pub. Co., 1997)

The Germans of Colonial Georgia, 1733–1783
by George F. Jones (Baltimore, MD: Genealogical Pub. Co., 1986)

Great Georgians
by Zell Miller (Franklin Springs, GA: Advocate Press, 1983)

A Guide to Native American (Indian) Research Sources at the Georgia Department of Archives and History
By Robert Scott Davis Jr. (Jasper, GA: R.S. Davis, 1985)

Guide to Genealogical Research in the National Archives of the United States
edited by Anne Bruner Eales and Robert M. Kvasnicka (Washington, D.C.: National Archives and Records Administration, 2000

Historical Collections of the Georgia Chapters, Daughters of the American Revolution, Vol. 1: Seventeen Georgia Counties
(Atlanta, GA: C.P. Byrd, state printer, 1926)

Historical Collections of Georgia: Containing the Most Interesting Facts, Traditions, Biographical Sketches, Anecdotes, etc., Relating to its History and Antiquities, from its first Settlements to the Present Time
by Rev. George White (New York: Pudney & Russell, 1854)

History of the Baptist Denomination in Georgia
(Atlanta, GA: J.P. Harrison & Co., 1881)

History of Georgia, 4 vols.
by Clark Howell (Chicago-Atlanta: The S.J. Clarke Publishing Co., 1926)

An Index to Georgia Tax Digests
(Spartanburg, SC: Reprint Co., 1986)

Index to Georgia's 1867–1868 Returns of Qualified Voters and Registration Oath Books (White)
compiled by John David Brandenburg and Rita Binkley Worthy (Atlanta, GA: J.D. Brandenburg, 1995)

Joe Brown's Army: the Georgia State Line, 1862–1865
by William Harris Bragg (Macon, GA: Mercer University Press, 1987)

Leon S. Hollingsworth Genealogical Card File
(Atlanta, GA: R.J. Taylor Jr., Foundation, ca. 1979)

A List of the Early Settlers of Georgia
by E. Merton Coulter and Albert B. Saye (Athens, GA: Univ. of Georgia Press, 1949)

Memoirs of Georgia; Containing Historical Accounts of the State's Civil, Military, Industrial, and Professional Interests, and Personal Sketches of Many of its People, 2 vols.
(Atlanta, GA: The Southern Historical Association, 1895)

Men of Mark in Georgia; a Complete and Elaborate History of the State from its Settlement to the Present Time, 6 vols.
by William J. Northen (Atlanta, GA: A.B. Caldwell, 1907–1912)

Methodist Preachers in Georgia, 1783–1900
edited and compiled by Harold Lawrence (Tignall, GA: Boyd Pub. Co., 1984)

The Moravians in Georgia, 1735–1740
by Adelaide L. Fries (Raleigh NC: Edwards & Broughton, 1905)

National Archives Microfilm Catalogs online:
<www.archives.gov/publica tions/genealogy_microfilm_ catalogs.html>

Old Bible Records and Land Lotteries, Published Under the Auspices of the Lucy Cook Peel Memorial Committee
compiled and edited by Lelia Thorton Gentry (Atlanta, GA: Stein Printing Co., 1932)

Pioneers of Wiregrass Georgia; a Biographical Account of some of the Early Settlers of that portion of Wiregrass Georgia Embraced in the Original Counties of Irwin, Appling, Wayne, Camden, and Glynn, 11 vols.
by Folks Huxford (Homerville, GA: 1951–ca. 2002)

Research in Georgia
compiled by Robert Scott Davis Jr. (Greenville, SC: Southern Historical Press, 1981)

A Researcher's Library of Georgia History, Genealogy, and Records Sources, Vol. 1
by Robert Scott Davis Jr. (Easley SC: Southern Historical Press, 1987)

A Researcher's Library of Georgia History, Genealogy, and Records Sources Vol. 2
by Robert Scott Davis, Jr. (Easley SC: Southern Historical Press, 1991)

The Reuben King Journal, 1800–1806
edited by Virginia Steele Wood and Ralph Van Wood (Savannah, GA: Georgia Historical Society, 1971)

The Salzburgers and their Descendants: Being the History of a Colony of German (Lutheran) Protestants
by Philip A. Strobel (Baltimore, MD: T.N. Kurtz, 1855)

The Search for Georgia's Colonial Records
edited by Lilla Mills Hawes and Albert S. Britt Jr. (Savannah, GA: Georgia Historical Society, 1976)

The Seed that was Sown in the Colony of Georgia, the Harvest and the Aftermath, 1740–1870
By Charles Spalding Wylly (New York and Washington: The Neale Publishing Company, 1910)

Some Early Tax Digests of Georgia
collected and edited by Ruth Blair (Atlanta, GA: Department of Archives and History, 1926)

Some Georgia County Records, 10 vols.
Compiled by Silas Emmett Lucas Jr. (Easley, SC: Southern Historical Press, 1977–2002)

A Standard History of Georgia and Georgians
by Lucian Lamar Knight (Chicago, IL: The Lewis Publishing Co., 1917)

The Story of Georgia and the Georgia People, 1732 to 1860, 2d ed.
by George Gillman Smith (Baltimore, MD: Genealogical Pub. Co., 1968)

Whites Among the Cherokees: Georgia 1828–1838
collected and edited by Mary B. Warren and Eve B. Weeks (Danielsville, GA: Heritage Papers, 1987)

■ **CENSUS RECORDS**

1864 Census for Re-Organizing the Georgia Militia
abstracted and compiled by Nancy J. Cornell (Baltimore, MD: Genealogical Pub. Co. 2000)

The American Census Handbook
by Thomas Jay Kemp (Eilmington, DE: Scholary Resources, 2001)

The Census Book: A Genealogist's Guide to Federal Census Facts, Schedules, and Indexes
by William Dollarhide (Bountiful, UT: Heritage Quest, 2000)

Finding Answers in U.S. Census Records
by Loretto Dennis Szucs and Matthew Wright (Orem, UT: Ancestry Pub., 2002)

Map Guide to the U.S. Federal Censuses, 1790–1920
by William Thorndale and William Dollarhide (Baltimore MD: Genealogical Pub. Co., 1987)

The Reconstructed 1790 Census of Georgia: Substitutes for Georgia's Lost 1790 Census
compiled by Marie De Lamar and Elisabeth Rothstein (Baltimore,

MD: Genealogical Pub. Co., 1985)

State Census Records
by Ann S. Lainhart (Baltimore, MD: Genealogical Publishing, 1992)

Your Guide to the Federal Census
by Kathleen W. Hinckley (Cincinnati: Betterway Books, 2002)

■ IMMIGRATION RECORDS

American Naturalization Records, 1790–1990: What They Are and How to Use Them
by John J. Newman (North Salt Lake, UT: HeritageQuest, 1998)

American Passenger Arrival Records
by Michael Tepper (Baltimore: Genealogical Publishing Co., 1993)

The Bench and Bar of Georgia: Memoirs and Sketches
by Stephen Franks Miller (Philadelphia, PA: J.B. Lippincott & Co., 1858)

Federal Naturalization Oaths, Savannah, Georgia, 1790–1860
compiled by Marion R. Hemperley (Georgia Historical Society Quarterly, Vol. 51, no. 4: 1967)

They Became Americans: Finding Naturalization Records and Ethnic Origins
by Loretto Dennis Szucs (Salt Lake City: Ancestry, Inc., 1998)

They Came in Ships: A Guide to Finding Your Immigrant Ancestor's Arrival Records, 2d ed.
by John P. Colletta (Salt Lake City: Ancestry, Inc., 1993)

■ LAND RECORDS

1805 Georgia Land Lottery
transcribed and indexed by Virginia S. Woof and Ralph V. Wood (Cambridge, MA: Greenwood Press, 1964)

1832 Cherokee Land Lottery: Index to Revolutionary Soldiers, Their Widows, and Orphans Who were Fortunate Drawers
compiled by Marian M. Richardson and Jessie J. Mize (Danielsville, GA: Heritage Papers, 1969)

The 1832 Gold Lottery of Georgia: Containing a List of the Fortunate Drawers in Said Lottery
compiled by Silas Emmett Lucas Jr. (Easley SC: Southern Historical Press 1988)

Abstracts of Georgia Land Plat Books A and B, 1779–1785
by Nathan and Kaydee Mathews (Fayetteville, GA: N. and K. Mathews, 1995)

Authentic List of all Land Lottery Grants Made to Veterans of the Revolutionary War by the State of Georgia, 2d ed.
compiled by Alex M. Hitz (Atlanta, GA: Secretary of State of Georgia, 1966)

The Cherokee Land Lottery: Containing a Numerical List of the Names of the Fortunate Drawers in Said Lottery, with an Engraved Map of Each District
by James F. Smith (Greenville, SC: Southern Historical Press, Inc., 1991)

Colonial Plats and Warrants, 1755–1775
(Georgia Surveyor General Dept.: 1755–1775)

Entry of Claims for Georgia Landholders, 1733–1755
compiled by Pat Bryant (Atlanta, GA: State Printing Office, 1975)

The First One Hundred Years of Town Planning in Georgia
by Joan Niles Sears (Atlanta, GA: Cherokee Pub. Co., 1979)

The Fourth or 1821 Land Lottery of Georgia
compiled by Silas Emmett Lucas Jr. (Easley, SC: Southern Historical Press 1986)

The Georgia Land Lottery Papers, 1805–1914: Genealogical Data from the Loose Papers Filed in the Georgia Surveyor General Office, Concerning the Lots Won in the State Land Lotteries and the People Who Won Them
compiled by Robert S. Davis Jr. and Silas Emmett Lucas Jr. (Easley, SC: Southern Historical Press, 1979)

Georgia Land Surveying History and Law
by Farris W. Cadle (Athens, GA: University of Georgia Press, 1991)

The Georgia Surveyor General Department: a History and Inventory of Georgia's Land Office
by Marion R. Hemperley (Atlanta, GA: State Printing Office, 1982)

Index to the Headright and Bounty Grants of Georgia, 1756–1909
(Vidalia, GA: Georgia Genealogical Reprints, 1970)

Land and Property Research in the United States
by E. Wade Hone (Salt Lake City, UT: Ancestry 1997)

Locating Your Roots: Discover Your Ancestors Using Land Records
by Patricia Law Hatcher (Cincinnati: Betterway Books, 2003)

Reprint of Official Register of Land Lottery of Georgia, 1827
(Columbus, GA: Walton-Forbes Co. 1929)

Revolutionary Soldiers' Receipts for Georgia Bounty Grants
by the Georgia State Department of Archives and History (Atlanta, GA: Foote and Davis Company, 1928)

The Second or 1807 Land Lottery of Georgia
compiled by Silas Emmett Lucas, Jr. (Easley, SC: Southern Historical Press, 1986)

The Third or 1820 Land Lottery of Georgia
compiled by Silas Emmett Lucas, Jr. (Easley, SC: Southern Historical Press, 1986)

■ MAPS

Atlas for Georgia History
by James C. Bonner (Milledgeville, GA: Georgia Duplicating Department, 1969)

The Atlas of Georgia
by Thomas W. Hodler and Howard A. Schretter (Athens, GA: Institute of Community and Area Development, University of Georgia, 1986)

Cities, Towns, and Communities of Georgia Between 1847–1962: 8500 Places and the County in which Located
compiled by Marion R. Hemperley (Easley, SC: Southern Historical Press, 1980)

Georgia: Comprising Sketches of Counties, Towns, Events, Institutions, and Persons Arranged in Cyclopedic Form, 4 vols.
edited by Allen D. Candler and Clement A. Evans (Atlanta, GA: State Historical Association, 1906)

Georgia Counties, Their Changing Boundaries, 2d ed.
by Pat Bryant, revised by Ingrid Shields (Atlanta, GA: State Printing Office, 1983)

Georgia Place-names, 1st ed.
by Kenneth K. Krakow (Macon, GA: Winship Press, 1975)

Hall's Original County Map of Georgia: Showing Present and Original Counties and Land Districts
compiled from state records by Hall Brothers, Civil and Mining Engineers, 1895 (Atlanta, GA: Dept. of Archives and History, ca. 1980)

Nineteenth Century Maps in the Collection of the Georgia Surveyor General Department, 1800–1849
compiled by Margaret A. Johnsen (Atlanta, GA: State Printing Office, 1981)

Placenames of Georgia: Essays of John H. Goff
edited by Francis Lee Utley and Marion R. Hemperley (Athens, GA: University of Georgia Press, 1975)

Pre-nineteenth Century Maps in the Collection of the Georgia Surveyor General Department: a Catalog
compiled by Janice Gayle Blake (Atlanta, GA: State Printing Office, 1975)

■ MILITARY RECORDS

Colonial Soldiers of the South, 1732–1774
by Murtie June Clark with an index by Judith McGhan (Baltimore, MD: Genealogical Pub. Co., 1983)

Compendium of the Confederate Armies, 11 vols.
by Stewart Sifakis (New York, NY: Facts on File ca. 1992–ca. 1995)

Georgia

The Confederate Records of the State of Georgia, 6 vols.
compiled by Allen D. Candler (Atlanta, GA: C.P. Byrd, state printer, 1909–1911)

Georgia Citizens and Soldiers of the American Revolution
by Robert S. Davis Jr. (Easley, SC: Southern Historical Press, ca. 1979)

Georgia Civil War Sites
by Jim Miles (Warner Robins, GA: J & R Graphics, ca. 1987)

Georgia Revolutionary War Soldiers' Graves, 2 vols.
compiled by H. Ross Arnold Jr. and H. Clifton Burnham (Athens, GA: Iberian Pub. Co., ca. 1993)

The Georgia State Memorial Book, Adopted as the Official Record by the Military Department, State of Georgia
by Bert E. Boss (American Memorial Publishing Co.: 1921)

Georgia's Roster of the Revolution
compiled by Lucian Lamar Knight (Baltimore, MD: Genealogical Pub. Co., 1967)

Index to War of 1812 Service Records for Volunteer Soldiers from Georgia
abstracted by Judy Swaim Kratovil (Atlanta, GA: J. S. Kratovil, 1986)

Military Certificates of Georgia, 1776–1800, on File in the Surveyor General Department, semiquincentenary ed.
compiled by Marion R. Hemperley (Atlanta, GA: State Printing Office, 1983)

Militiamen, Rangers, and Redcoats: the Military in Georgia, 1754–1776
by James M. Johnson (Macon, GA: Mercer University Press, 1992)

The Revolutionary Records of the State of Georgia
compiled by Allen D. Candler (Atlanta, GA: The Franklin-Turner Company, 1908)

Revolutionary Soldiers' Receipts for Georgia Bounty Grants
issued by the Georgia State Department of Archives and History (Atlanta, GA: Foote and Davies Company, 1928)

Roster of the Confederate Soldiers of Georgia, 1861–1865, 4 vols.
by Georgia State Division of Confederate Pensions and Records (Hapeville, GA: Longino & Porter, 1959–)

Roster of the Confederate Soldiers of Georgia, 1861–1865, 6 vols.
compiled by Lillian Henderson (Hapeville, GA: Longina and Porter, 1959–)

Roster of the Confederate Soldiers of Georgia, 1861–1865: Index
compiled by Juanita S. Brightwell, Eunices S. Lee, Elise C. Fulghum (Spartanburg, SC: Reprint Co., 1982)

Roster of Revolutionary Soldiers in Georgia, 3 vols.
compiled by Mrs. Howard H. McCall (Atlanta, GA: Genealogical Pub. Co., 1968–1969)

A Roster of Spanish American War Soldiers from Georgia
edited and arranged by Carlton J. Thaxton, Donna B. Thaxton, Stan Thaxton (Americus, GA: Thaxton Co., 1984)

Uncle, We Are Ready! Registering America's Men, 1917–1918: A Guide to Researching World War I Draft Registration Cards
by John J. Newman (North Salt Lake, UT: HeritageQuest, 2001)

U.S. Military Records: A Guide to Federal & State Sources, Colonial America to the Present
by James C. Neagles (Salt Lake City: Ancestry, Inc., 1994)

Volunteer Soldiers in the Cherokee War, 1836–1839
(Signal Mountain, TN: Mountain Press, 1995)

World War II: A Family Historian's Guide
by Debra Johnson Knox (Spartanburg, SC: MIE Publishing, 2003)

■ PROBATE RECORDS

Abstracts of Colonial Wills of the State of Georgia, 1733–1777
indexed by Willard E. Wight (Spartanburg, SC: Reprint Co., 1981)

Georgia Intestate Records
compiled by Jeannette Holland Austin (Baltimore, MD: Genealogical Pub. Co., 1986)

Georgia Wills, 1733–1860: an Index of Testators to Wills of Georgia Recorded in Colonial Will Books and in Loose Will Collections, 1733–1777, and Wills Recorded or on File in County and State Offices, 1777–1860
compiled by Ted O. Brooke (Atlanta, GA: Pilgrim Press, 1976)

Index to Georgia Wills
by Jeannette Holland Austin (Baltimore, MD: Genealogical Pub. Co., 1985)

Index to Georgia's Federal Naturalization Records to 1950 (Excluding Military Petitions)
by Linda Woodward Geiger (Bowie, MD: Heritage Books, 1995)

Index to Probate Records of Colonial Georgia, 1733–1778
(Atlanta, GA: R.J. Taylor Jr., Foundation, 1983)

Statutes Enacted by the Royal Legislature of Georgia from its first Session in 1754 to 1768, 3 vols.
compiled and pub. by Allen D. Candler (Atlanta, GA: C.P. Byrd, state printer, 1910–1911)

■ VITAL RECORDS

30,638 Burials in Georgia
by Jeannette Holland Austin (Baltimore, MD: Genealogical Pub. Co., ca. 1995)

37,000 Early Georgia Marriages
by Joseph T. Maddox (Irwinton, GA: J.T. Maddox, 1975)

1850 Georgia Mortality Schedules or Census
compiled and published by Aurora C. Shaw (Jacksonville, FL: Shaw, 1982)

Colonial Georgia Marriage Records from 1760–1810
by Frances T. Ingmire (St. Louis, MO: F.T. Ingmire, ca. 1985)

Early Georgia Marriages, 4 vols.
compiled by Joseph T. Maddox, and Mary Carter (Irwinton, GA: J. T. Maddox, 1975)

Georgia Cemetery Directory and Bibliography of Georgia Cemetery Reference Sources
by Ted O. Brooke (Marietta, GA: T.O. Brooke, ca. 1985)

Georgia Marriages: Early to 1800: a Research Tool
compiled, extracted, and transcribed by Liahona Research, Inc., edited by Jordan R. Dodd (Bountiful, UT: Precision Indexing Publishers, ca. 1990)

Georgia Marriages 1811 Through 1820: Prepared from Extant Legal Records and Published Sources
edited by Mary Bondurant Warren, abstracted by Frances H. Beckemeyer, et al. (Danielsville, GA: Heritage Papers, ca. 1988)

Guide to Public Vital Statistics Records in Georgia
prepared by the Georgia Historical Records Survey, Division of Community Service Programs, Work Projects Administration (Atlanta, GA: The Historical Records Survey, 1941)

Marriages and Deaths, 1820 to 1830: Abstracted from Extant Georgia Newspapers
by Mary Bondurant Warren with Sarah Fleming White (Danielsville, GA: Heritage Papers ca. 1972)

Marriages and Obituaries from Early Georgia Newspapers
abstracted by Folks Huxford (Easley, SC: Southern Historical Press, ca. 1989)

Marriages and Obituaries from the Macon Messenger, 1815–1865
by Willard R. Rocker (Easley, SC: Southern Historical Press, ca. 1988)

Obituaries Published by the Christian Index, 2 vols.
abstracted and edited by Mary Overby (Macon, GA: Georgia Baptist Historical Society, Mercer University, 1975–1982)

Roll of Honor: Names of Soldiers who Died in Defense of the American Union, Interred in the National Cemeteries, 27 vols.
U.S. Quartermaster's Department (Baltimore, MD: Genealogical Pub. Co., 1994)

Georgia

Some Early Epitaphs in Georgia compiled by the Georgia Society of the Colonial Dames of America, with a foreword and sketches by Mrs. Peter W. Meldrim (Durham, NC: The Seeman Printery, Inc., ca. 1924)

Your Guide to Cemetery Research by Sharon DeBartolo Carmack (Cincinnati: Betterway Books, 2002)

■ Appling 15 Dec. 1818
36 S. Main St., Suite B, Baxley, GA 31513
Phone: (912)367-8114
Web site: http://plant.sgc.peachnet.edu/~jbellis/genweb/appling/appling.html
Parent County: Creek Indian Lands
Comments/research tips: Records begin in 1879, some 1859.

Record Type	Year Begun	Jurisdiction
Birth	na	Probate Court
Marriage	1869	Probate Court
Death	na	Probate Court
Burial	na	Probate Court
Divorce	na	Clerk/Superior Ct.
Probate	1879	Clerk/Superior Ct.
Court	1879	Clerk/Superior Ct.
Land	1828	Clerk/Superior Ct.

■ Atkinson 15 Aug. 1917
P.O. Box 855, Pearson, GA 31642
Phone: (912)422-3552
Web site: www.geocities.com/Heartland/Lane/3390/
Parent County: Coffee, Clinch

Record Type	Year Begun	Jurisdiction
Divorce	1919	Clerk/Superior Ct.
Probate	1919	Probate Court
Court	1919	Clerk/Superior Ct.
Birth	1919	Dept./Health
Death	1919	Dept./Health
Marriage	1919	Probate Court
Land	1919	Clerk/Superior Ct.

■ Bacon 1914
P.O. Box 389, Alma, GA 31510
Phone: (912)632-7661
Web site: www.rootsweb.com/~gagenweb/
Parent County: Appling, Pierce, Ware

Record Type	Year Begun	Jurisdiction
Divorce	1919	Clerk/Superior Ct.
Court	1919	Clerk/Superior Ct.
Land	1919	Clerk/Superior Ct.
Birth	1919	Dept./Health
Marriage	1919	Probate Court
Death	1919	Dept./Health
Probate	1919	Probate Court

■ Baker 12 Dec. 1825
P.O. Box 548, Newton, GA 31770
Phone: (229)734-3007
Web site: www.rootsweb.com/~gabaker/
Parent County: Early

Record Type	Year Begun	Jurisdiction
Birth	1919	Dept./Health
Death	1919	Dept./Health
Marriage	1820	Probate Court
Probate	1868	Probate Court
Land	1850	Clerk/Superior Ct.
Divorce	na	Clerk/Superior Ct.
Court	1879	Clerk/Superior Ct.

■ Baldwin 11 May 1803
121 N. Wilkinson St., Suite 109, Milledgeville, GA 31061
Phone: (478)445-4807
Web site: www.genealogy-quest.com/Georgia/Baldwin/
Parent County: Creek Indian Lands

Record Type	Year Begun	Jurisdiction
Birth	1919	Dept./Health
Marriage	1806	Probate Court
Death	1919	Dept./Health
Burial	na	Probate Court
Probate	1808	Probate Court
Divorce	1861	County Clerk
Court	1861	Superior Court
Land	1861	Superior Court

■ Banks 11 Dec. 1858
P.O. Box 7, Homer, GA 30547
Phone: (706)677-6250
Web site: www.rootsweb.com/~gabanks/
Parent County: Franklin, Habersham

Record Type	Year Begun	Jurisdiction
Birth	1919	Dept./Health
Marriage	1859	Probate Court
Probate	1859	Probate Court
Court	1859	Clerk/Superior Ct.
Land	1859	Clerk/Superior Ct.

■ Barrow 7 July 1914
30 N. Broad St., Winder, GA 30680
Phone: (770)307-3045
Web site: www.rootsweb.com/~gabarrow/
Parent County: Jackson, Walton, Gwinnett

Record Type	Year Begun	Jurisdiction
Burial	na	Probate Court
Birth	1919	Dept./Health
Marriage	1915	Probate Court
Death	1919	Dept./Health
Probate	1915	Probate Court
Divorce	1915	Clerk/Superior Ct.
Court	1915	Clerk/Superior Ct.
Land	1915	Clerk/Superior Ct.

■ Bartow 3 Dec. 1832
135 W. Cherokee Ave. Suite 243A, Cartersville, GA 30120
Phone: (770)387-5075
Web site: www.geocities.com/Heartland/Park/9465/bartowcoga.html
Parent County: Cherokee
Comments/research tips: Formerly Cass County. Name changed to Bartow 3 December 1832.

Record Type	Year Begun	Jurisdiction
Birth	1919	Dept./Health

Marriage .... 1836 .... Probate Court
Probate .... 1853 .... Probate Court
Divorce .... 1862 .... Clerk/Superior Ct.
Court .... 1853 .... Clerk/Superior Ct.
Land .... 1837 .... Clerk/Superior Ct.
Military .... na .... Clerk/Superior Ct.

■ Ben Hill   31 July 1906
111 S. Sheridan St., Fitzgerald, GA 31750
Phone: (229)426-5137
Web site: www.benhillcounty.com/
Parent County: Irwin, Wilcox

Record Type	Year Begun	Jurisdiction
Divorce	1907	County Clerk
Court	1906	Clerk/Superior Ct.
Land	1906	Clerk/Superior Ct.
Birth	1919	Dept./Health
Marriage	1906	Probate Judge
Death	1919	Dept./Health
Burial	na	Probate Judge
Probate	1906	Probate Judge

■ Berrien   25 Feb. 1856
101 E. Marion Ave., Suite 2, Nashville, GA 31639
Phone: (229)686-5213
Web site: www.rootsweb.com/~gaberrie/
Parent County: Lowndes, Coffee, Irwin

Record Type	Year Begun	Jurisdiction
Divorce	1856	Clerk/Superior Ct.
Land	1850	Clerk/Superior Ct.
Court	1856	Clerk/Superior Ct.
Birth	1919	Dept./Health
Death	1919	Dept./Health
Marriage	1856	Probate Court
Probate	1855	Probate Court

■ Bibb   9 Dec. 1822
207 Bibb, County Courthouse, P.O. Box 6518, Macon, GA 31208
Phone: (478)749-6400
Web site: www.rootsweb.com/~gabibb/
Parent County: Jones, Monroe, Twiggs, Houston

Record Type	Year Begun	Jurisdiction
Birth	1919	Dept./Health
Death	1919	Dept./Health
Burial	na	Dept./Health
Marriage	1823	Probate Court
Probate	1823	Probate Court
Divorce	1823	County Clerk
Court	1823	Clerk/Superior Ct.
Land	1823	Clerk/Superior Ct.

■ Bleckley   30 July 1912
306 SE Second St., Cochran, GA 31014
Phone: (478)934-3204
Web site: www.rootsweb.com/~gableckl/
Parent County: Pulaski

Record Type	Year Begun	Jurisdiction
Birth	1919	Dept./Health

Marriage .... 1912 .... Probate Court
Death .... 1919 .... Dept./Health
Divorce .... na .... Clerk/Superior Ct.
Probate .... 1912 .... Probate Court
Court .... 1912 .... Clerk/Superior Ct.
Land .... 1912 .... Clerk/Superior Ct.

■ Brantley   14 Aug. 1920
P.O. Box 398, Nahunta, GA 31553-0387
Phone: (912)462-5256
Web site: www.rootsweb.com/~gabrantl/
Parent County: Charlton, Pierce, Wayne

Record Type	Year Begun	Jurisdiction
Marriage	1921	Probate Court
Death	1919	Dept./Health
Land	1921	Clerk/Superior Ct.
Birth	1919	Dept./Health
Divorce	1921	Clerk/Superior Ct.
Probate	1921	Probate Court
Court	1921	Clerk/Superior Ct.

■ Brooks   11 Dec. 1858
P.O. Box 665, Quitman, GA 31643
Phone: (229)263-5567
Web site: www.rootsweb.com/~gabrooks/
Parent County: Lowndes, Thomas

Record Type	Year Begun	Jurisdiction
Land	1857	Clerk/Superior Court
Divorce	na	Clerk of Courts
Court	1859	Clerk/Superior Court
Marriage	1859	Probate Court
Probate	1859	Probate Court
Birth	1919	Dept./Health
Death	1919	Dept./Health

■ Bryan   19 Dec. 1793
Courthouse, P.O. Box 418, Pembroke, GA 31321
Phone: (912)653-3856
Web site: www.rootsweb.com/~gabryan/
Parent County: Effingham, Chatham

Record Type	Year Begun	Jurisdiction
Marriage	1865	Probate Court
Probate	1790	Probate Court
Birth	1919	Dept./Health
Death	1919	Dept./Health
Divorce	1920	County Clerk
Court	1794	Clerk/Superior Court
Land	1793	Clerk/Superior Court

■ Bulloch   8 Feb. 1796
P.O. Box 1005, Statesboro, GA 30459
Phone: (912)489-8749
Web site: www.rootsweb.com/~gabulloc/
Parent County: Bryan, Screven

Record Type	Year Begun	Jurisdiction
Birth	1919	Dept./Health
Marriage	1796	Probate Court
Probate	1816	Probate Court
Divorce	1891	Clerk/Superior Ct.

Court .... 1806 .... Clerk/Superior Ct.
Land .... 1796 .... Clerk/Superior Ct.

■ Burke 5 Feb. 1777
111 E. Sixth St., P.O. Box 322, Waynesboro, GA 30830
Phone: (770)554-3000
Web site: members.aol.com/J2525/index.html
Parent County: Original county organized from St. George Parish
Comments/research tips: Courthouse burned in January 1856. All records prior to that date destroyed.

Record Type	Year Begun	Jurisdiction
Land	1843	Clerk/Superior Ct.
Court	1856	Clerk/Superior Ct.
Birth	1919	Dept./Health
Death	1919	Dept./Health
Marriage	1855	Probate Court
Probate	1856	Probate Court

■ Butts 24 Dec. 1825
25 Third St., Suite 7, Jackson, GA 30233
Phone: (770)775-8204
Web site: www.rootsweb.com/~gabutts/
Parent County: Henry, Monroe

Record Type	Year Begun	Jurisdiction
Birth	1919	Dept./Health
Marriage	1826	Probate Court
Death	1919	Dept./Health
Probate	1826	Probate Court
Divorce	1825	Clerk/Superior Ct.
Court	1826	Clerk/Superior Ct.
Land	1825	Clerk/Superior Ct.

■ Calhoun 20 Feb. 1854
P.O. Box 87, Morgan, GA 31766
Phone: (229)849-2115
Web site: members.tripod.com/~rakmun/
Parent County: Baker, Early

Record Type	Year Begun	Jurisdiction
Divorce	1854	Clerk/Superior Ct.
Land	1854	Clerk/Superior Ct.
Military	1854	Clerk/Superior Ct.
Court	1854	Clerk/Superior Ct.
Birth	1919	Dept./Health
Marriage	1854	Probate Court
Death	1919	Dept./Health
Burial	na	Probate Court
Probate	1854	Probate Court

■ Camden 5 Feb. 1777
P.O. Box 818, Woodbine, GA 31569-0000
Phone: (912)576-3785
Web site: www.rootsweb.com/~gacamden/
Parent County: Original county organized from St. Thomas and St. Mary Parishes
Comments/research tips: Fire 1870, few records lost.

Record Type	Year Begun	Jurisdiction
Divorce	na	Clerk/Superior Ct.
Court	1790	Clerk/Superior Ct.

Land	1773	Clerk/Superior Ct.
Birth	1919	Dept./Health
Marriage	1819	Probate Court
Death	1919	Dept./Health
Probate	1795	Probate Court

■ Campbell 20 Dec. 1828
Web site: www.rootsweb.com/~gacampbe/
Parent County: Carroll, Coweta, De Kalb, Fayette
Comments/research tips: (See Fulton) Merged into Fulton County 1 January 1932.

■ Candler 1914
Courthouse Square, Metter, GA 30439
Phone: (912)685-2357
Web site: www.rootsweb.com/~gacandle/
Parent County: Bulloch, Emanuel, Tattnall

Record Type	Year Begun	Jurisdiction
Probate	1915	Probate Court
Birth	1919	Dept./Health
Marriage	1915	Probate Court
Death	1919	Dept./Health
Divorce	1914	County Clerk
Court	1915	Clerk/Superior Court
Land	1915	Clerk/Superior Court

■ Carroll 11 Dec. 1826
Courthouse, Room 204, Carrollton, GA 30117
Phone: (770)830-5840
Web site: www.rootsweb.com/~gacarrol/
Parent County: Creek Indian Lands
Comments/research tips: 1828 Confederate Pension Applications with Clerk of Superior Court.

Record Type	Year Begun	Jurisdiction
Divorce	1900	Clerk/Superior Ct.
Land	1827	Clerk/Superior Ct.
Court	1827	Clerk/Superior Ct.
Marriage	1827	Probate Court
Probate	1827	Probate Court
Birth	1919	Dept./Health
Death	1919	Dept./Health

■ Cass 1832
Web site: www.geocities.com/Heartland/Park/9465/bartowcoga.html
Parent County: Cherokee
Comments/research tips: (See Bartow) Name changed to Bartow 6 December 1861.

■ Catoosa 5 Dec. 1853
875 LaFayette St., Ringgold, GA 30736
Phone: (706)935-3511
Web site: www.rootsweb.com/~gacatoos/
Parent County: Walker, Whitfield

Record Type	Year Begun	Jurisdiction
Court	1853	Clerk/Superior Ct.
Divorce	1853	Clerk/Superior Ct.
Land	1853	Clerk/Superior Ct.
Marriage	1853	Probate Court
Probate	1853	Probate Court

Georgia

■ Charlton 18 Feb. 1854
100 S. Third St., Folkston, GA 31537
Phone: (912)496-2230
Web site: www.rootsweb.com/~gacharlt/
Parent County: Camden
Comments/research tips: Courthouse burned in 1877.

Record Type	Year Begun	Jurisdiction
Birth	1919	Dept./Health
Marriage	1854	Probate Court
Death	1919	Dept./Health
Burial	na	Probate Judge
Probate	1878	Probate Court
Divorce	1877	Clerk/Superior Ct.
Court	1879	Clerk/Superior Ct.
Land	1878	Clerk/Superior Ct.

■ Chatham 5 Feb. 1777
133 Montgomery St., Room 509 Savannah, GA 31412
Phone: (912)652-7264
Web site: www.rootsweb.com/~gachatha/
Parent County: Original county organized from St. Phillip and Christ Church Parishes

Record Type	Year Begun	Jurisdiction
Birth	1919	Dept./Health
Marriage	1806	Probate Court
Death	1919	Dept./Health
Probate	1777	Probate Court
Divorce	1783	Clerk/Superior Ct.
Court	1783	Clerk/Superior Ct.
Land	1785	Clerk/Superior Ct.
Nat.	1801	Clerk/Superior Ct.

■ Chattahoochee 13 Feb. 1854
P.O. Box 219, Cusseta, GA 31805
Phone: (706)989-3603
Web site: www2.netdoor.com/~cch/CHA/
Parent County: Muscogee, Marion

Record Type	Year Begun	Jurisdiction
Marriage	1854	Probate Court
Probate	1854	Probate Court
Birth	1919	Dept./Health
Death	1919	Dept./Health
Divorce	1854	Clerk/Superior Ct.
Court	1854	Clerk/Superior Ct.
Land	1854	Clerk/Superior Ct.

■ Chattooga 28 Dec. 1838
P.O. Box 467, Summerville, GA 30747
Phone: (706)857-0709
Web site: www.rootsweb.com/~gachatto/
Parent County: Floyd, Walker

Record Type	Year Begun	Jurisdiction
Land	1839	Clerk/Superior Ct.
Divorce	ca. 1900	Clerk/Courts
Court	1839	Clerk/Superior Ct.
Birth	1919	Dept./Health
Marriage	1839	Probate Court
Death	1919	Dept./Health
Burial	na	Ordinary Office
Probate	1839	Probate Court

■ Cherokee 26 Dec. 1831
90 North St., Canton, GA 30114-2794
Phone: (770)479-0538
Web site: www.rootsweb.com/~gacherok/
Parent County: Cherokee Lands

Record Type	Year Begun	Jurisdiction
Divorce	1833	Clerk/Superior Ct.
Court	1832	Clerk/Superior Ct.
Land	1833	Clerk/Superior Ct.
Birth	1919	Dept./Health
Marriage	1841	Probate Court
Death	1919	Dept./Health
Burial	na	Probate Court
Probate	1833	Probate Court

■ Clarke 5 Dec. 1801
325 E. Washington St., Room 215, Athens, GA 30601
Phone: (706)613-3320
Web site: www.rootsweb.com/~gaclarke/
Parent County: Jackson

Record Type	Year Begun	Jurisdiction
Divorce	1801	Clerk/Superior Ct.
Land	1801	Clerk/Superior Ct.
Court	1801	Clerk/Superior Ct.
Military	1922	Clerk/Superior Ct.
Birth	1919	Dept./Health
Death	1919	Dept./Health
Marriage	1801	Probate Court
Probate	1801	Probate Court

■ Clay 16 Feb. 1854
210 S. Washington, P.O. Box 498, Fort Gaines, GA 39851
Phone: (229)768-2445
Web site: www.rootsweb.com/~gaclay/
Parent County: Early, Randolph

Record Type	Year Begun	Jurisdiction
Marriage	1854	Probate Court
Probate	1854	Probate Court
Court	1854	Clerk/Superior Ct.
Divorce	na	Clerk/Superior Ct.
Land	1854	Clerk/Superior Ct.

■ Clayton 30 Nov. 1858
Courthouse, Annex 3, 121 S. McDonough St., Jonesboro, GA 30236
Phone: (770)477-3299
Web site: www.rootsweb.com/~gaclayto/
Parent County: Fayette, Henry

Record Type	Year Begun	Jurisdiction
Birth	1919	Dept./Health
Marriage	1859	Probate Court
Death	1919	Dept./Health
Probate	1859	Probate Court
Divorce	1859	Clerk/Superior Ct.
Land	1859	Clerk/Superior Ct.
Court	1859	Clerk/Superior Ct.

■ Clinch 14 Feb. 1850
P.O. Box 364, Homerville, GA 31634
Phone: (912)487-5523

Georgia

Web site: www.rootsweb.com/~gaclinch
Parent County: Ware, Lowndes
Comments/research tips: All records burned in 1856 and 1867.

Record Type	Year Begun	Jurisdiction
Birth	1919	Dept./Health
Death	1919	Dept./Health
Marriage	1867	Probate Court
Probate	1867	Probate Court
Divorce	1867	Clerk/Superior Ct.
Court	1868	Clerk/Superior Ct.
Land	1868	Clerk/Superior Ct.
Voters List	1890	Clerk/Superior Ct.
Newspapers	1895	Clerk/Superior Ct.

■ Cobb   3 Dec. 1832
32 Waddell St., Marietta, GA 30060
Phone: (770)528-1990
Web site: www.rootsweb.com/~gacobb/
Parent County: Cherokee
Comments/research tips: Fire in 1864, records lost.

Record Type	Year Begun	Jurisdiction
Birth	1919	Dept./Health
Marriage	1865	Probate Court
Death	1919	Dept./Health
Probate	1865	Probate Court
Land	1865	Clerk/Superior Ct.
Divorce	na	Clerk/Superior Ct.
Court	1865	Clerk/Superior Ct.

■ Coffee   9 Feb. 1854
109 S. Peterson Ave., Douglas, GA 31533
Phone: (912)384-5213
Web site: www.geocities.com/Heartland/Prairie/5941/
Parent County: Clinch, Irwin, Ware, Telfair
Comments/research tips: Clerk of Superior Court has some Military Discharge records from 1919.

Record Type	Year Begun	Jurisdiction
Divorce	1854	Clerk/Superior Ct.
Court	1854	Clerk/Superior Ct.
Land	1854	Clerk/Superior Ct.
Marriage	1854	Probate Court
Probate	1854	Probate Court
Birth	1919	Dept./Health
Death	1919	Dept./Health

■ Colquitt   25 Feb. 1856
P.O. Box 264, Moultrie, GA 31776
Phone: (912)891-7400
Web site: www.rootsweb.com/~gacolqu2/
Parent County: Lowndes, Thomas
Comments/research tips: Fire in 1881, records lost.

Record Type	Year Begun	Jurisdiction
Birth	1919	Dept./Health
Marriage	1881	Probate Court
Death	1919	Dept./Health
Probate	1881	Probate Court
Divorce	na	Clerk/Superior Ct.
Court	1881	Clerk/Superior Ct.
Land	1881	Clerk/Superior Ct.

■ Columbia   10 Dec. 1790
P.O. Box 525, Appling, GA 30802
Phone: (760)541-1254
Web site: www.rootsweb.com/~gacolumb/
Parent County: Richmond

Record Type	Year Begun	Jurisdiction
Land	1790	Clerk/Superior Ct.
Court	1790	Clerk/Superior Ct.
Divorce	1945	Clerk of Courts
Birth	1919	Dept./Health
Marriage	1787	Probate Court
Death	1919	Dept./Health
Probate	1790	Probate Court

■ Cook   30 July 1918
212 N. Hutchinson Ave., Adel, GA 31620
Phone: (229)896-3941
Web site: www.rootsweb.com/~gacook/
Parent County: Berrien

Record Type	Year Begun	Jurisdiction
Divorce	1919	Clerk/Superior Ct.
Land	1919	Clerk/Superior Ct.
Court	1919	Clerk/Superior Ct.
Birth	1919	Dept./Health
Marriage	1919	Probate Court
Death	1919	Dept./Health
Probate	1919	Probate Court

■ Coweta   11 Dec. 1826
200 Court Sq., Newnan, GA 30263
Phone: (770)254-2690
Web site: www.rootsweb.com/~gacoweta/
Parent County: Creek Indian Lands

Record Type	Year Begun	Jurisdiction
Birth	1919	Dept./Health
Death	1919	Dept./Health
Marriage	1828	Probate Court
Probate	1828	Probate Court
Divorce	1828	Clerk/Superior Ct.
Court	1828	Clerk/Superior Ct.
Land	1827	Clerk/Superior Ct.

■ Crawford   9 Dec. 1822
P.O. Box 1028, Roberta, GA 31078
Phone: (478)836-3313
Web site: www.rootsweb.com/~gacrawfo/
Parent County: Houston

Record Type	Year Begun	Jurisdiction
Marriage	1823	Probate Court
Probate	1830	Probate Court
Divorce	1850	Clerk/Superior Ct.
Court	1830	Clerk/Superior Ct.
Land	1830	Clerk/Superior Ct.

■ Crisp   17 Aug. 1905
210 Seventh St. S., Cordele, GA 31015
Phone: (229)276-2616
Web site: www.rootsweb.com/~gacrisp/
Parent County: Dooly

Record Type	Year Begun	Jurisdiction
Divorce	1905	Clerk/Superior Ct.
Court	1905	Clerk/Superior Ct.
Land	1905	Clerk/Superior Ct.
Marriage	1905	Probate Court
Probate	1905	Probate Court
Birth	1919	Dept./Health
Death	1919	Dept./Health

■ **Dade** 25 Dec. 1837
P.O. Box 605, Trenton, GA 30752
Phone: (706)657-4414
Web site: www.rootsweb.com/~gadade/
Parent County: Walker

Record Type	Year Begun	Jurisdiction
Marriage	1866	Probate Court
Divorce	na	County Clerk
Court	1854	Clerk/Superior Ct.
Land	1849	Clerk/Superior Ct.

■ **Dawson** 3 Dec. 1857
25 Tucker Ave., Suite 102, Dawsonville, GA 30534
Phone: (706)344-3580
Web site: www.rootsweb.com/~gadawson/
Parent County: Lumpkin, Gilmer

Record Type	Year Begun	Jurisdiction
Burial	1858	Probate Court
Probate	1858	Probate Court
Divorce	1857	Clerk/Superior Ct.
Court	1858	Clerk/Superior Ct.
Land	1858	Clerk/Superior Ct.
Birth	1919	Dept./Health
Marriage	1858	Probate Court
Death	1919	Dept./Health

■ **De Kalb** 9 Dec. 1822
Courthouse, Decatur, GA 30030
Phone: (404)371-2718
Web site: www.rootsweb.com/~gadekalb/
Parent County: Fayette, Gwinett, Henry
Comments/research tips: Courthouse burned 1842 and 1916.

Record Type	Year Begun	Jurisdiction
Divorce	1842	Clerk/Superior Ct.
Court	1842	Clerk/Superior Ct.
Land	1842	Clerk/Superior Ct.
Marriage	1842	Probate Court
Probate	1842	Probate Court

■ **Decatur** 8 Dec. 1823
P.O. Box 234, Bainbridge, GA 31718
Phone: (229)248-3016
Web site: www.rootsweb.com/~gadecatu/
Parent County: Early

Record Type	Year Begun	Jurisdiction
Marriage	1824	Probate Court
Probate	1823	Probate Court
Divorce	1823	Clerk/Superior Ct.
Court	1823	Clerk/Superior Ct.
Land	1823	Clerk/Superior Ct.

■ **Dodge** 26 Oct. 1870
5401 Anson Ave., Eastman, GA 31023
Phone: (478)374-2871
Web site: www.rootsweb.com/~gadodge/
Parent County: Montgomery, Pulaski, Telfair

Record Type	Year Begun	Jurisdiction
Birth	1919	Dept./Health
Marriage	1871	Probate Court
Death	1919	Dept./Health
Probate	1871	Probate Court
Divorce	na	Clerk/Superior Ct.
Court	1871	Clerk/Superior Ct.
Land	1871	Clerk/Superior Ct.

■ **Dooly** 15 May 1821
P.O. Box 326, Vienna, GA 31092
Phone: (229)268-4234
Web site: www.rootsweb.com/~gadooly/
Parent County: Creek Indian Lands
Comments/research tips: Fire destroyed early records.

Record Type	Year Begun	Jurisdiction
Divorce	1846	Clerk/Superior Ct.
Court	1847	Clerk/Superior Ct.
Land	1847	Clerk/Superior Ct.
Birth	1919	Dept./Health
Marriage	1846	Probate Court
Death	1919	Dept./Health
Burial	na	Probate Court
Probate	1847	Probate Court

■ **Dougherty** 15 Dec. 1853
225 Pine Ave., Albany, GA 31701
Phone: (229)431-2198
Web site: www.rootsweb.com/~gadoughe/
Parent County: Baker

Record Type	Year Begun	Jurisdiction
Divorce	1856	Clerk/Superior Ct.
Court	1854	Clerk/Superior Ct.
Land	1854	Clerk/Superior Ct.
Birth	1919	Dept./Health
Marriage	1854	Probate Court
Death	1919	Dept./Health
Probate	1849	Probate Court

■ **Douglas** 17 Oct. 1870
8700 Hospital Dr., Douglasville, GA 30134
Phone: (770)920-7252
Web site: www.rootsweb.com/~gadougla/
Parent County: Carroll, Campbell

Record Type	Year Begun	Jurisdiction
Birth	1919	Dept./Health
Marriage	1871	Probate Court
Death	1919	Dept./Health
Probate	1871	Probate Court
Divorce	1870	Clerk/Superior Ct.
Court	1871	Clerk/Superior Ct.
Land	1871	Clerk/Superior Ct.

■ **Early** 15 Dec. 1818
P.O. Box 849, Blakely, GA 31723
Phone: (229)723-3033

Web site: www.rootsweb.com/~gaearly/
Parent County: Creek Indian Lands
Comments/research tips: Many records lost, first marriage book 1854.

Record Type	Year Begun	Jurisdiction
Marriage	1820	Probate Court
Probate	1824	Probate Court
Cemetery	na	Clerk of Courts
Divorce	na	Clerk of Courts
Land	1821	Clerk/Superior Ct.
Military	na	Clerk of Courts
Court	1820	Clerk/Superior Ct.

■ **Echols**   13 Dec. 1858
P.O. Box 213, Statenville, GA 31648
Phone: (229)559-5642
Web site: www.rootsweb.com/~gaechols/
Parent County: Clinch, Lowndes
Comments/research tips: Most records burned 1897.

Record Type	Year Begun	Jurisdiction
Marriage	1898	Probate Court
Probate	1897	Probate Court
Divorce	na	Clerk/Superior Ct.
Court	1898	Clerk/Superior Ct.
Land	1897	Clerk/Superior Ct.

■ **Effingham**   5 Feb. 1777
901 N. Pine St., Springfield, GA 31329
Phone: (912)754-2118
Web site: www.rootsweb.com/~gaeffing/
Parent County: Original county organized from St. Mathew and St. Phillip Parishes
Comments/research tips: Some records lost in Civil War and fire 1890.

Record Type	Year Begun	Jurisdiction
Land	1786	Clerk/Superior Ct.
Birth	1919	Dept./Health
Death	1919	Dept./Health
Marriage	1791	Probate Court
Probate	1796	Probate Court
Divorce	1777	Clerk/Superior Ct.
Court	1791	Clerk/Superior Ct.

■ **Elbert**   10 Dec. 1790
12 S. Oliver St., Elberton, GA 30635
Phone: (706)283-2005
Web site: www.arches.uga.edu/~laaron/
Parent County: Wilkes

Record Type	Year Begun	Jurisdiction
Divorce	1790	Clerk/Superior Ct.
Court	1791	Clerk/Superior Ct.
Land	1791	Clerk/Superior Ct.
Cemetery	1790	Clerk/Superior Ct.
Military	1922	Clerk/Superior Ct.
Birth	1919	Dept./Health
Marriage	1791	Probate Court
Death	1919	Dept./Health
Burial	na	Probate Court
Probate	1791	Probate Court

■ **Emanuel**   10 Dec. 1812
201 W. Main St., P.O. Box 627, Swainsboro, GA 30401
Phone: (478)237-8911
Web site: www.rootsweb.com/~gaemanue/
Parent County: Montgomery, Bulloch

Record Type	Year Begun	Jurisdiction
Birth	1919	Dept./Health
Marriage	1812	Probate Court
Death	1919	Dept./Health
Probate	1812	Probate Court
Divorce	1812	Clerk/Superior Ct.
Court	1810	Clerk/Superior Ct.
Land	1812	Clerk/Superior Ct.

■ **Evans**   11 Aug. 1914
123 W. Main St., Claxton, GA 30417-0000
Phone: (912)739-3868
Web site: www.rootsweb.com/~gaevans/
Parent County: Bulloch, Tattnall

Record Type	Year Begun	Jurisdiction
Birth	1919	Dept./Health
Marriage	1915	Probate Court
Death	1919	Dept./Health
Burial	na	Probate Court
Probate	1915	Probate Court
Divorce	1915	Clerk/Superior Ct.
Court	1915	Clerk/Superior Ct.
Land	1915	Clerk/Superior Ct.

■ **Fannin**   21 Jan. 1854
420 W. Main St., P.O. Box 1300, Blue Ridge, GA 30513
Phone: (706)632-2039
Web site: www.rootsweb.com/~gafannin/
Parent County: Gilmer, Union

Record Type	Year Begun	Jurisdiction
Birth	1919	Dept./Health
Marriage	1854	Probate Court
Death	1919	Dept./Health
Probate	1854	Probate Court
Divorce	1854	Clerk/Superior Ct.
Court	1854	Clerk/Superior Ct.
Land	1854	Clerk/Superior Ct.

■ **Fayette**   15 May 1821
One Center Drive, Fayetteville, GA 30214
Phone: (770)716-4290
Web site: www.rootsweb.com/~gafayett/
Parent County: Creek Indian Lands

Record Type	Year Begun	Jurisdiction
Birth	1919	Dept./Health
Marriage	1823	Probate Court
Death	1919	Dept./Health
Probate	1823	Probate Court
Divorce	na	Clerk/Superior Ct.
Court	1823	Clerk/Superior Ct.
Land	1823	Clerk/Superior Ct.

■ **Floyd**   3 Dec. 1832
3 Government Plaza, Rome, GA 30161
Phone: (706)291-5190

Georgia

Web site: www.rootsweb.com/~gafloyd/
Parent County: Cherokee

Record Type	Year Begun	Jurisdiction
Marriage	1834	Probate Court
Probate	1837	Probate Court
Divorce	1883	Clerk/Superior Ct.
Court	1840	Clerk/Superior Ct.
Land	1840	Clerk/Superior Ct.

■ **Forsyth** 3 Dec. 1832
100 Courthouse Sq., Cumming, GA 30040
Phone: (770)781-2120
Web site: www.rootsweb.com/~gaforsyt/
Parent County: Cherokee

Record Type	Year Begun	Jurisdiction
Land	1832	Clerk/Superior Ct.
Divorce	na	Clerk of Courts
Court	1832	Clerk/Superior Ct.
Birth	1919	Dept./Health
Marriage	1833	Probate Court
Death	1919	Dept./Health
Probate	1832	Probate Court

■ **Franklin** 25 Feb. 1784
Courthouse Sq., P.O. Box 207, Carnesville, GA 30521
Phone: (706)384-2403
Web site: www.rootsweb.com/~gafrankl/
Parent County: Cherokee Indian Lands
Comments/research tips: Some records prior to 1850 in Georgia State Archives.

Record Type	Year Begun	Jurisdiction
Marriage	1806	Probate Court
Probate	1786	Probate Court
Divorce	1900	Clerk/Superior Ct.
Court	1786	Clerk/Superior Ct.
Land	1786	Clerk/Superior Ct.

■ **Fulton** 20 Dec. 1853
136 Pryor St. SW, Atlanta, GA 30303
Phone: (404)730-5313
Web site: www.rootsweb.com/~gafulton/
Parent County: De Kalb, Campbell, Milton

Record Type	Year Begun	Jurisdiction
Marriage	1854	Probate Court
Probate	1854	Probate Court
Divorce	1854	Clerk/Superior Ct.
Court	1854	Clerk/Superior Ct.
Land	1854	Clerk/Superior Ct.

■ **Gilmer** 3 Dec. 1832
1 Westside Sq., Ellijay, GA 30540
Phone: (706)635-4462
Web site: www.rootsweb.com/~gagilmer/
Parent County: Cherokee

Record Type	Year Begun	Jurisdiction
Birth	1919	Dept./Health
Death	1919	Dept./Health
Marriage	1836	Probate Court
Probate	1833	Probate Court

Divorce	1909	Clerk/Superior Ct.
Land	1833	Clerk/Superior Ct.
Military	1902	Clerk/Superior Ct.
Court	1833	Clerk/Superior Ct.

■ **Glascock** 19 Dec. 1857
62 E. Main St., Gibson, GA 30810
Phone: (706)598-2084
Web site: www.rootsweb.com/~gaglasco/
Parent County: Warren

Record Type	Year Begun	Jurisdiction
Court	1858	Clerk/Superior Ct.
Land	1858	Clerk/Superior Ct.
Birth	1919	Dept./Health
Marriage	1858	Probate Court
Death	1919	Dept./Health
Probate	1858	Probate Court
Divorce	na	Clerk/Superior Ct.

■ **Glynn** 5 Feb. 1777
701 H St., Brunswick, GA 31520
Phone: (912)554-7272
Web site: www.rootsweb.com/~gaglynn/
Parent County: Original county organized from St. David and St. Patrick Parishes
Comments/research tips: Clerk of Superior Courts has Land records. Records 1824-1829 burned, all records to 1818 damaged.

Record Type	Year Begun	Jurisdiction
Marriage	1818	Probate Court
Probate	1792	Probate Court
Divorce	1792	Clerk/Superior Ct.
Court	1810	Clerk/Superior Ct.

■ **Gordon** 13 Feb. 1850
100 Wall St., Suite 102, Calhoun, GA 30701
Phone: (706)629-9533
Web site: www.rootsweb.com/~gagordon/
Parent County: Bartow (Cass), Floyd
Comments/research tips: Records destroyed 1864.

Record Type	Year Begun	Jurisdiction
Court	1850	Clerk/Superior Ct.
Land	1850	Clerk/Superior Ct.
Birth	1919	Dept./Health
Marriage	1864	Probate Court
Death	1919	Dept./Health
Burial	na	Probate Court
Probate	1856	Probate Court
Divorce	1864	Clerk/Superior Ct.

■ **Grady** 17 Aug. 1905
250 N. Broad St., Cairo, GA 31728
Phone: (229)377-4621
Web site: www.rootsweb.com/~gagrady/
Parent County: Decatur, Thomas

Record Type	Year Begun	Jurisdiction
Marriage	1906	Probate Court
Probate	1906	Probate Court
Divorce	1906	Clerk/Superior Ct.

Court .... 1906 .... Clerk/Superior Ct.
Land .... 1906 .... Clerk/Superior Ct.

■ **Greene**   3 Feb. 1786
113 N. Main, Greensboro, GA 30642
Phone: (706)453-3340
Web site: www.rootsweb.com/~gagreene
Parent County: Washington

Record Type	Year Begun	Jurisdiction
Marriage	1805	Probate Court
Death	1919	Dept./Health
Probate	1785	Probate Court
Divorce	1790	Clerk/Superior Ct.
Court	1785	Clerk/Superior Ct.
Land	1785	Clerk/Superior Ct.
Birth	1919	Dept./Health

■ **Gwinnett**   15 Dec. 1818
P.O. Box 880, Lawrenceville, GA 30046
Phone: (770)822-8100
Web site: www.rootsweb.com/~gagwinne/
Parent County: Cherokee Lands
Comments/research tips: Courthouse burned 1871, few records saved.

Record Type	Year Begun	Jurisdiction
Marriage	1871	Probate Court
Probate	1818	Probate Court
Divorce	na	Clerk/Superior Ct.
Court	1858	Clerk/Superior Ct.
Land	1871	Clerk/Superior Ct.

■ **Habersham**   15 Dec. 1818
555 Monroe St. Unit 35, Clarkesville, GA 30523
Phone: (706)754-2923
Web site: www.rootsweb.com/~gahabers/
Parent County: Cherokee Indian Lands

Record Type	Year Begun	Jurisdiction
Marriage	1824	Probate Court
Probate	1819	Probate Court
Birth	1919	Dept./Health
Death	1919	Dept./Health
Divorce	1819	Clerk/Superior Ct.
Court	1819	Clerk/Superior Ct.
Land	1819	Clerk/Superior Ct.

■ **Hall**   15 Dec. 1818
116 Spring St., Gainesville, GA 30501
Phone: (770)531-6925
Web site: www.rootsweb.com/~gahall/
Parent County: Cherokee Indian Lands
Comments/research tips: Tornado destroyed courthouse in 1936, most records lost, except deeds.

Record Type	Year Begun	Jurisdiction
Divorce	1900	Clerk/Superior Ct.
Court	1819	Clerk/Superior Ct.
Land	1819	Clerk/Superior Ct.
Marriage	1819	Probate Court
Probate	1819	Probate Court

■ **Hancock**   17 Dec. 1793
P.O. Box 451, Sparta, GA 31087
Phone: (706)444-6644
Web site: www.rootsweb.com/~gahancoc/index.html
Parent County: Greene, Washington

Record Type	Year Begun	Jurisdiction
Birth	1919	Dept./Health
Death	1919	Dept./Health
Marriage	1806	Probate Court
Probate	1794	Probate Court
Divorce	1919	Clerk/Superior Ct.
Court	1794	Clerk/Superior Ct.
Land	1794	Clerk/Superior Ct.

■ **Haralson**   26 Jan. 1856
P.O. Box 849, Buchanan, GA 30113
Phone: (770)646-2005
Web site: www.rootsweb.com/~gaharals/
Parent County: Carroll, Polk

Record Type	Year Begun	Jurisdiction
Birth	1919	Dept./Health
Marriage	1856	Probate Court
Death	1919	Dept./Health
Burial	na	Probate Court
Probate	1856	Probate Court
Divorce	na	Clerk/Superior Ct.
Court	1856	Clerk/Superior Ct.
Land	1856	Clerk/Superior Ct.

■ **Harris**   14 Dec. 1827
P.O. Box 528, Hamilton, GA 31811-0528
Phone: (706)628-4944
Web site: www.rootsweb.com/~gaharris/
Parent County: Muscogee, Troup

Record Type	Year Begun	Jurisdiction
Marriage	1828	Probate Court
Probate	1828	Probate Court
Land	1828	Clerk/Superior Ct.
Divorce	1927	Clerk/Superior Ct.
Court	1828	Clerk/Superior Ct.
Birth	1919	Dept./Health
Death	1919	Dept./Health

■ **Hart**   7 Dec. 1853
P.O. Box 386, Hartwell, GA 30643
Phone: (706)376-7189
Web site: www.geocities.com/RainForest/9478/hartcoga.html
Parent County: Elbert, Franklin

Record Type	Year Begun	Jurisdiction
Birth	1919	Dept./Health
Marriage	1856	Probate Court
Death	1919	Dept./Health
Burial	na	Probate Court
Probate	1856	Probate Court
Divorce	1856	Clerk/Superior Ct.
Court	1856	Clerk/Superior Ct.
Land	1856	Clerk/Superior Ct.

Georgia

Heard 22 Dec. 1830

P.O. Box 249, Franklin, GA 30217
Phone: (770)675-3301
Web site: www.rootsweb.com/~gaheard/
Parent County: Carroll, Coweta, Troup
Comments/research tips: Fire in 1894.

Record Type	Year Begun	Jurisdiction
Land	1894	Clerk/Superior Ct.
Court	1894	Clerk/Superior Ct.
Birth	1919	Dept./Health
Death	1919	Dept./Health
Marriage	1886	Probate Court
Probate	1894	Probate Court

Henry 15 May 1821

One Courthouse Sq., McDonough, GA 30253
Phone: (770)954-2121
Web site: www.rootsweb.com/~gahenry/
Parent County: Creek Indian Lands

Record Type	Year Begun	Jurisdiction
Marriage	1822	Probate Court
Probate	1822	Probate Court
Divorce	1821	Clerk/Superior Ct.
Court	1822	Clerk/Superior Ct.
Land	1822	Clerk/Superior Ct.

Houston 15 May 1821

201 Perry Pkwy., Perry, GA 31069
Phone: (478)218-4720
Web site: www.rootsweb.com/~gahousto/
Parent County: Creek Indian Lands

Record Type	Year Begun	Jurisdiction
Birth	1919	Dept./Health
Death	1919	Dept./Health
Marriage	1822	Probate Court
Probate	1822	Probate Court
Divorce	1822	Clerk/Superior Ct.
Court	1822	Clerk/Superior Ct.
Land	1822	Clerk/Superior Ct.

Irwin 15 Dec. 1818

202 S. Irwin Ave., Ocilla, GA 31774
Phone: (229)468-5138
Web site: www.geocities.com/Heartland/Plains/2604/Irwnx.htm
Parent County: Creek Indian Lands

Record Type	Year Begun	Jurisdiction
Divorce	1821	Clerk/Superior Ct.
Land	1821	Clerk/Superior Ct.
Court	1820	Clerk/Superior Ct.
Military	1900	Clerk/Superior Ct.
Birth	1919	Dept./Health
Marriage	1838	Probate Court
Death	1919	Dept./Health
Burial	1920	Probate Court
Probate	1821	Probate Court

Jackson 11 Feb. 1796

P.O. Box 78, Jefferson, GA 30549
Phone: (706)367-6360
Web site: www.rootsweb.com/~gajackso/
Parent County: Franklin

Record Type	Year Begun	Jurisdiction
Court	1796	Clerk/Superior Ct.
Land	1796	Clerk/Superior Ct.
Probate	1796	Probate Court
Marriage	1805	Probate Court
Birth	1919	Dept./Health
Death	1919	Dept./Health
Tax	1800	Clerk/Superior Ct.

Jasper 10 Dec. 1807

Courthouse, Monticello, GA 31064
Phone: (706)468-4903
Web site: www.rootsweb.com/~gajasper/
Parent County: Baldwin
Comments/research tips: Formerly Randolph County. Name changed to Jasper 10 December 1812.

Record Type	Year Begun	Jurisdiction
Marriage	1808	Probate Court
Probate	1809	Probate Court
Land	1808	Clerk/Superior Ct.
Divorce	1900	Clerk/Superior Ct.
Military	1900	Clerk/Superior Ct.
Court	1808	Clerk/Superior Ct.

Jeff Davis 18 Aug. 1905

14 Jeff Davis St., P.O. Box 429, Hazlehurst, GA 31539
Phone: (912)375-6615
Web site: plant.sgc.peachnet.edu/~jbellis/genweb/jeffdavis/jd.html
Parent County: Appling, Coffee

Record Type	Year Begun	Jurisdiction
Marriage	1905	Probate Court
Probate	1905	Probate Court
Divorce	1905	Clerk/Superior Ct.
Court	1905	Clerk/Superior Ct.
Land	1905	Clerk/Superior Ct.

Jefferson 20 Feb. 1796

202 E. Broad St., P.O. Box 151, Louisville, GA 30434
Phone: (478)625-7922
Web site: members.aol.com/J2525/jeff.htm
Parent County: Burke, Warren, Montgomery, Washington

Record Type	Year Begun	Jurisdiction
Land	1865	Clerk/Superior Ct.
Court	1796	Clerk/Superior Ct.
Divorce	ca.1900	Clerk of Courts
Marriage	1803	Probate Court
Probate	1796	Probate Court
Birth	1919	Dept./Health
Death	1919	Dept./Health

Jenkins 17 Aug. 1905

Harvey St., P.O. Box 659, Millen, GA 30442
Phone: (478)982-4683
Web site: www.lineages.com/usa/ga/JenkinsCounty.html
Parent County: Bullock, Burke, Emanuel, Screven

Record Type	Year Begun	Jurisdiction
Marriage	1905	Probate Court

Probate .... 1905 .... Probate Court
Divorce .... 1905 .... Clerk/Superior Ct.
Court .... 1905 .... Clerk/Superior Ct.
Land .... 1905 .... Clerk/Superior Ct.

■ Johnson 11 Dec. 1858

P.O. Box 264, Wrightsville, GA 31096
Phone: (478)864-3484
Web site: www.rootsweb.com/~gajohnso/
Parent County: Emanuel, Laurens, Washington

Record Type	Year Begun	Jurisdiction
Marriage	1859	Probate Court
Probate	1859	Probate Court
Divorce	1858	Clerk/Superior Ct.
Court	1859	Clerk/Superior Ct.
Land	1859	Clerk/Superior Ct.

■ Jones 10 Dec. 1807

P.O. Box 1359, Gray, GA 31032-1359
Phone: (478)986-6668
Web site: www.lineages.com/usa/ga/JonesCounty.html
Parent County: Baldwin

Record Type	Year Begun	Jurisdiction
Birth	1919	Dept./Health
Death	1919	Dept./Health
Marriage	1811	Probate Court
Probate	1808	Probate Court
Land	1808	Clerk/Superior Ct.
Court	1808	Clerk/Superior Ct.

■ Kinchafoonee 16 Dec. 1853

Parent County: Stewart
Comments/research tips: (See Webster) Name changed to Webster 21 February 1856.

■ Lamar 17 Aug. 1920

326 Thomaston St., Barnesville, GA 30204
Phone: (770)358-5145
Web site: www.rootsweb.com/~galamar/
Parent County: Monroe, Pike

Record Type	Year Begun	Jurisdiction
Marriage	1921	Probate Court
Birth	1921	Dept./Health
Death	1921	Dept./Health
Divorce	1921	Clerk/Superior Ct.
Court	1921	Clerk/Superior Ct.
Land	1921	Clerk/Superior Ct.

■ Lanier 7 Aug. 1920

100 Main St., Lakeland, GA 31635
Phone: (912)482-3594
Web site: www.rootsweb.com/~galanier/
Parent County: Berrien, Lowndes, Clinch

Record Type	Year Begun	Jurisdiction
Divorce	1921	Clerk/Superior Ct.
Court	1921	Clerk/Superior Ct.
Land	1921	Clerk/Superior Ct.
Birth	1919	Dept./Health
Marriage	1921	Probate Court

Death .... 1919 .... Dept./Health
Probate .... 1921 .... Probate Court

■ Laurens 10 Dec. 1807

101 N. Jefferson St., Dublin, GA 31040
Phone: (478)272-3210
Web site: www.rootsweb.com/~galauren/
Parent County: Wilkinson

Record Type	Year Begun	Jurisdiction
Marriage	1809	Probate Court
Probate	1808	Probate Court
Divorce	1807	Clerk/Superior Ct.
Court	1808	Clerk/Superior Ct.
Land	1807	Clerk/Superior Ct.
Birth	1919	Dept./Health
Death	1919	Dept./Health

■ Lee 11 Dec. 1826

P.O. Box 597, Leesburg, GA 31763
Phone: (229)579-6018
Web site: www.rootsweb.com/~galee/
Parent County: Creek Indian Lands
Comments/research tips: Courthouse fire 1858, all records lost.

Record Type	Year Begun	Jurisdiction
Land	1858	Clerk/Superior Ct.
Probate	1858	Probate Court
Marriage	1867	Probate Court
Divorce	na	Clerk/Superior Ct.
Court	1858	Clerk/Superior Ct.

■ Liberty 5 Feb. 1777

Courthouse Sq., Hinesville, GA 31313
Phone: (912)876-3625
Web site: www.rootsweb.com/~galibert/
Parent County: Original county organized from St. Andrew, St. James and St. John Parishes

Record Type	Year Begun	Jurisdiction
Marriage	1784	Probate Court
Probate	1784	Probate Court
Birth	1919	Dept./Health
Death	1927	Dept./Health
Divorce	1756	Clerk of Courts
Court	1784	Clerk/Superior Ct.
Land	1784	Clerk/Superior Ct.

■ Lincoln 20 Feb. 1796

210 Humphrey St., P.O. Box 340, Lincolnton, GA 30817
Phone: (706)359-5505
Web site: www.rootsweb.com/~galincol/
Parent County: Wilkes

Record Type	Year Begun	Jurisdiction
Birth	1919	Dept./Health
Marriage	1796	Probate Court
Death	1919	Dept./Health
Probate	1796	Probate Court
Divorce	1796	Clerk/Superior Ct.
Court	1796	Clerk/Superior Ct.
Land	1796	Clerk/Superior Ct.

Georgia

■ **Long** 14 Aug. 1920
49 S. McDonald St., Ludowici, GA 31316
Phone: (912)545-2123
Web site: www.rootsweb.com/~usgenweb/ga/long.htm
Parent County: Liberty

Record Type	Year Begun	Jurisdiction
Birth	1919	Dept./Health
Marriage	1920	Probate Court
Death	1919	Dept./Health
Burial	na	Probate Court
Probate	1920	Probate Court
Divorce	1920	Clerk/Superior Ct.
Court	1920	Clerk/Superior Ct.
Land	1920	Clerk/Superior Ct.
Adoption	1920	Clerk/Superior Ct.

■ **Lowndes** 23 Dec. 1825
P.O. Box 1349, Valdosta, GA 31601
Phone: (229)333-5126
Web site: www.rootsweb.com/~galownde/
Parent County: Irwin

Record Type	Year Begun	Jurisdiction
Marriage	1870	Probate Court
Probate	1862	Probate Court
Divorce	1858	Clerk/Superior Ct.
Court	1862	Clerk/Superior Ct.
Land	1858	Clerk/Superior Ct.

■ **Lumpkin** 3 Dec. 1832
99 Courthouse Hill, Suite D, Dahlonega, GA 30533
Phone: (706)864-3736
Web site: www.rootsweb.com/~galumpki/
Parent County: Cherokee, Habersham, Hall

Record Type	Year Begun	Jurisdiction
Birth	1919	Dept./Health
Marriage	1833	Probate Court
Death	1919	Dept./Health
Burial	na	Probate Court
Probate	1833	Probate Court
Divorce	1833	Clerk/Superior Ct.
Court	1833	Clerk/Superior Ct.
Land	1833	Clerk/Superior Ct.

■ **Macon** 14 Dec. 1837
121 N. Sumter St., P.O. Box 337, Oglethorpe, GA 31068
Phone: (478)472-7661
Web site: www.rootsweb.com/~gamacon/index.html
Parent County: Houston, Marion
Comments/research tips: Courthouse burned 1857, all records were lost.

Record Type	Year Begun	Jurisdiction
Divorce	na	Clerk/Superior Ct.
Court	1856	Clerk/Superior Ct.
Land	1857	Clerk/Superior Ct.
Marriage	1858	Probate Court
Probate	1857	Probate Court
Birth	1919	Dept./Health
Death	1919	Dept./Health

■ **Madison** 5 Dec. 1811
91 Albany Ave., Danielsville, GA 30633
Phone: (706)795-3352
Web site: www.rootsweb.com/~gamadiso/
Parent County: Clarke, Elbert, Franklin, Jackson, Oglethorpe

Record Type	Year Begun	Jurisdiction
Birth	1919	Dept./Health
Marriage	1812	Probate Court
Death	1919	Dept./Health
Burial	na	Probate Court
Probate	1811	Probate Court
Divorce	1812	Clerk/Superior Ct.
Court	1812	Clerk/Superior Ct.
Land	1812	Clerk/Superior Ct.

■ **Marion** 14 Dec. 1827
P.O. Box 41, Buena Vista, GA 31803
Phone: (229)649-7321
Web site: www.vitalrec.com/ga.html
Parent County: Lee, Muscogee
Comments/research tips: Courthouse fire 1845, all records lost.

Record Type	Year Begun	Jurisdiction
Divorce	na	Clerk/Superior Ct.
Court	1846	Clerk/Superior Ct.
Land	1846	Clerk/Superior Ct.

■ **McDuffie** 18 Oct. 1870
337 Main St., P.O. Box 101, Thomson, GA 30824
Phone: (706)595-2134
Web site: www.rootsweb.com/~gamcduff/
Parent County: Columbia, Warren

Record Type	Year Begun	Jurisdiction
Birth	1919	Dept./Health
Marriage	1871	Probate Court
Death	1919	Dept./Health
Probate	1871	Probate Court
Divorce	1872	Clerk/Superior Ct.
Court	1871	Clerk/Superior Ct.
Land	1871	Clerk/Superior Ct.

■ **McIntosh** 19 Dec. 1793
P.O. Box 1661, Darien, GA 31305
Phone: (912)437-6641
Web site: www.rootsweb.com/~gamcinto/
Parent County: Liberty
Comments/research tips: Many records lost during Civil War, courthouse fire 1931.

Record Type	Year Begun	Jurisdiction
Marriage	1873	Probate Court
Divorce	na	Clerk/Superior Ct.
Court	1873	Clerk/Superior Ct.
Probate	1873	Probate Court
Land	1873	Clerk/Superior Ct.

■ **Meriwether** 14 Dec. 1827
P.O. Box 608, Greenville, GA 30222
Phone: (706)672-4416
Web site: bellsouthpwp.net/m/s/msaffold/meriweth.htm

Georgia

Parent County: Troup

Record Type	Year Begun	Jurisdiction
Birth	1919	Dept./Health
Marriage	1828	Probate Court
Death	1919	Dept./Health
Probate	1825	Probate Court
Divorce	1827	Clerk/Superior Ct.
Court	1828	Clerk/Superior Ct.
Land	1827	Clerk/Superior Ct.

■ Miller 26 Feb. 1856

155 S. First St., Colquitt, GA 31737
Phone: (229)758-4102
Web site: www.rootsweb.com/~gamiller/
Parent County: Baker, Early
Comments/research tips: Courthouse fire 1873, all records lost.

Record Type	Year Begun	Jurisdiction
Birth	1919	Dept./Health
Marriage	1893	Probate Court
Death	1950	Dept./Health
Probate	1873	Probate Court
Land	1873	Clerk/Superior Ct.
Divorce	na	Clerk/Superior Ct.
Court	1873	Clerk/Superior Ct.

■ Milton 18 Dec. 1847

Web site: www.vitalsearch-ca.com/gen/ga/ga_.htm
Parent County: Cherokee, Cobb, Forsyth
Comments/research tips: (See Fulton) Merged into Fulton County 1 January 1832.

■ Mitchell 21 Dec. 1857

P.O. Box 427, Camilla, GA 31730
Phone: (229)336-2022
Web site: www.rootsweb.com/~gamitche/
Parent County: Baker
Comments/research tips: Courthouse fire 1869, Superior Court records and some other records were saved.

Record Type	Year Begun	Jurisdiction
Marriage	1867	Probate Court
Probate	1858	Probate Court
Land	1858	Clerk/Superior Ct.
Divorce	1857	Clerk/Superior Ct.
Court	1858	Clerk/Superior Ct.

■ Monroe 15 May 1821

P.O. Box 187, Forsyth, GA 31029
Phone: (478)994-7036
Web site: www.rootsweb.com/~gamonroe/
Parent County: Creek Indian Lands

Record Type	Year Begun	Jurisdiction
Marriage	1824	Probate Court
Probate	1824	Probate Court
Birth	1919	Dept./Health
Death	1919	Dept./Health
Court	1824	Clerk/Superior Ct.
Land	1822	Clerk/Superior Ct.
Divorce	na	Clerk/Superior Ct.

■ Montgomery 19 Dec. 1793

P.O. Box 311, Mount Vernon, GA 30445
Phone: (912)583-4401
Web site: plant.sgc.peachnet.edu/~jbellis/genweb/
montgomery/montgomery.html
Parent County: Washington
Comments/research tips: Most original records prior to 1890 are in State Archives.

Record Type	Year Begun	Jurisdiction
Birth	1919	Dept./Health
Death	1919	Dept./Health
Marriage	1807	Probate Court
Probate	1806	Probate Court
Divorce	1800	Clerk/Superior Ct.
Court	1794	Clerk/Superior Ct.
Land	1793	Clerk/Superior Ct.

■ Morgan 10 Dec. 1807

Courthouse, Madison, GA 30650
Phone: (706)343-6500
Web site: www.rootsweb.com/~gamorgan/
Parent County: Baldwin

Record Type	Year Begun	Jurisdiction
Birth	1919	Dept./Health
Marriage	1808	Probate Court
Death	1919	Dept./Health
Burial	na	Probate Court
Probate	1808	Probate Court
Divorce	1807	Clerk/Superior Ct.
Court	1808	Clerk/Superior Ct.
Land	1807	Clerk/Superior Ct.

■ Murray 3 Dec. 1832

121 N. Third Ave., Chatsworth, GA 30705
Phone: (706)695-2932
Web site: www.rootsweb.com/~gamurray/
Parent County: Cherokee

Record Type	Year Begun	Jurisdiction
Birth	1919	Dept./Health
Death	1919	Dept./Health
Marriage	1842	Probate Court
Probate	1840	Probate Court
Court	1833	Clerk/Superior Ct.

■ Muscogee 11 Dec. 1826

P.O. Box 1340, Columbus, GA 31902
Phone: (706)653-4333
Web site: www.rootsweb.com/~gamuscog/
Parent County: Creek Indian Lands

Record Type	Year Begun	Jurisdiction
Marriage	1838	Probate Court
Probate	1838	Probate Court
Divorce	1838	Clerk/Superior Ct.
Court	1838	Clerk/Superior Ct.
Land	1838	Clerk/Superior Ct.

■ Newton 24 Dec. 1821

1132 Usher St., Covington, GA 30014
Phone: (770)784-2050

Web site: www.rootsweb.com/~ganewton/
Parent County: Henry, Jasper, Walton

Record Type	Year Begun	Jurisdiction
Marriage	1822	Probate Court
Death	1819	Dept./Health
Probate	1822	Probate Court
Divorce	1822	Clerk/Superior Ct.
Court	1822	Clerk/Superior Ct.
Land	1822	Clerk/Superior Ct.
Military	1917	Clerk/Superior Ct.

■ Oconee 25 Feb. 1875
P.O. Box 54, Watkinsville, GA 30677
Phone: (706)769-3936
Web site: www.rootsweb.com/~gaoconee/
Parent County: Clarke

Record Type	Year Begun	Jurisdiction
Birth	1919	Dept./Health
Marriage	1875	Probate Court
Death	1919	Dept./Health
Probate	1875	Probate Court
Divorce	1875	Clerk/Superior Ct.
Court	1875	Clerk/Superior Ct.
Land	1875	Clerk/Superior Ct.

■ Oglethorpe 19 Dec. 1793
P.O. Box 70, Lexington, GA 30648
Phone: (706)743-5350
Web site: www.rootsweb.com/~gaogleth/
Parent County: Wilkes
Comments/research tips: Courthouse fire 1941.

Record Type	Year Begun	Jurisdiction
Birth	1919	Dept./Health
Marriage	1795	Probate Court
Death	1919	Dept./Health
Probate	1794	Probate Court
Divorce	1794	Clerk/Superior Ct.
Court	1794	Clerk/Superior Ct.
Land	1794	Clerk/Superior Ct.

■ Paulding 3 Dec. 1832
25 Courthouse Sq., Dallas, GA 30132
Phone: (770)445-7541
Web site: www.rootsweb.com/~gapauldi/
Parent County: Cherokee

Record Type	Year Begun	Jurisdiction
Marriage	1833	Probate Court
Probate	1850	Probate Court
Divorce	1876	Clerk/Superior Ct.
Court	1859	Clerk/Superior Ct.
Land	1848	Clerk/Superior Ct.

■ Peach 18 July 1924
P.O. Box 327, Fort Valley, GA 31030
Phone: (478)825-2313
Web site: www.rootsweb.com/~gapeach/
Parent County: Houston, Macon

Record Type	Year Begun	Jurisdiction
Birth	1925	Dept./Health
Marriage	1925	Probate Court
Death	1925	Dept./Health
Probate	1925	Probate Court
Divorce	1925	Clerk/Superior Ct.
Court	1925	Clerk/Superior Ct.
Land	1925	Clerk/Superior Ct.

■ Pickens 5 Dec. 1853
50 N. Main St., Jasper, GA 30143
Phone: (706)253-8756
Web site: www.marblevalley.org/research.htm
Parent County: Cherokee, Gilmer

Record Type	Year Begun	Jurisdiction
Birth	1919	Dept./Health
Marriage	1854	Probate Court
Death	1919	Dept./Health
Burial	na	Probate Court
Probate	1854	Probate Court
Divorce	1854	Clerk/Superior Ct.
Court	1854	Clerk/Superior Ct.
Land	1854	Clerk/Superior Ct.

■ Pierce 18 Dec. 1857
P.O. Box 406, Blackshear, GA 31516
Phone: (912)449-2029
Web site: bellsouthpwp.net/r/s/rskhdr/Pierce
Parent County: Appling, Ware
Comments/research tips: Courthouse fire 1874.

Record Type	Year Begun	Jurisdiction
Birth	1919	Dept./Health
Marriage	1875	Probate Court
Death	1919	Dept./Health
Probate	1875	Probate Court
Divorce	1875	Clerk/Superior Ct.
Court	1875	Clerk/Superior Ct.
Land	1875	Clerk/Superior Ct.

■ Pike 9 Dec. 1822
P.O. Box 324, Zebulon, GA 30295
Phone: (770)567-8734
Web site: www.rootsweb.com/~gapike/index.htm
Parent County: Monroe

Record Type	Year Begun	Jurisdiction
Marriage	1822	Probate Court
Probate	1823	Probate Court
Court	1824	Clerk/Superior Ct.
Land	1823	Clerk/Superior Ct.

■ Polk 20 Dec. 1851
Courthouse, Room 102, Cedartown, GA 30125
Phone: (770)749-2128
Web site: www.rootsweb.com/~gapolk/
Parent County: Paulding, Floyd

Record Type	Year Begun	Jurisdiction
Birth	1919	Dept./Health
Marriage	1852	Probate Court
Death	1919	Dept./Health
Probate	1852	Probate Court
Divorce	1852	Clerk/Superior Ct.

Court .... 1852 .... Clerk/Superior Ct.
Land .... 1852 .... Clerk/Superior Ct.

■ Pulaski   13 Dec. 1808
Hawkinsville, GA 31036-0029
Phone: (478)783-2061
Web site: www.rootsweb.com/~gapulask/
Parent County: Laurens

Record Type	Year Begun	Jurisdiction
Court	1809	Clerk/Superior Ct.
Divorce	1850	Clerk/Superior Ct.
Land	1807	Clerk/Superior Ct.
Marriage	1810	Probate Court
Probate	1810	Probate Court
Birth	1919	Dept./Health
Death	1919	Dept./Health

■ Putnam   10 Dec. 1807
100 S. Jefferson Ave., Eatonton, GA 31024
Phone: (706)485-5476
Web site: www.rootsweb.com/~gaputnam/
Parent County: Baldwin
Comments/research tips: Probate Court has Tax Digest records 1812–1848.

Record Type	Year Begun	Jurisdiction
Land	1806	Clerk/Superior Ct.
Divorce	1807	Clerk/Superior Ct.
Court	1807	Clerk/Superior Ct.
Birth	1919	Dept./Health
Marriage	1919	Probate Court
Probate	1808	Probate Court
Death	1919	Dept./Health

■ Quitman   10 Dec. 1858
P.O. Box 7, Georgetown, GA 31754
Phone: (229)334-2224
Web site: home.earthlink.net/~bwjohnson/quit_mn.htm
Parent County: Randolph, Stewart
Comments/research tips: Courthouse burned.

Record Type	Year Begun	Jurisdiction
Probate	1879	Probate Court
Birth	1919	Dept./Health
Marriage	1879	Probate Court
Death	1919	Dept./Health
Divorce	1923	Clerk/Superior Ct.
Court	1879	Clerk/Superior Ct.
Land	1879	Clerk/Superior Ct.

■ Rabun   21 Dec. 1819
25 Courthouse Sq., Clayton, GA 30525
Phone: (706)782-3614
Web site: www.usgennet.org/usa/region/southeast/garabun/
Parent County: Cherokee Indian Lands

Record Type	Year Begun	Jurisdiction
Marriage	1820	Probate Court
Probate	1826	Probate Court
Divorce	na	Clerk/Superior Ct.
Court	1829	Clerk/Superior Ct.
Land	1821	Clerk/Superior Ct.

■ Randolph   20 Dec. 1828
P.O. Box 424, Cuthbert, GA 31740
Phone: (229)732-2671
Web site: home.earthlink.net/~bwjohnson/rand_mn.htm
Parent County: Lee

Record Type	Year Begun	Jurisdiction
Birth	1919	Dept./Health
Probate	1835	Probate Court
Marriage	1835	Probate Court
Divorce	1835	Clerk/Superior Ct.
Court	1838	Clerk/Superior Ct.
Land	1830	Clerk/Superior Ct.

■ Randolph, old   10 Dec. 1807
Parent County: Baldwin
Comments/research tips: (See Jasper) Name changed to Jasper 10 December 1812.

■ Richmond   5 Feb. 1777
530 Green St., Augusta, GA 30911
Phone: (760)821-2434
Web site: www.rootsweb.com/~garichmo/
Parent County: Original county created from St. Paul Parish

Record Type	Year Begun	Jurisdiction
Land	1789	Clerk/Superior Ct.
Court	1782	Clerk/Superior Ct.
Marriage	1785	Probate Court
Probate	1782	Probate Court

■ Rockdale   18 Oct. 1870
922 Court St., Conyers, GA 30012
Phone: (770)929-4058
Web site: www.rootsweb.com/~garockda/
Parent County: Henry, Newton

Record Type	Year Begun	Jurisdiction
Marriage	1871	Probate Court
Probate	1871	Probate Court
Death	1919	Dept./Health
Land	1871	Clerk/Superior Ct.
Divorce	na	Clerk/Superior Ct.
Court	1871	Clerk/Superior Ct.

■ Schley   22 Dec. 1857
P.O. Box 385, Ellaville, GA 31806
Phone: (229)937-2905
Web site: www.rootsweb.com/~gaschley/
Parent County: Marion, Sumter

Record Type	Year Begun	Jurisdiction
Birth	1919	Dept./Health
Death	1919	Dept./Health
Burial	1927	Probate Court
Marriage	1858	Probate Court
Probate	1857	Probate Court
Divorce	1857	Clerk/Superior Ct.
Court	1857	Clerk/Superior Ct.
Land	1857	Clerk/Superior Ct.

■ Screven   14 Dec. 1793
216 Mims Rd., Sylvania, GA 30467
Phone: (912)564-2614

Web site: www.rootsweb.com/~gascreve/
Parent County: Burke, Effingham

Record Type	Year Begun	Jurisdiction
Birth	1919	Dept./Health
Death	1919	Dept./Health
Marriage	1817	Probate Court
Probate	1790	Probate Court
Divorce	1816	Clerk/Superior Ct.
Court	1811	Clerk/Superior Ct.
Land	1794	Clerk/Superior Ct.

■ Seminole 8 July 1920

200 S. Knox Ave., Donalsonville, GA 31745
Phone: (229)524-2525
Web site: www.rootsweb.com/~gasemino/
Parent County: Decatur, Early

Record Type	Year Begun	Jurisdiction
Birth	1921	Dept./Health
Marriage	1921	Probate Court
Death	1921	Dept./Health
Probate	1921	Probate Court
Divorce	1921	Clerk/Superior Ct.
Court	1921	Clerk/Superior Ct.
Land	1921	Clerk/Superior Ct.

■ Spalding 20 Dec. 1851

132 E. Solomon St., Griffin, GA 30223
Phone: (770)467-4356
Web site: www.rootsweb.com/~gaspaldi/
Parent County: Fayette, Henry, Pike

Record Type	Year Begun	Jurisdiction
Divorce	1852	Clerk/Superior Ct.
Court	1852	Clerk/Superior Ct.
Land	1852	Clerk/Superior Ct.
Marriage	1852	Probate Court
Probate	1852	Probate Court

■ St. Andrew Parish 1758

Parent County: Creek Cession of 1733
Comments/research tips: (See Liberty) Organized as an early parish and became part of Liberty County 5 February 1777.

■ St. David Parish 1765

Parent County: Creek Cession of 1763
Comments/research tips: (See Glynn) Organized as an early parish and became part of Glynn County 5 February 1777.

■ St. George Parish 1758

Parent County: Creek Cession of 1733
Comments/research tips: (See Burke) Organized as an early parish and became Burke County 5 February 1777.

■ St. James Parish 1758

Parent County: Creek Cession of 1733
Comments/research tips: (See Liberty) Organized as an early parish and became part of Liberty County 5 February 1777.

■ St. John Parish 1758

Parent County: Creek Cession of 1733
Comments/research tips: (See Liberty) Organized as an early parish and became part of Liberty County 5 February 1777.

■ St. Mary Parish 1765

Parent County: Creek Cession of 1763
Comments/research tips: (See Camden) Organized as an early parish and became part of Camden County 5 February 1777.

■ St. Matthew Parish 1758

Parent County: Creek Cession of 1733
Comments/research tips: (See Effingham) Organized as an early parish and became part of Effingham County 5 February 1777.

■ St. Patrick Parish 1765

Parent County: Creek Cession of 1763
Comments/research tips: (See Glynn) Organized as an early parish and became part of Glynn County 5 February 1777.

■ St. Paul Parish 1758

Parent County: Creek Cession of 1733
Comments/research tips: (See Richmond) Organized as an early parish and became Richmond County 5 February 1777.

■ St. Philip Parish 1758

Parent County: Creek Cession of 1733
Comments/research tips: (See Chatham and Effingham) Organized as an early parish and became part of Chatham and Effingham Counties 5 February 1777.

■ St. Thomas Parish 1765

Parent County: Creek Cession of 1763
Comments/research tips: (See Camden) Organized as an early parish and became part of Camden County 5 February 1777.

■ Stephens 18 Aug. 1905

205 N. Alexander St., Toccoa, GA 30577
Phone: (706)886-9496
Web site: www.rootsweb.com/~gastephe/
Parent County: Franklin, Habersham

Record Type	Year Begun	Jurisdiction
Birth	1919	Dept./Health
Death	1919	Dept./Health
Marriage	1906	Probate Court
Probate	1906	Probate Court
Divorce	1906	Clerk/Superior Ct.
Court	1906	Clerk/Superior Ct.
Land	1906	Clerk/Superior Ct.

■ Stewart 23 Dec. 1830

P.O. Box 910, Lumpkin, GA 31815
Phone: (912)838-6220
Web site: home.earthlink.net/~bwjohnson/stew_mn.htm
Parent County: Randolph

Record Type	Year Begun	Jurisdiction
Birth	1919	Dept./Health
Death	1919	Dept./Health

Georgia

Burial	1927	Probate Court
Marriage	1828	Probate Court
Probate	1830	Probate Court
Divorce	1830	Clerk/Superior Ct.
Court	1830	Clerk/Superior Ct.
Land	1830	Clerk/Superior Ct.

■ Sumter 26 Dec. 1831
P.O. Box 333, Americus, GA 31709
Phone: (229)928-4537
Web site: www.rootsweb.com/~gasumter/
Parent County: Lee

Record Type	Year Begun	Jurisdiction
Birth	1919	Dept./Health
Death	1919	Dept./Health
Burial	na	Dept./Health
Marriage	1831	Probate Court
Probate	1831	Probate Court
Divorce	1831	Clerk/Superior Ct.
Court	1831	Clerk/Superior Ct.
Land	1831	Clerk/Superior Ct.

■ Talbot 14 Dec. 1827
Courthouse Sq., P.O. Box 325, Talbotton, GA 31827
Phone: (706)665-3239
Web site: www.rootsweb.com/~gatalbo2/
Parent County: Muscogee

Record Type	Year Begun	Jurisdiction
Birth	1919	Dept./Health
Marriage	1828	Probate Court
Death	1919	Dept./Health
Probate	1828	Probate Court
Divorce	na	Clerk/Superior Ct.
Court	1828	Clerk/Superior Ct.
Land	1828	Clerk/Superior Ct.

■ Taliaferro 24 Dec. 1825
113 Monument St., P.O. Box 182, Crawfordville, GA 30631
Phone: (706)456-2123
Web site: www.rootsweb.com/~gataliaf/
Parent County: Green, Hancock, Oglethorpe, Warren, Wilkes

Record Type	Year Begun	Jurisdiction
Birth	1919	Dept./Health
Death	1919	Dept./Health
Marriage	1826	Probate Court
Probate	1826	Probate Court
Land	1750	Probate Court
Church	1802	Probate Court
Divorce	1826	Clerk/Superior Ct.
Court	1826	Clerk/Superior Ct.
Land	1826	Clerk/Superior Ct.

■ Tattnall 5 Dec. 1801
P.O. Box 39, Reidsville, GA 30453
Phone: (912)557-6716
Web site: www.rootsweb.com/~gatattna/
Parent County: Montgomery

Record Type	Year Begun	Jurisdiction
Birth	1919	Dept./Health

Marriage	1806	Probate Court
Death	1919	Dept./Health
Probate	1802	Probate Court
Divorce	1880	Clerk/Superior Ct.
Court	1805	Clerk/Superior Ct.
Land	1802	Clerk/Superior Ct.

■ Taylor 15 Jan. 1852
P.O. Box 536, Butler, GA 31006
Phone: (478)862-3357
Web site: www.rootsweb.com/~gataylo2/
Parent County: Macon, Marion, Talbot

Record Type	Year Begun	Jurisdiction
Marriage	1852	Probate Court
Probate	1852	Probate Court
Divorce	1852	Clerk/Superior Ct.
Land	1852	Clerk/Superior Ct.
Court	1852	Clerk/Superior Ct.
Birth	1919	Dept./Health
Death	1919	Dept./Health

■ Telfair 10 Dec. 1807
128 E. Oak St., McRae, GA 31055
Phone: (229)868-6525
Web site: plant.sgc.peachnet.edu/~jbellis/genweb/telfair/telfair.html
Parent County: Wilkinson

Record Type	Year Begun	Jurisdiction
Marriage	1810	Probate Judge
Probate	1831	Probate Judge
Divorce	na	Clerk/Superior Ct.
Court	1810	Clerk/Superior Ct.
Land	1809	Clerk/Superior Ct.
Birth	1919	Dept./Health
Death	1919	Dept./Health

■ Terrell 16 Feb. 1856
513 S. Main St., Dawson, GA 31742
Phone: (229)995-2631
Web site: home.earthlink.net/~bwjohnson/terr_mn.htm
Parent County: Lee, Randolph

Record Type	Year Begun	Jurisdiction
Divorce	1856	Clerk/Superior Ct.
Court	1856	Clerk/Superior Ct.
Land	1856	Clerk/Superior Ct.
Marriage	1856	Probate Court
Probate	1856	Probate Court

■ Thomas 23 Dec. 1825
225 N. Broad St., Thomasville, GA 31792
Phone: (229)225-4108
Web site: www.rootsweb.com/~gathomas/
Parent County: Decatur, Irwin

Record Type	Year Begun	Jurisdiction
Birth	1919	Dept./Health
Death	1919	Dept./Health
Marriage	1826	Probate Court
Probate	1826	Probate Court
Divorce	1919	Clerk/Superior Ct.

Georgia

Record Type	Year Begun	Jurisdiction
Court	1826	Clerk/Superior Ct.
Land	1826	Clerk/Superior Ct.

■ Tift 17 Aug. 1905
P.O. Box 354, Tifton, GA 31793
Phone: (229)386-7816
Web site: www.rootsweb.com/~gatift/
Parent County: Berrien, Irwin, Worth

Record Type	Year Begun	Jurisdiction
Marriage	1905	Probate Court
Probate	1905	Probate Court
Divorce	1905	Clerk/Superior Ct.
Court	1905	Clerk/Superior Ct.
Land	1905	Clerk/Superior Ct.
Birth	1919	Dept./Health
Death	1919	Dept./Health

■ Toombs 18 Aug. 1905
100 Courthouse Sq., Lyons, GA 30436
Phone: (912)526-3501
Web site: plant.sgc.peachnet.edu/~jbellis/genweb/toombs/toombs.html
Parent County: Emanuel, Tattnall, Montgomery

Record Type	Year Begun	Jurisdiction
Birth	1919	Dept./Health
Marriage	1905	Probate Court
Death	1919	Dept./Health
Burial	1905	Probate Court
Probate	1905	Probate Court
Divorce	1905	Clerk/Superior Ct.
Court	1905	Clerk/Superior Ct.
Land	1905	Clerk/Superior Ct.

■ Towns na
48 River St., Suite E, Hiawassee, GA 30546
Phone: (706)896-2130
Web site: www.rootsweb.com/~gatowns/
Parent County: Rabun, Union

Record Type	Year Begun	Jurisdiction
Birth	1919	Dept./Health
Death	1919	Dept./Health
Marriage	1856	Probate Court
Probate	1856	Probate Court
Divorce	1865	Clerk/Superior Ct.
Land	1856	Clerk/Superior Ct.
Military	1865	Clerk/Superior Ct.
Court	1856	Clerk/Superior Ct.

■ Treutlen 21 Aug. 1917
200 Georgia Ave., Soperton, GA 30457
Phone: (912)529-4515
Web site: www.rootsweb.com/~gatreutl/
Parent County: Emanuel, Montgomery

Record Type	Year Begun	Jurisdiction
Birth	1919	Dept./Health
Marriage	1919	Probate Court
Death	1919	Dept./Health
Probate	1919	Probate Court
Divorce	1919	Clerk/Superior Ct.

Record Type	Year Begun	Jurisdiction
Court	1919	Clerk/Superior Ct.
Land	1919	Clerk/Superior Ct.

■ Troup 11 Dec. 1826
P.O. Box 866, LaGrange, GA 30241
Phone: (706)883-1740
Web site: www.rootsweb.com/~gatroup/
Parent County: Creek Indian Lands
Comments/research tips: County Archives has Military records 1890–1936 and Naturalization records 1843–1908.

Record Type	Year Begun	Jurisdiction
Marriage	1828	Probate Court
Burial	1827	County Archives
Divorce	1827	County Archives
Land	1827	Clerk/Superior Ct.
Probate	1827	Probate Court
Court	1827	Clerk/Superior Ct.
Birth	1919	Dept./Health
Death	1919	Dept./Health

■ Turner 18 Aug. 1905
219 E. College Ave., Ashburn, GA 31714
Phone: (229)567-2011
Web site: www.rootsweb.com/~gaturner/
Parent County: Dooly, Irwin, Wilcox, Worth

Record Type	Year Begun	Jurisdiction
Divorce	1906	Clerk/Superior Ct.
Court	1906	Clerk/Superior Ct.
Land	1906	Clerk/Superior Ct.
Birth	1919	Dept./Health
Marriage	1906	Probate Court
Death	1919	Dept./Health
Burial	na	Probate Court
Probate	1906	Probate Court

■ Twiggs 14 Dec. 1809
P.O. Box 234, Jeffersonville, GA 31044
Phone: (478)945-3350
Web site: www.rootsweb.com/~gatwiggs/
Parent County: Wilkinson

Record Type	Year Begun	Jurisdiction
Land	1901	Clerk/Superior Ct.
Court	1901	Clerk/Superior Ct.
Divorce	na	Clerk/Superior Ct.
Birth	1919	Dept./Health
Marriage	1901	Probate Court
Death	1919	Dept./Health
Probate	1901	Probate Court

■ Union 3 Dec. 1832
114 Courthouse St., Blairsville, GA 30512
Phone: (706)439-6006
Web site: www.rootsweb.com/~gaunion/
Parent County: Cherokee

Record Type	Year Begun	Jurisdiction
Birth	1919	Dept./Health
Marriage	1833	Probate Court
Death	1919	Dept./Health
Probate	1851	Probate Court

Georgia

Divorce .... na .... Clerk/Superior Ct.
Court .... 1854 .... Clerk/Superior Ct.
Land .... 1860 .... Clerk/Superior Ct.

■ Upson 15 Dec. 1824
P.O. Box 906, Thomaston, GA 30286
Phone: (706)647-7015
Web site: www.rootsweb.com/~gaupson/
Parent County: Crawford, Pike

Record Type	Year Begun	Jurisdiction
Marriage	1825	Probate Court
Probate	1825	Probate Court
Divorce	1825	Clerk/Superior Ct.
Court	1825	Clerk/Superior Ct.
Land	1825	Clerk/Superior Ct.
Newspapers	1870	Clerk/Superior Ct.

■ Walker 18 Dec. 1833
103 S. Duke St., Lafayette, GA 30728
Phone: (706)638-1742
Web site: www.rootsweb.com/~gawalker/
Parent County: Murray
Comments/research tips: Courthouse fire 1883.

Record Type	Year Begun	Jurisdiction
Divorce	1883	Clerk/Superior Ct.
Court	1883	Clerk/Superior Ct.
Land	1883	Clerk/Superior Ct.
Marriage	1883	Probate Court
Probate	1883	Probate Court
Birth	1919	Dept./Health
Death	1919	Dept./Health

■ Walton 15 Dec. 1818
P.O. Box 745, Monroe, GA 30655
Phone: (770)267-1307
Web site: www.rootsweb.com/~gawalton/
Parent County: Creek Indian Lands

Record Type	Year Begun	Jurisdiction
Marriage	1825	Probate Court
Probate	1820	Probate Court
Land	1819	Clerk/Superior Ct.
Divorce	1900	Clerk/Superior Ct.
Court	1819	Clerk/Superior Ct.
Birth	1919	Dept./Health
Death	1919	Dept./Health

■ Ware 15 Dec. 1824
800 Church St., Waycross, GA 31501
Phone: (912)287-4340
Web site: www.rootsweb.com/~gaware/
Parent County: Appling
Comments/research tips: Records burned 1854.

Record Type	Year Begun	Jurisdiction
Marriage	1874	Probate Court
Probate	1879	Probate Court
Land	1874	Clerk/Superior Ct.
Court	1874	Clerk/Superior Ct.

■ Warren 19 Dec. 1793
100 Warren St., Warrenton, GA 30828-0000
Phone: (706)465-2262
Web site: www.rootsweb.com/~gawarren/
Parent County: Columbia, Richmond, Wilkes, Burke

Record Type	Year Begun	Jurisdiction
Birth	1919	Dept./Health
Marriage	1794	Probate Court
Death	1919	Dept./Health
Probate	1794	Probate Court
Divorce	na	Clerk/Superior Ct.
Court	1794	Clerk/Superior Ct.
Land	1796	Clerk/Superior Ct.

■ Washington 25 Feb. 1784
P.O. Box 669, Sandersville, GA 31082
Phone: (478)552-3304
Web site: gagen.i-found-it.net/washington.html
Parent County: Creek Indian Lands

Record Type	Year Begun	Jurisdiction
Birth	1919	Dept./Health
Marriage	1828	Probate Court
Probate	1865	Probate Court
Divorce	1865	Clerk/Superior Ct.
Court	1865	Clerk/Superior Ct.
Land	1865	Clerk/Superior Ct.

■ Wayne 11 May 1803
P.O. Box 918, Jesup, GA 31598
Phone: (912)427-5930
Web site: www.rootsweb.com/~gawayne/
Parent County: Creek Indian Lands

Record Type	Year Begun	Jurisdiction
Birth	1919	Dept./Health
Marriage	1809	Probate Court
Death	1919	Dept./Health
Probate	1809	Probate Court
Divorce	na	Clerk/Superior Ct.
Court	1809	Clerk/Superior Ct.
Land	1809	Clerk/Superior Ct.

■ Webster 16 Dec. 1853
P.O. Box 117, Preston, GA 31824
Phone: (229)828-3525
Web site: www.rootsweb.com/~gawebste/
Parent County: Stewart
Comments/research tips: Formerly Kinchafoonee County. Name changed to Webster 21 February 1856.

Record Type	Year Begun	Jurisdiction
Birth	1919	Dept./Health
Marriage	1878	Probate Court
Death	1919	Dept./Health
Burial	na	Probate Court
Probate	1854	Probate Court
Divorce	na	Clerk/Superior Ct.
Court	1854	Clerk/Superior Ct.
Land	1860	Clerk/Superior Ct.

■ Wheeler 14 Aug. 1912
P.O. Box 38, Alamo, GA 30411
Phone: (912)568-7137
Web site: www.angelfire.com/ga/WheelerC.html

Parent County: Montgomery

Record Type	Year Begun	Jurisdiction
Birth	1919	Dept./Health
Death	1919	Dept./Health
Marriage	1913	Probate Court
Probate	1913	Probate Court
Divorce	1913	Clerk/Superior Ct.
Court	1913	Clerk/Superior Ct.
Land	1913	Clerk/Superior Ct.

■ **White** 22 Dec. 1857

1650 S. Main St. #B, Cleveland, GA 30528

Phone: (706)865-2613

Web site: www.rootsweb.com/~gawhite/

Parent County: Habersham

Record Type	Year Begun	Jurisdiction
Birth	1919	Dept./Health
Marriage	1858	Probate Court
Death	1919	Dept./Health
Probate	1858	Probate Court
Divorce	1858	Clerk/Superior Ct.
Court	1858	Clerk/Superior Ct.
Land	1858	Clerk/Superior Ct.

■ **Whitfield** 30 Dec. 1851

P.O. Box 868, Dalton, GA 30720

Phone: (706)275-7450

Web site: www.geocities.com/Heartland/Plains/3242/whtfld.htm

Parent County: Murray

Record Type	Year Begun	Jurisdiction
Birth	1919	Dept./Health
Death	1919	Dept./Health
Marriage	1852	Probate Court
Probate	1852	Probate Court
Divorce	1852	Clerk/Superior Ct.
Court	1852	Clerk/Superior Ct.
Land	1852	Clerk/Superior Ct.

■ **Wilcox** 22 Dec. 1857

103 N. Broad St., Abbeville, GA 31001

Phone: (229)467-2442

Web site: www.rootsweb.com/~gawilcox/

Parent County: Dooly, Irwin, Pulaski

Record Type	Year Begun	Jurisdiction
Birth	1919	Dept./Health
Death	1919	Dept./Health

Marriage	1858	Probate Court
Probate	1858	Probate Court
Land	1858	Clerk/Superior Ct.
Divorce	1900	Clerk/Superior Ct.
Court	1858	Clerk/Superior Ct.
Military	1917	Clerk/Superior Ct.

■ **Wilkes** 5 Feb. 1777

23 E. Court St., Room 205, Washington, GA 30673

Phone: (706)678-2423

Web site: www.rootsweb.com/~gawilkes/

Parent County: Creek and Cherokee Indian Lands

Record Type	Year Begun	Jurisdiction
Birth	1919	Dept./Health
Marriage	1790	Probate Court
Death	1919	Dept./Health
Probate	1777	Probate Court
Divorce	1778	Clerk/Superior Ct.
Court	1778	Clerk/Superior Ct.
Land	1777	Clerk/Superior Ct.

■ **Wilkinson** 11 May 1803

P.O. Box 250, Irwinton, GA 31042

Phone: (478)946-2221

Web site: hometown.aol.com/johnstien/Wilkinso/gawilkin.html

Parent County: Creek Indian Lands

Comments/research tips: Courthouse burned in 1852 and 1924; Land records were not burned in 1924. Clerk of Superior Court has some Divorce records from 1852.

Record Type	Year Begun	Jurisdiction
Marriage	1854	Probate Court
Land	1855	Clerk/Superior Ct.
Probate	1854	Probate Court

■ **Worth** 20 Dec. 1853

201 N. Main St., Sylvester, GA 31791

Phone: (229)776-8205

Web site: www.rootsweb.com/~gaworth/

Parent County: Dooly, Irwin

Record Type	Year Begun	Jurisdiction
Birth	1919	Dept./Health
Marriage	1854	Probate Court
Death	1919	Dept./Health
Probate	1879	Probate Court
Divorce	na	Clerk/Superior Ct.
Court	1879	Clerk/Superior Ct.
Land	1892	Clerk/Superior Ct.

Georgia

Hawaii

By David A. Fryxell

HISTORICAL OVERVIEW

No one who's visited the beautiful islands of Hawaii should be surprised that the world's great powers vied for this tropical paradise for centuries after its discovery by Europeans. Spanish sailors visited in 1627, but it was Captain James Cook who put Hawaii on the map with his third voyage; he was killed at Kealakekua Bay in 1779. Britain claimed Hawaii in 1794, though that didn't deter incursions by the Russians in 1815 and the French in 1849.

Missionary fervor rather than imperialism sparked early American visits. Protestant missionaries came in 1820 and eventually codified the written Hawaiian language. Mormon missionaries began making numerous converts after 1850.

Despite Western interventions, King Kamehameha I established a monarchy in 1810 that survived until 1893. After a short-lived republic, Hawaii was annexed by the United States in 1898 and organized as a territory in 1900. The islands' modern face—sugar and pineapple growing, plus tourism—began to take shape soon after. Chinese laborers had been coming as early as 1852 to work on plantations, followed by Japanese beginning in 1865. The 1876 Reciprocity Act opened American sugar markets to Hawaiian growers. But James Drummond Dole's creation of a pineapple plantation in 1901 signaled a new day for Hawaii. In 1903, a Joint Tourism Committee was formed to promote Hawaii to the world; the first flight across the Pacific from San Francisco arrived in 1935.

Hawaii burst into the awareness of all Americans with the 1941 Japanese attack on Pearl Harbor. As the islands became a staging ground for the U.S. response, the way was paved for Hawaii to become the fiftieth state in 1959.

Today Hawaii is among the most multicultural states, combining vibrant native culture with Western and Asian influences. Other Asian and Pacific populations added

© PhotoDisc/Getty Images

HAWAII AT A GLANCE

Motto: The Life of the the Land Is Perpetuated in Righteousness

Population: 1.2 million

Prevalent Religions: Christianity, mostly Roman Catholicism and Congregationalism, also Buddhism, Shinto, Hinduism, Taoism, Judaism, and Muslim

Major Industries: Sugarcane, pineapples, nursery stock, livestock, macadamia nuts, tourism, food processing, apparel, fabricated metal products, stone, clay, and glass products

Ethnic Makeup (in percent): Caucasian 24.3%, African American 1.8%, Hispanic 7.2%, Asian 41.6%, Native American 0.3%, Other 1.3%

Famous Hawaiians: Tia Carrere, Steve Case, Don Ho, Bette Midler, Ellison Onizuka, Harold Sakata, James Shigeta, Don Stroud

Above: Pu'uhonua o Honaunau Historical Park

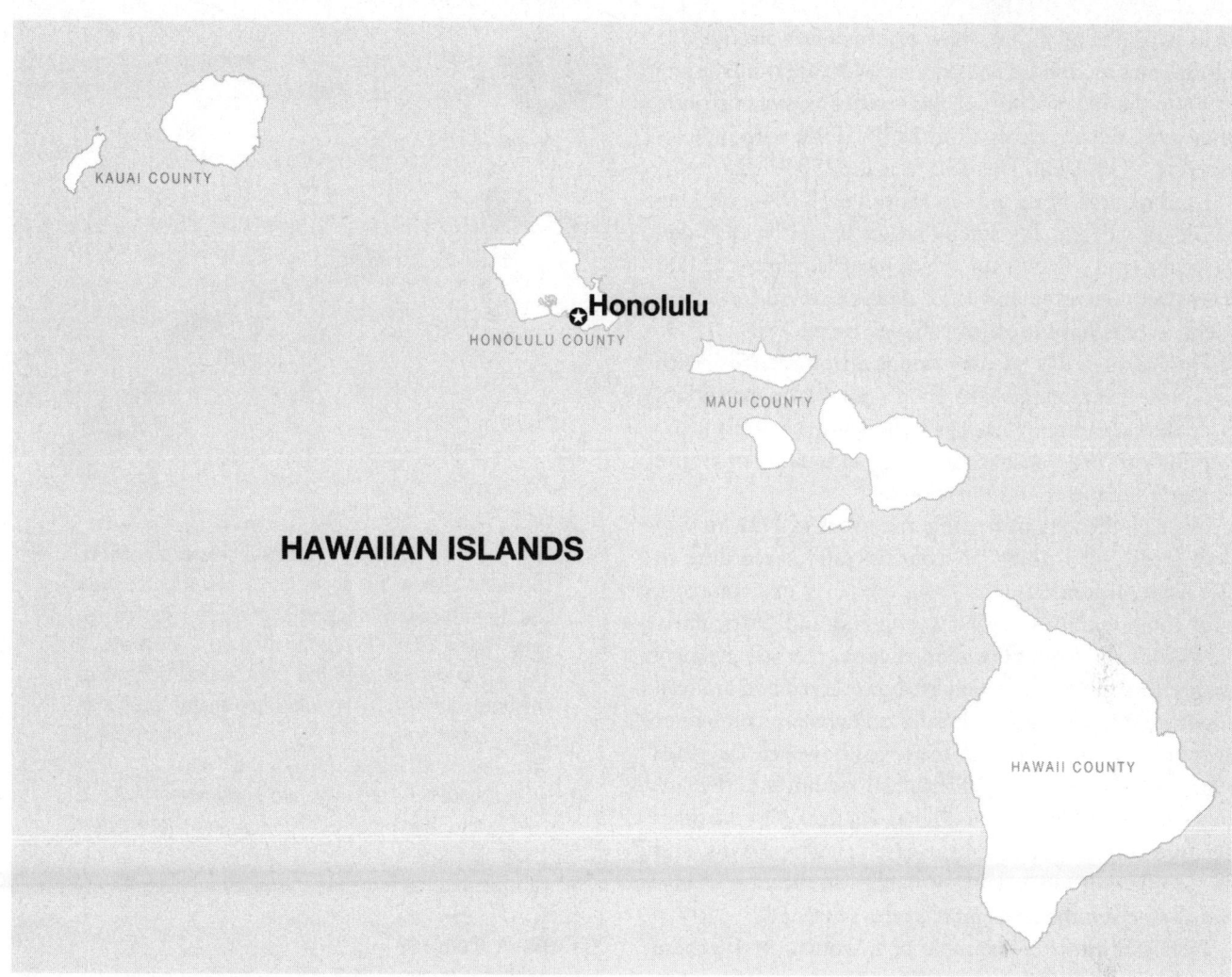

HAWAIIAN ISLANDS

KAUAI COUNTY

Honolulu
HONOLULU COUNTY

MAUI COUNTY

HAWAII COUNTY

to this mix in the 1960s, including Koreans, Filipinos, Tongans, and Samoans.

RECORD HIGHLIGHTS

Parts of Hawaii were enumerated well before it became a territory, and microfilm of these censuses is available through the FHL, including 1840–43 (index only), 1866 (fragment), 1878 (island of Hawaii), 1890 and 1896 (Oahu). The 1900 census was the first federal census to cover the new territory.

You can fill in some blanks in nineteenth-century Hawaiian enumerations using two groups of files in the state archives loosely labeled "census." These files, covering 1840–1866 (available on FHL microfilm) and 1847–1896, include a mixed bag of records such as school census statistics, population census statistics, and summaries of births, marriages, and deaths.

For such a new state Hawaii's vital records go back a long way, beginning with records kept by missionaries from 1826. Vital records at the state archives cover 1832 to 1949; official birth and death records began in 1853,

though records at the state health department are incomplete prior to 1896. Marriage records collected at the state archives cover 1826 to 1929 and are indexed to 1910. For copies of any records held at the state level, write to the State Department of Health, Office of Health Status Monitoring, Vital Records Section, P.O. Box 3378, Honolulu, Hawaii 96801-9984.

An important addition to Hawaii's vital records is the delayed birth record. Kathy McConnell DeFoster, librarian at the NSDAR Aloha Chapter Memorial Library and treasurer of the Honolulu County Genealogical Society, describes these as "an absolute gift" to researchers. As DeFoster explains it, a birth certificate could be created by the state for those lacking one through testimony from relatives, friends, and/or neighbors. These records are sometimes several pages long and may contain pictures and/or signatures of the applicant. "Many are veritable treasure troves of genealogical information—everything you wanted to know about your family in their own words!" she says, adding, "I have seen some people brought to tears when they discover a delayed birth document on one of their ancestors." Although the primary

Hawaii

focus is on the applicant, these records often also include information on siblings and parents. Most are from the late 1890s to the 1920s. The FHL has seventy reels of microfilm of delayed birth records from 1859–1903, with indexes covering 1859–1938, plus 132 reels for 1904–1925.

Land records didn't exist in Hawaii until 1840; the king owned all the land. Foreign influences led to the 1845 creation of a land commission, which recorded almost 12,000 claims between 1848 and 1852. Many of these and subsequent records have been microfilmed by the FHL.

Hawaii also has its own immigration records, with passenger lists from 1843 to 1900 available on microfilm. Note that separate indexes as well as some entirely separate entry records exist according to nationality of origin: Chinese, Japanese, and Portuguese.

Your challenges in tracing ancestors in Hawaii will vary greatly depending on your ancestry, according to DeFoster. If you descend from the early missionaries, who came mainly from New England and particularly New York, or from Hawaiian royalty, the task is fairly simple, as most records have been preserved and are well documented. If your search is for a Hawaiian commoner or for ancestors of Asian immigrants, however, DeFoster warns that it can be very difficult. In addition to the language barrier, she notes, you'll have to deal with the practice of changing names, in the case of many Asians, and the problem of not having surnames, in the case of Hawaiians before the latter part of the 1800s.

DeFoster cites the example of a woman of Japanese ancestry she's been helping: When the woman's grandparents married in Hawaii, her grandfather took his wife's surname. She doesn't know the names of her grandmother's parents or her grandfather's original name. In such cases, DeFoster recommends the state library's collection of vital records in its Hawaiiana section. Since the woman knows when her grandparents married, information at the library may give her the record number that she can then take to the Department of Health for a copy of the marriage application.

When researching native Hawaiians, DeFoster says, keep in mind that written records on the native population date only to the early 1800s. Some family histories, however, contain traditional oral genealogies, so in rare cases it's possible to link to pre-European contact ancestors.

STATE RESOURCES

■ ARCHIVES, LIBRARIES, AND SOCIETIES

Bernice P. Bishop Museum Library
1525 Bernice St., Honolulu, HI 96817-2704
Tel: (808) 848-4182

Fax: (808) 847-8241
E-mail: library@bishopmuseum.org
Web site: <www.bishopmuseum.org>

Bureau of Conveyances
1151 Punchbowl St., P.O. Box 2867, Honolulu, HI 96813
Tel: (808) 587-0120

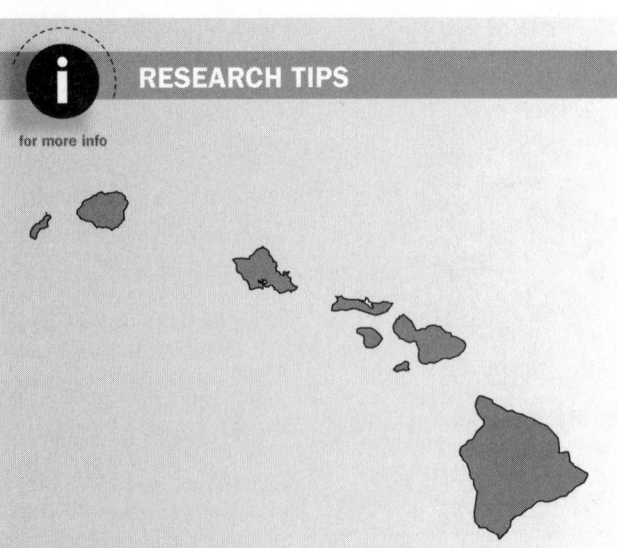

RESEARCH TIPS
for more info

- Written records for native Hawaiians date only to the early 1800s, but some family histories contain traditional oral genealogies so it's possible, though rare, to link to pre-European contact ancestors.
- The 1900 census was the first federal census of the area, but parts of Hawaii were enumerated well before it became a territory and microfilm of these censuses is available through the FHL.
- Vital records at the state archives cover 1832 to 1949, and marriage records housed there cover 1826 to 1929.
- Land records didn't exist in Hawaii until 1840.

Census Records
- Federal Census: 1900, 1910, 1920, 1930
- Royal Census Enumerations of the Kingdom of Hawaii: 1866 (mostly Maui), 1878, 1890, 1896 (part of Honolulu only)

Web site: <www.state.hi.us/dlnr/bc/bc.html>

Friends of Moku'ula
505 Front St., Suite 234, Lahaina, Maui, HI 96761
Tel: (808) 661-3659
Fax: (808) 661-1676
E-mail: friends@mokuula.com
Web site: <www.mokuula.com>

Hawaii Chinese History Center
111 N. King St., Suite 410, Honolulu, HI 96817
Tel: (808) 521-5948

Hawaii County Genealogical Society
P.O. Box 831, Keaau, HI 96749

Hawaii Maritime Center
Pier 7, Honolulu Harbor, Honolulu, HI 96813

Tel: (808) 536-6373
Web site: <holoholo.org/maritime/>

Hawaii State Archives, Historical Records Branch
Kekauluohi Building, Iolani Palace Grounds, Honolulu, HI 96813
Tel: (808) 586-0329
Fax: (808) 586-0330
E-mail: archives@Hawaii.gov
Web site: <www.state.hi.us/gags/archives/>

Hawaii State Department of Health
Office of Health Status Monitoring, Issuance/Vital Statistics Section
P.O. Box 3378, Honolulu, HI 96801
Tel: (808) 586-4733

Hawaii State Library
478 S. King St., Honolulu, HI
96813-2901
Tel (808) 586-3500
Web site: <www.librarieshawaii
.org>

Hawaiian Historical Society
560 Kawaiahao St., Honolulu, HI
96813
Tel: (808) 323-2222
Web site: <www.hawaiianhistory
.org>

**Honolulu County Genealogical
Society**
P.O. Box 235039, Honolulu, HI
96823-3500
Web site: <www.rootsweb.com/
~hihcgs/>

**Immigration and Naturalization
Service, Honolulu District
Office**
595 Ala Moana Blvd., Honolulu,
HI 96813
Tel: (800) 375-5283
Web Site: <uscis.gov/graphics/fie
ldoffices/honolulu/aboutus.htm
#anchor1658746>

**Kapi'olani Community College
Library, Char Asian-Pacific
study room**
4303 Diamond Head Rd., Honolulu, HI 96816
Tel: (808) 734-9758
E-mail: char@library.kcc.hawaii
.edu
Web site: <library.kcc.hawaii
.edu/main/char/index.htm>

Kaua'i Historical Society
P.O. Box 1778, Lihue'e, HI 96766
Tel: (808) 245-3373
Fax: (808) 245-8683
E-mail: khs@hawaiilink.net
Web site: <www.kauaihistoricals
ociety.org>

Kona Historical Society
P.O. Box 398, Captain Cook, HI
96704
Tel: (808) 323-2222
Fax: (808) 323-2398
E-mail: khs@konahistorical.org
Web site: <www.konahistorical
.org>

Land Court
777 Punchbowl St., Honolulu, HI
96813-5093
Tel: (808) 539-4777
Fax: (808) 539-4713
Web site: <www.courts.state.hi
.us/index.jsp>

**Lyman House Museum and
Mission House**
276 Haili St., Hilo, HI 96720
Tel: (808) 935-5021
Fax: (808) 969-7685
E-mail: <info@lymanmuseum
.org>
Web site: <www.lymanmuseum
.org>

Maui Genealogical Society
38A Alania Place, Kihei, HI
96753
E-mail: mauifun@maui.net
Web site: <www.maui.net/~maui
fun/mgs.htm>

Maui Historical Society
2375-A Main St., Wailuku, HI
96793
Tel: (808) 244-3326
Web site: <www.mauimuseum
.org>

**National Archives and Records
Administration, Pacific Region**
1000 Commodore Dr., San Bruno,
CA 94066-2350
Tel: (650) 238-3500
Fax: (650) 238-3511

**National Memorial Cemetery of
the Pacific**
2177 Puowaina Dr., Honolulu, HI
96813-1729
Tel: (808) 566-3720
Fax: (808) 532-3756

**Okinawan Genealogical Society
of Hawaii**
Hawaii Okinawa Center, 94-587
Ukee St., Waipahu, HI 96797
Tel: (808) 676-5400
Web site: <www.huoa.org/pa
ges/clubs/oy/ogsh.htm>

**Portuguese Genealogical
Society of Hawaii**
810 N. Vineyard Blvd., Honolulu,
HI 96817
Tel: (808) 841-5044

**Roman Catholic Diocese of
Honolulu, Chancery Office**
1184 Bishop St., Honolulu HI
96813
Tel: (808) 533-1791

**Joseph F. Smith Library,
Brigham Young
University-Hawaii**
55-220 Kulanui St., Laie, HI
96762
Tel: (808) 293-3850
Fax: (808) 293-3877
Web site: <w3.byuh.edu/library/>

**United Puerto Rican
Association of Hawaii, Inc.**
Tel: (808) 941-5216

**University of Hawaii at Manoa,
Hamilton Library**
2550 The Mall, Honolulu, HI
96822
Tel: (808) 956-8264
Fax: (808) 956-5968
E-mail: speccoll@hawaii.edu
Web site: <www2.hawaii.edu/~s
peccoll/arch/>

BIBLIOGRAPHY

■ GENERAL RESOURCES

*Buddhism in Hawaii: Its Impact
on a Yankee Community*
by Louise H. Hunter (Honolulu, HI:
University of Hawaii Press, 1971)

*Chinese Genealogy and Family
Book Guide: Hawaiian and
Chinese Sources*
by Jean B. Ohai (Honolulu, HI:
Hawaii Chinese History Center,
1975)

*The Chinese in Hawaii: an
Annotated Bibliography*
by Nancy Foon Young (Honolulu,
HI: Social Science Research Institute, University of Hawaii, 1973)

*Descendants of New England
Protestant Missionaries to the
Sandwich Islands (Hawaiian
Islands), 1820-1900: an
Alphabetically Arranged Copy
of Births, Marriages, and
Deaths from the Records of the
Hawaiian Mission Children
Society's Library, Honolulu,
Hawaii*
compiled by R.G. Rigler (Hono-
lulu, HI: G.R. Greenwood, 1984)

*A Directory of Libraries and
Information Sources in Hawaii
and the Pacific Islands, Rev. ed.*
compiled by Arlene D.C. Luster, edited by Yvonne Bartko and Beth
Madinger (Honolulu, HI: Hawaii Library Association, 1977)

*The Filipinos in Hawaii: an
Annotated Bibliography*
by Ruben R. Alcantara with Nancy
S. Alconcel, John Berger, and
Cesar Wycoo (Honolulu, HI: Social
Sciences and Linguistics Institute,
University of Hawaii, 1977)

Genealogical Sources in Hawaii
by Agnes C. Conrad (Honolulu, HI:
Hawaii Library Association,
1987)

*The Genealogist's Companion
and Sourcebook, 2d ed.*
by Emily Anne Croom (Cincinnati:
Betterway Books, 2003)

*A Genealogist's Guide to
Discovering Your African-
American Ancestors*
by Franklin Carter Smith and
Emily Anne Croom (Cincinnati:
Betterway Books, 2003)

*Guide to Genealogical
Research in the National
Archives of the United States*
edited by Anne Bruner Eales and
Robert M. Kvasnicka (Washing-
ton, D.C.: National Archives and
Records Administration, 2000)

*Hawaii Genealogy Project:
Directory of Secondary Sources*
by Jean Kadooka Mardfin (Honolulu, HI: Office of Hawaiian Affairs,
1993)

Hawaii Research Outline
by The Church of Jesus Christ of
Latter-day Saints (Salt Lake City,
UT: Corp. of the President of the
Church of Jesus Christ of L.D.S.
ca. 1997)

*Hawaiian Genealogies:
Extracted from Hawaiian
Language Newspapers, 2 vols.*
by Edith Kawelohea McKinzie, ed-
ited by Ishmael W. Stagner, II
(Laie, HI: Institute for Polynesian
Studies, Brigham Young
University-Hawaii Campus, ca.
1986)

*The Hawaiian Journal of History
vols. 1*
(Honolulu, HI: Hawaiian Historical
Society, 1967–)

The Hawaiian Kingdom, 3 vols.
by Ralph S. Kuykendall (Honolulu,
HI: University of Hawaii,
1938–1967)

Hawaiian Newspapers
by Esther K. Mookini (Honolulu,
HI: Topgallant Pub. Co., 1974)

*Hawaiian Royal Genealogies:
Charts and Comments*
by His Royal and Imperial Maj-
esty, the Oukah, Emperor of Tsa-
lagi, the Cherokee Nations (Dallas, TX: Triskelion Press, 1988)

Hawaii's People, 4th ed.
by Andrew W. Lind (Honolulu, HI:
University Press of Hawaii, ca.
1980)

Hawaii's Religions
by John F. Mulholland (Rutland, VT: C.E. Tuttle Co., 1970)

History Makers of Hawaii: a Biographical Dictionary
by Arthur Grove Day (Honolulu, HI: Mutual Publishing of Hawaii, 1984)

An Island Kingdom Passes: Hawaii Becomes American
by Kathleen Dickenson Mellen (New York: Hastings House, 1958)

The Japanese in Hawaii, 1868–1967: a Bibliography of the First Hundred Years
by Mitsugu Matsuda (Honolulu, HI: Social Science Research Institute, University of Hawaii, 1968)

Kanyaku Imin: a Hundred Years of Japanese Life in Hawaii
edited and produced by Leonard Lueras, designed by Kunio Hayashi (Honolulu, HI: International Savings and Loan Association, ca. 1985)

Ke Au Okoa weekly newspaper, 8 vols.
edited by J.M. Kapena 1870–1873 (Honolulu, HI: Hale Paipalapala Aupuni, 1865–1873)

The Koreans in Hawaii: an Annotated Bibliography
by Arthur L. Gardner (Honolulu, HI: Social Science Institute, University of Hawaii, 1970)

Men of Hawaii: a Biographical Reference Library, Complete and Authentic, of the Men of Note and Substantial Achievement in the Hawaiian Islands, 9 vols.
(Honolulu, HI: Honolulu Star-Bulletin, limited, 1917–1972)

Men and Women of Hawaii: 1954, a Biographical Encyclopedia of Persons of Notable Achievement and Historical Account of the Peoples who have Distinguished Themselves Through Personal Success and Through Public Service
by Henry P. Judd, edited by Perry Edward Hilleary (Honolulu, HI: Business Consultants, 1954)

Moramona: the Mormons in Hawaii
by R. Lanier Britsch (Laie, HI: Institute for Polynesian Studies, ca. 1989)

National Archives Microfilm Catalogs online:
<www.archives.gov/publications/genealogy_microfilm_catalogs.html>

Notable Women of Hawaii
edited by Barbara Bennett Peterson (Honolulu, HI: University of Hawaii press, ca. 1984)

The Pacific Islands, 3d ed.
by Douglas L. Oliver, illustrations by Sheila Mitchell Oliver (Honolulu, HI: University of Hawaii Press, ca. 1989)

The Peopling of Hawaii
by Eleanor C. Nordyke (Honolulu, HI: University Press of Hawaii, ca. 1977)

Portraits of American Protestant Missionaries to Hawaii
published by the Hawaiian Mission Children's Society (Honolulu, HI: Hawaiian Gazette Co., 1901)

Portuguese-Hawaiian Memories
by J. F. Freitas (Pearl City, HI: Portuguese Genealogical Society of Hawaii, ca. 1992)

Target Your Hawaiian Genealogy, and Others as Well: a Family Guide
by Maria Kaina (Honolulu, HI: Hawaii State Public Library System, 1991)

Under Hawaiian Skies: a Narrative of the Romance, Adventure and History of the Hawaiian Islands
by Albert Pierce Taylor (Honolulu, HI: Advertiser Publishing Co., ltd., 1926)

Voyages to Hawaii Before 1860: a Record based on Historical Narratives in the Libraries of the Hawaiian Mission Children's Society and the Hawaiian Historical Society, Extended to March 1860
by Bernice Judd, edited by Helen Yonge Llind (Honolulu, HI: University Press of Hawaii for Hawaiian Mission Children's Society, 1974)

■ CENSUS RECORDS

The American Census Handbook
by Thomas Jay Kemp (Wilmington, DE: Scholarly Resources, 2001)

The Census Book: A Genealogist's Guide to Federal Census Facts, Schedules, and Indexes
by William Dollarhide (Bountiful, UT: Heritage Quest, 2000)

Finding Answers in U.S. Census Records
by Loretto Dennis Szucs and Mathew Wright (Orem, UT: Ancestry Pub., ca. 2002)

Map Guide to the U.S. Federal Censuses, 1790–1920
by William Thorndale and William Dollarhide (Baltimore, MD: Genealogical Pub. Co., 1987)

State Census Records
by Ann S. Lainhart (Baltimore, MD: Genealogical Publishing, 1992)

Your Guide to the Federal Census
by Kathleen W. Hinckley (Cincinnati: Betterway Books, 2002)

■ IMMIGRATION RECORDS

American Naturalization Records, 1790–1990: What They Are and How to Use Them
by John J. Newman (North Salt Lake, UT: HeritageQuest, 1998)

American Passenger Arrival Records
by Michael Tepper (Baltimore: Genealogical Publishing Co., 1993)

They Became Americans: Finding Naturalization Records and Ethnic Origins
by Loretto Dennis Szucs (Salt Lake City: Ancestry, Inc., 1998)

They Came in Ships: A Guide to Finding Your Immigrant Ancestor's Arrival Records, 2d ed.
by John P. Colletta (Salt Lake City: Ancestry, Inc., 1993)

■ LAND RECORDS

The Great Mahele: Hawaii's Land Division of 1848
by Jon J. Chinen (Honolulu, HI: University of Hawaii Press, 1958)

Land and Property Research in the United States
by E. Wade Hone (Salt Lake City, UT: Ancestry, ca. 1997)

Locating Your Roots: Discover Your Ancestors Using Land Records
by Patricia Law Hatcher (Cincinnati: Betterway Books, 2003)

Native American Estate: the Struggle Over Indian and Hawaiian Lands
by Linda S. Parker (Honolulu, HI: University of Hawaii Press, ca. 1989)

Original Land Titles in Hawaii
by Jon J. Chinen, n.p., ca. 1961

■ MAPS

Atlas of Hawaii, 3d ed.
edited by Sonia P. Juvik and Hames O. Juvik, chief cartographer Thomas R. Paradise (Honolulu, HI: University of Hawaii Press, ca. 1998)

A Gazetteer of the Territory of Hawaii
compiled by John Wesley Coulter (Honolulu, HI: University of Hawaii, 1935)

Hawaiian Geographic Names
compiled by W.D. Alexander (Washington, DC: Government Printing Office, 1903)

Hawaiian Islands: Official Standard Names Approved by the United States Board on Geographic Names
(Washington DC: United States Office of Geography, 1956)

Leslie's Official History of the Spanish-American War: a Pictorial and Descriptive Record of the Cuban Rebellion, the Causes that Involved the United States, and a Complete Narrative of our Conflict with Spain on Land and Sea, Supplemented with Fullest Information Respecting Cuba, Porto Rico, the Philippines and Hawaii.
(Washington, DC: Leslie's Weekly, 1899)

Place Names of Hawaii, Revised and Enlarged ed.
by Mary Kawena Pukui, Samuel H. Elbert, and Esther T. Mookini (Honolulu, HI: University Press of Hawaii, 1974)

■ MILITARY RECORDS

Uncle, We Are Ready! Registering America's Men, 1917–1918: A Guide to Researching World War I Draft Registration Cards
by John J. Newman (North Salt Lake, UT: HeritageQuest, 2001)

Hawaii

Unlikely Liberators: the Men of the 100th and 442d
by Masayo Umezawa Duus, translated by Peter Duus (Honolulu, HI: University of Hawaii Press, ca. 1987)

U.S. Military Records: A Guide to Federal & State Sources, Colonial America to the Present
by James C. Neagles (Salt Lake City: Ancestry, Inc., 1994)

World War II: A Family Historian's Guide
by Debra Johnson Knox (Spartanburg, SC: MIE Publishing, 2003)

■ PROBATE RECORDS

Probate, divorce, criminal, civil, equity, law, and admiralty case files, minute books and wills: ca. 1847–1916
Hawaii State Archives, original records

■ VITAL RECORDS

Hawaiian Cemetery Records, 2 vols.
vol. 1 was typed by Mrs. Jessie H. Lindsey, vol. 2 was typed by the Hawaiian Mission, 1942–1954

Index to burial records of Lockview Cemetery: Pearl City, Island of Oahu, Hawaii, 1901–1937
compiled by Hawaii Archives Division (Honolulu, HI: Hawaii State Archives, 1991)

Index to burial records of Makiki Cemetery: Honolulu, island of Oahu, Hawaii, 1896–1954
compiled by Hawaii Archives Division (Honolulu, HI: Hawaii State Archives, 1991)

Tombstone Inscriptions from the Royal Mausoleum
by George Olin Zabriskie (n.p., 1969)

Your Guide to Cemetery Research
by Sharon DeBartolo Carmack (Cincinnati: Betterway Books, 2002)

■ Hawaii 1905
25 Aupuni St., Hilo, HI 96720
Phone: (808)961-8255
Web site: www.hawaii-county.com/
Parent County: Original county
Comments/research tips: State Health Department has Marriage records 1826–1929.

Record Type	Year Begun	Jurisdiction
Divorce	1951	Dept./Health
Death	1853	Dept./Health
Birth	1853	Dept./Health
Wills	na	Dept./Health
Probate	na	Dept./Health
Land	na	Dept./Health

■ Honolulu 1905
530 S. King St., Honolulu, HI 96813
Phone: (808)547-7000
Web site: www.co.honolulu.hi.us/

Parent County: Original county

Record Type	Year Begun	Jurisdiction
Marriage	na	Dept./Health
Death	1853	Dept./Health
Birth	1853	Dept./Health
Wills	na	Dept./Health
Probate	na	Dept./Health
Land	na	Dept./Health
Divorce	1951	Dept./Health

■ Kalawao 1905
Comments/research tips: Kalawao County was created in 1905 along with the other four original counties, but has been politically absorbed by Maui County. Maui does not claim jurisdiction over the villages of Kalaupapa, Kalawao, or Waikolu. Contact the State Health Department or Maui County for Kalawao records.

■ Kauai 1905
4444 Rice St., Lihue, HI 96766
Phone: (808)241-6371
Web site: www.kauaigov.org/
Parent County: Original county

Record Type	Year Begun	Jurisdiction
Marriage	na	Dept./Health
Death	1853	Dept./Health
Birth	1853	Dept./Health
Wills	na	Dept./Health
Probate	na	Dept./Health
Land	na	Dept./Health
Divorce	1951	Dept./Health

■ Maui 1905
200 S. High St., Wailuku, HI 96793
Phone: (808)270-7838
Web site: www.co.maui.hi.us/
Parent County: Original county

Record Type	Year Begun	Jurisdiction
Marriage	na	Dept./Health
Death	1853	Dept./Health
Birth	1853	Dept./Health
Wills	na	Dept./Health
Probate	na	Dept./Health
Land	na	Dept./Health
Divorce	1951	Dept./Health

Hawaii

Idaho

By David A. Fryxell

HISTORICAL OVERVIEW

Though native peoples came to Idaho as long as 14,000 years ago, it wasn't until after the Louisiana Purchase in 1803 that Europeans and Americans started to explore the area, beginning with Lewis and Clark in 1805. Fur traders dominated the early nineteenth century, establishing Fort Henry—the first American fur-trading post west of the Rockies—in 1810. Henry H. Spalding planted Idaho's first potatoes in 1836, though agriculture wouldn't grow to be the leading industry until after 1900.

Pioneers began crossing Idaho on the Oregon Trail in 1843 and then, with the 1849 gold rush, on the California Trail. After Idaho's own mineral riches were discovered in 1860, people started coming to stay instead of just passing through. Mining took over as the largest industry and in 1863, Idaho became a territory. The Idaho Territory included all of today's Montana and most of Wyoming.

Jobs in the mines drew waves of immigrants—first thousands of Chinese, then miners from Wales and Eastern Europe. Idaho also attracted many defeated Confederates after the Civil War. Subsequent migrations brought Scandinavians, a large influx of Basques, and Japanese. They formed a sometimes-uneasy melting pot with the Mormon settlers who'd dominated eastern Idaho since the state's first permanent settlement at Franklin in 1860.

Native tribes—including the Shoshone, Snake, Nez Perce, Bannock, and Sheepeater—resisted white settlement, sparking a series of wars from 1863 to 1879. Defeated, the tribes were eventually relocated to reservations. If you have native roots here, records of Idaho's various Indian agencies and schools are available at the state historical society and the National Archives' Pacific-Alaska regional facility in Seattle, as well as on FHL microfilm.

© PhotoDisc/Getty Images

IDAHO AT A GLANCE

Motto: It Is Perpetual

Population: 1.29 million

Prevalent Religions: Christianity, especially Roman Catholic, Baptist, and Methodist, also a small portion of Lutheran, Presbyterian, and Church of Jesus Christ of Latter-day Saints, and even fewer Pentecostal and Episcopalian

Major Industries: Cattle, dairy goods, potatoes, hay, wheat, peas, beans, sugar beets, electronic and computer equipment, processed foods, lumber, chemical manufacturing, tourism

Ethnic Makeup (in percent): Caucasian 91.0%, African American 0.4%, Hispanic 7.9%, Asian 0.9%, Native American 1.4%, Other 4.2%

Famous Idahoans: Gutzon Borglum, Carol Ryrie Brink, Frank F. Church, Fred Dubois, Vardis Fisher, Ezra Pound, Robert E. Smylie, Henry Spalding, Picabo Street, Lana Turner

Above: Idaho's Snake River

Idaho

Idaho

Idaho had an unusually long road to statehood, finally joining the union in 1890. Its post-statehood settlement was fueled in part by silver mining—the Coeur d'Alene mining district, first tapped in 1884, became the nation's richest source of silver—and by timber, with the United States' largest sawmill opening in Potlatch in 1906. Today Idaho is again enjoying a population boom. A new rush of migration from disenchanted Californians and others attracted by its low-key lifestyle and natural beauty has made Idaho one of the fastest-growing states.

RECORD HIGHLIGHTS

Idaho's protracted territorial period meant it was covered by the 1850 Oregon Territory census, the 1860 Washington Territory census (in Spokane County), and 1870 and 1880 Idaho Territory enumerations. Parts of southern Idaho were also included in the 1860 and 1870 censuses of Cache County, Utah. The earliest extant federal state census is that of 1900.

When looking for Idaho ancestors in the census, be aware of shifting county boundaries—and even disappearing counties, such as Alturas. Juvanne Martin, CGRS, owner of the Research Network and Idaho Connections and Southwest Coordinator of the Idaho Chapter of the Association of Professional Genealogists, advises, "Know when each of the forty-four Idaho counties were formed, including the counties that no longer exist. For instance, Canyon County started March 7, 1891. Before that time, it was part of Ada County. Thus, records for the Caldwell/Nampa area would be filed in Boise." She recommends several Web sites for tracing Idaho's counties: Idaho State Homepage <www.accessidaho.org/aboutidaho/county>, Idaho GenWeb <www.rootsweb.com/~idgenweb>, and a page on her own site <www.researchnetwork.net/idaho/idaholinks.shtml>.

Idaho was also a latecomer to statewide vital records. Birth and death registrations were first required on the county level in 1907, switching to a state responsibility in 1911. State marriage and divorce records didn't commence until 1947. Records before these dates were sometimes kept by churches, midwives or physicians, and mortuaries or, for marriages, the person performing the ceremony or making a marriage contract.

Cemetery records may offer clues when death records are unavailable: Volunteers from the Church of Jesus Christ of Latter-day Saints have transcribed records for cemeteries representing most Idaho counties. These are available in a set of twelve books or on five microfilm reels from the FHL.

Land records can also be useful in this public-lands state. Records from the land offices located in Boise, Blackfoot, Hailey, Lewiston, Coeur d'Alene, and Oxford

RESEARCH TIPS

for more info

- In Idaho, it's best to look for information in the county where the event occurred—contact county clerks and read through old newspapers.
- The Western States Historical Marriage Record Index <abish.byui.edu/specialCollections/fhc/gbsearch.htm> includes nearly all recorded pre-1900 Idaho marriages, which are housed at BYU-Idaho's David O. McKay Library
- The Idaho Death Index, which covers the years 1911–1951, can be found free of charge on the Idaho GenWeb site <www.rootsweb.com/~idgenweb/deaths/search.htm>. The actual death records are on microfilm at the Idaho State Historical Library and Archives (1911 through 1937) or can be ordered from the Idaho Vital Records Office in Boise.
- Most Idaho land records are kept by the National Archives in Seattle and by the Bureau of Land Management in Boise.
- www.vitalrec.com/id.html

Census Records
- Federal Census: 1850 (Oregon Territory), 1860 (Washington Territory), 1870, 1880, 1900, 1910, 1920, 1930
- Federal Mortality Schedules: 1870, 1880

(later known as Blackfoot) are kept by the National Archives in Seattle and by the Bureau of Land Management in Boise. The FHL has microfilmed land records covering 1868–1913 on twenty-three reels. Martin adds that a patent land search is available through the Bureau of Land Management's Web site <www.glorecords.blm.gov>. For county land records, she says, you can consult microfilm at the state historical society library or contact the assessor's office at each county courthouse.

The biggest challenge facing Idaho researchers, Martin

warns, is documenting sources prior to the state's requirement to file vital records. Her suggestion for working on this "brick wall" is to look for information in the county where the event occurred. In addition to contacting county clerks, don't overlook old newspapers as a source of local information. Fortunately, Idaho enjoys well-preserved collections of early newspapers in both the Idaho State Historical Society Library and Archives and the University of Idaho's library. You can borrow microfilm of these historic newspapers via interlibrary loan. For a list of early Idaho newspapers available on microfilm, see <www.lib.uidaho.edu/periodicals/microfilm>.

The Internet can also help with vital records, Martin notes. The Idaho Death Index, covering 1911–1951, with deaths listed by surname, can be found on the Idaho GenWeb site <www.rootsweb.com/~idgenweb/deaths/search.htm> and on the subscription Ancestry.com site. Once you've found a deceased ancestor in the index, you can view the actual death records on microfilm at the Idaho State Historical Library and Archives (1911 through 1937) or order copies from the Idaho Vital Records Office in Boise.

Another useful site, Martin adds, is the Western States Historical Marriage Record Index <abish.byui.edu/specialCollections/fhc/gbsearch.htm>, which covers an enormous collection of early marriage records housed at BYU-Idaho's David O. McKay Library in Rexburg. Virtually all of the pre-1900 Idaho marriages with available records are included in the index, and many Idaho counties have been extracted into the 1930s or later. Once you've identified an ancestor's marriage record in the index, it can be found on microfilm at the Idaho State Historical Society Library or by contacting the county clerk where the marriage was recorded.

STATE RESOURCES

■ ARCHIVES, LIBRARIES, AND SOCIETIES

Adams County Historical Society
P.O. Box 352, New Meadows, ID 83654

Albertson College Library
2112 Cleveland Blvd., Caldwell, ID 83605
Tel: (208) 459-5505
Fax: (208) 459-5299
Web site: <www.albertson.edu/library/>

Bannock County Historical Society
300 Alvord Loop, P.O. Box 253, Pocatello, ID 83204-0253
Tel: (208) 233-0434

Bonner County Genealogical Society
P.O. Box 27, Dover, ID 83825

Bonneville County Historical Society
P.O. Box 1784, Idaho Falls, ID 83401
Tel: (208) 522-1400

Boundary County Historical Society
P.O. Box 808, Bonners Ferry, ID 83805

Caldwell Genealogical Group
3504 S. Illinois St., Caldwell, ID 83605

Camas County Historical Society
General Delivery, Fairfield, ID 83327

Canyon County Historical Society and Museum
1200 Front St., P.O. Box 595, Nampa, ID 83651
Tel: (208) 467-7611

Caribou County Historical Society
290 W. Third S., Soda Springs, ID 83276
Tel: (208) 547-3506

Cascade Public Library
105 Front St., P.O. Box 10, Cascade, ID 83611
Tel: (208) 382-4757
E-mail: casclib@ctcweb.com
Web site: <www.lili.org/cascade/>

Cassis County Historical Society, Inc.
P.O. Box 331, Burley, ID 83318
Tel: (208) 678-7172

Clearwater County Historical Society
315 College Ave., P.O. Box 1154, Orofino, ID 83544
Tel: (208) 476-5033

Eagle Rock Railroad Historical Society, Inc.
P.O. Box 2685, Idaho Falls, ID 83404
Tel: (208) 522-3125
E-mail: errhsi@ida.net
Web site: <www.ida.net/org/errhsi/>

Elmore County Historical Foundation
180 S. Third E., P.O. Box 204, Mountain Home, ID 83647
Tel: (208) 587-9041

Gem County Historical Society
501 E. First, P.O. Box 312, Emmett, ID 83617
Tel: (208) 365-9530 or (208) 365-2990
E-mail: gemcohs@bigskytel.com

Idaho Department of Health and Welfare
450 W. State St., P.O. Box 83720, Boise, ID 83720-0036
Tel: (208) 334-5500
Fax: (208) 334-4921
Web site: <www2.state.id.us/dhw/>

Idaho Genealogical Society, Inc.
4620 Overland Rd. #204, P.O. Box 1854, Boise, ID 83701-1854
Tel: (208) 384-0542
E-mail: idahogenealogy@hotmail.com

Web site: <www.lili.org/idahogenealogy/>

Idaho State Historical Society and Library
1109 Main St., Suite 250, Boise, ID 83702
Tel: (208) 334-2682
Fax: (208) 334-2774
Web site: <idahohistory.net/index.html/>

Idaho State Library
325 W. State St., Boise, ID 83702
Tel: (208) 334-2150
Fax: (208) 334-4016
Web site: <www.lili.org>

Idaho State Office of the Bureau of Land Management
1387 S. Vinnell Way, Boise, ID 83709
Tel: (208) 373-4000
Web site: <www.id.blm.gov>

Idaho State University, Eli M. Oboler Library
850 S. Ninth St., Pocatello, ID 83209
Tel: (208) 282-2958
Web site: <www.isu.edu/library/home.htm>

Ilo-Volmer Historical Society
P.O. Box 61, Craigmont, ID 83523
Tel: (208) 924-5475

Jefferson County Historical Society
P.O. Box 284, Rigby, ID, 83442
Tel: (208) 745-8423

Jerome County Historical Society
220 N. Lincoln, P.O. Box 50, Jerome, ID 83338
Tel: (208) 324-5641
Fax: (208) 324-7694
E-mail: info@historicaljeromecounty.com
Web site: <www.historicaljeromecounty.com>

Kamiah Genealogical Society
Box 322, Kamiah, ID 83536

Kootenai County Genealogical Society, Hayden Lake Library
8385 N. Government Way, Hayden, ID 83835
Web site: <www.usgennet.org/usa/id/county/kootenai/kcgs/>

Latah County Historical Society
327 E. Second St., Moscow, ID 83843

Idaho

Tel: (208) 882-1004
Fax: (208) 882-0759
E-mail: lchlibrary@moscow.com
Web site: <users.Moscow.com/lchs/>

Lemhi County Historical Society
P.O. Box 645, Salmon, ID 83467

Lewis-Clark State College Library
500 Eighth Ave., Lewiston, ID 83501
Tel: (208) 792-2396
Fax: (208) 792-2831
Web site: <www.lcsc.edu/library>

Lewis County Historical Society
Route 2, P.O. Box 10, Kamiah, ID 83536

Luna House Historical Museum, and Nez Perce County Historical Society
0306 Third St., Lewiston, ID 83501
Tel: (208) 743-2535

Minidoka County Historical Society
P.O. Box 21, Rupert, ID 83350
Tel: (208) 436-0336

National Archives and Records Administration-Pacific Alaska Region
6125 Sand Point Way NE, Seattle, WA 98115-7999
Tel: (206) 336-5115
Fax: (206) 336-5112

Nez Perce Historical Society
P.O. Box 86, Nez Perce, ID 83542

North Idaho College, Molstead Library
100 W. Garden Ave., Coeur d'Alene, ID 83814
Tel: (208) 769-3355
Fax: (208) 769-3428

Northwest Nazarene College, John E. Riley Library
623 Holly, Nampa, ID 83686
Tel: (208) 467-8608
Fax: (208) 467-8605
Web site: <www.nnu.edu/academics/schools/libraryservices/>

Old Fort Boise Historical Society
Old Fort Boise Park, P.O. Box 924, Parma, ID 83660
Tel: (208) 722-5573

Owyhee County Historical Society
P.O. Box 67, Murphy, ID 83660
Tel: (208) 495-2319

Web site: <owyhee.county.net/museum/>

Payette County Historical Society
P.O. Box 476, Payette, ID 83661
Tel: (208) 642-4883
E-mail: payettemuseum@fmtc.com
Web site: <www.geocities.com/payettehistory/homepage.html>

Pocatello Branch Genealogical Society
P.O. Box 4272, Pocatello, ID 83201

Presbyterian Historical Society
425 Lombard St., Philadelphia, PA 19147-1516
Tel: (215) 627-1852
Fax: (215) 627-0509
E-mail: refdesk@history.pcusa.org
Web site: <www.history.pcusa.org>

Pullman, Washington Branch Genealogical Library
865 Bitterroot, Moscow, ID 84843

Roman Catholic Chancery Office, Diocese of Boise
303 Federal Way, Boise, ID 83705
Tel: (208) 342-1311
Fax: (208) 342-0224
Web site: <www.catholicidaho.org/chancery.cfm>

Shoshone County Genealogical Society
P.O. Box 183, Kellogg, ID 83837

South Bannock County Historical Society and Museum
110 E. Main St., P.O. Box 387, Lava Hot Springs, ID 83246
Tel: (208) 776-5254

South Custer County Historical Society
P.O. Box 355, Mackay, ID 83251

Spirit Lake Historical Society
P.O. Box 186, Spirit Lake, ID 83869

Treasure Valley Chapter of the Idaho Genealogical Society
325 W. State St., Boise, ID 83702

Twin Rivers Genealogical Society
P.O. Box 386, Lewiston, ID 83501

United Methodist Archives Center, Drew University Library
36 Madison Ave., P.O. Box 127, Madison, NJ 07940
Tel: (973) 408-3588
Fax: (973) 408-3770
Web site: <www.depts.drew.edu/lib/>

University of Idaho Library
Rayburn St., P.O. Box 442350, Moscow, ID 83844-2350
Tel: (208) 885-6584
Fax: (208) 855-6817
Web site: <www.lib.uidaho.edu>

Upper Snake River Valley Historical Society
51 N. Center St., P.O. Box 244, Rexburg, ID 83440
Tel: (208) 356-9101

Valley County Genealogical Society
P.O. Box 697, Cascade, ID 83611
Tel: (208) 382-4757

BIBLIOGRAPHY

■ GENERAL RESOURCES

The Basques in Idaho
by Pat Bieter (Boise, ID: Idaho State Historical Society, ca. 1970)

Blackrobes Journey, 1840–1990
compiled by Joan Drexler, et al. (Idaho Falls, ID: Holy Rosary Parish, Historical Committee, ca. 1990)

The Brethren Along the Snake River: A History of the Church of the Brethren in Idaho and Western Montana
by Roger E. Sappington (Elgin, IL: Brethren Press, 1966)

Citizens of North Idaho, 2 vols.
by Barbera V. Powell (Medical Lake, WA: B.V. Powell, ca. 1986–)

Cumulative Baptism Index to the Catholic Church Records of the Pacific Northwest
indexed by Sharon E. Osborn-Ryan (Portland, OR: Oregon Heritage Press, ca. 1999)

Directory of Churches and Religious Organizations of Idaho
prepared by the Idaho Historical Records Survey (Boise, ID: Historical Records Survey, 1940)

Directory of Oral History Resources in Idaho
compiled and edited by Madeline Buckendorf and Elizabeth P. Jacox (Boise, ID: Idaho Oral History Center, Idaho State Historical Society, 1982)

Discovering Idaho, a History
by Dwight William Jensen (Caldwell, ID: Caxton Printers, 1977)

Early Methodism in Idaho: Extracts from News Articles and Historic Note; Oregon-Idaho Conference of the United Methodist Church
compiled by Lila Hill, edited by John and Charlotte Hook (Salem, OR: United Methodist Church, Oregon-Idaho Conference, Commission on Archives and History, 1996)

Education in the Upper Snake River Valley: the Public Schools, 1880–1950
by Harold S. Forbush (Rexburg, ID: H.S. Forbush, Ricks College Press, ca. 1992)

The First One Hundred years: Cassia-Oakley Idaho Stake, 1887–1987
Church of Jesus Christ of Latter-day Saints, Cassia and Cassia-Oakley Stakes (Burley, ID: Burley Reminder, 1987)

Footprints Through Idaho: a Centennial Tribute to the Pioneer by their Descendents, 3 vols.
by the Idaho Genealogical Society (Boise, ID: Idaho Genealogical Society, 1989–)

Ghost Towns of Idaho
by Donald C. Miller (Boulder, CO: Pruett Pub. Co., ca. 1976)

The Genealogist's Companion and Sourcebook, 2d ed.
by Emily Anne Croom (Cincinnati: Betterway Books, 2003)

A Genealogist's Guide to Discovering Your African-American Ancestors
by Franklin Carter Smith and Emily Anne Croom (Cincinnati: Betterway Books, 2003)

The Gold Seekers: A 200 Year History of Mining in Washington, Idaho, Montana and Lower British Columbia
by Pauline Battien (Colville, WA: P. Battien, ca. 1989)

Guide to Genealogical Research in the National Archives of the United States
edited by Anne Bruner Eales and Robert M. Kvasnicka (Washington, DC: National Archives and Records Administration, 2000)

Guide to the Idaho Folklore Archives
by Elaine J. Lawless (Boise, ID: Idaho Folklife Center, Idaho State Historical Society, ca. 1983)

A History of the Catholic Church in the Pacific Northwest, 1743–1983
by Wilfred P. Schoenberg (Washington, DC: Pastoral Press, ca. 1987)

History of Idaho, 2 vols.
by Leonard J. Arrington (Moscow, ID: University of Idaho Press, 1994)

History of Idaho, 3 vols.
by Merrill D. Beal and Merle W. Wells (New York: Lewis Historical Pub. Co., 1959)

The History of Idaho
by John Hailey (Boise, ID: Press of Syms-York Company, Inc., 1910)

History of Idaho, the Gem of the Mountains, 4 vols.
by James Henry Hawley (Chicago, IL: The S. J. Clarke Publishing Company, 1920)

History of the Jews in Utah and Idaho
by Juanita Brooks (Salt Lake City, UT: Western Epics, 1973)

History of Idaho: a Narrative Account of its Historical Progress, its People and its Principal Interests, 3 vols.
by Hiram T. French (Chicago, IL: Lewis Publishing Co., 1914)

A History of Magic Valley
by Larry Quinn (Twin Falls, ID: Publishing West Associates, 1996)

A History of Southeastern Idaho: an Intimate Narrative of Peaceful Conquest by Empire Builders
by M.D. Beal (Caldwell, ID: The Caxton Printers, ltd., 1942)

Idaho 100: Stories from Idaho Century Citizens
by John Ohara Kirk (Helena, MT: Falcon Press, ca. 1989)

The Idaho Encyclopedia
compiled by the Federal Writers' Project of the Work Progress Administration (Caldwell, ID: Caxton Printers, 1938)

Idaho Ethnic Heritage, 3 vols.
By Laurie Mercier and Carole Simon-Smolinski (Idaho Centennial Commission and Idaho State Historical Society, 1990)

Idaho Folk Life: Homesteads to Headstones
edited by Louie W. Attebery, foreword by Wayland D. Hand, contributions by Brian Attebery, et al. (Boise, ID: Idaho State Historical Society, ca. 1985)

Idaho History: a Bibliography
by Richard W. Etulain and Merwin Swanson (Pocatello, ID: Idaho State University Press, ca. 1975)

Idaho Local History: a Bibliography with a Checklist of Library Holdings
edited by Milo G. Nelson and Charles A. Webbert (Moscow, ID: University Press of Idaho, 1976)

Idaho; the Place and its People; a History of the Gem State from Prehistoric to Present Days, 3 vols.
by Byron Defenbach (New York, NY: The American Historical Society, Inc., 1933)

Idaho Research Outline
by the Church of Jesus Christ of Latter-day Saints (Salt Lake City, UT: Corp. of the President of the Church of Jesus Christ of L.D.S., ca. 1988)

Idaho Surname Index
compiled by Judy Schmick (Boise, ID: Idaho Genealogical Society, 1989)

Idaho Women in History: Big and Little Biographies and Other Gender Stories
by Betty Penson-Ward (Boise, ID: Legendary Pub. Co., ca. 1991–)

An Illustrated History of North Idaho, Embracing Nez Perces, Idaho, Latah, Kootenai and Shoshone Counties State of Idaho
(Western Publishing Company, 1903)

An Illustrated History of the State of Idaho: Containing a History of the State of Idaho from the Earliest Period of its Discovery to the Present Time, Together with Glimpses of its Auspicious Future; Illustrations . . . and Biographical Mention of Many Pioneers and Prominent Citizens of Today, 4 vols.
(Chicago, IL: Lewis Pub. Co., 1899)

Indian Peoples of Idaho, 2d ed.
(Boise, ID: Boise State University Press, 1979)

Indian Wars of Idaho
by R. Ross Arnold (Caldwell, ID: The Caxton Printers, 1932)

Indians of Idaho
by Deward E. Walker Jr. (Moscow, ID: University Press of Idaho, ca. 1978)

Lineages of the Members, Past and Present, 1909 through 1961, Sons of the American Revolution, Idaho Society
by John Robert Gobble (Idaho Falls, ID: J.R. Gobble, ca. 1962)

Lives of the Saints in Southeast Idaho: an Introduction to Mormon Pioneer Life Story Writing
by Susan Hendricks Swetnam (Boise, ID: Idaho State Historical Society, ca. 1991)

Methodism in the Northwest
by Erle Howell, edited by Chapin D. Foster (Nashville, TN: Parthenon Press, Printers, 1966)

The Mining Industry in Idaho: a Short Bibliography of Sources on Mines and Mining in the Idaho State Historical Society library and Archives
by the Idaho State Historical Society (Boise, ID: Idaho State Historical Society, 1992)

Mormons and their Neighbors: an Index to Over 75,000 Biographical Sketches from 1820 to the Present, 2 vols.
compiled by Marvin E. Wiggins (Provo, UT: Harold B. Lee Library, Brigham Young University, ca. 1984)

National Archives Microfilm Catalogs online:
<www.archives.gov/publications/genealogy_microfilm_catalogs.html>

Newspapers in the Idaho Historical Society Microfilm Collection
by the Idaho State Historical Society (Boise, ID: Idaho State Historical Society ca. 1999)

Panhandle Personalities, Biographies from the Idaho Panhandle
compiled by Claude Simpson and Catherine Simpson (Moscow, ID: University Press of Idaho, ca. 1984)

Roman Catholic Diocese of Boise, Catholic Chancery Records of Idaho, Master Index, 26 vols.
compiled by the Idaho Genealogical Society (Boise, Idaho: Idaho Genealogical Society, ca. 1980)

Sketches of the Inter-mountain States: Together with Biographies of Many Prominent and Progressive Citizens who have Helped in the Development and History-making of this Marvelous Region: 1847–1909: Utah, Idaho, Nevada
(Salt Lake City, UT: Salt Lake Tribune, 1909)

Steamboats in the Timber
by Ruby El Hult (Caldwell, ID: Caxton Printers, 1952)

Thousands of Idaho Surnames: Abstracted from Rejected Federal Land Applications, 5 vols.
(Portland, OR: Genealogical Forum of Portland, Oregon, 1980–1987)

Zest for Living: Southern Idaho Senior Profiles
by Lorayne Orton Smith (Dallas, TX: Taylor Publishing, ca. 1991)

■ CENSUS RECORDS

The 1863 Census of Some Prominent Men of the Idaho Territory
by Sherman Lee Pompey (Charleston, OR: Pacific Specialties, 1974)

1910 Idaho Census Index
compiled by the Upper Snake River Valley Family History Center volunteers and McKay Library employees at Ricks College (Bountiful, UT: Heritage Quest, 1998)

Idaho

The American Census Handbook
by Thomas Jay Kemp (Wilmington, DE: Scholarly Resources, 2001)

The Census Book: A Genealogist's Guide to Federal Census Facts, Schedules, and Indexes
by William Dollarhide (Bountiful, UT: Heritage Quest, 2000)

Finding Answers in U.S. Census Records
by Loretto Dennis Szucs and Mathew Wright (Orem, UT: Ancestry Pub., ca. 2002)

Idaho Territorial Voters Poll Lists, 1863
transcribed, edited, and indexed by Gene F. Williams (Boise, ID: Williams Printing, ca. 1996)

Map Guide to the U.S. Federal Censuses, 1790–1920
by William Thorndale and William Dollarhide (Baltimore, MD: Genealogical Pub. Co., 1987)

Reconstructed 1890 Census
By Idaho State Historical Society Library and Archives, ongoing project

State Census Records
by Ann S. Lainhart (Baltimore, MD: Genealogical Publishing, 1992)

Your Guide to the Federal Census
by Kathleen W. Hinckley (Cincinnati: Betterway Books, 2002)

■ IMMIGRATION RECORDS

American Naturalization Records, 1790–1990: What They Are and How to Use Them
by John J. Newman (North Salt Lake, UT: HeritageQuest, 1998)

American Passenger Arrival Records
by Michael Tepper (Baltimore: Genealogical Publishing Co., 1993)

Emigrant Trails of Southeastern Idaho
by the U.S. Bureau of Land Management (Boise, ID: U.S. Dept. of the Interior, Bureau of Land Management, 1976)

They Became Americans: Finding Naturalization Records and Ethnic Origins
by Loretto Dennis Szucs (Salt Lake City: Ancestry, Inc., 1998)

They Came in Ships: A Guide to Finding Your Immigrant Ancestor's Arrival Records, 2d ed.
by John P. Colletta (Salt Lake City: Ancestry, Inc., 1993)

■ LAND RECORDS

Idaho State Brand Records and Indexes, 4 vols.
abstracted by the Idaho Genealogical Society (Boise, ID: Idaho Genealogical Society, ca. 1988)

Land and Property Research in the United States
by E. Wade Hone (Salt Lake City, UT: Ancestry, ca. 1997)

Locating Your Roots: Discover Your Ancestors Using Land Records
by Patricia Law Hatcher (Cincinnati: Betterway Books, 2003)

Stockman's Guide
compiled by J.A. Avery (Downey, ID: Downey Idahoan, 1913)

Thousands of Idaho Surnames: Abstracted from Rejected Federal Land Applications, 5 vols.
(Portland, OR: Genealogical Forum of Portland, OR, 1980–1987)

■ MAPS

An Atlas of Idaho Territory, 1863–1890
annotated by Merle W. Wells (Boise, ID: Idaho Historical Society, 1978)

A Checklist of Idaho Post Offices
by Alan H. Patera and John S. Gallagher (Burtonsville, MD: The Depot, ca. 1984)

Gazetteer of Cities, Villages, Unincorporated Communities, and Landmark Sites in the State of Idaho, 3d ed.
Idaho Highway Planning Survey, prepared in cooperation with U.S. Bureau of Public Roads (Boise, ID: 1966)

Ghost Towns and Live Ones: A Chronology of the Post Office Dept. in Idaho, 1861–1973
by Frank R. Schell (Twin Falls, ID: 1973)

Idaho Place Names: A Geographical Dictionary
by Lalia Boone (Moscow, ID: University of Idaho Press, ca. 1988)

"Idaho Town Names"
by Fritz L. Kramer, published in the Idaho State Historical Department Bienneal Report 23, 1951–1952

Maps of Early Idaho: Old Gold Mines, Indian Battle Grounds, Old Military Roads, Old Forts, Overland Stage Routes, Early Towns
prepared by R.N. Preston (Corvallis, OR: Western Guide Publishers, 1972)

Route of the Oregon Trail in Idaho
Idaho Department of Highways, historical data furnished by the Idaho Historical Society (Boise, ID: 1963)

A Short History and Postal Record of Idaho Towns: Ada County Thru Washington County, 1 vol.
by Art Randall (Hayden, ID: A. Randall, 1994)

■ MILITARY RECORDS

Soldiers of the Great War, 3 vols.
compiled by W.M. Haulsee, F.G. Howe, and A.C. Doyle (Washington, DC: Soldiers Record Publishing Association, ca. 1920)

Uncle, We Are Ready! Registering America's Men, 1917–1918: A Guide to Researching World War I Draft Registration Cards
by John J. Newman (North Salt Lake, UT: HeritageQuest, 2001)

U.S. Military Records: A Guide to Federal & State Sources, Colonial America to the Present
by James C. Neagles (Salt Lake City: Ancestry, Inc., 1994)

World War II: A Family Historian's Guide
by Debra Johnson Knox (Spartanburg, SC: MIE Publishing, 2003)

■ PROBATE RECORDS

Justice for the Times: A Centennial History of the Idaho State Courts
edited by Carl F. Bianchi (Boise, ID: Idaho Law Foundation, ca. 1990)

■ VITAL RECORDS

AZ, CA, ID, NV, 1850–1951
(S.I.: Brøderbund, ca. 1996. CD-ROM)

Guide to Public Vital Statistics Records in Idaho, State and County
prepared by the Idaho Historical Records Survey Projects (Boise, ID: Idaho Historical Records Survey Projects, 1942)

Western States Historical Marriage Index Online
compiled by the BYU-Idaho Family History Center
Web site: <abish.byui.edu/specialCollections/fhc/gbsearch.htm>

Your Guide to Cemetery Research
by Sharon DeBartolo Carmack (Cincinnati: Betterway Books, 2002)

■ Ada   22 Dec. 1864
200 W. Fourth St., Boise, ID 83702
Phone: (208)287-6840
Web site: www.rootsweb.com/~idada/
Parent County: Boise

Record Type	Year Begun	Jurisdiction
Marriage	1890	County Clerk/Aud./Rec.
Divorce	na	County Clerk/Aud./Rec.
Land	1864	County Clerk/Aud./Rec.
Probate	na	County Clerk/Aud./Rec.
Court	na	County Clerk/Aud./Rec.

■ **Adams** 3 Mar. 1911
P.O. Box 48, Council, ID 83612
Phone: (208)253-4561
Web site: www.co.adams.id.us/
Parent County: Washington

Record Type	Year Begun	Jurisdiction
Marriage	1911	County Clerk/Aud./Rec.
Divorce	1911	County Clerk/Aud./Rec.
Land	1911	County Clerk/Aud./Rec.
Probate	1911	County Clerk/Aud./Rec.
Court	1911	County Clerk/Aud./Rec.

■ **Alturas** 4 Feb. 1864
Parent County: Original county
Comments/research tips: (See Blaine) Abolished 5 March 1896 to create Blaine County.

■ **Bannock** 6 Mar. 1893
624 E. Center St., Pocatello, ID 83201-6274
Phone: (208)236-7340
Web site: www.co.bannock.id.us/
Parent County: Bingham
Comments/research tips: County Clerk has Birth and Death records 1893–1912.

Record Type	Year Begun	Jurisdiction
Land	1893	County Clerk
Marriage	1893	County Clerk
Divorce	1893	County Archives
Probate	1893	County Archives
Court	1893	County Archives

■ **Bear Lake** 5 Jan. 1875
P.O. Box 190, 7 E. Center St., Paris, ID 83261-0190
Phone: (208)945-2212
Web site: www.bearlakecounty.info
Parent County: Oneida
Comments/research tips: County Clerk has Birth and Death records 1907–1911.

Record Type	Year Begun	Jurisdiction
Marriage	1875	County Clerk
Land	1875	County Clerk
Divorce	1875	County Clerk
Court	1875	County Clerk
Probate	1875	County Clerk

■ **Benewah** 23 Jan. 1915
701 College Ave., Saint Maries, ID 83861-1886
Phone: (208)245-3212
Web site: www.rootsweb.com/~idbenewa/
Parent County: Kootenai

Record Type	Year Begun	Jurisdiction
Marriage	na	County Clerk
Divorce	na	County Clerk
Land	na	County Clerk
Court	na	Clerk/District Ct.
Probate	na	Clerk/District Ct.

■ **Bingham** 13 Jan. 1885
501 N. Maple St., Blackfoot, ID 83221-1028
Phone: (208)785-8040

Web site: www.co.bingham.id.us/
Parent County: Oneida
Comments/research tips: County Clerk has Birth and Death records 1907–1911.

Record Type	Year Begun	Jurisdiction
Marriage	1885	County Clerk
Land	1885	County Clerk
Divorce	1885	County Clerk
Court	1885	County Clerk
Probate	1885	County Clerk

■ **Blaine** 5 Mar. 1895
206 First Ave. S., P.O. Box 400, Hailey, ID 83333-0400
Phone: (208)788-5505
Web site: www.co.blaine.id.us/
Parent County: Alturas, Logan

Record Type	Year Begun	Jurisdiction
Marriage	1895	County Aud./Rec.
Divorce	1921	Clerk/District Ct.
Probate	1921	Clerk/District Ct.
Court	1921	Clerk/District Ct.
Land	1895	County Aud./Rec.

■ **Boise** 4 Feb. 1864
420 Main St., P.O. Box 1300, Idaho City, ID 83631
Phone: (208)392-4431
Web site: www.co.boise.id.us/
Parent County: Original county
Comments/research tips: County Clerk has very few Birth and Death records prior to 1911. Some records are not complete due to fires.

Record Type	Year Begun	Jurisdiction
Marriage	1868	County Clerk
Divorce	ca. 1930	Clerk/District Ct.
Land	1864	County Clerk
Probate	1862	State Archives
Court	1862	State Archives

■ **Bonner** 21 Feb. 1907
215 S. First Ave., Sandpoint, ID 83864
Phone: (208)265-1432
Web site: www.co.bonner.id.us/
Parent County: Kootenai

Record Type	Year Begun	Jurisdiction
Birth	na	County Clerk
Death	na	County Clerk
Probate	1890	County Clerk
Land	na	County Clerk
Marriage	na	County Clerk
Divorce	na	County Clerk
Court	na	County Clerk

■ **Bonneville** 7 Feb. 1911
605 N. Capital Ave., Idaho Falls, ID 83402-3582
Phone: (208)529-1350 ext. 1355
Web site: www.co.bonneville.id.us
Parent County: Bingham

Record Type	Year Begun	Jurisdiction
Marriage	1911	County Clerk

Idaho

Divorce	1911	Court Archives
Land	1911	County Clerk
Probate	1911	Court Archives
Court	1911	Court Archives

■ **Boundary** 23 Jan. 1915
P.O. Box 419, Bonners Ferry, ID 83805
Phone: (208)267-5504
Web site: www.boundary-idaho.com/
Parent County: Bonner

Record Type	Year Begun	Jurisdiction
Marriage	ca. 1890	County Clerk
Land	ca. 1890	County Clerk
Probate	1915	Clerk/District Ct.
Court	1915	Clerk/District Ct.
Divorce	1915	Clerk/District Ct.

■ **Butte** 6 Feb. 1917
248 W. Corand, P.O. Box 737, Arco, ID 83213-0737
Phone: (208)527-3021
Web site: www.rootsweb.com/~idbutte/
Parent County: Bingham, Blaine, Jefferson

Record Type	Year Begun	Jurisdiction
Marriage	1917	County Clerk
Divorce	1930	Clerk/District Ct.
Probate	1930	Clerk/District Ct.
Court	1930	Clerk/District Ct.
Land	1890	County Clerk

■ **Camas** 6 Feb. 1917
501 Soldier Rd., P.O. Box 430, Fairfield, ID 83327-0430
Phone: (208)764-2242
Web site: www.rootsweb.com/~idcamas/
Parent County: Blaine

Record Type	Year Begun	Jurisdiction
Court	ca. 1927	County Clerk
Probate	ca. 1927	County Clerk
Marriage	ca. 1917	County Clerk
Divorce	ca. 1917	County Clerk
Land	ca. 1917	County Clerk

■ **Canyon** 7 Mar. 1891
1115 Albany, Caldwell, ID 83605-3542
Phone: (208)454-7504
Web site: www.canyoncounty.org/
Parent County: Ada

Record Type	Year Begun	Jurisdiction
Marriage	1895	County Recorder
Land	1892	County Recorder
Divorce	ca. 1900	County Clerk
Probate	ca. 1900	County Clerk
Court	ca. 1900	County Clerk

■ **Caribou** 11 Feb. 1919
159 S. Main St., P.O. Box 775, Soda Springs, ID 83276
Phone: (208)547-4324
Web site: www.rootsweb.com/~idcaribo/
Parent County: Bannock

Record Type	Year Begun	Jurisdiction
Marriage	1919	County Clerk

Divorce	1919	Mag./District Ct.
Land	1919	County Clerk
Probate	1919	Mag./District Ct.
Court	1919	Mag./District Ct.

■ **Cassia** 20 Feb. 1879
1459 Overland Ave., Burley, ID 83318
Phone: (208)878-5240
Web site: www.cassiacounty.org/
Parent County: Owyhee
Comments/research tips: County Clerk/Recorder has Birth and Death records 1907–1911.

Record Type	Year Begun	Jurisdiction
Marriage	1878	County Recorder
Divorce	1879	County Recorder
Land	1878	County Recorder
Probate	1878	County Recorder
Court	1878	County Recorder

■ **Clark** 1 Feb. 1919
320 W. Main St., P.O. Box 205, Dubois, ID 83423
Phone: (208)374-5304
Web site: www.rootsweb.com/~idclark/
Parent County: Fremont

Record Type	Year Begun	Jurisdiction
Marriage	1919	County Clerk
Divorce	1919	County Clerk
Land	1919	County Clerk
Court	1919	County Clerk

■ **Clearwater** 27 Feb. 1911
150 Michigan Ave., P.O. Box 586, Orofino, ID 83544
Phone: (208)476-5615
Web site: www.clearwatercounty.org
Parent County: Nez Perce

Record Type	Year Begun	Jurisdiction
Marriage	1911	County Aud./Rec.
Divorce	1911	County Aud./Rec.
Land	1911	County Aud./Rec.
Probate	1911	County Aud./Rec.
Court	1911	County Aud./Rec.

■ **Custer** 8 Jan. 1881
P.O. Box 385, Challis, ID 83226
Phone: (208)879-2360
Web site: www.co.custer.id.us/
Parent County: Alturas, Lemhi
Comments/research tips: County Clerk has Marriage from the late 1800s.

Record Type	Year Begun	Jurisdiction
Divorce	1872	Off. of the Court
Land	1881	County Clerk
Probate	1881	Off. of the Court
Court	1881	Off. of the Court

■ **Elmore** 7 Feb. 1889
150 S. Fourth E St., Suite 3, Mountain Home, ID 83647
Phone: (208)587-2130
Web site: www.rootsweb.com/~idelmore/

Parent County: Alturas
Comments/research tips: County Auditor/Recorder has Birth and Death records 1907–1911.

Record Type	Year Begun	Jurisdiction
Marriage	1889	County Aud./Rec.
Divorce	1889	County Aud./Rec.
Land	1889	County Aud./Rec.
Probate	1889	County Aud./Rec.
Court	1889	County Aud./Rec.

■ **Franklin** 20 Jan. 1913
20 W. Oneida St., Preston, ID 83263-1234
Phone: (208)852-1090
Web site: www.rootsweb.com/~idfrankl/
Parent County: Oneida
Comments/research tips: Clerk of District Court has Naturalization records 1913–1928.

Record Type	Year Begun	Jurisdiction
Divorce	1913	Clerk/County Ct.
Probate	1913	Clerk/County Ct.
Marriage	1913	County Clerk
Land	ca. 1890	County Clerk
Court	1913	Clerk/County Ct.

■ **Fremont** 4 Mar. 1893
151 W. First St. N. Room 12, St. Anthony, ID 83445
Phone: (208)624-7332
Web site: www.rootsweb.com/~idfremon/
Parent County: Bingham, Lemhi
Comments/research tips: County Clerk has Birth and Death records 1907–1911.

Record Type	Year Begun	Jurisdiction
Marriage	1893	County Clerk
Divorce	1893	Mag. Court Clerk
Land	1893	County Clerk
Probate	1893	Mag. Court Clerk
Court	1893	Mag. Court Clerk

■ **Gem** 15 Mar. 1915
415 E. Main St., Emmett, ID 83617-3096
Phone: (208)365-4561
Web site: www.co.gem.id.us/
Parent County: Boise, Canyon
Comments/research tips: County Clerk has Land records from the late 1800s.

Record Type	Year Begun	Jurisdiction
Marriage	1915	County Clerk
Divorce	ca. 1915	Mag. Court Clerk
Probate	ca. 1915	Mag. Court Clerk
Court	ca. 1915	Mag. Court Clerk

■ **Gooding** 28 Jan. 1913
624 Main St., P.O. Box 417, Gooding, ID 83330
Phone: (208)934-4221
Web site: www.rootsweb.com/~idgoodin/
Parent County: Lincoln

Record Type	Year Begun	Jurisdiction
Marriage	1913	County Clerk
Divorce	1913	County Clerk
Land	1913	County Clerk
Probate	1913	County Clerk
Court	1913	County Clerk

■ **Idaho** 4 Feb. 1864
320 W. Main St., Grangeville, ID 83530-1992
Phone: (208)983-2751
Web site: www.idahocounty.org
Parent County: Original county
Comments/research tips: County Clerk/Auditor/Recorder has Birth and Death records 1907–1911.

Record Type	Year Begun	Jurisdiction
Probate	na	Clerk/District Ct.
Land	ca. 1860	County Clerk/Aud./Rec.
Court	na	Clerk/District Ct.
Marriage	ca. 1890	County Clerk/Aud./Rec.
Divorce	na	Clerk/District Ct.

■ **Jefferson** 18 Feb. 1913
134 N. Clark St., P.O. Box 275, Rigby, ID 83442
Phone: (208)745-7756
Web site: www.co.jefferson.id.us/
Parent County: Fremont

Record Type	Year Begun	Jurisdiction
Marriage	1914	County Clerk
Divorce	1914	Mag. Court Clerk
Land	1914	County Clerk
Probate	1914	Mag. Court Clerk
Court	1914	Mag. Court Clerk

■ **Jerome** 8 Feb. 1919
300 N. Lincoln Ave., Jerome, ID 83338
Phone: (208)324-8811
Web site: www.jeromecounty.org
Parent County: Gooding, Lincoln

Record Type	Year Begun	Jurisdiction
Marriage	1919	County Clerk
Divorce	1919	Mag. Court Clerk
Land	1919	County Clerk
Probate	1919	Mag. Court Clerk
Court	1919	Mag. Court Clerk

■ **Kootenai** 22 Dec. 1864
501 N. Government Way, Coeur d'Alene, ID 83816
Phone: (208)446-1650
Web site: www.co.kootenai.id.us/
Parent County: Nez Perce
Comments/research tips: County Recorder has Birth and Death records 1907–1912. Created in 1864, but not organized until 1881.

Record Type	Year Begun	Jurisdiction
Marriage	1881	County Recorder
Divorce	1895	Clerk/District Ct.
Probate	1895	Clerk/District Ct.
Court	1895	Clerk/District Ct.
Land	1881	County Recorder

■ **Latah** 14 May 1888
522 S. Adams, P.O. Box 8068, Moscow, ID 83843
Phone: (208)882-8580 ext. 3379

Idaho

Web site: www.latah.id.us/
Parent County: Nez Perce
Comments/research tips: County Clerk/Auditor/Recorder has Birth and Death records 1907–1911. Clerk of District Court has Court and Probate records from the early 1900s.

Record Type	Year Begun	Jurisdiction
Marriage	1888	County Clerk/Aud./Rec.
Land	1888	County Clerk/Aud./Rec.

■ Lemhi 9 Jan. 1869
206 Courthouse Dr., Salmon, ID 83467
Phone: (208)756-2815
Web site: www.rootsweb.com/~idlemhi/
Parent County: Idaho
Comments/research tips: County Clerk/Recorder has Birth and Death records 1907–1911.

Record Type	Year Begun	Jurisdiction
Marriage	1869	County Recorder
Divorce	1869	Mag. Court Clerk
Land	1869	County Recorder
Probate	1869	Mag. Court Clerk
Court	1869	Mag. Court Clerk

■ Lewis 3 Mar. 1911
P.O. Box 39, 510 Oak St., Nezperce, ID 83543
Phone: (208)937-2661
Web site: www.lewiscountyid.org
Parent County: Nez Perce

Record Type	Year Begun	Jurisdiction
Marriage	1911	County Auditor
Divorce	1911	Clerk/District Ct.
Land	1911	County Auditor
Probate	1911	Clerk/District Ct.
Court	1911	Clerk/District Ct.

■ Lincoln 18 Mar. 1895
P.O. Drawer A, 111 W. B St., Shoshone, ID 83352
Phone: (208)886-7641
Web site: www.rootsweb.com/~idlincol/
Parent County: Alturas, Blaine
Comments/research tips: Fire destroyed many early records. Some nineteenth-Century records are kept in Blaine and Gooding Counties.

Record Type	Year Begun	Jurisdiction
Marriage	1895	County Clerk
Divorce	1895	County Clerk
Land	1895	County Clerk
Probate	1895	County Clerk
Court	1895	County Clerk

■ Logan 7 Feb. 1889
Comments/research tips: Combined with Alturas County to form Blaine County 5 March 1895.

■ Madison 18 Feb. 1913
134 E. Main, P.O. Box 389, Rexburg, ID 83440-0389
Phone: (208)356-3662
Web site: www.co.madison.id.us/
Parent County: Fremont

Record Type	Year Begun	Jurisdiction
Marriage	1919	County Clerk
Divorce	1914	Mag./District Ct. Clerk
Land	1919	County Clerk
Probate	1914	Mag./District Ct. Clerk
Court	1914	Mag./District Ct. Clerk

■ Minidoka 28 Jan. 1913
715 G St., P.O. Box 368, Rupert, ID 83350
Phone: (208)436-9511
Web site: www.minidoka.id.us/
Parent County: Lincoln

Record Type	Year Begun	Jurisdiction
Marriage	1915	County Recorder
Divorce	1913	Mag. Court Clerk
Land	1915	County Recorder
Probate	1913	Mag. Court Clerk
Court	1913	Mag. Court Clerk

■ Nez Perce 4 Feb. 1864
1230 Main St., P.O. Box 896, Lewiston, ID 83501-0896
Phone: (208)799-3020
Web site: www.co.nezperce.id.us/
Parent County: Original County
Comments/research tips: County Auditor has Birth and Death records 1900–1911. Organized while part of Washington Territory in 1861.

Record Type	Year Begun	Jurisdiction
Marriage	1860	County Auditor
Divorce	1874	Clerk/District Ct.
Land	1860	County Auditor
Probate	1890	Clerk/District Ct.
Court	1874	Clerk/District Ct.

■ Oneida 22 Jan. 1864
10 Court St., Malad, ID 83252-0191
Phone: (208)766-4116
Web site: www.rootsweb.com/~idoneida/
Parent County: Original County
Comments/research tips: County Recorder has Birth and Death records 1907–1911. Magistrate Court Clerk has Court, Divorce, and Probate records from the late 1800s.

Record Type	Year Begun	Jurisdiction
Marriage	1866	County Recorder
Land	na	County Recorder

■ Owyhee 31 Dec. 1863
P.O. Box 128, Murphy, ID 83650
Phone: (208)495-2421
Web site: owyheecounty.net/
Parent County: Original County
Comments/research tips: County Clerk has Birth and Death records 1907–1913 and Naturalization records 1893–1911. Organized while part of Washington Territory.

Record Type	Year Begun	Jurisdiction
Marriage	1895	County Clerk
Divorce	na	County Court Clerk
Court	na	County Court Clerk
Land	1895	County Court Clerk
Probate	na	County Court Clerk

■ **Payette** 28 Feb. 1917
1130 Third Ave. N., P.O. Drawer D, Payette, ID 83661
Phone: (208)642-6000
Web site: www.rootsweb.com/~idpayett/
Parent County: Canyon

Record Type	Year Begun	Jurisdiction
Marriage	1917	County Clerk
Divorce	1917	County Clerk
Land	1865	County Clerk
Probate	1917	County Clerk
Court	1917	County Clerk
Nat.	1930	County Clerk

■ **Power** 30 Jan. 1913
543 Bannock Ave., American Falls, ID 83211-1200
Phone: (208)226-7611
Web site: www.co.power.id.us
Parent County: Bingham, Blaine, Oneida

Record Type	Year Begun	Jurisdiction
Marriage	1913	County Clerk
Divorce	1913	Clerk/District Ct.
Probate	1913	Mag. Court Clerk
Court	1913	Mag. Court Clerk

■ **Shoshone** 4 Feb. 1864
700 Bank St., Wallace, ID 83873
Phone: (208)752-1264
Web site: www.rootsweb.com/~idshosho/
Parent County: Original County
Comments/research tips: County Recorder has Birth and Death records 1907–1911. Organized while part of Washington Territory in 1861.

Record Type	Year Begun	Jurisdiction
Marriage	ca. 1890	County Recorder
Divorce	1887	County Clerk
Land	ca. 1890	County Recorder
Probate	1885	County Clerk
Court	1885	County Clerk

■ **Teton** 26 Jan. 1915
89 N. Main St., Driggs, ID 83422-0070
Phone: (208)354-2905
Web site: www.rootsweb.com/~idteton/
Parent County: Madison

Record Type	Year Begun	Jurisdiction
Marriage	1924	County Clerk
Divorce	1916	Mag. Court Clerk
Land	1924	County Clerk
Probate	1916	Mag. Court Clerk
Court	1916	Mag. Court Clerk

■ **Twin Falls** 21 Feb. 1907
425 Shoshone St. N., P.O. Box 126, Twin Falls, ID 83303
Phone: (208)736-4004
Web site: www.twinfallscounty.org
Parent County: Cassia

Record Type	Year Begun	Jurisdiction
Marriage	1907	County Recorder
Divorce	1907	Court Records
Land	1907	County Recorder
Probate	1907	Court Records
Court	1907	Court Records

■ **Valley** 26 Feb. 1917
219 N. Main St., P.O. Box 737, Cascade, ID 83611
Phone: (208)382-4297
Web site: www.rootsweb.com/~idvalley/
Parent County: Boise, Idaho

Record Type	Year Begun	Jurisdiction
Marriage	1917	County Recorder
Divorce	ca. 1960	Court Clerk
Land	1917	County Recorder
Probate	ca. 1960	Court Clerk
Court	ca. 1960	Court Clerk

■ **Washington** 20 Feb. 1879
256 E. Court St., P.O. Box 670, Weiser, ID 83672
Phone: (208)414-2092
Web site: www.ruralnetwork.net/~wcassr/
Parent County: Boise
Comments/research tips: County Clerk has Birth and Death records 1907–1911.

Record Type	Year Begun	Jurisdiction
Marriage	1879	County Clerk
Divorce	1879	Mag. Court Clerk
Land	1879	County Clerk
Probate	1879	Mag. Court Clerk
Court	1879	Mag. Court Clerk

Illinois

By James W. Warren

HISTORICAL OVERVIEW

Three hundred years ago, the land on which Chicago's glittering Michigan Avenue and the Sears Tower now stand was a quiet wilderness. Illinois' non-Indian beginnings were along the state's southern waterways. In 1699 French priests founded the oldest permanent white settlement in Illinois, a mission at Cahokia, in what is now St. Clair County. In 1703, Kaskaskia, now in Randolph county, was also founded by the French and eventually became the British seat of government. In 1763, France ceded the area to the British after the French and Indian War.

In 1778, the area that the Winnebago, Miami, Illinois, Kickapoo, Pottawatomie, Fox, and Sac Indians had long occupied became part of the United States. Illinois became a county of Virginia after Americans captured Kaskaskia from the British. Virginia relinquished its claim in 1784, and three years later Congress made Illinois part of the Northwest Territory. In 1800, the Northwest Territory was divided and what is now Illinois became part of Indiana Territory. When that was divided in 1809, Illinois Territory was formed. Prestatehood settlers were primarily from Virginia, Tennessee, Kentucky, and the Carolinas by way of the Ohio River.

In 1818 Illinois became the twenty-first state, after the Wisconsin region was transferred to Michigan Territory. At this point, most of the population lived near the waterways in the southern part of the state. The Black Hawk War of 1832 saw the Sauk and Fox Indians driven from the state and the last remaining Indian lands relinquished. Migration to Illinois during the 1830s was largely from New York and New England via the National Road or the Erie Canal to the Great Lakes. In the 1840s that migration continued, and large numbers of German and Irish also began to arrive. While many soon moved on to land opening up farther west, many remained in Illinois.

ILLINOIS AT A GLANCE

Motto: State Sovereignty, National Union

Population: 12.4 million

Prevalent Religions: Christianity, particularly Roman Catholic, Church of Jesus Christ of Latter-day Saints, Baptist, Methodist, Lutheran, and Pentecostal, also Judaism

Major Industries: Corn, soybeans, hogs, cattle, dairy products, wheat, machinery, food processing, electrical equipment, chemical products, printing and publishing, fabricated metal products, transportation equipment, petroleum, coal

Ethnic Makeup (in percent): Caucasian 73.5%, African American 15.1%, Hispanic 12.3%, Asian 3.4%, Native American 0.2%, Other 5.8%

Famous Illinoisans: Jane Addams, John Bardeen, Bonnie Blair, Gwendolyn Brooks, Dick Butkus, Al Capone, John Chancellor, Hillary Clinton, Richard Daley, Roger Ebert, Benny Goodman, Gene Hackman, Hugh Hefner, Charlton Heston, David Mamet, Carl Sandburg, James Tobin, Dick and Jerry Van Dyke, Charles Rudolph Walgreen, Frank Lloyd Wright

Above: Cityscape of downtown Chicago

© PhotoDisc/Getty Images

Illinois

So did many of the Poles, Italians, Austrians, Hungarians, Russians, and Scandinavians who arrived after the Civil War. More than a quarter-million Illinois troops served the Union during the Civil War.

In 1871, Mrs. O'Leary's pyromaniac cow kicked over a lantern and started the great Chicago fire. Much of the city and its records were destroyed. This makes thorough research in alternate records important for those with early Chicago ancestors. A helpful guide for locating such records is *Chicago and Cook County: Guide to Research* by Loretto Dennis Szucs.

In the decades after the Civil War, Illinois and the rapidly-growing Chicago area drew many African Americans north. Newcomers from around the world continued to migrate to Illinois throughout the twentieth century. Today's Illinois contrasts Chicago and surrounding counties, one of the country's largest commercial centers, with rich agricultural farmlands to the south.

RECORD HIGHLIGHTS

The available federal census for Illinois begins with 1820. (The exception is Randolph County, for which the 1810 census survived.) Mortality schedules exist for 1850, 1860, 1870 (partial), and 1880. Various territorial and state censuses exist. The 1810, 1818, and 1820 territorial censuses have been indexed and published. State censuses for 1825, 1835, 1845, 1855, and 1865 are held by the Illinois State Archives and are partially indexed, but many counties are missing or incomplete for the censuses through 1845.

Illinois county-level court records include probate, civil, and criminal cases, divorce, adoption, naturalization, and guardianship. The records are held by the clerks of the county court and the circuit court for each county. However, the older court and vital records are frequently available via microfilm (through the Family History Library) or may have been transferred to an Illinois Regional Archives Depository (IRAD) location.

Illinois law required the filing of vital records beginning in 1877, but statewide registration did not begin until 1916. Compliance with either was not always immediate. Post-1916 birth and death records are available from the State Department of Public Health in Springfield. Earlier records (sometimes including pre-1877 records) can be obtained from the county clerk.

Marriages are all at the county level. For divorces, a statewide index exists only from 1962. Divorce records are part of the civil court records at the county level.

Pre-1877 marriage records provide little information. But in 1877, preprinted marriage books went into use, and they included columns for such details as ages, residences, birthplaces, and often the names of the parents of the bride and groom. Couples were required to obtain

RESEARCH TIPS

for more info

- The Illinois State Archives and the Illinois State Genealogical Society have compiled an Illinois Marriage Records Index, 1763–1900, online at <www.sos.state.il.us/departments/archives/marriage.html>.
- Two online, statewide indexes to death records exist for Illinois: the index to death certificates from 1916–1950 <www.sos.state.il.us/departments/archives/idphdeathindex.html> and the pre-1916 Statewide Death Index <www.sos.state.il.us/departments/archives/death.html>.
- The Illinois State Historical Library has a biographical index of over 10,000 Illinois individuals in local histories and other sources.
- The Illinois Regional Archives Depository (IRAD) system houses older county and local government records at seven regional archives and is online at <www.sos.state.il.us/departments/archives/irad/iradholdings.html>.

Census Records
- Federal Census: 1810 (Randolph County), 1820, 1830, 1840, 1850, 1860, 1870, 1880, 1890, 1900, 1910, 1920, 1930
- Federal Mortality Schedules: 1850, 1860, 1870 (partial), 1880
- State/Territorial Census: 1810, 1818, 1820 (Edwards County missing), 1825 (Edwards, Fulton Randolph counties only), 1830 (Morgan), 1835, 1840, 1845, 1855, 1865
- 1835 (Fayette, Fulton, Jasper, Morgan), 1840 (35 of 87 counties), 1845 (Cass, Putnam, Tazewell), 1855, 1865 (all counties except Gallatin, Mason, Monroe; for Tazewell, only Elm Grove Township)

a marriage license, and marriage returns filed by the minister or JP indicated where the marriage took place and may provide the couple's religious denomination.

Another useful statewide resource provided by the Illinois State Genealogical Society is their "Cemetery Location Project." It is available online at <www.tbox.com/isgs/ilcemetery.html>. The Illinois USGenWeb site includes a county-by-county list of cemeteries, as well as an index to cemetery tombstone transcriptions and abstracts.

Church records can provide vital information for Illinois researchers. Sacramental records for the Roman Catholic Archdiocese of Chicago to 1915 are available through the Family History Library in Salt Lake City. The Evangelical Lutheran Church in America Archives in Chicago is the central archive and reference point for American Lutheran Church records research.

Online help for Illinois research is abundant. The Illinois State Archives and the Illinois State Genealogical Society have worked in unison for years to compile the Illinois Marriage Records Index, 1763–1900. The most up-to-date edition of this enormous ongoing project is available online from the Illinois State Archives at <www.sos.state.il.us/departments/archives/marriage.html>. The State Archives also provides two online statewide indexes to death records. The index to death certificates from 1916–1950 can be found at <www.sos.state.il.us/departments/archives/idphdeathindex.html>. The pre-1916 Statewide Death Index is a project the Archives is coordinating with volunteers worldwide. The site lists the counties and time periods completed to date <www.sos.state.il.us/departments/archives/death.html>.

Many nineteenth- and early twentieth-century immigrants lived in Chicago for awhile before migrating farther west. The Family History Library's microfilmed holdings for Chicago and Cook County are strong, easing the burden of big-city research. Vital records for Chicago include births to 1933, deaths to 1945, and marriages to 1920. (These records begin in 1871, after the Chicago Fire.) Chicago voting records (which can serve as a substitute for the missing 1890 census) are indexed for 1888, 1888–90, and 1892. The Chicago Historical Society is also an important resource for those with ancestors from the Chicago area.

The Illinois State Historical Library has a biographical index of over 10,000 Illinois individuals in local histories and other sources. Newberry Library is a private library in downtown Chicago with extensive reference materials and special collections for Illinois and beyond.

The Illinois Regional Archives Depository (IRAD) system houses older county and local government records at seven regional archives. The Web site, <www.sos.state.il.us/depts/archives/data_loc.html>, provides a listing of the records available at each of the seven IRADS, which are located on various Illinois University campuses.

STATE RESOURCES

■ ARCHIVES, LIBRARIES, AND SOCIETIES

Addison Historical Society and Museum
131 W. Lake St., Addison, IL 60101
Tel: (630) 628-1433

Afro-American Historical and Genealogical Society of Chicago, Inc.
P.O. Box 974, Carbondale, IL 62903-0974

Alton Area Historical Society, Inc.
239 W. Elm St., P.O. Box 971, Alton, IL 62002
Tel: (618) 466-5853

Archdiocese of Chicago's Joseph Cardinal Bernardin Archives and Records Center
711 W. Monroe St., Chicago, IL 60661
Tel: (312) 831-0711
Fax: (312) 831-0610
Web site: <http://archives.archchicago.org>

Arlington Heights Memorial Library
500 N. Dunton Ave., Arlington Heights, IL 60004
Tel: (847) 392-0100
Fax: (847) 506-2650
Web site: <www.ahml.lib.us>

Assumption Public Library
205 N. Oak St., Assumption, IL 62510-1137
Tel: (217) 226-3915

Augustana Historical Society
639-38th St., Rock Island, IL 61201-2296
Web site: <www.augustana.edu/Historical/AHS_member.htm>

Aurora Historical Society
P.O. Box 905, Aurora, IL 60507

Balzekas Museum of Lithuanian Culture
6500 S. Pulaski Rd., Chicago, IL 60629
Tel: (773) 582-6500
Fax: (773) 582-5133

Barrington Area Historical Society
212 W. Main St., Barrington, IL 60010
Tel: (847) 381-1730

Bartlett Historical Society
P.O. Box 8257, Bartlett, IL 60103-8257
Tel: (312) 837-2501

Batavia Historical Society
155 Houston St., P.O. Box 14, Batavia, IL 60510
E-mail: information@bataviahistoricalsociety.org
Web site: <www.bataviahistoricalsociety.org>

Belleville Public Library
121 E. Washington St., Belleville, IL 62220-2205
Tel: (618) 234-0441
Fax: (618) 234-9474

Bellflower Genealogical and Historical Society
Route 1, P.O. Box 17, Bellflower, IL 61724
Tel: (309) 722-3467

Blackhawk Genealogical Society
P.O. Box 3912, Rock Island, IL 61204-3912

Blue Island Historical Society
2433 York St., Blue Island, IL 60406
Tel: (708) 338-1078
E-mail: bis@sls.lib.il.us
Web site: <www.blueislan.org/Historical.html>

Bond County Genealogical Society
P.O. Box 172, Greenville, IL 62246

Bond County Historical Society
P.O. Box 327, Greenville, IL 62246
Tel: (618) 664-1606
Web site: <www.greenvilleusa.org/historical.htm>

Boone County Historical Society and Museum
311 Whitney Blvd., Belvidere, IL 61008
Tel: (815) 544-8391

E-mail: info@boonecountyhistoric almuseum.org
Web site: <www.boonecountyhist oricalmuseum.org>

Gail Borden Public Library
270 N. Grove Ave., Elgin, IL 60120
Tel: (847) 742-2411
Fax: (847) 742-0485
Web site: <www.elgin.lib.il.us>

C.E. Brehm Memorial Public Library District
101 S. Seventh St., Mt. Vernon, IL 62864
Tel: (618) 242-6322
Web site: <www.sirin.lib.il.us/ docs/bml/docs/lib/index.html

Brethren Historical Library and Archives
1451 Dundee Ave., Elgin, IL 60 120
Tel: (847) 742-5100 ext. 294
Fax: (847) 742-6103
Web site: <www.cob-net.org/ fobg/library.htm>

Brookfield Historical Society
8820 Brookfield Ave., Brookfield, IL 60513-1670
Tel: (708) 485-3420
Web site: <www.galia.com/bhs/>

Bryan-Bennett Library
217 W. Main St., Salem, IL 62881
Tel: (618) 548-7784
Fax: (618) 548-9593
Web site: <www.salembbl.lib.il .us>

Bureau County Genealogical Society
629 S. Main St., Princeton, IL 61356-2012
Tel: (815) 879-3133
Web site: <www.rootsweb.com/ ~ilbcgs/>

Bureau County Historical Society and Museum
109 Park Ave., West Princeton, IL 61356
Tel: (815) 875-2184

Bushnell Area Historical Society
300 Miller St., Bushnell, IL 61422

Cairo Historical Association
2700 Washington Ave., Cairo IL 62914

Calhoun County Historical Society
P.O. Box 327, Hardin, IL 62047-0327

Calumet City Historical Society Museum
760 Wentworth Ave., P.O. Box 1917, Calumet City, IL 60409-3515
Tel: (708) 891-8203 or (708) 862-8662

Cambridge Historical Society
R.R. #2, Box 96, Cambridge, IL 61238-9633

Carol Stream Historical Society
391 Illini Dr., Gretna Museum, Carol Stream, IL 60188-1962

Carroll County Genealogical Society
326 Third St., Savannah, IL 61074
Tel: (815) 273-3714
Web site: <www.internetni.com/ ~ahaliotis>

Carroll County Historical Society
P.O. Box 65, Mounty Carroll, IL 61053

Cass County Historical/ Genealogical Society
P.O. Box 11, Virginia, IL 62691
Web site: <www.rootsweb.com/ ~ilcchgs/>

Catlin Historical Society
210 N. Paris St., Catlin, IL 61817
Tel: (217) 424-5766
Web site: <www.rootsweb.com/ ~ilchs/>

Champaign Genealogical Society
% Champaign County Historical Archives
201 S. Race St., Urbana, IL 61801

Chatsworth Historical Society
424 E. Locust St., P.O. Box 755, Chatsworth, IL 60921
Tel: (815) 635-3124

Chicago Genealogical Society
P.O. Box 1160, Chicago, IL 60690-1160
Web site: <www.chgogs.org>

Chicago Heights Historical Society
3893 Merioneth Dr., Crete, IL 60417
Tel: (708) 672-5543

Chicago Historical Society
Clark St. at Narth Ave., Chicago, IL 60614-6071
Tel: (312) 642-4600

Fax: (312) 266-2077
Web site: <www.chicagohs.org>

Chillicothe Historical Society
P.O. Box 181, Chillicothe, IL 61523-0181
Tel: (309) 274-9076
E-mail: chillicothehistorical@yah oo.com
Web site: <www.Chillicothe.org>

Christian County Genealogical Society
P.O. Box 28, Taylorville, IL 62568-0028
Web site: <www.homepage.Mac omb.com/~tkuntz/ christianco.htm>

Christian County Historical Society
P.O. Box 254, Taylorville, IL 62568
Tel: (217) 824-6922

Clark County Genealogical Society
309 Maple, P.O. Box 153, Marshall, IL 62441
Tel: (217) 826-2864

Clay County Genealogical Society
P.O. Box 94, Louisville, IL 62858-0094
Tel: (618) 665-4544

Clinton County Historical Society
1091 Franklin St., Carlyle, IL 62231
Web site: <www.carlyle.il.us/mu s.htm>

Coles County Historical Society, Greenwood School Museum
800 Hayes Ave., P.O. Box 225, Charleston, IL 61920
Tel: (217) 345-2057

Coles County Illinois Genealogical Society
P.O. Box 592, Charleston, IL 61920-0592
E-mail: crngenealogy@yahoo .com
Web site: <www.rootsweb.com/ ~iltccgs/>

Columbia Historical Society
Rt. 1, P.O. Box 160A, Columbia, IL 62236

Cook Memorial Library
413 N. Milwaukee Ave., Libertyville, IL 60048
Tel: (847) 362-2330
Web site: <www.cooklib.org>

Crawford County Genealogical Society
803 N. Madison, Robinson, IL 62454

Crawford County Historical Society and Museum
P.O. Box 554, Robinson, IL 62454-0554
Tel: (618) 544-3087
E-mail: oldcrawf@frsb.net
Web site: <www.rootsweb.com/ ~ilcchs/>

Cumberland County Historical Society of Illinois
P.O. Box 393, Greenup, IL 62428

Czech and Slovak American Genealogy Society of Illinois
P.O. Box 313, Sugar Grove, IL 60554
Web site: <www.csagsi.org>

Czech and Slovak Library
% T.G. Masaryk School
5701 Twenty-second Place, Cicero, IL 60804

Danville Public Library
319 N. Vermilion St., Danville, IL 61832
Tel: (217) 447-5220
Fax: (217) 477-5230
Web site: <www.danville.lib.il .us>

Darien Historical Society
7422 Cass Ave., Darien, IL 60561
Tel: (847) 323-8926

Decatur Genealogical Library
1255 W. South Side Dr., Decatur, IL 62523
Tel: (217) 429-0135

DeKalb County Historical and Genealogical Society
P.O. Box 295, Sycamore, IL 60178

DeLavan Community Historical Society
Locust St., DeLavan, IL 61734

Des Plaines Historical Society
789 Pearson St., Des Plaines, IL 60016
Tel: (847) 391-5399
E-mail: dphslibrary@juno.com
Web site: <http://dpkhome.nort hstarnet.org/DPHS/>

DeWitt County Genealogical Society
P.O. Box 632, Clinton, IL 61727-0632

Illinois

Web site: <www.rootsweb.com/~idlewitt/id72.htm>

Douglas County Illinois Genealogical Society
P.O. Box 113, Tuscola, IL 61953

Downers Grove Historical Society
831 Downers Grove, IL 60515
Tel: (630) 963-1309

Dundee Township Historical Society
426 Highland Ave., West Dundee, IL 60118
Tel: (847) 428-6996
Web site: <http://dukhome.northstarnet.org/DTHS/>

Dunton Genealogical Society
500 N. Dunton, Arlington Heights, IL 60004

DuPage County Genealogical Society
P.O. Box 3, Wheaton, IL 60189-0003
Web site: <www.dcgs.org>

DuPage County Historical Museum
102 E. Wesley St., Wheaton, IL 60187
Tel: (630) 407-2888
E-mail: historical.museum@dupageco.org
Web site: <www.co.dupage.il.us/museum/>

Eastern Illinois University, Booth Library
600 Lincoln Ave., Charleston, IL 61920
Tel: (217) 581-6072 or (866) 862-6684
Web site: <www.eiu.edu/~booth/>

Edgar County Genealogical Society
P.O. Box 304, Paris, IL 61944-0304
Tel: (217) 463-4209

Edgar County Historical Society
414 N. Main St., Paris, IL 61944
Tel: (217) 463-5305

Edgewater Historical Society
358 N. Ashland, Chicago IL 60640
Tel: (773) 506-4849
Web site: <edgewaterhistory.org/index.htm>

Edwards County Historical Society
212 W. Main St., Albion, IL 62806
Tel: (618) 445-2631

Edwardsville Public Library
112 S. Kansas, Edwardsville, IL 62025-1708
Tel: (618) 692-7556
Fax: (618) 692-9566

Effingham County Genealogical and Historical Society
P.O. Box 1166, Effingham, IL 62401
Tel: (217) 342-2210

Ela Historical Society
95 E. Main St., Lake Zurich, IL 60047
Web site: <www.lzarea.org/ehs/>

Elgin Area Historical Society
360 Park St., Elgin, IL 60120
E-mail: elginhistory@foxvalley.net
Web site: <www.elginhistory.org>

Elgin Genealogical Society
P.O. Box 1418, Elgin, IL 60121-1418
Tel: (630) 833-1457
E-mail: ElginGS@aol.com
Web site: <www.elginarea.org/egs/page1.html>

Elk Grove Historical Society
499 Biesterfield Rd., Elk Grove Village, IL 60007
E-mail: heritage@northstarnet.org
Web site: <www.elkgrove.org/heritage/elk_grove_historical_society.htm>

Ellwood House Museum
509 N. First St., DeKalb, IL 60115
Tel: (815) 756-4609
Fax: (815) 756-4645
Web site: <www.elwoodhouse.org/barb_wire/>

Elmwood Historical Society
302 N. Magnolia, Elmwood, IL 61529
Tel: (309) 742-7791 or (309) 742-2431

Elmwood Park Historical Society
4 Conti Pkwy., Elmwood Park, IL 60635-4506
Tel: (630) 453-7645

Essley Noble Museum, Mercer County Historical Society
1406 Second Ave., Aledo, IL 61234
Tel: (309) 582-2280
Web site: <www.geocities.com/mchs_61231/>

Evangelical Lutheran Church in America Archives
321 Bonnie Lane, Elk Grove Village, IL 60007
Tel: (847) 690-9410
E-mail: archives@elca.org
Web site: <www.elca.org/archives/index.html>

Evangelical Lutheran Church in America Library
8765 W. Higgins Rd., Chicago, IL 60631
Tel: (773) 380-2811
Web site: <www.elca.org/os/library.html>

Evans Public Library
215 S. Fifth St., Vandalia, IL 62471
Tel: (618) 283-2824
Fax: (618) 283-4705
E-mail: evanspl@shawls.lib.il.us
Web site: < www.epl.lib.il.us>

Evanston Historical Society
225 Greenwood, Evanston, IL 60201
Tel: (847) 475-3410
E-mail: EvanstonHS@Northwestern.edu

Fayette County Genealogical and Historical Society
215 S. Fifth St., P.O. Box 177, Vandalia, IL 62471
Tel: (618) 423-2625

Fern Dell Historic Association
502 Chicago Rd., P.O. Box 254, Newark, IL 60541
Tel: (815) 695-5328

Ford County Historical Society
P.O. Box 115, Paxton, IL 60957
E-mail: FordCoHistSoc@hotmail.com
Web site: <www.rootsweb.com/~ilfchs/>

Forest Park Historical Society
% Forest Park Library, 7555 Jackson Ave., Forest Park, IL 60130

Fox Lake-Grant Township Area Historical Society
411 Washington St., P.O. Box 224, Ingleside, IL 60041
Tel: (847) 587-0544
E-mail: FLGrantHall@yahoo.com
Web site: <www.rootsweb.com/%7eiflahs/index.html>

Fox Valley Genealogical Society
P.O. Box 5435, Nashville, IL 60567-5433
E-mail: ilfvgs@yahoo.com

Web site: <www.rootsweb.com/~ilfvgs/index.htm>

Frankfort Area Genealogical Society
2000 E. St. Louis St., P.O. Box 427, West Frankfort, IL 62896
Tel: (618) 932-6159
Web site: <www.geocities.com/Heartland/Lane/4030/>

Franklin County Historical Society
304 E. Webster, St., Benton, IL 62812
Tel: (618) 435-6947

Freeburg Historical and Genealogical society
P.O. Box 69, Freeburg, IL 62243
Tel: (618) 539-5771

Freeport Public Library
100 E. Douglas, Freeport, IL 61032
Tel: (815) 233-3000
Fax: (815) 233-1099
E-mail: freeportlibrary@yahoo.com
Web site: <www.freeportpubliclibrary.org>

Fulton County Historical and Genealogical Society
45 N. Park Dr., P.O. Box 583, Canton, IL 61520
Tel: (309) 647-0771

Galena/Jo Daviess County Historical Society and Museum
211 S. Bench St., Galena, IL 61036
Tel: (815) 777-9129
Fax: (815) 777-9131
E-mail: ghmuseum@galenalink.net
Web site: <www.galenahistorymuseum.org>

Galewood-MontClare Historical Society
1705 N. Nashville Ave., Chicago, IL 60635
Tel: (312) 237-8960

Gallatin County Historical Society
P.O. Box 693, Shawneetown, IL 62984
Tel: (618) 269-3716

Garrett-Evangelical Theological Seminary
2121 Sheridan Rd., Evanston, IL 60201
Tel: (847) 866-3900
Fax: (847) 866-3957
Web site: <www.garrett.northwestern.edu>

Genealogical Forum of Elmhurst
% Elmhurst Historical Museum, 120 E. Park Ave., Elmhurst, IL 60126
Web site: <www.elmhurstespress .com/FORUM/>

The Genealogical Society of Southern Illinois
% John A. Logan College, Rte. 2, P.O. Box 145, Carterville, IL 62918-9599
Tel: (618) 985-6213

Genealogy Society of White County
P.O. Box 142, Carmi, IL 6281-0142
Web site: <www.rootsweb.com/ ~ilgswc/index.html>

Geneseo Historical Association
212 S. State St., Geneseo, IL 61254
Tel: (309) 944-3043

Geneva Historical Society
P.O. Box 345, Geneva, IL 60134
Tel: (630) 232-4951

Glen Ellyn Historical Society
P.O. Box 283, Glen Ellyn, IL 60138
Tel: (630) 858-8696
E-mail: historical@glen-ellyn.com
Web site: <www.glen-ellyn.com/ historical>

Glencoe Historical Society at the Eklund History Center and Garden
3777 Park Ave., Glencoe, IL 60022
Web site: <www.glencoehistoric alsociety.org/home/>

Glenview Area Historical Society
1121 Waukegan Rd., Glenview, IL 60025
Web site: <http://gvkhome.nort hstarnet.org/gvhist/ index.html>

Glenview Public Library
1930 Glenview Rd., Glenview, IL 60025
Tel: (847) 729-7500
Fax: (847) 729-7682
E-mail: info@glenview.lib.il.us
Web site: <www.glenview.lib.il .us>

Great River Genealogical Society
% Quincy Public Library, 526 Jersey St., Quincy, IL 62301-3996

Tel: (217) 222-0226
Web site: <www.outfitters.com/ ~grgs/>

Greater Harvard Area Historical Society
308 N. Hart St., P.O. Box 505, Harvard, Il 60033-3018
Tel: (815) 943-6141

Green Hills Genealogical Society
% Green Hills Public Library 8611 W. Thirteenth St., Palos Hills, IL 60465
Tel: (708) 598-8446

Greene County Historical and Genealogical Society
221 N. Fifth St., P.O. Box 137, Carrollton, IL 62016
Web site: <www.rootsweb.com/ ~ilgreene/gcgs.htm>

Greenville Public Library
414 W. Main St., Greenville, IL 62246-1615
Tel: (618) 664-3115
Fax: (618) 664-9442

Griggsville Area Genealogical and Historical Society
P.O. Box 75, Griggsville, IL 62340
Web site: <www.pikecoilgenweb. org/societies/griggsville.html>

Hancock County Historical Society
P.O. Box 68, Carthage, IL 62321-0068
Tel: (217) 357-0043
E-mail: hancockhistory@yahoo .com
Web site: <www.carthage.lib.il.us/ community/clubs/historical/>

Hardin County Historical and Genealogical Society
P.O. Box 72, Elizabethtown, IL 62931
Tel: (618) 287-2361

Henry County Genealogical Society
P.O. Box 346, Kewanee, IL 61443
Web site: <www.rootsweb.com/ ~ilhcgs/index.html>

Henry Historical and Genealogical Society
610 N. St., Henry, IL 61537
Tel: (309) 364-3272

Henry County Historical Society
P.O. Box 48, Bishop Hill, IL 61419
Tel: (309) 927-3528

Highland Park Historical Society
326 Central Ave., P.O. Box 56, Highland Park, IL, 60035
Tel: (847) 432-7090

Hinsdale Historical Society
P.O. Box 336, Hinsdale, IL 60522-0336
Tel: (630) 789-2600
E-mail Info@HinsdaleHistory.org
Web site: <www.hinsdalehistory .org>

Historical Society of the Fort Hill Country
432 W. Hillside Drive, Mundelein, IL 60060
Tel: (847) 566-7743

Historical Society of Greater Peotone
213 W. North St., Peotone, IL 60468
Tel: (708) 258-3436

Historical Society of Montgomery County
% City of Hillsboro, P.O. Box 556, Hillsboro, IL 62049

The Historical Society of Oak Park and River Forest
P.O. Box 771, Oak Park, IL 60303-0771
Tel: (708) 848-6755
E-mail: oprfhistory@aol.com
Web site: <www.oprf.com/OPRF HIST/>

Historical Society of Quincy and Adams County
425 S. Twelfth, Quincy, IL 62301
Tel: (217) 222-1835

Homer Historical Society
105 N. Main St., Homer, IL 61849

Hutsonville Historical and Genealogical Society
10953 E. 1825th Ave., Hutson- ville, IL 62433

The Hyde Park Historical Society
5529 S. Lake Park Ave., Chicago, IL 60637
E-mail: information@hydeparkhis tory.org
Web site: <www.hydeparkhistory .org>

Ida Public Library
320 N. State St., Belvidere, IL 61008
Tel: (815) 544-3838
Fax: (815) 544-8908

Illiana Genealogical and Historical Society
P.O. Box 207, Danville, IL 61834-0207
Tel: (217) 431-8733

Illiana Jewish Genealogical Society
P.O. Box 384, Flassmoor, IL 60422-0384
E-mail: ijgs@Comcast.net
Web site: <www.lincolnnet.net/ ijgs/>

Illinois Department of Public Health
Division of Vital Records, 605 W. Jefferson St., Springfield, IL 62702-5097
Tel: (217) 782-6553
Fax: (217) 785-3209
E-mail: vitalrecords@idph.state.il .us
Web site: <www.idph.state.il.us/ vitalrecords/index.htm>

Illinois Great Rivers Area Conference Archives and Special Collections
% Henry Pfeiffer Library— MacMurray College, 447 E. Jack- son Ave., Jacksonville, IL 62650
Tel: (217) 479-7694
Fax: (217) 245-5214
E-mail: archives@igrac.org
Web site: <www.igrac.org/archi ves/index.html>

Illinois Heritage Association
602 E. Green St., Champaign, IL 61820
Tel: (217) 359-5600

Illinois Historic Preservation Society
E-mail: info@ihpa.state.il.us
Web site: <www.illinoishistory .gov>

Illinois Mennonite Historical and Genealogical Society
675 State Rte. 116, Metamora, IL 61548-7732
E-mail: info@imhgs.org
Web site: <www.imhgs.org>

Illinois Regional Archives Depository
Illinois State Archives, Spring- field, IL 62756
Tel: (217) 785-1266
Fax: (217) 524-3930
Web site: <www.sos.state.il.us/ departments/archives/irad/ iradhome.html>

Illinois State Archives, Norton Building
Capitol Complex, Springfield, IL 627566

Tel: (217) 782-4682
Fax: (217) 524-3930
Web site: <www.sos.state.il.us/
departments/archives/archives
.html>

**Illinois State Genealogical
Society**
P.O. Box 10195, Springfield, IL
62791-0195
Tel: (217) 789-1968
E-mail: ISGSOffice@a5.com
Web site: <www.rootsweb.com/
ilgs/index.html>

Illinois State Historical Society
210 S. Sixth, Springfield, IL
62701-1503
Tel: (217) 525-2781
Fax: (217) 525-2783
E-mail: ishs@eosinc.com
Web site: <www.historyillinois
.org>

Illinois Veterans Home
1707 N. Twelfth St., Quincy, IL
62301
Tel: (217) 222-8641 ext. 248

**Iroquois County Genealogical
Society**
Old Courthouse Museum, 103 W.
Cherry St., Watseka, IL:
60970-1524
Tel: (815) 432-3730
E-mail: iroqgene@techinter.com
Web site: <www.rootsweb.com/
~ilicgs/>

**Jackson County Historical
Society**
1616 Edith St., Murphysboro IL
62966
E-mail: jchs@globaleyes.net
Web site: <home.globaleyes.net/
loganmus/JCHSEgypt.htm>

**Jacksonville Area Genealogical
and Historical Society**
416 S. Main St., Jacksonville, IL
62650-2904
Tel: (217) 245-5911 or (217)
245-9623
E-mail: jaghs@csj.net

**Jasper County Historical and
Genealogical Society**
% Newton Public Library, 100 S.
Van Buren St., Newton, IL 62448
Tel: (618) 783-8141

**Jefferson County Genealogical
Society**
P.O. Box 1131, Mt. Vernon, IL
628864-4187
Web site: <www.rootsweb.com/
~iljeffer/gensociety.htm>

**Jersey County Genealogical
Society**
P.O. Box 12, Jerseyville, IL 62052

**Jersey County Historical
Society**
601 N. State, Jerseyville, IL
62052
Tel: (618) 498-3514

**Jewish Genealogical Society of
Illinois**
P.O. Box 515, Northbrook, IL
60065-0515
Tel: (312) 666-0100
Web site: <www.jewishgen.org/
jgsi/>

**Johnson County Genealogical
and Historical Society**
P.O. Box 1207, Vienna, IL 62995
E-mail: jcghs@shawneelink.net
Web site: <www.jhohnsoncountyi
l.net>

**Kanakee County Historical
Society**
Eighth Ave. and Walter St.,
Kanakee, IL 60901
Tel: (815) 932-5279

**Kanakee Valley Genealogical
Society**
P.O. Box 442, Bourbonnais, IL
60914
Web site: <www.kvgs.org>

**Kane County Genealogical
Society**
P.O. Box 504, Geneva, IL 60134
E-mail: kcgsinfo@wideopenwest
.com
Web site: <www.rootsweb.com/
~ilkcgs/>

**Kane County Genealogical
Society**
P.O. Box 509, Geneva, IL 60134

**Kendall County Genealogical
Society**
P.O. Box 1086, Oswego, IL
60543
Tel: (630) 554-8342

**Kendall County Historical
Society**
P.O. Box 123, Yorkville, IL 60560
Tel: (630) 553-6777

Kenilworth Historical Society
415 Kenilworth Ave., P.O. Box
181, Kenilworth, IL 60043
Tel: (847) 251-2565

Kewanee Historical Society
211 N. Chestnut St., Kewanee, IL
61443
Tel: (309) 854-9701

**Kishwaukee Valley Heritage
Society**
700 W. Park Ave., Hwy. 72 W.,
P.O. Box 59, Genoa, IL
60135-0059
Tel: (815) 784-5498

**Knox County Genealogical
Society**
P.O. Box 13, Galesburg, IL
61402-0013
Tel: (309) 343-1466
Web site: <www.rootsweb.com/
ilknox/home/kcgs.htm>

Knox County Historical Society
P.O. Box 1757, Galesburg, IL
61402-1757
Web site: <knoxchs.homestead
.com>

LaGrange Public Library
10 W. Cossitt, LaGrange, IL
60525-2391
Tel: (708) 352-0576
Web site: <www.lagrangelibrary
.org>

**LaHarpe Historical and
Genealogical Society**
P.O. Box 289, LaHarpe, IL 61450

**Lake County Genealogical
Society**
1170 N. Midlothian Rd., Mendel-
ein, IL 60060
Tel: (847) 918-3208
E-mail: lcigs@yahoo.com
Web site: <www.rootsweb.com/
~illcgs/>

Lansing Historical Society
2750 Indiana Ave., P.O. Box
1776, Lansing, IL 60438
Tel: (708) 474-6160

**LaSalle County Genealogical
Guild**
115 W. Glover St., Ottawa, IL
61350
Tel: (815) 433-5261
Web site: <www.lscgg.org>

**Lawrence County Genealogical
Society**
R.R.1, Box 44, Bridgeport, IL
62417
Tel: (618) 945-7181

**Lawrence County Historical
Society**
P.O. Box 425, Lawrenceville, IL
62439
Tel: (618) 943-2300
E-mail: history@umfleet.net
Web site: <www.lawrencecountyi
llinois.com/history/index.html>

Lebanon Historical Society
309 W. St. Louis St., Lebanon, IL
62254
Tel: (618) 537-4498

**Lee County Genealogical
Society**
P.O. Box 63, Dixon, IL
61021-0063
Web site: <www.rootsweb.com/
~illee/genealogical_society
.htm>

Lemont Area Historical Society
P.O. Box 126, Lemont, IL 60439
Web site: < www.township.com/
lemont/historical/index.htm>

LeRoy Historical Society
301 E. Cedar, LeRoy, IL 61752

**Lewis and Clark Genealogical
Society**
P.O. Box 485, Godfrey, IL 62035

**Lexington Genealogical and
Historical Society**
318 W. Main St., Lexington, IL
61753
Tel: (309) 365-4591
Web site: <www.lexingtonillinois
.org/fort/>

**Libertyville-Mundelein
Historical Society**
413 N. Milwaukee Ave., Libertyville, IL 60048-2280
Tel: (847) 362-2330 or (847)
362-3130

Litchfield Carnegie Library
400 N. State St., Litchfield, IL
62056
Tel: (217) 324-3866
Fax: (217) 324-3884

**Lithuanian American
Genealogical Society**
% Balzekas Museum, 6500 S. Pu-
laski Rd., Chicago, IL 60629

**Logan County Illinois
Genealogical and Historical
Society**
114 N. Chicago St., Lincoln, IL
62656
Tel: (217) 732-3200
E-mail: LCGHS1@aol.com
Web site: <www.rootsweb.com/
~illcghs/>

Lombard Historical Society
23 W. Maple St., Lombard, IL
60148
Tel: (630) 629-1885

Long Grove Historical Society
RDF Box 3110, Long Grove, IL
60047
Tel: (847) 634-9440

Lyndon Historical Society
405 First St., Lyndon, IL 61261

Lyons Public Library
4209 Joliet Ave., Lyons, IL
60534-1597
Tel: (708) 447-3577
Web site: <www.lyons.lib.il.us>

Macon County Historical Society
5580 N. Fork Rd., Decatur, IL
62521
Tel: (217) 422-4919

Macoupin County Genealogical Society
P.O. Box 95, Staunton, IL
62088-0095
Web site: <www.rootsweb.com/
~ilmacoup/mcgs/index.htm>

Macoupin County Historical Society
P.O. Box 432, Carlinville, IL
62626
Tel: (217) 854-2850

Madison County Genealogical Society
P.O. Box 631, Edwardsville, IL
62025-0631
E-mail: mcgsil@hotmail.com
Web site: <www.rootsweb.com/
~ilmadcgs/index.html>

Madison County Historical Museum and Library
715 N. Main St., Edwardsville, IL
62025
Tel: (618) 656-7562

Manhattan Township Historical Society
240 Whitson, Manhattan, IL
60442
Tel: (815) 478-3374

Manito Historical Society
P.O. Box 304, Manito, IL 61546
Tel: (309) 968-6416

Marion County Genealogical and Historical Society
P.O. Box 342, Salem, IL 62881
Web site: <www.rootsweb.com/
~ilmarion/margenie.htm>

Marissa Historical and Genealogical Society
P.O. Box 47, Marissa, IL
62257-0047
Web site: <www.marissahgs
.org>

Marshall County Historical Society
314 Fifth St., Lacon, IL
61540-0123

Tel: (309) 246-2349
Web site: <www.il-mchs.org>

Mascoutah Historical Society
504 N. Jefferson St., Mascoutah,
IL 62258

Mason County Genealogical and Historical Society
P.O. Box 446, Havana, IL 62644
Web site: <www.havana.lib.il.us/
community/mcghs.html>

Massac County Genealogical Society
P.O. Box 1043, Metropolis, IL
62960-1043
Web site: <www.rootsweb.com/
~ilmcgs/>

Massac County Historical Society
P.O. Box 245, Brookport, IL
62910-0248

Matteson Historical Society
813 School Ave., Matteson, IL
60443
Web site: <www.vil.matteson.il
.us/Museum/historical_society
.htm>

Mattoon Public Library
1600 Charleston Ave., P.O. Box
809, Mattoon, IL 61938
Tel: (217) 234-2621
Fax: (217) 234-2660
E-mail: info@mattoonlibrary.org
Web site: <www.mattoonlibrary
.org>

McDonough County Genealogical Society
P.O. Box 202, Macomb, IL 61455
E-mail: mcgs@macomb.com
Web site: <www.Macomb.com/
mcgs/>

McHenry County Historical Society
6422 Main St., Union, IL 60180
Tel: (815) 923-2267

McHenry County Genealogical Society
P.O. Box 184, Crystal Lake, IL
60039-0184
Web site: <www.mcigs.org>

McLean County Genealogical Society
P.O. Box 488, Normal, IL
61761-0488
Web site: <http://home1.gte.
net/vzn05w35/index.html>

McLean County Genealogical Society Library
% McLean County Museum of
History, 200 N. Main St.,
Bloomington, IL 61701

Tel: (309) 827-0428 ext. 28
Fax: (309) 827-0100
E-mail: mcmh@mchistory.org
Web site: <www.mchistory.org>

Melrose Park Historical Society
P.O. Box 1453, Melrose Park, IL
60161

Menard County Historical Society
125 S. Seventh St., Petersburg,
IL 62675
Web site: <www.rootsweb.com/
~ilmenard/mchs.html>

Mercer County Historical Society
% Essley-Noble Museum, 1406
SE Second Ave., Aledo, IL 61231
Web site: <www.rootsweb.com/
~ilmercer/mchs.htm>

Meredosia Area Historical and Genealogical Society
P.O. Box 304, Meredosia, IL
62265

Metropolis Public Library
317 Metropolis St., Metropolis, IL
62960-2196
Tel: (618) 524-4312
Fax: (618) 524-3675
Web site: <www.sirin.lib.il.us/
docs/met/docs/lib/>

Monroe County Genealogical Society
P.O. Box 381, Columbia, IL
62236
Web site: <www.rootsweb.com/
~ilmcghs/>

Montgomery County Genealogical Society
P.O. Box 212, Litchfield, IL
62056-0212
Web site: <www.rootsweb.com/
~ilgreene/gensoc.htm>

Morgan County Historical Society
P.O. Box 1033, Jacksonville, IL
62651-1033
Tel: (217) 245-5390

Morris Library, Southern Illinois University Carbondale
Special Collections Research
Center, 605 Agriculture Dr., Mail-
code 6632, Carbondale, IL 62901
Tel: (618) 453-2516
Web site: <www.lib.siu.edu/sp
col/>

Morrison Historical Society
P.O. Box 1, Morrison, IL 61270
Tel: (815) 772-8889

Web site: <www.communitycouri
er.com/historical_society.htm>

John Mosser Public Library
106 W. Meek St., Abingdon, IL
61410-1451
Tel: (309) 462-3129

Moultrie County Historical and Genealogical Society
P.O. Box 588, Sullivan, IL
61951-0588
Tel: (217) 728-4085
Web site: <www.354.com/beth
any/genealogy.htm>

Mount Prospect Historical Society
101 S. Maple, Mount Prospect, IL
60056-3203
Tel: (847) 392-9006
Fax: (847) 392-8995
E-mail: mphist@wowway.com
Web site: <www.mphist.org/mph
shome.htm>

Mount Pulaski Township Historical Society
104 E. Cooke St., Mount Pulaski,
IL 62548
Tel: (217) 792-3719
Web site: <www.rootsweb.com/
~ilmpths/>

Mount Vernon Genealogical Society
101 S. Seventh, Mount Vernon, IL
62864

Mulkeytown Area Historical Society
P.O. Box 485, Mulkeytown, IL
62865

National Archives Records Administration, Great Lakes Branch
7358 S. Pulaski Rd., Chicago, IL
60629-5898
Tel: (773) 948-9019
Fax: (773) 948-9050

Nauvoo Historical Society
1380 Mulholland St., P.O. Box
69, Nauvoo, IL 62354
Tel: (217) 453-2528

The Newberry Library
60 W. Walton St., Chicago, IL
60610-7324
Tel: (312) 943-9090
Web site: <www.newberry.org/
general/abouthome.html>

Newport Township Historical Society
P.O. Box 98, Wadsworth, IL
60083

North Central Illinois Genealogical Society
P.O. Box 4635, Rockford, IL 61110-4635
Web site: <www.rootsweb.com/~ilwinneb/ncengen.htm>

North Suburban Genealogical Society
% Winnetka Public Library
768 Oak St., Winnetka, IL 60093-2583

Northbrook Historical Society
1776 Walter's Ave., Northbrook, IL 60062
Tel: (847) 498-3404

Northern Illinois Chapter, American Historical Society of Germans from Russia
847 S. Home Ave., Oak Park, IL 60304
Web site: <www.ahsgr.org/northern_illinois_chapter.htm>

Northwest Suburban Council of Genealogists
P.O. Box AC, Mount Prospect, IL 60056
Web site: <www.mtprospect.org/nsgs>

Norwood Park Historical Society
5624 N. Newark Ave., Chicago, IL 60631
Tel: (312) 631-4633

Oak Lawn Historical Society
4332 W. 109th St., Oak Lawn, IL 60453
Tel: (708) 425-3424

Odell Prairie Trails Genealogical and Historical Society
P.O. Box 82, Odell, IL 60460
Tel: (815) 998-2324

O'Fallon Historical Society
101 W. State St., P.O. Box 344, O'Fallon, IL 62269-0344
Tel: (618) 624-8409
E-mail: ohs@ofallonhistory.org
Web site: <www.ofallonhistory.org/index.shtml>

Ogle County Genealogical Society
P.O. Box 251, Oregon, IL 61061-0251
Web site: <www.rootsweb.com/~ilogle/societies.htm>

Ogle County Historical Society
111 N. Sixth St., Oregon, IL 61061

Web site: <www.rootsweb.com/~ilogle/historical.htm>

Oglesby Historical Society
100 Oak St., Oglesby, IL 61348

Old Six Mile Historical Society
3279 Maryville Road, P.O. Box 483, Granite City, IL 62040

Orland Historical Society
P.O. Box 324, Orland Park, IL 60543
Tel: (708) 349-0065
E-mail: orlandhistory@Comcast.net
Web site: <www.orlandhistory.org/index.htm>

Ostfriesian Heritage Society of East Central Illinois
3154 CR 2000E, Rantoul, IL 61866
Tel: (217) 896-4776

Oswego Roots Genealogical Society
P.O. Box 726, Oswego, IL 60543

Palatine Historical Society
P.O. Box 134, Palatine, IL 60078

Palatines to America, Illinois Chapter
P.O. Box 3884, Quincy, IL 62305

Palestine Historical Society
413 S. Lincoln, Palestine, IL 62451

Palos Historical Society
12332 S. Forest Glen Blvd., Palos Park, IL 60464-1707
Tel: (708) 361-3118

Park Forest Historical Society
400 Lakewood Blvd., Park Forest, IL 60466
Tel: (708) 748-3731
Web site: <www.lincolnnet.net/users/lrpfhs/>

Park Ridge Historical Society and Museum
41 S. Prairie, Park Ridge, IL 60068
Tel: (847) 696-1973

Peoria County Genealogical Society
P.O. Box 1489, Peoria, IL 61655-14/9
E-mail: PCGS@Prodigy.net
Web site: <www.usgennet.org/usa/il/county/peoria1>

Peoria Historical Society and Museum
611 SW Washington St., Peoria, IL 61602-5104
Tel: (309) 674-1921

Peoria Public Library
107 NE Monroe St., Peoria, IL 61602-1070
Tel: (309) 497-2000
Web site: <www.peoria.lib.il.us/INDEX.HTM>

Perry County Historical Society
108 W. Jackson St., Pickneyville, IL 62274.
Web site: <www.fnbpville.com/perrycounty.html>

Piatt County Historical and Genealogical Society
P.O. Box 111, Monticello, IL 61856
Web site: <www.monticello.net/html/genealogy.html>

Pike and Calhoun Counties Genealogical Society
P.O. Box 104, Pleasant Hill, IL 62366
Tel: (217) 734-2221

Pike County Historical Society and Museum
P.O. Box 44, Pittsfield, IL 62363
Tel: (217) 285-4618

Polish Genealogical Society and Museum of America
984 N. Milwaukee Ave., Chicago, IL 60622
Tel: (773) 384-3352
Fax: (773) 384-3799
E-mail: PGSAmerica@aol.com
Web site: <www.pgsa.org/index.htm>

Pontiac Public Library
211 E. Madison, Pontiac, IL 61764
Tel: (815) 844-7229
Fax; (815) 844-3475
E-mail: pontiac@davesworld.net
Web site: <www.pontiac.lib.il.us/library/>

Pope County Historical Society
P.O. Box 837, Golconda, IL 62938
Web site: <www.rootsweb.com/~ilpope/pchs.htm>

Putnam County Historical Society
P.O. Box 74, Hennepin, IL 61327
Tel: (815) 925-7560
E-mail: pchs61327@yahoo.com
Web site: <www.piperspages.com/putnamhistoricalsociety/>

Randolph County Genealogical Society
600 State St., Suite 306, Chester, IL 62233
Tel: (618) 826-3807
Web site: <www.rootsweb.com/~ilrcgs/index.htm>

Ravenswood-Lakeview Historical Association
% Conrad Sulzer Regional Library, 4455 N. Lincoln Ave., Chicago, IL 60625-2192
Tel: (312) 744-7616

Richland County Genealogical and Historical Society
P.O. Box 202, Olney, IL 62450

Ridge Historical Society
10621 S. Seeley Ave., Chicago, IL 60643
Tel: (773) 881-1675
E-mail: ridgehistory@hotmail.org
Web Page: <www.ridgehistoricalsociety.org>

Riverside Historical Commission and Museum
27 Riverside Rd., Riverside Village, IL 60546
Tel: (630) 447-2542
E-mail: riversidehistory@aol.com

Rock Island County Historical Society
822 Eleventh Ave., Moline, IL 61265-1221
Tel: (309) 764-8590
E-mail: Information@RICHS.cc
Web site: <www.richs.cc>

Rockford Historical Society
P.O. Box 4387, Rockford, IL 61101

Rockford Public Library
215 N. Wyman St., Rockford, IL 61101
Tel: (815) 965-6731
Fax: (815) 965-0866
Web site: <www.rpl.Rockford.org.index.asp>

Rogers Park/West Ridge Historical Society
7344 N. Western, Chicago, IL 60645
Tel: (773) 764-4078 or (773) 764-2401
Fax: (773) 764-2824
E-mail: rphistory@aol.com
Web site: <www.rpwrhs.org/rpwrhs/socinfo.htm>

Roselle Public Library
40 S. Park St., Roselle, IL 60172
Tel: (630) 529-1641
Web site: <www.roselle.lib.il.us>

Rossville Historical Museum
108 W. Attica St., Rossville, Il 60933
Tel: (217) 748-4080
E-mail: roshisoc@cooketech.net
Web site: <rossvilleshops.com/society.html>

Saint Charles Heritage Center
215 E. Main St., St. Charles, IL 60174
Tel: (630) 584-6967
Fax: (630) 584-6077
E-mail: info@stcmuseum.org
Web site: <www.stcmuseum .org/index.html>

Saint Clair County Genealogical Society
P.O. Box 431, Belleville, IL 62222-0431
Web site: <www.compu-type.net/rengen/stclair/stchome.htm>

Saint Clair County Historical Society
701 E. Washington St., Belleville, IL 62220
Tel: (618) 234-0600

Saline County Genealogical Society
P.O. Box 4, Harrisburg, IL 62946

Sangamon County Genealogical Society
P.O. Box 1829, Springfield, IL 62705-1829
Web site: <www.rootsweb.com/~ilsangam/scgs/scgs.htm>

Sangamon County Historical Society
308 E. Adams St., Springfield, IL 62701
E-mail: schs@eosinc.com
Web site: <www.sancohis.org>

Schuyler-Brown County Genealogical Society
200 S. Congress, Ruchville, IL 62681

David C. Shapiro Memorial Law Library
Swen Parson Hall, Northern Illinois University, DeKalb, IL 60625
Tel: (815) 753-0507
Web site: <http://law.niu.edu>

Shelby County Illinois Historical and Genealogical Society
151 S. Washington, P.O. Box 286, Shelbyville, IL 62565
E-mail: shgensoc@bmmhnet .com
Web site: <www.shelbycohistgen .org>

Skokie Historical Society
8031 Floral Ave., Skokie, IL 60077
Tel: (847) 673-1888

The Society of Colonial Wars in the State of Illinois
Web site: <http://my.execpc. com/~sril/ilcw.html>

South Holland Historical Society
P.O. Box 48, South Holland, IL 60473
Tel: (708) 596-2722

South Suburban Genealogical and Historical Society
3000 W. 170th Place, Hazel Crest, Illinois 6029-1174
Tel: (708) 335-3340
E-mail: SSGHS@usa.net
Web site: <www.rootsweb.com/~ssghs/>

Stark County Genealogical Society
P.O. Box 83, Toulon, IL 61483-0083
Web site: <www.rootsweb.com/~ilscgs/>

Staunton Public Library
306 W. Main St., Staunton, IL 62088
Tel: (618) 635-3852
Fax: (618) 635-2246

Stephenson County Genealogical Society
P.O. Box 514, Freeport, IL 61032-0514
E-mail: stephcogen@yahoo.com
Web site: <www.rootsweb.com/~ilstephe/HISTORYandMUSE UMS/Gensociety.html>

Stephenson County Historical Society
1440 S. Carroll Ave., Freeport, IL 61032
Tel: (815) 232-8419
Fax: (815) 297-0313
E-mail: Director@StephCoHS.Org
Web site: <www.stephcohs.org>

Sterling-Rock Falls Historical Society and Museum
P.O. Box 65, Sterling, IL 61081
Tel: (815) 625-6215

Streatorland Historical Society, Inc.
306 S. Vermillion St., Streator, IL 61364
Tel: (815) 672-2443

Swedish-American Historical Society, Inc.
3225 W. Foster Ave., Box 48, Chicago, IL 60625
Tel: (773) 583-5722
E-mail: info@swedishamericanhis t.org
Web site: <www.swedishamerica nhist.org>

Swenson Swedish immigration Research Center
% Augustana College, 639 Thirty-eighth St., Rock Island, Il 61201-2296
Tel: (309) 794-7204
Fax: (309) 794-7443
E-mail: sag@augustana.edu
Web site: <www.augustana.edu/administration/swenson/>

Sycamore Public Library
103 E. State St., Sycamore, IL 60178
Tel: (815) 895-7271

Tazewell County Genealogical and Historical Society
P.O. Box 312, Pekin, IL 61555-0312
Tel: (309) 477-3044
E-mail: tcghs cghs.org
Web site: <www.tcghs.org>

Thorton Township Historical Society/Genealogical Section
154 E. 154th St., Harvey, IL 60426
Tel: (708) 331-4247

Three Rivers Public Library District, Minooka Branch
109 N. Wabena, Minooka, IL 60447
Tel: (815) 467-1600
Fax: (815) 467-01632
E-mail: mhouchens@htls.lib.il.us

Tinely Moraine Genealogists
P.O. Box 521, Tinley Park, IL 60477
Tel: (708) 532-6594

Tinley Park Historical Society
P.O. Box 325, Tinley Park, IL 60477
Tel: (708) 429-4210

Tri-County Genealogical Society
P.O. Box 355, Augusta, IL 62311

Union County Genealogical and Historical Research Committee
101 E. First St., P.O. Box 92, Versailles, IL 62378
Tel: (217) 225-9094

University of Illinois at Springfield
One University Plaza, MS BRK 140, Springfield, IL 62703-5407
Tel: (217) 206-6520
Web site: <www.uis.edu/archi ves/>

Urbana Free Library Archives
201 S. Race St., Urbana, IL 61801
Tel: (217) 367-4025
E-mail: archives@urbanafreelibrar y.org
Web Site: <urbanafreelibrary .org>

Vandalia Historical Society
307 N. Sixth, Vandalia, IL 621471
Tel: (618) 283-0024

Vermilion County Museum
116 N. Gilbert, Danville, IL 61832
Tel: (217) 442-2922
Web site: <www.vermilioncounty museum.org/index.htm>

Versailles Area Genealogical and Historical Society
P.O. Box 92, Versailles, IL 62378

Villa Park Historical Society Museum
220 S. Villa Ave., Villa Park, IL 60181
Tel: (630) 941-0223
E-mail: contactus@vphistoricalso ciety.com
Web site: <www.vphistoricalsoci ety.com>

Village of Thornton Historical Society
114 N. Hunter St., Thorton, IL 60476
Tel: (708) 877-6569
Web site: <www.thornton60476 .com/history.html>

Vogel Genealogical Research Library
305 First St., Box 132, Holcomb, IL 61043

Wabash County Historical Society
P.O. Box 911, Mount Carmel, IL 62863
Web site: <www.rootsweb.com/~ilwabash/whistsoc.html>

Warren County Genealogical Society
P.O. Box 761, Monmouth, IL 61462-0761
Tel: (309) 734-6789

Warren County Historical Society
RR 2, Avon, IL, 61415
Tel: (309) 465-3361

Warren County Library
60-62 Public Square, Monmouth, IL 61462
Tel: (309) 734-3166
Fax: (309) 734-5955
E-mail: wcpl@monmouthnet.net
Web site: <http://wcpl.monmouthnet.net>

Warsaw Historical Society and Museum
401 Main St., Warsaw, IL 62379

Washington County Genealogical Society
Rt. 1, Nashville, IL 62263

Harold Washington Library Research Center, Chicago Public Library
Chicago Public Library's Central Library, 400 S. State St., Chicago, IL 60605
Tel: (312) 747-4526
Web site: <www.chipublib.org/001hwlc/001hwlc.html>

Wauconda Township Historical Society
711 N. Main St., P.O. Box 256, Wauconda, IL 60084
Tel: (847) 526-9303

Waukegan Historical Society, J. L. Raymond Memorial Research Library
1911 N. Sheridan Rd., P.O. Box 857, Waukegan, IL 60087
Tel: (847) 360-4772
Web site: <www.waukeganhistorical.org>

Waverly Genealogical and Historical Society
359 E. Tremont St., Waverly, IL 62692
Tel: (217) 435-4961

West Chicago Historical Society
Kruse House Museum
527 Main St., P.O. Box 246, West Chicago, IL 60186
Tel: (630) 231-0564 or (630) 231-8472

Western Illinois University Library
Illinois Regional Archives Depository, 1 University Circle, Macomb, IL 61455
Tel: (309) 298-2716
Web site: <www.wiu.edu/users/milibo/wiu/units/archives/irad/>

Westmont Historical Society, W.L. Gregg Museum
117 S. Linden, Westmont, IL 60559

Wheaton Public Library
225 N. Cross St., Wheaton, IL 60187
Tel: (630) 668-1374
Web site: <www.wheaton.lib.il.us/library/wpl.html>

Wheeling Historical Society
P.O. Box 3, Wheeling, IL 60090

White County Historical Society
P.O. Box 121, Carmi, IL 62821
Tel: (618) 381-8425
E-mail: WCHSgenealogylib@surffirst.net
Web Site: <www.rootsweb.com/~ilwcohs/>

Will County Historical Society
803 S. State St., Lockport, IL 60441
Tel: (815) 838-5080

Will-Grundy Counties Genealogical Society
P.O. Box 24, Wilmington, IL 60481-0024
Web site: <www.wggs.org>

Ronald Williams Library, Northeastern Illinois University
5500 N. St. Louis Ave., Chicago, IL 60625-4699
Tel: (773) 442-4506

Williamson County Historical Society
105 S. Van Buren St., Marion, IL 62959
Tel: (618) 997-5863
Web site: <www.thewchs.com>

Wilmette Historical Museum and Society
609 Ridge Rd., Wilmette, IL 60091
Tel: (847) 853-7666
Fax: (847) 853-7706
Web site: <www.wilmettehistory.org>

Winfield Historical Society
ON 555 Winfield Rd., P.O. Box 315, Winfield, IL 60190

Winnebago and Boone Counties Genealogical Society
P.O. Box 10166, Rockford, IL 61131-0616

Web site: <www.rootsweb.com/~ilwinneb/winbngen.htm>

Winnetka Historical Society
P.O. Box 365, Winnetka, IL 60093
Tel: (847) 501-6025
Web site: <www.winnetkahistory.org/index1.htm>

Winnetka-Northfield Public Library District, Main Library
768 Oak St., Winnetka, IL 60093
Tel: (847) 446-7220
Web site: <www.wpld.alibrary.com>

Withers Public Library
202 E. Washington, Bloomington, IL 61701

Woodford County Historical Society
203 S. Main St., Eureka, IL 61530-1618

Wyanet Historical Society
Main St., P.O. Box 169, Wyanet, IL 61379
Tel: (815) 699-2531

Zion Genealogical Society
% Zion Public Library, 2400 Gabriel Ave., Zion, IL 60099
E-mail: ziongenealogy@aol.com
Web site: <wkkhome.northstarnet.org/zion/>

Zion Historical Society
1300 Shiloh Blvd., Zion, IL 60099-2622
Tel: (847) 746-2427

BIBLIOGRAPHY

■ GENERAL RESOURCES

The Biographical Encyclopedia of Illinois of the Nineteenth Century
(Philadelphia, PA: Galaxy Publishing Company, 1875)

Brethren in Northern Illinois and Wisconsin
by John Heckman (Elgin, IL: Brethren Publishing House, 1941)

A Brief History of the Regular Baptists, Principally of Southern Illinois
by Achilles Coffey (Paducah, KY: Martin Steam Printers and Binders, 1877)

Chicago and Cook County: A Guide to Research
by Loretto Dennis Szucs (Salt Lake City, UT: Ancestry, ca. 1996)

A Complete History of Illinois from 1673–1968
by Alexander Davidson (Springfield, IL: Illinois Journal Company, 1874)

Descriptive Inventory of the Archives of the State of Illinois, 2d ed.
edited by Robert E. Bailey and Elaine Shemoney Evans (Springfield, IL: Illinois State Archives, Office of the Secretary of State, 1997)

Encyclopedia of Biography of Illinois, 3 vols.
(Chicago, IL: Century Publishing and Engraving Co., 1892–1902)

Finding Your Chicago Ancestors
by Grace DuMelle (Chicago, IL: Lake Claremont Press, 2004)

The Frontier State, 1818–1848
by Theodore Calvin Pease (Springfield, IL: Centennial Commission, 1918)

Genealogical Sources in Chicago, Illinois, 1835–1900
compiled by the Bicentennial Committee, Virginia M. Meyer, chairman (Chicago, IL: Chicago Genealogical Society, 1982)

The Genealogist's Companion and Sourcebook, 2d ed.
by Emily Anne Croom (Cincinnati: Betterway Books, 2003)

A Genealogist's Guide to Discovering Your African-American Ancestors
by Franklin Carter Smith and Emily Anne Croom (Cincinnati: Betterway Books, 2003)

Guide to Church Vital Statistics Records in Illinois, Preliminary ed.
prepared by Illinois Historical Records Survey (Chicago, IL: Illinois Historical Records Survey, Illinois Public Records Project, 1942)

A Guide to County Records in the Illinois Regional Archives
by Roy C. Turnbaugh, Jr. (Springfield, IL: Illinois State Archives, ca. 1983)

Illinois

Guide to Depositories of Manuscript Collection in Illinois, Preliminary ed.
prepared by the Illinois Historical Records Survey Project (Chicago, IL: Illinois Historical Records Survey Project, 1940)

Guide to Genealogical Research in the National Archives of the United States
edited by Anne Bruner Eales and Robert M. Kvasnicka (Washington, DC: National Archives and Records Administration, 2000

A Guide to the History of Illinois
edited by John Hoffman (New York, NY: Greenwood Press, 1991)

A Guide to Illinois Area Genealogical Societies and Illinois Researchers
by the Illinois State Genealogical Society (Lincoln, IL: Illinois State Genealogical Society, 1986)

Historical Encyclopedia of Illinois, 3 vols.
edited by Newton Bateman, Paul Selby, and David McCulloch (La Crosse, WI: Brookhaven Press, ca. 2001)

A History of Illinois from its Commencement as a State in 1818 to 1847
by Thomas Ford (Chicago, IL: S.C. Griggs and Co., 1854)

History of Illinois and Her People, 6 vols.
by Professor George W. Smith (Chicago, IL: The American Historical Society, Inc., 1927)

History of the Presbyterian Church, in the State of Illinois
by A.T. Norton (St. Louis, MO: W.S. Bryan, 1879)

How to Research a Family with Illinois Roots
by Lowell M. Volkel and Marjorie Smith (Thomson, IL: Heritage House, ca. 1977)

Illinois Biographical Dictionary: People of all Times and all Places Who have been Important to the History and Life of the State
(New York, NY: Somerset, ca. 1993)

Illinois: Crossroads of a Continent
by Lois Carrier (Urbana, IL: University of Illinois Press, ca. 1993)

The Illinois Fact Book and Historical Almanac, 1673–1968
by John Clayton (Carbondale, IL: Southern Illinois University Press, 1970)

Illinois Genealogical Research
by George K. Schweitzer; word processing by Anne M. Smalley (Knoxville, IN: G.K. Schweitzer, ca. 1997)

Illinois, the Heart of the Nation, 5 vols.
by Edward F. Dunne (Chicago, IL: Lewis Publishing Co., 1933)

Illinois; A History of the Prairie State
by Robert P. Howard (Grand Rapids, MI: W.B. Eerdmans Pub. Co., 1972)

Illinois Libraries with Genealogical Collections
edited by Lowell M. Volkel (Springfield, IL: Illinois State Genealogical Society, 1992)

Illinois Quaker Meeting Records
compiled and indexed by Shelby Publishing & Printing (Kokomo, IN: Shelby Pub. and Printing, ca. 1996)

Illinois Research Outline, 2d ed.
by Church of Jesus Christ of Latter-day Saints (Salt Lake City, UT: Corp of the President of the Church of Jesus Christ of LDS, ca. 1988, ca. 1999)

Illinois State Genealogical Society Surname Index, 1981
compiled by Mrs. O.B. Lunde (Decatur, IL: the Illinois State Genealogical Society, 1982)

The Indians of Illinois: A History and Genealogy
by Helen Cox Tregillis (S.1.: H.C. Tregillis, ca. 1983)

Log Cabins to Steeples: The Complete Story of the United Methodist Way in Illinois, Including all Constituent Elements of the United Methodist Church
by J. Gordon Melton (Chicago, IL: Commissions on Archives and History, Northern, Central, and Southern Illinois Conferences, 1974)

Manual for Illinois Genealogical Research
by Pat and Ray Gooldy (Indianapolis, IN: Ye Olde Genealogie Shoppe, ca. 1994)

Men of Illinois
(Chicago, IL: H. Witherspoon, 1902)

Mennonites in Illinois
by Willard H. Smith (Scottdale, PA: Herald Press, 1983)

The Methodist Movement in Northern Illinois
by Almer M. Pennewell (Sycamore, IL: The Sycamore Tribune, 1942)

National Archives Microfilm Catalogs online:
<www.archives.gov/publications/genealogy_microfilm_catalogs.html>

Newspapers in the Illinois State Historical Library
by the Illinois State Historical Library (Springfield, IL: 1964)

Newspapers and Periodicals of Illinois, 1814–1879, rev. and enl. ed.
by Franklin William Scott (Springfield, IL: Illinois State Historical Library 1910)

The Patriotism of Illinois. A Record of the Civil and Military History of the State in the War for the Union, with a History of the Campaigns in which Illinois Soldiers have been Conspicuous, Sketches of Distinguished Officers, the Roll of the Illustrious Dead, Movements of the Sanitary and Christian Commissions, 2 vols.
by T. M. Eddy (Chicago, IL: Clarke and Co., 1865–1866)

Plains People; the Midwest (Indiana, Illinois, Iowa, Missouri): Research Sources and Bibliographies
prepared by Fiske Genealogical Foundation (Seattle, WA: Fiske Genealogical Foundation, 1990)

Prairie Pioneers of Illinois, 2 vols.
edited by Beth Rochefort (Lincoln, IL: Illinois State Genealogical Society, 1986–1988)

A Reference Guide for Genealogical and Historical Research in Illinois
by Joseph C. Wolf (Detroit, MI: Detroit Society for Genealogical Research, 1963)

Searching in Illinois: A Reference Guide to Public and Private Records
by Gayle Beckstead and Mary Lou Kozub (Costa Mesa, CA: ISC Publications, ca. 1984)

Sources of Mormon History in Illinois, 1839–48; an Annotated Catalog of the Microfilm Collection at Southern Illinois University, 2d ed.
compiled by Stanley B. Kimball (Carbondale, IL: Central Publications, Southern Illinois University, 1966)

A Summary Guide to Local Government Records in the Illinois Regional Archives
edited by Robert E. Bailey, et al. (Springfield, IL: Illinois State Archives, Office of the Secretary of State, ca. 1992)

Travel and Description, 1765–1865: Together with a List of County Histories, Atlases, and Biographical Collections and a List of Territorial and State Laws
by Solon J. Buck (New York: B. Franklin, 1971)

The United States Biographical Dictionary and Portrait Gallery of Eminent and Self-made Men: Illinois Volume
(Chicago, IL: American Pub. Co., 1883)

We Were There: An Oral History of the Illinois Baptist State Association, 1907–1976
edited by Robert J. Hastings (Springfield, IL: the Illinois Baptist State Association, 1976)

Who's Who in Illinois, Women, Makers of History
by Agness Geneva Gilman, A.B. and Gertrude Marcelle Gilman, A.M. (Chicago, IL: The Electric Publishers, 1927)

The Women of Illinois
by Henry McCormick (Bloomington, IL: Pantagraph Printing and Stationery Company, 1913)

■ CENSUS RECORDS

The American Census Handbook
by Thomas Jay Kemp (Wilmington, DE: Scholarly Resources, 2001)

The Census Book: A Genealogist's Guide to Federal Census Facts, Schedules, and Indexes
by William Dollarhide (Bountiful, UT: Heritage Quest, 2000)

Finding Answers in U.S. Census Records
by Loretto Dennis Szucs and Mathew Wright (Orem, UT: Ancestry Pub., ca. 2002)

Map Guide to the U.S. Federal Censuses, 1790–1920
by William Thorndale and William Dollarhide (Baltimore, MD: Genealogical Pub. Co., 1987)

State Census Records
by Ann S. Lainhart (Baltimore, MD: Genealogical Publishing, 1992)

Your Guide to the Federal Census
by Kathleen W. Hinckley (Cincinnati: Betterway Books, 2002)

■ IMMIGRATION RECORDS

American Naturalization Records, 1790–1990: What They Are and How to Use Them
by John J. Newman (North Salt Lake, UT: HeritageQuest, 1998)

American Passenger Arrival Records
by Michael Tepper (Baltimore: Genealogical Publishing Co., 1993)

They Became Americans: Finding Naturalization Records and Ethnic Origins
by Loretto Dennis Szucs (Salt Lake City: Ancestry, Inc., 1998)

They Came in Ships: A Guide to Finding Your Immigrant Ancestor's Arrival Records, 2d ed.
by John P. Colletta (Salt Lake City: Ancestry, Inc., 1993)

■ LAND RECORDS

The Illinois Military Tract; a Study of Land Occupation, Utilization, and Tenure
by Theodore Leonard Carlson (Urbana, IL: University of Illinois Press, 1951)

Land and Property Research in the United States
by E. Wade Hone (Salt Lake City, UT: Ancestry, ca. 1997)

Locating Your Roots: Discover Your Ancestors Using Land Records
by Patricia Law Hatcher (Cincinnati: Betterway Books, 2003)

Original Land Grants, 1824–1870, photocopies of original records at Williamson county circuit court clerk's office
compiled by Charla Murphy, Mary Jo Moore, Jean Burke (Marion, IL: Williamson County Historical Society, 1997)

Record of the Services of Illinois Soldiers in the Black Hawk War, 1831–32, and in the Mexican War, 1846–48, Containing a Complete Roster of Commissioned officers and Enlisted Men of both Wars, Taken from the Official Rolls on File in the War Department, Washington, D.C.
prepared by Issac H. Elliott (Springfield, IL: H.W. Rokker, State Printer, 1882)

War of 1812 Bounty Lands in Illinois
indexed by James D. Walker with an introduction by Lowell M. Volkel (Thomson, IL: Heritage House, 1977)

■ MAPS

Counties of Illinois: Their Origin and Evolution, with Twenty-three Maps Showing the Original and present Boundary Lines of Each County of the State
compiled by Edward J. Hughes (Springfield, IL: E.J. Hughes, 1941)

County and Township Gazetteer; Notes on the Location of Illinois County Seats
compiled by Sheila Kelly, notes by Lori Lovett (Springfield, IL: Illinois State Archives, 1988)

A Gazetteer of Illinois in Three Parts, 2d ed.
John Mason Peck (Philadelphia, PA: Grigg and Elliott, 1837)

A Gazetteer of the States of Illinois and Missouri
by Lewis C. Beck (Albany, NY: C.R. and G. Webster, 1823)

Illinois Atlas and Gazetteer
(Yarmouth, ME: DeLorme Mapping Company, ca. 1991)

Illinois Place Names
compiled by James N. Adams, edited by William E. Keller with an addendum by Lowell M. Volkel (Springfield, IL: Illinois State Historical Society, 1989)

Indian Place Names in Illinois
by Virgil Vogel Jr. (Springfield, IL: 1963)

Maps of Illinois Counties in 1876, Together with the Plat of Chicago and other Cities and a Sampling of Illustrations
(Knightstown, IN: Mayhill Publications, 1972)

Origin and Evolution of Illinois Counties
by Jessie White, Secretary of State (Springfield, IL: The State, 2000)

■ MILITARY RECORDS

Biographical Sketches of Illinois Officers Engaged in the War Against the Rebellion of 1861
by James Grant Wilson (Chicago, IL: J. Barnet, 1862)

Fighting Men of Illinois: an Illustrated Historical Biography
edited by Publishers Subscription Co. (Tucson, AZ: W.C. Cox, 1974)

Illinois in the Civil War, 2d ed.
by Victor Hicken, foreword by E.B. Long (Urbana, IL: University of Illinois Press, ca. 1991)

Illinois Soldier's and Sailor's Home at Quincy, 2 vols.
indexed by Lowell M. Volkel (Thomson, IL: Heritage House, 1975–1980)

Index to War of 1812 Pension Files, revised edition, 2 vols.
transcribed by Virgil D. White (Waynesboro, TN: National Historical Pub. Co., 1992)

The Martyrs and Heroes of Illinois in the Great Rebellion. Biographical Sketches
edited by James Barnet (Chicago, IL: Press of J. Barnet, 1865)

Record of the Service of Illinois Soldiers in the Black Hawk War, 1831–32, and the Mexican War, 1846–48
by the Illinois Military and Naval Department (Springfield, IL: H.W. Rokker, State printer, 1882)

Remembering Illinois Veterans
sponsored by Illinois State Archives and the Illinois State Genealogical Society (Springfield, IL: the Illinois State Archives, 1992)

Report of the Adjutant General of the State of Illinois, 9 vols.
revised by J. N. Reece (Springfield IL: Phillips Brothers, 1900–1902)

Revolutionary Soldiers buried in Illinois
by Harriett J. Walker (Baltimore, MD: Genealogical Pub. Co., 1967)

Soldiers of the American Revolution Buried in Illinois: a Bicentennial Project of the Illinois State Genealogical Society
(Springfield, IL: the Illinois State Genealogical Society, 1976)

Soldiers' and Patriots' Biographical Album: Containing Biographies and Portraits of Soldiers and Loyal Citizens in the American Conflict, Together with the Great Commanders of the Union Army, also a History of the Organizations Growing out of the War
(Chicago, IL: Union Veteran Publishing Co., 1892)

Uncle, We Are Ready! Registering America's Men, 1917–1918: A Guide to Researching World War I Draft Registration Cards
by John J. Newman (North Salt Lake, UT: HeritageQuest, 2001)

U.S. Military Records: A Guide to Federal & State Sources, Colonial America to the Present
by James C. Neagles (Salt Lake City: Ancestry, Inc., 1994)

Illinois

World War II: A Family Historian's Guide
by Debra Johnson Knox (Spartanburg, SC: MIE Publishing, 2003)

■ PROBATE RECORDS

The Bench and Bar of Illinois: Historical and Reminiscent, 2 vols.
edited by John M. Palmer (Chicago, IL: Lewis Pub., 1899)

Courts and Lawyers, 3 vols.
by Frederic B. Crossley (Chicago, IL: The American Historical Society, 1916)

The Illinois Fact Book and Historical Almanac, 1673–1968
by John Clayton (Carbondale, IL: Southern Illinois University Press, 1970)

■ VITAL RECORDS

1820 Federal Census of Illinois
compiled by Lowell M. Volkel and James V. Gill (Danville, IL: Illiana Genealogical Pub. Co., 1966)

1850 Illinois Mortality Schedule, 3 vols.
transcribed and indexed by Lowell M. Volkel (n.p., 1972–ca. 1973)

1860 Illinois Mortality Schedule, 3 vols.
transcribed and indexed by Lowell M. Volkel (Indianapolis, IN: Heritage House, ca. 1979)

The Era of the Civil War: 1848–1870
by Arthur Charles Cole with an introduction by John Y. Simon (Urbana, IL: University of Illinois Press, ca. 1987)

Guide to Public Vital Statistics Records in Illinois
prepared by Illinois Historical Records Survey, Division of Community Service Programs, Works Projects Administration with an introduction by Aaron Vangeison (Thomson, IL: Heritage House, 1976)

Index of Illinois Marriages, earliest to 1900
(Springfield, IL: Illinois State Genealogical Society. CD-ROMs)

Marriages from Illinois Counties, 6 vols.
by Walter R. Sanders (Litchfield, IL: W.R. Sanders, 1976)

Vital Records from Chicago Newspapers
compiled by the Newspaper Research Committee, Mrs. Edward Rickie, Chairman (Chicago, IL: Chicago Genealogical Society, 1971–1981)

Your Guide to Cemetery Research
by Sharon DeBartolo Carmack (Cincinnati: Betterway Books, 2002)

■ Adams 13 Jan. 1825
521 Vermont St., Quincy, IL 62301-2934
Phone: (217)277-2100
Web site: www.co.adams.il.us/
Parent County: Pike

Record Type	Year Begun	Jurisdiction
Birth	1878	County Clerk
Marriage	1825	County Clerk
Death	1878	County Clerk
Divorce	na	Clerk/Circuit Ct.
Probate	1826	Clerk/Circuit Ct.
Court	1825	Clerk/Circuit Ct.

■ Alexander 4 Mar. 1819
2000 Washington Ave., Cairo, IL 62914
Phone: (618)734-7000
Web site: www.rootsweb.com/~ilalexan/
Parent County: Union

Record Type	Year Begun	Jurisdiction
Birth	1851	County Clerk
Marriage	1819	County Clerk
Death	1851	County Clerk
Divorce	na	Clerk/Circuit Ct.
Land	1818	County Recorder
Probate	1819	Clerk/Circuit Ct.
Court	1821	Clerk/Circuit Ct.

■ Bond 4 Jan. 1817
200 W. College, Greenville, IL 62246
Phone: (618)664-0449
Web site: www.rootsweb.com/~ilbond/
Parent County: Madison

Record Type	Year Begun	Jurisdiction
Birth	1877	County Clerk
Marriage	1817	County Clerk
Death	1877	County Clerk
Divorce	na	Clerk/Circuit Ct.
Land	na	County Recorder
Probate	na	Clerk/Circuit Ct.
Court	na	Clerk/Circuit Ct.
Military	na	County Clerk

■ Boone 4 Mar. 1837
601 N. Main St., Belvidere, IL 61008
Phone: (815)544-3103
Web site: www.rootsweb.com/~ilboone/boone.htm
Parent County: Winnebago

Record Type	Year Begun	Jurisdiction
Birth	1877	County Clerk
Marriage	1838	County Clerk
Death	1877	County Clerk
Divorce	na	Clerk/Circuit Ct.
Land	1838	County Recorder
Probate	1840	Clerk/Circuit Ct.
Court	1838	Clerk/Circuit Ct.

■ Brown 1 Feb. 1839
Courthouse Bldg., 200 W. Court, Mount Sterling, IL 62353
Phone: (217)773-3421

Web site: www.rootsweb.com/~ilbrown/brown.htm
Parent County: Schuyler

Record Type	Year Begun	Jurisdiction
Birth	1878	County Clerk
Marriage	1839	County Clerk
Death	1878	County Clerk
Divorce	na	Clerk/Circuit Ct.
Land	1817	County Recorder
Probate	1839	Clerk/Circuit Ct.
Court	1837	Clerk/Circuit Ct.
Nat.	na	Clerk/Circuit Ct.
Military	1918	County Clerk

■ Bureau 28 Feb. 1837
700 S. Main St., Princeton, IL 61356
Phone: (815)875-2001
Web site: www.rootsweb.com/~ilbureau/
Parent County: Putnam

Record Type	Year Begun	Jurisdiction
Birth	1878	County Clerk
Marriage	1837	County Clerk
Death	1878	County Clerk
Land	1817	County Recorder
Probate	1837	Clerk/Circuit Ct.
Court	1837	Clerk/Circuit Ct.

■ Calhoun 10 Jan. 1825
P.O. Box 187, Hardin, IL 62047
Phone: (618)576-2451
Web site: www.rootsweb.com/~ilcalhou/
Parent County: Pike

Record Type	Year Begun	Jurisdiction
Birth	1878	County Clerk
Marriage	1825	County Clerk
Death	1878	County Clerk
Land	1825	County Recorder
Probate	1833	Clerk/Circuit Ct.
Court	1825	Clerk/Circuit Ct.

■ Carroll 22 Feb. 1839
301 N. Main, Mount Carroll, IL 61053
Phone: (815)244-0230
Web site: www.rootsweb.com/~ilcarrol
Parent County: Jo Daviess

Record Type	Year Begun	Jurisdiction
Birth	1877	County Clerk
Marriage	1839	County Clerk
Death	1877	County Clerk
Land	1837	County Recorder
Probate	1839	Clerk/Circuit Ct.
Court	1837	Clerk/Circuit Ct.

■ Cass 30 Mar. 1837
100 E. Springfield St., Virginia, IL 62691
Phone: (217)452-7225
Web site: www.rootsweb.com/~ilcass/cass.htm
Parent County: Morgan

Record Type	Year Begun	Jurisdiction
Birth	1878	County Clerk
Marriage	1837	County Clerk
Death	1878	County Clerk
Land	1826	County Recorder
Probate	1837	Clerk/Circuit Ct.
Court	1837	Clerk/Circuit Ct.

■ Champaign 20 Feb. 1833
1776 E. Washington St., Urbana, IL 61802
Phone: (217)384-3725
Web site: www.rootsweb.com/~ilchampa/
Parent County: Vermilion

Record Type	Year Begun	Jurisdiction
Birth	1878	County Clerk
Marriage	1833	County Clerk
Death	1878	County Clerk
Land	1833	County Recorder
Probate	1833	Clerk/Circuit Ct.
Court	1836	Clerk/Circuit Ct.

■ Christian 15 Feb. 1839
P.O. Box 647, Taylorville, IL 62568
Phone: (217)824-4966
Web site: www.rootsweb.com/~ilchrist/
Parent County: Montgomery, Sangamon, Shelby
Comments/research tips: Formerly Dane County. Name changed to Christian in 1840.

Record Type	Year Begun	Jurisdiction
Birth	1877	County Clerk
Marriage	1839	County Clerk
Death	1877	County Clerk
Land	1828	County Recorder
Probate	1839	Clerk/Circuit Ct.
Court	1839	Clerk/Circuit Ct.

■ Clark 23 Mar. 1819
501 Archer Ave., Marshall, IL 62441
Phone: (217)826-2811
Web site: www.clarkcountyil.org/
Parent County: Crawford

Record Type	Year Begun	Jurisdiction
Birth	1865	County Clerk
Marriage	1819	County Clerk
Death	1865	County Clerk
Land	1816	County Recorder
Probate	1820	Clerk/Circuit Ct.
Court	1821	Clerk/Circuit Ct.

■ Clay 23 Dec. 1824
P.O. Box 160, Louisville, IL 62858
Phone: (618)665-3523
Web site: www.rootsweb.com/~ilclay/
Parent County: Wayne, Fayette, Crawford

Record Type	Year Begun	Jurisdiction
Birth	1877	County Clerk
Marriage	1825	County Clerk
Death	1877	County Clerk
Land	1825	County Recorder
Probate	1827	Clerk/Circuit Ct.
Court	1825	Clerk/Circuit Ct.

Illinois

Illinois

■ **Clinton**   27 Dec. 1824
850 Fairfax St., Carlyle, IL 62231
Phone: (618)594-2464
Web site: www.rootsweb.com/~ilclint2/
Parent County: Washington, Bond

Record Type	Year Begun	Jurisdiction
Birth	1877	County Clerk
Marriage	1825	County Clerk
Death	1877	County Clerk
Land	1818	County Recorder
Probate	1825	Clerk/Circuit Ct.
Court	1825	Clerk/Circuit Ct.

■ **Coles**   25 Dec. 1830
651 Jackson Ave., Charleston, IL 61920
Phone: (217)348-0516
Web site: www.rootsweb.com/~ilcoles/coles.htm
Parent County: Clark, Edgar

Record Type	Year Begun	Jurisdiction
Birth	1877	County Clerk
Marriage	1831	County Clerk
Death	1877	County Clerk
Land	1830	County Recorder
Probate	1830	Clerk/Circuit Court
Court	1830	Clerk/Circuit Court

■ **Cook**   15 Jan. 1831
118 N. Clark St., Chicago, IL 60602
Phone: (312)603-6601
Web site: www.co.cook.il.us/
Parent County: Putnam

Record Type	Year Begun	Jurisdiction
Birth	1871	County Clerk
Marriage	1856	County Clerk
Death	1871	County Clerk
Probate	1871	Clerk/Circuit Ct.
Court	1871	Clerk/Circuit Ct.
Land	1871	County Recorder

■ **Crawford**   31 Dec. 1816
One Courthouse Sq., P.O. Box 602, Robinson, IL 62454
Phone: (618)544-3512
Web site: www.rootsweb.com/~ilcrawfo/
Parent County: Edwards

Record Type	Year Begun	Jurisdiction
Birth	1877	County Clerk
Marriage	1817	County Clerk
Death	1877	County Clerk
Land	1816	County Recorder
Probate	1818	Clerk/Circuit Ct.
Court	1817	Clerk/Circuit Ct.

■ **Cumberland**   2 Mar. 1843
P.O. Box 146, Toledo, IL 62468
Phone: (217)849-3601
Web site: www.rootsweb.com/~ilcumber/
Parent County: Coles

Record Type	Year Begun	Jurisdiction
Birth	1885	County Clerk

Marriage	1880	County Clerk
Death	1885	County Clerk
Land	1885	County Recorder
Probate	1884	Clerk/Circuit Ct.
Court	1885	Clerk/Circuit Ct.

■ **Dane**   15 Feb. 1839
Parent County: Montgomery, Sangamon, Shelby
Comments/research tips: (See Christian) Name changed to Christian in 1840.

■ **De Kalb**   4 Mar. 1837
110 E. Sycamore St., Sycamore, IL 60178
Phone: (815)895-7138
Web site: www.dekalbcounty.org/
Parent County: Kane

Record Type	Year Begun	Jurisdiction
Marriage	1837	County Clerk
Death	1877	County Clerk
Land	1838	County Recorder
Probate	1837	Clerk/Circuit Ct.
Court	1838	Clerk/Circuit Ct.
Birth	1877	County Clerk

■ **De Witt**   1 Mar. 1839
201 W. Washington St., Clinton, IL 61727
Phone: (217)935-2195
Web site: www.rootsweb.com/~ildewitt/
Parent County: Macon, McLean

Record Type	Year Begun	Jurisdiction
Birth	1877	County Clerk
Marriage	1839	County Clerk
Death	1877	County Clerk
Land	1828	County Recorder
Probate	1839	Clerk/Circuit Ct.
Court	1839	Clerk/Circuit Ct.

■ **Douglas**   8 Feb. 1859
401 S. Center St., P.O. Box 467, Tuscola, IL 61953
Phone: (217)253-2352
Web site: www.sos.state.il.us/departments/archives/irad/douglas.html
Parent County: Coles

Record Type	Year Begun	Jurisdiction
Birth	1851	County Clerk
Marriage	na	County Clerk
Death	1851	County Clerk
Land	na	County Recorder
Probate	na	Clerk/Circuit Ct.
Court	na	Clerk/Circuit Ct.

■ **Du Page**   9 Feb. 1839
421 N. County Farm Rd., Wheaton, IL 60189
Phone: (630)682-7111
Web site: www.dupageco.org/
Parent County: Cook

Record Type	Year Begun	Jurisdiction
Birth	1877	County Clerk
Marriage	1839	County Clerk

Death .... 1877 .... County Clerk
Land .... 1828 .... County Recorder
Probate .... 1839 .... Clerk/Circuit Court
Court .... 1839 .... Clerk/Circuit Court

■ Edgar 3 Jan. 1823
115 W. Court St., Paris, IL 61944
Phone: (217)466-7447
Web site: www.rootsweb.com/~iledgar/
Parent County: Clark

Record Type	Year Begun	Jurisdiction
Birth	1877	County Clerk
Marriage	1823	County Clerk
Death	1877	County Clerk
Land	1823	County Recorder
Probate	1823	Clerk/Circuit Ct.
Court	1823	Clerk/Circuit Ct.

■ Edwards 28 Nov. 1814
50 E. Main St., Albion, IL 62806
Phone: (618)445-2016
Web site: www.rootsweb.com/~iledward/
Parent County: Madison, Gallatin

Record Type	Year Begun	Jurisdiction
Birth	1877	County Clerk
Marriage	1815	County Clerk
Death	1877	County Clerk
Land	1815	County Recorder
Probate	1815	Clerk/Circuit Ct.
Court	1815	Clerk/Circuit Ct.

■ Effingham 15 Feb. 1831
101 N. Fourth St., P.O. Box 628, Effingham, IL 62401
Phone: (217)342-4065
Web site: www.co.effingham.il.us/
Parent County: Fayette, Crawford

Record Type	Year Begun	Jurisdiction
Birth	1877	County Clerk
Marriage	1833	County Clerk
Death	1871	County Clerk
Land	1833	County Recorder
Probate	1838	Clerk/Circuit Ct.
Court	1833	Clerk/Circuit Ct.

■ Fayette 14 Feb. 1821
221 S. Seventh, Vandalia, IL 62471
Phone: (618)283-5009
Web site: www.rootsweb.com/~ilfayett/ilfayette.htm
Parent County: Bond, Clark, Crawford, Jefferson

Record Type	Year Begun	Jurisdiction
Birth	1877	County Clerk-Recorder
Marriage	1821	County Clerk-Recorder
Death	1877	County Clerk-Recorder
Land	1816	County Recorder
Probate	1821	Clerk/Circuit Ct.
Court	1821	Clerk/Circuit Ct.

■ Ford 17 Feb. 1859
200 W. State St., Paxton, IL 60957
Phone: (217)379-2641

Web site: www.prairienet.org/fordiroq/ford.htm
Parent County: Vermilion

Record Type	Year Begun	Jurisdiction
Birth	1877	County Clerk
Marriage	1859	County Clerk
Death	1877	County Clerk
Land	1834	County Recorder
Probate	1850	Clerk/Circuit Ct.
Court	1859	Clerk/Circuit Ct.

■ Franklin 2 Jan. 1818
P.O. Box 607, Benton, IL 62812
Phone: (618)439-2011
Web site: www.rootsweb.com/~ilfrankl/index2.html
Parent County: White, Gallatin

Record Type	Year Begun	Jurisdiction
Birth	1877	County Clerk
Marriage	1837	County Clerk
Death	1877	County Clerk
Probate	1837	Clerk/Circuit Ct.
Court	1836	Clerk/Circuit Ct.
Land	1835	County Recorder

■ Fulton 28 Jan. 1823
100 N. Main St., Lewistown, IL 61542
Phone: (309)547-3041
Web site: www.outfitters.com/illinois/fulton/
Parent County: Pike

Record Type	Year Begun	Jurisdiction
Birth	1877	County Clerk
Marriage	1824	County Clerk
Death	1877	County Clerk
Land	1817	County Recorder
Probate	1827	Clerk/Circuit Ct.
Court	1824	Clerk/Circuit Ct.

■ Gallatin 14 Sep. 1812
P.O. Box 550, Shawneetown, IL 62984
Phone: (618)269-3140
Web site: www.rootsweb.com/~ilgalla2/
Parent County: Randolph

Record Type	Year Begun	Jurisdiction
Birth	1877	County Clerk
Marriage	1813	County Clerk
Death	1877	County Clerk
Land	1813	County Recorder
Probate	1814	Clerk/Circuit Ct.
Court	1813	Clerk/Circuit Ct.

■ Greene 20 Jan. 1821
519 N. Main St., Carrollton, IL 62016
Phone: (217)942-3421
Web site: www.rootsweb.com/~ilgreene/green.htm
Parent County: Madison

Record Type	Year Begun	Jurisdiction
Birth	1877	County Clerk
Marriage	1821	County Clerk
Death	1877	County Clerk
Land	1821	County Recorder

Illinois

Probate .... 1821 .... Clerk/Circuit Ct.
Court .... 1821 .... Clerk/Circuit Ct.

■ Grundy 17 Feb. 1841
111 E. Washington St., Morris, IL 60450
Phone: (815)941-3256
Web site: www.rootsweb.com/~ilgrundy/
Parent County: LaSalle

Record Type	Year Begun	Jurisdiction
Birth	1877	County Clerk
Marriage	1841	County Clerk
Death	1877	County Clerk
Land	1832	County Recorder
Probate	1841	Clerk/Circuit Ct.
Court	1837	Clerk/Circuit Ct.

■ Hamilton 8 Feb. 1821
100 S. Jackson St., McLeansboro, IL 62859
Phone: (618)643-3224
Web site: www.rootsweb.com/~ilhamilt/
Parent County: White

Record Type	Year Begun	Jurisdiction
Birth	1877	County Clerk
Marriage	1821	County Clerk
Death	1877	County Clerk
Land	1823	County Recorder
Probate	1821	Clerk/Circuit Ct.
Court	1821	Clerk/Circuit Ct.

■ Hancock 13 Jan. 1825
P.O. Box 39, Carthage, IL 62321
Phone: (217)357-2616
Web site: www.rootsweb.com/~ilhancoc/
Parent County: Pike

Record Type	Year Begun	Jurisdiction
Birth	1877	County Clerk
Marriage	1829	County Clerk
Death	1877	County Clerk
Land	1817	County Recorder
Probate	1830	Clerk/Circuit Ct.
Court	1829	Clerk/Circuit Ct.

■ Hardin 2 Mar. 1839
P.O. Box 187, Elizabethtown, IL 62931
Phone: (618)287-2735
Web site: www.rootsweb.com/~ilhardi2/
Parent County: Gallatin, Pope

Record Type	Year Begun	Jurisdiction
Birth	1877	County Clerk
Marriage	1884	County Clerk
Death	1877	County Clerk
Land	1814	County Recorder
Probate	1884	Clerk/Circuit Ct.
Court	1841	Clerk/Circuit Ct.

■ Henderson 20 Jan. 1841
P.O. Box 308, Oquawka, IL 61469
Phone: (309)867-3121
Web site: www.outfitters.com/illinois/henderson/

Parent County: Warren

Record Type	Year Begun	Jurisdiction
Birth	1877	County Clerk
Marriage	1841	County Clerk
Death	1877	County Clerk
Land	1818	County Recorder
Probate	1839	Clerk/Circuit Ct.
Court	1841	Clerk/Circuit Ct.

■ Henry 13 Jan. 1825
307 W. Center St., Cambridge, IL 61238
Phone: (309)937-3578
Web site: www.henrycty.com/
Parent County: Fulton

Record Type	Year Begun	Jurisdiction
Birth	1877	County Clerk
Death	1877	County Clerk
Marriage	1837	County Clerk
Divorce	1880	Clerk/Circuit Ct.
Land	1836	County Recorder
Probate	1839	Clerk/Circuit Ct.
Court	1837	Clerk/Circuit Ct.

■ Iroquois 26 Feb. 1833
1001 E. Grant St., Watseka, IL 60970
Phone: (815)432-6950
Web site: www.rootsweb.com/~iliroquo
Parent County: Vermilion

Record Type	Year Begun	Jurisdiction
Birth	1877	County Clerk
Marriage	1866	County Clerk
Death	1877	County Clerk
Land	1834	County Recorder
Probate	1834	Clerk/Circuit Ct.
Court	1834	Clerk/Circuit Ct.

■ Jackson 10 Jan. 1816
1001 Walnut St., Murphysboro, IL 62966
Phone: (618)687-7300
Web site: www.co.jackson.il.us/
Parent County: Randolph, Johnson

Record Type	Year Begun	Jurisdiction
Birth	1877	County Clerk
Marriage	1843	County Clerk
Death	1877	County Clerk
Land	1814	County Recorder
Probate	1840	Clerk/Circuit Ct.
Court	1843	Clerk/Circuit Ct.
Burial	1872	County Clerk

■ Jasper 15 Feb. 1831
100 W. Jourdan St., Newton, IL 62448
Phone: (618)783-2524
Web site: www.rootsweb.com/~iljasper/
Parent County: Clay, Crawford

Record Type	Year Begun	Jurisdiction
Birth	1877	County Clerk
Marriage	1835	County Clerk
Death	1877	County Clerk

Illinois

Land .... 1835 ....County Recorder
Probate .... 1835 ....Clerk/Circuit Ct.
Court..................... 1835 ....Clerk/Circuit Ct.

■ **Jefferson** 26 Mar. 1819
100 S. Tenth St., Mount Vernon, IL 62864
Phone: (618)244-8007
Web site: www.rootsweb.com/~iljeffer/
Parent County: Edwards, White

Record Type	Year Begun	Jurisdiction
Birth	1851	County Clerk
Marriage	na	County Clerk
Death	1851	County Clerk
Land	na	County Recorder
Probate	na	Clerk/Circuit Ct.
Court	na	Clerk/Circuit Ct.

■ **Jersey** 28 Feb. 1839
102 W. Pearl St., Jerseyville, IL 62052
Phone: (618)498-5571
Web site: www.rootsweb.com/~iljersey/
Parent County: Greene

Record Type	Year Begun	Jurisdiction
Birth	1877	County Clerk
Marriage	1839	County Clerk
Death	1877	County Clerk
Land	1822	County Recorder
Probate	1839	Clerk/Circuit Ct.
Court	1839	Clerk/Circuit Ct.

■ **Jo Daviess** 17 Feb. 1827
330 N. Bench St., Galena, IL 61036
Phone: (815)777-0037
Web site: www.rootsweb.com/~iljodavi/index.html
Parent County: Henry, Putnam

Record Type	Year Begun	Jurisdiction
Birth	1877	County Clerk
Marriage	1830	County Clerk
Death	1877	County Clerk
Land	1828	County Recorder
Probate	1828	Clerk/Circuit Ct.
Court	1827	Clerk/Circuit Ct.

■ **Johnson** 14 Sep. 1812
P.O. Box 96, Vienna, IL 62995
Phone: (618)658-4751
Web site: www.rootsweb.com/~iljohnso/
Parent County: Randolph

Record Type	Year Begun	Jurisdiction
Birth	1877	County Clerk
Marriage	1835	County Clerk
Death	1877	County Clerk
Land	1809	County Recorder
Probate	1821	Clerk/Circuit Ct.
Court	1827	Clerk/Circuit Ct.

■ **Kane** 16 Jan. 1836
719 S. Batavia Ave., Geneva, IL 60134
Phone: (630)232-3413

Web site: www.rootsweb.com/~ilkane/
Parent County: Cook, LaSalle

Record Type	Year Begun	Jurisdiction
Birth	1877	County Clerk
Marriage	1836	County Clerk
Death	1877	County Clerk
Land	1836	County Recorder
Probate	1836	Clerk/Circuit Ct.
Court	1836	Clerk/Circuit Ct.

■ **Kankakee** 11 Feb. 1853
189 E. Court St., Kankakee, IL 60901
Phone: (815)937-2905
Web site: www.co.kankakee.il.us/
Parent County: Ford, Iroquois, Will

Record Type	Year Begun	Jurisdiction
Birth	1851	County Clerk
Marriage	na	County Clerk
Death	1851	County Clerk
Land	na	County Recorder
Probate	na	Clerk/Circuit Ct.
Court	na	Clerk/Circuit Ct.

■ **Kendall** 19 Feb. 1841
807 W. John St., Yorkville, IL 60560
Phone: (630)553-4183
Web site: www.rootsweb.com/~ilkendal/
Parent County: LaSalle, Kane

Record Type	Year Begun	Jurisdiction
Death	1877	County Clerk
Birth	1877	County Clerk
Marriage	1837	County Clerk
Land	1839	County Recorder
Probate	1847	Clerk/Circuit Ct.
Court	1841	Clerk/Circuit Ct.

■ **Knox** 13 Jan. 1825
200 S. Cherry St., Galesburg, IL 61401
Phone: (309)345-3859
Web site: www.outfitters.com/illinois/knox/knox.html
Parent County: Fulton, Henry

Record Type	Year Begun	Jurisdiction
Birth	1877	County Clerk
Marriage	1830	County Clerk
Death	1877	County Clerk
Land	1878	County Recorder
Probate	1830	Clerk/Circuit Ct.
Court	1836	Clerk/Circuit Ct.

■ **La Salle** 15 Jan. 1831
707 Etna Rd., Ottawa, IL 61350
Phone: (815)434-8202
Web site: www.outfitters.com/illinois/lasalle/
Parent County: Putnam, Tazewell

Record Type	Year Begun	Jurisdiction
Birth	1877	County Clerk
Marriage	1831	County Clerk
Death	1877	County Clerk
Land	1831	County Recorder

Illinois

Probate .... 1831 .... Clerk/Circuit Ct.
Court .... 1831 .... Clerk/Circuit Ct.

■ Lake 1 Mar. 1839
18 N. County St., Waukegan, IL 60085
Phone: (847)377-3380
Web site: www.rootsweb.com/~illake/
Parent County: McHenry

Record Type	Year Begun	Jurisdiction
Birth	1877	County Clerk
Marriage	1839	County Clerk
Death	1877	County Clerk
Land	1839	County Recorder
Probate	1839	Clerk/Circuit Ct.
Court	1840	Clerk/Circuit Ct.

■ Lawrence 16 Jan. 1821
1100 State St., Lawrenceville, IL 62439
Phone: (618)943-2815
Web site: www.rootsweb.com/~illawren/index.htm
Parent County: Crawford, Edwards

Record Type	Year Begun	Jurisdiction
Birth	1877	County Clerk
Marriage	1821	County Clerk
Death	1877	County Clerk
Land	1818	County Recorder
Probate	1821	Clerk/Circuit Ct.
Court	1820	Clerk/Circuit Ct.

■ Lee 27 Feb. 1839
P.O. Box 329, Dixon, IL 61021
Phone: (815)284-5234
Web site: www.outfitters.com/illinois/lee/
Parent County: Ogle

Record Type	Year Begun	Jurisdiction
Birth	1877	County Clerk
Marriage	1839	County Clerk
Death	1877	County Clerk
Land	1838	County Recorder
Probate	1839	Clerk/Circuit Ct.
Court	1840	Clerk/Circuit Ct.

■ Livingston 27 Feb. 1837
112 W. Madison St., Pontiac, IL 61764
Phone: (815)844-2602
Web site: www.iltrails.org/livingston
Parent County: La Salle, McLean

Record Type	Year Begun	Jurisdiction
Marriage	1837	County Clerk
Death	1877	County Clerk
Land	1835	County Recorder
Probate	1837	Clerk/Circuit Ct.
Court	1839	Clerk/Circuit Ct.
Birth	1877	County Clerk

■ Logan 15 Feb. 1839
P.O. Box 278., Lincoln, IL 62656
Phone: (217)735-2376
Web site: www.rootsweb.com/~illogan/

Parent County: McLean, Sangamon, Tazewell

Record Type	Year Begun	Jurisdiction
Birth	1877	County Clerk
Marriage	1857	County Clerk
Death	1877	County Clerk
Land	1829	County Recorder
Probate	1855	Clerk/Circuit Ct.
Court	1857	Clerk/Circuit Ct.

■ Macon 19 Jan. 1829
253 E. Wood St., Decatur, IL 62523
Phone: (217)424-1454
Web site: www.rootsweb.com/~ilmacon/
Parent County: Shelby

Record Type	Year Begun	Jurisdiction
Birth	1877	County Clerk
Marriage	1839	County Clerk
Death	1877	County Clerk
Probate	1831	Clerk/Circuit Ct.
Court	1829	Clerk/Circuit Ct.

■ Macoupin 17 Jan. 1829
210 E. Main St., Carlinville, IL 62626
Phone: (217)854-3211
Web site: www.rootsweb.com/~ilmacoup/macoupin.htm
Parent County: Madison, Greene

Record Type	Year Begun	Jurisdiction
Birth	1877	County Clerk
Marriage	1829	County Clerk
Death	1877	County Clerk
Land	1829	County Recorder
Probate	1829	Clerk/Circuit Ct.
Court	1829	Clerk/Circuit Ct.

■ Madison 14 Sep. 1812
155 N. Main St., Suite 120, Edwardsville, IL 62025
Phone: (618)692-6240
Web site: www.co.madison.il.us/
Parent County: St. Clair

Record Type	Year Begun	Jurisdiction
Birth	1877	County Clerk
Marriage	1813	County Clerk
Death	1877	County Clerk
Probate	1813	Clerk/Circuit Ct.
Court	1803	Clerk/Circuit Ct.
Land	1802	County Recorder

■ Marion Jan. 1816
100 S. Main St., Waterloo, IL 62298
Phone: (618)939-8681
Web site: www.rootsweb.com/~ilmarion/marionco.htm
Parent County: Fayette, Jefferson

Record Type	Year Begun	Jurisdiction
Birth	1851	County Clerk
Marriage	na	County Clerk
Death	1851	County Clerk
Land	na	County Recorder
Probate	na	Clerk/Circuit Ct.
Court	na	Clerk/Circuit Ct.

Illinois

Marshall 19 Jan. 1839
122 N. Prairie St., Lacon, IL 61540
Phone: (309)246-6435
Web site: www.rootsweb.com/~ilmarsha/index.htm
Parent County: La Salle, Putnam

Record Type	Year Begun	Jurisdiction
Birth	1877	County Clerk
Marriage	1830	County Clerk
Death	1877	County Clerk
Land	1839	County Recorder
Probate	1830	Clerk/Circuit Ct.
Court	1840	Clerk/Circuit Ct.

Mason 20 Jan. 1841
100 N. Broadway, P.O. Box 90, Havana, IL 62644
Phone: (309)543-6619
Web site: www.outfitters.com/~masonch/
Parent County: Tazewell, Menard

Record Type	Year Begun	Jurisdiction
Birth	1877	County Clerk
Marriage	1841	County Clerk
Death	1878	County Clerk
Land	1827	County Recorder
Probate	1841	Clerk/Circuit Ct.
Court	1841	Clerk/Circuit Ct.

Massac 8 Feb. 1843
P.O. Box 429, Metropolis, IL 62960
Phone: (618)524-9359
Web site: www.rootsweb.com/~ilmassac/
Parent County: Pope, Johnson

Record Type	Year Begun	Jurisdiction
Birth	1877	County Clerk
Marriage	1843	County Clerk
Death	1877	County Clerk
Land	1843	County Recorder
Probate	1843	Clerk/Circuit Ct.
Court	1843	Clerk/Circuit Ct.

McDonough 25 Jan. 1826
1 Courthouse Sq., Macomb, IL 61455
Phone: (309)837-4889
Web site: www.outfitters.com/illinois/mcdonough/
Parent County: Schuyler

Record Type	Year Begun	Jurisdiction
Birth	1877	County Clerk
Marriage	1830	County Clerk
Death	1877	County Clerk
Land	1817	County Recorder
Probate	1833	Clerk/Circuit Ct.
Court	1830	Clerk/Circuit Ct.

McHenry 16 Jan. 1836
2200 N. Seminary Ave., Woodstock, IL 60098
Phone: (815)334-4310
Web site: www.co.mchenry.il.us/
Parent County: Cook

Record Type	Year Begun	Jurisdiction
Birth	1877	County Clerk

Record Type	Year Begun	Jurisdiction
Marriage	1837	County Clerk
Death	1877	County Clerk
Land	1839	County Recorder
Probate	1840	Clerk/Circuit Ct.
Court	1838	Clerk/Circuit Ct.

McLean 25 Dec. 1830
104 W. Front St., Bloomington, IL 61701
Phone: (309)888-5001
Web site: www.mclean.gov/
Parent County: Tazewell, Unorganized Territory

Record Type	Year Begun	Jurisdiction
Birth	1887	County Clerk
Marriage	1831	County Clerk
Death	1877	County Clerk
Land	1931	County Recorder
Probate	1831	Clerk/Circuit Ct.
Court	1831	Clerk/Circuit Ct.

Menard 15 Feb. 1839
P.O. Box 456, Petersburg, IL 62675
Phone: (217)632-2615
Web site: www.rootsweb.com/~ilmenard/index.html/
Parent County: Sangamon

Record Type	Year Begun	Jurisdiction
Birth	1877	County Clerk
Marriage	1839	County Clerk
Death	1877	County Clerk
Land	1821	County Recorder
Probate	1839	Clerk/Circuit Ct.
Court	1839	Clerk/Circuit Ct.

Mercer 13 Jan. 1825
P.O. Box 66, Aledo, IL 61231
Phone: (309)582-7122
Web site: www.rootsweb.com/~ilmercer/
Parent County: Pike

Record Type	Year Begun	Jurisdiction
Birth	1877	County Clerk
Marriage	1835	County Clerk
Death	1877	County Clerk
Land	1834	County Recorder
Probate	1837	Clerk/Circuit Ct.
Court	1836	Clerk/Circuit Ct.

Monroe 6 Jan. 1816
100 S. Main St., Waterloo, IL 62298
Phone: (618)939-8681
Web site: www.rootsweb.com/~ilmonroe/
Parent County: Randolph, St. Clair

Record Type	Year Begun	Jurisdiction
Birth	1878	County Clerk
Marriage	1816	County Clerk
Death	1877	County Clerk
Land	1816	County Recorder
Probate	1820	Clerk/Circuit Ct.
Court	1816	Clerk/Circuit Ct.

Montgomery 21 Feb. 1821
1 Courthouse Sq., Hillsboro, IL 62049
Phone: (217)532-9546

Illinois

Web site: www.rootsweb.com/~ilmontgo/
Parent County: Bond, Madison

Record Type	Year Begun	Jurisdiction
Birth	1877	County Clerk
Marriage	1821	County Clerk
Death	1877	County Clerk
Land	1819	County Recorder
Probate	1821	Clerk/Circuit Ct.
Court	1821	Clerk/Circuit Ct.

■ Morgan 31 Jan. 1823
300 W. State St., Jacksonville, IL 62650
Phone: (217)243-2009
Web site: www.rootsweb.com/~ilmorgan/morgan.htm
Parent County: Greene, Sangamon

Record Type	Year Begun	Jurisdiction
Birth	1851	County Clerk
Marriage	1827	County Clerk
Death	1851	County Clerk
Land	1824	County Recorder
Probate	1824	County Clerk
Court	1827	County Clerk

■ Moultrie 16 Feb. 1843
10 S. Main St., Sullivan, IL 61951
Phone: (217)728-4622
Web site: www.rootsweb.com/~ilmoult2/
Parent County: Shelby, Macon

Record Type	Year Begun	Jurisdiction
Birth	1877	County Clerk
Marriage	1843	County Clerk
Death	1877	County Clerk
Land	1831	County Recorder
Probate	1845	Clerk/Circuit Ct.
Court	1840	Clerk/Circuit Ct.

■ Ogle 16 Jan. 1836
P.O. Box 357, Oregon, IL 61061
Phone: (815)732-1130
Web site: www.oglecounty.org/
Parent County: Jo Daviess, La Salle

Record Type	Year Begun	Jurisdiction
Birth	1878	County Clerk
Marriage	1837	County Clerk
Death	1878	County Clerk
Land	1836	County Recorder
Probate	1836	Clerk/Circuit Ct.
Court	1837	Clerk/Circuit Ct.

■ Peoria 13 Jan. 1825
324 Main St. Room 101, Peoria, IL 61602
Phone: (309)672-6015
Web site: www.co.peoria.il.us/
Parent County: Fulton

Record Type	Year Begun	Jurisdiction
Birth	1877	County Clerk
Marriage	1825	County Clerk
Death	1877	County Clerk
Land	1818	County Recorder

| Probate | 1825 | Clerk/Circuit Ct. |
| Court | 1825 | Clerk/Circuit Ct. |

■ Perry 29 Jan. 1827
P.O. Box 438, Pinckneyville, IL 62274
Phone: (618)357-6726
Web site: www.rootsweb.com/~ilperry/
Parent County: Randolph, Jackson

Record Type	Year Begun	Jurisdiction
Death	1878	County Clerk
Marriage	1827	County Clerk
Land	1817	County Recorder
Probate	1828	Clerk/Circuit Ct.
Court	1827	Clerk/Circuit Ct.
Birth	1878	County Clerk

■ Piatt 27 Jan. 1841
101 W. Washington St., P.O. Box 558, Monticello, IL 61856
Phone: (217)762-4966
Web site: www.rootsweb.com/~ilpiatt/
Parent County: DeWitt, Macon

Record Type	Year Begun	Jurisdiction
Birth	1877	County Clerk
Marriage	1841	County Clerk
Death	1877	County Clerk
Land	1840	County Recorder
Probate	1843	Clerk/Circuit Ct.
Court	1841	Clerk/Circuit Ct.

■ Pike 31 Jan. 1821
100 E. Washington St., Pittsfield, IL 62363
Phone: (217)285-6612
Web site: www.pikeil.org/
Parent County: Madison

Record Type	Year Begun	Jurisdiction
Birth	1877	County Clerk
Marriage	1827	County Clerk
Death	1877	County Clerk
Land	1818	County Recorder
Probate	1821	Clerk/Circuit Ct.
Court	1819	Clerk/Circuit Ct.

■ Pope 10 Jan. 1816
P.O. Box 216, Golconda, IL 62938
Phone: (618)683-3941
Web site: www.rootsweb.com/~ilpope/
Parent County: Gallatin, Johnson

Record Type	Year Begun	Jurisdiction
Birth	1877	County Clerk
Marriage	1813	County Clerk
Death	1877	County Clerk
Land	1816	County Recorder
Probate	1816	Clerk/Circuit Ct.
Court	1817	Clerk/Circuit Ct.

■ Pulaski 3 Mar. 1843
P.O. Box 218, Mound City, IL 62963
Phone: (618)748-9300
Web site: www.rootsweb.com/~ilpulask/

Parent County: Alexander, Johnson

Record Type	Year Begun	Jurisdiction
Birth	1882	County Clerk
Marriage	1861	County Clerk
Death	1882	County Clerk
Probate	1862	Clerk/Circuit Ct.
Court	1857	Clerk/Circuit Ct.
Land	1843	County Recorder

■ **Putnam** 13 Jan. 1825
120 N. Fourth St., Hennepin, IL 61327
Phone: (815)925-7016
Web site: www.rootsweb.com/~ilputnam/
Parent County: Fulton

Record Type	Year Begun	Jurisdiction
Birth	1877	County Clerk
Marriage	1831	County Clerk
Death	1877	County Clerk
Probate	1831	Clerk/Circuit Ct.
Court	1831	Clerk/Circuit Ct.
Land	1831	County Recorder

■ **Randolph** 5 Oct. 1795
1 Taylor St., Chester, IL 62233
Phone: (618)826-5000
Web site: www.rootsweb.com/~ilrandol/
Parent County: NW Territory, St. Clair

Record Type	Year Begun	Jurisdiction
Birth	1877	County Clerk
Marriage	1824	County Clerk
Death	1877	County Clerk
Land	1724	County Recorder
Probate	1722	Clerk/Circuit Ct.
Court	1722	Clerk/Circuit Ct.

■ **Richland** 24 Feb. 1841
103 W. Main St., Olney, IL 62450
Phone: (618)392-2151
Web site: www.rootsweb.com/~ilrichla/index.htm
Parent County: Clay, Lawrence

Record Type	Year Begun	Jurisdiction
Birth	1877	County Clerk
Marriage	1841	County Clerk
Death	1877	County Clerk
Probate	1841	Clerk/Circuit Ct.
Court	1842	Clerk/Circuit Ct.
Land	1836	County Recorder

■ **Rock Island** 9 Feb. 1831
1504 Third Ave., Rock Island, IL 61201
Phone: (309)558-3570
Web site: www.co.rock-island.il.us/
Parent County: Jo Daviess

Record Type	Year Begun	Jurisdiction
Birth	1877	County Clerk
Marriage	1833	County Clerk
Death	1877	County Clerk
Land	1835	County Recorder
Probate	1835	Clerk/Circuit Ct.
Court	1834	Clerk/Circuit Ct.

■ **Saline** 25 Feb. 1847
10 E. Poplar St., Harrisburg, IL 62946
Phone: (618)253-5096
Web site: www.rootsweb.com/~ilsaline/
Parent County: Gallatin

Record Type	Year Begun	Jurisdiction
Birth	1877	County Clerk
Marriage	1845	County Clerk
Death	1877	County Clerk
Land	1817	County Recorder
Probate	1847	Clerk/Circuit Ct.
Court	1848	Clerk/Circuit Ct.

■ **Sangamon** 30 Jan. 1821
200 S. Ninth St., Springfield, IL 62701-1629
Phone: (217)753-6674
Web site: www.co.sangamon.il.us/
Parent County: Bond, Madison

Record Type	Year Begun	Jurisdiction
Birth	1877	County Clerk
Marriage	1821	County Clerk
Death	1877	County Clerk
Land	1822	County Recorder
Probate	1821	Clerk/Circuit Ct.
Court	1821	Clerk/Circuit Ct.

■ **Schuyler** 13 Jan. 1825
100 S. Congress St., P.O. Box 200, Rushville, IL 62681
Phone: (217)322-4633
Web site: www.rootsweb.com/~ilschuyl/
Parent County: Pike

Record Type	Year Begun	Jurisdiction
Birth	1877	County Clerk
Marriage	1825	County Clerk
Death	1877	County Clerk
Land	1817	County Recorder
Probate	1825	Clerk/Circuit Ct.
Court	1825	Clerk/Circuit Ct.

■ **Scott** 16 Feb. 1839
101 E. Market St., Winchester, IL 62694
Phone: (217)742-5217
Web site: www.rootsweb.com/~ilscott/scott.htm
Parent County: Morgan

Record Type	Year Begun	Jurisdiction
Birth	1877	County Clerk
Marriage	1839	County Clerk
Death	1877	County Clerk
Land	1823	County Recorder
Probate	1839	Clerk/Circuit Ct.
Court	1839	Clerk/Circuit Ct.

■ **Shelby** 23 Jan. 1827
301 E. Main St., Shelbyville, IL 62565
Phone: (217)774-4212
Web site: www.rootsweb.com/~ilshelb2/shelby.htm
Parent County: Fayette

Record Type	Year Begun	Jurisdiction
Birth	1877	County Clerk

Illinois

Marriage .... 1827 .... County Clerk
Death .... 1877 .... County Clerk
Probate .... 1831 .... Clerk/Circuit Ct.
Land .... 1827 .... County Recorder
Court .... 1827 .... Clerk/Circuit Ct.

■ St. Clair 27 Apr. 1790
10 Public Sq., Belleville, IL 62220
Phone: (618)277-6600
Web site: www.rootsweb.com/~ilstclai/stclair.htm
Parent County: NW Territory

Record Type	Year Begun	Jurisdiction
Birth	1832	County Clerk
Marriage	1763	County Clerk
Death	1832	County Clerk
Land	1786	County Recorder
Probate	1772	Clerk/Circuit Ct.
Court	1778	Clerk/Circuit Ct.

■ Stark 2 Mar. 1839
130 W. Main St., Toulon, IL 61483
Phone: (309)286-5941
Web site: www.outfitters.com/illinois/stark/
Parent County: Knox, Putnam

Record Type	Year Begun	Jurisdiction
Birth	1877	County Clerk
Marriage	1839	County Clerk
Death	1877	County Clerk
Probate	1839	Clerk/Circuit Ct.
Court	1839	Clerk/Circuit Ct.
Land	1817	County Recorder

■ Stephenson 4 Mar. 1837
15 N. Galena Ave., Freeport, IL 61032
Phone: (815)235-8266
Web site: www.rootsweb.com/~ilstephe/
Parent County: Jo Daviess, Winnebago

Record Type	Year Begun	Jurisdiction
Birth	1877	County Clerk
Marriage	1837	County Clerk
Death	1877	County Clerk
Land	1837	County Recorder
Probate	1837	County Clerk
Court	1837	County Clerk

■ Tazewell 31 Jan. 1827
McKenzie Bldg., Fourth and Court Sts., Second Floor, Pekin, IL 61554
Phone: (309)477-2214
Web site: www.rootsweb.com/~iltazewe/
Parent County: Fayette, Peoria

Record Type	Year Begun	Jurisdiction
Birth	1877	County Clerk
Marriage	1827	County Clerk
Death	1877	County Clerk
Land	1825	County Recorder
Probate	1827	Clerk/Circuit Ct.
Court	1827	Clerk/Circuit Ct.

■ Union 2 Jan. 1818
311 W. Market St., P.O. Box H, Jonesboro, IL 62952
Phone: (618)833-5711
Web site: www.rootsweb.com/~ilunion
Parent County: Johnson, Jackson

Record Type	Year Begun	Jurisdiction
Birth	1877	County Clerk
Marriage	1818	County Clerk
Death	1877	County Clerk
Land	1818	County Recorder
Probate	1818	Clerk/Circuit Ct.
Court	1817	Clerk/Circuit Ct.

■ Vermilion 18 Jan. 1826
6 N. Vermilion St., Danville, IL 61832
Phone: (217)431-2540
Web site: www.co.vermilion.il.us/
Parent County: Edgar

Record Type	Year Begun	Jurisdiction
Birth	1877	County Clerk
Marriage	1826	County Clerk
Death	1877	County Clerk
Land	1826	County Recorder
Probate	1826	Clerk/Circuit Ct.
Court	1826	Clerk/Circuit Ct.

■ Wabash 27 Dec. 1824
401 Market St., P.O. Box 277, Mount Carmel, IL 62863
Phone: (618)262-4561
Web site: www.rootsweb.com/~ilwabash/
Parent County: Edwards

Record Type	Year Begun	Jurisdiction
Birth	1877	County Clerk
Marriage	1857	County Clerk
Death	1877	County Clerk
Land	1857	County Recorder
Probate	1851	Clerk/Circuit Ct.
Court	1851	Clerk/Circuit Ct.

■ Warren 13 Jan. 1825
100 W. Broadway, Monmouth, IL 61462
Phone: (309)734-8592
Web site: www.outfitters.com/illinois/warren/
Parent County: Pike

Record Type	Year Begun	Jurisdiction
Birth	1877	County Clerk
Marriage	1831	County Clerk
Death	1877	County Clerk
Land	1800	County Recorder
Probate	1830	Clerk/Circuit Ct.
Court	1832	Clerk/Circuit Ct.

■ Washington 2 Jan. 1818
101 E. St. Louis St., Nashville, IL 62263
Phone: (618)327-4800
Web site: www.iltrails.org/washington/
Parent County: St. Clair

Record Type	Year Begun	Jurisdiction
Court	1818	Clerk/Circuit Ct.

Illinois

Record Type	Year Begun	Jurisdiction
Birth	1877	County Clerk
Marriage	1831	County Clerk
Death	1877	County Clerk
Land	1815	County Recorder
Probate	1818	Clerk/Circuit Ct.

■ Wayne 26 Mar. 1819

301 E. Main St., P.O. Box 187, Fairfield, IL 62837
Phone: (618)842-5182
Web site: www.rootsweb.com/~ilwayne/
Parent County: Edwards

Record Type	Year Begun	Jurisdiction
Birth	1886	County Clerk
Marriage	1850	County Clerk
Death	1886	County Clerk
Land	1865	County Recorder
Probate	1886	Clerk/Circuit Ct.
Court	1819	Clerk/Circuit Ct.

■ White 9 Dec. 1815

P.O. Box 339, Carmi, IL 62821
Phone: (618)382-7211
Web site: www.rootsweb.com/~ilwhite2/
Parent County: Madison

Record Type	Year Begun	Jurisdiction
Birth	1877	County Clerk
Marriage	1816	County Clerk
Death	1877	County Clerk
Probate	1816	Clerk/Circuit Ct.
Court	1816	Clerk/Circuit Ct.
Land	1816	County Recorder

■ Whiteside 16 Jan. 1836

200 E. Knox St., Morrison, IL 61270-2698
Phone: (815)772-5188
Web site: www.whiteside.org/
Parent County: Jo Daviess, Henry

Record Type	Year Begun	Jurisdiction
Birth	1877	County Clerk
Marriage	1857	County Clerk
Death	1877	County Clerk
Land	1838	County Recorder
Probate	1839	Clerk/Circuit Ct.
Court	1838	Clerk/Circuit Ct.

■ Will 12 Jan. 1836

14 W. Jefferson St., Joliet, IL 60432
Phone: (815)727-8592
Web site: www.willcountyillinois.com/
Parent County: Cook, Iroquois

Record Type	Year Begun	Jurisdiction
Birth	1877	County Clerk
Marriage	1836	County Clerk
Death	1877	County Clerk
Land	1835	County Recorder
Probate	1837	Clerk/Circuit Ct.
Court	1836	Clerk/Circuit Ct.

■ Williamson 28 Feb. 1839

200 W. Jefferson St., Marion, IL 62959
Phone: (618)997-1301
Web site: www.people.ku.edu/~place/williamson.html
Parent County: Franklin

Record Type	Year Begun	Jurisdiction
Birth	1877	County Clerk
Marriage	1839	County Clerk
Death	1877	County Clerk
Land	1818	County Recorder
Probate	1836	Clerk/Circuit Ct.
Court	1840	Clerk/Circuit Ct.

■ Winnebago 16 Jan. 1836

400 W. State St., Room 101, Rockford, IL 61101
Phone: (815)987-2510
Web site: www.rootsweb.com/~ilwinneb/winncnty.htm
Parent County: Jo Daviess, La Salle

Record Type	Year Begun	Jurisdiction
Birth	1877	County Clerk
Marriage	1836	County Clerk
Death	1877	County Clerk
Land	1836	County Recorder
Probate	1837	Clerk/Circuit Ct.
Court	1836	Clerk/Circuit Ct.

■ Woodford 27 Feb. 1841

115 N. Main St., Eureka, IL 61530
Phone: (309)467-2822
Web site: www.rootsweb.com/~ilwoodfo/
Parent County: Tazewell, McLean

Record Type	Year Begun	Jurisdiction
Birth	1877	County Clerk
Marriage	1841	County Clerk
Death	1877	County Clerk
Land	1831	County Recorder
Probate	1841	Clerk/Circuit Ct.
Court	1841	Clerk/Circuit Ct.

Illinois

Indiana

By James W. Warren

HISTORICAL OVERVIEW

Famous Hoosiers? Larry Bird. William Henry Harrison. And, of course, Indiana Jones. The Miami, Wyandot, Wea, Potawatomis, and Delaware Indians gave the state its name. The earliest European settlers in Indiana were the French, who established trading outposts at Fort Wayne, Vincennes, and Lafayette in the early 1700s. The British took control of the area in 1763. There were a few hundred French settled in the area then. In 1764, Clarksville (across the Ohio from present-day Louisville, Kentucky) was established, the first authorized American settlement in Indiana. The United States established the Northwest Territory in 1787.

In 1800, Indiana Territory was organized. It was reduced in 1805 when Michigan Territory was created, and again in 1809 with the creation of Illinois Territory. The Battle of Tippecanoe in 1811 was the last major Indian battle in Indiana. After the War of 1812 Indiana settlement increased, with people who migrated from the Carolinas, Virginia, Kentucky, Tennessee, and Maryland.

Indiana became the nineteenth state admitted to the union in 1816. The National Road reached Indianapolis in 1834, and brought an influx of settlers from Ohio, Pennsylvania, and New York. Until 1850 most of the settlement was in the southern half of the state, and Indiana did not draw the large numbers of overseas immigrants that other midwest states did in the mid-nineteenth century. But in the last half of the century, the development of roads, canals, and railroads brought more settlers from the east. The industrial growth of the northern towns began to populate the north and attract foreign immigrants. The inexpensive farmland still drew many immigrants as well. Quakers who left Tennessee and the Carolinas came to Indiana, away from slavery.

During the Civil War, Indiana provided more than 224,000 Union troops. Former slaves came north to settle

INDIANA AT A GLANCE

Motto: The Crossroads of America

Population: 6.1 million

Prevalent Religions: Christianity, particularly Roman Catholic, and also Baptist, Methodist, Lutheran, Presbyterian, Pentecostal, Jewish, Mennonite, and Amish

Major Industries: Corn, soybeans, hogs, cattle, dairy products, eggs, steel, electrical equipment, transportation equipment, chemical products, petroleum and coal products, machinery

Ethnic Makeup (in percent): Caucasian 87.5%, African American 8.4%, Hispanic 3.5%, Native American 0.3%, Asian 1.0%, Other 1.6%

Famous Hoosiers: Larry Bird, Hoagy Carmichael, James Dean, Eugene Debs, Theodore Dreiser, Jimmy Hoffa, The Jacksons, David Letterman, Eli Lilly, Shelley Long, John Mellencamp, Joaquin Miller, Jim Nabors, Cole Porter, Ernie Pyle, Dan Quayle, Red Skelton, Rex Stout, Booth Tarkington, Kurt Vonnegut Jr.

Above: The Sim Smith Bridge in Parke County

© PhotoDisc/Getty Images

in Indiana. During the next century, Indiana's economy became increasingly industrial.

RECORD HIGHLIGHTS

The first extant federal population census for the State of Indiana is 1820. All of the 1800 and most of the 1810 territorial censuses for Indiana were lost. The 1890 census for Indiana was destroyed in a fire, and the 1890 Veterans' Schedule for Indiana was also lost. Mortality schedules exist for 1850, 1860, 1870, and 1880. Other territorial and state censuses (including 1807, 1853, 1866, 1871, and 1877) are largely incomplete or their content is sparse. Those enumerations are at the Indiana State Archives.

Indiana birth and death records were to be recorded by the counties beginning in 1882. The statewide registration of deaths began in 1899, and births followed in 1907. Marriage records have been kept by the clerk of the circuit court since 1807, and there was no statewide registration until 1958. WPA (Works Progress Administration) workers extracted and compiled birth, death, and marriage records up to 1920, and those typescripts are available at the Family History Library and other facilities. Birth and death certificates can be ordered from the Vital Records Office in Indianapolis. Marriage records can be ordered from the clerk of circuit court in the county where the marriage took place.

Divorces were handled by different courts at different time periods. There may be a special ledger book of divorces, or they may be incorporated with other civil case files or in order books.

The Indiana State Library's Genealogy Division has a searchable database of Indiana marriages though 1850 available on its Web site. The index was originally created by WPA workers. It is *not* without errors and omissions, but is a quick check <http://199.8.200.229/db/marriages_search.asp>.

In 1814, the circuit court became the basic county-level court in Indiana, and still is today. Superior Courts were established around 1871 as the case load became too heavy for a Circuit Court judge. In researching old records you may come across courts with other names. In territorial times, there were three courts: Common Pleas, General Court, and Quarter Sessions of the Peace. Circuit court replaced all three in 1814. The court of common pleas appeared again from roughly 1849–1873 and handled probate cases and sometimes divorce and naturalization. The records these courts generated will usually be recorded in court order books and case files. Most of the court order books and often other records have been or are being filmed, and are available through the Family History Library.

The county recorder's office handles land transactions

RESEARCH TIPS
for more info

- The Indiana State Library has two divisions important to Indiana researchers—the Genealogy Division and the Indiana Division. The Genealogy Division has an extensive genealogical reference library, and the Indiana Division houses manuscripts, state documents, newspapers, photographs, and oral history collections <www.statelib.lib.in.us>.
- The Indiana State Archives is the official repository of Indiana government records <www.state.in.us/icpr/archives>.
- The Allen County Public Library in Ft. Wayne has one of the largest genealogical collections in the country.
- Another important repository is the Indiana Historical Society, which houses a large collection of published materials as well as many photographs and important manuscripts.
- www.negenealogy.com

Census Records
- Territorial Census: 1807 (Dearborn, Knox, and Randolph Counties)
- Federal Censuses: 1820, 1830, 1840, 1850, 1860, 1870, 1880, 1900, 1910, 1920, 1930
- State/Territorial Censuses: 1820, 1830, 1840, 1850, 1860 (enumerations of eligible voters only)
- Indiana Mortality Schedules: 1850, 1860, 1870, 1880

in Indiana courthouses. Copies of deeds and mortgages can be ordered from there. Because research in land records can be time-consuming, and because indexes are often incomplete, whenever possible make use of microfilmed indexes and records. The Family History Library has filmed the county land records for more than two-thirds of the ninety-two Indiana counties.

Probate records are in the custody of the circuit court in almost all Indiana counties. Many of the probate records have been microfilmed. The Genealogy Division of the Indiana State Library has many of the microfilmed probate records. The Family History Library also has films for many Indiana counties.

During most time periods, naturalization could take place in any court of record. So do not overlook any of the "categories" of courts in Indiana counties when searching for naturalization records. The naturalization records from many of Indiana's counties have been transferred to the Indiana State Archives and microfilmed there. The Archives Web site includes a Naturalization Database Search. Using this, you can do a search online with no more information required than a surname <www.in.gov/serv/icpr_naturalization>. The Family History Library also has many of the Indiana counties naturalization records available.

The largest newspaper collection in the state is at the Indiana Division of the Indiana State Library. The microfilmed newspapers circulate on interlibrary loan. A county-by-county listing of the 16,500 reels of newspaper microfilm is accessible online at <www.statelib.lib.in.us/www/isl/whoweare/indiana.html>.

The Indiana State Archives has an interesting array of online databases available. This includes a database to the Indiana Soldier's and Sailor's Children's Home <www.in.gov/icpr/archives/databases/issch/index.html>.

Indiana's religious history is richly varied and can be very important in researching Indiana ancestors. Church records are abundant, and the best capsule description of where and how to look for them is included in John Beatty's *Research in Indiana*, a publication of the National Genealogical Society that first appeared as an article in the *National Genealogical Society Quarterly*, June 1991.

The Indiana State Library, Indiana Division manages the manuscript and state document collections of the state library, as well as the photographs, newspapers, and oral history collections. The Indiana Biography Index is an online finding aid to books, periodicals, newspaper clippings, obituaries, and other sources. It contains more than 250,000 names. You can search the index at <http://199.8.200.229/db/bio_cards_search.asp>.

Another branch of the Indiana State Library, the Genealogy Division, has an excellent genealogical reference library for Indiana research and beyond. Their collection includes more than 40,000 printed items, electronic resources, and microfilm. Their Web site offers an array of information and some online databases as well <www.statelib.lib.in.us/www/isl/whoweare/genealogy.html>.

The Indiana Historical Society is one more respository that should not be overlooked. In addition to its published reference and historical material, it has a huge collection of photographs and important manuscript materials <www.indianahistory.org>.

The Allen County Public Library's collection of local and family history covers all fifty states and Canada, and some resources for foreign research as well. With friendly, expert staff, extensive hours, and one of the largest genealogical collections in the country, it's not surprising that this is a popular research destination for genealogists across the U.S. and Canada.

STATE RESOURCES

■ ARCHIVES, LIBRARIES, AND SOCIETIES

Alexandria-Monroe Township Historical Society
313 N. Harrison St., Alexandria, IN 46001
Tel: (765) 724-2993
Web site: <www.rootsweb.com/~inmadiso/alexandria.htm>

Allen County Genealogical Society of Indiana
P.O. Box 12003, Fort Wayne, IN 46862
Web site: <www.ipfw.edu/ipfwhist/historgs/acgsi.htm>

Allen County Public Library
200 E. Berry St., Fort Wayne, IN 46801
Tel: (260) 421-1200
Web site:

Anderson Public Library
111 E. Twelfth St., Anderson, IN 46016
Tel: (765) 641-2456
Web site: <www.and.lib.in.us>

Bartholomew County Genealogical Society
P.O. Box 2455, Columbus, IN 47202

Benton County Historical Society
711 E. Third St., Fowler, IN 47944

Blackford County Historical Society
P.O. Box 264, Hartford City, IN 47348
Web site: <www.bchs-in.org>

Boone County Historical Society
P.O Box 141, Lebanon, IN 46052-0141

Tel: (765) 483-9414
Web site: <www.bccn.boone.in.us/bchs>

Brown County Genealogical Society
P.O. Box 1202, Nashville, IN 47448-1202
Web site: <www.rootsweb.com/~inbcgs/title.htm>

Brown County Historical Society
P.O. Box 668, Nashville, IN 47448
Tel: (812) 988-6089
Web site: <www.browncounty.org/bchistoric.html>

Carroll County Historical Society
Ground Floor Court House, P.O. Box 277, Delphi, IN 46923
Tel: (765) 564-3152
E-mail: cchs@dcwi.com
Web site: <dcwi.com/~cchs>

Cass County Genealogical Society
P.O. Box 373, Logansport, IN 46947

Clark County Historical Society
P.O. Box 606, Jeffersonville, IN 47130

Clay County Genealogical Society, Inc.
P.O. Box 56, Center Point, IN 47840-0056
Tel: (812) 835-5005
E-mail: research@ccgsilib.org
Web site: <www.ccgsilib.org>

Clinton County Genealogical Society
% Frankfort Community Public Library, 208 W. Clinton St., Frankfort, IN 46041

Clinton County Historical Society
301 E. Clinton St., Frankfort, IN 46041
E-mail: cchsm@geetel.net

Danville Public Library
101 S. Indiana St., Danville, IN 46122
Tel: (317) 745-2604
Web site: <www.dpl.lib.in.us>

DeKalb County Indiana Genealogy Society
P.O. Box 6085, Auburn, IN 46706
Web site: <www.rootsweb.com/ ~indkigs/main_page.html>

Delaware County Historical Society
120 E. Washington St., Muncie, IN 47305-1734
Tel: (765) 282-1550
E-mail: dchs@tmcsmail.com
Web site: <www.dchsmunciein .org>

Dubois County Genealogical Society
P.O. Box 84, Ferdinand, IN 47532-0084
Web site: <www.rootsweb.com/ ~indubois/dubges.htm>

Elkhart County Genealogy Society
P.O. Box 1031, Elkhart, IN 46515-1031
Web site: <www.rootsweb.com/ ~inelkhar/ecgs.htm>

Elwood Pipecreek Genealogy Society
1600 Main St., Elwood, IN 46036
Web site: <www.rootsweb.com/ ~inmadiso/Elwood.htm>

Fountain County Genealogical Society, Inc.
P.O. Box 273, Veedersburg, IN 47987
E-mail: focogensoc@netscape .net
Web site: <www.tctc.com/~emo yhbo/fcgs.html>

Fountain County Historical Society
P.O. Box 148, Kingman, IN 47952

Frankfort Community/Clinton County Contractual Public Library
208 W. Clinton St, Frankfort, IN 46041
Tel: (765) 654-8746
E-mail: fcpl@accs.net
Web site: <www.accs.net/fcpl>

Fulton County Historical Society
37 E. 375 N., Rochester, IN 46975
Tel: (574) 223-4436

Web site: <http://icss.net/ ~fchs/index.htm>

Fulton Library
504 Wright St., P.O. Box 206, Fulton, IN 46931
Tel: (574) 857-3895
E-mail: fulton@fulco.lib.in.us
Web site: <www.fulco.lib.in.us>

Genealogical Society of Marion County
P.O. Box 2292, Indianapolis, IN 46206-2292
Web site: <www.rootsweb.com/ ~ingsmc>

Genealogical Society of Whitley County
P.O. Box 224, Columbia City, IN 46725-0224
Web site: <genealogy.whitleynet .org>

Gibson County Historical Society, Inc.
P.O. Box 516, Princeton, IN 47670-4946

Greene County Genealogical Society
P.O. Box 164, Bloomfield, IN 47424
Web site: <www.greenecountyin .org/gcgs.htm>

Hamilton County Historical Society
P.O. Box 397, Noblesville, IN 46061
Tel: (317) 770-0775
Web site: <www.rootsweb.com/ ~inhchs/>

Hancock County Historical Society
P.O. Box 375, Greenfield, IN 46140
Tel: (317) 462-7780
Web site: <brandywine.newpal.k 12.in.us/bjhs/hancock_county_ historical_society.htm>

Harrison County Historical Society
117 W. Beaver St., Corydon, IN 47112

Henry County Historical Society
606 S. Fourteenth St., New Castle, IN 47362
Web site: <www.kiva.net/~hchi soc/museum.htm>

Historical Committee and Archives of the Mennonite Church
1700 S. Main St., Goshen, IN 46526

Tel: (574) 535-7477
Web site: <www.mcusa-archives .org>

Howard County Genealogical Society
P.O. Box 2, Oakford, IN 46965
Web site: <www.rootsweb.com/ ~inhoward/gensoc.html>

Huntington City-Township Public Library
200 W. Market St., Huntington, IN 46750
Tel: (260) 356-0824
Web site: <www.huntingtonpub.li b.in.us>

Indiana African American Historical and Genealogical Society
502 Clover Terrace, Bloomington, IN 47404-1809

Indiana Genealogical Society
P.O. Box 10507, Fort Wayne, IN 46852
Web site: <www.indgensoc.org>

Indiana Historical Society
William Henry Smith Memorial Library, 450 W. Ohio St. Indianapolis, IN 46202
Tel: (317) 232-1882

Indiana State Archives
6440 E. Thirtieth St., Indianapolis, IN 46219
Tel: (317) 591-5222
E-mail: arc@icpr.state.in.us
Web site: <www.in.gov/icpr/arc hives/databases>

Indiana State Library, Genealogy Division
140 N. Senate Ave., Indianapolis IN 46204-2296
Tel: (317) 232-3689

Jackson County Genealogical Society, Inc.
415 S. Poplar St., Brownstown, IN 47220-1939
Tel: (812) 358-2118
Web site: <www.rootsweb.com/ ~injackso/gensoc.html>

Jasper County Historical Society
479 N. Van Rensselaer, Rensselaer, IN 47978

Jay County Genealogy Society
109 S. Commerce St., Portland, IN 47371
Tel: (260) 726-4323
E-mail: jaycogen@jayco.net

Web site: <www.rootsweb.com/ ~injay/research/jaygene.htm>

Jay County Historical Society
P.O. Box 1282, Portland, IN 47371
Tel: (260) 726-7168

Jefferson County Historical Society
615 W. First St., Madison, IN 47250
Tel: (812) 265-2335
E-mail: jchs@seidata.com
Web site: <www.jcohs.org>

Kokomo-Howard County Public Library
220 N. Union St., Kokomo, IN 46901-4614
Tel: (765) 457-3242
E-mail: khcpl@kokomo.lib.in.us
Web site: <www.kokomo.lib.in .us>

Kosciusko County Historical Society
P.O. Box 1071, Warsaw, IN 46580-1071
Web site: <culture.kconline. com/kchs>

LaGrange County Historical Society
P.O. Box 134, LaGrange, IN 46761

LaPorte County Genealogical Society
% LaPorte County Public Library, 904 Indiana Ave., LaPorte, IN 46350
Web site: <www.rootsweb.com/ ~inlcigs>

LaPorte County Historical Society & Museum
809 State St., LaPorte, IN 46350-3329
Tel: (219) 326-6808
Web site: <www.lapcohistsoc .org>

Lexington Historical Society, Inc.
P.O. Box 238, Lexington, IN 47138-0238
Web site: <www.scottinhistory. com/societies/lhs.html>

Logansport-Cass County Public Library
616 E. Broadway, Logansport, IN 46947
Tel: (574) 753-6383
Web site: <www.logan.lib.in.us>

Madison-Jefferson Co. Public Library
420 W. Main St., Madison, IN 47250
Tel: (812) 265-2744
Web site: <www.madison-jeffco.lib.in.us>

Marion-Adams Historical & Genealogical Society
308 Main St., Sheridan, IN 46069

Marion Public Library
600 S. Washington St., Marion, IN 46953-1992
Tel: (765) 668-2900
Web site: <www.marion.lib.in.us>

Marshall County Historical Society and Museum
123 N. Michigan St., Plymouth, IN 46563
Tel: (574) 936-2306
E-mail: mchistory@mchistoricalsociety.org
Web site: <www.mchistoricalsociety.org>

Mennonite Historical Library, Goshen College
1700 S. Main St., Goshen, IN 46526
Tel: (574) 535-7418
E-mail: mhl@goshen.edu
Web site: <www.goshen.edu/mhl>

Merrillville-Ross Township Historical Museum
13 W. 73rd Ave., Merrillville, IN 46410
Web site: <www.rootsweb.com/~inlake/ross.htm>

Miami County Genealogical Society
P.O. Box 542, Peru, IN 46970
Web site: <www.rootsweb.com/~inmiami/gensoc.html>

Miami County Historical Society and Museum
51 N. Broadway, Peru, IN 46970
Tel: (765) 473-9183
E-mail: archivist@miamicountymuseum.com
Web site: <www.miamicountymuseum.com>

Michigan City Public Library
100 E. Fourth St., Michigan City, IN 46360
E-mail: reference@mclib.org
Web site: <www.mclib.org>

Middletown Public Library
554 Locust St., Middletown, IN 47356

Mishawaka-Penn-Harris Public Library
209 Lincoln Way E., Mishawaka, IN 46544
Tel: (574) 259-5277
Web site: <www.mppl.lib.in.us/home.html>

Monroe County Historical Society, Inc.
202 E. Sixth St., Bloomington, IN 47408
Tel: (812) 332-2517
Web site: <www.kiva.net/~mchm/monroe.html>

Monroe County Public Library
303 E. Kirkwood Ave., Bloomington, IN 47408
Web site: <www.monroe.lib.in.us>

Montgomery County Historical Society
212 S. Water St., Crawfordsville, IN 47933
Tel: (765) 362-3416

Morgan County History & Genealogy Association
P.O. Box 1012, Martinsville, IN 46151-0012
Web site: <www.rootsweb.com/~inmchaga/mchagai.html>

Morgan County Public Library
110 S. Jefferson St., Martinsville, IN 46151
Tel: (765) 342-3451
E-mail: morglib@scican.net
Web site: <http://morg.lib.in.us>

The National Archives, Great Lakes Region
7358 S. Pulaski Road, Chicago, IL 60629-5898
Tel: (773) 581-7816
E-mail: chicago.archives@nara.gov
Web site: <www.archives.gov/facilities/il/chicago.html>

Noble County Genealogical Society
813 E. Main St., Albion, IN 46701

Noblesville-Southeastern Public Library
One Library Plaza, Noblesville, IN 46701
Tel: (317) 773-1384

North Central Indiana Genealogical Society
2300 Canterbury Dr., Kokomo, IN 46901

Northern Indiana Historical Society
112 S. Lafayette Blvd., South Bend, IN 46601

Northwest Indiana Genealogical Society
% Valparaiso Public Library, 103 Jefferson St., Valparaiso, IN
Web site: <www.rootsweb.com/~innwigs>

Northwest Territory Genealogical Society
Lewis Historical Library-LCR 22, Vincennes University, Vincennes, IN 47591
Tel: (812) 885-4330

University of Notre Dame Archives
607 Hesburgh Library, Notre Dame, IN 46556
Tel: (574) 631-6448
E-mail: archives@nd.edu
Web site: <www.nd.edu/~archives>

Ohio County Indiana Historical Society and Museum
212 S. Walnut, Rising Sun, IN 47040
Tel: (812) 438-4915
E-mail: museum@ohiocountyinmuseum.org
Web site: <www.ohiocountyinmuseum.org>

Orange County Genealogical Society
P.O. Box 344, Paoli, IN 47454
Web site: <www.usgennet.org/usa/in/county/orange/gensoc.htm>

Owen County Historical & Genealogical Society
P.O. Box 569, Spencer, IN 47460
Web site: <www.owen.in.us/owenhist/owen.htm>

Owen County Public Library
10 S. Montgomery St., Spencer, IN 47460
Tel: (812) 829-3392
Web site: <www.owenlib.org>

Palatines to America, Indiana Chapter
1801 N. Duane Rd., Muncie, IN 47304-2649
Tel: (317) 284-1841

Paoli Public Library
10 NE Court, Paoli IN 47454
Tel: (812) 723-3841

Plainfield-Guilford Township Public Library
1120 Stafford Rd., Plainfield, IN 46168
Tel: (317) 839-6602
Web site: <www.plainfield.lib.in.us>

Plymouth Public Library
201 N. Center St, Plymouth, IN 46563
Tel: (574) 936-2324
E-mail: info@plymouth.lib.in.us
Web site: <www.plymouth.lib.in.us>

Porter County Public Library System
103 Jefferson St., Valparaiso, IN 46383
Tel: (219) 462-0524
Web site: <www.publiclibraries.com/indiana.htm>

Posey County Historical Society
P.O. Box 171, Mt. Vernon, IN 47620
Web site: <www.rootsweb.com/~inposey/society.htm>

Pulaski County Genealogical Society
Rural Rte. 4, Box 121, Winamac, IN 46996

Pulaski County Public Library
121 S. Riverside Dr., Winamac, IN 46996
Tel: (219) 946-3432

Randolph County Genealogical Society
Rte. 3, Box 60, Winchester, IN 47394

Randolph County Historical Society
416 S. Meridian, Winchester, IN 47394

Ripley County Historical Society
P.O. Box 525, Versailles, IN 47042
Tel: (812) 689-3031
Web site: <www.seidata.com/~rchslib>

Rockville Public Library
106 N. Market St., Rockville, IN 47872
Tel: (765) 569-5544
E-mail: rocklib@ticz.com
Web site: <http://rockvillepl.lib.in.us/index.htm>

Indiana

St. Joseph County Public Library
304 S. Main St., South Bend, IN 46601
Web site: <sjcpl.lib.in.us>

Scott County Genealogical Society
P.O. Box 258, Lexington, IN 47138-0258

Shelby County Historical Society
52 W. Broadway St, Shelbyville, IN 46176
Tel: (317) 392-4634

Shelbyville-Shelby County Public Library
57 W. Broadway, Shelbyville, IN 46176
Tel: (317) 398-7121
Web site: <www.sscpl.lib.in.us/library>

Society of Indiana Pioneers
450 W. Ohio St., Indianapolis, IN 46202
Tel: (317) 233-6588
Web site: <www.indianapioneers.com>

South Bend Area Genealogical Society
% The Mishawaka-Penn Public Library, 209 Lincoln Way E., Mishawaka, IN 46544
E-mail: mailsbags@go.com
Web site: <www.rootsweb.com/~insbags>

The Southern Indiana Genealogical Society
P.O. Box 665, New Albany, IN 47151-0665
Web site: <www.ka.net/spcarpenter/SIGserve.htm>

Spencer County Historical Society
% Spencer County Public Library, 210 Walnut St., Rockport, IN 47635-1398
Tel: (812) 649-4866

Starke County Genealogical Society
152 W. Culver Rd., Knox, IN 46534
E-mail: starkegen@myvine.com
Web site: <www.rootsweb.com/~inscgs/>

Steuben County Genealogical Society
P.O. Box 884, Angola, IN 46703
Web site: <www.rootsweb.com/~insteube/scgs>

The Sullivan County Historical Society
10 S. Court St., Sullivan, IN 47882
Tel: (812) 268-6253
Web site: <www.rootsweb.com/~inschs/schsplus/society.htm>

P.H. Sullivan Museum & Genealogy Library
225 W. Hawthorne St., Zionsville, IN 46077
Tel: (317) 873-4900
Web site: <www.sullivanmunce.org>

Switzerland County Public Library
205 Ferry St., Vevay, IN 47043
Tel: (812) 427-3363
E-mail: info@switzcpl.lib.in.us
Web site: <www.switzcpl.lib.in.us>

Tippecanoe County Area Genealogical Society
P.O. Box 2464, West Lafayette, IN 47996
Web site: <www.rootsweb.com/~intcags>

Tippecanoe County Historical Association
909 South St., Lafayette, IN 47901
Tel: (765) 476-8411
E-mail: mail@tcha.mus.in.us
Web site: <www.tcha.mus.in.us>

Tipton County Public Library
127 E. Madison St., Tipton, IN 46072
Tel: (765) 675-8761
E-mail: tipton@tiptonpl.lib.in.us
Web site: <www.tiptonpl.lib.in.us>

Tri-State Genealogical Society
% Willard Library, 21 First Ave., Evansville, IN 47710

Union City Public Library
408 N. Columbia St., Union City, IN 47390-1097
Tel: (765) 964-4748

Union County Historical Society
P.O. Box 143, Liberty, IN 47353

Union County Public Library
2 E. Seminary, Liberty, IN 47353
Tel: (765) 458-5355
Web site: <www.union-county.lib.in.us>

Valparaiso Public Library
103 Jefferson St., Valparaiso, IN 46383
Tel: (219) 462-0524

Vigo County Historical Society
1411 S. Sixth St., Terre Haute, IN 47802
Tel: (812) 235-9717
E-mail: vchs@vigohistory.com
Web site: <http://web.indstate.edu/community/vchs>

Wabash Carnegie Public Library
188 W. Hill St., Wabash, IN 46992
Tel: (260) 563-2972
E-mail: general@wabash.lib.in.us
Web site: <www.wabash.lib.in.us/index.htm>

Wabash County Genealogical Society
P. O. Box 825, Wabash, IN 46992
Web site: <www.rootsweb.com/~inwabash/wcgs.html>

Wabash Valley Genealogical Society
P.O. Box 85, Terre Haute, IN 47808

Warren County Historical Society
P.O. Box 176, Williamsport, IN 47993

Warsaw Community Public Library
310 E. Main St., Warsaw, IN 46580
Tel: (574) 267-6011
Web site: <www.wcpl.lib.in.us>

Washington Township Public Library
106 N. Main St., Lynn, IN 47355
Tel: (765) 874-1488

Wayne County Genealogical Society
P.O. Box 2599, Richmond IN 47375-2599
Web site: <www.waynet.org/nonprofit/wcgs.htm>

Wells County Historical Society
P.O. Box 143, Bluffton, IN 46714-0143
Web site: <www.wchs-museum.org/museum.htm>

White County Genealogical Society
101 S. Bluff St., Monticello, IN 47960
Tel: (574) 583-3998
Web site: <www.rootsweb.com/~inwhite/whgen.htm>

Willard Library of Evansville
21 First Ave., Evansville, IN 47710
Tel: (812) 425-4309

E-mail: willard@willard.lib.in.us
Web site: <www.willard.lib.in.us/location.html>

Winchester Community Public Library
125 N. East St, Winchester, IN 47394
Tel: (317) 584-4824

BIBLIOGRAPHY

■ GENERAL RESOURCES

Abstracts of the Records of the Society of Friends in Indiana
by Ruth Dorrel (Indianapolis: Indiana Historical Society, ca. 1996–1999)

Biographical and Historical Sketches of Early Indiana
by William Wesley Woollen (Tucson, AZ: W.C. Cox, 1974)

A Biographical History of Eminent and Selfmade Men of the State of Indiana
(Cincinnati: Western Biographical Pub. Co., 1880)

The Black Women in the Middle West Project: A Comprehensive Resource Guide, Illinois and Indiana; Historical Essays, Oral Histories, Biographical Profiles, and Document Collections
by Darlene Clark Hine (Indianapolis: Indiana Historical Bureau, 1986)

A Directory of Churches and Religious Organizations in Indiana
by the Historical Records Survey (Indianapolis: Indiana Historical Records Survey, 1941–)

Executive Journal of Indiana Territory, 1800–1816
by William Wesley Woollen, Daniel Wait Howe, and Jacob Piatt Dunn (Indianapolis: Indiana Historical Society, Family History Section, 1985)

Genealogical Sources: Reprinted from the Genealogy Section, Indiana Magazine of History
by Dorothy L. Riker (Indianapolis, IN: Family History & Genealogy Section, Indiana Historical Society, 1979)

The Genealogist's Companion and Sourcebook, 2d ed.
by Emily Anne Croom (Cincinnati: Betterway Books, 2003)

A Genealogist's Guide to Discovering Your African-American Ancestors
by Franklin Carter Smith and Emily Anne Croom (Cincinnati: Betterway Books, 2003)

A Genealogist's Guide to the Ft. Wayne, Indiana, Public Library
by Karen B. Cavanaugh (Owensboro, KY: McDowell Publications, ca. 1980)

A Guide to Genealogical Records in Indiana
by Malinda E.E. Newhard (Harlan, IN: M.E.E. Newhard, ca. 1979)

Guide to Genealogical Research in the National Archives of the United States
edited by Anne Bruner Eales and Robert M. Kvasnicka (Washington, DC: National Archives and Records Administration, 2000)

A Guide to the Manuscript Collections of the Indiana Historical Society and the Indiana State Library
by Eric Pumroy and Paul Brockman (Indianapolis: Indiana Historical Society, ca. 1986)

History of the Catholic Church in Indiana
by Charles Blanchard (Logansport, IN: A.W. Bowen & Co., 1898)

A History of Indiana: From its Earliest Exploration by Europeans to the Close of the Territorial Government, in 1816; Comprehending a History of the Discovery, Settlement, and Civil and Military Affairs of the Territory of the U.S. Northwest of the River Ohio
by John B. Dillon (Indianapolis: Bingham & Doughty, 1859)

Hoosier Faiths: A History of Indiana Churches and Religious Groups
by L.C. Rudolph (Bloomington, IN: Indiana University Press, ca. 1995)

Illiana Ancestors: Genealogy Column in the Commercial-news, Danville, Illinois
by Joan A. Griffis (Danville, IL: J. Griffis, ca. 1984–1996)

Index to Encyclopedia of American Quaker Genealogy
by William Wade Hinshaw (Baltimore: Genealogical Pub. Co., ca. 1999)

Index, Indiana Source Books
by Dorothy Riker (Indianapolis, IN: Indiana Historical Society, Family History Section, 1983)

Index to Indiana Wills: Phase 1, through 1850; Phase 2, 1850 through 1880
by Charles M. Franklin (Indianapolis: Heritage House, ca. 1986–1987)

Indiana Friends Heritage, 1821–1996: The 175th Anniversary History of Indiana Yearly Meeting of Friends (Quakers)
by Gregory P. Hinshaw (Muncie, IN: Indiana Yearly Meeting, 1996)

Indiana Genealogical Resource
by George K. Schweitzer (Knoxville, TN: G.K. Schweitzer, ca. 1996)

Indiana Genealogy and Local History Sources Index
by Stuart Harter (Ft. Wayne, IN: Stuart Harter, ca. 1985)

Indiana and Indianans: A History of Aboriginal and Territorial Indiana and the Century of Statehood
by Jacob Piatt Dunn (Chicago, IL: American Historical Society, 1919)

Indiana Negro Registers, 1852–1865
by Coy D. Robbins (Bowie, MD: Heritage Books, ca. 1994)

Indiana Newspaper Bibliography: Historical Accounts of All Indiana Newspapers Published from 1804 to 1980 and Locational Information for All Available Copies, Both Original and Microfilm
by John W. Miller (Indianapolis: Indiana Historical Society, 1982)

Indiana Research Outline
by the Church of Jesus Christ of Latter-day Saints (Salt Lake City, UT: Corp. of the President of The Church of Jesus Christ of L.D.S., ca. 1988, ca. 1999)

Indiana Source Book: Genealogical Material from The Hoosier Genealogist
by Willard Heiss, Rebah M. Fraustein, and Ruth Dorrel (Indianapolis: Indiana Historical Society, Family History Section, 1977–)

Indiana Sources for Genealogical Research in the Indiana State Library
by Carolynne L. Wendel Miller (Indianapolis: Indiana Historical Society, ca. 1984)

Indiana Territorial Pioneer Records, 1801–1820
by Charles M. Franklin (Heritage House, ca. 1983–1985)

Indiana's African-American Heritage: Essays from Black History News and Notes
by Wilma L. Gibbs (Indianapolis: Indiana Historical Society, ca. 1993)

Manual for Indiana Genealogical Research
by Pat and Ray Gooldy (Indianapolis: Ye Olde Genealogie Shoppe, ca. 1991)

National Archives Microfilm Catalogs online:
<www.archives.gov/publications/genealogy_microfilm_catalogs.html>

The Negro in Indiana before 1900: A Study of a Minority
by Emma Lou Thornbrough (Bloomington, IN: Indiana University Press, 1993)

The Old Northwest: Pioneer Period, 1815–1840
by R. Carlyle Buley (Bloomington: Indiana University Press in association with the Indiana Historical Society, ca. 1978)

The Old Northwest: Studies in Regional History, 1787–1910
by Harry N. Scheiber (Lincoln, NE: University of Nebraska Press, ca. 1969)

The Origin and Development of the Missionary Baptist Church in Indiana
by John Frank Cady (Franklin, IN: Franklin College, 1942)

Peopling Indiana: The Ethnic Experience
by Robert M. Taylor, Jr., and Connie A. McBirney (Indianapolis: Indiana Historical Society, ca. 1996)

Pioneer Ancestors of Members of the Society of Indiana Pioneers
by Ruth Dorrel (Indianapolis: Indiana Historical Society, ca. 1983)

Preliminary Checklist of Archives and Manuscripts in Indiana Repositories
by Donald E. Thompson (Indianapolis: Indiana Historical Society, 1980)

Religion in Indiana: A Guide to Historical Resources
by L.C. Rudolph and Judith E. Endelman (Bloomington, IN: Indiana University Press, ca. 1986)

Research in Indiana
by John D. Beatty (Arlington, VA: National Genealogical Society Bookstore, 1992)

Searching in Indiana: A Reference Guide to Public and Private Records
by Mickey Dimon Carty (Costa Mesa, CA: ISC Publications, ca. 1985)

Who's Your Hoosier Ancestor: Genealogy for Beginners
by Mona Robinson (Bloomington, IN: Indiana University Press, ca. 1992)

■ CENSUS RECORDS

1820 Federal Census for Indiana
by Willard Heiss (Indianapolis: Indiana Historical Society, Genealogical Section, 1966)

The American Census Handbook
by Thomas Jay Kemp (Wilmington, DE: Scholarly Resources Inc., ca. 2001)

The Census Book: A Genealogist's Guide to Federal Census Facts, Schedules and Indexes; with Master Extraction Forms for Federal Census Schedules, 1790–1930
by William Dollarhide (Bountiful, UT: Heritage Quest, ca. 1999)

Census of Indiana Territory for 1807
(Indianapolis: Indiana Historical Society, 1980)

Finding Answers in U.S. Census Records
by Loretto Dennis Szucs and Matthew Wright (Orem, UT: Ancestry Pub., ca. 2001)

Indiana Territorial Pioneer Records, 1801–1820
by Charles M. Franklin (Heritage House, ca. 1983–1985)

Map Guide to the U.S. Federal Censuses, 1790–1920
by William Thorndale and William Dollarhide (Baltimore, MD: Genealogical Pub. Co., ca. 1987)

State Census Records
by Ann S. Lainhart (Baltimore, MD: Genealogical Pub. Co., ca. 1992)

Your Guide to the Federal Census
by Kathleen W. Hinckley (Cincinnati: Betterway Books, 2002)

■ IMMIGRATION RECORDS

American Naturalization Records, 1790–1990: What They Are and How to Use Them
by John J. Newman (North Salt Lake, UT: HeritageQuest, 1998)

American Passenger Arrival Records
by Michael Tepper (Baltimore: Genealogical Publishing Co., 1993)

From A to B: Migration Research: Birds of a Feather
by Richard A. Enochs (Fort Wayne, IN: Indiana Genealogical Society, ca. 1994)

An Index to Indiana Naturalization Records Found in Various Order Books of the Ninety-two Local Courts Prior to 1907
by John J Newman (Indianapolis: Indiana Historical Society, 1981)

The National Road in Indiana
by Lee Burns (Indianapolis: C.E. Pauley, ca. 1920)

They Became Americans: Finding Naturalization Records and Ethnic Origins
by Loretto Dennis Szucs (Salt Lake City: Ancestry, Inc., 1998)

They Came in Ships: A Guide to Finding Your Immigrant Ancestor's Arrival Records, 2d ed.
by John P. Colletta (Salt Lake City: Ancestry, Inc., 1993)

■ LAND RECORDS

French and British Land Grants in the Post Vincennes (Indiana) District, 1750–1784
by Clifford Neal Smith (McNeal, AZ: Westland, 1996)

Indiana Land Entries
by Margaret R. Waters (Knightstown, IN: The Bookmark, 1977–1979)

Jeffersonville Land Entries, 1808–1818
by Janet C. Cowen (Indianapolis: J.C. Cowen, ca. 1984)

Land & Property Research in the United States
by E. Wade Hone (Salt Lake City, UT: Ancestry, ca. 1997)

Locating Your Roots: Discover Your Ancestors Using Land Records
by Patricia Law Hatcher (Cincinnati: Betterway Books, 2003)

This Land of Ours: The Acquisition and Disposition of the Public Domain; Papers Presented at an Indiana American Revolution Bicentennial Symposium, Purdue University, West Lafayette, Indiana, April 29 and 30, 1978
Indiana Historical Society (Indianapolis: The Society, ca. 1978)

The Vincennes Donation Lands
by Leonard Lux (Indianapolis: Indiana Historical Society, 1949)

■ MAPS

Early Indiana Trails and Surveys
by George R. Wilson (Indianapolis: C.E. Pauley, 1919)

Genealogical Atlas of Indiana
by Charles M. Franklin (Indianapolis: Heritage House, ca. 1985)

Illustrated Historical Atlas of the State of Indiana
(Indianapolis: Indiana Historical Society, 1968)

Indiana: Atlas of Historical County Boundaries
by Peggy Tuck Sinko (New York: Charles Scribner's Sons, Simon & Schuster Macmillan, ca. 1996)

Indiana Boundaries: Territory, State and County
by George Pence (Indianapolis: Indiana Historical Bureau, 1967, ca. 1933)

The Indiana Gazetteer, or, Topographical Dictionary
by John Scott (Indianapolis: Indiana Historical Society, 1954)

Indiana Place Names
by Ronald L. Baker (Bloomington, IN: Indiana University Press, ca. 1975)

Maps of Indiana Counties in 1876: Together with the Plat of Indianapolis and a Sampling of Illustrations
by the Indiana Historical Society (Indianapolis: Indiana Historical Society, 1979)

New Topographical Atlas and Gazetteer of Indiana: Comprising a Topographical View of the Several Counties of the State, Together with a Railroad Map of Ohio, Indiana, and Illinois; An Alphabetical Gazetteer, Giving a Concise Description and the Location of Cities, Villages, Post Offices, Railroad Stations, Landings etc. . . . .
(Evansville, IN: Unigraphic, 1975)

Northwestern Indiana from 1800 to 1900, or, A View of Our Region through the Nineteenth Century
by Timothy Horton (Tucson, AZ: W.C. Cox, 1974)

■ MILITARY RECORDS

Enrollment of the Late Soldiers, Their Widows & Orphans, of the Late Armies of the United States Residing in the State of Indiana, Kosciusko County, 1886, 1890, 1894
by Anne Laurie Austin Smith (Warsaw, IN: Kosciusko County Historical Society, 1992)

Index to Admission Book, Indiana Soldiers and Sailors Home, 1868 through 1995
by Ruth Dorrel (Indianapolis: Indiana Historical Society, 1997)

Index to the Report of the Adjutant General of the State of Indiana: An Every Name Index to Volumes I, II and III
by Glenda K. Trapp (Evansville, IN: Trapp Publishing Service, ca. 1986)

Index to Revolutionary Soldiers of Indiana and Other Patriots
by Barbara Schull Wolfe (Indianapolis: Ye Olde Genealogie Shoppe, ca. 1983)

Indiana, War of 1812 Soldiers: Militia
by Charles M. Franklin (Indianapolis: Ye Olde Genealogie Shoppe, 1984)

Uncle, We Are Ready! Registering America's Men, 1917–1918: A Guide to Researching World War I Draft Registration Cards
by John J. Newman (North Salt Lake, UT: HeritageQuest, 2001)

U.S. Military Records: A Guide to Federal & State Sources, Colonial America to the Present
by James C. Neagles (Salt Lake City: Ancestry, Inc., 1994)

World War II: A Family Historian's Guide
by Debra Johnson Knox (Spartanburg, SC: MIE Publishing, 2003)

■ PROBATE RECORDS

Biographical Sketches and Review of the Bench and Bar of Indiana: Containing Biographies and Sketches of Eminent Judges and Lawyers of Indiana, Together with a History of the Judiciary of the State and Review of the Bar from the Earliest Times to the Present with Anecdotes, Reminiscences, etc. . . . .
by Charles W. Taylor (Indianapolis: Bench and Bar Pub. Co., 1895)

Directory, Wills and Estates Information in Genealogy Dept., Indiana State Library
by Vera Mae (Ginder) Moudy (Indianapolis: Ye Olde Genealogie Shoppe, 1981)

Index to Indiana Wills: Phase 1, through 1850; Phase 2, 1850 through 1880
by Charles M. Franklin (Indianapolis: Heritage House, ca. 1986–1987)

The Laws and Courts of Northwest and Indiana Territories
by Daniel Wait Howe (Indiana Historical: Bowen-Merrill Co., 1886)

The Laws of Indiana Territory, 1801–1809
(Springfield, IL: Trustees of the Ill. State Historical Library, ca. 1930)

Preliminary Inventory, Records of the United States Courts for the District of Indiana
by the United States National Archives and Records Service and Warren B. Griffin (Chicago, IL: Federal Records Center, 1967)

Research in Indiana Courthouses: Judicial and Other Records
by John J. Newman (Indianapolis: Indiana Historical Society, 1981)

■ VITAL RECORDS

1850 Indiana Mortality Schedule
by Lowell M. Volkel (L.M. Volkel, ca. 1971)

1870 Illinois Mortality Schedules
by Lowell M. Volkel (Indianapolis: Heritage House, ca. 1985–1987)

Guide to Public Vital Statistics Records in Indiana
by the Historical Records Survey (Indianapolis: Indiana Historical Records Survey, 1941)

Illinois Mortality Schedule, 1860
by Lowell M. Volkel (Indianapolis: Heritage House, 1979)

Indiana, 1851–1900
(Brøderbund, ca. 1998. CD-ROM)

Indiana Marriages, Early to 1825: A Research Tool
by Jordan R. Dodd and Norman L. Moyes (Bountiful, UT: Precision Indexing, Inc., ca. 1991)

Miscellaneous Records of Indiana, 1827–1922
by the Historical Records Survey (Indiana, 1968)

Pre-1882 Indiana Births, from Secondary Sources
by Dawne Slater-Putt (Fort Wayne, IN: Heritage Pathways, Inc., ca. 1999)

Southern Seed, Northern Soil: African-American Farm Communities in the Midwest 1765–1900
by Stephen A. Vincent (Bloomington, IN: Indiana University Press, ca. 1999)

Your Guide to Cemetery Research
by Sharon DeBartolo Carmack (Cincinnati: Betterway Books, 2002)

■ Adams 1 Mar. 1836
112 S. Second St., Decatur, IN 46733
Phone: (219)724-2600
Web site: www.rootsweb.com/~inadams/
Parent County: Adam's New Purchase
Comments/research tips: Formed 1820 as Delaware New Purchase, renamed 1827 and abolished 1844.

Record Type	Year Begun	Jurisdiction
Marriage	1836	County Clerk
Probate	1838	County Clerk
Court	na	County Clerk

■ Allen 1 Apr. 1824
Courthouse #200, Fort Wayne, IN 46802
Phone: (260)449-7245
Web site: www.rootsweb.com/~inallen
Parent County: Delaware New Purchase
Comments/research tips: Formed 1829 as Delaware New Purchase, renamed 1827 and abolished 1844.

Record Type	Year Begun	Jurisdiction
Birth	1882	Dept./Health
Marriage	1824	County Clerk
Death	1882	Dept./Health
Divorce	1823	Clerk/Circuit Ct.
Land	1824	County Recorder
Probate	1825	County Clerk
Court	1824	County Clerk
Burial	na	County Board of Health

■ Bartholomew 8 Jan. 1821
234 Washington St., Columbus, IN 47202
Phone: (812)379-1600

Web site: www.rootsweb.com/~inbartho/barth.html
Parent County: Delaware New Purchase, Jackson

Record Type	Year Begun	Jurisdiction
Birth	1882	Dept./Health
Marriage	1821	County Clerk
Death	1882	Dept./Health
Divorce	1821	County Clerk
Land	1822	County Recorder
Probate	1821	County Clerk
Court	1821	County Clerk
Military	na	County Clerk
Nat.	na	County Clerk
Cemetery	na	County Clerk

■ Benton 18 Feb. 1840
706 E. Fifth St. Room 23, Fowler, IN 47944
Phone: (317)884-0930
Web site: www.roots.web.com/~inbenton/
Parent County: Jasper

Record Type	Year Begun	Jurisdiction
Birth	1882	Dept./Health
Marriage	1840	County Clerk
Death	1882	Dept./Health
Divorce	ca.1800	Clerk/Circuit Ct.
Land	1840	County Recorder
Probate	1840	County Clerk
Court	1840	County Clerk
Military	na	County Recorder
Nat.	na	Clerk/Circuit Ct.

■ Blackford 18 Feb. 1839
110 W. Washington St., Hartford City, IN 47348
Phone: (765)348-1130
Web site: www.rootsweb.com/~inblackf/
Parent County: Jay

Record Type	Year Begun	Jurisdiction
Birth	1882	Dept./Health
Marriage	1839	County Clerk
Death	1882	Dept./Health
Divorce	1839	County Clerk
Land	na	County Recorder
Probate	1839	County Clerk
Court	1839	County Clerk
Burial	na	County Coroner

■ Boone 1 Apr. 1830
212 Courthouse Sq., Lebanon, IN 46052
Phone: (765)482-3510
Web site: www.rootsweb.com/~inboone
Parent County: Adams New Purchase, Wabash New Purchase

Record Type	Year Begun	Jurisdiction
Birth	1882	Dept./Health
Marriage	1831	County Clerk
Death	1882	Dept./Health
Divorce	1830	County Clerk
Land	1856	County Recorder
Probate	1846	County Clerk
Court	1846	County Clerk

■ **Brown** 4 Feb. 1836
Main St. and Van Buren St., Nashville, IN 47448
Phone: (812)988-5510
Web site: www.rootsweb.com/~inbrown
Parent County: Monroe, Bartholomew, Jackson
Comments/research tips: Some records lost in 1873 fire.
County Clerk has court ordered Birth records from 1942.

Record Type	Year Begun	Jurisdiction
Birth	1882	Dept./Health
Marriage	1836	County Clerk
Death	1882	Dept./Health
Divorce	1850	County Clerk
Land	1873	County Recorder
Probate	1837	County Clerk
Court	1837	County Clerk

■ **Carroll** 7 Jan. 1828
101 W. Main St., Delphi, IN 46923
Phone: (765)564-4485
Web site: www.rootsweb.com/~incarrol
Parent County: Adam's New Purchase, Wabash New
Purchase, Unorganized Land

Record Type	Year Begun	Jurisdiction
Burial	1882	Dept./Health
Newspapers	1841	Pub. Lib./Delphi
Birth	1882	Dept./Health
Marriage	1828	County Clerk
Death	1882	Dept./Health
Divorce	1828	County Clerk
Land	1829	County Recorder
Probate	1829	County Clerk
Court	1829	County Clerk
Burial	na	County Historical Society

■ **Cass** 13 Apr. 1829
103 Cass County Government Bldg., Logansport, IN 46947
Phone: (574)753-7740
Web site: www.rootsweb.com/~incass/
Parent County: Unorganized Land

Record Type	Year Begun	Jurisdiction
Birth	1882	Dept./Health
Marriage	1829	County Clerk
Death	1882	Dept./Health
Divorce	1894	County Clerk
Land	1830	County Recorder
Probate	1829	County Clerk
Court	1829	County Clerk

■ **Clark** 3 Feb. 1801
501 E. Court Ave., Room 105, Jeffersonville, IN 47130
Phone: (812)285-6235
Web site: www.rootsweb.com/~inclark/
Parent County: Knox

Record Type	Year Begun	Jurisdiction
Birth	1882	Dept./Health
Marriage	1807	County Clerk
Death	1882	Dept./Health
Land	1801	County Recorder
Probate	1801	County Clerk
Court	1801	County Clerk

■ **Clay** 1 Apr. 1825
609 E. National Ave., Brazil, IN 47834
Phone: (812)448-9024
Web site: www.rootsweb.com/~inclay/
Parent County: Owen, Putnam, Vigo, Sullivan
Comments/research tips: County Recorder has some Burial
and some Naturalization records.

Record Type	Year Begun	Jurisdiction
Birth	1882	Dept./Health
Marriage	1851	County Clerk
Death	1882	Dept./Health
Divorce	1851	County Clerk
Land	1825	County Recorder
Probate	1873	County Clerk
Court	na	County Clerk

■ **Clinton** 1 Mar. 1830
265 Courthouse Sq., Frankfort, IN 46041
Phone: (765)659-6335
Web site: www.rootsweb.com/~inclinto/
Parent County: Adams New Purchase, Wabash New Purchase

Record Type	Year Begun	Jurisdiction
Birth	1882	Dept./Health
Marriage	1830	County Clerk
Death	1882	Dept./Health
Divorce	1888	County Clerk
Land	1829	County Recorder
Probate	1830	County Clerk
Court	1830	County Clerk

■ **Crawford** 29 Jan. 1818
Courthouse, P.O. Box 375, English, IN 47118
Phone: (812)338-2565
Web site: www.rootsweb.com/~incrawfo/
Parent County: Orange, Harrison, Perry

Record Type	Year Begun	Jurisdiction
Birth	1882	Dept./Health
Marriage	1818	County Clerk
Death	1882	Dept./Health
Divorce	1860	County Clerk
Land	1818	County Recorder
Probate	1818	County Clerk
Court	1818	County Clerk

■ **Daviess** 15 Feb. 1817
County Courthouse, P.O. Box 739, Washington, IN 47501
Phone: (812)254-8664
Web site: http://indaviess.freeservers.com
Parent County: Knox

Record Type	Year Begun	Jurisdiction
Marriage	1817	County Clerk
Divorce	1817	County Clerk
Probate	1817	County Clerk
Court	1817	County Clerk

■ **Dearborn** 7 Mar. 1803
215 W. High St., Lawrenceburg, IN 47025
Phone: (812)537-8867
Web site: www.rootsweb.com/~indearbo

Parent County: Clark

Record Type	Year Begun	Jurisdiction
Marriage	1806	County Clerk
Death	1882	Dept./Health
Divorce	na	Clerk/Circuit Ct.
Land	1824	County Recorder
Probate	1824	County Clerk
Court	1824	County Clerk
Birth	1882	Dept./Health

■ Decatur 31 Dec. 1821

150 Courthouse Sq., Suite 1, Greensburg, IN 47240
Phone: (812)663-8223
Web site: www.rootsweb.com/~indecatu/indecatu.html
Parent County: Unorganized Land, Delaware New Purchase

Record Type	Year Begun	Jurisdiction
Birth	1882	Dept./Health
Marriage	1822	County Clerk
Death	1882	Dept./Health
Divorce	na	County Clerk
Probate	1822	County Clerk
Court	1822	County Clerk

■ Delaware 1 Apr. 1827

100 W. Main St., Muncie, IN 47305
Phone: (765)747-7726
Web site: www.rootsweb.com/~indelawa
Parent County: Delaware New Purchase
Comments/research tips: Delaware New Purchase formed 1820 from Unorganized Land, renamed Adams New Purchase 1827. Some records may exist in Fayette, Franklin, Jackson, Jennings, Randolph, Ripley, Wayne, and Bartholomew Counties.

Record Type	Year Begun	Jurisdiction
Marriage	1827	County Clerk
Divorce	1827	County Clerk
Probate	1830	County Clerk
Court	na	County Clerk

■ De Kalb 1 May 1837

100 S. Main St., P.O. Box 810, Auburn, IN 46706
Web site: www.rootsweb.com/~indekalb
Parent County: Unorganized Land
Comments/research tips: County Clerk has School records 1903–1932.

Record Type	Year Begun	Jurisdiction
Birth	1882	Dept./Health
Marriage	1837	County Clerk
Death	1882	Dept./Health
Land	1837	County Recorder
Probate	1847	County Clerk
Court	na	County Clerk

■ Dubois 1 Feb. 1818

1 Courthouse Sq., Jasper, IN 47546
Phone: (812)481-7035
Web site: www.rootsweb.com/~indubois/
Parent County: Pike

Record Type	Year Begun	Jurisdiction
Birth	1882	Dept./Health

Record Type	Year Begun	Jurisdiction
Marriage	1839	County Clerk
Death	1882	Dept./Health
Divorce	1839	Records Library
Land	1839	County Recorder
Probate	1840	County Clerk
Court	na	County Clerk
Military	1864	Records Library
Nat.	1839	Records Library

■ Elkhart 1 Apr. 1830

101 N. Main St., Goshen, IN 46526
Phone: (574)535-6433
Web site: www.rootsweb.com/~inelkhar
Parent County: Unorganized Land

Record Type	Year Begun	Jurisdiction
Birth	1882	Dept./Health
Marriage	1830	County Clerk
Death	1882	Dept./Health
Divorce	1830	County Clerk
Land	1831	County Recorder
Probate	1830	County Clerk
Court	na	County Clerk

■ Fayette 28 Dec. 1818

P.O. Box 607, Connersville, IN 47331
Phone: (765)825-1813
Web site: www.rootsquest.com/~indiana/fayette
Parent County: Wayne, Franklin, Unorganized Land

Record Type	Year Begun	Jurisdiction
Marriage	1819	County Clerk
Divorce	1819	Clerk/Circuit Ct.
Probate	1819	County Clerk
Court	na	County Clerk
Nat.	1924	Clerk/Circuit Ct.

■ Floyd 2 Jan. 1819

P.O. Box 878, New Albany, IN 47150
Phone: (812)948-5430
Web site: www.rootsweb.com/~infloyd/floydigw.html
Parent County: Harrison, Clark

Record Type	Year Begun	Jurisdiction
Birth	1882	Dept./Health
Marriage	1819	County Clerk
Death	1882	Dept./Health
Divorce	1863	County Clerk
Probate	1819	County Clerk
Court	na	County Clerk

■ Fountain 1 Apr. 1826

301 Fourth St., P.O. Box 183, Covington, IN 47932
Phone: (765)793-2192
Web site: www.tctc.com/~emoyhbo
Parent County: Montgomery, Wabash New Purchase

Record Type	Year Begun	Jurisdiction
Birth	1882	Dept./Health
Marriage	1826	County Clerk
Death	1882	Dept./Health
Divorce	1830	County Clerk
Land	1827	County Recorder

Indiana

Probate .... 1827 ....County Clerk
Court .... na ....County Clerk

■ Franklin 1811
634 Main St., Brookville, IN 47012
Phone: (765)647-3322
Web site: www.rootsweb.com/~infrankl/
Parent County: Clark, Dearborn

Record Type	Year Begun	Jurisdiction
Birth	1882	Dept./Health
Marriage	1811	County Clerk
Death	1882	Dept./Health
Divorce	1811	County Clerk
Land	1811	County Recorder
Probate	1811	County Clerk
Court	1811	County Clerk
Nat.	1820	Public Library
Cemetery	1817	Public Library

■ Fulton 1835
815 Main St., Rochester, IN 46975
Phone: (219)223-2911
Web site: www.rootsweb.com/~infulton
Parent County: Unorganized Land

Record Type	Year Begun	Jurisdiction
Birth	1882	Dept./Health
Marriage	1836	County Clerk
Death	1882	Dept./Health
Divorce	1836	County Clerk
Land	1826	County Recorder
Probate	1828	County Clerk
Court	1826	County Clerk

■ Gibson 1 Apr. 1813
101 N. Main St., Princeton, IN 47670
Phone: (812)386-8401
Web site: www.rootsquest.com/~jmurphy/gibson/gibson.htm
Parent County: Knox

Record Type	Year Begun	Jurisdiction
Birth	1882	Dept./Health
Marriage	na	County Clerk
Death	1882	Dept./Health
Divorce	1820	County Clerk
Probate	na	County Clerk
Court	na	County Clerk

■ Grant 1 Apr. 1832
100 E. Fourth St., Marion, IN 46953
Phone: (765)668-8121
Web site: http://resources.rootsweb.com/USA/IN/Grant
Parent County: Madison, Adams New Purchase, Unorganized Land

Record Type	Year Begun	Jurisdiction
Birth	1882	Dept./Health
Marriage	1831	County Clerk
Death	1882	Dept./Health
Divorce	1831	County Clerk
Land	1831	County Recorder

Probate .... 1831 ....County Clerk
Court .... na ....County Clerk

■ Greene 5 Feb. 1821
P.O. Box 229, Bloomfield, IN 47424
Phone: (812)384-8532
Web site: www.rootsweb.com/~ingreene/greenegw.htm
Parent County: Sullivan, Unorganized Land
Comments/research tips: County Clerk has Naturalization records 1854–1906. County Recorder has some Cemetery records.

Record Type	Year Begun	Jurisdiction
Birth	1882	Dept./Health
Marriage	1821	County Clerk
Death	1882	Dept./Health
Divorce	1821	County Clerk
Land	1822	County Recorder
Probate	1823	County Clerk
Court	na	County Clerk
Military	na	County Recorder

■ Hamilton 7 Apr. 1823
One Hamilton County Sq., Suite 106, Noblesville, IN 46060
Phone: (317)776-9629
Web site: www.countyhistory.com/hamilton
Parent County: Delaware New Purchase

Record Type	Year Begun	Jurisdiction
Marriage	1833	County Clerk
Death	1882	Dept./Health
Divorce	1833	County Clerk
Land	1825	County Recorder
Probate	1823	County Clerk
Court	na	County Clerk
Birth	1882	Dept./Health

■ Hancock 1 Mar. 1828
9 E. Main St., Greenfield, IN 46140
Phone: (317)462-1109
Web site: www.rootsquest.com/~indiana/hancock
Parent County: Madison

Record Type	Year Begun	Jurisdiction
Birth	1882	Dept./Health
Marriage	1828	County Clerk
Death	1882	Dept./Health
Divorce	1828	County Clerk
Land	1827	County Recorder
Probate	1828	County Clerk
Court	na	County Clerk

■ Harrison 1 Dec. 1808
300 N. Capitol Ave., Corydon, IN 47112
Phone: (812)738-4289
Web site: www.jbntelco.com/~straub/
Parent County: Knox, Clark

Record Type	Year Begun	Jurisdiction
Birth	1882	Dept./Health
Marriage	1809	County Clerk
Death	1882	Dept./Health
Divorce	1815	County Clerk

Indiana

Land	1807	County Recorder
Probate	1809	County Clerk
Court	na	County Clerk

■ Hendricks 28 Dec. 1823
355 S. Washington St., Danville, IN 46122
Phone: (317)745-9224
Web site: www.rootsweb.com/~inhendri
Parent County: Delware New Purchase, Wabash New Purchase

Record Type	Year Begun	Jurisdiction
Birth	1882	Dept./Health
Marriage	1824	County Clerk
Death	1882	Dept./Health
Divorce	1823	County Clerk
Land	1823	County Auditor
Probate	1822	County Clerk
Court	na	County Clerk

■ Henry 1 June 1822
P.O. Box B, New Castle, IN 47362
Phone: (765)529-9310
Web site: www.rootsweb.com/~inhenry
Parent County: Delaware New Purchase

Record Type	Year Begun	Jurisdiction
Birth	1882	Dept./Health
Marriage	1823	County Clerk
Death	1882	Dept./Health
Divorce	1822	County Clerk
Land	1824	County Recorder
Probate	1822	County Clerk
Court	na	County Clerk
Cem. Deeds	1925	County Recorder

■ Howard 1 May 1844
P.O. Box 9004, Kokomo, IN 46904
Phone: (765)456-2204
Web site: www.rootsweb.com/~inhoward
Parent County: Unorganized Land
Comments/research tips: Formerly Richardville County. Name changed to Howard 28 December 1846.

Record Type	Year Begun	Jurisdiction
Birth	1882	Dept./Health
Marriage	1844	County Clerk
Death	1882	Dept./Health
Divorce	1844	County Clerk
Land	1846	County Recorder
Probate	1844	County Clerk
Court	na	County Clerk
Burial	na	Dept./Health

■ Huntington 2 Dec. 1834
P.O. Box 228, Huntington, IN 46750
Phone: (219)358-4818
Web site: www.rootsweb.com/~inhuntin
Parent County: Adams New Purchase, Unorganized Land

Record Type	Year Begun	Jurisdiction
Birth	1882	Dept./Health
Marriage	1837	County Clerk

Death	1882	Dept./Health
Divorce	1850	County Clerk
Land	1834	County Recorder
Probate	1841	County Clerk
Court	na	County Clerk

■ Jackson 1 Jan. 1816
Courthouse, Brownstown, IN 47220
Phone: (812)358-6116
Web site: www.rootsweb.com/~injackso/
Parent County: Washington, Clark, Jefferson

Record Type	Year Begun	Jurisdiction
Birth	1882	Dept./Health
Marriage	1816	County Clerk
Death	1882	Dept./Health
Divorce	1816	County Clerk
Land	1815	County Recorder
Probate	1817	County Clerk
Court	na	County Clerk

■ Jasper 15 Mar. 1838
Courthouse, Recorder's Office, Rensselaer, IN 47978
Phone: (219)866-4681
Web site: www.lanewood.com/
Parent County: Wabash New Purchase, Unorganized Land
Comments/research tips: Courthouse burned in 1862, all records destroyed.

Record Type	Year Begun	Jurisdiction
Birth	1882	Dept./Health
Marriage	1850	County Clerk
Death	1882	Dept./Health
Divorce	1865	County Clerk
Probate	1864	County Clerk
Court	na	County Clerk

■ Jay 1 Mar. 1836
120 W. Main St., Portland, IN 47371
Phone: (219)726-4572
Web site: www.rootsweb.com/~injay
Parent County: Adams New Purchase

Record Type	Year Begun	Jurisdiction
Birth	1882	Dept./Health
Marriage	1837	County Clerk
Death	1882	Dept./Health
Divorce	1882	County Clerk
Land	1836	County Recorder
Probate	na	County Clerk
Court	na	County Clerk

■ Jefferson 23 Nov. 1810
Main & Jefferson St., Madison, IN 47250
Phone: (812)265-8922
Web site: http://myindianahome.net/gen/jeff
Parent County: Dearborn, Clark

Record Type	Year Begun	Jurisdiction
Birth	1882	Dept./Health
Marriage	1811	County Clerk
Death	1882	Dept./Health
Divorce	na	County Clerk

Land .... 1811 .... County Recorder
Probate .... 1811 .... County Clerk
Court .... 1811 .... County Clerk
Burial...................... na .... Dept./Health

■ Jennings 1 Feb. 1817
275 E. Main St., North Vernon, IN 47265
Phone: (812)352-3073
Web site: www.rootsweb.com/~injennin/
Parent County: Jefferson, Jackson

Record Type	Year Begun	Jurisdiction
Birth	1882	Dept./Health
Marriage	1818	County Clerk
Death	1882	Dept./Health
Land	1817	County Recorder
Probate	1818	County Clerk

■ Johnson 5 May 1823
County Courthouse, 1st Floor, Franklin, IN 46131
Phone: (317)736-3708
Web site: www.rootsweb.com/~injohnso/johnson.html
Parent County: Delaware New Purchase

Record Type	Year Begun	Jurisdiction
Birth	1882	Dept./Health
Marriage	1830	County Clerk
Death	1882	Dept./Health
Divorce	1830	County Clerk
Land	1825	County Recorder
Probate	1821	County Clerk
Court	na	County Clerk
Burial	1882	Dept./Health

■ Knox 20 June 1790
101 N. Seventh St., Vincennes, IN 47591
Phone: (812)885-2521
Web site: www.rootsweb.com/~inknox
Parent County: Indiana Territory

Record Type	Year Begun	Jurisdiction
Birth	1882	Dept./Health
Marriage	1806	County Clerk
Death	1882	Dept./Health
Divorce	1806	County Clerk
Land	1783	County Recorder
Probate	1790	County Clerk
Court	1801	County Clerk

■ Kosciusko 1 June 1837
121 N. Lake St., Warsaw, IN 46580
Phone: (574)372-2334
Web site: www.rootsweb.com/~inkosciu/
Parent County: Unorganized Land

Record Type	Year Begun	Jurisdiction
Birth	1882	Dept./Health
Marriage	1830	County Clerk
Death	1882	Dept./Health
Divorce	1836	County Clerk
Land	1834	County Recorder
Probate	1836	County Clerk

■ La Grange 1 Apr. 1832
105 N. Detroit St., La Grange, IN 46761
Phone: (260)499-6377
Web site: www.rootsweb.com/~inlagran
Parent County: Unorganized Land

Record Type	Year Begun	Jurisdiction
Birth	1882	Dept./Health
Marriage	1832	County Clerk
Death	1882	Dept./Health
Divorce	1832	County Clerk
Land	1832	County Recorder
Probate	1832	County Clerk
Court	na	County Clerk

■ La Porte 9 Jan. 1832
813 Lincoln Way, La Porte, IN 46350
Phone: (219)326-6808
Web site: www.alco.org
Parent County: St. Joseph, Unorganized Land

Record Type	Year Begun	Jurisdiction
Birth	1882	Dept./Health
Marriage	1832	County Clerk
Death	1882	Dept./Health
Divorce	1834	County Clerk
Land	1831	County Recorder
Probate	1832	County Clerk
Court	na	County Clerk
Burial	na	Dept./Health

■ Lake 15 Feb. 1837
2293 N. Main St., Crown Point, IN 46307
Phone: (219)755-3465
Web site: www.rootsweb.com/~inlake
Parent County: Porter, Newton

Record Type	Year Begun	Jurisdiction
Birth	1882	Dept./Health
Marriage	1837	County Clerk
Death	1882	Dept./Health
Divorce	1837	Clerk/Circuit Ct.
Land	1837	County Recorder
Probate	1854	County Clerk
Court	na	County Clerk

■ Lawrence 1 Mar. 1818
P.O. Box 99, Bedford, IN 47421
Phone: (812)275-7543
Web site: www.rootsweb.com/~inlawren/lawrengw.htm
Parent County: Orange

Record Type	Year Begun	Jurisdiction
Land	1819	County Recorder
Probate	1819	County Clerk
Court	na	County Clerk
Military	na	County Recorder
Birth	1882	Dept./Health
Marriage	1818	County Clerk
Death	1882	Dept./Health
Divorce	1818	County Clerk

■ Madison 1 July 1823
16 E. Ninth, Anderson, IN 46015
Phone: (765)641-9443

Web site: www.rootsweb.com/~inmadiso/
Parent County: Delaware New Purchase
Comments/research tips: County Board of Health has School records 1904–1932.

Record Type	Year Begun	Jurisdiction
Birth	1882	Dept./Health
Marriage	1853	County Clerk
Death	1882	Dept./Health
Divorce	1880	County Clerk
Land	1822	County Recorder
Probate	1879	County Clerk
Court	na	County Clerk

■ Marion 1 Apr. 1822
200 E. Washington St., Indianapolis, IN 46204
Phone: (317)327-4740
Web site: www.rootsweb.com/~inmarion
Parent County: Delaware New Purchase

Record Type	Year Begun	Jurisdiction
Birth	1882	Dept./Health
Marriage	1822	County Clerk
Death	1882	Dept./Health
Divorce	na	County Clerk
Land	1822	County Recorder
Probate	1822	County Clerk

■ Marshall 7 Feb. 1835
211 W. Madison St., Plymouth, IN 46563
Phone: (574)936-8922
Web site: www.rootsweb.com/~inmarsha
Parent County: St. Joseph, Unorganized Land

Record Type	Year Begun	Jurisdiction
Birth	1882	Dept./Health
Marriage	1836	County Clerk
Death	1882	Dept./Health
Divorce	1836	County Clerk
Land	1834	County Recorder
Probate	1834	County Clerk
Court	na	County Clerk
Burial	1882	Dept./Health

■ Martin 1 Feb. 1820
P.O. Box 120, Shoals, IN 47581
Phone: (812)247-3651
Web site: www.rootsweb.com/~inmartin/
Parent County: Daviess, Dubois

Record Type	Year Begun	Jurisdiction
Birth	1882	Dept./Health
Marriage	1820	County Clerk
Death	1882	Dept./Health
Divorce	1842	County Clerk
Land	1820	County Recorder
Probate	1821	County Clerk
Court	na	County Clerk

■ Miami 1 Mar. 1834
P.O. Box 184, Peru, IN 46970
Phone: (765)472-3901
Web site: www.rootsweb.com/~inmiami/

Parent County: Cass, Unorganized Land

Record Type	Year Begun	Jurisdiction
Birth	1882	Dept./Health
Marriage	1843	County Clerk
Death	1882	Dept./Health
Divorce	1843	County Clerk
Probate	1843	County Clerk
Court	na	County Clerk
Burial	na	Dept./Health

■ Monroe 10 Apr. 1818
301 N. College Ave., Room 201, Bloomington, IN 47404
Phone: (812)349-2600
Web site: www.rootsweb.com/~inmonroe/monroegw.html
Parent County: Orange

Record Type	Year Begun	Jurisdiction
Birth	1882	Dept./Health
Marriage	1818	County Clerk
Death	1882	Dept./Health
Divorce	1818	County Clerk
Land	1817	County Recorder
Probate	1818	County Clerk
Court	1854	County Clerk
Burial	1882	Dept./Health

■ Montgomery 1 Mar. 1823
Vital Records Office, Crawfordsville, IN 47933
Phone: (765)364-6440
Web site: www.rootsweb.com/~inmontgo
Parent County: Wabash New Purchase
Comments/research tips: County Clerk has some Naturalization records.

Record Type	Year Begun	Jurisdiction
Birth	1882	Dept./Health
Marriage	1823	County Clerk
Death	1882	Dept./Health
Divorce	1823	County Clerk
Land	1821	County Recorder
Probate	1822	County Clerk
Court	na	County Clerk
Cemetery	1823	Public Library

■ Morgan 15 Feb. 1822
County Courthouse, 10 E. Washington St., Martinsville, IN 46151
Phone: (765)342-1025
Web site: www.rootsweb.com/~inmorgan
Parent County: Delaware New Purchase, Wabash New Purchase

Record Type	Year Begun	Jurisdiction
Birth	1882	Dept./Health
Marriage	1822	County Clerk
Death	1882	Dept./Health
Land	1822	County Recorder
Probate	1822	County Clerk
Court	na	County Clerk

■ Newton 9 Dec. 1859
P.O. Box 49, Kentland, IN 47951
Phone: (219)474-6081

Indiana

Web site: www.rootsweb.com/~innewton/
Parent County: Jasper
Comments/research tips: Attached to St. Joseph, Warren, and White Counties before re-creation and organization from Jasper County 8 December 1859. Old Newton County was formed in 1835 from Unorganized land and abolished in 1839.

Record Type	Year Begun	Jurisdiction
Birth	1882	Dept./Health
Marriage	1860	County Clerk
Death	1882	Dept./Health
Divorce	1860	County Clerk
Land	1838	County Recorder
Probate	1860	County Clerk
Court	na	County Clerk

■ Noble 1 Mar. 1836
101 N. Orange St., Albion, IN 46701
Phone: (260)636-2736
Web site: www.rootsweb.com/~innoble
Parent County: Unorganized Land

Record Type	Year Begun	Jurisdiction
Birth	1882	Dept./Health
Marriage	1859	County Clerk
Death	1882	Dept./Health
Divorce	1859	County Clerk
Land	1834	County Recorder
Probate	1854	County Clerk
Court	na	County Clerk
Burial	na	City Clerk

■ Ohio 15 Jan. 1844
413 Main St., Rising Sun, IN 47040
Phone: (812)438-2610
Web site: www.rootsweb.com/~inohio
Parent County: Dearborn

Record Type	Year Begun	Jurisdiction
Marriage	1844	County Clerk
Divorce	1844	County Clerk
Probate	1844	County Clerk
Court	na	County Clerk

■ Orange 1 Feb. 1816
Court St., Paoli, IN 47454
Phone: (812)723-2649
Web site: www.usgennet.org/usa/in/county/orange
Parent County: Washington, Knox, Gibson

Record Type	Year Begun	Jurisdiction
Birth	1882	Dept./Health
Marriage	1816	County Clerk
Death	1882	Dept./Health
Divorce	1816	County Clerk
Land	1816	County Recorder
Probate	1816	County Clerk
Court	na	County Clerk
Burial	na	Dept./Health

■ Owen 1 Jan. 1819
P.O. Box 146, Spencer, IN 47460
Phone: (812)829-5015

Web site: www.rootsweb.com/~inowen/owenindx.html
Parent County: Daviess, Sullivan

Record Type	Year Begun	Jurisdiction
Birth	1882	Dept./Health
Marriage	1819	County Clerk
Death	1882	Dept./Health
Divorce	1832	County Clerk
Land	1819	County Recorder
Probate	1819	County Clerk
Court	na	County Clerk

■ Parke 2 Apr. 1821
116 W. High St. #204, Rockville, IN 47872
Phone: (765)569-5132
Web site: www.rootsweb.com/~inparke/
Parent County: Unorganized Land, Vigo, Wabash New Purchase

Record Type	Year Begun	Jurisdiction
Birth	1882	Dept./Health
Marriage	1829	County Clerk
Death	1882	Dept./Health
Divorce	1833	County Clerk
Land	1816	County Recorder
Probate	1833	County Clerk
Court	na	County Clerk

■ Perry 1 Nov. 1814
2219 Payne St., Tell City, IN 47586
Phone: (812)547-3741
Web site: www.usroots.com/~jmurphy/perry/perry.htm
Parent County: Warrick, Gibson

Record Type	Year Begun	Jurisdiction
Birth	1882	Dept./Health
Marriage	1814	County Clerk
Death	1882	Dept./Health
Divorce	1813	County Clerk
Land	1815	County Recorder
Probate	1813	County Clerk
Court	1815	County Clerk

■ Pike 1 Feb. 1817
801 Main St., Petersburg, IN 47567
Phone: (812)354-6025
Web site: www.rootsweb.com/~inpike/Pikegen.htm
Parent County: Gibson, Perry, Knox
Comments/research tips: County Clerk has Probate records from early 1805.

Record Type	Year Begun	Jurisdiction
Birth	1882	Dept./Health
Marriage	1817	County Clerk
Death	1882	Dept./Health
Divorce	1817	County Clerk
Land	1817	County Recorder
Court	1817	County Clerk

■ Porter 1 Feb. 1836
16 Lincolnway, Suite 211, Valparaiso, IN 46383
Phone: (219)465-3450
Web site: www.ingenweb.org/porter

Parent County: Unorganized Land
Comments/research tips: Attached to St. Joseph County prior to organization 6 February 1836.

Record Type	Year Begun	Jurisdiction
Birth	1882	Dept./Health
Marriage	1836	County Clerk
Death	1882	Dept./Health
Divorce	1836	County Clerk
Land	1833	County Recorder
Probate	1839	County Clerk
Court	na	County Clerk

■ **Posey** 1 Nov. 1814
P.O. Box 606, Mt. Vernon, IN 47620
Phone: (812)838-1306
Web site: www.rootsweb.com/~inposey/
Parent County: Warrick
Comments/research tips: County Recorder has some Military Discharge records.

Record Type	Year Begun	Jurisdiction
Birth	1882	Dept./Health
Marriage	1814	County Clerk
Death	1882	Dept./Health
Divorce	1815	County Clerk
Land	1812	County Recorder
Probate	1815	County Clerk
Court	1815	County Clerk

■ **Pulaski** 6 May 1840
112 E. Main St., Winamac, IN 46996
Phone: (574)946-3313
Web site: www.rootsweb.com/~inpulask/
Parent County: Unorganized Land

Record Type	Year Begun	Jurisdiction
Birth	1882	Dept./Health
Marriage	1839	County Clerk
Death	1882	Dept./Health
Divorce	1839	County Clerk
Land	1840	County Recorder
Probate	1839	County Clerk
Court	na	County Clerk

■ **Putnam** 1 Apr. 1822
P.O. Box 546, Greencastle, IN 46135
Phone: (765)653-2648
Web site: www.rootsweb.com/~inputnam/
Parent County: Vigo, Owen, Wabash New Purchase

Record Type	Year Begun	Jurisdiction
Birth	1882	Dept./Health
Marriage	1820	County Clerk
Death	1882	Dept./Health
Divorce	1825	County Clerk
Land	1824	County Recorder
Probate	1825	County Clerk
Court	na	County Clerk

■ **Randolph** 10 Aug. 1818
100 S. Main St., Winchester, IN 47394
Phone: (765)584-0465
Web site: www.rootsweb.co/~inrandol/
Parent County: Wayne
Comments/research tips: Formed from St. Clair County. Became part of Indiana Territory 1800, absorbed by Illinois Territory 1809.

Record Type	Year Begun	Jurisdiction
Birth	1882	Dept./Health
Marriage	1819	County Clerk
Death	1882	Dept./Health
Divorce	na	County Clerk
Land	1820	County Recorder
Probate	1819	County Clerk
Court	na	County Clerk
Newspapers	1876	County Recorder

■ **Richardville** 15 Jan. 1844
Parent County: Unorganized Land
Comments/research tips: Name changed to Howard 28 December 1846.

■ **Ripley** 10 Apr. 1818
P.O. Box 177, Versailles, IN 47042
Phone: (812)689-6115
Web site: www.rootsweb.com/~inripley
Parent County: Dearborn, Jefferson

Record Type	Year Begun	Jurisdiction
Birth	1882	Dept./Health
Marriage	1818	County Clerk
Death	1882	Dept./Health
Divorce	1818	County Clerk
Land	1818	County Recorder
Probate	1818	County Clerk
Court	1818	County Clerk

■ **Rush** 1 Apr. 1822
P.O. Box 429, Rushville, IN 46173
Phone: (765)932-2086
Web site: www.rootsweb.com/~inrush/
Parent County: Delaware New Purchase

Record Type	Year Begun	Jurisdiction
Birth	1882	Dept./Health
Marriage	1822	County Clerk
Death	1882	Dept./Health
Divorce	1822	County Clerk
Land	1822	County Recorder
Probate	1822	County Clerk
Court	1822	County Clerk
Burial	1882	Dept./Health

■ **Scott** 1 Feb. 1820
1 E. McClain Ave., Scottsburg, IN 47170
Phone: (812)752-8442
Web site: www.rootsweb.com/~inscott
Parent County: Clark, Jefferson, Jennings, Jackson, Washington

Record Type	Year Begun	Jurisdiction
Birth	1882	Dept./Health
Marriage	1820	County Clerk
Death	1882	Dept./Health

Divorce	1820	County Clerk
Land	1819	County Recorder
Probate	na	County Clerk
Court	na	County Clerk

■ Shelby 1 Apr. 1822
P.O. Box 198, Shelbyville, IN 46176
Phone: (317)392-6320
Web site: www.rootsweb.com/~inshelby
Parent County: Delaware New Purchase

Record Type	Year Begun	Jurisdiction
Birth	1882	Dept./Health
Marriage	1822	County Clerk
Death	1882	Dept./Health
Divorce	na	County Clerk
Land	1822	County Recorder
Probate	1822	County Clerk
Court	na	County Clerk
Burial	na	Dept./Health

■ Spencer 1 Feb. 1818
Rockport, IN 47635
Phone: (812)649-6027
Web site: www.ingenweb.org/spencer
Parent County: Warrick, Perry
Comments/research tips: County Clerk has Naturalization records 1852–1929.

Record Type	Year Begun	Jurisdiction
Birth	1882	Dept./Health
Marriage	1818	County Clerk
Death	1882	Dept./Health
Divorce	1883	County Clerk
Land	1818	County Recorder
Probate	1818	County Clerk
Court	na	County Clerk
Burial	na	Cemetery Trustees

■ St. Clair
Parent County: Unorganized Land
Comments/research tips: Became part of the Indiana Territory in 1800, absorbed by the Illinois Territory 1809.

■ St. Joseph 29 Jan. 1830
1000 Michigan St., South Bend, IN 46601
Phone: (574)235-9635
Web site: www.rootsweb.com/~instjose/
Parent County: Unorganized Land

Record Type	Year Begun	Jurisdiction
Birth	1882	Dept./Health
Marriage	1830	County Clerk
Death	1882	Dept./Health
Divorce	na	County Clerk
Land	1830	County Recorder
Probate	1830	County Clerk
Court	na	County Clerk
Burial	na	Dept./Health

■ Starke 15 Jan. 1844
P.O. Box 395, Knox, IN 46534
Phone: (574)772-9128

Web site: www.rootsweb.com/~instarke/
Parent County: St. Joseph, Unorganized Land

Record Type	Year Begun	Jurisdiction
Birth	1882	Dept./Health
Marriage	1840	County Clerk
Death	1882	Dept./Health
Divorce	1850	County Clerk
Land	1850	County Recorder
Probate	1850	County Clerk
Court	na	County Clerk

■ Steuben 1 May 1837
55 S. Public Sq., Angola, IN 46703
Phone: (260)668-1000
Web site: www.rootsweb.com/~insteube
Parent County: Unorganized Land
Comments/research tips: County Clerk has Land records from mid-1800s.

Record Type	Year Begun	Jurisdiction
Birth	1882	Dept./Health
Marriage	1832	County Clerk
Death	1882	Dept./Health
Divorce	1837	County Clerk
Probate	1845	County Clerk
Court	na	County Clerk

■ Sullivan 15 Jan. 1817
Courthouse, Room 304, Sullivan, IN 47882
Phone: (812)268-4657
Web site: www.rootsweb.com/~insulliv/
Parent County: Knox

Record Type	Year Begun	Jurisdiction
Marriage	1850	County Clerk
Divorce	1850	County Clerk
Probate	1844	County Clerk
Court	na	County Clerk

■ Switzerland 1 Oct. 1814
212 W. Main St., Vevay, IN 47043
Phone: (812)427-3175
Web site: http://myindianahome.net/gen/switz/index.html
Parent County: Dearborn, Jefferson

Record Type	Year Begun	Jurisdiction
Birth	1882	Dept./Health
Marriage	1814	County Clerk
Death	1882	Dept./Health
Divorce	1814	County Clerk
Land	1814	County Recorder
Probate	1814	County Clerk
Court	na	County Clerk
Burial	na	Dept./Health

■ Tippecanoe 1 Mar. 1826
301 Main St., Lafayette, IN 47901
Web site: www.rootsweb.com/~intippec
Parent County: Unorganized Land, Wabash New Purchase

Record Type	Year Begun	Jurisdiction
Marriage	1826	County Clerk
Death	1882	Dept./Health

'

Divorce .... 1850 .... Clerk/Circuit Ct.
Probate .... 1825 .... County Clerk
Court .... na .... County Clerk
Nat. .... na .... Clerk/Circuit Ct.

■ Tipton   1 May 1844
101 E. Jefferson, Tipton, IN 46072
Phone: (765)675-2795
Web site: www.rootsweb.com/~intipton/
Parent County: Adams New Purchase, Unorganized Land

Record Type	Year Begun	Jurisdiction
Marriage	1844	County Clerk
Divorce	1850	County Clerk
Probate	1844	County Clerk
Court	na	County Clerk

■ Union   1 Feb. 1821
26 W. Union St., Liberty, IN 47353
Phone: (765)458-6121
Web site: www.rootsweb.com/~inunion
Parent County: Wayne, Franklin, Fayette

Record Type	Year Begun	Jurisdiction
Birth	1882	Dept./Health
Marriage	1821	County Clerk
Death	1882	Dept./Health
Divorce	1821	Clerk/Circuit Ct.
Probate	1821	County Clerk
Court	na	County Clerk

■ Vanderburgh   1 Feb. 1818
P.O. Box 3356, Evansville, IN 47732
Phone: (812)435-5160
Web site: www.rootsweb.com/~invander
Parent County: Gibson, Posey, Warrick
Comments/research tips: Willard Library has many older records.

Record Type	Year Begun	Jurisdiction
Birth	1882	Dept./Health
Marriage	1818	County Clerk
Death	1882	Dept./Health
Divorce	1969	County Clerk
Land	1818	County Recorder
Probate	1821	County Clerk
Court	1825	County Clerk
Military	1865	County Recorder

■ Vermillion   2 Jan. 1824
Courthouse Sq., Newport, IN 47966
Phone: (765)492-3500
Web site: www.rootsweb.com/~invermil/
Parent County: Parke, Unorganized Land, Wabash New Purchase

Record Type	Year Begun	Jurisdiction
Birth	1882	Dept./Health
Marriage	1824	County Clerk
Death	1882	Dept./Health
Divorce	1824	County Clerk
Land	1824	County Recorder
Probate	1827	County Clerk
Court	1825	County Clerk

■ Vigo   21 Mar. 1818
P.O. Box 8449, Terre Haute, IN 47807
Phone: (812)462-3211
Web site: www.rootsweb.com/~invigo/vigo.htm
Parent County: Sullivan

Record Type	Year Begun	Jurisdiction
Marriage	1818	County Clerk
Divorce	1825	County Clerk
Probate	1818	County Clerk
Court	na	County Clerk

■ Wabash   1 Mar. 1835
1 W. Hill St., Wabash, IN 46992
Phone: (219)563-0661
Web site: www.rootsweb.com/~inwabash/
Parent County: Adams New Purchase, Unorganized Land
Comments/research tips: Formed from territorial Knox County and Unorganized Land abolished 1835. Some early records may be found in Monroe, Owen, Vigo, and Parke Counties.

Record Type	Year Begun	Jurisdiction
Birth	1882	Dept./Health
Marriage	1835	County Clerk
Death	1882	Dept./Health
Divorce	1835	County Clerk
Probate	1847	County Clerk
Court	na	County Clerk
Burial	na	Co. Rec./Museum

■ Warren   1 Mar. 1827
125 N. Monroe St., Williamsport, IN 47993
Phone: (765)762-3510
Web site: www.rootsweb.com/~inwarren
Parent County: Wabash New Purchase, Unorganized Land

Record Type	Year Begun	Jurisdiction
Birth	1882	Dept./Health
Marriage	1827	County Clerk
Death	1882	Dept./Health
Divorce	1827	County Clerk
Land	1830	County Recorder
Probate	1829	County Clerk
Court	na	County Clerk

■ Warrick   9 Mar. 1813
County Judicial Center, Box 28 One County Sq., Boonville, IN 47601
Phone: (812)897-6165
Web site: www.rootsweb.com/~inwarric
Parent County: Knox

Record Type	Year Begun	Jurisdiction
Birth	1882	Dept./Health
Marriage	1813	County Clerk
Death	1882	Dept./Health
Divorce	1813	County Clerk
Land	1813	County Recorder
Probate	1814	County Clerk
Court	1813	County Clerk
Burial	na	Dept./Health

Indiana

■ **Washington** 21 Dec. 1813
99 Public Sq., Salem, IN 47167
Phone: (812)883-5748
Web site: http://jerry.vigo.lib.in.us/washington
Parent County: Clark, Harrison
Comments/research tips: County Historical Society has many Family records.

Record Type	Year Begun	Jurisdiction
Birth	1882	Dept./Health
Marriage	1815	County Clerk
Death	1882	Dept./Health
Divorce	1814	County Clerk
Land	1814	County Recorder
Probate	1814	County Clerk
Court	1814	County Clerk
Newspapers	1891	County Clerk

■ **Wayne** 27 Nov. 1810
301 E. Main St., Richmond, IN 47374
Phone: (765)973-9220
Web site: www.waynet.org/people/genealogy/default.htm
Parent County: Clark, Dearborn, Knox
Comments/research tips: Wayne (old) formed from Unorganized Land in the Northwest Territory which included parts of modern Illinois, Michigan, Ohio, and Wisconsin.

Record Type	Year Begun	Jurisdiction
Birth	1882	Dept./Health
Marriage	1811	County Clerk
Death	na	Dept./Health
Divorce	1873	County Clerk
Probate	1812	County Clerk
Court	1811	County Clerk
Burial	na	Dept./Health

■ **Wells** 17 Feb. 1837
102 W. Market St., Bluffton, IN 46714
Phone: (219)824-6482

Web site: www.rootsweb.com/~inwells/
Parent County: Adams New Purchase

Record Type	Year Begun	Jurisdiction
Birth	1882	Dept./Health
Marriage	1837	County Clerk
Death	1882	Dept./Health
Divorce	1837	County Clerk
Land	1838	County Recorder
Probate	1838	County Clerk
Court	na	County Clerk

■ **White** 1 Apr. 1834
P.O. Box 350, Monticello, IN 47960
Phone: (219)583-7032
Web site: www.rootsweb.com/~inwhite/
Parent County: Wabash New Purchase

Record Type	Year Begun	Jurisdiction
Birth	1882	Dept./Health
Marriage	1834	County Clerk
Death	1882	Dept./Health
Divorce	1834	County Clerk
Land	1834	County Recorder
Probate	1835	County Clerk
Court	na	County Clerk
Burial	na	Dept./Health

■ **Whitley** 29 Jan. 1839
101 W. Van Buren St., Columbia City, IN 46725
Phone: (260)248-3102
Web site: www.countyhistory.com/whitley
Parent County: Unorganized Land

Record Type	Year Begun	Jurisdiction
Birth	1882	Dept./Health
Marriage	1835	County Clerk
Death	1882	Dept./Health
Divorce	1853	County Clerk
Land	1813	County Recorder
Probate	1839	County Clerk
Court	na	County Clerk

Indiana

Iowa

By James W. Warren

HISTORICAL OVERVIEW

There were others who hailed from Iowa before John Deere, Herbert Hoover, and John Wayne. The early French explorers who traveled through the area in the late 1600s encountered the Fox, Sauk, and Pottawatomie Indians. France ceded the land to Spain in 1762. In 1798, Julien Dubuque was able to negotiate with the Fox Indians and begin a lead mining operation. Though his fellow French-Canadians would abandon that settlement upon Dubuque's death in 1810, a city would later rise there and bear his name.

The land came back to France in 1800, but was acquired in 1803 by the United States as part of the Louisiana Purchase. In 1808, Iowa was part of Illinois Territory. Fort Madison was built by the Army that same year. In 1812, Iowa was made part of Missouri Territory. That lasted until 1821. Iowa was not attached to any territory for the next thirteen years.

In 1831 the Sauk and Fox, who had earlier been driven east off their lands by the French and other Indians, returned to Iowa. The next year the Black Hawk War broke out. When it was over the Fox and Sauk were forced to merge and were relocated to Kansas, leaving the area open for legal settlement. The first settlements were made in Eastern Iowa in 1833. The Indian claims to the land were extinguished in a series of treaties that would not be completed until 1851. During the next fifteen years, settlers poured into the area. The southern part of the state saw arrivals mostly from Kentucky and Tennessee. Those settling in the north were primarily from the New England and Mid-Atlantic States, Ohio, Indiana, and Illinois.

Iowa was made part of Michigan Territory in 1834 and Wisconsin Territory in 1836. In 1838, Iowa Territory was formed and included what would become Minnesota and parts of the Dakotas.

© PhotoDisc/Getty Images

IOWA AT A GLANCE

Motto: Our Liberties We Prize and Our Rights We Will Maintain

Population: 2.92 million

Prevalent Religions: Christianity, particularly Roman Catholic, Methodist, and Lutheran, some Presbyterian, Pentecostal, and Baptist

Major Industries: Hogs, corn, soybeans, oats, cattle, dairy products, food processing, machinery, electric equipment, chemical products, printing and publishing, primary metal

Ethnic Makeup (in percent): Caucasian 93.9%, African American 2.1%, Hispanic 2.2%, Asian 1.3%, Native American 0.3%, Other 1.3%

Famous Iowans: Tom Arnold, Buffalo Bill (William F. Cody), Johnny Carson, Mamie Eisenhower, George H. Gallup, Susan Glaspell, Herbert Hoover, Ann Landers, Glenn Miller, Harriet Nelson, Radar O'Riley, David Rabe, Harry Reasoner, Wallace Stegner, James A. Van Allen, Abigail Van Buren, John Wayne, Andy Williams

Above: An aerial view of Iowa's farmland

Iowa

In 1846 Iowa achieved statehood as the twenty-ninth state, and its boundaries have not changed since—but the capital has. Iowa City was the capital at statehood, but in 1857 Des Moines became the capital city.

During the 1850s more people moved into Iowa from Ohio and Indiana, and many immigrants from Germany, Britain, and Ireland arrived. Iowa's population tripled. The Amana colonists settled in Iowa. The last part of the nineteenth century saw heavy immigration from the Scandinavian countries.

RECORD HIGHLIGHTS

The first available federal census for the state of Iowa is 1850. Sequent federal censuses through 1930 are available, except 1890, which was destroyed by fire. Mortality Schedules exist for 1850, 1860, 1870, and 1880. A large number of territorial and state censuses were taken between 1836 and 1854 which do not give much detail, and generally only a few counties have survived. The same is true of state censuses taken between 1881 and 1893. However, there are a few wonderful exceptions. The

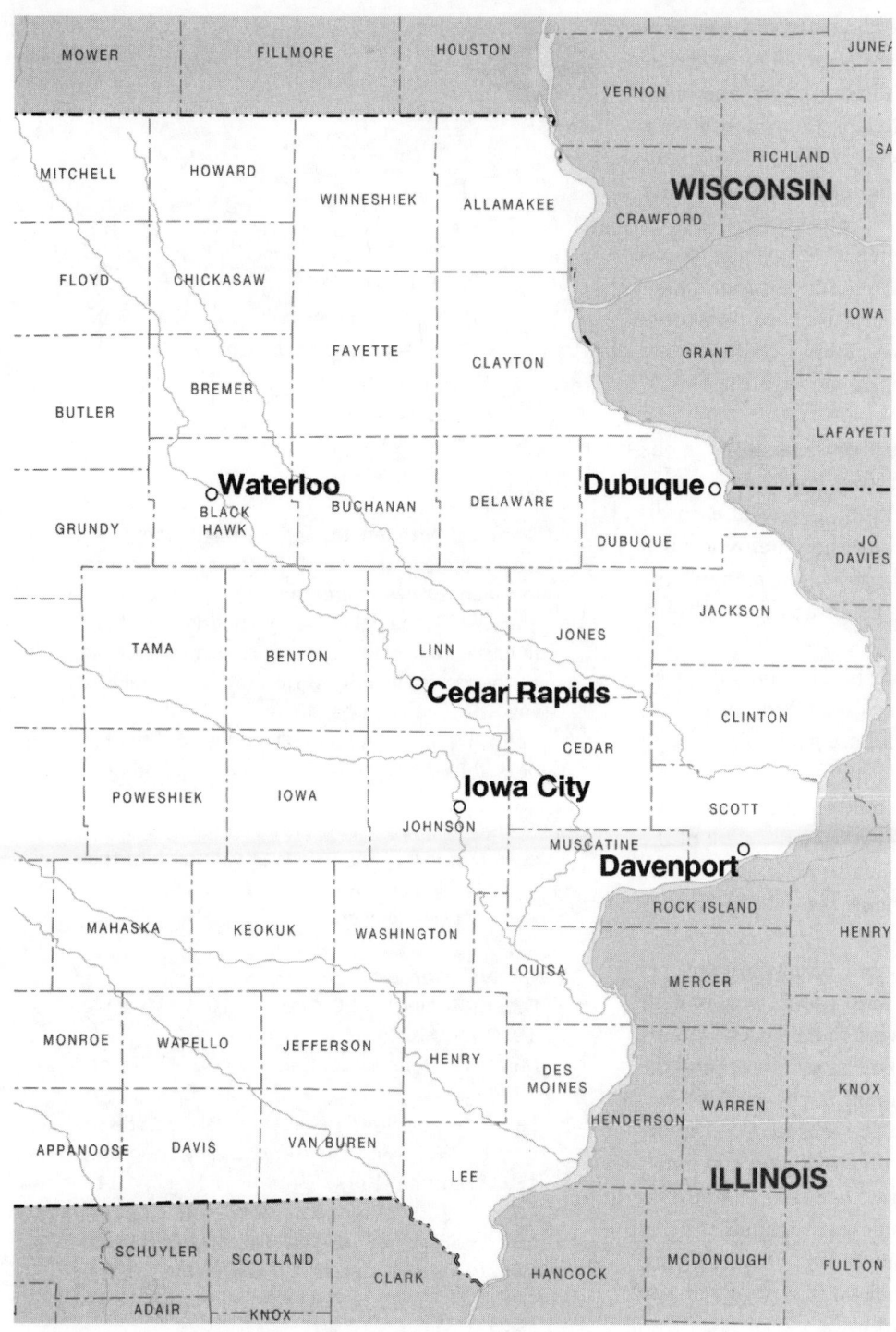

1856, 1885, 1895, 1905, 1915, and 1925 Iowa state censuses list every person in the household, and provide much detail. These censuses are available at the State Historical Society in Des Moines and, except the 1905, at the State Historical Society in Iowa City.

Iowa marriage records begin just after county formation, some as early as 1830. Registration of births and deaths became mandatory in Iowa in 1880, and compliance was basically complete by 1924. Some counties began recording births and deaths in the 1870s. County copies of the birth, death, and marriage records are with the clerk of the district court. The state copies of births and marriages begin in July 1880 and the deaths in January 1881. They are available from the Iowa Department of Public Health, Vital Records Bureau in Des Moines. Online information: <www.idph.state.ia.us/pa/vr.htm>.

The State Historical Society of Iowa has two collections of cemetery transcriptions, as well as two collections of Daughters of the American Revolution (DAR) volumes that contain many cemetery transcriptions. Lo-

Iowa

cal cemetery, church, and funeral home records can provide connections and clues not easily found elsewhere.

Iowa county-level courts are district courts, and operated under that name as early as 1836. Other courts were also active in the past. County courts (1851–1868) handled probate, marriage licenses, liquor permits, and other lesser civil and criminal cases. Circuit courts (1868–1887) had county-level jurisdiction over juvenile, criminal, civil, and probate cases. When the circuit courts were abolished in 1887, the district courts assumed their jurisdiction. The court records for many Iowa counties have been microfilmed and are available through the Family History Library.

Divorce records are civil court cases recorded in the proceedings of each county's district court, where they can be researched. Starting in 1906, a copy of each divorce record was made and sent to the state. Not much has been filmed for the early divorces, but many of the divorces from 1906 to the mid-1950s are at the Family History Library.

Land records are in the custody of the county recorder in each county. In addition, many county's deeds and indexes have been microfilmed and are available through the Family History Library.

Naturalization was usually handled in the local district court, and the records are available from the clerk of the district court. Most Iowa county naturalizations are also microfilmed and available through the Family History Library.

Naturalization could be performed during most time periods in any court of law. While most people went to their local county courthouse, some went to the Federal Courthouse for this process. The Family History Library and the National Archives have a National Archives-produced Soundex Index to Naturalization Petitions for U.S. District and Circuit Courts, Northern District of Illinois and Immigration and Naturalization Service District 9, 1840–1850. On 183 rolls of microfilm, this indexes thousands of naturalizations that were processed in *Federal* District Court, including naturalizations for people in Illinois, Wisconsin, and forty-four counties in Eastern Iowa.

Probate courts were created in each county when Iowa Territory was organized, but were eventually discontinued. Some county courts and some circuit courts took responsibility for probate matters until 1887, but after that all probate matters normally go through district court. Many of the Iowa county probate records are available on microfilm through the Family History Library.

The State Historical Society of Iowa (formerly named the Iowa Historical Society) Library and Archives has several extensive indexes and collections. Their collections of biographical indexes, Bible records, more than

RESEARCH TIPS

for more info

- Copies of birth, death, and marriage records are with the clerk of the district court in the county in which they were created.
- The Iowa Genealogical Society has dozens of published volumes of local record abstracts, transcriptions, and indexes. They are all available at the IGS Library in Des Moines.
- Extensive indexes and collections of Bible records, individuals in local histories, and other resources are available from the State Historical Society of Iowa <www.iowahistory.org>. For research in Iowa, you'll want to visit both of their facilities, in Iowa City and Des Moines.
- www.negenealogy.com

Census Records
- Federal Census: 1850, 1860, 1870, 1880, 1900, 1910 and 1920
- Mortality Schedules: 1850, 1860, 1870, and 1880
- Territorial and State Census: 1836 and 1838 (as part of Wisconsin Territory), 1844 (Keokuk), 1846 (Louisa, Polk, Wapello), 1847, 1849, 1851, 1852, 1853 (part of Warren County), 1854, 1856, 1859, 1863 and 1869 (Henry County), 1881 and 1882 (fragments), 1885, 1888, 1889, 1891–1893 (fragments), 1895–1897 (fragments), 1905, 1915, 1925

10,000 Iowa individuals in local histories, and other resources are just examples of the material available. The Historical Society has two locations: Iowa City and Des Moines. Some material is duplicated in the two facilities, but most is not. The largest collection of Iowa newspapers on microfilm is held by the State Historical Society at the Iowa City facility <www.iowahistory.org>.

In Iowa, the County Board of Supervisors records can

be significant. Usually dating back to the creation of the county, these records document the functioning of the county boards, whose responsibilities include roads, care of the poor, blind, and elderly, levying taxes, and setting salaries for county officials. The Family History Library has some copies of such records. They would normally be cataloged under the locality (state and county) with the keywords "Public Records."

School records for many Iowa school districts are on microfilm at the FHL. They often include school censuses that identify birth dates and places as well as parents. Coroner's records for some counties are also on film at the FHL, some starting as early as 1855.

The Iowa Genealogical Society has worked hand-in-hand with local genealogical societies around the state for many years in a record-publishing program. Local societies prepare a publication, such as tombstone transcriptions, courthouse record abstracts, or an index to local records. The IGS then prints the publication "on demand" using their own equipment and volunteer labor. This has resulted in the production of literally dozens of volumes of local record abstracts, transcriptions, and indexes. To make it even better, they are all at the IGS Library in downtown Des Moines, right across the street from the State Historical Society. And the IGS Library is an excellent research facility in itself, with an extensive collection that goes far beyond Iowa material.

STATE RESOURCES

■ ARCHIVES, LIBRARIES, AND SOCIETIES

Adair County Anquestors Genealogy Society
% Greenfield Public Library, P.O. Box 328, Greenfield, IA 50849-0328
Web site: <www.rootsweb.com/~iaaags/>

Adams County Genealogical Society
P.O. Box 177, Prescott, IA 50859

Allamakee County Historical Society
P.O. Box 95, Waukon, IA 52172
Tel: (319) 568-3210
Web site: <www.rootsweb.com/~iaachs/>

American/Schleswig-Holstein Heritage Society
121 W. Bryant St., Walcott, IA
Web site: <www.ashhs.org/index.html>

Ankeny Genealogical Society
P.O. Box 136, Ankeny, IA 50021-0136

Appanoose County Genealogical Society
1601 S. Sixteenth St., Centerville, IA 52544-3040

Audubon County Genealogical Society
505 Brayton St., Audubon, IA 50025-1301
E-mail: exxtian@metc.net
Web site: <http://metc.net/exiracc/acgs/>

Benton County Genealogical Society
1808 Ninth Ave., Belle Plaine, IA 52208
Web site: <www.rootsweb.com/~iabenton/bcgs.htm>

Benton County Historical Society
P.O. Box 22, Vinton, IA 52349
Tel: (319) 472-4325
Web site: <www.rootsweb.com/~iabenton/bchs/bchs.htm>

Boone County Genealogical Society
P.O. Box 453, Boone, IA 50036
Web site: <www.rootsweb.com/~iabcgs/index.htm>

Boone County Historical Center
602 Story St., Boone, IA 50036
Tel: (515) 432-1907
E-mail: bchs@opencominc.com
Web site: <http://homepages.opencominc.com/bchs/>

Botna Valley Genealogical Society (East Pottawattamie)
P.O. Box 633, Oakland, IA 51560-0633

Bremer County Genealogical Society
426 Washington St., Denver, IA 50622
Web site: <www.rootsweb.com/~iabremer/GenealogicalSociety.html>

Buchanan County Genealogical Society
P.O. Box 4, Independence, IA 50644-0004
Tel: (319) 334-9333
Web site: <www.rootsweb.com/~iabuchan/gensociety.htm>

Buena Vista County Genealogical Society and Library
221 W. Railroad, Storm Lake, IA 50588
Tel: (712) 732-7111
E-mail: famhisbv@ncn.net
Web site: <www.stormlake-ia.com/bvchs/gen1.htm>

Buena Vista County Historical Society
214 W. Fifth St., Storm Lake, IA 50598
Tel: (712) 732-4955

Burlington Public Library
501 N. Fourth St., Burlington, IA 52601
Tel: (319) 753-1647
Web site:

Butler County Genealogy Society
P.O. Box 534, Allison, IA 50602-0534
Tel: (319) 267-2427
Web site: <www.pafways.org/genealogy/societies/butler.htm>

Calhoun County Genealogical Society
426 Fifth St., Rockwell City, IA 50579-1415

Carroll County Genealogical Society
P.O. Box 21, Carroll, IA 51401

Cass County Genealogical Society
% Atlantic Carnegie Public Library, 507 Poplar St., Atlantic, IA 50022-1241
Tel: (712) 243-5466
Web site: <www.rootsweb.com/~iacassgs/cassgen1.html>

Cedar County Genealogical Society
P.O. Box 52, Tipton, IA 52772-0052
Web site: <www.rootsweb.com/~iacedar/ccgs.htm>

Central Community Historical Society
628 Sixth Ave., DeWitt, IA 52742
Tel: (563) 659-3686
Web site: <www.rootsweb.com/~iaclinto/resources/soc/central.htm>

Central Iowa Genealogical Society (Marshall County)
P.O. Box 945, Marshalltown, IA 50158-0945

Chadwick Library, Iowa Wesleyan College
107 W. Broad St., Mt. Pleasant, IA 52641
E-mail: reference@iwc.edu
Web site: <http://chadwick.iwc.edu/>

Charter-Pierce Memorial Internet Genealogical Society and Library
3221 Villa Vista Dr., Des Moines, IA 50316-1338
Tel: (515) 266-5326
Web site:

Cherokee County Historical Society
P.O. Box 247, Cleghorn, IA 51014-0247
Tel: (712) 436-2624

Chickasaw County Genealogical Society
P.O. Box 434, New Hampton, IA 50659
Web site: <www.chickasawcoiageniesoc.org/CK_CCGS.htm>

Clarke County Genealogical Society
% Osceola Public Library
300 S. Fillmore, Osceola, IA 50213

Web site: <www.rootsweb.com/
~iaclarke/ccgs.html>

**Clarke County Historical
Society**
Hwy. 69 S., Osceola, IA 50213
Tel: (515) 342-3550
Web site: <www.rootsweb.com/
~iaclarke/hist.html>

**Clayton County Genealogical
Society**
P.O. Box 846, Elkader, IA
52043-0846
Web site: <www.rootsweb.com/
~iaccgs/>

**Clinton County Genealogical
Chapter**
P.O. Box 2062, Clinton, IA
52732-2062

**Conrad Public Library, Grundy
County Genealogical Society**
P.O. Box 189, 102 Grundy, Con-
rad, IA 50621

**Crawford County Genealogical
Society**
2704 Hwy. 59, Denison, IA
51442-7415
E-mail: ccigs24@yahoo.com

Cresco Public Library
320 N. Elm St., Cresco, IA 52136
Tel: (563) 547-2540

**Dallas County Genealogical
Society**
P.O. Box 264, Dallas Center, IA
50063-0246

**Danish American Heritage
Society**
4105 Stone Brooke Rd., Ames, IA
50010
Web site: <www.dana.edu/
dahs/>

The Danish Immigrant Museum
2212 Washington St., Elk Horn,
IA 51531-0470
Tel: (712) 764-7001
Web site:

**Decorah Genealogy
Association**
202 Winnebago (Lower Level),
Decorah, IA 52101-1812
Tel: (563) 382-8559
E-mail: ddiggers@decorah.lib.ia
.us
Web site:
**Delaware County Genealogical
Society**
304 N. Franklin, Manchester, IA
52057

Web site: <www.rootsweb.com/
~iadelawa/gensociety.htm>

**Des Moines County
Genealogical Society**
P.O. Box 493, Burlington, IA
52601-0493

Donnellson Public Library
500 Park, Donnellson IA 52625
Tel: (319) 835-5545

**Dubuque County-Key City
Genealogical Society**
P.O. Box 13, Dubuque, IA
52004-0013
E-mail: dckcgs_library@hotmail
.com
Web site: <www.rootsweb.com/
~iadckcgs/>

**Dyersville Area Historical
Society**
120 Third St. SW, Dyersville, IA
52040
Tel: (563) 875-2504

**Mamie Doud Eisenhower
Birthplace Foundation, Inc.**
P.O. Box 55, Boone, IA 50036
Tel: (515) 432-1896
Web site:
Elliott Public Library
401 Main St., Elliott, IA 51532
Tel: (712) 767-2355

**Emmet County Genealogical
Society**
% Estherville Public Library, 613
Central Ave., Estherville, IA
51334-2294

Emmetsburg Public Library
707 Superior, Emmetsburg, IA
50536
Tel: (712) 852-4009
E-mail: publib@iowalakes.edu
Web site:
Ericson Public Library
702 Greene St, Boone, IA 50036
Tel: (515) 432-3727

**Evangelical Lutheran Church of
America, Wartburg Theological
Seminary**
P.O. Box 5004, Dubuque, IA
52004-5004
Tel: (563) 589-0200
Web site: <www.wartburgsemina
ry.edu/welcome/about.htm>

Fairfield Public Library
104 W. Adams, Fairfield, IA
52556

Tel: (641) 472-6551
E-mail: fplib@fairfield.lib.ia.us
Web site:
**Fayette County Helpers Club
and Historical Society**
100 N. Walnut, West Union, IA
52175
Tel: (563) 422-5797
Web site: <www.rootsweb.com/
~iafayett/iafirst6.htm>

**Franklin County Genealogical
Society**
4 Federal St., Hampton, IA
50441-1934

**Free Public Library, Family
History Department**
8th and Braden, Chariton, IA
50049

**Fremont County Historical
Society**
P.O. Box 671, Sidney, IA
51652-0337

Gateway Genealogical Society
618 Fourteenth Ave., Camanche,
IA 52730

**German American Heritage
Center**
712 W. Second St., Davenport, IA
52802-1410
Tel: (563) 322-8844
Web site: <www.wiu.edu/users/
mfbdw/gahc_web/>

Gibson Memorial Library
200 W. Howard St., Creston, IA
50801
Tel: (641) 782-2277
Web site:
Glenwood Public Library
109 N. Vine St., Glenwood, IA
51534
Tel: (712) 527-5252
Web site:
**Greater Sioux County
Genealogical Society**
102 S. Main Ave., Sioux Center,
IA 51250
E-mail: query@mtcnet.net
Web site: <www.rootsweb.com/
~iasioux/GSCGS/GSCGS.htm>

**Greene County Genealogical
Society**
P.O. Box 133, Jefferson, IA
50129-0133

**Grout Museum of History &
Science**
503 South St., Waterloo, IA
50701
Tel: (319) 234-6357

**Grundy County Genealogical
Society**
708 West St., Reinbeck, IA
50668-1365

**Guthrie County Genealogical
Society**
P.O. Box 96B, Jamaica, IA
50128-0096
Web site: <www.rootsweb.com/
~iaguthri/html/society.html>

**Hamilton Heritage Hunters
Genealogical Society**
943 First St., Webster City, IA
50595-2001
Web site: <www.rootsweb.com/
~iahamilt/HHH.htm>

Hampton Public Library
4 Federal S., Hampton, IA 50441
Tel: (641) 456-4451

**Hancock County Genealogy
Society**
P.O. Box 81, Klemme, IA
50449-0081
Web site: <www.pafways.org/ge
nealogy/societies/hancock
.htm>

**Harrison County Genealogical
Society**
% Merry Brook School Museum,
212 Lincoln Way, Woodbine, IA
Tel: (712) 642-4191

**Henry County Genealogical
Society**
P.O. Box 81, Mount Pleasant, IA
52641

**Howard-Winneshiek Genealogy
Society**
P.O. Box 362, Cresco, IA 52136

**Humboldt County Genealogical
Society**
30 Sixth St. N., Humboldt, IA
50548-1799

**Ida County Genealogical
Society**
1111 S. Main St., Ida Grove, IA
51445

Iowa City Genealogical Society
P.O. Box 822, Iowa City, IA
52244-0822

Iowa County Historical Society
% Pioneer Heritage Museum,
P.O. Box 288, Marengo, IA
52301
Tel: (319) 642-7018

Iowa Department of Public Health, Bureau of Vital Statistics
Lucas State Office Building, 1st Floor, Des Moines, IA 50319
Tel: (515) 281-4944

Iowa Genealogical Society
628 E. Grand Ave., Des Moines, IA 50309-1924
Tel: (515) 276-0287
E-mail: igs@iowagenealogy.org
Web site: <www.iowagenealogy.org >

Iowa Lakes Genealogical Society
% Spencer Public Library, 21 E. Third St., Spencer, IA 51301
Tel: (712) 580-7290
E-mail: info@spencerlibrary.com
Web site: <spencerlibrary.com/genealogy.htm>

Jackson County Genealogical Chapter
P.O. Box 1065, Maquoketa, IA 52060
Tel: (563) 652-5020
Web site: <www.rootsweb.com/~iajackso/JCGenie.html>

Jasper County Genealogical Society
P.O. Box 163, Newton, IA 50208-2707
Web site: <www.usgennet.org/usa/ia/county/jasper1/jcgs/>

Jefferson County Genealogical Society
2791 240th St., Fairfield, IA 52556
Web site: <www.rootsweb.com/~iajeffer/JCGS.htm>

Johnson County Historical Society
P.O. Box 5081, Coralville, IA 52241-5081
Tel: (319) 351-5738
Web site: <www.jccniowa.org/~JCHSWEB/>

Jones County Genealogical Society
P.O. Box 174, Anamosa, IA 52205
Web site: <www.rootsweb.com/~iajones/research/research.htm>

KeoMah Genealogical Society
P.O. Box 616, Oskaloosa, IA 52577
Tel: (641)673-9373
Web site: <www.geocities.com/Heartland/Acres/2263/>

Keosauqua Public Library
First and Van Buren, Keosauqua, IA 52565
Tel: (319) 293-3766
Web site: <http://showcase.netins.net/web/keolibrary/>

Lee County Genealogical Society
P.O. Box 303, Keokuk, IA 52632-0303
Web site: <www.rootsweb.com/~ialeecgs/>

Le Mars Public Library
46 First St., SW, Le Mars, IA 51031
Tel: (712) 546-5004

Lime Creek/Winnebago County Genealogical Society
135 N. Eleventh St., Forest City, IA 50436-1630
Tel: (641) 585-2584
Web site: <www.pafways.org/genealogy/societies/winnebago.htm>

Linn County Genealogical Society
P.O. Box 175, Cedar Rapids, IA 52406
Tel: (319) 369-0022
Web site: <www.usgennet.org/usa/ia/county/linn/gen_soc.htm>

The Louisa County Genealogical Society
P.O. Box 202, Wapello, IA 52653
Web site: <www.rootsweb.com/~ialcgs/>

Lucas County Genealogical Society
% Chariton Public Library, 803 Braden Ave., Chariton, IA 50049-1742
Tel: 641-774-5514
E-mail: lucasgene@hotmail.com
Web site: <www.rootsweb.com/~ialucas/Lucasinfor.htm>

Madison County Genealogical Society
P.O. Box 26, Winterset, IA 50273-0026

Marion County Genealogical Society
P.O. Box 385, Knoxville, IA 50138
Web site: <www.rootsweb.com/~iamcgs/Index.html>

Marshalltown Public Library
36 N. Center St., Marshalltown, IA 50158

Tel: (641) 754-5738
E-mail: library@marshallnet.com
Web site: <www.marshallnet.net/library.htm>

Mason City Public Library
225 Second St. SE, Mason City, IA 50401
Tel: (641) 421-3668
Web site:

Mid-America Genealogical Society
P.O. Box 316, Davenport, IA 52801

Mills County Genealogical Society
% Glenwood Public Library, 109 N. Vine St., Glenwood, IA 51534
Web site: <www.rootsweb.com/~iamills/Helps/genhelps.htm#society>

Monona County Genealogical Society
P.O. Box 16, Onawa, IA 51040-0016

Monroe County Genealogical Society
% Albia Public Library, 203 Benton Ave. E., Albia, IA 52531-2036
Web site: <www.iamonroe.org/monroeco.htm>

Montgomery County Genealogical Society
320A Coolbaugh, Red Oak, IA 51566-2416

Muscatine County Genealogical Society
323 Main St., Muscatine, IA 52761-2867

The National Archives-Central Plains Region
2312 E. Bannister Rd., Kansas City, MO 64131-3011
Tel: (816) 926-6920
E-mail: kansascity.archives@nara.gov
Web site: <www.archives.gov/facilities/mo/kansas_city.html>

Nishnabotna Genealogical Society
847 Rd. M56, Harlan, IA 51537
Web site: <www.rootsweb.com/~iashelby/scgs.htm>

North American Baptist Conference
1 S. 210 Summit Ave., Oakbrook Terrace, IL 60181
Tel: (630) 495-2000
E-mail: serve@nabconf.org

Web site: <www.nabconference.org/whoweare/assocreps.shtml>

North Central Iowa Genealogy Society
P.O. Box 237, Mason City, IA 50402-0237
Web site: <www.pafways.org/genealogy/societies/northcentraliowa/index.htm>

Northeast Iowa Genealogical Society
P.O. Box 7735, Des Moines, IA 50322-7735
Tel: (515) 276-0287
E-mail: egs@digiserve.com
Web site: <www.rootsweb.com/~iablackh/neigsbooklist.html>

Northwest Iowa Genealogical Society (Plymouth County)
46 First St. SW, LeMars, IA 51031-3696

Oelwein Area Genealogical Society
P.O. Box 389, Oelwein, IA 50662-0389
Web site: <www.rootsweb.com/~iaoags/>

Oelwein Area Historical Society Museum
P.O. Box 445, Oelwein, IA 50662
Tel: (319) 283-4203

Old Fort Genealogical Society
P.O. Box 1, Fort Madison, IA 52627
E-mail: ofgensoc@interl.net
Web site: <http://freepages.genealogy.rootsweb.com/~oldfort/>

Oskaloosa Public Library
301 S. Market St., Oskaloosa, IA 52577
Tel: (641) 673-0441
E-mail: OPL@wmpenn.edu

Ostfriesen Heritage Society
905 East Ave., Grundy Center, IA 50638
Tel: (319) 824-6321
Web site: <http://iagenweb.org/grundy/ostfriesian_heritage_society.htm>

Page County Genealogical Society
RR 2, P.O. Box 236, Shenandoah, IA 51610

Palo Alto County Genealogical Society
% Emmetsburg Public Library, 707 N. Superior St., Emmetsburg, IA 50536
Web site: <www.rootsweb.com/~iapaloal/pageone.htm>

Iowa

Pocahontas County Genealogical Society
14 Second Ave. NW, Pocahontas, IA 50574-1611

Pottawattamie County Genealogical Society
P.O. Box 394, Council Bluffs, IA 51502-0394
E-mail: pcgs@pcgs.omhcoxmail.com
Web site: <www.rootsweb.com/~iapottaw/PCGS.htm>

Poweshiek County Historical & Genealogical Society
P.O. Box 280, Montezuma, IA 50171
Tel: (641) 623-3322
Web site: <http://showcase.netins.net/web/powshk/>

Ringgold County Genealogical Society
202 Adams St., Diagonal, IA 50845-1001

Sac County Genealogical Society
P.O. Box 54, Sac City, IA 50583
Web site: <www.rootsweb.com/~iasac/gensociety/gensoc.htm>

Scott County Genealogical Society
P.O. Box 3132, Davenport, IA 52808-3132
Web site: <www.rootsweb.com/~iascott/scigs.htm>

Sioux City Public Library
529 Pierce St., Sioux City, IA 51101
Tel: (712) 255-2933

Spencer Public Library
21 E. Third St., Spencer, IA 51301
Tel: (712) 580-7290
E-mail: info@spencerlibrary.com
Web site: <http://spencerlibrary.com/libinfo.htm>

State Historical Society of Iowa
600 E. Locust, Des Moines, IA 50319-0290
Tel: (515) 281-6200
Web site: <www.iowahistory.org>

Story County Genealogical Society
P.O. Box 692, Ames, IA 50010-0692
Web site: <www.rootsweb.com/~iastory/chapter.htm>

Tama County Tracers Genealogical Society
200 N. Broadway, Toledo, IA 52342-0084

Taylor County Genealogical Society
P.O. Box 8, Gravity, IA 50848

Union County Genealogical Society
200 W. Howard, Creston, IA 50801

Urbandale Public Library
3520 86th St., Urbandale, IA 50322
Tel: (515) 278-3945
Web site:

Van Buren County Genealogical Society
P.O. Box 158, Keosauqua, IA 52565
Web site: <www.rootsweb.com/~iavanbur/>

Vesterheim Norwegian-American Museum
P.O. Box 379, Decorah, IA 52101
Tel: (563) 382-9681
E-mail: vesterheim@vesterheim.org
Web site:

Wapello County, Iowa Genealogical Society
P.O. Box 163, Ottumwa, IA 52501
Web site: <www.rootsweb.com/~iawapegs/>

Warren County Genealogical Society
Rt. 2, 802 Kennedy St., Indianola, IA 50125

Washington County Genealogical Society Library
P.O. Box 446, Washington, IA 52353
E-mail: washlib@lisco.net
Web site: <www.washlib.net/genealogy.html>

Wayne County Genealogical Society
% LeCompte Memorial Library, 110 S. Franklin St., Corydon, IA 50060-1518
Tel: (515) 872-1621
E-mail: lecompte@grm.net
Web site: <http://freepages.history.rootsweb.com/~rkross/wayne_gen_society.html>

Webster County Iowa Genealogical Society and Library
P.O.Box 1584, Fort Dodge, IA 50501
Web site: <www.rootsweb.com/~iawebste/webgenso.htm>

Woodbury County Genealogical Society
P.O. Box 624, Sioux City, IA 51102-0624
Web site: <www.rootsweb.com/~iawoodbu/WCGS.htm>

Wright County Genealogical Searchers
P.O. Box 225, Clarion, IA 50525-0225
Web site: <www.pafways.org/genealogy/societies/wright.htm>

BIBLIOGRAPHY

■ GENERAL RESOURCES

A Bibliography of Iowa Newspapers, 1836–1976
(Iowa: Iowa State Historical Dept., Division of the State Historical Society, 1979)

Biographical Index to the County Histories of Iowa
by Charles Morford (Baltimore, MD: Gateway Press, ca. 1979)

Biographies and Portraits of the Progressive Men of Iowa: Leaders in Business, Politics and the Professions; Together with an Original and Authentic History of the State
by B.F. Gue and Benjamin Franklin Shambaugh (Des Moines: Conaway & Shaw, 1899)

The First Century of Congregationalism in Iowa, 1840–1940
by P. Adelstein Johnson (Congregational Christian Conference of Iowa, ca. 1945)

The Genealogist's Companion and Sourcebook, 2d ed.
by Emily Anne Croom (Cincinnati: Betterway Books, 2003)

A Genealogist's Guide to Discovering Your African-American Ancestors
by Franklin Carter Smith and Emily Anne Croom (Cincinnati: Betterway Books, 2003)

German Settlers of Iowa: Their Descendants & Their European Ancestors
by Margaret Krug Palen (Bowie, MD: Heritage Books, ca. 2000)

Guide to Depositories of Manuscript Collections in the United States, Iowa
by the Historical Records Survey (Des Moines: Iowa Historical Records Survey, 1940)

Guide to Genealogical Research in the National Archives of the United States
edited by Anne Bruner Eales and Robert M. Kvasnicka (Washington, DC: National Archives and Records Administration, 2000)

Guide to Manuscripts
by Katherine Harris (Iowa City, IA: State Historical Society of Iowa, 1973)

A History of the Danes in Iowa
by Thomas Peter Christensen (New York, NY: Arno Press, Inc., 1979)

History of Iowa from the Earliest Times to the Beginning of the Twentieth Century
by Benjamin F. Gue (New York, NY: Century History Co., ca. 1903)

History of Western Iowa: Its Settlement and Growth; A Comprehensive Compilation of Progressive Events Concerning the Counties, Cities, Towns and Villages . . . with an Authentic History of the State of Iowa
(Tucson, AZ: W.C. Cox, 1974)

Iowa Biographical Dictionary: People of All Times and Places Who Have Been Important to the History and Life of the State
(New York, NY: Somerset, ca. 1996)

Iowa County Records Manual
by Becki Peterson (Iowa City: State Historical Society of Iowa, ca. 1987)

Iowa History and Culture: A Bibliography of Materials Published between 1952 and 1986
by Patricia Dawson (Ames, IA: Iowa State University Press, ca. 1989)

Iowa History Reference Guide
by William J. Petersen (Iowa City, IA: State Historical Society of Iowa, ca. 1952)

Iowa: Research Outline
by the Church of Jesus Christ of Latter-day Saints (Salt Lake City, UT: Corp. of the President of the Church of Jesus Christ of L.D.S., ca. 1988)

A Memorial and Biographical Record of Iowa
by Merrill D. Anthony (Marceline, MO: Walsworth Pub. Co., 1978)

The Mennonites in Iowa: Marking the One Hundredth Anniversary of the Coming of the Mennonites to Iowa
by Melvin Gingerich (Iowa City, IA: State Historical Society of Iowa, 1939)

A Narrative History of the People of Iowa: With Special Treatment of their Chief Enterprises in Education, Religion, Valor, Industry, Business, etc.
by Edgar Rubey Harlan (Tucson, AZ: W.C. Cox, 1974)

National Archives Microfilm Catalogs online:
<www.archives.gov/publications/genealogy_microfilm_catalogs.html>

Personal Name Index to the 1856 City Directories of Iowa
by Elsie L. Sopp (Detroit, MI: Gale Research Company, 1980)

The Story of Iowa: The Progress of an American State
by William John Petersen (New York, NY: Lewis Historical Pub. Co., 1952)

Swedish Settlements in Iowa and Western Illinois
by Norma Goedeke & Shirley Graham (Galesburg, IL: Knox County Genealogical Society, 1992)

The United States Biographical Dictionary and Portrait Gallery of Eminent and Self-made Men
(Chicago, IL: American Biographical Pub. Co., 1878)

Upper Midwest German Biographical Index
by Don Heinrich Tolzmann (Bowie, MD: Heritage Books, ca. 1993)

The William Wade Hinshaw Index to Iowa Quaker Meeting Records
by William Wade Hinshaw (Kokomo, IN: Selby Pub. & Print., ca. 1990)

■ CENSUS RECORDS

The American Census Handbook
by Thomas Jay Kemp (Wilmington, DE: Scholarly Resources Inc., ca. 2001)

The Census Book: A Genealogist's Guide to Federal Census Facts, Schedules and Indexes; with Master Extraction Forms for Federal Census Schedules, 1790–1930
by William Dollarhide (Bountiful, UT: Heritage Quest, ca. 1999)

Finding Answers in U.S. Census Records
by Loretto Dennis Szucs and Matthew Wright (Orem, UT: Ancestry Pub., ca. 2001)

Map Guide to the U.S. Federal Censuses, 1790–1920
by William Thorndale and William Dollarhide (Baltimore, MD: Genealogical Pub. Co., ca. 1987)

State Census Records
by Ann S. Lainhart (Baltimore: Genealogical Pub. Co., ca. 1992)

Your Guide to the Federal Census
by Kathleen W. Hinckley (Cincinnati: Betterway Books, 2002)

■ IMMIGRATION RECORDS

American Naturalization Records, 1790–1990: What They Are and How to Use Them
by John J. Newman (North Salt Lake, UT: HeritageQuest, 1998)

American Passenger Arrival Records
by Michael Tepper (Baltimore: Genealogical Publishing Co., 1993)

Amsterdamse Emigranten: Onbekende Brieven uit de Prairie van Iowa, 1846–1873
by J. Stellingwerff (Amsterdam: Buijten & Schipperheijn, 1975)

German Settlers of Iowa: Their Descendants & Their European Ancestors
by Margaret Krug Palen (Bowie, MD: Heritage Books, ca. 2000)

They Became Americans: Finding Naturalization Records and Ethnic Origins
by Loretto Dennis Szucs (Salt Lake City: Ancestry, Inc., 1998)

They Came in Ships: A Guide to Finding Your Immigrant Ancestor's Arrival Records, 2d ed.
by John P. Colletta (Salt Lake City: Ancestry, Inc., 1993)

■ LAND RECORDS

Iowa, Public Land Disposal
by Roscoe L. Lokken (Iowa City, IA: State Historical Society of Iowa, ca. 1942)

Land & Property Research in the United States
by E. Wade Hone (Salt Lake City, UT: Ancestry, ca. 1997)

Locating Your Roots: Discover Your Ancestors Using Land Records
by Patricia Law Hatcher (Cincinnati: Betterway Books, 2003)

Pioneers and Profits: Land Speculation on the Iowa Frontier
by Robert P. Swierenga (Ames, IA: Iowa State University Press, ca. 1968)

■ MAPS

Abandoned Towns, Villages and Post Offices of Iowa
by David C. Mott (Council Bluffs, IA: J.W. Hoffman & S.L. Purington Pub., 1973)

From Ackley to Zwingle: The Origins of Iowa Place Names
by Harold E. Dilts (Ames, IA: Iowa State University Press, ca. 1993)

Iowa Post Offices, 1833–1986
by Alan H. Patera (Lake Oswego, OR: The Depot, ca. 1986)

Iowa State Gazetteer
by James T. Hair (Chicago, IL: Bailey & Hair, 1865)

Postmarked Iowa: A List of Discontinued and Renamed Post Offices
by Guy Reed Ramsey (Crete, NE: J-B Publishing, ca. 1976)

■ MILITARY RECORDS

Iowa in the Civil War: A Reference Guide
by James J. Robertson Jr. (Iowa City, IA: State Historical Society of Iowa, ca. 1970)

The Iowa Department of the Grand Army of the Republic
by Jacob A. Swisher (Iowa City, IA: State Historical Society of Iowa, ca. 1936)

List of Ex-Soldiers, Sailors and Marines Living in Iowa
by William L. Alexander (Decorah, IA: Decorah Genealogy Association, 1997)

Roster and Record of Iowa Soldiers in the War of the Rebellion: Together with Historical Sketches of Volunteer Organizations, 1861–1866
by the Iowa Adjutant General's Office (Des Moines: E.H. English, 1908–1911)

Uncle, We Are Ready! Registering America's Men, 1917–1918: A Guide to Researching World War I Draft Registration Cards
by John J. Newman (North Salt Lake, UT: HeritageQuest, 2001)

U.S. Military Records: A Guide to Federal & State Sources, Colonial America to the Present
by James C. Neagles (Salt Lake City: Ancestry, Inc., 1994)

World War II: A Family Historian's Guide
by Debra Johnson Knox (Spartanburg, SC: MIE Publishing, 2003)

■ VITAL RECORDS

Guide to Public Records of Iowa Counties
by John P. Dolan Jr. (Des Moines: Connie Wimer, ca. 1986)

Guide to Public Vital Statistics Records in Iowa
by the Historical Records Survey Division of Community Service Programs (Georgia) (Des Moines: Iowa Historical Records Survey, 1941)

Iowa Marriages Before Statehood, 1835–1846
by Shela S. Fretwell (Waterloo, IA: 1985)

Iowa Marriages, Early to 1850: A Research Tool
by Liahona Research (Orem, UT: Liahona Research, Inc., ca. 1990)

Your Guide to Cemetery Research
by Sharon DeBartolo Carmack (Cincinnati: Betterway Books, 2002)

Iowa

■ Adair 15 Jan. 1851
400 Public Sq., P.O. Box L, Greenfield, IA 50849
Phone: (641)743-2445
Web site: http://iagenweb.org/adair/
Parent County: Pottawattamie
Comments/research tips: Attached to Pottawattamie and Cass Counties prior to organization 6 May 1854.

Record Type	Year Begun	Jurisdiction
Birth	1880	Clerk/District Ct.
Marriage	1854	Clerk/District Ct.
Death	1880	Clerk/District Ct.
Divorce	1852	Clerk/District Ct.
Probate	1852	Clerk/District Ct.
Court	1852	Clerk/District Ct.

■ Adams 15 Jan. 1851
500 Ninth St., P.O. Box 484, Corning, IA 50841
Phone: (641)322-4711
Web site: http://iagenweb.org/adams/
Parent County: Pottawattamie
Comments/research tips: Organized 7 March 1853.

Record Type	Year Begun	Jurisdiction
Birth	1880	Clerk/District Ct.
Marriage	1855	Clerk/District Ct.
Death	1880	Clerk/District Ct.
Divorce	1910	Clerk/District Ct.
Land	1853	County Recorder
Probate	1868	Clerk/District Ct.
Court	1857	Clerk/District Ct.

■ Allamakee 20 Feb. 1847
110 Allamakee St., P.O. Box 248, Waukon, IA 52172
Phone: (563)568-6351
Web site: http://iagenweb.org/allamakee/
Parent County: Unorganized Territory
Comments/research tips: Attached to Clayton County prior to organization 6 March 1849.

Record Type	Year Begun	Jurisdiction
Birth	1880	County Recorder
Marriage	1845	County Recorder
Death	1880	County Recorder
Divorce	1852	Clerk of Courts
Land	1851	County Recorder
Probate	1854	Clerk of Courts
Court	1852	Clerk of Courts
Nat.	1849	Clerk of Courts

■ Appanoose 17 Feb. 1843
P.O. Box 400, Centerville, IA 52544
Phone: (641)856-6101
Web site: http://iagenweb.org/appanoose/
Parent County: Unorganized Territory
Comments/research tips: Attached to Davis and Van Buren Counties prior to organization 3 August 1846. Clerk of District Court has Naturalization records 1868–1953.

Record Type	Year Begun	Jurisdiction
Birth	1880	Clerk/District Ct.
Marriage	1846	Clerk/District Ct.
Death	1880	Clerk/District Ct.
Divorce	1847	Clerk/District Ct.
Land	1850	County Recorder
Probate	1847	Clerk/District Ct.
Court	1847	Clerk/District Ct.
Military	1850	County Recorder

■ Audubon 15 Jan. 1851
318 Leroy St. #6, Audubon, IA 50025
Phone: (712)563-4275
Web site: http://iagenweb.org/audubon/
Parent County: Pottawattamie
Comments/research tips: Attached to Cass County prior to organization 9 July 1855.

Record Type	Year Begun	Jurisdiction
Birth	1880	Clerk/District Ct.
Marriage	1856	Clerk/District Ct.
Death	1880	Clerk/District Ct.
Divorce	1867	Clerk/District Ct.
Land	1853	County Recorder
Probate	1855	Clerk/District Ct.
Court	1861	Clerk/District Ct.
Burial	1880	Clerk/District Ct.

■ Bancroft 15 Jan. 1851
Parent County: Unorganized Territory
Comments/research tips: Attached to Boone County. Eliminated 24 January 1855 and absorbed by Kossuth County.

■ Benton 21 Dec. 1837
111 E. Fourth St., P.O. Box 719, Vinton, IA 52349
Phone: (319)472-2766
Web site: www.rootsweb.com/~iabenton/
Parent County: Dubuque
Comments/research tips: Attached to Jackson and Linn Counties prior to organization 1 March 1846.

Record Type	Year Begun	Jurisdiction
Birth	1880	Clerk/District Ct.
Marriage	1851	Clerk/District Ct.
Death	1880	Clerk/District Ct.
Divorce	1900	Clerk/District Ct.
Land	1846	Clerk/District Ct.
Probate	1872	Clerk/District Ct.
Court	1850	Clerk/District Ct.
Burial	1880	Clerk/District Ct.

■ Black Hawk 17 Feb. 1843
316 E. Fifth St., Waterloo, IA 50703
Phone: (319)833-3331
Web site: www.rootsweb.com/~iablackh/
Parent County: Buchanan
Comments/research tips: Attached to Buchanan, Benton, and Delaware Counties prior to organization 17 August 1853.

Record Type	Year Begun	Jurisdiction
Birth	1880	Clerk/District Ct.
Marriage	1853	Clerk/District Ct.
Death	1880	Clerk/District Ct.
Land	1853	Clerk/District Ct.
Probate	1880	Clerk/District Ct.

■ Boone 13 Jan. 1846

201 State St., Boone, IA 50036
Phone: (515)433-0561
Web site: www.rootsweb.com/~iaboone/
Parent County: Unorganized Territory
Comments/research tips: Attached to Polk and Linn Counties prior to organization 1 October 1849.

Record Type	Year Begun	Jurisdiction
Nat.	1867	Clerk/District Ct.
Birth	1880	Clerk/District Ct.
Marriage	1851	Clerk/District Ct.
Death	1880	Clerk/District Ct.
Divorce	1900	Clerk/District Ct.
Land	1849	County Recorder
Probate	1850	Clerk/District Ct.
Court	1851	Clerk/District Ct.
School	1889	Clerk/District Ct.

■ Bremer 15 Jan. 1851

415 E. Bremer Ave., P.O. Box 328, Waverly, IA 50677
Phone: (319)352-5661
Web site: www.rootsweb.com/~iabremer/
Parent County: Unorganized Territory
Comments/research tips: Attached to Buchanan County prior to organization 15 August 1853.

Record Type	Year Begun	Jurisdiction
Birth	1800	County Recorder
Marriage	1853	County Recorder
Death	1800	County Recorder
Divorce	1852	Clerk of Courts
Land	1852	County Recorder
Probate	na	Clerk of Courts
Court	1853	Clerk of Courts

■ Buchanan 21 Dec. 1837

210 Fifth Ave., P.O. Box 259, Independence, IA 50644
Phone: (319)334-2196
Web site: www.rootsweb.com/~iabuchan/
Parent County: Dubuque
Comments/research tips: Attached to Dubuque and Delaware Counties prior to organization 4 October 1847.

Record Type	Year Begun	Jurisdiction
Birth	1880	Clerk/District Ct.
Marriage	1848	Clerk/District Ct.
Death	1880	Clerk/District Ct.
Divorce	1845	Clerk/District Ct.
Probate	1845	Clerk/District Ct.
Court	1845	Clerk/District Ct.

■ Buena Vista 15 Jan. 1851

215 E. Fifth St., P.O. Box 1186, Storm Lake, IA 50588
Phone: (712)749-2546
Web site: www.rootsweb.com/~iabuenav/
Parent County: Unorganized Territory
Comments/research tips: Attached to Woodbury County prior to organization 20 November 1858.

Record Type	Year Begun	Jurisdiction
Birth	1880	Clerk/District Ct.
Marriage	1877	Clerk/District Ct.
Death	1880	Clerk/District Ct.
Divorce	1877	Clerk/District Ct.
Probate	1880	Clerk/District Ct.
Court	1877	Clerk/District Ct.
Land	1869	Clerk/District Ct.

■ Buncombe 15 Jan. 1851

Parent County: Unorganized Territory
Comments/research tips: (See Lyon) Name changed to Lyon 11 September 1862.

■ Butler 15 Jan. 1851

428 Sixth St., P.O. Box 307, Allison, IA 50602
Phone: (319)267-2487
Web site: www.rootsweb.com/~iabutler/
Parent County: Unorganized Territory
Comments/research tips: Attached to Buchanan and Black Hawk Counties prior to organization 2 October 1854.

Record Type	Year Begun	Jurisdiction
Birth	1880	Clerk/District Ct.
Marriage	1854	Clerk/District Ct.
Death	1880	Clerk/District Ct.
Divorce	1861	Clerk/District Ct.
Probate	1864	Clerk/District Ct.
Court	1861	Clerk/District Ct.
Land	1854	Clerk/District Ct.

■ Calhoun 15 Jan. 1851

P.O. Box 273, Rockwell City, IA 50579-1428
Phone: (712)297-8122
Web site: www.rootsweb.com/~iacalhou/
Parent County: Unorganized Territory
Comments/research tips: Formerly Fox County. Name changed to Calhoun 22 January 1853. Attached to Greene and Boone Counties prior to organization 7 November 1855.

Record Type	Year Begun	Jurisdiction
Birth	1880	Clerk/District Ct.
Marriage	1857	Clerk/District Ct.
Death	1880	Clerk/District Ct.
Divorce	1906	Clerk/District Ct.
Probate	1880	Clerk/District Ct.
Court	1872	Clerk/District Ct.
Burial	1900	Clerk/District Ct.

■ Carroll 15 Jan. 1851

Sixth & Main Sts., P.O. Box 867, Carroll, IA 51401
Phone: (712)792-4327
Web site: http://iagenweb.org/carroll/
Parent County: Pottawattamie
Comments/research tips: Attached to Shelby and Guthrie Counties prior to organization 17 August 1855.

Record Type	Year Begun	Jurisdiction
Birth	1880	Clerk/District Ct.
Marriage	1855	Clerk/District Ct.
Death	1880	Clerk/District Ct.
Divorce	1923	Clerk/District Ct.
Probate	1858	Clerk/District Ct.
Tax	1934	Clerk/District Ct.

Iowa

Court .... 1871 .... Clerk/District Ct.
Nat. .... 1873 .... Clerk/District Ct.

■ Cass 15 Jan. 1851
5 W. Seventh St., Atlantic, IA 50022
Phone: (712)243-2105
Web site: www.rootsweb.com/~usgenweb/ia/cass/cass.htm
Parent County: Pottawattamie
Comments/research tips: Organized 7 March 1853.

Record Type	Year Begun	Jurisdiction
Birth	1880	Clerk/District Ct.
Marriage	1853	Clerk/District Ct.
Death	1880	Clerk/District Ct.
Divorce	1906	Clerk/District Ct.
Probate	1870	Clerk/District Ct.
Court	1865	Clerk/District Ct.

■ Cedar 21 Dec. 1837
400 Cedar St., P.O. Box 111, Tipton, IA 52772
Phone: (563)886-2101
Web site: www.rootsweb.com/~iacedar/
Parent County: Dubuque

Record Type	Year Begun	Jurisdiction
Birth	1880	County Recorder
Marriage	1841	County Recorder
Death	1880	County Recorder
Divorce	1850	Clerk/District Ct.
Land	1838	County Recorder
Probate	1839	Clerk/District Ct.
Court	1839	Clerk/District Ct.
Burial	1880	County Recorder

■ Cerro Gordo 15 Jan. 1851
220 N. Washington, Mason City, IA 50401
Phone: (641)424-6431
Web site: http://iagenweb.org/cerrogordo/
Parent County: Unorganized Territory
Comments/research tips: Attached to Floyd County prior to organization 29 December 1855.

Record Type	Year Begun	Jurisdiction
Birth	1880	County Recorder
Marriage	1855	County Recorder
Death	1880	County Recorder
Land	1882	County Recorder
Probate	1857	Clerk of Courts
Court	1880	Clerk of Courts

■ Cherokee 15 Jan. 1851
520 W. Main St., Cherokee, IA 51012
Phone: (712)225-6744
Web site: http://iagenweb.org/cherokee/
Parent County: Unorganized Territory
Comments/research tips: Attached to Woodbury County prior to organization 2 October 1858. Clerk of District Court has some Cemetery records.

Record Type	Year Begun	Jurisdiction
Birth	1880	Clerk/District Ct.
Marriage	1859	Clerk/District Ct.
Death	1880	Clerk/District Ct.

Probate .... 1859 .... Clerk/District Ct.
Court .... 1872 .... Clerk/District Ct.
Land .... 1856 .... Clerk/District Ct.

■ Chickasaw 15 Jan. 1851
8 E. Prospect, P.O. Box 467, New Hampton, IA 50659
Phone: (641)394-2106
Web site: http://iagenweb.org/chickasaw/
Parent County: Unorganized Territory
Comments/research tips: Attached to Fayette County prior to organization 12 September 1853.

Record Type	Year Begun	Jurisdiction
Birth	1880	County Recorder
Marriage	1853	County Recorder
Death	1880	County Recorder
Land	1851	County Recorder
Probate	1854	Clerk of Courts
Court	1865	Clerk of Courts
Nat.	1880	Clerk of Courts

■ Clarke 13 Jan. 1846
100 S. Main, Osceola, IA 50213
Phone: (641)342-6096
Web site: http://iagenweb.org/clarke/
Parent County: Unorganized Territory
Comments/research tips: Attached to Lucas and Kishkekosh Counties prior to organization 21 August 1851.

Record Type	Year Begun	Jurisdiction
Birth	1880	Clerk/District Ct.
Marriage	1852	Clerk/District Ct.
Death	1880	Clerk/District Ct.
Divorce	1905	Clerk/District Ct.
Land	1849	County Recorder
Probate	1865	Clerk/District Ct.
Court	1865	Clerk/District Ct.

■ Clay 15 Jan. 1851
215 W. Fourth St., Spencer, IA 51301-3890
Phone: (712)262-4335
Web site: http://iagenweb.org/clay/
Parent County: Unorganized Territory
Comments/research tips: Attached to Woodbury County prior to organization 15 October 1858.

Record Type	Year Begun	Jurisdiction
Birth	1880	Clerk/District Ct.
Marriage	1864	Clerk/District Ct.
Death	1880	Clerk/District Ct.
Divorce	1906	Clerk/District Ct.
Land	1858	Clerk/District Ct.
Probate	1871	Clerk/District Ct.
Court	1869	Clerk/District Ct.

■ Clayton 21 Dec. 1837
111 High St. NE, Elkader, IA 52043
Phone: (563)245-2204
Web site: http://iagenweb.org/clayton/
Parent County: Dubuque
Comments/research tips: Clerk of District Court has Death records 1880–1921 and from 1941.

Iowa

Record Type	Year Begun	Jurisdiction
Birth	1880	Clerk/District Ct.
Marriage	1850	Clerk/District Ct.
Divorce	1880	Clerk/District Ct.
Land	1839	County Recorder
Probate	1840	Clerk/District Ct.
Court	1840	Clerk/District Ct.
Nat.	1858	Clerk/District Ct.
Death	1880	Clerk/District Ct.

■ Clinton 21 Dec. 1837

612 N. Second St., P.O. Box 2957, Clinton, IA 52732

Phone: (563)243-6210

Web site: http://iagenweb.org/clinton/

Parent County: Dubuque

Comments/research tips: Attached to Scott County prior to organization 5 January 1841. Clerk of District Court has Divorce records from mid-1800s.

Record Type	Year Begun	Jurisdiction
Marriage	1840	Clerk/District Ct.
Land	1840	County Recorder
Probate	1840	Clerk/District Ct.
Court	1851	Clerk/District Ct.
Birth	1880	Clerk/District Ct.
Death	1880	Clerk/District Ct.

■ Cook 7 Dec. 1836

Parent County: Des Moines

Comments/research tips: Attached to Muscatine. Absorbed 18 January 1838 into Muscatine.

■ Crawford 1 Jan. 1851

1202 Broadway, Denison, IA 51442

Phone: (712)263-2242

Web site: http://iagenweb.org/crawford/

Parent County: Pottawattamie, Unorganized Territory

Comments/research tips: Attached to Shelby County prior to organization 3 September 1855. Clerk of Courts has some Naturalization records.

Record Type	Year Begun	Jurisdiction
Birth	1880	County Recorder
Marriage	1853	County Recorder
Death	1880	County Recorder
Divorce	1906	Clerk of Courts
Land	1859	County Recorder
Probate	1869	Clerk of Courts
Court	1866	Clerk of Courts

■ Crocker 12 May 1870

Parent County: Kossuth

Comments/research tips: Absorbed 11 December 1871 into Kossuth.

■ Dallas 13 Jan. 1846

801 Court St., Adel, IA 50003

Phone: (515)993-5816

Web site: www.rootsweb.com/~iadallas/

Parent County: Unorganized Territory

Comments/research tips: Attached to Polk and Mahaska Counties prior to organization 1 March 1847.

Record Type	Year Begun	Jurisdiction
Birth	1880	Clerk/District Ct.
Marriage	1851	Clerk/District Ct.
Death	1880	Clerk/District Ct.
Divorce	1881	Clerk/District Ct.
Land	1859	County Recorder
Probate	1863	Clerk/District Ct.
Court	1866	Clerk/District Ct.

■ Davis 17 Feb. 1843

100 Courthouse Sq., Bloomfield, IA 52537

Phone: (641)664-2011

Web site: http://iagenweb.org/davis/

Parent County: Unorganized Territory

Comments/research tips: Attached to Van Buren County prior to organization 1 March 1844.

Record Type	Year Begun	Jurisdiction
Birth	1880	Clerk/District Ct.
Marriage	1844	Clerk/District Ct.
Death	1880	Clerk/District Ct.
Divorce	1844	Clerk/District Ct.
Probate	1844	Clerk/District Ct.
Court	1844	Clerk/District Ct.

■ Decatur 13 Jan. 1846

207 N. Main St., Leon, IA 50144

Phone: (641)446-4331

Web site: www.rootsweb.com/~iadecatu/

Parent County: Unorganized Territory

Comments/research tips: Attached to Davis County prior to organization 6 May 1850. Courthouse burned in 1874. County Clerk has some Military Discharge records.

Record Type	Year Begun	Jurisdiction
Birth	1880	County Clerk
Marriage	1874	County Clerk
Death	1880	County Clerk
Divorce	1880	County Clerk
Land	1874	County Clerk
Probate	1880	County Clerk
Court	1871	County Clerk

■ Delaware 21 Dec. 1837

301 E. Main St., P.O. Box 527, Manchester, IA 52057

Phone: (563)927-4942

Web site: www.rootsweb.com/~iadelawa/

Parent County: Dubuque

Comments/research tips: Organized 19 November 1841.

Record Type	Year Begun	Jurisdiction
Birth	1880	Clerk/District Ct.
Marriage	1861	Clerk/District Ct.
Death	1880	Clerk/District Ct.
Divorce	1851	Clerk/District Ct.
Probate	1849	Clerk/District Ct.
Court	1851	Clerk/District Ct.

■ Des Moines 1 Oct. 1834

513 Main St., P.O. Box 158, Burlington, IA 52601

Phone: (319)753-8262

Web site: www.rootsweb.com/~iadesmoi/

Iowa

Parent County: Michigan Territory

Record Type	Year Begun	Jurisdiction
Birth	1880	Clerk/District Ct.
Marriage	1835	Clerk/District Ct.
Divorce	1835	Clerk/District Ct.
Probate	1835	Clerk/District Ct.
Court	1835	Clerk/District Ct.
Nat.	1840	Clerk/District Ct.

■ **Dickinson** 15 Jan. 1851
18th & Hill County Courthouse, Spirit Lake, IA 51360
Phone: (712)336-1138
Web site: www.rootsweb.com/~iadickin/
Parent County: Unorganized Territory
Comments/research tips: Attached to Woodbury County prior to organization 3 August 1857.

Record Type	Year Begun	Jurisdiction
Birth	1880	Clerk/District Ct.
Marriage	1871	Clerk/District Ct.
Death	1880	Clerk/District Ct.
Divorce	1880	Clerk/District Ct.
Probate	1880	Clerk/District Ct.
Court	1880	Clerk/District Ct.
Burial	1880	Clerk/District Ct.

■ **Dubuque** 1 Oct. 1834
720 Central Ave., Dubuque, IA 52001
Phone: (563)589-4418
Web site: www.rootsweb.com/~iadubuqu/
Parent County: Michigan Territory

Record Type	Year Begun	Jurisdiction
Birth	1880	Clerk/District Ct.
Marriage	1840	Clerk/District Ct.
Death	1880	Clerk/District Ct.
Divorce	1900	Clerk/District Ct.
Land	1836	County Recorder
Probate	1835	Clerk/District Ct.
Court	1836	Clerk/District Ct.

■ **Emmet** 15 Jan. 1851
609 First Ave. N., Estherville, IA 51334
Phone: (712)362-3325
Web site: http://iagenweb.org/emmet/
Parent County: Unorganized Territory
Comments/research tips: Attached to Boone and Webster Counties prior to organization 7 February 1859.

Record Type	Year Begun	Jurisdiction
Birth	1880	Clerk/District Ct.
Marriage	1876	Clerk/District Ct.
Death	1880	Clerk/District Ct.
Divorce	1915	Clerk/District Ct.
Probate	1885	Clerk/District Ct.

■ **Fayette** 21 Dec. 1837
114 N. Vine St., West Union, IA 52175
Phone: (563)422-3234
Web site: http://iagenweb.org/fayette/
Parent County: Dubuque
Comments/research tips: Attached to Clayton County prior to organization 26 August 1850.

Record Type	Year Begun	Jurisdiction
Birth	1880	County Recorder
Marriage	1861	County Recorder
Death	1880	County Recorder
Divorce	1897	Clerk of Courts
Land	1855	County Recorder
Probate	1869	Clerk of Courts
Court	1852	Clerk of Courts

■ **Floyd** 15 Jan. 1851
101 S. Main St., Charles City, IA 50616
Phone: (641)228-7111
Web site: http://iagenweb.org/floyd/
Parent County: Unorganized Territory
Comments/research tips: Attached to Fayette & Chickasaw Counties prior to organization 4 September 1854.

Record Type	Year Begun	Jurisdiction
Birth	1880	Clerk/District Ct.
Marriage	1854	Clerk/District Ct.
Death	1880	Clerk/District Ct.
Divorce	1860	Clerk/District Ct.
Probate	1854	Clerk/District Ct.
Court	1854	Clerk/District Ct.

■ **Fox** 15 Jan. 1851
Parent County: Unorganized Territory
Comments/research tips: (See Calhoun) Name changed to Calhoun 22 January 1853.

■ **Franklin** 15 Jan. 1851
12 First Ave. NW, Hampton, IA 50441
Phone: (641)456-5626
Web site: www.rootsweb.com/~iafrankl/
Parent County: Unorganized Territory
Comments/research tips: Attached to Chickasaw, Fayette, and Hardin Counties prior to organization 3 March 1856.

Record Type	Year Begun	Jurisdiction
Birth	1880	Clerk/Circuit Ct.
Marriage	1855	Clerk/Circuit Ct.
Death	1880	Clerk/Circuit Ct.
Divorce	1869	Clerk/Circuit Ct.
Probate	1864	Clerk/Circuit Ct.
Court	1869	Clerk/Circuit Ct.

■ **Fremont** 24 Feb. 1847
P.O. Box 549, Sidney, IA 51652
Phone: (712)374-2232
Web site: www.rootsweb.com/~iafremon/
Parent County: Unorganized Territory
Comments/research tips: Attached to Appanoose County prior to organization 10 September 1849. Clerk of District Court has limited Marriage records from 1948.

Record Type	Year Begun	Jurisdiction
Land	1849	County Recorder
Probate	1880	Clerk/District Ct.
Court	1850	Clerk/District Ct.
Birth	1880	Clerk/District Ct.
Death	1880	Clerk/District Ct.

■ **Greene** 15 Jan. 1851
114 N. Chestnut, Jefferson, IA 50129
Phone: (515)386-2516
Web site: www.rootsweb.com/~iagreene
Parent County: Unorganized Territory
Comments/research tips: Attached to Dallas County prior to organization 25 August 1853.

Record Type	Year Begun	Jurisdiction
Birth	1880	Clerk/District Ct.
Marriage	1855	Clerk/District Ct.
Death	1880	Clerk/District Ct.
Land	1854	Clerk/District Ct.
Probate	1854	Clerk/District Ct.
Court	1880	Clerk/District Ct.

■ **Grundy** 15 Jan. 1851
706 G Ave., P.O. Box 345, Grundy Center, IA 50638
Phone: (319)824-5229
Web site: www.rootsweb.com/~iagrundy/
Parent County: Unorganized Territory
Comments/research tips: Attached to Buchanan and Black Hawk Counties prior to organization 25 December 1856.

Record Type	Year Begun	Jurisdiction
Birth	1880	Clerk/District Ct.
Marriage	1856	Clerk/District Ct.
Death	1880	Clerk/District Ct.
Divorce	1881	Clerk/District Ct.
Land	1863	County Recorder
Probate	1870	Clerk/District Ct.
Court	1871	Clerk/District Ct.

■ **Guthrie** 15 Jan. 1851
200 N. Fifth St., Guthrie Center, IA 50115
Phone: (641)747-3415
Web site: http://iagenweb.org/guthrie/
Parent County: Unorganized Territory

Record Type	Year Begun	Jurisdiction
Birth	1880	Clerk/District Ct.
Marriage	1852	Clerk/District Ct.
Death	1880	Clerk/District Ct.
Divorce	1883	Clerk/District Ct.
Probate	1881	Clerk/District Ct.
Court	1916	Clerk/District Ct.

■ **Hamilton** 8 Jan. 1857
P.O. Box 845, Webster City, IA 50595
Phone: (515)832-9600
Web site: www.rootsweb.com/~iahamilt/
Parent County: Webster

Record Type	Year Begun	Jurisdiction
Birth	1880	Clerk/District Ct.
Marriage	1857	Clerk/District Ct.
Death	1880	Clerk/District Ct.
Divorce	1880	Clerk/District Ct.
Probate	1880	Clerk/District Ct.
Court	1880	Clerk/District Ct.

■ **Hancock** 15 Jan. 1851
855 State St., P.O. Box 70, Garner, IA 50438
Phone: (641)923-2532

Web site: http://iagenweb/hancock/
Parent County: Unorganized Territory
Comments/research tips: Attached to Boone and Webster Counties prior to organization 25 November 1858.

Record Type	Year Begun	Jurisdiction
Birth	1880	Clerk/District Ct.
Marriage	1861	Clerk/District Ct.
Death	1880	Clerk/District Ct.
Divorce	1880	Clerk/District Ct.
Probate	1856	Clerk/District Ct.
Court	1856	Clerk/District Ct.
Burial	1880	Clerk/District Ct.

■ **Hardin** 15 Jan. 1851
Pioneer Plaza, P.O. 495, Eldora, IA 50627
Phone: (641)858-2328
Web site: www.rootsweb.com/~iahardin/
Parent County: Unorganized Territory
Comments/research tips: Attached to Marshall County prior to organization 2 March 1853.

Record Type	Year Begun	Jurisdiction
Birth	1880	Clerk/District Ct.
Marriage	1853	Clerk/District Ct.
Death	1880	Clerk/District Ct.
Divorce	1889	Clerk/District Ct.
Land	1853	Clerk/District Ct.
Probate	1853	Clerk/District Ct.
Court	1853	Clerk/District Ct.

■ **Harrison** 15 Jan. 1851
111 N. Second Ave., Logan, IA 51546
Phone: (712)644-2665
Web site: www.rootsweb.com/~iaharris/
Parent County: Pottawattamie
Comments/research tips: Organized 7 March 1853. Clerk of District Court has some Burial records.

Record Type	Year Begun	Jurisdiction
Birth	1880	Clerk/District Ct.
Marriage	1853	Clerk/District Ct.
Death	1880	Clerk/District Ct.
Divorce	1853	Clerk/District Ct.
Probate	1869	Clerk/District Ct.
Court	1850	Clerk/District Ct.

■ **Henry** 7 Dec. 1836
100 E. Washington St., P.O. Box 176, Mt. Pleasant, IA 52641
Phone: (319)385-2632
Web site: www.rootsweb.com/~iahenry/
Parent County: Des Moines

Record Type	Year Begun	Jurisdiction
Birth	1880	Clerk/District Ct.
Marriage	1836	Clerk/District Ct.
Death	1880	Clerk/District Ct.
Land	1836	County Recorder
Probate	1836	Clerk/District Ct.
Adoption	1836	Clerk/District Ct.
Court	1836	Clerk/District Ct.

Iowa

■ **Howard** 15 Jan. 1851
137 N. Elm St., Cresco, IA 52136
Phone: (563)547-2661
Web site: http://iagenweb.org/howard/
Parent County: Unorganized Territory
Comments/research tips: Attached to Floyd County prior to organization 15 September 1855.

Record Type	Year Begun	Jurisdiction
Birth	1880	Clerk/District Ct.
Marriage	1875	Clerk/District Ct.
Death	1880	Clerk/District Ct.
Divorce	1876	Clerk/District Ct.
Land	1855	County Recorder
Probate	1877	Clerk/District Ct.
Court	1876	Clerk/District Ct.

■ **Humboldt** 31 Aug. 1857
P.O. Box 100, Dakota City, IA 50529
Phone: (515)332-1806
Web site: www.rootsweb.com/~iahumbol/
Parent County: Webster, Kossuth

Record Type	Year Begun	Jurisdiction
Birth	1880	Clerk/District Ct.
Marriage	1858	Clerk/District Ct.
Death	1885	Clerk/District Ct.
Divorce	1890	Clerk/District Ct.
Probate	1873	Clerk/District Ct.
Court	1892	Clerk/District Ct.

■ **Humboldt, old** 15 Jan. 1851
Parent County: Unorganized Territory
Comments/research tips: Attached to Boone. Abolished 24 January 1855 and absorbed by Kossuth and Webster Counties.

■ **Ida** 15 Jan. 1851
401 Moorehead St., Ida Grove, IA 51445
Phone: (712)364-2628
Web site: www.rootsweb.com/~iaida/
Parent County: Unorganized Territory
Comments/research tips: Attached to Woodbury County prior to organization 1 January 1859.

Record Type	Year Begun	Jurisdiction
Birth	1880	Clerk/District Ct.
Marriage	1868	Clerk/District Ct.
Death	1880	Clerk/District Ct.
Divorce	1880	Clerk/District Ct.
Probate	1880	Clerk/District Ct.
Court	1880	Clerk/District Ct.

■ **Iowa** 17 Feb. 1843
901 Court Ave., P.O. Box 266, Marengo, IA 52301
Phone: (319)642-3914
Web site: www.rootsweb.com/~iaiowa/
Parent County: Keokuk
Comments/research tips: Attached to Poweshiek and Johnson Counties prior to organization 1 July 1845.

Record Type	Year Begun	Jurisdiction
Birth	1880	County Recorder
Marriage	1847	County Recorder
Death	1880	County Recorder
Cemetery	1867	County Recorder

■ **Jackson** 21 Dec. 1837
201 W. Platt St., Maquoketa, IA 52060
Phone: (563)652-4946
Web site: www.rootsweb.com/~iajackso/
Parent County: Dubuque

Record Type	Year Begun	Jurisdiction
Birth	1880	Clerk/District Ct.
Marriage	1847	Clerk/District Ct.
Death	1890	Clerk/District Ct.
Divorce	1906	Clerk/District Ct.
Probate	1869	Clerk/District Ct.
Court	1858	Clerk/District Ct.

■ **Jasper** 13 Jan. 1846
101 First St. N. Room 104, Newton, IA 50208
Phone: (641)792-3255
Web site: http://iagenweb.org/jasper/
Parent County: Unorganized Territory
Comments/research tips: Attached to Mahaska County prior to organization 1 March 1846.

Record Type	Year Begun	Jurisdiction
Birth	1880	County Recorder
Marriage	1846	County Recorder
Death	1880	County Recorder
Land	1855	County Recorder
Probate	1882	Clerk/District Ct.
Court	1857	Clerk/District Ct.
Military	1855	County Recorder

■ **Jefferson** 21 Jan. 1839
51 W. Briggs, P.O. Box 984, Fairfield, IA 52556
Phone: (641)472-3454
Web site: www.rootsweb.com/~iajeffer/
Parent County: Henry, Unorganized Territory

Record Type	Year Begun	Jurisdiction
Birth	1880	Clerk/District Ct.
Marriage	1839	Clerk/District Ct.
Death	1880	Clerk/District Ct.
Divorce	1880	Clerk/District Ct.
Probate	1850	Clerk/District Ct.
Court	1880	Clerk/District Ct.

■ **Johnson** 21 Dec. 1837
417 S. Clinton St., P.O. Box 2510, Iowa City, IA 52240
Phone: (319)356-6060
Web site: www.rootsweb.com/~iajohnso/
Parent County: Dubuque, Cook, Muscatine
Comments/research tips: Attached to Cedar County prior to organization 4 July 1838.

Record Type	Year Begun	Jurisdiction
Birth	1880	County Recorder
Marriage	1839	County Recorder
Death	1880	County Recorder

■ **Jones** 21 Dec. 1837
Main St., P.O. Box 19, Anamosa, IA 52205
Phone: (319)462-4341

Iowa

Web site: www.rootsweb.com/~iajones/
Parent County: Dubuque
Comments/research tips: Attached to Jackson County prior to organization 1 June 1839.

Record Type	Year Begun	Jurisdiction
Birth	1880	Clerk/District Ct.
Marriage	1833	Clerk/District Ct.
Death	1880	Clerk/District Ct.
Divorce	1895	Clerk/District Ct.
Military	1864	County Recorder

■ **Keokuk** 21 Dec. 1837
101 S. Main St., Sigourney, IA 52591
Phone: (641)622-2210
Web site: www.rootsweb.com/~iakeokuk/
Parent County: Dubuque
Comments/research tips: Attached to Johnson, Washington and Cedar Counties prior to organization 1 March 1844.

Record Type	Year Begun	Jurisdiction
Birth	1880	Clerk/District Ct.
Marriage	1844	Clerk/District Ct.
Death	1880	Clerk/District Ct.
Divorce	1845	Clerk/District Ct.
Probate	1845	Clerk/District Ct.
Court	1845	Clerk/District Ct.

■ **Kishkekosh** 17 Feb. 1843
Parent County: Unorganized Territory
Comments/research tips: (See Monroe) Name changed to Monroe 1 August 1846.

■ **Kossuth** 15 Jan. 1851
114 W. State St., Algona, IA 50511
Phone: (515)295-3240
Web site: http://iagenweb.org/kossuth/
Parent County: Unorganized Territory
Comments/research tips: Attached to Boone and Webster Counties prior to organization 1 March 1856.

Record Type	Year Begun	Jurisdiction
Marriage	1857	Clerk/District Ct.
Death	1880	Clerk/District Ct.
Birth	1880	Clerk/District Ct.
Probate	1877	Clerk/District Ct.
Burial	1880	Clerk/District Ct.

■ **Lee** 7 Dec. 1836
P.O. Box 1443, Fort Madison, IA 52627
Phone: (319)372-3523
Web site: www.rootsweb.com/~ialee/
Parent County: Des Moines

Record Type	Year Begun	Jurisdiction
Birth	1880	Cl./Dis. Ct., Ft. Madison
Death	1880	Cl./Dis. Ct., Ft. Madison
Birth	1880	Cl./Dis. Ct., Keokuk
Probate	1873	Cl./Dis. Ct., Ft. Madison
Probate	1838	Cl./Dis. Ct., Keokuk
Court	1898	Cl./Dis. Ct., Keokuk
Marriage	1837	Cl./Dis. Ct., Ft. Madison
Death	1867	Cl./Dis. Ct., Keokuk
Divorce	1906	Cl./Dis. Ct., Keokuk

■ **Linn** 21 Dec. 1837
Third Ave. Bridge, P.O. Box 1468, Cedar Rapids, IA 52406
Phone: (319)398-3411
Web site: www.rootsweb.com/~ialinn/
Parent County: Dubuque
Comments/research tips: Attached to Jackson County prior to organization 1 June 1839.

Record Type	Year Begun	Jurisdiction
Marriage	1840	Clerk/District Ct.
Divorce	1860	Clerk/District Ct.
Probate	1860	Clerk/District Ct.
Court	1860	Clerk/District Ct.
Birth	1880	Clerk/District Ct.
Death	1880	Clerk/District Ct.

■ **Louisa** 7 Dec. 1836
P.O. Box 268, Wapello, IA 52653
Phone: (319)523-4541
Web site: www.rootsweb.com/~ialouisa/
Parent County: Des Moines

Record Type	Year Begun	Jurisdiction
Birth	1880	Clerk/District Ct.
Marriage	1842	Clerk/District Ct.
Death	1880	Clerk/District Ct.

■ **Lucas** 13 Jan. 1846
916 Braden Ave., Chariton, IA 50049
Phone: (641)774-4421
Web site: http://iagenweb.org/lucas/
Parent County: Unorganized Territory
Comments/research tips: Attached to Monroe County prior to organization 4 July 1849.

Record Type	Year Begun	Jurisdiction
Nat.	1900	Clerk/District Ct.
Divorce	1900	Clerk/District Ct.
Probate	1850	Clerk/District Ct.
Court	1900	Clerk/District Ct.
Birth	1880	Clerk/District Ct.
Marriage	1849	Clerk/District Ct.
Death	1880	Clerk/District Ct.

■ **Lyon** 15 Jan. 1851
206 S. Second Ave., Rock Rapids, IA 51246
Phone: (712)472-2623
Web site: www.rootsweb.com/~ialyon/
Parent County: Unorganized Territory
Comments/research tips: Formerly Buncombe County. Name changed to Lyon 11 September 1862. Attached to Woodbury County prior to organization 1 January 1872.

Record Type	Year Begun	Jurisdiction
Birth	1880	Clerk/District Ct.
Marriage	1872	Clerk/District Ct.
Death	1880	Clerk/District Ct.
Divorce	1880	Clerk/District Ct.
Land	1880	Clerk/District Ct.
Probate	1880	Clerk/District Ct.
Court	1880	Clerk/District Ct.

■ **Madison** 13 Jan. 1846
P.O. Box 152, Winterset, IA 50273
Phone: (515)462-4451

Iowa

Web site: www.rootsweb.com/~iamadiso/
Parent County: Unorganized Territory
Comments/research tips: Attached to Mahaska County prior to organization 19 February 1849.

Record Type	Year Begun	Jurisdiction
Birth	1880	Clerk/District Ct.
Marriage	1855	Clerk/District Ct.
Death	1880	Clerk/District Ct.
Divorce	1861	Clerk/District Ct.
Probate	1852	Clerk/District Ct.
Court	1861	Clerk/District Ct.
Burial	1849	Clerk/District Ct.

■ Mahaska   17 Feb. 1843
106 S. First St., Oskaloosa, IA 52577
Phone: (641)673-7786
Web site: www.rootsweb.com/~iamahask/
Parent County: Unorganized Territory
Comments/research tips: Attached to Washington County prior to organization 1 March 1844.

Record Type	Year Begun	Jurisdiction
Birth	1880	Clerk/District Ct.
Marriage	1844	Clerk/District Ct.
Death	1880	Clerk/District Ct.
Divorce	1844	Clerk/District Ct.
Probate	1844	Clerk/District Ct.
Court	1844	Clerk/District Ct.

■ Marion   4 Aug. 1845
P.O. Box 497, Knoxville, IA 50138
Phone: (641)828-2207
Web site: www.rootsweb.com/~iamarion/
Parent County: Unorganized Territory

Record Type	Year Begun	Jurisdiction
Birth	1880	Clerk/District Ct.
Marriage	1845	Clerk/District Ct.
Death	1880	Clerk/District Ct.
Divorce	1845	Clerk/District Ct.
Probate	1845	Clerk/District Ct.

■ Marshall   13 Jan. 1846
17 E. Main St., Marshalltown, IA 50158
Phone: (641)754-1603
Web site: www.rootsweb.com/~iamarsha/
Parent County: Unorganized Territory
Comments/research tips: Attached to Jasper and Linn Counties prior to organization 1 October 1849.

Record Type	Year Begun	Jurisdiction
Birth	1880	Clerk/District Ct.
Marriage	1850	Clerk/District Ct.
Death	1880	Clerk/District Ct.
Divorce	1850	Clerk/District Ct.
Probate	1850	Clerk/District Ct.
Court	1850	Clerk/District Ct.

■ Mills   15 Jan. 1851
418 Sharp St., Glenwood, IA 51534
Phone: (712)527-4880
Web site: www.rootsweb.com/~iamills/

Parent County: Pottawattamie

Record Type	Year Begun	Jurisdiction
Birth	1880	County Recorder
Marriage	1852	County Recorder
Death	1880	County Recorder

■ Mitchell   15 Jan. 1851
508 Eighth St., Osage, IA 50461
Phone: (641)732-3726
Web site: www.rootsweb.com/~iamitche/
Parent County: Unorganized Territory
Comments/research tips: Attached to Chickasaw and Fayette Counties prior to organization 2 October 1854.

Record Type	Year Begun	Jurisdiction
Birth	1880	County Recorder
Marriage	1885	County Recorder
Death	1880	County Recorder
Divorce	1880	Clerk of Courts
Probate	1880	Clerk of Courts
Court	1880	Clerk of Courts

■ Monona   15 Jan. 1851
610 Iowa Ave., Onawa, IA 51040
Phone: (712)423-2491
Web site: www.rootsweb.com/~iamonona/
Parent County: Pottawattamie
Comments/research tips: Attached to Harrison County prior to organization 3 April 1854.

Record Type	Year Begun	Jurisdiction
Birth	1880	Clerk/District Ct.
Marriage	1856	Clerk/District Ct.
Death	1880	Clerk/District Ct.
Divorce	1856	Clerk/District Ct.
Probate	1858	Clerk/District Ct.
Court	1856	Clerk/District Ct.
Burial	1950	Clerk/District Ct.

■ Monroe   17 Feb. 1843
10 Benton Ave. E., Albia, IA 52531
Phone: (641)932-5212
Web site: www.iamonroe.org/
Parent County: Unorganized Territory
Comments/research tips: Formerly Kishkekosh County. Name changed to Monroe 1 August 1846. Attached to Wapello and Jefferson Counties prior to organization 1 July 1845.

Record Type	Year Begun	Jurisdiction
Birth	1880	Clerk/District Ct.
Marriage	1845	Clerk/District Ct.
Death	1880	Clerk/District Ct.
Divorce	1845	Clerk/District Ct.
Probate	1845	Clerk/District Ct.
Court	1845	Clerk/District Ct.

■ Montgomery   15 Jan. 1851
105 Coolbaugh St., P.O. Box 469, Red Oak, IA 51566
Phone: (712)623-4986
Web site: www.rootsweb.com/~iamontgo/
Parent County: Pottawattamie

Comments/research tips: Attached to Adams County prior to organization 5 August 1853.

Record Type	Year Begun	Jurisdiction
Birth	1880	Clerk/District Ct.
Marriage	1855	Clerk/District Ct.
Death	1880	Clerk/District Ct.
Divorce	1873	Clerk/District Ct.
Probate	1860	Clerk/District Ct.
Court	1873	Clerk/District Ct.

■ Muscatine 7 Dec. 1836
400 E. Third St., P.O. Box 8010, Muscatine, IA 52761
Phone: (563)263-6511
Web site: www.rootsweb.com/~iamuscat/
Parent County: Des Moines

Record Type	Year Begun	Jurisdiction
Marriage	1837	County Recorder
Death	1880	County Recorder
Birth	1880	County Recorder

■ O'Brien 15 Jan. 1851
155 S. Hayes Ave., Primghar, IA 51245
Phone: (712)757-3255
Web site: www.rootsweb.com/~iaobrien/
Parent County: Unorganized Territory
Comments/research tips: Attached to Woodbury County prior to organization 7 April 1860.

Record Type	Year Begun	Jurisdiction
Birth	1880	County Recorder
Marriage	1860	County Recorder
Death	1880	County Recorder
Divorce	1880	Clerk of Courts
Land	1857	County Recorder
Probate	1880	Clerk of Courts
Court	1880	Clerk of Courts
Military	1917	County Recorder

■ Osceola 15 Jan. 1851
300 Seventh Ave., P.O. Box 156, Sibley, IA 51249
Phone: (712)754-3595
Web site: www.rootsweb.com/~iaosceol/
Parent County: Unorganized Territory
Comments/research tips: Attached to Woodbury County prior to organization 1 January 1872.

Record Type	Year Begun	Jurisdiction
Birth	1880	Clerk/District Ct.
Marriage	1872	Clerk/District Ct.
Death	1880	Clerk/District Ct.
Divorce	1880	Clerk/District Ct.
Probate	1880	Clerk/District Ct.
Court	1880	Clerk/District Ct.

■ Page 24 Feb. 1847
112 E. Main St., P.O. Box 263, Clarinda, IA 51632
Phone: (712)542-3214
Web site: www.rootsweb.com/~iapage/
Parent County: Unorganized Territory
Comments/research tips: Attached to Appanoose County prior to organization 22 March 1852.

Record Type	Year Begun	Jurisdiction
Birth	1880	County Recorder
Marriage	1852	County Recorder
Death	1880	County Recorder

■ Palo Alto 15 Jan. 1851
1010 Broadway, P.O. Box 387, Emmetsburg, IA 50536
Phone: (712)852-3603
Web site: http://iagenweb.org/paloalto/
Parent County: Unorganized Territory
Comments/research tips: Attached to Boone and Webster Counties prior to organization 29 December 1858.

Record Type	Year Begun	Jurisdiction
Marriage	1860	Clerk/District Ct.
Birth	1880	Clerk/District Ct.
Death	1880	Clerk/District Ct.

■ Plymouth 15 Jan. 1851
215 Fourth Ave. SE, Le Mars, IA 51031
Phone: (712)546-4215
Web site: www.rootsweb.com/~iaplymou/
Parent County: Unorganized Territory
Comments/research tips: Attached to Woodbury County prior to organization 27 October 1858.

Record Type	Year Begun	Jurisdiction
Birth	1880	Clerk/District Ct.
Marriage	1871	Clerk/District Ct.
Death	1880	Clerk/District Ct.
Court	1869	Clerk/District Ct.

■ Pocahontas 15 Jan. 1851
99 Court Sq., Pocahontas, IA 50574
Phone: (712)335-4208
Web site: www.rootsweb.com/~iapocaho/
Parent County: Unorganized Territory
Comments/research tips: Attached to Boone and Webster Counties prior to organization 11 May 1859.

Record Type	Year Begun	Jurisdiction
Birth	1880	County Recorder
Marriage	1859	County Recorder
Death	1880	County Recorder
Divorce	1860	Clerk/District Ct.
Probate	1872	Clerk/District Ct.

■ Polk 13 Jan. 1846
500 Mulberry St. #201, Des Moines, IA 50309
Phone: (515)286-3772
Web site: http://iagenweb.org/polk/
Parent County: Unorganized Territory

Record Type	Year Begun	Jurisdiction
Marriage	1846	County Recorder
Death	1880	County Recorder
Divorce	1870	Clerk of Courts
Probate	1855	Clerk of Courts
Court	1850	Clerk of Courts
Nat.	1870	Clerk of Courts
Birth	1880	County Recorder

■ Pottawattamie 21 Sep. 1848
227 S. Sixth St., Council Bluffs, IA 51501
Phone: (712)328-5604

Web site: www.rootsweb.com/~iapottaw/
Parent County: Unorganized Territory

Record Type	Year Begun	Jurisdiction
Death	1882	Clerk of Courts
Marriage	1848	Clerk of Courts
Divorce	1907	Clerk of Courts
Probate	1898	Clerk of Courts
Birth	1880	Clerk of Courts

■ Poweshiek 17 Feb. 1843
302 E. Main St., P.O. Box 218, Montezuma, IA 50171
Phone: (641)623-5644
Web site: www.rootsweb.com/~iapowesh/
Parent County: Keokuk
Comments/research tips: Attached to Mahaska and Iowa Counties prior to organization 3 April 1848.

Record Type	Year Begun	Jurisdiction
Birth	1880	Clerk/District Ct.
Marriage	1848	Clerk/District Ct.
Death	1880	Clerk/District Ct.
Divorce	1880	Clerk/District Ct.
Probate	1860	Clerk/District Ct.

■ Ringgold 24 Feb. 1847
109 W. Madison, P.O. 523, Mount Ayr, IA 50854
Phone: (641)464-3234
Web site: www.rootsweb.com/~iaringgo/
Parent County: Unorganized Territory
Comments/research tips: Attached to Taylor and Appanoose Counties prior to organization 31 January 1855.

Record Type	Year Begun	Jurisdiction
Birth	1880	Clerk/District Ct.
Marriage	1855	Clerk/District Ct.
Death	1880	Clerk/District Ct.
Divorce	1880	Clerk/District Ct.
Probate	1880	Clerk/District Ct.
Court	1880	Clerk/District Ct.

■ Risley 15 Jan. 1851
Parent County: Unorganized Territory
Comments/research tips: (See Webster County) Lost to Webster County 22 January 1853.

■ Sac 15 Jan. 1851
P.O. Box 368, Sac City, IA 50583
Phone: (712)662-7791
Web site: www.rootsweb.com/~iasac/
Parent County: Unorganized Territory
Comments/research tips: Attached to Woodbury and Greene Counties prior to organization 7 April 1856. Courthouse burned 1888, some charred records recovered.

Record Type	Year Begun	Jurisdiction
Birth	1880	Clerk/District Ct.
Marriage	1863	Clerk/District Ct.
Divorce	1880	Clerk/District Ct.
Probate	1888	Clerk/District Ct.
Court	1888	Clerk/District Ct.
Burial	1888	Clerk/District Ct.

■ Scott 21 Dec. 1837
416 W. Fourth St., Davenport, IA 52801
Phone: (563)326-8786
Web site: http://iagenweb.org/scott/
Parent County: Dubuque, Cook, Muscatine

Record Type	Year Begun	Jurisdiction
Birth	1880	Clerk/District Ct.
Marriage	1840	Clerk/District Ct.
Death	1880	Clerk/District Ct.
Divorce	1838	Clerk/District Ct.
Probate	1838	Clerk/District Ct.
Court	1851	Clerk/District Ct.

■ Shelby 15 Jan. 1851
612 Court St., P.O. Box 431, Harlan, IA 51537
Phone: (712)755-5543
Web site: www.rootsweb.com/~iashelby/
Parent County: Pottawattamie
Comments/research tips: Organized 7 March 1853.

Record Type	Year Begun	Jurisdiction
Birth	1880	County Recorder
Marriage	1853	County Recorder
Death	1880	County Recorder
Divorce	1869	Clerk of Courts
Land	1854	County Recorder
Probate	1869	Clerk of Courts
Court	1869	Clerk of Courts
Military	1919	County Recorder

■ Sioux 15 Jan. 1851
P.O. Box 47, Orange City, IA 51041
Phone: (712)737-2286
Web site: www.rootsweb.com/~iasioux/
Parent County: Unorganized Territory
Comments/research tips: Attached to Woodbury County prior to organization 1 January 1860.

Record Type	Year Begun	Jurisdiction
Birth	1880	Clerk/District Ct.
Marriage	1871	Clerk/District Ct.
Death	1880	Clerk/District Ct.
Divorce	1908	Clerk/District Ct.
Probate	1870	Clerk/District Ct.

■ Slaughter 18 Jan. 1838
Parent County: Henry, Louisa, Muscatine
Comments/research tips: (See Washington) Name changed to Washington 25 January 1839.

■ Story 13 Jan. 1846
1315 S. B Ave., P.O. Box 408, Nevada, IA 50201
Phone: (515)382-7410
Web site: www.rootsweb.com/~iastory/
Parent County: Unorganized Territory
Comments/research tips: Attached to Boone, Polk, and Linn Counties prior to organization 1 June 1853.

Record Type	Year Begun	Jurisdiction
Birth	1880	Clerk/District Ct.
Marriage	1854	Clerk/District Ct.
Death	1880	Clerk/District Ct.

Iowa

Divorce .... 1854 .... Clerk/District Ct.
Probate .... 1854 .... Clerk/District Ct.
Court .... 1854 .... Clerk/District Ct.

■ Tama   17 Feb. 1843
100 W. High St., P.O. Box 306, Toledo, IA 52342
Phone: (641)484-3721
Web site: www.rootsweb.com/~iatama/
Parent County: Benton
Comments/research tips: Attached to Benton & Linn Counties prior to organization 4 July 1853.

Record Type	Year Begun	Jurisdiction
Birth	1880	Clerk/District Ct.
Marriage	1853	Clerk/District Ct.
Death	1880	Clerk/District Ct.
Divorce	1908	Clerk/District Ct.
Probate	1895	Clerk/District Ct.
Court	1859	Clerk/District Ct.

■ Taylor   24 Feb. 1847
403 Jefferson St., P.O. Box 306, Bedford, IA 50833
Phone: (712)523-2095
Web site: www.rootsweb.com/~iataylor/
Parent County: Unorganized Territory
Comments/research tips: Attached to Appanoose County prior to organization 26 February 1851.

Record Type	Year Begun	Jurisdiction
Birth	1880	Clerk/District Ct.
Marriage	1851	Clerk/District Ct.
Death	1880	Clerk/District Ct.
Divorce	1858	Clerk/District Ct.
Probate	1863	Clerk/District Ct.
Court	1858	Clerk/District Ct.

■ Union   15 Jan. 1851
300 N. Pine St., Creston, IA 50801
Phone: (641)782-7315
Web site: http://iagenweb.org/union/
Parent County: Pottawattamie
Comments/research tips: Organized 1 March 1853.

Record Type	Year Begun	Jurisdiction
Birth	1880	Clerk/District Ct.
Marriage	1864	Clerk/District Ct.
Death	1880	Clerk/District Ct.
Probate	1880	Clerk/District Ct.
Court	1880	Clerk/District Ct.

■ Van Buren   7 Dec. 1836
4th St. & Dodge Sts., Keosauqua, IA 52565
Phone: (319)293-3108
Web site: www.rootsweb.com/~iavanbur/
Parent County: Des Moines

Record Type	Year Begun	Jurisdiction
Birth	1880	Clerk/District Ct.
Marriage	1837	Clerk/District Ct.
Death	1880	Clerk/District Ct.
Divorce	1837	Clerk/District Ct.
Probate	1837	Clerk/District Ct.
Court	1837	Clerk/District Ct.

■ Wahkaw   15 Jan. 1851
Parent County: Unorganized Territory
Comments/research tips: (See Woodbury) Name changed to Woodbury 22 January 1853.

■ Wapello   17 Feb. 1843
101 W. Fourth St., Ottumwa, IA 52501
Phone: (641)683-0060
Web site: www.rootsweb.com/~iawapell/
Parent County: Unorganized Territory
Comments/research tips: Attached to Jefferson County prior to organization 1 March 1844.

Record Type	Year Begun	Jurisdiction
Birth	1880	County Recorder
Marriage	1844	County Recorder
Death	1880	County Recorder
Divorce	1844	Clerk of Courts
Probate	1844	Clerk of Courts
Court	1844	Clerk of Courts

■ Warren   13 Jan. 1846
P.O. Box 379, Indianola, IA 50125
Phone: (515)961-1033
Web site: www.rootsweb.com/~iawarren/
Parent County: Unorganized Territory
Comments/research tips: Attached to Mahaska County prior to organization 10 February 1849.

Record Type	Year Begun	Jurisdiction
Birth	1880	Clerk/District Ct.
Marriage	1850	Clerk/District Ct.
Death	1880	Clerk/District Ct.
Divorce	1880	Clerk/District Ct.
Probate	1880	Clerk/District Ct.
Court	1880	Clerk/District Ct.

■ Washington   18 Jan. 1838
P.O. Box 391, Washington, IA 52353
Phone: (319)653-7741
Web site: www.rootsweb.com/~iawashin/
Parent County: Henry, Louisa, Muscatine
Comments/research tips: Formerly Slaughter County. Name changed to Washington 25 January 1839. Clerk of District Court has some Naturalization records.

Record Type	Year Begun	Jurisdiction
Birth	1880	Clerk/District Ct.
Marriage	1844	Clerk/District Ct.
Death	1880	Clerk/District Ct.
Divorce	1836	Clerk/District Ct.
Probate	1836	Clerk/District Ct.
Court	1836	Clerk/District Ct.

■ Wayne   13 Jan. 1846
P.O. Box 424, Corydon, IA 50060
Phone: (641)872-2264
Web site: www.rootsweb.com/~iawayne/
Parent County: Unorganized Territory
Comments/research tips: Attached to Davis County prior to organization 27 January 1851.

Record Type	Year Begun	Jurisdiction
Birth	1880	Clerk/District Ct.

Marriage .... 1851 .... Clerk/District Ct.
Death .... 1880 .... Clerk/District Ct.
Divorce .... 1906 .... Clerk/District Ct.
Probate .... 1891 .... Clerk/District Ct.
Court .... 1875 .... Clerk/District Ct.

■ Webster   15 Jan. 1851
701 Central Ave., Fort Dodge, IA 50501
Phone: (515)576-7115
Web site: www.rootsweb.com/~iawebste/
Parent County: Yell, Risley
Comments/research tips: Formerly Risley and Yell Counties. Name changed to Webster 22 January 1853.

Record Type	Year Begun	Jurisdiction
Birth	1880	Clerk/District Ct.
Marriage	1853	Clerk/District Ct.
Death	1880	Clerk/District Ct.
Divorce	1870	Clerk/District Ct.
Probate	1855	Clerk/District Ct.
Court	1860	Clerk/District Ct.

■ Winnebago   15 Jan. 1851
126 W. Clark, P.O. Box 468, Forest City, IA 50436
Phone: (641)585-4520
Web site: www.rootsweb.com/~iawinneb/
Parent County: Unorganized Territory
Comments/research tips: Attached to Boone and Webster Counties prior to organization 1 November 1857.

Record Type	Year Begun	Jurisdiction
Birth	1880	Clerk of Courts
Marriage	1868	Clerk of Courts
Death	1880	Clerk of Courts
Divorce	1865	Clerk of Courts
Probate	1865	Clerk of Courts
Court	1865	Clerk of Courts

■ Winneshiek   20 Feb. 1847
201 W. Main St., Decorah, IA 52101
Phone: (563)382-2469
Web site: www.rootsweb.com/~iawinnes/
Parent County: Unorganized Territory
Comments/research tips: Attached to Clayton County prior to organization 1 March 1851.

Record Type	Year Begun	Jurisdiction
Birth	1880	Clerk/District Ct.
Marriage	1851	Clerk/District Ct.
Death	1880	Clerk/District Ct.
Divorce	1855	Clerk/District Ct.
Probate	1853	Clerk/District Ct.
Court	1855	Clerk/District Ct.

■ Woodbury   15 Jan. 1851
620 Douglas #101, Sioux City, IA 51101
Phone: (712)279-6611
Web site: www.rootsweb.com/~iawoodbu/
Parent County: Unorganized Territory
Comments/research tips: Formerly Wahkaw County. Name changed to Woodbury 22 January 1853. Organized 7 March 1853.

Record Type	Year Begun	Jurisdiction
Birth	1880	Clerk/District Ct.
Death	1880	Clerk/District Ct.
Divorce	1857	Clerk/District Ct.
Probate	1868	Clerk/District Ct.
Court	1850	Clerk/District Ct.
Adoption	1920	Clerk/District Ct.
Marriage	1854	Clerk/District Ct.

■ Worth   15 Jan. 1851
1000 Central Ave., Northwood, IA 50459
Phone: (641)324-2840
Web site: www.rootsweb.com/~iaworth/
Parent County: Unorganized Territory
Comments/research tips: Attached to Fayette, Chickasaw, Floyd, and Mitchell Counties prior to organization 13 October 1857.

Record Type	Year Begun	Jurisdiction
Marriage	1853	Clerk/District Ct.
Death	1880	Clerk/District Ct.
Land	1879	Clerk/District Ct.
Probate	1857	Clerk/District Ct.
Court	1857	Clerk/District Ct.
Birth	1880	Clerk/District Ct.

■ Wright   15 Jan. 1851
115 N. Main St., P.O. Box 306, Clarion, IA 50525
Phone: (515)532-3113
Web site: www.rootsweb.com/~iawright/
Parent County: Unorganized Territory
Comments/research tips: Attached to Boone and Webster Counties prior to organization 1 October 1855.

Record Type	Year Begun	Jurisdiction
Birth	1880	Clerk/District Ct.
Marriage	1855	Clerk/District Ct.
Death	1880	Clerk/District Ct.
Divorce	1873	Clerk/District Ct.
Nat.	1857	Clerk/District Ct.
Probate	1880	Clerk/District Ct.
Court	1873	Clerk/District Ct.

■ Yell   15 Jan. 1851
Parent County: Unorganized Territory
Comments/research tips: (See Webster) Lost to Webster County 22 January 1853.

Kansas

By Maureen Taylor

HISTORICAL OVERVIEW

Kansas, once part of land claimed in 1682 by Frenchman Rene-Robert Cavelier, Sieur de La Salle, became part of the United States through the Louisiana Purchase in 1803. At the time of exploration by Lewis and Clark, Omaha, Pawnee, Apache, and Wichita tribes populated the area. The state derives its name from the Kansa tribe.

In the 1820s steamboats traveled the rivers in the area and thousands of people passed through, on their way west following the Sante Fe and Oregon Trails. No permanent settlements existed except for military outposts at Fort Riley, Fort Scott, and Fort Leavenworth, religious missions, or trading posts until the Kansas-Nebraska Act (1854) opened the region to settlers and conveyed territorial status to the region. The Act also allowed citizens to vote on the slavery issue. Antislavery Free Soilers opened a territorial government at Lawrence in 1855, while pro-slavers founded another government in the southeastern part of the state. Resulting conflicts between the two groups gave the region the nickname Bleeding Kansas.

Kansas became a state in 1861, with Topeka as the capital and a constitution that prohibited slavery. The next year immigration to the area increased with the Homestead Act, which provided citizens or those intending to become citizens a chance to claim 160 acres for farming if they stayed five years. Individuals from Germany, Russia, Sweden, England, and Mexico settled in the area, while African Americans known as Exodusters moved to the state because of its antislavery status. Mennonites from Russia arrived in the 1870s. Throughout the nineteenth century, towns grew along the Chisholm Trail from Texas to Abilene, Kansas. Residents of the region relied on farming or cattle, and remained despite devastating weather and plagues of insects. In the 1930s, the Kansas Dust Bowl epitomized the misery of the rest of the country during

© Kansas Travel and Tourism/Teresa Garrison

KANSAS AT A GLANCE

Motto: To the Stars Through Difficulties

Population: 2.68 million

Prevalent Religions: Roman Catholic, Baptist, Methodist, some Lutheran and Presbyterian, and fewer Pentecostal and Episcopalian, also Church of Jesus Christ of Latter-day Saints and Jewish

Major Industries: Cattle, transportation equipment, food processing, printing and publishing, chemical products, machinery, apparel, wheat, sorghum, soybeans, hogs, corn, petroleum, mining

Ethnic Makeup (in percent): Caucasian 86.1%, African American 5.7%, Hispanic 7.0%, Asian 1.7%, Native American 0.9%, Other 3.4%

Famous Kansans: Walter P. Chrysler, Bob Dole, Amelia Earhart, Dwight D. Eisenhower, Dennis Hopper, William Inge, Buster Keaton, Harold Lloyd, Edgar Lee Masters, Gordon Parks, Charles "Buddy" Rogers, Damon Runyon, Barry Sanders, W. Eugene Smith, William E. Stafford, William Allen White

Above: Sunset on the Missouri river, northeastern Kansas

Kansas

the Depression. In the late nineteenth and early twentieth century the state's economy relied on oil production, mineral mines, and aircraft manufacturing, as well as farming.

Kansas citizens made many important military contributions. Members of the Kansas Twenty-Third Colored Regiment fought during the Spanish-American War. During the twentieth century, Camp Funston and Camp Leavenworth became important military training facilities. Kansas manufacturing plants supplied aircraft to the war effort during World War II.

RECORD HIGHLIGHTS

Researchers with ancestors who lived during the territorial period will have to rely on federal and state census records for 1855, 1859, and 1860. In addition to the federal census, there are state census records from 1865 to 1925. "The 1865 and 1875 censuses are indexed, and volunteers are working on an index to the 1895 census to fill in for the destroyed 1890 federal census," according to William Grace, of the Kansas State Historical Society. Partial indexes exist for other years.

The statewide recording of births and deaths didn't occur until July 1911. According to the Web site of the Kansas State Historical Society <www.kshs.org>, "before 1911, births and deaths *may* have been recorded in the town/city or county clerk's office where the event occurred." Original documents may be located where recorded or in the collections of a historical or genealogical

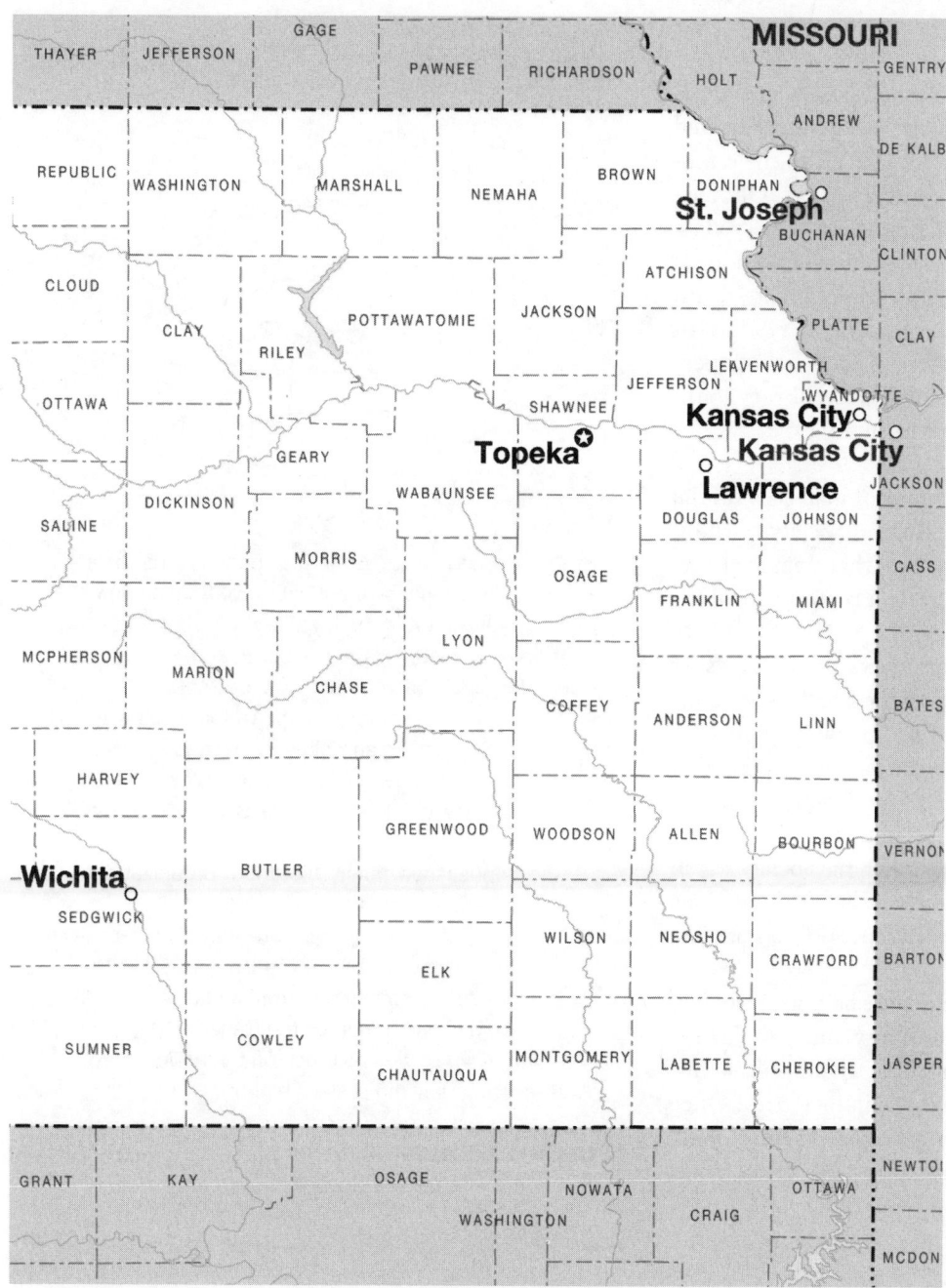

society. The historical society's Web site suggests consulting church records, newspapers, cemetery records, or school records.

Marriage licenses exist for the territorial period, but weren't legally recorded until 1867. The Kansas State Historical Society has an index to marriage licenses before 1867. Statewide registration began in 1913. Birth and death records after 1911 and marriages after 1913 may be obtained from the Office of Vital Statistics.

The Kansas State Archive has records from the office of the Kansas Adjutant General's Office, including muster rolls. The Kansas State Historical Society is collecting war letters of men and women in the military from the Civil War to the present.

As a public domain state, the federal government handled land sales and grants. Initial land transfers appear in the Kansas Tract Books and are available on microfilm from the National Archives and Records Administration (NARA). Other land records occur on the county level and can be found at the Register of Deeds. Originals of all federal land records for Kansas are at the National Archives.

William Grace from the Kansas State Historical Society suggests that, before delving into the records, "researchers first verify birth and death dates as well as places of residence for their Kansas ancestors." Genealogical research is more successful if the researcher has an idea of when and where the family lived. These details

Kansas

will help determine the type of records in existence and where they are located.

In 1875, a group of newspaper publishers in Kansas sought a repository to preserve all the newspapers printed in the state. Their desire for an archive led to the establishment of the Kansas State Historical Society. Obituaries located in newspapers, including those that predate civil registration of vital records, can contain additional family details. Researchers need an approximate death date, since the papers are unindexed. The KSHS has an almost comprehensive collection of Kansas newspapers available at their facility or through interlibrary loan. Their Web site <www.kshs.org> includes a database of available newspapers.

The KSHS also collects microfilm of materials on the county level filmed by the Genealogical Society of Utah, as well as those on the national level that document the state's history. Their goal is to create a central repository for research on Kansas.

An online catalog exists that covers the holdings of seven libraries in Topeka, including the KSHS <lib.wuacc.edu>. Search it for both printed and manuscript materials cataloged since 1995. You'll find maps, directories, published and unpublished family histories, organizational papers, and county histories in their library. Additional details on the holdings appear on the Society's Web site. If you're unable visit the state, contact the Kansas State Historical Society for their reference policies or view them on their Web site.

Most of the 105 counties in the state have genealogical societies that participate in the Kansas Council of Genealogical Societies. Volunteers for these organizations undertake indexing projects for records in their area. Once you've determined where your ancestors lived, contact the appropriate county genealogical society to see what materials might be available on the local level.

RESEARCH TIPS

for more info

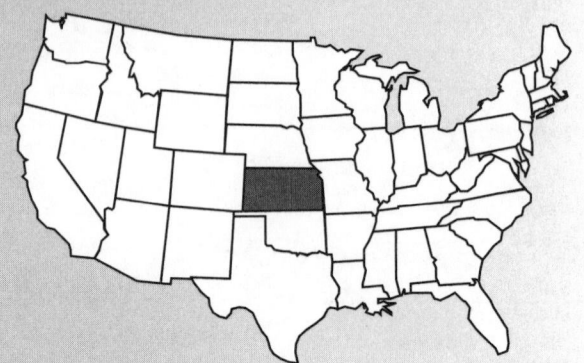

- The Kansas State Historical Society has an almost comprehensive collection of Kansas newspapers available at their facility or through interlibrary loan—check their Web site <www.kshs.org> for a database of available newspapers.
- ATLAS, the Associated Topeka Libraries Automated System, is an online catalog that covers the holdings of seven libraries in Topeka, including the Kansas State Historical Society <lib.wuacc.edu>. It contains maps, directories, published and unpublished family histories, organizational papers, and county histories.
- In it's ongoing quest to create a central repository for Kansas research, the Kansas State Historical Society collects microfilm of materials on the county level filmed by the Genealogical Society of Utah, as well as those on the national level that document the state's history.

Census Records
- Federal Censuses—1870, 1880, 1900, 1910, 1920, 1930
- Territory/State Censuses—1865, 1875, 1885, 1895, 1905, 1915, and 1925
- Mortality schedules—1860, 1870, 1880

STATE RESOURCES

■ ARCHIVES, LIBRARIES, AND SOCIETIES

Anderson County Genealogical Society
P.O. Box 194, Garnett, KS 66032
Web site: <www.grapevine.net/~swguinn/acgs.html>

Arkansas City Public Library
213 W. Fifth Ave., Arkansas City, KS 67705

Atchison County Genealogical Society
P.O. Box 303, Atchison, KS 66002-0303
Web site: <http://skyways.lib.ks.us/genweb/society/atchison/ackgs.htm>

Barton County Genealogical Society
P.O. Box 425, Great Bend, KS 67530

Bluestem Genealogical Society
P.O. Box 582, Eureka, KS 67045

Branches and Twigs Genealogical Society
℅ Kingman Carnegie Library, 455 N. Main, Kingman, KS 67068-1395
Tel: (620) 532-3061
Web site: <http://skyways.lib.ks.us/genweb/kingman/branches.html>

Brown County Genealogical Society
116 S. Seventh St., Hiawatha, KS 66434
Tel: (785) 742-7511

Chanute Genealogical Society
800 W. Fourteenth St., Chanute, KS 66720-2699
Web site: <www.rootsweb.com/~kscgs/>

Chautauqua County Historical and Genealogical Society
115 W. Main, Sedan, KS 67361
Tel: (620) 725-3408

Cherokee County Genealogical-Historical Society, Inc.
P.O. Box 33, Columbus, KS 66725-0033
Tel: (620) 429-2992
E-mail: cckghs@columbus-ks.com

Cloud County Genealogical Society
E-mail: CloudGen@care2.com
Web site: <www.dustdevil.com/towns/concordia/history/ccgs/>

Cowley County Genealogical Society
1518 E. Twelfth, Winfield, KS 67156
Tel: (620) 221-4591

Crawford County Genealogy Society and Library
308 N. Walnut, Pittsburg, KS 66762
Web site: <http://skyways.lib.ks.us/genweb/crawford/society.html>

Decatur County Genealogical Society
% The Decatur County Museum, 258 S. Penn Ave., Oberlin, KS
Web site: <http://skyways.lib.ks.us/genweb/decatur/genealogy_society_files/genealogical_society.htm>

Disciples of Christ Historical Society
1101 Nineteenth Ave. S., Nashville, TN 37212
Web site:

The Douglas County Genealogical Society
P.O. Box 3664, Lawrence, KS 66046-0664
Web site: <http://skyways.lib.ks.us/kansas/genweb/douglas/dckgs.htm>

Douglas County Historical Society
% The Watkins Community Museum of History, 1047 Massachusetts St., Lawrence, KS 66044
Tel: (785) 841-4109

Finney County Genealogical Society
P.O. Box 592, Garden City, KS 67846-0592

Flint Hills Genealogical Society
P.O. Box 555, Emporia, KS 66801-0555
Web site: <http://skyways.lib.ks.us/genweb/society/emporia/index.html>

Franklin County Genealogical Society
P.O. Box 353, Ottawa, KS 66067
Web site: <www.ukans.edu/heritage/chs/franklin/>

Garden City Public Library
210 N. Seventh, Garden City, KS 67846

Girard Public Library
128 W. Prairie, Girard, KS 66743-1498
Tel: (620) 724-4317

Golden Wheat Chapter, American Historical Society of Germans from Russia
E-mail: gwahsgr@rocketmail.com
Web site: <www.ahsgr.org/GoldenWheatChapter/ksgolden.html>

The Greenwood County Historical Society
120 W. Fourth St., Eureka, KS 67045-1445
Tel: (620) 583-6682
E-mail: gwhistory@correct-connect.com
Web site: <http://skyways.lib.ks.us/genweb/greenwoo/gchs.htm>

Halstead Historical Society
P.O. Box 88, Halstead, KS 67056
Tel: (316) 835-2267
Web site: <www.halsteadkansas.com/historical/>

Hamilton County Historical Society
108 E. Hwy. 50, Syracuse, KS 67878
Tel: (620) 384-7496

Hamilton County Library
P.O.Box 1307, Syracuse, KS 67878-1307
Tel: (620) 384-5622
E-mail: hamcolib@yahoo.com
Web site: <http://skyways.lib.ks.us/library/hamilton/>

Harper County Genealogical Society
Web site: <http://skyways.lib.ks.us/kansas/genweb/society/harper/index.html>

Heart of America Chapter, American Historical Society of Germans from Russia
117 E. Minneapolis St., Salina, KS 67401-6024
Tel: (913) 827-0782
Web site: <www.ahsgr.org/heart_of_america_chapter.htm>

Heritage Seekers of SW Kansas Chapter, American Historical Society of Germans from Russia
511 Baughman, Ulysses, KS 67880
Tel: (316) 356-2228

Historical Society of the Downs Carnegie Library
S. Morgan Ave., Downs, KS 67437

Hodgeman County Genealogical Society
P.O. Box 608, Jetmore, KS 67854
Tel: (620) 357-6594
E-mail: hcgs18m@hotmail.com

Iola Public Library
218 E. Madison, Iola, KS 66749
Tel: (620) 365-3262
E-mail: iolaref@alltel.net
Web site: <www.iola.lib.ks.us>

Jefferson County Genealogical Society
P.O. Box 174, Oskaloosa, KS, 66066-0174
E-mail: jcgs1979@yahoo.com
Web site: <http://skyways.lib.ks.us/kansas/genweb/jefferso/jfcogen.html>

Johnson County Genealogical Society and Library, Inc.
P.O. Box 12666, Shawnee Mission, KS 66282-2666
Tel: (913) 780-4764
Web site: <www.johnsoncountykansasgenealogy.org>

Kansas City Area Chapter, American Historical Society of Germans from Russia
4441 W. Fifty-second Terrace, Roeland Park, KS 66205
Web site: <www.ahsgr.org/kansas_city_area_chapter.htm>

Kansas Council of Genealogical Societies
P.O. Box 3858, Topeka, KS 66604-6858
Web site: <http://skyways.lib.ks.us/genweb/kcgs/>

Kansas Department of Health & Environment, Office of Vital Statistics
1000 SW Jackson, Topeka, KS 66612
Tel: (785) 296-1400
E-mail: Vital.Records@kdhe.state.ks.us
Web site: <www.kdhe.state.ks.us/vital/>

Kansas Genealogical Society Library
Village Square Mall, 2601 Central Ave., Dodge City, KS 67801

Kansas Public Library
625 Minnesota Ave., Kansas City, KS 66101

Kansas State Historical Society
6425 SW Sixth Ave., Topeka, KS 66615
Tel: (785) 272-8681
Web site: <www.kshs.org>

Kansas State Library
State Capitol Building, Topeka, KS 66612-1593
Tel: (785) 296-3296 or (800) 432-3919

Web site: <http://skyways.lib.ks.us/KSL>

Labette County Genealogical Society, Inc.
P.O. Box 544, Parsons, KS 67357-0544
Web site: <http://skyways.lib.ks.us/genweb/society/parsons/>

Nora E. Larabee Memorial Library
108 N. Union St., Stafford, KS 67578
Tel: (620) 234-5762
Web site: <http://skyways.lib.ks.us/towns/Stafford/library>

Liberal Area Genealogical Society
P.O. Box 1094, Liberal, KS 67905-1094

Marion County Genealogical Society
Web site: <http://skyways.lib.ks.us/genweb/marion/>

Marshall County Historical Society and Museum
Web site: <www.mchistoricalsociety.org>

Mennonite Library and Archives
% Bethel College, 300 E. Twenty-seventh St., North Newton, KS 67117
Web site: <www.bethelks.edu/services/mla/>

Miami County Genealogy Society
P.O. Box 123, Paola, KS 66071
Tel: (913) 294-4940
Web site:

Midwest Historical and Genealogical Society
P.O. Box 1121, Wichita, KS 67201-1121
Tel: (316) 264-3611
E-mail: mhgs1121@aol.com
Web site: <http://skyways.lib.ks.us/kansas/genweb/mhgs/>

Montgomery County Genealogical Society
P.O. Box 444, Coffeyville, KS 67337
Web site: <www.rootsweb.com/~ksmontgo/>

Nemaha County Genealogical Society
Sixth and Nemaha, Seneca, KS 66538
Web site: <raven.cc.ukans.edu/kansas/seneca/gensoc.html>

The North Central Kansas Genealogical Society, Inc.
P.O. Box 251, Cawker City, KS 67430
Web site: <http://skyways.lib.ks.us/towns/Cawker/library.html>

Northeastern Kansas Chapter, American Historical Society of Germans from Russia
2938 SE Peck Rd., Topeka, KS 66605-1925
Web site: <www.ahsgr.org/north eastern_kansas_chapter.htm>

Northwest Kansas Genealogical And Historical Society
700 W. Third, Oakley, KS 67748

Norton County Historical Society & Museum
P.O. Box 303, Norton, KS 67654
Tel: (785) 877-5107
E-mail: Norton County Historical Society
Web site: <www.nex-tech.com/clients/nchistory/index.htm>

Old Fort Genealogical Society of Southeastern Kansas, Inc.
P.O. Box 786, Fort Scott, KS 66701
Tel: (620) 223-3300
Web site: <http://skyways.lib.ks.us/genweb/society/ftscott/>

Osage County Historical Society, Inc. & Genealogical Research Center
P.O. Box 361, Lyndon, KS 66451
Tel: (785) 828-3477
Web site:

Phillips County Genealogical Society
P.O. Box 114, Phillipsburg, KS 67661
Web site: <http://skyways.lib.ks.us/genweb/phillips/plgensoc.html>

Pittsburg Public Library
308 N. Walnut, Pittsburg, KS 66762
Tel: (620) 231-8110
Web site: <http://skyways.lib.ks.us/library/pittsburg/>

Post Rock Chapter, American Historical Society of Germans from Russia
18350 Homer Rd., Russell, KS 67665
Tel: (785) 483-3976
Web site: <www.ahsgr.org/post_rock_chapter.htm>

Presbyterian Historical Society
425 Lombard St., Philadelphia, PA 19147-1516
Tel: (215) 627-1852
Web site: <www.history.pcusa.org>

Rawlins County Genealogical Society
Web site: <http://skyways.lib.ks.us/genweb/rawlins/rawgenesoc.html>

Reno County Genealogical Society
P.O. Box 0005, Hutchinson, KS 67504-0005
Web site: <rootsweb.com/~ksrcgs/renocokansas.html>

Riley County Genealogical Society
2005 Claflin, Manhattan, KS 66502-3415
Web site: <www.rileycgs.com>

Santa Fe Trail Genealogical Society
P.O. Box 528, Syracuse, KS 67878

Smoky Valley Genealogical Society and Library, Inc.
211 W. Iron, Suite 205, Salina, KS 67401-2613
Web site: <http://skyways.lib.ks.us/genweb/saline/society/gensoc.html>

Southeast Kansas Genealogy Society
P.O. Box 393, Iola, KS 66749

Southwestern College Memorial Library
100 College St., Winfield, KS 67156
Tel: (800) 846-1543
Web site: <www.sckans.edu/library/introd.html>

Kenneth Spencer Research Library
1450 Poplar Lane, The University of Kansas, KS 66045-7616
Tel: (785) 864-4334
Web site: <http://spencer.lib.ku.edu/kc>

St. Mary's Historical Society
106 E. Mission, St. Marys, NV 66536

Stanton County Historical Society
P.O. Box 806, Johnson, KS 67855

Sumner County Historical & Genealogical Society
P.O. Box 402, Wellington, KS 67152
E-mail: scgs67152@yahoo.com
Web site: <www.rootsweb.com/~ksscgs>

Topeka Genealogical Society, Inc.
P.O. Box 4048, Topeka, KS 66604-0048
Web site: <www.tgstopeka.org>

Topeka Public Library
1515 SW Tenth Ave., Topeka, KS 66604

Wichita County Genealogical Society
P.O. Box 1561, Leoti, KS 67861
Tel: (620) 375-2316
Web site: <www.wichitacountymuseum.org/gensociety.htm>

The Wichita Genealogical Society
P.O. Box 3705, Wichita, KS 67201-3705
Web site: <http://skyways.lib.ks.us/orgs/wgs>

Wichita Public Library
223 S. Main, Wichita, KS 67202
Tel: (316) 721-6794
E-mail: wichita.gen.soc@mail.com
Web site: <www.wichita.lib.ks.us>

Wyandotte County Genealogical Society
P.O. Box 4228, Kansas City, KS 66104-0228
Web site: <http://kcgenealogy.com/wyandotte_county_genealogical_so.htm>

Wyandotte County Historical Society and Museum
631 N. 126th St., Bonner Springs, KS 66012
Tel: (913) 721-1078
Web site: <www.wycokck.org/museum/index.html>

BIBLIOGRAPHY

■ GENERAL RESOURCES

The Beginning of the West: Annals of the Kansas Gateway to the American West, 1540–1854
by Louise Barry (Topeka, KS: Kansas State Historical Society, ca. 1972)

A Biographical History of Central Kansas
(New York, NY: Lewis Pub. Co., 1902)

Black, Buckskin and Blue: African American Scouts and Soldiers on the Western Frontier
by Arthur T. Burton (Austin, TX: Eaton Press, ca. 1999)

A Century of Congregationalism in Kansas, 1854–1954
by Charles M. Correll (Topeka, KS: The Kansas Congregational and Christian Conference, ca. 1953)

Early Kansas Churches
by Edward Robert DeZurko (Manhattan, KS: The College, 1949)

The First Protestant Osage Missions, 1820–1837
by William Whites Graves (Oswego, KS: Carpenter Press, ca. 1949)

The Genealogist's Companion and Sourcebook, 2d ed.
by Emily Anne Croom (Cincinnati: Betterway Books, 2003)

A Genealogist's Guide to Discovering Your African-American Ancestors
by Franklin Carter Smith and Emily Anne Croom (Cincinnati: Betterway Books, 2003)

Guide to Genealogical Research in the National Archives of the United States
edited by Anne Bruner Eales and Robert M. Kvasnicka (Washington, DC: National Archives and Records Administration, 2000)

Guide to the Microfilm Collections of the Kansas State Historical Society
by David A. Haury (Topeka, KS: Kansas State Historical Society, 1991)

Guide to Public Vital Statistics Records in Kansas
by the Historical Records Survey (Topeka, KS: The Survey, 1942)

History of Kansas Newspapers: A History of the Newspapers and Magazines Published in Kansas from the Organization of Kansas Territory, 1854, to January 1, 1916 Together with Brief Statistical Information of the Counties, Cities and Towns of the State
by the Kansas State Historical Society (Topeka, KS: Kansas State Printing Plant, 1916)

History of the State of Kansas: Containing a Full Account of its Growth from an Uninhabited Territory to a Wealthy and Important State, of its Early Settlement, a Supplementary History and Description of its Counties, Cities, Towns and Villages, Their Advantages, Industries and Commerce, to which are Added Biographical Sketches and Portraits of Prominent Men and Early Settlers
by A.T. Andreas (Marceline, MO: Walsworth Pub. Co., 1976)

Illustriana Kansas: Biographical Sketches of Kansas Men and Women of Achievement Who Have Been Awarded Life Membership in Kansas Illustriana Society
by Robert Morton Baldwin and Sara Mullin Baldwin (Tucson, AZ: W.C. Cox, 1974)

The Kansa Indians, A History of the Wind People, 1673–1873
by William E. Unrau (Norman, OK: University of Oklahoma Press, 1971)

Kansas Biographical Index: State-Wide and Regional Histories: Citing More Than 35,500 Biographies from Sixty-eight Volumes of Kansas Biographical Sources
by Patricia Douglass Smith (Garden City, KS: P.D. Smith, ca. 1994)

Kansas: A Cyclopedia of State History, Embracing Events, Institutions, Industries, Counties, Cities, Towns, Prominent Persons, etc . . . With a Supplementary Volume Devoted to Selected Personal History and Reminiscence
by Frank Wilson Blackmar (Chicago, IL: Standard Pub. Co., ca. 1912)

Kansas, the First Century
by John D. Bright (New York, NY: Lewis Historical Pub. Co., ca. 1956)

Kansas Genealogical Society Six Generation Ancestor Tables
by Doris Dockstader Rooney (Dodge City, KS: Kansas Genealogical Society, 1976)

Kansas Newspapers: A Directory of Newspaper Holdings in Kansas
by Eileen Anderson (Topeka, KS: The Board, 1984)

Kansas Orphan Train Riders— These We Know
by Robert A. Hodge (Emporia, KS: R.A. Hodge, ca. 1996)

Kansas Research Outline
by the Church of Jesus Christ of Latter-day Saints (Salt Lake City, UT: Corp. of the President of The Church of Jesus Christ of L.D.S., ca. 1988, ca. 1997)

Narratives of African Americans in Kansas, 1870–1992: Beyond the Exodust Movement
by Jacob U. Gordon (Lewiston, NY: E. Mellen Press, ca. 1993)

National Archives Microfilm Catalogs online:
<www.archives.gov/publications/genealogy_microfilm_catalogs.html>

A New Centennial History of the State of Kansas: Being a Full and Complete Civil, Political and Military History of the State, from its Earliest Settlement to the Present Time
by Charles Richard Tuttle (Madison, WI: Inter-state Book Co., 1876)

Peopling the Plains: Who Settled Where in Frontier Kansas
by James R. Shortridge (Lawrence, KS: University Press of Kansas, ca. 1995)

Pioneer Women: Voices from the Kansas Frontier
by Joanna L. Stratton (New York, NY: Simon and Schuster, ca. 1981)

Portrait and Biographical Record of Southeastern Kansas: Containing Biographical Sketches of Prominent and Representative Citizens of the Counties, Together with Biographies and Portraits of All the Presidents of the United States and the Governors of the State of Kansas
(Chicago, IL: Biographical Pub. Co., 1894)

The Sod House Frontier, 1854–1890: A Social History of the Northern Plains from the Creation of Kansas & Nebraska to the Admission of the Dakotas
by Everett Dick (Lincoln, NE: University of Nebraska, 1979, ca. 1954)

A Standard History of Kansas and Kansans
by William Elsey Connelley (Chicago, IL: Lewis Pub. Co., 1918)

Territorial Papers of Kansas, 1854–1861
by the United States Department of State (Washington, DC: The National Archives, 1953)

The United States Biographical Dictionary: Kansas Volume, Containing Accurately Compiled Biographical Sketches into which is Woven the History of the State and its Leading Interests
(Chicago and Kansas City: S. Lewis and Co., 1879)

West of Wichita: Settling the High Plains of Kansas, 1865–1890
by Craig Miner (Lawrence, KS: University Press of Kansas, ca. 1986)

The William Wade Hinshaw Index to Kansas Quaker Meeting Records
by William Wade Hinshaw (Kokomo, IN: Selby Publishing & Printing, ca. 1991)

■ CENSUS RECORDS

The American Census Handbook
by Thomas Jay Kemp (Wilmington, DE: Scholarly Resources Inc., ca. 2001)

The Census Book: A Genealogist's Guide to Federal Census Facts, Schedules and Indexes; with Master Extraction Forms for Federal Census Schedules, 1790–1930
by William Dollarhide (Bountiful, UT: HeritageQuest, ca. 1999)

Finding Answers in U.S. Census Records
by Loretto Dennis Szucs and Matthew Wright (Orem, UT: Ancestry Pub., ca. 2001)

Map Guide to the U.S. Federal Censuses, 1790–1920
by William Thorndale and William Dollarhide (Baltimore, MD: Genealogical Pub. Co., ca. 1987)

State Census Records
by Ann S. Lainhart (Baltimore, MD: Genealogical Pub. Co., ca. 1992)

Your Guide to the Federal Census
by Kathleen W. Hinckley (Cincinnati: Betterway Books, 2002)

■ IMMIGRATION RECORDS

American Naturalization Records, 1790–1990: What They Are and How to Use Them
by John J. Newman (North Salt Lake, UT: HeritageQuest, 1998)

American Passenger Arrival Records
by Michael Tepper (Baltimore: Genealogical Publishing Co., 1993)

Kansas Territorial Settlers of 1860 Who Were Born in Tennessee, Virginia, North Carolina and South Carolina: A Compilation with Historical Annotations and Editorial Comment
by Clara Hamlett Robertson (Baltimore, MD: Genealogical Pub. Co., ca. 1976)

They Became Americans: Finding Naturalization Records and Ethnic Origins
by Loretto Dennis Szucs (Salt Lake City: Ancestry, Inc., 1998)

They Came in Ships: A Guide to Finding Your Immigrant Ancestor's Arrival Records, 2d ed.
by John P. Colletta (Salt Lake City: Ancestry, Inc., 1993)

■ LAND RECORDS

Land & Property Research in the United States
by E. Wade Hone (Salt Lake City, UT: Ancestry, ca. 1997)

Locating Your Roots: Discover Your Ancestors Using Land Records
by Patricia Law Hatcher (Cincinnati: Betterway Books, 2003)

■ MAPS

1001 Kansas Place Names
by Sondra Van Meter McCoy (Lawrence, KS: University Press of Kansas, ca. 1989)

Historical Atlas of Kansas
by Homer E. Socolofsky and Huber Self (Norman, OK: University of Oklahoma Press, ca. 1972, 1988)

Kansas in Maps
by Robert W. Baughman (Topeka, KS: Kansas State Historical Society, 1961)

Kansas Place-Names
by John Rydjord (Norman, OK: University of Oklahoma Press, ca. 1972)

Kansas Post Offices, May 29, 1828–Aug 3, 1961
by Robert W. Baughman (Topeka, KS: Kansas Postal History Society, ca. 1961)

Kansas Towns & Cities as of 1912: Includes a List of Extinct towns [and a] Bonus Index of Biographies from Volumes 1, 2 & 3 Extracted from "Kansas"
by Debra Graden (Leavenworth, KS: Grey Ink, ca. 1997)

The Official State Atlas of Kansas
(Kansas Council of Genealogical Societies, 1982)

■ MILITARY RECORDS

Fighting Twentieth, History and Official Souvenir: An Account of the Kansas Volunteers in the Spanish American War, 1898–1899
(St. Joseph, MO: Copied by John A. Ostertag, 1989)

The History of the Kansas Department of the American Legion
by Richard J. Loosbrock (Topeka, KS: Kansas Dept. of the American Legion, ca. 1968)

An Honor Roll of Kansas Civil War Veterans
by Sherman Lee Pompey (Kingsburg, CA: Pacific Specialties, 1972)

Records of Indians in World War I
by the United States Bureau of Indian Affairs, Potawatomi Agency (Kansas City, MO: Federal Archives and Records Center, 1977)

Uncle, We Are Ready! Registering America's Men, 1917–1918: A Guide to Researching World War I Draft Registration Cards
by John J. Newman (North Salt Lake, UT: HeritageQuest, 2001)

U.S. Military Records: A Guide to Federal & State Sources, Colonial America to the Present
by James C. Neagles (Salt Lake City: Ancestry, Inc., 1994)

World War II: A Family Historian's Guide
by Debra Johnson Knox (Spartanburg, SC: MIE Publishing, 2003)

■ VITAL RECORDS

Abandoned and Semi-Active Cemeteries of Kansas
by Don L. Ford (Decorah, IA: Anundsen, ca. 1983–1985)

Births, Marriages, Deaths and Other News Items and Events
by John Ostertag and Enid Ostertag (St. Joseph, MO: J.A. Ostertag, 1989–1999)

Guide to Public Vital Statistics Records in Kansas
by the Historical Records Survey (Topeka, KS: The Survey, 1942)

Mortality Schedule, Kansas 1860
by Ronald Vern Jackson (Bountiful, UT: Accelerated Indexing Systems, ca. 1980)

Mortality Schedule, Kansas 1870
by Ronald Vern Jackson (Bountiful, UT: Accelerated Indexing Systems, 1979)

Mortality Schedule, Kansas 1880
by Ronald Vern Jackson (Bountiful, UT: Accelerated Indexing Systems, 1979)

Your Guide to Cemetery Research
by Sharon DeBartolo Carmack (Cincinnati: Betterway Books, 2002)

■ Allen 7 May 1856
1 N. Washington St., Iola, KS 66749
Phone: (620)365-1407
Web site: www.allencounty.org
Parent County: Original county
Comments/research tips: Clerk of District Court has Divorce records for late 1800s.

Record Type	Year Begun	Jurisdiction
Marriage	1856	County Clerk
Land	1861	Registrar/Deeds
Probate	1858	Probate Court
Court	1858	Probate Court
Military	1860	Registrar/Deeds
Nat.	1871	Clerk/District Ct.

■ Anderson 7 Jan. 1856
100 E. Fourth St., P.O. Box 305, Garnett, KS 66032-1503
Phone: (785)448-6841
Web site: http://skyways.lib.ks.us/genweb/anderson/index.html
Parent County: Original county

Record Type	Year Begun	Jurisdiction
Marriage	1856	County Clerk
Land	1857	Registrar/Deeds
Probate	1855	Probate Court
Court	1860	Clerk/District Ct.
Wills	1869	Probate Court
Nat.	1903	Clerk/District Ct.

■ Arapahoe 1873
Parent County: Original county
Comments/research tips: (See Haskell) Arapahoe County was absorbed by Finney County in 1883 and name changed to Haskell County 1887.

■ Atchison 17 Sep. 1855
423 N. Fifth St., Atchison, KS 66002
Phone: (913)367-1653
Web site: http://skyways.lib.ks.us/genweb/atchison/index.html
Parent County: Original county
Comments/research tips: County Clerk has Birth and Death records 1891–1911. Registrar of Deeds has Military Discharge records 1943–1990. Kansas Genealogical Society has Naturalization records 1858–1953, 1914–1929.

Record Type	Year Begun	Jurisdiction
Divorce	1859	Clerk/District Ct.
Land	1855	Registrar/Deeds
Probate	1855	Probate Court
Court	1858	Clerk/District Ct.
Marriage	1855	County Clerk

■ Barber 7 July 1873
120 E. Washington St., Medicine Lodge, KS 67104
Phone: (620)886-3961
Web site: http://skyways.lib.ks.us/genweb/barber/index.html
Parent County: Marion
Comments/research tips: County Clerk has Birth and Death records 1891–1911.

Record Type	Year Begun	Jurisdiction
Court	1874	Clerk/District Ct.
Marriage	1874	County Clerk
Land	1867	Registrar/Deeds
Probate	1867	Probate Court

■ Barton 16 May 1872
P.O. Box 1089, Great Bend, KS 67530
Phone: (620)793-1835
Web site: www.bartonks.com/
Parent County: Marion
Comments/research tips: County Clerk has Birth and Death records 1892–1911.

Record Type	Year Begun	Jurisdiction
Marriage	1872	County Clerk
Land	1872	County Clerk
Probate	1872	County Clerk
Court	1873	County Clerk

■ Billings 20 Mar. 1873
Parent County: Original county
Comments/research tips: (See Norton) Created in 1859 as Oro County, name changed to Norton County in 1867. In 1873 name changed to Billings and changed back to Norton in 1874.

■ Bourbon 12 Sep. 1855
210 S. National Ave., Fort Scott, KS 66701
Phone: (316)223-3800
Web site: www.bourboncountyks.org
Parent County: Original county
Comments/research tips: District Court has Naturalization records 1868–1933. Military records are available 1861–1865. Probate Court has Wills 1858–1925.

Record Type	Year Begun	Jurisdiction
Marriage	1855	Probate Court
Land	1856	Registrar/Deeds
Probate	1864	Probate Court
Court	1864	Probate Court

■ Breckenridge 25 Aug. 1855
Parent County: Original county
Comments/research tips: (See Lyon) Name changed to Lyon 5 February 1862. Was attached to Madison County for civil and criminal purposes. In 1861 Madison County was abolished and the northern part was given to Breckenridge.

■ Brown 25 Aug. 1855
601 Oregon St., Hiawatha, KS 66434
Phone: (785)742-2581
Web site: http://skyways.lib.ks.us/genweb/brown/index.html
Parent County: Original county
Comments/research tips: District Court has Naturalization records 1873–1954. Military Draft Registration Cards 1914–1918 available.

Record Type	Year Begun	Jurisdiction
Marriage	1857	Probate Court
Land	1857	Registrar/Deeds
Probate	1857	Probate Court

Court	1859	Clerk/District Ct.
Birth	1885	County District Ct.
Death	1895	County District Ct.

■ Buffalo 20 Mar. 1873
Parent County: Unorganized Territory
Comments/research tips: (See Gray, old) In 1881 the northern tier of Buffalo County was added to Lane County. The remainder was added to Gray County and later to Finney County.

■ Butler 25 Aug. 1855
205 W. Central Ave., El Dorado, KS 67042
Phone: (316)322-4232
Web site: www.bucoks.com/
Parent County: Original county
Comments/research tips: Registrar of Deeds has Military Discharge records 1943–1950. County Clerk has Birth and Death records 1887–1912.

Record Type	Year Begun	Jurisdiction
Marriage	1861	Clerk/District Ct.
Land	1868	Registrar/Deeds

■ Calhoun 24 Sep. 1855
Parent County: Original county
Comments/research tips: (See Jackson) Name changed to Jackson 11 February 1859. Early Marriage records are in Molton and Jackson Counties.

■ Chase 15 Mar. 1859
Courthouse Sq., Box 547, Cottonwood Falls, KS 66845
Phone: (620)273-6423
Web site: http://skyways.lib.ks.us/genweb/chase/index.html
Parent County: Butler, Wise
Comments/research tips: Military records 1861–1865 are available. Circuit Court has Naturalization records 1872–1941.

Record Type	Year Begun	Jurisdiction
Land	1859	Registrar/Deeds
Probate	1864	Probate Court
Marriage	1860	Clerk/District Ct.
Court	1861	Clerk/District Ct.

■ Chautauqua 1 June 1875
215 N. Chautauqua, Sedan, KS 67361
Phone: (620)725-5800
Web site: http://skyways.lib.ks.us/genweb/chautauq/index.html
Parent County: Howard, Godfrey
Comments/research tips: Clerk of District Court has Divorce records 1884–1949. Probate Judge has Probate records 1871–1900.

Record Type	Year Begun	Jurisdiction
Marriage	1870	Probate Judge
Land	1871	Registrar/Deeds
Court	1871	Clerk/District Ct.

■ Cherokee 3 Aug. 1866
100 W. Maple, P.O. Box 14, Columbus, KS 66725
Phone: (620)429-2042

Web site: http://skyways.lib.ks.us/genweb/cherokee/index.html
Parent County: Unorganized Territory
Comments/research tips: Formerly McGee County. Name changed to Cherokee 18 February 1860.

Record Type	Year Begun	Jurisdiction
Birth	1894	County Clerk
Nat.	1870	Probate Court
Marriage	1867	Probate Court
Death	1894	County Clerk
Land	1866	Registrar/Deeds
Probate	1870	Probate Court
Wills	1870	Probate Court

■ Cheyenne 1886

P.O. Box 985, St. Francis, KS 67756
Phone: (785)332-8800
Web site: http://skyways.lib.ks.us/genweb/cheyenne/index.html
Parent County: Unorganized Territory

Record Type	Year Begun	Jurisdiction
Marriage	1886	Clerk/District Ct.
Divorce	1892	Clerk/District Ct.
Probate	1892	Clerk/District Ct.
Court	1892	Clerk/District Ct.
Land	1873	Registrar/Deeds

■ Clark 5 May 1885

913 Highland St., Ashland, KS 67831
Phone: (620)635-2813
Web site: http://skyways.lib.ks.us/genweb/clark/index.html
Parent County: Marion, Ford

Record Type	Year Begun	Jurisdiction
Marriage	1885	Probate Judge
Divorce	1885	Probate Judge
Land	1872	Registrar/Deeds
Probate	1885	Probate Judge
Court	1885	Probate Judge

■ Clay 1866

712 Fifth St., P.O. Box 98, Clay Center, KS 67432
Phone: (785)632-2552
Web site: http://skyways.lib.ks.us/genweb/clay/index.html
Parent County: Original county
Comments/research tips: Registrar of Deeds has Military Discharge records 1919–1957. Probate Court has Birth and Death records 1885–1911.

Record Type	Year Begun	Jurisdiction
Land	1866	Registrar/Deeds
Probate	1872	Probate Court
Court	1868	Clerk/District Ct.
Marriage	1867	Probate Court
Wills	1867	Probate Court
Nat.	1868	District Court

■ Cloud 27 Mar. 1867

811 Washington St., Concordia, KS 66901
Phone: (785)243-8110
Web site: www.dustdevil.com/towns/concordia/courthouse

Parent County: Shirley
Comments/research tips: County Clerk has Birth and Death records 1885–1911. Formerly Shirley County, name changed to Cloud 27 March 1867.

Record Type	Year Begun	Jurisdiction
Divorce	ca. 1860	Clerk/District Ct.
Land	1869	Registrar/Deeds
Probate	ca. 1860	Clerk/Circuit Ct.
Court	ca. 1860	Clerk/District Ct.
Marriage	1867	Probate Judge

■ Coffey 25 Aug. 1855

110 S. Sixth St., Burlington, KS 66839
Phone: (620)364-2191
Web site: www.coffeycountyks.org/
Parent County: Original county
Comments/research tips: Registrar of Deeds has Military Discharge records 1869–1885. Historical Society has a master index to Cemeteries of Coffey County.

Record Type	Year Begun	Jurisdiction
Marriage	1856	County Clerk
Divorce	1861	Clerk/District Ct.
Land	1857	Registrar/Deeds
Probate	1857	Probate Court
Court	1861	Clerk/District Ct.
Death	1886	County Clerk
Birth	1892	County Clerk
Nat.	1869	District Court
Wills	1861	Probate Court

■ Comanche 1885

201 S. New York, P.O. Box 776, Coldwater, KS 67029
Phone: (620)582-2361
Web site: http://skyways.lib.ks.us/genweb/comanche/index.html
Parent County: Marion
Comments/research tips: County Clerk has Birth records 1891–1911, Death records 1891–1908, and Marriage records 1891–1913.

Record Type	Year Begun	Jurisdiction
Divorce	1867	Clerk/District Ct.
Land	1885	Registrar/Deeds
Probate	1867	Clerk/District Ct.
Court	1867	Clerk/District Ct.

■ Cowley 28 Feb. 1870

311 E. Ninth Ave., Winfield, KS 67156
Phone: (620)221-5495
Web site: www.cowleycounty.org/
Parent County: Butler
Comments/research tips: Registrar of Deeds has Marriage records 1870–1911. Name was Hunter, changed to Cowley in 1870.

Record Type	Year Begun	Jurisdiction
Birth	1911	State Vital Records
Death	1911	State Vital Records
Divorce	1870	Registrar/Deeds
Land	1871	Registrar/Deeds
Probate	1870	Clerk/District Ct.
Court	1870	Clerk/District Ct.

Crawford 13 Feb. 1867

P.O. Box 249, Girard, KS 66743-0249
Phone: (620)724-6115
Web site: www.crawfordcountykansas.org/
Parent County: Bourbon, Cherokee
Comments/research tips: County Clerk has Birth and Death records 1887–1911.

Record Type	Year Begun	Jurisdiction
Marriage	1867	Probate Court
Divorce	1867	Clerk/District Ct.
Land	1867	Registrar/Deeds
Probate	1868	Probate Court
Court	1867	Clerk/District Ct.
Nat.	1868	Clerk/District Ct.

Davis 25 Aug. 1855

Parent County: Original county
Comments/research tips: (See Geary) Name changed to Geary 7 March 1889.

Decatur 15 Dec. 1879

P.O. Box 28, Oberlin, KS 67749
Phone: (785)475-8102
Web site: http://skyways.lib.ks.us/genweb/decatur/index.html
Parent County: Unorganized Territory
Comments/research tips: Clerk of District Court has Birth and Death records 1885–1911 and Marriage records 1881–1912, 1917–1926.

Record Type	Year Begun	Jurisdiction
Divorce	1881	Clerk/District Ct.
Land	1855	Registrar/Deeds
Probate	1891	Clerk/District Ct.
Court	1881	Clerk/District Ct.
Nat.	1880	Clerk/District Ct.

Dickinson 20 Feb. 1857

109 E. First St., P.O. Box 248, Abilene, KS 67410-0248
Phone: (785)263-3774
Web site: www.dkcoks.com
Parent County: Davis, Unorganized Territory
Comments/research tips: County Clerk has Birth, Death and Marriage records 1895–1911.

Record Type	Year Begun	Jurisdiction
Land	1859	Registrar/Deeds
Court	1882	District Clerk
Probate	1882	District Clerk

Doniphan 18 Sep. 1855

P.O. Box 278, Troy, KS 66087
Phone: (785)985-3513
Web site: http://skyways.lib.ks.us/genweb/doniphan/index.html
Parent County: Original county
Comments/research tips: A yearly county census is taken.

Record Type	Year Begun	Jurisdiction
Marriage	1856	Probate Court
Land	1856	Registrar/Deeds
Probate	1852	Probate Court

Court	1858	Clerk/District Ct.
Birth	1898	County Health Officer
Death	1898	County Health Officer
Nat.	1868	District Court

Dorn 25 Aug. 1855

Parent County: Original county
Comments/research tips: (See Neosho) Name changed to Neosho 3 June 1861.

Douglas 24 Sep. 1855

1100 Massachusetts, Lawrence, KS 66044
Phone: (785)832-5281
Web site: www.douglas-county.com/
Parent County: Original county
Comments/research tips: Clerk of District Court has Naturalization records 1867–1954 and Genealogical Society has Marriage records 1854–1884. Records destroyed 21 August 1863 in Quantrill's raid. Some marriage records reconstructed.

Record Type	Year Begun	Jurisdiction
Land	1856	Registrar/Deeds
Probate	1855	Clerk/District Ct.
Court	1863	Clerk/District Ct.
Divorce	1864	District Court

Edwards 18 Mar. 1874

312 Massachusetts Ave., Kinsley, KS 67547-1099
Phone: (620)659-3000
Web site: http://skyways.lib.ks.us/genweb/edwards/index.html
Parent County: Kiowa

Record Type	Year Begun	Jurisdiction
Divorce	1874	Clerk/District Ct.
Land	1874	Registrar/Deeds
Probate	1874	Clerk/District Ct.
Court	1874	Clerk/District Ct.

Elk 25 Mar. 1875

127 N. Pine St., P.O. Box 606, Howard, KS 67349
Phone: (620)374-2490
Web site: http://skyways.lib.ks.us/genweb/elk/index.html
Parent County: Howard
Comments/research tips: Clerk of District Court has Birth and Death records 1885–1889, 1892–1911. Courthouse burned in 1906.

Record Type	Year Begun	Jurisdiction
Marriage	1878	Registrar/Deeds
Land	1871	Registrar/Deeds
Probate	1906	Probate Judge
Court	1906	Clerk/District Ct.

Ellis 26 Feb. 1867

1204 Fort St., P.O. Box 720, Hays, KS 67601
Phone: (785)628-9410
Web site: www.ellisco.org/
Parent County: Unorganized Territory
Comments/research tips: County Clerk has Birth, Death, and Marriage records 1886–1912.

Kansas

Record Type	Year Begun	Jurisdiction
Divorce	1871	Clerk/District Ct.
Land	ca. 1880	Registrar/Deeds
Probate	1871	Clerk/District Ct.
Court	1871	Clerk/District Ct.

■ Ellsworth 26 Feb. 1867

210 N. Kansas Ave., P.O. Box 396, Ellsworth, KS 67439
Phone: (785)472-4161
Web site: http://skyways.lib.ks.us/genweb/ellswort/
index.html
Parent County: Marion, Unorganized Territory, Peketon
Territory

Record Type	Year Begun	Jurisdiction
Divorce	1868	Clerk/District Ct.
Land	1867	Registrar/Deeds
Probate	1868	Clerk/District Ct.
Court	1868	Clerk/District Ct.

■ Finney 22 Feb. 1883

P.O. Box M, Garden City, KS 67846
Phone: (620)272-3522
Web site: www.finneycounty.org/
Parent County: Marion
Comments/research tips: Formerly Sequoyah County. Name
changed to Finney 21 February 1883.

Record Type	Year Begun	Jurisdiction
Marriage	1885	Clerk/District Ct.
Divorce	1885	Clerk/District Ct.
Probate	1885	Clerk/District Ct.
Court	1885	Clerk/District Ct.
Nat.	1885	Clerk/District Ct.

■ Foote 20 Mar. 1873

Parent County: Marion
Comments/research tips: (See Gray, old) Became Gray
County 1881 and disappeared 1883.

■ Ford 5 Apr. 1873

100 Gunsmoke, Dodge City, KS 67801
Phone: (620)227-4550
Web site: www.fordcounty.net/
Parent County: Marion
Comments/research tips: County Clerk has Birth, Death, and
Marriage records 1905–1911. Probate Judge has
Naturalization records 1874–1906.

Record Type	Year Begun	Jurisdiction
Divorce	1873	Clerk/District Ct.
Land	1873	Registrar/Deeds
Probate	1873	Probate Judge
Court	1873	Probate Judge

■ Franklin 25 Aug. 1855

315 S. Main, Ottawa, KS 66067
Phone: (785)229-3410
Web site: www.co.franklin.ks.us/
Parent County: Original county

Record Type	Year Begun	Jurisdiction
Marriage	1858	Clerk/District Ct.

Record Type	Year Begun	Jurisdiction
Divorce	1860	Clerk/District Ct.
Land	1857	Registrar/Deeds
Probate	1859	Clerk/District Ct.
Court	1859	Clerk/District Ct.
Wills	1863	Probate Court
Nat.	1869	Clerk/District Ct.

■ Garfield 23 Mar. 1889

Parent County: Finney, Hodgeman
Comments/research tips: Annexed to Finney 18 March 1893.

■ Geary 7 Mar. 1889

139 E. Eighth St., P.O. Box 927, Junction City, KS 66441
Phone: (785)238-3912
Web site: http://skyways.lib.ks.us/genweb/geary/index.html
Parent County: Original county
Comments/research tips: Formerly Davis County. Name
changed to Geary 28 February 1889.

Record Type	Year Begun	Jurisdiction
Marriage	1860	Probate Court
Divorce	1867	Clerk/District Ct.
Land	1858	Registrar/Deeds
Probate	1856	Probate Court
Court	1861	Clerk/District Ct.
Nat.	1865	Clerk/District Ct.

■ Godfrey 30 Aug. 1855

Parent County: Original county
Comments/research tips: (See Seward, old) Name changed to
Seward 3 June 1861.

■ Gove 1886

520 Washington St., P.O. Box 128, Gove, KS 67736-0128
Phone: (785)938-2300
Web site: http://skyways.lib.ks.us/genweb/gove/index.html
Parent County: Unorganized Territory

Record Type	Year Begun	Jurisdiction
Land	1885	Registrar/Deeds
Probate	1886	Clerk/District Ct.
Court	1886	Clerk/District Ct.

■ Graham 1880

410 N. Pomeroy, Hill City, KS 67642-1645
Phone: (785)421-3453
Web site: http://skyways.lib.ks.us/genweb/graham/
index.html
Parent County: Unorganized Territory
Comments/research tips: County Clerk has Birth, Death, and
Marriage records 1892–1904.

Record Type	Year Begun	Jurisdiction
Divorce	1887	Clerk/District Ct.
Land	1886	Registrar/Deeds
Probate	1887	Clerk/District Ct.
Court	1887	Clerk/District Ct.

■ Grant 1889

108 S. Glenn, Ulysses, KS 67880-2551
Phone: (620)356-1335
Web site: www.grantcoks.org/

Parent County: Unorganized Territory
Comments/research tips: Local census taken every year.

Record Type	Year Begun	Jurisdiction
Marriage	na	Clerk/District Ct.
Divorce	na	Clerk/District Ct.
Land	1887	Registrar/Deeds
Probate	na	Clerk/District Ct.
Court	na	Clerk/District Ct.

■ Gray 20 July 1887
300 S. Main, P.O. Box 487, Cimarron, KS 67835-0487
Phone: (620)855-3618
Web site: http://skyways.lib.ks.us/genweb/gray/index.html
Parent County: Finney, Ford

Record Type	Year Begun	Jurisdiction
Marriage	1887	Clerk/District Ct.
Divorce	1887	Clerk/District Ct.
Land	1887	Registrar/Deeds
Probate	1885	Clerk/District Ct.

■ Gray, Old 13 Mar. 1881
Parent County: Foote, Buffalo
Comments/research tips: Disappeared in 1883; reorganized 20 July 1887.

■ Greeley 9 July 1888
208 Harper St., P.O. Box 277, Tribune, KS 67879-0277
Phone: (620)376-4256
Web site: http://skyways.lib.ks.us/genweb/greeley/index.html
Parent County: Unorganized Territory

Record Type	Year Begun	Jurisdiction
Marriage	1888	Probate Judge
Land	1886	Registrar/Deeds
Probate	1887	Clerk/District Ct.
Court	1888	Clerk/District Ct.

■ Greenwood 25 Aug. 1855
311 N. Main, P.O. Box 268, Eureka, KS 67045-1321
Phone: (620)583-8121
Web site: http://skyways.lib.ks.us/genweb/greenwoo/index.html
Parent County: Original county
Comments/research tips: County Historical Society has Marriage records 1856–1985.

Record Type	Year Begun	Jurisdiction
Divorce	na	Clerk/District Ct.
Land	1858	Registrar/Deeds
Probate	1911	Clerk/District Ct.
Court	na	Clerk/District Ct.

■ Hamilton 20 Mar. 1873
P.O. Box 1167, Syracuse, KS 67878
Phone: (620)384-5629
Web site: http://skyways.lib.ks.us/genweb/hamilton/index.html
Parent County: Unorganized Territory

Record Type	Year Begun	Jurisdiction
Court	1886	Clerk/District Ct.

Divorce	1886	Clerk/District Ct.
Land	1884	Registrar/Deeds
Probate	1886	Clerk/District Ct.

■ Harper 1873
201 N. Jennings Ave., Anthony, KS 67003
Phone: (620)842-5555
Web site: www.harpercounty.org/
Parent County: Marion

Record Type	Year Begun	Jurisdiction
Marriage	1878	Clerk/District Ct.
Land	1878	Registrar/Deeds
Probate	1883	Clerk/District Ct.
Court	1883	Clerk/District Ct.

■ Harvey 7 Mar. 1872
800 N. Main, P.O. Box 687, Newton, KS 67114
Phone: (316)284-6842
Web site: http://skyways.lib.ks.us/genweb/harvey/index.html
Parent County: McPherson, Sedgwick, Marion
Comments/research tips: Clerk of District Court has Divorce records 1877–1917 and Marriage records 1872–1951. Registrar of Deeds has Military Discharge records 1919–1945.

Record Type	Year Begun	Jurisdiction
Land	1862	Registrar/Deeds
Probate	1872	Clerk/District Ct.
Court	1877	Clerk/District Ct.

■ Haskell 1 July 1887
P.O. Box 518, Sublette, KS 67877
Phone: (620)675-2263
Web site: www.haskellcounty.org/
Parent County: Finney

Record Type	Year Begun	Jurisdiction
Marriage	1887	Probate Judge
Court	1875	Clerk/District Ct.
Divorce	1887	Clerk/District Ct.
Probate	1875	Clerk/District Ct.

■ Hodgeman 26 Feb. 1867
500 Main St., P.O. Box 247, Jetmore, KS 67854
Phone: (620)357-6421
Web site: http://skyways.lib.ks.us/genweb/hodgeman/index.html
Parent County: Marion

Record Type	Year Begun	Jurisdiction
Divorce	1887	Clerk/District Ct.
Land	1879	Registrar/Deeds
Probate	1887	Clerk/District Ct.
Court	1887	Clerk/District Ct.

■ Howard 26 Feb. 1867
Parent County: Original county
Comments/research tips: (See Elk and Chautauqua) Originated as Godfrey County. Name changed to Seward, old in 1861. Name changed to Howard in 1867. Howard divided to form Elk and Chautauqua Counties in 1875.

■ **Hunter** 1855
Parent County: Original county
Comments/research tips: Annexed into Butler County 1864.

■ **Jackson** 11 Feb. 1859
400 New York Ave., Holton, KS 66436
Phone: (785)364-2891
Web site: http://skyways.lib.ks.us/genweb/jackson/
index.html
Parent County: Original county
Comments/research tips: County Clerk has Birth and Death records 1902–1911. Registrar of Deeds has Military Discharge records 1862–1965. Formerly Calhoun County. Name changed to Jackson 11 February 1859.

Record Type	Year Begun	Jurisdiction
Marriage	1855	County Clerk
Divorce	1859	Clerk/District Ct.
Land	1857	Registrar/Deeds
Probate	1855	Probate Court
Court	1858	Clerk/District Ct.
Nat.	1868	Clerk/District Ct.

■ **Jefferson** 25 Aug. 1855
300 W. Jefferson St., P.O. Box 321, Oskaloosa, KS 66066
Phone: (785)863-2272
Web site: www.jfcountyks.com
Parent County: Original county

Record Type	Year Begun	Jurisdiction
Marriage	1856	County Clerk
Divorce	na	Clerk/District Ct.
Land	1856	Registrar/Deeds
Probate	1855	Clerk/District Ct.

■ **Jewell** 1870
307 N. Commercial, Mankato, KS 66956
Phone: (785)378-4020
Web site: http://skyways.lib.ks.us/counties/JW
Parent County: Unorganized Territory
Comments/research tips: Registrar of Deeds has Birth and Death records 1886–1908.

Record Type	Year Begun	Jurisdiction
Marriage	1871	Clerk/District Ct.
Divorce	1813	Clerk/District Ct.
Land	1871	Registrar/Deeds
Probate	1813	Clerk/District Ct.
Court	1813	Clerk/District Ct.

■ **Johnson** 25 Aug. 1855
111 S. Cherry, Suite 1200, Olathe, KS 66061
Phone: (913)715-0780
Web site: www.jocoks.com/
Parent County: Original county

Record Type	Year Begun	Jurisdiction
Marriage	1857	Probate Court
Divorce	1860	Clerk/District Ct.
Probate	1857	Probate Court
Court	1861	Clerk/District Ct.
Land	1857	Registrar/Deeds
Nat.	1870	Clerk/District Ct.

■ **Kansas** 1873
Parent County: Unorganized Territory
Comments/research tips: Created in 1873 from unorganized lands, absorbed into Seward County in 1883. In 1886 it was reorganized under the name of Morton County.

■ **Kearny** 27 Mar. 1888
305 N. Main St., P.O. Box 86, Lakin, KS 67860
Phone: (620)355-6422
Web site: http://skyways.lib.ks.us/genweb/kearny
Parent County: Unorganized Territory
Comments/research tips: County Clerk has Birth, Marriage, and Death records 1900–1910. You can find Newspapers with County Clerk and Historical Society. Created in 1873 from the unorganized lands. It was absorbed by Finney and Hamilton Counties in 1883. In 1887 it was re-created with its same boundaries and was formally organized in 1889. A fire in 1904 destroyed many county records.

Record Type	Year Begun	Jurisdiction
Divorce	1894	Clerk/District Ct.
Land	1894	Registrar/Deeds
Probate	1895	Clerk/District Ct.
Court	1894	Clerk/District Ct.
Local Census	1913	County Appraiser

■ **Kingman** 7 Mar. 1872
138 N. Spruce St., Kingman, KS 67068
Phone: (620)523-2521
Web site: http://skyways.lib.ks.us/counties/KM
Parent County: Reno

Record Type	Year Begun	Jurisdiction
Marriage	1875	Clerk/District Ct.
Divorce	1874	Clerk/District Ct.
Land	1874	Registrar/Deeds
Probate	1874	Clerk/District Ct.
Court	1874	Clerk/District Ct.

■ **Kiowa** 25 Mar. 1886
211 E. Florida, Greensburg, KS 67054
Phone: (620)723-3366
Web site: http://skyways.lib.ks.us/genweb/kiowa
Parent County: Comanche, Edwards

Record Type	Year Begun	Jurisdiction
Land	1886	Registrar/Deeds
Probate	1886	Clerk/District Ct.
Court	1886	Clerk/District Ct.

■ **Kiowa, old** 26 Feb. 1867
Parent County: Marion
Comments/research tips: Kiowa County absorbed by Edwards and Comanche Counties in 1875. Kiowa re-created 10 February 1886 from parts of Edwards and Comanche.

■ **Labette** 26 Feb. 1867
517 Merchant St., P.O. Box 387, Oswego, KS 67356
Phone: (620)795-2138
Web site: www.labettecounty.com/
Parent County: Neosho

Comments/research tips: County Clerk has Birth records 1885–1891 and Death records 1885–1889. Registrar of Deeds has Land records 1868–1919. Probate Court has Marriage records 1867–1920. A yearly county census taken 1915–1979.

Record Type	Year Begun	Jurisdiction
Divorce	1870	Clerk/District Ct.
Probate	1868	Probate Court
Court	1870	Clerk/District Ct.
Wills	1868	Probate Court

■ Lane 3 June 1886
144 S. Lane, P.O. Box 788, Dighton, KS 67839
Phone: (620)397-5356
Web site: http://skyways.l.b.ks.usLE/
Parent County: Unorganized Territory, Pekedon Territory

Record Type	Year Begun	Jurisdiction
Divorce	1887	Clerk/District Ct.
Land	1887	Registrar/Deeds
Probate	1887	Clerk/District Ct.
Court	1887	Clerk/District Ct.

■ Leavenworth 25 Aug. 1855
300 Walnut, Leavenworth, KS 66048
Phone: (913)684-0422
Web site: www.leavenworthcounty.org/
Parent County: Original county
Comments/research tips: City Hall has Death records 1891–1911. Clerk of District Court has Divorce records 1868–1917 and Naturalization records 1859–1906. Registrar of Deeds has Military records 1861–1865, 1919–1920, 1935–1946.

Record Type	Year Begun	Jurisdiction
Marriage	1855	Probate Judge
Land	1857	Registrar/Deeds
Probate	1855	Probate Court
Court	1855	Clerk/District Ct.
Wills	1857	Probate Court

■ Lincoln 1870
216 E. Lincoln, Lincoln, KS 67455-2097
Phone: (785)524-4757
Web site: http://skyways.lib.ks.us/genweb/lincoln/
Parent County: Unorganized Territory
Comments/research tips: Lincoln City Hall has Death records 1886–1989.

Record Type	Year Begun	Jurisdiction
Marriage	1871	Clerk/District Ct.
Land	1871	Registrar/Deeds
Probate	1880	Clerk/District Ct.
Court	1880	Clerk/District Ct.
Divorce	1880	Clerk/District Ct.
Birth	1886	Lincoln City Hall

■ Linn 30 Aug. 1855
315 Main St., P.O. Box 350, Mound City, KS 66056
Phone: (913)795-2668
Web site: http://skyways.lib.ks.us/genweb/linn/
Parent County: Original county

Comments/research tips: Registrar of Deeds has Military records 1919–1960.

Record Type	Year Begun	Jurisdiction
Birth	1885	County Clerk
Marriage	1855	County Clerk/Probate Judge
Death	1885	County Clerk
Divorce	1856	County Clerk
Probate	1856	Probate Court
Court	1856	County Clerk
Land	1857	Registrar/Deeds
Nat.	1868	District Court
Wills	1866	Probate Court

■ Logan 17 Sep. 1887
710 W. Second, Oakley, KS 67748
Phone: (785)672-4244
Web site: http://skyways.lib.ks.us/genweb/logan/index.html
Parent County: St. John
Comments/research tips: Clerk of District Court has Naturalization records 1908–1926. Formerly St. John County. Name changed to Logan 24 February 1887.

Record Type	Year Begun	Jurisdiction
Marriage	1888	Clerk/District Ct.
Divorce	1887	Clerk/District Ct.
Land	1885	Registrar/Deeds
Probate	1887	Clerk/District Ct.
Court	1887	Clerk/District Ct.

■ Lykins 25 Aug. 1855
Parent County: Original county
Comments/research tips: (See Miami) Name changed to Miami 3 June 1861.

■ Lyon 1858
430 Commercial, Emporia, KS 66801
Phone: (620)341-3245
Web site: www.lyoncounty.org/
Parent County: Original County
Comments/research tips: Formerly Breckenridge County. Name changed to Lyon 5 February 1862.

Record Type	Year Begun	Jurisdiction
Birth	1885	County Historical Society
Marriage	1856	Clerk/District Ct.
Death	1885	County Historical Society
Divorce	1860	Clerk/District Ct.
Land	1856	Registrar/Deeds
Probate	1859	Clerk/District Ct.
Court	1858	Clerk/District Ct.

■ Madison 1855
Parent County: Original county
Comments/research tips: Created in 1855. In 1861 it was divided between Greenwood and and Breckinridge (now Lyon).

■ Marion 30 Aug. 1855
P.O. Box 219, Madison, KS 66861
Phone: (620)382-2185
Web site: http://skyways.lib.ks.us/genweb/marion/

Kansas

Parent County: Original county

Comments/research tips: County Clerk has Birth and Death records 1885–1902. Registrar of Deeds has School records 1873–1964. Created 30 August 1855 as an original county but disappeared with the Act of 1857 (or 1859). It was organized in 1860 as a much smaller county and was enlarged in 1865 to include Peketon area. It was reduced in area as other counties were formed from it.

Record Type	Year Begun	Jurisdiction
Marriage	1866	Probate Court
Divorce	na	Clerk/District Ct.
Land	1870	Registrar/Deeds
Probate	1870	Probate Court
Court	1867	Clerk/District Ct.
Nat.	1870	District Court

■ **Marshall** 25 Aug. 1855

1201 Broadway, Marysville, KS 66508-1844

Phone: (785)562-5361

Web site: http://skyways.lib.ks.us/genweb/marshall/

Parent County: Original county

Comments/research tips: County Clerk has Birth records 1885–1911 and Death records 1889–1911.

Record Type	Year Begun	Jurisdiction
Marriage	1857	Probate Court
Divorce	1863	Clerk/District Ct.
Land	1859	Probate Court
Probate	1857	Probate Court
Court	1858	Clerk/District Ct.

■ **McGee** 30 Aug. 1855

Parent County: Unorganized Territory

Comments/research tips: Created 25 August 1855 as an original county. Name changed to Cherokee County 18 February 1860.

■ **McPherson** 1 Mar. 1870

P.O. Box 425, McPherson, KS 67460

Phone: (620)241-3656

Web site: www.mcphersoncountyks.us

Parent County: Peketon, Marion

Comments/research tips: County Clerk has Birth and Death records 1874–1911. Clerk of District Court has Marriage records 1870–1951, Naturalization records 1908–1929, and Probate records 1859–1923. Originally part of Peketon County. Became a township of Marion County when Peketon was abolished. Organized as a county in 1870.

Record Type	Year Begun	Jurisdiction
Divorce	1871	Clerk/District Ct.
Land	1870	Registrar/Deeds
Court	1871	Clerk/District Ct.

■ **Meade** 30 Mar. 1873

200 N. Fowler St., P.O. Box 278, Meade, KS 67864

Phone: (620)873-8700

Web site: http://skyways.lib.ks.us/genweb/meade/

Parent County: Unorganized Territory

Comments/research tips: Created 30 March 1873 from unorganized lands. It was divided in 1883 between Seward, Finney, and Ford Counties. On 3 November 1885 it was reorganized in the same area but with slightly different boundaries.

Record Type	Year Begun	Jurisdiction
Birth	ca. 1900	Clerk/District Ct.
Marriage	ca. 1900	Probate Judge
Divorce	ca. 1900	Clerk/District Ct.
Land	1884	Registrar/Deeds
Probate	ca. 1900	Clerk/District Ct.
Court	ca. 1900	Clerk/District Ct.

■ **Miami** 30 Aug. 1855

201 S. Pearl St., Suite 102, Paola, KS 66071

Phone: (913)294-3976

Web site: www.miamicountyks.org/

Parent County: Original county

Comments/research tips: Formerly Lykins County. Name changed to Miami 3 June 1861.

Record Type	Year Begun	Jurisdiction
Birth	1885	Probate Court
Marriage	1857	Probate Court
Death	1885	Probate Court
Land	1857	Registrar/Deeds
Probate	1857	Probate Court
Court	1858	Clerk/District Ct.
Nat.	1867	Clerk/District Ct.
Wills	1857	Probate Court
Divorce	1857	Clerk/District Ct.

■ **Mitchell** 26 Feb. 1867

111 S. Henry, P.O. Box 190, Beloit, KS 67420

Phone: (785)738-3652

Web site: http://skyways.lib.ks.us/genweb/mitchell/

Parent County: Unorganized Territory

Record Type	Year Begun	Jurisdiction
Marriage	1870	Clerk/District Ct.
Divorce	1875	Clerk/District Ct.
Land	1871	Registrar/Deeds
Probate	ca. 1870	Clerk/District Ct.
Court	ca. 1875	Clerk/District Ct.

■ **Montgomery** 26 Feb. 1867

217 E. Myrtle, P.O. Box 446, Independence, KS 67301

Phone: (620)330-1200

Web site: http://skyways.lib.ks.us/genweb/montgome/index.html

Parent County: Wilson

Comments/research tips: County Clerk has Birth records 1888–1911 and Death records 1887–1911. Registrar of Deeds has Land records 1870–1886. Clerk of District Court has Marriage records 1870–1918 and Naturalization records 1870–1917.

Record Type	Year Begun	Jurisdiction
Divorce	1871	Clerk/District Ct.
Probate	1870	Clerk/District Ct.
Court	1871	Clerk/District Ct.
Wills	1870	Clerk/District Ct.

■ **Morris** 30 Aug. 1855

501 W. Main St., Council Grove, KS 66846

Phone: (620)767-5518

Web site: http://skyways.lib.ks.us/genweb/morris/
Parent County: Original county
Comments/research tips: County Clerk has Military Discharge records 1917–1999. Clerk of District Court has Naturalization records 1907–1929. Formerly Wise County, name changed to Morris 11 February 1859.

Record Type	Year Begun	Jurisdiction
Marriage	1859	Clerk/District Ct.
Divorce	1860	Clerk/District Ct.
Land	1858	Registrar/Deeds
Probate	1856	Probate Court
Court	1860	Clerk/District Ct.

■ Morton   18 Feb. 1886
1025 Morton St., P.O. Box 1116, Elkhart, KS 67950-1116
Phone: (620)697-2157
Web site: www.mtcoks.org
Parent County: Seward

Record Type	Year Begun	Jurisdiction
Marriage	1887	Clerk/District Ct.
Divorce	ca. 1900	Clerk/District Ct.
Land	1886	Registrar/Deeds
Court	ca. 1900	County Clerk
Probate	ca. 1900	Clerk/District Ct.

■ Nemaha   30 Aug. 1855
607 Nemaha, P.O. Box 186, Seneca, KS 66538
Phone: (785)336-2170
Web site: http://skyways.lib.ks.us/genweb/nemaha/
Parent County: Original county
Comments/research tips: County Clerk has Birth, Marriage, and Death records 1885–1911. Courthouse burned in 1876. Some records were destroyed.

Record Type	Year Begun	Jurisdiction
Divorce	1857	Clerk/District Ct.
Marriage	1861	Probate Court
Probate	1857	Probate Court
Court	1859	Clerk/District Ct.
Nat.	1859	Clerk/District Ct.
Land	1858	Registrar/Deeds

■ Neosho   3 June 1861
100 S. Main St., P.O. Box 138, Erie, KS 66733
Phone: (620)244-3811
Web site: http://skyways.lib.ks.us/genweb/neosho/
Parent County: Dorn
Comments/research tips: Registrar of Deeds has Military Discharge records 1883–1947. Formerly Dorn County. Name changed to Neosho in 1861 and formally organized in 1864.

Record Type	Year Begun	Jurisdiction
Marriage	1864	Probate Court
Land	1866	Registrar/Deeds
Probate	1867	Probate Court
Nat.	1868	Clerk/District Ct.
Birth	1892	County Clerk
Death	1892	County Clerk
Court	1867	Probate Court
Wills	1867	Probate Court

■ Ness   26 Feb. 1867
202 W. Sycamore St., Ness City, KS 67560
Phone: (785)798-2401
Web site: http://skyways.lib.ks.us/genweb/ness/index.html
Parent County: Unorganized Territory, Peketon Territory
Comments/research tips: Created in 1867 from unorganized lands. It was first organized in 1873, then disorganized in 1874, and reorganized 14 April 1880.

Record Type	Year Begun	Jurisdiction
Marriage	1876	Clerk/District Ct.
Divorce	1876	Clerk/District Ct.
Land	1874	Registrar/Deeds
Probate	1876	Clerk/District Ct.
Court	1876	Clerk/District Ct.

■ Norton   26 Feb. 1867
105 S. Kansas, P.O. Box 70, Norton, KS 67654-0070
Phone: (785)877-5710
Web site: http://skyways.lib.ks.us/genweb/norton/index.html
Parent County: Unorganized Territory
Comments/research tips: Name changed to Billings 6 March 1873. Name changed back to Norton 19 February 1874. Registrar of Deeds has some Cemetery records. Courthouse destroyed by fire 1 December 1926. Records prior to 1926 are incomplete.

Record Type	Year Begun	Jurisdiction
Birth	1874	County Clerk
Marriage	1875	Clerk/District Ct.
Death	1874	County Clerk
Divorce	1874	Clerk/District Ct.
Land	1874	Registrar/Deeds
Probate	1872	Clerk/District Ct.
Court	1874	Clerk/District Ct.

■ Old Arapahoe   1855
Parent County: Original county
Comments/research tips: Was under the territory of Kansas. Became part of the Colorado territory in 1861.

■ Oro   7 Feb. 1859
Parent County: Original county
Comments/research tips: Now part of Colorado.

■ Osage   11 Feb. 1859
717 Topeka Ave., P.O. Box 226, Lyndon, KS 66451-0226
Phone: (785)828-4812
Web site: www.osage.kansasgov.com
Parent County: Original County
Comments/research tips: County Clerk has Birth records 1886–1921 and Death records 1885–1909. Formerly Weller County. Name changed to Osage 11 February 1859.

Record Type	Year Begun	Jurisdiction
Divorce	1861	District Court
Land	1858	Registrar/Deeds
Court	1861	District Court
Marriage	1889	District Court
Nat.	1870	District Court
Probate	1859	Probate Court
Wills	1861	Probate Court

Kansas

■ **Osborne** 26 Feb. 1867
423 W. Main , P.O. Box 160, Osborne, KS 67473
Phone: (785)346-2431
Web site: http://skyways.lib.ks.us/genweb/osborne/
index.html
Parent County: Unorganized Territory
Comments/research tips: Created in 1867 from unorganized
lands in Kansas. It was formally organized in 1871.

Record Type	Year Begun	Jurisdiction
Marriage	1872	Probate Judge
Divorce	1872	Probate Judge
Land	1872	Registrar/Deeds
Probate	1872	Probate Judge
Court	1872	Probate Judge

■ **Otoe** 17 Feb. 1860
Parent County: Marion
Comments/research tips: Became part of Butler County 24
February 1864.

■ **Ottawa** 27 Feb. 1860
307 N. Concord, Minneapolis, KS 67467
Phone: (785)392-2279
Web site: www.ottawacounty.org
Parent County: Unorganized Territory
Comments/research tips: Clerk of District Court has
Marriage records 1868–1890. Created in 1860 from
unorganized lands. It was formally organized in 1866.

Record Type	Year Begun	Jurisdiction
Birth	1890	Clerk/District Ct.
Death	1890	Clerk/District Ct.
Divorce	1890	Clerk/District Ct.
Land	1867	Registrar/Deeds
Probate	1890	Clerk/District Ct.

■ **Pawnee** 26 Feb. 1867
715 Broadway, Larned, KS 67550-3098
Phone: (620)285-3721
Web site: http://skyways.lib.ks.us/genweb/pawnee/
index.html
Parent County: Marion

Record Type	Year Begun	Jurisdiction
Marriage	1873	Clerk/District Ct.
Divorce	ca. 1867	Clerk/District Ct.
Land	1867	Registrar/Deeds
Probate	ca. 1867	Clerk/District Ct.
Court	ca. 1867	Clerk/District Ct.

■ **Peketon** 1854
Parent County: Original territory
Comments/research tips: Abolished in 1867.

■ **Phillips** 26 Feb. 1867
301 State St., Phillipsburg, KS 67661
Phone: (785)543-6825
Web site: www.phillipscounty.org
Parent County: Unorganized Territory
Comments/research tips: Clerk of District Court has Birth,
Death, Marriage records 1872–1924, and Naturalization

records 1876–1906. Phillips County Genealogical Society
has Military records 1861–1865. County formally
organized in 1872.

Record Type	Year Begun	Jurisdiction
Divorce	1867	Clerk/District Ct.
Land	1867	Registrar/Deeds
Probate	1867	Clerk/District Ct.
Court	1867	Clerk/District Ct.

■ **Pottawatomie** 20 Feb. 1857
207 N. First, P.O. Box 187, Westmoreland, KS 66549-0187
Phone: (785)457-3314
Web site: www.pottcounty.org/
Parent County: Riley
Comments/research tips: County Clerk has Birth and Death
records 1885–1911. Registrar of Deeds has Military
Discharge records 1919–1970.

Record Type	Year Begun	Jurisdiction
Divorce	na	Unified Court System
Land	1858	Registrar/Deeds
Probate	1857	Probate Court
Court	1861	County Court
Marriage	1858	Probate Court
Nat.	1866	District Court

■ **Pratt** 26 Feb. 1867
300 S. Ninnescah St., P.O. Box 885, Pratt, KS 67124
Phone: (620)672-4110
Web site: www.prattcounty.org/
Parent County: Marion
Comments/research tips: Clerk of District Court has
Marriage records 1878–1911.

Record Type	Year Begun	Jurisdiction
Divorce	ca. 1879	Clerk/District Ct.
Land	ca. 1879	Registrar/Deeds
Probate	ca. 1979	Clerk/District Ct.
Court	ca. 1879	Clerk/District Ct.

■ **Rawlins** 20 Mar. 1873
607 Main St., Atwood, KS 67730
Phone: (785)626-3351
Web site: http://skyways.lib.ks.us/genweb/rawlins/
Parent County: Unorganized Territory
Comments/research tips: Clerk of District Court has
Marriage records 1880–1920.

Record Type	Year Begun	Jurisdiction
Land	1881	Registrar/Deeds
Probate	1881	Clerk/District Ct.
Court	1881	Clerk/District Ct.

■ **Reno** 1873
206 W. First, Hutchinson, KS 67501
Phone: (620)694-2514
Web site: www.renogov.com
Parent County: Marion
Comments/research tips: County Clerk has Birth and Death
records 1890–1911 and Cemetery records 1865–1978.

Record Type	Year Begun	Jurisdiction
Divorce	1872	Clerk/District Ct.

Record Type	Year Begun	Jurisdiction
Probate	1872	Clerk/District Ct.
Court	1872	Clerk/District Ct.
Marriage	1872	County Clerk
Land	1872	Registrar/Deeds

■ Republic 1867

P.O. Box 429, Belleville, KS 66935
Phone: (785)527-5691
Web site: http://skyways.lib.ks.us/genweb/republic/
Parent County: Original county, unorganized land

Record Type	Year Begun	Jurisdiction
Land	1865	Registrar/Deeds
Probate	ca. 1868	Clerk/District Ct.
Court	ca. 1868	Clerk/District Ct.
Marriage	1872	Clerk/District Ct.

■ Rice 1871

101 W. Commercial St., Lyons, KS 67554
Phone: (620)257-2232
Web site: http://skyways.lib.ks.us/genweb/rice/
Parent County: Marion
Comments/research tips: Lyons City Clerk has Birth records 1890–1911. Clerk of District Court has Naturalization records 1907–1929.

Record Type	Year Begun	Jurisdiction
Marriage	1872	Clerk/District Ct.
Divorce	1898	Clerk/District Ct.
Land	1872	Registrar/Deeds
Probate	1898	Clerk of Probate Court
Court	1898	Clerk/District Ct.

■ Richardson 25 Aug. 1855

Parent County: Original county
Comments/research tips: Name changed to Wabaunsee 11 February 1859.

■ Riley 25 Aug. 1855

110 Courthouse Plaza, Manhattan, KS 66502
Phone: (785)537-6300
Web site: www.co.riley.ks.us/
Parent County: Original county
Comments/research tips: County Clerk has Birth and Death records 1892–1909. Registrar of Deeds has Military Discharge records 1919–1953.

Record Type	Year Begun	Jurisdiction
Court	1859	District Court
Land	1859	Registrar/Deeds
Probate	1857	Probate Court
Divorce	1859	District Court
Nat.	1859	District Court
Marriage	1856	Probate Court

■ Rooks 1872

115 N. Walnut St., Stockton, KS 67669-1663
Phone: (785)425-6391
Web site: http://skyways.lib.ks.us/genweb/rooks/
Parent County: Unorganized Territory
Comments/research tips: Clerk of District Court has Birth and Death records 1888–1901.

Record Type	Year Begun	Jurisdiction
Marriage	1874	Clerk/District Ct.
Divorce	1872	Clerk/District Ct.
Land	1872	Registrar/Deeds
Probate	1872	Clerk/District Ct.
Court	1872	Clerk/District Ct.

■ Rush 1874

715 Elm, P.O. Box 220, La Crosse, KS 67548
Phone: (785)222-2731
Web site: http://skyways.lib.ks.us/genweb/rush/
Parent County: Unorganized Territory

Record Type	Year Begun	Jurisdiction
Marriage	ca. 1876	Clerk/District Ct.
Divorce	1874	Clerk/District Ct.
Land	1874	Registrar/Deeds
Probate	1874	Clerk/District Ct.
Court	1874	Clerk/District Ct.

■ Russell 1872

P.O. Box 113, Russell, KS 67665
Phone: (785)483-4641
Web site: http://skyways.lib.ks.us/genweb/russell/
Parent County: Unorganized Territory

Record Type	Year Begun	Jurisdiction
Marriage	1873	Clerk/District Ct.
Divorce	1872	Clerk/District Ct.
Probate	1872	Clerk/District Ct.
Court	1872	Clerk/District Ct.

■ Saline 15 Feb. 1860

300 W. Ash, Salina, KS 67401
Phone: (785)309-5820
Web site: www.co.saline.ks.us/
Parent County: Unorganized land

Record Type	Year Begun	Jurisdiction
Marriage	1860	Clerk/District Ct.
Land	ca. 1860	Registrar/Deeds
Probate	ca. 1860	Clerk/District Ct.
Court	1870	Clerk/District Ct.

■ Scott 1886

303 Court St., Scott City, KS 67871
Phone: (620)872-2420
Web site: http://skyways.lib.ks.us/genweb/scott/
Parent County: Unorganized Territory

Record Type	Year Begun	Jurisdiction
Marriage	1886	Probate Judge
Divorce	1886	Clerk/District Ct.
Probate	1886	Clerk/District Ct.
Court	1886	Clerk/District Ct.
Land	1886	Registrar/Deeds

■ Sedgwick 1870

515 N. Main, Suite 211, Wichita, KS 67203
Phone: (316)383-7666
Web site: http://skyways.lib.ks.us/genweb/sedgwick/
Parent County: Butler, Marion
Comments/research tips: Clerk of District Court has Naturalization records 1870–1926.

Kansas

Record Type	Year Begun	Jurisdiction
Marriage	1870	Clerk/District Ct.
Land	1870	Registrar/Deeds
Probate	1870	Clerk/District Ct.
Court	1870	District Court

■ Sequoyah 1873
Parent County: Marion
Comments/research tips: (See Finney) Name changed to Finney 21 February 1883.

■ Seward 17 Jan. 1886
415 N. Washington, Liberal, KS 67901
Phone: (620)626-3204
Web site: www.seward.kansasgov.com
Parent County: Unorganized land
Comments/research tips: Created in 1873 from the unorganized lands in southwestern Kansas (not the old Seward County in eastern Kansas). It was absorbed in 1883 by Kansas, Stevens, and part of Meade Counties. In 1886 it was organized and reduced as counties were divided from it.

Record Type	Year Begun	Jurisdiction
Marriage	ca. 1886	Clerk/District Ct.
Divorce	ca. 1886	Clerk/District Ct.
Land	1886	Registrar/Deeds
Probate	ca. 1886	Clerk/District Ct.
Court	ca. 1886	Clerk/District Ct.

■ Seward, Old 30 Aug. 1855
Parent County: Original county
Comments/research tips: Created in 1855 as Godfrey County. In 1861 its name was changed to Seward (not the modern southwestern county of Seward). Its name was changed again in 1867 to Howard County. In 1875 Howard County was divided into Elk and Chautauqua Counties.

■ Shawnee 25 Aug. 1855
200 E. Seventh, Room 107, Topeka, KS 66603
Phone: (785)233-8200
Web site: www.co.shawnee.ks.us/
Parent County: Original county
Comments/research tips: County Clerk has Birth, Marriage, and Death records 1894–1911. Third Judicial District Court has Marriage records 1856–1913.

Record Type	Year Begun	Jurisdiction
Land	1859	Registrar/Deeds
Probate	1859	Probate Court
Nat.	1865	District Court

■ Sheridan 1880
925 Eighth St., P.O. Box 899, Hoxie, KS 67740
Phone: (785)675-3361
Web site: http://skyways.lib.ks.us/genweb/sheridan/
Parent County: Unorganized Territory

Record Type	Year Begun	Jurisdiction
Marriage	ca. 1885	Clerk/District Ct.
Divorce	ca. 1885	Clerk/District Ct.
Land	1880	Registrar/Deeds

Probate	1881	Clerk/District Ct.
Court	ca. 1885	Clerk/District Ct.

■ Sherman 1886
813 Broadway, Room 102, Goodland, KS 67735
Phone: (785)899-4802
Web site: http://skyways.lib.ks.us/genweb/sherman/
Parent County: Unorganized Territory
Comments/research tips: County Clerk has Birth and Death records 1888–1892 and Marriage records 1886–1923.

Record Type	Year Begun	Jurisdiction
Divorce	1887	Clerk/District Ct.
Land	1886	Registrar/Deeds
Probate	1886	Clerk/District Ct.
Court	1887	Clerk/District Ct.

■ Shirley 6 Sep. 1866
Parent County: Original county
Comments/research tips: Shirley County was attached to Marshall County for judicial purposes prior to its organization. Name changed to Cloud 26 February 1867.

■ Smith 1872
218 S. Grant St., Smith Center, KS 66967
Phone: (785)282-5110
Web site: http://skyways.lib.ks.us/genweb/smith/
Parent County: Unorganized Territory

Record Type	Year Begun	Jurisdiction
Marriage	1875	Probate Judge
Divorce	1875	Clerk/District Ct.
Land	1872	County Clerk
Probate	1875	Probate Judge
Court	1875	Clerk/District Ct.

■ St. John 13 Mar. 1881
Parent County: Wallace
Comments/research tips: Name changed to Logan 25 February 1887.

■ Stafford 1879
209 N. Broadway St., St. John, KS 67576
Phone: (620)549-3509
Web site: www.staffordcounty.org
Parent County: Marion
Comments/research tips: County Court has Birth and Death records 1885–1894.

Record Type	Year Begun	Jurisdiction
Land	1879	Registrar/Deeds
Probate	1879	Probate Judge
Court	1879	Probate Judge
Marriage	1879	Probate Judge

■ Stanton 1887
210 N. Main, P.O. Box 190, Johnson, KS 67855-0190
Phone: (620)492-2140
Web site: http://skyways.lib.ks.us/genweb/stanton/
Parent County: Unorganized Territory
Comments/research tips: Absorbed by Hamilton County 1883. Reorganized February 1887.

Record Type	Year Begun	Jurisdiction
Marriage	1887	Clerk/District Ct.
Divorce	1887	Clerk/District Ct.
Land	1887	Registrar/Deeds
Probate	1887	Clerk/District Ct.
Court	1887	Clerk/District Ct.

■ Stevens 1886

200 E. Sixth St., Hugoton, KS 67951-2652

Phone: (620)544-2541

Web site: http://skyways.lib.ks.us/genweb/stevens/index.html

Parent County: Unorganized land

Comments/research tips: Registrar of Deeds has Military records 1914–1918. Stevens County was absorbed by Seward County in 1883. In 1886 it was reorganized with the same boundaries as it had in 1873.

Record Type	Year Begun	Jurisdiction
Land	1888	Registrar/Deeds
Probate	1887	Probate Court
Court	1887	Clerk/District Ct.
Nat.	1887	District Court

■ Sumner 1871

501 N. Washington, Wellington, KS 67152

Phone: (620)326-3395

Web site: co.sumner.ks.us/

Parent County: Butler, Marion

Comments/research tips: County Court has Birth records 1887–1911 and Death records 1893–1911. Clerk of District Court has Marriage records 1871–1899.

Record Type	Year Begun	Jurisdiction
Land	1873	Registrar/Deeds
Probate	1871	Clerk/District Ct.
Court	1871	Clerk/District Ct.

■ Thomas 6 Mar. 1873

300 N. Court St., Colby, KS 67701

Phone: (785)462-4500

Web site: http://skyways.lib.ks.us/genweb/thomas/

Parent County: Unorganized Territory

Comments/research tips: County Clerk has Birth and Death records 1885–1910. Probate Court has Marriage records 1885–1910.

Record Type	Year Begun	Jurisdiction
Divorce	1885	Clerk/District Ct.
Land	1885	Registrar/Deeds
Probate	1885	Clerk/District Ct.
Court	1885	Clerk/District Ct.

■ Trego 26 Feb. 1867

216 Main St., WaKeeney, KS 67672-2189

Phone: (785)743-5773

Web site: http://skyways.lib.ks.us/genweb/trego/

Parent County: Unorganized Territory

Record Type	Year Begun	Jurisdiction
Land	1879	Registrar/Deeds
Marriage	1878	Clerk/District Ct.
Divorce	ca. 1900	Clerk/District Ct.
Probate	ca. 1900	Clerk/District Ct.
Court	ca. 1900	Clerk/District Ct.

■ Wabaunsee 30 Aug. 1855

215 Kansas St., Alma, KS 66401

Phone: (785)765-3414

Web site: http://skyways.lib.ks.us/genweb/wabaunse/

Parent County: Original county

Comments/research tips: County Clerk has Birth and Death records 1892–1911. Clerk of District Court has Divorce records 1857–1917 and Probate records 1857–1937. Created in 1855 as Richardson County and was an original county. Name changed to Wabaunsee in 1859.

Record Type	Year Begun	Jurisdiction
Court	1860	Clerk/District Ct.
Land	1858	Registrar/Deeds

■ Wallace 2 Mar. 1868

P.O. Box 70, Sharon Springs, KS 67758

Phone: (785)852-4282

Web site: http://skyways.lib.ks.us/genweb/wallace/

Parent County: Unorganized Territory

Comments/research tips: Clerk of District Court has Birth and Death records 1889–1911.

Record Type	Year Begun	Jurisdiction
Divorce	1889	Clerk/District Ct.
Land	1889	Registrar/Deeds
Probate	1889	Clerk/District Ct.
Court	1889	Clerk/District Ct.
Marriage	1887	Clerk/District Ct.

■ Washington 1859

214 C St., Washington, KS 66968-1928

Phone: (785)325-2974

Web site: http://skyways.lib.ks.us/genweb/washingt/index.html

Parent County: Unorganized Territory

Comments/research tips: County Clerk has Birth records 1887–1911 and Death records 1885–1911. Clerk of District Court has Marriage records 1862–1955 and Naturalization records 1907–1928.

Record Type	Year Begun	Jurisdiction
Land	1870	Registrar/Deeds
Probate	1862	Probate Court
Court	1872	Clerk/District Ct.

■ Washington, old 1855

Parent County: Original county

Comments/research tips: County absorbed by Peketon in 1860.

■ Weller 30 Aug. 1855

Parent County: Original county

Comments/research tips: (See Osage) Name changed to Osage 11 February 1859.

■ Wichita 6 Mar. 1873

206 S. Fourth St., P.O. Drawer 968, Leoti, KS 67861-0279

Phone: (620)375-2731

Web site: http://skyways.lib.ks.us/genweb/wichita/
Parent County: Indian Lands

Record Type	Year Begun	Jurisdiction
Marriage	1887	Clerk/District Ct.
Divorce	1887	Clerk/District Ct.
Land	1886	Registrar/Deeds
Probate	1887	Clerk/District Ct.
Court	1887	Clerk/District Ct.

■ Wilson 1867

615 Madison St., Fredonia, KS 66736
Phone: (626)378-2186
Web site: www.wilson.kansasgov.com
Parent County: Original county
Comments/research tips: Probate Judge has Probate records 1869–1918.

Record Type	Year Begun	Jurisdiction
Marriage	1864	Probate Court
Divorce	1869	Clerk/District Ct.
Land	1868	Registrar/Deeds
Court	1869	Probate Court

■ Wise 30 Aug. 1855

Parent County: Original county
Comments/research tips: (See Morris) Name changed to Morris 11 February 1859.

■ Woodson 30 Aug. 1855

105 W. Rutledge, Yates Center, KS 66783-1497
Phone: (620)625-8605
Web site: www.woodsoncounty.net/
Parent County: Original county
Comments/research tips: County Clerk has Birth and Death records 1853–1926.

Record Type	Year Begun	Jurisdiction
Marriage	1860	Probate Court
Land	1858	Registrar/Deeds
Probate	1864	Probate Court
Court	1864	Clerk/District Ct.

■ Wyandotte 29 Jan. 1859

710 N. Seventh St., Kansas City, KS 66101
Phone: (913)573-2867
Web site: www.wycokck.org/
Parent County: Leavenworth, Johnson
Comments/research tips: Clerk of District Court has Divorce records 1871–1918. District Court and Probate Court have Marriage records 1859–1917. Registrar of Deeds has Military Discharge records 1919–1929. District Court has Naturalization records 1859–1947.

Record Type	Year Begun	Jurisdiction
Court	1871	District Court
Land	na	Registrar/Deeds
Probate	1857	Probate Court Clerk

Kentucky

By Emily Anne Croom

HISTORICAL OVERVIEW

Long the home of Indian tribes, Kentucky lay within territory claimed but not settled by France in 1682. In the 1750s, British colonials began exploring west of the Appalachian Mountains, moving down the Ohio River or through the Cumberland Gap into Kentucky. Britain's Proclamation of 1763 forbidding settlement west of the crest of the Appalachian Mountains was largely ignored by land speculators and adventurous North Carolinians and Virginians, who began building stockaded settlements in Kentucky in the 1770s. The region fell within the jurisdiction of Fincastle County, Virginia, in 1772 and became Kentucky County, Virginia, in 1776. During the American Revolution, Indians allied with the British raided throughout the western frontiers, killing or driving out many Kentucky settlers.

After the Revolution, bounty land for military veterans and the lure of cheap, fertile soil attracted numerous settlers from the east, especially from the worn-out tobacco lands of Virginia, North Carolina, and Maryland. From Maryland, Pennsylvania, Virginia, and later from Ohio and Indiana, they often came via the Ohio River. Thousands from Virginia and the Carolinas traveled along the Wilderness Trail to the Cumberland Gap. Others arrived from neighboring Tennessee, and a few from Europe. After several calls for separation from Virginia, Kentucky became the fifteenth state in 1792.

The Ohio River became an avenue of commerce, with towns springing up along its banks. Some textile, timber, and mining industries developed in Kentucky. However, the majority of the state's residents were farmers and planters. Tobacco was king, and corn and wheat were staple crops of smaller farmers. By 1860, the state's population included about 20 percent slaves, about 5 percent

KENTUCKY AT A GLANCE

Motto: United We Stand, Divided We Fall

Population: 4.1 million

Prevalent Religions: Christianity, particularly Southern Baptist, Pentecostal, Lutheran, and Roman Catholic

Major Industries: Horses, tobacco, cattle, dairy products, hogs, soybeans, corn, transportation equipment, car manufacturing, petroleum, natural gas, electrical equipment, machinery, food processing, aluminum, coal, tourism

Ethnic Makeup (in percent): Caucasian 90.1%, African American 7.3%, Hispanic 1.5%, Asian 0.7%, Native American 0.2%, Other 0.6%

Famous Kentuckians: Muhammad Ali, Wendell Berry, Kit Carson, the Clooneys (Rosemary, Nick, and George), Johnny Depp, Crystal Gayle, Sue Grafton, David W. Griffith, bell hooks, the Judds, Barbara Kingsolver, Abraham Lincoln, Loretta Lynn, Thomas Merton, Bill Monroe, Patricia Neal, Diane Sawyer, Adlai Stevenson, Allen Tate, Hunter S. Thompson, Robert Penn Warren

Above: One of Kentucky's many country roads

© PhotoDisc/Getty Images

foreign-born immigrants, and less than 1 percent free blacks.

In spite of the presence of slavery, Kentucky had a large anti-slavery population. Choosing not to secede and with numerous families split over the issue, the state furnished troops to both sides during the Civil War. In this border state, many Kentuckians preferred neutrality in the war, but military engagements took place within its boundaries.

Important in the state's economy before the war, railroads, coal mining, and tobacco farming invigorated the economy after the war. The development of the Tennessee Valley Authority in the 1930s and the coming of World War II encouraged manufacturing growth in Kentucky. While coal and tobacco remained the leading industries, others gaining importance since World War II include lumber, whiskey, and food processing. By 1970, Kentucky's urban population surpassed the rural population by a small margin.

RECORD HIGHLIGHTS

Kentucky first attempted statewide vital registration from 1852 to 1862, but some cities and counties again created these records in the late nineteenth century. The Office of Vital Statistics maintains birth and death records from 1911 forward and marriage and divorce certificates after mid-1958. Online indexes and options for obtaining record copies are on the Web site <http://chs.ky.gov/publichealth/vital.htm>. The Kentucky Historical Society in Frankfort <http://history.ky.gov/> and the Filson Historical Society in Louisville <www.filsonhistorical.org> hold microfilm of nineteenth- and early twentieth-century vital records.

Until 1809, only the General Assembly could grant divorces; between 1809 and 1849 both the legislature and circuit courts had jurisdiction in these cases. The legislature was prohibited from handling divorces after 1849.

More than half of Kentucky's counties have suffered some degree of record loss from fire and storms. Alternate sources cannot replace all the information lost in disasters, but check for surviving records, resources of

Kentucky

parent and neighboring counties, and records created in local, state, and federal jurisdictions.

Kentucky has not taken state censuses. Although the 1790, 1800, and 1890 federal enumerations for Kentucky are lost, tax rolls provide important documentation of households from 1782 forward. Besides some published abstracts in libraries nationwide, microfilmed tax records are available at the Kentucky Historical Society, the Kentucky Department for Libraries and Archives <www.kdla.ky.gov/collections.htm>, the Filson Historical Society, the Family History Library, and Clayton Library in Houston, Texas <www.hpl.lib.tx.us/clayton/clmca9.html#Kentucky>.

Other Kentucky-specific records available at the state archives, Kentucky Historical Society, Filson Historical Society, or other research libraries include these:

- Draper manuscripts at the State Historical Society of Wisconsin and major libraries elsewhere, especially Series CC, Kentucky Papers, described in *Calendar of the Kentucky Papers of the Draper Collection of Manuscripts*, Mabel Clare Weaks, ed.

(Madison, Wis.: The State Historical Society of Wisconsin, 1925).

- Shane manuscripts, other than those in the Draper collection, at the Presbyterian Historical Society, Philadelphia, and on microfilm at major libraries; described in *The Shane Manuscript Collection: A Genealogical Guide to the Kentucky and Ohio Papers*, by William K. Hall (Galveston, Tex.: Frontier Press, 1990).

- *Index of Economic Material in Documents of the States of the United States: Kentucky, 1792–1904* Adelaide R. Hasse, ed. (Washington, D.C.: Carnegie Institution of Washington, 1910). This book can help identify material in state government documents.

- Kentucky militia records, 1786–1864.

- School censuses from 1888 forward.

- Confederate pensions to veterans or their widows from 1912 forward.

- records of depositors in Kentucky's two branches of the Freedman's Savings and Trust Company (FHL microfilm 928581).

Kentucky

STATE RESOURCES

■ ARCHIVES, LIBRARIES, AND SOCIETIES

Adair County Genealogical Society
P.O. Box 613, Columbia, KY 42728

Adair County Public Library
307 Greensburg St., Columbia, KY 42728-1488
Tel: (270) 384-2472
E-mail: adairlibrary@yahoo.com
Web site: <www.geocities.com/adairlibrary/>

Ancestral Trails Historical Society, Inc.
P.O. Box 573, Vine Grove, KY 40175
E-mail: info@aths.com
Web site: <www.aths.com>

Ballard-Carlisle Historical-Genealogical Society
P.O. Box 279, Wickliffe, KY 42087
Web site: <www.ballardconet.com/bchgs/>

Bell County Historical Society & Museum
P.O. Box 1344, Middlesboro, KY 40965
Web site: <www.geocities.com/bellhistorical/>

Boyd County Public Library
1740 Central Ave., Ashland, KY 41101
Tel: (606) 329-0090
Web site:

Breathitt County Public Library
1024 College Ave., Jackson, KY 41339-1016
Tel: (606) 666-5541
Web site:

Breckinridge County Public Library
112 S. Main St., P.O. Box 248, Hardinsburg, KY 40143-0248
Tel: (270) 756-2323

Bullitt County Genealogical Society
P.O. Box 960, Shepherdsville, KY 40165-0960

Butler County Historical & Genealogical Society
P.O. Box 435, Morgantown KY 42261-0435

Web site: <www.rootsweb.com/~kybutler/butler_books.html>

Cadiz, John L. Street Library
244 Main St., Cadiz, KY 42211-9153
Tel: (270) 522-6301

Campbell County Historical and Genealogical Society
19 E. Main St., Alexandria KY, 41001
Tel: (859) 635-6407
Web site: <www.rootsweb.com/~kycchgs/>

Christian County Genealogical Society
1101 Bethel St., Hopkinsville, KY 42240
Web site: <www.kyseeker.com/christian/ccgsbks.htm>

Clay County Genealogical and Historical Society
P.O. Box 394, Manchester, KY 40962
Web site: <members.tripod.com/~Sue_1/clay.html>

Corbin Genealogical Society
99 Boone Ave., Corbin, KY 40701

Crittenden County Genealogical Society
P.O. Box 61, Marion, KY 42054

Cynthiana-Harrison County Public Library
104 N. Main St., Cynthiana, KY 41031
Tel: (859) 234-4881
Web site:

Daviess County Public Library
450 Griffith Ave., Owensboro, KY 42301
Tel: (270) 684-0211
Web site:

Department for Health Services, Office of Vital Statistics
275 E. Main St., Frankfort, KY 40621
Tel: (502) 564-4212

Eastern Kentucky Genealogical Society
P.O. Box 1544, Ashland, KY 41101

Eastern Kentucky University Libraries
521 Lancaster Ave., 103 Libraries Complex, Richmond, KY 40475

RESEARCH TIPS

for more info

- Remember that someone reportedly born in Virginia before 1792 may have been born in what is now Kentucky.
- The state archives, state historical society, and Filson History Society hold numerous Kentucky research materials, including censuses, county records, and Kentucky newspapers.
- Because of its colonial beginnings, Kentucky was never federal public domain; land grants originated with the colonial and state governments. However, the process of acquiring land was confusing and inconsistent until after statehood. Microfilm of numerous Kentucky land grant records are available at the state archives and the Kentucky Historical Society. Subsequent land transactions between individuals were recorded at any court of record. Some of the early colonial Kentucky land entries are in the Fincastle County records, maintained with records of Montgomery County, Virginia, after Fincastle was abolished in 1777. No records of Kentucky County, Virginia, are known to survive.
- www.segenealogy.com

Census Records

- Federal Census Population Schedules: 1810, 1820, 1830, 1840, 1850, 1860, 1870, 1880, 1900, 1910, 1920, 1930
- Federal Census Soundex or Miracode: 1880, 1900, 1910, 1920, 1930 (currently 7 counties)
- Federal Mortality Schedules: 1850, 1860, 1870, 1880
- Federal Slave Schedules: 1850, 1860. Schedules name slaveholders but rarely name slaves. Special Census of Civil War Union Veterans and Widows: 1890 (incomplete coverage)

Tel: (859) 622-1790
Web site:

Fayette County Genealogical Society
P.O. Box 8113, Lexington, KY 40533-8113
Web site: <www.rootsweb.com/~kyekg/fayette.htm>

Filson Historical Society
1310 S. Third St., Louisville, KY 40208
Tel: (502) 635-5083
Web site:

Fulton County Genealogical Society
P.O. Box 1031, Fulton, KY 42041-1031
Web site: <www.rootsweb.com/~kyfulcgs/>

Fulton County Public Library
312 Main St., Fulton, KY 42041
Tel: (270) 472-3439
Web site:

Gallatin County Public Library
209 W. Market St., P.O. Box 848, Warsaw, KY 41095
Tel: (859) 567-2786
E-mail: Info@GallatinCountyLibrary.org
Web site:

Grant County Public Library
201 Barnes Rd., Williamstown, KY 41097
Tel: (859) 824-2080

Graves County Genealogical Society
P.O. Box 245, Mayfield, KY 42066
Web site: <www.rootsweb.com/~kygraves/gravesghs.html>

Grayson County Historical Society
P.O. Box 84, Leitchfield, KY 42755

Green County Historical Society
P.O. Box 276, Greensburg, KY 42743
Web site: <www.greensburgky.com/historicsoc.htm>

Greenup Public Library
614 Main St., Greenup, KY
Tel: (606) 473-6514
Web site:

Harlan County Genealogical Society
P.O. Box 1498, Harlan, KY 40831

Harlan Heritage Seekers
P.O. Box 853, Harlan, KY 40831

Harrodsburg Historical Society
220 S. Chiles St., Harrodsburg, KY 40330
Tel: (606) 734-5985

Hart County Historical Society
P.O. Box 606, Munfordville, KY 42765
Tel: (270) 524-0101
E-mail: Museum@historichart.org

Hawesville, Genealogical Society of Hancock County
P.O. Box 667, Hawesville, KY 42348
Tel: (270) 927-8095

Henderson County Historical and Genealogical Society
132-B Green St., P.O. Box 303, Henderson, KY 42419-0303
Tel: (270) 830-7514
E-mail: hendersoncounty@hotmail.com
Web site: <www.rootsweb.com/~kyhender/HCHGS/HCHGSpg.htm>

Henderson County Public Library
101 S. Main St., Henderson, KY 42420-3599
Tel: (270) 826-3712
Web site:

Hickman County Historical Society
Route 3, Box 255, Clinton, KY 42031

Hopkins County Genealogical Society
P.O. Box 51, Madisonville, KY 42431
Web site: <www.rootsweb.com/~kyhopkin/hcgs/index.html>

Jewish Genealogical Society of Louisville
3304 Furman Blvd., Louisville, KY 40220

Johnson County Historical and Genealogical Society
444 Main St., P.O. Box 788, Paintsville, KY 41240
Tel: (606) 789-4355

Kenton County Public Library, Covington Branch
502 Scott Blvd., Covington, KY 41011
Tel: (859) 962-4060

Kentucky Department for Libraries & Archives
300 Coffee Tree Rd., Frankfort, KY 40601
Web site:

Kentucky Genealogical Society
P.O. Box 153, Frankfort, KY 40602
Web site:

Kentucky History Center and Historical Society
100 W. Broadway, Frankfort, KY 40601
Tel: (502) 564-1792
E-mail: KHS@ky.gov
Web site:

Knott County Historical & Genealogical Society & Library, Inc.
P.O. Box 1023, Carew Dr., Duke's Branch, Hindman, KY 41822
Tel: (606) 785-5751
Web site: <www.geocities.com/Athens/Oracle/5468/>

Knox County Historical Society
P.O. Box 528, Barbourville, KY 40906-0528

Laurel County Historical Society
P.O. Box 816, London, KY 40743
Tel: (606) 864-0607
E-mail: lchistsoc@alltel.net
Web site:

Laurel County Public Library
120 College Park Dr., London, KY 40741
Tel: (606) 864-5759
Web site:

Leslie County Public Library
22065 Main St, Hyden, KY 41749
Tel: (606) 672-2460

Letcher County Historical and Genealogical Society
P.O. Box 312, Whitesburg, KY 41858
Web site: <www.rootsweb.com/~kyletch/lchgs/>

Lewis County Historical Society
P.O. Box 212, Vanceburg, KY 41179

Lexington Public Library Central Library
140 E. Main St., Lexington, KY 40507
Tel: (859) 231-5530
Web site:

Logan County Genealogical Society, Inc.
P.O. Box 853, Russellville, KY 42276-0853

Louisville Free Public Library
301 York St., Louisville, KY 40203
Tel: (502) 574-1611
Web site:

Louisville Genealogical Society
P.O. Box 5164, Louisville, KY 40255-0164
E-mail: lougensoc@yahoo.com
Web site: <www.rootsweb.com/~kylgs/>

Louisville Presbyterian Theological Seminary
1044 Alta Vista Rd., Louisville, KY 40205
Tel: (800) 264-1839
Web site: <www.lpts.edu/default.asp>

Magoffin County Historical Society
P.O. Box 222, Salyersville, KY 41465
Tel: (606) 349-1607
Web site: <www.rootsweb.com/~kymhs/>

Marshall County Historical and Genealogical Society
P.O. Box 373, Benton, KY 42025
Tel: (502) 527-4749

Mason County Genealogical Society
P.O. Box 266, Maysville KY 41056

Mason County Museum and Library
215 Sutton St., Maysville, KY 41056
Tel: (606) 564-5865
E-mail: museum@masoncountymuseum.org

McCracken County Genealogical Society
4640 Buckner Lane, Paducah, KY 42001

Metcalfe County Historical Society
P.O. Box 910, Edmonton, KY 42129

Muhlenberg County Genealogical Society
% Central City Public Library, Broad St., Central City, KY 42330

Kentucky

Kentucky

National Archives-Southeast Region
1557 St. Joseph Ave., East Point, GA 30344-2593
Web site: <www.archives.gov/fa cilities/ga/atlanta.html>

Nelson County Genealogical Roundtable
P.O. Box 409, Bardstown, KY 40004
Tel: (502) 348-5652
Web site: <www.rootsweb.com/ ~kyncgr/>

Paris, John Fox Jr. Memorial Library
Duncan Tavern, Paris, KY 40361
Tel: (859) 987-1788

Pendleton County Historical & Genealogical Society
P.O. Box 130, Falmouth, KY 41040
Web site: <www.rootsweb.com/ ~kypendle/historicalsociety .htm>

Perry County Public Library
479 High St., Hazard, KY 41701
Tel: (606) 436-2475
E-mail: pcpl479@gtemail.net
Web site: <www.geocities.com/ pcpl479/>

Pike County Public Library District
119 College St, Pikeville, KY 41501-1787
Tel: (606) 432-9977

Pike County Society for Historical & Genealogical Research
P.O. Box 97, Pikesville, KY 41502

Pikesville College, Frank M. Allard Library, Special Collections
214 Sycamore, Pikeville, KY 41501
Tel: (606) 432-9698
Web site: <www.rootsweb.com/ ~kypike2/pikeaddys.html>

Princeton, George Coon Public Library
114 S. Harrison St., P.O. Box 230, Princeton, KY 42445
Tel: (270) 365-2884
Web site: <www.youseemore. com/georgecoon/default.asp>

Pulaski County Historical Society
P.O. Box 36, Somerset, KY 42502-0036

Tel: (606) 679-8401
Web site: <www.rootsweb.com/ ~kypchs/>

Rowan County Historical Society
P.O. Box 60, Morehead, KY 40351

Russell County Historical Society
P.O. Box 544, Jamestown, KY 42629

Scott County Genealogical Society
% Scott County Public Library, 230 E. Main St., Georgetown, KY 40324

Simpson County Archives and Museum
206 N. College St., Franklin, KY 42134
Tel: (270) 586-4228
E-mail: Information@SimpsonCou ntyKyArchives.com
Web site: <www.rootsweb.com/ ~kyschs/>

Southern Kentucky Genealogical Society
P.O. Box 1782, Bowling Green, KY 42102-1782
Web site: <members.aol.com/ky gen/skgs/>

Spencer County Historical Society
P.O. Box 266, Taylorsville, KY 40071

Van Lear Historical Society, Inc.
P.O. Box 369, Van Lear, KY 41265-0369
E-mail: coalcamp@yahoo.com
Web site: <www.geocities.com/ coalcamp/>

Wayne County Public Library District
159 S. Main St., Monticello, KY 42633
Tel: (606) 348-8565

Webster County Historical & Genealogical Society
P.O. Box 215, Dixon, KY 42409-0215
Web site: <www.rootsweb.com/ ~kywebste/wch_gs.htm>

West-Central Kentucky Family Research Association
P.O. Box 1932, Owensboro, KY 42302-1932
Web site: <www.rootsweb.com/ ~kywckfra/>

Western Kentucky University Libraries
1 Big Red Way, Bowling Green, KY 42101-3576
Web site: <www.wku.edu/Libr ary/>

Woodford County Historical Society
121 Rose Hill Ave., Versailles, KY 40383
Tel: (859) 873-6786
Web site:

BIBLIOGRAPHY

■ GENERAL RESOURCES

Bibliography of County Resources
by the Kentucky Historical Society (Frankfort, KY: Kentucky Historical Society, 1990)

A Bibliography of Kentucky History
by John Winston Coleman (Lexington, KY: University of Kentucky Press, 1949)

Biographical Cyclopedia of the Commonwealth of Kentucky: Embracing Biographies of Many of the Prominent Men and Families of the State
by Eileene Sandlin (Easley, S.C.: Southern Historical Press, ca. 1980)

The Biographical Encyclopaedia of Kentucky of the Dead and Living Men of the Nineteenth Century
(Cincinnati, OH: J.M. Armstrong, 1878)

The Centenary of Catholicity in Kentucky
by Ben J. Webb (Utica, KY: McDowell Publications, ca. 1980)

Early Families of Eastern and Southeastern Kentucky and their Descendants
by William C. Kozee (Baltimore, MD: Genealogical Pub. Co., 1973)

Early Kentucky Tax Records, from the Register of the Kentucky Historical Society
(Baltimore, MD: Genealogical Pub. Co., 1984)

The Fascinating Story of Black Kentuckians: Their Heritage and Traditions
by Alice Allison Dunnigan (Washington, DC: Associated Pub., 1982)

Genealogies of Kentucky Families: From the Register of the Kentucky Historical Society
by James C. Klotter (Baltimore, MD: Genealogical Pub. Co., 1981)

The Genealogist's Companion and Sourcebook, 2d ed.
by Emily Anne Croom (Cincinnati: Betterway Books, 2003)

A Genealogist's Guide to Discovering Your African-American Ancestors
by Franklin Carter Smith and Emily Anne Croom (Cincinnati: Betterway Books, 2003)

Guide to Genealogical Research in the National Archives of the United States
edited by Anne Bruner Eales and Robert M. Kvasnicka (Washington, DC: National Archives and Records Administration, 2000)

Guide to Kentucky Archival and Manuscript Collections
by Barbara Teague and Jane A. Minder (Frankfort, KY: Kentucky Department for Libraries and Archives, Public Records Div., ca. 1988–)

A History of Kentucky Baptists: from 1769 to 1885, including more than 800 biographical sketches
by John H. Spencer (Cincinnati: J.R. Baumes, 1886)

The History of Kentucky: From its Earliest Discovery and Settlement, to the Present Date . . .
by Zachariah Frederick Smith (Louisville, KY: Prentice Press, 1886; reprint: Louisville: Courier-Journal Job Printing Co., 1980)

A History of Kentucky, Embracing Gleanings, Reminiscences, Antiquities, Natural Curiosities, Statistics, and Biographical Sketches
by William B. Allen (Louisville, KY: Bradley and Gilbert, 1872; reprint: Green County Historical Society, 1972)

A History of Kentucky and Kentuckians: The Leaders and Representative Men in Commerce, Industry and Modern Activities, 3 vols.
by E. Polk Johnson (Chicago, NY: Lewis, 1912)

Kentucky Bible Records from the Files of the Genealogical Records Committee, Kentucky Society, Daughters of the American Revolution
by the Daughters of the American Revolution (Lexington, KY: KSDAR, ca. 1962–1981)

Kentucky Family Records
edited by Mrs. Edgar L. Cox (Owensboro, KY: West Central Kentucky Family Research Association, 1969; reprint; Owensboro: McDowell Publications, 1991)

Kentucky Genealogical Research
by George K. Schweitzer (Knoxville, TN: The Author, 1981)

"Kentucky." In Genealogical Research: Methods and Sources
chapter by John Frederick Dorman and James Robert Bentley, Kenn Stryker-Rodda, ed. (Vol. II. Rev. ed. Washington, DC: The American Society of Genealogists, 1983)

Kentucky; A History of the State: Embracing a Concise Account of the Origin and Development of the Virginia Colony
by W.H. Perrin, J.H. Battle, G.C. Kniffin (Reprint: Easley, SC: Southern Historical Press, 1979)

Kentucky Index of Biographical Sketches in State, Regional and County Histories
by Michael L. Cook (Evansville, IN: Cook Publications, 1986)

Kentucky Research Outline
by the Church of Jesus Christ of Latter-day (Salt Lake City, UT: Corp. of the President of The Church of Jesus Christ of L.D.S., 1988)

National Archives Microfilm Catalogs online:
<www.archives.gov/publica tions/genealogy_microfilm_ catalogs.html>

A Sesqui-Centennial History of Kentucky: A Narrative Historical Edition
by Frederick A. Wallis (Hopkinsville, KY: Historical Record Association, 1945)

■ **CENSUS RECORDS**

The 1787 Census of Virginia
by Netti Schreiner-Yantis (Springfield, VA: Genealogical Books in Print, 1987)

The American Census Handbook
by Thomas Jay Kemp (Wilmington, DE: Scholarly Resources Inc., 2001)

The Census Book: A Genealogist's Guide to Federal Census Facts, Schedules and Indexes; with Master Extraction Forms for Federal Census Schedules, 1790–1930
by William Dollarhide (Bountiful, UT: Heritage Quest, 1999)

Finding Answers in U.S. Census Records
by Loretto Dennis Szucs and Matthew Wright (Orem, UT: Ancestry Pub., ca. 2001)

Map Guide to the U.S. Federal Censuses, 1790–1920
by William Thorndale and William Dollarhide (Baltimore, MD: Genealogical Pub. Co., ca. 1987)

State Census Records
by Ann S. Lainhart (Baltimore: Genealogical Pub. Co., ca. 1992)

Your Guide to the Federal Census
by Kathleen W. Hinckley (Cincinnati: Betterway Books, 2002)

■ **IMMIGRATION RECORDS**

American Naturalization Records, 1790–1990: What They Are and How to Use Them
by John J. Newman (North Salt Lake, UT: HeritageQuest, 1998)

American Passenger Arrival Records
by Michael Tepper (Baltimore: Genealogical Publishing Co., 1993)

They Became Americans: Finding Naturalization Records and Ethnic Origins
by Loretto Dennis Szucs (Salt Lake City: Ancestry, Inc., 1998)

They Came in Ships: A Guide to Finding Your Immigrant Ancestor's Arrival Records, 2d ed.
by John P. Colletta (Salt Lake City: Ancestry, Inc., 1993)

■ **LAND RECORDS**

A Calendar of the Warrants for Land in Kentucky, Granted for Service in the French and Indian War
by Philip Fall Taylor (Baltimore, MD: Clearfield Co., 1995)

Index for Old Kentucky Survey's and Grants; Index for Tellico Surveys and Grants
by the Kentucky Historical Society (Frankfort, KY: Kentucky Historical Society, ca. 1975)

Kentucky Court of Appeals Deed Books
by Michael L. Cook (Evansville, IN: Cook Publications, 1985)

The Kentucky Land Grants: A Systematic Index to All of the Land Grants Recorded in the State Land Office at Frankfort, Kentucky, 1782–1924
by Willard Rouse Jillson (Louisville: Standard Printing Co., 1925)

Land & Property Research in the United States
by E. Wade Hone (Salt Lake City, UT: Ancestry, ca. 1997)

Locating Your Roots: Discover Your Ancestors Using Land Records
by Patricia Law Hatcher (Cincinnati: Betterway Books, 2003)

Old Kentucky Entries and Deeds: A Complete Index to All of the Earliest Land Entries, Military Warrants, Deeds and Wills of the Commonwealth of Kentucky
by Willard Rouse Jillson (Louisville, KY: 1926; reprint: Baltimore, MD: Genealogical Pub. Co., 1999)

■ **MAPS**

Atlas of Historical County Boundaries, Kentucky
by John H. Long and Gordon DenBoer (New York, NY: Charles Scribner's Sons, ca. 1995)

Atlas of Kentucky
by Richard Ulack (Lexington, KY: University of Kentucky Press, ca. 1998)

A Checklist of Kentucky Post Offices
by Alan H. Patera and John S. Gallagher (Lake Grove, OR: The Depot, ca. 1989)

A Guide to Kentucky Place Names
by Thomas P. Field (Lexington, KY: University of Kentucky, 1961)

Historic Maps of Kentucky
by Thomas D. Clark (Lexington, KY: University Press of Kentucky, 1979)

An Historical Atlas of Kentucky and Her Counties
by Wendell H. Rone Sr. (Owensboro, KY: Progress Print. Co., 1965)

The Kentucky Encyclopedia
by John E. Kleber (Lexington, KY: University Press of Kentucky, ca. 1992)

Kentucky Geographic Names
by the United States Office of Geographic Research Branch of Geographic Names (Reston, VA: United States. Branch of Geographic Names, 1981)

Kentucky Place Names
by Robert M. Rennick (Lexington, KY: University Press of Kentucky, 1984)

Kentucky Post Offices, 1794–1819
by Thelma M. Murphy (Indianapolis: The Author: 1975)

Kentucky State Gazetteer and Business Directory for 1895–96
by R.L. Polk and Company (1895; reprint: Vine Grove, KY: Ancestral Trails Historical Society, 2000)

Kentucky's Bluegrass: A Survey of the Post Offices
by Robert M. Rennick (Lake Grove, OR: Depot, 1993–)

Kentucky

Pioneer Kentucky: an outline of its exploration and settlement, its early cartography and primitive geography coupled with a brief presentation of the principal trails, traces, forts, stations, springs, licks, fords and ferries used prior to the year 1800
by Willard Rouse Jillson (Frankfort, KY: State Journal, 1934)

■ MILITARY RECORDS

Compendium of the War of the Revolution
by Frederick H. Dyer (1908; reprint: Dayton, OH: Morningside Bookshop, 1978)

The Corn Stalk Militia of Kentucky, 1792–1800: a brief statutory history of the militia and records of commissions of officers in the organization from the beginning of statehood to the commencement of the War of 1812
by Garrett Gleen Clift (Frankfort, KY: Kentucky Historical Society, 1957)

Index to Veterans of American Wars from Kentucky
by the Kentucky Historical Society (Frankfort, KY: Kentucky Historical Society, 1966)

Kentucky Confederate Veteran and Widows Pension Index
by Michael L. Cook and Alicia Simpson (Utica, KY: Cook & McDowell Publications, ca. 1979)

Kentucky Soldiers of the War of 1812
by Minnie S. Wilder (Baltimore, MD: Genealogical Pub. Co., 1969)

Kentucky in the War of 1812
by Anderson Chenault Quisenberry (Baltimore, MD: Genealogical Pub. Co., 1969)

Kentucky's Revolutionary War Pensioners, Under Acts 1818–1832
by Kenneth Gene Lindsay (Evansville, IN: Kenma Pub. Co., ca. 1977)

List of the Revolutionary Soldiers of Virginia
H.J. Eckenrode (Richmond, VA: Virginia State Library, Archives Division, 1912)

Report of the Adjutant General of the State of Kentucky, Confederate Kentucky Volunteers, War 1861–1865
by the Kentucky Adjutant General (1915; reprint: Utica, KY: Cook and McDowell, 1980)

Report of the Adjutant General of the State of Kentucky: Kentucky Volunteers, War with Spain, 1898–1899
by the Kentucky Adjutant General (Frankfort, KY: Globe Print Co., 1908)

Revolutionary Soldiers in Kentucky: containing a roll of the officers of Virginia line who received land bounties, a roll of the revolutionary pensioners in Kentucky
by Anderson Chenault Quisenberry (Baltimore: Southern Book Co., 1959)

Uncle, We Are Ready! Registering America's Men, 1917–1918: A Guide to Researching World War I Draft Registration Cards
by John J. Newman (North Salt Lake, UT: HeritageQuest, 2001)

The Union Army: A History of Military Affairs in the Loyal States, 1861–1865, 9 vols.
(Broadfoot Pub. Co., 1997–1998)

The Union Regiments of Kentucky
by Thomas Speed and Alfred Pirtle (1897; reprint: Dayton, OH: Morningside House, ca. 1984)

U.S. Military Records: A Guide to Federal & State Sources, Colonial America to the Present
by James C. Neagles (Salt Lake City: Ancestry, Inc., 1994)

World War II: A Family Historian's Guide
by Debra Johnson Knox (Spartanburg, SC: MIE Publishing, 2003)

■ PROBATE RECORDS

Abstract of Early Kentucky Wills and Inventories: Copied from Original and Recorded Wills and Inventories
by J. Estelle Stewart King (Baltimore: Clearfield Co., 1993)

The County Courts in Antebellum Kentucky
by Robert M. Ireland (Lexington, KY: University Press of Kentucky, ca. 1972)

Federal Courts in the Early Republic: Kentucky 1789–1816
by Mary K. Bonsteel Tachau (Princeton: Princeton University Press, 1978)

Index to Kentucky Wills to 1851, the Testators
by Ronald Vern Jackson and David Schaefermeyer (Salt Lake City: Accelerated Indexing Systems, ca. 1977)

Kentucky Pioneer and Court Records: abstracts of early wills, deeds, and marriages
by Ednah Wilson McAdams (1929; reprint: Baltimore, MD: Genealogical Pub. Co., 1975)

Virginia Supreme Court; District of Kentucky, Order Books, 1783–1792
by Michael L. Cook (Evansville, IN: Cook Pub., ca. 1988)

■ VITAL RECORDS

Cemetery Records of Kentucky
by Robert C. Jobson (Jeffersontown, KY: the author, 1988–)

Guide to Public Vital Statistics Records in Kentucky
by the Historical Records Survey (Louisville, KY: Historical Records Survey, Kentucky, 1942)

Inventory of Kentucky Birth, Marriage, and Death records 1852–1910
by Jeffrey Michael Duff (Frankfort, KY: Department of Library and Archives, 1980)

The Kentucky Gazette . . . : Genealogical and Historical Abstracts
by Karen Mauer Green (Baltimore, MD: Gateway Press, 1983–)

Kentucky Marriage Records, From the Register of the Kentucky Historical Society
(Baltimore, MD: Genealogical Pub. Co., 1983)

Kentucky Marriages, 1797–1865
by G. Glenn Clift (Baltimore: Genealogical Pub. Co., 1974)

Kentucky Obituaries, 1787–1854
by Garrett Glenn Clift (Baltimore, MD: Genealogical Pub. Co., ca. 1977)

Kentucky Records: early wills and marriages
by Julia Spencer Ardery (1926; reprint: Baltimore: Genealogical Pub. Co., 1965)

Wilderness Road Cemeteries in Kentucky, Tennessee and Virginia
by Robert Foster Johnson (Owensboro, KY: McDowell Publications, 1981)

Your Guide to Cemetery Research
by Sharon DeBartolo Carmack (Cincinnati: Betterway Books, 2002)

■ Adair 11 Dec. 1801
424 Public Sq., Columbia, KY 42728
Phone: (270)384-2801
Web site: http://columbia-adaircounty.com/
Parent County: Green

Record Type	Year Begun	Jurisdiction
Marriage	1802	County Clerk
Land	1801	County Clerk
Probate	1804	Clerk/Circuit Ct.
Court	1802	Clerk/Circuit Ct.
Military	1802	County Clerk

■ Allen 11 Jan. 1815
201 W. Main St., Scottsville, KY 42164
Phone: (270)237-3706
Web site: www.rootsweb.com/~kyallen
Parent County: Barren, Warren

Record Type	Year Begun	Jurisdiction
Marriage	1815	County Clerk

Record Type	Year Begun	Jurisdiction
Divorce	1902	Clerk/Circuit Ct.
Probate	1815	Clerk/Circuit Ct.

■ Anderson 16 Jan. 1827
151 S. Main St., Lawrenceburg, KY 40342
Phone: (502)839-3041
Web site: www.rootsweb.com/~kyanders
Parent County: Franklin, Mercer, Washington

Record Type	Year Begun	Jurisdiction
Marriage	1831	County Clerk
Land	1827	County Clerk
Probate	1827	Clerk/Circuit Ct.
Court	1827	Clerk/Circuit Ct.
School	na	County Clerk

■ Ballard 15 Feb. 1842
P.O. Box 145, Wickliffe, KY 42087-0145
Phone: (270)335-5168
Web site: www.ballardconet.com/
Parent County: Hickman, McCracken
Comments/research tips: Courthouse burned in 1880.

Record Type	Year Begun	Jurisdiction
Marriage	1852	County Clerk
Divorce	na	Clerk/Circuit Ct.
Land	1873	County Clerk
Probate	1879	Clerk/Circuit Ct.

■ Barren 20 Dec. 1798
Courthouse, 100 Courthouse Sq., Glasgow, KY 42141
Phone: (270)651-3763
Web site: www.rootsweb.com/~kybarren/
Parent County: Green, Warren

Record Type	Year Begun	Jurisdiction
Marriage	1799	County Clerk
Divorce	na	Clerk/Circuit Ct.
Land	1795	County Clerk
Probate	1799	Clerk/Circuit Ct.
Court	1799	Clerk/Circuit Ct.

■ Bath 15 Jan. 1811
P.O. Box 609, Owingsville, KY 40360
Phone: (606)674-2613
Web site: www.rootsweb.com/~kybath/bathcounty.html
Parent County: Montgomery

Record Type	Year Begun	Jurisdiction
Birth	1911	KY/Vital Statistics
Marriage	1811	County Clerk
Death	1911	KY/Vital Statistics
Divorce	na	Clerk/Circuit Ct.
Land	1811	County Clerk
Probate	1811	Clerk/Circuit Ct.
Court	1811	Clerk/Circuit Ct.
Military	na	County Clerk

■ Bell 1 Aug. 1867
Courthouse Sq. Floor 1, P.O. Box 157, Pineville, KY 40977
Phone: (606)337-6143
Web site: www.rootsweb.com/~kybell/
Parent County: Knox, Harlan

Record Type	Year Begun	Jurisdiction
Marriage	1867	County Clerk
Land	1867	County Clerk

■ Boone 1799
2950 E. Washington Sq., Burlington, KY 41005
Phone: (859)334-2112
Web site: www.boonecountyky.org/
Parent County: Campbell

Record Type	Year Begun	Jurisdiction
Marriage	1798	County Clerk
Probate	1800	Clerk/Circuit Ct.

■ Bourbon 1786
P.O. Box 312, Paris, KY 40361
Phone: (859)987-2142
Web site: www.parisky.com/
Parent County: Fayette

Record Type	Year Begun	Jurisdiction
Marriage	1786	County Clerk
Divorce	na	Clerk/Circuit Ct.
Probate	1786	Clerk/Circuit Ct.
Court	1786	Clerk/Circuit Ct.

■ Boyd 1860
P.O. Box 523, Catlettsburg, KY 41129
Phone: (606)739-5116
Web site: www.rootsweb.com/~kyboyd/
Parent County: Carter, Lawrence, Greenup

Record Type	Year Begun	Jurisdiction
Marriage	1860	County Clerk
Divorce	na	Clerk/Circuit Ct.
Land	1860	County Clerk
Probate	1860	Clerk/Circuit Ct.
Court	1860	Clerk/Circuit Ct.
Military	1860	County Clerk

■ Boyle 15 Feb. 1842
321 W. Main St. 123, Danville, KY 40422
Phone: (859)238-1110
Web site: www.danville-ky.com/
Parent County: Mercer, Lincoln

Record Type	Year Begun	Jurisdiction
Marriage	1842	County Clerk
Divorce	na	Clerk/Circuit Ct.
Land	1842	County Clerk
Probate	1842	Clerk/Circuit Ct.
Court	1842	Clerk/Circuit Ct.
Military	1797	County Clerk

■ Bracken 1797
P.O. Box 147, Brooksville, KY 41004
Phone: (606)735-2952
Web site: http://resources.rootsweb.com/USA/KY/Bracken
Parent County: Campbell, Mason

Record Type	Year Begun	Jurisdiction
Marriage	1797	County Clerk
Land	1797	County Clerk
Probate	1797	Clerk/Circuit Ct.

■ **Breathitt** 1839
1137 Main St., Jackson, KY 41339
Phone: (606)666-3810
Web site: www.breathittcounty.com/
Parent County: Clay, Estill, Perry

Record Type	Year Begun	Jurisdiction
Marriage	1852	County Clerk
Divorce	na	Clerk/Circuit Ct.
Land	1850	County Clerk
Probate	1884	Clerk/Circuit Ct.
Court	1873	Clerk/Circuit Ct.

■ **Breckinridge** 7 Dec. 1799
Courthouse Sq., P.O. Box 538, Hardinsburg, KY 40143
Phone: (270)756-2246
Web site: www.geocities.com/dabugman.geo/breck.html
Parent County: Hardin
Comments/research tips: County Archives has some Marriage records from 1800, some Birth records 1853–1969, some Death records 1853–1993.

Record Type	Year Begun	Jurisdiction
Land	1800	County Archives
Probate	1800	Clerk/Circuit Ct.
Court	1800	Clerk/Circuit Ct.

■ **Bullitt** 1797
P.O. Box 6, Shepherdsville, KY 40165
Phone: (502)543-2513
Web site: www.rootsweb.com/~kybullit/
Parent County: Jefferson, Nelson
Comments/research tips: County Clerk has Military Discharge records 1921–1997.

Record Type	Year Begun	Jurisdiction
Marriage	1797	County Clerk
Divorce	na	Clerk/Circuit Ct.
Land	1797	County Clerk
Probate	1796	Clerk/District Ct.
Court	1797	Clerk/Circuit Ct.

■ **Butler** 1810
P.O. Box 449, Morgantown, KY 42261-0448
Phone: (270)526-5676
Web site: www.rootsweb.com/~kybutler/
Parent County: Logan, Ohio

Record Type	Year Begun	Jurisdiction
Marriage	1814	County Clerk
Divorce	na	Clerk/Circuit Ct.
Land	1809	County Clerk
Court	1810	Clerk/Circuit Ct.

■ **Caldwell** 1809
100 E. Market St., Room 23, Princeton, KY 42445
Phone: (270)365-6754
Web site: http://home.hiwaay.net/~woliver/caldwell.html
Parent County: Livingston

Record Type	Year Begun	Jurisdiction
Marriage	1809	County Clerk
Divorce	na	Clerk/Circuit Ct.
Land	1809	County Clerk
Probate	1809	Clerk/Circuit Ct.
Court	1809	Clerk/Circuit Ct.
Military	na	County Clerk

■ **Calloway** 1821
101 S. Fifth St., Murray, KY 42071
Phone: (270)753-3923
Web site: http://users.arn.net/~billco/calloway.html
Parent County: Hickman

Record Type	Year Begun	Jurisdiction
Marriage	1823	County Clerk
Divorce	na	Clerk/Circuit Ct.
Land	1823	County Clerk
Probate	1836	Clerk/Circuit Ct.
Military	na	County Clerk
Election	na	County Clerk

■ **Campbell** 17 Dec. 1794
340 York St., Newport, KY 41071
Phone: (859)292-3845
Web site: www.campbellcountyky.org/
Parent County: Harrison, Mason, Scott

Record Type	Year Begun	Jurisdiction
Marriage	1795	County Clerk
Land	1795	County Clerk
Probate	1794	Clerk/Circuit Ct.

■ **Carlisle** 3 May 1886
P.O. Box 176, Bardwell, KY 42023
Phone: (270)628-3233
Web site: www.ballardconet.com/GenWeb/carlisle.html
Parent County: Ballard

Record Type	Year Begun	Jurisdiction
Marriage	1886	County Clerk
Land	1886	County Clerk
Probate	1886	Clerk/Circuit Ct.

■ **Carroll** 1838
440 Main St., Carrollton, KY 41008
Phone: (502)732-7005
Web site: www.rootsweb.com/~kycarroll/Carroll.html/
Parent County: Gallatin, Henry, and Trimble

Record Type	Year Begun	Jurisdiction
Marriage	1837	County Clerk
Divorce	na	Clerk/Circuit Ct.
Land	1795	County Clerk
Probate	1838	Clerk/Circuit Ct.
Court	1838	Clerk/Circuit Ct.

■ **Carter** 10 Apr. 1838
300 W. Main St., Grayson, KY 41143
Phone: (606)474-5188
Web site: www.rootsweb.com/~kycarter/
Parent County: Greenup, Lawrence
Comments/research tips: County Clerk has both Birth and Death records 1911–1954.

Record Type	Year Begun	Jurisdiction
Marriage	1838	County Clerk

Divorce .... na ....Clerk/Circuit Ct.
Probate .... 1835 ....Clerk/Circuit Ct.
Court .... 1838 ....Clerk/Circuit Ct.

■ **Casey** 14 Nov. 1806
P.O. Box 310, Liberty, KY 42539
Phone: (606)787-6471
Web site: www.rootsweb.com/~kycasey/caseypge.htm
Parent County: Lincoln
Comments/research tips: Probate records can be found with County Clerk (1806) and Clerk of Circuit Court (1978).

Record Type	Year Begun	Jurisdiction
Birth	1911	KY/Vital Statistics
Marriage	1807	County Clerk
Death	1911	KY/Vital Statistics
Divorce	na	Clerk/Circuit Ct.
Land	1807	County Clerk
Court	1807	Clerk/Circuit Ct.

■ **Christian** 1 Mar. 1797
511 S. Main St., Hopkinsville, KY 42240
Phone: (270)887-4105
Web site: www.kyseeker.com/christian/index.html
Parent County: Logan
Comments/research tips: Probate records can be found with Clerk of Circuit Court (1797).

Record Type	Year Begun	Jurisdiction
Marriage	1797	County Clerk
Divorce	na	Clerk/Circuit Ct.
Land	1797	County Clerk
Court	1797	Clerk/Circuit Ct.

■ **Clark** 1793
P.O. Box 4060, Winchester, KY 40392
Phone: (859)745-0280
Web site: www.rootsweb.com/~kyclark/
Parent County: Bourbon, Fayette

Record Type	Year Begun	Jurisdiction
Marriage	1793	County Clerk
Divorce	na	Clerk/Circuit Ct.
Land	1793	County Clerk
Probate	1793	Clerk/Circuit Ct.
Court	1993	Clerk/Circuit Ct.

■ **Clay** 1 Apr. 1807
123 Town Sq., Suite 3, Manchester, KY 40962
Phone: (606)598-2544
Web site: www.rootsweb.com/usgenweb/ky/clay/clayar.html
Parent County: Madison, Floyd, Knox

Record Type	Year Begun	Jurisdiction
Marriage	1806	County Clerk
Divorce	1955	Clerk/Circuit Ct.
Land	1807	County Clerk
Probate	1826	Clerk/Circuit Ct.

■ **Clinton** 20 Feb. 1835
100 S. Cross Street, Albany, KY 42602
Phone: (859)387-5943

Web site: www.rootsweb.com/~kyclinto/
Parent County: Wayne, Cumberland

Record Type	Year Begun	Jurisdiction
Marriage	1852	County Clerk
Land	1853	County Clerk
Probate	1863	Clerk/Circuit Ct.

■ **Crittenden** 1 Apr. 1842
107 S. Main St., Marion, KY 42064
Phone: (270)965-3403
Web site: http://home.hiwaay.net/~woliver/crittenden.html
Parent County: Livingston

Record Type	Year Begun	Jurisdiction
Marriage	1842	County Clerk
Divorce	na	Clerk/Circuit Ct.
Land	1842	Clerk/Circuit Ct.
Probate	1843	Clerk/Circuit Ct.
Court	1843	Clerk/Circuit Ct.

■ **Cumberland** 14 Dec. 1798
P.O. Box 275, Burkesville, KY 42717
Phone: (270)864-3726
Web site: www.geocities.com/Heartland/Trail/1794/
Parent County: Green
Comments/research tips: County Clerk has some Marriage records 1882–1923 and from 1927. Clerk of Circuit Court has Probate records from 1815.

Record Type	Year Begun	Jurisdiction
Divorce	na	Clerk/Circuit Ct.
Land	1799	County Clerk
Court	1820	Clerk/Circuit Ct.

■ **Daviess** 14 Jan. 1815
P.O. Box 609, Owensboro, KY 42302
Phone: (270)685-8434
Web site: www.rootsweb.com/~kydavies/
Parent County: Ohio

Record Type	Year Begun	Jurisdiction
Marriage	1815	County Clerk
Divorce	na	Clerk/Circuit Ct.
Land	1815	County Clerk
Probate	1815	Clerk/Circuit Ct.
Court	1815	Clerk/Circuit Ct.

■ **Edmonson** 12 Jan. 1825
P.O. Box 830, Brownsville, KY 42210
Phone: (270)597-2624
Web site: http://users.rootsweb.com/~kyedmons/
Parent County: Grayson, Hart, Warren

Record Type	Year Begun	Jurisdiction
Marriage	1825	County Clerk

■ **Elliott** 1 Apr. 1869
Main St., P.O. Box 225, Sandy Hook, KY 41171-0225
Phone: (606)738-5421
Web site: http://home.zoomnet.net/~cbarker/elliott.htm
Parent County: Carter, Lawrence, Morgan

Record Type	Year Begun	Jurisdiction
Birth	1911	KY/Vital Statistics

Record Type	Year Begun	Jurisdiction
Marriage	1874	County Clerk
Death	1911	KY/Vital Statistics
Divorce	1957	Clerk/Circuit Ct.
Land	1869	County Clerk
Probate	1966	Clerk/Circuit Ct.
Court	1858	Clerk/Circuit Ct.

■ Estill 19 Feb. 1808
P.O. Box 59, Irvine, KY 40336
Phone: (606)723-5156
Web site: www.estill.net/
Parent County: Clark, Madison

Record Type	Year Begun	Jurisdiction
Marriage	1808	County Clerk
Divorce	na	Clerk/Circuit Ct.
Land	1808	County Clerk
Probate	1808	Clerk/Circuit Ct.
Court	1808	Clerk/Circuit Ct.
Burial	1808	County Clerk

■ Fayette 30 June 1780
162 E. Main St., Lexington, KY 40507
Phone: (859)253-3344
Web site: www.lfucg.com/
Parent County: Kentucky County, Virginia

Record Type	Year Begun	Jurisdiction
Marriage	1785	County Clerk
Divorce	na	Clerk/Circuit Ct.
Land	1782	County Clerk
Probate	1793	Clerk/Circuit Ct.
Court	1782	Clerk/Circuit Ct.

■ Fleming 1798
P.O. Box 324, Flemingsburg, KY 41041
Phone: (606)845-8461
Web site: www.flemingcounty.org/
Parent County: Mason

Record Type	Year Begun	Jurisdiction
Marriage	1798	County Clerk
Land	1798	County Clerk
Probate	1798	Clerk/Circuit Ct.

■ Floyd 1 June 1800
P.O. Box 1089, Prestonburg, KY 41653
Phone: (606)886-3816
Web site: www.rootsweb.com/~kyfloyd/floyd.htm
Parent County: Fleming, Mason, Montgomery

Record Type	Year Begun	Jurisdiction
Marriage	1808	County Clerk
Land	1810	County Clerk

■ Franklin 7 Dec. 1794
P.O. Box 338, Frankfort, KY 40602
Phone: (502)875-8702
Web site: www.rootsweb.com/~kyfrankl/franklin.html
Parent County: Woodford, Mercer, Shelby

Record Type	Year Begun	Jurisdiction
Marriage	1795	County Clerk
Divorce	na	Clerk/Circuit Ct.

Record Type	Year Begun	Jurisdiction
Land	1794	County Clerk
Probate	1795	Clerk/Circuit Ct.
Court	1795	Clerk/Circuit Ct.

■ Fulton 15 Jan. 1845
P.O. Box 126, Hickman, KY 42050-0126
Phone: (270)236-2727
Web site: www.rootsweb.com/~kyfulton/5642.html
Parent County: Hickman

Record Type	Year Begun	Jurisdiction
Marriage	1845	County Clerk
Divorce	na	Clerk/Circuit Ct.
Land	1845	County Clerk
Probate	1845	Clerk/Circuit Ct.
Court	1845	Clerk/Circuit Ct.

■ Gallatin 14 Dec. 1798
P.O. Box 1309, Warsaw, KY 41095
Phone: (859)567-5411
Web site: www.rootsweb.com/~kygallat/Gallatin.html
Parent County: Franklin, Shelby

Record Type	Year Begun	Jurisdiction
Marriage	1799	County Clerk
Divorce	na	Clerk/Circuit Ct.
Land	1798	County Clerk
Probate	1800	Clerk/Circuit Ct.
Court	1799	Clerk/Circuit Ct.

■ Garrard 17 Dec. 1796
15 Public Sq., Suite 5, Lancaster, KY 40444
Phone: (859)792-3071
Web site: www.kycourts.net/Counties/Garrard.asp?County=Garrard
Parent County: Madison, Lincoln, Mercer

Record Type	Year Begun	Jurisdiction
Marriage	1797	County Clerk
Land	1797	County Clerk
Probate	1797	Clerk/Circuit Ct.
Court	1797	Clerk/Circuit Ct.

■ Grant 1820
107 N. Main St., Williamstown, KY 41097
Phone: (859)824-3321
Web site: www.kycourts.net/Counties/Grant.asp?County=Grant
Parent County: Pendleton

Record Type	Year Begun	Jurisdiction
Marriage	1820	County Clerk
Land	1820	County Clerk
Probate	1820	Clerk/Circuit Ct.

■ Graves 1824
101 E. South St., Suite 2, Mayfield, KY 42066
Phone: (270)247-1676
Web site: www.rootsweb.com/~kygraves/graves.htm
Parent County: Hickman

Record Type	Year Begun	Jurisdiction
Marriage	1852	County Clerk
Divorce	na	Clerk/Circuit Ct.

Kentucky

Land	1887	County Clerk
Probate	1887	Clerk/Circuit Ct.
Court	1853	Clerk/Circuit Ct.

■ Grayson 25 Jan. 1810

10 Public Sq., Leitchfield, KY 42754
Phone: (270)259-3201
Web site: www.rootsweb.com/~kygrayson3.htm
Parent County: Hardin, Ohio

Record Type	Year Begun	Jurisdiction
Marriage	1852	County Clerk
Divorce	na	Clerk/Circuit Ct.
Land	1896	County Clerk
Probate	1896	Clerk/Circuit Ct.
Court	1906	Clerk/Circuit Ct.
Military	1896	County Clerk

■ Green 20 Dec. 1792

203 W. Court St., Greensburg, KY 42743
Phone: (270)932-5386
Web site: www.rootsweb.com/~kygreen/
Parent County: Lincoln, Nelson

Record Type	Year Begun	Jurisdiction
Birth	1911	KY/Vital Statistics
Marriage	1793	County Clerk
Death	1911	KY/Vital Statistics
Divorce	na	Clerk/Circuit Ct.
Land	1793	County Clerk
Probate	1793	Clerk/Circuit Ct.
Court	1794	Clerk/Circuit Ct.

■ Greenup 1803

Main & Harrison, Greenup, KY 41144-1055
Phone: (606)473-7394
Web site: www.rootsweb.com/~kygreen2/
Parent County: Mason
Comments/research tips: Kenutcky Office of Vital Statistics has both Birth and Death records 1911–present.

Record Type	Year Begun	Jurisdiction
Marriage	1803	County Clerk
Divorce	1803	Clerk/Circuit Ct.
Probate	1822	Clerk/Circuit Ct.
Court	1838	Clerk/Circuit Ct.

■ Hancock 3 Jan. 1829

P.O. Box 146, Hawesville, KY 42348
Phone: (270)927-6117
Web site: www.rootsweb.com/~kyhancoc/
Parent County: Daviess, Ohio, Breckinridge

Record Type	Year Begun	Jurisdiction
Marriage	1829	County Clerk
Divorce	na	Clerk/Circuit Ct.
Land	1829	County Clerk
Probate	1830	Clerk/Circuit Ct.
Court	1834	Clerk/Circuit Ct.

■ Hardin Nov. 1792

P.O. Box 1030, Elizabethtown, KY 42701
Phone: (270)765-2171

Web site: www.geocities.com/dabugman.geo/hardin.html
Parent County: Nelson

Record Type	Year Begun	Jurisdiction
Marriage	1793	County Clerk
Land	1793	County Clerk

■ Harlan 1819

P.O. Box 670, Harlan, KY 40831
Phone: (606)573-3636
Web site: www.rootsweb.com/~kyharlan/
Parent County: Knox

Record Type	Year Begun	Jurisdiction
Marriage	1820	County Clerk
Divorce	na	Clerk/Circuit Ct.
Land	1820	County Clerk
Court	1820	Clerk/Circuit Ct.

■ Harrison 21 Dec. 1793

313 Oddville Ave., Cynthiana, KY 41031
Phone: (859)234-7130
Web site: http://home.netcom.com/~jog1/harrison.html
Parent County: Bourbon, Scott

Record Type	Year Begun	Jurisdiction
Marriage	1794	County Clerk
Divorce	na	Clerk/Circuit Ct.
Land	1794	County Clerk
Probate	1794	Clerk/Circuit Ct.
Court	1794	Clerk/Circuit Ct.

■ Hart 28 Jan. 1819

P.O. Box 277, Munfordville, KY 42765
Phone: (270)524-2751
Web site: www.hartcounty.com/
Parent County: Hardin, Barren

Record Type	Year Begun	Jurisdiction
Birth	1911	KY/Vital Statistics
Marriage	1852	County Clerk
Death	1911	KY/Vital Statistics
Land	1819	County Clerk
Probate	1819	Clerk/Circuit Ct.
Court	1819	Clerk/Circuit Ct.

■ Henderson 1798

P.O. Box 374, Henderson, KY 42419
Phone: (270)826-3906
Web site: www.go-henderson.com/
Parent County: Christian
Comments/research tips: County Clerk has both Birth and Death records 1911-1949. Probate records can be found with County Clerk (1800) and Clerk of District Court (1979).

Record Type	Year Begun	Jurisdiction
Marriage	1808	County Clerk
Divorce	na	Clerk/Circuit Ct.
Land	1797	County Clerk
Court	1816	Clerk/Circuit Ct.

■ Henry 1799

30 N. Main St., P.O. Box 615, New Castle, KY 40050-0202
Phone: (502)845-5705

Web site: www.henryweb.com/
Parent County: Shelby

Record Type	Year Begun	Jurisdiction
Marriage	1800	County Clerk
Divorce	na	Clerk/Circuit Ct.
Land	1799	County Clerk
Probate	1800	Clerk/Circuit Ct.
Court	1800	Clerk/Circuit Ct.

■ Hickman 1821

110 E. Clay St., Clinton, KY 42031
Phone: (270)653-2131
Web site: www.rootsweb.com/~kyhickma/
Parent County: Caldwell, Livingston
Comments/research tips: County Clerk has some Birth records 1854-1909, some Death records 1856–1909, and Tax lists 1825–1829.

Record Type	Year Begun	Jurisdiction
Divorce	na	Clerk/Circuit Ct.
Land	1822	County Clerk
Probate	1822	Clerk/Circuit Ct.
Court	1822	Clerk/Circuit Ct.

■ Hopkins 1806

10 S. Main St., Room 23, Madisonville, KY 42431
Phone: (270)821-7361
Web site: www.rootsweb.com/~kyhopkin/
Parent County: Henderson

Record Type	Year Begun	Jurisdiction
Marriage	1807	County Clerk
Land	1807	County Clerk
Probate	1806	Clerk/Circuit Ct.
Court	1807	Clerk/Circuit Ct.

■ Jackson 1858

P.O. Box 339, McKee, KY 40447
Phone: (606)287-7800
Web site: www.rootsweb.com/~kyjackso/
Parent County: Rockcastle, Owsley, Madison, Clay, Estill, Laurel

Record Type	Year Begun	Jurisdiction
Birth	1911	KY/Vital Statistics
Marriage	1858	County Clerk
Death	1911	KY/Vital Statistics
Land	1858	County Clerk

■ Jefferson May 1780

527 W. Jefferson St., Louisville, KY 40202
Phone: (502)574-5680
Web site: www.rootsweb.com/~kyjeffer/
Parent County: Kentucky County, Virginia

Record Type	Year Begun	Jurisdiction
Marriage	1780	County Clerk
Divorce	1850	Clerk/Circuit Ct.
Probate	1784	Clerk/Circuit Ct.
Court	1780	Clerk/Circuit Ct.

■ Jessamine 19 Dec. 1798

100 N. Main St., Nicholasville, KY 40356
Phone: (859)885-4161

Web site: www.kycourts.net/Counties/Jessamine.asp?County=Jessamine
Parent County: Fayette

Record Type	Year Begun	Jurisdiction
Marriage	1799	County Clerk
Divorce	na	Clerk/Circuit Ct.
Land	1799	County Clerk
Probate	1799	Clerk/Circuit Ct.

■ Johnson 1843

230 Court St., Paintsville, KY 41240
Phone: (606)789-2557
Web site: www.rootsweb.com/~kyjohnso/johnson.htm
Parent County: Floyd, Morgan, Lawrence

Record Type	Year Begun	Jurisdiction
Birth	1911	KY/Vital Statistics
Marriage	1843	County Clerk
Death	1911	KY/Vital Statistics
Land	1843	County Clerk
Probate	1859	Clerk/Circuit Ct.
Court	1843	Clerk/Circuit Ct.

■ Kenton 29 Jan. 1840

P.O. Box 1109, Covington, KY 41012
Phone: (859)392-1652
Web site: www.kentoncounty.org/
Parent County: Campbell

Record Type	Year Begun	Jurisdiction
Marriage	1840	County Clerk
Divorce	na	Clerk/Circuit Ct.
Land	1840	County Clerk
Probate	1840	Clerk/Circuit Ct.
Court	1840	Clerk/Circuit Ct.

■ Knott 1884

P.O. Box 446, Hindman, KY 41822
Phone: (606)785-5651
Web site: www.rootsweb.com/~kyknott/
Parent County: Perry, Breathitt, Floyd, Letcher

Record Type	Year Begun	Jurisdiction
Marriage	1844	County Clerk
Land	1883	County Clerk
Court	1888	Clerk/Circuit Ct.

■ Knox 19 Dec. 1799

401 Court Sq., Suite 102, Barbourville, KY 40906
Phone: (606)546-3568
Web site: www.rootsweb.com/~knknox/
Parent County: Lincoln

Record Type	Year Begun	Jurisdiction
Marriage	1800	County Clerk
Land	1800	County Clerk

■ Larue 4 Mar. 1843

209 W. High St., Hodgenville, KY 42748
Phone: (270)358-3544
Web site: www.rootsweb.com/~kylarue/larue4.htm
Parent County: Hardin
Comments/research tips: Clerk of Circuit Court has Probate records 1843–1979.

Kentucky

Record Type	Year Begun	Jurisdiction
Marriage	1843	County Clerk
Divorce	1979	Clerk/Circuit Ct.
Land	1843	County Clerk

■ Laurel 12 Dec. 1825
101 S. Main St., London, KY 40741
Phone: (606)864-5158
Web site: www.rootsweb.com/~kylaurel/
Parent County: Whitley, Clay, Knox, Rockcastle

Record Type	Year Begun	Jurisdiction
Marriage	1826	County Clerk
Land	1826	County Clerk
Probate	1826	Clerk/Circuit Ct.
Court	1826	Clerk/Circuit Ct.

■ Lawrence 1822
122 S. Main Cross St., Louisa, KY 41230
Phone: (606)638-4108
Web site: www.rootsweb.com/~kylawren/lawrence.html
Parent County: Floyd, Greenup
Comments/research tips: Clerk of Circuit Court has Probate records 1822–1977.

Record Type	Year Begun	Jurisdiction
Marriage	1822	County Clerk
Divorce	na	Clerk/Circuit Ct.
Land	1822	County Clerk

■ Lee 1870
P.O. Box 551, Beattyville, KY 41311
Phone: (606)464-4115
Web site: www.usgennet.org/usa/ky/county/lee/index.html
Parent County: Owsley, Breathitt, Wolfe, Estill

Record Type	Year Begun	Jurisdiction
Marriage	1870	County Clerk
Divorce	na	Clerk/Circuit Ct.
Land	1870	County Clerk
Probate	1873	Clerk/Circuit Ct.
Court	1870	Clerk/Circuit Ct.

■ Leslie 29 Mar. 1878
P.O. Box 916, Hyden, KY 41749
Phone: (606)672-2193
Web site: www.rootsweb.com/~kyleslie
Parent County: Clay, Harlan, Perry

Record Type	Year Begun	Jurisdiction
Marriage	1878	County Clerk
Divorce	na	Clerk/Circuit Ct.
Land	1879	County Clerk
Probate	1884	Clerk/Circuit Ct.
Court	1878	Clerk/Circuit Ct.

■ Letcher 1842
156 W. Main St., Whitesburg, KY 41858
Phone: (606)633-2432
Web site: www.rootsweb.com/~kyletch/
Parent County: Perry, Harlan

Record Type	Year Begun	Jurisdiction
Marriage	1842	County Clerk

Land	1844	County Clerk
Probate	1871	County Clerk

■ Lewis 1807
P.O. Box 129, Vanceburg, KY 41179
Phone: (606)796-3062
Web site: www.rootsweb.com/~kylewis/
Parent County: Mason

Record Type	Year Begun	Jurisdiction
Marriage	1807	County Clerk
Land	1807	County Clerk
Probate	1807	Clerk/Circuit Ct.
Court	1807	Clerk/Circuit Ct.

■ Lincoln 1780
102 E. Main St., Stanford, KY 40484
Phone: (606)365-4570
Web site: www.rootsweb.com/~kylincol/
Parent County: Kentucky County, Virginia

Record Type	Year Begun	Jurisdiction
Marriage	1781	County Clerk
Divorce	1792	County Clerk
Probate	1781	Clerk/Circuit Ct.
Court	1781	Clerk/Circuit Ct.

■ Livingston 1798
P.O. Box 400, Smithland, KY 42081
Phone: (270)928-2162
Web site: http://home.hiwaay.net/~woliver/livingston.html
Parent County: Christian
Comments/research tips: Records through 1865 have been microfilmed.

Record Type	Year Begun	Jurisdiction
Marriage	1799	County Clerk
Divorce	na	Clerk/Circuit Ct.
Land	1800	County Clerk
Probate	1799	Clerk/Circuit Ct.
Court	1799	Clerk/Circuit Ct.

■ Logan 1792
P.O. Box 358, Russellville, KY 42276
Phone: (270)726-6061
Web site: www.rootsweb.com/~kylogan/
Parent County: Lincoln

Record Type	Year Begun	Jurisdiction
Marriage	1790	County Clerk
Land	1792	County Clerk
Probate	1795	Clerk/Circuit Ct.
Court	1793	Clerk/Circuit Ct.

■ Lyon 1854
P.O. Box 310, Eddyville, KY 42038
Phone: (270)388-2331
Web site: http://home.hiwaay.net/~woliver/lyon.html
Parent County: Caldwell

Record Type	Year Begun	Jurisdiction
Birth	1912	KY/Vital Statistics
Marriage	1854	County Clerk
Divorce	na	Clerk/Circuit Ct.
Land	1854	County Clerk

Kentucky

Kentucky

■ **Madison**   15 Dec. 1785
101 W. Main St., Richmond, KY 40475-1415
Phone: (859)624-4703
Web site: www.rootsweb.com/~kymadiso/madison/html
Parent County: Lincoln

Record Type	Year Begun	Jurisdiction
Marriage	1786	County Clerk
Divorce	na	Clerk/Circuit Ct.
Land	1787	County Clerk
Court	1787	Clerk/Circuit Ct.
Probate	1787	Clerk/Circuit Ct.

■ **Magoffin**   22 Feb. 1860
P.O. Box 530, Salyersville, KY 41465
Phone: (606)349-2216
Web site: www.rootsweb.com/~kymagoff/
Parent County: Floyd, Johnson, Morgan

Record Type	Year Begun	Jurisdiction
Marriage	1860	County Clerk

■ **Marion**   25 Jan. 1834
120 W. Main, Lebanon, KY 40033
Phone: (270)692-2651
Web site: www.kycourts.net/Counties/Marion.asp?County=Madison
Parent County: Washington
Comments/research tips: Probate records are with Clerk of Circuit Court 1863–present.

Record Type	Year Begun	Jurisdiction
Birth	1911	KY/Vital Statistics
Marriage	1852	County Clerk
Death	1911	KY/Vital Statistics
Divorce	na	Clerk/Circuit Ct.
Land	1863	County Clerk
Court	1863	Clerk/Circuit Ct.

■ **Marshall**   1 June 1842
1101 Main St., Benton, KY 42025
Phone: (270)527-4740
Web site: http://home.hiwaay.net/~woliver/marshall.html
Parent County: Calloway

Record Type	Year Begun	Jurisdiction
Marriage	1848	County Clerk
Land	1848	County Clerk

■ **Martin**   1 Sep. 1870
P.O. Box 460, Inez, KY 41224
Phone: (606)298-2810
Web site: www.kycourts.net/Counties/Martin.aspCounty=Martin
Parent County: Lawrence, Floyd, Pike, Johnson
Comments/research tips: Kentucky Office of Vital Statistics has Birth records 1911–1949 and Death records 1911–1949.

Record Type	Year Begun	Jurisdiction
Marriage	1871	County Clerk
Divorce	na	Clerk/Circuit Ct.
Probate	1861	Clerk/Circuit Ct.
Court	1870	Clerk/Circuit Ct.

■ **Mason**   1789
P.O. Box 234, Maysville, KY 41056
Phone: (606)564-3341
Web site: www.rootsweb.com/~kymason/mason.htm
Parent County: Bourbon

Record Type	Year Begun	Jurisdiction
Marriage	1789	County Clerk
Divorce	1929	Clerk/Circuit Ct.
Land	1789	County Clerk
Probate	1791	Clerk/Circuit Ct.
Court	1789	Clerk/Circuit Ct.

■ **McCracken**   15 Jan. 1825
P.O. Box 609, Paducah, KY 42002
Phone: (270)444-4700
Web site: www.co.mccracken.ky.us/
Parent County: Hickman

Record Type	Year Begun	Jurisdiction
Marriage	1825	County Clerk
Land	1825	County Clerk
Probate	1826	Clerk/Circuit Ct.

■ **McCreary**   1912
P.O. Box 699, Whitley City, KY 42653
Phone: (606)376-2411
Web site: www.kycourts.net/Counties/McCreary.asp?County=McCreary
Parent County: Wayne, Pulaski, Whitley
Comments/research tips: Records from 1923–1927 burned.

Record Type	Year Begun	Jurisdiction
Marriage	1912	County Clerk
Land	1912	County Clerk

■ **McLean**   28 Jan. 1854
P.O. Box 57, Calhoun, KY 42327
Phone: (270)273-3082
Web site: www.kycourts.net/Counties/McLean.asp?County=McLean
Parent County: Muhlenberg, Daviess, Ohio

Record Type	Year Begun	Jurisdiction
Marriage	1854	County Clerk
Divorce	na	Clerk/Circuit Ct.
Land	1854	County Clerk
Probate	1854	Clerk/Circuit Ct.
Court	1854	Clerk/Circuit Ct.
Military	1854	County Clerk

■ **Meade**   17 Dec. 1823
P.O. Box 614, Brandenburg, KY 40108
Phone: (270)422-2152
Web site: www.rootsweb.com/~kymeade/
Parent County: Hardin, Breckinridge
Comments/research tips: County Clerk has some Marriage and Land records from 1824. Clerk of Circuit Court has Probate records from 1824.

Record Type	Year Begun	Jurisdiction
Divorce	na	Clerk/Circuit Ct.
Tax	na	County Clerk

■ Menifee 29 May 1869
P.O. Box 123, Frenchburg, KY 40322
Phone: (606)768-3512
Web site: www.rootsweb.com/~kymenife/
Parent County: Powell, Wolfe, Bath, Morgan, Montgomery

Record Type	Year Begun	Jurisdiction
Marriage	1869	County Clerk
Divorce	1869	Clerk/Circuit Ct.

■ Mercer 15 Dec. 1785
P.O. Box 426, Harrodsburg, KY 40330
Phone: (859)734-6310
Web site: www.rootsweb.com/~kymercer/
Parent County: Lincoln

Record Type	Year Begun	Jurisdiction
Marriage	1786	County Clerk
Divorce	na	Clerk/Circuit Ct.
Land	1786	County Clerk
Probate	1786	Clerk/Circuit Ct.
Court	1786	Clerk/Circuit Ct.
Military	1919	County Clerk

■ Metcalfe 1 May 1860
P.O. Box 25, Edmonton, KY 42129
Phone: (270)432-4821
Web site: www.rootsweb.com/~kymetca2/
Parent County: Monroe, Adair, Barren, Cumberland, Green

Record Type	Year Begun	Jurisdiction
Marriage	1867	County Clerk
Land	1868	County Clerk

■ Monroe 19 Jan. 1820
P.O. Box 188, Tompkinsville, KY 42167
Phone: (270)487-5471
Web site: www.geocities.com/Heartland/Plains/4335/
Monroeco/index.html
Parent County: Barren, Cumberland

Record Type	Year Begun	Jurisdiction
Marriage	1863	County Clerk
Divorce	na	Clerk/Circuit Ct.
Land	1863	County Clerk
Probate	1863	County Clerk
Court	na	Clerk/Circuit Ct.

■ Montgomery 14 Dec. 1796
P.O. Box 414, Mount Sterling, KY 40353
Phone: (859)498-8700
Web site: www.rootsweb.com/~kymontgo/montgo.html
Parent County: Clark

Record Type	Year Begun	Jurisdiction
Birth	1911	KY/Vital Statistics
Marriage	1852	County Clerk
Death	1911	KY/Vital Statistics
Divorce	na	Clerk/Circuit Ct.
Land	1797	County Clerk
Probate	1797	Clerk/Circuit Ct.
Court	1841	Clerk/Circuit Ct.

■ Morgan 1823
P.O. Box 26, West Liberty, KY 41472
Phone: (606)743-3949

Web site: www.rootsweb.com/~kymorgan/
Parent County: Floyd, Bath
Comments/research tips: Kentucky Office of Vital Statistics has Birth records 1911–present.

Record Type	Year Begun	Jurisdiction
Marriage	1823	County Clerk
Land	1823	County Clerk
Probate	1866	Clerk/Circuit Ct.

■ Muhlenberg 1799
P.O. Box 525, Greenville, KY 42345
Phone: (270)338-1441
Web site: www.geocities.com/Heartland/Plains/4708/index-1.html
Parent County: Christian, Logan

Record Type	Year Begun	Jurisdiction
Marriage	1799	County Clerk
Divorce	na	Clerk/Circuit Ct.
Land	1798	County Clerk
Probate	1801	Clerk/Circuit Ct.

■ Nelson 29 Nov. 1784
P.O. Box 312, Bardstown, KY 40004
Phone: (502)348-1820
Web site: www.pastracks.org/states/kentucky/nelson
Parent County: Jefferson

Record Type	Year Begun	Jurisdiction
Marriage	1785	County Clerk
Probate	1784	Clerk/Circuit Ct.

■ Nicholas 1799
P.O. Box 227, Carlisle, KY 40311
Phone: (859)289-3730
Web site: www.rootsweb.com/~usgenweb/ky/nicholas/toc.html
Parent County: Bourbon, Mason

Record Type	Year Begun	Jurisdiction
Marriage	1800	County Clerk
Divorce	na	Clerk/Circuit Ct.
Land	1800	County Clerk
Probate	1800	Clerk/Circuit Ct.
Court	1800	Clerk/Circuit Ct.

■ Ohio 17 Dec. 1798
P.O. Box 85, Hartford, KY 42347
Phone: (270)298-4422
Web site: www.1bigparty.com/h/myfamily/ohioco.html
Parent County: Hardin

Record Type	Year Begun	Jurisdiction
Marriage	1808	County Clerk
Death	1911	KY/Vital Statistics
Divorce	na	Clerk/Circuit Ct.
Land	1799	County Clerk
Military	1861	County Clerk
Probate	1801	Clerk/Circuit Ct.

■ Oldham 15 Dec. 1823
100 W. Jefferson St., La Grange, KY 40031
Phone: (502)222-0047

Web site: www.rootsweb.com/~kyoldham
Parent County: Henry, Shelby, Jefferson

Record Type	Year Begun	Jurisdiction
Marriage	1824	County Clerk
Divorce	na	Clerk/Circuit Ct.
Land	1824	County Clerk
Probate	1824	Clerk/Circuit Ct.
Court	1824	Clerk/Circuit Ct.

■ Owen   6 Feb. 1819

135 W. Bryan St., Owenton, KY 40359
Phone: (502)484-2213
Web site: www.rootsweb.com/~kyowen
Parent County: Scott, Franklin, Gallatin, Pendleton
Comments/research tips: Kentucky Office of Vital Statistics has Birth and Death records 1911–present.

Record Type	Year Begun	Jurisdiction
Marriage	1819	County Clerk
Divorce	na	State Archives-Frankfort
Land	1819	County Clerk
Probate	1820	Clerk/Circuit Ct.
Court	1819	Clerk/Circuit Ct.

■ Owsley   1843

P.O. Box 500, Booneville, KY 41314
Phone: (606)593-5735
Web site: www.rootsweb.com/~usgenweb/ky/owsley/owsleyar.html
Parent County: Clay, Estill, Breathitt

Record Type	Year Begun	Jurisdiction
Marriage	1852	County Clerk
Divorce	na	Clerk/Circuit Ct.
Land	1929	County Clerk
Probate	1929	Clerk/Circuit Ct.
Court	1923	Clerk/Circuit Ct.

■ Pendleton   13 Dec. 1798

P.O. Box 112, Falmouth, KY 41040
Phone: (859)654-3380
Web site: www.rootsweb.com/~kypendle/
Parent County: Bracken, Campbell

Record Type	Year Begun	Jurisdiction
Marriage	1799	County Clerk
Divorce	na	Clerk/Circuit Ct.
Land	1798	County Clerk
Probate	1841	Clerk/Circuit Ct.
Court	1799	Clerk/Circuit Ct.

■ Perry   2 Nov. 1820

P.O. Box 150, Hazard, KY 41702
Phone: (606)436-4614
Web site: www.rootsweb.com/~kyperry/
Parent County: Clay, Floyd

Record Type	Year Begun	Jurisdiction
Marriage	1821	County Clerk
Divorce	na	Clerk/Circuit Ct.
Land	1821	County Clerk
Probate	1901	Clerk/District Ct.
Court	1822	Clerk/District Ct.

■ Pike   19 Dec. 1821

P.O. Box 631, Pikeville, KY 41501
Phone: (606)432-6211
Web site: www.rootsweb.com/~kypike/
Parent County: Floyd
Comments/research tips: County Clerk has School records 1895–1934.

Record Type	Year Begun	Jurisdiction
Birth	1911	KY/Vital Statistics
Death	1911	KY/Vital Statistics
Marriage	1822	County Clerk
Land	1820	County Clerk
Probate	1839	Clerk/Circuit Ct.

■ Powell   7 Jan. 1852

P.O. Box 548, Stanton, KY 40380
Phone: (606)663-6444
Web site: www.rootsweb.com/~kypowell
Parent County: Clark, Estill, Montgomery

Record Type	Year Begun	Jurisdiction
Marriage	1852	County Clerk
Divorce	na	Clerk/Circuit Ct.
Land	1864	County Clerk
Probate	1864	Clerk/Circuit Ct.
Court	1864	Clerk/Circuit Ct.
Military	1864	County Clerk

■ Pulaski   1799

P.O. Box 724, Somerset, KY 42501
Phone: (606)679-2042
Web site: www.rootsweb.com/~kypulask/
Parent County: Green, Lincoln

Record Type	Year Begun	Jurisdiction
Marriage	1799	County Clerk
Divorce	na	Clerk/Circuit Ct.
Land	1799	County Clerk
Probate	1801	Clerk/Circuit Ct.
Court	1799	Clerk/Circuit Ct.

■ Robertson   1 Aug. 1867

P.O. Box 75, Mount Olivet, KY 41064
Phone: (606)724-5212
Web site: http://frontierfolk.org/robco.htm
Parent County: Nicholas, Bracken, Mason, Harrison

Record Type	Year Begun	Jurisdiction
Marriage	1867	County Clerk
Divorce	1867	Clerk/Circuit Ct.
Land	1868	County Clerk
Probate	1864	Clerk/Circuit Ct.
Court	1867	Clerk/Circuit Ct.

■ Rockcastle   1810

205 E. Main St., Mount Vernon, KY 40456
Phone: (606)256-2831
Web site: www.rootsweb.com/~kyrockca
Parent County: Pulaski, Lincoln, Madison, Knox

Record Type	Year Begun	Jurisdiction
Marriage	1852	County Clerk
Divorce	1873	Clerk/Circuit Ct.

Kentucky

Land .... 1865 ....County Clerk
Probate .... 1855 ....Clerk/Circuit Ct.
Court .... 1873 ....Clerk/Circuit Ct.

■ Rowan 1856
627 E. Main St., Morehead, KY 40351
Phone: (606)784-5212
Web site: www.rootsweb.com/~kyrowan/
Parent County: Fleming, Morgan

Record Type	Year Begun	Jurisdiction
Marriage	1881	County Clerk
Divorce	na	Clerk/Circuit Ct.
Land	1880	County Clerk
Probate	1853	Clerk/Circuit Ct.
Court	1880	Clerk/Circuit Ct.

■ Russell 14 Dec. 1825
P.O. Box 579, Jamestown, KY 42629
Phone: (270)343-2125
Web site: www.rootsweb.com/~kyrussel/russell.html
Parent County: Cumberland, Adair, Wayne

Record Type	Year Begun	Jurisdiction
Marriage	1826	County Clerk
Divorce	na	Clerk/Circuit Ct.
Land	1826	County Clerk
Probate	1826	Clerk/Circuit Ct.
Court	1826	Clerk/Circuit Ct.

■ Scott 1 June 1792
101 E. Main St., Georgetown, KY 40324
Phone: (502)863-7875
Web site: www.rootsweb.com/~kyscott/scottco.htm
Parent County: Woodford

Record Type	Year Begun	Jurisdiction
Marriage	1837	County Clerk
Divorce	na	Clerk/Circuit Ct.
Land	1783	County Clerk
Probate	1792	Clerk/Circuit Ct.
Court	1792	Clerk/Circuit Ct.

■ Shelby 23 June 1792
501 Main St., Shelbyville, KY 40065-1133
Phone: (502)663-4410
Web site: www.rootsweb.com/~kyshelby
Parent County: Jefferson

Record Type	Year Begun	Jurisdiction
Birth	1911	KY/Vital Statistics
Marriage	1792	County Clerk
Probate	1792	Clerk/Circuit Ct.

■ Simpson 28 Jan. 1819
P.O. Box 268, Franklin, KY 42134
Phone: (270)586-8161
Web site: http://simpsonco.bizland.com/index.html
Parent County: Allen, Logan, Warren

Record Type	Year Begun	Jurisdiction
Marriage	1852	County Clerk
Land	1822	County Clerk

■ Spencer 7 Jan. 1824
P.O. Box 544, Taylorsville, KY 40071
Phone: (502)477-3215
Web site: www.rootsweb.com/~kyspence/kyspenc.htm
Parent County: Shelby, Bullitt, Nelson

Record Type	Year Begun	Jurisdiction
Marriage	1824	County Clerk
Divorce	na	Clerk/Circuit Ct.
Land	1824	County Clerk
Probate	1824	Clerk/Circuit Ct.
Court	1824	Clerk/Circuit Ct.

■ Taylor 1 Mar. 1848
203 N. Court St., Campbellsville, KY 42718
Phone: (270)465-6677
Web site: www.rootsweb.com/~usgenweb/ky/taylor/taylor.html
Parent County: Green

Record Type	Year Begun	Jurisdiction
Birth	1911	KY/Vital Statistics
Marriage	1848	County Clerk
Death	1911	KY/Vital Statistics
Land	1848	County Clerk
Probate	1848	Clerk/Circuit Ct.
Court	1848	Clerk/Circuit Ct.

■ Todd 30 Dec. 1819
P.O. Box 307, Elkton, KY 42220
Phone: (270)265-2363
Web site: www.rootsweb.com/~kytodd
Parent County: Christian, Logan

Record Type	Year Begun	Jurisdiction
Marriage	1820	County Clerk
Divorce	na	County Clerk
Land	1820	County Clerk
Probate	1820	Clerk/Circuit Ct.
Court	1820	Clerk/Circuit Ct.

■ Trigg 27 Jan. 1820
P.O. Box 1310, Cadiz, KY 42211
Phone: (270)552-6661
Web site: www.kyseeker.com/trigg/index.html
Parent County: Christian, Caldwell

Record Type	Year Begun	Jurisdiction
Birth	1911	KY/Vital Statistics
Marriage	1820	County Clerk
Death	1911	KY/Vital Statistics
Divorce	na	Clerk/Circuit Ct.
Land	1820	County Clerk
Court	1820	Clerk/Circuit Ct.
Probate	1820	Clerk/Circuit Ct.

■ Trimble 9 Feb. 1837
P.O. Box 262, Bedford, KY 40006
Phone: (502)255-7174
Web site: www.ole.net/~maggie/trimble/index.htm
Parent County: Henry, Oldham, Gallatin

Record Type	Year Begun	Jurisdiction
Birth	1911	KY/Vital Statistics

Kentucky

Death.....................1911.......KY/Vital Statistics
Marriage................1837.......County Clerk
Land ....1837.......County Clerk

■ Union 15 Jan. 1811
P.O. Box 119, Morganfield, KY 42437
Phone: (270)389-1334
Web site: www.rootsweb.com/~kyunion
Parent County: Henderson

Record Type	Year Begun	Jurisdiction
Marriage	1811	County Clerk
Land	1811	County Clerk
Probate	1811	Clerk/Circuit Ct.

■ Warren 19 Dec. 1796
429 E. Tenth St., Bowling Green, KY 42101-2250
Phone: (270)842-1535
Web site: www.rootsweb.com/~kywarren/
Parent County: Logan

Record Type	Year Begun	Jurisdiction
Birth	1911	KY/Vital Statistics
Marriage	1797	County Clerk
Land	1797	County Clerk
Military	1917	County Clerk
Probate	1796	Clerk/Circuit Ct.

■ Washington 2 June 1792
P.O. Box 446, Springfield, KY 40069
Phone: (859)336-5425
Web site: www.pastracks.org/states/kentucky/washington
Parent County: Nelson
Comments/research tips: County Clerk has School Census 1893–1917. Clerk of Circuit Court has some Naturalization records and some Military Discharge records.

Record Type	Year Begun	Jurisdiction
Marriage	1792	County Clerk
Divorce	1792	Clerk/Circuit Ct.
Land	1792	County Clerk
Probate	1792	Clerk/Circuit Ct.
Court	1792	Clerk/Circuit Ct.

■ Wayne 13 Dec. 1800
P.O. Box 565, Monticello, KY 42633
Phone: (606)348-5721
Web site: www.rootsweb.com/~kywayne/wayne.html
Parent County: Pulaski, Cumberland

Record Type	Year Begun	Jurisdiction
Marriage	1801	County Clerk

Land ....1800.......County Clerk
Probate ....1801.......Clerk/Circuit Ct.

■ Webster 1 July 1860
P.O. Box 19, Dixon, KY 42409
Phone: (270)639-7006
Web site: www.rootsweb.com/~kywebste/
Parent County: Hopkins, Union, Henderson

Record Type	Year Begun	Jurisdiction
Marriage	1860	County Clerk
Divorce	na	Clerk/Circuit Ct.
Land	1860	County Clerk
Court	1860	Clerk/Circuit Ct.
Probate	1860	Clerk/Circuit Ct.

■ Whitley 17 Jan. 1818
P.O. Box 8, Williamsburg, KY 40769
Phone: (606)549-6002
Web site: http://resources.rootsweb.com/USA/KY/Whitley
Parent County: Knox

Record Type	Year Begun	Jurisdiction
Birth	1911	KY/Vital Statistics
Death	1911	KY/Vital Statistics
Marriage	1860	County Clerk
Land	1818	County Clerk
Probate	1818	Clerk/Circuit Ct.

■ Wolfe 1860
P.O. Box 400, Campton, KY 41301
Phone: (606)668-3515
Web site: www.rootsweb.com/~kywolfe
Parent County: Owsley, Breathitt, Powell, Morgan

Record Type	Year Begun	Jurisdiction
Marriage	1861	County Clerk
Divorce	na	Clerk/Circuit Ct.
Land	1887	County Clerk
Probate	1887	Clerk/Circuit Ct.
Court	1818	Clerk/Circuit Ct.

■ Woodford 12 Nov. 1788
103 S. Main St., Versailles, KY 40383
Phone: (859)873-3421
Web site: www.rootsweb.com/~kywoodfo/
Parent County: Fayette

Record Type	Year Begun	Jurisdiction
Marriage	1789	County Clerk
Divorce	na	Clerk/Circuit Ct.
Land	1789	County Clerk
Probate	1789	Clerk/Circuit Ct.
Court	1789	Clerk/Circuit Ct.

Louisiana

By Emily Anne Croom

HISTORICAL OVERVIEW

Louisiana's history is a mixture of American Indian, Spanish, French, German, English, and African experience and culture. Although Spaniards reached the area in 1541, the earliest European claim came from French explorers at the mouth of the Mississippi River in 1682 and settlements at Biloxi (1699), Natchitoches (1714), and New Orleans (1718). France ceded to Spain its vast territory west of the Mississippi and the port of New Orleans in a secret treaty in 1762. French territory east of the Mississippi River, except for New Orleans, went to Britain at the end of the Seven Years War (1763). New-World-born descendants of European and African colonists, called Creoles, still live in the region. The Acadians, exiles from French Canada and ancestors of today's Cajuns, settled in southern Louisiana in the mid-1700s. Other eighteenth-century European immigrants included Palatinate Germans and Canary Islanders.

Learning that France was to regain Louisiana from Spain, President Jefferson sent envoys to try to buy New Orleans, a port of growing importance to U.S. commerce. Instead, the United States accepted Napoleon's offer to sell the entire territory of Louisiana in 1803. After several years as Orleans Territory, the southern portion of this Louisiana Purchase became the eighteenth state—Louisiana—in 1812. The United States was able to hold the port of New Orleans by defeating the British at the Battle of New Orleans in 1815.

Because Louisiana lies in the coastal plains, agriculture using slave labor dominated the early economy, from coastal sugar cane and rice plantations to cotton farms and plantations throughout most of the rest of the state. By 1860, the state's 708,000 people included about 47 percent slaves and 53 percent free inhabitants, of whom about 11 percent were foreign-born and just over 2 percent were free blacks.

© PhotoDisc/Getty Images

LOUISIANA AT A GLANCE

Motto: Union, Justice, and Confidence

Population: 4.68 million

Prevalent Religions: Primarily French Catholic in the south, Protestant, Pentecostal, and nondenominational in the north, Buddhism, Voodooism, and other fringe religions in and around New Orleans

Major Industries: Tourism, chemical products, petroleum and coal products, food processing, transportation equipment, paper products, seafood, cotton, soybeans, cattle, sugarcane, poultry and eggs, dairy products, rice

Ethnic Makeup (in percent): Caucasian 63.9%, African American 32.5%, Hispanic 2.4%, Asian 1.2%, Native American 0.6%, Other 0.7%

Famous Louisianians: Louis Armstrong, Truman Capote, Van Cliburn, Fats Domino, Louis Moreau Gottschalk, Bryant Gumbel, Lillian Hellman, Dorothy Lamour, Jerry Lee Lewis, the Marsalis brothers, Jelly Roll Morton, Huey Newton, Cokie Roberts, Kordell Stewart

Above: The swampy Atchafalaya Basin in Cajun Country

Louisiana

Louisiana seceded in January 1861, and numerous Civil War engagements took place on its soil. After New Orleans and Baton Rouge fell into northern hands in the spring of 1862, the Union controlled the eastern portion of the state. Louisiana was readmitted to the Union in 1868.

After the Civil War, farm labor was largely comprised of tenant farmers and sharecroppers. Urban Louisiana grew during the early twentieth century and by 1950 was almost 55 percent of the state's population. Especially after World War II, petrochemical, timber, fishing, and related industries became major factors in Louisiana's economy, along with food processing based on agricultural diversity. However, the traditional cotton, sugar cane, and

rice farming, as well as the related manufacturing, remained important cornerstones in the state's economy. The port of New Orleans has been a significant commercial and immigration center for over two hundred years.

RECORD HIGHLIGHTS

Louisiana began statewide birth and death registration in 1914. Information on obtaining copies is on the Office of Public Health's Web site, <www.oph.dhh.state.la.us/recordsstatistics/vitalrecords/index.html>. The state archives houses early nineteenth-century vital records from New Orleans. For more information, see the Web site

<www.sec.state.la.us/archives/archives/archives-library.htm> under "Vital Records." Also check the Family History Library catalog, using a place search under Louisiana-parish name-vital records. Consult Catholic church registers for ecclesiastical vital records.

Because of its French and Spanish roots southern Louisiana has traditionally been strongly Roman Catholic, and civil records are based on French Napoleonic civil law practices. The state is divided into parishes rather than counties. Deed records are called conveyances; probate records are successions. Important components of succession papers are records of any "family meeting" during the probate process.

Notaries traditionally wrote legal documents for individuals and businesses; thus, the notarial records are important resources. Because of the large French population, most of these documents were in French in the eighteenth and early-nineteenth centuries. Over time after U.S. acquisition, records were more consistently written in English. The Family History Library has microfilm and indexes of numerous notarial records; use a "place search" for Louisiana-parish name-notarial records.

New Orleans notarial records have been centralized in the New Orleans Notarial Archives <www.notarialarchives.org/>. No master index exists, but many volumes have internal indexes. To streamline your research, try to identify the notary who created your ancestor's records. For example, a land transaction that was filed in the parish courthouse may name the notary the family hired for that document; check that notary's records for other family documents. Also an alphabetical list of New Orleans notaries and their dates of service is online at <www.notarialarchives.org/Notaries/lista.htm>.

Additional Louisiana-specific research materials include:

- Colonial civil and ecclesiastical archives (original, microform, and published abstracts) in various repositories, including the Louisiana State Archives; Historic New Orleans Collection; Louisiana State Museum/Louisiana Historical Center Library, New Orleans; New Orleans Public Library; Louisiana State University; Tulane University; the University of Texas, Center for American History, Austin; and Clayton Library, Houston.
- *American State Papers: Public Lands.* 8 vols. Washington, D.C.: Gales and Seaton, from 1832. Land claims of early settlers. See also FHL film 908743.
- *The Territorial Papers of the United States, Territorial Papers of the United States Senate,* and *State Department Territorial Papers* for Orleans Territory.
- Confederate pensions from 1898; online index at the state archives Web site <www.sec.state.la.us/archives/gen/cpa-index.htm>.

- City archives for New Orleans, housed at the New Orleans Public Library <http://nutrias.org/~nopl/spec/speclist.htm>.

STATE RESOURCES

■ ARCHIVES, LIBRARIES, AND SOCIETIES

Alexandria Historical & Genealogical Library
503 Washington St., Alexandria, LA 71301
Tel: (318) 487-8556

Allen Genealogical & Historical Society
P.O. Box 789, Kinder, LA 70648-0789

Amite Genealogical Club
739 W. Oak, Amite, LA 70422-2734

Archdiocese of New Orleans, Archives
1100 Chartres St., New Orleans, LA 70116-2505
Tel: (504) 529-2651
Fax: (504) 529-3075
E-mail: archives@archdiocese-no.org
Web site: <www.archdioces-no.org/archives/index>

The Archives of the Diocese of Shreveport
3500 Fairfield Ave., Shreveport, LA 71104
Tel: (318) 868-4441
Fax: (318) 868-4605
E-mail: criverss@dioshpt.org
Web site: <www.dioshpt.org/archives/srchives>

Ark-La-Tex Genealogical Association
P.O. Box 4463, Shreveport, LA 71134-0463
Web site: <www.rootsweb.com/~laaltga/>

Association for Preservation and Promotion of Iberville
602 Main St., Plaquemine, LA 70764

Attakapas Historical Association
P.O. Box 43010 USL, Lafayette, LA 70504-3010

Baton Rouge Genealogical & Historical Society
P.O. Box 80565, Southeast Station, Baton Rouge, LA 70898-0565

Beauregard Historical Society
P.O. Box 658, De Ridder, LA 70634-0658

Bienville Historical Society
Rt. 1, Box 9, Bienville, LA 71008-9653

Bluebonnet Regional Branch Library
9200 Bluebonnet Blvd., Baton Rouge, LA 70810
Tel: (225) 763-2283

Bossier Restoration Foundation
231 Mercy Lane, Benton, LA 71006

Brimstone Historical Society
P.O. Box 242, Sulphur, LA 70663

Calcasieu Historical Preservation Society
1635 Hodges St., Lake Charles, LA 70601-6016

Cameron Parish Historical & Genealogical Society
P.O. Box 1107, Cameron, LA 70631

Centenary College Archives, Magale Library
P.O. Box 41188, Shreveport, LA 71134-1188
Tel: (318) 869-5462
E-mail: archives@centenary.edu
Web site: <www.centenary.edu/library/archives/index.html>

Central Louisiana Genealogical Society
P.O. Box 12206, Alexandria, LA 71315-2206
Web site: <www.rootsweb.com/~laclgs/>

Claiborne Historical Association
931 N. Main St., Homer, LA 71040

Le Circle Historique
734 Main St., New Roads, LA 70760-3522

Le Comite des Archives de la Louisiane
P.O. Box 1547, Baton Rouge, LA 70821-1547
Web site: <www.sec.state.la.us/archives/archives/archives-comite.htm>

Louisiana

Commission des Avoyelles
P.O. Box 28, Hamburg, LA
71339-0028

Desoto Historical Society
P.O. Box 300, Stonewall, LA
71078
Web site: <www.rootsweb.com/
~ladesoto/society.htm>

**Diocese of Baton Rouge,
Archives Department**
P.O. Box 2028, Baton Rouge, LA
70821-2028
Tel: (225) 387-0561 ext. 220
Fax: (225) 242-0299
E-mail: archives@diobr.org
Web site: <www.diobr.org>

**Dorcheat Historical
Association**
Webster Parish, P.O. Box 774,
Minden, LA 71055-0774

**East Ascension Genealogical &
Historical Society**
P.O. Box 1006, Gonzales, LA
70707-1006

**East Baton Rouge Parish
Library**
7711 Goodword Blvd., Baton
Rouge, LA 70806-7625
Tel: (225) 231-3700

**Edward Livingston Historical
Association**
P.O. Box 67, Livingston, LA
70754-0067

**Evangeline Genealogical &
Historical Society**
P.O. Box 664, Ville Platte, LA
70586-0664

**Foundation for Historical
Louisiana**
P.O. Box 908, Baton Rouge, LA
70821
Tel: (225) 387-2464
Fax: (225) 343-3989
E-mail: fhla@bellsouth.net
Web site: <www.fhl.org>

Francaise Comite Louisiana
2717 Massachusetts, Matairie,
LA 70003-5213

**Franklin Parish Genealogical &
Historical Society**
Rt. 4, Box 150, Winnsboro, LA
71295

**French Settlement Historical
Society**
P.O. Box 365, French Settlement,
LA 70733-0365

**Genealogical Research Society
of New Orleans**
P.O. Box 51791, New Orleans, LA
70151-1791
Web site: <www.rootsweb.com/
~lagrsno>

Genealogy West
5644 Abbey Dr., New Orleans, LA
70131-3808

**The German-Acadian Coast
Historical & Genealogical
Society**
P.O. Box 517, Destrehan, LA
70047
Web site: <www.rootsweb.com/
~lastjohn/geracadn.htm>

**Germantown Commission
Association**
P.O. Box 389, Minden, LA
71055-0389

Grant Genealogical Society
300 Main St., Colfax, LA
71417-1830

Gretna Historical Society
P.O. Box 115, Gretna, LA
70054-0115

Historical Society of Grand Isle
P.O. Box 275, Grand Isle, LA
70358-0275

**Historical Society of North
Caddo**
P.O. Box 31, Vivian, LA 71082
Web site: <http://pages.prodigy.
net/scollier/hsnc/>

Iberia Cultural Resources
924 E. Main St., New Iberia, LA
70560-3866

**The Jackson Assembly of the
Felicianas**
P.O. Box 494, Jackson, LA
70748-0494

**Jefferson Genealogical Society
Inc.**
P.O. Box 961, Metairie, LA
70004-0961
E-mail: jeffersongenealogicalsoci
ety@yahoo.com
Web site: <www.geocities.com/
jeffersongenealogicalsociety/>

Jefferson Parish Library
4747 W. Napoleon Ave., Metairie,
LA 70001
Tel: (504) 838-1190
Fax: (504) 838-1110
E-mail: helpdesk@jefferson.lib.la
.us

RESEARCH TIPS

for more info

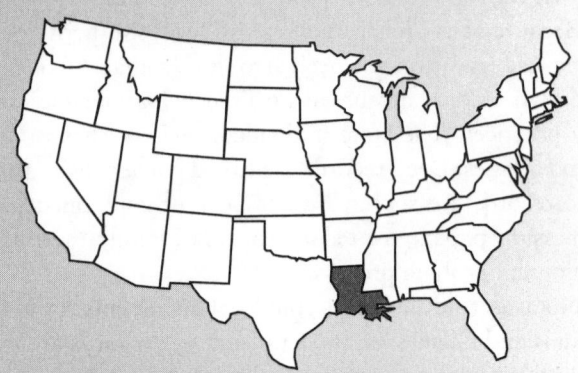

- Louisiana has not taken state censuses.
- Louisiana's first federal census is 1810, although numerous earlier residents lists have been published or microfilmed.
- Louisiana's federal land patents are searchable online at <www.glorecords.blm.gov>. Subsequent land transactions between individuals are filed at parish courthouses.
- Some parish courthouses have lost records to fires or storms; check for surviving records, resources in neighboring or parent parishes, and local, state, and federal records.

Census Records
- Federal Census Population Schedules: 1810, 1820, 1830, 1840, 1850, 1860, 1870, 1880, 1900, 1910, 1920, 1930
- Federal Census Soundex or Miracode: 1880, 1900, 1910, 1920, 1930
- Federal Mortality Schedules: 1850, 1860, 1870, 1880
- Federal Slave Schedules: 1850, 1860. Schedules named slaveholders but rarely named slaves.
- Special Census of Civil War Union Veterans and Widows: 1890
- Colonial Censuses: 1699–1796, various years and places

Web site: <www.Jefferson.lib.la
.us>

**Jefferson Parish Library, West
Bank Regional Library**
2751 Manhattan Blvd., Harvey,
LA 70058
Tel: (504) 364-2660
Fax: (504) 364-3739

Jennings Genealogical Society
136 Greenwood Dr., Jennings, LA
70546

**Jewish Genealogical Society of
New Orleans**
P.O. Box 7811, Metairie, LA
70010
Tel: (504) 836-2720
Fax: (504) 836-2722
Web site: <www.jewishgen.org/
jgsno/>

Lafayette Genealogical Society
1021 Rosedown Lane, Lafayette,
LA 70593-5932

Lafourche Heritage Society
P.O. Box 567, Thibodaux, LA
70393-0567

Lake Providence Historical Society
1002 S. Lake St., Lake Providence, LA 71254-2428

Lincoln Parish Library
509 W. Alabama St., Ruston, LA
71270-4236
Tel: (318) 251-5030

Louisiana Czech Heritage Association
14 Locker Rd., DeVille, LA
71328-9318

Louisiana Genealogical & Historical Society
P.O. Box 82060, Baton Rouge, LA
70884
Web site: <www.rootsweb.com/
~la-lghs/>

Louisiana Historical Center
% Louisiana State Museum, located at the Old U.S. Mint, 400
Esplanade Ave., New Orleans, LA
70116
Tel: (504) 568-8214
Web site: <lsm.crt.state.la.us/
site/mintex.htm>

Louisiana Historical Society
5801 St. Charles Ave., New Orleans, LA 70115
Tel: (504) 866-3049
E-mail: president@louisianahistor
icalsociety.org
Web site: <www.louisianahistoric
alsociety.org>

Louisiana Office of Cultural Development
Tel: (225) 342-8200
Fax: (225) 342-8173
E-mail: ocd@crt.state.la.us
Web site: <www.crt.state.la.us/
crt/ocd/cultdev.htm>

Louisiana State Archives, Research Library
P.O. Box 94125, 3851 Essen
Lane, Baton Rouge, LA
70804-9125
Tel: (225) 922-1000 (main) or
(225) 922-2012 (vital records)
E-mail: library@sos.louisiana.gov
Web site: <www.sec.state.la.us/
archives/archives/archives-
library.htm>

Louisiana State University, Hill Memorial Library
Baton Rouge, LA 70803
Tel: (225) 578-6544

Fax: (225) 578-9425
Web site: <www.lib.lsu.edu/spec
ial/>

Madison Parish Historical Society
100 S. Chestnut St., Tallulah, LA,
71282-4202

Mount Lebanon Historical Society
12801 Hwy. 154, Gibsland, LA
71028
Web site: <mountlebanonlouisian
a.com/historicamountlebanonlo
uisiana/>

Natchitoches Genealogical & Historical Association Library
Old Courthouse Bldg., Corner of
Second and Church Sts., P.O. Box
1349, Natchitoches, LA
71458-1349
Tel: (318) 357-2235
E-mail: ngha@wnonline.net
Web site: <www.rootsweb.com/
~lanatchi/ngl.htm>

National Archives-Southwest Region
P.O. Box 6216, Fort Worth, TX
76115-0216
Tel: (817) 831-5920
Fax: (817) 334-5511
E-mail: ftworth.reference@nara
.gov

New Orleans, Historic New Orleans Collection
Williams Research Center, 410
Chartres St., New Orleans, LA
70130
Tel: (504) 598-7171
Fax: (504) 598-7168

New Orleans Notarial Archives, Research Center
1340 Poydras St., Suite 360,
New Orleans, LA 70112
Tel: (504) 680-9604
Fax: (504) 680-9607
E-mail: Archivist@NotarialArchive
s.org
Web site: <www.notarialarchives
.org>

New Orleans Public Library
219 Loyola Ave., New Orleans, LA
70112
Tel: (504) 596-7323
E-mail: weverard@gno.lib.la.us
Web site: <nutrias.org>

North Louisiana Genealogical Society
P.O. Box 324, Ruston, LA
71273-0324

North Louisiana Historical Association
P.O. Box 6701, Shreveport, LA
71106-6701

Office of Public Health, Vital Records Registry
P.O. Box 60630, New Orleans, LA
70160
Tel: (504) 568-5152 or
1-800-454-9570
Web site: <www.oph.dhh.state.la
.us/recordstatistics/vitalrec
ords>

Ouachita Genealogical Society
221 Riverbend, West Monroe, LA
71292-3627

Plaquemines Deep Delta Genealogical & Historical Society
% Plaquemines Parish Library,
203 Hwy. 11, South Buras, LA
70041
Tel: (504) 657-7121

Plaquemines Public Library
35572 Hwy. 11, Buras, LA
70041-1625
Tel: (985) 657-7121 or (985)
657-7122
Fax: (985) 657-6175
E-mail: admin.s1pq@pelican.stat
e.lib.la.us
Web site: <www.plaquemines.lib
.la.us>

Pointe Coupee Historical Society
P.O. Box 462, New Roads, LA
70760

Pointe Coupee Parish, Le Circle Historique
734 Main St., New Roads, LA
70760-3522

Pointe Coupee Parish Museum
State Hwy. 1, New Roads, LA
70760
Tel: (225) 638-7788

Pointe de l'Eglise: Acadia Genealogical and Historical Society, Inc.
P.O. Box 160, Church Point, LA
70505-0160
E-mail: quebedo1@msn.com

Rapides Parish Library
411 Washington St., Alexandria,
LA 71301
Tel: (318) 442-1858
Web site: <www.rpl.org>

Red River Heritage
Rt. 4, Box 364, Coushatta, LA
71019-8730

River Road Historical Society
P.O. Box 5, Destrehan, LA
70047-0005

St. Bernard Genealogical Society, Inc.
P.O. Box 271, Chalmette, LA
70044-0271
Web site: <www.ccugpc.org/
sbgs/sbgs.htm>

Saint Domingue Special Interest Group
1514 Saint Roch Ave., New Orleans, LA 70117-8347
Tel: (504) 944-4908
Fax: (504) 943-8150
Web site: <www.agh.qc.ca/fr/do
cuments/sig>

St. Helena Historical Association
Rt. 1, Box 131, Amite, LA
70422-9415

St. Mary Genealogical & Historical Society
P.O. Box 662, Morgan City, LA
70381

St. Tammany Genealogical Society
P.O. Box 1904, Covington, LA
70434-1904
Web site: <www.sttammanygs
.org>

St. Tammany Historical Society
P.O. Box 1001, Mandeville, LA
70470-1001

St. Tammany Parish Library
310 W. Twenty-first Ave., Covington, LA 70433-3100
Tel: (985) 871-1219

Shreve Memorial Library, Broadmoor Branch, Genealogy Dept.
1212 Captain Shreve Dr., Shreveport, LA 71105
Tel: (318) 219-3468
Fax: (318) 868-9464
E-mail: smlgenealogy@yahoo
.com
Web site: <www.shreve-lib
.org/images/genealogy.htm>

La Societe Des Cajuns
P.O. Box 433, Larose, LA 70373
E-mail: la_societe@vienici.com
Web site: <www.vienici.com/las
ociete/>

Southeast Louisiana Historical Society
P.O. Box 789, Hammond, LA
70401-0789

Louisiana

Southern Baptist Historical Library and Archives
901 Commerce St., Nashville, TN 37203-3630
Tel: (615) 244-0344
Fax: (615) 782-4821
Web site: <www.sbhla.org>

Southwest Louisiana Genealogical & Historical Library
411 Pujo St., Lake Charles, LA 70601
Tel: (337) 437-3490
Web site: <www.calcasieu.lib.la .us/SouthwestLouisianaGeneal ogicalandHistoricalLibrary>

Southwest Louisiana Genealogical Society, Inc.
P.O. Box 5652, Lake Charles, LA 70606-5652
Web site: <www.rootsweb.com/ ~laslgs/swlgs.htm>

Southwest Louisiana Historical Association
4201 Alma Lane, Lake Charles, LA 70605
Web site: <www.swlahistory .org>

State Land Office
P.O. Box 44124, Baton Rouge, LA 70804
Tel: (504) 342-4586
E-mail: Gwelch@doa.state.la.us
Web site: <www.state.la.us/slo/>

State Library of Louisiana
P.O. Box 131, Baton Rouge, LA 70821
Tel: (225) 342-4923
Fax: (225) 219-4804
E-mail: admin@state.lib.la.us
Web site: <www.state.lib.la .us>

Tangipahoa Parish Historical Society
739 W. Oak, Amite, LA 70422-2734

Tangipahoa Parish Library, Genealogy Department
200 E. Mulberry St., Amite, LA 70422
Tel: (985) 748-7559
Fax: (985) 748-2812
Web site: <www.tangipahoa.lib .la.us>

Terrebonne Genealogical Society
P.O. Box 20295, Houma, LA 70360-0295
Web site: <www.rootsweb.com/ ~laterreb/tgs.htm>

Tulane University, Special Collections
Jones Hall, New Orleans, LA 70118
Tel: (504) 865-5685
Fax: (504) 865-5761
E-mail: meneray@tulane.edu
Web site: <specialcollections.tul ane.edu>

University of Louisiana-Lafayette, Dupré Library, Louisiana Historical Association, Center for Louisiana Studies
P.O. Box 40831, 302 St. Bary Blvd., Lafayette, LA 70504
Tel: (337) 482-6027
Fax: (337) 482-6028
E-mail: cls@louisiana.edu
Web site: <cls.louisiana.edu/lahi st.html> and <cls.louisiana.edu/ collections-archives.html>

University of New Orleans, Earl K. Long Library
2000 Lakeshore Dr., New Orleans, LA 70148
Tel: (504) 280-6543
Fax: (504) 280-3173 or (504) 280-7277

Vermillion Genealogical Society
P.O. Box 117, Abbeville, LA 70511-0117

Vermillion Historical Society
P.O. Box 877, Abbeville, LA 70511-0877
Tel: (337) 893-7142
Fax: (337) 893-7145
Web site: <www.vermilionhistoric al.com>

Vernon Historical & Genealogical Society & Library
P.O. Box 159, Anacoco, LA 71403-0310

West Bank Genealogy Society
P.O. Box 872, Harvey, LA 70059-0872

West Baton Rouge Genealogical Society
P.O. Box 1126, Port Allen, LA 70767-1126

West Baton Rouge Historical Society
845 N. Jefferson Ave., Port Allen, LA 70767-2417

West Feliciana Historical Society
P.O. Box 338, St. Francisville, LA 70775

Tel: (225) 635-6330
E-mail: sf@audubonpilgrimage .info

Winn Parish Genealogical & Historical Association, Inc.
P.O. Box 652, Winnfield, LA 71483-0652
Web site: <www.rootsweb.com/ ~lawpgha/>

BIBLIOGRAPHY

■ GENERAL RESOURCES

Acadian-Cajun Genealogy: Step by Step
by Timothy Hebert (Lafayette, LA: Center for Louisiana Studies, University of Southwestern Louisiana, ca. 1993)

Acadian to Cajun: Transformation of a People, 1803–1877
by Carl A. Brasseaux (Jackson, MS: University Press of Mississippi, ca. 1992)

Acadian Odyssey
by Oscar William Winzerling (Baton Rouge, LA: Louisiana State University Press, 1955)

African-American Genealogy: A Bibliography and Guide to Sources
by Curt Bryan Witcher (Fort Wayne, IN: Round Tower Books, 2000. Includes white families' papers)

Africans in Colonial Louisiana: The Development of Afro-Creole Culture in the Eighteenth Century
by Gwendolyn Midlo Hall (Baton Rouge, LA: Louisiana State University Press, ca. 1992)

An Atlas of Louisiana Surnames of French and Spanish Origin
by Robert C. West (Baton Rouge, LA: Geoscience Publications, Louisiana State University, 1986)

Biographical and Historical Memoirs of Louisiana: Embracing an Authentic and Comprehensive Account of the Chief Events in the History of the State, A Special Sketch of Every Parish and a Record of the Lives of Many of the Most Worthy and Illustrious Families and Individuals, 2 vols.
(Chicago, IL: The Goodspeed Publishing Co., 1892)

Black Names in Louisiana
by Mary Eleanor Williams (LA: M. E. Williams, ca. 1992)

The Canary Islanders of Louisiana
by Gilbert C. Din (Baton Rouge, LA: Louisiana State University Press, ca. 1988)

The Catholic Church in Louisiana
by Roger Baudier (New Orleans: A.W. Hyatt Stationery Manufacturing Co., Ltd., 1939)

Cajun Sketches from the Prairies of Southwest Louisiana
by Lauren C. Post (Baton Rouge, LA: Louisiana State University Press, 1990)

Creoles of Color in the Bayou Country
by Carl A. Brasseaux, Keith P. Fontenot, and Claude F. Oubre (Jackson, MS: University Press of Mississippi, ca. 1994)

Creole New Orleans: Race and Americanization
edited by Arnold R. Hirsch and Joseph Logsdon (Baton Rouge, LA: Louisiana State University Press, ca. 1992)

A Dictionary of Louisiana Biography, 2 vols.
edited by Glenn R. Conrad (New Orleans, LA: Louisiana Historical Association, ca. 1988)

Dictionnaire Genealogique des Familles Canadiennes Depuis la Fondation de la Colonie jusqu'a nos jours, 7 vols.
by Cyprien Tanguay (Montreal: E. Senecal, 1871–1890)

Down the Old Spanish Trail
by Kitty Courts (New Iberia, LA: K. Courts, ca. 1999)

Forgotten People: Cane River's Creoles of Color
by Gary B. Mills (Baton Rouge, LA: Louisiana State University Press, ca. 1977)

Founding of New Acadia: The Beginning of Acadian Life in Louisiana, 1765–1803
by Carl A. Brasseaux (Baton Rouge, LA: Louisiana State University Press, ca. 1987)

The Free Negro in Ante-Bellum Louisiana
by H. E. Sterkc (Rutherford, NJ: Fairleigh Dickinson University Press, 1972)

The French Experience in Louisiana
edited by Glenn R. Conrad (Lafayette, LA: Center for Louisiana Studies, University of Southwestern Louisiana, 1995)

French and Spanish Records of Louisiana: A Bibliographical Guide to Archive and Manuscript Sources
by Henry Putney Beers (Baton Rouge: Louisiana State University Press, 1989)

Genealogical Encyclopedia of the Colonial Americas
by Christina K. Schaefer (Baltimore: Genealogical Publishing Co., 1998. Pages 589-598, Louisiana)

Genealogical Materials in the New Orleans Public Library
by Collin B. Hamer, Jr. (New Orleans, LA: Friends of the New Orleans Public Library, 1984)

The Genealogist's Companion and Sourcebook, 2d ed.
by Emily Anne Croom (Cincinnati: Betterway Books, 2003)

A Genealogist's Guide to Discovering Your African-American Ancestors
by Franklin Carter Smith and Emily Anne Croom (Cincinnati: Betterway Books, 2003)

German Coast Families: European Original and Settlement in Colonial Louisiana
by Albert J. Robichaux, Jr. (Rayne, LA: Hebert Publications, ca. 1997)

A Guide to the Acadians in Maryland in the Eighteenth and Nineteenth Centuries
by Gregory A. Wood (Baltimore, MD: Gateway Press, 1995)

A Guide to Church Records in Louisiana, 1720–1975
by Donald J. Hebert (Eunice, LA: 1975)

Guide to Genealogical Research in the National Archives of the United States
edited by Anne Bruner Eales and Robert M. Kvasnicka (Washington, DC: National Archives and Records Administration, 2000)

A Guide to the History of Louisiana
edited by Light Townsend Cummins and Glen Jeansonne (Westport, CN: Greenwood Press, 1982)

Guide to the Microfilm Edition of the Records of the Diocese of Louisiana and the Floridas, 1576–1803
by Thomas T. McAvoy, and Lawrence J. Bradley (Notre Dame, IN: University of Notre Dame Archives, 1967)

A Guide to Printed Sources for Genealogical and Historical Research in the Louisiana Parishes
compiled by Yvette Guillot Boling (Jefferson, LA: Y. G. Boling with the Louisiana Genealogical and Historical Society, ca. 1985)

Gulf Coast Colonials; A Compendium of French Families in Early Eighteenth Century Louisiana
by Winston De Ville (Baltimore, MD: Genealogical Pub. Co., 1968)

The Historic Indian Tribes of Louisiana: From 1542 to the Present
by Fred B. Kniffen, Hiram F. Gregory, and George A. Stokes (Baton Rouge, LA: Louisiana State University Press, ca. 1987)

A History of the German Churches in Louisiana
by J. Hanno Deiler, translated and edited by Marie Stella Condo (Lafayette, LA: Center for Louisiana Studies, University of Southwest Louisiana, ca. 1983)

A History of Louisiana, 4 vols.
by Alcee Fortier (New York, NY: Goupil & Co. of Paris, Manzi, Joyant, and Co., 1904)

The History of Louisiana, from the Earliest Period, 2 vols.
by Francois Xavier Martin (New Orleans, LA: Lyman and Beardslee, 1827–29)

Index to the Archives of Spanish West Florida, 1782–1810
introduction by Stanley Clisby Arthur (New Orleans, LA: Polyanthos, 1975)

Indians, Settlers & Slaves in a Frontier Exchange Economy: The Lower Mississippi Valley Before 1783
by Daniel H. Usner Jr. (Chapel Hill, NC: University of North Carolina Press, ca. 1992)

The Large Slaveholders of the Deep South, 1860
by Joseph Karl Menn (Ann Arbor, MI: UMI Dissertation Services, 1964)

"Louisiana." In Genealogical Research: Methods and Sources
by Winston DeVille (Kenn Stryker-Rodda, ed. Vol. 2. Rev. ed. Washington, D.C.: The American Society of Genealogists, 1983)

Louisiana Colonials: Soldiers and Vagabonds
translated and compiled by Winston De Ville (Mobile, AL: W. De Ville, 1963)

Louisiana History: The Journal of the Louisiana Historical Association, 42 vols.
by the Louisiana Historical Association (Lafayette, LA: The Louisiana Historical Association, 1968)

Louisiana, The Land and Its People
by Sue Eakin and Manie Culbertson, illustrations by James Forest Culbertson (Gretna, LA: Pelican Pub. Co., 1986)

Louisiana, A Narrative History, 3rd ed.
by Edwin Adams Davis (Baton Rouge, LA: Claitor's Pub. Division, 1971)

The Louisiana Purchase and Its Aftermath, 1800–1830
edited by Dolores Egger Labbe (Lafayette, LA: Center for Louisiana Studies, University of Southwestern Louisiana, 1998)

Louisiana Research Outline
(Salt Lake City, UT: Corp. of the President of the Church of Jesus Christ of L.D.S., ca. 1988)

Louisianans and Their State: A Historical And Biographical Text Book of Louisiana
by the Louisiana Historical and Biographical Association (New Orleans, LA: ca. 1919)

National Archives Microfilm Catalogs online:
<www.archives.gov/publications/genealogy_microfilm_catalogs.html>

Newspaper Files in Louisiana State University Library
(Baton Rouge, LA: Louisiana State University Library, 1961)

Old Families of Louisiana, 1608–1929
by Stanley Clisby Arthur (New Orleans, LA: Harmanson, 1931)

Old Louisiana Plantation Homes and Family Trees, 2 vols.
by Herman Boehm de Bachelle Seebold (New Orleans, LA: Pelican Press, Inc., ca. 1941)

South Louisiana Records: Church and Civil Records of Lafourche-Terrebonne Parishes, 12 vols.
by Donald J.Hebert (Cecilia, LA: D.J. Hebert, ca. 1978–ca. 1985)

A Southern Catholic Heritage
by Charles E. Nolan (New Orleans, LA: Archdiocese of New Orleans, 1976)

Southwest Louisiana: Biographical And Historical
edited by William Henry Perry (New Orleans, LA: Gulf Publishing Co., 1891)

Southwest Louisiana Records: Church and Civil Records, revised ed., 4 vols.
by Donald J. Hebert, art by Jan Lewis (Hebert Publications, ca. 1996-ca. 1997)

The Spanish Borderlands: A Chronicle of Old Florida and the Southwest
by Herbert Eugene Bolton (New Haven: Yale University Press, 1921)

Sweet Chariot: Slave Family and Household Structure in Nineteenth-Century Louisiana
by Ann Patton Malone (Chapel Hill, NC: University of North Carolina Press, ca. 1992)

Vignettes of Louisiana Church History
by George C. Poret (Mansura, LA: G. C. Poret, ca. 1985)

Louisiana

Who's Who in Colored Louisiana
edited by A. E. Perkins (Baton Rouge, LA: Douglas Loan Co., Inc., 1930)

Who's Who in Louisiana and Mississippi: Biographical Sketches of Prominent Men and Women of Louisiana and Mississippi
(New Orleans, LA: Times-Picayune, 1918)

Women in the Florida Parishes, 2 vols.
by Donna Burge Adams (Baton Rouge, LA: D.B. Adams, 1985–1986)

■ CENSUS RECORDS

The American Census Handbook
by Thomas Jay Kemp (Wilmington, DE: Scholarly Resources, 2001)

The Census Book: A Genealogist's Guide to Federal Census Facts, Schedules and Indexes
by William Dollarhide (Bountiful, UT: Heritage Quest, 2000)

The Census Tables for the French Colony of Louisiana from 1699 Through 1732
compiled and translated by Charles R. Maduell Jr. (Baltimore, MD: Genealogical Pub. Co., 1972)

Finding Answers in U.S. Census Records
by Loretto Dennis Szucs and Matthew Wright (Orem, UT: Ancestry Publishing, ca. 2002)

Louisiana Census and Militia Lists 1770–1789
compiled, translated, and edited by Albert J. Robichaux Jr. (Harvey, LA: 1973)

Map Guide to the U.S. Federal Censuses, 1790–1920
by William Thorndale and William Dollarhide (Baltimore, MD: Genealogical Publishing Co., 1987)

State Census Records
by Ann S. Lainhart (Baltimore, MD: Genealogical Publishing, 1992)

Your Guide to the Federal Census
by Kathleen W. Hinckley (Cincinnati: Betterway Books, 2002)

■ IMMIGRATION RECORDS

The Acadian Exiles in the American Colonies, 1755–1768
compiled, translated, and edited by Milton P. Reider Jr., and Norma Gaudet Rieder (Metairie, LA: Reider, ca. 1977)

American Naturalization Records, 1790–1990: What They Are and How to Use Them
by John J. Newman (North Salt Lake, UT: HeritageQuest, 1998)

American Passenger Arrival Records
by Michael Tepper (Baltimore: Genealogical Publishing Co., 1993)

The Canary Islands Migration to Louisiana, 1778–1783: The History and Passenger Lists of the Islenos Volunteer Recruits and Their Families
by Sidney Louis Viller'ae (Baltimore MD: Genealogical Publishing Co., 1972)

The First Families of Louisiana
translated and compiled by Glenn R. Conrad (Baton Rouge, LA: Claitor's Pub. Division, 1970)

The "Foreign French:" Nineteenth-Century French Immigration into Louisiana, 3 vols.
by Carl A. Brasseaux (Lafayette, LA: Center for Louisiana Studies, University of Southwestern Louisiana, 1990–1993)

From Palermo to New Orleans
compiled by Mary Ann Riviere (M. A. Riviere, ca. 1987)

Immigration Files of Southwest Louisiana, 1840–1929: Naturalization Records
by Donald J. Hebert (Mire, LA: Hebert Publications, 1990)

A Refuge For All Ages, Immigration In Louisiana History
edited by Carl A. Brasseaux (Lafayette, LA: Center for Louisiana Studies, University of Southwestern Louisiana, 1996)

They Became Americans: Finding Naturalization Records and Ethnic Origins
by Loretto Dennis Szucs (Salt Lake City: Ancestry, Inc., 1998)

They Came in Ships: A Guide to Finding Your Immigrant Ancestor's Arrival Records, 2d ed.
by John P. Colletta (Salt Lake City: Ancestry, Inc., 1993)

■ LAND RECORDS

English Land Grants in West Florida: A Register for the States of Alabama, Mississippi, and Parts of Florida and Louisiana, 1766–1776
by Winston De Ville (Ville Platte, LA: Winston De Ville, 1986)

Federal Land Grants in the Territory of Orleans: The Delta Parishes, adapted from American State Papers, Public Lands volume II, and Arranged by Counties as they Existed in 1812
by Charles R. Maudell, Jr. (New Orleans, LA: Polyanthose, 1975)

First Settlers of the Louisiana Territory: Orleans Territory Grants from American State Papers, Class VIII, Public Lands
(Nacogdoches, TX: Ericson Books; and St. Louis, MO: Ingmire Publications, ca. 1983)

Index To U.S. Tract Books, Northwestern Land District, Old Natchitoches District, In The Louisiana State Land Office, Baton Rouge, Louisiana
compiled by Ennis Mayfield Tipton (Bossier City, LA: Tipton Printing & Pub. Co., 1980)

Land Claims in the Eastern District of the Oreleans Territory
by Walter Lowrie (Greenville, SC: Southern Historical Press, 1986)

Land and Property Research in the United States
by E. Wade Hone (Salt Lake City, UT: Ancestry, ca. 1997)

Locating Your Roots: Discover Your Ancestors Using Land Records
by Patricia Law Hatcher (Cincinnati: Betterway Books, 2003)

Louisiana Land Titles: An Inventory of State Land Office Records from the Early Nineteenth Century on File at the State Archives of Louisiana
compiled by Orgy G. Poret and John Spencer Howell (Ville Platte, LA: Provincial Press, 1998)

Papers of Vicente Sebastian Pintado, 1781–1842
by Vicente Sebastian Pintado, (1781–1842)

Survey of Federal Archives in Louisiana: From U.S. Land Office Archives
Historical Records Survey (Baton Rouge, LA: Work Progress Administration of Louisiana, 1930)

■ MAPS

County-Parish Boundaries in Louisiana
prepared by the Historical Records Survey (New Orleans, LA: The Department of Archives, Louisiana State University, 1939)

Historical Atlas of Louisiana
by Charles Robert Goins and John Michael Caldwell (Norman, OK: University of Oklahoma Press, ca. 1995)

Index to Louisiana Place Names Mentioned in the War of the Rebellion: A Compilation of the Official Records of the Union and Confederate Armies
edited by Dennis A. Gibson, indexed by Jeffrey A. Baker, et al. (Lafayette, LA: University of Southwestern Louisiana, 1975)

Louisiana, A Geographical Portrait
by M.B. Newton, Jr. (Baton Rouge, LA: Geoforensics, 1987)

Louisiana: A Guide to the State, rev. ed.
edited by Harry Hansen (New York: Hastings House, ca. 1971)

Louisiana Post Offices
by John J. Germann with Alan H. Patera and John S. Gallagher (Lake Grove, OR: The Depot, ca. 1990)

■ MILITARY RECORDS

The Confederate Cherokees: John Drew's Regiment of Mounted Rifles
by W. Craig Gaines (Baton Rouge, LA: Louisiana State University Press, ca. 1989)

Doctors in Gray: The Confederate Medical Service, Louisiana
by H.H. Cunningham (Baton Rouge, LA: Louisiana State University Press, 1993)

Guide to Louisiana Confederate Military Units, 1861–1865
by Arthur W. Bergeron Jr. (Baton Rouge, LA: Louisiana State University Press, ca. 1989)

The Life of Johnny Reb: The Common Soldier of the Confederacy
by Bell Irvin Wiley (Baton Rouge, LA: Louisiana State University Press, 1978)

Louisiana Soldiers in the War of 1812
by Marion John Bennett Pierson (Baton Rouge, LA: Louisiana Genealogical and Historical Society, 1963)

Louisiana Troops, 1720–1770
by Winston De Ville (Fort Worth American Reference Publishers, ca. 1965, 1967)

Louisiana Volunteers In The War of 1898
compiled by Nancy Lowrie Wright and Cathy Dantin Shannon (Houma, LA: Wright Shannon Publications, 1989)

Louisiana in the War of 1812
by Powell A. Casey (Baton Rouge, LA: 1963)

Military Records of Louisiana: Including Biographical and Historical Papers Relating to the Military Organizations of the State
by Napier Bartlett (New Orleans, LA: L. Graham & Co., Printers, 1875)

More Generals in Gray
by Bruce S. Allardice (Baton Rouge, LA: Louisiana State University Press, ca. 1995)

Records of Louisiana Confederate Soldiers and Louisiana Confederate Commands, 3 vols.
compiled by Andrew B. Booth (Spartanburg, SC: Reprint Co., 1984)

Uncle, We Are Ready! Registering America's Men, 1917–1918: A Guide to Researching World War I Draft Registration Cards
by John J. Newman (North Salt Lake, UT: HeritageQuest, 2001)

U.S. Military Records: A Guide to Federal & State Sources, Colonial America to the Present
by James C. Neagles (Salt Lake City: Ancestry, Inc., 1994)

World War II: A Family Historian's Guide
by Debra Johnson Knox (Spartanburg, SC: MIE Publishing, 2003)

■ PROBATE RECORDS

The Calendar of Louisiana Colonial Documents, 3 vols.
by Elizabeth Becker Gianelloni and Winston De Ville (S.I.: The Louisiana State Archives and Records Comission, 1961–ca. 1967)

■ VITAL RECORDS

Be It Known and Remembered: Bible Records
by the Louisiana Genealogical and Historical Society (Baton Rouge, LA: 1960)

Death Notices from Louisiana Newspapers, 4 vols.
compiled by LaGroue Mayers and Gloria Lambert Kerns (Baker, LA: Folk Finders, ca. 1984)

Guide to Public Vital Statistics Records in Louisiana
prepared by the Historical Records Survey and the War Services Program, Service Division, Work Projects Administration (New Orleans, LA: The Louisiana State Board of Health, 1942)

Guide to Vital Statistics Records of Church Archives in Louisiana, 2 vols.
prepared by War Service Program, Service Division, Works Projects Administration (New Orleans, LA: The Louisiana State Board of Health, 1942)

Louisiana Marriage Contracts: A Compilation of Abstracts From Records of the Superior Council of Louisiana During the French Regime, 1725–1769, 2 vols.
by Alice Daly Forsyth and Ghislaine Pleasonton; introduction by Hans W. Baade; with an index by Yvette Guillot Boling (New Orleans, LA: Polyanthos, 1980–1989)

Marriage Dispensations in the Diocese of Louisiana and the Floridas: 1786–1803
by Shiley Chaisson Gourgard (New Orleans, LA: Polyanthose, 1980)

The New Orleans French, 1720–1733, A Collection of Marriage Records Relating to the First Colonists of the Louisiana Province
by Winston De Ville (Baltimore, MD: Genealogical Publishing Co., 1973)

Southwest Louisiana Records: Church and Civil Records, rev. ed., 4 vols.
by Donald J. Hebert, art by Jan Lewis (Rayne, LA: Herbert Publications, ca. 1996–ca. 1997)

Tombstone Inscriptions of Northwest Louisiana Cemeteries
compiled by John Purnell Frazier (Pittsburg, TX: John Purnell Frazier, 1986)

Your Guide to Cemetery Research
by Sharon DeBartolo Carmack (Cincinnati: Betterway Books, 2002)

■ Acadia Parish 10 Apr. 1805
Parent Parish: Original parish
Comments/research tips: Discontinued. Became Ascension and St. James Parishes 31 March 1807.

■ Acadia Parish 30 June 1886
P.O. Box 922, Crowley, LA 70527-0922
Phone: (337)788-8881
Web site: www.rootsweb.com/~lapehgs/
Parent Parish: St. Landry

Record Type	Year Begun	Jurisdiction
Probate	1886	Parish Clerk
Court	1886	Parish Clerk
Marriage	1886	Parish Clerk
Divorce	1886	Parish Clerk

■ Allen Parish 12 Jan. 1912
P.O. Box 248, Oberlin, LA 70655-2007
Phone: (337)639-4351
Web site: www.rootsweb.com/~laallen/
Parent Parish: Calcasieu

Record Type	Year Begun	Jurisdiction
Marriage	1913	Parish Clerk
Divorce	1913	Parish Clerk
Probate	1913	Parish Clerk
Court	1913	Parish Clerk

■ Ascension Parish 31 Mar. 1807
300 Houmas St., P.O. Box 192, Donaldsonville, LA 70346
Phone: (225)773-9866
Web site: www.ascensionparish.net/
Parent Parish: Acadia, St. James

Record Type	Year Begun	Jurisdiction
Marriage	1763	Parish Clerk
Divorce	1800	Parish Clerk
Land	1770	Parish Clerk
Probate	1800	Parish Clerk
Court	1800	Parish Clerk

■ Assumption Parish 31 Mar. 1807
4809 Hwy. 1, P.O. Box 249, Napoleonville, LA 70390
Phone: (985)369-6653
Web site: www.rootsweb.com/~laassump/

Parent Parish: Original parish

Record Type	Year Begun	Jurisdiction
Probate	1841	Parish Clerk
Marriage	1800	Parish Clerk
Divorce	1868	Parish Clerk
Land	1788	Parish Clerk
Court	1868	Parish Clerk

■ Attakapas Parish 10 Apr. 1805
Parent Parish: Original parish
Comments/research tips: Discontinued and divided into St. Martin and St. Mary 17 April 1811, Lafayette, 17 February 1823, and Vermilion 25 March 1844.

■ Avoyelles Parish 31 Mar. 1807
P.O. Box 219, Marksville, LA 71351
Phone: (318)253-7523
Web site: www.mindspring.com/~jwbarron/avoyeles.htm
Parent Parish: Original parish

Record Type	Year Begun	Jurisdiction
Marriage	1908	Parish Clerk
Divorce	1939	Parish Clerk
Land	1908	Parish Clerk
Probate	1925	Parish Clerk
Court	1925	Parish Clerk
Military	1886	Parish Clerk

■ Baton Rouge Parish 31 Mar. 1807
Parent Parish: Pointe Coupee
Comments/research tips: (See East Baton Route and West Baton Rouge.) Became East and West Baton Rouge Parishes in 1810.

■ Beauregard Parish 12 Jan. 1913
214 W. First St., P.O. Box 100, De Ridder, LA 70634-0310
Phone: (337)463-8595
Web site: www.rootsweb.com/~labeaure/beaurega.htm
Parent Parish: Calcasieu

Record Type	Year Begun	Jurisdiction
Marriage	1913	Parish Clerk
Divorce	1913	Parish Clerk
Court	1913	Parish Clerk
Land	1913	Parish Clerk
Probate	1913	Parish Clerk

■ Bienville Parish 14 Mar. 1848
100 Courthouse Dr., P.O. Box 746, Arcadia, LA 71001
Phone: (318)263-2123
Web site: www.rootsweb.com/~labienvi/
Parent Parish: Claiborne

Record Type	Year Begun	Jurisdiction
Marriage	1848	Parish Clerk
Divorce	1848	Parish Clerk
Probate	1848	Parish Clerk
Court	1848	Parish Clerk

■ Bossier Parish 24 Feb. 1843
240 Burt Blvd., P.O. Box 430, Benton, LA 71006
Phone: (318)965-2336

Web site: www.mybossier.com/index.htm
Parent Parish: Claiborne

Record Type	Year Begun	Jurisdiction
Marriage	1843	Parish Clerk
Divorce	1843	Parish Clerk
Land	1843	Parish Clerk
Probate	1843	Parish Clerk
Court	1843	Parish Clerk
Military	1917	Parish Clerk

■ Caddo Parish 18 Jan. 1838
501 Texas St., Room 103, Shreveport, LA 71101
Phone: (318)226-6786
Web site: www.caddo.org/parish_comm.cFm
Parent Parish: Natchitoches

Record Type	Year Begun	Jurisdiction
Marriage	1835	Parish Clerk
Divorce	1835	Parish Clerk
Probate	1835	Parish Clerk
Land	1835	Parish Clerk
Court	1835	Parish Clerk

■ Calcasieu Parish 24 Mar. 1840
1000 Ryan St., P.O. Box 1030, Lake Charles, LA 70601
Phone: (337)437-3550
Web site: www.cppj.net/
Parent Parish: St. Landry

Record Type	Year Begun	Jurisdiction
Marriage	1910	Parish Clerk
Divorce	1910	Parish Clerk
Probate	1910	Parish Clerk
Land	1910	Parish Clerk
Court	1910	Parish Clerk

■ Caldwell Parish 6 Mar. 1838
200 Main St., Columbia, LA 71418
Phone: (318)649-2681
Web site: www.rootsweb.com/~lacaldwe/
Parent Parish: Catahoula, Ouachita

Record Type	Year Begun	Jurisdiction
Marriage	1838	Parish Clerk
Divorce	1838	Parish Clerk
Probate	1838	Parish Clerk
Land	1838	Parish Clerk
Court	1838	Parish Clerk

■ Cameron Parish 15 Mar. 1870
119 Smith Circle, P.O. Box 549, Cameron, LA 70631-0549
Phone: (337)775-5316
Web site: www.cameronparish.net/
Parent Parish: Calcasieu, Vermilion

Record Type	Year Begun	Jurisdiction
Marriage	1870	Parish Clerk
Divorce	1870	Parish Clerk
Probate	1870	Parish Clerk
Land	1870	Parish Clerk
Court	1870	Parish Clerk
Military	1918	Parish Clerk

■ **Carroll Parish** 14 Mar. 1832

Parent Parish: Concordia, Ouachita

Comments/research tips: (See East and West Carroll) Divided into East and West Carroll 28 March 1877.

■ **Catahoula Parish** 23 Mar. 1808

301 Bushley St., Room 101, Harrisonburg, LA 71340-0198

Phone: (318)744-5497

Web site: www.rootsweb.com/~lacataho/catahoula.htm

Parent Parish: Rapides

Record Type	Year Begun	Jurisdiction
Marriage	1830	Parish Clerk
Divorce	ca. 1800	Parish Clerk
Land	1808	Parish Clerk
Probate	ca. 1800	Parish Clerk
Burial	ca. 1800	Parish Clerk
Military	na	Parish Clerk

■ **Claiborne Parish** 13 Mar. 1828

512 E. Main St., P.O. Box 330, Homer, LA 71040

Phone: (318)927-9601

Web site: www.rootsweb.com/~laclaib2/claibla.htm

Parent Parish: Natchitoches

Comments/research tips: Courthouse burned in 1849.

Record Type	Year Begun	Jurisdiction
Marriage	1850	Parish Clerk
Divorce	1850	Parish Clerk
Probate	1850	Parish Clerk
Land	1850	Parish Clerk
Court	1850	Parish Clerk

■ **Concordia Parish** 10 Apr. 1805

4001 Carter St., P.O. Box 790, Vidalia, LA 71373-0790

Phone: (318)336-4204

Web site: www.rootsweb.com/~laconcor/

Parent Parish: Original parish (Ayoelles)

Record Type	Year Begun	Jurisdiction
Marriage	1840	Parish Clerk
Divorce	1850	Parish Clerk
Probate	1850	Parish Clerk
Land	1850	Parish Clerk
Court	1850	Parish Clerk

■ **DeSoto Parish** 1 Apr. 1843

Parish Courthouse, P.O. Box 1206, Mansfield, LA 71052

Phone: (318)872-3110

Web site: www.rootsweb.com/~ladesoto/

Parent Parish: Natchitoches, Caddo

Record Type	Year Begun	Jurisdiction
Marriage	1843	Parish Clerk
Divorce	na	Parish Clerk
Land	1843	Parish Clerk
Probate	na	Parish Clerk
Court	na	Parish Clerk

■ **East Baton Rouge Parish** 22 Dec. 1810

222 St. Louis St., Baton Rouge, LA 70802-5817

Phone: (225)383-0378

Web site: www.ebrclerkofcourt.org/

Parent Parish: Baton Rouge

Record Type	Year Begun	Jurisdiction
Land	1782	Parish Clerk
Court	1782	Parish Clerk
Marriage	1840	Parish Clerk
Divorce	1782	Parish Clerk
Probate	1782	Parish Clerk

■ **East Carroll Parish** 28 Mar. 1877

400 First St., Lake Providence, LA 71254-2616

Phone: (318)559-2399

Web site: www.eastcarroll.net/home.htm

Parent Parish: Carroll

Record Type	Year Begun	Jurisdiction
Marriage	na	Parish Clerk
Land	na	Parish Clerk
Probate	na	Parish Clerk

■ **East Feliciana Parish** 17 Feb. 1824

12305 St. Helena St., P.O. Drawer 599, Clinton, LA 70722

Phone: (225)683-5145

Web site: www.rootsweb.com/~laeastfe/eastfeliciana.htm

Parent Parish: Feliciana

Record Type	Year Begun	Jurisdiction
Marriage	1824	Parish Clerk
Divorce	1824	Parish Clerk
Probate	1824	Parish Clerk
Land	1824	Parish Clerk
Court	1824	Parish Clerk

■ **Evangeline Parish** 15 June 1911

200 Court St., Ville Platte, LA 70586

Phone: (337)363-5671

Web site: www.evangelineparish.com/

Parent Parish: St. Landry Parish

Record Type	Year Begun	Jurisdiction
Marriage	1911	Parish Clerk
Divorce	1911	Parish Clerk
Probate	1911	Parish Clerk
Land	1911	Parish Clerk
Court	1911	Parish Clerk

■ **Feliciana Parish** 7 Dec. 1810

Parent Parish: Spanish West Florida

Comments/research tips: (See East and West Feliciana) Dissolved to form East and West Feliciana 17 February 1824.

■ **Franklin Parish** 1 Mar. 1843

210 Main St., Winnsboro, LA 71295

Phone: (318)435-9429

Web site: www.rootsweb.com/~lafrankl/

Parent Parish: Catahoula, Ouachita, Madison

Record Type	Year Begun	Jurisdiction
Marriage	1843	Parish Clerk
Divorce	1843	Parish Clerk
Land	1843	Parish Clerk
Probate	1843	Parish Clerk
Court	1843	Parish Clerk

Louisiana

■ German Coast Parish 10 Apr. 1805
Parent Parish: Original parish
Comments/research tips: Discontinued. Divided to form parishes of St. Charles and St. John the Baptist 31 March 1807.

■ Grant Parish 4 Mar. 1869
200 Main St., Colfax, LA 71417
Phone: (318)627-3157
Web site: www.rootsweb.com/~lagrant/
Parent Parish: Rapides, Winn

Record Type	Year Begun	Jurisdiction
Marriage	1878	Parish Clerk
Divorce	1878	Parish Clerk
Land	1878	Parish Clerk
Probate	1878	Parish Clerk
Court	1878	Parish Clerk
Military	1878	Parish Clerk

■ Iberia Parish 30 Oct. 1868
300 Iberia St., Suite 400, New Iberia, LA 70560
Phone: (337)365-3221
Web site: www.intersurf.com/~johnjanr/iberia.htm
Parent Parish: St. Martin, St. Mary

Record Type	Year Begun	Jurisdiction
Marriage	1868	Parish Clerk
Divorce	1868	Parish Clerk
Land	1868	Parish Clerk
Probate	1868	Parish Clerk
Court	1868	Parish Clerk

■ Iberville Parish 10 Apr. 1805
P.O. Box 423, Plaquemine, LA 70765-0423
Phone: (225)687-5160
Web site: www.parish.iberville.la.us/
Parent Parish: Original parish

Record Type	Year Begun	Jurisdiction
Marriage	1770	Parish Clerk
Divorce	1807	Parish Clerk
Land	1770	Parish Clerk
Probate	1807	Parish Clerk
Court	1807	Parish Clerk

■ Jackson Parish 27 Feb. 1845
500 E. Court St., P.O. Box 730, Jonesboro, LA 71251
Phone: (318)259-2424
Web site: www.rootsweb.com/~lajackso/jacksonIndex.htm
Parent Parish: Claiborne, Ouachita, Union

Record Type	Year Begun	Jurisdiction
Marriage	1880	Parish Clerk
Divorce	1880	Parish Clerk
Land	1880	Parish Clerk
Probate	1880	Parish Clerk
Court	1880	Parish Clerk
Military	1880	Parish Clerk

■ Jefferson Davis Parish 12 June 1912
P.O. Box 1409, Jennings, LA 70546-1409
Phone: (337)824-1161

Web site: www.rootsweb.com/~lajeffda/
Parent Parish: Calcasieu

Record Type	Year Begun	Jurisdiction
Marriage	1913	Parish Clerk
Divorce	1913	Parish Clerk
Land	1913	Parish Clerk
Probate	1913	Parish Clerk
Court	1913	Parish Clerk

■ Jefferson Parish 11 Feb. 1825
200 Derbigny St., Gretna, LA 70053
Phone: (504)364-2800
Web site: www.jeffparish.net/
Parent Parish: Orleans

Record Type	Year Begun	Jurisdiction
Marriage	1863	Parish Clerk
Divorce	1825	Parish Clerk
Land	1827	Parish Clerk
Probate	1825	Parish Clerk
Court	1825	Parish Clerk

■ Lafayette Parish 17 Jan. 1823
P.O. Box 4508, Lafayette, LA 70502-4508
Phone: (337)291-6400
Web site: www.lafayettegov.org/
Parent Parish: St. Martin, Attakapas

Record Type	Year Begun	Jurisdiction
Marriage	1823	Parish Clerk
Divorce	1823	Parish Clerk
Land	1823	Parish Clerk
Probate	1823	Parish Clerk
Court	1823	Parish Clerk

■ Lafourche Parish 10 Apr. 1805
309 W. Third St., Thibodaux, LA 70301-3021
Phone: (985)447-4841
Web site: www.lapage.com/parishes/lafou.htm
Parent Parish: Original parish

Record Type	Year Begun	Jurisdiction
Birth	1808	Parish Clerk
Marriage	1808	Parish Clerk
Divorce	1808	Parish Clerk
Land	1808	Parish Clerk
Probate	1808	Parish Clerk
Court	1808	Parish Clerk

■ LaSalle Parish 3 July 1908
P.O. Box 1372, Jena, LA 71342-0057
Phone: (318)992-2101
Web site: www.rootsweb.com/~lalasall/
Parent Parish: Catahoula

Record Type	Year Begun	Jurisdiction
Marriage	1910	Parish Clerk
Divorce	1910	Parish Clerk
Land	1910	Parish Clerk
Probate	1910	Parish Clerk
Court	1910	Parish Clerk

■ Lincoln Parish 27 Feb. 1873
100 W. Texas Ave., Ruston, LA 71270
Phone: (318)255-3663

Louisiana

Web site: www.lincolnparish.org/
Parent Parish: Bienville, Jackson, Union, Claiborne

Record Type	Year Begun	Jurisdiction
Marriage	1873	Parish Clerk
Divorce	1873	Parish Clerk
Probate	1873	Parish Clerk
Court	1873	Parish Clerk

■ **Livingston Parish** 10 Feb. 1832
20180 Iowa St., P.O. Box 427, Livingston, LA 70754
Phone: (225)686-2266
Web site: www.lapage.com/parishes/livin.htm
Parent Parish: St. Helena

Record Type	Year Begun	Jurisdiction
Marriage	1875	Parish Clerk
Divorce	1875	Parish Clerk
Land	1875	Parish Clerk
Probate	1875	Parish Clerk
Court	1875	Parish Clerk

■ **Madison Parish** 19 Jan. 1838
100 N. Cedar St., Tallulah, LA 71282
Phone: (318)574-0655
Web site: www.rootsweb.com/~lamadiso/
Parent Parish: Concordia

Record Type	Year Begun	Jurisdiction
Marriage	1866	Parish Clerk
Divorce	1839	Parish Clerk
Land	1839	Parish Clerk
Probate	1850	Parish Clerk
Court	1882	Parish Clerk

■ **Morehouse Parish** 25 Mar. 1844
125 E. Madison St., Bastrop, LA 71221
Phone: (318)281-3343
Web site: www.rootsweb.com/~usgenweb/la/morehous.htm
Parent Parish: Ouachita
Comments/research tips: Parish Clerk has Cemetery
Abstracts 1867–1957.

Record Type	Year Begun	Jurisdiction
Marriage	1870	Parish Clerk
Divorce	1870	Parish Clerk
Land	1844	Parish Clerk
Probate	1870	Parish Clerk
Court	1870	Parish Clerk

■ **Natchitoches Parish** 10 Apr. 1805
P.O. Box 799, Natchitoches, LA 71458-0799
Phone: (318)352-2714
Web site: www.rootsweb.com/~lanatchi/
Parent Parish: Original parish

Record Type	Year Begun	Jurisdiction
Marriage	1780	Parish Clerk
Divorce	na	Parish Clerk
Probate	na	Parish Clerk
Court	na	Parish Clerk

■ **Opelousas Parish** 1807
Parent Parish: Original parish
Comments/research tips: (See St. Landry) St. Landry formed
from Opelousas County 31 March 1807.

■ **Orleans Parish** 10 Apr. 1805
1300 Perdido St., New Orleans, LA 70112
Phone: (504)568-5152
Web site: www.nocitycouncil.com/content/
Parent Parish: Original parish
Comments/research tips: Public library has Voter
Registration records 1895–1941 and Precinct books
1895–1952. Public Library has City Directories from 1805.

Record Type	Year Begun	Jurisdiction
Divorce	1805	Clerk/Civil District Ct.
Probate	1805	Clerk/Civil District Ct.
Court	1805	Clerk/Civil District Ct.
Land	1832	Register/Conveyances

■ **Ouachita Parish** 10 Apr. 1805
300 St. John St., Monroe, LA 71201
Phone: (318)327-1444
Web site: www.bayou.com/~suelynn/ouachita.html
Parent Parish: Original parish
Comments/research tips: Parish Clerk has some Military
records.

Record Type	Year Begun	Jurisdiction
Marriage	ca. 1800	Parish Clerk
Divorce	1900	Parish Clerk
Land	ca. 1790	Parish Clerk
Probate	1900	Parish Clerk
Court	1900	Parish Clerk

■ **Plaquemines Parish** 31 Mar. 1807
Hwy. 39, Pointe a la Hache, LA 70082-9999
Phone: (504)333-4343
Web site: www.rootsweb.com/~laplaque/laplaque.htm
Parent Parish: Orleans

Record Type	Year Begun	Jurisdiction
Marriage	1809	Parish Clerk
Divorce	1800	Parish Clerk
Land	1800	Parish Clerk
Probate	1800	Parish Clerk
Court	1800	Parish Clerk

■ **Pointe Coupee Parish** 10 Apr. 1805
160 E. Main St., New Roads, LA 70760
Phone: (225)638-9596
Web site: www.pcpolicejury.org/
Parent Parish: Original parish

Record Type	Year Begun	Jurisdiction
Marriage	1735	Clerk of Courts
Divorce	1800	Clerk of Courts
Land	1780	Clerk of Courts
Probate	1780	Clerk of Courts
Court	1780	Clerk of Courts

■ **Rapides Parish** 10 Apr. 1805
700 Murray St., P.O. Box 952, Alexandria, LA 71301
Phone: (318)473-8153
Web site: www.rppj.com/
Parent Parish: Original parish

Record Type	Year Begun	Jurisdiction
Marriage	1864	Parish Clerk

Louisiana

Record Type	Year Begun	Jurisdiction
Divorce	1864	Parish Clerk
Land	1864	Parish Clerk
Probate	1864	Parish Clerk
Court	1864	Parish Clerk

■ Red River Parish 2 Mar. 1871
615 E. Carroll St., Coushatta, LA 71019
Phone: (318)932-6741
Web site: www.rootsweb.com/~laredriv/
Parent Parish: Caddo, Bienville, Bossier, DeSoto, Natchitoches

Record Type	Year Begun	Jurisdiction
Marriage	1871	Clerk of Courts
Divorce	1904	Clerk of Courts
Probate	1871	Clerk of Courts
Court	1904	Clerk of Courts

■ Richland Parish 29 Sep. 1868
108 Courthouse Sq., P.O. Box 119, Rayville, LA 71269
Phone: (318)728-4171
Web site: www.rootsweb.com/~larichla/home.html
Parent Parish: Ouachita, Carroll, Franklin, Morehouse

Record Type	Year Begun	Jurisdiction
Marriage	1869	Parish Clerk
Divorce	1869	Parish Clerk
Land	1869	Parish Clerk
Probate	1869	Parish Clerk
Court	1869	Parish Clerk

■ Sabine Parish 7 Mar. 1843
400 Court St., P.O. Box 419, Many, LA 71449-0419
Phone: (318)256-6223
Web site: www.pastracks.com/states/louisiana/sabine/
Parent Parish: Natchitoches

Record Type	Year Begun	Jurisdiction
Marriage	1843	Parish Clerk
Divorce	1843	Parish Clerk
Land	1843	Parish Clerk
Probate	1843	Parish Clerk
Court	1843	Parish Clerk

■ St. Bernard Parish 31 Mar. 1807
8201 W. Judge Perez Dr., Chalmette , LA 70043
Phone: (504)278-1500
Web site: www.st-bernard.la.us/
Parent Parish: Original parish

Record Type	Year Begun	Jurisdiction
Marriage	na	Clerk of Courts
Land	na	Clerk of Courts
Probate	na	Clerk of Courts
Court	na	Clerk of Courts

■ St. Charles Parish 31 Mar. 1807
15045 Hwy. 18, P.O. Box 302, Hahnville, LA 70057
Phone: (985)783-6632
Web site: www.st-charles.la.us/
Parent Parish: German Coast

Record Type	Year Begun	Jurisdiction
Marriage	na	Parish Clerk

Record Type	Year Begun	Jurisdiction
Land	na	Parish Clerk
Probate	na	Parish Clerk
Court	na	Parish Clerk

■ St. Helena Parish 27 Oct. 1810
Court Sq., Greensburg, LA 70441
Phone: (225)222-4521
Web site: www.rootsweb.com/~lasthele/
Parent Parish: Spanish West Florida
Comments/research tips: Parish Clerk has records from 1804.

■ St. James Parish 31 Mar. 1807
River Rd., P.O. Box 106, Convent, LA 70723
Phone: (225)562-7497
Web site: www.stjamesla.com/James/index.asp
Parent Parish: Original parish

Record Type	Year Begun	Jurisdiction
Marriage	1846	Parish Clerk
Divorce	1809	Parish Clerk
Probate	1809	Parish Clerk
Court	1809	Parish Clerk

■ St. John the Baptist Parish 31 Mar. 1807
1801 W. Airline Hwy., La Place, LA 70065
Phone: (985)652-9569
Web site: www.sjbparish.com/
Parent Parish: German Coast

Record Type	Year Begun	Jurisdiction
Marriage	na	Parish Clerk
Divorce	na	Parish Clerk
Land	na	Parish Clerk
Probate	na	Parish Clerk
Court	na	Parish Clerk

■ St. Landry Parish 31 Mar. 1807
Court & Landry St., Opelousas, LA 70570
Phone: (337)942-5606
Web site: www.slpolicejury.org/
Parent Parish: Opelousas

Record Type	Year Begun	Jurisdiction
Marriage	1808	Parish Clerk
Divorce	1813	Parish Clerk
Probate	1809	Parish Clerk
Court	1813	Parish Clerk

■ St. Martin Parish 17 Apr. 1811
County Courthouse, P.O. Box 9, Saint Martinville, LA 70582
Phone: (337)332-4136
Web site: www.intersurf.com/~johnjanr/stmartin.htm
Parent Parish: Attakapas

Record Type	Year Begun	Jurisdiction
Marriage	na	Parish Clerk
Land	na	Parish Clerk
Probate	na	Parish Clerk
Court	na	Parish Clerk

■ St. Mary Parish 17 Apr. 1811
101 Wilson St., P.O. Box 1231, Franklin, LA 70538-6198
Phone: (337)828-4238

Web site: www.parish.st-mary.la.us/
Parent Parish: Attakapas

Record Type	Year Begun	Jurisdiction
Marriage	1800	Parish Clerk
Divorce	1800	Parish Clerk
Land	1800	Parish Clerk
Probate	1800	Parish Clerk
Court	1800	Parish Clerk

■ St. Tammany Parish 27 Oct. 1810

510 E. Boston St., P.O. Box 1090, Covington, LA 70434-1090
Phone: (985)646-4077
Web site: www.rootsweb.com/~lasttamm/
Parent Parish: Spanish West Florida

Record Type	Year Begun	Jurisdiction
Marriage	1812	Parish Clerk
Divorce	1812	Parish Clerk
Land	1810	Parish Clerk
Probate	1812	Parish Clerk
Tax	1810	Parish Clerk
Court	1812	Parish Clerk
Military	na	Parish Clerk

■ Tangipahoa Parish 6 Mar. 1869

110 N. Bay St., P.O. Box 667, Amite, LA 70422-0215
Phone: (985)748-8015
Web site: www.tangicouncil.com/
Parent Parish: Livingston, St. Tammany, St. Helena, Washington

Record Type	Year Begun	Jurisdiction
Marriage	1869	Parish Clerk
Divorce	1869	Parish Clerk
Probate	1869	Parish Clerk
Land	1869	Parish Clerk
Court	1869	Parish Clerk

■ Tensas Parish 17 Mar. 1843

Courthouse Sq., P.O. Box 78, Saint Joseph, LA 71366
Phone: (318)766-3921
Web site: www.rootsweb.com/~latensas/
Parent Parish: Concordia

Record Type	Year Begun	Jurisdiction
Marriage	1843	Parish Clerk
Divorce	1843	Parish Clerk
Probate	1843	Parish Clerk
Court	1843	Parish Clerk

■ Terrebonne Parish 22 Mar. 1822

301 Goode St., Houma, LA 70360-4513
Phone: (985)868-5660
Web site: www.terrebonneparish.com/
Parent Parish: Lafourche

Record Type	Year Begun	Jurisdiction
Marriage	na	Parish Clerk
Probate	na	Parish Clerk
Land	na	Parish Clerk

■ Union Parish 13 Mar. 1839

Courthouse Bldg., 100 E. Bayou St. #105, Farmerville, LA 71241

Phone: (318)368-3055
Web site: www.rootsweb.com/~launion/
Parent Parish: Ouachita

Record Type	Year Begun	Jurisdiction
Marriage	1839	Parish Clerk
Divorce	1839	Parish Clerk
Probate	1839	Parish Clerk
Court	na	Parish Clerk

■ Vermilion Parish 25 Mar. 1844

100 N. State St. #101, P.O. Box 790, Abbeville, LA 70511
Phone: (337)898-1992
Web site: www.vermilion.org/
Parent Parish: Lafayette

Record Type	Year Begun	Jurisdiction
Marriage	1885	Parish Clerk
Divorce	1885	Parish Clerk
Land	1885	Parish Clerk
Probate	1885	Parish Clerk
Court	1885	Parish Clerk

■ Vernon Parish 30 Mar. 1871

201 S. Third St., P.O. Box 40, Leesville, LA 71496
Phone: (337)238-1384
Web site: www.rootsweb.com/~lavernon/
Parent Parish: Natchitoches, Rapides, Sabine

Record Type	Year Begun	Jurisdiction
Marriage	1890	Parish Clerk
Divorce	1871	Parish Clerk
Probate	1871	Parish Clerk
Court	1871	Parish Clerk

■ Washington Parish 6 Mar. 1819

Courthouse, P.O. Box 607, Franklinton, LA 70438
Phone: (985)839-4663
Web site: www.rootsweb.com/~lawashin/
Parent Parish: St. Tammany

Record Type	Year Begun	Jurisdiction
Marriage	1897	Parish Clerk
Divorce	1897	Parish Clerk
Land	1897	Parish Clerk
Probate	1897	Parish Clerk
Court	1897	Parish Clerk

■ Webster Parish 27 Feb. 1871

410 Main St., P.O. Box 370, Minden, LA 71058-0370
Phone: (318)371-0366
Web site: www.rootsweb.com/~lawebste/
Parent Parish: Claiborne, Bienville, Bossier

Record Type	Year Begun	Jurisdiction
Marriage	1871	Parish Clerk
Divorce	1871	Parish Clerk
Land	1871	Parish Clerk
Probate	1871	Parish Clerk
Court	1871	Parish Clerk

■ West Baton Rouge Parish 31 Mar. 1807

P.O. Box 107, Port Allen, LA 70767-0757
Phone: (225)383-0378

Web site: www.wbrcouncil.org/
Parent Parish: Baton Rouge

Record Type	Year Begun	Jurisdiction
Birth	na	Clerk of Courts
Marriage	na	Clerk of Courts
Land	na	Clerk of Courts
Probate	na	Clerk of Courts

■ West Carroll Parish 28 Mar. 1877

P.O. Box 630, Oak Grove, LA 71263-0630
Phone: (318)428-3390
Web site: www.rootsweb.com/~lawestca/
Parent Parish: Carroll

Record Type	Year Begun	Jurisdiction
Marriage	1877	Parish Clerk
Divorce	1833	Parish Clerk
Land	1833	Parish Clerk
Probate	1833	Parish Clerk
Court	1833	Parish Clerk

■ West Feliciana Parish 17 Feb. 1824

4789 Prosperity St., P.O. Box 1845, St. Francisville, LA 70775

Phone: (225)635-3794
Web site: www.segenealogy.com/louisiana/la_county/wf.htm
Parent Parish: Feliciana

Record Type	Year Begun	Jurisdiction
Marriage	1879	Parish Clerk
Divorce	1900	Parish Clerk
Land	1811	Parish Clerk
Probate	1900	Parish Clerk
Court	1900	Parish Clerk

■ Winn Parish 24 Feb. 1852

100 Main St. #103, P.O. Box 951, Winnfield, LA 71483-0951
Phone: (318)628-3515
Web site: www.rootsweb.com/~lawinn/
Parent Parish: Natchitoches, Catahoula, Rapides

Record Type	Year Begun	Jurisdiction
Marriage	1886	Parish Clerk
Divorce	1886	Parish Clerk
Land	1886	Parish Clerk
Probate	1886	Parish Clerk
Court	1886	Parish Clerk

Louisiana

Maine

By Maureen Taylor

HISTORICAL OVERVIEW

Maine is both the largest state in New England and the most sparsely populated, in spite of being settled in the seventeenth century. In 1622, King Charles I of England gave John Mason and Sir Fernando Gorges land that encompassed part of present-day Maine and New Hampshire. Gorges established the first colonial government in the region. He sold his land parcel to Massachusetts in 1677, which it remained a part of until 1820.

Emigrants from Massachusetts Bay established the first permanent communities along the coast, gaining control of the region, while the French inhabited the area near the Penobscot River. Colonial conflicts between the French, the English, and native populations resulted in Massachusetts declaring war on all Native Americans in Maine in 1703. After the French and Indian War (1754–1763) France had to give up its claim to the region. While early settlers were primarily English, a wide variety of ethnic groups—French Canadians, Scot-Irish, Acadians, and African Americans—populated the area along with the native people.

Maine became a separate state in 1820 under the Missouri Compromise. Missouri entered the Union as a slave state, and Maine a free one. Boundary disputes with Canada in 1839 resulted in the Aroostook War, which was eventually settled by the Webster-Ashburton Treaty of 1842.

Farming, fishing, logging, shipbuilding, and fur trading supported area residents for much of Maine's early history. However, employment opportunities changed in the nineteenth century. Steamships began to be produced at Maine's shipyards, followed by battleships. Textile mills attracted girls from all over the area, while urban dwellers escaped the cities to enjoy the state's natural charms—creating the tourism industry that is still thriving today.

MAINE AT A GLANCE

Motto: *Dirigo* (I lead)

Population: 1.3 million

Prevalent Religions: Roman Catholic, Baptist, and Methodist

Major Industries: Wood-product manufacturing, fishing and fishing-related industries, tourism, agriculture (primarily fruit, vegetables, and dairy)

Ethnic Makeup (in percent): Caucasian 96.9%, African-American 0.5%, Hispanic 0.7%, Asian 0.7%, Native American 0.6%, Other 0.6%

Famous Mainers: "L.L." Bean, Dorothea Dix, John Ford, Sarah Orne Jewett, Stephen King, Henry Wadsworth Longfellow, Edna St. Vincent Millay, Judd Nelson, Edward Arlington Robinson, Joan Benoit Samuelson

Above: Old lobster buoys in eastern Maine

© PhotoDisc/Getty Images

RECORD HIGHLIGHTS

Searching for records in Maine is challenging. The recording practices lack the completeness found in other New England states, due to later civil registration and the remoteness of some towns. Only five towns (Biddeford, Kittery, Kennebunkport, York, and Wells) have vital records from the seventeenth century. State legislation in

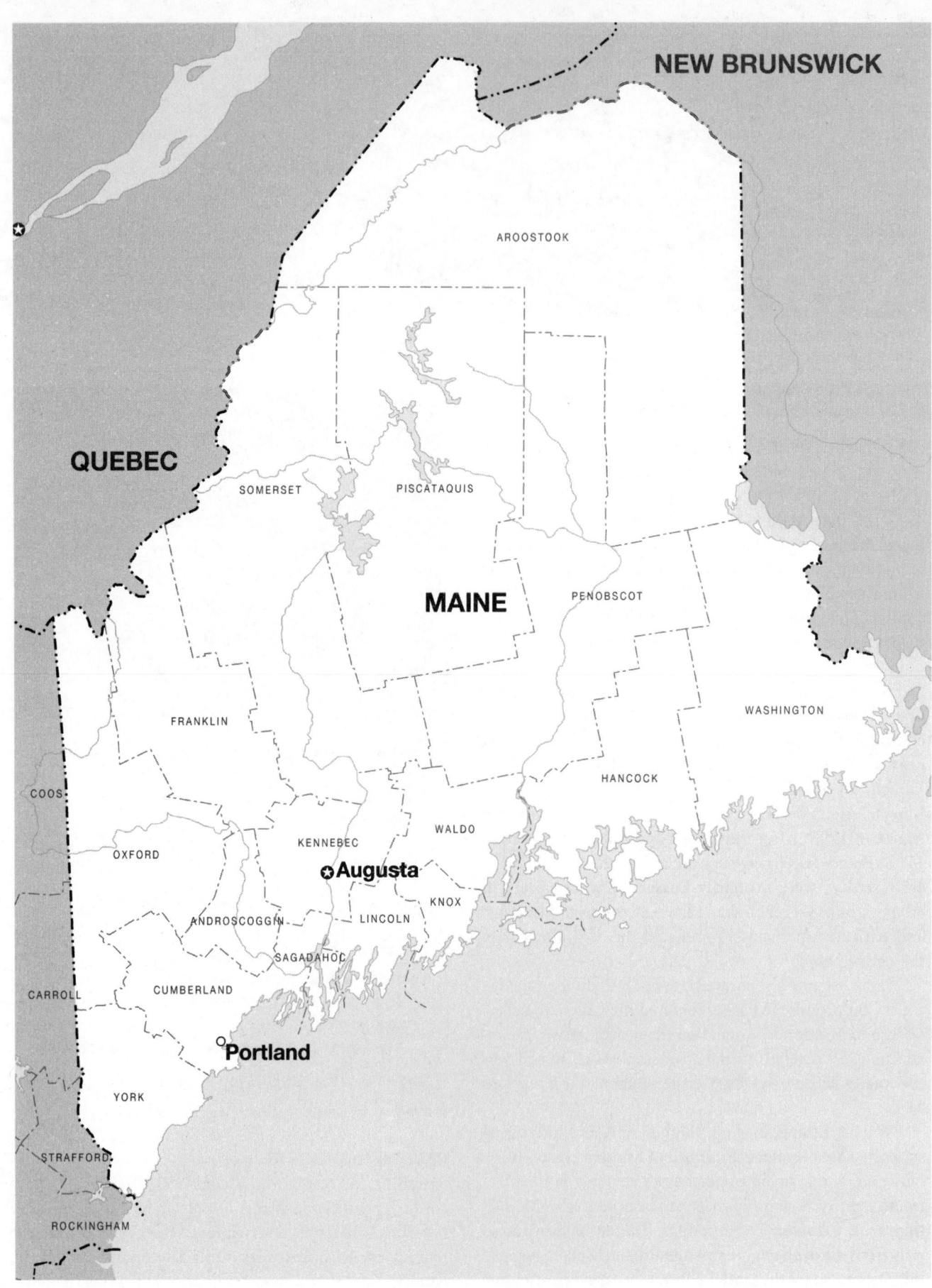

NEW BRUNSWICK

QUEBEC

AROOSTOOK

SOMERSET

PISCATAQUIS

MAINE

PENOBSCOT

FRANKLIN

COOS

WASHINGTON

OXFORD

HANCOCK

KENNEBEC

WALDO

Augusta

KNOX

ANDROSCOGGIN

LINCOLN

SAGADAHOC

CARROLL

CUMBERLAND

Portland

YORK

STRAFFORD

ROCKINGHAM

Maine

1864 specified that town clerks provide the Secretary of State with birth, marriage, and death records, but total compliance didn't happen until 1892 with the establishment of the State Board of Vital Statistics. Marriage records from 1892 to 1996 are accessible on online from the Maine State Archives <www.state.me.us/sos/arc/general/admin/mawww001.htm>. According to Art Dostie, Research Room Supervisor at the Maine State Archives, "as late as 1944, as many as one out of ten births were not recorded." Dostie continued, "You have a fifty/fifty chance of finding a birth record before 1892, and only a 20 percent chance of locating a death record." The Maine Historical Society <www.mainehistory.org> has published compilations of births, marriages, and deaths extracted from diaries, church records, newspapers, gravestones, and vital records for eighteen towns. Their library has vital records for 1892–1955 on microfilm, and has an index to the towns listed in the vital records pre-1892. Picton Press <www.pictonpress.com> has published vital records for many Maine towns.

Deaths records are being supplemented by the cemetery transcription project of the Maine Old Cemetery Association <www.rootsweb.com/~memoca/moca.htm>. A list of cemeteries covered by this project is available via their Web site.

The lack of centralized records means that you'll have to look for resources in a variety of locations: probate records—wills, adoptions, and guardianships—are on the county level, as are deeds; court documents are mostly at the Maine State Archives; and military records prior to statehood are in the Massachusetts State Archives or at the National Archives.

Church records require lots of effort both to locate and use. The majority are unpublished and unindexed. The Maine Historical Society has manuscript and published records for Baptist, Congregational, Methodist, Quaker, and Unitarian denominations.

Researching your Maine ancestors can present challenges for the novice genealogist. Identify when your ancestor was in Maine, determine what type of record you need to reference, and visit the appropriate repository. According to David Allen Lambert, Reference Library Manager of the New England Historic Genealogical Society's Microtext Library, "Maine is the worst New England state for town hall fires. Researchers should not expect to always find their ancestors neatly arranged in published town histories in Maine."

Maine was part of Massachusetts for close to 150 years, which means you'll need to look outside Maine for records pre-statehood. The Massachusetts State Archives and Massachusetts Historical Society contain material on Maine.

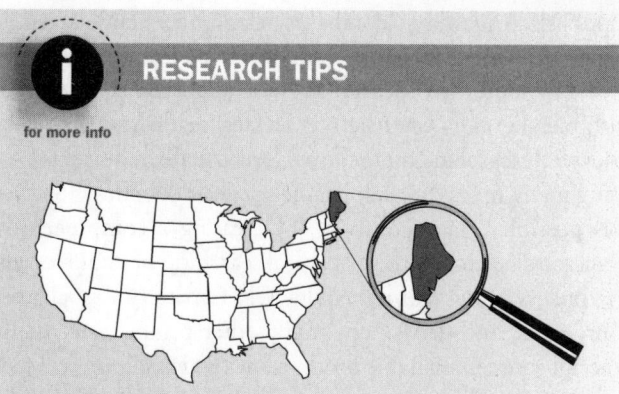

RESEARCH TIPS

for more info

- The Massachusetts State Archives and Massachusetts Historical Society contain information on Maine, which was a part of their state for more than one hundred years.
- In Maine research, it's best to conduct the majority of your research on the state level—working in town records can be disappointing.
- The Maine State Archivesc <www.state.me.us/sos/arc> and the Maine Historical Society <www.mainehistory.org> are the best places to begin your Maine research.

Census Records
- Federal Census: 1790, 1800, 1810, 1820, 1830, 1840, 1850, 1860, 1870, 1880, 1900, 1910, 1920, 1930
- Federal Mortality Schedules: 1850, 1860, 1870, 1880
- Union Veterans and Widows: 1890
- State Census: 1837 (fragments for Bangor, Portland, and unincorporated towns; town of Eliot). No statewide censuses.

The Maine State Archives <www.state.me.us/sos/arc/> has one of the largest collections of resources in the state. Availability and completeness depend on the time period.

The Maine Historical Society has manuscripts, indexed vital records, and Bible records, as well as an online guide to their genealogical holdings. Of particular note are the more than two million unpublished items in their collection, in particular "the early records of the Kennebec Purchase, the Pejepscot Proprietors and the Pownalborough Courthouse collection." An ongoing retrospective conversion project has created online cataloguing records for about half the book collection and less than half the manuscript collection, so patrons should consult the card catalogs or call to verify additional holdings.

Although located in Boston, the New England Historic Genealogical Society has many manuscripts relating to Maine families, including the Direct Tax of 1798. They also

Maine

publish articles and databases relating to Maine research on their Web site <www.newenglandancestors.org>.

The materials located at these libraries and archives should be exhausted before seeking records at the town level. Researching on the town level usually requires traveling many miles through Maine's sixteen counties. "Success is possible," says Lambert "by creating a comprehensive ancestral sketch with the careful searching of vital records, cemetery records of the Maine Old Cemetery Association, probates, and deeds. The many other printed and manuscript sources available on the state and local level will aide you in rounding out any and all Maine problems easily."

STATE RESOURCES

■ ARCHIVES, LIBRARIES, AND SOCIETIES

Acton-Shapleigh Historical Society
P.O. Box 545, Acton, ME 04001-0545
Web site: <www.actonmaine .com/histscty/histscty.htm>

Albion Historical Society
P.O. Box 68, Albion, ME 04910
Web site: <www.albionmaine.org>

Allagash Historical Society
Web site: <http://aroostook.me .us/allagash/historical.html>

Androscoggin Historical Society
Web site: <www.rootsweb.com/ ~meandrhs>

The Archives of the Diocese of Portland (Roman Catholic)
P.O. Box 11559, 510 Ocean Ave., Portland, ME 04104-7559

Arnold Expedition Historical Society
RR 4, Box 6895, Gardiner, ME 04345-9112
Web site: <www.rootsweb.com/ ~aehs/aehs.htm>

Auburn Public Library
Court & Spring Sts., Auburn, ME 04210

Bangor Public Library
145 Harlow St., Bangor, ME 04401
Tel: (207) 947-8336
Fax: (207) 945-6694

Bath Historical Society
Patten Free Library, 33 Summer St., Bath, ME 04530-2687

Bethel Historical Society
P.O. Box 12, Bethel, ME 04217
Tel: (207) 824-0882
Web site: <www.bethelhistorical .org/>

Bridgton Historical Society
P.O. Box 44, Bridgton, ME 04009
Web site: <www.megalink.net/ ~bhs/index.html>

Buckfield Historical Society
R.R. 4, Box 780, Turner, ME 04282-9604

Camden Historical Society
80 Mechanic St., Camden, ME 04843

Camden-Rockport Historical Society
P.O. Box 747, Rockport, ME 04856
Web site: <http://members.mint .net/chmuseum/>

Cherryfield-Narraguagus Historical Society
PO Box 96, Cherryfield, ME 04622

Cushing Historical Society, Inc.
P.O. Box 110, Cushing, ME 04563
Web site: <www.rootsweb.com/ ~usgenweb/me/knox/cushing .htm>

Dexter Historical Society
P.O. Box 481, Dexter, ME 04930
Web site: <www.dextermaine .org/museum/index.html>

Episcopal Archives of the Diocesan House
143 State St., Portland, ME 04101
Tel: (800) 244-6062

Falmouth Historical Society
Falmouth Memorial Library, 5 Lunt Rd., Falmouth, ME 04105

Web site: <www.falmouth.lib.me .us./historical.html>

Finnish American Heritage Society of Maine
P.O. Box 294, West Paris, ME 04289

Finnish American Society of Mid-Coast Maine
P.O. Box 488, Warren, ME 04864

Gorham Historical Society
28 School St., Gorham, ME 04038
Web site: <www.gorhamcu.com/ ghs/home.html>

Gray Historical Society
P.O. Box 544, Gray, ME 04039
Web site: <www.graymaine.org/ history.htm>

Hancock Genealogical Society
P.O. Box 243, Bass Harbor, ME 04653
Web site: <http://ellsworthme. org/hcgs/>

Hiram Historical Society
158 Sebago Rd., Hiram, ME 04041
Tel: (207) 625-4663
Web site: <www.rootsweb.com/ ~mechiram>

Kennebeck Historical Society
P.O. Box 5582, Augusta, ME 04332-5582
Web site: <www.kennebechistori cal.org/>

Kennebunk Free Library
112 Main St., Kennebunk, ME 04043

Kennebunkport Historical Society
P.O. Box 1173, Kennebunkport, ME 04046
Tel: (207) 967-1205
Web site: <www.kporthistory .org/>

Madison Historical and Genealogical Society
165 Main St., Madison, ME 04950
Web site: <www.wtrl.net/sba las/mhs.htm>

Maine Department of Health and Human Services
Office of Vital Statistics, 221 State St., Station 11, Augusta, ME 04333-0011

Maine Franco-American Genealogical Society
115 High St., Auburn, ME 04210
Tel: (207) 782-7939
Web site: <www.avcnet.org/be gin/>

Maine Genealogical Society
P.O. Box 221, Farmington, ME 04938
Web site: <www.rootsweb.com/ ~megs/MaineGS.htm>

Maine Historical Society
489 Congress St., Portland, ME 04111
Tel: (207) 775-4301
Web site: <www.mainehistory .org/>

Maine State Archives
84 State House Station, Augusta, ME 04333-0084
Tel: (207) 287-5739
Web site: <www.state.me.us/ sos/arc/>

Maine State Library
64 State House Station, Augusta, ME 04333-0064
Tel: (207) 287-5600
Web site: <www.state.me.us/ msl>

Milo Historical Society
12 High St., Milo, ME 04463
Tel: (207) 943-2268
Web site: <www.milohistorical .org>

Mount Desert Island Historical Society
P.O. Box 653, Mount Desert, ME 04660
Web site: <www.milohistory.org/ about.html>

National Archives-New England Region
380 Trapelo Rd., Waltham, MA 02452-6399
Tel: (866) 406-2379
Web site: <www.archives.gov/fa cilities/ma/boston.html>

New England Historic Genealogical Society
101 Newbury St., Boston, MA 02116
Tel: (617) 536-5740
Fax: (617) 536-7307
Web site: <www.nehgs.org>

Old Broad Bay Family History Association
P.O. Box 1242, Waldoboro, ME 04572
Web site: <www.rootsweb.com/ ~meobbfha/>

Old York Historical Society Library
P.O. Box 312, 207 York St., York, ME 03909
Tel: (207) 363-4974
Web site: <www.oldyork.org>

Otisfield Historical Society
Web site: <www.rootsweb.com/ ~mecotisf/otis8.htm>

Patton Free Library
33 Summer St., Bath, ME 04530
Tel: (207) 443-5141

Pejepscot Historical Society
159 Park Row, Brunswick, ME 04011
Tel: (207) 729-6606
Web site: <www.curtislibrary .com/pejepscot.htm>

The Sandy River Valley Chapter of the Maine Genealogical Society
Web site: <www.rootsweb.com/ ~mesrvmgs/mgsindex.htm>

Scarborough Historical Society
P.O. Box 156, Scarborough, ME 04070-0156
Web site: <www.scarboroughmai ne.com/historical/>

Stephen Phillips Memorial Library
Penobscot Marine Museum, P.O. Box 498, Searsport, ME 04974
Tel: (207) 548-2529
Fax: (207) 548-2520

Sullivan & Sorrento Historical Society
P.O. Box 44, Sullivan, ME 04664
Tel: (207) 422-6816
Web site: <http://ellsworthme .org/sshs/>

Thomaston Historical Society
P.O. Box 384, Thomaston, ME 04861
Web site: <www.thomastonhistor icalsociety.com>

Union Historical Society
P.O. Box 154, Union, ME 04862
Web site: <www.midcoast.com/ comespring/>

University of Maine at Orono, Raymond H. Fogler Library
P.O. Box 5729, Orono, ME 04469-5729
Tel: (207) 581-1661
Web site: <www.library.umaine .edu>

Vinalhaven Historical Society
P.O. Box 339, Vinalhaven, ME 04863

Web site: <www.midcoast.com/ ~vhhissoc/home.html>

Walker Memorial Library
800 Main St., Westbrook, ME 04092
Tel: (207) 854-0630
Web site: <www.westbrookmaine .com/departments/library>

Windham Historical Society
Web site: <www.rootsweb.com/ ~mewhs/>

Woolwich Historical Society
P.O. Box 98, Woolwich, ME 04579
Tel: (207) 443-4833
Web site: <www.woolwichhistory .org/>

BIBLIOGRAPHY

■ GENERAL REOURCES

Agencies of the State Government, 1820–1971
from the Maine State Archives (Augusta, ME: Maine State Archives)

The American Genealogical-Biographical Index
(Middletown, CT: Godfrey Memorial Library, 2000–2003)

Ancient Dominions of Maine: Embracing the Earliest Facts
by R.K. Sewall (Bowie, MD: Heritage Books, 1998)

Bibliographical Reference List of Manuscripts Relating to the History of Maine
by Elizabeth Ring (Salem, MA: Higginson Books, 1992)

Bibliography of the State of Maine, 2 vols.
(Rockport, ME: Picton Press, 1985)

A Bibliography of the State of Maine from the Earliest Period to 1891, 2 vols.
by Joseph Williamson (Portland, ME: Thurston Print, 1896)

Brief Biographies, Maine: A Biographical Dictionary of Who's Who in Maine, Vol. 1
by Theodore Roosevelt Hodgkins (Lewiston, ME: Lewiston Journal, 1926–1927)

Directory of Churches and Religious Organizations in Maine
from the Historical Records Survey (Portland, ME: Historical Records Survey Project, 1940)

Early New England Settlers, 1600s–1800s
(Brøderbund, 1999. CD-ROM)

English Origins of New England Families: From the New England Historical and Genealogical Register. Second Series, 3 vols.
(Baltimore: Genealogical Publishing, 1985)

Franco-Americans of the State of Maine, U.S.A., and Their Achievements: Historical, Descriptive and Biographical
by R.J. Lawton (Lewiston, ME: H.F. Roy, 1915)

A Genealogical Dictionary of the First Settlers of New England Showing Three Generations of Those Who Came Before May 1692, on the Basis of Farmer's Register, 4 vols.
by James Savage (Baltimore: Genealogical Publishing Co., 1969)

Genealogical Dictionary of Maine and New Hampshire
by Sybil Noyes, Charles T. Libby, and Walter G. Davis (Baltimore: Genealogical Publishing, 1996)

Genealogical and Family History of the State of Maine, 4 vols.
edited by George Thomas Little (New York: Lewis Historical Publishing, 1909)

Genealogical Research in New England
edited by Ralph J. Crandall (Baltimore: Genealogical Publishing Co., 1984)

The Genealogist's Companion and Sourcebook, 2d ed.
by Emily Anne Croom (Cincinnati: Betterway Books, 2003)

A Genealogist's Guide to Discovering Your African-American Ancestors
by Franklin Carter Smith and Emily Anne Croom (Cincinnati: Betterway Books, 2003)

Genealogist's Handbook for New England Research, 3rd ed.
by Marcia Wiswall Lindberg (Boston, MA: New England Historic Genealogical Society, 1993)

The Greenlaw Index of the New England Historic Genealogical Society, 2 vols.
by William Prescott Greenlaw (Boston: G.K. Hall, 1979)

Guide to Genealogical Research in the National Archives of the United States
edited by Anne Bruner Eales and Robert M. Kvasnicka (Washington, DC: National Archives and Records Administration, 2000)

Historic Trails and Waterways of Maine
by William Otis Sawtelle (Augusta, ME: Maine Development Commission, 1932)

A History of the Discovery of Maine
by J.G. Kohl (Portland, ME: Maine Historical Society, 1869)

An Index and Guide to the Microfilm Edition of the Massachusetts and Maine Direct Tax Census of 1798
edited by Michael H. Gorn (Boston: New England Historic Genealogical Society, 1979)

The Indians of Maine and the Atlantic Provinces: A Bibliographical Guide
by Roger B. Ray (Portland, ME: Maine Historical Society, 1977)

Liberty Men and Great Proprietors: The Revolutionary Settlement on the Maine Frontier, 1760–1820
by Alan Taylor (Galveston, TX: Frontier Press, 1990)

Maine Becomes a State: The Movement to Separate Maine from Massachusetts, 1785–1820
by Ronald F. Banks (Middletown, CT: Published for the Maine Historical Society by Wesleyan University Press, 1970)

Maine, A Bibliography of Its History
from the Committee for a New England Bibliography, edited by John D. Haskell Jr. (Boston: G.K. Hall, 1977)

Maine Families in 1790, 6 vols.
(Camden, ME: Picton Press,
1988–1998)

*The Maine Frontier, 1607 to
1763*
by Robert Earle Moody (Ann
Arbor, MI: University Microfilms,
1980)

*Maine Genealogy: A
Bibliography Guide*, rev. ed.
by John Eldridge Frost (Portland,
ME: Maine Historical Society,
1985)

Maine Historical Sketches
by Augustus F. Moulton (Lewiston, ME: Printed for the State by
the Lewiston Journal Printshop,
1929)

Maine: A History, 5 vols.
edited by Louis Clinton Hatch
(New York: American Historical
Society, 1919)

*Maine & New Hampshire
Settlers, 1600s–1900s*
(Brøderbund, 2000. CD-ROM)

Maine Pioneer Settlements,
5 vols.
by Herbert Milton Sylvester (Boston: W.B. Clark, 1909)

Maine Research Outline
(Salt Lake City: Family History Library, 1988)

*Massachusetts and Maine
Families*
by Walter Goodwin David (Baltimore: Genealogical Pub. Co.,
1996)

*Men of Progress: Biographical
Sketches and Portraits of
Leaders in Business and
Professional Life in and of the
State of Maine*
by Richard Herdon, et al. (Boston:
New England Magazine, 1897)

*Name Index to Maine Local
Histories*
by Marie Estes (Portland: Maine
Historical Society, 1985)

*National Archives Microfilm
Catalogs online:*
<www.archives.gov/publica
tions/genealogy_microfilm_
catalogs.html>

*New England Families:
Genealogical and Memorial*,
4 vols.
by William Richard Cutter (New
York: Lewis Historical Publishing,
1914)

*New England Family Histories:
States of Maine and Rhode
Island*
by LuVerne V. Hall (Bowie, MD:
Heritage Books, 2000)

Penobscot Pioneers, 4 vols.
by Philip Howard Gray (Camden,
ME: Penobscot Press, 1992–
1994)

*The Pioneers of Maine and New
Hampshire, 1623–1660*
by Charles Henry Pope (Baltimore: Clearfield Co., 1997)

Pioneers on Maine Rivers
by Wilbur D. Spencer (Baltimore:
Clearfield Co., 1995)

*Public Record Repositories in
Maine*
from the Maine State Archives
(Augusta, ME: Maine State Archives, 1976)

*Representative Men of Maine:
A Collection of Portraits with
Biographical Sketches of
Residents of the State, Who
Have Achieved Success . . . to
Which is Added the Portraits
and Sketches of all the
Governors Since the Formation
of the State*
by Henry Chase (Portland, ME:
Lakeside Press, 1893)

*Sketches of the Ecclesiastical
History of the State of Maine
from the Earliest Settlement to
the Present Time*
by Jonathan Greenleaf (Portsmouth, NH: H. Gray, 1821)

Town Government in Maine
from the Historical Records Survey (Portland, ME: The Survey,
1940)

■ CENSUS RECORDS

*The American Census
Handbook*
by Thomas Jay Kemp (Wilmington, DE: Scholarly Resources,
Inc., 2001)

*The Census Book: A
Genealogist's Guide to Federal
Census Facts, Schedules and
Indexes*
by William Dollarhide (Bountiful,
UT: Heritage Quest, 1996)

1790 Census of Maine
from the Maine Genealogical Society (Farmington, ME: The Society, 1995)

*Finding Answers in U.S. Census
Records*
by Loretto Dennis Szucs and Matthew Wright (Salt Lake City: Ancestry Publishing, 2001)

*An Index and Guide to the
Microfilm Edition of the
Massachusetts and Maine
Direct Tax Census of 1798*
by Michael H. Gorn (Boston: New
England Historic Genealogical Society, 1979)

*Map Guide to the U.S. Federal
Censuses, 1790–1920*
by William Thorndale and William
Dollarhide (Baltimore: Genealogical Publishing Co., 1987)

*Massachusetts and Maine
Direct Tax Census of 1798*
from the United States Secretary
of the Treasury (Cambridge, MA:
New England Historic Genealogical Society, 1978)

*The Massachusetts Tax
Valuation List of 1771*
edited by Betty Hobbs Pruitt (Boston: G.K. Hall, 1978)

State Census Records
by Ann S. Lainhart (Baltimore: Genealogical Publishing, 1992)

*Your Guide to the Federal
Census*
by Kathleen W. Hinckley (Cincinnati: Betterway Books, 2002)

■ IMMIGRATION RECORDS

*American Naturalization
Records, 1790–1990: What
They Are and How to Use Them*
by John J. Newman (North Salt
Lake, UT: HeritageQuest, 1998)

*American Passenger Arrival
Records*
by Michael Tepper (Baltimore:
Genealogical Publishing Co.,
1993)

*The Complete Book of
Emigrants, 1607–1776, and
Emigrants in Bondage,
1614–1775*
by Peter Wilson Coldham (Broderbund, 1996. CD-ROM)

*Immigrants to New England,
1700–1775*
by Ethel Stanwood Bolton (Salem, MA: Essex Institute, 1931)

*They Became Americans:
Finding Naturalization Records
and Ethnic Origins*
by Loretto Dennis Szucs (Salt
Lake City: Ancestry, Inc., 1998)

*They Came in Ships: A Guide to
Finding Your Immigrant
Ancestor's Arrival Records*, 2d
ed.
by John P. Colletta (Salt Lake
City: Ancestry, Inc., 1993)

■ LAND RECORDS

*Black House Papers—A Guide
to Certain Microfilmed Land
Records*
from the Maine State Archives
(Augusta, ME: Maine State
Archives)

*Land and Property Research in
the United States*
by Wade E. Hone (Salt Lake City:
Ancestry Inc., 1997)

*Locating Your Roots: Discover
Your Ancestors Using Land
Records*
by Patricia Law Hatcher (Cincinnati: Betterway Books, 2003)

*Names of Soldiers of the
American Revolution Who
Applied for State Bounty, 1893*
by Charles J. House (Baltimore:
Genealogical Publishing Co.,
1967)

■ MAPS

*Connecticut, Maine,
Massachusetts, and Rhode
Island Atlas of Historical
County Boundaries*
edited by John H. Long (New York:
Simon & Schuster, 1994)

*Counties, Cities, Towns, and
Plantations of Maine*
from the Historical Records Survey (Portland, ME: The Survey,
1940)

*The Dictionary of Maine
Place-Names*
by Phillip R. Rutherford (Freeport,
ME: Bond Wheelwright Co.,
1970)

*A Gazetteer of the State of
Maine: With Numerous
Illustrations*
by George J. Varney (Bowie, MD:
Heritage Books, 1991)

Indian Place Names of the Penobscot Valley and the Maine Coast
by Fannie Hardy Eckstorm (Orono, ME: University of Maine, 1978)

The Length and Breadth of Maine
by Stanley Bearce Attwood (Orono, ME: University of Maine, 1977)

Maine County Subdivisions, Towns, Plantations, Unorganized Territories, and Places
(Washington, D.C.: U.S. Government Printing Office, 1977)

Maine Geographic Names: Alphabetical Finding List
from the United States Office of Geographic Research (Reston, VA: U.S. Geological Survey, 1985)

Maine Place Names and the Peopling of its Towns
by Ava Harrie Shadbourne (Portland, ME: Bond Wheelwright Co., 1955)

Maine Postal History and Postmarks
by Sterling T. Dow (Lawrence, MA: Quarterman Publications, 1976)

Maine Towns and Counties: What Was What, Where and When
by Michael J. Denis (Oakland, ME: Danbury House Books, 1981)

Map Exhibiting the Principal Original Grants and Sales of Lands in the State of Maine
By Moses Greenleaf (Ellsworth, ME: Ellsworth American, 1977)

■ MILITARY RECORDS

An Alphabetical Index of Revolutionary Pensioners Living in Maine
by Charles A. Flagg (Reprint: Baltimore: Genealogical Publishing Co., 1967)

The American Civil War: the Service Records of Atlantic Canadians with the State of Maine Volunteers, 2 vols.
by Daniel F. Johnson (Saint John, NE: D.F. Johnson, 1995)

Aroostook War: Historical Sketch and Roster of Commissioned Officers and Enlisted Men
(Augusta, ME: Kennebec Journal Print, 1904)

Dubros Times: Depositions of Revolutionary War Veterans
from the Maine State Archives (Augusta, ME: Maine State Archives)

Genealogical Abstracts of the Revolutionary War Pension Files, 4 vols.
by Virgil D. White (Waynesboro, TN: National Historical Publishing, 1990)

Index to Revolutionary War Service Records, 4 vols.
by Virgil D. White (Waynesboro, TN: National Historical Publishing, 1995)

Maine in the Civil War: A Bibliographical Guide
compiled by William B. Jordan (Portland, ME: Maine Historical Society, 1976)

Maine in the War for the Union
by William E.S. Whitman and Charles H. True (Lewiston, ME: Nelson Dingley, Jr., 1865)

Military Records and Related Sources
from the Maine State Archives (Augusta, ME: Maine State Archives, 2000)

Names of Soldiers of the American Revolution Who Applied for State Bounty under the Resolves of March 17, 1835, March 24, 1836, and March 20, 1838, as Appears of Record in Land Office
compiled by Charles L. House (Baltimore: Genealogical Publishing Co., 1967)

Red Diamond Regiment: The 17th Maine Infantry, 1862–1865
by William B. Jordan (Galveston, TX: Frontier Press, 1995)

Soldiers, Sailors, and Patriots of the Revolutionary War, Maine
by Carleton E. Fisher (Louisville, KY: National Society of the Sons of the American Revolution, 1982)

Uncle, We Are Ready! Registering America's Men, 1917–1918: A Guide to Researching World War I Draft Registration Cards
by John J. Newman (North Salt Lake, UT: HeritageQuest, 2001)

U.S. Military Records: A Guide to Federal & State Sources, Colonial America to the Present
by James C. Neagles (Salt Lake City: Ancestry, Inc., 1994)

World War II: A Family Historian's Guide
by Debra Johnson Knox (Spartanburg, SC: MIE Publishing, 2003)

■ PROBATE RECORDS

History Of the Court System Of The State Of Maine
by David Q. Whittier (Augusta, ME: Maine State Archives, ca. 1980)

Maine Probate Abstracts. Vol. 1, 1687–1775; vol. 2, 1775–1800
by Frost, John Eldridge Frost (Rockport, ME: Picton Press, 1991)

Maine Wills, 1640–1760
by William M. Sargent (Baltimore: Clearfield Co., 1996)

Province and Court Records of Maine, 6 vols.
edited by Charles T. Libby, Robert E. Moody, and Neal W. Allen (Portland, ME: Maine Historical Society, 1928–1975)

York County, Maine Wills Abstracts 1801–1858, 2 vols.
from the Maine Genealogical Society (Rockport, ME: Picton Press, 1997)

■ VITAL RECORDS

Cemetery Inscriptions and Odd Information of Various Towns in the State of Maine: In the Counties of Lincoln, Oxford, Penobscot, Somerset, Waldo
edited by Charles D. Townsend (Sarasota, FL: Aceto Bookmen, 1995)

Index to Maine Deaths, 1960–1996
from the Maine State Archives (Augusta, ME: Maine State Archives, 2002)

Index to Maine Marriages, 1892–1966, 1976–1996
from the Maine State Archives (Augusta, ME: Maine State Archive, 2002)

The Maine Historical and Genealogical Recorder, 9 vols.
(Portland, OR: S.M. Watson, 1884–98)

Maine Marriages 1892–1966: A Complete List
edited by Lewis Bunker Rohrbach (Rockport, ME: Picton Press, 1996. CD-ROM)

Maine Old Cemetery Association Cemetery Inscription Project: Series One, Two and Three
by Katherine W. Trickey (Bangor, ME: Northeast Reprographics, 1982)

Maine Town Microfilm List: Town and Vital Records, and Census Reports
from the Maine State Archives (Augusta, ME: Maine State Archives)

New England Marriages Prior to 1700
by Clarence Almon Torrey (Baltimore: Genealogical Publishing Company, ca. 1985)

Vital Records (Births, Marriages, Deaths) before 1892
from the Maine State Archives (Augusta, ME: Maine State Archives, 2002)

Vital Records from 1892–1922
from the Maine State Archives (Augusta, ME: Maine State Archives, 2002)

Vital Records, 1923–Present
from the Maine State Archives (Augusta, ME: Maine State Archives, 2002)

Vital Records from Maine Newspapers 1785–1820, 2 vols.
by David C. Young and Elizabeth Keene Young (Bowie, MD: Heritage Books, 1993)

Your Guide to Cemetery Research
by Sharon DeBartolo Carmack (Cincinnati: Betterway Books, 2002)

■ **Androscoggin** 18 Mar. 1854

2 Turner St., Auburn, ME 04210-5953

Phone: (207)784-8390

Web site: www.rootsweb.com/~meandrhs/

Parent County: Cumberland, Oxford, Kennebec, Lincoln

Comments/research tips: Androscoggin Historical Society has Military records 1775–1785. Towns organized before 1800: Durham 1789, Greene 1788, Lewiston 1795, Lisbon 1799, Livermore 1795, Turner 1786.

Record Type	Year Begun	Jurisdiction
Birth	na	City Clerk
Marriage	na	City Clerk
Death	na	City Clerk
Divorce	1854	Clerk/District Ct.
Land	1854	Registrar/Deeds
Probate	1854	Probate Court
Court	1854	County Comm. Office
Burial	na	City Clerk
Wills	1854	Probate Court

■ **Aroostook** 16 Mar. 1839

County Courthouse, 144 Swenden St., P.O. Box 846, Caribou, ME 04736

Phone: (207)532-7317

Web site: www.aroostook.me.us/

Parent County: Washington, Penobscot

Record Type	Year Begun	Jurisdiction
Birth	na	Town Clerks
Marriage	na	Town Clerks
Death	na	Town Clerks
Divorce	1839	Clerk/District Ct.
Land	1839	Registrar/Deeds
Probate	1839	Probate Court
Court	1839	Probate Court

■ **Cumberland** 28 May 1760

142 Federal St., Portland, ME 04101-4151

Phone: (207)871-8380

Web site: www.cumberlandcounty.org/

Parent County: York

Comments/research tips: Towns organized before 1800: Bridgton 1794, Brunswick 1739, Cape Elizabeth 1765, Falmouth 1718, Freeport 1789, Gorham 1764, Gray 1778, Harpswell 1758, New Gloucester 1774, North Yarmouth 1732, Otisfield 1798, Portland 1786, Scarborough 1658, Standish 1785, Windham 1762.

Record Type	Year Begun	Jurisdiction
Birth	na	City/Town Clerks
Marriage	na	City/Town Clerks
Death	na	City/Town Clerks
Land	1760	Registrar/Deeds
Probate	1908	Registrar of Probate
Court	1760	Court/County Comm.

■ **Franklin** 20 Mar. 1838

140 Main St., Farmington, ME 04938

Phone: (207)778-6614

Web site: www.rootsweb.com/~mefrankl/

Parent County: Kennebec, Oxford, Somerset

Comments/research tips: Towns organized before 1800: Farmington 1794, Jay 1795, New Sharon 1794.

Record Type	Year Begun	Jurisdiction
Birth	na	Town Clerks
Marriage	na	Town Clerks
Death	na	Town Clerks
Divorce	1852	Clerk/District Ct.
Land	1838	Registrar/Deeds
Probate	1838	Probate Court

■ **Hancock** 25 June 1789

60 State St., Ellsworth, ME 04605-1926

Phone: (207)667-9542

Web site: www.co.hancock.me.us/

Parent County: Lincoln

Comments/research tips: Towns organized before 1800: Bar Harbor 1796, Blue Hill 1789, Bucksport 1792, Castine 1796, Deer Isle 1789, Gouldsboro 1789, Mount Desert 1789, Penobscot 1787, Sedgwick 1789, Sullivan 1789, Trenton 1789.

Record Type	Year Begun	Jurisdiction
Birth	na	Town Clerks
Marriage	na	Town Clerks
Death	na	Town Clerks
Divorce	na	Clerk/District Ct.
Land	1791	Registrar/Deeds
Probate	1791	Probate Court

■ **Kennebec** 20 Feb. 1799

125 State St., Augusta, ME 04330

Phone: (207)622-0971

Web site: www.rootsweb.com/~mekenneb/

Parent County: Lincoln, Cumberland

Comments/research tips: Towns organized before 1800: Augusta 1797, Belgrade 1796, China 1796, Clinton 1795, Fayette 1795, Hallowell 1771, Litchfield 1798, Monmouth 1792, Mount Vernon 1792, Pittsdon 1779, Readfield 1791, Sidney 1792, Vassalboro 1771, Wayne 1798, Winslow 1771, Winthrop 1771.

Record Type	Year Begun	Jurisdiction
Birth	na	Town Clerks
Marriage	na	Town Clerks
Death	na	Town Clerks
Land	1799	Registrar/Deeds
Probate	1799	Probate Court

■ **Knox** 9 Mar. 1860

62 Union St., P.O. Box 885, Rockland, ME 04841-0885

Phone: (207)594-9379

Web site: http://members.aol.com/vsena/knox/KnoxGenWeb.html

Parent County: Lincoln, Waldo

Comments/research tips: Towns organized before 1800: Camden 1791, Cushing 1789, Thomaston 1777, Union 1786, Vinalhaven 1789, Warren 1776.

Record Type	Year Begun	Jurisdiction
Probate	1860	Probate Court
Court	1860	Court/County Comm.
Birth	na	Town Clerks

Marriage .... na .... Town Clerks
Death .... na .... Town Clerks
Divorce .... na .... Clerk/District Ct.
Land .... 1860 ...... Registrar/Deeds

■ Lincoln   21 June 1760

County Courthouse, High St., P.O. Box 249, Wiscasset, ME 04578-0000
Phone: (207)882-6311
Web site: www.rootsweb.com/~melincol/
Parent County: York
Comments/research tips: Supreme Judicial Court has Military Discharge records 1866–1890. Towns organized before 1800: Alna 1794, Boothbay 1764, Bristol 1765, Dresden 1794, Newcastle 1753, Nobleboro 1788, Waldoboro 1773, Wiscasset 1760.

Record Type	Year Begun	Jurisdiction
Marriage	na	Clerk of Courts
Land	1761	Registrar/Deeds
Probate	1769	Probate Court
Court	1761	Court/County Comm.

■ Oxford   4 Mar. 1805

26 Western Ave., P.O. Box 179, South Paris, ME 04281
Phone: (207)743-6359
Web site: www.rootsweb.com/~meoxford/
Parent County: York, Cumberland
Comments/research tips: Towns organized before 1800: Bethel 1796, Buckfield 1793, Buxton 1762, Fryeburg 1777, Hartford 1798, Hebron 1792, Norway 1797, Paris 1793, Sumner 1798, Waterford 1797.

Record Type	Year Begun	Jurisdiction
Birth	na	Town Clerks
Marriage	na	Town Clerks
Death	na	Town Clerks
Divorce	1930	Clerk/District Ct.
Probate	1805	Probate Court
Land	1805	Registrar/Deeds

■ Penobscot   15 Feb. 1816

97 Hammond St., Bangor, ME 04401
Phone: (207)942-8535
Web site: www.rootsweb.com/~mepenobs/mepenobs.htm
Parent County: Hancock
Comments/research tips: Towns organized before 1800: Hampden 1794, Orrington 1788.

Record Type	Year Begun	Jurisdiction
Divorce	1900	Clerk/District Ct.
Land	1814	Registrar/Deeds
Probate	1816	Probate Court
Nat.	1821	Clerk of Courts

■ Piscataquis   23 Mar. 1838

51 E. Main St., Dover-Foxcroft, ME 04426-1306
Phone: (207)564-2161
Web site: www.rootsweb.com/~mepiscat/
Parent County: Penobscot, Somerset

Record Type	Year Begun	Jurisdiction
Birth	na	Town Clerks

Marriage .... na .... Town Clerks
Death .... na .... Town Clerks
Divorce .... na .... Clerk/District Ct.
Land .... 1838 ...... Registrar/Deeds
Probate .... 1838 ...... Probate Court
Court .... 1838 ...... Clerk/District Ct.

■ Sagadahoc   4 Apr. 1854

752 High, P.O. Box 246, Bath, ME 04530
Phone: (207)443-9332
Web site: www.rootsweb.com/~mesagada/
Parent County: Lincoln
Comments/research tips: Towns organized before 1800: Bath 1781, Bowdoin 1788, Bowdoinham 1762, Georgetown 1716, Topsham 1764, Woolwich 1759.

Record Type	Year Begun	Jurisdiction
Birth	na	Town Clerks
Marriage	na	Town Clerks
Death	na	Town Clerks
Divorce	na	Clerk/District Ct.
Land	1826	Registrar/Deeds
Probate	1854	Probate Court Clerk

■ Somerset   1 Mar. 1809

Court St., Skowhegan, ME 04976
Phone: (207)474-9861
Web site: www.rootsweb.com/~mesomers/
Parent County: Kennebec
Comments/research tips: Towns organized before 1800: Canaan 1788, Cornville 1798, Fairfield 1788, Norridgewock 1788, Starks 1795.

Record Type	Year Begun	Jurisdiction
Probate	1830	Probate Court
Land	1804	Registrar/Deeds

■ Waldo   7 Feb. 1827

73 Church St., Belfast, ME 04915
Phone: (207)338-8282
Web site: www.rootsweb.com/~mewaldo/
Parent County: Hancock
Comments/research tips: Towns organized before 1800: Belfast 1773, Frankfort 1789, Northport 1796, Prospect 1794.

Record Type	Year Begun	Jurisdiction
Birth	na	City/Town Clerks
Marriage	na	City/Town Clerks
Death	na	City/Town Clerks
Divorce	1828	Clerk/District Ct.
Land	1789	Registrar/Deeds
Probate	1827	Probate Court Clerk

■ Washington   25 June 1789

Court St., P.O. Box 297, Machias, ME 04654
Phone: (207)255-3127
Web site: www.rootsweb.com/~mewashin/
Parent County: Lincoln
Comments/research tips: Towns organized before 1800: Addison 1797, Columbia 1796, Eastport 1798, Harrington 1797, Machias 1784, Steuben 1795.

Record Type	Year Begun	Jurisdiction
Birth	na	Town Clerks
Marriage	na	Town Clerks
Death	na	Town Clerks
Divorce	na	Clerk of Courts
Land	1784	Registrar/Deeds
Probate	1785	Probate Court Clerk

■ York(shire) 20 Nov. 1652

45 Kennebank Rd., Alfred, ME 04002

Phone: (207)324-1571

Web site: www.raynorshyn.com/megenweb/york/

Parent County: Original county

Comments/research tips: Towns organized before 1800: Berwick 1713, Biddeford 1718, Cornish 1794, Hollis 1798, Kennebunkport 1653, Kittery 1652, Lebanon 1767, Limington 1792, Lyman 1778, Newfield 1794, Parsonfield 1785, Saco 1762, Sanford 1768, Shapleigh 1785, Waterboro 1787, Wells 1653, York 1652.

Record Type	Year Begun	Jurisdiction
Birth	na	Town Clerks
Marriage	na	Town Clerks
Death	na	Town Clerks
Divorce	na	Clerk/District Ct.
Land	1642	Registrar/Deeds
Probate	1689	Probate Court Clerk

Maryland

By Rhonda R. McClure

HISTORICAL OVERVIEW

Like many of the colonial territories, Maryland was a giant land-grant, given to Cecil Calvert, Second Baron of Baltimore, in 1632. Cecil was the son of George Calvert, who was the secretary of state under King James I of England—a title he was stripped of when he converted to Catholicism. The grant was given to Cecil after his father passed away. However, it was another son, Leonard, who was responsible for the first colonists—Catholic and Protestant English—to what became St. Mary's, the first capital. Maryland, or "Terra Mary," was named for the wife of King Charles I, Henrietta Maria, and was also known as Maria's Land and Mariland.

Of particular note in Maryland's history is the Act of Toleration that was passed in 1649. The act encouraged settlement by "nonconformists" including Catholics, Virginian dissenters, and Quakers by guaranteeing that those who were intolerant would be fined, and if they couldn't pay the fine, jailed. Unfortunately, this did not last long—the government of Maryland was overthrown in 1689 in a Protestant coup and the Anglican church became the state church of Maryland. In 1715 Lord Baltimore converted to Protestantism and the proprietary government was restored, though the Catholics found themselves disfranchised in 1781.

Migrations in and out of Maryland during the 1700s may help you in tracing your ancestors. Germans from Pennsylvania began to enter the counties of Baltimore and Frederick in the 1730s. Quakers migrated from New Jersey at about the same time. Not all of those coming into the state were from other colonies, however—in the mid-1700s there was an influx of Jacobites, servants, and felons from England. As these people were coming into Maryland, many Catholics were heading for Kentucky and the Moravians were heading for North Carolina.

© PhotoDisc/Getty Images

MARYLAND AT A GLANCE

Motto: Strong Deeds, Gentle Words

Population: 5.3 million

Prevalent Religions: Roman Catholic, Baptist, and Methodist, smaller portions of Lutheran, Presbyterian, Pentecostal, Episcopalian, Judaism, Muslim, and Church of Jesus Christ of Latter-day Saints

Major Industries: Seafood, poultry and eggs, dairy products, nursery stock, cattle, soybeans, corn, electrical equipment, food processing, chemical products, printing and publishing, transportation equipment, machinery, primary metals, coal, tourism

Ethnic Makeup (in percent): Caucasian 64.0%, African American 27.9%, Hispanic 4.3%, Asian 4.0%, Native American 0.3%, Other 1.8%

Famous Marylanders: Spiro T. Agnew, John Barth, Eubie Blake, John Wilkes Booth, James M. Cain, Samuel Chase, Frederick Douglass, Philip Glass, Billie Holliday, Johns Hopkins, Francis Scott Key, Thurgood Marshall, H.L. Mencken, Babe Ruth, Harriet Tubman, Leon Uris, Frank Zappa

Above: Coastal Maryland at its finest

Maryland

And don't forget that, once the National Road was completed from Cumberland to Wheeling, it gave Marylanders a route to the recently opened West.

RECORD HIGHLIGHTS

Don't assume you're out of luck for census records before 1790. Maryland took a colonial census in 1776 for most counties. Unlike many other early censuses, this one lists the name, age, and race of each family member for some of the counties. Two years later, in 1778, almost all the males eighteen years old and older took an oath of fidelity. This list has been published in Bettie Stirling Carothers' *Maryland Oaths of Fidelity,* two vols. (Lutherville, Maryland: B.S. Carothers, 1971). Those males who did not take the oath were primarily Friends (Quakers) and others who objected to oaths on religious basis. For those who have Quaker ancestors or others who did not participate, there are some surviving records of adult males who did not take the oath. These have also been compiled by Bettie Stirling Carothers in the *1778 Census of Maryland* (Chesterfield, Missouri: B.S. Carothers, 1975).

From 1633 to 1683, the Calverts—who originally owned all of Maryland—issued headrights or land grants to encourage immigrants to settle in Maryland. A valuable resource to these early settlers is Gust Skordas' *Early Settlers of Maryland: An Index to Names of Immigrants Compiled from Records of Land Patents, 1633–1680* (Baltimore, Maryland: Genealogical Publishing Company, Inc., 1968). A continuation of this work is Peter

Wilson Coldham's *Settlers of Maryland,* 5 vols. (Baltimore, Maryland: Genealogical Publishing Company, Inc., 1995–1996).

Birth records in Maryland from 1898 until 1950 and those for Baltimore City from 1875 until 1941 are on microfilm at the Maryland State Archives. Death records cover the years beginning in 1898 for the state and 1875 for the city of Baltimore, and go through 1982. While the birth records for the last one hundred years are restricted, you can write to the Maryland State Archives, 350 Rowe Boulevard, Annapolis, MD 21401. The Archives can supply:

- Copies of death records through 1978 for the state and 1942 for the City of Baltimore.
- Unofficial transcripts of genealogical information from birth and death records that are restricted.
- Copies of restricted birth and death records to those individuals who are entitled to them.

Marriage records from 1914 to 1950 are also at the Archives. Earlier ones from the late 1700s through 1919 may be found at the clerk of court's office, but you may also want to check the Archives, as they may have what you need. The Family History Library has marriages from the 1850s on microfilm, though they do not have the indexes.

Divorces before the American Revolution were not granted, and after that they were only granted by the state legislature until 1842. Divorce records can be found at the circuit court in the county where the divorce was granted, or they may be in the state archives.

STATE RESOURCES

■ ARCHIVES, LIBRARIES, AND SOCIETIES

Allegany County Historical Society
218 Washington St., Cumberland, MD 21502
Web site: <http://historyhouse.allconet.org>

American Latvian Association
400 Hurley Ave., Rockville, MD 20850-3121
Web site: <www.alausa.org>

Anne Arundel Genealogical Society
P.O. Box 221, Pasadena, MD 21123
Web site: <www.aagensoc.org>

Appalachian Collection, Allegany Community College Library
12401 Willowbrook Rd. SE, Cumberland, MD 21502-2596
Tel: (301) 784-5005

Baltimore Afro-American Historical and Genealogical Society
P.O. Box 66265, Baltimore, MD 21218

Baltimore City Archives
211 E. Pleasant St., Room 201, Baltimore, MD 21202
Tel: (410) 396-4861

Baltimore County Genealogical Society
P.O. Box 10085, Towson, MD 21285-0085
Web site: <www.serve.com/bcgs/bcgs.html>

Baltimore County Historical Society
9811 Van Buren Lane, Cockeysville, MD 21030
Tel: (410) 666-1878
Web site: <www.baltocohistsoc.org>

Baptist Convention of Maryland/Delaware
10255 Old Columbia Rd., Columbia, MD 21046
Tel: (410) 290-5290
Web site: <www.bcmd.org/home.asp>

Calvert County Genealogical Historical Society
P.O. Box 358, Prince Frederick, MD 20678
Tel: (410) 535-2452
Web site: <www.somd.lib.md.us/CALV/cchs/>

Carroll County Genealogical Society
P.O. Box 1752, Westminster, MD 21158
Web site: <www.carr.org/ccgs/ccgs.html>

Catonsville Historical Society, Inc.
P.O. Box 9311, Catonsville, MD 21228-0311
Web site: <www.catonsvillehistory.org/>

Central Maryland Afro-American Historical & Genealogical Society
P.O. Box 2774, Columbia, MD 21045

Crisfield Heritage Foundation
P.O. Box 253, Crisfield, MD 21817
Web site: <www.crisfield.org/Crisfieldheritage.htm>

Division of Vital Records
6550 Reisterstown Rd., Baltimore, MD 21215
Tel: (410) 764-3038

Dorchester County Public Library
303 Gay St., Cambridge, MD 21613
Tel: (410) 228-7331

Dorchester County Historical Society
902 LaGrange Ave., Cambridge, MD 21613
Tel: (410) 228-7953
Web site: <http://bluecrab.org/dchs/>

Dundalk Patapsco Neck Historical Society
P.O. Box 21781, Dundalk, MD 21222

Enoch Pratt Free Library
400 Cathedral St., Baltimore, MD 21201-4484
Tel: (410) 396-5430
Web site: <www.pratt.lib.md.us>

Frederick County Genealogical Society
P.O. Box 234, Monrovia, MD 21770
Tel: (301) 831-5781
Web site: <www.members.aol.com/frecogs>

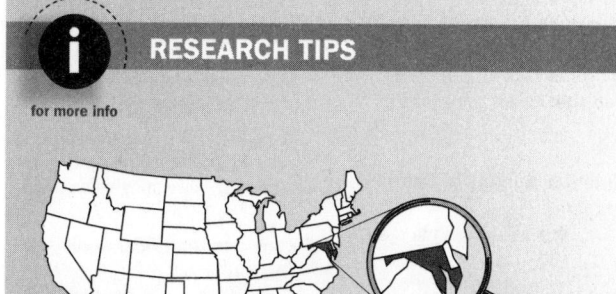

RESEARCH TIPS

for more info

- Baltimore is an independent city. It began keeping court, land, and probate records separate from Baltimore County in 1851.
- When looking for Civil War records, be sure to check both Union and Confederate records—Maryland residents fought on both sides.
- Check all the different repositories when it comes to records in Maryland. Many county records are now housed at the state archives, a repository that many genealogists turn to only as a last resort.

Census Records
- Federal Census: 1790, 1800, 1810, 1820, 1830, 1840, 1850, 1860, 1870, 1880, 1900, 1910, 1920, 1930
- Federal Mortality Schedules: 1850, 1860, 1870, 1880
- Union Veterans and Widows: 1890

Garrett County Historical Society Museum
P.O. Box 28, Oakland, MD 21550
Tel: (301) 334-3226
Web site: <www.deepcreektimes.com/gchs.html>

Genealogical Society of Allegany County
P.O. Box 3103, LaVale, MD 21504-3103
Web site: <www.rootsweb.com/~mdallegh/acgs.html>

Genealogical Society of Cecil County
P.O. Box 11, Charlestown, MD 21914

George Peabody Library, John Hopkins University
17 E. Mt. Vernon Pl., Baltimore, MD 21202
Tel: (410) 659-8179

Germantown Historical Society
P.O. Box 475, Germantown, MD 20875
Tel: (301) 972-0795

Granite Historical Society
P.O. Box 43, Granite, MD 21163-0043
Web site: <www.granitehistory.org/natlhistoric.html>

Harford County Genealogical Society
P.O. Box 15, Aberdeen, MD 21001
Web site: <www.rtis.com/reg/md/org/hcgs/default.htm>

Harford County Historical Society, Inc.
P.O. Box 366, Bel Air, MD 21014
Tel: (410) 838-7691
Web site: <www.harfordhistory.net>

Maryland

Historic Annapolis Foundation
18 Pinkney St., Annapolis, MD 21401
Tel: (800) 603-4020
Web site: <www.annapolis .org>

Historical Society of Carroll County
210 E. Main St., Westminster, MD 21157
Tel: (410) 848-6494
Web site: <http://hscc.carr.org/>

Historical Society of Cecil County
135 E. Main St., Elkton, MD 21921
Tel: (410) 398-1790
Web site: <http://cchistory.org/>

Historical Society of Frederick County, Inc.
24 E. Church St., Frederick, MD 21701
Web site: <www.hsfcinfo.org/index.htm>

Historical Society of Talbot County
29 S. Washington St., Easton, MD 21601
Tel: (410) 822-0773
Web site:

Howard County Genealogical Society
Box 274, Columbia, MD 21045
Web site: <http://users.aol.com/castlewrks/hcgs>

Jewish Genealogical Society of Greater Washington D.C.
P.O. Box 31122, Bethesda, MD 20824-1122
Web site: <www.jewishgen.org/jgsgw/>

Jewish Historical Society Library of Maryland
15 Lloyd St., Baltimore, MD 21202
Tel: (410) 732-6400
Web site: <www.ohwy.com/md/j/jehisoma.htm>

Lower Delmarva Genealogical Society
P.O. Box 3602, Salisbury, MD 21802-3602
Web site: <http://bay.intercom.net/ldgs/index.html>

Lutheran Archives of the Delaware-Maryland Synod Evangelical Lutheran Church of America
7604 York Rd., Towson, MD 21204-7570

Tel: (410) 825-9520
Fax: (410) 825-6745

Maryland Genealogical Society
201 W. Monument St., Baltimore, MD 21201-4674
Tel: (410) 685-3750
Web site:

Maryland Historical Society Library
201 W. Monument St., Baltimore, MD 21201-4674
Tel: (410) 685-3750
Web site:

Maryland State Archives
350 Rowe Blvd., Annapolis, MD 21401
Tel: (800) 235-4045
Web site: <www.mdarchives.state.md.us>

Maryland State Law Library
361 Row Blvd., Annapolis, MD 21401-1697
Tel: (410) 260-1430
Web site:

Mid-Atlantic Germanic Society
P.O. Box 2642, Kensington, MD 20891-2642
Web site: <www.rootsweb.com/~usmags/>

Montgomery County Historical Society
103 W. Montgomery Ave., Rockville, MD 20850
Tel: (301) 340-2825
Web site:

National Archives and Records Administration
8601 Adelphi Rd., College Park, MD 20740-6001
Tel: (866) 272-6272
Web site: <www.archives.gov/facilities/md/archives_2.html>

Prince George County Genealogical Society
Box 819, Bowie, MD 20718-0819
Tel: (301) 262-2063
Web site: <his.com/~krutar/PGCGS/>

Prince George's County Afro-American Historical and Genealogical Society
P.O. Box 44252, Ft. Washington, MD 20744
Web site: <http://pgcm.aahgs.org/index.html>

Prince George County Historical Society
5626 Bell Station Rd., Glenn Dale, MD 20769
Web site: <www.pghistory.org>

Saint Mary's City Historical Society
11 Courthouse Dr., P.O. Box 212, Leonardtown, MD 20650

Saint Mary's County Genealogical Society, Inc.
P.O. Box 1109, Leonardtown, MD 20650
Web site: <www.smcgsi.org>

Silver Spring Historical Society
P.O. Box 1160, Silver Spring, MD 20910-1160
Web site: <www.homestead.com/silverspringhistory/>

Society for the History of the Germans in Maryland
P.O. Box 22595, Baltimore, MD 22585

Theodore R. McKeldin Library, University of Maryland
College Park, MD 20742-7011
Tel: (301) 405-0800
Web site: <www.lib.umd.edu/mck/mckeldin.html>

United Methodist Historical Society
% Lovely Lane Museum Library, 2200 St. Paul St., Baltimore, MD 21218-5897
Tel: (410) 889-4458

Upper Shore Genealogical Society of Maryland
23602 Canvasback Rd., Chestertown, MD 21620
Web site: <www.chronography.com/usgs/>

Washington County Historical Society
P.O. Box 1281, Hagerstown, MD 21741-1281
Tel: (301) 797-8782
Web site: <www.rootsweb.com/~mdwchs/>

Washington, D.C. Temple Branch Genealogical Library
P.O. Box 49, 10000 Stoneybrook Dr., Kensington, MD 20895

Worcester County Library
307 N. Washington St., Snow Hill, MD 21869
Tel: (410) 632-2600
Web site: <www.worc.lib.md.us/library/home.html>

BIBLIOGRAPHY

■ GENERAL RESOURCES

American Genealogical–Biographical Index. Vols. 1-186+
edited by Fremont Rider (Middletown, CT: Godfrey Memorial Library, 1952–)

Anglican Maryland, 1692–1792
by Canon Arthur Pierce Middleton (Virginia Beach: The Donning Company/Publishers, 1992)

Archives of Maryland, New Series, Vol. 1
from the Maryland State Archives (Annapolis, MD: Maryland State Archives Publications, 1990–)

Baltimore County Families, 1659–1759
by Robert W. Barnes (Baltimore, MD: Genealogical Publishing Company, Inc., 1989)

Biographical Cyclopedia of Representative Men of Maryland and District of Columbia.
(Baltimore: National Biographical Publishing Co., 1879)

A Biographical Dictionary of the Maryland Legislature, 1635–1789, 2 vols.
by Edward C. Papenfuse, et al. (Baltimore: Johns Hopkins University Press, 1985)

British Roots of Maryland Families
by Robert Barnes (Baltimore: Genealogical Publishing Co., 1999)

Calendar of Maryland State Papers: No. 1—The Black Books
from the Maryland Hall of Records (Baltimore: Clearfield Company, 1995)

The Calvert Papers: Calender and Guide to the Microfilm Edition
by Donna M. Ellis and Karen A. Stuart (Baltimore: Maryland Historical Society, 1973)

Captains and Mariners of Early Maryland
by Raphael T. Semmes (Baltimore: The John Hopkins Press, 1937)

Chronicles of Colonial Maryland
by James Walter Thomas (Baltimore: Clearfield Company, 1900, 1995)

Church Records at the Maryland State Archives
from the Maryland State Archives (Annapolis, MD: Maryland State Archives, 2002)

Colonial Chesapeake Society
by Lois Green Carr, et al. (Galveston, TX: Frontier Press, 1988)

Colonial Families of the Eastern Shore of Maryland, Vol. 2.
by Robert W. Barnes and F. Edward Wright (Westminster, MD: Family Line Publications, 1996)

Directory of Maryland Church Records
compiled by Edna Agatha Kanely (Westminster, MD: Family Line Publications, 1987)

Directory of Ministers and the Maryland Churches They Served, 1634–1990, 2 vols.
by Edna Agatha Kanely (Westminster, MD: Family Line Publications, 1991)

Early Families of Southern Maryland, 5 vols.
by Elise Greenup Jordan (Westminster, MD: Family Line Publications, 1995)

The Early Settlers of Maryland
by Gust Skordas (Baltimore: Genealogical Publishing Co., Inc., 1968, 1995)

The First Parishes of the Province of Maryland
by Percy G. Skirven (Baltimore: Clearfield Company, 1692, 1923, 1997)

The Flowering of the Maryland Palatinate
by Harry Wright Newman (Baltimore: Clearfield Co., 1985)

The Free State of Maryland: A History of the State and Its People, 1634–1941, 4 vols.
by Frederic Arnold Kummer (Ft. Wayne: Allen County Public Library, ca. 1980)

Genealogical and Memorial Encyclopedia of the State of Maryland
by Richard Henry Spencer (Baltimore: Clearfield Company, 1919, 1992)

Genealogical Research in Maryland: A Guide, 4th ed.
by Mary Keysor Meyer (Baltimore: Maryland Historical Society, 1992)

The Genealogist's Companion and Sourcebook, 2d ed.
by Emily Anne Croom (Cincinnati: Betterway Books, 2003)

A Genealogist's Guide to Discovering Your African-American Ancestors
by Franklin Carter Smith and Emily Anne Croom (Cincinnati: Betterway Books, 2003)

Guide to Genealogical Research in the National Archives of the United States
edited by Anne Bruner Eales and Robert M. Kvasnicka (Washington, DC: National Archives and Records Administration, 2000)

A Guide to Government Records at the Maryland State Archives: A Comprehensive List by Agency and Record Series
from the Maryland State Archives (Annapolis, MD: Maryland State Archives, 1992)

A Guide to the Microfilm Collection of Newspapers at the Maryland State Archives
by Les White (Annapolis: MD State Archives, 1990)

Guide to the Research Collections of the Maryland Historical Society
edited by Richard J. Cox and Larry E. Sullivan (Baltimore: Maryland Historical Society, 1981)

Guide to State Agency Records–Histories and Series Descriptions
from the Maryland State Archives (Annapolis, MD: Maryland State Archives Publications, 1994)

A History of Baltimore Yearly Meeting of Friends: Three Hundred Years of Quakerism in Maryland, Virginia, the District of Columbia, and Central Pennsylvania
by Bliss A. Forbush (Sandy Spring, MD: Baltimore Yearly Meeting of Friends, 1972)

History of the Church of the Brethren in Maryland
by J. Maurice Henry (Elgin, IL: Brethren Publishing, 1936)

History of Maryland, 3 vols.
(Hatboro, PA: Tradition Press, 1967, reprint)

The History of Maryland, from Its First Settlement in 1633 to the Restoration in 1660, Vol. 1
by John Leeds Bozeman (Baltimore: Heritage Books, Inc., 1990)

History of Western Maryland: Being a History of Frederick, Montgomery, Carroll, Washington, Allegany, and Garrett Counties from the Earliest Period to the Present Day, 2 vols.
by John T. Scharf (Baltimore: Regional Publishing Co., 1968)

An Index to the Source Records of Maryland: Genealogical and Historical
by Eleanor P. Passano (Baltimore, MD: Genealogical Publishing Company, Inc., 1967, 1984)

Inside the Great House: Planter Family Life in Eighteenth-Century Chesapeake Society
by Daniel Blake Smith (Galveston, TX: Frontier Press, 1994)

Inventory of the Church Archives of Maryland: Protestant Episcopal Diocese of Maryland
(Baltimore: Historical Records Survey, 1940)

Inventory of Maryland Bible Records
from the Genealogical Council of Maryland (Westminster, MD: Family Line Publications, 1989)

The Manuscript Collections of the Maryland Historical Society
compiled by Avril J.M. Pedley (Baltimore: MD Historical Society, 1969)

Maryland Biographical Sketch Index
by Samuel M. Andrusko (Silver Spring, MD: Samuel M. Adrusko, 1983)

Maryland and Delaware Genealogies and Family Histories: A Bibliography of Books about Maryland and Delaware Families
by Donald Odell Virdin (Bowie, MD: Heritage Books, 1993)

Maryland Deponents, 1634–1799
by Henry C. Peden Jr. (Westminster, MD: Family Line Publications, 1991)

The Maryland Gazette, 1727–1761: Genealogical and Historical Abstracts
By Karen M. Green (Galveston, TX: Frontier Press, 1990)

Maryland Genealogical Library Guide
by John W. Heisey (Morgantown, PA: Masthof Press, 1998)

Maryland Genealogical Research
by George K. Schweitzer (Knoxville, TN: George K. Schweitzer, 1991)

Maryland: A History, 1632–1974
edited by Richard Walsh and William Lloyd Fox (Baltimore: MD Historical Society, 1974)

Maryland, A History of Its People
edited by Suzanne Ellery Greene Chapelle (Baltimore, MD: Johns Hopkins University Press, 1986)

Maryland Lost and Found: People and Places from Chesapeake to Appalacia
by Eugene L. Meyer (Baltimore: John Hopkins University Press, 1986)

Maryland: A Middle Tempermant, 1634–1980
by Robert J. Brugger (Galveston, TX: Frontier Press, 1990)

Maryland Records: Colonial Revolutionary, County and Church from Original Sources, 2 vols.
by Gaius Marcus Brumbaugh (Baltimore: Genealogical Publishing Co., 1993)

Maryland Research Guide
by John W. Heisey (Indianapolis: Heritage House, 1986)

Maryland Research Outline
(Salt Lake City: Family History Library, 1988)

Marylanders to Kentucky, 1775–1825
by Henry C. Peden Jr. (Westminster, MD: Family Line Publications, 1991)

Maryland

Men of Mark in Maryland: Biographies of Leading Men in the State, 4 vols.
(Washington, D.C.: Johnson-Wynne Co., 1907–12)

More Maryland Deponents, 1716–1799
by Henry C. Peden Jr. (Westminster, MD: Family Line Publications, 1992)

National Archives Microfilm Catalogs online:
<www.archives.gov/publications/genealogy_microfilm_catalogs.html>

Newspapers in Maryland Libraries: A Union List
by Eleanor O. Hofstetter (Baltimore: Division of Library Development Services, Maryland State Department of Education, 1977)

Newspapers at the Maryland State Archives
from the Maryland State Archives (Annapolis, MD: Maryland State Archives, 2002)

Old Kent: The Eastern Shore of Maryland
by George A. Hanson (Baltimore: Clearfield Company, 1996)

The Old Line State: A History of Maryland
by Morris Leon Radoff (Annapolis, MD: Hall of Records Commission, 1971)

Old Somerset on the Eastern Shore of Maryland
by Clayton Torrence (Baltimore: Clearfield Company, 1935, 1996)

The Pennsylvania-German in the Settlement of Maryland
by Daniel Wunderlich Nead (Genealogical Publishing Co., 1975)

Pioneers of Old Monocacy: The Early Settlement of Frederick County, Maryland, 1721–1743
by Grace L. Tracey and John P. Dern (Baltimore, MD: Genealogical Publishing Company, Inc., 1987)

The Price of Freedom: Slavery and Manumission in Baltimore and Early National Maryland
by T. Stephen Whitman (Lexington, KY: The University Press of Kentucky, 1997)

Quaker Records in Maryland
by Phebe R. Jacobsen (Annapolis, MD: Hall of Records Commission, 1966)

Quaker Records of Southern Maryland, 1658–1800
by Henry C. Peden Jr. (Westminster, MD: Family Line Publications, 1992)

Register of Maryland's Heraldic Families 1634–1935, 2 vols.
by Alice Parran (Baltimore: Parran, 1937)

Robert Cole's World: Agriculture & Society in Early Maryland
by Lois Green Carr, et al. (Galveston, TX: Frontier Press, 1991)

Scots on the Chesapeake, 1607–1830
by David Dobson (Baltimore: Genealogical Publishing Co., 1985)

Selected Maryland Bibliographies and Resources, 2 vols.
by Barbara S. Giles (Seattle: B.S. Giles, ca. 1988–1989)

Settlers of Maryland, 5 vols.
by Peter Wilson Coldham (Baltimore: Genealogical Publishing Co., 1995–1996)

Side-lights on Maryland History with Sketches of Early Maryland Families, 2 vols.
by Hester Dorsey Richardson (Baltimore: Genealogy Publishing Co., 1995)

Sketches of Maryland Eastern Shoremen
(Westminster, MD: Family Line Publications, 1898, 1992)

Sources of Genealogical Help in Maryland
from the Southern California Genealogical Society (Burbank, CA: Southern California Genealogical Society)

Sources for Genealogical Searching in Maryland
by Betty L. McCay (Indianapolis: B.L. McCay, 1972)

To Maryland from Overseas
by Harry Wright Newman (Baltimore: Genealogical Publishing Co., (1991)

CENSUS RECORDS

The American Census Handbook
by Thomas Jay Kemp (Wilmington, DE: Scholarly Resources, Inc., 2001)

The Census Book: A Genealogist's Guide to Federal Census Facts, Schedules and Indexes
By William Dollarhide (Bountiful, UT: Heritage Quest, 1996)

1776 Census of Maryland
compiled by Bettie Stirling Carothers (Westminster, MD: Family Line Publications, 1989)

1778 Census of Maryland
by Bettie Stirling Carothers (Chesterfield, MI: B.S. Carothers, 1975)

Finding Answers in U.S. Census Records
by Loretto Dennis Szucs and Matthew Wright (Salt Lake City: Ancestry Publishing, 2001)

Map Guide to the U.S. Federal Censuses, 1790–1920
by William Thorndale and William Dollarhide (Baltimore: Genealogical Publishing Co., 1987)

State Census Records
by Ann S. Lainhart (Baltimore: Genealogical Publishing, 1992)

Your Guide to the Federal Census
by Kathleen W. Hinckley (Cincinnati: Betterway Books, 2002)

IMMIGRATION RECORDS

American Naturalization Records, 1790–1990: What They Are and How to Use Them
by John J. Newman (North Salt Lake, UT: HeritageQuest, 1998)

American Passenger Arrival Records
by Michael Tepper (Baltimore: Genealogical Publishing Co., 1993)

Citizens of the Eastern Shore of Maryland, 1659–1750
by F. Edward Wright (Westminster, MD: Family Line Publications, 1986)

Colonial Maryland Naturalizations
by Jeffrey A. Wyand and Florence L. Wyand (Baltimore: Genealogical Publishing Co., 1986)

The Early Settlers of Maryland: An Index to the Names of Immigrants Compiled from Records of Land Patents, 1633–1680, in the Hall of Records, Annapolis, Maryland
by Gust Skordas (Baltimore: Genealogical Publishing Co., 1986)

A Guide to the Acadians in Maryland in the 18th and 19th Centuries
by Gregory A. Wood (Wheaton, MD: Maryland Acadian Studies, 1995)

The King's Passengers To Maryland And Virginia
by Peter Wilson Coldham (Westminster, MD: Family Line, 1997)

Maryland in Africa: The Maryland State Colonization Society, 1831–1857
by Penelope Campbell (Urbana, IL: University of Illinois Press, 1971)

Maryland Naturalization Abstracts, Vol. 2.
by Robert A. Oszakiewski (Westminster, MD: Family Line Publications, 1996)

Marylanders to Carolina: Migrations of Marylanders to North and South Carolina Prior to 1800
by Henry C. Peden (Westminster, MD: Family Line Publications, 1994)

They Became Americans: Finding Naturalization Records and Ethnic Origins
by Loretto Dennis Szucs (Salt Lake City: Ancestry, Inc., 1998)

They Came in Ships: A Guide to Finding Your Immigrant Ancestor's Arrival Records, 2d ed.
by John P. Colletta (Salt Lake City: Ancestry, Inc., 1993)

LAND RECORDS

Land Office and Prerogative Court Records of Colonial Maryland
by Elisabeth Hartsook and Gust Skordas (Baltimore: Clearfield Company, 1968, 1996)

Land and Property Research in the United States
by Wade E. Hone (Salt Lake City: Ancestry Inc., 1997)

Land Records at the Maryland State Archives
from the Maryland State Archives (Annapolis, MD: Maryland State Archives, 2002)

Locating Your Roots: Discover Your Ancestors Using Land Records
by Patricia Law Hatcher (Cincinnati: Betterway Books, 2003)

Old Manors in the Colony of Maryland, 2 vols.
by Annie Middleton Sioussat (Ft. Wayne: Allen County Public Library, ca. 1980)

Settlers of Maryland, 1679–1783, 5 vols.
by Peter Wilson Coldham (Baltimore: Genealogical Publishing Company, 1995–1996)

■ MAPS

Atlas of Maryland
edited by Derek Thompson (College Park: University of Maryland, 1977)

The Counties of Maryland and Baltimore City: Their Origin, Growth, and Development, 1634–1967
from the Maryland State Planning Department (Baltimore: Staff Planning Commission, 1968)

A Gazetteer of Maryland and Delaware
by Henry Gannett (Baltimore: Clearfield Co., 1904, 1994)

Gazetteer of the State of Maryland: Compiled from the Returns of the Seventh Census of the United States and Other Official Documents to Which is Added, A General Account of the District of Columbia
by Richard Swainson Fisher (New York: J.H. Colton, 1852)

The Hammond-Harwood House Atlas of Historical Maps of Maryland, 1608–1908
by Edward C. Pappenfuse and Joseph M. Coale (Baltimore: John Hopkins University Press, 1982)

Historical Atlas and Chronology of County Boundaries, 1788–1980
edited by John H. Long (Boston, MA: G.K. Hall, 1984)

An Illustrated Genealogy of the Counties of Maryland and the District of Columbia as a Guide to Locating Records
by Mary R. Brown (Baltimore: French Bray Printing, 1967)

Maryland A to Z: A Topographical Dictionary
by Marion J. Kaminkow (Baltimore: Magna Carta Book Co., 1985)

Maryland-Delaware Atlas & Gazetteer
(Freeport, MA: DeLorme Mapping, 1993)

Place Names of the Eastern Shore of Maryland
by J. Kenneth Keatley (Queenstown, MD: Queen Anne Press, 1987)

The Place Names of Maryland: Their Origin and Meaning
by Hamill Kenny (Baltimore: Maryland Historical Society)

The Postal History of Maryland, the Delmarva Peninsula and the District of Columbia: The Post Offices and First Postmasters from 1775 To 1984
by Chester M. Smith (Burtonsville, MD: The Depot, 1984)

■ MILITARY RECORDS

The British Invasion of Maryland: 1812–1815
by William M. Marine (Baltimore: Genealogical Publishing Co., 1913, 1977)

Colored Volunteers of Maryland, Civil War, 7th Regiment, United States Colored Troops, 1863–1866
by Agnes Kane Callum (Baltimore: Mullac Publishers, 1990)

Compendium of the Confederate Armies: Kentucky, Maryland, Missouri, the Confederate Units and the Indian Units, 10 vols.
by Stewart Sifakis (New York: Facts on File, ca. 1992–1995)

Dartmoor Prison
by Thomas V. and Joanne M. Huntsberry (Baltimore: J. Mart Publishers, 1984)

German Regiment of Maryland and Pennsylvania
by Henry J. Retzler (Westminster, MD: Family Line Publications, 1996)

Maryland in the Civil War, 2 vols.
by Thomas V. and Joanne M. Huntsberry (Edgemere, MD: J. Mart Publishers, 1985)

Maryland and District of Columbia Volunteers in the Mexican War
by Charles J. Wells (Westminster, MD: Family Line Publications, 1991)

The Maryland Line in the Confederate Army, 1861–1865
by William W. Goldborough (Gaithersburg, MD: Olde Soldier Books, 1987)

The Maryland Militia in the Revolutionary War
by S. Eugene Clements (Westminster, MD: Family Line Publications, 1987)

Maryland Militia, War of 1812, 8 vols.
by F. Edward Wright (Silver Spring, MD: Family Line Publications, 1979–92)

Maryland Revolutionary Records
by Harry Wright Newman (Baltimore: Genealogical Publishing Co., 1993)

Maryland in the World War I, 1917–19. Military and Naval Service Records, 2 vols.
from the Maryland War Records Commission (Baltimore: Maryland War Records Commission, 1933)

Marylanders in the Confederacy
by Daniel D. Hrtzler (Silver Spring, MD: Family Line Publications, 1986)

Marylanders Who Served the Nation: A Biographical Dictionary of Federal Officials from Maryland
by Gerson G. Eisenberg (Annapolis, MD: Maryland State Archives Publications, 1992)

Muster Rolls and Other Records of Service of Maryland Troops in the American Revolution, 1775–1783
from the Maryland Historical Society (Baltimore: Genealogical Publishing Co., 1972)

Revolutionary Records of Maryland
by Gaius Marcus Brumbaugh (Washington, D.C.: Rufus H.

Darby, 1924; Reprint: Baltimore: Clearfield Co., 1996)

Roster of the Soldiers and Sailors Who Served in Organizations from Maryland During the Spanish-American War
(Westminster, MD: Family Line Publications, 1990)

A Short History of the Maryland Line in the Continental Army
by John Dwight Kilbourne (Baltimore: The Society of the Cincinnati of Maryland, 1992)

Uncle, We Are Ready! Registering America's Men, 1917–1918: A Guide to Researching World War I Draft Registration Cards
by John J. Newman (North Salt Lake, UT: HeritageQuest, 2001)

U.S. Military Records: A Guide to Federal & State Sources, Colonial America to the Present
by James C. Neagles (Salt Lake City: Ancestry, Inc., 1994)

Westward of Fort Cumberland; Military Lots Set Off for Maryland's Revolutionary Soldiers
by Mary K. Meyer (Finksburg, MD: Pipe Creek, 1993)

World War II: A Family Historian's Guide
by Debra Johnson Knox (Spartanburg, SC: MIE Publishing, 2003)

■ PROBATE RECORDS

Abstracts of Chancery Court Records of Maryland, 1669–1782
by Debbie Hooper (Westminster, MD: Family Line Publications, 1996)

Abstracts of the Inventories and Accounts of the Prerogative Court of Maryland
by Vernon L. Skinner (Westminster, MD: Family Line Publications, 1988–91)

The County Courthouses and Records of Maryland, Part Two: The Records
by Morris Leon Radoff, et al. (Annapolis: Hall of Records Commission, 1963)

Courts of Admiralty in Colonial America: The Maryland Experience, 1634–1776
by David R. Owen and Michael C. Tolley (Baltimore: Maryland Historical Society)

First Laws of the State of Maryland
(Washington, DE: Scholarly Resources, 1787, 1981)

A Guide To The Maryland Hall Of Records: Local, Judicial And Administrative Records On Microform
by Edward C. Papenfuse (Annapolis: Archives Division, Hall of Records Commission, 1978)

Index to Inventories of Estates, 1718–1777
(Annapolis, MD: Hall of Records Commission, 1947)

Index to Wills of the Colonial Period, Books 1–41, 1634–1777
by Jane Baldwin Cotton (Annapolis: Hall of Records Commission, 1947)

Judgements and Decrees
from the Maryland Court of Appeals (Annapolis: Hall of Records Commission, 1947)

Judicial and Testamentary Business of the Provincial Court: 1637–1683
from the Maryland Provincial Court (Baltimore: Maryland Historical Society, 1887–1964)

Orderly Book of the "Maryland Loyalists Regiment," June 18, 1778 to October 12, 1778
compiled by Caleb Jones (Baltimore: Clearfield Company, 1891, 1996)

Provincial Court Judgements
from the Maryland Provincial Court (Annapolis: Hall of Records Commission, 1947)

■ VITAL RECORDS

Directory of Maryland Burial Grouds
(Westminster, MD: Family Line Publications, 1996)

Divorces And Name Changes In Maryland: By Act Of The Legislature, 1634–1867
by Mark K. Meyer (Mt. Airy, MD: Pipe Creek, 1991)

Historic Graves of Maryland and the District of Columbia
edited by Helen West Ridgely (Baltimore: Genealogical Publishing Co., 1967)

An Illustrated Genealogy of the Counties of Maryland and the District of Columbia as a Guide to Locating Records
by Mary Ross Brown (Baltimore: French-Bray Printing Co., 1967)

Marriages and Deaths from the Maryland Gazette, 1727–1839
by Robert W. Barnes (Baltimore: Genealogical Publishing Co., 1973)

Maryland Eastern Shore Vital Records: 1648–1825, 5 vols.
by F. Edward Wright (Silver Spring, MD: Family Line Publications, 1986)

Maryland Genealogies And Marriages, 1634–1820
(Brøderbund, 1998. CD-ROM)

Maryland Marriages, 1634–1777
by Robert W. Barnes (Baltimore: Genealogical Publishing Co., 1975)

Maryland Marriages, 1778–1800
by Robert W. Barnes (Baltimore: Genealogical Publishing Co., 1975)

Maryland Marriages, 1801–1820
by Robert W. Barnes (Baltimore: Genealogical Publishing Co., 1978)

Maryland Marriage Records, 23 vols.
by Annie W.B. Bell (Annapolis, MD: Annie W.B. Bell, 1938–39)

Maryland Records: Colonial, Revolutionary, County and Church from Original Sources, 2 vols.
by Gaius Marcus Brumbaugh (Baltimore: Genealogical Publishing Co., 1967)

Maryland Records of Deaths, 1718–1777
by Annie W.B. Bell (Annapolis, MD: Annie W.B. Bell, 1936)

Names in Stone: 75,000 Cemetery Inscriptions from Frederick County, Maryland, 2 vols.
by Jacob Mehrling Holdcraft (Baltimore: Genealogical Publishing Co., 1985)

Vital and Probate Records at the Maryland State Archives
from the Maryland State Archives (Annapolis, MD: Maryland State Archives, 2002)

Your Guide to Cemetery Research
by Sharon DeBartolo Carmack (Cincinnati: Betterway Books, 2002)

■ Allegany   25 Dec. 1789
701 Kelly Rd., Suite 407, Cumberland, MD 21502
Phone: (301)777-5911
Web site: www.allconet.org/
Parent County: Washington
Comments/research tips: State Archives has Birth records 1898–1972, Court records 1791–1954, Death records 1865–1882, 1898–1972, Marriage records 1791–1972, and Probate records 1790–1964. Department of Health and Mental Hygiene, has Birth records 1973–1978, Death records 1972–1987, and Marriage records 1973–1987. Clerk of Circuit Court has Naturalization records 1854–1904.

Record Type	Year Begun	Jurisdiction
Marriage	1987	Clerk/Circuit Ct.

■ Anne Arundel   9 Apr. 1650
7 Church Circle, P.O. Box 71, Annapolis, MD 21401-0071
Phone: (410)222-1397
Web site: www.aacounty.org
Parent County: Original county
Comments/research tips: State Archives has Birth records 1804–1877, 1898–1972, Court records 1775–1910, Death records 1865–1880, 1898–1972, Marriage records 1777–1972, and Probate records 1777–1980. Clerk of Circuit Court has Naturalization records 1899–1929. Department of Health and Mental Hygiene, has Birth records 1973–1978, Death records 1972–1987, and Marriage recods 1973–1987.

Record Type	Year Begun	Jurisdiction
Marriage	1987	Clerk/Circuit Ct.
Divorce	1851	Clerk/Circuit Ct.
Land	1653	Clerk/Circuit Ct.

■ Baltimore   30 June 1659
401 Bosley Ave., Towson, MD 21204
Phone: (410)887-2601
Web site: www.co.ba.md.us/
Parent County: Anne Arundel
Comments/research tips: State Archives has Birth records 1865–1883, 1898–1972, Court records 1755–1964, Death records 1898–1972, Divorce records 1851–1973, Marriage records 1777–1851, 1865–1972, Naturalization records 1796–1851, 1868–1906, and Probate records 1664–1979. Department of Health and Mental Hygiene, has Birth records 1973–1978, Death records 1972–1987, and Marriage records 1973–1987.

Record Type	Year Begun	Jurisdiction
Marriage	1987	Clerk/Circuit Ct.
Land	1659	State Archives

■ Baltimore City 4 July 1851
111 N. Calvert St., Baltimore, MD 21202
Phone: (410)333-3733
Web site: www.ci.baltimore.md.us
Parent County: Baltimore
Comments/research tips: State Archives has Birth records 1875–1972, Court records 1821–1849, 1852–1959, Death records 1875–1972, Divorce records 1851–1982, Marriage records 1851–1972, Naturalization records 1845–1906, 1911–1933, and Probate records 1850–1970. Department of Health and Mental Hygiene, has Birth records 1973–1978, Death records 1972–1987, and Marriage records 1973–1987.

Record Type	Year Begun	Jurisdiction
Marriage	1987	Clerk/Circuit Ct.
Land	1851	State Archives

■ Calvert July 1654
175 Main St., Prince Frederick, MD 20678
Phone: (410)535-1600
Web site: www.co.cal.md.us
Parent County: Original county
Comments/research tips: State Archives has Birth records 1898–1972, Court records 1882–1966, Death records 1898–1972, Divorce records 1881–1993, Marriage records 1812–1972, Military Discharge records 1954–1972, Naturalization records 1908–1920, and Probate records 1882–1983. Department of Health and Mental Hygiene has Birth records 1973–1978, Death records 1972–1987, and Marriage records 1973–1987. Called Patuxent County until 1658. Courthouse burned in 1882, destroying most county records.

Record Type	Year Begun	Jurisdiction
Marriage	1987	Clerk/Circuit Ct.
Land	1812	State Archives

■ Caroline Dec. 1773
P.O. Box 458, Denton, MD 21629
Phone: (410)479-1811
Web site: www.caroline.md.org
Parent County: Dorchester, Queen Anne
Comments/research tips: State Archives has Birth and Death records 1865–1884, 1898–1972, Court records 1775–1947, Divorce records 1969–1984, Marriage records 1774–1972, and Probate records 1685–1981. Department of Health and Mental Hygiene has Birth records 1973–1978, Death records 1972–1987, and Marriage records 1973–1987.

Record Type	Year Begun	Jurisdiction
Land	1774	State Archives
Marriage	1987	Clerk/Circuit Ct.

■ Carroll Dec. 1837
225 N. Center St., Westminster, MD 21157
Phone: (410)386-2026
Web site: www.carr.org
Parent County: Baltimore, Frederick
Comments/research tips: State Archives has Birth records 1865–1891, 1898–1972, Court records 1842–1905, Death records 1898–1972, Divorce records 1837–1983, Marriage records 1837–1972, and Probate records 1837–1975. Department of Health and Mental Hygiene has Birth records 1973–1978, Death records 1972–1987, and Marriage records 1973–1987.

Record Type	Year Begun	Jurisdiction
Marriage	1987	Clerk/Circuit Ct.
Land	1812	State Archives

■ Cecil Dec. 1674
129 E. Main St., Room 108, Elkton, MD 21921
Phone: (410)996-5376
Web site: www.ccgov.org
Parent County: Baltimore, Kent
Comments/research tips: State Archives has Birth records 1865–1891, 1898–1972, Court records 1750–1856, Death records 1898–1972, Divorce records 1972–1976, Marriage records 1777–1972, Probate records 1674–1977. Department of Health and Mental Hygiene has Birth records 1973–1978, Death records 1972–1987, and Marriage records 1973–1987.

Record Type	Year Begun	Jurisdiction
Marriage	1987	Clerk/Circuit Ct.
Land	1674	State Archives

■ Charles July 1658
200 Charles St., P.O. Box 970, La Plata, MD 20646
Phone: (301)932-3202
Web site: www.charlescounty.org
Parent County: Original county
Comments/research tips: State Archives has Birth records 1654–1706, 1865–1877, 1898–1972, Court records 1658–1780, Death records 1654–1706, 1865–1866, 1898–1972, Divorce records 1829–1885, 1949–1992, Marriage records 1654–1706, 1865–1921, Military Discharge records 1957–1995, and Probate records 1665–1981. Department of Health and Mental Hygiene has Birth records 1973–1978, Death records 1972–1987, and Marriage records 1973–1987.

Record Type	Year Begun	Jurisdiction
Marriage	1987	Clerk/Circuit Ct.
Land	1658	State Archives

■ Charles, old 1650
Comments/research tips: Abolished in 1653.

■ Dorchester 16 Feb. 1669
206 High St., P.O. Box 150, Cambridge, MD 21613
Phone: (410)228-0480
Web site: www.commissioners.net/
Parent County: Somerset, Talbot
Comments/research tips: State Archives has Birth and Death records 1898–1972, Court records 1743–1902, Divorce records 1820–1827, 1852–1948, Marriage records 1780–1841, 1851–1972, and Probate records 1688–1976.

Record Type	Year Begun	Jurisdiction
Marriage	1987	Clerk/Circuit Ct.
Nat.	1860	Clerk/Circuit Ct.
Land	1669	State Archives

■ **Frederick**   10 June 1748
100 W. Patrick St., Frederick, MD 21701
Phone: (301)694-1976
Web site: www.co.frederic.md.us
Parent County: Prince George's, Baltimore
Comments/research tips: State Archives has Birth records 1865–1873, 1898–1972, Court records 1748–1936, Death records 1865–1881, 1898–1972, Divorce records 1807–1988, Marriage records 1779–1975, Naturalization records 1785–1836, 1854–1958, and Probate records 1745–1963. Department of Health and Mental Hygiene has Birth records 1973–1978, Death records 1972–1987, and Marriage records 1976–1987.

Record Type	Year Begun	Jurisdiction
Marriage	1987	Clerk/Circuit Ct.
Land	1748	State Archives

■ **Garrett**   1 Apr. 1872
203 S. Fourth St., Room 301, Oakland, MD 21550
Phone: (301)334-1941
Web site: www.garrettcounty.org
Parent County: Allegany
Comments/research tips: State Archives has Birth and Death records 1898–1972, Divorce records 1874–1904, Marriage records 1873–1972, and Probate records 1873–1996. Department of Health and Mental Hygiene has Birth records 1973–1978, Death records 1972–1987, and Marriage records 1973–1987.

Record Type	Year Begun	Jurisdiction
Marriage	1987	Clerk/Circuit Ct.
Land	1872	State Archives

■ **Harford**   Mar. 1773
20 W. Courtland St., Bel Air, MD 21014-3833
Phone: (410)838-6000
Web site: www.co.ha.md.us/
Parent County: Baltimore
Comments/research tips: State Archives has Birth and Death records 1898–1972, Court records 1774–1788, Divorce records 1851–1972, Marriage records 1782–1886, 1914–1972, and Probate records 1774–1976. Department of Health and Mental Hygiene has Birth records 1973–1978, Death records 1972–1987, and Marriage records 1973–1987.

Record Type	Year Begun	Jurisdiction
Marriage	1987	Clerk/Circuit Ct.
Land	1774	State Archives

■ **Howard**   4 July 1851
3430 Courthouse Dr., Ellicott City, MD 21043-4300
Phone: (410)313-2111
Web site: co.ho.md.us/
Parent County: Anne Arundel
Comments/research tips: State Archives has Birth records 1898–1972, Court records 1851–1933, Death records 1865–1878, 1898–1972, Marriage records 1840–1972, Military Discharge records 1957–1978, Naturalization records 1903–1945, and Probate records 1840–1976. Department of Health and Mental Hygiene has vital records has Birth records 1973–1978, Death records 1972–1987, and Marriage records 1973–1987. Howard District formed in 1838, didn't become a county until 1851.

Record Type	Year Begun	Jurisdiction
Marriage	1987	Clerk/Circuit Ct.
Land	1839	State Archives

■ **Kent**   2 Aug. 1642
103 N. Cross St., Chestertown, MD 21620
Phone: (410)778-7460
Web site: www.kentcounty.com/
Parent County: Original county
Comments/research tips: State Archives has Birth records 1865–1873, 1898–1972, Court records 1654–1850, Death records 1865–1871, 1898–1972, Marriage records 1675–1707, 1796–1792, and Probate records 1669–1977. Department of Health and Mental Hygiene has Birth records 1973–1978, Death records 1972–1987, and Marriage records 1973–1987.

Record Type	Year Begun	Jurisdiction
Marriage	1987	Clerk/Circuit Ct.
Land	1648	State Archives

■ **Montgomery**   6 Sep. 1776
50 Maryland Ave., Rockville, MD 20850
Phone: (240)777-9466
Web site: www.montgomerycountymd.gov
Parent County: Frederick
Comments/research tips: State Archives has Birth records 1865–1972, Court records 1779–1820, Death records 1898–1972, Divorce records 1851–1940, Marriage records 1798–1839, 1867–1899, 1939–1980, and Probate records 1777–1953. Department of Health and Mental Hygiene has Birth records 1973–1978, Death records 1972–1987, and Marriage records 1973–1987.

Record Type	Year Begun	Jurisdiction
Marriage	1993	State Archives
Land	1777	State Archives

■ **Patuxent**   July 1654
Parent County: Original county
Comments/research tips: (See Calvert) Name changed to Calvert in 1658.

■ **Prince George's**   20 May 1695
14735 Main St., Upper Marlboro, MD 20772
Phone: (301)952-4576
Web site: www.goprincegeorgescounty.com/
Parent County: Charles, Calvert
Comments/research tips: State Archives has Birth records 1865–1867, 1898–1972, Court records 1696–1870, Death records 1865–1866, 1898–1972, Divorce records 1851–1868, 1965–1969, Marriage records 1777–1972, Naturalization records 1799–1845, 1865–1910, and Probate records 1698–1984. Department of Health and Mental Hygiene has Birth records 1973–1978, Death records 1972–1987, and Marriage records 1973–1987.

Record Type	Year Begun	Jurisdiction
Land	1696	State Archives
Marriage	1987	Clerk/Circuit Ct.

Maryland *(side tab)*

■ **Queen Anne's** 18 Apr. 1706
107 N. Liberty, Centreville, MD 21617
Phone: (410)758-1773
Web site: www.qac.org/
Parent County: Kent, Dorchester, Talbot
Comments/research tips: State Archives has Birth records 1865–1881, 1898–1972, Court records 1734–1905, Death records 1898–1972, Marriage records 1817–1972, Military Discharge records 1966–1984, and Probate records 1667–1984. Department of Health and Mental Hygiene has Birth records 1973–1978, Death records 1972–1987, and Marriage records 1973–1987.

Record Type	Year Begun	Jurisdiction
Marriage	1987	Clerk/Circuit Ct.
Land	1707	State Archives

■ **Somerset** 22 Aug. 1666
30512 Prince William St., Princess Anne, MD 21853
Phone: (410)651-1555
Web site: www.rootsweb.com/~mdsomers/
Parent County: Original county
Comments/research tips: State Archives has Birth records 1649–1720, 1865–1870, 1894, 1898–1972, Court records 1698–1899, Death records 1649–1720, 1898–1972, Divorce records 1816–1983, Marriage records 1649–1720, 1796–1972, Military Discharge records 1956–1973, and Probate records 1664–1977. Department of Health and Mental Hygiene has Birth records 1973–1978, Death records 1972–1987, and Marriage records 1973–1987.

Record Type	Year Begun	Jurisdiction
Marriage	1987	Clerk/Circuit Ct.
Land	1665	State Archives

■ **St. Mary's** 9 Feb. 1637
41605 Courthouse Dr., Leonardtown, MD 20650
Phone: (301)475-4567
Web site: www.co.saint-marys.md.us
Parent County: Original county
Comments/research tips: State Archives has Birth and Death records 1865–1867, 1898–1972, Court records 1795–1949, Marriage records 1794–1863, 1865–1972, and Probate records 1658–1976. Department of Health and Mental Hygiene has Birth records 1973–1978, Death records 1972–1987, and Marriage records 1973–1987.

Record Type	Year Begun	Jurisdiction
Marriage	1987	Clerk/Circuit Ct.
Land	1777	Registrar of Wills
Military	1944	State Archives
Divorce	1815	State Archives

■ **Talbot** 18 Feb. 1662
11 N. Washington St., Easton, MD 21601-0816
Phone: (410)822-2401
Web site: www.talbgov.org/
Parent County: Original county
Comments/research tips: State Archives has Birth and Death records 1657–1691, 1898–1972, Court records 1662–1916, Divorce records 1870–1973, Marriage records 1657–1691, 1794–1972, Military Discharge records 1959–1976, and Probate records 1665–1990. Department of Health and Mental Hygiene has Birth records 1973–1978, Death records 1972–1987, and Marriage records 1973–1987.

Record Type	Year Begun	Jurisdiction
Marriage	1987	Clerk/Circuit Ct.
Land	1662	State Archives

■ **Washington** 6 Sep. 1776
95 Washington St., Hagerstown, MD 21740
Phone: (301)733-8660
Web site: www.washco-md.net
Parent County: Frederick
Comments/research tips: State Archives has Birth and Death records 1865–1867, 1898–1972, Court records 1782–1818, Marriage records 1799–1981, and Probate records 1749–1977. Department of Health and Mental Hygiene has Birth records 1973–1978, Death records 1972–1987, and Marriage records 1973–1987.

Record Type	Year Begun	Jurisdiction
Marriage	1987	Clerk/Circuit Ct.
Divorce	1815	State Archives
Land	1777	State Archives

■ **Wicomico** 17 Aug. 1867
P.O. Box 198, Salisbury, MD 21803-0198
Phone: (410)543-6551
Web site: www.wicomicocounty.org
Parent County: Somerset, Worcester
Comments/research tips: State Archives has Birth and Death records 1898–1972, Court records 1868–1984, Divorce records 1908–1988, Marriage records 1868–1981, Naturalization records 1912–1975, and Probate records 1867–1984. Department of Health and Mental Hygiene has Birth records 1973–1978, Death records 1972–1987, and Marriage records 1973–1987.

Record Type	Year Begun	Jurisdiction
Marriage	1987	Clerk/Circuit Ct.
Land	1867	State Archives

■ **Worcester** 29 Oct. 1742
1 W. Market St., Snow Hill, MD 21863
Phone: (401)632-1194
Web site: www.co.worcester.md.us
Parent County: Somerset
Comments/research tips: State Archives has Birth records 1865–1889, 1898–1972, Court records 1825–1900, 1959–1969, Death records 1898–1972, Marriage records 1795–1972, and Probate records 1777–1963. Department of Health and Mental Hygiene has Birth records 1973–1978, Death records 1972–1987, and Marriage records 1973–1987.

Record Type	Year Begun	Jurisdiction
Marriage	1987	Clerk/Circuit Ct.
Divorce	1818	State Archives
Land	1742	State Archives

Massachusetts

By Maureen Taylor

HISTORICAL OVERVIEW

Massachusetts is one of the earliest settlements, but it was actually two separate colonies for most of the seventeenth century. Plymouth Colony was the first settlement, founded by a group of Pilgrims seeking religious freedom in 1620, and it eventually expanded to include Plymouth, Barnstable, and Bristol counties. Reverend John White and his New England Company arrived at Cape Ann in 1628 and established the Massachusetts Bay Colony, which consisted of the towns north of the Merrimack River, plus New Hampshire and Suffolk Counties. In 1691, a charter united the Plymouth and Massachusetts Bay colonies and added parts of Maine and Nova Scotia. Individuals seeking freedom to worship differently than the original settlers, such as Quakers and Baptists, either left the area voluntarily or were banished to other parts of New England, where they created new towns.

Military conflicts characterize Massachusetts' colonial period, from King Philip's War of 1675–76 between settlers and the Narragansett tribe, to European campaigns fought on American soil, such as the French and Indian War. Massachusetts residents sparked the American Revolution with the Boston Tea Party, and the first skirmish of the war happened in the colony. Massachusetts became the sixth state in 1788.

Trade for goods produced in Massachusetts was a critical part of the colony's economy throughout the colonial period, but in the nineteenth century it became global with new markets like South America and the Orient. The Industrial Revolution gave rise to textile and shoe factories that employed girls from nearby farms and later immigrants from Europe, especially Ireland, Italy, and Germany. By the twentieth century newcomers from all over the world sought opportunities in the business, educational, and cultural offerings of the area.

© PhotoDisc / Getty Images

MASSACHUSETTS AT A GLANCE

Motto: By the Sword We Seek Peace, But Peace Only Under Liberty

Population: 6.4 million

Prevalent Religions: Roman Catholicism rules the state, but small pockets of other Christians are here as well.

Major Industries: Seafood, scientific instruments, printing and publishing, nursery stock, dairy products, cranberries, vegetables, machinery, electrical equipment, tourism

Ethnic Makeup (in percent): Caucasian 84.5%, African American 5.4%, Hispanic 6.8%, Asian 3.8%, Native American 0.2%, Other 3.7%

Famous Bay Staters: Henry Adams, John Adams, Samuel Adams, Louisa May Alcott, Horatio Alger, Susan B. Anthony, F. Lee Bailey, Clara Barton, Alexander Graham Bell, William Cullen Bryant, e.e. cummings, Emily Dickinson, Ralph Waldo Emerson, Benjamin Franklin, Margaret Fuller, Erle Stanley Gardner, Robert H. Goddard, John Hancock, Nathaniel Hawthorne, Oliver Wendell Holmes, Jack Kerouac, Amy Lowell, James Russell Lowell, Robert Lowell, Samuel Morse, Sylvia Plath, Paul Revere, Norman Rockwell, Dr. Seuss (Theodor Geisel), Anne Sexton, Lesley Stahl, Paul Theroux, Henry David Thoreau, Mike Wallace, Barbara Walters, John Greenleaf Whittier, James Whistler, Eli Whitney.

Above: The famed House of Seven Gables

RECORD HIGHLIGHTS

Extensive resources exist for the Massachusetts researcher. The Puritan leaders modeled their record keeping after those in England, so early records are orderly and plentiful.

Town clerks kept books of meeting records, earmarks, tax rolls, and vital records. An exception is the city of Boston, where birth records were not recorded from 1800–1849. Vital records date from the founding of the colony and many are in print up to 1850. Unfortunately, no statewide index exists for those records. Lists of freemen, males of legal age at least sixteen to twenty-one years of age, and church members who participated in government and the military can also be found on the town level, on microfilm or in print.

Between 1620 and 1642, more than twenty thousand individuals migrated to present-day New England in what is known as the Great Migration. Robert Charles Anderson, FASG, is researching those immigrants and compiling his findings in a series of books, *The Great Migration Begins*, being published by the New England Historic Genealogical Society. The Massachusetts Society of Mayflower Descendants is in the process of publishing material on individuals that arrived on the *Mayflower*. It is estimated that a quarter of the population of the present-day United States can trace their ancestry back to these early immigrants.

Massachusetts records contain material on early settlers in Maine, which was part of the area until 1820, and the adjacent states of Rhode Island and New Hampshire due to boundary changes. According to the Web site of the The Massachusetts State Archives <www.state.ma.us/sec/arc/arcidx.htm>, their collection includes "land grants, early divorces, military records from 1643 through 1775, and tax valuations for 1738–1786."

Census records include federal population schedules with two exceptions: the 1800 census lacks Boston and parts of Suffolk County, and only the veterans enumeration exists from the destroyed 1890 census. There were state enumerations in 1855 and 1865, for which a partial index exists.

Several cities in Massachusetts served as ports of immigration in the nineteenth century. Passenger lists and naturalization papers are at the National Archives in Washington, with some originals at the Northeast facility in Waltham, Massachusetts.

Massachusetts records are a tremendous resource. David Dearborn, FASG and a librarian at the New England Historic Genealogical Society, states that "because of the excellent quality and abundance of its records, Massachusetts is, arguably, the best place from which to have ancestors." There is one myth that needs to be dispelled— not everything is in print. Many family genealogies, vital

RESEARCH TIPS
for more info

- Before delving into town or county records, explore the holdings of one of the major research repositories in Boston, such as the Massachusetts State Archives <www.state.ma.us/sec/arc/arcidx.htm>.
- There is a wealth of published material on Massachusetts history, genealogies, and records— make sure you look into these books and periodicals before venturing into the unpublished manuscripts held in state and local collections.
- Boundary and land disputes can affect where your ancestor's records are held—don't discount the possibility that they can be found in a neighboring state.

Census Records
- Federal census: 1790, 1800, 1810, 1820, 1830, 1840, 1850, 1860, 1870, 1880, 1900, 1910, 1920, 1930
- Federal Mortality Schedules: 1850, 1860, 1870, 1880
- State Census: 1855 and 1865

records, court documents, and colonial documents appear in book form or in periodicals, but there are still manuscripts in state and local repositories that await publication. Because so much is in print, it is important to start your research by looking at those sources first, before surveying the repositories for relevant unpublished material. The sheer abundance of records on the town and county level, combined with the fact that no single agency is responsible for all the records, makes it necessary to be organized and methodical.

Whether you're looking for early Massachusetts residents or those from the nineteenth century, be aware of boundary and land disputes in the area your ancestor lived. Records might be in an adjacent state.

Start at one of the major research facilities in Boston, such as the Massachusetts State Archives or the New England Historic Genealogical Society (NEHGS). The Massachusetts State Archives collects public records such as judicial records, state papers, and materials on state institutions. The holdings of the NEHGS are more varied,

Massachusetts

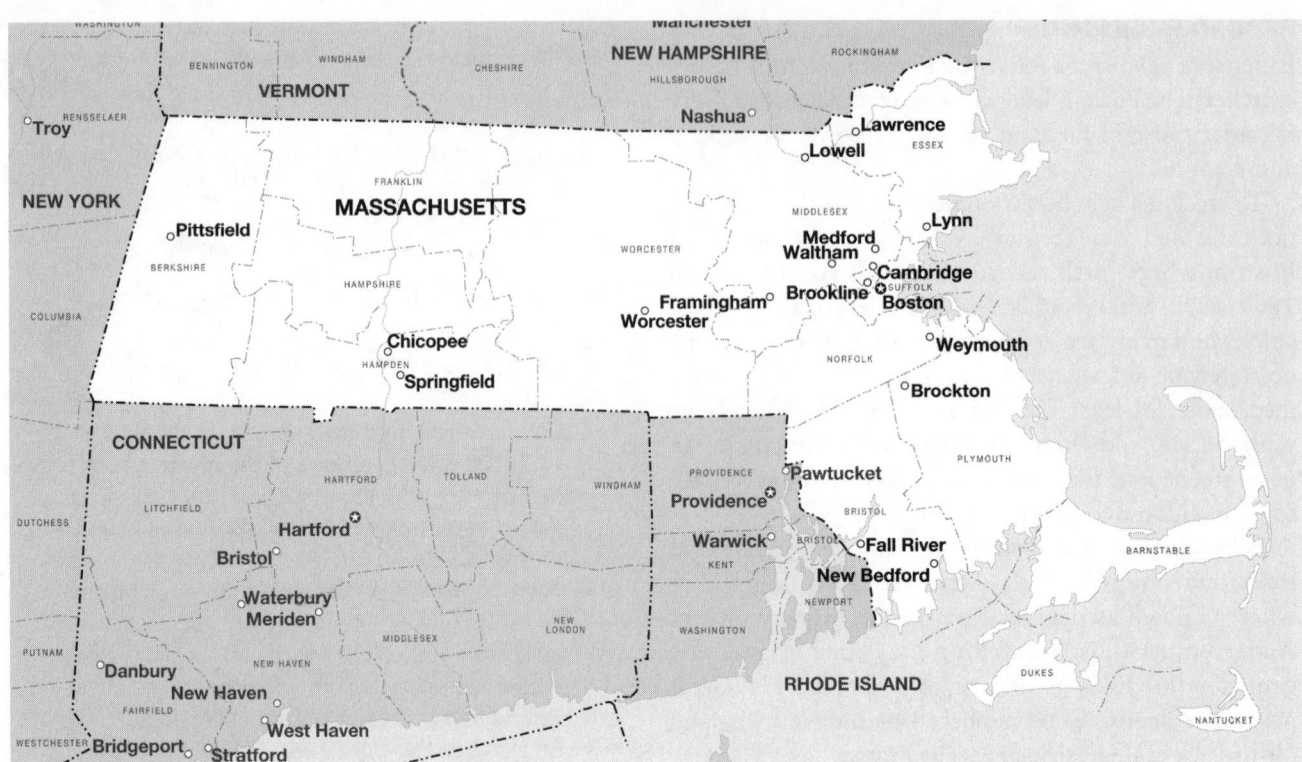

containing unpublished family genealogies, private letters and diaries, transcriptions, and the papers of leading genealogists. They also maintain an extensive research library of printed materials.

Once you've exhausted the resources kept in centralized locations, venture to the town or city from which your ancestor hailed. You'll find more than can be imagined in the town clerk's office, at the local historical society, and even the public library. In Massachusetts there are additional sources to explore around every corner.

STATE RESOURCES

■ ARCHIVES, LIBRARIES, AND SOCIETIES

American Jewish Historical Society
160 Herrick Rd., Newton Centre, MA 02459
Tel: (617) 559-8880
Web site:

American-Portuguese Genealogical Society
P.O. Box 644, Taunton, MA 02780-0644
Tel: (508) 823-3330

Andover-Harvard Theological Library
Harvard Divinity School, 45 Francis Ave., Cambridge, MA 02138
Tel: (617) 496-5153

Web site: <www.hds.harvard.edu/library/bms/>

Andover Historical Society
97 Main St., Andover, MA 01810
Tel: (978) 475-2236
E-mail: info@andhist.org
Web site: <www.andhist.org>

Association for Gravestone Studies
278 Main St., Suite 207, Greenfield, MA 01301
Tel: (413) 772-0836
E-mail: info@gravestonestudies.org
Web site:

Berkshire Historical Society
780 Holmes Rd., Pittsfield, MA 01201
Tel: (413) 442-1793

E-mail: info@berkshirehistory.org
Web site:

Beverly Historical Society
117 Cabot St., Beverly, MA 01915
Tel: (978) 922-1186
E-mail: info@beverlyhistory.org
Web site:

The Boston Public Library
700 Boylston St., Boston, MA 02116
Tel: (617) 536-5400
E-mail: info@bpl.org
Web site:

The Braintree Historical Society
786 Washington St., Braintree, MA 02184
Tel: (617) 848-1640
Web site: <www.key-biz.com/ssn/Braintree/hist_soc.html>

Brockton Historical Society
216 Pearl St., Brockton, MA 02301
Tel: (508) 583-1039
Web site: <www.brocktonma.com/bhs/bhs_mus.html>

Canton Historical Society
1400 Washington St., Canton, MA 02021
Web site:

Cape Cod Genealogical Society, Inc.
P.O. Box 1394, Harwich, MA 02645
Web site:

Danvers Historical Society
P.O. Box 381, Danvers, MA 01923
Tel: (978) 777-1666
E-mail: dhs@danvershistory.org
Web site:

Dedham Historical Society
P.O. Box 215, Dedham, MA 02027
Tel: (781) 326-1385
Web site:

Eastham Historical Society
P.O. Box 8, Eastham, MA 02642
Web site:

The Episcopal Diocese of Massachusetts
138 Tremont St., Boston MA 02111
Web site:

Essex Institute Museum
132 Essex St., Salem, MA 01970
Tel: (978) 745-1876

Essex Society of Genealogists, Inc.
P.O. Box 313, Lynnfield, MA 01940-0313
Web site:

Falmouth Genealogical Society
P.O. Box 2107, Falmouth, MA 02536
Web site:

Finlandia Foundation-Boston, Inc.
P.O. Box 308, Arlington, MA 02476
Web site: <www.finlandiafoundation.org/MA/boston/>

The Finnish American Society of Cape Cod
P.O. Box 220, West Barnstable, MA 02668

General Society of Mayflower Descendants
P.O. Box 3297, Plymouth, MA 02361-3297
Tel: (508) 746-3188
Web site:

Harwich Historical Society
P.O. Box 5217, Harwich, MA 02645-2507
Tel: (508) 432-8089
E-mail: hhs@capecodhistory.org

The Irish Ancestral Research Association
Dept. W, P.O. Box 619, Sudbury, MA 01776
E-mail: president@tiara.ie
Web site: <http://tiara.ie/>

Italian Genealogical Society of America
P.O. Box 3572, Peabody, MA 01961-3572
Web site: <64.252.159.163/igsa/Default.htm>

The Jamaica Plain Historical Society
P.O. Box 2924, Jamaica Plain, MA 02130-0024
Tel: (617) 522-1150
Web site: <www.geocities.com/jphistoricalsociety/>

Jewish Genealogical Society of Greater Boston, Inc.
P.O. Box 610366, Newton, MA 02461-0366
Tel: (617) 796-8522
E-mail: info@jgsgb.org
Web site: <www.jewishgen.org/boston/>

Martha's Vineyard Historical Society
P.O. Box 1310, Edgartown, MA 02539
Tel: (508) 627-4441
E-mail: mvhist@vineyard.net
Web site:

Massachusetts Archives
220 Morrissey Blvd., Boston, MA 02125
Tel: (617) 727-2816
E-mail: archives@sec.state.ma.us
Web site: <www.sec.state.ma.us/arc/arcgen/genidx.htm>

Massachusetts Genealogical Council
P.O. Box 5393, Cochituate, MA 01778
Web site: <http://home.comcast.net/~massgencouncil/>

Massachusetts Historical Society
1154 Boylston St., Boston, MA 02215-3695
Tel: (617) 536-1608
Web site: <www.masshist.org/welcome/>

Massachusetts Society of Genealogists, Inc.
P.O. Box 215, Ashland, MA 01721-0215
Tel: (508) 892-1225
Web site: <www.rootsweb.com/~masgi/>

The Massachusetts Society of Mayflower Descendants
100 Boylston St., #750, Boston, MA 02116-4610
Tel: (617) 338-1991
E-mail: MSMDassmayflower.org
Web site:

Massachusetts Society, Sons of the American Revolution
255 Main St., Marlborough, MA 01752
Tel: (508) 229-1776
Web site:

Medford Historical Society
10 George St., Medford, MA 02155

Middleborough Historical Association
Jackson St., Middleborough, MA 2346
Tel: (508) 947-3394

Natick Historical Society & Museum
58 Eliot St., South Natick, MA 01760
Tel: (508) 647-4841
E-mail: info@natickhistory.com
Web site:

National Archives-New England Region
380 Trapelo Rd., Waltham, MA 02452-6399
Tel: (781) 663-0130
Fax: (781) 663-0154
Web site: <www.archives.gov/facilities/ma/boston.html>

National Society Daughters of the American Revolution
1776 D St. NW, Washington, DC 20006-5392

Needham Historical Society
53 Glendoon Rd., Needham, MA 02492
Tel: (781) 455-8860
Web site: <http://greisnet.com/needhist.nsf/>

New England Historic Genealogical Society
101 Newbury St. Boston, MA 02116-3007
Tel: (617) 536-5740
E-mail: nehgreditor@aol.com
Web site:

New England Lutheran Archives
Trinity Lutheran Church, 292 Orange St., New Haven, CT 06510
Tel: (203) 787-6521

Old Colony Historical Society
66 Church Green, Taunton, MA 02780
Tel: (508) 822-1622
Web site:

The Peabody Essex Museum
East India Square, Salem, MA 01970
Tel: (978) 745-9500
Web site: <www.pem.org/homepage/>

Peabody Historical Society
35 Washington St., Peabody, MA 01960
Tel: (978) 531-0805

Plymouth County Genealogists, Inc.
P.O. Box 7025, Brockton, MA. 02301-7025
Web site: <www.rootsweb.com/~maplymou/pcgs/pcgsmain.htm>

Plympton Historical Society
189 Main St., Plympton, MA 02367-1112
Tel: (781) 585-2725

Quincy Historical Society
8 Adams St., Quincy, MA 02169
Tel: (617) 773-1144
E-mail: qhist@ci.quincy.ma.us
Web site: <www.key-biz.com/ssn/Quincy/hist_soc.html>

Registrar of Vital Statistics
470 Atlantic Ave., Boston, MA 02110
Tel: (617) 753-8600
Web site: <http://vitalrec.com/ma.html>

Roman Catholic Archives of the Archdiocese of Boston
2121 Commonwealth Ave., Boston, MA 02135-3193
Tel: (617) 254-0100

The Saugus Historical Society
P.O. Box 1209, Saugus, MA 01906-1209
Tel: (781) 233-7232
Web site: <www.saugus.org/HistoricalSociety/>

Sheffield Historical Society
159-161 Main St., P.O. Box 747, Sheffield, MA 01257
Tel: (413) 229-2694
E-mail: shs@sheffieldhistory.org
Web site:

Shirley Historical Society and Museum
182 Center Rd., P.O. Box 217, Shirley, MA 01464-0217
Tel: (978) 425-9328
E-mail: shs1.ma.ultranet@rcn.com
Web site: <http://users.rcn.com/shs1.ma.ultranet/>

South Shore Genealogical Society
P.O. Box 396, Norwell, MA 02061
E-mail: soshoregen@yahoo.com
Web site: <http://rootsweb.com/~massgs/>

Southborough Historical Society
P.O. Box 364, 25 Common St., Southborough, MA 01772
Tel: (508) 229-8055
E-mail: info@southboroughhistory.org
Web site:

Massachusetts

Massachusetts

The State Library of Massachusetts
State House, Room 341, Boston, MA 02133
Tel: (617) 727-2590
Web site: <www.mass.gov/lib/>

Swedish Ancestry Research Association
P.O. Box 70603, Worcester, MA 01607-0603

Walpole Historical Society, Inc.
P.O. Box 100, Walpole MA 02081
E-mail: walpolehistoricalsociety @yahoo.com
Web site:

Western Massachusetts Genealogical Society
P.O. Box 206, Springfield, MA 01108

Winchester Historical Society
P.O. Box 127, Winchester, MA 01890-0127
Web site:

BIBLIOGRAPHY

■ GENERAL RESOURCES

Baptists in Massachusetts
by John Woolman Brush (Valley Forge, PA: Judson Press, 1970)

Biographical History of Massachusetts: Biographies and autobiographies of the leading men in the state
by Samuel Atkins Eliot (Boston, MA: Massachusetts Biographical Society, 1911–1918)

Catalog of Manuscripts of the Massachusetts Historical Society
(Boston, MA: G.K. Hall, 1969)

Chronicles of the First Planters of the Colony of Massachusetts Bay from 1623 to 1636
by Alexander Young (Boston, MA: C.C. Little and J. Brown, 1846)

Chronicles of the Pilgrim Fathers of the Colony of Plymouth, from 1602 to 1625
by Alexander Young (Boston, MA: C.C. Little and J. Brown, 1844)

Commonwealth History of Massachusetts: Colony, Province, and State, 5 vols.
by Albert Bushnell Hart (New York: States History, ca. 1927–ca. 1930)

Encyclopedia of Massachusetts, Biographical-Genealogical
(New York, NY: American Historical Society, ca. 1916)

The English Ancestry and Homes of the Pilgrim Fathers: Who Came to Plymouth on the "Mayflower" in 1620, the "Fortune" in 1621, and the "Anne" and the "Little James" in 1623
by Charles Edward Banks (Baltimore, MD: Genealogical Pub. Co., 1962)

English Origins of New England Families: From The New England Historical and Genealogical Register, first series
by Gary Boyd Roberts (Baltimore, MD: Genealogical Pub. Co., 1984)

The Episcopal Diocese of Massachusetts, 1784–1984: A Mission to Remember, Proclaim, and Fulfill
by Mark J. Duffy (Boston: Episcopal Diocese of Massachusetts, 1984)

Families of the Pilgrims
by Huber Kinney Shaw (Boston, MA: The Society, ca. 1956)

Genealogical and Personal Memoirs Relating to the Families of the State of Massachusetts
by William F. Adams and William R. Cutter (New York, NY: Lewis Historical Pub. Co., 1910)

Genealogical Research in New England
by Ralph J. Crandall (Baltimore, MD: Genealogical Pub. Co., ca. 1984)

Genealogies of Mayflower Families: From The New England Historical and Genealogical Register
by Gary Boyd Roberts (Baltimore, MD: Genealogical Pub. Co., ca. 1985)

The Genealogist's Companion and Sourcebook, 2d ed.
by Emily Anne Croom (Cincinnati: Betterway Books, 2003)

A Genealogist's Guide to Discovering Your African-American Ancestors
by Franklin Carter Smith and Emily Anne Croom (Cincinnati: Betterway Books, 2003)

Genealogist's Handbook for New England Research
by Marcia Wiswall Lindberg (Boston, MA: New England Historic Genealogical Society, ca. 1993)

Guide to Genealogical Research in the National Archives of the United States
edited by Anne Bruner Eales and Robert M. Kvasnicka (Washington, DC: National Archives and Records Administration, 2000)

A Guide to the History of Massachusetts
by Martin Kaufman, John W. Ifkovic, and Joseph Carvalho (New York, NY: Greenwood Press, ca. 1988)

A Guide to Massachusetts Local History
by Charles A. Flagg (Salem, MA: Salem Press Co., ca. 1907)

Historical Collections: Being a general collection of interesting facts, traditions, biographical sketches, anecdotes, etc., relating to the history and antiquities of every town in Massachusetts, with geographical descriptions
by John Warner Barber (Worcester, MA: Dorr, Howland, 1839)

King and People in Provincial Massachusetts
by Richard L. Bushman (Chapel Hill, NC: University of North Carolina Press, ca. 1985)

Massachusetts, 1620–1930
(Brøderbund, ca. 1998. CD-ROM)

Massachusetts Bay Connections: Historical and Biographical Sketches of the Towns and Communities of the Massachusetts Bay Colony
by Judy Jacobson (Baltimore, MD: Clearfield Co., ca. 1992)

Massachusetts, A Bibliography of its History
by John D. Haskell (Hanover, NH: University Press of New England, ca. 1983)

Massachusetts Biographical Dictionary
(Wilmington, DE: American Historical Publications, ca. 1988)

Massachusetts Episcopalians, 1607–1957
by Dudley Tyng (Episcopal Diocese of Massachusetts, ca. 1960)

Massachusetts Genealogical Research
by George K. Schweitzer (Knoxville, TN: G.K. Schweitzer, ca. 1990)

Massachusetts and Maine Families: In the ancestry of Walter Goodwin Davis (1885–1966): a reprinting, in alphabetical order by surname, of the sixteen multi-ancestor compendia: (plus Thomas Haley of Winter Harbor and his descendants)
by Walter Goodwin Davis (Baltimore, MD: Genealogical Pub. Co., ca. 1996)

Massachusetts Research Outline
from the Church of Jesus Christ of Latter-day Saints Family (Salt Lake City, UT: Corp. of the President of The Church of Jesus Christ of L.D.S., ca. 1988, ca. 1997)

The Mayflower Reader: A selection of articles from The Mayflower Descendant
by George Ernest Bowman (Baltimore, MD: Genealogical Pub. Co., 1996)

National Archives Microfilm Catalogs online:
<www.archives.gov/publica tions/genealogy_microfilm_ catalogs.html>

Pilgrim Genealogies and Histories
(Brøderbund, ca. 1999. CD-ROM)

The Planters of the Commonwealth: A Study of the Emigrants and Emigration in Colonial Times, to which are Added Lists of Passengers to Boston and to the Bay Colony, the Ships which Brought Them, their English Homes, and the Places of their Settlement in Massachusetts, 1620–1640
by Charles Edward Banks (Baltimore, MD: Genealogical Pub. Co., 1961)

Plymouth Colony, Its History & People 1620–1691
by Eugene Aubrey Stratton (Salt Lake City, UT: Ancestry Pub., ca. 1986)

The Plymouth Scrap Book: The oldest original documents extant in Plymouth archives printed verbatim, some repoduced, with a review of Bradford's History of Plymouth Plantation
by Charles Henry Pope (Boston, MA: C.E. Goodspeed, 1918)

The Quaker Invasion of Massachusetts
by Richard P. Hallowell (Bowie, MD: Heritage Books, 1987)

Records of the Colony of New Plymouth in New England
edited by Nathaniel B. Shurtleff (Bowie, MD: Heritage Books, 1998)

A Surname Guide to Massachusetts Town Histories
by Phyllis O. Longver (Bowie, MD: Heritage Books, ca. 1993)

■ CENSUS RECORDS

The American Census Handbook
by Thomas Jay Kemp (Wilmington, DE: Scholarly Resources Inc., ca. 2001)

The Census Book: A Genealogist's Guide to Federal Census Facts, Schedules and Indexes
by William Dollarhide (Bountiful, UT: Heritage Quest, ca. 1999)

Finding Answers in U.S. Census Records
by Loretto Dennis Szucs and Matthew Wright (Orem, UT: Ancestry Pub., ca. 2001)

List of Freemen of Massachusetts, 1630–1691
by Lucius R. Paige (Baltimore: Genealogical Pub. Co., 1978)

Map Guide to the U.S. Federal Censuses, 1790–1920
by William Thorndale and William Dollarhide (Baltimore, MD: Genealogical Pub. Co., ca. 1987)

Massachusetts and Maine Direct Tax Census of 1798
by the United States Secretary of the Treasury (Cambridge, MA: New England Historic Genealogical Society, 1978)

The Massachusetts Tax Valuation List of 1771
by Betty Hobbs Pruitt (Camden, ME: Picton Press, ca. 1998)

A Research Aid for the Massachusetts 1910 Federal Census
by Mary Lou Craver Mariner (Sudbury, MA: Computerized Assistance, ca. 1988)

State Census Records
by Ann S. Lainhart (Baltimore: Genealogical Pub. Co., ca. 1992)

Your Guide to the Federal Census
by Kathleen W. Hinckley (Cincinnati: Betterway Books, 2002)

■ IMMIGRATION RECORDS

American Naturalization Records, 1790–1990: What They Are and How to Use Them
by John J. Newman (North Salt Lake, UT: HeritageQuest, 1998)

American Passenger Arrival Records
by Michael Tepper (Baltimore: Genealogical Publishing Co., 1993)

The Complete Book of Emigrants, 1661–1699
by Peter Wilson Coldham (Baltimore, MD: Genealogical Pub. Co., ca. 1990)

The Complete Book of Emigrants, 1700–1750
by Peter Wilson Coldham (Baltimore, MD: Genealogical Pub. Co., ca. 1992)

Founders of Early American Families: Emigrants from Europe, 1607–1657
by Meredith B. Colket (Cleveland, OH: General Court of the Order of Founders and Patriots of America, ca. 1985)

The Great Migration Begins: Immigrants to New England, 1620–1633
by Robert Charles Anderson (Boston, MA: New England Historic Genealogical Society, ca. 1995)

Immigrants to New England, 1700–1775
by Ethel Stanwood Bolton (Salem, MA: The Essex Institute, 1931)

A List of Alien Passengers, Bonded, from January 1, 1847 to January 1, 1851
by J.B. Munroe (Baltimore, MD: Genealogical Pub. Co., 1971)

Passenger and Immigration Lists Index: A Guide to Published Arrival Records of about 500,000 Passengers Who Came to the United States and Canada in the Seventeenth, Eighteenth, and Nineteenth Centuries
by P. William Filby and Mary K. Meyer (Detroit, MI: Gale Research, ca. 1981–)

Port Arrivals and Immigrants to the City of Boston, 1715–1716 and 1762 and 1769
by William H. Whitmore (Baltimore, MD: Genealogical Pub. Co., 1973)

The Search for Missing Friends: Irish Immigrant Advertisements Placed in The Boston Pilot
by Ruth-Ann M. Harris, Donald M. Jacobs, and B.E. O'Keeffe (Boston, MA: New England Historic Genealogical Society, 1989–1997)

They Became Americans: Finding Naturalization Records and Ethnic Origins
by Loretto Dennis Szucs (Salt Lake City: Ancestry, Inc., 1998)

They Came in Ships: A Guide to Finding Your Immigrant Ancestor's Arrival Records, 2d ed.
by John P. Colletta (Salt Lake City: Ancestry, Inc., 1993)

The Winthrop Fleet of 1630: An account of the vessels, the voyage, the passengers and their English home from original authorities
by Charles Edward Banks (Baltimore, MD: Genealogical Pub. Co., 1961)

■ LAND RECORDS

Land & Property Research in the United States
by E. Wade Hone (Salt Lake City, UT: Ancestry, ca. 1997)

Locating Your Roots: Discover Your Ancestors Using Land Records
by Patricia Law Hatcher (Cincinnati: Betterway Books, 2003)

Records of the Colony of New Plymouth, in New England
by the New Plymouth (Boston, MA: William White, 1855–61)

Records of the Governor and Company of the Massachusetts Bay in New England: Printed by Order of the Legislature
by Nathaniel Bradstreet Shurtleff (Boston, MA: W. White, 1853–1854)

■ MAPS

Atlas of Historical County Boundaries: Connecticut, Maine, Massachusetts, Rhode Island
edited by John H. Long (New York: Simon & Schuster, 1994)

Directory of Massachusetts Place Names
by Charlotte Pease Davis (Lexington, MA: Bay State News, ca. 1987)

A Gazetteer of the State of Massachusetts
by Elias Nason (Boston, MA: B.B. Russell, 1874)

A Geographic Dictionary of Massachusetts
by Henry Gannett (Baltimore, MD: Genealogical Pub. Co., 1978)

Historical Atlas of Massachusetts
by Richard W. Wilkie, Jack Tager, and Roy Doyon (Amherst. MA: The University of Massachusetts Press, ca. 1991)

Search for the Passengers of the Mary & John, 1630
by Burton W. Spear (Toledo, OH: B.W. Spear, ca. 1985–)

Topographic Maps of Massachusetts, Rhode Island and Connecticut
by the United States Geological Survey (Washington, DC: United States Geological Survey, 1950, 1964–1965)

■ MILITARY RECORDS

The Loyalists of Massachusetts and the Other Side of the American Revolution
by James H. Stark (Bowie, MD: Heritage Books, 1988)

The Loyalists of Massachusetts: Their Memorials, Petitions and Claims
by E. Alfred Jones (Baltimore, MD: Genealogical Pub. Co., 1969)

Massachusetts in the Army and Navy During the War of 1861–65
by Thomas Wentworth Higginson (Boston, MA: Wright & Potter Printing, 1895–1896)

Massachusetts Officers in the French and Indian Wars, 1748–1763
by Nancy S. Voye (Boston: Society of Colonial Wars in the Commonwealth of Massachusetts, ca. 1975)

Massachusetts

Massachusetts Officers and Soldiers, 1702–1722: Queen Anne's War to Dummer's War by Mary E. Donahue (Boston: Society of Colonial Wars in the Commonwealth of Massachusetts, ca. 1980)

Massachusetts Officers and Soldiers, 1723–1743: Dummer's War to the War of Jenkins' Ear by Myron O. Stachiw (Boston: Society of Colonial Wars in the Commonwealth of Massachusetts, ca. 1979)

Massachusetts Officers and Soldiers in the Seventeenth Century Conflicts by Carole Doreski (Society of Colonial Wars in the Commonwealth of Massachusetts, New England Historic Genealogical Society, ca. 1982)

Massachusetts Privateers of the Revolution by Gardner Weld Allen (Boston: Massachusetts Historical Society, 1927)

Massachusetts Soldiers in the French and Indian Wars, 1744–1755 by Robert E. MacKay (Boston: Society of Colonial Wars in the Commonwealth of Massachusetts, ca. 1978)

Massachusetts Soldiers, Sailors, and Marines in the Civil War by Charles H. Cole (Bethesda, MD: University Publications of America, ca. 1991)

Pierce's Colonial Lists: Civil, military and professional lists of Plymouth and Rhode Island colonies, comprising colonial, county and town officers, clergymen, physicians and lawyers: with extracts from colonial laws defining their duties, 1621–1700 by Ebenezer W. Pierce (Baltimore, MD: Genealogical Pub. Co., 1968)

Record of the Massachusetts Volunteers, 1861–1865 by the Massachusetts Adjutant General (Bethesda, MD: University Publications of America, ca. 1991)

Uncle, We Are Ready! Registering America's Men, 1917–1918: A Guide to Researching World War I Draft Registration Cards by John J. Newman (North Salt Lake, UT: HeritageQuest, 2001)

U.S. Military Records: A Guide to Federal & State Sources, Colonial America to the Present by James C. Neagles (Salt Lake City: Ancestry, Inc., 1994)

World War II: A Family Historian's Guide by Debra Johnson Knox (Spartanburg, SC: MIE Publishing, 2003)

■ **PROBATE RECORDS**

Abstracts of Bristol County, Massachusetts, Probate Records by H.L. Peter Rounds (Baltimore, MD: Genealogical Pub. Co., 1987–1988)

Essex County, Massachusetts, Probate Index, 1638–1840 by Melinde Lutz Sanborn (Boston, MA: M.L. Sanborn, ca. 1987)

Index to the Probate Records of the County of Middlesex, Massachusetts: first series, from 1648 to 1871 by the Massachusetts Probate Court (Cambridge, MA: 1914)

List of Freemen of Massachusetts, 1630–1691 by Lucius R. Paige (Baltimore, MD: Genealogical Pub. Co., 1978)

List of Persons Whose Names Have Been Changed in Massachusetts, 1780–1892 (Baltimore, MD: Genealogical Pub. Co., 1972)

Mayflower Deeds & Probates: from the files of George Ernest Bowman at the Massachusetts Society of Mayflower Descendants by Susan E. Roser (Baltimore, MD: Genealogical Pub. Co., ca. 1994)

Mayflower Source Records: Primary Data Concerning Southeastern Massachusetts, Cape Cod, and the Islands of Nantucket and Martha's Vineyard by Gary Boyd Roberts (Baltimore, MD: Genealogical Pub. Co., ca. 1986)

Plymouth Colony Probate Guide: Where to Find Wills and Related Data for 800 people of Plymouth Colony, 1620–1691 by Ruth Wilder Sherman (Warwick, R.I.: Plymouth Colony Research Group, 1983)

Plymouth County, Massachusetts Probate Index, 1686–1881 by Ralph V. Wood (Camden, ME: Picton Press, ca. 1988)

Plymouth Court Records, 1686–1859 by David Thomas Konig and William E. Nelson (Wilmington, DE: Michael Glazier, Inc., in association with the Pilgrim Society, 1978–1981)

Suffolk County Wills: Abstracts of the Earliest Wills upon Record in the County of Suffolk, Massachusetts by Judith McGhan (Baltimore, MD: Genealogical Pub. Co., 1984)

■ **VITAL RECORDS**

Bibliography of Massachusetts Vital Records 1620–1905: An Inventory of the Original Volumes of Births, Marriages, and Deaths by Jay Mack Holbrook (Oxford, MA: Holbrook Research Institute, 1999)

Early Massachusetts Marriages Prior to 1800: With the addition of Plymouth County Marriages, 1692–1746 by Frederic W. Bailey (Baltimore, MD: Genealogical Pub. Co., 1968)

Index of Marriages in Massachusetts Centinel and Columbian Centinel, 1784 to 1840 by the American Antiquarian Society (Boston, MA: G.K. Hall, 1961)

The Massachusetts Magazine: Marriage and Death Notices, 1789–1796 by C.J. Stevens (New Orleans: Polyanthos, Inc., ca. 1978)

Mayflower Descendants and Their Marriages for Two Generations After the Landing: Including a Short History of the Church of the Pilgrim Founders of New England by John T. Landis (Baltimore, MD: Southern Book Company, 1956)

Mayflower Source Records: Primary Data Concerning Southeastern Massachusetts, Cape Cod, and the Islands of Nantucket and Martha's Vineyard by Gary Boyd Roberts (Baltimore, MD: Genealogical Pub. Co., ca. 1986)

New England Marriages Prior to 1700 by Clarence Almon Torrey (Andover, MA: Northeast Document Conservation Center, ca. 1983)

Your Guide to Cemetery Research by Sharon DeBartolo Carmack (Cincinnati: Betterway Books, 2002)

■ **Barnstable** 2 June 1685
P.O. Box 346, Barnstable, MA 02630
Phone: (508)375-6725
Web site: www.barnstablecounty.org/
Parent County: New Plymouth Colony
Comments/research tips: State Archives has Birth, Death, and Marriage records 1841–1910 (contact City and Town Clerks for records prior to 1841), Divorce records 1639–1887. Clerk of Superior Court has Divorce records 1887–1922. Towns organized before 1800: Barnstable 1639, Chatham 1712, Dennis 1793, Eastham 1646, Falmouth 1686, Harwich 1694, Mashpee 1763, Orleans 1797, Provincetown 1727, Truro 1709, Wellfleet 1763, Yarmouth 1639. Fire destroyed nearly all early deed books and probate files, but probate books survived. The official deed books begin in 1827. Many deeds were rerecorded back to 1783, though these are far from complete.

Record Type	Year Begun	Jurisdiction
Divorce	1922	County Probate
Land	1783	Registrar/Deeds
Probate	1674	Register/Probate
Court	1827	Court/Common Pleas
Wills	1637	Register/Probate
Nat.	1907	Superior Court
Birth	1911	MA Registry/Vital Records
Death	1911	MA Registry/Vital Records
Marriage	1911	MA Registry/Vital Records

■ Berkshire   28 May 1760
780 Holmes Rd., Pittsfield, MA 01201
Phone: (413)448-8424
Web site: www.rootsweb.com/~maberksh/
Parent County: Hampshire
Comments/research tips: State Archives has Birth, Death, and Marriage records 1841–1910 (for records prior to 1841 contact City/Town Clerks), Divorce records 1639–1887. Clerk of Superior Court has Divorce records 1887–1922. Court of Common Pleas has Revolutionary War records 1775–1783. Towns organized before 1800: Adams 1778, Alford 1773, Becket 1765, Chasire 1793, Clarksburg 1798, Dalton 1784, Egremont 1775, Great Barrington 1761, Hancock 1776, Lanesborough 1765, Lee 1777, Lenox 1767, Mount Washington 1779, New Ashford 1781, New Marlborough 1759, Otis 1773, Peru 1771, Pittsfield 1761, Richmond 1765, Savoy 1797, Sheffield 1733, Sandisfield 1762, Stockbridge 1739, Tyringham 1762, Washington 1777, West Stockbridge 1774, Williamstown 1765.

Record Type	Year Begun	Jurisdiction
Divorce	1847	Clerk/Superior Ct.
Land	1761	Registrar/Deeds
Probate	1761	Probate Court
Court	1760	Court/Common Pleas
Nat.	1815	Common Pleas
Birth	1911	MA Registry/Vital Records
Death	1911	MA Registry/Vital Records
Marriage	1911	MA Registry/Vital Records

■ Bristol   2 June 1685
11 Court St., Taunton, MA 02780-3223
Phone: (508)822-0502
Web site: http://home.att.net/~Local_History/MA-Bristol-Co.htm
Parent County: New Plymouth Colony
Comments/research tips: State Archives has Birth, Death, and Marriage records 1841–1910 (for records prior to 1841 contact City/Town Clerks, and Divorce records 1639–1887. Clerk of Superior Court has Divorce records 1887–1922. Towns organized before 1800: Attleboro 1694, Berkley 1735, Dartmouth 1652, Dighton 1712, Easton 1725, Freetown 1683, Mansfield 1775, New Bedford 1787, Norton 1710, Raynham 1731, Rehoboth 1645, Sandwich 1639, Somerset 1790, Swansea 1667, Taunton 1639, Westport 1787.

Record Type	Year Begun	Jurisdiction
Nat.	1805	Court/Common Pleas
Birth	1911	MA Registry/Vital Records

Marriage	1911	MA Registry/Vital Records
Death	1911	MA Registry/Vital Records
Divorce	1862	Supreme Judicial Court
Probate	1687	Probate Court
Court	1696	Court/Common Pleas
Land	1686	Registrar's Office

■ Dukes   22 June 1695
P.O. Box 237, Edgartown, MA 02539
Phone: (508)627-4703
Web site: www.vineyard.net/vineyard/history/dukes/
Parent County: Martha's Vineyard
Comments/research tips: State Archives has Birth, Death, and Marriage records 1841–1911 (for records prior to 1841 contact City/Town Clerks), Divorce records 1639–1887, and Probate records 1690–1938. Clerk of Superior Court has Divorce records 1887–1922. Towns organized before 1800: Chilmark 1694, Edgartown 1671, Tisbury 1671.

Record Type	Year Begun	Jurisdiction
Birth	1911	MA Registry/Vital Records
Marriage	1911	MA Registry/Vital Records
Death	1911	MA Registry/Vital Records
Divorce	1922	County Probate
Probate	1790	Probate Court
Land	1641	Registrar/Deeds

■ Essex   10 May 1643
36 Federal St., Salem, MA 01970
Phone: (978)741-0201
Web site: www.rootsweb.com/~maessex
Parent County: Original county
Comments/research tips: County Court has Birth, Marriage, and Death records 1636–1795. State Archives has Birth, Death, and Marriage records 1841–1910 (for records prior to 1841 contact City/Town Clerks), Divorce records 1639–1887. Clerk of Superior Court has Divorce records 1887–1922. Essex Institute has Military records 1755–1761. Towns organized before 1800: Amesbury 1668, Andover 1646, Beverly 1668, Boxford 1694, Danvers 1752, Hamilton 1793, Haverhill 1641, Ipswich 1634, Lynn 1635, Lynnfield 1782, Manchester 1645, Marblehead 1633, Methuen 1725, Middleton 1728, Newbury 1635, Newburyport 1764, Rowley 1639, Salem 1630, Salisbury 1639, Topsfield 1648, Wenham 1643.

Record Type	Year Begun	Jurisdiction
Birth	1911	MA Registry/Vital Records
Marriage	1911	MA Registry/Vital Records
Death	1911	MA Registry/Vital Records
Land	1639	Registrar/Deeds
Probate	1638	Probate Court
Court	1636	Quarterly Court
Nat.	1794	Superior Court
Divorce	1922	County Probate

■ Franklin   24 June 1811
425 Main St, Greenfield, MA 01301
Phone: (413)774-7011
Web site: www.kindredtrails.com/MA_Franklin.html
Parent County: Hampshire

Massachusetts

Comments/research tips: State Archives has Birth, Death, and Marriage records 1841–1910 (for records prior to 1841 contact City/Town Clerks), Divorce records 1639–1887. Clerk of Superior Court has Divorce records 1887–1922. Supreme Judicial Court has Court records 1816–1823. Towns organized before 1800: Ashfield 1765, Bernardston 1762, Buckland 1779, Charlemont 1765, Colrain 1761, Conway 1767, Deerfield 1677, Gil 1793, Greenfield 1753, Hawley 1792, Heath 1785, Leverett 1774, Leyden 1784, Montague 1754, New Salem 1753, Northfield 1714, Orange 1783, Rowe 1785, Shelburne 1768, Shuetesbury 1761, Sunderland 1714, Warwick 1763, Wendell 1781, Whately 1771, Williamsburg 1771.

Record Type	Year Begun	Jurisdiction
Marriage	1911	MA Registry/Vital Records
Divorce	1922	County Probate
Court	1823	Court/Common Pleas
Birth	1911	MA Registry/Vital Records
Death	1911	MA Registry/Vital Records
Land	1787	Registrar/Deeds
Nat.	1811	Superior Court
Probate	1810	Probate Court

■ Hampden 25 Feb. 1812

50 State St., Springfield, MA 01103
Phone: (413)748-6058
Web site: www.kindredtrails.com/MA_Hampden.html
Parent County: Hampshire
Comments/research tips: State Archives has Birth, Death, and Marriage records 1841–1910 (for records prior to 1841 contact City/Town Clerks), Divorce records 1639-1887. Clerk of Superior Court has Divorce records 1887–1922. Court of General Sessions of the Peace has Court records 1638–1812. Towns organized before 1800: Blandford 1741, Brimfield 1714, Chester 1765, Granville 1754, Holland 1783, Longmeadow 1783, Monson 1760, Montgomery 1780, Palmer 1752, Southwick 1770, Springfield 1641, Wales 1645, West Springfield 1636, Westfield 1669, Wilbraham 1763.

Record Type	Year Begun	Jurisdiction
Land	1628	Registrar/Deeds
Probate	1812	Probate Court
Court	1812	Court/Common Pleas
Divorce	1831	Clerk/Superior Ct.
Wills	1812	Probate Court
Birth	1911	MA Registry/Vital Records
Death	1911	MA Registry/Vital Records
Marriage	1911	MA Registry/Vital Records

■ Hampshire 7 May 1662

33 King St., Northampton, MA 01060
Phone: (413)586-8500
Web site: www.rootsweb.com/~mahampsh/
Parent County: Middlesex
Comments/research tips: State Archives has Birth, Death, and Marriage records 1841–1910 (for records prior to 1841 contact City/Town Clerks), Divorce records 1639–1887. Clerk of Superior Court has Divorce records 1887–1922. Towns organized before 1800: Amherst 1759, Belchertown 1761, Chesterfield 1762, Cummington 1779, Easthampton 1785, Goshen 1781, Granby 1768, Hadley 1661, Middlefield 1783, Northampton 1656, Pelham 1743, Plainfield 1785, Russell 1792, South Hadley 1753, Southampton 1753, Ware 1761, Westhampton 1778, Worthington 1768.

Record Type	Year Begun	Jurisdiction
Birth	1911	MA Registry/Vital Records
Marriage	1758	Court of Sessions, NH
Death	1911	MA Registry/Vital Records
Divorce	1758	Clerk/Superior Ct.
Land	1628	Registrar/Deeds
Probate	1660	Probate Court
Court	1638	Court/General Sessions
Nat.	1836	Superior Court

■ Middlesex 10 May 1643

208 Cambridge St., East Cambridge, MA 02141
Phone: (617)768-5808
Web site: www.rootsweb.com/~mamiddle/
Parent County: Original county
Comments/research tips: Clerk of Courts has Birth, and Death records, Wills 1600–1799, Court records 1648–1798. Superior Court has Birth, Death, and Marriage records 1651–1793. City Clerk has Proprietors records 1634–1697, 1751–1773, and 1784–1829. Towns organized before 1800: Acton 1735, Ashby 1767, Bedford 1729, Billerica 1655, Boxborough 1783, Burlington 1799, Cambridge 1638, Carlisle 1754, Chelmsford 1655, Concord 1635, Dracut 1702, Dunstable 1673, Everett 1630, Framingham 1700, Groton 1655, Holliston 1724, Hopkinton 1715, Lexington 1713, Lincoln 1754, Littleton 1716, Malden 1649, Marlborough 1660, Medford 1630, Natick 1651, Newton 1688, Pepperell 1753, Reading 1644, Sherborn 1674, Shirley 1786, Stoneham 1725, Stow 1683, Sudbury 1639, Tewksbury 1734, Townsend 1732, Tyngsboro 1789, Waltham 1738, Watertown 1630, Wayland 1780, Westford 1729, Weston 1713, Wilmington 1730, Woburn 1642.

Record Type	Year Begun	Jurisdiction
Divorce	1851	Supreme Judicial Court
Nat.	1800	Clerk of Courts
Probate	1648	Probate Court
Land	1649	Registrar/Deeds

■ Nantucket 22 June 1695

16 Broad St., Nantucket, MA 02554
Phone: (508)228-2669
Web site: www.mdwsweb.com/magenweb/nantucket.html
Parent County: Dukes
Comments/research tips: State Archives has Birth, Marriage, and Death records 1841–1910 (for records prior to 1841 contact City/Town Clerks), Divorce records 1639–1887. Clerk of Superior Court has Divorce records 1887–1922. Towns organized before 1800: Nantucket 1687.

Record Type	Year Begun	Jurisdiction
Birth	1911	MA Registry/Vital Records
Marriage	1911	MA Registry/Vital Records
Death	1911	MA Registry/Vital Records
Divorce	1922	Probate/Family Court

Massachusetts

Land	1657	Registrar/Deeds
Probate	1706	Probate Court
Court	1721	Court/Common Pleas
Nat.	1908	State Archives

■ Norfolk 26 Mar. 1793

649 High St., Dedham, MA 02026-1855
Phone: (781)461-6122
Web site: www.rootsweb.com/~manorfol/manorfol.htm
Parent County: Suffolk
Comments/research tips: Town Clerk has Birth, Death, and Marriage records 1635–1845. State Archives has Birth, Death, and Marriage records 1841–1910, Divorce records 1639–1887. Towns organized before 1800: Bellingham 1719, Braintree 1640, Brookline 1705, Canton 1797, Cohasset 1770, Dedham 1636, Dover 1784, Franklin 1778, Medfield 1651, Milton 1662, Needham 1711, Quincy 1792, Randolph 1793, Sharon 1765, Walpole 1724, Weymouth 1635, Wrentham 1673.

Record Type	Year Begun	Jurisdiction
Divorce	1887	Superior Court
Land	1793	Registrar/Deeds
Probate	1793	Probate Court
Court	1793	Court/Common Pleas
Nat.	1806	Superior Court
Birth	1911	MA Registry/Vital Records
Death	1911	MA Registry/Vital Records
Marriage	1911	MA Registry/Vital Records

■ Plymouth 2 June 1685

7 Russell St., Plymouth, MA 02361
Phone: (508)830-9200
Web site: www.seeplymouth.com/
Parent County: New Plymouth Colony
Comments/research tips: Registrar of Deeds has Plymouth Colony Birth, Death, and Marriage records 1636–1686 and 1699–1756. State Archives has Birth, Death and Marriage records 1841–1910. Court of General Sessions has Court records 1686–1817. Court of Common Pleas has Court records 1702–1859. State Archives has Divorce records 1639–1887. Clerk of Superior Court has Divorce records 1887–1922. Inferior Court of Common Pleas and Court of General Sessions of the Peace has Marriage records 1692–1746. Fourth District Court, District Court Clerk, Wareham has Naturalization records and applications 1885–1906. Superior Court, Massachusetts State Archives, Boston has Naturalization declarations and petitions 1907–1945. Superior Court records at Massachusetts State Archives has Plymouth County declarations of intention index 1906–1984. Towns organized before 1800: Abington 1712, Bridgewater 1656, Brockton 1700, Carver 1790, Duxbury 1637, Halifax 1734, Hanover 1727, Hingham 1635, Hull 1644, Kingston 1726, Marshfield 1640, Middleborough 1669, Pembroke 1712, Plymouth 1620, Plympton 1707, Rochester 1686, Scituate 1636, Wareham 1739.

Record Type	Year Begun	Jurisdiction
Birth	1911	MA Registry/Vital Records

Marriage	1911	MA Registry/Vital Records
Death	1911	MA Registry/Vital Records
Divorce	1922	County Probate
Land	1664	Registrar/Deeds

■ Suffolk 10 May 1643

24 New Chardon St., Boston, MA 02114
Phone: (617)788-8300
Web site: www.geocities.com/masuffolk/
Parent County: Original county
Comments/research tips: State Archives has Birth, Death, Marriage records 1841–1910 (for records prior to 1841 contact City and Town Clerks), Divorce records 1639–1887. County Court, Court of Common Pleas, Court of General Sessions of Peace, Superior Court of Judicature, and Supreme Judicial Court have Court records spanning 1629–1827. Clerk of Superior Court has Divorce records 1887–1922. Towns organized before 1800: Boston 1630, Chelsea 1739, Dorchester 1630, Roxbury 1630.

Record Type	Year Begun	Jurisdiction
Birth	1911	MA Registry/Vital Records
Marriage	1911	MA Registry/Vital Records
Death	1911	MA Registry/Vital Records
Divorce	1922	County Probate
Land	1639	Registrar/Deeds
Probate	1636	Probate Court
Nat.	1782	Court/Common Pleas

■ Worcester 5 Apr. 1731

2 Main St., Worcester, MA 01608
Phone: (508)770-0825
Web site: www.rootsweb.com/~maworces/
Parent County: Suffolk, Middlesex
Comments/research tips: State Archives has Birth, Death, Marriage records 1841–1910, Divorce records 1639–1887, and Naturalization records 1885–1949. Superior Court has Divorce records 1887–1936. Towns organized before 1800: Ashburnham 1765, Athol 1762, Auburn 1778, Barre 1753, Berlin 1784, Bolton 1738, Boylston 1786, Brookfield 1673, Charlton 1755, Douglas 1746, Fitchburg 1764, Gardner 1785, Grafton 1735, Greenwich 1754, Hardwick 1739, Harvard 1732, Hubbardston 1767, Lancaster 1653, Leicester 1722, Leominister 1740, Lunenburg 1726, Mendon 1667, Milford 1780, New Braintree 1751, Northborough 1766, Northbridge 1772, Oakham 1762, Oxford 1713, Paxton 1765, Petersham 1754, Phillipston 1786, Princeton 1759, Royalston 1763, Rutland 1713, Shrewsbury 1727, Southborough 1727, Spencer 1753, Sterling 1781, Sturbridge 1738, Sutton 1716, Templeton 1762, Upton 1735, Uxbridge 1727, Warren 1741, Westbourough 1717, Westminister 1759, Winchendon 1764, Worcester 1722.

Record Type	Year Begun	Jurisdiction
Birth	1911	MA Registry/Vital Records
Marriage	1911	MA Registry/Vital Records
Death	1911	MA Registry/Vital Records
Land	1722	Registrar/Deeds
Probate	1731	Probate Court

Massachusetts

Michigan

By James W. Warren

HISTORICAL OVERVIEW

French explorers were the first Europeans into the area that is present-day Michigan, an area that the Ojibway, Saginaw, Menominee, Wyandot, Ottawa, and other Indian tribes had long occupied. In 1688, Jacques Marquette organized the first permanent settlement at Sault Ste. Marie. Fort Pontchartrain, established in 1701, would later be renamed Detroit. The French gave up possession of the area in 1763 to the British, who discouraged settlement just as the French had.

In 1787 the United States acquired the area and it became part of the Northwest Territory, but the British retained control of Detroit and Mackinac. It was 1796 before the U.S. had control over all of Michigan, when General Anthony Wayne took Detroit. Michigan became part of Indiana Territory in 1800.

In 1805, Michigan Territory was formed. During the War of 1812, Detroit was lost temporarily to British forces in Canada. The early settlers of Michigan came mainly from Canada, New York, Ohio, and the New England states. In 1836, a disputed strip of land five to seven miles wide on Michigan's southern border, known as the "Toledo Strip," was granted to Ohio by Congress.

Michigan became the twenty-sixth state in 1837, and the population continued to expand. By 1850, large numbers of German and Dutch immigrants were arriving. In subsequent years immigrants continued to pour into Michigan. Scandinavian, Irish, Cornish, Polish, and Italian immigrants choose the state, many working in the mining and lumbering camps. Over the decades, the growth of Detroit and its auto industry would pace the industrial growth of the country.

RECORD HIGHLIGHTS

Except for a few surviving fragments of the 1810 census, the first available federal population census for Michigan

MICHIGAN AT A GLANCE

Motto: If You Seek a Pleasant Peninsula, Look About You

Population: 9.9 million

Prevalent Religions: Roman Catholic, Baptist, Methodist, and Lutheran

Major Industries: Automobile and other motor vehicles, motor vehicle parts, fabricated metal and chemical products, food processing, agriculture (primarily dairy products, fruits, and vegetables), tourism

Ethnic Makeup (in percent): Caucasian 80.2%, African American 14.2%, Hispanic 3.3%, Asian 1.8%, Native American 0.6%, Other 1.3%

Famous Michiganders: Ellen Burstyn, Francis Ford Coppola, Thomas E. Dewey, Gerald Ford, Henry Ford, Julie Harris, Magic Johnson, Ring Lardner, Madonna, Terry McMillan, Ted Nugent, Iggy Pop, Gilda Radner, Della Reese, Martha Reeves, Diana Ross, Steven Seagal, Bob Seger, Tom Selleck, David Spade, Potter Stewart, Lily Tomlin, Danny Thomas, Jackie Wilson, Stevie Wonder

Above: A "superior" lakeshore view

is the 1820. The 1890 census was destroyed in a fire, but the 1890 Veterans' Schedule for Michigan survived. There were more than twenty territorial censuses taken of various parts of Michigan Territory, but in many cases, the census for only a few counties is extant. Territorial and state census enumerations were taken in 1827, 1834, 1837, 1845, 1854, 1864, 1874, 1884, 1894, and 1904. Indexes to the 1827, 1837, and 1845 have been published. The most complete collections are the 1884 and 1894 censuses, which list every member of the household and are a good substitute for the lost 1890 federal census. These schedules are available at the Archives of Michigan.

Registration of births and deaths by the counties began in 1867, and was generally complied with by 1915. Registration of marriages was required by law starting in 1805, and most counties kept marriage records from the date the county was formed. Copies of birth, death, and marriage records may be ordered from the county clerk of the appropriate county, or from the Michigan Department of Community Health (MDCH), which has copies of the county records from 1867. The MDCH Web site <www.michigan .gov/mdch/0,1607,7-132-4645---,00.html> allows online ordering of records and provides additional information on requirements and restrictions. The Family History Library has microfilm of birth, death, and marriage records for most counties into the twentieth century. The Library of Michigan has statewide indexes to births from 1867 to 1915 and deaths from 1867 to 1914.

Early divorce records were handled by the Michigan supreme court. Later divorces will usually be found in the circuit court's civil case files. The Michigan Department of Community Health has copies of divorce records from about 1897, and those can also be ordered online at the MDCH Web site.

Michigan's county-level courts are district courts, but have jurisdiction over only minor matters. Circuit courts, which serve one to four counties, handle most matters. A list of circuit records that have been turned over to the Archives of Michigan can be found at <www.michigan .gov/documents/mhc_sa_circular37_49972_7.pdf>.

Naturalization Records are held by the county clerk in each county. Indexes to the records for thirteen Michigan counties are online (PDF format). The naturalization indexes have been created by the generous efforts of volunteers at the State Archives of Michigan <www.michigan .gov/hal/0,1607,7-160-17449_18635_20684---,00.html>.

The Family History Library also has 188 rolls of National Archives microfilm of federal district court naturalizations for Michigan.

Probate records are handled by the probate court in each county, and date either from the formation of the county or 1817. Wayne County's records start in 1797. Probate files from most Michigan counties through

roughly 1900 are microfilmed and available through the Family History Library <www.michigan.gov/documents/ mhc_sa_circular06_49689_7.pdf>.

The Michigan Cemetery Sources Web site is a compilation of published cemetery transcriptions located at the Library of Michigan and links to Michigan cemetery Web sites. This database also identifies the location of more than 3,700 cemeteries in Michigan. It was not intended to include a list of personal names, but now individual burials are being included in the database. This is an ongoing project, so check back regularly to see what's being added <http://michigancemeteries.libraryofmichigan.org/>.

The Library of Michigan's record collection includes many church and cemetery abstracts, transcriptions, and indexes, as well as original records or microfilm copies. The FHL has microfilmed records from some Michigan churches. Most churches and cemeteries still have their original records.

STATE RESOURCES

■ ARCHIVES, LIBRARIES, AND SOCIETIES

Albion Historical Society
Gardner House Museum, 509 S. Superior St., Albion, MI 49224
Tel: (517) 629-5100
Web site: <www.forks.org/hist ory/albion.htm>

Archdiocese of Detroit
305 Michigan Ave., Detroit, MI 48226
Tel: (313) 237-5800
Web site: <www.aodonline.org>

Bay City Branch Library
708 Center Ave., Bay City, MI 48708
Tel: (989) 893-9566
Web site: <www.baycountylibrary .org/bbc.htm>

Berrien County Genealogical Society
P.O. Box 8808, Benton Harbor, MI 49023-8808
Web site: <w3.qtm.net/bcgen soc/>

Bigelow Genealogical Society
P.O. Box 4115, Flint, MI 49504

Branch County Genealogical Society
P.O. Box 443, Coldwater, MI 49036
Web site: <www.geocities.com/ TheTropics/1050/Gensociety .html>

Branch County Historical Society
% The Wing House Museum, 27 S. Jefferson, Coldwater, MI 49036
Web site: <www.wingmuseum .org>

Burton Historical Collection
Detroit Public Library, 5201 Woodward Avenue, Detroit, MI 48202
Tel: (313) 833-1480
Web site: <www.detroit.lib.mi .us/index.htm>

Calhoun County Genealogical Society
P.O. Box 879, Marshall, MI 49068
Web site: <www.rootsweb.com/ ~micalhou/ccgs.htm>

Cass River Genealogy Society
359 S. Franklin, Frankenmuth, MI 48734
Web site: <www.frankenmuthcity .com/library/genealogy.htm>

Cedar Springs Historical Society/Museum
60 Cedar St., P.O. Box 296, Cedar Springs, MI 49319
Tel: (616) 696-3335
Web site: <www.cedar-springs.mi .us/history.htm>

Central Michigan University Library
300 E. Preston St., Mount Pleasant, MI 48859
E-mail: library.reference@cich .edu
Web site: <www.lib.cmich.edu>

Charlevoix County Genealogical Society
201 E. Main St., Boyne City, MI 49712
Web site: <www.rootsweb.com/~micharle/cx-03.htm>

Cheboygan County Genealogical Society
P.O. Box 51, Cheboygan, MI 49721
Web site: <www.rootsweb.com/~miccgs/CCGSmainx.html>

Chippewa County Genealogical Society
P.O. Box 1686, Sault Ste. Marie, MI 49783-1686
Web site: <www.rootsweb.com/~michcgs/>

Chippewa County Historical Society
P.O. Box 1686, Sault Ste. Marie, MI 49783
Web site: <www.rootsweb.com/~michcgs>

Dearborn Genealogical Society
P.O. Box 1112, Dearborn, MI 48121-1112
Web site: <www.rootsweb.com/~midgs/>

Delta County Genealogical Society
Box 442, Escanaba, MI 49829-0442
Web site: <www.grandmastree.com/society/>

Detroit Health Department
1151 Taylor St., Detroit, MI 48202
Tel: (313) 876-4133
Web site: <www.ci.detroit.mi.us/health/default.htm>

Detroit Public Library
5201 Woodward Ave., Detroit, MI 48202
Tel: (313) 833-1000
Web site: <www.detroit.lib.mi.us>

Grace A. Dow Memorial Library
1710 W. St. Andrews, Midland, MI 48657
Tel: (989) 837-3430
Web site: <www.midland-mi.org/gracedowlibrary>

Downriver Genealogical Society
P.O. Box 476, Lincoln Park, MI 49146
Tel: (313) 381-0507
Web site: <www.rootsweb.com/~midrgs/drgs.html>

Eaton County Genealogical Society
P.O. Box 337, Charlotte, MI 48813-0337
Web site: <www.rootsweb.com/~miecgs>

Farmington Genealogical Society
Farmington Community Library, 23500 Liberty St., Farmington, MI 48335
Web site: <www.farmlib.org/gensoc.html>

Finnish American Historical Society of Michigan
19995 Melrose, Southfield, MI 49075

Flint Genealogical Society
P.O. Box 1217, Flint, MI 48501-1217
Web site: <www.rootsweb.com/~mifgs/>

Flint Public Library
1026 E. Kearsley, Flint, MI 48502
Web site: <www.flint.lib.mi.us>

Ford Genealogy Club
P.O. Box 1652, Dearborn, MI 48121-1652
Web site: <www.wwnet.com/~krugman1/fgc/>

Four Flags Area Genealogical Society
P.O. Box 414, Niles, MI 49120
Web site: <www.fourflagsgenealogicalsociety.com>

French Canadian Heritage Society of Michigan
9513 Whipple Shores Dr., Clarkston, MI 48348
Web site: <http://fchsm.habitant.org/>

Gaylord Fact Finders Genealogical Society
P.O. Box 1524, Gaylord, MI 49734-5524
Web site: <www.ofsego.org/factfinders>

Genealogical Society of Flemish Americans
18740 Thirteen Mile Rd., Roseville, MI 48066
Web site: <www.rootsweb.com/~gsfa/>

Genealogical Society of Monroe County
P.O. Box 1428, Monroe, MI 48161

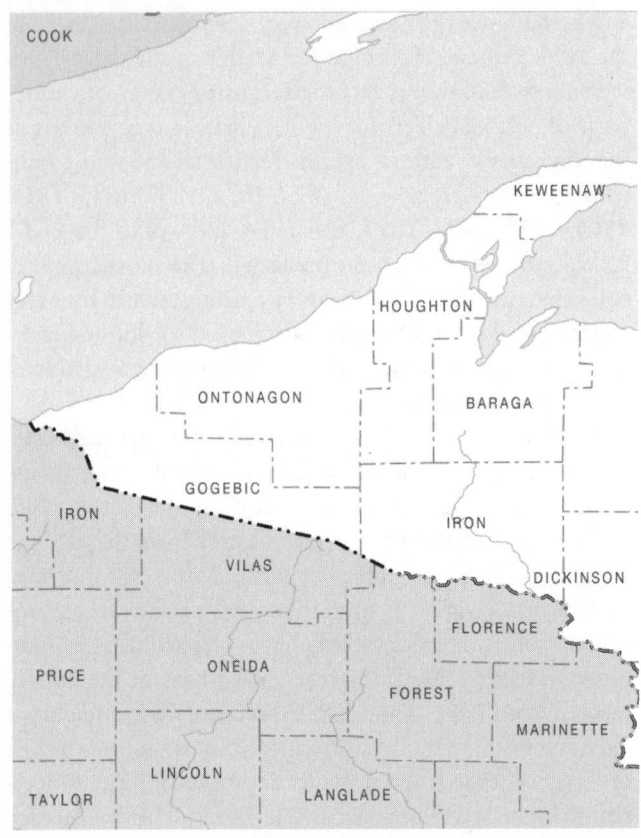

Genealogical Society of Washtenaw County
Web site: <www.hvcn.org/info/gswc/>

Grand Haven Genealogical Society
% Loutit Library, 407 Columbus St., Grand Haven, MI 49417
Tel: (616) 842-5560

Grand Rapids Public Library
111 Library St., NE, Grand Rapids, MI 49503
Web site: <www.grpl.org>

Grand Traverse Area Genealogical Society
P.O. Box 2015, Traverse City, MI 49685-2015
Web site: <www.rootsweb.com/~migtags/gtag.htm>

Gratiot County Historical and Genealogical Society
P.O. Box 73, Ithaca, MI 48847
Web site: <www.rootsweb.com/~migratio/gchgs/>

Harrison Area Genealogy Society
P.O. Box 796, Harrison, MI 48625
Web site: <www.rootsweb.com/~miclare/harrison.htm>

Herrick Public Library
300 River Ave., Holland, MI 49423
Web site: <www.herrickdl.org>

Holland Genealogical Society
% Herrick Public Library, 300 S. River Ave., Holland, MI 49423
Web site: <www.macatawa.org/~brianter/familyties.htm>

Huron County Genealogical Society
2843 Electric Ave., Port Huron, MI 48060
Web site: <www.rootsweb.com/~mihuron/societies/societies.html>

Huron Shores Genealogical Society
% Robert J. Parks Public Library, 6010 N. Skeel Ave., Oscoda, MI 48750-1577
Tel: (989) 362-5425
Web site: <www.rootsweb.com/~miiosco2/huronpage.html>

Ingham County Genealogical Society
P.O. Box 85, Mason, MI 48854
Web site: <www.ingcogenesoc.org>

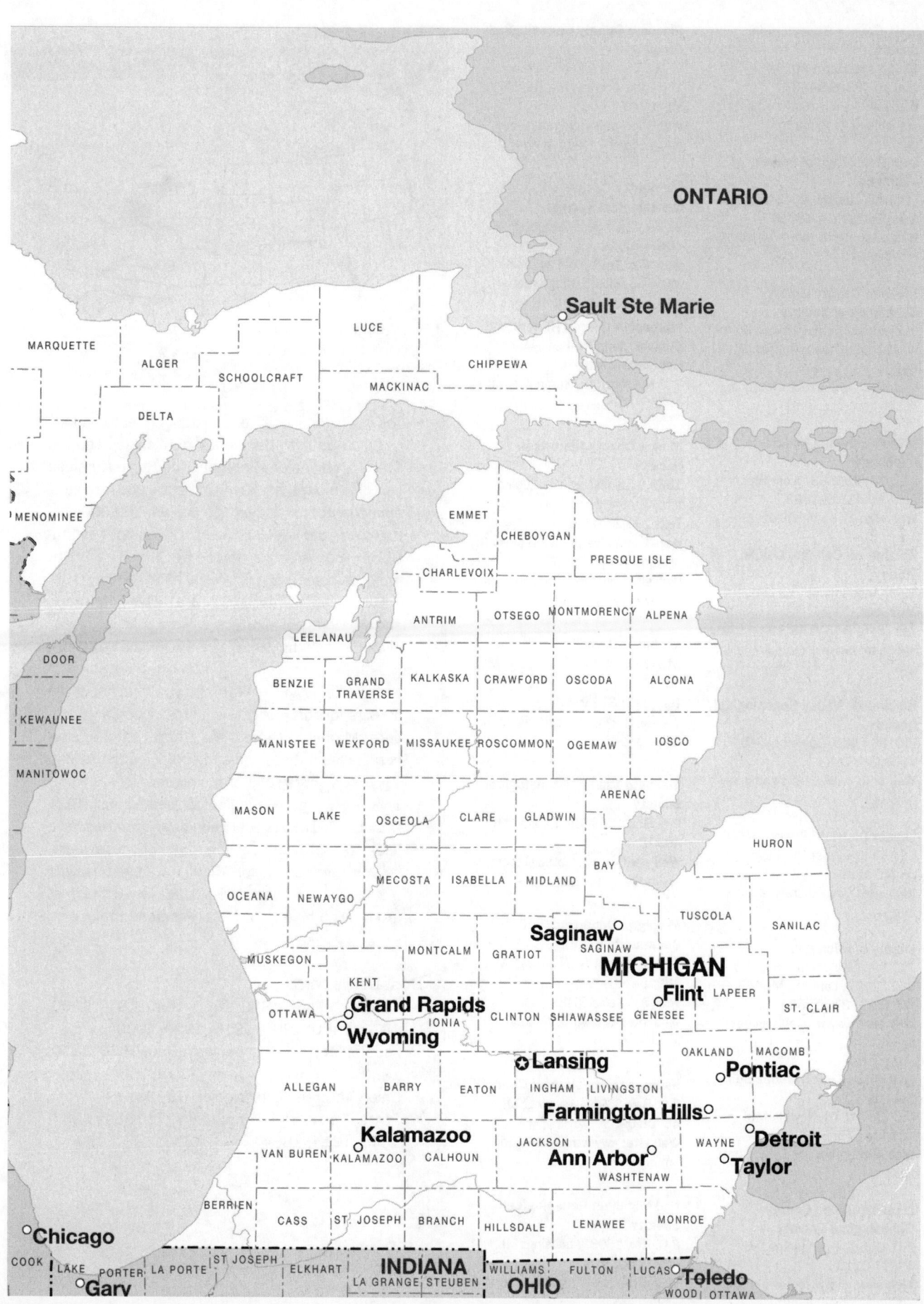

ONTARIO

MARQUETTE

ALGER

SCHOOLCRAFT

DELTA

LUCE

CHIPPEWA

MACKINAC

Sault Ste Marie

MENOMINEE

EMMET

CHEBOYGAN

PRESQUE ISLE

CHARLEVOIX

ANTRIM

OTSEGO

MONTMORENCY

ALPENA

LEELANAU

DOOR

BENZIE

GRAND
TRAVERSE

KALKASKA

CRAWFORD

OSCODA

ALCONA

KEWAUNEE

MANISTEE

WEXFORD

MISSAUKEE

ROSCOMMON

OGEMAW

IOSCO

MANITOWOC

MASON

LAKE

OSCEOLA

CLARE

GLADWIN

ARENAC

HURON

OCEANA

NEWAYGO

MECOSTA

ISABELLA

MIDLAND

BAY

TUSCOLA

SANILAC

MUSKEGON

MONTCALM

Saginaw

SAGINAW

MICHIGAN

KENT

GRATIOT

Flint

LAPEER

ST. CLAIR

OTTAWA

Grand Rapids

IONIA

CLINTON

SHIAWASSEE

GENESEE

Wyoming

OAKLAND

MACOMB

Lansing

Pontiac

ALLEGAN

BARRY

EATON

INGHAM

LIVINGSTON

Farmington Hills

Kalamazoo

JACKSON

WAYNE

Detroit

VAN BUREN

KALAMAZOO

CALHOUN

Ann Arbor

WASHTENAW

Taylor

BERRIEN

CASS

ST. JOSEPH

BRANCH

HILLSDALE

LENAWEE

MONROE

Chicago

COOK

LAKE

PORTER

LA PORTE

ST JOSEPH

ELKHART

INDIANA

LA GRANGE

STEUBEN

WILLIAMS

FULTON

LUCAS

Toledo

Gary

OHIO

WOOD

OTTAWA

Michigan

Michigan

Ionia County Genealogical Society
13051 Ainsworth Rd., Lake Odessa, MI 48849-9406
Web site: <www.rootsweb.com/~miionia/icgshom.htm>

Irish Genealogical Society of Michigan
% Gaelic League, 2068 Michigan Ave., Detroit, MI 48216
Web site: <www.rootsweb.com/~miigsm/>

Jackson County Library/ Genealogical Society
% Jackson District Library, 244 W. Michigan Ave., Jackson, MI 49201
Web site: <www.rootsweb.com/~mijackso/jcgs.htm>

Jewish Genealogical Society of Michigan
P.O. Box 251693, West Bloomfield, MI 48325-1693
Web site:

Kalamazoo College, Upjohn Library
1200 Academy St., Kalamazoo, MI 49006
Tel: (616) 337-7153
Web site: <www.kzoo.edu/is/library>

Kalamazoo Valley Genealogical Society
P.O. Box 405, Comstock, MI 49041
Web site: <www.rootsweb.com/~mikvgs/>

Lapeer District Library
201 Village West Dr., Lapeer, MI 48446-1699
Web site: <www.library.lapeer.org>

Library of Michigan
717 West Kalamazoo St., P.O. Box 30007, Lansing, MI 48909
Tel: (517) 373-1580
Web site: <www.michigan.gov/hal>

Livingston County Genealogical Society
P.O. Box 1073, Howell, MI 48844-1073
Web site: <www.rootsweb.com/milcgs>

Luce-Mackinac County Genealogical Society
P.O. Box 113, Engadine, MI 49827-0113
Web site: <www.rootsweb.com/~miluce/luce-mac.htm>

Macomb County Genealogical Group
% Mt. Clemens Public Library, 150 Cass Avenue, Mt. Clemens, MI 48043
Web site: <www.ole.net/~maggie/macomb/mcgroup.htm/>

Marquette County Genealogical Society
217 N. Front St., Marquette, MI 49855-3710
Web site: <members.aol.com/MQTCGS/MCGS/mcgs.html>

Marquette County Historical Society, John M. Longyear Research Library
213 N. Front St., Marquette, MI 49855

Mason County Historical Society
1687 S. Lakeshore Dr., Ludington, MI 49431
Tel: (231)843-4808
E-mail: info@historicwhitepinevillage.org
Web site: <www.historicwhitepinevillage.org/mchs.html>

Michigan Catholic Conference
510 S. Capitol Ave., Lansing, MI 48933
Tel: (517) 372-9310
Web site: <www.micatholicconference.org>

Mecosta County Genealogical Society
P.O. Box 1068, Big Rapids, MI 49307
Web site: <www.rootsweb.com/~mimecost/mecgen.html>

Michigan Department of Community Health
320 S. Walnut St., Lansing, MI 48913
Tel: (517) 373-3740
Web site: <www.michigan.gov/mdch>

Michigan Genealogical Council
P.O. Box 80953, Lansing, MI 48908-0953
Web site: <www.rootsweb.com/~mimgc>

Mid-Michigan Genealogical Society
P.O. Box 16033, Lansing, MI 48901-6033
Web site: <www.rootsweb.com/~mimmgs>

RESEARCH TIPS

for more info

- The Michigan Library and Historical Center in Lansing houses both the Library of Michigan and the State Archives of Michigan. The State Archives contains more than 80 million state and local government records and private papers, 300,000 photographs, and 500,000 maps. Check both institutions' Web sites for more details. The State Archives home page is: <www.michigan.gov/hal/0,1607,7-160-17445_19273_19313—,00.html>, and the Library of Michigan's home page is: <www.michigan.gov/hal/0,1607,7-160-17449_18635—,00.html>.
- At the Michigan GenWeb site you'll find updated listings for three of the volunteers' ongoing projects: Michigan tombstone transcriptions, a funeral home listing, and a Michigan cemetery listing <www.rootsweb.com/~migenweb/>.
- Try the Michigan Genealogical Death Index (GENDIS) 1867–1882. Local genealogy societies have been transcribing death records for these years, so you can search for Michigan ancestors who died during the years 1867–1882 <www.mdch.state.mi.us/pha/osr/gendisx/search2.htm>.
- www.negenealogy.com

Census Records
- Federal Census: 1820, 1830, 1840, 1850, 1860, 1870, 1880, 1900, 1910, 1920, 1930
- Federal Mortality Schedules: 1850, 1860, 1870, 1880
- Union Veterans and Widows: 1890
- State/Territorial Census: 1827, 1834, 1837, 1845, 1854, 1864, 1874, 1884, 1894, 1904

Midland County Historical Society
℅ Midland Center for the Arts, 1901 W. St. Andrews Dr., Midland, MI 48640
Web site: <www.mcfta.org>

Mt. Clemens Public Library
150 Cass Ave., Mt. Clemens, MI 48043
Web site: <www.macomb.lib.mi.us/mountclemens>

Muskegon County Genealogical Society
℅ Hackley Library, 316 W. Webster Ave., Muskegon, MI 49440
Web site: <www.rootsweb.com/~mimcgs/>

National Archives and Records Administration, Great Lakes Region
7358 S. Pulaski Rd., Chicago, IL 60629-5898
Tel: (773) 948-9019
Web site: <www.archives.gov/facilities/il/chicago.html>

Newaygo County Society of History and Genealogy
P.O. Box 68, White Cloud, MI 49349
Tel: (231) 689-6631
Web site: <www.rootsweb.com/~minewayg/society.html>

North Oakland Genealogical Society
℅ Orion Township Library, 825 Joslyn Rd., Lake Orion, MI 48362
Web site: <www.pontiac.lib.mi.us/genealog.htm>

Northville Genealogical Society
P.O. Box 932, Northville, MI 48167-0932
Web site: <www.rootsweb.com/~mings/>

Northwestern Michigan College
Mark Osterlin Library, 1704 E. Front St., Traverse City, MI 49684

Northwestern Michigan Genealogical Society
Mark and Helen Osterlin Library, 1704 E. Front St., Traverse City, MI 49684
Tel: (231) 995-1540
Web site: <www.nmc.edu>

Oakland County Genealogical Society
P.O. Box 1094, Birmingham, MI 48012-1094
Web site: <www.metronet.lib.mi.us/ROCH/OCGS/>

Oceana County Historical & Genealogical Society
114 Dryden St., Hart, MI 49420
Tel: (231) 873-2600
Web site: <www.oceanacountyhistoricalgenealogysociety.org>

Ogemaw District Library
107 W. Main St., Rose City, MI 48654
Tel: (989) 685-3300

Ogemaw Genealogical and Historical Society
P.O. Box 734, West Branch, MI 48661
Tel: (989) 345-1643
Web site: <www.rootsweb.com/~mioghs/sgt/f10000.htm>

Onaway Library
P.O. Box 742, Onaway, MI 49767
Tel: (989) 733-6621

Orion Township Public Library
825 Joslyn, Lake Orion, MI 48362
Web site: <www.orion.lib.mi.us>

Polish Genealogical Society of Michigan
℅ Burton Historical Collection, Detroit Public Library, 5201 Woodward Ave., Detroit, MI 48202-4007
Web site: <www.pgsm.org>

Pontiac Area Historical and Genealogical Society
P.O. Box 430901, Pontiac, MI 48343-0901
Web site: <www.pontiac.lib.mi.us/genealog.htm>

Reed City Area Genealogical Society (Osceola County)
780 Park St., P.O. Box 27, Reed City, MI 49677
Web site: <www.infomi.com/city/reedcity/museum.html>

Sage Branch Library
4101 E. Wilder Rd., Bay City, MI 48706
Web site: <http://baycountylibrary.org>

Saginaw Genealogical Society
℅ Saginaw Public Library, 505 Janes Ave., Saginaw, MI 48607
Web site: <www.saginaw.lib.mi.us>

Saginaw Valley Chapter, American Historical Society of Germans From Russia
6910 Trowbridge Circle, Saginaw, MI 48603
Tel: (989) 799-4266

Web site: <www.ahsgr.org/saginaw.html>

Shiawassee County Genealogical Society
P.O. Box 841, Owosso, MI 48867
Web site: <www.shianet.org/community/orgs/scgs/>

South Side Branch Library
311 Lafayette Ave., Bay City, MI 48708
Web site: <www.baycountylibrary.org/bss.htm>

St. Clair County Library
210 McMorran Blvd., Port Huron, MI 48060
Tel: (877) 987-READ

St. Joseph Genealogical Society
P.O. Box 486, White Pigeon, MI 49099
Web site: <www.famgen.net/sjcgs>

State Archives of Michigan, Michigan Library and Historical Center
702 W. Kalamazoo St., Lansing, MI 48909-8240
Web site: <www.michigan.gov/hal/0,1607,7-160-17445_19273--_,00.html>

Sterling Heights Genealogical and Historical Society
P.O. Box 1154, Sterling Heights, MI 48311-1154
Web site: <www.rootsweb.com/~mishghs/>

Sturgis Public Library
130 N. Nottawa, Sturgis, MI 49091
Web site: <www.ci.sturgis.mi.us/library.htm>

Then & Now Historical & Genealogical Society of East Allegan County
532 N. Main, Wayland, MI 49348
Tel: (269) 792-9970

Three Oaks Township Library
3 N. Elm St., Three Oaks, MI 49128
Tel: (269) 756-5621

University of Michigan
Ann Arbor, MI 48109
Tel: (734) 764-1817
Web site: <www.umich.edu>

Van Buren District Library
200 N. Phelps St., Decatur, MI 49045
Tel: (269) 423-4771

Van Buren Regional Genealogical Society
P.O. Box 143, Decatur, MI 49045
Web site: <http://cwic1.jackson.lib.mi.us/van/vbrgs.htm>

Waterford Township Public Library
5168 Civic Center Dr., Waterford, MI 48329
Tel: (248) 674-4831
Web site: <http://waterford.lib.mi.us>

Western Michigan Genealogical Society
℅ Grand Rapids Public Library, 111 Library St. NE, Grand Rapids, MI 49503-3268
Web site: <www.wmgs.org/>

Western Wayne County Genealogical Society
P.O. Box 530063, Livonia, MI 48153

White Pine Library Cooperative
3210 Davenport Ave., Saginaw, MI 48602
Web site: <www.wplc.org>

Willard Library
7 W. Van Buren St., Battle Creek, MI 49017
Tel: (269) 968-8166

Ypsilanti Historical Society Museum
220 N. Huron St., Ypsilanti, MI 48197
Web site: <www.hvcn.org/info/gswc/society/socypsi/antihtm>

BIBLIOGRAPHY

■ GENERAL RESOURCES

American Biographical History of Eminent and Self-Made Men: Michigan Volume
(Cincinnati, OH: Western Biographical Pub. Co., 1878)

Bench and Bar of Michigan: A Volume of History and Biography
by George Irving Reed (Century Publishing and Engraving, ca. 1897)

Church Record Index, 2 vols.
(Grand Rapids: The Society, 1993)

County Evolution in Michigan, 1790–1897
by Richard Warren Welch (Lansing, MI: Department of Education, 1972)

Directory of Historical Collections and Societies in Michigan
by Wystan Stevens (Ann Arbor: Historical Society of Michigan, 1973)

Early Michigan Settlements, 3 vols.
by Warren Washburn Florer (Ann Arbor: W.W. Florer, ca. 1941–1953)

Genealogical Materials in the Eddy Historical Collection of the Public Libraries of Saginaw
by Nelda M. Hinz (Saginaw, MI: Public Libraries, 1975)

The Genealogist's Companion and Sourcebook, 2d ed.
by Emily Anne Croom (Cincinnati: Betterway Books, 2003)

A Genealogist's Guide to Discovering Your African-American Ancestors
by Franklin Carter Smith and Emily Anne Croom (Cincinnati: Betterway Books, 2003)

Genealogist's Guide to the Capitol Region of Michigan
compiled by Victoria Wilson (Grawn, MI: Kinseeker Publications, 1987)

Genealogist's Guide to the Middle of Michigan
compiled by Victoria Wilson (Grawn, MI: Kinseeker Publications, 1987)

Genealogist's Guide to Northeastern Michigan
compiled by Victoria Wilson (Grawn, MI: Kinseeker Publications, 1987)

Genealogist's Guide to Southwestern Michigan
compiled by Victoria Wilson (Grawn, MI: Kinseeker Publications, 1987)

Genealogist's Guide to the Thumb Area of Michigan
compiled by Victoria Wilson (Grawn, MI: Kinseeker Publications, 1987)

Genealogist's Guide to Upper Penninsula Michigan
compiled by Victoria Wilson (Grawn, MI: Kinseeker Publications, 1987)

Genealogy in Michigan: What, When, Where, 2d ed.
by Alloa Caviness Anderson (Ann Arbor, MI: A. Anderson, P. Bender, 1978)

General History of the State of Michigan: With Biographical Sketches, Portrait Engraving and Numerous Illustrations; A Complete History of the Peninsular State from Its Earliest Settlement to the Present Time
by Charles Richard Tuttle (Detroit: R.D.S. Tyler, 1873)

A Guide to Ancestral Trails in Michigan, 4th ed.
by Lucy Mary Kellogg (Detroit: Detroit Society for Genealogical Research, 1975)

Guide to Genealogical Research in the National Archives of the United States
edited by Anne Bruner Eales and Robert M. Kvasnicka (Washington, DC: National Archives and Records Administration, 2000)

Guide to the Manuscripts in the Burton Historical Collection
by Bernice Cox Sprenger (Detroit: Detroit Public Library, 1985)

Guide to the Michigan Genealogical and Historical Collections at the Library of Michigan and the State Archives of Michigan
from the Michigan Genealogical Council (Lansing, MI: Michigan Genealogical Council, 1996)

History of Michigan, 4 vols.
by Charles Moore (Chicago: Lewis Pub. Co., 1915)

A History of Northern Michigan and Its People, 3 vols.
by Perry F. Powers (Chicago: Lewis Pub. Co, 1912)

A History of the Northern Peninsula of Michigan and Its People, Its Mining, Lumber and Agricultural Industries, 3 vols.
by Alvah Littlefield Sawyer (Chicago: Lewis Publishing Co., 1911)

Inventory of the Church Archives of Michigan, The Roman Catholic Church, Archdiocese of Detroit
from the Historical Records Survey (Detroit: Michigan Historical Records Survey, 1941)

Men of Progress: Embracing Biographical Sketches of Representative Michigan Men, With an Outline History of the State
(Detroit: Evening New Assoc., 1900)

Michigan Biographies, Including Members of Congress, Elective State Officers, Justices of the Supreme Court, Members of the Michigan Legislature, Board of Regents of the University of Michigan, State Board of Agriculture and State Board of Education
(Baltimore: Clearfield Co., 1924, 1999)

Michigan, A Centennial History of the State and Its People, 5 vols.
by George Newman Fuller (Lewis Publishing Co., 1939)

Michigan County Histories: A Bibliography
from the Michigan Bureau of Library Services (Lansing: Michigan Department of Education, Bureau of Library Services, 1978)

Michigan Genealogy Sources and Resources
by Carol McGinnis (Baltimore: Genealogical Publishing Co., 1987)

Michigan's German Heritage, John Russell's History of the German Influence in the Making of Michigan
by Don Heinrich Tolzman (Bowie, MD: Heritage Books, 1994)

Michigan Historical Collections, 40 vols.
from the Michigan State Historical Society (Lansing, MI: W.S. George & Co., 1877–1929)

Michigan Research Outline
(Salt Lake City: Family History Library, 1988)

The Michigan Surname Index
edited by Donald J. DeZeeuw (Lansing, MI: Michigan Genealogical Council, 1984)

Midwest Pioneers, 1600s–1800s
(Brøderbund, 1999. CD-ROM)

National Archives Microfilm Catalogs online:
<www.archives.gov/publications/genealogy_microfilm_catalogs.html>

Portrait and Biographical Records of Northern Michigan: Containing Portraits and Biographical Sketches of Prominent and Representative Citizens, Together with Biographies and Portraits of All the Presidents of the United States
by Rev. E.H. Pilcher (Chicago: Record Pub., 1895)

The Red Book of Michigan; A Civil, Military, and Biographical History
by Charles Lanman (Detroit: E.B. Smith, 1871)

Settling the Great Lakes Frontier: Immigration to Michigan, 1837–1924
by C. Warren Vander Hill (Lansing, MI: Michigan Historical Commission, 1970)

Sourcebook of Michigan Census, County Histories, and Vital Records
edited by Carole Callard (Lansing, MI: Library; of Michigan, 1986)

■ CENSUS RECORDS

The American Census Handbook
by Thomas Jay Kemp (Wilmington, DE: Scholarly Resources, 2001)

The Census Book: A Genealogist's Guide to Federal Census Facts, Schedules and Indexes
by William Dollarhide (Bountiful, UT: Heritage Quest, 1999)

Finding Answers in U.S. Census Records
by Loretto Dennis Szucs and Matthew Wright (Salt Lake City: Ancestry Publishing, 2001)

Index to 1840 Federal Population Census of Michigan
edited by Estelle A. McGlynn (Detroit: Detroit Society for Genealogical Research, 1977)

Map Guide to the U.S. Federal Censuses, 1790–1920
by William Thorndale and William Dollarhide (Baltimore: Genealogical Publishing Co., 1987)

Michigan Censuses 1710–1830 Under the French, British, and Americans
by Donna Valley Russell (Detroit: Detroit Society for Genealogical Research, 1982)

State Census Records
by Ann S. Lainhart (Baltimore: Genealogical Publishing Co., Inc., 1992)

Your Guide to the Federal Census
by Kathleen W. Hinckley (Cincinnati: Betterway Books, 2002)

■ IMMIGRATION RECORDS

American Naturalization Records, 1790–1990: What They Are and How to Use Them
by John J. Newman (North Salt Lake, UT: HeritageQuest, 1998)

American Passenger Arrival Records
by Michael Tepper (Baltimore: Genealogical Publishing Co., 1993)

They Became Americans: Finding Naturalization Records and Ethnic Origins
by Loretto Dennis Szucs (Salt Lake City: Ancestry, Inc., 1998)

They Came in Ships: A Guide to Finding Your Immigrant Ancestor's Arrival Records, 2d ed.
by John P. Colletta (Salt Lake City: Ancestry, Inc., 1993)

■ LAND RECORDS

American State Papers
from the United States Congress (La Crosse, WI: Brookhaven Press, 1959, 1975, 1977)

Grassroots of America
by Phillip W. McMullin (Salt Lake City: Gendex Corp., 1972)

Land Records: AL, AR, FL, LA, MI, MN, OH, WI
(Brøderbund, 1996. CD-ROM)

Locating Your Roots: Discover Your Ancestors Using Land Records
by Patricia Law Hatcher (Cincinnati: Betterway Books, 2003)

Private Land Claims, Illinois, Indiana, Michigan and Wisconsin
by Fern Ainsworth (Natchitoches, LA: Fern Ainsworth, 1985)

■ MAPS

Along the Tracks: A Directory of Named Places on Michigan Railroads
by Graydon M. Meints (Mount Pleasant, MI: Central Michigan University, Clarke Historical Library, 1987)

Bowen's Michigan State Atlas: Containing a Separate Map of Each County, Showing Section, Township and Range Lines, Railroad and Interurban Lines
by F.F. Bowen (Indianapolis: B.F. Bowen, 1916)

Gazetteer of the State of Michigan
by John T. Blois (Detroit: S.L. Rood, 1939)

Historical Atlas and Chronology of County Boundaries, 1788–1980, 5 vols.
edited by John H. Long (Boston: G.K. Hall, 1984)

Indian Names in Michigan
by Virgil J. Vogel (Ann Arbor: The University of Michigan Press, 1986)

Michigan; Atlas of Historical County Boundaries
by Peggy Tuck Sinko (New York: Charles Scribner's Sons, 1997)

Michigan Atlases and Plat Books: A Checklist, 1872–1973
by William Miles (Lansing: State Library Service, 1975)

Michigan County Map Guide
by C.J. Puetz (Lyndon Station, WI: Thomas Publications, 1990)

Michigan Gazetteer
(Wilmington, DE: American Historical Publications, 1991)

Michigan Place Names: The History of the Founding and the Naming of More Than Five Thousand Past and Present Michigan Communities
by Walter Romig (Grosse Point, MI: Romig, ca. 1970)

Michigan Postal History: The Post Offices, 1805–1986
by David M. Ellis (Lake Grove, OR: The Depot, 1993)

Upper Michigan Postal History and Postmarks
by William J. Taylor (Lake Grove, OR: The Depot, 1988)

■ MILITARY RECORDS

Annual Report of the Adjutant General 1865–1866, 3 vols.
from the Michigan Adjutant General's Office (Lansing, MI: John A. Kerr & Co., 1866)

Michigan Military Records
by Sue Silliman (Baltimore, MD: Genealogical Publishing Co., 1969)

Michigan in the War
by John Robertson (Lansing, MI: W.S. George, 1882)

Michigan in the World War: Military and Naval Honors of Michigan Men and Women
by Charles H. Landrum (Michigan Historical Commission, 1924)

Record of Service of Michigan Volunteers in the Civil War
from the Michigan Adjutant General's Office (Lansing: Michigan Secretary of State, 1915)

Soldiers of the War of 1812 Who Died in Michigan
by Alice Turner Miller (Ithaca, MI: Alice Turner Miller, 1962)

Uncle, We Are Ready! Registering America's Men, 1917–1918: A Guide to Researching World War I Draft Registration Cards
by John J. Newman (North Salt Lake, UT: HeritageQuest, 2001)

United States Civil War Soldiers Living in Michigan in 1894
(St. Johns, MI: Genealogists of Clinton County Historical Society, 1988)

U.S. Military Records: A Guide to Federal & State Sources, Colonial America to the Present
by James C. Neagles (Salt Lake City: Ancestry, Inc., 1994)

World War II: A Family Historian's Guide
by Debra Johnson Knox (Spartanburg, SC: MIE Publishing, 2003)

World War II Honor List of Dead and Missing, State of Michigan
from the United States War Department, Bureau of Public Relations (Washington, DC: War Dept. Bureau of Public Relations, 1946)

■ VITAL RECORDS

Cemetery Inscriptions, Michigan, 3 vols.
by Edward H. Mohnecke (Grand Rapids, MI: Edward H. Mohnecke, 1939–44)

Michigan Cemetery Compendium
(Spring Arbor, MI: Har-Al, 1979)

Michigan Cemetery Source Book
from the State Library of Michigan (Lansing, MI: State Library of Michigan, 1994)

Michigan Death Index, 1867–1874, 3 vols.
from the Michigan Department of Community Health (Lansing, MI: Michigan Dept. of Community Health, ca. 1997)

Michigan Quakers, Abstracts of Fifteen Meetings of the Society of Friends 1831–1860
by Ann and Conrad Burton (Glyndwr Resources, 1989)

Vital Statistics Holdings by Government Agencies in Michigan; Birth Records
from the Historical Records Survey (Detroit, MI: The Project, 1941)

Vital Statistics Holdings by Government Agencies in Michigan; Death Records
from the Historical Records Survey (Detroit, MI: The Project, 1942)

Vital Statistics Holdings by Government Agencies in Michigan; Marriage Records
from the Historical Records Survey (Detroit, MI: The Project, 1941)

Your Guide to Cemetery Research
by Sharon DeBartolo Carmack (Cincinnati: Betterway Books, 2002)

Michigan

■ **Aishcum** 1 Apr. 1840
Parent County: Mackinac
Comments/research tips: (See Lake) Name changed to Lake 8 March 1843.

■ **Alcona** 1 Apr. 1840
P.O. Box 308., Harrisville, MI 48740
Phone: (983)724-6807
Web site: www.rootsweb.com/~mialcona/index.htm
Parent County: Unorganized Territory
Comments/research tips: Formerly Neewago County. Name changed to Alcona 8 March 1843. Attached to Mackinac, Cheboygan, Iosco, and Alpena Counties prior to organization 12 March 1869.

Record Type	Year Begun	Jurisdiction
Birth	1869	County Clerk
Marriage	1869	County Clerk
Death	1869	County Clerk
Divorce	1869	County Clerk
Probate	1869	Probate Court
Court	1872	Clerk/Circuit Ct.
Military	1900	County Clerk
Nat.	1869	County Clerk

■ **Alger** 17 Mar. 1885
101 Court St., Munising, MI 49862
Phone: (906)387-2076
Web site: www.rootsweb.com/~mialger
Parent County: Schoolcraft

Record Type	Year Begun	Jurisdiction
Birth	1884	County Clerk
Marriage	1887	County Clerk
Death	1884	County Clerk
Divorce	1885	County Clerk
Land	1884	Reg./Deeds
Probate	1889	Probate Court
Court	1885	Clerk/Circuit Ct.

■ **Allegan** 2 Mar. 1831
113 Chestnut St., Allegan, MI 49010
Phone: (269)673-0450
Web site: www.rootsweb.com/~miallega
Parent County: Barry, Unorganized Land

Record Type	Year Begun	Jurisdiction
Birth	1867	County Clerk
Marriage	1836	County Clerk
Death	1867	County Clerk
Divorce	1900	County Clerk
Land	1835	Reg./Deeds
Probate	1839	Probate Court
Court	1837	Clerk/Circuit Ct.

■ **Alpena** 1 Apr. 1840
720 W. Chisholm St., Alpena, MI 49707
Phone: (517)356-0115
Web site: www.rootsweb.com/~mialpena
Parent County: Mackinac
Comments/research tips: Formerly Anamickee County. Name changed to Alpena 8 March 1843.

Record Type	Year Begun	Jurisdiction
Birth	1869	County Clerk
Marriage	1871	County Clerk
Death	1871	County Clerk
Divorce	1871	County Clerk
Land	1858	Registrar/Deeds
Probate	1858	Probate Judge
Court	1871	Clerk/Circuit Ct.

■ **Anamickee** 1 Apr. 1840
Parent County: Mackinac, Unorganized Territory
Comments/research tips: (See Alpena) Name changed to Alpena 8 March 1843.

■ **Antrim** 1 Apr. 1840
203 E. Cayugoa St., Bellaire, MI 49615
Phone: (231)533-6353
Web site: www.ole.net/~maggie/antrim
Parent County: Mackinac
Comments/research tips: Formerly Meegisee County. Name changed to Antrim 8 March 1843.

Record Type	Year Begun	Jurisdiction
Birth	1866	County Clerk
Marriage	1866	County Clerk
Death	1867	County Clerk
Divorce	1866	County Clerk
Land	1867	Registrar/Deeds
Probate	1863	Probate Court
Court	1867	Clerk/Circuit Ct.
Military	1868	County Clerk

■ **Arenac** 21 Apr. 1883
120 N. Grove St., Standish, MI 48658
Phone: (989)846-4626
Web site: www.rootsweb.com/~miarennac/index.htm
Parent County: Bay, Saginaw
Comments/research tips: Originally created from Unorganized Land. 2 March 1831. It was abolished in 1857 and re-created in 1883. Some early records before 1883 may be located in Saginaw County.

Record Type	Year Begun	Jurisdiction
Birth	1883	County Clerk
Marriage	1883	County Clerk
Death	1883	County Clerk
Divorce	1883	County Clerk
Court	1883	Clerk/Circuit Ct.
Burial	1952	County Clerk

■ **Baraga** 19 Feb. 1875
16 N. Third St., L'Anse, MI 49946
Phone: (906)524-6183
Web site: www.rootsweb.com/~mibaraga/
Parent County: Houghton

Record Type	Year Begun	Jurisdiction
Birth	1875	County Clerk
Marriage	1875	County Clerk
Death	1875	County Clerk
Divorce	1875	County Clerk
Land	1875	County Clerk

Court	1875	County Clerk
Burial	1950	County Clerk

■ Barry 29 Oct. 1829
220 W. State St., Hastings, MI 49058
Phone: (616)945-1285
Web site: www.rootsweb.com/~mibarry
Parent County: Unorganized Territory

Record Type	Year Begun	Jurisdiction
Birth	1867	County Clerk
Marriage	1839	County Clerk
Death	1867	County Clerk
Land	1834	Registrar/Deeds
Probate	1862	Probate Court
Court	1850	Clerk/Circuit Ct.

■ Bay 17 Feb. 1857
515 Center Ave., Bay City, MI 48708
Phone: (989)895-4280
Web site: www.rootsweb.com/~mibay/
Parent County: Saginaw, Midland, Arenac

Record Type	Year Begun	Jurisdiction
Birth	1868	County Clerk
Marriage	1867	County Clerk
Death	1867	County Clerk
Divorce	1869	County Clerk
Land	1835	Registrar/Deeds
Probate	1857	Probate Court
Court	1883	Clerk/Circuit Ct.

■ Benzie 27 Feb. 1863
P.O. Box 377, Beulah, MI 49617
Phone: (231)882-9671
Web site: www.rootsweb.com/~mibenzie
Parent County: Leelanau

Record Type	Year Begun	Jurisdiction
Birth	1868	County Clerk
Marriage	1869	County Clerk
Death	1868	County Clerk
Divorce	1869	County Clerk
Probate	1870	Probate Court
Court	1869	Clerk/Circuit Ct.
Nat.	1871	County Clerk

■ Berrien 29 Oct. 1829
701 Main St., St. Joseph, MI 49085
Phone: (616)983-7111
Web site: www.rootsweb.com/~miberrie
Parent County: Unorganized Territory
Comments/research tips: County Clerk has Naturalization records 1835–1985.

Record Type	Year Begun	Jurisdiction
Birth	1867	County Clerk
Marriage	1831	County Clerk
Death	1867	County Clerk
Land	1831	Registrar/Deeds
Probate	1834	Probate Court
Court	1833	Clerk/Circuit Ct.

■ Bleeker 15 Mar. 1861
Parent County: Unorganized Territory
Comments/research tips: (See Menominee) Name changed to Menominee 19 March 1863.

■ Branch 29 Oct. 1829
31 Division St., Coldwater, MI 49036
Phone: (517)279-4306
Web site: www.geocities.com/TheTropics/1050
Parent County: Unorganized Territory

Record Type	Year Begun	Jurisdiction
Birth	1867	County Clerk
Marriage	1833	County Clerk
Death	1867	County Clerk
Divorce	1867	County Clerk
Land	1833	Registrar/Deeds
Probate	1833	Probate Court
Court	1850	Clerk/Circuit Ct.
Nat.	1847	County Clerk

■ Calhoun 29 Oct. 1829
315 W. Green St., Marshall, MI 49068
Phone: (616)781-0730
Web site: www.rootsweb.com/~micalhou
Parent County: Unorganized Territory

Record Type	Year Begun	Jurisdiction
Birth	1867	County Clerk
Marriage	1867	County Clerk
Death	1867	County Clerk
Probate	1835	Probate Court
Court	1867	Clerk/Circuit Ct.

■ Cass 29 Oct. 1829
P.O. Box 355, Cassopolis, MI 49031
Phone: (616)445-8621
Web site: www.rootsweb.com/~micass
Parent County: Lenawee
Comments/research tips: County Clerk has Naturalization records from 1924–1941.

Record Type	Year Begun	Jurisdiction
Birth	1867	County Clerk
Marriage	1837	County Clerk
Death	1867	County Clerk
Divorce	1831	County Clerk
Land	1829	Registrar/Deeds
Probate	1829	Probate Court
Court	1831	Clerk/Circuit Ct.

■ Charlevoix 1869
203 W. Antrim St., Charlevoix, MI 49720
Phone: (231)547-7200
Web site: www.rootsweb.com/~micharle/cx-03.htm
Parent County: Emmet, Antrim, Otsego

Record Type	Year Begun	Jurisdiction
Birth	1868	County Clerk
Marriage	1868	County Clerk
Death	1868	County Clerk
Divorce	1868	County Clerk
Land	1869	Registrar/Deeds

Michigan

Probate .... 1881 .... Probate Court
Court .... 1869 .... Clerk/Circuit Ct.

■ Charlevoix, old 1841

Parent County: Mackinac
Comments/research tips: Formed Keskkauko County 1840. Name changed to Charlevoix 8 March 1843. Merged with Emmet 1853. Re-created 2 April 1869.

■ Cheboygan 1 Apr. 1840

P.O. Box 70, Cheboygan, MI 49721
Phone: (231)627-8808
Web site: www.rootsweb.com/~micheboy
Parent County: Mackinac

Record Type	Year Begun	Jurisdiction
Birth	1867	County Clerk
Marriage	1867	County Clerk
Death	1867	County Clerk
Land	1854	Registrar/Deeds
Probate	1854	Probate Court
Court	1884	Clerk/Circuit Ct.

■ Cheonoquet 1 Apr. 1840

Web site: Future Web site at www.rootsweb.com/~migenweb/county_list.htm
Parent County: Mackinac
Comments/research tips: (See Montmorency) Name changed to Montmorency 8 March 1843.

■ Chippewa 26 Dec. 1826

319 Court St., Sault Ste. Marie, MI 49783
Phone: (906)635-6300
Web site: www.rootsweb.com/~michippe
Parent County: Michilimackinac

Record Type	Year Begun	Jurisdiction
Birth	1869	County Clerk
Marriage	1827	County Clerk
Death	1869	County Clerk
Land	1826	Registrar/Deeds
Probate	1828	Probate Court
Court	1860	Clerk/Circuit Ct.

■ Clare 1 Mar. 1840

P.O. Box 438, Harrison, MI 48625
Phone: (989)539-7131
Web site: www.rootsweb.com/~miclare/index.htm
Parent County: Mackinac
Comments/research tips: Formerly Kaykakee County. Name changed to Clare 8 March 1843.

Record Type	Year Begun	Jurisdiction
Birth	1871	County Clerk
Marriage	1871	County Clerk
Death	1871	County Clerk
Divorce	1871	County Clerk
Land	1865	County Clerk
Court	1871	County Clerk

■ Clinton 2 Mar. 1831

P.O. Box 69, St. Johns, MI 48879
Phone: (989)224-5140

Web site: www.rootsweb.com/~miclinto
Parent County: Unorganized Territory

Record Type	Year Begun	Jurisdiction
Birth	1867	County Clerk
Marriage	1839	County Clerk
Death	1867	County Clerk
Court	1860	Clerk/Circuit Ct.

■ Crawford 10 Sep 1822

200 W. Michigan Ave., Grayling, MI 49738
Phone: (989)344-3200
Web site: www.rootsweb.com/~micrawfo/
Parent County: Mackinac
Comments/research tips: Formerly Shawano County. Name changed to Crawford 8 March 1843. Some early records may be located in Cheboygan, Iosco, Antrim, and Kalkaska Counties.

Record Type	Year Begun	Jurisdiction
Birth	1873	County Clerk
Marriage	1873	County Clerk
Death	1873	County Clerk
Divorce	1878	County Clerk
Land	1863	Registrar/Deeds
Probate	1881	Probate Court
Court	1881	Clerk/Circuit Ct.

■ Delta 9 Mar. 1843

310 Ludington St., Escanaba, MI 49829
Phone: (906)789-5105
Web site: www.grandmastree.com/migenweb/
Parent County: Mackinac, Unorganized Territories

Record Type	Year Begun	Jurisdiction
Birth	1867	County Clerk
Marriage	1867	County Clerk
Death	1867	County Clerk
Divorce	1867	County Clerk
Land	1843	Registrar/Deeds
Probate	1843	Probate Court
Court	1869	Clerk/Circuit Ct.

■ Des Moines 1 Oct. 1834

Parent County: Unorganized Territory
Comments/research tips: Became part of Wisconsin Territory 3 July 1836.

■ Dickinson 21 Mar. 1891

705 S. Stephenson Ave., Iron Mountain, MI 49801
Phone: (906)774-0988
Web site: www.rootsweb.com/~midickin
Parent County: Marquette, Menominee, Iron

Record Type	Year Begun	Jurisdiction
Birth	1891	County Clerk
Marriage	1891	County Clerk
Death	1891	County Clerk
Divorce	1891	County Clerk
Land	1891	Registrar/Deeds
Probate	1891	Probate Court
Court	1891	Clerk/Circuit Ct.
Nat.	1892	County Clerk

■ Eaton 29 Oct. 1829

1045 Independence Blvd., Charlotte, MI 48813

Phone: (517)543-7500

Web site: www.rootsweb.com/~mieaton/eatonmn.htm

Parent County: Unorganized Territory

Comments/research tips: County Clerk has some Naturalization records.

Record Type	Year Begun	Jurisdiction
Birth	1867	County Clerk
Marriage	1838	County Clerk
Death	1867	County Clerk
Divorce	1847	County Clerk
Land	1835	Registrar/Deeds
Probate	1835	Probate Court
Court	1848	Clerk/Circuit Ct.

■ Emmet 1 Apr. 1840

200 Division St., Petoskey, MI 49770

Phone: (231)348-1744

Web site: www.rootsweb.com/~miemmet

Parent County: Mackinac

Comments/research tips: County Clerk has some Military records. Formerly Tonedagana County. Name changed to Emmet 8 March 1843.

Record Type	Year Begun	Jurisdiction
Birth	1867	County Clerk
Marriage	1867	County Clerk
Death	1867	County Clerk
Divorce	ca. 1800	County Clerk
Court	1867	Clerk/Circuit Ct.

■ Genesee 8 Mar. 1836

900 S. Saginaw St., Flint, MI 48502

Phone: (810)257-3282

Web site: www.rootsweb.com/~migenese

Parent County: Lapeer, Saginaw, Shiawassee

Record Type	Year Begun	Jurisdiction
Birth	1867	County Clerk
Marriage	1867	County Clerk
Death	1867	County Clerk
Divorce	1871	County Clerk
Probate	1836	Probate Court
Court	1835	Clerk/Circuit Ct.

■ Gladwin 2 Mar. 1831

401 W. Cedar Ave., Gladwin, MI 48624

Phone: (517)426-7351

Web site: www.rootsweb.com/~migladwi/

Parent County: Unorganized Territory

Comments/research tips: County Clerk has birth records 1875–1972.

Record Type	Year Begun	Jurisdiction
Marriage	1875	County Clerk
Death	1875	County Clerk
Divorce	1875	County Clerk
Land	1886	Registrar/Deeds
Probate	1889	Probate Court
Court	1880	Clerk/Circuit Ct.
Military	1917	County Clerk

■ Gogebic 7 Feb. 1881

200 N. Moore St., Bessemer, MI 49911

Phone: (906)663-4518

Web site: www.rootsweb.com/~migogebi/

Parent County: Ontonagon

Record Type	Year Begun	Jurisdiction
Birth	1887	County Clerk
Marriage	1887	County Clerk
Death	1887	County Clerk
Divorce	1887	County Clerk
Land	1887	Registrar/Deeds
Probate	1887	Probate Court
Court	1887	Clerk/Circuit Ct.

■ Grand Traverse 1 Apr. 1840

400 Boardman Ave., Traverse City, MI 49684

Phone: (231)922-4760

Web site: www.grandtraverseregion.com/grandtraverse

Parent County: Omeena

Record Type	Year Begun	Jurisdiction
Birth	1856	County Clerk
Marriage	1853	County Clerk
Death	1867	County Clerk
Divorce	1857	County Clerk
Land	1853	Registrar/Deeds
Court	1882	Clerk/Circuit Ct.

■ Gratiot 2 Mar. 1831

214 E. Center St., Ithaca, MI 48847

Phone: (517)875-5215

Web site: www.mfhn.com/gratiot

Parent County: Unorganized Territory

Comments/research tips: County Clerk has Birth records 1867–1880 (after 1880 staff check in computer files). Staff also does research for Divorce records.

Record Type	Year Begun	Jurisdiction
Marriage	1867	County Clerk
Death	1867	County Clerk
Land	1847	Registrar/Deeds
Probate	1867	Probate Court
Court	1867	Clerk/Circuit Ct.

■ Hillsdale 29 Oct. 1829

29 N. Howell St., Hillsdale, MI 49242

Phone: (517)437-3391

Web site: www.rootsweb.com/~mihillsd

Parent County: Unorganized Territory

Record Type	Year Begun	Jurisdiction
Birth	1867	County Clerk
Marriage	1835	County Clerk
Death	1867	County Clerk
Divorce	1844	County Clerk
Land	1835	Registrar/Deeds
Probate	1835	Probate Court
Court	1846	Clerk/Circuit Ct.

■ Houghton 9 Mar. 1845

401 E. Houghton Ave., Houghton, MI 49931-2016

Phone: (906)482-1150

Web site: www.rootsweb.com/~mihought
Parent County: Marquette, Ontonagon

Record Type	Year Begun	Jurisdiction
Birth	1867	County Clerk
Marriage	1855	County Clerk
Death	1867	County Clerk
Divorce	1853	County Clerk
Land	1847	Registrar/Deeds
Probate	1872	Probate Court
Court	1848	Clerk/Circuit Ct.

■ **Huron** 1 Apr. 1840
250 E. Huron Ave., Bad Axe, MI 48413
Phone: (989)269-9942
Web site: www.rootsweb.com/~mihuron/
Parent County: Sanilac

Record Type	Year Begun	Jurisdiction
Birth	1867	County Clerk
Marriage	1867	County Clerk
Death	1867	County Clerk
Divorce	1867	County Clerk
Land	1837	Registrar/Deeds
Probate	1861	Probate Court
Court	1867	Clerk/Circuit Ct.

■ **Ingham** 29 Oct. 1829
315 S. Jefferson St., Mason, MI 48854
Phone: (517)676-7201
Web site: www.rootsweb.com/~miingham
Parent County: Washtenaw, Shiawassee, Unorganized Territory

Record Type	Year Begun	Jurisdiction
Birth	1867	County Clerk
Marriage	1837	County Clerk
Death	1867	County Clerk
Probate	1835	Probate Court
Court	1839	Clerk/Circuit Ct.

■ **Ionia** 2 Mar. 1831
100 E. Main St., Ionia, MI 48846
Phone: (616)527-5322
Web site: www.rootsweb.com/~miionia
Parent County: Michilimackinac

Record Type	Year Begun	Jurisdiction
Birth	1867	County Clerk
Marriage	1837	County Clerk
Death	1867	County Clerk
Divorce	1858	County Clerk
Court	1839	Clerk/Circuit Ct.

■ **Iosco** 1 Feb. 1840
P.O. Box 838, Tawas City, MI 48764
Phone: (989)362-3497
Web site: www.rootsweb.com/~miiosco
Parent County: Unorganized Territory
Comments/research tips: County Clerk has Burial records 1961–1978 and Naturalization records 1859–1906. Formerly Kanotin County. Name changed to Iosco 8 March 1843. Some early records may be located in Cheboygan and

Saginaw Counties. Note: Researchers are not allowed to search Birth records.

Record Type	Year Begun	Jurisdiction
Marriage	1862	County Clerk
Death	1868	County Clerk
Court	1859	Clerk/Circuit Ct.

■ **Iron** 3 Apr. 1885
2 S. Sixth St., Crystal Falls, MI 49920
Phone: (906)875-3221
Web site: www.rootsweb.com/~miiron
Parent County: Marquette, Menominee

Record Type	Year Begun	Jurisdiction
Birth	1895	County Clerk
Marriage	1895	County Clerk
Death	1895	County Clerk
Divorce	1895	County Clerk
Land	1855	Registrar/Deeds
Court	1895	Clerk/Circuit Ct.

■ **Isabella** 2 Mar. 1831
200 N. Main St., Mount Pleasant, MI 48858
Phone: (517)772-0911
Web site: www.rootsweb.com/~miisabel/isabella.html
Parent County: Michilimackinac, Unorganized Territory

Record Type	Year Begun	Jurisdiction
Birth	1867	County Clerk
Marriage	1859	County Clerk
Death	1867	County Clerk
Divorce	1900	County Clerk
Court	1880	Clerk/Circuit Ct.

■ **Isle Royal** 4 Mar. 1875
Parent County: Keweenaw
Comments/research tips: Attached to Houghton 13 March 1885. Absorbed by Keweenaw 9 April 1897.

■ **Jackson** 29 Oct. 1829
312 S. Jackson St., Jackson, MI 49201
Phone: (517)788-4265
Web site: www.rootsweb.com/~mijackso/jackson.htm
Parent County: Washtenaw, Unorganized Territory

Record Type	Year Begun	Jurisdiction
Birth	1867	County Clerk
Marriage	1830	County Clerk
Death	1867	County Clerk
Divorce	1800	County Clerk
Land	1830	Registrar/Deeds
Probate	1834	Probate Court
Court	1830	Clerk/Circuit Ct.

■ **Kalamazoo** 29 Oct. 1829
201 W. Kalamazoo Ave., Kalamazoo, MI 49007
Phone: (269)383-8840
Web site: www.rootsweb.com/~mikalama
Parent County: Unorganized Territory
Comments/research tips: Contact Circuit Court Clerk for Divorce records.

Record Type	Year Begun	Jurisdiction
Birth	1867	County Clerk

Marriage .... 1831 .... County Clerk
Death .... 1867 .... County Clerk
Land .... 1824 ...... Registrar/Deeds
Probate .... 1830 ...... Probate Court
Court .... 1847 .... Clerk/Circuit Ct.

■ Kalkaska 1 Apr. 1840
605 N. Birch St., Kalkaska, MI 49646
Phone: (231)258-3300
Web site: resources.rootsweb.com/USA/MI/kalkaska
Parent County: Mackinac
Comments/research tips: Formerly Wabassee County. Name changed to Kalkaska 8 March 1843.

Record Type	Year Begun	Jurisdiction
Birth	1871	County Clerk
Marriage	1871	County Clerk
Death	1871	County Clerk
Land	1853	Registrar/Deeds
Probate	1874	Probate Court
Court	1871	Clerk/Circuit Ct.

■ Kanotin 1 Feb. 1840
Parent County: Unorganized Territory
Comments/research tips: See Iosco. Name changed to Iosco 8 March 1843.

■ Kautawaubet 1 Apr. 1840
Parent County: Mackinac
Comments/research tips: (See Wexford) Name changed to Wexford 8 March 1843.

■ Kayakee 1 Apr. 1840
Parent County: Mackinac, Saginaw, Unorganized Territory
Comments/research tips: (See Clare) Name changed to Clare 8 March 1843.

■ Kent 2 Mar. 1831
300 Monroe Ave. NW, Grand Rapids, MI 49503
Phone: (616)336-3550
Web site: www.rootsweb.com/~mikent
Parent County: Michilimackinac, Unorganized Territory
Comments/research tips: Organized 4 April 1836. The State Archives of Michigan has Naturalization/Citizenship records 1860–1920 for Kent County.

Record Type	Year Begun	Jurisdiction
Birth	1867	County Clerk
Marriage	1845	County Clerk
Death	1867	County Clerk
Land	1860	Registrar/Deeds
Probate	1898	Probate Court
Court	1854	Clerk/Circuit Ct.

■ Keweenaw 11 Mar. 1861
County Courthouse, HC1, Box 607, Eagle River, MI 49950
Phone: (906)337-2229
Web site: Future Web site at www.rootsweb.com/~migenweb/county_list.htm
Parent County: Houghton

Record Type	Year Begun	Jurisdiction
Birth	1869	County Clerk

Marriage .... 1869 .... County Clerk
Death .... 1869 .... County Clerk
Land .... 1861 ...... Registrar/Deeds
Probate .... 1866 ...... Probate Court
Court .... 1861 .... Clerk/Circuit Ct.

■ Lake 1 Apr. 1840
800 Tenth St., Baldwin, MI 49304
Phone: (231)745-4641
Web site: www.rootsweb.com/~milake/
Parent County: Mackinac
Comments/research tips: Formerly Aishcum County. Name changed to Lake 8 March 1843.

Record Type	Year Begun	Jurisdiction
Birth	1870	County Clerk
Marriage	1870	County Clerk
Death	1870	County Clerk
Divorce	1874	County Clerk
Land	1872	Registrar/Deeds
Probate	1872	Probate Court
Court	1871	Clerk/Circuit Ct.

■ Lapeer 10 Sep. 1822
255 Clay St., Lapeer, MI 48446
Phone: (810)667-0356
Web site: www.rootsweb.com/~milapeer
Parent County: Oakland, St. Clair, Unorganized Territory

Record Type	Year Begun	Jurisdiction
Birth	1867	County Clerk
Marriage	1831	County Clerk
Death	1867	County Clerk
Divorce	1837	County Clerk
Court	1835	Clerk/Circuit Ct.

■ Leelanau 1 Apr. 1840
P.O. Box 467, Leland, MI 49654
Phone: (231)256-9824
Web site: www.rootsweb.com/~mileelan
Parent County: Mackinac

Record Type	Year Begun	Jurisdiction
Birth	1867	County Clerk
Marriage	1867	County Clerk
Death	1867	County Clerk
Divorce	1867	County Clerk
Probate	1882	Probate Court
Court	1879	Clerk/Circuit Ct.

■ Lenawee 10 Sep. 1822
425 N. Main St., Adrian, MI 49221
Phone: (517)264-4606
Web site: www.geocities.com/lenaweemi
Parent County: Monroe

Record Type	Year Begun	Jurisdiction
Birth	1867	County Clerk
Marriage	1853	County Clerk
Death	1867	County Clerk
Divorce	1853	County Clerk
Court	1870	Clerk/Circuit Ct.

Michigan

Michigan

■ **Livingston**   24 Mar. 1836
200 E. Grand River Ave., Howell, MI 48843
Phone: (517)546-0500
Web site: www.rootsewb.com/~miliving
Parent County: Shiawassee, Washtenaw

Record Type	Year Begun	Jurisdiction
Birth	1867	County Clerk
Marriage	1836	County Clerk
Death	1867	County Clerk
Divorce	1847	County Clerk
Land	1834	Registrar/Deeds
Probate	1837	Probate Court
Court	1837	Clerk/Circuit Ct.

■ **Luce**   1 Mar. 1887
407 W. Harrie St., Newberry, MI 49868
Phone: (906)293-5521
Web site: www.rootsweb.com/~miluce/
Parent County: Chippewa, Mackinac

Record Type	Year Begun	Jurisdiction
Birth	1887	County Clerk
Marriage	1887	County Clerk
Death	1887	County Clerk
Land	1887	Registrar/Deeds
Probate	1887	Probate Court
Court	1887	Clerk/Circuit Ct.

■ **Mackinac**   26 Oct. 1818
100 N. Marley St., St. Ignace, MI 49781
Phone: (906)643-7300
Web site: www.rootsweb.com/~mimackin/
Parent County: Wayne
Comments/research tips: Formerly Michilimackinac County. Name changed to Mackinac 26 January 1837.

Record Type	Year Begun	Jurisdiction
Birth	1873	County Clerk
Marriage	1867	County Clerk
Death	1873	County Clerk
Court	1808	Clerk/Circuit Ct.

■ **Macomb**   11 Mar. 1818
40 N. Main, Mount Clemens, MI 48043
Phone: (586)469-5120
Web site: www.online-isp.com/~maggie/macomb
Comments/research tips: County Clerk has birth records 1867–1900. Records from 1900 to present must be applied for. Death records from 1867 to 1934 are open for inspection but are stored off-site. Marriage records 1819 to 1925 are open for inspection.
Parent County: Wayne

Record Type	Year Begun	Jurisdiction
Divorce	1857	County Clerk
Land	1818	Registrar/Deeds
Probate	1849	Probate Court

■ **Manistee**   1 Apr. 1840
415 Third St., Manistee, MI 49660
Phone: (231)723-3331
Web site: www.rootsweb.com/mimanist/Index/html

Parent County: Mackinac

Record Type	Year Begun	Jurisdiction
Birth	1867	County Clerk
Marriage	1867	County Clerk
Death	1867	County Clerk
Land	1868	Registrar/Deeds
Probate	1881	Probate Court
Court	1855	Clerk/Circuit Ct.

■ **Manitou**   12 Feb. 1855
Parent County: Emmet, Leelanau
Comments/research tips: Disorganized. Elimiated 4 April 1895 and absorbed by Charlevoix and Leelanau Counties.

■ **Marquette**   9 Mar. 1843
232 W. Baraga Ave., Marquette, MI 49855
Phone: (906)225-8330
Web site: www.rootsweb.com/~mimarque
Parent County: Chippewa, Mackinac

Record Type	Year Begun	Jurisdiction
Birth	1867	County Clerk
Marriage	1850	County Clerk
Death	1867	County Clerk
Divorce	1852	County Clerk
Court	1852	Clerk/Circuit Ct.

■ **Mason**   1 Apr. 1840
304 E. Ludington Ave., Ludington, MI 49431
Phone: (231)843-8202
Web site: www.rootsweb.com/~mimason/county.html
Parent County: Mackinac
Comments/research tips: Formerly Notipekago County. Name changed to Mason 8 March 1843.

Record Type	Year Begun	Jurisdiction
Birth	1867	County Clerk
Marriage	1867	County Clerk
Death	1867	County Clerk
Land	1840	Registrar/Deeds
Probate	1855	Probate Court
Court	1867	Clerk/Circuit Ct.

■ **Mecosta**   1 Apr. 1840
400 Elm St., Big Rapids, MI 49307
Phone: (231)592-0783
Web site: www.rootsweb.com/~mikeween
Parent County: Mackinac, Oceana
Comments/research tips: Attached to Newaygo and Kent Counties prior to organization 11 February 1858.

Record Type	Year Begun	Jurisdiction
Birth	1867	County Clerk
Marriage	1859	County Clerk
Death	1867	County Clerk
Divorce	1867	County Clerk
Land	1867	Registrar/Deeds
Probate	1867	Probate Court
Court	1859	Clerk/Circuit Ct.

■ **Meegisee**   1 Apr. 1840
Parent County: Mackinac
Comments/research tips: (See Antrim) Name changed to Antrim 8 March 1843.

■ Menominee 1861

839 Tenth Ave., Menominee, MI 49858
Phone: (906)863-9968
Web site: www.menomineecounty.com/
Parent County: Unorganized Territory
Comments/research tips: Formerly Bleeker County. Name changed to Menominee 19 March 1863.

Record Type	Year Begun	Jurisdiction
Birth	1863	County Clerk
Marriage	1867	County Clerk
Death	1860	County Clerk
Land	1850	Registrar/Deeds
Probate	1868	Probate Judge
Court	1861	Clerk/Circuit Ct.

■ Michilimackinac 26 Oct. 1818

Parent County: Wayne
Comments/research tips: (See Mackinac) Name changed to Mackinac 8 March 1843.

■ Midland 2 Mar. 1831

220 W. Ellsworth St., Midland, MI 48640
Phone: (517)832-6739
Web site: resources..rootsweb.com/USA/MI/Midland
Parent County: Saginaw, Unorganized Territory
Comments/research tips: County Clerk has Naturalization records 1855–1965 and Burial records from mid 1800s.

Record Type	Year Begun	Jurisdiction
Birth	1867	County Clerk
Marriage	1867	County Clerk
Death	1867	County Clerk
Divorce	1916	County Clerk
Land	1855	Registrar/Deeds
Probate	1856	Probate Court
Court	1839	Clerk/Circuit Ct.

■ Mikenauk 1 Apr. 1840

Parent County: Mackinac
Comments/research tips: (See Roscommon) Name changed to Roscommon 8 March 1843.

■ Missaukee 1 Apr. 1840

111 S. Canal St., Lake City , MI 49651
Phone: (231)839-4967
Web site: www.mifamilyhistory.org/missaukee
Parent County: Mackinac
Comments/research tips: Some records were destroyed by fire in 1944.

Record Type	Year Begun	Jurisdiction
Birth	1870	County Clerk
Marriage	1871	County Clerk
Death	1870	County Clerk
Divorce	1872	County Clerk
Land	1871	Registrar/Deeds
Probate	1871	Probate Court
Court	1871	Clerk/Circuit Ct.

■ Monroe 14 July 1817

106 E. First St., Monroe, MI 48161
Phone: (734)240-7020

Web site: www.geocities.com/Athens/4105
Parent County: Wayne

Record Type	Year Begun	Jurisdiction
Birth	1874	County Clerk
Marriage	1818	County Clerk
Death	1867	County Clerk
Divorce	1897	County Clerk
Land	1806	Registrar/Deeds
Probate	1817	Probate Court
Court	1805	Clerk/Circuit Ct.

■ Montcalm 2 Mar. 1831

P.O. Box 368, Stanton, MI 48888
Phone: (989)831-7339
Web site: www.rootsweb.com/~mimontca
Parent County: Michilimackinac

Record Type	Year Begun	Jurisdiction
Birth	1867	County Clerk
Marriage	1867	County Clerk
Death	1867	County Clerk
Divorce	1867	County Clerk
Land	1837	Registrar/Deeds
Probate	1855	Probate Court
Court	1860	Clerk/Circuit Ct.

■ Montmorency 1 Apr. 1840

P.O. 789, Atlanta, MI 49709
Phone: (517)785-8022
Web site: www.rootsweb.com/~mimontmo/
Parent County: Mackinac, Unorganized Land
Comments/research tips: Formerly Cheonoquet County. Name changed to Montmorency 8 March 1843. Most records lost in fire, 1942.

Record Type	Year Begun	Jurisdiction
Birth	1881	County Clerk
Marriage	1881	County Clerk
Death	1881	County Clerk
Divorce	1940	County Clerk
Court	1940	Clerk/Circuit Ct.
Military	1920	County Clerk

■ Muskegon 4 Feb. 1859

990 Terrace St., Muskegon, MI 49442
Phone: (231)724-6221
Web site: www.rootsweb.com/~mimuskeg
Parent County: Ottawa, Unorganized Territory

Record Type	Year Begun	Jurisdiction
Birth	1867	County Clerk
Marriage	1867	County Clerk
Death	1867	County Clerk
Divorce	1867	County Clerk
Land	1839	Registrar/Deeds
Probate	1867	Probate Court
Court	1856	Clerk/Circuit Ct.

■ Negweon 1 Apr. 1840

Parent County: Unorganized Territory
Comments/research tips: (See Alcona) Name changed to Alcona 8 March 1843. AKA Neewago.

■ **Newaygo** 1 Apr. 1840
1087 Newell St., White Cloud, MI 49349
Phone: (231)689-7235
Web site: www.rootsweb.com/~minewayg
Parent County: Mackinac, Oceana

Record Type	Year Begun	Jurisdiction
Birth	1867	County Clerk
Marriage	1851	County Clerk
Death	1867	County Clerk
Divorce	1854	Clerk/Circuit Ct.
Land	1840	Registrar/Deeds
Probate	1880	Probate Court
Court	1893	Clerk/Circuit Ct.

■ **Notipekago** 1840
Parent County: Mackinac, Ottawa
Comments/research tips: (See Mason) Name changed to Mason 8 March 1843.

■ **Oakland** 12 Jan. 1819
1200 N. Telegraph Rd., Pontiac, MI 48341
Phone: (248)858-0572
Web site: www.miprofgenic.com/genweb/mioakland
Parent County: Macomb

Record Type	Year Begun	Jurisdiction
Birth	1867	County Clerk
Marriage	1827	County Clerk
Death	1867	County Clerk
Nat.	1827	County Clerk

■ **Oceana** 2 Mar. 1831
P.O. Box 653, Hart, MI 49420
Phone: (231)873-4328
Web site: www.rootsweb.com/~mioceana
Parent County: Michilimackinac

Record Type	Year Begun	Jurisdiction
Birth	1867	County Clerk
Marriage	1867	County Clerk
Death	1867	County Clerk
Divorce	1859	County Clerk
Land	1846	Registrar/Deeds
Probate	1900	Probate Court
Court	1859	Clerk/Circuit Ct.

■ **Ogemaw** 27 Feb. 1875
806 W. Houghton Ave., West Branch, MI 48661
Phone: (517)345-0215
Web site: www.rootsweb.com/~miogemaw/index.htm
Parent County: Unorganized Territory
Comments/research tips: Eliminated 7 March 1867 to Iosco. Re-created 28 March 1873 from Iosco and organized 27 April 1875. Some records before 1875 may be located in Mackinac, Cheboygan, and Iosco Counties. Staff of County Clerk officer will research Divorce and Naturalization records.

Record Type	Year Begun	Jurisdiction
Birth	1876	County Clerk
Marriage	1876	County Clerk
Death	1876	County Clerk
Land	1876	Registrar/Deeds

Probate	1877	Probate Court
Court	1876	Clerk/Circuit Ct.

■ **Okkuddo** 1840
Parent County: Mackinac
Comments/research tips: (See Otsego) Name changed to Otsego 8 March 1843.

■ **Omeena** 1840
Parent County: Mackinac
Comments/research tips: (See Grand Traverse) Absorbed by Grand Traverse County 3 February 1843.

■ **Ontonagon** 3 Apr. 1848
725 Greenland Rd., Ontonagon, MI 49953
Phone: (906)884-4255
Web site: www.rootsweb.com/~miontona
Parent County: Chippewa, Mackinac

Record Type	Year Begun	Jurisdiction
Birth	1868	County Clerk
Marriage	1853	County Clerk
Death	1868	County Clerk
Divorce	1856	County Clerk
Land	1850	Registrar/Deeds
Probate	1853	Probate Court
Court	1854	Clerk/Circuit Ct.

■ **Osceola** 1 Apr. 1840
301 W. Upton Ave., Reed City, MI 49677
Phone: (231)832-6104
Web site: www.rootsweb.com/~miosceol/
Parent County: Mackinac
Comments/research tips: Formerly Unwattin County. Name changed to Osceola 8 March 1843.

Record Type	Year Begun	Jurisdiction
Birth	1869	County Clerk
Marriage	1869	County Clerk
Death	1869	County Clerk
Divorce	1882	County Clerk
Land	1853	Registrar/Deeds
Probate	1870	Probate Court
Court	1870	Clerk/Circuit Ct.

■ **Oscoda** 1 Apr. 1840
P.O. Box 399, Mio, MI 48647
Phone: (989)826-1110
Web site: www.rootsweb.com/~mioscoda/
Parent County: Mackinac

Record Type	Year Begun	Jurisdiction
Birth	1880	County Clerk
Marriage	1881	County Clerk
Death	1880	County Clerk
Divorce	1881	County Clerk
Land	1850	Registrar/Deeds
Probate	1881	Probate Court
Court	1881	Clerk/Circuit Ct.

■ **Otsego** 1 Apr. 1840
225 W. Main St., Gaylord, MI 49735
Phone: (517)732-6484

Web site: www.rootsweb.com/~miotsego/index.html
Parent County: Mackinac
Comments/research tips: Formerly Okkuddo County. Name changed to Otsego 8 March 1843.

Record Type	Year Begun	Jurisdiction
Death	1875	County Clerk
Divorce	1895	County Clerk
Land	1864	Registrar/Deeds
Court	1875	Clerk/Circuit Ct.
Birth	1875	County Clerk
Marriage	1895	County Clerk

■ Ottawa 2 Mar. 1831
414 Washington Ave., Grand Haven, MI 49417
Phone: (616)846-8310
Web site: www.rootsweb.com/~miottawa
Parent County: Michilimackinac, Unorganized Territory

Record Type	Year Begun	Jurisdiction
Birth	1866	County Clerk
Marriage	1848	County Clerk
Death	1866	County Clerk
Divorce	1898	County Clerk
Court	1839	Clerk/Circuit Ct.

■ Presque Isle 1 Apr. 1840
151 E. Huron Ave., P.O. Box 110, Rogers City, MI 49779-1316
Phone: (517)734-3288
Web site: members.aol.com/alpenaco/presque/index.htm
Parent County: Mackinac
Comments/research tips: Attached to Cheboygan and Alpena Counties prior to organization 31 March 1871.

Record Type	Year Begun	Jurisdiction
Birth	1871	County Clerk
Marriage	1842	County Clerk
Death	1871	County Clerk
Divorce	1900	County Clerk

■ Roscommon 1 Apr. 1840
P.O. Box 98, Roscommon, MI 48653
Phone: (989)275-5923
Web site: www.rootsweb.com/~miroscom/
Parent County: Mackinac
Comments/research tips: Formerly Mikenauk County. Name changed to Roscommon 8 March 1843.

Record Type	Year Begun	Jurisdiction
Birth	1874	County Clerk
Marriage	1887	County Clerk
Death	1874	County Clerk
Divorce	1887	County Clerk
Land	1875	Registrar/Deeds
Probate	1875	Probate Court
Court	1875	Clerk/Circuit Ct.

■ Saginaw 10 Sep. 1822
111 S. Michigan Ave., Saginaw, MI 48602
Phone: (989)790-5251
Web site: www.rootsweb.com/~misagina
Parent County: St. Clair, Unorganized Territory

Comments/research tips: Staff of County Clerks office will research Divorce records.

Record Type	Year Begun	Jurisdiction
Birth	1867	County Clerk
Marriage	1867	County Clerk
Death	1867	County Clerk
Land	1836	Registrar/Deeds
Probate	1800	Probate Court
Court	1843	Clerk/Circuit Ct.

■ Sanilac 10 Sep. 1822
60 W. Sanilac Rd. Room 203, Sandusky, MI 48471
Phone: (810)648-3212
Web site: www.rootsweb.com/~misanila/
Parent County: St. Clair, Unorganized Territory

Record Type	Year Begun	Jurisdiction
Birth	1867	County Clerk
Marriage	1867	County Clerk
Death	1867	County Clerk
Divorce	1898	County Clerk
Land	1834	Registrar/Deeds
Probate	1857	Probate Court
Court	1850	Clerk/Circuit Ct.

■ Schoolcraft 9 Mar. 1843
300 Walnut St. #164, Manistique, MI 49854
Phone: (906)341-3618
Web site: www.rootsweb.com/~mischool/
Parent County: Chippewa, Mackinac
Comments/research tips: County Clerk has Divorce records late 1800s.

Record Type	Year Begun	Jurisdiction
Birth	1870	County Clerk
Marriage	1870	County Clerk
Death	1870	County Clerk
Land	1871	Registrar/Deeds
Probate	1874	Probate Court
Court	1881	Clerk/Circuit Ct.

■ Shawono 26 Oct. 1818
Parent County: Mackinac
Comments/research tips: (See Crawford) Name changed to Crawford 8 March 1843. AKA Shawano and Shawona.

■ Shiawassee 10 Sep. 1822
208 N. Shiawasee St., Corunna, MI 48817
Phone: (989)743-2242
Web site: www.rootsweb.com/~mishiawa/mishiawa.html
Parent County: Oakland, St. Clair, Unorganized Territory

Record Type	Year Begun	Jurisdiction
Birth	1867	County Clerk
Marriage	1867	County Clerk
Death	1867	County Clerk
Divorce	1861	County Clerk
Land	1836	Registrar/Deeds
Probate	1840	Probate Court
Court	1848	Clerk/Circuit Ct.

■ St. Clair 10 Sep. 1820
201 McMorran Blvd., Port Huron, MI 48060
Phone: (810)985-2200

Web site: www.rootsweb.com/~mistclai/index.html
Parent County: Macomb
Comments/research tips: Attached to Macomb County prior to organization 8 May 1821.

Record Type	Year Begun	Jurisdiction
Birth	1868	County Clerk
Marriage	1837	County Clerk
Death	1868	County Clerk
Divorce	1933	County Clerk
Court	1833	Clerk/Circuit Ct.

■ St. Joseph   29 Oct. 1829
125 W. Main St., Centreville, MI 49032
Phone: (616)467-5602
Web site: members.tripod.com/~tfred/mistjo.html
Parent County: Unorganized Territory

Record Type	Year Begun	Jurisdiction
Birth	1867	County Clerk
Marriage	1832	County Clerk
Death	1867	County Clerk
Divorce	1900	County Clerk
Land	1830	Registrar/Deeds
Probate	1832	Probate Court
Court	1842	Clerk/Circuit Ct.
Nat.	1854	County Clerk

■ Tonedagana   1 Apr. 1840
Parent County: Mackinac
Comments/research tips: (See Emmet) Name changed to Emmet 8 March 1843.

■ Tuscola   1 Apr. 1840
440 N. State St., Caro, MI 48723
Phone: (517)672-3780
Web site: www.rootsweb.com/~mituscol
Parent County: Sanilac

Record Type	Year Begun	Jurisdiction
Birth	1867	County Clerk
Marriage	1851	County Clerk
Death	1867	County Clerk
Divorce	1850	County Clerk
Court	1887	Clerk/Circuit Ct.

■ Unwattin   1 Apr. 1840
Parent County: Mackinac
Comments/research tips: (See Osceola) Name changed to Osceola 8 March 1843.

■ Van Buren   29 Oct. 1829
212 E. Paw Paw St., Paw Paw, MI 49079
Phone: (616)657-8218
Web site: www.rootsweb.com/~mivanbur/Mivanbur.html
Parent County: Unorganized Territory

Record Type	Year Begun	Jurisdiction
Court	1837	County Clerk
Birth	1867	County Clerk
Marriage	1836	County Clerk
Death	1867	County Clerk
Divorce	1857	County Clerk

Land	1837	Registrar/Deeds
Probate	1837	Probate Court

■ Wabassee   1 Apr. 1840
Parent County: Mackinac
Comments/research tips: (See Kalkaska) Name changed to Kalkaska 8 March 1843.

■ Washington   1867
Parent County: Marquette
Comments/research tips: Was declared constitutional.

■ Washtenaw   10 Sep. 1822
P.O. Box 8645, Ann Arbor, MI 48107
Phone: (734)222-6700
Web site: www.rootsweb.com/~miwashte
Parent County: Wayne, Oakland
Comments/research tips: Naturalization records available at State Archives, Michigan Historical Center.

Record Type	Year Begun	Jurisdiction
Birth	1867	County Clerk
Marriage	1833	County Clerk
Death	1867	County Clerk
Divorce	1838	County Clerk
Land	1835	Registrar/Deeds
Court	1835	Clerk/Circuit Ct.

■ Wayne   18 Aug. 1766
201 City County Bldg., Detroit, MI 48226
Phone: (313)224-6262
Web site: www.rootsweb.com/~miwayne
Parent County: Original county
Comments/research tips: The County Clerk has record books open to public inspection of Marriage records 1842–1848. For years 1848–1937 are on microfilm and staff will conduct search.

Record Type	Year Begun	Jurisdiction
Birth	1867	County Clerk
Death	1867	County Clerk
Land	1703	Registrar/Deeds
Probate	1797	Probate Court

■ Wexford   1 Apr. 1840
437 E. Division St., Cadillac, MI 49601
Phone: (231)779-9450
Web site: www.rootsweb.com/~miwexfor
Parent County: Mackinac
Comments/research tips: Formerly Kautawaubet County. Name changed to Wexford 8 March 1843.

Record Type	Year Begun	Jurisdiction
Birth	1867	County Clerk
Marriage	1864	County Clerk
Death	1867	County Clerk
Court	1869	Clerk/Circuit Ct.

■ Wyandiot   1840
Parent County: Mackinac
Comments/research tips: (See Cheboygan) Wyandiot was abolished in 1853 and became a part of Cheboygan County in 1853.

Michigan

Minnesota

By James W. Warren

HISTORICAL OVERVIEW

Centuries before Bob Dylan, Sinclair Lewis, or Betty Crocker could claim Minnesota as their birthplace, the area was inhabited by the Dakota (Sioux) and Ojibway (Chippewa) Indians. Early French traders and missionaries arrived by 1680, including Father Hennepin, who discovered the headwaters of the Mississippi River at Lake Itasca. The trading area came under English control in 1763.

The eastern part of what would become Minnesota was acquired from the English in 1783. It was part of the Northwest Territory from 1787 until 1800, and of Indiana Territory until 1809. In 1803, the western part of Minnesota was acquired from the French as part of the Louisiana Purchase. All of present-day Minnesota was subsequently part of Illinois, Michigan, and Wisconsin Territories. After Fort Snelling was established in 1820 and Indian lands east of the Mississippi were purchased in 1837, large-scale settlement of that area began. Minnesota itself became a Territory in 1849. In the early 1850s the Dakota and Ojibway sold almost all their lands west of the Mississippi, the railroads reached the territory, and immigrants flocked to the area.

Minnesota's varied terrain made a variety of settlers feel at home. The Northeast corner of the state is a pine and glacial lake paradise. A band of hardwood forest arcs across the state to the rolling "great plains," which commence along Minnesota's Southwest quarter and western border. After becoming the thirty-second state in 1858, Minnesota was the first to answer Lincoln's 1861 call for Civil War volunteer regiments. A year later, war erupted within Minnesota itself. Broken treaty promises and starvation pushed Dakota Indians to attack several settlements. With hundreds of casualties on each side, the Dakota Conflict caused temporary panic among settlers across the Midwest.

© PhotoDisc / Getty Images

MINNESOTA AT A GLANCE

Motto: The Star of the North

Population: 5 million

Prevalent Religions: Roman Catholic, Lutheran, Baptist, and Methodist

Major Industries: Food processing, dairy products, agriculture (primarily corn, wheat, and soybeans), printing and publishing, mining (primarily iron ore), manufacturing of industrial machinery

Ethnic Makeup (in percent): Caucasian 89.4%, African American 3.5%, Hispanic 2.9%, Asian 2.9%, Native American 1.1%, Other 0.2%

Famous Minnesotans: Loni Anderson, Warren Berger, Bob Dylan, F. Scott Fitzgerald, Judy Garland, J. Paul Getty, Garrison Keillor, Jessica Lange, Sinclair Lewis, John Madden, Kate Millett, Walter Mondale, Prince, Jane Russell, Winona Ryder, Charles Schultz, Dave Winfield

Above: Bridges of the Twin Cities

Early pioneers had come mostly from New England, New York, Pennsylvania, or French Canada. After statehood there were large waves of Irish and German immigration, followed by Swedes, Norwegians, and Danes in the last third of the nineteenth century. Discovery of the world's richest iron ore deposits brought many Eastern European immigrants to Minnesota's "Iron Range" towns. New arrivals may have come up the Mississippi by steamboat from Iowa, Illinois, St. Louis, or even New Orleans. For many Irish, English, and Scandinavian immigrants, the cheapest ocean passage was to Quebec or another Canadian port. From there, they traveled up the Great Lakes and on by train or wagon to Minnesota.

In modern times, Southeast Asians fleeing the Vietnam War made St. Paul's Hmong community the second largest in America, and many Somali refugees have arrived in recent years. Today half of the state's population lives in the Greater Metropolitan area of the Twin Cities, St. Paul, and Minneapolis.

RECORD HIGHLIGHTS

Federal censuses start in 1850 (territorial) and 1860 (state). Only tiny fragments of the 1890 federal census have survived for Minnesota, but the full 1890 Veterans Census is available for the state. Mortality schedules exist for 1850, 1860, 1870, and 1880, and a portion of the 1900 Mortality Schedule survives. The 1856 territorial census and state censuses for 1865, 1875, 1885, 1895, and 1905 are available on microfilm. Partial indexes to some state censuses are available as ongoing projects of the Minnesota Historical Society (MHS).

Legislation in recent years gave individual Minnesota counties authority over which office handles specific records, and in establishing ease of access to those records. The District Court for each county has civil and criminal cases, including divorce. Divorce proceedings are usually indexed with the other civil cases for that county. The Minnesota Department of Health has a statewide index to divorces that begins with 1970. Each county's Probate Court handles probate, guardianship, incompetency, and sometimes juvenile cases. Land and vital records are usually found in the recorder's office. WPA Inventories were completed for a number of Minnesota counties and are a shopping list for other, lesser-used courthouse records.

While some county-level records start much earlier, birth registration on a statewide basis began in 1900, and deaths in 1908. Any Minnesota courthouse can now provide any post-1900/1908 Minnesota birth or death record, as each county courthouse has online access to the Minnesota Department of Health's birth and death record database and indexes. The documents that result, however, are computer-generated certificates that include

Minnesota

only the information in the database, not necessarily all the detail contained on the original document. Access to Minnesota marriages is a different story, as there is no statewide registration and no central index to Minnesota marriages except those after 1957. It is necessary to identify the county where the marriage likely took place in order to track down the record.

For later immigrants, alien registration records from February 1918 list non-US citizens residing in Minnesota with their name, place of birth, port of entry and date of arrival, names of children, and occupation. They are indexed and microfilmed, available at the Minnesota Historical Society.

The Minnesota Historical Society offers a wealth of resources, including the State Archives collections. Minnesota law requires all counties, state agencies, and local governments, including school districts, to offer any records they no longer use or plan to retain to the State Archives. The older land, probate, and other court records from many county courthouses have been transferred to MHS. For example, the naturalization records (with indexes) from all eighty-seven Minnesota counties have been transferred to MHS and microfilmed. Along with microfilmed state census and Minnesota newspapers, those films are available for purchase and on interlibrary loan. Examples of state agency records at MHS are the records of Stillwater State Prison, the various state hospitals, the Minnesota Veterans Home, and microfilmed application records for military service bonuses. (Minnesota has paid a bonus to its veterans for service during every conflict since the Civil War.) MHS has an online index <www.mnhs.org> to some years of the death records from the Minnesota Department of Health, with more being added.

The Minnesota Genealogical Society Library was founded to complement, not duplicate, the holdings of MHS. The MGS Library collection has material for many other states and foreign countries, including exceptional collections for Canadian (particularly French-Canadian) and Irish research. Special resources include the MGS Cemetery Project, which lists many cemetery locations in Minnesota, and identifying who holds any records, transcriptions or indexes.

Local libraries, county historical societies and museums, and genealogical societies should never be overlooked. They may hold unique resources or indexes, including helpful staff or volunteers.

Other resources in specialized collections include Celtic and Luxembourg collections at the University of St. Thomas in St. Paul, the Roberg Collection of Norwegian materials at St. Olaf University in Northfield, the Swedish Institute in Minneapolis, and mining and northern Minnesota immigration and history at the Iron Range Research Center in Chisholm. The Immigration History Research Center in Minneapolis is a major repository for American immigration research, containing more than 880 manuscript collections, 25,000 books, and 4,000 newspapers and serials.

The Minnesota USGenWeb Project <www.rootsweb.com/~mngenweb/> is an indispensable resource for the resources, indexes, and links it provides at both the state and county levels. The Family History Library in Salt Lake City holds microfilmed records for a number of Minnesota counties, primarily in the southern tier of the state, as well as some for Ramsey (St. Paul) and Hennepin (Minneapolis) counties. Active microfilming continues in Minnesota.

STATE RESOURCES

■ ARCHIVES, LIBRARIES, AND SOCIETIES

Gustavus Adolphus College
800 W. College Ave., Saint Peter, MN 56082
Tel: (507) 933-8000
Web site: <www.gustavus.edu/>

Aitkin County Historical Society
P.O. Box 215, Aitkin, MN 56431
Web site: <www.aitkin.com/achs/>

American Swedish Institute
2600 Park Ave., Minneapolis, MN 55407
Tel: (612) 871-4907
Web site: <www.americanswedishinst.org>

Anoka County Genealogical Society
2135 Third Ave. N., Coon Rapids, MN 55303
Web site: <http://freepages.genealogy.rootsweb.com/~relativememory/>

Anoka County Historical Society
2135 Third Ave., Anoka, MN 56431
Web site: <www.ac-hs.org>

Becker County Historical Society
P.O. Box 622, Detroit Lakes, MN 56502
Tel: (218) 847-2938
Web site: <www.beckercountyhistory.org>

Benton County Historical Society
218 First St. N., Sauk Rapids, MN 56379

Web site: <http://members.aol.com/bchsmus>

Blue Earth County Historical Society
415 E. Cherry St., Mankato, MN 56001
Web site: <www.rootsweb.com/~mnbechs>

Brown County Historical Society
2 N. Broadway, New Ulm, MN 56073
Tel: (507) 233-2616
Web site: <http://browncountyhisotrymnusa.org/>

Bureau of Land Management, Eastern States Office
7450 Boston Blvd., Springfield, VA 22153
Tel: (703) 440-1600
Web site: <www.es.blm.gov>

Carver County Historical Society
555 W. First St., Waconia, MN, 55387
Tel: (952) 442-4234
Web site: <www.co.carver.mn.us/HistoricalSociety/HistSoc.htm>

Chippewa County Genealogical Society
151 Pioneer Dr., P.O. Box 303, Montevideo, MN 56265

Chippewa County Historical Society
Junction Hwy. 7 & Hwy. 59, Montevideo, MN 56265
Web site: <www.montechamber.com/cchs/cchshp.htm>

Clearwater County Historical Society
P.O. Box 241, Bagley, MN 56621
Web site: <www.rrv.net/bagleymn/hstSoc.htm>

Crow River Genealogical Society
380 School Rd. N., Hutchinson, MN 55350

Crow Wing County Genealogical Society
2103 Graydon Ave., Brainerd, MN 56401

Crow Wing County Historical Society
P.O. Box 722, Brainerd, MN 56401

Cuyuna Country Heritage Preservation Society
P.O. Box 68, Ironton, MN 56455
Web site: <www.cuyunaheritage.org/>

Czechoslovak Genealogical Society International
P.O. Box 16225, St. Paul, MN 55116-0225
Web site: <www.cgsi.org/>

Dakota County Genealogical Society
130 Third Ave. N., South St. Paul, MN 55075
Web site: <www.geocities.com/Heartland/Flats/9284/>

Danish American Fellowship
4200 Cedar Ave. S., Minneapolis, MN 55407
Web site: <www.daf-mn.org/>

Dodge County Genealogical Society
Box 683, Dodge Center, MN 55927-0683

Dodge County Historical Society
P.O. Box 433, Mantorville, MN 55955
Tel: (507) 635-5508

Douglas County Historical Society
1219 Nokomis St., Alexandria, MN 56308
Tel: (320) 762-0382
Web site: <www.rea-alp.com/~historic>

Evangelical Lutheran Church of America
2481 Como Ave., St. Paul, MN 55108
Tel: (651) 641-3456
Web site: <www.luthersem.edu>

Fillmore County Historical Center
202 County Rd. 8, Fountain, MN 55935
Tel: (507) 268-4449

Fort Snelling National Cemetery
7601 Thirty-fourth Ave. S., Fort Snelling, MN 55450
Tel: (612) 726-1127

Freeborn County Genealogical Society
1033 Bridge Ave., Albert Lee, MN 56007-2205
Web site: <www.fcgs.org>

Freeborn County Historical Society Library
1031 Bridge St., Albert Lea, MN 56007
Tel: (507) 373-8003
Web site: <www.smig.net/fchm>

Genealogical Society of Carlton County
P.O. Box 204, Cloquet, MN 55720

German-Bohemian Heritage Society
P.O. Box 822, New Ulm, MN 56073-0822
Web site: <www.rootsweb.com/~gbhs/>

Germanic Genealogy Society
P.O. Box 16312, St. Paul, MN 55116-0312
Web site: <www.rootsweb.com/~mnggs/GGS.html>

Heart O'Lakes Genealogical Library
P.O. Box 622, Detroit Lakes, MN 56502
Web site: <www.geocities.com/heartolakes>

Hubbard County Historical Society
P.O. Box 327, Park Rapids, MN 56470
Web site: <www.rootsweb.com/~mnhchs/>

Irish Genealogical Society, Int'l
P.O. Box 16585, St. Paul, MN 55116-0585
Web site: <www.rootsweb.com/~irish/>

Iron Range Historical Society
19 S. Broadway, Gilbert, MN 55741

Jewish Historical Society of the Upper Midwest
4330 S. Cedar Lake Rd., Minneapolis, MN 55416
Web site: <www.tc.umn.edu/~schlo006>

RESEARCH TIPS

for more info

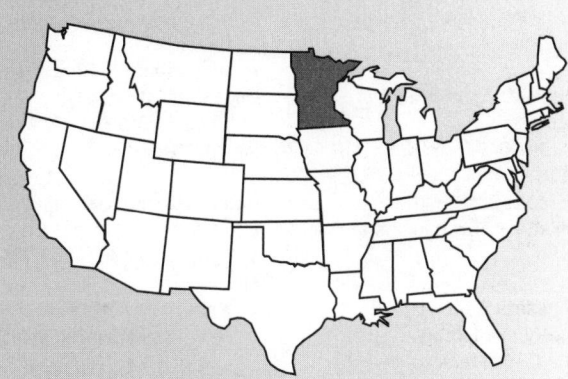

- The Minnesota Historical Society also acts as the official state archives, and it contains many records from state agencies and local governments <www.mnhs.org>.
- The Minnesota USGenWeb site can help you with your online research in the state, with links and indexes for records and resources across Minnesota <www.rootsweb.com/~mngenweb/>.
- If you're looking for information on other states and foreign countries the Minnesota Genealogical Society Library has lots of helpful resources, particularly for Canadian and Irish research.

Census Records
- Federal Census: 1850, 1860, 1870, 1880, 1900, 1910, 1920, 1930
- Federal Mortality Schedules: 1850, 1860, 1870, 1880, 1900
- Union Veterans and Widows: 1890
- State/Territorial Census: 1836, 1838, 1849, 1853, 1857, 1865, 1875, 1885, 1895, 1905

Kanabec County Historical Society & History Center
805 W. Forest Ave., Mora, MN 55051
Web site: <www.kanabechistory.org>

Kandiyohi County Historical Society
617 NE Hwy. 71, Willman, MN 56201
Tel: (320) 235-1881

Le Sueur County Historical Society and Museum
301 NE Second St., Elysian, MN 56028
Web site: <www.frontier.net/~lchsmuseum/>

Maplewood Area Historical Society
1890 Barclay St., Maplewood, MN 55109

Martin County Genealogical Society
222 E. Blue Earth Ave., Fairmont, MN 56031
Web site: <www.geocities.com/Heartland/Hills/4091/>

McLeod County Historical Society Library
380 School Rd. NW, Hutchinson, MN 55350
Tel: (320) 587-2109
Web site: <www.mcleodhistory.org>

Military Historical Society of Minnesota
15000 Hwy. 115, Little Falls, MN 56345-4173
Tel: (320) 632-7374
Web site: <www.dma.state.mn.us/cpripley/SpecFeatures/muse1.htm>

Minnesota Department of Health
P.O. Box 64975, St. Paul, MN 55164
Tel: (651) 215-5800
Web site: <www.health.state.mn.us>

Minnesota Genealogical Society and Library
5768 Olson Memorial Hwy., Golden Valley, MN 55422
Tel: (763) 595-9347
Web site: <http://mngs.org>

Minnesota Historical Depository, United Methodist Conference
122 W. Franklin Ave., Suite 400, Minneapolis, MN 55404
Tel: (612) 870-0058
Web site: <www.minnesotaumc.org>

Minneapolis Public Library
250 Marquette Ave., Minneapolis, MN 55401
Web site: <www.mplib.org>

Minnesota State Historical Society and Archives
345 W. Kellogg Blvd., St. Paul, MN 55102-1906
Tel: (651) 297-4562
Web site: <www.mnhs.org/preserve/records/>

Minnetonka Historical Society
14600 Minnetonka Blvd., Minnetonka, MN 55345
Tel: (952) 930-3962
Web site: <www.minnetonka.history.org/>

Morrison County Historical Society
P.O. Box 239, 2151 S. Lindberg Drive, Little Falls, MN 56345
Web site: <www.upstel.net/johns/History/MorrisonCo.html>

Mower County Genealogical Society
P.O. Box 145, Austin, MN 55912

Mower County Historical Society
P.O. Box 804, Austin, MN 55912
Web site: <www2.smig.net/mchistory/>

National Archives-Central Plains Region (Kansas City)
2312 E. Bannister Rd., Kansas City, MO 64131
Tel: (816) 268-8000
Web site: <www.archives.gov/facilities.mo/kansas-city.html>

Nobles County Historical and Genealogical Society
407 Twelfth St., Suite 2, Worthington, MN 56187

Norman County Genealogical Society
100 First St. E., Apt. 202, Ada, MN 56510
Web site: <www.rootsweb.com/~mnnorman/NCGenSoc.html>

Norwegian-American Historical Association
1510 St. Olaf Ave., Northfield, MN 55057-1097
Web site: <www.naha.stolaf.edu/>

Olmsted County Genealogical Society
P.O. Box 6411, Rochester, MN 55903
Web site: <http://olmstedhistory.com/ocgs.htm>

Olmsted County Historical Society Library
1195 W. Circle Dr., SW, Rochester, MN 55902
Web site: <http://olmstedhistory.com>

Ostfriesen Genealogical Society of Minnesota
Box 474, Wyoming, MN 55092
Web site: <www.rootsweb.com/~mnogsm/>

Otter Tail County Genealogical Society
1110 Lincoln Ave. W., Fergus Falls, MN 56537

Pennington County Historical Society
P.O. Box 127, Thief River Falls, MN 56701
Web site: <http://pvillage.org>

Pipestone County Historical Society and Museum
113 S. Hiawatha, Pipestone, MN 56164
Web site: <www.pipestoneminnesota.com/museum>

Polish Genealogical Society of Minnesota
3487 Darrow Ave. SE, Buffalo, MN 55313

Web site: <www.rootsweb.com/~mnpolgs/pgs-mn.html>

Prairieland Genealogical Society Historical Center
Room 141, Social Science Building, Southwest State University, Marshall, MN 56258
Web site: <http://freepages.genealogy.rootsweb.com/~cmolitor/>

Ramsey County Historical Society
323 Landmark Center, 75 West Fifth St., Saint Paul, MN 55102
Tel: (651) 223-8539
Web site: <www.rchs.com/>

Ramsey County Vital Records
555 Cedar St., St. Paul, MN 55101
Tel: (651) 266-1333

Range Genealogical Society
P.O. Box 388, Chisholm, MN 55719

Redwood County Genealogical Society
217 W. Flynn St., Redwood Falls, MN 56268
Tel: (507) 637-3529

Renville County Genealogical Society
Box 331, Renville, MN 56284
Web site: <www.ci.renville.mn.us/rcgs/>

Renville County Historical Society and Museum
411 N. Park Dr., P.O. Box 266, Morton, MN 56270
Web site: <www.rootsweb.com/~mnrenvil/mus-rchs.htm>

Rice County Genealogical Society
408 Division St. S., Northfield, MN 55057

Rice County Museum of History
1814 Second Ave. NW, Faribault, MN 55021
Tel: (507) 332-2121

Rochester Public Library
101 Second St. SE, Rochester, MN 55904
Web site: <www.rochesterpubliclibrary.org>

Rolvaag Memorial Library
1510 St. Olaf Ave., Northfield, MN 55057

Roseau County Historical Society and Museum
110 Second Ave NE, Roseau, MN 56751
Tel: (218) 463-1918
Web site: <www.roseaucohistoricalsociety.org>

Sherburne County Historical Society
13122 First St., Becker, MN 55308
Tel: (763) 261-4433
Web site: <www.rootsweb.com/~mnschs/home.htm>

Sibley County Historical Society
P.O. Box 407, 700 Main St., Henderson, MN 56044

Sons of Norway
1455 W. Lake St., Minneapolis, MN 55408-2666
Tel: (612) 827-3611

St. Cloud Area Genealogists, Inc.
P.O. Box 213, St. Cloud, MN 56302-0213
Web site: <www.rootsweb.com/~mnscag/SCAG/>

St. Paul Public Library
90 W. Fourth, St. Paul, MN 55102
Web site: <www.stpaul.lib.mn.us>

Stearns County Historical Society
235 Thirty-third Ave. S., St. Cloud, MN 56301-3752
Tel: (866) 253-8424
E-mail: info@stearns-museum.org
Web site: <www.stearns-museum.org>

Swedish Genealogical Society of Minnesota
5768 Olson Memorial Hwy., Golden Valley, MN 55422
Web site: <www.rootsweb.com/~mnsgsm>

Swift County Historical Society
1135 Minnesota Ave, Bldg. 2, Benson, MN 56215
Tel: (612) 843-4467

Twin Ports Genealogical Society
P.O. Box 16895, Duluth, MN 55816-0895

Upsala Area Historical Society
P.O. Box 35, Upsala, MN 56384
Web site: <www.upsala.K12.mn.us/uahs>

Verndale Historical Society
N. Third St. and Main, Verndale, MN 56481

Veterans Service Building
20 W. Twelfth St., St. Paul, MN 55155
Tel: (612) 296-2562

Vital Records Office, Hennepin County
300 S. Sixth St., Minneapolis, MN 55487
Web site: <www.rootsweb.com/~mnhenneplvital.htm>

Waseca County Historical Society
P.O. Box 314, Waseca, MN 56093
Tel: (507) 835-7700
Web site:

Washington County Historical Society
P.O. Box 167, Stillwater, MN 55082
Tel: (651) 439-5956
Web site: <http://wchsmn.org/>

Watertown Area Historical Society
309 Lewis Ave. S., P.O. Box 836, Watertown, MN 55388-0836
Web site: <http://home.earthlink.net/~lahtinen/wahs.htm>

White Bear Lake Genealogical Society
P.O. Box 10555, White Bear Lake, MN 55110

Winona County Genealogical Roundtable
P.O. Box 363, Winona, MN 55987

Winona County Historical Society
160 Johnson St., Winona, MN 55987
Tel: (507) 454-2723
Web site: <www.winona.msus.edu/historicalsociety/>

Wright County Genealogical Society
2001 Hwy. 25 N., Buffalo, MN 55313
Tel: (763) 682-7323

Yankee Genealogical Society of Minnesota
5768 Olson Memorial Hwy., Golden Valley, MN 55422

Carl B. Ylvisaker Library, Concordia College
901 Eighth St. S., Moorhead, MN 56562

Tel: (218) 299-4640
Web site: <www4.cord.edu/library/default.asp>

BIBLIOGRAPHY

■ GENERAL RESOURCES

A Bibliography of Books and Pamphlets Held in the Northeast Minnesota Historical Center
by D. Gaynon (Duluth, MN: St. Louis County Historical Society, 1981)

A Bibliography of Minnesota Territorial Documents
by Esther Jerabek (St. Paul, MN: Minnesota Historical Society, 1936)

Blacks in Minnesota: A Preliminary Guide to Historical Sources
by David Vassar Taylor (St. Paul: Minnesota Historical Society, 1976)

The Book of Minnesotans: A Biographical Dictionary of Leading Living Men of the State of Minnesota
by Albert Nelson Marquis (Chicago: A.N. Marquis, 1907)

Check List of Minnesota State Documents, 1858–1923
by Esther Jerabek (St. Paul: Minnesota Historical Society, 1972)

Chippewa and Dakota Indians: A Subject Catalog of Books, Pamphlets, Periodical Articles, and Manuscripts in the Minnesota Historical Society
from the Minnesota Historical Society (St. Paul: Minnesota Historical Society, 1969)

Church Records in Minnesota: A Guide Parish Records of Congregational, Evangelical, Reformed, and United Church of Christ Churches 1851–1981
by Anne A. Hage (Minneapolis: Minnesota Conference, United Church of Christ, 1983)

Commemorative Biographical Record of the Upper Lake Region: Containing Biographical Sketches of Prominent and Representative Citizens and Many of the Early Settled Families
(Chicago: J.H. Beers, 1905)

Compendium of History and Biography of Central and Northern Minnesota
(Chicago: George A. Ogle, 1904)

Continuing Your Genealogical Research in Minnesota
by Marilyn Lind (Cloquet, MN: The Linden Tree, 1986)

Directory of Churches and Religious Organizations in Minnesota
edited by Antona Hawkins Richardson (St. Paul, MN: Paduan Press, 1977)

Early Presbyterian Church Records from Minnesota 1835–1871
by Mary Hawker Bakeman (Roseville, MN: Park Genealogical Books, 1992)

Every Name Index to Pioneer Chronicles, Stories of Minnesota Territorial Pioneers
by Ann H. Peterson (St. Paul: Warren Research & Marketing, 1990)

French-Canadian Families of the North Central States: A Genealogical Dictionary, 8 vols.
by Paul J. Lareau and Elmer Courteau (St. Paul, MN: Northwest Territory French and Canadian Heritage Institute, 1980)

Genealogical Resources of the Minnesota Historical Society: A Guide, 2d ed.
from the Minnesota Historical Society (St. Paul: Minnesota Historical Society Press, 1993)

The Genealogist's Companion and Sourcebook, 2d ed.
by Emily Anne Croom (Cincinnati: Betterway Books, 2003)

A Genealogist's Guide to Discovering Your African-American Ancestors
by Franklin Carter Smith and Emily Anne Croom (Cincinnati: Betterway Books, 2003)

Guide to Depositories of Manuscript Collections in the United States: Minnesota
from the Historical Records Survey (Saint Paul, MN: Historical Records Survey, 1941)

Guide to the Northwest Minnesota Historical Center Collections
from the Northwest Minnesota Historical Center (Moorhead, MN: Livingston Lord Library, Moorhead State University, 1988)

Guide to Genealogical Research in the National Archives of the United States
edited by Anne Bruner Eales and Robert M. Kvasnicka (Washington, DC: National Archives and Records Administration, 2000)

Guide to the Public Affairs Collection of the Minnesota Historical Society
by Lucille M. Kane (St. Paul: Minnesota Historical Society, 1968)

Guide to Public Vital Statistics Records in Minnesota
from the Historical Records Survey (St. Paul, MN: The Survey, 1941)

Historic Resources in Minnesota: A Report on Their Extent, Location, and Need for Preservation
from the Minnesota Historical Society (St. Paul: Minnesota Historical Society, 1979)

History of the Finns in Minnesota
by Hans R. Wasasjerna (Duluth, MN: Minnesota Finnish-American Historical Society, 1957)

History of the Great Northwest and Its Men of Progress: A Select List of Biographical Sketches and Portraits of the Leaders in Business, Professional and Official Life
by C. W. G. Hyde (Minneapolis: Minneapolis Journal, 1901)

History of Methodism in Minnesota
by Chauncey Hobart (Roseville, MN: Park Genealogical Books, 1887, 1992)

The History of Minnesota, 4 vols.
by Val Bjornson (West Palm Beach, FL: Lewis Historical Pub., Co., 1969)

History of the St. Croix Valley, 2 vols.
edited by Augustus B. Easton, et al. (Salem, MA: Higginson Books, 1996)

History of the Swedish-Americans of Minnesota, 3 vols.
by A.E. Strand (Salem, MA: Higginson Books, 1910, 1994)

Minnesota

History of the Synod of Minnesota—Presbyterian Church
by Rev. Maurice Dwight Edwards (Roseville, MN: Park Genealogical Books, 1924, 1993)

History of the Upper Mississippi Valley
by Newton Horace Winchell (Minneapolis: Minnesota Historical Co., 1881)

Holdings of Genealogical Value in Minnesota's County Museums
by Lucille L. Kirkeby (Brainerd, MN: L. Kirkeby, 1986)

Illustrated Historical Atlas of the State of Minnesota
(Chicago: A.T. Andreas, 1874)

An Introduction to Minnesota Research Sources
by Ann H. Peterson (St. Paul, MN: Minnesota Genealogical Society, 1988)

Minnesota: A Bicentennial History
by William E. Lass (New York: W.W. Norton & Co., 1977)

Minnesota Biographies, 1655–1912
compiled by Warren Upham (St. Paul: Minnesota Historical Society, 1912)

Minnesota in a Century of Change: The State and Its People Since 1900
by Clifford Edward Clark (St. Paul: Minnesota Historical Society Press, 1989)

Minnesota Genealogical Index
by Wiley R. Pope (St. Paul: Minnesota Family Trees, 1984)

Minnesota Genealogical Reference Guide
by Paula Stewart Warren (St. Paul, MN: Warren Research & Publishing, 1994)

Minnesota Research Outline
by the Church of Jesus Christ of Latter-day Saints (Salt Lake City, UT: Corp. of the President of the Church of Jesus Christ of L.D.S., 1988)

Minnesota State Archives Preliminary Checklist
(St. Paul: Minnesota Historical Society, Division of Archives and manuscripts, 1979)

Minnesota: Its Story and Biography, 3 vols.
by Henry Anson Castle (Chicago: Lewis Publishing Co., 1915)

Minnesota in Three Centuries, 1655–1908, 4 vols.
by Lucius Frederick Hubbard (New York: Society of Minnesota, 1908)

National Archives Microfilm Catalogs online:
<www.archives.gov/publications/genealogy_microfilm_catalogs.html>

Newspapers on the Minnesota Frontier, 1849–1860
by George Sigrud Hage (St. Paul: Minnesota Historical Society, 1967)

The Oral History Collections of the Minnesota Historical Society
(St. Paul: Minnesota Historical Society Press, 1984)

Reference Guide to Minnesota History
by Michael Brook (St. Paul: Minnesota Historical Society, 1974)

Research in Minnesota
by Paula Stewart Warren (Arlington, VA: National Genealogical Society, 1992)

Tracing Your Ancestors in Minnesota: A Guide to the Sources
by Wiley R. Pope (St. Paul: Pope Families Association, 1978–)

The United States Biographical Dictionary and Portrait Gallery of Eminent and Self-Made Men: Minnesota Volume
(Tuscon, AZ: W.C. Cox Co., 1974)

Women's History in Minnesota: A Survey of Published Sources and Dissertations
by Jo Blatti (St. Paul: Minnesota Historical Society Press, 1993)

Women of Minnesota: Selected Biographical Essays
by Barbara Stuhler (St. Paul: Minnesota Historical Society Press, ca. 1977, 1979)

■ CENSUS RECORDS

The American Census Handbook
by Thomas Jay Kemp (Wilmington, DE: Scholarly Resources, Inc., 2001)

The Census Book: A Genealogist's Guide to Federal Census Facts, Schedules and Indexes
by William Dollarhide (Bountiful, UT: Heritage Quest, 1999)

Finding Answers in U.S. Census Records
by Loretto Dennis Szucs and Matthew Wright (Salt Lake City: Ancestry Publishing, 2001)

Guide to the Minnesota State Census Microfilm
by Mary Hawker Bakeman (Roseville, MN: Park Genealogical Books, 1992)

Map Guide to the U.S. Federal Censuses, 1790–1920
by William Thorndale and William Dollarhide (Baltimore: Genealogical Publishing Co., 1987)

State Census Records
by Ann S. Lainhart (Baltimore: Genealogical Publishing Co., 1992)

Your Guide to the Federal Census
by Kathleen W. Hinckley (Cincinnati: Betterway Books, 2002)

■ IMMIGRATION RECORDS

American Naturalization Records, 1790–1990: What They Are and How to Use Them
by John J. Newman (North Salt Lake, UT: HeritageQuest, 1998)

American Passenger Arrival Records
by Michael Tepper (Baltimore: Genealogical Publishing Co., 1993)

Declarations of Intention (1847–1852) of 262 Minnesota Pioneers
by James E. Erickson (Roseville, MN: Park Genealogical Books, 1997)

For Sale-Minnesota: Organized Promotion of Scandinavian Immigration, 1866–1873
by Lars Ljungmark (Chicago: Swedish Pioneer Historical Society, 1971)

They Became Americans: Finding Naturalization Records and Ethnic Origins
by Loretto Dennis Szucs (Salt Lake City: Ancestry, Inc., 1998)

They Came in Ships: A Guide to Finding Your Immigrant Ancestor's Arrival Records, 2d ed.
by John P. Colletta (Salt Lake City: Ancestry, Inc., 1993)

They Chose Minnesota: A Survey of the State's Ethnic Groups
edited by June D. Holmquist (St. Paul: Minnesota Historical Society, 1981)

■ LAND RECORDS

Federal Land Grants to the States with Special Reference to Minnesota
by Matthias N. Orfield (Minnesota: Matthias N. Orfield, 1915)

A Guide to the Records of Minnesota's Public Lands
by Gregory Kinney (St. Paul: Minnesota Historical Society, 1985)

Land and Property Research in the United States
by Wade E. Hone (Salt Lake City: Ancestry Inc., 1997)

Land Records: AL, AR, FL, LA, MI, MN, OH, WI
(Brøderbund, 1996. CD-ROM)

Locating Your Roots: Discover Your Ancestors Using Land Records
by Patricia Law Hatcher (Cincinnati: Betterway Books, 2003)

Minnesota, 1820-1908: Cash and Homestead Entries
from the United States Department of the Interior, Bureau of Land Management (Springfield, VA: BLM Eastern States, 1995. CD-ROM)

Minnesota Land Owner Maps and Directories
by Mary Hawker Bakeman (Roseville, MN: Park Genealogical Books, 1994)

■ MAPS

Comprehensive Index to A.T. Andreas' Illustrated Historical Atlas of Minnesota—1874
by Mary Hawker Bakeman (Roseville, MN: Park Genealogical Books, 1992)

Every Person's Name Index to An Illustrated Atlas of the State of Minnesota
by Paul J. Ostendorf (Winona, MN: St. Mary's College, 1979)

Gazetteer of Minnesota Railroad Towns, 1861–1997
by Hudson Leighton (Roseville, MN: Park Genealogical Books, 1992)

German Place Names in Minnesota—Deutsche Ortsnamen in Minnesota
by LaVern J. Rippley (Northfield, MN: St. Olaf College, 1989)

Illustrated Historical Atlas of the State of Minnesota
by Alfred T. Andreas (Evansville, IN: Unigraphic, 1874, 1976)

Minnesota Atlas and Gazetteer, 2d ed.
(Freeport, ME: DeLorme Mapping Co., 1995)

Minnesota Geographic Names: Their Origin and Historic Significance
by Warren Upham (St. Paul: Minnesota Historical Society, 1920, 1969)

Minnesota's Boundary with Canada: Its Evolution since 1783
by William E. Lass (St. Paul: Minnesota Historical Society Press, 1980)

The Post Offices of Minnesota
by Alan H. Patera and John S. Gallagher (Burtonville, MD: The Depot, 1978)

Windows to the Past: A Bibliography of Minnesota County Atlases
by Mai Treude (Minnesota: Center for Urban and Regional Affairs, University of Minnesota, 1980)

■ MILITARY RECORDS

History of the Fourth Regiment of Minnesota Infantry Volunteers During the Great Rebellion
by Alonzo L. Brown (Salem, MA: Higginson Books, 1892, 1995)

Known War of 1812 Veterans Buried in Minnesota
by Arthur Louis Finnell (Bloomington, MN: A.L. Finnell, 1996)

Minnesota in the Civil and Indian Wars, 1861–1865
(St. Paul: Pioneer Press, 1891)

Minnesota in the Spanish-American War and the Philippine Insurrection
by Franklin F. Holbrook (St. Paul: Minnesota War Records Commission, 1923)

Minnesota's World War II Army Dead
(Roseville, MN: Park Genealogical Books, 1994)

Uncle, We Are Ready! Registering America's Men, 1917–1918: A Guide to Researching World War I Draft Registration Cards
by John J. Newman (North Salt Lake, UT: HeritageQuest, 2001)

U.S. Military Records: A Guide to Federal & State Sources, Colonial America to the Present
by James C. Neagles (Salt Lake City: Ancestry, Inc., 1994)

World War II: A Family Historian's Guide
by Debra Johnson Knox (Spartanburg, SC: MIE Publishing, 2003)

■ PROBATE RECORDS

Adoptions & Name Changes: Minnesota Territory & State, 1851–1881
by Stina B. Green (Roseville, MN: Park Genealogical Books, 1994)

■ VITAL RECORDS

Church Records in Minnesota: Guide to Parish Records of Congregational, Evangelical, Reformed & United Church of Christ Churches 1851–1891
by Anne A. Hage (Roseville, MN: Park Genealogical Books, 1983)

Early Presbyterian Church Records from Minnesota 1825–1871
by the Pond Brothers, transcribed by Mary Hawker Bakeman (Roseville, MN: Park Genealogical Books, 1992)

Guide to Church Vital Statistics Records in Minnesota: Baptisms, Marriages, Funerals
(St. Paul: Historical Records Survey, 1942)

Guide to Public Vital Statistics Records in Minnesota
(St. Paul: Historical Records Survey, 1941)

Minnesota Cemeteries in Print: A Bibliography of Minnesota Published Cemetery Inscriptions, Burials, Etc.
by Wiley R. Pope (St. Paul: Minnesota Family Trees, 1986)

Your Guide to Cemetery Research
by Sharon DeBartolo Carmack (Cincinnati: Betterway Books, 2002)

■ Aitkin   23 May 1857
209 Second St. NW, Aitkin, MN 56431
Phone: (218)927-7336
Web site: www.rootsweb.com/~mnaitkin
Parent County: Pine, Ramsey
Comments/research tips: Attached to Crow Wing and Morrison Counties prior to organization 6 February 1885.

Record Type	Year Begun	Jurisdiction
Birth	1883	Clerk/District Ct.
Marriage	1885	Clerk/District Ct.
Death	1887	Clerk/District Ct.
Divorce	1886	Clerk/District Ct.
Probate	1885	Clerk/District Ct.
Court	1885	Clerk/District Ct.
Nat.	1885	Clerk/District Ct.

■ Andy Johnson   18 Mar. 1858
Parent County: Pembina
Comments/research tips: (See Wilkin) Formerly Toombs County. Name changed to Andy Johnson 8 March 1862. Name changed to Wilkin 6 March 1868.

■ Anoka   23 May 1857
325 E. Main St., Anoka, MN 55303
Phone: (763)422-7399
Web site: www.rootsweb.com/~mnanoka/intro.htm
Parent County: Ramsey

Record Type	Year Begun	Jurisdiction
Birth	1870	Clerk/District Ct.
Marriage	1865	Clerk/District Ct.
Death	1870	Clerk/District Ct.
Divorce	1866	Clerk/District Ct.
Land	1866	Clerk/District Ct.
Court	1866	Clerk/District Ct.

■ Becker   18 Mar. 1858
913 Lake Ave., P.O. Box 702, Detroit Lakes, MN 56501
Phone: (218)846-7304
Web site: www.rootsweb.com/~mnbecker
Parent County: Cass, Pembina
Comments/research tips: Attached to Stearns, Crow Wing and Douglas counties prior to organization 1 March 1871.

Record Type	Year Begun	Jurisdiction
Birth	1871	County Recorder
Marriage	1871	County Recorder
Death	1871	County Recorder
Divorce	1940	County Recorder
Probate	1940	County Recorder
Court	1940	County Recorder

■ **Beltrami** 28 Feb. 1866
619 Beltrami Ave. NW, Bemidji, MN 56601
Phone: (218)759-4174
Web site: www.rootsweb.com/~mnbeltra/
Parent County: Unorganized Territory, Itasca, Pembina, Polk
Comments/research tips: Attached to Becker County prior to organization 6 April 1897. Historical Society has Land records prior to 1969.

Record Type	Year Begun	Jurisdiction
Military	na	Recorder Office
Birth	1896	Court Administrator
Marriage	1896	Court Administrator
Death	1896	Court Administrator
Divorce	1951	Clerk/Courts
Probate	na	Clerk/Courts
Court	na	Clerk/Courts

■ **Benton** 27 Oct. 1849
531 Dewey St., P.O. Box 129, Foley, MN 56329
Phone: (320)968-5037
Web site: www.rootsweb.com/~mnbenton/
Parent County: St. Croix

Record Type	Year Begun	Jurisdiction
Birth	1870	County Recorder
Marriage	1887	County Recorder
Death	1871	County Recorder
Divorce	1900	Court Administrator
Land	1850	County Recorder
Probate	1850	Court Administrator
Court	1900	Court Administrator

■ **Big Sioux** 23 May 1857
Parent County: Brown
Comments/research tips: (See South Dakota) Attached to Pipestone County. Eliminated 11 May 1858 when Minnesota state was created.

■ **Big Stone** 20 Feb. 1862
20 SE Second St., Ortonville, MN 56278
Phone: (320)839-2308
Web site: www.rootsweb.com/~mnbigsto/index.html
Parent County: Pierce
Comments/research tips: Attached to Renville and Stevens Counties prior to organization 8 February 1881.

Record Type	Year Begun	Jurisdiction
Birth	1881	County Recorder
Marriage	1881	County Recorder
Death	1881	County Recorder
Divorce	1885	County Recorder
Land	1881	County Recorder
Probate	na	Court Judge
Court	1885	County Recorder

■ **Blue Earth** 5 Mar. 1853
204 S. Fifth St., P.O. Box 3524, Mankato, MN 56001
Phone: (507)389-8343
Web site: www.rootsweb.com/~mnblueea/
Parent County: Unorganized Territory, Dakota

Record Type	Year Begun	Jurisdiction
Birth	1870	Clerk/District Ct.
Marriage	1865	Clerk/District Ct.
Death	1870	Clerk/District Ct.
Divorce	1854	Clerk/District Ct.
Land	na	Registrar/Deeds
Probate	1858	Clerk/District Ct.
Court	1854	Clerk/District Ct.

■ **Breckenridge** 18 Mar. 1858
Parent County: Pembina
Comments/research tips: (See Clay) Name changed to Clay 6 March 1862.

■ **Brown** 20 Feb. 1855
Center & State Sts., P.O. Box 248, New Ulm, MN 56073
Phone: (507)233-6657
Web site: www.rootsweb.com/~mnbrown
Parent County: Blue Earth
Comments/research tips: Organized 11 February 1856.

Record Type	Year Begun	Jurisdiction
Birth	1870	County Recorder
Marriage	1857	County Recorder
Death	1870	County Recorder
Divorce	1856	Clerk/District Ct.
Land	na	County Recorder
Probate	1856	Clerk/District Ct.
Court	1885	Clerk/District Ct.
Nat.	na	Historical Society

■ **Buchanan** 23 May 1857
Parent County: Pine
Comments/research tips: (See Pine) Attached to Chisago and St. Louis Counties. Eliminated and absorbed by Pine County 8 October 1861.

■ **Carlton** 23 May 1857
301 Walnut Ave., Carlton, MN 55718
Phone: (218)384-9195
Web site: www.mjpdan.com/genweb/carlton/carlton.htm
Parent County: Pine, St. Louis
Comments/research tips: Organized 18 February 1870.

Record Type	Year Begun	Jurisdiction
Birth	1872	Clerk/District Ct.
Marriage	1872	Clerk/District Ct.
Death	1872	Clerk/District Ct.
Divorce	1872	Clerk/District Ct.
Land	1872	Clerk/District Ct.
Probate	1872	Clerk/District Ct.
Court	1872	Clerk/District Ct.
Nat.	1872	Clerk/District Ct.
Burial	1872	Clerk/District Ct.

■ **Carver** 20 Feb. 1855
600 E. Fourth St., Chaska, MN 55318
Phone: (612)361-1930
Web site: www.rootsweb.com/~mncarver/
Parent County: Hennepin, Sibley

Record Type	Year Begun	Jurisdiction
Birth	1870	County Recorder
Marriage	1870	County Recorder

Record Type	Year Begun	Jurisdiction
Death	1870	County Recorder
Divorce	1856	Court Administrator
Land	1870	County Recorder
Probate	1856	Court Administrator
Court	1856	Court Administrator

■ Cass   31 Mar. 1851

300 Minnesota Ave., P.O. Box 3000, Walker, MN 56484
Phone: (218)547-7247
Web site: www.rootsweb.com/~mncass
Parent County: Dakota, Pembina, Mahkato, Wahrahta
Comments/research tips: Attached to Benton, Stearns, Crow Wing and Morrison Counties prior to organization 4 May 1872.

Record Type	Year Begun	Jurisdiction
Birth	1896	County Treasurer
Marriage	1897	County Treasurer
Death	1896	County Treasurer
Divorce	1899	Clerk/District Ct.
Probate	na	Clerk/District Ct.
Court	1898	Clerk/District Ct.
Burial	na	Town/City Clerks
Nat.	na	Clerk/District Ct.

■ Chippewa   20 Feb. 1862

629 N. Eleventh St., Montevideo, MN 56265
Phone: (320)269-9431
Web site: www.rootsweb.com/~mnchippe
Parent County: Pierce, Davis
Comments/research tips: Attached to Renville County prior to organization 9 January 1869.

Record Type	Year Begun	Jurisdiction
Birth	1870	Clerk/District Ct.
Marriage	1870	Clerk/District Ct.
Death	1870	Clerk/District Ct.
Divorce	1870	Clerk/District Ct.
Land	1870	County Recorder
Probate	1870	Clerk/District Ct.
Court	1870	Clerk/District Ct.
Burial	na	City Clerk

■ Chisago   31 Mar. 1851

313 N. Main St., Center City, MN 55012
Phone: (612)213-0438
Web site: www.rootsweb.com/~mnchisag
Parent County: Washington, Ramsey
Comments/research tips: Organized 1 January 1852.

Record Type	Year Begun	Jurisdiction
Birth	1870	Clerk/District Ct.
Marriage	1852	Clerk/District Ct.
Death	1870	Clerk/District Ct.
Divorce	na	Clerk/District Ct.
Land	na	Registrar/Deeds
Probate	na	Probate Judge
Court	1880	Clerk/District Ct.

■ Clay   18 Mar. 1858

807 Eleventh St., Moorhead, MN 56561
Phone: (218)299-5031

Web site: www.rootsweb.com/~mnclay/
Parent County: Pembina
Comments/research tips: Formerly Breckenridge County. Name changed to Clay 6 March 1862. Attached to Stearns, Crow Wing, Douglas and Becker Counties prior to organization 27 February 1872.

Record Type	Year Begun	Jurisdiction
Birth	1872	County Recorder
Marriage	1872	County Recorder
Death	1872	County Recorder
Divorce	1931	Court Administrator
Land	1872	County Recorder
Probate	1885	Court Administrator
Court	1931	Court Administrator
Military	1917	County Recorder

■ Clearwater   20 Dec. 1902

213 Main Ave. N., Bagley, MN 56621
Phone: (218)694-6129
Web site: www.rootsweb.com/~mnclearw
Parent County: Beltrami

Record Type	Year Begun	Jurisdiction
Birth	1903	County Recorder
Marriage	1903	County Recorder
Death	1903	County Recorder
Divorce	na	Court Administrator
Land	1903	County Recorder
Probate	na	Court Administrator
Court	na	Court Administrator
Military	1903	County Recorder
Nat.	na	Court Administrator

■ Cook   3 Nov. 1874

P.O. Box 1150, Grand Marais, MN 55604
Phone: (218)387-3000
Web site: www.rootsweb.com/~mncook
Parent County: Lake
Comments/research tips: Attached to Lake and St. Louis Counties prior to organization 6 April 1897.

Record Type	Year Begun	Jurisdiction
Birth	1900	County Recorder
Marriage	1901	County Recorder
Death	1900	County Recorder
Divorce	na	Court Administrator
Land	1886	County Recorder
Probate	na	Court Administrator
Court	na	Court Administrator
Military	1919	County Recorder

■ Cottonwood   23 May 1857

900 Third Ave., Windom, MN 56101
Phone: (507)831-1458
Web site: www.rootsweb.com/~mncotton
Parent County: Brown
Comments/research tips: Attached to Brown, Redwood, and Watonwan Counties prior to organization 4 July 1873.

Record Type	Year Begun	Jurisdiction
Birth	1871	Clerk/District Ct.
Marriage	1871	Clerk/District Ct.

Record Type	Year Begun	Jurisdiction
Death	1871	Clerk/District Ct.
Divorce	1871	Clerk/District Ct.
Court	1871	Clerk/District Ct.

■ Crow Wing 23 May 1857
326 Laurel St., Brainerd, MN 56401
Phone: (218)824-1300
Web site: www.mjpdan.com/genweb/crowwing/
crowwing.htm
Parent County: Ramsey

Record Type	Year Begun	Jurisdiction
Birth	1873	County Treasurer
Marriage	1871	County Treasurer
Death	1874	County Treasurer
Divorce	na	Court Administrator
Land	1867	County Recorder
Probate	na	Court Administrator
Court	na	Court Administrator
Military	1919	County Recorder

■ Dakota 27 Oct. 1849
1560 Hwy. 55 W., Hastings, MN 55033
Phone: (612)438-4313
Web site: www.tc.umn.edu/~bluhmoo2/Dakota/
public_html/index.html
Parent County: Unorganized Territory
Comments/research tips: Attached to Ramsey County prior to organization 5 March 1853.

Record Type	Year Begun	Jurisdiction
Birth	1870	Clerk/District Ct.
Marriage	1857	Clerk/District Ct.
Death	1870	Clerk/District Ct.
Divorce	1853	Clerk/District Ct.
Court	1853	Clerk/District Ct.

■ Davis 20 Feb. 1855
Parent County: Cass, Nicollet, Pierce, Sibley
Comments/research tips: Attached to Stearns County. Eliminated 20 February 1862. Lost to Chippewa and Lac Qui Parle Counties.

■ Dodge 20 Feb. 1855
22 E. Sixth St., P.O. Box 128, Mantorville, MN 55955
Phone: (507)635-6250
Web site: www.rootsweb.com/~mndodge/
Parent County: Rice, Unorganized Territory

Record Type	Year Begun	Jurisdiction
Birth	1870	Clerk/District Ct.
Marriage	1865	Clerk/District Ct.
Death	1870	Clerk/District Ct.
Divorce	1870	Clerk/District Ct.
Probate	1858	Clerk/District Ct.
Court	1870	Clerk/District Ct.
School	1917	Clerk/District Ct.

■ Doty 20 Feb. 1855
Parent County: Itasca
Comments/research tips: (See St. Louis) Name changed to Newton 3 March 1855. Eliminated to St. Louis County 1 March 1856.

■ Douglas 8 Mar. 1858
305 Eighth Ave. W., Alexandria, MN 56308
Phone: (320)762-3877
Web site: www.rootsweb.com/~mndougla
Parent County: Cass, Pembina
Comments/research tips: County Recorder has Land records late 1800s.

Record Type	Year Begun	Jurisdiction
Birth	1890	County Recorder
Marriage	1890	County Recorder
Death	1890	County Recorder
Divorce	na	Clerk/Courts
Probate	na	Clerk/Courts
Court	na	Clerk/Courts
Military	na	County Recorder

■ Faribault 20 Feb. 1855
415 N. Main St., P.O. Box 130, Blue Earth, MN 56013
Phone: (507)526-6252
Web site: www.rootsweb.com/~mnfariba
Parent County: Blue Earth
Comments/research tips: Attached to Blue Earth County prior to organization 1 May 1857.

Record Type	Year Begun	Jurisdiction
Birth	1870	Court Administrator
Marriage	1870	Court Administrator
Death	1870	Court Administrator
Divorce	1870	Court Administrator
Land	na	Registrar/Deeds
Probate	1870	Court Administrator
Court	1950	Court Administrator
Nat.	na	Court Administrator

■ Fillmore 5 Mar. 1853
101 Fillmore St., Preston, MN 55965
Phone: (507)765-4701
Web site: www.rootsweb.com/~mnfillmo
Parent County: Wabasha

Record Type	Year Begun	Jurisdiction
Birth	1870	Court Administrator
Marriage	1865	Court Administrator
Death	1870	Court Administrator
Divorce	1885	Court Administrator
Land	na	County Recorder
Probate	1858	Court Administrator
Court	1885	Court Administrator

■ Freeborn 20 Feb. 1855
411 S. Broadway Ave., Albert Lea, MN 56007
Phone: (507)377-5153
Web site: www.rootsweb.com/~mnfreebo
Parent County: Blue Earth, Rice
Comments/research tips: Organized 6 March 1857.

Record Type	Year Begun	Jurisdiction
Birth	1870	Clerk/District Ct.
Marriage	1857	Clerk/District Ct.
Death	1870	Clerk/District Ct.
Land	1854	County Recorder
Probate	1866	Probate Office
Court	1857	Clerk/District Ct.

■ **Goodhue** 5 Mar. 1853
509 Fifth St. W., Red Wing, MN 55066
Phone: (651)385-3148
Web site: www.rootsweb.com/~mngoodhu
Parent County: Wabasha, Dakota
Comments/research tips: Minnesota Historical Society has
Divorce and Court records from 1854–1950. Attached to
Wabasha County prior to organization 15 June 1854.

Record Type	Year Begun	Jurisdiction
Birth	1870	Court Administrator
Marriage	1854	Court Administrator
Death	1870	Court Administrator
Divorce	1951	Court Administrator
Probate	1854	Court Administrator
Court	1951	Court Administrator

■ **Grant** 6 Mar. 1868
County Courthouse, Elbow Lake, MN 56531
Phone: (218)685-4520
Web site: www.rootsweb.com/~mngrant/
Parent County: Stevens, Wilkin, Traverse
Comments/research tips: Attached to Douglas County prior
to organization 1 March 1883.

Record Type	Year Begun	Jurisdiction
Birth	1877	Clerk/District Ct.
Marriage	1869	Clerk/District Ct.
Death	1877	Clerk/District Ct.
Divorce	1883	Clerk/District Ct.
Land	na	Registrar/Deeds
Probate	na	Probate Judge
Court	1883	Clerk/District Ct.

■ **Hennepin** 6 Mar. 1852
300 S. Sixth St., Minneapolis, MN 55487
Phone: (612)348-8241
Web site: www.rootsweb.com/~mnhennep
Parent County: Dakota

Record Type	Year Begun	Jurisdiction
Birth	1870	Clerk/District Ct.
Marriage	1853	Clerk/District Ct.
Death	1870	Clerk/District Ct.
Divorce	1853	Clerk/District Ct.
Court	1853	Clerk/District Ct.

■ **Houston** 4 Apr. 1854
304 S. Marshall St., Caledonia, MN 55921
Phone: (507)724-5813
Web site: www.rootsweb.com/~mnhousto
Parent County: Fillmore

Record Type	Year Begun	Jurisdiction
Birth	1870	Clerk/District Ct.
Marriage	1854	Clerk/District Ct.
Death	1870	Clerk/District Ct.
Divorce	na	Clerk/District Ct.
Land	na	Registrar/Deeds
Probate	na	Probate Judge
Court	1856	Clerk/District Ct.

■ **Hubbard** 26 Feb. 1883
301 Court St., Park Rapids, MN 56470
Phone: (218)732-3552
Web site: www.rootsweb.com/~mnhubbar
Parent County: Cass
Comments/research tips: Attached to Wadena County prior
to organization 3 March 1887.

Record Type	Year Begun	Jurisdiction
Birth	na	County Recorder
Marriage	na	License Center
Death	na	County Recorder
Divorce	na	Clerk/District Ct.
Land	na	County Recorder
Probate	na	Clerk/District Ct.
Court	na	Clerk/District Ct.

■ **Isanti** 13 Feb. 1857
555 Eighteenth Ave. SW, Cambridge, MN 55008
Phone: (763)689-1191
Web site: www.rootsweb.com/~mnisanti/Isanti/
Parent County: Ramsey
Comments/research tips: Clerk of District Court has Burial
records from 1900–1908 and 1941–1979.

Record Type	Year Begun	Jurisdiction
Birth	1869	Clerk/District Ct.
Marriage	1871	Clerk/District Ct.
Death	1873	Clerk/District Ct.
Divorce	1872	Clerk/District Ct.
Land	na	County Recorder
Probate	1892	Clerk/District Ct.
Court	1872	Clerk/District Ct.

■ **Itasca** 27 Oct. 1849
123 Fourth St. NE, Grand Rapids, MN 55744
Phone: (218)327-2856
Web site: www.rootsweb.com/~mnitasca
Parent County: Unorganized Territories
Comments/research tips: Attached to Washington, Benton,
and Chisago Counties prior to organization 6 March 1857.
Minnesota Historical Society has Divorce and Court records
to 1950.

Record Type	Year Begun	Jurisdiction
Birth	1891	County Recorder/Registrar
Marriage	1891	County Recorder/Registrar
Death	1894	County Recorder/Registrar
Divorce	1950	Court Administrator
Land	1883	County Recorder/Registrar
Probate	1896	Court Administrator
Court	1950	Court Administrator
Burial	1900	County Recorder/Registrar
Military	1919	County Recorder/Registrar

■ **Jackson** 23 May 1857
405 Fourth St., P.O. Box 209, Jackson, MN 56143
Phone: (507)847-2580
Web site: www.rootsweb.com/~mnjackso/
Parent County: Brown

Record Type	Year Begun	Jurisdiction
Birth	1870	Court Administrator
Marriage	1868	Court Administrator
Death	1870	Court Administrator
Divorce	1870	Court Administrator

Minnesota

Land .... 1870 ....County Recorder
Probate .... 1870 ....Court Administrator
Court .... 1870 ....Court Administrator

■ Kanabec 12 Oct. 1858

18 Vine St. N., Mora, MN 55051

Phone: (320)679-6466

Web site: www.rootsweb.com/~mnkanabe/

Parent County: Pine

Comments/research tips: Attached to Pine County prior to organization 4 November 1881.

Record Type	Year Begun	Jurisdiction
Birth	1883	Clerk/District Ct.
Marriage	1882	Clerk/District Ct.
Death	1883	Clerk/District Ct.
Divorce	1882	Clerk/District Ct.
Land	na	County Recorder
Probate	1891	Clerk/District Ct.
Court	1882	Clerk/District Ct.
Burial	na	Mora City Hall

■ Kandiyohi 20 Mar. 1858

400 Benson Ave. SW, Willmar, MN 56201

Phone: (320)231-6532

Web site: www.rootsweb.com/~mnkandiy

Parent County: Meeker, Renville, Pierce, Davis, Stearns

Record Type	Year Begun	Jurisdiction
Birth	1870	Clerk/District Ct.
Marriage	1870	Clerk/District Ct.
Death	1870	Clerk/District Ct.
Divorce	1870	Clerk/District Ct.
Court	1870	Clerk/District Ct.

■ Kittson 27 Oct. 1849

410 S. Fifth St., P.O. Box 39, Hallock, MN 56728

Phone: (218)843-3632

Web site: www.rootsweb.com/~mnkittso/

Parent County: Unorganized Territory

Comments/research tips: Formerly Pembina County. Name changed to Kittson 9 March 1878. Attached to Benton prior to organization 4 March 1852. Disorganized 5 March 1853. Recreated 24 April 1862 from Benton. Attached to Benton, Morrison, Crow Wing, Douglas Becker, Clay, and Polk Counties prior to organization 6 April 1897.

Record Type	Year Begun	Jurisdiction
Probate	ca. 1880	Clerk/District Ct.
Court	ca. 1880	Clerk/District Ct.
Birth	ca. 1880	Clerk/District Ct.
Marriage	ca. 1880	Clerk/District Ct.
Death	ca. 1880	Clerk/District Ct.
Divorce	ca. 1880	Clerk/District Ct.

■ Koochiching 19 Dec. 1906

715 Fourth St., International Falls, MN 56649

Phone: (218)283-6260

Web site: www.rootsweb.com/~mnkoochi/

Parent County: Itasca

Comments/research tips: Attached to Redwood County prior to organization 7 January 1873.

Record Type	Year Begun	Jurisdiction
Birth	1907	Clerk/District Ct.
Marriage	1907	Clerk/District Ct.
Death	1907	Clerk/District Ct.
Divorce	1907	Clerk/District Ct.
Probate	1907	Clerk/District Ct.
Court	1907	Clerk/District Ct.

■ Lac Qui Parle 7 Nov. 1871

600 Sixth St., Madison, MN 56256

Phone: (320)598-3724

Web site: www.rootsweb.com/~mnlacqui/index.htm

Parent County: Redwood

Comments/research tips: Attached to Redwood County prior to organization 7 January 1873.

Record Type	Year Begun	Jurisdiction
Birth	na	County Recorder
Marriage	na	County Recorder
Death	na	County Recorder
Divorce	na	Court Administrator
Land	na	County Assessor
Probate	na	Court Administrator
Court	na	Court Administrator
Military	na	County Recorder

■ Lac Qui Parle, old 20 Feb. 1862

Parent County: Davis, Pierce

Comments/research tips: Attached to Renville County. Eliminated 3 November 1868, and absorbed by Chippewa County.

■ Lake 20 Feb. 1855

601 Third Ave., Two Harbors, MN 55616

Phone: (218)834-8347

Web site: www.rootsweb.com/~mnlake

Parent County: Itasca

Comments/research tips: Formerly Superior County. Name changed to St. Louis (old) 3 March 1855. Name changed to Lake 1 March 1856. Attached to Benton and St. Louis Counties prior to organization 27 February 1891.

Record Type	Year Begun	Jurisdiction
Birth	1898	County Registrar
Marriage	1891	County Registrar
Death	1891	County Registrar
Divorce	1892	County Registrar
Probate	na	Probate Judge
Court	1892	County Registrar
Burial	na	City Clerk

■ Lake of the Woods 28 Nov. 1922

206 SE Eighth Ave., P.O. Box 808, Baudette, MN 56623

Phone: (218)634-1902

Web site: www.rootsweb.com/~mnlakeof/

Parent County: Beltrami

Record Type	Year Begun	Jurisdiction
Birth	1923	Court Administrator
Marriage	1923	Court Administrator
Death	1923	Court Administrator
Divorce	1923	Court Administrator

Probate .... 1923 .... Court Administrator
Court .... 1923 .... Court Administrator

■ Le Sueur 5 Mar. 1853
88 S. Park Ave., Le Center, MN 56057
Phone: (507)357-2251
Web site: www.rootsweb.com/~mnlesueu/
Parent County: Dakota
Comments/research tips: Clerk of District Court has some School records from 1920–1945.

Record Type	Year Begun	Jurisdiction
Birth	1870	Clerk/District Ct.
Marriage	1854	Clerk/District Ct.
Death	1870	Clerk/District Ct.
Divorce	1880	Clerk/District Ct.
Land	1850	Registrar/Deeds
Probate	1855	Probate Judge
Court	1880	Clerk/District Ct.

■ Lincoln 4 Nov. 1873
319 N. Rebecca, Ivanhoe, MN 56142
Phone: (507)694-1360
Web site: www.rootsweb.com/~mnlincol/
Parent County: Lyon
Comments/research tips: Attached to Lyon and Redwood Counties prior to organization 9 February 1881.

Record Type	Year Begun	Jurisdiction
Birth	1879	Clerk/District Ct.
Marriage	1879	Clerk/District Ct.
Death	1880	Clerk/District Ct.
Divorce	1891	Clerk/District Ct.
Land	1873	Registrar/Deeds
Probate	1877	Probate Judge
Court	1880	Clerk/District Ct.

■ Lincoln, old 8 Oct. 1861
Parent County: Renville
Comments/research tips: Attached to McLeod County. Eliminated 3 November 1868, for Renville County.

■ Lyon 2 Nov. 1869
607 W. Main, Marshall, MN 56258
Phone: (507)537-6722
Web site: www.rootsweb.com/~mnlyon
Parent County: Redwood
Comments/research tips: Organized 12 April 1870.

Record Type	Year Begun	Jurisdiction
Birth	1874	Clerk/District Ct.
Marriage	1872	Clerk/District Ct.
Death	1874	Clerk/District Ct.
Divorce	1880	Clerk/District Ct.
Land	na	County Recorder
Probate	1880	Clerk/District Ct.
Court	1880	Clerk/District Ct.

■ Mahnomen 27 Dec. 1906
P.O. Box 379, Mahnomen, MN 56557
Phone: (218)935-2251
Web site: www.rootsweb.com/~mnmahnom/

Parent County: Norman

Record Type	Year Begun	Jurisdiction
Birth	1908	Clerk/District Ct.
Marriage	1908	Clerk/District Ct.
Death	1908	Clerk/District Ct.
Divorce	1908	Clerk/District Ct.
Court	1908	Clerk/District Ct.

■ Mankahto 27 Oct. 1849
Parent County: Unorganized Territories
Comments/research tips: Attached to Ramsey. Eliminated 1 September 1851. Lost to Cass and Pembina Counties.

■ Manomin 23 May 1857
Parent County: Ramsey
Comments/research tips: Eliminated 2 November 1869, for Anoka County.

■ Marshall 25 Feb. 1879
208 E. Colvin Ave., Warren, MN 56762
Phone: (218)745-4816
Web site: www.rootsweb.com/~mnmarsha/
Parent County: Kittson
Comments/research tips: Attached to Polk County prior to organization 11 March 1881.

Record Type	Year Begun	Jurisdiction
Birth	1882	Court Administrator
Marriage	1882	Court Administrator
Death	1882	Court Administrator
Divorce	1891	Court Administrator
Land	1883	County Recorder
Probate	1891	Court Administrator
Court	na	Court Administrator
Military	1919	County Recorder

■ Martin 23 May 1857
201 Lake Ave., Fairmont, MN 56031
Phone: (507)238-3213
Web site: www.rootsweb.com/~mnmartin
Parent County: Faribault, Brown

Record Type	Year Begun	Jurisdiction
Birth	1874	County Recorder
Marriage	1864	County Recorder
Death	1879	County Recorder
Divorce	na	Court Administrator
Land	na	County Recorder
Probate	na	Court Administrator
Court	na	Court Administrator

■ McLeod 1 Mar. 1856
830 Eleventh St., P.O. Box 127, Glencoe, MN 55336
Phone: (320)864-1216
Web site: www.rootsweb.com/~mnmcleod
Parent County: Carver, Sibley

Record Type	Year Begun	Jurisdiction
Birth	1870	County Recorder
Marriage	1865	County Recorder
Death	1870	County Recorder
Divorce	na	County Administrator

Land .... na ....County Recorder
Probate .... na ....County Administrator
Court .... na ....County Administrator
Military .... na ....Veterans Service
School Census.......... na ....County Recorder

■ Meeker 23 Feb. 1856
325 N. Sibley Ave., Litchfield, MN 55355
Phone: (320)693-5345
Web site: www.rootsweb.com/~mnmeeker
Parent County: Davis

Record Type	Year Begun	Jurisdiction
Birth	1870	Clerk/District Ct.
Marriage	1870	Clerk/District Ct.
Death	1870	Clerk/District Ct.
Divorce	1870	Clerk/District Ct.
Land	na	County Recorder
Probate	1858	Clerk/District Ct.
Court	1870	Clerk/District Ct.
Nat.	1884	Clerk/District Ct.
School	1884	Clerk/District Ct.

■ Mille Lacs 23 May 1857
635 Second St. SE, Milaca, MN 56353
Phone: (320)983-8308
Web site: www.rootsweb.com/~mnmillel
Parent County: Ramsey
Comments/research tips: Attached to Morrison County prior to organization 30 April 1860.

Record Type	Year Begun	Jurisdiction
Birth	na	County Recorder
Marriage	na	County Recorder
Death	na	County Recorder
Divorce	na	Court Administrator
Land	na	County Recorder
Probate	na	Court Administrator
Court	na	Court Administrator

■ Monongalia 8 Mar. 1861
Parent County: Davis, Pierce
Comments/research tips: Discontinued 8 November 1870 and became part of Kandyohi County.

■ Morrison 25 Feb. 1856
213 First Ave. SE, Little Falls, MN 56345
Phone: (320)632-1045
Web site: www.rootsweb.com/~mnmorris/
Parent County: Benton
Comments/research tips: County Recorder has some Cemetery records.

Record Type	Year Begun	Jurisdiction
Birth	na	County Recorder
Marriage	na	County Recorder
Death	na	County Recorder
Divorce	na	Court Administrator
Land	na	County Recorder
Probate	na	Court Administrator
Court	na	Court Administrator
Military	na	County Recorder

■ Mower 20 Feb. 1855
201 First St. NE, Austin, MN 55912
Phone: (507)437-9456
Web site: www.rootsweb.com/~mnmower/
Parent County: Rice
Comments/research tips: Organized 1 March 1856.

Record Type	Year Begun	Jurisdiction
Birth	1870	Clerk/District Ct.
Marriage	1865	Clerk/District Ct.
Death	1870	Clerk/District Ct.
Divorce	1900	Clerk/District Ct.
Land	na	County Recorder
Probate	1856	Clerk/District Ct.
Court	1900	Clerk/District Ct.

■ Murray 23 May 1857
2500 Twenty-eighth St., Slayton, MN 56172
Phone: (507)836-6148
Web site: www.rootsweb.com/~mnmurray
Parent County: Brown
Comments/research tips: Attached to Brown, Redwood, Watonwan, and Cottonwood Counties prior to organization 5 March 1879.

Record Type	Year Begun	Jurisdiction
Birth	na	Clerk/District Ct.
Marriage	na	Clerk/District Ct.
Death	na	Clerk/District Ct.
Divorce	na	Clerk/District Ct.
Land	na	County Recorder
Probate	na	Clerk/District Ct.
Court	na	Clerk/District Ct.

■ Newton 20 Feb. 1855
Parent County: Itasca
Comments/research tips: Formerly Doty County. Name changed to Newton 3 March 1855. Eliminated to St. Louis County 1 March 1856.

■ Nicollet 5 Mar. 1853
501 S. Minnesota Ave., P.O. Box 493, St. Peter, MN 56082
Phone: (507)931-6800
Web site: www.rootsweb.com/~mnnicoll
Parent County: Dakota

Record Type	Year Begun	Jurisdiction
Divorce	1853	Clerk/District Ct.
Land	na	County Recorder
Probate	1853	Clerk/District Ct.
Court	1853	Clerk/District Ct.
Birth	1870	Clerk/District Ct.
Marriage	1856	Clerk/District Ct.
Death	1870	Clerk/District Ct.

■ Nobles 23 May 1857
315 Tenth St., Worthington, MN 56187
Phone: (507)372-8263
Web site: www.rootsweb.com/~mnnobles
Parent County: Brown
Comments/research tips: Attached to Brown and Martin Counties prior to organization 19 October 1870.

Record Type	Year Begun	Jurisdiction
Birth	1872	County Recorder
Marriage	1872	County Recorder
Death	1872	County Recorder
Divorce	1882	Court Administrator
Land	na	County Recorder
Probate	na	Court Administrator
Court	1874	Court Administrator

■ Norman 8 Nov. 1881

16 E. Third Ave., Ada, MN 56510
Phone: (218)784-7131
Web site: www.rootsweb.com/~mnnorman/
Parent County: Polk
Comments/research tips: Clerk of District Court has some Divorce and Court records.

Record Type	Year Begun	Jurisdiction
Birth	1881	Clerk/District Ct.
Marriage	1882	Clerk/District Ct.
Death	1881	Clerk/District Ct.
Probate	na	Probate Judge

■ Olmsted 20 Feb. 1855

151 SE Fourth St., Rochester, MN 55904
Phone: (507)287-1444
Web site: www.rootsweb.com/~mnolmste
Parent County: Fillmore, Wabasha, Rice
Comments/research tips: Clerk of District Court has incomplete Birth and Death records from 1871.

Record Type	Year Begun	Jurisdiction
Marriage	1855	Clerk/District Ct.
Divorce	1860	Clerk/District Ct.
Probate	na	County Court
Court	1858	Clerk/District Ct.
Burial	na	Coroner and Department of Health

■ Otter Tail 18 Mar. 1858

121 W. Junis Ave., Fergus Falls, MN 56537
Phone: (218)739-2271
Web site: http://resources.rootsweb.com/USA/MN/ottertail
Parent County: Pembina, Cass
Comments/research tips: Attached to Stearns, Crow Wing, and Douglas Counties prior to organization 28 February 1870.

Record Type	Year Begun	Jurisdiction
Birth	1870	Clerk/District Ct.
Marriage	1869	Clerk/District Ct.
Death	1870	Clerk/District Ct.
Divorce	1897	Clerk/District Ct.
Probate	1872	Clerk/District Ct.
Court	1872	Clerk/District Ct.

■ Pembina 27 Oct. 1849

Parent County: Unorganized Territory
Comments/research tips: (See Kittson) Name changed to Kittson 9 March 1878.

■ Pennington 23 Nov. 1910

101 Main Ave., P.O. Box 616, Thief River Falls, MN 56701
Phone: (218)681-2522

Web site: www.rootsweb.com/~mnpennin/mnpennin.htm
Parent County: Red Lake

Record Type	Year Begun	Jurisdiction
Birth	1910	County Recorder
Marriage	1910	County Recorder
Death	1910	County Recorder
Divorce	na	Court Administrator
Land	1910	County Recorder
Probate	na	Court Administrator
Court	na	Court Administrator
Burial	1910	County Recorder
Military	1910	County Recorder

■ Pierce 5 Mar. 1853

Parent County: Dakota
Comments/research tips: Eliminated 20 February 1862, for Big Stone, Chippewa, Lac Qui Parle, Pope, Stevens, and Traverse Counties.

■ Pine 1 Mar. 1856

315 Sixth St., Pine City, MN 55063
Phone: (320)629-5662
Web site: www.rootsweb.com/~mnpine
Parent County: Chisago, Ramsey
Comments/research tips: Organized 1 April 1857.

Record Type	Year Begun	Jurisdiction
Birth	1874	Clerk/District Ct.
Marriage	1871	Clerk/District Ct.
Death	1879	Clerk/District Ct.
Divorce	1871	Clerk/District Ct.
Land	na	Registrar/Deeds
Probate	na	Probate Judge
Court	1871	Clerk/District Ct.

■ Pipestone 23 May 1857

416 S. Hiawatha, Pipestone, MN 56164
Phone: (507)825-6755
Web site: www.rootsweb.com/~mnpipest
Parent County: Brown
Comments/research tips: Attached to Big Sioux, Brown, Redwood, Watonwan, Rock, and Cottonwood Counties prior to organization 27 January 1879.

Record Type	Year Begun	Jurisdiction
Birth	1877	Clerk/District Ct.
Marriage	1877	Clerk/District Ct.
Death	1877	Clerk/District Ct.
Divorce	1877	Clerk/District Ct.
Land	na	County Recorder
Probate	1877	Clerk/District Ct.
Court	1877	Clerk/District Ct.

■ Polk 20 July 1858

612 N. Broadway, Crookston, MN 56716
Phone: (218)281-3464
Web site: www.rootsweb.com/~mnpolk/
Parent County: Pembina
Comments/research tips: Attached to Crow Wing, Douglas, Becker, and Clay Counties prior to organization 27 February 1879.

Record Type	Year Begun	Jurisdiction
Birth	1875	Court Administrator
Marriage	1875	Court Administrator
Death	1875	Court Administrator
Land	na	County Recorder
Probate	1875	Court Administrator
Court	1875	Court Administrator

■ Pope 20 Feb. 1862

130 Minnesota Ave. E., Glenwood, MN 56334
Phone: (320)634-5723
Web site: www.rootsweb.com/~mnpope
Parent County: Pierce, Cass, Unorganized Territory
Comments/research tips: Organized 28 February 1866.

Record Type	Year Begun	Jurisdiction
Birth	1870	Clerk/District Ct.
Marriage	1870	Clerk/District Ct.
Death	1870	Clerk/District Ct.
Divorce	1880	Clerk/District Ct.
Probate	1867	Clerk/District Ct.
Court	1880	Clerk/District Ct.

■ Ramsey 27 Oct. 1849

15 Kellogg Blvd. W., St. Paul, MN 55102
Phone: (651)266-4444
Web site: www.mtn.org/quack/local/ramsey/ramsey.htm
Parent County: St. Croix
Comments/research tips: The Historical Society has Court records from 1858–1899.

Record Type	Year Begun	Jurisdiction
Birth	1870	Clerk/District Ct.
Marriage	1850	Clerk/District Ct.
Death	1870	Clerk/District Ct.
Divorce	1900	Clerk/District Ct.
Land	na	Historical Society
Probate	1849	Clerk/District Ct.
Court	1900	Clerk/District Ct.

■ Red Lake 24 Dec. 1896

124 Langevin Ave., P.O. Box 3, Red Lake Falls, MN 56750
Phone: (218)253-2997
Web site: www.rootsweb.com/~mnredlak/mnredlak.htm
Parent County: Polk
Comments/research tips: Organized 6 April 1897. Court Administrator has School records from 1900–1955.

Record Type	Year Begun	Jurisdiction
Birth	1897	Court Administrator
Marriage	1897	Court Administrator
Death	1897	Court Administrator
Divorce	1897	Court Administrator
Land	na	County Recorder
Probate	1897	Court Administrator
Court	1897	Court Administrator

■ Redwood 4 Nov. 1862

P.O. Box 130, Redwood Falls, MN 56283
Phone: (507)637-4032
Web site: www.rootsweb.com/~mnredwoo/rwindex.htm
Parent County: Brown

Comments/research tips: Attached to Brown County prior to organization 23 February 1865.

Record Type	Year Begun	Jurisdiction
Birth	1865	Court Administrator
Marriage	1865	Court Administrator
Death	1865	Court Administrator
Divorce	1871	Court Administrator
Land	na	County Recorder
Probate	1877	Court Administrator
Court	1867	Court Administrator

■ Renville 20 Feb. 1855

500 DePue Ave. E., Olivia, MN 56277
Phone: (320)523-3669
Web site: http://resources.rootsweb.com/USA/MN/renville
Parent County: Nicollet, Pierce, Sibley
Comments/research tips: Attached to Nicollet County prior to organization 31 July 1866.

Record Type	Year Begun	Jurisdiction
Birth	1870	Clerk/District Ct.
Marriage	1870	Clerk/District Ct.
Death	1870	Clerk/District Ct.
Divorce	na	Clerk/District Ct.
Land	na	County Recorder
Probate	na	Clerk/District Ct.
Court	na	Clerk/District Ct.

■ Rice 5 Mar. 1853

320 NW Third St., Faribault, MN 55021
Phone: (507)332-6114
Web site: www.rootsweb.com/~mnrice
Parent County: Dakota, Wabasha
Comments/research tips: Attached to Dakota County prior to organization 9 October 1855.

Record Type	Year Begun	Jurisdiction
Birth	1870	Clerk/District Ct.
Marriage	1856	Clerk/District Ct.
Death	1870	Clerk/District Ct.
Divorce	1870	Clerk/District Ct.
Land	na	County Recorder
Probate	1870	Clerk/District Ct.
Court	1870	Clerk/District Ct.
Burial	na	Clerk/District Ct.

■ Rock 23 May 1857

204 E. Brown, P.O. Box 509, Luverne, MN 56156
Phone: (507)283-5060
Web site: www.rootsweb.com/~mnrock
Parent County: Brown
Comments/research tips: Attached to Brown, Martin and Nobles Counties prior to organization 7 February 1874.

Record Type	Year Begun	Jurisdiction
Birth	1875	County Auditor/Treasurer
Marriage	1875	County Auditor/Treasurer
Death	1875	County Auditor/Treasurer
Divorce	1872	Clerk/District Ct.
Court	1872	Clerk/District Ct.

■ Roseau 28 Feb. 1894

606 Fifth Ave. SW Room 20, Roseau, MN 56751
Phone: (218)463-2541

Web site: www.rootsweb.com/~mnroseau/
Parent County: Kittson, Beltrami
Comments/research tips: Organized 6 April 1896.

Record Type	Year Begun	Jurisdiction
Birth	1895	Clerk/District Ct.
Marriage	1895	Clerk/District Ct.
Death	1895	Clerk/District Ct.
Divorce	1895	Clerk/District Ct.
Land	na	Registrar/Deeds
Probate	1895	Clerk/District Ct.
Court	1895	Clerk/District Ct.

■ **Scott** 5 Mar. 1853
428 S. Holmes St., Shakopee, MN 55379
Phone: (952)496-8150
Web site: www.rootsweb.com/~mnscott
Parent County: Dakota

Record Type	Year Begun	Jurisdiction
Birth	1871	County Recorder
Marriage	1856	County Recorder
Death	1871	County Recorder
Court	1880	Clerk/Courts
Military	1950	County Recorder
Divorce	ca. 1850	Clerk/Courts
Land	ca. 1850	County Recorder
Probate	ca. 1850	Clerk/Courts

■ **Sherburne** 25 Feb. 1856
13880 Hwy. 10, Elk River, MN 55330
Phone: (763)241-2915
Web site: www.rootsweb.com/~mnsherbu
Parent County: Benton
Comments/research tips: Attached to Benton County prior to organization 6 March 1862.

Record Type	Year Begun	Jurisdiction
Birth	1870	Court Administrator
Marriage	1858	Court Administrator
Death	1870	Court Administrator
Divorce	1884	Court Administrator
Land	na	County Recorder
Probate	1893	Court Administrator
Court	1877	Court Administrator

■ **Sibley** 5 Mar. 1853
400 Court St., P.O. Box 44, Gaylord, MN 55334
Phone: (507)237-4080
Web site: www.rootsweb.com/~mnsibley
Parent County: Dakota
Comments/research tips: Attached to Hennepin County prior to organization 10 October 1854.

Record Type	Year Begun	Jurisdiction
Birth	1860	Court Administrator
Marriage	1856	Court Administrator
Death	1860	Court Administrator
Divorce	1860	Court Administrator
Land	1855	County Recorder
Probate	1870	Court Administrator
Court	1870	Court Administrator

■ **St. Croix** 3 Aug. 1840
Parent County: Wisconsin Territories
Comments/research tips: Eliminated to Benton, Ramsey, and Washington Counties 27 October 1849.

■ **St. Louis** 1 Mar. 1856
100 N. Fifth Ave. W., Duluth, MN 55802
Phone: (218)726-2559
Web site: www.rootsweb.com/~mnstloui
Parent County: Itasca, Newton
Comments/research tips: Attached to Benton County prior to organization 23 May 1857.

Record Type	Year Begun	Jurisdiction
Birth	1870	Clerk/District Ct.
Marriage	1870	Clerk/District Ct.
Death	1870	Clerk/District Ct.
Divorce	1859	Clerk/District Ct.
Land	1859	Clerk/District Ct.
Probate	na	County Court
Court	1859	Clerk/District Ct.
Burial Permits	1938	Clerk/District Ct.

■ **St. Louis, old** 20 Feb. 1855
Parent County: Itasca
Comments/research tips: Formerly Superior County. Name changed to St. Louis (old) 3 March 1855. Abolished 1 March 1856, and became part of Lake County.

■ **Stearns** 20 Feb. 1855
705 Courthouse Sq., St. Cloud, MN 56303
Phone: (320)656-3855
Web site: www.rootsweb.com/~mnstearn
Parent County: Cass, Nicollet, Pierce, Sibley

Record Type	Year Begun	Jurisdiction
Birth	na	License Center
Marriage	na	License Center
Death	na	License Center
Divorce	na	Court Administrator
Land	na	County Recorder
Probate	na	Court Administrator
Court	na	Court Administrator

■ **Steele** 20 Feb. 1855
111 E. Main St., Owatonna, MN 55060
Phone: (507)444-7450
Web site: www.rootsweb.com/~mnsteele
Parent County: Rice, Blue Earth, Le Sueur
Comments/research tips: Organized 29 February 1856.

Record Type	Year Begun	Jurisdiction
Birth	1870	Clerk/District Ct.
Marriage	1855	Clerk/District Ct.
Death	1870	Clerk/District Ct.
Divorce	1858	Clerk/District Ct.
Land	1858	County Recorder
Probate	1858	Clerk/District Ct.
Court	1858	Clerk/District Ct.

■ **Stevens** 20 Feb. 1862
400 Colorado Ave., P.O. Box 530, Morris, MN 56267
Phone: (320)589-7414

Web site: www.rootsweb.com/~mnsteven/newindex.htm
Parent County: Pierce, Unorganized Territory
Comments/research tips: Attached to Stearns, Douglas, and Pope Counties prior to organization 31 December 1871.

Record Type	Year Begun	Jurisdiction
Birth	1872	Clerk/District Ct.
Marriage	1869	Clerk/District Ct.
Death	1872	Clerk/District Ct.
Divorce	1873	Clerk/District Ct.
Land	1871	County Recorder
Probate	1901	Clerk/District Ct.
Court	1873	Clerk/District Ct.

■ Superior 20 Feb. 1855
Parent County: Itasca
Comments/research tips: (See Lake) Name changed to Saint Louis (old) 3 March 1855. Name changed to Lake 1 March 1856.

■ Swift 8 Nov. 1870
301 Fourteenth St. N., P.O. Box 50, Benson, MN 56215
Phone: (320)843-3377
Web site: www.rootsweb.com/~mnswift/
Parent County: Chippewa
Comments/research tips: Attached to Pope and Chippewa Counties prior to organization 6 April 1897.

Record Type	Year Begun	Jurisdiction
Birth	1870	County Treasurer
Marriage	1871	County Treasurer
Death	1872	County Treasurer
Divorce	na	Clerk/Courts
Land	na	County Recorder
Probate	na	Clerk/Courts
Court	na	Clerk/Courts

■ Todd 20 Feb. 1855
215 First Ave. S., Long Prairie, MN 56347
Phone: (320)732-4428
Web site: www.rootsweb.com/~mntodd
Parent County: Cass
Comments/research tips: Attached to Stearns and Morrison Counties prior to organization 21 February 1873.

Record Type	Year Begun	Jurisdiction
School Census	1914	County Recorder
Birth	1870	County Recorder
Marriage	1867	County Recorder
Death	1870	County Recorder
Divorce	1880	Clerk/District Ct.
Land	na	County Recorder
Probate	na	Clerk/District Ct.
Court	1874	Clerk/District Ct.

■ Toombs 18 Mar. 1858
Parent County: Pembina
Comments/research tips: (See Wilkin) Name changed to Andy Johnson 8 March 1862. Name changed to Wilkin 6 March 1868.

■ Traverse 20 Feb. 1862
702 Second Ave. N., P.O. Box 487, Wheaton, MN 56296
Phone: (320)563-4266

Web site: www.rootsweb.com/~mntraver/index.html
Parent County: Pierce, Unorganized Territory
Comments/research tips: Attached to Stearns, Douglas, Pope, and Stevens Counties prior to organization 14 February 1881.

Record Type	Year Begun	Jurisdiction
Birth	1881	Clerk/District Ct.
Marriage	1881	Clerk/District Ct.
Death	1881	Clerk/District Ct.
Divorce	1881	Clerk/District Ct.
Land	1881	Clerk/District Ct.
Probate	1881	Clerk/District Ct.
Court	1881	Clerk/District Ct.

■ Wabasha 27 Oct. 1849
625 Jefferson Ave., Wabasha, MN 55981
Phone: (651)565-3018
Web site: www.rootsweb.com/~mnwabash
Parent County: Unorganized Territory
Comments/research tips: Attached to Washington County prior to organization 5 March 1853.

Record Type	Year Begun	Jurisdiction
Birth	1870	County Recorder
Marriage	1865	County Recorder
Death	1870	County Recorder
Divorce	1858	Court Administrator
Land	1855	County Recorder
Probate	1858	Court Administrator
Court	1858	Court Administrator
Military	na	Veteran Service Office

■ Wadena 11 June 1858
415 S. Jefferson, P.O. Box 415, Wadena, MN 56482
Phone: (218)631-7622
Web site: www.rootsewb.com/~mnwadena
Parent County: Cass, Todd
Comments/research tips: Attached to Crow Wing and Morrison Counties prior to organization 17 February 1881.

Record Type	Year Begun	Jurisdiction
Birth	1873	Clerk/District Ct.
Marriage	1873	Clerk/District Ct.
Death	1873	Clerk/District Ct.
Divorce	1881	Clerk/District Ct.
Court	1881	Clerk/District Ct.

■ Wahnata 27 Oct. 1849
Parent County: Unorganized Territory
Comments/research tips: Eliminated 1 September 1851 to Cass, Dakota, and Pembina Counties.

■ Waseca 27 Feb. 1857
307 N. State St., Waseca, MN 56093
Phone: (507)835-0670
Web site: www.rootsweb.com/~mnwaseca/
Parent County: Steele

Record Type	Year Begun	Jurisdiction
Birth	1870	Clerk/District Ct.
Marriage	1858	Clerk/District Ct.
Death	1870	Clerk/District Ct.

Minnesota

Divorce .... 1858 ....Clerk/District Ct.
Probate .... 1870 ....Clerk/District Ct.
Court .... 1870 ....Clerk/District Ct.

■ Washington 27 Oct. 1849
14949 Sixty-second St. N., Stillwater, MN 55082
Phone: (651)430-6755
Web site: www.rootsweb.com/~mnwashin
Parent County: St. Croix

Record Type	Year Begun	Jurisdiction
Birth	1870	Clerk/District Ct.
Marriage	1845	Clerk/District Ct.
Death	1870	Clerk/District Ct.
Divorce	1847	Clerk/District Ct.
Probate	1850	Clerk/District Ct.
Court	1847	Clerk/District Ct.

■ Watonwan 6 Nov. 1860
710 Second Ave. S., P.O. Box 518, St. James, MN 56081
Phone: (507)375-1216
Web site: www.rootsweb.com/~mnwatanw
Parent County: Brown
Comments/research tips: Attached to Brown and Blue Earth Counties to organization 15 June 1871.

Record Type	Year Begun	Jurisdiction
Birth	1863	Clerk/District Ct.
Marriage	1863	Clerk/District Ct.
Death	1863	Clerk/District Ct.
Divorce	1865	Clerk/District Ct.
Land	na	Registrar/Deeds
Probate	na	Probate Judge
Court	1865	Clerk/District Ct.

■ Wilkin 18 Mar. 1858
300 S. Fifth St., Breckenridge, MN 56520
Phone: (218)643-5112
Web site: www.rootsweb.com/~mnwilkin
Parent County: Cass, Pembina
Comments/research tips: Formerly Toombs and Andy Johnson Counties. Name changed to Andy Johnson 8 March 1862. Name changed to Wilkin 6 March 1868. Attached to Stearns, Crow Wing, Douglas, and Otter Tail Counties prior to organization 4 March 1872.

Record Type	Year Begun	Jurisdiction
Birth	1874	Clerk/District Ct.
Marriage	1890	Clerk/District Ct.
Death	1875	Clerk/District Ct.

Divorce .... 1890 ....Clerk/District Ct.
Probate .... na ....Probate Judge
Court .... 1858 ....Clerk/District Ct.

■ Winona 4 Apr. 1854
171 W. Third St., Winona, MN 55987
Phone: (507)457-6340
Web site: www.rootsweb.com/~mnwinona/
Parent County: Fillmore, Wabasha
Comments/research tips: Clerk of District Court has School records from 1909–1939.

Record Type	Year Begun	Jurisdiction
Birth	1870	Clerk/District Ct.
Marriage	1854	Clerk/District Ct.
Death	1870	Clerk/District Ct.
Divorce	1854	Clerk/District Ct.
Probate	1871	Clerk/District Ct.
Court	1854	Clerk/District Ct.

■ Wright 20 Feb. 1855
10 Second St. NW, Buffalo, MN 55313
Phone: (763)682-7357
Web site: www.rootsweb.com/~mnwright
Parent County: Cass, Sibley

Record Type	Year Begun	Jurisdiction
Birth	1871	License Bureau
Marriage	1866	License Bureau
Death	1871	License Bureau
Divorce	1870	Court Administrator
Land	na	Registrar/Deeds
Probate	na	Court Administrator
Court	1870	Court Administrator

■ Yellow Medicine 7 Nov. 1871
415 Ninth Ave., Granite Falls, MN 56241
Phone: (320)564-2529
Web site: www.rootsweb.com/~mnyellow/
Parent County: Redwood
Comments/research tips: Organized 25 February 1874.

Record Type	Year Begun	Jurisdiction
Birth	1872	Clerk/District Ct.
Marriage	1872	Clerk/District Ct.
Death	na	Clerk/District Ct.
Divorce	na	Clerk/District Ct.
Land	na	County Recorder
Probate	na	Clerk/District Ct.
Court	na	Clerk/District Ct.
Nat.	1872	Clerk/District Ct.

Mississippi

By Emily Anne Croom

HISTORICAL OVERVIEW

For more than two centuries, Spain, France, and Britain vied for a foothold in Mississippi because control of the Mississippi River valley meant dominance in much of North America. Although Spaniards explored Mississippi in 1540, France founded the first European settlement in 1699 near present-day Biloxi. At the end of the Seven Years War (1763), France ceded its territory east of the Mississippi River to Britain, which controlled it for about twenty years. Spain occupied the coastal area in the last years of the American Revolution. After that war, the 1783 Treaty of Paris gave to the new United States the British territory north of the thirty-first parallel.

Though largely Indian lands, much of present Mississippi and Alabama became Mississippi Territory in 1798. In 1802 Georgia gave up her claim to the northernmost Mississippi-Alabama land along the Tennessee boundary, and the War of 1812 brought the coastal area under U.S. control. From all directions, by road, river, and sea, land-hungry settlers flocked to the fertile coastal plains, and Mississippi became the twentieth state in 1817. Forced Indian removal in the early 1830s opened the northern portion of the state to white settlement. Early residents came mostly, but not exclusively, from older Southern states.

Along with river commerce, cotton agriculture on farms and plantations—worked largely with slave labor—dominated Mississippi's pre–Civil War economy. By 1860 the state's population was just over 55 percent slaves; of the free population, 1 percent were foreign-born and less than one-tenth of 1 percent were free blacks.

In January 1861, Mississippi became the second state to secede. The state experienced numerous Civil War engagements, including the year-long siege of strategic

MISSISSIPPI AT A GLANCE

Motto: By Valor and Arms

Population: 2.85 million

Prevalent Religions: Christianity, particularly Southern Baptist, Pentecostal, Methodist, Lutheran, and Roman Catholic

Major Industries: Cotton, poultry, cattle, catfish, gaming, soybeans, dairy products, rice, gaming, clothing, furniture, lumber, food processing, electrical machinery

Ethnic Makeup (in percent): Caucasian 61%, African American 36%, Hispanic 1.4%, Asian 0.4%, Native American 0.7%

Famous Mississippians: Bo Diddley, William Faulkner, Richard Ford, John Grisham, Jim Henson, Faith Hill, James Earl Jones, B.B. King, Elvis Presley, Eudora Welty, Tennessee Williams, Oprah Winfrey

Above: Monument in the Vicksburg National Military Park

Courtesy Vicksburg Convention/Visitors Bureau

CRITTENDEN
ST. FRANCIS
Memphis
LAUDERDALE
PRAIRIE
DE SOTO
BENTON
ALCORN
LEE
ARKANSAS
MARSHALL
TIPPAH
TISHOMINGO
COLBERT
LONOKE
MONROE
TATE
PRENTISS
TUNICA
PHILLIPS
UNION
FRANKLIN
JEFFERSON
ARKANSAS
PANOLA
LAFAYETTE
PONTOTOC
LEE
ITAWAMBA
LINCOLN
COAHOMA
QUITMAN
MARION
DESHA
YALOBUSHA
CALHOUN
CHICKASAW
MONROE
CLEVELAND
TALLAHATCHIE
MONROE
LAMAR
FAYETTE
BOLIVAR
GRENADA
CLAY
DREW
LEFLORE
WEBSTER
SUNFLOWER
MONTGOMERY
OKTIBBEHA
LOWNDES
BRADLEY
CARROLL
CHOCTAW
PICKENS
CHICOT
WASHINGTON
ASHLEY
HUMPHREYS
HOLMES
ATTALA
Tuscaloosa
WINSTON
NOXUBEE
SHARKEY
MISSISSIPPI
GREENE
MOREHOUSE
WEST
CARROLL
YAZOO
LEAKE
NESHOBA
KEMPER
HALE
UNION
EAST
CARROLL
ISSAQUENA
MADISON
OUACHITA
SUMTER
RICHLAND
WARREN
MADISON
SCOTT
NEWTON
LAUDERDALE
HINDS
Jackson ✪
RANKIN
MARENGO
CALDWELL
FRANKLIN
TENSAS
CLAIBORNE
SMITH
JASPER
CLARKE
CHOCTAW
CATAHOULA
COPIAH
SIMPSON
CLARKE
LA SALLE
JEFFERSON
COVINGTON
JONES
WAYNE
ALABAMA
CONCORDIA
ADAMS
FRANKLIN
LINCOLN
JEFFERSON
DAVIS
WASHINGTON
LAWRENCE
WILKINSON
AMITE
PIKE
MARION
LAMAR
FORREST
PERRY
GREENE
WALTHALL
WEST
FELICIANA
EAST
FELICIANA
ST.
HELENA
WASHINGTON
MOBILE
LOUISIANA
STONE
GEORGE
POINTE
COUPEE
TANGIPAHOA
PEARL RIVER
Mobile
BALDWIN
ST. LANDRY
EAST
BATON
ROUGE
LIVINGSTON
ST. TAMMANY
HARRISON
JACKSON
WEST
BATON
ROUGE
✪**Baton Rouge**
ST. TAMMANY
HANCOCK
ST. MARTIN
IBERVILLE
ASCENSION
ST. JOHN
THE BAPTIST
LAFAYETTE
ST. JAMES
ORLEANS
IBERIA
ASSUMPTION
Kenner Metairie

Mississippi

Vicksburg that ended in July 1863 with the Union controlling the Mississippi River corridor. Mississippi was readmitted to the Union in 1870. In this predominantly agricultural state, sharecropping replaced slavery and included numerous poor white farmers. The state remained impoverished long after Reconstruction.

During the twentieth century manufacturing grew, especially in food processing, textile, timber, and petroleum industries. In 1900, the state's urban population was 8 percent of the total; by 2000, it was still the minority at 49 percent.

RECORD HIGHLIGHTS

The Mississippi Department of Health maintains statewide birth and death records from November 1912. Statewide marriage records and an index to divorces date from 1926, except for the period of 1938–1941, when only the county circuit courts kept marriage records. In the counties, check circuit and chancery courts for earlier marriage records. The state legislature had jurisdiction over early divorce cases; check county chancery courts for divorces after the mid-nineteenth century. Pre-1955 adoption records are open; check court records in the county where the adopting parents lived.

More than a third of Mississippi's eighty-two counties have experienced record losses due to storms or fires, very few of which occurred during the Civil War. Since courthouse disasters rarely destroy everything, check for surviving records and those of parent and neighboring counties. Also consult records created in the family and in colonial, territorial, local, state, and federal jurisdictions. Mississippi is a federal land state, with land patents searchable at <www.glorecords.blm.gov/>.

Mississippi began granting Confederate pensions in 1888 to indigent veterans or their widows. The state archives Web site, <http://mdah.state.ms.us/arlib/faqs.html #civilwar>, contains information on requesting copies.

Other Mississippi-specific records of genealogical use include these:

- Natchez Trace Papers, primarily for early Mississippi, Louisiana, and Arkansas, at the University of Texas, Center for American History, Austin.
- *Territorial Papers of the United States* (includes some early censuses) and *Territorial Papers of the U.S. Senate* for Mississippi Territory.
- Colonial and territorial censuses, various years; see PERSI for those published in periodicals.
- State censuses, various counties, various years (1822–1825, 1837, 1841, 1845, 1853, 1866); see FHL microfilms 899868-70 for censuses between 1792 and 1866; some are statistical only. Some state censuses of the 1820s contain statistics on births and deaths among slaves and white family members in reporting households.

RESEARCH TIPS

for more info

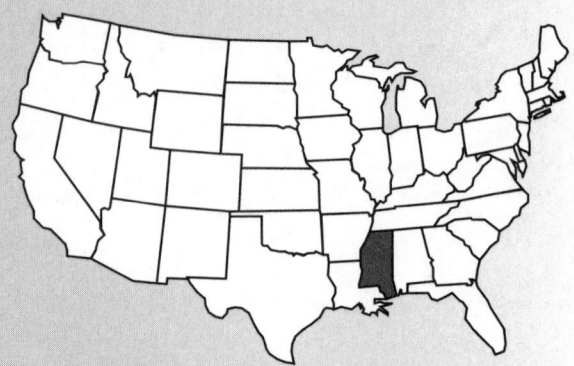

- Ancestors reporting their birthplace as Florida or West Florida before about 1813 could have been born in what is now Mississippi. Someone reportedly born in Mississippi before 1817 may have been born in what is now Alabama.
- Mississippi's federal censuses date from 1820, but investigate surviving fragments, state or territorial censuses, and county tax lists for evidence of family presence in earlier years or when schedules are missing.
- The Mississippi Department of Archives and History <www.mdah.state.ms.us/>, in its new facility, is the state's major genealogical research site.
- The University of Southern Mississippi, Hattiesburg, has a sizeable genealogy collection, a large archive of family and historical manuscripts, and a large oral history collection. The University of Mississippi holds special collections dealing with all periods of state history.
- www.segenealogy.com

Census Records
- Federal Census: 1820, 1830, 1840, 1850, 1860, 1870, 1880, 1900, 1910, 1920, 1930
- Federal Census Soundex: 1880, 1900, 1910, 1920, 1930
- Federal Mortality Schedules: 1850, 1860, 1870, 1880
- Federal Slave Schedules: 1850, 1860 (schedules name slaveholders but rarely name slaves.)
- Special Census of Civil War Union Veterans and Windows: 1890
- State Census: 1822–1825, 1837, 1841, 1845, 1853, 1866
- Territorial Census: 1805, 1808, 1810, 1813, 1816

- Records of ante-bellum plantations, on microfilm at the University of Mississippi and the University of Southern Mississippi.
- Records of the three Mississippi branches of the Freedman's Savings and Trust Company, 1865–1874; see FHL microfilm 928584.
- Indentures, marriages, and labor contracts in the records of the Freedmen's Bureau (FHL microfilm, beginning with film 491557 and film 1616481).
- Enumerations of Confederate soldiers and widows, 1907, 1925–1933.
- School censuses for the late-nineteenth and early-twentieth centuries, at the state archives, various counties, various years.
- Armstrong Roll of 1831, enumerating Choctaw Indians.

STATE RESOURCES

■ ARCHIVES, LIBRARIES, AND SOCIETIES

Aberdeen, Evans Memorial Library
105 North Long St., Aberdeen, MS 39730
Tel: (601) 369-4601
Fax: (601) 372-2959

Alcorn County Genealogical Society
P.O. Box 1808, Corinth, MS 38835-1808
Web site: <www.rootsweb.com/~msacgs/index.html>

Attala County Library
328 Goodman St., Kosciusko, MS 39090

Batesville, Historical and Genealogical Society of Panola County
105 Church St., Batesville, MS 38606

Batesville Public Library
106 College St., Batesville, MS 38606

Biloxi, Mississippi Coast Genealogical and Historical Society
P.O. Box 513, Biloxi, MS 39530

Biloxi Public Library
P.O. Box 467, Biloxi, MS 39533

Bolivar County Historical Society
1615 Terrace Rd., Cleveland, MS 38732

J.B. Cain Archives of Mississippi Methodism
Millsaps-Wilson Library, Millsaps College, 1701 N. State St., Jackson, MS 39210
Tel: (601) 974-1073
Fax: (601) 974-1082

Chickasaw County Historical and Genealogical Society
P.O. Box 42, Houston, MS 38851
Web site: <www.rootsweb.com/~mschchgs/>

Claiborne-Jefferson Genealogical Society
P.O. Box 1017, Port Gibson, MS 39150

Clarksdale, Carnegie Public Library
114 Delta Ave., P.O. Box 280, Clarksdale, MS 38614
Tel: (601) 624-4461
Fax: (601) 627-4344

Columbus and Lowndes County Historical Society
916 College St., Columbus, MS 39701

Columbus Public Library
314 N. Seventh St., Columbus, MS 39701

Corinth, Northeast Regional Library
1023 Fillmore, Corinth, MS 38834

Family Research Association of Mississippi
P.O. Box 13334, Jackson, MS 39236-3334
Tel: (601) 372-2959

Genealogical Society of Desoto County
P.O. Box 607, Hernando, MS 38632-0632
Web site: <www.rootsweb.com/~msdesoto/gsdcm.htm>

Greenville Public Library
341 Main St., Greenville, MS 38701

Greenwood-Leflore Public Library
408 W. Washington, Greenwood, MS 38930

Gulf Port-Harrison Co. Public Library
Box 4018, Fourteenth St. & Twenty-first Ave., Gulf Port, MS 39501

Gulf Port, L.W. Anderson Genealogical Library
P.O. Box 1647, Gulf Port, MS 39502

Hancock County Historical Society
113 Citizen St., P.O. Box 1340, Bay Saint Louis, MS 39520

Hattiesburg Area Historical Society
127 W Front St., Hattiesburg, MS 39401-3461

Hattiesburg, South Mississippi Genealogical Society
Box 15271, Hattiesburg, MS 39404-5271
Web site:

Homichitto Valley Historical Society
P.O. Box 337, Crosby, MS 39633

Houston, West Chickasaw County Genealogical and Historical Society
P.O. Box 42, Houston, MS 38851

Itawamba County Historical Society
P.O. Box 7G, Mantachie, MS 38855
Web site: <www.rootsweb.com/~msichs/>

Jackson County Genealogical Society
P.O. Box 994, Pascagoula, MS 39567

Jackson-George Regional Library System, Pascagoula City Library
P.O. Box 937, 3214, Pascagoula St., Pascagoula, MS 39567

Jefferson County Library
3033 High Ridge Blvd., High Ridge, MS 63049
Tel: (636) 677-8186

Jones County Genealogical and Historical Organization
P.O. Box 2644, Laurel, MS 39442-2644

Lafayette County-Oxford Public Library
401 Bramlett Blvd., Oxford, MS 38655

Laurel-Jones County Library
530 Commerce St., Laurel, MS 39440
Tel: (601) 428-4313
Web site: <www.laurel.lib.ms.us>

Marion County Historical Society
John Ford Home, Sandy Hook Community, P.O. Box 430, Columbia, MS 39429

Marks-Quitman County Library
315 E. Main, Marks, MS 38646

Marshall County Historical Society
220 E. College Ave., P.O. Box 806, Holly Springs, MS 38635

Meridian Public Library
2517 Seventh St., Meridian, MS 30301

Mississippi Archives and Library, William F. Winters Archives and History Building
200 North St., P.O. Box 571, Jackson, MS 39205-0571
Tel: (610) 576-6876
Web site: <www.mdah.state.ms.us/arlib/arlib_index.html>

Mississippi Baptist Historical Commission
Mississippi College Library, P.O. Box 51, Clinton, MS 39060
Tel: (601) 924-3434
Fax: (601) 924-3435

Mississippi Department of Archives and History
P.O. Box 571, Jackson, MS 39205-0571
Tel: (601) 576-6850
Web site: <www.mdah.state.ms.us/admin/contact.html>

Mississippi Genealogical Society
P.O. Box 5301, Jackson, MS 39216

Mississippi

Mississippi Historical Society
P.O. Box 571, Jackson, MS
39205-0571
Web site: <www.mdah.state.ms
.us/admin/mhistsoc.html>

**Mississippi State Department
of Health**
2423 N. State St., Jackson, MS
39216
Tel: (601) 960-7981
Web site: <www.msdh.state.ms
.us>

**Mississippi State
University-Mitchel Memorial,
Special Collections-
Genealogical Library**
P.O. Box 5408, Mississippi State,
MS 39762
Tel: (601) 325-7679
Fax: (601) 325-3560
Web site: <www.lib.usm.edu/~ar
chives>

Natchez Historical Society
307 S. Wall St., P.O. Box 49,
Natchez, MS 39120

**National Archives-Southeast
Region (Atlanta)**
1557 St. Joseph Ave., East Point,
Georgia 30344-2593
Tel: (404) 763-7477
Fax: (404) 763-7033
Web site: <www.archives.gov/fa
cilities/ga/atlanta.html>

Neshoba Ancestral Group
Route 1, Box 284.D, Philadel-
phia, Mississippi 39350
Tel: (601) 656-4787
Web site: <www.rootsweb.com/
~msneshgg/>

**Ocean Springs Genealogical
Society**
P.O. Box 1765, Ocean Springs,
MS 39566-1765
Web site: <www.rootsweb.com/
~msosgs/>

**Oxford, Skipwith Historical and
Genealogical Society, Inc.**
P.O. Box 1392, Oxford, MS
38655

**Philadelphia-Neshoba Co.
Public Library**
230 Beacon St., Philadelphia, MS
39350

**Prentiss County Historical &
Genealogical Society**
P.O. Box 491, Booneville, MS
38829
Web site <www.rootsweb.com/
~mspcgs/Index.html>

**Rankin County Historical
Society**
P.O. Box 841, Brandon, MS
39042

**Scott County Genealogical
Society**
P.O. Box 7373, Forest, MS
39074-0737
Tel: (601) 469-4799
Web site: <www.geocities.com/
scottcogensoc>

**Smith County Genealogical
Society**
Route 1, Box 4B-1, Raleigh, MS
39153

**Southern Baptist Historical
Library and Archives**
901 Commerce St. #400, Nash-
ville, TN 37203-3630
Tel: (615) 244-0344
Fax: (615) 782-4821
Web site: <www.sbhla.org>

**Sunflower County Historical
Society**
Sunflower County Library, 201 Cy-
press Dr., Indianola, MS 38751

**Tate County Genealogical
Library**
102B Robinson St., Senatobia,
MS 38668

**Tate County Genealogical and
Historical Society**
P.O. Box 974, Senatobia, MS
38668

**Tippah County Historical and
Genealogical Society**
Ripley Public Library, 308 N. Com-
merce St., Ripley, MS 38663

**Tishomingo County Historical &
Genealogical Society**
204 N. Main St, Iuka, MS
38852-2311
Tel: (662) 423-2543
Web site: <www.rootsweb.com/
~mstchgs/index.htm>

**Tupelo, Northeast Mississippi
Historical and Genealogical
Society**
P.O. Box 434, Tupelo, MS
38802-0434

Union County Library
P.O. Box 846, New Albany, MS
38652-0846

**Vicksburg Genealogical
Society, Inc.**
P.O. Box 1161, Vicksburg, MS
39181-1161

Web site: <www.rootsweb.com/
~msvgs/index.htm>

**Wayne County Genealogical
Organization, Inc.**
712 Wayne St., Waynesboro, MS
39367

**Webster County Historical
Society**
Rt. 3, Box 14, Elepora, MS 39744

Wilkinson County Museum
P.O. Box 1055, Woodville, MS
39669
Tel: (601) 888-3998

**Winston County Historical and
Genealogical Society**
P.O. Box 428, Louisville, MS
39339

**Yalobusha County Historical
Society**
P.O. Box 258, Coffeeville, MS
38922

Yazoo Historical Society
332 N. Main St., P.O. Box 575,
Yazoo City, MS 39194
Tel: (601) 746-2273

BIBLIOGRAPHY

■ GENERAL RESOURCES

*Abstract History of the
Mississippi Baptist Association
for One Hundred Years,
1806–1906*
by T.C. Schilling (New Orleans:
J.G. Hauser, 1908)

*African American Genealogy: A
Bibliography and Guide to
Sources*
by Curt Bryan Witcher (Fort
Wayne, IN: Round Tower Books,
2000. Includes white families'
papers)

*Anglo-Americans in Spanish
Archives: Lists of
Anglo-American Settlers in the
Spanish Colonies of America; A
Finding Aid*
by Lawrence H. Feldman (Balti-
more: Genealogical Publishing
Co., 1991)

*Biographical and Historical
Memoirs of Mississippi,
Embracing an Authentic and
Comprehensive Account of the
Chief Events in the History of
the State and a Record of the
Lives of many of the Most
Worthy and Illustrious Families
and Individuals, 2 vols.*
(Chicago: Goodspeed Publishing
Co, 1891. Reprint: Spartanburg,
SC: Reprint Company, 1978)

*Choctaws And Missionaries In
Mississippi, 1818–1918*
by Clara Sue Kidwell (Norman,
OK: University of Oklahoma
Press, 1995)

*The Episcopal Church in
Mississippi, 1763–1992*
from the Episcopal Diocese of
Mississippi (Jackson, MS: The Diocese, 1992)

*First Settlers of the Mississippi
Territory: Grants Taken from
the American State Papers*
by Frances Terry Ingmire (Nacogdoches, TX: Distributed by Ericson Books; St. Louis, MO: Ingmire
Publications, 1982)

*Forgotten Time: The
Yazoo-Mississippi Delta after
the Civil War*
by John C. Willis (Charlottesville,
VA: University Press of Virginia,
2000)

*Four Centuries on the
Pascagoula, 2 vols.*
by Cyril Edward Cain (State Col-
lege, MS: C.E. Cain, 1953, 1962;
Reprint: Spartanburg, SC: Reprint
Co., 1983)

*"Genealogical Research in
Mississippi"*
by Ruth Land Hatten (*National Genealogical Society Quarterly* 77
(March 1988): 22-50)

*The Genealogist's Companion
and Sourcebook, 2d ed.*
by Emily Anne Croom (Cincinnati:
Betterway Books, 2003)

*A Genealogist's Guide to
Discovering Your African-
American Ancestors*
by Franklin Carter Smith and
Emily Anne Croom (Cincinnati:
Betterway Books, 2003. Con-
tains case studies of Mississippi
research before and after 1865)

*Guide to Genealogical
Research in the National
Archives of the United States*
edited by Anne Bruner Eales and
Robert M. Kvasnicka (Washing-
ton, DC: National Archives and
Records Administration, 2000)

*Guide to Official Records in the
Mississippi Department of
Archives and History*
compiled by Thomas W. Henderson and Ronald E. Tomlin (Jackson: Mississippi Department of
Archives and History, 1975)

Mississippi

A History of Mississippi from the Discovery of the Great River by Hernando Desoto, Including the Earliest Settlement made by The French, Under Iberville, to the Death of Jefferson Davis by Robert Lowry and William H. McCardle (Chicago: Goodspeed Publishing Co., 1891; Reprint: Spartanburg, SC: Reprint Company, 1978)

History of Mississippi, the Heart of the South, 4 vols. by Dunbar Rowland (Originally published in 1925; Reprint: Spartanburg, SC: The Reprint Co., 1978)

History of the Primitive Baptists of Mississippi by Benjamin Griffin (Originally published in 1853; Reprint: Jonesboro, AR: Sammons Printing, 1958)

The Large Slaveholders of the Deep South, 1860, 2 vols. by Joseph Karl Menn (Ph.D Thesis: University of Texas, 1964)

Lutheranism In The Southeastern States, 1860–1886: A Social History by Hugh George Anderson (Minneapolis: Augsburg, 1992)

Methodism in the Mississippi Conference [1894–1919] by J. Allen Lindsey (Jackson, MS: Hawkins Foundation, Mississippi Conference Historical Society, 1964)

"Mississippi" by Richard Stephen Lackey (In *Genealogical Research: Methods and Sources.* Kenn Stryker-Rodda, ed. Vol. 2. Rev. ed. Washington, DC: The American Society of Genealogists, 1983)

Mississippi Biographical Abstracts by Jean Strickland (Moss Point, MS: J. Strickland, 1990)

Mississippi Newspapers, 1805–1940: A Preliminary Union List . . . (Jackson, MS: Mississippi Historical Records Survey, 1942)

Mississippi as a Province, Territory, and State, with Biographical Notices of Eminent Citizens by J.F.H. Claiborne (Chicago: Goodspeed Publishing Co., 1880;

Reprint: Spartanburg, SC: Reprint Company, 1978)

Mississippi Provincial Archives, 1701–1763, French Dominion edited by Dunbar Rowland and A. G. Sanders (Jackson, MS: Department of Archives and History, 1927–1984)

Mississippi Research Outline by the Church of Jesus Christ of Latter-day Saints (Salt Lake City, UT: Corp. of the President of the Church of Jesus Christ of L.D.S., 1988)

Mississippi, United Methodist Churches: Two Hundred Years of Heritage and Hope by William L. Jenkins (Franklin, TN: Providence House Pub., 1998)

National Archives Microfilm Catalogs online: <www.archives.gov/publications/genealogy_microfilm_catalogs.html>

The Order of the First Families of Mississippi 1699–1817 edited by Charles Owen Johnson (Ann Arbor, MI: Edwards Brothers, Inc., 1981)

A Postal History of Mississippi, Stampless Period, 1799–1860 by Bruce C. Oakley (Baldwyn, MS: Magnolia Pub., 1969)

Redskins, Ruffleshirts and Rednecks: Indian Allotments in Alabama and Mississippi, 1830–1860 by Mary Elizabeth Young (Norman: University of Oklahoma Press, 1961, 2002)

The Removal of the Choctaw Indians by Arthur H. DeRosier (Knoxville: University of Tennessee Press, 1989)

Residents of the Mississippi Territory Miscellaneous, 2 vols. by Jean Strickland and Patricia N. Edwards (Moss Point, MS: Ben Strickland)

Residents of the Southeastern Mississippi Territory, 5 vols. by Jean Strickland and Patricia N. Edwards (Moss Point, MS: J. Strickland, 1995–1999)

A Southern Catholic Heritage by Charles E. Nolan (New Orleans: Archdiocese of New Orleans, 1976)

Steamboats and the Cotton Economy: River Trade in the Yazoo-Mississippi Delta by Harry P. Owens (Jackson, MS: University Press of Mississippi, 1990)

Tracing Your Mississippi Ancestors by Anne S. Lipscomb and Kathleen S. Hutchison Jackson (University Press of Mississippi, 1994)

Twelve Flags—Triumphs And Tragedies, 3 vols. by Dale Greenwell (Ocean Springs, MS: D. Greenwell, 1968)

Who's Who in Mississippi by Thomas E. Kelly (Jackson, MS: Tucker Printing House, 1914)

Women in the Florida Parishes, 5 vols. by Donna Burge Adams (Baton Rouge, LA: D.B. Adams, 1985–1991)

■ CENSUS RECORDS

The American Census Handbook by Thomas Jay Kemp (Wilmington, DE: Scholarly Resources, Inc., 2001)

The Census Book: A Genealogist's Guide to Federal Census Facts, Schedules and Indexes by William Dollarhide (Bountiful, UT: Heritage Quest, 1999)

Finding Answers in U.S. Census Records by Loretto Dennis Szucs and Matthew Wright (Salt Lake City: Ancestry Publishing, 2001)

Map Guide to the U.S. Federal Censuses, 1790–1920 by William Thorndale and William Dollarhide (Baltimore: Genealogical Publishing Co., 1987)

State Census Records by Anne S. Lainhart (Baltimore: Genealogical Publishing Co., Inc., 1992)

Your Guide to the Federal Census by Kathleen W. Hinckley (Cincinnati: Betterway Books, 2002)

■ IMMIGRATION RECORDS

American Naturalization Records, 1790–1990: What They Are and How to Use Them by John J. Newman (North Salt Lake, UT: HeritageQuest, 1998)

American Passenger Arrival Records by Michael Tepper (Baltimore: Genealogical Publishing Co., 1993)

Old Law Naturalization Records Project (Jackson, MS: Works Projects Administration, 1942)

They Became Americans: Finding Naturalization Records and Ethnic Origins by Loretto Dennis Szucs (Salt Lake City: Ancestry, Inc., 1998)

They Came in Ships: A Guide to Finding Your Immigrant Ancestor's Arrival Records, 2d ed. by John P. Colletta (Salt Lake City: Ancestry, Inc., 1993)

■ LAND RECORDS

Early Settlers of Mississippi as Taken from Land Claims in the Mississippi Territory by Walter Lowrie (Originally published in 1834; Reprint: Southern Historical Press, 1986)

English Land Grants in West Florida: A Register for the States of Alabama, Mississippi, and Parts of Florida and Louisiana, 1766–1776 by Winston DeVille (Ville Platte, LA: Winston DeVille, 1986)

Land and Property Research in the United States by Wade E. Hone (Salt Lake City: Ancestry Inc., 1997)

Locating Your Roots: Discover Your Ancestors Using Land Records by Patricia Law Hatcher (Cincinnati: Betterway Books, 2003)

Private Land Claims of Mississippi and Missouri by Fern Ainsworth (Natchitoches, LA: Fern Ainsworth, 1980s)

Mississippi

Spanish and British Land Grants in Mississippi Territory, 1750–1784, 3 vols.
by Clifford Neal Smith (McNeal, AZ: Westland, 1996)

■ MAPS

Atlas of Historical County Boundaries, Mississippi
edited by John H. Long and compiled by Peggy Tuck Sinko (New York: Simon & Schuster, 1993)

Hometown, Mississippi, 2d ed.
by James Brieger (Jackson, MS: Town Square Books, 1997)

Mississippi: Comprising Sketches of Counties, Towns, Events, Institutions, and Persons, Arranged in Cylopedic Form, 4 vols.
by Dunbar Rowland (Atlanta: Southern Historical Publishing Association, 1907; Reprint: Spartanburg, SC: Reprint Co., 1976)

Mississippi Post Offices
by John S. Gallagher (Lake Grove, OR: The Depot, 1996)

■ MILITARY RECORDS

Military Annals of Mississippi: Military Organizations Which Entered the Service of the Confederate States of America from the State of Mississippi
by John C. Rietti (Originally published in 1896; Reprint: Spartanburg, SC: Reprint Co., 1988)

Military History of Mississippi, 1803–1898
by Dunbar Rowland (Originally published in 1908; Reprint: Spartanburg, SC: Reprint Co., 1978)

Mississippi Confederate Grave Registrations, 2 vols.
by Betty Couch Wiltshire (Bowie, MD: Heritage Books, 1991)

Mississippi Confederate Pension Applications, 3 vols.
by Betty Couch Wiltshire (Carrollton, MS: Pioneer Publishing Co., 1994–)

Mississippi Territory in the War of 1812
by Eron Opha Rowland (Originally published in 1921; Reprint: Baltimore: Clearfield Co., 1996)

Official & Statistical Register of the State of Mississippi, Military History Only
by Dunbar Rowland (Originally published in 1908; Reprint: Salem, MA: Higginson Co., 1995)

Uncle, We Are Ready! Registering America's Men, 1917–1918: A Guide to Researching World War I Draft Registration Cards
by John J. Newman (North Salt Lake, UT: HeritageQuest, 2001)

U.S. Military Records: A Guide to Federal & State Sources, Colonial America to the Present
by James C. Neagles (Salt Lake City: Ancestry, Inc., 1994)

World War II: A Family Historian's Guide
by Debra Johnson Knox (Spartanburg, SC: MIE Publishing, 2003)

■ PROBATE RECORDS

Courts, Judges, and Lawyers of Mississippi, 1798–1935
by Dunbar Rowland (Jackson: Mississippi Dept. of Archives and History, 1935)

Mississippi County Court Records
compiled by May Wilson McBee (Originally published in 1958; Reprint: Baltimore: Clearfield Co., 1994)

Mississippi Court Records 1799–1835
compiled by J. Estelle King (Originally published in 1936; Reprint: Baltimore: Genealogical Publishing Co., 2002)

Mississippi Index of Wills, 1800–1900
compiled by Betty Couch Wiltshire (Bowie, MD: Heritage Books, 1989)

The Natchez Court Records, 1767–1805
by May Wilson McBee (Originally published in 1953; Reprint: Baltimore: Clearfield Co., 1994)

■ VITAL RECORDS

Guide to Vital Statistics Records in Mississippi, 2 vols.
(Jackson, MS: Historical Records Survey, 1942)

Mississippi Cemetery and Bible Records, 23 vols.
(Jackson, MS: Mississippi Genealogical Society, 1954)

Your Guide to Cemetery Research
by Sharon DeBartolo Carmack (Cincinnati: Betterway Books, 2002)

■ Adams 2 Apr. 1799
115 S. Wall St., P.O. Box 1008, Natchez, MS 39120
Phone: (601)446-6684
Web site: www.rootsweb.com/~msadams/
Parent County: Natchez District
Comments/research tips: Clerk of Circuit Court has Marriage records 1802–1866.

Record Type	Year Begun	Jurisdiction
Birth	1912	Health Dept.
Death	1912	Health Dept.
Land	1780	Clerk/Chancery Ct.
Probate	1800	Clerk/Chancery Ct.
Court	1781	Clerk/Chancery Ct.

■ Alcorn 1870
P.O. Box 69, Corinth, MS 38834
Phone: (601)286-7702
Web site: www.freedom2000net.com/userpages/genealogy/alcorn/index.html
Parent County: Tippah, Tishomingo
Comments/research tips: The Clerk of Circuit Court has Marriage records 1876 and 1871.

Record Type	Year Begun	Jurisdiction
Land	1870	Clerk/Chancery Ct.
Probate	1870	Clerk/Chancery Ct.
Birth	1912	Health Dept.
Death	1912	Health Dept.
Court	1881	Clerk/Circuit Ct.

■ Amite 24 Feb. 1809
P.O. Box 680, Liberty, MS 39645
Phone: (601)657-8022
Web site: www.rootsweb.com/~msamite/
Parent County: Wilkinson
Comments/research tips: The Clerk of Circuit Court has Marriage records 1809–1866.

Record Type	Year Begun	Jurisdiction
Birth	1912	Health Dept.
Death	1912	Health Dept.
Land	1809	Clerk/Chancery Ct.
Probate	1809	Clerk/Chancery Ct.
Court	1809	Clerk/Circuit Ct.

■ Attala 23 Dec. 1833
230 W. Washington St., Kosciusko, MS 39090
Phone: (662)289-2921
Web site: www.rootsweb.com/msattala/
Parent County: Choctaw Cession

Mississippi

Comments/research tips: The Clerk of Circuit Court has Marriage records for 1892.

Record Type	Year Begun	Jurisdiction
Birth	1912	Health Dept.
Death	1912	Health Dept.
Land	1858	Clerk/Chancery Ct.
Probate	1858	Clerk/Chancery Ct.
Court	1858	Clerk/Circuit Ct.

■ Bainbridge 17 Jan. 1823
Parent County: Lawrence, Wayne
Comments/research tips: (See Covington) Discontinued 21 January 1824 and became Covington County.

■ Benton 21 July 1870
P.O. Box 218, Ashland, MS 38603
Phone: (662)224-6300
Web site: www.rootsweb.com/~msbenton/
Parent County: Marshall, Tippah
Comments/research tips: The Clerk of Circuit Court has Marriage records 1870–1909.

Record Type	Year Begun	Jurisdiction
Birth	1912	Health Dept.
Death	1912	Health Dept.
Land	1870	Clerk/Chancery Ct.
Probate	1871	Clerk/Chancery Ct.
Court	na	Clerk/Circuit Ct.

■ Bolivar 9 Feb. 1836
P.O. Box 789, Cleveland, MS 38732
Phone: (601)843-2071
Web site: www.rootsweb.com/~msboliva/
Parent County: Choctaw Cession
Comments/research tips: Check records in both Cleveland and Rosedale.

Record Type	Year Begun	Jurisdiction
Birth	1912	Health Dept.
Death	1912	Health Dept.
Marriage	1866	Clerk/Circuit Ct.
Land	1836	Clerk/Chancery Ct.
Probate	1861	Clerk/Chancery Ct.
Court	1836	Clerk/Circuit Ct.

■ Calhoun 8 June 1852
P.O. Box 8, Pittsboro, MS 38951
Phone: (662)983-3122
Web site: www.rootsweb.com/~mscalhou/
Parent County: Lafayette, Yalobusha, Chickasaw
Comments/research tips: Courthouse burned in 1922.

Record Type	Year Begun	Jurisdiction
Birth	1912	Health Dept.
Death	1912	Health Dept.
Marriage	na	Clerk/Circuit Ct.
Land	na	Clerk/Chancery Ct.
Probate	na	Clerk/Chancery Ct.
Court	na	Clerk/Circuit Ct.

■ Carroll 23 Dec. 1833
P.O. Box 60, Carrollton, MS 38917
Phone: (662)237-9274

Web site: www.rootsweb.com/~mscarrol/
Parent County: Choctaw Cession
Comments/research tips: The Clerk of Circuit Court has Marriage records 1834–1915.

Record Type	Year Begun	Jurisdiction
Birth	1912	Health Dept.
Death	1912	Health Dept.
Land	1834	Clerk/Chancery Ct.
Probate	1834	Clerk/Chancery Ct.
Court	1834	Clerk/Circuit Ct.

■ Chickasaw 9 Feb. 1836
101 N. Jefferson, Houston, MS 38851
Phone: (662)456-2513
Web site: www.rootsweb.com/~mschicka/
Parent County: Chickasaw Cession 1832
Comments/research tips: Check records in both Houston and Okalona. The Clerk of Circuit Court has Marriage records 1863.

Record Type	Year Begun	Jurisdiction
Birth	1912	Health Dept.
Death	1912	Health Dept.
Land	1836	Clerk/Chancery Ct.
Probate	1863	Clerk/Chancery Ct.
Court	1863	Clerk/Circuit Ct.

■ Choctaw 23 Dec. 1833
P.O. Box 736, Ackerman, MS 39735
Phone: (662)285-6329
Web site: www.rootsweb.com/~mschocta/
Parent County: Choctaw Cession
Comments/research tips: The Clerk of Circuit Court has Marriage records 1870–1909.

Record Type	Year Begun	Jurisdiction
Birth	1912	Health Dept.
Death	1912	Health Dept.
Land	1880	Clerk/Chancery Ct.
Probate	1879	Clerk/Chancery Ct.
Court	1881	Clerk/Circuit Ct.

■ Claiborne 27 Jan. 1802
P.O. Box 449, Port Gibson, MS 39150
Phone: (601)437-4992
Web site: www.rootsweb.com/~msclaib2/
Parent County: Jefferson
Comments/research tips: The Clerk of Circuit Court has Marriage records 1802–1805.

Record Type	Year Begun	Jurisdiction
Birth	1912	Health Dept.
Death	1912	Health Dept.
Probate	1802	Clerk/Chancery Ct.
Court	1805	Clerk/Circuit Ct.
Land	1802	Clerk/Chancery Ct.

■ Clarke 1833
P.O. Box 689, Quitman, MS 39355
Phone: (662)776-2126
Web site: www.rootsweb.com/~msclarke/
Parent County: Choctaw Cession

Mississippi

Comments/research tips: The Clerk of Circuit Court has Marriage records 1853–1865.

Record Type	Year Begun	Jurisdiction
Birth	1912	Health Dept.
Death	1912	Health Dept.
Probate	1837	Clerk/Chancery Ct.
Court	1867	Clerk/Circuit Ct.
Land	1834	Clerk/Chancery Ct.

■ **Clay** 12 May 1871
P.O. Box 815, West Point, MS 39773
Phone: (662)494-3124
Web site: www.rootsweb.com/~msclay/
Parent County: Chickasaw, Lowndes, Monroe, Oktibbeha
Comments/research tips: Formerly Colfax County. Name changed to Clay 10 April 1876.

Record Type	Year Begun	Jurisdiction
Birth	1912	Health Dept.
Death	1912	Health Dept.
Marriage	1872	Clerk/Circuit Ct.
Land	1872	Clerk/Chancery Ct.
Probate	1872	Clerk/Chancery Ct.
Court	1872	Clerk/Circuit Ct.

■ **Coahoma** 1836
P.O. Box 98, Clarksdale, MS 38614
Phone: (662)624-3000
Web site: www.rootsweb.com/~mxcoahom
Parent County: Choctaw Cession

Record Type	Year Begun	Jurisdiction
Birth	1912	Health Dept.
Death	1912	Health Dept.
Marriage	1949	Clerk/Circuit Ct.
Land	1839	Clerk/Chancery Ct.
Probate	1856	Clerk/Chancery Ct.
Court	1839	Clerk/Circuit Ct.

■ **Colfax** 12 May 1871
Parent County: Chickasaw, Lowndes, Monroe, Oktibbeha
Comments/research tips: (See Clay) Name changed to Clay 10 April 1876.

■ **Copiah** 21 Jan. 1823
P.O. Box 507, Hazlehurst, MS 39083
Phone: (601)894-3021
Web site: www.rootsweb.com/~mscopiah/
Parent County: Choctaw Cession

Record Type	Year Begun	Jurisdiction
Birth	1912	Health Dept.
Death	1912	Health Dept.
Marriage	1823	Clerk/Circuit Ct.
Land	1823	Clerk/Chancery Ct.
Probate	1823	Clerk/Chancery Ct.
Court	1856	Clerk/Circuit Ct.

■ **Covington** 5 Feb. 1819
P.O. Drawer 1679, Collins, MS 39428
Phone: (601)765-6132
Web site: www.rootsweb.com/~mscoving/

Parent County: Lawrence, Wayne
Comments/research tips: The Clerk of Circuit Court has Marriage records 1904.

Record Type	Year Begun	Jurisdiction
Birth	1912	Health Dept.
Death	1912	Health Dept.
Land	1853	Clerk/Chancery Ct.
Probate	1854	Clerk/Chancery Ct.
Court	1857	Clerk/Circuit Ct.

■ **De Soto** 9 Feb. 1836
2535 Hwy. Fifty-One S., Room 5, Hernando, MS 38632
Phone: (662)429-1317
Web site: www.desotoms.com/
Parent County: Chickasaw Cession
Comments/research tips: The Clerk of Circuit Court has Marriage records 1845–1866.

Record Type	Year Begun	Jurisdiction
Birth	1912	Health Dept.
Death	1912	Health Dept.
Land	1836	Clerk/Chancery Ct.
Probate	1836	Clerk/Chancery Ct.
Court	1854	Clerk/Circuit Ct.

■ **Forrest** 19 Apr. 1906
P.O. Box 951, Hattiesburg, MS 39401
Phone: (601)545-6014
Web site: www.rootsweb.com/~msforres
Parent County: Perry

Record Type	Year Begun	Jurisdiction
Birth	1912	Health Dept.
Death	1912	Health Dept.
Marriage	1906	Clerk/Circuit Ct.
Land	1906	Clerk/Chancery Ct.
Probate	1906	Clerk/Chancery Ct.
Court	1906	Clerk/Circuit Ct.

■ **Franklin** 21 Dec. 1809
P.O. Box 297, Meadville, MS 39653
Phone: (601)384-2330
Web site: www.rootsweb.com/~msfrankl/
Parent County: Adams

Record Type	Year Begun	Jurisdiction
Birth	1912	Health Dept.
Death	1912	Health Dept.
Marriage	1825	Clerk/Circuit Ct.
Land	1842	Clerk/Chancery Ct.
Probate	1842	Clerk/Chancery Ct.
Court	1836	Clerk/Circuit Ct.

■ **George** 16 Mar. 1910
355 Cox St., Suite A, Lucedale, MS 39452
Phone: (601)947-4801
Web site: www.rootsweb.com/~msgeorge/
Parent County: Greene, Jackson

Record Type	Year Begun	Jurisdiction
Birth	1912	Health Dept.
Death	1912	Health Dept.
Marriage	1910	Clerk/Circuit Ct.

Land .... 1910 .... Clerk/Chancery Ct.
Probate .... 1910 .... Clerk/Chancery Ct.
Court .... 1910 .... Clerk/Circuit Ct.

■ Greene 9 Dec. 1811

P.O. Box 610, Leakesville, MS 39451
Phone: (601)394-2377
Web site: www.rootsweb.com/~msgreene/
Parent County: Amite, Franklin, Wayne
Comments/research tips: The Clerk of Circuit Court has Marriage records 1874–1910.

Record Type	Year Begun	Jurisdiction
Birth	1912	Health Dept.
Death	1912	Health Dept.
Land	1876	Clerk/Chancery Ct.
Probate	1878	Clerk/Chancery Ct.
Court	1898	Clerk/Circuit Ct.

■ Grenada 9 May 1870

P.O. Drawer 1208, Grenada, MS 38902
Phone: (662)226-1821
Web site: www.rootsweb.com/~msgrenad/
Parent County: Carroll, Yalobuska, Choctaw, Tallahatchie
Comments/research tips: The Clerk of Circuit Court has Marriage records 1870–1880.

Record Type	Year Begun	Jurisdiction
Birth	1912	Health Dept.
Death	1912	Health Dept.
Land	1834	Clerk/Chancery Ct.
Probate	1870	Clerk/Chancery Ct.
Court	1870	Clerk/Circuit Ct.

■ Hancock 18 Dec. 1812

150 Main St., Bay St. Louis, MS 39520
Phone: (601)467-5404
Web site: www.rootsweb.com/~mshancoc/
Parent County: Mobile District

Record Type	Year Begun	Jurisdiction
Birth	1912	Health Dept.
Death	1912	Health Dept.
Marriage	1853	Clerk/Circuit Ct.
Land	1853	Clerk/Chancery Ct.
Probate	1853	Clerk/Chancery Ct.
Court	1853	Clerk/Circuit Ct.

■ Harrison 5 Feb. 1841

P.O. Drawer CC, Gulfport, MS 39502
Phone: (228)865-4118
Web site: www.co.harrison.ms.us/
Parent County: Hancock, Jackson, Perry
Comments/research tips: The Clerk of Circuit Court has Marriage records 1841–1907.

Record Type	Year Begun	Jurisdiction
Birth	1912	Health Dept.
Death	1912	Health Dept.
Land	1841	Clerk/Chancery Ct.
Probate	1853	Clerk/Chancery Ct.
Court	na	Clerk/Circuit Ct.

■ Hinds 12 Feb. 1821

P.O. Box 686, Jackson, MS 39205
Phone: (601)968-6508
Web site: www.co.hinds.ms.us/pgs/index.asp
Parent County: Choctaw Cession 1820
Comments/research tips: Check records in both Jackson and Raymond. The Clerk of Circuit Court has Marriage records 1815–1930 and Court records 1821–1930. The Chancery Court Clerk has Land records 1821–1930 and Probate records 1823–1930.

Record Type	Year Begun	Jurisdiction
Birth	1912	Health Dept.
Death	1912	Health Dept.

■ Holmes 1833

P.O. Box 239, Lexington, MS 39095
Phone: (662)834-2281
Web site: www.rootsweb.com/~msholmes/
Parent County: Yazoo

Record Type	Year Begun	Jurisdiction
Birth	1912	Health Dept.
Death	1912	Health Dept.
Marriage	1884	Clerk/Circuit Ct.
Land	1833	Clerk/Chancery Ct.
Probate	1833	Clerk/Chancery Ct.
Court	na	Clerk/Circuit Ct.

■ Humphreys 1918

P.O. Box 547, Belzoni, MS 39038
Phone: (601)247-1740
Web site: www.rootsweb.com/~mshumphr/
Parent County: Holmes, Washington, Yazoo, Sunflower

Record Type	Year Begun	Jurisdiction
Birth	1912	Health Dept.
Death	1912	Health Dept.
Marriage	1918	Clerk/Circuit Ct.
Land	1918	Clerk/Chancery Ct.
Probate	1918	Clerk/Chancery Ct.
Court	1918	Clerk/Circuit Ct.

■ Issaquena 1844

P.O. Box 27, Mayersville, MS 39113
Phone: (662)873-2761
Web site: www.rootsweb.com/~msissaqu/
Parent County: Washington

Record Type	Year Begun	Jurisdiction
Birth	1912	Health Dept.
Death	1912	Health Dept.
Marriage	1866	Clerk/Circuit Ct.
Land	1843	Clerk/Chancery Ct.
Probate	1849	Clerk/Chancery Ct.
Court	1849	Clerk/Circuit Ct.

■ Itawamba 1836

P.O. Box 776, Fulton, MS 38843
Phone: (601)862-3421
Web site: www.rootsweb.com/~msitawam/
Parent County: Chickasaw Cession 1832

Record Type	Year Begun	Jurisdiction
Birth	1912	Health Dept.

Record Type	Year Begun	Jurisdiction
Death	1912	Health Dept.
Marriage	1837	Clerk/Circuit Ct.
Land	1836	Clerk/Chancery Ct.
Probate	1854	Clerk/Chancery Ct.
Court	1854	Clerk/Circuit Ct.

■ Jackson 18 Dec. 1812

P.O. Box 998, Pascagoula, MS 39567
Phone: (228)769-3499
Web site: www.co.jackson.ms.us/
Parent County: Mobile District

Record Type	Year Begun	Jurisdiction
Birth	1912	Health Dept.
Death	1912	Health Dept.
Marriage	1875	Clerk/Circuit Ct.
Probate	1874	Clerk/Chancery Ct.
Court	1875	Clerk/Circuit Ct.
Probate	1874	Clerk/Chancery Ct.

■ Jasper 23 Dec. 1833

P.O. Box 1047, Bay Springs, MS 39422
Phone: (601)764-3368
Web site: www.rootsweb.com/~msjasper/
Parent County: Choctaw Cession 1830
Comments/research tips: The Clerk of Circuit Court has Marriage records 1906.

Record Type	Year Begun	Jurisdiction
Birth	1912	Health Dept.
Death	1912	Health Dept.
Probate	1904	Clerk/Chancery Ct.
Court	na	Clerk/Circuit Ct.
Land	1904	Clerk/Chancery Ct.

■ Jefferson 2 Apr. 1799

P.O. Box 145, Fayette, MS 39069
Phone: (601)786-3021
Web site: www.rootsweb.com/~msjeffer/
Parent County: Natchez District
Comments/research tips: Formerly Pickering County. Name changed to Jefferson 11 January 1802. The Clerk of Circuit Court has Marriage records 1805–1869.

Record Type	Year Begun	Jurisdiction
Birth	1912	Health Dept.
Death	1912	Health Dept.
Land	1798	Clerk/Chancery Ct.
Probate	1805	Clerk/Chancery Ct.
Court	1802	Clerk/Circuit Ct.

■ Jefferson Davis 31 Mar. 1906

P.O. Box 1137, Prentiss, MS 39474
Phone: (601)792-4204
Web site: www.rootsweb.com/~msjdavis/
Parent County: Covington, Lawrence

Record Type	Year Begun	Jurisdiction
Birth	1912	Health Dept.
Death	1912	Health Dept.
Marriage	na	Clerk/Circuit Ct.
Land	na	Clerk/Chancery Ct.
Probate	na	Clerk/Chancery Ct.
Court	na	Clerk/Circuit Ct.

■ Jones 24 Jan. 1826

P.O. Box 1468, Laurel, MS 39441
Phone: (601)428-0527
Web site: www.rootsweb.com/~msjones
Parent County: Covington, Wayne
Comments/research tips: The Clerk of Circuit Court has Marriage records 1882–1888.

Record Type	Year Begun	Jurisdiction
Birth	1912	Health Dept.
Death	1912	Health Dept.
Probate	1894	Clerk/Chancery Ct.
Land	1828	Clerk/Chancery Ct.
Court	1857	Clerk/Circuit Ct.

■ Kemper 23 Dec. 1833

P.O. Box 188, De Kalb, MS 39328
Phone: (601)743-2560
Web site: www.rootsweb.com/~mskemper/
Parent County: Choctaw Cession 1830
Comments/research tips: The Clerk of Circuit Court has Marriage records 1912.

Record Type	Year Begun	Jurisdiction
Birth	1912	Health Dept.
Death	1912	Health Dept.
Land	1881	Clerk/Chancery Ct.
Probate	1881	Clerk/Chancery Ct.
Court	1881	Clerk/Circuit Ct.

■ Lafayette 1836

P.O. Box 1240, Oxford, MS 38655
Phone: (662)234-2131
Web site: www.rootsweb.com/~mslafaye/
Parent County: Chickasaw Cession
Comments/research tips: The Clerk of Circuit Court has Marriage records 1850–1876.

Record Type	Year Begun	Jurisdiction
Birth	1912	Health Dept.
Death	1912	Health Dept.
Probate	1836	Clerk/Chancery Ct.
Court	1836	Clerk/Circuit Ct.
Land	1836	Clerk/Chancery Ct.

■ Lamar 1904

P.O. Box 247, Purvis, MS 39475
Phone: (601)544-4410
Web site: www.lamarcounty.com/
Parent County: Marion, Pearl River

Record Type	Year Begun	Jurisdiction
Birth	1912	Health Dept.
Death	1912	Health Dept.
Marriage	1903	Clerk/Circuit Ct.
Land	1836	Clerk/Chancery Ct.
Probate	1901	Clerk/Chancery Ct.
Court	na	Clerk/Circuit Ct.

■ Lauderdale 23 Dec. 1833

P.O. Box 1587, Meridian, MS 39302
Phone: (601)482-9704
Web site: www.lauderdalecounty.org/

Parent County: Choctaw Cession
Comments/research tips: The Clerk of Circuit Court has Marriage records 1839–1870.

Record Type	Year Begun	Jurisdiction
Birth	1912	Health Dept.
Death	1912	Health Dept.
Land	1837	Clerk/Chancery Ct.
Probate	1849	Clerk/Chancery Ct.
Court	1856	Clerk/Circuit Ct.

■ Lawrence 22 Dec. 1814
P.O. Box 40, Monticello, MS 39654
Phone: (601)587-7162
Web site: www.rootsweb.com/~mslawren/
Parent County: Marion
Comments/research tips: The Clerk of Circuit Court has Marriage records 1818–1910.

Record Type	Year Begun	Jurisdiction
Birth	1912	Health Dept.
Death	1912	Health Dept.
Land	1815	Clerk/Chancery Ct.
Probate	1836	Clerk/Chancery Ct.
Court	1815	Clerk/Circuit Ct.

■ Leake 23 Dec. 1833
P.O. Box 72, Carthage, MS 39051
Phone: (601)267-7371
Web site: www.rootsweb.com/~msleake/
Parent County: Choctaw Cession

Record Type	Year Begun	Jurisdiction
Birth	1912	Health Dept.
Death	1912	Health Dept.
Marriage	1836	Clerk/Circuit Ct.
Land	1834	Clerk/Chancery Ct.
Probate	1844	Clerk/Chancery Ct.
Court	1852	Clerk/Circuit Ct.

■ Lee 10 Dec. 1866
P.O. Box 7127, Tupelo, MS 38802
Phone: (662)841-9100
Web site: www.rootsweb.com/~mslee/
Parent County: Itawamba, Pontotoc
Comments/research tips: The Clerk of Circuit Court has Marriage records 1867.

Record Type	Year Begun	Jurisdiction
Birth	1912	Health Dept.
Death	1912	Health Dept.
Land	1867	Clerk/Chancery Ct.
Probate	1867	Clerk/Chancery Ct.
Court	1867	Clerk/Circuit Ct.

■ Leflore 15 Mar. 1871
P.O. Box 250, Greenwood, MS 38935
Phone: (662)453-6203
Web site: www.rootsweb.com/~msleflor/
Parent County: Carroll, Sunflower, Tallahatchie
Comments/research tips: The Clerk of Circuit Court has Marriage records 1844–1894.

Record Type	Year Begun	Jurisdiction
Birth	1912	Health Dept.

Death	1912	Health Dept.
Land	1837	Clerk/Chancery Ct.
Probate	na	Clerk/Chancery Ct.
Court	1845	Clerk/Circuit Ct.

■ Lincoln 7 Apr. 1870
P.O. Box 555, Brookhaven, MS 39602
Phone: (601)835-3411
Web site: www.rootsweb.com/~mslincol/
Parent County: Franklin, Lawrence, Copiah, Pike, Amite

Record Type	Year Begun	Jurisdiction
Birth	1912	Health Dept.
Death	1912	Health Dept.
Marriage	1893	Clerk/Circuit Ct.
Land	1894	Clerk/Chancery Ct.
Probate	1893	Clerk/Chancery Ct.
Court	na	Clerk/Circuit Ct.

■ Lowndes 30 Jan. 1830
P.O. Box 684, Columbus, MS 39703
Phone: (662)329-5805
Web site: www.rootsweb.com/~mslownde/
Parent County: Monroe

Record Type	Year Begun	Jurisdiction
Birth	1912	Health Dept.
Death	1912	Health Dept.
Marriage	1821	Clerk/Circuit Ct.
Court	1825	Clerk/Circuit Ct.
Land	1821	Clerk/Chancery Ct.
Probate	1825	Clerk/Chancery Ct.

■ Madison 29 Jan. 1828
P.O. Box 404, Canton, MS 39046
Phone: (601)859-1177
Web site: www.rootsweb.com/~msmadiso/
Parent County: Yazoo

Record Type	Year Begun	Jurisdiction
Birth	1912	Health Dept.
Death	1912	Health Dept.
Marriage	1830	Clerk/Circuit Ct.
Land	1828	Clerk/Chancery Ct.
Probate	1828	Clerk/Chancery Ct.
Court	1828	Clerk/Circuit Ct.

■ Marion 9 Dec. 1811
250 Broad St., Suite 2, Columbia, MS 39429
Phone: (601)736-2691
Web site: www.rootsweb.com/~msmarion/
Parent County: Amite, Wayne, Franklin
Comments/research tips: The Clerk of Circuit Court has Marriage records 1812–1908.

Record Type	Year Begun	Jurisdiction
Birth	1912	Health Dept.
Death	1912	Health Dept.
Land	1821	Clerk/Chancery Ct.
Probate	1812	Clerk/Chancery Ct.
Court	1812	Clerk/Circuit Ct.

■ Marshall 9 Feb. 1836
P.O. Box 219, Holly Springs, MS 38635
Phone: (662)252-4431

Web site: www.rootsweb.com/~msmarsha/
Parent County: Chickasaw Cession 1832

Record Type	Year Begun	Jurisdiction
Birth	1912	Health Dept.
Death	1912	Health Dept.
Court	1836	Clerk/Circuit Ct.
Land	1856	Clerk/Chancery Ct.
Probate	1836	Clerk/Chancery Ct.
Marriage	1836	Clerk/Circuit Ct.

■ Monroe   9 Feb. 1821
P.O. Box 578, Aberdeen, MS 39730
Phone: (662)369-8143
Web site: www.rootsweb.com/~msmonroe/index.htm
Parent County: Chickasaw Cession

Record Type	Year Begun	Jurisdiction
Birth	1912	Health Dept.
Death	1912	Health Dept.
Marriage	1821	Clerk/Circuit Ct.
Land	1821	Clerk/Chancery Ct.
Probate	1825	Clerk/Chancery Ct.
Court	1825	Clerk/Circuit Ct.

■ Montgomery   13 May 1871
P.O. Box 71, Winona, MS 38967
Phone: (662)283-2333
Web site: www.rootsweb.com/~msmontgo/
Parent County: Carroll, Choctaw
Comments/research tips: The Clerk of Circuit Court has Marriage records 1891–1901.

Record Type	Year Begun	Jurisdiction
Birth	1912	Health Dept.
Death	1912	Health Dept.
Land	1871	Clerk/Chancery Ct.
Probate	1872	Clerk/Chancery Ct.
Court	1821	Clerk/Circuit Ct.

■ Neshoba   23 Dec. 1833
401 E. Beacon St., Suite 107, Philadelphia, MS 39350
Phone: (601)656-3581
Web site: www.neshoba.org/
Parent County: Chocktaw Cession 1830
Comments/research tips: The Clerk of Circuit Court has Marriage records 1877–1895.

Record Type	Year Begun	Jurisdiction
Birth	1912	Health Dept.
Death	1912	Health Dept.
Court	1859	Clerk/Circuit Ct.
Land	1835	Clerk/Chancery Ct.
Probate	1837	Clerk/Chancery Ct.

■ Newton   25 Feb. 1836
P.O. Box 68, Decatur, MS 39327
Phone: (601)635-2367
Web site: www.rootsweb.com/~msnewton/
Parent County: Neshoba
Comments/research tips: The Clerk of Circuit Court has Marriage records 1772–1876.

Record Type	Year Begun	Jurisdiction
Birth	1912	Health Dept.

Death	1912	Health Dept.
Land	1876	Clerk/Chancery Ct.
Probate	1876	Clerk/Chancery Ct.
Court	1876	Clerk/Circuit Ct.

■ Noxubee   23 Dec. 1833
P.O. Box 147, Macon, MS 39341
Phone: (662)726-4243
Web site: www.rootsweb.com/~msnoxube/
Parent County: Choctaw Cession, 1830
Comments/research tips: The Clerk of Circuit Court has Marriage records 1834.

Record Type	Year Begun	Jurisdiction
Birth	1912	Health Dept.
Death	1912	Health Dept.
Land	1834	Clerk/Chancery Ct.
Probate	1834	Clerk/Chancery Ct.
Court	1834	Clerk/Circuit Ct.

■ Oktibbeha   23 Dec. 1833
Courthouse, E. Main St., Starkville, MS 39759
Phone: (662)323-5834
Web site: www.rootsweb.com/~msokibb/
Parent County: Choctaw Cession 1830
Comments/research tips: The Clerk of Circuit Court has Marriage records 1861.

Record Type	Year Begun	Jurisdiction
Birth	1912	Health Dept.
Death	1912	Health Dept.
Land	1834	Clerk/Chancery Ct.
Probate	1845	Clerk/Chancery Ct.
Court	1836	Clerk/Circuit Ct.

■ Panola   9 Feb. 1836
151 Public Sq., Batesville, MS 38606
Phone: (601)563-6205
Web site: www.rootsweb.com/~mspanola
Parent County: Chickasaw Cession 1832
Comments/research tips: The Clerk of Circuit Court has Marriage records 1871–1884.

Record Type	Year Begun	Jurisdiction
Birth	1912	Health Dept.
Death	1912	Health Dept.
Land	1836	Clerk/Chancery Ct.
Probate	1845	Clerk/Chancery Ct.
Court	1836	Clerk/Circuit Ct.

■ Pearl River   22 Feb. 1890
P.O. Box 431, Poplarville, MS 39470
Phone: (601)795-2237
Web site: www.rootsweb.com/~mspearlr/
Parent County: Hancock, Marion
Comments/research tips: The Clerk of Circuit Court has Marriage records 1890–1909.

Record Type	Year Begun	Jurisdiction
Birth	1912	Health Dept.
Death	1912	Health Dept.
Land	1890	Clerk/Chancery Ct.
Probate	1899	Clerk/Chancery Ct.
Court	1890	Clerk/Circuit Ct.

■ **Perry** 3 Feb. 1820
P.O. Box 198, New Augusta, MS 39462
Phone: (601)964-8398
Web site: www.rootsweb.com/~msperry
Comments/research tips: The Clerk of Circuit Court has Marriage records 1877–1892.
Parent County: Greene

Record Type	Year Begun	Jurisdiction
Birth	1912	Health Dept.
Death	1912	Health Dept.
Land	1862	Clerk/Chancery Ct.
Probate	na	Clerk/Chancery Ct.
Court	1889	Clerk/Circuit Ct.

■ **Pickering** 2 Apr. 1799
Parent County: Natchez District
Comments/research tips: (See Jefferson) Name changed to Jefferson 11 January 1802.

■ **Pike** 9 Dec. 1815
P.O. Box 309, Magnolia, MS 39652
Phone: (601)783-3362
Web site: http://resources.rootsweb.com/USA/MS/Pike
Parent County: Marion
Comments/research tips: The Clerk of Circuit Court has Marriage records 1882.

Record Type	Year Begun	Jurisdiction
Birth	1912	Health Dept.
Death	1912	Health Dept.
Land	1882	Clerk/Chancery Ct.
Probate	1882	Clerk/Chancery Ct.
Court	1882	Clerk/Circuit Ct.

■ **Pontotoc** 9 Feb. 1836
P.O. Box 209, Pontotoc, MS 38863
Phone: (662)489-3900
Web site: www.rootsweb.com/~mspontot
Parent County: Chickasaw Cession 1832
Comments/research tips: The Clerk of Circuit Court has Marriage records 1849–1880.

Record Type	Year Begun	Jurisdiction
Birth	1912	Health Dept.
Death	1912	Health Dept.
Land	1836	Clerk/Chancery Ct.
Probate	1836	Clerk/Chancery Ct.
Court	1872	Clerk/Circuit Ct.

■ **Prentiss** 15 Apr. 1870
P.O. Box 477, Booneville, MS 38829
Phone: (662)728-8151
Web site: www.rootsweb.com/~msprenti/
Parent County: Tishomingo

Record Type	Year Begun	Jurisdiction
Birth	1912	Health Dept.
Death	1912	Health Dept.
Court	1872	Clerk/Circuit Ct.
Marriage	1870	Clerk/Circuit Ct.
Land	1836	Clerk/Chancery Ct.
Probate	1870	Clerk/Chancery Ct.

■ **Quitman** 1 Feb. 1877
230 Chestnut St., Marks, MS 38646
Phone: (662)326-2661
Web site: www.rootsweb.com/~msquitma
Parent County: Panola, Coahoma, Tunica, Tallahatchie

Record Type	Year Begun	Jurisdiction
Birth	1912	Health Dept.
Death	1912	Health Dept.
Marriage	1877	Clerk/Circuit Ct.
Land	1877	Clerk/Chancery Ct.
Probate	1878	Clerk/Chancery Ct.
Court	1878	Clerk/Circuit Ct.

■ **Rankin** 4 Feb. 1828
P.O. Box 700, Brandon, MS 39042
Phone: (601)825-1469
Web site: www.rootsweb.com/~msrankin/
Parent County: Hinds

Record Type	Year Begun	Jurisdiction
Birth	1912	Health Dept.
Death	1912	Health Dept.
Court	1819	Clerk/Circuit Ct.
Land	1824	Clerk/Chancery Ct.
Probate	1828	Clerk/Chancery Ct.
Marriage	1828	Clerk/Circuit Ct.

■ **Scott** 23 Dec. 1833
100 E. Main St., P.O. Box 630, Forest, MS 39074
Phone: (601)469-1922
Web site: www.rootsweb.com/~msscott/
Parent County: Choctaw Cession 1830
Comments/research tips: The Clerk of Circuit Court has Marriage records 1865–1872.

Record Type	Year Begun	Jurisdiction
Birth	1912	Health Dept.
Death	1912	Health Dept.
Land	1835	Clerk/Chancery Ct.
Probate	1835	Clerk/Chancery Ct.
Court	1867	Clerk/Circuit Ct.

■ **Sharkey** 29 Mar. 1876
P.O. Box 218, Rolling Fork, MS 39159
Phone: (662)873-2755
Web site: www.rootsweb.com/~mssharke/
Parent County: Washington, Issaquena

Record Type	Year Begun	Jurisdiction
Birth	1912	Health Dept.
Death	1912	Health Dept.
Marriage	1876	Clerk/Circuit Ct.
Land	1876	Clerk/Chancery Ct.
Probate	1877	Clerk/Chancery Ct.
Court	1877	Clerk/Circuit Ct.

■ **Simpson** 23 Jan. 1824
P.O. Box 367, Mendenhall, MS 39114
Phone: (601)847-2626
Web site: www.rootsweb.com/~mssimpso/
Parent County: Choctaw Cession 1820

Record Type	Year Begun	Jurisdiction
Birth	1912	Health Dept.

Death	1912	Health Dept.
Marriage	1872	Clerk/Circuit Ct.
Land	1872	Clerk/Chancery Ct.
Court	1872	Clerk/Circuit Ct.
Probate	1872	Clerk/Chancery Ct.

■ Smith 23 Dec. 1833

P.O. Box 39, Raleigh, MS 39153
Phone: (601)782-9811
Web site: www.rootsweb.com/~mssmith/
Parent County: Choctaw Cession

Record Type	Year Begun	Jurisdiction
Birth	1912	Health Dept.
Death	1912	Health Dept.
Marriage	1912	Clerk/Circuit Ct.
Land	1892	Clerk/Chancery Ct.
Court	1893	Clerk/Circuit Ct.

■ Stone 1917

P.O. Drawer 7, Wiggins, MS 39577
Phone: (601)928-5266
Web site: www.rootsweb.com/~msstone
Parent County: Harrison

Record Type	Year Begun	Jurisdiction
Birth	1912	Health Dept.
Death	1912	Health Dept.
Marriage	na	Clerk/Circuit Ct.
Land	1917	Clerk/Chancery Ct.
Probate	1917	Clerk/Chancery Ct.
Court	1917	Clerk/Circuit Ct.

■ Sumner 6 Apr. 1874

Parent County: Montgomery, Choctaw
Comments/research tips: (See Webster) Name changed to Webster 30 January 1882.

■ Sunflower 15 Feb. 1844

P.O. Box 988, Indianola, MS 38751
Comments/research tips: The Clerk of Circuit Court has Marriage records 1871.
Phone: (662)887-4703
Web site: www.rootsweb.com/~mssunflo/
Parent County: Bolivar, Washington

Record Type	Year Begun	Jurisdiction
Birth	1912	Health Dept.
Death	1912	Health Dept.
Land	1817	Clerk/Chancery Ct.
Probate	1844	Clerk/Chancery Ct.
Court	1844	Clerk/Circuit Ct.

■ Tallahatchie 1830

P.O. Drawer 350, Charleston, MS 38921
Phone: (662)647-5551
Web site: www.rootsweb.com/~mstallah/
Parent County: Choctaw Cession
Comments/research tips: The Clerk of Circuit Court has Marriage records 1856–1880.

Record Type	Year Begun	Jurisdiction
Birth	1912	Health Dept.

Death	1912	Health Dept.
Court	1841	Clerk/Circuit Ct.
Land	1835	Clerk/Chancery Ct.
Probate	1834	Clerk/Chancery Ct.

■ Tate 15 Apr. 1873

201 Ward St., Senatobia, MS 38668
Phone: (662)562-5661
Web site: www.rootsweb.com/~mstate/
Parent County: Marshall, Tunica, DeSoto
Comments/research tips: The Clerk of Circuit Court has Marriage records 1873.

Record Type	Year Begun	Jurisdiction
Birth	1912	Health Dept.
Death	1912	Health Dept.
Land	1873	Clerk/Chancery Ct.
Probate	1873	Clerk/Chancery Ct.
Court	1873	Clerk/Circuit Ct.

■ Tippah 9 Feb. 1836

P.O. Box 99, Ripley, MS 38663
Phone: (662)837-7374
Web site: www.rootsweb.com/~mstippah/
Parent County: Chickasaw Cession 1832
Comments/research tips: Courthouse burned in 1863. Clerk of Circuit Court has Marriage records from 1858–1888.

Record Type	Year Begun	Jurisdiction
Birth	1912	Health Dept.
Death	1912	Health Dept.
Court	1836	Clerk/Circuit Ct.
Land	1836	Clerk/Chancery Ct.
Probate	1836	Clerk/Chancery Ct.

■ Tishomingo 9 Feb. 1836

1008 Battleground Dr., Iuka, MS 38852
Phone: (662)423-7010
Web site: www.tishomingo.org
Parent County: Chickasaw Cession 1832
Comments/research tips: The Clerk of Circuit Court has Marriage records 1842–1866.

Record Type	Year Begun	Jurisdiction
Birth	1912	Health Dept.
Death	1912	Health Dept.
Land	1836	Clerk/Chancery Ct.
Probate	1836	Clerk/Chancery Ct.
Court	1836	Clerk/Circuit Ct.

■ Tunica 9 Feb. 1836

P.O. Box 217, Tunica, MS 38676
Phone: (662)363-2451
Web site: www.rootsweb.com/~mstunica/
Parent County: Chickasaw Cession 1832

Record Type	Year Begun	Jurisdiction
Birth	1912	Health Dept.
Death	1912	Health Dept.
Marriage	1858	Clerk/Circuit Ct.
Land	1836	Clerk/Chancery Ct.
Probate	1839	Clerk/Chancery Ct.
Court	1839	Clerk/Circuit Ct.

■ **Union** 7 July 1870
P.O. Box 847, New Albany, MS 38652
Phone: (662)534-1900
Web site: www.rootsweb.com/~msunion/
Parent County: Pontotoc, Tippah
Comments/research tips: The Clerk of Circuit Court has
Marriage records 1878–1892.

Record Type	Year Begun	Jurisdiction
Birth	1912	Health Dept.
Death	1912	Health Dept.
Land	1872	Clerk/Chancery Ct.
Probate	na	Clerk/Chancery Ct.
Court	na	Clerk/Circuit Ct.

■ **Walthall** 1914
P.O. Box 351, Tylertown, MS 39667
Phone: (601)876-3553
Web site: www.rootsweb.com/~mswaltha/waltmain.html
Parent County: Marion, Pike
Comments/research tips: The Clerk of Circuit Court has
Marriage records 1914.

Record Type	Year Begun	Jurisdiction
Birth	1912	Health Dept.
Death	1912	Health Dept.
Land	1913	Clerk/Chancery Ct.
Probate	1913	Clerk/Chancery Ct.
Court	1913	Clerk/Circuit Ct.

■ **Warren** 22 Dec. 1809
P.O. Box 351, Vicksburg, MS 39180
Phone: (601)636-4415
Web site: www.rootsweb.com/~mswarren/
Parent County: Natchez District
Comments/research tips: The Clerk of Circuit Court has
Marriage records 1846–1860.

Record Type	Year Begun	Jurisdiction
Birth	1912	Health Dept.
Death	1912	Health Dept.
Land	1810	Clerk/Chancery Ct.
Probate	1810	Clerk/Chancery Ct.
Court	1810	Clerk/Circuit Ct.

■ **Washington** 29 Jan. 1827
P.O. Box 309, Greenville, MS 38701
Phone: (662)332-1595
Web site: www.rootsweb.com/~mswashin
Parent County: Warren, Yazoo
Comments/research tips: The Clerk of Circuit Court has
Marriage records 1858–1891.

Record Type	Year Begun	Jurisdiction
Birth	1912	Health Dept.
Death	1912	Health Dept.
Land	1828	Clerk/Chancery Ct.
Probate	1839	Clerk/Chancery Ct.
Court	na	Clerk/Circuit Ct.

■ **Washington, old** 4 June 1800
Parent County: Unorganized Territory
Comments/research tips: (Now in Alabama)

■ **Wayne** 21 Dec. 1809
Courthouse, Waynesboro, MS 39367
Phone: (601)735-2873
Web site: www.rootsweb.com/~mswayne
Parent County: Washington, old

Record Type	Year Begun	Jurisdiction
Birth	1912	Health Dept.
Death	1912	Health Dept.
Marriage	1881	Clerk/Circuit Ct.
Land	na	Clerk/Chancery Ct.
Probate	1879	Clerk/Chancery Ct.
Court	na	Clerk/Circuit Ct.

■ **Webster** 6 Apr. 1874
P.O. Box 398, Walthall, MS 39771
Phone: (662)258-4131
Web site: www.rootsweb.com/~mswebst2/
Parent County: Montgomery, Choctaw
Comments/research tips: Formerly Sumner County. Name
changed to Webster 30 January 1882. The Clerk of Circuit
Court has Marriage records 1874–1909.

Record Type	Year Begun	Jurisdiction
Birth	1912	Health Dept.
Death	1912	Health Dept.
Land	1873	Clerk/Chancery Ct.
Probate	1874	Clerk/Chancery Ct.
Court	1879	Clerk/Circuit Ct.

■ **Wilkinson** 30 Jan. 1802
P.O. Box 516, Woodville, MS 39669
Phone: (601)888-4381
Web site: www.rootsweb.com/~mswilkin/
Parent County: Adams
Comments/research tips: The Clerk of Circuit Court has
Marriage records 1804–1823.

Record Type	Year Begun	Jurisdiction
Birth	1912	Health Dept.
Death	1912	Health Dept.
Land	1803	Clerk/Chancery Ct.
Probate	1806	Clerk/Chancery Ct.
Court	1822	Clerk/Circuit Ct.

■ **Winston** 23 Dec. 1833
P.O. Drawer 69, Louisville, MS 39339
Phone: (662)773-3631
Web site: www.rootsweb.com/~mswinsto/
Parent County: Choctaw Cession 1830
Comments/research tips: The Clerk of Circuit Court has
Marriage records 1834–1908.

Record Type	Year Begun	Jurisdiction
Birth	1912	Health Dept.
Death	1912	Health Dept.
Land	1835	Clerk/Chancery Ct.
Probate	1834	Clerk/Chancery Ct.
Court	1856	Clerk/Circuit Ct.

■ **Yalobusha** 23 Dec. 1833
P.O. Box 664, Water Valley, MS 38965
Phone: (662)473-2091

Mississippi

Web site: www.rootsweb.com/~msyalobu/
Parent County: Choctaw Cession 1830
Comments/research tips: Check records in both Water Valley and Coffeeville. The Clerk of Circuit Court has Marriage records 1847–1866.

Record Type	Year Begun	Jurisdiction
Birth	1912	Health Dept.
Death	1912	Health Dept.
Land	1834	Clerk/Chancery Ct.
Probate	1834	Clerk/Chancery Ct.
Court	1834	Clerk/Circuit Ct.

■ **Yazoo** 21 Jan. 1823
P.O. Box 68, Yazoo City, MS 39194
Phone: (601)746-2661
Web site: www.rootsweb.com/~msyazoo
Parent County: Choctaw Cession 1830

Record Type	Year Begun	Jurisdiction
Birth	1912	Health Dept.
Death	1912	Health Dept.
Marriage	1845	Clerk/Circuit Ct.
Land	1824	Clerk/Chancery Ct.
Probate	1824	Clerk/Chancery Ct.
Court	1867	Clerk/Circuit Ct.

Missouri

By James W. Warren

HISTORICAL OVERVIEW

It was the Gateway to the West—the jumping-off point for Lewis and Clark's expedition, the Santa Fe and Oregon trails, and for those heading to the California Gold Rush. Missouri was notorious for being a way station, a stopping point en route to a final destination, but many adventurers remained and made it their home. Whether your ancestors passed through or stayed, Missouri has an incredible history and offers wonderful records and resources to help you find your ancestors' stories.

The area was home to the Missouri, Osage, Delaware, and Shawnee Indians long before Europeans ventured there. Early explorers through the area were DeSoto in 1541, Marquette and Joliet in 1673, and Robert Cavelier, Sieur de la Salle, who claimed the Mississippi River Valley for France in 1682. The first permanent white settlement was established in 1735 at Ste. Genevieve by French lead miners. In 1763, France ceded the area to Spain. French fur traders founded St. Louis the following year, word of the cession to Spain not having reached them yet, as they had no e-mail.

Settlement by Americans in the Spanish territory began as early as 1787 in Ste. Genevieve County. Spain offered free land, and after 1795, large numbers of Americans from Kentucky, Tennessee, Virginia, and the Carolinas were in the area. In 1800 Spain returned the area to France, and in 1803 the United States acquired the land as part of the Louisiana Purchase.

Missouri became part of Louisiana Territory in 1805, and in 1812 Congress created the Missouri Territory. Migration continued, but many people left due to earthquakes, ongoing Indian raids, and other problems. When Missouri became the twenty-fourth state in 1821, the population was about 57,000. The descendants of the early French and American settlers were joined by immigrants from Ireland, Switzerland, Italy, Poland, England,

MISSOURI AT A GLANCE

Motto: The Welfare of the People Shall be the Supreme Law

Population: 5.6 million

Prevalent Religions: Christianity, particularly Roman Catholic, Baptist, Methodist, Lutheran, Pentecostal, and non/inter-denominational, small segments of Judaism and Church of Jesus Christ of Latter-day Saints

Major Industries: Cattle, soybeans, hogs, dairy products, corn, poultry and eggs, transportation equipment, food processing, chemical products

Ethnic Makeup (in percent): Caucasian 84.9%, African American 11.2%, Hispanic 2.1%, Asian 1.1%, Native American 0.4%, Other 0.8%

Famous Missourians: Thomas Hart Benton, Yogi Berra, Bill Bradley, Martha Jane Canary (Calamity Jane), Dale Carnegie, George Washington Carver, Walter Cronkite, T.S. Eliot, Eugene Field, Redd Foxx, James W. Fulbright, Betty Grable, Edwin Hubble, Langston Hughes, John Huston, Marianne Moore, Vincent Price, Ginger Rogers, Harry Truman, Mark Twain

Above: The famous Gateway Arch

© PhotoDisc/Getty Images

Switzerland, and Bohemia. During the 1830s, the foreign immigration became large-scale. The Platte Purchase of 1837 added six northwestern counties to the state. In the 1840s large numbers of German immigrants continued to arrive, as did many Irish fleeing the Potato Famine. Many of the new arrivals were settling in Missouri's growing cities.

Missouri provided many soldiers to both the Union and Confederacy during the Civil War, and many critical battles of that war were fought within the state. During the remainder of the nineteenth century, Missouri's cities saw increasing immigration from Greece, Poland, Italy, and East European Jews.

RECORD HIGHLIGHTS

The first federal census population schedule available for the state of Missouri is the 1830. The 1890 census was destroyed, but the 1890 Union Veterans' Schedule survives. The 1850, 1860, 1870, and 1880 Mortality Schedules are also extant.

Statewide registration of births and deaths began in 1863, but it was not mandatory until 1910 (except for 1883–1893, when it *was* required, but repealed when no one was complying.) Pre-1910 records are available from the county clerk, while later records can be ordered from the Bureau of Vital Records in Jefferson City. In addition, the Missouri State Archives Web site has a searchable Birth and Death Records Database of 185,000 pre-1910 birth and death records from eighty-seven counties that are available on microfilm at the Missouri State Archives <www.sos.mo.gov/archives/resources/birthdeath/>.

Marriage records are kept by the county clerks. Statewide registration of marriages began in 1881. The Bureau of Vital Records in Jefferson City has an index to marriages starting 1 July 1948, and issues certificates of proof of marriage. Copies of actual marriage licenses can be obtained from the county recorder of deeds or from microfilm at the Missouri State Archives. The Family History Library has microfilm of marriage licenses from each Missouri county, often up to the 1920s. Divorce records are available from the circuit court clerk for each county, and the Bureau of Vital Records has copies of divorce records from 1948 to the present.

Two county-level courts exist today in Missouri: probate and county. (The county courts usually have the records for past county-level courts that went by other names: chancery, common-pleas, and justice-of-the-peace.) At the district-level is the circuit court; there are forty-five judicial circuits covering Missouri's one hundred and fourteen counties. Missouri has had an excellent state archives microfilming program for many years. More than fifty-five thousand rolls of microfilmed county-level records, circuit court civil case files, and other significant collections are available for use at the State Archives. The microfilm is available for sale, and much of it is also available through the Family History Library. You can view the listing of filmed records for any county at the Archives Web site <www.sos.mo.gov/archives/resources/county/croll.asp>.

Naturalization records are generally held by the circuit courts and can be ordered from the clerk's office at the courthouse. Some county naturalizations are available through the Family History Library. Land records are held by the recorder of deeds in each county. Pre-1900 deeds for almost all Missouri counties are available through the Family History Library. Probate records are generally maintained by the clerk of the probate court in each county. The FHL has films of probate records for many Missouri counties from the date the county was created to about 1925.

Many Missouri cemetery and church records have been abstracted, indexed, or microfilmed, and many original records and church histories are available at archives, historical societies, or from the church or cemetery association where they originated. Check the Web sites and catalogs of the major repositories in Missouri, as well as the Family History Library catalog. For example, the FHL holds the microfilmed parish registers of the Roman Catholic Archdiocese of St. Louis, and has a collection of alphabetized parish register transcripts from the Roman Catholic Archdiocese of Kansas City covering the years 1830 to 1900.

Newspapers are available at many of the larger libraries, historical societies, and colleges. The state's major newspaper collection is at the State Historical Society of Missouri in Columbia.

STATE RESOURCES

■ ARCHIVES, LIBRARIES, AND SOCIETIES

Adair County Historical Society, Inc.
211 S. Elson St., Kirksville, MO 63501-3466
Tel: (660) 665-6502
Web site: <www.webmoondance.com/ACHS/ACHS.htm>

Afro-American Historical & Genealogical Society
3700 Blue Pkwy., Kansas City, MO 64130

Andrew County Historical Society
℅ Andrew County Museum, P.O. Box 12, Savannah, MO 64485-0012

E-mail: andcomus@ccp.com
Web site: <www.rootsweb.com/~moandrew/and-society.html>

Audrain County Area Genealogical Society
℅ Mexico-Audrain County Library, 305 W. Jackson St., Mexico, MO 65265
Web site: <http://members.sockets.net/~macld/genealogy.htm>

Audrain County Historical Society
501 S. Muldrow, Mexico, MO 65265
Tel: (573) 581-3910
E-mail: info@audrain.org
Web site: <www.audrain.org/index.php>

Barry County Genealogical & Historical Society
P.O. Box 291, Cassville, MO 65625

RESEARCH TIPS

for more info

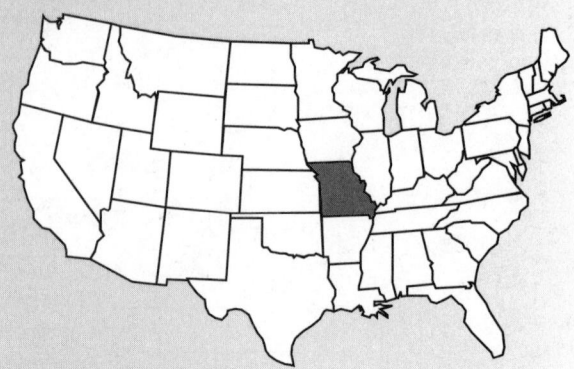

- The St. Louis Genealogical Society's Web site provides details on their many resources, projects, and benefits of membership <www.stlgs.org/index.shtml>.
- The Missouri State Archives in Jefferson City is the state's official repository for original historical records from the colonial era through statehood <www.sos.mo.gov/archives>.
- The State Historical Society of Missouri is located at Ells Library at the University of Missouri in Columbia and it is a state-supported society that has a major collection of available Missouri newspapers, as well as significant indexes, maps, and library collections <www.umsystem.edu/shs/>.
- The Missouri Historical Society in St. Louis has holdings that pertain to the colonial, territorial, and state history of Missouri, but are particularly strong for the colonial period <www.mohistory.org/content/HomePage/HomePage.aspx>.
- The Mercantile Library at the University of Missouri—St. Louis specializes in the history of the Mississippi Valley.
- The results of more than a decade of research will soon be published. *Opening the Ozarks: 1835–1839*, by Marsha Hoffman Rising, CG, FASG, is a study of the first one thousand men and women to patent land at the Springfield (Missouri) Land Office.

Census Records
- Federal Censuses: 1830, 1840, 1850, 1860, 1870, 1880, 1900, 1910, 1920, 1930
- Federal Mortality Schedules: 1850, 1860, 1870, and 1880
- Union Veterans and Widows: 1890
- State Censuses: 1844, 1852, and 1856 (Callaway and Greene Counties), 1876

Web site: <www.rootsweb.com/ ~mobarry/society.html>

Boone County Historical Society
3801 Ponderosa St., Columbia, MO 65201
Tel: (573) 443-8936
E-mail: bchs@socket.net
Web site: <http://members.sock et.com/~bchs/index.htm>

Camden County Museum-Historical Society
P.O. Box 19, 204 Locust St., Linn Creek, MO 65052
Tel: (573) 346-7191

Cape Girardeau County Archive Center
112 E. Washington, Jackson, MO 63755
Tel: (573) 204-2331
E-mail: archive@capecounty.us
Web site: <www.showme.net/Ca peCounty/archive/index.htm>

Cape Girardeau County Genealogical Society
P.O. Box 389, Jackson, MO 63755
E-mail: hummingbird@clas.net
Web site: <www.rootsweb.com/ ~mocgcgs/index.htm>

Carroll County Genealogical Association
P.O. Box 354, Carrollton, MO 64633-0354
E-mail: root-tracking@centurytel .net
Web site: <www.carolnet.com/ ccga/>

Carthage Genealogical Society and Southwest Missouri Genealogical Library
Rt. 3, Box 117, Carthage, MO 64836
Tel: (417) 358-6494

Cass County Historical Society
P.O. Box 406, 400 E. Mechanic, Harrisonville, MO 64701-0406
Tel: (816) 380-4396
Web site: <www.rootsweb.com/ ~mocass/cashist.html>

Commerce Historical Society
P.O. Box 93, Commerce, MO 63742-0093
Web site: <www.rosecity.net/co mmerce/books.html>

Concordia Historical Institute
801 DeMun Ave., Saint Louis, MO 63105
Tel: (314) 505-7900
Web site: <http://chi.lcms.org/>

Cooper County Historical Society
5236 Hwy. A, Bunceton, MO 65237
Tel: (660) 834-4581
Web site: <www.mo-river.net/Co mmunity/social-services/cooper/ historical-society.htm>

Dade County Genealogical Society
P.O. Box 155, Greenfield, MO 65661
Web site: <www.rootsweb.com/ ~modade/dcgs.htm>

Dallas County Historical Society, Inc.
P.O. Box 594, Buffalo, MO 65622
Tel: (417) 345-8694
Web site: <www.rootsweb.com/ ~modallas/DCHS.html>

DeKalb County Historical Society
P.O. Box 467, Maysville, MO 64469-0467
Tel: (816) 449-5451
E-mail: dchs@cameron.net
Web site: <www.rootsweb.com/ ~modekalb/dchs.html>

Disciples of Christ Historical Society
1101 Nineteenth Ave. S., Nashville, TN 37212
Web site:

Dunklin County Genealogical Society
% Dunklin County Library, 209 N. Main, Kennett, MO 63857
Tel: (573) 888-3561

Edson Genealogical Association
724 S. Whitmer St., Richmond, MO 64085-2154
Tel: (816) 776-3257
E-mail: EdsonEGA@aol.com
Web site: <http://members.aol. com/genee76689/>

Excelsior Springs Genealogical Society
1000 Magnolia W., Excelsior Springs, MO 64024

Four Rivers Genealogy Society
P.O. Box 146, Washington, MO 63090
Web site: <www.rootsweb.com/ ~mofrankl/hsfourrivers.htm>

Genealogical Society of Butler County
P.O. Box 426, Poplar Bluff, MO 63902-0426

Web site: <www.rootsweb.com/ ~mobcgs/>

Genealogical Society of Central Missouri
P.O. Box 26, Columbia, MO 65205-0026
Web site: <www.gscm.gen.mo .us/GSCM.HTM>

Genealogical Society of Pulaski County
P.O. Box 144, Waynesville, MO 65583

Genealogy Friends of the Library
P.O. Box 314, Neosho, MO 64850
Tel: (417) 451-4231
E-mail: Genealogy@neosho.lib .mo.us
Web site: <www.rootsweb.com/ ~monewton/gf.html>

Graham Historical Society
417 S. Walnut, Marysville, MO 64468

Grundy County Genealogical Society
P.O. Box 223, Trenton, MO 64683
Web site: <www.rootsweb.com/ ~mogrundy/gcgen.html>

Harrison County Genealogical Society
2307 Central Bethany, MO 64424
Tel: (660) 425-2459
Web site: <www.rootsweb.com/ ~moharris/hcgen.html>

Heart of America Genealogical Society and Library, Inc.
% Kansas City Public Library, 311 E. Twelfth St., Kansas City, MO 64106-2412
Tel: (816) 221-2685

Historical Society of Maries County
P.O. Box 289, Vienna, MO 65582
Web site: <www.rootsweb.com/ ~momaries/marihiso.htm>

Howard County Genealogical Society
% Fayette Public Library, 201 S. Main St., Fayette, MO 65248
Web site: <www.rootsweb.com/ ~mohoward/local.html>

Iron County Genealogical Society
P.O. Box 343, Arcadia, MO 63621
Web site: <www.rootsweb.com/ ~moicgs/icgs_home.html>

Jackson County Genealogical Society
420 S. Main St., Box 1133, Independence, MO 64055

Jackson County Historical Society
129 W. Lexington, Independence, MO 64050
Tel: (816) 461-1897
Web site:

Jefferson County Historical Society
% De Soto Public Library, 712 S. Main, De Soto, MO 63020-2401
Tel: (636) 586-3858
Web site: <www.rootsweb.com/ ~mojeffer/jchs/>

Jefferson County Genealogical Society
P.O. Box 1342, High Ridge, MO 63049
Tel: (636) 677-8186
E-mail: dlanghistory@earthlink .net
Web site: <www.rootsweb.com/ ~mojcgs/Jcgs_Info.html>

Jewish Genealogical Society of St. Louis
% United Hebrew Congregation, 13788 Conway Rd., St. Louis, MO
Web site:

Joplin Genealogical Society
P.O. Box 152, Joplin, MO 64801

Kansas City Public Library
14 W. Tenth St., Kansas City, MO 64105
Tel: (816) 701-3400
Web site:

Kimmswick Historical Society
Burgess-How House, P.O. Box 41, 6000 Third St., Kimmswick, MO 63053
Tel: (314) 464-8687
Web site: <http://library.wustl. edu/units/spec/archives/aslaa/ directory/kimmswick.html>

Laclede County Genealogical Society
P.O. Box 350 , Lebanon, MO 65536
Web site: <www.llion.org/~mola cled>

Landon Creek Chapter, Afro-American Historical & Genealogical Society
P.O. Box 231804, St. Louis, MO 63121-0804

Missouri

Missouri

Lawrence County Historical Society
P.O. Box 406, Mt. Vernon, MO 65712
Web site: <www.rootsweb.com/~molawre2/society.htm>

Lewis County Historical Society, Inc.
112 N. Fourth St., Canton, MO 63435-1313
Tel: (573) 288-5713

Lincoln County Genealogical Society & Library
125 W. Second, St., Moscow Mills, MO 63362
Web site: <www.rootsweb.com/~molincol/research/lcsociety.htm>

Livingston County Genealogical Society
% Livingston County Library, 450 Locust St., Chillicothe, MO 64601-2597
Tel: (816) 646-0547
Web site: <http://ghlin2.greenhills.net/~fwoods/pages/lcgs.htm>

Mercer County Genealogical & Historical Society
P.O. Box 97, Princeton, MO 64673
Web site: <www.rootsweb.com/~momercer/mcghs.html>

Mid-Continent Public Library
15616 E. Twenty-four Hwy., Independence, MO 64050
Tel: (816) 836-5200
Web site:

Mid-Missouri Genealogical Society
P.O. Box 387, Jefferson City, MO 65101

Mine Au Breton Historical Society
10205 Weber Lane, Potosi, MO 63664
Web site: <www.rootsweb.com/~mowashin/mabhs.html>

Mississippi County Genealogical Society
P.O. Box 5, Charleston, MO 63834

Missouri Baptist Historical Commission
William E. Partee Center, William Jewel College, 500 College Hill, Liberty, MO 64068
Tel: (816) 781-7700

Missouri Department of Health and Senior Services, Bureau of Vital Records
P.O. Box 570, Jefferson City, MO 65102

Missouri Historical Society
P.O. Box 11940, St. Louis, MO 63112
Tel: (314) 746-4511
E-mail: photo@mohistory.org
Web site: <www.mohistory.org>

Missouri State Archives
600 W. Main St., P.O. Box 1747, Jefferson City, MO 65102
Tel: (573) 751-3280
E-mail: archref@sos.mo.gov
Web site: <www.sos.mo.gov/archives/Default.asp>

Missouri State Genealogical Association
P.O. Box 833, Columbia, MO 65205-0833
E-mail: mosga@mosga.org
Web site:

Missouri Territorial Pioneers
3929 Milton Dr., Independence, MO 64055
Web site: <http://kinnexions.com/ancestries/pioneer/mo.htm>

The Missouri United Methodist Archives
Central Methodist University, Fayette, MO 65248
E-mail: MUMA@cmc.edu
Web site: <www.cmc.edu/library/Archives/ARCHIVES.html>

Moniteau County Historical Society
201 N. High, California, MO 65018
Tel: (573) 796-3563

Montgomery County Genealogical Society
112 W. Second St., Montgomery City, MO 63361

Morgan County Historical Society
P.O. Box 181, Versailles, MO 65084
E-mail: mocohist@advertisnet.com

National Archives-Central Plains Region
2312 E. Bannister Rd., Kansas City, MO 64131-3011
Tel: (816) 268-8000
Web site: <www.archives.gov/facilities/mo/kansas_city.html>

Newton County Historical Society/Genealogical Study Group
P.O. Box 675, Neosho, MO 64850

Nodaway County Genealogical Society
P.O. Box 214, Maryville, MO 64468
Web site: <www.rootsweb.com/~monodawa/ncgs.htm>

Northland Genealogical Society
P.O. Box 14121, Parkville, MO 64152
Web site: <http://homepages.rootsweb.com/~kcngs/>

Northwest Missouri Genealogical Society
P.O. Box 382, St. Joseph, MO 64502
Tel: (816) 233-0524
Web site: <www.rootsweb.com/~monwmgs/index.htm>

Old Mines Area Historical Society
Rt. 1, Box 1466, Old Mines, MO 63630
Web site: <www.rootsweb.com/~mowashin/omahs.html>

Oregon County Genealogical Society
P.O. Box 324, Alton, MO 65606
Tel: (417) 778-6414
Web site: <www.rootsweb.com/~mooregon/ocgs.htm>

Osage County Historical Society
P.O. Box 402, Linn, MO 65051
Web site:

Ozark County Genealogical and Historical Society
HCR 2, Box 88, Gainsville, MO 65655

Ozarks Genealogical Society, Inc.
P.O. Box 3945, Springfield, MO 65808-3945
E-mail: ogso@sbcglobal.net
Web site: <www.rootsweb.com/~ozarksgs/>

Perry County Historical Society
P.O. Box 97, Perryville, MO 63775
Web site: <www.perryvillemissouri.com/perrycountyhistoricalsociety.htm>

Phelps County Genealogical Society
P.O. Box 571, Rolla, MO 65402-0571

E-mail: pcgs@rollanet.org
Web site: <www.rollanet.org/~pcgs/>

Phelps County Historical Society
P.O. Box 1535, Rolla, MO 65402-1535
Tel: (573) 364-5977
Web site: <http://web.umr.edu/~whmcinfo/pchs/>

Pike County Historical Society
304 W. Georgia St., Louisiana, MO 63353

Pike County Genealogical Society
P.O. Box 313, Bowling Green, MO 63334-0313
Web site: <www.pastracks.com/pcgs/index.html>

Platte County Historical & Genealogical Society
P.O. Box 103, Platte City, MO 64079-0103
Web site: <www.rootsweb.com/~mopchgs/>

Polk County Genealogical Society
P.O. Box 632, Bolivar, MO 65613-0632
Tel: (417) 777-2820
E-mail: pcgs@microcore.net
Web site: <www.rootsweb.com/~mopolkgs/>

Randolph County Historical Society
223 N. Clark, Moberly, MO 65270
Tel: (660) 263-9396
Web site: <www.rootsweb.com/~morandol/rchs.htm>

Ray County Genealogical Association
901 W. Royle St., Richmond, MO 64085-1545
Web site: <www.rootsweb.com/~morcga/>

Ray County Historical Society
P.O. Box 2, Richmond, MO 64085
Tel: (816) 776-2305

Reynolds County Genealogy and Historical Society
P.O. Box 281, Ellington, MO 63638
Tel: (573) 663-7289

Ripley County Historical Society
101 Washington St., Doniphan, MO 63935
Tel: (573) 996-5298

Scotland County Historical Society
P.O. Box 263, Memphis, MO 63555
Web site: <www.rootsweb.com/~moscotla/>

Scott County Historical & Genealogy Society
P.O. Box 151, Benton, MO 63736
Web site:

S. Vernon Genealogical Society
Rt. 2, Box 280, Sheldon, MO 64784

South Central Missouri Genealogical Society
1043 W. Fifth St., West Plains, MO 65775

St. Charles County Genealogical Society
P.O. Box 715, St. Charles, MO 63302-0715
Web site: <www.rootsweb.com/~mosccgs/>

St. Louis Genealogical Society
P.O. Box 43010, St. Louis, MO 63143-0010
Tel: (314) 647-8547
Web site: <www.stlgs.org/index.shtml>

St. Louis Public Library
1301 Olive St., St. Louis, MO 63103
Tel: (314) 241-2288
Web site: <www.slpl.lib.mo.us/libsrc/h&gdept.htm>

State Historical Society of Missouri
1020 Lowry St., Columbia, MO 65201-7298
Tel: (573) 882-7083
Web site: <www.umsystem.edu/shs/>

Stone County Missouri Historical & Genealogical Society
P.O. Box 63, Galena, MO 65656
Web site: <www.rootsweb.com/~mostone/society/society.html>

Texas County Genealogical and Historical Society
P.O. Box 12, 300 S. Grand Ave., Houston, MO 65483
Tel: (417) 967-3126

Thrailkill Genealogical Society
2018 Gentry, North Kansas City, MO 64116

Tri-County Genealogical Society
P.O. Box B, 218 W. Walnut St., Nevada, MO 64772
E-mail: TriCountyGenealogy@starband.net

Union Cemetery Historical Society
227 E. Twenty-eighth Terrace, Kansas City, MO 64108-3277
Tel: (816) 472-4990

United Centenary Methodist Church
55 Plaza Sq., Saint Louis, MO 63103
Tel: (314) 588-1450

Vernon County Historical Society
231 N. Main St., Nevada, MO 64772
E-mail: bushwhackerjail@sbcglobal.net
Web site:

Warren County Historical Society
P.O. Box 12, Warrenton, MO 63383

Webb City Area Genealogical Society
101 S. Liberty St., Webb City, MO 64870
Tel: (417) 673-4326

West Central Missouri Genealogical Society
P.O. Box 4, Warrensburg, MO, 64093-2032
Web site: <www.rootsweb.com/~mojohnso/library/Society.htm>

Westport Historical Society
4000 Baltimore, Kansas City, MO, 64111
Tel: (816) 561-1821
Web site:

White River Valley Historical Society
P.O. Box 555, Pt. Lookout, MO 65726-0555
Web site: <http://homepages.rootsweb.com/~moarwrv/>

Wright County Historical and Genealogical Society
P.O. Box 66, Hartville MO 65667

BIBLIOGRAPHY

■ GENERAL RESOURCES

Bible Records of Missouri
by Elizabeth B. Langley (Billings, MO: Langley, 1968)

A Bibliography of Missouri County Histories and Atlases
by Paul O. Selby (Kirksville, MO: Northeast Missouri State Teachers College, 1966)

A Centennial History of the State Historical Society of Missouri, 1898–1998
by Alan R. Havig (Columbia, MO: University of Missouri Press, ca. 1998)

Directory of Local Historical, Museum, and Genealogical Agencies in Missouri
(Columbia, MO: State Historical Society of Missouri, ca. 1993)

Early Missourians and Kin, A Genealogical Compilation of Interrelated Early Missouri Settlers, Their Ancestors, Descendants and Other Kin
by Roy Burgess (Venice, FL: R. Burgess, 1984–1987)

Encyclopedia of the History of Missouri, A Compendium of History and Biography for Ready Reference
by Howard Louis Conard (New York: Southern History Co., 1901)

Genealogical Material and Local Histories in the St. Louis Public Library
by the St. Louis Public (St. Louis, MO: St. Louis Public Library, 1953–)

The Genealogist's Companion and Sourcebook, 2d ed.
by Emily Anne Croom (Cincinnati: Betterway Books, 2003)

A Genealogist's Guide to Discovering Your African-American Ancestors
by Franklin Carter Smith and Emily Anne Croom (Cincinnati: Betterway Books, 2003)

A Guide to County Records on Microfilm
(Jefferson City, MO: Missouri State Archives, 1990)

Guide to Genealogical Research in the National Archives of the United States
edited by Anne Bruner Eales and Robert M. Kvasnicka (Washington, DC: National Archives and Records Administration, 2000)

A Guide to Genealogical Research in St. Louis
by Edward E. Steele (St. Louis, MO: St. Louis Genealogical Society, 1995)

Guide to Public Vital Statistics Records in Missouri
by the Historical Records Survey (St. Louis, MO: Historical Records Survey, 1941)

Historical and Biographical Sketches of the Early Churches and Pioneer Preachers of the Christian Church in Missouri
by T.P. Haley (Kansas City: J.H. Smart, ca. 1888)

A History of the Baptists in Missouri, Embracing an Account of the Organization and Growth of Baptist Churches and Associations
by R.S. Duncan (St. Louis, MO: Scammell, 1882)

A History of Missouri from the Earliest Explorations and Settlements until the Admission of the State into the Union
by Louis Houck (Chicago: R.R. Donnelley, ca. 1908)

A History of the Pioneer Families of Missouri, with Numerous Sketches, Anecdotes, Adventures, etc., Relating to Early Days in Missouri: also the Lives of Daniel Boone and the Celebrated Indian Chief Black Hawk, with Numerous Biographies and Histories of Primitive Institutions
by William S. Bryan (St. Louis, MO: Bryan Brand, 1876)

History of the United Methodist Churches of Missouri
by Richard A. Seaton (Fayette, MO: Missouri Methodist Historical Society, 1984)

A List of Manuscript Collections in the Archives of the Missouri Historical Society
by Beverly D. Biship (St. Louis, MO: Missouri Historical Society, ca. 1982)

Missouri

The Methodist Church in Missouri: 1798–1939, A Brief History
by Frank C. Tucker (F.C. Tucker, ca. 1966)

Midwest Pioneers, 1600s-1800s
(Brøderbund, ca. 1999. CD-ROM)

Missouri Family Histories and Genealogies: A Bibliography
by Donald M. Hehir (Bowie, MD: Heritage Books, ca. 1996)

Missouri, A History of the Crossroads State
by Edwin C. McReynolds (Norman, OK: University of Oklahoma Press, ca. 1962)

Missouri, Mother of the West
by Walter Williams (Chicago: American Historical Society, 1930)

Missouri Pioneers, County and Genealogical Records
compiled and published by Nadine Hodges, Mrs. John Vineyard, and Mrs. Howard W. Woodruff (Missouri: N. Hodges, 1967–1976)

Missouri Research Outline
by the Church of Jesus Christ of Latter-day Saints (Salt Lake City, UT: Corp. of the President of The Church of Jesus Christ of L.D.S., ca. 1988, ca. 1997)

National Archives Microfilm Catalogs online:
<www.archives.gov/publications/genealogy_microfilm_catalogs.html>

The Organization of Missouri Counties
by the Historical Records Survey (St. Louis, MO: Historical Records Survey, 1941)

Orphan Trains to Missouri
by Michael D. Patrick (Columbia, MO: University of Missouri Press, ca. 1997)

People of Color: Black Genealogical Records and Abstracts from Missouri Sources
by Teresa Blattner (Bowie, MD: Heritage Books, ca. 1993, ca. 1998)

Pioneer Kentuckians with Missouri Cousins
by Linda Barber Brooks (St. Louis, MO: Ingmire Publications, ca. 1985)

The Refiner's Fire: The Significance of Events Transpiring in Missouri
by Alvin R. Dyer (Salt Lake City: Deseret Books, 1968)

"Research in Missouri"
by Pamela Boyer Porter and Ann Carter Fleming (*National Genealogical Society Quarterly*, June 1999)

Robert E. Parkin's Guide to Tracing Your Family Tree in Missouri
by Robert E. Parkin (St. Louis, MO: Genealogical Research & Productions, ca. 1979)

Southeast Missouri, A Narrative Account of its Historical Progress, its People and its Principal Interests
by Robert Sidney Douglass (Chicago: Lewis Pub. Co., 1912)

The Trail of Tears Across Missouri
by Joan Gilbert (Columbia, MO: University of Missouri Press, ca. 1996)

Who's What and Why in Missouri: Library of American lives; a reference edition recording the biographies of contemporary leaders in Missouri with special emphasis on their achievements in making the "show me" state one of America's greatest
by the Jefferson City, Missouri Chamber of Commerce (Hopkinsville, KY: Historical Record Association, 1959)

■ CENSUS RECORDS

The American Census Handbook
by Thomas Jay Kemp (Wilmington, DE: Scholarly Resources Inc., ca. 2001)

Anglo-Americans in Spanish Archives: Lists of Anglo-American Settlers in the Spanish Colonies of America; A Finding Aid
by Lawrence H. Feldman (Baltimore, MD: Genealogical Pub. Co., ca. 1991)

The Census Book: A Genealogist's Guide to Federal Census Facts, Schedules and Indexes; With Master Extraction Forms for Federal Census Schedules, 1790–1930
by William Dollarhide (Bountiful, UT: Heritage Quest, ca. 1999)

Enumeration of the County of St. Charles, Missouri Territory for the Years 1817 and 1819, With Some Selected Marriage and Cemetery Records . . .
by Melvin B. Goe (Owensboro, KY: Cook-McDowell Publications, 1980)

Finding Answers in U.S. Census Records
by Loretto Dennis Szucs and Matthew Wright (Orem, UT: Ancestry Pub., ca. 2001)

Map Guide to the U.S. Federal Censuses, 1790–1920
by William Thorndale and William Dollarhide (Baltimore: Genealogical Pub. Co., ca. 1987)

Missouri Taxpayers, 1819–1826
by Lois Stanley (Greenville, SC: Southern Historical Press, ca. 1990)

State Census Records
by Ann S. Lainhart (Baltimore, MD: Genealogical Pub. Co., ca. 1992)

Ten Thousand Missouri Taxpayers
by Sherida K. Eddlemon (Bowie, MD: Heritage Books, ca. 1996)

Your Guide to the Federal Census
by Kathleen W. Hinckley (Cincinnati: Betterway Books, 2002)

■ IMMIGRATION RECORDS

American Naturalization Records, 1790–1990: What They Are and How to Use Them
by John J. Newman (North Salt Lake, UT: HeritageQuest, 1998)

American Passenger Arrival Records
by Michael Tepper (Baltimore: Genealogical Publishing Co., 1993)

German Settlement in Missouri: New Land, Old Ways
by Robyn Burnett (Columbia, MO: University of Missouri Press, ca. 1996)

Immigrants in the Ozarks: A Study in Ethnic Geography
by Russel L. Gerlach (Columbia, MO: University of Missouri Press, ca. 1976)

Settlement Patterns in Missouri, A Study of Population Origins
by Russel L. Gerlach (Columbia, MO: University of Missouri Press, ca. 1986)

They Became Americans: Finding Naturalization Records and Ethnic Origins
by Loretto Dennis Szucs (Salt Lake City: Ancestry, Inc., 1998)

They Came in Ships: A Guide to Finding Your Immigrant Ancestor's Arrival Records, 2d ed.
by John P. Colletta (Salt Lake City: Ancestry, Inc., 1993)

Virginia Settlers in Missouri
by A. Maxim Coppage (Owensboro, KY: Cook & McDowell Pub., 1979)

The Westfalians: from Germany to Missouri
by Walter D. Kamphoefner (Princeton: Princeton University Press, ca. 1987)

■ LAND RECORDS

Citizens of Missouri
by Frances Terry Ingmire (St. Louis, MO: F.T. Ingmire, ca. 1984)

Early Settlers of Missouri as Taken from Land Claims in the Missouri Territory
by Walter Lowrie (Easley, SC: Southern Historical Press, 1986)

First Settlers of the Missouri Territory
(Nacogdoches, TX: Ericson Books, ca. 1983)

Land Patents, 1800's–early 1900's
by the Missouri Governor (Jefferson City, MO: State of Missouri, 1971)

Land & Property Research in the United States
by E. Wade Hone (Salt Lake City, UT: Ancestry, ca. 1997)

Locating Your Roots: Discover Your Ancestors Using Land Records
by Patricia Law Hatcher (Cincinnati: Betterway Books, 2003)

Miscellaneous Records Relating to Missouri lands, 1700's, 1800's, 1900's
by the Missouri State Archives (Jefferson City, MO: State of Missouri, 1969–1972)

Missouri Military Land Warrants, War of 1812
by Maxine Dunaway (Springfield, MO: M. Dunaway, ca. 1985)

Missouri Plat Books in the State Historical Society of Missouri
by Laurel Boeckman (Columbia, MO: State Historical Society of Missouri, 1989)

Record Books, 1795–1808; Index to French and Spanish Land Grants, 1795–1812
by the Louisiana Territory Recorder of Land Titles (Jefferson City, MO: State of Missouri, 1970)

Records of Missouri Swamp Lands: Original Selections, New Selections, and Sales, 1800's
by the United States General Land Office (Jefferson City, MO: State of Missouri, 1969)

United States Land Sales in Missouri, 1827–1903; Index to Land Sales, 1818–1893
by the United States General Land Office (Jefferson City, MO: State of Missouri, 1969)

■ MAPS

A Bibliography of Missouri County Histories and Atlases
by Paul O. Selby (Kirksville, MO: Northeast Missouri State Teachers College, 1966)

A Gazetteer of the States of Illinois and Missouri
by Lewis Caleb Beck (New York: Arno Press, Inc., 1975)

Gazetteer of the State of Missouri
by Alphonso Wetmore (New York: Arno Press, Inc., 1975)

Historical Atlas of Missouri
by Milton D. Rafferty (Norman, OK: University of Oklahoma Press, ca. 1982)

Interesting Missouri Place Names
by Gerald Leonard Cohen (Rolla, MO: G. Cohen, ca. 1982)

Missouri Atlas and Gazetteer
by the DeLorme Mapping Company (Yarmouth, ME: DeLorme Mapping Co., ca. 1998)

Our Storehouse of Missouri Place Names
by Robert Lee Ramsay (Columbia: University of Missouri, 1952)

■ MILITARY RECORDS

The Forgotten Men: Missouri State Guards
by Carolyn M. Bartels (Shawnee Mission, KS: Two Trails Pub., ca. 1995)

Grand Army of the Republic, Missouri Division, Index to Death Rolls 1882–1940: Taken from the Proceedings of the Annual Encampments
by Marie Concannon (Columbia, MO: State Historical Society of Missouri, 1995)

Index of Residents, State Federal Soldiers' Home of Missouri, St. James, Missouri, 1899–1946
by Marie C. Concannon (Columbia, MO: State Historical Society of Missouri, 1998)

Missouri Confederate Pensions and Confederate Home Applications Index
by Peggy Barnes Fox (Hillsboro, TX: Hill College Press, ca. 1996)

The 24th Missouri Volunteer Infantry "Lyon's Legion"
by J. Randall Houp (Alma, AR: J.R. Houp, ca. 1997)

Revolutionary Soldiers Buried in Missouri
by Alice Kinyoun Houts (Kansas City, MO: Houts, ca. 1966)

Uncle, We Are Ready! Registering America's Men, 1917–1918: A Guide to Researching World War I Draft Registration Cards
by John J. Newman (North Salt Lake, UT: HeritageQuest, 2001)

U.S. Military Records: A Guide to Federal & State Sources, Colonial America to the Present
by James C. Neagles (Salt Lake City: Ancestry, Inc., 1994)

World War II: A Family Historian's Guide
by Debra Johnson Knox (Spartanburg, SC: MIE Publishing, 2003)

■ PROBATE RECORDS

A Digest of all the Decisions of the Supreme Court of the State of Missouri, Contained in the First Fifteen Volumes of the Missouri Reports
by Evans Casselberry (Saint Louis: Fisher & Bennett, 1853)

French and Spanish Archives, 1766–1816
by the St. Louis, Missouri Archival Library (St. Louis, MO: City of St. Louis, 1962)

Gentry County, Missouri Probate Index, 1885–1902
by the Northwest Missouri Genealogical Society (St. Joseph, MO: Northwest Missouri Genealogy Society, ca. 1980)

■ VITAL RECORDS

Death Records from Missouri Newspapers: the Civil War Years, January 1861–December 1865
by Lois Stanley (Decorah, IA: Anundsen, 1983)

Death Records from Missouri Newspapers: January 1854-December 1860
by Lois Stanley (Decorah, IA: Anundsen, 1982)

Death Records of Pioneer Missouri Women, 1808–1853
by Lois Stanley (Greenville, SC: Southern Historical Press, ca. 1990)

Divorces, Separations and Annulments in Missouri 1769 to 1850
by Teresa Blattner (Bowie, MD: Heritage Books, ca. 1993)

Divorces and Separations in Missouri: 1808–1853
by Lois Stanley (Greenville, SC: Southern Historical Press, ca. 1990)

Early Bibles and Graveyard Records
by Kathryn H. Campbell (1972–)

Early Missouri Ancestors: From Newspapers
by George F. Wilson (Decorah, IA: The Anundsen Pub. Co., 1986–1987)

East Central Missouri Cemetery and Bible Records
by the Daughters of the American Revolution, John Sappington Chapter (Affton, MO: 1974)

Guide to Public Vital Statistics Records in Missouri
by the Historical Records Survey (St. Louis, MO: Historical Records Survey, 1941)

1300 "Missing" Missouri Marriage Records from Newspapers, 1812–1853
by George F. Wilson (Decorah, IA: Anundsen, 1982)

Missouri, 1851–1900
by the Liahona Research, Orem, UT (Brøderbund, ca. 1998. CD-ROM)

Missouri Birth and Death Records
by Sherida K. Eddlemon (Bowie, MD: Heritage Books, ca. 1995, ca. 1999, ca. 2001)

Missouri Cemetery Inscription Sources; Print and Microform
by Elizabeth Gorrell Kot (Vallejo, CA: Indices Pub., ca. 1995)

Missouri Marriages to 1850
by Linda Barber Brooks (St. Louis, MO: Distributed by Ingmire Publications, ca. 1983–)

Missouri Marriages Before 1840
by Susan Ormesher (Baltimore: Genealogical Pub. Co., ca. 1982)

Missouri Marriages, Early (ca. 1754) to 1825: A Research Tool
by Jordon R. Dodd (Bountiful, UT: Precision Indexing, ca. 1990)

Missouri Taxpayers, 1819–1826
by Lois Stanley (Greenville, SC: Southern Historical Press, ca. 1990)

More Death Records from Missouri Newspapers, 1810–1857
by Lois Stanley (Decorah, IA: Anundsen, 1985)

Selected Union Burials, Missouri Units
by Edward Parker (Columbia, MO: The State Historical Society of Missouri, 1988, 1993)

Missouri

Your Guide to Cemetery Research
by Sharon DeBartolo Carmack
(Cincinnati: Betterway Books, 2002)

■ **Adair** 29 Jan. 1841
P.O. Box 690, Kirksville, MO 63501
Phone: (660)665-2552
Web site: www.rootsweb.com/~moadair/
Parent County: Macon
Comments/research tips: County Clerk has Birth records 1883–1893.

Record Type	Year Begun	Jurisdiction
Marriage	1841	County Recorder
Divorce	na	Clerk/Circuit Ct.
Land	1841	County Recorder
Probate	1841	Probate Clerk
Court	1841	County Clerk

■ **Allen** 23 Feb. 1843
Parent County: Holt
Comments/research tips: (See Atchison) Name changed to Atchison 14 February 1845.

■ **Andrew** 29 Jan. 1841
P.O. Box 208, Savannah, MO 64485
Phone: (816)324-4221
Web site: www.rootsweb.com/~moandrew/
Parent County: Platte Purchase
Comments/research tips: County Clerk has Birth records 1883–1895 and Death records 1883–1893.

Record Type	Year Begun	Jurisdiction
Marriage	1841	County Recorder
Divorce	1841	Clerk/Circuit Ct.
Land	1841	County Recorder
Probate	1841	Probate Clerk
Court	1841	Clerk/Circuit Ct.
Military	na	Clerk/Circuit Ct.

■ **Arkansas** 1813
Parent County: New Madrid
Comments/research tips: Abolished in 1819 when Territory of Arkansas was formed.

■ **Ashley** 17 Feb. 1843
Parent County: Shannon, Wright
Comments/research tips: (See Texas) Name changed to Texas 14 February 1845.

■ **Atchison** 23 Feb. 1845
P.O. Box 280, Rock Port, MO 64482
Phone: (660)744-2707
Web site: www.rootsweb.com/~moatchis/atchison.html
Parent County: Holt/Platte Purhchase
Comments/research tips: Formerly Allen County. Name changed to Atchison 14 February 1845, part of Platte Purchase, attached to Holt County until 1854, lost 10-mile strip to Iowa in 1848. County Clerk has Birth and Death records 1883–1893.

Record Type	Year Begun	Jurisdiction
Marriage	1845	County Recorder
Divorce	na	Clerk/Circuit Ct.
Land	1845	County Recorder
Probate	1845	Probate Clerk
Court	1845	County Clerk

■ **Audrain** 12 Jan. 1831
101 N. Jefferson, Mexico, MO 65265
Phone: (573)473-5840
Web site: www.rootsweb.com/~moaudrai/
Parent County: Ralls
Comments/research tips: Created in 1831, but remained attached to Callaway, Monroe, and Ralls Counties until 1836. In 1842 gained an additional 31 square miles from Monroe County. County Clerk has Birth and Death records 1883–1886.

Record Type	Year Begun	Jurisdiction
Probate	1837	Probate Clerk
Court	1837	County Clerk
Marriage	1837	County Recorder
Divorce	na	Clerk/Circuit Ct.
Land	1837	County Recorder

■ **Barry** 5 Jan. 1835
102 West St. #1, Cassville, MO 65625
Phone: (417)847-2361
Web site: www.rootsweb.com/~mobarry/barry.htm
Parent County: Greene
Comments/research tips: Fire in 1872 destroyed many records in the Circuit Clerks office. County Clerk has Birth and Death records 1883–1885.

Record Type	Year Begun	Jurisdiction
Marriage	1837	County Recorder
Divorce	na	Clerk/Circuit Ct.
Land	1835	County Recorder
Probate	1835	Probate Clerk
Court	1872	County Clerk

■ **Barton** 12 Dec. 1855
1007 Broadway, Lamar, MO 64759
Phone: (417)682-2444
Web site: www.rootsweb.com/~mobarton/
Parent County: Jasper
Comments/research tips: Courthouse burned in 1860. County Clerk has Birth records 1883–1896 and Death records 1883–1899.

Record Type	Year Begun	Jurisdiction
Divorce	na	Clerk/Circuit Ct.
Land	1857	County Recorder
Probate	1866	Probate Clerk
Court	1866	County Clerk
Marriage	1866	County Recorder

■ **Bates** 29 Jan. 1841
1 N. Delaware, Butler, MO 64730
Phone: (660)679-5171

Web site: www.rootsweb.com/~mobates/
Parent County: Cass
Comments/research tips: 22 February 1855 three southern tiers of townships in Cass County were added to Bates. Courthouse burned in 1861. County Clerk has Birth records 1883–1907 and Death records 1883–1893.

Record Type	Year Begun	Jurisdiction
Marriage	1860	County Recorder
Divorce	1860	Clerk/Circuit Ct.
Land	1839	County Recorder
Probate	1845	Probate Clerk
Court	1858	County Clerk

■ Benton   3 Jan. 1835

P.O. Box 37, Warsaw, MO 65355
Phone: (660)438-7712
Web site: http://members.aol.com/hrftx/index.htm
Parent County: Pettis/Greene
Comments/research tips: Benton remained unorganized until January 1837, in 1845, 24 square miles of the northwest part of Benton became part of Pettis County and Hickory County was created, reducing Benton to its present size. County Clerk has Birth and Death records 1883–1890.

Record Type	Year Begun	Jurisdiction
Marriage	1839	County Recorder
Divorce	na	Clerk/Circuit Ct.
Land	1837	County Recorder
Probate	1836	Probate Clerk
Court	1835	County Clerk

■ Bollinger   1 Mar. 1851

P.O. Box 949, Marble Hill, MO 63764
Phone: (573)238-1900
Web site: www.rootsweb.com/~mobollin
Parent County: Cape Girardeau, Stoddard, Wayne/Madison
Comments/research tips: Courthouse burned in 1866 and 1884, while occupied only by the County Clerk's office. County Clerk has Birth records 1883–1891 and Death records 1883–1892.

Record Type	Year Begun	Jurisdiction
Marriage	1865	County Recorder
Divorce	na	Clerk/Circuit Ct.
Land	1851	County Recorder
Probate	1866	Probate Clerk
Court	1866	County Clerk

■ Boone   16 Nov. 1820

705 E. Walnut St., Columbia, MO 65201
Phone: (573)886-4000
Web site: www.showmeboone.com/
Parent County: Howard

Record Type	Year Begun	Jurisdiction
Marriage	1821	County Recorder
Divorce	1821	Clerk/Circuit Ct.
Land	1821	County Recorder
Probate	1821	Probate Clerk
Court	1821	County Clerk

■ Buchanan   31 Dec. 1838

411 Jules St., Room 331, St. Joseph, MO 64501
Phone: (816)271-1462

Web site: www.rootsweb.com/~mobuchan/
Parent County: Platte Purchase
Comments/research tips: County Clerk has Death records 1883–1893.

Record Type	Year Begun	Jurisdiction
Marriage	na	Recorder/Deeds
Probate	na	Probate Judge
Court	na	Magistrate Court
Land	na	County Assayer
Divorce	na	Clerk/Circuit Ct.

■ Butler   27 Feb. 1849

100 N. Main, Poplar Bluff, MO 63901
Phone: (573)686-8082
Web site: www.rootsweb.com/~mobutle2/
Parent County: Wayne
Comments/research tips: County Clerk has Birth and Death records 1883–1893.

Record Type	Year Begun	Jurisdiction
Marriage	1849	Recorder/Deeds
Land	1849	County Recorder
Probate	1849	Probate Clerk

■ Caldwell   29 Dec. 1836

49 E. Main St., P.O. Box 68, Kingston, MO 64650
Phone: (816)586-2581
Web site: www.rootsweb.com/~mocaldwe/
Parent County: Ray
Comments/research tips: 19 April 1860 courthouse destroyed by fire, all records destroyed except those of the Probate Court. 28 November 1896 courthouse destroyed by fire.

Record Type	Year Begun	Jurisdiction
Marriage	na	Clerk/Circuit Ct.
Land	na	Clerk/Circuit Ct.
Probate	1856	Circuit Ct., Div. 2
Court	1859	Circuit Ct., Div. 1

■ Callaway   25 Nov. 1820

10 E. Fifth St., Fulton, MO 65251
Phone: (573)642-0780
Web site: www.rootsweb.com/~mocallaw/
Parent County: Montgomery, Boone, Howard
Comments/research tips: County Clerk has Birth and Death records 1883–1888.

Record Type	Year Begun	Jurisdiction
Marriage	na	County Recorder
Land	na	County Recorder
Probate	na	Probate Judge
Divorce	na	Clerk/Circuit Ct.

■ Camden   29 Jan. 1841

1 Court Circle, Suite 8, Camdenton, MO 65020
Phone: (573)346-4440
Web site: www.rootsweb.com/~mocamden/page1.htm
Parent County: Benton, Pulaski, Morgan
Comments/research tips: Formerly Kinderhook County. Name changed to Camden 23 February 1843. Line between Camden and Miller changed 1845. Courthouse burned 1902.

Record Type	Year Begun	Jurisdiction
Marriage	1902	County Recorder
Probate	1902	Probate Judge
Court	1902	Clerk/Circuit Ct.
Land	na	Abstract Office
Divorce	1902	County Recorder

■ Cape Girardeau 1 Oct. 1812
44 N. Lorimier, P.O. Box 2047, Cape Girardeau, MO 63702
Phone: (573)335-8253
Web site: www.showme.net/CapeCounty/
Parent County: Original District
Comments/research tips: Present size of county since 5 March 1849. Courthouse burned in 1870. County Clerk has Birth and Death records 1883–1893. Riverside Regional Library has all records on microfilm.

Record Type	Year Begun	Jurisdiction
Marriage	na	County Recorder
Court	1815	Clerk/Circuit Ct.
Probate	1805	Probate Judge
Divorce	na	Clerk/Circuit Ct.

■ Carroll 3 Jan. 1833
County Courthouse, Carrollton, MO 64633
Phone: (816)542-0615
Web site: http://us-gen.com/mo/carroll/
Parent County: Ray
Comments/research tips: County Clerk has Birth records 1883–1885 and Death records 1883–1890.

Record Type	Year Begun	Jurisdiction
Marriage	1833	Recorder/Deeds
Land	1833	Recorder/Deeds
Probate	1833	Probate Office

■ Carter 10 Mar. 1859
P.O. Box 578, Van Buren, MO 63965
Phone: (573)323-4513
Web site: www.rootsweb.com/~mocarter/
Parent County: Oregon, Reynolds, Ripley, Shannon

Record Type	Year Begun	Jurisdiction
Marriage	na	Recorder/Deeds
Land	na	Recorder/Deeds
Probate	1859	Probate Court

■ Cass 3 Mar. 1835
102 E. Wall, Harrisonville, MO 64701
Phone: (816)380-8226
Web site: www.rootsweb.com/~mocass/
Parent County: Jackson
Comments/research tips: Formerly Van Buren County. Named changed to Cass 19 February 1949. Three southern tiers of townships relinquished to Bates 22 February 1855. County Clerk has Birth records 1883–1903.

Record Type	Year Begun	Jurisdiction
Marriage	1836	Recorder/Deeds
Land	1837	County Recorder
Probate	1835	Associate Dir.
Divorce	1835	Recorder/Deeds

■ Cedar 14 Feb. 1845
1113 South St., P.O. Box 158, Stockton, MO 65785
Phone: (417)276-3514
Web site: www.rootsweb.com/~mocedar/
Parent County: Dade, St. Clair
Comments/research tips: County Clerk has Birth records 1883–1889, Death records 1883–1886.

Record Type	Year Begun	Jurisdiction
Marriage	1845	County Clerk
Divorce	1845	County Clerk
Land	1845	County Clerk
Probate	na	County Clerk
Court	na	County Clerk

■ Chariton 16 Nov. 1820
306 S. Cherry, Keytesville, MO 65261
Phone: (660)288-3602
Web site: www.rootsweb.com/~mocharit/
Parent County: Howard
Comments/research tips: Courthouse burned 20 September 1864, only a few records lost. County Clerk has Birth and Death records 1883–1887.

Record Type	Year Begun	Jurisdiction
Marriage	1821	Clerk/Circuit Ct.
Court	1872	County Clerk
Land	1827	County Recorder
Probate	1861	Cir. Ct./Probate Div.
Divorce	1872	Clerk/Circuit Ct.

■ Christian 8 Mar. 1859
100 W. Church, P.O. Box 278, Ozark, MO 65721
Phone: (417)581-6372
Web site: www.rootsweb.com/~mochrist/
Parent County: Greene, Taney, Webster
Comments/research tips: Courthouse burned 1865. County Clerk has Birth records 1840–1904, Death recods 1883–1884.

Record Type	Year Begun	Jurisdiction
Marriage	1866	Clerk/Circuit Ct.
Divorce	na	Clerk/Circuit Ct.
Land	1861	Clerk/Circuit Ct.
Probate	1864	Clerk/Circuit Ct.
Court	1865	Clerk/Circuit Ct.

■ Clark 16 Dec. 1836
111 E. Court St. #2, Kahoka, MO 63445
Phone: (660)727-3292
Web site: www.rootsweb.com/~moclark/clark.htm
Parent County: Lewis
Comments/research tips: County Clerk has Birth records 1830–1840, 1883–1892, Death records 1883–1892.

Record Type	Year Begun	Jurisdiction
Marriage	1836	County Recorder
Divorce	1836	Clerk/Circuit Ct.
Land	1833	County Recorder
Probate	1836	Probate Clerk
Court	1837	County Clerk

■ Clark (old) 1818
Parent County: Arkansas
Comments/research tips: Never organized; abolished in 1819 when territory of Arkansas was created.

■ **Clay**   2 Jan. 1822
11 S. Water St., P.O. Box 218, Liberty, MO 64069
Phone: (816)792-7706
Web site: www.claycogov.com/
Parent County: Ray
Comments/research tips: County Clerk has Birth and Death records 1883–1884.

Record Type	Year Begun	Jurisdiction
Marriage	1822	Recorder/Deeds
Divorce	1822	Clerk/Circuit Ct.
Land	1822	County Recorder
Probate	1821	Probate Clerk
Court	1822	County Clerk

■ **Clinton**   2 Jan. 1833
P.O. Box 245, Plattsburg, MO 64477
Phone: (816)539-3731
Web site: www.rootsweb.com/~moclinto/
Parent County: Clay
Comments/research tips: County Clerk has Birth records 1863–1879, 1883–1888, Death records 1883–1888.

Record Type	Year Begun	Jurisdiction
Marriage	1847	County Recorder
Divorce	1833	Clerk/Circuit Ct.
Land	1833	County Recorder
Probate	1833	Parish Clerk
Court	1836	County Clerk
Military	1919	County Clerk

■ **Cole**   16 Nov. 1820
301 E. High St., Jefferson City, MO 65101
Phone: (573)634-9100
Web site: www.rootsweb.com/~mocole/
Parent County: Cooper
Comments/research tips: County Clerk has Birth and Death records 1883–1906.

Record Type	Year Begun	Jurisdiction
Marriage	1821	Recorder/Deeds
Divorce	1821	Clerk/Circuit Ct.
Land	1821	County Recorder
Probate	1834	Probate Clerk
Court	1821	County Clerk

■ **Cooper**   17 Dec. 1818
200 Main St., Booneville, MO 65233
Phone: (660)882-2232
Web site: www.rootsweb.com/~mocooper/
Parent County: Howard
Comments/research tips: County Clerk has Birth records 1883–1894, Death records 1883–1889.

Record Type	Year Begun	Jurisdiction
Marriage	1819	County Recorder
Divorce	1819	Clerk/Circuit Ct.
Land	1819	County Recorder
Probate	1819	Probate Clerk
Court	1821	County Clerk
Burial	na	County Clerk
Nat.	1819	Circuit Clerk/Recorder

■ **Crawford**   23 Jan. 1829
302 W. Main St., Steelville, MO 65565
Phone: (573)775-2376
Web site: www.rootsweb.com/~mocrawfo/
Parent County: Gasconade
Comments/research tips: County Court records lost 1829–1835; Courthouse burned 15 February 1873; Courthouse burned 5 January 1884. County Clerk has Birth records 1879–1903, Death records 1883–1891 and 1941–1943.

Record Type	Year Begun	Jurisdiction
Marriage	1829	County Recorder
Divorce	1832	Clerk/Circuit Ct.
Land	1832	County Recorder
Probate	1832	Probate Clerk
Court	1831	County Clerk

■ **Dade**   29 Jan. 1841
Main St., Greenfield, MO 65661
Phone: (417)637-2724
Web site: www.rootsweb.com/~modade/modade.htm
Parent County: Barry, Polk
Comments/research tips: Lost 10-mile strip on northern boundary to Cedar County and 9-mile strip on southern boundary to Lawrence, reducing it to its present size 28 March 1845. County Clerk has Birth and Death records 1883–1885.

Record Type	Year Begun	Jurisdiction
Marriage	1863	County Recorder
Divorce	1867	Clerk/Circuit Ct.
Land	1841	County Recorder
Probate	1841	Probate Clerk
Court	1846	County Clerk

■ **Dallas**   29 Jan. 1841
107 Maple St., P.O. Box 436, Buffalo, MO 65622
Phone: (417)345-2632
Web site: www.rootsweb.com/~modallas/
Parent County: Polk
Comments/research tips: Formerly Niangua County. Name changed to Dallas 16 December 1844. Courthouse burned 18 October 1863; second courthouse burned 30 July 1864 and records destroyed. The replaced records burned 3 September 1867. County Clerk has Birth records 1883–1908, Death records 1883–1924.

Record Type	Year Begun	Jurisdiction
Marriage	1867	County Recorder
Divorce	na	Clerk/Circuit Ct.
Land	1867	County Recorder
Probate	1867	Probate Clerk
Court	1867	County Clerk
Burial	na	County Recorder

■ **Daviess**   29 Dec. 1836
102 N. Main St., Gallatin, MO 64640
Phone: (660)663-2641
Web site: www.rootsweb.com/~modavies/
Parent County: Ray
Comments/research tips: County Library has Birth and

Death records on microfilm 1883–1893. County Clerk has Birth and Death records 1883–1891.

Record Type	Year Begun	Jurisdiction
Court	1837	County Clerk
Land	1838	County Recorder
Probate	1890	Probate Clerk
Marriage	1837	County Recorder

■ De Kalb   25 Feb. 1845
109 W. Main St., P.O. Box 248, Maysville, MO 64469
Phone: (816)449-2602
Web site: www.rootsweb.com/~modekalb/
Parent County: Clinton
Comments/research tips: Courthouse burned in 1878, many records lost, but records of Circuit Clerk's Office were preserved along with a few records from other offices. County Clerk has Birth records 1883–1893, Death records 1883–1891 and 1942–1943.

Record Type	Year Begun	Jurisdiction
Marriage	1845	County Recorder
Divorce	na	Clerk/Circuit Ct.
Probate	1877	Probate Clerk
Court	1856	County Clerk
Land	1836	County Recorder

■ Dent   10 Feb. 1851
112 E. Fifth St., Salem, MO 65560
Phone: (573)729-3931
Web site: www.rootsweb.com/~modent/
Parent County: Crawford, Shannon
Comments/research tips: Courthouse burned in 1864, destroying some records. County Clerk has Birth and Death records 1883–1884.

Record Type	Year Begun	Jurisdiction
Marriage	1851	County Recorder
Divorce	na	Clerk/Circuit Ct.
Land	1851	County Recorder
Probate	1866	Probate Clerk
Court	1866	County Clerk

■ Dodge   18 Dec. 1846
Parent County: Putnam
Comments/research tips: Discontinued in 1853. Lost territory when Iowa boundary was established 13 February 1849, bringing its area below the constitutional limit of 400 square miles. Its territory was added to Putnam County 16 March 1853.

■ Douglas   29 Oct. 1857
203 SE Second Ave., P.O. Box 398, Ava, MO 65608
Phone: (417)683-4713
Web site: www.rootsweb.com/~modougla/
Parent County: Ozark
Comments/research tips: Territory increased in 1864 by addition of portions of Taney and Webster Counties. County Clerk has Death records 1886–1894.

Record Type	Year Begun	Jurisdiction
Marriage	1877	County Recorder
Divorce	na	Clerk/Circuit Ct.

Probate	1886	Probate Clerk
Court	1886	County Clerk
Land	1858	County Recorder

■ Dunklin   14 Feb. 1845
P.O. Box 567, Kennett, MO 63857
Phone: (573)888-2456
Web site: www.rootsweb.com/~modunkl2/dcgenweb.htm
Parent County: Stoddard
Comments/research tips: In 1853, a strip one mile wide was taken from Stoddard and added to the northern boundary of Dunklin County. Courthouse burned in 1872.

Record Type	Year Begun	Jurisdiction
Marriage	1872	Recorder/Deeds
Divorce	na	Clerk/Circuit Ct.
Land	1859	County Recorder
Probate	1865	Probate Clerk
Court	1872	County Clerk

■ Franklin   11 Dec. 1818
P.O. Box 311, Union, MO 63084
Phone: (636)583-6303
Web site: www/rootsweb.com/~mofrankl/
Parent County: St. Louis
Comments/research tips: Boundaries not accurately defined until 1845. County Clerk has Birth records 1862–1892 and Death records 1883–1887.

Record Type	Year Begun	Jurisdiction
Marriage	1819	Recorder/Deeds
Divorce	na	Clerk/Circuit Ct.
Land	1819	County Recorder
Probate	1819	Probate Clerk

■ Gasconade   25 Nov. 1820
110 E. First St. #2, P.O. Box 295, Hermann, MO 65041
Phone: (573)486-2632
Web site: www.rootsweb.com/~mogascon/
Parent County: Franklin
Comments/research tips: In 1869, relinquished 36 sq. miles to Crawford County. County Clerk has Birth records 1867–1896 and Death records 1883–1896.

Record Type	Year Begun	Jurisdiction
Land	1821	County Recorder
Probate	1825	Probate Clerk
Court	1821	County Clerk
Marriage	1822	County Recorder

■ Gentry   12 Feb. 1845
200 Clay St., Albany, MO 64402
Phone: (660)726-3525
Web site: www.rootsweb.com/~mogentry/
Parent County: Clinton
Comments/research tips: Organization completed 1843. Courthouse burned 1885. County Clerk has Birth records 1867–1893 and Death records 1883–1893.

Record Type	Year Begun	Jurisdiction
Land	1885	County Recorder
Marriage	1859	County Recorder
Divorce	1885	Clerk/Circuit Ct.

Probate .... 1885 ....Probate Clerk
Court .... 1885 ....County Clerk

■ Greene 2 Jan. 1833
940 Boonville, Springfield, MO 65802
Phone: (417)868-4074
Web site: www.rootsweb.com/~mogreene/
Parent County: Crawford
Comments/research tips: Courthouse burned 1861, few records lost. County Clerk has Birth records 1883–1901, Death records 1883–1902, and Divorce records 1837–1950.

Record Type	Year Begun	Jurisdiction
Land	1833	County Recorder
Probate	1832	Probate Clerk
Tax	1833	Archives/Record Center
Court	1833	County Clerk
Local Census	1876	Archives/Record Center
Marriage	1833	County Recorder
Military	na	Archives/Record Center

■ Grundy 29 Jan. 1841
700 Main St., Trenton, MO 64683
Phone: (660)359-6605
Web site: www.rootsweb.com/~mogrundy/
Parent County: Livingston
Comments/research tips: County Clerk has Birth and Death records 1883–1893.

Record Type	Year Begun	Jurisdiction
Marriage	1841	County Recorder
Divorce	na	Clerk/Circuit Ct.
Land	1841	County Recorder
Probate	1863	Probate Clerk
Court	1841	County Clerk

■ Harrison 14 Feb. 1845
1500 Central St., Bethany, MO 64424
Phone: (660)425-6425
Web site: www.rootsweb.com/~moharris/
Parent County: Daviess
Comments/research tips: Courthouse burned January 1874, most records saved, tax records destroyed. County Clerk has Birth records 1883–1889 and Death records 1883–1893.

Record Type	Year Begun	Jurisdiction
Land	1845	County Recorder
Marriage	1845	County Recorder
Divorce	1858	Clerk/Circuit Ct.
Probate	1853	Probate Clerk
Court	1845	County Clerk

■ Hempstead 1818
Parent County: New Madrid
Comments/research tips: Abolished 1819 when territory of Arkansas was created.

■ Henry 13 Dec. 1834
100 W. Franklin St., Box 478, Clinton, MO 64735
Phone: (660)885-7200
Web site: www.rootsweb.com/~mohenry/henryco.html
Parent County: Lillard

Comments/research tips: Formerly Rives County. Name changed to Henry 15 February 1841. Death records are scattered. County Clerk has Birth records 1883–1890.

Record Type	Year Begun	Jurisdiction
Marriage	1835	County Recorder
Divorce	na	Clerk/Circuit Ct.
Land	1835	County Recorder
Probate	1834	Probate Clerk
Court	1835	County Clerk
Burial	na	County Museum
Military	na	County Recorder

■ Hickory 14 Feb. 1845
P.O. Box 101, Hermitage, MO 65668
Phone: (417)745-6421
Web site: www.rootsweb.com/~mohickor/
Parent County: Benton, Polk
Comments/research tips: Courthouse burned 1852 and 1881, many records lost. County Clerk has Birth and Death records 1883–1898.

Record Type	Year Begun	Jurisdiction
Marriage	1872	County Recorder
Divorce	1858	Clerk/Circuit Ct.
Probate	1845	Probate Clerk
Court	1845	County Clerk
Land	1846	County Recorder

■ Holt 29 Jan. 1841
100 W. Nodaway St., Oregon, MO 64473
Phone: (660)446-3303
Web site: www.rootsweb.com/~holt
Parent County: Platte Purchase
Comments/research tips: Formerly Nodaway County. Name changed to Holt 15 February 1841. Courthouse burned 30 January 1965, most records undamaged. County Clerk has Birth and Death records 1883–1889.

Record Type	Year Begun	Jurisdiction
Marriage	1841	County Recorder
Divorce	1841	Clerk/Circuit Ct.
Land	1841	County Recorder
Probate	1837	Probate Judge
Court	1841	County Clerk

■ Howard 13 Jan. 1816
#1 Courthouse Sq., Fayette, MO 65248
Phone: (660)248-2194
Web site: www.rootsweb.com/~mohoward/
Parent County: St. Charles, St. Louis
Comments/research tips: Courthouse burned 1887; few records lost. County Clerk has Birth records 1883–1893 and Death Records 1883–1888.

Record Type	Year Begun	Jurisdiction
Marriage	1816	County Recorder
Divorce	1900	Clerk/Circuit Ct.
Land	1816	County Recorder
Probate	1818	Parish Clerk
Court	1816	County Clerk
Burial	1820	Clerk/Circuit Ct.
Military	1900	Clerk/Circuit Ct.

■ Howell 2 Mar. 1857
County Courthouse Sq., West Plains, MO 65775
Phone: (417)256-3741
Web site: www.rootsweb.com/~mohowell/
Parent County: Oregon
Comments/research tips: Courthouse destroyed during Civil War. County Clerk has Birth and Death records 1883–1895.

Record Type	Year Begun	Jurisdiction
Marriage	1867	County Recorder
Divorce	na	Clerk/Circuit Ct.
Land	1866	County Recorder
Probate	1862	Probate Clerk
Court	1857	County Clerk

■ Iron 17 Feb. 1857
P.O. Box 42, Ironton, MO 63650
Phone: (573)546-2811
Web site: www.rootsweb.com/~moiron2/
Parent County: Madison, Reynolds, St. Francis, Washington, Wayne
Comments/research tips: County Clerk has Birth records 1883–1896 and Death records 1883–1887.

Record Type	Year Begun	Jurisdiction
Marriage	1857	County Recorder
Divorce	na	Clerk/Circuit Ct.
Land	1814	County Recorder
Probate	1857	Probate Clerk
Court	1857	County Clerk

■ Jackson 15 Dec. 1826
415 E. Twelfth St., 3rd Floor, Kansas City, MO 64106
Phone: (816)881-3926
Web site: www.rootsweb.com/~mojackso/
Parent County: Lillard
Comments/research tips: Nearly all its territory was acquired from Osage and Kansas Indians 2 June 1825. County Clerk has Birth records 1883–1895 and Death records 1883–1893.

Record Type	Year Begun	Jurisdiction
Marriage	1827	County Recorder
Divorce	na	Clerk/Circuit Ct.
Land	1827	County Recorder
Probate	1828	Probate Clerk
Court	1828	County Clerk

■ Jasper 29 Jan. 1841
302 S. Main St., Carthage, MO 64836
Phone: (417)358-0441
Web site: www.rootsweb.com/~mojasper/
Parent County: Barry
Comments/research tips: Courthouse destroyed in 1863; records had been removed and were returned in 1865. County Clerk has Birth records 1883–1900 and Death records 1883–1897.

Record Type	Year Begun	Jurisdiction
Marriage	1841	Recorder/Deeds
Land	1841	County Recorder
Probate	1841	Probate Judge

■ Jefferson 8 Dec. 1818
P.O. Box 100, Hillsboro, MO 63050
Phone: (636)797-5443
Web site: www.rootsweb.com/~mojeffer/
Parent County: St. Genevieve, St. Louis
Comments/research tips: County Clerk has Birth and Death records 1883–1892.

Record Type	Year Begun	Jurisdiction
Marriage	1825	Recorder/Deeds
Land	1819	County Recorder
Probate	1820	Probate Clerk
Court	1819	County Clerk

■ Johnson 13 Dec. 1834
300 N. Holden St., Warrensburg, MO 64093
Phone: (660)422-7413
Web site: www.rootsweb.com/~mojohnso/
Parent County: Lillard
Comments/research tips: County Clerk has Birth and Death records 1883–1894.

Record Type	Year Begun	Jurisdiction
Marriage	1835	Recorder/Deeds
Divorce	ca.1860	Clerk/Circuit Ct.
Land	1832	County Recorder
Probate	1835	Probate Clerk
Court	1835	County Clerk

■ Kinderhook 29 Jan. 1841
Parent County: Benton, Pulaski, Morgan
Comments/research tips: (See Camden) Name changed to Camden 23 February 1843.

■ Knox 14 Feb. 1845
107 N. Fourth St., Edina, MO 63537
Phone: (660)397-2688
Web site: www.rootsweb.com/~moknox/
Parent County: Scotland
Comments/research tips: County Clerk has Birth records 1883–1939 and Death records 1883–1893.

Record Type	Year Begun	Jurisdiction
Marriage	1845	County Recorder
Divorce	na	Clerk/Circuit Ct.
Land	1845	County Recorder
Probate	1845	Probate Clerk
Court	1845	County Clerk

■ Laclede 24 Feb. 1849
200 N. Adams St., Lebanon, MO 65536
Phone: (417)532-2471
Web site: http://laclede.county.missouri.org/
Parent County: Camden, Pulaski, Wright
Comments/research tips: County Clerk has Birth records 1883–1893.

Record Type	Year Begun	Jurisdiction
Marriage	1855	County Recorder
Divorce	na	Clerk/Circuit Ct.
Land	1849	County Assessor
Probate	1848	Probate Judge
Court	1845	Clerk/Circuit Ct.

Missouri

■ Lafayette 16 Nov. 1820
1001 Main St., P.O. Box 357, Lexington, MO 64067
Phone: (660)259-4315
Web site: www.rootsweb.com/~molafaye/
Parent County: Cooper
Comments/research tips: Formerly Lillard County. Name changed to Lafayette 16 February 1825.

Record Type	Year Begun	Jurisdiction
Marriage	1821	County Recorder
Divorce	1821	County Recorder
Land	1820	County Recorder
Probate	1821	County Recorder
Court	1821	County Recorder

■ Lawrence 14 Feb. 1845
P.O. Box 309, Mount Vernon, MO 65712
Phone: (417)466-2471
Web site: www.rootsweb.com/~molawre2/
Parent County: Barry, Dade
Comments/research tips: County Clerk has Birth and Death records 1883–1893.

Record Type	Year Begun	Jurisdiction
Marriage	1845	Recorder/Deeds
Divorce	1846	Clerk/Circuit Ct.
Land	1845	Recorder/Deeds
Probate	1843	Probate Judge
Court	1845	Clerk/Circuit Ct.

■ Lawrence, old 1 Mar. 1815
Parent County: New Madrid
Comments/research tips: Lost territory to Wayne 1 February 1819. Abolished 16 February 1825.

■ Lewis 2 Jan. 1833
100 E. Lafayette St., Monticello, MO 63457
Phone: (573)767-5352
Web site: www.rootsweb.com/~molewis/
Parent County: Marion
Comments/research tips: County Clerk has Birth and Death records 1883–1887.

Record Type	Year Begun	Jurisdiction
Marriage	1833	Clerk/Circuit Ct.
Divorce	na	Clerk/Circuit Ct.
Land	1833	Clerk/Circuit Ct.
Probate	1833	Probate Judge
Court	1833	Clerk/Circuit Ct.

■ Lillard 16 Nov. 1820
Parent County: Cooper
Comments/research tips: (See Lafayette) Name changed to Lafayette 16 February 1825.

■ Lincoln 14 Dec. 1818
201 Main St., Troy, MO 63379
Phone: (636)528-6300
Web site: www.rootsweb.com/~molincol/
Parent County: St. Charles
Comments/research tips: County Clerk has Death records 1883–1884.

Record Type	Year Begun	Jurisdiction
Marriage	1825	County Recorder
Divorce	na	Clerk/Circuit Ct.
Land	1819	County Recorder
Probate	1820	Probate Judge
Burial	na	County Recorder
Court	1819	County Clerk

■ Linn 6 Jan. 1837
108 N. High, Linneus, MO 64653
Phone: (660)895-5409
Web site: www.rootsweb.com/~molinn/
Parent County: Chariton
Comments/research tips: County Clerk has Birth records 1822–1888 and Death records 1883–1887.

Record Type	Year Begun	Jurisdiction
Marriage	1857	County Recorder
Divorce	1837	Clerk/Circuit Ct.
Land	1836	County Recorder
Probate	1840	Probate Clerk
Court	1857	County Clerk

■ Livingston 6 Jan. 1837
700 Webster St., Chillicothe, MO 64601
Phone: (660)646-1718
Web site: http://ghlin2.greenhills.net/~fwoods/
Parent County: Carroll
Comments/research tips: County Clerk has Birth records 1883–1891 and Death records 1883–1890.

Record Type	Year Begun	Jurisdiction
Marriage	1837	Recorder/Deeds
Land	1837	Recorder/Deeds
Probate	1837	Probate Clerk
Court	1837	Clerk/Circuit Ct.

■ Macon 6 Jan. 1837
101 E. Washington St., Macon, MO 63552
Phone: (660)385-4631
Web site: www.rootsweb.com/~momacon/
Parent County: Randolph, Chariton
Comments/research tips: County Clerk has Birth and Death records 1883–1893.

Record Type	Year Begun	Jurisdiction
Marriage	1837	County Recorder
Divorce	na	Clerk/Circuit Ct.
Land	1837	County Recorder
Probate	1838	Circuit Ct., Div. 2
Court	1837	County Clerk

■ Madison 14 Dec. 1818
1 Courthouse Sq., Fredericktown, MO 63645
Phone: (573)783-2176
Web site: www.rootsweb.com/~momadiso/
Parent County: Cape Giradeau, St. Genevieve
Comments/research tips: County Clerk has Birth and Death records 1883–1900.

Record Type	Year Begun	Jurisdiction
Marriage	1821	Clerk/Circuit Ct.
Divorce	1821	Clerk/Circuit Ct.

Land	1819	County Assessor
Probate	1821	County Magistrate
Court	1827	Clerk/Circuit Ct.
Military	1943	Clerk/Circuit Ct.
Local Census	1876	County Clerk

■ Maries 2 Mar. 1855

P.O. Box 205, Vienna, MO 65582
Phone: (573)422-3338
Web site: www.rootsweb.com/~momaries/maries.htm
Parent County: Osage, Pulaski
Comments/research tips: In 1859 and 1868 small tracts of land were exchanged with Phelps County. Courthouse burned 6 November 1868, nearly all records destroyed. County Clerk has Birth records 1883–1884 and Death records for 1883.

Record Type	Year Begun	Jurisdiction
Marriage	1869	Clerk/Circuit Ct.
Divorce	1866	Clerk/Circuit Ct.
Land	1855	Clerk/Circuit Ct.
Probate	1866	Probate Div.
Court	1866	Clerk/Circuit Ct.
School	1911	Clerk/Circuit Ct.

■ Marion 14 Dec. 1826

100 S. Main St., Palmyra, MO 63461
Phone: (573)769-2318
Web site: www.rootsweb.com/~momarion/
Parent County: Ralls
Comments/research tips: County Clerk has Birth records 1883–1890, Death records 1883–1889, and Birth and Death records 1927–1930.

Record Type	Year Begun	Jurisdiction
Marriage	1827	Clerk/Circuit Ct.
Divorce	1827	Clerk/Circuit Ct.
Land	1827	Clerk/Circuit Ct.
Probate	1827	Probate Clerk
Court	1827	Clerk/Circuit Ct.
Military	na	Clerk/Circuit Ct.

■ McDonald 3 Mar. 1849

Hwy. W, Pineville, MO 64856
Phone: (417)223-7515
Web site: www.rootsweb.com/~momcdona/momcdon.htm
Parent County: Newton
Comments/research tips: Changed from Seneca to McDonald in 1849. In 1876 an error in survey was corrected, establishing a new eastern line which annexed a 2 1/2 mile strip previously included in Barry County. Courthouse and records burned in 1863. County Clerk has Birth records 1856–1894.

Record Type	Year Begun	Jurisdiction
Marriage	1865	Recorder/Deeds
Divorce	na	Clerk/Circuit Ct.
Land	1853	Clerk/Circuit Ct.
Probate	1865	Probate Judge
Court	1855	Clerk/Circuit Ct.

■ Mercer 14 Feb. 1845

802 E. Main St., Princeton, MO 64673
Phone: (660)748-3425

Web site: www.rootsweb.com/~momercer/
Parent County: Grundy
Comments/research tips: Courthouse burned 24 March 1898 and nearly all records of the Circuit Clerk and Recorder, Treasurer and Sheriff were destroyed or badly damaged; records in office of Probate Judge and County Clerk were saved but many were badly damaged. County Clerk has Birth records 1883–1894 and Death records 1883–1894.

Record Type	Year Begun	Jurisdiction
Marriage	1898	County Recorder
Court	1868	County Clerk
Land	1846	County Recorder
Probate	1849	Probate Clerk

■ Miller 6 Feb. 1837

P.O. Box 12, Tuscumbia, MO 65082
Phone: (573)369-2303
Web site: www.rootsweb.com/~momiller/miller.htm
Parent County: Cole, Pulaski
Comments/research tips: Line between Camden and Miller changed 1845. Territory from Morgan County annexed 1860. Minor changes in 1868. County Clerk has Birth records 1883–1891 and Death records 1883–1904.

Record Type	Year Begun	Jurisdiction
Land	1837	County Recorder
Marriage	1837	County Recorder
Probate	1837	Probate Clerk
Court	1837	County Clerk

■ Mississippi 14 Feb. 1845

P.O. Box 304, Charleston, MO 63834
Phone: (573)683-2146
Web site: www.rootsweb.com/~momissis/
Parent County: Scott

Record Type	Year Begun	Jurisdiction
Marriage	1845	County Recorder
Court	1845	County Clerk
Probate	1845	Probate Clerk
Land	1823	County Recorder

■ Moniteau 14 Feb. 1845

200 E. Main St., California, MO 65018
Phone: (573)796-2071
Web site: www.rootsweb.com/~momonite/
moniteauhomepage.htm
Parent County: Cole, Morgan
Comments/research tips: County Clerk has Birth records 1883–1894 and Death records 1883–1887.

Record Type	Year Begun	Jurisdiction
Court	1845	County Clerk
Marriage	1845	Recorder/Deeds
Land	1845	County Recorder
Probate	1845	Probate Clerk

■ Monroe 6 Jan. 1831

300 N. Main St., Paris, MO 65275
Phone: (660)327-5204
Web site: www.rootsweb.com/~momonroe/
Parent County: Ralls

Missouri

Comments/research tips: County Clerk has Birth and Death records 1883–1885.

Record Type	Year Begun	Jurisdiction
Marriage	1831	County Recorder
Court	1831	County Clerk
Probate	1832	Probate Clerk
Land	1831	County Recorder

■ Montgomery 14 Dec. 1818
211 E. Third St., Montgomery City, MO 63361
Phone: (573)564-3341
Web site: www.rootsweb.com/~momontgo/
Parent County: St. Charles
Comments/research tips: County records burned 1864.

Record Type	Year Begun	Jurisdiction
Land	1839	County Recorder
Marriage	1864	County Recorder
Probate	1889	Probate Clerk

■ Morgan 5 Jan. 1833
100 E. Newton St., Versailles, MO 65084-1298
Phone: (573)378-5436
Web site: www.rootsweb.com/~momorgan/
Parent County: Cooper
Comments/research tips: County Clerk has Birth records 1841–1863 and Birth and Death records 1883–1886.

Record Type	Year Begun	Jurisdiction
Court	1833	County Clerk
Probate	1834	Probate Clerk
Marriage	1833	Recorder/Deeds
Land	1837	County Recorder

■ New Madrid 1 Oct. 1812
P.O. Box 68, New Madrid, MO 63869
Phone: (573)748-2228
Web site: www.rootsweb.com/~monewmad/
Parent County: Original district

Record Type	Year Begun	Jurisdiction
Marriage	1847	Recorder/Deeds
Land	1805	County Recorder
Probate	1800	Probate Clerk
Court	1805	County Clerk

■ Newton 30 Dec. 1838
101 S. Wood St., Neosho, MO 64850
Phone: (417)451-8257
Web site: www.rootsweb.com/~monewton/
Parent County: Barry
Comments/research tips: In 1846 a strip two miles wide was detached from Newton and attached to Jasper. Courthouse burned 1862. County Clerk has Birth and Death records 1883–1885.

Record Type	Year Begun	Jurisdiction
Marriage	1865	County Recorder
Probate	1839	Probate Clerk
Court	1839	County Clerk
Land	1839	County Recorder

■ Niangua 29 Jan. 1841
Parent County: Polk
Comments/research tips: (See Dallas) Boundaries slightly changed and name changed to Dallas 16 December 1844.

■ Nodaway 2 Jan. 1845
305 N. Main St., Maryville, MO 64468-0218
Phone: (660)582-2251
Web site: www.rootsweb.com/~monodawa/nodaway.html
Parent County: Andrew
Comments/research tips: Attached to Andrew County until organization 14 February 1845. County Clerk has Birth records 1883–1890 and Death records 1883–1893.

Record Type	Year Begun	Jurisdiction
Court	1845	County Clerk
Land	1845	County Recorder
Marriage	1845	County Recorder
Probate	1845	Probate Clerk

■ Oregon 14 Feb. 1845
P.O. Box 406, Alton, MO 65606
Phone: (417)778-7460
Web site: www.rootsweb.com/~mooregon/
Parent County: Ripley
Comments/research tips: Courthouse burned during Civil War; records were removed and most of them saved. County Clerk has Birth records 1883–1890, Court records 1845–1859, and Death records 1883–1889. County Recorder has Marriage records 1845–1861.

Record Type	Year Begun	Jurisdiction
Marriage	1877	County Recorder
Court	1872	County Clerk
Probate	1854	Probate Clerk
Land	1845	County Recorder

■ Osage 29 Jan. 1841
106 E. Main St., Linn, MO 65051
Phone: (573)897-3114
Web site: www.rootsweb.com/~moosage/vosage.htm
Parent County: Gasconade
Comments/research tips: 1 March 1855 boundaries between Osage and Pulaski defined. Courthouse burned 15 November 1880, records saved. County Clerk has Birth records 1883–1898 and Death records 1883–1894.

Record Type	Year Begun	Jurisdiction
Marriage	1841	Recorder/Deeds
Land	1841	County Recorder
Probate	1841	Probate Clerk
Court	1841	County Clerk

■ Ozark 29 Jan. 1841
P.O. Box 416, Gainesville, MO 65655-0416
Phone: (417)679-3516
Web site: www.rootsweb.com/~moozark/oz.htm
Parent County: Taney
Comments/research tips: Name changed to Decatur 22 February 1843; changed back to Ozark 24 March 1845. County Clerk has Birth records 1884–1890 and Death records 1887–1889.

Record Type	Year Begun	Jurisdiction
Marriage	1858	County Recorder
Court	1858	County Clerk
Probate	1865	Probate Clerk
Land	1858	County Recorder

■ Pemiscot   19 Feb. 1851
610 Ward Ave., Caruthersville, MO 63830
Phone: (573)333-0182
Web site: www.rootsweb.com/~mopemis2/
Parent County: New Madrid
Comments/research tips: Courthouse and records burned 1883. County Clerk has Birth records 1883–1884.

Record Type	Year Begun	Jurisdiction
Marriage	1882	Recorder/Deeds
Land	1881	County Recorder
Probate	1865	Probate Clerk
Court	1883	County Clerk

■ Perry   16 Nov. 1820
321 N. Main St., Perryville, MO 63775
Phone: (573)547-6581
Web site: www.rootsweb.com/~moperry/
Parent County: St. Genevieve
Comments/research tips: County Clerk has birth and death records 1883–1894.

Record Type	Year Begun	Jurisdiction
Marriage	1830	County Recorder
Divorce	na	Clerk/Circuit Ct.
Land	1821	Clerk/Circuit Ct.
Probate	1821	Clerk/Circuit Ct.
Court	1821	County Clerk
Military	na	County Recorder
Nat.	1821	County Clerk

■ Pettis   26 Jan. 1833
415 S. Ohio Ave., Sedalia, MO 65301
Phone: (660)826-0617
Web site: www.rootsweb.com/~mopettis/pettis.htm
Parent County: Cooper, Saline
Comments/research tips: County Clerk has Birth and Death records 1883–1885.

Record Type	Year Begun	Jurisdiction
Marriage	1833	Recorder/Deeds
Land	1833	Recorder/Deeds
Probate	1833	Probate Clerk
Court	1833	Clerk/Circuit Ct.

■ Phelps   13 Nov. 1857
200 N. Main, Rolla, MO 65401
Phone: (573)364-1891
Web site: www.rootsweb.com/~mophelps/phelps.htm
Parent County: Crawford, Pulaski, Maries
Comments/research tips: County Clerk has Birth and Death records 1883–1890.

Record Type	Year Begun	Jurisdiction
Marriage	1857	County Clerk
Divorce	1857	County Clerk
Land	1857	County Clerk
Probate	1858	County Clerk
Court	1857	County Clerk

■ Pike   14 Dec. 1818
115 W. Main, Bowling Green, MO 63334
Phone: (573)324-3112
Web site: www.pastracks.com/states/missouri/pike/
Parent County: St. Charles
Comments/research tips: Courthouse burned 1864. County Clerk has Birth records 1883–1884.

Record Type	Year Begun	Jurisdiction
Marriage	1825	Recorder/Deeds
Land	1819	Recorder/Deeds
Probate	1825	Probate Clerk
Court	1819	Clerk/Circuit Ct.

■ Platte   31 Dec. 1838
415 Third St. #5, Platte City, MO 64079
Phone: (816)858-2232
Web site: www.rootsweb.com/~moplatte/
Parent County: Platte Purchase
Comments/research tips: Attached to Clay County for civil and military purposes from December 1836 to December 1838. County Clerk has Birth and Death records 1883–1887.

Record Type	Year Begun	Jurisdiction
Marriage	1839	Recorder/Deeds
Divorce	na	Clerk/Circuit Ct.
Land	1839	Recorder/Deeds
Probate	1839	Probate Judge
Court	1839	Probate Judge

■ Polk   5 Jan. 1835
102 E. Broadway St., Room 14, Bolivar, MO 65613
Phone: (417)326-4912
Web site: www.rootsweb.com/~mopolk/
Parent County: Greene
Comments/research tips: County Clerk has Birth records 1872–1900 and Death records 1883–1890.

Record Type	Year Begun	Jurisdiction
Marriage	1836	County Recorder
Divorce	1857	Clerk/Circuit Ct.
Land	1837	County Recorder
Probate	1835	Probate Judge
Court	1836	Clerk/Circuit Ct.

■ Pulaski   19 Jan. 1833
301 Historic Rt. 66 E., Room 202, Waynesville, MO 65583
Phone: (573)774-4755
Web site: www.rootsweb.com/~mopulask/
Parent County: Crawford

Record Type	Year Begun	Jurisdiction
Marriage	1903	County Clerk
Divorce	1903	County Clerk
Probate	1833	County Clerk
Court	1903	County Clerk
Land	1903	County Recorder

■ Pulaski, old   1818
Parent County: Franklin
Comments/research tips: Organization not perfected and much of its territory became Gasconade in 1820. Abolished in 1819 when territory of Arkansas was created.

■ Putnam   22 Feb. 1845
County Courthouse Main St., Room 204, Unionville, MO 63565

Phone: (660)947-2674
Web site: www.rootsweb.com/~moputnam/
Parent County: Adair, Sullivan
Comments/research tips: When the Iowa boundary was established, the areas of both Putnam and Dodge Counties were below the constitutional limit. Dodge was disorganized in 1853 and its territory was regained by Putnam. County Clerk has Birth records 1878–1907 and Death records 1887–1907.

Record Type	Year Begun	Jurisdiction
Marriage	1849	Clerk/Circuit Ct.
Divorce	1855	Clerk/Circuit Ct.
Land	1847	Clerk/Circuit Ct.
Probate	1853	Probate Judge
Court	1855	Clerk/Circuit Ct.

■ Ralls 16 Nov. 1820

311 S. Main St., New London, MO 63459
Phone: (573)985-5633
Web site: www.rootsweb.com/~moralls
Parent County: Pike
Comments/research tips: County Clerk has Birth records 1883–1893 and Death records 1883–1886.

Record Type	Year Begun	Jurisdiction
Marriage	1821	Clerk/Circuit Ct.
Divorce	1821	Clerk/Circuit Ct.
Land	1821	Clerk/Circuit Ct.
Probate	1821	Probate Judge
Court	1821	Clerk/Circuit Ct.

■ Randolph 22 Jan. 1829

110 S. Main St., Huntsville, MO 65259
Phone: (660)277-4717
Web site: www.rootsweb.com/~morandol/
Parent County: Chariton, Ralls
Comments/research tips: Courthouse burned 1880; a few records lost. County Clerk has Birth and Death records 1883–1889.

Record Type	Year Begun	Jurisdiction
Marriage	1829	County Recorder
Divorce	na	Clerk/Circuit Ct.
Land	1841	County Recorder
Probate	1829	Probate Clerk
Court	1858	County Clerk

■ Ray 14 Nov. 1820

100 W. Main St., Richmond, MO 64085
Phone: (816)776-3377
Web site: www.rootsweb.com/~moray/
Parent County: Howard
Comments/research tips: County Clerk has Birth records 1883–1890 and Death records 1883–1889. Records of interest to genealogists obtainable from Ray County Historical Society, Richmond MO 64085.

Record Type	Year Begun	Jurisdiction
Marriage	1820	Recorder/Deeds
Divorce	na	Clerk/Circuit Ct.
Land	1820	Recorder/Deeds
Court	1821	Clerk/Circuit Ct.
Probate	1821	Probate Clerk

■ Reynolds 25 Feb. 1845

Courhouse Square, Centerville, MO 63633
Phone: (573)648-2494
Web site: www.rootsweb.com/~moreynol/
Parent County: Shannon
Comments/research tips: Courthouse burned 1872; all records lost. County Clerk has Birth and Death records 1883–1886.

Record Type	Year Begun	Jurisdiction
Marriage	1872	County Clerk
Divorce	1872	County Clerk
Probate	1872	County Clerk
Court	1872	County Clerk
Land	1872	County Recorder

■ Ripley 5 Jan. 1833

County Courthouse, Doniphan, MO 63935
Phone: (573)996-2818
Web site: www.rootsweb.com/~moripley/
Parent County: Wayne
Comments/research tips: County Clerk has Birth records 1883–1897 and Death records 1883–1893.

Record Type	Year Begun	Jurisdiction
Court	1867	County Clerk
Marriage	1833	Recorder/Deeds
Land	1833	Recorder/Deeds
Probate	1856	Probate Clerk

■ Rives 13 Dec. 1834

Parent County: Lafayette
Comments/research tips: (See Henry) Name changed to Henry 15 February 1841.

■ Saline 25 Nov. 1820

101 E. Arrow St., Marshall, MO 65340
Phone: (660)886-3331
Web site: www.rootsweb.com/~mosaline/
Parent County: Cooper, Howard
Comments/research tips: Courthouse burned 1864, but records were saved. County Clerk has Birth and Death records 1883–1885.

Record Type	Year Begun	Jurisdiction
Cemetery	na	Marshall Public Library
Genealogy	na	Marshall Public Library
Court	1821	County Clerk
Land	1821	County Recorder
Marriage	1835	County Recorder
Probate	1821	Probate Clerk

■ Schuyler 14 Feb. 1845

Hwy. 136, Lancaster, MO 63548-0187
Phone: (660)457-3842
Web site: www.rootsweb.com/~moschuy2/
Parent County: Adair
Comments/research tips: County Clerk has Birth records 1883–1893 and Death records 1883–1891.

Record Type	Year Begun	Jurisdiction
Marriage	1845	Clerk/Circuit Ct.
Divorce	na	Clerk/Circuit Ct.

Probate .... 1845 ....Probate Judge
Court .... 1846 ....Probate Judge
Land .... 1845 ....County Recorder

■ **Scotland** 29 Jan. 1841
117 S. Market St. #106, Memphis, MO 63555
Phone: (660)465-8605
Web site: www.rootsweb.com/~moscotla/
Parent County: Lewis, Clark, Shelby
Comments/research tips: County Clerk has Birth and Death records 1883–1889.

Record Type	Year Begun	Jurisdiction
Marriage	1841	Clerk/Circuit Ct.
Divorce	1841	Clerk/Circuit Ct.
Land	1836	Clerk/Circuit Ct.
Probate	1842	Probate Judge
Court	1841	Clerk/Circuit Ct.

■ **Scott** 28 Dec. 1821
P.O. Box 188, Benton, MO 63736
Phone: (573)545-3596
Web site: www.rootsweb.com/~moscott/moscott-index.htm
Parent County: New Madrid
Comments/research tips: County Clerk has Birth and Death records 1883–1886.

Record Type	Year Begun	Jurisdiction
Marriage	1840	Recorder/Deeds
Divorce	na	Clerk/Circuit Ct.
Land	1822	Recorder/Deeds
Probate	1825	Probate Judge
Court	1822	Clerk/Circuit Ct.

■ **Shannon** 29 Jan. 1841
P.O. Box 187, Eminence, MO 65466
Phone: (573)226-3315
Web site: www.rootsweb.com/~moshanno/
Parent County: Ripley
Comments/research tips: Courthouse destroyed during Civil War, burned 1863, 1871, and 1938. Recorder Office burned 1893, some land records in Ironton, Missouri prior to 1872.

Record Type	Year Begun	Jurisdiction
Marriage	1881	County Clerk
Divorce	1872	County Clerk
Land	1859	County Clerk
Probate	1869	County Clerk
Court	1872	County Clerk

■ **Shelby** 2 Jan. 1835
P.O. Box 186, Shelbyville, MO 63469
Phone: (573)633-2151
Web site: www.rootsweb.com/~moshelby/
Parent County: Marion
Comments/research tips: County Clerk has Birth and Death records 1883–1887.

Record Type	Year Begun	Jurisdiction
Marriage	1835	Recorder/Deeds
Divorce	na	Clerk/Circuit Ct.
Land	1835	Recorder/Deeds
Probate	1836	Probate Judge
Court	1835	Clerk/Magistrate Ct.

■ **St. Charles** 1 Oct. 1812
300 N. Second St., St. Charles, MO 63301
Phone: (636)949-7900
Web site: www.rootsweb.com/~mostchar/
Parent County: Original district
Comments/research tips: County Clerk has Birth records 1867–1890.

Record Type	Year Begun	Jurisdiction
Marriage	1807	Recorder/Deeds
Land	1804	Recorder/Deeds
Probate	1805	Probate Clerk
Court	1808	Clerk/Circuit Ct.

■ **St. Clair** 16 Jan. 1833
P.O. Box 525, Osceola, MO 64776
Phone: (417)646-2315
Web site: www.rootsweb.com/~mostclai/
Parent County: Rives
Comments/research tips: Lost land to Pettis 26 January 1833 and attached to Rives until formally organized from Rives County 29 January 1841. County Clerk has Birth records 1883–1903 and Death records 1883–1890.

Record Type	Year Begun	Jurisdiction
Marriage	1855	County Recorder
Divorce	na	Clerk/Circuit Ct.
Land	1841	County Recorder
Probate	1865	Probate Clerk
Court	1841	County Clerk

■ **St. Francois** 19 Dec. 1821
County Courthouse Square, Farmington, MO 63640
Phone: (573)756-4511
Web site: www.rootsweb.com/~mostfran/
Parent County: Jefferson, St. Genevieve, Washington
Comments/research tips: County Clerk has Birth records 1883–1893 and Death records 1883–1890.

Record Type	Year Begun	Jurisdiction
Marriage	1836	County Recorder
Divorce	na	Clerk/Circuit Ct.
Land	1822	County Recorder
Probate	1822	Clerk/Circuit Ct.

■ **St. Genevieve** 1 Oct. 1812
55 S. Third St., St. Genevieve, MO 63670
Phone: (573)883-2705
Web site: www.segenealogy.com/missouri/mo_county/sg.htm
Parent County: Original district
Comments/research tips: County Clerk has birth and death records 1883–1892.

Record Type	Year Begun	Jurisdiction
Marriage	1807	Circuit Clerk/Recorder
Divorce	na	Circuit Clerk/Recorder
Land	1804	Circuit Clerk/Recorder
Probate	1807	Circuit Ct. Judge
Court	1804	Circuit Clerk/Recorder

■ **St. Louis** 1 Oct. 1876
41 S. Central Ave., Clayton, MO 63105
Phone: (314)615-8029

Web site: www.rootsweb.com/~mocstlou/
Parent County: Original district, St. Louis City

Record Type	Year Begun	Jurisdiction
Marriage	1876	Recorder/Deeds
Divorce	na	Clerk/Circuit Ct.
Land	1876	Recorder/Deeds
Court	1876	Clerk/Circuit Ct.
Birth	1876	County Clerk
Death	1883	County Clerk
Probate	1876	Probate Clerk

■ St. Louis City 5 Mar. 1804
1200 Market St., St. Louis, MO 63101
Phone: (314)622-4405
Web site: www.rootsweb.com/~mocstlou/
Parent County: Original county

Record Type	Year Begun	Jurisdiction
Marriage	1766	City Recorder
Land	1766	City Recorder
Probate	1766	Probate Clerk
Tax	na	Assessor
Birth	1825	County Clerk
Death	1825	County Clerk
Court	1766	County Clerk

■ Stoddard 2 Jan. 1835
P.O. Box 110, Bloomfield, MO 63825
Phone: (573)568-4640
Web site: www.rootsweb.com/~mostodd2/
Parent County: New Madrid
Comments/research tips: Courthouse burned 1864 but records were removed safely. County Clerk has Birth records 1883–1887 and Death records 1883–1886.

Record Type	Year Begun	Jurisdiction
Marriage	1863	Recorder/Deeds
Divorce	na	Clerk/Circuit Ct.
Land	1835	Recorder/Deeds
Probate	1835	Probate Clerk
Court	1835	Clerk/Magistrate Ct.

■ Stone 10 Feb. 1851
PO Box 45, Galena, MO 65656
Phone: (417)357-6127
Web site: www.rootsweb.com/~mostone/stone.htm
Parent County: Taney

Record Type	Year Begun	Jurisdiction
Marriage	1851	County Clerk
Land	1854	County Clerk
Probate	1848	County Clerk
Court	1851	County Clerk
Military	1918	County Clerk

■ Sullivan 14 Feb. 1845
109 N. Main, Milan, MO 63556
Phone: (660)265-4717
Web site: www.rootsweb.com/~mosulliv/
Parent County: Linn
Comments/research tips: Recorder of Deeds has Birth records 1835–1871, 1883–1892 and Death records 1883–1899.

Record Type	Year Begun	Jurisdiction
Marriage	1845	Recorder/Deeds
Divorce	1845	Clerk/Circuit Ct.
Land	1845	Recorder/Deeds
Probate	1849	Probate Judge
Court	1845	Clerk/Circuit Ct.

■ Taney 6 Jan. 1837
132 David St., Forsyth, MO 65653-0156
Phone: (417)546-7200
Web site: www.rootsweb.com/~motaney/
Parent County: Greene
Comments/research tips: Courthouse burned 1885.

Record Type	Year Begun	Jurisdiction
Marriage	1885	Clerk/Circuit Ct.
Divorce	na	Clerk/Circuit Ct.
Land	1881	Clerk/Circuit Ct.
Probate	1888	Probate Judge
Court	1887	Clerk/Circuit Ct.
Voter Reg.	1961	County Clerk

■ Texas 14 Feb. 1845
210 N. Grand Ave., Houston, MO 65483
Phone: (417)967-3742
Web site: www.rootsweb.com/~usgenweb/mo/texas/texas.htm
Parent County: Shannon, Wright
Comments/research tips: Formerly Ashley County. Name changed to Texas 14 February 1845. County Clerk has Birth records 1883–1887 and Death records 1883–1890.

Record Type	Year Begun	Jurisdiction
Marriage	1855	Recorder/Deeds
Divorce	1855	Clerk/Circuit Ct.
Land	1843	Recorder/Deeds
Probate	1870	Clerk/Circuit Ct.
Court	1858	Clerk/Circuit Ct.

■ Van Buren 3 Mar. 1835
Parent County: Jackson
Comments/research tips: (See Cass) Name changed to Cass 19 February 1849.

■ Vernon 27 Feb. 1855
100 W. Cherry St., Nevada, MO 64772
Phone: (417)448-2550
Web site: www.rootsweb.com/~movernon/
Parent County: Bates
Comments/research tips: Vernon created 17 February 1851, but act was declared unconstitutional since its territory was exactly that of Bates County; legally created 27 February 1855. Reorganized 17 October 1865 after total suspension of civil order during Civil War. Courthouse destroyed during that period, but clerk had taken the records with him when he joined the army and all records were later recovered, except the deed book. County Clerk has Birth records 1883–1897 and Death records 1883–1904.

Record Type	Year Begun	Jurisdiction
Marriage	1855	Recorder/Deeds
Divorce	na	Clerk/Circuit Ct.

Land .... 1855 ....Recorder/Deeds
Probate .... 1855 ....Probate Clerk
Court .... 1856 ....Clerk/Circuit Ct.
Burial..................... na ....County Health Office

■ Warren 5 Jan. 1833
104 W. Market St., Warrenton, MO 63383
Phone: (636)456-3363
Web site: www.rootsweb.com/~mowarren/
Parent County: Montgomery
Comments/research tips: County Clerk has Birth records 1883–1889 and Death records 1883–1894.

Record Type	Year Begun	Jurisdiction
Marriage	1833	Recorder/Deeds
Land	1833	Recorder/Deeds
Probate	1833	Probate Judge
Court	1833	Clerk/Circuit Ct.

■ Washington 21 Aug. 1813
102 N. Missouri St., Potosi, MO 63664
Phone: (573)438-4171
Web site: www.rootsweb.com/~mowashin/
Parent County: St. Genevieve
Comments/research tips: County Clerk has Birth records 1883–1895, Death records 1883–1895 and 1974–1976.

Record Type	Year Begun	Jurisdiction
Marriage	1815	Clerk/Circuit Ct.
Divorce	1825	Clerk/Circuit Ct.
Land	1813	Clerk/Circuit Ct.
Probate	1813	Probate Judge
Court	1819	Clerk/Circuit Ct.

■ Wayne 11 Dec. 1818
County Courthouse, Greenville, MO 63944
Phone: (573)224-3052
Web site: www.rootsweb.com/~mowayne/
Parent County: Cape Girardeau, Lawrence
Comments/research tips: Courthouse and all records burned 1854 and again in 1892. County Clerk has Birth and Death records 1914–1940.

Record Type	Year Begun	Jurisdiction
Marriage	1892	Clerk/Circuit Ct.
Divorce	na	Clerk/Circuit Ct.
Land	1849	County Recorder
Probate	1869	Clerk/Circuit Ct.
Court	1893	County Clerk

■ Webster 3 Mar. 1855
100 Crittenden St., Marshfield, MO 65706
Phone: (417)859-2006
Web site: www.rootsweb.com/~mowebste/webster.htm
Parent County: Greene
Comments/research tips: Courthouse burned 1863, but records were saved, except tax rolls and election returns. County Clerk has Birth records 1883–1893 and Death records 1883–1884.

Record Type	Year Begun	Jurisdiction
Marriage	1855	County Recorder
Divorce	na	Clerk/Circuit Ct.
Land	1854	County Recorder
Probate	1856	Probate Judge
Court	1855	Clerk/Circuit Ct.

■ Worth 8 Feb. 1861
4th & Front St., Grant City, MO 64456
Phone: (660)564-2210
Web site: www.rootsweb.com/~moworth/worth.html
Parent County: Gentry
Comments/research tips: County clerk has Birth and Death records 1883–1893.

Record Type	Year Begun	Jurisdiction
Marriage	1861	County Clerk
Divorce	1861	County Clerk
Land	1849	County Clerk
Probate	1861	County Clerk
Court	1861	County Clerk

■ Wright 29 Jan. 1841
P.O. Box 39, Hartville, MO 65667
Phone: (417)741-7121
Web site: www.rootsweb.com/~mowright/
Parent County: Pulaski
Comments/research tips: Courthouse burned in 1864, destroying many records; courthouse and records destroyed in 1897.

Record Type	Year Begun	Jurisdiction
Marriage	1897	Clerk/Circuit Ct.
Divorce	na	Clerk/Circuit Ct.
Land	1853	County Recorder
Probate	1853	Probate Judge
Court	1895	Clerk/Circuit Ct.

Missouri

Montana

By Rhonda R. McClure

HISTORICAL OVERVIEW

Montana's roots begin in the early 1800s, when the United States acquired the part of Montana east of the mountains from France. It was another forty years before Britain relinquished its claim to the western section of the state. However, during the 1850s, the only inhabitants besides the wild life were Native Americans, adventurous explorers, fur trappers, and some missionaries. St. Mary's, the first mission, was founded by Jesuit priests in 1841 and would become the center for ranching in the Bitterroot Valley.

The trading post, Fort Benton, was established in 1846. It was the only trading post to become a permanent settlement, and was the point to which steamboats brought early travelers, a trip that took months on the Missouri River from St. Louis or Sioux City.

The early influx of settlers in the 1850s came from all over the world. Homesteaders appeared from the east, the south, and even the west, including Chinese and others who had originally settled in California and Oregon. The first major migration to Montana began in 1862 with the discovery of gold. The miners who came also began to farm, and some of their earliest settlements include Missoula, Deer Lodge, and Bozeman.

As a result of the gold rush, the territory of Montana was established in 1864. The railroads got to the territory in the 1880s, and in 1889 it became a state. In the early 1900s many homesteaders moved into the eastern part of the state, but drought in the late 1920s and 1930 forced many of the settlers to move out of the state.

RECORD HIGHLIGHTS

Montana was a public-domain state, so as settlers came into the territory and then the state, land was purchased from the government. Homesteading was another way to

© PhotoDisc/Getty Images

MONTANA AT A GLANCE

Motto: Gold and Silver

Population: 902,195

Prevalent Religions: Christianity, with particularly large numbers of Roman Catholic and Lutheran, also Baptist, Methodist, Presbyterian, and Church of Jesus Christ of Latter-day Saints

Major Industries: Mining, lumber and wood products, food processing, tourism, cattle, wheat, barley, sugar beets, hay, hogs

Ethnic Makeup (in percent): Caucasian 90.6%, African American 0.3%, Hispanic 2.0%, Asian 0.5%, Native American 6.2%, Other 0.6%

Famous Montanans: Dorothy Baker, Dana Carvey, Gary Cooper, Chet Huntley, Evel Knievel, Myrna Loy, David Lynch, George Montgomery, Martha Raye.

Above: A waterfall at Clements Mountain in West Glacier

earn the land—living on the acreage and making improvements on it over a period of time, which in this case was five years. You can search the initial land patents through the Bureau of Land Management—General Land Office Records <www.glorecords.blm.gov>. If the entry on the Web site is anything other than a Cash Sale, you will want to order a copy of the land file. You can order the necessary forms from the National Archives. They offer e-mail ordering options via the National Archives' Web site, Research Room pages at <www.archives .gov/research_room/obtain_copies/reproductions_ overview.html>. Once land was transferred to individuals, future sales were recorded in the deeds in the county where the sale took place. You will also find patents on

timber and mining claims at the county level in the office of the county recorder.

Because Montana did not become a territory until 1864, federal census records do not begin until 1870, though early residents may be listed in Washington or Nebraska. There was an early list of settlers, mostly miners, that has been compiled and listed in "List of Early Settlers: A List of All Persons (Except Indians) Who Were in What is Now Montana During the Winter of 1862–1863" found in *Contributions to the Historical Society of Montana*, vol. 1 (Helena, Montana: Rocky Mountain Publishing Company, 1902).

Vital records for Montana are not as complete as researchers would like. Though there were nine counties

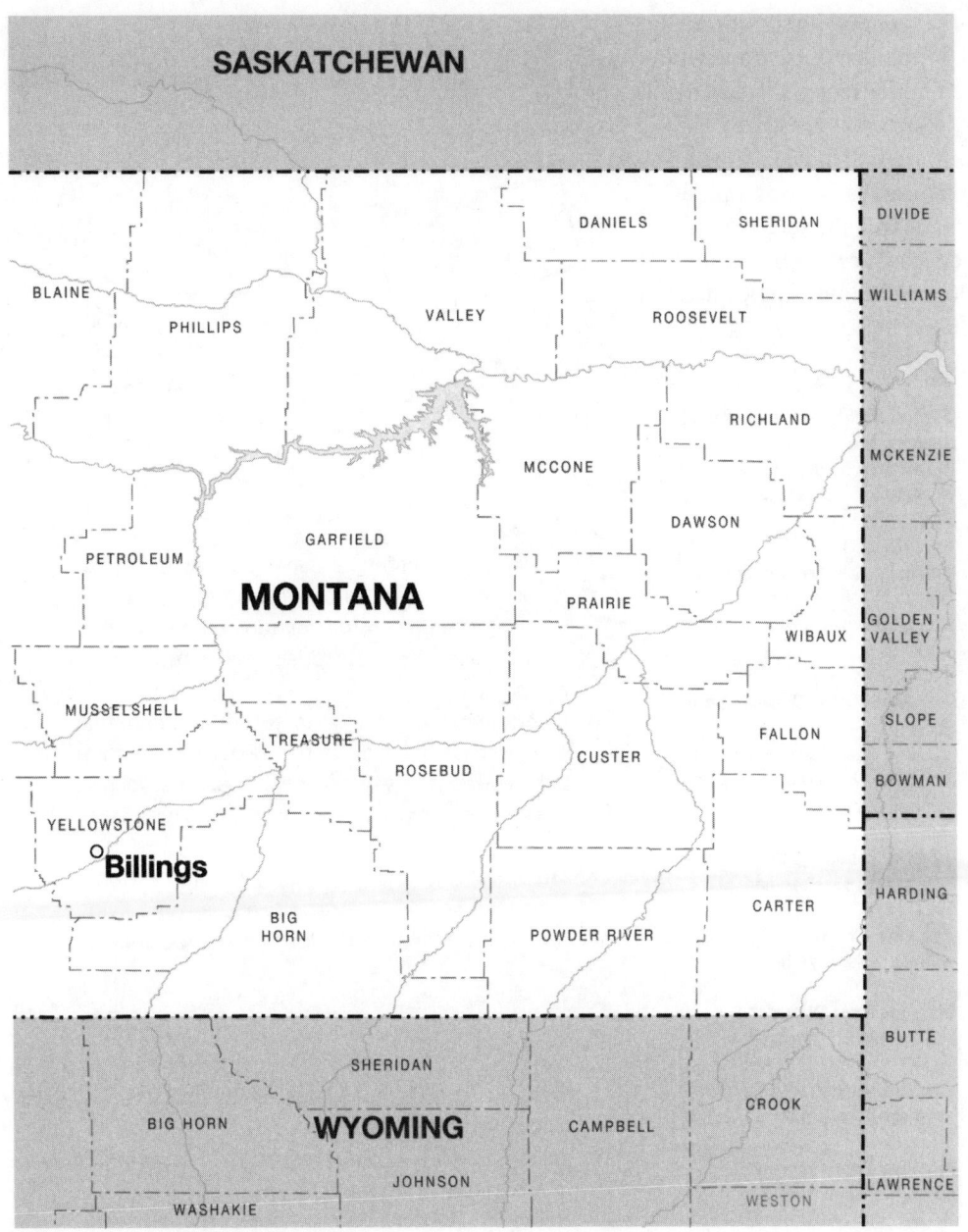

when the territory was formed, births and deaths were not recorded until 1895. It wasn't until 1907 that statewide registration began, and it would be another twenty-five years before 90 percent of births were being reported. Death records reached good reporting a little sooner, reaching more than 90 percent complete by 1915.

Probate records were originally held by probate courts for the years 1864 through 1889. These courts handled marriages, minor civil and criminal matters, adoptions, and probate. Once they were disbanded, the functions and records were transferred to district courts. District courts now serve as the major trial courts, each covering one to seven counties, with court sessions held in each county and most of the records dating to the year each county was founded.

In the 1860s the western part of Montana was originally Missoula County, Washington, and the eastern section was part of Nebraska Territory. You will want to consider this if your ancestors were some of the earliest settlers of Montana.

Anyone who was living in the area that was set aside as Yellowstone National Park in 1872 will be found in the Wyoming census of 1880. Another early census to look into is the 1864 Montana poll list, which lists the eligible voters living in the territory.

The Montana Historical Society, located at 225 North Roberts, Helena, Montana 59601 <www.his.state.mt.us>, has been amassing records on Montana's history and residents since 1969. Their records include papers of the governors, various prison and institution records, and a large collection of manuscripts. You will find all types of records housed in the society, including church and military records, territorial censuses, and poll lists. The society has been compiling indexes by subject, name, and place to aid researchers in using the records in their collection. You can search the society's collection online, and many of the records can also be found in the National Union Catalog of Manuscript Collections <http://lcweb.loc.gov/coll/nucmc>.

STATE RESOURCES

■ ARCHIVES, LIBRARIES, AND SOCIETIES

Beaverhead Hunters Genealogical Society/County Museum
15 S. Montana, Dillon, MT 59725
Web site: <www.rootsweb.com/ ~mtmsgs/soc_bhh.htm>

Big Horn County Genealogical Society
P.O. Box 51, Hardin, MT 59034
Web site: <www.rootsweb.com/ ~mtmsgs/soc_bhcgs.htm>

Bitterroot Genealogical Society
P.O. Box 941, Corvallis, MT 59828
Web site: <www.rootsweb.com/ ~mtmsgs/soc_bvgs.htm>

Broken Mountain Genealogical Society
P.O. Box 261, Chester, MT 59522
Web site: <www.rootsweb.com/ ~mtmsgs/soc_bmgs.htm>

Bureau of Land Management, Montana State Office
5001 Southgate Dr., Billings, MT 59101
Tel: (406) 896-5000
E-mail: MT_SO_Information@blm .gov
Web site: <www.mt.blm.gov>

Butte-Silver Bow Public Library
226 W. Broadway, Butte, MT 59701
Tel: (406) 723-3361
E-mail: bplref@mtlib.org

Cascade County Historical Museum
1400 First Ave. N., Great Falls, MT 59401
Tel: (406) 452-3462

Central Montana Genealogical Society, Inc.
℅ Lewistown Public Library, 701 W. Main, Lewistown, MT 59457-2501
Tel: (406) 538-5212
E-mail: gen@lewistownlibrary .org
Web site: <www.lewistownlibrary .org>

Fort Assiniboine Genealogical Society
P.O. Box 321, Havre, MT 59531
Web site: <www.rootsweb.com/ ~mtmsgs/soc_fags.htm>

Gallatin Genealogical Society
P.O. Box 1783, Bozeman, MT 59771-1783
Web site: <www.rootsweb.com/ ~mtmsgs/soc_ggs.htm>

Glasgow Root Diggers
102 Bonnie St., Glasgow, MT 59230
Web site: <www.rootsweb.com/ ~mtmsgs/soc_grd.htm>

Glendive Public Library
200 S. Kendrick Ave., Glendive, MT 59330
Tel: (406) 377-3633
E-mail: booksrus@midrivers.com
Web site: <www.dawsoncountym ontana.org/library.htm>

Great Falls Genealogy Society
422 Second St. S., Great Falls, MT 59405
Tel: (406) 727-3922
E-mail: gfgs@mt.net
Web site: <www.mt.net/~gfgs>

Havre-Hill County Library
402 Third St., Havre, MT 59501
Tel: (406) 265-2123
Web site: <www.mtha.mt.lib .org>

Historian Archivist, Diocese of Helena
515 N. Ewing, Helena, MT 59624
Tel: (406) 442-5820

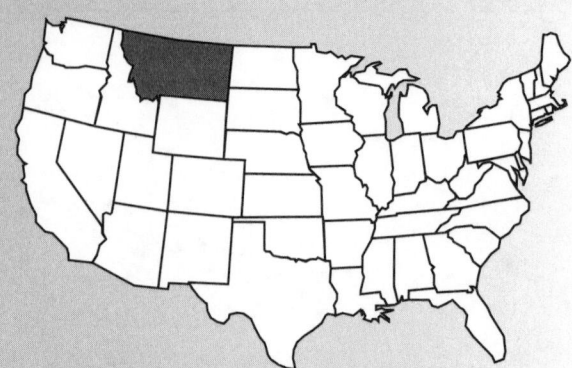

RESEARCH TIPS

for more info

- The Montana Historical Society <www.his.state. mt.us> has a massive collection of records that includes church records, military records, territorial censuses, poll lists, prison and institution records, etc.
- If your ancestors helped to settle Montana, find out where they lived—in the 1860s the western part of Montana was originally Missoula County, Washington, and the eastern section was part of Nebraska Territory.
- The land that comprises Yellowstone National Park was set aside in 1872, and anyone living there will be found in the 1880 Wyoming census.

Census Records
- Federal Census: 1870, 1880, 1900, 1910, 1920, 1930
- Federal Mortality Schedules: 1870, 1880
- Union Veterans Schedule: 1890
- Washington Territory Census (includes what is now western Montana): 1860
- Nebraska Territory Census (includes what is now eastern Montana): 1860

Lewis & Clark County Genealogical Library
120 S. Last Chance Gulch, Helena, MT 59601
Web site: <www.lewisandclarklib rary.org>

Lewis & Clark County Genealogical Society
P.O. Box 5313, Helena, MT 59604
Tel: (406) 447-1690
Web site: <www.lewisandclarklib rary.org>

Liberty County Library
100 E. First St., P.O. Box 458, Chester, MT 59522
Tel: (406) 759-5445

The Mansfield Library, University of Montana-Missoula
32 Campus Dr., Missoula, MT 59812-9936
Tel: (406) 243-6800
Web site: <www.lib.umt.edu>

Miles City Genealogical Society
P.O. Box 711, Miles City, MT 59301

Montana

E-mail: milescity@geocities.com
Web site: <www.geocities.com/
Heartland/Fields/6175/>

Miles City Public Library
One S. Tenth St., Miles City, MT
59301
E-mail: mcpl@midrivers.com
Web site: <http://milescitypubli
clibrary.org>

**Milk River Genealogical
Society**
P.O. Box 1000, Chinook, MT
59523
Web site: <www.rootsweb.com/
~mtmsgs/soc_mrgs.htm>

Missoula Public Library
301 E. Main, Missoula, MT
59802
Tel: (406) 721-2665
E-mail: mslaplib@missoula.lib.mt
.us
Web site: <www.missoula.lib.mt
.us>

**Montana Historical Society,
Library and Archives**
225 N. Roberts, P.O. Box
201201, Helena, MT
59620-1201
Tel: (406) 444-2694
E-mail: archives@mon.net
Web site: <www.his.state.mt
.us>

**Montana State Genealogical
Society**
P.O. Box 555, Chester, MT
59522
E-mail: msgs@iname.com
Web site: <www.rootsweb.com/
~mtmsgs/index.htm>

Montana State Library
1515 E. Sixth Ave., P.O. Box
201800, Helena, MT
59620-1800
Tel: (406) 444-3004 (reference)
Web site: <http://msl.state.mt
.us/>

**Montana State University
Libraries**
P.O. Box 173320, Bozeman, MT
59717-3320
Tel: (406) 994-3119
Web site: <www.lib.montana.edu>

**Montana State Vital Records
Office**
P.O. Box 4210, 111 N. Sanders,
Helena, MT 59604-4210
Tel: (406) 444-2685
Web site: <www.vitalrec.com/mt
.html>

**National Archives and Record
Administration, Rocky
Mountain Region**
Bldg. 48, Denver Federal Center,
W. Sixth Ave. and Kipling St., P.O.
Box 25307, Denver, CO
80225-0307
E-mail: denver.archives@nara
.gov
Web site: <www.archives.gov/fa
cilities/co/denver.html>

Parmly Billings Library
510 N. Broadway, Billings, MT
59101
Tel: (406) 657-8257
E-mail: refdesk@billings.lib.mt
.us
Web site: <www.billings.lib.mt
.us>

**Phillips County Genealogical
Society**
P.O. Box 334, Malta, MT 59538
Web site: <www.rootsweb.com/
~mtmsgs/soc_phcgs.htm>

**Powell County Genealogical
Society**
652 Greenhouse Rd., Deer Lodge,
MT 59722
Web site: <www.rootsweb.com/
~mtmsgs/soc_pcgs.htm>

**Roman Catholic Archives,
Diocese of Great Falls-Billings**
Web site: <www.dioceseofgfb
.org>

**Sheridan County Daybreakers
Genealogical Society**
E-mail: daybreakers@petersnn
.org
Web site: <www.petersnn.org/da
ybreakers/scdgsindex.htm>

**Tangled Roots Genealogical
Society**
P.O. Box 1992, Cut Bank, MT
59427
Web site: <www.rootsweb.com/
~mtmsgs/soc_trgs.htm>

The Tree Branches
P.O. Box 1275, Glendive, MT
59330-1275
Web site: <www.cheyenneancest
ors.com/dawson/dwsgens
.html>

**Western Montana Genealogical
Society**
P.O. Box 2714, Missoula, MT
59806-2714
E-mail: jalf@marsweb.com
Web site: <www.rootsweb.com/
~mtwmgs>

Yellowstone Genealogy Forum
% Parmly Billings Library, 510 N.
Broadway, Billings, MT 59101
Web site: <www.rootsweb.com/
~mtmsgs/soc_ygf.htm>

**Yellowstone Valley Chapter,
American Historical Society of
Germans from Russia (AHSGR)**
715 W. Fifth St., Laurel, MT
59044
Tel: (406) 628-6795
E-mail: howros717@juno.com
Web site: <www.ahsgr.org/yello
wstone_valley_chapter.htm>

BIBLIOGRAPHY

■ GENERAL RESOURCES

*Bibliography of Montana Local
Histories*
by Coburn Johnson (Montana:
Montana Library Association,
1977)

*The Bloody Bozeman: The
Perilous Trail to Montana's
Gold*
by Dorothy M. Johnson (Missoula,
MT: Mountain Press, 1983)

*The Bridger Trail: A Viable
Alternative to the Gold Fields of
Montana Territory in 1864,
With Excerpts From Emigrant
Diaries, Letters, and
Comparitive Material From
Oregon and Bozeman Trail
Diaries*
by James A. Lowe (Spokane, WA:
Arthur H. Clark Co., 1999)

*A Directory of Churches &
Religious Organizations in
Montana*
prepared by the Historical Records Survey, Division of Community Service Programs, Works
Progress Administration (Bozeman, MT: 1941)

*First Families of Montana and
Early Settlers*
by Al Stoner (Lewistown, MT:
Montana State Genealogical Society, 2000)

*The Genealogist's Companion
and Sourcebook, 2d ed.*
by Emily Anne Croom (Cincinnati:
Betterway Books, 2003)

*A Genealogist's Guide to
Discovering Your African-
American Ancestors*
by Franklin Carter Smith and
Emily Anne Croom (Cincinnati:
Betterway Books, 2003)

*Golden Opportunities: A
Biographical History of
Montana's Jewish
Communities*
by Julie L. Coleman (Billings, MT:
J.L. Coleman; Helena, MT: Sky-
House Publishers, distributed by
Falcon Press, ca. 1994)

*Go With Haste Into the
Mountains: A History of the
Diocese of Helena*
by Cornelia M. Flaherty (Helena,
MT: Catholic Diocese of Helena,
1984)

*Guide to Genealogical
Research in the National
Archives of the United States*
edited by Anne Bruner Eales and
Robert M. Kvasnicka (Washing-
ton, DC: National Archives and
Records Administration, 2000)

*A History of the Catholic
Church in the Pacific
Northwest, 1743–1983*
by Wilfred P. Schoenberg (Washington, DC: Pastoral Press, 1987)

*History of the Great Northwest
and Its Men of Progress: A
Select List of Biographical
Sketches and Portraits of the
Leaders in Business,
Professional and Official Life*
edited by C.W.G. Hyde and William Stoddard (Minneapolis: Minneapolis Journal, 1901)

A History of Montana, 3 vols.
edited by Merrill G. Burlingame
and K. Ross Toole, et al (New
York: Lewis Historical Publishing
Company, 1957)

A History of Montana, 3 vols.
by Helen Fitzgerald Sanders (Chicago: Lewis Publishing Co.,
1913)

*Indian and White in the
Northwest, or, A History of
Catholicity in Montana*
by L.B. Palladino (Baltimore, MD:
J. Murphy, 1894)

Jesuits in Montana 1840–1960
by Wilfred P. Schoenberg (Portland, OR: Jesuits, 1960)

*Men and Trade on the
Northwest Frontier as Shown by
the Fort Owen Ledger*
edited by George Ferdinand
Weisel (Missoula, MT: Montana
State University Press, 1955)

Montana

Montana Data Index: A Reference Guide to Historical and Genealogical Resources
compiled by Paulette K. Parpart and Donald E. Spritzer (Missoula, MT: Montana Library Association, 1992)

The Montana Historical and Genealogical Data Index
compiled by Paulette K. Parpart and Donald E. Spritzer (Missoula, MT: Montana Library Association Indexing Special Interest Group, 1987)

Montana, Its Story and Biography: A History of Aboriginal and Territorial Montana and Three Decades of Statehood, 3 vols.
edited by Tom Stout (Chicago: American Historical Society, 1921)

Montana Legislators, 1864–1979: Profiles and Biographical Directory
by Ellis Waldron (Missoula, MT: Bureau of Government Research, University of Montana, 1980)

The Montana Locator: A Directory of Public Records for Locating People Dead or Alive in Montana
by Laurie Nicklas (Modesto, CA: L. Nicklas, 1999)

Montana Pay Dirt: A Guide to Mining Camps of the Treasure State
by Muriel Vincent Sibell Wolle (Denver: Sage, 1963)

Montana Research Outline
by the Church of Jesus Christ of Latter-day Saints Family History Library (Salt Lake City, UT: Corp. of the President of the Church of Jesus Christ of L.D.S., 1988)

Montana's Genealogical and Local History Records, A Selected List of Books, Manuscripts, and Periodicals
by Dennis L. Richards (Detroit: Gale Research Company, 1981)

More Than Petticoats: Remarkable Montana Women
by Gayle C. Shirley (Helena, MT: Falcon Press, 1995)

Names on the Face of Montana: the Story of Montana's Place Names
by Roberta Carkeek Cheney (Missoula, MT: Mountain Press Pub. Co., 1984)

National Archives Microfilm Catalogs online:
<www.archives.gov/publications/genealogy_microfilm_catalogs.html>

The Pioneer Work of the Presbyterian Church in Montana
edited by Rev. George Edwards (Helena, MT: Independent Publishing Company, 1907)

Plains, Peaks, and Pioneers; Eighty Years of Methodism in Montana
by Edward Laird Mills (Portland, OR: Binfords & Mort, 1947)

Speaking of Montana: A Guide to the Oral History Collection at the Montana Historical Society, Through 1996
compiled by Patricia Borneman, et al, edited by Jodie Foley and Dave Walter (Helena, MT: Montana Historical Society Press, 1997)

Twentieth-Century Montana: A State of Extremes
by K. Ross Toole (Norman, OK: University of Oklahoma Press, 1972)

■ CENSUS RECORDS

The American Census Handbook
by Thomas Jay Kemp (Wilmington, DE: Scholarly Resources, 2001)

The Census Book: A Genealogist's Guide to Federal Census Facts, Schedules and Indexes
by William Dollarhide (Bountiful, UT: Heritage Quest, 2000)

Finding Answers in U.S. Census Records
by Loretto Dennis Szucs and Matthew Wright (Orem, UT: Ancestry Publishing, 2002)

Map Guide to the U.S. Federal Censuses, 1790–1920
by William Thorndale and William Dollarhide (Baltimore, MD: Genealogical Pub. Co., 1987)

State Census Records
by Ann S. Lainhart (Baltimore, MD: Genealogical Publishing, 1992)

Your Guide to the Federal Census
by Kathleen W. Hinckley (Cincinnati: Betterway Books, 2002)

■ IMMIGRATION RECORDS

American Naturalization Records, 1790–1990: What They Are and How to Use Them
by John J. Newman (North Salt Lake, UT: HeritageQuest, 1998)

American Passenger Arrival Records
by Michael Tepper (Baltimore: Genealogical Publishing Co., 1993)

They Became Americans: Finding Naturalization Records and Ethnic Origins
by Loretto Dennis Szucs (Salt Lake City: Ancestry, Inc., 1998)

They Came in Ships: A Guide to Finding Your Immigrant Ancestor's Arrival Records, 2d ed.
by John P. Colletta (Salt Lake City: Ancestry, Inc., 1993)

■ LAND RECORDS

After Barbed Wire: A Pictorial History of the Homestead Rush Into the Northern Great Plains, 1900–1919
by Marie Peterson MacDonald (Glendive, MT: Frontier Gateway Museum, 1983)

Homesteading
by Percy Wollaston (New York: Lyons & Burford, 1997)

Land and Property Research in the United States
by E. Wade Hone (Salt Lake City, UT: Ancestry, 1997)

Locating Your Roots: Discover Your Ancestors Using Land Records
by Patricia Law Hatcher (Cincinnati: Betterway Books, 2003)

■ MAPS

Atlas of the Pacific Northwest
edited by Richard M. Highsmith and A. Jon Kimerling (Corvallis, OR: University of Oregon Press, 1979)

Catalog of the Map Collection
by the Montana Historical Society (Helena, MT: The Society, 1983)

Military Posts in Montana
by Michael J. Koury, illustrated by Derek Fitz James, photography by Clark Babcock (Bellvue, Nebraska: Old Army Press, 1970)

■ MILITARY RECORDS

Men With Custer: Biographies of the 7th Cavalry, 25 June, 1876
by Kenneth Hammer (Fort Collins, CO: Old Army Press, 1972)

Roll Call on the Little Big Horn, 28 June 1876
compiled by John M. Carroll and Byron Price (Ft. Collins, CO: Old Army Press, 1974)

Uncle, We Are Ready! Registering America's Men, 1917–1918: A Guide to Researching World War I Draft Registration Cards
by John J. Newman (North Salt Lake, UT: HeritageQuest, 2001)

U.S. Military Records: A Guide to Federal & State Sources, Colonial America to the Present
by James C. Neagles (Salt Lake City: Ancestry, Inc., 1994)

World War II: A Family Historian's Guide
by Debra Johnson Knox (Spartanburg, SC: MIE Publishing, 2003)

■ VITAL RECORDS

Cemetery Inscriptions and Church Records From Hingham, Rudyard, Inverness, Whitlash, Lothair, Joplin, and Chester, Montana
compiled and typed by Una Moog (Chester, MT: Broken Mountains Genealogical Society, 1986)

Inventory of the Vital Statistics Records of Church and Religious Organizations in Montana, 1942
by the Historical Records Survey (Bozeman, MT: The Inventory of Public Archives, Montana Historical Records Survey, 1942)

Your Guide to Cemetery Research
by Sharon DeBartolo Carmack (Cincinnati: Betterway Books, 2002)

Montana

■ **Beaverhead** 2 Feb. 1865
2 S. Pacific St., Cluster #3, Dillon, MT 59725
Phone: (406)683-2642
Web site: www.rootsweb.com/~mtbeaver/
Parent County: Original county

Record Type	Year Begun	Jurisdiction
Birth	1901	County Clerk
Death	1901	County Clerk
Marriage	1877	County Clerk
Deeds	1876	County Clerk
Probate	1865	Clerk/District Ct.
Court	1865	Clerk/District Ct.

■ **Big Horn** 13 Jan. 1913
121 W. Third St., Room 221, P.O. Box 908, Hardin, MT 59034
Phone: (406)665-1506
Web site: www.kindredtrails.com/MT_Big_Horn.html
Parent County: Rosebud, Yellowstone

Record Type	Year Begun	Jurisdiction
Marriage	1913	Clerk/District Ct.
Deeds	1913	County Clerk
Probate	1913	Clerk/District Ct.
Court	1913	Clerk/District Ct.
Nat.	1913	County Clerk

■ **Blaine** 29 Feb. 1912
P.O. Box 908, Chinook, MT 59523
Phone: (406)357-3240
Web site: www.rootsweb.com/~mtblaine/
Parent County: Chouteau

Record Type	Year Begun	Jurisdiction
Marriage	1912	Clerk/District Ct.
Deeds	1912	County Clerk
Probate	1912	Clerk/District Ct.
Court	1912	Clerk/District Ct.

■ **Broadwater** 9 Feb. 1897
515 Broadway, Townsend, MT 59644
Phone: (406)266-3443
Web site: www.rootsweb.com/~mtbroadw/
Parent County: Jefferson, Meagher

Record Type	Year Begun	Jurisdiction
Birth	1894	County Recorder
Marriage	1897	Clerk of Courts
Death	1903	County Recorder
Deeds	1866	County Recorder
Probate	1897	Clerk of Courts
Court	1897	Clerk of Courts

■ **Carbon** 4 Mar. 1895
P.O. Box 887, Red Lodge, MT 59068
Phone: (406)446-1220
Web site: www.rootsweb.com/~mtcarbon/_crb.html
Parent County: Park, Yellowstone, Custer

Record Type	Year Begun	Jurisdiction
Birth	1904	County Clerk
Marriage	1895	County Clerk
Death	1895	County Clerk

Deeds	1888	County Clerk
Probate	1895	County Clerk
Court	1895	County Clerk

■ **Carter** 22 Feb. 1917
P.O. Box 315, Ekalaka, MT 59324
Phone: (406)775-8749
Web site: www.rootsweb.com/~mtcarter/
Parent County: Custer

Record Type	Year Begun	Jurisdiction
Marriage	1917	Clerk of Courts
Deeds	1917	County Clerk
Probate	1917	Clerk of Courts
Court	1917	Clerk of Courts

■ **Cascade** 12 Sep. 1887
415 Second Ave. N., Room 203, P.O. Box 2305, Great Falls, MT 59401
Phone: (406)454-6801
Web site: www.rootsweb.com/~mtcascad/
Parent County: Chouteau, Meagher, Lewis & Clark

Record Type	Year Begun	Jurisdiction
Birth	1892	County Recorder
Marriage	1888	Clerk of Courts
Death	1893	County Recorder
Deeds	1889	County Recorder
Probate	1889	Clerk of Courts
Court	1889	Clerk of Courts

■ **Chouteau** 2 Feb. 1865
1308 Franklin St., P.O. Box 459, Fort Benton, MT 59442
Phone: (406)622-5151
Web site: www.kindredtrails.com/MT_Chouteau.html
Parent County: Original county

Record Type	Year Begun	Jurisdiction
Birth	1895	County Clerk
Marriage	1882	Clerk of Courts
Death	1895	County Clerk
Deeds	1872	County Clerk
Probate	1880	Clerk of Courts
Court	1895	Clerk of Courts

■ **Custer** 2 Feb. 1865
1010 Main St., Miles City, MT 59301
Phone: (406)233-3457
Web site: www.rootsweb.com/~mtcuster/
Parent County: Original county
Comments/research tips: Formerly Big Horn County. Name changed to Custer 16 February 1877.

Record Type	Year Begun	Jurisdiction
Birth	1895	County Clerk
Marriage	1887	Clerk/District Ct.
Death	1895	County Clerk
Deeds	1877	County Clerk
Probate	1883	Clerk/District Ct.
Court	1879	Justice of the Peace

■ **Daniels** 30 Aug. 1920
P.O. Box 247, Scobey, MT 59263
Phone: (406)487-5561

Web site: www.kindredtrails.com/MT_Daniels.html
Parent County: Valley, Sheridan

Record Type	Year Begun	Jurisdiction
Marriage	1920	Clerk of Courts
Deeds	1920	County Recorder
Probate	1920	Clerk of Courts
Court	1910	Clerk/District Ct.

■ Dawson 15 Jan. 1869

207 W. Bell St., Glendive, MT 59330
Phone: (406)377-3058
Web site: www.dawsoncountymontana.org
Parent County: Original county

Record Type	Year Begun	Jurisdiction
Marriage	1882	Clerk of Courts
Death	1895	County Clerk
Deeds	1881	County Clerk
Probate	1883	Clerk of Courts
Court	1883	Clerk of Courts
Birth	1895	County Clerk

■ Deer Lodge 2 Feb. 1865

800 S. Main St., Anaconda, MT 59711
Phone: (406)563-4060
Web site: www.mtech.edu/silverbow/deerlodge.htm
Parent County: Original county

Record Type	Year Begun	Jurisdiction
Birth	1903	County Clerk
Marriage	1865	Clerk of Courts
Death	1895	County Clerk
Deeds	1864	County Clerk
Probate	1871	Clerk of Courts
Court	1865	Clerk of Courts

■ Edgerton 2 Feb. 1865

Parent County: Original county
Comments/research tips: (See Lewis and Clark) Name changed to Lewis and Clark 20 December 1867.

■ Fallon 9 Dec. 1913

712 W. Fallon Ave., P.O. Box 846, Baker, MT 59313
Phone: (406)788
Web site: www.rootsweb.com/~mtfallon/_fll.html
Parent County: Custer

Record Type	Year Begun	Jurisdiction
Marriage	1912	Clerk of Courts
Deeds	1889	County Recorder
Probate	1914	Clerk of Courts
Court	1914	Clerk of Courts

■ Fergus 12 Mar. 1885

712 W. Main St., Lewistown, MT 59457-2562
Phone: (406)538-5242
Web site: www.rootsweb.com/~mtfergus/
Parent County: Meagher, Chouteau

Record Type	Year Begun	Jurisdiction
Birth	1904	County Clerk
Marriage	1885	Clerk of Courts
Death	1904	County Clerk

Record Type	Year Begun	Jurisdiction
Deeds	1888	County Assessor
Probate	1888	Clerk of Courts
Court	1888	Clerk of Courts

■ Flathead 6 Feb. 1893

800 S. Main St., Kalispell, MT 59901
Phone: (406)758-5526
Web site: www.genealogylinks.net/usa/montana/Flathead.htm
Parent County: Missoula

Record Type	Year Begun	Jurisdiction
Birth	1896	County Recorder
Marriage	1892	Clerk/District Ct.
Deeds	1884	County Recorder
Probate	1893	Clerk/District Ct.
Court	1893	Clerk/District Ct.

■ Gallatin 2 Feb. 1865

311 W. Main St., Bozeman, MT 59715
Phone: (406)582-3050
Web site: www.rootsweb.com/~mtgallat/Gallatin.htm
Parent County: Original county

Record Type	Year Begun	Jurisdiction
Birth	1895	County Recorder
Marriage	1865	Clerk/District Ct.
Death	1895	County Recorder
Deeds	1862	County Recorder
Probate	1886	Clerk/District Ct.
Court	1886	Clerk/District Ct.

■ Garfield 7 Feb. 1919

P.O. Box 7, Jordan, MT 59337
Phone: (406)557-2760
Web site: www.rootsweb.com/~mtgarfie/
Parent County: Dawson

Record Type	Year Begun	Jurisdiction
Marriage	1919	Clerk of Courts
Deeds	1919	County Clerk
Probate	1919	Clerk of Courts
Court	1919	Clerk of Courts

■ Glacier 17 Feb. 1919

512 E. Main St., Cut Bank, MT 59427
Phone: (406)873-5063
Web site: www.rootsweb.com/~mtglacie/
Parent County: Teton

Record Type	Year Begun	Jurisdiction
Marriage	1910	Clerk of Courts
Deeds	1919	County Clerk
Probate	1919	Clerk of Courts
Court	1919	Clerk of Courts

■ Golden Valley 4 Oct. 1920

P.O. Box 10, Ryegate, MT 59074
Phone: (406)568-2231
Web site: www.rootsweb.com/~mtgolden/
Parent County: Musselshell, Sweet Grass

Record Type	Year Begun	Jurisdiction
Deeds	1920	County Recorder

Probate .... 1920 ....County Recorder
Court .... 1920 ....County Recorder

■ Granite 2 Mar. 1893
P.O. Box 925, Phillipsburg, MT 59858
Phone: (406)859-3771
Web site: www.rootsweb.com/~mtgranit/
Parent County: Deer Lodge

Record Type	Year Begun	Jurisdiction
Birth	1895	County Recorder
Marriage	1893	Clerk of Courts
Death	1895	County Recorder
Deeds	1866	County Recorder
Probate	1893	Clerk of Courts
Court	1893	Clerk of Courts

■ Hill 28 Feb. 1912
315 Fourth St., Havre, MT 59501
Phone: (406)265-5481, Ext.
Web site: www.kindredtrails.com/MT_Hill.html
Parent County: Chouteau

Record Type	Year Begun	Jurisdiction
Birth	1898	County Recorder
Marriage	1912	Clerk of Courts
Death	1897	County Recorder
Deeds	1912	County Recorder
Probate	1912	Clerk of Courts
Court	1912	Clerk of Courts

■ Jefferson 2 Feb. 1865
P.O. Box H, Boulder, MT 59632
Phone: (406)225-4020
Web site: www.rootsweb.com/~mtjeffer/
Parent County: Original county

Record Type	Year Begun	Jurisdiction
Birth	1895	County Clerk
Marriage	1887	Clerk/District Ct.
Deeds	1865	County Clerk
Probate	1869	Clerk/District Ct.
Court	1869	Clerk/District Ct.
Death	1895	Clerk/District Ct.

■ Judith Basin 10 Dec. 1920
P.O. Box 427, Stanford, MT 59479
Phone: (406)566-2277
Web site: www.rootsweb.com/~mtjudith/
Parent County: Fergus, Cascade

Record Type	Year Begun	Jurisdiction
Marriage	1920	Clerk of Courts
Deeds	1921	County Recorder
Probate	1921	Clerk of Courts
Court	1921	Clerk of Courts

■ Lake 11 May 1923
106 Fourth Ave. E., Polson, MT 59860
Phone: (406)883-7215
Web site: www.rootsweb.com/~mtlake/
Parent County: Flathead, Missoula

Record Type	Year Begun	Jurisdiction
Marriage	1923	Clerk of Courts

Deeds.................... 1923 ....County Recorder
Probate .... 1923 ....Clerk of Courts
Court .... 1923 ....Clerk of Courts

■ Lewis & Clark 2 Feb. 1865
316 N. Park, P.O. Box 1721, Helena, MT 59601
Phone: (406)447-8334
Web site: www.genealogylinks.net/usa/montana/
Lewis_and_Clark.htm
Parent County: Original county
Comments/research tips: Formerly Edgerton County. Name changed to Lewis & Clark 20 December 1867.

Record Type	Year Begun	Jurisdiction
Birth	1895	County Clerk
Marriage	1865	Clerk/District Ct.
Death	1895	County Clerk
Deeds	1865	County Clerk
Probate	1895	Clerk/District Ct.
Court	1867	Clerk/District Ct.

■ Liberty 11 Feb. 1920
111 First St. E., Chester, MT 59522
Phone: (406)759-5365
Web site: www.genealogylinks.net/usa/montana/
Liberty.htm
Parent County: Chouteau, Hill

Record Type	Year Begun	Jurisdiction
Marriage	1920	Clerk/District Ct.
Deeds	1920	County Clerk
Probate	1920	Clerk/District Ct.
Court	1920	Clerk/District Ct.

■ Lincoln 9 Mar. 1909
512 California Ave., Libby, MT 59923
Phone: (406)293-7781
Web site: www.libby.org/
Parent County: Flathead

Record Type	Year Begun	Jurisdiction
Birth	1897	County Clerk
Marriage	1896	Clerk/District Ct.
Death	1897	County Clerk
Deeds	1909	County Clerk
Probate	1909	Clerk/District Ct.
Court	1909	Clerk/District Ct.

■ Madison 2 Feb. 1865
110 W. Wallace St., Virginia City, MT 59755
Phone: (406)843-4270
Web site: www.rootsweb.com/~mtmadiso/
Parent County: Original county

Record Type	Year Begun	Jurisdiction
Birth	1903	County Recorder
Marriage	1887	Clerk of Courts
Death	1903	County Recorder
Deeds	1863	County Recorder
Probate	1864	Clerk of Courts
Court	1864	Clerk of Courts

■ McCone 20 Feb. 1919
P.O. Box 199, Circle, MT 59215
Phone: (406)485-3505

Web site: www.rootsweb.com/~mtmccone/
Parent County: Dawson, Richland

Record Type	Year Begun	Jurisdiction
Marriage	1919	Clerk of Courts
Deeds	1919	County Recorder
Probate	1919	Clerk of Courts
Court	1919	Clerk of Courts

■ Meagher 16 Nov. 1867
15 W. Main St., P.O. Box 309, White Sulphur Springs, MT 59645
Phone: (406)547-3612
Web site: www.rootsweb.com/~mtmeaghe/
Parent County: Original county

Record Type	Year Begun	Jurisdiction
Birth	1895	County Recorder
Marriage	1866	Clerk of Courts
Deeds	1866	County Recorder
Probate	1866	Clerk of Courts
Court	1867	Clerk of Courts

■ Mineral 7 Aug. 1914
P.O. Box 550, Superior, MT 59872
Phone: (406)822-3521
Web site: www.rootsweb.com/~mtminera/mineral.htm
Parent County: Missoula

Record Type	Year Begun	Jurisdiction
Marriage	1887	Clerk/District Ct.
Deeds	1914	County Recorder
Probate	1914	Clerk/District Ct.
Court	1914	Clerk/District Ct.

■ Missoula 2 Feb. 1865
200 W. Broadway, Missoula, MT 59802
Phone: (406)721-5700
Web site: www.rootsweb.com/~mtmissou/
Parent County: Original county

Record Type	Year Begun	Jurisdiction
Birth	1895	County Clerk
Marriage	1865	Clerk of Courts
Death	1895	County Clerk
Deeds	1868	County Clerk
Probate	1867	Clerk of Courts
Court	1865	Clerk of Courts

■ Musselshell 11 Feb. 1911
506 S. Main St., P.O. Box 686, Roundup, MT 59072
Phone: (406)323-1104
Web site: www.rootsweb.com/~mtmussel/
Parent County: Fergus, Yellowstone

Record Type	Year Begun	Jurisdiction
Marriage	1895	Clerk of Courts
Deeds	1911	County Recorder
Probate	1911	Clerk of Courts
Court	1911	Clerk of Courts

■ Park 23 Feb. 1887
414 E. Callender, Livingston, MT 59047
Phone: (406)222-4110

Web site: www.rootsweb.com/~mtpark/Park.htm
Parent County: Gallatin

Record Type	Year Begun	Jurisdiction
Birth	1889	County Clerk
Marriage	1887	Clerk/District Ct.
Death	1892	County Clerk
Deeds	1887	County Clerk
Probate	1886	Clerk/District Ct.
Court	1886	Clerk/District Ct.

■ Petroleum 24 Nov. 1924
201 E. Main St., P.O. Box 226, Winnett, MT 59087
Phone: (406)429-5311
Web site: www.rootsweb.com/~mtpetrol/
Parent County: Fergus

Record Type	Year Begun	Jurisdiction
Marriage	1925	Director of Records
Deeds	1925	Director of Records
Probate	1925	Director of Records
Court	1925	Director of Records

■ Phillips 5 Feb. 1915
314 Second Ave. W., P.O. Box 306, Malta, MT 59538
Phone: (406)654-2423
Web site: www.rootsweb.com/~mtphilli/
Parent County: Valley, Blaine

Record Type	Year Begun	Jurisdiction
Marriage	1915	Clerk of Courts
Deeds	1915	County Clerk
Probate	1915	Clerk of Courts
Court	1915	Clerk of Courts

■ Pondera 17 Feb. 1919
20 Fourth Ave. SW, Conrad, MT 59425
Phone: (406)278-4000
Web site: www.rootsweb.com/~mtponder/
Parent County: Chouteau, Teton

Record Type	Year Begun	Jurisdiction
Marriage	1919	Clerk of Courts
Deeds	1919	County Clerk
Probate	1919	Clerk of Courts
Court	1919	Clerk of Courts

■ Powder River 7 Mar. 1919
P.O. Box 270, Broadus, MT 59317
Phone: (406)436-2361
Web site: www.rangeweb.net/~emmov/prc.html/
Parent County: Custer

Record Type	Year Begun	Jurisdiction
Marriage	1919	Clerk/District Ct.
Deeds	1919	County Clerk
Probate	1919	Clerk/District Ct.
Court	1919	Clerk/District Ct.

■ Powell 31 Jan. 1901
409 Missouri Ave., P.O. Box 125, Deer Lodge, MT 59722
Phone: (406)846-3680
Web site: www.mtech.edu/silverbow/powell.htm
Parent County: Deer Lodge

Montana

Record Type	Year Begun	Jurisdiction
Marriage	1901	Clerk of Courts
Deeds	1901	County Clerk
Probate	1901	Clerk of Courts
Court	1901	Clerk of Courts

■ Prairie 5 Feb. 1915
309 S. Garfield, Terry, MT 59349
Phone: (406)637-5575
Web site: www.rangeweb.net/~emmov/prairie/index2.html
Parent County: Custer

Record Type	Year Begun	Jurisdiction
Birth	1915	County Clerk
Death	1915	County Clerk
Marriage	1915	Clerk of Courts
Deeds	1915	County Clerk
Probate	1915	Clerk of Courts
Court	1915	Clerk of Courts
Divorce	1915	Clerk of Courts

■ Ravalli 16 Feb. 1893
205 Bedford St., Hamilton, MT 59840
Phone: (406)375-6213
Web site: www.rootsweb.com/~mtravall/
Parent County: Missoula

Record Type	Year Begun	Jurisdiction
Marriage	1893	Clerk of Courts
Deeds	1866	County Clerk
Probate	1893	Clerk of Courts
Court	1893	Clerk of Courts

■ Richland 27 May 1914
201 W. Main St., Sidney, MT 59270
Phone: (406)482-1708
Web site: www.midrivers.com/~wyldrose/
Parent County: Dawson

Record Type	Year Begun	Jurisdiction
Marriage	1914	Clerk/District Ct.
Deeds	1914	County Clerk
Probate	1914	Clerk/District Ct.
Court	1914	Clerk/District Ct.

■ Roosevelt 18 Feb. 1919
400 Second Ave. S, Wolf Point, MT 59201
Phone: (406)653-6229
Web site: www.genealogylinks.net/usa/montana/
Roosevelt.htm
Parent County: Sheridan

Record Type	Year Begun	Jurisdiction
Marriage	1913	Clerk/District Ct.
Deeds	1919	County Recorder
Probate	1919	Clerk/District Ct.
Court	1919	Clerk/District Ct.

■ Rosebud 11 Feb. 1901
P.O. Box 48, Forsyth, MT 59327
Phone: (406)356-7318
Web site: www.rootsweb.com/~mtrosebu/
Parent County: Custer

Record Type	Year Begun	Jurisdiction
Birth	1893	County Clerk
Marriage	1901	Clerk/District Ct.
Death	1909	County Clerk
Deeds	1877	County Clerk
Probate	1901	Clerk/District Ct.
Court	1901	Clerk/District Ct.

■ Sanders 7 Feb. 1905
P.O. Box 519, Thompson Falls, MT 59873
Phone: (406)827-4392
Web site: www.rootsweb.com/~mtsander/
Parent County: Missoula

Record Type	Year Begun	Jurisdiction
Marriage	1906	County Recorder
Deeds	1885	County Recorder
Probate	1906	County Recorder
Court	1906	County Recorder

■ Sheridan 24 Mar. 1913
100 W. Laurel Ave., Plentywood, MT 59254
Phone: (406)765-2310
Web site: www.petersnn.org/daybreakers/scdgsindex.htm
Parent County: Valley

Record Type	Year Begun	Jurisdiction
Marriage	1913	Clerk of Courts
Deeds	1913	County Clerk
Probate	1913	Clerk of Courts
Court	1913	Clerk of Courts

■ Silver Bow 16 Feb. 1881
155 W. Granite St., Box 585, Butte, MT 59701
Phone: (406)723-6335
Web site: http://resources.rootsweb.com/USA/MT/
SilverBow/
Parent County: Deer Lodge
Comments/research tips: 2 May 1977 the city of Butte and county of Silver Bow were unified to form the Butte-Silver Bow government.

Record Type	Year Begun	Jurisdiction
Birth	1878	County Recorder
Marriage	1881	Clerk of Courts
Death	1890	County Recorder
Deeds	1881	County Recorder
Probate	1881	Clerk of Courts
Court	1881	Clerk of Courts

■ Stillwater 24 Mar. 1913
400 E. Third Ave. N., P.O. Box 149, Columbus, MT 59019
Phone: (406)322-8000
Web site: www.rootsweb.com/~mtstillw/
Parent County: Sweet Grass, Yellowstone, Carbon

Record Type	Year Begun	Jurisdiction
Birth	1887	County Recorder
Deeds	1913	County Recorder
Probate	1913	Clerk of Courts
Court	1913	Clerk of Courts
Marriage	1913	Clerk of Courts

Montana

■ Sweet Grass 5 Mar. 1895
200 W. First Ave., P.O. Box 460, Big Timber, MT 59011
Phone: (406)932-5152
Web site: www.rootsweb.com/~mtsweetg/
Parent County: Meagher, Park, Yellowstone

Record Type	Year Begun	Jurisdiction
Birth	1895	County Recorder
Marriage	1895	Clerk/District Ct.
Death	1895	County Recorder
Deeds	1895	County Recorder
Probate	1895	Clerk/District Ct.
Court	1895	Clerk/District Ct.

■ Teton 7 Feb. 1893
P.O. Box 610, Choteau, MT 59422
Phone: (406)466-2693
Web site: www.rootsweb.com/~mtteton/
Parent County: Chouteau

Record Type	Year Begun	Jurisdiction
Birth	1897	County Clerk
Marriage	1893	Clerk/District Ct.
Deeds	1893	County Clerk
Probate	1890	Clerk/District Ct.
Court	1895	Clerk/District Ct.

■ Toole 7 May 1914
226 First St. S., Shelby, MT 59474
Phone: (406)434-2232
Web site: www.rootsweb.com/~mttoole/
Parent County: Teton, Hill

Record Type	Year Begun	Jurisdiction
Marriage	1914	Clerk of Courts
Deeds	1914	County Recorder
Probate	1914	Clerk of Courts
Court	1914	Clerk of Courts

■ Treasure 7 Feb. 1919
P.O. Box 392, Hysham, MT 59038
Phone: (406)342-5547
Web site: www.rootsweb.com/~mttreasu/
Parent County: Rosebud

Record Type	Year Begun	Jurisdiction
Marriage	1919	Clerk/District Ct.
Deeds	1879	County Recorder
Probate	1919	Clerk/District Ct.
Court	1919	Clerk/District Ct.

■ Valley 6 Feb. 1893
501 Court Sq. #2, Glasgow, MT 59230
Phone: (406)228-8221
Web site: www.petersnn.org/nemontana/nemont/Valley-main.html
Parent County: Dawson

Record Type	Year Begun	Jurisdiction
Marriage	1893	Clerk of Courts
Deeds	1893	County Recorder
Probate	1893	Clerk of Courts
Court	1893	Clerk of Courts

■ Wheatland 22 Feb. 1917
201 A Ave. NW, Harlowton, MT 59036
Phone: (406)632-4891
Web site: www.rootsweb.com/~mtwheatl/
Parent County: Meagher, Sweet Grass

Record Type	Year Begun	Jurisdiction
Marriage	1917	Clerk of Courts
Deeds	1917	County Recorder
Probate	1917	Clerk of Courts
Court	1917	Clerk of Courts

■ Wibaux 17 Aug. 1914
200 S. Wibaux St., Box 199, Wibaux, MT 59353
Phone: (406)796-2481
Web site: www.rootsweb.com/~mtwibaux
Parent County: Dawson, Fallon

Record Type	Year Begun	Jurisdiction
Marriage	1914	Clerk/District Ct.
Probate	1914	Clerk/District Ct.
Court	1914	Clerk/District Ct.
Deeds	1914	County Recorder

■ Yellowstone 26 Feb. 1883
217 N. Twenty-seventh St., Billings, MT 59101
Phone: (406)256-2785
Web site: www.co.yellowstone.mt.us
Parent County: Gallatin, Custer

Record Type	Year Begun	Jurisdiction
Birth	1884	County Recorder
Marriage	1895	Clerk/District Ct.
Death	1884	County Recorder
Deeds	1881	County Recorder
Probate	1890	Clerk/District Ct.
Court	1884	Clerk/District Ct.

Montana

Nebraska

By Maureen Taylor

HISTORICAL OVERVIEW

The area that encompasses present-day Nebraska was sold to the United States as part of the Louisiana Purchase in 1803. Lewis and Clark explored the region in 1804. At that time, Native Americans from the Cheyenne, Dakota, Omaha, Oto, Pawnee, and Ponca tribes inhabited the plains of the future state. Fort Atkinson, a military outpost, was established in 1819. Fur traders and missionaries moved into the area during the 1820s and 1830s. Emigrants following the Oregon and Mormon Trails traveled across it along the Platte River.

The Kansas-Nebraska Act of 1854 gave those regions territorial status. The Nebraska territory included not only the present boundaries of Nebraska, but also Montana and portions of Wyoming, Colorado, and the Dakotas. Omaha was the territorial capitol.

The promise of free land and the emergence of railroads encouraged immigrants and settlers from the eastern part of the United States to move to Nebraska. The Homestead Act of 1862 gave 160 acres to families that farmed and lived on the land for five years. The region was settled mostly by European immigrants, Civil War veterans, and, to a lesser extent, African-Americans. Nebraska became the thirty-seventh state in 1867. Indian conflicts and harsh living conditions caused many settlers to move on, but others arrived to take their place, mainly from other countries. By 1900, half of the state's population was foreign-born.

Agriculture and cattle ranching became mainstays of the state's economy. During World Wars I and II, much of the grain produced in the United States came from Nebraska.

RECORD HIGHLIGHTS

Vital records in Nebraska were not mandated for births and deaths until 1904, and marriages and divorces followed in 1909. Copies are available from the Bureau of

NEBRASKA AT A GLANCE

Motto: Equality Before the Law

Population: 1.7 million

Prevalent Religions: Christianity, particularly Roman Catholic, also Lutheran, Methodist, Presbyterian, Pentecostal, Baptist, Episcopalian, and Church of Jesus Christ of Latter-day Saints

Major Industries: Cattle, corn, hogs, soybeans, wheat, sorghum, food processing, machinery, electrical equipment, printing and publishing

Ethnic Makeup (in percent): Caucasian 89.6%, African American 4.0%, Hispanic 5.5%, Asian 1.3%, Native American 0.9%, Other 2.8%

Famous Nebraskans: Fred Astaire, Marlon Brando, William Jennings Bryan, Buffalo Bill (William F. Cody), Warren Buffett, Johnny Carson, Willa Cather, Dick Cavett, Loren Eisley, Henry Fonda, Gerald Ford, Robert Henri, Malcolm X, Wright Morris, Nick Nolte, Mari Sandoz, Standing Bear

Above: Nebraska's famed Eagle Rock

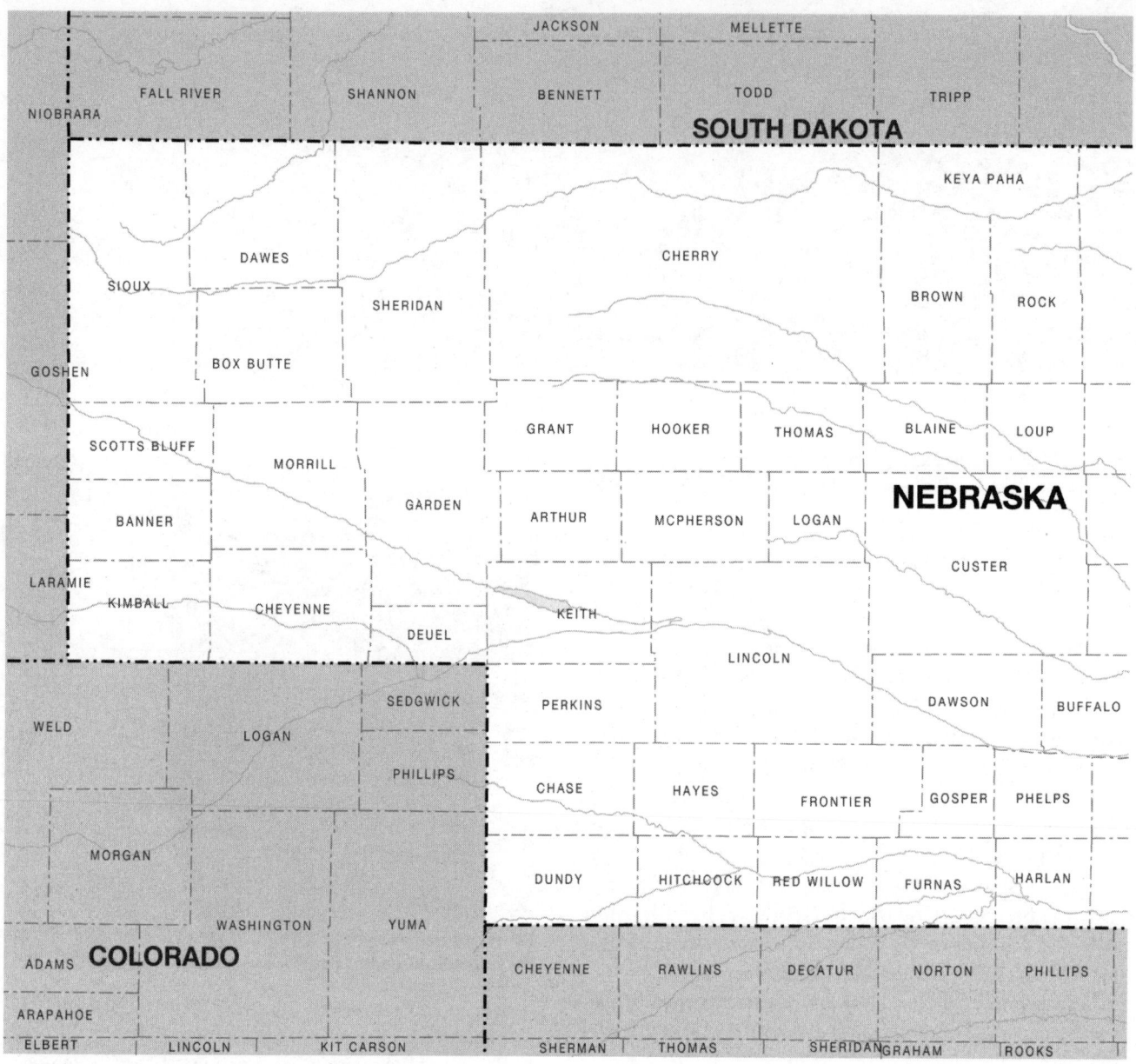

Vital Records. Marriages and divorces before and after 1909 are on file with the individual counties. Recording errors or a lack of total compliance characterize the first decades after civil registration. Doctors submitted records to the state via the county clerk, who then contacted the parents to verify the information.

It is possible to fill in the gaps with church records, but completeness varies depending on the denomination. Most church records are still housed at the church, but researchers need to verify what happened to registers when churches merged or disbanded, or when different denominations occupied the same structure. Researchers should begin by checking with the church, then contacting the denomination headquarters on the state or regional level to locate records. A list is available of all microfilmed church records held by the Nebraska State Historical Society.

Newspaper accounts for obituaries, marriages, etc. may also fill in the gaps when vital records do not exist. In the 1890s, the Nebraska Press Association agreed to send copies of all their papers to the Nebraska State Historical Society. Newspapers from the territorial period to the present are on microfilm at the Nebraska Historical Society, and most can be borrowed via interlibrary loan through public libraries.

All existing Nebraska census records are available at the Nebraska State Historical Society. This includes the federal censuses from 1860 to 1930, with the exception of the 1890 census, for which only the Veterans Schedules remain. The one state census for 1885 is unindexed, but

partial indexing is available. Territorial census originals and transcriptions (1854, 1855, and 1856) are at the Historical Society. County census records exist for some counties during the 1860s, 1870s, and 1880s. There is a special census of Germans from Russia living in Lincoln 1913–1914.

If school census records exist, they are either at the county level or at the Nebraska State Historical Society. School censuses, taken annually from the 1870s to the present, can supply data for families prior to the recording of vital records.

In the office of the county clerk researchers will discover a variety of helpful documents, including motor vehicle registrations, military discharges, voter registrations, and school registers. Also on the county level are probate documents including wills and guardianships.

District court proceedings cover civil and criminal proceedings, divorces, and naturalizations. In some cases, certain county records have been transferred to the Nebraska State Historical Society.

Between 1854 and 1863, the most common type of land entry in Nebraska was the pre-emption claim under the Act of 1841, which was followed with the Homestead Act of 1862. The Nebraska Historical Society has the U.S. General Land Office Tract Books on microfilm for Nebraska and indexes for some counties. Check this resource to locate information—date, description, type of acquisition, and final certificate number—necessary to request files in the National Archives that include data on the citizenship status of the applicant. Only the initial transfer of ownership appears in government records. After that date land records are in the registers of deeds in the county. County boundaries have changed over the years, so it is necessary to verify the county borders at the time of the land transaction.

"Many researchers come to Nebraska to pinpoint where their ancestors came from overseas, but whether or not we can help them depends on the completeness of the records left behind," explained Cindy Drake, Library Curator at the Nebraska State Historical Society. "Researchers with emigrants from the eastern United States end up following them across the state backward along their migration trails."

Family historians shouldn't expect to find a lot of original and printed material on cemeteries—there are so many small cemeteries that tracking them all down would be a monumental task. On the county level volunteer groups are trying to change that by walking the cemeteries and transcribing inscriptions. These projects enable genealogists to find a date of death prior to vital records.

You'll quickly discover that the Nebraska State Historical Society is a researcher's first stop. In addition to private collections and printed materials, in 1905 the state legislature named the Society the official repository of state and local public records, and it became the state archives in 1969. Holdings cover records from 1854 to the present. A guide to genealogical materials on their Web site <www.nebraskahistory.org>, as well as reviewing the Table of Contents for references to sources <www.nebraskahistory.org/oversite/research.htm>, will help researchers identify appropriate materials before visiting.

STATE RESOURCES

■ ARCHIVES, LIBRARIES, AND SOCIETIES

Adams County Genealogical Society
P.O. Box 424, Hastings, NE 68902-0424
Tel: (402) 463-5838
Web site: <http://incolor.inetnebr.com/achs/acgs.html>

Adams County Historical Society
P.O. Box 102, Hastings, NE 68902
Tel: (402) 463-5838
Web site: <http://incolor.inetnebr.com/achs/>

Alliance Public Library
1750 Sweetwater Ave., Alliance, NE 69301
Tel: (308) 762-1387
Web site: <www.cityofalliance.net/id55.htm>

American Historical Society of Germans from Russia
631 D St., Lincoln, NE 68502-1199
Tel: (402) 474-3363
E-mail: ahsgr@ahsgr.org
Web site: <http://ahsgr.org/>

Boone-Nance Genealogical Society
P.O.Box 231, Belgrade, NE 68623
Web site: <www.rootsweb.com/~nenance/bngensoc.html>

Buffalo County Historical Society
P.O. Box 523, Kearney, NE 68848-0523
Tel: (308) 234-3041
E-mail: BCHS@kearney.net
Web site: <http://bchs.kearney.net/index.html>

Bureau of Land Management, Wyoming
5353 Yellowstone Rd., Cheyenne, WY 82009
Tel: (307) 775-6256
E-mail: state_office_wymail@blm.gov
Web site:

Butler County Historical Society
200 D St., David City, NE 68632

Cairo Roots
Route 1, P.O. Box 42, Cairo, NE 68824

Chase County Genealogical Society
P.O. Box 303, Imperial, NE 69033

Chase County Historical Society
73989 320th Ave., Imperial, NE 69033-8616
Web site: <http://freepages.genealogy.rootsweb.com/~chasecountyne/>

Cherry County Genealogical Society
P.O. Box 1380, Valentine, NE 69201
Web site: <www.rootsweb.com/~necherry/>

Cheyenne County Genealogical Society
P.O. Box 802, Sidney, NE 69162

Cravath Memorial Library
P.O. Box 309, Hay Springs, NE 69347-0309
Tel: (308) 638-4541

Cuming County Historical Society
130 N. River, West Point, NE 68788

Custer County Historical Society, Inc.
P.O. Box 334, Broken Bow, NE 68822
Tel: (308) 872-2203
E-mail: custer.county.history@navix.net
Web site: <www.rootsweb.com/~necuster/index.htm>

Dakota County Genealogical Society
P.O. Box 18, Dakota City, NE 68850
Web site: <www.geocities.com/Heartland/Flats/9284/>

Danish Immigrant Archive/ Dana College
2848 College Dr., Blair, NE 68008
Tel: (402) 426-7300

Web site: <www.dana.edu/library/archive.html>

Dawson County Genealogical Society
514 E. Eighth St., Cozad, NE 69130

Dawson County Historical Society
P.O. Box 369, Lexington, NE 68850
Tel: (308) 324-5340
E-mail: dchs@nebi.com

Denton Community Historical Society
P.O. Box 405, Denton, NE 68339
Web site: <www.rootsweb.com/~nedchs/>

Dixon County Historical Society
P.O. Box 95, Allen, NE 68710
Web site: <www.homestead.com/DixonCoNEGenWebProject/Dixoncomuseum.html>

Douglas County Health Department
1819 Farnam St., Omaha, NE 68183
Tel: (402) 444-7213
Web site: <www.co.douglas.ne.us/dept/health/index.php>

Eastern Nebraska Genealogical Society
P.O. Box 541, Fremont, NE 68026
Web site: <www.connectfremont.org/CLUB/ENGS.HTM>

Elkhorn Valley Genealogical Society
341 E. Walnut, West Point, NE 68788
Web site: <www.rootsweb.com/~necuming/evgs.html>

Fillmore Heritage Genealogical Society
Rte. 2, P.O. Box 28, Exeter, NE 68351

Fort Kearney Genealogical Society
P.O. Box 22, Kearney, NE 68847
Web site: <www.rootsweb.com/~nebuffal/fkgs.htm>

Frontier County Historical Society
P.O. Box 242, Curtis, NE 69025

Furnas County Genealogical Society
P.O. Box 391, Beaver City, NE 68926

Web site: <www.rootsweb.com/
~nefurnas/GenSocResources
.html>

Gage County Historical Society
Second & Court Sts., Beatrice,
NE 68310
Tel: (402) 228-1679
Web site: <www.infoanalytic.com/
gage/#society>

Genealogical Society of Wayne
1108 Walnut St., Wayne, NE
68787

Grand Island Public Library
211 N. Washington St., Grand Is-
land, NE 68801
Tel: (308) 385-5333
E-mail: sf@gi.lib.ne.us
Web site:

**Greater Omaha Genealogical
Society**
P.O. Box 4011, Omaha, NE
68104-0011
E-mail: GrOmahaGenSoc@aol
.com
Web site: <http://hometown.aol.
com/gromahagensoc/myhome
page/>

**Greater York Area Genealogical
Society/Kilgore Memorial
Library**
Sixth and Nebraska, York, NE
68467
Tel: (402) 362-3039

**Holt County Genealogical
Society**
P.O. Box 376, O'Neill, NE 68763

Holt County Historical Society
402 E. Douglas, O'Neill, NE
68763
Web site: <www.usgennet.org/
usa/ne/county/holt1/index
.html>

**Hooker County Genealogical
Society**
P.O. Box 280, Mullen, NE 69152
Web site:
**Howard County Historical
Society**
P.O. Box 1, Saint Paul, NE 68873
Tel: (308) 754-4901
Web site:

J.A. Stahl Library
330 N. Colfax St., West Point, NE
68788
Tel: (402) 372-3831
Web site: <www.rootsweb.com/
~necuming/lsbuffet.html>

**Jefferson County Genealogical
Society**
P.O. Box 163, Fairbury NE 68352
E-mail: JCGS@neb.rr.com
Web site: <www.rootsweb.com/
~nejeffgs/>

Jensen Memorial Library
443 N. Kearney, Minden, NE
68959
Tel: (308) 832-2648

**Johnson County Historical
Society & Museum**
Third and Lincoln Sts., Tecumseh,
NE 68450
Web site: <www.rootsweb.com/
~nejohnso/jchstsoc.htm>

Lexington Genealogical Society
P.O. Box 778, Lexington, NE
68850-0778
Web site: <www.rootsweb.com/
~nedawson/lexsoc.html>

**Lincoln Nebraska Chapter,
American Historical Society of
Germans from Russia (AHSGR)**
2111 Kingswood Circle, Lincoln,
NE 68521-5037
Tel: (402) 438-3814
Web site: <www.ahsgr.org/lincol
n_nebraska_chapter.htm>

**Lincoln-Lancaster County
Genealogical Society**
P.O. Box 30055, Lincoln, NE
68503-0055
Web site: <www.rootsweb.com/
~nellcgs/>

**Nebraska Synod, Evangelical
Lutheran Church in America**
4980 S. 118th St., Suite D,
Omaha, NE 68137-2220
Tel: (402) 896-5311
Web site: <www.nebraskasynod.
org/index.html>

**Madison County Genealogical
Society**
P.O. Box 1031, Norfolk, NE
68702-1031
E-mail: madisoncgs@cableone
.net
Web site: <www.rootsweb.com/
~nemadiso/>

Nebraska Wesleyan University
5000 St. Paul Ave., Lincoln, NE
68504-2794
Tel: (402) 466-2371 and (800)
541-3818
Web site: <www.nebrwesleyan.
edu/university/methodist.php>

Midlands Chapter, AHSGR
9373 Maplewood Blvd., Omaha,
NE 68134-4663

RESEARCH TIPS
for more info

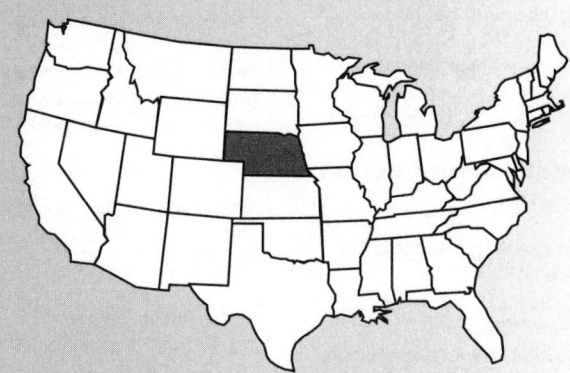

- Your first stop for Nebraska research should be the State Historical Society <www.nebraskahistory.or g>. It's officially considered the state archives.
- Newspapers from the territorial period to the present are on microfilm at the Nebraska Historical Society—these can help fill in the gaps when vital records do not exist.
- The office of the county clerk in each county holds a variety of helpful documents, including motor vehicle registrations, school registers, and probate documents including wills and guardianships.

Census Records
- Federal Census: 1860, 1870, 1880, 1890 (only Veterans Schedules) 1900, 1910, 1920, 1930
- State and Territorial Censuses: 1854, 1855, 1856, 1885

Tel: (402) 572-8871
E-mail: ahsgr@ahsgr.org
Web site: <www.ahsgr.org/midla
nds_chapter.htm>

**Nancy Fawcett Memorial
Library**
P.O. Box 318, Lodgepole, NE
69149
Tel: (308) 483-5714

Naponee Historical Society
P.O. Box 128, Naponee, NE
68960
Tel: (308) 269-2791
Web site: <http://home.alltel.
net/ps60313/naponeehist
.html>

**The National Archives—Central
Plains Region**
2312 E. Bannister Rd., Kansas
City, MO 64131-3011

Tel: (816) 926-6920
E-mail: kansascity.archives@nar
a.gov
Web site: <www.archives.gov/fa
cilities/mo/kansas_city.html>

**Nebraska Department of Health
and Human Services**
P.O. Box 95044, Lincoln, NE
68509-5044
Tel: (402) 471–2306
Web site:
Nebraska Panhandle Chapter
2430 Ave. C, Scottsbluff, NE
69361
Tel: (308) 632-2459
Web site: <www.ahsgr.org/nebra
ska_panhandle_chapter.htm>

Nebraska

Nebraska State Historical Society and Nebraska State Archives
P.O. Box 82554, Lincoln, NE 68501
Web site: <www.nebraskahistory.org/lib-arch/index.htm>

Nebraska State Genealogical Society
P.O. Box 5608, Lincoln, NE 68505-0608
Web site: <www.rootsweb.com/~nesgs/>

Nemaha Valley Genealogical Society
P.O. Box 25, Auburn, NE 68305-0025
Web site: <www.rootsweb.com/~nenemaha/nvgs.html>

Norfolk Public Library
308 Prospect Ave, Norfolk, NE 68701
Tel: (402) 844-2100
Web site: <www.ci.norfolk.ne.us/library/>

North Platte Genealogical Society
P.O. Box 1452, North Platte, NE 69101

Northeast Nebraska Chapter, AHSGR
314 S. Thirteenth Place, Norfolk, NE 68701-4809
Tel: (402) 371–0693
Web site: <www.ahsgr.org/northeast_nebraska_chapter.htm>

Northeastern Nebraska Genealogical Society
P.O. Box 169, Lyons, NE 68038

Northern Antelope County Genealogical Society
P.O. Box 56, Orchard, NE 68764

Northern Nebraska Genealogical Society
P.O. Box 362, O'Neill, NE 68763

Northwest Genealogical Society
P.O. Box 6, Alliance, NE 69301
Tel: (308) 762-1387
Web site: <www.rootsweb.com/~neboxbut/northwestgensociety.html>

Nuckolls County Genealogical Society
P.O. Box 441, Superior, NE 68978-0441

Omaha Public Library
215 S. Fifteenth St., Omaha, NE 68102

Tel: (402) 444-4800
Web site:

Perkins County Genealogical Society
P.O. Box 418, Grant, NE 69140

Phelps County Museum Library (Holdrege Area Genealogy)
P.O. Box 164, Holdrege, NE 68949

Plains Genealogical Society
208 S. Walnut St., Kimball, NE 69145

Potter Public Library
P.O. Box 317, Potter, NE 69156-0317
Tel: (308) 879-4345

Prairie Pioneer Genealogical Society
P.O. Box 1122, Grand Island, NE 68802
Web site: <www.rootsweb.com/~nehall/ppgen.html>

Lincoln City Library
136 S. Fourteenth St., Lincoln, Nebraska 68508
Tel: (402) 441-8500

Pastfinders Library
730 E. Thirteenth St., Crete, NE 68333-2308
Tel: (402) 826-3462
E-mail: pastfinder-library@alltel.net
Web site: <http://members.tripod.com/~PastfinderLibrary/>

Saline County Genealogical Society
P.O. Box 24, Crete, NE 68333-0024
Tel: (402) 821-2430
Web site: <www.co.saline.ne.us/content/Genealogical.htm>

Sarpy County Genealogical Society
2402 Sac Pl., Bellevue, NE 68005-3932

Saunders County Historical Society & Museum
240 N. Walnut, Wahoo, NE 68066
Tel: (402) 443-3090
Web site: <www.visitsaunderscounty.org/attractions/museum/>

Schuyler Historical Society and Museum
1005 B St., Schuyler, NE 68661
Tel: (402) 352-3219

Seward County Genealogical Society
P.O. Box 72, Seward, NE 68434-0072

South Central Genealogical Society
Rte. 2, Box 57, Minden, NE 68959

Southeast Nebraska Genealogical Society
P.O. Box 562, Beatrice, NE 68301

Southwest Nebraska Genealogical Society
P.O. Box 156, McCook, NE 69001-0156
Web site: <www.rootsweb.com/~neswngs/>

Thayer County Genealogical Society
P.O. Box 388, Belvidere, NE 68315

Thomas County Genealogical Society
P.O. Box 136, Thedford, NE 69166

United Methodist Historical Center, Nebraska Conference
P.O. Box 4553, Lincoln, NE 68504-0553
Tel: (402) 464-5994 or (800) 435-6107
E-mail: info@umcneb.org
Web site: <www.umcneb.org>

Valley County Genealogical Society
619 S. Tenth, Ord, NE 68862

Washington County Genealogical Society
% Blair Public Library, 210 S. Seventeenth St., Blair, NE 68008
Tel: (402) 426-2013
Web site: <www.blairpubliclibrary.com/cemetery/ContactUs.asp>

Washington County Historical Association
P.O. Box 25, Fort Calhoun, NE 68023
Tel: (402) 468-5740
E-mail: info@newashcohist.org
Web site:

Wayne Public Library
410 Pearl St., Wayne, NE 68787
Tel: (402) 375-3135
Web site: <http://city.waynene.org/Library__Senior_Center/Library/>

Wilson Public Library
910 Meridian, Cozad, NE 69130
Tel: (308) 784-2019

BIBLIOGRAPHY

■ GENERAL RESOURCES

Broken Hoops and Plains People
by Galen Buller (Lincoln, NE: Nebraska Curiculum Development Center, 1976)

Early Pioneers of Nebraska: with Allied Lines as Taken from Family Recognation [sic] Records
by Beth Haring (Lincoln, NE: Nebraska State Genealogical Society, ca. 1980)

The Genealogist's Companion and Sourcebook, 2d ed.
by Emily Anne Croom (Cincinnati: Betterway Books, 2003)

A Genealogist's Guide to Discovering Your African-American Ancestors
by Franklin Carter Smith and Emily Anne Croom (Cincinnati: Betterway Books, 2003)

Germans and German-Russians in Nebraska: a Research Guide to Nebraska Ethnic Studies
by Janet Warkentin Rife (Lincoln, NE: Nebraska Curriculum Development Center, University of Nebraska-Lincoln, 1980)

Guide to Genealogical Research in the National Archives of the United States
edited by Anne Bruner Eales and Robert M. Kvasnicka (Washington, DC: National Archives and Records Administration, 2000)

A Guide to the Manuscript Division of the State Archives, Nebraska State Historical Society
by Nebraska State Historical Society, State Archives: (Lincoln, NE: The Society, 1974)

A Guide to the Newspaper Collection of the State Archives
(Lincoln, NE: Nebraska State Historical Society, 1969)

Historical Resources for Genealogists in the Nebraska State Historical Society
by Nebraska State Historical Society: (Lincoln, NE: Nebraska State Historical Society, 1986)

History of the Catholic Church in Nebraska
by Henry Weber Casper (Milwaukee: Catholic Life Publications, 1960–1966)

A History of Czechs (Bohemians) in Nebraska
by Rose Rosicky (Evansville, IN: Unigraphic, Inc., 1977)

History of Nebraska
by James C. Olson (Lincoln, NE: University of Nebraska Press, 1966)

Illustrated History of Nebraska
by J. Sterling Morton, succeeded by Albert Watkins and Dr. George L. Miller (Lincoln, NE: Jacob North & Co., ca. 1905–1913)

National Archives Microfilm Catalogs online:
<www.archives.gov/publications/genealogy_microfilm_catalogs.html>

Nebraska, A Guide to Genealogical Research
by Georgene Morris Sones (Lincoln, NE: Nebraska State Genealogical Society, 1984)

Nebraska: the Land and the People
by Addison Erwin Sheldon (Chicago: Lewis Publishing Co., 1931)

Nebraska Local History and Genealogy Reference Guide: A Bibliography of County Research Materials in Selected Repositories
by Sylvia Nimmo and Mary Cutler (Papillion, NE: S. Nimmo, 1987)

Nebraska Newspaper Abstracts: A Computer Index to Names and Events Abstracted from Selected Nebraska Newspapers
by Nebraska State Genealogical Society (Alliance, NE: Nebraska State Genealogical Society, 1983)

Nebraska: Research Outline
by Church of Jesus Christ of Latter-day Saints: (Salt Lake City, Utah: Corp. of the President of the Church of Jesus Christ of L.D.S., 1988)

Preliminary Edition of Guide to Depositories of Manuscript Collections in the United States-Nebraska
prepared by the Nebraska Historical Records Survey Project (Lincoln, NE: Nebraska Historical Records Survey Project, 1940)

Sittler Index of Surnames
by Melvin Sittler (Lincoln, NE: Lincoln-Lancaster County Genealogical Society, 1983–1984, 1993)

■ CENSUS RECORDS

The American Census Handbook
by Thomas Jay Kemp (Wilmington, DE: Scholarly Resources Inc., 2001)

The Census Book: A Genealogist's Guide to Federal Census Facts, Schedules and Indexes
by William Dollarhide (Bountiful, UT: Heritage Quest, 1999)

Finding Answers in U.S. Census Records
by Loretto Dennis Szucs and Matthew Wright (Orem, UT: Ancestry Pub., 2001)

Map Guide to the U.S. Federal Censuses, 1790–1920
by William Thorndale and William Dollarhide (Baltimore: Genealogical Pub. Co., 1987)

■ IMMIGRATION RECORDS

111 days to Zion
by Hal Knight and Dr. Stanley B. Kimball: (Salt Lake City, UT: Deseret News, 1978)

American Naturalization Records, 1790–1990: What They Are and How to Use Them
by John J. Newman (North Salt Lake, UT: HeritageQuest, 1998)

American Passenger Arrival Records
by Michael Tepper (Baltimore: Genealogical Publishing Co., 1993)

Czech Immigrant Passenger List (for Nebraska) 1879
compiled by Margie Sobotka (Omaha: Eastern Nebraska Genealogical Society, 1982)

They Became Americans: Finding Naturalization Records and Ethnic Origins
by Loretto Dennis Szucs (Salt Lake City: Ancestry, Inc., 1998)

They Came in Ships: A Guide to Finding Your Immigrant Ancestor's Arrival Records, 2d ed.
by John P. Colletta (Salt Lake City: Ancestry, Inc., 1993)

■ LAND RECORDS

Land & Property Research in the United States
by E. Wade Hone (Salt Lake City, UT: Ancestry, 1997)

Locating Your Roots: Discover Your Ancestors Using Land Records
by Patricia Law Hatcher (Cincinnati: Betterway Books, 2003)

■ MAPS

Nebraska Atlas
by N.D. Searcy and A.R. Longwell (Kearney, NE: Nebraska Atlas Pub Co. 1964)

Nebraska Atlas & Gazetteer
(Yarmouth, ME: DeLorme, 1996)

Nebraska Place-Names
by Lilian L. Fitzpatrick (Lincoln, NE: University of Nebraska Press, 1960)

Perkey's Nebraska Place-Names
by Elton Perkey (Lincoln, NE: Nebraska State Historical Society, 1982)

The Post Offices of Nebraska: part 1, Territorial Post Offices
by William F. Rapp and Janet L. C. Rapp (Crete, NE: J-B Pub., 1992)

■ MILITARY RECORDS

Nebraska Born Veterans Buried in Colorado, 1862–1949
by Gerald E. Sherard (Lakewood, CO: G.E. Sherard, 1997)

A Nebraska Civil War Ancestor
by Gerald E. Sherard (Lakewood, CO: G.E. Sherard, 1994)

Nebraska's Militia: the History of the Army and Air National Guard, 1854–1991
by Douglas R. Hartman (Virginia Beach, VA: Donning, 1994)

Roster and Indexes of Soldiers, 1911
by Grand Army of the Republic. Department of Nebraska (Lincoln, NE: Nebraska State Historical Society, 1974)

Roster of Soldiers, Sailors and Marines of the War of 1812, the Mexican War, and the War of the Rebellion, Residing in Nebraska as of June 1, 1891, Who Enlisted from the State of Illinois
by John C. Allen (Lincoln, NE: Nebraska State Genealogical Society, 2000)

Uncle, We Are Ready! Registering America's Men, 1917–1918: A Guide to Researching World War I Draft Registration Cards
by John J. Newman (North Salt Lake, UT: HeritageQuest, 2001)

U.S. Military Records: A Guide to Federal & State Sources, Colonial America to the Present
by James C. Neagles (Salt Lake City: Ancestry, Inc., 1994)

World War II: A Family Historian's Guide
by Debra Johnson Knox (Spartanburg, SC: MIE Publishing, 2003)

■ VITAL RECORDS

Guide to Public Vital Statistics Records in Nebraska
by Historical Records Survey (Lincoln, NE: The Survey, 1941)

Nebraska Cemeteries and Burial Sites: in Two Parts
by Georgene Morris Sones, Omaha Norvell, and Dennis Norvell (Lincoln, NE: Nebraska State Geneal. Society, 1996)

Vital Statistics: Births, Marriages and Deaths, 1863–1947
by United States. Bureau of Indian Affairs, Winnebago Agency (Kansas City, MO: Federal Archives and Records Center, 1977)

Your Guide to Cemetery Research
by Sharon DeBartolo Carmack (Cincinnati: Betterway Books, 2002)

Nebraska

■ Adams 16 Feb. 1867
500 W. Fifth, Hastings, NE 68901
Phone: (402)461-7107
Web site: www.rootsweb.co/~neadams/
Parent County: Unorganized Territory

Record Type	Year Begun	Jurisdiction
Marriage	na	County Judge
Divorce	na	Clerk/District Ct.
Land	na	Clerk/District Ct.
Probate	na	County Judge

■ Antelope 1 Mar. 1871
501 Main St., Neligh, NE 68756
Phone: (402)887-4410
Web site: www.rootsweb.com/~neantelo/
Parent County: L'Eau Qui Court, Unorganized Territory

Record Type	Year Begun	Jurisdiction
Marriage	na	County Judge
Land	na	County Clerk
Probate	na	County Judge

■ Arthur 31 Mar. 1887
Main St., Arthur, NE 69121
Phone: (308)764-2203
Web site: www.rootsweb.com/~nearthur/
Parent County: Unorganized Territory
Comments/research tips: Arthur County was formed in 1887, but did not become a county until 1913. Before 1913, records were kept at McPherson County.

Record Type	Year Begun	Jurisdiction
Marriage	1913	County Court
Divorce	1913	Clerk/District Ct.
Land	1913	County Clerk
Probate	1913	County Court
Court	1913	County Court
Burial	na	County Cemetery Sexton

■ Banner 6 Nov. 1888
State St., P.O. Box 67, Harrisburg, NE 69345
Phone: (308)436-5265
Web site: www.rootsweb.com/~nebanner/
Parent County: Cheyenne

Record Type	Year Begun	Jurisdiction
Birth	1920	County Clerk
Marriage	1890	County Court
Divorce	na	Dept./Health
Land	1890	County Clerk
Probate	1890	County Court
Court	1890	County Court
Burial	na	Dept./Health

■ Blackbird 7 Nov. 1855
Parent County: Burt
Comments/research tips: (See Thurston) Name changed to Thurston 28 March 1889.

■ Blaine 5 Mar. 1885
P.O. Box 136, Brewster, NE 68821
Phone: (308)547-2222

Web site: www.rootsweb.com/~neblaine/
Parent County: Custer

Record Type	Year Begun	Jurisdiction
Divorce	1887	County Clerk
Land	1887	County Clerk
Probate	na	County Judge
Court	na	County Judge

■ Boone 1 Mar. 1871
222 S. Fourth St., Albion, NE 68620
Phone: (402)395-2055
Web site: www.rootsweb.com/~neboone/
Parent County: Unorganized Territory
Comments/research tips: State Archives, 1500 R St., P.O. Box 82554, Lincoln, NE 68501 has Marriage records to 1932.

Record Type	Year Begun	Jurisdiction
Marriage	1932	County Clerk
Divorce	na	County Clerk
Land	na	Recorder/Deeds
Probate	na	County Clerk
Court	na	County Clerk

■ Box Butte 23 Mar. 1887
515 Box Butte Ave. #203, Alliance, NE 69301
Phone: (308)762-6565
Web site: www.rootsweb.com/~neboxbut/
Parent County: Dawes

Record Type	Year Begun	Jurisdiction
Marriage	na	County Clerk
Divorce	na	Clerk/District Ct.
Land	na	County Clerk
Probate	na	County Judge
Court	na	County Judge

■ Boyd 20 Apr. 1891
401 Thayer St., Butte, NE 68722
Phone: (402)775-2391
Web site: www.rootsweb.com/~neboyd/
Parent County: Holt

Record Type	Year Begun	Jurisdiction
Marriage	na	County Clerk
Divorce	na	County Clerk
Land	na	County Clerk
Probate	na	Clerk/County Ct.
Court	na	Clerk/District Ct.
Military	na	County Clerk
Nat.	na	County Clerk

■ Brown 19 Feb. 1883
148 W. Fourth St., Ainsworth, NE 69210
Phone: (402)387-2705
Web site: www.rootsweb.com/~nebrown
Parent County: Unorganized Territory
Comments/research tips: County Clerk has Naturalization records 1884–1922. Attached to Holt County prior to 1883.

Record Type	Year Begun	Jurisdiction
Marriage	1883	County Clerk
Divorce	na	Clerk/District Ct.

Land .... 1883 ....County Clerk
Probate .... na ....County Judge
Court .... na ....Clerk/District Ct.
Military .... 1919 ....County Clerk

■ Buffalo   14 Mar. 1855

Fifteenth & Central Ave., P.O. Box 1270, Kearney, NE 68848
Phone: (308)236-1226
Web site: www.rootsweb.com/~nebuffal
Parent County: Original county

Record Type	Year Begun	Jurisdiction
Marriage	1872	County Clerk
Divorce	na	Clerk/District Ct.
Land	na	Registrar/Deeds
Probate	1872	County Judge
Court	1872	County Judge

■ Burt   23 Nov. 1854

111 N. Thirteenth St., Tekamah, NE 68061
Phone: (402)374-2955
Web site: www.rootsweb.com/~neburt/
Parent County: Original county

Record Type	Year Begun	Jurisdiction
Marriage	na	County Clerk
Divorce	na	Clerk/District Ct.
Land	na	County Clerk
Probate	na	County Judge
Court	na	County Judge

■ Butler   26 Jan. 1856

451 Fifth St., David City, NE 68632
Phone: (402)367-7430
Web site: www.rootsweb.com/~nebutler/
Parent County: Greene

Record Type	Year Begun	Jurisdiction
Marriage	na	County Court
Divorce	na	Clerk/District Ct.
Land	1869	County Clerk
Probate	na	County Court
Court	na	Clerk/District Ct.

■ Calhoun   26 Jan. 1856

Parent County: Lancaster, Douglas
Comments/research tips: (See Saunders) Name changed to Saunders 8 January 1862.

■ Cass   23 Nov. 1854

346 Main St. #202, Plattsmouth, NE 68048
Phone: (402)296-9300
Web site: www.rootsweb.com/~necass
Parent County: Original County

Record Type	Year Begun	Jurisdiction
Marriage	1855	County Clerk
Divorce	1855	Clerk/District Ct.
Land	na	Registrar/Deeds
Probate	1854	County Court
Court	1854	County Court
Burial	na	Cemetery Board

■ Cedar   12 Feb. 1857

101 S. Broadway Ave., P.O. Box 47, Hartington, NE 68739
Phone: (402)254-7411
Web site: www.rootsweb.com/~necedar/
Parent County: Dixon, Pierce

Record Type	Year Begun	Jurisdiction
Marriage	na	County Clerk
Divorce	na	Clerk/District Ct.
Land	na	County Clerk
Probate	na	County Judge
Court	na	County Judge

■ Chase   27 Feb. 1873

921 Broadway, Imperial, NE 69033
Phone: (308)882-5266
Web site: http://resources.rootsweb.com/USA/NE/chase
Parent County: Unorganized Territory

Record Type	Year Begun	Jurisdiction
Marriage	1886	County Judge
Divorce	1886	Clerk/District Ct.
Land	1886	County Clerk
Probate	1886	County Judge
Court	1886	County Judge

■ Cherry   23 Feb. 1883

365 N. Main St., P.O. Box 120, Valentine, NE 69201
Phone: (402)376-2771
Web site: www.rootsweb.com/~necherry/
Parent County: Unorganized Territory

Record Type	Year Begun	Jurisdiction
Marriage	na	County Clerk
Divorce	na	Clerk/District Ct.
Land	na	County Clerk
Probate	na	County Court
Court	na	County Court

■ Cheyenne   22 June 1867

1000 Tenth Ave., P.O. Box 217, Sidney, NE 69162
Phone: (308)254-2141
Web site: www.rootsweb.com/~necheyen
Parent County: Unorganized Territory

Record Type	Year Begun	Jurisdiction
Marriage	na	County Clerk
Divorce	na	Clerk/District Ct.
Land	na	County Clerk
Probate	na	County Court

■ Clay   16 Feb. 1867

111 W. Fairfield St., Clay Center, NE 68933
Phone: (402)762-3463
Web site: www.rootsweb.com/~neclay/
Parent County: Unorganized Territory
Comments/research tips: County Clerk has Birth and Death records 1917–1918.

Record Type	Year Begun	Jurisdiction
Marriage	1871	County Clerk
Divorce	na	Clerk/District Ct.
Land	1871	County Clerk
Probate	na	County Court

Court .... na ....Clerk/District Ct.
Military .... 1921 ....County Clerk
Nat. .... na ....Clerk/District Ct.

■ **Clay, old** 7 Mar. 1855
Parent County: Original County
Comments/research tips: Absorbed by Gage County in 1864.

■ **Colfax** 15 Feb. 1869
411 E. Eleventh St., Schuyler, NE 68661
Phone: (402)352-3434
Web site: www.rootsweb.com/~necolfax/
Parent County: Platte

Record Type	Year Begun	Jurisdiction
Marriage	1869	County Judge
Divorce	1881	Clerk/District Ct.
Land	1860	County Clerk
Probate	1886	County Judge
Court	1885	County Judge

■ **Cuming** 16 Mar. 1855
200 S. Lincoln St., West Point, NE 68788
Phone: (402)372-6002
Web site: www.rootsweb.com/~necuming/
Parent County: Burt

Record Type	Year Begun	Jurisdiction
Marriage	1866	County Judge
Divorce	1869	Clerk/District Ct.
Probate	1866	County Judge
Court	1960	County Judge

■ **Custer** 17 Feb. 1877
431 S. Tenth Ave., Broken Bow, NE 68822
Phone: (308)872-5701
Web site: www.rootsweb.com/~necuste2/
Parent County: Unorganized Territory
Comments/research tips: County Historical Society has many records.

Record Type	Year Begun	Jurisdiction
Birth	1910	County Clerk
Marriage	1878	County Judge
Death	1915	County Clerk
Divorce	1881	Clerk/District Ct.
Land	1880	Registrar/Deeds
Probate	1887	County Judge
Court	1887	County Judge

■ **Dakota** 7 Mar. 1855
1601 Broadway St., Dakota City, NE 68731
Phone: (402)987-2126
Web site: www.rootsweb.com/~nedakota
Parent County: Burt

Record Type	Year Begun	Jurisdiction
Marriage	1856	County Clerk
Divorce	1862	Clerk/District Ct.
Land	1856	Registrar/Deeds
Probate	1858	County Court
Court	1862	Clerk/District Ct.
Military	1921	County Clerk
Nat.	na	Clerk/District Ct.

■ **Dawes** 19 Feb. 1885
451 Main St., Chadron, NE 69337-2649
Phone: (308)432-0100
Web site: http://resources.rootsweb.com/USA/NE/Dawes
Parent County: Sioux

Record Type	Year Begun	Jurisdiction
Marriage	na	County Judge
Divorce	na	Clerk/District Ct.
Land	1880	County Clerk
Probate	na	County Judge

■ **Dawson** 11 Jan. 1860
P.O. Box 370, Lexington, NE 68850
Phone: (308)324-2127
Web site: www.rootsweb.com/~nedawson/
Parent County: Unorganized Territory

Record Type	Year Begun	Jurisdiction
Marriage	1873	County Clerk
Divorce	na	Clerk/District Ct.
Land	na	Registrar/Deeds
Probate	na	County Court
Court	na	County Court
Military	na	Veterans Service Office
Nat.	na	Clerk/District Ct.

■ **Deuel** 6 Nov. 1888
Third & Vincent, Chappell, NE 69129
Phone: (308)874-3308
Web site: www.rootsweb.com/~nedeuel/
Parent County: Cheyenne

Record Type	Year Begun	Jurisdiction
Marriage	na	County Judge
Divorce	na	County Clerk
Land	na	County Clerk
Probate	na	County Judge
Court	1890	County Clerk
Burial	na	County Clerk

■ **Dixon** 26 Jan. 1856
302 Third St., Ponca, NE 68770
Phone: (402)755-2208
Web site: www.co.dixon.ne.us
Parent County: Blackbird, Izard, Unorganized Territory

Record Type	Year Begun	Jurisdiction
Birth	1919	County Clerk
Death	1919	County Clerk
Land	1871	County Clerk
Burial	1919	County Clerk

■ **Dodge** 23 Nov. 1854
435 N. Park Ave., Fremont, NE 68025
Phone: (402)727-2767
Web site: www.rootsweb.com/~nedodge/
Parent County: Original County

Record Type	Year Begun	Jurisdiction
Marriage	na	County Clerk
Divorce	na	Clerk/District Ct.
Land	na	Registrar/Deeds
Probate	na	County Judge

Douglas 23 Nov. 1854
1819 Farman St., Omaha, NE 68102
Phone: (402)444-7143
Web site: www.rootsweb.com/~nedougla
Parent County: Original County

Record Type	Year Begun	Jurisdiction
Marriage	na	County Judge
Divorce	na	Clerk/District Ct.
Probate	na	County Judge
Military	na	County Clerk

Dundy 27 Feb. 1873
P.O. Box 506, Benkelman, NE 69021
Phone: (308)423-2058
Web site: www.rootsweb.com/~nedundy/
Parent County: Unorganized Territory

Record Type	Year Begun	Jurisdiction
Birth	1907	County Clerk
Death	1904	County Clerk
Divorce	na	County Clerk
Probate	na	County Judge
Court	na	County Clerk
Burial	na	County Clerk

Emmet 10 Feb. 1857
Parent County: Pierce, Unorganized Territory
Comments/research tips: (See Knox) Formerly L'Eau Qui Court County. Name changed to Emmet 18 February 1867. Name changed to Knox 21 February 1873.

Fillmore 26 Jan. 1856
900 G St., Geneva, NE 68361
Phone: (402)759-4931
Web site: www.rootsweb.com/~nefillmo
Parent County: Unorganized Territory
Comments/research tips: County Clerk has delayed Birth records.

Record Type	Year Begun	Jurisdiction
Marriage	1872	County Clerk
Divorce	na	Clerk/District Ct.
Land	1872	County Clerk
Probate	na	County Court
Court	na	County Court

Forney 23 Nov. 1854
Parent County: Original County
Comments/research tips: (See Nemaha) Name changed to Nemaha 7 March 1855.

Franklin 16 Feb. 1867
405 Fifteenth Ave., P.O. Box 146, Franklin, NE 68939
Phone: (308)425-6202
Web site: www.rootsweb.com/~nefrankl/
Parent County: Kearney

Record Type	Year Begun	Jurisdiction
Marriage	1872	County Clerk
Divorce	na	County Clerk
Land	na	County Clerk

Frontier 17 Jan. 1872
1 Wellington St., P.O. Box 40, Stockville, NE 69042
Phone: (308)367-8641
Web site: www.rootsweb.com/~nefronti/
Parent County: Unorganized Territory

Record Type	Year Begun	Jurisdiction
Marriage	na	County Clerk
Divorce	na	County Judge
Land	na	Registrar/Deeds
Probate	na	County Judge
Court	na	County Judge
Military	na	County Clerk
Nat.	na	County Judge

Furnas 27 Feb. 1873
912 R St., P.O. Box 387, Beaver City, NE 68926
Phone: (308)268-4145
Web site: www.rootsweb.com/~nefurnas/
Parent County: Unorganized Territory

Record Type	Year Begun	Jurisdiction
Marriage	na	County Judge
Divorce	na	Clerk/District Ct.
Land	1873	County Clerk
Probate	na	County Judge
Court	na	County Judge

Gage 16 Mar. 1855
612 Grant St., P.O. Box 429, Beatrice, NE 68310
Phone: (402)223-1300
Web site: www.usgennet.org/usa/ne/county/gage/index.html
Parent County: Original County

Record Type	Year Begun	Jurisdiction
Marriage	1860	County Judge
Divorce	na	Clerk/District Ct.
Probate	1860	County Judge

Garden 2 Nov. 1909
611 Main St., P.O. Box 486, Oshkosh, NE 69154
Phone: (308)772-3924
Web site: www.rootsweb.com/~negarden/
Parent County: Deuel

Record Type	Year Begun	Jurisdiction
Marriage	na	County Clerk
Divorce	na	Clerk/District Ct.
Land	na	County Clerk
Probate	na	County Judge
Court	na	County Judge

Garfield 8 Nov. 1884
250 S. Eighth St., P.O. Box 218, Burwell, NE 68823
Phone: (308)346-4161
Web site: www.rootsweb.com/~negarfie/
Parent County: Wheeler

Record Type	Year Begun	Jurisdiction
Marriage	na	County Judge
Divorce	na	County Judge
Probate	na	County Judge

Gosper 26 Nov. 1873
507 Smith Ave., P.O. Box 136, Elwood, NE 68937
Phone: (308)785-2611

Web site: www.rootsweb.com/~negosper/
Parent County: Unorganized Territory, Kearney

Record Type	Year Begun	Jurisdiction
Marriage	1891	County Judge
Divorce	1880	County Clerk
Land	na	County Clerk
Probate	1891	County Judge
Court	1920	County Judge

■ Grant 31 Mar. 1887
P.O. Box 139, Hyannis, NE 69350
Phone: (308)458-2488
Web site: www.rootsweb.com/~negrant/
Parent County: Unorganized Territory
Comments/research tips: County Clerk has Naturalization records 1891–1912.

Record Type	Year Begun	Jurisdiction
Marriage	1888	County Clerk
Divorce	1890	County Clerk
Land	1888	County Clerk
Probate	na	County Judge
Court	1897	County Clerk
Military	1921	County Clerk

■ Greeley 1 Mar. 1871
P.O. Box 287, Greeley, NE 68842
Phone: (308)428-3625
Web site: www.rootsweb.com/~negreele/
Parent County: Unorganized Territory

Record Type	Year Begun	Jurisdiction
Marriage	na	County Clerk
Divorce	na	Clerk/District Ct.
Land	na	County Clerk
Probate	na	County Court
Court	na	Clerk/District Ct.
Military	na	County Clerk
Nat.	na	County Clerk

■ Greene 6 Mar. 1855
Parent County: Cass, Pierce, old
Comments/research tips: (See Seward) Name changed to Seward 3 January 1862.

■ Hall 4 Nov. 1858
121 S. Pine St., Grand Island, NE 68801
Phone: (308)385-5080
Web site: www.rootsweb.com/~nehall/
Parent County: Original County

Record Type	Year Begun	Jurisdiction
Marriage	1869	County Clerk
Divorce	na	Clerk/District Ct.
Land	na	Registrar/Deeds
Probate	na	County Judge
Court	na	Clerk/District Ct.

■ Hamilton 16 Feb. 1867
1111 Thirteenth St., Suite 1, Aurora, NE 68818
Phone: (402)694-3443
Web site: www.rootsweb.com/~nehamilt

Parent County: Unorganized Territory

Record Type	Year Begun	Jurisdiction
Marriage	1870	County Clerk
Divorce	na	Clerk/District Ct.
Land	1870	County Clerk
Probate	na	County Judge
Court	na	County Judge

■ Harlan 3 June 1871
706 W. Second St., Alma, NE 68920
Phone: (308)928-2173
Web site: www.rootsweb.com/~neharlan/
Parent County: Kearney

Record Type	Year Begun	Jurisdiction
Marriage	na	County Clerk
Divorce	na	Clerk/District Ct.
Probate	na	County Judge
Court	na	County Judge

■ Hayes 19 Feb. 1877
Troth St., P.O. Box 370, Hayes Center, NE 69032
Phone: (308)286-3413
Web site: www.rootsweb.com/~nehayes/
Parent County: Unorganized Territory

Record Type	Year Begun	Jurisdiction
Death	na	County Clerk
Land	na	County Clerk
Burial	na	County Clerk

■ Hitchcock 27 Feb. 1873
229 E. D St., P.O. Box 248, Trenton, NE 69044
Phone: (308)334-5646
Web site: www.rootsweb.com/~nehitchc
Parent County: Unorganized Territory

Record Type	Year Begun	Jurisdiction
Marriage	na	County Clerk
Divorce	na	County Clerk
Land	na	County Clerk
Probate	na	County Judge
Court	na	County Clerk

■ Holt 13 Jan. 1860
204 N. Fourth St., P.O. Box 329, O'Neill, NE 68763
Phone: (402)336-1762
Web site: www.rootsweb.com/~neholt/
Parent County: Unorganized Territory
Comments/research tips: Formerly West County. Name changed to Holt 9 January 1862.

Record Type	Year Begun	Jurisdiction
Marriage	1878	County Clerk
Divorce	1879	Clerk/District Ct.
Land	1879	Registrar/Deeds
Probate	1882	County Judge
Court	1882	County Judge

■ Hooker 29 Mar. 1889
303 NE First St., P.O. Box 184, Mullen, NE 69152
Phone: (308)546-2244
Web site: www.rootsweb.com/~nehooker/

Nebraska

Parent County: Unorganized Territory

Record Type	Year Begun	Jurisdiction
Birth	1919	County Clerk
Marriage	na	County Judge
Death	1919	County Clerk
Land	1889	County Clerk
Probate	na	County Judge

■ **Howard** 1 Mar. 1871

612 Indian, P.O. Box 25, St. Paul, NE 68873

Phone: (308)754-4343

Web site: www.rootsweb.com/~nehoward/

Parent County: Hall

Record Type	Year Begun	Jurisdiction
Marriage	1872	County Judge
Divorce	1873	County Judge
Land	1872	County Judge
Probate	1872	County Judge
Court	1872	County Judge
Nat.	1872	County Judge

■ **Izard** 6 Mar. 1855

Parent County: Unorganized Territory

Comments/research tips: (See Stanton) Name changed to Stanton 10 January 1862.

■ **Jackson** 1855

Parent County: Unorganized Territory

Comments/research tips: (See Fillmore) Never organized. Changed to Fillmore 26 January 1856.

■ **Jefferson** 26 Jan. 1856

411 Fourth St., Fairbury, NE 68352

Phone: (402)729-2323

Web site: www.rootsweb.com/~nejeffer/

Parent County: Unorganized Territory

Comments/research tips: Formerly Jones County. Name changed to Jefferson 1864. Boundaries redefined 1867 and 1871.

Record Type	Year Begun	Jurisdiction
Marriage	na	County Clerk
Divorce	na	Clerk/District Ct.
Land	na	Registrar/Deeds
Probate	na	County Judge
Court	na	County Judge

■ **Johnson** 2 Mar. 1855

Fourth & Broadway, P.O. Box 416, Tecumseh, NE 68450

Phone: (402)335-3246

Web site: www.rootsweb.com/~nejohnso/

Parent County: Nemaha

Record Type	Year Begun	Jurisdiction
Marriage	1858	County Clerk
Divorce	1858	Clerk/District Ct.
Land	1858	County Clerk
Probate	na	County Judge
Court	na	County Judge

■ **Jones** 26 Jan. 1856

Parent County: Unorganized Territory

Comments/research tips: (See Jefferson) Absorbed by Jefferson in 1867.

■ **Kearney** 10 Jan. 1860

424 N. Colorado, P.O. Box 339, Minden, NE 68959

Phone: (308)832-2723

Web site: www.rootsweb.com/~nekearne/

Parent County: Unorganized Territory

Record Type	Year Begun	Jurisdiction
Marriage	1872	County Clerk
Divorce	na	Clerk/District Ct.
Land	na	County Clerk
Probate	na	County Judge
Court	na	County Judge

■ **Keith** 27 Feb. 1873

511 N. Spruce St., P.O. Box 149, Ogallala, NE 69153

Phone: (308)284-4726

Web site: www.rootsweb.com/~nekeith/

Parent County: Unorganized Territory

Record Type	Year Begun	Jurisdiction
Birth	na	County Clerk
Marriage	na	County Judge
Death	na	County Clerk
Divorce	na	Clerk/District Ct.
Land	na	County Clerk
Probate	na	Clerk/District Ct.
Court	na	Clerk/District Ct.

■ **Keya Paha** 4 Nov. 1884

P.O. Box 349, Springview, NE 68778

Phone: (402)497-3791

Web site: www.rootsweb.com/~nekeyapa/

Parent County: Brown

Record Type	Year Begun	Jurisdiction
Marriage	1886	County Clerk
Divorce	1886	County Clerk
Land	1886	County Clerk
Probate	1886	County Clerk
Court	1886	County Clerk

■ **Kimball** 6 Nov. 1888

114 E. Third St., Kimball, NE 69145

Phone: (308)235-2241

Web site: www.rootsweb.com/~nekimbal/

Parent County: Cheyenne

Record Type	Year Begun	Jurisdiction
Marriage	na	County Judge
Divorce	na	County Clerk
Probate	na	County Clerk
Court	na	County Judge

■ **Knox** 10 Feb. 1857

P.O. Box 166, Center, NE 68724

Phone: (402)288-4282

Web site: www.rootsweb.com/~neknox

Parent County: Pierce, Unorganized Territory

Comments/research tips: Formerly L'Eau Qui Court and Emmet Counties. Created as L'Eau Qui Court County. Name changed to Emmet 18 February 1867. Name changed to Knox 21 February 1873.

Record Type	Year Begun	Jurisdiction
Marriage	na	County Clerk
Divorce	na	Clerk/District Ct.
Land	na	Registrar/Deeds
Probate	na	County Judge
Court	na	County Judge

■ L'Eau Qui Court 10 Feb. 1857
Parent County: Pierce, Unorganized Territory
Comments/research tips: (See Knox) Name changed to Emmet 18 February 1867. Name changed to Knox 21 February 1873.

■ Lancaster 6 Mar. 1855
555 S. Tenth St., Lincoln, NE 68508
Phone: (402)441-7484
Web site: www.rootsweb.com/~nelancas
Parent County: Cass, Pierce, old

Record Type	Year Begun	Jurisdiction
Marriage	na	County Judge
Land	na	County Clerk
Probate	na	County Judge

■ Lincoln 7 Jan. 1860
301 N. Jeffers, North Platte, NE 69101
Phone: (308)532-4051
Web site: http://resources.rootsweb.com/USA/NE/Lincoln
Parent County: Unorganized Territory
Comments/research tips: Formerly Shorter County. Name changed to Lincoln 11 December 1861.

Record Type	Year Begun	Jurisdiction
Marriage	na	County Clerk
Divorce	na	Clerk/District Ct.
Land	na	Registrar/Deeds
Probate	na	County Court
Court	na	County Court

■ Logan 24 Feb. 1885
317 Main St., P.O. Box 8, Stapleton, NE 69163
Phone: (308)636-2311
Web site: www.rootsweb.com/~nelogan/
Parent County: Unorganized Territory
Comments/research tips: County Judge has partial Burial records.

Record Type	Year Begun	Jurisdiction
Marriage	1885	County Judge
Divorce	1885	County Judge
Land	na	County Clerk
Probate	1885	County Judge
Court	1885	County Judge

■ Loup 23 Feb. 1883
Fourth St., P.O. Box 187, Taylor, NE 68879
Phone: (308)942-3135
Web site: www.rootsweb.com/~neloup/

Parent County: Unorganized Territory

Record Type	Year Begun	Jurisdiction
Marriage	na	County Judge
Divorce	1887	County Clerk
Land	1887	County Clerk
Probate	na	County Judge
Court	1887	County Clerk

■ Loup, old 6 Mar. 1855
Parent County: Burt
Comments/research tips: Disorganized in 1856 and became part of Izard, Madison, Monroe and Platte Counties.

■ Madison 26 Jan. 1856
110 Clara Davis Dr., P.O. Box 290, Madison, NE 68748
Phone: (402)454-3311
Web site: www.rootsweb.com/~nemadiso
Parent County: McNeale, Loup, old

Record Type	Year Begun	Jurisdiction
Marriage	1868	County Clerk
Divorce	1907	County Clerk
Land	1868	County Clerk
Probate	1863	County Clerk
Court	1907	County Clerk

■ McNeale 1855
Parent County: Burt
Comments/research tips: Absorbed by Madison and Izard (now Stanton) in 1856.

■ McPherson 31 Mar. 1887
Fifth & Anderson, P.O. Box 122, Tryon, NE 69167
Phone: (308)587-2363
Web site: www.rootsweb.com/~nemcpher/
Parent County: Lincoln, Keith, Logan

Record Type	Year Begun	Jurisdiction
Marriage	na	County Clerk
Divorce	na	County Clerk
Land	na	County Clerk
Probate	na	County Judge
Court	na	County Judge

■ Merrick 4 Nov. 1858
1510 Eighteenth St., P.O. Box 27, Central City, NE 68826
Phone: (308)946-2881
Web site: www.rootsweb.com/~nemerric/
Parent County: Unorganized Territory

Record Type	Year Begun	Jurisdiction
Birth	na	County Clerk
Marriage	na	County Judge
Death	na	County Clerk
Divorce	na	County Judge
Land	1873	Registrar/Deeds
Probate	na	County Judge
Court	na	County Judge

■ Monroe 1856
Parent County: Loup, old
Comments/research tips: Absorbed by Platte County in 1860.

■ Morrill   12 Nov. 1908
P.O. Box 610, Bridgeport, NE 69336-0610
Phone: (308)262-0860
Web site: www.rootsweb.com/~nemorril/
Parent County: Cheyenne

Record Type	Year Begun	Jurisdiction
Birth	1917	County Clerk
Marriage	na	County Judge
Death	1917	County Clerk
Land	1909	County Clerk
Probate	na	County Judge
Burial	1917	County Clerk

■ Nance   13 Feb. 1879
209 Esther St., Fullerton, NE 68638
Phone: (308)536-2331
Web site: www.rootsweb.com/~nenance/
Parent County: Pawnee Indian Reservation

Record Type	Year Begun	Jurisdiction
Marriage	1890	County Clerk
Divorce	1882	Clerk/District Ct.
Land	1879	County Clerk
Probate	na	County Judge
Court	1882	Clerk/District Ct.

■ Nemaha   23 Nov. 1854
1824 N St., Auburn, NE 68305
Phone: (402)274-4213
Web site: www.rootsweb.com/~nenemaha/
Parent County: Original County
Comments/research tips: Formed as Forney County, name changed to Nemaha 7 Mar 1855.

Record Type	Year Begun	Jurisdiction
Marriage	1856	County Clerk
Divorce	na	Clerk/District Ct.
Land	na	County Clerk
Probate	na	County Judge
Court	na	County Judge
Military	na	County Clerk

■ Nuckolls   13 Jan. 1860
150 S. Main St., P.O. Box 366, Nelson, NE 68961
Phone: (409)225-4361
Web site: www.rootsweb.com/~nenuckol/
Parent County: Unorganized Territory

Record Type	Year Begun	Jurisdiction
Marriage	na	County Judge
Divorce	na	Clerk/District Ct.
Land	1900	County Clerk
Probate	na	County Judge
Court	na	Clerk/District Ct.

■ Otoe   23 Nov. 1854
1021 Central Ave., P.O. Box 249, Nebraska City, NE 68410
Phone: (402)873-9505
Web site: www.rootsweb.com/~neotoe
Parent County: Cass, Pierce, old
Comments/research tips: Formerly Pierce, old. Name changed to Otoe.

Record Type	Year Begun	Jurisdiction
Marriage	na	County Clerk
Divorce	na	County Clerk
Land	na	Registrar/Deeds
Probate	na	County Judge
Court	na	County Clerk

■ Pawnee   6 Mar. 1855
625 Sixth St., P.O. Box 431, Pawnee City, NE 68420
Phone: (402)852-2962
Web site: www.rootsweb.com/~nepawnee/
Parent County: Richardson

Record Type	Year Begun	Jurisdiction
Marriage	1858	County Clerk
Divorce	na	County Clerk
Land	na	County Clerk
Probate	na	County Judge
Court	na	County Clerk

■ Perkins   8 Nov. 1887
200 Lincoln Ave., P.O. Box 156, Grant, NE 69140
Phone: (308)352-4643
Web site: www.rootsweb.com/~neperkin/
Parent County: Keith

Record Type	Year Begun	Jurisdiction
Marriage	na	County Clerk
Divorce	na	County Clerk
Land	na	County Clerk
Probate	na	County Judge
Court	na	County Clerk

■ Phelps   11 Feb. 1873
P.O. Box 404, Holdrege, NE 68949
Phone: (308)995-4469
Web site: www.rootsweb.com/~nephelps/
Parent County: Kearney

Record Type	Year Begun	Jurisdiction
Marriage	na	County Clerk
Divorce	na	Clerk/District Ct.
Land	na	County Clerk
Probate	na	County Judge

■ Pierce   26 Jan. 1856
111 W. Court St., Room 1, Pierce, NE 68767
Phone: (402)329-4225
Web site: www.rootsweb.com/~nepierce
Parent County: Izard, Unorganized Territory
Comments/research tips: Formerly Otoe County.

Record Type	Year Begun	Jurisdiction
Marriage	na	County Clerk
Divorce	na	Clerk/District Ct.
Land	na	County Clerk
Probate	na	County Court
Military	na	County Clerk
Nat.	na	Clerk/District Ct.

■ Pierce, old   1854
Parent County: Original County
Comments/research tips: (See Otoe) Became part of Otoe County 1855.

■ Platte   26 Jan. 1856
2610 Fourteenth St., Columbus, NE 68601
Phone: (402)563-4904
Web site: www.rootsweb.com/~neplatte/
Parent County: Loup, old

Record Type	Year Begun	Jurisdiction
Marriage	na	County Judge
Divorce	na	Clerk/District Ct.
Land	na	County Assessor
Probate	na	County Judge
Court	na	Clerk/District Ct.

■ Polk   26 Jan. 1856
P.O. Box 276, Osceola, NE 68651
Phone: (402)747-5431
Web site: www.wathenadesigns.com/Polk/index.html
Parent County: York, Unorganized Territory

Record Type	Year Begun	Jurisdiction
Marriage	na	County Judge
Land	na	County Clerk
Probate	na	County Judge

■ Red Willow   27 Feb. 1873
502 Norris Ave., McCook, NE 69001
Phone: (308)345-1552
Web site: www.rootsweb.com/~neredwil/
Parent County: Unorganized Territory

Record Type	Year Begun	Jurisdiction
Marriage	1874	County Clerk
Divorce	na	Clerk/District Ct.
Land	1888	County Clerk
Probate	na	County Court
Court	na	Clerk/District Ct.
Military	na	Veteran Service Office

■ Richardson   23 Nov. 1854
1700 Stone St., Falls City, NE 68355
Phone: (402)245-2911
Web site: www.rootsweb.com/~nerichar/
Parent County: Original County

Record Type	Year Begun	Jurisdiction
Birth	1918	County Clerk
Marriage	ca.1800	County Judge
Death	1918	County Clerk
Divorce	na	Clerk/District Ct.
Land	na	Registrar/Deeds
Probate	na	County Judge
Court	na	County Judge

■ Rock   6 Nov. 1888
400 State St., P.O. Box 367, Bassett, NE 68714
Phone: (402)684-3933
Web site: www.rootsweb.com/~nerock
Parent County: Brown

Record Type	Year Begun	Jurisdiction
Marriage	na	County Judge
Divorce	1889	County Clerk
Land	1889	County Clerk
Probate	1889	County Clerk
Court	1889	County Clerk

■ Saline   6 Mar. 1855
215 S. Court St., P.O. Box 865, Wilber, NE 68465
Phone: (402)821-2374
Web site: www.rootsweb.com/~nesaline/
Parent County: Original County

Record Type	Year Begun	Jurisdiction
Birth	1976	County Clerk
Marriage	1886	County Court
Death	1976	County Clerk
Divorce	1886	Clerk/District Ct.
Land	1886	County Clerk
Probate	1870	County Court
Court	1886	Clerk/District Ct.

■ Sarpy   7 Feb. 1857
1210 Golden Gate Dr., Papillion, NE 68046
Phone: (402)593-2100
Web site: www.rootsweb.com/~nesarpy
Parent County: Douglas

Record Type	Year Begun	Jurisdiction
Marriage	na	County Judge
Land	na	County Clerk
Probate	na	County Judge

■ Saunders   26 Jan. 1856
P.O. Box 61, Wahoo, NE 68066
Phone: (402)443-8101
Web site: www.rootsweb.com/~nesaunde
Parent County: Lancaster, Douglas
Comments/research tips: Formerly Calhoun County. Name changed to Saunders 8 January 1862.

Record Type	Year Begun	Jurisdiction
Marriage	na	County Clerk
Divorce	na	County Clerk
Land	na	County Clerk
Probate	na	County Clerk
Court	na	County Clerk
Burial	na	County Clerk

■ Scotts Bluff   6 Nov. 1888
1825 Tenth St., Gering, NE 69341
Phone: (308)436-6600
Web site: www.rootsweb.com/~nescotts
Parent County: Cheyenne

Record Type	Year Begun	Jurisdiction
Marriage	na	County Clerk
Divorce	na	County Judge
Probate	na	County Judge
Court	na	County Judge

■ Seward   6 Mar. 1855
529 Seward St., P.O. Box 190, Seward, NE 68434
Phone: (402)643-2883
Web site: http://resources.rootsweb.com/USA/NE/Seward
Parent County: Cass, Pierce, old
Comments/research tips: Formerly Greene County. Name changed to Seward 3 January 1862.

Record Type	Year Begun	Jurisdiction
Marriage	1866	County Clerk

Nebraska

Divorce................. 1868 ....Clerk/District Ct.
Land .... 1866 ....County Clerk
Probate .... 1869 ....County Court
Court..................... 1869 ....Clerk/District Ct.

■ Sheridan 25 Feb. 1885
301 E. Second St., P.O. Box 39, Rushville, NE 69360
Phone: (308)327-2633
Web site: www.rootsweb.com/~nesherid/
Parent County: Sioux

Record Type	Year Begun	Jurisdiction
Marriage.................. na ....County Judge
Divorce.................... na ....Clerk/District Ct.
Probate .... na ....County Judge
Court....................... na ....County Judge

■ Sherman 1 Mar. 1871
630 O St., P.O. Box 456, Loup City, NE 68853
Phone: (308)745-1513
Web site: www.rootsweb.com/~nesherma/
Parent County: Buffalo, Unorganized Territory
Comments/research tips: County Clerk has Naturalization records 1882–1920.

Record Type	Year Begun	Jurisdiction
Marriage................ 1883 ....County Clerk
Divorce................. 1882 ....County Clerk
Land .... 1873 ....County Clerk
Probate .... na ....County Clerk Magistrate
Court..................... 1882 ....County Clerk

■ Shorter 7 Jan. 1860
Parent County: Unorganized Territory
Comments/research tips: (See Lincoln) Name changed to Lincoln 11 December 1861.

■ Sioux 19 Feb. 1877
325 Main St., P.O. Box 158, Harrison, NE 69346
Phone: (308)668-2443
Web site: www.rootsweb.com/~nesioux/
Parent County: Unorganized Territory

Record Type	Year Begun	Jurisdiction
Marriage.................. na ....County Judge
Divorce.................... na ....Clerk/District Ct.
Land .... na ....County Clerk
Probate .... na ....County Judge
Court....................... na ....County Judge

■ Stanton 6 Mar. 1855
804 Ivy St., P.O. Box 347, Stanton, NE 68779
Phone: (402)439-2222
Web site: www.rootsweb.com/~nestanto
Parent County: Unorganized Territory
Comments/research tips: Formerly Izard County. Name changed to Stanton 20 January 1862.

Record Type	Year Begun	Jurisdiction
Marriage................ 1869 ....County Clerk
Divorce................. 1875 ....Clerk/District Ct.
Land .... 1868 ....County Clerk
Probate .... na ....County Court

Court..................... 1875 ....Clerk/District Ct.
Military .... na ....County Clerk
Nat. .... na ....County Clerk

■ Taylor
Comments/research tips: Unorganized county in southwest corner of state enumerated with Lincoln in 1870 census. Became the counties Garden, Deuel, and parts of Morrill and Cheyenne.

■ Thayer 26 Jan. 1871
225 N. Fourh St., P.O. Box 208, Hebron, NE 68370
Phone: (402)768-6126
Web site: www.rootsweb.com/~nethayer/
Parent County: Jefferson

Record Type	Year Begun	Jurisdiction
Marriage.................. na ....County Judge
Divorce.................... na ....Clerk/District Ct.
Land .... na ....County Clerk
Probate .... na ....County Judge
Court....................... na ....County Judge

■ Thomas 31 Mar. 1887
503 Main St., Thedford, NE 69166
Phone: (308)645-2261
Web site: www.rootsweb.com/~nethomas/
Parent County: Unorganized territory

Record Type	Year Begun	Jurisdiction
Marriage................ 1887 ....County Clerk
Divorce.................... na ....Clerk/District Ct.
Land .... na ....County Clerk
Probate .... na ....County Judge
Court....................... na ....Clerk/District Ct.

■ Thurston 28 Mar. 1889
106 S. Fifth St., P.O. Box G, Pender, NE 68047
Phone: (402)385-2343
Web site: www.rootsweb.com/~nethurst/
Parent County: Burt
Comments/research tips: Thurston County was originally an Indian reservation and prior to organization was called Blackbird County, created 7 March 1855. From 1884–1889 it was administered by Dakota County. Name changed to Thurston 28 March 1889.

Record Type	Year Begun	Jurisdiction
Marriage................ 1889 ....County Judge
Divorce................. 1889 ....Clerk/District Ct.
Land .... 1885 ....County Clerk
Probate .... 1889 ....County Judge
Court..................... 1889 ....Clerk/District Ct.

■ Valley 1 Mar. 1871
125 S. Fifteenth St., Ord, NE 68862
Phone: (308)728-3700
Web site: www.rootsweb.com/~nevalley/
Parent County: Unorganized Territory

Record Type	Year Begun	Jurisdiction
Marriage................ 1883 ....County Clerk
Divorce.................... na ....Clerk/District Ct.

Land .... 1883 ....County Clerk
Probate .... na ....County Judge
Court .... na ....Clerk/District Ct.

■ **Washington** 23 Nov. 1854
1555 Colfax St., Blair, NE 68008
Phone: (402)426-6822
Web site: www.rootsweb.com/~newashin
Parent County: Original County

Record Type	Year Begun	Jurisdiction
Birth	na	County Clerk
Marriage	1856	County Judge
Death	na	County Clerk
Divorce	na	Clerk/District Ct.
Land	1857	County Clerk
Probate	1855	County Judge
Court	1855	County Judge
Burial	na	County Clerk

■ **Wayne** 4 Mar. 1871
510 N. Pearl St., P.O. Box 248, Wayne, NE 68787
Phone: (402)375-2288
Web site: www.rootsweb.com/~newayne/
Parent County: Unorganized Territory

Record Type	Year Begun	Jurisdiction
Marriage	1871	County Judge
Divorce	na	Clerk/District Ct.
Land	1870	County Clerk
Probate	1871	County Judge
Court	1871	County Judge

■ **Webster** 16 Feb. 1867
621 N. Cedar St., Red Cloud, NE 68970
Phone: (402)746-2716

Web site: www.rootsweb.com/~newebste/
Parent County: Unorganized Territory

Record Type	Year Begun	Jurisdiction
Marriage	1871	County Clerk
Divorce	1871	County Clerk
Land	1871	County Clerk
Probate	1871	County Clerk
Court	1871	County Clerk
Nat.	1874	County Clerk

■ **West** 13 Jan. 1860
Parent County: Unorganized Territory
Comments/research tips: (See Holt) Name changed to Holt 9 January 1862.

■ **Wheeler** 17 Feb. 1877
Third and Main Sts., P.O. Box 127, Bartlett, NE 68622
Phone: (308)654-3235
Web site: www.rootsweb.com/~newheele/
Parent County: Unorganized Territory

Record Type	Year Begun	Jurisdiction
Land	na	County Clerk
Court	na	County Clerk

■ **York** 13 Mar. 1855
510 Lincoln Ave., York, NE 68467
Phone: (402)362-7759
Web site: www.rootsweb.com/~neyork/
Parent County: Cass, Pierce, old

Record Type	Year Begun	Jurisdiction
Marriage	na	County Clerk
Divorce	na	Clerk/District Ct.
Land	na	Registrar/Deeds
Probate	na	County Court
Military	na	Veteran Service Office

Nevada

By David A. Fryxell

HISTORICAL OVERVIEW

Nevada's history is far more compressed than that of its Southwestern neighbors, with native settlements dating only to 900 BC and little Spanish colonization. Not until the 1833–34 expedition of John C. Fremont, in which he discovered Lake Tahoe, did the outside world pay much attention to Nevada. But that began to change with the 1847 arrival of Brigham Young in Utah and the 1849 discovery of gold in California. Both Mormon faithful and fortune-seekers soon spilled over into Nevada, which had come under U.S. control with the 1848 Treaty of Guadalupe Hidalgo. Most of Nevada became part of the new Utah Territory in 1850, with the southern tip assigned to the New Mexico Territory. The first permanent European-American settlement in Nevada was established in 1851 at Mormon Station, thirteen miles south of what would soon become Carson City. That same year, gold was discovered at Dalton.

With the 1859 gold and silver find dubbed the Comstock Lode, Nevada jumped onto the fast track to settlement and statehood. Virginia City sprang up almost overnight. A separate Nevada Territory was established in 1861, the same year journalist Mark Twain arrived in Carson City, beginning an adventure he'd dramatize in *Roughing It* (1872). Statehood came in 1864. (The longest Morse Code telegram ever sent was the new state constitution, dash-dotted from Carson City to Washington, DC, at a cost of $3,000.)

But bust soon followed boom, and Nevada slid into a depression that saw its population decline by a third from 1880 to 1900, when gold was found at Tonopah.

What most think of as modern Nevada began in 1927 with the re-legalization of gambling and the six-week divorce law. Soon Reno and Las Vegas were "wide open" cities. In 1941, just a decade after Las Vegas' first traffic

NEVADA AT A GLANCE

Motto: All for Our Country

Population: 1.9 million

Prevalent Religions: Christianity, with particularly large numbers of Roman Catholic and Baptist, and smaller numbers of Lutheran, Methodist, Presbyterian, also Jewish and Church of Jesus Christ of Latter-day Saints

Major Industries: Tourism, mining, machinery, printing and publishing, food processing, electrical equipment, cattle, hay, dairy products, potatoes

Ethnic Makeup (in percent): Caucasian 75.2%, African American 6.8%, Hispanic 19.7%, Asian 4.5%, Native American 1.3%, Other 8.0%

Famous Nevadans: Andre Agassi, Ben Alexander, Helen Delich Bentley, Hobart Cavanaugh, Abby Dalton, James A. Gibbons, Jack Kramer, Paul Laxalt, Pat Nixon, Jack Wilson Paiute, Edna Purviance, Harry M. Reid, David Derek Stacton, Sarah Hopkins Winnemucca

Above: Vegas at night—no other city quite like it

Nevada

light, Tommy Hull opened the first hotel on what would become the Las Vegas Strip.

RECORD HIGHLIGHTS

Nevada's records essentially begin with the 1860 census, in which the counties of Carson, Humboldt, and St. Mary's were enumerated with the Utah Territory. There were partial territorial censuses in 1862 and 1863. Note that post-statehood, in 1866, Arizona Territory ceded lands to Nevada that, along with land from Utah Territory, became Lincoln County. In addition to the regular federal census in 1870, there was a special 1875 state census.

Nevada census researchers are unusually fortunate: The Nevada State Historic Preservation Office has put 310,000 entries, the state's entire 1860, 1870, 1880, 1900, 1910, and 1920 censuses online at <http://dmla.clan.lib.nv.us/docs/shpo/NVCENSUS>. It's the first state to undertake such a massive endeavor.

Despite its early statehood, Nevada didn't begin statewide records of births and deaths until 1911 and marriages until 1968. Some Nevada counties have birth and death records beginning in 1887 in their county recorder's office. Nevada is a tough state to research in, warns Nevada genealogist and author Patricia A. Hall Scott, in part because death records are not open to the public. Obituary files are now being placed online to assist researchers, however; see the Nevada Obituary Project at <www.rootsweb.com/~usgenweb/obits/obitsnv.htm>.

If your ancestors went to Nevada for a "quickie divorce," you can obtain those records from the clerk of the district court in the county.

With the transient nature of mining work and out-of-the-way desert locales, Scott adds, your ancestors' final resting place may be equally tricky to find. Volunteers are also working to put data on "lost" Nevada cemeteries online, she says. Extant cemetery records from almost every county can be accessed on microfilm from the FHL. And Nevada cemetery researchers shouldn't miss Richard B. Taylor's *The Nevada Tombstone Record Book* (Las Vegas: BeeHive Books, 1994) and *The Nevada Tombstone Record Book: Southern Nevada* (Las Vegas: BeeHive Books, 1986).

On the bright side, miners often left records because of the nature of their work. Miners traveled from boom to boom, each of which lasted from a few months to several decades, but most only a few years, explains David A. Davis, newsletter editor of the Nevada State Genealogical Society. After the Comstock Lode, more than two hundred mining districts were established that recorded deeds and claims. These records, along with mining corporation papers and state mine inspection records, can be found at the state archives. Who cares about mine

RESEARCH TIPS

for more info

- The *Nevada Guide to Genealogical Records* by Diane E. Greene is a good place to start your Nevada research—it can point you to the source of records and is a guide to published histories of the state.
- In Nevada, it's important to check the history and formation of the counties you're researching in; county names and boundaries changed often.
- State censuses from 1860 through 1910 are online at <dmla.clan.lib.nv.us/docs/shpo/NVCENSUS>.

Census Records

- Federal Census Records: 1870, 1880, 1900, 1910, 1920, 1930
- Statewide and Territorial Censuses Index: 1860 (Carson, Humboldt, and St. Mary's counties), 1862 (Douglas, Humboldt, Lyon, Ormsby, Storey, and Washoe counties), 1863 (Lander county), 1875
- Mortality Schedules: 1870, 1880
- Mortality Schedules for Utah Territory: 1850, 1860

inspections? You might—if your ancestor was mentioned in the lists of mine supervisors, hoist operators, or accident victims.

Records of the massive irrigation projects began in 1902, and though scattered among several archives they can also prove useful, according to professional researcher Barbara L. Hodges, CGRS.

And don't forget military records. Nevada joined the Union during the Civil War—hence its motto, "Battle Born"—and a dozen Army companies were raised there even before statehood, though they served only locally.

Census records are great for Nevada, says Scott, but keep in mind that since Nevadans moved so often, they

Nevada

can be found in various locations. Always check the history and formation of a county when you are looking for an ancestor, she adds: Your ancestor may live in the same spot, but it will now be a different county name. In a state like Nevada, ten years between censuses is a long time.

Newspapers of the period can also reveal "pieces of gold" about your ancestors, says Scott. According to Hodges, there is a project underway to index these old papers.

Davis recommends the book *Nevada Guide to Genealogical Records* by Diane E. Greene (Baltimore: Clearfield Co., 1998). It's a useful starting point for sources of records and as a guide to the histories of Nevada published in 1881 (Thompson and West), 1904 (Wren), 1913 (Davis), and 1932 (Scrugham). The book is also a handy guide to courthouse records, which Davis says are fairly complete; the only courthouse to have burned down, as far as he knows, was in Storey County in 1875.

Besides the state genealogical society, Davis mentions the Clark County Genealogical Society, which has a genealogical library in Henderson. The Northeastern Nevada Historical Society in Elko is also a good source of information, he says, as are the historical societies in Reno and Las Vegas. The University of Nevada-Reno has a good collection of Nevada newspapers on microfilm. Small towns such as Elko, Winnemucca, and Eureka have their own museums, Davis adds, and each of these has its own collection of records that might have the clues you need to solve your Nevada puzzles.

STATE RESOURCES

■ ARCHIVES, LIBRARIES, AND SOCIETIES

Bureau of Land Management
P.O. Box 12000, Reno, NV 89520
Tel: (775) 861-6400
Web site: <www.nv.blm.gov>

Carson City Historical Society
P.O. Box 1864, Carson City, NV 89702
Tel: (775) 882-5694

Carson Valley Historical Society
1477 Hwy. 395 N., Gardnerville, NV 89410
Tel: (775) 782-2555

Churchill County Historical and Genealogical Society
% Churchill County Museum, 1050 S. Main St., Fallon, NV 89406-8824
Tel: (702) 423-3677

Clark County Heritage Museum
1830 S. Boulder Hwy., Henderson, NV 89015
Tel: (702) 455-7955

Clark County Genealogical Society
P.O. Box 1929, Las Vegas, NV 89125-1929
Tel: (702) 225-5838
Web site: <www.rootsweb.com/~nvccngs/>

Elko Genealogical Society
3001 N. Fifth St., Elko, NV 89801

Eureka Historical Society
P.O. Box 82, Eureka, NV 89316

Goldfield Historical Society
P.O. Box 178, Goldfield, NV 89013

Humboldt County Genealogical Society
% Humboldt County Library, 85 E. Fifth St., Winnemucca, NV 89445

The Las Vegas Family History Center
509 S. Ninth St., Las Vegas, NV 89101
Web site: <www.lvccld.org/ref_info/virtual_tours/family_history/location.htm>

Las Vegas Public Library
833 Las Vegas Blvd. N., Las Vegas, NV 89101
Tel: (702) 382-3493
Web site: <www.lvccld.org>

Lincoln County Historical Society
P.O. Box 515, Pioche, NV 89043

National Archives Pacific Region (Laguna Niguel)
24000 Avila Rd., 1st Fl., Laguna Niguel, CA 92677-3497
Tel: (949) 360-2640
Web site: <www.archives.gov/facilities/ca/laguna_niguel>

The National Archives Pacific Sierra Region (San Bruno)
1000 Commodore Drive, San Bruno, CA 94066-2350
Tel: (650) 876-9001
E-mail: sanbruno.archives@nara.gov
Web site: <www.archives.gov/facilities/ca/san_francisco.html>

Nevada Historical Society
1650 N. Virginia St., Reno, NV 89503
Tel: (775) 688-1190
E-mail: <http://dmla.clan.lib.nv.us/docs/museums/reno/his-soc.htm>

Nevada State Genealogical Society
P.O. Box 20666, Reno, NV 89515-0666
Web site: <www.rootsweb.com/~nvsgs/>

Nevada State Library & Archives
100 N. Stewart St., Carson City, NV 89701-4285
Tel: Archives (775) 684-3310; Library (775) 684-3360
E-mail: nslref@clan.lib.nv.us
Web site: <http://dmla.clan.lib.nv.us/docs/nsla/>

Nevada State Museum and Historical Society
700 Twin Lakes Dr., Las Vegas, NV 89107
Tel: (702) 486-5205
Web site: <http://dmla.clan.lib.nv.us/docs/museums/lv/vegas.htm>

Nevada State Office Vital Records
505 E. King St., Rm. 102, Carson City, NV 89710-4749
Tel: (775) 654-4242
Web site: <www.vitalrec.com/nv.html#state>

North Las Vegas Library
2300 Civic Center Dr., North Las Vegas, NV 89030
Tel: (702) 633-1070
Web site: <www.ci.north-las-vegas.nv.us/Departments/Library/Library.cfm>

Northeastern Nevada Historical Society and Museum
1515 Idaho St., Elko, NV 89801
Tel: (775) 738-3418
Web site: <www.rootsweb.com/~nvnengs/>

Protestant Episcopal Church
% the Nevada Historical Society, 1650 N. Virginia St., Reno, NV 89503
Tel: (775) 688-1190

Sparks Heritage Society
814 Victorian Ave., Sparks, NV 89431

University of Nevada-Reno, Special Collections Department
% University Library, University of Nevada-Reno, Reno, NV 89557-0044
Tel: (775) 784-6500
Web site: <www.library.unr.edu/specoll/Default.htm>

Washoe County Library
P.O. Box 2151, Reno, NV 89505
Tel: (775) 327-8349
Web site: <www.washoe.lib.nv.us>

Wellington Historical Society
P.O. Box 36, Wellington, NV 89444

White Pine Historical and Archaeological Society
P.O. Box 151725, Ely, NV 89315
Web site: <www.webpanda.com/white_pine_county/historical_society>

BIBLIOGRAPHY

■ GENERAL RESOURCES

200 Years in Nevada: a Story of People Who Opened, Explored and Developed the Land
by Elbert B Edwards (Salt Lake City, UT: Publishers Press, 1978)

Beyond This Place There Be Dragons: the Routes of the Tragic Trek of the Death Valley 1849ers Through Nevada, Death Valley, and onto Southern California
by George Koenig (Glendale, CA: Arthur Clark, 1984)

Carson Valley: Historical Sketches of Nevada's First Settlement
by Grace Dangberg (Reno, NV: Carson Valley Historical Society, 1979, 1972)

Covered Wagon Women: Diaries & Letters from the Western Trails, 1840–1890
by Kenneth L. Holmes (Glendale, CA: Arthur H. Clark Co., ca. 1983–1991)

Desert Between the Mountains: Mormons, Miners, Padres, Mountain Men, and the Opening of the Great Basin, 1772–1869
by Michael S. Durham (New York, NY: Henry Holt, 1997)

First Directory of Nevada Territory: Containing the Names of Residents in the Principal Towns, a Historical Sketch
by J. Wells Kelly (Tucson, AZ: W.C. Cox Co., 1974)

Founding the Far West; California, Oregon, and Nevada, 1840–1890
by David Allen Johnson (Berkeley, CA: University of California Press, ca. 1992)

Genealogical Guide to Arizona and Nevada
by Joyce V. Hawley (Gallup, NM: Verlene Publishing, ca. 1983)

Genealogical Prospecting in Nevada: a Guide to Nevada Directories
by Joyce C. Lee (Henderson, NV: Nevada Library Association, 1984)

The Genealogist's Companion and Sourcebook, 2d ed.
by Emily Anne Croom (Cincinnati: Betterway Books, 2003)

A Genealogist's Guide to Discovering Your African-American Ancestors
by Franklin Carter Smith and Emily Anne Croom (Cincinnati: Betterway Books, 2003)

Guide to Genealogical Research in the National Archives of the United States
edited by Anne Bruner Eales and Robert M. Kvasnicka (Washington, DC: National Archives and Records Administration, 2000)

History of Nevada
by Russell R Elliott (Lincoln, NE: University of Nebraska Press, 1984, 1973)

History of Nevada, Colorado and Wyoming, 1540–1888
by Hubert Howe Bancroft (San Francisco, CA: History Co., 1890)

History of Nevada: with illustrations and biographical sketches of its prominent men and pioneers
by Myron Angel (Tucson, AZ: W.C. Cox, 1974)

Inventory of the Church Archives of Nevada, Protestant Episcopal Church
prepared by the Division of Professional and Service Projects, Work Projects Administration (Reno, NV: Historical Records Survey, 1941)

Inventory of the Church Archives of Nevada, Roman Catholic Church
prepared by the Division of Professional and Service Projects, Work Projects Administration (Reno, NV: Historical Records Survey, 1939)

Mormons and Their Neighbors: an Index to Over 75,000 Biographical Sketches From 1820 To the Present
by Marvin E. Wiggins (Provo, UT: Harold B. Lee Library, Brigham Young University, ca. 1984)

National Archives Microfilm Catalogs online:
<www.archives.gov/publications/genealogy_microfilm_catalogs.html>

Nevada Biographical and Genealogical Sketch Index
by Carlyle J. Parker and Janet G. Parker (Turlock, CA: Marietta Publishing Co., ca. 1986)

Nevada Guide to Genealogical Records
by Diane E. Greene (Baltimore, MD: Genealogical Pub. Co., 1998)

Nevada, a Guide to the Silver State
compiled by workers of the Writer's Program of the Work Projects Administration (Tucson, AZ: W.C. Cox Co., 1974)

Nevada: a History of the State From the Earliest Times Through the Civil War
by Effie Mona Mack (Glendale, CA: Arthur H. Clark Co., 1936)

Nevada: A Narrative of the Conquest of a Frontier Land Comprising the Story of Her People From the Dawn of History to the Present Time . . .
by James Graves Scrugham (Chicago: American Historical Society, 1935)

Nevada's Northeast Frontier
by Edna B. Patterson, Louise A. Ulph, and Victor Goodwin (Reno, NV: University of Nevada Press, ca. 1991)

Nevada State Children's Home, Admission Records, 1870–1920
by Doreen Robinson (Pawtucket, R.I.: Quintin Publications, ca. 2000)

The Newspapers of Nevada: a History and Bibliography, 1854–1979
by Richard E. Lingenfelter and Karen Rix Gash (Reno, NV: University of Nevada Press, 1984)

Reproduction of Thompson and West's "History of Nevada, 1881": With Illustrations and Biographical Sketches of its Prominent Men and Pioneers
by Thomas Hinckley Thompson (Berkeley, CA: Howell-North, 1958)

Steeples Among the Sage, a Centennial Story of Nevada's Churches
by Leonidas Latimer Loofbourow (Oakland, CA: Lake Park Press, ca. 1964)

The Story of the Mine: As Illustrated by the Great Comstock Lode of Nevada
by Charles Howard Shinn (New York, NY: D. Appleton, 1897)

Territorial Lawmen of Nevada: Vol. One, the Utah Territorial Period, 1851–1861
by Robert W. Ellison (Minden, NV: Hot Springs Mountain Press, ca. 1999)

■ CENSUS RECORDS

The American Census Handbook
by Thomas Jay Kemp (Wilmington, DE: Scholarly Resources Inc., ca. 2001)

The Census Book: A Genealogist's Guide to Federal Census Facts, Schedules and Indexes
by William Dollarhide (Bountiful, UT: Heritage Quest, ca. 1999)

Finding Answers in U.S. Census Records
by Loretto Dennis Szucs and Matthew Wright (Orem, UT: Ancestry Pub., ca. 2001)

Map Guide to the U.S. Federal Censuses, 1790–1920
by William Thorndale and William Dollarhide (Baltimore, MD: Genealogical Pub. Co., ca. 1987)

State Census Records
by Ann S. Lainhart (Baltimore, MD: Genealogical Pub. Co., ca. 1992)

Your Guide to the Federal Census
by Kathleen W. Hinckley (Cincinnati: Betterway Books, 2002)

■ IMMIGRATION RECORDS

American Naturalization Records, 1790–1990: What They Are and How to Use Them
by John J. Newman (North Salt Lake, UT: HeritageQuest, 1998)

American Passenger Arrival Records
by Michael Tepper (Baltimore: Genealogical Publishing Co., 1993)

The Basques in the Northwest: A Dissertation
by Flavina Maria McCullough (San Francisco, CA: R and E Research Associates, 1974)

The Mormons in Nevada
by Leonard J. Arrington (Las Vegas, NV: Las Vegas Sun, 1979)

Nevada

They Became Americans: Finding Naturalization Records and Ethnic Origins
by Loretto Dennis Szucs (Salt Lake City: Ancestry, Inc., 1998)

They Came in Ships: A Guide to Finding Your Immigrant Ancestor's Arrival Records, 2d ed.
by John P. Colletta (Salt Lake City: Ancestry, Inc., 1993)

■ LAND RECORDS

An Inventory & Index to the Records of Carson County, Utah & Nevada Territories, 1855–1861
by Marion Ellison (Reno, NV: Grace Dangberg Foundation, 1984)

Land & Property Research in the United States
by E. Wade Hone (Salt Lake City, UT: Ancestry, 1997)

Locating Your Roots: Discover Your Ancestors Using Land Records
by Patricia Law Hatcher (Cincinnati: Betterway Books, 2003)

■ MAPS

Directory of Southern Nevada Place Names
by Walter R. Averett ([S.l.]: W.R. Averett, ca. 1962)

Nevada Atlas & Gazetteer
(Freeport, ME: DeLorme, 1996)

Nevada Ghost Towns & Mining Camps
by Stanley W. Paher (Las Vegas, NV: Nevada Publications, ca. 1970)

Nevada Place Names: A Geographical Dictionary
by Helen S. Carlson (Reno, NV: University of Nevada Press, 1974)

Nevada Place Names: Their Origin and Significance
by Rufus Wood Leigh (Salt Lake City, UT: Manufactured by Deseret News Press, ca. 1964)

Nevada Post Offices: An Illustrated History
by James Gamett (Las Vegas, NV: Nevada Publications, ca. 1983)

Nevada Postal History, 1861 to 1972
by Robert P. Harris (Santa Cruz, CA: Bonanza Press, 1973)

■ MILITARY RECORDS

Uncle, We Are Ready! Registering America's Men, 1917–1918: A Guide to Researching World War I Draft Registration Cards
by John J. Newman (North Salt Lake, UT: HeritageQuest, 2001)

U.S. Military Records: A Guide to Federal & State Sources, Colonial America to the Present
by James C. Neagles (Salt Lake City: Ancestry, Inc., 1994)

World War II: A Family Historian's Guide
by Debra Johnson Knox (Spartanburg, SC: MIE Publishing, 2003)

■ VITAL RECORDS

AZ, CA, ID, NV, 1850–1951
(Brøderbund, 1996. CD-ROM)

Guide To Public Vital Statistics Records in Nevada
by the Historical Records Survey (Reno, NV: University of Nevada, Las Vegas, 1941)

Nevada State Cemeteries
by Jean Winters Ferral and Roger Ferrel (S.l.: s.n., ca. 1997)

The Nevada Tombstone Record Book
by Richard B. Taylor (Las Vegas, NV: Nevada Families Project, ca. 1986)

Your Guide to Cemetery Research
by Sharon DeBartolo Carmack (Cincinnati: Betterway Books, 2002)

■ Carson   17 Jan. 1854
Parent County: Original county
Comments/research tips: Organized as a county in Utah Territory. Discontinued 2 March 1861 when Nevada Territory was created. Became part of Douglas, Lyon, Ormsby, Storey, Churchill, Pershing, Humboldt, and Washoe Counties.

■ Carson City   25 Nov. 1861
885 E. Musser St., Carson City, NV 89701
Phone: (775)887-2260
Web site: www.rootsweb.com/~nvgenweb/carson/carson.htm
Parent County: Original county
Comments/research tips: Organized as Ormsby County. Consolidated into Carson City 1969 and Ormsby County discontinued.

Record Type	Year Begun	Jurisdiction
Birth	1887	County Recorder
Death	1891	County Recorder
Marriage	1855	County Clerk
Divorce	na	County Clerk
Land	1862	County Recorder
Probate	1864	County Clerk
Court	1864	County Clerk

■ Churchill   25 Nov. 1861
155 N. Taylor St. #110, Fallon, NV 89406
Phone: (775)423-6028
Web site: www.rootsweb.com/~nvchurch
Parent County: Original county

Record Type	Year Begun	Jurisdiction
Birth	1888	County Clerk
Death	1888	County Clerk
Land	1864	County Clerk
Marriage	1864	County Clerk
Probate	1904	County Clerk
Court	1904	County Clerk

■ Clark   5 Feb. 1909
200 S. Third St., Las Vegas, NV 89155
Phone: (702)455-3156
Web site: www.rootsweb.com/~nvclark/
Parent County: Lincoln

Record Type	Year Begun	Jurisdiction
Birth	1909	Dept./Health
Marriage	1909	County Recorder
Death	1909	Dept./Health
Land	1909	County Recorder
Probate	1909	County Clerk
Court	1909	County Clerk

■ Douglas   25 Nov. 1861
1594 Esmeralda Ave., Room 105, Minden, NV 89423
Phone: (775)782-9014

Web site: www.rootsweb.com/~nvdougla/douglas.htm
Parent County: Original county

Record Type	Year Begun	Jurisdiction
Birth	1887	County Clerk
Death	1887	County Clerk
Land	1855	County Clerk
Marriage	1802	County Clerk
Probate	1887	County Clerk
Court	1887	County Clerk

■ Elko 5 Mar. 1869
571 Idaho St., Third Floor, Elko, NV 89801
Phone: (775)738-4600
Web site: www.rootsweb.com/~nvelko/
Parent County: St. Mary's

Record Type	Year Begun	Jurisdiction
Marriage	1869	County Recorder
Birth	1887	County Recorder
Death	1887	County Recorder
Land	1869	County Recorder
Probate	1869	County Clerk
Court	1869	County Clerk

■ Esmeralda 25 Nov. 1861
P.O. Box 547, Goldfield, NV 89013
Phone: (775)485-6367
Web site: www.rootsweb.com/~nvesmera/
Parent County: Original county

Record Type	Year Begun	Jurisdiction
Land	1863	County Clerk/Treas.
Birth	1907	County Clerk/Treas.
Marriage	1898	County Clerk/Treas.
Probate	1881	County Clerk/Treas.
Court	1908	County Clerk/Treas.
Death	1907	County Clerk/Treas.

■ Eureka 1 Mar. 1873
10 S. Main St., P.O. Box 677, Eureka, NV 89316
Phone: (775)237-5262
Web site: www.rootsweb.com/~nveureka/
Parent County: Lander

Record Type	Year Begun	Jurisdiction
Birth	1873	County Recorder
Marriage	1873	County Recorder
Death	1887	County Recorder
Land	1873	County Recorder
Probate	1873	County Clerk
Court	1873	County Clerk

■ Humboldt 25 Nov. 1861
50 W. Fifth St., Winnemucca, NV 89445
Phone: (775)623-6343
Web site: www.rootsweb.com/~nvhumbol/
Parent County: Original county
Comments/research tips: See 1860 Utah census.

Record Type	Year Begun	Jurisdiction
Birth	1888	County Clerk
Land	1861	County Assessor
Probate	1863	County Clerk

Court	1862	County Clerk
Marriage	1862	County Clerk
Death	1888	County Clerk

■ Lander 19 Dec. 1862
315 S. Humboldt St., Battle Mountain, NV 89820
Phone: (775)635-5738
Web site: www.rootsweb.com/~nvlander/
Parent County: Original county
Comments/research tips: County Auditor has some Birth records.

Record Type	Year Begun	Jurisdiction
Probate	1862	County Clerk
Court	1862	County Clerk
Land	1862	County Auditor

■ Lincoln 26 Feb. 1866
P.O. Box 90, Pioche, NV 89043
Phone: (775)962-5390
Web site: www.rootsweb.com/~nvlincol/
Parent County: Nye

Record Type	Year Begun	Jurisdiction
Death	1887	County Clerk
Marriage	1872	County Clerk
Land	1865	County Clerk
Probate	1855	County Clerk
Court	1873	County Clerk
Birth	1887	County Clerk

■ Lyon 25 Nov. 1861
27 S. Main St., Yerington, NV 89447
Phone: (775)463-6501
Web site: www.rootsweb.com/~nvlyon/lyon.htm
Parent County: Original county

Record Type	Year Begun	Jurisdiction
Death	1887	County Recorder
Marriage	1862	County Recorder
Land	1862	County Recorder
Probate	1867	County Clerk
Court	1867	County Clerk
Birth	1887	County Recorder

■ Mineral 10 Feb. 1911
P.O. Box 1450, Hawthorne, NV 89415
Phone: (775)945-2446
Web site: www.rootsweb.com/~nvminera/mineral.htm
Parent County: Esmeralda
Comments/research tips: County Clerk has (some earlier) Divorce, Probate, and Court records before 1911, and Naturalization records 1911–1956.

Record Type	Year Begun	Jurisdiction
Land	1911	County Treasurer
Probate	1911	County Clerk
Court	1911	County Clerk
Birth	1911	County Clerk
Death	1911	County Clerk
Marriage	1911	County Clerk

■ Nye 16 Feb. 1864
101 Radar Rd., P.O. Box 1031, Tonopah, NV 89049
Phone: (775)482-8127

Nevada

Web site: www.rootsweb.com/~nvnye/
Parent County: Esmeralda

Record Type	Year Begun	Jurisdiction
Death	1887	County Clerk
Marriage	1864	County Clerk
Land	1864	County Recorder
Probate	1865	County Clerk
Court	1864	County Clerk
Birth	1887	County Clerk

■ Ormsby 25 Nov. 1861
Parent County: Original county
Comments/research tips: Consolidated with Carson City 1969 and discontinued.

■ Pahute 1864
Parent County: Arizona Territory
Comments/research tips: Abolished 1871, became part of Lincoln County, now Clark. (See Lincoln County, now Clark)

■ Pershing 18 Mar. 1919
P.O. Box 820, Lovelock, NV 89419
Phone: (775)273-2208
Web site: www.rootsweb.com/~nvpershi/
Parent County: Humboldt

Record Type	Year Begun	Jurisdiction
Death	1919	County Clerk
Marriage	1919	County Clerk
Probate	1919	County Clerk
Court	1919	County Clerk
Birth	1919	County Clerk
Land	1919	County Clerk

■ Roop 1860
Comments/research tips: (See Washoe) Discontinued after a boundary dispute with California. Territory absorbed by Plumas County, California, and Washoe County.

■ St. Mary's 1856
Parent County: Original county
Comments/research tips: Organized as a county in Utah

Territory. Discontinued 2 March 1861 when Nevada Territory was created.

■ Storey 25 Nov. 1861
P.O. Box D, Virginia City, NV 89440
Phone: (755)847-0969
Web site: www.rootsweb.com/~nvstorey/
Parent County: Original county

Record Type	Year Begun	Jurisdiction
Birth	1887	County Recorder
Marriage	1874	County Recorder
Land	1876	County Recorder
Probate	1886	County Clerk
Court	1861	County Clerk
Death	1887	County Recorder

■ Washoe 25 Nov. 1861
75 Court St., P.O. Box 11130, Reno, NV 89520
Phone: (775)328-3260
Web site: www.rootsweb.com/~nvwashoe/
Parent County: Original county

Record Type	Year Begun	Jurisdiction
Birth	1887	Dept./Health
Marriage	1861	County Recorder
Death	1887	Dept./Health
Land	1870	County Recorder
Probate	1870	County Clerk
Court	1870	County Clerk

■ White Pine 2 Mar. 1869
801 Clark St., Ely, NV 89301
Phone: (775)289-2341
Web site: www.rootsweb.com/~nvwhitep/
Parent County: Millard, Utah Territory

Record Type	Year Begun	Jurisdiction
Marriage	1869	County Clerk
Land	1885	County Recorder
Probate	1885	County Clerk
Court	1885	County Clerk
Birth	1887	County Clerk
Death	1887	County Clerk

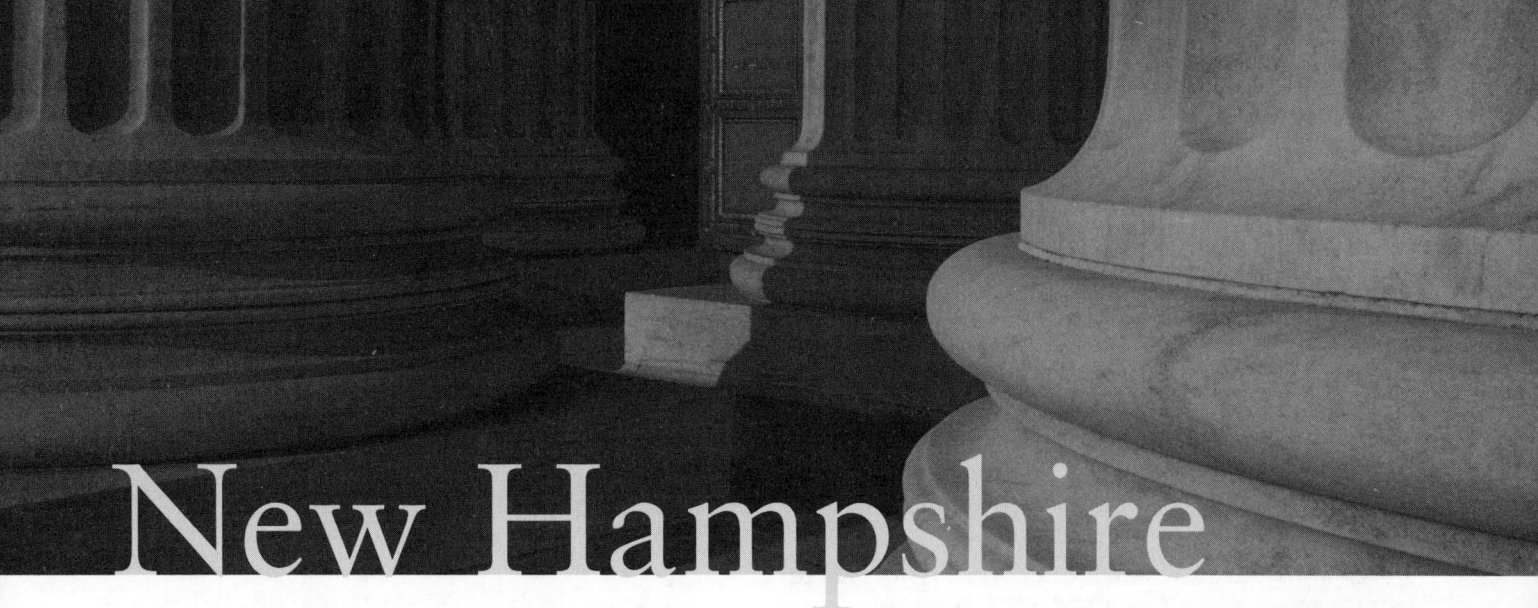

New Hampshire

By Maureen Taylor

HISTORICAL OVERVIEW

Four towns founded by migrants from Essex County, Massachusetts—Portsmouth, Dover, Exeter, and Hampton—clustered near the New Hampshire shoreline. Massachusetts governed the area from 1642–1679 and again during 1690–1692, even though the area became a royal province in 1679. New Hampshire's border disputes with adjacent states weren't settled until the mid-eighteenth century, when present-day New Hampshire's boundaries were established.

More than 18,000 men from New Hampshire joined forces to fight the British in the American Revolution. Shortly thereafter, in 1781, thirty-six towns declared themselves part of Vermont, not New Hampshire, but the rift was temporary. New Hampshire ratified the Constitution in 1788 to become the ninth state.

In the seventeenth century residents settled in the area to fish, farm, and trade furs, with Portsmouth being the center of trade, shipbuilding, and logging. Textile manufacturing became a major industry in the nineteenth and early twentieth century with Amoskeag Manufacturing Co. of Manchester. European immigrants came to New Hampshire from many countries, including England, France, Germany, Greece, Ireland, Poland, Russia, Scotland, and Sweden to work in the fabric and shoe industries, as did laborers from French Canada. During the twentieth century, World War I and II kept these factories and the Portsmouth Navy Yard busy producing goods for the war effort.

RECORD HIGHLIGHTS

Like Massachusetts', Connecticut's, and Rhode Island's, New Hampshire's records date from the early colonial period. Town and city clerks kept track of vital records, but coverage is spotty. An every name index to early vital

NEW HAMPSHIRE AT A GLANCE

Motto: Live Free or Die
Population: 1.24 million
Prevalent Religions: Christianity, particularly Roman Catholic, followed by Baptist, Methodist, and Episcopalian (smaller portions of Lutheran, Presbyterian, Pentecostal), also Judaism and Buddhism
Major Industries: Dairy products, electrical equipment, rubber and plastic products, tourism nursery stock, cattle, apples, eggs, machinery
Ethnic Makeup (in percent): Caucasian 96%, African American 0.7%, Hispanic 1.7%, Asian 1.3%, Native American 0.2%, Other 0.6%
Famous New Hampshirians: Bill Bryson, Salmon P. Chase, Robert Frost, Horace Greeley, Sarah Josepha Hale, John Irving, Franklin Pierce, Adam Sandler, Alan Shepard, John Stark, Steven Tyler (Aerosmith), Daniel Webster

Above: One of New Hampshire's many tiny, steepled churches

New Hampshire

records exists, but doesn't include seventeen towns. Microfilm copies can be found at the New Hampshire State Library, the New England Historic Genealogical Society in Boston, and through the Church of Jesus Christ of Latter-day Saints <www.familysearch.org>.

Civil Registration in 1866 required cities and towns to send copies of their birth and death records to the state, but total compliance didn't occur until 1905 with the establishment of the Bureau of Vital Records. Originals remain in most town and city halls. Births prior to 1901 and marriages, divorces, and deaths before 1949 are open to the public.

Colonial resources include provincial tax lists for 1732, 1744, 1767, and 1776. With the exception of 1732, they all appear in the forty volume *Documents and Records Relating to New Hampshire, 1623–1800* (1867–1943), known as the *New Hampshire State Papers*. The State Papers are a good resource for lists of Revolutionary War soldiers and probate documents prior to statehood.

Land records provide clues to early families, but recording was inconsistent and didn't always occur at the time of the transaction. Deeds prior to 1771 are indexed and available. After the establishment of counties in 1769, land records reside in the registrar's office of each county. Some land transactions appear in probate records (also kept in the county seat), especially if the transfer occurred between family members.

The New Hampshire State Archives has extensive military papers, including a Revolutionary War Index, an index for the War of 1812, and Civil War enlistment cards and pension records.

Town histories are in print for most communities and often include genealogies of founding families. The largest collection of these is at the New Hampshire Historical Society's Tuck Library <www.nhhistory.org>.

New Hampshire resources are plentiful, so preparing for your research trip beforehand will help you identify the appropriate facility to visit. Researchers with families in the southern part of the state will find a greater variety of records to search than those in the north. However, the relatively small size of the state makes it easy to visit multiple facilities, wherever you need to conduct research.

The state capital, Concord, is the center for New Hampshire research. Three major repositories are there—The New Hampshire Historical Society's Tuck Library, The New Hampshire State Library, and the New Hampshire Division of Records Management and Archives. Each one contains pieces of New Hampshire's history.

At the New Hampshire Historical Society, discover town reports, unpublished genealogies, city directories, newspapers, letters, diaries, and papers for a wide variety of the state's residents. While the Society also has a collection of manuscripts for many New Hampshire churches,

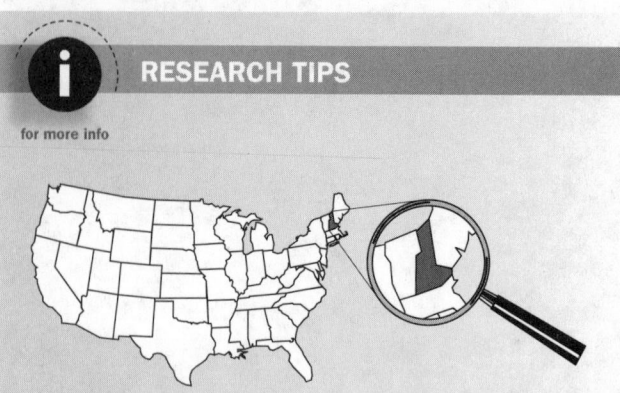

RESEARCH TIPS

for more info

- Start your New Hampshire research in Concord, the state capitol—it's home to The New Hampshire Historical Society's Tuck Library, The New Hampshire State Library, and the New Hampshire Division of Records Management and Archives.
- Town reports, unpublished genealogies, city directories, letters, diaries, and some church manuscripts can be found at the New Hampshire Historical Society <nhhistory.library.net>.
- The New England Historic Genealogical Society <www.newenglandancestors.org> has material on New Hampshire families collected by prominent genealogists, as well as some town documents and cemetery transcriptions.
- www.negenealogy.com

Census Records
- Federal Census: 1790, 1800, 1810, 1820, 1830, 1840, 1850, 1860, 1870, 1880, 1900, 1910, 1920, 1930
- Veterans Schedules: 1840, 1890
- Mortality Schedules: 1850, 1860, 1870, 1880
- Colonial Census: 1732, 1742, 1776

it only represents a small number of congregations. Papers for the rest might be at the church itself, in the hands of descendants of the ministers, or in libraries or historical societies. Unfortunately, many are missing. Search their online catalog for resources relevant to your research <nhhistory.library.net>.

Fill in gaps in the vital records by consulting probate and land records on the county level. Probate records on the county level offer additional genealogical clues for some families by listing children and wives. Individuals with ancestors in southern New Hampshire and Northern Massachusetts have to look at land and other records on both sides of the border for families in the area prior to boundary decisions.

Original court records can be found at the New Hampshire Division of Records Management and Archives.

Provincial records from the period before 1771 are organized and indexed. Some appear in the *New Hampshire State Papers*. County court records are not indexed and difficult to use. These records are an underutilized resource.

Also at the New Hampshire Division of Records Management and Archives are legislative petitions beginning in the seventeenth century. They contain a miscellaneous assortment of material, including petitions for release from prison, divorces, and name changes. Organized by year, they are currently being indexed by Archives staff. Approximately 20 percent of them appear in the *New Hampshire State Papers*.

Not all New Hampshire material is located instate. The New England Historic Genealogical Society's manuscript department contains material on New Hampshire families collected by prominent genealogists, as well as some town documents and cemetery transcriptions. Their website <www.newenglandancestors.org> features databases and a research column on the state.

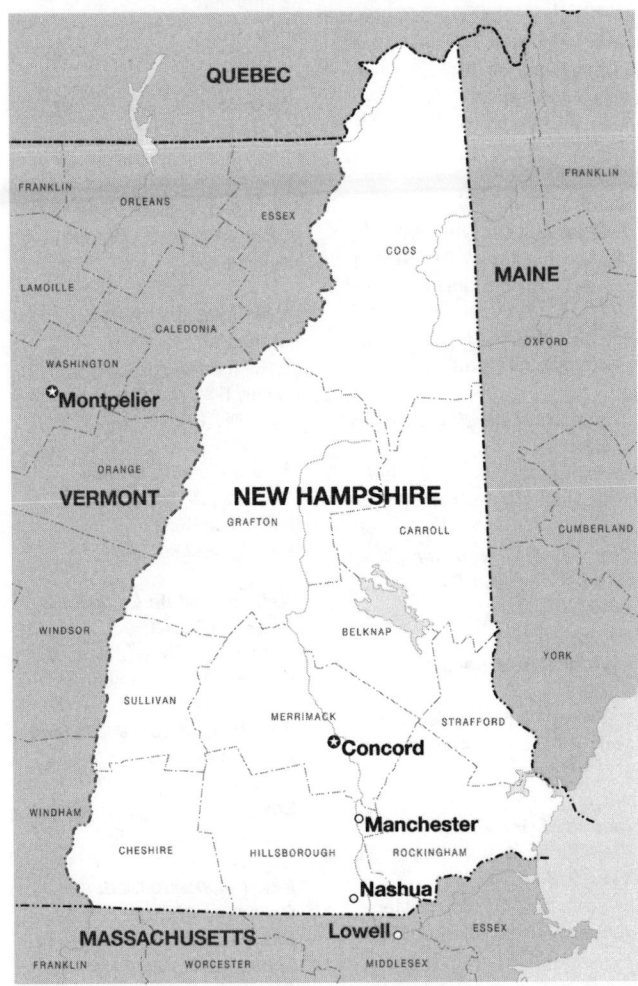

STATE RESOURCES

■ ARCHIVES, LIBRARIES, AND SOCIETIES

Acadian Genealogical and Historical Association
P.O. Box 668, Manchester, NH 03105

American Baptist Churches of Vermont and New Hampshire
P.O. Box 1206, Lebanon, NH 03766
Tel: (603) 643-4201
Web site: <www.abcvnh.org>

American-Canadian Genealogical Society
P.O. Box 6478, Manchester, NH 03108-6478
E-mail: ACGS@acgs.org
Web site: <www.acgs.org>

Baker Memorial Library, Dartmouth College
Hanover, NH 03755
Tel: (603) 646-1110
Web site: <www.dartmouth.edu>

Berlin & Coos County Historical Society
P.O. Box 52, Berlin, NH 03570
Tel: (603) 752-4590

Bureau of Vital Records, Health and Welfare Building
29 Hazen Dr., Concord, NH 03301-6508
Web site: <http://vitalrec.com/nh.html>

Conway Historical Society
100 Main St., P.O. Box 1949, Conway, NH 03818
Tel: (603) 447-5551
E-mail: info@conwayhistory.org
Web site: <www.conwayhistory.org>

Dover Public Library
73 Locust St., Dover, NH 03820
Tel: (603) 516-6050
Web site: <www.dover.lib.nh.us>

Exeter Public Library
1 Founders Park, Exeter, NH 03833
Tel: (603) 772-3101
E-mail: pnd@exeterpl.org
Web site: <www.exeterpl.org>

Hancock Historical Society
P.O. Box 138, 7 Main St., Hancock, NH 03449
Tel: (603) 525-9379
E-mail: hancockhistsoc@webryders.net

Web site: <www.mv.com/ipusers/hancocknh/hhs/home.htm>

Historical Society of Cheshire County
P.O. Box 803, 246 Main St., Keene, NH 03431
Tel: (603) 352-1895
E-mail: hscc@hsccnh.org
Web site: <www.hsccnh.org>

Hollis Historical Society
P.O. Box 754, Hollis, NH 03079
Web site: <www.hollis-history.org>

Manchester City Library
405 Pine St., Manchester, NH 03104
Tel: (603) 624-6550
Web site: <www.manchesternh.gov/CityGov/LIB/Home.html>

Merrimack Historical Society
520 Boston Post Rd., Merrimack, NH 03054
Tel: (603) 880-4343
E-mail: mmkhistsoc@adelphia.net
Web site: <www.mmkhistsoc.org>

Merrimack Society of Genealogists
P.O. Box 1035, Concord, NH 03302

National Archives and Record Administration (NARA) Northeast Region (Boston)
Frederick C. Murphy Federal Center, 380 Trapelo Rd., Waltham, MA 02452-6399
Tel: (781) 663-0127
Web site: <www.archives.gov/facilities/ma/boston.html>

New Hampshire Division of Archives and Records Management
71 S. Fruit St., Concord, NH 03301
Tel: (603) 271-2236
Web site: <www.sos.nh.gov/archives/>

New Hampshire Historical Society, NHHS Tuck Library
30 Park St., Concord, NH 03301-6384
Tel: (603) 228-6688
Web site: <www.nhhistory.org/>

New Hampshire Old Graveyard Association
P.O. Box 1016, Goshen, NH 03752
Web site: <www.rootsweb.com/~nhoga/>

New Hampshire

New Hampshire

New Hampshire Society of Genealogists
P.O. Box 2316, Concord, NH 03302-2316
Web site: <www.nhsog.org>

New Hampshire State Library
20 Park St., Concord, NH 03301
Tel: (603) 271-2144
Web site: <www.state.nh.us/nhsl/>

Northwood Historical Society
P.O. Box 114, Northwood, NH 03261-0114
Web site: <www.rootsweb.com/~nhnhs/>

Portsmouth Athenaeum
6-8 Market Sq., Third Floor, Portsmouth, NH 03801
Tel: (603) 431-2538
Web site: <www.tfaoi.com/newsmu/nmus108.htm>

Rindge Historical Society
47 School St., Rindge, NH 03461
Web site: <www.town.rindge.nh.us/Public_Documents/Rindge NH_Historical/index>

Roman Catholic Diocese of Manchester
153 Ash St., P.O. Box 310, Manchester, NH 03105
Tel: (603) 669-3100
Web site:

University of New Hampshire Library
18 Library Way, Durham, NH 03824-3592
Tel: (603) 862-1535
Web site:

BIBLIOGRAPHY

■ GENERAL RESOURCES

The Baptists of New Hampshire
by William Hurlin (Manchester, NH: Printed by the John B. Clarke Company, 1902)

Bent's Bibliography of the White Mountains
by Allen H. Bent, edited by E.J. Hanrahan (Somersworth, NH: New Hampshire Pub. Co., 1971)

Biographical Sketches of Representative Citizens of the State of New Hampshire
(Boston, MA: New England Historical Pub., 1902)

Check List of New Hampshire History
by Otis Grant Hammond, edited by E.J. Hanrahan (Somersworth, NH: New Hampshire Pub. Co., 1971)

Descriptive Inventory of the New Hampshire Collection
by Randall C. Carpenter (Salt Lake City, UT: University of Utah Press, 1983)

Directory of Repositories of Family History in New Hampshire
by Scott E. Green (Baltimore: Clearfield Company, 1993)

The First Laws of the State of New Hampshire
(Wilmington, DE: Michael Glazier, Inc., 1981)

Gathered Sketches From the Early History of New Hampshire and Vermont: Containing Vivid and Interesting Accounts of a Great Variety of the Adventures of our Forefathers, and of Other Incidents of Olden Time, Original and Selected
edited by Francis Chase (Bowie, MD: Heritage Books, ca. 1987)

Genealogical Dictionary of Maine and New Hampshire
by Sybil Noyes, Charles T. Libby, and Walter Goodwin Davis (Baltimore, MD: Genealogical Pub. Co., 1983)

Genealogical and Family History of the State of New Hampshire: A Record of the Achievements of Her People in the Making of a Commonwealth and the Founding of a Nation, 4 vols.
by Ezra S. Stearns, William F. Whitcher, and Edward Everett Parker (New York: Lewis Publishing Co., 1908)

Genealogical Research in New England
edited by Ralph J. Crandall (Baltimore, MD: Genealogical Pub. Co., 1984)

The Genealogist's Companion and Sourcebook, 2d ed.
by Emily Anne Croom (Cincinnati: Betterway Books, 2003)

A Genealogist's Guide to Discovering Your African-American Ancestors
by Franklin Carter Smith and Emily Anne Croom (Cincinnati: Betterway Books, 2003)

God, Grace, and Granite: The History of Methodism in New Hampshire, 1768–1988
by Charles W. Kern (Canaan, NH: Published for the New Hampshire United Methodist Conference by Phoenix Pub., 1988)

Guide to Church Vital Statistics Records in New Hampshire
by the Historical Records Survey (Manchester, NH: The Survey, 1942)

Guide to Depositories of Manuscript Collections in the United States, New Hampshire
by the Historical Records Survey (Manchester, NH: The Survey, 1940)

Guide to Early Documents (ca. 1680–ca. 1900) at the New Hampshire Records Management and Archives Center
by the New Hampshire Department of State, Division of Records Management and Archives; compiled by Frank C. Mevers (Concord, NH: Division of Records Management and Archives, 1981)

Guide to Genealogical Research in the National Archives of the United States
edited by Anne Bruner Eales and Robert M. Kvasnicka (Washington, DC: National Archives and Records Administration, 2000)

The Heart of the White Mountains
by Samuel Adams Drake (New York: Harper & Brothers, 1882)

The History of New Hampshire
by Jeremy Belknap (New York: Arno Press, 1972)

History of New Hampshire, 4 vols.
by Everett S. Stackpole (New York: American Historical Society, 1916)

History of New Hampshire, From its First Discovery to the Year 1830;
by Edwin David Sanborn (Manchester, NH: J.B. Clarke, 1875)

Index to Genealogies in New Hampshire Town Histories
by William Copeley (Concord, NH: New Hampshire Historical Society, ca. 1988)

Inhabitants of New Hampshire, 1776
by Emily S. Wilson (Baltimore, MD: Genealogical Pub., 1993)

Inventory of the Church Archives of New Hampshire, Protestant Episcopal Diocese of New Hampshire
by the Historical Records Survey (Manchester, NH: The Survey, 1942)

Inventory of the Roman Catholic Church Records in New Hampshire
by the Historical Records Survey (Manchester, NH: Diocese of Manchester, 1938)

National Archives Microfilm Catalogs online:
<www.archives.gov/publications/genealogy_microfilm_catalogs.html>

The Native Ministry of New Hampshire
by Rev. N.F. Carter (Concord, NH: Rumford Printing Co., 1906)

New Hampshire, a Bibliography of Its History
prepared by the Committee for a New England Bibliography, edited by John D. Haskell Jr., and T.D. Seymour Bassett (Boston: G.K. Hall, 1979)

New Hampshire Family Histories
by Rich Rollock (Laconia, NH: Family Histories Directory; Concord, NH: Capital Copy, 1993)

New Hampshire Family Records, 2 vols.
by William Copeley (Bowie, MD: Heritage Books, 1994)

New Hampshire Genealogical Digest, 1623–1900
by Glenn C. Towle (Bowie, MD: Heritage Books, 1986–)

New Hampshire Genealogical Research Guide
by Laird C. Towle and Ann N. Brown (Bowie, MD: Heritage Books, 1983)

New Hampshire Men: A Collection of Biographical Sketches, With Portraits, of Sons and Residents of the State who Have Become Known in Commercial, Professional, and Political Life
compiled and edited by George H. Moses (Concord, NH: The New

Hampshire Publishing Company, 1893)

New Hampshire Name Changes, 1768–1923
by Richard P. Roberts (Bowie, MD: Heritage Books, Inc., 1996)

New Hampshire Research Outline
by the Church of Jesus Christ of Latter-day Saints, Family History Library (Salt Lake City, UT: Corp. of the President of the Church of Jesus Christ of L.D.S., 1988)

New Hampshire Women: A Collection of Portraits and Biographical Sketches of Daughters and Residents of the Granite State, who are Worthy Representatives of Their Sex in the Various Walks and Conditions of Life
by Henry Harrison Metcalf (Concord, NH: The New Hampshire Publishing Co., 1895)

The Pastors of New Hampshire, Congregational and Presbyterian
by Henry Allen Hazen (Bristol, NH: Printed by R.W. Musgrove, 1878)

The Pioneers of Maine and New Hampshire, 1623 to 1660
by Charles Henry Pope (Baltimore, MD: Genealogical Pub. Co., 1965)

The Records of American Baptists in New Hampshire and Related Organizations
by the American Baptist Historical Society and Susan M. Eltscher (Rochester, NY: American Baptist Historical Society, 1981)

State Builders; an Illustrated Historical and Biographical Record of the State of New Hampshire at the Beginning of the Twentieth Century
edited by George Franklyn Willey (Manchester, NH: The New Hampshire Publishing Corporation, 1903)

The Statistics and Gazetteer of New Hampshire Containing Descriptions of all the Counties, Towns, and Villages . . . Statistical Tables . . . With a List of State Officers, etc.
compiled by Alonzo J. Fogg (Concord, NH: D.L. Guernsey, 1874)

They Paved the Way: A History of New Hampshire Women
by Olive Tardiff (Exeter, NH: Women for Women Weekly Publishing, 1980)

The Yankee Pioneers: A Saga of Courage
by Samuel B. Pettengill (Hanover, NH: Regional Center for Educational Training, 1977)

■ CENSUS RECORDS

The American Census Handbook
by Thomas Jay Kemp (Wilmington, DE: Scholarly Resources, 2001)

The Census Book: A Genealogist's Guide to Federal Census Facts, Schedules and Indexes
by William Dollarhide (Bountiful, UT: Heritage Quest, 2000)

Finding Answers in U.S. Census Records
by Loretto Dennis Szucs and Matthew Wright (Orem, UT: Ancestry Publishing, 2002)

Map Guide to the U.S. Federal Censuses, 1790–1920
by William Thorndale and William Dollarhide (Baltimore, MD: Genealogical Pub. Co., 1987)

New Hampshire 1732 Census
by Jay Mack Holbrook (Oxford, MA: Holbrook Research Institute, 1981)

New Hampshire 1776 Census
by Jay Mack Holbrook (Oxford, MA: Holbrook Research Institute, 1976)

New Hampshire Residents, 633–1699
by Jay Mack Holbrook (Oxford, MA: Holbrook Research Institute, 1979)

State Census Records
by Ann S. Lainhart (Baltimore, MD: Genealogical Publishing, 1992)

Your Guide to the Federal Census
by Kathleen W. Hinckley (Cincinnati: Betterway Books, 2002)

■ IMMIGRATION RECORDS

American Naturalization Records, 1790–1990: What They Are and How to Use Them
by John J. Newman (North Salt Lake, UT: HeritageQuest, 1998)

American Passenger Arrival Records
by Michael Tepper (Baltimore: Genealogical Publishing Co., 1993)

Immigrants to New England, 1700–1775
by Ethel Bolton (Baltimore, MD: Genealogical Pub. Co., 1966)

They Became Americans: Finding Naturalization Records and Ethnic Origins
by Loretto Dennis Szucs (Salt Lake City: Ancestry, Inc., 1998)

They Came in Ships: A Guide to Finding Your Immigrant Ancestor's Arrival Records, 2d ed.
by John P. Colletta (Salt Lake City: Ancestry, Inc., 1993)

■ LAND RECORDS

Land & Property Research in the United States
by Wade E. Hone (Salt Lake City, UT: Ancestry, 1997)

Locating Your Roots: Discover Your Ancestors Using Land Records
by Patricia Law Hatcher (Cincinnati: Betterway Books, 2003)

■ MAPS

Atlas of Historical County Boundaries. New Hampshire, Vermont
edited by John H. Long, compiled by Gordon DenBoer and George E. Goodridge Jr. (New York: Simon & Schuster, 1993)

Communities, Settlements, and Neighborhood Centers in the State of New Hampshire: An Inventory
by the New Hampshire State Planning and Development Commission (Concord, NH: The Commission, 1937)

A Gazetteer of the State of New Hampshire
by John Farmer and Jacob B. Moore (Bowie, MD: Heritage Books, Inc., 1997)

New Hampshire as it is
compiled by Edwin A. Charlton (Claremont, NH: Tracy and Sanford, 1855)

The New Hampshire Atlas and Gazetteer
by the DeLorme Mapping Company (Freeport, ME: DeLorme Mapping Company, 1987)

New Hampshire Maps to 1900: An Annotated Checklist
by David A. Cobb (Hanover, NH: New Hampshire Historical Society: Distributed by University Press of New England, 1981)

New Hampshire Town Names and Whence They Came
by Elmer Munson Hunt (Peterborough, NH: Noone House, 1971)

The Place Names of the White Mountains: History and Origins
by Robert and Mary Hixon (Camden, ME: Down East Books, 1980)

The Postal History of New Hampshire: The Post Offices and First Postmasters From 1775 to 1985
by Chester M. Smith Jr. and John L. Kay (Lake Grove, OR: Depot, 1986)

Town and City Atlas of the State of New Hampshire
(Boston: D.H. Hurd Company, 1892)

■ MILITARY RECORDS

Military History of New Hampshire, From its Settlement, in 1623, to the Year 1861
by Chandler Eastman Potter (Concord, NH: 1868)

New Hampshire in the Great Rebellion. Containing Histories of the Several New Hampshire Regiments, and a Biographical Notices of Many of the Prominent Actors in the Civil War of 1861–65.
by Otis F.R. Waite (Claremont, NH: Tracy, Chase & Co., 1870)

New Hampshire's Role in the American Revolution, 1763–1789: A Bibliography
by the New Hampshire American Revolution Bicentennial Commission (Concord, NH: The Commission, 1974)

Revised Register of the Soldiers and Sailors of New Hampshire in the War of the Rebellion, 1861–1866
by the New Hampshire Adjutant General's Office and Augustus D.

Ayling (Concord, NH: Ira C. Evans, 1895)

State of New Hampshire. Rolls of the Soldiers in the Revolutionary War, 4 vols.
by Isaac Weare Hammond (New York: AMS Press, 1973)

Uncle, We Are Ready! Registering America's Men, 1917–1918: A Guide to Researching World War I Draft Registration Cards
by John J. Newman (North Salt Lake, UT: HeritageQuest, 2001)

U.S. Military Records: A Guide to Federal & State Sources, Colonial America to the Present
by James C. Neagles (Salt Lake City: Ancestry, Inc., 1994)

World War II: A Family Historian's Guide
by Debra Johnson Knox (Spartanburg, SC: MIE Publishing, 2003)

■ PROBATE RECORDS

The Bench and Bar of New Hampshire, Including Biographical Notices of Deceased Judges of the Highest Court, and Lawyers of the Province and State, and a List of Names of Those Now Living
by Charles H. Bell (Boston, New York: Houghton, Mifflin and Company, 1894)

New Hampshire Provincial and State Papers, 40 vols.
(Concord, NH: George E. Jenks, 1867–1943)

Probate Records of the Province of New Hampshire . . ., 9 vols.
by Albert Stillman Batchellor (Concord, NH: Rumford Printing Co., 1907–41)

■ VITAL RECORDS

Bride's Index, 1640–1900
by the New Hampshire Division of Vital Statistics (SI: Division of Vital Statistics, ca. 1970)

Colonial Gravestone Inscriptions in the State of New Hampshire
compiled by Winifred Lane Goss (Baltimore, MD: Genealogical Pub. Co., 1974)

Guide to Church Vital Statistics Records in New Hampshire
by the New Hampshire Historical Records Survey (Manchester, NH: The Survey, 1942)

New Hampshire Marriage Licenses and Intentions, 1709–1961
by Pauline Johnson Oesterlin (Bowie, MD: Heritage Books, 1991)

Northern New Hampshire Graveyards and Cemeteries: Transcriptions and Indexes of Burial Sites in the Towns of Clarksville, Colebrook, Columbia, Dixville, Pittsburg, Stewartstown, and Stratford
by Nancy L. Dodge (Salem, MA: Higginson Books, 1985)

Your Guide to Cemetery Research
by Sharon DeBartolo Carmack (Cincinnati: Betterway Books, 2002)

■ Belknap   22 Dec. 1840
64 Court St., Laconia, NH 03246
Phone: (603)524-3570
Web site: www.belknapcounty.org/
Parent County: Strafford, Merrimac
Comments/research tips: Towns organized before 1800: Alton 1796, Barnstead 1727, Centre Harbor 1797, Gilmanton 1727, Meredith 1768, New Hampton 1777, Sanbornton 1770.

Record Type	Year Begun	Jurisdiction
Probate	1841	Probate Court
Nat.	1842	County Courthouse
Land	1841	Registrar/Deeds
Court	1841	Clerk/Superior Ct.
Birth	na	Town/City Clerks
Marriage	na	Town/City Clerks
Death	na	Town/City Clerks
Divorce	1808	Bur./Vital Rec.

■ Carroll   22 Dec. 1840
Rt. 171, Ossipee, NH 03864
Phone: (603)539-7751
Web site: www.rootsweb.com/~nhcarrol/
Parent County: Strafford
Comments/research tips: Towns organized before 1800: Albany 1766, Brookfield 1794, Chatham 1767, Conway 1765, Eaton 1766, Effingham 1778, Moultonborough 1777, Ossipee 1785, Sandwich 1763, Tamworth 1766, Tuftonboro 1795, Wakefield 1774, Wolfeborough 1770.

Record Type	Year Begun	Jurisdiction
Probate	1840	Probate Court
Court	1861	County Courthouse
Nat.	1871	County Courthouse
Land	1841	Registrar/Deeds
Birth	na	Town/City Clerks
Marriage	na	Town/City Clerks
Death	na	Town/City Clerks
Divorce	1808	Bur./Vital Rec.

■ Cheshire   29 Apr. 1769
12 Court St., Keene, NH 03431
Phone: (603)352-6902
Web site: www.co.cheshire.nh.us/
Parent County: Original County
Comments/research tips: Towns organized before 1800: Alstead 1763, Chesterfield 1752, Dublin 1771, Fitzwilliam 1773, Gilsum 1787, Hinsdale 1753, Jaffrey 1773, Keene 1753, Marlborough 1776, Marlow 1761, Nelson 1774, Richmond 1752, Rindge 1768, Stoddard 1774, Sullivan 1787, Surry 1769, Swanzey 1753, Walpole 1752, Winchester 1753.

Record Type	Year Begun	Jurisdiction
Probate	1769	Probate Court
Wills	1771	Probate Court
Court	1771	County Courthouse
Nat.	1860	County Courthouse
Land	1770	Registrar/Deeds
Birth	na	Town/City Clerks
Marriage	na	Town/City Clerks

Death...................... na ....Town/City Clerks
Divorce .... 1808 ....Bur./Vital Rec.

■ Coos 24 Dec. 1803
P.O. Box 309, Lancaster, NH 03584
Phone: (603)788-4900
Web site: http://freepages.genealogy.rootsweb.com/
~dickmarston/Coos.html
Parent County: Grafton
Comments/research tips: Towns organized before 1800:
Bartlett 1790, Cambridge 1773, Colebrook 1790, Columbia
1797, Dalton 1784, Dummer 1773, Jefferson 1796,
Kilkenny 1774, Lancaster 1763, Millsfield 1774,
Northumberland 1779, Stratford 1773, Stewartstown 1799,
Success 1773, Whitefield 1774.

Record Type	Year Begun	Jurisdiction
Court	1886	County Courthouse
Probate	1885	Probate Court
Land	1772	Registrar/Deeds
Birth	na	Town/City Clerks
Marriage	na	Town/City Clerks
Death	na	Town/City Clerks
Nat.	1888	County Courthouse
Divorce	1808	Bur./Vital Rec.

■ Grafton 29 Apr. 1769
RR 1 Box 67, North Haverhill, NH 03774
Phone: (603)787-6941
Web site: www.geocities.com/Yosemite/2821/grafton.htm
Parent County: Original County
Comments/research tips: Towns organized before 1800:
Alexandria 1782, Bath 1761, Benton 1764, Bethlehem
1799, Bridgewater 1788, Campton 1761, Canaan 1761,
Danbury 1795, Dorchester 1761, Enfield 1761, Franconia
1764, Grafton 1778, Groton 1796, Hanover 1761,
Haverhill 1763, Hebron 1792, Hill 1778, Holderness 1761,
Landaff 1764, Lebanon 1761, Lisbon 1768, Lincoln 1764,
Littleton 1784, Lyman 1761, Lyme 1761, Orange 1780,
Orford 1761, Plymouth 1763, Rumney 1761, Thornton
1781, Warren 1763, Wentworth 1766, Woodstock 1784.

Record Type	Year Begun	Jurisdiction
Probate	1773	Probate Court
Court	1773	County Courthouse
Nat.	1840	County Courthouse
Land	1773	Registrar/Deeds
Divorce	1773	State Archives
Birth	na	Town/City Clerks
Marriage	na	Town/City Clerks
Death	na	Town/City Clerks

■ Hillsborough 29 Apr. 1769
19 Temple St., Nashua, NH 03060
Phone: (603)882-9471
Web site: www.hillsboroughcountynh.org/
Parent County: Original County
Comments/research tips: State Archives has Divorce records
1783–ca. 1836. Towns organized before 1800: Amherst
1760, Antrim 1777, Bedford 1750, Brookline 1789, Deering
1774, Francestown 1772, Goffstown 1761, Greenfield

1791, Hancock 1779, Hillsborough 1772, Hollis 1746,
Hudson 1746, Litchfield 1749, Lyndeborough 1764,
Manchester 1751, Mason 1768, Merrimack 1746, Milford
1794, Nashua 1746, New Ipswich 1762, New Boston 1763,
Pelham 1746, Peterborough 1760, Sharon 1791, Temple
1768, Weare 1764, Wilton 1762, Windsor 1798.

Record Type	Year Begun	Jurisdiction
Probate	1771	Probate Court
Court	1772	County Courthouse
Nat.	1842	County Courthouse
Land	1771	Registrar/Deeds
Birth	na	Town/City Clerks
Marriage	na	Town/City Clerks
Death	na	Town/City Clerks

■ Merrimack 1 July 1823
163 N. Main St., Concord, NH 03301
Phone: (603)225-5501
Web site: www.ci.concord.nh.us/
Parent County: Rockingham, Hillsborough
Comments/research tips: State Archives has Divorce records
1824–1880. Towns organized before 1800: Andover 1779,
Bradford 1771, Bow 1727, Boscawen 1760, Canterbury
1727, Chichester 1727, Concord 1765, Dunbarton 1765,
Epsom 1727, Henniker 1768, Hopkinton 1765, Loudon
1773, New Bradford 1787, Newbury 1778, New London
1779, Northfield 1780, Pembroke 1759, Pittsfield 1782,
Salisbury 1768, Sutton 1784, Warner 1774.

Record Type	Year Begun	Jurisdiction
Probate	1823	Probate Court
Court	1840	County Courthouse
Nat.	1846	County Courthouse
Land	1823	Registrar/Deeds
Birth	na	Town/City Clerks
Marriage	na	Town/City Clerks
Death	na	Town/City Clerks
Burial	na	Town/City Clerks

■ Rockingham 29 Apr. 1769
99-119 North Rd., Brentwood, NH 03833
Phone: (603)679-2256
Web site: www.co.rockingham.nh.us/
Parent County: Original County
Comments/research tips: Towns organized before 1800:
Atkinson 1767, Brentwood 1742, Candia 1763, Chester
1722, Danville 1760, Deerfield 1766, East Kingston 1738,
Epping 1741, Exeter 1638, Gosport 1715, Greenland 1704,
Hampstead 1749, Hampton 1639, Hampton Falls 1723,
Kensington 1737, Kingston 1694, Londonderry 1722, New
Castle 1693, Newington 1764, Newmarket 1727, Newton
1749, North Hampton 1742, Northwood 1773,
Nottingham 1722, Plaistow 1749, Poplin 1764, Portsmouth
1653, Raymond 1764, Rye 1726, Salem 1750, Sandown
1756, Seabrook 1768, South Hampton 1742, Stratham
1716, Windham 1741.

Record Type	Year Begun	Jurisdiction
Probate	1771	Probate Court
Land	1770	Registrar/Deeds
Divorce	ca. 1920	State Archives

Nat. .... 1771 ....Clerk/Superior Ct.
Birth .... na ....Town/City Clerks
Marriage................. na ....Town/City Clerks
Death...................... na ....Town/City Clerks
Court .... 1772 ....Clerk/Common Pleas Ct.

■ **Strafford**   29 Apr. 1769
County Farm Rd., P.O. Box 799, Dover, NH 03820
Phone: (603)742-3065
Web site: www.usgennet.org/usa/nh/county/strafford/
Parent County: Original County
Comments/research tips: State Archives has Divorce records 1780–1859, 1870–1874. Towns organized before 1800: Barrington 1722, Dover 1623, Durham 1732, Farmington 1798, Lee 1766, Madbury 1755, Middleton 1778, New Durham 1762, Rochester 1722, Somersworth 1754.

Record Type	Year Begun	Jurisdiction
Probate	1773	Probate Court
Land	1773	Registrar/Deeds
Court	1773	County Courthouse
Birth	na	Town/City Clerks
Marriage	na	Town/City Clerks

Death...................... na ....Town/City Clerks
Nat. .... 1842 ....County Courthouse

■ **Sullivan**   5 July 1827
22 Main St., P.O. Box 45, Newport, NH 03773
Phone: (603)863-3450
Web site: www.usgennet.org/usa/nh/county/sullivan/
Parent County: Cheshire
Comments/research tips: State Archives has Divorce records 1828–1919. Towns organized before 1800: Acworth 1766, Charlestown 1753, Claremont 1764, Cornish 1763, Croydon 1763, Goshen 1791, Grantham 1761, Langdon 1787, Lempster 1761, Newport 1761, Plainfield 1761, Springfield 1794, Unity 1764, Washington 1776, Wendell 1781.

Record Type	Year Begun	Jurisdiction
Probate	1827	Probate Court
Land	1827	Registrar/Deeds
Court	1827	Clerk/Superior Ct.
Birth	na	Town/City Clerks
Marriage	na	Town/City Clerks
Death	na	Town/City Clerks
Nat.	1838	County Courthouse

New Hampshire

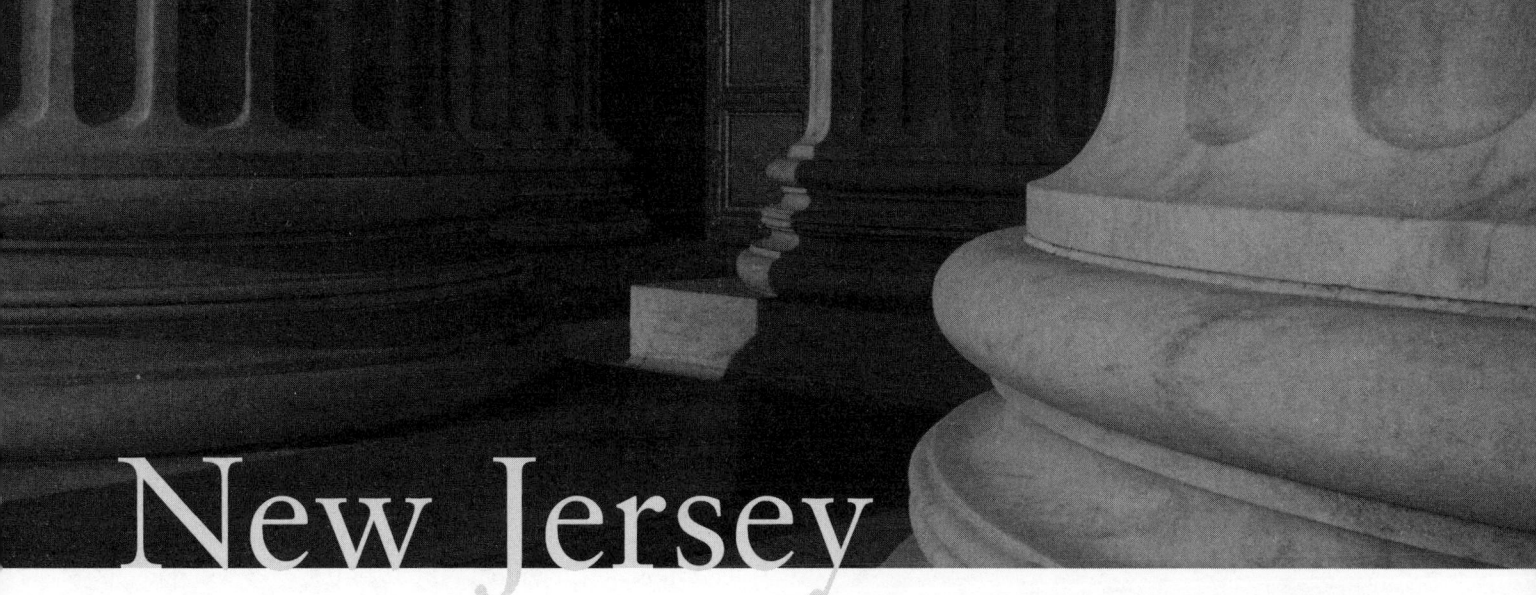

New Jersey

By Rhonda R. McClure

HISTORICAL OVERVIEW

Attempts by the Dutch to settle the area that became New Jersey can be traced to the early 1600s, but it wasn't until the Swedes and Finns settled along the Delaware River as part of New Sweden that things began to take hold. Some of the settlers living in New Netherland (what eventually became New York) gained control, and Dutch farmers began to move into New Jersey.

Official New Jersey history is generally accepted to have started in 1664, when the British conquered New Netherland and the land that was New Jersey was divided and granted to two proprieters—individuals who received land for a town or colony from the king or monarch. East Jersey went to Sir George Carteret and West Jersey was granted to Lord John Berkeley. Within a year, there was a major influx of settlers from New England and New York, specifically Long Island.

You will also find a number of Quakers in New Jersey. In fact, William Penn and some other early Quakers purchased the proprietorships from Berkeley and Carteret between 1672 and 1682.

RECORD HIGHLIGHTS

Mug books were popular late-nineteenth century publications, and New Jersey has many of them on the state and county levels. Mug books—so named because of the photos that accompanied the biographies of those who subscribed to the publication—should always be used with caution. Because people paid to be included in these books, the facts are sometimes suspiciously complete— with maiden names for all the females and complete dates of events. Mug books can be great places to begin when you are in need of clues, but remember, these books usually only include the well-respected and prosperous members of the state or community.

NEW JERSEY AT A GLANCE

Motto: Liberty and Prosperity

Population: 8.4 million

Prevalent Religions: Christianity, particularly Roman Catholic (some Baptist, Methodist, Lutheran, Presbyterian, Episcopalian)

Major Industries: Chemical products, food processing, electrical equipment, printing and publishing, tourism, nursery stock, horses, vegetables, fruits and nuts, seafood, dairy products

Ethnic Makeup (in percent): Caucasian 72.6%, African American 13.6%, Hispanic 13.3%, Asian 5.7%, Native American 0.2%, Other 5.4%

Famous New Jerseyans: Alan Alda, Judy Blume, Jon Bon Jovi, Stephen Crane, Olympia Dukakis, Allen Ginsberg, Whitney Houston, Jerry Lewis, Norman Mailer, Joe Pesci, Susan Sarandon, General Norman Schwarzkopf, Bruce Springsteen, John Travolta, Dionne Warwick, Phyllis Whitney, William Carlos Williams

Above: A boat on the beach near Atlantic City

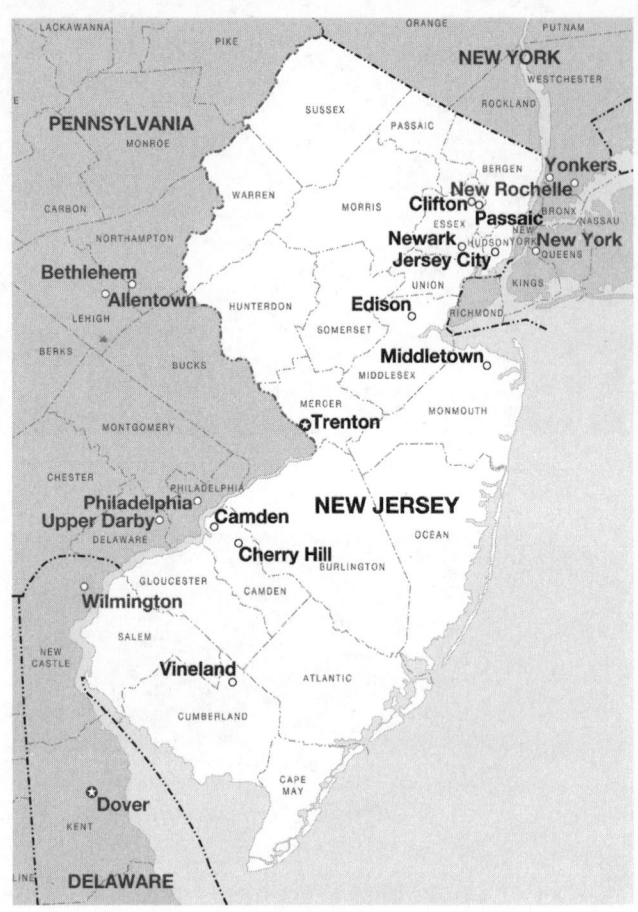

New Jersey took state census records decennially from 1855 to 1915, offering genealogists another census in between federal censuses. Like early federal census records, the 1855 and 1865 censuses only name the head of household, with all others enumerated by gender. In addition, the 1855, 1865, and 1875 censuses are not complete—some counties are missing in the 1855 and 1865 censuses, and enumerations of other counties are incomplete. The 1875 census only has two counties that survived, Sussex and Essex. The 1885, 1895, 1905, and 1915 have all of the counties available, and considering the destruction of the 1890 federal census, having the 1885 and 1895 state censuses—which list everyone in the household by name—is a blessing for researchers. The state census records are unindexed and the state archives' staff will not search then for you, but they are available on microfilm through the Family History Library.

Land records have not always been recorded in county courts. The land sales before 1785 were recorded in the capitals of East and West Jersey—Perth Amboy and Burlington, respectively. In 1795 these were transferred to Trenton, where you will want to look into the Secretary of State's Deeds. However, mortgages can be found in the county court records from 1766, and other deeds from 1785. Proprietary records, the first distribution of land by the proprietors, are handled differently. Some of them have been published, while others are available on microfilm or in transcriptions of the surveys. The records were kept separately by individual boards of proprietors for East and West Jersey.

Second only to Massachusetts, New Jersey required statewide registration of births and deaths beginning in 1848, though it wasn't until 1920 that the county clerks recorded them consistently. If you are searching for a birth or death record from 1848 to 1878, the death returns from 1 May 1848 to 31 May 1878 are on microfilm at the New Jersey State Archives, 225 West State Street, P.O. Box 307, Trenton, NJ 08625-0307, <www.state.nj.us/state/darm/links/archives.html>, as well as from the Family History Library. For those births that took place from 1878 to 1900, the state archives has microfilms of the original certificates as well as copies in registers. The Family History Library has only the registers. You can only get birth and death records for the years 1901 to 1940 from the state archives.

There are provincial marriages that were supposed to begin in 1673, though they are incomplete in the early years. Marriage licenses or the publishing of banns for three weeks were required from 1719 until 1795, when the marriage license requirement was eliminated. After 1795, marriage certificates were moved to the county courts of common pleas. Unfortunately, these records seldom mention parents' names, but the good news is that you can access the marriages from 1795 to 1900 on microfilm through the Family History Library and its branch Family History Centers.

STATE RESOURCES

■ ARCHIVES, LIBRARIES, AND SOCIETIES

Anglican Diocese of New Jersey
808 W. State St., Trenton, NJ 08618-5326
Tel: (609) 394-5281
Web site: <http://newjersey.anglican.org/>

Archibald S. Alexander Library, Rutgers, The State University of New Jersey
169 College Ave., New Brunswick, NJ 08901-1163
Tel: (732) 932-7851
Web site: <www.libraries.rutgers.edu/rul/libs/alex_lib/alex_lib.shtml>

Atlantic County Historical Society
P.O. Box 301, Somers Point, NJ 08244
Tel: (609) 927-5218
Web site: <www.aclink.org/achs>

Atlantic Highlands Historical Society
P.O. Box 108, Atlantic Highlands, NJ 07716
Web site: <www.atlantichighlandshistory.org>

Bergen County Historical Society
P.O. Box 55, River Edge, NJ 07661
Tel: (201) 343-9492
Web site: <www.bergencountyhistory.org>

The Boonton Historical Society & Museum
The John Taylor Building, 210 Main St., Boonton, NJ 07005
Tel: (973) 402-8840
Web site: <www.boonton.org/historical/>

Bureau of Vital Statistics, Department of Health and Senior Services
P.O. Box 360, Trenton, NJ 08625-0360
Web site: <www.state.nj.us/health/vital/vital.shtml>

Burlington County Historical Society
451 High St., Burlington City, NJ 08016-4514
Tel: (609) 386-4773
Web site: <http://08016.com/bchs.html>

Camden County Historical Society
P.O. Box 378, Collingswood, NJ 08108-0378
Tel: (856) 964-3333
E-mail: cchsnj@voicenet.com
Web site:

Central Jersey Genealogy Club
P.O. Box 9903, Hamilton, NJ 08650-1903
Web site: <www.rootsweb.com/~njcjgc/>

Cranford Historical Society
The Hanson House, 38 Springfield Ave., Cranford, NJ 07016
Tel: (908) 276-0489
Web site: <www.bobdevlin.com/crhissoc.html>

The Cumberland County Historical Society
P.O. Box 16, Greenwich, NJ 08323
Tel: (856) 455-4055
Web site:

Genealogical Society of Bergen County
P.O. Box 432, Midland Park, NJ 07432
Web site: <www.rootsweb.com/~njgsbc/>

The Genealogical Society of New Jersey
P.O. Box 1291, New Brunswick, NJ 08903
Web site:

Genealogical Society of Salem County
P.O. Box 231, Woodstown, NJ 08098
Web site: <www.rootsweb.com/~njsalem/gsscnj.html>

Genealogical Society of the West Fields
℅ Westfield Memorial Library, 550 E. Broad St., Westfield, NJ 07090-2116

Web site: <www.westfieldnj.com/gswf/>

Gloucester County Historical Society
17 Hunter St., Woodbury, NJ 08096-4605
Web site: <www.rootsweb.com/~njglouce/gchs/>

Greater Cape May Historical Society
P.O. Box 495, Cape May, NJ 08204
Tel: (609) 884-9100
Web site:

Highland Park Historical Society
P.O. Box 4255, Highland Park, NJ 08904-4255
Web site: <www.monmouth.com/~ricekolva/>

Historical Society of Moorestown
P.O. Box 477, Moorestown, NJ 08057
Tel: (856) 235-0353
E-mail: historic08057@hotmail.com
Web site: <www.moorestown.com/community/history/>

Howell Historical Society
427 Lakewood-Farmingdale Rd., Howell, NJ 07731-8723
Tel: (732) 938-2212
Web site: <www.howellnj.com/historic/>

Hunterdon County Historical Society
114 Main St., Flemington, NJ 08822
Tel: (908) 782-1091
Web site: <www.rootsweb.com/~njhunter/hchs.htm>

Jewish Genealogical Society of North Jersey
℅ YM-YWHA of Wayne, 1 Pike Dr., Wayne, NJ 07470
Tel: (973) 595-0100
Web site: <http://mysite.verizon.net/vze2gnpn/>

Jewish Historical Society of Central Jersey
228 Livingston Ave., New Brunswick, NJ 08901
Tel: (732) 249-4894
E-mail: jhscj@cs.com
Web site: <www.jewishgen.org/jhscj/>

RESEARCH TIPS

for more info

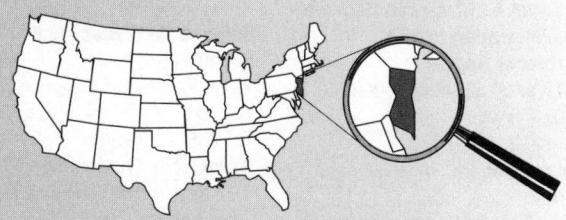

- Some of New Jersey's earliest records were lost as a result of the battles and troop movements through the state during the American Revolution.
- If your New Jersey ancestors just seem to up and appear there, check other New England states, as this was a natural migration route in the latter 1600s—especially to East Jersey.
- When New Englanders went to East Jersey, their record keeping practices came with them. Look for town records, in which you may find vital records and other entries with genealogical value.
- Some marriage records are hiding in the deed books. These are indexed in *Index of Names to Various Records in Various New Jersey Counties, 1600–1800s*, which is on six microfilm reels through the Family History Library.
- www.segenealogy.com

Census Records
- Federal Census: 1830, 1840, 1850, 1860, 1870, 1880, 1900, 1910, 1920, 1930
- Federal Mortality Schedules: 1850, 1860, 1870, 1880
- Union Veterans and Widows: 1890
- State/Territorial Census: 1855 (incomplete), 1865 (incomplete), 1875 (Essex and Sussex counties only), 1885, 1895, 1905, 1915

Jewish Historical Society of Metrowest
901 Route 10, Whippany, NJ 07981-1156
Tel: (973) 929-2995
Web site:

The Metuchen-Edison Historical Society
P.O. Box 61, Metuchen, NJ 08840-0061
Web site: <www.jhalpin.com/metuchen/met-ed98.htm>

Monmouth County Genealogy Society
P.O. Box 5, Lincroft, NJ 07738-0005
Web site: <www.rootsweb.com/~njmcgs/>

Monmouth County Historical Association
70 Court St., Freehold, NJ 07728
Web site: <www.monmouth.com/~mcha/>

New Jersey

Morris Area Genealogy Society
P.O. Box 105, Convent Station,
NJ 07961-0105
Web site: <www.rootsweb.com/
~njmags/>

**National Archives and Records
Administration (NARA),
Northeast Region**
201 Varick St., New York, NY
10014-4811
Tel: (212) 401-1620
E-mail: newyork.archives@nara
.gov
Web site: <www.archives.gov/fa
cilities/ny/new_york_city.html>

**Navy Lakehurst Historical
Society, Inc.**
P.O. Box 328, Lakehurst, NJ
08733-0328
Web site:

**The New Jersey Historical
Society**
52 Park Pl., Newark, NJ 07102
Tel: (973) 596-8500
Web site:
New Jersey State Archives
P.O. Box 307, Trenton, NJ
08625-0307
Tel: (609) 292-6260
E-mail: archives.reference@sos
.state.nj.us
Web site: <www.state.nj.us/st
ate/darm/links/archives.html>

New Jersey State Library
P.O. Box 520, Trenton, NJ
08625-0520
Tel: (609) 292-6220
Web site:

Newark Public Library
P.O. Box 630, Newark, NJ
07101-0630
Tel: (973) 733-7784
Web site: <www.npl.org>

**Ocean County Historical
Society**
P.O. Box 2191, Toms River, NJ
08754-2191
Tel: (732) 341-1880
E-mail: oceancounty.history@veri
zon.net
Web site: <www.oceancountyhist
ory.org>

**Passaic County Historical
Society**
Lambert Castle, Valley Rd., Pater-
son, NJ 07503
Tel: (973) 247-0085
Web site:
Plainsboro Historical Society
641 Plainsboro Rd., Plainsboro,
NJ 08536
Tel: (609) 799-9040
Web site:
**Salem County Historical
Society**
79-83 Market St., Salem, NJ
08079
Tel: (856) 935-5004
E-mail: schs@verizon.net
Web site:
**The Scandinavian American
Heritage Society of New Jersey
(SAHS)**
E-mail: sahsnj@aol.com
Web site:

**Seton Hall University Libraries,
Seton Hall University**
400 S. Orange Ave., South Orange, NJ 07079-2671
Tel: (973) 761-9435
Web site: <http://library.shu
.edu/>

**Township of Neptune Historical
Society**
P.O. Box 1125, Neptune, NJ
07754-1125
Tel: (908) 775-8241

**United Methodist Archives
Center, Drew University Library**
Tel: (973) 408-3486
Web site: <www.depts.drew
.edu/lib/uma.html>

**United Methodist Church
Commission on Archives and
History, Northern New Jersey
Conference**
% The Meckler Library, Penning-
ton School, 112 W. Delaware
Ave., Pennington, NJ 08534

**Vineland Historical and
Antiquarian Society**
P.O. Box 35, Vineland, NJ 08360
Tel: (856) 691-1111
Web site: <www.vineland.org/his
tory/society/>

Westfield Historical Society
P.O. Box 613, Westfield, NJ
07091-0613

**Westfield Historical Society
Museum**
Town Hall, 425 E. Broad St.,
Westfield, NJ 07090-2196
Tel: (908) 789-4047
E-mail: history@westfieldnj.com
Web site: <www.westfieldnj.com/
history/contents.htm>

BIBLIOGRAPHY

■ GENERAL RESOURCES

*The Catholic Church in New
Jersey*
by Joseph M. Flynn (Morristown,
NJ: 1904)

*The Complete Public Records
Guide: Central and Northern
New Jersey Region*
by Fred D. Knapp (New Rochelle,
NY: Reyn, 1993)

*Cyclopedia of New Jersey
Biography: Memorial and
Biographical*
compiled with the assistance of
the Advisory Committee (New
York: American Historical Society, 1923)

*Directory of Churches in New
Jersey*, 10 vols.
prepared by the Historical Records Survey (Newark, NJ: Historical Records Survey, 1940–1941)

*Directory of New Jersey
Newspapers, 1765–1970*
edited by William C. Wright and
Paul A. Stellhorn (Trenton, NJ:
New Jersey Historical Commis-
sion, 1977)

*Documents Relating to the
Colonial History of the State of
New Jersey*
(Newark, NJ: The Daily Journal Es-
tablishment, 1880–1949)

*Documents Relating to the
Colonial History of the State of
New Jersey, Marriage Records,
1665–1800*
edited by William Nelson (Archives of the State of New Jersey,
First Series, vol. 22, 1900), reprinted as *New Jersey Marriage
Records* (Baltimore, MD: Genealogical Publishing Company, Inc.,
1967)

*Dutch Systems in Family
Naming, New York-New Jersey*
by Rosalie Fellows Bailey (Washington, DC: National Genealogical
Society Bookstore, 1965)

*The Early Germans of New
Jersey; Their History, Churches,
and Genealogies*
by Theodore Frelinghuysen Chambers (Baltimore: Genealogical
Pub. Co., 1969)

*Family Records: Or,
Genealogies of the First
Settlers of Passaic Valley (and
Vicinity)*
by John Littell (Baltimore: Geneal
Pub. Co., 1976)

*The First Laws of the State of
New Jersey*
edited by John D. Cushing (Wilmington, DE: Michael Glazier,
Inc., 1981)

*First Settlers of Ye Plantations
of Piscataway and Woodbridge,
olde East New Jersey,
1664–1714, a Period of Fifty
Years*
by Orra Eugene Monette (Los
Angeles, CA: The Leroy Carman
Press, 1930)

*Genealogical Resources in
Southern New Jersey*
by Edith Hoelle (Woodbury, NJ:
Gloucester County Historical Society, 1989)

*The Genealogist's Companion
and Sourcebook*, 2d ed.
by Emily Anne Croom (Cincinnati:
Betterway Books, 2003)

*A Genealogist's Guide to
Discovering Your African-
American Ancestors*
by Franklin Carter Smith and
Emily Anne Croom (Cincinnati:
Betterway Books, 2003)

*Genealogy of Early Settlers in
Trenton and Ewing, "Old
Hunterdon County," New
Jersey*
by Eli F. and William Cooley (Baltimore: Genealogical Pub. Co.,
1977)

*General Index to the
Documents Relating to the
Colonial History of the State of
New Jersey*, 10 vols.
prepared by Frederick W. Ricord
(Baltimore: Genealogical Re-
search Society of New Orleans,
1994)

*Guide to Depositories of
Manuscript Collections in the
United States: New Jersey*
compiled by the Historical Records Survey (Newark, NJ: Historical Records Survey, 1941)

*Guide to Family History Sources
in the New Jersey State
Archives*, 2d ed.
compiled by Bette Marie Barker,
Daniel P. Jones, and Karl J. Nied-
erer (Trenton, NJ: Division of Archives and Records Management, 1990)

Guide to Genealogical Research in the National Archives of the United States
edited by Anne Bruner Eales and Robert M. Kvasnicka (Washington, DC: National Archives and Records Administration, 2000)

Guide to Local Church Records in the Archives of the Reformed Church in America and to Genealogical Resources in the Gardner Sage Library: New Brunswick Theological Seminary
edited by Russell L. Gasero (New Brunswick, NJ: Historical Society of the Reformed Church in America, 1979)

Guide to the Manuscript Collections of the New Jersey Historical Society
compiled by Don C. Skemer and Robert C. Morris (Newark: The Society, 1979)

Guide to the Manuscript Collection of the Rutgers University Library
compiled by Herbert F. Smith (New Brunswick, NJ: Rutgers University Library, 1964)

Guide to Vital Statistics Records in New Jersey, 2 vols.
prepared by the Historical Records Survey (Newark, NJ: Historical Records Survey, 1941)

Historical and Genealogical Miscellany; Data Relating to the Settlement and Settlers of New York and New Jersey, 5 vols.
by John E. Stillwell (Baltimore: Genealogical Pub. Co., 1970)

Historical Organizations in New Jersey: A Directory
compiled by Mary Alice Quigley, Judith A. Fullerton, and Diane E. Kauffman (Trenton, NJ: League of Historical Societies of New Jersey: New Jersey Historical Commission, 1983)

History and Genealogy of Fenwick's Colony
by Thomas Shourds (Baltimore: Genealogical Pub. Co., 1976)

The Judicial and Civil History of New Jersey
by John Whitehead (Clark, NJ: Lawbook Exchange, 2004)

Memorial Cyclopedia of New Jersey, 3 vols.
by Mary Depue Ogden (Newark, NJ: Memorial History Company, 1915–17)

A Narrative and Descriptive Bibliography of New Jersey
by Nelson R. Burr (Princeton, NJ: Van Nostrand, 1964)

National Archives Microfilm Catalogs online:
<www.archives.gov/publications/genealogy_microfilm_catalogs.html>

Nelson's Biographical Cyclopedia of New Jersey
edited by William Nelson (New York: Eastern Historical Pub. Society, 1913)

New Jersey Biographical and Genealogical Notes From the Volumes of the New Jersey Archives, With Additions and Supplements
by William Nelson (Newark, NJ: The Society, 1916)

A New Jersey Biographical Index: Covering Some 100,000 Biographies and Associated Portraits in 237 New Jersey Cyclopedias, Histories, Yearbooks, Periodicals, and Other Collective Biographical Sources Published to About 1980
compiled by Donald Arleigh Sinclair (Baltimore: Genealogical Pub. Co., 1993)

New Jersey from Colony to State, 1609–1789
by Richard Patrick McCormick (New Brunswick, NJ: Rutgers, 1964)

New Jersey: Digging for Ancestors in the Garden State
by Kenn Stryker-Rodda (Detroit, MI: Detroit Society for Genealogical Research, 1984)

New Jersey Ethnic History: A Bibliography
compiled by David Steven Cohen (Trenton, NJ: New Jersey Historical Commission, Dept. of State, 1986)

New Jersey Historical Manuscripts: A Guide to Collections in the State
compiled by Mary R. Murrin (Trenton, NJ: New Jersey Historical Commission, 1987)

New Jersey, a History, 6 vols.
edited by Irving S. Kull (New York: American Historical Society, 1930–1932)

New Jersey: Research Outline
by the Church of Jesus Christ of Latter-day Saints, Family History Library (Salt Lake City, UT: Corp. of the President of the Church of Jesus Christ of L.D.S., 1991)

Northwest New Jersey: A History of Somerset, Morris, Hunterdon, Warren and Sussex Counties, 4 vols.
by Abraham Van Doren Honeyman (New York, Chicago: Lewis Publishing Company, Inc., 1927)

Notices From New Jersey Newspapers, 2 vols.
by Thomas B. Wilson and Dorothy Agans Stratford (Lambertville, NJ: Hunterdon House, ca. 1988, ca. 2002)

Pioneer Families of Northwestern New Jersey
by William C. Armstrong (Lambertville, NJ: Hunterdon House, 1979)

Religion in New Jersey: A Brief History
by Wallace N. Jamison (Princeton: D. Van Nostrand, 1964)

South Jersey, a History, 1664–1924, 5 vols.
by Alfred Miller Heston (New York and Chicago: Lewis Historical Publishing Company, Inc., 1924)

The Story of New Jersey, 5 vols.
edited by William Starr Myers (New York: Lewis Historical Publishing Company, Inc., 1945)

The Story of New Jersey's Civil Boundaries 1606–1968
by John P. Snyder (Trenton, NJ: Bureau of Geology and Topography, 1969)

■ CENSUS RECORDS

The American Census Handbook
by Thomas Jay Kemp (Wilmington, DE: Scholarly Resources, 2001)

The Census Book: A Genealogist's Guide to Federal Census Facts, Schedules and Indexes
by William Dollarhide (Bountiful, UT: Heritage Quest, 2000)

The 1693 Census of the Swedes on the Delaware: Family Histories of the Swedish Lutheran Church Members Residing in Pennsylvania, Delaware, West New Jersey and Cecil County, Maryland, 1638–1693
by Peter Stebbins Craig (Winter Park, FL: SAG Publications, 1993)

Map Guide to the U.S. Federal Censuses, 1790–1920
by William Thorndale and William Dollarhide (Baltimore, MD: Genealogical Pub. Co., 1987)

New Jersey 1850 Mortality Schedule Index
compiled by Shirley J. George and Sandra E. Glenn (Columbus, NJ: G. & G. Genealogical Book Co., 1982)

Revolutionary Census of New Jersey; an Index, Based on Ratables, of the Inhabitants of New Jersey During the Period of the American Revolution
by Kenn Stryker-Rodda (Cottonport, Polyanthos, 1972)

State Census Records
by Ann S. Lainhart (Baltimore, MD: Genealogical Publishing, 1992)

Your Guide to the Federal Census
by Kathleen W. Hinckley (Cincinnati: Betterway Books, 2002)

■ IMMIGRATION RECORDS

American Naturalization Records, 1790–1990: What They Are and How to Use Them
by John J. Newman (North Salt Lake, UT: HeritageQuest, 1998)

American Passenger Arrival Records
by Michael Tepper (Baltimore: Genealogical Publishing Co., 1993)

The Early Germans of New Jersey: Their History, Churches and Genealogies
by Theodore Frelinghuysen Chambers (Baltimore, MD: Genealogical Pub. Co., 1969)

New Jersey

Mayflower Pilgrim Descendants in Cape May County, New Jersey: A Memorial of the Three Hundreth Anniversary of the Landing of the Pilgrims at Plymouth, 1620-1920
by Paul Sturtevant Howe (Baltimore: Genealogical Pub. Co., 1977)

More Palatine Families: Some Immigrants to the Middle Colonies, 1717–1776, and Their European Origins, Plus New Discoveries on German Families who Arrived in Colonial New York in 1710
by Henry Z. Jones (Universal City, CA: H.Z. Jones, 1991)

They Became Americans: Finding Naturalization Records and Ethnic Origins
by Loretto Dennis Szucs (Salt Lake City: Ancestry, Inc., 1998)

They Came in Ships: A Guide to Finding Your Immigrant Ancestor's Arrival Records, 2d ed.
by John P. Colletta (Salt Lake City: Ancestry, Inc., 1993)

■ LAND RECORDS

Land Ownership Maps, a Checklist of Nineteenth Century United States County Maps in the Library of Congress
compiled by Richard W. Stephenson (Washington, DC: 1967)

Land & Property Research in the United States
by Wade E. Hone (Salt Lake City, UT: Ancestry, 1997)

Locating Your Roots: Discover Your Ancestors Using Land Records
by Patricia Law Hatcher (Cincinnati: Betterway Books, 2003)

Minutes of the Board of Proprietors of the Eastern Division of New Jersey, 4 vols.
by the Board of Proprietors of the Eastern Division of New Jersey (Perth Amboy, NJ: The Board, 1949–1985)

Patents and Deeds and Other Early Records of New Jersey, 1664–1703
edited by William Nelson (Baltimore: Genealogical Pub. Co., 1976)

■ MAPS

A Gazetteer of the State of New Jersey: Comprehending a General View of its Physical and Moral Condition, Together With a Topographical and Statistical Account of its Counties, Towns, Villages, Canals, Railroads etc., Accompanied by a Map
by Thomas F. Gordon (Trenton, NJ: D. Fenton, 1834)

A Geographic Dictionary of New Jersey
by Henry Gannett (Baltimore: Genealogical Pub. Co., 1978)

Historical Atlas and Chronology of County Boundaries, 1788–1980, 5 vols.
edited John H. Long (Boston, MA: G.K. Hall, 1984)

The National Gazetteer of the United States of America—New Jersey, 1983
prepared by the U.S. Geological Survey in cooperation with the U.S. Board on Geographic Names (Washington, DC: United States Government Printing Office, 1983)

New Jersey Historic Map Portfolio
edited by Don C. Skemer (Florham Park, NJ: Afton Pub., 1983)

New Jersey Postal History: The Post Offices and First Postmasters, 1776–1976
by John L. Kay and Chester Smith, Jr. (Lawrence, MA: Quarterman Publications, 1977)

The Origin of New Jersey Place Names
compiled by workers of the Federal Writer's Program (Trenton, NJ: New Jersey Public Library Commission, 1945)

The Story of New Jersey's Civil Boundaries, 1606–1968
by John P. Snyder (Trenton, NJ: New Jersey Dept. of Environmental Protection, Division of Water Resources, Geological Survey, 1988)

■ MILITARY RECORDS

A Bibliography: The Civil War and New Jersey
by Donald A. Sinclair (New Brunswick, NJ: Friends of the Rutgers University Library for the New Jersey Civil War Centennial Commission, 1968)

Certificates and Receipts of Revolutionary New Jersey
by Dorothy Agans Stratford and Thomas B. Wilson (Lambertville, NJ: Hunterdon House, 1996)

Genealogical Abstracts of Revolutionary War Pension Files, 4 vols.
abstracted by Virgil D. White (Waynesboro, TN: National Historical Pub. Co., 1990–1992)

Index to Revolutionary War Service Records, 4 vols.
transcribed by Virgil D. White (Waynesboro, TN: The National Historical Publishing Company, 1995)

The Loyalists of New Jersey, Their Memorials, Petitions, Claims, etc., From English Records
by Edward Alfred Jones (Newark, NJ: New Jersey Historical Society, 1927)

New Jersey Civil War Records, Books 1–829
by the New Jersey State Library (Trenton, NJ: State Library of Archives and History, 1969)

New Jersey and the Revolutionary War
by Alfred Hoyt Bill (New Brunswick, NJ: Rutgers University, 1964)

Official Register of the Officers and Men of New Jersey in the Revolutionary War
compiled by James W.S. Campbell (Baltimore: Genealogical Pub. Co., 1967)

Record of Officers and Men of New Jersey in the Civil War, 1861–1865
by the New Jersey Adjutant General's Office (Trenton, NJ: J.L. Murphy, 1876)

Register of the Commissioned Officers and Privates of the New Jersey Volunteers in the Service of the United States
by the New Jersey Adjutant General's Office (Bethesda, MD: University Publications of America, 1991)

Revolutionary War Pensioners Living in New Jersey Before 1834
by Inez Raney Waldenmaier (Tulsa, OK: Inez Waldenmaier, 1983)

Uncle, We Are Ready! Registering America's Men, 1917–1918: A Guide to Researching World War I Draft Registration Cards
by John J. Newman (North Salt Lake, UT: HeritageQuest, 2001)

U.S. Military Records: A Guide to Federal & State Sources, Colonial America to the Present
by James C. Neagles (Salt Lake City: Ancestry, Inc., 1994)

World War II: A Family Historian's Guide
by Debra Johnson Knox (Spartanburg, SC: MIE Publishing, 2003)

■ PROBATE RECORDS

Calender of New Jersey Wills, 7 vols.
by William Nelson and Abraham Van Doren Honeyman (Bowie, MD: Heritage Books, 1994–1997)

The Law and Practice of New Jersey From the Earliest Times: Concerning the Probate of Wills, the Administration of Estates, the Protection of Orphans and Minors, and the Control of Their Estates; the Perogative Court, the Ordinary, and the Surrogates
by William Nelson (Paterson, NJ: Paterson History Club, 1909)

New Jersey Index to Wills, 3 vols.
by the New Jersey Secretary of State (Baltimore: Genealogical Pub. Co., 1969)

■ VITAL RECORDS

Guide to Vital Statistics Records in New Jersey
by the Historical Records Survey (Newark, NJ: Historical Records Survey, 1941)

New Jersey Catholic Baptismal Records From 1759 to 1781
by Janet Drumm Dirnberger (Seabrook, TX: Brambles, 1981)

New Jersey Marriage Records, 1665–1800
edited by William Nelson (Baltimore, MD: Genealogical Pub. Co., 1967, 1973, 1982)

Your Guide to Cemetery Research
by Sharon DeBartolo Carmack (Cincinnati: Betterway Books, 2002)

■ **Atlantic** 7 Feb. 1837
P.O. Box 2005, Mays Landing, NJ 08330
Phone: (609)625-4011
Web site: www.aclink.org/
Parent County: Gloucester
Comments/research tips: State Archives has Birth and Death records 1848–1878, Court records 1838–1905, Land records 1837–1900, Marriage records 1875–1897 and microfilm records of Marriage records 1837–1876, Naturalization records 1837–1951, and Probate records and Wills 1837–1922. County Clerk has Marriage records 1837–1876. Superior Court Public Information Center has Divorce records 1901–1992.

Record Type	Year Begun	Jurisdiction
Marriage	1878	Dept./Health/Vital Stats.

■ **Bergen** 7 Mar. 1683
1 Bergen County Plaza, Hackensack, NJ 07601
Phone: (201)336-7000
Web site: www.co.bergen.nj.us/
Parent County: Prov. East Jersey
Comments/research tips: State Archives has Birth and Death records 1848–1878, Land records 1715–1901, Marriage records 1795–1877, Naturalization records 1804–1906, Probate records 1785–1962, and Wills 1698–1900. Superior Court Public Information Center has Divorce records 1901–1992.

Record Type	Year Begun	Jurisdiction
Court	na	County Clerk
Marriage	1878	Dept./Health/Vital Stats.

■ **Burlington** 17 May 1694
49 Rancocas Rd., P.O. Box 6000, Mount Holly, NJ 08060
Phone: (609)265-5122
Web site: http://co.burlington.nj.us/
Parent County: Province of West Jersey
Comments/research tips: State Archives has Birth and Death records 1848–1878, Court records 1681–1937, Land records 1718–1901, Marriage records 1795–1878, Naturalization records 1790–1956, Probate records 1785–1970, and Wills 1688–1900. Superior Court Public Information Center has Divorce records 1901–1992.

■ **Camden** 13 Mar. 1844
Camden County Courthouse, Room 102, 520 Market St., Camden, NJ 08102-1375
Phone: (856)225-5300

Web site: www.co.camden.nj.us/
Parent County: Gloucester
Comments/research tips: State Archives has Birth and Death records 1848–1878, Court records 1844–1961, Land records 1759–1840, 1844–1900, Marriage records 1848–1878, and Probate records 1844–1946. Superior Court Public Information Center has Divorce records 1901–1992. Land records prior to 1844 are from parts of Gloucester County that became Camden County.

■ **Cape May** 12 Nov. 1692
7 N. Main St., DN 109, P.O. Box 5000, Cape May Court House, NJ 08210-5000
Phone: (609)465-1010
Web site: www.capemaycountygov.net
Parent County: West Jersey
Comments/research tips: State Archives has Birth and Death records 1848–1878, Court records 1790–1964, Land records 1692–1926, Marriage records 1795–1878, Probate records 1786–1980, and Wills 1704–1900. Superior Court Public Information Center has Divorce records 1901–1992.

■ **Cumberland** 19 Jan. 1748
60 W. Broad St., Bridgeton, NJ 08302
Phone: (856)451-8000
Web site: www.co.cumberland.nj.us/
Parent County: Salem
Comments/research tips: State Archives has Birth and Death records 1848–1878, Court records 1745–1937, Land records 1785–1952, Marriage records 1795–1878, Naturalization records 1802–1931, Probate records 1785–1904, and Wills 1747–1900. Superior Court Public Information Center has Divorce records 1901–1992.

■ **Essex** 1 Mar. 1683
Hall of Records, Room 247, Dr. Martin Luther King Jr. Blvd., Newark, NJ 07102
Phone: (973)621-4920
Web site: www.co.essex.nj.us/
Parent County: Prov. East Jersey
Comments/research tips: State Archives has Birth and Death records 1848–1878, Court records 1709–1911, Land records 1728–1909, Marriage records 1795–1893, Naturalization records 1698–1931, Probate records 1793–1907, and Wills 1697–1900. Superior Court Public Information Center has Divorce records 1901–1992. Fire destroyed records of Deeds 1688–1728.

■ **Gloucester** 17 May 1694
P.O. Box 129, Woodbury, NJ 08096
Phone: (856)853-3237
Web site: www.co.gloucester.nj.us/
Parent County: Prov. West Jersey
Comments/research tips: State Archives has Birth and Death records 1848–1878, Court records 1686–1887, Land records 1650–1703, 1714–1779, 1786–1901, Naturalization records 1808–1932, Probate records 1785–1897, and Wills 1691–1922. Superior Court Public Information Center has Divorce records 1901–1992.

County Historical Society has Marriage records 1686–1939. Courthouse burned 1786, early records preserved at Surveyor General's Office, Burlington, and Secretary of State's Office, Trenton.

■ Hudson 22 Feb. 1840
583 Newark Ave., Jersey City, NJ 07306
Phone: (201)795-6112
Web site: www.hudsoncountynj.org/
Parent County: Bergen
Comments/research tips: State Archives has Birth and Death records 1848–1878, Court records 1842–1927, Land records 1805–1901, Marriage records 1848–1878, and Probate records 1840–1953. Superior Court Public Information Center has Divorce records 1901–1992.

■ Hunterdon 13 Mar. 1714
P.O. Box 2900, Flemington, NJ 08822
Phone: (908)788-1221
Web site: www.co.hunterdon.nj.us/
Parent County: Burlington
Comments/research tips: State Archives has Birth and Death records 1848–1878, Court records 1713–1916, Land records 1705–1955, Marriage records 1795–1900, Naturalization records 1803–1906, Probate records 1785–1906, and Wills 1704–1919. Superior Court Public Information Center has Divorce records 1901–1992.

■ Mercer 22 Feb. 1838
209 S. Broad St., Trenton, NJ 08608
Phone: (609)989-6465
Web site: www.mercercounty.org/
Parent County: Somerset, Middlesex, Hunterdon, Burlington
Comments/research tips: State Archives has Birth and Death records 1848–1878, Land records 1795–ca. 1930s, Marriage records 1815, 1832, 1841–1887, Naturalization records 1838–1940, and Probate records 1838–1939. Superior Court Public Information Center has Divorce records 1901–1992.

Record Type	Year Begun	Jurisdiction
Court	1838	County Clerk

■ Middlesex 7 Mar. 1683
P.O. Box 1100, New Brunswick, NJ 08901
Phone: (732)745-4399
Web site: co.middlesex.nj.us/
Parent County: Prov. East Jersey
Comments/research tips: State Archives has Birth and Death records 1848–1878, Court records 1792–1871, Marriage records 1795–1928, Naturalization records 1794–1906, Probate records 1786–1971, and Wills 1683–1913. Superior Court Public Information Center has Divorce records 1901–1992.

Record Type	Year Begun	Jurisdiction
Land	1683	County Clerk

■ Monmouth 1 Mar. 1683
P.O. Box 1251, Freehold, NJ 07728
Phone: (732)431-7324

Web site: http://shore.co.monmouth.nj.us/
Parent County: Prov. East Jersey
Comments/research tips: State Archives has Birth and Death records 1848–1878, Land records 1665–1899, Marriage records 1789–1880, Naturalization records 1824–1908, Probate records 1785–1969, and Wills 1695–1900. Superior Court Public Information Center has Divorce records 1901–1992.

■ Morris 15 Mar. 1739
Court St., P.O. Box 315, Morristown, NJ 07963
Phone: (973)285-6125
Web site: www.co.morris.nj.us/
Parent County: Hunterdon
Comments/research tips: State Archives has Birth and Death records 1848–1878, Court records 1740–1866, Land records 1785–1962, Marriage records 1795–1919, Naturalization records 1816–1906, and Wills 1740–1900. Superior Court Public Information Center has Divorce records 1901–1992.

Record Type	Year Begun	Jurisdiction
Probate	na	County Surrogate

■ Ocean 15 Feb. 1850
P.O. Box 2191, Toms River, NJ 08754
Phone: (732)929-2018
Web site: www.oceancountygov.com/
Parent County: Monmouth
Comments/research tips: State Archives has Birth and Death records 1848–1878, Land records 1850–1960, Marriage records 1850–1908, Probate records 1850–1955, and Wills 1850–1900. Superior Court Public Information Center has Divorce records 1901–1992.

Record Type	Year Begun	Jurisdiction
Court	1850	County Clerk

■ Passaic 7 Feb. 1837
401 Grand St., Paterson, NJ 07505
Phone: (973)225-3632
Web site: www.passaiccountynj.org/
Parent County: Bergen, Essex
Comments/research tips: State Archives has Birth and Death records 1848–1878, Court records 1837–1946, Land records 1837–1901, Marriage records 1837–1902, Naturalization records 1837–1906, Probate records 1835–1919, and Wills 1835–1911. Superior Court Public Information Center has Divorce records 1901–1992.

■ Salem 17 May 1694
92 Market St., Salem, NJ 08079
Phone: (856)935-7510
Web site: www.salemco.org
Parent County: Salem Tenth
Comments/research tips: State Archives has Birth and Death records 1848–1878, Court records 1706–1953, Land records 1664–1710, 1786–1900, Marriage records 1680–1956, Naturalization records 1800–1929, and Wills 1678–1703, 1712–1923, Probate records 1748–1908, Superior Court Public Information Center has Divorce records 1901–1992.

■ **Somerset**   14 May 1688
20 Grove St., P.O. Box 3000, Somerville, NJ 08876
Phone: (908)231-7006
Web site: www.co.somerset.nj.us/
Parent County: Middlesex
Comments/research tips: State Archives has Birth and Death records 1848–1878, Court records 1776–1926, Land records 1779–1901, Marriage records 1778–1887, Naturalization records 1805–1922, Probate records 1794–1972, and Wills 1702–1900. Superior Court Public Information Center has Divorce records 1901–1992.

■ **Sussex**   8 June 1753
4 Park Pl., Newton, NJ 07860
Phone: (973)579-0900
Web site: www.sussex.nj.us
Parent County: Morris
Comments/research tips: State Archives has Birth and Death records 1848–1878, Court records 1798–1907, Land records 1785–1901, Marriage records 1795–1878, Naturalization records 1855–1902, Probate records 1779–1924, and Wills 1754–1905. Superior Court Public Information Center has Divorce records 1901–1992.

■ **Union**   19 Mar. 1857
2 Broad St., Elizabeth, NJ 07207
Phone: (908)527-4966
Web site: www.unioncountynj.org/
Parent County: Essex
Comments/research tips: State Archives has Birth and Death records 1848–1878, Court records 1819–1933, Marriage records 1850–1878, Naturalization records 1845–1945, Probate records 1854–1902, and Wills 1854–1911. Superior Court Public Information Center has Divorce records 1901–1992.

Record Type	Year Begun	Jurisdiction
Land	1857	County Clerk

■ **Warren**   20 Nov. 1824
413 Second St., Belvidere, NJ 07823
Phone: (908)475-6211
Web site: www.co.warren.nj.us
Parent County: Sussex
Comments/research tips: State Archives has Birth and Death records 1848–1878, Court records 1825–1941, Land records 1823–1901, Marriage records 1825–1902, Naturalization records 1825–1906, Probate records 1825–1956, and Wills 1824–1901. Superior Court Public Information Center has Divorce records 1901–1992.

New Jersey

New Mexico

By David A. Fryxell

HISTORICAL OVERVIEW

New Mexico is among the most recent stars on the American flag, not gaining statehood until 1912, and many non-New Mexicans still don't seem to realize the "Land of Enchantment" is part of the United States. ("One of Our States Is Missing" is a regular feature in *New Mexico Magazine*.) Yet New Mexico's history, both native and European, is among the longest on the continent. Evidence of habitation by the Sandia people dates to 25000 BC. Other native cultures evolved in turn, among them the Mogollon, the Anasazi, and, about 1130–1180, the Pueblo Indians who were here when Coronado came in 1540. Don Juan de Oñate founded the first Spanish settlements in 1598. Santa Fe, founded in 1610, will soon celebrate its quadcentennial; Albuquerque marks its tricentennial in 2006. Except for Pueblo Indian revolts in 1680 and 1696 that briefly sent colonists fleeing, the Spanish held sway for centuries. For a brief period following Mexican independence in 1821, the Spanish flag was replaced by that of the new nation.

With the outbreak of the Mexican-American War in 1846, the Stars and Stripes arrived in New Mexico. In 1848, the Treaty of Guadalupe Hidalgo ended the war and fixed the boundaries between the US and Mexico at the Rio Grande, the Gila River, and the Colorado River. The Gadsden Purchase, signed in Mesilla, New Mexico, in 1854, would add the rest of southwestern New Mexico and southern Arizona.

The Compromise of 1850 created the New Mexico Territory, which encompassed today's New Mexico plus southern Nevada and Arizona, which split off in 1863. The arrival of the telegraph in 1877 and the joining of the second transcontinental railroad at Deming, New Mexico, in 1881 began to bring the rough-and-tumble territory into the American family. New Mexico attracted miners and ranchers; some of the latter battled in

NEW MEXICO AT A GLANCE

Motto: It Grows As It Goes
Population: 1.8 million
Prevalent Religions: Christianity, particularly Roman Catholicism, Baptist, Presbyterian, Lutheran, and Pentecostal
Major Industries: Scientific research, mining, electrical equipment, petroleum and coal products, food processing, printing and publishing, stone, glass, clay, tourism, cattle, dairy products, hay, nursery stock, chiles
Ethnic Makeup (in percent): Caucasian 56%, African American 1.9%, Hispanic 42.1%, Asian 1.1%, Native American 1.9%, Other 0.7%
Famous New Mexicans: Dennis Chavez, Robert Crichton, John Denver, Pete Domenici, Harvey Fergusson, Neil Patrick Harris, Conrad Hilton, Peter Hurd, Ralph Kiner, John Madden, Demi Moore, Kim Stanley Robinson, Harrison Schmitt, Slim Summerville, Al and Bobby Unser, Thomas Weaver, Linda Wertheimer

Above: An aerial view of picturesque Albuquerque

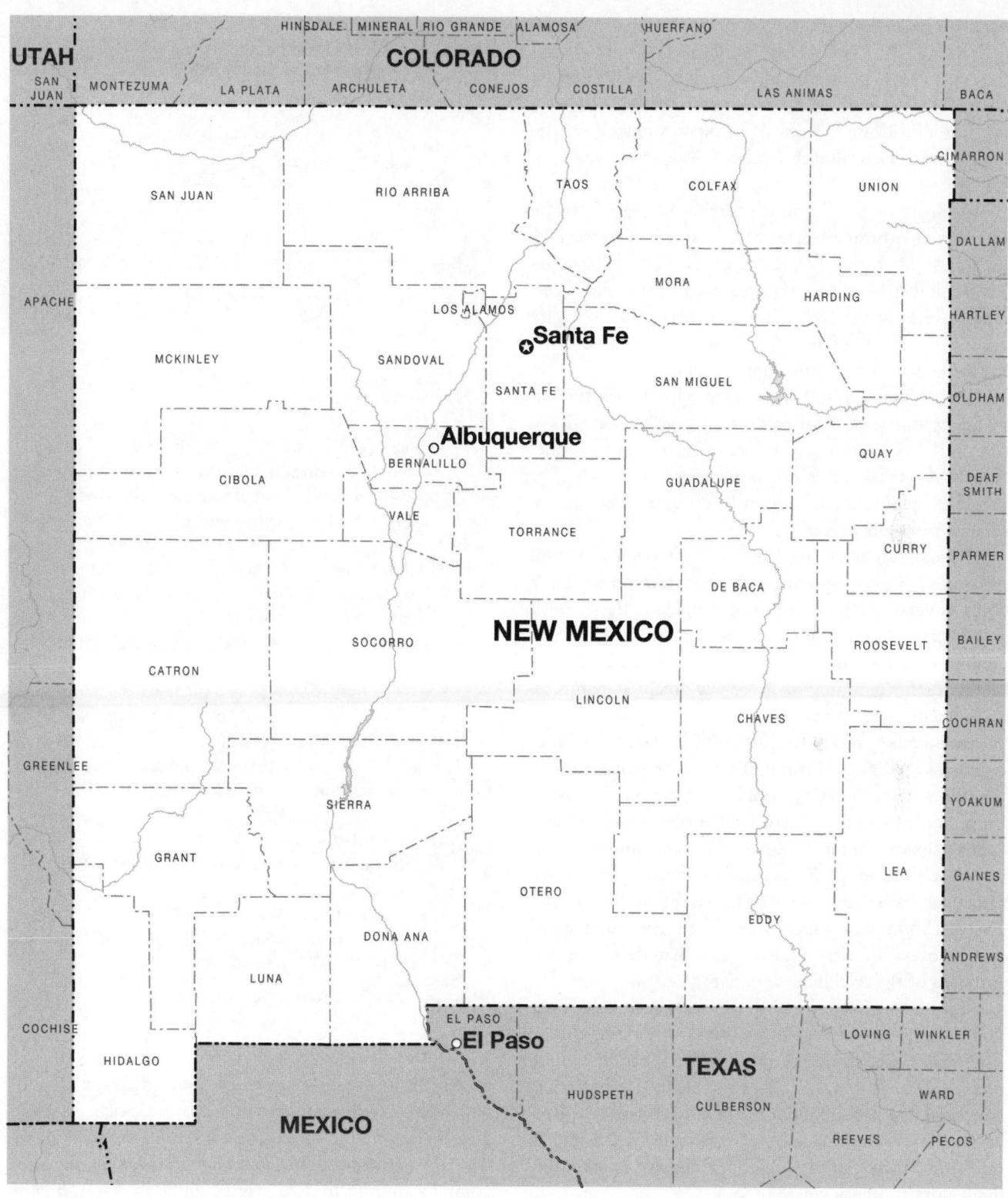

UTAH

COLORADO

HINSDALE | MINERAL | RIO GRANDE | ALAMOSA | HUERFANO

SAN JUAN

MONTEZUMA   LA PLATA   ARCHULETA   CONEJOS   COSTILLA   LAS ANIMAS   BACA

CIMARRON

SAN JUAN

RIO ARRIBA   TAOS   COLFAX   UNION

DALLAM

APACHE

MCKINLEY

LOS ALAMOS

SANDOVAL

SANTA FE ★Santa Fe

MORA   HARDING

HARTLEY

OLDHAM

SAN MIGUEL

CIBOLA

Albuquerque
BERNALILLO

VALE

TORRANCE

GUADALUPE

QUAY

DEAF SMITH

NEW MEXICO

DE BACA

CURRY   PARMER

CATRON

SOCORRO

LINCOLN

ROOSEVELT   BAILEY

CHAVES

COCHRAN

GREENLEE

SIERRA

YOAKUM

GRANT

OTERO

LEA   GAINES

EDDY

DONA ANA

ANDREWS

LUNA

COCHISE

HIDALGO

EL PASO
○El Paso

TEXAS

HUDSPETH   CULBERSON

LOVING | WINKLER

WARD

MEXICO

REEVES   PECOS

the Lincoln County Wars, which made a legend of Billy the Kid.

Though New Mexico was not yet a state, its soldiers formed Teddy Roosevelt's Rough Riders in the Spanish-American War. During World War II the atomic age was born at Los Alamos and Alamogordo, beginning a new, high-tech era for this ancient land.

RECORD HIGHLIGHTS

If your roots go back to the Spanish and Mexican era, you can find colonial censuses from 1750–1830 at the state archives, and in a collection published by the New Mexico Genealogical Society. The archives also has Spanish land records from 1693–1821 and Mexican records from 1821–1845. Catholic church records from the

Archdiocese of Santa Fe, now at the archives, also extend to this time; the Family History Library has microfilmed these back to 1726. Karen Stein Daniel, CG, editor of the *New Mexico Genealogist*, recommends the guide "Locating Catholic Church Records in New Mexico" on the New Mexico Genealogical Society's Web site <www.nmgs.org>.

Ancestors living during the territorial period can be found in territorial censuses, taken as part of the regular federal enumeration beginning in 1850. Note that the 1860 count covered only the area south of the Gila River. Don't overlook the 1885 state census, actually federally administered, which listed all household members; it's available on microfilm through the FHL.

As a latecomer to statehood, New Mexico was the last to adopt statewide vital records and health statistics—not until 1920, prompted by war and the flu epidemic. Access to records is restricted to immediate family. For pre-1920 vital records, look at the county level; church records may substitute.

The state archives contains a wide variety of helpful records, such as land grants, early probates, and pre-1912 court papers. Military records here include the Spanish and Mexican era, the Indian Wars, and the Civil War (including Confederate data). See the archives' helpful online guide for genealogists at <www.nmcpr.state.nm.us/archives/ancestors.htm>.

The other key repository, according to Daniel, is Albuquerque's Special Collections Library, a branch of the Rio Grande Valley Library System. This easily-overlooked library holds the Spanish Archives of New Mexico I and II, the Mexican Archives of New Mexico, land grant records, and portions of the territorial records, all on microfilm. You'll also find a large collection of family genealogies, territorial newspapers, city directories, vital records and indexes, obituary indexes, and materials from the Archives of the Archdiocese of Santa Fe.

New Mexico's long history represents both a challenge and an opportunity for researchers, spanning Native American, Spanish, Mexican, territorial, and statehood periods. Daniel says the most valuable tip for beginning researchers is to read about the history of the area. Records are typically divided and catalogued according to the period in which they fall, meaning you must know the history to know where to look.

Be prepared to find many records in Spanish—more so as you go further back in time. Many have now been translated or partially translated into English, says Daniel, but she cautions that translations may contain inaccuracies or gaps.

Once you've familiarized yourself with the history, discover the New Mexico Genealogical Society's award-winning Web site <www.nmgs.org>. You'll find a

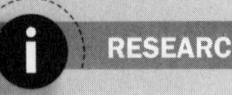

RESEARCH TIPS

for more info

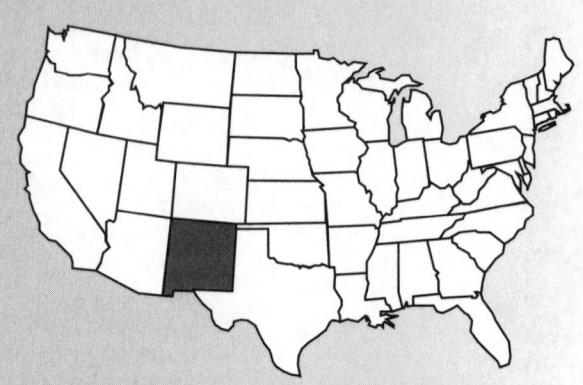

- ¿Habla usted español? The farther back you go, the more records you will find in Spanish—and though many have been translated, the translations may contain inaccuracies or gaps.
- Arguably, the key to being successful in your New Mexico research is knowing the history of the records for which you are searching. Read up on the many phases of the state's past.
- Two indispensable New Mexico Web sites are the Online Archives of New Mexico <http://elibrary.unm.edu/oanm>, which is a guide to several of the state's major archival holdings, and the New Mexico Genealogical Society's site <www.nmgs.org>, which contains tons of helpful tips and tools to help you in your search.

Census Records
- Federal Census: 1820, 1860, 1870, 1880, 1900, 1910, 1920, 1930
- Union Veterans and Widows: 1890
- Spanish/Mexican Census: 1790, 1823, 1845
- State/Territorial Census: 1885

myriad of links and suggestions, plus articles, abstracts, and other information from the *New Mexico Genealogist*. If you join the society, you'll receive the second edition of *Genealogical Resources in New Mexico*, the most complete and up-to-date printed guide to research here. You can also purchase a CD collection of the first forty years of the society's quarterly journal.

Another useful site is the Online Archives of New Mexico <elibrary.unm.edu/oanm>, a valuable research tool for several of the state's primary repositories of manuscript and major archival holdings.

Finally, Daniel advises, if at first you don't succeed, don't give up—look somewhere else. You may have to scour several locations for the records you need. For example, some county records are now housed in the archives in Santa Fe. The best chance of success, says Daniel, comes from doing your homework, preparing a research plan, and establishing the location of records you seek prior to setting out.

STATE RESOURCES

■ ARCHIVES, LIBRARIES, AND SOCIETIES

Albuquerque Public Library
423 E. Central Ave., Albuquerque, NM 87101

Albuquerque Public Library
501 Copper Ave. NW, Albuquerque, NM 87102
Tel: (505) 768-5100
Fax: (505) 768-5191

Artesia Genealogical Society
P.O. Box 803, Artesia, NM 88210

Thomas Branigan Memorial Library
200 E. Picacho Ave., Las Cruces, NM 88001

Bureau of Land Management, New Mexico State Office
Federal Building, 1474 Rodeo Rd., P.O. Box 27115, Santa Fe, NM 87502-0115
Tel: (505) 438-7450
Fax: (505) 438-7452

Chaves County Genealogical Society
P.O. Box 51, Roswell, NM 88201

Eddy County Genealogical Society
P.O. Box 461, Carlsbad, NM 88220

Genealogical Club of the Albuquerque Public Library
423 Central Ave. NE, Albuquerque, NM 87102

Genealogy Club of Angel Fire
P.O. Box 503, Angel Fire, New Mexico 87710

Historical Society of New Mexico
P.O. Box 1912, Santa Fe, NM 87504
Tel: (505) 827-7332
Fax: (505) 827-7331

History Library Museum of New Mexico
Palace of the Governors, Santa Fe, NM 87501

Lea County Genealogical Society
P.O. Box 1044, Lovington, NM 88260

Los Alamos Family History Society
P.O. Box 900l Los Alamos, NM 87544

Lovington Public Library
103 N. First St., Lovington, NM 88260

National Archives-Southwest Region (Fort Worth)
501 W. Felix St., P.O. Box 6216, Fort Worth, TX 76115-0216
Tel: (817) 334-5525

New Mexico Genealogical Society
P.O. Box 8283, Albuquerque, NM 87198-8283
Tel: (505) 828-2514
Web site: <www.nmgs.org>

New Mexico Health Services
1190 St. Francis Dr., Santa Fe, NM 87505
Tel: (505) 827-2338
Fax: (505) 984-1048

New Mexico Records Center and Archives
404 Montezuma, Santa Fe, NM 87502
Tel: (505) 827-7332
Fax: (505) 827-7331

New Mexico State Library Commission
301 Don Gaspar, Santa Fe, NM 87501

New Mexico State University Library
Box 30006, Dept. 3475, Las Cruces, NM 88003-8006
Tel: (505) 646-2932
Web site: <http://lib.nmsu.edu/>

New Mexico State Library
325 Don Gaspar, Santa Fe, NM 87501-2777
Tel: (505) 827-3800
Fax: (505) 827-3888

Portales Public Library
218 S. Ave. B, Portales, NM 88130

Roman Catholic Archdiocese of Santa Fe
4000 St. Joseph Place NW, Albuquerque, NM 87120
Tel: (505) 831-8100
Fax: (505) 831-8345

Roman Catholic Diocese of Gallup
711 S. Puerco Dr., P.O. Box 1338, Gallup, NM 87301
Tel: (505) 863-4406
Fax: (505) 722-9131

Roman Catholic Diocese of Las Cruces
1280 Med Park, P.O. Box 16318, Las Cruces, NM 88004
Tel: (505) 523-7577
Fax: (505) 524-3874

Roswell Genealogical Society
807 N. Missouri, Roswell, NM 88201

Roswell Public Library
301 N. Pennsylvania Ave., Roswell, NM 88201

Salmon Ruins Museum
% Totah Tracers Genealogy, 6131 U.S. Hwy. 64, P.O. Box 125, Bloomfield, NM 87413-0125

Sierra County Genealogical Society
% Truth or Consequences Public Library
P.O. Box 311, Truth or Consequences, NM 87901

Socorro County Genealogical Society
Web site: <www.rootsweb.com/~nmscgs/>

Socorro County Historical Society, Inc.
P.O. Box 923, Socorro, NM 87801-0923
Web site: <www.rootsweb.com/~nmschs/>

Sons of the American Revolution, NM Society
12429 Chelwood Court NW, Albuquerque, NM 87112

Southeastern New Mexico Genealogical Society
P.O. Box 5725, Hobbs, NM 88240

Southern New Mexico Genealogical Society
P.O. Box 2563, Las Cruces, NM 88004

Totah Tracers Genealogical Society
% Salmon Ruins Museum, P.O. Box 125, Bloomfield, NM 87413-0125

Wilson-Cobb History and Genealogy Research Library
2212 W. Second, P.O. Box 2964, Roswell, NM 88202

BIBLIOGRAPHY

■ GENERAL RESOURCES

Archives of the Archdiocese of Santa Fe, 1678–1900
by Angelico Chavez (Washington, DC: Academy of American Franciscan History, 1957)

Caronado's Land: Daily Life in Colonial New Mexico
by Marc Simons (Galveston, TX: Frontier Press, 1996)

Foreigners in their Native Land: Historical Roots Of the Mexican Americans
by David J. Weber (Albuquerque, NM: University of New Mexico Press, 1972)

A Forgotten Kingdom: The Spanish Frontier In Colorado and New Mexico 1540–1821
by Frederic J. Athern (Denver: Bureau of Land Management, Colorado State Office, 1989)

Genealogical Resources in New Mexico
by Robert E. Esterly (Albuquerque: New Mexico Genealogical Society, 1997)

The Genealogist's Companion and Sourcebook, 2d ed.
by Emily Anne Croom (Cincinnati: Betterway Books, 2003)

A Genealogist's Guide to Discovering Your African-American Ancestors
by Franklin Carter Smith and Emily Anne Croom (Cincinnati: Betterway Books, 2003)

Guide to Genealogical Research in the National Archives of the United States
edited by Anne Bruner Eales and Robert M. Kvasnicka (Washington, DC: National Archives and Records Administration, 2000)

*Handy Genealogical Guide to
New Mexico*
by Joyce V. Hawley Spiros (Gallup, NM: Verlene Publishing,
1981)

*A History of the Church of Jesus
Christ of Latter-Day Saints in
New Mexico, 1876–1989*
by Lyle K. Porter (Albuquerque:
L.K. and W.H. Porter, 2001)

*A History of the Italians In New
Mexico*
by Frederick G. Bohme (New
York: Arno Press, 1975)

*History of Mormon Settlements
in Mexico and New Mexico*
by H. Mannie Foster (Logan, UT:
Utah State Agricultural College,
1955)

*A History of New Mexico, 3
vols.*
by Charles F. Coan (Chicago: The
American Historical Society,
1925)

*History of New Mexico: Its
Resources and People, 2 vols.*
(Los Angeles: Pacific States Pub-
lishing Co., 1907)

*An Illustrated History of New
Mexico*
by Thomas E. Chavez (Albuquerque: University of New Mexico
Press, 2002)

*An Illustrated History of New
Mexico: Containing a History of
this Important Section of the
Great Southwest, from the
Earliest Period of its Discovery to
the Present Time . . . Portraits of
Some of its Eminent Men, and
Biographical Mention of Many of
its Pioneers and Prominent
Citizens of Today*
(Chicago: Lewis Pub. Co., 1895)

*Leading Facts of New Mexican
History, 2 vols.*
by Ralph Emerson Twitchell (Salem, MA: Higginson Book Co.,
1994)

*Los Primeros Pobladores:
Antecesores De Los Chicanos
En Nuevo Mexico*
by Frances Leon Swadesh (Mexico: Fondo de Cultura Economica,
1977)

*The Missions of New Mexico,
1776*
by Francisco A. Dominquez (Albuquerque: University of New Mexico Press, 1956)

*Mormons and Their Neighbors:
an Index to Over 75,000
Biographical Sketches from
1820 to the Present, 2 vols.*
by Marvin E. Wiggins (Provo, UT:
Harold B. Lee Library, Brigham
Young University, 1984)

*National Archives Microfilm
Catalogs online:*
<www.archives.gov/publica
tions/genealogy_microfilm_
catalogs.html>

*Navajos in the Catholic Church
Records of New Mexico,
1694–1875*
by David M. Brugge (Window
Rock, AZ: Parks and Recreation
Dept., 1968)

*The Navajos: The Past and
Present of a Great People*
by John Upton Terrell (NY: Wey-
bright and Talley, 1970)

*Origins of New Mexico Families
in the Spanish Colonial Period
in Two Parts: The Seventeenth
(1598–1693) and the
Eighteenth (1693–1821)
Centuries*
by Fray Angelico Chavez (Albuquerque: the University of Albuquerque, 1973)

*The Plains Indians and New
Mexico, 1751–1778: A
Collection of Documents
Illustrative of the History of the
Eastern Frontier of New Mexico*
by Alfred Barnaby Thomas (Ann
Arbor, MI: University Microfilms
International, 1978)

*Pobladores: Hispanic
Americans of the Ute Frontier*
by Frances Leon Swadesh (Notre
Dame, IN: University of Notre
Dame Press, 1991)

*Protestantism in the Sangre De
Cristos, 1850–1920*
by Randi Jones Walker (Albuquerque: University of New Mexico
Press, 1991)

*Sanctuaries of Spanish New
Mexico*
by Marc Treib (Berkeley, CA: University of California Press, 1933)

*Soldiers of the Cross: notes on
the Ecclesiastical History of
New Mexico, Arizona and
Colorado*
by Jean Baptiste Salpointe (Banning, CA: St. Boniface's Industrial
School, 1898)

*Sources for New Mexican
History, 1821–1848*
by Daniel Tyler (Santa Fe, NM:
Museum of New Mexico Press,
1984)

*The Southern Utes: A Tribal
History*
by James Jefferson (Ignacio, CO:
Southern Ute Tribe, ca. 1972)

Southwestern Indian Tribes
by Tom Bahti (Las Vegas, NV: KC
Publications, 1968)

*The Spanish Archives of New
Mexico: Compiled and
Chronologically Arrange With
Historical, Genealogical,
Geographical, and Other
Annotations, By Authority of
the State of New Mexico*
by Ralph Emerson Twitchell (Ce-
dar Rapids, IA: Torch Press,
1914)

*The Spanish Borderlands: A
Chronicle of Old Florida and the
Southwest*
by Herbert E. Bolton (Galveston,
TX: Frontier Press, 1996)

*Spanish and Mexican Records
of the American Southwest: A
Bibliographic Guide to Archive
and Manuscript Sources*
by Henry P. Beers (Tucson, AZ:
University of Arizona Press,
1979)

*Spanish Mission Churches of
New Mexico*
by Le Baron Bradford Prince (Glorieta, NM: Rio Grande Press,
1977)

The Taos Indians
by Blanche Chloe Grant (Glorieta,
NM: Rio Grande Press, 1976)

*The Territorial press of New
Mexico, 1834–1912*
by Porter A. Stratton (Albuquerque: University of New Mexico
Press, 1969)

The Ute Mountain Utes
by Robert W. Delaney (Albuquerque: University of New Mexico
Press, 1989)

*Voices of the Territory of New
Mexico: and Oral History of
People of Spanish Descent and
Early Settlers born During the
Territorial Days*
by Alfonso Griego (S.l.: Griego,
1985)

*Women of the New Mexico
Frontier; 1846–1912*
by Cheryl J. Foote (Niwot, CO: University Press of Colorado, 1990)

*20,000 Years of History: A New
Mexico Bibliography*
by Frances Leon Swadesh (Santa
Fe: Sunstone Press, 1973)

■ CENSUS RECORDS

*The American Census
Handbook*
by Thomas Jay Kemp (Wilmington, DE: Scholarly Resources,
Inc., 2001)

*The Census Book: A Genealo-
gist's Guide to Federal Census
Facts, Schedules and Indexes*
by William Dollarhide (Bountiful,
UT: Heritage Quest, 1999)

*Finding Answers In U.S. Census
Records*
by Loretto Dennis Szucs and Matthew Wright (Salt Lake City: Ancestry Publishing, 2001)

*Latin American Census
Records, 2d ed.*
by Lyman D. Platt (Salt Lake City:
Instituto Genealogico e Historico
Latinoamericano, 1992)

*Map Guide to the U.S. Federal
Censuses 1790–1920*
by William Thorndale and William
Dollarhide (Baltimore: Genealogical Publishing Co., 1987)

*Spanish and Mexican Censuses
of New Mexico: 1750–1830*
by Virginia L. Olmsted (Albuquerque: New Mexico Genealogical
Society, 1981)

*Spanish and Mexican Colonial
Censuses of New Mexico:
1790, 1823, 1845*
by Virginia L. Olmsted (Albuquerque: New Mexico Genealogical
Society, 1975)

State Census Records
by Ann S. Lainhart (Baltimore: Genealogical Publishing Co, Inc.,
1992)

*Your Guide to the Federal
Census*
by Kathleen W. Hinckley (Cincinnati: Betterway Books, 2002)

■ IMMIGRATION RECORDS

*American Naturalization
Records, 1790–1990: What
They Are and How to Use Them*
by John J. Newman (North Salt
Lake, UT: HeritageQuest, 1998)

New Mexico

American Passenger Arrival Records
by Michael Tepper (Baltimore: Genealogical Publishing Co., 1993)

The Juan Paez Hurtado Expedition of 1865: Fraud in Recruiting colonists for New Mexico
by John B. Colligan (Albuquerque: University of New Mexico Press, 1995)

Let There be Towns: Spanish Municipal Origins in the American Southwest, 1610–1810
by Gilberto Rafael Cruz (College Station, TX: Texas A & M University Press, 1988)

Mexican Immigrant: His Life-Story
by Manuel Gamio (New York: Arno Press and the New York Times, 1969)

Mexican Immigration to the United States: A Study of Human Migration and Adjustment
by Manuel Gamio (New York: Arno Press and the New York Times, 1969)

Over 1400 Naturalization Records for Various Courts of New Mexico: 1882–1917, Denver Federal Archives
Lakewood, CO: Foothills Genealogical Society of Colorado, 1998)

They Became Americans: Finding Naturalization Records and Ethnic Origins
by Loretto Dennis Szucs (Salt Lake City: Ancestry, Inc., 1998)

They Came in Ships: A Guide to Finding Your Immigrant Ancestor's Arrival Records, 2d ed.
by John P. Colletta (Salt Lake City: Ancestry, Inc., 1993)

■ LAND RECORDS

A Guide to the Microfilm of Papers Relating to New Mexico Land Grants
by Albert James Diaz (Albuquerque: University of New Mexico Press, 1960)

Land and Property Research in the United States
by Wade E. Hone (Salt Lake City: Ancestry Inc., 1997)

Locating Your Roots: Discover Your Ancestors Using Land Records
by Patricia Law Hatcher (Cincinnati: Betterway Books, 2003)

Miscellaneous Archives Relating to New Mexico Land Grants, 1695–1842
(Albuquerque: University of New Mexico Library, 1955–1957)

Press Copies of Grant Papers
from the Surveyor General's office of the New Mexico Territory (Santa Fe: University of New Mexico Library, 1955–57)

The Public Domain in New Mexico, 1854–1891
by Victor Westphall (Albuquerque: University of New Mexico, 1965)

Record of Private Land Claims Adjudicated By the U.S. Surveyor General, 1855–1890
from the Surveyor General's office of the New Mexico Territory (Albuquerque: University of New Mexico Library, 1955–1957)

Records of Land Titles, 1847–1852
from the secretary's office of the New Mexico Territory (Albuquerque: University of New Mexico Library, 1955–1957)

Spanish & Mexican Land Grants in New Mexico and Colorado
by John R. Van Ness and Christine M. Van Ness (Manhattan, KN: AG Press, ca. 1980)

Vigil's Index, 1681–1846
by Donaciano Vigil (Albuquerque: University of New Mexico Library, 1955–1957)

■ MAPS

"The County Boundaries of New Mexico"
by Charles F. Coan (*Southwestern Political Science Quarterly*, December 1922: 252-86; Reprint: Santa Fe, NM: Legislative Council Service, 1965)

Historical Atlas of New Mexico
by Warren A. Beck and Ynez D. Haase (Norman, OK: University of Oklahoma Press, 1969)

New Mexico in Maps
edited by Jerry L. Williams (Albuquerque: University of New Mexico Press, 1986)

New Mexico Place Names: A Geographical Dictionary
by T.M. Pearce (Albuquerque: University of New Mexico Press, 1985)

The Place Names of New Mexico, 2d ed.
by Robert Hixson Julyan (Albuquerque: University of New Mexico Press, 1998)

Post Offices of New Mexico
by Richard W. Helbock (Las Cruces, NM: R.W. Helbock, 1981)

"The Territorial Post Offices of New Mexico"
by Sheldon H. Dike (*New Mexico Historical Review*, October 1958)

■ MILITARY RECORDS

The History of the Military Occupation of the Territory of New Mexico from 1846 to 1851 by the Government Of the United States: Together with Biographical Sketches of Men Prominent in the Conduct of the Government During that Period
by Ralph E. Twitchell (Tucson, AZ: W.C. Cox, 1974)

It Tolled for New Mexico: New Mexicans Captured by the Japanese, 1941–1945
by Eva Jane Matson (Las Cruces, NM: Yucca Tree Press, 1994)

New Mexico's Buffalo Soldiers, 1866–1900
by Monroe Lee Billington (Niwot, CO: University Press of Colorado, 1991)

Soldiers and Settlers: Military Supply in the Southwest, 1861–1885
by Darlis A. Miller (Albuquerque: University of New Mexico Press, 1989)

Uncle, We Are Ready! Registering America's Men, 1917–1918: A Guide to Researching World War I Draft Registration Cards
by John J. Newman (North Salt Lake, UT: HeritageQuest, 2001)

U.S. Military Records: A Guide to Federal & State Sources, Colonial America to the Present
by James C. Neagles (Salt Lake City: Ancestry, Inc., 1994)

World War II: A Family Historian's Guide
by Debra Johnson Knox (Spartanburg, SC: MIE Publishing, 2003)

■ VITAL RECORDS

Cemetery Records from Southern New Mexico
by Lee Myers (Lee Myers, 1982)

New Mexico Roots LTD: A Demographic Perspective from Genealogical, Historical, and Geographical Data Found in the Diligencia Matrimoniales or Pre-nuptial Investigations (1678–1869) of the Archives of the Archdiocese of Santa Fe
by Angelico Chavez (Santa Fe: Angelico Chavez, 1982)

Some Marriages of the State of New Mexico, ca. 1880–1920, 2 vols.
(New Mexico Chapter, Daughters of the American Revolution, 1971–73)

Your Guide to Cemetery Research
by Sharon DeBartolo Carmack (Cincinnati: Betterway Books, 2002)

■ **Bernalillo** 9 Jan. 1852
1 Civic Plaza NW, Albuquerque, NM 87102
Phone: (505)768-4090
Web site: www.rootsweb.com/~nmbernal/
Parent County: Original county

Record Type	Year Begun	Jurisdiction
Marriage	1885	County Clerk
Land	1873	County Clerk

■ **Catron** 25 Feb. 1921
P.O. Box 197, Reserve, NM 87830
Phone: (505)533-6400
Web site: bombaci.rootsweb.com/Catron/
Parent County: Socorro

Record Type	Year Begun	Jurisdiction
Marriage	1921	County Clerk
Land	1921	County Clerk
Probate	1921	County Clerk

■ **Chaves** 25 Feb. 1887
P.O. Box 580, Roswell, NM 88202
Phone: (505)624-6614
Web site: www.rootsweb.com/~nmchaves/
Parent County: Lincoln

Record Type	Year Begun	Jurisdiction
Probate	1900	Clerk/District Ct.

■ **Cibola** 1981
P.O. Box 190, Grants, NM 87020
Phone: (505)285-2535
Web site: bombaci.rootsweb.com/Cibola/
Parent County: Valencia

Record Type	Year Begun	Jurisdiction
Marriage	1981	County Clerk
Land	1981	County Clerk
Probate	1981	County Clerk

■ **Colfax** 25 Jan. 1869
P.O. Box 159, Raton, NM 87740
Phone: (505)445-5551
Web site: www.rootsweb.com/~nmcolfax/
Parent County: Taos

Record Type	Year Begun	Jurisdiction
Land	1864	County Clerk

■ **Curry** 25 Feb. 1909
P.O. Box 1168, Clovis, NM 88102
Phone: (505)763-5591
Web site: www.rootsweb.com/~nmcurry/
Parent County: Quay, Roosevelt

■ **De Baca** 28 Feb. 1917
P.O. Box 347, Fort Sumner, NM 88119
Phone: (505)355-2601
Web site: www.rootsweb.com/~nmdebaca/
Parent County: Chaves, Guadalupe, Roosevelt

■ **Doña Ana** 9 Jan. 1852
251 W. Amador Ave. Room 103, Las Cruces, NM 88005
Phone: (505)647-7421

Web site: www.rootsweb.com/~nmdonaan/
Parent County: Original county

■ **Eddy** 25 Feb. 1889
101 W. Greene, Carlsbad, NM 88220
Phone: (505)885-3383
Web site: www.rootsweb.com/~nmeddy/eddyfiles.html
Parent County: Lincoln

■ **Grant** 30 Jan. 1868
P.O. Box 898, Silver City, NM 88062
Phone: (505)574-0042
Web site: www.rootsweb.com/~nmgrant/
Parent County: Doña Ana

■ **Guadalupe** 26 Feb. 1891
420 Parker Ave., Santa Rosa, NM 88435
Phone: (505)472-3791
Web site: www.rootsweb.com/~nmguadal/
Parent County: Lincoln, San Miguel

■ **Harding** 4 Mar. 1921
P.O. Box 1002, Mosquero, NM 87733
Phone: (505)673-2301
Web site: www.rootsweb.com/~nmhardin/
Parent County: Mora, Union

■ **Hidalgo** 25 Feb. 1919
300 S. Shakespeare St., Lordsburg, NM 88045
Phone: (505)542-9213
Web site: www.rootsweb.com/~nmhidalg/
Parent County: Grant

■ **Lea** 7 Mar. 1917
P.O. Box 1507, Lovington, NM 88260
Phone: (505)396-8619
Web site: www.rootsweb.com/~nmlea/
Parent County: Chaves, Eddy

■ **Lincoln** 16 Jan. 1869
300 Central Ave., P.O. Box 338, Carrizozo, NM 88301
Phone: (505)648-2394
Web site: www.rootsweb.com/~nmlincol/
Parent County: Socorro, Doña Ana

■ **Los Alamos** 16 Mar. 1949
2300 Trinity Dr., P.O. Box 30, Los Alamos, NM 87544
Phone: (505)662-8010
Web site: www.rootsweb.com/~nmlosala/
Parent County: Sandoval, Santa Fe

■ **Luna** 16 Mar. 1901
P.O. Box 1838, Deming, NM 88031
Phone: (505)546-0491
Web site: www.rootsweb.com/~nmluna/
Parent County: Doña Ana, Grant

■ **McKinley** 23 Feb. 1899
P.O. Box 1268, Gallup, NM 87305
Phone: (505)863-6866

Web site: bombaci.rootsweb.com/McKinley/
Parent County: Valencia, San Juan, Río Arriba

■ **Mora** 1 Feb. 1860
P.O. Box 360, Mora, NM 87732
Phone: (505)387-2448
Web site: www.rootsweb.com/~nmmora/
Parent County: Taos

■ **Otero** 30 Jan. 1899
1000 New York Ave., Alamogordo, NM 88310
Phone: (505)437-4942
Web site: www.rootsweb.com/~nmotero/
Parent County: Doña Ana, Lincoln, Socorro

■ **Quay** 28 Feb. 1903
P.O. Box 1225, Tucumcari, NM 88401
Phone: (505)461-0510
Web site: www.rootsweb.com/~nmquay/
Parent County: Guadalupe

■ **Río Arriba** 9 Jan. 1852
County Courthouse P.O. Box 158, Tierra Amarilla, NM 87575
Phone: (505)588-7724
Web site: www.rootsweb.com/~nmrioarr/
Parent County: Original county

■ **Roosevelt** 28 Feb. 1903
109 W. First St., Portales, NM 88130
Phone: (505)356-8562
Web site: www.rootsweb.com/~nmroosev/
Parent County: Chaves, Guadalupe

■ **San Juan** 24 Feb. 1887
P.O. Box 550, Aztec, NM 87410
Phone: (505)334-9471
Web site: bombaci.rootsweb.com/SanJuan/
Parent County: Río Arriba

■ **San Miguel** 9 Jan. 1852
500 W. National St., Las Vegas, NM 87701
Phone: (505)425-9331
Web site: www.rootsweb.com/~nmsanmig/index.html
Parent County: Original county

■ **Sandoval** 10 Mar. 1903
P.O. Box 40, Bernalillo, NM 87004
Phone: (505)867-7572
Web site: www.rootsweb.com/~nmsandov/
Parent County: Bernalillo

Record Type	Year Begun	Jurisdiction
Marriage	1926	County Clerk
Land	1903	County Recorder
Probate	1903	County Clerk
Death	1925	Bureau/Public Health

■ **Santa Ana** 1844
Parent County: Original county
Comments/research tips: Became part of Bernalillo County, 1876.

■ **Santa Fe** 9 Jan. 1852
P.O. Box 276, Santa Fe, NM 87504
Phone: (505)986-6280
Web site: www.rootsweb.com/~nmsantaf/
Parent County: Original county

■ **Sierra** 3 Apr. 1884
100 N. Date St., Truth or Consequences, NM 87901
Phone: (505)894-2840
Web site: www.rootsweb.com/~nmsierra/
Parent County: Socorro

■ **Socorro** 9 Jan. 1852
200 Church St., P.O. Box 1, Socorro, NM 87801
Phone: (505)835-0423
Web site: www.rootsweb.com/~nmsocorr/
Parent County: Original county

Record Type	Year Begun	Jurisdiction
Land	1851	County Clerk
Probate	1874	County Clerk
Court	1851	County Recorder
Death	1907	Bureau/Public Health

■ **Taos** 9 Jan. 1852
105 Albright St. Suite D, Taos, NM 87571
Phone: (505)737-6380
Web site: http://resources.rootsweb.com/USA/NM/Taos/
Parent County: Original county

■ **Torrance** 16 Mar. 1903
P.O. Box 767, Estancia, NM 87016
Phone: (505)384-2221
Web site: www.usgennet.org/usa/nm/county/torrance/
Parent County: Lincoln, San Miguel, Socorro, Santa Fe, Valencia
Comments/research tips: Courthouse burned in 1910.

■ **Union** 23 Feb. 1893
P.O. Box 430, Clayton, NM 88415-0430
Phone: (505)374-9491
Web site: www.rootsweb.com/~nmunion/
Parent County: Colfax, Mora, San Miguel

■ **Valencia** 9 Jan. 1852
P.O. Box 969, Los Lunas, NM 87031
Phone: (505)866-2073
Web site: www.rootsweb.com/~nmvalenc/
Parent County: Original county

Record Type	Year Begun	Jurisdiction
Probate	1871	County Clerk
Land	1873	City Clerk
Death	1907	City Clerk

New York

By Rhonda R. McClure

HISTORICAL OVERVIEW

Originally New Netherland, New York was founded by the Dutch West India Company, a merchant company founded in 1621 and chartered by the Dutch government. The colony would remain New Netherland until 1664, when the English separated it into what became the British colonies of New York and New Jersey.

After the American Revolutionary War ended in 1783, Loyalists from New York were relocated to Nova Scotia, New Brunswick, and the British West Indies. If your ancestor seems to have disappeared about this time, you may want to investigate these areas.

The Reorganization Act of 1788 divided the state into 120 towns, and these towns became the level at which many records are recorded. Cities are not part of towns. In fact, New York City is in many ways almost a separate entity, exempt from some of the state laws, which can affect record keeping.

New York began to really grow in many different ways after the American Revolutionary War. When its port was chosen by many of the shipping lines to be a major stop, this increased the traffic of immigrants and cargo, giving New York City an opportunity to become a thriving metropolis. The completion of the Erie Canal in 1825 further enhanced travel through the state of New York.

RECORD HIGHLIGHTS

Land records in New York have gone through a number of different systems. The first Dutch owners enacted patroonship—manorial—records, which was changed to patents and surveys by the British, and finally to the more modern system of deeds and mortgages. To get a true sense all of these different records and what exists, you will want to check out the Land Records section of the

NEW YORK AT A GLANCE

Motto: Excelsior

Population: 18.9 million

Prevalent Religions: Roman Catholicism rules in New York State, followed by Judaism, with smaller numbers of Methodist, Lutheran, Presbyterian, Pentecostal, Baptist, and Episcopalian. Muslim, Buddhism, and all world religions are also present.

Major Industries: Printing and publishing, scientific instruments, electrical equipment, machinery, chemical products, tourism, dairy products, cattle and other livestock, vegetables, nursery stock, apples

Ethnic Makeup (in percent): Caucasian 67.9%, African American 15.9%, Hispanic 15.1%, Asian 5.5%, Native American 0.4%, Other 7.1%

Famous New Yorkers: Lucille Ball, Humphrey Bogart, James Cagney, Aaron Copland, Sammy Davis Jr., George Eastman, Millard Fillmore, Lou Gehrig, George Gershwin, Washington Irving, Henry James, Jerome Kern, Marx Brothers, Herman Melville, Ogden Nash, Eugene O'Neill, Red Jacket, Christopher Reeve, John D. Rockefeller, Norman Rockwell, Franklin D. Roosevelt, Margaret Sanger, Barbra Streisand, Mae West, George Westinghouse, Edith Wharton, Walt Whitman

Above: Traffic in downtown Manhattan

© PhotoDisc/Getty Images

New York Research Outline published by the Family History Library and located on their Web site <www.familysearch.org> under the Research Helps section.

Probate records for New York can be a wealth of information. Instead of just concentrating on the wills—though you certainly want to locate that item—you want to look for the probate packets, handled by the Surrogate Court in each county. These probate packets offer many different documents generated during the estate settlement process that can offer you insight into where heirs are presently living, married names of women, and much more.

State census records for New York offer lots of useful information and are available from 1825 through 1855 for some counties, with many more counties available from 1865 through 1925. Those taken from 1855 to 1875 not only list where the person was born, but if they were born in the state of New York, the enumerator listed the county of birth. Some of them offer insight into how long the family or individual had been living in the given county.

Vital records for New York are not as encompassing as some other states. In fact, it wasn't until the mid-nineteenth century that the state even began to attempt to enforce the keeping of vital records. And it was not until the latter 1800s that the state attempted again and made progress. As a result, you will find that many times it is necessary to use vital record substitutes such as tombstones, newspapers, and church records to get the dates of birth, marriage, or death that you are seeking. While the towns originate the records, a copy is sent to the New York Department of Health in Albany, with the exception of New York City's boroughs. When trying to determine if vital records exist, it's a good idea to search Albany as well as the individual town. You can request copies from the Department of Health by writing to the Genealogy Unit, Vital Records Section, P.O. Box 2602, Albany, NY 12220-2602. Be prepared to be patient, as requests to this unit can take up to ten months to process. They suggest contacting the local town registrar if you know the exact place of birth, death, or marriage.

Vital records for New York City's boroughs are filed in the New York City Municipal Archives, 31 Chambers Street, New York, NY 10007. Record availability varies from borough to borough. Many of them have been microfilmed and are available through the Family History Library.

STATE RESOURCES

■ ARCHIVES, LIBRARIES, AND SOCIETIES

Adirondack Genealogical Historical Society
100 Main St., Saranac Lake, NY 12983
E-mail: mtucker@northnet.org
Web site: <http://freepages.genealogy.rootsweb.com/~adkghs/>

Adriance Memorial Library
93 Market St., Poughkeepsie, NY 12601
Tel: (845) 485-3445
Web site: <http://poklib.org/html/adriance.php>

African-Atlantic Genealogical Society (AAGS)
P.O. Box 7385, Freeport, NY 11520
Web site:

Albany County Hall of Records
95 Tivoli St., Albany, NY 12207
Tel: (518) 436-3663
Web site: <www.albanycounty.com/departments/records/>

Allegany Area Historical Association (AAHA)
P.O. Box 162, Allegany, NY 14706
E-mail: oep31@juno.com
Web site: <http://bfn.org/~aaha/>

Almond Historical Society
7 Main St., Almond, NY 14804
Web site: <www.rootsweb.com/~nyahs/AlmondHS.html>

American Baptist-Samuel Colgate Historical Library
1106 S. Goodman St., Rochester, NY 14620-2532
Tel: (716) 473-1740
E-mail: abhs@creds.edu
Web site: <www.crds.edu/abhs/default.htm>

American Irish Historical Society
991 Fifth Ave., New York, NY 10028
Web site:

American Jewish Historical Society
15 W. Sixth St., New York, NY 10011
Tel: (212) 294-6160
Web site:

American Scandinavian Foundation
58 Park Ave., New York, NY 10016
Tel: (212) 879-9779
E-mail: info@amscan.org
Web site:

Archdiocese of New York
1011 First Ave., New York, NY 10022-4134
Tel: (212) 371-1000
Web site:

Lee Baeck Institute German-Jewish Families
129 E. 73 St., New York, NY 10021

Bethlehem Historical Association
1003 River Rd., Selkirk, NY 12158

Blauvelt Free Library
541 Western Hwy., Blauvelt, NY 10913-2014
Web site: <www.rcls.org/blv/>

Bridge Line Historical Society
P.O. Box 13324, Albany, NY 12212
Web site:

Bronx County Historical Society
3309 Bainbridge Ave., The Bronx, NY 10467
Web site: <www.bronxhistoricalsociety.org/index86.html>

Brooklyn Historical Society
128 Pierrepont St., Brooklyn, NY 11201
Web site: <www.brooklynhistory.org/indexWeb.html>

Buffalo Irish Genealogical Society (BIGS)
GAAA Library Buffalo Irish Center, 245 Abbott Rd., Buffalo, NY 14220
Tel: (716) 662-1164
Web site: <www.buffalonet.org/army/bigs.htm>

Capital District Genealogical Society
P.O. Box 2175, Albany, NY 12220-0175

Cayuga County Historian's Office
Historic Old Post Office Bldg., 3d Floor, 157 Genesee St., Auburn, NY 13021
Tel: (315) 253-1300

New York

Ottawa

ONTARIO

Kingston

JEFFERSON

LEWIS

Toronto

OSWEGO

ONEIDA

ORLEANS

Rochester

NIAGARA

WAYNE

Utica

Niagara Falls

MONROE

Syracuse

GENESEE

ONONDAGA

MADISON

ONTARIO

Buffalo

West Seneca

SENECA CAYUGA

ERIE

WYOMING

LIVINGSTON

YATES

CORTLAND

CHENANGO

TOMPKINS

SCHUYLER

CHAUTAUQUA

CATTARAUGUS

ALLEGANY

STEUBEN

TIOGA

BROOME

CHEMUNG

Binghamton

ERIE

PENNSYLVANIA

WARREN

MCKEAN

POTTER

TIOGA

BRADFORD

SUSQUEHANNA

CRAWFORD

WAYNE

WYOMING

LACKAWANNA

FOREST

SULLIVAN

Scranton

VENANGO

ELK

CAMERON

LYCOMING

Wilkes-Barre

CLARION

JEFFERSON

CLINTON

LUZERNE

MONROE

COLUMBIA

CLEARFIELD

CENTRE

UNION

MONTOUR

CARBON

BUTLER

NORTHAMPTON

ARMSTRONG

NORTHUMBERLAND

SNYDER

INDIANA

MIFFLIN

SCHUYLKILL

Allentown

CAMBRIA

BLAIR

JUNIATA

LEHIGH

Altoona

DAUPHIN

BERKS

PERRY

LEBANON

Reading

WESTMORELAND

HUNTINGDON

Harrisburg

MONTGOMERY

CUMBERLAND

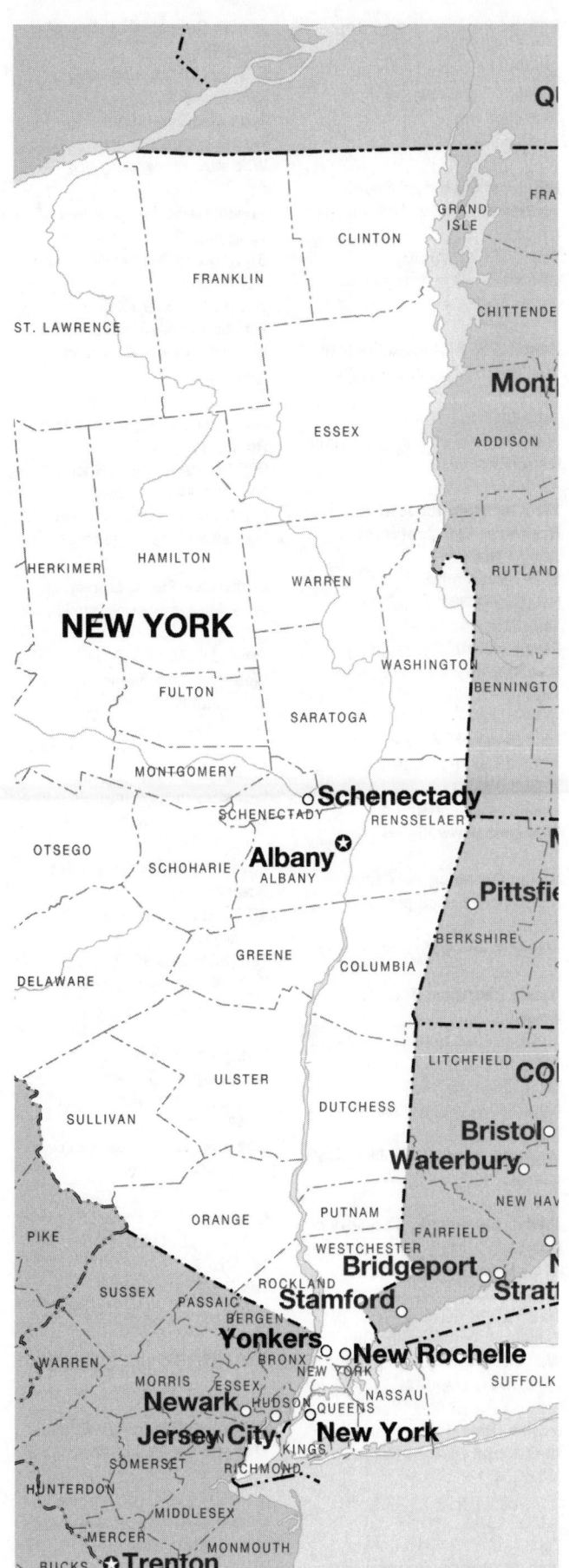

E-mail: historian@co.cayuga.ny.us
Web site: <www.co.cayuga.ny.us/history/>

Cayuga-Owasco Lakes Historical Society
P.O. Box 247, 14 W. Cayuga St., Moravia, NY 13118
Web site: <www.rootsweb.com/~nycayuga/colhs.htm>

Central New York Genealogical Society
P.O. Box 104, Colvin Station, Syracuse, NY 13205
Web site: <www.rootsweb.com/~nycnygs/>

Cheektowgo Historical Association
3329 Broadway, Cheektowga, NY 14227
Tel: (716) 683-5589

Chemung Valley History Museum/Chemung County Historical Society
415 E. Water St., Elmira, NY 14901
Tel: (607) 734-4167
E-mail: cchs@chemungvalleymuseum.org
Web site:

Chenango Historical Society
45 Rexford St., Norwich, NY 13815
Web site: <www.chenangocounty.org/chencohistso/>

The Children's Aid Society
105 E. 22nd St.; New York, NY 10010
Tel: (212) 949-4800
Web site:

Columbia County Historical Society
5 Albany Ave., P.O. Box 311, Kinderhook, NY 12106
Tel: (518) 758-9265
Web site: <www.berkshire.net/OnlineArchives/columbia/cchs.html>

Columbia University, Journalism Library
203 Journalism, 2950 Broadway, New York, NY 10027
Tel: (212) 854-0390
E-mail: journalism@ibraries.cul.columbia.edu
Web site: <www.columbia.edu/cu/lweb/indiv/jour/>

Commission on History, Reformed Church in America
New Brunswick Theological Seminary, Gardner A. Sage Library, 21 Seminary Pl., New Brunswick, NJ 08901
Tel: (732) 246-1779

Congregational Library and Archives
14 Beacon St., Boston, MA 02108
Tel: (617) 523-0470
Web site:

Cortland County Historical Society, Inc.
25 Homer Ave., Cortland, NY 13045
Tel: (607) 756-6071
Web site: <www.rootsweb.com/~nycortla/chsfe.htm>

Cow Neck Peninsula Historical Society
336 Port Washington Blvd., Port Washington, NY 11050–4530
Tel: (516) 365-9074
E-mail: curator@cowneck.org
Web site:

Creole-American Genealogical Society, Inc.
P.O. Box 2666, Church Street Station, New York, NY 10008

East Greenbush Community Library
10 Community Way, East Greenbush, NY 12061
Tel: (518) 447-7476
Web site:

East Hampton Library
159 Main St., East Hampton, NY 11937
Tel: (631) 324-0222
E-mail: ehamlib@suffolk.lib.ny.us
Web site: <www.easthamptonlibrary.org/index.html>

East Hampton Historical Society
101 Main St., East Hampton, NY 11937
Tel: (631) 324-6850
Web site:

Eastchester Historical Society
P.O. Box 37, Eastchester, NY 10709
Web site: <www.museumsusa.org/data/museums/NY/22461.htm>

Episcopal Diocese of New York
1047 Amsterdam Ave., New York, NY 10025

New York

Tel: (212) 316-7400
E-mail: info@dioceseny.org
Web site:

Essex County Historical Society/Adirondack History Center Museum
P.O. Box 428, 7590 Court St., Elizabethtown, NY 12932
Tel: (518) 873-6466
E-mail: echs@northnet.org
Web site:

Evangelical Lutheran Church in America, Metropolitan New York Synod
Interchurch Center, 475 Riverside Dr., Suite 1620, New York, NY 10115
Tel: (212) 665-0732
Web site: <www.elca.org>

Family History Library
35 NW Temple St., Salt Lake City, UT 84150–3400
Tel: (801) 240-2331 or (800) 453-3860 x.22331
Web site: <www.familysearch.org>

Finger Lake Finns
Web site:

Roswell P. Flower Memorial Library
229 Washington St., Watertown, NY 13601
Tel: (315) 788-2352
E-mail: flower@northnet.org
Web site:

Genealogical Society of Rockland County
P.O. Box 444, New City, NY 10956
Web site: <www.rootsweb.com/~nyrockla/GSRC/>

General Society of Colonial Wars Archives
Langsdale Library, 1420 Maryland Ave., Baltimore, MD 21201
E-mail: gscw@ubmail.ubalt.edu
Web site:

Genesse County Genealogy Society
Web site: <www.rootsweb.com/~nygags/index.htm>

Geneva Free Library
244 Main St., Geneva, NY 14456
Tel: (315) 789-5303
E-mail: geneva@pls-net.org
Web site: <http://geneva.pls-net.org/>

Geneva Historical Society
543 S. Main St., Geneva, NY 14456
Tel: (315) 789-5151
E-mail: info@genevahistoricalsociety.com
Web site:

German Genealogical Group
P.O. Box 1004, Kings Park, NY 11754
Web site:

Goshen Public Library and Historical Society
203 Main St., Goshen, NY 10924
Tel: (845) 294-6606
Web site: <http://ansernet.rcls.org/gplhs/>

Greater Ridgewood Historical Society
1820 Flushing Ave., Ridgewood, NY 11385
Web site: <http://members.aol.com/ondrdnkhse/grhs.htm>

Guernsey Memorial Library
3 Court St., Norwich, NY 13815
Tel: (607) 334-4034
Web site: <www.4cls.org/webpages/members/Norwich/NORWICH.HTML>

Hebrew Immigrant Aid Society (HIAS)
333 Seventh Ave., 17th Floor, New York, NY 10001-5004
Tel: (212) 967-4100
Web site: <www.hias.org/splash.html>

Heritage Hunters
P.O. Box 270, Sarasota Springs, NY 12866-0270
Web site: <www.rootsweb.com/~nysarato/gwsarhh.html>

Herkimer County Historical Society
400 N. Main St., Herkimer, NY 13350
Tel: (315) 866-6413
E-mail: herkimerhistory@yahoo.com
Web site: <www.rootsweb.com/~nyhchs/info.htm/odyframe.htm>

Hispanic Genealogical Society of New York
309 W. 105th St., New York, NY 10025
Web site:

Holland Society of New York
122 E. 58th St., New York, NY 10022
E-mail: hollsoc@aol.com
Web site: <http://members.aol.com/hollsoc/>

Huguenot Historical Society
18 Broadhead Ave., New Paltz, NY 12561
Tel: (845) 255-1660
Web site:

Huntington Historical Society
209 Main St., Huntington, NY 11743
Tel: (631) 427-7045
Web site:

YIVO Institute for Jewish Research, The Center for Jewish History
15 W. Sixteenth St., New York, NY 10011-6301
Tel: (212) 246-6080
E-mail: yivomail@yivo.cjh.org
Web site:

Irish Family History Forum
P.O. Box 67, Plainview, NY 11803-0067
E-mail: president@ifhf.org
Web site:

Italian Genealogical Group
P.O. Box 626, Bethpage, NY 11714-0626
Web site:

Italian Historical Society of America
111 Columbia Heights, Brooklyn, NY 11201
Tel: (718) 852-2929
E-mail: society1@italianhistorical.org
Web site:

Jewish Genealogical Society of Buffalo
3700 Main St., Amherst, NY 14226-3233
Tel: (716) 833-0743
E-mail: lefcourt@localnet.com
Web site: <www.jewishgen.org/iajgs/members.html>

Jewish Genealogical Society of the Capital District (NY), (JGSCD)
58 Edgecomb St., Albany, NY 12209-1306
Tel: (518) 462-4815
Web site: <www.jewishgen.org/iajgs/members.html>

Jewish Genealogical Society, Inc. (NY)
P.O. Box 6398, New York, NY 10128–0004
Tel: (212) 294-8326
E-mail: info@jgsny.org
Web site:

Jewish Genealogy Society of Long Island
37 Westcliff Dr., Dix Hills, NY 11746-5627
Tel: (631) 549-9532
E-mail: JGSLI@suffolk.lib.ny.us
Web site: <www.jewishgen.org/jgsli/>

Jewish Genealogical Society of Rochester
265 Viennawood Dr., Rochester, NY 14618-4465
Tel: (585) 271-2118
Web site: <http://jgsr.org/>

Johnstown Public Library
38 S. Market St., Johnstown, NY 12095
Tel: (518) 762-8317
Web site: <www.johnstown.com/library.html>

Lancaster New York Historical Society
Web site: <http://intotem.buffnet.net/lancasterpast/society/>

Livingston County Historical Society
30 Center St., Geneseo, NY 14454-1204
Tel: (585) 243-9147
Web site:

Livingston-Steuben County Genealogical Society
5 Elizabeth St., Dansville, NY 14437-1719
Web site: <www.rootsweb.com/~nyliving/lscgs.htm>

Long Beach Historical Society
P.O. Box 286, Long Beach, NY 11561
Tel: (515) 432-1192
E-mail: info@longbeachhistory.org
Web site:

Longwood Genealogy Group
Web site: <www.rootsweb.com/~nygglshp/>

Lynbrook Historical and Preservation Society
28 Hart St., Lynbrook, NY 11563–1711

E-mail: lynhistory@aol.com
Web site: <http://members.aol.com/lynhistory/lhps/lynindex.htm>

Madison County Historical Society
435 Main St., Oneida, NY 13421
Tel: (315) 363-4136
Web site: <www.dreamscape.com/mchs1900/>

Malverne Historical and Preservation Society
P.O. Box 393, Malverne, NY 11565
Tel: (516) 887-9727
Web site: <http://hometown.aol.com/lynhistory/malverne/malindex.htm>

Manlius Historical Society
109 Pleasant St., P.O. Box 28, Manlius, NY 13104
Tel: (315) 682-6660
E-mail: MHSDirector@aol.com
Web site: <www.manliushistory.org>

Margaret Reaney Memorial Library & Museum
19 Kingsbury Ave., St. Johnsville, NY 13452
Tel: (518) 568-7822
Web site: <www2.telenet.net/community/mvla/stjo/>

Minisink Valley Historical Society
125–133 W. Main St., P.O. Box 659, Port Jervis, NY 12771
Tel: (845) 856-2375
E-mail: history@minisink.org
Web site: <www.minisink.org>

Montgomery County Department of History and Archives
Old Courthouse, P.O. Box 1500, Fonda, NY 12068-1500
Tel: (518) 853-8186
Web site: <www.amsterdam-ny.com/mcha/>

Moore Memorial Library
59 Genesee St., Greene, NY 13778
Tel: (607) 656-9349
Web site: <www.4cls.org/Greene/Greene.html>

National Archives and Record Administration (NARA), Northeast Region (New York City)
201 Varick St., New York, NY 10014-4811
Tel: (212) 401-1620
E-mail: newyork.archives@nara.gov

Web site: <www.archives.gov/facilities/ny/new_york_city.html>

New Castle Historical Society
100 King St., Chappaqua, NY 10514
Tel: (914) 238-4666
E-mail: newcastlehs@aol.com
Web site:

New City Library
220 N. Main St., New City, NY 10956
Tel: (845) 634-4997
Web site:

New York City Board of Elections
32 Broadway, 7th Floor, New York, NY 10004-1609
Tel: (212) 487-5300
Web site: <www.vote.nyc.ny.us/index.jsp>

NYC Department of Records, Municipal Archives
31 Chambers St., Room 103, New York, NY 10007
Tel: (212) NEW-YORK
Web site: <www.nyc.gov/html/records/html/about/archives.shtml>

New York Family History Center
125 Columbus Ave. at 65th St., New York, NY 10023
Tel: (212) 873-1690

New York Foundling Hospital
590 Avenue of the Americas, New York, NY 10011
Tel: (212) 633-9300
Web site:

New York Genealogical and Biographical Society
122 E. 58th St., New York, NY 10022-1939
Tel: (212) 755-8532
Web site:

New York Historical Association
P.O. Box 800, Cooperstown, NY 13326
Tel: (607) 547-1400
Web site: <www.nysha.org/about/index.htm>

New York Orange County Genealogical Society
1841 Court House, 101 Main St., Goshen, NY 10924
Web site: <www.rootsweb.com/~nozell/ocgs/>

RESEARCH TIPS

for more info

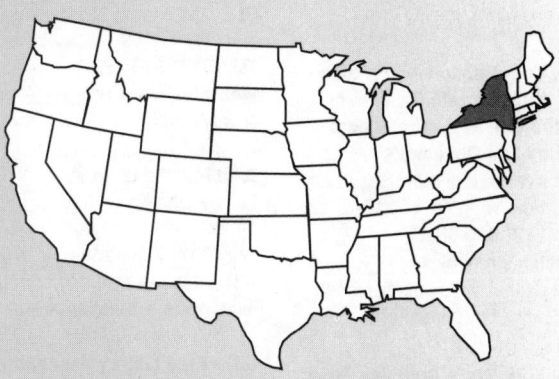

- When working with the state census records, see if there is a compiled index for the county of interest. For instance, Steuben County, New York, has an index of every name found on early federal census pages, plus the state censuses from 1825 through 1925. Other counties have similar compiled indexes, though whether they are every-name or head of household indexes will vary.
- A number of border disputes with Connecticut, New Jersey, Massachusetts, and Vermont during the mid-to-late 1700s may affect where you search for records. Some of the records created may be in one of these other states.
- New York is the only state that has historians at the town and county level. These individuals have amassed a lot of information for their respective towns or counties, including valuable genealogical information. Contact information for those currently serving as historians can be found on the Web site of the Association of Public Historians of New York State <www.tier.net/~aphnys/cohistorians.html>.
- www.negenealogy.com

Census Records
- Federal Census: 1790, 1800, 1810, 1820, 1830, 1840, 1850, 1860, 1870, 1880, 1890 (only counties Eastchester, Westchester, Brookhaven, and Suffolk), 1900, 1910, 1920
- Federal Mortality Schedules: 1850, 1860, 1870, 1880
- Union Veterans and Widows: 1890
- Agricultural, Industrial (Manufacturing), and Social Schedules: 1850, 1860, 1870, 1880

New York Public Library, Dorot Jewish Division
Fifth Ave. and 42nd St., New York, NY 10018-2788
Tel: (212) 930-0601
Web site: <www.nypl.org/research/chss/jws/jewish.html>

New York Public Library, Irma and Paul Milstein Division of United States History, Local History and Genealogy
Fifth Avenue and 42nd St., Room 121, New York, NY 10018–2788
Tel: (212) 930-0828
E-mail: histref@nypl.org
Web site: <www.nypl.org/research/chss/lhg/genea.html>

New York State Archives, New York State Education Dept.
Cultural Education Center, Albany, NY 12230
Tel: (518) 474-6926
E-mail: ARCHINFO@mail.nysed.gov
Web site: <www.archives.nysed.gov/aindex.shtml>

New York State Library Cultural Education Center, Albany, NY 12230
Tel: (518) 474-5355
Web site:

New York State Museum
3040 Cultural Education Center, Albany, NY 12230
Web site:

Newburgh Free Library
124 Grand St., Newburgh, NY 12550
Tel: (845) 563-3601
Web site:

Niagara County Genealogical Society
215 Niagara St., Lockport, NY 14094
Tel: (716) 433-1033
E-mail: genealogy@niagaracounty.org
Web site: <www.niagaracounty.org/genealogical_society_home.htm>

Northern New York American-Canadian Genealogical Society
P.O. Box 1256, Plattsburgh, NY 12901
E-mail: grcp@juno.com
Web site:

Office of Vital Records, City of New York
Web site: <www.nyc.gov/html/doh/html/vr/vr.html>

Ogdensburg Public Library
312 Washington St., Ogdensburg, NY 13669
Tel: (315) 393-4325
Web site: <www.nc3r.org/ogdensburg/>

John M. Olin Library
Cornell University, Ithaca, NY 14853
Tel: (607) 255-4144
Web site: <www.library.cornell.edu/olinuris/index.html>

Olive Free Library Association
4033 Rte. 28-A, West Shokan, NY 12494
Tel: (845) 657-2482
E-mail: olivelib@netscape.net
Web site: <http://olive.westshokan.lib.ny.us/>

Oneida County Historical Society
1608 Genesee St., Utica, NY 13502-5425
Tel: (315) 735-3642
E-mail: ochs@midyork.org
Web site: <www.midyork.org/ochs/>

Oneida Public Library
220 Broad St., Oneida, NY 13421
Tel: (315) 363-3050
E-mail: oneida@midyork.org
Web site: <www.midyork.org/oneida/>

Onondaga Historical Association
311 Montgomery St., Syracuse, NY 13202
Tel: (315) 428-1862
Web site:

Onondaga Public Library
447 S. Salina St., Syracuse, NY 13202-2494
Tel: (315) 435-1900
Web site:

Ontario County Genealogical Society
55 N. Main St., Canandaigua, NY 14424
Web site: <www.ochs.org/Genealogy/Ocgs/>

Ontario County Historical Society
55 N. Main St., Canandaigua, NY 14424
Tel: (585) 394-4975

E-mail: museum@ochs.org
Web site: <www.ochs.org/Menu/frame.html>

Oyster Bay Historical Society
P.O. Box 297, 20 Summit St., Oyster Bay, NY 11771-0297
Tel: (516) 922-5032
E-mail: OBHistory@aol.com
Web site: <http://users.aol.com/OBHistory/>

Palatines to America
611 E. Weber Rd., Columbus, OH 43211-1097
Tel: (614) 267-4700
E-mail: Pal-Am@Juno.com
Web site: <http://palam.org/welcome.html>

Philadelphia Jewish Archives Center
18 S. Seventh St., Philadelphia, PA 19106
Tel: (215) 925-8090
Web site: <www.gophila.com/culturefiles/libraries/jewisharchives/>

Polish Genealogical Society of New York State
12645 Rt. 78, East Aurora, NY 14052
Web site:

Port Chester Public Library
1 Haseco Ave., Port Chester, NY 10573
Tel: (914) 939-6710
Web site:

Puerto Rican/Hispanic Genealogical Society
P.O. Box 260118, Bellerose, NY 11426-0118
Tel: (516) 834-2511
E-mail: prhgs@yahoo.com
Web site: <www.rootsweb.com/~prhgs/>

Queens Borough Public Library
89-11 Merrick Blvd., Jamaica, NY 11432
Tel: (718) 990-0700
Web site:

Queens Historical Society
143–35 37th Ave., Flushing, NY 11354
Tel: (718) 939-0647 x17
E-mail: info@queenshistoricalsociety.org
Web site: <www.queenshistoricalsociety.org/index.html>

Registrar, City of Albany Vital Statistics
Room 254M, City Hall, Albany, NY 12207
Web site: <www.albanyny.org/government/departments/d_cityclerk5.asp>

Rennsselaer County Historical Society
57 Second St., Troy, NY 12180
Tel: (518) 272-7232
Web site:

Richmond Memorial Library
19 Ross St., Batavia, NY 14020
Tel: (585) 343-9550
Web site: <www.batvialibrary.org>

Rochester Genealogical Society
P.O. Box 10501, Rochester, NY 14610-0501
Web site: <www.rootsweb.com/~nyrgs/>

Rochester Public Library, Local History Division
115 South Ave., Rochester, NY 14604
Tel: (585) 428-8370
Web site: <www.rochester.lib.ny.us/rochimag/lochist.html>

Saint Lawrence County Historical Association
3 E. Main St., P.O. Box 8, Canton, NY 13617-0008
Tel: (315) 386-8133
E-mail: slcha@northnet.org
Web site: <http://slcha.org/>

Scarsdale Historical Society
P.O. Box 431, Scarsdale, NY 10583-0431
Tel: (914) 723-1744
Web site: <www.scarsdalenet.com/historicalsociety/>

Schenectady County Historical Society
32 Washington Ave., Schenectady, NY 12305
Tel: (518) 374-0263
Web site:

Schulyer County Historical Society and Museum
108 N. Catharine St., P.O. Drawer 651, Montour Falls, NY 14865
Tel: (607) 535-9741
Web site: <www.rootsweb.com/~nyschuyl/address1.htm>

Shaker Heritage Society
875 Watervliet Shaker Rd., Suite 2, Albany, NY 12211

Tel: (518) 456-7890
E-mail: shakerwv@crisny.org
Web site: <www.crisny.org/not-for-profit/shakerwv/>

Slovak Heritage and Folklore Society International
151 Colebrook Dr., Rochester, NY 14617-2215
Tel: (716) 342-9383
E-mail: helenezx@aol.com
Web site: <www.iarelative.com/shfsinfo.htm>

Southern Tier Genealogical Society
P.O. Box 680, Vestal, NY 13850
Web site: <www.rootsweb.com/~nybroome/stgs/stgs.htm>

Southold Historical Society
54325 Main Rd., P.O. Box 1, Southold, NY 11971
Tel: (631) 765-5500
E-mail: sohissoc@optonline.net
Web site:

St. George's Society of New York
216 E. 45th St., Suite 901, New York, NY 10017-3304
Tel: (212) 682-6110
E-mail: info@stgeorgesociety.org
Web site:

Staten Island Historical Society
Historic Richmond Town, 441 Clarke Ave., Staten Island, NY 10306
Tel: (718) 351-1611
Web site: <www.newyorkled.com/Staten-Island-Historical.htm>

Steele Memorial Library
101 E. Church St., Elmira, NY 14901
Tel: (607) 733-9173
Web site:

Suffolk County Historical Society
300 W. Main St., Riverhead, NY 11901-2894
Tel: (631) 727-2881
Web site: <www.riverheadli.com/rmuseum.html>

Sullivan County Historical Society
P.O. Box 247W, Hurleyville, NY 12747
Tel: (914) 434-8044
E-mail: schs@warwick.net
Web site:

Three Village Historical Society
P.O. Box 76, East Setauket, NY 11733
Tel: (631) 751-3730
E-mail: info@tvhs.org
Web site:

Tioga County Historical Society
110 Front St., Owego, NY 13827
Tel: (607) 687-2460
E-mail: info@tiogahistory.org
Web site:

Town of Watertown Historical Society
22867 County Road 67, Watertown, NY 13601
E-mail: TWHS@imcnet.net
Web site: <www.usgennet.org/usa/ny/town/watertown/twhsmain.html>

Troy Public Library
100 Second St., Troy, NY 12180
Tel: (518) 274-7071
E-mail: troyref@uhls.lib.ny.us
Web site: <www.uhls.org/troy/>

Twin Tiers Genealogical Society, Inc.
P.O. Box 763, Elmira, NY 14902
Web site: <www.rootsweb.com/~nychemun/tths.htm>

Ulster County Elting Memorial Library
93 Main St., New Paltz, NY 12561-1593
E-mail: newpaltzeltingLibrary@yahoo.com
Web site: <www.co.ulster.ny.us/libraries.htm>

Ulster County Genealogical Society
P.O. Box 536, Hurley, NY 12443
Web site: <www.rootsweb.com/~nyucgs/>

United Methodist Archives Center, Drew University Library
Tel: (973) 408-3486
Web site: <www.depts.drew.edu/lib/uma.html>

Utica Public Library
303 Genesee St., Utica, NY 13501
Tel: (315) 735-2279
Web site: <www.uticapubliclibrary.org/home.html>

Wayne County Historical Society
21 Butternut St., Lyons, NY 14489

Tel: (315) 946-4943
E-mail: WCHS4943@aol.com
Web site: <www.cgazette.com/common/standing/WC-historical_society/waynecountyhistorical.htm/>

Westchester County Historical Society
2199 Saw Mill River Rd., Elmsford, NY 10523
Tel: (914) 592-4323
Web site:

Western New York Genealogical Society, Inc.
P.O. Box 338, Hamburg, NY 14075-0338
Web site:

Yates County Genealogical and Historical Society, Inc.
200 Main St., Penn Yan, NY 14527
Tel: (315) 536-7318
Web site:

Yorktown Historical Society
P.O. Box 355, Yorktown Heights, NY 10598
Tel: (914) 962-5722 ext. 440
Web site:

BIBLIOGRAPHY

■ GENERAL RESOURCES

A Bibliography of New York State Communities, 3d ed.
compiled by Harold Nestler (Bowie, MD: Heritage Books, Inc., 1990)

The Book of Names Especially Relating to the Early Palatines and the First Settlers in the Mohawk Valley
compiled and arranged by Lou D. MacWethy (Baltimore, MD: Genealogical Pub. Co., 1981)

Colonial Families of Long Island, New York and Connecticut: Being the Ancestry & Kindred of Herbert Furman Seversmith, 5 vols.
by Herbert Furman Seversmith (Washington, DC: H.F. Seversmith, 1939–1958)

Contributions for the Genealogies of the Descendants of the First Settlers of the Patent and City of Schenectady, From 1662 to 1800
by Jonathan Pearson (Baltimore, MD: Genealogical Pub. Co., 1976)

Cutter Index: A Consolidated Index of Cutter's 9 Genealogy Series
by Norma Olin Ireland and Winifred Irving (Fallbrook, CA: Ireland Indexing Service, ca. 1970)

Dutch Houses in the Hudson Valley Before 1776
by Helen Wilkinson Reynolds (New York: Dover Publications, 1965)

Famous Families of New York, 2 vols.
by Margherita Arlina Hamm (New York: G.P. Putnam's Sons, 1902)

Genealogical Data From New York Administration Bonds, 1753–1799 and Hithero Unpublished Letters of Administration
abstracted by Kenneth Scott (New York: New York Genealogical and Biographical Society, 1969)

Genealogical Data From the New York Post-Boy, 1743–1773
by Kenneth Scott (Washington: National Genealogical Society, 1970)

Genealogical and Family History of Southern New York and the Hudson River Valley: A Record of the Achievements of her People in the Making of a Commonwealth and the Building of a Nation, 3 vols.
compiled under the editorial supervision of Cuyler Reynolds (New York: Lewis Historical Pub. Co., 1914)

Genealogical Notes of New York and New England Families
by S.V. Talcott (Baltimore, MD: Genealogical Pub. Co., 1973)

Genealogical Resources in New York
edited by Estelle M. Guzik (New York, NY: Jewish Genealogical Society, 2003)

Genealogical Resources in the New York Metropolitan Area
edited by Estelle M. Guzik (New York: Jewish Genealogical Society, 1989)

The Genealogist's Companion and Sourcebook, 2d ed.
by Emily Anne Croom (Cincinnati: Betterway Books, 2003)

New York

A Genealogist's Guide to Discovering Your African-American Ancestors
by Franklin Carter Smith and Emily Anne Croom (Cincinnati: Betterway Books, 2003)

Genealogy of the French Settlers of New Paltz
by Louis Bevier (Baltimore, MD: Genealogical Pub. Co., 1965)

Guide to Genealogical and Biographical Sources for New York City (Manhattan) 1783–1898
by Rosalie Fellows Bailey (New York, 1954)

Guide to Genealogical Research in the National Archives of the United States
edited by Anne Bruner Eales and Robert M. Kvasnicka (Washington, DC: National Archives and Records Administration, 2000)

A Guide to the Manuscript Collections of the New-York Historical Society, 2 vols.
by Arthur J. Breton (Westport, CT: Greenwood Press, 1972)

A Handy Guide to Record-Searching in the Larger Cities of the United States
by E. Kay Kirkham (Logan, UT: Everton, 1974)

History of the Mohawk Valley: Gateway to the West, 1614–1925, Covering the six Counties of Schenectady, Schoharie, Montgomery, Fulton, Herkimer, and Oneida, 4 vols.
edited by Nelson Greene (Chicago, IL: S.J. Clarke, 1925)

A History of New York State
by David M. Ellis. et al. (Ithaca, N.Y.: Cornell University Press, 1983)

Inhabitants of New York, 1774–1776
by Thomas B. Wilson (Baltimore, MD: Genealogical Pub. Co., 1993)

Land Papers
translated and edited by Charles T. Gehring (Baltimore, MD: Genealogical Pub. Co., 1980)

Lists of Inhabitants of Colonial New York: Excerpted From the Documentary History of the State of New York
by E.B. O'Callaghan (Edmund Bailey) (Baltimore, MD: Genealogical Pub. Co., 1979)

Long Island Genealogical Source Material, a Bibliography
by Herbert F. Seversmith and Kenn Stryker-Rodda (Washington, DC: National Genealogical Society Bookstore, 1962)

National Archives Microfilm Catalogs online:
<www.archives.gov/publications/genealogy_microfilm_catalogs.html>

New Netherland Roots
by Gwen F. Epperson (Baltimore, MD: Genealogical Pub. Co., 1994)

New York State Towns, Villages, and Cities: A Guide to Genealogical Sources
by Gordon L. Remington (Boston: New England Historic Genealogical Society, 2002)

Searching in New York: A Reference Guide to Public and Private Records
by Kate Burke (Costa Mesa, CA: ISC Publications, 1987)

■ CENSUS RECORDS

The American Census Handbook
by Thomas Jay Kemp (Wilmington, DE: Scholarly Resources, 2001)

The Census Book: A Genealogist's Guide to Federal Census Facts, Schedules and Indexes
by William Dollarhide (Bountiful, UT: Heritage Quest, 2000)

Map Guide to the U.S. Federal Censuses, 1790–1920
by William Thorndale and William Dollarhide (Baltimore, MD: Genealogical Pub. Co., 1987)

Your Guide to the Federal Census
by Kathleen W. Hinckley (Cincinnati: Betterway Books, 2002)

■ IMMIGRATION RECORDS

American Naturalization Records, 1790–1990: What They Are and How to Use Them
by John J. Newman (North Salt Lake, UT: HeritageQuest, 1998)

American Passenger Arrival Records
by Michael Tepper (Baltimore: Genealogical Publishing Co., 1993)

Landholders of Northeastern New York, 1739–1802
by Fred Q. Bowman (Baltimore, MD: Genealogical Pub. Co., 1983)

New York State—Confiscations of Loyalists
copied by H.C. Burleigh (Toronto: United Empire Loyalists' Association of Canada, 1970)

The Palatine Families of New York: A Study of the German Immigrants who Arrived in Colonial New York in 1710, 2 vols.
by Henry Z. Jones (Universal City, CA: H.Z. Jones, 1985)

Palatine Roots: The 1710 German Settlement in New York as Experienced by Johann Peter Wagner
by Nancy Wagoner Dixon (Camden, ME: Picton Press, 1994)

Reports of Joseph Ellicott as Chief of Survey (1797–1800): and as Agent (1800–1821) of the Holland Land Company's Purchases in Western New York, 2 vols.
edited by Robert Warwick Bingham (Buffalo: The Buffalo Historical Society, 1937–41)

Ship Passenger Lists, New York and New Jersey, 1600–1825
edited and indexed by Carl Boyer (Newhall, CA: C. Boyer, 1978)

They Became Americans: Finding Naturalization Records and Ethnic Origins
by Loretto Dennis Szucs (Salt Lake City: Ancestry, Inc., 1998)

They Came in Ships: A Guide to Finding Your Immigrant Ancestor's Arrival Records, 2d ed.
by John P. Colletta (Salt Lake City: Ancestry, Inc., 1993)

■ LAND RECORDS

Calender of N.Y. Colonial Manuscripts, Indorsed Land Papers: In the Office of the Secretary of State of New York, 1643–1803
compiled by E.B. O'Callaghan (Harrison, NY: Harbor Hill Books, 1987)

Denizations, Naturalizations, and Oaths of Allegiance in Colonial New York
by Kenneth Scott and Kenn Stryker-Rodda (Baltimore, MD: Genealogical Pub. Co., 1975)

The Disposition of Loyalist Estates in the Southern District of the State of New York
by Harry Beller Yoshpe (New York: Columbia University, 1999)

Dutch New York
by Esther Singleton (New York: B. Blom, 1968)

Inventory of the Archives of the Holland Land Company: Including the Related Amsterdam Companies and Negotiations Dealing With the Purchase of Land and State Funds in the United States of America 1789–1869
by Wilhelmina C. Pierterse, English translation by Sytha Hart (Amsterdam: Municipal Print. Office, 1976)

Locating Your Roots: Discover Your Ancestors Using Land Records
by Patricia Law Hatcher (Cincinnati: Betterway Books, 2003)

Western New York Land Transactions, 1825–1835: Extracted From the Archives of the Holland Land Company
by Karen E. Livsey (Baltimore, MD: Genealogical Pub. Co., 1996)

■ MAPS

Atlas of Historical County Boundaries. New York
edited by John H. Long and compiled by Kathryn Ford Thorne (New York: Simon & Schuster, 1993)

Gazetteer of the State of New York
by John Homer French (Baltimore, MD: Genealogical Pub. Co., 1995)

Gazetteer of the State of New York
by Thomas Francis Gordon (Philadelphia: Printed for the Author, 1836)

Gazetteer of the State of New York: Embracing a Comprehensive Account of the History and Statistics of the State, With Geological and Topographical Descriptions, and Recent Statistical Tables Representing the Present Condition of Each County, City, Town and Village in the State
by Franklin B. Hough (Albany, NY: Van Benthuysen Printing House, 1990s)

■ MILITARY RECORDS

A History of the 134th New York Volunteer Infantry Regiment in the American Civil

War, 1862–1865: Long Night's Journey Into Day
by Charles H. Cosgrove (Lewiston, NY: E. Mellen Press, 1997)

Inhabitants of New York, 1774–1776
by Thomas B. Wilson (Baltimore, MD: Genealogical Pub. Co., 1993)

New York in the American Revolution: A Bibliography
by Milton M. Klein (Albany, NY: New York State American Revolution Bicentennial Commission, 1974)

New York in the Revolution
by Berthold Fernow (Cottonport, LA: Polyanthos, Inc., 1972)

New York in the Revolution as Colony and State
by James A. Roberts (Baltimore, MD: Genealogical Pub. Co., 1996)

New York, World War I Selective Service System Draft Registration Cards, 1917–1918
by the United States Selective Service System (Washington, DC: The National Archives, 1987–1988)

Uncle, We Are Ready! Registering America's Men, 1917–1918: A Guide to Researching World War I Draft Registration Cards
by John J. Newman (North Salt Lake, UT: HeritageQuest, 2001)

U.S. Military Records: A Guide to Federal & State Sources, Colonial America to the Present
by James C. Neagles (Salt Lake City: Ancestry, Inc., 1994)

World War II: A Family Historian's Guide
by Debra Johnson Knox (Spartanburg, SC: MIE Publishing, 2003)

■ PROBATE RECORDS

Calender of Wills on File and Recorded in the Offices of the Clerk of the Court of Appeals, of the County Clerk at Albany, and of the Secretary of State, 1626–1836
by Berthold Fernow (Baltimore, MD: Genealogical Pub. Co., 1967)

Genealogical Data From Further New York Administration Bonds, 1791–1798
abstracted by Kenneth Scott (New York: New York Genealogical and Biographical Society, 1971)

Genealogical Data From Inventories of New York Estates, 1666–1825
by Kenneth Scott and James A. Owre (New York: New York Genealogical and Biographical Society, 1970)

Genealogical Data From New York Administration Bonds, 1753–1799 and Hithero Unpublished Letters of Administration
abstracted by Kenneth Scott (New York: New York Genealogical and Biographical Society, 1969)

New York Alien Residents, 1825–1848
compiled by Kenneth Scott & Rosanne Conway (Baltimore, MD: Genealogical Pub. Co., 1978)

■ VITAL RECORDS

Marriages and Deaths From the New Yorker (Double Quarto Edition), 1836–1841
by Kenneth Scott (Washington, DC: National Genealogical Society, 1980)

New York State Cemeteries Name/Location Inventory, 1995–1997, 3 vols.
compiled by the Association of Municipal Historians of New York State (Bowie, MD: Heritage Books, 1999)

Your Guide to Cemetery Research
by Sharon DeBartolo Carmack (Cincinnati: Betterway Books, 2002)

■ Albany   1 Nov. 1683
95 Tivoli St., Albany, NY 12207
Phone: (518)436-3663
Web site: www.rootsweb.com/~nyalbany/
Parent County: Original county

Record Type	Year Begun	Jurisdiction
Land	1630	Hall of Records
Probate	1629	Surrogate Court
Court	1652	County Clerk
Tax Rolls	1850	Hall of Records
Nat.	1895	County Court
City Direct.	1829	Hall of Records

■ Allegany   7 Apr. 1806
7 Court St., Belmont, NY 14813-1039
Phone: (585)268-9270
Web site: www.rootsweb.com/~nyallega/
Parent County: Genesee
Comments/research tips: County Clerk has Marriage records 1908-1935.

Record Type	Year Begun	Jurisdiction
Land	1807	County Clerk
Probate	1807	Clerk/Surrogate Ct.
Court	1807	County Clerk
Nat.	1866	Supreme Court

■ Bronx   19 Apr. 1912
851 Grand Concourse Room 118, Bronx, NY 10451
Phone: (718)590-3645
Web site: www.rootsweb.com/~nybronx/
Parent County: New York

Record Type	Year Begun	Jurisdiction
Marriage	1897	Dept./Health
Birth	1898	Dept./Health
Death	1898	Dept./Health
Nat.	1914	County Clerk

■ Broome   28 Mar. 1806
44 Hawley St., P.O. Box 2062, Binghamton, NY 13902
Phone: (607)778-2451
Web site: www.rootsweb.com/~nybroome/
Parent County: Tioga

Record Type	Year Begun	Jurisdiction
Birth	1847	Town/City Clerks
Marriage	1847	Town/City Clerks
Death	1847	Town/City Clerks
Land	1791	County Clerk
Probate	1806	Surrogate Court
Nat.	1820	Supreme Court
Court	1808	County Court

■ Cattaraugus   11 Mar. 1808
303 Court St., Little Valley, NY 14755
Phone: (716)938-9111
Web site: www.rootsweb.com/~nycattar
Parent County: Genesee

Record Type	Year Begun	Jurisdiction
Marriage	1808	Town/City Clerks
Land	1800	County Clerk

New York

■ **Cayuga** 8 Mar. 1799
160 Genesee St. 1st Floor, Auburn, NY 13021
Phone: (315)253-1271
Web site: www.rootsweb.com/~nycayuga/
Parent County: Onondaga

Record Type	Year Begun	Jurisdiction
Nat.	1879	County Court
Marriage	1908	Town/City Clerks
Land	1794	County Clerk
Probate	1799	Surrogate Court
Court	1794	County Clerk

■ **Charlotte** 12 Mar. 1772
Parent County: Albany
Comments/research tips: (See Washington) Name changed to Washington 2 April 1784.

■ **Chautauqua** 11 Mar. 1808
One N. Erie St., P.O. Box 170, Mayville, NY 14757
Phone: (716)753-4331
Web site: www.rootsweb.com/~nychauta/
Parent County: Genesee

Record Type	Year Begun	Jurisdiction
Marriage	1908	County Clerk
Nat.	1837	Supreme Court
Land	1811	County Clerk
Probate	1811	Surrogate Court

■ **Chemung** 29 Mar. 1836
210 Lake St., P.O. Box 588, Elmira , NY 14902
Phone: (607)737-2920
Web site: www.rootsweb.com/~nychemun/chemweb.htm
Parent County: Tioga

Record Type	Year Begun	Jurisdiction
Marriage	1908	County Clerk
Land	1791	County Clerk
Probate	1836	Surrogate Court
Court	1836	County Clerk

■ **Chenango** 15 Mar. 1798
5 Court St., Norwich, NY 13815
Phone: (607)337-1450
Web site: www.rootsweb.com/~nychenan/
Parent County: Herkimer, Tioga

Record Type	Year Begun	Jurisdiction
Marriage	1908	Town Clerks
Nat.	1859	Supreme Court
Land	1798	County Clerk
Probate	1792	Surrogate Court
Court	1799	County Clerk

■ **Clinton** 7 Mar. 1788
137 Margaret St., Plattsburgh, NY 12901
Phone: (518)565-4700
Web site: www.rootsweb.com/~nyclinto/
Parent County: Washington

Record Type	Year Begun	Jurisdiction
Marriage	1908	Town/City Clerks
Court	1789	Ct./Common Pleas

Nat.	1820	County Court
Land	1788	County Clerk
Probate	1790	Surrogate Court

■ **Columbia** 4 Apr. 1786
560 Warren St., Hudson, NY 12534
Phone: (518)828-3339
Web site: www.rootsweb.com/~nycolumb/
Parent County: Albany

Record Type	Year Begun	Jurisdiction
Marriage	1908	Town Clerks
Land	1786	County Clerk
Probate	1786	Surrogate Court
Court	1830	Surrogate Court
Nat.	1835	County Court

■ **Cortland** 8 Apr. 1808
46 Greenbush St. Suite 101, Cortland, NY 13045
Phone: (607)753-5021
Web site: www.rootsweb.com/~nycortla/
Parent County: Onondaga

Record Type	Year Begun	Jurisdiction
Marriage	1908	Town/City Clerks
Nat.	1816	County Court
Land	1808	County Clerk
Probate	1809	Surrogate Court
Court	1808	County Clerk

■ **Delaware** 10 Mar. 1797
P.O. Box 426, Delhi, NY 13753
Phone: (607)746-2123
Web site: www.rootsweb.com/~nydelawa/
Parent County: Ulster, Otsego

Record Type	Year Begun	Jurisdiction
Birth	1847	Town Clerks
Marriage	1847	Town Clerks
Death	1847	Town Clerks
Land	1792	County Clerk
Probate	1797	Surrogate Court
Court	1797	Ct./Common Pleas
Nat.	1810	Ct./Common Pleas

■ **Dutchess** 1 Nov. 1683
22 Market St., Poughkeepsie, NY 12601
Phone: (845)486-2120
Web site: www.rootsweb.com/~nydutche/
Parent County: Original county

Record Type	Year Begun	Jurisdiction
Nat.	1802	County Court
Land	1697	Surrogate Court
Probate	1721	County Court
Court	1721	County Clerk

■ **Erie** 2 Apr. 1821
25 Delaware Ave., Buffalo, NY 14202
Phone: (716)858-8785
Web site: www.rootsweb.com/~nyerie/
Parent County: Niagara

Record Type	Year Begun	Jurisdiction
Nat.	1831	County Court

Record Type	Year Begun	Jurisdiction
Land	1808	County Clerk
Court	1808	County Clerk

■ Essex 1 Mar. 1799
7559 Court St., P.O. Box 247, Elizabethtown, NY 12932
Phone: (518)873-3600
Web site: www.rootsweb.com/~nyessex/
Parent County: Clinton

Record Type	Year Begun	Jurisdiction
Marriage	1908	Town/City Clerks
Land	1799	County Clerk
Probate	1799	Surrogate Court
Court	1799	Supreme Court
Nat.	1856	County Court

■ Franklin 11 Mar. 1808
355 W. Main St., P.O. Box 70, Malone, NY 12953
Phone: (518)481-1681
Web site: www.rootsweb.com/~nyFrankl/
Parent County: Clinton

Record Type	Year Begun	Jurisdiction
Land	1808	County Clerk
Probate	1809	Surrogate Court
Court	1808	County Clerk
Nat.	1832	County Court

■ Fulton 18 Apr. 1838
P.O. Box 485, Johnstown, NY 12095
Phone: (518)736-5555
Web site: www.rootsweb.com/~nyfulton/
Parent County: Montgomery

Record Type	Year Begun	Jurisdiction
Land	1772	County Clerk
Probate	1789	Surrogate Court
Death	1847	County Clerk
Birth	1847	County Clerk
Marriage	1847	County Clerk
Nat.	1839	County Court

■ Genesee 30 Mar. 1802
Box 379, Batavia, NY 14021
Phone: (585)344-2550
Web site: www.rootsweb.com/~nygenese/
Parent County: Ontario

Record Type	Year Begun	Jurisdiction
Marriage	1908	Town/City Clerks
Land	1792	County Clerk
Probate	1805	Surrogate Court
Court	1865	Supreme Court
Nat.	1849	Supreme Court

■ Greene 25 Mar. 1800
P.O. Box 446, Catskill, NY 12414
Phone: (518)943-2050
Web site: www.hopefarm.com/geneatop.htm
Parent County: Ulster, Albany

Record Type	Year Begun	Jurisdiction
Marriage	1908	Town Clerks
Nat.	1850	Clerk/County Ct.

Record Type	Year Begun	Jurisdiction
Land	1800	County Clerk
Probate	1800	Surrogate Court

■ Hamilton 12 Apr. 1816
Rt. 8, Box 204, Lake Pleasant, NY 12108
Phone: (518)548-7111
Web site: www.rootsweb.com/~nyhamilt/
Parent County: Montgomery

Record Type	Year Begun	Jurisdiction
Marriage	1908	Town/City Clerks
Nat.	1854	County Court
Land	1797	County Clerk
Probate	1861	Surrogate Court
Court	1880	Supreme Court

■ Herkimer 16 Feb. 1791
109 Mary St. Suite 1111, Herkimer, NY 13350
Phone: (315)867-1137
Web site: www.rootsweb.com/~nyherkim/
Parent County: Montgomery
Comments/research tips: County Clerk has Vital records 1847-1849.

Record Type	Year Begun	Jurisdiction
Marriage	1908	County Clerk
Land	1791	County Clerk
Probate	1792	Surrogate Court
Court	1804	Ct./Oyer/Terminer
Nat.	1818	Ct./Common Pleas

■ Jefferson 28 Mar. 1805
175 Arsenal St., Watertown, NY 13601
Phone: (315)785-3081
Web site: www.rootsweb.com/~nyjeffer/
Parent County: Oneida

Record Type	Year Begun	Jurisdiction
Land	1805	County Clerk
Probate	1805	Surrogate Court
Court	1817	Ct./Common Pleas
Marriage	1908	County Clerk
Nat.	1896	County Clerk
Coroner Rpt.	1878	County Coroner

■ Kings 1 Nov. 1683
360 Adams St. Room 188, Brooklyn, NY 11201
Phone: (718)643-5256
Web site: www.rootsweb.com/~nykings/
Parent County: Original county

Record Type	Year Begun	Jurisdiction
Birth	1866	Dept./Health
Marriage	1866	Board/Health
Death	1898	Dept./Health
Land	1724	County Registrar
Probate	1787	Surrogate Court
Nat.	1792	County Court

■ Lewis 28 Mar. 1805
7660 State St., Box 232, Lowville, NY 13367
Phone: (315)376-5333
Web site: www.rootsweb.com/~nylewis/

Parent County: Oneida
Comments/research tips: County Clerk has Birth and Death records 1848-1851.

Record Type	Year Begun	Jurisdiction
Land	1788	County Clerk
Probate	1805	Surrogate Court
Court	1805	Supreme Court
Nat.	1808	County Court
Marriage	1908	County Clerk

■ Livingston 23 Feb. 1821
6 Court St., Room 201, Geneseo, NY 14454
Phone: (585)243-7000
Web site: www.rootsweb.com/~nyliving/
Parent County: Genesee, Ontario

Record Type	Year Begun	Jurisdiction
Nat.	1821	Supreme Court
Land	1820	County Clerk
Probate	1821	Surrogate Court
Court	1821	Ct./Common Pleas
Marriage	1908	County Clerk

■ Madison 21 Mar. 1806
P.O. Box 668, Wampsville, NY 13163
Phone: (315)366-2261
Web site: www.rootsweb.com/~nymadiso/
Parent County: Chenango

Record Type	Year Begun	Jurisdiction
Nat.	1853	County Court
Marriage	1806	Town Clerks
Land	1806	County Clerk
Probate	1806	Surrogate Court
Court	1808	Ct./Oyer/Terminer

■ Monroe 23 Feb. 1821
39 Main St. W. Room 101, Rochester, NY 14614
Phone: (585)428-5151
Web site: www.rootsweb.com/~nymonroe/
Parent County: Genesee, Ontario

Record Type	Year Begun	Jurisdiction
Land	1821	County Clerk
Probate	1826	Surrogate Court
Court	1821	County Clerk
Nat.	1821	County Court

■ Montgomery 12 Mar. 1772
P.O. Box 1500, Fonda, NY 12068
Phone: (518)853-8115
Web site: www.rootsweb.com/~nyherkim/
Parent County: Albany

Record Type	Year Begun	Jurisdiction
Marriage	1908	Town/City Clerks
Land	1772	County Clerk
Court	1772	Ct./General Session
Nat.	1810	Supreme Court

■ Nassau 27 Apr. 1898
240 Old Country Rd., Mineola, NY 11501
Phone: (516)571-2861

Web site: www.rootsweb.com/~nynassau/
Parent County: Queens

Record Type	Year Begun	Jurisdiction
Nat.	1899	County Court
Marriage	1908	Town Clerks

■ New York 1 Nov. 1683
60 Centre St. Room 161, New York, NY 10007
Phone: (212)374-8589
Web site: www.rootsweb/~nymanhat/
Parent County: Original county

Record Type	Year Begun	Jurisdiction
Death	1795	Dept./Health
Probate	1665	Surrogate Court
Marriage	1830	County Clerk
Birth	1866	Dept./Health
Land	1680	County Registrar
Nat.	1784	Ct./Common Pleas
Court	1665	Ct./Assizes

■ Niagara 11 Mar. 1808
175 Hawley St., P.O. Box 461, Lockport, NY 14094
Phone: (716)439-7022
Web site: www.rootsweb.com/~nyniagar/
Parent County: Genesee

Record Type	Year Begun	Jurisdiction
Marriage	1908	Town/City Clerks
Land	1800	County Clerk
Probate	1820	Surrogate Court
Court	1831	Supreme Court
Nat.	1830	County Court

■ Oneida 15 Mar. 1798
800 Park Ave., Utica, NY 13501
Phone: (315)798-5773
Web site: www.rootsweb.com/~nyoneida/mainpage.html
Parent County: Herkimer

Record Type	Year Begun	Jurisdiction
Marriage	1908	Town Clerks
Nat.	1805	Ct./Common Pleas
Land	1791	County Clerk
Probate	1798	Surrogate Court
Court	1830	Surrogate Court

■ Onondaga 5 Mar. 1794
401 Montgomery St. Room 200, Syracuse, NY 13202
Phone: (315)435-2226
Web site: www.rootsweb.com/~nyononda/
Parent County: Herkimer

Record Type	Year Begun	Jurisdiction
Marriage	1908	Town/City Clerks
Land	1794	County Clerk
Probate	1796	Surrogate Court
Court	1807	Ct./Common Pleas
Nat.	1802	County Court

■ Ontario 27 Jan. 1789
20 Ontario St., Canandaigua, NY 14424
Phone: (585)396-4200

Web site: www.rootsweb.com/~nyontari/
Parent County: Montgomery

Record Type	Year Begun	Jurisdiction
Marriage	1908	Rec. Manage. Officer
Land	1789	Rec. Manage. Officer
Nat.	1803	Ct./Common Pleas

■ Orange 1 Nov. 1683
255 Main St., Goshen, NY 10924
Phone: (845)291-2690
Web site: www.rootsweb.com/~nyorange/
Parent County: Original county

Record Type	Year Begun	Jurisdiction
Land	1703	County Clerk
Probate	1785	Surrogate Court
Court	1727	Ct./Common Pleas
Marriage	1908	County Clerk

■ Orleans 12 Nov. 1824
3 S. Main St., Albion, NY 14411
Phone: (585)589-5334
Web site: www.rootsweb.com/~nyorlean/
Parent County: Genesee
Comments/research tips: Town/City Clerks have Birth, Marriage and Death records 1847-1849.

Record Type	Year Begun	Jurisdiction
Marriage	1908	Town/City Clerks
Nat.	1830	County Court
Land	1810	County Clerk
Probate	1825	Surrogate Court
Court	1864	Supreme Court

■ Oswego 1 Mar. 1816
46 E. Bridge St., Oswego, NY 13126
Phone: (315)349-8385
Web site: www.rootsweb.com/~nyoswego/
Parent County: Oneida, Onondaga

Record Type	Year Begun	Jurisdiction
Land	1791	County Clerk
Probate	1816	Surrogate Court
Court	1816	County Clerk
Nat.	1830	County Court

■ Otsego 16 Feb. 1791
197 Main St., P.O. Box 710, Cooperstown, NY 13326
Phone: (607)547-4276
Web site: www.rootsweb.com/~nyotsego/
Parent County: Montgomery

Record Type	Year Begun	Jurisdiction
Marriage	1908	Town/City Clerks
Nat.	1806	Ct./Common Pleas
Land	1791	County Clerk
Probate	1781	Surrogate Court
Court	1791	Ct./Common Pleas

■ Putnam 12 June 1812
40 Gleneida Ave., Carmel, NY 10512
Phone: (845)225-3641
Web site: www.rootsweb.com/~nyputnam/

Parent County: Dutchess

Record Type	Year Begun	Jurisdiction
Marriage	1908	Town Clerks
Land	1812	County Clerk
Nat.	1861	County Court
Court	1824	Supreme Court

■ Queens 1 Nov. 1683
88-11 Sutphin Blvd., Jamaica, NY 11435
Phone: (718)520-0499
Web site: www.rootsweb.com/~nyqueens/
Parent County: Original county

Record Type	Year Begun	Jurisdiction
Birth	1898	NYC Mun. Arch.
Marriage	1881	NYC Mun. Arch.
Death	1898	NYC Mun. Arch.
Land	1686	County Registrar
Probate	1787	Surrogate Court
Court	1701	Chancery Ct. Clerk
Nat.	1794	County Court

■ Rensselaer 7 Feb. 1791
105 Third St., Troy, NY 12180
Phone: (518)270-4080
Web site: www.rootsweb.com/~nyrensse/
Parent County: Albany

Record Type	Year Begun	Jurisdiction
Land	1791	County Clerk
Probate	1791	Surrogate Court
Nat.	1827	Justice Court
Court	1843	Court/Common Pleas

■ Richmond 1 Nov. 1683
130 Stuyvesant Pl., Staten Island, NY 10301
Phone: (718)390-5386
Web site: www.rootsweb.com/~nyrichmo/
Parent County: Original county
Comments/research tips: Town Clerks have Marriage records 1847-1897.

Record Type	Year Begun	Jurisdiction
Birth	1847	Town Clerks
Death	1847	Town Clerks
Nat.	1820	County Court
Court	1711	Ct./Common Pleas
Land	1683	County Clerk
Probate	1664	Surrogate Court

■ Rockland 23 Feb. 1798
One S. Main St. Suite 100, New City, NY 10956
Phone: (845)638-5221
Web site: www.rootsweb.com/~nyrockla/
Parent County: Orange

Record Type	Year Begun	Jurisdiction
Nat.	1817	County Clerk
Marriage	1908	County Clerk
Land	1703	County Clerk
Probate	1798	Surrogate Court
Court	1798	Surrogate Court

■ **Saratoga** 7 Feb. 1791
40 McMasters St., Ballston Spa, NY 12020
Phone: (518)885-2213
Web site: www.rootsweb.com/~nysarato/
Parent County: Albany

Record Type	Year Begun	Jurisdiction
Nat.	1791	County Court
Marriage	1908	County Clerk
Land	1774	County Clerk
Probate	1791	Surrogate Court
Court	1791	Ct./Oyer/Terminer

■ **Schenectady** 7 Mar. 1809
620 State St., 3d Floor, Schenectady, NY 12305
Phone: (518)388-4225
Web site: www.schenectadyhistory.org
Parent County: Albany

Record Type	Year Begun	Jurisdiction
Nat.	1810	Ct./Common Pleas
Land	1809	County Clerk
Probate	1809	Surrogate Court
Court	1809	Ct./Common Pleas
Marriage	1908	County Clerk

■ **Schoharie** 6 Apr. 1795
300 Main St., P.O. Box 549, Schoharie, NY 12157
Phone: (518)295-8316
Web site: www.rootsweb.com/~nyschoha/
Parent County: Albany, Otsego
Comments/research tips: Town Clerks have Marriage records 1847-1852.

Record Type	Year Begun	Jurisdiction
Marriage	1908	Town Clerks
Nat.	1810	County Court
Land	1795	County Clerk
Probate	1795	Surrogate Court
Court	1796	Ct./Common Pleas

■ **Schuyler** 17 Apr. 1854
105 Ninth St., Box 8, Watkins Glen, NY 14891
Phone: (607)535-8133
Web site: www.rootsweb.com/~nyschuyl/
Parent County: Tompkins, Steuben, Chemung

Record Type	Year Begun	Jurisdiction
Marriage	1908	Town Clerks
Land	1799	County Clerk
Probate	1829	Surrogate Court
Court	1855	Supreme Court
Nat.	1864	Supreme Court

■ **Seneca** 24 Mar. 1804
One Di Pronio Dr., Waterloo, NY 13165
Phone: (315)539-1770
Web site: www.rootsweb.com/~nyseneca/
Parent County: Cayuga

Record Type	Year Begun	Jurisdiction
Marriage	1908	Town/City Clerks
Nat.	1827	Supreme Court
Land	1804	County Clerk

Probate	1804	Surrogate Court
Court	1804	County Clerk

■ **St. Lawrence** 3 Mar. 1802
48 Court St., Canton, NY 13617
Phone: (315)379-2237
Web site: www.rootsweb.com/~nystlawr/
Parent County: Clinton, Herkimer, Montgomery
Comments/research tips: County Clerk has Birth, Marriage and Death records 1847-1849.

Record Type	Year Begun	Jurisdiction
Nat.	1816	Surrogate Court
Land	1787	County Clerk
Probate	1830	Surrogate Court
Court	1802	Ct./General Session

■ **Steuben** 18 Mar. 1796
3 E. Pulteney Sq., Bath, NY 14810
Phone: (607)776-9631
Web site: www.rootsweb.com/~nysteube/
Parent County: Ontario

Record Type	Year Begun	Jurisdiction
Birth	1908	Town/City Clerks
Land	1796	County Clerk
Probate	1796	Surrogate Court
Court	1841	Surrogate Court
Nat.	1820	Ct./Common Pleas

■ **Suffolk** 1 Nov. 1683
310 Center Dr., Riverhead, NY 11901
Phone: (631)852-2048
Web site: www.rootsweb.com/~nysuffol/
Parent County: Original county

Record Type	Year Begun	Jurisdiction
Nat.	1853	County Court
Birth	1847	County Clerk
Marriage	1847	County Clerk
Death	1847	County Clerk
Land	1660	County Clerk
Probate	1669	County Clerk
Court	1669	County Clerk

■ **Sullivan** 27 Mar. 1809
100 North St., Monticello, NY 12701
Phone: (845)794-3000
Web site: www.rootsweb.com/~nysulliv/
Parent County: Ulster

Record Type	Year Begun	Jurisdiction
Marriage	1908	Town Clerks
Land	1809	County Clerk
Nat.	1835	Ct./Oyer/Terminer
Court	1835	Ct./Oyer/Terminer

■ **Tioga** 16 Feb. 1791
16 Court, P.O. Box 307, Owego, NY 13827
Phone: (607)687-8660
Web site: www.rootsweb.com/~nytioga/
Parent County: Montgomery
Comments/research tips: Town Clerks have Marriage records 1847-1850.

Record Type	Year Begun	Jurisdiction
Nat.	1854	County Clerk
Land	1791	County Clerk
Probate	1798	Surrogate Court
Court	1790	Circuit Court

■ Tompkins   7 Apr. 1817

320 N. Tioga St., Ithaca, NY 14850
Phone: (607)274-5431
Web site: www.rootsweb.com/~nytompki/
Parent County: Cayuga, Seneca

Record Type	Year Begun	Jurisdiction
Marriage	1908	County Clerk
Land	1799	County Clerk
Nat.	1818	Supreme Court
Court	1817	County Clerk

■ Tryon   12 Mar. 1772

Parent County: Albany
Comments/research tips: (See Montgomery) Name changed to Montgomery 2 April 1784.

■ Ulster   1 Nov. 1683

244 Fair St., P.O. Box 1800, Kingston, NY 12402
Phone: (845)340-3000
Web site: www.hopefarm.com/geneatop.htm
Parent County: Original county

Record Type	Year Begun	Jurisdiction
Marriage	1908	County Clerk
Land	1685	County Clerk
Probate	1662	Surrogate Court
Court	1844	Circuit Court
Nat.	1812	County Clerk

■ Warren   12 Mar. 1813

1340 State Rt. 9, Lake George, NY 12845
Phone: (518)761-6429
Web site: www.rootsweb.com/~nywarren/
Parent County: Washington

Record Type	Year Begun	Jurisdiction
Marriage	1908	Town/City Clerks
Land	1813	County Clerk
Probate	1813	Surrogate Court
Court	1813	County Clerk
Nat.	1821	Supreme Court

■ Washington   12 Mar. 1772

383 Broadway Bldg. A, Fort Edward, NY 12828
Phone: (518)746-2170
Web site: www.rootsweb.com/~nywashin/
Parent County: Albany
Comments/research tips: Town Clerks have Birth, Death, and Marriage records 1847-1849.

Record Type	Year Begun	Jurisdiction
Nat.	1793	Ct./Common Pleas
Land	1773	County Clerk
Court	1830	Surrogate Court
Probate	1778	Surrogate Court

■ Wayne   11 Apr. 1823

9 Pearl St., P.O. Box 608, Lyons, NY 14489
Phone: (315)946-7470
Web site: www.rootsweb.com/~nywayne/
Parent County: Ontario, Seneca

Record Type	Year Begun	Jurisdiction
Marriage	1908	Town Clerks
Land	1823	County Clerk
Probate	1823	Surrogate Court
Court	1836	Supreme Court
Nat.	1855	County Clerk

■ Westchester   1 Nov. 1683

110 Dr. Martin Luther King Jr. Blvd., White Plains, NY 10601
Phone: (914)995-3080
Web site: www.rootsweb.com/~nywestch/
Parent County: Original county

Record Type	Year Begun	Jurisdiction
Probate	1775	Surrogate Court
Marriage	1908	Town Clerks
Land	1684	County Archives
Court	1657	Court/Sessions
Nat.	1844	County Court

■ Wyoming   19 May 1841

143 N. Main St., Warsaw, NY 14569
Phone: (585)786-8810
Web site: www.rootsweb.com/~nywyomin/
Parent County: Genesee

Record Type	Year Begun	Jurisdiction
Marriage	1908	Town Clerks
Land	1841	County Clerk
Probate	1841	Surrogate Court
Court	1841	County Clerk
Nat.	1841	County Court

■ Yates   5 Feb. 1823

417 Liberty St. Suite 1107, Penn Yan, NY 14527
Phone: (315)536-5120
Web site: www.kindredtrails.com/NY_Yates.html
Parent County: Ontario

Record Type	Year Begun	Jurisdiction
Birth	1908	Town Clerks
Land	1823	County Clerk
Probate	1823	Surrogate Court
Court	1823	County Clerk
Nat.	1823	County Court

North Carolina

By Emily Anne Croom

HISTORICAL OVERVIEW

In the 1650s, before Carolina was an official colony, Virginians began seeking new tobacco-farming land around Albemarle Sound in the northeast corner of what is now North Carolina. Ten years later, the British king granted eight proprietors the region south of Virginia, between latitude 31, and 36, and from sea to sea. By 1691, when the northern part of the proprietary province acquired the name North Carolina, it had developed a different, more diverse economy and society from its southern counterpart and was in effect a separate colony. Official separation occurred in 1712, and Parliament made both Carolinas royal colonies in 1729.

Many of the early settlers came from Barbados, Virginia, and Europe, including Swiss, German, French (Huguenots), and English immigrants. Along with tobacco and some rice, North Carolina farmers also produced foodstuffs for neighboring colonies and the West Indies, and a naval stores industry developed. Because the long barrier islands and lack of natural harbors discouraged ocean-going vessels, trade and passengers generally went through the harbors at Charles Town and Norfolk. Slavery, though present, developed more slowly in North Carolina than in other southern or Caribbean colonies. Most of the Indians eventually died of disease or in war with the newcomers, or were forced westward.

As a royal colony, North Carolina saw its population mushroom. From the 1730s, Ulster Scots, Germans, Virginians, and other British colonists arrived in large numbers, many coming via the Great Philadelphia Wagon Road through Maryland and Virginia and settling in the Piedmont. By the 1760s, North Carolinians were spilling over the mountains into eastern Tennessee.

North Carolina's Continental Congress delegates

NORTH CAROLINA AT A GLANCE

Motto: To Be Rather Than to Seem
Population: 8.1 million
Prevalent Religions: Christianity, particularly Lutheran, Pentecostal, Baptist, and Roman Catholic
Major Industries: Tobacco, textiles, chemical products, electrical equipment, machinery, tourism, poultry and eggs, tobacco, hogs, milk, nursery stock, cattle, soybeans
Ethnic Makeup (in percent): Caucasian 72.1%, African American 21.6%, Hispanic 4.7%, Asian 1.4%, Native American 1.2%, Other 4.7%
Famous North Carolinians: Doris Betts, David Brinkley, Howard Cosell, Roberta Flack, Eileen Fulton, Ava Gardner, Billy Graham, Paul Green, Andy Griffith, O. Henry (William Sidney Porter), Hatcher Hughes, Andrew Jackson, Andrew Johnson, Michael Jordan, Charles Kuralt, Sugar Ray Leonard, Ronnie Milsap, Edward R. Murrow, Guy Owen, James K. Polk, Reynolds Price, Sequoyah, Betty Smith, James Taylor, Doc Watson, Thomas Wolfe

Above: The Bodie Island Lighthouse

voted for independence, but during the Revolution conflict raged between the colony's patriots and loyalists, who included many Highland Scots. Wary of a strong central government, North Carolina did not ratify the new Constitution until late 1789, after President Washington was inaugurated and the Bill of Rights was proposed as amendments. North Carolina permanently relinquished claim to Tennessee in 1790.

Between 1760 and 1860, political and economic rifts developed between Piedmont farmers and coastal planters, who basically controlled the state. As cotton production increased and farmland wore out, many North Carolinians moved west and southwest to newer states. In spite of large emigrations, by 1860 North Carolina had almost one million residents, of whom one-third were slaves, about 3 percent were free blacks, and about three-tenths of 1 percent were foreign-born immigrants.

Not strongly secessionist, North Carolina did not secede until after Civil War hostilities began. Sending and losing large numbers of men to the war, the state saw limited engagements but experienced a significant peace movement. The state was readmitted to the Union in 1868.

From the Civil War forward, industries developed around the state's natural resources and dominant crops—forests (especially the furniture industry), minerals, commercial fishing, tobacco, and cotton (textile industry). The 1990 census was the first to show the urban population barely surpassing the rural.

RECORD HIGHLIGHTS

North Carolina began statewide registration of births and deaths in October 1913, marriages in 1962, and divorces in 1958. Records of these events are also kept in the county where the event occurred: birth (before 1960), death, and marriage records with the register of deeds; divorces with the superior court clerk. Before the twentieth century, legislative divorces (before 1835) or court-granted divorces (after 1814) were rare. The state archives holds surviving pre-1868 marriage bonds; few early marriage licenses exist.

For vital records copies, try the county office first. At this writing, the state archives holds death records from 1913 to 1956 but periodically receives later records from the Vital Records Registrar. The Web site <http://vitalrecords.dhhs.state.nc.us/vr/holdings/genealogy.html> contains information on obtaining copies from the state Vital Records Unit.

The state archives Web site, <www.ah.dcr.state.nc.us/sections/archives/arch/gen-res.htm>, contains valuable information on its genealogical holdings. For detailed guides to manuscripts and county records held at the archives, see <www.ah.dcr.state.nc.us/sections/archives/arch/FindingAids/findaids.htm>.

State-specific records of genealogical value include these:

- Colonial records, including some abstracted or microfilmed tax lists and estate records
- Early North Carolina papers in several series, especially series KK, of the Draper Manuscripts, which are housed at the State Historical Society of Wisconsin and available on microfilm at major research libraries
- 1785–1787 state census, various counties, not complete; no state censuses after 1787
- Pre-Civil War records of ante-bellum plantations and industries (see Witcher's book cited below)
- Post-Civil War African-American cohabitation (marriage) records and slave narratives
- Records of the three North Carolina branches of the Freedman's Savings and Trust Company (FHL film 928586)
- North Carolina Confederate pension records from 1885, at the state archives

STATE RESOURCES

■ ARCHIVES, LIBRARIES, AND SOCIETIES

Afro-American Heritage Society of North Carolina
P.O. Box 26334, Raleigh, NC 27611

The Alamance County Genealogical Society
P.O. Box 3052, Burlington, NC 27215-3052
Tel: (336) 584-8381
E-mail: alamancecogen@yahoo.com
Web site: <www.rootsweb.com/~ncacgs/>

Alexander County Genealogical Society, Inc.
P.O. Box 545, Hiddenite, NC 28636

Alleghany Historical-Genealogical Society (AHGS)
P.O. Box 817, Sparta, NC 28675
Web site: <www.ls.net/~ahgs/>

Anson County Genealogical Society
Web site: <http://freepages.genealogy.rootsweb.com/~stevebailey/society.htm>

Ashe County Historical Society
% Ashe County Public Library, 148 Library Dr., West Jefferson, NC 28694

Asheville, Pack Memorial Public Library
67 Haywood St., Asheville, NC 28801
Tel: (828) 255-5203
Web site: <www.buncombecounty.org/governing/depts/Library>

Beaufort County Genealogical Society
P.O. Box 1089, Washington, NC 27889-1089
Web site: <www.beaufort-county.com/Genealogy>

Bladen County Historical Society
P.O. Box 848; Elizabethtown, NC 28337
Web site: <www.rootsweb.com/~ncbladen/bchs.htm>

Braswell Memorial Library
727 N. Grace St., Rocky Mount, NC 27804
Tel: (252) 442-1951
Web site: <www.braswell-library.org>

Broad River Genealogical Society, Inc.
P.O. Box 2261, Shelby, NC 28151-2261
Web site: <www.rootsweb.com/~ncbrgs/>

Burke County Genealogical Society
536 Liberty St., Waynesboro, GA 30830

Web site: <http://members.aol.com/J2525/gen.htm>

Burke County Public Library, Inc., Morganton Branch
204 S. King St., Morganton, NC 28655
Tel: (828) 437-5638
Web site: <www.bcpls.org>

Cabarrus Genealogy Society
P.O. Box 2981, Concord, NC 28025
Web site: <www.rootsweb.com/~nccgs>

Carolinas Genealogical Society
P.O. Box 397, Monroe, NC 28111
Web site: <www.rootsweb.com/~ncunion/Genealogical_society.htm>

Carteret County Historical Society, The History Place
1008 Arendell St., Morehead City, NC 28557
E-mail: historyplace@starfishnet.com
Web site: <www.thehistoryplace.org>

Catawba County Genealogical Society
P.O. Box 2406, Hickory, NC 28603-2406
Web site: <www.rootsweb.com/~nccatawb/ccgsmain.htm>

Charlotte Jewish Historical Society
Web site: <http://users.vnet.net/lsstein/cjhs/cjhs.html>

Chatham County Historical Association, Inc.
P.O. Box 93, Pittsboro, NC 27312
E-mail: history@chathamhistory.org
Web site: <http://chathamhistory.org>

Cumberland County Genealogical Society
P.O. Box 53299, Fayetteville, NC 28305
Web site: <www.rootsweb.com/~nccumber/society.htm>

Davidson County Public Library
602 S. Main St., Lexington, NC 27292
Tel: (336) 242-2040

Web site: <www.co.davidson.nc.us/library>

Davie County Historical & Genealogical Society
371 N. Main St., Mocksville, NC 27028

Duke University, Rare Book, Manuscript, and Special Collections Library
Duke University, Durham, NC 27708-0185
Tel: (919) 660-5822
Web site: <http://scriptorium.lib.duke.edu>

Durham-Orange Genealogical Society
P.O. Box 4703, Chapel Hill, NC 27515-4703
E-mail: NCDOGS-adminootsweb.com
Web site: <www.rootsweb.com/~ncdogs>

Evangelical Lutheran Church in America, North Carolina Synod Archives
1988 Lutheran Synod Dr., Salisbury, NC 28144
Tel: (704) 633-4861

Family Research Society of Northeastern North Carolina
P.O. Box 1425, Elizabeth City, NC 27906-1425
Tel: (252) 333-1640
E-mail: frsnnc2@hotmail.com
Web site: <www.geocities.com/heartland/farm/7890>

Forsyth County Genealogical Society
P.O. Box 5715, Winston-Salem, NC 27113-5715
Web site: <www.rootsweb.com/~ncfcgs/>

Free Will Baptist Collection, Moye Library
Mount Olive College, 634 Henderson St., Mount Olive, NC 28365
Tel: (919) 658-2502 or 1-800-653-0854
Web site: <www.moc.edu/request.cfm?dept=moyelibrary&PageName=Special%20Collection>

Gaston Lincoln Genealogical Society
P.O. Box 584, Mount Holly, NC 28120

Web site: <www.rootsweb.com/~ncglgs/Index.htm>

Gates County Historical Society
P.O. Box 98, Gates, NC 27937
Web site: <www.throughwire.net/gchs/>

Genealogical Society of Davidson County
P.O. Box 1665, Lexington, NC 27293-1665
Web site: <www.rootsweb.com/~ncdavids/gsdcpub.htm>

Genealogical Society of Iredell County
P.O. Box 946, Statesville, NC 28687
Tel: (704) 878-5384
Web site: <www.iredell.com/iredellgensoc.htm>

Genealogical Society of Old Tryon County
P.O. Box 938, Forest City, NC 28043
Tel: (828) 247-8700
Web site: <http://rfci.net/wdfloyd/gsotc.html>

Genealogical Society of Rockingham and Stokes Counties, Inc.
P.O. Box 152, Mayodan, NC 27027-0152
Web site: <http://ns.netmcr.com/~lonabec/gsrs.html>

Genealogical Society of Rowan County
P.O. Box 4305, Salisbury, NC 28145-4305
Web site: <www.lib.co.rowan.nc.us/HistoryRoom/html/gsrc.htm>

Granville County Genealogical Society 1746, Inc.
P.O. Box 1746, Oxford, NC 27565-1746
Web site: <www.gcgs.org/Default.asp>

Guilford College, Friends Historical Collection
5800 W. Friendly Ave., Greensboro, NC 27410
Tel: (336) 316-2301 or (336) 316-2000
Web site: <www.guilford.edu>

Guilford County Genealogical Society
P.O. Box 49104, Greensboro, NC 27419-1104
Web site: <www.greensboro.com/gcgs>

Haywood County Genealogical Society
P.O. Box 1331, Waynesville, NC 28786
E-mail: hcgs_nc@yahoo.com
Web site: <www.rootsweb.com/~nchcgs>

Henderson County Genealogical and Historical Society, Inc.
400 N. Main St., Hendersonville, NC 28792-4901
Tel: (828) 693-1531
E-mail: hcgenhis@brinet.com
Web site: <www.brinet.com/~hcgenhis/>

Hyde County Historical and Genealogical Society
Web site: <www.rootsweb.com/~nchyde/HCHGS.HTM>

Jackson County Genealogical Society
P.O. Box 2108, Cullowhee, NC 28723
Web site: <www.jcncgs.com>

Johnston County Genealogical and Historical Society
P.O. Box 2373, Smithfield, NC 27577
Web site: <www.rootsweb.com/~ncjohnst>

Lincoln County Charles R. Jonas Public Library
306 W. Main St., Lincolnton, NC 28092
Tel: (704) 735-8044
Web site: <www.glrl.lib.nc.us/index.htm>

Moravian Archives
457 S. Church St., Winston-Salem, NC 27101
Web site: <www.moravianarchives.org>

National Archives and Record Administration (NARA), Southeast Region
1557 St. Joseph Ave., East Point, GA 30344-2593
Tel: (404) 763-7383
Web site: <www.archives.gov/facilities/ga/atlanta.html>

North Carolina Department of Health and Human Services, Vital Records
1903 Mail Service Center, Raleigh, NC 27699-1903
Tel: (919) 733-3526
Web site: <http://vitalrecords.dhhs.state.nc.us/vr/index.html>

North Carolina Genealogical Society
P.O. Box 22, Greenville, NC 27835-0022
Web site: <www.ncgenealogy.org>

North Carolina State Archives
4614 Mail Service Center, Raleigh, NC 27699-4614
Tel: (919) 807-7310
E-mail: archives@ncmail.net
Web site: <www.ah.dcr.state.nc.us/sections/archives/arch/default.htm>

North Carolina State Library
Archives and History/State Library Building, 109 E. Jones St., Raleigh, NC 27601
Tel: (919) 733-5679
Web site: <http://statelibrary.dcr.state.nc.us/ncslhome.htm>

North Carolina

Old Buncombe County Genealogical Society
P.O. Box 2122, Asheville, NC 28802-2122
Tel: (828) 253-1894
Web site: <http://obcgs.com>

Old Dobbs County Genealogical Society
P.O. Box 617, Goldsboro, NC 27533-0617
Web site: <www.usgennet.org/usa/nc/county/wayne/gensform.htm>

Old Mecklenburg Genealogical Society
P.O. Box 32453, Charlotte, NC 28232-2453
E-mail: OMGS1775@yahoo.com
Web site: <www.rootsweb.com/~ncomgs>

Old New Hanover Genealogical Society
P.O. Box 2536, Wilmington, NC 28402-2536
E-mail: info@onhgs.org
Web site: <www.onhgs.org>

Oxford, Richard H. Thornton Library
P.O. Box 339, Oxford, NC 27565
Tel: (919) 693-1121
E-mail: reference@gloryroad.net
Web site: <www.granville.lib.nc.us>

PAF-Finders Club
P.O. Box 17494, Raleigh, NC 27619-7494
Tel: (919) 876-6456
Web site: <http://freepages.genealogy.rootsweb.com/~paffinders>

Pitt County Family Researchers, Inc.
P.O. Box 20339, Greenville, NC 27858-0339
Web site: <www.rootsweb.com/~ncpcfr>

Presbyterian Historical Society, Montreat Office
P.O. Box 849, Montreat, NC 28757
Tel: (828) 669-7061
E-mail: refdesk@history.pcusa.org
Web site: <www.history.pcusa.org>

Public Library of Charlotte and Mecklenburg County
310 N. Tryon St., Charlotte, NC 28202
Tel: (704) 336-2725
Web site: <www.plcmc.org>

Rowan Public Library, Main Branch
201 W. Fisher St., Salisbury, NC 28144
Tel: (704) 638-3001
Web site: <www.lib.co.rowan.nc.us>

Southeastern North Carolina Genealogical Society
P.O. Box 468, Chadbourn, NC 28431
Web site: <www.spiritdesign.net/columbus/sencgs.htm>

Southport Historical Society
501 N. Atlantic Ave., Southport, NC 28461

Toe Valley Genealogical Society
491 Beaver Creek Rd., Spruce Pine, NC 28777
Web site: <www.rootsweb.com/~ncmitche/tvgs.html>

Union County Public Library, Main Branch
316 E. Windsor St., Monroe, NC 28112
Tel: (704) 283-8184
Web site: <www.union.lib.nc.us>

United Methodist Church, Western North Carolina Conference Archives
P.O. Box 18005, Charlotte, NC 28218
Tel: (704) 535-2260
E-mail: archives@wnccumc.org
Web site: <www.wnccumc.org>

University of North Carolina, Wilson Library
Chapel Hill, NC 27514-8890
Tel: (919) 962-1172
E-mail: nccref@email.unc.edu
Web site: <www.lib.unc.edu/ncc>

Wake County Genealogical Society
P.O. Box 17713, Raleigh, NC 27619-7713
Web site: <www.rootsweb.com/~ncwcgs>

Wake Forest University, Baptist Historical Collection, Z. Smith Reynolds Library
Wake Forest University, P.O. Box 7777, Reynolda Station, Winston-Salem, NC 27109
Tel: (336) 758-5480
E-mail: zsr@wfu.edu
Web site: <www.wfu.edu/Library/baptist>

RESEARCH TIPS

for more info

- Due to its colonial beginnings, North Carolina is a state land state.
- Marriage license applications, often made by a friend or relative of the groom, may not provide completely accurate information.
- The boundaries of North Carolina were established after settlement began: the Virginia border about 1728; the South Carolina border, 1772. Researchers should consult land records on both sides of the current border when studying ancestors from the border counties.
- Although numerous church records exist for North Carolina research, no eighteenth-century Anglican parish registers survive.
- Someone reporting a North Carolina birth prior to 1796 may have been born in what is now Tennessee.
- Major archival collections are housed at the North Carolina Division of Archives and History; University of North Carolina, Chapel Hill; and Duke University, Durham.
- www.segenealogy.com

Census Records

- Federal Census Population Schedules: 1790 (incomplete), 1800, 1810 (incomplete), 1820 (incomplete), 1830, 1840, 1850, 1860, 1870, 1880, 1890 (fragments/only: parts of Gaston and Cleveland counties), 1900, 1910, 1920, 1930
- Federal Census Soundex or Miracode: 1880, 1900, 1910, 1920, 1930
- Federal Mortality Schedules: 1850, 1860, 1870, 1880
- Federal Slave Schedules: 1850, 1860
- State Census: 1784–1787
- Special Census of Civil War Veterans or their Widows: 1890

Wayne County Historical Association and Museum
116 N. William St., Goldsboro, NC 27530
Tel: (919) 734-5023
E-mail: museum@esn.net
Web site: <www.historicalwayne nc.com>

Wilkes Genealogical Society, Inc.
P.O. Box 1629, North Wilkesboro, NC 28659
Web site: <www.angelfire.com/ nc/wwwjmd/wgs.html>

Wilson County Genealogical Society
E-mail: ancestor@wcgs.org
Web site: <www.wcgs.org>

BIBLIOGRAPHY

■ GENERAL RESOURCES

African American Genealogy: A Bibliography and Guide to Sources
Curt Bryan Witcher (Fort Wayne, IN: Round Tower Books, 2000. Includes white families' papers.)

The American Indian in North Carolina
by Douglas L. Rights (Winston-Salem, J.F. Blair, 1957)

Archival and Manuscript Repositories in North Carolina: A Directory
by the Society of North Carolina Archivists (Raleigh, NC: Society of North Carolina Archivists, 1993)

A Bibliography of North Carolina, 1589–1956
by Mary Lindsay Thornton (Westport, CT: Greenwood Press, 1973, ca. 1958)

Biographical History of North Carolina From Colonial Times to the Present
edited by Samuel A'Court Ashe (Greensboro, NC: C.L. Van Noppen, 1905–1917)

The Carolina Backcountry on the Eve of the Revolution
by Charles Woodmason (Chapel Hill, NC: Published for the Institute of Early American History and Culture at Williamsburg, VA, by the University of North Carolina Press, 1953)

Carolina Cradle; Settlement of the Northwest Carolina Frontier, 1747–1762
by Robert W. Ramsey (Chapel Hill, NC: University of North Carolina Press, 1964)

Carolina Families: A Bibliography of Books About North and South Carolina Families
by Donald M. Hehir (Bowie, MD: Heritage Books, 1994)

The Colonial Records of North Carolina, 10 vols.
collected and edited by William L. Saunders (Raleigh, NC: P.M. Hale State Printer, 1886–90)

The Country Church in North Carolina
by Jesse Marvin Ormond (Durham, NC: Duke University Press, 1931)

Dictionary of North Carolina Biography, 6 vols.
by William Stevens Powell (Chapel Hill, NC: University of North Carolina Press, ca. 1979–1996)

Directory of Scots in the Carolinas, 1680–1830
by David Dobson (Baltimore, MD: Genealogical Pub. Co., 1986)

Early Methodism in the Carolinas
by A.M. Chreitzberg (Spartanburg, SC: Reprint Co., 1972)

Encyclopedia of American Quaker Genealogy
by William Wade Hinshaw, compiled by Thomas W. Marshall (Baltimore, MD: Genealogical Pub. Co., 1969)

The Episcopal Church in North Carolina, 1701–1959
edited by Lawrence Foushee London and Sarah McCulloh Lemmon (Raleigh, NC: Episcopal Diocese of North Carolina, 1987)

Exploring Your Cherokee Ancestry: A Basic Genealogical Research Guide
by Thomas G. Mooney (Tahlequah, OK: Cherokee National Historical Society, 1988, ca. 1990)

The Flowering of Methodism in Western North Carolina
by George William Bumgarner and James Elwood Carroll (Charlotte,

NC: Commission on Archives and History of the Western North Carolina Conference of the United Methodist Church, 1984)

The Formation of North Carolina Counties, 1663–1943
by David Leroy Corbitt (Raleigh, NC: State Department of Archives and History, 1969)

Genealogical Encyclopedia of the Colonial Americas
by Christina K. Schaefer (Baltimore: Genealogical Publishing Co., 1998. Pages 517-536, North Carolina; 617-620, Tennessee)

The Genealogist's Companion and Sourcebook, 2d ed.
by Emily Anne Croom (Cincinnati: Betterway Books, 2003)

A Genealogist's Guide to Discovering Your African-American Ancestors
by Franklin Carter Smith and Emily Anne Croom (Cincinnati: Betterway Books, 2003)

Guide to Genealogical Research in the National Archives of the United States
edited by Anne Bruner Eales and Robert M. Kvasnicka (Washington, DC: National Archives and Records Administration, 2000)

Guide to Genealogical Research in North Carolina
by Wendy L. Elliott (Bountiful, UT: W.L. Elliott, 1988)

Guide to Private Manuscript Collections in the North Carolina State Archives
compiled and edited by Barbara T. Cain, Ellen Z. McGrew, and Charles E. Morris (Raleigh, NC: North Carolina Dept. of Cultural Resources, Division of Archives and History, 1981)

The Heritage of Blacks in North Carolina
project director Linda Simmons-Henry; edited by Phillip N. Henry and Carol M. Speas (Raleigh, NC: North Carolina African-American Heritage Foundation in Cooperation with the Delmar Company, Charlotte, NC, 1990)

A History of African Americans in North Carolina
by Jeffrey J. Crow, Paul D. Escott, and Flora J. Hatley (Raleigh, NC:

Dept. of Cultural Resources, Divions of Archives and History, 1992)

History of the German Settlements and of the Lutheran Church in North and South Carolina, From the Earliest Period of the Colonization of the Dutch, German and Swiss Settlers to the Close of the First Half of the Present Century
by Gotthardt Dellmann Bernheim (Philadelphia: The Lutheran Book Store, 1872)

History of North Carolina, 4 vols.
by Hugh Talmage Leffer (New York: Lewis Historical Pub. Co., 1956)

History of the North Carolina Baptists
by George Washington Paschal (Gallatin, TN: Church History Research & Archives, 1990, ca. 1955)

History of the Protestant Episcopal Church in North Carolina
by the Prostestant Episcopal Church (North Carolina) (Raleigh, NC: North Carolina Dept. of Archives and History, 1961)

I Have Called You Friends; the Story of Quakerism in North Carolina
by Francis Charles Anscombe (Boston: Christopher Pub. House, 1959)

King's Mountain and Its Heroes; History of the Battle of King's Mountain, October 7th, 1780, and the Events Which Led to It
by Lyman Copeland Draper (Spartanburg, SC: Reprint Co., 1967)

Lawson's History of North Carolina: Containing the Exact Description and Natural History of That Country, Together With the Present State Thereof and a Journal of a Thousand Miles Traveled Through Several Nations of Indians, Giving a Particular Account of Their Customs, Manners, etc., etc.
by John Lawson and Frances Latham Harriss (Richmond, VA: Garrett and Massie, 1937)

Lost Tribes of North Carolina. Where did They Come From? Where did They go?
by Worth Stickley Ray (Austin, TX: 1947)

The Loyalists in North Carolina During the Revolution
by Robert O. DeMond (Baltimore, MD: Genealogical Pub. Co., 1979, ca. 1940)

"A Master Plan for North Carolina Research"
by Helen F.M. Leary (*National Genealogical Society Quarterly* 75 (March 1987): 15-36)

The Melungeons: Notes on the Origin of a Race
by Bonnie Ball (Johnson City, TN: Overmountain Press, 1992)

Melungeons Yesterday and Today
by Jean Patterson Bible (Tennessee: J.P. Bible, 1975)

More Than Petticoats. Remarkable North Carolina Women
by Scotti Kent (Helena, MT: Two-Dot, 2000)

National Archives Microfilm Catalogs online:
<www.archives.gov/publications/genealogy_microfilm_catalogs.html>

The North Carolina Experience, an Interpretive and Documentary History
edited by Lindley S. Butler and Alan D. Watson (Chapel Hill, NC: University of North Carolina Press, 1984)

North Carolina Genealogical Reference: A Research Guide for all Genealogists, Both Amateur and Professional
compiled and edited by Wallace R. Draughon and William Perry Johnson (Durham, NC: s.n., 1966)

North Carolina Genealogical Research
by George K. Schweitzer (Knoxville, TN: G.K. Schweitzer, 1984)

North Carolina Higher Court Records
edited by Mattie Erma Parker (Raleigh, NC: State Dept. of Archives and History, 1968-1981)

North Carolina Local History, a Select Bibliography
compiled by George Stevenson (Raleigh, NC: North Carolina Dept. of Cultural Resources, Division of Archives and History, 1984)

North Carolina Portraits of Faith: A Pictorial History of Religions
by Anne Russell and Marjorie Megivern (Norfolk, VA: Donning Co., 1986)

North Carolina Research: Genealogy and Local History, 2d ed.
Helen F.M. Leary, ed. (Raleigh: North Carolina Genealogical Society, 1996)

North Carolina Taxpayers
compiled by Clarence E. Ratcliff (Baltimore, MD: Genealogical Pub. Co., 1987-1989)

North Carolina Through Four Centuries
by William Stevens Powell (Chapel Hill, NC: University of North Carolina Press, ca. 1989)

Old Cherokee Families: Notes of Dr. Emmet Starr, 3 vols.
edited and annotated by Jack D. Baker and David Keith Hampton (Oklahoma City, Baker Pub. Co., 1987)

One Dozen Pre-Revolutionary War Families of Eastern North Carolina, and Some of Their Descendants
by Primrose Watson Fisher (New Bern, NC: New Bern Historical Society Foundation, 1958)

Paths Towards Freedom: A Biographical History of Blacks and Indians in North Carolina
by Frank Emory (Raleigh, NC: Center for Urban Affairs, North Carolina State University, 1976)

Quaker Women of Carolina: Freedom, Achievement
by Seth B. Hinshaw and Mary Edith Hinshaw (Greensboro, NC: North Carolina United Society of Friends Women, 1994)

Reminiscences and Memoirs of North Carolina and Eminent North Carolinians
by John H. Wheeler (Baltimore, MD: Genealogical Pub. Co., 1966)

Sketches of the Pioneers of Methodism in North Carolina and Virginia
by M.H. Moore (Nashville: Southern Methodist Publishing House, 1884)

Sketches of Western North Carolina, Historical and Biographical; Illustrating Principally the Revolutionary Period of Mecklenburg, Rowan, Lincoln, and Adjoining Counties, Accompanied With Miscellaneous Information
by C.L. Hunter (Baltimore, MD: Regional Pub. Co., 1970)

Slavery in the State of North Carolina
by John Spencer Bassett (New York: AMS Press, 1972)

Sojourners no More: The Quakers in the New South, 1865-1920
by Damon D. Hickey (Greensboro, NC: North Carolina Friends Historical Society: North Carolina Yearly Meeting of Friends, 1997)

Some Colonial and Revolutionary Families of North Carolina, 3 vols.
by Marilu Burch Smallwood (Washington, NC: 1964-1976)

The Southern Historical Collection; a Guide to Manuscripts
by Susan Sokol Blosser and Clyde Norman Wilson Jr. (Chapel Hill, NC: 1970)

Union Lists of North Carolina Newspapers, 1751-1900
edited by H.G. Jones and Julius H. Avant (Raleigh, NC: State Dept. of Archives & History, 1963)

■ CENSUS RECORDS

The American Census Handbook
by Thomas Jay Kemp (Wilmington, DE: Scholarly Resources, 2001)

The Census Book: A Genealogist's Guide to Federal Census Facts, Schedules and Indexes
by William Dollarhide (Bountiful, UT: Heritage Quest, 2000)

The Eastern Cherokees, a Census of the Cherokee Nation in North Carolina, Tennessee, Alabama and Georgia in 1851
compiled by David W. Siler (Cottonport, LA: Polyanthos, Inc., 1972)

Map Guide to the U.S. Federal Censuses, 1790-1920
by William Thorndale and William Dollarhide (Baltimore, MD: Genealogical Pub. Co., 1987)

North Carolina Extant Voter Registrations of 1867
by Frances Holloway Wynne (Bowie, MD: Heritage Books, 1992)

State Census Records
by Ann S. Lainhart (Baltimore, MD: Genealogical Publishing, 1992)

Your Guide to the Federal Census
by Kathleen W. Hinckley (Cincinnati: Betterway Books, 2002)

■ IMMIGRATION RECORDS

American Naturalization Records, 1790-1990: What They Are and How to Use Them
by John J. Newman (North Salt Lake, UT: HeritageQuest, 1998)

American Passenger Arrival Records
by Michael Tepper (Baltimore: Genealogical Publishing Co., 1993)

Explorations, Descriptions and Attempted Settlements of Carolina, 1584-1590
by Richard Hakluyt, edited by David Leroy Corbitt (Raleigh, NC: State Dept. of Archives and History, 1948)

The Highland Scots of North Carolina
by Duane Gilbert Meyer (Raleigh, NC: Carolina Charter Tercentenary Commission, 1963)

Marylanders to Carolina: Migration of Marylanders to North Carolina and South Carolina Prior to 1800
by Henry C. Peden Jr. (Westminster, MD: Family Line Publications, 1994)

The Moravians in North Carolina; an Authentic History
by Levin Theodore Reichel (Baltimore, MD: Genealogical Pub. Co., 1968)

They Became Americans: Finding Naturalization Records and Ethnic Origins
by Loretto Dennis Szucs (Salt Lake City: Ancestry, Inc., 1998)

They Came in Ships: A Guide to Finding Your Immigrant Ancestor's Arrival Records, 2d ed.
by John P. Colletta (Salt Lake City: Ancestry, Inc., 1993)

Westward From Virginia: The Exploration of the Virginia-Carolina Frontier, 1650–1710
by Alan Vance Briceland (Charlotteville, VA: University Press of Virginia, 1987)

LAND RECORDS

Colonial Land Entries in North Carolina, 3 vols.
by A.B. Pruitt (North Carolina: A.B. Pruitt, 1994–1995)

Colony of North Carolina: Abstracts of Land Patents, 2 vols.
by Margaret M. Hofmann (Weldon, NC: Roanoke News Co., 1982–1984)

The Granville District of North Carolina, 1748-1763: Abstracts of Land Grants, 4 vols.
by Margaret M. Hofmann (Weldon, NC: Roanoke News Co., 1986–1993)

The History of Land Titles in Western North Carolina: A History of the Cherokee Land Laws Affecting the Title to Land Lying West of the Meigs and Freeman Line, and Laws Affecting the Title of Land Lying East of the Meigs and Freeman Line Back to the Top of Blue Ridge
by George Henry Smathers (Asheville, NC: Miller Printing Co., 1938)

Land & Property Research in the United States
by Wade E. Hone (Salt Lake City, UT: Ancestry, 1997)

Locating Your Roots: Discover Your Ancestors Using Land Records
by Patricia Law Hatcher (Cincinnati: Betterway Books, 2003)

North Carolina Land Grants in Tennessee, 1778-1791
compiled by Goldene Fillers Burgner (Sl: Southern Historical Press, 1981)

The Proprietors of Carolina
by William Stevens Powell (Raleigh, NC: Carolina Charter Tercentenary Commission, 1963)

Province of North Carolina, 1663-1729: Abstracts of Land Patents
by Margaret M. Hofmann (Weldon, NC: Roanoke News Co., 1979)

MAPS

The Formation of North Carolina Counties, 1663–1943
by David Leroy Corbitt (Raleigh, NC: Division of Archives and History, North Carolina Department of Cultural Resources, 1950)

Index to Maps of North Carolina in Books and Periodicals Illustrating the History of the State From the Voyage of Verrazzano in 1524 to 1975
by David Sanders Clark (Fayetteville, NC: Clark, 1976)

The National Post Road
by Virginia Greene DePriest (Shelby, NC: V.G. DePriest, 1990)

North Carolina Atlas and Gazetteer: Topo Maps of the Entire State
by the Delorme Mapping Company (Yarmouth, ME: Delorme, ca. 1997)

North Carolina Atlas: Portrait of a Changing Southern State
edited by James W. Clay, Douglas M. Orr, and Alfred W. Stuart (Chapel Hill, NC: University of North Carolina Press, 1975)

North Carolina County Maps
compiled by C.J. Puetz (Lyndon Station, WI: Puetz Place, ca. 1980)

North Carolina, Her Counties, Her Townships, and Her Towns
compiled by Joan Colbert Gioe (Indianapolis: Researchers, 1981)

North Carolina in Maps
by William P. Cumming (Raleigh, NC: State Department of Archives and History, 1966)

Statistical Gazetteer of the States of Virginia and North Carolina: Embracing Important Topographical and Historical Information, From Recent and Original Sources Together With the Results of the Last Census, Population and Statistics in Many Cases to 1855
edited by Richard Edwards (Richmond: Published for the Proprietor, 1856)

MILITARY RECORDS

Abstracts and Letters of Resignations of Militia Officers in North Carolina, 1779–1840
compiled and abstracted by Timothy Kearney (Raleigh, NC: North Carolina Genealogical Society, 1992 (Raleigh, NC: Walsworth Pub.)

Abstracts of Pensions of North Carolina Soldiers of the Revolution, War of 1812 & Indian Wars
by Annie W. Burns (Washington, DC: ca. 1960)

The Black Experience in Revolutionary North Carolina
by Jeffrey J. Crow (Raleigh, NC: Department of Cultural Resources, Division of Archives and History, 1977)

Compendium of the Confederate Armies, 11 vols.
by Stewart Sifakis (New York: Facts on File, 1992–1995)

Histories of the Several Regiments and Battalions From North Carolina in the Great War, 1861–'65, 5 vols.
edited by Walter Clark (Wilmington, NC: Broadfoot Pub., 1996)

The King's Mountain Men; the Story of the Battle, With Sketches of the American Soldiers who Took Part
by Katherine Keogh White (Baltimore, MD: Genealogical Pub. Co., 1966)

Muster Roles of the Soldiers of the War of 1812 Detached From the Militia of North Carolina in 1812 and 1814
by Maurice S. Toler (Baltimore, MD: Genealogical Pub. Co., 1976)

North Carolina Civil War Documentary
edited by W. Buck Yearns and John G. Barrett (Chapel Hill, NC:

University of North Carolina Press, 2002)

North Carolina Revolutionary Soldiers, Sailors, Patriots & Descendants
compiled by Joseph T. Maddox & Mary Carter (Albany, GA: Georgia Pioneers Publications, ca. 1970)

North Carolina Troops, 1861–1865: A Roster, 15 vols.
compiled by Louis H. Manarin (Raleigh, NC: State Department of Archives and History, 1966–2003)

North Carolina's Role in the First World War
by Sarah McCulloh Lemmon (Raleigh, NC: State Dept. of Archives and History, 1966)

North Carolina's Role in the Spanish-American War
by Joseph S. Steelman (Raleigh, NC: Department of Cultural Resources, Division of Archives and History, 1975)

This Destructive War: The British Campaign in the Carolinas, 1780–1782
by John S. Pancake (Tuscaloosa, AL: University of Alabama Press, 2003)

Uncle, We Are Ready! Registering America's Men, 1917–1918: A Guide to Researching World War I Draft Registration Cards
by John J. Newman (North Salt Lake, UT: HeritageQuest, 2001)

U.S. Military Records: A Guide to Federal & State Sources, Colonial America to the Present
by James C. Neagles (Salt Lake City: Ancestry, Inc., 1994)

Volunteer Soldiers in the Cherokee War, 1836–39
by James L. Douthat (Signal Mountain, TN: Mountain Press, 1995)

World War II: A Family Historian's Guide
by Debra Johnson Knox (Spartanburg, SC: MIE Publishing, 2003)

PROBATE RECORDS

An Abstract of North Carolina Wills From About 1760 to About 1800
by Fred A. Olds (Baltimore, MD: Genealogical Pub. Co., 1965)

The County Court in North Carolina Before 1750
by Paul Moffatt McCain (Durham, NC: Duke University Press, 1954)

The First Laws of the State of North Carolina, 2 vols.
by John D. Cushing (Wilmington, DE: M. Clazier, 1984)

North Carolina Wills and Inventories, Copied From Original and Recorded Wills and Inventories in the Office of the Secretary of State
by J. Bryan Grimes (Baltimore, MD: Genealogical Pub. Co., 1967)

North Carolina Wills, a Testator Index 1665–1900, 2 vols.
by Thornton W. Mitchell (Raleigh, NC: T.W. Mitchell, 1987)

■ VITAL RECORDS

Marriage and Death Notices in Raleigh Register and North Carolina State Gazette (1799–1867), 4 vols.
compiled by Carrie L. Broughton (Baltimore, MD: Genealogical Pub. Co., 1949)

Somebody Knows My Name: Marriages of Freed People in North Carolina County by County, 3 vols.
compiled by Barnetta McGee White (Athens, GA: Iberian Publishing Co., 1995)

Tar Heel Tombstones and the Tales They Tell
by Henry King (Asheboro, NC: Down Home Press, 1990)

Your Guide to Cemetery Research
by Sharon DeBartolo Carmack (Cincinnati: Betterway Books, 2002)

■ Alamance   Apr. 1849
P.O. Box 837, 118 W. Harden St., Graham, NC 27253-2802
Phone: (336)570-6565
Web site: www.alamance-nc.com/
Parent County: Orange
Comments/research tips: State Archives has Court records 1849–1920, Divorce records 1889–1917, Land records 1793–1905, Probate records 1856–1949, and Wills 1832–1900.

Record Type	Year Begun	Jurisdiction
Land	1905	Registrar/Deeds
Birth	1913	Registrar/Deeds
Marriage	1849	Registrar/Deeds
Death	1913	Registrar/Deeds
Divorce	1917	Clerk/Superior Ct.
Probate	1949	Clerk/Superior Ct.
Court	1920	Clerk/Superior Ct.

■ Albemarle   1664
Parent County: Original county
Comments/research tips: County divided into Chowan, Currituck, Pasquotank, and Perquimans Precincts in 1668. County discontinued in 1689.

■ Alexander   15 Jan. 1847
201 First St. SW, Suite 1, Taylorsville, NC 28681
Phone: (828)632-3152

Web site: www.co.alexander.nc.us
Parent County: Iredell, Caldwell, Wilkes
Comments/research tips: State Archives has Court records 1866–1900, Divorce records 1867–1905, Probate records 1858–1939, and Wills 1847–1949. Courthouse burned in 1865, destroying many records.

Record Type	Year Begun	Jurisdiction
Land	1847	Registrar/Deeds
Birth	1913	Registrar/Deeds
Marriage	1866	Registrar/Deeds
Death	1913	Registrar/Deeds

■ Alleghany   1859
12 N. Main St., P.O. Box 186, Sparta, NC 28675
Phone: (336)372-4342
Web site: www.alleghanycoungy-nc.gov
Parent County: Ashe
Comments/research tips: State Archives has Court records 1862–1928, Divorce recods 1862–1932, Land records 1837–1908, Probate records 1859–1928, and Wills 1859–1912. Courthouse fire in 1932 destroyed some county records.

Record Type	Year Begun	Jurisdiction
Birth	1913	Registrar/Deeds
Marriage	1859	Registrar/Deeds
Death	1913	Registrar/Deeds

■ Anson   1750
N. Green St., P.O. Box 352, Wadesboro, NC 28170
Phone: (704)694-3212
Web site: www.co.anson.nc.us
Parent County: Bladen
Comments/research tips: State Archives has Court records 1771–1777, 1848–1905, Divorce records 1872–1925, Land records 1749–1838, Naturalization records 1913–1924, Probate records 1805–1953, and Wills 1754–1946. Courthouse burned 1868.

Record Type	Year Begun	Jurisdiction
Birth	1914	Registrar/Deeds
Marriage	1869	Registrar/Deeds
Death	1914	Registrar/Deeds

■ Archdale   1705
Parent County: Bath
Comments/research tips: (See Craven) Name changed to Craven, 1712. Known as a precinct then declared a County.

■ Ashe   1799
150 Government Circle, Suite 2300, Jefferson, NC 28640
Phone: (336)219-2540
Web site: www.ashecountygov.com
Parent County: Wilkes
Comments/research tips: State Archives has Court records 1807–1938, Divorce records 1822–1912, Land records 1778–1954, Probate records 1819–1935 and Wills 1801–1912. Fire in 1865 destroyed many court records.

Record Type	Year Begun	Jurisdiction
Birth	1913	Registrar/Deeds
Death	1913	Registrar/Deeds
Marriage	1799	Clerk/Superior Ct.

North Carolina

■ Avery 1911
200 Montezuma St., Newland, NC 28657
Phone: (828)733-8260
Web site: www.rootsweb.com/ncavery/
Parent County: Caldwell, Mitchell, Watauga

Record Type	Year Begun	Jurisdiction
Marriage	1859	Registrar/Deeds
Land	1911	Registrar/Deeds
Birth	1913	Registrar/Deeds
Death	1913	Registrar/Deeds
Divorce	1911	Clerk/Superior Ct.
Probate	1911	Clerk/Superior Ct.
Court	1911	Clerk/Superior Ct.

■ Bath 1696
Parent County: Original county
Comments/research tips: Divided into Archdale, Pamptecough, and Wickham Precincts 1705, county discontinued in 1724.

■ Beaufort 1705
112 W. Second St., Washington, NC 27889
Phone: (252)946-2323
Web site: www.co.beaufort.nc.us
Parent County: Bath
Comments/research tips: State Archives has Court records 1756–1902, Divorce records 1868–1902, Land records 1695–1881, Probate records 1760–1949, and Wills 1720–1903.

Record Type	Year Begun	Jurisdiction
Death	1913	Registrar/Deeds
Marriage	1850	Registrar/Deeds
Birth	1913	Registrar/Deeds

■ Berkeley 1668
Parent County: Precinct in Albemarle County
Comments/research tips: (See Perquimans) Perquimans County known as Berkeley Precinct from 1670–1682.

■ Bertie 1722
P.O. Box 340, Windsor, NC 27983
Phone: (252)794-5309
Web site: www.co.bertie.nc.us/
Parent County: Chowan
Comments/research tips: State Archives has Court records 1724–1915, Land records 1723–1820, Marriage records 1762–1868, 1870–1903, Probate records 1728–1920, and Wills 1749–1897.

Record Type	Year Begun	Jurisdiction
Marriage	1902	Registrar/Deeds
Birth	1913	Registrar/Deeds
Death	1913	Registrar/Deeds
Divorce	na	Clerk/Superior Ct.

■ Bladen 1734
101 E. Broad St., Elizabethtown, NC 28337
Phone: (910)862-6713
Web site: www.bladeninfo.org
Parent County: New Hanover

Comments/research tips: State Archives has Court records 1866–1890, 1893–1956, Divorce records 1893–1955, Land records 1738–1804, Marriage records 1892–1904, and Probate records 1761, 1862, and 1868–1956. Courthouse burned 1800 and 1893.

Record Type	Year Begun	Jurisdiction
Birth	1913	Registrar/Deeds
Death	1913	Registrar/Deeds

■ Brunswick 1764
P.O. Box 87, Bolivia, NC 28422
Phone: (910)253-2690
Web site: www.brunsco.net
Parent County: New Hanover, Bladen
Comments/research tips: State Archives has Court records 1782–1912, Divorce records 1844, 1866, 1869–1905, Probate records 1783–1920, and Wills 1765–1912. Many records were destroyed in 1865.

Record Type	Year Begun	Jurisdiction
Land	1764	Registrar/Deeds
Birth	1913	Registrar/Deeds
Marriage	1804	Registrar/Deeds
Death	1913	Registrar/Deeds

■ Buncombe 1791
60 Court Plaza, Room 110, Asheville, NC 28801
Phone: (828)250-4300
Web site: www.buncombecounty.org
Parent County: Burke, Rutherford
Comments/research tips: State Archives has Court records 1792–1892, Divorce records 1830–1918, Land records 1789–1919, Marriage records 1842–1867, Probate records 1815–1924, and Wills 1826–1909. Courthouse burned 1830 and 1835.

Record Type	Year Begun	Jurisdiction
Land	1919	Registrar/Deeds
Birth	1913	Registrar/Deeds
Death	1913	Registrar/Deeds

■ Burke 1 June 1777
201 S. Green St., P.O. Box 219, Morganton, NC 28680
Phone: (828)438-5450
Web site: www.co.burke.nc.us
Parent County: Rowan
Comments/research tips: State Archives has Court records 1791–1907, Divorce records 1828–1911, Marriage records 1780–1865, Probate records 1776–1934, and Wills 1790–1905. Many records prior to 1865 were destroyed during the Civil War.

Record Type	Year Begun	Jurisdiction
Land	1865	Registrar/Deeds
Birth	1913	Registrar/Deeds
Death	1913	Registrar/Deeds

■ Bute 1764
Parent County: Granville
Comments/research tips: Became Warren and Franklin Counties in 1779.

North Carolina

■ **Cabarrus** 1792
65 Church St. SE, Concord, NC 28025
Phone: (704)920-2112
Web site: www.co.cabarrus.nc.us/
Parent County: Mecklenburg
Comments/research tips: State Archives has Court records 1793–1943, Divorce records 1866, 1868, and 1873–1930, Probate records 1793–1953, and Wills 1794–1921. Courthouse burned 1874.

Record Type	Year Begun	Jurisdiction
Land	1792	Registrar/Deeds
Birth	1913	Registrar/Deeds
Marriage	1856	Registrar/Deeds
Death	1913	Registrar/Deeds

■ **Caldwell** 1841
905 West Ave. NW, Lenoir, NC 28645
Phone: (828)757-1310
Web site: www.co.caldwell.nc.us
Parent County: Burke, Wilkes
Comments/research tips: State Archives has Court records 1841–1911, Divorce records 1850–1925, Probate records 1841–1934, and Wills 1830–1925.

Record Type	Year Begun	Jurisdiction
Land	1840	Registrar/Deeds
Birth	1914	Registrar/Deeds
Marriage	1850	Registrar/Deeds
Death	1914	Registrar/Deeds
Divorce	1926	Clerk/Superior Ct.

■ **Camden** 1777
117 North Hwy. 343, Camden, NC 27921
Phone: (252)331-4871
Web site: www.rootsweb.com/~nccamden/camden.htm
Parent County: Pasquotank
Comments/research tips: State Archives has Court records 1853–1911, Land records 1739–1912, and Probate records 1790–1929.

Record Type	Year Begun	Jurisdiction
Death	1913	Registrar/Deeds
Marriage	1848	Registrar/Deeds
Birth	1913	Registrar/Deeds
Divorce	na	Clerk/Superior Ct.

■ **Carteret** 1722
Courthouse Sq., Beaufort, NC 28516
Phone: (252)728-8474
Web site: www.carteret.co.nc.us
Parent County: Craven
Comments/research tips: State Archives has Court records 1723–1907, Divorce records 1877–1939, Land records 1721–1952, Marriage records 1746–1872, Probate records 1744–1957, and Wills 1744–1921.

Record Type	Year Begun	Jurisdiction
Birth	1913	Registrar/Deeds
Death	1913	Registrar/Deeds

■ **Caswell** 8 Apr. 1777
P.O. Box 98, 139 E. Church St., Yanceyville, NC 27379
Phone: (336)694-4197

Web site: www.caswell.countync.org
Parent County: Orange
Comments/research tips: State Archives has Court records 1777–1924, Divorce records 1818–1928, Land records 1780–1884, Marriage records 1778–1868, and Probate records 1772–1941.

Record Type	Year Begun	Jurisdiction
Birth	1913	Registrar/Deeds
Death	1913	Registrar/Deeds

■ **Catawba** 1842
P.O. Box 65, Newton, NC 28658
Phone: (828)465-1573
Web site: www.co.catawba.nc.us
Parent County: Lincoln
Comments/research tips: State Archives has Court records 1843–1886, Divorce records 1869–1927, Probate records 1843–1922, and Wills 1843–1966.

Record Type	Year Begun	Jurisdiction
Land	1842	Registrar/Deeds
Birth	1913	Registrar/Deeds
Death	1913	Registrar/Deeds
Marriage	1842	Registrar/Deeds

■ **Chatham** 1771
12 East Rd., Pittsboro, NC 27312
Phone: (919)542-8235
Web site: www.co.chatham.nc.us
Parent County: Orange
Comments/research tips: State Archives has Court records 1774–1931, Divorce records 1829–1934, Marriage records 1778–1876, Probate records 1771–1948, and Wills 1771–1964.

Record Type	Year Begun	Jurisdiction
Birth	1913	Registrar/Deeds
Death	1913	Registrar/Deeds
Land	1771	Registrar/Deeds

■ **Cherokee** 1839
53 Peachtree, Murphy, NC 28906
Phone: (282)837-2613
Web site: www.main.nc.us/cherokee/index.html
Parent County: Macon
Comments/research tips: State Archives has Court records 1865–1913, Divorce records 1869–1914, and 1942, Probate records 1843–1940, and Wills 1857–1941. A portion of Cherokee County lies in Cherokee land. For information regarding the genealogy of the Eastern band of the Cherokee of North Carolina contact the Qualla Public Library, Acauoni Road, Cherokee North Carolina.

Record Type	Year Begun	Jurisdiction
Land	1838	Registrar/Deeds
Birth	1913	Registrar/Deeds
Death	1913	Registrar/Deeds
Marriage	1865	Registrar/Deeds

■ **Chowan** 1670
101 S. Broad St., Edenton, NC 27932
Phone: (252)482-2619

Web site: www.chowancounty-nc.gov
Parent County: Albemarle
Comments/research tips: State Archives has Court records 1714–1910, Divorce records 1823–1909, and Marriage records 1747–1868.

Record Type	Year Begun	Jurisdiction
Land	1678	Registrar/Deeds
Birth	1913	Registrar/Deeds
Death	1913	Registrar/Deeds
Probate	1694	Clerk/Superior Ct.

■ Clarendon 1664
Parent County: Original county
Comments/research tips: Abandoned in 1667.

■ Clay 1861
P.O. Box 118, Hayesville, NC 28904
Phone: (828)389-0087
Web site: www.rootsweb.com/~ncclay/
Parent County: Cherokee
Comments/research tips: State Archives has Court records 1870–1902, Land records 1845–1937, Probate records 1862–1943, and Wills 1870–1928.

Record Type	Year Begun	Jurisdiction
Birth	1913	Registrar/Deeds
Marriage	1877	Registrar/Deeds
Death	1913	Registrar/Deeds

■ Cleveland Jan. 1841
311 E. Marion St., P.O. Box 1210, Shelby, NC 28150
Phone: (704)484-4834
Web site: www.clevelandcounty.com/nav/index.htm
Parent County: Rutherford, Lincoln
Comments/research tips: State Archives has Court records 1841–1910, Divorce records 1842–1907, Land records 1775–1898, Probate records 1795–1915, and Wills 1841–1919.

Record Type	Year Begun	Jurisdiction
Birth	1913	Registrar/Deeds
Marriage	1851	Registrar/Deeds
Death	1913	Registrar/Deeds

■ Columbus 1808
P.O. Box 1086, Whiteville, NC 28472
Phone: (910)640-6625
Web site: www.columbusco.org
Parent County: Bladen, Brunswick
Comments/research tips: State Archives has Court records 1817–1968, Probate records 1812–1923, and Wills 1808–1917.

Record Type	Year Begun	Jurisdiction
Land	1802	Registrar/Deeds
Birth	1913	Registrar/Deeds
Marriage	1867	Registrar/Deeds
Death	1913	Registrar/Deeds
Divorce	1817	Clerk/Superior Ct.

■ Craven 1705
226 Pollock St., New Bern, NC 28560
Phone: (252)636-6617

Web site: www.cravencounty.com
Parent County: Precinct of Bath County
Comments/research tips: State Archives has Court records 1712–1715, 1730–1914, Divorce records 1828–1897, Probate records 1745–1945, and Wills 1737–1868. Formerly Archdale Precinct of Bath County. Named changed to Craven, 1712.

Record Type	Year Begun	Jurisdiction
Land	1710	Registrar/Deeds
Birth	1914	Registrar/Deeds
Marriage	1740	Registrar/Deeds
Death	1914	Registrar/Deeds

■ Cumberland 1754
117 Dick St. Room 114, Fayetteville, NC 28301
Phone: (910)678-7775
Web site: www.co.cumberland.nc.us
Parent County: Bladen
Comments/research tips: State Archives has Court records 1755–1913, Marriage records 1868–1906, Probate records 1758–1930, and Wills 1757–1955.

Record Type	Year Begun	Jurisdiction
Land	1754	Registrar/Deeds
Birth	1913	Registrar/Deeds
Death	1913	Registrar/Deeds
Divorce	na	Clerk/Superior Ct.

■ Currituck 1668
P.O. Box 71, Currituck, NC 27929
Phone: (252)232-3297
Web site: www.co.currituck.nc.us
Parent County: Albemarle
Comments/research tips: State Archives has Court records 1799–1907, Probate records 1812–1926, and Wills 1841–1924.

Record Type	Year Begun	Jurisdiction
Land	1696	Registrar/Deeds
Birth	1913	Registrar/Deeds
Marriage	1850	Registrar/Deeds
Death	1913	Registrar/Deeds
Divorce	na	Clerk/Superior Ct.

■ Dare 1870
962 Marshall C. Collins Dr., Manteo, NC 27954
Phone: (252)475-5970
Web site: www.co.dare.nc.us
Parent County: Currituck, Tyrell, Hyde
Comments/research tips: State Archives has Court records 1870–1966, Divorce records 1882–1969, Probate records 1832–1964, and Wills 1872–1959.

Record Type	Year Begun	Jurisdiction
Land	1880	Registrar/Deeds
Birth	1913	Registrar/Deeds
Marriage	1880	Registrar/Deeds
Death	1913	Registrar/Deeds

■ Davidson 1822
P.O. Box 464, Lexington, NC 27293
Phone: (336)242-2150

North Carolina

Web site: www.co.davidson.nc.us
Parent County: Rowan
Comments/research tips: State Archives has Court records 1823–1910, Divorce records 1831–1944, Land records 1808–1922, Probate records 1817–1948, and Wills 1823–1940. Courthouse fire in 1866 destroyed some records.

Record Type	Year Begun	Jurisdiction
Birth	1822	Registrar/Deeds
Marriage	1822	Registrar/Deeds
Death	1823	Registrar/Deeds

■ Davie 1836
123 S. Main St., Mocksville, NC 27028
Phone: (336)751-2513
Web site: www.co.davie.nc.us
Parent County: Rowan
Comments/research tips: State Archives has Court records 1837–1905, Divorce records 1849–1908, Probate records 1809–1936, and Wills 1808–1902.

Record Type	Year Begun	Jurisdiction
Death	1913	Registrar of Probate
Birth	1913	Registrar/Deeds
Marriage	1836	Registrar/Deeds
Land	1836	Registrar/Deeds

■ Dobbs 1759
Parent County: Johnston
Comments/research tips: Discontinued and became part of Wayne County in 1779 and Glasgow and Lenoir Counties in 1791.

■ Duplin 7 Apr. 1750
118 Duplin St., Kenansville, NC 28349
Phone: (910)296-2108
Web site: www.duplincounty.org
Parent County: New Hanover
Comments/research tips: State Archives has Court records 1784–1908, Divorce records 1869–1952, Marriage records 1755–1869, Probate records 1752–1930, and Wills 1759–1913.

Record Type	Year Begun	Jurisdiction
Land	1749	Registrar/Deeds
Birth	1913	Registrar/Deeds
Death	1913	Registrar/Deeds

■ Durham Feb. 1881
P.O. Box 1107, Durham, NC 27707
Phone: (919)560-0480
Web site: www.co.durham.nc.us
Parent County: Orange, Wake
Comments/research tips: State Archives has Court records 1887–1924, Naturalization records 1882–1904, and Probate records 1875–1926.

Record Type	Year Begun	Jurisdiction
Birth	1913	Dept./Health
Death	1913	Dept./Health
Marriage	1881	Registrar/Deeds
Land	1881	Registrar/Deeds
Divorce	1881	Clerk/Superior Ct.

■ Edgecombe 1741
301 Saint Andrews St., P.O. Box 386, Tarboro, NC 27886
Phone: (252)641-7924
Web site: www.edgecombe.cc.nc.us/county/
Parent County: Bertie
Comments/research tips: State Archives has Court records 1744–1746, 1757–1910, Divorce records 1835–1901, Land records 1732–1741, Probate records 1748–1917, and Wills 1750–1945. Records prior to 1759 are found in Halifax County.

Record Type	Year Begun	Jurisdiction
Land	1759	Registrar/Deeds
Death	1913	Registrar/Deeds
Birth	1913	Registrar/Deeds
Marriage	1866	Registrar/Deeds

■ Forsyth 1849
P.O. Box 20639, Winston-Salem, NC 27120
Phone: (336)727-2903
Web site: www.co.forsyth.nc.us
Parent County: Stokes
Comments/research tips: State Archives has Court records 1848–1941, Divorce records 1871–1929, Probate records 1845–1956, and Wills 1840–1900.

Record Type	Year Begun	Jurisdiction
Land	1849	Registrar/Deeds
Birth	1913	Registrar/Deeds
Marriage	1849	Registrar/Deeds
Death	1913	Registrar/Deeds

■ Franklin 1779
113 S. Main St., P.O. Box 545, Louisburg, NC 27549
Phone: (919)496-3500
Web site: www.co.franklin.nc.us
Parent County: Bute
Comments/research tips: State Archives has Court records 1785–1883, Divorce records 1820–1928, Marriage records 1789–1868, Probate records 1781–1934, and Wills 1787–1929.

Record Type	Year Begun	Jurisdiction
Land	1776	Registrar/Deeds
Birth	1913	Registrar/Deeds
Marriage	1869	Registrar/Deeds
Death	1913	Registrar/Deeds

■ Gaston Dec. 1846
325 N. Marietta St., P.O. Box 1578, Gastonia, NC 28053
Phone: (704)868-7684
Web site: www.co.gaston.nc.us
Parent County: Lincoln
Comments/research tips: State Archives has Court records 1847–1941, Divorce records 1859–1910, Probate records 1839–1928, and Wills 1849–1924. Many recores were destroyed in courthouse in 1874.

Record Type	Year Begun	Jurisdiction
Land	1846	Registrar/Deeds
Birth	1913	Registrar/Deeds
Marriage	1948	Registrar/Deeds
Death	1913	Registrar/Deeds

Gates 1779
P.O. Box 471, Gatesville, NC 27938
Phone: (252)357-0850
Web site: www.throughwire.net/gatesgenweb
Parent County: Chowan, Hertford, Perquimans
Comments/research tips: State Archives has Court records 1779–1868, Divorce records 1817–1911, Marriage records 1779–1868, Probate records 1765–1920, and Wills 1762–1904.

Record Type	Year Begun	Jurisdiction
Land	1779	Registrar/Deeds
Birth	1913	Registrar/Deeds
Marriage	1869	Registrar/Deeds
Death	1913	Registrar/Deeds
Court	1869	Clerk/Superior Ct.

Glasgow 1791
Parent County: Dobbs
Comments/research tips: Name changed to Greene County in 1799.

Graham 1872
P.O. Box 406, Robbinsville, NC 28771
Phone: (828)479-7971
Web site: www.main.nc.us/graham/
Parent County: Cherokee
Comments/research tips: State Archives has Court records 1873–1908, Land records 1789–1921, Marriage records 1873–1926, and Probate records 1847–1930. A portion of Graham County lies in Cherokee land. Contact Eastern Band of the Cherokee at Cherokee Qualla Public Library for genealogy information.

Record Type	Year Begun	Jurisdiction
Birth	1913	Registrar/Deeds
Death	1913	Registrar/Deeds
Divorce	1872	Clerk/Superior Ct.

Granville 1746
101 Main St., Oxford, NC 27565
Phone: (919)693-6314
Web site: www.granvillecounty.org
Parent County: Edgecombe
Comments/research tips: State Archives has Court records 1754–1900, Divorce records 1819–1895, Probate records 1746–1919, and Wills 1749–1968.

Record Type	Year Begun	Jurisdiction
Birth	1913	Registrar/Deeds
Land	1746	Registrar/Deeds
Death	1913	Registrar/Deeds
Marriage	1869	Registrar/Deeds
Divorce	1896	Clerk/Superior Ct.

Greene 1791
P.O. Box 86, Snow Hill, NC 28580
Phone: (252)747-3620
Web site: www.rootsweb.com/~ncgreene/
Parent County: Glasgow
Comments/research tips: State Archives has Court records 1868–1959, Divorce records 1875–1959, Probate records 1809–1962, and Wills 1846–1944. Established as Glasgow County in 1791. Name changed to Greene County in 1799. Courthouse burned in 1876.

Record Type	Year Begun	Jurisdiction
Land	1875	Registrar/Deeds
Birth	1913	Registrar/Deeds
Marriage	1875	Registrar/Deeds
Death	1913	Registrar/Deeds

Guilford 1771
201 S. Eugene St., P.O. Box 3427, Greensboro, NC 27402
Phone: (336)641-7556
Web site: www.rootsweb.com/~ncguilfo/
Parent County: Rowan, Orange
Comments/research tips: State Archives has Court records 1781–1924, Divorce records 1820–1929, Probate records 1778–1942, and Wills 1771–1968. Courthouse burned 1872; many older records still available.

Record Type	Year Begun	Jurisdiction
Land	1771	Registrar/Deeds
Birth	1913	Registrar/Deeds
Marriage	1865	Registrar/Deeds
Death	1913	Registrar/Deeds

Halifax 1758
King St., P.O. Box 67, Halifax, NC 27839
Phone: (252)583-2101
Web site: www.halifaxnc.com
Parent County: Edgecombe
Comments/research tips: State Archives has Court records 1759–1902, Divorce records 1870–1922, Naturalization records 1916–1925, Probate records 1762–1924, and Wills 1772–1916.

Record Type	Year Begun	Jurisdiction
Land	1732	Registrar/Deeds
Birth	1913	Registrar/Deeds
Marriage	1825	Registrar/Deeds
Death	1913	Registrar/Deeds

Harnett 1855
305 W. Cornelius Harnett Blvd., Suite 200, Lillington, NC 27546
Phone: (910)893-7542
Web site: www.harnett.org
Parent County: Cumberland
Comments/research tips: Many Court and Land records were destroyed in courthouse fires in 1892 and 1894.

Record Type	Year Begun	Jurisdiction
Land	1855	Registrar/Deeds
Birth	1913	Registrar/Deeds
Marriage	1862	Registrar/Deeds
Death	1913	Registrar/Deeds
Divorce	na	Clerk/Superior Ct.
Probate	1884	Clerk/Superior Ct.
Court	1892	Clerk/Superior Ct.

Haywood 1808
215 N. Main St., Waynesville, NC 28786
Phone: (828)452-6635

Web site: www.gov.co.haywood.nc.us
Parent County: Buncombe
Comments/research tips: State Archives has Court records 1815–1913, Divorce records 1829–1944, Land records 1801–1942, Marriage records 1808–1868, Probate records 1809–1942, and Wills 1803–1937.

Record Type	Year Begun	Jurisdiction
Birth	1913	Registrar/Deeds
Death	1913	Registrar/Deeds
Marriage	1869	Registrar/Deeds

■ **Henderson** Dec. 1838
200 N. Grove St. Suite 129, Hendersonville, NC 28792
Phone: (828)697-4901
Web site: www.hendersoncountync.org
Parent County: Buncombe
Comments/research tips: State Archives has Court records 1808–1959, Divorce records 1842–1931, Marriage records 1838–1967, Probate records 1838–1968, and Wills 1797, 1817, and 1835-1969.

Record Type	Year Begun	Jurisdiction
Land	1893	Registrar/Deeds
Birth	1914	Registrar/Deeds
Death	1914	Registrar/Deeds

■ **Hertford** 1 May 1760
701 N. King St., P.O. Box 36, Winton, NC 27986
Phone: (252)358-7850
Web site: www.co.hertford.nc.us
Parent County: Bertie, Chowan, Northampton
Comments/research tips: State Archives has Court records 1830–1915, Divorce records 1871–1914, Land records 1775–1940, Probate records 1830–1914, and Wills 1763, and 1861–1903. Courthouse burned in 1832 and 1862.

Record Type	Year Begun	Jurisdiction
Military	1928	Registrar/Deeds
Birth	1913	Registrar/Deeds
Marriage	1868	Registrar/Deeds
Death	1913	Registrar/Deeds

■ **Hoke** 1911
304 N. Main St., Raeford, NC 28376
Phone: (910)875-2035
Web site: www.hokecounty.org/hokehome.html
Parent County: Cumberland, Robeson

Record Type	Year Begun	Jurisdiction
Land	1911	Registrar/Deeds
Birth	1913	Registrar/Deeds
Marriage	1911	Registrar/Deeds
Death	1913	Registrar/Deeds
Divorce	1911	Clerk/Superior Ct.
Probate	1911	Clerk/Superior Ct.
Court	1911	Clerk/Superior Ct.

■ **Hyde** 1705
P.O. Box 294, Swan Quarter, NC 27885
Phone: (252)926-4181
Web site: www.hydecounty.org/government/
Parent County: Bath County

Comments/research tips: State Archives has Court records 1736–1914, Divorce records 1829–1914, Probate records 1735–1933, and Wills 1760–1908. Formerly Wickham, Precinct of Bath County. Name changed to Hyde, 1712.

Record Type	Year Begun	Jurisdiction
Land	1736	Registrar/Deeds
Birth	1913	Registrar/Deeds
Marriage	1850	Registrar/Deeds
Death	1913	Registrar/Deeds

■ **Iredell** 1788
201 E. Water St., P.O. Box 904, Statesville, NC 28677
Phone: (704)872-7468
Web site: www.co.iredell.nc.us
Parent County: Rowan
Comments/research tips: State Archives has Court records 1788–1909, Divorce records 1855–1934, Marriage records 1788–1868, Probate records 1790–1970, and Wills 1787–1917. Courthouse burned in 1854.

Record Type	Year Begun	Jurisdiction
Land	1788	Registrar/Deeds
Birth	1913	Registrar/Deeds
Marriage	1869	Registrar/Deeds
Death	1913	Registrar/Deeds

■ **Jackson** 1851
401 Grindstass Rd. Room 103, Sylva, NC 28779
Phone: (828)586-7535
Web site: www.jacksonnc.org
Parent County: Haywood, Macon
Comments/research tips: A portion of Jackson County lies in Cherokee land. Contact Cherokee Qualla Public Library for genealogy information. State Archives has Court records 1853–1910 and Probate records 1853–1879.

Record Type	Year Begun	Jurisdiction
Land	ca. 1890	Registrar/Deeds
Birth	1913	Registrar/Deeds
Marriage	ca. 1890	Registrar/Deeds
Death	1913	Registrar/Deeds
Divorce	1853	Clerk/Superior Ct.
Probate	1880	Clerk/Superior Ct.

■ **Johnston** 1746
P.O. Box 118, Smithfield, NC 27577
Phone: (919)989-5160
Web site: www.co.johnston.nc.us
Parent County: Craven
Comments/research tips: State Archives has Court records 1759–1913, Land records 1748–1939, Marriage records 1746–1868, and Probate records 1771–1962.

Record Type	Year Begun	Jurisdiction
Birth	1913	Registrar/Deeds
Death	1913	Registrar/Deeds
Marriage	1869	Registrar/Deeds

■ **Jones** 19 Jan. 1779
P.O. Box 189, Trenton, NC 28585
Phone: (252)448-2551
Web site: www.co.jones.nc.us

North Carolina

Parent County: Craven
Comments/research tips: State Archives has Court records 1807–1932, Marriage records 1851–1874, Probate records 1780–1854, and Wills 1779–1935. Courthouse burned in 1862.

Record Type	Year Begun	Jurisdiction
Land	1779	Registrar/Deeds
Birth	1913	Registrar/Deeds
Marriage	1875	Registrar/Deeds
Death	1913	Registrar/Deeds
Divorce	1906	Clerk/Superior Ct.
Probate	1855	Clerk/Superior Ct.

■ **Lee** 1 Apr. 1908
1400 S. Horner Blvd., P.O. Box 2040, Sanford, NC 27330
Phone: (919)718-4585
Web site: www.leecountync.com
Parent County: Chatham, Moore

Record Type	Year Begun	Jurisdiction
Land	1908	Registrar/Deeds
Birth	1913	Registrar/Deeds
Marriage	1908	Registrar/Deeds
Death	1913	Registrar/Deeds
Divorce	1908	Clerk/Superior Ct.
Probate	1908	Clerk/Superior Ct.
Court	1908	Clerk/Superior Ct.

■ **Lenoir** 1791
P.O. Box 3289, Kinston, NC 28502
Phone: (252)559-6420
Web site: www.co.lenoir.nc.us
Parent County: Dobbs
Comments/research tips: State Archives has Court records 1866–1939, Divorce records 1880–1914, Marriage records 1791–1868, and Probate records 1830–1956. Registrar of Deeds has Wills 1824–1916. Courthouse burned in 1878 and 1880.

Record Type	Year Begun	Jurisdiction
Death	1913	Registrar/Deeds
Marriage	1896	Registrar/Deeds
Land	1896	Registrar/Deeds
Birth	1913	Registrar/Deeds

■ **Lincoln** 1779
115 W. Main St., P.O. Box 218, Lincolnton, NC 28093
Phone: (704)736-8530
Web site: www.co.lincoln.nc.us
Parent County: Tryon
Comments/research tips: State Archives has Court records 1781–1911, Divorce records 1811–1921, Marriage records 1779–1868, and Probate records 1779–1925.

Record Type	Year Begun	Jurisdiction
Land	1763	Registrar/Deeds
Birth	1913	Registrar/Deeds
Marriage	1869	Registrar/Deeds
Death	1913	Registrar/Deeds

■ **Macon** 1828
5 W. Main St., Franklin, NC 28734
Phone: (828)349-2095

Web site: www.maconnc.org
Parent County: Haywood
Comments/research tips: State Archives has Court records 1829–1914, Divorce records 1835–1913, Marriage records 1828–1891, Probate records 1831–1920, and Wills 1830–1905, and 1933.

Record Type	Year Begun	Jurisdiction
Death	1913	Registrar/Deeds
Marriage	1892	Registrar/Deeds
Land	1820	Registrar/Deeds
Birth	1913	Registrar/Deeds

■ **Madison** 1851
P.O. Box 66, 75 Blannahassett Island, Marshall, NC 28753
Phone: (828)649-3131
Web site: www.rootsweb.com/~ncmadiso/
Parent County: Buncombe, Yancey
Comments/research tips: State Archives has Court records 1837–1925, Divorce records 1854–1926, Marriage records 1851–1945, Probate records 1833–1943, and Wills 1851–1912.

Record Type	Year Begun	Jurisdiction
Land	1851	Registrar/Deeds
Birth	1913	Registrar/Deeds
Death	1913	Registrar/Deeds

■ **Martin** 1774
P.O. Box 348, Williamston, NC 27892
Phone: (252)792-1683
Web site: www.rootsweb.com/~ncmartin/
Parent County: Halifax, Tyrrell
Comments/research tips: State Archives has Court records 1838–1912, Divorce records 1882–1903, and Probate records 1820–1906. Courthouse burned in 1884.

Record Type	Year Begun	Jurisdiction
Land	1776	Registrar/Deeds
Birth	1913	Registrar/Deeds
Marriage	1872	Registrar/Deeds
Death	1913	Registrar/Deeds

■ **McDowell** 1842
21 S. Main St. Suite A, Marion, NC 28752
Phone: (828)652-4727
Web site: www.main.nc.us/mcdowell/index.html
Parent County: Burke, Rutherford
Comments/research tips: State Archives has Court records 1843–1925, Divorce records 1849–1941, Land records 1813–1916, Marriage records 1842–1868, and Probate records 1830–1832, 1842–1939, and Wills 1841–1920.

Record Type	Year Begun	Jurisdiction
Birth	1913	Registrar/Deeds
Marriage	1869	Registrar/Deeds
Death	1913	Registrar/Deeds

■ **Mecklenburg** 1 Feb. 1763
720 E. Fourth St., Charlotte, NC 28202
Phone: (704)336-2443
Web site: www.charmeck.org
Parent County: Anson

North Carolina

Comments/research tips: State Archives has Court records 1774–1885, Divorce records 1846–1969, Marriage records 1783–1868, Naturalization records 1822, 1886–1927, Probate records 1762–1957, and Wills 1749–1918.

Record Type	Year Begun	Jurisdiction
Birth	1913	Dept./Health
Death	1913	Dept./Health
Marriage	1869	Registrar/Deeds
Land	1763	Registrar/Deeds

■ Mitchell Feb. 1861

26 Crimson Laurel Circle Suite #4, Bakersville, NC 28705
Phone: (828)688-2139
Web site: www.mitchellcounty.org
Parent County: Burke, Caldwell, McDowell, Watauga, Yancey
Comments/research tips: State Archives has Court records 1861–1910, Divorce records 1867–1915, Land records 1846–1951, Probate records 1826–1946, and Wills 1823–1927.

Record Type	Year Begun	Jurisdiction
Death	1913	Registrar/Deeds
Marriage	1861	Registrar/Deeds
Birth	1913	Registrar/Deeds

■ Montgomery 1779

102 E. Main St., Troy, NC 27371
Phone: (910)576-4271
Web site: www.montgomery-county-nc.gov
Parent County: Anson
Comments/research tips: State Archives has Court records 1843–1912, Divorce records 1856–1907, Marriage records 1779–1868, Probate records 1818–1970, and Wills 1785–1970. Courthouse burned in 1835.

Record Type	Year Begun	Jurisdiction
Land	1843	Registrar/Deeds
Birth	1913	Registrar/Deeds
Marriage	1869	Registrar/Deeds
Death	1913	Registrar/Deeds

■ Moore 1784

P.O. Box 1210, Carthage, NC 28327
Phone: (910)947-6370
Web site: www.moorecountync.gov
Parent County: Cumberland
Comments/research tips: State Archives has Court records 1784–1873, Divorce records 1887–1915, Land records 1797–1923, Naturalization records 1887–1914, Probate records 1828–1921, and Wills 1831, 1859–1921. Courthouse burned in 1889.

Record Type	Year Begun	Jurisdiction
Birth	1913	Registrar/Deeds
Marriage	1889	Registrar/Deeds
Death	1913	Registrar/Deeds
Court	1874	Clerk/Superior Ct.

■ Nash 1777

P.O. Box 974, Nashville, NC 27856
Phone: (252)459-9836

Web site: www.co.nash.nc.us
Parent County: Edgecombe
Comments/research tips: State Archives has Court records 1778–1915, Divorce records 1818–1866, Marriage records 1777–1868, Probate records 1770–1909, and Wills 1778–1922.

Record Type	Year Begun	Jurisdiction
Marriage	1867	Registrar/Deeds
Land	1777	Registrar/Deeds
Death	1913	Registrar/Deeds
Divorce	1867	Registrar/Deeds
Birth	1913	Registrar/Deeds

■ New Hanover 1729

216 N. Second St., Room 4, Wilmington, NC 28401
Phone: (910)341-4530
Web site: www.co.new-hanover.nc.us
Parent County: Craven
Comments/research tips: State Archives has Court records 1738–1910, Divorce records 1858–1945, Marriage records 1741–1868, Probate records 1741–1939, and Wills 1732–1961.

Record Type	Year Begun	Jurisdiction
Land	1729	Registrar/Deeds
Birth	1913	Registrar/Deeds
Marriage	1869	Registrar/Deeds
Death	1913	Registrar/Deeds

■ Northampton 1741

P.O. Box 128, Jackson, NC 27845
Phone: (252)534-2511
Web site: www.northamptonnc.com
Parent County: Bertie
Comments/research tips: State Archives has Court records 1792–1908, Divorce records 1818–1951, Marriage records 1811–1868, Probate records 1781–1929, and Wills 1764–1950.

Record Type	Year Begun	Jurisdiction
Land	1741	Registrar/Deeds
Birth	1913	Registrar/Deeds
Marriage	1869	Registrar/Deeds
Death	1913	Registrar/Deeds

■ Onslow 1734

109 Old Bridge St., Jacksonville, NC 28540
Phone: (910)347-3451
Web site: www.co.onslow.nc.us
Parent County: New Hanover
Comments/research tips: State Archives has Court records 1732–1909, Divorce records 1866–1906, Marriage records 1745–1868, Probate records 1735–1914, and Wills 1746–1968. Many records were destroyed in storms in 1752 and 1786.

Record Type	Year Begun	Jurisdiction
Land	1734	Registrar/Deeds
Birth	1914	Registrar/Deeds
Marriage	1869	Registrar/Deeds
Death	1914	Registrar/Deeds

■ Orange Mar. 1752

200 S. Cameron St., P.O. Box 8181, Hillsborough, NC 27278
Phone: (919)245-2675
Web site: www.co.orange.nc.us
Parent County: Bladen, Granville, Johnston
Comments/research tips: State Archives has Court records 1752–1889, Divorce records 1824–1908, Probate records 1754–1944, and Wills 1753–1968. Courthouse burned in 1789.

Record Type	Year Begun	Jurisdiction
Land	1752	Registrar/Deeds
Birth	1913	Registrar/Deeds
Marriage	1752	Registrar/Deeds
Death	1913	Registrar/Deeds
Court	1890	Clerk/Superior Ct.

■ Pamlico 1872

P.O. Box 433, Bayboro, NC 28515
Phone: (252)745-4421
Web site: www.co.pamlico.nc.us
Parent County: Beaufort, Craven
Comments/research tips: State Archives has Court records 1872–1968, Divorce records 1874–1915, Probate records 1872–1939, and Wills 1872–1921.

Record Type	Year Begun	Jurisdiction
Land	1872	Registrar/Deeds
Birth	1913	Registrar/Deeds
Marriage	1872	Registrar/Deeds
Death	1913	Registrar/Deeds

■ Pamptecough 1705

Parent County: Bath
Comments/research tips: (See Beaufort) Name changed to Beaufort in 1712.

■ Pasquotank 1668

206 E. Main, P.O. Box 154, Elizabeth City, NC 27907
Phone: (252)335-4367
Web site: www.co.pasquotank.nc.us
Parent County: Albemarle
Comments/research tips: State Archives has Court records 1737–1922, Divorce records 1838–1910, Land records 1666–1947, Marriage records 1741–1868, Probate records 1712–1931, and Wills 1709–1917.

Record Type	Year Begun	Jurisdiction
Birth	1913	Registrar/Deeds
Marriage	1869	Registrar/Deeds
Death	1913	Registrar/Deeds

■ Pender 1875

300 E. Freemont St., P.O. Box 43, Burgaw, NC 28425
Phone: (910)259-1225
Web site: www.pender-county.com
Parent County: New Hanover
Comments/research tips: State Archives has Marriage records 1875–1936, Probate records 1866–1969, and Wills 1832, 1875–1969.

Record Type	Year Begun	Jurisdiction
Land	1873	Registrar/Deeds

Birth	1913	Registrar/Deeds
Death	1913	Registrar/Deeds
Divorce	1875	Clerk/Superior Ct.
Court	1875	Clerk/Superior Ct.

■ Perquimans 1668

P.O. Box 74, Hertford, NC 27944
Phone: (252)426-5660
Web site: www.co.perquimans.nc.us
Parent County: Albemarle
Comments/research tips: State Archives has Court records 1688–1908, Divorce records 1824–1912, Marriage records 1742–1868, Probate records 1714–1930, and Wills 1711–1909. Perquimans County was known as Berkeley Precinct 1670–1682.

Record Type	Year Begun	Jurisdiction
Marriage	1869	Registrar/Deeds
Land	1681	Registrar/Deeds

■ Person Dec. 1791

105 S. Main St., Roxboro, NC 27573
Phone: (336)597-1733
Web site: http://web.personcounty.net/nuke/DesktopDefault.aspx
Parent County: Caswell
Comments/research tips: State Archives has Court records 1792–1909, Divorce records 1821–1939, Land records 1777–1918, Marriage records 1791–1868, Probate records 1791–1951, and Wills 1790–1943.

Record Type	Year Begun	Jurisdiction
Birth	1913	Registrar/Deeds
Marriage	1913	Registrar/Deeds
Death	1913	Registrar/Deeds

■ Pitt 1760

W. Third St., P.O. Box 35, Greenville, NC 27835
Phone: (252)902-1650
Web site: www.co.pitt.nc.us
Parent County: Beaufort
Comments/research tips: State Archives has Court records 1858–1921, Divorce records 1861, 1866, 1870–1906, Marriage records 1826–1833, 1867–1875, Probate records 1791, 1827–1947, and Wills 1805, 1808, 1817, 1836–1930, and 1938. Courthouse burned 1857.

Record Type	Year Begun	Jurisdiction
Land	1762	Registrar/Deeds
Birth	1913	Registrar/Deeds
Death	1913	Registrar/Deeds

■ Polk 1847

P.O. Box 308, Columbus, NC 28722
Phone: (828)894-8450
Web site: www.polkcounty.org/
Parent County: Henderson, Rutherford
Comments/research tips: State Archives has Court records 1847–1848, 1855–1942, Divorce records 1856–1909, and Probate records 1851–1913. Polk County was originally established in 1847 from Henderson and Rutherford Counties. In 1848 the act was appealed. Polk was reestablished in 1855.

North Carolina

Record Type	Year Begun	Jurisdiction
Land	1855	Registrar/Deeds
Birth	1913	Registrar/Deeds
Death	1913	Registrar/Deeds
Marriage	1855	Registrar/Deeds

■ Randolph 1779

158 Worth St., Asheboro, NC 27203

Phone: (336)318-6960

Web site: www.co.randolph.nc.us

Parent County: Guilford

Comments/research tips: State Archives has Court records 1783–1939, Divorce records 1804–1927, Marriage records 1779–1868, Probate records 1781–1928, and Wills 1775–1902.

Record Type	Year Begun	Jurisdiction
Land	1779	Registrar/Deeds
Birth	1913	Registrar/Deeds
Death	1913	Registrar/Deeds

■ Richmond 1779

114 E. Franklin St. #101, Rockingham, NC 28379

Phone: (910)997-8250

Web site: www.co.richmond.nc.us

Parent County: Anson

Comments/research tips: State Archives has Court records 1779–1913, Divorce records 1816–1910, Marriage records 1791–1872, Probate records 1772–1933, and Wills 1779–1915.

Record Type	Year Begun	Jurisdiction
Land	1784	Registrar/Deeds
Birth	1913	Registrar/Deeds
Marriage	1900	Registrar/Deeds
Death	1913	Registrar/Deeds

■ Robeson 6 Jan. 1787

500 N. Elm St., Lumberton, NC 28358

Phone: (910)671-3044

Web site: www.co.robeson.nc.us

Parent County: Bladen

Comments/research tips: State Archives has Court records 1797–1912, Divorce records 1841–1920, Marriage records 1803–1868, Probate records 1801–1935, and Wills 1783–1918, 1930, 1933, and 1935.

Record Type	Year Begun	Jurisdiction
Land	1787	Registrar/Deeds
Birth	1913	Registrar/Deeds
Marriage	1869	Registrar/Deeds
Death	1916	Registrar/Deeds

■ Rockingham 29 Dec. 1785

P.O. Box 56, Wentworth, NC 27375

Phone: (336)342-8820

Web site: www.co.rockingham.nc.us

Parent County: Guilford

Comments/research tips: State Archives has Court records 1786–1868, Divorce records 1824–1921, Marriage records 1785–1868, Probate records 1780–1926, and Wills 1772–1925, 1936, and 1938.

Record Type	Year Begun	Jurisdiction
Land	1787	Registrar/Deeds
Birth	1913	Registrar/Deeds
Marriage	1869	Registrar/Deeds
Death	1913	Registrar/Deeds
Court	1869	Clerk/Superior Ct.

■ Rowan 1753

P.O. Box 2568, Salisbury, NC 28145

Phone: (704)638-3102

Web site: www.co.rowan.nc.us

Parent County: Anson

Comments/research tips: State Archives has Court records 1753–1910, Divorce records 1805–1900, Naturalization records 1823–1915, Probate records 1753–1929, and Wills 1743–1900. Federal troops destroyed some records in 1865.

Record Type	Year Begun	Jurisdiction
Land	1755	Registrar/Deeds
Birth	1913	Registrar/Deeds
Marriage	1753	Registrar/Deeds
Death	1913	Registrar/Deeds

■ Rutherford 14 Apr. 1779

229 N. Main St., P.O. Box 551, Rutherfordton, NC 28139

Phone: (828)287-6155

Web site: www.rutherfordcountync.gov

Parent County: Tryon

Comments/research tips: State Archives has Court records 1783–1911, Divorce records 1870–1940, Probate records 1802–1968, and Wills 1784–1968. Courthouse burned in 1907.

Record Type	Year Begun	Jurisdiction
Land	1779	Registrar/Deeds
Birth	1913	Registrar/Deeds
Marriage	1779	Registrar/Deeds
Death	1913	Registrar/Deeds

■ Sampson 1784

P.O. Box 256, Courthouse, Main St., Clinton, NC 28329

Phone: (910)592-8026

Web site: www.sampsonnc.com

Parent County: Duplin

Comments/research tips: State Archives has Court records 1794–1925, Divorce records 1869–1921, Probate records 1784–1923, and Wills 1778–1953. Courthouse burned 1921.

Record Type	Year Begun	Jurisdiction
Land	1784	Registrar/Deeds
Birth	1913	Registrar/Deeds
Death	1913	Registrar/Deeds
Marriage	1865	Registrar/Deeds

■ Scotland 20 Feb. 1899

212 Biggs St., P.O. Box 769, Laurinburg, NC 28353

Phone: (910)277-2577

Web site: www.scotlandcounty.org

Parent County: Richmond

Comments/research tips: State Archives has Divorce records 1901–1948, Probate records 1887–1951, and Wills, 1893, 1896, and 1900–1937.

Record Type	Year Begun	Jurisdiction
Land	1900	Registrar/Deeds
Birth	1913	Registrar/Deeds
Marriage	1900	Registrar/Deeds
Death	1913	Registrar/Deeds
Court	1900	Clerk/Superior Ct.

■ Stanly 11 Jan. 1841

201 S. Second St., Albemarle, NC 28001
Phone: (704)986-3640
Web site: www.co.stanly.nc.us/
Parent County: Montgomery
Comments/research tips: State Archives has Divorce records 1854-1920 and Probate records 1820, 1839–1952.

Record Type	Year Begun	Jurisdiction
Land	1841	Registrar/Deeds
Birth	1913	Registrar/Deeds
Death	1913	Registrar/Deeds
Marriage	1865	Registrar/Deeds

■ Stokes 1789

1014 Main St., Danbury, NC 27016
Phone: (336)593-2811
Web site: www.co.stokes.nc.us
Parent County: Surry
Comments/research tips: State Archives has Court records 1790–1912, Divorce records 1816–1941, Land records 1760–1929, Marriage records 1790–1868, Probate records 1753–1941, and Wills 1775–1925.

Record Type	Year Begun	Jurisdiction
Birth	1913	Registrar/Deeds
Death	1913	Registrar/Deeds
Marriage	1869	Registrar/Deeds

■ Surry 1 Apr. 1771

201 E. Kapp St., P.O. Box 303, Dobson, NC 27017
Phone: (336)401-8150
Web site: www.co.surry.nc.us
Parent County: Rowan
Comments/research tips: State Archives Court records 1778–1910, Divorce records 1826–1927, Probate records 1771–1943, and Wills 1770–1970.

Record Type	Year Begun	Jurisdiction
Land	1771	Registrar/Deeds
Birth	1913	Registrar/Deeds
Marriage	1771	Registrar/Deeds
Death	1913	Registrar/Deeds

■ Swain 1871

101 Mitchell St., P.O. Box 1183, Bryson, NC 28713
Phone: (828)488-9273
Web site: www.swaincounty.org
Parent County: Jackson, Macon
Comments/research tips: State Archives has Court records 1871–1907. A portion of Swain County lies in Cherokee land. For genealogy information on the Eastern Band of the Cherokee Indians contact the Cherokee Qualla Public Library. Many records were destroyed in a courthouse fire in 1879.

Record Type	Year Begun	Jurisdiction
Land	1871	Registrar/Deeds
Birth	1913	Registrar/Deeds
Marriage	1871	Registrar/Deeds
Death	1913	Registrar/Deeds
Divorce	1871	Clerk/Superior Ct.
Probate	1871	Clerk/Superior Ct.

■ Transylvania 1861

12 E. Main St., Brevard, NC 28712
Phone: (828)884-3162
Web site: www.transylvaniacounty.org
Parent County: Henderson, Jackson
Comments/research tips: State Archives has Court records 1861–1910, Divorce records 1866–1921, Land records 1827–1923, Marriage records 1861–1872, Probate records 1810–1951, and Wills 1838–1926.

Record Type	Year Begun	Jurisdiction
Birth	1913	Registrar/Deeds
Marriage	1885	Registrar/Deeds
Death	1913	Registrar/Deeds

■ Tryon 1768

Parent County: Mecklenburg
Comments/research tips: (See Lincoln and Rutherford) Discontinued 1779. Split into Lincoln and Rutherford Counties.

■ Tyrrell 1729

P.O. Box 449, Columbia, NC 27925
Phone: (252)796-2901
Web site: http://patriot.net/~cpbarnes/TYRELL.HTM
Parent County: Chowan, Currituck, Pasquotank
Comments/research tips: State Archives has Court records 1735–1883, Divorce records 1815–1925, Probate records 1738–1935, and Wills 1744–1925.

Record Type	Year Begun	Jurisdiction
Land	1736	Registrar/Deeds
Birth	1913	Registrar/Deeds
Marriage	1742	Registrar/Deeds
Death	1913	Registrar/Deeds
Court	1884	Clerk/Superior Ct.

■ Union 1842

P.O. Box 248, Monroe, NC 28111
Phone: (704)283-3727
Web site: www.co.union.nc.us
Parent County: Anson, Mecklenburg
Comments/research tips: State Archives has Court records 1843–1920, Divorce records 1865–1928, Probate records 1818–1969, and Wills 1837–1968, 1977, 1978.

Record Type	Year Begun	Jurisdiction
Land	1842	Registrar/Deeds
Birth	1913	Registrar/Deeds
Marriage	1842	Registrar/Deeds
Death	1913	Registrar/Deeds

■ Vance 1881

122 Young St. Suite F, Henderson, NC 27536
Phone: (252)738-2110

North Carolina

Web site: www.vancecounty.org
Parent County: Franklin, Granville, Warren

Record Type	Year Begun	Jurisdiction
Land	1881	Registrar/Deeds
Birth	1913	Registrar/Deeds
Death	1913	Registrar/Deeds
Marriage	1881	Registrar/Deeds
Divorce	1881	Clerk/Superior Ct.
Probate	1881	Clerk/Superior Ct.
Court	1881	Clerk/Superior Ct.

■ Wake 1771

P.O. Box 1897, Raleigh, NC 27602
Phone: (919)856-5490
Web site: www.wakegov.com
Parent County: Cumberland, Johnston, Orange
Comments/research tips: State Archives has Court records 1777–1941, Death records 1900–1909, Divorce records 1831–1952, Marriage records 1790–1865, Naturalization records 1821–1908, Probate records 1771–1952, and Wills 1771–1966. Fire at the Registrar's office in 1832 destroyed some deed books.

Record Type	Year Begun	Jurisdiction
Land	1774	Registrar/Deeds
Birth	1913	Registrar/Deeds
Death	1913	Registrar/Deeds
Marriage	1866	Registrar/Deeds

■ Warren 20 Jan. 1779

P.O. Box 506, Warrenton, NC 27589
Phone: (252)257-3265
Web site: www.rootsweb.com/~ncwarren/
Parent County: Bute
Comments/research tips: State Archives has Court records 1780–1931, Divorce records 1874–1914, 1922, Marriage records 1779–1868, Probate records 1772–1940, and Wills 1779–1931.

Record Type	Year Begun	Jurisdiction
Land	1778	Registrar/Deeds
Birth	1914	Registrar/Deeds
Marriage	1869	Registrar/Deeds
Death	1914	Registrar/Deeds

■ Washington 1799

120 Adams St., P.O. Box 1007, Plymouth, NC 27962
Phone: (252)793-2325
Web site: www.washingtoncountygov.com
Parent County: Tyrrell
Comments/research tips: State Archives has Court records 1822–1921, Divorce records 1851, 1873–1903, Probate records 1795–1933, and Wills 1856–1964. Courthouse burned 1862, 1869, and 1873.

Record Type	Year Begun	Jurisdiction
Land	1799	Registrar/Deeds
Birth	1913	Registrar/Deeds
Marriage	1851	Registrar/Deeds
Death	1913	Registrar/Deeds

■ Watauga 1849

842 W. King St. Suite 9, Boone, NC 28607
Phone: (828)265-8052

Web site: www.wataugacounty.org
Parent County: Ashe, Caldwell, Wilkes, Yancey
Comments/research tips: State Archives has Court records 1873–1924, Divorce records 1874–1948, Land records 1858–1976, Probate records 1858–1948, and Wills 1859, 1872–1947. A courthouse fire in 1873 destroyed all of the Land records and most of the Court records.

Record Type	Year Begun	Jurisdiction
Birth	1914	Registrar/Deeds
Marriage	1872	Registrar/Deeds
Death	1914	Registrar/Deeds

■ Wayne 1779

224 E. Walnut St., P.O. Box 267, Goldsboro, NC 27533
Phone: (919)731-1449
Web site: www.waynegov.com
Parent County: Dobbs
Comments/research tips: State Archives has Court records 1787–1968, Divorce records 1822–1930, Marriage records 1790–1859, Probate records 1782–1937. Clerk of Superior Court has Wills 1776–1927.

Record Type	Year Begun	Jurisdiction
Land	1779	Registrar/Deeds
Birth	1913	Registrar/Deeds
Marriage	1860	Registrar/Deeds
Death	1913	Registrar/Deeds

■ Wickham 1705

Parent County: Bath
Comments/research tips: (See Hyde) Name changed to Hyde, 1712.

■ Wilkes 15 Feb. 1778

110 North St., Wilkesboro, NC 28697
Phone: (336)651-7351
Web site: www.rootsweb.com/~ncwilkes/
Parent County: Surry, District of Washington
Comments/research tips: State Archives has Court records 1778–1931, Divorce records 1820–1912, Probate records 1777–1945, and Wills 1778–1948.

Record Type	Year Begun	Jurisdiction
Land	1778	Registrar/Deeds
Birth	1913	Registrar/Deeds
Marriage	1778	Registrar/Deeds
Death	1913	Registrar/Deeds

■ Wilson 1855

101 N. Goldsboro St., Wilson, NC 27893
Phone: (252)399-2935
Web site: www.wilson-co.com
Parent County: Edgecombe, Johnston, Nash, Wayne
Comments/research tips: State Archives has Court records 1855–1914, Divorce records 1859–1912, Probate records 1854-1959, and Wills 1840–1925.

Record Type	Year Begun	Jurisdiction
Land	1855	Registrar/Deeds
Birth	1913	Registrar/Deeds
Marriage	1855	Registrar/Deeds
Death	1913	Registrar/Deeds

North Carolina

■ Yadkin 1850

P.O. Box 211, 101 State St., Yadkinville, NC 27055
Phone: (336)679-4225
Web site: www.yadkincounty.gov
Parent County: Surry
Comments/research tips: State Archives has Court records 1851–1898, Divorce records 1851–1931, Land records 1793–1951, Probate records 1850–1920, and Wills 1836–1942.

Record Type	Year Begun	Jurisdiction
Birth	1913	Registrar/Deeds
Marriage	1850	Registrar/Deeds
Death	1913	Registrar/Deeds
Court	1899	Clerk/Superior Ct.

■ Yancey 1833

County Courthouse, Burnsville, NC 28714
Phone: (828)682-2174
Web site: http://pages.xtn.net/~nute/
Parent County: Buncombe, Burke
Comments/research tips: State Archives has Court records 1834–1915, Divorce records 1866–1914, Probate records 1853–1915, and Wills 1885–1909.

Record Type	Year Begun	Jurisdiction
Land	1833	Registrar/Deeds
Birth	1913	Registrar/Deeds
Marriage	1855	Registrar/Deeds
Death	1913	Registrar/Deeds

North Carolina

North Dakota

By James W. Warren

HISTORICAL OVERVIEW

Teddy Roosevelt loved the state, Lawrence Welk was born here, and Lewis and Clark spent the winter here during their great expedition. From the endless flat plains along the Red River that form its eastern border, North Dakota's lands gradually rise to the spectacular badlands on its western border. The area's original settlers were the Dakota (Sioux), Arapaho, Cheyenne, Mandan, Hidatsa, and Assiniboine Indians.

Fur traders from the Missouri Fur Company paved the way for settlers to come to the area. The U.S. acquired half of the state in the Louisiana Purchase in 1803, and the other half from Britain in 1818. The first settlement was along the Red River, made by Scottish settlers from Canada on what became the Red River Ox Cart Trail. Early white settlers to the area were primarily from Canada, states directly to the east (Minnesota, Iowa, or Wisconsin), New York, or Norway.

Dakota Territory was created in 1861 and included what would become North Dakota, South Dakota, Montana, and Wyoming. In 1864 Montana Territory was split off, as was Wyoming Territory in 1868.

In 1871 the railroads extending across Minnesota reached the Dakota's eastern boundary, the Red River. Settlement began to boom, and through 1888 large numbers of immigrants poured into the eastern part of the state. They included many Norwegians, Germans, and Germans from Russia, as well as smaller numbers of people from other European and British Isles countries. Cycles of boom and bust, fueled partly by land speculators and partly by the inherent risks of farm yields, weather, and prices, saw many settlers leave the area after a few years. The temporary successes of the Bonanza Farms, huge tracts of land owned by eastern speculators and worked by immigrant laborers, fueled some of the speculation. In 1889, North and South Dakota were admitted

NORTH DAKOTA AT A GLANCE

Motto: Liberty and Union, Now and Forever: One and Inseparable

Population: 642,200

Prevalent Religions: Christianity, mostly Lutheran, Roman Catholic, Methodist, and Baptist

Major Industries: Wheat, cattle, barley, sunflowers, milk, sugar beets, food processing, machinery, mining

Ethnic Makeup (in percent): Caucasian 92.4%, African American 0.6%, Hispanic 0.6%, Asian 0.6%, Native American 4.9%, Other 0.4%

Famous North Dakotans: Angie Dickinson, Ivan Dmitre, Phyllis Frelich, William Gass, Phil D. Jackson, Louis L'Amour, Peggy Lee, Arthur Peterson, Eric Sevareid, Ann Sothern, Dorothy Stickney, Edward K. Thompson, Era Bell Thompson, Lawrence Welk, Larry Woiwode

Above: The North Dakota horizon

© PhotoDisc/Getty Images

to the Union. Homesteaders again moved into the state in large numbers through 1915.

RECORD HIGHLIGHTS

The federal censuses for the state of North Dakota start with 1900. There were territorial censuses and mortality schedules taken in 1860, 1870, 1880, and 1885 for Dakota Territory. State censuses for 1905, 1915, and 1925 are available at the State Historical Society of North Dakota <www.state.nd.us/hist>.

The Division of Vital Records in Bismarck holds statewide birth certificates from 1870, death certificates from 1881, and marriages from July 1925. Online ordering is available at <www.vitalnd.com>. Earlier marriages, if registered, will be found with the county recorder in the county in which the marriage license was issued. All divorces are also in the hands of the pertinent county recorder. The legal requirement to register vital events was generally complied with by the mid-1920s.

County courthouse records include land, naturalization, probate, guardianship, and civil and criminal cases. Most of these records and their indexes remain in the county, and little has been microfilmed. While some counties are beginning to put a few indexes online, in most cases it is necessary to contact the courthouse directly or plan to have research done on-site. The newspapers that are available at the State Historical Society in Bismarck have largely been microfilmed.

Compared to the rest of the country, North Dakota was settled and populated relatively late and is rather lacking in record resources. Few of its county records are available on microfilm. This makes using local resources the key to successful research. Some records at the county level can be accessed by using the Web, and you can get some by mail. Local church and cemetery records may be important to fill the research gaps. Local or church newspapers may provide details or clues not recorded elsewhere.

Some church, cemetery, and newspaper abstracts and indexes have been published or mounted on the Web. Genealogical society publications may also hold clues and provide contacts to put you on the right track. Check for links to such resources at Cyndi's List <www.cyndislit .com> and the USGenWeb site for North Dakota <www .rootsweb.com/~ndgenweb/>. The North Dakota State Genealogical Society's Web site is another contact point <www.rootsweb.com/~ndsgs/index.html>.

By the time the State Historical Society of North Dakota was founded in Bismarck, significant historical and genealogical resources had already been gathered at both the University of North Dakota (UND) in Grand Forks and North Dakota State University (NDSU) in Fargo. All three facilities have excellent published genealogy and manuscript collections, much of which is not duplicated

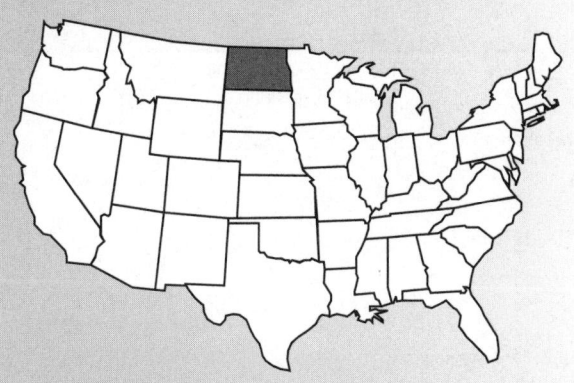

- The three most important repositories containing North Dakota records and collections are the University of North Dakota in Grand Forks, North Dakota State University in Fargo, and the State Historical Society in Bismarck.
- Local county resources such as church records and newspapers are particularly important to North Dakota research, due to the late settlement of the state and the relatively few record resources available. Genealogical society publications can also be helpful.
- The Web can be extremely useful for North Dakota researchers—look for links to county sources on Cyndi's List and the North Dakota GenWeb.
- www.kindredtrails.com

Census Records

- Federal Census: 1900, 1910, 1920
- Union Veterans Schedule: 1890
- State Censuses: 1836 (included in the Wisconsin census), 1840 (Iowa), 1850 (Minnesota)
- Dakota Territory Census: 1860, 1870, 1880, 1885, 1905, 1915, 1925 (all records are located at the State Historical Society of North Dakota)
- Mortality Schedules: 1860, 1870, 1880, 1885

by the other institutions. So none of the three repositories should be overlooked when researching North Dakota ancestors.

The State Historical Society of North Dakota's Web site <www.state.nd.us/hist/> includes basic information about the Society's holdings, which includes library, newspaper, and manuscript collections, as well as the State Archives. The Society also holds two important collections of oral history interviews. Also available at the Web site is the North Dakota Naturalization Records

North Dakota

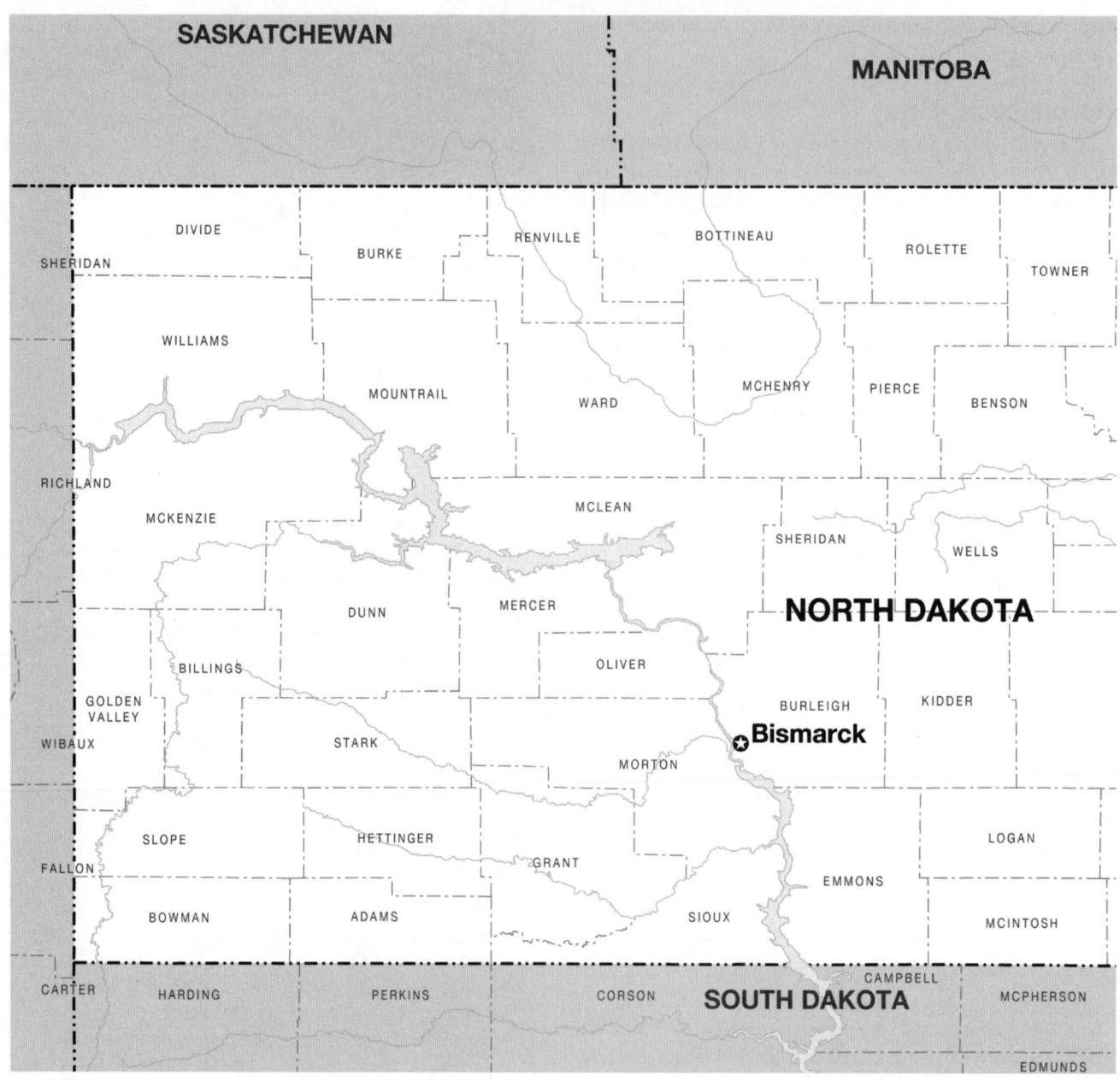

Database. It lists the 212,000 name entries for the first and second naturalization papers recorded at the county level, and is complete for all North Dakota counties. The records themselves have all been transferred from the counties to the Historical Society.

The University of North Dakota's Department of Special Collections at the Chester Fritz Library holds the genealogy and history collections. Online information about their collection, including some useful online indexes, is available at <www.und/nodak/edu/dept/library/Collections>. For example, recently added databases include an index to the Grand Forks County Coroner Records, 1881–1989, and a keyword searchable index to the UND student newspaper covering 1888 to the present.

The North Dakota Institute for Regional Studies collection at NDSU in Fargo has an extensive collection of North Dakota county, town, and church histories available. All those volumes acquired prior to 1980 are indexed by every name, and available online at the North Dakota Biography Index on the NDIRS Web site <www.lib.sdsu.nodak.edu/ndirs/bio&genealogy/ndbioindes.html>. The NDIRS also holds extensive collections on the Germans from Russia, a very active present-day historical and genealogical society for descendants of an important portion of the North Dakota settlers.

STATE RESOURCES

■ ARCHIVES, LIBRARIES, AND SOCIETIES

Bismarck Mandan Historical and Genealogical Society, Inc. (BMHGS)
P.O. Box 485, Bismarck, ND 58502-0485
Web site: <www.rootsweb.com/~ndbmhgs/>

Bowman County Genealogical Society/Pioneer Trails Regional Museum
12 First Ave. NE, Bowman, ND 58623
Tel: (701) 523-3600
E-mail: ptrm@ptrm.org
Web site: <www.ptrm.org>

Dakotas Conference of the United Methodist Church
Box 460; 1331 W. University Ave., Mitchell, SD 57301
Tel: (605) 996-6552
Web site: <www.santel.net/~dumcc/archives_history.html>

Family History Library
35 NW Temple St., Salt Lake City, UT 84150-3400
Tel: (801) 240-2331 or (800) 453-3860 x.22331
Web site: <www.familysearch.org>

Chester Fritz Library; University of North Dakota
P.O. Box 9000, Grand Forks, ND 58202
Tel: (701) 777-2617
E-mail: library@mail.und.nodak.edu
Web site: <www.und.nodak.edu/dept/library/>

Germans from Russia Heritage Society
1125 W. Turnpike Ave., Bismark, ND 58501
Tel: (701) 223-6167
Web site:

Institute for Regional Studies, North Dakota State University
P.O. Box 5599, Fargo, ND 58105-5599
Tel: (701) 231-8914
E-mail: archives@www.lib.ndsu.nodak.edu
Web site: <www.lib.ndsu.nodak.edu/ndirs/>

James River Genealogy Club
651 Fourth St., Carrington, ND 58421
Web site: <www.rootsweb.com/~ndjrgc/>

Minot Public Library
516 Second Ave. SW, Minot, ND 58701
Tel: (701) 852-1045
Web site:

Mouse River Loop Genealogical Society
P.O. Box 1391, Minot, ND 58702-1391
Web site:

National Archives and Records Administration, Central Plains Region
2312 E. Bannister Rd., Kansas City, MO 64131-3011
Tel: (816) 268-8000
E-mail: kansascity.reference@nara.gov
Web site: <www.archives.gov/facilities/mo/kansas_city.html>

National Archives and Records Administration, Rocky Mountain Region
Denver Federal Center, W. Sixth Ave. and Kipling St., Denver, CO 80225
Tel: (303) 407-5700
Web site: <www.archives.gov/facilities/co/denver.html>

North Dakota Division of Vital Records
600 E. Boulevard Ave., Bismark, ND 58505-0200
Tel: (701) 328-2360
E-mail: vitalrec@state.nd.us
Web site:

North Dakota Genealogical Society
Web site: <www.rootsweb.com/~ndsgs/>

North Dakota State Archives and Library
612 E. Boulevard Ave., Bismarck, ND 58505-0830
Tel: (701) 328-2091
E-mail: archives@state.nd.us
Web site: <www.state.nd.us/hist/sal.htm>

North Dakota State Water Commission
900 E. Boulevard Ave., Bismarck, ND 58505-0850
Tel: (701) 328-2750
Web site:

Presbyterian Church (USA), Department of History
425 Lombard St., Philadelphia, PA 19147
Tel: (215) 627-1852

Red River Valley Genealogical Society
P.O. Box 9284, Fargo, ND 58106
Web site: <www.fargocity.com/~rrvgs/htmls/info.htm>

Roman Catholic Diocese of Bismarck
Chancery Office, P.O Box 1575, Bismarck, ND 58502-1575
Tel: (701) 223-1347
Web site: <http://bismarckdiocese.com/default.asp>

Roman Catholic Diocese of Fargo
5201 Bishops Blvd., Suite A, Fargo, ND 58104
Tel: (701) 356-7900
E-mail: webadmin2004@fargodiocese.org
Web site:

State Historical Society of North Dakota
612 E. Boulevard Ave., Bismarck, ND 58505-0830
Tel: (701) 328-2666
Web site: <www.state.nd.us/hist/>

North Dakota

University of North Dakota, Chester Fritz Library
P.O. Box 9000, Grand Forks, ND 58202
Tel: (701) 777-2617
E-mail: library@mail.und.nodak .edu
Web site: <www.und.nodak.edu/ dept/library/>

BIBLIOGRAPHY

■ GENERAL RESOURCES

The Black Sea Germans in the Dakotas
by George Rath (Freeman, SD: Pine Hills Press, 1977)

Chronology and Documentary Handbook of the State of North Dakota
by Robert I. Vexler, State editor (Dobbs Ferry, NY: Oceana Publications, 1978)

Compendium of History and Biography of North Dakota Containing a History of North Dakota: Embracing an Account of Early Explorations, Early Settlement, Indian Occupancy . . . and a Concise History of Growth and Development of the State Also a Compendium of Biography of North Dakota
(Chicago: Geo. A. Ogle & Co., 1900)

French-Canadian Families of the North Central States: A Genealogical Dictionary, 8 vols.
compiled by Paul J. Lareau & Elmer Courteau (St. Paul, MN: 1980–1981)

The Genealogist's Companion and Sourcebook, 2d ed.
by Emily Anne Croom (Cincinnati: Betterway Books, 2003)

A Genealogist's Guide to Discovering Your African-American Ancestors
by Franklin Carter Smith and Emily Anne Croom (Cincinnati: Betterway Books, 2003)

Guide to Genealogical Research in the National Archives of the United States
edited by Anne Bruner Eales and Robert M. Kvasnicka (Washington, DC: National Archives and Records Administration, 2000)

Guide to the Orin G. Libby Manuscript Collection & Related Research Collections, 3 vols.
compiled by John B. Davenport, Colleen A. Oihus, and Sandra J. Beidler (Grand Forks, ND: University of North Dakota, 1975–1985)

Historical Data Project; Pioneer Biography Files
by the State Historical Society of North Dakota (Bismark, ND: State Historical Society of North Dakota, 1988–1989)

History of North Dakota
by Elwyn B. Robinson (Lincoln, NE: University of Nebraska Press, 1966)

History of North Dakota, 3 vols.
by Lewis F. Crawford (Chicago and New York: The American Historical Society, Inc., 1931)

History of the Red River Valley Past and Present, 2 vols.
(Grand Forks, ND: Herald Printing Co., Chicago: C.F. Cooper, 1909)

National Archives Microfilm Catalogs online:
<www.archives.gov/publica tions/genealogy_microfilm_ catalogs.html>

North Dakota History and People, Outlines of American History, 3 vols.
by C.A. Lounsberry (Chicago: S.J. Clarke, 1916)

Pioneers and Their Sons: One Hundred Sixty Five Family Histories, 2 vols.
by George P. Aberle (Bismark, ND: Tumbleweed Press, 1980)

Plains Folk: North Dakota's Ethnic History
edited by Playford V. Thorson and William C. Sherman (Fargo, ND: in cooperation with the ND Humanities Council and the University of North Dakota, 1988)

Reference Guide to North Dakota History and North Dakota Literature
compiled by Dan Rylance and J.F.S. Smeall (Grand Forks, ND: Chester Fritz Library, University of North Dakota, 1979)

Steppes to Neu Odessa: Germans From Russia who Settled in Odessa Township, Dakota Territory, 1872–1876
by Cynthia Anne Frank Stupnik (Bowie, MD: Heritage Books, 2002)

The Way it Was: The North Dakota Frontier Experience: Book Four: Germans From Russia Settlers
edited by Everett C. Albers (Fessenden, ND: Grass Roots Press, 1999)

■ CENSUS RECORDS

The American Census Handbook
by Thomas Jay Kemp (Wilmington, DE: Scholarly Resources, 2001)

The Census Book: A Genealogist's Guide to Federal Census Facts, Schedules and Indexes
by William Dollarhide (Bountiful, UT: Heritage Quest, 2000)

Map Guide to the U.S. Federal Censuses, 1790–1920
by William Thorndale and William Dollarhide (Baltimore, MD: Genealogical Pub. Co., 1987)

Your Guide to the Federal Census
by Kathleen W. Hinckley (Cincinnati: Betterway Books, 2002)

■ IMMIGRATION RECORDS

American Naturalization Records, 1790–1990: What They Are and How to Use Them
by John J. Newman (North Salt Lake, UT: HeritageQuest, 1998)

American Passenger Arrival Records
by Michael Tepper (Baltimore: Genealogical Publishing Co., 1993)

Ethnic Group Files, ca. 1935–1942
by the Writers' Program (North Dakota) (Bismark, ND: State Historical Society of North Dakota, 1989)

North Dakota Pioneers From the Banat
by John M. Michels (Bismark, ND: University of Mary Press, 1992)

Prairie Mosaic: An Ethnic Atlas of Rural North Dakota
by William C. Sherman (Fargo, ND: North Dakota Institute for Regional Studies, 1983)

Red River Trails: Oxcart Routes Between St. Paul and the Selkirk Settlement, 1820–1870
by Rhoda R. Gilman, Carolyn Gilman, and Deborah M. Stultz (St. Paul, MN: Minnesota Historical Society, 1979)

They Became Americans: Finding Naturalization Records and Ethnic Origins
by Loretto Dennis Szucs (Salt Lake City: Ancestry, Inc., 1998)

They Came in Ships: A Guide to Finding Your Immigrant Ancestor's Arrival Records, 2d ed.
by John P. Colletta (Salt Lake City: Ancestry, Inc., 1993)

■ LAND RECORDS

Land in Her Own Name: Women as Homesteaders in North Dakota
by H. Elaine Lindgren (Fargo, ND: North Dakota Institute for Regional Studies, 1991)

Locating Your Roots: Discover Your Ancestors Using Land Records
by Patricia Law Hatcher (Cincinnati: Betterway Books, 2003)

Sioux Personal Property Claims: From the Original Ledger
by Ruth Brown (Medford, OR: Rogue Valley Genealogical Society, 1987)

■ MAPS

The Atlas of North Dakota
by L.R. Goodman and R.J. Eidem (Fargo, ND: North Dakota Studies, 1976)

North Dakota Place Names
by Douglas A. Wick (Bismark, ND: Hedemarken Collectibles, 1988)

North Dakota Post Offices, 1850–1982
by Alan H. Patera and John S. Gallagher (Burtonsville, MD: The Depot, 1982)

Origins of North Dakota Place Names
by Mary Ann Barnes Williams (Washburn, ND: Bismark Tribune, 1966)

Postoffices and Postmarks of Dakota Territory
by George H. Phillips (Crete, NE: J-B Pub. Co., 1973)

■ **MILITARY RECORDS**

General Index to Pension Files, 1861–1934
by the United States Veterans Administration (Washington, DC: Veterans Administration, Publications Service, 1953)

Index to Compiled Service Records of Volunteer Union Soldiers who Served in Organizations From the Territory of Dakota
by the United States General Adjutant's Office (Washington, DC: The National Archives, 1964)

North Dakota, World War I Selective Service System Draft Registration Cards, 1917–1918
by the United States Selective Service System (Washington, DC: The National Archives, 1987–1988)

Uncle, We Are Ready! Registering America's Men, 1917–1918: A Guide to Researching World War I Draft Registration Cards
by John J. Newman (North Salt Lake, UT: HeritageQuest, 2001)

U.S. Military Records: A Guide to Federal & State Sources, Colonial America to the Present
by James C. Neagles (Salt Lake City: Ancestry, Inc., 1994)

World War II: A Family Historian's Guide
by Debra Johnson Knox (Spartanburg, SC: MIE Publishing, 2003)

■ **VITAL RECORDS**

Births, Marriages and Deaths, 1880–1942 [Standing Rock Agency]
by the United States Bureau of Indian Affairs, Standing Rock Agency (Kansas City, MO: Federal Archives and Records Center, 1977)

North Dakota Cemeteries, 32 vols.
compiled and edited by the Fargo Genealogical Society (Fargo, ND: Fargo Genealogical Society, 1972–1977, 1986–1998)

Your Guide to Cemetery Research
by Sharon DeBartolo Carmack (Cincinnati: Betterway Books, 2002)

■ **Adams** 17 Apr. 1907
602 Adams Ave., Hettinger, ND 58639
Phone: (701)567-2468
Web site: www.rootsweb.com/~ndadams/
Parent County: Hettinger
Comments/research tips: Division of Vital Records in Bismarck holds Birth and Death records from 1870.

Record Type	Year Begun	Jurisdiction
Marriage	1907	Clerk/District Ct.
Divorce	1907	Clerk/District Ct.
Land	1907	Clerk/District Ct.
Probate	1907	Clerk/District Ct.
Court	1907	Clerk/District Ct.

■ **Allred** 9 Mar. 1883
Parent County: Howard
Comments/research tips: (See McKenzie) Eliminated 16 March 1905 and absorbed by McKenzie.

■ **Barnes** 4 Jan. 1873
230 Fourth St. NE, Valley City, ND 58072
Phone: (701)845-8512
Web site: www.rootsweb.com/~ndbarnes/
Parent County: Pembina
Comments/research tips: Formerly Burbank County. Name changed to Barnes 14 January 1875. Organized 5 August 1878.

Record Type	Year Begun	Jurisdiction
Birth	na	Clerk/District Ct.
Marriage	1880	County Judge
Death	na	Clerk/District Ct.
Probate	na	County Judge
Court	na	Clerk/District Ct.

■ **Benson** 9 Mar. 1883
311 B Ave. S., Box 213, Minnewaukan, ND 58351
Phone: (701)473-5345
Web site: www.rootsweb.com/~ndbenson/
Parent County: De Smet, Ramsey

Record Type	Year Begun	Jurisdiction
Death	1895	Clerk/District Ct.
Divorce	1895	Clerk/District Ct.
Land	1885	Registrar/Deeds
Probate	1895	Clerk/District Ct.
Court	1895	Clerk/District Ct.
Birth	ca. 1890	Clerk/District Ct.
Marriage	1889	Clerk/District Ct.

■ **Billings** 10 Feb. 1879
495 Fourth St., P.O. Box 138, Medora, ND 58645
Phone: (701)623-4492
Web site: www.geocities.com/Athens/Forum/2079/BILLINGS.HTM
Parent County: Unorganized Territory, Howard
Comments/research tips: Organized 30 April 1886.

Record Type	Year Begun	Jurisdiction
Marriage	1893	Clerk/District Ct.
Divorce	1895	Clerk/District Ct.
Land	1886	Clerk/District Ct.

North Dakota

Record Type	Year Begun	Jurisdiction
Probate	1895	Clerk/District Ct.
Court	1890	Clerk/District Ct.
Burial	1922	Clerk/District Ct.

■ Bottineau   4 Jan. 1873

314 W. Fifth St., Bottineau, ND 58318
Phone: (701)228-3983
Web site: www.geocities.com/Athens/Forum/2079/bottine.html
Parent County: Buffalo
Comments/research tips: Organized 22 July 1884.

Record Type	Year Begun	Jurisdiction
Birth	1943	Clerk/District Ct.
Marriage	1887	Clerk/District Ct.
Death	1943	Clerk/District Ct.
Divorce	1889	Clerk/District Ct.
Land	1889	Registrar/Deeds
Probate	1889	Clerk/District Ct.
Court	1889	Clerk/District Ct.
Burial	1943	Clerk/District Ct.
Nat.	1884	Historical Society

■ Bowman   8 Mar. 1883

104 First St. NW, Bowman, ND 58623
Phone: (701)523-3450
Web site: www.rootsweb.com/~ndbowman/
Parent County: Billings
Comments/research tips: Eliminated 30 November 1896. Re-created 24 May 1901. Attached to Stark County prior to organization 17 April 1907.

Record Type	Year Begun	Jurisdiction
Marriage	1907	Clerk/District Ct.
Divorce	1908	Clerk/District Ct.
Land	1896	Clerk/District Ct.
Probate	1908	Clerk/District Ct.
Court	1908	Clerk/District Ct.

■ Buffalo   6 Jan. 1864

Parent County: Brugier, Charles Mix and Unorganized Territory, South Dakota
Comments/research tips: Now in South Dakota. (See Burleigh, Kidder, Logan, McHenry, Rolette and Sheridan)

■ Buford   9 Mar. 1883

Parent County: Wallette
Comments/research tips: (See Williams) Eliminated 30 November 1892 and added to Williams.

■ Burbank   4 Jan. 1873

Parent County: Pembina
Comments/research tips: (See Barnes) Named changed to Barnes 14 January 1875. Lost to Trail County 12 January 1875 and Griggs County 18 February 1881 and discontinued.

■ Burke   8 Feb. 1910

103 Main St. SW, P.O. Box 219, Bowbells , ND 58721
Phone: (701)377-2718
Web site: www.rootsweb.com/~ndburke/burke2.htm

Parent County: Ward
Comments/research tips: Vital Statistics in Bismarck has Birth and Death records.

Record Type	Year Begun	Jurisdiction
Marriage	1910	Clerk/District Ct.
Divorce	1910	Clerk/District Ct.
Land	1910	Clerk/District Ct.
Probate	1910	Clerk/District Ct.
Court	1910	Clerk/District Ct.
Burial	1910	Clerk/District Ct.
Homestd. Pat.	1903	Clerk/District Ct.

■ Burleigh   4 Jan. 1873

514 E. Thayer Ave., P.O. Box 1055, Bismarck, ND 58502
Phone: (701)222-6690
Web site: www.rootsweb.com/~ndburlei/index.htm
Parent County: Buffalo
Comments/research tips: Recorder's Office has Land and Marriage records from late 1800s.

Record Type	Year Begun	Jurisdiction
Probate	1873	Clerk/District Ct.
Court	1873	Clerk/District Ct.
Burial	ca.1950	Recorder's Office
Divorce	1876	Clerk/District Ct.

■ Cass   4 Jan. 1873

211 Ninth St. S., P.O. Box 2806, Fargo , ND 58103
Phone: (701)241-5646
Web site: www.lib.ndsu.nodak.edu/archives
Parent County: Pembina
Comments/research tips: The Institute for Regional Studies at North Dakota University has Divorce, Civil Court, and Probate records 1870–1942. Mariage records 1870–1944. Naturalization records ca. 1870.

Record Type	Year Begun	Jurisdiction
Divorce	ca. 1940	Clerk/District Ct.
Court	ca. 1940	Clerk/District Ct.
Wills	1988	Recorder's Office
Marriage	1945	Treasurer's Office

■ Cavalier   4 Jan. 1873

901 Third St., Langdon, ND 58249
Phone: (701)256-2124
Web site: www.ccjda.org/
Parent County: Pembina
Comments/research tips: Clerk of District has Township Books from late 1800s–1940s. Organized 8 July 1884.

Record Type	Year Begun	Jurisdiction
Marriage	1890	Clerk/District Ct.
Divorce	1900	Clerk/District Ct.
Land	1883	Recorder's Office
Probate	1900	Clerk/District Ct.
Court	1900	Clerk/District Ct.
Military	1943	Clerk/District Ct.

■ Chippewa   24 Apr. 1862

Parent County: Unorganized Territory
Comments/research tips: Eliminated 17 December 1863 to Unorganized Territory.

■ **Church** 11 Mar. 1887
Parent County: McHenry, Sheridan, old
Comments/research tips: (See Sheridan) Attached to McHenry. Lost to McHenry, McLean and Pierce Counties. Eliminated 30 November 1892 to Sheridan.

■ **De Smet** 4 Jan. 1873
Parent County: Buffalo
Comments/research tips: (See Pierce) Formerly French County. Name changed to De Smet 14 January 1875. Eliminated 11 March 1887 to Pierce.

■ **Dickey** 5 Mar. 1881
309 N. Second St., P.O. Box 336, Ellendale, ND 58436
Phone: (701)349-3249
Web site: www.rootsweb.com/~nddickey/dickey.htm
Parent County: La Moure, Ransom, Unorganized Territory
Comments/research tips: *The Oakes Times* newspaper has Birth announcements 1888–1921, 1932, and 1934. Organized 31 August 1882.

Record Type	Year Begun	Jurisdiction
Marriage	1887	Clerk/District Ct.
Divorce	1881	Clerk/District Ct.
Land	1882	Recorder's Office
Probate	1881	Clerk/District Ct.
Court	1881	Clerk/District Ct.

■ **Divide** 8 Nov. 1910
300 N. Main St., P.O. Box 68, Crosby, ND 58730
Phone: (701)965-6831
Web site: www.rootsweb.com/~nddivide/divide97.htm
Parent County: Williams
Comments/research tips: Township Birth and Death records turned over to the county in 1943. Divide County Library has county newspapers (obituaries, birth announcements etc.) back to 1916, Tombstone recordings back to 1909, and Family History books compiled in 1964 and 1974.

Record Type	Year Begun	Jurisdiction
Marriage	1910	Clerk/District Ct.
Divorce	1910	Clerk/District Ct.
Land	1910	Registrar/Deeds
Probate	1910	Clerk/District Ct.
Court	1910	Clerk/District Ct.
Burial	1910	Clerk/District Ct.
Military	1919	Clerk/District Ct.

■ **Dunn** 24 May 1901
205 Owens St., P.O. Box 136, Manning, ND 58642
Phone: (701)573-4447
Web site: www.dunnjda.com/
Parent County: Stark
Comments/research tips: Recorder's Office has Land records from late 1800s. Organized 17 January 1908. Dunn County Historical Museum has homestead records, old city records books, county family history books, voting records, Service records, etc.

Record Type	Year Begun	Jurisdiction
Marriage	1908	Clerk/District Ct.
Divorce	1914	Clerk/District Ct.
Land	1900	Registrar/Deeds
Probate	1931	Clerk/District Ct.
Court	1914	Clerk/District Ct.
Military	1919	Clerk/District Ct.
Tax	1908	Auditor's Office
School	1908	Auditor's Office

■ **Dunn, old** 9 Mar. 1883
Web site: www.rootsweb.com/~nddunn/
Parent County: Howard
Comments/research tips: Discontinued and annexed to Stark 30 November 1896.

■ **Eddy** 31 Mar. 1885
524 Central Ave., New Rockford, ND 58356
Phone: (701)947-2813
Web site: www.rootsweb.com/~ndeddy/
Parent County: Foster
Comments/research tips: Burial permits can be destroyed after one year.

Record Type	Year Begun	Jurisdiction
Marriage	1887	Clerk/District Ct.
Land	ca. 1880	Recorder's Office
Probate	1887	Clerk/District Ct.
Court	1887	Clerk/District Ct.
Military	1919	Clerk/District Ct.
Divorce	1887	Clerk/District Ct.

■ **Emmons** 10 Feb. 1879
100 Fourth St. NW, Linton, ND 58552
Phone: (701)254-4812
Web site: www.rootsweb.com/~ndemmons/index.htm
Parent County: Unorganized Territory, Burleigh, Campbell Co, SD
Comments/research tips: Military records are not open to public. Would need to go through Veteran Service Officer. Court records (not Probate) are destroyed after so many years. Organized 9 November 1883.

Record Type	Year Begun	Jurisdiction
Birth	1889	Clerk/District Ct.
Marriage	1888	Clerk/District Ct.
Death	1890	Clerk/District Ct.
Divorce	1890	Clerk/District Ct.
Land	1890	Recorder's Office
Probate	1885	Clerk/District Ct.
Court	1930	Clerk/District Ct.
Burial	ca. 1950	Clerk/District Ct.

■ **Flannery** 9 Mar. 1883
Parent County: Wallette
Comments/research tips: (See Williams) Eliminated 30 November 1892 and added to Williams.

■ **Foster** 4 Jan. 1873
1000 Fifth St. N., P.O. Box 257, Carrington, ND 58421
Phone: (701)652-1001
Web site: www.rootsweb.com/~ndfoster/
Parent County: Pembina
Comments/research tips: Auditor's office keeps the old

county newspapers in a basement vault. Organized 11 October 1883.

Record Type	Year Begun	Jurisdiction
Birth	1900	Clerk/District Ct.
Marriage	1896	Clerk/District Ct.
Death	1900	Clerk/District Ct.
Divorce	1896	Clerk/District Ct.
Probate	1896	Clerk/District Ct.
Court	1896	Clerk/District Ct.
Military	1917	Clerk/District Ct.
Nat.	1883	Clerk/District Ct.
Land	1890	Registrar/Deeds

■ **French** 4 Jan. 1873
Parent County: Buffalo
Comments/research tips: (See Pierce) Name changed to De Smet 14 January 1875. Eliminated 11 March 1887 to Pierce.

■ **Garfield** 13 Mar. 1885
Parent County: Mountrail, Stevens
Comments/research tips: Eliminated 30 November 1892 to McLean and Ward.

■ **Gingras** 4 Jan. 1873
Parent County: Buffalo
Comments/research tips: (See Wells) Name changed to Wells 26 February 1881.

■ **Golden Valley** 19 Nov. 1912
150 First Ave. SE. P.O. Box 9, Beach , ND 58621
Phone: (701)872-3713
Web site: www.rootsweb.com/~ndgolden/
Parent County: Billings

Record Type	Year Begun	Jurisdiction
Marriage	1912	Clerk/District Ct.
Divorce	1912	Clerk/District Ct.
Land	1912	Recorder's Office
Probate	1912	Clerk/District Ct.
Court	1912	Clerk/District Ct.
Burial	1912	Clerk/District Ct.

■ **Grand Forks** 4 Jan. 1873
151 S. Fouth St., P.O. Box 5066, Grand Forks, ND 58201
Phone: (701)780-8221
Web site: www.grandforkscountygov.com/homepage.htm
Parent County: Pembina
Comments/research tips: Organized 12 January 1875. Lost most older records in flood of 1997. Best bet is State Historical Society.

Record Type	Year Begun	Jurisdiction
Marriage	1887	County Judge
Divorce	1878	Clerk/District Ct.
Land	ca. 1880	Recorder's Office
Probate	1880	County Judge
Court	na	Clerk/District Ct.

■ **Grant** 7 Nov. 1916
P.O. Box 258, Carson, ND 58529
Phone: (701)622-3615

Web site: www.rootsweb.com/~ndgrant/
Parent County: Morton

Record Type	Year Begun	Jurisdiction
Marriage	1916	Clerk/District Ct.
Divorce	1916	Clerk/District Ct.
Land	1916	Recorder's Office
Probate	1916	Clerk/District Ct.
Court	1916	Clerk/District Ct.
Burial	1916	Clerk/District Ct.
School	na	Auditor's Office

■ **Griggs** 18 Feb. 1881
P.O. Box 326, Cooperstown, ND 58425
Phone: (701)797-2772
Web site: www.cooperstownnd.com/
Parent County: Foster, Burbank, Traill
Comments/research tips: Organized 16 June 1882.

Record Type	Year Begun	Jurisdiction
Birth	1901	Clerk/District Ct.
Marriage	1884	Clerk/District Ct.
Death	1901	Clerk/District Ct.
Divorce	1887	Clerk/District Ct.
Land	1880	Recorder's Office
Probate	1883	Clerk/District Ct.
Court	1887	Clerk/District Ct.
School	ca. 1880	Super./Schools

■ **Hettinger** 24 May 1901
336 Pacific Ave., Mott, ND 58646
Phone: (701)824-2645
Web site: www.hettcnty.com/
Parent County: Stark
Comments/research tips: Attached to Stark County prior to organization 17 April 1907.

Record Type	Year Begun	Jurisdiction
Birth	1907	Clerk/District Ct.
Marriage	1907	Clerk/District Ct.
Death	1907	Clerk/District Ct.
Divorce	1907	Clerk/District Ct.
Land	1907	Recorder's Office
Probate	1907	Clerk/District Ct.
Court	1907	Clerk/District Ct.
Burial	1943	Clerk/District Ct.
School	na	Super./Schools
Newspapers	na	Auditor's Office

■ **Hettinger, old** 29 Mar. 1883
Parent County: Stark
Comments/research tips: Eliminated 30 November 1896 to Stark.

■ **Howard** 8 Jan. 1873
Parent County: Unorganized Territory
Comments/research tips: Eliminated 9 March 1883 to Allred, Dunn, McKenzie, old and Wallace.

■ **Kidder** 4 Jan. 1873
120 E. Broadway, P.O. Box 66, Steele, ND 58482
Phone: (701)475-2651

Web site: www.rootsweb.com/~ndkidder/
Parent County: Buffalo
Comments/research tips: Organized 22 March 1881.

Record Type	Year Begun	Jurisdiction
Birth	1943	Clerk/District Ct.
Marriage	1887	Clerk/District Ct.
Death	1943	Clerk/District Ct.
Divorce	1885	Clerk/District Ct.
Land	1881	Recorder's Office
Probate	1883	Clerk/District Ct.
Court	1885	Clerk/District Ct.
Burial	1943	Clerk/District Ct.
School	na	Super./Schools
Newspapers	na	Recorder's Office

■ Kittson 24 Apr. 1862

Parent County: Unorganized Territory
Comments/research tips: Organized 1 June 1862. Eliminated 17 December 1863 to Unorganized Territory.

■ La Moure 4 Jan. 1873

202 Fourth Ave. NE, P.O. Box 128, La Moure, ND 58458
Phone: (701)883-5301
Web site: www.rootsweb.com/~ndlamour/
Parent County: Pembina
Comments/research tips: Organized 27 October 1881.

Record Type	Year Begun	Jurisdiction
Birth	1881	Clerk/District Ct.
Marriage	1881	Clerk/District Ct.
Death	1881	Clerk/District Ct.
Divorce	1881	Clerk/District Ct.
Land	ca. 1890	Recorder's Office
Probate	1881	Clerk/District Ct.
Court	1881	Clerk/District Ct.
Burial	ca. 1930	Clerk/District Ct.
Newspapers	na	Auditor's Office
School	na	Super./Schools

■ Logan 4 Jan. 1873

301 Broadway, Napoleon, ND 58561
Phone: (701)754-2751
Web site: www.rootsweb.com/~ndlogan/
Parent County: Buffalo
Comments/research tips: Clerk of District Court has incomplete Birth and Death records from 1893, Court Probate records from late 1800s, and Marriage records from 1890 or 1900. Organized 1 September 1884.

Record Type	Year Begun	Jurisdiction
Divorce	1920	Clerk/District Ct.
Land	1884	Recorder's Office
Burial	1950	Clerk/District Ct.
Military	1920	Clerk/District Ct.
School	na	Super./Schools

■ McHenry 4 Jan. 1873

407 Main St., Towner, ND 58788
Phone: (701)537-5729
Web site: www.rootsweb.com/~ndmchenr/
Parent County: Buffalo

Comments/research tips: Recorder's Office has Land records from late 1800s. Organized 14 May 1885.

Record Type	Year Begun	Jurisdiction
Marriage	1920	Clerk/District Ct.
Divorce	1920	Clerk/District Ct.
School	na	Super./Schools
Probate	1900	Clerk/District Ct.
Court	ca. 1910	Clerk/District Ct.
Newspapers	na	Social Services

■ McIntosh 9 Mar. 1883

112 NE First St., Ashley, ND 58413
Phone: (701)288-3450
Web site: www.rootsweb.com/~ndmcinto/
Parent County: Logan, Unorganized Territory, McPherson Co, SD
Comments/research tips: Organized 4 October 1884.

Record Type	Year Begun	Jurisdiction
Birth	1899	Clerk/District Ct.
Marriage	1885	Clerk/District Ct.
Death	1899	Clerk/District Ct.
Divorce	1937	Clerk/District Ct.
Land	na	Recorder's Office
Probate	1889	Clerk/District Ct.
Court	1883	Clerk/District Ct.

■ McKenzie 24 May 1901

201 Fifth St. NW, P.O. Box 524, Watford City, ND 58854
Phone: (701)444-3452
Web site: www.4eyes.net/
Parent County: Billings
Comments/research tips: Attached to Stark County prior to organization 16 March 1905.

Record Type	Year Begun	Jurisdiction
Birth	1910	Clerk/District Ct.
Marriage	1905	Clerk/District Ct.
Death	1910	Clerk/District Ct.
Divorce	1905	Clerk/District Ct.
Land	1905	Recorder's Office
Probate	1905	Clerk/District Ct.
Court	1905	Clerk/District Ct.
Military	na	Recorder's Office
School	na	Super./Schools

■ McKenzie, old 9 Mar. 1883

Parent County: Howard
Comments/research tips: Annexed to Billings 30 November 1896.

■ McLean 8 Mar. 1883

712 Fifth Ave., Washburn, ND 58577
Phone: (701)462-8541
Web site: www.visitmcleancounty.com/
Parent County: Stevens, Burleigh, Sheridan, old

Record Type	Year Begun	Jurisdiction
Marriage	1898	Clerk/District Ct.
Divorce	1900	Clerk/District Ct.
Land	1883	Recorder's Office
Probate	1900	Clerk/District Ct.

North Dakota

Court .... 1900 .... Clerk/District Ct.
Burial .... 1920 .... Clerk/District Ct.
School .... na .... Auditor's Office
Homestead .... 1883 .... Recorder's Office
Newspapers .... na .... Co. Hist. Society

■ **Mercer** 14 Jan. 1875
1021 Arthur St., Stanton, ND 58571
Phone: (701)745-3262
Web site: www.rootsweb.com/~ndmercer/
Parent County: Unorganized Territory
Comments/research tips: Organized 22 August 1884.

Record Type	Year Begun	Jurisdiction
Marriage	1894	Clerk/District Ct.
Death	1942	Clerk/District Ct.
Divorce	1940	Clerk/District Ct.
Land	1908	Recorder's Office
Probate	1898	Clerk/District Ct.
Court	1906	Clerk/District Ct.

■ **Morton** 8 Jan. 1873
210 Second Ave. NW, Mandan, ND 58554
Phone: (701)667-3355
Web site: www.rootsweb.com/%7endmorton/
Parent County: Unorganized Territory
Comments/research tips: Clerk of District Court has Court records from late 1800s. Recorder's Office has Land records from late 1800s. Organized 28 February 1881.

Record Type	Year Begun	Jurisdiction
School	na	Super./Schools
Marriage	1882	Recorder's Office
Divorce	ca.1900	Clerk/District Ct.
Probate	ca.1900	Clerk/District Ct.

■ **Mountrail** 4 Jan. 1873
P.O. Box 69, Stanley, ND 58784
Phone: (701)628-2915
Web site: www.rootsweb.com/~ndmountr/mountrail.htm
Parent County: Buffalo
Comments/research tips: Clerk of District Court has incomplete Burial records. Annexed to Ward in 1891 and eliminated 30 November 1892. Re-created 29 January 1909 from Ward.

Record Type	Year Begun	Jurisdiction
Birth	1909	Clerk/District Ct.
Marriage	1909	Clerk/District Ct.
Death	1909	Clerk/District Ct.
Divorce	1909	Clerk/District Ct.
Land	1908	Records Office
Probate	1909	Clerk/District Ct.
Court	1909	Clerk/District Ct.
Nat.	1909	St. Hist. Society
Military	1919	Clerk/District Ct.

■ **Nelson** 2 Mar. 1883
210 B Ave. W., P.O. Box 565, Lakota, ND 58344
Phone: (701)247-2462
Web site: www.rootsweb.com/~ndnelson/
Parent County: Foster, Grand Forks, Ramsey, Unorganized Territory

Comments/research tips: Clerk of District Court has Burial records from mid 1900s.

Record Type	Year Begun	Jurisdiction
Birth	1903	Clerk/District Ct.
Marriage	1883	Clerk/District Ct.
Death	1903	Clerk/District Ct.
Divorce	1883	Clerk/District Ct.
Land	1880	Clerk/District Ct.
Probate	1880	Clerk/District Ct.
Court	na	Clerk/District Ct.

■ **Oliver** 14 Apr. 1885
115 W. Main, Center, ND 58530
Phone: (701)794-8777
Web site: www.rootsweb.com/~ndoliver/
Parent County: Mercer

Record Type	Year Begun	Jurisdiction
Marriage	1915	Clerk/District Ct.
Death	ca. 1920	Clerk/District Ct.
Land	ca. 1900	Recorder's Office
Probate	ca. 1900	County Judge
Court	ca. 1900	County Judge

■ **Pembina** 9 Jan. 1867
301 Dakota St. W. #10, Cavalier, ND 58220
Phone: (701)265-4275
Web site: www.rootsweb.com/~ndpembin/pembina.htm
Parent County: Unorganized Territory

Record Type	Year Begun	Jurisdiction
Birth	1893	Clerk/District Ct.
Marriage	1881	Clerk/District Ct.
Death	1893	Clerk/District Ct.
Divorce	1883	Clerk/District Ct.
Land	ca. 1880	Recorder's Office
Probate	1883	Clerk/District Ct.
Court	1883	Clerk/District Ct.
Burial	1943	Clerk/District Ct.
Military	1945	Vet. Serv. Officer

■ **Pierce** 11 Mar. 1887
240 SE Second St., Rugby, ND 58368
Phone: (701)776-6161
Web site: www.rootsweb.com/~ndpierce/
Parent County: De Smet, Bottineau, McHenry, Rolette
Comments/research tips: Organized 11 April 1889.

Record Type	Year Begun	Jurisdiction
Birth	1945	Clerk/District Ct.
Marriage	1890	Clerk/District Ct.
Death	1945	Clerk/District Ct.
Divorce	1910	Clerk/District Ct.
Land	1884	Recorder's Office
Probate	1898	Clerk/District Ct.
Court	1900	Clerk/District Ct.
Burial Permits	1943	Clerk/District Ct.
Military	ca. 1940	Vet. Serv. Officer

■ **Ramsey** 4 Jan. 1873
524 Fourth Ave. #4, Devils Lake, ND 58301
Phone: (701)662-1309

Web site: www.rootsweb.com/~ndramsey/ramsey.htm
Parent County: Pembina
Comments/research tips: Clerk of District Court has Court and Divorce records from late 1800s. County Judge has Probate records from late 1800s. Organized 25 January 1885.

Record Type	Year Begun	Jurisdiction
Military	na	Recorder's Office
School	na	Super./Schools
Birth	1900	Recorder's Office
Marriage	1887	Recorder's Office
Death	1900	Recorder's Office
Land	1885	Recorder's Office
Burial Permits	na	Recorder's Office

■ Ransom 4 Jan. 1873
204 Fifth Ave. W., P.O. Box 626, Lisbon, ND 58054
Phone: (701)683-5823
Web site: www.rootsweb.com/~ndransom/
Parent County: Pembina
Comments/research tips: Organized 4 April 1881.

Record Type	Year Begun	Jurisdiction
Marriage	1908	Clerk/District Ct.
Divorce	1908	Clerk/District Ct.
Land	1870	Recorder's Office
Probate	1908	Clerk/District Ct.
Court	1908	Clerk/District Ct.
Military	1919	Clerk/District Ct.

■ Renville 3 June 1910
205 Main St. E., P.O. Box 68, Mohall, ND 58761
Phone: (701)756-6398
Web site: www.upstel.net/~johns/Renville/renv.html
Parent County: Ward
Comments/research tips: Clerk of District Court has incomplete Birth and Death records from (township).

Record Type	Year Begun	Jurisdiction
Marriage	1910	Clerk/District Ct.
Divorce	1910	Clerk/District Ct.
Land	1910	Registrar/Deeds
Probate	1910	Clerk/District Ct.
Court	1910	Clerk/District Ct.
Military	1910	Clerk/District Ct.

■ Renville, old 4 Jan. 1873
Parent County: Buffalo
Comments/research tips: Part taken to form Ward County 14 April 1885. Attached to Ward. Eliminated 30 November 1892 to Bottineau and Ward. Recreated 3 June 1910.

■ Richland 4 Jan. 1873
418 Second Ave. N., Wahpeton, ND 58075
Phone: (701)671-1524
Web site: www.rootsweb.com/~ndrichla/
Parent County: Pembina
Comments/research tips: County Recorder has Marriage records fro late 1800s. Organized 25 November 1875.

Record Type	Year Begun	Jurisdiction
Divorce	na	County Recorder
Land	na	County Recorder
Probate	na	County Judge
Court	na	Clerk/District Ct.
Burial	na	County Recorder
School	na	Super./Schools

■ Rolette 4 Jan. 1873
102 Second St. NE, P.O. Box 460, Rolla, ND 58367
Phone: (701)477-3816
Web site: www.rootsweb.com/~ndrolett/
Parent County: Buffalo
Comments/research tips: Clerk of District Court has Death records from late 1800s. Organized 14 October 1884.

Record Type	Year Begun	Jurisdiction
Marriage	1887	Clerk/District Ct.
School	na	Super./Schools
Divorce	1889	Clerk/District Ct.
Land	1884	Recorder's Office
Probate	1896	Clerk/District Ct.
Court	1889	Clerk/District Ct.
Military	1944	Clerk/District Ct.

■ Sargent 9 Apr. 1883
355 Main St., P.O. Box 176, Forman, ND 58032
Phone: (701)724-6241
Web site: www.rootsweb.com/~ndsargen/index.htm
Parent County: Ransom

Record Type	Year Begun	Jurisdiction
Birth	ca. 1900	Clerk/District Ct.
Marriage	1886	Clerk/District Ct.
Death	1903	Clerk/District Ct.
Divorce	na	Clerk/District Ct.
Land	1886	Recorder's Office
Probate	1883	Clerk/District Ct.
Court	na	Clerk/District Ct.
Burial	1948	Clerk/District Ct.

■ Sheridan 24 Dec. 1908
215 E. Second St., P.O. Box 409, McClusky, ND 58463
Phone: (701)363-2207
Web site: www.rootsweb.com/~ndsherid/
Parent County: McLean
Comments/research tips: Birth and Death records prior to 1908 were held by townships.

Record Type	Year Begun	Jurisdiction
Birth	1943	Clerk/District Ct.
Marriage	1909	Clerk/District Ct.
Death	1943	Clerk/District Ct.
Divorce	1909	Clerk/District Ct.
Land	1909	Registrar/Deeds
Burial	na	Clerk/District Ct.
Military	1918	Clerk/District Ct.
School	na	County Auditor
Probate	1909	Clerk/District Ct.
Court	1909	Clerk/District Ct.

■ Sheridan, old 4 Jan. 1873
Parent County: Buffalo
Comments/research tips: Part taken to form part of Church 11 March 1887. Eliminated 30 November 1892 to McLean.

■ Sheyenne 24 Apr. 1862
Parent County: Unorganized Territory
Comments/research tips: Eliminated 17 December 1863 to Unorganized Territory.

■ Sioux 3 Sep. 1914
303 Second Ave., Fort Yates, ND 58538
Phone: (701)854-3853
Web site: www.rootsweb.com/~ndsioux/
Parent County: Standing Rock Reservation
Comments/research tips: This county is an American Indian reservation. The Tribal Court has been keeping records since 1970s. Bureau of Indian Affairs has reservation Birth and Death records.

Record Type	Year Begun	Jurisdiction
Marriage	1916	Clerk/District Ct.
Divorce	na	Clerk/District Ct.
Land	na	Clerk/District Ct.
Probate	na	Clerk/District Ct.
Court	na	Clerk/District Ct.
Burial	na	Clerk/District Ct.
School	na	Auditor's Office
Military	ca. 1880	Clerk/District Ct.

■ Slope 3 Nov. 1914
206 S. Main, Amidon, ND 58620
Phone: (701)879-6275
Web site: www.rootsweb.com/~ndslope/
Parent County: Billings
Comments/research tips: Organized 14 January 1915.

Record Type	Year Begun	Jurisdiction
Marriage	1915	Clerk/District Ct.
Death	1915	Clerk/District Ct.
Divorce	1915	Clerk/District Ct.
Land	1915	Clerk/District Ct.
Probate	1915	Clerk/District Ct.
Court	1915	Clerk/District Ct.
Burial	1915	Clerk/District Ct.
School	na	Super./Schools

■ Stark 10 Feb. 1879
51 Third St. E., P.O. Box 130, Dickinson, ND 58602
Phone: (701)456-7645
Web site: www.rootsweb.com/~ndstark/
Parent County: Unorganized Territory, Howard, William (old)
Comments/research tips: Recorder's Office has Land records from late 1800s. State Historical Center has Divorce records prior to 1950. Clerk of District Court has Naturalization records 1887–1963. Organized 30 May 1883.

Record Type	Year Begun	Jurisdiction
Birth	1898	Recorder's Office
Death	1898	Recorder's Office
Court	na	Clerk/District Ct.
School	na	Auditor's Office

■ Steele 2 June 1883
201 Washington Ave. W., P.O. Box 296, Finley, ND 58230
Phone: (701)524-2152

Web site: www.rootsweb.com/~ndsteele/steele.htm
Parent County: Griggs, Traill

Record Type	Year Begun	Jurisdiction
Marriage	1883	County Judge
Divorce	1886	Clerk/District Ct.
Probate	1886	County Judge
Court	1886	Clerk/District Ct.

■ Stevens 4 Jan. 1873
Parent County: Buffalo
Comments/research tips: Eliminated 30 November 1892 to McLean and Ward.

■ Stevens, old 24 Apr. 1862
Parent County: Unorganized Territory
Comments/research tips: Eliminated 17 December 1863 to Unorganized Territory.

■ Stutsman 4 Jan. 1873
511 Second Ave. SE, Jamestown, ND 58401
Phone: (701)252-9042
Web site: www.rootsweb.com/~ndstutsm/
Parent County: Pembina, Buffalo
Comments/research tips: The state has Birth and Death records.

Record Type	Year Begun	Jurisdiction
Marriage	1884	Recorder's Office
Divorce	na	Clerk/District Ct.
Land	1874	Recorder's Office
Probate	na	Clerk of Courts
Court	na	Clerk/District Ct.

■ Towner 8 Mar. 1883
315 Second St., P.O. Box 517, Cando, ND 58324
Phone: (701)968-4343
Web site: www.rootsweb.com/~ndtowner/
Parent County: Rolette, Cavalier
Comments/research tips: Organized 24 January 1884.

Record Type	Year Begun	Jurisdiction
Marriage	1889	Clerk/District Ct.
Divorce	1884	Clerk/District Ct.
Land	1884	Clerk/District Ct.
Probate	1886	Clerk/District Ct.
Court	1884	Clerk/District Ct.
School	na	Super./Schools
Birth	ca. 1940	Clerk of Courts
Death	ca. 1940	Clerk of Courts

■ Traill 12 Jan. 1875
13 First St. NW., Hillsboro, ND 58045
Phone: (701)636-4454
Web site: www.rootsweb.com/~ndtraill/
Parent County: Grand Forks, Burbank, Cass
Comments/research tips: Recorder's Office has Land records from mid–1800s.

Record Type	Year Begun	Jurisdiction
Marriage	1872	Clerk/District Ct.
Divorce	1890	Clerk/District Ct.
Probate	1882	Clerk/District Ct.

■ **Villard** 8 Mar. 1883
Parent County: Billlings
Comments/research tips: Eliminated 10 March 1887 to Billings and Stark.

■ **Wallace** 9 Mar. 1883
Parent County: Howard
Comments/research tips: (See McKenzie) Eliminated 30 November 1896 to Billings and Stark. Re-created 24 May 1901 from Billings and Stark and attached to Stark County. Eliminated 16 March 1905 to McKenzie.

■ **Wallette** 4 Jan. 1873
Parent County: Buffalo
Comments/research tips: Eliminated 9 March 1883 to Buford and Flannery.

■ **Walsh** 20 May 1881
600 Cooper Ave., Grafton, ND 58237
Phone: (701)352-0350
Web site: www.rootsweb.com/~ndwalsh/walsh.htm
Parent County: Grand Forks, Pembina

Record Type	Year Begun	Jurisdiction
Marriage	1884	Clerk/District Ct.
Divorce	na	Clerk/District Ct.
Land	1878	County Recorder
Probate	na	Clerk/District Ct.
Court	na	Clerk/District Ct.
School	na	Super./Schools

■ **Ward** 14 Apr. 1885
315 Third St. SE, Minot, ND 58701
Phone: (701)857-6460
Web site: www.geocities.com/Athens/Forum/2079/
Parent County: Stevens, Wynn, Renville, old
Comments/research tips: County Recorder has Land records from late 1800s.

Record Type	Year Begun	Jurisdiction
Military	ca. 1930	County Recorder
Marriage	na	County Judge
Divorce	na	Clerk/District Ct.
School	na	Auditor's Office

Probate	na	County Judge
Burial	na	County Recorder

■ **Wells** 4 Jan. 1873
700 Railway St. N., P.O. Box 155, Fessenden, ND 58438
Phone: (701)547-3122
Web site: www.rootsweb.com/~ndwells/
Parent County: Buffalo
Comments/research tips: Clerk of District Court has Probate records from late 1800s. Formerly Gingras County. Name changed to Wells 26 February 1881. Organized 24 August 1884.

Record Type	Year Begun	Jurisdiction
Marriage	1890	Clerk/District Ct.
Divorce	na	Clerk/District Ct.
Land	1884	Recorder's Office
Court	na	Clerk/District Ct.

■ **Williams** 30 Nov. 1892
Box 2047, Williston, ND 58802
Phone: (701)774-4374
Web site: www.rootsweb.com/~ndwillia/
Parent County: Buford, Flannery
Comments/research tips: Divorce records prior to 1926 are held in Bismark. Superintendant of Schools has township books. Organized 10 March 1903.

Record Type	Year Begun	Jurisdiction
Land	ca. 1900	County Treasurer
Probate	1903	Clerk of Courts
Court	1903	Clerk/District Ct.
Marriage	1892	Auditor's Office
Divorce	1926	Clerk of Courts

■ **Williams, old** 8 Jan. 1873
Parent County: Unorganized Territory
Comments/research tips: Eliminated 30 November 1892 to Mercer.

■ **Wynn** 9 Mar. 1883
Parent County: Bottineau, Renville, old
Comments/research tips: Eliminated 11 March 1887 to Bottineau, McHenry, old Renville, and Ward.

Ohio

By Rhonda R. McClure

HISTORICAL OVERVIEW

While many consider the establishment of the Northwest Territory in 1787 to be the magical event responsible for the foundation of Ohio, the history of the state can be traced even further back. In 1747, the Ohio Company of Virginia was organized with the intent of settling in the Ohio River Valley. Among the members of this land speculation is Lawrence Washington, brother of George, who would one day become President of the newly formed United States. Because of Lawrence's involvement in this land, George Washington was recruited to take some soldiers to the area to warn off the French who had settled there. This incident launched the French and Indian War, a war which ignited the Seven Year War in Europe. When it was all over, the British had possession of the land that became Ohio, though they did not encourage settlement.

After the American Revolution, colonies whose charters included land west of the Appalachian Mountains were encouraged to "donate" this land to the newly formed government to aid them in creating revenues, thus preventing the need for taxes. The Northwest Territory and the Ordinance of 1787 are crucial moments in American history—the Ordinance established how all other territories and states would be created. The Northwest Territory was eventually divided into what we now know as the states of Ohio (1803), Indiana (1816), Illinois (1818), Michigan (1837), Wisconsin (1848), and Minnesota (1858).

Maps of early Ohio show land that was divided and set aside for certain land bounties and other promised land entitlements. In addition to bounty land given to soldiers for fighting in the American Revolution, there were also areas reserved for repaying individuals who lost their land in support of the patriots. Understanding each

© PhotoDisc/Getty Images

OHIO AT A GLANCE

Motto: With God, All Things Are Possible

Population: 11.4 million

Prevalent Religions: Roman Catholicism, Protestantism (mainly Baptist and Methodist), and Judaism

Major Industries: Transportation equipment, fabricated metal products, machinery, food processing, electrical equipment, soybeans, dairy products, corn, tomatoes, hogs, cattle, poultry, eggs

Ethnic Makeup (in percent): Caucasian 85%, African American 11.5%, Hispanic 1.9%, Asian 1.2%, Native American 0.2%, Other 0.2%

Per Capita Income: $27,081

Famous Ohioans: Neil Armstrong, Halle Berry, Erma Bombeck, Dorothy Dandridge, Doris Day, Paul Laurence Dunbar, Thomas Alva Edison, John Glenn, Bob Hope, Dean Martin, Toni Morrison, Paul Newman, Annie Oakley, Jesse Owens, Norman Vincent Peale, Arthur M. Schlesinger Jr., Steven Spielberg, Gloria Steinem, Orville Wright

Above: Amish road sign in Northeastern Ohio

section's history will aid you in discovering where your ancestors may have come from before arriving in Ohio.

RECORD HIGHLIGHTS

County-level registration of births and deaths began in 1867 and was the responsibility of the probate court. Statewide registration of births and deaths would not begin until the end of 1908. Marriage records are generally from the creation of the state, though they often list only the names of the bride and groom, the date of the marriage, and the individual who performed the marriage.

Indexes to the death records from 1908 to 1937 are available online through the Ohio Historical Society's Web site <www.ohiohistory.org>. The Society also has copies of the actual death certificates from 1908 to 1944, and you can request copies of these records for a fee. Details on the information you need to supply have been made available at the OHS Web site. Births after 1908 and deaths after 1945 must be requested from the Ohio Department of Health, Division of Vital Statistics, P.O. Box 15098, Columbus, OH 43215–0098, <www.odh.sta te.oh.us/VitStats/vsmain1.htm>. Death certificates from 1908 to 1944 are also available on microfilm through the Family History Library.

When it comes to land records, remember that the various land tracts mentioned earlier affect where you will find the earliest land records. Some of the Ohio land was sold by the federal government, while other tracts were used to satisfy federal and state bounty lands. In all, there were thirteen land tracts that were earmarked. Understanding where a given tract lay and the corresponding counties is a good clue to where your ancestors may have lived before Ohio.

From 1797 until 1851, probate records were the responsibility of the court of common pleas. In 1852, separate probate courts were created. Genealogists will want to concentrate on finding the estate file. This file includes much more than the will. In addition to a will—if one existed—you may find settlement papers, inventories, and receipts. Estate files were sometimes known as case files or probate packets. For those estates before 1850, a valuable statewide resource is Carol Willsey Bell's *Ohio Wills and Estates to 1850: An Index* (Columbus, Ohio, Carol Willsey Bell, 1981).

An excellent resource for Ohio history and the division of the land, including useful maps, is the *Official Ohio Lands Book* by Dr. George W. Knepper (Columbus, Ohio: The Auditor of State, 2002). This book is available online at the Auditor of State's Web site <www.auditor.st ate.oh.us/publications/along_the_ohio_trail/pdf/ ohio_lands_book/ohio_lands.pdf>.

An excellent place to begin your Ohio research is the Ohio Historical Society, 1982 Velma Avenue, Columbus, Ohio 43211. Another valuable society is the Ohio Genealogical Society, which has published many Ohio records over the years and offers some searchable databases to its members through their Web site <www.ogs.org>.

The Western Reserve Historical Society, 10825 East Boulevard, Cleveland, Ohio 44106, <www.wrhs.org/>, has an extensive manuscript collection, as well as Revolutionary War Pension records.

Ohio has established eight research centers, each responsible for amassing materials related to Ohio history. Each center collects records for the counties in its region. To find out more about each center and the counties it is responsible for, visit the Ohio Historical Society's Web site <www.ohiohistory.org/resource/lgr/networkl.html>.

STATE RESOURCES

■ ARCHIVES, LIBRARIES, AND SOCIETIES

Adams County OGS
1982 Velma Ave., Columbus OH 43211
Tel: (614) 297-2300

African-American Genealogical Society of Cleveland, Ohio
P.O. Box 201476, Cleveland, OH 44120-8107

Tel: (513) 221-1875
Fax: (513) 221-7812

Ashland Genealogical Society
P.O. Box 681, Ashland, OH 44805-0681

Ashtabula County Genealogical Society, Geneva Public Library
860 Sherman St., Geneva, OH 44041-9101
Web site:

Athens County Genealogical Society, Athens County Historical Society & Museum
65 N. Court St., Athens, OH 45701.2506
Tel: (740) 698-3551
Web site: <www.frognet.net/~ac hsm/>

Auglaize County Genealogical Society
P.O. Box 2021, Wapakoneta, OH 45895-0521
Web site: <www.rootsweb.com/ ~hangdogs/index.html>

Bedford Historical Society Museum and Library
P.O. Box 46282, Bedford, OH 44146
Tel: (440) 232-0796

Belmont County Chapter OGS
P.O. Box 285, Barnesville, OH 43713
Tel: (740) 695-3660
Web site: <www.rootsweb.com/ ~ohbelogs/>

Bowling Green State University, Center for Archival Collections, Jerome Library
Bowling Green, OH 43403-0175
Tel: (419) 372-2411
Fax: (419) 372-0155

Brookville, Historical Society Library
P.O. Box 82, Brookville, OH 45309

Brown County Chapter, OGS
P.O. Box 83, Georgetown, OH 45121-0083

Butler County Chapter, OGS
Ohio Public Library, P.O. Box 2011, Middletown, OH 45042-2011
Tel: (513) 523-3580
Web site:

Carnegie Library
520 Sycamore St., Greensville, OH 45331

Allen County Genealogical Society
P.O. Box 1104, Lima, OH 45802

Allen County Historical Society and Museum
620 W. Market St., Lima, OH 45801

Akron Public Library
55 S. Main St., Akron, OH 44309

American Jewish Archives
3101 Clifton Ave., Cincinnati, OH 45220

Carnegie Public Library
127 S. North St., Washington Court House, OH 43160
Tel: (740) 335-2540

Carroll County Genealogical Society
P.O. Box 36, Carrollton, OH 44615
Tel: (330) 627-9411
Web site: <www.rootsweb.com/ ~ochcarcgs/>

Champaign County Genealogical Society
P.O. Box 682, Urbana, OH 43078-0680
Web site: <www.rootsweb.com/ ~ohchampa/society.htm>

Champaign County Historical Society
809 E. Lawn, Urbana OH 43078

Champaign County Library
160 W. Market St., Urbana, OH 43078
Tel: (513) 653-3811

Chillicothe & Ross County, Public Library
140 S. Paint St., Chillicothe, OH 45601

Cincinnati Historical Society Library, The Museum Center at Cincinnati Union Terminal
1301 Western Ave., Cincinnati, OH 45203

George Rogers Clark Chapter, OHSSAR
Springfield, OH
Web site: <grccsar.homestead .com/grccsar.html>

Clark County Friends of the Library Genealogy Research Group
1268 Kenwood Ave., Springfield, OH 45505
Tel: (937) 323-2905

Clark County Genealogical Society
P.O. Box 2524, Springfield, OH 45501-2524
Tel: (937) 323-4728
Web site: <www.rootsweb.com/ ~occurs/>

Clark County Public Library
201 S. Fountain Ave., P.O. Box 1080, Springfield, OH 45501-1080

Clermont County Genealogical Society
P.O. Box 394, Batavia, OH 45103-0394

Tel: (513) 522-8458
Web site: <www.rootsweb.com/~ohclecgs/>

Cleveland Public Library
325 Superior Ave., Cleveland, OH 44114

Clinton County Historical Society
P.O. Box 529, Wilmington, OH 45177-0529
Tel: (937) 382-5209

Columbiana County Historical Society
P.O. Box 221, Lisbon, OH 44432

Columbiana County, O.G.S.
P.O. Box 861, Salem OH 44460-0861
Tel: (330) 223-1447
Web site: <www.rootsweb.com/~hoodlum/>

Columbus Jewish Historical Society
1175 College Ave., Columbus, OH 43209-2890
Web site: <www.gcis.net/cjhs>

Columbus Metropolitan Library, Biography & History
96 S. Grant Ave., Columbus, OH 43215
Web site: <www.cml.lib.oh.us>

Coshocton County, OGS
P.O. Box 128, Coshocton, OH 43812-0128

Coshocton Public Library, Miriam C. Hunter Local History Rom
655 Main St., Coshocton, OH 43812-1697
Tel: (614) 622-0956

Crawford County Genealogical Society
P.O. Box 92, Galion, OH 44833-0092

Cumberland Trail Genealogical Society
P.O. Box 576, St. Clairesville, OH 43905
Tel: (740) 676-4132

Cuyahoga East
P.O. Box 24182, Lyndhurst OH 44124-0182

Cuyahoga-Parma Chapter/OGS
P.O. Box 29509, Parma, OH 44129-0509

Cuyahoga Southwest County OGS
13305 Pearl Rd., Strongville OH 44136

Cuyahoga Valley, OGS
P.O. Box 41414, Brecksville, Ohio 44141-0414

Cuyahoga West, OGS
P.O. Box 26196, Fairview Park, Ohio 44126

Darke County Genealogical Society
P.O. Box 908, Greenville, OH 45331-0908

Dayton & Montgomery County Public Library
215 E. Third St., Dayton, OH 45402-2103
Tel: (513) 227-9531

Defiance County, OGS
P.O. Box 7006, Defiance, OH 43512-7006
Web site: <www.rootsweb.com/~ohdcgs/>

Delaware County Genealogical Society
P.O. Box 1126, Delaware, OH 43015-3126

Delaware County Historical Society
157 E. William St.; Delaware, OH 43015-0317
Web site: <www.midohio.net/dchsdchs/>

Division of Vital Statistics, Ohio Department of Health
P.O. Box 15098, Columbus, OH 43215-0098
Tel: (614) 446-2531

East Liverpool Historical Society
305 Walnut St., East Liverpool, OH 43920

East Palestine Historical Society
555 Bacon Ave., East Palestine, OH 44413

Ebenezer Zane Chapter, OHSSAR
2101 County Rd. 1, Rayland, OH 43943-7866

Erie County Chapter, OGS
P.O. Box 1301, Sandusky, OH 44871-1301

RESEARCH TIPS
for more info

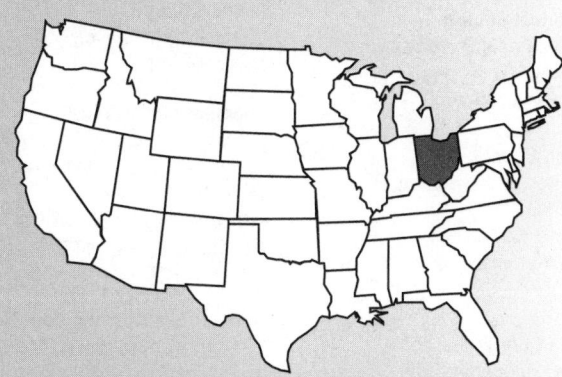

- Ohio has eight regional research centers, each responsible for the records and resources concerning the counties in their district. Visit <www.ohiohistory.org/resource/lgr/networkl.html> to find the center you need.
- The best place to begin your Ohio research is the Ohio Historical Society in Columbus, where you'll find primary resources as well as research tools to help you find the actual records you need <www.ohiohistory.org>.
- The Ohio Genealogical Society <www.ogs.org>, the largest state genealogical society in the U.S., has published many Ohio records and offers searchable online databases. Visit them in person in Mansfield.
- www.negenealogy.com

Census Records
- Federal Census: 1820, 1830, 1840, 1850, 1860, 1870, 1880, 1900, 1910, 1920, 1930
- Federal Mortality Schedules: 1850, 1860, 1870
- Union Veterans and Widows: 1890

Ethan Allen Chapter, OHSSAR
1379 Bradford St., Warren, OH 44485-1963
Tel: (330) 395-0310

Evangelical Friends Church, Eastern Division
5350 Broadmoor Circle, NW, Canton, OH 44709
Tel: (330) 493-1660
Fax: (330) 493-0852

Ewings Chapter, OHSSAR
18660 State Rt. 550, Amesville, OH 45711
Tel: (740) 448-7269
Web site: <www.frognet.net/~assar/>

Fairfield County District Library
219 N. Broad St., Lancaster, OH 43130

Fairfield County, OGS
P.O. Box 1470, Lancaster, OH 43130-0570
Web site:

Fayette County Chapter, OGS
P.O. Box 342, Washington Courthouse, OH 43130-0570

Firelands Historical Society Library
4 Case Ave., Norwalk, Ohio 44857

Flesh Public Library
124 W. Greene St., Piqua, OH
45356
Tel: (937) 773-6753

**Franklin County Genealogical &
Historical Society**
P.O. Box 44309, Columbus, OH
43204-0309
Tel: (614) 469-1300

Fulton County, OGS
P.O. Box 337, Swanton, OH
43558-0337
Tel: (419) 335-0898
Web site: <www.rootsweb/~ohfu
lton/>

**Gallia County Historical/
Genealogical Society**
P.O. Box 295, Gallipolis, OH
45631-0295
Tel: (740) 446-7200
Web site: <www.zoomnet.net/
~histosco>

**Garst Museum, Genealogical
Library**
205 N. Broadway, Greenville, OH
45331

Geauga County, OGS
110 E. Park St., Chardon, OH
44024-1213

Geauga West Library
13445 Chilicothe Rd., Chester-
land, OH 44026

**Glendover Warren County
Museum**
Lebanon, OH 45036

Granville Public Library
217 E. Broadway, Granville, OH
43023

Greater Cleveland
P.O. Box 40254, Cleveland, OH
44140-0254

**The Greater Cleveland
Genealogical Society**
P.O. Box 40234, Cleveland, OH
44140-0254
Web site: <www.rootsweb.com/
~ohgcgg/>

Greene County Library
76 E. Market St., Xenia, Ohio
45385

Greene County, OGS
P.O. Box 706, Xenia, Ohio
45385-0706
Web site: <www.rootsweb.com/
~ohgccogs/main.htm>

**Greenville Public Library,
Genealogy Department**
520 Sycamore St., Greenville, OH
45331

**Guernsey County District
Public Library**
800 Steubenville Ave., Cambridge, OH 43725

Guernsey County, OGS
P.O. Box 661, 125 N. Seventh St.,
Cambridge, OH 43725-0661
Tel: (740) 432-9249
Web site: <www.usgenet.orgr/
usa/oh/county/Guernsey/
gcgspub.html>

Nathan Hale Chapter, OHSSAR
30 Babic St., Struthers, Ohio
44471-3108
Tel. (330) 755-8590

Hamilton County, OGS
P.O. Box 15865, Cincinnati, OH
45215-0865
Tel: (513) 956-7078
Web site: <members.aol.com/
gosh/>

Hancock County, OGS
P.O. Box 672, Findlay, OH
45839-0672
Web site: <www.rootsweb.com/
~ohhccogs>

**Hanover Township Historical
Society**
P.O. Box 381, Hanoverton, OH
44423

**Hardin County Historic
Museums**
P.O. Box 521, Kenton, OH 43326

Hardin County, OGS
P.O. Box 520, Kenton, OH
43326-0520
Tel: (419) 674-4088
Web site: <www.kenton.com/us
ers/chuck/soc.htm>

**Harrison County Genealogical
Society**
45507 Unionvale Rd., Cadiz, OH
43907-9723
Web site: <www.rootsweb.com/
~ohharris/>

**Hayes Presidential Center
Library**
1337 Hayes Ave., Fremont, OH
43420

Henry County OGS
P.O. Box 231, Deshler, OH 43516

Highland County, OGS
713 S. Main St., Mansfield, OH
44907-1644
Tel: (419) 756-7294

**Historical Society of
Columbiana and Fairfield
Townships, Dept. I**
10 Park Ave., Columbiana, OH
44408

Hocking County, OGS
P.O. Box 115, Rockbridge, Ohio
43149-0115

Homes County, OGS
P.O. Box 136, Millersburg, OH
44654-0136

**Hudson Genealogical Study
Group, Hudson Library and
Historical Society, Dept. G.**
22 Aurora St., Hudson, Ohio
44236-2947
Tel: (330) 653-6658
Web site: <www.rootsweb.com/
~ohhudogs/Hudson.htm>

**Samuel Huntington Chapter,
OHSSAR**
6366 Indian Point Rd., Painesville, OH 44077-8844
Web site: <www.sar.org/ohssar/
samuel_Huntington_chapter
.htm>

Huron County, OGS
P.O. Box 923, Norwalk, OH
44857-0923
Web site: <www.rootsweb.com/
~ohhuron/>

Jackson County, OGS
P.O. Box 807, Jackson, OH
45640-0807
Web site: <scioto.org/OGS/Jack
son/>

**Jefferson County Historical
Society Library**
P.O. Box 268, Steubenville, OH
43952

Jefferson County, OGS
P.O. Box 4712, Steubenville, OH
43952-8712
Web site: <www.rootsweb.com/
~ohjefogs/>

Johnson St. Paris Library
E. Main St., St. Paris, Ohio 43072
Tel: (513) 663-4349

Knox County, OGS
P.O. Box 1098, Mt. Vernon, OH
43050-1098

Lafayette Chapter, OHSSAR
899 Hancock Ave., Akron, OH
44314-1044
Tel: (330) 745-1532
Web site:
**Lake County Genealogical
Society**
184 Phelps St., Painesville, OH
44077-3927
Web site: <131.187.173.99/gen
ealogy_lcgs.htm>

Lakewood Public Library
15425 Detroit Ave., Lakewood,
Ohio 44107

Lawrence County, OGS
P.O. Box 1035, Proctorville, OH
45669-1035
Tel: (304) 525-5720

**Licking County Genealogical
Society**
101 W. Main St., Newark, OH
43055-5054
Tel: (740) 349-5510
Web site: <www.npls.org/lcgs/>

Lisbon Historical Society
P.O. Box 221, Lisbon, OH 44432
Web site: <http://countypage.
com/lhs/>

Logan County, OGS
P.O. Box 36, Bellefontaine, OH
43311-0036
Tel: (937) 593-7811

Lorain County, OGS
P.O. Box 865, Elyria, OH
44036-0865
Web site:
Lorain Public Library
351 Sixth St., Lorain, OH 44052

Lucas County Public Library
235 N. Michigan St., Toledo, OH
43624-1614
Tel: (419) 259-5207
Web site: <www.toledolibrary
.org>

Lucasville, Historical Society
P.O. Box 761, Lucasville, OH
45648-0761

Madison County, OGS
P.O. Box 102, London, OH
43140-0102

Mahoning County, OGS
P.O. Box 9333, Youngstown, OH
44513-0333

**Mansfield/Richland County
Public Library**
43 W. Third St., Mansfield, OH
44902

Marion County, OGS
P.O. Box 844, Marion, OH
43301-0844

Web site: <www.genealogy.org/
~smoore/marion/>

Medina County, OGS
P.O. Box 804, Medina, OH
44258-0804

**Meigs County Historical
Society**
P.O. Box 346, Pomeroy, OH
45769

Meigs County, OGS
P.O. Box 346, Pomeroy, OH
45769-0345

Mennonite Historical Library
Bluffton College, Bluffton, OH
45817

Mercer County, OGS
P.O. Box 437, Celina, OH
45822-0437
Web site: <www.calweb.com/~w
ally/mercer/society.htm>

**Methodist Historical
Commission, Ohio Wesleyan
University**
Delaware, Ohio 43015

**Miami County Historical &
Genealogical Society**
P.O. Box 305, Troy, OH
45373-0305
Web site: <www.TDS.NET.com/
mchgs>

Miami Valley, OGS
P.O. Box 1364, Dayton, OH
45401-1364

Miamisburg Historical Society
P.O. Box 774, Miamisburg, Ohio
45343-0774

Middletown Public Library
1320 First Ave., Middletown, OH
45042

Milan Public Library
P.O. Box 1550, Milan, OH 44846

**Monroe County Genealogical
Society**
P.O. Box 641, Woodsfield, OH
43793-0641
Tel: (740) 483-1481
Web site: <www.rootsweb.com/
~ohmccogs/>

Montgomery County, OGS
P.O. Box 1584, Dayton, OH
45401-1584
Tel: (937) 253-2503

Morgan County, OGS
P.O. Box 418, McConnelsville, OH
43756-0418

Morley Library
184 Phelps St., Painesville, OH
44077
Tel: (440) 352-3383

**Morrow County, Ohio
Genealogical Society**
P.O. Box 401, Mt. Gilead, OH
43338-0401
Web site: <www.rootsweb.com/
~ohmorrow/>

**Muskingum County,
Genealogical Society**
P.O. Box 3066, Zanesville, OH
43702-3066

**National Archives-Great Lakes
Region**
7358 S. Pulaski Rd., Chicago, IL
60629
(312) 581-7816
Fax: (312) 353-1294

Noble County, OGS
P.O. Box 174, Caldwell, OH
43724-0174

**North American Baptist,
General Conference**
7308 Madison St., Forest Park, IL
60130

**Northeastern Chapter #12,
SAR**
1659 Chapel Rd., Jefferson, OH
44047-8716

Norwalk Public Library
46 W. Main St., Norwalk, OH
44857

Ohio Genealogical Society
713 Main St., Mansfield, Ohio
44907-1644
Tel: (419) 756-7294
Fax: (419) 522-0224

**Ohio Historical Society
Archives/Library Division**
1982 Velma Ave., Columbus, OH
43211
Tel: (614) 297-8300
Web site: <www.ohiohistory.org/
resource/statearc/>

**Ohio Historical Society, Ohio
Historical Center**
1982 Velma Ave., Columbus, OH
43211-2497
Tel: (614) 297-2510
Fax: (614) 297-2546

**Ohio Land Office, Auditor of
State**
P.O. Box 1140, 88 E. Broad St.,
Columbus, OH 43266-0040

Tel: (614) 466-4514
Fax: (614) 466-6228

Ohio State Library
65 S. Front St., Columbus, OH
43215

**Ohio University, Archives, and
Special Collections**
Alden Library, Athens, OH
45701-2978
Tel: (614) 593-2710
Fax: (614) 593-0138

**Old Northwest Historical
Society**
P.O. Box 6235, Cincinnati, OH
45262
Tel: (513) 530-9546
Web site: <home.fuse.net/rro
wan/>

**Ottawa County Genealogical
Society**
P.O. Box 193, Port Clinton, OH
43452-0193
Tel: (419) 734-3895
Web site: <www.rootseb.com/~o
hoccgs/>

**Palatine Library, Palatines to
America, Capital University**
Box 101, Columbus, OH
43209-2394
Tel: (614) 236-8281
Web site: <genealogy.org/~pa
lam/>

Palatines to America
611 E. Weber Rd., Columbus, OH
43211
Tel: (614) 267-4888
Web site: <http://palam.org/>

**Paulding County Carnegie
Library**
205 S. Main St., Paulding, OH
45879-1492

Paulding County, OGS
205 E. Main St., Paulding, OH
45879-1492

Pemberville Public Library
375 E. Front St., Pemberville,
Ohio 43450
Tel: (419) 287-4012
Fax: (419) 287-4620

Perry County, OGS
P.O. Box 275, Junction City, OH
43748-0275
Web site: <www.perrygenealogy
.net/perryogs.htm>

**Pickaway County Historical &
Genealogical Society**
P.O. Box 85, Circleville, OH
43113

Web site: <www.rootsweb.com/
~ohpickaw/gen.html>

Pike County Genealogy Society
P.O. Box 224, Waverly, OH
45690-0224
Web site: <www.rootsweb.com/
~ohpcgs/pike.htm>

**Polish Genealogical Society of
Greater Cleveland, Ohio**
105 Pleasant View Dr., Seville,
OH 44273

Portage County, OGS
P.O. Box 821, Ravenna, OH
44266

Portsmouth Public Library
1220 Gallia St., Portsmouth, OH
45662

**Preble County District Library,
Preble Room., Eaton Branch**
301 N. Barren St., Eaton, OH
45320

**Preble County Genealogical
Society, Preble County District
Library**
450 S. Barron St., Eaton, OH
45320
Web site: <www.pcdl.lib.oh.us/
pcgs/>

**Preble County Historical
Society**
7693 Swartsel Rd., Easton, Ohio
45320
Tel: (937) 787-9662

Presbyterian Historical Society
425 Lombard St., Philadelphia,
PA 19147-1516
Tel: (215) 627-1852

**The Public Library of Cincinnati
and Hamilton County**
800 Vine St., Cincinnati, OH
45202-2071
Tel: (513) 369-6900
Web site: <www.cincinnatilibrary
.org>

Putnam County, OGS
P.O. Box 403, Ottawa, OH
45875-0403

**Randolph Township Historical
Society, Inc.**
P.O. Box 355, Clayton, OH 45315

**Richland County Genealogical
Society**
P.O. Box 3823, Mansfield, OH
44907-3823
Web site: <www.rootsweb.com/
~enriches/>

Ohio

Roman Catholic, Archdiocese of Cincinnati
Chancery, 100 E. Eighth St., Cincinnati, OH 45202
Tel: (513) 421-3131
Fax: (513) 421-6225

Roman Catholic, Diocese of Cleveland
Chancery Building, 1027 Superior Ave., Cleveland, OH 44114
Tel: (216) 696-6525
Fax: (216) 621-7332

Roman Catholic, Diocese of Columbus
Chancery Office, 198 E. Broad St., Columbus, OH 43215
Tel: (614) 224-2251
Fax: (614) 224-6306

Roman Catholic, Diocese of Steubenville
422 Washington St., P.O. Box 969, Steubenville, OH 43952
Tel: (614) 282-3631
Fax: (614) 282-3327

Roman Catholic, Diocese of Toledo
Chancery, P.O. Box 985, Toledo, OH 43697-0985
Tel: (419) 244-6711
Fax: (419) 244-4791

Roman Catholic, Diocese of Youngstown
Chancery Office, 144 W. Wood St., Youngstown, OH 44503
Tel: (216) 744-8451
Fax: (330) 742-6448

Ross County Genealogical Society Library
P.O. Box 6325, Chillicothe, OH 45601

Ross County, OGS
P.O. Box 6352, Chillicothe, OH 45601-6352
Tel: (740) 775-0420
Web site: <www.bright.net/~rcgs>

Salem Historical Society
208 S. Broadway Ave., Salem, OH 44460

Sandusky County Kin Hunters
Spiegle Grove, Fremont, OH 43420-2796

Schiappa Branch Library
4141 Mall Dr., Steubenville, OH 43952

Scioto County, OGS
P.O. Box 812, Portsmouth, OH 45662-0812

Seneca County Genealogical Society
P.O. Box 157, Tiffin, Ohio 44883-0157
Web site: <www.senecasearchers.org/index.html>

Shelby Genealogical Society
P.O. Box 766, Shelby, OH 44875-0766
Web site: <www.rootsweb.com/~scogs/>

Sidney Public Library
230 E. North St., Sidney, OH 45365

Society of Friends, Olney Friends School
61830 Sandy Ridge Rd., Barnesville, OH 43713
Tel: (614) 425-3655

Southern Ohio, OGS
P.O. Box 414, Hillsboro, OH 45133

John Stark Chapter, OHSSAR
5220 Woodlynn Dr., East Canton, OH 44730-1756
Tel: (330) 488-2227

Stark County District Library
715 Market Ave., North Canton, OH 44702

Stark County, Ohio, OGS
1950 Market Ave. N., Apt. B2, Canton, OH 44714-2242

State Library of Ohio Genealogical Section
65 S. Front St., Room 308, Columbus, Ohio 43215-4163
Tel: (614) 644-6966
Fax: (614) 728-2789

Summit County, OGS
239 N. Highland Ave., Akron, OH 44303
Tel: (330) 836-6518
Web site: <spot.acorn.net/gen/>

Toledo Area Genealogical Society
P.O. Box 352258, Toledo, OH 43635-2258

Toledo Public Library, Local History & Genealogy Dept.
325 Michigan St., Toledo, OH 43624

Tri-County Lineage Research Society (Hancock, Seneca, Wood)
Kaubisch Library, Fostoria, OH 44830

Trumbull County, OGS
P.O. Box 309, Warren, OH 44482-0309

Tuscarawas County Genealogical Society
P.O. Box 141, New Philadelphia, OH

Union County Genealogical Society
P.O. Box 438
Marysville, OH 43040-0438

United Methodist Church
601 W. Riverview Ave., Dayton, OH 45406

University of Cincinnati, Archives Department, Blegen Library
Cincinnati, OH 45221-0113
Tel: (513) 556-1959
Fax: (513) 556-2113

University of Cincinnati Library
P.O. Box 21033, Cincinnati, Ohio 45221-0033
Tel: (513) 556-1424
Web site:

Van Wert County, OGS
P.O. Box 485, Van Wert, Ohio 45891-0485
Web site: <www.rootsweb.com/~ohvanwer/vwc_ogs.htm>

Vinton County Historical and Genealogical Society
P.O. Box 306, Hamden, OH 45634-0306
Web site: <www.rootsweb.com/~ohvinton/oxcart.htm>

Warder Public Library
137 E. High St., Springfield, OH 45502

Warren County Genealogy Resource Center
300 E. Silver, Lebanon, OH 45036

Warren County, OGS
406 Justice Dr., Lebanon, OH 45036

Warren-Trumbull County Public Library
444 Mahoning Ave., NW, Warren, OH 44483-4692

Washington County Public Library
418 Washington St., Marietta, OH 45750
Tel: (740) 373-1057

Web site: <www.wcplib.oh.us/lhg.htm>

Washington County, OGS
P.O. Box 2174, Marietta, Ohio 45750-2174

Wayne County Genealogical Society
P.O. Box 856, Wooster, OH 44691
Web site: <www.rootsweb.com/~ohwayne/wcgs.htm>

Wayne County Public Library
304 N. Market St., Wooster, OH 44691

Wellsville Historical Society
1003 Riverside Ave., Wellsville, OH 43968

Western Reserve Historical Society
10825 East Blvd., Cleveland, OH 44106-1788
Tel: (216) 721-5722
Fax: (216) 721-0645

Williams County Genealogical Society
P.O. Box 293, Bryan, OH 43506-0293
Web site: <www.wcgs-ogs.com>

Wood County Chapter of the Ohio Genealogical Society
P.O. Box 722, Bowling Green, OH 43402-0722
Web site: <www.rootsweb.com/~ohwood/searchwd.htm#Woods>

Wright State University, Special Collections and Archives
Paul Laurence Dunbar Library, Dayton, OH 45435-001
Tel: (937) 775-2092
Fax: (937) 775-4109

Wyandot Tracers OGS
P.O. Box 414, Upper Sanducky, OH 43351-0414
Web site: <www.udata.com/users/hsbaker/tracers.htm>

Youngstown Historical Center of Industry and Labor Archives-Library
P.O. Box 533, 151 W. Wood St., Youngstown, OH 44501
Tel: (330) 743-5934
Fax: (330) 743-2999

Youngstown & Mahoning Counties Public Library
305 Wick Ave., Youngstown, OH 44503

Ohio

BIBLIOGRAPHY

■ GENERAL RESOURCES

Bench and Bar of Ohio: A Compendium of History and Biography, 2 vols.
by George Irving Reed (Chicago: Century Publishing and Engraving Co., 1897)

Bibliography of the State of Ohio, Being a Catalog of the Books and Pamphlets Relating to the History of the State, the West and Northwest
by Peter G. Thomson (Salem, MA: Higginson Book Co., 1993)

The Biographical Encyclopedia of Ohio of the Nineteenth Century
by Charles Robson (Cincinnati: Galaxy Pub. Co., 1876)

Black Ohio and the Color Line, 1860–1915
by David Allison Gerber (Urbana, IL: University of Illinois Press, 1976)

Early History of the Disciples in the Western Reserve 1875
by A.S. Hayden (Reprint. Knightstown, IN: The Bookmark, 1979)

The Encyclopedia Of Quaker Genealogy 1750–1930
(Brøderbund, 1998: CD-ROM)

Frontier Republic: Ideology and Politics in the Ohio Country 1780–1825
by Andrew Cayton (Galveston, TX: Frontier Press, 1986)

Gateway to the West, 2 vols.
by Ruth Bowers and Anita Short (Reprint. Baltimore, MD: Genealogical Publishing Co., 1989)

Genealogical Data Relating to Women in the Western Reserve Before 1840 (1850)
compiled by the Cleveland Centennial Commission (Columbus, OH: Ohio Historical Society, 1973)

Genealogical Research in Ohio, 2d ed.
by Kip Sperry (Baltimore, Maryland: Genealogical Publishing Company, Inc., 2003)

Genealogical Researcher's Manual: With Special References for Using the Ohio Historical Society Library
compiled by Suzanne Wolfe Mettle and Nova Anderson Weller (Columbus, OH: Ohio Genealogical Society, 1981)

The Genealogist's Companion and Sourcebook, 2d ed.
by Emily Anne Croom (Cincinnati: Betterway Books, 2003)

A Genealogist's Guide to Discovering Your African-American Ancestors
by Franklin Carter Smith and Emily Anne Croom (Cincinnati: Betterway Books, 2003)

Guide to Genealogical Research in the National Archives of the United States
edited by Anne Bruner Eales and Robert M. Kvasnicka (Washington, DC: National Archives and Records Administration, 2000)

Guide to the Manuscript Collection of Early Ohio Methodism: United Methodist Church of Ohio
by Frances D. Harter (Delaware, OH: United Methodist Archives Center, 1980)

A Guide to Shaker Manuscripts in the Library of The Western Reserve Historical Society, with an Inventory of its Shaker Photographs
(Cleveland: Western Reserve Historical Society, 1974)

Historical Collections of Ohio, 2 vols.
by Henry Howe (Salem, MA: Higginson Book Co., 1994)

History of Ohio, 5 vols.
by Charles Burleigh Galbreath (Chicago: American Historical Society, 1925)

A History of the Ohio Conference of the Churches of God, General Conferences, 1836–1986
by Richard Kern (Findlay, OH: Richard Kern, 1986)

The History of the State of Ohio, 6 vols.
edited by Carl F. Wittke (Columbus, OH: The Society, 1941–1944)

History of West Central Ohio, 3 vols.
by Orton G. Rust (Indianapolis, IN: Historical Pub. Co., 1934)

History of the Western Reserve, 3 vols.
by Harriet T. Upton (Salem, MA: Higginson Book Co., 1995)

Local History And Genealogy Resources Guide To Southeastern Ohio
by Linda L. Harfst (Wellston, OH: Ohio Valley Area Libraries, 1984)

Log Construction in the Ohio Country, 1750–1850
by Donald A. Hutslar (Galveston, TX: Frontier Press, 1992)

Memoirs of the Early Pioneer Settlers of Ohio, with Narratives of Incidents and Occurrences in 1775
by S.P. Hildreth (Reprint. Baltimore, MD: Clearfield Company, 1995)

Memoirs of the Lower Ohio Valley: Personal and Genealogical with Portraits, 2 vols.
(Madison, WI: Federal Publishing, 1905)

Memoirs of the Miami Valley, 3 vols.
by John Calvin Hover (Chicago: R.O. Law Co., 1919)

National Archives Microfilm Catalogs online:
<www.archives.gov/publications/genealogy_microfilm_catalogs.html>

Ohio Families: A Bibliography of Books About Ohio Families
by Donald M. Hehir (Bowie, MD: Heritage books, 1993)

Ohio; The Future Great State: Her Manufacturers and a History of Her Commercial Cities, Cincinnati and Cleveland with Portraits and Biographies of Some of the Old Settlers, and Many of The Most Prominent Business Men.
by W.J. Comley and W. D'Eggville (Cincinnati, OH: Comley Brothers Manufacturing and Publishing Co., 1875)

Ohio Genealogical Research
by George K. Schweitzer (Knoxville, TN: George K. Schweitzer, 1995)

The Ohio Hundred Year book: A Hand-Book of the Public Men and Public Institutions of Ohio from the Formation of the North-West Territory (1787) to July 1, 1901
by Elliot Howard Gilkey (Columbus OH: F.J. Heer, 1901)

The Ohio River: A Course of Empire
by Archer Butler Hulbert (Salem, MA: Higginson Book Co., 1996)

Ohio's Progressive Sons, A History of the State: Sketches of Those Who Have Helped to Build Up the Commonwealth
(Cincinnati: Queen City Publishing, 1905)

The Old Northwest: Pioneer Period, 1815–1840, 2 vols.
by R. Carlyle Buley (Bloomington: Indiana University Press in association with the Indiana Historical Society, 1978)

Pioneer Ohio Newspapers, 1793–1810 and 1802–1818: Genealogical and Historical Abstracts, 2 vols.
by Karen Mauer Green (Galveston, TX: Frontier Press, 1988)

Pioneer Sketches: Scenes and Incidents of Former Days
by M.P. Sargent (Salem, MA: Higginson Book Co., 1993)

Progressive Men Of Northern Ohio
(Cleveland: Plain Dealer Pub. Co., 1906)

The Shane Manuscript Collection: A Genealogical Guide to the Kentucky and Ohio Papers
by William K. Hall (Galveston, TX: Frontier Press, 1990)

Six Thousand Country Churches
by Charles Otis Gill and Gifford Pinchot (New York: Macmillan, 1919)

Sketches of Western Methodism: Biographical, Historical & Miscellaneous, Illustrative Of Pioneer Life
by James Bradley Finley (Cincinnati: Methodist Book Concern, 1856)

Ohio

*Southern Ohio And Its Builders:
A Biographical Record of Those
Personalities, Who by Reason
of Their Achievements Have
Merited a Permanent Place in
the Story of Twentieth Century
Southern Ohio*
(Southern Ohio Biographical Association, 1927)

*State Centennial History of
Ohio, Covering The Period of
Indian, French and British
Dominion, the Territory
Northwest, and the Hundred
Years of Statehood*
by Rowland H. Rerick (Salem,
MA: Higginson Book Co., 1995)

*The Western Reserve: The
Story of New Connecticut in
Ohio*
by Harlan Hatcher (Galveston, TX:
Frontier Press, 1991)

■ CENSUS RECORDS

*The American Census
Handbook*
by Thomas Jay Kemp (Wilmington, DE: Scholarly Resources,
Inc., 2001)

*The Census Book: A
Genealogist's Guide to Federal
Census Facts, Schedules and
Indexes*
by William Dollarhide (Bountiful,
UT: Heritage Quest, 1999)

*Map Guide to the U.S. Federal
Censuses, 1790–1920.*
by William Thorndale and William
Dollarhide (Baltimore: Genealogical Publishing Co., 1987)

*Your Guide to the Federal
Census*
by Kathleen W. Hinckley (Cincinnati: Betterway Books, 2002)

■ IMMIGRATION RECORDS

*American Naturalization
Records, 1790–1990: What
They Are and How to Use Them*
by John J. Newman (North Salt
Lake, UT: HeritageQuest, 1998)

*American Passenger Arrival
Records*
by Michael Tepper (Baltimore:
Genealogical Publishing Co.,
1993)

*County Naturalizations Held by
OHS.*
by the Ohio Historical Society
(Columbus, OH: Ohio Historical
Society, 1996–2001)

*Gone to Ohio: Ashland, Brown,
Columbiana, Harrison,
Jefferson, Richland,
Champaign, Crawford, Wood,
Logan, Mahoning, Stark and
Trumbull Counties, From the
Pennsylvania Counties: Adams,
Cumberland, Dauphin, Franklin,
Lancaster, and York, 3 vols.*
by Gloria L. Aughenbaugh (York,
PA: South Central Pennsylvania
Genealogical Society,
1990–1996)

*Mountain People in a Flat Land
A Popular History of
Appalachian Migration to
Northeast Ohio 1940–1965*
by Carl E. Feather (Athens, OH:
Ohio University Press, 1998)

*The Origin and Distribution of
Settlement Groups*
by Hubert G.H. Wilhelm (Athens,
OH: Ohio University, 1982)

*The Politics of Community:
Migration and Politics in
Antebellum Ohio*
by Kenneth J. Winkle (New York:
Press Syndicate of the University
of Cambridge, 1988)

*They Became Americans:
Finding Naturalization Records
and Ethnic Origins*
by Loretto Dennis Szucs (Salt
Lake City: Ancestry, Inc., 1998)

*They Came in Ships: A Guide to
Finding Your Immigrant
Ancestor's Arrival Records,
2d ed.*
by John P. Colletta (Salt Lake
City: Ancestry, Inc., 1993)

■ LAND RECORDS

*The Bounty Lands of the
American Revolution in Ohio*
by William Thomas Hutchinson
(New York: Arno Press, 1979)

*Early Ohio Settlers Purchasers
of Land in Southwestern Ohio,
1800–1840*
by Ellen T. Berry and David Berry
(Baltimore, MD: Genealogical
Publishing, 1993)

First Ownership of Ohio Lands
by Albion Morris Dyer (Baltimore:
Genealogical Publishing Co.,
1982)

*Locating Your Roots: Discover
Your Ancestors Using Land
Records*
by Patricia Law Hatcher (Cincinnati: Betterway Books, 2003)

*Ohio Lands: A Short History, 6th
ed.*
by Thomas E. Ferguson (Columbus, OH: Auditor's Office, State of
Ohio, 1995)

*Ohio Lands South of the Indian
Boundary Line*
(Chillicothe, OH: Marie Taylor
Clark, 1984)

Ohio Lands and Their History
by William Edwards Peters (Athens, OH: W.E. Peters, 1930)

*Ohio Lands and Their
Subdivision, 2d ed.*
by William Edwards Peters (Athens, OH: W.E. Peters, 1918)

*Original Ohio Land Subdivision
Being Volume III: Final Report
Ohio Cooperative Topographic
Survey*
by C.E. Sherman (Columbus:
State Reformatory Press, 1925)

*U.S. Revolutionary War Bounty
Land Warrants Used in the U.S.
Military District of Ohio and
Related Papers, Acts of 1788,
1803, 1806*
from the United States General
Land Office (Washington, D.C.:
National Archives, 1971)

■ MAPS

Atlas of Ohio
(Madison, WI: American Publishing Co., 1975)

Atlas of the State of Ohio.
by H.F. Walling (Knightstown, IN:
The Bookmark, 1868, reprint
1995)

*The Development of Ohio's
Counties And Their Historic
Courthouses*
by Lawrence J. Marzulli (Columbus, OH: County Commissioners
Assoc. Of Ohio, ca. 1980)

Early Maps of the Ohio Valley
by Lloyd Arnold Brown (Pittsburgh: University of Pittsburgh
Press, 1959)

*Historical Atlas and Chronology
of County Boundaries,
1788–1980*
by John H. Long (Boston, MA:
G.K. Hall, 1984)

*Jurisdictional Histories For
Ohio's Eighty-Eight Counties,
1788–1985*
by W. Louis Phillips (Bowie, MD:
Heritage Books, 1986)

*Maps Of Ohio Showing The
Development Of Its Counties*
by W.L. Howison & Associates
(Columbus, OH: W.L. Howison &
Assoc., ca. 1980)

*Ohio Atlas and Gazetteer, 4th
ed.*
(Freeport, ME: DeLorme Mapping
Co., 1996)

Ohio County Maps
compiled by C.J Puetz (Lyndon
Station, WI: Thomas Publishing
Co., 1992)

The Ohio Gazetteer
by John Kilbourn (Knightstown,
IN: The Bookmark, 1981)

*The Ohio Gazetteer And
Traveler's Guide: Containing A
Description Of The Several
Towns, Townships And
Counties. With Their Water
Courses, Roads,
Improvements, Mineral
Productions*
by Warren Jenkins (Columbus,
OH: Isaac N. Whiting, 1837)

*Ohio Lands: A Short History,
3d ed.*
by Thomas A. Burke (Columbus,
OH: Auditor of the State, 1991)

Ohio Place Names
by Larry L. Miller (Bloomington,
IN: Indiana University Press,
1996)

Ohio Town Names
by William D. Overman (Akron,
OH: Atlantic Press, 1958)

The Post Offices Of Ohio
by John S. Gallagher (Burtonsville, MD: The Depot, 1979)

■ MILITARY RECORDS

*Annotated Bibliography of Ohio
Patriots: Revolutionary War &
War of 1812*
by William Louis Phillips (Bowie,
MD: Heritage Books, 1985)

Civil War Documents
from the Ohio Historical Society
(Columbus, OH: Ohio Historical
Society, 1996–2001)

*Genealogical Abstracts of the
Revolutionary War Pension
Files, 4 vols.*
by Virgil D. White (Waynesboro,
TN: National Historical Publishing, 1990)

History of the 21st Regiment, Ohio Volunteer Infantry, in the War of the Rebellion
(Salem, MA: Higginson Book Co., 1893, reprint 1995)

The Official Roster of Ohio Soldiers in the War with Spain 1898–1899
from the Ohio Adjutant General's Department (Columbus, OH: Edward T. Miller, Co., 1916)

The Official Roster of the Soldiers of the American Revolution Buried in the State of Ohio
from the Ohio Adjutant General's Office (Columbus, OH: F.J. Heer Printing Co., 1929–1959)

The Official Roster of the Soldiers of the American Revolution Who Lived in the State of Ohio: Vol. 2, A-Z
by Mrs. Orville D. Dailey (Columbus, OH: State Society DAR, State of Ohio, ca. 1938)

Official Roster of the Soldiers of the State of Ohio in the War of the Rebellion, 1861–1866
from the Ohio Roster Commission (Akron, OH: Werner Co., 1886–1895)

Ohio Indian, Revolutionary War, and War of 1812 Trails
by Fay Maxwell (St. Peter, MN: Ohio Genealogy Center, 1974)

Ohio Revolutionary War Soldiers 1840 Census and Grave Locations
by Fay Maxwell (St. Peter, MN: Ohio Genealogy Center, 1985)

Ohio, World War I Selective Service System Draft Registration Cards, 1917–1918
from the United States Selective Service System (Washington, D.C.: National Archives, 1987–1988)

Ohio's Virginia Military Tract Settlers, Also 1801 Tax List
by Fay Maxwell (St. Peter, MN: Ohio Genealogy Center, 1991)

Revolutionary War Pension and Bounty-Land-Warrant Application Files
from the United States Veterans Administration (Washington, D.C.: National Archives, 1969)

Roster of Ohio Soldiers in The War of 1812
from the Ohio Adjutant General's Department (Baltimore, MD: Clearfield Company, 1968, reprint 1989)

Roster of the Soldiers of the State of Ohio in the War with Mexico 1846–1848
(Mansfield, OH: Ohio Genealogical Society, 1897, reprint 1991)

Two Hundred Years the Military History of Ohio: Its Border Annals, Its Part in the Indian Wars, in the War of 1812, in the Mexican War, and in the War of the rebellion, with a Prefix, Giving a Compendium of the History of the United States, History of the Declaration of Independence, Sketches of its Signers, and of the Presidents, with Portraits and Autographs
(New York: H.H. Hardesty, 1886)

Uncle, We Are Ready! Registering America's Men, 1917–1918: A Guide to Researching World War I Draft Registration Cards
by John J. Newman (North Salt Lake, UT: HeritageQuest, 2001)

U.S. Military Records: A Guide to Federal & State Sources, Colonial America to the Present
by James C. Neagles (Salt Lake City: Ancestry, Inc., 1994)

War of 1812, Roster of Ohio Soldiers
from the Ohio Historical Society (Columbus, OH: Ohio Historical Society, 1996–2001)

World War II: A Family Historian's Guide
by Debra Johnson Knox (Spartanburg, SC: MIE Publishing, 2003)

Young American Patriots: The Youth of Ohio in World War II
(Richmond, VA: National Publishing Co., 1947)

■ PROBATE RECORDS

Abstracts and Extracts of the Legislative Acts And Resolutions of the State of Ohio: 1803–1821
by Mary L. Bowman (Mansfield, OH: Ohio Genealogical Society, 1994)

Guide to Local Government Records at the Ohio University Library
by the Ohio Historical Society (Athens, OH: Ohio University Library, 1986)

A History of the Courts and Lawyers of Ohio, 4 vols.
edited by Carrington Tanner Marshall (New York: American Historical Society, 1934)

Ohio Federal Court Orders, 1803–1807
(Miami Beach, FL: TLC Genealogy, 1998)

Ohio Marriages Recorded in County Courts Through 1820: An Index
by Jean Nathan (Mansfield, OH: the Society, 1996)

Ohio Wills and Estates to 1850: An Index
by Carol Willsey Bell (Youngstown, OH: Bell Books, 1981)

Wills, 1655–1871, 1917
by the Daughters of the American Revolution (Independence, MO: the D.A.R. chapter, 1970–1971)

■ VITAL RECORDS

Certificates of Death, 1908–1944; Index, 1908–1911
from the Ohio Department of Health (Columbus, OH: Ohio Historical Society, 1983, 1994–1995)

Death Certificate Index, 1913–1937
from the Ohio Historical Society (Columbus, OH: Ohio Historical Society, 1992)

Marriage Notices From the Ohio Observer Series 1827–1855
by James F. Caccamo (Apollo, PA: Closson Press, 1994)

Official Roster of the Soldiers of the American Revolution Buried in the State of Ohio, 3 vols.
(Columbus, OH: F.J. Heer Printing, 1929–59)

Ohio Cemeteries
edited by Maxine Hartmann Smith (Mansfield, OH: Ohio Genealogical Society, 1978)

Ohio Divorces: The Early Years
by Carol Willsey Bell (Boardman, OH: Bell Books, ca. 1994)

Ohio Marriages: Extracted form the Old Northwest Genealogical Quarterly
edited by Marjorie Smith (Baltimore: Genealogical Publishing Co., 1980)

Your Guide to Cemetery Research
by Sharon DeBartolo Carmack (Cincinnati: Betterway Books, 2002)

■ Adams 10 July 1797
110 W. Main St., West Union, OH 45693
Phone: (937)544-2921
Web site: www.rootsweb.com/~ohadams/
Parent County: Hamilton, Washington
Comments/research tips: Probate Court has Birth and Death records 1888–1893, Marriage records 1803–1833, Wills 1849–1860, and a book by the genealogy society of Marriages 1834–1910. Courthouse burned in 1910, some records saved, some as early as 1796. records of several adjacent counties prior to their formation included.

Record Type	Year Begun	Jurisdiction
Divorce	1910	Clerk of Courts
Land	1797	County Recorder
Probate	1910	Probate Court
Court	1910	Clerk of Courts

■ Allen 12 Feb. 1820
301 N. Main St., Lima, OH 45801
Phone: (419)223-8517
Web site: www.co.allen.oh.us/

Parent County: Shelby, Logan, Mercer
Comments/research tips: Probate Court has Birth and Death records 1867–1908. County Museum has Naturalization records 1830s–1870s.

Record Type	Year Begun	Jurisdiction
Marriage	1831	Probate Court
Divorce	1831	Clerk of Courts
Probate	1831	Probate Court
Court	1831	Clerk of Courts

■ Ashland   24 Feb. 1846

Second St., Ashland, OH 44805
Phone: (419)289-0000
Web site: www.ashlandcounty.org/
Parent County: Wayne, Richland, Huron, Lorain
Comments/research tips: Probate Court has Birth records 1879–1908 and Death records 1867–1908. Clerk of Courts has Court and Divorce records from mid 1800s.

Record Type	Year Begun	Jurisdiction
Marriage	1846	Probate Court
Land	1846	County Recorder
Probate	1846	Probate Court

■ Ashtabula   10 Feb. 1808

25 W. Jefferson St., Jefferson, OH 44047
Phone: (440)576-3637
Web site: www.co.ashtabula.oh.us/
Parent County: Trumbull, Geauga
Comments/research tips: Probate Court has Birth and Death records 1867–1908.

Record Type	Year Begun	Jurisdiction
Marriage	1812	Probate Court
Divorce	1811	Clerk of Courts
Land	1798	County Recorder
Probate	1811	Probate Court
Court	1811	Clerk of Courts

■ Athens   20 Feb. 1805

Court & Washington Sts., P.O. Box 290, Athens, OH 45701-0000
Phone: (740)592-3242
Web site: www.seorf.ohiou.edu/athens_county.html
Parent County: Washington
Comments/research tips: Probate Court has Birth and some Death records 1867–1908.

Record Type	Year Begun	Jurisdiction
Marriage	1817	Probate Court
Divorce	ca. 1800	Alden Library Archives
Land	1792	County Recorder
Probate	1800	Probate Court
Court	1807	Clerk of Courts

■ Auglaize   14 Feb. 1848

201 Willipie St. Suite 103, Wapakoneta, OH 45895
Phone: (419)738-7710
Web site: www.genweb.brightusa.net/index.html
Parent County: Allen, Mercer
Comments/research tips: Probate Court has Birth and Death records 1867–1908.

Record Type	Year Begun	Jurisdiction
Marriage	1848	Probate Court
Divorce	1848	Clerk of Courts
Land	ca. 1830	County Recorder
Probate	1852	Probate Court
Court	1848	Clerk of Courts

■ Belmont   7 Sep. 1801

101 W. Main St., St. Clairsville, OH 43950-1225
Phone: (740)699-2169
Web site: www.belmontcountyohio.org/
Parent County: Jefferson, Washington
Comments/research tips: Probate Court has Birth and Death records 1867–1908. Divorce records will be in journals from 1803–1897. St. Clairsville Library has Cemetery/Tombstone records.

Record Type	Year Begun	Jurisdiction
Marriage	1803	Probate Court
Probate	1804	Probate Court
Court	1804	Clerk of Courts

■ Brown   27 Dec. 1818

101 S. Main St., Georgetown, OH 45121
Phone: (937)378-6549
Web site: www.rootsweb.com/~ohbrown/index/htm
Parent County: Adams, Clermont
Comments/research tips: Probate Court has Birth and Death records 1867–1908.

Record Type	Year Begun	Jurisdiction
Marriage	1818	Probate Court
Divorce	ca.1800	Clerk of Courts
Land	1818	County Recorder
Probate	1817	Probate Court
Court	1818	Clerk of Courts

■ Butler   24 Mar. 1803

315 S. High St., Hamilton, OH 45011
Phone: (513)887-3278
Web site: www.butlercountyohio.org/
Parent County: Hamilton
Comments/research tips: Butler County Health Department has Birth and Death records 1914–present, City of Hamilton Health Department 1913–present, and City of Middletown 1885–present. City of Hamilton and County Birth and Death records 1909–1912 were lost in a flood. Probate Court has Birth and Death records 1867–1908 plus other record types prior to 1976.

Record Type	Year Begun	Jurisdiction
Marriage	1803	Probate Court
Divorce	1976	Clerk of Courts
Land	1803	County Recorder
Probate	1851	Probate Court

■ Carroll   25 Dec. 1833

119 S. Lisbon St., Carrollton, OH 44615
Phone: (330)627-2323
Web site: pages.eohio.net/carrcomm/
Parent County: Columbiana, Stark, Harrison, Jefferson, Tuscarawas

Comments/research tips: Probate Court has Birth and Death records 1867–1909. All public records other than Land records prior to years noted are housed at the Genealogy Building on Second Street.

Record Type	Year Begun	Jurisdiction
Divorce	1833	Clerk of Courts
Land	1826	County Recorder
Probate	1833	Probate Court
Court	1833	Probate Court
Marriage	1833	Court Clerk

■ **Champaign** 20 Feb. 1805
200 N. Main St., Urbana, OH 43078
Phone: (937)652-2108
Web site: www.rootsweb.com/~ohchampa/
Parent County: Greene, Franklin
Comments/research tips: Court Clerk has Birth and Death records 1867–1908.

Record Type	Year Begun	Jurisdiction
Marriage	1805	Court Clerk
Divorce	ca. 1800	Clerk of Courts
Land	1806	County Recorder
Probate	1804	Circuit Court Clerk
Court	1805	Circuit Court Clerk

■ **Clark** 26 Dec. 1818
31 N. Limestone St., Springfield, OH 45501
Phone: (937)328-2445
Web site: www.rootsweb.com/~ohclark/
Parent County: Champaign, Madison, Greene
Comments/research tips: Court Clerk has Birth and Death records 1867–1908 and Naturalization records 1861–1904. Clerk of Courts has Divorce records late 1880s–1990. The Heritage Center houses the Clark County Historical Society, a genealogy department and library.

Record Type	Year Begun	Jurisdiction
Marriage	1818	Court Clerk
Land	1818	County Recorder
Probate	1818	Circuit Court Clerk
Court	1818	Circuit Court Clerk

■ **Clermont** 6 Dec. 1800
101 E. Main St., Batavia, OH 45103
Phone: (513)732-7236
Web site: www.co.clermont.oh.us/
Parent County: Hamilton
Comments/research tips: Court Clerk has Birth and Death records 1867–1908.

Record Type	Year Begun	Jurisdiction
Marriage	1800	Court Clerk
Divorce	1861	Clerk of Courts
Probate	1801	Circuit Court Clerk
Court	1801	Circuit Court Clerk
Nat.	ca.1860	Probate Court
Land	1800	County Recorder

■ **Clinton** 19 Feb. 1810
46 S. South St., Wilmington, OH 45177
Phone: (937)382-2280

Web site: www.rootsweb.com/~ohclinto/
Parent County: Highland, Warren
Comments/research tips: Court Clerk has Birth and Death records 1867–1908. A lot of the original Birth, Death and Marriage records are kept at the Records Center on Nelson Avenue.

Record Type	Year Begun	Jurisdiction
Birth	1908	Dept./Health
Marriage	1817	Court Clerk
Death	1908	Dept./Health
Divorce	1810	Clerk of Courts
Land	1806	County Recorder
Probate	1810	Circuit Court Clerk
Court	1810	Circuit Court Clerk

■ **Columbiana** 25 Mar. 1803
105 S. Market St., Lisbon, OH 44432
Phone: (330)424-9511
Web site: www.rootsweb.com/~ohcolumb/index.htm
Parent County: Jefferson
Comments/research tips: Probate has Birth and Death records 1867–1908. Birth and Death records from 1909 to the present are located at the City or County Health Departments of Salem City, East Liverpool City, or East Palestine City. Clerk of Courts has Naturalization records 1840–1970.

Record Type	Year Begun	Jurisdiction
Marriage	1803	Court Clerk
Divorce	na	Clerk of Courts
Land	1798	County Recorder
Probate	1803	Circuit Court Clerk
Court	1803	Circuit Court Clerk

■ **Coshocton** 31 Jan. 1810
426 Main St., Coshocton, OH 43812
Phone: (740)622-1837
Web site: www.co.coshocton.oh.us/
Parent County: Tuscarawas, Muskingum
Comments/research tips: Probate has Birth and Death records 1867–1908. Common Pleas has some Naturalization records from 1912.

Record Type	Year Begun	Jurisdiction
Marriage	1811	Court Clerk
Divorce	1811	Clerk of Courts
Land	1800	County Recorder
Probate	1811	Circuit Court Clerk
Court	1811	Circuit Court Clerk

■ **Crawford** 12 Feb. 1820
112 E. Mansfield St., Bucyrus, OH 44820
Phone: (419)562-8891
Web site: www.rootsweb.com/~ohcrawfo/index.htm
Parent County: Seneca, Sandusky, Marion
Comments/research tips: Probate Judge has Birth and Death records 1867–1908. Galion City Health Department has Birth and Death records for the city only from 1909 to the present. The County Health Department has all others.

Record Type	Year Begun	Jurisdiction
Marriage	1831	Court Clerk

Ohio

Record Type	Year Begun	Jurisdiction
Divorce	1834	Clerk of Courts
Land	1816	County Recorder
Probate	1831	Circuit Court Clerk
Court	1831	Circuit Court Clerk

■ Cuyahoga 10 Feb. 1808

1 Lakeside Ave., Cleveland, OH 44113
Phone: (216)443-8764
Web site: www.cuyahoga.oh.us/home/default.asp
Parent County: Geauga
Comments/research tips: Probate Court has Birth and Death records 1868–1908. Western Reserve Historical Society has Marriage records 1810–1941 and Tax records 1819–1869. County County Archives has Naturalization records 1818–1971. Clerk of Courts has Divorce records 1837–1925.

Record Type	Year Begun	Jurisdiction
Land	1810	County Recorder
Probate	1811	Probate Court

■ Darke 3 Jan. 1809

504 S. Broadway St., Greenville, OH 45331
Phone: (937)547-7390
Web site: www.calweb.com/~wally/ohdarke/index.htm
Parent County: Miami
Comments/research tips: Court Clerk has Birth and Death records 1867–1908. County Recorder has Burial records (veterans graves) from 1832.

Record Type	Year Begun	Jurisdiction
Marriage	1817	Court Clerk
Divorce	ca. 1800	Clerk of Courts
Land	1822	County Recorder
Probate	1818	Circuit Court Clerk
Court	1817	Circuit Court Clerk

■ Defiance 4 Mar. 1845

221 Clinton St., Defiance, OH 43512
Phone: (419)782-4181
Web site: www.rootsweb.com/~ohdefian/index.html
Parent County: Williams, Henry, Paulding
Comments/research tips: Court Clerk has Birth and Death records 1867–1908, Naturalization records 1872–1903, Military Discharge records 1865–1974, and Circuit Court Clerk Probate and Court records of closed cases from 1845 to the present. Active cases are at the courts.

Record Type	Year Begun	Jurisdiction
Marriage	1845	Court Clerk
Divorce	1845	County Records Center
Land	1823	County Recorder

■ Delaware 10 Feb. 1808

91 N. Sandusky St., Delaware, OH 43015
Phone: (740)369-8761
Web site: www.co.delaware.oh.us/
Parent County: Franklin
Comments/research tips: Court Clerk has Birth and Death records 1867–1908, Marriage records 1835–1995. Genealogical Society has Court records 1835–1883.

Record Type	Year Begun	Jurisdiction
Divorce	1825	Records Center

Record Type	Year Begun	Jurisdiction
Land	na	County Recorder
Probate	1812	Circuit Court Clerk

■ Erie 15 Mar. 1838

323 Columbus Ave., Sandusky, OH 44870
Phone: (419)627-7750
Web site: www.erie-county-ohio.net/
Parent County: Huron, Sandusky
Comments/research tips: Probate Court has Birth and Death records 1856–1908.

Record Type	Year Begun	Jurisdiction
Marriage	1838	Probate Court
Divorce	1838	Clerk of Courts
Land	1837	County Recorder
Probate	1838	Probate Court
Court	1838	Circuit Court Clerk

■ Fairfield 9 Dec. 1800

224 E. Main St., Lancaster, OH 43130
Phone: (740)687-7090
Web site: www.co.fairfield.oh.us/
Parent County: Ross, Washington
Comments/research tips: Probate Court has Birth records 1867–1909.

Record Type	Year Begun	Jurisdiction
Marriage	1803	Probate Court
Divorce	1803	Clerk of Courts
Land	1801	County Recorder
Probate	1803	Probate Court
Court	1801	Clerk of Courts

■ Fayette 19 Feb. 1810

110 E. Court St., Washington Court House, OH 43160
Phone: (740)333-0720
Web site: www.fayette-co-oh.com/
Parent County: Ross, Highland
Comments/research tips: Probate Court has Birth and Death records 1867–1908. Records lost in 1828 court house fire.

Record Type	Year Begun	Jurisdiction
Divorce	na	County Archives
Land	1810	County Recorder
Probate	1810	Probate Court
Court	1882	Clerk of Courts
Marriage	1810	Probate Court

■ Franklin 30 Mar. 1803

373 S. High St., Columbus, OH 43215
Phone: (614)462-3322
Web site: www.co.franklin.oh.us/
Parent County: Ross, Unorganized land
Comments/research tips: Probate Court has Birth and Death records before 1867–1908 and Probate records 1803–1944.

Record Type	Year Begun	Jurisdiction
Marriage	1803	Probate Court
Divorce	1820	Clerk of Courts
Land	1800	County Recorder
Court	1803	Clerk of Courts

■ Fulton 28 Feb. 1850

210 S. Fulton St., Wauseon, OH 43567
Phone: (419)337-9242

Web site: www.fultoncountyoh.com/
Parent County: Lucas, Henry, Williams
Comments/research tips: Probate Court has Birth and Death records 1867–1908 and Naturalization records ca. 1867–1908.

Record Type	Year Begun	Jurisdiction
Marriage	1864	Probate Court
Divorce	1850	Clerk of Courts
Land	1835	County Recorder
Probate	1853	Probate Court
Court	na	Clerk of Courts
Military Bur.	ca. 1850	County Recorder

■ Gallia 25 Mar. 1803

18 Locust St., Gallipolis, OH 45631
Phone: (740)446-3842
Web site: www.rootsweb.com/~ohgallia/gallia.htm
Parent County: Washington
Comments/research tips: Probate Judge has Birth and Death records 1867–1908.

Record Type	Year Begun	Jurisdiction
Divorce	1870	Clerk of Courts
Land	1803	County Recorder
Probate	1803	Probate Court
Court	1811	Clerk of Courts
Marriage	1803	Probate Court

■ Geauga 31 Dec. 1806

100 Short Ct., Chardon, OH 44024
Phone: (440)285-2222
Web site: www.co.geauga.oh.us/
Parent County: Trumbull
Comments/research tips: Probate Court has Birth and Death records 1867–1908.

Record Type	Year Begun	Jurisdiction
Marriage	1806	Probate Court
Divorce	1806	Clerk of Courts
Land	1795	County Recorder
Probate	1806	Probate Court
Court	1806	Clerk of Courts

■ Greene 24 Mar. 1803

45 N. Detroit St., Xenia, OH 45385
Phone: (937)562-5280
Web site: www.co.greene.oh.us/
Parent County: Hamilton, Ross
Comments/research tips: Probate Court has Birth and Death records 1869–1908. Greene County Library (www.gcpl.lib.oh.us) has more than 85,000 Obituaries, Birth and Death records 1869–1908, Marriage records 1803–1968, Wills and Estates 1803–1950, and Land records 1803–1940.

Record Type	Year Begun	Jurisdiction
Marriage	1803	Probate Court
Divorce	1802	Clerk of Courts
Land	1798	County Recorder
Probate	1803	Probate Court
Tax	1803	County Auditor
Court	1802	Clerk of Courts

■ Guernsey 31 Jan. 1810

801 Wheeling Ave., Cambridge, OH 43725
Phone: (740)432-9200
Web site: www.usgennet.org/usa/oh/county/guernsey/
Parent County: Belmont, Muskingum
Comments/research tips: Probate Court has Birth and Death records 1867–1909.

Record Type	Year Begun	Jurisdiction
Marriage	1810	Probate Court
Divorce	1850	Clerk of Courts
Land	1802	County Recorder
Probate	1812	Probate Court
Court	1802	Clerk of Courts

■ Hamilton 2 Jan. 1790

1000 Main St., Cincinnati, OH 45202
Phone: (513)632-6500
Web site: www.hamilton-co.org/
Parent County: Original county
Comments/research tips: Probate Court has Birth records 1867–1908 and has Death records 1882–1908. Clerk of Courts has Court records from mid 1800s. Records 1791–1884 incomplete due to fire etc.

Record Type	Year Begun	Jurisdiction
Marriage	1808	Probate Court
Divorce	ca. 1830	Clerk of Courts
Land	1787	County Recorder
Probate	1790	Probate Court

■ Hancock 12 Feb. 1820

300 S. Main St., Findlay, OH 45840
Phone: (419)424-7037
Web site: www.co.hancock.oh.us/
Parent County: Logan, Delaware, Wood
Comments/research tips: Probate Judge has Birth and Death records 1867–1908.

Record Type	Year Begun	Jurisdiction
Marriage	1828	Probate Court
Land	1820	County Recorder
Probate	1828	Probate Court
Divorce	ca. 1830	Clerk of Courts
Court	1828	Clerk of Courts

■ Hardin 12 Feb. 1820

1 Courthouse Sq. Suite 210, Kenton, OH 43326
Phone: (419)674-2252
Web site: www.kenton.com/users/chuck/index.htm
Parent County: Logan, Delaware
Comments/research tips: Probate Court has Birth and Death records 1867–1908. Clerk of Courts has Court and Divorce records from mid 1800s.

Record Type	Year Begun	Jurisdiction
Marriage	1833	Probate Court
Death	na	Probate Court
Divorce	1864	Clerk of Courts
Land	1831	County Recorder
Probate	1830	Probate Court
Court	1833	Clerk of Courts

Ohio

■ Harrison 2 Jan. 1813

100 W. Market St., Cadiz, OH 43907-1132

Phone: (740)942-8863

Web site: Future website at scioto.org/OHGenWeb/ohiomap.html

Parent County: Jefferson, Tuscarawas

Comments/research tips: Probate Court has Birth and Death records 1867–1990.

Record Type	Year Begun	Jurisdiction
Marriage	na	Probate Court
Divorce	1819	Clerk of Courts
Land	na	County Recorder
Probate	na	Probate Court
Court	na	Clerk of Courts

■ Henry 12 Feb. 1820

660 N. Perry St., Napoleon, OH 43545

Phone: (419)592-4876

Web site: www.rootsweb.com/~ohhenry/

Parent County: Shelby, Logan, Wood, Williams

Comments/research tips: Probate Court has Birth and Death records 1867–1908. Henry County was attached to Wood and Williams Counties from 1820–1834. Early Court records could be found there.

Record Type	Year Begun	Jurisdiction
Marriage	1847	Probate Court
Divorce	1860	Clerk of Courts
Land	1846	County Recorder
Probate	1847	Probate Court
Court	1847	Clerk of Courts

■ Highland 18 Feb. 1805

105 N. High St., Hillsboro, OH 45133

Phone: (937)393-1941

Web site: www.usgennet.org/usa/oh/county/highland/

Parent County: Ross, Adams, Clermont

Comments/research tips: Probate Court has Birth and Death records 1867–1908. Clerk of Courts has some Naturalization. Recorder's office has some Military Discharge and some Burial records. Probate Court has Probate records ca. 1800–ca. 1810.

Record Type	Year Begun	Jurisdiction
Birth	1909	Dept./Health
Marriage	1805	Probate Court
Death	1909	Dept./Health
Divorce	1805	Clerk of Courts
Land	1804	County Recorder
Court	1805	Clerk of Courts

■ Hocking 3 Jan. 1818

1 E. Main St., Logan, OH 43138

Phone: (740)385-3022

Web site: www.co.hocking.oh.us/

Parent County: Athens, Ross, Fairfield

Comments/research tips: Probate Court has Birth records 1867–1909, Death records 1867–1908, and Marriage records 1818–1990.

Record Type	Year Begun	Jurisdiction
Divorce	1873	Clerk of Courts

Land	1818	County Recorder
Probate	1819	Probate Court
Court	1818	Clerk of Courts

■ Holmes 20 Jan. 1824

1 E. Jackson St., Millersburg, OH 44654

Phone: (330)674-0286

Web site: www.holmescounty.com/gov/

Parent County: Coshocton, Wayne, Tuscarawas

Comments/research tips: Probate Court has Birth and Death records 1867–1908.

Record Type	Year Begun	Jurisdiction
Marriage	na	Probate Court
Land	na	County Recorder
Probate	na	Probate Court
Court	na	Clerk of Courts
Burial	ca. 1825	County Library
Military	1825	County Recorder

■ Huron 7 Feb. 1809

2 E. Main St., Norwalk, OH 44857

Phone: (419)668-5113

Web site: www.hccommissioners.com/homepage.htm

Parent County: Portage, Geauga

Comments/research tips: Probate Court has Birth and Death records 1867–1908, Name Changes and Clergy records 1823–1976, and Naturalization records 1859–1899. County Recorder has Connecticut Fire Sufferers records 1792–1808. County Auditor has Infirmary records 1848–1974, Tax records 1815–1825, Land Partition records 1815–1920, County Militia lists 1864–1865, and Indigent Soldier Burial records 1880–1920. County Clerk has Divorce records 1815–1859.

Record Type	Year Begun	Jurisdiction
Marriage	1816	Probate Court
Land	1809	County Recorder
Probate	1815	Probate Court
Tax	1820	County Auditor
Court	1818	Clerk of Courts
Military	1865	County Recorder

■ Jackson 12 Jan. 1816

226 E. Main St., Jackson, OH 45640

Phone: (740)286-3301

Web site: www.rootsweb.com/~ohjackso/jackson.htm

Parent County: Scioto, Gallia, Athens, Ross

Comments/research tips: Probate Court has Birth and Death records 1867–1908.

Record Type	Year Begun	Jurisdiction
Marriage	1816	Probate Court
Divorce	ca. 1800	Clerk of Courts
Land	1816	County Recorder
Probate	1819	Probate Court
Court	1816	Clerk of Courts

■ Jefferson 27 July 1797

301 Market St., Steubenville, OH 43952

Phone: (740)283-8583

Web site: www.rootsweb.com/~ohjeffer/

Parent County: Washington
Comments/research tips: Probate Judge has Birth and Death records 1867–1908 and Naturalization records 1863–1903. Kent State University Library has Naturalization records 1800–1863. Clerk of Courts has Naturalization records 1903–1939.

Record Type	Year Begun	Jurisdiction
Marriage	1816	Probate Court
Divorce	1797	Clerk of Courts
Land	1816	County Recorder
Probate	1819	Probate Court
Court	1816	Clerk of Courts

■ Knox   30 Jan. 1808
111 E. High St., Mount Vernon, OH 43050
Phone: (740)393-6796
Web site: www.knoxcountyohio.org/
Parent County: Fairfield, Franklin
Comments/research tips: Probate Court has Birth and Death records 1867–1908.

Record Type	Year Begun	Jurisdiction
Marriage	1808	Probate Court
Divorce	1808	Clerk of Courts
Land	1808	County Recorder
Probate	1808	Probate Court
Court	1808	Clerk of Courts

■ Lake   6 Mar. 1840
25 N. Park Pl., Painesville, OH 44077
Phone: (440)350-2626
Web site: www.rootsweb.com/~ohlake/
Parent County: Geauga, Cuyahoga
Comments/research tips: Probate Court has Birth and Death records 1867–1908.

Record Type	Year Begun	Jurisdiction
Marriage	1840	Probate Court
Land	1839	County Recorder
Probate	1853	Probate Court
Court	1840	Clerk of Courts
Divorce	1840	Clerk of Courts

■ Lawrence   21 Dec. 1815
1 Veterans Sq., Ironton, OH 45638
Phone: (740)533-4300
Web site: www.db.k12.oh.us/community/lcc_1.htm
Parent County: Gallia, Scioto
Comments/research tips: Probate Court has Birth records 1868–1938 and Death records 1868–1933.

Record Type	Year Begun	Jurisdiction
Marriage	na	Probate Court
Land	na	County Recorder
Probate	na	Probate Court
Court	na	Clerk of Courts

■ Licking   30 Jan. 1808
Public Sq. First Floor, Newark, OH 43055
Phone: (740)349-6125
Web site: www.lcounty.com/
Parent County: Fairfield

Comments/research tips: Probate Court has Birth records 1867–1908 and Marriage records 1808–1828. County Health Department has Death recordss 1882–1908.

Record Type	Year Begun	Jurisdiction
Divorce	1876	Clerk of Courts
Land	1800	County Recorder
Probate	1875	Probate Court
Court	1809	Clerk of Courts

■ Logan   30 Dec. 1818
101 S. Main St. Courthouse, Bellefontaine, OH 43311
Phone: (937)599-7275
Web site: www.co.logan.oh.us/
Parent County: Champaign
Comments/research tips: Probate Court has Birth and Death records 1867–1908.

Record Type	Year Begun	Jurisdiction
Marriage	1818	Probate Court
Divorce	1942	Domestic Court
Land	1810	County Recorder
Probate	1851	Probate Court
Court	1804	Clerk of Courts

■ Lorain   26 Dec. 1822
226 Middle Ave., Elyria, OH 44035
Phone: (440)329-5176
Web site: www.centurytel.net/lorgen/
Parent County: Elyria
Comments/research tips: Probate Court has Birth and Death records 1867–1908 and Indigent Soldier Burial records 1926–1927. Elyria Public Library and Lorain County Historical Society have books of genealogical interest.

Record Type	Year Begun	Jurisdiction
Marriage	1824	Probate Court
Divorce	1854	Clerk of Courts
Land	na	County Recorder
Probate	1840	Probate Court
Court	1824	Clerk of Courts

■ Lucas   20 June 1835
700 Adams St., Toledo, OH 43624
Phone: (419)213-4775
Web site: co.lucas.oh.us/
Parent County: Wood, Sandusky
Comments/research tips: Probate Court has Birth records 1865–1908 and Death records 1867–1908.

Record Type	Year Begun	Jurisdiction
Marriage	1835	Probate Court
Divorce	1835	Clerk of Courts
Land	1808	County Recorder
Probate	1835	Probate Court
Court	1835	Clerk of Courts

■ Madison   16 Feb. 1810
1 N. Main St., London, OH 43140
Phone: (740)852-2972
Web site: www.co.madison.oh.us/
Parent County: Franklin
Comments/research tips: Probate Court has Birth and Death records 1865–1908.

Record Type	Year Begun	Jurisdiction
Marriage	1810	Probate Court
Divorce	na	Clerk of Courts
Land	1810	County Recorder
Probate	1810	Probate Court
Court	1810	Clerk of Courts
Nat.	1860	Probate Court
Military	1865	County Recorder

■ Mahoning 16 Feb. 1846
120 Market St., Youngstown, OH 44503
Phone: (330)740-2130
Web site: mahoningcountygov.com/
Parent County: Columbiana, Trumbull
Comments/research tips: Probate Court has Birth and Death records 1847–1908.

Record Type	Year Begun	Jurisdiction
Marriage	1846	Probate Court
Divorce	1846	Clerk of Courts
Land	1795	County Recorder
Probate	1846	Probate Court
Court	1847	Clerk of Courts

■ Marion 12 Feb. 1820
114 N. Main St., Marion, OH 43302
Phone: (740)223-4260
Web site: www.mariononline.com/county/
Parent County: Delaware
Comments/research tips: Probate Court has Birth and Death records 1867–1908 and Marriage certificates 1824–1920. Ohio Historical Society in Columbus has original Marriage certificates.

Record Type	Year Begun	Jurisdiction
Divorce	na	Clerk of Courts
Land	1821	County Recorder
Probate	1825	Probate Court
Court	1824	Clerk of Courts

■ Medina 18 Feb. 1812
93 Public Sq., Medina, OH 44256
Phone: (330)725-9703
Web site: www.co.medina.oh.us/
Parent County: Portage
Comments/research tips: Probate Court has Birth and Death records 1867–1908.

Record Type	Year Begun	Jurisdiction
Marriage	1818	Probate Court
Land	1818	County Recorder
Probate	1818	Probate Court
Court	1818	Clerk of Courts
Divorce	1818	Clerk of Courts

■ Meigs 21 Jan. 1819
100 E. Second St., Pomeroy, OH 45769
Phone: (740)992-3096
Web site: genealogy.rootsweb.com/~baf/meigs.html
Parent County: Gallia, Athens
Comments/research tips: Probate Court has Birth and Death records 1865–1909 and Marriage records 1819–1930.

Record Type	Year Begun	Jurisdiction
Divorce	ca. 1800	Clerk of Courts
Land	1819	County Recorder
Probate	1820	Probate Court
Court	1819	Clerk of Courts

■ Mercer 12 Feb. 1820
101 N. Main St., Celina, OH 45822
Phone: (419)586-8779
Web site: www.mercercountyohio.org/
Parent County: Darke, Shelby
Comments/research tips: Probate Court has Birth and Death records 1867–1908. Wright State University in Dayton has some Naturalization records 1852–1930 and some Supreme Court cases 1825–1873.

Record Type	Year Begun	Jurisdiction
Marriage	1838	Probate Court
Divorce	1850	Clerk of Courts
Land	1823	County Recorder
Probate	1824	Probate Court
Court	1824	Clerk of Courts

■ Miami 16 Jan. 1807
201 W. Main St., Troy, OH 45373
Phone: (937)332-6823
Web site: www.co.miami.oh.us/
Parent County: Montgomery
Comments/research tips: Probate Court has Birth and Death records 1853–1908. City of Piqua Health Department has Birth and Death records for the city of Piqua.

Record Type	Year Begun	Jurisdiction
Marriage	1807	Probate Court
Divorce	1807	Clerk of Courts
Land	1807	County Recorder
Probate	1807	Probate Court
Court	1804	Clerk of Courts

■ Monroe 29 Jan. 1813
101 N. Main St., Woodsfield, OH 43793
Phone: (740)472-0873
Web site: www.rootsweb.com/~ohmonroe/
Parent County: Belmont
Comments/research tips: Probate Court has Birth and Death records 1867–1908.

Record Type	Year Begun	Jurisdiction
Marriage	1866	Probate Court
Land	1836	County Recorder
Probate	na	Probate Court

■ Montgomery 24 Mar. 1803
41 N. Perry, Dayton, OH 45402
Phone: (937)225-4400
Web site: www.mcohio.org
Parent County: Hamilton
Comments/research tips: The Records Center in the Riebold Building in Dayton has all old records. Probate Court has Birth and Death records 1867–1908.

Record Type	Year Begun	Jurisdiction
Marriage	1803	Probate Court

Ohio

Divorce	1991	Clerk of Courts
Land	1805	County Recorder
Probate	1803	Probate Court
Court	1803	Clerk of Courts

■ Morgan 29 Dec. 1817
19 E. Main St., McConnelsville, OH 43756
Phone: (740)962-3183
Web site: www.rootsweb.com/~ohmorgan/index.htm
Parent County: Washington, Guernsey, Muskingum
Comments/research tips: Probate Court has Birth and Death records 1867–1908.

Record Type	Year Begun	Jurisdiction
Marriage	1819	Probate Court
Land	1795	County Recorder
Probate	1819	Probate Court

■ Morrow 24 Feb. 1848
48 E. High St., Mount Gilead, OH 43338
Phone: (419)947-5575
Web site: www.rootsweb.com/~ohmorrow/
Parent County: Knox, Marion, Delaware, Richland
Comments/research tips: Probate Court has Birth and Death records 1867–1908 and random Naturalization records. Common Pleas Court records prior to February 1970 need to be pulled and sent from Mansfield.

Record Type	Year Begun	Jurisdiction
Marriage	1848	Probate Court
Divorce	ca. 1850	Common Pleas Court
Land	1848	County Recorder
Probate	1848	Probate Court
Court	1848	Clerk of Courts
Military	1846	County Recorder

■ Muskingum 7 Jan. 1804
401 Main St., Zanesville, OH 43701
Phone: (740)455-7104
Web site: www.rootsweb.com/~ohmuskin/
Parent County: Washington, Fairfield
Comments/research tips: Probate Court has Birth and Death records 1867–1908. Probate Court has Naturalization records 1860–1940.

Record Type	Year Begun	Jurisdiction
Marriage	1804	Probate Court
Divorce	1846	Clerk of Courts
Land	1800	County Recorder
Probate	1804	Probate Court
Court	1804	Clerk of Courts
Military	1864	County Recorder

■ Noble 11 Mar. 1851
270 Courthouse Sq., Caldwell, OH 43724
Phone: (614)732-2969
Web site: www.rootsweb.com/~ohnoble/index.htm
Parent County: Monroe, Washington, Morgan, Guernsey
Comments/research tips: Probate has Birth and Death records 1867–1908.

Record Type	Year Begun	Jurisdiction
Marriage	1851	Probate Court

Divorce	1851	Clerk of Courts
Land	1851	County Recorder
Probate	1851	Probate Court
Court	1851	Clerk of Courts

■ Ottawa 6 Mar. 1840
315 Madison St. Room 304, Port Clinton, OH 43452
Phone: (419)734-6830
Web site: www.co.ottawa.oh.us/OCHome/OCFrameset.htm
Parent County: Erie, Sandusky, Lucas
Comments/research tips: Probate Court has Birth and Death records 1867–1908. Ohio Historical Society has Death records 1908–1944. Clerk of Courts has Naturalization records 1905–1929.

Record Type	Year Begun	Jurisdiction
Marriage	1840	Probate Court
Divorce	1840	Clerk of Courts
Land	1820	County Recorder
Probate	1840	Probate Court
Court	1840	Clerk of Courts

■ Paulding 12 Feb. 1820
115 N. Williams, Paulding, OH 45879
Phone: (419)399-2051
Web site: Future website at scioto.org/OHGenWeb/ohiomap.html
Parent County: Darke, Shelby, Williams, Darke
Comments/research tips: Probate has Birth and Death records 1867–1908. County Recorder has some Civil War Military Discharge records.

Record Type	Year Begun	Jurisdiction
Marriage	1839	Probate Court
Divorce	1820	Clerk of Courts
Land	1835	County Recorder
Probate	1842	Probate Court
Court	1839	Clerk of Courts

■ Perry 26 Dec. 1818
105 N. Main St., New Lexington, OH 43764
Phone: (740)342-1493
Web site: www.perrygenealogy.net/
Parent County: Washington, Fairfield, Muskingum
Comments/research tips: Probate Court has Birth and Death records 1867–1908.

Record Type	Year Begun	Jurisdiction
Marriage	1818	Probate Court
Land	1818	County Recorder
Probate	1817	Probate Court
Divorce	ca. 1800	Clerk of Courts
Court	1818	Clerk of Courts

■ Pickaway 12 Jan. 1810
217 S. Court St., Circleville, OH 43113
Phone: (740)474-1524
Web site: www.rootsweb.com/~ohpickaw/index.html
Parent County: Ross, Fairfield, Franklin
Comments/research tips: Probate Court has Birth and Death records 1867–1908. Court and Divorce records ca. 1800s.

Record Type	Year Begun	Jurisdiction
Marriage	1810	Probate Court
Land	1810	County Recorder
Probate	1810	Probate Court

■ **Pike** 4 Jan. 1815
100 E. Second St., Waverly, OH 45690
Phone: (740)947-2715
Web site: www.scioto.org/Pike/
Parent County: Ross, Scioto, Adams
Comments/research tips: Probate has Birth and Death records 1867–1909. Ohio Department of Health/Vital Statistics Department has Birth and Death records 1909–ca. 1932.

Record Type	Year Begun	Jurisdiction
Marriage	1815	Probate Court
Divorce	1815	Clerk of Courts
Land	1799	County Recorder
Probate	1817	Probate Court
Court	1815	Clerk of Courts

■ **Portage** 10 Feb. 1808
203 W. Main St., Ravenna, OH 44266
Phone: (330)297-3849
Web site: www.portageworkforce.org/portagecountydirectory/
Parent County: Trumbull
Comments/research tips: Probate Court has Birth and Death records 1867–1908.

Record Type	Year Begun	Jurisdiction
Marriage	1808	Probate Court
Divorce	1885	Clerk of Courts
Land	1795	County Recorder
Probate	1803	Probate Court
Court	1809	Clerk of Courts

■ **Preble** 15 Feb. 1808
100 Main St., Eaton, OH 45320
Phone: (937)456-8160
Web site: www.calweb.com/~wally/preble/index.htm
Parent County: Montgomery, Butler
Comments/research tips: Probate Court has Birth and Death records 1867–1908.

Record Type	Year Begun	Jurisdiction
Marriage	1808	Probate Court
Divorce	ca. 1853	Clerk of Courts
Land	1805	County Recorder
Probate	1808	Probate Court
Court	1808	Clerk of Courts

■ **Putnam** 12 Feb. 1820
245 E. Main St., Ottawa, OH 45875
Phone: (419)523-3656
Web site: www.rootsweb.com/~ohputnam/
Parent County: Shelby, Logan, Wood, Williams
Comments/research tips: Probate Court has Birth and Death records 1867–1920.

Record Type	Year Begun	Jurisdiction
Marriage	1834	Probate Court

Divorce	1834	Clerk of Courts
Land	1830	County Recorder
Probate	1835	Probate Court
Court	1834	Clerk of Courts

■ **Richland** 30 Jan. 1808
50 Park Ave. E., Mansfield, OH 44902
Phone: (419)774-5550
Web site: www.rootsweb.com/~ohrichla/
Parent County: Fairfield, Knox
Comments/research tips: Probate Court has Birth and Death records 1867–1908.

Record Type	Year Begun	Jurisdiction
Marriage	1813	Probate Court
Divorce	1920	Clerk of Courts
Land	1814	County Recorder
Probate	1813	Probate Court
Court	1819	Clerk of Courts

■ **Ross** 20 Aug. 1798
2 N. Paint St., Chillicothe, OH 45601
Phone: (740)702-3010
Web site: www.co.ross.oh.us/
Parent County: Adams, Washington, Hamilton
Comments/research tips: Probate Judge has Birth and Death records 1867–1908.

Record Type	Year Begun	Jurisdiction
Marriage	1798	Probate Court
Land	1797	County Recorder
Probate	1797	Probate Court
Court	1798	Clerk of Courts

■ **Sandusky** 12 Feb. 1820
100 N. Park Ave., Fremont, OH 43420
Phone: (419)334-6377
Web site: www.sandusky-county.org/
Parent County: Huron
Comments/research tips: Probate has Birth and Death records 1867–1908.

Record Type	Year Begun	Jurisdiction
Marriage	1820	Probate Court
Divorce	1868	Clerk of Courts
Land	1822	County Recorder
Probate	1820	Probate Court
Court	1820	Clerk of Courts

■ **Scioto** 24 Mar. 1803
602 Seventh St., Portsmouth, OH 45662
Phone: (740)355-5111
Web site: www.sciotocountyohio.com/
Parent County: Adams
Comments/research tips: Probate has Birth and Death records 1856–1908. Portsmouth Board of Health has Birth and Death records for the city from 1909 while the County Board of Health has Birth and Death records for the rest of the county from 1909.

Record Type	Year Begun	Jurisdiction
Marriage	1804	Probate Court
Divorce	1835	Clerk of Courts

Land .... 1803 ....County Recorder
Probate .... 1804 ....Probate Court
Court .... 1809 ....Clerk of Courts

■ **Seneca**   12 Feb. 1820
103 S. Washington St., Tiffin, OH 44883
Phone: (419)447-4550
Web site: www.rootsweb.com/~ohseneca/seneca.html
Parent County: Huron, Sandusky
Comments/research tips: Probate Court has Birth and Death records 1867–1908.

Record Type	Year Begun	Jurisdiction
Marriage	1841	Probate Court
Divorce	ca. 1800	Clerk of Courts
Land	1821	County Recorder
Probate	1836	Probate Court
Court	1824	Clerk of Courts

■ **Shelby**   7 Jan. 1819
129 E. Court St., Sidney, OH 45365
Phone: (937)498-7226
Web site: www.co.shelby.oh.us/
Parent County: Miami

Record Type	Year Begun	Jurisdiction
Marriage	1824	Probate Court
Land	1819	County Recorder
Probate	1825	Probate Court
Court	1819	Clerk of Courts

■ **Stark**   13 Feb. 1808
110 Central Plaza S., Canton, OH 44702
Phone: (330)438-9904
Web site: www.co.stark.oh.us/
Parent County: Columbiana, Muskingham
Comments/research tips: Probate Court has Birth and Death records 1867–1908.

Record Type	Year Begun	Jurisdiction
Marriage	1809	Probate Court
Land	1809	County Recorder
Probate	1810	Probate Court
Court	1809	Clerk of Courts

■ **Summit**   3 Mar. 1840
209 S. High St., Akron, OH 44308
Phone: (330)379-2512
Web site: www.co.summit.oh.us/
Parent County: Portage, Medina, Stark
Comments/research tips: Probate Court has Birth and Death records 1869–1908. Clerk of Court has Court records from late 1800s.

Record Type	Year Begun	Jurisdiction
Marriage	1840	Probate Court
Land	1840	County Recorder
Probate	1839	Probate Court
Divorce	1902	Domestic Court

■ **Trumbull**   10 July 1800
160 High St. NW, Warren, OH 44481
Phone: (330)675-2557

Web site: www.co.trumbull.oh.us/
Parent County: Jefferson, Wayne, old
Comments/research tips: Probate Court has Birth and Death records 1867–1908.

Record Type	Year Begun	Jurisdiction
Marriage	1803	Probate Court
Divorce	1800	Clerk of Courts
Land	1795	County Recorder
Probate	1803	Probate Court
Court	1807	Clerk of Courts
Nat.	1800	Clerk of Courts

■ **Tuscarawas**   13 Feb. 1808
101 E. High Ave., New Philadelphia, OH 44663
Phone: (330)364-8811
Web site: web1.tusco.net/tuscgen/
Parent County: Muskingum
Comments/research tips: Probate Court has Birth and Death records 1867–1908. Clerk of Courts has Naturalization records 1908–1980.

Record Type	Year Begun	Jurisdiction
Marriage	na	Probate Court
Divorce	1808	Clerk of Courts
Land	na	County Recorder
Probate	na	Probate Court
Court	1808	Clerk of Courts

■ **Union**   10 Jan. 1820
233 W. Sixth St., Marysville, OH 43040
Phone: (937)645-3032
Web site: www.co.union.oh.us/
Parent County: Franklin, Madison, Logan, Delaware
Comments/research tips: Probate Court has Birth and Death records 1867–1908

Record Type	Year Begun	Jurisdiction
Marriage	1820	Probate Court
Land	1811	County Recorder
Probate	1820	Probate Court
Court	1820	Clerk of Courts
Divorce	1821	Clerk of Courts

■ **Van Wert**   12 Feb. 1820
121 E. Main St. 2d Floor, Van Wert, OH 45891
Phone: (419)238-6159
Web site: www.rootsweb.com/~ohvanwer/
Parent County: Darke, Shelby, Mercer
Comments/research tips: Probate Judge has Birth and Death records 1867–1908.

Record Type	Year Begun	Jurisdiction
Marriage	1840	Probate Court
Divorce	na	Clerk of Courts
Land	1824	County Recorder
Probate	1840	Probate Court
Court	1837	Clerk of Courts

■ **Vinton**   23 Mar. 1850
100 E. Main St., McArthur, OH 45651
Phone: (740)596-5480
Web site: www.rootsweb.com/~ohvinton/vinton.htm

Ohio

Parent County: Gallia, Athens, Ross, Jackson, Hocking
Comments/research tips: Probate Court has Birth and Death records 1867–1908.

Record Type	Year Begun	Jurisdiction
Marriage	1850	Probate Court
Divorce	1850	Clerk of Courts
Land	1850	County Recorder
Probate	1852	Probate Court
Court	1850	Clerk of Courts

■ Warren 24 Mar. 1803
570 Justice Dr., Lebanon, OH 45036
Phone: (513)695-1181
Web site: www.co.warren.oh.us/geninfo/index.htm
Parent County: Hamilton
Comments/research tips: Probate Court has Birth and Death records 1867–1908.

Record Type	Year Begun	Jurisdiction
Marriage	1803	Probate Court
Divorce	1803	Clerk of Courts
Land	1795	County Recorder
Probate	1803	Probate Court
Court	1803	Clerk of Courts

■ Washington 27 July 1788
205 Putnam St., Marietta, OH 45750
Phone: (740)373-6623
Web site: www.washingtongov.org/
Parent County: Original County
Comments/research tips: Probate Court has Birth and Death records 1867–1908

Record Type	Year Begun	Jurisdiction
Marriage	1789	Probate Court
Divorce	1787	Clerk of Courts
Land	1788	County Recorder
Probate	1789	Probate Court
Court	1790	Clerk of Courts

■ Wayne 13 Feb. 1808
107 W. Liberty St., Wooster, OH 44691
Phone: (330)287-5575
Web site: www.wooster-wayne.com/county/
Parent County: Columbiana, Stark
Comments/research tips: Probate Court has Birth and Death records 1867–1908.

Record Type	Year Begun	Jurisdiction
Marriage	1813	Probate Court
Divorce	1812	Clerk/Common Pleas Ct.
Land	1813	County Recorder
Probate	1817	Probate Court
Court	1812	Clerk of Courts

■ Wayne, old 15 Aug. 1786
Parent County: Original County
Comments/research tips: This county disappeared from Ohio in 1803 when Ohio became a state. It ultimately became Wayne County, Michigan.

■ Williams 12 Feb. 1820
100 S. Main St., Bryan, OH 43506
Phone: (419)636-1548
Web site: www.co.williams.oh.us/
Parent County: Columbiana, Stark
Comments/research tips: Probate Court has Birth and Death records 1867–1908; Civil Court, Domestic Court and Divorce records 1824–1980; Criminal Court records 1824–1999; Marriage and Probate records 1824–1996; and Naturalization records 1835–1877.

■ Wood 12 Feb. 1820
1 Courthouse Sq., Bowling Green, OH 43402
Phone: (419)354-9280
Web site: www.wcnet.org/wcgovt/
Parent County: Logan
Comments/research tips: Probate Court has Birth and Death records 1867–1908.

Record Type	Year Begun	Jurisdiction
Marriage	1820	Probate Court
Divorce	1851	Clerk of Courts
Land	1820	County Recorder
Probate	1820	Probate Court
Court	1823	Clerk of Courts

■ Wyandot 3 Feb. 1845
County Courthouse, Upper Sandusky, OH 43351
Phone: (419)294-1432
Web site: www.co.wyandot.oh.us/
Parent County: Marion, Crawford, Hardin, Hancock
Comments/research tips: Probate Court has Birth and Death records 1867–1908.

Record Type	Year Begun	Jurisdiction
Marriage	1845	Probate Court
Divorce	1848	Clerk of Courts
Land	1826	County Recorder
Probate	1845	Probate Court
Court	1845	Clerk of Courts

Oklahoma

By Rhonda R. McClure

HISTORICAL OVERVIEW

Oklahoma has the distinction of being the only state that was originally two separate territories. The land that became Oklahoma was originally among the acres purchased by Thomas Jefferson in the Louisiana Purchase, though the panhandle was still under Spanish control in 1803. Oklahoma was then part of Missouri Territory in 1812 and Arkansas Territory in 1819.

In 1830 the western part of the Louisiana Purchase, which included Arkansas Territory (and thus what became Oklahoma), was set aside as Indian Territory. The Indian Removal Act resulted in the resettlement of many Native Americans from the south and southeast into this territory, with the promise that it would be their home, in essence, forever. Of course, after the Civil War, partly in response to the Five Civilized Tribes' support of the Confederacy, the treaties were renegotiated. During this negotiation, approximately two million acres were designated as "Unassigned Lands." In 1889, these lands were purchased from the Native Americans by the federal government and opened up for white settlement, the birth of what would become Oklahoma Territory. From 1890 to 1906 Oklahoma Territory began to absorb a number of reservations and other Native American lands, and in 1907, the "twin territories" were combined to form the new state of Oklahoma.

Though the "Unassigned Lands" were not open for white settlement until 1889, there were many whites who settled in Indian Territory from 1865 to 1889, using loopholes in the law that allowed artisans and professionals to contract with the Native Americans for labor.

RECORD HIGHLIGHTS

Though Oklahoma required statewide registration of births and death from 1908, many of the counties did not comply until 1930. You may discover some county

OKLAHOMA AT A GLANCE

Motto: Labor Conquers All Things

Population: 3.45 million

Prevalent Religions: Baptists by far, also Methodist, Roman Catholic, Lutheran, Presbyterian, Pentecostal, and Episcopalian

Major Industries: Cattle, wheat, milk, poultry, cotton, transportation equipment, machinery, electrical products, rubber and plastic products, food processing

Ethnic Makeup (in percent): Caucasian 76.2%, African American 7.6%, Hispanic 5.2%, Asian 1.4%, Native American 7.9%, Other 2.4%

Famous Oklahomans: Johnny Bench, John Berryman, Garth Brooks, Ralph Ellison, James Garner, Vince Gill, Woody Guthrie, Paul Harvey, Tony Hillerman, Ron Howard, Mickey Mantle, Reba McEntire, Shannon Miller, Bill Moyers, Brad Pitt, Tony Randall, Oral Roberts, Will Rogers, Jim Thorpe, Jeanne Tripplehorn

Above: Skyline of Oklahoma City

© PhotoDisc/Getty Images

Oklahoma

vital records from before 1930, but they are highly incomplete. To request births and deaths from the state, contact the Vital Records Section, State Department of Health, P.O. Box 53551, Oklahoma City, OK 73152, <www.health.state.ok.us/program/vital/brec.html>. They offer Portable Document Format (PDF) versions of their order forms on their Web site.

Marriage records began around 1890 for existing counties, and at the date of creation in counties created later. In the territorial years (1890–1907) a lot of marriages were not recorded, and you will need to check county courthouses in Arkansas, Texas, and Kansas as well.

Land records for whites who settled in the territory before 1889 (the year it became legal for whites to own land there) will be found in the Bureau of Indian Affairs

in the land records for the nation of the Five Civilized Tribes.

In April 1889 the first "land run" offered people the opportunity to race to claim a surveyed section of land on a first-come basis. It is estimated that fifty thousand people settled tracts on the first day of the run. Additional runs would follow in September 1891, April 1892, September 1893, and May 1895. Homestead records can be searched through the Bureau of Land Management-General Land Office's Web site <www.glorecords.blm.gov>, which supplies you with a digitized image of the final patent and all the information necessary to order the land case file from the National Archives. Later land records are found in the county courthouses.

When researching Native American ancestry in Okla-

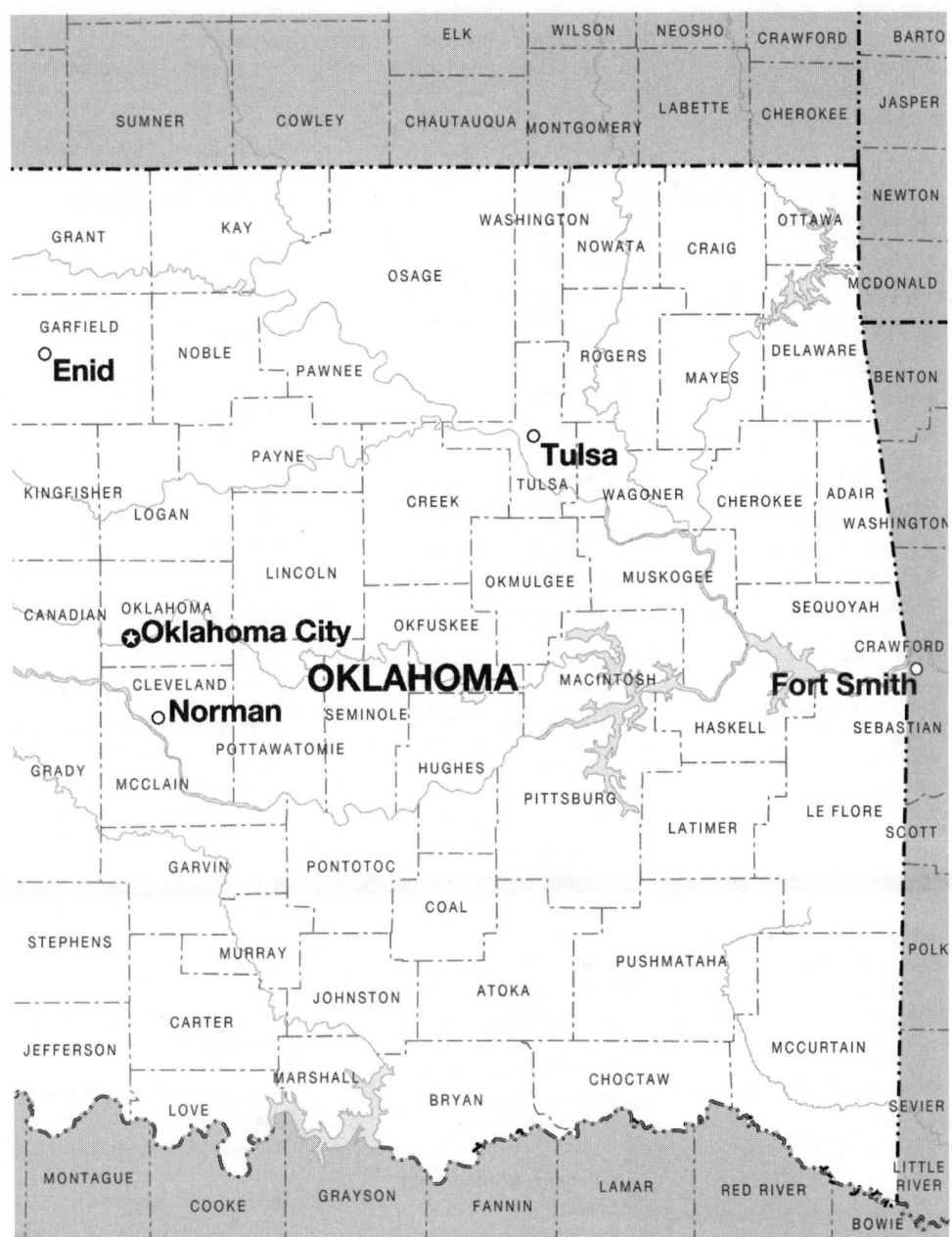

homa, it is important to know the tribe to which your ancestor belonged. Remember that the tribes were self-governing entities for many years, though the federal government did conduct censuses. Other records include land allotment records, which required the applicant to show documentation of Native American descent. The Dawes Commission was established in 1898 to enroll those living in Indian Territory in one of the five tribes. Because of intermarriage of whites and Native Americans, when the U.S. Government began to grant land after the governments of the Five Civilized Tribes dissolved in 1908, there were many whites entitled to receive a portion. The records of the Dawes Commission were used to establish the right to receive land.

STATE RESOURCES

■ ARCHIVES, LIBRARIES, AND SOCIETIES

American Heritage Library
P.O. Box 176, Davis, OK 73030

American Indian Institute
University of Oklahoma, 555 E. Constitution St., Suite 237, Norman, OK 73072-7820
Tel: (405) 325-4127
Web site: <http://tel.occe.ou.edu/aii>

Arbuckle Historical Society
12 Main St., Davis, OK 73030
Tel: (580) 369-2518

Web site: <www.rootsweb.com/~okahs>

Atoka County Library
205 E. A St., Atoka, OK 74525
Tel: (580) 889-3555

Atoka County Genealogical Society
P.O. Box 245, Atoka, OK 74525

Bartlesville Genealogical Society
Sixth and Johnstone Ave., Bartlesville, OK 74003

Bartlesville Public Library
600 S. Johnstone, Bartlesville, OK 74003
Tel: (918) 337-5353
Web site: <www.bartlesville.lib.ok.us>

Beaver River Genealogical and Historical Society
Rt. 1, P.O. Box 79, Hooker, OK 73945

Broken Arrow Genealogical Society Library
P.O. Box 1244, Broken Arrow, OK 74013-1244

Bryan County Heritage Society
P.O. Box 153, Calera, OK 74730

Canadian County Genealogical Society
P.O. Box 866, El Reno, OK 73036
Web site: <www.rootsweb.com/~okccgs>

Carter County Genealogical Society
P.O. Box 1326, Ardmore, OK 73402

Catholic Archdiocese of Oklahoma City
7501 NW Expressway, Oklahoma city, OK 73132
Tel: (405) 721-5651
Web site: <www.catharchdioceseokc.org>

Cherokee City-County Public Library
602 S. Grand Ave., Cherokee, OK 73728
Tel: (580) 596-2366

Chickasha Public Library
527 Iowa Ave., Chickasha, OK 73018
Tel: (405) 222-6075

Choctaw County Genealogical Society
P.O. Box 1056, Hugo, OK 74743
Tel: (580) 326-7359

Web site: <www2.1starnet.com/
choctaw>

**Cleveland County Genealogical
Society**
P.O. Box 6176, Norman, OK
73070

**Coal County Historical and
Genealogical Society**
P.O. Box 436, Coalgate, OK
74538
Tel: (580) 927-3103
Web site: <www.rootsweb.com/
~okcoalgs>

**Craig County Genealogical
Society**
P.O. Box 484, Vinita, OK 74301

Cushing Public Library
P.O. Box 551, 215 N. Steele,
Cushing, OK 74203

**Delaware County Genealogical
Society**
℅ Grove Public Library, 206 S.
Elk St., Grove, OK 74344
Tel: (918) 786-4127

Edmond Genealogical Society
P.O. Box 1984, Edmond, OK
73093-1984
Web site: <www.rootsweb.com/
~okegs>

**Federation of Oklahoma
Genealogical Societies**
P.O. Box 26151, Oklahoma City,
OK 73126

Five Civilized Tribes Museum
Agency Hill, Honor Heights Dr.,
Muskogee, OK 74401
Tel: (918) 683-1701
Web site: <www.fivetribes.com>

**Fort Gibson Genealogical and
Historical Society**
P.O. Box 416, Fort Gibson, OK
74434

**Garfield County Genealogists,
Inc.**
P.O. Box 1106, Enid, OK 73703
Web site: <http://bjsbytes.com/
garfield>

**Grady County Genealogical
Society**
P.O. Box 792, Chickasha, OK
73023

Grant County Historical Society
P.O. Box 127, Medford, OK
73759

**Greer County Genealogical &
Historical Society**
℅ Margaret Carder Library, 201
W. Lincoln, Mangum, OK 73554
Web site: <www.rootsweb.com/
~okgcghs>

**Haskell County Historical and
Genealogical Society**
P.O. Box 481, Stigler, OK 74462
Tel: (918) 967-8681
Web site: <www.rootsweb.com/
~okhaskel/hasksoc.htm>

**Kiowa County Genealogical
Society**
P.O. Box 191, Hobart, OK 73651

Lawton Public Library
110 SW Fourth St., Lawton, OK
73501
Tel: (580) 581-3450
Web site: <www.cityoflawton.ok
.us/library>

**Logan County Genealogical
Society Inc. Library**
P.O. Box 1419, Guthrie, OK
73044
Web site: <www.rootsweb.com/
~oklcgs>

Love County Historical Society
P.O. Box 134, Marietta, OK
73448

**Major County Genealogical
Society and Research Library**
P.O. Box 74, Fairview OK 73737
Web site: <www.rootsweb.com/
~okmajor/mcgs.htm>

**Mayes County Genealogical
Society**
P.O. Box 924, Chouteau, OK
74337

**McClain County Historical and
Genealogical Society**
203 W. Washington St., Purcell,
OK 73080
Tel: (405) 527-5894
Web site: <www.rootsweb.com/
~okmcclai/mchg.htm>

**McCurtain County
Genealogical Society**
P.O. Box 1832, Idebel, OK 74745
Web site: <www.rootsweb.com/
~okmcgs>

Metropolitan Library System
131 Dean McGee Ave., Oklahoma
City, OK 73102
Tel: (405) 231-8650
Web site: <www.mls.lib.ok.us>

Muldrow Genealogical Society
P.O. Box 1253, Muldrow, OK
74938

Muldrow Public Library
711 W. Shawntel Blvd., P.O. Box
449, Muldrow, OK 74948

Museum of the Great Plains
601 NW Ferris, Lawton, OK
73502

**Muskogee County
Genealogical Society**
℅ Muskogee Public Library, 801
W. Okmulgee, Muskogee, OK
74401
Web site: <www.rootsweb.com/
~okmuscgs>

**National Archives-Central
Plains Region (Kansas City)**
2312 E. Bannister Rd., Kansas
City, Missouri 64131
Tel: (816) 926-6272
Web site: <www.archives.gov/fa
cilities/mo/kansas_city.html>

**Noble County Genealogical
Society**
P.O. Box 785, Perry, OK 73077
Web site: <www.rootsweb.com/
~oknoble/histsoci.htm>

**Northwest Oklahoma
Genealogical Society**
P.O. Box 834, Woodward, OK
73802

**Oklahoma Department of
Libraries and State Archives**
200 NE Eighteenth St., Oklahoma
City, OK 73105-3298
Tel: (405) 522-3217
Web site: <www.odl.state.ok.us/
go/pl.asp>

**Oklahoma Genealogical
Society**
P.O. Box 314, Oklahoma City, OK
73101
Web site: <www.rootsweb.com/
~okgs>

Oklahoma Historical Society
2100 N. Lincoln Blvd., Oklahoma
City, OK 73105-4997
Tel: (405) 522-5242
Web site:
**Okmulgee County Genealogical
Society**
P.O. Box 805, Okmulgee, OK
74447

**Ottawa County Genealogical
Society**
P.O. Box 1383, Miami, OK
74355-1383

**Pawhuska Genealogical
Society**
P.O. Box 807, Pawhuska, OK
74056

**Payne County Genealogical
Society**
P.O. Box 2708, Stillwater, OK
74076
Web site: <www.pcgsok.org>

Pioneer Genealogical Society
P.O. Box 1965, Ponca City, OK
74602

**Pittsburg County Genealogical
and Historical Society, Inc.**
113 E. Carl Albert Pkwy., McAlester, OK 74501
Tel: (918) 426-0388
Web site: <www.oil.cwis.net/tob
ucksy/hints.htm>

Ponca City Library
515 E. Grand, Ponca, OK 74601
Tel: (405) 767-0354

**Pontotoc County Historical and
Genealogical Society**
221 W. Sixteenth St., Ada, OK
74820
Web site: <www.rootsweb.com/
~okpontgs>

**Poteau Valley Genealogical
Society**
P.O. Box 1031, Poteau, OK
74953
Web site: <www.rootsweb.com/
~okleflor/pvgs.htm>

**Pushmataha County Historical
Society**
P.O. Box 285, Antler, OK 74523

Ralph Ellison Library
2000 NE Twenty-third St., Oklahoma City, OK 73111
Tel: (405) 424-1437
Web site: <www.mls.lib.ok.us/Li
brary/RE.htm>

**Rogers County Genealogical
Society**
P.O. Box 2493, Claremore, OK
74018

Rudisill North Regional Library
1520 N. Hartford, Tulsa, OK
74106
Tel: (918) 596-7280

Sapulpa Public Library
27 W. Dewey Ave., Sapulpa, OK
74066
Tel: (918) 224-5624
Web site: <www.rootsweb.com/
~okcreek/sapulpa.html>

Seminole Public Library
424 N. Main, Seminole, OK
74868
Tel: (405) 382-4221
E-mail: seminolepl@onenet.net

**Southwest Oklahoma
Genealogical Society**
P.O. Box 148, Lawton, OK
73502-0148
Web site: <www.sirinet.net/~lga
rris/swogs>

State Department of Health
1000 NE Tenth St., P.O. Box
53551, Okalahoma City, OK
73152
Tel: (405) 271-5600
Web site: <www.health.state.ok
.us>

**Stephens County Oklahoma
Genealogical Society**
301 N. Eighth St., Duncan, OK
73533
Tel: (580) 255-8718

Talbot Library & Museum
P.O. Box 349, Colcord, OK 74338

**Three Forks Genealogical
Society**
102 S. State St., Wagoner, OK
74467

**Tulsa City-County Public
Library, Schusterman-Benson
Branch**
3333 E. Thirty-second Pl., Tulsa,
OK 74135
Tel: (918) 746-5024

**Tulsa Genealogical Society and
Library**
P.O. Box 585, Tulsa, OK 74101
Web site: <www.tulsagenealogy
.org>

Tulsa Public Library
220 S. Cheyenne, Tulsa, OK
74103
Web site: <www.tulsalibrary
.org>

Vinita Public Library
215 W. Illinois, Vinita, OK 74301
Tel: (918) 256-2115
Web site: <www.vinitapl.okpls
.org>

Weatherford Public Library
219 E. Franklin, Weatherford, OK
73096
Tel: (580) 772-3591

**Western Trails Genealogical
Society**
P.O. Box 70, Altus, OK 73521
Web site: <www.rootsweb.com/

~okjackso/wtgsweb/wtgshome
.html>

Woods County Genealogists
P.O. Box 234, Alva, OK 73717

BIBLIOGRAPHY

■ GENERAL RESOURCES

*All Along the Chisholm Trail,
2 vols.*
by James W. Parker (Yukon, OK:
J.W. Parker, 1988)

*American Indian Resource
Materials in the Western
History Collections, University
Of Oklahoma*
by Donald L. Dewitt (Norman, OK:
University of Oklahoma Press,
1990)

*An Annotated Guide to the
Chronicles of Oklahoma,
1921–1994*
by Carol Welsh (Oklahoma City:
Oklahoma Historical Society,
1996)

*Bible Belt Catholicism: A
History of The Roman Catholic
Church in Oklahoma,
1905–1945*
by Thomas E. Brown (New York:
United States Catholic Historical
Society, 1977)

*Black Indian Genealogy
Research: African-American
Ancestors Among the Five
Civilized Tribes*
by Angela Y. Walton-Raji (Bowie,
MD: Heritage Books, 1993)

Boundaries of Oklahoma
edited by John W. Morris (Oklahoma City, OK: Oklahoma Historical Society, 1980)

*Catalog Of Microfilm Holdings
in the Archives & Manuscripts
Division of the Oklahoma
Historical Society 1976–1989:
Native American tribal records
and special collections*
from the Oklahoma Historical So-
ciety, Indian Archives Division
(Oklahoma City: the Oklahoma
Historical Society, 1976–1989)

Cherokee Notes
by James Manford Carselowey
(Tulsa, OK: Yesterdays Publications, 1980)

RESEARCH TIPS

for more info

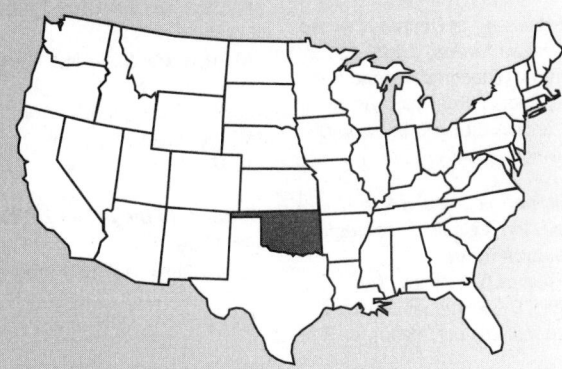

- When working in the 1900 federal census, do not assume that your white ancestors were not in Indian Territory. Exhaust both of the "twin territories" through the Soundex.
- The Indian Archives Division of the Oklahoma Historical Society, 2100 N. Lincoln Blvd., Oklahoma City, OK 73105, <www.ok-history.mus.ok.us/>, should be consulted when researching your Native American ancestry. However, they cannot work miracles, so you must have identifying information—in most cases, the tribe is the first step in that research.
- The Dawes Rolls Database-Final Rolls is searchable online at <www.accessgenealogy.com/native/da wes.php>. The site allows you to search for your ancestors and get the necessary identifying information to lead you to the actual enrollment cards, which will then take you to the census and other records that will offer genealogical information.

Census Records
- Federal Census: 1860 (with Arkansas), 1900, 1910, 1920, 1930
- Civil War Union Veterans and Widows: 1890
- Territorial Census: 1890 (Unassigned lands, not Indian Territory)

Cherokee Pioneers
by James Manford Carselowey
(Adair, OK: J.M. Carselowey,
1961)

*The Cherokee Strip of
Oklahoma: A Hundred
Yesteryears*
by Robert N. Gray (Enid, OK: Sons
and Daughters of the Cherokee
Strip Pioneers Museum, 1992)

*The Chickasaw Freemen: A
People Without A Country*
by Daniel F. Littlefield (Westport,
CT: Greenwood Press, 1980)

The Chisholm Trail
by Wayne Gard (Norman, OK: University Of Oklahoma Press, 1976)

The Czechs in Oklahoma
by Karel D. Bicha (Norman, OK:
University of Oklahoma Press,
1980)

Directory of Oklahoma Sources
from the Federation of Oklahoma Genealogical Societies (Oklahoma City: Federation of Oklahoma Genealogical Societies, 1993)

Establishing of Churches in the Cherokee Nation, 1866–1908
from the Oklahoma Historical Society, Indian Archives Division (Oklahoma City: the Oklahoma Historical Society, 1976–)

Exploring Your Cherokee Ancestry: A Basic Genealogical Research Guide
by Thomas G. Mooney (Tahlequah, OK: Cherokee National Historical Society, 1990)

Family History: A Bibliography of the Collection In the Oklahoma Historical Society
by Mary Huffman (Oklahoma City: the Oklahoma Historical Society, 1992)

First Families of the Twin Territories: Our Ancestors in Oklahoma Before Statehood
from the Oklahoma Genealogical Society (Oklahoma City, OK: the Oklahoma Genealogical Society, 1997)

The Five Civilized Tribes: A Bibliography
by Mary Huffman (Oklahoma City: Oklahoma Historical Society, Library Resources Division, 1991)

The Genealogist's Companion and Sourcebook, 2d ed.
by Emily Anne Croom (Cincinnati: Betterway Books, 2003)

A Genealogist's Guide to Discovering Your African-American Ancestors
by Franklin Carter Smith and Emily Anne Croom (Cincinnati: Betterway Books, 2003)

Genealogy of Old and New Cherokee Indian Families
by George Bell (Bartlesville, OK: George Bell, 1972)

Growing Faith: General Conference Mennonites In Oklahoma
by Wilma McKee (Newton, KS: Faith and Life Press, 1988)

Guide to Cherokee Indian Records Microfilm Collection: Archives and Manuscripts Division, Oklahoma Historical Society
by Sharron Standifer Aston (Norman, OK: Ashton Books, 1996)

Guide to Genealogical Research in the National Archives of the United States
edited by Anne Bruner Eales and Robert M. Kvasnicka (Washington, DC: National Archives and Records Administration, 2000)

Guide to the Historical Records of Oklahoma
by Bradford Koplowitz (Bowie, MD: Heritage Books, 1990, 1997)

A Guide to the Indian Tribes of Oklahoma
by Muriel Hazel Wright (Norman, OK: University of Oklahoma Press, 1951, 1986)

Guide to Manuscript Collections Western History Collections University of Oklahoma
by Donald L. Dewitt (Bowie, MD: Heritage Books, 1994)

Guide to Records in the National Archives Relating to American Indians
compiled by Edward E. Hill (Washington, DC: National Archives, 1981)

A Guide to Regional Manuscript Collections in the Division of Manuscripts, University of Oklahoma Library
by Arrell M. Gibson (Norman, OK: University of Oklahoma Press, 1960)

A History of the Church of Jesus Christ of Latter-day Saints in Eastern Oklahoma: From Oklahoma and Indian Territories to 1980
by Lynetta K. Bingha (Tulsa: Tulsa Oklahoma Stake, c.1980)

History of Oklahoma, 4 vols.
by Gatson Litton (New York: Lewis Historical Publishing Co., 1957)

A History of the State of Oklahoma, 2 vols.
by Luther B. Hill (Chicago: Lewis Publishing Co., 1908)

Index to Oklahoma Newspapers
from the Oklahoma Historical Society (Oklahoma City, OK: Oklahoma Historical Society 2002)

Indian Leaders: Oklahoma's First Statesmen
by H. Glenn Jordan (Oklahoma City: Oklahoma Historical Society, 1979)

The Indian Territory: Its' Chiefs, Legislators and Leading Men
by Harry F. and Edward S. O'Beirne (St. Louis: C.B. Woodward Co., 1892)

The Intruders: The Illegal Residents of Cherokee Nation, 1866–1907
by Nancy Hope Sober (Ponca City, OK: Cherokee Books, 1991)

The Jews in Oklahoma
by Henry J. Tobias (Norman, OK: University of Oklahoma Press, 1980)

Journey Toward Hope: A History of Blacks In Oklahoma
by Jimmie L. Franklin (Norman, OK: University of Oklahoma Press, 1982)

The Kiowa Indians: Their History & Life Stories
by Hugh D. Corwin (Lawton, OK: H.D. Corwin, 1958)

Leaders and Leading Men of the Indian Territory wit Interesting Biographical Sketches Choctawas and Cickasaws
by Harry F. O'Beirne (Chicago: American Publishers Association, 1891)

Like A Prairie Fire: A History of the Assemblies of God in Oklahoma
by Bob Burke (Oklahoma City: Oklahoma District Council of the Assemblies of God, 1994)

A List of the Records of the State of Oklahoma
from the Historical Records Survey (Oklahoma City: Historical Records Survey, 1938)

Missions and Missionaries of Indian Territory
by C.W. West (Muskogee, OK: Muscogee Pub., 1990)

National Archives Microfilm Catalogs online:
<www.archives.gov/publica tions/genealogy_microfilm_ catalogs.html>

Oklahoma Christians: A History of Christian Churches and of the Start of the Christian Church (Disciples of Christ) in Oklahoma
by Stephen J. England (Minneapolis, MN: Bethany Press, 1975)

Oklahoma Genealogical Research
by Mary Metzger O'Brien (Sand Springs, OK: M. O'Brien Bookshop, 1986)

Oklahoma: A History of Five Centuries, 2nd ed.
by Arrell Morgan Gibson (Originally published in 1965; Reprint: Norman, OK: Harlow Publishing Corporation, 1981)

Oklahoma, A History of the State and its People, 4 vols.
by Joseph Bradfield Thorburn (New York: Lewis Historical Pub. Co., 1929)

The Oklahoma Land Rush of 1889
by Stan Hoig (Oklahoma City, OK: Oklahoma Historical Society, 1984)

Oklahoma Marriages: A Bibliography
by Laura Martin (Oklahoma City: Library Resources Division, 1996)

Oklahoma: Records and Archives
by Patrick J. Blessing (Tulsa, OK: Universitory of Tulsa Publications, 1978)

Oklahoma Research Outline
by the Church of Jesus Christ of Latter-Day Saints (Salt Lake City, UT: Corp. of the President of the Church of Jesus Christ of L.D.S., 1988)

Oklahoma Research: The Twin Territories
by Jean C. Brown (Sapulpa, OK: Jean C. Brown, 1975)

The Oklahoma Spirit of '17: Biographical Volume
by W.E. Welch (Oklahoma City: Historical Pub., 1920)

Oklahoma State, County and Town Records
from the Oklahoma Historical Society (Oklahoma City: the Oklahoma Historical Society, 2002)

Oklahoma: A Student's Guide to Localized History
by Arrell M. Gibson (New York: Columbia University, 1965)

The Poles in Oklahoma
by Richard M. Bernard (Norman, OK: University of Oklahoma Press, 1980)

Portraits and Biographical Record of Oklahoma: Commemorating the Achievements of Citizens Who Have Contributed to the Progress Of Oklahoma and the Development of its Resources (Chicago: Chapman Publishing Co., 1901)

Prairie Fire: A Pioneer History of Western Oklahoma
from the Western Oklahoma Historical Society (Elk City, OK: Western Oklahoma Historical Society, 1978)

Preliminary List of Churches and Religious Organizations in Oklahoma
by James W. Parker (Oklahoma City: Historical Records Survey, 1942)

A Seminole Sourcebook
by William C. Sturtevant (New York: Garland Pub., 1987)

Smith's First Directory of Oklahoma Territory, for the Year Commencing August 1st, 1890
from the Oklahoma Historical Society (Oklahoma City: Oklahoma Historical Society, Research Library, 1986)

The Souls of the Just: A Necrology of the Catholic Church in Oklahoma
by James D. White (Tulsa, OK: Sarto Press, 1983)

Southwest Oklahoma Keys
by Willie Reeves Hardin Bivins (Oklahoma City: Southwest Oklahoma Genealogical Society, 1982

A Standard History of Oklahoma: An Authentic Narrative of its Development form the Date of the First European Exploration Down to the Present Time, Including Accounts of the Indian Tribes, Both Civilized and Wild, of the Cattle Range, of the Land Openings and the Achievements of the Most Recent Period, 5 vols.
by Joseph Bradfield Thorburn (Chicago: American Historical Society, 1916)

State Records, Manuscripts, and Newspapers at the Oklahoma State Archives and Oklahoma Historical Society
by John Stewart and Kenny A. Franks (Oklahoma City: State Department Of Libraries and Oklahoma Historical Society, 1975)

The Story of Oklahoma
by W. David Baird (Norman, OK: University of Oklahoma Press, 1994)

The Story of Oklahoma Baptists
by E.C. Routh (Oklahoma City: Baptist General Convention, 1932)

They Carried the Torch: the Story of Oklahoma's Pioneer Newspapers
by Mrs. Tom B. Ferguson (Norman, OK: Levite Of Apache, 1989)

Tracing Indian Family Histories
by Duane Kendall Hale (Norman, OK: OCCE Copy Service, University of Oklahoma, 1983)

Where Are My Cherokees
by Sandi Garrett (Spavinaw, OK: Cherokee Woman Pub., 1997)

Women of Oklahoma, 1890–1920
by Linda Williams Reese (Norman, OK: University of Okla., 1997)

■ CENSUS RECORDS

The American Census Handbook
by Thomas Jay Kemp (Wilmington, DE: Scholarly Resources, Inc., 2001)

The Census Book: A Genealogist's Guide to Federal Census Facts, Schedules and Indexes
by William Dollarhide (Bountiful, UT: Heritage Quest, 1999)

Finding Answers In U.S. Census Records
by Loretto Dennis Szucs and Matthew Wright (Salt Lake City: Ancestry Publishing, 2001)

Map Guide to the U.S. Federal Censuses, 1790–1920
William Thorndale and William Dollarhide (Baltimore: Genealogical Publishing Co., 1987)

State Census Records
by Ann S. Lainhart (Baltimore: Genealogical Publishing Co., Inc. 1992)

Your Guide to the Federal Census
by Kathleen W. Hinckley (Cincinnati: Betterway Books, 2002)

■ IMMIGRATION RECORDS

American Naturalization Records, 1790–1990: What They Are and How to Use Them
by John J. Newman (North Salt Lake, UT: HeritageQuest, 1998)

American Passenger Arrival Records
by Michael Tepper (Baltimore: Genealogical Publishing Co., 1993)

Choctaw Emigration Records, 2 vols.
by Monty Olsen (Calera, OK: Bryan County Heritage Association, 1990)

German-Russian Heritage, Steppes to America
American Historical Society of Germans from Russia, Oklahoma Harvester Chapter (Oklahoma: AHSGR, 1991)

They Became Americans: Finding Naturalization Records and Ethnic Origins
by Loretto Dennis Szucs (Salt Lake City: Ancestry, Inc., 1998)

They Came in Ships: A Guide to Finding Your Immigrant Ancestor's Arrival Records, 2d ed.
by John P. Colletta (Salt Lake City: Ancestry, Inc., 1993)

■ LAND RECORDS

Boundaries of Oklahoma
edited by John W. Morris (Oklahoma City: Oklahoma Historical Society, 1980)

El Reno District 1901 Land Lottery: Index to Names of Homesteaders Filings
by Julie Peterson Hinton and Louise F. Wilcox (El Reno, OK: J.P. Hinton, 1985)

Land and Property Research in the United States
by Wade E. Hone (Salt Lake City: Ancestry Inc., 1997)

Locating Your Roots: Discover Your Ancestors Using Land Records
by Patricia Law Hatcher (Cincinnati: Betterway Books, 2003)

Oklahoma Land Records.
from the Oklahoma Historical Society (Oklahoma City, OK: Oklahoma Historical Society)

The Oklahoma Land Rush of 1889
by Stan Hoig (Oklahoma City: Oklahoma Historical Society, 1984)

■ MAPS

Boundaries of Oklahoma
by John W. Morris (Oklahoma City: Oklahoma Historical Society, 1980)

A Gazetteer of Indian Territory
by Henry A. Gannett (Washington, DC: U.S. Government Printing Office, 1905; Reprint: Tulsa, OK: Oklahoma Yesterday Pub., 1980)

Ghost Towns of Oklahoma
by John W. Morris (Norman, OK: University of Oklahoma Press, 1977)

Historical Atlas of Oklahoma
by John W. Morris and Edwin C. McReynolds (Norman, OK: University of Oklahoma Press, 1976)

Oklahoma Place Names, 2d ed.
by George H. Shirk (Norman, OK: University of Oklahoma Press, 1974)

Town and Place Locations
from the Oklahoma Department of Transportation (Oklahoma City: Oklahoma Department of Transportation, 1991)

■ MILITARY RECORDS

Black, Buckskin And Blue: African American Scouts And Soldiers On The Western Frontier
by Arthur T. Burton (Austin, TX: Eaton Press, 1999)

Early Military Forts and Posts in Oklahoma
edited by Odie B. Faulk, Kenny A. Franks, and Paul F. Lambert (Oklahoma City: Oklahoma Historical Society, 1978)

A History of the Second World War: A Remembrance, An Appreciation, A Memorial
(Oklahoma City: Victory Publishing Co., 1946)

Index to Applications for Pensions From the State of Oklahoma Submitted by Confederate Soldiers, Sailors and their Widows
(Oklahoma City: Oklahoma Genealogical Society, 1969)

Master Lists of the Cherokee Confederate Indians
by Sherman Lee Pompey (Independence, CA: Historical and Genealogical Publishing Co., 1965)

Muster Lists of the Creek and Other Confederate Indians
by Sherman Lee Pompey (Independence, CA: Historical and Genealogical Publishing Co., 1996)

Oklahoma Air National Guard Pilots in the Korean War
Newman, Stanley Newman (Oklahoma City: 45th Infantry Division Museum, 1990)

Soldiers of the Great War, 3 vols.
by W.M. Haulsee (Washington, D.C.: Soldiers Record Publishing Association, 1920)

Uncle, We Are Ready! Registering America's Men, 1917–1918: A Guide to Researching World War I Draft Registration Cards
by John J. Newman (North Salt Lake, UT: HeritageQuest, 2001)

U.S. Military Records: A Guide to Federal & State Sources, Colonial America to the Present
by James C. Neagles (Salt Lake City: Ancestry, Inc., 1994)

World War II: A Family Historian's Guide
by Debra Johnson Knox (Spartanburg, SC: MIE Publishing, 2003)

■ PROBATE RECORDS

Probate Records, 1892–1908, Northern District Cherokee Nation, 3 vols.
by Orpha Jewell Wever (Vinita, OK: Northeast Oklahoma Genealogical Society, 1982–83)

■ VITAL RECORDS

Birth And Death Notices In Oklahoma And Indian Territories From 1871
by N. Dale Talkington (Houston, TX: N.D. Talkington, 1999)

Cherokee National Births and Deaths, 1884–1901
by Dixie Bogle (Utica, KY: Cook and McDowell Publishers, 1980)

Cherokee Nation Marriages, 1884–1901
by Dixie Bogle (Utica, KY: Cook and McDowell Publishers, 1980)

Guide to Public Vital Statistics Records in Oklahoma
(Oklahoma City: Historical Records Survey, 1941)

Oklahoma Cemeteries: A Bibliography of the Collections in the Oklahoma Historical Society
Barbara Pierce and Brian Basore (Oklahoma City: Library Resources Division, The Society, 1993)

Oklahoma Marriage Records, Choctaw Nation, Indian Territory, 10 vols.
by Ellen Tifee and Gloryann Hankins Young (Norman, OK: University of Oklahoma, 1969–78)

Oklahoma Territory Weddings
by Frances M. Bode (Geary, OK: Pioneer Book Committee, 1983)

Our People and Where They Rest, 12 vols.
by James W. Tyner and Alice Tyner Timmons (Norman, OK: University of Oklahoma, 1969–78)

Relocated Cemeteries in Oklahoma and Parts of Arkansas, Kansas, Texas
by Madeline S. Mills and Helen R. Mullenax (Tulsa, OK: Mills and Mullenax, 1974)

Union List of Oklahoma Cemeteries
(Oklahoma city, OK: Oklahoma Genealogical Society, 1969)

Your Guide to Cemetery Research
by Sharon DeBartolo Carmack (Cincinnati: Betterway Books, 2002)

■ A   1891
Parent County: Iowa-Sac-Fox and Pottawatomie-Shawnee Lands
Comments/research tips: (See Lincoln) Name changed to Lincoln.

■ Adair   16 July 1907
P.O. Box 169, Stilwell, OK 74960
Phone: (918)696-7633
Web site: www.rootsweb.com/~okadair/adaircty.htm
Parent County: Cherokee Lands

Record Type	Year Begun	Jurisdiction
Military	1906	County Clerk
Probate	1907	Clerk of Courts
Court	1907	Clerk of Courts
Marriage	1907	Clerk of Courts
Divorce	1907	Clerk of Courts
Land	1906	County Clerk

■ Alfalfa   16 July 1907
County Courthouse, 300 S. Grand St., Cherokee, OK 73728
Phone: (580)596-3523
Web site: www.rootsweb.com/~okalfalf/main-alfalfa.htm
Parent County: Woods

Record Type	Year Begun	Jurisdiction
Marriage	1894	Clerk of Courts
Divorce	1893	Clerk of Courts
Land	1893	County Clerk
Probate	1893	Clerk of Courts
Court	1893	Clerk of Courts

■ Atoka   16 July 1907
200 E. Court St., Atoka, OK 74525
Phone: (580)889-5157
Web site: www.rootsweb.com/~okatoka/
Parent County: Choctaw Lands

Record Type	Year Begun	Jurisdiction
Marriage	1897	Clerk of Courts
Divorce	na	Clerk of Courts
Land	1903	County Clerk
Probate	na	Clerk of Courts
Court	na	Clerk of Courts

■ B   1891
Parent County: Original County (Pottawatomie-Shawnee Lands)
Comments/research tips: (See Pattawatomie) Name changed to Pottawatomie.

■ Beaver   1890
111 W. Second St., P.O. Box 338, Beaver, OK 73932
Phone: (580)625-3191
Web site: www.rootsweb.com/~okbeaver/
Parent County: Original County (Public Lands)

Record Type	Year Begun	Jurisdiction
Marriage	1890	Clerk of Courts
Divorce	1890	Clerk of Courts

Probate	1891	Clerk of Courts
Court	1890	Clerk of Courts
Land	ca. 1890	County Clerk
Military	1917	County Clerk

■ Beckham 16 July 1907
302 E. Main St., P.O. Box 428, Sayre, OK 73662
Phone: (580)928-3330
Web site: www.rootsweb.com/~okbeckha/
Parent County: Roger Mills, Greer Territory

Record Type	Year Begun	Jurisdiction
Marriage	1907	Clerk of Courts
Land	1907	County Clerk
Probate	1907	Clerk of Courts
Court	1907	Clerk of Courts

■ Blaine 1892
212 N. Weigle Ave., P.O. Box 138, Watonga, OK 73772
Phone: (580)623-5970
Web site: www.rootsweb.com/~okblaine/
Parent County: Original County
Comments/research tips: Formerly C County. Name changed to Blaine.

Record Type	Year Begun	Jurisdiction
Marriage	1892	Clerk of Courts
Divorce	1892	Clerk of Courts
Land	1892	County Clerk
Probate	1892	Clerk of Courts
Court	1892	Clerk of Courts
Military	1918	County Clerk

■ Bryan 16 July 1907
402 W. Evergreen St., Durant, OK 74701
Phone: (580)924-1446
Web site: www.rootsweb.com/~okbryan/
Parent County: Choctaw Lands

Record Type	Year Begun	Jurisdiction
Marriage	1907	Clerk of Courts
Divorce	1907	Clerk of Courts
Land	1903	County Clerk
Probate	1907	Clerk of Courts
Court	1907	Clerk of Courts
Military	1919	County Clerk

■ C 1892
Parent County: Original County
Comments/research tips: (See Blaine) Name changed to Blaine.

■ Caddo 1901
SW Second St. & Oklahoma Ave., P.O. Box 68, Anadarko, OK 73005
Phone: (405)247-3393
Web site: www.rootsweb.com/~okcaddo/ccpage.htm
Parent County: Original Lands
Comments/research tips: Formerly I County. Name changed to Caddo 8 November 1902.

Record Type	Year Begun	Jurisdiction
Marriage	1901	Clerk of Courts

Divorce	1901	Clerk of Courts
Probate	1901	Clerk of Courts
Court	1901	Clerk of Courts
Land	1907	County Clerk

■ Canadian 1889
201 N. Choctaw Ave., P.O. Box 458, El Reno, OK 73036
Phone: (405)262-1070
Web site: www.canadiancounty.org/
Parent County: Original County

Record Type	Year Begun	Jurisdiction
Marriage	1890	Clerk of Courts
Divorce	1890	Clerk of Courts
Land	1889	County Clerk
Probate	1890	Clerk of Courts
Court	1890	Clerk of Courts
Military	1919	County Clerk

■ Carter 16 July 1907
First & B St. SW, P.O. Box 1236, Ardmore, OK 73401
Phone: (580)223-8162
Web site: www.brightok.net/chickasaw//ardmore/county
Parent County: Chickasaw Lands

Record Type	Year Begun	Jurisdiction
Marriage	1895	Clerk of Courts
Land	1907	County Clerk
Probate	1907	Clerk of Courts
Court	1907	Clerk of Courts
Divorce	1907	Clerk of Courts
Military	na	County Clerk

■ Cherokee 16 July 1907
213 W. Delaware St., Tahlequah, OK 74464
Phone: (918)456-3171
Web site: www.rootsweb.com/~okchero2/
Parent County: Cherokee Lands

Record Type	Year Begun	Jurisdiction
Marriage	1907	Clerk of Courts
Divorce	1907	Clerk of Courts
Land	1907	County Clerk
Probate	1907	Clerk of Courts
Court	1907	Clerk of Courts
Military	1918	County Clerk

■ Choctaw 16 July 1907
300 E. Duke St., Hugo, OK 74743
Phone: (580)326-7554
Web site: www.rootsweb.com/~okchocta/
Parent County: Choctaw Lands

Record Type	Year Begun	Jurisdiction
Marriage	1907	Clerk of Courts
Divorce	1907	Clerk of Courts
Land	1907	County Clerk
Probate	1907	Clerk of Courts
Court	1907	Clerk of Courts

■ Cimarron 16 July 1907
P.O. Box 145, Boise City, OK 73933-0145
Phone: (580)544-2251

Web site: www.rootsweb.com/~okcimarr/cimarron.htm
Parent County: Beaver

Record Type	Year Begun	Jurisdiction
Marriage	1908	Clerk of Courts
Land	1907	County Clerk
Probate	1908	Clerk of Courts
Court	1908	Clerk of Courts
Divorce	1908	Clerk of Courts

■ **Cleveland** 1890
641 E. Robinson, Norman, OK 73071
Phone: (405)366-0240
Web site: www.telepath.com/dataman/okcleveland.html
Parent County: Unassigned Lands

Record Type	Year Begun	Jurisdiction
Marriage	1890	Clerk of Courts
Divorce	na	Clerk of Courts
Land	1889	County Clerk
Probate	na	Clerk of Courts
Court	na	Clerk of Courts

■ **Coal** 16 July 1907
4 N. Main St., Suite 1, Coalgate, OK 74538
Phone: (580)927-2103
Web site: www.rootsweb.com/~okcoal/
Parent County: Cherokee Lands

Record Type	Year Begun	Jurisdiction
Marriage	1907	Clerk of Courts
Divorce	1907	Clerk of Courts
Land	1907	County Clerk
Probate	1907	Clerk of Courts
Court	1907	Clerk of Courts

■ **Comanche** 1901
315 SW Fifth St., Lawton, OK 73501
Phone: (580)355-5214
Web site: www.comancheco.gen.ok.us/
Parent County: Kiowa-Comanche-Apache and Whichita-Caddo Lands

Record Type	Year Begun	Jurisdiction
Marriage	1900	Clerk of Courts
Divorce	1900	Clerk of Courts
Land	1901	County Clerk
Probate	1900	Clerk of Courts
Court	1900	Clerk of Courts
Military	1918	County Clerk

■ **Cotton** 22 Aug. 1912
301 N. Broadway St., Walters, OK 73572
Phone: (580)875-3029
Web site: www.rootsweb.com/~okcotton/
Parent County: Comanche, Oklahoma Territory
Comments/research tips: County Clerk has Birth records 1912–1945.

Record Type	Year Begun	Jurisdiction
Marriage	1912	Clerk of Courts
Death	1912	Clerk of Courts
Divorce	1912	Clerk of Courts
Land	1912	County Clerk

Probate	1912	Clerk of Courts
Court	1912	Clerk of Courts

■ **Craig** 16 July 1907
301 W. Canadian Ave., Vinita, OK 74301
Phone: (918)256-6451
Web site: www.rootsweb.com/~okcraig/
Parent County: Cherokee Lands

Record Type	Year Begun	Jurisdiction
Marriage	1902	Clerk of Courts
Divorce	1907	Clerk of Courts
Land	1907	County Clerk
Probate	1907	Clerk of Courts
Court	1907	Clerk of Courts

■ **Creek** 16 July 1907
222 E. Dewey Suite 201, Sapulpa, OK 74067
Phone: (918)227-2525
Web site: www.rootsweb.com/~okcreek/
Parent County: Creek Lands
Comments/research tips: District Court in Bristow and the County Court Clerk in Drumright have the Marriage and Divorce records for their respective towns.

Record Type	Year Begun	Jurisdiction
Marriage	1907	Clerk of Courts
Divorce	1907	Clerk of Courts
Land	1907	County Clerk
Probate	1907	Clerk of Courts
Court	1907	Clerk of Courts

■ **Custer** 1892
Seventh & B Sts., Arapaho, OK 73620
Phone: (580)323-3233
Web site: www.rootsweb.com/~okcuster/custer.htm
Parent County: Cheyenne-Arapaho Lands
Comments/research tips: Formerly G County. Name changed to Custer 8 November 1892. Cemetery Association has Burial records for each city.

Record Type	Year Begun	Jurisdiction
Marriage	1895	Clerk of Courts
Divorce	1899	Clerk of Courts
Land	1896	Clerk of Courts
Probate	1900	Clerk of Courts
Court	1896	Clerk of Courts
Military	1892	County Clerk

■ **D** 1892
Parent County: Original County (Cheyenne-Arapaho Lands)
Comments/research tips: (See Dewey) Name changed to Dewey 8 November 1898.

■ **Day** 19 Apr. 1892
Web site: http://freepages.genealogy.rootsweb.com/~swokla/day/daycounty.html
Parent County: Cheyenne-Arapaho Lands
Comments/research tips: Formerly E County. Name changed to Day. Discontinued 16 November 1907 and became part of Ellis and Roger Mills Counties.

■ **Delaware** 16 July 1907
P.O. Box 309, Jay, OK 74346
Phone: (918)253-4420
Web site: www.rootsweb.com/~okdelawa/
Parent County: Cherokee Lands

Record Type	Year Begun	Jurisdiction
Marriage	1907	Clerk of Courts
Land	1907	County Clerk
Probate	1906	Clerk of Courts

■ **Dewey** 1892
P.O. Box 278, Taloga, OK 73667
Phone: (580)328-5521
Web site: www.rootsweb.com/~okdewey/
Parent County: Original County (Cheyenne-Arapaho Lands)
Comments/research tips: Formerly D County. Name changed to Dewey 8 November 1898.

Record Type	Year Begun	Jurisdiction
Marriage	1893	Clerk of Courts
Divorce	1894	Clerk of Courts
Land	1892	County Clerk
Probate	1893	Clerk of Courts
Court	1893	Clerk of Courts

■ **E** 1892
Parent County: Cheyenne-Arapaho Lands
Comments/research tips: (See Day) Name changed to Day.

■ **Ellis** 16 July 1907
Courthouse Sq., 100 S. Washington, Arnett, OK 73832
Phone: (580)885-7301
Web site: www.rootsweb.com/~okellis/ellis.htm
Parent County: Day, Woodward

Record Type	Year Begun	Jurisdiction
Marriage	1892	Clerk of Courts
Probate	1908	Clerk of Courts
Divorce	1893	Clerk of Courts
Land	1898	County Clerk
Court	1896	Clerk of Courts

■ **F** 1892
Parent County: Cheyenne-Arapaho Lands
Comments/research tips: (See Roger Mills) Name changed to Roger Mills 8 November 1892.

■ **G** 1892
Parent County: Cheyenne-Arapaho Lands
Comments/research tips: (See Custer) Name changed to Custer 8 November 1892.

■ **Garfield** 1893
County Courthouse, Room 101, Enid, OK 73701
Phone: (580)237-0232
Web site: www.rootsweb.com/~okgarfie/gar.htm
Parent County: Original County (Cherokee Outlet)
Comments/research tips: Originally O County. Name changed to Garfield 6 November 1894.

Record Type	Year Begun	Jurisdiction
Marriage	1893	Clerk/District Ct.
Divorce	1893	Clerk/District Ct.
Land	1893	Registrar/Deeds
Probate	1893	Clerk/District Ct.
Court	1893	Clerk/District Ct.

■ **Garvin** 16 July 1907
P.O. Box 239, Pauls Valley, OK 73075
Phone: (405)238-5596
Web site: www.rootsweb.com/~okgarvin/garvin.htm
Parent County: Chickasaw Lands

Record Type	Year Begun	Jurisdiction
Marriage	1907	Clerk of Courts
Divorce	1907	Clerk of Courts
Land	1907	County Clerk
Probate	1907	Clerk of Courts
Court	1907	Clerk of Courts

■ **Grady** 16 July 1907
320 E. Choctaw, Chickasha, OK 73018
Phone: (405)224-7446
Web site: www.rootsweb.com/~okgrady/
Parent County: Chickasaw Lands

Record Type	Year Begun	Jurisdiction
Marriage	1907	Clerk of Courts
Divorce	1907	Clerk of Courts
Land	1907	Clerk of Courts
Probate	1907	Clerk of Courts
Court	1907	Clerk of Courts
Burial	1907	County Clerk
Military	1907	County Clerk

■ **Grant** 1893
Grant County Courthouse, P.O. Box 167, Medford, OK 73759
Phone: (580)395-2828
Web site: www.rootsweb.com/~okgrant/okgrant.htm
Parent County: Original County (Cherokee Outlet)
Comments/research tips: Formerly L County. Name changed to Grant 6 November 1894.

Record Type	Year Begun	Jurisdiction
Marriage	1893	Clerk of Courts
Divorce	1893	Clerk of Courts
Land	1894	County Clerk
Probate	1893	Clerk of Courts
Court	1893	Clerk of Courts
Military	na	County Clerk

■ **Greer** 1886
Greer County Courthouse, P.O. Box 216, Mangum, OK 73554
Phone: (580)782-3665
Web site: www.rootsweb.com/~okgreer/
Parent County: Organized by Texas, transferred to Oklahoma by court decision
Comments/research tips: Organized as Greer County, Texas in 1886; an act of Congress on 4 May 1896 declared it Greer County, Oklahoma. A fire in 1901 destroyed the county records.

Record Type	Year Begun	Jurisdiction
Marriage	1901	Clerk of Courts

Divorce .... 1901 ....Clerk of Courts
Land .... ca. 1898 ....County Clerk
Probate .... 1901 ....Clerk of Courts
Court .... 1901 ....Clerk of Courts

■ H 1892
Parent County: Cheyenne-Arapaho Lands
Comments/research tips: (See Washita) Name changed to
Washita 8 November 1892.

■ Harmon 2 June 1909
County Courthouse 114 W. Hollis, Hollis, OK 73550
Phone: (580)688-3617
Web site: www.rootsweb.com/~okharmon/
Parent County: Greer

Record Type	Year Begun	Jurisdiction
Land	1909	County Clerk
Marriage	1909	Clerk of Courts
Divorce	1909	Clerk of Courts
Probate	1909	Clerk of Courts
Court	1909	Clerk of Courts

■ Harper 16 July 1907
P.O. Box 347, Buffalo, OK 73834
Phone: (580)735-2010
Web site: www.rootsweb.com/~okharper/
Parent County: Woodward, Woods, Indian Lands
Comments/research tips: County Clerk has School records
1907–1963.

Record Type	Year Begun	Jurisdiction
Marriage	1907	Clerk of Courts
Divorce	1907	Clerk of Courts
Land	1907	County Clerk
Probate	1907	Clerk of Courts
Court	1907	Clerk of Courts

■ Haskell 16 July 1907
202 E. Main St., Stigler, OK 74462
Phone: (918)967-3323
Web site: www.rootsweb.com/~okhaskel/
Parent County: Choctaw Lands

Record Type	Year Begun	Jurisdiction
Marriage	1907	Clerk of Courts
Divorce	1907	Clerk of Courts
Land	1905	County Clerk
Probate	1907	Clerk of Courts
Court	1907	Clerk of Courts

■ Hughes 16 July 1907
Hughes County Courthouse, P.O. Box 32, Holdenville, OK
74848
Phone: (405)379-3384
Web site: www.rootsweb.com/~okhughes/
Parent County: Creek Lands (Creek & Choctaw Lands)

Record Type	Year Begun	Jurisdiction
Marriage	1907	Clerk of Courts
Divorce	1907	Clerk of Courts
Land	1907	County Clerk
Probate	1907	Clerk of Courts
Court	1907	Clerk of Courts

■ I 1901
Parent County: Original Lands
Comments/research tips: (See Caddo) Name changed to
Caddo 8 November 1902.

■ Jackson 16 July 1907
101 N. Main St., Altus, OK 73521
Phone: (580)482-0448
Web site: www.rootsweb.com/~okjackso/jackson.htm
Parent County: Greer

Record Type	Year Begun	Jurisdiction
Marriage	1907	Clerk of Courts
Divorce	1907	Clerk of Courts
Land	1907	County Clerk
Probate	1907	Clerk of Courts
Court	1907	Clerk of Courts

■ Jefferson 16 July 1907
220 N. Main St., Room 101, Waurika, OK 73573
Phone: (580)228-2961
Web site: www.rootsweb.com/~okjeffer/
Parent County: Comanche (Chickasaw Lands)

Record Type	Year Begun	Jurisdiction
Marriage	1907	Clerk of Courts
Divorce	1907	Clerk of Courts
Land	1907	County Clerk
Probate	1907	Clerk of Courts
Court	1907	Clerk of Courts

■ Johnston 16 July 1907
403 W. Main, Suite 201, Tishomingo, OK 73460
Phone: (580)371-3281
Web site: www.rootsweb.com/~okjohnst/
Parent County: Chickasaw Lands

Record Type	Year Begun	Jurisdiction
Marriage	1907	Clerk of Courts
Divorce	1907	Clerk of Courts
Land	1907	County Clerk
Probate	1907	Clerk of Courts
Court	1907	Clerk of Courts
Military	1917	County Clerk

■ K 1893
Parent County: Original County
Comments/research tips: (See Kay) Name changed to Kay.

■ Kay 1893
P.O. Box 450, Newkirk, OK 74647
Phone: (580)362-3350
Web site: www.courthouse.kay.ok.us/home.html
Parent County: Original County (Cherokee Outlet)
Comments/research tips: Formerly K County. Name changed
to Kay.

Record Type	Year Begun	Jurisdiction
Marriage	1893	Clerk of Courts
Divorce	1893	Clerk of Courts
Land	1893	County Clerk
Probate	1893	Clerk of Courts
Court	1893	Clerk of Courts

Kingfisher May 1890
P.O. Box 328, Kingfisher, OK 73750
Phone: (405)375-3813
Web site: www.rootsweb.com/~okkingfi/
Parent County: Original County

Record Type	Year Begun	Jurisdiction
Marriage	1900	Clerk of Courts
Divorce	1900	Clerk of Courts
Land	1890	County Clerk
Probate	1900	Clerk of Courts
Court	1900	Clerk of Courts

Kiowa May 1901
P.O. Box 73, Hobart, OK 73651
Phone: (580)726-5125
Web site: http://rebelcherokee.labddiva.com/okkiowa.html
Parent County: Kiowa-Comanche-Apache & Caddo-Wichita Lands

Record Type	Year Begun	Jurisdiction
Marriage	1901	Clerk of Courts
Divorce	1901	Clerk of Courts
Land	1901	County Clerk
Probate	1901	Clerk of Courts
Court	1901	Clerk of Courts
Burial	1901	County Clerk
Military	1901	County Clerk

L 1893
Parent County: Chickasaw Lands
Comments/research tips: (See Grant) Name changed to Grant 6 November 1894.

Latimer 1902
109 N. Central St., Room 200, Wilburton, OK 74578
Phone: (918)465-2011
Web site: www.rootsweb.com/~oklatime/
Parent County: Choctaw Lands

Record Type	Year Begun	Jurisdiction
Marriage	1906	Clerk of Courts
Divorce	1907	Clerk of Courts
Probate	1907	Clerk of Courts
Court	1907	Clerk of Courts

Le Flore 16 July 1907
Courthouse, P.O. Box 218, Poteau, OK 74953
Phone: (918)647-3181
Web site: www.rootsweb.com/~okleflor/
Parent County: Choctaw Lands
Comments/research tips: Clerk of Courts has some Probate records as early as 1895.

Record Type	Year Begun	Jurisdiction
Marriage	1897	Clerk of Courts
Divorce	1907	Clerk of Courts
Land	1907	County Clerk
Probate	1907	Clerk of Courts
Court	1907	Clerk of Courts

Lincoln 1891
P.O. Box 307, Manvel Ave., Chandler, OK 74834
Phone: (405)258-1309

Web site: www.rootsweb.com/~oklincol/
Parent County: Iowa-Sac-Fox & Pottawatomie-Shawnee Lands
Comments/research tips: (See Lincoln) Formerly A County. Name changed to Lincoln.

Record Type	Year Begun	Jurisdiction
Marriage	1892	Clerk/District Ct.
Divorce	1892	Clerk/District Ct.
Land	1892	County Clerk
Probate	1892	Clerk/District Ct.
Court	1892	Clerk/District Ct.

Logan May 1890
301 E. Harrison Ave., Guthrie, OK 73044
Phone: (405)282-0123
Web site: www.rootsweb.com/~oklogan/oklogan.htm
Parent County: Original County

Record Type	Year Begun	Jurisdiction
Marriage	1889	Clerk of Courts
Divorce	na	Clerk of Courts
Land	1889	County Clerk
Probate	ca. 1900	Clerk of Courts
Court	ca. 1900	Clerk of Courts

Love 16 July 1907
405 W. Main St., Marietta, OK 73448
Phone: (580)276-2235
Web site: www.rootsweb.com/~oklove/
Parent County: Chickasaw Lands

Record Type	Year Begun	Jurisdiction
Birth	1908	County Clerk
Marriage	1907	Clerk of Courts
Death	1908	County Clerk
Divorce	1907	Clerk of Courts
Land	1903	County Clerk
Probate	1907	Clerk of Courts
Court	1907	Clerk of Courts

M 1893
Parent County: Cherokee Outlet
Comments/research tips: (See Woods) Name changed to Woods 6 November 1894.

Major 16 July 1907
P.O. Box 379, E. Broadway, Fairview, OK 73737
Phone: (580)227-4712
Web site: www.rootsweb.com/~okmajor/major.htm
Parent County: Woods
Comments/research tips: Clerk of Court has Marriage records from late 1800's.

Record Type	Year Begun	Jurisdiction
Divorce	1907	Clerk of Courts
Land	1907	County Clerk
Probate	1907	Clerk of Courts
Court	1907	Clerk of Courts

Marshall 16 July 1907
P.O. Box 58, Madill, OK 73446
Phone: (580)795-3278

Oklahoma

Web site: www.rootsweb.com/~okmarsha/
Parent County: Chickasaw Lands

Record Type	Year Begun	Jurisdiction
Marriage	1907	Clerk of Courts
Divorce	1907	Clerk of Courts
Land	1907	County Clerk
Probate	1907	Clerk of Courts
Court	1907	Clerk of Courts
Military	na	County Clerk

■ Mayes 16 July 1907

P.O. Box 97, Pryor, OK 74361
Phone: (918)825-2185
Web site: www.rootsweb.com/~okmayes/
Parent County: Cherokee Lands

Record Type	Year Begun	Jurisdiction
Marriage	1907	Clerk of Courts
Divorce	1907	Clerk of Courts
Land	1907	County Clerk
Probate	1907	Clerk of Courts
Tax	na	County Treasurer
Court	1907	Clerk of Courts

■ McClain 16 July 1907

121 N. Second St., Suite 231, Purcell, OK 73080
Phone: (405)527-3221
Web site: www.rootsweb.com/~okmcclai/
Parent County: Chickasaw Lands

Record Type	Year Begun	Jurisdiction
Land	1891	County Clerk
Marriage	1907	Clerk of Courts
Death	1883	Clerk of Courts
Court	1895	Clerk of Courts
Probate	1895	Clerk of Courts

■ McCurtain 16 July 1907

P.O. Box 1378, Idabel, OK 74745
Phone: (580)286-3693
Web site: www.rootsweb/~okmccurt/mccurt.htm
Parent County: Choctaw Lands

Record Type	Year Begun	Jurisdiction
Marriage	1907	Clerk of Courts
Divorce	1907	Clerk of Courts
Probate	1907	Clerk of Courts
Court	1907	Clerk of Courts
Birth	1908	County Clerk
Death	1908	County Clerk
Land	1907	County Clerk

■ McIntosh 16 July 1907

P.O. Box 426, Eufaula, OK 74432
Phone: (918)689-2282
Web site: www.rootsweb.com/~okmcinto/
Parent County: Creek Lands, Cherokee Nations
Comments/research tips: Birth and Death records are held at the State Health Department.

Record Type	Year Begun	Jurisdiction
Marriage	1907	Clerk of Courts
Divorce	1907	Clerk of Courts

Record Type	Year Begun	Jurisdiction
Land	1907	County Clerk
Probate	1907	Clerk of Courts
Court	1907	Clerk of Courts

■ Murray 16 July 1907

P.O. Box 578, Sulphur, OK 73086
Phone: (580)622-3223
Web site: www.rootsweb.com/~okmurray/
Parent County: Chickasaw Lands

Record Type	Year Begun	Jurisdiction
Marriage	1907	Clerk of Courts
Divorce	1907	Clerk of Courts
Land	1908	County Clerk
Probate	1907	Clerk of Courts
Court	1907	Clerk of Courts

■ Muskogee 1898

P.O. Box 1008, Muskogee, OK 74401
Phone: (918)682-7873
Web site: www.rootsweb.com/~okmuskog/
Parent County: Creek Lands, Cherokee Nations
Comments/research tips: Clerk of Courts has Court and Probate records 1890–1907.

Record Type	Year Begun	Jurisdiction
Marriage	1890	Clerk of Courts
Divorce	1907	Clerk of Courts
Land	1907	County Clerk

■ N 1893

Parent County: Cherokee Outlet
Comments/research tips: (See Woodward) Name changed to Woodward 6 November 1894.

■ Noble 1893

300 Courthouse Dr. #14, Perry, OK 73077
Phone: (580)336-5187
Web site: www.rootsweb.com/~oknoble/
Parent County: Cherokee Outlet
Comments/research tips: Formerly P County. Name changed to Noble 6 November 1893.

Record Type	Year Begun	Jurisdiction
Marriage	1893	Clerk of Courts
Divorce	1893	Clerk of Courts
Land	1893	County Clerk
Probate	1893	Clerk of Courts
Court	1893	Clerk of Courts

■ Nowata 16 July 1907

229 N. Maple St., Nowata, OK 74048
Phone: (918)273-0127
Web site: www.rootsweb.com/~oknowata/
Parent County: Cherokee Lands

Record Type	Year Begun	Jurisdiction
Marriage	1907	Clerk/District Ct.
Divorce	1907	Clerk/District Ct.
Land	1911	County Clerk
Probate	1907	Clerk/District Ct.
Court	1907	Clerk/District Ct.

■ O 1893
Parent County: Cherokee Outlet
Comments/research tips: (See Garfield) Name changed to Garfield 6 November 1894.

■ Okfuskee 16 July 1907
Third & Atlanta, P.O. Box 30, Okemah, OK 74859
Phone: (918)623-0525
Web site: www.rootsweb.com/~okokfusk/
Parent County: Creek Lands
Comments/research tips: County Historical Society has incomplete Birth records 1909–1923 and incomplete Death records 1911–1923.

Record Type	Year Begun	Jurisdiction
Marriage	1907	Clerk of Courts
Divorce	1907	Clerk of Courts
Land	1907	County Clerk
Probate	1907	Clerk of Courts
Court	1907	Clerk of Courts

■ Oklahoma May 1890
320 Robert S. Kerr Ave., Office 409, Oklahoma City, OK 73102
Phone: (405)713-1708
Web site: www.oklahomacounty.org/
Parent County: Original County

Record Type	Year Begun	Jurisdiction
Marriage	1890	Clerk of Courts
Divorce	1907	Clerk of Courts
Probate	1920	Clerk of Courts
Court	1890	Clerk of Courts

■ Okmulgee 16 July 1907
314 W. Seventh St., Okmulgee, OK 74447
Phone: (918)756-3042
Web site: www.rootsweb.com/~okokmulg/
Parent County: Creek Lands

Record Type	Year Begun	Jurisdiction
Marriage	1907	Clerk of Courts
Divorce	1907	Clerk of Courts
Land	1900	County Clerk
Probate	1907	Clerk of Courts
Court	1907	Clerk of Courts

■ Osage 16 July 1907
600 Grandview Ave., Pawhuska, OK 74056
Phone: (918)287-4104
Web site: www.rootsweb.com/~okosage2/
Parent County: Osage Indian Lands

Record Type	Year Begun	Jurisdiction
Marriage	1907	Clerk of Courts
Divorce	1907	Clerk of Courts
Land	1907	County Clerk
Probate	1907	Clerk of Courts
Court	1907	Clerk of Courts

■ Ottawa 16 July 1907
102 E. Central, Miami, OK 74354
Phone: (918)542-2801
Web site: www.rootsweb.com/~okottawa/
Parent County: Cherokee Lands

Record Type	Year Begun	Jurisdiction
Marriage	1907	Clerk of Courts
Divorce	1907	Clerk of Courts
Land	1890	County Clerk
Probate	1907	Clerk of Courts
Court	1907	Clerk of Courts

■ P 1893
Parent County: Cherokee Outlet
Comments/research tips: (See Noble) Name changed to Noble 6 November 1894.

■ Pawnee 1893
500 Harrison St., Room 300, Pawnee, OK 74058
Phone: (918)762-2547
Web site: www.rootsweb.com/~okpawnee/pawnee.htm
Parent County: Pawnee Lands, Cherokee Outlet
Comments/research tips: Formerly Q County. Name changed to Pawnee.

Record Type	Year Begun	Jurisdiction
Marriage	1893	Clerk of Courts
Divorce	1893	Clerk of Courts
Land	1893	County Clerk
Probate	1893	Clerk of Courts
Court	1893	Clerk of Courts

■ Payne May 1890
308 Payne County Courthouse, Stillwater, OK 74074
Phone: (405)372-4744
Web site: www.paynecounty.org/
Parent County: Unassigned lands

Record Type	Year Begun	Jurisdiction
Court	1894	Clerk of Courts
Marriage	1894	Clerk of Courts
Divorce	1894	Clerk of Courts
Land	1894	County Clerk
Probate	1894	Clerk of Courts

■ Pittsburgh 16 July 1907
P.O. Box 460, McAlester, OK 74502
Phone: (918)423-4859
Web site: www.rootsweb.com/~okpitts2/
Parent County: Choctaw Lands
Comments/research tips: Clerk of Courts has Naturalization records 1890–1908.

Record Type	Year Begun	Jurisdiction
Birth	1908	Dept./Health
Marriage	1907	Clerk of Courts
Death	1908	Dept./Health
Divorce	1907	Clerk of Courts
Land	1907	County Clerk
Probate	1907	Clerk of Courts
Court	1907	Clerk of Courts

■ Pontotoc 16 July 1907
P.O. Box 427, Ada, OK 74820
Phone: (580)332-5763

Web site: www.rootsweb.com/~okpontot/pontotoc.htm
Parent County: Chickasaw Lands

Record Type	Year Begun	Jurisdiction
Marriage	1907	Clerk of Courts
Divorce	1907	Clerk of Courts
Probate	1907	Clerk of Courts
Court	1907	Clerk of Courts
Land	1907	Clerk of Courts

■ Pottawatomie 1891

325 N. Broadway St., Shawnee, OK 74801
Phone: (405)273-3624
Web site: www.usgennet.org/usa/ok/county/pottawatomie
Parent County: Original County (Pottawatomie-Shawnee Lands)
Comments/research tips: Formerly B County. Name changed to Pottawatomie 1892.

Record Type	Year Begun	Jurisdiction
Marriage	1892	Clerk of Courts
Divorce	1892	Clerk of Courts
Land	1895	County Clerk
Probate	1892	Clerk of Courts
Court	1892	Clerk of Courts
Birth	1908	Clerk of Courts
Death	1908	Clerk of Courts

■ Pushmataha 16 July 1907

302 SW B, Antlers, OK 74523
Phone: (580)298-2274
Web site: www.rootsweb.com/~okpushma/
Parent County: Choctaw Lands

Record Type	Year Begun	Jurisdiction
Marriage	1907	Clerk of Courts
Land	1907	County Clerk
Probate	1907	Clerk of Courts
Court	1907	Clerk of Courts

■ Q 1893

Parent County: Pawnee Lands, Cherokee Outlet
Comments/research tips: (See Pawnee) Name changed to Pawnee.

■ Roger Mills 1892

P.O. Box 409, Cheyenne, OK 73628
Phone: (580)497-3361
Web site: www.rootsweb.com/~okrogerm/
Parent County: Cheyenne-Arapaho Lands
Comments/research tips: Formerly F County. Name changed to Roger Mills 8 November 1892.

Record Type	Year Begun	Jurisdiction
Marriage	1897	Clerk of Courts
Divorce	1892	Clerk of Courts
Land	1892	County Clerk
Probate	1892	Clerk of Courts
Court	1892	Clerk of Courts

■ Rogers 26 Jan. 1907

P.O. Box 839, 219 S. Missouri Ave., Claremore, OK 74018
Phone: (918)341-5711

Web site: users.rootsweb.com/~okrogers/
Parent County: Cherokee Nation

Record Type	Year Begun	Jurisdiction
Marriage	1907	Clerk of Courts
Divorce	1907	Clerk of Courts
Probate	1907	Clerk of Courts
Court	1907	Clerk of Courts

■ Seminole 16 July 1907

120 S. Wewoka Ave., P.O. Box 130, Wewoka, OK 74884
Phone: (405)257-6236
Web site: www.usgennet.org/usa/ok/county/seminole/
Parent County: Seminole Indian Lands

Record Type	Year Begun	Jurisdiction
Marriage	1907	Clerk of Courts
Divorce	1907	Clerk of Courts
Probate	1907	Clerk of Courts
Court	1907	Clerk of Courts
Land	1907	County Recorder

■ Sequoyah 16 July 1907

120 E. Chickasaw Ave., Sallisaw, OK 74955
Phone: (918)775-4411
Web site: www.rootsweb.com/~oksequo2/
Parent County: Cherokee Indian Lands

Record Type	Year Begun	Jurisdiction
Marriage	1907	Clerk of Courts
Divorce	1907	Clerk of Courts
Probate	1907	Clerk of Courts
Court	1907	Clerk of Courts
Land	1907	County Clerk

■ Stephens 16 July 1907

101 S. Eleventh St., Duncan, OK 73533
Phone: (580)470-2000
Web site: www.rootsweb.com/~okstephe/stephens.htm
Parent County: Comanche, Chickasaw Lands, Oklahoma Territory

Record Type	Year Begun	Jurisdiction
Marriage	1907	Clerk of Courts
Land	1907	County Clerk
Probate	1907	Clerk of Courts
Court	1907	Clerk of Courts

■ Texas 1907

P.O. Box 1081, Guymon, OK 73942
Phone: (580)338-3003
Web site: www.geocities.com/Heartland/Estates/7166
Parent County: Beaver, Oklahoma Territory
Comments/research tips: Part of the panhandle area known as no man's land 1850-1890.

Record Type	Year Begun	Jurisdiction
Marriage	1907	Clerk of Courts
Divorce	1907	Clerk of Courts
Land	1889	County Clerk
Probate	1907	Clerk of Courts
Court	1907	Clerk of Courts

■ Tillman 16 July 1907

P.O. Box 116, Frederick, OK 73542
Phone: (580)335-3023

Oklahoma

Web site: www.rootsweb.com/~oktillma/
Parent County: Comanche, Kiowa

Record Type	Year Begun	Jurisdiction
Marriage	1907	Clerk of Courts
Divorce	1907	Clerk of Courts
Land	1907	County Clerk
Probate	1907	Clerk of Courts
Court	1907	Clerk of Courts

■ Tobucksy ca. 1876

Parent County: Choctaw Lands of the Moshulatubee District
Comments/research tips: (See Pittsburgh and Atoka) Became extinct after Oklahoma statehood, 1907. For more information on the history of Choctaw lands visit www.rootsweb.com/~itchocta/.

■ Tulsa 1905

500 S. Denver Ave., Room 200, Tulsa, OK 74103
Phone: (918)596-5000
Web site: www.rootsweb.com/~oktulsa/
Parent County: Creek Lands

Record Type	Year Begun	Jurisdiction
Marriage	1907	Clerk of Courts
Divorce	1907	Clerk of Courts
Probate	1907	Clerk of Courts
Court	1907	Clerk of Courts

■ Wagoner July 1908

P.O. Box 249, Wagoner, OK 74477
Phone: (918)485-4508
Web site: www.rootsweb.com/~okwagone/
Parent County: Creek Nation Lands

Record Type	Year Begun	Jurisdiction
Marriage	1908	Clerk of Courts
Divorce	1907	Clerk of Courts
Probate	1907	Clerk of Courts
Court	1907	Clerk of Courts
Birth	1908	Clerk of Courts
Death	1908	Clerk of Courts
Land	1906	County Clerk

■ Washington 1907

420 S. Johnstone Ave., Bartlesville, OK 74003
Phone: (918)337-2870
Web site: www.co.washington.ok.us/
Parent County: Cherokee Lands

Record Type	Year Begun	Jurisdiction
Marriage	1907	Clerk of Courts
Divorce	1907	Clerk of Courts
Probate	1907	Clerk of Courts
Court	1907	Clerk of Courts
Land	1907	County Clerk

■ Washita 1900

P.O. Box 397, Cordell, OK 73632
Phone: (580)832-3836
Web site: www.rootsweb.com/~okwashit/
Parent County: Cheyenne-Arapaho Lands
Comments/research tips: Formerly H County. Name changed to Washita after statehood in 1907.

Record Type	Year Begun	Jurisdiction
Marriage	1900	Clerk of Courts
Divorce	1900	Clerk of Courts
Probate	1900	Clerk of Courts
Court	1900	Clerk of Courts

■ Woods 1893

P.O. Box 924, Alva, OK 73717
Phone: (580)327-3119
Web site: www.rootsweb.com/~okwoods/main-woods.html
Parent County: Cherokee Outlet
Comments/research tips: Formerly M County. Name changed to Woods 6 November 1894.

Record Type	Year Begun	Jurisdiction
Marriage	1894	Court Clerk
Divorce	1893	Court Clerk
Land	1893	County Clerk
Probate	1901	Court Clerk
Court	1893	Court Clerk

■ Woodward 1893

1600 Main St., Woodward, OK 73801
Phone: (580)256-3413
Web site: www.rootsweb.com/~okwoodwa/woodward.htm
Parent County: Cherokee Outlet
Comments/research tips: Formerly N County. Name changed to Woodward 6 November 1894.

Record Type	Year Begun	Jurisdiction
Marriage	1897	Clerk of Courts
Land	1894	County Clerk
Probate	1900	Clerk of Courts
Court	1894	Court Clerk

Oregon

By David A. Fryxell

HISTORICAL OVERVIEW

Spanish mariners, Sir Francis Drake, and, two centuries later, Captain James Cook and even Russian fur traders all had their eyes on Oregon in its earliest history. The arrival of the first American, Robert Gray, in 1792 set off a fifty-four-year tussle with the British over Oregon. Lewis and Clark came in 1805, soon followed by agents of John Jacob Astor's fur company, who founded the first permanent American settlement on the Pacific Coast, Astoria, in 1811. Dr. John McLoughlin of the Hudson's Bay Company established the first real city, Willamette Falls, later renamed Oregon City, in 1829. That same year, missionaries led by Hall J. Kelley, Nathaniel J. Wyeth, and, later, Marcus Whitman began to encourage farmers from the Mississippi, Missouri, and Ohio River valleys to migrate to Oregon. That trickle became a flood with the wagon trains of the Oregon Trail beginning in 1842: 53,000 newcomers arrived between 1840 and 1860.

The boundary disputes with the British were finally settled in 1846. The Oregon Territory was established in 1848, partly in response to the massacre of Whitman and other settlers by Indians. The territory originally included everything west of the Rockies and north of the 42nd parallel, but a separate Washington Territory was carved out in 1853. Oregon became a state in 1859.

In turn, gold strikes, the railroads, farming and ranching, and then logging drove subsequent waves of settlement. Chinese came to work the mines and the railroads. In the 1870s Scandinavians began to arrive, with many Finns settling in Astoria. Swiss immigrants to Tillamook began the state's cheese industry. Basques settled in southeast Oregon in the late 1800s and early 1900s.

By 1880, a spate of Indian uprisings had been quelled and the state's Native American tribes—including the Chinookan, Shahaptian, Athapascan, Molala, Klamath,

OREGON AT A GLANCE

Motto: She Flies With Her Own Wings

Population: 3.47 Million

Prevalent Religion: Christianity, particularly Methodist, Lutheran, and Roman Catholic

Major Industries: Manufacturing, semiconductors, computers, services, trade, finance, insurance, real estate, government, construction, lumber and wood products, metals, transportation equipment, farming (hay, wheat, potatoes, berries, onions, Christmas trees), commercial fishing

Ethnic Makeup (in percent): Caucasian 86.6%, African-American 1.6%, Hispanic 8.0%, Asian 3.0%, Native American 1.4%, Other 4.2%

Famous Oregonians: Chief Joseph, Ken Kesey, Edwin Markham, Joaquin Miller, Linus Pauling, John Reed, Alberto Salazar, Mary Decker Slaney

Above: Picturesque Crater Lake

Umpqua, Kalapooian, Salishan, Kusan, Yakonan, Modoc, and Northern Paiutes—were exiled to reservations in Oregon, Washington, and as far away as Oklahoma. If you have Native American roots in Oregon, the records of the various Indian agencies and of the Chemawa Indian School may help you trace them.

RECORD HIGHLIGHTS

Oregon's boom years were tracked by a succession of territorial censuses beginning in 1842 and repeated almost annually until statehood; the Family History Library has indexes to the surviving portions of these censuses. These and subsequent state censuses in 1865, 1875, and 1885 typically name only the head of the household. State censuses in 1895 and 1905 list all family members. The first federal census to include the Oregon Territory was in 1850; it was enumerated as a state beginning in 1860.

Oregon didn't begin statewide birth and death registration until 1903, marriages in 1906, and divorces in 1925. Many of these records, along with earlier local vital records, are kept at the state archives, whose online Oregon Historical Records Index <http://arcweb.sos.state.or.us/banners/genealogy.htm> totals more than half a million entries, including Portland births (1881–1902) and deaths (1881–1917). The archives also has some early probate records, though these largely remain at county courthouses.

Land records can also provide clues to ancestors who joined the nineteenth century rush to Oregon. Territorial land records have been indexed and are kept in the state archives. Look for Donation Land Claims, which document those who arrived by 1855 and contain records that are rich in details about the settler family. Federal land records are available on microfilm from the FHL; later records, post-1908, are being added to the Bureau of Land Management's database at <www.glorecords.blm.gov>.

Don't forget that Oregon had joined the Union by the time of the Civil War, so its military records go back to that conflict. The FHL has microfilms of service and burial records of Oregon soldiers in the Civil War.

The biggest challenge for Oregon researchers, according to Connie Lenzen, CGRS, a member of the Genealogical Forum of Oregon, is that many of the records you'll seek are still in courthouses, archives, and libraries. Generally, she warns, they are not in published form or on the Internet. But Lenzen notes two online exceptions to this that can help researchers get started long-distance: the Oregon Death Index, included in the Ancestry.com subscription service, and the aforementioned Oregon State Archives' Historical Records Index.

Because so many Oregon records are located at the county level, Lenzen advises, it's crucial to first locate your ancestors in the censuses so you know where they were living. Records in the county courthouses may be difficult to access from a distance, she adds: "Due to budget cuts, most offices are short-staffed. The day-to-day business of running a county government takes precedence over answering queries by mail."

Ferne Kellow, president of the Oregon Genealogical Society, adds that many records may not be filed where you would normally expect to find them. For example, Kellow found the pioneer cemetery records for a county-owned cemetery in Josphine County in the county's Parks and Recreation Department. The Oregon Historical County Records Guide <http://arcweb.sos.state.or.us/county/cphome.html> can help you figure out what's where.

The number-one research repository, according to Lenzen, is the Oregon State Archives in Salem. You may not even have to leave home to tap the archives' holdings: In the past five years, Lenzen says, the FHL has microfilmed many records at the Oregon State Archives and other state repositories <www.familysearch.org>.

For published resources, she adds, the holdings of the Genealogical Forum of Oregon (GFO) are among the best in the state. The GFO has a research service and will look up materials in its library for a nominal fee. See the research policy at <www.gfo.org/respol.htm>.

The largest collection of Oregon historical materials belongs to the Oregon Historical Society Library in Portland, which holds more than 100,000 volumes, two million photographs, 15,000 maps, and 8,000 linear feet of original documents. You can search its catalog of book and serial holdings online at <http://librarycatalog.ohs.org/WebOPAC/index.asp>.

For more advice on getting started with Oregon research, consult Lenzen's online Guide to Oregon Records <www.oregonvos.net/~clenzen/oregonguide.html>. This will give you background information on the type of records you can expect to find and information about where they are located.

STATE RESOURCES

■ ARCHIVES, LIBRARIES, AND SOCIETIES

Alsi Historical and Genealogical Society, Inc.
P.O. Box 822, Waldport, OR 97394

Astoria Public Library
450 Tenth St., Astoria, OR 97103

Baker County Genealogical Group
% Baker County Public Library, 2400 Resort St., Baker City, OR 97814

Bend Genealogical Society
P.O. Box 8254, Bend, OR 97708-8254
Web site: <www.rootsweb.com/~ordeschu/BGS/bgsindex.htm>

Benton County Genealogical Society
P.O. Box 1646, Philomath, OR 97370-1646
Tel: (541) 752-6425

Blue Mountain Genealogical Society
P.O. Box 1801, Pendleton, OR 97801
Web site: <www.ucinet.com/~sandral>

Oregon

Clackamas County Family History Society
P.O. Box 995, 211 Tumwater Dr., Oregon City, OR 97045
Web site: <www.rootsweb.com/~genepool/ccfhs.htm>

Clatsop County Genealogical Society
% Astoria Public Library, 450 Tenth St., Astoria, OR 97103

Clatsop County Historical Society
1618 Exchange St., Astoria, OR 97103

Columbia Gorge Genealogical Society
% The Dalles-Wasco Public Library, 722 Court St., The Dalles, OR 97058

Cottage Grove Genealogical Society

P.O. Box 399, Cottage Grove, OR 97424
Web site: <www.rootsweb.com/~orlane/links/cggs.htm>

Crook County Genealogical Society
246 N. Main St., Prineville, OR 97754-1852

Curry County Historical Society
29410 Ellensburg Ave., Gold Beach, OR 97444

Dalles-Wasco County Public Library
722 Court St., The Dalles, OR 97058
Tel: (541) 296-2815

Deschutes County Historical Society
P.O. Box 5252, Bend, OR 97708

Eugene City Library
100 W. Thirteenth Ave., Eugene, OR 97401

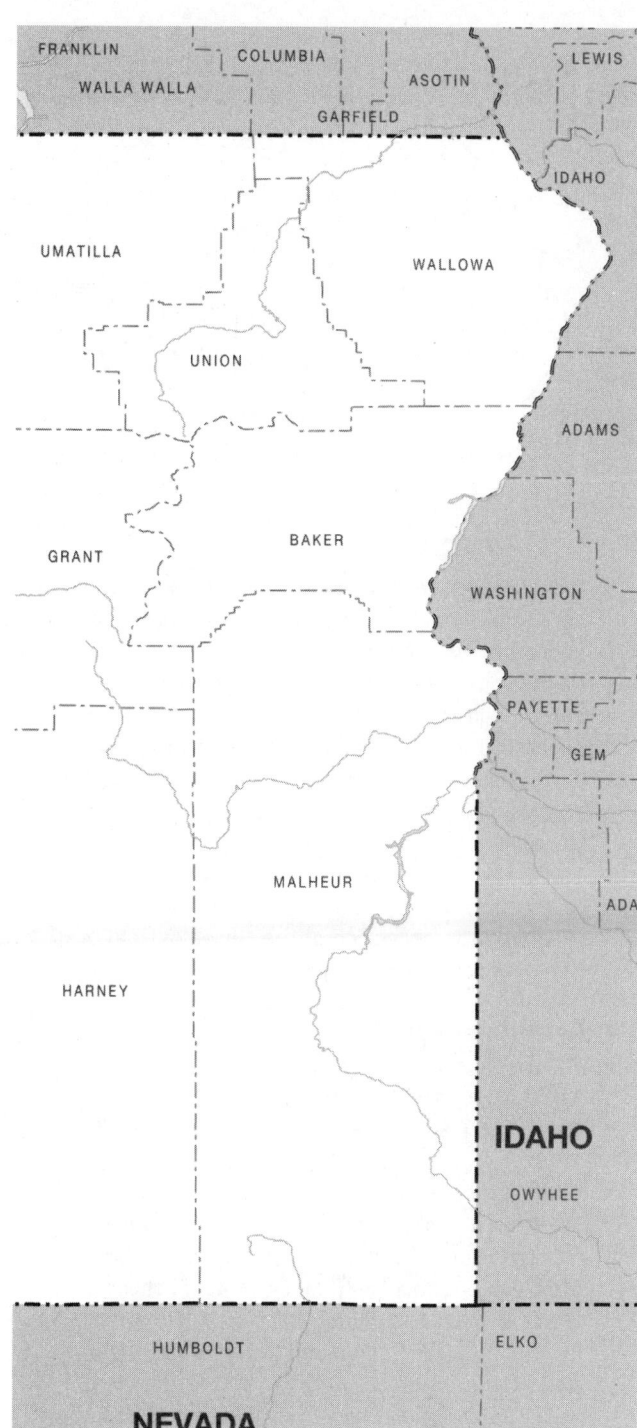

Grants Pass Genealogical Society
P.O. Box 1934, Grants Pass, OR 97526

Harney County Genealogical Society
426 E. Jefferson, Burns, OR 97720

Jewish Genealogical Society of Oregon
% Mittleman Jewish Community Center, 6651 SW Capitol Highway, Portland, OR 97219
Web site: <www.rootsweb.com/~origs/>

Klamath Basin Library and Genealogical Society
126 S. Third St., Klamath Falls, OR 97601

Lake County Historical Society
P.O. Box 49, Lakeview, OR 97630

LaPine Genealogical Society
P.O. Box 1081, LaPine, OR 97739

Lebanon Genealogical Society
% Lebanon Public Library, 626 Second St., Lebanon, OR 97355

Linn Genealogical Society
P.O. Box 1222, Albany, OR 97321
Web site: <www.rootsweb.com/~orlinngs/>

Madras Genealogical Society
671 SW Fairgrounds, Madras, OR 97741

Mennonite Historical and Genealogical Society of Oregon
675 Elma Ave. SE, Salem, OR 97301

Milton-Freewater Genealogical Club
127 SE Sixth St., Milton-Freewater, OR 97962

Mt. Hood Genealogical Forum
950 S. End Rd., Oregon City, OR 97045

Multnomah County Library
801 SW Tenth Avenue, Portland, OR 97205
Tel:
Web site: <www.multcolib.org>

National Archives-Pacific Northwest Region
6125 Sand Point Way NE, Seattle, WA 98115

Tel: (206) 526-6407
Fax: (206) 526-6545
Web site: <www.archives.gov/facilities/wa/seattle.html>

Northrup Library, Linfield College
900 S. Baker, McMinnville, OR 97128-9989
Tel: (503) 434-2262
Fax: (503) 434-2566

Oregon Chapter, American Historical Society of Germans from Russia (AHSGR)
8618 SE Thirty-sixth Ave., Portland, OR 97222-5522
Tel: (503) 659-8248
Web site: <www.ahsgr.org/orportla.html>

Oregon Genealogical Society, Inc.
P.O. Box 10306, Eugene, OR 97449-2306
Tel: (541) 345-0399
Web site: <www.rootsweb.com/~orlncogs/ogsinfo.htm>

Oregon Historical Society
1200 SW Park Ave., Portland, OR 97205-2483
Tel: (503) 222-1741
Web site: <www.ohs.org>

Oregon State Archives
800 Summer St. NE, Salem, OR 97310
Tel: (503) 373-0701
Fax: (503) 373-0953
Web site: <http://arcweb.sos.state.or.us/>

Oregon State Health Division, Center for Health Statistics
P.O. Box 14050, Portland, OR 97293-0050
Tel: (503) 731-4095
Fax: (503) 731-4084
Web site: <www.dhs.state.or.us/publishealth/chs>

Oregon State Library
250 Winter St. NE, Salem, OR 97310-3950
Tel: (503) 378-4243 x221
Fax: (503) 588-7119
Web site: <www.osl.state.or.us/home/>

Oregon State Office of the Bureau of Land Management
1515 SW Fifth Ave., P.O. Box 2965, Portland, OR 97208-2965
Tel: (503) 952-6287
Fax: (503) 952-6333
Web site: <www.or.blm.gov>

Web site: <www.ci.eugene.or.us/Library>

Genealogical Forum of Oregon, Inc.
2130 SW Fifth Ave., Suite 220, Portland, OR 97201-4934
Tel: (503) 227-2398
Web site:

Genealogical Forum of Oregon Library
1 SW Morrison #812, Portland, OR 97201
Web site: <www.gfo.org/library.htm>

Grant County Museum
P.O. Box 416, Canyon City, OR 97820

Grant County Genealogical Society
P.O. Box 419, Canyon City, OR 97820

Oregon

Oregon

Polk County Genealogical Society
535 SE Ash St., The Dalles, OR 97338

Port Orford Genealogical Society
℅ Port Orford Public Library, 555 W. Twentieth St., Port Orford, OR 97465

Portland Library Association
801 SW Tenth Ave., Portland, OR 97205

Rogue Valley Genealogical Society and Library
P.O. Box 1468, 95 Houston Rd., Phoenix, OR 97535
Tel: (541) 512-2340

Roman Catholic Archdiocese of Portland
Chancery Office, 2838 E. Burnside St., P.O. Box 351, Portland, OR 97214-1895
Tel: (503) 234-5334
Fax: (503) 234-2545

Scandinavian Genealogical Society
9143 Olney St. SE, Salem, OR 97301

Sherman County Historical Society
P.O. Box 173, Moro, OR 97039

Siuslaw Genealogical Society
℅ Siuslaw Public Library, P.O. Box 1540, Florence, OR 97439

Sweet Home Genealogical Society
℅ Sweet Home Library, P.O. Box 279, Sweet Home, OR 97386

Tillamook County Historical Society Genealogical Study Group
P.O. Box 123, Tillamook, OR 97141

Umatilla County Historical Society
P.O. Box 253, Pendleton, OR 97801

Waldport Heritage Museum
P.O. Box 882, Waldport, OR 97394
Tel: (541) 563-7092

Willamette Valley Genealogical Society
P.O. Box 2093, Salem, OR 97308

Yamhill County Genealogical Society
P.O. Box 569, McMinnville, OR 97128

Yaquina Genealogical Society
℅ Toledo Public Library, 173 NW Seventh St., Toledo, OR 97391
Web site: <www.rootsweb.com/~orygs/>

BIBLIOGRAPHY

■ GENERAL RESOURCES

Apart and Together, Mennonites in Oregon And Neighboring States, 1876–1976
by Hope Kauffman Lind (Scottdale, PA: Herald Press, 1990)

Baptist Annals of Oregon, 1844–1900, 2 vols.
by Charles Hiram Mattoon (McMinnville, OR: Telephone Register Pub. Co., 1913)

Capitol Names: Individuals Woven into Oregon's History
by Philip Cogswell (Portland, OR: Oregon Historical Society, 1977)

Capitol's Who's Who For Oregon, 1936–1944, 2 vols.
(Portland, OR: Capitol Pub. Co., 1936–1942)

Catholic Church Records of the Pacific Northwest: Grand Ronde Register I (1860–1885), Grand Ronde Register II (1886–1898): St. Michael the Archangel Parish, Grand Ronde Indian Reservation, Grand Ronder, Oregon; St. Patrick's Parish, Muddy Valley, Oregon
by Harriet Duncan Munnick (Portland, OR: Binford & Mort, 1987)

Catholic Church Records of the Pacific Northwest: Missions of St. Ann and St. Rose of the Cayuse, 1847–1888; Walla Walla and Frenchtown, 1858–1872, Frenchtown, 1872–1888
by Harriet Duncan Munnick (Portland, OR: Binford & Mort, 1989)

The Centennial History of Oregon, 1811–1912, 4 vols.
by Joseph Gaston (Chicago: S.J. Clarke Publishing Co., 1912)

Christians on the Oregon Trail: Churches of Christ And Christian Churches in Early Oregon, 1842–1882
by Jerry Rushford (Joplin, MO: College Press Pub. Co., 1997)

RESEARCH TIPS

for more info

- Many Oregon records can only be found at the county level, so it's crucial to pinpoint where your ancestors were living in order to find the documents you need.
- The Oregon Death Index, part of Ancestry.com's subscription service, and the Oregon State Archives' Historical Records Index <http://arcweb.sos.state.or.us/banners/genealogy.htm> can help you start your Oregon research from a distance.
- The Oregon State Archives in Salem is the best research repository in the state, but you'll want to search the collection of the Genealogical Forum of Oregon for published resources.

Census Records
- Federal Census: 1850, 1860, 1870, 1880, 1900, 1910, 1920, 1930
- Federal Mortality Schedules: 1850, 1860, 1870, 1880
- Union Veterans and Widows: 1890
- State/Territorial Census: 1842–1846 (a few counties), 1849 (males over age twenty-one), 1850–1859 (various counties), 1865 (Benton, Columbia, Marion, Umatilla counties), 1870 and 1875 (Umatilla county), 1885 (Linn and Umatilla counties), 1895 (Linn, Morrow, Multnomah, Marion counties), 1905 (Baker, Lane, Linn, Marion counties)

Covered Wagon Women: Diaries & Letters From the Western Trails, 1840–1890, 11 vols.
by Kenneth L. Holmes (Glendale, CA: Arthur H. Clark Co., 1983–1991)

Directory of Churches and Religious Organizations, State of Oregon

(Portland: Historical Records Survey, 1940)

The Genealogist's Companion and Sourcebook, 2d ed.
by Emily Anne Croom (Cincinnati: Betterway Books, 2003)

A Genealogist's Guide to Discovering Your African-American Ancestors
by Franklin Carter Smith and

Emily Anne Croom (Cincinnati: Betterway Books, 2003)

Give all to Oregon: Missionary Pioneers of The Far West
by Cecil Pearl Dryden (New York: Hastings House, 1968)

Guide to Depositories of Manuscript Collections in the United States: Oregon-Washington
(Portland: Oregon Historical Records Survey, 1940)

Guide to Genealogical Sources
by Connie Miller Lenzen (Portland: Genealogical Forum of Oregon, 1994)

Guide to Genealogical Research in the National Archives of the United States
edited by Anne Bruner Eales and Robert M. Kvasnicka (Washington, DC: National Archives and Records Administration, 2000)

Guide to the Manuscript Collections of the Oregon Historical Society
(Portland: Oregon Historical Records Survey, 1940)

History of the Columbia River Valley from The Dalles To the Sea, 3 vols.
by Fred Lockley (Chicago: S.J. Clarke Publishing Co., 1928)

History of Oregon, 2 vols.
by Hubert Howe Bancroft (San Francisco: The History Co., 1886–1888)

History of Oregon, 3 vols.
by Charles Henry Carey (Chicago: Pioneer History Publishing Co., 1922)

History of Oregon: The Growth of an American State
by Horace Sumner Lyman (New York: North Pacific Pub. Society, 1903)

A History of Oregon Methodism
by Thomas D. Yarnes (Portland: Oregon Methodist Conference Historical Society, 1957)

A History of the Oregon Trail, Santa Fe Trail, And Other Trails
by Jacob Ray Gregg (Portland, OR: Binfords & Mort, ca. 1955)

History Of The Pacific Northwest: Oregon and Washington; Embracing an Account of the Original Discoveries On the Pacific Coast of North American, and A Description of the Conquest, Settlement and Subjugation of the . . . Original Territory Of Oregon; Also Interesting Biographies of the Earliest Settlers, 2 vols.
by Elwood Evans (Portland, OR: North Pacific History Co., 1889)

An Illustrated History of Central Oregon: Embracing Wasco, Sherman, Gilliam, Wheeler, Crook, Lake, and Klamath Counties
F.A. Shaver, Arthur P. Rose, R.F. Steele, and A.E. Adams (Spokane, WA: Western Historical Pub. Co., 1905)

An Illustrated History of the State of Oregon: Containing a History of Oregon from the Earliest Period of its Discovery to the Present Time, Together with Glimpses of its Auspicious Future
by Harvey K. Hines (Chicago: Lewis Pub. Co., 1893)

Index to Oregon Newspaper Clippings, 1895–1952
by Alice Stansfield Herzberg (Medford, OR: Rogue Valley Genealogical Society, 1995)

Indians of Oregon Bibliography, 1966–1983
by Betty Book (Portland, OR: Genealogical Council of Oregon, 1991)

Mantle of Elias, The Story of Fathers Blanchet And Demers in Early Oregon
by M. Leona Nichols (Portland: Binfords and Mort, 1941)

National Archives Microfilm Catalogs online:
<www.archives.gov/publications/genealogy_microfilm_catalogs.html>

Oregon Biography Index
edited by Patricia Brandt and Nancy Guilford (Corvallis, OR: Oregon State University, 1976)

Oregon: Comprising a Brief History and Full Description of the Territories of Oregon and Washington: Together with Remarks Upon the Social Position, Productions, Resources and Prospects of the country a Dissertation Upon the Climate, and a Full Description of the Indian Tribes of the Pacific Slope . . . Interspersed with Incidents of Travel and Adventure
by A.N. Armstrong (Washington, DC: Library of Congress, 1989)

Oregon History and Early Literature: A Pictorial Narrative of the Pacific Northwest
by John B. Horner (Portland, OR: The J.K. Gill Company, 1931)

Oregon Pioneers
from the Oregon Genealogical Society (Eugene, OR: the Oregon Historical Society, ca. 1980)

Oregon Research Outline
by the Church of Jesus Christ of Latter-Day Saints (Salt Lake City, UT: Corp. of the President of the Church of Jesus Christ of L.D.S., 1988)

Oregon Trail: Last of the Pioneers
by Rick Steber (Prineville, OR: Bonanza Publishing, 1993)

Paths to the Northwest: A Jesuit History of The Oregon Province
by Wilfred P. Schoenberg (Chicago: Loyola University Press, 1982)

Portrait and Biographical Record of Western Oregon: Containing Original Sketches of Many Well Known Citizens of the Past and Present
(Chicago: Chapman Publishing Co., 1904)

Portrait and Biographical Record of the Willamette Valley, Oregon
(Chicago: Chapman Publishing Co., 1903)

Presbyterianism in Southern Oregon: A History of The Presbytery of Southwest Oregon and its Forebears 1851–1949
by Lawrence H. Mitchelmore (North Bend, OR: L.H. Mitchelmore, 1949)

Research in Oregon
by Connie Miller Lenzen (Arlington, VA: National Genealogical Society, 1992)

Rolls of Certain Indian Tribes in Oregon and Washington
by Charles E. McChesney (Fairfield, WA: Ye Galleon Press, 1969)

Saints to the Columbia: A History of The Church of Jesus Christ of Latter-day Saints in Oregon and Southwestern Washington, 1850–1990
by Louis G. Gassaway Kullberg (Vancouver, WA: L-K Publications, 1991)

The Story of Oregon: A History With Portraits and Biographies, 2 vols.
by Julian Hawthorne (New York: American Historical Pub. Co., 1892)

Terrible Trail: The Meek Cutoff, 1845
by Keith Clark (Caldwell, ID: Caxton Printers, 1966)

These Valiant Women: History of the Sisters of St. Mary of Oregon, 1886–1986
by Wilfred P. Schoenberg (Beaverton, OR: Sisters of St. Mary of Oregon, 1986)

Who's Who for Idaho, Combined With Who's Who for Oregon and Who's Who for the Western States
(Portland, OR: Capitol Publishing Co., 1970)

■ CENSUS RECORDS

The American Census Handbook
by Thomas Jay Kemp (Wilmington, DE: Scholarly Resources, Inc., 2001)

The Census Book: A Genealogist's Guide to Federal Census Facts, Schedules and Indexes
by William Dollarhide (Bountiful, UT: Heritage Quest, 1999)

Finding Answers in U.S. Census Records
by Loretto Dennis Szucs and Matthew Wright (Salt Lake City: Ancestry Publishing, 2001)

Oregon

Oregon

Map Guide to the U.S. Federal Censuses, 1790–1920
by William Thorndale and William Dollarhide (Baltimore: Genealogical Publishing Co., 1987)

State Census Records
by Ann S. Lainhart (Baltimore: Genealogical Publishing Co., Inc. 1992)

Your Guide to the Federal Census
by Kathleen W. Hinckley (Cincinnati: Betterway Books, 2002)

■ IMMIGRATION RECORDS

American Naturalization Records, 1790–1990: What They Are and How to Use Them
by John J. Newman (North Salt Lake, UT: HeritageQuest, 1998)

American Passenger Arrival Records
by Michael Tepper (Baltimore: Genealogical Publishing Co., 1993)

How to Find Oregon Naturalization Records
by Connie Lenzen (Portland, OR: C. Lenzen, 1990)

Oregon Naturalization Records Index: Declaration of Intention, 2 vols.
by W. David Samuelsen (Salt Lake City: Sampubco, 1995)

Overland Passages: A Guide to Overland Documents in the Oregon Historical Society
by Kris White (Portland, OR: Oregon Historical Society Press, 1993)

They Became Americans: Finding Naturalization Records and Ethnic Origins
by Loretto Dennis Szucs (Salt Lake City: Ancestry, Inc., 1998)

They Came in Ships: A Guide to Finding Your Immigrant Ancestor's Arrival Records, 2d ed.
by John P. Colletta (Salt Lake City: Ancestry, Inc., 1993)

The Willamette Valley: Migration and Settlement on the Oregon Frontier
by William Adrian Bowen (Seattle: University of Washington Press, 1978)

■ LAND RECORDS

The Frontier: The Agricultural Opening of the Oregon Country, 1786–1846
by James R. Farming Gibson (Vancouver: University of British Columbia Press, 1985)

Genealogical Material in Oregon Donation Land Claims, 5 vols.
(Portland: Genealogical Forum of Portland, 1957–1975)

Index of Oregon Donation Land Claims, 2d ed.
compiled by the Oregon State Archives (Portland: Genealogical Forum of Portland, 1987)

Land and Property Research in the United States
by Wade E. Hone (Salt Lake City: Ancestry Inc., 1997)

Locating Your Roots: Discover Your Ancestors Using Land Records
by Patricia Law Hatcher (Cincinnati: Betterway Books, 2003)

Preliminary Inventory of the Land-Entry Papers of the General Land Office
compiled by Harry P. Yoshpe and Philip P. Brower (Seattle: National Archives Pacific Alaska Region, 1949)

■ MAPS

Historical Maps of Oregon: Overland Stage Routes, Old Military Roads, Indian Battle Grounds, Old Forts, and Old Gold Mines
by Ralph N. Preston (Corvallis, OR: Western Guide Publishers, 1972)

Oregon Atlas and Gazetteer, 2d ed.
(Freeport, ME: DeLorme Mapping Co., 1995)

Oregon County Boundary Change Maps, 1843–1916
by Erma Skyles Brown (Lebanon, OR: End of Trail Researchers, 1970)

Oregon Geographic Names, 6th ed.
by Lewis A. McArthur (Portland: Oregon Historical Society, 1992)

Oregon Post Offices, 1847–1982
by Richard W. Helbock (Las Cruces, NM: La Posta, ca. 1982)

Places Names of the Pacific Northwest Coast: Origins, Histories and Ancedotes in Bibliographic Form About the Coast of British Columbia, Washington and Oregon
by Lynn Middleton (Seattle, WA: Superior Pub. Co, 1969)

A Preliminary Atlas of Oregon
by William G. Loy (Eugene, OR: Geography Dept., University of Oregon, 1972)

R.L. Polk & Co., Oregon and Washington Gazetteer and Business Directory, 1909–1910
(Seattle: R.L. Polk, 1909)

■ MILITARY RECORDS

An Account of the Origin and Early Prosecution Of the Indian War in Oregon
by Charles S. Drew (Fairfield, WA: Ye Galleon Press, 1972)

Honor Roll of Oregon Grand Army of the Republic, 1881–1935
by Jane Myers (Cottage Grove, OR: Cottage Grove Genealogical Society, 1980)

The Official Records of the Oregon Volunteers In the Spanish War and Philippine Insurrection, 2nd ed.
by C. U. Gantenbein (Salem, OR: J.R. Whitney, 1903)

A Partial List of Military Casualties and MIA's From the State of Oregon During World War II
by Spencer Leonard (Portland, OR: Genealogical Forum of Oregon, Inc., 1993)

Soldiers Who Served in the Oregon Volunteers: Civil War Period, Infantry and Cavalry
by M.A. Pekar (Portland, OR: Genealogical Forum of Portland, 1961)

Uncle, We Are Ready! Registering America's Men, 1917–1918: A Guide to Researching World War I Draft Registration Cards
by John J. Newman (North Salt Lake, UT: HeritageQuest, 2001)

U.S. Military Records: A Guide to Federal & State Sources, Colonial America to the Present
by James C. Neagles (Salt Lake City: Ancestry, Inc., 1994)

World War II: A Family Historian's Guide
by Debra Johnson Knox (Spartanburg, SC: MIE Publishing, 2003)

■ VITAL RECORDS

Cumulative Baptism Index to the Catholic Church Records of the Pacific Northwest
by Sharon E. Osborn-Ryan (Oregon Heritage Press, 1999)

Cumulative Death Index to the Catholic Church Records of the Pacific Northwest Northwest
by Sharon E. Osborn-Ryan (Portland, OR: S. Osborn-Ryan, 1998)

Cumulative Marriage Index to the Catholic Church Records of the Pacific Northwest Northwest
by Sharon E. Osborn-Ryan (Oregon Heritage Press, 1998)

Episcopal Marriages of the Southern Oregon Coast, 1884–1940
by Barbara Brown Eakley (Coos Bay, OR: Bayview Publishers, 1997)

Guide to Public Vital Statistics Records in Oregon
(Portland, OR: Historical Records Survey, 1942)

Oregon Cemetery Directory
(Salem, OR: Oregon Heritage Council, 1976)

Your Guide to Cemetery Research
by Sharon DeBartolo Carmack (Cincinnati: Betterway Books, 2002)

■ **Baker** 22 Sep. 1862
1995 Third St., Baker, OR 97814
Phone: (541)523-8207
Web site: www.bakercounty.org/
Parent County: Wasco
Comments/research tips: Oregon State Archives has Birth records 1871–1929 and Death records 1905–1944. County Clerk has Circuit Court records 1862–1988, Divorce records 1862–1988, Nauturalization records 1897–1928, and Probate records 1863–1984. Since 1965, Marriage records and Military Discharge records have been recorded in the Baker County Records. Since 1987, County Probate Court records have been filed in the Oregon Judicial Information Network (OJIN).

Record Type	Year Begun	Jurisdiction
Marriage	1862	County Clerk
Land	1865	County Clerk
Military	1891	County Clerk

■ **Benton** 23 Dec. 1847
120 NW Fourth St., Corvallis, OR 97330
Phone: (541)766-6800
Web site: www.co.benton.or.us/
Parent County: Polk
Comments/research tips: County Clerk has Birth records ca. 1868–1950, Benton County Historical Museum has Birth records 1907–1916, and Oregon State Archives has Birth records 1907–1929. County Clerk has Circuit Court records 1853–1984, Death records 1907–1948, Divorce records 1853–1984, Land records ca. 1865–1971, Marriage records 1852–1878, and Naturalization records ca. 1864–1950.

Record Type	Year Begun	Jurisdiction
Probate	1880	Benton County Courthouse
Military	1920	County Clerk

■ **Clackamas** 5 July 1843
104 Eleventh St., Oregon City, OR 97045
Phone: (503)722-2745
Web site: www.co.clackamas.or.us/
Parent County: Original County
Comments/research tips: County Clerk has Birth and Death records 1902–1920, Land records 1906–1972, Marriage records 1853–1966, and Naturalization records 1890–1905. Oregon State Archives has Birth and Death records 1915–1945, Circuit Court records 1846–1986, Divorce records 1850–1949, Marriage records 1848–1948, and Naturalization records 1887–1926. From 1967–1977 Military discharges were entered by the County Clerk in the Recording Instruments. Since 1977, the County Clerk has filed Military discharges in the Recording Index.

Record Type	Year Begun	Jurisdiction
Military	1920	County Clerk
Land	ca. 1851	Oregon State Archives
Probate	1850	County Clerk

■ **Clark** 27 June 1844
Parent County: Original County
Comments/research tips: (See Washington State) Now part of the state of Washington.

■ **Clatsop** 22 June 1844
749 Commercial St., P.O. Box 178, Astoria, OR 97103
Phone: (503)325-8511
Web site: www.co.clatsop.or.us/
Parent County: Tuality
Comments/research tips: County Clerk has Birth records 1894–1937, Circuit Court and Divorce records 1855–1987, Death records 1903–1937, Marriage records 1851–1985, Military records 1892–1900, and Naturalization records 1907–1924. Clatsop County Historical Society has Birth records 1915–1949 and Death records 1915–1949. Oregon State Archives has Circuit Court and Divorce records 1849–1858 and 1860–1935, Naturalization records 1907–1970, and Probate records 1848–1930.

Record Type	Year Begun	Jurisdiction
Land	1860	County Clerk
Probate	ca. 1850	County Clerk
Military	1919	County Clerk

■ **Columbia** 16 Jan. 1854
230 Strand St., St. Helens, OR 97051-0010
Phone: (503)397-3796
Web site: www.co.columbia.or.us/
Parent County: Washington
Comments/research tips: County Clerk has Birth records 1907–1929, Circuit Court and Divorce records 1854–1987, Death records 1907–1929, Land records 1854–1860 and 1872–1991, Marriage records 1854–1961, Military records 1887–1900 and 1919–1958, and Naturalization records 1891–1926. Oregon State Archives has Probate records 1850–1930. In 1987, Columbia County started filing county probate cases with the OJIN.

Record Type	Year Begun	Jurisdiction
Probate	1874	County Clerk

■ **Coos** 22 Dec. 1853
250 N. Baxter St., Coquille, OR 97423
Phone: (541)396-3121 ext. 3
Web site: www.co.coos.or.us/
Parent County: Umpqua, Jackson
Comments/research tips: County Clerk has Birth and Death records 1906–1929, Circuit Court records 1854–1983, Divorce records 1854–1983, Marriage records 1853–1968, Military records 1875–1906, Naturalization records 1907–1929, and Probate records 1852–1989. Prior to 1946 Military Discharges were filed by the County Clerk in the Miscellaneous Record. Since 1965, the County Clerk has filed Military Discharges in the Clerk's Book of Records. After 1987, all Coos County Probate Court cases have been filed in OJIN.

Record Type	Year Begun	Jurisdiction
Land	1854	County Clerk
Military	1946	County Clerk
Probate	1990	County Clerk

■ **Crook** 24 Oct. 1882
300 E. Third St., Prineville, OR 97754
Phone: (541)447-6553
Web site: www.co.crook.or.us

Oregon

Parent County: Wasco
Comments/research tips: County Clerk has Birth and Death records 1907–1939, Circuit Court records 1882–1919, Divorce records 1882–1919, Marriage records 1882–1975, Naturalization records 1903–1925, and Probate records 1882–1943 and 1971–1982. Trial Court Administrator has Circuit Court and Divorce records 1883–1985. A.R. Bowman Museum has Land records 1869–1997. The County Clerk has recorded military discharges in the clerk's Microfiche Records since 1982. After 1986, all Crook County probate court cases have been filed in OJIN.

Record Type	Year Begun	Jurisdiction
Military	1883	County Clerk
Land	1883	County Clerk
Probate	1883	Trial Court Administrator

■ **Curry**   18 Dec. 1855
29821 Ellensburg Ave., GoldBeach, OR 97444
Phone: (541)247-7011
Web site: www.co.curry.or.us/
Parent County: Coos
Comments/research tips: Oregon State Archives has Circuit Court records 1872–1939 and Naturalization records 1904, 1909–1913, and 1916–1928. Oregon Historical Records Index has Divorce records 1866–1929. State Courts Civil-Domestic-Probate Office has Divorce records 1903–1987. County Clerk has Marriage records 1856–1964 and Military records 1887–1902. The County Clerk has recorded military discharges in the clerk's Book of Records since 1966. After 1987, all Curry County probate court cases have been filed in OJIN.

Record Type	Year Begun	Jurisdiction
Land	1865	County Clerk
Probate	1888	Curry County Courthouse
Military	1920	County Clerk

■ **Deschutes**   13 Dec. 1916
1340 NW Wall St., Bend, OR 97701
Phone: (541)388-6549
Web site: www.deschutes.org/
Parent County: Crook
Comments/research tips: Circuit Court Clerk has Circuit Court records 1917–1985 and Divorce records 1917–1986. County Clerk has Marriage records 1916–1975. Oregon State Archives has Naturalization records 1917–1969. The Crook County surveyor's office has provided a computer database of subdivision plats dating from 1904 to the present, and partition plats dating from 1977 to the present. The clerk's Miscellaneous Record contains Military Discharge records before 1945. After 1983 the County Clerk has Military Discharge records. After 1986, all Deschutes County Probate Court cases have been filed in OJIN.

Record Type	Year Begun	Jurisdiction
Land	1900	County Clerk
Military	1916	County Clerk
Probate	1916	Circuit Court Clerk

■ **Douglas**   7 Jan. 1852
1036 SE Douglas St., Room 221, Roseburg, OR 97470
Phone: (541)440-4324

Web site: www.co.douglas.or.us/
Parent County: Umpqua
Comments/research tips: County Clerk has Birth records 1903–1933, Circuit Court records 1852–1978, Death records 1903–1933, Divorce records 1852–1978, Marriage records 1852–1969, and Naturalization records 1907–1927. Trial Court Administrator has Circuit Court records 1852–1983, Divorce records 1852–1983, and Probate records 1852–1989. Oregon State Archives has Marriage records 1852–1983. Absorbed Umpqua County 1862.

Record Type	Year Begun	Jurisdiction
Land	1851	County Clerk
Military	1887	County Clerk

■ **Gilliam**   14 Oct. 1864
221 S. Oregon St., Condon, OR 97823
Phone: (541)384-2311
Web site: www.rootsweb.com/~orgillia/
Parent County: Wasco
Comments/research tips: County Clerk has Birth records 1903–1920, Circuit Court and Divorce records 1885–1985, Death records for 1914 only, Marriage records 1885–1984, and Naturalization records 1885–1928. Oregon State Archives has Birth records 1913–1933 and Death records 1912–1933. Miscellaneous Record has Military records before 1945.

Record Type	Year Begun	Jurisdiction
Military	1871	County Clerk
Land	1882	County Clerk
Probate	1885	County Clerk

■ **Grant**   14 Oct. 1864
200 S. Humbolt St., Canyon City, OR 97820
Phone: (541)575-1675
Web site: www.grantcounty.cc/
Parent County: Wasco, Umatilla
Comments/research tips: County Clerk has Birth records 1894–1929 and 1940–1941, Death records 1915–1929, Marriage records 1864–1970, Military records 1887–1901, and Naturalization records 1862–1948. Circuit Court Clerk has Circuit Court records 1887–1888 and 1893–1986. Oregon State Archives has Circuit Court records 1864–1923 and Military records 1872–1898. Oregon Historical Records Index has Divorce records 1872–1922.

Record Type	Year Begun	Jurisdiction
Land	ca. 1877	County Clerk
Probate	1864	County Clerk
Military	1920	County Clerk

■ **Harney**   25 Feb. 1889
450 N. Buena Vista Ave., Burns, OR 97720
Phone: (541)573-6641
Web site: www.co.harney.or.us/
Parent County: Grant
Comments/research tips: County Clerk has Circuit Court and Divorce records 1886–1976, Land records for 1885 and 1902, Marriage records 1889–1966, Military records 1889–1900, and Naturalization records 1889–1929. Circuit

Courtroom Cabinet has Circuit Court records 1947–1985.

Record Type	Year Begun	Jurisdiction
Land	1911	County Clerk
Probate	1898	County Clerk
Military	1942	County Clerk

■ Hood River 23 June 1908
309 State St., Hood River, OR 97031
Phone: (541)386-1442
Web site: www.hoodriver.org/
Parent County: Wasco
Comments/research tips: Oregon State Archives has Birth and Death records 1907–1921 and Naturalization records 1913–1928. Hood River County Trial Court Clerk has Circuit Court and Divorce records 1896–1898 and 1908–1983. Hood River County Assessment Office has Marriage records 1908–1961. Oregon Historical Records Index has Naturalization records 1880–1940. Probate, Land, and Circuit Court case records from Wasco County prior to the creation of Hood River County are included.

Record Type	Year Begun	Jurisdiction
Military	1919	County Clerk
Land	ca. 1890	County Clerk
Probate	1868	Trial Court Clerk
Military	1919	County Clerk

■ Jackson 12 Jan. 1852
10 S. Oakdale Ave., Medford, OR 67501
Phone: (541)774-6147
Web site: www.co.jackson.or.us/
Parent County: Lane
Comments/research tips: County Clerk has Birth records 1907–1929, Death records 1906–1929, Land records for 1887 and 1905–1971, and Marriage records 1855–1964. Oregon State Archives has Birth records 1906–1915, Circuit Court records 1856–1914, Military records 1868–1873, and Naturalization records 1859–1981. Circuit Court Clerk has Circuit Court records 1860–1983, Divorce records 1856–1978, and Probate records ca. 1853–1987. University of Oregon, Knight Library has Circuit Court records 1858–1918, Land records ca. 1867–1892, and Military records for 1864 and 1874. Southern Oregon Historical Society has Marriage records 1854–1930. Oregon Historical Society has Military records 1863, 1868–1875, 1877, 1879–1880, and 1882–1883. County Court Clerk has Naturalization records 1907–1929. Military discharges were recorded in the clerk's Miscellaneous Record before 1966.

Record Type	Year Begun	Jurisdiction
Probate	1988	OJIN
Circuit Court	1983	OJIN
Military	1966	Clerk's Official Records

■ Jefferson 12 Dec. 1914
75 SE C St., Madras, OR 97741
Phone: (541)475-4451
Web site: www.rootsweb.com/~orjeffer/
Parent County: Crook
Comments/research tips: County Clerk has Birth records 1886–1944, Death records 1915–1944, Marriage records 1882–1961, Military records 1920–1982, and Naturalization records 1915–1928. Trial Court Administrator has Circuit Court and Divorce records 1915–1984, Probate records 1893–1985. Jefferson County Public Works Department has Land records 1918–1949. Jefferson County Probate records have been filed on OJIN since 1985.

Record Type	Year Begun	Jurisdiction
Military	1983	County Clerk
Land	1870	Hist. Soc. Museum
Probate	1893	Trial Court Administrator

■ Josephine 22 Jan. 1856
500 NW Sixth St., Grants Pass, OR 97526
Phone: (541)474-5243
Web site: www.co.josephine.or.us/
Parent County: Jackson
Comments/research tips: Josephine County Public Health Department has Birth and Death records 1906–1925. County Clerk has Circuit Court records 1958–1981, Divorce records 1925–1949 and 1959–1978, Marriage records 1857–1971, and Military records 1863–1893 and 1896–1900. Oregon State Archives has Naturalization records 1907–1936 and Probate records 1848–1944. Josephine County Court Civil Unit Office has Probate records 1939–1986.

Record Type	Year Begun	Jurisdiction
Land	1854	County Clerk
Probate	1987	OJIN
Military	1919	County Clerk

■ Klamath 17 Oct. 1882
305 Main St., Klamath Falls, OR 97601-6385
Phone: (541)883-5134
Web site: www.co.klamath.or.us/
Parent County: West part of Lake County
Comments/research tips: Clerk of Circuit Court has Circuit Court records 1883–1987 and Divorce records 1883–1988. County Clerk has Marriage records 1882–1990 and Military records 1887–1888. Clerk of County Court has Naturalization records 1889–1981. Military Discharge records were recorded in the Miscellaneous Record before 1920 and filed in the clerk's Book of Records since 1965. Clerk of County Court has Probate records ca. 1882–1987.

Record Type	Year Begun	Jurisdiction
Land	1875	County Clerk
Probate	1988	OJIN
Military	1919	County Clerk

■ Lake 24 Oct. 1874
513 Center St., Lakeview, OR 97630
Phone: (541)947-6051
Web site: www.rootsweb.com/~orlake/
Parent County: Jackson, Wasco
Comments/research tips: Trial Court Administrator has Circuit Court records 1875–1983 and Divorce records 1875–1984. County Clerk has Marriage records 1875–1968, Naturalization records ca. 1882–1957, and

Oregon

Probate records 1875–1930. Lake County Museum has Military records 1887–1888. Planning and Building Department has Naturalization records ca. 1875–1940.

Record Type	Year Begun	Jurisdiction
Military	1944	County Clerk
Land	ca. 1879	County Clerk
Probate	ca. 1892	Trial Court Administrator

■ Lane 28 Jan. 1851
125 E. Eighth, Eugene, OR 97401
Phone: (541)682-3654
Web site: www.co.lane.or.us/
Parent County: Benton, Linn
Comments/research tips: Deeds/Records Research Library has Birth and Death records 1882–1915, Marriage records 1852–1965, Military records 1918–1966, and Naturalization records 1926–1980. State Archives has Birth and Death records 1915–1928. Court Archives has Circuit Court records 1854–1989, Divorce records 1854–1989, and Probate records 1853–1982. Lane County Historical Museum has Military records 1857–1894.

Record Type	Year Begun	Jurisdiction
Land	1856	Deeds/Records Lib.
Probate	1988	Court Archives
Military	1905	Historical Museum

■ Lewis 21 Dec. 1845
Parent County: Original County
Comments/research tips: (See Washington state) Now part of state of Washington.

■ Lincoln 20 Feb. 1893
225 W. Olive St., Newport, OR 97365
Phone: (541)265-4131
Web site: www.co.lincoln.or.us/
Parent County: Benton, Polk
Comments/research tips: County Clerk has Birth and Death records 1907–1920 and Marriage records 1893–1989. Trial Court Administrator has Circuit Court and Divorce records 1893–1983, Military records 1945–1986, and Probate records 1893–1989. Community Corrections Clerk has Military records 1894–1899. Public Service Building Clerk has Naturalization records 1903–1929. Military Discharge records after 1968 are filed in the Book of Records. Circuit and Probate Court records after 1983 are filed on OJIN.

Record Type	Year Begun	Jurisdiction
Land	1869	County Clerk
Probate	1992	Trial Court Admin.

■ Linn 28 Dec. 1847
300 Fourth Ave. SW, P.O. Box 100, Albany, OR 97321
Phone: (541)967-3831
Web site: www.co.linn.or.us/
Parent County: Marion
Comments/research tips: State Archives has Birth and Death records 1903–1949, Military records 1874–1893, and Naturalization records 1891–1956. Circuit Court Clerk has Circuit Court and Divorce records 1861–1974. County Clerk has Marriage records 1850–1969 and Military

records 1888–1901 and 1919–1970. Historical Records Index contains Naturalization records 1850–1856.

Record Type	Year Begun	Jurisdiction
Land	1856	County Surveyor
Divorce	1983	Circuit Court Clerk
Probate	1863	Circuit Court Clerk
Circuit Court	1983	Circuit Court Clerk

■ Malheur 17 Feb. 1887
251 B St. W., Vale, OR 97918
Phone: (541)473-5151
Web site: www.malheurco.org
Parent County: Baker
Comments/research tips: Trial Court Administrator has Birth and Death records 1907–1939. State Archives has Circuit Court and Divorce records 1886–1930. County Clerk has Marriage records 1880–1986, Military records 1944–1973, and Naturalization records 1861–1908.

Record Type	Year Begun	Jurisdiction
Military	1983	County Clerk
Land	1887	County Clerk
Probate	1886	County Clerk
Nat.	1932	County Clerk
Divorce	1931	Trial Court Admin.
Circuit Court	1931	Trial Court Admin.

■ Marion 5 July 1843
100 High St. NW, Room 1331, Salem, OR 97301
Phone: (503)588-5225
Web site: www.co.marion.or.us/
Parent County: Original County
Comments/research tips: County Clerk has Birth records 1871–1932, Death records 1907–1929, and Marriage records 1849–1967. Circuit Court Clerk has Circuit Court records 1848–1984 and Divorce records 1848–1984. State Archives has Military records 1891–1893, 1896–1902, 1917, and 1940. Probate Court records after 1987 filed on OJIN. Originally Champooick District. Name changed to Marion 3 September 1849.

Record Type	Year Begun	Jurisdiction
Military	1913	County Clerk
Land	1850	County Clerk
Probate	1843	Circuit Court Clerk

■ Morrow 16 Feb. 1885
100 Court St., Heppner, OR 97836
Phone: (541)676-9061
Web site: www.morrowcounty.oregon.com
Parent County: Umatilla, Wasco
Comments/research tips: County Clerk has Birth and Death records 1905–1929, Land records 1861–1915, Marriage records 1885–1901 and 1905–1988, Military records 1887–1898, and Naturalization records 1906–1953. Circuit Court Clerk has Circuit Court and Divorce records 1885–1985.

Record Type	Year Begun	Jurisdiction
Military	1945	County Clerk
Land	1935	County Clerk
Probate	1885	Circuit Court Clerk

■ **Multnomah** 22 Dec. 1854
1120 SW Third Ave., Portland, OR 97204
Phone: (503)988-3957
Web site: www.co.multnomah.or.us
Parent County: Washington, Clackamas
Comments/research tips: Circuit Court has Circuit Court records 1855–1860, 1906–1929, 1972–1982, and Divorce records 1855–1860, 1906–1929, 1972–1983. County Assessment/Taxation Division has Marriage records 1855–1968 and Military records for 1893. Circuit Court Clerk has Naturalization records 1887–1940. Oregon Historical Society has Probate records 1850–1873 and 1896. Book of Records has Military Discharge records before 1964.

Record Type	Year Begun	Jurisdiction
Military	1909	Assessment/Tax. Div.
Land	1851	Assessment/Tax. Div.
Probate	1855	Circuit Court Clerk

■ **Polk** 22 Dec. 1845
850 Main St., Room 201, Dallas, OR 97338
Phone: (503)623-9217
Web site: www.co.polk.or.us/
Parent County: Yamhill
Comments/research tips: State Archives has Birth records 1903–1915, Death records 1903–1906, Military records 1892–1901, Naturalization records 1872–1906 and 1908–1925, and Probate records 1847–1921. County Clerk has Birth records 1915–1921, Death records 1907–1921, and Marriage records 1848–1980. Circuit Court Clerk has Circuit Court records 1846–1983, Divorce records 1846–1983, and Probate records 1921–1971. Public Works Department has Military records for 1877. County Assessor's Office has Land records 1853–1889.

Record Type	Year Begun	Jurisdiction
Probate	1986	Circuit Court Clerk
Land	1890	County Clerk
Military	1919	County Clerk

■ **Sherman** 25 Feb. 1889
500 Court St., Moro, OR 97039
Phone: (541)565-3606
Web site: www.sherman-county.com
Parent County: Wasco
Comments/research tips: County Clerk has Birth records 1904–1941, Circuit Court records 1889–1933, Death records 1905–1952, Divorce records 1889–1933, Marriage records 1889–1977 and 1982–1987, Military records 1921–1955, 1960–1977, and for 1982, and Naturalization records 1889–1901 and 1907–1929. Circuit Court Clerk has Circuit Court and Divorce records 1933–1987.

Record Type	Year Begun	Jurisdiction
Land	1885	County Clerk
Probate	1889	County Clerk
Military	1987	Clerk's Recordings

■ **Tillamook** 15 Dec. 1853
201 Laurel Ave., Tillamook, OR 97141
Phone: (503)842-3402

Web site: www.co.tillamook.or.us
Parent County: Clatsop, Polk, Yamhill
Comments/research tips: State Archives has Birth and Death records 1903–1943, Circuit Court records 1862–1969, Divorce records 1862–1969, and Naturalization records 1907–1927. Tillamook County Pioneer Museum has Death records 1918–1945. Trial Court Administrator has Divorce records ca. 1868–1983 and Probate records 1859–1987. County Clerk has Marriage records 1854–1964. Circuit Court civil and criminal records dating before 1904 were recorded separately. Recorded Instruments has Military Discharge records before 1968. Direct and Indirect Alpha Indexes has Military Discharge records after 1994 as part of the recorded instruments.

Record Type	Year Begun	Jurisdiction
Military	1918	County Clerk
Probate	1988	OJIN
Land	1860	County Clerk

■ **Twality** 5 July 1843
Parent County: Original County
Comments/research tips: (See Washington) Name changed to Washington 3 September 1849.

■ **Umatilla** 27 Sep. 1862
216 SE Fourth St., Pendleton, OR 97801-2590
Phone: (541)276-7111
Web site: www.co.umatilla.or.us/
Parent County: Wasco
Comments/research tips: County Clerk has Birth records 1890–1897 and 1914–1926, Death records 1892–1897 and 1914–1926, Marriage records 1862–1962, and Naturalization records ca. 1863–1974. State Archives has Birth records 1906–1945 and Death records 1907–1944. Trial Court Administrator has Circuit Court records 1863–ca. 1997, Divorce records 1863–ca. 1997, and Probate records 1863–1986. County Surveyor's office has Military records 1889–1902 and 1942–1976. The clerk's Miscellaneous Record has Military Discharge records before 1942.

Record Type	Year Begun	Jurisdiction
Military	1910	County Clerk
Land	1862	County Clerk
Probate	1987	OJIN

■ **Umpqua** 1851
Parent County: Benton, Linn
Comments/research tips: (See Douglas) Absorbed by Douglas County 1862.

■ **Union** 14 Oct. 1864
1106 K Ave., LaGrande, OR 97850
Phone: (541)963-1006
Web site: www.union-county.org
Parent County: Baker
Comments/research tips: County Clerk has Birth and Death records 1905–1906, Marriage records 1864–1968, Military records 1864–1991, Military Discharge records 1919–1944, and Naturalization records 1865–1926. Trial Court

Administrator has Circuit Court records 1864–1986, Divorce records 1864–1986, and Probate records 1865–1986.

Record Type	Year Begun	Jurisdiction
Military	1989	County Clerk
Land	1865	County Clerk
Probate	1987	OJIN

■ Wallowa 11 Feb. 1887
101 S. River St., Enterprise, OR 97828-1300
Phone: (541)426-4543
Web site: www.co.wallowa.or.us/
Parent County: Union
Comments/research tips: County Clerk has Birth and Death records 1905–1944, Circuit Court and Divorce records 1887–1983, Marriage records 1887–1970, Military records for 1878, 1888–1900 and 1919–1990, Naturalization records 1897–1906, and Probate records 1886–1995.

Record Type	Year Begun	Jurisdiction
Land	1906	County Clerk
Probate	1987	OJIN
Military	1990	County Clerk

■ Wasco 11 Jan. 1854
511 Washington St., The Dalles, OR 97058
Phone: (541)296-2207
Web site: www.historysavers.com/orwasco/
Parent County: Clackamas, Marion, Linn, Lane
Comments/research tips: County Clerk has Birth and Death records 1865–1891, Marriage records 1854–1962, and Military records 1855–1856, 1889–1905, 1918–1962, and 1975–1986. Oregon State Archives has Birth and Death records 1915–1941, Circuit Court records 1848–1963, Divorce records 1848–1963, and Naturalization records 1885–1962. Circuit Court Clerk has Circuit Court and Divorce records 1854–1989.

Record Type	Year Begun	Jurisdiction
Land	1854	County Clerk
Probate	1854	Court Operations Office

■ Washington 5 July 1843
155 N. First Ave., Suite 130, Hillsboro, OR 97124-3072
Phone: (503)846-8601
Web site: www.co.washington.or.us/cgi/home/washco.pl
Parent County: Original County
Comments/research tips: Assessment/Taxation Department has Birth and Death records 1907–1946, Marriage records 1842–1961, Military records 1895–1917 and 1919–1977, and Naturalization records 1903–1906. Clerk of Circuit Court has Circuit Court and Divorce records 1850–1982 and Probate records 1848–1986. State Archives has Circuit Court and Divorce records 1844–1939, Military records for 1864, 1867–1873, 1884–1900 and 1917–1918, Naturalization records 1907–1927, and Probate records 1842–1921. Washington County Historical Museum has Land records ca. 1850–1985. Formerly Twality (or Falatine) County. Name changed to Washington 3 September 1849.

Record Type	Year Begun	Jurisdiction
Land	1868	Assessment/Tax. Dept.
Probate	1987	OJIN
Military	1964	Book of Records

■ Wheeler 17 Feb. 1889
701 Adams St., P.O. Box 327, Fossil, OR 97830
Phone: (541)763-2400
Web site: www.wheelerinfo.com
Parent County: Crook, Gilliam, Grant
Comments/research tips: State Archives has Birth and Death records 1915–1930. Trial Court Coordinator has Circuit Court and Divorce records 1898–1988. County Clerk has Marriage records 1896–1977 and Naturalization records 1899–1927.

Record Type	Year Begun	Jurisdiction
Land	1884	County Clerk
Probate	1887	County Clerk
Military	1899	County Clerk

■ Yamhill 5 July 1843
535 NE Fifth St., McMinnville, OR 97128
Phone: (503)434-7518
Web site: www.co.yamhill.or.us/
Parent County: Original County
Comments/research tips: State Archives has Birth records 1871–1944, Circuit Court and Divorce records 1854–1943, Death records 1907–1928, and Naturalization records 1853–1959. County Clerk has Birth records 1903–1906 and 1908–1925, and Marriage records 1856–1978. Trial Court Administrator has Circuit Court and Divorce records 1894–1979. Yamhill County Museum has Death records ca. 1919–ca. 1928. Yamhill Public Works/Surveyor's office has Land records 1852–1899. Oregon Historical Society has Military records 1864–1870.

Record Type	Year Begun	Jurisdiction
Military	1919	County Clerk
Land	ca. 1858	County Clerk
Probate	1852	Trial Court Admin.

Pennsylvania

By Maureen Taylor

HISTORICAL OVERVIEW

William Penn received a Royal Charter in 1681 giving him the right to establish a colony on land taken from the Dutch. Initially known as Penn's Woods, the official name of the colony would eventually become Pennsylvania. Penn opened the area to individuals of diverse religious beliefs and published advertisements in European newspapers encouraging immigration. By the early eighteenth century, Philadelphia was already a bustling city.

In 1749, the Ohio Company claimed land from Virginia north through the Ohio valley, including what is now western Pennsylvania. Pennsylvania had major land disputes with Maryland to the south and Connecticut in the northeast that lasted through the Revolutionary War. Many of the early immigrants to the western part of the colony came from the eastern Pennsylvania settlements and other colonies, generally not from other countries.

Philadelphia became one of the centers of the Revolutionary War when other colonies sent representatives to the First Continental Congress held there. The city was the site of the reading of the Declaration of Independence on July 4, 1776. In 1787, representatives again met in Philadelphia for a Constitutional Convention to establish the United States government. Pennsylvania was the second state to ratify the Constitution. Philadelphia served as the capital of the United States from 1790 to 1800.

Canals built during the early 1800s—like the three hundred-mile Pennsylvania Main Line Canal—traversed the state. Philadelphia and Pittsburgh acted as shipping hubs due to their access to major transportation routes and waterways. Philadelphia merchants imported goods from foreign ports and shipped them west to Pittsburgh. In the nineteenth century, multiple railroad lines encouraged transportation and trade between the eastern and western parts of the state.

PENNSYLVANIA AT A GLANCE

Motto: Virtue, Liberty, and Independence

Population: 12.3 million

Prevalent Religions: Quakers, Lutherans, Mennonites, Amish, Baptist Brethren, Catholics, Presbyterians, Jews, Swedenborgians, Schwenkfelders, Moravians, and Methodists, among others.

Major Industries: Health care, banking, education, pharmaceuticals, manufacturing, food processing (ketchup, chocolate, ice cream, potato chips), agribusiness (dairy products, cattle, mushrooms, poultry, apples, sweet corn), coal, steel, hardwood forestry, tourism, shipping

Ethnic Makeup (in percent): Caucasian 85.4%, African American 10.0%, Hispanic 3.2%, Asian 1.8%, Native American 0.1%, Other 1.5%

Famous Pennsylvanians: Marian Anderson, Samuel Barber, Pearl S. Buck, Alexander Calder, Rachel Carson, Bill Cosby, Stephen Foster, Martha Graham, Alexander Haig, Lee Iacocca, Reggie Jackson, General George Marshall, Margaret Mead, Man Ray, B.F. Skinner, Gertrude Stein, Jimmy Stewart, John Updike, August Wilson, Andrew Wyeth

Above: Cannons at Gettysburg Battlefield

Ulster Scots, Dutch, Finns, Germans, French, and Swedes brought religious denominations including the Amish, Mennonites, Moravians, Schwenkfelders, Reformed, and Lutherans to Pennsylvania, taking advantage of the religious freedom encouraged by William Penn. Some of these newcomers settled in the eastern regions or moved into the western state lands, joined by immigrants from other colonies. In the nineteenth century, immigrants from southern and eastern Europe established residence. Today the state contains individuals from all over the world, including Southeast Asia and Latin America.

Pennsylvania is known for agriculture, tourism, and manufacturing, including Hershey's chocolate factories and Pittsburgh's Heinz Company's pickles and ketchup. Manufactured goods include steel, chemicals, clothing, and petroleum products.

RECORD HIGHLIGHTS

Aside from what exists in the published *Pennsylvania Archives*, few vital records are extant before the mid-nineteenth century, and it wasn't until 1 January 1906 that birth and death records were officially recorded by the state. From 1852 to 1854, the Register of Wills in each county recorded births, marriages, and deaths. The records are not complete for all the counties in existence during those years. According to the Archives Web site <www.phmc.state.pa.us>, the Clerk of the Orphan's

Court in each county recorded vital records: births and deaths from 1893 to 1906 and marriages from 1885. Compliance varied from county to county. Because of the lack of civil registration in the nineteenth century, church records are the main source for vital information, especially for German and Quaker congregations.

Many types of records are available on the county level, including estate papers (wills, orphan court records, inventories, and affidavits of death); land records (deeds, mortgages, and tax records); as well as court records (criminal and civil cases, naturalization, and divorces).

Land records date from 1682. Transactions between individuals and the Commonwealth of Pennsylvania are at the Pennsylvania State Archives. Deeds can also be found in the Office of the Recorder of Deeds for each county. The Archives Web site states that the 1706 "act for the acknowledgment and recording of deeds" provided that, within six months, every deed or conveyance of real property had to be acknowledged by two witnesses before a justice of the peace or the recorder of deeds or his deputy.

Tax records are particularly good for Pennsylvania and can substitute for state census records and missing vital records. Every seven years a taxpayer list known as the "Septennial Census" was compiled. Unfortunately, only a small percentage of the original documents have survived. The amount of information enumerated depends on the county and time period, but usually included taxable inhabitants and freemen. According to the Archives Web site, "Commencing in 1800, the age, name, gender, and place of residence of each slave is also frequently given, and occasionally the name of the slave's owner." In addition to the Septennial Census to determine political representation, Pennsylvania counties compiled yearly tax rolls which are available at county courthouses or historical societies. Tax records generally cover from the mid-1700s through the present day (in one form or another), depending upon the county. Many of the early county tax lists are in the published *Pennsylvania Archives*.

The Pennsylvania State Archives has military papers from 1775 to 1985, but their Web site cautions that "most of the records of military service created prior to 1861 contain scant genealogical or descriptive data." A fairly good listing of service prior to the Civil War is in the published *Pennsylvania Archives*. The State Archives has card files online for service in various wars.

According to Jane Addams Clark of the Genealogical Society of Pennsylvania, "finding genealogical records depends on establishing an ancestor's place of residence in a particular county." Many counties were carved out of the three original counties, Philadelphia, Buck, and Chester. Also, the counties of Bedford, Cumberland, Westmoreland, and the northern county of Northumberland served as the mother counties for many western and northern counties. Clark advises that a researcher "really needs to know the genealogies of the counties and townships" in order to locate the appropriate county.

The Web sites of the Genealogical Society of Pennsylvania (GSP) <www.libertynet.org/gspa/> and the Historical Society of Pennsylvania (HSP) <www.hsp.org> contain helpful information for genealogists. Researchers can start their search in Philadelphia at either of these two major research libraries. In the early 1900s, volunteers at the GSP abstracted wills for Philadelphia County and others counties in southeastern Pennsylvania to create an every name index. The GSP Web site has this index online, as well as an index to manuscript collections in their holdings. Researchers can access the HSP catalog online as well. Peruse the collections of these two institutions before proceeding to the county level. For Western Pennsylvania, researchers really need to visit the Carnegie Library of Pittsburgh and the Blair County Genealogical Society in Hollidaysburg. Because the state is so large geographically, even these regional libraries do not comprehensively cover all areas of the state. Thus, you will need to look into the holdings of local public libraries and historical societies.

STATE RESOURCES

■ ARCHIVES, LIBRARIES, AND SOCIETIES

Adams County Pennsylvania Historical Society
P.O. Box 4325, Gettysburg, PA 17325
Tel: (717) 334-4723
Web site: <www.emmitsburg.net/achs>

Allegheny Valley Community Library
400 Lock St., Tarentum, PA 15084
Tel: (724) 226-0770
Web site: <www.einpgh.org/ein/alvalley>

Altoona Public Library
1600 Fifth Ave., Altoona, PA 16602-3693
Tel: (814) 946-0417
Web site: <www.altoonalibrary.org>

American Swedish Historical Museum
1900 Pattison Ave., Philadelphia, PA 19145
Tel: (215) 389-1776
Web site: <www.americanswedish.org/>

Annie Halenbake Ross Library
232 W. Main St., Lock Haven, PA 17745
Tel: (570) 748-3321
Web site: <www.rosslibrary.org>

Armstrong County Genealogical Society
300 N. McKean St., P.O. Box 735, Kittanning, PA 16201-1345
Tel: (724) 548-5707
Web site: <www.angelfire.com/pa2/acgs/>

Beaver County Genealogical Society
P.O. Box 640, Beaver Falls, PA 15010
Web site: <www.rootsweb.com/~pabecgs/>

Bedford County, Pioneer Historical Society, Inc.
242 E. John St., Bedford, PA 15522
Tel: (814) 623-2011
Web site: <www.rootsweb.com/~paphsbc>

Berks County Genealogical Society
3618 Kutztown Rd., Laureldale, PA 19605

Web site: <www.berksgenes.org/>

Berks County Historical Society
940 Centre Ave., Reading, PA 19601
Tel: (610) 375-4375
Web site: <www.berkshistory.org>

Berwick Historical Society
102 E. Second St., Berwick, PA 18603-4827
Tel: (570) 759-8020
Web site: <www.berwickhistoricalsociety.org>

Blair County Genealogical Society
431 Scotch Valley Rd., Hollidaysburg, PA 16648
Tel: (814) 696-3492
Web site: <www.rootsweb.com/~pabcgs/>

Blair County Historical Society
P.O. Box 1083, Altoona, PA 16603
Tel: (814) 942-3916
Web site: <www.blaircohistoricalsociety.homestead.com>

Bloomsburg Public Library
225 Market St., Bloomsburg, PA 17815
Tel: (570) 784-0883
Web site: <www.bloomsburgpl.org>

Bradford Landmark Society
45 E. Corydon, Bradford, PA 16701
Tel: (801) 362-3906
Web site: <www.bradfordlandmark.org>

Bucks County Historical Society
84 S. Pine St., Doylestown, PA 18901
Tel: (215) 345-0210
Web site: <www.mercermuseum.org/>

Cambria County Historical Society
615 N. Center St., P.O. Box 278, Ebensburg, PA 15931
Tel: (814) 472-6674
Web site: <www.cambriacountyhistorical.com>

Cameron County Historical Society
P.O. Box 433, Emporium, PA 15834
Tel: (814) 486-6355

Web site: <www.thelittlemuseum
.org>

**Capital Area Genealogical
Society**
P.O. Box 4502, Harrisburg, PA
17111-0502
Web site: <http://maley.net/
cags/>

Carnegie Library of Pittsburgh
4400 Forbes Ave., Pittsburgh, PA
15213
Tel: (412) 622-3144
Web site: <www.clpgh.org/>

**Centre County Library &
Historical Museum**
200/203 N. Allegheny St., Bellefonte, PA 16823
Tel: (814) 355-1516
Web site: <www.centrecountylibr
ary.org>

**Centre County Genealogical
Society**
P.O. Box 1135, State College, PA
16804-1135
Web site: <www.rootsweb.com/
~paccgs/>

**Centre County Historical
Society**
1001 E. College Ave., State College, PA 16801
Tel: (814) 234-4779
Web site: <www.centrecountyhis
tory.org>

**Chester County Archives &
Records Service**
601 Westtown Rd., Suite 080,
P.O. Box 2747, West Chester, PA
19380
Web site: <www.chesco.org/arc
hives.html>

**Chester County Historical
Society**
225 N. High St., West Chester,
PA 19380-2691
Tel: (610) 692-4800
Web site: <www.chestercohistori
cal.org>

Citizens Library
55 S. College St., Washington,
PA 15301
Tel: (724) 222-2400
Web site: <www.citlib.org>

City Archives of Philadelphia
3101 Market St., Suite 150, Philadelphia, PA 19104
Tel: (215) 685-9401
E-mail: archives@phila.gov
Web site: <www.phila.gov/phils/
carchive.htm>

**Clarion County Historical and
Genealogical Society**
17 S. Fifth Ave., Clarion, PA
16214-1501
Tel: (814) 226-4450
Fax: (814) 226-7106
E-mail: cchs@csonline.net
Web site: <www.csonline.net/
cchs/>

**Clearfield County Historical
Society**
104 E. Pine St., Clearfield, PA
16830
Tel: (814) 765-6125
Web site: <www.rootsweb.com/
~pacchsm>

**Clinton County Genealogical
Society**
P.O. Box 393, Lock Haven, PA
17745
Web site: <www.clintoncogensoc
iety.org>

**Clinton County Historical
Society**
362 E. Water St., Lock Haven, PA
17745
Tel: (570) 748-7254
Web site: <www.clintoncountyhis
tory.com>

**Cocalico Valley Historical
Society**
P.O. Box 193, 249 W. Main St.,
Ephrata, PA 17522
Tel: (717) 733-1616
Web site: <www.cocalicovalleyhs
.org>

**Columbia County Historical and
Genealogical Society**
225 Market St., P.O. Box 360,
Bloomsburg, PA 17815-0360
Tel: (570) 784-1600
Web site: <www.colcohist-genso
c.org/CCHGShome.html>

**Cornerstone Genealogical
Society**
P.O. Box 547, Waynesburg, PA
15370
Tel: (724) 627-5653
Web site: <www.vicoa.com/corn
erstone/>

Coyle Free Library
102 N. Main St., Chambersburg,
PA 17201
Tel: (717) 263-1054
Web site: <http://fclspa.org/co
yle/coyle.htm>

**Crawford County Genealogical
Society**
P.O. Box 514, Meadville, PA
16335

Web site: <www.rootsweb.com/
~pacrawgs>

**Cumberland County Historical
Society**
21 N. Pitt St., Carlisle, PA 17013
Web site: <www.historicalsociety
.com>

**Delaware County Historical
Society/Museum**
408 E. Avenue of the States,
Chester, PA 19013
Tel: (610) 872-0502
Web site: <www.delcohistory
.org/dchs>

Easton Area Public Library
515 Church St., Easton, PA
18042
Tel: (610) 258-2917
Web site: <www.eastonpl.org>

**Elizabeth Township Historical
Society**
5811 Smithfield St., Boston, PA
15135
Tel: (412) 754-2030
Web site: <www.15122.com/
ETHS>

**Episcopal Diocese of
Pennsylvania**
240 S. Forth St., Philadelphia, PA
19106
Tel: (215) 627-6434
Web site: <www.diopa.org/diop
a>

Erie County Historical Society
417 State St., Erie, PA 16501
Tel: (814) 454-1813
Web site: <www.eriecountyhistor
y.org>

Erie County Library
160 E. Front St., Erie, PA 16507
Tel: (814) 451-6900
Web site: <www.ecls.lib.pa.us>

**Erie Society for Genealogical
Research**
P.O. Box 1403, Erie, PA 16512
Web site: <www.pa-roots.com/
~erie>

**Evangelical and Reformed
Historical Library**
555 W. James St., Lancaster, PA
17603
Tel: (717) 290-8711
Web site: <www.erhs.info>

**Fayette County Genealogical
Society**
24 Jefferson St., Uniontown, PA
15401

Web site: <www.hhs.net/sss/fay
ette/fcgsinfo.htm>

**Forest County Historical
Society**
206 Elm St., P.O. Box 546, Ti-
onesta, PA 16353
Tel: (814) 755-4422
E-mail: FCHS@usachoice.net
Web site: <http://forestcounty
.com/historyhouse.html>

**Frackville Area Historical
Society**
104 Broad Mountain Ave., Frack-
ville, PA 17931
Web site: <www.geocities.com/
Heartland/Acres/5200/>

Franklin Public Library
421 Twelfth St., Franklin, PA
16323
Tel: (814) 432-5062
Web site: <www.csonline.net/fpl>

The Free Library of Philadelphia
1901 Vine St., Philadelphia, PA
19103
Tel: (215) 686-5322
Web site: <www.library.phila.gov>

**Friends Historical Library of
Swarthmore College**
500 College Ave., Swarthmore,
PA 19081
Tel: (610) 328-8497
Fax: (610) 328-7329
Web site: <www.swathmore.
edu/Library/friends>

**Fulton County Historical
Society**
P.O. Box 115, McConnellsburg,
PA 17233
Web site: <www.fultonhistory
.org>

**Genealogical Research Society
of Northeastern Pennsylvania**
P.O. Box 1, Olyphant, PA
18447-0001
Tel: (570) 383-7661
Web site: <www.cfrobbins.com/
grsnp/>

**Genealogical Society of
Pennsylvania**
215 S. Broad St., Seventh Floor,
Philadelphia, PA 19107-5325
Tel: (215) 545-0391
Web site: <www.libertynet.org/
gspa/>

**Genealogical Society of
Southwestern Pennsylvania**
P.O. Box 894, Washington, PA
15301
Web site: <http://jock.cobweb.
net/~gssp>

Pennsylvania

German Society of Pennsylvania
P.O. Box 244, Kutztown, PA 19530
Tel: (610) 894-9551
Web site: <www.pgs.org>

Green Free Library
134 Main St., Wellsboro, PA 16901
Tel: (570) 724-4876
Web site: <http://home.epix.net/~greenlib>

Greene County Historical Society
P.O. Box 127, Waynesburg, PA 15370
Tel: (724) 627-3204
Web site: <www.greenepg.net/~museum>

Heritage Society of Pennsylvania
300 North St., Harrisburg, PA 17120
Tel: (717) 787-2407
Web site: <www.paheritage.org>

Historic Schaefferstown, Inc.
P.O. Box 307, Schaefferstown, PA 17088
Tel: (717) 949-2244
Web site: <www.hsimuseum.org>

Historical & Genealogical Society of Indiana County
200 S. Sixth St., Indiana, PA 15701
Tel: (724) 463-9600
Web site: <www.rootsweb.com/~paicgs/>

Historical and Genealogical Society of Somerset County
10649 Somerset Pike, Somerset, PA 15501
Tel: (814) 445-6077
Web site: <www.somersetcounty.com/historicalcenter>

Historical Society of Dauphin County
219 S. Front St., Harrisburg, PA 17104
Tel: (717) 233-3462
Web site: <www.dauphincountyhistoricalsociety.org>

Historical Society of Green Tree
10 W. Manilla Ave., Pittsburgh, PA 15220
Tel: (412) 921-9292
Web site: <www.einetwork.net/ein/greentree>

Historical Society of Pennsylvania Library
1300 Locust St., Philadelphia, PA 19107
Tel: (215) 732-6200
Web site: <www.hsp.org>

Historical Society of Schuylkill County
14 N. Centre St., Pottsville, PA 17901
Tel: (570) 622-7540
Web site: <www.rootsweb.com/~paschuyl>

Historical Society of Westmoreland
41 W. Otterman St., Suite 310, Greensburg, PA 15601
Tel: (724) 836-1800
Web site: <www.starofthewest.org>

Huntingdon County Historical Society
P.O. Box 305, Huntingdon, PA 16652
Tel: (814) 643-5449
Web site: <www.huntingdonhistory.org>

Jewish Genealogical Society of Philadelphia
P.O. Box 335, Exton, PA 19341
Web site: <www2.jewishgen.org/jgsp>

Jewish Genealogical Society of Pittsburgh
2131 Fifth Ave., Pittsburgh, PA 15219
Web site: <http://feefhs.org/jg/frgjgspi.html>

Juaniata County Historical Society
498B Jefferson St., Mifflintown, PA 17059
Tel: (717) 436-5152
Web site: <www.rootsweb.com/~pajchs>

Lackawanna County Historical Society
The Catlin House, 232 Monroe Ave., Scranton, PA 18510
Tel: (570) 344-3841
Web site: <www.lackawannahistory.org>

Lancaster County Historical Society
230 N. President Ave., Lancaster, PA 17603
Tel: (717) 392-4633
Web site: <www.lancasterhistory.org/index.html>

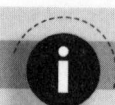

RESEARCH TIPS
for more info

- Start your Pennsylvania research from your living room with the Web sites of the Genealogical Society of Pennsylvania <www.libertynet.org/gspa> and the Historical Society of Pennsylvania <www.hsp.org>.
- Before chasing your ancestors in county records across this large state, make sure you know exactly where you ancestors were living and when in order to find the records you need—most Pennsylvania records are held at the county level.
- If you're researching in Western Pennsylvania, visit the Carnegie Library of Pittsburgh <www.clpgh.org/> and the Blair County Genealogical Society in Hollidaysburg <www.rootsweb.com/~pabcgs/>. Those these two regional resources will help you on your way, they do not thoroughly cover the entire state—you'll need to delve into the collections of local public libraries and societies.

Census Records
- Federal Census: 1790, 1800, 1810, 1820, 1830, 1840, 1850, 1860, 1870, 1880, 1900, 1910, 1920, 1930
- Federal Mortality Schedules: 1850, 1860, 1870, 1880
- Union Veterans and Widows: 1890
- Septennial Census: 1779–1863

Lancaster Mennonite Historical Society
2215 Millstream Rd., Lancaster, PA 17602-1499
Tel: (717) 393-9745
Web site: <www.lmhs.org>

Lebanon County Historical Society
924 Cumberland St., Lebanon, PA 17042

Web site: <www.lebanonhistory.org>

Lehigh County Historical Society
P.O. Box 1548, Allentown, PA 18105
Web site: <www.lehighcountyhistoricalsociety.org>

Ligonier Valley Historical Society

P.O. Box 167, Ligonier, PA 15655
Tel: (724) 238-6818
Web site: <www.compassinn
.com/lvhs.html>

**Lycoming County Genealogical
Society**
P.O. Box 3625, Williamsport, PA
17701
Web site: <http://members.aol.
com/LCGSgen/lcgs.htm>

**Lycoming County Historical
Society**
858 W. Forth St., Williamsport,
PA 17754
Web site: <www.lycoming.org/lc
hsmuseum>

**James P. Magill Library,
Haverford College (Orthodox
Quaker records)**
370 Lancaster Ave., Haverford,
PA 19041
Tel: (610) 896-1175
Web site: <www.haverford.edu/li
brary/web/library.html>

**Mahanoy and Mahantongo
Historical & Preservation
Society**
P.O. Box 143, Dalmatia, PA
17017
Web site: <www.mahantongo
.org/>

**McKean County Genealogical
Society**
201 Fullerton Rd., R.R. Box 46,
Derrick City, PA 16727
Web site: <http://happeningsint
hehills.com/mcgs>

**Mercer County Genealogical
Society**
P.O. Box 812, Sharon, PA 16146
Web site: <www.rootsweb.com/
~pamercer/PA/MCGS/MCGS
.htm>

**Mercer County Historical
Society**
119 S. Pitt St., Mercer, PA 16137
Tel: (724) 662-3490
Web site: <www.mchspa.org>

**Mifflin County Historical
Society**
1 W. Market St., Suite 1, Lewistown, PA 17044
Tel: (717) 242-1022
Web site: <www.rootsweb.com/
~pamchs/home.htm>

**Montgomery County Historical
Society**
1654 Dekalb St., Norristown, PA
19401

Tel: (610) 272-0297
Web site: <www.hsmcpa.org>

**Montour County Genealogical
Society**
205 Ferry St., Danville, PA 17821
Tel: (570) 275-6177
Web site: <www.rootsweb.com/
~pamcgs>

**Muncy Historical Society and
Museum of History**
40 N. Main St., P.O. Box 11,
Muncy, PA 17756
Tel: (570) 546-5917
Web site: <www.muncyhistorical
society.org>

Myerstown Community Library
199 N. College St., Myerstown,
PA 17067
Web site: <www.lebanoncountyli
braries.org/myerstown>

**National Archives, Mid-Atlantic
Region (Philadelphia)**
900 Market St., Philadelphia, PA
19107
Tel: (215) 606-0100
Fax: (215) 597-2303
Web site: <www.archives.gov/mi
datlantic/>

New Castle Public Library
207 E. North St., New Castle, PA
16101
Tel: (724) 658-6659
Web site: <www.newcastle.lib.pa
.us>

**Northampton County Historical
and Genealogical Society**
107 S. Fourth St., Easton, PA
18042
Tel: (610) 253-1222
Web site: <www.northamptoncty
museum.org>

**Northeast Pennsylvania
Genealogical Society, Inc.**
P.O. Box 1776, Shavertown, PA
18708-0776
Web site: <www.rootsweb.com/
~panepgs/>

**Northeast Regional Archives of
the Evangelical Lutheran
Church in America**
Krauth Memorial Library, 7301
Germantown Ave., Philadelphia,
PA 19119
Tel: (215) 248-6383

**Northumberland County
Historical Society**
1150 N. Front St., Sunbury, PA
17801
Tel: (570) 286-4083

Web site: <www.mahantongo
.org/nchs.htm>

Oil City Library
2 Central Ave., Oil City, PA 16301
Tel: (814) 678-3072

**Old York Road Genealogical
Society**
1030 Old York Road, Abington,
PA 19001
Web site: <www.oyrgs.org>

**Palatines to America,
Pennsylvania Chapter**
P.O. Box 280, Strasburg, PA
17579-0280
Tel: (717) 244-7358

Pennsylvania German Society
P.O. Box 244, Kutztown, PA
19530-0244
Tel: (610) 894-9808
Web site: <www.pgs.org/>

Pennsylvania State Archives
350 North Street, Harrisburg, PA
17120
Tel: (717) 783-3281
Web site: <www.phmc.state.pa
.us/bah/dam/
overview.htm?secid=31>

Pike County Historical Society
608 Broad St., Milford, PA 18337
Tel: (570) 296-8126
Web site: <www.pikehistory.org>

Pinegrove Historical Society
P.O. Box 65, Pine Grove, PA
17963
Tel: (570) 345-0157
Web site: <www.rootsweb.com/
~papghs/>

**Pioneer Historical Society of
Bedford County**
242 E. John St., Bedford, PA
15522
Tel: (814) 623-2011
Web site: <www.rootsweb.com/
~paphsbc>

**Potter County Historical
Society**
308 N. Main St., P.O. Box 605,
Coudersport, PA 16915
Tel: (814) 274-4410
Web site: <http://pottercountyp
a.net/history>

**Presbyterian Historical
Society, Northern Region**
425 Lombard St., Philadelphia,
PA 19147-1516
Tel: (215) 627-1852
Fax: (215) 627-0509

Web site: <www.history.pcusa
.org>

**Punxsutawney Area Historical
and Genealogical Society**
401 W. Mahoning St., Punxsutawney, PA 15767
Tel: (814) 938-2555
Web site: <http://users.penn.
com/~mweimer/historcl.html>

Reading Public Library
100 S. Fifth St., Reading, PA
19602
Tel: (610) 655-6350
Web site: <www.reading.lib.pa
.us>

**Resource & Research Center
for Beaver County & Local
History**
Carnegie Free Library, 1301 Sev-
enth Ave., Beaver Falls, PA
15010
Tel: (724) 846-4340
Web site: <www.bchistory.org>

**Roman Catholic Archives of the
American Catholic Historical
Society of Philadelphia**
St. Charles Borromeo Seminary,
100 E. Wynnewood Rd., Wynne-
wood, PA 19096

Schlow-Memorial Library
118 S. Fraser St., State College,
PA 16801
Tel: (814) 237-6236
Web site: <www.schlowlibrary
.org>

**Snyder County Historical
Society**
30 E. Market St., P.O. Box 276,
Middleburg, PA 17842
Tel: (570) 837-6191
Web site: <www.rootsweb.com/
~pasnyder/histsoc.htm>

**South Central Pennsylvania
Genealogical Society, Inc.**
P.O. Box 1824, York, PA 17405
Tel: (717) 843-6169
Web site: <www.scpgs.org>

**Spruance Library, Bucks
County Historical Society**
84 S. Pine St., Doylestown, PA
18901-4999
Tel: (215) 345-0210
Web site: <www.mercermuseum.
org/spruancelibrary>

State Department of Health
P.O. Box 90, Harrisburg, PA
17108
Web site: <www.dsf.health.state.
pa.us>

State Library of Pennsylvania
333 Market St., Harrisburg, PA 17126
Tel: (717) 787-4440
Web site: <www.statelibrary.state.pa.us>

Sullivan County Historical Society
Web site: <www.rootsweb.com/~pasulliv/SullivanCountyHistoricalSociety/SCHS.html>

Susquehanna County Historical Society and Library
2 Monument Square, Montrose, PA 18801
Web site: <www.susqcohistsoc.org/>

Tioga County Historical Society
P.O. Box 724, Wellsboro, PA 16901
Tel: (570) 724-6116
Web site: <www.rootsweb.com/~patioga/tchs.htm>

Tri-county Heritage Society
P.O. Box 352, Morgantown, PA 19543
Tel: (610) 286-7477
Web site: <www.tchslibrary.com>

Tulpehocken Settlement Historical Society
116 N. Front St., P.O. Box 53, Womelsdorf, PA 19567
Tel: (610) 589-2527
Web site: <www.berksmuseums.org/tulpe>

Union County Historical Society
% Union County Courthouse, St. Louis and S. Second Sts., Lewisburg, PA 17837
Tel: (570) 524-8666
E-mail: Hstoricl@ptd.net
Web site: <www.rootsweb.com/~paunion/society.html>

Venango County Genealogy Club
2 Central Ave., Oil City, PA 16301
Tel: (814) 678-3077
Web site: <www.csonline.net/vengen>

Venango County Historical Society
P.O. Box 101, 301 S. Park St., Franklin, PA 16323
Tel: (814) 437-2275
Web site: <www.franklinpa.net/vchs.htm>

Warren County Historical Society
210 Fourth Ave., Warren, PA 16365

Web site: <ws2.kinzua.net/warrenhistory>

Wattsburg Historical Society Museum
14438 Main St., Wattsburg, PA 16442
Tel: (814) 739-2952
Web site: <www.goerie.com/erie yesterday/wattsburg_museum.html>

Wayne County Historical Society
810 Main St., P.O. Box 446, Honesdale, PA 18431
Tel: (570) 253-3240
Web site: <www.waynehistorypa.org>

Western Pennsylvania Genealogical Society
4400 Forbes Ave., Pittsburgh, PA 15213-4080
Tel: (412) 687-6811
Web site: <www.wpgs.org>

Wyoming County Historical Society
P.O. Box 309, Tunkhannock, PA 18657
Tel: (570) 836-5303
Web site: <www.rootsweb.com/~pawyomin/WCHS.html>

York County Archives
150 Pleasant Acres Rd., York, PA 17402
Tel: (717) 840-7222
Web site: <www.york-county.org>

York County Historical Society
250 E. Market St., York, PA 17403
Tel: (717) 848-1587
Web site: <www.fieldtrip.com/pa/78481587.htm>

BIBLIOGRAPHY

■ GENERAL RESOURCES

African Americans in Pennsylvania
by Charles L. Blockson (Baltimore, MD: RB Books, 2001)

Bibliography on the Colonial Germans of North American: Especially the Pennsylvania Germans and their Descendants
by Emil Meyen (Reprint: Baltimore, MD: Genealogical Publishing, 1982)

Bibliography of Pennsylvania History, 2d ed.
compiled by Norman B. Wilkinson, edited by Sylvester Kirby Stevens and Donald H. Kent (Harrisburg, PA: Pennsylvania Historical and Museum Commission, 1957)

The Biographical Encyclopedia of Pennsylvania of the Nineteenth Century
edited by Charles Robson (Philadelphia: Galaxy, 1874)

A Checklist Of Pennsylvania Newspapers, Philadelphia County
from the Pennsylvania Historical Survey, Division of Community Service Programs (Harrisburg, PA: Pennsylvania Historical Commission, 1944)

Church and Pastoral Records in the Archives of the United Church of Christ and the Evangelical and Reformed Historical Society, Lancaster Pennsylvania
by Florence M. Bricker (Lancaster, PA: The Society, 1982)

Colonial and Revolutionary Families of Pennsylvania, 11 vols.
by John W. Jordan, et al. (New York: Lewis Publishing, 1911–65)

A Country Between: The Upper Ohio Valley and Its Peoples, 1724–1774
by Michael N. McConnell (Lincoln, NE: University of Nebraska Press, 1992)

County Government and Archives in Pennsylvania
from the Pennsylvania Historical Survey (Harrisburg, PA: Pennsylvania Historical and Museum Commission, 1947)

Directory of Museums and Historical Organizations in Pennsylvania
by Jean H. Cutler (Harrisburg, PA: The Federation, 1991)

Encyclopedia of Pennsylvania Biography, 32 Vols.
by John W. Jordan, et al. (New York: Lewis Historical Publishing Co, 1914–67)

Genealogical Abstracts from Newspapers of the German Reformed Church, 1830–1839
by Barbara Manning (Bowie, MD: Heritage Books, 1992)

Genealogical Abstracts from Newspapers of the German Reformed Church 1840–1843
by Barbara Manning (Bowie, MD: Heritage Books, Inc., 1995)

Genealogical and Personal History of the Allegheny Valley, Pennsylvania, 3 vols.
by John W. Jordan (New York: Lewis Historical Publishing, 1913)

Genealogical and Personal History of Northern Pennsylvania, 3 vols.
edited by John W. Jordan (New York: Lewis Historical Publishing, 1913)

Genealogies of Pennsylvania Families: From the Pennsylvania Genealogical Magazine, 3 vols.
(Baltimore, MD: Genealogical Publishing, 1982)

The Genealogist's Companion and Sourcebook, 2d ed.
by Emily Anne Croom (Cincinnati: Betterway Books, 2003)

A Genealogist's Guide to Discovering Your African-American Ancestors
by Franklin Carter Smith and Emily Anne Croom (Cincinnati: Betterway Books, 2003)

A Genealogist's Guide to Pennsylvania Records
compiled by Helen Hutchison Woodroofe (Reprinted from the *Pennsylvania Genealogical Magazine*; Philadelphia: Genealogical Society of Pennsylvania, 1995)

Guide to Depositories of Manuscript Collections in Pennsylvania
by Margaret Sherburne Elliot (Harrisburg, PA: Pennsylvania Historical Commission, 1939)

Guide to Genealogical and Historical Research in Pennsylvania
by Floyd G. Hoenstine (Hollidaysburg, PA: Floyd G. Hoenstine, 1978)

Guide to Genealogical Research in the National Archives of the United States
edited by Anne Bruner Eales and Robert M. Kvasnicka (Washington, DC: National Archives and Records Administration, 2000)

A Guide to the History of Pennsylvania
by Dennis B. Downey and Francis J. Bremer (Westport, CT: Greenwood Press, 1993)

Guide to the Microfilm of the Records of Pennsylvania's Revolutionary Governments, 1775–1790 (Record Group 27) in the Pennsylvania State Archives
by Roland M. Baumann (Harrisburg: Pennsylvania Historical and Museum Commission, 1978, 1979)

Guide to the Records Groups in the Pennsylvania State Archives
by Frank M. Suran (Harrisburg, PA: Pennsylvania Historical and Museum Commission, 1980)

Handbook for Genealogical Research in Pennsylvania
by John W. Heisey (Indianapolis: Heritage House, 1985)

Historical Manuscript Depositories in Pennsylvania
by Irwin Richman (Harrisburg: The Pennsylvania Historical and Museum Commission, 1965)

Historic Background and Annals of the Swiss And German Pioneer Settlers of Southeastern Pennsylvania and of Their Remote Ancestors from the Middle of the Dark Ages, Down To the Time of the Revolutionary War
by Frank Eshleman (Originally published in 1917; Reprint: Baltimore: Genealogical Publishing Co., 1969)

An Illustrated History of the Commonwealth Of Pennsylvania: Civil, Political, and Military from its Earliest Settlement to the Present Time, Including Historical Descriptions Of Each County in the State, Their Towns, and Industrial Resources
by William Henry Egle (Philadelphia: E.M. Gardner, 1880)

Index to the Encyclopedia of Pennsylvania Biography
by Frederic Antes Godcharles (Philadelphia: W.D. Stock, 1996)

Memorials of the Huguenots in America, With Special Reference to Their Emigration [sic] to Pennsylvania
by Ammon Stapleton (Originally published in 1901: Reprint: Baltimore: Genealogical Publishing, 1969)

Merion in the Welsh Tract: With Sketches Of the Townships of Haverford and Radnor, Historical and Genealogical Collections concerning the Welsh Barony in the Province of Pennsylvania, Settled by the Cymric Quaker in 1682
by Thomas Allen Glenn (Norristown, PA: Herald Press, 1896)

National Archives Microfilm Catalogs online:
<www.archives.gov/publications/genealogy_microfilm_catalogs.html>

The Negro in Pennsylvania: Slavery-Servitude-Freedom, 1639–1861
by Edward Raymond Turner (New York: Negro Universities Press, 1969)

Notes and Queries: Historical, Biographical, and Genealogical, Relating Chiefly to Interior Pennsylvania 1894–1904
edited by William Henry Egle (Reprint: Baltimore: Genealogical Publishing, 1971)

Penn's Example to the Nations: 300 Years of the Holy Experiment
by Robert Grant Crist (Harrisburg, PA: Pennsylvania Council of Churches, Inc. for the Pennsylvania Religious Tercentenary Committee, 1987)

Pennsylvania Archives
by J. Severns (Philadelphia: J. Severns, 1852–1856, 1874–1935)

Pennsylvania Area Key: A Guide to the Genealogical Records of the State of Pennsylvania
by Florence Clint (Denver: Area Keys, 1976)

Pennsylvania Biographical Dictionary: People of All Times and Places Who Have Been Important to the History and Life of the State
by William T. Parsons (Wilmington, DE: American Historical Publications, 1989)

Pennsylvania Directory of Historical Organizations, 1970
by Gail M. Gibson (Harrisburg, PA: Pennsylvania Historical and Museum Commission, 1970)

The Pennsylvania Dutch: A Persistent Minority
by William T. Parsons (Boston: Twayne Publishers, 1976)

Pennsylvania Family Histories and Genealogies
by Donald Odell Virdin (Bowie, MD: Heritage Books, 1992)

Pennsylvania Genealogical Research
by George K. Schweitzer (Knoxville, TN: G. Schweitzer, 1986)

Pennsylvania Genealogies, Chiefly Scotch-Irish and German
by William Henry Egle (Reprint: Baltimore: Genealogical Publishing, 1969)

The Pennsylvania Germans, 1891–1965, Frequently Known as the "Pennsylvania Dutch"
by Homer Tope Rosenberger (Lancaster, PA: H.T. Rosenberger, 1966)

Pennsylvania: The Heritage of a Commonwealth, 4 vols.
by Sylvester Kirby Stevens (West Palm Beach, FL: The American Historical Company, 1968)

Pennsylvania Historical Bibliography, Vols. 1-6.
by John B. Trussell Jr. (Harrisburg, PA: Pennsylvania Historical and Museum Commission, 1979–1989)

Pennsylvania; A History, 9 vols.
by George P. Donehoo (New York: Lewis Historical Pub. Co., 1926–1931)

Pennsylvania Line: A Research Guide to Pennsylvania Genealogy And Local History, 4th ed.
edited by William L. Iscrupe and Shirley G. M. Iscrupe Laughlintown (Pennsylvania: Southwest Pennsylvania Genealogical Services, 1990)

Pennsylvania and Middle Atlantic States Genealogical Manuscripts: A User's Guide to the Manuscript Collections of the Genealogical Society of Pennsylvania
by J. Carlyle Parker (Turlock, CA: Marietta Publishing, 1986)

Pennsylvania Newspapers, a Bibliography and Union List
edited by Ruth Salisbury (Pittsburgh: Pennsylvania Library Association, 1969)

The Scotch-Irish of Colonial Pennsylvania
by Wayland Fuller Dunaway (Chapel Hill, NC: The University Of North Carolina Press, 1944)

Summary Guide To the Pennsylvania State Archives
edited by Frank B. Evans and Martha L. Simonetti (Harrisburg, PA: Pennsylvania Historical and Museum Commission, 1970)

Welsh Founders of Pennsylvania, 2 vols.
by Thomas Allen Glenn (Oxford: Fox, Jones and Co., 1911–1913)

Welsh Settlement of Pennsylvania
by Charles Henry Browning (Philadelphia, PA: William J. Campbell, 1912)

Writing on Pennsylvania History: A Bibliography
by Arthur C. Bining (Harrisburg, PA: Pennsylvania Historical and Museum Commission, 1946)

■ CENSUS RECORDS

The American Census Handbook
by Thomas Jay Kemp (Wilmington, DE: Scholarly Resources, Inc., 2001)

The Census Book: A Genealogist's Guide to Federal Census Facts, Schedules and Indexes
by William Dollarhide (Bountiful, UT: Heritage Quest, 1999)

Finding Answers in U.S. Census Records
by Loretto Dennis Szucs and Matthew Wright (Salt Lake City: Ancestry Publishing, 2001)

Map Guide to the U.S. Federal Censuses, 1790–1920
by William Thorndale and William Dollarhide (Baltimore: Genealogical Publishing Co., 1987)

Your Guide to the Federal Census
by Kathleen W. Hinckley (Cincinnati: Betterway Books, 2002)

Pennsylvania

■ IMMIGRATION RECORDS

American Naturalization Records, 1790–1990: What They Are and How to Use Them
by John J. Newman (North Salt Lake, UT: HeritageQuest, 1998)

American Passenger Arrival Records
by Michael Tepper (Baltimore: Genealogical Publishing Co., 1993)

Emigrants to Pennsylvania, 1641–1819: A Consolidation of Ship Passenger Lists from the Pennsylvania Magazine of History and Biography
(Baltimore, MD: Genealogical Publishing, 1975)

Immigrants to Pennsylvania, 1600's–1800's
(Brøderbund, 1999. CD-ROM)

Names of Foreigners Who Took the Oath of Allegiance to the Province and State of Pennsylvania, 1727–1775, with Foreign Arrivals, 1786–1808
by William Henry Egle (Baltimore: Genealogical Publishing Co., 1967)

Names of Persons Who Took the Oath of Allegiance to the State of Pennsylvania Between the Years 1777 And 1789: With a History of the "Test Laws" of Pennsylvania
by Thompson Westcott (Originally published in 1865; Reprint: Baltimore: Genealogical Pub. Co., 1965)

Passenger Arrivals at the Port of Philadelphia, 1800–1819
by Elizabeth P. Bentley and Michael H. Tepper (Baltimore, MD: Genealogical Publishing, 1986)

Pennsylvania German Pioneers: A Publication of the Original Lists of Arrivals in The Port of Philadelphia from 1727 to 1808
by Ralph Beaver Strassburger and William John Hinke (Norristown, PA: Pennsylvania German Society, 1934)

Philadelphia Naturalization Records, and Index to Records of Aliens 'Declarations of Intentions and/or Oaths of Allegiance, 1789–1880
edited by P. William Filby and Mary K. Meyer (Detroit, MI: Gale Research, 1982)

Ship Passenger Lists, Pennsylvania and Delaware, 1641–1825
by Carl Boyer (Newhall, CA: C. Boyer, 1980)

They Became Americans: Finding Naturalization Records and Ethnic Origins
by Loretto Dennis Szucs (Salt Lake City: Ancestry, Inc., 1998)

They Came in Ships: A Guide to Finding Your Immigrant Ancestor's Arrival Records, 2d ed.
by John P. Colletta (Salt Lake City: Ancestry, Inc., 1993)

The Trail of the Black Walnut
by George Elmore Reaman (Baltimore, MD: Genealogical Pub. Co., Inc., 1993)

■ LAND RECORDS

Early Pennsylvania Land Records: Minutes of The Board of Property
edited by William Henry Egle (Baltimore: Genealogical Publishing, 1976)

Land and Property Research in the United States
by Wade E. Hine (Salt Lake City: Ancestry Inc., 1997)

Locating Your Roots: Discover Your Ancestors Using Land Records
by Patricia Law Hatcher (Cincinnati: Betterway Books, 2003)

Pennsylvania Land Records: A History and Guide for Research
by Donna Bingham Munger (Wilmington, DE: Scholarly Resources, 1991)

Susquehanna Company Papers, 11 vols.
by Julian P. Boyd and Robert J. Taylor (Ithaca, NY: Cornell University Press, 1962–71)

Warrantees of Land in Several Counties Of the State of Pennsylvania, 1730–1898, 3 vols.
edited by William Henry Egle (Harrisburg, PA: W.S. Ray, State Printer, 1897)

■ MAPS

Atlas of Pennsylvania
(Philadelphia: Temple University, 1989)

Atlas of the State of Pennsylvania: From Original Surveys and Various Local Surveys Revised and Corrected
by Joseph R. Bien (New York: Julius Bein & Co., 1900)

Descriptive List of the Map Collection in the Pennsylvania State Archives
compiled by Martha L. Simonetti, edited by Donald H. Kent and Harry E. Whipkey (Harrisburg, PA: Pennsylvania Historical and Museum Commission, 1976)

A Gazetteer of the State of Pennsylvania
by Thomas F. Gordon (Philadelphia: T. Belknap, 1932)

Historical Atlas and Chronology of County Boundaries, 1788–1980, Vol. 1.
edited by John H. Long (Boston: G.K. Hall, 1984)

Historical Topographical Atlas of The State of Pennsylvania
by H. F. Walling and O.W. Gray (Originally published in 1872; Reprint: Knightstown, IN: Bookmark, 1977)

How Pennsylvania Acquired Its Present Boundaries
by William A. Russ Jr. (University Park: Pennsylvania Historical Association, 1966)

Pennsylvania: Atlas of Historical County Boundaries
by John H. Long (New York: Charles Scribner's Sons, Simon and Schuster Macmillan, 1996)

Pennsylvania Gazetteer
(Wilmington, DE: American Historical Publications, 1989)

Pennsylvania: Index to Topographic and Other Map Coverage
from the United States Geological Survey (Reston, VA: The Survey, ca. 1983)

Pennsylvania Place Names
by Abraham H. Espenschade (Originally published in 1925; Reprint: Baltimore, MD: Genealogical Publishing, 1970)

Pennsylvania Postal History
by John L. Kay and Chester M. Smith Jr. (Lawrence, MA: Quarterman Publications, 1976)

■ MILITARY RECORDS

Colonial Records, 16 vols.
from the Provincial Council (Philadelphia: The State, 1853)

Genealogical War Abstracts of the Revolutionary Pension Files, 4 vols.
by Virgil D. White (Waynesboro, TN: National Historical Publishing, 1990)

History of Pennsylvania Volunteers
by Samuel P. Bates (Harrisburg, PA: State Printer, 1869–71)

Index to Revolutionary War Service Records, 4 vols.
by Virgil D. White (Waynesboro, TN: National Historical Publishing, 1995)

Officers and Soldiers in the Service of the Province Of Pennsylvania, 1744–1764
by James B. Nolan (Philadelphia: University of Pennsylvania, 1936)

Pennsylvania Archives, 138 vols.
from the State of Pennsylvania (Harrisburg, PA: Pennsylvania Historical and Museum Commission, 1857–1914)

The Pennsylvania Line, Regimental Organization and Operations, 1776–1783
by John B. Trussell Jr. (Harrisburg, PA: Pennsylvania Historical and Museum Commission, 1977)

Pennsylvania Military History: A Bibliography. Part II, The Civil War.
by Dan A. Nettling (Carlisle Barracks, PA: U.S. Army Military History Institute, 1992)

Pennsylvania and the War of 1812
by Harold L. Myers (Harrisburg, PA: Pennsylvania Historical and Museum Commission, 1964)

Pennsylvania in the War with Mexico
by Randy W. Hackenburg (Shippensburg, PA: White Mane Pub. Co., 1992)

Pennsylvania in the War of the Revolution, Battalions and Line 1775–1783
by John Blair Linn (Harrisburg, PA: State printer, 1880)

Record of Pennsylvania Volunteers in the Spanish-American War, 1898, 2nd ed.
by Thomas J. Stewart (Harrisburg, PA: Wm. Stanley Ray, 1901)

Uncle, We Are Ready! Registering America's Men, 1917–1918: A Guide to Researching World War I Draft Registration Cards
by John J. Newman (North Salt Lake, UT: HeritageQuest, 2001)

U.S. Military Records: A Guide to Federal & State Sources, Colonial America to the Present
by James C. Neagles (Salt Lake City: Ancestry, Inc., 1994)

World War II: A Family Historian's Guide
by Debra Johnson Knox (Spartanburg, SC: MIE Publishing, 2003)

■ PROBATE RECORDS

Guide to Records of the Court of Common Pleas, Chester County, Pennsylvania, 1681–1900: Records of the Prothonotary, Civil Records of the Sheriff, Select Civil Records of The Circuit Court of Chester County and the Supreme Court of Pennsylvania
by Lynn Ann Catanese (West Chester, PA: Chester County Historical Society, 1987)

Guide to Records of the Court of Quarter Sessions, Chester County, Pennsylvania, 1681–1969: Records of the Clerk of Courts, Records of the Court of Oyer and Terminer and General Jail Deliver, Criminal Records of the Sheriff
by Lynn Ann Catanese (West Chester, PA: Chester County Historical Society, 1988)

Pennsylvania in the 1700's: An Index to Who Was There and Where
by Donna Beers (Warrensburg, MO: D. Beers, 1998)

Registrar's Book of Governor Keith's Court of Chancery of the Province of Pennsylvania, 1720–1735
(Harrisburg, PA: Pennsylvania Bar Association, 1941)

■ VITAL RECORDS

Abstracts (Mainly Deaths) From the Pennsylvania Gazette, 1775–1783
by Kenneth Scott (Baltimore: Genealogical Publishing Co., 1976)

Catholic Vital Records of Central Pennsylvania, 4 vols.
by Albert H. Ledoux (Altoona, PA: A.H. Ledoux, 1993–1996)

Early Pennsylvania Births: 1675–1875
by Charles Adam Fisher (Originally published in 1947; Reprint: Baltimore: Genealogical Publishing Co., 1979)

Inventory of Vital Statistics within Each County
(Harrisburg, PA: Historical Records Survey)

Pennsylvania Marriages Prior to 1790
(Reprint: Baltimore: Genealogical Publishing Co., 1968)

Pennsylvania Vital Records From the Pennsylvania Genealogical Magazine and the Pennsylvania Magazine of History and Biography, 3 vols.
(Baltimore: Genealogical Publishing Co., 1983)

Your Guide to Cemetery Research
by Sharon DeBartolo Carmack (Cincinnati: Betterway Books, 2002)

■ Adams 22 Jan. 1800
111 Baltimore St., Gettysburg, PA 17325-2312
Phone: (717)334-6781
Web site: www.rootsweb.com/~paadams/adams.htm
Parent County: York
Comments/research tips: Clerk of Courts has Birth and Death records 1852–1855, 1893–1905, and Marriage records 1852–1855, 1893. Register/Recorder has Land records 1800–1937.

Record Type	Year Begun	Jurisdiction
Marriage	1893	Clerk of Court
Divorce	1800	Prothonotary Office
Probate	1800	Register/Recorder
Court	1800	Prothonotary Office

■ Allegheny 24 Sep. 1788
436 Grant St., Pittsburgh, PA 15219-2403
Phone: (412)350-5313
Web site: www.county.allegheny.pa.us/
Parent County: Westmoreland, Washington
Comments/research tips: PA Room of the Carnegie Main Library has Birth records 1852–1854. Registrar of Wills has Birth records 1893–1905, Death records 1870–1905, Naturalization records 1798–1891, and Marriage records 1885–1925. PA State Archives has Land records 1788–1904.

Record Type	Year Begun	Jurisdiction
Divorce	na	Prothonotary Office
Land	1787	Recorder/Deeds
Probate	1789	Register of Wills
Court	na	Clerk of Court

■ Armstrong 12 Mar. 1800
500 E. Market St., Kittanning, PA 16201
Phone: (724)543-2500
Web site: www.armstrongcounty.com/
Parent County: Allegheny, Lycoming, Westmoreland
Comments/research tips: County Recorder/Registrar has Birth and Death records 1893–1905.

Record Type	Year Begun	Jurisdiction
Marriage	1885	County Recorder/Registrar
Land	1805	County Recorder/Registrar
Probate	1805	County Recorder/Registrar

■ Beaver 12 Mar. 1800
810 Third St., Beaver, PA 15009-2187
Phone: (724)728-5700
Web site: www.co.beaver.pa.us/
Parent County: Allegheny, Washington
Comments/research tips: Registrar of Wills has Birth records 1893–1906, Marriage records 1852–1854 and 1886, and Death records 1893–1906.

Record Type	Year Begun	Jurisdiction
Divorce	1802	Clerk of Courts
Land	1800	Recorder/Deeds
Probate	1800	Registrar of Wills
Court	1802	Clerk of Courts
Military	1862	Veterans Office
Nat.	1800	Prothonotary

■ **Bedford** 9 Mar. 1771
200 S. Juliana St., Bedford, PA 15522
Phone: (814)623-4836
Web site: www.bedfordcounty.net
Parent County: Cumberland
Comments/research tips: Prothonotary has Birth and Death records 1852–1854 and 1894–1906, Marriage records 1852–1854 and 1885–1963, and Naturalization records 1802–1934. State Archives has Military records 1775–1791.

Record Type	Year Begun	Jurisdiction
Land	1771	Recorder/Deeds
Military	1775	State Archives
Divorce	1804	Prothonotary
Court	1771	Prothonotary

■ **Berks** 11 Mar. 1752
633 Court St., Reading, PA 19601
Phone: (610)478-6600
Web site: www.co.berks.pa.us
Parent County: Lancaster, Philadelphia, Chester
Comments/research tips: Registrar of Wills has Birth records 1876–1906, Death records 1852–1855 and 1876–1906, and Probate records 1752–1914. Prothonotary Office has Divorce records 1754–1950 and Court records 1754–1950 and 1770–1956.

Record Type	Year Begun	Jurisdiction
Nat.	1795	Prothonotary
Marriage	1885	Registrar of Wills
Land	1752	Recorder/Deeds

■ **Blair** 20 Feb. 1848
423 Allegheny St., Hollidaysburg, PA 16648-2022
Phone: (814)693-3082
Web site: http://blair.sapdc.org/
Parent County: Huntingdon, Bedford
Comments/research tips: Prothonotary Office has Birth and Death records 1893–1905.

Record Type	Year Begun	Jurisdiction
Marriage	1885	Prothonotary Office
Divorce	1846	Prothonotary Office
Probate	1846	Prothonotary Office
Court	1846	Prothonotary Office
Nat.	1848	Prothonotary Office

■ **Bradford** 21 Feb. 1810
301 Main St., Towanda, PA 18848-1884
Phone: (570)265-1727
Web site: www.rootsweb.com/~pabradfo/bradweb.htm
Parent County: Luzerne, Lycoming
Comments/research tips: Registrar/Recorder has Birth and Death records 1893–1905. Prothonotary/Clerk of Courts has Naturalization records 1832–1960. Formerly Ontario County. Name changed to Bradford 24 March 1812.

Record Type	Year Begun	Jurisdiction
Marriage	1885	Registrar/Recorder
Divorce	1878	Prothonotary/Clerk/Courts
Land	1812	Registrar/Recorder
Probate	1812	Registrar/Recorder
Court	1812	Prothonotary/Clerk/Courts
Military	1940	Registrar/Recorder

■ **Bucks** 10 Mar. 1682
55 E. Court St., Doylestown, PA 18901
Phone: (215)348-6000
Web site: www.buckscounty.org/
Parent County: Original County
Comments/research tips: Registrar of Wills/Orphan's Court has Birth records 1893–1906 and 1852–1854, Death records 1852–1855 and 1893–1906, Marriage records 1812–1842, 1852–1859 and 1885–1906, Military records 1776–1802, and Probate records 1682–1906. Prothonotary has Court records 1733–1923, Divorce records 1733–1923, and Naturalization records 1802–1906. Recorder of Deeds has Land records 1684–1866.

■ **Butler** 12 Mar. 1800
124 W. Diamond St. PO Box 1208, Butler, PA 16001
Phone: (724)284-5348
Web site: www.co.butler.pa.us/
Parent County: Allegheny
Comments/research tips: Registrar of Wills has Birth and Death records 1893–1906, Marriage records 1885 and 1893–1905, and Probate records 1800–1971. Prothonotary has Court records 1804–1866 and Naturalization records 1804–1903.

Record Type	Year Begun	Jurisdiction
Divorce	1805	Prothonotary
Land	1804	Recorder/Deeds

■ **Cambria** 26 Mar. 1804
200 S. Center St., Edensburg, PA 15931-1936
Phone: (814)472-5440
Web site: www.co.cambria.pa.us/
Parent County: Somerset, Bedford, Huntingdon
Comments/research tips: Registrar of Wills has Birth and Death records 1893–1906. Prothonotary has Naturalization records 1835–1906.

Record Type	Year Begun	Jurisdiction
Marriage	1885	Registrar of Wills
Divorce	1866	Prothonotary
Land	1804	Recorder/Deeds
Probate	1805	Registrar of Wills
Court	1849	Clerk of Courts

■ **Cameron** 29 Mar. 1860
20 E. Fifth St., Emporium, PA 15834
Phone: (814)486-3349
Web site: www.rootsweb.com/~pacamero/
Parent County: Clinton, Elk, McKean, Potter
Comments/research tips: County Clerk has Birth records 1894–1906 and Death records 1860–1905.

Record Type	Year Begun	Jurisdiction
Nat.	1860	County Clerk
Marriage	1860	County Clerk
Divorce	1860	County Clerk
Land	1860	County Clerk
Probate	1860	County Clerk
Court	1860	County Clerk

Pennsylvania

■ **Carbon** 13 Mar. 1843
Broadway Lock Box 129, Jim Thorpe, PA 18229-0129
Phone: (570)325-9124
Web site: www.rootsweb.com/~pacarbon/
Parent County: Northampton, Monroe
Comments/research tips: Courthouse Archivist/Records
Coordinator has Birth records 1892–1905, Death records
1894–1905, Naturalization records 1843–1958, and
Probate records 1843–1990.

Record Type	Year Begun	Jurisdiction
Marriage	1885	Courthouse Archivist
Divorce	1843	Courthouse Archivist
Land	1843	Recorder/Deeds
Probate	1843	County Clerk
Court	1843	Courthouse Archivist

■ **Centre** 13 Feb. 1800
County Courthouse, Bellefonte, PA 16823-1488
Phone: (814)355-6724
Web site: www.co.centre.pa.us
Parent County: Lycoming, Mifflin, Northumberland
Comments/research tips: Registrar of Wills/Clerk of
Orphan's Court has Birth and Death records 1893–1905.

Record Type	Year Begun	Jurisdiction
Marriage	1885	Registrar of Wills
Divorce	1890	Prothonotary Office
Land	1801	Recorder/Deeds
Probate	1800	Registrar of Wills
Court	1800	Prothonotary Office
Nat.	1800	Prothonotary Office

■ **Chester** 10 Mar. 1682
2 N. High St., P.O. Box 2748, West Chester, PA 19380
Phone: (610)344-6000
Web site: www.chesco.org/
Parent County: Original County
Comments/research tips: County Archives has Birth and
Death records 1852–1855 and 1893–1906, Court records
1681–1900, Divorce records 1681–1900, Land records
1688–1905, Marriage records 1852–1855 and 1885–1930,
Naturalization records 1798–1989, Probate records
1714–1923, and Tax records 1715–1939.

Record Type	Year Begun	Jurisdiction
Marriage	1931	Clerk of Orphan's Court
Probate	1923	Registrar of Wills

■ **Clarion** 11 Mar. 1839
421 Main St., Clarion, PA 16214-1028
Phone: (814)226-4000
Web site: www.co.clarion.pa.us/
Parent County: Venango, Armstrong
Comments/research tips: Registrar/Recorder has Birth
records 1893–1906, Death records 1852–1854, 1893–1906,
and Marriage records 1852–1854.

Record Type	Year Begun	Jurisdiction
Marriage	1885	Registrar/Recorder
Divorce	1880	Prothonotary Clerk
Land	1840	Registrar/Recorder
Probate	1840	Registrar/Recorder
Court	1874	Prothonotary Clerk

■ **Clearfield** 26 Mar. 1804
230 Market St., Clearfield, PA 16830
Phone: (814)765-2641
Web site: www.clearfieldco.org/
Parent County: Huntingdon, Lycoming
Comments/research tips: County Registrar/Recorder has
Birth and Death records 1893–1905.

Record Type	Year Begun	Jurisdiction
Marriage	1885	County Registrar/Recorder
Divorce	1828	Prothonotary Office
Land	1805	County Commissioner
Probate	1875	County Recorder
Court	1828	Prothonotary Office

■ **Clinton** 21 June 1839
230 E. Water St., Lock Haven, PA 17745
Phone: (570)893-4010
Web site: www.clintoncountypa.com/
Parent County: Lycoming, Centre
Comments/research tips: County Registrar/Recorder has
Birth and Death records 1893–1905. Prothonotary has
Naturalization records 1839–1982.

Record Type	Year Begun	Jurisdiction
Marriage	1885	County Registrar/Recorder
Divorce	1839	Prothonotary
Land	na	County Registrar/Recorder
Probate	na	County Registrar/Recorder
Court	na	Prothonotary

■ **Columbia** 22 Mar. 1813
35 W. Main St., P.O. Box 380, Bloomsburg, PA 17815
Phone: (570)389-5600
Web site: www.columbiapa.org/
Parent County: Northumberland
Comments/research tips: Prothonotary has Birth and Death
records 1893–1905 and Marriage records 1885–1907.
Columbia County Genealogy Society has Death and
Marriage records 1837–1870.

Record Type	Year Begun	Jurisdiction
Divorce	1814	Prothonotary
Court	1814	Prothonotary

■ **Crawford** 12 Mar. 1800
903 Diamond Park, Meadville, PA 16335
Phone: (814)336-1151
Web site: www.co.crawford.pa.us/
Parent County: Allegheny
Comments/research tips: Clerk of Courts has Birth records
1893–1905, Court records 1800–1859, Death records
1852–1854 and 1893–1905, and Marriage records
1852–1854.

Record Type	Year Begun	Jurisdiction
Marriage	1885	Clerk of Courts
Divorce	1800	Prothonotary
Land	1800	Registrar/Recorder
Probate	1800	Registrar/Recorder

■ **Cumberland** 27 Jan. 1750
1 Courthouse Sq., Carlisle, PA 17013
Phone: (717)240-6370

Pennsylvania

Web site: www.ccpa.net/cumberland
Parent County: Lancaster
Comments/research tips: Rigistrar of Wills has Birth and Death records 1894–1906.

Record Type	Year Begun	Jurisdiction
Marriage	1885	Registrar of Wills
Divorce	1751	Prothonotary Office
Land	1751	Recorder/Deeds
Probate	1750	Registrar of Wills
Court	1750	Registrar of Wills

■ **Dauphin** 4 Mar. 1785
Front & Market Sts., Harrisburg, PA 17101-2012
Phone: (717)255-2692
Web site: http://dsf.pacounties.org/dauphin
Parent County: Lancaster
Comments/research tips: Registrar of Wills/Clerk of Orphan's Court has Birth records 1852–1854 and 1893–1906, Death records 1852–1855 and 1893–1906, and Marriage records 1852–1855.

Record Type	Year Begun	Jurisdiction
Divorce	1785	Prothonotary Office
Land	1785	Recorder/Deeds
Probate	1785	Registrar of Wills
Court	1785	Prothonotary Office

■ **Delaware** 26 Sep. 1789
201 W. Front St., Media, PA 19063
Phone: (610)891-4260
Web site: www.co.delaware.pa.us/
Parent County: Chester
Comments/research tips: Registrar of Wills/Clerk of Orphan's Court has Birth and Death records 1893–1906. County Clerk has Delayed Birth records 1875–1900.

Record Type	Year Begun	Jurisdiction
Marriage	1885	Registrar of Wills
Divorce	1927	Prothonotary
Land	1789	Recorder/Deeds
Probate	1790	Registrar of Wills
Court	1897	Prothonotary
Orph. Court	1865	County Clerk

■ **Elk** 18 Apr. 1843
240 Main St., Ridgway, PA 15853
Phone: (814)776-1161
Web site: www.co.elk.pa.us/
Parent County: Jefferson, McKean, Clearfield
Comments/research tips: Registrar/Recorder has Birth and Death records 1893–1906.

Record Type	Year Begun	Jurisdiction
Marriage	1885	Registrar/Recorder
Divorce	1844	Prothonotary Office
Land	1844	Registrar/Recorder
Probate	1844	Registrar/Recorder
Court	1844	Prothonotary Office

■ **Erie** 12 Mar. 1800
140 W. Sixth St., Erie, PA 16501
Phone: (814)451-6080

Web site: www.eriecountygov.org/
Parent County: Allegheny
Comments/research tips: Clerk of Records has Birth and Death records 1893–1906. Courthouse burned in 1823; all records destroyed.

Record Type	Year Begun	Jurisdiction
Marriage	1885	Clerk of Records
Divorce	1823	Prothonotary Office
Land	1823	Recorder/Deeds
Probate	1823	Registrar of Wills
Court	1823	Prothonotary Office

■ **Fayette** 26 Sep. 1783
61 E. Main St., Uniontown, PA 15401-3514
Phone: (724)430-1206
Web site: www.fforward.com/
Parent County: Westmoreland
Comments/research tips: Clerk of Orphans Court has Birth and Death records 1893–1905.

Record Type	Year Begun	Jurisdiction
Marriage	1885	Clerk/Orphans Court
Divorce	1784	Prothonotary Office
Land	1784	Recorder/Deeds
Probate	1784	Registrar of Wills
Court	1784	Prothonotary Office

■ **Forest** 11 Apr. 1848
526 Elm St., P.O. Box 423, Tionesta, PA 16353
Phone: (814)755-3526
Web site: www.forestcounty.com/
Parent County: Jefferson
Comments/research tips: Prothonotary has Birth records 1893–1906 and Death records 1893–1907. Part of Venango County was added to Forest 31 October 1886. All records are kept in the Prothonotary's Office.

Record Type	Year Begun	Jurisdiction
Marriage	1885	Prothonotary
Divorce	1857	Prothonotary
Land	1857	Prothonotary

■ **Franklin** 9 Sep. 1784
157 Lincoln Way E., Chambersburg, PA 17201-2211
Phone: (717)261-3805
Web site: www.franklinco.pa.net/
Parent County: Cumberland
Comments/research tips: County Clerk has Birth and Death records 1894–1906.

Record Type	Year Begun	Jurisdiction
Marriage	1885	County Clerk
Divorce	1884	County Clerk
Land	1785	Registrar/Recorder
Probate	1785	Registrar/Recorder

■ **Fulton** 19 Apr. 1851
201 N. Second St., McConnellsburg, PA 17233
Phone: (717)485-4212
Web site: www.rootsweb.com/~pafulton/
Parent County: Bedford
Comments/research tips: Clerk of Orphans Court has Birth

records 1895–1905, Death records 1852–1854 and 1895–1905, and Marriage records 1852–1854.

Record Type	Year Begun	Jurisdiction
Marriage	1885	Clerk/Orphans Court
Divorce	1850	Prothonotary Office
Land	1850	Recorder/Deeds
Probate	1850	Registrar of Wills
Court	1850	Prothonotary Office
Orph. Court	1850	Clerk/Orphans Court

■ Greene 9 Feb. 1796

10 E. High St., Waynesburg, PA 15370
Phone: (724)852-5281
Web site: http://county.greenepa.net/
Parent County: Washington
Comments/research tips: Prothonotary has Birth and Death records 1893–1915.

Record Type	Year Begun	Jurisdiction
Marriage	1885	Registrar/Recorder
Divorce	1816	Prothonotary
Land	1796	Registrar/Recorder
Probate	1796	Registrar/Recorder
Court	1797	Prothonotary

■ Huntingdon 20 Sep. 1787

223 Penn St., P.O. Box 39, Huntingdon, PA 16652
Phone: (814)643-2740
Web site: www.huntingdoncounty.net/
Parent County: Bedford
Comments/research tips: Registrar/Recorder Clerk has Birth records 1894–1906 and Death records 1894–1905.

Record Type	Year Begun	Jurisdiction
Marriage	1885	Registrar/Recorder
Divorce	1787	Prothonotary
Probate	1787	Registrar/Recorder
Court	1787	Prothonotary

■ Indiana 30 Mar. 1803

825 Philadelpia St., Indiana, PA 15701-3934
Phone: (724)465-3860
Web site: www.indianapa.info
Parent County: Westmoreland, Lycoming
Comments/research tips: Registrar/Recorder has Birth and Death records 1852–1855 and 1893–1906, and Marriage records 1852–1855. Prothonotary has Naturalization records 1807–1959.

Record Type	Year Begun	Jurisdiction
Marriage	1887	Registrar/Recorder
Divorce	1807	Prothonotary
Land	1807	Registrar/Recorder
Probate	1807	Registrar/Recorder
Court	1807	Prothonotary

■ Jefferson 26 Mar. 1804

200 Main St., Brookville, PA 15825
Phone: (814)849-1607
Web site: www.jeffersoncountypa.com
Parent County: Lycoming
Comments/research tips: Registrar/Recorder has Birth and

Death records 1893–1906 and Marriage records 1852–1855.

Record Type	Year Begun	Jurisdiction
Marriage	1885	Registrar/Recorder
Divorce	1885	Prothonotary/Clerk/Courts
Land	1828	Registrar/Recorder
Probate	1830	Registrar/Recorder
Court	1940	Prothonotary/Clerk/Courts

■ Juniata 2 Mar. 1831

Bridge St., P.O. Box 68, Mifflintown, PA 17059-0068
Phone: (717)436-8991
Web site: www.co.juniata.pa.us/
Parent County: Mifflin
Comments/research tips: County Clerk has Birth records 1893–1907, Death records 1852–1878 and 1893–1907, and Naturalization records early 1800–1930. Juniata County Historical Society has Marriage records 1800–1995.

Record Type	Year Begun	Jurisdiction
Marriage	1885	County Clerk
Divorce	1900	County Clerk
Land	1831	County Clerk
Probate	1831	County Clerk
Court	1831	County Clerk

■ Lackawanna 21 Aug. 1878

200 N. Washington Ave., Scranton, PA 18503
Phone: (570)963-6723
Web site: www.rootsweb.com/~palackaw/
Parent County: Luzerne
Comments/research tips: Registrar of Wills has Birth and Death records 1893–1905. Clerk of Judicial Records has Naturalization records.

Record Type	Year Begun	Jurisdiction
Land	1878	Recorder/Deeds
Marriage	1885	Marriage License Bureau
Divorce	1878	Clerk of Judicial Records
Probate	1878	Registrar of Wills
Court	1878	Clerk of Judicial Records

■ Lancaster 10 May 1729

50 N. Duke St., P.O. Box 3480, Lancaster, PA 17602-2805
Phone: (717)299-8319
Web site: www.co.lancaster.pa.us/
Parent County: Chester
Comments/research tips: Registrar of Wills has Birth records 1881–1906. Office of Records has Death records 1894–1927.

Record Type	Year Begun	Jurisdiction
Marriage	1885	Office of Records
Divorce	na	Office of Records
Land	1729	Office of Records
Probate	1729	Office of Records
Court	1729	Office of Records
Orph. Court	1742	Office of Records

■ Lawrence 20 Mar. 1849

433 Court St., New Castle, PA 16101-3599
Phone: (724)656-2127

Web site: www.rootsweb.com/~palawren
Parent County: Beaver, Mercer
Comments/research tips: Prothonotary has Birth and Death records 1893–1905.

Record Type	Year Begun	Jurisdiction
Marriage	1885	Prothonotary
Divorce	1885	Prothonotary
Land	1849	Registrar/Recorder
Probate	1849	Registrar/Recorder
Court	1855	Prothonotary

■ Lebanon 16 Feb. 1813
400 S. Eighth St., Lebanon, PA 17042-6794
Phone: (717)274-2801
Web site: http://dsf.pacounties.org/lebanon/site/default.asp
Parent County: Lancaster & Dauphin
Comments/research tips: Registrar of Wills has Birth records 1893–1906.

Record Type	Year Begun	Jurisdiction
Marriage	1885	Registrar of Wills
Divorce	1888	Prothonotary Office
Probate	1813	Registrar of Wills

■ Lehigh 6 Mar. 1812
455 W. Hamilton St., Allentown, PA 18101
Phone: (610)782-3148
Web site: www.lehighcounty.org/
Parent County: Northampton
Comments/research tips: Clerk of Orphans Court has Birth records 1895–1905 and Death records 1893–1904.

Record Type	Year Begun	Jurisdiction
Marriage	1885	Clerk/Orphans Court
Divorce	1812	Clerk of Courts
Land	1812	Recorder/Deeds
Probate	1812	Registrar of Wills
Court	1812	Clerk of Courts

■ Luzerne 25 Sep. 1786
200 N. River St., Wilkes-Barre, PA 18711
Phone: (570)825-1585
Web site: www.luzernecounty.org
Parent County: Northumberland
Comments/research tips: Registrar of Wills has Birth and Death records 1890–1906.

Record Type	Year Begun	Jurisdiction
Marriage	1885	Registrar of Wills
Divorce	1878	Prothonotary Office
Land	1786	Recorder/Deeds
Probate	1786	Registrar of Wills
Court	1878	Prothonotary Office

■ Lycoming 13 Apr. 1795
48 W. Third St., Williamsport, PA 17701
Phone: (570)327-2200
Web site: www.lyco.org/
Parent County: Northumberland
Comments/research tips: Registrar/Recorder has Birth records 1893–1905 and Death records 1893–1898. Prothonotary has Naturalization records 1804–1956. The

James V. Brown Library, 19 E. Fourth St., Williamsport, PA is the major source of Lycoming County genealogical information.

Record Type	Year Begun	Jurisdiction
Marriage	1885	Registrar/Recorder
Divorce	1795	Prothonotary
Land	1795	Registrar/Recorder
Probate	1850	Registrar/Recorder
Court	1795	Prothonotary

■ McKean 26 Mar. 1804
500 W. Main St., Smethport, PA 16749
Phone: (814)887-5571
Web site: www.rootsweb.com/~pamckean/
Parent County: Lycoming
Comments/research tips: Registrar of Wills has Birth and Death records 1892–1905.

Record Type	Year Begun	Jurisdiction
Court	1804	Prothonotary
Divorce	1804	Prothonotary
Marriage	1885	Registrar of Wills
Land	1804	Recorder/Deeds
Probate	1827	Registrar of Wills

■ Mercer 12 Mar. 1800
103 N. Diamond St., Mercer, PA 16137
Phone: (724)662-3800
Web site: www.mcc.co.mercer.pa.us/
Parent County: Allegheny
Comments/research tips: Clerk of Orphan's Court has Birth records 1893–1905. Registrar of Wills has Death records 1893–1905. County courthouse does not research records.

Record Type	Year Begun	Jurisdiction
Marriage	1885	County Clerk
Divorce	na	Prothonotary Office
Land	1800	Recorder/Deeds
Probate	1800	Registrar of Wills
Court	na	Prothonotary Office

■ Mifflin 19 Sep. 1789
20 N. Wayne St., Lewistown, PA 17044
Phone: (717)248-6733
Web site: www.co.mifflin.pa.us
Parent County: Cumberland, Northumberland
Comments/research tips: Registrar/Recorder has Birth records 1853, 1854, 1893–1905, and 1941–1969, Death records 1852–1855 and 1896–1905, Land records 1789–1953, Marriage records 1852–1853, and Probate records 1789–1899. Prothonotary Office has Court and Divorce records 1792–1809 and 1826–1834.

Record Type	Year Begun	Jurisdiction
Marriage	1885	Registrar/Recorder

■ Monroe 1 Apr. 1836
7 Monroe St., Stroudsburg, PA 18360
Phone: (570)420-3400
Web site: www.co.monroe.pa.us/
Parent County: Pike, Northampton
Comments/research tips: Prothonotary has Birth records 1892–1905.

Record Type	Year Begun	Jurisdiction
Marriage	1885	County Clerk
Divorce	1900	County Clerk
Land	1836	Recorder/Deeds
Probate	na	Registrar of Wills
Court	1845	County Clerk

■ Montgomery   10 Sep. 1784
Airy & Swede St., P.O. Box 311, Norristown, PA 19404
Phone: (610)270-3000
Web site: www.montcopa.org/
Parent County: Philadelphia
Comments/research tips: County Records Department has Birth and Death records 1852–1855 and 1893–1913 and Marriage records 1852–1855.

Record Type	Year Begun	Jurisdiction
Marriage	1885	County Records Dept.
Divorce	1784	Prothonotary Office
Land	1784	County Records Dept.
Probate	1784	County Records Dept.
Court	1784	Prothonotary Office

■ Montour   3 May 1850
29 Mill St., Danville, PA 17821-1945
Phone: (570)271-3000
Web site: www.montourco.org/
Parent County: Columbia
Comments/research tips: Prothonotary has Birth and Death records 1893–1905 and Naturalization records 1850–1940.

Record Type	Year Begun	Jurisdiction
Marriage	1885	Prothonotary
Divorce	1850	Prothonotary
Land	1850	Recorder/Deeds
Probate	1850	Registrar/Recorder
Court	1850	Prothonotary

■ Northampton   11 Mar. 1752
669 Washington St., Easton, PA 18042
Phone: (610)559-3000
Web site: www.northamptoncounty.org/
Parent County: Bucks
Comments/research tips: Clerk of Orphans Court has Birth and Death records 1893–1936.

Record Type	Year Begun	Jurisdiction
Marriage	1885	County Archives
Divorce	1752	Prothonotary Office
Land	1752	County Archives
Probate	1752	Registrar of Wills
Court	1752	Prothonotary Office

■ Northumberland   21 Mar. 1772
201 Market St., Sunbury, PA 17801
Phone: (570)988-4100
Web site: www.northumberlandco.org/
Parent County: Lancaster, Berks, Cumberland, Bedford, Northampton
Comments/research tips: Registrar/Recorder has Birth and Death records 1893–1905.

Record Type	Year Begun	Jurisdiction
Marriage	1885	Registrar/Recorder
Divorce	1772	Prothonotary Office
Land	1772	Registrar/Recorder
Probate	1772	Registrar/Recorder
Court	1772	Prothonotary Office

■ Ontario   21 Feb. 1810
Parent County: Luzerne, Lycoming
Comments/research tips: (See Bradford) Name changed to Bradford 24 March 1812.

■ Perry   22 Mar. 1820
25 W. Main St., P.O. Box 37, New Bloomfield, PA 17068
Phone: (717)582-2131
Web site: www.perryco.org/
Parent County: Cumberland
Comments/research tips: Registrar/Recorder has Birth records 1893–1918, Death records 1894–1914, and Marriage records 1870–1885.

Record Type	Year Begun	Jurisdiction
Land	1820	Registrar/Recorder
Probate	1820	Registrar/Recorder

■ Philadelphia   10 Mar. 1682
Broad & Market Sts., Philadelphia, PA 19107
Phone: (215)686-1776
Web site: www.phila.gov
Parent County: Original County
Comments/research tips: Philadelphia City Archives has Birth records 1860–1915, Court records 1810–1811 and 1819–1874, Divorce records 1851–1875, Land records 1683–1952, and Naturalization records 1793–1930.

Record Type	Year Begun	Jurisdiction
Marriage	1885	Clerk/Orphans Court
Probate	na	Registrar of Wills

■ Pike   26 Mar. 1814
506 Broad St., Milford, PA 18337-1511
Phone: (570)296-7613
Web site: www.pa-roots.com/~pike and www.pikepa.org
Parent County: Wayne
Comments/research tips: Prothonotary has Birth and Death records 1893–1905.

Record Type	Year Begun	Jurisdiction
Marriage	1884	Prothonotary
Divorce	1814	Prothonotary
Land	1814	Prothonotary
Probate	1814	Prothonotary
Court	1814	Prothonotary

■ Potter   26 Mar. 1804
1 E. Second St., Coudersport, PA 16915
Phone: (814)274-8290
Web site: www.pottercountypa.net/
Parent County: Lycoming
Comments/research tips: Prothonotary has Birth, Death, and Burial records 1893–1905.

Record Type	Year Begun	Jurisdiction
Marriage	1885	Prothonotary
Divorce	1885	Prothonotary

Pennsylvania

Land .... na ....Registrar/Recorder
Probate .... na ....Registrar/Recorder

■ **Schuylkill** 1 Mar. 1811
401 N. Second St., Pottsville, PA 17901
Phone: (570)622-5570
Web site: www.co.schuylkill.pa.us/
Parent County: Berks, Northampton
Comments/research tips: Registrar of Wills has Birth and Death records 1893–1905. County Archives has Naturalization records 1828–1988.

Record Type	Year Begun	Jurisdiction
Marriage	1885	Registrar of Wills
Divorce	1878	County Archives
Land	1811	Recorder/Deeds
Probate	1811	Registrar of Wills
Court	1811	County Archives

■ **Snyder** 2 Mar. 1855
9 W. Market St., P.O. Box 217, Middleburg, PA 17842
Phone: (570)837-4208
Web site: www.snydercounty.org
Parent County: Union
Comments/research tips: Prothonotary has Birth and Death records 1893–1905. Susquehanna University Library in Selinsgrove has Census records for 1910 and 1920.

Record Type	Year Begun	Jurisdiction
Marriage	1885	Prothonotary
Divorce	1855	Prothonotary
Land	1855	County Registrar/Recorder
Probate	1855	County Registrar/Recorder
Court	1855	Prothonotary

■ **Somerset** 17 Apr. 1795
111 E. Union St., Somerset, PA 15501
Phone: (814)445-5154
Web site: www.co.somerset.pa.us
Parent County: Bedford
Comments/research tips: Registrar of Wills has Birth and Death records 1893–1906. Prothonotary Office has Naturalization records 1795–1955.

Record Type	Year Begun	Jurisdiction
Marriage	1885	Registrar of Wills
Divorce	1795	Prothonotary Office
Land	1795	Recorder/Deeds
Probate	1795	Registrar of Wills
Court	1795	Prothonotary Office
Military	1865	Recorder/Deeds

■ **Sullivan** 15 Mar. 1847
Main & Muncy, Laporte, PA 18626
Phone: (570)946-5201
Web site: www.sullivancounty-pa.us
Parent County: Lycoming
Comments/research tips: Prothonotary has Birth and Death records 1893–1905.

Record Type	Year Begun	Jurisdiction
Marriage	1874	Prothonotary
Divorce	1847	Prothonotary
Land	1847	Prothonotary
Probate	1847	Prothonotary
Court	1847	Prothonotary

■ **Susquehanna** 21 Feb. 1810
11 Maple St., P.O. Box 218, Montrose, PA 18801
Phone: (570)278-4600
Web site: www.susquehanna.pa.us/
Parent County: Luzerne
Comments/research tips: Registrar/Recorder has Birth and Death records 1893–1905. Prothonotary has Naturalization records 1844–1956.

Record Type	Year Begun	Jurisdiction
Marriage	1885	Registrar/Recorder
Divorce	1877	Prothonotary
Probate	1810	Registrar/Recorder
Court	1812	Prothonotary
Military	1918	Registrar/Recorder
Land	1810	Registrar/Recorder

■ **Tioga** 26 Mar. 1804
116 Main St., Wellsboro, PA 16901
Phone: (717)724-1906
Web site: www.rootsweb.com/~patioga/tiogaweb.htm
Parent County: Lycoming
Comments/research tips: Registrar/Recorder has Birth and Death records 1893–1905.

Record Type	Year Begun	Jurisdiction
Orph. Court	1812	Registrar/Recorder
Marriage	1885	Registrar/Recorder
Divorce	1813	Prothonotary
Land	1807	Registrar/Recorder
Probate	1803	Registrar/Recorder
Court	1813	Prothonotary
Military	1868	Registrar/Recorder
Nat.	1818	Prothonotary

■ **Union** 22 Mar. 1813
103 S. Second St., Lewisburg, PA 17837
Phone: (717)524-8600
Web site: www.seda-cog.org/union
Parent County: Northumberland
Comments/research tips: Prothonotary has Birth records 1893–1905.

Record Type	Year Begun	Jurisdiction
Marriage	1885	Prothonotary
Divorce	1813	Prothonotary
Land	1813	Registrar/Recorder
Probate	1813	Registrar/Recorder
Court	1813	Prothonotary

■ **Venango** 12 Mar. 1800
1168 Liberty St., Franklin, PA 16323-1295
Phone: (814)432-9539
Web site: www.co.venango.pa.us/
Parent County: Allegheny, Lycoming
Comments/research tips: Clerk of Courts/Recorder of Deeds has Birth and Death records 1893–1905.

Record Type	Year Begun	Jurisdiction
Marriage	1885	Clk. of Courts/Rec. of Deeds

Pennsylvania

Divorce	na	Clk. of Courts/Rec. of Deeds
Land	1806	Clk. of Courts/Rec. of Deeds
Probate	1806	Clk. of Courts/Rec. of Deeds
Court	na	Clk. of Courts/Rec. of Deeds

■ Warren 12 Mar. 1800

204 Fourth Ave., Warren, PA 16365-2399
Phone: (814)723-7550
Web site: www.warren-county.net/
Parent County: Allegheny, Lycoming
Comments/research tips: Registrar/Recorder has Birth and Death records 1893–1906. Fire destroyed some court and divorce records.

Record Type	Year Begun	Jurisdiction
Marriage	1885	Registrar/Recorder
Divorce	ca. 1800	Prothonotary
Land	1819	Registrar/Recorder
Probate	1819	Registrar/Recorder
Court	ca. 1800	Prothonotary

■ Washington 28 Mar. 1781

1 S. Main St., Washington, PA 15301
Phone: (724)228-6723
Web site: www.co.washington.pa.us/
Parent County: Westmoreland
Comments/research tips: Registrar of Wills has Birth and Death records 1893–1906. Prothonotary has Naturalization records 1802–1905 and 1918–1984.

Record Type	Year Begun	Jurisdiction
Marriage	1885	Registrar of Wills
Divorce	1781	Prothonotary/Clerk of Courts
Land	1781	Recorder/Deeds
Probate	1785	Registrar of Wills
Court	1781	Prothonotary
Military	1781	Recorder/Deeds

■ Wayne 21 Mar. 1798

925 Court St., Honesdale, PA 18431-1922
Phone: (570)253-5970
Web site: www.co.wayne.pa.us
Parent County: Northampton
Comments/research tips: Prothonotary has Birth and Death records 1893–1906.

Record Type	Year Begun	Jurisdiction
Marriage	1885	Prothonotary
Divorce	1900	Prothonotary

Land	1798	Recorder/Deeds
Probate	1798	Registrar of Wills
Court	1798	Prothonotary

■ Westmoreland 26 Feb. 1773

2 N. Main St., Greensburg, PA 15601-2405
Phone: (724)830-3000
Web site: www.co.westmoreland.pa.us/
Parent County: Bedford
Comments/research tips: Registrar of Wills has Birth and Divorce records 1893–1905.

Record Type	Year Begun	Jurisdiction
Marriage	1885	County Clerk
Land	1773	Recorder/Deeds
Probate	1773	Registrar of Wills
Court	1773	Clerk of Courts
Nat.	1804	Prothonotary

■ Wyoming 4 Apr. 1842

1 Courthouse Sq., Tunkhannock, PA 18657
Phone: (570)836-3200
Web site: www.pacounties.org/wyoming
Parent County: Luzerne
Comments/research tips: Prothonotary has Birth and Death records 1893–1906.

Record Type	Year Begun	Jurisdiction
Marriage	1885	Prothonotary
Divorce	1842	Prothonotary
Land	1842	Reg. of Wills/Rec. of Deeds
Probate	1842	Reg. of Wills/Rec. of Deeds
Court	1842	Prothonotary

■ York 19 Aug. 1749

28 E. Market St., York, PA 17401
Phone: (717)771-9675
Web site: www.york-county.org/
Parent County: Lancaster
Comments/research tips: Clerk of Orphan's Court has Birth and Death records 1893–1906. County Archives has Court and Divorce records 1749–1989 and Probate records 1749–1967. Prothonotary has Naturalization records 1795–1992.

Record Type	Year Begun	Jurisdiction
Marriage	1885	County Clerk
Divorce	1749	County Clerk
Land	1749	Recorder/Deeds
Probate	1967	Registrar of Wills
Court	1749	County Clerk

Rhode Island

By Maureen Taylor

HISTORICAL OVERVIEW

Rhode Island is a small state with a long name—State of Rhode Island and Providence Plantations. The original four separate towns were clustered around Narragansett Bay. Roger Williams, a banished minister from Massachusetts Bay, established Providence; another religious free thinker, Samuel Gorton, founded Warwick; Anne Hutchinson's followers settled in Portsmouth; and Thomas Coddington's followers populated Newport. The colony became a haven for those seeking freedom to worship, attracting Baptists, French Huguenots, French Calvinists, Jews, and Quakers. King Philip's War of 1675–1676 devastated the colony and resulted in the destruction of the Native American's in the area. At war's end, only a small tribe remained in what is now Charlestown. Both Massachusetts and Connecticut claimed ownership of parts of the colony in the seventeenth century.

In the eighteenth century, the close proximity of Narragansett Bay enabled Rhode Island traders to lead the Colonies in imports and exports. Many Rhode Island families today have connections in the West Indies as a direct result of the colony's prominence in the Triangle trade of slaves, rum, and sugar. Inhabitants of coastal areas participated in whaling and fishing. The reputation of Rhode Island mariners led to Newport becoming home to the United States Naval War College.

The American Industrial Revolution began with Samuel Slater, an English immigrant who constructed the first American factory for the manufacture of cotton thread. Textile manufacturing attracted immigrants in waves—Irish, Scots, French-Canadians, and Italians. Germans found employment in the jewelry and silver trades.

As the factories moved away, Rhode Islanders turned their coastline into a playground for the rich and famous

RHODE ISLAND AT A GLANCE

Motto: Hope

Population: 1.04 million

Prevalent Religions: Largely Roman Catholic, and small pockets of Baptist, Episcopalian, Methodist, and Buddhist

Major Industries: Nursery stock, vegetables, dairy products, eggs, jewelry, fabricated metal products, electrical equipment, machinery, shipbuilding and boat building, tourism

Ethnic Makeup (in percent): Caucasian 85.0%, African American 4.5%, Hispanic 8.7%, Asian 2.3%, Native American 0.5%, Other 5.0%

Famous Rhode Islanders: Harry Anderson, George M. Cohan, Eddie Dowling, Peter Farrelly, Spalding Gray, David Hartman, Ruth Hussey, Thomas H. Ince, Van Johnson, Galway Kinnell, H.P. Lovecraft, Dana C. Munro, Gilbert Stuart

Above: Sailboats and a bridge at sunset in Newport

from New York and elsewhere—today, tourism attracts visitors from all over the world.

RECORD HIGHLIGHTS

Rhode Island is a gold mine for genealogical research. Records date back to 1636 with most material located in two major repositories—The Rhode Island State Archives and the Rhode Island Historical Society.

Town governments maintained town meeting minutes, vital records, land transactions, and probate and tax valuations. While originals are located in town clerk's offices, researchers can also find vital records in print, on microfilm, or online. Indexes are available. Civil registration occurred in 1853, but discrepancies exist between those kept by the town and those submitted to the state. Prior to total compliance coverage is spotty in the rural parts of the state, but it is possible to fill the gaps with other types of documents.

A wealth of census material exists in print for the colonial period. Check out *Rhode Island Freemen, 1747–1755: A Census of Registered Voters*, edited by Bruce C. Mac-Gunnigle (Baltimore: Genealogical Publishing Co., 1977); *Census of the Inhabitants of the Colony of Rhode Island and Providence Plantations, 1774*, edited by John R. Bartlett (Baltimore: Genealogical Publishing Co., 1969); *The Rhode Island 1777 Military Census*, edited by Mildred Mosher Chamberlain (Baltimore: GPC, 1985; includes men sixteen and older); and *Rhode Island 1782 Census*, edited by Jay Mack Holbrook (Oxford, Mass.: Holbrook Research Institute, 1979). State census records were taken every ten years from 1865 to 1935 and are available at the Rhode Island State Archives. These can supplement the federal population and special schedules—with the exception of the 1890 census, for which only the veterans schedule is extant.

Volunteers for the Rhode Island Cemetery Transcription Project have created a cemetery database of all known stones and are actively looking for transcriptions and additional cemeteries.

The Rhode Island Historical Society <www.rihs.org> holds the largest manuscript, map, and photograph collections in the state. Their library also contains unpublished genealogical manuscripts and a complete set of all newspapers published in the state.

Church records are spread throughout the state in archives and churches. The records of the Episcopal Diocese are at the University of Rhode Island. The Rhode Island Historical Society has on deposit the New England Yearly Meeting collection of Quaker records. Their manuscript department also contains church registers for miscellaneous denominations.

Rhode Islanders participated in every military conflict with record coverage, which varies depending on the war.

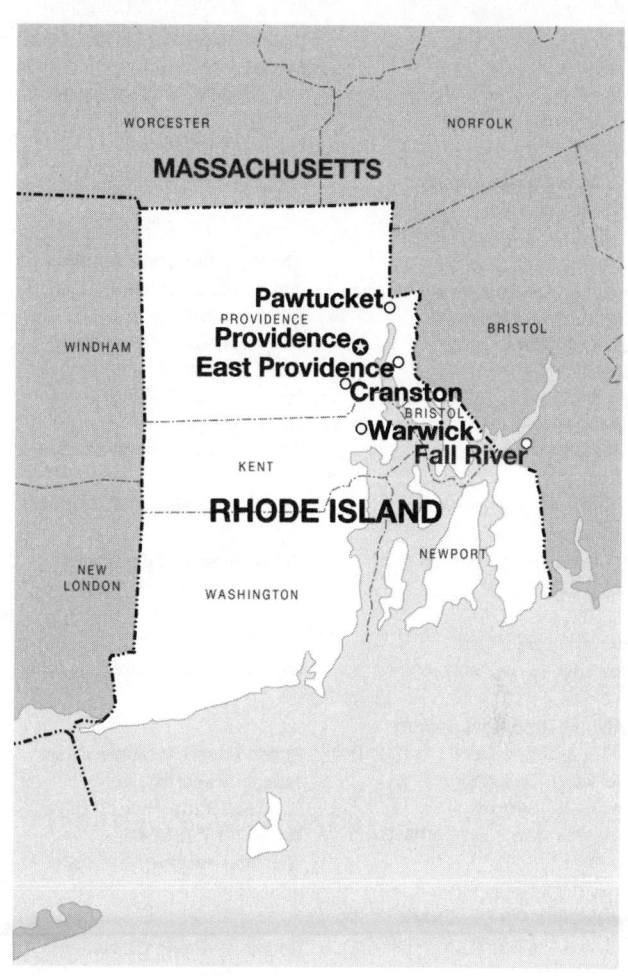

Original military records are located at the Rhode Island State Archives and the Rhode Island Historical Society, as well as the National Archives. For the American Revolution, muster rolls, pay rosters, and hospital records are available but unindexed. The Rhode Island State Archives has a guide to their Civil War materials, including enlistment rosters. They also have records relating to colonial militia and the National Guard.

Court records—civil and criminal—are stored in the Judicial Records Center in Pawtucket. A guide to their holdings and the accessibility of those materials is online at <www.judicial-records.state.ri.us>.

STATE RESOURCES

■ ARCHIVES, LIBRARIES, AND SOCIETIES

American-French Genealogical Society
78 Earle St., Woonsocket, RI 02895
Tel: (401) 765-6141
Fax: (401) 765-6141
Web site:

Clerk of Family Court
1 Dorrance Plaza, Providence, RI 02903
Tel: (401) 227-3340

East Greenwich Free Library
82 Pierce St., East Greenwich, RI 02818

John Hay Library, Brown University
20 Prospect St., Box A, Providence, RI 02912
Tel: (401) 863-3723

Fax: (401) 863-2093
E-mail: hay@brown.edu
Web site: <www.brown.edu/Facilit
ies/University_Library/libs/hay/>

Knight Memorial Library
275 Elmwood Ave., Providence,
RI 02907

**National Archives-New England
Region (Massachusetts)**
380 Trapelo Rd., Waltham, MA
02154
Tel: (781) 663-0130
Web site: <www.archives.gov/fa
cilties/ma/boston.html>

**New England Historic
Genealogical Society**
101 Newbury St., Boston, MA
02116-3007
Tel: (617) 536-5740
Fax: (617) 536-7307
Web site: <www.nehgs.org>

Newport Historical Society
82 Touro St., Newport, RI 02840
Tel: (401) 846-0813
Fax: (401) 846-1853
Web site: <www.newporthistoric
al.org>

Providence Public Library
225 Washington St., Providence,
RI 02903
Tel: (401) 455-8000
Web site: <www.provlib.org>

**Rhode Island Black Heritage
Society**
65 Weybosset St. at the Arcade,
Providence, RI 02903
Tel: (401) 751-3490
Web site: <http://providenceri.
com/RI_BlackHeritage>

**Rhode Island Department of
Health**
3 Capitol Hill, Providence, RI
02908
Tel: (401) 222-2231
Web site: <www.heath.state.ri
.us>

**Rhode Island Genealogical
Society**
P.O. Box 433, Greenville, RI
02828
Web site: <http://users.ids.net/
~ricon/rigs.html>

Rhode Island Historical Society
121 Hope St., Providence, RI
02906
Tel: (401) 331-8575
Fax: (401) 351-0127
Web site: <www.rihs.org>

**Rhode Island Jewish Historical
Association**
130 Sessions St., Providence, RI
02906
Tel: (401) 272-6729
Web site: <www.dowtech.com/
rijha>

**Rhode Island State Archives
and Public Records
Administration**
337 Westminster St., Provi-
dence, RI 02903
Tel: (401) 222-2353
Fax: (401) 222-3199
E-mail: reference@archives.state
.ri.us
Web site: <www.sec.state.ri.us>

Rhode Island State Library
State House, Room 208, Provi-
dence, RI 02903
Tel: (401) 222-2473
Web site: <www.state.ri.us/libra
ry>

**Rhode Island Supreme Court
Judicial Records**
5 Hill St., Pawtucket, RI 02860
Tel: (401) 721-2640
Web site: <www.courts.state.ri
.us>

**Roman Catholic Diocese of
Providence**
The Chancery Office, 34 Fenner
Street, Providence, RI
02903-3695
Tel: (401) 278-4500
Fax: (401) 278-4548

Westerly Public Library
P.O. Box 356, Broad St., Westerly, RI 02891

BIBLIOGRAPHY

■ GENERAL RESOURCES

***An Album of Rhode Island
History, 1636–1986***
by Patrick T. Conley (Norfolk, VA:
Donning, 1986)

***Biographical Cyclopedia of
Representative Men of Rhode
Island, 2 vols.***
(Providence: National Biographi-
cal Publishing Co., 1881)

***The Catholic Church in Rhode
Island***
by Thomas F. Cullen (North Providence, RI: Franciscan Missionaries of Mary, 1936)

 **RESEARCH TIPS**

for more info

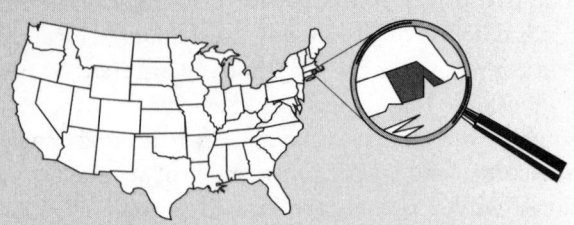

- Even in a state as small as Rhode Island, it is important to know the history of your ancestral town or
village. Town boundaries act as political divisions
for record keeping purposes, but individuals usually
claim allegiance to one of the more than one hundred villages in Rhode Island, not the town where
they were born. Orientation is possible by using a
gazetteer of place names for the state.
- Start your research at the Rhode Island Historical
Society, the fourth oldest historical society in the
United States, for the broadest possible selection
of resources from family genealogies to immigration records. The reference materials are open to
the public, but use of the manuscript and photo
departments requires an appointment.
- Once you've covered the resources available in
the two major repositories, take your search to
the town of your ancestors. Every public library
has a local history collection worth mining for genealogical treasures. Outside the major cities,
towns are small and you can easily connect with
a town historian.
- Regardless of the time period you're researching,
you will discover basic sources and little known
collections to help you trace your family through
Rhode Island's colorful past. This tiny state can
be traversed in a day, enabling genealogists to
visit town clerks, public libraries, and state
repositories.

Census Records
- Federal Census: 1790, 1800, 1810, 1820, 1830,
1840, 1850, 1860, 1870, 1880, 1900, 1910,
1920, 1930
- Union Veteran and Widows: 1890
- State Census: 1865, 1875, 1885, 1905, 1915,
1925, 1935

Rhode Island

Civil, Military and Professional Lists of Plymouth and Rhode Island Colonies: Comprising Colonial, County, and Town Officers, Clergymen, Physicians and Lawyers
by Ebenezer Weaver Pierce (Originally published in 1881; Reprint: Baltimore: Genealogical Publishing Co., 1968)

Documentary History of Rhode Island, 2 vols.
by Howard Millar Chapin (Providence: Preston and Rounds, 1916, 1919)

The Early Records of the Town of Providence, 21 vols.
(Providence: Snow and Farnham, City Printers, 1892–1915)

English Origins of New England Families: From the New England Historical and Genealogical Register, 3 vols.
from the New England Historic Genealogical Society (Baltimore: Genealogical Publishing Co., 1985)

The Genealogical Dictionary of Rhode Island: Comprising Three Generations of Settlers Who Came Before 1690 (with Many Families Carried to the Fourth Generation)
by John Osborne Austin (Baltimore: Genealogical Publishing Co., 1978)

A Genealogical Dictionary of the First Settlers of New England, 4 vols.
by James Savage (Originally published ca. 1860; Reprint: Baltimore: Genealogical Publishing Co., 1965)

Genealogies of Rhode Island Families: From Rhode Island Periodicals, 2 vols.
(Baltimore: Genealogical Publishing Co., 1983)

The Genealogist's Companion and Sourcebook, 2d ed.
by Emily Anne Croom (Cincinnati: Betterway Books, 2003)

A Genealogist's Guide to Discovering Your African-American Ancestors
by Franklin Carter Smith and Emily Anne Croom (Cincinnati: Betterway Books, 2003)

The Greenlaw Index of the New England Historic Genealogical Society, 2 vols.
by William Prescott Greenlaw (Boston: G.K. Hall, 1979)

Guide to Genealogical Research in the National Archives of the United States
edited by Anne Bruner Eales and Robert M. Kvasnicka (Washington, DC: National Archives and Records Administration, 2000)

A Guide to Newspaper Indexes in New England
(Holden, MA: New England Library Association, 1978)

History of the State of Rhode Island and Providence Plantations: 1636–1790, 2 vols.
by Samuel Green Arnold (Spartanburg, SC: The Reprint Co., 1970)

Inventory of Church Archives in Rhode Island: Baptist Bodies
from the Works Projects Administration (Providence: Historical Records Survey, 1939)

Inventory of the Church Archives of Rhode Island; Society of Friends
(Providence: The Historical Records Survey, 1939)

Memorial Encyclopedia of the State of Rhode Island
by Wilfred H. Munro (Boston: American Historical Society, 1916)

Men of Progress: Biographical Sketches and Portraits of Leaders in Business and Professional Life in the State of Rhode Island and Providence Plantations
by Richard Herndon (Boston: *New England Magazine*, 1896)

National Archives Microfilm Catalogs online:
<www.archives.gov/publications/genealogy_microfilm_catalogs.html>

New England Families: Genealogical and Memorial, 4 vols.
by William Richard Cutter (Originally published in 1913; Reprint: New York: Lewis Historical Publishing Co., 1914)

New England Family Histories: States of Maine and Rhode Island
by LuVerne V. Hall (Bowie, MD: Heritage Books, 2000)

The Records of American Baptists in Rhode Island and Related Organizations
from the American Baptist Historical Society (Rochester, NY: American Baptist Historical Society, 1981)

Representative Men and Old Families of Rhode Island: Genealogical And Historical Sketches of Prominent and Representative Citizens And Many of the Old Families, 3 vols.
(Chicago: J.H. Beers & Co., 1908)

Rhode Island: A Bibliography of Its History
edited by Roger Parks (Hanover, NH: University Press of New England, 1983)

Rhode Island Biographical and Genealogical Sketch Index
by J. Carlyle Parker (Turlock, CA: Marietta Pub. Co., 1991)

Rhode Island Genealogies
(Brøderbund, 1996. CD-ROM)

Rhode Island Research Outline
by the Church of Jesus Christ of Latter-Day Saints (Salt Lake City, UT: Corp. of the President of the Church of Jesus Christ of L.D.S., 1988)

Rhode Island Sources for Family Historians and Genealogists
by Kip Sperry (Logan, UT: Everton Publishers, 1986)

State of Rhode Island and Providence Plantations at the End of the Century, 3 vols.
edited by Edward Feld (Boston: Mason Publishing Co., 1902)

■ CENSUS RECORDS

The American Census Handbook
by Thomas Jay Kemp (Wilmington, DE: Scholarly Resources, Inc., 2001)

Atlas of the State of Rhode and Providence Plantations
by Daniel G. Beers (Philadelphia: Pomeroy & Beers, 1870)

The Census Book: A Genealogist's Guide to Federal Census Facts, Schedules and Indexes
by William Dollarhide (Bountiful, UT: Heritage Quest, 1999)

Census of the Inhabitants of the Colony of Rhode Island and Providence Plantations, 1774
compiled by John R. Bartlett (Baltimore: Genealogical Publishing Co., 1969)

Finding Answers in U.S. Census Records
by Loretto Dennis Szucs and Matthew Wright (Salt Lake City: Ancestry Publishing, 2001)

Map Guide to the U.S. Federal Censuses, 1790–1920
by William Thorndale and William Dollarhide (Baltimore: Genealogical Publishing Co., 1987)

The Rhode Island 1777 Military Census
by Mildred M. Chamberlain (Baltimore: Genealogical Publishing Co., 1985)

State Census Records
by Ann S. Lainhart (Baltimore: Genealogical Publishing Co., Inc. 1992)

Your Guide to the Federal Census
by Kathleen W. Hinckley (Cincinnati: Betterway Books, 2002)

■ IMMIGRATION RECORDS

American Naturalization Records, 1790–1990: What They Are and How to Use Them
by John J. Newman (North Salt Lake, UT: HeritageQuest, 1998)

American Passenger Arrival Records
by Michael Tepper (Baltimore: Genealogical Publishing Co., 1993)

Immigrants to New England, 1700–1775
by Ethel Stanwood Bolton (Salem, MA: The Essex Institute, 1931)

Passenger and Immigration Lists Index, 15 vols.
by P. William Filby (Detroit: Gale Research, 1981–)

Rhode Island

Rhode Island Passenger Lists: Port of Providence 1798–1808; 1820–1872 and Port of Bristol and Warren 1820–1871
by Maureen A. Taylor (Baltimore: Genealogical Publishing Co., 1993)

They Became Americans: Finding Naturalization Records and Ethnic Origins
by Loretto Dennis Szucs (Salt Lake City: Ancestry, Inc., 1998)

They Came in Ships: A Guide to Finding Your Immigrant Ancestor's Arrival Records, 2d ed.
by John P. Colletta (Salt Lake City: Ancestry, Inc., 1993)

■ LAND RECORDS

Land and Property Research in the United States
by Wade E. Hone (Salt Lake City: Ancestry Inc., 1997)

Locating Your Roots: Discover Your Ancestors Using Land Records
by Patricia Law Hatcher (Cincinnati: Betterway Books, 2003)

The Records of the Properties of the Narragansett, Otherwise Called the Fones Record
by James N. Arnold (Providence, RI: Narragansett Historical Publishing, 1894)

Rhode Island Land Evidences, vol. I, 1648–96
compiled by Dorothy Worthington (Providence, RI: Rhode Island Historical Society, 1921; Reprint: Baltimore: Genealogical Publishing Co., 1970)

■ MAPS

Connecticut, Maine, Massachusetts, Rhode Island, Atlas of Historical County Boundaries
by John H. Long (New York: Simon & Schuster, 1994)

A Gazetteer of the State of Connecticut and Rhode Island
by John Chauncey Pease and John M. Niles (Hartford, CT: Heritage Books, 1991)

A Geographic Dictionary of Connecticut and Rhode Island
by Henry Gannett (Originally published in 1894; Reprint: Baltimore: Genealogical Publishing Co., 1978)

The Post Offices of Rhode Island
by Johns S. Gallagher (Burtonsville, MD: The Depot, 1977)

Rhode Island Atlas
by Marion I. Wright and Robert J. Sullivan (Providence: Rhode Island Publications Society, 1982)

Rhode Island Boundaries, 1636–1936
by John H. Cady (Providence: State of Rhode Island and Providence Plantations, 1936)

Rhode Island—A Guide to the Smallest State
(Boston: Houghton Mifflin Co., 1937)

Rhode Island Postal History: The Post Office
by Lawrence M. Merolla, Arthur B. Jackson, and Frank M. Crowther (Providence: Rhode Island Postal History Society, 1977)

■ MILITARY RECORDS

Civil and Military List of Rhode Island, 1647–1800, 3 vols.
by Joseph J. Smith (Providence, RI: Preston and Rounds, 1901)

Rhode Island in the Colonial Wars: A List of Rhode Island Soldiers and Sailors in King George's War, 1740–1748
by Howard Miller Chapin (Providence, RI: Rhode Island Historical Society, 1920)

Rhode Island in the Colonial Wars: A List of Rhode Island Soldiers and Sailors in the Old French and Indian Wars, 1755–1762
by Howard Miller Chapin (Providence, RI: Rhode Island Historical Society, 1918)

So Few the Brave: Rhode Island Continentals, 1775–1783
by Anthony Walker (Newport, RI: Seafield, 1981)

Spirit of '76 in Rhode Island
by Benjamin Cowell (Boston: A.J. Wright, 1850)

Uncle, We Are Ready! Registering America's Men, 1917–1918: A Guide to Researching World War I Draft Registration Cards
by John J. Newman (North Salt Lake, UT: HeritageQuest, 2001)

U.S. Military Records: A Guide to Federal & State Sources, Colonial America to the Present
by James C. Neagles (Salt Lake City: Ancestry, Inc., 1994)

World War II: A Family Historian's Guide
by Debra Johnson Knox (Spartanburg, SC: MIE Publishing, 2003)

■ PROBATE RECORDS

Index to the Probate Records of the Municipal Court of the city of Providence, Rhode Island: From 1646 to and Including the Year 1899
edited by Edward Field (Providence, RI: Providence Press, 1902)

Index of Wills, 1636–1850
by Nellie M.C. Beaman (Princeton, MA: Rhode Island Families Association, 1992)

Index to Wills in Rhode Island Genealogical Register, Vol. 1-4
by Robert S. Wakefield (Warwick, RI: Plymouth Colony Research Group, 1982)

Records of the Colony of Rhode Island and Providence Plantations in New England, 10 vols.
by John R. Bartlett (Providence: A.C. Green, 1856–1865)

Records of the Vice-Admiralty Court of Rhode Island: 1716–1752
(Millwood, NY: Kraus Reprint, 1975)

Rhode Island Court Records: Records of the Court of Trials of the Colony of Providence Plantations, 1647–1670, 2 vols.
(Providence: Rhode Island Historical Society, 1920–1922)

Rhode Island General Court of Trials, 1671–1704
(Boxford, MA: J.F. Fiske, 1998)

■ VITAL RECORDS

Guide to the Public Vital Statistics Records (Births, Marriages, Deaths) in the State of Rhode Island and Providence Plantations
from the Rhode Island Department of State (Providence: the Historical Records Survey, 1941)

New England Marriages Prior to 1700
by Clarence Almon Torrey (Baltimore: Genealogical Publishing Co., 1985)

Vital Records of Rhode Island, 1636–1850: A Family Register for the People, 20 vols.
by James N. Arnold (Providence, RI: Narragansett Historical Publishing Co., 1891–1912)

Vital Records of Rhode Island, New Series, 13 Vols.
compiled by Alden G. Beaman (Princeton, MA: Alden G. Beaman, 1975–87)

Your Guide to Cemetery Research
by Sharon DeBartolo Carmack (Cincinnati: Betterway Books, 2002)

Rhode Island

■ Bristol   17 Feb. 1747

1 Dorrance Plaza, Bristol, RI 02809
Phone: (508)823-6588
Web site: www.rootsweb.com/~ribristo/
Parent County: Created from Bristol, MA
Comments/research tips: There is no County Clerk in Bristol County. Towns organized before 1800: Barrington 1717, Bristol 1681, Warren 1746–1747. Block Island was transferred from Newport County to Washington County on 6 May 1963. There are four town in the county.

Record Type	Year Begun	Jurisdiction
Birth	na	Town/City Clerks
Marriage	na	Town/City Clerks
Death	na	Town/City Clerks
Burial	na	Town/City Clerks
Probate	na	Town/City Clerks
Court	na	Clerk/District Ct.

■ Kent   11 June 1750

222 Quaker Lane, East Greenwich, RI 02818
Phone: (401)841-8350
Web site: www.rootsweb.com/~rikent/
Parent County: Providence
Comments/research tips: Five Towns in Kent County. Towns organized before 1800: Coventry 1741, East Greenwich 1677, Warwick 1642–1643, West Greenwich 1741.

Record Type	Year Begun	Jurisdiction
Birth	na	Town/City Clerks
Marriage	na	Town/City Clerks
Death	na	Town/City Clerks
Burial	na	Town/City Clerks
Probate	na	Town/City Clerks
Land	na	Town/City Clerks

■ King's   3 June 1729

Parent County: Providence Plantations
Comments/research tips: (See Washington) Name changed to Washington 29 October 1781.

■ Newport   16 June 1729

8 Washington Sq., Newport, RI 02840-7199
Phone: (401)841-8350
Web site: www.rootsweb.com/~rinewpor/ or www.gonewport.com
Parent County: Rhode Island
Comments/research tips: 1746–1747 eastern boundary adjusted under decree of the King of England. Five towns and one city in Newport County. Towns organized before 1800: Jamestown 1678, Little Compton 1746–1747, Middletown 1743, Portsmouth 1638, Newport 1939, Tiverton 1746–1747. Newport Historical Society has early Church, Land, and Probate records.

Record Type	Year Begun	Jurisdiction
Birth	na	Town/City Clerks
Marriage	na	Town/City Clerks
Death	na	Town/City Clerks
Burial	na	Town/City Clerks
Divorce	na	Family & Superior Courts
Probate	1784	Probate Court
Court	na	District Court
Land	1780	Town/City Clerks

■ Providence   22 June 1703

250 Benefit Street, Providence, RI 02903
Phone: (401)277-6710
Web site: www.rootsweb.com/~riprovid/
Parent County: Providence Plantations
Comments/research tips: Formerly Providence Plantations. Name changed to Providence County 16 June 1729. Twenty-two towns in Providence County. Towns organized before 1800: Cranston 1754, Cumberland 1746–1747, Foster 1781, Gloucester 1730–1731, Johnston 1759, North Providence 1765, Providence 1636, Scituate 1730–1731, Smithfield 1730–1731.

Record Type	Year Begun	Jurisdiction
Probate	na	Probate Judge
Divorce	na	Family Court
Court	na	Municipal Court
Land	na	Recorder/Deeds
Birth	na	Town/City Clerks
Marriage	na	Town/City Clerks
Death	na	Town/City Clerks

■ Providence Plantations   22 June 1703

Parent County: Original County
Comments/research tips: (See Providence) Name changed to Providence County 16 June 1729.

■ Rhode Island   22 June 1703

Parent County: Original County
Comments/research tips: (See Newport) Name changed to Newport 16 June 1729.

■ Washington   29 Oct. 1781

4800 Tower Hill Road, Wakefield, RI 02879
Phone: (401)841-8350
Web site: www.rootsweb.com/~riwashin/
Parent County: Newport
Comments/research tips: Formerly King's County. Name changed to Washington 29 October 1781. Twenty towns in Washington County. Towns Organized before 1800: Charlestown 1738, Exeter 1742–1743, Hopkinton 1757, North Kingstown 1641, Richmond 1747, South Kingstown (Pettaquamscutt) 1656–1657, Westerly 1669.

Record Type	Year Begun	Jurisdiction
Birth	na	Town/City Clerks
Marriage	na	Town/City Clerks
Death	na	Town/City Clerks
Probate	na	Town/City Clerks
Land	na	Town/City Clerks

South Carolina

By Emily Anne Croom

HISTORICAL OVERVIEW

Although Spaniards explored and established missions along the Atlantic coast in the early sixteenth century, Spain, France, and England all desired a permanent foothold there. In 1663, Britain's Charles II granted a charter to eight proprietors to colonize between 31, and 36, north latitude from sea to sea. English colonists built Charles Town, the first permanent European settlement, near present-day Charleston in 1670. Early settlers—mostly from Virginia and Barbados, other British Caribbean and New England colonies, the British Isles, and France (Huguenots)—created an economy based on fur and deer-skin trade and production of foodstuffs and forest products for Barbados and other Caribbean colonies. In 1712 North and South Carolina became separate provinces. Political discontent led Parliament to establish both Carolinas as royal colonies in 1729.

South Carolina experienced remarkable growth in its first century. In the coastal lowcountry, plantations growing rice (after 1700) and indigo (from the 1740s) using slave labor began to dominate the economy. In the 1750s, settlement in the upcountry—the inland area and highlands in the northwest—began with an influx of yeomen farmers, some recruited from Europe and others moving overland from or through Pennsylvania, Virginia, and North Carolina.

During the American Revolution, the British occupied Charleston from May 1780 to late 1782. More than two hundred engagements took place in South Carolina, including conflicts between its numerous loyalists and its patriots, who frequently waged guerilla warfare.

By the 1820s, cotton culture dominated the state's economy and slaves were the majority of the population, as they had been in the late colonial years. By 1860, the state had almost 704,000 residents, of whom more than 57 percent

SOUTH CAROLINA AT A GLANCE

Mottoes: Prepared in Mind and Resources *and* While I Breathe, I Hope

Population: 4 million

Prevalent Religions: Christianity, particularly Protestant (Lutheran, Methodist, Presbyterian, Episcopalian, and Southern Baptist), and a small percentage of Roman Catholics

Major Industries: Tobacco, poultry, cattle, dairy products, soybeans, hogs, textile goods, chemical products, paper products, machinery, tourism

Ethnic Makeup (in percent): Caucasian 67.2%, African American 29.5%, Hispanic 2.4%, Asian 0.9%, Native American 0.3%, Other 1.0%

Famous South Carolinians: Whispering Bill Anderson, James Brown, John C. Calhoun, Dizzy Gillespie, Andrew Jackson, Jesse Jackson, Andie MacDowell, Ronald McNair, Micky Spillane, Strom Thurmond, General William Westmoreland, Vanna White, Woodrow Wilson

Above: The glorious Boone Hall Plantation

© PhotoDisc/Getty Images

were slaves; the free black and the foreign-born populations were each about 1.4 percent.

Shortly after Lincoln's election in 1860, decades of economic and political tension came to a head and South Carolina seceded. The Civil War began in April 1861 when Confederate forces fired on Fort Sumter in Charleston harbor. The city was under siege during much of the war. Sherman's march to the sea in 1865 destroyed most of the state capital, Columbia, and left the state charred and impoverished. Numerous ex-slaves and white farmers became sharecroppers after the war. South Carolina was readmitted to the Union in June 1868.

Between the Civil War and World War II agricultural domination declined, and the state's economy diversified to include textile mills, food and forest products, fishing, and mineral industries. However, poverty still gripped much of the state. By 1922, large numbers of African Americans had migrated to northern cities, leaving the black population a minority in the state. In the 1970s,

the urban population of the state surpassed the rural population.

RECORD HIGHLIGHTS

South Carolina began statewide registration of births and deaths in 1915, marriages in July 1950, and divorces in July 1962. The Division of Vital Records <www.scdhec. com/vr/index.htm> can supply copies of all four kinds of records. The vital records offices in the county health departments handle birth and death records only. Several county health departments or courthouses hold birth and death records from the late nineteenth century. Vital records at the state archives are listed at <www.state.sc.us/scdah/vit.htm>.

The state did not require marriage licenses until July 1911. Some pre-1911 marriage records and settlements (prenuptial agreements) exist, and evidence of marriages can be found in numerous other county records and newspapers. For marriage records created between 1911

South Carolina

and July 1950, contact the county probate office that issued the license. Before 1949, divorce was illegal and rarely granted. For divorce records created since April 1949, contact the county clerk where the case was filed.

State-specific records available at the state archives and/or other research facilities include the following:

- *Mills' Atlas of the State of South Carolina, 1825*
- Several series of the Draper Manuscripts, especially series V, TT, and UU, dealing with South Carolina, housed at the State Historical Society of Wisconsin and available on microfilm at major libraries
- Voter registrations, 1867–1868
- Records of depositors in South Carolina's two branches of the Freedman's Savings and Trust Company (FHL microfilm 928587-89)
- Confederate pension applications, 1919–1938; some Confederate Home records
- Searchable indexes to various records series, including Confederate pensions, online at <www.archivesindex.sc.gov/search/default.asp>
- Agricultural censuses (1868, 1875) and state censuses (1829, 1839, 1869, 1875), various counties, various years

STATE RESOURCES

■ ARCHIVES, LIBRARIES, AND SOCIETIES

Abbeville-Greenwood Regional Library
106 N. Main St., Greenwood, SC 29646
Tel: (864) 941-4650

Aiken-Barnwell Genealogical Society
P.O. Box 415, Aiken, SC 29802
Web site: <www.abgs.org>

Allendale County Historical Society
P.O. Box 523, Allendale, SC 29810

Anderson County Chapter of the South Carolina Genealogical Society
P.O. Box 74, Anderson, SC 29622-0074
Web site: <www.rootsweb.com/~scandeers/andgensoc.html>

Catawba Wateree Genealogical Society, Camden Archives and Museum
E-mail: CatawbaWatereeGS@aol.com
Web site: <http://hometown.aol.com/catawbawatereegs/>

Catholic Diocese of Charleston, Archives
119 Broad St., P.O. Box 818, Charleston, SC 29402
Tel: (843) 724-8372
Web site: <www.catholic-doc.org/archives>

Charleston Chapter of the South Carolina Genealogical Society
P.O. Box 20266, Charleston, SC 29413-0266
Web site: <http://scgen.org/charlestonmain.htm>

Charleston Library Society
164 King St., Charleston, SC 29401
Tel: (803) 723-9912

Chester District Genealogical Society
P.O. Box 336, Richburg, SC 29729

Chesterfield District Chapter of the South Carolina Genealogical Society
P.O. Box 167, Chesterfield, SC 29709-0167

Clarendon County Genealogical Society, Clarendon County Archives
211 N. Brooks St., Manning, SC 29102

RESEARCH TIPS

for more info

- The state archives is South Carolina's major research facility <www.state.sc.us/scdah/guide/guide.htm#guide>. Other important research locations are the South Caroliniana Library of the University of South Carolina in Columbia and the South Carolina Historical Society, Charleston.
- In the eighteenth century, parishes registered life events and provided assistance to the poor, mostly in the lowcountry where the majority of the population lived. Many surviving parish records have been published or placed at the South Carolina Historical Society.
- Before 1785, most legal documents were recorded centrally in Charleston. Between 1785 and 1800 and since 1868, South Carolina's civil divisions have been counties. Between 1800 and 1868, records were created in districts. An important step in South Carolina research is to identify the ancestral parish, district, and/or county.
- The late establishment of the North-South Carolina boundary (1772) suggests that researchers consult records on both sides of the current line.

Census Records
- Federal Census Population Schedules: 1790, 1800, 1810, 1830, 1840, 1850, 1860, 1870, 1880, 1900, 1910, 1920, 1930
- Federal Census Soundex: 1880, 1900, 1910, 1920, 1930
- Federal Slave Schedules: 1850, 1860 (schedules name slaveholders but rarely name slaves)
- Federal Mortality Schedules: 1850, 1860, 1870, 1880
- Special Census of Civil War Union Veterans and Widows: 1890
- State Census: (all incomplete) 1829, 1839, 1869, 1875

Web site: <www.rootsweb.com/ ~scclaren/archives.html>

Columbia Chapter of the South Carolina Genealogical Society
P.O. Box 11353, Columbia, SC 29211

Darlington County Historical Commission
204 Hewitt St., Darlington, SC 29532

Division of Vital Records, South Carolina Department of Health and Environmental Control
2600 Bull St., Columbia, SC 29201-1708
Tel: (803) 898-3630
Web site: <www.scdhec.com/rr/ index.htm>

Greenville County Library
300 College St., Greenville, SC 29601

Greenville County Historical Society
P.O. Box 10472, Greenville, SC 29603-0472
Web site: <www.greenvillehistory .org/>

Hilton Head Island Genealogical Society
32 Office Park Rd., Ste. 300, Hilton Head Island, SC 29928-4640
Tel: (843) 785-6834 or (843) 341-6493
Web site: <http://ourtown.island packet.com/32/>

Horry County Historical Society
606 Main St., Conway, SC 29526-4340
Web site: <www.hchsonline.org/>

Huguenot Society of South Carolina
138 Logan St., Charleston, SC 29401
Tel: (843) 853-8476

Jasper County Historical Society
P.O. Box 2111, Ridgeland, SC 29936

Kershaw County Historical Society
811 Fair St., P.O. Box 501, Camden, SC 29020
Web site: <www.mindspring .com/~ekchistory/>

Laurens County Library
1017 W. Main St., Laurens, SC 29360-2647

Laurens District Chapter of the South Carolina Genealogical Society
P.O. Box 1217, Laurens, SC 29360-1217

Lexington Genealogical Association
P.O. Box 1442, Lexington, SC 29072
Web site: <www.homestead. com/lexingtongenealogy/ main.html>

National Archives-Southeast Region
1557 St. Joseph Ave., East Point, GA 30344
Tel: (404) 763-7477
Fax: (404) 763-7033
Web site: <www.archives.gov/fa cilities/ga/atlanta.html>

Old Darlington District Chapter of the South Carolina Genealogical Society
307 Kings Place, Hartsville, SC 29550
Web site: <www.geocities.com/ Heartland/Estates/7212/>

Old Edgefield District Archives Chapter of the South Carolina Genealogical Society
P.O. Box 468, Edgefield, SC 29824
Web site: <www.rootsweb.com/ ~scedgegi/oedgs.html>

Old Pendleton District Chapter of the South Carolina Genealogical Society
228 Ivydale Dr., Greenville, SC 29609
Web site: <http://oldpendleton .homestead.com/>

Old St. Bartholomew Chapter of the South Carolina Genealogical Society
104 Wade Hampton Ave., Walterboro, SC 29488

Orangeburg German-Swiss Genealogical Society
P.O. Box 974, Orangeburg, SC 29119-0974
Web site: <www.netside.com/~g enealogy/orangeburgh.htm>

Parris Island Historical and Museum Society
P.O. Box 5202, Parris Island, SC 29905-5202
Web site: <www.parrisisland .com/historic.htm>

Pee Dee Chapter of the South Carolina Genealogical Society
P.O. Box 236, Latta, SC 29565
Web site: <www.scgen.org/peed ee.htm>

Piedmont Historical Society
P.O. Box 8096, Spartanburg, SC 29305
Web site: <www.piedmont-histori cal-society.org>

Pinckney District Chapter of the South Carolina Genealogical Society
P.O. Box 5281, Spartanburg, SC 29304

Richland County Public Library
1431 Assembly St., Columbia, SC 29201-3101
Tel: (803) 799-9084

Rock Hill Public Library
Box 32, 325 S. Oakland Ave., Rock Hill, SC 29730

Saluda County Historical Society
P.O. Box 22, Saluda, SC 29138
Web site: <www.saludaschisoric al.org/>

South Carolina Baptist Historical Collection
James B. Duke Library, Furman University, 3300 Poinsett Hwy., Greenville, SC 29613-0600
Tel: (864) 294-2192
Fax: (864) 294-2194

South Carolina Genealogical Society
2910 Duncan St., Columbia, SC 29205
Web site: <www.scgen.org>

South Carolina Historical Society
100 Meeting St., Charleston, SC 29401-2299
Tel: (803) 723-3225
Fax: (803) 723-8584
Web site: <www.schistory.org>

South Carolina United Methodist Collection
℅ Sandor Teszler Library, Wofford College, 429 N. Church St., Spartanburg, SC 29303
Tel: (864) 597-4309
Web site: <www.wofford.edu/Sa ndorTeszlerLibrary/archives/ default.asp>

South Carolina Department of Archives and History, State Archives
P.O. Box 11469, 8301 Parklane Rd., Columbia, SC 29211

Tel: (803) 896-6100
Web site: <www.state.sc.us/sc dah/research.htm>

Southern Wesleyan University, Rickman Library
Faith Clayton Research Center, P.O. Box 1020, 907 Wesleyan Dr., Central, SC 29630-1020
Tel: (864) 644-5000
Web site: <www.swu.edu/libr ary/index.php>

Spartanburg County Historical Association
P.O. Box 887, Spartanburg, SC 29304
Web site: <www.spartanarts .org/history/>

Three Rivers Historical Society
414 N. Main St., Hemingway, SC 29554
Web site: <www.threerivershists oc.org/index.htm>

University of South Carolina, Thomas Cooper Library
1322 Greene St., University of South Carolina, Columbia, SC 29208
Tel: (803) 777-3142
Fax: (803) 777-4661
Web site: <www.sc.edu/library/ tcl.html>

BIBLIOGRAPHY

■ GENERAL RESOURCES

African-American Genealogy: A Bibliography and Guide to Sources
by Curt Bryan Witcher (Fort Wayne, IN: Round Tower Books, 2000. Lists numerous white families' papers)

Bible Records, 7 vols.
compiled by Memory Aldridge Lester (Chapel Hill, NC: Memory Aldridge Lester, 1956–62)

Books and Articles on South Carolina History
by Lewis P. Jones (Columbia, SC: University of South Carolina Press, 1991)

Carolina Families: A Bibliography of Books About North and South Carolina Families
by Donald M. Hehir (Bowie, MD: Heritage Books, 1994)

A Collection of Upper South Carolina Genealogical and Family Records, 3 vols.
edited by James E. Wooley (Easley, SC: Southern Historical Press, 1979–82)

Correct Mispronunciations of Some South Carolina Names
by Claude Neuffer and Irene Neuffer (Columbia, SC: University of South Carolina Press, 1983)

Cyclopedia of Eminent and Representative Men of the Carolinas of the Nineteenth Century
by Edward McCrady and Samuel A. Ashe (Madison, WI: Brant & Fuller, 1892)

Dictionary of South Carolina Biography
edited by Richard N. Cote and Patricia H. Williams (Easley, SC: Southern Historical Press, 1985)

Genealogical Encyclopedia of the Colonial Americas
by Christina K. Schaefer (Baltimore: Genealogical Publishing Co., 1998. Pages 537-547, South Carolina)

"Genealogical Research in South Carolina"
by Ge Lee C. Hendrix (*National Genealogical Society Quarterly* 75, Dec. 1987: 249-270)

The Genealogist's Companion and Sourcebook, 2d ed.
by Emily Anne Croom (Cincinnati: Betterway Books, 2003)

A Genealogist's Guide to Discovering Your African-American Ancestors
by Franklin Carter Smith and Emily Anne Croom (Cincinnati: Betterway Books, 2003)

The Growth and Distribution of Population in South Carolina
by Julian J. Petty (Originally published in 1943; Reprint: Spartanburg, SC: The Reprint Co., 1975)

Guide to Genealogical Research in the National Archives of the United States
edited by Anne Bruner Eales and Robert M. Kvasnicka (Washington, DC: National Archives and Records Administration, 2000)

A Guide To Local Government Records in the South Carolina Archives
South Carolina Department of Archives and History (Columbia, SC: University of South Carolina Press, 1988)

A Guide to the Manuscript Collection of the South Caroliniana Library
by Allen H. Stokes (Columbia, SC: the South Caroliniana Library, 1982)

A Guide to South Carolina Genealogical Research and Records
by Brent Holcomb (Columbia, S.C.: Brent H. Holcomb, 1998)

Guide to the Study and Reading of South Carolina History: A General Classified Bibliography, 2 vols.
by James H. Easterby (Columbia, SC: Historical Commission of South Carolina, 1949–1950)

History of South Carolina, 5 vols.
edited by Yates Snowden and Harry G. Cutler (Chicago: Lewis Publishing Co., 1920)

An Index to Some of the Family Records of the Southern States
by E. Kay Kirkham (Logan, UT: Everton Publishers, 1979)

Journal of the Commons House of Assembly, 1736–1750
edited by James H. Easterby (Columbia, SC: Historical Commission of South Carolina, 1951–)

Local and Family History in South Carolina: A Bibliography
by Richard N. Cote (Easley, SC: Southern Historical Press, 1981)

Men of Mark in South Carolina . . . A Collection of Biographies of Leading Men of the State, 4 vols.
by James C. Hemphill (Washington, D.C.: Men of Mark Publishing Co., 1907–1909)

National Archives Microfilm Catalogs online:
<www.archives.gov/publications/genealogy_microfilm_catalogs.html>

North Carolina-South Carolina Bible Records
by Jeannette H. Austin (Westminster, MD: Willow Bend Books, 2000)

Records in the British Public Records Office Relating to South Carolina, 1663–1782
by Helen C. Carson (Columbia, SC: South Carolina Department of Archives and History, 1973)

Research Materials in South Carolina: A Guide
by John Hammond Moore (Columbia, SC: University of South Carolina Press, 1967)

A Sketch of the History of South Carolina To the Close of the Proprietary Government by the Revolution of 1719
by William James Rivers (Originally published in 1856; Reprint: Spartanburg, SC: Reprint Co., 1972)

The South Carolina Archives: A Temporary Summary Guide, 2d ed.
by Marion C. Chandler and Earl W. Wade (Columbia: SC: Department of Archives and History, 1976)

South Carolina Genealogical Research
by George K. Schweitzer (Knoxville: George K. Schweitzer, 1985)

South Carolina: A Guide for Genealogists
by Theresa Hicks (Columbia, SC: Columbia Chapter, South Carolina Genealogical Society, 1995)

South Carolina Newspapers
by John Hammond Moore (Columbia, SC: University of South Carolina Press, 1988)

South Carolina Research Outline
by the Church of Jesus Christ of Latter-Day Saints (Salt Lake City, UT: Corp. of the President of the Church of Jesus Christ of L.D.S., 1988)

South Carolina: A Short History, 1520–1948
by David Duncan Wallace (Columbia, SC: University of South Carolina Press, 1951)

South Carolina Women, 2d ed.
by Idella Bodie (Orangeburg, SC: Sandlapper Pub., 1991)

The Story of the South Carolina Lowcountry, 3 vols.
by Herbert Ravenel Sass (West Columbia, SC: J.F. Hyer Pub., 1956)

■ **CENSUS RECORDS**

The American Census Handbook
by Thomas Jay Kemp (Wilmington, DE: Scholarly Resources, Inc. 2001)

The Census Book: A Genealogist's Guide to Federal Census Facts, Schedules and Indexes
by William Dollarhide (Bountiful, UT: Heritage Quest, 1999)

Finding Answers in U.S. Census Records
by Loretto Dennis Szucs and Matthew Wright (Salt Lake City: Ancestry Publishing, 2001)

Map Guide to the U.S. Federal Censuses, 1790–1920
by William Thorndale and William Dollarhide (Baltimore: Genealogical Publishing Co., 1987)

State Census Records
by Ann S. Lainhart (Baltimore: Genealogical Publishing Co., Inc., 1992)

Your Guide to the Federal Census
by Kathleen W. Hinckley (Cincinnati: Betterway Books, 2002)

■ **IMMIGRATION RECORDS**

American Naturalization Records, 1790–1990: What They Are and How to Use Them
by John J. Newman (North Salt Lake, UT: HeritageQuest, 1998)

American Passenger Arrival Records
by Michael Tepper (Baltimore: Genealogical Publishing Co., 1993)

Citizens and Immigrants— South Carolina, 1768
by Mary Bondurant Warren (Danielsville, GA: Heritage Papers, 1980)

A Compilation of the Original Lists of Protestant Immigrants to South Carolina, 1763–1773
by Janie Revill (Originally published in 1939; Reprint: Baltimore: Genealogical Publishing Co., 1999)

First Settlers of South Carolina 1670–1700
by Agnes Leland Baldwin (Easley, SC: Southern Historical Press, 1985)

Passenger and Immigration Lists Index
by P. William Filby (Detroit: Gale Research Co., 1980–)

Scotch-Irish Migration to South Carolina, 1772
by Jean Stephenson (Originally published in 1971; Reprint: Baltimore: Genealogical Publishing Co., 1999)

South Carolina Immigrants, 1760 to 1770
by Jack Moreland Jones and Mary Bondurant Warren (Danielsville, GA: Heritage Papers, 1988)

South Carolina Naturalizations, 1783–1850
by Brent H. Holcomb (Baltimore: Genealogical Publishing Co., 1997)

They Became Americans: Finding Naturalization Records and Ethnic Origins
by Loretto Dennis Szucs (Salt Lake City: Ancestry, Inc., 1998)

They Came in Ships: A Guide to Finding Your Immigrant Ancestor's Arrival Records, 2d ed.
by John P. Colletta (Salt Lake City: Ancestry, Inc., 1993)

■ LAND RECORDS

An Index to Deeds of the Province and State of South Carolina, 1719–1785, and Charleston District, 1785–1800
by Silas Emmett Lucas Jr. (Easley, SC: Southern Historical Press, 1977)

Land and Property Research in the United States
by Wade E. Hone (Salt Lake City: Ancestry Inc., 1997)

Locating Your Roots: Discover Your Ancestors Using Land Records
by Patricia Law Hatcher (Cincinnati: Betterway Books, 2003)

North Carolina Land Grants in South Carolina
by Brent H. Holcomb (Originally published in 1975; Reprint: Baltimore: Genealogical Publishing Co., 1999)

Petitions for Land from the South Carolina Council Journals, 7 vols.
by Brent H. Holcomb (Columbia, SC: South Carolina Magazine of Ancestral Research, ca. 1996–ca. 1999)

The Promised Land: The History of The South Carolina Land Commission 1869–1890
by Carol K. Rothrock Bleser (Columbia, SC: University of South Carolina Press, 1969)

Records of the Secretary of the Province and The Register of the Province of South Carolina, 1671–1675
by Alexander S. Salley (Columbia, SC: Historical Commission of South Carolina, 1944)

South Carolina Deed Abstracts, 3 vols.
by Brent H. Holcomb (Columbia, SC: South Carolina Magazine of Ancestral Research, 1996)

South Carolina Deed Abstracts, 1719–1772, 4 vols.
by Clara A. Langley (Easley, SC: Southern Historical Press, 1983–1984)

South Carolina Memorials: Abstracts of Land Titles
by Jesse Hogan Motes (Greenville, SC: Southern Historical Press, 1996)

South Carolina Memorials, 1731–1776: Abstracts of Selected Land Records from a Collection in the Department of Archives and History, 2 vols.
by Katie-Prince Ward Esker (New Orleans: Polyanthos, 1973–1977)

South Carolina as a Royal Province, 1719–1776
by William Roy Smith (Originally published New York: Macmillan, 1903; Reprint: Freeport, NY: Books for Libraries Press, 1970)

Warrants for Land in South Carolina, 1672–1711
edited by A.S. Salley Jr. (Originally published in 1910; Reprint: Baltimore: Genealogical Publishing Co., 1998)

■ MAPS

Atlas of Historical County Boundaries, South Carolina
edited by John H. Long and Gordon DenBoer (NY: Charles Scribner's Sons, 1997)

"The Counties and Districts of South Carolina"
by James Black (Genealogical Journal, vol 5, no. 3, pp. 100–113. Salt Lake City: Utah Genealogical Association, 1976)

Mills' Atlas of the State of South Carolina, 1825
by Robert Mills (Easley, SC: Southern Historical Press, 1980)

Names of South Carolina, vols. 1–12
edited by Claude H. Neuffer (Columbia: University of South Carolina, 1967; Reprint: Spartanburg, SC: Reprint Co., 1976)

Palmetto Place Names
from the Work Projects Administration (Originally published in 1941; Reprint: Spartanburg, SC: The Reprint Co., 1975)

South Carolina County Maps
compiled by C.J. Puetz (Lyndon Station, WI: County Maps, 1994)

South Carolina Waterways As They Appear in Mill's Atlas
by Mariam D. Cropper (Bountiful, UT: Accelerated Indexing Systems, 1977)

■ MILITARY RECORDS

Compendium of the Confederate Armies, 11 vols.
by Stewart Sifakis (NY: Facts on File, 1992–1995)

Colonial Soldiers of the South, 1732–1774
compiled by Murtie June Clark (Baltimore: Genealogical Publishing Co., 1983)

Copy of the Original Index Book Showing the Revolutionary Claims Filed in South Carolina Between August 20, 1783 and August 31, 1786
by Janie Revill (Originally published in 1941; Reprint: Baltimore: Genealogical Publishing Co., 1990)

The Militia in Antebellum South Carolina Society
by Jean Martin Flynn (Spartanburg, SC: The Reprint Co., 1991)

Records of the Regiments of the South Carolina Line in the Revolutionary War
compiled by Alexander S. Salley (Baltimore: Clearfield Co., 1991)

Roster of South Carolina Patriots in the American Revolution
by Bobby Gilmer Moss (Baltimore: Genealogical Publishing Co., 1994)

Soldiers of The Great War, 3 vols.
by W.M. Haulsee, F.G. Howe, and Alfred C. Doyle (Washington, DC: Soldiers Record Publishing Association, 1920)

South Carolina in the Mexican War: A History of the Palmetto Regiment of Volunteers, 1846–1917
by Jack Allen Meyer (Columbia, SC: South Carolina Dept. of Archives and History, 1996)

South Carolinians in the Revolution, with Service Records and Miscellaneous Data . . . 1775–1855
edited by Sara A. Ervin (Originally published in 1949, Ypsilanti, MI; Reprint: Baltimore: Genealogical Publishing Co., 1971)

South Carolina Revolutionary Records, Selected Final Pension Payment Vouchers, 1818–1864
by Alycon Trubey Pierce (Athens, GA: Iberian Pub. Co., 1996)

South Carolina Troops in Confederate Service, 3 vols.
by A.S. Salley Jr. (Columbia, SC: R.L. Bryan, 1913–30)

Uncle, We Are Ready! Registering America's Men, 1917–1918: A Guide to Researching World War I Draft Registration Cards
by John J. Newman (North Salt Lake, UT: HeritageQuest, 2001)

U.S. Military Records: A Guide to Federal & State Sources, Colonial America to the Present
by James C. Neagles (Salt Lake City: Ancestry, Inc., 1994)

World War II: A Family Historian's Guide
by Debra Johnson Knox (Spartanburg, SC: MIE Publishing, 2003)

■ PROBATE RECORDS

Abstracts of the Wills of the State of South Carolina, 3 vols.
compiled by Carolina T. Moore and Agatha Aimar Simmons (Columbia, SC: the compilers, 1960–69)

A Genealogical Collection of South Carolina Wills and Records, 2 vols.

by Willie Pauline Young (Originally published in 1955; Reprint: Easley, SC: Southern Historical Press, 1981)

Indexes to the County Wills of South Carolina

compiled by Martha Lou Houston (Originally published in 1939; Reprint: Baltimore: Clearfield Co., 1994)

Probate Records of South Carolina, 3 vols.

by Brent H. Holcomb (Originally published 1977; Reprint: Greenville, SC: Southern Historical Press, 1992)

Records of the Secretary of the Province of South Carolina, 1692–1721

compiled by Caroline T. Moore (Originally published 1978; Reprint: Columbia, SC: South Carolina Magazine of Ancestral Research, 2003)

South Carolina Begins: The Records of a Proprietary Colony, 1663–1721

by Charles H. Lesser (Columbia, SC: South Carolina Dept. of Archives and History, 1995)

South Carolina Jury Lists, 1718 through 1783

compiled by Mary Bondurant Warren (Danielsville, GA: Heritage Papers, 1977)

South Carolina Wills, 1670–1853, or Later

by Mary Bondurant Warren (Danielsville, GA: Heritage Papers, 1981)

■ VITAL RECORDS

Marriage and Death Notices from the (Charleston) Times, 1800–1821

compiled by Brent Holcomb (Baltimore: Genealogical Publishing Co., 1979)

North and South Carolina Marriage Records: From the Earliest Colonial Days to the Civil War

by William M. Clemens (Baltimore, MD: Genealogical Publishing Company, 1981)

South Carolina Marriages: 1688–1820, 3 Vols.

by Brent H. Holcomb (Baltimore: Genealogical Publishing Co., 1980–81, 1984)

South Carolina Marriages, Volume I, 1749–1867: Implied in South Carolina Equity Reports

by Barara R. Langdon (Aiken, SC: Langdon & Langdon Genealogical Research, 1991)

South Carolina Marriages, 1735–1885: Implied in South Carolina Law Reports, vol. 2

by Barara R. Langdon (Aiken, SC: Langdon & Langdon Genealogical Research, 1992)

South Carolina Marriages, 1671–1791, Implied in Provincial and Miscellaneous Records of South Carolina, vol. 3

by Barara R. Langdon (Aiken, SC: Langdon & Langdon Genealogical Research, 1993)

South Carolina Marriages, 1787–1875, Implied in the Miscellaneous Records of South Carolina, vol. 4

by Barara R. Langdon (Aiken, SC: Langdon & Langdon Genealogical Research, 1994)

South Carolina Marriages, 1749–1853, Implied in South Carolina Marriage Settlements, vol. 5

by Barara R. Langdon (Aiken, SC: Langdon & Langdon Genealogical Research, 1995)

South Carolina Marriages, 1753–1843, Implied in the Miscellaneous Records of South Carolina, vol. 6

by Barara R. Langdon (Aiken, SC: Langdon & Langdon Genealogical Research, 1997)

South Carolina Marriages, 1794–1877, Implied in the Miscellaneous Records and Marriage Settlements of South Carolina, vol. 7

by Barara R. Langdon (Aiken, SC: Langdon & Langdon Genealogical Research, 1999)

Your Guide to Cemetery Research

by Sharon DeBartolo Carmack (Cincinnati: Betterway Books, 2002)

■ Abbeville 12 Mar. 1785

102 Court Sq., P.O. Box 99, Abbeville, SC 29620

Phone: (864)459-5074

Web site: www.sccounties.org/counties/abbeville.htm

Parent County: District 96

Comments/research tips: Probate Judge has Land records 1840–1875, Marriage records 1911–1950, and Probate records 1782–1950. Fire destroyed most pre-1872 county records.

Record Type	Year Begun	Jurisdiction
Divorce	1873	Clerk of Court
Birth	1915	Dept./Health
Court	1873	Clerk of Court
Death	1915	Dept./Health

■ Aiken 10 Mar. 1871

828 Richland Ave. W., Aiken, SC 29801

Phone: (803)642-1715

Web site: www.aikencounty.net/

Parent County: Edgefield, Orangeburg, Barnwell, Lexington

Record Type	Year Begun	Jurisdiction
Birth	1901	Dept./Health
Death	1999	Dept./Health
Marriage	1911	Probate Judge
Probate	1872	Probate Judge
Divorce	1873	Clerk of Court
Court	1873	Clerk of Court
Land	1872	Registrar Mesne Conveyance

■ Allendale 6 Feb. 1919

526 Memorial Ave., P.O. Box 126, Allendale, SC 29810

Phone: 803-584-2737

Web site: www.allendalecounty.com/

Parent County: Barnwell, Hampton

Comments/research tips: County Board of Health has Birth and Death records 1915–1958. Probate Judge has Marriage records 1919-2000 and Probate records 1919–1951. Pre-1919 Birth and Death records include Barnwell County.

Record Type	Year Begun	Jurisdiction
Court	1919	Clerk of Courts
Land	1919	Clerk of Courts

■ Anderson 20 Dec. 1826

100 S Main St., P.O. Box 8002, Anderson, SC 29622

Phone: (864)260-4053

Web site: www.andersoncountysc.org/

Parent County: Pendleton District

Comments/research tips: Anderson County Public Library has Land records 1719–1772. Registrar of Deeds has Land records 1828–1942. Probate Judge has Marriage records 1911–1955 and Probate records 1828–1907.

Record Type	Year Begun	Jurisdiction
Birth	1915	Dept./Health
Death	1915	Dept./Health
Divorce	1949	Clerk of Court
Court	1828	Clerk of Court

■ **Bamberg**   25 Feb. 1897

110 N Main St., P.O. Box 150, Bamberg, SC 29003
Phone: (803)245-3025
Web site: www.sccounties.org/counties/Bamberg.htm
Parent County: Barnwell

Record Type	Year Begun	Jurisdiction
Divorce	1898	Clerk of Court
Court	1898	Clerk of Court
Land	1898	Clerk of Court
Marriage	1904	Probate Judge
Probate	1904	Probate Judge
Birth	1915	Dept./Health
Death	1915	Dept./Health

■ **Barnwell**   1800

Main St., P.O. Box 723, Barnwell, SC 29812
Phone: (803)541-1020
Web site: www.barnwellcountysc.com
Parent County: Orangeburg District
Comments/research tips: Probate Judge has Marriage records 1911–1959 and Probate records 1787–1932. Probate records 1781–1787 and Clerk of Courts records 1791–1799 were destroyed with Orangeburg County records in February 1865.

Record Type	Year Begun	Jurisdiction
Land	1779	County Clerk
Court	ca. 1800	County Clerk
Divorce	ca. 1800	County Clerk

■ **Beaufort**   1769

100 Ribaut Rd., Beaufort, SC 29902
Phone: (843)470-5218
Web site: www.co.beaufort.sc.us/
Parent County: Beaufort District (name changed 1785)
Comments/research tips: Records prior to 1785 are filed in Charleston. Many records pre-1865 were lost during reconstruction.

Record Type	Year Begun	Jurisdiction
Land	1885	Registrar/Deeds
Birth	1915	Dept./Health
Death	1915	Dept./Health
Marriage	na	Probate Judge
Probate	na	Probate Judge

■ **Berkeley**   31 Jan. 1882

223 N. Live Oak Dr., Moncks Corner, SC 29461
Phone: (843)719-4234
Web site: www.co.berkeley.sc.us
Parent County: Charleston
Comments/research tips: Registrar of Deeds has Land records 1885–1926. Probate Judge has Probate records 1883–1939.

Record Type	Year Begun	Jurisdiction
Divorce	na	Clerk of Court
Court	na	Clerk of Court
Marriage	1920	Probate Judge
Birth	1915	Dept./Health
Death	1915	Dept./Health
Burial	na	Dept./Health

■ **Berkeley, old**   1682

Parent County: Original county (not present Berkeley County)
Comments/research tips: One of four original counties. Discontinued 1769. Became part of Charleston District.

■ **Calhoun**   14 Feb. 1908

302 S. Huff Dr., St. Matthews, SC 29135
Phone: (803)874-3524
Web site: www.sccounties.org/counties/calhoun.htm
Parent County: Lexington, Orangeburg
Comments/research tips: Probate Judge has Marriage records 1911–1956 and Probate records 1908–1950.

Record Type	Year Begun	Jurisdiction
Birth	1915	Dept./Health
Death	1915	Dept./Health
Marriage	1911	Probate Judge
Probate	1908	Probate Judge
Court	1908	Clerk of Court
Divorce	1949	Clerk of Court
Land	1735	Hist. Commission
Bible	1735	Hist. Commission
Cemetery	1735	Hist. Commission

■ **Camden District**   1769

Parent County: Craven, Berkeley, old
Comments/research tips: Created as one of seven original judicial districts. Discontinued in 1798 to form Chester, Claremont, Clarendon, Fairfield, Kershaw, and Lancaster Counties.

■ **Charleston**   1769

2144 Melbourne Ave., Charleston, SC 29405
Phone: (843)958-5000
Web site: www.charlestoncounty.org/
Parent County: Colleton, Berkeley, old
Comments/research tips: County Health Department has Birth records 1877–1926 and Death records 1866–1914. Registrar of Mense Conveyance has Land records 1680–1929. Probate Judge has Probate records 1671–1874. Created in 1769 as one of seven original judicial districts; split in 1880 to form Charleston and Colleton Counties.

Record Type	Year Begun	Jurisdiction
Marriage	1879	Probate Judge
Court	1867	Clerk of Courts
Divorce	na	Clerk of Court

■ **Cheraws**   1769

Parent County: Original district
Comments/research tips: Created in 1769 as one of seven original judicial districts. Discontinued in 1798 to form Chesterfield, Darlington, and Marlboro Counties.

■ **Cherokee**   25 Feb. 1897

125 E. Floyd Baker Blvd., P.O. Drawer 3380, Gaffney, SC 29342
Phone: (864)487-2574
Web site: www.cherokeecounty-sc.org
Parent County: Union, York, Spartanburg
Comments/research tips: Clerk of Courts has Court and

Divorce records 1897–1937. Probate Judge has Marriage records 1911–1950 and Probate records 1897–1950.

Record Type	Year Begun	Jurisdiction
Birth	1915	Dept./Health
Death	1915	Dept./Health
Land	1897	Clerk of Court

■ Chester 1785

140 Main St., P.O. Box 580, Chester, SC 29342
Phone: (803)385-2605
Web site: www.chestercountysc.com
Parent County: Camden District
Comments/research tips: Probate Judge has Marriage records 1911–1962 and Probate records 1787–1950.

Record Type	Year Begun	Jurisdiction
Death	1915	Dept./Health
Birth	1915	Dept./Health
Land	1776	Clerk of Court
Divorce	1962	Clerk of Court
Court	1785	Clerk of Court

■ Chesterfield 1785

200 W. Main St., Chesterfield, SC 29709
Phone: (843)623-2574
Web site: www.sccounties.org/counties/chesterfield
Parent County: Cheraws District
Comments/research tips: Probate Judge has Marriage records 1911–1962 and Probate records 1787–1950. Sherman's army burned the county courthouse containing almost all public records in March 1865.

Record Type	Year Begun	Jurisdiction
Court	1865	Clerk of Courts
Birth	1915	Dept./Health
Death	1915	Dept./Health

■ Claremont 1785

Parent County: Camden
Comments/research tips: (See Sumter) Functioned 1785–1800, absorbed by Sumter District 1801.

■ Clarendon 1785

W. Boyce St., P.O. Drawer E, Manning, SC 29102
Phone: (803)435-4443
Web site: www.clarendoncounty.com/
Parent County: Camden District
Comments/research tips: Clerk of Courts has Court records 1840–1964. Probate Judge has Marriage records 1911–1950 and Probate records 1875–1915. Absorbed by Sumter District 1800, then recreated from Sumter 1855. Census schedules missing for 1820, 1830, 1840, and 1850. Clarendon's loose Probate records begin in 1875.

Record Type	Year Begun	Jurisdiction
Birth	1915	Dept./Health
Death	1915	Dept./Health
Divorce	1947	Clerk of Court
Land	1908	Registrar Mesne Conveyance

■ Colleton 1798

P.O. Box 620, Walterboro, SC 29488
Phone: (843)549-5791

Web site: www.sccounties.org/counties/Colleton.htm
Parent County: Charleston District
Comments/research tips: Clerk of Courts has Court records 1824–1861. Probate Court has Marriage records 1911–1973 and Probate records 1865–1972. Almost all records prior to 1865 were destroyed in Columbia fire of February 1865.

Record Type	Year Begun	Jurisdiction
Birth	1915	Dept./Health
Death	1915	Dept./Health
Divorce	1949	Clerk of Court
Land	1865	Registrar/Deeds
Military	1865	Veterans Office

■ Colleton, old 1683

Parent County: Original county
Comments/research tips: One of four original counties. Discontinued 1769.

■ Craven, old 1683

Parent County: Original county
Comments/research tips: One of four original counties. Discontinued 1769.

■ Darlington 1785

1 Public Sq., Darlington, SC 29532
Phone: (843)398-4330
Web site: www.sccounties.org/counties/Darlington.htm
Parent County: Cheraws District
Comments/research tips: County Historical Commission has Court records 1841–1875, Land records 1806–1900, and Probate records 1840–1895. Probate Judge has Marriage records 1911–1941. Most of Darlington County's pre-1806 records were destroyed in a courthouse fire 19 March 1806. This fire also destroyed most of Cheraw judicial district's records.

Record Type	Year Begun	Jurisdiction
Probate	1900	Probate Judge
Divorce	1950	County Clerk
Land	1910	County Clerk
Birth	1915	Dept./Health
Death	1915	Dept./Health

■ Dillon 5 Feb. 1910

P.O. Drawer 1220, Dillon, SC 29536
Phone: (843)774-1425
Web site: www.sccounties.org/counties/Dillon.htm
Parent County: Marion
Comments/research tips: Probate Judge has Probate records 1910–1950.

Record Type	Year Begun	Jurisdiction
Death	1915	Dept./Health
Court	1910	Clerk of Courts
Land	1910	Clerk of Courts
Marriage	1913	Probate Judge
Birth	1915	Dept./Health

■ Dorchester 25 Feb. 1897

P.O. Box 158, St. George, SC 29477
Phone: (843)563-0120

Web site: www.dorchestercounty.net
Parent County: Berkeley, Colleton
Comments/research tips: County Clerk has Court records 1897–1960. Registrar of Mesne Conveyances has Land records 1847–1920. Probate Judge has Marriage records 1911–1957 and Probate records 1897–1915.

Record Type	Year Begun	Jurisdiction
Birth	1915	Dept./Health
Death	1915	Dept./Health

■ Edgefield 1785

129 Courthouse Sq., Edgefield, SC 29824
Phone: (803)637-4080
Web site: www.edgefieldcounty.sc.gov
Parent County: District 96
Comments/research tips: County Clerk has Court records 1800–1922. Probate Judge has Marriage records 1911–1976 and Probate records 1787–1905. Small portion of Aiken County added to Edgefield in 1966.

Record Type	Year Begun	Jurisdiction
Birth	1915	Dept./Health
Death	1915	Dept./Health
Land	1839	County Clerk
Divorce	na	County Clerk

■ Fairfield 1785

P.O. Drawer 299, Winnsboro, SC 29180
Phone: (803)712-6526
Web site: www.sccounties.org/counties/Fairfield.htm
Parent County: Camden District
Comments/research tips: Clerk of Courts has Court records 1800–1907. Probate Judge has Marriage records 1911–1993 and Probate records 1840–1904.

Record Type	Year Begun	Jurisdiction
Divorce	na	Clerk of Courts
Land	1918	Clerk of Courts
Birth	1915	Dept./Health
Death	1915	Dept./Health

■ Florence 22 Dec. 1888

180 N. Irby St., Florence, SC 29501
Phone: (843)665-3031
Web site: www.florenceco.org
Parent County: Marion, Darlington, Clarendon, Williamsburg
Comments/research tips: Clerk of Courts has Court records 1889–1965. Probate Judge has Marriage records 1911–1955 and Probate records 1888–1916.

Record Type	Year Begun	Jurisdiction
Birth	1915	Dept./Health
Death	1915	Dept./Health
Divorce	na	Clerk of Court
Land	1889	Clerk of Courts

■ Georgetown 1800

715 Prince St., Georgetown, SC 29442
Phone: (843)545-3215
Web site: www.georgetowncountysc.org
Parent County: Craven, Georgetown District

Comments/research tips: Clerk of Courts has Court records 1850–1984. Created in 1769 from Craven County as one of seven original judicial districts. Records prior to 1785 are filed in Charleston. Union soldiers destroyed Georgetown County records in March 1865.

Record Type	Year Begun	Jurisdiction
Birth	1915	Dept./Health
Death	1915	Dept./Health
Marriage	1911	Probate Judge
Probate	1865	Probate Judge
Divorce	1949	Clerk of Court
Land	1866	Registrar/Deeds

■ Granville 1686

Parent County: Original county
Comments/research tips: Discontinued 1769.

■ Greenville 1786

301 University Ridge, Suite 100, Greenville, SC 29601
Phone: (864)467-8554
Web site: www.greenvillecounty.org
Parent County: Cherokee lands
Comments/research tips: Registrar of Deeds has Land records 1787–1940. Probate Judge has Probate records 1787–1951. From 1791–1800 Greenville County was part of Washington District.

Record Type	Year Begun	Jurisdiction
Birth	1915	Dept./Health
Death	1915	Dept./Health
Marriage	1911	Probate Judge
Divorce	na	Clerk of Court

■ Greenwood 2 Mar. 1897

528 Monument St., Greenwood, SC 29646
Phone: (864)942-8546
Web site: www.co.greenwood.sc.us/
Parent County: Abbeville, Edgefield
Comments/research tips: Clerk of Courts has Land records 1899–1945. Probate Judge has Marriage records 1911–1970.

Record Type	Year Begun	Jurisdiction
Birth	1915	Dept./Health
Death	1915	Dept./Health
Probate	1897	Probate Judge
Divorce	1937	Clerk of Courts
Court	1897	Clerk of Courts

■ Hampton 18 Feb. 1878

1 Courthouse Sq., P.O. Box 7, Hampton, SC 29924
Phone: (803)943-7510
Web site: www.hamptoncountysc.org
Parent County: Beaufort
Comments/research tips: Clerk of Courts has Land records 1918–1930. Probate Judge has Marriage records 1911–1951.

Record Type	Year Begun	Jurisdiction
Birth	1915	Dept./Health
Death	1915	Dept./Health
Court	na	Clerk of Court
Probate	1878	Probate Judge

South Carolina

■ Horry 19 Dec. 1801
1301 Second Ave., Conway, SC 29526
Phone: (843)915-5080
Web site: www.horrycounty.org/
Parent County: Georgetown District
Comments/research tips: Clerk of Courts has Court records 1803–1944. Probate Judge has Marriage records 1911–1950 and Probate records 1819–1907. Horry was known as Kingston County 1785–1800.

Record Type	Year Begun	Jurisdiction
Birth	1915	Dept./Health
Death	1915	Dept./Health
Divorce	1947	Clerk of Court
Land	1803	Registrar/Deeds

■ Jasper 30 Jan. 1912
305 Russell St., P.O. Box 248, Ridgeland, SC 29936
Phone: (843)726-7781
Web site: www.sccounties.org/counties/Jasper.htm
Parent County: Beaufort, Hampton
Comments/research tips: Probate Judge has Marriage records 1912–1950 and Probate records 1912–1967. Due to negligence, a majority of equity (old criminal court) records were lost pre-1829.

Record Type	Year Begun	Jurisdiction
Court	1912	Clerk of Courts
Land	1912	Clerk of Courts
Birth	1915	Dept./Health
Death	1915	Dept./Health
Divorce	na	Clerk of Courts

■ Kershaw 1791
1121 Broad St., Camden, SC 29020
Phone: (803)425-1500
Web site: www.camden-sc.org/
Parent County: Parts of Claremont, Fairfield, Lancaster, and Richland Counties
Comments/research tips: Clerk of Courts has Court records 1783–1908 and Land records 1791–1934. Probate Judge has Marriage records 1911–1960 and Probate records 1791–1911. Camden Archives and Museum has Wills 1775–1853.

Record Type	Year Begun	Jurisdiction
Divorce	1949	Clerk of Court
Birth	1915	Dept./Health
Death	1915	Dept./Health

■ Lancaster 1785
P.O. Box 1809, Lancaster, SC 29721
Phone: (803)285-1581
Web site: www.lancastercountysc.net
Parent County: Camden District
Comments/research tips: Clerk of Courts has Court records 1800–1962 and Divorce records 1958–1976. Probate Judge has Marriage records 1911–1950 and Probate records 1865–1919. Most of Lancaster County's loose equity papers and Probate records were destroyed during the Civil War.

Record Type	Year Begun	Jurisdiction
Birth	1915	Dept./Health
Death	1915	Dept./Health
Divorce	1977	Family Court Clerk
Land	1719	Registrar/Deeds

■ Laurens 1785
P.O. Box 287, Laurens, SC 29360
Phone: (864)984-3538
Web site: www.laurenscounty.org/lc/index.html
Parent County: District 96
Comments/research tips: Clerk of Courts has Court records 1800–1937. County Library has Death records 1915–1944 and Probate records 1785–1900. Probate Judge has Marriage records 1911–1951.

Record Type	Year Begun	Jurisdiction
Probate	1901	Probate Judge
Birth	1915	Dept./Health
Divorce	na	Clerk of Court
Death	1915	Dept./Health
Land	1785	Clerk of Court

■ Lee 25 Feb. 1902
11 Courthouse Sq., P.O. 387, Bishopville, SC 29010
Phone: (803)484-1632
Web site: www.rootsweb.com/~sclee/index.html
Parent County: Darlington, Sumter, Kershaw

Record Type	Year Begun	Jurisdiction
Birth	1915	Dept./Health
Death	1915	Dept./Health
Marriage	1902	Probate Judge
Probate	1902	Probate Judge
Court	1902	Clerk of Court
Land	1902	Clerk of Court

■ Lexington 1785
139 E. Main St., Lexington, SC 29072
Phone: (803)359-8212
Web site: www.lex-co.com/my_lex.html
Parent County: Orangeburg District
Comments/research tips: Clerk of Courts has Court records 1806–1954. Probate Judge has Marriage records 1911–1973 and Probate records 1865–1908. 1791 county was re-absorbed into Orangeburg District. In 1804 Lexington became a separate county. Union troops destroyed Clerk of Courts' records prior to 1839. Destroyed records included Deeds and almost all Probate records.

Record Type	Year Begun	Jurisdiction
Birth	1915	Dept./Health
Death	1915	Dept./Health
Divorce	1949	Clerk of Courts
Land	1839	Registrar/Deeds

■ Liberty 1785
Parent County: Original county
Comments/research tips: (See Marion) Used briefly as a subdivision of Marion County.

■ Marion 1798
P.O. Box 295, Marion, SC 29571
Phone: (843)423-8240

Web site: www.co.marion.sc.us
Parent County: Georgetown District
Comments/research tips: Clerk of Courts has Court records 1800–1873. County Archives/History Center has Land records 1800–1906 and Probate records 1800–1900. Probate Judge has Marriage records 1800–1859 and 1911–1950.

Record Type	Year Begun	Jurisdiction
Birth	1915	Dept./Health
Death	1915	Dept./Health
Marriage	na	Probate Judge
Probate	1900	Probate Judge
Divorce	1948	Clerk of Courts
Land	1907	Clerk of Courts

■ Marlboro 1785
205 Usher St., Bennetsville, SC 29512
Phone: (843)479-5613
Web site: www.rootsweb.com/~scmarlbo/
Parent County: Cheraws District
Comments/research tips: County Clerk has Court records 1800–1933. Probate Judge has Marriage records 1788–1950 and Probate records 1787–1902.

Record Type	Year Begun	Jurisdiction
Birth	1915	Dept./Health
Death	1915	Dept./Health
Land	1786	County Clerk
Divorce	1950	County Clerk

■ McCormick 19 Feb. 1916
133 S. Mine St., McCormick, SC 29835
Phone: (864)465-2195
Web site: www.mccormickcountysc.com
Parent County: Greenwood, Abbeville, Edgefield
Comments/research tips: Clerk of Courts has Court records 1917–1960. Probate Judge has Probate records 1917–1966.

Record Type	Year Begun	Jurisdiction
Divorce	1950	Clerk of Courts
Land	1916	Clerk of Courts
Marriage	1916	Probate Judge
Birth	1916	Dept./Health
Death	1916	Dept./Health

■ Newberry 1785
1226 College St., P.O. Box 278, Newberry, SC 29108
Phone: (803)321-2110
Web site: www.newberrycounty.net
Parent County: District 96
Comments/research tips: Clerk of Courts has Court records 1785–1798 and 1816–1956. Probate Court has Probate records 1787–1913. Pre-1818 Equity Rolls, pre-1881 General Sessions indictments, and pre-1870 Judgement rolls were lost.

Record Type	Year Begun	Jurisdiction
Birth	1915	Dept./Health
Death	1915	Dept./Health
Marriage	1911	Probate Court
Divorce	1950	Clerk of Courts
Probate	1776	Clerk of Court

| Court | 1776 | Clerk of Court |
| Land | 1785 | Clerk of Courts |

■ Ninety-Six District 1769
Parent County: Original district, area northwest of Camden District
Comments/research tips: One of seven original judicial districts. Discontinued in 1785 to form Abbeville, Edgefield, Newberry, Laurens, Spartanburg, and Union Counties.

■ Oconee 29 Jan. 1868
W Main St., P.O. Box 678, Walhalla, SC 29691
Phone: (864)638-4280
Web site: www.oconeesc.com
Parent County: Pickens
Comments/research tips: Clerk of Courts has Court records 1868–1976. Registrar of Deeds has Land records 1868–1926. Probate Judge has Probate records 1868–1928.

Record Type	Year Begun	Jurisdiction
Birth	1915	Dept./Health
Death	1915	Dept./Health
Marriage	1911	Probate Judge
Divorce	1950	Clerk of Court

■ Orange 1785
Parent County: Orangeburg District
Comments/research tips: Former County in Orangeburg District, abolished 1791. Pre-1865 public records were burned by Sherman's troops.

■ Orangeburg 1769
190 Gibson St., Orangeburg, SC 29115
Phone: (803)533-6243
Web site: www.orangeburgcounty.org
Parent County: Orangeburg District
Comments/research tips: Clerk of Courts has Court records 1824–1837. Recorder of Deeds has Land records 1865–1957, 1974–1978. Probate Judge has Probate records 1864–1957. Created as one of seven original judicial districts.

Record Type	Year Begun	Jurisdiction
Divorce	1950	Clerk of Court
Birth	1915	Dept./Health
Death	1915	Dept./Health
Marriage	1911	Probate Judge

■ Pendleton 1789
Parent County: Cherokee Lands
Comments/research tips: (See Pickens and Anderson) Pendleton County was known as Washington District 1791–1800. Discontinued in 1826 to form Pickens and Anderson Counties.

■ Pickens 20 Dec. 1826
214 E. Main St., Pickens, SC 29671
Phone: (864)898-5866
Web site: www.co.pickens.sc.us
Parent County: Pendleton District
Comments/research tips: Clerk of Court has Court records

1828–1907. Probate Judge has Probate records 1828–1884. Anderson County Registrar of Deeds office has Pickens area land records 1789–1826.

Record Type	Year Begun	Jurisdiction
Birth	1915	Dept./Health
Death	1915	Dept./Health
Divorce	1950	Clerk of Court
Land	1826	Registrar/Deeds
Marriage	1911	Probate Judge

■ Pickney District 1791
Parent County: 96 District
Comments/research tips: (See Union and York) Discontinued in 1800 to form Union and York Counties.

■ Richland 1785
1701 Main St. #205, Columbia, SC 29202
Phone: (803)748-4684
Web site: www.richlandonline.com
Parent County: Camden District
Comments/research tips: County Clerk has Court records 1781–1957. Registrar of Deeds has Land records 1865–1951. Probate Judge has Marriage records 1911–1965. Fire February 1865 destroyed the courthouse and most public records. However, most Equity and Probate records were removed prior to the fire.

Record Type	Year Begun	Jurisdiction
Death	1915	Dept./Health
Probate	1787	Probate Judge
Birth	1915	Dept./Health

■ Salem 1791
Parent County: Parts of Claremont and Clarendon
Comments/research tips: In 1800 Claremont, Clarendon, and Salem Counties were combined to create Sumter District. Clarendon (1857), Lee (1902), and Sumter Counties were created out of Sumter District.

■ Saluda 1895
100 E. Church St., Saluda, SC 29138
Phone: (864)445-3303
Web site: www.saludasc.com
Parent County: Edgefield
Comments/research tips: Clerk of Courts has Court records 1929–1964 and Land records 1896–1928. Probate Judge has Marriage records 1911–1950 and Probate records 1896–1963.

Record Type	Year Begun	Jurisdiction
Divorce	na	Clerk of Court
Birth	1915	Dept./Health
Death	1915	Dept./Health

■ Spartanburg 1785
180 Magnolia St., Spartanburg, SC 29301
Phone: (864)596-2591
Web site: www.spartanburgcounty.org
Parent County: 96 District
Comments/research tips: From 1791–1799 Spartanburg was part of Pickney District. Clerk of Courts has Court records 1785–1960. Registrar of Deeds has Land records 1785–1911. Probate Judge has Probate records 1787–1968. Spartanburg County Public Library has County Estate papers (probate) 1787–1900, County Land records 1785–1900, and Death register 1895–1896 and 1903–1914.

Record Type	Year Begun	Jurisdiction
Birth	1915	Dept./Health
Death	1915	Dept./Health
Marriage	1911	Probate Judge
Divorce	na	Clerk of Court

■ Sumter 1800
141 N. Main St., Sumter, SC 29150
Phone: (803)436-2227
Web site: www.sumtercountysc.org
Parent County: Claremont, Clarendon, Salem
Comments/research tips: 27 November 1801 fire destroyed most of the county's deeds and probate records. Probate Judge has Marriage records 1911–1950 and Probate records 1800–1963. Clerk of Court has Court records 1802–1953 and Military records 1918–1953.

Record Type	Year Begun	Jurisdiction
Birth	1915	Dept./Health
Death	1915	Dept./Health
Divorce	1950	Clerk of Court
Land	1795	Registrar of Deeds

■ Union 1785
210 W. Main St., P.O. Box 703, Union, SC 29379
Phone: (864)429-1630
Web site: www.countyofunion.com
Parent County: 96 District
Comments/research tips: Union County was a part of Pickney District 1791–1800. Clerk of Court has Court records 1785–1957, Divorce records 1962–1967, and Land records 1785–1901. Probate Judge has Marriage records 1911–1950 and Probate records 1787–1928.

Record Type	Year Begun	Jurisdiction
Birth	1915	Dept./Health
Death	1915	Dept./Health

■ Williamsburg 1804
125 W. Main St., Kingstree, SC 29556
Phone: (843)355-9321
Web site: www.williamsburgsc.com
Parent County: Georgetown District
Comments/research tips: Clerk of Courts has Court records 1806–1909 and Land records 1806–1929. Probate Judge has Marriage records 1911–1950 and Probate records 1802–1915.

Record Type	Year Begun	Jurisdiction
Divorce	1948	Clerk of Court
Birth	1915	Dept./Health
Death	1915	Dept./Health

■ Winyah 1785
Parent County: Original county
Comments/research tips: (See Georgetown) Formerly a county in Georgetown District, later became Georgetown County.

■ **York** 1785
S. Congress, P.O. Box 649, York, SC 29745
Phone: (803)684-8506
Web site: www.yorkcountygov.com
Parent County: Camden District
Comments/research tips: Clerk of Courts has Court records 1786–1797 and 1800–1950 and Land records 1786–1950. Probate Judge has Marriage records 1911–1950 and

Probate records 1787–1977. Historical Center of York County has Court records 1750–1979. From 1791–1800 York County was part of Pickney District.

Record Type	Year Begun	Jurisdiction
Birth	1915	Dept./Health
Death	1915	Dept./Health
Divorce	1942	Clerk of Court

South Dakota

By James W. Warren

HISTORICAL OVERVIEW

Pioneers to South Dakota hoped to be rewarded at the end of their arduous journey to the state, but instead they found the enormous challenge of surviving life on its unforgiving, endless plains. The area's original settlers were the Dakota, Arapaho, Cheyenne, Mandan, Hidatsa, and Assiniboine Indians. The area was remote and often unwelcoming, settled late, and the worst of the land was eventually assigned as reservation land for Indians.

Present-day South Dakota became part of the United States with the Louisiana Purchase in 1803. Shortly after, Lewis and Clark traveled through the center of the region during their expedition. Throughout the first half of the nineteenth century, the South Dakota region was inhabited primarily by Dakota (Sioux) Indians, and there was relatively little white settlement. The land at various times was part of the territories of Missouri, Michigan, Wisconsin, Iowa, Minnesota, and Nebraska.

Army posts were established in the 1850s, and in 1858 the Yankton Sioux ceded lands to the U.S. Settlement between the Big Sioux and Missouri Rivers began, with towns being established at Yankton and Vermillion. Dakota Territory was created in 1861, including what would become North Dakota, South Dakota, Montana, and Wyoming. (Montana Territory was split off in 1864, and Wyoming became a separate territory in 1868.)

After the Homestead Act of 1863, newcomers from Iowa, Minnesota, Illinois, and Wisconsin, largely of Norwegian descent, began to settle the southern part of Dakota Territory. Further migrations from the Midwestern and Eastern states continued the settlement, as well as arriving immigrant Czechs, Danes, Swedes, and Germans from Russia.

In 1875, gold was discovered in the sacred Indian land of the Black Hills and thousands of settlers poured in.

© PhotoDisc/Getty Images

SOUTH DAKOTA AT A GLANCE

Motto: Under God the People Rule

Population: 755,000

Prevalent Religions: Lutheran, Roman Catholic, and Methodist

Major Industries: Tourism, manufacturing (predominately food processing), agriculture (wheat, corn, oats, soybeans, sunflowers), mining, banking (credit card processing)

Ethnic Makeup (in percent): Caucasian 88.7%, African American 0.6%, Hispanic 1.4%, Asian 0.6%, Native American 8.3%, Other 0.5%

Famous South Dakotans: Sparky Anderson, Tom Brokaw, Crazy Horse, Mary Hart, Cheryl Ladd, Russell Means, George McGovern, Dorothy Provine, Red Cloud, Joe Foss, Tom Daschle

Above: Mount Rushmore

Between 1877 and 1887, the influx of settlers peaked as railroads were completed through the northeast and central part of what would become South Dakota.

In 1889 Dakota Territory was split into South Dakota and North Dakota, and both states were admitted to the Union. During the first decade of the twentieth century, western South Dakota was settled after the railroads were extended to that region.

RECORD HIGHLIGHTS

The first available federal census for the state of South Dakota is the 1900 census. There were territorial censuses and mortality schedules taken in 1860, 1870, 1880, and 1885 for Dakota Territory. South Dakota's state censuses are true research gems. Taken every ten years beginning in 1895, they are available through 1945 and include details not usually found on other census enumerations.

For example, the 1925 through 1945 enumerations gathered the following information: Name; County; Post Office where person received mail; Town or Township name; If in a town, Ward Number; Age; Occupation; Owner or Renter; Place of birth; Years lived in South Dakota; Years living in U.S.; If foreign born, naturalized?; Birthplace of father and mother; Extent of Education; Military Service, including Wars fought, state, company, regiment, and division; Marital status; Maiden Name of wife; Year Married; Church Affiliation; Sex; Ethnicity (color); Misc. (Read, write, blind, deaf, idiotic, insane); Enumerator.

These censuses, recorded primarily on index cards that have been filed alphabetically, are available at the South Dakota State Historical Society <www.sdhistory.org>. Microfilming of these records by the Family History Library is in progress.

South Dakota began keeping birth, death, marriage, and divorce records on a statewide basis in 1905. This registration requirement was usually complied with by the early 1930s. Some records prior to 1905 may be found at county courthouses with the registrar of deeds.

State birth, death, marriage, and divorce records (1905 and later) are on file with the State Health Department at the Office of Vital Records in the capitol building in Pierre. A fee is charged for each search. When South Dakota's Vital Records System was started in July of 1905, individuals who were born before its inception were given the opportunity to file delayed birth records. Although many records from the 1800s and early 1900s have been filed throughout the years, the records before 1905 are not complete. Birth Records more than one hundred years old can be searched online at <www.state.sd.us/applications/PH14Over100BirthRec/index.asp>. At this time this site contains 114,195 records.

Marriages prior to 1905 that were recorded in an individual town or county are available from that county's treasurer. Pre-1905 divorces will be on file with the clerk of courts in the county where the divorce case was tried.

County level courts in South Dakota include District County Court and Circuit Court. Their records include probate, guardianship, and civil and criminal cases. Land records are held by the registrar of deeds in each county. Most of these records and their indexes remain in the county courthouses, and little has been microfilmed.

The State Archives, part of the South Dakota State Historical Society, currently has naturalization records from all South Dakota county courts except Brule and Campbell. It also holds Territorial Probate Court records and some local and county records. It has more than one thousand newspaper articles microfilmed and available through interlibrary loan. The Archives holds the book, periodical, manuscript, map, and sound recording collections for the State Historical Society, as well as the State Archives government documents. However, because the State Archives was not created by the State Legislature until 1975, the collection of government records and other manuscript materials is not as extensive as that of many state archives. For a fee, you can request online searches of the Archives' naturalization records, newspapers, and federal and state census collections.

STATE RESOURCES

◼ ARCHIVES, LIBRARIES, AND SOCIETIES

Aberdeen Area Genealogical Society
P.O. Box 493, Aberdeen, SD 57402-0493

Alexander Mitchell Public Library
519 S. Kline St., Aberdeen, SD 57401

Bennett County Genealogical Society
P.O. Box 483, Allen, SD 57714

Brookings Area Genealogical Society
524 Fourth St., Brookings, SD 57006

Bureau of Land Management (BLM)
222 N. Thirty-second St., P.O. Box 36800, Billings, MT 59101
Tel: (406) 255-2940
Fax: (406) 255-2894

Center for Western Studies
P.O. Box 727, Augustana College, Sioux Falls, SD 57197
Tel: (605) 336-4921
Fax: (605) 336-5447

Center of the Nation, American Historical Society of Germans from Russia
7 Swan Lane, Spearfish, SD 57783
Tel: (605) 642-1149

East River Genealogical Forum
R.R. 2, P.O. Box 148, Wolsey, SD 57394

Evangelical Lutheran Church of American (ELCA Archives)
8765 W. Higgins Rd., Chicago, IL 60631-4198
Tel: (773) 380-2818

Family Tree Genealogical Society
P.O. Box 202, Winner, SD 57580-0202

Heritage Club-Platte
Rt. 2, P.O. Box 128, Platte, SD 57369-0128

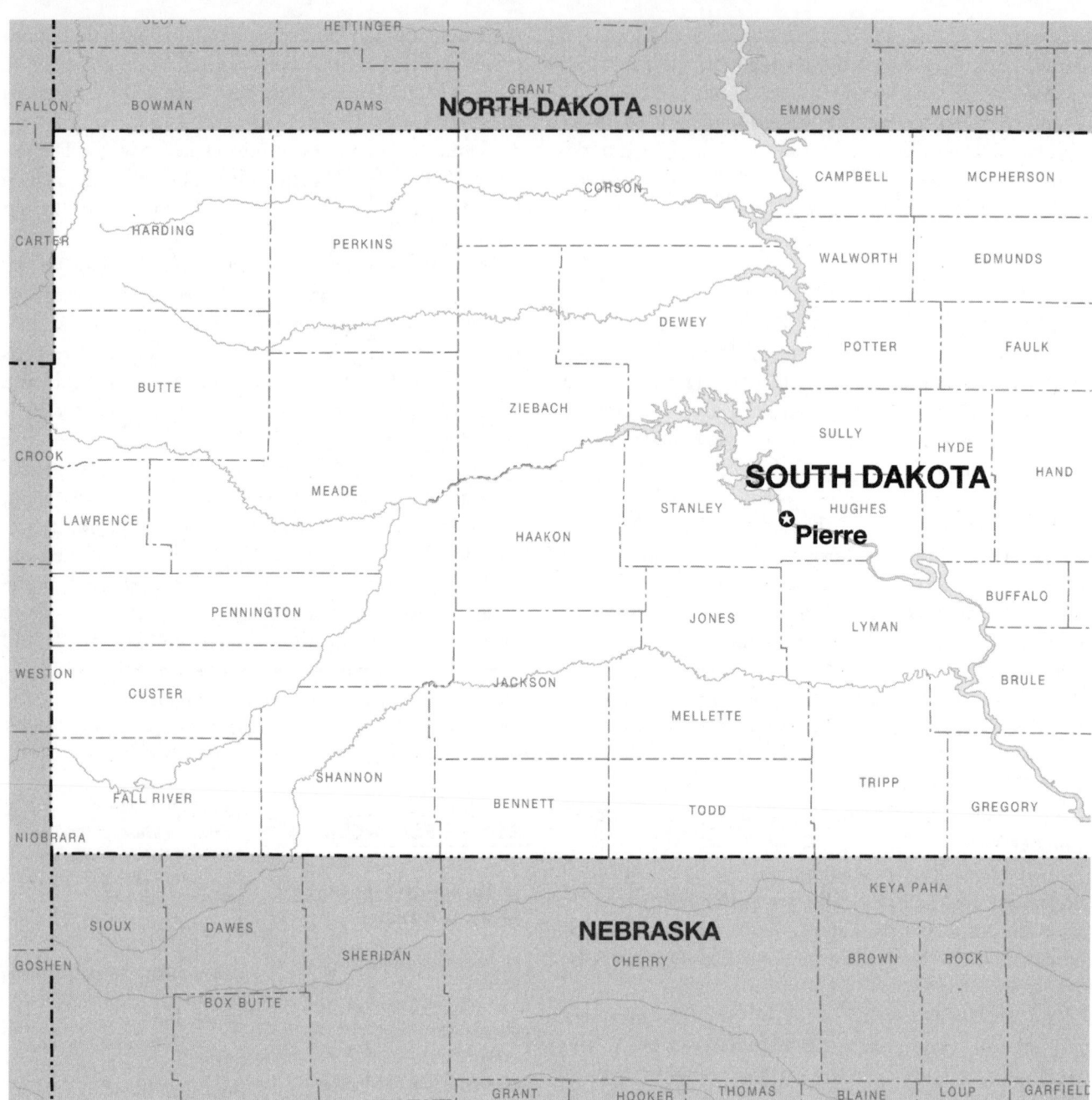

South Dakota

Homestead Chapter, American Historical Society of Germans from Russia
P.O. Box 98, Freeman, SD 57029-0098
Tel: (605) 925-7834

Hyde County Historical & Genealogical Society
P.O. Box 392, Highmore, SD 57345-0392

I.D. Weeks Library, University of South Dakota
414 E. Clark St., Vermillion, SD 57069
Tel: (605) 677-5371
Fax: (605) 677-5488

Web site: <www.usd.edu/libr ary/>

Kingsbury Genealogical Society
P.O. Box 330, DeSmet, SD 57231-0330

Lake County Genealogical Society
% Karl Mundt Library, Dakota State College, Madison, SD 57042

Lyman-Brule Genealogical Society
110 E. Lawler, Chamdberlain, SD 57325

Methodist Archives and History Library
1331 W. University Blvd., P.O. Box 460, Mitchell, SD 57301
Tel: (605) 996-6552
Fax: (605) 996-1766

Mitchell Area Genealogical Society
620 N. Edmunds, Mitchell, SD 57301

Moody County Genealogical Society
501 W. First Ave., Flandreau, SD 57028-1003

Murdo Genealogical Society
P.O. Box 441, Murdo, SD 57559-0441

National Archives and Records Administration-Rocky Mountain Region (Colorado)
P.O. Box 25307, Denver, Colorado 80225
Tel: (303) 236-0817
Fax: (303) 236-9297
Web site: <www.archives.gov/fa cilities/co/denver.html>

North Central South Dakota Genealogical Society
178 Southshore Dr., Mina, SD 57462-3000

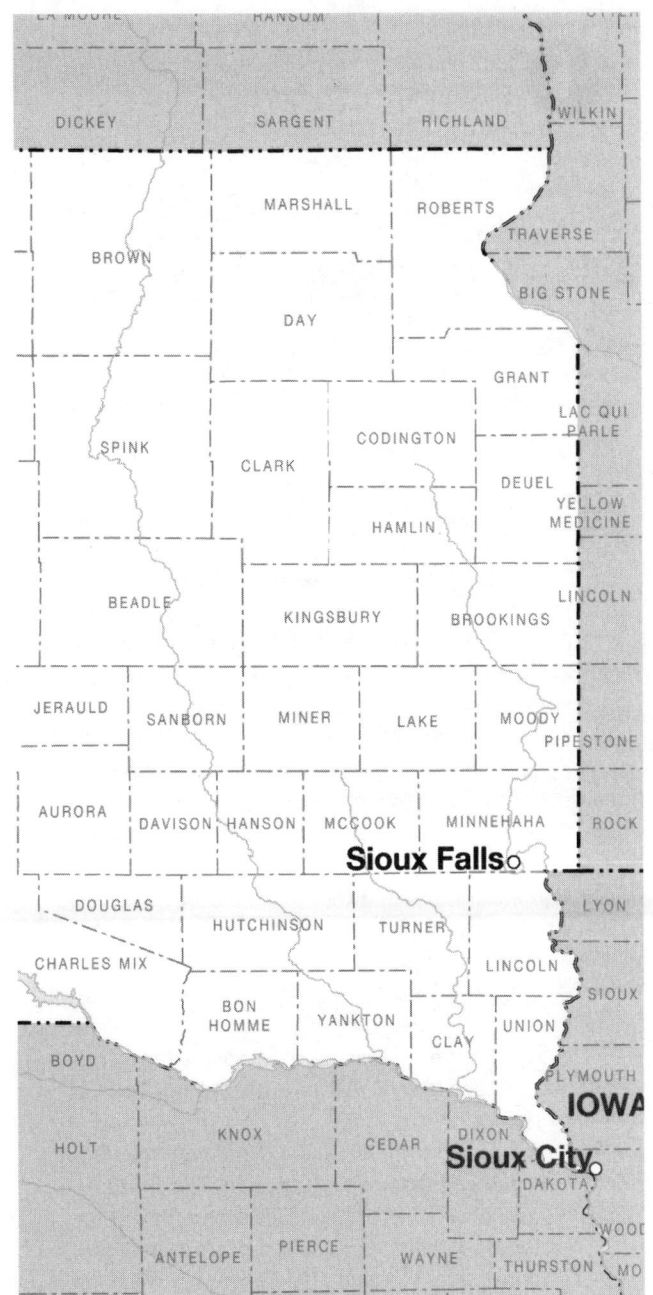

Pierre-Ft. Pierre Genealogical Society
P.O. Box 925, Pierre, SD
57501-0925

Platte Heritage Club
Rt. 2, P.O. Box 128, Platte, SD
57369

Rapid City Society for Genealogical Research
P.O. Box 1495, Rapid City, SD
57709-1495

Roman Catholic Diocese of Rapid City
Chancery Office, 606 Cathedral Dr., P.O. Box 678, Rapid City, SD
57709

Tel: (605) 343-3541
Fax: (605) 348-7985

Roman Catholic Diocese of Sioux Falls
Chancery Office, 3100 W. Forty-first St., Sioux Falls, SD
57105
Tel: (605) 334-9861
Fax: (605) 333-3346

Sioux Valley Genealogical Society
200 W. Sixth S., Sioux Falls, SD
57104-6001

South Dakota Genealogical Society
P.O. Box 1101, Pierre, SD
57501-1101

Web site: <www.rootsweb.com/~sdgenweb/gensoc/stenos.html>

South Dakota State Historical Society
900 Governors Dr., Pierre, SD
57501-2217
Tel: (605) 773-3458
Fax: (605) 773-6041
Web site:

State Department of Health
445 E. Capitol, Pierre, SD
57501-3185
Tel: (605) 773-3355

Tri-State Genealogical Society
% Public Library, 905 Fifth St., Belle Fourche, SD 57717-1705
Web site: <scream.iw.net/~shepherd/>

Union County Historical Society
P.O. Box 552, Elk Point, SD
57025

Watertown Genealogical Society
611 NE B Ave., Watertown, SD
57201

Yankton Genealogical Society
P.O. Box 71, Missions Hills, SD
57406

BIBLIOGRAPHY

■ GENERAL RESOURCES

Daughters of Dakota, 6 vols.
by Sally Roesch Wagner (Yankton, SD: Daughters of Dakota, ca. 1989)

Fox's Who's Who Among South Dakotans: A Biographical Directory of citizens Who Are Prominent in Professional, Political, Business and Civic Affairs of the State, 2 vols.
(Pierre, SD: Fox Kindley, 1929)

The Genealogist's Companion and Sourcebook, 2d ed.
by Emily Anne Croom (Cincinnati: Betterway Books, 2003)

A Genealogist's Guide to Discovering Your African-American Ancestors
by Franklin Carter Smith and Emily Anne Croom (Cincinnati: Betterway Books, 2003)

Guide to Genealogical Research in the National Archives of the United States
edited by Anne Bruner Eales and Robert M. Kvasnicka (Washington, DC: National Archives and Records Administration, 2000)

Historical Data Project; Pioneer Biography Files
from the State Historical Society of North Dakota (Bismarck, ND: State Historical Society of North Dakota, 1988–1989)

History of Dakota Territory and South Dakota: Its History and Its People, 5 vols.
by George Martin Smith (Chicago: S.J. Clarke Co., 1915)

History of South Dakota
by Herbert S. Schell (Lincoln, NE: University of Nebraska Press, 1968)

National Archives Microfilm Catalogs online:
<www.archives.gov/publications/genealogy_microfilm_catalogs.html>

Once Their Home: or Our Legacy From the Dahkotahs
by Frances Chamberlain Holley (Chicago: Donohue & Henneberry, 1892)

Prairie Progress in West Central South Dakota
(Sioux Falls, SD: Historical Society of Old Stanley County, South Dakota, 1968)

South Dakota: Changing, Changeless, 1889–1989
compiled by Ruth A. Alexander, et al. (Rapid City, SD: South Dakota Library Association, 1985)

South Dakota Research Outline
by the Church of Jesus Christ of Latter-Day Saints (Salt Lake City, UT: Corp. of the President of the Church of Jesus Christ of L.D.S., 1988)

■ CENSUS RECORDS

The American Census Handbook
by Thomas Jay Kemp (Wilmington, DE: Scholarly Resources, Inc., 2001)

The Census Book: A Genealogist's Guide to Federal Census Facts, Schedules and Indexes
by William Dollarhide (Bountiful, UT: Heritage Quest, 1999)

Finding Answers in U.S. Census Records
by Loretto Dennis Szucs and Matthew Wright (Salt Lake City: Ancestry Publishing, 2001)

Map Guide to the U.S. Federal Censuses, 1790–1920
by William Thorndale and William Dollarhide (Baltimore: Genealogical Publishing Co., 1987)

State Census Records
by Ann S. Lainhart (Baltimore: Genealogical Publishing Co., Inc., 1992)

Your Guide to the Federal Census
by Kathleen W. Hinckley (Cincinnati: Betterway Books, 2002)

■ IMMIGRATION RECORDS

American Naturalization Records, 1790–1990: What They Are and How to Use Them
by John J. Newman (North Salt Lake, UT: HeritageQuest, 1998)

American Passenger Arrival Records
by Michael Tepper (Baltimore: Genealogical Publishing Co., 1993)

French-Canadian Families of the North Central Sates: A Genealogical Dictionary, 8 vols.
Paul J. Lareau and Elmer Courteau (St Paul, MN: Northwest Territory French and Canadian Heritage Institute, 1980)

The Immigration History Research Center: A Guide to Collections
from the University of Minnes (New York: Greenwood Press, 1991)

They Became Americans: Finding Naturalization Records and Ethnic Origins
by Loretto Dennis Szucs (Salt Lake City: Ancestry, Inc., 1998)

They Came in Ships: A Guide to Finding Your Immigrant Ancestor's Arrival Records, 2d ed.
by John P. Colletta (Salt Lake City: Ancestry, Inc., 1993)

■ LAND RECORDS

The Administration of the Public Domain in South Dakota
by Charles L. Green (Pierre, SD: Hipple Printing, 1939)

Fifty Million Acres: Conflicts Over Kansas Land Policy, 1854–1890
by Paul Wallace Gates (Norman, OK: University of Oklahoma Press, 1997)

A History of the Public Land Policies
by Benjamin Horace Hibbard (Madison: University of Wisconsin Press, 1965)

Indian Depredation Claims, 1796–1920
by Larry C. Skogen (Norman, OK: University of Oklahoma Press, ca. 1996)

Land and Property Research in the United States
by Wade E. Hone (Salt Lake City: Ancestry Inc., 1997)

Locating Your Roots: Discover Your Ancestors Using Land Records
by Patricia Law Hatcher (Cincinnati: Betterway Books, 2003)

■ MAPS

Northwestern Gazetteer: Minnesota, North and South Dakota and Montana Gazetteer and Business Directory
from R.L. Polk & Company (St. Paul, MN: R.L. Polk & Company, 1914)

Postoffices and Postmarks of Dakota Territory
by George H. Phillips (Crete, NE: J-B Publishing, 1973)

The Postoffices of South Dakota, 1861–1930
by George H. Phillips (Crete, NE: J-B Publishing, 1975)

South Dakota Place Names
from the Federal Writer's Project (Vermillion: University of South Dakota, 1940)

■ MILITARY RECORDS

Soldiers of the Great War, 3 vols.
by W.M. Haulsee, F.G. Howe, and A.C. Doyle (Washington, D.C.: Soldiers Record Publishing Association, 1920)

Uncle, We Are Ready! Registering America's Men, 1917–1918: A Guide to Researching World War I Draft Registration Cards
by John J. Newman (North Salt Lake, UT: HeritageQuest, 2001)

RESEARCH TIPS
for more info

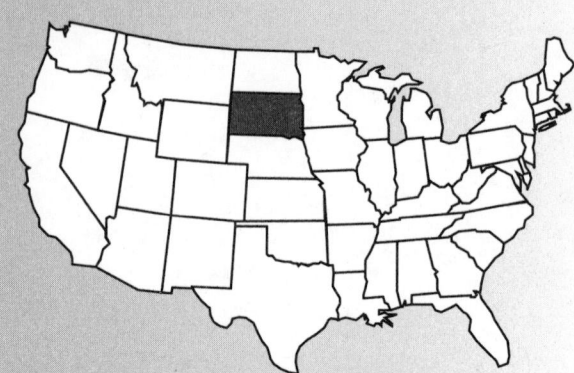

- South Dakota was settled late and is relatively recordless, making it important to track down the existing local resources. While some local church and cemetery records have been published, in many cases you will need to contact them directly to obtain information. Newspapers as well as published county, town, church, or organizational histories can also provide vital clues.
- The South Dakota Genealogical Society's Web site <www.rootsweb.com/~sdgenweb/gensoc/sdgensoc.html> and the South Dakota GenWeb site <www.rootsweb.com/~sdgenweb/> are good places to begin your research.
- Because the State Archives was founded recently, state university and college collections, town libraries, local museums, and historical societies are important sources for historical materials.
- American Indians make up a significant percentage of South Dakota's population. The State Archives holds Indian census rolls and extensive microfilmed federal records and correspondence. Special collections at the Center for Western Studies at Augustana College in Sioux Falls, and at the University of South Dakota at Vermillion, are also significant. The University of South Dakota's Institute of American Indian Studies has important collections and ongoing projects.

Census Records
- Federal Census: 1860, 1870, 1880, 1900, 1910, 1920, 1930
- Federal Mortality Schedules: 1860, 1870, 1880
- Union Veterans and Widows: 1890
- State/Territorial Census: 1836, 1885, 1895, 1905, 1915, 1925, 1935, 1945

U.S. Military Records: A Guide to Federal & State Sources, Colonial America to the Present
by James C. Neagles (Salt Lake City: Ancestry, Inc., 1994)

World War II: A Family Historian's Guide
by Debra Johnson Knox (Spartanburg, SC: MIE Publishing, 2003)

■ **VITAL RECORDS**

Some Black Hills Area Cemeteries, South Dakota, 6 vols.
from the Rapid City Society for Genealogical Research (Rapid

City, SD: Rapid City Society for Genealogical Research, 1993)

South Dakota Cemeteries, 1990
by Maurice Krueger and Florence Krueger (Mina, SD: Maurice and Florence Krueger, 1990)

Your Guide to Cemetery Research
by Sharon DeBartolo Carmack (Cincinnati: Betterway Books, 2002)

■ **Armstrong** 1895
Parent County: Pratt
Comments/research tips: (See Dewey) Formerly Pyatt County. Eliminated 1952 to Dewey, Haakon, and Ziebach.

■ **Armstrong, old** 1873
Parent County: Dakota territory
Comments/research tips: (See Hutchinson) Eliminated 1879 to Hutchinson.

■ **Ashmore** 1875
Parent County: Buffalo
Comments/research tips: (See Potter) Name changed to Potter 1877.

■ **Aurora** 1879
P.O. Box 397, Plankinton, SD 57368-0397
Phone: (605)942-7161
Web site: www.rootsweb.com/~sdaurora/
Parent County: Brule
Comments/research tips: Registrar of Deeds has incomplete Marriage records 1883-1904. State Archives has Naturalization records 1882-1953.

Record Type	Year Begun	Jurisdiction
Divorce	1883	Clerk of Courts
Probate	1882	Clerk of Courts
Court	1882	Clerk of Courts
Burial	1941	Registrar/Deeds
Land	1882	Registrar/Deeds
Birth	1905	Registrar/Deeds
Death	1905	Registrar/Deeds
Marriage	1905	Registrar/Deeds

■ **Beadle** 1879
P.O. Box 55, Huron, SD 57350-0055
Phone: (605)353-8412
Web site: www.beadlecounty.org
Parent County: Spink, Clark
Comments/research tips: Officially organized 1880. State Archives has Naturalization records 1880-1956.

Record Type	Year Begun	Jurisdiction
Divorce	1881	Clerk of Courts
Probate	1882	Clerk of Courts
Court	1882	Clerk of Courts
Death	1905	Registrar/Deeds
Burial	1925	Registrar/Deeds
Land	1886	Registrar/Deeds
Birth	1905	Registrar/Deeds
Marriage	1880	Registrar/Deeds

■ **Beadle, old** 1873
Parent County: Hanson
Comments/research tips: (See Brown) Eliminated 1879 to Brown.

■ **Bennett** 1909
P.O. Box 433, Martin, SD 57551-0433
Phone: (605)685-6054
Web site: www.rootsweb.com/~sdbennet/
Parent County: Indian lands
Comments/research tips: Attached to Fall River County prior to organization 1912. State Archives has Naturalization records 1912-1952.

Record Type	Year Begun	Jurisdiction
Divorce	1912	Clerk of Courts
Probate	1912	Clerk of Courts
Court	1912	Clerk of Courts
Death	1912	Registrar/Deeds
Burial	1940	Registrar/Deeds
Land	1907	Registrar/Deeds
Marriage	1912	Registrar/Deeds
Birth	1912	Registrar/Deeds

■ **Bon Homme** 1862
P.O. Box 3, Tyndall, SD 57066-003
Phone: (605)589-4217
Web site: www.rootsweb.com/~sdbonhom/
Parent County: Charles Mix
Comments/research tips: State Archives has Naturalization records 1871-1944.

Record Type	Year Begun	Jurisdiction
Probate	1877	Clerk of Courts
Court	1871	Clerk of Courts
Divorce	1870	Clerk of Courts
Marriage	1885	Registrar/Deeds
Death	1905	Registrar/Deeds
Burial	1940	Registrar/Deeds
Land	1890	Registrar/Deeds
Birth	1905	Registrar/Deeds

■ **Boreman** 1873
Parent County: Unorganized Territory
Comments/research tips: (See Corson) Attached to Campbell County. Eliminated 1909 to Corson.

■ **Bramble** 1873
Parent County: Hanson
Comments/research tips: Eliminated 1879 to Miner.

■ **Brookings** 1862
314 Sixth Ave., Brookings, SD 57006-2084
Phone: (605)692-2724

Web site: www.rootsweb.com/~sdbrooki/
Parent County: Unorganized Territory
Comments/research tips: Organized 3 July 1871. Registrar of Deeds has incomplete Marriage records 1887–1905. State Archives has Naturalization records 1880–1954.

Record Type	Year Begun	Jurisdiction
Divorce	1870	Clerk of Courts
Probate	ca. 1870	Clerk of Courts
Court	ca. 1870	Clerk of Courts
Land	1871	Registrar/Deeds
Birth	1905	Registrar/Deeds
Marriage	1905	Registrar/Deeds
Death	1905	Registrar/Deeds

■ Brown   20 July 1880

P.O. Box 1307, Aberdeen, SD 57402-1307
Phone: (605)626-7140
Web site: www.brown.sd.us/
Parent County: Mills, Stone, Beadle, old
Comments/research tips: Registrar of Deeds has incomplete Marriage records 1892–1905. State Archives has Naturalization records 1881–1954.

Record Type	Year Begun	Jurisdiction
Divorce	1884	Clerk of Courts
Probate	ca. 1880	Clerk of Courts
Court	ca. 1880	Clerk of Courts
Death	1905	Registrar/Deeds
Burial	1885	Registrar/Deeds
Land	1880	Registrar/Deeds
Military	1917	Registrar/Deeds
Birth	1905	Registrar/Deeds
Marriage	1905	Registrar/Deeds

■ Bruguier   1862

Parent County: Unorganized Territory
Comments/research tips: Attached to Charles Mix. Eliminated 1864 to Buffalo and Charles Mix.

■ Brule   Jan. 1875

300 S. Courtland St., Suite 110, Chamberlain, SD 57325-1599
Phone: (605)734-5310
Web site: www.rootsweb.com/~sdbrule/
Parent County: Charles Mix
Comments/research tips: Registrar of Deeds has incomplete Burial records 1888–1941.

Record Type	Year Begun	Jurisdiction
Court	ca. 1875	Clerk of Courts
Divorce	1883	Clerk of Courts
Probate	ca. 1875	Clerk of Courts
Nat.	1882	Clerk of Courts
Land	1879	Registrar/Deeds
Marriage	1882	Registrar/Deeds
Birth	1905	Registrar/Deeds
Death	1905	Registrar/Deeds
Burial	1941	Registrar/Deeds

■ Buffalo   1864

P.O. Box 174, Gann Valley, SD 57341-0174
Phone: (605)293-3239

Web site: www.geocities.com/lynettet.geo/buffalo/buffalo.html
Parent County: Brugier, Charles Mix, Unorganized Territory
Comments/research tips: Attached to Bon Homme County prior to organization 1871. State Archives has Naturalization records 1885–1938.

Record Type	Year Begun	Jurisdiction
Divorce	1889	Clerk of Courts
Probate	1884	Clerk of Courts
Court	1890	Clerk of Courts
Burial	1941	Registrar/Deeds
Land	1885	Registrar/Deeds
Marriage	1887	Registrar/Deeds
Military	1919	Registrar/Deeds
Birth	1905	Registrar/Deeds
Death	1905	Registrar/Deeds

■ Burchard   1873

Parent County: Hanson
Comments/research tips: Eliminated 1879 to Beadle and Hand.

■ Burdick   1883

Parent County: Dakota territory
Comments/research tips: Eliminated 1889 to Harding.

■ Butte   1883

839 Fifth Ave., Belle Fourche, SD 57717-1796
Phone: (605)892-2912
Web site: www.rootsweb.com/~sdbutte/
Parent County: Lawrence, Mandan
Comments/research tips: State Archives has Naturalization records 1876–1955.

Record Type	Year Begun	Jurisdiction
Divorce	1893	Clerk of Courts
Probate	ca. 1883	Clerk of Courts
Court	ca. 1883	Clerk of Courts
Land	1883	Registrar/Deeds
Marriage	1890	Registrar/Deeds
Birth	1905	Registrar/Deeds
Death	1905	Registrar/Deeds
Burial	1907	Registrar/Deeds

■ Campbell   1873

P.O. Box 148, Mound City, SD 57646-0148
Phone: (605)955-3505
Web site: www.ehrman.net/campbell/
Parent County: Buffalo
Comments/research tips: Organized 1884. Registrar of Deeds has incomplete Burial records 1923–1934.

Record Type	Year Begun	Jurisdiction
Nat.	1884	Clerk of Courts
Divorce	1884	Clerk of Courts
Court	1884	Clerk of Courts
Probate	1884	Clerk of Courts
Death	1905	Registrar/Deeds
Land	1898	Registrar/Deeds
Birth	1905	Registrar/Deeds
Burial	1941	Registrar/Deeds
Marriage	1888	Registrar/Deeds

■ Charles Mix 1862
P.O. Box 206, Lake Andes, SD 57356-0206
Phone: (605)487-7141
Web site: www.rootsweb.com/~sdcharle/
Parent County: Unorganized Territory
Comments/research tips: County was dissolved in 1864 and was attached to Bon Homme county. County was reorganized in 1879. State Archives has Naturalization records 1879–1955.

Record Type	Year Begun	Jurisdiction
Divorce	1886	Clerk of Courts
Probate	ca. 1875	Clerk of Courts
Court	ca. 1875	Clerk of Courts
Death	1905	Registrar/Deeds
Land	ca. 1890	Registrar/Deeds
Birth	1905	Registrar/Deeds
Marriage	1883	Registrar/Deeds

■ Cheyenne 1875
Parent County: Pratt, Rusk, Stanley, Unorganized Territory
Comments/research tips: Eliminated 1883 to Jackson, Nowlin, Pyatt, and Sterling.

■ Choteau 1883
Parent County: Martin
Comments/research tips: Attached to Lawrence County. Eliminated 1898 to Butte and Meade.

■ Clark 1873
P.O. Box 294, Clark, SD 57225-0294
Phone: (605)532-5363
Web site: www.rootsweb.com/~sdclark/
Parent County: Hanson
Comments/research tips: Officially organized 1881. Registrar of Deeds has incomplete Marriage records 1883–1905. State Archives has Naturalization records 1881–1945.

Record Type	Year Begun	Jurisdiction
Divorce	1882	Clerk of Courts
Probate	1882	Clerk of Courts
Court	1885	Clerk of Courts
Burial	1940	Registrar/Deeds
Land	1881	Registrar/Deeds
Marriage	1905	Registrar/Deeds
Birth	1905	Registrar/Deeds
Death	1905	Registrar/Deeds

■ Clay 1862
211 W Main St., P.O. Box 202, Vermillion, SD 57069
Phone: (605)677-7130
Web site: www.rootsweb.com/~sdclay/
Parent County: Unorganized Territory
Comments/research tips: Burial records are kept by each individual cemetery. State Archives has Naturalization records 1867–1929.

Record Type	Year Begun	Jurisdiction
Court	ca. 1862	Clerk of Courts
Divorce	1866	Clerk of Courts
Land	1863	Registrar/Deeds
Birth	1905	Registrar/Deeds
Death	1905	Registrar/Deeds
Marriage	1860	Registrar/Deeds
Probate	ca. 1862	Clerk of Court

■ Codington 1877
14 First Ave. SE, Watertown, SD 57201
Phone: (605)882-6278
Web site: http://sweb.lakeareatech.edu/derbyc/county/index.htm
Parent County: Clark, Grant, Hamlin
Comments/research tips: Organized 19 July 1878. Registrar of Deeds has incomplete Birth records 1884–1905 and Marriage records 1887–1905. State Archives has Naturalization records 1879–1930.

Record Type	Year Begun	Jurisdiction
Divorce	1887	Clerk of Courts
Probate	1878	Clerk of Courts
Court	1878	Clerk of Courts
Death	1905	Registrar/Deeds
Burial	1892	Registrar/Deeds
Marriage	1905	Registrar/Deeds
Land	1877	Registrar/Deeds
Military	1919	Registrar/Deeds
Birth	1905	Registrar/Deeds

■ Cole 1862
Parent County: Unorganized Territory
Comments/research tips: (See Union) Name changed to Union 1864.

■ Corson 1909
P.O. Box 256, McIntosh, SD 57641-0247
Phone: (605)273-4395
Web site: www.rootsweb.com/~sdcorson/
Parent County: Boreman, Dewey, Schnasse
Comments/research tips: State Archives has Naturalization records 1909–1951.

Record Type	Year Begun	Jurisdiction
Divorce	1909	Clerk of Courts
Probate	ca. 1909	Clerk of Courts
Court	ca. 1909	Clerk of Courts
Marriage	1909	Registrar/Deeds
Birth	1909	Registrar/Deeds
Death	1909	Registrar/Deeds
Land	1909	Registrar/Deeds

■ Cragin 1873
Parent County: Hanson
Comments/research tips: Eliminated 1879 to Aurora.

■ Custer 1875
420 Mt. Rushmore Rd., Custer, SD 57730-1934
Phone: (605)673-2784
Web site: www.rapidnet.com/~saj/custer/
Parent County: Unorganized Territory
Comments/research tips: Organized 1877. State Archives has Naturalization records 1880–1942.

Record Type	Year Begun	Jurisdiction
Divorce	1880	Clerk of Courts

Record Type	Year Begun	Jurisdiction
Probate	ca. 1877	Clerk of Courts
Court	ca. 1877	Clerk of Courts
Marriage	1890	Registrar/Deeds
Land	1875	Registrar/Deeds
Birth	1905	Registrar/Deeds
Death	1905	Registrar/Deeds

■ Davison 1873

200 E. Fourth Ave., Mitchell, SD 57301-2692
Phone: (605)995-8616
Web site: www.davisoncounty.org/
Parent County: Hanson
Comments/research tips: Organized 1874. State Archives has Naturalization records 1878–1956.

Record Type	Year Begun	Jurisdiction
Divorce	1882	Clerk of Courts
Probate	ca. 1873	Clerk of Courts
Court	ca. 1833	Clerk of Courts
Land	1873	Registrar/Deeds
Birth	1905	Registrar/Deeds
Death	1905	Registrar/Deeds
Marriage	1887	Registrar/Deeds

■ Day 1879

710 W. First St., Webster, SD 57274-1396
Phone: (605)345-4162
Web site: www.rootsweb.com/~sdday/
Parent County: Greeley, Stone
Comments/research tips: Officially organized 1882. State Archives has Naturalization records 1882–1942.

Record Type	Year Begun	Jurisdiction
Divorce	1881	Clerk of Courts
Court	ca. 1882	Clerk of Courts
Probate	ca. 1882	Clerk of Courts
Burial	1905	Registrar/Deeds
Marriage	1882	Registrar/Deeds
Birth	1905	Registrar/Deeds
Death	1905	Registrar/Deeds
Land	1879	Registrar/Deeds

■ Delano 1875

Parent County: Unorganized Territory
Comments/research tips: Attached to Lawrence County. Eliminated 1898 to Meade.

■ Deuel 1862

P.O. Box 307, Clear Lake, SD 57226-0307
Phone: (605)874-2268
Web site: www.rootsweb.com/~sddeuel/
Parent County: Unorganized Territory
Comments/research tips: Officially organized 1878. Registrar of Deeds has incomplete Birth records 1880–1905 and Burial records 1930–1941. State Archives has Naturalization records 1878–1930.

Record Type	Year Begun	Jurisdiction
Divorce	1879	Clerk of Courts
Probate	ca. 1878	Clerk of Courts
Court	ca. 1878	Clerk of Courts
Burial	1941	Registrar/Deeds

Record Type	Year Begun	Jurisdiction
Marriage	1879	Registrar/Deeds
Land	1885	Registrar/Deeds
Birth	1905	Registrar/Deeds
Death	1905	Registrar/Deeds

■ Dewey 1873

P.O. Box 117, Timber Lake, SD 57656-0017
Phone: (605)865-3661
Web site: www.rootsweb.com/~sddewey/
Parent County: Unorganized Territory
Comments/research tips: Formerly Rusk County. Name changed to Dewey 1883. Attached to Walworth County prior to organization 1910. State Archives has Naturalization records 1911–1955.

Record Type	Year Begun	Jurisdiction
Divorce	1910	Clerk of Courts
Probate	ca. 1910	Clerk of Courts
Court	ca. 1910	Clerk of Courts
Death	1905	Registrar/Deeds
Burial	1941	Registrar/Deeds
Birth	1905	Registrar/Deeds
Marriage	1910	Registrar/Deeds
Land	1912	Registrar/Deeds

■ Douglas 1873

P.O. Box 267, Armour, SD 57313-0267
Phone: (605)724-2204
Web site: www.rootsweb.com/~sddougla/
Parent County: Charles Mix
Comments/research tips: Officially organized 1882. State Archives has Naturalization records 1882–1943.

Record Type	Year Begun	Jurisdiction
Court	ca. 1882	Clerk of Courts
Divorce	1885	Clerk of Courts
Probate	ca. 1882	Clerk of Courts
Marriage	1883	Registrar/Deeds
Birth	1905	Registrar/Deeds
Death	1905	Registrar/Deeds
Land	1882	Registrar/Deeds

■ Edmunds 1873

P.O. Box 386, Ipswich, SD 57451-0386
Phone: (605)426-6431
Web site: www.rootsweb.com/~sdedmund/
Parent County: Buffalo
Comments/research tips: Officially organized 1883. State Archives has Naturalization records 1884–1954.

Record Type	Year Begun	Jurisdiction
Divorce	1884	Clerk of Courts
Court	1884	Clerk of Courts
Probate	1884	Clerk of Courts
Burial	1941	Registrar/Deeds
Marriage	1887	Registrar/Deeds
Birth	1905	Registrar/Deeds
Death	1905	Registrar/Deeds
Land	1883	Registrar/Deeds

■ Ewing 1883

Parent County: Harding
Comments/research tips: Elimnated 1894 to Harding.

South Dakota

■ Fall River 1883

906 N. River St., Hot Springs, SD 57747-1399
Phone: (605)745-5139
Web site: www.rootsweb.com/~sdfallsr/
Parent County: Custer
Comments/research tips: State Archives has Naturalization records 1905–1954.

Record Type	Year Begun	Jurisdiction
Divorce	1882	Clerk of Courts
Probate	ca. 1883	Clerk of Courts
Court	ca. 1883	Clerk of Courts
Marriage	1905	Registrar/Deeds
Land	1907	Registrar/Deeds
Birth	1905	Registrar/Deeds
Death	1905	Registrar/Deeds

■ Faulk 1873

P.O. Box 309, Faulkton, SD 57438-0309
Phone: (605)598-6228
Web site: www.rootsweb.com/~sdfaulk/findex.htm
Parent County: Buffalo
Comments/research tips: Officially organized 1883. Registrar of Deeds has incomplete Marriage records 1883–1887. State Archives has Naturalization records 1884–1944.

Record Type	Year Begun	Jurisdiction
Divorce	1883	Clerk of Courts
Court	1883	Clerk of Courts
Probate	1884	Clerk of Courts
Burial	1890	Registrar/Deeds
Land	1888	Registrar/Deeds
Birth	1905	Registrar/Deeds
Marriage	1890	Registrar/Deeds
Death	1905	Registrar/Deeds

■ Forsythe 1875

Parent County: Unorganized Territory
Comments/research tips: Eliminated 1881 to Custer.

■ Grant 1873

210 E. Fifth Ave., Milbank, SD 57252-2499
Phone: (605)432-4752
Web site: ww.rootsweb.com/~sdgrant/
Parent County: Deuel, Hanson
Comments/research tips: Officially organized 1878. Fire in early 1900's destroyed many records. State Archives has Naturalization records 1881–1955.

Record Type	Year Begun	Jurisdiction
Divorce	1895	Clerk of Courts
Probate	1878	Clerk of Courts
Court	1878	Clerk of Courts
Land	1878	Registrar/Deeds
Birth	1905	Registrar/Deeds
Death	1905	Registrar/Deeds
Marriage	1905	Registrar/Deeds

■ Greely 1873

Parent County: Hanson
Comments/research tips: Eliminated 1879 to Day.

■ Gregory 1862

P.O. Box 415, Burke, SD 57523-0415
Phone: (605)775-2624
Web site: www.rootsweb.com/~sdgregor/
Parent County: Unorganized Territory
Comments/research tips: Attached to Todd and Charles Mix Counties prior to organization 1898. State Archives has Naturalization records 1898–1952.

Record Type	Year Begun	Jurisdiction
Divorce	1899	Clerk of Courts
Probate	1862	Clerk of Courts
Court	1862	Clerk of Courts
Land	1862	Registrar/Deeds
Burial	1905	Registrar/Deeds
Marriage	1898	Registrar/Deeds
Birth	1905	Registrar/Deeds
Death	1905	Registrar/Deeds

■ Haakon 1914

P.O. Box 100,, Philip, SD 57567-0100
Phone: (605)859-2785
Web site: www.rootsweb.com/~sdhaakon/
Parent County: Stanley
Comments/research tips: Officially organized 1915.

Record Type	Year Begun	Jurisdiction
Divorce	1915	Clerk of Courts
Probate	1915	Clerk of Courts
Court	1915	Clerk of Courts
Death	1915	Registrar/Deeds
Burial	1941	Registrar/Deeds
Land	1893	Registrar/Deeds
Birth	1915	Registrar/Deeds
Marriage	1915	Registrar/Deeds

■ Hamlin 1873

P.O. Box 56, Hayti, SD 57241-0056
Phone: (605)783-3206
Web site: www.rootsweb.com/~sdhamlin/
Parent County: Deuel, Hanson
Comments/research tips: Officially organized 1878. State Archives has Naturalization records 1880–1945.

Record Type	Year Begun	Jurisdiction
Court	ca. 1878	Clerk of Courts
Divorce	1885	Clerk of Courts
Probate	ca. 1878	Clerk of Courts
Marriage	1887	Registrar/Deeds
Birth	1905	Registrar/Deeds
Death	1905	Registrar/Deeds
Land	1885	Registrar/Deeds

■ Hand 1873

415 W. First Ave., Miller, SD 57362-1346
Phone: (605)853-3512
Web site: www.geocities.com/lynettet.geo/hand/hand.html
Parent County: Buffalo
Comments/research tips: Officially organized 1882. State Archives has Naturalization records 1882–1945.

Record Type	Year Begun	Jurisdiction
Divorce	1882	Clerk of Courts

Probate .... 1873 ...... Clerk of Courts
Court .... 1873 ...... Clerk of Courts
Land .... 1881 ...... Registrar/Deeds
Marriage .... 1883 ...... Registrar/Deeds
Birth .... 1905 ...... Registrar/Deeds
Death .... 1905 ...... Registrar/Deeds
Burial .... 1932 ...... Registrar/Deeds

■ Hanson 1871
P.O. Box 500, Alexandria, SD 57311-0500
Phone: (605)239-4512
Web site: www.rootsweb.com/~sdhanson/
Parent County: Buffalo, Deuel, Brookings, Charles Mix, Hutchinson, Jayne, Minnehaha, Unorganized Land
Comments/research tips: Officially organized 1873. State Archives has Naturalization records 1901–1946.

Record Type	Year Begun	Jurisdiction
Divorce	1896	Clerk of Courts
Probate	ca. 1873	Clerk of Courts
Court	ca. 1873	Clerk of Courts
Birth	1905	Registrar/Deeds
Marriage	1901	Registrar/Deeds
Death	1905	Registrar/Deeds

■ Harding 1881
P.O. Box 101,, Buffalo, SD 57720-0101
Phone: (605)375-3321
Web site: www.rootsweb.com/~sdhardin/
Parent County: Unorganized Territory
Comments/research tips: Attached to Butte County 1881–1898. Eliminated 1898 to Butte. Re-created 1908 from Butte. Officially organized 1911. State Archives has Naturalization records 1909–1944.

Record Type	Year Begun	Jurisdiction
Divorce	1909	Clerk of Courts
Probate	ca. 1911	Clerk of Courts
Court	ca. 1911	Clerk of Courts
Land	1909	Registrar/Deeds
Marriage	1909	Registrar/Deeds
Birth	1909	Registrar/Deeds
Death	1909	Registrar/Deeds
Military	1917	Registrar/Deeds

■ Hughes 1873
104 E. Capitol Ave., Pierre, SD 57501
Phone: (605)773-7495
Web site: www.rootsweb.com/~sdhughes/
Parent County: Buffalo
Comments/research tips: Officially organized 1880. State Archives has Naturalization records 1881–1956.

Record Type	Year Begun	Jurisdiction
Divorce	1909	Clerk of Courts
Court	ca. 1880	Clerk of Courts
Probate	ca. 1880	Clerk of Courts
Burial	1951	Registrar/Deeds
Land	1885	Registrar/Deeds
Birth	1905	Registrar/Deeds
Marriage	1905	Registrar/Deeds
Death	1905	Registrar/Deeds

■ Hutchinson 1862
140 Euclid St., Room 37, Olivet, SD 57032-4217
Phone: (605)387-2838
Web site: www.rootsweb.com/~sdhutchi/
Parent County: Unorganized Territory
Comments/research tips: Officially organized 1871. State Archives has Naturalization records 1876–1948.

Record Type	Year Begun	Jurisdiction
Court	ca. 1871	Clerk of Courts
Probate	ca. 1871	Clerk of Courts
Death	1905	Registrar/Deeds
Land	1876	Registrar/Deeds
Marriage	1887	Registrar/Deeds
Birth	1905	Registrar/Deeds

■ Hyde 1873
P.O. Box 342, Highmore, SD 57345-0342
Phone: (605)852-2517
Web site: www.rootsweb.com/~sdhyde/
Parent County: Buffalo
Comments/research tips: Officially organized 1883. State Archives has Naturalization records 1883–1944.

Record Type	Year Begun	Jurisdiction
Court	ca. 1883	Clerk of Courts
Probate	ca. 1883	Clerk of Courts
Land	ca. 1883	Registrar/Deeds
Birth	1905	Registrar/Deeds
Death	1905	Registrar/Deeds
Marriage	1890	Registrar/Deeds

■ Jackson 1883
P.O. Box 248, Kadoka, SD 57543-0248
Phone: (605)837-2420
Web site: www.rootsweb.com/~sdjackso/
Parent County: Cheyenne, Lugenbeel, White River
Comments/research tips: Eliminated 1909 to Mellette and Washabaugh. Recretated 1914 from Stanley. Organized 1915. State Archives has Naturalization records 1916–1948.

Record Type	Year Begun	Jurisdiction
Probate	1915	Clerk of Courts
Court	1915	Clerk of Courts
Burial	1915	Registrar/Deeds
Land	1907	Registrar/Deeds
Birth	1915	Registrar/Deeds
Marriage	1915	Registrar/Deeds
Death	1915	Registrar/Deeds

■ Jayne 1862
Parent County: Unorganized Territory
Comments/research tips: Eliminated 1871 to Hanson, Hutchinson, and Turner Counties.

■ Jerauld 1883
P.O. Box 452, Wessington Springs, SD 57382-0452
Phone: (605)539-1221
Web site: www.rootsweb.com/~sdjeraul/jindex.htm
Parent County: Aurora, Buffalo
Comments/research tips: Registrar of Deeds has incomplete

Marriage records 1884–1887. State Archives has
Naturalization records 1906–1947.

Record Type	Year Begun	Jurisdiction
Probate	ca. 1883	Clerk of Courts
Court	ca. 1883	Clerk of Courts
Marriage	1888	Registrar/Deeds
Land	ca. 1910	Registrar/Deeds
Birth	1905	Registrar/Deeds
Death	1905	Registrar/Deeds

■ Jones 1916

P.O. Box 446, Murdo, SD 57559-0446
Phone: (605)669-7104
Web site: www.rootsweb.com/~sdjones/
Parent County: Lyman
Comments/research tips: State Archives has Naturalization
records 1903–1959.

Record Type	Year Begun	Jurisdiction
Probate	ca. 1917	Clerk of Courts
Court	ca. 1917	Clerk of Courts
Death	1917	Registrar/Deeds
Land	1906	Registrar/Deeds
Burial	1917	Registrar/Deeds
Birth	1917	Registrar/Deeds
Marriage	1917	Registrar/Deeds

■ Kingsbury 1873

P.O. Box 146, DeSmet, SD 57231-0146
Phone: (605)854-3591
Web site: www.rootsweb.com/~sdkingsb/
Parent County: Hanson
Comments/research tips: Officially organized 1880. State
Archives has Naturalization records 1883–1945.

Record Type	Year Begun	Jurisdiction
Court	ca. 1880	Clerk of Courts
Probate	ca. 1880	Clerk of Courts
Burial	1941	Registrar/Deeds
Marriage	1887	Registrar/Deeds
Land	ca. 1880	Registrar/Deeds
Birth	1905	Registrar/Deeds
Death	1905	Registrar/Deeds

■ Lake 1873

P.O. Box 266, Madison, SD 57042-0266
Phone: (605)256-7614
Web site: www.rootsweb.com/~sdlake/
Parent County: Brookings, Hanson, Minnehaha
Comments/research tips: State Archives has Naturalization
records 1881–1944.

Record Type	Year Begun	Jurisdiction
Court	ca. 1880	Clerk of Courts
Probate	ca. 1880	Clerk of Courts
Marriage	1880	Registrar/Deeds
Burial	1941	Registrar/Deeds
Land	1878	Registrar/Deeds
Birth	1905	Registrar/Deeds
Death	1905	Registrar/Deeds

■ Lawrence 1875

P.O. Box 565, Deadwood, SD 57732-0565
Phone: (605)578-3930

Web site: www.lawrence.sd.us/
Parent County: Unorganized Territory
Comments/research tips: Officially organized 1877. State
Archives has Naturalization records 1879–1954.

Record Type	Year Begun	Jurisdiction
Probate	ca. 1877	Clerk of Courts
Court	ca. 1877	Clerk of Courts
Marriage	1880	Registrar/Deeds
Land	ca. 1880	Registrar/Deeds
Military	1921	Registrar/Deeds
Birth	1905	Registrar/Deeds
Death	1877	Registrar/Deeds
Burial	1870	Registrar/Deeds

■ Lincoln 1862

100 E. Fifth St., Carton, SD 57013-1789
Phone: (605)764-5661
Web site: www.rootsweb.com/~sdlincol/
Parent County: Unorganized Territory
Comments/research tips: Officially organized 1867.
Registrar of Deeds has incomplete Marriage records
1873–1905. State Archives has Naturalization records
1871–1945.

Record Type	Year Begun	Jurisdiction
Probate	ca. 1867	Clerk of Courts
Court	ca. 1867	Clerk of Courts
Burial	1941	Registrar/Deeds
Marriage	1905	Registrar/Deeds
Birth	1905	Registrar/Deeds
Death	1905	Registrar/Deeds
Land	ca. 1870	Registrar/Deeds

■ Lugenbeel 1875

Parent County: Meyer, Pratt, Unorganized Land
Comments/research tips: Eliminated 1909 to Bennett and
Todd.

■ Lyman 1873

P.O. Box 98, Kennebec, SD 57544-0098
Phone: (605)869-2297
Web site: www.rootsweb.com/~sdlyman/
Parent County: Gregory, Unorganized Territory
Comments/research tips: Officially organized 1893. State
Archives has Naturalization records 1893–1950.

Record Type	Year Begun	Jurisdiction
Probate	ca. 1893	Clerk of Courts
Court	ca. 1893	Clerk of Courts
Land	1893	Registrar/Deeds
Marriage	1893	Registrar/Deeds
Birth	1905	Registrar/Deeds
Death	1905	Registrar/Deeds
Burial	1944	Registrar/Deeds

■ Mandan 1875

Parent County: Unorganized Territory
Comments/research tips: Eliminated 1887 to Lawrence.

■ Marshall 1885

P.O. Box 130, Britton, SD 57430-0130
Phone: (605)448-2352

Web site: www.rootsweb.com/~sdmarsha/mindex.htm
Parent County: Day
Comments/research tips: State Archives has Naturalization records 1885–1944.

Record Type	Year Begun	Jurisdiction
Probate	ca. 1885	Clerk of Courts
Court	ca. 1885	Clerk of Courts
Land	ca. 1885	Registrar/Deeds
Birth	1905	Registrar/Deeds
Death	1905	Registrar/Deeds
Marriage	1887	Registrar/Deeds

■ Martin 1881

Parent County: Unorganized Territory
Comments/research tips: Eliminated 1898 to Butte.

■ McCook 1873

P.O. Box 338, Salem, SD 57058-0338
Phone: (605)425-2701
Web site: www.rootsweb.com/~sdmccook/
Parent County: Hanson
Comments/research tips: Officially organized 1878. State Archives has Naturalization records 1870–1945.

Record Type	Year Begun	Jurisdiction
Court	ca. 1878	Clerk of Courts
Probate	ca. 1878	Clerk of Courts
Land	1878	Registrar/Deeds
Birth	1880	Registrar/Deeds
Marriage	1887	Registrar/Deeds
Death	1905	Registrar/Deeds

■ McPherson 1873

P.O. Box 129, Leola, SD 57456-0129
Phone: (605)439-3151
Web site: www.rootsweb.com/~sdmcpher/
Parent County: Buffalo
Comments/research tips: Officially organized 1884. State Archives has Naturalization records 1884–1944.

Record Type	Year Begun	Jurisdiction
Probate	ca. 1884	Clerk of Courts
Court	ca. 1884	Clerk of Courts
Land	ca. 1890	Registrar/Deeds
Birth	1905	Registrar/Deeds
Death	1905	Registrar/Deeds
Marriage	1884	Registrar/Deeds

■ Meade 1889

1425 Sherman St., Sturgis, SD 57785-0447
Phone: (605)347-2356
Web site: www.rootsweb.com/~sdmeade/Meade%20Co/
Parent County: Lawrence
Comments/research tips: State Archives has Naturalization records 1889–1943.

Record Type	Year Begun	Jurisdiction
Probate	ca. 1889	Clerk of Courts
Court	ca. 1889	Clerk of Courts
Marriage	1905	Registrar/Deeds
Land	1889	Registrar/Deeds
Birth	1905	Registrar/Deeds

Death	1905	Registrar/Deeds
Burial	1905	Registrar/Deeds

■ Mellette 1909

P.O. Box 183, White River, SD 57579
Phone: (605)259-3371
Web site: www.rootsweb.com/~sdmellet/
Parent County: Jackdon, Meyer, Washabaugh, Unorganized Territory
Comments/research tips: Organized 1911. State Archives has Naturalization records 1912–1946.

Record Type	Year Begun	Jurisdiction
Probate	1912	Clerk of Courts
Court	1912	Clerk of Courts
Marriage	1912	Registrar/Deeds
Birth	1912	Registrar/Deeds
Death	1912	Registrar/Deeds
Land	1907	Registrar/Deeds

■ Meyer 1873

Parent County: Unorganized Territory
Comments/research tips: Eliminated 1909 to Mellette and Todd.

■ Miner 1873

P.O. Box 546, Howard, SD 57349
Phone: (605)772-5621
Web site: www.geocities.com/lynettet.geo/miner/miner.html
Parent County: Hanson
Comments/research tips: Organized 1880. State Archives has Naturalization records 1881–1944.

Record Type	Year Begun	Jurisdiction
Probate	1883	Clerk of Courts
Court	1881	Clerk of Courts
Land	1881	Registrar/Deeds
Birth	1905	Registrar/Deeds
Death	1905	Registrar/Deeds
Marriage	1887	Registrar/Deeds

■ Minnehaha 1862

415 N. Dakota Ave., Sioux Falls, SD 57104
Phone: (605)367-4223
Web site: www.minnehahacounty.org/
Parent County: Unorganized Territory
Comments/research tips: Attached to Union County prior to organization 1868. State Archives has Naturalization records 1868–1954.

Record Type	Year Begun	Jurisdiction
Probate	1873	Clerk of Courts
Court	1862	Clerk of Courts
Death	1867	Registrar/Deeds
Land	1870	Registrar/Deeds
Burial	1941	Registrar/Deeds
Marriage	1872	Registrar/Deeds
Birth	1856	Registrar/Deeds

■ Moody 1873

P.O. Box 247, Flandreau, SD 57028
Phone: (605)997-3151

Web site: www.rootsweb.com/~sdmoody/
Parent County: Brookings, Minnehaha
Comments/research tips: State Archives has Naturalization records 1877–1944.

Record Type	Year Begun	Jurisdiction
Divorce	1891	Clerk of Courts
Probate	ca. 1873	Clerk of Courts
Court	ca. 1873	Clerk of Courts
Land	1873	Registrar/Deeds
Marriage	1887	Registrar/Deeds
Birth	1905	Registrar/Deeds
Death	1905	Registrar/Deeds
Burial	1941	Registrar/Deeds

■ Nowlin 1883
Parent County: Dakota territory
Comments/research tips: Eliminated 1898 to Haakon and Jackson.

■ Pennington 1875
315 St. Joseph St., Rapid City, SD 57701
Phone: (605)394-2177
Web site: www.co.pennington.sd.us/
Parent County: Unorganized Territory
Comments/research tips: Organized 1877. State Archives has Naturalization records 1879–1975.

Record Type	Year Begun	Jurisdiction
Divorce	1877	Clerk of Courts
Court	ca. 1877	Clerk of Courts
Probate	ca. 1877	Clerk of Courts
Marriage	1887	Registrar/Deeds
Birth	1905	Registrar/Deeds
Death	1905	Registrar/Deeds
Land	1883	Registrar/Deeds

■ Perkins 1908
P.O. Box 127, Bison, SD 57620
Phone: (605)244-5620
Web site: www.rootsweb.com/~sdperkin/
Parent County: Butte
Comments/research tips: Organized 1909. State Archives has Naturalization records 1909–1955.

Record Type	Year Begun	Jurisdiction
Probate	ca. 1909	Clerk of Courts
Court	ca. 1909	Clerk of Courts
Divorce	1909	Clerk of Courts
Marriage	1909	Registrar/Deeds
Birth	1909	Registrar/Deeds
Death	1909	Registrar/Deeds
Land	1908	Registrar/Deeds

■ Potter 1873
201 S. Exene St., Gettysburg, SD 57442
Phone: (605)765-9467
Web site: www.rootsweb.com/~sdpotter/potterindex.htm
Parent County: Buffalo
Comments/research tips: Formerly Ashmore County. Name changed to Potter 1875. Organized 1883. State Archives has Naturalization records 1884–1943.

Record Type	Year Begun	Jurisdiction
Probate	ca. 1883	Clerk of Courts
Divorce	1884	Clerk of Courts
Court	ca. 1883	Clerk of Courts
Death	1905	Registrar/Deeds
Land	ca. 1875	Registrar/Deeds
Marriage	1890	Registrar/Deeds
Burial	1941	Registrar/Deeds
Birth	1905	Registrar/Deeds

■ Pratt 1883
Parent County: Unorganized Territory
Comments/research tips: Eliminated 1895 to Jones, Lyman, Mellette, and Stanley.

■ Pyatt 1883
Parent County: Cheyenne, Rusk, Stanley
Comments/research tips: Attached to Lawrence county. Name changed to Armstrong 1895. Armstrong eliminated 1952 to Dewey.

■ Rinehart 1883
Parent County: Unorganized Territory
Comments/research tips: Eliminated 1897 to Perkins.

■ Roberts 1883
411 Second Ave. E., Sisseton, SD 57262
Phone: (605)698-7152
Web site: www.rootsweb.com/~sdrobert/
Parent County: Grant, Sisseton/Wahpeton Indian Reserve
Comments/research tips: State Archives has Naturalization records 1884–1946.

Record Type	Year Begun	Jurisdiction
Divorce	1884	Clerk of Courts
Probate	ca. 1883	Clerk of Courts
Court	ca. 1883	Clerk of Courts
Marriage	1887	Registrar/Deeds
Land	ca. 1800	Registrar/Deeds
Birth	1905	Registrar/Deeds
Death	1905	Registrar/Deeds
Burial	1941	Registrar/Deeds

■ Rusk 1873
Parent County: Unorganized Territory
Comments/research tips: (See Dewey) Name changed to Dewey 1883.

■ Sanborn 1883
P.O. Box 295, Woonsocket, SD 57385
Phone: (605)796-4516
Web site: www.rootsweb.com/~sdsanbor/
Parent County: Miner
Comments/research tips: State Archives has Naturalization records 1885–1930.

Record Type	Year Begun	Jurisdiction
Divorce	1884	Clerk of Courts
Probate	ca. 1883	Clerk of Courts
Court	ca. 1883	Clerk of Courts
Burial	1894	Registrar/Deeds

Land	1883	Registrar/Deeds
Birth	1905	Registrar/Deeds
Marriage	1887	Registrar/Deeds
Death	1905	Registrar/Deeds

■ Schnasse 1883
Parent County: Boreman, Unorganized Territory
Comments/research tips: Eliminated 1911 to Ziebach.

■ Scobey 1883
Parent County: Dakota territory
Comments/research tips: Eliminated 1897 to Meade.

■ Shannon 1875
906 N. River St., Hot Springs, SD 57747
Phone: (605)745-5139
Web site: www.rotosweb.com/~sdshanno/
Parent County: Unorganized Territory
Comments/research tips: Attached to Fall River County.

Record Type	Year Begun	Jurisdiction
Probate	ca. 1883	Clerk of Courts
Court	ca. 1883	Clerk of Courts
Land	1907	Registrar/Deeds
Birth	1905	Registrar/Deeds
Death	1905	Registrar/Deeds
Marriage	1905	Registrar/Deeds

■ Spink 1873
210 E. Seventh Ave., Redfield, SD 57469
Phone: (605)472-0150
Web site: www.rootsweb.com/~sdspink/sindex.htm
Parent County: Hanson
Comments/research tips: Organized 1879. State Archives has Naturalization records 1879–1945.

Record Type	Year Begun	Jurisdiction
Divorce	1882	Clerk of Courts
Court	ca. 1879	Clerk of Courts
Probate	ca. 1879	Clerk of Courts
Death	1905	Registrar of Wills
Land	ca. 1883	Registrar/Deeds
Birth	1905	Registrar/Deeds
Marriage	1880	Registrar/Deeds
Burial	1941	Registrar/Deeds

■ Stanley 1873
P.O. Box 596, Ft. Pierre, SD 57532
Phone: (605)223-2673
Web site: www.rootsweb.com/~sdstanle/
Parent County: Unorganized Territory
Comments/research tips: Organized 1890. Registrar of Deeds has incomplete Marriage records 1892–1905. State Archives has Naturalization records 1892–1927.

Record Type	Year Begun	Jurisdiction
Divorce	1890	Clerk of Courts
Probate	ca. 1890	Clerk of Courts
Court	ca. 1890	Clerk of Courts
Land	na	Registrar/Deeds
Marriage	1905	Registrar/Deeds
Birth	1905	Registrar/Deeds
Death	1905	Registrar/Deeds

■ Sterling 1883
Parent County: Cheyenne
Comments/research tips: Attached to Lawrence County. Eliminated 1911 to Ziebach.

■ Stone 1873
Parent County: Hanson
Comments/research tips: Eliminated 1879 to Brown, and Day Counties

■ Sully 1873
P.O. Box 265, Onida, SD 57564
Phone: (605)258-2331
Web site: www.rootsweb.com/~sdsully/sullyindex.htm
Parent County: Buffalo
Comments/research tips: Organized 1883.

Record Type	Year Begun	Jurisdiction
Divorce	1885	Clerk of Courts
Probate	ca. 1883	Clerk of Courts
Court	ca. 1883	Clerk of Courts
Land	1883	Registrar/Deeds
Birth	1905	Registrar/Deeds
Marriage	1883	Registrar/Deeds
Death	1905	Registrar/Deeds

■ Todd 1909
200 E. Third St., Winner, SD 57580
Phone: (605)842-2208
Web site: www.rootsweb.com/~sdtodd/
Parent County: Lugenbeel, Meyer, Washabaugh, Unorganized Territory
Comments/research tips: Though created by legislative act 1909, Todd has never been fully organized. Attached to Lyman and Trip Counties.

Record Type	Year Begun	Jurisdiction
Divorce	1928	Clerk of Courts
Probate	ca. 1909	Clerk of Courts
Court	ca. 1909	Clerk of Courts
Land	1909	Registrar/Deeds
Birth	1905	Registrar/Deeds
Death	1905	Registrar/Deeds
Marriage	1905	Registrar/Deeds

■ Todd, old 1862
Parent County: Unorganized Territory
Comments/research tips: Disorganized 1890 and attached to Charles Mix County. Eliminated 1897 to Gregory.

■ Tripp 1873
200 E. Third St., Winner, SD 57580
Phone: (605)842-2208
Web site: www.rootsweb.com/~sdtripp/
Parent County: Unorganized Territory, Gregory, Todd (old)
Comments/research tips: Organized 1909. State Archives has Naturalization records 1908–1952.

Record Type	Year Begun	Jurisdiction
Divorce	1909	Clerk of Courts
Probate	ca. 1909	Clerk of Courts
Court	ca. 1909	Clerk of Courts
Marriage	1905	Registrar/Deeds

Death .... 1905 ....Registrar/Deeds
Birth .... 1905 ....Registrar/Deeds
Land .... 1909 ....Registrar/Deeds

■ Turner 1871
P.O. Box 485, Parker, SD 57053
Phone: (605)297-3443
Web site: www.rootsweb.com/~sdturner/
Parent County: Lincoln, Jayne
Comments/research tips: Registrar of Deeds has incomplete Marriage records 1872–1905, and Burial records 1941 to the present. State Archives has Naturalization records 1873–1945.

Record Type	Year Begun	Jurisdiction
Divorce	1880	Clerk of Courts
Probate	ca. 1871	Clerk of Courts
Court	ca. 1871	Clerk of Courts
Land	1871	Registrar/Deeds
Birth	1905	Registrar/Deeds
Death	1905	Registrar/Deeds
Marriage	1905	Registrar/Deeds

■ Union 1862
P.O. Box 290, Elk Point, SD 57025
Phone: (605)356-2191
Web site: www.rootsweb.com/~sdunion/
Parent County: Unorganized Territory
Comments/research tips: Formerly Cole County. Name changed to Union 1864. State Archives has Naturalization records 1873–1946.

Record Type	Year Begun	Jurisdiction
Court	ca. 1862	Clerk of Courts
Divorce	1875	Clerk of Courts
Death	1905	Registrar/Deeds
Land	1862	Registrar/Deeds
Cemetery	1880	Registrar/Deeds
Birth	1905	Registrar/Deeds
Marriage	1866	Registrar/Deeds
Probate	ca. 1862	Clerk of Court

■ Wagner 1883
Parent County: Dakota teritory
Comments/research tips: Eliminated 1897 to Perkins.

■ Walworth 1873
P.O. Box 159, Selby, SD 57472
Phone: (605)649-7057
Web site: www.rootsweb.com/~sdwalwor/
Parent County: Buffalo
Comments/research tips: Organized 1883. State Archives has Naturalization records 1883–1954.

Record Type	Year Begun	Jurisdiction
Divorce	1889	Clerk of Courts
Probate	ca. 1883	Clerk of Courts
Court	ca. 1883	Clerk of Courts
Land	ca. 1873	Registrar/Deeds
Marriage	1890	Registrar/Deeds
Birth	1905	Registrar/Deeds
Death	1905	Registrar/Deeds
Burial	1941	Registrar/Deeds

■ Washabaugh 1883
Parent County: Lugenbeel
Comments/research tips: Unorganized, attached to Custer and Jackson Counties.

■ Washington 1883
Parent County: Shannon, Lugenbeel
Comments/research tips: Unorganized, attached to Custer county. Eliminated 1943 to Shannon.

■ Wetmore 1873
Parent County: Hanson
Comments/research tips: Eliminated 1879 to Aurora and Miner.

■ White River 1875
Parent County: Pratt, Unorganized Territory
Comments/research tips: Eliminated 1883 to Jackson.

■ Yankton 1862
P.O. Box 694, Yankton, SD 57078
Phone: (605)665-2422
Web site: www.co.yankton.sd.us
Parent County: Unorganized Territory
Comments/research tips: Registrar of Deeds has incomplete Marriage records 1889–1905. State Archives has Naturalization records 1874–1955.

Record Type	Year Begun	Jurisdiction
Divorce	1874	Clerk of Courts
Probate	ca. 1862	Clerk of Courts
Court	ca. 1862	Clerk of Courts
Marriage	1905	Registrar/Deeds
Land	1862	Registrar/Deeds
Birth	1905	Registrar/Deeds
Death	1905	Registrar/Deeds
Burial	1950	Registrar/Deeds

■ Ziebach 1911
P.O. Box 68, Dupree, SD 57623
Phone: (605)365-5165
Web site: www.rootsweb.com/~sdziebac/
Parent County: Schnasse, Sterling, Armstrong
Comments/research tips: Within limits of Cheyenne River Indian Reservation. State Archives has Naturalization records 1911–1951.

Record Type	Year Begun	Jurisdiction
Divorce	1911	Clerk of Courts
Probate	ca. 1911	Clerk of Courts
Court	ca. 1911	Clerk of Courts
Burial	1910	Registrar/Deeds
Land	1911	Registrar/Deeds
Birth	1910	Registrar/Deeds
Marriage	1910	Registrar/Deeds
Death	1910	Registrar/Deeds

■ Ziebach, old 1877
Parent County: Pennington
Comments/research tips: Eliminated 1898 to Pennington.

South Dakota

Tennessee

By Emily Anne Croom

HISTORICAL OVERVIEW

Spaniards explored the fringes of Tennessee in the 1540s, but the French claimed the region in 1673, established trade with the Indians, and built Fort Assumption at present-day Memphis in 1739. Although explored and claimed by both Britain and France in the early eighteenth century, the French lands east of the Mississippi became British in the 1763 Treaty of Paris. Thus, while technically still Indian land, Tennessee became British on European maps and by the king's proclamation was off-limits to settlement from the east-coast colonies.

Ignoring the ban, pioneers from North Carolina and Virginia settled along the Watauga River in the northeastern Tennessee highlands in the 1770s. In 1777, Tennessee came under the jurisdiction of Washington County, North Carolina, since the original Carolina charter had not specified a western boundary. North Carolinians established a settlement in the winter of 1779–1780 at a trading spot on the Cumberland River called French Lick, now Nashville. In 1783, that area became Davidson County, North Carolina.

After several years of turbulence from Indian raids, lack of stable local government, and apparent lack of concern from national and state governments, Tennesseeans wanted to govern themselves. In 1788 North Carolina ceded its claim to the area to the new federal government. Two years later, Congress established the Territory South of the River Ohio, commonly called the Southwest Territory; and Tennessee became the sixteenth state in 1796.

Via rivers and trails and through the Cumberland Gap, settlers flocked into Tennessee, especially from the Carolinas and Virginia. For several decades, considerable numbers came also from Georgia, Kentucky, Maryland, and Pennsylvania. Indian land cessions and forced removal had opened all of Tennessee to white settlement by the 1830s.

© PhotoDisc / Getty Images

TENNESSEE AT A GLANCE

Motto: Agriculture and Commerce

Population: 5.7 million

Prevalent Religions: Christianity, particularly Pentecostals, Southern Baptists, and a few Roman Catholics

Major Industries: Soybeans, cotton, tobacco, livestock and livestock products, dairy products, cattle, hogs, chemicals, transportation equipment, rubber, plastics

Ethnic Makeup (in percent): Caucasian 80.2%, African American 16.4%, Hispanic 2.2%, Asian 1.0%, Native American 0.3%, Other 1.0%

Famous Tennesseans: James Agee, Chet Atkins, Davy Crockett, Morgan Freeman, Tennessee Ernie Ford, Aretha Franklin, Nikki Giovanni, Al Gore, Isaac Hayes, Benjamin L. Hooks, Dolly Parton, Minnie Pearl, Wilma Rudolph, Cybill Shepherd, Dinah Shore, Tina Turner

Above: The Pioneer Farmstead in the Great Smoky Mountains

Farmers and planters introduced tobacco and cotton culture, often with slave labor, while the Mississippi, Cumberland, and Tennessee Rivers encouraged river commerce. By 1860 Tennessee had over one million residents, of whom 25 percent were slaves, less than 1 percent were free blacks, and nearly 2 percent were foreign-born.

Tennessee seceded after hostilities began in 1861, sent soldiers to both sides during the Civil War, and saw numerous military engagements on its soil. The Union army occupied much of the state during the first year of the war and virtually all of the state by 1863. In 1866, without going through Reconstruction but impoverished like the rest of the South, Tennessee was the first former Confederate state readmitted to the Union. Until the 1940s the state remained largely agricultural, dedicated to cotton and tobacco, but with growing industries for food, wood, textile, mineral, and chemical products. By 1960, the urban population surpassed the rural with 52 percent of the state's total.

RECORD HIGHLIGHTS

More than fifty Tennessee counties have lost some records in fires or storms. County-by-county lists of the disasters and their effect on records are online at the state archives Web site, <www.state.tn.us/sos/statelib/pubsvs/intro.htm>, along with numerous indexes and information about other holdings. Courthouse disasters rarely destroy all records. Therefore, investigate surviving county materials, resources of parent and neighboring counties, and family, local, state, and federal records.

Tennessee first tried statewide birth and death registration between 1908 and 1912, but some counties and cities have nineteenth-century records. For information on pre-1908 records and death, marriage, and divorce records more than fifty years old, see <www.state.tn.us/sos/statelib/pubsvs/vital3.htm>. The state Department of Health <www2.state.tn.us/health/vr/> holds birth records from 1914 and death, marriage, and divorce records less than fifty years old. Usually, county clerks hold marriage records dating from the formation of their counties. Although county circuit courts have handled divorces since 1834, the legislature had jurisdiction to grant divorces until 1834. Birth and death indexes and records, 1908–1912, and death records, 1914–1950, are available on microfilm from the Family History Library; there are no records for 1913.

Other Tennessee-specific records of genealogical value include these:

- Several series of the Draper Manuscripts, especially series XX, Tennessee Papers, housed at the State Historical Society of Wisconsin and on microfilm at research libraries
- *Territorial Papers of the United States* and *Territorial Papers of the U.S. Senate* for the Territory South of the River Ohio
- Confederate pensions; index to applications for pensions and the Confederate Soldiers Home, and list of Tennessee Confederate physicians at <www.state.tn.us/sos/statelib/pubsvs/intro.htm> under military records; pension index and applications available on microfilm from the Family History Library
- Civil War Veterans Questionnaires, 1914–1920, at the Tennessee State Library and Archives; compiled into 5 volumes by Gustavus W. Dyer and John Trotwood Moore, published by the Southern Historical Press in 1985; online index at <www.state.tn.us/sos/statelib/pubsvs/quest.htm>
- County tax lists; list of existing records, by county, available at the state archives, <www.state.tn.us/sos/statelib/pubsvs/taxlist.htm>
- School censuses, various counties, most from the twentieth century; online list at <www.state.tn.us/sos/statelib/pubsvs/school.htm>
- Records of depositors in Tennessee's two branches of the Freedman's Savings and Trust Company (FHL microfilm 928590)
- 1869 and 1897 censuses of Memphis (FHL microfilm 375237)

STATE RESOURCES

■ ARCHIVES, LIBRARIES, AND SOCIETIES

Bedford County Historical Society
624 S. Brittain St., Shelbyville, TN 37160

Blount County Genealogical and Historical Society
P.O. Box 4986, Maryville, TN 37902-4986

Blount County Library
509 N. Cusick St., Maryville, TN 37804
Tel: (865) 982-0981

Bradley County Genealogical Society
P.O. Box 1384, Cleveland, TN 37364-1384

Campbell County Historical Society
101 Sixth St., LaFollette, TN 37766

Carroll County Library
625 High St., Huntingdon, TN 38344
Tel: (731) 986-1919

Chattanooga-Hamilton County Bicentennial Library, Local History and Genealogy Dept.
1001 Broad St. Chattanooga, TN 37402
Tel: (423) 757-5317

Cheatham County Historical and Genealogical Association
P.O. Box 703, Ashland city, TN 37015
Web site: <www.rootsweb.com/~tncchga>

Claiborne County Historical and Genealogical Society
P.O. Box 32, Tazewell, TN 37879
Web site: <www.rootsweb.com/~tnccths>

Cleveland Public Library History Branch
833 N. Ocoee St., Cleveland, TN 37311
Tel: (423) 479-8367

Clinton, Pellissippi Genealogical and Historical Society
% Clinton Public Library, Anderson County, 118 S. Hicks, Clinton, TN 37716

Coffee County Historical Society
P.O. Box 524, Manchester, TN 37355

Crossville, Art Circle Public Library
154 E. First St., Crossville, TN 38555
Tel: (931) 484-6790

Dandridge Memorial Library
1235 Circle Dr., P.O. Box 339, Dandridge, TN 37725
Tel: (865) 397-9758

Dayton, Clyde W. Roddy Library
371 First Ave., Dayton, TN 37321
Tel: (423) 775-8406

Delta Genealogical Society (NW Georgia, NE Alabama, SE Tennessee)
504 McFarland Ave., Rossville, GA 30741-1255
Web site: <www.rootsweb.com/~gadgs/index.htm>

Disciples of Christ Historical Society
1101 Nineteenth Ave. S., Nashville, TN 37212
Tel: (615) 327-1444
Fax: (615) 327-1445

East Tennessee Historical Society
500 W. Church Ave., Knoxville, TN 37902-2505

Fayetteville-Lincoln County Public Library
400 Rocky Knob Lane, Fayetteville, TN 37334
Tel: (931) 433-3286

Fentress County Genealogical Society
P.O. Box 178, Jamestown, TN 38556

Franklin County Historical Society
P.O. Box 130, Winchester, TN 37398

Giles County Historical Society
P.O. Box 693, Pulaski, TN 38478

Greene County Genealogical Society
P.O. Box 1903, Greeneville, TN 37744

Hamblen County Genealogical Society
P.O. Box 1213, Morristown, TN 37816-1213

Hancock County Historical & Genealogical Society
P.O. Box 307, Sneedville, TN 37869
Web site: <www.kornet.org/overhome/page3.html>

Hawkins County Genealogical and Historical Society
P.O. Box 429, Rogersville, TN 37857-3424

Hendersonville Genealogy Friends
P.O. Box 863, Hendersonville, TN 37077

Henry County Genealogical Society of Tennessee
P.O. Box 1411, Paris, TN 38242

Highland Rim Regional Library Center
2118 E. Main St., Murfreesboro, TN 37130
Tel: (615) 893-3380
Fax: (615) 895-6727
Web site: <http://state.tn.us/sos/statelib/ptd/highrim/index.htm>

Jackson-Madison County Library
433 E. Lafayette, Jackson, TN 38301
Tel: (731) 425-8600

Jefferson County Genealogical Society
P.O. Box 267, Jefferson City, TN 37760

Jonesborough Genealogical Society
% Washington County-Jonesborough Library, 200 Sabine Dr., Jonesborough, TN 37659

Kingsport Public Library & Archives
J. Fred Johnson Memorial Library, 400 Broad St., Kingsport, TN 37660-4208

Tel: (423) 224-2559
Fax: (423) 224-2558
Web site: <www.kingsportlibrary.org>

Knox County-Lawson McGhee Library
500 W. Church Ave., Knoxville, TN 37902-2505
Tel: (865) 215-8750
Fax: (865) 215-8742

Lambuth University, Memphis Conference United Methodist Archives
Luther L. Gobbel Library, 705 Lambuth Blvd., Jackson, TN 38301
Tel: (731) 425-3290

Lawrence County Genealogical Society
218 N. Military Ave., Suite B-1, Lawrenceburg, TN 38464

Lincoln County Genealogical Society
1508 W. Washington St., Fayetteville, TN 37334

Macon County Historical Society
P.O. Box 231, Lafayette, TN 37083
Web site: <www.rootsweb.com/~tnmchs>

Marion County Genealogical Group
6611 Old Dunlap Rd., Whitewell, TN 37397

Marshall County, Tennessee Historical Society
224 Third Ave. N., Lewisburg, TN 37091

Maury County Historical Society
P.O. Box 147, Columbia, TN 38401

Maury County Public Library
211 W. Eighth St., Columbia, TN 38402

McClung Historical Collection and Knox County Archives, East Tennessee History Center
500 W. Church Ave., Knoxville, TN 37902
Tel: (865) 215-8800
E-mail: archives@knoxlib.org
Web site: <www.knoxcounty. org/library/history.html>

McMinnville, Magness Memorial Library
118 W. Main St., McMinnville, TN 37110
Tel: (931) 473-2428

Memphis/Shelby County Public Library and Information Center
3030 Poplar Ave., Memphis, TN 38111-3527
Tel: (901) 415-2742
Web site: <www.memphislibrary. org/history/index.html>

Middle Tennessee Genealogical Society
P.O. Box 190625, Nashville, TN 37219-0625

Mid-West Tennessee Genealogical Society
P.O. Box 3343, Jackson, TN 38301

Morgan County Genealogical and Historical Society
Rt. 2, Box 992, Wartburg, TN 37887

Morristown-Hamblen Library
417 W. Main St., Morristown, TN 37814
Tel: (423) 586-6410

Mount Juliet Public Library
P.O. Box 319, 2765 N. Mt. Juliet Rd., Mt. Juliet, TN 37122
Tel: (615) 758-7051

Mount Juliet-West Wilson County Historical Society
P.O. box 337, Mt. Juliet, TN 37122
Web site: <www.rootsweb.com/ ~tngenny1/mtjuliet.html>

Mt. Pleasant Public Library
200 Hay Long Ave., P.O. Box 71, Mt. Pleasant, TN 38474
Tel: (931) 379-3752

Nashville & Davidson County Public Library, Special Collections
615 Church St., Nashville, TN 37219
Tel: (615) 862-5782
Web site: <www.library.nashville. org/Library/Depts/Nashroom .html>

National Archives and Federal Record Center Southeast Region (Atlanta)
1557 St. Joseph Ave., East Point, GA 30344
Tel: (404) 763-7477
Fax: (404) 763-7477
Web site: <www.archives.gov/fa cilities/ga/atlanta.html>

Obion County Genealogical Society
P.O. Box 241, Union City, TN 38261

Old James County Historical Society
P.O. Box 203, Ooltewah, TN 37363

Polk County Historical & Genealogical Society Library
P.O. Box 636, Benton, TN 37307-0636
Tel: (423) 338-1005

Roane County Genealogical Society
P.O. Box 297, Kingston, TN 37763-0297

Rogersville, H.B. Stamps Memorial Library
407 E. Main St., Rogersville, TN 37857
Tel: (423) 272-8710

Signal Mountain Genealogical Society, Inc.
103 Florida Ave., Signal Mountain, TN 37377

Southern Baptist Historical Library and Archives
901 Commerce, Suite 400, Nashville, TN 37203
Tel: (615) 224-0344
Web site: <www.sbhla.org>

Sumner County Archives
155 E. Main St., Gallatin, TN 37066
Tel: (615) 452-0037

Tennessee Department of Health
425 Fifth Ave., North Cordell Hull Building, 3d Floor, Nashville, TN 37247
Tel: (800) 852-2187
E-mail: TN.health@state.tn.us
Web site: <www.state.tn.us/hea lth/>

Tennessee Genealogical Society and Library
9114 Davies Plantation Rd., P.O. Box 247, Brunswick, TN 38014
Tel: (901) 381-1447
Web site: <www.rootsweb.com/ ~tngs/>

Tennessee State Library and Archives
403 Seventh Ave. N., Nashville, TN 37243-0312
Tel: (615) 741-2764
Fax: (615) 741-6471
E-mail: reference.tsla@state .tn.us
Web site: <www.state.tn.us/ sos/statelib>

Trousdale County Historical Society
4233 Green Grove Rd., Hartsville, TN 37074

Union County Historical Society, Inc.
P.O. Box 95, Maynardville, TN 37807

University of Memphis, McWherter Library
Special Collections Dept., 126 Ned R. McWherter Library, Campus Box 526500, Memphis, TN 38152-3250

Tennessee

Tel: (901) 678-2210
Fax: (901) 678-8218
Web site: <exlibris.memphis.
edu/about/depts/special/
index.html>

**University of Tennessee,
Knoxville, Hoskins Library**
1401 Cumberland Ave., Special
Collections, Room 200, Knox-
ville, TN 37996-4000
Tel: (865) 974-4480
Fax: (865) 974-0560
E-mail: special@aztec.lib.utk.edu
Web site: <www.lib.utk.edu/spc
oll/>

**Upper Cumberland
Genealogical Association**
Putnam County Library, P.O. Box
575, Cookeville, TN 38503-0575
Web site: <www.rootsweb.com/
~tnucga>

**Van Buren County Historical
Society**
P.O. Box 126, Spencer, TN 38585

**Vanderbilt University, Special
Collections and University
Archives, Heard Library**
419 Twenty-first Ave. S., Nash-
ville, TN 37240
Tel: (615) 322-2407
Fax: (615) 343-8279
E-mail: archives@vanderbilt.edu
Web site: <www.library.vanderbil
t.edu>

**Vardy Community Historical
Society**
P.O. Box 554, Sneedville, TN
37869
Web site: <hometown.aol.com/
vardyvalley/index.html

**Watauga Association of
Genealogists, Northeast
Tennessee**
P.O. Box 117, Johnson City, TN
37605-0117
Web site: <www.rootsweb.com/
~tnwag>

**Weakley County Genealogical
Society**
P.O. Box 92, Martin, TN 38237

**White County Genealogical-
Historical Society**
P.O. Box 721, Sparta, TN
38583-0721

**Williamson County Public
Library**
Special Collections Dept., 1314
Columbia Ave., Franklin, TN
37064

Tel: (615) 595-1246
Web site: <http://lib.williamson-
tn.org/gen.htm>

BIBLIOGRAPHY

■ GENERAL RESOURCES

*African-American Genealogy: A
Bibliography and Guide to
Sources*
by Curt Bryan Witcher (Fort
Wayne, IN: Round Tower Books,
2000. Includes white families'
papers)

*Bible Records of Families of
East Tennessee and Their
Connections From Other Areas,
4 vols.*
compiled by Adele Weiss Sneed
(Tennessee: Knoxville Chapter of
the Daughters of the American
Colonists and James White Chapter of the Daughters of the American Revolution, 1959–63)

*Check List of Tennessee
Imprints, 1841–1850*
from the Historical Records Survey (Nashville: Tennessee Historical Records Survey, 1941)

*The Civil and Political History of
the State of Tennessee: From
It's Earliest Settlement Up to
the Year 1796 . . .*
by John Haywood and A.S. Colyar
(Originally published in 1891; Reprint: Johnson City, TN: Overmountain Press, 1999)

*Early Times in Middle
Tennessee*
by John Carr (Nashville: Parthenon Press, 1958)

East Tennessee Tax Lists
compiled by Mary Barnett Curtis
(Fort Worth, TX: Arrow Printing
Co., 1964)

*The Genealogist's Companion
and Sourcebook, 2d ed.*
by Emily Anne Croom (Cincinnati:
Betterway Books, 2003)

*A Genealogist's Guide to
Discovering Your African-
American Ancestors*
by Franklin Carter Smith and
Emily Anne Croom (Cincinnati:
Betterway Books, 2003)

*Guide to County Records and
Genealogical Resources in
Tennessee*
by Richard Carlton Fulcher (Balti-
more: Genealogical Publishing
Co., 1987)

RESEARCH TIPS

for more info

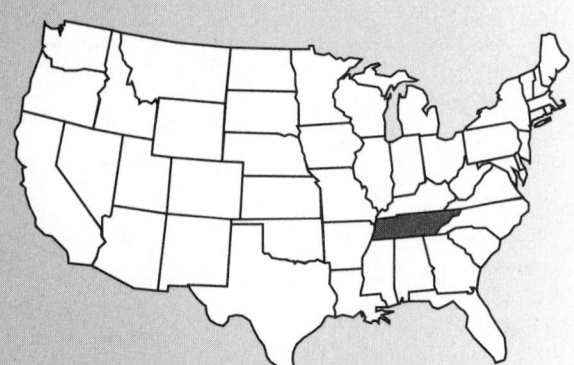

- Substitutes cannot fully replace lost census
  schedules, but tax lists and other contemporary
  records can help identify early residents. Partial
  substitutes for the lost 1890 census are the
  1891 enumerations of males over twenty-one,
  available for most counties, at the state archives
  and on microfilm elsewhere.
- Although Tennessee was briefly a territory, it is
  not a federal land state. However, some North
  Carolina Revolutionary veterans or their heirs received bounty land in the state.
- Because Tennessee was considered an off-shoot
  of North Carolina, people reporting they were born
  in North Carolina before 1796 might have been
  born in what is now Tennessee.
- The Tennessee State Library and Archives participates in interlibrary loan of some materials. See
  <www.state.tn.us/sos/statelib/pubsvs/
  mailill.htm> for information.
- Visit <www.gbmuseum.tn.org/books/GEN_HIST
  .htm> and <www.state.tn.us/sos/statelib/pub
  svs/#tn_bibliographies> for extensive Tennessee bibliographies.

Census Records
- Federal Census Population Schedules: 1810
  (Rutherford and Grainger Counties Only), 1820
  (26 counties), 1830, 1840, 1850, 1860, 1870,
  1880, 1900, 1910, 1920, 1930
- Federal Census Soundex: 1880, 1900, 1910,
  1920, 1930
- Federal Mortality Schedules: 1850, 1860, 1880
- Federal Slave Schedules: 1850, 1860 (Schedules
  name slaveholders but rarely name slaves.)
- Special Census of Civil War Union Veterans and
  Widows: 1890

Guide to Genealogical Research in the National Archives of the United States
edited by Anne Bruner Eales and Robert M. Kvasnicka (Washington, DC: National Archives and Records Administration, 2000)

Guide to Microfilmed Manuscript Holdings of the Tennessee State Library and Archives, 3d ed.
(Nashville: Tennessee State Library and Archives, 1983)

A History of Tennessee and Tennesseans, 8 vols.
by William T. Hale and Dixon L. Merritt (Chicago: Lewis Publishing Co., 1913)

Inventory of the Church Archives of Tennessee
from the Historical Records Survey (Nashville: Historical Records Survey, WPA, 1939)

List of Tennessee Imprints, 1793–1840, in Tennessee Libraries
from the Historical Records Survey (Nashville: Tennessee Historical Records Survey, 1941)

National Archives Microfilm Catalogs online:
<www.archives.gov/publications/genealogy_microfilm_catalogs.html>

Notable Men of Tennessee: Personal and Genealogical, With Portraits, 2 vols.
by John Roy V. Allison (Atlanta: Southern Historical Association, 1905)

"Research in Tennessee"
by Gale Williams Baumann (*National Genealogical Society Quarterly* 81, June 1993: 99-125)

Sketches of Prominent Tennesseans
by William S. Speer (Originally published in 1888; Reprint: Baltimore: Genealogical Publishing Co., 2003)

"Tennessee"
by James R. Johnson (in *Genealogical Research: Methods and Sources*. Kenn Stryker-Rodda, ed. Vol. 2. Rev. ed. Washington, DC: The American Society of Genealogists, 1983)

Tennessee County Records Manual
(Nashville: Tennessee State Library and Archives, 1968)

Tennessee Cousins: A History of Tennessee People
by Worth Stickley Ray (Originally published in 1950; Reprint: Baltimore: Genealogical Publishing Co., 2002)

Tennessee Genealogical Records: Records Of Early Settlers from State and County Archives
compiled by Edythe Rucker Whitley (Baltimore: Genealogical Publishing Co., 1989)

Tennessee Genealogical Research
by George K. Schweitzer (Knoxville: George K. Schweitzer, 1986)

Tennessee History: A Bibliography
compiled and edited by Sam B. Smith (Knoxville: University of Tennessee Press, 1974)

Tennessee Newspapers: A Cumulative List of Microfilmed Tennessee Newspapers in the Tennessee State Library
(Nashville: Tennessee State Library and Archives, 1978)

Tennessee Research Outline
(Salt Lake City, UT: Corp. of the President of the Church of Jesus Christ of L.D.S., 1988)

Tennessee: A Short History, 2d ed.
by Robert Ewing Corlew, Stanley John Folmsbee, and Enoch L. Mitchell (Knoxville: University of Tennessee Press, 1990)

Tennessee, the Volunteer State, 1760–1923, 4 vols.
by John Trotwood Moore and Austin P. Foster (Chicago: S.J. Clark Publishing Co., 1923)

Timeless Tennesseans
by James Andrew Crutchfield (Huntsville, AL: Strode Publishers, 1984)

■ CENSUS RECORDS

The American Census Handbook
by Thomas Jay Kemp (Wilmington, DE: Scholarly Resources, Inc., 2001)

The Census Book: A Genealogist's Guide to Federal Census Facts, Schedules and Indexes
by William Dollarhide (Bountiful, UT: Heritage Quest, 1999)

Eastern Cherokees: A Census of the Cherokee Nation in North Carolina, Tennessee, Alabama and Georgia in 1851
by David W. Siler (Cottonport, LA: Polyanthos, 1972)

Map Guide to the U.S. Federal Censuses, 1790–1920
by William Thorndale and William Dollarhide (Baltimore: Genealogical Publishing Co., 1987)

State Census Records
by Ann S. Lainhart (Baltimore: Genealogical Publishing Co., Inc., 1992)

Your Guide to the Federal Census
by Kathleen W. Hinckley (Cincinnati: Betterway Books, 2002)

■ IMMIGRATION RECORDS

American Naturalization Records, 1790–1990: What They Are and How to Use Them
by John J. Newman (North Salt Lake, UT: HeritageQuest, 1998)

American Passenger Arrival Records
by Michael Tepper (Baltimore: Genealogical Publishing Co., 1993)

They Became Americans: Finding Naturalization Records and Ethnic Origins
by Loretto Dennis Szucs (Salt Lake City: Ancestry, Inc., 1998)

They Came in Ships: A Guide to Finding Your Immigrant Ancestor's Arrival Records, 2d ed.
by John P. Colletta (Salt Lake City: Ancestry, Inc., 1993)

■ LAND RECORDS

Earliest Tennessee Land Records & Earliest Tennessee Land History
by Irene M. Griffey (Baltimore: Clearfield Co., 2003)

The Hidden Revolutionary War Land Grants in the Tennessee Military Reservation
by Shirley Hollis Rice (Lawrenceburg, TN: Family Tree Press, 1992)

Locating Your Roots: Discover Your Ancestors Using Land Records
by Patricia Law Hatcher (Cincinnati: Betterway Books, 2003)

North Carolina Land Grants in Tennessee, 1778–1791, Rev. ed.
compiled by Goldene F. Burgner and Betty Goff Cook Cartwright (Greenville, SC: Southern Historical Press, 1990)

Tennessee Land: Its Early History and Laws
by Billie R. McNamara (Knoxville, TN: B.R. McNamara, 1997)

Tennessee Land Entries: John Armstrong's Office, 2 vols.
by Albert Bruce Pruitt (Whitakers, NC: A. Bruce Pruitt, 1995)

Tennessee Land Entries: Military Bounty Land Warrents, Martin Armstrong's Office, 7 vols.
by Albert Bruce Pruitt (Whitakers, NC: A. Bruce Pruitt, 1996)

Tennessee Land Grants. Surnames A-Z, 17 vols. and cross index
by Barbara Sistler, Byron Sistler, and Samuel Sistler (Nashville: B. Sistler and Associates, 1997–1998)

■ MAPS

Atlas of Historical County Boundaries, Tennessee
edited by John H. Long, compiled by Peggy Tuck Sinko (New York: Charles Scribner's Sons, 2000)

Counties of Tennessee
by Austin P. Foster (Originally published 1923; Reprint: Baltimore: Clearfield Co. 1992)

Eastin Morris' Tennessee Gazetteer 1834 and Matthew Rhea's Map of the State Of Tennessee, 1832
edited by Robert M. McBride and Owen Meredith (Nashville: The Gazetteer Press, 1971)

Place Names of Tennessee
by Ralph O. Fullerton (Nashville: Tennessee Department of Conservation, Division of Geology, 1974)

Tennessee Atlas and Gazetteer, 5th ed.
(Freeport, ME: DeLorme Mapping Co., 1995)

Tennessee

Tennessee County Maps
compiled by C.J. Puetz (Lyndon Station, WI: County Maps, 1999)

■ MILITARY RECORDS

1890 Civil War Veterans Census: Tennesseans in Texas
by Byron Sistler and Barbara Sistler (Nashville: B. Sistler and Associates, 1978)

Index to Tennessee Confederate Pension Applications
by Samuel Sistler (Nashville: Byron Sistler, 1995)

Record of Commissions of Officers in the Tennessee Militia, 1796–1815
by Mary Brown Daniel Moore (Baltimore: Genealogical Publishing Co., 1977)

Soldiers of the War of 1812 Buried in Tennessee, Rev. ed.
compiled by Mary Hardin McCown and Inez E. Burns (Johnson City, TN: McCown, 1977)

Some Tennessee Heroes of the Revolution Compiled from Pension Statements
compiled by Zella Armstrong (Baltimore: Clearfield Co., 1989)

Tennesseeans in the Civil War
(Nashville: Civil War Centennial Commission, 1964–1965, 1985)

The Tennessee Civil War Veterans Questionnaires, 5 vols.
by Gustavus Dyer et al. (Easley SC: Southern Historical Press, 1985)

Tennessee Confederate Widows and Their Families: Abstracts of 11,190 Confederate Widows' Applications
by Edna Wiefering and Charles A. Sherrill (Cleveland, TN: Cleveland Public Library, 1992)

Tennessee Soldiers in the Revolution
by Penelope J. Allen (Baltimore: Genealogical Publishing Co., 1996)

Twenty-four Hundred Tennessee Pensioners: Revolution, War of 1812
compiled by Zella Armstrong (Originally published in 1937; Reprint: Baltimore: Genealogical Publishing Co, 1996)

Uncle, We Are Ready! Registering America's Men, 1917–1918: A Guide to Researching World War I Draft Registration Cards
by John J. Newman (North Salt Lake, UT: HeritageQuest, 2001)

U.S. Military Records: A Guide to Federal & State Sources, Colonial America to the Present
by James C. Neagles (Salt Lake City: Ancestry, Inc., 1994)

Volunteers: Tennesseans in the War with Mexico, 2 vols.
by Reid Brock (Chattanooga: Kitchen Table Press, 1986)

World War II: A Family Historian's Guide
by Debra Johnson Knox (Spartanburg, SC: MIE Publishing, 2003)

■ PROBATE RECORDS

Index to Tennessee Wills and Administrations, 1779–1861
by Byron Sistler and Barbara Sistler (Nashville: Byron Sistler & Associates, 1990)

Tennessee Tidbits, 1778–1914, 4 vols.
by Marjorie Hood Fischer and Ruth Blake Burns (Originally published in 1988; Reprint of vols. 2, 4: Bowie, MD: Heritage Books, 1999, 2000)

■ VITAL RECORDS

Early East Tennessee Marriages, 2 vols.
by Byron Sistler and Barbara Sistler (Nashville: Byron Sistler & Associates, 1987)

Early Middle Tennessee Marriages, 2 vols.
by Byron Sistler and Barbara Sistler (Nashville: Byron Sistler and Associates, 1988)

Early West Tennessee Marriages, 2 vols.
by Byron Sistler and Barbara Sistler (Nashville: B. Sistler and Associates, 1989)

Guide to Church Vital Statistics in Tennessee
(Nashville: War Services Section, WPA, 1942)

Marriages from Early Tennessee Newspapers, 1794–1851
by S. Emmett Lucas (Easley, SC: Southern Historical Press, 1978)

Obituaries and Marriage Notices From the Tennessee Baptist: 1844–1862
by Russell Pierce Baker (Easley, SC: Southern Historical Press, 1979)

Obituaries from Tennessee Newspapers
by Jill L. Garrett (Greenville, SC: Southern Historical Press, 1995)

Tennessee Divorces, 1797–1858
by Gale Williams Bamman and Debbie Williams Spers (Originally published in 1985; Reprint: Thorndike, MA: Van Volumes, 1997)

Tennessee Records: Bible Records and Marriage Bonds
by Jeannette T. Acklen (Originally published in 1933; Reprint: Baltimore: Clearfield Co., 2001)

Tennessee Records: Tombstone Inscriptions and Manuscripts, Historical and Biographical
by Jeannette T. Acklen (Originally published in 1933; Reprint: Baltimore: Clearfield Co., 1995)

35,000 Tennessee Marriage Records and Bonds, 1783–1870, 3 vols.
by S. Emmett Lucas and Ella Lee Sheffield (Easley, SC: Southern Historical Press, 1981)

Vital Statistics from Nineteenth Century Tennessee Church Records
by Byron Sistler and Barbara Sistler (Nashville: B. Sistler and Assoc., 1979)

Your Guide to Cemetery Research
by Sharon DeBartolo Carmack (Cincinnati: Betterway Books, 2002)

■ Anderson   6 Nov. 1801
100 N. Main St., Clinton, TN 37716
Phone: (865)457-6228
Web site: www.andersoncountyclerk.com
Parent County: Knox, Grainger
Comments/research tips: Clerk of Circuit Court has Divorce records 1947–1951. TSLA (Tennessee State Library and Archives) has Birth and Death records.

Record Type	Year Begun	Jurisdiction
Land	1802	Registrar/Deeds
Marriage	1838	County Clerk
Probate	1830	County Clerk
Court	1811	County Clerk

■ Bedford   31 Dec. 1807
1 Public Sq., Shelbyville, TN 37160
Phone: (931)684-1921
Web site: www.shelbyvilletn.com
Parent County: Rutherford
Comments/research tips: County Clerk has Marriage records 1861–1987 and Probate records 1861–1988. Registrar of Deeds has Military Discharge records 1919–1988. Courthouse destroyed by fire in 1863.

Record Type	Year Begun	Jurisdiction
Land	1808	Registrar/Deeds
Birth	1949	Dept./Health
Divorce	na	Clerk/Circuit Ct.
Court	1840	Clerk/Circuit Ct.

■ Benton   19 Dec. 1835
Court Sq., Camden, TN 38320
Phone: (901)584-6053
Web site: www.tngenweb.org/benton/

Parent County: Henry, Humphreys
Comments/research tips: County Clerk has Birth and Death records 1881–1882 and 1900–1901.

Record Type	Year Begun	Jurisdiction
Birth	1914	TN Vital Record
Death	1914	TSLA
Marriage	1838	County Clerk
Divorce	na	Clerk/Circuit Ct.
Land	1836	Registrar/Deeds
Probate	1836	County Court Clerk
Circuit Court	1836	Clerk/Circuit Ct.

■ Bledsoe 30 Nov. 1807

127 Hwy. N. Courthouse St., P.O. Box 149, Pikeville, TN 37367
Phone: (423)447-2137
Web site: www.tngenweb.org/bledsoe/
Parent County: Roane
Comments/research tips: Courthouse burned 9 December 1909. Birth and Death records held by state.

Record Type	Year Begun	Jurisdiction
Court	1845	Clerk/Circuit Ct.
Marriage	1909	County Clerk
Land	1808	Registrar/Deeds
Probate	1909	County Clerk

■ Blount 11 July 1795

345 Court St., Maryville, TN 37804
Phone: (865)273-5800
Web site: www.blounttn.org
Parent County: Knox
Comments/research tips: County Health Department has Birth and Death records 1881–1882, 1908–1912 and 1925–1938.

Record Type	Year Begun	Jurisdiction
Court	1852	Clerk/Circuit Ct.
Marriage	1795	County Clerk
Divorce	na	Clerk & Master
Land	1795	Registrar/Deeds
Probate	1795	County Clerk

■ Bradley 10 Feb. 1836

155 N. Ocoee St., P.O. Box 846 (37364-0846), Cleveland, TN 37311
Phone: (423)476-0520
Web site: www.bradleyco.net/
Parent County: Cherokee Indian Lands
Comments/research tips: Courthouse records destroyed by fire in November 1864. Cleveland Public Library has early Birth, Court, Census, Land, Probate, Marriage, and Death records. County Clerk has Birth records 1908–1912, Death records 1908–1912 and 1914–1925, and Marriage records 1864–1912 and 1914–1957.

Record Type	Year Begun	Jurisdiction
Divorce	1864	Clerk & Master
Land	1862	Registrar/Deeds
Probate	1859	Clerk & Master
Court	1838	Clerk/Circuit Ct.
Military	1864	Registrar/Deeds

■ Campbell 11 Sep. 1806

195 Kentucky St., Jacksboro, TN 37757
Phone: (423)562-3496
Web site: www.rootsweb.com/~tncampbe/
Parent County: Anderson, Claiborne
Comments/research tips: Registrar of Deeds has Land records 1806–1986 and Military Discharge records 1919–1974. County Clerk has Marriage records 1838–1986. Clerk & Master has Probate records 1806–1841 and 1848–1983.

■ Cannon 31 Jan. 1836

County Courthouse, Woodbury, TN 37190
Phone: (615)563-4278
Web site: www.cafes.net/jlewis/cannon.htm
Parent County: Warren, Rutherford, Smith, Wilson
Comments/research tips: Clerk of Circuit Court has Court records 1840–1987. Registrar of Deeds has Land records 1836–1985 and Military Discharge records 1917–1987. County Clerk has Marriage records 1838–1989. Clerk & Master has Probate records 1836–1926, 1935–1970, and 1974–1987. Birth and Death records held by state.

■ Carroll 7 Nov. 1821

625 High St., P.O. Box 110, Huntingdon, TN 38344
Phone: (731)986-1960
Web site: www.rootsweb.com/~tncarrol/
Parent County: Chickasaw Indian Lands
Comments/research tips: County Clerk has Marriage records 1838–1986. Chancery Court Clerk has Divorce records 1826–1900. Registrar of Deeds has Land records 1822–1989 and Military Discharge records 1919–1988. Clerk & Master has Probate records 1822–1986. Microfilm copies of earlier records (except Birth and Death) are archived at the Gordon Browning Museum.

Record Type	Year Begun	Jurisdiction
Court	1839	County Clerk

■ Carter 9 Apr. 1796

801 E. Elk Ave., Elizabethton, TN 37643
Phone: (423)542-1814
Web site: www.netvaly.org/carter.htm
Parent County: Washington
Comments/research tips: County Clerk has Birth and Death records 1907–1962 and Marriage records 1790–1993. Chancery & Circuit Court has Court records 1848–2000. Registrar of Deeds has Land records 1796–1976 and Military Discharge records 1920–1976. County or Chancery Court has Probate records 1794–1985.

Record Type	Year Begun	Jurisdiction
Divorce	na	Chancery & Circuit Court

■ Cheatham 28 Feb. 1856

100 Public Sq., Ashland City, TN 37015
Phone: (615)792-5179
Web site: www.cheathamcounty.net/
Parent County: Davidson, Dickson, Montgomery, Robertson
Comments/research tips: County Clerk has Birth records 1881–1882 and 1908–1912, Death records 1881–1882,

1908–1912 and 1925–1941, and Marriage records 1856–1996. Clerk of Circuit Court has Court records 1877–1996. Chancery Clerk has Marriage records 1856–1996 and Probate records 1856–1994. Registrar of Deeds has Land records 1856–1996 and Military Discharge records 1919–1997.

■ Chester 1879
159 E. Main St., Henderson, TN 38340
Phone: (731)989-2233
Web site: www.rootsweb.com/~tncheste/chester.htm
Parent County: Hardeman, Madison, Henderson, McNairy
Comments/research tips: Clerk of Circuit Court has Court records 1882–1993. Registrar of Deeds has Land records 1891–1994 and Military Discharge records 1945–1987. County Clerk has Marriage records 1891–1994. Chancery Court Clerk has Probate records 1891–1990.

Record Type	Year Begun	Jurisdiction
Divorce	na	Clerk/Chancery Ct.

■ Claiborne 29 Oct. 1801
P.O. Box 173, Tazewell, TN 37879
Phone: (423)626-3283
Web site: www.claibornecounty.com
Parent County: Grainger, Hawkins
Comments/research tips: Clerk of Circuit Court has Court and Divorce records 1837–1842 and 1916–1994. Registrar of Deeds has Land records 1801–1994 and Military Discharge records 1919–1996. County Clerk has Marriage records 1838–1995. Chancery Court Clerk has Probate records 1812–1992.

■ Clay 24 June 1870
100 Courthouse Sq., Celina, TN 38551
Phone: (931)243-2249
Web site: www.tngenweb.org/clay/
Parent County: Jackson, Overton
Comments/research tips: County Clerk has Birth and Death records 1908–1912. TSLA has Death records 1908–1949. Registrar of Deeds has Military Discharge records 1919–1995.

Record Type	Year Begun	Jurisdiction
Marriage	1871	County Clerk
Divorce	1871	County Clerk
Land	1871	Registrar/Deeds
Probate	1871	County Clerk
Court	1871	Clerk/Circuit Ct.
Birth	1914	TN Vital Record

■ Cocke 9 Oct. 1797
111 Court Ave., Newport, TN 37821
Phone: (423)623-6176
Web site: www.rootsweb.com/~tncocke/Index.html
Parent County: Jefferson
Comments/research tips: County Clerk has Birth records 1909–1911 and 1925–1938, Death records 1909–1911 and 1926–1938, and Marriage records 1877–1994. Clerk of Circuit Court has Court records 1877–1993. Clerk & Master has Divorce records 1886–1899 and Probate records

1877–1996. Registrar of Deeds has Land records 1865–1996. Stokely Memorial Library has Birth records 1908–1912 and 1925–1938, records of all county courts, probate, deed, etc. Some records were lost in courthouse fire 31 Dec. 1876.

■ Coffee 8 Jan. 1836
300 Hillsboro Blvd., P.O. Box 8, Manchester, TN 37355
Phone: (931)723-5106
Web site: www.cafes.net/jlewis/
Parent County: Franklin, Warren, Bedford
Comments/research tips: TSLA has Birth records 1881–1882 and 1908–1912. Clerk of Circuit Court has Court records 1852–1988. Registrar of Deeds has Land records 1836–1973 and Military Discharge records 1919–1988. County Clerk has Marriage records 1853–1989 and Probate records 1836–1987. Birth and Death records held by TSLA and TN vital records.

Record Type	Year Begun	Jurisdiction
Divorce	na	Clerk/Circuit Ct.

■ Crockett 1872
1 S. Bells St., Alamo, TN 38001
Phone: (731)696-5452
Web site: www.rootsweb.com/~tncrocke/
Parent County: Dyer, Madison, Gibson, Haywood
Comments/research tips: County Clerk has Birth and Death records 1908–1911 and 1925–1938, Marriage records 1872–1987, and Probate records 1872–1980. Clerk of Circuit Court has Court records 1872–1986. Registrar of Deeds has Land records 1872–1980 and Military Discharge records 1917–1970. Many early Census records of residents of Crockett County can be found in surrounding counties. Crockett County formed and dissolved several times between 20 December 1845 and 1872.

Record Type	Year Begun	Jurisdiction
Divorce	1872	County Clerk

■ Cumberland 16 Nov. 1855
2 N. Main St., Crossville, TN 38555
Phone: (931)484-6442
Web site: www.upper-cumberland.net/users/mboniol/
Parent County: Bledsoe, Morgan, Roane, White, Rhea, Van Buren, Putnam
Comments/research tips: Clerk of Circuit Court has Court records 1907–1995. Registrar of Deeds has Land records 1855–1969 and Military Discharge records 1920–1992. County Clerk has Marriage records 1905–1996. Clerk & Master has Probate records 1905–1997. Cumberland Courthouse fire of 1905 destroyed many early records except deeds. The Art Circle Public Library has census, marriages, land records, court and probate records, birth and state records.

Record Type	Year Begun	Jurisdiction
Divorce	na	Clerk/Master/Circuit Ct.

■ Davidson 18 Apr. 1783
1 Public Sq., Nashville, TN 37201
Phone: (615)862-6251

Web site: www.rootsweb.com/~tndavids/nashgene.htm
Parent County: Washington

Record Type	Year Begun	Jurisdiction
Birth	na	TSLA/TN Vital Rec.
Death	na	TSLA/TN Vital Rec.
Marriage	1789	County Clerk
Divorce	1803	Clerk/Circuit Ct.
Land	1784	Registrar/Deeds
Probate	1783	Probate Court Clerk
Court	1803	Clerk/Circuit Ct.

■ De Kalb   2 Dec. 1837
County Courthouse, Room 205, Smithville, TN 37166
Phone: (615)597-5177
Web site: www.tngenweb.org/dekalb/
Parent County: Cannon, Warren, White, and Smith
Comments/research tips: Clerk of Circuit Court has Court and Divorce records 1860–1995. Registrar of Deeds has Military Discharge records 1919–1995. County Clerk has Probate records 1846–1995.

Record Type	Year Begun	Jurisdiction
Marriage	1848	County Clerk
Land	1838	Registrar/Deeds

■ Decatur   Nov. 1845
P.O. Box 488, Decaturville, TN 38329
Phone: (731)852-3417
Web site: www.netease.net/decatur/
Parent County: Perry
Comments/research tips: Clerk of Circuit Court has Court records 1927–1994. Registrar of Deeds has Land records 1846–1995 and Military Discharge records 1943–1994. County Clerk has Marriage records 1869–1990. Clerk/Master has Probate records 1869–1992. In 1927 and on 3 July 1869 fire destroyed the county courthouse and all documents except Registrar of Deeds and Clerk and Masters' records. Birth and Death records are kept by the state at TSLA and TN vital records.

■ Dickson   25 Oct. 1803
4 Court Sq., Charlotte, TN 37036
Phone: (615)789-4171
Web site: www.rootsweb.com/~tndickso/
Parent County: Montgomery, Robertson
Comments/research tips: County Clerk has Birth records 1908–1930, Death records 1908–1939, and Divorce records 1849–1932. Clerk of Circuit Court has Court records 1810–1827 and 1839–1996. Registrar of Deeds has Military Discharge records 1920–1981. Courthouse was destroyed by tornado around 1835, many records were destroyed. County Clerk has Birth and Death records 1908–1912 and 1925–1939.

Record Type	Year Begun	Jurisdiction
Marriage	1817	County Clerk
Land	1804	Registrar/Deeds
Probate	1803	Clerk & Master

■ Dyer   16 Oct. 1823
P.O. Box 1360, Dyersburg, TN 38025
Phone: (731)286-7814

Web site: www.rootsweb.com/~tndyer/
Parent County: Chickasaw Indian Lands
Comments/research tips: County Clerk has Birth and Death records 1908–1912 and Probate records 1850–1976. Registrar of Deeds has Land records 1822–1976 and Military Discharge records 1918–1976.

Record Type	Year Begun	Jurisdiction
Marriage	1860	County Clerk
Divorce	na	Clerk/Circuit Ct.
Court	1863	Clerk/Circuit Ct.

■ Fayette   29 Sep. 1824
1 Court Sq., County Courthouse, Somerville, TN 38068
Phone: (901)465-5213
Web site: www.wdbj.net/fayette/
Parent County: Shelby, Hardeman
Comments/research tips: County Clerk has Birth and Death records 1925–1929 and Marriage records 1838–1917. Registrar of Deeds has Military Discharge records 1943–1988. Marriage records 1918–1925 lost in fire.

Record Type	Year Begun	Jurisdiction
Court	1829	Clerk/Circuit Ct.
Marriage	1926	County Clerk
Land	1825	Registrar/Deeds
Probate	1836	Clerk & Master

■ Fentress   28 Nov. 1823
101 S. Main St., P.O. Box 699, Jamestown, TN 38556
Phone: (931)879-8014
Web site: www.rootsweb.com/~tnfentre/fent.htm
Parent County: Morgan, Overton, White
Comments/research tips: County Clerk has Birth and Death records 1909–1939. For other Birth and Death records see State Archives (TSLA and Vital Records). Registrar of Deeds has Military Discharge records 1943–1972. Many county records were destroyed in courthouse fire of 1905.

Record Type	Year Begun	Jurisdiction
Court	1854	Clerk/Circuit Ct.
Probate	1905	Clerk & Master
Marriage	1905	County Clerk
Land	1820	Registrar/Deeds

■ Franklin   3 Dec. 1807
1 Jefferson St., Winchester, TN 37398
Phone: (931)967-2541
Web site: www.tngenweb.org/franklin/
Parent County: White
Comments/research tips: County Clerk has Birth and Death records 1881–1883 and 1908–1912 and Divorce records 1860–1930. Registrar of Deeds has Military records 1917–1919 and 1944–1987. County boundaries have changed thirteen times since 1807, check neighboring counties for records. Minute books for county court before 1832 have been destroyed or lost. Circuit Court records begin in 1824.

Record Type	Year Begun	Jurisdiction
Marriage	1838	County Clerk
Land	1808	Registrar/Deeds
Probate	1808	Clerk & Master
Court	1832	Clerk/Circuit Ct.

■ **Gibson** 21 Oct. 1823
County Courthouse, P.O. Box 228, Trenton, TN 38382
Phone: (731)855-7639
Web site: www.rootsweb.com/~tngibson/
Parent County: Chickasaw Indian Lands
Comments/research tips: County Clerk has Birth records 1881–1882 and 1909–1911, Death records 1909–1911, and Probate records 1824–1981. Registrar of Deeds has Military Discharge records 1943–1988.

Record Type	Year Begun	Jurisdiction
Marriage	1824	County Clerk
Land	1819	Registrar/Deeds
Court	1824	Clerk/Circuit Ct.

■ **Giles** 14 Nov. 1809
P.O. Box 678, Pulaski, TN 38478
Phone: (931)363-1509
Web site: www.rootsweb.com/~tngiles/
Parent County: Maury
Comments/research tips: County Clerk has Marriage records 1818–1862. Registrar of deeds has Military Discharge records 1919–1990. Courthouse burned 20 April 1907.

Record Type	Year Begun	Jurisdiction
Death	1936	County Clerk
Marriage	1865	County Clerk
Birth	1936	County Clerk
Land	1790	Registrar/Deeds
Probate	1860	County Clerk
Court	1817	Clerk/Circuit Ct.

■ **Grainger** 22 Apr. 1796
County Courthouse, P.O. Box 116, Rutledge, TN 37861
Phone: (865)828-3511
Web site: www.rootsweb.com/~tngraing/
Parent County: Hawkins, Knox
Comments/research tips: County Clerk has Birth and Death records 1908–1912. Registrar of Deeds has Military Discharge records 1943–1982.

Record Type	Year Begun	Jurisdiction
Court	1826	Clerk/Circuit Ct.
Probate	1831	County Clerk
Marriage	1796	County Clerk
Land	1796	Registrar/Deeds

■ **Greene** 18 Apr. 1783
101 S. Main St., Greenville, TN 37743
Phone: (423)798-1768
Web site: www.tngenweb.org/greene
Parent County: Washington
Comments/research tips: County Clerk has Birth and Death records 1908–1912 and 1925–1939 and Probate records 1780–1986. Clerk of Circuit Court has Court records 1809–1986. Registrar of Deeds has Military Discharge records 1865–1882 and 1916–1988. The T. Elmer Cox Library has Marriage, Death, Court, Land, and Probate records.

Record Type	Year Begun	Jurisdiction
Marriage	1780	County Clerk
Land	1785	Registrar/Deeds

■ **Grundy** 29 Jan. 1844
Cumberland St., Altamont, TN 37301
Phone: (931)692-3622
Web site: www.tngenweb.org/grundy/
Parent County: Warren, Franklin
Comments/research tips: County Clerk has Birth and Death records 1908–1912. Clerk of Circuit Court has Court records 1848–1986. Registrar of Deeds has Military Discharge records 1919–1988.

Record Type	Year Begun	Jurisdiction
Marriage	1850	County Clerk
Land	1852	Registrar/Deeds
Probate	1838	County Clerk

■ **Hamblen** 8 June 1870
511 W. Second N. St., Morristown, TN 37814
Phone: (423)586-1993
Web site: www.tngenweb.org/hamblen/
Parent County: Grainger, Jefferson, Greene
Comments/research tips: County Clerk has Birth records 1909–1912 and Death records 1909–1912 and 1925–1939. The Morristown-Hamblen County Library has Hamblen County Census (1830–1880) and Marriage records.

Record Type	Year Begun	Jurisdiction
Marriage	1863	County Clerk
Land	1870	Registrar/Deeds
Probate	1870	County Clerk
Court	1870	Clerk/Circuit Ct.
Military	1919	Registrar of Deeds

■ **Hamilton** 25 Oct. 1819
County Courthouse, Room 201, Chattanooga, TN 37402
Phone: (423)209-6500
Web site: www.hamiltontn.gov/
Parent County: Cherokee Indian Lands and Rhea County

Record Type	Year Begun	Jurisdiction
Divorce	na	Clerk/Circuit Ct.
Land	1796	Registrar/Deeds
Probate	1862	Clerk & Master
Court	1860	Clerk/Circuit Ct.
Military	na	Registrar/Deeds
Birth	1949	Dept./Health
Marriage	1857	County Clerk
Death	1972	Dept./Health

■ **Hancock** 7 Jan. 1844
P.O. Box 347, Sneedville, TN 37869
Phone: (423)733-2519
Web site: www.tngenweb.org/hancock
Parent County: Claiborne, Hawkins
Comments/research tips: Registrar of Deeds has Military Discharge records 1919–1944.

Record Type	Year Begun	Jurisdiction
Marriage	1930	County Clerk
Land	1879	Registrar/Deeds
Probate	1924	County Clerk
Court	1930	Clerk/Circuit Ct.

■ **Hardeman** 16 Oct. 1823
100 N. Main St., Bolivar, TN 38008
Phone: (731)658-3541

Web site: www.rootsweb.com/~tnhardem/
Parent County: Chickasaw Indian Lands and Hardin County
Comments/research tips: County Clerk has Birth and Death records 1828–1939.

Record Type	Year Begun	Jurisdiction
Court	1833	Clerk/Circuit Ct.
Military	1919	Registrar/Deeds
Marriage	1823	County Clerk
Land	1822	Registrar/Deeds
Probate	1824	Clerk & Master

■ **Hardin**   13 Nov. 1819
601 Main St., Savannah, TN 38372
Phone: (901)925-3921
Web site: www.tngenweb.org/hardin
Parent County: Chickasaw Indian Lands
Comments/research tips: County Library has Birth records 1908–1912 and Death records 1908–1912 and 1914–1939. Registrar of Deeds has Military Discharge records 1919–1970.

Record Type	Year Begun	Jurisdiction
Marriage	1863	County Clerk
Land	1835	Registrar/Deeds
Probate	1836	County Clerk
Court	1840	Clerk/Circuit Ct.

■ **Hawkins**   18 Nov. 1786
100 E. Main St., Rogersville, TN 37857
Phone: (423)272-7002
Web site: www.rootsweb.com/~tnhawkin/
Parent County: Sullivan
Comments/research tips: County Clerk has Birth and Death records 1925–1938 and Military Discharge records 1920–1978. Clerk of Circuit Court has Court records 1810–1829.

Record Type	Year Begun	Jurisdiction
Marriage	1789	County Clerk
Land	1787	Registrar/Deeds
Probate	1797	County Clerk
Court	1837	Clerk/Circuit Ct.

■ **Haywood**   3 Nov. 1823
100 N. Washington St., Brownsville, TN 38012
Phone: (731)772-2362
Web site: www.rootsweb.com/~tnhaywoo/
Parent County: Chickasaw Indian Lands
Comments/research tips: County Clerk has Birth and Death records 1881–1882, 1908–1912 and 1937–1939, Divorce records 1941–1965, Marriage records 1859–1986, and Probate records 1826–1983. Clerk of Circuit Court has Court records 1840–1985. Clerk & Master has Divorce records 1860–1936. Registrar of Deeds has Land records 1823–1986 and Military Discharge records 1943–1972.

■ **Henderson**   7 Nov. 1821
17 Monroe St., Lexington, TN 38351
Phone: (731)968-2856
Web site: www.tngenweb.org/henderson/
Parent County: Chickasaw Indian Lands

Comments/research tips: County Clerk has Birth and Death records 1908–1912 and 1925–1938, Marriage records 1893–1991, and Probate records 1895–1986. Clerk of Circuit Court has Court records 1893–1943. Clerk & Master has Divorce records 1896–1950. Registrar of Deeds has Land records 1856–1878, 1880–1884 and 1892–1894, and Military Discharge records 1933–1994. Courthouse burned 1863 and 1895, many county records were lost.

Record Type	Year Begun	Jurisdiction
Land	1895	Registrar/Deeds

■ **Henry**   7 Nov. 1821
100 W. Washington St., Paris, TN 38242
Phone: (731)642-2412
Web site: www.rootsweb.com/~tnhenry/
Parent County: Stewart
Comments/research tips: County Clerk has Birth records 1914–1936, Death records 1925–1939, Marriage records 1838–1987, and Probate records 1822–1987. Clerk of Circuit Court has Court records 1834–1986. Registrar of Deeds has Land records 1822–1986 and Military Discharge records 1864–1978. Rhea Public Library has Birth records 1908–1912 and 1914–1946, Death records 1908–1939 and microfilm copies of Court, Land, and Probate records.

■ **Hickman**   3 Dec. 1807
South Public Sq., Centerville, TN 37033
Phone: (931)729-2621
Web site: www.rootsweb.com/~tnhickma/
Parent County: Dickson
Comments/research tips: County Clerk has Birth and Death records 1908–1912 and 1925–1939, Marriage records 1868–1992, and Probate records 1866–1944. Registrar of Deeds has Military Discharge records 1967–1990. Courthouse burned in 1865, all records were lost. Hickman County Library has Census records for 1850, 1860, 1870, and Marriage records 1865–1907.

Record Type	Year Begun	Jurisdiction
Divorce	na	Clerk & Master
Land	1808	Registrar/Deeds
Court	1841	Clerk/Circuit Ct.

■ **Houston**   23 Jan. 1871
100 Main St., P.O. Box 388, Erin, TN 37061
Phone: (931)289-3141
Web site: www.rootsweb.com/~tnhousto/
Parent County: Dickson, Humphreys, Montgomery
Comments/research tips: County Clerk has Birth records 1881–1882, Marriage records 1871–1991, and Probate records 1869–1994. Clerk of Circuit Court has Court records 1871–1994. Registrar of Deeds has Military Discharge records 1945–1979.

Record Type	Year Begun	Jurisdiction
Land	1871	Registrar/Deeds

■ **Humphreys**   9 Oct. 1809
102 Thompson St., Waverly, TN 37185
Phone: (931)296-7681
Web site: www.tngenweb.org/humphreys/

Parent County: Stewart
Comments/research tips: County Clerk has Birth records 1908–1912 and 1925–1939 and Death records 1908–1912 and 1925–1935. Courthouse burned in 1876 and 1898, many records were lost. Only Land records are complete.

Record Type	Year Begun	Jurisdiction
Court	1898	Clerk/Circuit Ct.
Military	1919	Registrar/Deeds
Marriage	1864	County Clerk
Land	1810	Registrar/Deeds
Probate	1837	County Clerk

■ Jackson   6 Nov. 1801
101 E. Hill Rd., P.O. Box 346, Gainesboro, TN 38562
Phone: (931)268-9212
Web site: www.jacksonco.com
Parent County: Smith County and Indian Lands
Comments/research tips: County Clerk has Death records 1881–1883 and 1909–1912. County, Chancery, and Circuit Courts have Divorce records 1839–1915. Birth records available from TN Vital records and TSLA.

Record Type	Year Begun	Jurisdiction
Court	1839	Clerk/Circuit Ct.
Marriage	1870	County Clerk
Land	1872	Registrar/Deeds
Probate	1872	Clerk & Master

■ James   1871
Parent County: Bradley, Hamilton
Comments/research tips: (See Hamilton) Abolished in 1919 and absorbed into Hamilton County. All James County records are in Hamilton County.

■ Jefferson   11 June 1792
204 W. Main St., Dandridge, TN 37725
Phone: (865)397-2935
Web site: www.tnhillbillie.net/tn/jefferson/index.html
Parent County: Greene, Hawkins
Comments/research tips: County Clerk has Birth records 1881–1882, 1908–1909 and 1925–1939 and Death records 1881–1882 and 1925–1939. Registrar of Deeds has Military Discharge records 1919–1993.

Record Type	Year Begun	Jurisdiction
Marriage	1792	County Clerk
Land	1792	Registrar/Deeds
Probate	1792	County Clerk
Court	1810	Clerk/Circuit Ct.

■ Johnson   2 Jan. 1836
222 Main St., Mountain City, TN 37683
Phone: (423)727-9633
Web site: www.rootsweb.com/~tnjohnso/
Parent County: Carter
Comments/research tips: TSLA and Vital records have Birth and Death records.

Record Type	Year Begun	Jurisdiction
Marriage	1838	County Clerk
Divorce	na	Clerk/Chancery Ct.
Land	1836	Registrar/Deeds

Probate	1836	County Clerk
Court	1836	Clerk/Circuit Ct.

■ Knox   11 June 1792
400 Main St., Knoxville, TN 37902
Phone: (865)215-8800
Web site: www.knoxcounty.org
Parent County: Greene, Hawkins
Comments/research tips: County Archives has Birth and Death records 1881–1913 and Land records 1792–1931. County Archives are at Knoxville Public Library, 300 Main Ave., Knoxville, TN 37902.

Record Type	Year Begun	Jurisdiction
Marriage	1792	County Archives
Divorce	1793	County Archives
Land	1932	Registrar/Deeds
Probate	1792	County Archives
Tax	1806	County Archives
Court	1792	County Archives

■ Lake   24 June 1870
116 S. Court, Tiptonville, TN 38079
Phone: (731)253-7582
Web site: www.ecsis.net/lakecounty/history/
Parent County: Obion
Comments/research tips: County Clerk has Birth and Death records 1925–1939, Marriage records 1883–1953, and Probate records 1871–1975. Clerk of Circuit Court has Court records 1892–1947. Registrar of Deeds has Military Discharge records 1945–1953.

Record Type	Year Begun	Jurisdiction
Divorce	na	Clerk/Chancery/Circuit Ct.
Land	1870	Registrar

■ Lauderdale   24 Nov. 1835
100 Court Sq., Ripley, TN 38063
Phone: (731)635-2561
Web site: www.rootsweb.com/~tnlauder/
Parent County: Dyer, Tipton, Haywood
Comments/research tips: County Clerk has Birth and Death records 1881–1882, 1908–1912 and 1925–1938, Marriage records 1838–1962, and Probate records 1837–1966. Circuit Court has Court records 1836–1956. Registrar of Deeds has Land records 1835–1952 and Military Discharge records 1943–1968. Sugarhill Library has a collection of microfilmed records that includes Census, Marriage, Probate, and Land records.

Record Type	Year Begun	Jurisdiction
Divorce	na	Clerk/Chancery Ct.

■ Lawrence   21 Oct. 1817
240 W. Gaines St., Lawrenceburg, TN 38464
Phone: (931)762-7700
Web site: www.co.lawrence.tn.us
Parent County: Hickman and Indian Lands
Comments/research tips: County Archives has Birth records 1908–1912, Death records 1908–1938, Land records 1818–1909, Marriage records 1818–1838, and Probate records 1829–1847.

Record Type	Year Begun	Jurisdiction
Military	1919	Registrar/Deeds
Court	1826	Clerk/Circuit Ct.
Divorce	na	Clerk/Circuit Ct.
Land	1909	Registrar/Deeds
Probate	1847	County Clerk
Marriage	1866	County Clerk

■ Lewis 23 Dec. 1843

110 N. Park St., Hohenwald, TN 38462
Phone: (931)796-3378
Web site: www.tngenweb.org/lewis/
Parent County: Hickman, Maury, Wayne, Lawrence
Comments/research tips: County Clerk has Birth and Death records 1908–1912. Registrar of Deeds has Military Discharge records 1930–1979. County completely abolished for one year following the Civil War, for that year records will be found in Maury, Lawrence, Hickman, and Wayne Counties.

Record Type	Year Begun	Jurisdiction
Marriage	1847	County Clerk
Divorce	na	Clerk/Circuit Ct.
Land	1844	Registrar/Deeds
Probate	1842	County Clerk
Court	1844	Clerk/Circuit Ct.

■ Lincoln 14 Nov. 1809

112 Main Ave. S., Fayetteville, TN 37334
Phone: (931)433-2454
Web site: www.rootsweb.com/~tnlincol/
Parent County: Bedford
Comments/research tips: County Clerk has Birth records 1881–1883 and Probate records 1809–1986. County Archives has Court records 1855–1940. Fayetteville-Lincoln Public Library has Death records 1908–1912 and 1914–1926. Registrar of Deeds has Military Discharge records 1921–1988. All unbound records are kept in County Archives.

Record Type	Year Begun	Jurisdiction
Marriage	1838	County Clerk
Divorce	na	Clerk/Circuit Ct.
Land	1810	Registrar/Deeds
Court	1941	Clerk/Circuit Ct.

■ Loudon 2 June 1870

101 Mulberry St., Loudon, TN 37774
Phone: (423)458-3314
Web site: www.rootsweb.com/~tnloudon/
Parent County: Blount, Monroe, Roane, McMinn
Comments/research tips: County Clerk has Birth and Death records 1908–1936 and Military Discharge records 1920–1988. Clerk of Circuit Court has Divorce records 1963–1986.

Record Type	Year Begun	Jurisdiction
Marriage	1870	County Clerk
Probate	1870	County Clerk
Land	1870	County Clerk
Court	1870	Clerk/Circuit Ct.

■ Macon 18 Jan. 1842

104 Courthouse Public Sq., Lafayette, TN 37083
Phone: (615)666-2333
Web site: www.maconcountytn.com
Parent County: Smith, Sumner
Comments/research tips: County Clerk has Birth records 1908–1910 and Death records 1920–1939. Clerk of Circuit Court has Divorce records 1907–1996 and Court records 1901–1996. Registrar of Deeds has Military Discharge records 1919–1972.

Record Type	Year Begun	Jurisdiction
Marriage	1901	County Clerk
Land	1901	Registrar/Deeds
Probate	1901	County Clerk

■ Madison 6 Nov. 1821

100 E. Main St., Room 105, Jackson, TN 38301
Phone: (731)423-6022
Web site: www.co.madison.tn.us/
Parent County: Chickasaw Indian Lands
Comments/research tips: County Clerk has Birth and Death records 1925–1939 and Marriage records 1823–1832.

Record Type	Year Begun	Jurisdiction
Marriage	1846	County Clerk
Probate	1825	Clerk & Master
Divorce	1846	Clerk/Master/Chancery Ct.
Court	1821	Clerk/Circuit Ct.
Land	1821	Registrar/Deeds

■ Marion 20 Nov. 1817

1 County Courthouse Sq., Jasper, TN 37347
Phone: (423)942-2515
Web site: www.rootsweb.com/~tnmarion/
Parent County: Cherokee Indian Lands
Comments/research tips: Clerk of Circuit Court has Court records 1922–1986. Registrar of Deeds has Military Discharge records 1919–1969. Courthouse burned in 1822, many Marriage records destroyed.

Record Type	Year Begun	Jurisdiction
Marriage	1881	County Clerk
Land	1819	Registrar/Deeds
Probate	1875	County Clerk

■ Marshall 20 Feb. 1836

207 Marshall County Courthouse, Lewisburg, TN 37091
Phone: (931)359-1072
Web site: www.tngenweb.org/marshall/
Parent County: Bedford, Lincoln, Maury
Comments/research tips: County Clerk has Birth records 1909–1912 and 1927–1938 and Death records 1909–1911. Clerk of Circuit Court has Court records 1836–1986. Registrar of Deeds has Military Discharge records 1920–1967.

Record Type	Year Begun	Jurisdiction
Marriage	1836	County Clerk
Land	1836	Registrar/Deeds
Probate	1835	County Clerk

■ Maury 16 Nov. 1807

Courthouse, P.O. Box 769, Columbia, TN 38401
Phone: (931)381-3690

Tennessee

Web site: www.tngenweb.org/maury/
Parent County: Williamson, Indian lands
Comments/research tips: County Clerk has Birth and Death records 1908–1910 and 1914–1940. County Archives has Marriage records 1807–ca. 1950 and Probate records 1807–ca. 1900. Registrar of Deeds has Military Discharge records 1943–1967.

Record Type	Year Begun	Jurisdiction
Divorce	1810	Clerk/Circuit Ct.
Land	1808	Registrar/Deeds
Court	1810	Clerk/Circuit Ct.
Marriage	1950	County Clerk
Probate	1900	Clerk/Circuit Ct.

■ McMinn 13 Nov. 1819
6 E. Madison Ave., Athens, TN 37303
Phone: (423)745-4440
Web site: www.rootsweb.com/~tnmcminn
Parent County: Cherokee Indian Lands
Comments/research tips: County Clerk has Birth and Death records 1908–1912 and 1914–1925. Registrar of Deeds has Military Discharge records 1919–1970.

Record Type	Year Begun	Jurisdiction
Marriage	1820	County Clerk
Land	1820	Registrar/Deeds
Probate	1819	County Clerk
Court	1860	Clerk/Circuit Ct.

■ McNairy 8 Oct. 1823
County Courthouse, Room 102, Selmer, TN 38375
Phone: (731)645-3511
Web site: www.rootsweb.com/~tnmcnair/
Parent County: Hardin
Comments/research tips: County Clerk has Birth records 1881–1882. Registrar of Deeds has Military Discharge records 1919–1994.

Record Type	Year Begun	Jurisdiction
Probate	1861	Clerk/Circuit Ct.
Marriage	1861	County Clerk
Death	na	County Clerk
Divorce	1856	Clerk/Circuit Ct.
Land	1823	Registrar/Deeds
Court	1856	Clerk/Circuit Ct.

■ Meigs 20 Jan. 1836
Main St., P.O. Box 218, Decatur, TN 37322
Phone: (423)334-5747
Web site: www.tngenweb.org/meigs/
Parent County: Rhea
Comments/research tips: County Clerk has Birth records 1908–1912 and Death records 1908–1912 and 1925–1937. Registrar of Deeds has Military Discharge records 1919–1969.

Record Type	Year Begun	Jurisdiction
Marriage	1838	County Clerk
Divorce	1836	County Clerk
Land	1876	Registrar/Deeds
Probate	1836	County Clerk
Court	1836	County Clerk

■ Monroe 13 Nov. 1819
103 College St., Madisonville, TN 37354
Phone: (423)442-2220
Web site: www.monroegovernment.org/
Parent County: Cherokee Indian Lands
Comments/research tips: County Clerk has Birth records 1881–1889 and 1909–1911 and Death records 1909–1911. Registrar of Deeds has Military Discharge records 1919–1956. Wills are filed with the Registrar of Deeds.

Record Type	Year Begun	Jurisdiction
Marriage	1838	County Clerk
Land	1820	Registrar/Deeds
Probate	1833	County Clerk
Court	1827	Clerk/Circuit Ct.

■ Montgomery 9 Apr. 1796
350 Pagent Ln., Clarksville, TN 37040
Phone: (931)648-5711
Web site: www.tngenweb.org/montgomery/
Parent County: Tennessee
Comments/research tips: County Archives has Court records 1808–1825 and Land records 1784–1804, Marriage records 1799–1836 and 1838–1975, Military records 1798–1900, and Probate records 1796–1819. TSLA and TN Vital Records have Birth and Death records.

Record Type	Year Begun	Jurisdiction
Marriage	1975	County Clerk
Divorce	1930	Clerk/Circuit Ct.
Land	1804	Registrar/Deeds
Probate	1819	County Clerk
Court	1825	Clerk/County Ct.

■ Moore 14 Dec. 1871
Public Sq., P.O. Box 206, Lynchburg, TN 37352
Phone: (931)759-7346
Web site: www.knology.net/~jparkes/genealogy/moretn/moore.htm
Parent County: Bedford, Franklin, Lincoln
Comments/research tips: County Clerk has Birth and Death records 1881–1882 and 1908–1912. Registrar of Deeds has Military Discharge records 1918–1980.

Record Type	Year Begun	Jurisdiction
Marriage	1872	County Clerk
Land	1872	Registrar/Deeds
Probate	1872	County Clerk
Court	1872	Clerk/Circuit Ct.

■ Morgan 15 Oct. 1817
Main St., Wartburg, TN 37887
Phone: (423)346-3105
Web site: www.tngenweb.org/morgan/
Parent County: Anderson, Roane
Comments/research tips: County Clerk has Birth and Death records 1908–1912 and 1925–1940. Registrar of Deeds has Military Discharge records 1945–1984. Fires occured at county courthouse in 1826, 1870, and 1904.

Record Type	Year Begun	Jurisdiction
Marriage	1862	County Clerk
Divorce	1905	Clerk/Circuit Ct.

Land	1818	Registrar/Deeds
Probate	1866	County Clerk
Court	1840	Clerk/Circuit Ct.

■ Obion 24 Oct. 1823
2 Bill Burnett Circle, Union City, TN 38261
Phone: (731)885-3831
Web site: www.rootsweb.com/~tnobion/
Parent County: Chickasaw Indian Lands
Comments/research tips: County Clerk has Birth records 1925–1938 and Death records 1881–1882. Circuit Court has Divorce records 1823–1950. Registrar of Deeds has Military Discharge records 1920–1968.

Record Type	Year Begun	Jurisdiction
Marriage	1838	County Clerk
Land	1824	Registrar/Deeds
Probate	1834	County Clerk
Court	1826	Circuit/General Sessions Ct.

■ Overton 12 Sep. 1806
317 E. University St., Livingston, TN 38570
Phone: (931)823-2631
Web site: www.rootsweb.com/~tnoverto/overton.htm
Parent County: Jackson, Indian lands
Comments/research tips: County Clerk has Birth and Death records 1908–1938. Registrar of Deeds has Military Discharge records 1943–1966. Almost all pre–1865 records were lost in courthouse fire of April 1865.

Record Type	Year Begun	Jurisdiction
Marriage	1867	County Clerk
Divorce	1907	Clerk/Circuit Ct.
Land	1801	Registrar/Deeds
Probate	1870	County Clerk
Court	1815	Clerk/Circuit Ct.

■ Perry Nov. 1819
Main St., P.O. Box 16, Linden, TN 37096
Phone: (931)589-2216
Web site: www.netease.net/perry/
Parent County: Hickman, Humphreys
Comments/research tips: County Clerk has Birth records 1881–1882 and 1908–1912 and Death records 1881–1882, 1908–1912 and 1926–1938. Registrar of Deeds has Military Discharge records 1920–1988. County courthouse burned during the Civil War.

Record Type	Year Begun	Jurisdiction
Marriage	1865	County Clerk
Land	1841	Registrar/Deeds
Court	1834	Clerk/Circuit Ct.
Probate	1847	County Clerk

■ Pickett 27 Feb. 1879
1 Courthouse Sq., Byrdstown, TN 38549
Phone: (931)864-3879
Web site: www.rootsweb.com/~tnpicket/pick.htm
Parent County: Fentress, Overton
Comments/research tips: County Clerk has Birth and Death records 1934–1938. Registrar of Deeds has Military Discharge records 1945–1995.

Record Type	Year Begun	Jurisdiction
Marriage	1934	County Clerk
Divorce	1934	Clerk/Master/Circuit Ct.
Land	1934	Registrar/Deeds
Probate	1933	County Clerk
Court	1935	Clerk/Circuit Ct.

■ Polk 28 Nov. 1839
Hwy. 411, Benton, TN 37307
Phone: (423)338-4526
Web site: www.tngenweb.org/polk/
Parent County: Bradley, McMinn
Comments/research tips: Registrar of Deeds has Military Discharge records 1945–1989. TSLA and TN Vital Records have Birth and Death records.

Record Type	Year Begun	Jurisdiction
Marriage	1894	County Clerk
Land	1894	Registrar/Deeds
Probate	1873	County Clerk
Court	1886	Clerk/Circuit Ct.

■ Putnam 2 Feb. 1842
29 Washington, Cookeville, TN 38501
Phone: (931)526-7106
Web site: www.putnamcountytn.gov
Parent County: White, Jackson, Overton, Smith, Fentress
Comments/research tips: County Clerk has Birth records 1908–1912 and 1925–1931 and Death records 1908–1912 and 1925–1937. Registrar of Deeds has Military Discharge records 1918–1994. Courthouse burned in 1899.

Record Type	Year Begun	Jurisdiction
Marriage	1879	County Clerk
Divorce	1900	Clerk & Master
Land	1854	Registrar/Deeds
Probate	1876	County Clerk
Chancery Ct.	1895	Clerk & Master
Circuit Ct.	1842	Clerk/Circuit Ct.

■ Rhea 30 Nov. 1807
1475 Market St., Dayton, TN 37321
Phone: (423)775-7808
Web site: www.tngenweb.org/rhea/
Parent County: Roane
Comments/research tips: County Clerk has Birth records 1908–1912 and 1924–1939 and Death records 1925–1939. Registrar of Deeds has Military Discharge records 1919–1996.

Record Type	Year Begun	Jurisdiction
Court	1809	Clerk/Circuit Ct.
Probate	1825	County Clerk
Marriage	1808	County Clerk
Land	1809	Registrar/Deeds

■ Roane 6 Nov. 1801
200 W. Race St., Kingston, TN 37763
Phone: (865)376-5578
Web site: www.tngenweb.org/roane/
Parent County: Knox, Indian lands
Comments/research tips: Registrar of Deeds has Military

Discharge records 1944–1968. TSLA and TN Vital Records have Birth and Death records.

Record Type	Year Begun	Jurisdiction
Court	1810	Clerk/Circuit Ct.
Marriage	1801	County Clerk
Land	1801	Registrar/Deeds
Probate	1802	County Clerk

■ Robertson   9 Apr. 1796
101 Fifth Ave. W., Springfield, TN 37172
Phone: (615)384-5895
Web site: http://members.aol.com/tngenweb/robtco.htm
Parent County: Tennessee, Sumner
Comments/research tips: County Clerk has Birth and Death records 1908–1912, Court records 1832–1993, Land records 1796–1899, Marriage records 1839–ca. 1980, and Probate records 1796–1975. Registrar of Deeds has Military Discharge records 1922–1989.

Record Type	Year Begun	Jurisdiction
Marriage	1980	County Clerk
Divorce	1935	Clerk/Circuit Ct.
Land	1899	Registrar/Deeds
Probate	1975	County Clerk
Court	1993	Clerk/Circuit Ct.

■ Rutherford   25 Oct. 1803
26 N. Public Sq., Murfreesboro, TN 37130
Phone: (615)898-7798
Web site: www.rutherfordcounty.org/
Parent County: Davidson, Williamson, Wilson
Comments/research tips: County Archives has Naturalization records 1922–1924. TSLA and TN Vital Records have Birth and Death records.

Record Type	Year Begun	Jurisdiction
Court	1849	Clerk/Circuit Ct.
Marriage	1804	County Clerk
Land	1804	Registrar/Deeds
Probate	1804	County Clerk

■ Scott   17 Dec. 1849
283 Court St., P.O. Box 69, Huntsville, TN 37756
Phone: (423)663-2588
Web site: www.scottcounty.com/
Parent County: Fentress, Morgan, Anderson, Campbell
Comments/research tips: Scott County Historical Society, 198 Woodland Place, Huntsville, TN 37756, (423)663-3887, has Court records 1850–1987, Death records 1901–1968, Land records 1850–1972, Marriage records 1854–1972, Military Discharge records 1919–1987, and Probate records 1850–1927.

■ Sequatchie   9 Dec. 1857
308 Cherry St., Dunlap, TN 37327
Phone: (423)949-2522
Web site: www.tngenweb.org/sequatchie/
Parent County: Hamilton, Marion, Warren
Comments/research tips: County Clerk has Birth records 1880–1940 and Death records 1881–1938. Registrar of Deeds has Military Discharge records 1919–1968.

Record Type	Year Begun	Jurisdiction
Marriage	1858	County Clerk
Divorce	1898	Clerk/Circuit Ct.
Land	1858	Registrar/Deeds
Probate	1858	County Clerk
Court	1898	Clerk/Circuit Ct.

■ Sevier   28 Sep. 1794
125 Court Ave. #202, Sevierville, TN 37862
Phone: (423)453-5502
Web site: www.tngenweb.org/sevier/
Parent County: Jefferson
Comments/research tips: TSLA and TN Vital Records office have Birth and Death records available. Courthouse fire of 1856 destroyed all county records except one surveyor's book.

Record Type	Year Begun	Jurisdiction
Court	1850	Clerk/Circuit Ct.
Marriage	1856	County Clerk
Land	1845	Registrar/Deeds
Probate	1849	County Clerk

■ Shelby   24 Nov. 1819
140 Adams Ave., Memphis, TN 38103
Phone: (901)545-4244
Web site: www.co.shelby.countytn.gov
Parent County: Indian lands
Comments/research tips: County Archives has Death records 1848–1951, Marriage records 1820–1999, Naturalization records 1856–1906, and Probate records 1820–1900.

Record Type	Year Begun	Jurisdiction
Birth	1914	Dept./Health
Marriage	2000	County Clerk
Death	1950	Dept./Health
Divorce	1895	Clerk/Circuit Ct.
Land	1788	County Archives
Probate	1900	Probate Court Clerk
Court	1828	Clerk/Circuit Ct.
Nat.	1907	US Immigration/Nat.

■ Smith   26 Oct. 1799
211 Main St. W., Carthage, TN 37030
Phone: (615)735-9833
Web site: www.rootsweb.com/~tnsmith/
Parent County: Sumner, Indian Lands
Comments/research tips: County Clerk has Birth and Death records 1881–1882 and 1908–1912. Registrar of Deeds has Military Discharge records 1919–1988.

Record Type	Year Begun	Jurisdiction
Court	1811	Clerk/Circuit Ct.
Marriage	1838	County Clerk
Land	1799	Registrar/Deeds
Probate	1805	County Clerk

■ Stewart   1 Nov. 1803
Main St., P.O. Box 67, Dover, TN 37058
Phone: (931)232-7616
Web site: www.rootsweb.com/~tnstewar/index.htm
Parent County: Montgomery

Comments/research tips: County Clerk has Birth records 1881–1912 and Death records 1881–1912 and 1914–1925. Registrar of Deeds has Military Discharge records 1917–1994. Courthouse burned during Civil War.

Record Type	Year Begun	Jurisdiction
Court	1821	Clerk/Circuit Ct.
Marriage	1849	County Clerk
Land	1796	Registrar/Deeds
Probate	1812	County Clerk

■ Sullivan 18 Oct. 1779
3411 Hwy. 126, Blountville, TN 37617
Phone: (423)323-6428
Web site: www.sullivancounty.org/
Parent County: Washington
Comments/research tips: TSLA and TN Vital Records office have Birth and Death records.

Record Type	Year Begun	Jurisdiction
Court	1879	Clerk/Circuit Ct.
Marriage	1863	County Clerk
Land	1770	Registrar/Deeds
Probate	1867	Clerk/Chancery Ct.

■ Sumner 18 Nov. 1786
Courthouse, Public Sq., Gallatin, TN 37066
Phone: (615)452-4063
Web site: www.sumnertn.org/
Parent County: Davidson
Comments/research tips: County Archives has Death records 1908–1925, Land records 1793–1965, Loose Court Papers 1786–1930, Marriage records 1787–1998, and Probate records 1789–1985.

Record Type	Year Begun	Jurisdiction
Marriage	1998	County Clerk
Land	1965	Registrar/Deeds
Probate	1985	Clerk/Chancery Ct.

■ Tennessee 1788
Comments/research tips: County surrendered name when state became Tennessee, 1796. Portions of Tennessee County now found in Robertson and Montgomery Counties. Records in Robertson County.

■ Tipton 1 Dec. 1823
P.O. Box 528, Covington, TN 38019
Phone: (901)476-2438
Web site: www.rootsweb.com/~tntipton/
Parent County: Chickasaw Indian Lands
Comments/research tips: County Clerk has Birth records 1908–1912 and 1925–1939, Death records 1925–1939, and Divorce records 1911–1950. Registrar of Deeds has Military Discharge records 1919–1976.

Record Type	Year Begun	Jurisdiction
Marriage	1840	County Clerk
Land	1824	Registrar/Deeds
Probate	1824	Clerk/Chancery Ct.
Court	1832	Clerk/Circuit Ct.

■ Trousdale 5 Sep. 1870
200 E. Main St., Hartsville, TN 37074
Phone: (615)374-2906

Web site: www.rootsweb.com/~tntrousd/
Parent County: Macon, Smith, Wilson, Sumner
Comments/research tips: County Clerk has Birth records 1917–1940. Registrar of Deeds has Military Discharge records 1917–1919 and 1948–1981. Courthouse documents were damaged in fires 1900 and 1904.

Record Type	Year Begun	Jurisdiction
Marriage	1905	County Clerk
Divorce	1906	Clerk/Circuit Ct.
Land	1905	Registrar/Deeds
Probate	1905	County Clerk
Court	1906	Clerk/Circuit Ct.

■ Unicoi 23 Mar. 1875
100 N. Main Ave., P.O. Box 340, Erwin, TN 37650
Phone: (423)743-3381
Web site: www.rootsweb.com/~tnunicoi/
Parent County: Carter, Washington
Comments/research tips: County Clerk has Birth and Death records 1908–1912 and 1924–1939. Registrar of Deeds has Military Discharge records 1919–1996.

Record Type	Year Begun	Jurisdiction
Marriage	1876	County Clerk
Divorce	na	Clerk/Chancery/Circuit Ct.
Land	1876	Registrar/Deeds
Probate	1876	County Clerk
Court	1876	Clerk/Chancery/Circuit Ct.

■ Union 3 Jan. 1850
901 Main St., P.O. Box 395, Maynardville, TN 37807
Phone: (865)992-8043
Web site: www.rootsweb.com/~tnunion
Parent County: Anderson, Campbell, Claiborne, Grainger, Knox
Comments/research tips: County Clerk has Birth and Death records 1881–1882. Registrar of Deeds has Military Discharge records 1949–1984.

Record Type	Year Begun	Jurisdiction
Court	1854	Clerk/County Ct.
Marriage	1864	County Clerk
Land	1856	Registrar/Deeds
Probate	1856	County Clerk

■ Van Buren 3 Jan. 1840
Veterans' Sq., P.O. Box 126, Spencer, TN 38585
Phone: (931)946-2121
Web site: www.rootsweb.com/~tnvanbur/
Parent County: Warren, White
Comments/research tips: County Clerk has Birth and Death records 1908–1911 and 1925–1935. Registrar of Deeds has Military Discharge records 1919–1968.

Record Type	Year Begun	Jurisdiction
Marriage	1840	County Clerk
Divorce	1840	Clerk/Circuit Ct.
Land	1840	Registrar/Deeds
Probate	1840	County Clerk
Court	1840	Clerk/Circuit Ct.

■ Warren 26 Nov. 1807
P.O. Box 231, McMinnville, TN 37111
Phone: (615)473-2623

Tennessee

Web site: www.tngenweb.org/warren/
Parent County: White
Comments/research tips: County Clerk has Birth and Death records 1881–1912. Registrar of Deeds has Military Discharge records 1919–1983.

Record Type	Year Begun	Jurisdiction
Marriage	1852	County Clerk
Divorce	na	Clerk/Chancery/Circuit Ct.
Land	1814	Registrar/Deeds
Probate	1827	County Clerk
Court	1842	Clerk/Circuit Ct.

■ Washington   1 June 1796
P.O. Box 219, Jonesborough, TN 37659
Phone: (423)753-1621
Web site: www.rootsweb.com/~tnwashin/
Parent County: Washington County, NC
Comments/research tips: TSLA and TN Vital Records have Birth and Death records. East Tennessee State University Archives has Chancery Court records 1836–1886 and Circuit Court records 1810–1886. Circuit Court Clerk has Divorce records 1799–1945. County Clerk has Marriage records 1787–1945. Eighteenth century Court records are kept at the Archives of Appalachia collection at East Tennessee State University. Covered present state. Many counties formed from it. This county also embraced parts of present North Carolina counties. County Clerk has Birth records 1908–1912 and 1925–1938.

Record Type	Year Begun	Jurisdiction
Land	1782	Registrar/Deeds
Probate	1779	County Clerk

■ Wayne   24 Nov. 1817
100 Court Cir., P.O. Box 185, Waynesboro, TN 38485
Phone: (931)722-5544
Web site: www.netease.net/wayne/
Parent County: Hickman
Comments/research tips: County Clerk has Birth and Death records 1881–1883 and 1908–1921. Registrar of Deeds has Military Discharge records 1914–1975.

Record Type	Year Begun	Jurisdiction
Court	1848	Clerk/County Ct.
Marriage	1857	County Clerk
Land	1821	Registrar/Deeds
Probate	1848	County Clerk

■ Weakley   21 Oct. 1823
1 Courthouse Sq. #107, P.O. Box 587, Dresden, TN 38225
Phone: (731)364-2285
Web site: www.rootsweb.com/~tnweakle/
Parent County: Chickasaw Indian Lands
Comments/research tips: County Clerk has Birth records 1908–1912. Registrar of Deeds has Military Discharge

records 1917–1989. For more Birth and Death records (current) see TSLA and TN Vital Records.

Record Type	Year Begun	Jurisdiction
Marriage	1843	County Clerk
Divorce	na	Clerk/Chancery/Circuit Ct.
Land	1822	Registrar/Deeds
Probate	1828	County Clerk
Court	1827	Clerk/Chancery Ct.

■ White   11 Sep. 1806
County Courthouse, Room 205, Sparta, TN 38583
Phone: (931)836-3712
Web site: www.tngenweb.org/white/
Parent County: Smith
Comments/research tips: Registrar of Deeds has Military Discharge records 1943–1992.

Record Type	Year Begun	Jurisdiction
Land	1806	Registrar/Deeds
Probate	1806	County Clerk
Birth	1881	County Clerk
Death	1881	County Clerk
Marriage	1809	County Clerk
Court	1806	County Clerk

■ Williamson   26 Oct. 1799
1320 W. Main St., Franklin, TN 37064
Phone: (615)790-5712
Web site: www.williamson-tn.org
Parent County: Davidson
Comments/research tips: County Clerk has Birth and Death records 1881–1882 and 1908–1912. County Archives has Divorce records 1900–1950, Land records 1800–1950, Marriage records 1800–2000, and Probate records 1800–1899. Registrar of Deeds has Military Discharge records 1918–1966.

Record Type	Year Begun	Jurisdiction
Land	1950	Registrar/Deeds
Probate	1899	County Clerk

■ Wilson   26 Oct. 1799
228 E. Main St., Lebanon, TN 37087
Phone: (615)444-2835
Web site: www.wilsoncountytn.com/
Parent County: Sumner
Comments/research tips: County Archives has Birth records 1881–1886 and 1907–1912, Court records 1803–1964, Death records 1907–1912 and 1925–1939, Marriage records 1802–1953, and Probate records 1802–1964. Registrar of Deeds has Military Discharge records 1919–1986.

Record Type	Year Begun	Jurisdiction
Marriage	1953	County Clerk
Divorce	na	Clerk/Master/Circuit Ct.
Land	1789	Registrar/Deeds

Texas

By Emily Anne Croom

HISTORICAL OVERVIEW

Sixteenth-century Spaniards exploring in Texas found indigenous people, but not the gold they sought. Later Spanish missions, presidios, and villages became the nuclei for modern cities, including El Paso (1682), San Antonio (1718), and Nacogdoches (1779)—the latter well situated for trade with the Indians and with Natchitoches, Louisiana. French settlement on the Texas Gulf coast in 1685 was short-lived, and French cession to Spain of greater Louisiana in 1762 brought Texas and Louisiana under the same crown. In 1803, the United States tried to claim Texas as part of the loosely defined Louisiana Purchase.

Anglo-American settlement was negotiated but not begun when Mexico gained independence from Spain in 1821. Under a renegotiated Mexican contract, Stephen F. Austin recruited several hundred families to settle the river valleys near his San Felipe de Austin headquarters. Other *empresarios* also settled colonies in the Mexican State of Coahuila and Texas. Newcomers had to swear allegiance to Mexico and Catholicism.

Fueled by a restless sense of Manifest Destiny to see Texas as part of the United States, adventurers and would-be land speculators became disgruntled by the centralist Mexican government and its 1830 attempt to halt Anglo-American settlement. Many colonists became alarmed at Mexican preparations to send their army to occupy Texas. After several military engagements, Texans declared themselves an independent republic on 2 March 1836. The war for independence was short. The Republic of Texas existed for nine years before the U.S. Congress adopted a resolution of annexation in late 1845, accepting Texas as the twenty-eighth state. Annexation led to war with Mexico from 1846 to 1848, after which Mexico relinquished its claim to Texas and the United States gained most of its present Southwest.

© PhotoDisc/Getty Images

TEXAS AT A GLANCE

Motto: Friendship

Population: 20.8 million

Prevalent Religions: Baptist, Roman Catholic, Pentecostal, Methodist, and Lutheran

Major Industries: Energy, oil production and refining, natural gas, chemical and petrochemical products, computer and high-tech-related industry, agriculture (primarily cattle, sheep, and cotton), machinery, tourism

Ethnic Makeup (in percent): Caucasian 71%, African American 11.5%, Hispanic 32.0%, Asian 2.7%, Native American 0.6%, Other 11.7%

Famous Texans: Gene Autry, Clyde Barrow, Carol Burnett, George W. Bush, Joan Crawford, Dwight D. Eisenhower, A.J. Foyt, Larry Hagman, Ben Hogan, Buddy Holly, Howard Hughes, Jack Johnson, Lyndon Johnson, George Jones, Tommy Lee Jones, Janis Joplin, Mary Martin, Roger Miller, Willie Nelson, Roy Orbison, Bonnie Parker, Ross Perot, Katherine Ann Porter, Wiley Post, Dan Rather, Gene Roddenberry, Stevie Ray Vaughn, Mildred "Babe" Didrikson Zaharias

Above: An oil pump in Texas

CIMARRON   TEXAS   BEAVER

RIO ARRIBA   TAOS   COLFAX   UNION

DALLAM   SHERMAN   OCHILTREE   LIPSCOMB
HANSFORD

MORA   HARDING

LOS ALAMOS   HARTLEY   MOORE   HUTCHINSON   ROBERTS   HEMPHILL

SAN MIGUEL   OLDHAM   POTTER   CARSON   WHEELER

Santa Fe ☆
SANDOVAL   SANTA FE   GRAY
DONLEY
Albuquerque ○   ○ **Amarillo**
BERNALILLO   DEAF SMITH   ARMSTRONG   COLLINGSWORTH
RANDALL
VALENCIA   QUAY   GUADALUPE
PARMER   CASTRO   BRISCOE   CHILDRESS
SWISHER   HALL
TORRANCE   DE BACA

BAILEY   LAMB   HALE   FLOYD   MOTLEY   COTTLE
NEW MEXICO
SOCORRO   ROOSEVELT
LINCOLN   CROSBY
COCHRAN   HOCKLEY   LUBBOCK   DICKENS   KING
CHAVES   ○ **Lubbock**
STONEWALL
SIERRA   YOAKUM   TERRY   LYNN   GARZA   KENT

LEA   GAINES   DAWSON   SCURRY   FISHER
BORDEN
OTERO   HOWARD   NOLAN
EDDY   MITCHELL
DONA ANA   ANDREWS   MARTIN
○ **Midland**
ECTOR   MIDLAND
○ **Odessa** ○   STERLING   COKE
EL PASO   LOVING   WINKLER   GLASSCOCK
○   UPTON   **San Angelo** ○
El Paso   CULBERSON   WARD   CRANE   REAGAN   IRION   TOM
HUDSPETH   GREEN
REEVES
SCHLEICHER
JEFF DAVIS   PECOS   CROCKETT
SUTTON
PRESIDIO   TERRELL   VAL VERDE   EDWARDS

BREWSTER   KINNEY

Chihuahua ○
☆   MAVERICK

MEXICO

Monterrey

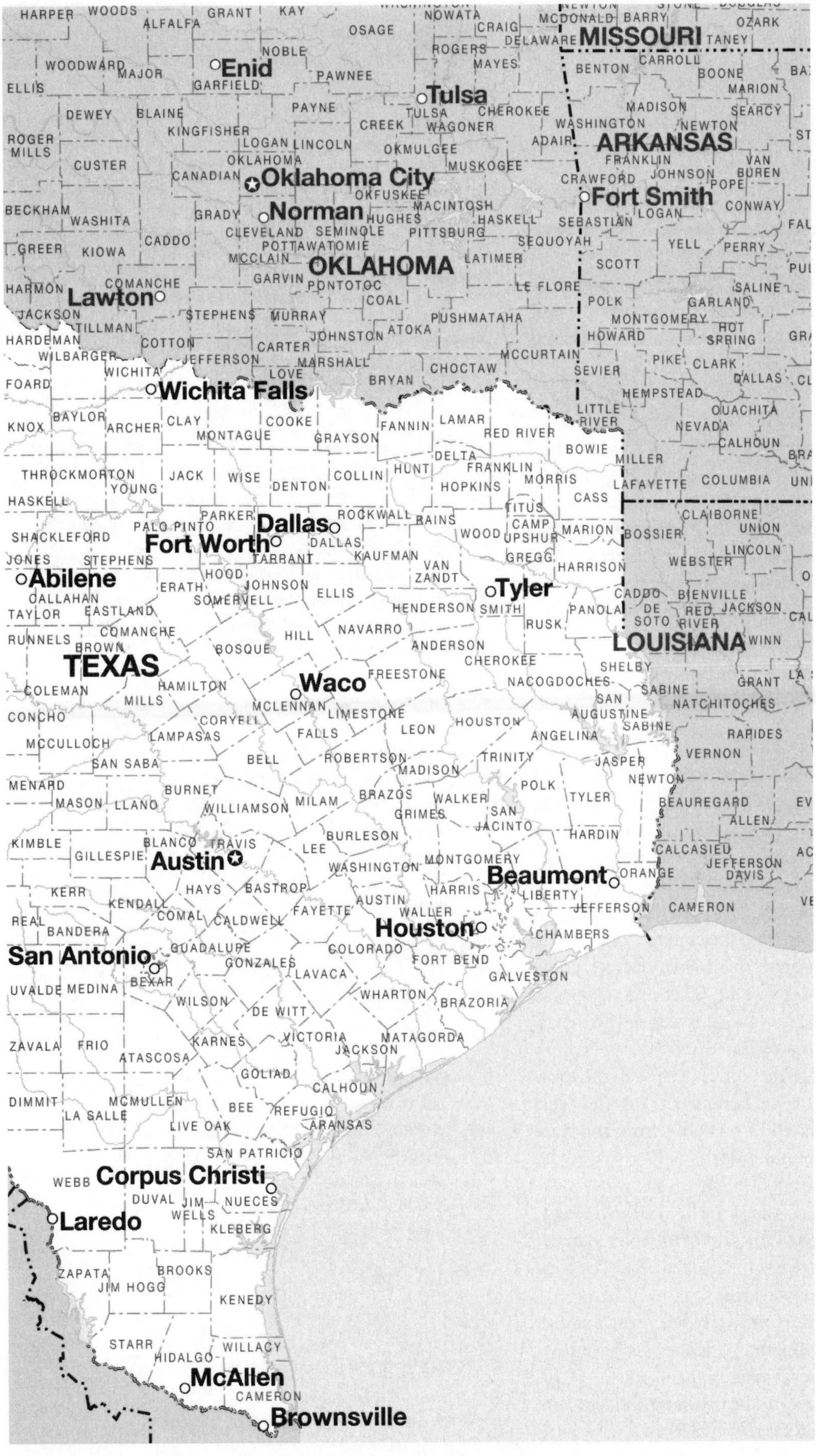
HARPER
WOODS
ALFALFA
GRANT
KAY
NOWATA
MCDONALD
BARRY
OZARK
OSAGE
CRAIG
DELAWARE
MISSOURI
TANEY
NOBLE
ROGERS
MAYES
WOODWARD
MAJOR
Enid
PAWNEE
BENTON
CARROLL
BOONE
ELLIS
GARFIELD
Tulsa
MARION
DEWEY
BLAINE
PAYNE
MADISON
SEARCY
TULSA
CHEROKEE
KINGFISHER
CREEK
WAGONER
WASHINGTON
NEWTON
ROGER MILLS
LOGAN
LINCOLN
ADAIR
ARKANSAS
OKMULGEE
FRANKLIN
VAN BUREN
CUSTER
OKLAHOMA
MUSKOGEE
CANADIAN
Oklahoma City
CRAWFORD
JOHNSON
POPE
OKFUSKEE
Fort Smith
BECKHAM
MACINTOSH
CONWAY
GRADY
Norman
HUGHES
HASKELL
LOGAN
WASHITA
SEBASTIAN
CLEVELAND
SEMINOLE
PITTSBURG
CADDO
SEQUOYAH
YELL
PERRY
POTTAWATOMIE
GREER
KIOWA
MCCLAIN
OKLAHOMA
LATIMER
SCOTT
GARVIN
PONTOTOC
HARMON
COMANCHE
LE FLORE
SALINE
Lawton
COAL
POLK
GARLAND
JACKSON
STEPHENS
MURRAY
PUSHMATAHA
TILLMAN
MONTGOMERY
HOT SPRING
ATOKA
HARDEMAN
COTTON
JOHNSTON
HOWARD
CARTER
WILBARGER
JEFFERSON
MARSHALL
MCCURTAIN
PIKE
CLARK
WICHITA
CHOCTAW
SEVIER
LOVE
FOARD
Wichita Falls
BRYAN
DALLAS
HEMPSTEAD
LITTLE RIVER
OUACHITA
BAYLOR
COOKE
LAMAR
NEVADA
KNOX
ARCHER
CLAY
FANNIN
MONTAGUE
GRAYSON
RED RIVER
CALHOUN
BOWIE
DELTA
MILLER
THROCKMORTON
JACK
WISE
COLLIN
HUNT
FRANKLIN
YOUNG
DENTON
HOPKINS
MORRIS
LAFAYETTE
COLUMBIA
HASKELL
CASS
TITUS
PARKER
ROCKWALL
CLAIBORNE
RAINS
CAMP
PALO PINTO
Dallas
UNION
SHACKLEFORD
WOOD
UPSHUR
MARION
BOSSIER
Fort Worth
DALLAS
LINCOLN
TARRANT
KAUFMAN
WEBSTER
JONES
STEPHENS
GREGG
HOOD
VAN ZANDT
HARRISON
Abilene
JOHNSON
Tyler
CADDO
BIENVILLE
CALLAHAN
ERATH
ELLIS
SOMERVELL
HENDERSON
SMITH
DE SOTO
RED RIVER
JACKSON
TAYLOR
EASTLAND
PANOLA
RUSK
RUNNELS
COMANCHE
HILL
NAVARRO
LOUISIANA
WINN
BROWN
BOSQUE
ANDERSON
TEXAS
CHEROKEE
SHELBY
FREESTONE
GRANT
Waco
NACOGDOCHES
COLEMAN
HAMILTON
SABINE
MILLS
MCLENNAN
SAN AUGUSTINE
NATCHITOCHES
CONCHO
CORYELL
LIMESTONE
HOUSTON
SABINE
LEON
RAPIDES
FALLS
MCCULLOCH
LAMPASAS
ANGELINA
VERNON
BELL
ROBERTSON
TRINITY
SAN SABA
MADISON
JASPER
MENARD
NEWTON
POLK
BURNET
BRAZOS
WALKER
TYLER
MASON
LLANO
BEAUREGARD
MILAM
WILLIAMSON
GRIMES
SAN JACINTO
ALLEN
BURLESON
KIMBLE
BLANCO
TRAVIS
HARDIN
LEE
GILLESPIE
CALCASIEU
Austin
MONTGOMERY
WASHINGTON
JEFFERSON DAVIS
Beaumont
ORANGE
KERR
HAYS
BASTROP
HARRIS
KENDALL
LIBERTY
AUSTIN
COMAL
JEFFERSON
CAMERON
REAL
WALLER
CALDWELL
FAYETTE
BANDERA
Houston
CHAMBERS
GUADALUPE
COLORADO
San Antonio
GONZALES
FORT BEND
LAVACA
BEXAR
GALVESTON
UVALDE
MEDINA
WHARTON
WILSON
BRAZORIA
DE WITT
VICTORIA
MATAGORDA
ZAVALA
FRIO
KARNES
JACKSON
ATASCOSA
GOLIAD
CALHOUN
DIMMIT
MCMULLEN
BEE
REFUGIO
LA SALLE
LIVE OAK
ARANSAS
SAN PATRICIO
WEBB
Corpus Christi
DUVAL
JIM WELLS
NUECES
Laredo
KLEBERG
ZAPATA
BROOKS
JIM HOGG
KENEDY
STARR
WILLACY
HIDALGO
McAllen
CAMERON
Brownsville

During the colonial and republic periods, land-hungry settlers arrived largely from Alabama, Mississippi, Tennessee, Arkansas, Georgia, Louisiana, and Missouri, as well as other U.S. states, Mexico, the British Isles, and German states. Czechs, Scandinavians, and Alsatians began arriving in the 1840s; Poles, in the 1850s. Most early settlers were small farmers, but cotton planters with slaves also migrated to Texas. By 1860, Texas had about 604,000 residents, of whom 30 percent were slaves, 7 percent were foreign-born immigrants, and only about 350 (.05 percent) were free blacks. Not counted in censuses were numerous Indians, some of whom raided frontier settlements through the 1870s and many of whom were eventually relocated to Indian Territory reservations.

Although divided over the issues of slavery and secession, Texas seceded in February 1861. The state saw limited military action during the Civil War and was readmitted to the Union in 1870.

From the 1820s to the early 1900s, cotton was the money crop, and corn sustained life. After the Civil War, cotton, railroads, and cattle and sheep industries expanded rapidly. The twentieth century saw economic diversification in agriculture and development of the petrochemical, timber-related, food-processing, and other industries. In the 1940s the urban population surpassed the rural.

RECORD HIGHLIGHTS

Texas began statewide civil registration of births and deaths in 1903, marriages in 1966, and divorces in 1968. Copies of birth and death certificates can be requested from the county clerk's office where the record originated or the state bureau of vital statistics. The county office is often a good first choice; fees vary. Certified copies of marriage licenses come only from the county clerk's office that issued the license; copies of divorce decrees come only from the district clerk's office where the case was heard. The state vital statistics office issues only a verification of marriage or divorce based on the application the court clerk submitted to that office. The Web site <www.tdh.state.tx.us/bvs/> provides instructions and fees; allow about three months for a response from the state office. The voluntary Central Adoption Registry is described at <www.tdh.state.tx.us/bvs/car/car.htm>.

Pre-1903 vital records exist for some locations. Marriage records often survive from the creation of the county; many pre-republic marriages have been published. The Congress of the Republic granted few divorces.

Texas has taken no state censuses, but most Spanish and Mexican town censuses and resident lists have been published. The first federal census for Texas is 1850. Good resources for republic and early state residents are county tax rolls, many dating from 1836.

RESEARCH TIPS

for more info

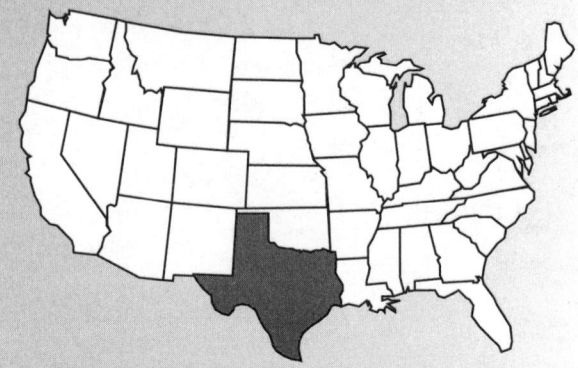

- The Texas State Library participates in interlibrary loan of microfilmed county records through a "regional historical resource depository" program. Lists of the regional depositories and the county records available on microfilm are online at <www.tsl.state.tx.us/arc/local/index.html>.
- Besides the state library and archives in Austin, major research facilities include the Center for American History, University of Texas, Austin, <www.cah.utexas.edu>; Clayton Library Center for Genealogical Research, a unit of the Houston Public Library, <www.houstonlibrary.org/clayton>; the Texas Room, Central Library, Houston Public Library; Dallas Public Library's genealogy department and Texas/Dallas history and archives department, <www.dallaslibrary.org/central.htm>; and various academic libraries with archival collections. Numerous Texas public libraries have genealogy collections.

Census Records
- Federal Census Population Schedules: 1850, 1860, 1870, 1880, 1900, 1910, 1920, 1930
- Federal Census Soundex: 1880, 1900, 1910, 1920
- Federal Mortality Schedules: 1850, 1860, 1870, 1880
- Federal Slave Schedules: 1850, 1860 (Schedules name slaveholders but rarely name slaves.)
- Special Census of Civil War Union Veterans and Widows: 1890
- Colonial: 1829–1836

Texas

Never federal public domain, Texas retained the land within its current boundaries after statehood. Colonial, republic, and state land grants and related records are at the Texas General Land Office <www.glo.state.tx.us/archives.html>.

In the state library, state archives, general land office, or other repositories, Texas-specific records of genealogical value include the following:

- Colonial collections such as the Bexar, Laredo, and Nacogdoches archives
- 1834–1835 character certificates, mostly for East Texans
- Confederate indigent families list <www.tsl.state.tx.us/arc/cif/index.html>
- Confederate pension applications from 1899; index available online at <www.tsl.state.tx.us/arc/pensions/introcpi.html>
- Republic of Texas claims for payment, reimbursement, or damages that citizens submitted to the Republic government, 1835–1846; republic pensions and claims submitted after 1846; index at <www2.tsl.state.tx.us/trail/RepublicSearch.jsp>
- 1854–1855 scholastic censuses of school-age children, various counties
- 1867 voter registrations

STATE RESOURCES

■ ARCHIVES, LIBRARIES, AND SOCIETIES

Note:
Visit <www.rootsweb.com/~txgenweb/society.htm> for more societies in the state.

Abilene Public Library
202 Cedar, Abilene, TX 79606
Tel: (915) 676-6029
Web site: <www.abilenetx.com/apl.>

Amarillo Genealogical Society
℅ Amarillo Public Library, 300 E. Fourth, P.O. Box 2171, Amarillo, TX 79189

Anderson County Genealogical Society
P.O. Box 2045, Palestine, TX 75802-2045
Web site: <users.tvec.net/bonniew/acgs/acgs2.htm>

Angelina County Genealogical Society
P.O. Box 150631, Lufkin, TX 75915-0631

Archer County Historical Commission
Rt. 1, Windthorst, TX 76389

Arlington Genealogical Society
℅ Arlington Public Library, 101 E. Abram St., Arlington, TX 76010
Tel: (817) 451-5764
Web site: <www.rootsweb.com/~txags/ags.htm>

Atascosa County Genealogical Society Library
Mummer Memorial Building, Fourth and H Aves., P.O. Box 93, Poteet, TX 78065
Web site: <http:members.aol.com/poteetlib/gen/index.html>

Athens Genealogical Organization
℅ Henderson Public Library, 121 Prairieville St., Athens, TX 75751

Atlanta Public Library
101 W. Hiram, Atlanta, TX 75551
Tel: (903) 796-2112

Austin County Historical Commission
206 S. Masonie St, Bellville, TX 77418

Austin Genealogical Society
P.O. Box 1507, Austin, TX 78767-1507

Tel: (512) 378-4735
Web site:

Austin History Center, Austin Public Library
P.O. Box 2287, 810 Guadalupe St., Austin, TX 78768-228
Tel: (512) 499-7480

Bay Area Genealogical Society
P.O. Box 891447, Houston, TX 7389-1447
Web site: <www.rootsweb.com/~txbags/baygen.html>

Bay Area Heritage Society
220 W. Defee Ave., Baytown, TX 77520-4010

Baylor University Institute for Oral History
Carroll Library, Suite 306, One Bear Place #97271, Waco, TX 76798-7271
Tel: (254) 710-3437
Fax: (254) 710-1571
Web site: <www3.baylor.edu/Oral_History/>

Baytown Genealogical Society
P.O. Box 2486, Baytown, TX 77522

Bear Creek Genealogical Society
8922 Rockhurst Dr., Houston, TX 77080-3018

Beaumont Heritage Society
2985 French Rd., Beaumont TX 77706

Beaumont, Tyrell Public Library
695 Pearl St., P.O. Box 3827, Beaumont, TX 77701-3827
Tel: (409) 883-2759

Bellville Historical Society
P.O. Box 67, Bellville, TX 77418

Big Bend Genealogy Society
P.O. Box 1251, Alpine, TX 79831
Web site: <www.rootsweb.com/~txbcgs/>

Boerne Area Historical Society
P.O. Box 178, Boerne, TX 78006

Boerne, Genealogical Society of Kendall County
P.O. Box 623, Boerne, TX 78006-0623

Borden County Historical Commission
P.O. Box 23, Gail, TX 79738

Bosque County Historical Commission
P.O. Box 534, Meridian, TX 76665

Brazos Genealogical Association
P.O. Box 5493, Bryan, TX 77805-5493
Web site: <http://user.txcyber.com/-bga/>

Brazosport Genealogical Society
P.O. Box 813, Lake Jackson, TX 77566

Brooks County Historical Commission
604 W. Blucher, Falfurrias, TX 78355

Brown County Historical Society
P.O. Box 146, Brownwood, TX 76801

Burkburnett Genealogical Society
℅ Burkburnett Library, 215 E. Fourth St., Burkburnett, TX 76354

Burnet County Genealogical Society
℅ Herman Brown Free Library, 100 E. Washington St., Burnet, TX 78611
Web site: <www.rootsweb.com/-txburnet/index.htm>

Caldwell County Genealogical and Historical Society
215 S. Pecan Ave., Luling, TX 78648
Web site: <www.rootsweb.com/-txcaldwe/socpage.htm>

Camp County Genealogical Society
P.O. Box 1083, Pittsburg, TX 75686-3083
Web site: <www.rootsweb.com/-txccgs/members.htm>

Cass County Genealogical Society
P.O. Box 880, Atlanta, TX 7551-0880
Web site: <http://homepages.rootsweb.com/-danasite/CCGS/>

Central Texas Genealogical Society
Waco-McLennan County Library System, 1717 Austin Ave., Waco, TX 76701

Texas

Web site: <www.rootsweb.com/
-txmclenn/>

Chaparral Genealogical Society
P.O. Box 606, Tomball, TX
77377-0606
Web site: <www.rootsweb.com/
-txwaller/chap.htm>

**Cherokee County Genealogical
Society**
P.O. Box 1332, Jacksonville, TX
75766

Childress Genealogical Society
17 Ave. B NE, Childress, TX
79201

**Clayton Library Center for
Genealogical Research**
5300 Caroline, Houston, TX
77004-6896
Tel: (832) 393-2600
Web site: <www.hpl.lib.tx.us/cla
yton/>

**Cleveland Area Genealogical
Enterprises (CAGE)**
Austin Memorial Library, 220 S.
Bonham, Cleveland, TX 77327

**Coastal Bend Genealogical
Society**
P.O. Box 2826, Corpus Christi, TX
78403

**Collin County Genealogical
Society**
P.O. Box 865052, Plano, TX
75086-5052

**Comal County Genealogy
Society**
P.O. Box 310583, New Brauns-
fels, TX 78130

Cooke County Heritage Society
P.O. Box 150, Gainesville, TX
76240

**Coryell County Genealogical
Society**
% Gatesville Public Library, 811
Main St., Gatesville, TX 76528

**Cross Timbers Genealogical
Society, Inc.**
P.O. Box 197, Gainesville, TX
76241

**Czech Heritage Society of
Texas**
7411 Kite Hill, Houston, TX
77041

**Dallas County East
Genealogical Society**
7637 Mary Dan Dr., Dallas, TX
75217-4603

Dallas Genealogical Society
P.O. Box 12446, Dallas, TX
75225-0446
Web site: <www.dallasgenealogy
.org>

**Dallas Jewish Historical
Society**
7900 Northaven Rd., Dallas, TX
75230
Web site: <www.dvjc.org/hist
ory/genealogy.shtml>

Dallas Public Library
1515 Young St., Dallas, TX
75201
Tel: (214) 670-1400
Web site: <http://dallaslibrary.o
rg>

**Daughters of the Republic of
Texas Library**
P.O. Box 1401, San Antonio, TX
78205-1401
Tel: (210) 225-1071
Fax: (210) 212-8514

**Deaf Smith County
Genealogical Society**
211 E. Fourth St., Hereford, TX
79045

Denison Library
300 W. Gandy., Denison, TX
75020-7117
Tel: (903) 465-1797
Web site: <www.barr.org/deniso
n.htm>

**Denton County Genealogical
Society**
P.O. Box 424707, Denton, TX
76204-4707
Web site: <www.iglobal.net/
pub/dcgs/>

**Disciples of Christ, Brite
Divinity School Collection**
Mary Couts Burnett Library,
Texas Christian University, 2913
W. Lowden, Fort Worth, TX 76129
Tel: (817) 921-7117
Fax: (817) 921-7447

**Donley County Genealogical
Society**
P.O. Box 116, Clarendon, TX
79226

**East Bell County Genealogical
Society**
3219 Meadow Oaks Dr., Temple,
TX 76502-1752

East End Historical Association
P.O. Box 2424, Galveston, TX
77550

**East Texas Genealogical
Society**
P.O. Box 6967, Tyler, TX 75711
Web site: <www.rootsweb.com/
~txetgs>

**Eastland County Genealogical
Society**
609 Marsh St., Eastland, TX
76448

El Paso Genealogical Society
% El Paso Main Public Library,
501 N. Oregon St., El Paso, TX
79901

**Ellis County Genealogical
Society**
P.O. Box 479, Waxahachie, TX
75168

**Erath County Genealogical
Society**
P.O. Box 1587, Stephenville, TX
76401
Web site: <www.rootsweb.com/
-txerath/gene_soc_temp.htm>

**Federation of Genealogical
Societies Business Office**
P.O. Box 200940, Austin, TX
78720-0940
Tel: (888) 347-1500
Web site: <www.fgs.org>

Forney Heritage Society
98 FM 2757, Forney, TX 75126

**Fort Bend County Genealogical
Society**
Web site: <www.ft.ftbendgensoci
ety.netfirms.com/index.html>

**Fort Brown Genealogical
Society**
608 E. Adams, Brownsville, TX
78520

Fort Clark Historical Society
P.O. Box 1061, Brackettville, TX
78832

**Fort Worth Genealogical
Society**
P.O. Box 9767, Fort Worth, TX
76147-2767

**Fredericksburg Genealogical
Society**
P.O. Box 164, 108 N. Edison St.,
Fredericksburg, TX 78624

**Freestone County Genealogical
Society**
P.O. Box 14, Fairfield, TX 75840

**Fulton, Genealogical Society of
Aransas County**
P.O. Box 1642, Fulton, TX 78358

**Galveston County Genealogical
Society**
P.O. Box 1141, Galveston, TX
77553-1141

**Galveston, Rosenberg Library
Archives**
2310 Sealy Ave., Galveston, TX
77550-2296
Tel: (409) 763-8854
Fax: (409) 763-0275

Garland Genealogical Society
P.O. Box 461882, Garland, TX
75046

**Genealogical Society of Big
Spring**
% Howard County Library, 810 E.
Twelfth St., Big Spring, TX 79720

**Genealogical Society of
Kerrville**
505 Water St., Kerrville, TX
78028

German Texan Heritage Society
507 E. Tenth St., P.O. Box
684171, Austin, TX 78768-4171

**Gillespie County Historical
Society**
312 W. San Antonio, Fredericksburg, TX 78624

**Golden Spread Chapter,
American Historical Society of
Germans from Russia**
P.O. Box 107, Darrouzett, TX
79024

**Grand Prairie Genealogical
Society**
P.O. Box 532026, Grand Prairie,
TX 75053

**Grayson County Genealogical
Society**
421 N. Travis, Sherman, TX
75090

**Gregg County Historical &
Genealogical Society**
P.O. Box 2985, Longview, TX
75606-2985

**Grimes County Heritage
Association**
1215 E. Washington Ave., Navasota, TX 77868

**Guadalupe County
Genealogical Society**
707 E. College St., Sequin, TX
78155

**Gulf Coast Ancestry
Researchers**
P.O. Box 16, Wallisville, TX
77597

Texas

Harris County Genealogical Society
P.O. Box 391, Pasadena, TX 77501

Harrison County Historical Old Courthouse Museum
Peter Whetstone Square, Marshall, TX 75670

Hemphill County Historical & Genealogical Society
Rt. 2, Canadian, TX 79014

Henderson County Historical Society
P.O. Box 943, Athens, TX 75751

Heritage Association of San Marcos
P.O. Box 1806, San Marcos, TX 78666

Heritage Society of Washington County
P.O. Box 1123, Brenham, TX 77833

High Plains Genealogical Society
1807 Ennis St., Plainview, TX 79072

Hill County Genealogical Society
P.O. Box 636, Hillsboro, TX 76645-0636

Hillsboro Heritage League
P.O. Box 2, Hillsboro, TX 76645

Hispanic Genealogical Society
2932 Barksdale, Houston, TX 77093

Hood County Genealogical Society
P.O. Box 1623, Granbury, TX 76048

Hood County Library
222 N. Travis, Granbury, TX 76048

Hopkins County Genealogical Society
P.O. Box 624, Sulphur Springs, TX 75483-0624

Houston Academy of Medicine Historical Research Center
1133 M.D. Anderson Blvd., Houston, TX 77030-2809
Tel: (713) 795-5183

Houston Afro-American Historical & Genealogical Society
302 Harbor Dr., Houston, TX 77062

Houston Genealogical Forum
P.O. Box 271466, Houston, TX 77277-1466

Houston Metropolitan Research Center
Julia B. Ideson Bldg., 500 McKinney St., Houston, TX 77002-2534
Tel: (713) 247-3557

Houston Polish Genealogical Society
3606 Maroneal, Houston TX 77025

Houston Public Library, Houston Metropolitan Research Center
500 McKinney St., Houston, TX 77002-2534
Tel: (713) 236-1313

Humble Area Genealogical Society
P.O. Box 2723, Humble TX 77347

Hunt County Genealogical Society
P.O. Box 398, Greenville, TX 75401

Huntsville Public Library
1216 Fourteenth St., Huntsville, TX 773401
Tel: (936) 291-5472

Hutchinson County Genealogical Society
Hutchinson County Library, 625 Weatherly St., Borger, TX 79007

Institute of Texas Cultures
Hemisfair Plaza, P.O. Box 1226, San Antonio, TX 78294-1226
Tel: (210) 226-7651

Iowa Park Genealogical and Historical Society
400 W. Alameda, Iowa Park, TX 76367

Irving Public Library
P.O. Box 152288, Irving, TX 75015-2288

Jewish Genealogical Society of Houston
11727 Riverview Dr., Houston, TX 77077

Jewish Holocaust Education Center and Memorial Museum of Houston
5401 Caroline, Houston, TX 77004-6804
Tel: (832) 789-9898

Johnson County Genealogical Society
P.O. Box 1256, Cleburne, TX 76033

Karnes County Historical Society
P.O. Box 162, Karnes City, TX 78118

Kaufman County Genealogical Society
P.O. Box 337, Terrell, TX 75160

Kent County Genealogical and Historical Society
P.O. Box 414, Jayton, TX 79528

Kingsland Genealogical Society
P.O. Box 952, Kingsland, TX 78639

Kingsland Library, Llano County Library System
125 W. Polk St., Kingsland, TX 78639

La Porte Library
526 San Jacinto, La Porte, TX 77571-5498
Tel: (281) 471-4022

La Retama Public Library
505 N. Mesquite St., Corpus Christi, TX 78401

Lake Cities Historical Society
P.O. Box 1222, Lake Dallas, TX 75065

Lake Jackson Historical Association
P.O. Box 242, Lake Jackson, TX 77566

Lamar County Genealogical Society
P.O. Box 18, 2400 Clarksville St., Paris, TX 75460

Lamesa Area Genealogical Society
P.O. Box 1264, Lamesa, TX 79331

Lancaster Public Library
1600 Veterans Memorial Pkwy., Lancaster, TX 75134
Tel: (927) 227-1080

Laredo Public Library Historical Collections
Dept. 1120, E. Calton Rd., Laredo, TX 78041
Tel: (956) 795-2400

Lee County Genealogical Society
Rt. 1, P.O. Box 8-D, Ledbetter, TX 78946

Leon County Genealogical Society
P.O. Box 400, Centerville, TX 75833-0400

Leonard, Tri-County Genealogical Society
P.O. Box 107, Leonard, TX 75452

Liberty County Historical Commission
P.O. Box 23, Liberty, TX 77575

Liberty, Sam Houston Regional Library Research Center
1011 Governor's Rd., P.O. Box 310, Liberty, TX 77575-0310
Tel: (409) 336-8821

Llano County Library
102 Haynie, Llano, TX 78643

Longview Public Library
222 W. Cotton St., Longview, TX 75601

Los Bexarenos Genealogical Society
P.O. Box 1935, San Antonio, TX 78297

Lubbock City-County Library
1306 Ninth St., Lubbock, TX 79401

Lubbock Heritage Society
P.O. Box 5443, Lubbock, TX 79417

Lufkin Genealogical & Historical Society
P.O. Box 150631, Lufkin, TX 75915-0631

Lufkin, Kurth Memorial Library
706 S. Raguet, Lufkin, TX 75904

Luling Public Library
215 S. Pecan Ave., Luling, TX 78648

MaBank, Root Seekers Genealogical Society
Tri-County Library, P.O. Box 1770, Mabank, TX 75147-1770

Madison County Genealogical Society
P.O. Box 26, Madisonville, TX 77864

Marion County Genealogical Society
P.O. Box 224, Jefferson, TX 75657

Matagorda County African-American Historical Society
P.O. Box 1386, Bay City, TX 77404-1386

Matagorda County Genealogical Society
P.O. Box 264, Bay City, TX 77404-0264
Web site: <www.rootsweb.com/~txmatago/gensoc.htm>

McAllen Genealogical Society
% McAllen Memorial Library, 601 N. Main St., McAllen, TX 78501

McKinney Memorial Public Library
200 N. Kentucky St., McKinney, TX 75069

McLennan County Library
1717 Austin Ave., Waco, TX 76701

Menard Genealogical Society
P.O. Box 714, Menard, TX 76859

Mesquite Historical and Genealogical Society
P.O. Box 850164, Mesquite, TX 75185-0165

Mesquite Public Library
300 Grubb Dr., Mesquite, TX 75149

Mid-Cities Genealogical Society
P.O. Box 407, Bedford, TX 76095-0407

Midland County Public Library, Redfern Genealogical Research Center
301 W. Missouri, Midland, TX 79701

Midland Genealogical Society
301 W. Missouri, Midland, TX 79701-5108

Milam County Genealogical Society
% Lucy Patterson Memorial Library, 201 Ackerman, Rockdale, TX 76567

Montague County Genealogical Society
P.O. Box 795, Bowie, TX 76230

Montgomery County Library
104 I-45 North, Conroe, TX 77301-2720
Tel: (409) 788-8363

Montgomery County Genealogical & Historical Society, Inc.
P.O. Box 867, Conroe, TX 77305-0867

Moody Texas Ranger Library
P.O. Box 2570, Waco, TX 76702-2570

Moore Memorial Library
1701 Ninth Ave. N., Texas City, TX 77590

Motley County Genealogical & Historical Society Library
P.O. Box 557, 1105 Main, Matador, TX 79244

Mt. Pleasant, Cypress Basin Genealogical and Historical Society
P.O. Box 403, Mt. Pleasant, TX 75455

Mt. Pleasant Municipal Library
P.O. Box 1285, 213 N. Madison, Mt. Pleasant, TX 75455

Nacogdoches Genealogical Society
P.O. Box 4634, Nacogdoches, TX 75962
Web site: <www.rootsweb.com/~txngs/>

National Archives-Southwest Regional Branch (Fort Worth)
501 W. Felix St., Building 1, Dock 1, Fort Worth, TX 76115
Tel: (817) 334-5524
Fax: (817) 334-5621
Web site: <www.archives.gov/facilities/tx/fort_worth.html>

Navarro County Genealogical Society
P.O. Box 2278, Corsicana, TX 75151

New Boston Genealogical Society
% New Boston Public Library, 127 North Ellis, New Boston, TX 75570-2905

Newton County Historical Commission
P.O. Box 56, Burkeville, TX 75932

Nicholson Memorial Library
625 Austin St., Garland, TX 75040

Nolan County Genealogical Association
% County City Library, P.O. Box 780, Sweetwater, TX 79556

North Texas Genealogical and Historical Association
P.O. Box 4602, Wichita Falls, TX 76308

Odessa, Ector County Library
321 W. Fifth St., Odessa, TX 79761
Tel: (432) 332-0633
Web site: <www.ector.lib.tx.us>

Orange County Historical Society
P.O. Box 1345, Orange, TX 77630

Palestine Public Library
1101 N. Cedar, Palestine, TX 75801

Palo Pinto County Historical Association
P.O. Box 42, Palo Pinto, TX 76072

Pampa Genealogical and Historical Society
430 N. Summer St., Pampa, TX 79065

Parker County Genealogical Society
1707 Third, Brownwood, TX 76801

Permian Basin Genealogical Society
321 W. Fifth St., Odessa, TX 79761
Web site: <www.permiangen.com>

Pilot Point Community Library
324 S. Washington St., P.O. Box 969, Pilot Point, TX 76258-0969

Plano Heritage Association
1900 W. Fifteenth St., Plano, TX 75075

Polk County Heritage Society
207 N. Beatty St., Livingston, TX 77351

Quitman Public Library
202 E. Goode St., P.O. Box 77, Quitman, TX 75783

Randolph Area Genealogical Society
P.O. Box 2134, Universal City, TX 78148-1134

Red River County Texas Genealogical Society
P.O. Drawer D, Clarksville, TX 75426

Refugio County Historical Society
Refugio County Museum, 102 West St., Refugio, TX 78377

Richmond, George Memorial Library
Genealogy and Local History Dept., 1001 Golfview Dr., Richmond, TX 77469
Tel: (281) 342-4455
Web site: <www.fortbend.lib.tx.us>

Roberts County Historical Commission
% Roberts County Museum, P.O. Box 306, Miami, TX 79059

Rochelle, Heart of Texas Genealogical Society
P.O. Box 133, Rochelle, TX 76872

Round Rock Public Library
216 E. Main, Round Rock, TX 78664

Rusk County Library
106 E. Main St., Henderson, TX 75652

Rusk County Historical Commission
P.O. Box 1773, Henderson, TX 75652

Salado Historical Society
P.O. Box 251, Salado, TX 76571

San Angelo Genealogical and Historical Society, Inc.
P.O. Box 3453, San Angelo, TX 76901

San Antonio Genealogical and Historical Society
P.O. Box 790087, San Antonio, TX 78279-0087

San Antonio Genealogical and Historical Society Library
911 Melissa Dr., San Antonio, TX 78213
Tel: (210) 342-5242

San Augustine Public Library
413 E. Columbia, San Augustine, TX 75972

San Jacinto County Heritage Society
P.O. Box 505, Coldspring, TX 77331

San Marcos/Hays County Genealogical Society
P.O. Box 503, San Marcos, TX 78666

Schleicher County Historical Society
P.O. Box 473, Eldorado, TX 76936

Scurry County Library
1916 Twenty-third St., Snyder, TX 79549

Scurry County Genealogical Society
P.O. Box 195, Snyder, TX 79550

Sherman Public Library
P.O. Box 1106, 421 N. Travis, Sherman, TX 75090-0190
Tel: (214) 892-7240

Smith County Historical Society
624 N. Broadway, Tyler, TX 75702

Somervell County Genealogical and Heritage Society
P.O. Box 1097, Glen Rose, TX 76043

Sophienburg Archives
200 N. Sequin St., New Braunfels, TX 78130

South Plains Genealogical Society
P.O. Box 6607, Lubbock, TX 79493

South Texas Genealogical Society
P.O. Box 754, Beeville, TX 78104

Southeast Texas Genealogical & Historical Society
℅ Tyrrell Historical Library, P.O. Box 3827, Beaumont, TX 77704

Southwest Genealogical Society & Library
412 W. College St. #A, Carthage, TX 75633-1406

Stephens County Genealogical Society
P.O. Box 350, Breckenridge, TX 76024

Stephens County Historical Association
01 N. Harding, Breckenridge, TX 76024

Sterling Municipal Library
#1 Mary Elizabeth Wilbanks Ave., Baytown, TX 77520-4258
Tel: (281) 427-7331

Tarrant County Black History & Genealogical Society
1020 E. Humboldt, Fort Worth, TX 76104

Taylor Heritage Society
P.O. Box 385, Taylor, TX 76574

Temple Public Library
101 N. Main St., Temple, TX 76501

Terrell County Historical Commission
P.O. Box 7, Sanderson, TX 79848

Texarkana Public Library
901 State Line Ave., Texarkana, TX 75501

Texarkana Genealogical Society
P.O. Box 2323, Texarkana, TX 75504

Texas Bureau of Vital Statistics
P.O. Box 12040, Austin, TX 78711
Tel: (512) 458-7111
Web site: <www.dshs.state.tx.us>

Texas City Ancestry Searchers
P.O. Box 3301, Texas City, TX 77592
Web site: <www.rootsweb.com/~txtcas>

Texas Czech Heritage and Cultural Center, Inc.
P.O. Box 6, La Grange, TX 78945
Tel: (409) 968-8373
Web site: <www.genealogy.org/czech/tchcc.html>

Texas General Land Office
Stephen F. Austin Bldg., 1700 N. Congress, Suite 800, Austin, TX 78701-1495
Tel: (512) 463-5277
Web site: <www.glo.state.tx.us>

Texas-Oklahoma Panhandle Genealogical Society
1010 S. Harvard St., Perryton, TX 79070

Texas State Archives
1201 St., P.O. Box 12927, Austin, TX 78711-2927
Tel: (512) 463-5480
Web site: <www.tsl.state.tx.us>

Texas State Genealogical Society
3219 Meadow Oaks Dr., Temple, TX 76502
Tel: (254) 778-2073
Web site: <www.rootsweb.com/~txsgs>

Texas State Library
1201 Brazos, P.O. Box 12927, Austin, TX 78711-2917
Web site: <www.tsl.state.tx.us>

Texas Wendish Heritage Society
P.O. Box 311, Giddings, TX 78942

Timpson Area Genealogical and Heritage Society
P.O. Box 726, Timpson, TX 75975

Tom Burnett Memorial Library
400 W. Alameda, Iowa Park, TX 76367

Tom Green County Historical Preservation League
P.O. Box 1625, San Angelo, TX 76902

Troup Genealogical/Historical Society
P.O. Box 173, Troup, TX 75789

Tyler Public Library
201 S. College Ave., Tyler, TX 75702
Tel: (903) 593-7323
Web site: <www.tylertexas.com/cot/departments/library>

University of Texas at Austin, The Center for American History
Sid Richardson Hall 2.101, 1 University Station D1100, Austin, TX 78712-0335
Tel: (512) 495-4515
Fax: (512) 495-4542
Web site:

Val Verde County Genealogical Society
P.O. Box 442052, DelRio, TX 78842

Van Alstyne Genealogical Society
P.O. Box 308, Van Alstyne, TX 75095

Van Zandt County Library of Genealogy & Local History
Van Zandt County Courthouse, Annex Bldg., Canton, TX 75103-0716
Tel: (903) 567-5012
Web site: <www.rootsweb.com/txvanzan/vzcpage.htm>

Van Zandt County Genealogical Society
P.O. Box 716, Canton, TX 75103-0716

Victoria County Genealogical Society
302 N. Main St., Victoria, TX 77901

Victoria Public Library
302 N. Main St., Victoria, TX 77901
Tel: (361) 572-2708

Waco Public Library
1717 Austin Ave., Waco, TX 76701

Walker County Genealogical Society
P.O. Box 1295, Huntsville, TX 77342-1295
Web site: <www.wcgen.com>

Walker County Historical Society
P.O. Box 235, Brookshire, TX 75455

Wallisville Heritage Library & Museum
Hwy. I-10, P.O. Box 16, Wallisville, TX 77597-0016
Tel: (409) 389-2252

Ward County Genealogical Society
400 E. Fourth St., Monahans, TX 79756

Weatherford Public Library
1014 Charles St., Weatherford, TX 76086
Tel: (817) 598-4156

Webb County Heritage Foundation
P.O. Drawer 29, Laredo, TX 78042

West Bell Genealogical Society
P.O. Box 851, Killeen, TX 76540

West Texas Genealogical Society
P.O. Box 2307, Abilene, TX 79604

Wharton County Chapter of the Texas German Society
P.O. Box 1236, El Campo, TX 77457

Wharton County Czech Society
Rt. 1, P.O. Box 23, Louise, TX 77455

Whitmeyer Genealogy Library and Heritage Village Museum
P.O. Box 888, Woodville, TX 75979-0888

Williamson County Genealogical Society
P.O. Box 585, Round Rock, TX 78680

Texas

Winkler County Genealogical Society
P.O. Box 1028, Kermit, TX 79745

Wise County Genealogical Society
P.O. Box 126, Rhome, TX 76078

Wise County Historical Society and Heritage Museum
1602 S. Trinity St., P.O. Box 427, Decatur, TX 76234
Tel: (940) 627-5586
Web site: <http://homepages.nt ws.net/sites/wisemuseum/ index.htm>

Wood County Genealogical Society
P.O. Box 832, Quitman, TX 75783

Yoakum County Historical Commission
P.O. Box 960, Plains, TX 79355

Zapata County Historical Commission
P.O. Box 6305, Zapata, TX 78076

BIBLIOGRAPHY

■ GENERAL RESOURCES

Bibliography of Texas, 1795–1845, 2d ed.
by Archibald Hanna (Woodbridge, CT: Research Pub., 1983)

Biographical Gazetteer of Texas: Publication of the Biographical Sketch File of the Texas Collection At Baylor University, an Ongoing Project . . ., 6 vols.
compiled by Virginia Ming and William L. Ming (Austin: Morrison Books, 1985–)

Biographical Souvenir of the State of Texas, 1889
(Easley, SC: Southern Historical Press, 1978)

Black Churches in Texas: A Guide to Historic Congregations
by Clyde McQueen (College Station, TX: Texas A&M University Press, 2000)

Catalog of Genealogical Materials in Texas Libraries
compiled by John Corbin (Austin: Texas State Library and Historical Commission, 1965–)

Citizens of the Republic of Texas
compiled by Mrs. Harry Joseph Morris (Dallas: Texas State Genealogical Society, 1979)

Cracker Barrel Chronicles: A Bibliography of Texas Town and County Histories
by John Holmes Jenkins (Austin: Pemberton Press, 1965)

Four Decades of Catholicism in Texas 1820–1860
by Sister Mary Angela Fitzmorris (Washington, DC: Catholic University of America, 1926)

Genealogical Records in Texas
by Imogene Kinard Kennedy and J. Leon Kennedy (Baltimore: Genealogical Publishing Co., 1987)

"Genealogical Research in Texas: A Bibliographical Guide"
by Lloyd DeWitt Bockstruck (*National Genealogical Society Quarterly* 75, Sept. 1987: 194-215)

The Genealogist's Companion and Sourcebook, 2d ed.
by Emily Anne Croom (Cincinnati: Betterway Books, 2003)

A Genealogist's Guide to Discovering Your African-American Ancestors
by Franklin Carter Smith and Emily Anne Croom (Cincinnati: Betterway Books, 2003)

Guide to Genealogical Research in the National Archives of the United States
edited by Anne Bruner Eales and Robert M. Kvasnicka (Washington, DC: National Archives and Records Administration, 2000)

Guide to Genealogical Resources in the Texas State Archives
by Jean Carefoot (Austin: Archives Division, Texas State Library, 1984)

A Guide to Texas Research
by Carolyn Reeves Ericson and Joe E. Ericson (Nacogdoches, TX: Ericson Books, 1994)

A Guide to the Texana Holdings of the Texas History Library of the Daughters of the Republic of Texas, 2 vols.
compiled by Catherine McDowell (San Antonio: Daughters of the Republic of Texas, 1978)

The Handbook of Texas Online
sponsored by the Texas State Historical Association and the General Libraries of the University of Texas <www.tsha.utexas.edu/ handbook/online>

The Historical Encyclopedia of Texas, 2 vols.
edited by Thomas S. Chamblin (Dallas: Texas Historical Institute, 1982)

History of Early Methodism in Texas, 1817–1866
by Macum Phelan (Nashville: Cokesbury Press, 1924)

A History of Texas Baptists
by James M. Carroll (Originally published in 1923; Reprint: Houston: Historical Pub. Society, 1977)

History of Texas and Texans, 5 vols.
by Frank W. Johnson, edited by Eugene C. Barker (Chicago: American Historical Society, 1914)

Indian Wars and Pioneers of Texas
by John Henry Brown (Originally published in 1880; Reprint: Greenville, SC: Southern Historical Press, 1978)

National Archives Microfilm Catalogs online:
<www.archives.gov/publica tions/genealogy_microfilm_ catalogs.html>

The New Handbook of Texas, 6 vols.
edited by Ron Tyler, et al. (Austin: Texas State Historical Association, 1996)

Residents of Texas, 1782–1836, 3 vols.
(San Antonio: The University of Texas, Institute of Texan Cultures, 1984)

Spanish and Mexican Records of the American Southwest: A Bibliographic Guide to Archive and Manuscript Sources
by Henry P. Beers (Tucson: University of Arizona Press, 1979)

Texas Family Land Heritage Registry, 13 vols.
(Austin: Texas Department of Agriculture, 1974–1997)

Texas Historical and Biographical Record with a Genealogical Study of Historical Family Records
by Ernest Emory Bailey (Austin: Texas Historical and Biographical Record, 1900)

Texas Local History: A Source Book for Available Town and County Histories, Local Memoirs and Genealogical Records
by Tom Munnerlyn (Austin: Eakin Press, 1983)

Texas Newspapers, 1813–1939: A Union List of Newspaper Files Available in Offices of Publishers, Libraries, and a Number of Private Collections
(Houston, TX: San Jacinto Museum of History Associations, 1941)

Texas Research Outline
(Salt Lake City, UT: Corp. of the President of the Church of Jesus Christ of L.D.S., 1988)

Who's Who in Texas
edited by Emory E. Bailey, et al. (Dallas: Who's Who Publishing, 1931)

Who's Who in Texas Today: A New Biographical Survey of Texas
by the International Biographical Research Corp. (Austin: Pemberton Press, 1968)

■ CENSUS RECORDS

The American Census Handbook
by Thomas Jay Kemp (Wilmington, DE: Scholarly Resources, Inc., 2001)

The Census Book: A Genealogist's Guide to Federal Census Facts, Schedules and Indexes
by William Dollarhide (Bountiful, UT: Heritage Quest, 1999)

1830 Citizens of Texas
by Gifford E. White (Austin: Eakin Press, 1999)

1840 Citizens of Texas, 3 vols.
compiled by Gifford E. White (Originally published in 1980s; Reprint: Nacogdoches, TX: Ericson Books, 1994)

Texas

Map Guide to the U.S. Federal Censuses, 1790–1920
by William Thorndale and William Dollarhide (Baltimore: Genealogical Publishing Co., 1987)

State Census Records
by Ann S. Lainhart (Baltimore: Genealogical Publishing Co., Inc., 1992)

Your Guide to the Federal Census
by Kathleen W. Hinckley (Cincinnati: Betterway Books, 2002)

■ IMMIGRATION RECORDS

American Naturalization Records, 1790–1990: What They Are and How to Use Them
by John J. Newman (North Salt Lake, UT: HeritageQuest, 1998)

American Passenger Arrival Records
by Michael Tepper (Baltimore: Genealogical Publishing Co., 1993)

Comal County, Texas, and New Braunfels, Texas, German Immigration Ships, 1845–1846
by J. McManus (St. Louis, MO: Frances T. Ingmire, 1985)

A New Land Beckoned: German Immigration to Texas, 1844–1847
by Chester W. Geue and Ethel H. Geue (Originally published in 1972; Reprint: Baltimore: Genealogical Publishing Co., 2002)

Passenger Lists for Galveston 1850–1855
by Albert J. Blaha (Houston, TX: A.J. Blaha, 1985)

Ships Passenger Lists, Port of Galveston, Texas, 1846–1871
(Easley, SC: Southern Historical Press, 1984)

Stephen F. Austin's Register of Families
edited by Villamae Williams (Originally published 1984; Reprint: Baltimore: Clearfield Co., 1996)

Tennesseans in Texas
by Helen Crawford Marsh and Timothy R. Marsh (Easley, SC: Southern Historical Press, 1986)

They Became Americans: Finding Naturalization Records and Ethnic Origins
by Loretto Dennis Szucs (Salt Lake City: Ancestry, Inc., 1998)

They Came in Ships: A Guide to Finding Your Immigrant Ancestor's Arrival Records, 2d ed.
by John P. Colletta (Salt Lake City: Ancestry, Inc., 1993)

■ LAND RECORDS

Abstract of Valid Land Claims, Complied From the Records of the General Land Office and Court of Claims of the State of Texas
by John Burlage, et al. (Austin: J. Marshall, 1859)

Abstract of Land Titles of Texas: Comprising the Titled, Parented, and Located Lands in the State
(Galveston: Shaw and Blaylock, 1878)

Bounty and Donation Land Grants of Texas, 1835–1888
by Thomas Lloyd Miller (Austin: University of Texas Press, 1967)

Character Certificates in the General Land Office of Texas
by Gifford E. White (Originally published in 1985; Reprint: Baltimore: Clearfield Co., 1993)

Claiming Their Land: Women Homesteaders in Texas
by Florence C. Gould and Patricia N. Pando (El Paso, TX: Texas Western Press, 1991)

First Settlers of the Republic of Texas: Headright Land Grants . . . , 1840, 2 vols.
by Carolyn Reeves Ericson and Frances Terry Ingmire (Originally published in 1841; Reprint: Nacogdoches, TX: Carolyn R. Ericson, 1982)

Index to Spanish and Mexican Land Grants in Texas
by Virginia H. Taylor (Originally published in 1956; Austin: Lone Star Press, 1995)

The Land Commissioners of Texas: 150 Years of the General Land Office
by Garry Mauro (Austin: Texas General Land Office, 1986)

Locating Your Roots: Discover Your Ancestors Using Land Records
by Patricia Law Hatcher (Cincinnati: Betterway Books, 2003)

The Public Lands of Texas 1519–1970
by Thomas Lloyd Miller (Norman, OK: University of Oklahoma Press, 1972)

Spanish and Mexican Land Grants in the Chihuahuan Acquisition
by J.J. Bowden (El Paso, TX: Texas Western Press, 1971)

■ MAPS

A Gazetteer of Texas
by Henry Gannett (Washington: Government Printing Office, 1904)

A Historical Atlas of Texas
by William C. Pool (Austin: Encino Press, 1975)

How Come It's Called That?: Place Names in the Big Bend Country
by Virginia Madison and Hallie Stillwell (Originally published in 1958; Reprint: Marathon, TX: Iron Mountain Press, 1997)

Maps of Texas, 1527–1900: The Map Collection of the Texas State Archives
compiled by James M. Day (Mansfield Centre, CT: Martino Fine Books, 1997)

Maps of Texas and the Southwest, 1513–1900
James C. Martin and Robert S. Martin (Austin: Texas State Historical Association, 1999)

Old Texas Trails
by J.W. Williams; edited and compiled by Kenneth F. Neighbours (Burnet, TX: Eakin Press, 1979)

Texas Atlas and Gazetteer
(Freeport, ME: DeLorme Mapping, 1995)

800 Texas Ghost Towns
by Ed Ellsworth Bartholomew (Fort Davis, TX: Frontier Book Publishers, 1974)

1001 Texas Place Names
by Fred Tarpley (Austin: University of Texas Press, 1980)

■ MILITARY RECORDS

The Heroes of San Jacinto
by Sam Houston Dixon and Louise Wiltz Kemp (Houston: The Anson Jones Press, 1932)

Index to Applications for Texas Confederate Pensions
by John M. Kinney (Austin: Archives Division, Texas State Library, 1977)

Index to Texas CSA Pension Files
by Virgil D. White (Waynesboro, TN: National Historical Publishing Co., 1989)

Lone Stars and State Gazettes: Texas Newspapers Before the Civil War
by Marilyn McAdams Sibley (College Station, TX: Texas A&M University Press, 1983)

Muster Lists of the Texas Confederate Troops
by Sherman L. Pompey (Independence, CA: Historical and Genealogical Publishing Co., 1966)

Muster Rolls of the Texas Revolution
(Austin, TX: Daughters of the Republic of Texas, Inc., 1986)

Republic of Texan Pension Application Abstracts
by John C. Barron, et al. (Austin: Austin Genealogical Society, 1987)

Roll Call at the Alamo
by Phil Rosenthal and Bill Groneman (Ft. Collins, CO: The Old Army Press, 1985)

Texas Frontiersman, 1839–1860: Minute Men, Militia, Home Guard, Indian Fighter
compiled by Frances Terry Ingmire (St. Louis: F.T. Ingmire, 1982)

Texas Rangers: Frontier Battalion, Minute Men, Commanding Officers, 1847–1900, 6 vols.
by Frances Terry Ingmire (St. Louis: F.T. Ingmire, 1982)

Texas Ranger Indian War Pensions
by Robert W. Stephens (Quanah, TX: Nortex Press, 1975)

Texas Volunteers in the Mexican War
by Henry W. Barton (Wichita Falls, TX: Texian Press, 1970)

Uncle, We Are Ready! Registering America's Men, 1917–1918: A Guide to Researching World War I Draft Registration Cards
by John J. Newman (North Salt Lake, UT: HeritageQuest, 2001)

Texas

U.S. Military Records: A Guide to Federal & State Sources, Colonial America to the Present
by James C. Neagles (Salt Lake City: Ancestry, Inc., 1994)

War of 1812 Veterans in Texas
by Mary Smith Fay (Greenville, SC: Southern Historical Press, 1994)

World War II: A Family Historian's Guide
by Debra Johnson Knox (Spartanburg, SC: MIE Publishing, 2003)

■ PROBATE RECORDS

Note:
Numerous books on county probate records exist for Texas counties. Check online library catalogs.

Index to Probate Cases, 1846–1900, Dallas County, Texas
by Helen M. Lu, et al. (Dallas: Dallas Genealogical Society, 1978)

Walker County, Texas Probate Records
compiled by Johnnie Jo Dickenson (Huntsville, TX: Dickenson Research, 1992–)

■ VITAL RECORDS

Early Texas Birth Records, 1838–1878, 2 vols.
by Alice D. Gracy, Emma G. S. Gentry, and Jane Sumner (Easley, SC: Southern Historical Press, 1991)

4000 Inscriptions from Texas, 1745–1870: Along the Old San Antonio Road and the Trail of Austin's Colonists
compiled by Inez Boswell Biggerstaff (Oklahoma City: Oklahoma Historical Society, 1952)

Lost, Abandoned, Family and Small Community Cemeteries: Along the Red River Valley in Northeast Texas . . .
edited by Patricia A. Newhouse (Honey Grove, TX: Newhouse Publications, 1992)

Marriage by Bond in Colonial Texas
by Bennett L. Smith (Fort Worth, TX: Branch-Smith, 1972)

Marriage Records of Early Texas, 1824–1846
by Norma R. Grammer (Fort Worth, TX: Fort Worth Genealogical Society, 1980)

Northeast Texas Cemeteries
by John P. Frazier (Shreveport, CA: J. and W. Enterprises, 1984)

A Reference to Texas Cemetery Records
by Kim Parsons (Humble, TX: Kim Parsons, 1988)

Texas Cemetery Inscriptions: A Source Index
by Sherry Crofford-Gould (San Antonio: Limited Editions, 1977)

8,800 Texas Marriages, 1824–1850, 2 vols.
by Helen S. Swenson (Nacogdoches, TX: Ericson Books, 1995)

Texas Marriages, Early to 1850: A Research Tool
by Jordan R. Dodd (Bountiful, UT: Precision Indexing, 1990)

Your Guide to Cemetery Research
by Sharon DeBartolo Carmack (Cincinnati: Betterway Books, 2002)

■ Anderson   24 Mar. 1846
500 N. Church St., Palestine, TX 75801-3024
Phone: (903)723-7432
Web site: www.rootsweb.com/~txanders
Parent County: Houston
Comments/research tips: County Clerk has Military Discharge records 1919–1947. District Clerk has Naturalization records 1874–1928.

Record Type	Year Begun	Jurisdiction
Birth	1903	District Court
Marriage	1846	County Clerk
Death	1903	County Clerk
Divorce	1898	District Clerk
Land	1846	County Clerk
Probate	1846	County Clerk
Court	1846	District Clerk

■ Andrews   21 Aug. 1876
215 NW First St., Andrews, TX 79714
Phone: (915)524-1426
Web site: www.rootsweb.com/~txandrew/
Parent County: Bexar Land District

Record Type	Year Begun	Jurisdiction
Birth	1910	County Clerk
Marriage	1910	County Clerk
Divorce	na	District Clerk
Land	1884	County Clerk
Probate	1911	County Clerk
Court	1910	County Clerk

■ Angelina   22 Apr. 1846
P.O. Box 908, Lufkin, TX 75902
Phone: (936)634-8339
Web site: www.rootsweb.com/~txangeli/
Parent County: Nacogdoches
Comments/research tips: County Clerk has Land records 1846–1887, Marriage records 1846–1917, and Probate records 1850–1934.

Record Type	Year Begun	Jurisdiction
Birth	1875	County Clerk
Death	1903	County Clerk
Divorce	1847	District Clerk
Court	1847	District Court

■ Aransas   18 Sep. 1871
301 N. Liveoak St., Rockport, TX 78382
Phone: (361)790-0122
Web site: www.rootsweb.com/~txaransa/
Parent County: Refugio
Comments/research tips: District Clerk has Naturalization records 1908–1913.

Record Type	Year Begun	Jurisdiction
Birth	1871	County Clerk
Marriage	1871	County Clerk
Death	1871	County Clerk
Land	1871	County Clerk
Probate	1860	County Clerk
Court	1871	County Clerk

Texas

■ Archer 22 Jan. 1858

112 E. Walnut, P.O. Box 815, Archer City, TX 76351
Phone: (940)574-4302
Web site: www.rootsweb.com/~txarcher/archer.htm
Parent County: Clay
Comments/research tips: County Clerk has Court records 1881–1941, Land records 1855–1901, Naturalization records 1811–1957, and Probate records 1875–1936.

Record Type	Year Begun	Jurisdiction
Birth	1903	County Clerk
Marriage	1927	County Clerk
Death	1903	County Clerk
Divorce	1881	District Clerk

■ Armstrong 21 Aug. 1876

P.O. Box 309, Claude, TX 79019
Phone: (806)226-2081
Web site: www.rootsweb.com/~txarmstr/
Parent County: Bexar

Record Type	Year Begun	Jurisdiction
Birth	1903	County Clerk
Marriage	1890	County Clerk
Death	1903	County Clerk
Divorce	na	District Clerk
Land	1883	County Clerk
Probate	1890	County Clerk
Court	1898	County Clerk

■ Atascosa 25 Jan. 1856

Circle Dr., Room 6-1, Jourdanton, TX 78026
Phone: (830)767-2511
Web site: www.pastracks.com/states/texas/atascosa/
Parent County: Bexar Land District
Comments/research tips: District Clerk has Court records 1857–1910 and Naturalization records 1888–1903. County Clerk has Land records 1856–1907, Marriage records 1856–1911, and Probate records 1873–1910.

Record Type	Year Begun	Jurisdiction
Birth	1856	County Clerk
Death	1903	County Clerk
Divorce	1857	District Clerk

■ Austin 1837

1 E. Main St., Bellville, TX 77418
Phone: (979)865-5911
Web site: www.rootsweb.com/~txaustin
Parent County: Old Mexican Municipality
Comments/research tips: County Clerk has Land records 1837–1920, Military Discharge records 1918–1951, Naturalization records 1849–1936, and Probate records 1837–1977. District Clerk has Court records 1839–1940.

Record Type	Year Begun	Jurisdiction
Birth	1903	County Clerk
Death	1903	County Clerk
Divorce	1839	District Court
Marriage	1824	County Clerk

■ Bailey 21 Aug. 1876

300 S. First St., Muleshoe, TX 79347-3621
Phone: (806)272-3044

Web site: www.rootsweb.com/~txbailey/
Parent County: Bexar Land District
Comments/research tips: Became an independent county in 1919. Previously Bailey County was attached to Jack County 1876–1881, Baylor County 1881–1887, Hale County 1887–1892, and Castro County 1892–1919.

Record Type	Year Begun	Jurisdiction
Birth	1919	County Clerk
Marriage	1919	County Clerk
Divorce	1919	District Clerk
Land	1919	County Clerk
Probate	1919	County Clerk
Court	1919	County Clerk

■ Bandera 26 Jan. 1856

County Courthouse, P.O. Box 823, Bandera, TX 78003
Phone: (830)796-3332
Web site: www.rootsweb.com/~txbander/
Parent County: Bexar, Uvalde
Comments/research tips: County Clerk has Birth records 1873–1876, Land records 1856–1906, Marriage records 1856–1931, and Probate records 1856–1970.

Record Type	Year Begun	Jurisdiction
Birth	1926	County Clerk
Death	1904	County Clerk
Divorce	1856	District Clerk
Court	1857	District Clerk

■ Bastrop 18 Dec. 1837

804 Pecan St., P.O. Box 577, Bastrop, TX 78602
Phone: (512)332-7234
Web site: www.rootsweb.com/~txbastro/bastrop.htm
Parent County: Old Mexican Municipality (Municipality of Mina)
Comments/research tips: District Clerk has Court records 1837–1952 and Divorce records 1901–1942. County Clerk has Land records 1837–1920, Marriage records 1851–1974, Military Discharge records 1917–1943, Naturalization records 1837–1941, and Probate records 1837–1974.

Record Type	Year Begun	Jurisdiction
Birth	1853	County Clerk
Death	1903	County Clerk

■ Baylor 1 Feb. 1858

101 S. Washington, P.O. Box 689, Seymour, TX 76380
Phone: (940)889-3322
Web site: www.rootsweb.com/~txbaylor/baylor.htm
Parent County: Fannin Land District
Comments/research tips: County Clerk has Marriage records 1879–1920.

Record Type	Year Begun	Jurisdiction
Birth	1903	County Clerk
Death	1903	County Clerk
Divorce	1881	County Clerk
Probate	1880	County Clerk
Court	1880	County Clerk

■ Bee 8 Dec. 1857

105 W. Corpus Christi St., Beeville, TX 78102
Phone: (361)362-3245

Web site: www.beeville.net/TXGenWeb/Bee/
Parent County: Goliad, Refugio, Live Oak, San Patricio, Karnes
Comments/research tips: District Clerk has Court and Divorce records 1858–1895. County Clerk has Land records 1858–1892, Marriage records 1860–1911, and Probate records 1859–1895.

Record Type	Year Begun	Jurisdiction
Birth	1903	County Clerk
Death	1903	County Clerk

■ **Bell** 22 Jan. 1850
550 E. Second St., P.O. Box 480, Belton, TX 76513
Phone: (254)933-5160
Web site: www.bellcountytx.com/
Parent County: Milam
Comments/research tips: County Clerk has Birth records 1873–1876. Clerk of District Court has Naturalization records 1886–1920.

Record Type	Year Begun	Jurisdiction
Death	1903	County Clerk
Marriage	1850	County Clerk
Probate	1850	County Clerk
Land	1850	County Clerk
Military	na	County Clerk
Divorce	1893	Clerk/District Ct.
Court	1852	Clerk/District Ct.

■ **Bexar** 20 Dec. 1836
100 Dolorosa St., Suite 108, San Antonio, TX 78205
Phone: (210)335-2216
Web site: www.co.bexar.tx.us/
Parent County: Old Mexican Municipality (established 1731), Department of Bejar
Comments/research tips: County Clerk has Birth records 1837–1967, Death records 1902–1967, and Naturalization records 1850–1906. County Clerk also has Spanish Church Records from 1737–1859 and Spanish City Council Minutes from 1815–1820.

Record Type	Year Begun	Jurisdiction
Court	1836	District Clerk
Marriage	1837	County Clerk
Military	1919	County Clerk
Probate	1837	County Clerk
Land	1736	County Clerk

■ **Blanco** 12 Feb. 1858
P.O. Box 65, Johnson City, TX 78636
Phone: (830)868-7357
Web site: www.rootsweb.com/~txblanco/
Parent County: Gillespie, Comal, Burnet, Hays
Comments/research tips: County Clerk has Divorce and Land records 1875–1959, Marriage records 1876–1974, Military records 1917–1943, and Naturalization records 1880–1924.

Record Type	Year Begun	Jurisdiction
Birth	1903	County Clerk
Death	1903	County Clerk
Probate	1876	County Clerk
Court	1876	County Clerk

■ **Borden** 21 Aug. 1876
117 E. Wasson, P.O. Box 124, Gail, TX 79738
Phone: (806)756-4312
Web site: www.rootsweb.com/~txborden/
Parent County: Bosque

Record Type	Year Begun	Jurisdiction
Birth	1900	County Clerk
Death	1900	County Clerk
Divorce	1891	County Clerk
Court	1891	County Clerk
Land	1880	County Clerk
Probate	1894	County Clerk
Marriage	1891	County Clerk

■ **Bosque** 4 Feb. 1854
P.O. Box 617, Meridian, TX 76665
Phone: (254)435-2201
Web site: http://users.htcomp.net/bosque/
Parent County: McLennan
Comments/research tips: District Clerk has Court records 1856–1980 and Naturalization records 1887–1914.

Record Type	Year Begun	Jurisdiction
Birth	1903	County Clerk
Marriage	1860	County Clerk
Death	1903	County Clerk
Probate	1860	County Clerk
Land	1860	County Clerk
Divorce	na	District Clerk

■ **Bowie** 17 Dec. 1840
P.O. Box 248, New Boston, TX 75570
Phone: (903)628-6742
Web site: www.usroots.com/~jmautrey/
Parent County: Red River
Comments/research tips: County Clerk has Birth records 1903–1941, Death records 1903–1966, Land records 1889–1908, Marriage records 1889–1952, and Probate records 1889–1931. Clerk of District Court has Court records 1883–1931 and Divorce records 1883–1942.

Record Type	Year Begun	Jurisdiction
Military	na	County Clerk

■ **Brazoria** 24 Mar. 1836
111 E. Locust St. Suite 200, Angleton, TX 77515
Phone: (979)849-5711
Web site: www.brazoria-county.com/
Parent County: Old Mexican Municipality
Comments/research tips: County Clerk has Court records 1867–1915, Marriage records 1829–1948, and Probate records 1826–1916.

Record Type	Year Begun	Jurisdiction
Birth	1901	County Clerk
Death	1903	County Clerk
Land	1837	County Clerk
Military	1919	County Clerk

■ **Brazos** 30 Jan. 1841
300 E. 26th St. Suite 120, Bryan, TX 77803
Phone: (409)361-4124

Web site: www.co.brazos.tx.us/
Parent County: Washington, Robertson
Comments/research tips: District Clerk has Court records 1841–1924. County Clerk has Naturalization records 1872–1941 and Probate records 1844–1947. Formerly Navasota County. Name changed to Brazos 28 January 1842.

Record Type	Year Begun	Jurisdiction
Marriage	1843	County Clerk
Birth	1900	County Clerk
Death	1900	County Clerk
Land	1841	County Clerk

■ Brewster 2 Feb. 1887
201 W. Ave. E., Alpine, TX 79831
Phone: (915)837-3366
Web site: www.rootsweb.com/~txbrewst/
Parent County: Presidio
Comments/research tips: County Clerk has Birth records 1903–1912 and 1915–1946, Death records 1903–1971, and Marriage records 1887–1965.

Record Type	Year Begun	Jurisdiction
Probate	1887	County Clerk
Military	1900	County Clerk
Court	1887	District Clerk
Land	1887	County Clerk
Divorce	1887	District Court

■ Briscoe 21 Aug. 1876
415 Main, P.O. Box 555, Silverton, TX 79257
Phone: (806)823-2134
Web site: www.rootsweb.com/~txbrisco/
Parent County: Bexar Land District

Record Type	Year Begun	Jurisdiction
Birth	1903	County Clerk
Land	1892	County Clerk
Marriage	1892	County Clerk
Death	1903	County Clerk
Probate	1892	County Clerk
Court	1892	County Clerk
Divorce	na	County Clerk

■ Brooks 11 Mar. 1911
P.O. Box 427, Falfurrias, TX 78355
Phone: (361)325-5604
Web site: www.rootsweb.com/~txbrooks
Parent County: Starr, Zapata, Hidalgo
Comments/research tips: County Clerk has Death records 1911–1971, Marriage records 1911–1951, Military Discharge records 1919–1947, and Probate records 1911–1990. Land records from 1848–1911 are transcribed from Hidalgo County records.

Record Type	Year Begun	Jurisdiction
Birth	1911	County Clerk
Land	1848	County Clerk
Court	1911	County Clerk

■ Brown 27 Aug. 1856
200 S. Broadway St., Brownwood, TX 76801
Phone: (915)643-2594

Web site: www.rootsweb.com/~txbrown/
Parent County: Travis, Comanche
Comments/research tips: County Clerk has Birth records 1903–1969, Death records 1903–1987, Land records 1880–1919, Marriage records 1880–1937, Military Discharge records 1917–1985, and Probate records 1880–1964. District Clerk has Divorce records 1906–1938.

Record Type	Year Begun	Jurisdiction
Military	1880	County Clerk
Court	1884	District Clerk

■ Burleson 24 Mar. 1846
P.O. Box 57, Caldwell, TX 77836
Phone: (979)567-2329
Web site: www.rootsweb.com/~txburles/burles.htm
Parent County: Milam, Washington
Comments/research tips: County Clerk has Death records 1903–1941. District Clerk has Divorce records 1856–1891 and 1899–1908.

Record Type	Year Begun	Jurisdiction
Birth	1903	County Clerk
Court	1845	County Clerk
Land	1846	County Clerk
Probate	1847	County Clerk
Marriage	1846	County Clerk

■ Burnet 5 Feb. 1852
220 S. Pierce St., Burnet, TX 78611-3196
Phone: (512)756-5406
Web site: www.rootsweb.com/~txburnet/
Parent County: Travis, Bell, Williamson
Comments/research tips: County Clerk has Death records 1903–1917, Land records 1852–1927, and Military Discharge records 1919–1968. District Clerk has Naturalization records 1852–1906.

Record Type	Year Begun	Jurisdiction
Birth	1903	County Clerk
Marriage	1852	County Clerk
Burial	1852	County Clerk
Probate	1852	County Clerk
Court	1854	District Clerk
Divorce	1867	District Clerk

■ Caldwell 6 Mar. 1848
110 S. Main St., Lockhart, TX 78644
Phone: (512)398-1804
Web site: www.rootsweb.com/~txcaldwe/
Parent County: Gonzales
Comments/research tips: County Clerk has Birth records 1873–1876 and 1903–1912, Death records 1903–1915, Military Discharge records 1918–1931, and Naturalization records 1853–1925. District Clerk has Divorce records 1896–1944.

Record Type	Year Begun	Jurisdiction
Birth	1915	County Clerk
Death	1915	County Clerk
Marriage	1848	County Clerk
Land	1846	County Clerk
Court	1848	District Clerk
Probate	1849	County Clerk

Texas

■ Calhoun 4 Apr. 1846
211 S. Ann St., Port Lavaca, TX 77979
Phone: (361)553-4411
Web site: www.rootsweb.com/~txcalhou/
Parent County: Victoria, Matagorda, Jackson
Comments/research tips: County Clerk has Marriage records 1846–1919 and Probate records 1846–1968. District Clerk has Court records 1847–1914 and Naturalization records 1851–1914.

Record Type	Year Begun	Jurisdiction
Land	1846	County Clerk
Birth	ca. 1850	County Clerk
Death	ca. 1850	County Clerk

■ Callahan 1 Feb. 1858
400 Market St., Baird, TX 79504
Phone: (325)854-1217
Web site: www.rootsweb.com/~txcallah/
Parent County: Bexar, Travis, Bosque

Record Type	Year Begun	Jurisdiction
Birth	1903	County Clerk
Death	1903	District/County Clerk
Marriage	1878	County Clerk
Probate	1879	County Clerk
Land	1878	County Clerk
Divorce	na	District Clerk
Court	1879	County Clerk

■ Cameron 12 Feb. 1848
964 E. Harrison, Brownsville, TX 78520
Phone: (956)554-0815
Web site: www.rootsweb.com/~txcamero/
Parent County: San Patricio
Comments/research tips: District Clerk has Divorce records 1849–1914. County Clerk has Land records 1848–1911, Marriage and Probate records 1848–1912, and Naturalization records 1876–1930.

Record Type	Year Begun	Jurisdiction
Birth	1903	County Clerk
Death	1903	County Clerk
Court	1849	District Clerk

■ Camp 6 Apr. 1874
126 Church St., Pittsburg, TX 75686
Phone: (903)856-2731
Web site: www.rootsweb.com/~txcamp/
Parent County: Upshur
Comments/research tips: District Clerk has Court records 1874–1974 and Divorce records 1911–1943.

Record Type	Year Begun	Jurisdiction
Birth	1903	County Clerk
Death	1903	County Clerk
Marriage	1874	County Clerk
Probate	1874	County Clerk
Land	1874	County Clerk

■ Carson 21 Aug. 1876
P.O. Box 487, Panhandle, TX 79068
Phone: (806)537-3873

Web site: www.rootsweb.com/~txcarson/
Parent County: Bexar Land District

Record Type	Year Begun	Jurisdiction
Birth	1903	County Clerk
Death	1903	County Clerk
Marriage	1888	County Clerk
Divorce	1902	County Clerk
Probate	1907	County Clerk
Land	1883	County Clerk

■ Cass 25 Apr. 1846
P.O. Box 449, Linden, TX 75563
Phone: (903)756-5071
Web site: www.rootsweb.com/~txcass/
Parent County: Bowie
Comments/research tips: Name changed to Davis 17 December 1861, changed back to Cass 16 May 1871. County Clerk has some Delayed Birth records from 1873.

Record Type	Year Begun	Jurisdiction
Death	1903	County Clerk
Marriage	1847	County Clerk
Probate	1846	County Clerk
Land	1846	County Clerk
Birth	1903	County Clerk
Divorce	1841	District Clerk
Court	1841	District Clerk

■ Castro 21 Aug. 1876
100 E. Bedford St., Dimmitt, TX 79027
Phone: (806)647-3338
Web site: www.rootsweb.com/~txcastro/castro/index.htm
Parent County: Bexar Land District

Record Type	Year Begun	Jurisdiction
Birth	1903	County Clerk
Death	1903	County Clerk
Marriage	1892	County Clerk
Divorce	1892	County Clerk
Court	1892	County Clerk
Land	1911	County Clerk
Probate	1948	County Clerk
Military	1917	County Clerk

■ Chambers 12 Feb. 1858
404 Washington, Anahuac, TX 77514
Phone: (409)267-8309
Web site: co.chambers.tx.us/
Parent County: Jefferson, Liberty
Comments/research tips: County Clerk has Land records 1875–1902, Marriage records 1876–1916, and Probate records 1876–1945.

Record Type	Year Begun	Jurisdiction
Birth	1903	County Clerk
Death	1908	County Clerk
Court	1875	County Clerk
Land	1875	County Clerk
Divorce	1910	County Clerk

■ Cherokee 11 Apr. 1846
520 N. Main St., P.O. Box 420, Rusk, TX 75785
Phone: (903)683-2350

Web site: www.tyler.net/ccgs/default.html
Parent County: Nacogdoches
Comments/research tips: County Clerk has Birth records 1903–1987, Death records 1903–1935, Land records 1846–1901, Marriage records 1846–1934, and Probate records 1839–1934.

Record Type	Year Begun	Jurisdiction
Court	1867	County Clerk
Divorce	1879	County Clerk

■ Childress   21 Aug. 1876
Courthouse Box 4, Childress, TX 79201
Phone: (940)937-6143
Web site: www.rootsweb.com/~txchildr/
Parent County: Donley
Comments/research tips: Courthouse fire 21 October 1891 destroyed many documents.

Record Type	Year Begun	Jurisdiction
Birth	1903	County Clerk
Death	1903	County Clerk
Marriage	1893	County Clerk
Divorce	1900	County Clerk
Court	1900	County Clerk
Probate	1894	County Clerk
Land	1895	County Clerk

■ Clay   24 Dec. 1857
100 N. Bridge St., Henrietta, TX 76365
Phone: (940)538-4631
Web site: www.rootsweb.com/~txclay/
Parent County: Cooke
Comments/research tips: District Clerk has Court records 1874–1945, Divorce records 1925–1943, and Naturalization records 1879–1917. County Clerk has Land records 1873–1891, Marriage records 1870–1946, and Probate records 1873–1961. County was dissolved in 1862, then reorganized in 1873.

Record Type	Year Begun	Jurisdiction
Birth	1903	County Clerk
Death	1903	County Clerk

■ Cochran   21 Aug. 1876
Courthouse, Morton, TX 79346
Phone: (806)266-5450
Web site: www.rootsweb.com/~txcochra/
Parent County: Bexar, Young

Record Type	Year Begun	Jurisdiction
Birth	1926	County Clerk
Death	1926	County Clerk
Divorce	1926	County Clerk
Probate	1926	County Clerk
Court	1926	County Clerk
Marriage	1924	County Clerk
Land	1884	County Clerk

■ Coke   13 Mar. 1889
P.O. Box 150, Robert Lee, TX 76945
Phone: (325)453-2631
Web site: www.rootsweb.com/~txcoke/

Parent County: Tom Green
Comments/research tips: County Clerk has Birth records 1903–1910, 1926–1990 and Marriage records 1890–2000.

Record Type	Year Begun	Jurisdiction
Death	1903	County Clerk
Divorce	1891	County Clerk
Probate	1891	County Clerk
Court	1891	County Clerk
Land	1872	County Clerk

■ Coleman   1 Feb. 1858
100 W. Liveoak St., Suite 105, P.O. Box 591, Coleman, TX 76834-0591
Phone: (325)625-2889
Web site: www.rootsweb.com/~txcolema/
Parent County: Travis, Brown

Record Type	Year Begun	Jurisdiction
Birth	1900	County Clerk
Death	1900	County Clerk
Marriage	1873	County Clerk
Land	1846	County Clerk
Probate	1876	County Clerk
Military	1918	County Clerk
Court	1876	County Clerk
Divorce	na	District/County Clerk

■ Collin   3 Apr. 1846
200 S. McDonald St., Suite 120, Annex A, McKinney, TX 75069
Phone: (972)548-4139
Web site: www.rootsweb.com/~txcolli2/
Parent County: Fannin
Comments/research tips: County Clerk has Military Discharge records 1919–1943. District Clerk has Naturalization records 1893–1902.

Record Type	Year Begun	Jurisdiction
Birth	1903	County Clerk
Death	1903	County Clerk
Court	1846	District Clerk
Marriage	1846	County Clerk
Probate	1846	County Clerk
Divorce	1846	District Clerk
Land	1846	County Clerk

■ Collingsworth   21 Aug. 1876
County Courthouse, Wellington, TX 79095
Phone: (806)447-2408
Web site: www.rootsweb.com/~txcollin/
Parent County: Bexar Land District, Youngland District

Record Type	Year Begun	Jurisdiction
Birth	1891	County Clerk
Marriage	1890	County Clerk
Death	1892	County Clerk
Divorce	1903	County Clerk
Court	1903	County Clerk
Land	na	County Clerk

■ Colorado   17 Mar. 1836
P.O. Box 68, Columbus, TX 78934
Phone: (979)732-2155

Web site: www.rootsweb.com/~txcolora/
Parent County: Old Mexican Municipality
Comments/research tips: County Clerk has Marriage records 1837–1879.

Record Type	Year Begun	Jurisdiction
Birth	1903	County Clerk
Death	1903	County Clerk
Marriage	1966	County Clerk
Probate	1837	County Clerk
Land	1908	County Clerk
Divorce	1837	District Clerk
Court	1937	District Clerk

■ **Comal**   24 Mar. 1846
150 N. Seguin, Room 101, New Braunfels, TX 78130
Phone: (830)620-5513
Web site: www.rootsweb.com/~txcomal
Parent County: Bexar, Gonzales, Travis
Comments/research tips: County Clerk has Land records 1846–1901, Marriage records 1846–1941, Military Discharge records 1919–1956, Naturalization records 1847–1926, and Probate records 1846–1981. District Clerk has Court records 1846–1944.

Record Type	Year Begun	Jurisdiction
Death	1903	County Clerk
Birth	1903	County Clerk

■ **Comanche**   25 Jan. 1856
County Courthouse, Comanche, TX 76442
Phone: (325)356-2655
Web site: www.rootsweb.com/~txcomanc/comanche.htm
Parent County: Bosque, Coryell

Record Type	Year Begun	Jurisdiction
Birth	1903	County Clerk
Death	1903	County Clerk
Marriage	1856	County Clerk
Probate	1897	County Clerk
Court	1858	County Clerk
Land	1859	County Clerk

■ **Concho**   1 Feb. 1858
P.O. Box 98, Paint Rock, TX 76866
Phone: (325)732-4322
Web site: www.rootsweb.com/~txconcho/
Parent County: Bexar

Record Type	Year Begun	Jurisdiction
Birth	1800	County Clerk
Marriage	1879	County Clerk
Probate	1879	County Clerk
Land	1879	County Clerk
Death	1903	County Clerk
Divorce	1907	County Clerk
Court	1907	County Clerk

■ **Cooke**   20 Mar. 1848
100 Dixon St., Gainesville, TX 76240
Phone: (940)668-5420
Web site: www.rootsweb.com/~txcooke/
Parent County: Fannin

Record Type	Year Begun	Jurisdiction
Birth	1903	County Clerk
Death	1903	County Clerk
Marriage	1849	County Clerk
Probate	1848	County Clerk
Court	1850	District Clerk
Land	1850	County Clerk
Divorce	1850	District Clerk

■ **Coryell**   4 Feb. 1854
P.O. Box 237, Gatesville, TX 76528
Phone: (254)865-5911
Web site: www.rootsweb.com/~txcoryel/
Parent County: Bell
Comments/research tips: District Clerk has Court records 1856–1978. County Clerk has Marriage records 1854–1956, Military Discharge records for 1919, Naturalization records 1887–1926, and Probate records 1854–1934.

Record Type	Year Begun	Jurisdiction
Birth	1903	County Clerk
Death	1903	County Clerk
Land	1852	County Clerk

■ **Cottle**   21 Aug. 1876
P.O. Box 717, Paducah, TX 79248
Phone: (806)492-3823
Web site: www.rootsweb.com/~txcottle/
Parent County: Fannin

Record Type	Year Begun	Jurisdiction
Birth	1892	County Clerk
Marriage	1892	County Clerk
Death	1892	County Clerk
Probate	1892	County Clerk
Court	1892	County Clerk
Land	1892	County Clerk
Divorce	1892	County Clerk

■ **Crane**   26 Feb. 1887
P.O. Box 578, Crane, TX 79731
Phone: (915)558-1148
Web site: www.rootsweb.com/~txcrane/
Parent County: Tom Green

Record Type	Year Begun	Jurisdiction
Birth	1928	County Clerk
Marriage	1927	County Clerk
Death	1927	County Clerk
Divorce	1927	County Clerk
Probate	1927	County Clerk
Court	1927	County Clerk
Land	1927	County Clerk

■ **Crockett**   1 July 1891
P.O. Drawer C, Ozona, TX 76943
Phone: (325)392-2022
Web site: www.rootsweb.com/~txcrocke/
Parent County: Bexar Land District

Record Type	Year Begun	Jurisdiction
Birth	1903	County Clerk
Death	1903	County Clerk

Record Type	Year Begun	Jurisdiction
Divorce	1892	County Clerk
Probate	1892	County Clerk
Court	1892	County Clerk
Marriage	1891	County Clerk

■ Crosby 21 Aug. 1876
201 W. Aspen, Suite 102, Crosbyton, TX 79322
Phone: (806)675-2334
Web site: www.rootsweb.com/~txcrosby/
Parent County: Bexar, Young
Comments/research tips: County Clerk has Birth records 1903–1946, Death records 1903–1971, and Marriage records 1886–1953.

Record Type	Year Begun	Jurisdiction
Probate	1887	County Clerk
Court	1887	District Clerk
Land	1886	County Clerk
Divorce	1887	District Clerk

■ Culberson 10 Mar. 1911
P.O. Box 158, Van Horn, TX 79855
Phone: (432)283-2058
Web site: www.rootsweb.com/~txculber/
Parent County: El Paso

Record Type	Year Begun	Jurisdiction
Birth	1911	County Clerk
Marriage	1911	County Clerk
Death	1911	County Clerk
Divorce	1911	County Clerk
Land	1911	County Clerk
Probate	1911	County Clerk
Court	1911	County Clerk

■ Dallam 21 Aug. 1876
P.O. Box 9395, Dalhart, TX 79022
Phone: (806)244-4751
Web site: www.dallam.org/county/
Parent County: Bexar Land District

Record Type	Year Begun	Jurisdiction
Birth	1903	County Clerk
Death	1903	County Clerk
Marriage	1891	County Clerk
Court	1891	County Clerk
Divorce	1892	County Clerk
Probate	1900	County Clerk
Land	1876	County Clerk

■ Dallas 30 Mar. 1846
509 Main St., Dallas, TX 75202
Phone: (214)653-7131
Web site: www.dallascounty.org/
Parent County: Nacogdoches, Robertson
Comments/research tips: District Clerk has Court records and Divorce records 1846–1939 and Naturalization records 1872–1912.

Record Type	Year Begun	Jurisdiction
Birth	1903	County Clerk
Death	1903	County Clerk
Marriage	1846	County Clerk

Record Type	Year Begun	Jurisdiction
Probate	1846	County Clerk
Land	1880	County Clerk

■ Dawson 13 Feb. 1905
P.O. Drawer 1268, Lamesa, TX 79331
Phone: (806)872-3778
Web site: www.rootsweb.com/~txdawson
Parent County: Howard
Comments/research tips: County Clerk has Death records 1918–1971 and Marriage records 1905–1953.

Record Type	Year Begun	Jurisdiction
Birth	1905	County Clerk
Probate	1905	County Clerk
Land	1905	County Clerk
Court	1920	District Clerk
Divorce	1920	District Clerk

■ De Witt 24 Mar. 1846
307 N. Gonzales St., Cuero, TX 77954
Phone: (361)275-3724
Web site: www.rootsweb.com/~txdewitt/
Parent County: Goliad, Gonzales, Victoria
Comments/research tips: District Clerk has Court records 1852–1912. County Clerk has Naturalization records 1851–1929 and Probate records 1846–1938.

Record Type	Year Begun	Jurisdiction
Birth	1903	County Clerk
Death	1903	County Clerk
Marriage	1846	County Clerk
Land	1846	County Clerk

■ Deaf Smith 21 Aug. 1876
235 E. Third Room 203, Hereford, TX 79045-5542
Phone: (806)363-7077
Web site: www.rootsweb.com/~txdeafsm/
Parent County: Bexar Land District

Record Type	Year Begun	Jurisdiction
Birth	1903	County Clerk
Death	1903	County Clerk
Marriage	1891	County Clerk
Probate	1891	County Clerk
Court	1891	District Clerk
Land	1882	County Clerk
Military	1919	County Clerk
Divorce	na	District Clerk

■ Delta 29 July 1870
200 W. Dallas Ave., P.O. Box 455, Cooper, TX 75432
Phone: (903)395-4400 ext. 223
Web site: http://gen.1starnet.com/delta/
Parent County: Hopkins, Lamar
Comments/research tips: County Clerk has Court records 1872–1918, Land records 1871–1886, Marriage records 1871–1970, and Probate records 1872–1946.

Record Type	Year Begun	Jurisdiction
Birth	1903	County Clerk
Death	ca. 1916	County Clerk

■ Denton 11 Apr. 1846
1415 E. McKinney, Suite 1100, Denton, TX 76209
Phone: (940)349-2010

Texas

Web site: http://dentoncounty.com/
Parent County: Fannin
Comments/research tips: District Clerk has Court records 1877–1954 and Divorce records 1876–1931. County Clerk has Land records 1854–1902, Marriage records 1875–1905, and Probate records 1876–1931. Courthouse burned in 1875, a few records were saved.

Record Type	Year Begun	Jurisdiction
Birth	1904	County Clerk
Death	1904	County Clerk

■ Dickens   21 Aug. 1876
P.O. Box 120, Dickens, TX 79229
Phone: (806)623-5531
Web site: www.rootsweb.com/~txdicken/
Parent County: Bexar Land District

Record Type	Year Begun	Jurisdiction
Birth	1892	County Clerk
Marriage	1891	County Clerk
Death	1892	County Clerk
Divorce	1891	County Clerk
Probate	1891	County Clerk
Court	1891	County Clerk
Land	1884	County Clerk

■ Dimmit   1 Feb. 1858
Courthouse Sq., Carrizo Springs, TX 78834
Phone: (830)876-2323 ext. 2
Web site: www.dimmitcountytx.com
Parent County: Uvalde, Bexar, Maverick, Webb
Comments/research tips: District Clerk has Court records, Divorce records, and Naturalization records 1881–1931. County Clerk has Land records 1880–1912 and Probate records 1881–1952.

Record Type	Year Begun	Jurisdiction
Birth	1903	County Clerk
Death	1903	County Clerk
Marriage	1880	County Clerk

■ Donley   21 Aug. 1876
300 S. Sally, Drawer U, Clarendon, TX 79226
Phone: (806)874-3436
Web site: www.rootsweb.com/~txdonley/
Parent County: Bexar Land District

Record Type	Year Begun	Jurisdiction
Birth	1903	County Clerk
Marriage	1882	County Clerk
Land	1882	County Clerk
Death	1903	County Clerk
Probate	1882	County Clerk
Court	1882	County Clerk

■ Duval   1 Feb. 1858
P.O. Box 248, San Diego, TX 78384
Phone: (512)279-3322
Web site: www.rootsweb.com/~txduval
Parent County: Live Oak, Starr, Neuces
Comments/research tips: District Clerk has Court records 1879–1908. County Clerk has Land records 1877–1919,

Probate records 1877–1883 and 1887–1901, and Marriage records 1877–1902.

Record Type	Year Begun	Jurisdiction
Birth	1903	County Clerk
Death	1903	County Clerk

■ Eastland   1 Feb. 1858
100 W. Main #102, P.O. Box 110, Eastland, TX 76448
Phone: (254)629-1583
Web site: www.rootsweb.com/~txeastla/
Parent County: Bosque, Coryell, Travis
Comments/research tips: County Clerk has Birth and Death records from 1903–1930 and 1940–1950.

Record Type	Year Begun	Jurisdiction
Marriage	1874	County Clerk
Land	1870	County Clerk
Probate	1882	County Clerk
Military	1919	County Clerk
Divorce	1903	District Court

■ Ector   26 Feb. 1887
300 N. Grant Ave., Odessa, TX 79761
Phone: (915)498-4130
Web site: www.historictexas.net/ector
Parent County: Tom Green
Comments/research tips: County Clerk has Death records 1903–1971, Marriage records 1891–1994, and Probate records 1891–1945.

Record Type	Year Begun	Jurisdiction
Birth	1903	County Clerk
Court	1896	County Clerk
Land	1896	County Clerk
Divorce	na	District Clerk

■ Edwards   1 Feb. 1858
P.O. Box 184, Rocksprings, TX 78880
Phone: (830)683-2235
Web site: www.rootsweb.com/~txedward/
Parent County: Bexar Land District

Record Type	Year Begun	Jurisdiction
Birth	1903	County Clerk
Death	1903	County Clerk
Marriage	1888	County Clerk
Divorce	1884	County Clerk
Probate	1888	County Clerk
Court	1888	County Clerk
Land	1888	County Clerk

■ El Paso   3 Jan. 1850
500 E. San Antonio St., El Paso, TX 79901
Phone: (915)546-2071
Web site: www.co.el-paso.tx.us
Parent County: Bexar Land District

Record Type	Year Begun	Jurisdiction
Birth	1903	County Clerk
Death	1903	County Clerk
Marriage	1866	County Clerk
Probate	1866	County Clerk
Court	1861	County Clerk
Land	1856	County Clerk

■ Ellis   20 Dec. 1849
117 W. Franklin, P.O. Box 250, Waxahachie, TX 75168
Phone: (972)923-5070
Web site: www.rootsweb.com/~txellis/
Parent County: Navarro
Comments/research tips: County Clerk has Birth records 1903–1936, Death records 1903–1982, Land records 1845–1901, Military Discharge records 1919–1980, and Probate records 1850–1946. District Clerk has Court records 1850–1931, Divorce records 1899–1936, and Naturalization records 1854–1935.

Record Type	Year Begun	Jurisdiction
Marriage	1850	County Clerk

■ Erath   25 Jan. 1856
100 W. Washington St., Stephenville, TX 76401
Phone: (254)965-1482
Web site: www.rootsweb.com/~txerath/erath.htm
Parent County: Bosque, Coryell
Comments/research tips: County Clerk has Birth records 1903–1942, Death records 1903–1992, Land records 1867–1902, Marriage records 1869–1956, Naturalization records 1886–1910, and Probate records 1866–1934. District Clerk has Court records 1866–1977 and Divorce records 1866–1985.

■ Falls   28 Jan. 1850
P.O. Box 458, Marlin, TX 76661
Phone: (254)883-1408
Web site: www.rootsweb.com/~txfalls/
Parent County: Limestone, Milam
Comments/research tips: District Clerk has Court records 1851–1906, Divorce records 1869–1950, and Naturalization records 1855–1926. County Clerk has Land records 1850–1904, Marriage records 1854–1946, and Probate records 1851–1935.

Record Type	Year Begun	Jurisdiction
Birth	1904	County Clerk
Death	1904	County Clerk

■ Fannin   14 Dec. 1837
101 Sam Rayburn Dr., Bonham, TX 75418
Phone: (903)583-7486
Web site: www.rootsweb.com/~txfannin/
Parent County: Red River
Comments/research tips: County Clerk has Birth Records 1874–1876, Court records 1840–1889, Death records 1903–1973, Land records 1838–1886, Marriage records 1852–1917, and Probate records 1838–1888.

Record Type	Year Begun	Jurisdiction
Birth	1903	County Clerk

■ Fayette   18 Jan. 1838
151 N. Washington, P.O. Box 59, La Grange, TX 78945
Phone: (979)968-3251
Web site: www.co.fayette.tx.us/
Parent County: Colorado, Mina
Comments/research tips: District Clerk has Court records and Divorce records 1838–1936. County Clerk has Land records 1838–1901, Marriage records 1838–1942, Naturalization records 1850–1936, and Probate records 1838–1934.

Record Type	Year Begun	Jurisdiction
Birth	1903	County Clerk
Death	1903	County Clerk

■ Fisher   21 Aug. 1876
County Courthouse, Room 101, Roby, TX 79543
Phone: (325)776-2401
Web site: www.rootsweb.com/~txfisher/
Parent County: Bexar Territory, Young Territory

Record Type	Year Begun	Jurisdiction
Birth	1903	County Clerk
Death	1903	County Clerk
Marriage	1886	County Clerk
Land	1886	County Clerk
Probate	1886	County Clerk
Court	1886	County Clerk

■ Floyd   21 Aug. 1876
100 S. Main St., P.O. Box 476, Floydada, TX 79235
Phone: (806)983-4900
Web site: www.rootsweb.com/~txfloyd/
Parent County: Bexar Territory, Young Territory
Comments/research tips: County Clerk has Birth records 1903–1946, Death records 1903–1971, and Marriage records 1890–1955.

Record Type	Year Begun	Jurisdiction
Probate	1890	County Clerk
Court	1890	County Clerk
Land	1890	County Clerk
Divorce	na	District Clerk

■ Foard   3 Mar. 1891
P.O. Box 539, Crowell, TX 79227
Phone: (940)684-1365
Web site: www.rootsweb.com/~txfoard/foard.htm
Parent County: Hardeman, Knox, King, Cottle

Record Type	Year Begun	Jurisdiction
Birth	1903	County Clerk
Death	1903	County Clerk
Marriage	1891	County Clerk
Divorce	1891	County Clerk
Probate	1891	County Clerk
Court	1891	County Clerk
Land	1891	County Clerk

■ Fort Bend   29 Dec. 1837
301 Jackson St., P.O. Box 520, Richmond, TX 77469
Phone: (281)341-8685
Web site: www.co.fort-bend.tx.us/
Parent County: Austin, Harris, Bazoria
Comments/research tips: District Clerk has Naturalization records 1854–1929.

Record Type	Year Begun	Jurisdiction
Birth	1903	County Clerk
Death	1903	County Clerk
Marriage	1838	County Clerk
Land	1838	County Clerk

Record Type	Year Begun	Jurisdiction
Probate	1838	County Clerk
Court	1838	County Clerk

■ Franklin 6 Mar. 1875

P.O. Box 68, Mount Vernon, TX 75457
Phone: (903)537-4252
Web site: www.mt-vernon.com/~skelly/
Parent County: Titus
Comments/research tips: County Clerk also has Deeds for Red River County.

Record Type	Year Begun	Jurisdiction
Birth	1903	County Clerk
Death	1903	County Clerk
Divorce	1875	District Clerk
Marriage	1875	County Clerk
Probate	1875	County Clerk
Land	1845	County Clerk

■ Freestone 6 Sep. 1850

P.O. Box 1010, Fairfield, TX 75840
Phone: (903)389-2635
Web site: www.rootsweb.com/~txfreest/
Parent County: Limestone

Record Type	Year Begun	Jurisdiction
Birth	1903	County Clerk
Death	1903	County Clerk
Marriage	1851	County Clerk
Land	1850	County Clerk
Probate	1851	County Clerk
Court	1851	County Clerk

■ Frio 1 Feb. 1858

500 E. San Antonio St., Box #6, Pearsall, TX 78601
Phone: (830)334-2214
Web site: www.rootsweb.com/~txfrio/
Parent County: Atascosa, Bexar, Uvalde
Comments/research tips: County Clerk has Naturalization records 1877–1916.

Record Type	Year Begun	Jurisdiction
Birth	1903	County Clerk
Death	1903	County Clerk
Marriage	1871	County Clerk
Probate	1871	County Clerk
Court	1873	County Clerk
Land	1871	County Clerk

■ Gaines 21 Aug. 1876

101 S. Main St., Room 107, Seminole, TX 79360
Phone: (432)758-3521
Web site: http://abq.com/txgaines/
Parent County: Bexar Territory, Young Territory

Record Type	Year Begun	Jurisdiction
Birth	1905	County Clerk
Marriage	1905	County Clerk
Death	1905	County Clerk
Probate	1905	County Clerk
Court	1906	County Clerk
Land	1905	County Clerk

■ Galveston 15 May 1838

722 Moody, P.O. Box 2450, Galveston, TX 77553
Phone: (409)766-2200
Web site: www.co.galveston.tx.us/
Parent County: Brazoria, Liberty, Harrisburg
Comments/research tips: County Clerk has Birth records 1903–1910, Land records 1838–1886, Marriage records 1838–1907, Naturalization records 1876–1906, and Probate records 1838–1930. District Clerk has Court records 1839–1909.

■ Garza 21 Aug. 1876

300 W. Main St., Post, TX 79356
Phone: (806)495-4430
Web site: www.rootsweb.com/~txgarza
Parent County: Bexar Land District, Young Territory

Record Type	Year Begun	Jurisdiction
Birth	1903	County Clerk
Marriage	1907	County Clerk
Death	1903	County Clerk
Divorce	1907	County Clerk
Probate	1907	County Clerk
Court	1907	County Clerk
Land	1907	County Clerk

■ Gillespie 23 Feb. 1848

101 W. Main St., P.O. Box 551, Fredericksburg, TX 78624
Phone: (830)997-6515
Web site: www.rootsweb.com/~txgilles/
Parent County: Bexar, Travis
Comments/research tips: District Clerk has Court records 1849–1946 and Divorce records 1850–1940. County Clerk has Marriage records 1850–1965, Military Discharge records 1917–1919, Naturalization records 1849–1936, and Probate records 1850–1936.

Record Type	Year Begun	Jurisdiction
Birth	1846	County Clerk
Death	1903	County Clerk
Land	1850	County Clerk

■ Glasscock 4 Apr. 1887

P.O. Box 190, Garden City, TX 79739
Phone: (915)354-2371
Web site: www.rootsweb.com/~txglassc/
Parent County: Tom Green
Comments/research tips: County Judge has recent Burial records.

Record Type	Year Begun	Jurisdiction
Birth	1903	County Clerk
Death	1903	County Clerk
Marriage	1893	County Clerk
Court	1893	County Clerk
Probate	1893	County Clerk
Land	1893	County Clerk
Divorce	na	County Clerk

■ Goliad 17 Mar. 1836

127 S. Courthouse Sq., P.O. Box 50, Goliad, TX 77963
Phone: (361)645-3294

Web site: www.rootsweb.com/~txgoliad
Parent County: Old Mexican Municipality
Comments/research tips: District Clerk has Court records 1855–1866 and 1870–1907. County Clerk has Divorce records 1855–1866 and 1870–1907, Land records 1870–1908, Marriage records 1876–1911, and Probate records 1871–1913.

Record Type	Year Begun	Jurisdiction
Birth	1903	County Clerk
Death	1903	County Clerk

■ Gonzales 14 Dec. 1837
1709 Dewitt Dr., P.O. Box 77, Gonzales, TX 78629
Phone: (830)672-2801
Web site: www.rootsweb.com/~txgonzal/
Parent County: Old Mexican Municipality
Comments/research tips: County Clerk has Birth and Death records 1903–1995, Land records 1837–1993, Marriage records 1839–1955, and Probate records 1838–1935. District Clerk has Divorce records 1927–1958 and Naturalization records 1887–1929. Archives and Records Center has all older records from County and District Clerks, Cemetery Records, and School Census. Guadalupe, Caldwell, Comal, Lavaca, Fayette, DeWitt, Victoria, and Jackson Counties formed out of Gonzales, contain old Gonzales county records.

■ Gray 21 Aug. 1876
200 N. Russell St., P.O. Box 1902, Pampa, TX 79065
Phone: (806)669-8004
Web site: www.rootsweb.com/~txgray/
Parent County: Bexar Land District

Record Type	Year Begun	Jurisdiction
Birth	1903	County Clerk
Marriage	1902	County Clerk
Death	1903	County Clerk
Probate	1902	County Clerk
Court	1903	County Clerk
Land	1902	County Clerk
Divorce	na	District Clerk

■ Grayson 17 Mar. 1846
100 W. Houston St., Sherman, TX 75090
Phone: (903)813-4243
Web site: www.co.grayson.tx.us/
Parent County: Fannin Land District
Comments/research tips: District Clerk has Court records 1836–1893. County Clerk has Naturalization records 1853–1906.

Record Type	Year Begun	Jurisdiction
Birth	1909	County Clerk
Death	1909	County Clerk
Marriage	1846	County Clerk
Probate	1846	County Clerk
Land	1846	County Clerk
Divorce	na	District Clerk

■ Gregg 12 Apr. 1873
101 E. Methvin St., P.O. Box 3049, Longview, TX 75601
Phone: (903)236-8430

Web site: www.co.gregg.tx.us/
Parent County: Rusk, Upshur
Comments/research tips: County Clerk has Birth records 1873–1946, Death records 1906–1915, Land records 1873–1901, and Marriage records 1873–1936. District Clerk has Court records 1848–1934 and Divorce records 1905–1935.

Record Type	Year Begun	Jurisdiction
Death	1964	County Clerk
Probate	1873	County Clerk

■ Grimes 6 Apr. 1846
P.O. Box 209, Anderson, TX 77830
Phone: (409)873-2606
Web site: www.rootsweb.com/~txgrimes/
Parent County: Montgomery
Comments/research tips: County Clerk has Birth records ca. 1850–1946, Land records 1846–1898, Marriage records 1848–1960, and Probate records 1838–1957. District Clerk has Court records 1848–1934 and Naturalization records 1890–1925. Four courthouses were destroyed, present courthouse was built in 1894.

Record Type	Year Begun	Jurisdiction
Death	1903	County Clerk

■ Guadalupe 30 Mar. 1846
101 E. Court St., Seguin, TX 78155
Phone: (830)303-4188 ext. 239
Web site: www.rootsweb.com/~txguadal/
Parent County: Bexar, Gonzales
Comments/research tips: County Clerk has Birth records 1903–1942 and Naturalization records 1887–1906.

Record Type	Year Begun	Jurisdiction
Death	1903	County Clerk
Marriage	1846	County Clerk
Probate	1846	County Clerk
Court	1848	District Clerk
Land	1840	County Clerk
Divorce	1846	District Clerk

■ Hale 21 Aug. 1876
500 Broadway, Plainview, TX 79072
Phone: (806)291-5261
Web site: www.texasonline.net/halecounty/
Parent County: Bexar Land District

Record Type	Year Begun	Jurisdiction
Birth	1903	County Clerk
Death	1903	County Clerk
Marriage	1888	County Clerk
Land	1888	County Clerk
Probate	1888	County Clerk
Divorce	na	District Clerk
Court	1888	County Clerk

■ Hall 21 Aug. 1876
County Courthouse, Box 8, Memphis, TX 79245
Phone: (806)259-2627
Web site: www.rootsweb.com/~txhall/
Parent County: Bexar Land District, Young

Record Type	Year Begun	Jurisdiction
Birth	1903	County Clerk
Marriage	1890	County Clerk
Death	1903	County Clerk
Divorce	1890	County Clerk
Probate	1890	County Clerk
Court	1890	County Clerk
Land	1890	County Clerk

■ Hamilton 22 June 1858

County Courthouse, Hamilton, TX 76531
Phone: (254)386-3518
Web site: www.rootsweb.com/~txhamilt/
Parent County: Bosque, Comanche, Lampasas
Comments/research tips: County Clerk has Birth records 1903–1985, Death records 1903–1941, Land records 1866–1899, Marriage records 1876–1935, and Probate records 1870–1948. District Clerk has Court records 1870–1930 and Naturalization records 1880–1927.

Record Type	Year Begun	Jurisdiction
Divorce	1870	District Clerk

■ Hansford 21 Aug. 1876

P.O. Box 397, Spearman, TX 79081
Phone: (806)659-4110
Web site: www.rootsweb.com/~txhansfo/
Parent County: Bexar Land District, Young

Record Type	Year Begun	Jurisdiction
Land	1889	County Clerk
Birth	1903	County Clerk
Marriage	1889	County Clerk
Death	1903	County Clerk
Divorce	na	County Clerk
Probate	1889	County Clerk
Court	1889	County Clerk

■ Hardeman 1 Feb. 1858

P.O. Box 30, Quanah, TX 79252
Phone: (940)663-2901
Web site: www.rootsweb.com/~txhardem/
Parent County: Fannin Land District

Record Type	Year Begun	Jurisdiction
Birth	1903	County Clerk
Death	1903	County Clerk
Marriage	1885	County Clerk
Probate	1885	County Clerk
Court	1885	County Clerk
Land	1884	County Clerk
Divorce	na	District Clerk

■ Hardin 22 Jan. 1858

P.O. Box 38, Kountze, TX 77625
Phone: (409)246-5185
Web site: www.rootsweb.com/~txhardin/
Parent County: Jefferson, Liberty
Comments/research tips: District Clerk has Court records 1871 and 1879–1925. County Clerk has Land records 1858–1894, Marriage records 1862–1920, and Probate records 1886–1936.

Record Type	Year Begun	Jurisdiction
Birth	1903	County Clerk
Death	1903	County Clerk
Divorce	na	District Clerk

■ Harris 30 Dec. 1835

1001 Preston, Houston, TX 77002
Phone: (713)755-6411
Web site: www.co.harris.tx.us/
Parent County: Old Mexican Municipality
Comments/research tips: District Clerk has Court records 1872–1910. County Clerk has Land records 1837–1886, Naturalization records 1855–1906, and Probate records 1837–1891. Name changed to Harrisburg County in 1836. Name changed to Harris 28 December 1839.

Record Type	Year Begun	Jurisdiction
Birth	1903	County Clerk
Death	1903	County Clerk
Marriage	1837	County Clerk
Divorce	na	District Clerk

■ Harrison 28 Jan. 1839

P.O. Box 1365, Marshall, TX 75671
Phone: (903)935-4858
Web site: www.rootsweb.com/~txharris/
Parent County: Shelby
Comments/research tips: County Clerk has Land records 1840–1886, Marriage records 1860–1936, and Probate records 1840–1934. District Clerk has Court records 1840–1934, Divorce records 1903–1943, and Naturalization records 1850–1916.

Record Type	Year Begun	Jurisdiction
Birth	1903	County Clerk
Death	1903	County Clerk

■ Hartley 21 Aug. 1876

P.O. Box 147, Channing, TX 79018
Phone: (806)235-3582
Web site: www.rootsweb.com/~txhartle/
Parent County: Bexar Land District, Young

Record Type	Year Begun	Jurisdiction
Birth	1903	County Clerk
Marriage	1891	County Clerk
Probate	1891	County Clerk
Death	1903	County Clerk
Land	1891	County Clerk
Divorce	1891	County Clerk
Court	1891	County Clerk

■ Haskell 1 Feb. 1858

P.O. Box 725, Haskell, TX 79521
Phone: (940)864-2451
Web site: www.rootsweb.com/~txhaskel/haskell.htm
Parent County: Fannin, Milam

Record Type	Year Begun	Jurisdiction
Birth	1903	County Clerk
Marriage	1885	County Clerk
Probate	1885	County Clerk
Death	1903	County Clerk

Texas

Land .... 1885 ....County Clerk
Court .... 1885 ....County Clerk
Divorce .... na ....District Court

■ Hays 1 Mar. 1848
137 N. Guadalupe St., San Marcos, TX 78666
Phone: (512)393-7330
Web site: www.co.hays.tx.us/
Parent County: Travis
Comments/research tips: District Clerk has Court records 1850–1864, 1874–1876 and 1881–1939, Divorce records 1896–1929, and Naturalization records 1876–1906. County Clerk has Death records 1903–1934, Land records 1848–1905, Marriage records 1848–1931, Military Discharge records 1908–1944, and Probate records 1848–1950.

Record Type	Year Begun	Jurisdiction
Birth	1865	County Clerk

■ Hemphill 21 Aug. 1876
P.O. Box 867, Canadian, TX 79014
Phone: (806)323-6212
Web site: www.rootsweb.com/~txhemphi/
Parent County: Bexar Territory, Young Territory, Clay County

Record Type	Year Begun	Jurisdiction
Birth	1903	County Clerk
Death	1903	County Clerk
Marriage	1887	County Clerk
Divorce	1887	County Clerk
Probate	1887	County Clerk
Court	1887	County Clerk
Land	1887	County Clerk

■ Henderson 27 Apr. 1846
Courthouse Sq., Room 107, Athens, TX 75751
Phone: (903)675-6140
Web site: www.co.henderson.tx.us
Parent County: Houston, Nacogdoches
Comments/research tips: County Clerk has Death records 1908–1938 and 1941–1965, Land records 1847–1901, Marriage records 1847–1854 and 1860–1941, and Probate records 1846–1936.

Record Type	Year Begun	Jurisdiction
Birth	1903	County Clerk
Court	1847	County Clerk

■ Hidalgo 24 Jan. 1852
100 N. Closner, Edinburg, TX 78539
Phone: (956)318-2100
Web site: www.co.hidalgo.tx.us/
Parent County: Cameron
Comments/research tips: District Clerk has Court records 1853–1912 and Divorce records 1853–1912. County Clerk has Marriage records 1852–1957 and Probate records 1852–1911.

Record Type	Year Begun	Jurisdiction
Birth	1903	County Clerk
Death	1903	County Clerk
Land	1852	County Clerk

■ Hill 7 Feb. 1853
P.O. Box 398, Hillsboro, TX 76645
Phone: (254)582-4030
Web site: www.rootsweb.com/~txhill/
Parent County: Navarro
Comments/research tips: County Clerk has Birth records 1903–1935, Land records 1857–1901, Death records 1903–1938, Marriage records 1873–1934, and Probate records 1853–1934. District Clerk has Court records 1867–1932, Divorce records 1896–1947, and Naturalization records 1896–1913. Courthouse burned between 1874 and 1878.

■ Hockley 21 Aug. 1876
802 Houston St., Box 1, Levelland, TX 79336
Phone: (806)894-3185
Web site: www.rootsweb.com/~txhockle/
Parent County: Bexar Land District, Young
Comments/research tips: Attached to Lubbock County 1891–1921.

Record Type	Year Begun	Jurisdiction
Birth	1903	County Clerk
Marriage	1921	County Clerk
Death	1903	County Clerk
Probate	1921	County Clerk
Court	1921	County Clerk
Land	1921	County Clerk

■ Hood 3 Nov. 1865
100 E. Pearl St., P.O. Box 339, Granbury, TX 76048
Phone: (817)579-3222
Web site: www.granburydepot.org/
Parent County: Johnson
Comments/research tips: County Clerk has Birth records 1903–1995, Death records 1903–1998, Divorce records 1908–1946, Land records 1875–1910, Marriage records 1854–2002, and Probate records 1873–1936. District Clerk has Court records 1875–1943. Hood Public Library in Granbury has many records of the late Judge Henry Davis.

■ Hopkins 25 Mar. 1846
P.O. Box 288, Sulphur Springs, TX 75482
Phone: (903)438-4074
Web site: www.hopkinscountytx.org
Parent County: Lamar, Nacogdoches
Comments/research tips: District Clerk has Court records 1846–1911. County Clerk has Divorce records 1846–1911, Land records 1846–1887, Marriage records 1846–1920, and Probate records 1846–1946.

Record Type	Year Begun	Jurisdiction
Birth	1903	County Clerk
Death	1903	County Clerk

■ Houston 12 June 1837
P.O. Box 370, Crockett, TX 75835
Phone: (936)544-3255 ext. 240
Web site: www.io.com/~dwhite/ more.html
Parent County: Nacogdoches
Comments/research tips: County Clerk has Land records 1865–1909 and Probate records 1859–1945. District Clerk has Naturalization records 1880–1925.

Texas

Record Type	Year Begun	Jurisdiction
Birth	1903	County Clerk
Marriage	1903	County Clerk
Death	1903	County Clerk
Court	1882	County Clerk
Divorce	1920	District Clerk

■ Howard 21 Aug. 1876
300 Main St., P.O. Box 1468, Big Spring, TX 79720
Phone: (915)264-2213
Web site: www.rootsweb.com/~txhoward/
Parent County: Bexar Land District, Young

Record Type	Year Begun	Jurisdiction
Birth	1903	County Clerk
Death	1903	County Clerk
Marriage	1882	County Clerk
Probate	1882	County Clerk
Land	1882	County Clerk
Divorce	1883	County Clerk
Court	1882	County Clerk

■ Hudspeth 16 Feb. 1917
P.O. Drawer A, Sierra Blanca, TX 79851
Phone: (915)369-2301
Web site: www.rootsweb.com/~txhudspe/
Parent County: El Paso
Comments/research tips: County Clerk has Birth records 1917–1937, Death records 1917–1971, and Marriage records 1917–1960.

Record Type	Year Begun	Jurisdiction
Divorce	1917	County Clerk
Probate	1917	County Clerk
Court	1917	County Clerk
Land	1836	County Clerk

■ Hunt 11 Apr. 1846
2500 Lee St., P.O. Box 1316, Greenville, TX 75403
Phone: (903)408-4130
Web site: www.rootsweb.com/~txhunt/
Parent County: Fannin, Nacogdoches
Comments/research tips: District Clerk has Court and Divorce records 1851–1930 and Naturalization records 1851–1926. County Clerk has Marriage records 1858–1912 and Probate records 1847–1927.

Record Type	Year Begun	Jurisdiction
Military	na	County Clerk
Birth	1903	County Clerk
Death	1903	County Clerk
Land	1846	County Clerk

■ Hutchinson 21 Aug. 1876
P.O. Box 1186, Stinnett, TX 79083
Phone: (806)878-4002
Web site: www.usroots.org/~hutchitx/
Parent County: Bexar Land District
Comments/research tips: County was attached to Wheeler and Carson Counties until it was officially organized on 13 May 1901.

Record Type	Year Begun	Jurisdiction
Marriage	1901	County Clerk

Probate	1901	County Clerk
Court	1901	County Clerk
Land	1901	County Clerk
Birth	1903	County Clerk
Death	1903	County Clerk
Divorce	1901	County Clerk

■ Irion 7 Mar. 1889
P.O. Box 736, Mertzon, TX 76941
Phone: (915)835-2421
Web site: www.rootsweb.com/~txirion/
Parent County: Tom Green

Record Type	Year Begun	Jurisdiction
Birth	1901	County Clerk
Marriage	1889	County Clerk
Death	1903	County Clerk
Divorce	1889	County Clerk
Land	1889	County Clerk
Probate	1889	County Clerk
Military	na	County Clerk
Court	1889	County Clerk

■ Jack 27 Aug. 1856
100 Main St., Jacksboro, TX 76458
Phone: (940)567-2111
Web site: www.rootsweb.com/~txjack/
Parent County: Cooke

Record Type	Year Begun	Jurisdiction
Birth	1903	County Clerk
Death	1903	County Clerk
Probate	1858	County Clerk
Land	1858	County Clerk
Marriage	1858	County Clerk
Court	1858	County Clerk
Divorce	na	County Clerk

■ Jackson 17 Mar. 1836
115 W. Main St., Room 101, Edna, TX 77957
Phone: (361)782-3563
Web site: www.historictexas.net/jackson/
Parent County: Old Mexican Municipality
Comments/research tips: District Clerk has Court records 1838–1944 and Naturalization records 1903–1906. County Clerk has Land records 1837–1886, Marriage records 1835–1976, and Probate records 1837–1944.

Record Type	Year Begun	Jurisdiction
Birth	1903	County Clerk
Death	1903	County Clerk
Divorce	na	District Clerk

■ Jasper 17 Mar. 1836
P.O. Box 2070, Jasper, TX 75951
Phone: (409)384-2632
Web site: www.rootsweb.com/~txjasper/
Parent County: Old Mexican Municipality known as Municipality of Bevil
Comments/research tips: County Clerk has Land records 1849–1888, Marriage records 1849–1921, and Probate records 1849–1920. Fire destroyed county courthouse and records in 1849.

Record Type	Year Begun	Jurisdiction
Birth	1903	County Clerk
Death	1903	County Clerk
Court	1850	County Clerk
Divorce	na	District/County Clerk

■ Jeff Davis 15 Mar. 1887
P.O. Box 398, Fort Davis, TX 79734
Phone: (915)426-3251
Web site: www.rootsweb.com/~txjeffda/
Parent County: Presidio
Comments/research tips: County Clerk has Birth records 1903–1950, Death records 1903–1971, and Marriage records 1887–1974.

Record Type	Year Begun	Jurisdiction
Divorce	na	County Clerk
Probate	1887	County Clerk
Court	1887	County Clerk
Land	1887	County Clerk

■ Jefferson 21 Dec. 1837
P.O. Box 1151, Beaumont, TX 77704
Phone: (409)835-8475
Web site: www.co.jefferson.tx.us/
Parent County: Old Mexican Municipality, Jefferson Municipality
Comments/research tips: District Clerk has Court records 1844–1896, Divorce records 1896–1908, and Naturalization records 1894–1906. County Court has Land records 1834–1887, Marriage records 1837–1926, and Probate records 1838–1965.

Record Type	Year Begun	Jurisdiction
Birth	1903	County Clerk
Death	1903	County Clerk
Military	na	County Clerk

■ Jim Hogg 31 Mar. 1913
102 E. Tilley, P.O. Box 878, Hebbronville, TX 78361
Phone: (361)527-4031
Web site: www.rootsweb.com/~txjimhog/
Parent County: Brooks, Duval

Record Type	Year Begun	Jurisdiction
Birth	1913	County Clerk
Marriage	1913	County Clerk
Death	1913	County Clerk
Divorce	1913	County Clerk
Land	1913	County Clerk
Probate	1913	County Clerk
Military	1913	County Clerk
Court	1913	County Clerk

■ Jim Wells 25 Mar. 1911
200 N. Almond St., P.O. Box 1459, Alice, TX 78332
Phone: (361)668-5702
Web site: www.rootsweb.com/~txjimwel/
Parent County: Nueces
Comments/research tips: County Clerk has Death records 1900–2003.

Record Type	Year Begun	Jurisdiction
Birth	1912	County Clerk

Record Type	Year Begun	Jurisdiction
Marriage	1912	County Clerk
Probate	1912	County Clerk
Court	1912	County Clerk
Land	1912	County Clerk
Divorce	na	District/County Clerk

■ Johnson 13 Feb. 1854
2 Main St., P.O. Box 662, Cleburne, TX 76031
Phone: (817)556-6323
Web site: www.rootsweb.com/~txjohnso/
Parent County: Ellis, Hill, Navarro
Comments/research tips: County Clerk has Birth records 1903–1985, Death records 1903–1966, Land records 1853–1911, Marriage records 1860–1867 and 1870–1942, Naturalization records 1898–1904, and Probate records 1854–1945. District Clerk has Court records 1856–1934 and Divorce records 1893–1936.

■ Jones 1 Feb. 1858
P.O. Box 552, Anson, TX 79501
Phone: (915)823-3762
Web site: www.rootsweb.com/~txjones/
Parent County: Bexar, Bosque

Record Type	Year Begun	Jurisdiction
Birth	1903	County Clerk
Death	1903	County Clerk
Marriage	1881	County Clerk
Land	1881	County Clerk
Probate	1881	County Clerk
Divorce	na	District/County Clerk
Court	1881	District/County Clerk

■ Karnes 4 Feb. 1854
101 N. Panna Maria St., Karnes City, TX 78118
Phone: (830)780-3938
Web site: www.rootsweb.com/~txkarnes
Parent County: Bexar, DeWitt, Goliad, San Patricio, Gonzales
Comments/research tips: District Clerk has Court records 1858–1910. County Clerk has Land records 1855–1905, Marriage records 1865–1910, Naturalization records 1892–1924, and Probate records 1865–1907.

Record Type	Year Begun	Jurisdiction
Divorce	na	District/County Clerk
Death	1903	County Clerk
Birth	1903	County Clerk

■ Kaufman 26 Feb. 1848
County Courthouse, 100 W. Mulberry St., Kaufman, TX 75142
Phone: (972)932-4331 ext. 213
Web site: www.rootsweb.com/~txkaufma/
Parent County: Henderson
Comments/research tips: District Clerk has Court records 1848–1931, Divorce records 1901–1945, and Naturalization records 1908–1913. County Clerk has Death records 1903–1966, Land records 1849–1911, Naturalization records 1892–1893, and Probate records 1848–1940.

Record Type	Year Begun	Jurisdiction
Birth	1848	County Clerk
Marriage	1848	County Clerk

■ Kendall 10 Jan. 1862

204 E. San Antonio St., Boerne, TX 78006
Phone: (830)249-9343 ext. 360
Web site: www.rootsweb.com/~txkendal/index.htm
Parent County: Kerr, Blanco
Comments/research tips: District Clerk has Court records 1869–1939 and Naturalization records 1876–1906. County Clerk has Land records 1862–1887, Marriage records 1862–1956, and Probate records 1862–1977.

Record Type	Year Begun	Jurisdiction
Death	1903	County Clerk
Birth	1903	County Clerk

■ Kenedy 2 Apr. 1921

P.O. Box 37, Sarita, TX 78385
Phone: (361)294-5220
Web site: www.rootsweb.com/~txkenedy/
Parent County: Willacy, Hidalgo, Cameron
Comments/research tips: County Clerk has Land records 1845–1911, Marriage records 1911–1965, and Probate records 1860–1911. Marriages 1911–1921 were recorded in Willacy County. Probate records and Land records are transcribed from parent counties' land records.

Record Type	Year Begun	Jurisdiction
Birth	1903	County Clerk
Death	1903	County Clerk
Divorce	1911	County Clerk
Court	1911	County Clerk

■ Kent 21 Aug. 1876

101 Main St., P.O. Box 9, Jayton, TX 79528
Phone: (806)237-3881
Web site: www.rootsweb.com/~txkent/
Parent County: Bexar Territory, Young Territory

Record Type	Year Begun	Jurisdiction
Birth	1903	County Clerk
Marriage	1892	County Clerk
Death	1903	County Clerk
Divorce	1892	County Clerk
Land	1892	County Clerk
Probate	1892	County Clerk
Court	1892	County Clerk

■ Kerr 26 Jan. 1856

700 Main St., Suite 122, Kerrville, TX 78028
Phone: (830)792-2255
Web site: www.rootsweb.com/~txkerr2/
Parent County: Bexar

Record Type	Year Begun	Jurisdiction
Birth	1903	County Clerk
Death	1903	County Clerk
Marriage	1856	County Clerk
Probate	1856	County Clerk
Land	1856	County Clerk
Court	1856	County Clerk
Divorce	1856	County Clerk

■ Kimble 22 Jan. 1858

501 Main St., Junction, TX 76849
Phone: (915)446-3353

Web site: www.rootsweb.com/~txkimble/
Parent County: Bexar Land District
Comments/research tips: Kimble County was attached to Gillespie County until 6 September 1875.

Record Type	Year Begun	Jurisdiction
Probate	1884	County Clerk
Birth	1874	County Clerk
Death	1903	County Clerk
Marriage	1884	County Clerk
Divorce	1884	County Clerk
Land	1884	County Clerk
Court	1884	County Clerk

■ King 21 Aug. 1876

P.O. Box 135, Guthrie, TX 79236
Phone: (806)596-4412
Web site: www.rootsweb.com/~txking/
Parent County: Bexar Land District

Record Type	Year Begun	Jurisdiction
Birth	1903	County Clerk
Divorce	na	County Clerk
Court	1914	County Clerk
Marriage	1914	County Clerk
Death	1903	County Clerk
Probate	1914	County Clerk
Land	1914	County Clerk

■ Kinney 28 Jan. 1850

P.O. Drawer 9, Brackettville, TX 78832
Phone: (830)563-2521
Web site: www.rootsweb.com/~txkinney/
Parent County: Bexar Land District
Comments/research tips: District Clerk has Court records 1873–1937 and Naturalization records 1887–1906. County Clerk has Land records 1872–1887, Marriage records 1872–1915, and Probate records 1874–1913. St. Mary's Catholic Church, Brackettville, Texas has Burial records.

Record Type	Year Begun	Jurisdiction
Birth	1903	County Clerk
Death	1903	County Clerk
Divorce	na	District/County Clerk

■ Kleberg 27 Feb. 1913

700 E. Kleberg, P.O. Box 1327, Kingsville, TX 78363
Phone: (361)595-8548
Web site: www.rootsweb.com/~txkleber/
Parent County: Nueces

Record Type	Year Begun	Jurisdiction
Birth	1913	County Clerk
Marriage	1913	County Clerk
Death	1913	County Clerk
Probate	1913	County Clerk
Court	1913	County Clerk
Land	1913	County Clerk
Divorce	na	District Clerk

■ Knox 1 Feb. 1858

P.O. Box 196, Benjamin, TX 79505
Phone: (940)454-2441

Texas

Web site: www.rootsweb.com/~txknox/knox.htm
Parent County: Young, Bexar
Comments/research tips: District Clerk has Court records 1886–1937 and Naturalization records 1906–1936. County Clerk has Probate records 1886–1975.

Record Type	Year Begun	Jurisdiction
Birth	1903	County Clerk
Marriage	1886	County Clerk
Death	1903	County Clerk
Divorce	na	County Clerk
Land	1886	County Clerk

■ La Salle 1 Feb. 1858
P.O. Box 340, Cotulla, TX 78014
Phone: (830)879-4432
Web site: www.historicdistrict.com/Genealogy/lasalle/lasalle.htm
Parent County: Bexar
Comments/research tips: District/County Clerk has Court records 1881–1910, Land records 1880–1896, Marriage records 1880–1940, Naturalization records 1882–1906, and Probate records 1881–1949.

Record Type	Year Begun	Jurisdiction
Death	1903	District/County Clerk
Divorce	na	District/County Clerk
Birth	1903	District/County Clerk

■ Lamar 17 Dec. 1840
119 N. Main St., Paris, TX 75460
Phone: (903)737-2420
Web site: http://gen.1starnet.com/
Parent County: Red River
Comments/research tips: District Clerk has Court records 1887–1927 and Naturalization records 1855–1925. County Clerk has Land records 1841–1889.

Record Type	Year Begun	Jurisdiction
Birth	1903	County Clerk
Death	1903	County Clerk
Marriage	1841	County Clerk
Probate	1841	County Clerk
Divorce	na	District/County Clerk

■ Lamb 21 Aug. 1876
100 Sixth St., Room 103, Box 3, Littlefield, TX 79339-3366
Phone: (806)385-4222 ext. 214
Web site: www.rootsweb.com/~txlamb/
Parent County: Bexar Land District

Record Type	Year Begun	Jurisdiction
Birth	1908	County Clerk
Marriage	1909	County Clerk
Death	1908	County Clerk
Probate	1909	County Clerk
Land	1908	County Clerk
Court	1909	County Clerk

■ Lampasas 1 Feb. 1856
P.O. Box 347, Lampasas, TX 76550
Phone: (512)556-8271 ext. 37
Web site: www.rootsweb.com/~txlampas/

Parent County: Bell, Travis, Coryell
Comments/research tips: District Clerk has Court records 1877–1926 and Naturalization records 1909–1914. County Clerk has Marriage records 1886–1937 and Probate records 1876–1937.

Record Type	Year Begun	Jurisdiction
Birth	1903	County Clerk
Death	1903	County Clerk
Land	1872	County Clerk

■ Lavaca 6 Apr. 1846
P.O. Box 326, Hallettsville, TX 77964
Phone: (361)798-3612
Web site: www.rootsweb.com/~txlavaca/index.htm
Parent County: Colorado, Victoria, Jackson, Gonzales, Fayette
Comments/research tips: County Clerk has Birth records 1870–1879, Land records 1846–1889, Marriage records 1847–1917, Naturalization records 1856–1935, and Probate records 1846–1916. District Clerk has Court records 1847–1974. From 1842–1846 area was known as La Baca County.

Record Type	Year Begun	Jurisdiction
Birth	1903	County Clerk
Death	1903	County Clerk

■ Lee 14 Apr. 1874
898 E. Richmond, P.O. Box 419, Giddings, TX 78942
Phone: (979)542-3684
Web site: www.rootsweb.com/~txlee
Parent County: Bastrop, Burleson, Washington, Fayette
Comments/research tips: County Clerk has Birth records 1873–1985, Death records 1903–1985, Land records 1874–1908, Marriage records 1874–1937, and Probate records 1874–1936. District Clerk has Court records 1874–1932, Divorce records 1901–1952, and Naturalization records 1876–1936.

■ Leon 17 Mar. 1846
P.O. Box 98, Centerville, TX 75833
Phone: (903)536-2352
Web site: www.rootsweb.com/~txleon/
Parent County: Robertson
Comments/research tips: District Clerk has Court records 1846–1937. County Clerk has Death records 1903–1934, Land records 1846–1903, Marriage records 1885–1935, and Probate records 1846–1933.

Record Type	Year Begun	Jurisdiction
Divorce	1884	District Clerk
Birth	1903	County Clerk

■ Liberty 17 Mar. 1836
1923 Sam Houston St., P.O. Box 369, Liberty, TX 77575
Phone: (936)336-4671
Web site: www.rootsweb.com/~txlibert/
Parent County: Old Mexican Municipality called Villa de la Santisima Trinidad de la Libertad
Comments/research tips: District Clerk has Court records 1874–1910. County Clerk has Land records 1875–1886, Marriage records 1875–1919, and Probate records 1873–1917. Courthouse burned 11 December 1874.

Record Type	Year Begun	Jurisdiction
Birth	1903	County Clerk
Death	1903	County Clerk
Divorce	na	District/County Clerk

■ Limestone 11 Apr. 1846
200 W. State St., P.O. Box 350, Groesbeck, TX 76642
Phone: (254)729-5504
Web site: www.rootsweb.com/~txlimest/
Parent County: Robertson
Comments/research tips: County Clerk has Land records 1873–1889, Marriage records 1873–1946, Probate records 1876–1918, and Military records for 1861 and 1936. Original county courthouse along with county records burned in 1873.

Record Type	Year Begun	Jurisdiction
Birth	1903	County Clerk
Death	1903	County Clerk
Court	1873	County Clerk
Divorce	na	District/County Clerk

■ Lipscomb 21 Aug. 1876
P.O. Box 70, Lipscomb, TX 79056
Phone: (806)862-3091
Web site: www.rootsweb.com/~txlipsco/
Parent County: Bexar Land District
Comments/research tips: County Clerk has Marriage records 1851–1900.

Record Type	Year Begun	Jurisdiction
Birth	1903	County Clerk
Death	1903	County Clerk
Divorce	1887	County Clerk
Probate	1887	County Clerk
Court	1887	County Clerk
Land	1887	County Clerk

■ Live Oak 2 Feb. 1856
301 Houston St., P.O. Box 280, George West, TX 78022
Phone: (361)449-2733
Web site: wwwrootsweb.com/~txliveoa/
Parent County: Nueces, San Patricio
Comments/research tips: County Clerk has Divorce records for 1860 and 1867–1868, Land records 1856–1886, Marriage records 1857–1926, and Probate records 1857–1903.

Record Type	Year Begun	Jurisdiction
Birth	1903	County Clerk
Death	1903	County Clerk
Court	1856	County Clerk

■ Llano 1 Feb. 1856
801 Ford, P.O. Box 40, Llano, TX 78643
Phone: (915)247-4455
Web site: www.rootsweb.com/~txllano/
Parent County: Bexar, Gillespie
Comments/research tips: District Clerk has Court and Divorce records 1882–1940 and Naturalization records 1882–1925. County Clerk has Death records 1903–1966, Land records 1880–1928, Marriage records 1880–1957, Military Discharge records 1919–1943, and Probate records 1881–1955.

Record Type	Year Begun	Jurisdiction
Birth	1903	County Clerk

■ Loving 26 Feb. 1887
P.O. Box 194, Mentone, TX 79754
Phone: (915)377-2441
Web site: www.rootsweb.com/~txloving/
Parent County: Tom Green
Comments/research tips: County Clerk has Death records 1931–1951 and Marriage records 1931–1974. Organized 8 July 1893, dissolved 12 May 1897, reorganized 1931.

Record Type	Year Begun	Jurisdiction
Birth	1886	County Clerk
Divorce	1931	County Clerk
Probate	1931	County Clerk
Court	1931	County Clerk
Land	1931	County Clerk

■ Lubbock 21 Aug. 1876
904 Broadway, P.O. Box 10536, Lubbock, TX 79408
Phone: (806)775-1043
Web site: www.rootsweb.com/~txlubboc/
Parent County: Bexar Land District
Comments/research tips: County Clerk has Marriage records 1891–1975. Attached to Crosby, Young, and Baylor Counties at one time, officially formed 10 March 1891.

Record Type	Year Begun	Jurisdiction
Birth	1903	County Clerk
Death	1903	County Clerk
Probate	1891	County Clerk
Court	1891	County Clerk
Land	1891	County Clerk

■ Lynn 21 Aug. 1876
P.O. Box 937, Tahoka, TX 79373
Phone: (806)998-4750
Web site: www.rootsweb.com/~txlynn/
Parent County: Bexar Land District
Comments/research tips: County Clerk has Birth records 1870–1946, Death records 1904–1971, and Marriage records 1903–1962.

Record Type	Year Begun	Jurisdiction
Land	1903	County Clerk
Probate	1903	County Clerk
Court	1903	County Clerk

■ Madison 27 Jan. 1853
101 W. Main St., Room 102, Madisonville, TX 77864
Phone: (936)348-2638
Web site: www.rootsweb,com/~txmadiso/
Parent County: Leon, Grimes, Walker
Comments/research tips: District Clerk has Court records 1873–1904. County Clerk has Marriage records 1874–1940.

Record Type	Year Begun	Jurisdiction
Birth	1903	County Clerk
Death	1903	County Clerk
Probate	1873	County Clerk
Land	1873	County Clerk

■ Marion 8 Feb. 1860
102 W. Austin St., Drawer 763, Jefferson, TX 75657
Phone: (903)665-3971

Web site: http://txgenes.com/TxMarion/index.html
Parent County: Cass
Comments/research tips: County Clerk has Birth records 1873–1876 and 1903–1940, Death records 1903–1940, Land records 1838–1850 and 1860–1900, Marriage records 1860–1937, Naturalization records 1871–1938, and Probate records 1860–1943. District Clerk has Court records 1860–1934. Land records 1838–1850 transcribed from Bowie, Cass, Harrison, Red River, and Titus Counties.

■ **Martin** 21 Aug. 1876
P.O. Box 906, Stanton, TX 79782
Phone: (915)756-3412
Web site: www.rootsweb.com/~txmartin/
Parent County: Bexar Land District
Comments/research tips: County Clerk has Birth records 1873–1950 and Marriage records 1885–1950. Martin County was attached to Mitchell County for five months after county formation, then to Howard County until 1884.

Record Type	Year Begun	Jurisdiction
Death	1910	County Clerk
Court	1885	County Clerk
Divorce	na	District/County Clerk
Probate	1885	County Clerk
Land	1885	County Clerk

■ **Mason** 22 Jan. 1858
P.O. Box 702, Mason, TX 76856
Phone: (915)347-5253
Web site: http://us-gen.com/tx/mason/
Parent County: Gillespie, Bexar Land District

Record Type	Year Begun	Jurisdiction
Birth	1903	County Clerk
Death	1903	County Clerk
Marriage	1877	County Clerk
Divorce	na	County Clerk
Probate	1877	County Clerk
Court	1877	County Clerk
Land	1877	County Clerk

■ **Matagorda** 17 Mar. 1836
1700 Seventh St., Room 202, Bay City, TX 77414
Phone: (979)244-7680
Web site: www.rootsweb.com/~txmatago/
Parent County: Old Mexican Municipality called Matagorda
Comments/research tips: District Clerk has Court records 1837–1947. County Clerk has Land records 1837–1898, Marriage records 1837–1927, and Probate records 1837–1913.

Record Type	Year Begun	Jurisdiction
Birth	1903	County Clerk
Death	1903	County Clerk

■ **Maverick** 2 Feb. 1856
500 Quarry St., P.O. Box 4050, Eagle Pass, TX 78852
Phone: (830)773-2829
Web site: www.rootsweb.com/~txmaveri/
Parent County: Kinney
Comments/research tips: District Clerk has Court records 1871–1905. County Clerk has Land records 1871–1923,

Marriage records 1871–1917, Naturalization records 1871–1926, and Probate records 1876–1913.

Record Type	Year Begun	Jurisdiction
Birth	1903	County Clerk
Death	1903	County Clerk

■ **McCulloch** 27 Aug. 1856
Courthouse Sq., Brady, TX 76825
Phone: (915)597-0733
Web site: www.rootsweb.com/~txmccull/
Parent County: Bexar

Record Type	Year Begun	Jurisdiction
Birth	1903	County Clerk
Death	1903	County Clerk
Marriage	1876	County Clerk
Land	1876	County Clerk
Court	1876	County Clerk
Probate	1876	County Clerk

■ **McLennan** 22 Jan. 1850
215 N. Fifth, P.O. Box 1727, Waco, TX 76701
Phone: (254)757-5078
Web site: www.rootsweb.com/~txmclenn/
Parent County: Milam, Limestone, Navarro
Comments/research tips: County Clerk has Birth records 1908–1917, Land records 1850–1906, Marriage records 1850–1916, Naturalization records 1855–1907, and Probate records 1861–1949. District Clerk has Court records 1893–1904 and Divorce records 1851–1907.

Record Type	Year Begun	Jurisdiction
Death	1903	County Clerk

■ **McMullen** 1 Feb. 1858
P.O. Box 235, Tilden, TX 78072
Phone: (512)274-3215
Web site: www.rootsweb.com/~txmcmull/
Parent County: Bexar, Live Oak, Atascosa
Comments/research tips: District Clerk has Court records 1879–1919 and Naturalization records 1892–1904. County Clerk has Land records 1871–1910, Marriage records 1877–1918, and Probate records 1877–1925. County officially organized in 1877.

Record Type	Year Begun	Jurisdiction
Birth	1903	County Clerk
Death	1903	County Clerk

■ **Medina** 12 Feb. 1848
County Courthouse 2516 McHaughten, Hondo, TX 78861
Phone: (830)741-6045
Web site: www.rootsweb.com/~txmedina/
Parent County: Bexar Land District
Comments/research tips: District Clerk has Court records 1849–1909. County Clerk has Land records 1848–1886 and Marriage and Probate records 1848–1977.

Record Type	Year Begun	Jurisdiction
Birth	1903	County Clerk
Death	1903	County Clerk

■ **Menard** 22 Jan. 1858
P.O. Box 1028, Menard, TX 76859
Phone: (915)396-4682

Texas

Web site: www.rootsweb.com/~txmenard/
Parent County: Bexar Land District

Record Type	Year Begun	Jurisdiction
Birth	1903	County Clerk
Court	1871	County Clerk
Marriage	1871	County Clerk
Death	1903	County Clerk
Divorce	na	County Clerk
Probate	1871	County Clerk
Land	1871	County Clerk

■ Midland 4 Mar. 1885
200 W. Wall, P.O. Box 211, Midland, TX 79701
Phone: (915)688-1070
Web site: www.co.midland.tx.us/
Parent County: Tom Green
Comments/research tips: District Clerk has Divorce records 1886–1900. County Clerk has Probate records 1886–1893.

Record Type	Year Begun	Jurisdiction
Birth	1903	County Clerk
Death	1903	County Clerk
Marriage	1885	County Clerk
Land	1885	County Clerk
Court	1886	County Clerk

■ Milam 17 Mar. 1836
107 W. Main, P.O. Box 191, Cameron, TX 76520
Phone: (254)697-7049
Web site: www.milamcounty.org/
Parent County: Old Mexican Municipality, Municipality of Milam
Comments/research tips: County Clerk has School Census 1909–1970.

Record Type	Year Begun	Jurisdiction
Birth	1903	County Clerk
Death	1903	County Clerk
Marriage	1874	County Clerk
Probate	1874	County Clerk
Court	1872	County Clerk
Land	1874	County Clerk

■ Mills 15 Mar. 1887
P.O. Box 646, Goldthwaite, TX 76844
Phone: (915)648-2711
Web site: www.rootsweb.com/~txmills/mills.html
Parent County: Comanche, Brown, Hamilton, Lampasas

Record Type	Year Begun	Jurisdiction
Birth	1903	County Clerk
Death	1903	County Clerk
Marriage	1887	County Clerk
Divorce	1887	County Clerk
Probate	1887	County Clerk
Court	1887	County Clerk
Land	1887	County Clerk

■ Mitchell 21 Aug. 1876
349 Oak St., Room 103, Colorado City, TX 79512
Phone: (915)728-3481
Web site: www.rootsweb.com/~txmitche/

Parent County: Bexar Land District

Record Type	Year Begun	Jurisdiction
Birth	1903	County Clerk
Marriage	1881	County Clerk
Death	1903	County Clerk
Probate	1881	County Clerk
Court	1881	County Clerk
Land	1881	County Clerk

■ Montague 24 Dec. 1857
P.O. Box 77, Montague, TX 76251
Phone: (940)894-2461
Web site: www.rootsweb.com/~txmontag/
Parent County: Cooke
Comments/research tips: County Clerk has Court records 1876–1985, Land records 1873–1926, Marriage records 1873–1940, and Probate records 1874–1950. District Clerk has Divorce records 1921–1946 and Naturalization records 1885–1927.

Record Type	Year Begun	Jurisdiction
Birth	1903	County Clerk
Death	1903	County Clerk

■ Montgomery 14 Dec. 1837
301 N. Main, P.O. Box 959, Conroe, TX 77305
Phone: (936)539-7885
Web site: www.co.montgomery.tx.us/
Parent County: Washington
Comments/research tips: District Clerk has Court records 1839–1912. County Clerk has Land records 1838–1887.

Record Type	Year Begun	Jurisdiction
Birth	1903	County Clerk
Death	1903	County Clerk
Marriage	1838	County Clerk
Probate	1839	County Clerk
Divorce	na	District Clerk

■ Moore 21 Aug. 1876
715 Dumas Ave., Room 105, Dumas, TX 79029
Phone: (806)935-6164
Web site: www.rootsweb.com/~txmoore/
Parent County: Bexar

Record Type	Year Begun	Jurisdiction
Birth	1903	County Clerk
Death	1903	County Clerk
Probate	1892	County Clerk
Court	1892	County Clerk
Marriage	1892	County Clerk
Land	1882	County Clerk
Divorce	na	District/County Clerk

■ Morris 13 Mar. 1875
500 Broadnax St., Daingerfield, TX 75638
Phone: (903)645-3911
Web site: www.rootsweb.com/~txmorris/
Parent County: Titus
Comments/research tips: District Clerk has Court records 1875–1954. County Clerk has Land records 1875–1910, Marriage records 1875–1940, and Probate records 1876–1955.

Record Type	Year Begun	Jurisdiction
Birth	1903	County Clerk
Death	1903	County Clerk
Divorce	na	District Clerk

■ Motley   21 Aug. 1876

701 Dundee, P.O. Box 66, Matador, TX 79244
Phone: (806)347-2621
Web site: www.rootsweb.com/~txmotley/
Parent County: Bexar Land District
Comments/research tips: Motley County was officially organized in 1891.

Record Type	Year Begun	Jurisdiction
Birth	1903	County Clerk
Death	1903	County Clerk
Marriage	1891	County Clerk
Divorce	1891	County Clerk
Probate	1891	County Clerk
Court	1891	County Clerk

■ Nacogdoches   17 Mar. 1836

101 W. Main St., Nacogdoches, TX 75961
Phone: (936)560-7733
Web site: www.rootsweb.com/~txnacogd/
Parent County: Old Mexican Municipality, Municipality of Nacogdoches
Comments/research tips: County Clerk has Land records 1826–1887, Marriage records 1820–1918, and Probate records 1838–1917. County Archives has Military records 1820–1830.

Record Type	Year Begun	Jurisdiction
Birth	1903	County Clerk
Death	1903	County Clerk
Court	1837	County Clerk
Divorce	na	District/County Clerk

■ Navarro   25 Apr. 1846

300 W. Third Ave., P.O. Box 423, Corsicana, TX 75151
Phone: (903)654-3035
Web site: www.rootsweb.com/~txnavarr/
Parent County: Robertson
Comments/research tips: County Clerk has Birth records 1873–1987, Death records 1903–1988, Land records 1846–1912, Marriage records 1846–1942, and Probate records 1847–1978. District Clerk has Court records 1855–1936, Divorce records 1905–1937, and Naturalization records 1894–1914.

■ Newton   22 Apr. 1846

P.O. Box 484, Newton, TX 75966
Phone: (409)379-5341
Web site: www.rootsweb.com/~txnewton
Parent County: Jasper
Comments/research tips: County Clerk has Land records 1846–1889, Marriage records 1846–1923, and Probate records 1846–1920.

Record Type	Year Begun	Jurisdiction
Birth	1903	County Clerk
Death	1903	County Clerk
Court	1846	County Clerk

■ Nolan   21 Aug. 1876

100 E. Third St., Sweetwater, TX 79556
Phone: (915)235-2462
Web site: www.rootsweb.com/~txnolan/
Parent County: Bexar Land District, Young

Record Type	Year Begun	Jurisdiction
Birth	1903	County Clerk
Death	1903	County Clerk
Court	1881	County Clerk
Marriage	1881	County Clerk
Probate	1881	County Clerk
Land	1881	County Clerk
Divorce	na	District/County Clerk

■ Nueces   18 Apr. 1846

901 Leopard St., Corpus Christi, TX 78401
Phone: (361)888-0580
Web site: www.rootsweb.com/~txnueces/
Parent County: San Patricio
Comments/research tips: District Clerk has Court records 1850–1910 and Naturalization records 1912–1914. County Clerk has Land records 1847–1902, Marriage records 1846–1906, Naturalization records 1852–1906, and Probate records 1846–1907.

Record Type	Year Begun	Jurisdiction
Birth	1903	County Clerk
Death	1903	County Clerk

■ Ochiltree   21 Aug. 1876

511 S. Main St., Perryton, TX 79070
Phone: (806)435-8039
Web site: www.rootsweb.com/~txochilt/
Parent County: Bexar Land District

Record Type	Year Begun	Jurisdiction
Birth	1903	County Clerk
Death	1903	County Clerk
Marriage	1889	County Clerk
Probate	1889	County Clerk
Land	1889	County Clerk
Court	1889	County Clerk
Divorce	na	District/County Clerk

■ Oldham   21 Aug. 1876

P.O. Box 360, Vega, TX 79092
Phone: (806)267-2667
Web site: www.rootsweb.com/~txoldham/index.html
Parent County: Bexar Land District

Record Type	Year Begun	Jurisdiction
Birth	1903	County Clerk
Death	1903	County Clerk
Marriage	1881	County Clerk
Divorce	1881	County Clerk
Probate	1881	County Clerk
Court	1881	County Clerk
Land	1881	County Clerk

■ Orange   5 Jan. 1852

801 W. Division St., P.O. Box 1536, Orange, TX 77630
Phone: (409)882-7055

Texas

Web site: www.co.orange.tx.us/
Parent County: Jefferson
Comments/research tips: District Clerk has Court records 1852–1909. County Clerk has Land records 1852–1905, Marriage records 1852–1921, Naturalization records 1871–1909, and Probate records 1852–1942.

Record Type	Year Begun	Jurisdiction
Birth	1903	County Clerk
Death	1903	County Clerk
Divorce	na	District Clerk

■ Palo Pinto   27 Aug. 1856
P.O. Box 219, Palo Pinto, TX 76484
Phone: (940)659-1277
Web site: www.rootsweb.com/~txpalopi/
Parent County: Navarro, Bosque

Record Type	Year Begun	Jurisdiction
Birth	1903	County Clerk
Death	1903	County Clerk
Marriage	1858	County Clerk
Land	1858	County Clerk
Probate	1858	County Clerk
Divorce	na	District/County Clerk
Court	1858	County Clerk

■ Panola   30 Mar. 1846
110 S. Sycamore St., Carthage, TX 75633
Phone: (903)693-0302
Web site: www.rootsweb.com/~txpanola/
Parent County: Harrison, Shelby
Comments/research tips: County Clerk has Land records 1846–1887, Marriage records 1846–1950, and Probate records 1846–1923.

Record Type	Year Begun	Jurisdiction
Birth	1903	County Clerk
Death	1903	County Clerk
Court	1846	County Clerk

■ Parker   12 Dec. 1855
1112 Santa Fe, P.O. Box 819, Weatherford, TX 76086
Phone: (817)594-7461
Web site: www.rootsweb.com/~txparker/
Parent County: Bosque, Navarro
Comments/research tips: District Clerk has Court records 1874–1931 and Divorce records 1900–1944. County Clerk has Land records 1874–1908, Marriage records 1874–1939, Naturalization records 1874–1930, and Probate records 1860–1935.

Record Type	Year Begun	Jurisdiction
Birth	1903	County Clerk
Death	1903	County Clerk

■ Parmer   21 Aug. 1876
401 Third St., P.O. Box 356, Farwell, TX 79325
Phone: (806)481-3691
Web site: www.rootsweb.com/~txparmer/
Parent County: Bexar Land District

Record Type	Year Begun	Jurisdiction
Birth	1903	County Clerk
Marriage	1907	County Clerk
Death	1903	County Clerk
Probate	1907	County Clerk
Court	1907	County Clerk
Land	1907	County Clerk
Divorce	na	District/County Clerk

■ Pecos   3 May 1871
103 W. Callaghan St., Fort Stockton, TX 79735
Phone: (915)336-7555
Web site: www.rootsweb.com/~txpecos/
Parent County: Presidio
Comments/research tips: County Clerk has Death records 1903–1965 and Marriage records for 1875–1951, 1983, 1991, and 1995.

Record Type	Year Begun	Jurisdiction
Birth	1903	County Clerk
Court	1875	District Clerk
Probate	1875	County Clerk
Land	1875	County Clerk

■ Polk   30 Mar. 1846
101 Church St. W., P.O. Drawer 2119, Livingston, TX 77351
Phone: (936)327-6804 ext. 1100
Web site: www.rootsweb.com/~txpolk/
Parent County: Liberty Municipality
Comments/research tips: District Clerk has Court records 1848–1868, 1872–1879, and 1883–1909. County Clerk has Land records 1846–1898, Marriage records 1846–1937, and Probate records 1840–1976.

Record Type	Year Begun	Jurisdiction
Birth	1903	County Clerk
Death	1903	County Clerk
Divorce	na	District/County Clerk

■ Potter   21 Aug. 1876
500 S. Filmore, P.O. Box 9638, Amarillo, TX 79101
Phone: (806)379-2275
Web site: www.co.potter.tx.us/home.html
Parent County: Bexar Land District
Comments/research tips: County Clerk has Birth and Death Records 1941–1951.

Record Type	Year Begun	Jurisdiction
Marriage	1887	County Clerk
Probate	1887	County Clerk
Court	1889	County Clerk
Land	1887	County Clerk
Divorce	na	District Clerk

■ Presidio   3 Jan. 1850
County Courthouse, 320 N. Highland St., P.O. Box 789, Marfa, TX 79843
Phone: (915)729-4812
Web site: www.rootsweb.com/~txpresid/
Parent County: Bexar Land District

Record Type	Year Begun	Jurisdiction
Birth	1903	County Clerk
Death	1903	County Clerk

Marriage	1875	County Clerk
Land	1876	County Clerk
Divorce	1876	County Clerk
Court	1876	County Clerk
Probate	1875	County Clerk

■ Rains 9 June 1870
100 Quitman St., P.O. Box 187, Emory, TX 75440
Phone: (903)473-2461
Web site: http://txgenes.com/txrains/rains.htm
Parent County: Hopkins, Hunt, Wood

Record Type	Year Begun	Jurisdiction
Birth	1903	County Clerk
Death	1903	County Clerk
Marriage	1879	County Clerk
Divorce	na	District/County Clerk
Land	1870	County Clerk
Probate	1880	County Clerk
Court	1880	County Clerk

■ Randall 21 Aug. 1876
401 Fifteenth St., P.O. Box 660, Canyon, TX 79015
Phone: (806)468-5505
Web site: www.rootsweb.com/~txrandal/
Parent County: Bexar Land District
Comments/research tips: County was unorganized until 1889. Randall County was attached to Jack County (1876–1879), Wheeler County (1879–1881), Oldham County (1881–1883), Donley County (1883–1885), and Oldham (1885–1889).

Record Type	Year Begun	Jurisdiction
Marriage	1889	County Clerk
Probate	1889	County Clerk
Court	1889	County Clerk
Land	1889	County Clerk
Divorce	na	District/County Clerk
Birth	1903	County Clerk
Death	1903	County Clerk

■ Reagan 7 Mar. 1903
P.O. Box 100, Big Lake, TX 76932
Phone: (915)884-2442
Web site: www.rootsweb.com/~txreagan/
Parent County: Tom Green
Comments/research tips: Some records from 1883 transferred from Tom Green County.

Record Type	Year Begun	Jurisdiction
Birth	1903	County Clerk
Marriage	1903	County Clerk
Death	1903	County Clerk
Divorce	1903	County Clerk
Probate	1903	County Clerk
Court	1903	County Clerk
Land	1903	County Clerk

■ Real 3 Apr. 1913
P.O. Box 750, Leakey, TX 78873
Phone: (830)232-5202
Web site: www.rootsweb.com/~txreal/

Parent County: Bandera, Kerr, Edwards

Record Type	Year Begun	Jurisdiction
Birth	1913	County Clerk
Marriage	1913	County Clerk
Death	1913	County Clerk
Divorce	1913	County Clerk
Probate	1913	County Clerk
Court	1913	County Clerk
Land	1913	County Clerk

■ Red River 14 Dec. 1837
Red River County Annex, 200 N. Walnut St., Clarksville, TX 75426
Phone: (903)427-2401
Web site: www.rootsweb.com/~txredriv/index.htm
Parent County: Red River District
Comments/research tips: District Clerk has Court records 1840–1910 and Naturalization records 1839–1927. County Clerk has Land records 1838–1886, Marriage records 1846–1934, and Probate records 1838–1887.

Record Type	Year Begun	Jurisdiction
Birth	1903	County Clerk
Death	1903	County Clerk
Divorce	na	District/County Clerk

■ Reeves 14 Apr. 1883
100 E. Fourteenth St., P.O. Box 867, Pecos, TX 79772
Phone: (432)445-5467
Web site: www.rootsweb.com/~txreeves/
Parent County: Pecos
Comments/research tips: County Clerk has some deferred Birth Records from the 1800s.

Record Type	Year Begun	Jurisdiction
Birth	1903	County Clerk
Death	1903	County Clerk
Marriage	1884	County Clerk
Probate	1884	County Clerk
Court	1885	County Clerk
Land	1884	County Clerk

■ Refugio 17 Mar. 1836
808 Commerce St., Room 112, P.O. Box 704, Refugio, TX 78377
Phone: (361)526-2233
Web site: www.rootsweb.com/~txrefugi/
Parent County: Refugio Municipality
Comments/research tips: County Clerk has Court records 1879–1922, Land records 1839–1904, Marriage records 1851–1956, Naturalization records 1854–1904, and Probate records 1840–1909.

Record Type	Year Begun	Jurisdiction
Birth	1903	County Clerk
Death	1903	County Clerk

■ Roberts 21 Aug. 1876
P.O. Box 477, Miami, TX 79059
Phone: (806)868-2341
Web site: www.rootsweb.com/~txrobert/
Parent County: Bexar County, Clay Land District

Comments/research tips: County was organized in January 1889. From 1876–1889 Roberts was officially attached to Wheeler County.

Record Type	Year Begun	Jurisdiction
Birth	1903	County Clerk
Death	1903	County Clerk
Marriage	1889	County Clerk
Divorce	1889	County Clerk
Probate	1889	County Clerk
Court	1889	County Clerk
Land	1889	County Clerk

■ Robertson 14 Dec. 1837
P.O. Box 1029, Franklin, TX 77856
Phone: (979)828-4130
Web site: www.rootsweb.com/~txrober2/
Parent County: Milam, Bexar, Nacogdoches
Comments/research tips: District Clerk has Court records 1838–1972 and Divorce records 1903–1972. County Clerk has Death records 1903–1934, Land records 1838–1901, Naturalization records 1874–1941, and Probate records 1838–1974.

Record Type	Year Begun	Jurisdiction
Birth	1903	County Clerk
Marriage	1838	County Clerk

■ Rockwall 1 Mar. 1873
1101 Ridge Rd., Suite 101, Rockwall, TX 75087
Phone: (972)882-0220
Web site: www.rootsweb.com/~txrockwa/
Parent County: Kaufman
Comments/research tips: District Clerk has Court records 1874–1978. County Clerk has Land records 1873–1901 and Probate records 1877–1938.

Record Type	Year Begun	Jurisdiction
Birth	1903	County Clerk
Marriage	1875	County Clerk
Death	1903	County Clerk

■ Runnels 1 Feb. 1858
600 Courthouse Sq., P.O. Box 189, Ballinger, TX 76821
Phone: (915)365-2720
Web site: www.rootsweb.com/~txrunnel/
Parent County: Bexar, Travis

Record Type	Year Begun	Jurisdiction
Birth	1903	County Clerk
Death	1903	County Clerk
Court	1881	County Clerk
Marriage	1880	County Clerk
Probate	1880	County Clerk
Land	1880	County Clerk
Divorce	na	District/County Clerk

■ Rusk 16 Jan. 1843
2115 N. Main St., P.O. Box 758, Henderson, TX 75653
Phone: (903)657-0330
Web site: www.rootsweb.com/~txrusk/
Parent County: Nacogdoches
Comments/research tips: County Clerk has Birth records 1873–1876 and 1903–1917, Land Records 1843–1845 and 1851–1887, Marriage records 1839–1917, and Probate records 1847–1930. District Clerk has Court records 1847–1930. Courthouse fire in 1878 destroyed some records.

Record Type	Year Begun	Jurisdiction
Death	1903	County Clerk
Divorce	1847	District Court

■ Sabine 14 Dec. 1837
P.O. Drawer 580, Hemphill, TX 75948
Phone: (409)787-3786
Web site: www.rootsweb.com/~txsabine/
Parent County: Sabine Municipality
Comments/research tips: County Clerk has Land records 1876–1891, Marriage records 1875–1919, and Probate records 1879–1923. Fire destroyed most pre-1875 records.

Record Type	Year Begun	Jurisdiction
Birth	1903	County Clerk
Death	1903	County Clerk
Divorce	na	District/County Clerk
Court	1876	County Clerk

■ San Augustine 17 Mar. 1836
106 Courthouse, San Augustine, TX 75972
Phone: (936)275-2452
Web site: www.rootsweb.com/~txsanaug/
Parent County: San Augustine Municipality
Comments/research tips: County Clerk has Land records 1833–1901, Marriage records 1837–1920, and Probate records 1837–1920.

Record Type	Year Begun	Jurisdiction
Birth	1903	County Clerk
Death	1903	County Clerk
Divorce	na	District/County Clerk
Court	1837	District Clerk

■ San Jacinto 13 Aug. 1870
P.O. Box 669, Cold Spring, TX 77331
Phone: (936)653-2324
Web site: www.geocities.com/Athens/Academy/2670/SANJAC-ol.htm
Parent County: Liberty, Polk, Montgomery, Walker
Comments/research tips: District Clerk has Court records 1872–1954 and Divorce records 1900–1931. County Clerk has Land records 1870–1886, Marriage records 1870–1965, and Probate records 1876–1926.

Record Type	Year Begun	Jurisdiction
Birth	1888	County Clerk
Death	1888	County Clerk

■ San Patricio 17 Mar. 1836
400 W. Sinton, Room 105, P.O. Box 578, Sinton, TX 78387
Phone: (361)364-6290
Web site: www.rootsweb.com/~txsanpat/
Parent County: San Patricio Municipality
Comments/research tips: District Clerk has Court records 1848–1896. County Clerk has Land records 1846–1896, Marriage records 1859–1958, and Probate records 1847–1976.

Record Type	Year Begun	Jurisdiction
Birth	1903	County Clerk
Death	1903	County Clerk

■ San Saba   1 Feb. 1856

County Courthouse, 500 E. Wallace, San Saba, TX 76877
Phone: (915)372-3614
Web site: www.rootsweb.com/~txssaba/
Parent County: Bexar Land District

Record Type	Year Begun	Jurisdiction
Birth	1903	County Clerk
Death	1903	County Clerk
Marriage	1857	County Clerk
Divorce	na	District/County Clerk
Court	1868	County Clerk
Land	1857	County Clerk
Probate	1868	County Clerk

■ Schleicher   1 Apr. 1887

P.O. Drawer 580, Eldorado, TX 76936
Phone: (915)853-2833
Web site: www.rootsweb.com/~txschlei/
Parent County: Crockett
Comments/research tips: Due to its small population, Schleicher County was attached to Kimble then Menard Counties. First election of county officials occured in 1901.

Record Type	Year Begun	Jurisdiction
Birth	1903	County Clerk
Death	1903	County Clerk
Marriage	1901	County Clerk
Divorce	1901	County Clerk
Probate	1901	County Clerk
Court	1901	County Clerk
Land	1901	County Clerk

■ Scurry   21 Aug. 1876

1806 Twenty-Fifth St., Suite 300, Snyder, TX 79549-2530
Phone: (325)573-5332
Web site: www.rootsweb.com/~txscurry/
Parent County: Bexar Land District
Comments/research tips: Scurry County was attached to Mitchell County until 1884.

Record Type	Year Begun	Jurisdiction
Birth	1903	County Clerk
Death	1903	County Clerk
Marriage	1884	County Clerk
Land	1884	County Clerk
Probate	1884	County Clerk
Court	1885	County Clerk
Divorce	na	District/County Clerk

■ Shackelford   1 Feb. 1858

225 S. Main, P.O. Box 247, Albany, TX 76430-0247
Phone: (915)762-2232
Web site: www.rootsweb.com/~txshacke/
Parent County: Bosque

Record Type	Year Begun	Jurisdiction
Birth	1903	County Clerk
Marriage	1874	County Clerk

Land	1874	County Clerk
Death	1903	County Clerk
Probate	1874	County Clerk
Court	1875	County Clerk
Divorce	na	County Clerk

■ Shelby   17 Mar. 1836

200 San Augustine St., P.O. Box 1987, Center, TX 75935
Phone: (936)598-6361
Web site: www.rootsweb.com/~txshelby/
Parent County: Tenehaw Municipality
Comments/research tips: County courthouse records were destroyed in fire of 1882.

Record Type	Year Begun	Jurisdiction
Birth	1903	County Clerk
Marriage	1882	County Clerk
Probate	1881	County Clerk
Court	1882	County Clerk
Land	1838	County Clerk
Death	1903	County Clerk
Divorce	na	District/County Clerk

■ Sherman   21 Aug. 1876

701 N. Third, P.O. Box 270, Stratford, TX 79084
Phone: (806)396-2371
Web site: www.rootsweb.com/~txsherma/
Parent County: Bexar

Record Type	Year Begun	Jurisdiction
Birth	1903	County Clerk
Death	1903	County Clerk
Probate	1889	County Clerk
Court	1889	County Clerk
Marriage	1889	County Clerk
Land	1889	County Clerk
Divorce	1889	County Clerk

■ Smith   July 1846

100 N. Broadway Ave., Tyler, TX 75702
Phone: (903)535-0630
Web site: www.rootsweb.com/~txsmith/
Parent County: Nacogdoches District
Comments/research tips: County Clerk has Birth records 1873–1876 and 1880–1992, Death records 1903–1965, Land records 1846–1901, Marriage records 1848–1951, and Probate records 1846–1931. District Clerk has Court records 1846–1941, Divorce records 1893–1951, and Naturalization records ca. 1854–1912.

■ Somervell   13 Mar. 1875

P.O. Box 1098, Glen Rose, TX 76043
Phone: (254)897-4427
Web site: vip.hpnc.com/~clerk/
Parent County: Hood

Record Type	Year Begun	Jurisdiction
Birth	1903	County Clerk
Death	1903	County Clerk
Marriage	1885	County Clerk
Divorce	na	District/County Clerk
Court	1875	County Clerk

Probate .... 1875 ....County Clerk
Land .... 1875 ....County Clerk

■ Starr 10 Feb. 1848
County Courthouse, 401 N. Britian, Room 201, Rio Grande City, TX 78582
Phone: (956)487-8032
Web site: www.rootsweb.com/~txstarr/
Parent County: Nueces
Comments/research tips: District Clerk has Court records 1848–1966. County Clerk has Land records 1848–1909, Marriage records 1858–1974, Naturalization records 1883–1902, and Probate records 1848–1939.

Record Type	Year Begun	Jurisdiction
Birth	1903	County Clerk
Death	1903	County Clerk

■ Stephens 22 Jan. 1858
County Courthouse, 200 W. Walker, Breckenridge, TX 76424
Phone: (254)559-3700
Web site: www.rootsweb.com/~txstephe/
Parent County: Bosque
Comments/research tips: Formerly Buchanan County. Name changed to Stephens 17 December 1861.

Record Type	Year Begun	Jurisdiction
Birth	1903	County Clerk
Death	1903	County Clerk
Marriage	1876	County Clerk
Probate	1876	County Clerk
Land	1876	County Clerk
Divorce	na	District/County Clerk
Court	1876	County Clerk

■ Sterling 4 Mar. 1891
615 Fourth, P.O. Box 55, Sterling City, TX 76951
Phone: (915)378-5191
Web site: www.rootsweb.com/~txsterli/
Parent County: Tom Green

Record Type	Year Begun	Jurisdiction
Birth	1903	County Clerk
Death	1903	County Clerk
Marriage	1891	County Clerk
Divorce	1891	County Clerk
Probate	1891	County Clerk
Court	1891	County Clerk
Land	1891	County Clerk

■ Stonewall 21 Aug. 1876
P.O. Drawer P, Aspermont, TX 79502
Phone: (940)989-2272
Web site: www.rootsweb.com/~txstonew/
Parent County: Bexar District, Young District

Record Type	Year Begun	Jurisdiction
Birth	1903	County Clerk
Marriage	1888	County Clerk
Death	1903	County Clerk
Divorce	ca. 1900	District/County Clerk
Probate	1888	County Clerk

Court .... 1889 ....County Clerk
Land .... 1887 ....County Clerk

■ Sutton 1 Apr. 1887
300 E. Oak St., Suite 3, Sonora, TX 76950
Phone: (915)387-3815
Web site: www.rootsweb.com/~txsutton/
Parent County: Crockett

Record Type	Year Begun	Jurisdiction
Birth	1903	County Clerk
Death	1903	County Clerk
Marriage	1890	County Clerk
Divorce	1890	County Clerk
Probate	1890	County Clerk
Court	1890	County Clerk
Land	1890	County Clerk

■ Swisher 21 Aug. 1876
County Courthouse, 119 S. Maxwell, Tulia, TX 79088
Phone: (806)995-3294
Web site: www.rootsweb.com/~txswishe/
Parent County: Bexar District, Young District

Record Type	Year Begun	Jurisdiction
Birth	1903	County Clerk
Marriage	1890	County Clerk
Death	1903	County Clerk
Divorce	1890	County Clerk
Probate	1890	County Clerk
Court	1890	County Clerk
Land	1890	County Clerk

■ Tarrant 20 Dec. 1849
100 W. Weatherford St., Fort Worth, TX 76196
Phone: (817)884-1195
Web site: www.rootsweb.com/~txtarran/
Parent County: Navarro
Comments/research tips: 1860 Census is missing. Many early records for Tarrant County were destroyed in courthouse fire of 1876.

Record Type	Year Begun	Jurisdiction
Birth	1903	County Clerk
Marriage	1876	County Clerk
Land	1850	County Clerk
Probate	1856	County Clerk
Death	1903	County Clerk
Divorce	1887	District Clerk
Court	1876	County Clerk

■ Taylor 1 Feb. 1858
300 Oak St., Abilene, TX 79602
Phone: (915)674-1202
Web site: www.rootsweb.com/~txtaylor/
Parent County: Bexar, Travis

Record Type	Year Begun	Jurisdiction
Birth	1903	County Clerk
Court	1878	County Clerk
Death	1903	County Clerk
Marriage	1878	County Clerk
Probate	1878	County Clerk
Land	1878	County Clerk

Texas

■ **Terrell** 8 Apr. 1905
P.O. Drawer 410, Sanderson, TX 79848
Phone: (915)345-2391
Web site: www.rootsweb.com/~txterrel/
Parent County: Pecos

Record Type	Year Begun	Jurisdiction
Birth	1905	County Clerk
Court	1905	County Clerk
Death	1905	County Clerk
Marriage	1905	County Clerk
Probate	1905	County Clerk
Land	1905	County Clerk

■ **Terry** 21 Aug. 1876
500 W. Main, Brownfield, TX 79316
Phone: (806)637-8551
Web site: www.rootsweb.com/~txterry/
Parent County: Bexar Land District
Comments/research tips: Attached to Young County 1876–1881, Throckmorton County 1881–1883, Howard County 1883–1889, Martin County 1889–1904.

Record Type	Year Begun	Jurisdiction
Birth	1904	County Clerk
Marriage	1904	County Clerk
Death	1904	County Clerk
Land	1904	County Clerk
Probate	1904	County Clerk
Court	1904	County Clerk

■ **Throckmorton** 13 Jan. 1858
P.O. Box 309, Throckmorton, TX 76483
Phone: (940)849-2501
Web site: www.rootsweb.com/~txthrock/throck.htm
Parent County: Fannin, Bosque
Comments/research tips: 1870 Census is missing. County was officially organized in 1879.

Record Type	Year Begun	Jurisdiction
Birth	1903	County Clerk
Marriage	1879	County Clerk
Death	1903	County Clerk
Divorce	1879	County Clerk
Probate	1879	County Clerk
Court	1879	County Clerk
Land	1879	County Clerk

■ **Titus** 11 May 1846
100 W. First St., Suite 204, Mt. Pleasant, TX 75455
Phone: (903)577-6796
Web site: www.rootsweb.com/~txtitus
Parent County: Red River, Bowie
Comments/research tips: County Clerk has Birth and Death records 1903–1984, Land records 1846–1906, Marriage records 1895–1973, and Probate records 1895–1935.

Record Type	Year Begun	Jurisdiction
Court	1895	County Clerk
Divorce	na	District Clerk

■ **Tom Green** 13 Mar. 1874
124 W. Beauregard Ave., San Angelo, TX 76903-5835
Phone: (915)659-6553

Web site: www.rootsweb.com/~txtomgre/
Parent County: Bexar Land District

Record Type	Year Begun	Jurisdiction
Birth	1903	County Clerk
Death	1903	County Clerk
Marriage	1875	County Clerk
Probate	1875	County Clerk
Court	1875	County Clerk
Land	1875	County Clerk

■ **Travis** 25 Jan. 1840
1000 Guadalupe St. #222, P.O. Box 1748, Austin, TX 78767
Phone: (512)854-9188
Web site: www.rootsweb.com/~txtravis/
Parent County: Bastrop
Comments/research tips: County Clerk has Court records 1876–1894, Land records 1840–1886, Marriage records 1840–1916, Naturalization records 1840–1907, and Probate records 1840–1918.

Record Type	Year Begun	Jurisdiction
Birth	1903	County Clerk
Death	1903	County Clerk

■ **Trinity** 11 Feb. 1850
P.O. Box 456, Groveton, TX 75845
Phone: (936)642-1208
Web site: www.rootsweb.com/~txtrinit/
Parent County: Houston
Comments/research tips: District Clerk has Court records 1887–1901 and Naturalization records 1886–1925. County Clerk has Land records 1873–1886 and Probate records 1876–1920. Courthouse burned in 1876, some Deeds were refiled.

Record Type	Year Begun	Jurisdiction
Birth	1903	County Clerk
Death	1903	County Clerk
Marriage	1876	County Clerk
Divorce	na	District/County Clerk

■ **Tyler** 3 Apr. 1846
100 W. Bluff St., Room 110, Woodville, TX 75979
Phone: (409)283-2281
Web site: www.rootsweb.com/~txtyler/
Parent County: Menard District
Comments/research tips: County Clerk has Marriage records 1849–1917, Probate records 1847–1939, and Land records 1846–1913.

Record Type	Year Begun	Jurisdiction
Birth	1903	County Clerk
Death	1903	County Clerk
Burial	1903	County Clerk
Divorce	na	District/County Clerk
Court	1847	County Clerk

■ **Upshur** 27 Apr. 1846
P.O. Box 730, Gilmer, TX 75644
Phone: (903)843-4015
Web site: www.txgenes.com/TxUpshur/index.html

Parent County: Harrison, Nacogdoches

Record Type	Year Begun	Jurisdiction
Birth	1873	County Clerk
Death	1903	County Clerk
Marriage	1873	County Clerk
Land	1846	County Clerk
Probate	1846	County Clerk
Court	1846	County Clerk

■ Upton 26 Feb. 1887

P.O. Box 465, Rankin, TX 79778

Phone: (915)693-2861

Web site: www.rootsweb.com/~txupton/

Parent County: Tom Green

Comments/research tips: County was officially organized in 1910.

Record Type	Year Begun	Jurisdiction
Birth	1910	County Clerk
Marriage	1910	County Clerk
Divorce	1910	County Clerk
Land	1910	County Clerk
Probate	1910	County Clerk
Death	1910	County Clerk
Court	1910	County Clerk

■ Uvalde 8 Feb. 1850

100 N. Getty St., P.O. Box 284, Uvalde, TX 78802

Phone: (830)278-6614

Web site: www.rootsweb.com/~txuvalde/

Parent County: Bexar

Comments/research tips: District Clerk has Court records 1857–1912 and Naturalization records 1884–1906. County Clerk has Land records 1856–1906, Marriage records 1856–1919, and Probate records 1857–1920. Recreated and reorganized 2 February 1856.

Record Type	Year Begun	Jurisdiction
Birth	1903	County Clerk
Death	1903	County Clerk

■ Val Verde 20 Feb. 1885

400 Pecan St., P.O. Box 1267, Del Rio, TX 78841-1267

Phone: (830)774-7564

Web site: www.historictexas.net/valverde/

Parent County: Crockett, Kinney, Pecos

Comments/research tips: County Clerk has Birth, Death, and Marriage records 1882–1995.

Record Type	Year Begun	Jurisdiction
Land	1885	County Clerk
Probate	1885	County Clerk
Court	1885	County Clerk

■ Van Zandt 20 Mar. 1848

121 E. Dallas St., Room 202, Canton, TX 75103

Phone: (903) 567-6503

Web site: www.rootsweb.com/~txvanzan/vzcpage.htm

Parent County: Henderson

Comments/research tips: County Clerk has Birth records 1872–1877 and 1903–1988, Death records 1903–1991, Land records 1848–1925, Marriage records 1848–1957,

and Probate records 1848–1936. District Clerk has Court records 1848–1935, Divorce records 1899–1935, and Naturalization records 1907–1920.

■ Victoria 17 Mar. 1836

115 N. Bridge, Victoria, TX 77901

Phone: (361)575-1478

Web site: www.viptx.net/vcgs/

Parent County: Guadalupe Victoria Municipality

Comments/research tips: District Clerk has Naturalization records 1849–1887, 1895, 1897, and 1904. County Clerk has Naturalization records 1888–1906.

Record Type	Year Begun	Jurisdiction
Birth	1902	County Clerk
Death	1902	County Clerk
Marriage	1838	County Clerk
Probate	1838	County Clerk
Land	1838	County Clerk
Court	1867	County Clerk
Divorce	1838	District Clerk

■ Walker 6 Apr. 1846

1100 University Ave., P.O. Box 210, Huntsville, TX 77340

Phone: (936)436-4922

Web site: www.rootsweb.com/~txwalker/

Parent County: Montgomery

Comments/research tips: District Clerk has Court records 1847–1902 and Naturalization records 1857–1920. County Clerk has Land records 1846–1886 and Probate records 1846–1948.

Record Type	Year Begun	Jurisdiction
Marriage	1846	County Clerk
Birth	1903	County Clerk
Death	1903	County Clerk

■ Waller 28 Apr. 1873

836 Austin St., Room 217, Hempstead, TX 77445

Phone: (979)826-7711

Web site: www.rootsweb.com/~txwaller/

Parent County: Austin, Grimes

Record Type	Year Begun	Jurisdiction
Birth	1903	County Clerk
Death	1903	County Clerk
Marriage	1873	County Clerk
Probate	1873	County Clerk
Court	1873	County Clerk
Land	1873	County Clerk

■ Ward 26 Feb. 1887

400 S. Allen St., Monahans, TX 79756

Phone: (915)943-3294

Web site: www.rootsweb.com/~txward/

Parent County: Tom Green

Comments/research tips: County Clerk has Death records 1893–1951 and Marriage records 1893–1951. County was officially organized in 1892.

Record Type	Year Begun	Jurisdiction
Land	1893	County Clerk
Birth	1882	County Clerk

Probate .... 1893 ....County Clerk
Court .... 1893 ....County Clerk

■ Washington 17 Mar. 1836
100 E. Main St., Suite 102, Brenham, TX 77833
Phone: (409)277-6200
Web site: www.alphal/net/~awhart/wgenweb/
washington.htm
Parent County: Texas Municipality
Comments/research tips: District Clerk has Divorce records 1895–1943. County Clerk has Military Discharge records 1917–1966 and Naturalization records 1850–1940.

Record Type	Year Begun	Jurisdiction
Court	1876	County Clerk
Birth	1903	County Clerk
Death	1903	County Clerk
Marriage	1836	County Clerk
Probate	1837	County Clerk
Land	1831	County Clerk

■ Webb 28 Jan. 1848
P.O. Box 29, Laredo, TX 78042
Phone: (956)721-2645
Web site: www.rootsweb.com/~txwebb/
Parent County: Nueces
Comments/research tips: District Clerk has Court records 1851–1914. County Clerk has Land records 1843–1890, Marriage records 1849–1909, Naturalization records 1881–1907, and Probate records 1851–1945.

Record Type	Year Begun	Jurisdiction
Death	1903	County Clerk
Birth	1903	County Clerk

■ Wharton 3 Apr. 1846
P.O. Box 69, Wharton, TX 77488
Phone: (979)532-2381
Web site: www.rootsweb.com/~txwharto/
Parent County: Matagorda, Jackson, Colorado
Comments/research tips: District Clerk has Court records 1847–1918 and Naturalization records 1880–1930. County Clerk has Land records 1837–1900, Marriage records 1847–1909, and Probate records 1846–1938.

Record Type	Year Begun	Jurisdiction
Birth	1903	County Clerk
Death	1903	County Clerk

■ Wheeler 21 Aug. 1876
P.O. Box 465, Wheeler, TX 79096
Phone: (806)826-5544
Web site: www.rootsweb.com/~txwheele/
Parent County: Bexar District, Young District

Record Type	Year Begun	Jurisdiction
Birth	1903	County Clerk
Death	1903	County Clerk
Marriage	1879	County Clerk
Probate	1879	County Clerk
Court	1879	County Clerk
Land	1881	County Clerk

■ Wichita 1 Feb. 1858
900 Seventh St., P.O. Box 1679, Wichita Falls, TX 76301
Phone: (940)766-8144
Web site: www.rootsweb.com/~txwichit/
Parent County: Cooke Land District
Comments/research tips: County Clerk has Birth and Death records 1860–1949, Land records 1873–1917, and Marriage and Probate records 1882–1934. District Clerk has Court records 1882–1943 and Naturalization records 1884–1917. Attached to Clay County until 21 June 1882.

Record Type	Year Begun	Jurisdiction
Divorce	na	District Clerk

■ Wilbarger 1 Feb. 1858
1700 Wilbarger St., Room 15, Vernon, TX 76384-4742
Phone: (940)552-5486
Web site: www.co.wilbarger.tx.us/
Parent County: Cooke
Comments/research tips: Wilbarger County was officially organized on 10 October 1881.

Record Type	Year Begun	Jurisdiction
Birth	1900	County Clerk
Marriage	1882	County Clerk
Death	1900	County Clerk
Probate	1882	County Clerk
Court	1900	County Clerk
Land	1900	County Clerk

■ Willacy 11 Mar. 1911
540 W. Hidalgo, Raymondville, TX 78580
Phone: (956)689-2710
Web site: www.rootsweb.com/~txwillac/
Parent County: Hidalgo, Cameron
Comments/research tips: Recreated and reorganized in 1921.

Record Type	Year Begun	Jurisdiction
Birth	1903	County Clerk
Marriage	1921	County Clerk
Death	1903	County Clerk
Probate	1921	County Clerk
Court	1921	County Clerk
Land	1891	County Clerk

■ Williamson 13 Mar. 1848
P.O. Box 18, Georgetown, TX 78627
Phone: (512)943-1515
Web site: www.williamson-county.org
Parent County: Milam
Comments/research tips: County Clerk has Birth records 1873–1876, Military Discharge records 1918–1945, and Naturalization records 1857–1938. District Clerk has Divorce records 1909–1938.

Record Type	Year Begun	Jurisdiction
Birth	1903	County Clerk
Death	1903	County Clerk
Marriage	1848	County Clerk
Land	1835	County Clerk
Probate	1848	County Clerk
Court	1848	District Clerk

■ **Wilson** 13 Feb. 1860
1420 Third St., P.O. Box 27, Floresville, TX 78114
Phone: (830)393-7308
Web site: www.pastracks.com/states/texas/wilson/
Parent County: Bexar, Karnes
Comments/research tips: District Clerk has Court records 1896–1908, Divorce records 1893–1985, and Naturalization records 1891–1924. County Clerk has Land records 1860–1976, Marriage records 1860–1908, and Probate records 1862–1915. From 1869–1874 Wilson County was called Cibilo County.

Record Type	Year Begun	Jurisdiction
Birth	1903	County Clerk
Death	1903	County Clerk

■ **Winkler** 26 Feb. 1887
120 E. Winkler, P.O. Box 1007, Kermit, TX 79745
Phone: (915)586-3401
Web site: www.rootsweb.com/~txwinkle/
Parent County: Tom Green
Comments/research tips: Winkler County was officially organized in 1910.

Record Type	Year Begun	Jurisdiction
Birth	1910	County Clerk
Death	1910	County Clerk
Probate	1910	County Clerk
Marriage	1910	County Clerk
Court	1910	County Clerk
Land	1910	County Clerk

■ **Wise** 23 Jan. 1856
200 N. Trinity St., P.O. Box 359, Decatur, TX 76234
Phone: (940)627-3351
Web site: www.rootsweb.com/~txwise/wise2.htm
Parent County: Cooke
Comments/research tips: District Clerk has Court records 1894–1940, Divorce records 1915–1940, and Naturalization records 1907–1914. County Clerk has Land records 1852–1982, Military Discharge records 1918–1943, and Probate records 1882–1991.

Record Type	Year Begun	Jurisdiction
Birth	1864	County Clerk
Death	1902	County Clerk
Marriage	1881	County Clerk

■ **Wood** 5 Feb. 1850
1 Main St., P.O. Box 1796, Quitman, TX 75783
Phone: (903)763-2711
Web site: www.rootsweb.com/~txwood/
Parent County: Van Zandt
Comments/research tips: County Clerk has Birth records 1903–1995, Death records 1903–1999, Land records 1878–1909, Marriage records 1879–2002, Military Discharge records 1918–1949, and Probate records 1878–1932. District Clerk has Court records 1860–1936 and Divorce records 1897–1935. County courthouse and records burned in 1878.

■ **Yoakum** 21 Aug. 1876
P.O. Box 309, Plains, TX 79355
Phone: (806)456-2721
Web site: www.rootsweb.com/~txyoakum/
Parent County: Bexar Land District
Comments/research tips: Attached to Martin County 1904–1907. Yoakum County was officially organized in 1907.

Record Type	Year Begun	Jurisdiction
Birth	1903	County Clerk
Marriage	1907	County Clerk
Death	1903	County Clerk
Probate	1907	County Clerk
Court	1907	County Clerk
Land	1907	County Clerk

■ **Young** 2 Feb. 1856
516 Fourth St., Room 104, Graham, TX 76450
Phone: (940)549-8432
Web site: www.rootsweb.com/~txyoung/young.htm
Parent County: Bosque, Fannin

Record Type	Year Begun	Jurisdiction
Birth	1903	County Clerk
Death	1903	County Clerk
Marriage	1856	County Clerk
Probate	1858	County Clerk
Court	1858	County Clerk
Land	1858	County Clerk

■ **Zapata** 22 Jan. 1858
P.O. Box 789, Zapata, TX 78076
Phone: (956)765-9915
Web site: www.rootsweb.com/~txzapata
Parent County: Starr, Webb
Comments/research tips: District Clerk has Court records 1874–1881 and 1884–1928. County Clerk has Land records 1868–1891, Marriage records 1873–1915, Naturalization records 1885–1906, and Probate records 1886–1944.

Record Type	Year Begun	Jurisdiction
Birth	1903	County Clerk
Death	1903	County Clerk

■ **Zavala** Feb. 1846
County Courthouse, Crystal City, TX 78839
Phone: (830)374-2331
Web site: www.historicdistric.com/Genealogy/zavala/zavala.htm
Parent County: Uvalde, Maverick
Comments/research tips: County was officially organized in 1858. From 1846–1858 county was attached to San Antonio Municipality.

Record Type	Year Begun	Jurisdiction
Birth	1903	County Clerk
Marriage	1884	County Clerk
Death	1903	County Clerk
Probate	1884	County Clerk
Court	1885	County Clerk
Land	1884	County Clerk

Texas

Utah

By Rhonda R. McClure

HISTORICAL OVERVIEW

The first white settlers in Utah were the pioneer Saints—members of the Church of Jesus Christ of Latter-day Saints—who were following Brigham Young, the newly recognized prophet of the church. Brigham Young led the first wagon train of Mormons into the Salt Lake Valley in 1847. In the next twelve years, some sixty-nine thousand Mormons would flock to Utah by wagon and handcart. In 1849, the provisional State of Deseret was organized with a constitution and system of government which was in effect until Utah became a U.S. territory in 1850.

Until statehood was granted in 1896, the federal government and the Mormons, who were the majority of Utah's settlers, would often come to disagreements. Most were a result of the unique practices of the religion, which included polygamy. Over the years, a number of anti-polygamy acts would be passed that had a direct affect on when, where, and how the territory's courts worked, in addition to altering their record-keeping practices.

Because of the overseas missionary efforts of the church, Utah had a large influx of immigrants as people in Europe began to convert to this new religion and head to "Zion"—Utah.

RECORD HIGHLIGHTS

Though registering births and deaths at the state level was required beginning in 1905, compliance would take another twelve years. For these records contact the Bureau of Vital Records, Utah State Department of Health, P.O. Box 141010, Salt Lake City, UT 84114, <http://health.utah.gov/vitalrecords/silver/>. The Web site offers information on how to order certificates and supplies the necessary forms. In addition to the state records, you will want to search at the county level. Some counties began to keep birth and death records as early as 1898. Salt

UTAH AT A GLANCE

Motto: Industry

Population: 2.3 million

Prevalent Religions: Church of Jesus Christ of Latter-day Saints, Roman Catholic, Methodist, Lutheran, Presbyterian, Muslim, and Episcopalian

Major Industries: Cattle, dairy products, hay, turkeys, machinery, aerospace, mining, food processing, electrical equipment, tourism

Ethnic Makeup (in percent): Caucasian 89.2%, African American 0.8%, Hispanic 9.0%, Asian 1.7%, Native American 1.3%, Other 4.2%

Famous Utahans: Frank Borzage, Butch Cassidy, Laraine Day, Bernard De Voto, Philo Farnsworth, John Gilbert, J. Willard Marriott, Merlin Olsen, The Osmonds, Reed Smoot, Mack Swain, Everett Thorpe, Robert Walker, James Woods, Loretta Young

Above: Salt Lake City's skyline

Utah

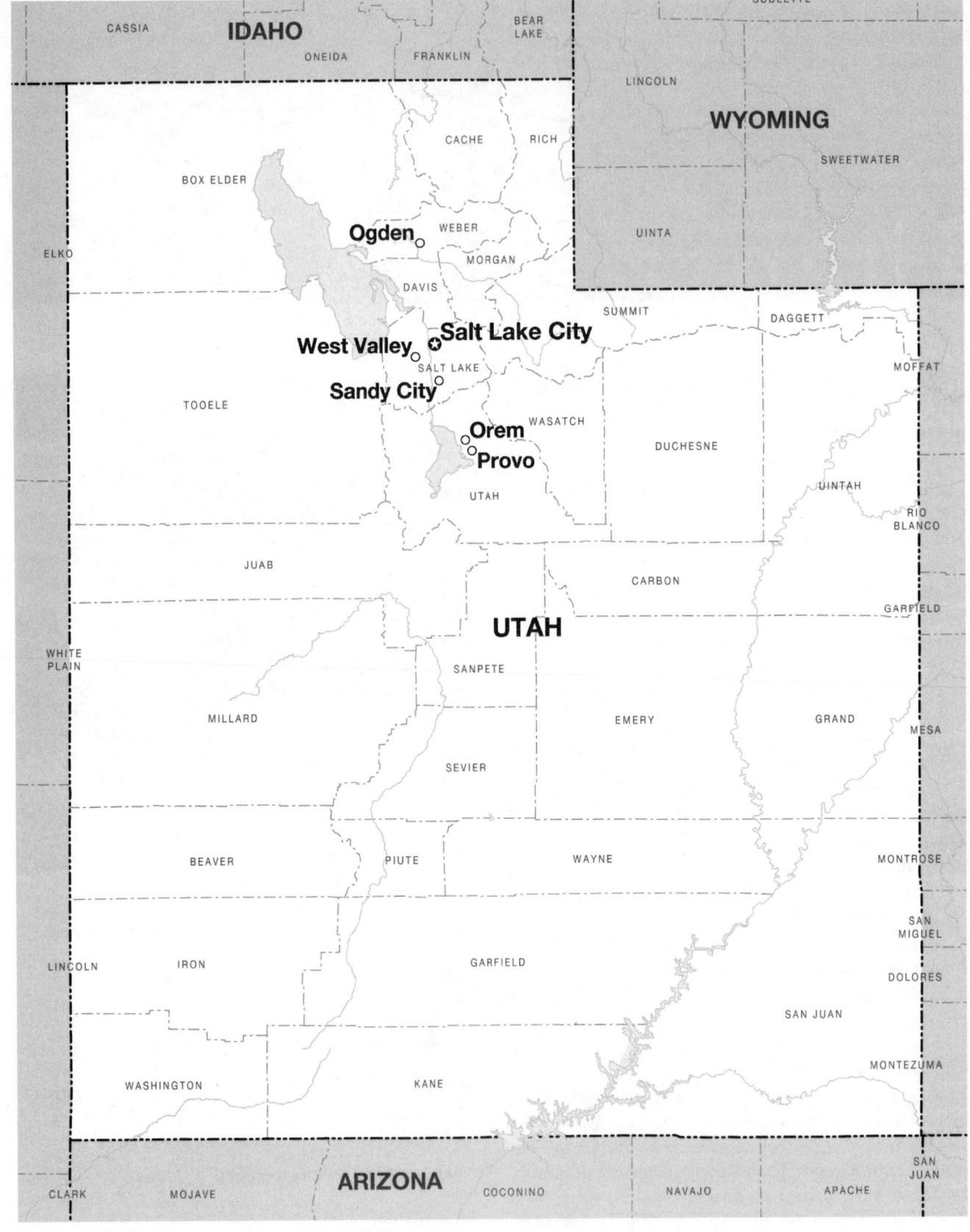

Lake City, Ogden, and Logan have also kept birth and death records at the city level.

Marriage records are kept on the county level, with a few existing before 1887 in the justice of the peace or probate court records. Marriages after 1887 were affected by the Edmunds-Tucker Act, an anti-polygamy law that had harsh effects on civil rights, woman's suffrage, voters, and officeholders. The Edmunds-Tucker Act required that all marriages be registered with the office of the probate court. In the 1890s, registration was moved to the county clerk. The Family History Library has microfilm copies of county marriages to about 1960.

Divorce records can be found in a number of different places. Early divorces had to be granted by church leaders. During the territorial period (1852–1895) the federal district courts had jurisdiction, although there is overlap with the probate courts, as they also had jurisdiction from 1852 to 1887. After statehood, divorces fell under the auspices of the state district courts.

In the early years of the settlement, LDS Bishops Courts, also known as Ecclesiastical courts, were responsible for criminal and civil cases for individuals in their wards or churches. These records are found in the Church History Library. If you need to access them, you will want to contact the Church History Library, 50 East North Temple Street, Room 227E, Salt Lake City, UT 84150-3420, <www.lds.org/churchhistory/library>.

At the same time that the Bishops Courts were in effect, there were also civil courts. These included county courts, which were replaced by probate courts in 1851, as well as justice of the peace courts for cases involving less than three hundred dollars. In 1874 many of the courts of Utah were restricted, as a result of the attempts to eliminate polygamy. Many civil, criminal, and probate matters were handled in federal district courts until statehood in 1896.

Once statehood was established, Utah was divided into seven districts and state district courts were instituted, with an eighth being added in 1988—though each county has a district court branch. The state district courts have jurisdiction over all criminal felonies and civil actions, including divorces, custody disputes, adoptions, probate, and naturalization.

County-level records for land, probate, and court usually begin with the creation of the county, though there are a few exceptions to this rule—for instance, Rich County was created in 1864 but its land, probate, and court records begin in 1872.

STATE RESOURCES

■ ARCHIVES, LIBRARIES, AND SOCIETIES

Bear River District Health Department
655 E. 1300 North St., Logan, UT 84341
Tel: (801) 752-3730

Brigham Carnegie Library
26 E. Forest, Brigham City, UT 84302

Bureau of Land Management, Utah State Office
324 S. State St., Suite 400, Salt Lake City, UT 84111-2303
Tel: (801) 539-4001
Fax: (801) 539-4260

Bureau of Vital Records, Utah State Department of Health
P.O. Box 141010, Salt Lake City, UT 84114
Tel: (801) 538-6105

Cuban Genealogical Society
P.O. Box 2650, Salt Lake City, UT 84110-2650
Web site: <www.rootsweb.com/~utcubangs/>

Episcopal Diocese of Utah
80 South 300 East St., Salt Lake City, UT 84111
Tel: (801) 322-4131

Everton's Genealogical Library
3223 S. Main St., Nibley, UT 84321

Family History Library
35 North West Temple St., Salt Lake City, UT 84150
Tel: (800) 346-6044 or (801) 240-2584
Web site: <www.familysearch.org>

Genealogical Society of Utah
50 East North Temple, Salt Lake City, UT 84150
Tel: (801) 538-2978
Fax: (801) 240-1448
Web site:

Harold B. Lee Library
P.O. Box 26800, Provo, UT, 84602-6800
Tel: (801) 422-2927
Web site:

HeritageQuest Lending Library
P.O. Box 329 Bountiful, UT 84011-0329

Icelandic Association of Utah
84 N. 1120 E., Spanish Fork, UT 84660

Institute of Genealogy and History for Latin America
2191 S. 2200 E., Mt. Springs, UT 84757
Tel: (435) 674-5787
Web site: <www.genealogy.com/00000140>

Jewish Genealogical Society of Salt Lake City
3510 Fleetwood Dr., Salt Lake City, UT 04109

Logan Public Library
255 N. Main, Logan, UT 84321

Marriott Library, University of Utah
295 S. 1500 E., Salt Lake City, UT 84112-0860
Tel: (801) 581-8558
Fax: (801) 585-3464
Web site:

Merrill Library, Utah State University
Logan, UT 84322
Tel: (801) 797-2678
Fax: (801) 797-2880
Web site: <http://library.usu.edu/Specol/>

National Archives & Record Administration-Rocky Mountain Region (Denver)
Bldg. 48, W. Sixth Ave. & Kipling, Denver Federal Center, Denver, CO 80225
Tel: (303) 236-0817
Web site: <www.archives.gov/facilities/co/denver.html>

Presbytery of Utah
342 West 200 South St., Suite 30, Salt Lake City, UT 84101
Tel: (801) 539-8446

Roman Catholic Pastoral Center, Diocese of Salt Lake City
27 C St., Salt Lake City, UT 84103
Tel: (801) 328-8641

Salt Lake City Public Library
209 East 500 South St., Salt Lake City, UT 84111
Tel: (801) 524-8200
Fax: (801) 524-8289

Salt Lake County Records Management and Archives
2001 S. State St. N. 4400, Salt Lake City, UT 84109

Utah

Tel: (801) 468-2330
Fax: (801) 468-3987

U.S. Mormon Battalion, Inc.
7321 S. State St., Midvale, UT 84047
Tel: (801) 255-3591

Uintah and Ouray Tribal Business Council
P.O. Box 190, Fort Duchesne, UT 84026
Tel: (801) 722-5141
Fax: (801) 722-2374

Utah Chapter, America Historical Society of Germans from Russia (AHSGR)
259 E. 500 North, Lehi, UT 84043-1638
Tel: (801) 731-3054

Utah Division of Indian Affairs
State Office Bldg., P.O. Box 140760, Salt Lake City, UT 84114-0760
Tel: (801) 538-8808
Web site: <http://dced.utah.gov/indian/>

Utah Genealogical Association
P.O. Box 1144, Salt Lake City, UT 84110
Tel: (888) 463-6842
Web site:

Utah State Archives and Record Services
Archives Building, State Capitol, Salt Lake City, UT 84114
Tel: (801) 538-3013
Fax: (801) 538-3354

Utah State Historical Society and Library
300 South Rio Grande, Salt Lake City, UT 84101-1143
Tel: (801) 533-3503
Web site: <www.dced.state.ut.us/history/>

BIBLIOGRAPHY

■ GENERAL RESOURCES

Early Utah Journalism
by J. Cecil Alter (Salt Lake City: Utah State Historical Society, 1938)

Encyclopedia History of the Church
by Andrew Jenson (Salt Lake City: Deseret News Publishing Company, 1941)

Genealogical Records in Utah
by Laureen Richardson Jaussi and Gloria Duncan Chaston (Salt Lake

City: Deseret Book Company, 1974)

The Genealogist's Companion and Sourcebook, 2d ed.
by Emily Anne Croom (Cincinnati: Betterway Books, 2003)

A Genealogist's Guide to Discovering Your African-American Ancestors
by Franklin Carter Smith and Emily Anne Croom (Cincinnati: Betterway Books, 2003)

Guide to Archives and Manuscript Collections in Selected Utah Repositories
from the Utah State Historical Society (Salt Lake City: Utah State Historical Society, 1990. CD-ROM)

Guide to Genealogical Research in the National Archives of the United States
edited by Anne Bruner Eales and Robert M. Kvasnicka (Washington, DC: National Archives and Records Administration, 2000)

Guide to Mormon Diaries and Autobiographies
by Davis Bitton (Provo, UT: Brigham Young University Press, 1977)

Guide to Newspapers Located in the Utah State Historical Society Library
by Linda Thatcher (Salt Lake City: Utah State Historical Society, 1985)

Here Are the Counties of Utah
by Betty R. Cook (Bountiful, UT: Betty R. Cook, 1983)

"The History of Marriage in Utah, 1847–1905"
by Lyman D. Platt (*Genealogical Journal* 12, Spring 1983: 28-41)

Inventory of the Church Archives of Utah, 3 vols.
from the Historical Records Survey (Salt Lake City: Utah Historical Records Survey, 1940)

History of the Church of Jesus Christ of Latter-day Saints, 7 vols.
by Joseph Smith (Originally published in 1902; Reprint: Salt Lake City: Deseret Book Co., 1970)

Latter-day Saint Biographical Encyclopedia
by Andrew Jenson (Salt Lake City: A. Jenson History Co., 1901–36)

RESEARCH TIPS

for more info

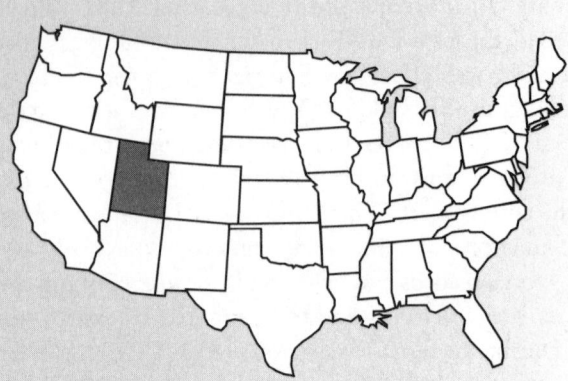

- There is an ongoing project of the Church of Jesus Christ of Latter-day Saints and the Church History Library to make information available about those pioneers who came to Utah from 1847 to 1868. The database is searchable online by name, and the project will eventually have history of each of the pioneer companies. You can access this database by visiting the Church's Web site <www.lds.org> and selecting the Church History link.
- While the Family History Library is under the auspices of the Church of Jesus Christ of Latter-day Saints, it is open to anyone interested in tracing their family history. To get the most from the Family History Library and its branches around the country, be sure to read *Your Guide to the Family History Library* by Paula Stuart Warren and James W. Warren (Cincinnati, Ohio: Betterway Books, 2001).
- When it comes to early births, you may want to see what midwives' records exist and if you can access them. The Family History Library is a good place to start, searching on the city and town level.

Census Records
- Federal Census: 1850, 1860, 1870, 1880, 1900, 1910, 1920, 1930
- Federal Mortality Schedules: 1870
- Special Census of Civil War Union Veterans and Widows: 1890
- State/Territorial Census: 1851, 1856

The Mormon Experience: A History of the Latter-day Saints
by Leonard J. Arrington (New York: Alfred A. Knopf, 1980)

Mormons and Their Neighbors: An Index of Over 75,000 Biographical Sketches from 1820 to the Present, 2 Vols.
by Marvin E. Wiggins (Provo, UT: Brigham Young Univ., 1984)

Name Index to the Library of Congress, Collection of Mormon Diaries.
(Logan, UT: Utah State University, 1971)

National Archives Microfilm Catalogs online:
<www.archives.gov/publica tions/genealogy_microfilm_ catalogs.html>

Pioneers and Prominent Men of Utah
by Frank Esshom (Originally published in 1913; Reprint: Salt Lake City: Western Epics Inc., 1966)

Portrait, Genealogical and Biographical Record of the State of Utah
(Chicago: National Historical Board, 1902)

Salt of the Earth
by Bernice Mooney (Salt Lake City: Catholic Diocese of Salt Lake City, 1987)

The Story of the Latter-day Saints
by James B. Allen and Glen M. Leonard (Salt Lake City: Deseret Book Co., 1976)

Treasures of Pioneer History, 6 vols.
compiled by Kate B. Carter (Salt Lake City: Daughters of the Utah Pioneers, 1952–1957)

Utah: A Centennial History, 3 vols.
edited by Wain Sutton (New York: Lewis Historical Publishing Co., 1949)

Utah's Newspapers–Traces of Her Past
edited by Robert P. Holley (Salt Lake City: University of Utah, 1984)

Utah: A People's History
by Dean L. May (Salt Lake City: University of Utah Press, 1987)

Utah Research Outline
(Salt Lake City, UT: Corp. of the President of the Church of Jesus Christ of L.D.S., 1988)

Utah, The Storied Domain, A Documentary History Of Utah's Eventful Career, 3 vols.
by J. Cecil Alter (Chicago & New York: American Historical Society, Inc., 1932)

Your Guide to the Family History Library
by Paula Stewart Warren and James W. Warren (Cincinnati: Betterway Books, 2001)

■ CENSUS RECORDS

The American Census Handbook
by Thomas Jay Kemp (Wilmington, DE: Scholarly Resources, Inc., 2001)

The Census Book: A Genealogist's Guide to Federal Census Facts, Schedules and Indexes
by William Dollarhide (Bountiful, UT: Heritage Quest, 1999)

Finding Answers In U.S. Census Records
by Loretto Dennis Szucs and Matthew Wright (Salt Lake City: Ancestry Publishing, 2001)

Map Guide to the U.S. Federal Census, 1790–1920
by William Thorndale and William Dollarhide (Baltimore: Genealogical Publishing Co., 1987)

State Census Records
by Ann S. Lainhart (Baltimore: Genealogical Publishing Co., Inc., 1992)

Your Guide to the Federal Census
by Kathleen W. Hinckley (Cincinnati: Betterway Books, 2002)

■ IMMIGRATION RECORDS

American Naturalization Records, 1790–1990: What They Are and How to Use Them
by John J. Newman (North Salt Lake, UT: HeritageQuest, 1998)

American Passenger Arrival Records
by Michael Tepper (Baltimore: Genealogical Publishing Co., 1993)

Handcarts to Zion: The Story of a Unique Western Migration, 1856–1860, with Contemporary Journals, Accounts, Reports, and Rosters of Members of the Ten Handcart Companies
by LeRoy R. Hafen and Ann W. Hafen (Glendale, CA: Arthur H. Clark, 1960)

Mormons on the High Seas: Ocean Voyage Narratives to American (1840–1890)
by Melvin L. Bashire and Linda L. Haslam (Salt Lake City: Historical Department of the Church of Jesus Christ of Latter-day Saints, 1990)

Mormon Pioneer Companies Crossing the Plains (1847–1868) Narratives: Guide to Sources in Utah Libraries and Archives
by Melvin Lee Bashire (Salt Lake City): The Church of Jesus Christ of Latter-day Saints, Historical Dept., 1990)

Saints on the Seas: A Maritime History of Mormon Migration, 1830–1890
by Conway B. Sonne (Salt Lake City: University of Utah Press, 1983)

Ships, Saints, and Mariners: A Maritime Encyclopedia of Mormon Migration, 1830–1890
by Conway B. Sonne (Salt Lake City: University of Utah Press, 1987)

They Became Americans: Finding Naturalization Records and Ethnic Origins
by Loretto Dennis Szucs (Salt Lake City: Ancestry, Inc., 1998)

They Came in Ships: A Guide to Finding Your Immigrant Ancestor's Arrival Records, 2d ed.
by John P. Colletta (Salt Lake City: Ancestry, Inc., 1993)

Worldwide LDS Ship Register 1840–1913
by Margery Taylor (Salt Lake City: Family History Library, 1991)

■ LAND RECORDS

"Establishing and Maintaining Land Ownership in Utah Prior to 1869"
by Lawrence, L. Linford (Salt Lake City: *Utah Historical Society Quarterly*, vol. 42, 1974: 126–43)

Locating Your Roots: Discover Your Ancestors Using Land Records
by Patricia Law Hatcher (Cincinnati: Betterway Books, 2003)

The Mormon Land System, A Study of the Settlement and Utilization of Land Under the Direction of the Mormon Church
by Feramorz Young Fox (Logan, UT: Utah State Agricultural College, 1955)

The Mormon Village: A Pattern and Technique of Land Settlement
by Lowry Nelson (Salt Lake City: University of Utah Press, 1952)

Preliminary Inventory of Land Management—Utah
by Joel Barker (Denver: Denver Archives and Records Center, 1979)

■ MAPS

Atlas of Utah
by Deon C. Greer, et al. (Ogden, UT: Weber State College, 1981)

Five Hundred Utah Place Names
by Rufus Wood Leigh (Salt Lake City: Deseret News Press, 1961)

A Gazetteer of Utah
by Henry A. Gannett (Washington, DC: U.S. Government Printing Office, 1900)

LDS Place Names Gazetteer
by Jill Anderson Ward (Salt Lake City: Family History Library, 1986)

Origins of Utah Place Names
from the Utah Writer's Project (Salt Lake City: State Department of Instruction, 1940)

Postal History of Utah, 1849–1976
by Ted Gruber (Crete, NE: J-B Publishing Co., 1978)

The Post Offices of Utah
by John S. Gallagher (Burtonsville, MD: The Depot, 1977)

Printed Maps of Utah to 1900: An Annotated Cartobibliography
by Riley Moore Moffat (Western Association of Map Librarians, 1981)

Utah Gazetteer and Directory of Logan, Ogden, Provo and Salt Lake City for 1884
by Robert W. Sloan (Salt Lake City: Herald Printing and Publishing Co., 1884)

Utah: A Guide to the State
(New York: Hastings House, 1941)

Utah Place Names: A Comprehensive Guide to the Origins of Geographic Names
compiled by John E. Van Cott (Salt Lake City: University of Utah Press, 1990)

■ MILITARY RECORDS

A Database of the Mormon Battalion
by Carl V. Larson (Providence, UT: K.W. Watkins, 1987)

Johnston, Connor and the Mormons: An Outline of Military History in Northern Utah
by Watson Hance and Irene Warr (Salt Lake City: Watson Hance and Irene Warr, 1962)

Uncle, We Are Ready! Registering America's Men, 1917–1918: A Guide to Researching World War I Draft Registration Cards
by John J. Newman (North Salt Lake, UT: HeritageQuest, 2001)

U.S. Military Records: A Guide to Federal & State Sources, Colonial America to the Present
by James C. Neagles (Salt Lake City: Ancestry, Inc., 1994)

Utah and the Civil War
by Margaret May Merrill Fisher (Salt Lake City: Deseret Book Co., 1929)

Utah in the World War
by Noble Warrum (Salt Lake City: Utah State Council of Defense, 1924)

World War II: A Family Historian's Guide
by Debra Johnson Knox (Spartanburg, SC: MIE Publishing, 2003)

■ VITAL RECORDS

Cemetery Records of Utah, 13 vols.
(Salt Lake City: Genealogical Society of Utah, 1953)

Cemeteries in Utah
by Irvin C. McClay (Salt Lake City: Utah State Archives and Records Service, 1980)

Guide to Public Vital Statistics of Utah
(Salt Lake City: Utah Historical Records Survey, 1941)

An Inventory and Index to the Records of Carson County, Utah and Nevada Territories, 1855–1861
by Marion Ellison (Reno, NV: Grace Dangberg Foundation, 1984)

Marriages in Utah Territory, 1850–1884: From the Deseret News, 1850–1872, and the Elias Smith Journals, 1850–1884
by Judith Woolstenhume Hansen (Salt Lake City: Utah Genealogical Association, 1998)

Your Guide to Cemetery Research
by Sharon DeBartolo Carmack (Cincinnati: Betterway Books, 2002)

■ Beaver 5 Jan. 1856
105 E. Center, P.O. Box 392, Beaver, UT 84713
Phone: (435)438-6463
Web site: http://archives.utah.gov/
Parent County: Iron, Millard
Comments/research tips: County Clerk has Birth records 1897–1905, Death records 1900–1905, and Probate records 1856–1897. Historical Society has Burial records 1865–1986. Clerk of 5th District Court Clerk has Divorce records 1870–1897 and Naturalization records 1846–1902.

Record Type	Year Begun	Jurisdiction
Land	1878	County Recorder
Marriage	1920	County Clerk
Court	1856	Clerk/5th District Ct.

■ Box Elder 5 Jan. 1856
1 S. Main St., Brigham City, UT 84302
Phone: (435)734-2031
Web site: http://archives.utah.gov/
Parent County: Weber
Comments/research tips: County Clerk has Birth and Death records 1898–1905 and Court records 1889–1895. Probate Court has Divorce records 1856–1877. County Recorder has Military Discharge records 1944–1952. County Clerk has Naturalization records 1868–1869. Clerk of 1st District Court has has Probate records 1856–1877.

Record Type	Year Begun	Jurisdiction
Marriage	1887	County Recorder
Land	1856	County Recorder

■ Cache 5 Jan. 1856
170 N. Main St., Logan, UT 84321
Phone: (435)716-7150
Web site: http://archives.utah.gov/
Parent County: Unorganized Territory Green River
Comments/research tips: Online Index available for Birth records. County Clerk has Birth and Death records 1898–1905. Clerk of 1st District Court has Court records 1889–1895, Divorce records 1860–1887, and Probate records 1876–1906.

Record Type	Year Begun	Jurisdiction
Marriage	1888	County Clerk
Land	1856	County Recorder

■ Carbon 8 Mar. 1894
120 E. Main St., Price, UT 84501
Phone: (435)636-3200
Web site: http://archives.utah.gov/
Parent County: Emery
Comments/research tips: County Clerk has Birth and Death records 1898–1905. Index available online. Clerk of 7th District Court has Probate records 1895–1966.

Record Type	Year Begun	Jurisdiction
Marriage	1894	County Clerk
Divorce	1895	Clerk/7th District Ct.
Court	1896	Clerk/7th District Ct.
Land	ca. 1890	County Recorder
Military	1944	County Recorder

■ Carson 17 Jan. 1854
Parent County: Tooele, Juab, Millard, Iron
Comments/research tips: (See Nevada State) Transferred to Nevada Territory 2 March 1861.

■ **Cedar** 5 Jan. 1856
Comments/research tips: (See Utah) Absorbed by Utah County 17 January 1862.

■ **Daggett** 7 Jan. 1918
95 N. First St. W., Manila, UT 84046
Phone: (435)784-3154
Web site: http://archives.utah.gov/
Parent County: Uintah
Comments/research tips: District Court has Probate records 1916–1966. See Unitah County for Birth and Death records.

Record Type	Year Begun	Jurisdiction
Marriage	1918	County Clerk
Divorce	1918	County Clerk
Court	1918	County Clerk
Land	1918	County Recorder

■ **Davis** 3 Mar. 1852
28 E. State St., P.O. Box 618, Farmington, UT 84025
Phone: (801)451-3200
Web site: http://archives.utah.gov/
Parent County: Original County
Comments/research tips: County Clerk has Birth and Death records 1898–1905. Birth Index online. Clerk of 2nd District Court has Divorce records 1875–1886 and Naturalization records 1902–1938. Probate Court has Probate records 1853–1896.

Record Type	Year Begun	Jurisdiction
Land	1870	County Recorder
Marriage	1887	County Clerk
Court	1853	Clerk/2d District Ct.

■ **Desert** 3 Mar. 1852
Comments/research tips: Absorbed by Tooele County, Nevada and Box Elder County, Utah 17 January 1862.

■ **Duchesne** 4 Jan. 1915
Drawer 270, 50 E. 100 South, Duchesne, UT 84021
Phone: (435)738-2435
Web site: http://archives.utah.gov/
Parent County: Wasatch
Comments/research tips: See Wasatch County for Birth and Death records.

Record Type	Year Begun	Jurisdiction
Marriage	1915	Clerk/Auditor
Divorce	1915	Clerk/8th District Ct.
Court	1915	Clerk/8th District Ct.
Land	1915	County Recorder
Probate	1915	Clerk/8th District Ct.

■ **Emery** 12 Feb. 1880
95 E. Main St., P.O. Box 629, Castle Dale, UT 84513
Phone: (435)381-5106
Web site: http://archives.utah.gov/
Parent County: Sanpete, Sevier
Comments/research tips: County Clerk has Birth and Death records 1898–1905. Birth Index online. Clerk of 7th District Court has Court and Divorce records 1896–1986 and Naturalization records 1904–1942. County Recorder has Military Discharge records 1923–1952.

Record Type	Year Begun	Jurisdiction
Marriage	1888	County Clerk
Probate	1886	Clerk/7th District Ct.
Land	ca. 1880	County Recorder

■ **Garfield** 9 Mar. 1882
55 S. Main St., P.O. Box 77, Panguitch, UT 84759
Phone: (435)676-8826
Web site: http://archives.utah.gov/
Parent County: Iron
Comments/research tips: County Clerk has Birth and Death records 1898–1905. Clerk of 6th District Court has Court records 1896–1966 and Divorce records 1883–1889.

Record Type	Year Begun	Jurisdiction
Divorce	1896	County Clerk
Marriage	1887	County Clerk
Land	1882	County Recorder
Probate	1896	Clerk/6th District Ct.

■ **Grand** 13 Mar. 1890
125 E. Center St., Moab, UT 84532
Phone: (435)259-1321
Web site: http://archives.utah.gov/
Parent County: Emery
Comments/research tips: County Clerk has Birth and Death records 1898–1905. Birth Index online. Clerk of 7th District Court has Probate records 1908–1975.

Record Type	Year Begun	Jurisdiction
Marriage	1890	County Clerk
Divorce	1896	Clerk/7th District Ct.
Court	1896	Clerk/7th District Ct.
Land	1890	County Recorder

■ **Greasewood** 5 Jan. 1856
Comments/research tips: (See Box Elder) Absorbed by Box Elder County 17 January 1862.

■ **Great Salt Lake** 3 Mar. 1852
Parent County: Original County
Comments/research tips: (See Salt Lake) Name changed to Salt Lake 29 January 1868.

■ **Green River** 3 Mar. 1852
Parent County: Original County
Comments/research tips: Green River County was dissolved 16 February 1872. Cache, Webber, Morgan, Davis, Wasatch, Summit, Duchesne, Carbon, and Utah Counties contain part of Green River County. Some parts of Green River County went to Wyoming Territory and Colorado Territory.

■ **Iron** 31 Jan. 1850
68 S. 100 East, P.O. Box 429, Parowan, UT 84761
Phone: (435)477-8341
Web site: http://archives.utah.gov/
Parent County: Original County
Comments/research tips: County Clerk has Birth and Death records 1898–1905. Birth Index online. Clerk of 5th District Court has Court records 1896–1948, Divorce records

Utah

1852–1896, Naturalization records 1853–1868, and Probate records 1854–1965. Formerly Little Salt Lake County. Name changed to Iron 3 December 1850.

Record Type	Year Begun	Jurisdiction
Land	1852	County Recorder
Marriage	1877	County Clerk

■ **Juab** 3 Mar. 1852
160 N. Main St., Nephi, UT 84648
Phone: (435)623-3410
Web site: http://archives.utah.gov/
Parent County: Original County
Comments/research tips: County Clerk has Birth and Death records 1898–1905, Marriage records 1887–1985, Divorce records 1852–1854, and Court records 1896–1985. Clerk of 4th District Court has Probate records 1862–1962 and Naturalization records 1904–1958. County Recorder has Military Discharge records 1944–1947.

Record Type	Year Begun	Jurisdiction
Land	1898	County Recorder

■ **Kane** 16 Jan. 1864
76 N. Main St., Kanab, UT 84741
Phone: (435)644-2551
Web site: http://archives.utah.gov/
Parent County: Washington
Comments/research tips: County Clerk has Birth records 1900–1905, Death records 1898–1905, Marriage records 1887–1966, and Land records 1872–1883. Birth Index online. Clerk of 6th District Court has Court and Divorce records 1864–1966. Probate Court has Probate records 1864–1896. County Recorder has Military Discharge records 1945–1994.

■ **Little Salt Lake** 31 Jan. 1850
Parent County: Original County
Comments/research tips: (See Iron) Name changed to Iron 3 December 1850.

■ **Millard** 4 Oct. 1851
P.O. Box 226, 50 S. Main St., Fillmore, UT 84631
Phone: (435)743-6223
Web site: http://archives.utah.gov/
Parent County: Iron
Comments/research tips: Clerk of 4th District Court has Probate records 1870–1966, Naturalization records 1896–1906, Divorce and Court records 1870–1966. County Recorder has Military Discharge records 1944–1960. No Death registration before 1905.

Record Type	Year Begun	Jurisdiction
Marriage	1887	County Clerk
Land	1891	County Recorder

■ **Morgan** 17 Jan. 1862
P.O. Box 886, 48 W. Young St., Morgan, UT 84050
Phone: (801)829-6811
Web site: archives.utah.gov/
Parent County: Summit, Weber, Cache
Comments/research tips: County Clerk has Birth and Death records 1897–1905 and Court records 1889–1895. Clerk of

2nd District Court has Probate records 1868–1966, and Divorce and Court records 1852–1865 and 1878–1916. County Recorder has Military Discharge records 1943–1951.

Record Type	Year Begun	Jurisdiction
Marriage	1888	County Clerk
Land	1862	County Recorder

■ **Piute** 16 Jan. 1865
550 N. Main St., Junction, UT 84740
Phone: (435)577-2840
Web site: http://archives.utah.gov/
Parent County: Beaver
Comments/research tips: Birth Index available online. County Clerk has Death records for 1898 and 1904, Birth records 1898–1900, and Marriage records 1872–1966. Clerk of 6th District Court has Naturalization records 1896–1920, and Probate records 1869–1910, Divorce and Court records 1869–1953.

■ **Rich** 16 Jan. 1864
P.O. Box 218, 20 S. Main St., Randolph, UT 84064
Phone: (435)793-2415
Web site: http://archives.utah.gov/
Parent County: Cache
Comments/research tips: County Clerk has Birth and Death records 1898–1905. Birth Index online. County Clerk has Court records 1889–1895 and Probate records 1865–1873 and 1875–1896. Clerk of 1st District Court has Naturalization records 1880–1896. Formerly Richland County. Name changed to Rich 29 January 1868.

Record Type	Year Begun	Jurisdiction
Marriage	1888	County Clerk
Land	1869	County Recorder

■ **Richland** 16 Jan. 1864
Parent County: Cache
Comments/research tips: (See Rich) Name changed to Rich 29 January 1868.

■ **Rio Virgin** 18 Feb. 1869
Comments/research tips: (See Washington) Absorbed by Washington County 16 February 1872. Parts of county went to Nevada and Arizona.

■ **Salt Lake** 3 Mar. 1852
2001 S. State St., Room S-2200, Salt Lake City, UT 84190
Phone: (801)468-3000
Web site: http://archives.utah.gov/
Parent County: Original County
Comments/research tips: County Clerk has Birth and Death records 1898–1905. Birth Index online. Salt Lake City Recorder has Death records 1848–1933. Clerk of 3rd District Court has Probate records 1852–1966 and Naturalization records 1896–1929. Formerly Great Salt Lake County. Name changed to Salt Lake 29 January 1868.

Record Type	Year Begun	Jurisdiction
Marriage	1887	County Archives
Court	1896	County Clerk
Land	1852	County Recorder
Divorce	1896	County Clerk

■ **San Juan**   17 Feb. 1880
117 S. Main St., P.O. Box 338, Monticello, UT 84535
Phone: (435)587-3223
Web site: http://archives.utah.gov/
Parent County: Kane, Iron, Piute
Comments/research tips: County Clerk has Birth and Death records 1898–1905. County Recorder has Military Discharge records 1944–1948 and Land records 1891–1952.

Record Type	Year Begun	Jurisdiction
Marriage	1888	County Clerk
Divorce	1888	Clerk/7th District Ct.
Court	1888	Clerk/7th District Ct.
Probate	1888	Clerk/7th District Ct.

■ **Sanpete**   3 Mar. 1852
160 N. Main St., Manti, UT 84642
Phone: (435)835-2131
Web site: http://archives.utah.gov/
Parent County: Original County
Comments/research tips: County Clerk has Birth and Death records 1898–1905. Clerk of 6th District has Probate records 1870–1901 and Divorce records 1873–1887. County Recorder has Military Discharge records 1944–1964.

Record Type	Year Begun	Jurisdiction
Marriage	1888	County Clerk
Court	1852	Clerk/6th District Ct.
Land	1872	County Clerk
Probate	1852	Clerk/6th District Ct.

■ **Sevier**   16 Jan. 1865
250 N. Main, Richfield, UT 84701
Phone: (435)896-9262
Web site: http://archives.utah.gov/
Parent County: Sanpete
Comments/research tips: County Clerk has Birth and Death records 1898–1905 and Naturalization records 1850–1898. County Recorder has Military Discharge records 1942–1970.

Record Type	Year Begun	Jurisdiction
Marriage	1887	County Clerk
Divorce	1865	Clerk/6th District Ct.
Probate	1865	Clerk/6th District Ct.
Court	1865	Clerk/6th District Ct.
Land	1865	County Recorder

■ **Summit**   13 Jan. 1854
P.O. Box 128, Coalville, UT 84017
Phone: (435)336-4451
Web site: http://archives.utah.gov/
Parent County: Green River, Great Salt Lake
Comments/research tips: County Clerk has Birth and Death records 1898–1905 and Marriage records 1887–1934. Clerk of 3rd District Court has Probate, Court, and Divorce records 1866–1963.

Record Type	Year Begun	Jurisdiction
Land	1895	County Recorder

■ **Tooele**   3 Mar. 1852
47 S. Main St., Tooele, UT 84074
Phone: (435)843-3100

Web site: www.co.tooele.ut.us/
Parent County: Original County
Comments/research tips: County Clerk has Birth and Death records 1898–1905. Clerk of 3rd District Court has Divorce records 1854–1892 and Probate records 1896–1966. County Recorder has Land records 1869–1978.

Record Type	Year Begun	Jurisdiction
Marriage	1888	County Clerk
Court	1852	Clerk/3rd District Ct.

■ **Uintah**   18 Feb. 1880
147 E. Main St., Vernal, UT 84078
Phone: (435)781-0770
Web site: www.lofthouse.com/USA/Utah/unitah/
Parent County: Wasatch
Comments/research tips: County Clerk has Birth records 1898–1905, Death records 1900–1901 and 1904–1905, and Marriage records 1888–1978. County Recorder has Military Discharge records 1944–1992. Clerk of 8th District Court has Probate records 1886–1966.

Record Type	Year Begun	Jurisdiction
Divorce	1886	Clerk/8th District Ct.
Court	1886	Clerk/8th District Ct.
Land	1894	County Recorder

■ **Utah**   3 Mar. 1852
100 E. Center St., Provo, UT 84606
Phone: (801)370-8000
Web site: http://archives.utah.gov/
Parent County: Original County
Comments/research tips: County Clerk has Birth and Death records 1898–1905. Clerk of 4th District Court has Naturalization records 1878–1896 and Probate records 1852–1900 and 1958–1964. County Recorder has Military Discharge records 1944–1992.

Record Type	Year Begun	Jurisdiction
Marriage	1887	County Clerk
Land	ca. 1890	County Recorder

■ **Wasatch**   17 Jan. 1862
25 N. Main St., Heber City, UT 84032
Phone: (435)654-3211
Web site: http://archives.utah.gov/
Parent County: Davis, Green River
Comments/research tips: County Clerk has Birth and Death records 1898–1905. Clerk of 4th District Court has Naturalization records 1896–1935 and Probate records 1862–1964. County Recorder has Military Discharge records 1919–1954.

Record Type	Year Begun	Jurisdiction
Marriage	1896	County Clerk
Land	1862	County Recorder
Court	1898	Clerk/4th District Ct.
Divorce	1898	Clerk/4th District Ct.

■ **Washington**   3 Mar. 1852
197 E. Tabernacle St., St. George, UT 84770
Phone: (435)634-5700
Web site: http://archives.utah.gov/
Parent County: Original County

Comments/research tips: County Clerk has Birth and Death records 1898–1905 and Marriage records 1862–1919. Clerk of 5th District Court has Naturalization records 1896–1940 and Probate records 1877–1981. County Recorder has Military Discharge records 1923–1967.

Record Type	Year Begun	Jurisdiction
Land	1892	County Recorder
Marriage	1898	County Clerk

■ **Wayne** 10 Mar. 1892
18 S. Main, Loa, UT 84747
Phone: (435)836-2731
Web site: www.rootsweb.com/~utwayne/ _Wayne_index.html
Parent County: Piute
Comments/research tips: County Clerk has some Birth and Death Records 1898–1905. Clerk of 6th District Court has Naturalization records 1896–1902 and Probate records 1889–1987. County Recorder has Military Discharge records 1945–1974.

Record Type	Year Begun	Jurisdiction
Marriage	1898	County Clerk
Land	1892	County Recorder

■ **Weber** 3 Mar. 1852
2380 Washington Blvd., Ogden, UT 84401
Phone: (801)399-8401
Web site: www.co.weber.ut.us/
Parent County: Original County
Comments/research tips: County Clerk has Birth and Death records 1898–1905. Birth Index online. Death records exclude Ogden.

Record Type	Year Begun	Jurisdiction
Probate	1851	Clerk/2d District Ct.
Marriage	1887	County Clerk
Nat.	1896	Clerk/2d District Ct.
Land	1852	County Recorder
Court	1852	Clerk/2d District Ct.

Vermont

By Maureen Taylor

HISTORICAL OVERVIEW

Geography and climate hindered the development of the second largest New England state—Vermont had no permanent settlements until 1760. Independent-minded Vermonters fought off land claims from New York State and New Hampshire to form their own republic in 1777. In 1791, Vermont became the fourteenth state. Montpelier was chosen as the capital in 1805. Vermont was the first state to provide voting rights to all males regardless of race or religion and to abolish the land-ownership requirement.

By the time of the American Revolution only twenty thousand people lived in the area, mostly emigrants from Connecticut and Massachusetts. Families from Connecticut traveled the Connecticut River to settle the region. Harsh living conditions and a depressed economy forced many to migrate to the northern part of the state or west into New York. New immigrants arrived to take their place. French Canadians moved down from Quebec. Scottish immigrants came to work Vermont's rock quarries and the Irish built its canals, including the 1823 Champlain Canal that connected Lake Champlain to the Hudson River.

Vermont's waterways provided transportation for the goods produced at its paper mills, sawmills, and tanneries, as well as their agricultural and dairy products. Today, Vermonter's can be proud of their rock quarries that supply marble throughout the world, their craftsmen who turn wood into furniture, the dairy products that appear on tables throughout the country, and the tourists who visit to ski Vermont's mountains.

RECORD HIGHLIGHTS

Like the rest of New England, vital records in Vermont are incomplete before civil registration in 1857. Before 1820, entire families sometimes appear together in the

VERMONT AT A GLANCE

Motto: Freedom and Unity
Population: 608,000
Prevalent Religions: Christianity, particularly Roman Catholic, Methodist, Lutheran, Presbyterian, Pentecostal, Baptist, and Episcopalian
Major Industries: Dairy products, cattle, hay, apples, maple products, electronical equipment, fabricated metal products, printing and publishing, paper products, tourism
Ethnic Makeup (in percent): Caucasian 96.8%, African American 0.5%, Hispanic 0.9%, Asian 0.9%, Native American 0.4%, Other 0.2%
Famous Vermonters: Chester A. Arthur, Orson Bean, Calvin Coolidge, John Deere, John Dewey, Stephen A. Douglas, Richard Morris Hunt, William Morris Hunt, Moses Pendleton, Joseph Smith, Ernest Thompson, Rudy Vallee, Brigham Young

Above: A wood shed in Vermont

records of the towns they lived in. Vermont's population was mobile, with families looking for economic opportunities in various areas—an additional challenge to your research.

Vermont ratified the Constitution in 1791, missing the first federal census by one year. There is a 1791 census for the state. The Genealogical Society of Vermont (GSV) <www.rootsweb.com/~vtgsv/> is compiling genealogies of families living there at the time in the series *Vermont Families in 1791* (GSV). Find out more about the project by contacting the GSV. Jay Mack Holbrook compiled names from land grants and other sources to produce the *1771 Census* (Holbrook Research, 1982). Examine the original sources cited to verify whether your ancestor actually lived in Vermont or was just awarded land.

Probate records, when they exist, were recorded on the district level. They are indexed, but only by district. Microfilm copies of probate proceedings do not include all the papers found in an original probate file. Use the indexes to locate a record, then track down the originals.

Land disputes in the colonial period dictate that pre-1777 land transactions could be in New York, New Hampshire, or Vermont. The *New Hampshire State Papers (see New Hampshire)* and the as yet unpublished manuscript *Vermont State Papers* contain information on original territorial proprietors, and a volume of *Vermont State Papers* has information on confiscated land. The Vermont State Archives has the Nye index, which indexes the signatories to petitions. After 1777, original land records are in the town clerk's office. Most records have been microfilmed and are available in central repositories like the Vermont Historical Society <www.vermonthistory.org>.

Two cemetery sources can help researchers. The Vermont Historical Society has an index of veteran's graves from the Civil War through World War I. Microfilms of vital records include cemetery cards serving as a statewide index to grave records.

Unfortunately, a fire destroyed some of Vermont's military records before 1920 that were stored on the state level. Miscellaneous records are available in town clerk's offices or at the Vermont State Archives. The records that were saved from the fire have been preserved and microfilmed by the Vermont Department of Public Records and are available there. A finding aid is online at www.bgs.state.vt.us/gsc/pubrec/referen/military.htm>.

A Works Progress Administration (WPA) inventory of church records at the Vermont Public Records Office enables you to locate original records, but some of the listings are out of date. Church registers that contain membership lists, baptisms, marriages, deaths, and removals provide documentation on Vermont families prior to civil registration.

Vermont's first published newspaper pre-dates statehood. The Vermont Department of Libraries has an extensive collection of papers printed since 1781 on microfilm.

A cooperative project between several libraries and archives, including the Vermont Historical Society and the University of Vermont, serves as a union list of manuscript collections in the state. Search the holdings by using the ArcCat catalog <http://arccat.uvm.edu>. You'll find unpublished manuscripts for individuals and organizations.

Genealogical research in Vermont is both challenging and rewarding. Incomplete colonial records, the lack of statewide indexes, and an extremely mobile population make locating material difficult. However, there are rewards for the persistent researcher willing to patiently search town records and multiple districts. following their ancestral travels. "Knowing the town is the primary access point for finding information," counsels Marjorie Strong, Assistant Librarian at the Vermont Historical Society. "Once you have the town you'll be able to consult cemetery records, published histories, and family genealogies."

According to Strong, "start looking at vital records at Vital Records in Montpelier to find life dates and towns of residence for family members." While your research plan will depend on the information you already know, a good next step is to visit Vital Records in Middlesex to find the dates and towns for the family. Then, visit the largest genealogical society in the state—the Vermont Historical Society Library in Barre. According to their Web site <www.vermonthistory.org> they "collect family histories, published vital records, cemetery inscriptions, town histories, census, published military records," as well as manuscripts and photographs on the history of the state. A guide to their genealogical resources appears on the Web site. The collection of the VHS will fill in the background information on your family.

If you're looking for a colonial Vermont ancestor, records of their settlement might be in New York or New Hampshire depending on where they lived and when. Learn the history of their town to determine where materials might be found. Families traveled together from town to town.

Since most early settlers emigrated from Connecticut, following the Connecticut River through Massachusetts and into Vermont, you can discover pre-Vermont information on the family in the records of towns near the river.

It is quite possible that at least some members of your Vermont family sought opportunities outside the state. During the 1820s, approximately half the state's population moved elsewhere to join communities established by ex-Vermonters. Poor agricultural conditions and harsh winters drove many individuals to New York, lower Canada, Pennsylvania, Ohio, Michigan, Illinois, Wisconsin, and elsewhere, seeking ways to support their family. These former Vermonters established Sons of Vermont chapters outside the state. Find evidence of their emigration in church removal records and insolvency cases in probate records.

Vermont ancestral research is complicated, but not impossible. The resources are easy to locate and accessible. Travel from major repositories to small towns looking for your ancestors, and don't forget to enjoy the beautiful scenery along the way.

RESEARCH TIPS

for more info

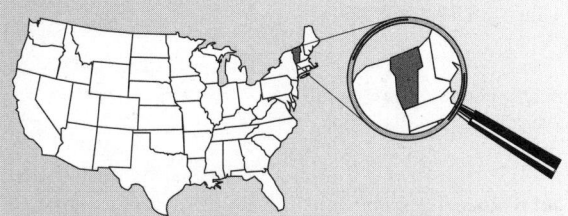

- Genealogical research in Vermont begins with knowing the town where your ancestor lived. Armed with that knowledge, begin consulting the cemetery records and published histories of that town.
- Visit the Vermont Historical Society Library <www. vermonthistory.org> for a large collection of state-wide resources such as vital records, census records, and family histories, as well as manuscripts and photographs documenting the history of the state.
- Search for ancestors who left the state for greener pastures—the freezing winters and rough farming environment chased many early settlers away.
- www.negenealogy.com

Census Records
- Federal Census: 1790, 1800, 1810, 1820, 1830, 1840, 1850, 1860, 1870, 1880, 1900, 1910, 1920, 1930
- Federal Mortality Schedules: 1880
- Union Veterans and Widows: 1890

STATE RESOURCES

■ ARCHIVES, LIBRARIES, AND SOCIETIES

Addison Town Historical Society
288 Cedar Dr., Addison, VT 05491-8732

Alburg Historical Society, Inc.
P.O. Box 453, Alburg, VT 05440

American Baptist, Samuel Colgate Historical Library
1106 S. Goodman, St., Rochester, NY 14620
Tel: (716) 473-1740

Archives of the Roman Catholic Diocese of Burlington
351 North Ave., Burlington, VT 05401
Tel: (802) 658-6110

Assemblee des Eveques du Quebec
1225 St. Joseph Blvd. E., Montreal, Quebec, Canada H2J 1L7

Bailey-Howe Library, University of Vermont
Burlington, VT 05405
Tel: (802)656-2022
Web site: <http://library.uvm .edu/>

Barnet Historical Society
RR 1, Box 241, Barnet, VT 05821

Bennington Historical Society
W. Main St., Bennington, VT 05201
Web site: <www.benningtonmuse um.com/BHS.html>

Berlin Historical Society, Inc.
1921 Scott Hill Rd., Berlin, VT 05602

Bethel Historical Society
Church St., Bethel, VT 05032

Bradford Historical Society
P.O. Box 301, Bradford, VT 05033

Braintree Historical Society
RFD 1, Thayer Brook Rd., Randolph, VT 05060
Web site:

Brattleboro Historical Society, Inc.
23 West St., Brattleboro, VT 05301

Bridport Historical Society
2947 Basin Harbor Rd., Bridport, VT 05734

Bristol Historical Society Museum
Howden Hall Community Center, Main St., Bristol, VT 05443

Brooks Memorial Library
224 Main St., Brattleboro, VT 05301

Burlington Genealogical Group
36 Franklin Square, Burlington, VT 05401

Cabot Historical Society
P.O. Box 63, Marshfield, VT 05658

Canaan Historical Society
P.O. Box 371, Canaan, VT 05903

Cavendish Historical Society
P.O. Box 110, Cavendish, VT 05142

Charleston Historical Society
1896 Vermont Route 105, W. Charleston, VT 05872

Charlotte Historical Society
613 Hill's Point Rd., Charlotte, VT 05445

Chelsea Historical Society
P.O. Box 206, Chelsea, VT 05038

Chester Historical Society
P.O. Box 118, Chester, VT 05143
Tel: (802) 875-6211

Concord Historical Society
P.O. Box 195, Concord, VT 05824-0195

Congregational Library
14 Beacon St., Boston, MA 02108
Tel: (617) 523-0470
Fax: (617) 523-0470

Crystal Lake Falls Historical Association
P.O. Box 253, Barton, VT 05822

Derby Historical Society
P.O. Box 357, Derby, VT 05829

Division of State Papers, Office of the Secretary of State
109 State St., Montpelier, VT 05609-1103
Tel: (802) 828-2308
Fax: (802) 828-5171

Dorset Historical Society
P.O. Box 52, Dorset, VT 05251
Web site:

Dover Historical Society
P.O. Box 53, East Dover, VT 05341-7705

Elmore Historical Society
P.O. Box 53, Lake Elmore, VT 05657

Enosburg Historical Society
P.O. box 98, Enosburg Falls, VT 05450

Episcopal Diocesan Center
#5 Rock Point Rd., Burlington, VT 05401-2735
Tel: (802) 863-3431
Fax: (802) 860-1562

Essex Historical Society
3 Browns River Rd., Essex Jct., VT 05452
Web site: <www.essex.org/esxhs/esxhsfindex.htm>

Fairfax Historical Society
P.O. Box 145, Fairfax, VT 05454
Tel: (802) 849-6638
Web site: <www.geocities.com/Heartland/Farm/9445/index.html>

Fairfield Historical Society
1345 Northrup Rd., Enosburg Falls, VT 05450

Fairlee Historical Society
P.O. Box 95, Fairlee, VT 05045

Family History Library
35 NW Temple St., Salt Lake City, UT 84150
Tel: (800) 346-6044 or (801) 240-2584
Web site: <www.familysearch.org>

Fletcher Free Library
235 College St., Burlington, VT 05401

Genealogical Society of Vermont
P.O. Box 1553, St. Albans, VT 05478-1006
Web site: <www.rootsweb.com/~vtgsv>

General Services Center, Reference Research
US Route 2, P.O. Drawer 33, Middlesex, VT 05633-7601
Tel: (802) 828-3286
Fax: (802) 828-3710

Georgia Historical Society Museum
P.O. Box 2072, Georgia, VT 05468

Glover Historical Society
Municipal Building, Glover, VT 05839
Tel: (802) 525-8855

Grafton Historical Society
P.O. Box 202, Grafton, VT 05146

Green Mountain College Library
One College Circle, Poultney, VT 05764
Tel: (802) 287-8225
Fax: (802) 287-8099

Greensboro Historical Society
P.O. Box 151, Greensboro, VT 05841

Groton Historical Society
P.O. Box 89, Groton, VT 05046
Tel: (802) 584-3417

Guilford Historical Society
236 School Rd., Guilford, VT 05301

Halifax Historical Society
RR 4, Box 531, Brattleboro, VT 05301

Hartford Historical Society
P.O. Box 547, Hartford, VT 05047

Historical Society of Peru
P.O. Box 153, Peru, VT 05152

Historical Society of Windham County
P.O. Box 246, Newfane, VT 05345

Holland Historical Society
RD 1, Box 37, Derby Line, Holland, VT 05830

Huntington Historical Society
P.O. Box 147, Huntington, VT 05462

Hyde Park Historical Society
97 Eden St., Hyde Park, VT 05655

Island Pond Historical Society
P.O. Box 408, Island Pond, VT 05846

Isle La Motte Historical Society
283 School St., Isle La Motte, VT 05463
Tel: (802) 928-3173

Jamaica Historical Foundation
P.O. Box 287, Jamaica, VT 05343

Jericho Historical Society
P.O. Box 35, Jericho, VT 05465
Web site: <http://snowflakeBentley.com/jhs.htm>

Lincoln Historical Society
88 Quaker St., Lincoln, VT 05443
Tel: (802) 453-7111

Londonderry Historical Society
P.O. Box 114, South Londonderry, VT 05155

Lowell Historical Society
636 Irish Hill Rd., Lowell, VT 05847

Lunenburg Historical Society
P.O. Box 5, Lunenburg, VT 05906

Lyndon Historical Society
P.O. Box 85, Lyndon Center, VT 05850
Tel: (802) 626-8746
Web site: <www.sover.net/~boerad/Historic.htm>

Manchester Historical Society
P.O. Box 363, Manchester, VT 05254

Marlboro Historical Society
P.O. Box 131, Marlboro, VT 05344

Memphremagog Historical Society
Goodrich Memorial Library, 70 Main St., Newport, VT 05855

Middlesex Historical Society
84 McCullough Hill Rd., Middlesex, VT 05602

Milton Historical Society
P.O. Box 2, Milton, VT 05468

Missiquoi Valley Historical Society
P.O. Box 237, North Troy, VT 05859
Tel: (802) 988-2397

Montgomery Historical Society
P.O. Box 47, Montgomery, VT 05470

Moretown Historical Society
800 South Hill Rd., Moretown, VT 05660
Tel: (802) 496-2090

National Archives-Northeast Region (Boston)
380 Trapelo Rd., Waltham, MA 02154
Tel: (617) 647-8100
Fax: (617) 647-8460
Web site: <www.archives.gov/facilities/ma/boston.html>

New England Historic Genealogical Society
101 Newbury St., Boston, MA 02116-3007

Tel: (617) 536-5740
Fax: (617) 536-7307

New Haven Historical Society
70 East St., New Haven, VT
05472

Northfield Historical Society
P.O. Box 88, Northfield, VT
05663

Norwich Historical Society
P.O. Box 1680, Norwich, VT
05055

**Peacham Historical
Association**
104 Thaddeus Stevens Rd.,
Peacham, VT 05862
Web site: <www.peacham.net/hi
storical/>

Pittsford Historical Society
P.O. Box 423, Pittsford, VT
05763
Web site:
Poultney Historical Society
148 Upper Rd., Poultney, VT
05764
Web site: <www.rootsweb.com/
~vtphs/>

Pownal Historical Society, Inc.
P.O. Box 313, Pownal, VT 05261
Web site:

Randolph Historical Society
P.O. Box 15, Randolph Center, VT
05061

Reading Historical Society
P.O. Box 252, Reading, VT 05062
Tel: (802) 484-5738 or (802)
484-7431

Readsboro Historical Society
P.O. Box 158, Readsboro, VT
05350

Richford Historical Society
186 S. Main St., Richford, VT
05476

Rochester Historical Society
P.O. Box 7, Rochester, VT 05767

Royalton Historical Society
4184 Route 14, Royalton, VT
05068

Rupert Historical Society
Box 2, Lewis Rd., Rupert, VT
05768

Rutland Historical Society
96 Center St., Rutland, VT 05701

Salisbury Historical Society
7 Forbes Circle, Middlebury, VT
05753

**Saxtons River Historical
Society**
P.O. Box 18, Saxtons River, VT
05154

Shaftsbury Historical Society
P.O. Box 401, Shaftsbury, VT
05262

Shoreham Historical Society
P.O. Box 235, Shoreham, VT
05770
Tel: (802) 897-2600

Shrewsbury Historical Society
996 Lincoln Hill Rd., Cuttings-
ville, VT 05738

**Springfield Art & Historical
Society**
P.O. Box 313, Springfield, VT
05156

St. Albans Historical Society
P.O. Box 722, St. Albans, VT
05478

St. Johnsbury Historical Society
106 Harvey Street, St. Johnsbury,
VT 05819
Tel: (802) 748-8281

Stannard Historical Society
9 Willey Rd., Greensboro Bend,
VT 05842

Stowe Historical Society
P.O. Box 822, Stowe, VT 05672
Tel: (802) 253-6360

Swanton Historical Society
11 Lake St., Swanton, VT 05488

Thetford Historical Society
P.O. Box 33, Thetford, VT 05074

**Tinmouth Historical &
Genealogical Society**
43 Chipmunk Crossing Dr., Tinmouth, VT 05773

Townshend Historical Society
P.O. Box 202, Townshend, VT
05353
Web site: <www.townshendvt
.com>

Tunbridge Historical Society
24 The Crossroad, Tunbridge, VT
05077

Vermont Department of Health
108 Cherry St., Burlington, VT
05402
Tel: (802) 863-7275
Fax: (802) 863-7425

**Vermont Department of
Libraries**
109 State St., Montpelier, VT
05609-0601
Tel: (802) 828-3268
Fax: (802) 828-2199
Web site: <http://dol.state.vt
.us/>

Vermont Finnish Society
RR1, Box 349A, Jamaica, VT
05343

**Vermont French Canadian
Genealogical Society**
P.O. Box 65128, Burlington, VT
05406-5128

Vermont Genealogical Society
P.O. Box 422, Pittsford, VT
05763

Vermont Historical Society
Pavilion Office Bldg., 109 State
St., Montpelier, VT 05609-0901
Tel: (802) 828-3638
Fax: (802) 828-3638
Web site: <www.state.vt.us/
vhs/>

**Vermont Public Records
Division**
P.O. Drawer 33, Montpielier, VT
05633-7601
Tel: (802) 828-3286
Fax: (802) 828-3710

Vermont State Archives
109 State St. Montpelier, VT
05609-1103
Tel: (802) 828-2308
Fax: (802) 828-5171

Vernon Historians
P.O. Box 282, Vernon, VT 05354

**Veterans' Affairs Office,
Vermont Adjutant General**
120 State St., Montpelier, VT
05620-4401
Tel: (802) 828-3379
Fax: (802) 828-3381

Waitsfield Historical Society
P.O. Box 816, Waitsfield, VT
05673

Wallingford Historical Society
P.O. Box 327, Wallingford, VT
05773

Waterbury Historical Society
28 N. Main St., Waterbury, VT
05676

**Weathersfield Historical
Society**
P.O. Box 126, Weathersfield, VT
05151

Wells Historical Society
8 Capron Lane, Wells, VT 05774

**Welsh-American Genealogical
Society**
60 Norton Ave., Poultney, VT
05764-1011
Web site: <www.rootsweb.com/
~vtwags>

**West Haven Historical Society,
Inc.**
834 Main St, West Haven, VT
05743

**West Windsor Historical
Society**
P.O. Box 12, Brownsville, VT
05037
Tel: (802) 484-7249

Westford Historical Society
P.O. Box 21, Westford, VT 05494
Web site: <www.geocities.com/
westford_05494/>

**Westminister Historical
Society, Inc.**
P.O. Box 2, Westminster, VT
05158-0002
Web site: <www.microserve.net/
~rduffalo/Wrhistsoc.html>

Whitingham Historical Society
P.O. Box 125, Jacksonville, VT
05342

**Williamstown Historical
Society**
498 Boyce Rd., Williamstown, VT
05679

Williston Historical Society
P.O. Box 995, Williston, VT
05495

Woodstock Historical Society
26 Elm St., Woodstock, VT
05091
Web site: <www.uvm.edu/~histp
res/vtiana/Woodstock's.html>

BIBLIOGRAPHY

■ GENERAL RESOURCES

*Basic Sources for Vermont
Historical Research*
(Montpelier, VT: Office of the Sec-
retary of State, ca. 1981)

Vermont (sidebar, right margin)

A Calendar of Manuscripts in Certain Boxes At the Vermont Historical Society
by Loriman S. Brigham (Montpelier, VT: Loriman S. Brigham, 1970)

Collecting Vermont Ancestors
by Alice Eichholz (Montpelier, VT: New Trails, 1986)

The Congregational Churches of Vermont and Their Ministry
by John Moore Comstock (St. Johnsbury, Vermont: Caledonian Co., 1915)

Encyclopedia, Vermont Biography
by Prentiss Cutler Dodge (Burlington, VT: Ullery Publishing Co., 1912)

English Origins of New England Families: From the New England Historical and Genealogical Register, 3 vols.
from the New England Historic Genealogical Society (Boston: The Society, 1984)

A Genealogical Dictionary of the First Settlers of New England: Showing Three Generations of Those Who Came Before May 1692, 4 vols.
by James Savage (Originally published 1860–62; Reprint: Baltimore: Genealogical Publishing Company, 1981)

Genealogical and Family History of the State of Vermont, 2 vols.
by Hiram Carleton (New York: Lewis Publishing Co., 1903)

Genealogical Research in New England
edited by Ralph J. Crandall (Baltimore: Genealogical Publishing Co., 1984)

The Genealogist's Companion and Sourcebook, 2d ed.
by Emily Anne Croom (Cincinnati: Betterway Books, 2003)

A Genealogist's Guide to Discovering Your African-American Ancestors
by Franklin Carter Smith and Emily Anne Croom (Cincinnati: Betterway Books, 2003)

Genealogist's Handbook for New England Research, 3d ed.
(Boston: New England Historic Genealogical Society, 1993)

Guide to Genealogical Research in the National Archives of the United States
edited by Anne Bruner Eales and Robert M. Kvasnicka (Washington, DC: National Archives and Records Administration, 2000)

Guide to the "Miscellaneous File" of Uncatalogued Material in the Vermont Historical Society
by Loriman S. Brigham (Montpelier, VT: Loriman S. Brigham, 1969)

A Guide to Vermont's Repositories
(Montpelier, VT: Vermont State Archives, 1986)

History of the Baptists in Vermont
by Henry Crocker (Bellows Falls, VT: P.H. Gobie Press, 1913)

History of Vermont
by Zadock Thompson (Burlington, VT: Thompson, 1853)

The History of Vermont, from its Discovery to its Administration into the Union in 1791
by Hiland Hall (Albany, New York: J. Munsell, 1868)

Men of Vermont
by Jacob G. Ullery (Brattleboro, VT: Transcript Publishing Co., 1894)

National Archives Microfilm Catalogs online:
<www.archives.gov/publications/genealogy_microfilm_catalogs.html>

New England Family Histories and Genealogies: States of New Hampshire and Vermont
by Lu Verne V. Hall (Bowie, MD: Heritage Books, 2000)

Vermont: A Bibliography of Its History
edited by T.D. Seymour Bassett (Boston: G.K. Hall & Co., 1981)

Vermont's First Settlers
by Jay Mack Holbrook (Oxford, MA: Holbrook Research Institute, 1976)

Vermont Historical Gazetteer: A Magazine Embracing a History of Each Town, Civil, Ecclesiastical, Biographical and Military, 6 vols.
edited by Abby Maria Hemenway (Burlington, VT: A.M. Hemenway, 1868–1891)

Vermont Newspaper Abstract: Vermont Gazette, The Vermont Gazette: Epitome of the World, The World, the Green-Mountain Farmer
by Marsh Hoffman Rising (Boston: The New England Historic Genealogical Society, 2001)

Vermonters
by Dorman B.E. Kent (Montpelier, VT: Vermont Historical Society, 1937)

■ CENSUS RECORDS

The American Census Handbook
by Thomas Jay Kamp (Wilmington, DE: Scholarly Resources, Inc., 2001)

Map Guide to the U.S. Federal Censuses, 1790–1920
by William Thorndale and William Dollarhide (Baltimore: Genealogical Publishing Co., 1987)

Vermont 1771 Census
by Jay Mack Holbrook (Oxford, MA: Holbrook Research Institute, 1982)

Your Guide to the Federal Census
by Kathleen W. Hinckley (Cincinnati: Betterway Books, 2002)

■ IMMIGRATION RECORDS

American Naturalization Records, 1790–1990: What They Are and How to Use Them
by John J. Newman (North Salt Lake, UT: HeritageQuest, 1998)

American Passenger Arrival Records
by Michael Tepper (Baltimore: Genealogical Publishing Co., 1993)

Migration from Vermont
by Lewis D. Stillwell (Montpelier, VT: Vermont Historical Society, 1948)

They Became Americans: Finding Naturalization Records and Ethnic Origins
by Loretto Dennis Szucs (Salt Lake City: Ancestry, Inc., 1998)

They Came in Ships: A Guide to Finding Your Immigrant Ancestor's Arrival Records, 2d ed.
by John P. Colletta (Salt Lake City: Ancestry, Inc., 1993)

■ LAND RECORDS

Locating Your Roots: Discover Your Ancestors Using Land Records
by Patricia Law Hatcher (Cincinnati: Betterway Books, 2003)

Massachusetts Land Grants in Vermont
by Herbert Williams Denio (Cambridge, MA: John Wilson and Son, University Press, 1920)

State Papers of Vermont
from the Vermont Secretary of State (Montpelier, VT: Published by authority of the Secretary of State, 1939–)

The Vermont Lease Lands
by Walter Thompson Bogart (Montpelier, VT: Vermont Historical Society, 1950)

Vermont's First Settlers
by Jay Mack Holbrook (Oxford, MA: Holbrook Research Institute, 1976)

■ MAPS

A Gazetteer of Vermont: Containing Descriptions Of all the Counties. Towns, and Districts in the State, and of its Principal Mountains, Rivers, Waterfalls, Harbors, Islands, and Curious Places
by John Hayward (Bowie, MD: Heritage books, 1990)

The Postal History of Vermont
by George C. Slawson, Arthur W. Bingham, and Sprague W. Drenan (Collectors Club Handbook, no. 21. New York: Collectors Club, 1969)

The Shaping of Vermont: 1749–1877
by J. Kevin Graffagnino (Rutland, VT: Vermont Heritage Press, 1983)

Vermont Atlas and Gazetteer
(Freeport, ME: DeLorme Mapping Co., 1996)

Vermont Place-Names: Footprints of History
by Ester Munroe Swift (Brattleboro, VT: Stephen Green Press, 1977)

■ MILITARY RECORDS

A List of Pensioners of the War of 1812. Vermont Claimants.
by Byron N. Clark (Baltimore: Genealogical Publishing Co., 1969)

Revised Roster of Vermont Volunteers: and Lists Of Vermonters Who Served in the Army and Navy of the United States During the War of the Rebellion, 1861–66
by Theodore S. Peck (Montpelier, VT: Watchman Publishing Co., 1892)

Revolutionary Soldiers Buried in Vermont
by Walter Hill Crockett (Baltimore: Genealogical Publishing Co., 1959)

Rolls of Soldiers in the Revolutionary War, 1775–1783
compiled and edited by John E. Goodrich (Rutland, VT: Tuttle Co., 1904)

Roster of Soldiers in the War Of 1812–1814
from the Vermont Adjutant Generals Office (Montpelier, VT: Herbert T. Johnson, Adjutant General, 1933)

Soldiers, Sailors and Patriots of the Revolutionary War, Vermont
by Carleton E. Fisher (Camden, ME: Picton Press, 1992)

Uncle, We Are Ready! Registering America's Men, 1917–1918: A Guide to Researching World War I Draft Registration Cards
by John J. Newman (North Salt Lake, UT: HeritageQuest, 2001)

U.S. Military Records: A Guide to Federal & State Sources, Colonial America to the Present
by James C. Neagles (Salt Lake City: Ancestry, Inc., 1994)

Vermont in the Spanish-American War
by Herbert T. Johnson (Montpelier, VT: Adjutant General, 1929)

World War II: A Family Historian's Guide
by Debra Johnson Knox (Spartanburg, SC: MIE Publishing, 2003)

■ PROBATE RECORDS

State Papers of Vermont
from the Vermont Secretary of State (Montpelier, VT: Published by authority of Secretary of State, 1939–)

■ VITAL RECORDS

Burial Grounds of Vermont
by Arthur L. Hyde (Townshend, VT: Vermont Old Cemetery Association, 1991)

Vermont Warnings Out, 2 vols.
by Alden M. Rollins (Camden, ME: Picton Press, 1995–1997)

Your Guide to Cemetery Research
by Sharon DeBartolo Carmack (Cincinnati: Betterway Books, 2002)

■ Addison 18 Oct. 1785

5 Court St., Middlebury, VT 05753
Phone: (802)388-7741
Web site: home.att.net/~swaitela/Default.htm
Parent County: Rutland
Comments/research tips: Towns chartered before 1800: Addison 1761, Bridport 1761, Cornwall 1761, Ferrisburgh 1762, Leicester 1761, Lincoln 1780, Middlebury 1761, Monkton 1762, New Haven 1761, Orwell 1763, Panton 1761, Ripton 1781, Salisbury 1761, Shoreham 1761, Starksboro 1780, Vergennes 1788, Waltham 1796, Weybridge 1761, Whiting 1763.

Record Type	Year Begun	Jurisdiction
Birth	na	Town Clerks
Marriage	na	Town Clerks
Death	na	Town Clerks
Divorce	1797	Dept./BGS
Probate	1824	Probate Office
Court	1797	District/Superior Clerk
Burial	na	Town Clerks

■ Bennington 11 Feb. 1779

207 South St., Bennington, VT 05201
Phone: (802)442-8528
Web site: www.rootsweb.com/~vtbennin/
Parent County: Original county
Comments/research tips: Towns Chartered Before 1800: Arlington 1761, Bennington 1749, Dorset 1761, Glastenbury 1761, Landgrove 1780, Manchester 1761, Peru 1761, Pownal 1760, Rupert 1761, Sandgate 1761, Shaftsbury 1761, Sunderland 1761, Winhall 1761. Bennington County has 2 probate districts: Bennington (Probate Office has records from 1778) and Manchester (Probate Office has records from 1779).

Record Type	Year Begun	Jurisdiction
Birth	na	Town Clerks
Marriage	na	Town Clerks
Death	na	Town Clerks
Divorce	1899	Dept./BGS
Court	1861	Dist./Sup. Clerk

■ Caledonia 5 Nov. 1792

27 Main St., P.O. Box 4129, St. Johnsbury, VT 05819
Phone: (802)748-6600
Web site: home.att.net/~local_history/Caledonia-Co-VT.htm
Parent County: Orange
Comments/research tips: Towns Chartered Before 1800: Barnet 1763, Burke 1782, Cabot 1780, Danville 1786, Groton 1789, Hardwick 1781, Lyndon 1780, Peacham 1763, Ryegate 1763, Sheffield 1780, St. Johnsbury 1786, Sutton 1782, Walden 1781, Waterford 1780, Wheelock 1785. City of Cabot became part of Washington County in 1855.

Record Type	Year Begun	Jurisdiction
Birth	na	Town Clerks
Marriage	na	Town Clerks
Death	na	Town Clerks
Divorce	ca. 1800	Dept./BGS

Vermont

Land .... na .... Town Clerks
Probate .... na .... Probate Office
Court .... ca. 1800 ....Dist./Sup. Clerk

■ Chittenden 22 Oct. 1787
175 Main St., Burlington, VT 05402
Phone: (802)863-3467
Web site: home.att.net/~local_history/Chittenden-Co-VT.htm
Parent County: Addison
Comments/research tips: Towns Chartered Before 1800:
Bolton 1763, Burlington 1763, Charlotte 1762, Colchester 1763, Essex 1763, Hinesburg 1762, Huntington 1763, Jericho 1763, Milton 1763, Richmond 1794, Shelburne 1763, St. George 1763, Underhill 1763, Williston 1763.

Record Type	Year Begun	Jurisdiction
Land	na	Town Clerks
Probate	na	Probate Office
Court	1969	Dist./Sup. Clerk
Birth	na	Town Clerks
Marriage	na	Town Clerks
Death	na	Town Clerks
Divorce	na	Dept./BGS

■ Essex 5 Nov. 1792
75 Courthouse Dr., P.O. Box 75, Guildhall, VT 05905
Phone: (802)676-3910
Web site: www.rootsweb.com/~vermont/GenWebEssexCounty.html
Parent County: Orange
Comments/research tips: Towns Chartered Before 1800:
Bloomfield 1762, Brunswick 1761, Canaan 1782, Concord 1780, Guildhall 1761, Lunenburg 1763, Maidstone 1761, Victory 1781.

Record Type	Year Begun	Jurisdiction
Birth	na	Town Clerks
Marriage	na	Town Clerks
Death	na	Town Clerks
Land	na	Town Clerks
Probate	1791	Probate Office
Court	na	Dept./BGS
Divorce	na	Dept./BGS

■ Franklin 5 Nov. 1792
Church St., P.O. Box 808, St. Albans, VT 05478
Phone: (802)828-3286
Web site: www.rootsweb.com/~vtfrankl/
Parent County: Chittenden
Comments/research tips: Town Clerks have Birth, Death and Marriage records 1760–1954. Towns Founded Before 1800: Bakersfield 1791, Berkshire 1781, Enosburg 1780, Fairfax 1763, Fairfield 1763, Fletcher 1781, Franklin 1789, Georgia 1763, Highgate 1762, Montgomery 1789, Richford 1780, Sheldon 1763, Swanton 1763, St. Albans 1763.

Record Type	Year Begun	Jurisdiction
Divorce	1900	Dept./BGS
Land	na	Town Clerks
Probate	ca. 1800	Probate Office
Court	ca. 1940	Dist./Sup. Clerk

■ Grand Isle 9 Nov. 1802
Rt. 2, P.O. Box 7, North Hero, VT 05474
Phone: (802)372-8350
Web site: www.rootsweb.com/~vermont/GenWebGrndisleCounty.html
Parent County: Franklin, Chittenden
Comments/research tips: Towns Chartered Before 1800:
Alburg 1781, Grand Isle 1779, Isles La Motte 1779, North Hero 1779, South Hero 1779.

Record Type	Year Begun	Jurisdiction
Birth	na	Town Clerks
Marriage	na	Town Clerks
Death	na	Town Clerks
Land	na	Town Clerks
Probate	1800	County Clerk
Court	1800	County Clerk

■ Jefferson 1 Nov. 1810
Parent County: Chittenden, Caledonia, Orange
Comments/research tips: (See Washington) Name changed to Washington 8 November 1814.

■ Lamoille 26 Oct. 1835
P.O. Box 303, Hyde Park, VT 05655
Phone: (802)888-2207
Web site: www.usgennet.org/usa/vt/county/lamoille1/index.htm
Parent County: Chittenden, Orleans, Franklin, Washington
Comments/research tips: Towns Chartered Before 1800:
Cambridge 1781, Elmore 1781, Hyde Park 1781, Johnson 1792, Morristown 1781, Stowe 1763, Wolcott 1781.

Record Type	Year Begun	Jurisdiction
Birth	na	Town Clerks
Marriage	na	Town Clerks
Death	na	Town Clerks
Divorce	na	Dept./BGS
Land	na	Town Clerks
Probate	1837	Probate Clerk
Court	1837	County Clerk

■ Orange 22 Feb. 1781
5 Court St., Chelsea, VT 05038
Phone: (802)685-4610
Web site: www.usgennet.org/usa/vt/county/orange/
Parent County: Cumberland
Comments/research tips: Towns Chartered Before 1800:
Bradford 1770, Braintree 1781, Brookfield 1781, Chelsea 1781, Corinth 1764, Fairlee 1761, Newbury 1763, Orange 1781, Randolph 1781, Straford 1761, Thetford 1761, Topsham 1763, Turnbridge 1761, Vershire 1781, Washington 1781, West Fairlee 1779, Williamstown 1781.

Record Type	Year Begun	Jurisdiction
Birth	na	Town Clerks
Marriage	na	Town Clerks
Death	na	Town Clerks
Divorce	na	Dept./BGS
Land	na	Town Clerks
Probate	1771	Probate Office
Court	1781	Superior Clerk

Vermont

■ Orleans 5 Nov. 1792
247 Main St., P.O. Box 787, Newport, VT 05855
Phone: (802)334-3344
Web site: users.rootsweb.com/~vtorlean/
VTGenWeb.SM.htm
Parent County: Chittenden, Orange
Comments/research tips: Towns Chartered Before 1800:
Barton 1789, Craftsbury 1781, Derby 1779, Glover 1783,
Greensboro 1781, Holland 1779, Jay 1792, Westfield 1780.

Record Type	Year Begun	Jurisdiction
Birth	na	Town Clerks
Marriage	na	Town Clerks
Death	na	Town Clerks
Divorce	na	Dept./BGS
Land	na	Town Clerks
Probate	1796	Probate Office
Court	na	Superior Clerk

■ Rutland 22 Feb. 1781
83 Center St., Rutland, VT 05701
Phone: (802)775-4394
Web site: home.att.net/~local_history/Rutland-Co-Vt.htm
Parent County: Bennington
Comments/research tips: Rutland County has two probate
districts: Fairhaven and Rutland. Towns Organized Before
1800: Benson 1780, Brandon 1761, Castleton 1761,
Chittenden 1780, Clarendon 1761, Danby 1761, Fair
Haven 1779, Hubbardton 1764, Ira 1780, Mendon 1781,
Middletown Springs 1784, Mt. Holly 1792, Mt. Tabor
1761, Pawlet 1761, Pittsford 1761, Poultney 1761, Rutland
1761, Sherburne 1761, Shrewsbury 1761, Sudbury 1763,
Wallingford 1761, Wells 1761, West Haven 1792.

Record Type	Year Begun	Jurisdiction
Land	na	Town Clerks
Probate	1780	Probate Office
Court	ca. 1775	Superior Clerk

■ Washington 1 Nov. 1810
P.O. Box 426, Montpelier, VT 05602
Phone: (802)223-2091
Web site: www.rootsweb.com/~vtwashin/
Parent County: Addison, Orange, Caledonia, Orleans
Comments/research tips: Formerly Jefferson County. Name
changed to Washington 8 November 1814. Towns
Organized Before 1800: Barre 1781, Berlin 1763, Cabot
1780, Calais 1781, Duxbury 1763, Marshfield 1782,
Middlesex 1763, Montpelier 1781, Moretown 1763,
Northfield 1781, Plainfield 1797, Roxbury 1781, Waitsfield
1782, Warren 1780, Waterbury 1763, Worcester 1763.

Record Type	Year Begun	Jurisdiction
Birth	na	Town Clerks
Marriage	na	Town Clerks
Death	na	Town Clerks
Divorce	na	Dept./BGS
Land	na	Town Clerks
Probate	1811	Probate Office
Court	na	Superior Clerk

■ Windham 22 Feb. 1781
Rt. 30, P.O. Box 207, Newfane, VT 05345
Phone: (802)365-7979
Web site: www.rootsweb.com/~vtwashin/
Parent County: Cumberland
Comments/research tips: Windham County has two probate
districts: Marlboro and Westminster. Probate Clerk has
Probate records for Marlboro District from 1790. Probate
Office has Probate records for Westminster District from
1781. Towns Chartered Before 1800: Athens 1780,
Brattleboro 1753, Brookline 1794, Grafton 1754, Guilford
1754, Halifax 1750, Jamaica 1780, Londonderry 1780,
Marlboro 1751, Newfane 1753, Putney 1753, Rockingham
1752, Townshend 1753, Woodbury 1781, Westminster
1752, Whitingham 1770, Wilmington 1751, Windham
1795.

Record Type	Year Begun	Jurisdiction
Birth	na	Town Clerks
Marriage	na	Town Clerks
Death	na	Town Clerks
Divorce	na	Dept./BGS
Land	na	Town Clerks
Court	na	Superior Clerk

■ Windsor 22 Feb. 1781
12 The Green, Woodstock, VT 05091
Phone: (802)457-2121
Web site: www.usgennet.org/usa/vt/county/windsor/
Parent County: Cumberland
Comments/research tips: Windsor has two probate districts:
Hartford and Windsor. Probate Offices in Hartford and
Windsor have Probate records. Towns Chartered Before
1800: Andover 1761, Baltimore 1793, Barnard 1761, Bethel
1779, Bridgewater 1761, Cavendish 1761, Chester 1754,
Hartford 1761, Hartland 1761, Ludlow 1761, Norwich
1761, Plymouth 1761, Pomfret 1761, Reading 1761,
Royalton 1769, Sharon 1761, Springfield 1761, Stockbridge
1761, Weathersfield 1761, Weston 1799, Windsor 1761,
Woodstock 1761.

Record Type	Year Begun	Jurisdiction
Birth	na	Town Clerks
Marriage	na	Town Clerks
Death	na	Town Clerks
Divorce	1782	Dept./BGS
Land	na	Town Clerks
Court	1782	Clerk/District Ct.

Vermont

Virginia

By Rhonda R. McClure

HISTORICAL OVERVIEW

Jamestown is often overshadowed by Plymouth Colony when it comes to the founding of what would eventually become the United States. Jamestown was founded in 1607, making it the second oldest community in the United States to St. Augustine, Florida, but was the first permanent English settlement. Unlike St. Augustine and Plymouth, however, Jamestown almost didn't survive its first five years. It took the experiments of John Rolfe with tobacco, especially his exportation of it to London, that began to make Virginia—named after the Virgin Queen, Elizabeth I—economically sustaining.

Early colonization of Virginia was encouraged through the use of headright grants, a method of giving public land—fifty acres in Virginia—to anyone who paid his own way to the new colony. These individuals could earn additional lots of fifty acres for each additional individual for whom they paid passage.

For what has become a small state, the original territory that was considered Virginia was enormous and was eventually was carved up to form parts of the following:

- 1779—a section became part of North Carolina
- 1786—a section became part of Pennsylvania
- 1792—a section became Kentucky and another became a part of Maryland
- 1803—a section became part of Tennessee and another area became Ohio and Indiana Territory
- 1816—a former part became Indiana
- 1818—a former part became Illinois
- 1863—a former part became West Virginia

Some of the divisions were enacted to settle border disputes. In the case of the midwest states of Ohio, Indiana, and Illinois, the land, originally known as the Northwest Territory, was ceded to the United States in the ratification of the Constitution which made Virginia a state.

VIRGINIA AT A GLANCE

Motto: Thus Always to Tyrants

Population: 7.1 million

Prevalent Religions: Mostly Baptist and Roman Catholic, with varieties of international religions in the Washington, D.C. area

Major Industries: Tobacco, cattle, poultry, dairy products, textiles, food processing, printing, electrical equipment, chemicals, hogs, soybeans, transportation equipment

Ethnic Makeup (in percent): Caucasian 72.3%, African American 19.6%, Hispanic 4.7%, Asian 3.7%, Native American 0.3%, Other 2.0%

Famous Virginians: Arthur Ashe, Pearl Bailey, Warren Beatty, Willa Cather, William Clark, Joseph Cotton, Ella Fitzgerald, William H. Harrison, Patrick Henry, Sam Houston, Thomas Jefferson, Robert E. Lee, Meriwether Lewis, John Marshall, James Madison, Shirley MacLaine, James Monroe, Opechancanough, Bill Bojangles Robinson, George C. Scott, Jeb Stuart, Thomas Sumter, Zachary Taylor, Nat Turner, John Tyler, Booker T. Washington, George Washington, Woodrow Wilson, Tom Wolfe

Above: George Washington's Mount Vernon

© PhotoDisc/Getty Images

Finally, West Virginia's counties broke away from Virginia because of their support of the Union during the Civil War.

RECORD HIGHLIGHTS

Though Virginia was one of the first states of the newly formed union and census enumerations were taken for the years 1790 and 1800, the records have not survived—only part of the 1810 census exists. This makes it necessary to turn your attention to census alternatives, including the Virginia tax lists from 1782 through 1785.

Tax lists are a wealth of information that are too often overlooked. Colonial taxes included the tithables and quit-rents described below. Pre-1783 tax records have been published in *Virginia Tax Records: From the Virginia Magazine of History and Biography, The William and Mary College Quarterly, and Tyler's Quarterly: with an index by Gary Parks* (Baltimore, Maryland: Genealogical Publishing Company, Inc., 1983).

Researching in Virginia court records is like running a maze made up of county courts, orphans' courts, courts of claim, quarter courts, general courts, a supreme court of appeals, a high court of chancery, a superior court of chancery, district courts, circuit superior courts of law and chancery, and circuit courts. Some of the courts overlap, others replaced earlier courts. To get more information about the different courts and their jurisdictions, refer to *A Preliminary Guide to Pre-1904 County Records in the Archives Branch, Virginia State Library and Archives* by Suzanne Smith Ray, Lyndon H. Hart III, and J. Christian Kolbe (Richmond, Virginia: Virginia State Library and Archives, 1987).

Virginia began early registration of births and deaths, requiring the counties to register these records in 1853. This continued until 1896, though there is a gap during the Civil War, when most of the counties abandoned registration. You will find another gap in the records from 1896 until statewide registration began in 1912. Just a few independent cities kept births and deaths during this time.

Pre-1853 marriages were done by posting a bond—a written agreement to forfeit an amount of money should the marriage not take place—or by banns, which were announced or published at three church meetings prior to the ceremony. Banns, therefore, are found in church records rather than county courthouse records.

Since 1853, a state law has required the counties and independent cities to issue a marriage license. The application for marriage, which was formalized in 1858, asks for full names, ages, places of birth and residence, proposed marriage date and place, if divorced or widowed, parents' names, groom's occupation, and minister's name. When the license was given to the state by the minister or other officiating individual, the clerk was required to enter the marriage in a marriage register. The Division of Vital Records has this marriage register, which dates from January 1853. The clerk of the county or city court has copies of all marriage records kept by that court. The Library of Virginia <www.lva.lib.va.us/> has many marriage records. You can search their catalog online. The Family History Library has microfilmed copies of marriage bonds and marriage registers up until about 1935.

STATE RESOURCES

■ ARCHIVES, LIBRARIES, AND SOCIETIES

Albemarle County Historical Society
220 Court Square, Charlottesville, VA 22901

Alderman Library, University of Virginia
P.O. Box 400114, Charlottesville, VA 22904-4114
Tel: (434) 924-3021
Web site: <www.lib.virginia.edu/alderman/>

Alexandria Library
717 Queen St., Alexandria, VA 22314

Alleghany Highlands Genealogical Society
1011 N. Rockbridge St., Covington, VA 24426

Arlington Central Library
1015 N. Quincy St., Arlington, VA 22201

Augusta County Genealogical Society
2002 Lyndhurst Rd., Waynesboro, VA 22980-5226

Augusta County Historical Society
P.O. Box 686, Staunton, VA 247401

Bath County Historical Society, Inc.
P.O. Box 212, Warm Springs, VA 24484

Bedford Historical Society, Inc.
P.O. Box 602, Bedford, VA 24523

Blue Ridge Regional Library
310 E. Church St., Martinsville, VA 24112

Bristol Public Library
701 Good St., Bristol, VA 24201

Caroline County Genealogical Society
P.O. Box 9, Bowling Green, VA 22427

Carroll County Historical Society
P.O. Box 937, Hillsville, VA 24343

Carroll County Historical Society Museum
307 N. Main St., Hillsville, VA 24343

Central Virginia Genealogical Association
P.O. Box 4483, Charlottesville, VA 22905-5583

Chesterfield Historical Society of Virginia
P.O. Box 40, Chesterfield, VA 23832

Claiborne County Historical Society
Rt. 1, Box 589, Jonesville, VA 24263

College of William and Mary, Earl Gregg Swem Library
P.O. Box 220, Williamsburg, VA 23187
Tel: (804) 221-3500
Fax: (804) 221-3088
Web site:

Culpeper Historical Society, Inc.
P.O. Box 785, Culpeper, VA 22701

Culpeper Town and County Library
271 Southgate Shopping Center, Culpeper, VA 22701
Tel: (540) 825-8691
Fax: (540) 825-7486
E-mail: ccl@cclva.org
Web site: <http://tlc.library.net/culpeper/default.asp>

Cumberland County Historical Society
Box 88, Cumberland, VA 23040

Danville Public Library
511 Patton St., Danville, VA 24541

Fairfax Genealogical Society
P.O. Box 2290, Merrifield, VA 22116-2290

Fairfax Historical Society
P.O. Box 415, Fairfax, VA 22030

Fauquier Heritage Society
P.O. Box 548, Marshall, VA 22115

Franklin County Genealogical Society
P.O. Box 316, Ferrum, VA 24088

Fredericksburg Regional Genealogical Society
P.O. Box 42013, Fredericksburg, VA 22404

Ft. Eustis Historical and Archaeological Association
P.O. Box 4408, Ft. Eustis, VA 23604

Genealogical Research Institute of Virginia
P.O. Box 29178, Richmond, VA 23242-0178

Genealogical Society of Page County
% Page Public Library, 100 Zerkel St., Luray, VA 22835

Goochland County Historical Society
P. O. Box 602, Goochland, VA 23063
Tel: (804) 556-3966
Web site: <www.goochlandhistory.org>

Grayson County Historical Society, Inc.
P.O. Box 529, Independence, VA 24348-0529

Green County Historical Society
P.O. Box 185, Stanardsville, VA 22973

Hampton Public Library
4205 Victoria Blvd., Hampton, VA 23669

Handley Library
P.O. Box 58, Winchester, VA 22601
Tel: (540) 662-9041
Fax: (540) 722-4769

Harrisonburg-Rockingham Historical Society and Library
3228 High St., P.O. Box 716, Dayton, VA 22821

Historical Society of Washington County
Box 484, Abingdon, VA 24210

Holston Territory Genealogical Society
P.O. Box 433, Bristol, VA 24203-0433

Isle of Wight County Historical Society
P.O. Box 121, Smithfield, VA 23431

James Monroe Museum & Memorial Library
908 Charles St., Fredericksburg, VA 22401

Jefferson/Madison Regional Library
201 E. Market St., Charlottesville, VA 22903

Jewish Genealogical Society of Tidewater
Jewish Community Center, 7300 Newport Ave., Norfolk, VA 23505

Jones Memorial Library
2311 Memorial Ave., Lynchburg, VA 24501
Tel: (804) 846-0501
Fax: (804) 846-0501

King George County Historical Society
P.O. Box 424, King George, VA 22485

Lee County Historical and Genealogical Society
P.O. Box 231, Jonesville, VA 24263

Library of Virginia
800 E. Broad St., Richmond, VA 23219-1905
Tel: (804) 692-3500

Pittsylvania Historical Society
P.O. Box 846, Chatham, VA
24531

Portsmouth Genealogical Society
P.O. Box 7062, Portsmouth, VA
23707-7062

Presbyterian Church Archives, Union Theological Seminary
34901 Brook Rd., Richmond, VA
23227
Tel: (804) 355-0671
Fax: (804) 355-3919

Prince William County Genealogical Society
P.O. Box 2019, Manassas, VA
20108-0812

Radford Public Library
30 W. Main St., Radford, VA
24141
Tel: (540) 731-3621
Fax: (540) 731-4857
Web site: <www.radford.va.us/library/>

Roanoke City Public Library
706 S. Jefferson St., Roanoke, VA
24016

Roanoke Valley Historical Society
P.O. Box 1904, Roanoke, VA
24008

Rockingham County Historical Society
301 S. Main St., Dayton, VA
22812

Rockingham Public Library
45 Newman Ave., Harrisonburg,
VA 22801

Shenandoah County Library
300 Stoney Creek Blvd., Edinburg, VA 22824
Tel: (504) 984-8200
Fax: (540) 984-8207
Web site: <www.shenandoah.co.lib.va.us>

Simpson Library, Mary Washington College
1801 College Ave., Fredericksburg, VA 22401-4664
Tel: (703) 899-4594
Fax: (703) 899-4499
Web site: <www.library.mwc.edu/cgi-bin/gw/chameleon>

Society of the Old Creek Cross
9501 Fourth Place, Lorton, VA
22079

Fax: (804) 692-3556
Web site:

Martinsville Henry County Historical Society
P.O. Drawer 432, Martinsville, VA
24114

Mary Ball Washington Museum & Library, Inc.
P.O. Box 97, Lancaster, VA
22503-0097

Mathews County Historical Society
P.O. Box 885, Mathews, VA
23109

Menno Simons Historical Library and Archives, Eastern Mennonite College
1200 Park Rd., Harrisonburg, VA
22801-2462
Tel: (540) 432-4177
Web site: <www.loc.gov/rr/main/religion/emu.html>

Mount Vernon Genealogical Society
1500 Shenandoah Rd., Alexandria, VA 22308

National Archives-Mid-Atlantic Region
900 Market St., Philadelphia, PA
19107-4292
Tel: (215) 606-0100
Fax: (215) 606-0116
Web site: <www.archives.gov/midatlantic/>

National Genealogical Society Library
4527 Seventeenth St. N., Arlington, VA 22207
Tel: (703) 525-0052
Web site: <http://genealogy.org/NGS/>

New River Historical Society
P.O. Box 373, Newborn, VA
24126

Norfolk County Historical Society
% Chesapeake Public Library,
298 Cedar Rd., Chesapeake, VA
23320-5512

Norfolk Genealogical Society
P.O. Box 12813, Norfolk, VA
23502-5309

Norfolk Public Library
301 E. City Hall Ave., Norfolk, VA
23510

Northern Neck Historical Society
43 Courthouse Square, P.O. Box
716, Montross, VA 22520
Tel: (804) 493-8440

Orange County Historical Society
130 Caroline St., Orange, VA
22960

Page Public Library
100 Zerkel St., Luray, VA 22835

Palatines to America, Virginia Chapter
3249 Cambridge Court, Fairfax,
VA 22032-1942

Patrick County Genealogical Society
P.O. Drawer 1016, Stuart, VA
24171

Petersburg Public Library
137 S. Sycamore St., Petersburg,
VA 23803

Southside Regional Library
P.O. Box 10, Boydton, VA 23917

Southwestern Virginia Genealogical Society
P.O. Box 12485, Roanoke, VA 24026

State Health Department
P.O. Box 1000, Richmond, VA 23208-1000
Tel: (804) 225-5000

Surry County Historical Society and Museum
P.O. Box 262, Surry, VA 23883

Thomas Balch Library
208 W. Market St., Leesburg, VA 22075
Tel: (703) 777-0132

Tidewater Genealogical Society
P.O. Box 7650, Hampton, VA 23666

Tidewater Afro-American Historical and Genealogical Society
2200 Crossroad Trail, Virginia Beach, VA 23456

United Daughters of the Confederacy, UDC General Headquarters
328 North Blvd., Richmond, VA 23220-4057
Tel: (804) 353-1396
Web site:

Virginia Baptist Historical Society
% Boatwright Memorial Library, P.O. Box 34, University of Richmond, Richmond, VA 23173
Tel: (804) 289-8434

Virginia Beach Genealogical Society
P.O. Box 62901, VA Beach, VA 23466-2901

Virginia Genealogical Society
5001 W. Broad St. #115, Richmond, VA 23230-3023
Web site:

Virginia Historical Library
P.O. Box 7311, Richmond, VA 23211

Virginia Historical Society
428 North Blvd., Richmond, VA 23220
Web site: <www.vahistorical. org/index.htm>

Virginia-North Carolina, Piedmont Genealogical Society
P.O. Box 2272, Danville, VA 24541-2272

Waynesboro Public Library
600 S. Waynes Ave., Waynesboro, VA 22980

Winchester-Frederick County Historical Society
% Handley Regional Library, P.O. Box 58, Winchester, VA 22604

BIBLIOGRAPHY

■ GENERAL RESOURCES

Adventurers Of Purse and Person, Virginia, 1607–1624/5
by Annie Lash Jester and Martha Woodruff Hiden (Order of the First Families of Virginia, 1987)

Annals of Southwest Virginia, 1769–1800
by Lewis Preston Summers (Baltimore: Genealogical Publishing Co., 1996)

Biographical Sketches of Virginia
by S. Bassett French (Richmond, VA: Virginia State Library, 1942)

The Colonial Church in Virginia
by Edward L. Goodwin (Milwaukee: Morehouse Pub., 1927)

Early Virginia Families Along the James River, 2 vols.
by Louise Pledge Heath Foley (Baltimore: Genealogical Publishing Co., 1990)

Encyclopedia of Virginia Biography, 5 vols.
by Lyn Gardiner Tyler (New York: Lewis Historical Pub., 1915)

English Duplicates of Lost Virginia Records
compiled by Louis Des Cognet Jr. (Baltimore: Genealogical Publishing Co., 1981)

The Genealogist's Companion and Sourcebook, 2d ed.
by Emily Anne Croom (Cincinnati: Betterway Books, 2003)

A Genealogist's Guide to Discovering Your African-American Ancestors
by Franklin Carter Smith and Emily Anne Croom (Cincinnati: Betterway Books, 2003)

A Guide to Church Records in the Archives Branch, Virginia State Library
by Jewell T. Clark and Elizabeth Terry Long (Richmond: Virginia State Library, Archives and Records Division, 1981)

A Guide to Episcopal Church Records in Virginia
by Edith F. Axelson (Athens, GA: Iberian Publishing, 1988)

A Guide to Genealogical Notes and Charts in the Archives Branch, Virginia State Library
compiled by Lyndon H. Hart (Richmond: Virginia State Library, 1983)

Guide to Genealogical Research in the National Archives of the United States
edited by Anne Bruner Eales and Robert M. Kvasnicka (Washington, DC: National Archives and Records Administration, 2000)

A Guide to State Records in the Archives Branch
compiled by John S. Salmon (Richmond: Virginia State Library, 1985)

History of Virginia, 6 vols.
(Chicago: American Historical Society, 1924)

The Handbook of Virginia History: A Ready Reference Guide to the Old Dominion's People, Places and Past, 4th ed.
by Emily J. Salmon and Edward D.C. Campbell (Richmond, VA: The Library of Virginia, 1994)

Index to Printed Virginia Genealogies
by Robert Armistead Stewart (Baltimore: Genealogical Publishing Co., 1970)

Men of Mark in Virginia, 5 vols.
(Washington, DC: Men of Mark Publishing Co., 1906–09)

National Archives Microfilm Catalogs online:
<www.archives.gov/publications/genealogy_microfilm_catalogs.html>

Old Churches, Ministers and Families of Virginia, 1857
by William Meade (Baltimore: Genealogical Publishing, 1966)

Research in Virginia
by Eric Grundset (Arlington, VA: National Genealogical Society, 1998)

Sketches of Virginia: Historical and Biographical, 2 vols.
by William Henry Foote (Philadelphia: William S. Marten, 1850–56)

Some Prominent Virginia Families, 4 Vols.
by Louise Pecquet du Bellet (Baltimore: Genealogical Publishing, 1976)

State Slavery Statutes: Guide to the Microfiche Collection
by Paul Finkelman (Frederick, MD: University Publications of America, 1989)

3rd Burned County Data 1809–1848: As Found in the Virginia Contested Elected Files
by Benjamin B. Weisiger (Richmond, VA: Benjamin B. Weisiger, 1986)

Timesaving Aid to Virginia-West Virginia Ancestors, 4 vols.
by Patrick G. Wardell (Athens, GA: Iberian Publishing Co., 1985–1990)

The Virginia Battles and Leaders Series
by H.E. Howard (Lynchburg, VA: H.E. Howard, 1984)

Virginia Colonial Abstracts, 34 vols.
by Beverley Fleet (Baltimore: Genealogical Publishing, 1988)

Virginia Genealogical Research
by George K. Schweitzer (Knoxville, TN: George K. Schweitzer, 1982)

Virginia Genealogical Resources
by Robert Young Clay (Detroit, MI: Detroit Society of Genealogical Research, 1980)

Virginia Genealogies: A Trial List of Printed Books and Pamphlets, 2 vols.
by Stuart E. Brown Jr. (Berryville, VA: Virginia Book, 1967, 1980)

Virginia Genealogy: A Guide to Resources in the University of Virginia Library
(Charlottesville, VA: the University Press of Virginia, 1983)

Virginia

Virginia Genealogy: Sources and Resources
by Carol McGinnis (Baltimore: Genealogical Publishing Co., 1993)

Virginia Historical Index, 2 vols.
by Earl Gregg Swen (Gloucester, MA: Peter Smith, 1965)

Virginia in the 1600's
compiled and edited by Harold Oliver (Riverside, CA: D&H Publishing Co., 1992)

Virginia Local History: A Bibliography
(Richmond: Virginia State Library, 1971)

Virginia: The New Dominion
by Virginius Dabney (Charlottesville: University Press of Virginia, 1971)

Virginia Newspapers 1821–1935: A Bibliography with Historical Introductions and Notes
by Lester J. Cappon (New York: D. Appleton Century, 1936)

Virginia Northern Neck Land Grants, 4 vols.
by Gertrude E. Gray (Baltimore, MD: Genealogical Pub. Co., 1993)

Virginia Research Outline
(Salt Lake City, UT: Corp. of the President of the Church of Jesus Christ of L.D.S., 1988)

Virginia Tithables from Burned Record Counties
by Robert F. and Isobel B. Woodson (Richmond, VA: Isobel B. Woodson, 1970)

Virginia and Virginians, 2 vols.
by Robert Alonzo Brock (Richmond, Virginia, and Toledo, OH: H.H. Hardesty, 1888)

Virginians and West Virginians, 1607–1870, 3 vols.
by Patrick G. Wardell (Bowie, MD: Heritage Books, 1986–1992)

■ CENSUS RECORDS

The American Census Handbook
by Thomas Jay Kemp (Wilmington, DE: Scholarly Resources, Inc., 2001)

The Census Book: A Genealogist's Guide to Federal Census Facts, Schedules and Indexes
by William Dollarhide (Bountiful, UT: HeritageQuest, 1999)

The 1787 Census of Virginia, 3 vols.
by Netti Schreiner-Yanits and Florence Speakman Love (Springfield, VA: Genealogical Books in Print, 1987)

Finding Answers In U.S. Census Records
by Loretto Dennis Szucs and Matthew Wright (Salt Lake City: Ancestry Publishing, 2001)

Map Guide to the U.S. Federal Censuses, 1790–1920
by William Thorndale and William Dollarhide (Baltimore: Genealogical Publishing Co., 1987)

The Quitrents of Virginia
by Annie Laurie Wright Smith (Richmond: Expert Letter Writing, 1957)

State Census Records
by Ann S. Lainhart (Baltimore: Genealogical Publishing Co., 1992)

A Supplement to the 1810 Census of Virginia: Tax Lists of the Counties for which the Census is Missing
by Netti Schreiner-Yanits (Springfield, VA: Genealogical Books in Print, 1971)

Virginia in 1740: A Reconstructed Census
(Miami Beach, FL: T.L. C. Genealogy, 1992)

Virginia Taxpayers, 1782–1787
by Augusta B. Fothergill (Baltimore: Genealogical Publishing, 1974)

Virginia Tax Records: From the Virginia Magazine of History and Biography, the William and Mary College Quarterly, and Tyler's Quarterly
(Baltimore: Genealogical Publishing Company, 1983)

Your Guide to the Federal Census
by Kathleen W. Hinckley (Cincinnati: Betterway Books, 2002)

RESEARCH TIPS
for more info

- When researching colonial ancestors, records such as tithables lists and quitrent rolls help to establish at least the head of the household. Tithables were close to head counts. Those who were considered tithable changed over the years from originally including only every male above sixteen to eventually covering all males, nonwhite females, and wives of free nonwhite males. Quitrents, on the other hand, were annual rents paid to the crown or to the proprietor who had granted the individual the land. Many of the tithables and quitrents have been published.
- Virginia has a number of independent cities. These cities have their own records, though they reside within a county. In some instances, the county has been absorbed by an independent city. There are forty-one independent cities in the state of Virginia. Before spending a lot of time digging in county records, verify that your ancestor was not living in one of these cities. For a list, visit the Virginia US-GenWeb site <www.rootsweb.com/~vagenweb/> and view their County Links. You will find links to the independent cities below the counties.

Census Records
- Federal Census: 1810, 1820, 1830. 1840, 1850, 1860, 1870, 1880, 1900, 1910, 1920, 1930
- Federal Mortality Schedules: 1850, 1860, 1870, 1880
- Tax Lists: 1782–1785

Virginia

■ IMMIGRATION RECORDS

American Naturalization Records, 1790–1990: What They Are and How to Use Them
by John J. Newman (North Salt Lake, UT: HeritageQuest, 1998)

American Passenger Arrival Records
by Michael Tepper (Baltimore: Genealogical Publishing Co., 1993)

The Complete Book of Emigrants, 1607–1776, and Emigrants In Bondage, 1614–1775
by Peter Wilson Coldham (Novato, CA: Brøderbund Software, 1996. CD-ROM)

Documents, Chiefly Unpublished, Relating to the Huguenot Emigration to Virginia and to the Settlement at Manakintown
by Robert A. Brock (Originally published in 1886; Reprint: Baltimore: Genealogical Publishing Co., 1987)

Early Child Immigrants to Virginia, 1618–1642
by Robert Hume (Baltimore: Magna Carta Book Co., 1986)

Early Virginia Immigrants, 1623–1666
by George C. Greer (Originally published in 1912; Reprint: Baltimore: Genealogical Publishing Co., 1982)

Some Emigrants to Virginia: Memoranda in Regard to Several Hundred Emigrants to Virginia During the Colonial Period Whose Parentage is Shown or Former Residence Indicated by Authentic Records
by William Glover Stanard (Originally published in 1911; Reprint: Baltimore: Genealogical Publishing Co., 1979)

They Became Americans: Finding Naturalization Records and Ethnic Origins
by Loretto Dennis Szucs (Salt Lake City: Ancestry, Inc., 1998)

They Came in Ships: A Guide to Finding Your Immigrant Ancestor's Arrival Records, 2d ed.
by John P. Colletta (Salt Lake City: Ancestry, Inc., 1993)

Virginia Gleanings in England: Abstracts of 17th and 18th Century English Wills and Administrations Relating to Virginia and Virginians
by Lathrop Withington (Baltimore: Genealogical Publishing, 1980)

■ LAND RECORDS

Abstract of Land Grant Surveys, 1761–1791
by Peter Cline Kaylor (Baltimore: Clearfield Co., 1991)

Cavaliers and Pioneers: Abstracts of Virginia Land Patents and Grants, 5 vols.
edited by Dennis Hudgins (Richmond: Virginia Genealogical Society, 1994)

Land and Property Research in the United States
by Wade E. Hone (Salt Lake City: Ancestry Inc., 1997)

Locating Your Roots: Discover Your Ancestors Using Land Records
by Patricia Law Hatcher (Cincinnati: Betterway Books, 2003)

Master Index to Virginia Surveys and Grants, 1774–1791
by Joan E. Brookes-Smith (Frankfort: Kentucky Historical Society, 1976)

Mother Earth—Land Grants in Virginia, 1607–1699
by W. Stitt Robinson (Williamsburg: 350th Anniversary Celebration Corp., 1957)

Old Rights, Property Rights, Virginia Entries and Soldiers Entitled to Donation Lands
by William Henry Egle (Harrisburg, VA: C.M. Busch, State Printer, 1896)

Turff and Twigg: The French Lands
by Priscilla Harriss Cabell (Richmond, VA: Priscilla Harriss Cabell, 1988)

Virginia Land Records: From the Virginia Magazine of History and Biography, the William and Mary College Quarterly, and Tyler's Quarterly
by Gary Parks (Baltimore: Genealogical Publishing Co., 1982)

Virginia Soldiers of 1776, Compiled from Documents on File in the Virginia Land Office, 3 vols.
compiled and edited by Louis A. Burgess (Spartanburg, SC: Reprint Co., 1973)

War of 1812 Virginia Bounty Land and Pension Applicants
by Patrick G. Wardell (Bowie, MD: Heritage Books, 1987)

■ MAPS

Approved Place Names in Virginia
by Mary Topping (Charlottesville, VA: University Press of Virginia, 1971)

Atlas of County Boundary Changes in Virginia, 1634–1895
by Michael F. Doran (Athens, GA: Iberian Publishing, 1987)

The Cartography of Northern Virginia: Facsimile Reproductions of Maps Dating From 1608 to 1915
by Richard W. Stephenson (Fairfax, VA: Fairfax County, Virginia, 1981)

A Gazetteer of Virginia and West Virginia
by Henry Gannett (Baltimore: Genealogical Publishing Co., 1975)

A Historical Atlas of Colonial Virginia
by John S. Hale (Staunton, VA: Old Dominion Publications, 1978)

How Justice Grew: Virginia Counties and Abstracts of Their Formation
by Martha W. Hiden (Charlottesville: University Press Of Virginia, 1957; Reprint: Baltimore: Clearfield Co., 1992)

Index of Kentucky and Virginia Maps, 1562 to 1900
by James W. Sames III (Frankfurt, KY: Kentucky Historical Society, 1976)

A New and Comprehensive Gazetteer of Virginia and the District of Columbia
by Joseph Martin (Charlottesville: J. Martin, 1835)

Virginia Atlas and Gazetteer
(Freeport, ME: Delorme Mapping Co., 1995)

Virginia Place Names
by Raus McDill Hanson (Verona, VA: McClure Press, 1969)

Virginia Postmasters and Post Offices, 1789–1832
by Edith F. Axelson (Athens, GA: Iberian Pub. Co., 1991)

■ MILITARY RECORDS

A Calendar of the Warrants for Land in Kentucky, Granted for Service in the French and Indian War
by Philip F. Taylor (Originally published in 1917; Reprint: Baltimore: Genealogical Publishing Company, 1967)

Catalogue of Revolutionary Soldiers and Sailors of the Commonwealth of Virginia: To Whom Land Bounty Warrants Were Granted By Virginia for Military Service in the War for Independence
by Samuel Mackay Wilson (Baltimore: Genealogical Publishing Co., 1967)

Gold Star Honor Roll of Virginians in The Second World War
edited by W. Edwin Hemphill (Charlottesville, VA: Virginia World War II History Commission, 1947)

A Guide to Virginia Military Organizations, 1860–1865
by Lee A. Wallace (Lynchburg, VA: H.E. Howard, 1986)

Guide to Virginia Militia Units in the War of 1812
by Stuart Lee Butler (Athens, GA: Iberian Publishing Co., 1988)

Historical Register of Virginians in the Revolution: Soldiers, Sailors, Marines: 1775–1783
by John H. Gwathmey (Richmond, VA: Deitz Press, 1938; Reprint: Baltimore: Genealogical Publishing Co., 1973)

Index to Saffell's List of Virginia Soldiers in the Revolution
by Joseph T. McCallister (Hot Springs, VA: McAllister Publishing Co., 1913)

List of the Colonial Soldiers of Virginia
by H.J. Eckenrod (Originally published in 1905; Reprint: Baltimore: Genealogical Publishing Co., 1974)

Virginia

List of the Revolutionary Soldiers of Virginia
by H.J. Eckenrod (Richmond: D. Bottom, 1912)

Old Rights, Property Rights, Virginia Entries and Soldiers Entitled to Donation Lands
by William Henry Egle (Harrisburg, VA: C.M. Busch, State Printer, 1896)

Revolutionary War Records: Virginia Army And Navy Forces with Bounty Land Warrants for Virginia Military District of Ohio and Virginia Scrip, From Federal and State Archives
by Gaius M. Brumbaugh (Originally published in 1936; Reprint: Baltimore: Genealogical Publishing Co., 1967)

Soldiers Of the Great War, 3 vols.
compiled by W.M. Haulsee, F.G. Howe, and A.C. Doyle (Washington, DC: Soldiers Records Publishing Association, 1920)

Uncle, We Are Ready! Registering America's Men, 1917–1918: A Guide to Researching World War I Draft Registration Cards
by John J. Newman (North Salt Lake, UT: HeritageQuest, 2001)

U.S. Military Records: A Guide to Federal & State Sources, Colonial America to the Present
by James C. Neagles (Salt Lake City: Ancestry, Inc., 1994)

Virginia Colonial Militia, 1651–1776
by William Armstrong Crozier (Originally published in 1905; Reprint: Baltimore: Genealogical Publishing Co., 1982)

Virginia's Colonial Soldiers
by Lloyd DeWitt Bockstruck (Baltimore: Genealogical Publishing Co., 1988)

Virginia Military Records: From the Virginia Magazine of History And Biography, the William and Mary College Quarterly, and Tyler's Quarterly
(Baltimore: Genealogical Publishing, 1983)

Virginia Public Claims, 3 vols.
by Janice L. Abercrombie (Athens, GA: Iberian Publishing Co., 1992)

Virginia Regimental History Series
by H.E. Howard (Lynchburg, VA: H.E. Howard, 1982)

Virginia Revolutionary War State Pensions
(Easley, SC: Southern Historical Press, 1982)

Virginia Soldiers in the United States Army, 1800–1815
by Stuart Lee Butler (Atlanta: Iberian Publishing Co., 1986)

War of 1812: Virginia Bounty Land and Pension Applications
by Patrick G. Wardell (Bowie, MD: Heritage Books 1987)

World War II: A Family Historian's Guide
by Debra Johnson Knox (Spartanburg, SC: MIE Publishing, 2003)

■ PROBATE RECORDS

Chronicles of the Scotch-Irish Settlement in Virginia: Extracted form the Original Court Records of Augusta County, 1754–1800, 3 vols.
by Lyman Chalkey (Originally published in 1912; Reprint: Baltimore: Genealogical Publishing, 1980)

Hanover county Chancery Wills and Notes: A Compendium of Genealogical, Biographical and Historical Material as Contained in Cases of the Chancery Suits Of Hanover County, Virginia
by William Ronald Crocke (Originally published in 1940; Reprint: Baltimore: Genealogical Publishing Co., 1978)

Minutes of the Council and General Court of Colonial Virginia
by H.R. McIlwaine (Richmond: Virginia State Library, 1979)

Some Wills from Burned Counties of Virginia and Other Wills Not Listed in the Virginia Wills and Administrations, 1632–1800
by William Lindsay Hopkins (Richmond, VA: W.L. Hopkins, 1987)

Virginia Settlers and English Adventurers: Abstracts of Wills, 1484–1798, and Legal Proceedings, 1560–1700, Relating to Early Virginia Families, 3 vols.
by Noel Currier-Briggs (Baltimore: Genealogical Publishing Co., 1970)

Virginia Wills and Administrations 1632–1800: An Index of Wills Recorded in Local Courts of Virginia, 1632–1800, and of Administration on Estates Shown By Inventories of the Estates of Intestates Recorded in Will (and Other) Books of Local Courts, 1632–1800
by Clayton Torrence (Originally published in 1931; Reprint: Baltimore: Genealogical Publishing Co., 1985)

Virginia Wills Before 1799: A Complete Abstract Register of All Names Mentioned in Over Six Hundred Recorded Wills
compiled by William Montgomery Clemens (Pompton Lakes, NJ: Biblio Co., 1924)

Virginia Will Records
by Judith McGhan (Baltimore: Genealogical Publishing, 1982)

Will and Estate Records In the Virginia State Library: A Researcher's Guide
by John Vogt and T. William Kethley Jr. (Athens, GA: Iberian Publishing Co., 1987)

■ VITAL RECORDS

Early Virginia Marriages
by William A. Crozier (Baltimore: Genealogical Publishing Co., 1982)

Index to Obituary Notices in the Richmond Enquirer from May 9, 1804 through 1828, and the Richmond Whig from January 1824 to 1838
by H.R. McIlwaine (Originally published in 1921; Reprint: Baltimore: Genealogical Publishing, 1974)

Marriage Records in the Virginia State Library: A Researcher's Guide
by John Vogt and T. William Kethley (Athens, GA: Iberian Press, 1984)

Marriages of Some Virginia Residents, 1607–1800, 2 vols.
by Dorothy F. Wulfeck (Baltimore: Genealogical Publishing Co., 1986)

Some Marriages in the Burned Record Counties of Virginia
(Richmond: Virginia Genealogical Society, 1979)

Some Virginia Marriages, 1700–1799, 25 vols.
by Cecil D. McDonald (Seattle: Cecil D. McDonald, 1972)

Some Virginia Marriages, 1800–1825, 12 vols.
by Cecil D. McDonald (Seattle: Cecil D. McDonald, 1973)

Some Virginia Marriages, 1826–1850, 2 vols.
by Ransom B. True (Seattle: Cecil D. McDonald, 1975)

Tombstone Inscriptions (Virginia), 9 vols.
by Duane L. Borden (Ozark, MO: Yates Pub. Co., 1986)

Virginia Cemeteries: A Guide to Resources
by Anne M. Hogg and Dennis A. Tosh. (Charlottesville: University of Virginia, 1986)

Virginia Marriage Records: From the Virginia Magazine of History And Biography, the William and Mary's College Quarterly, and The Tyler's Quarterly
(Baltimore: Genealogical Publishing Co., 1982)

Virginia Vital Records: From the Virginia Magazine of History and Biography, the William and Mary's College Quarterly, and the Tyler's Quarterly
(Baltimore: Genealogical Publishing Co., 1982)

Your Guide to Cemetery Research
by Sharon DeBartolo Carmack (Cincinnati: Betterway Books, 2002)

Virginia

■ **Accomac Shire** 1634
Parent County: Original Shire
Comments/research tips: (See Northampton) Name changed to Northampton 1642.

■ **Accomack** 1663
P.O. Box 126, Courthouse Rd., Accomac, VA 23301
Phone: (757)787-5776
Web site: www.co.accomack.va.us
Parent County: Accomac Shire
Comments/research tips: Clerk of Circuit Court has Birth records 1853–1896, Death records 1853–1871, and Military records 1823–1849, 1861–1865, and 1917–1967.

Record Type	Year Begun	Jurisdiction
Marriage	1774	Clerk/Circuit Ct.
Divorce	1848	Clerk/Circuit Ct.
Land	1663	Clerk/Circuit Ct.
Probate	1663	Clerk/Circuit Ct.
Court	1666	Clerk/Circuit Ct.

■ **Albemarle** 6 May 1744
501 E. Jefferson St., Charlottesville, VA 22902
Phone: (434)972-4084
Web site: www.albemarle.org/
Parent County: Goochland, Louisa

Record Type	Year Begun	Jurisdiction
Birth	1852	Clerk/Circuit Ct.
Death	1853	Clerk/Circuit Ct.
Marriage	1780	Clerk/Circuit Ct.
Divorce	1848	Clerk/Circuit Ct.
Land	1748	Clerk/Circuit Ct.
Probate	1748	Clerk/Circuit Ct.
Court	1744	Clerk/Circuit Ct.

■ **Alexandria (Ind. City)** 11 May 1749
520 King St. Suite 307, Alexandria , VA 22314
Phone: (703)838-4550
Web site: www.rootsweb.com/~vacalexa/alex1.htm
Parent County: Fairfax
Comments/research tips: Clerk of Circuit Court has Naturalization records 1909–1920. Alexandria was part of Fairfax County 1749–1801. Part of District of Columbia 1801–1847. Incorporated as a city in 1852. Alexandria is an independent city government.

Record Type	Year Begun	Jurisdiction
Birth	1853	Alexandria Health Center
Marriage	1870	Clerk/Circuit Ct.
Death	1863	Alexandria Health Center
Divorce	1870	Clerk/Circuit Ct.
Land	1783	Clerk/Circuit Ct.
Probate	1786	Clerk/Circuit Ct.
Court	1785	Clerk/Circuit Ct.

■ **Alleghany** 5 Jan. 1822
266 W. Main St., Covington, VA 24426
Phone: (540)965-1730
Web site: www.co.alleghany.va.us
Parent County: Bath, Botetourt, Monroe, West Virginia
Comments/research tips: Clerk of Circuit Court has Naturalization records 1908–1929.

Record Type	Year Begun	Jurisdiction
Marriage	1822	Clerk/Circuit Ct.
Divorce	1881	Clerk/Circuit Ct.
Land	1822	Clerk/Circuit Ct.
Probate	1822	Clerk/Circuit Ct.
Court	1822	Clerk/Circuit Ct.
Birth	1833	Clerk/Circuit Ct.
Death	1853	Clerk/Circuit Ct.

■ **Amelia** 1 Feb. 1734
16441 Court St., P.O. Box 237, Amelia Court House, VA 23002
Phone: (804)561-2128
Web site: www.rootsweb.com/~vaamelia/
Parent County: Brunswick, Prince George
Comments/research tips: Clerk of Circuit Court has Military records 1861–1865 and 1918–1966.

Record Type	Year Begun	Jurisdiction
Marriage	1735	Clerk/Circuit Ct.
Divorce	1848	Clerk/Circuit Ct.
Land	1734	Clerk/Circuit Ct.
Probate	1734	Clerk/Circuit Ct.
Court	1735	Clerk/Circuit Ct.
Birth	1853	Clerk/Circuit Ct.
Death	1853	Clerk/Circuit Ct.

■ **Amherst** Mar. 1761
P.O. Box 462, 113 Taylor St., Amherst, VA 24521
Phone: (434)946-9321
Web site: www.rootsweb.com/~vaamhers/
Parent County: Albemarle
Comments/research tips: Library of Virginia has Birth and Death records 1853–1896.

Record Type	Year Begun	Jurisdiction
Marriage	1763	Clerk/Circuit Ct.
Divorce	1761	Clerk/Circuit Ct.
Land	1761	Clerk/Circuit Ct.
Probate	1761	Clerk/Circuit Ct.
Court	1761	Clerk/Circuit Ct.
Birth	1912	Library of Virginia
Death	1912	Library of Virginia

■ **Appomattox** 8 Feb. 1845
P.O. Box 672, Appomattox, VA 24522
Phone: (434)352-5275
Web site: www.rootsweb.com/~vaappoma
Parent County: Buckingham, Campbell, Charlotte, Prince Edward
Comments/research tips: Birth and Death records held at the Library of Virginia.

Record Type	Year Begun	Jurisdiction
Marriage	1854	Clerk/Circuit Ct.
Divorce	1892	Clerk/Circuit Ct.
Land	1892	Clerk/Circuit Ct.
Probate	1892	Clerk/Circuit Ct.
Court	1892	Clerk/Circuit Ct.

■ **Arlington** 13 Mar. 1847
1425 N. Court House Rd., Arlington, VA 22201
Phone: (703)228-7010

Web site: www.co.arlington.va.us/homepage/default.asp
Parent County: Fairfax
Comments/research tips: Formerly Alexandria County. Name changed to Arlington 16 March 1920. Founded as Alexandria VA in 1789. In 1802 county became part of District of Columbia. In 1847 county rejoined Virginia. In 1920 changed name to Arlington.

Record Type	Year Begun	Jurisdiction
Birth	1853	Library of Virginia
Marriage	1801	Clerk/Circuit Ct.
Death	1853	Library of Virginia
Land	1801	Clerk/Circuit Ct.
Probate	1800	Clerk/Circuit Ct.
Court	1783	Clerk/Circuit Ct.

■ Augusta 1 Apr. 1738
6 E. Johnson St., Staunton, VA 24401
Phone: (540)245-5321
Web site: www.co.augusta.va.us/
Parent County: Orange
Comments/research tips: Clerk of Circuit Court has Birth records 1853–1896, Death records 1853–1912, Military records 1756–1796, 1807–1812, and 1861–1865, Naturalization records 1753–1902, Property Tax records 1800–1851, and Court Claims 1782–1785.

Record Type	Year Begun	Jurisdiction
Marriage	1785	Clerk/Circuit Ct.
Land	1745	Clerk/Circuit Ct.
Probate	1745	Clerk/Circuit Ct.
Court	1745	Clerk/Circuit Ct.

■ Barbour 3 Mar. 1843
Web site: www.rootsweb.com/~wvbarbou/
Comments/research tips: (See West Virginia) County formed from Harrison, Lewis, and Randolph Counties. Became part of West Virginia in 1863.

■ Bath 14 Dec. 1790
P.O. Box 180, Warm Springs, VA 24484
Phone: (540)839-7226
Web site: www.bathcountyva.org/
Parent County: Augusta, Botetourt, Greenbrier (West Virginia)
Comments/research tips: Clerk of Circuit Court has Birth and Death records 1853–1870 and Military records 1917–1918.

Record Type	Year Begun	Jurisdiction
Divorce	1791	Clerk/Circuit Ct.
Land	1791	Clerk/Circuit Ct.
Probate	1791	Clerk/Circuit Ct.
Court	1791	Clerk/Circuit Ct.
Marriage	1791	Clerk/Circuit Ct.

■ Bedford 13 Dec. 1753
123 E. Main St., Bedford, VA 24523
Phone: (540)586-7632
Web site: www.co.bedford.va.us/
Parent County: Albemarle, Lunenburg
Comments/research tips: Clerk of Circuit Court has Birth

records 1853–1897, Death records 1853–1917, and Military records 1861–1865 and 1917–1918.

Record Type	Year Begun	Jurisdiction
Marriage	1755	Clerk/Circuit Ct.
Divorce	1754	Clerk/Circuit Ct.
Land	1754	Clerk/Circuit Ct.
Probate	1754	Clerk/Circuit Ct.
Court	1753	Clerk/Circuit Ct.

■ Bedford (Ind. City) 1969
123 E. Main St., Bedford, VA 24523
Phone: (540)586-7632
Web site: www.ci.bedford.va.us
Parent County: Bedford
Comments/research tips: Established 1782 as Liberty. Name changed to Bedford City in 1890. Name changed to Bedford in 1912. Incorporated as a city in 1969. County seat of Bedford.

Record Type	Year Begun	Jurisdiction
Marriage	1969	Clerk/Circuit Ct.
Land	1969	Clerk/Circuit Ct.
Probate	1969	Clerk/Circuit Ct.
Court	1969	Clerk/Circuit Ct.

■ Berkeley 1772
Web site: www.rootsweb.com/~wvberkel/
Comments/research tips: (See West Virginia) Created from Frederick County, Virginia. Became part of West Virginia in November 1863.

■ Bland 30 Mar. 1861
1 Courthouse Sq., P.O. Box 295, Bland, VA 24315
Phone: (540)688-4562
Web site: www.rootsweb.com/~vabland/
Parent County: Giles, Tazewell, Wythe

Record Type	Year Begun	Jurisdiction
Marriage	1861	Clerk/Circuit Ct.
Divorce	1900	Clerk/Circuit Ct.
Land	1861	Clerk/Circuit Ct.
Probate	1861	Clerk/Circuit Ct.
Court	1861	Clerk/Circuit Ct.

■ Boone 11 Mar. 1847
Web site: www.rootsweb.com/~wvboone/
Comments/research tips: (See West Virginia) Formed from Cabell, Kanawha, and Logan Counties. Became part of West Virginia in 1863.

■ Botetourt 7 Nov. 1769
Main St., Box 219, Fincastle, VA 24090
Phone: (540)473-8274
Web site: co.botetourt.va.us/
Parent County: Augusta, Rockbridge
Comments/research tips: Clerk of Circuit Court has Birth and Death records 1853–1870.

Record Type	Year Begun	Jurisdiction
Marriage	1770	Clerk/Circuit Ct.
Divorce	1770	Clerk/Circuit Ct.
Land	1770	Clerk/Circuit Ct.

Probate .... 1770 .... Clerk/Circuit Ct.
Court .... 1770 .... Clerk/Circuit Ct.

■ Braxton 1786

Web site: www.rootsweb.com/~wvbraxto/
Comments/research tips: (See West Virginia) Became part of West Virginia in 1863.

■ Bristol (Ind. City) 12 Feb. 1890

497 Cumberland St., Bristol, VA 24201
Phone: (276)645-7321
Web site: www.bristolva.org/
Parent County: Washington
Comments/research tips: Bristol was known as Goodson 1850–1890. Incorporated as a city 12 February 1890.

Record Type	Year Begun	Jurisdiction
Marriage	1890	Clerk/Circuit Ct.
Divorce	1890	Clerk/Circuit Ct.
Land	1890	Clerk/Circuit Ct.
Probate	1890	Clerk/Circuit Ct.
Court	1890	Clerk/Circuit Ct.
Military	1890	Clerk/Circuit Ct.

■ Brooke 1794

Web site: www.rootsweb.com/~wvbrooke/index.htm
Parent County: Ohio
Comments/research tips: (See West Virginia) Became part of West Virginia in 1863.

■ Brunswick 2 Nov. 1720

216 N. Main St., Lawrenceville, VA 23868
Phone: (434)848-2215
Web site: www.rootsweb.com/~vabrunsw/
Parent County: Prince George, Isle of Wight, Surry
Comments/research tips: Clerk of Circuit Court has Birth records 1867–1896. County was not officially organized until 1732.

Record Type	Year Begun	Jurisdiction
Marriage	1750	Clerk/Circuit Ct.
Divorce	na	Clerk/Circuit Ct.
Land	1732	Clerk/Circuit Ct.
Probate	1732	Clerk/Circuit Ct.
Court	1732	Clerk/Circuit Ct.

■ Buchanan 13 Feb. 1858

P.O. Box 849, Grundy, VA 24614
Phone: (276)935-6567
Web site: www.silvermaple.net/buchanan/
Parent County: Russell, Tazewell
Comments/research tips: Courthouse burned in 1885.

Record Type	Year Begun	Jurisdiction
Marriage	1885	Clerk/Circuit Ct.
Divorce	1885	Clerk/Circuit Ct.
Land	1870	Clerk/Circuit Ct.
Probate	1874	Clerk/Circuit Ct.
Court	1885	Clerk/Circuit Ct.

■ Buckingham 1761

P.O. Box 252, Buckingham, VA 23921
Phone: (804)969-4242

Web site: www.rootsweb.com/~vabuckin/
Parent County: Albemarle
Comments/research tips: The courthouse and records were destroyed in 1869 fire.

Record Type	Year Begun	Jurisdiction
Court	1869	Clerk/Circuit Ct.
Birth	1896	Clerk/Circuit Ct.
Marriage	1869	Clerk/Circuit Ct.
Death	1896	Clerk/Circuit Ct.
Divorce	1869	Clerk/Circuit Ct.
Probate	1869	Clerk/Circuit Ct.

■ Buena Vista (Ind. City) 15 Feb. 1892

2039 Sycamore Ave., Buena Vista, VA 24416
Phone: (540)261-8627 ext. 127
Web site: www.buenavistavirginia.org
Parent County: Rockbridge
Comments/research tips: Clerk of Circuit Court has Military records 1926–1970.

Record Type	Year Begun	Jurisdiction
Marriage	1892	Clerk/Circuit Ct.
Divorce	1892	Clerk/Circuit Ct.
Land	1892	Clerk/Circuit Ct.
Probate	1892	Clerk/Circuit Ct.
Court	1892	Clerk/Circuit Ct.

■ Cabell 2 Jan. 1809

Web site: www.rootsweb.com/~wvcabell/cabell.htm
Parent County: Kanawha
Comments/research tips: (See West Virginia) Became part of West Virginia 20 June 1863.

■ Calhoun 5 Mar. 1856

Web site: www.rootsweb.com/~wvcalhou/index2.htm
Parent County: Gilmer
Comments/research tips: (See West Virginia)

■ Campbell 5 Nov. 1781

P.O. Box 7, Rustburg, VA 24588
Phone: (434)332-9517
Web site: www.co.campbell.va.us/index.htm
Parent County: Bedford
Comments/research tips: Clerk of Circuit Court has Birth records 1853–1865 and 1912–1932, Death records 1853–1865 and 1912–1930, and Military records 1854, 1855, 1917–1919, and 1953–1980.

Record Type	Year Begun	Jurisdiction
Probate	1782	Clerk/Circuit Ct.
Court	1782	Clerk/Circuit Ct.
Marriage	1782	Clerk/Circuit Ct.
Divorce	1782	Clerk/Circuit Ct.
Land	1782	Clerk/Circuit Ct.

■ Caroline 1728

Main & Courthouse Ln., P.O. Box 309, Bowling Green, VA 22427
Phone: (804)633-5800
Web site: www.co.caroline.va.us/
Parent County: Essex, King and Queen, King William

Comments/research tips: Clerk of Circuit Court has Birth records 1864–1867 and Death records 1865–1867.

Record Type	Year Begun	Jurisdiction
Marriage	1786	Clerk/Circuit Ct.
Military	1918	Clerk/Circuit Ct.
Divorce	1848	Clerk/Circuit Ct.
Land	1777	Clerk/Circuit Ct.
Probate	1742	Clerk/Circuit Ct.
Court	1732	Clerk/Circuit Ct.

■ Carroll 17 Jan. 1842

605 Pine St., P.O. Box 218, Hillsville, VA 24343
Phone: (276)728-3117
Web site: www.co.carroll.va.us/
Parent County: Grayson, Patrick
Comments/research tips: Clerk of Circuit Court has Death records 1855–1896.

Record Type	Year Begun	Jurisdiction
Court	1842	Clerk/Circuit Ct.
Marriage	1853	Clerk/Circuit Ct.
Divorce	1848	Clerk/Circuit Ct.
Land	1842	Clerk/Circuit Ct.
Probate	1842	Clerk/Circuit Ct.

■ Charles City 1634

P.O. Box 86, Charles City, VA 23030
Phone: (804)829-9212
Web site: www.co.charles-city.va.us
Parent County: Original shire
Comments/research tips: Clerk of Circuit Court has Birth and Death records 1853–1896 and Military records 1861–1865. County Center for local history has microfilmed vital records: (804) 829-5609.

Record Type	Year Begun	Jurisdiction
Court	1650	Clerk/Circuit Ct.
Marriage	1762	Clerk/Circuit Ct.
Land	1655	Clerk/Circuit Ct.

■ Charles River 1634

Web site: www.yorkcounty.gov
Parent County: Original Shire
Comments/research tips: (See York) Name changed to York 1643.

■ Charlotte 26 May 1764

115 LaGrande Ave., P.O. Box 38, Charlotte Court House, VA 23923
Phone: (804)542-5147
Web site: www.rootsweb.com/~vacharlo/indexcha.htm
Parent County: Lunenburg
Comments/research tips: Clerk of Circuit Court has Military records 1811–1822 and 1860–1868.

Record Type	Year Begun	Jurisdiction
Marriage	1765	Clerk/Circuit Ct.
Divorce	1848	Clerk/Circuit Ct.
Land	1765	Clerk/Circuit Ct.
Probate	1765	Clerk/Circuit Ct.
Court	1765	Clerk/Circuit Ct.

■ Charlottesville (Ind. City) 1762

315 E. High St., Charlottesville, VA 22901
Phone: (434)970-3766
Web site: www.charlottesville.org
Parent County: Albemarle
Comments/research tips: Established in 1762 and incorporated as a city in 1888. County seat of Albemarle County.

Record Type	Year Begun	Jurisdiction
Marriage	na	Clerk/Circuit Ct.
Land	na	Clerk/Circuit Ct.
Probate	na	Clerk/Circuit Ct.

■ Chesapeake (Ind. City) 1 Jan. 1963

307 Albemarle Dr. Suite 300A, Chesapeake, VA 23322
Phone: (757)382-3000
Web site: www.chesapeake.va.us
Parent County: Norfolk
Comments/research tips: Formerly Norfolk County. Norfolk County merged with city of South Norfolk to create Chesapeake 1 January 1963.

Record Type	Year Begun	Jurisdiction
Marriage	1850	Dept./Health
Divorce	1850	Clerk/Circuit Ct.
Land	1637	Clerk/Circuit Ct.
Probate	1637	Clerk/Circuit Ct.

■ Chesterfield 1 May 1749

9500 Courthouse Rd., P.O. Box 125, Chesterfield, VA 23832
Phone: (804)748-1241
Web site: www.co.chesterfield.va.us/
Parent County: Henrico
Comments/research tips: Clerk of Circuit Court has Military records for 1812 and 1861–1865.

Record Type	Year Begun	Jurisdiction
Marriage	1770	Clerk/Circuit Ct.
Divorce	1848	Clerk/Circuit Ct.
Land	1749	Clerk/Circuit Ct.
Probate	1749	Clerk/Circuit Ct.
Court	1749	Clerk/Circuit Ct.

■ Clarke 8 Mar. 1836

102 N. Church St., P.O. Box 189, Berryville, VA 22611
Phone: (540)955-5116
Web site: www.co.clarke.va.us/
Parent County: Frederick, Warren
Comments/research tips: Clerk of Circuit Court has Military records 1861–1865.

Record Type	Year Begun	Jurisdiction
Marriage	1836	Clerk/Circuit Ct.
Divorce	1848	Clerk/Circuit Ct.
Land	1836	Clerk/Circuit Ct.
Probate	1836	Clerk/Circuit Ct.
Court	1836	Clerk/Circuit Ct.

■ Clay 1858

Web site: www.rootsweb.com/~wvclay/
Parent County: Braxton, Nicholas, Kanawha
Comments/research tips: (See West Virginia)

Virginia

■ Clifton Forge (Ind. City) 1906

266 W. Main St., P.O. Box 670, Covington, VA 24426
Phone: (540)965-1730
Web site: www.ci.clifton-forge.va.us
Parent County: Alleghany
Comments/research tips: Clifton Forge records are kept in Alleghany County Circuit Court.

Record Type	Year Begun	Jurisdiction
Marriage	1906	Clerk/Circuit Ct.
Divorce	1906	Clerk/Circuit Ct.
Land	1906	Clerk/Circuit Ct.
Probate	1906	Clerk/Circuit Ct.

■ Colonial Heights (Ind. City) 1960

401 Temple Ave., Colonial Heights, VA 23834
Phone: (804)520-9364
Web site: www.colonial-heights.com
Parent County: Chesterfield
Comments/research tips: Incorporated as a town in 1926, incorporated as a city in 1948, and became an independent city in 1960.

Record Type	Year Begun	Jurisdiction
Marriage	1961	Clerk/Circuit Ct.
Divorce	1961	Clerk/Circuit Ct.
Land	1961	Clerk/Circuit Ct.
Probate	1961	Clerk/Circuit Ct.
Court	1961	Clerk/Circuit Ct.

■ Covington (Ind. City) 1952

266 W. Main St., P.O. Box 670, Covington, VA 24426
Phone: (540)965-1730
Web site: www.covington.va.us
Parent County: Alleghany
Comments/research tips: Established in 1819. Incorporated as a town 1873. Incorporated as a city 1952. County seat of Alleghany County.

Record Type	Year Begun	Jurisdiction
Marriage	na	Clerk/Circuit Ct.
Land	na	Clerk/Circuit Ct.
Probate	na	Clerk/Circuit Ct.

■ Craig 21 Mar. 1851

303 Main St., New Castle, VA 24127
Phone: (540)864-6141
Web site: www.co.craig.va.us/
Parent County: Botetourt, Giles, Roanoke, Monroe (West Virginia), Montgomery, Alleghany
Comments/research tips: Clerk of Circuit Court has Birth and Death records 1864–1869 and Military records 1861–1865 and 1917–1918.

Record Type	Year Begun	Jurisdiction
Marriage	1865	Clerk/Circuit Ct.
Divorce	1848	Clerk/Circuit Ct.
Land	1851	Clerk/Circuit Ct.
Probate	1851	Clerk/Circuit Ct.
Court	1851	Clerk/Circuit Ct.

■ Culpeper 23 Mar. 1748

135 W. Cameron St., Culpeper, VA 22701
Phone: (540)727-3438

Web site: www.rootsweb.com/~vaculpep/culp.htm
Parent County: Orange
Comments/research tips: Clerk of Circuit Court has Birth records 1864–1896 and 1912–1917 and Death records 1864–1896.

Record Type	Year Begun	Jurisdiction
Marriage	1781	Clerk/Circuit Ct.
Land	1749	Clerk/Circuit Ct.
Probate	1749	Clerk/Circuit Ct.
Court	1763	Clerk/Circuit Ct.

■ Cumberland 1749

County Courthouse, P.O. Box 8, Cumberland, VA 23040
Phone: (804)492-4442
Web site: www.rootsweb.com/~vacumber/
Parent County: Goochland
Comments/research tips: Clerk of Circuit Court has Birth records 1853–1872 and Death records 1853–1885.

Record Type	Year Begun	Jurisdiction
Land	1749	Clerk/Circuit Ct.
Marriage	1749	Clerk/Circuit Ct.
Divorce	1848	Clerk/Circuit Ct.
Probate	1749	Clerk/Circuit Ct.
Court	1749	Clerk/Circuit Ct.

■ Danville (Ind. City) 1890

401 Patton St., P.O. Box 3300, Danville, VA 24543
Phone: (434)799-5168
Web site: www.danville-va.gov/home.asp
Parent County: Pittsylvania
Comments/research tips: Established in 1793, incorporated as a town in 1830, and incorporated as a city in 1890.

Record Type	Year Begun	Jurisdiction
Marriage	1841	Clerk/Circuit Ct.
Divorce	1860	Clerk/Circuit Ct.
Land	1841	Clerk/Circuit Ct.
Probate	1841	Clerk/Circuit Ct.
Court	1859	Clerk/Circuit Ct.

■ Dickenson 3 Mar. 1880

P.O. Box 190, Clintwood, VA 24228
Phone: (276)926-1616
Web site: www.dickensoncty.va.com/
Parent County: Buchanan, Russell, Wise

Record Type	Year Begun	Jurisdiction
Birth	1912	Dept./Health/Library of VA
Marriage	1880	Clerk/Circuit Ct.
Death	1912	Dept./Health/Library of VA
Divorce	1880	Clerk/Circuit Ct.
Land	1880	Clerk/Circuit Ct.
Probate	1880	Clerk/Circuit Ct.
Court	1880	Clerk/Circuit Ct.

■ Dinwiddie 27 Feb. 1752

P.O. Box 63, Dinwiddie, VA 23841
Phone: (804)469-4540
Web site: www.rootsweb.com/~vadinwid/
Parent County: Prince George
Comments/research tips: Clerk of Circuit Court has Birth and Death records 1865–1896.

Record Type	Year Begun	Jurisdiction
Marriage	1850	Clerk/Circuit Ct.
Divorce	1832	Clerk/Circuit Ct.
Land	1833	Clerk/Circuit Ct.
Probate	1758	Clerk/Circuit Ct.
Court	1819	Clerk/Circuit Ct.

■ Doddridge 1845
Web site: www.rootsweb.com/~wvdoddri/
Parent County: Harrison, Tyler, Ritchie, Lewis
Comments/research tips: (See West Virginia)

■ Dunmore 24 Mar. 1772
Web site: www.rootsweb.com/~vashenan/vashenan.html
Parent County: Frederick
Comments/research tips: (See Shenandoah) Name changed to Shenandoah 1 February 1778.

■ Elizabeth City 1634
Web site: www.rootsweb.com/~vaelizab/
Parent County: Original Shire
Comments/research tips: (See Hampton) Absorbed by Hampton July 1952.

■ Essex 16 Apr. 1692
P.O. Box 445, Tappahannock, VA 22560
Phone: (804)443-3541
Web site: www.co.essex.va.us
Parent County: Rappahannock, old
Comments/research tips: Clerk of Circuit Court has Birth and Death records 1856–1916, Military records 1861–1865, and the Probate records of Rappahannock 1654–1692.

Record Type	Year Begun	Jurisdiction
Marriage	1804	Clerk/Circuit Ct.
Divorce	1852	Clerk/Circuit Ct.
Land	1692	Clerk/Circuit Ct.
Probate	1692	Clerk/Circuit Ct.
Court	1692	Clerk/Circuit Ct.

■ Fairfax 6 May 1742
4110 Chain Bridge Rd., Fairfax, VA 22030
Phone: (703)246-4168
Web site: www.rootsweb.com/~vafairfa/
Parent County: Prince William
Comments/research tips: Clerk of Circuit Court has Birth records 1853–1897 and 1912–1917 and Military records 1861–1865.

Record Type	Year Begun	Jurisdiction
Marriage	1853	Clerk/Circuit Ct.
Divorce	1852	Clerk/Circuit Ct.
Land	1742	Clerk/Circuit Ct.
Probate	1742	Clerk/Circuit Ct.
Court	1749	Clerk/Circuit Ct.

■ Fairfax (Ind. City) 1961
4110 Chain Bridge Rd., Fairfax, VA 22030
Phone: (703)246-4168
Web site: www.ci.fairfax.va.us

Parent County: Fairfax
Comments/research tips: Established as Providence in 1805, name changed to Fairfax in 1859, incorporated as a town in 1874, and incorporated as a city in 1961. County seat of Fairfax County.

Record Type	Year Begun	Jurisdiction
Marriage	1961	Clerk/Circuit Ct.
Land	1961	Clerk/Circuit Ct.
Probate	1961	Clerk/Circuit Ct.

■ Falls Church (Ind. City) 1948
300 Park Ave., Falls Church, VA 22046
Phone: (703)241-5014
Web site: www.ci.falls-church.va.us
Parent County: Fairfax
Comments/research tips: Fairfax County Courthouse has records prior to 1988. Arlington County Courthouse has records after 1988. Established 1850. Incorporated as a town 1875. Incorporated as a city 1948.

Record Type	Year Begun	Jurisdiction
Birth	na	Clerk/Circuit Ct.
Marriage	1853	Clerk/Circuit Ct.
Divorce	1852	Clerk/Circuit Ct.
Land	1742	Clerk/Circuit Ct.
Probate	1850	Clerk/Circuit Ct.
Court	1749	Clerk/Circuit Ct.

■ Fauquier 1 May 1759
40 Culpeper St., Warrenton, VA 20186
Phone: (540)347-8610
Web site: www.fauquiercounty.gov
Parent County: Prince William
Comments/research tips: Clerk of Circuit Court has Birth and Death records 1853–1896 and Military Muster Rolls 1861–1865.

Record Type	Year Begun	Jurisdiction
Marriage	1759	Clerk/Circuit Ct.
Divorce	1831	Clerk/Circuit Ct.
Land	1759	Clerk/Circuit Ct.
Probate	1759	Clerk/Circuit Ct.
Court	1759	Clerk/Circuit Ct.

■ Fayette 1831
Parent County: Kanawha, Nicholas, Greenbrier, Logan
Comments/research tips: (See West Virginia) Two Counties, Fayette 1, split to Kentucky, and Fayette 2, split to West Virginia.

■ Fincastle 1772
Parent County: Botetourt
Comments/research tips: (See Montgomery) Discontinued 1776. Divided into Kentucky, Montgomery, and Washington Counties.

■ Floyd 15 Jan. 1831
100 E. Main St., Room 200, Floyd, VA 24091
Phone: (540)745-9330
Web site: www.fin.org/
Parent County: Montgomery, Franklin

Virginia

Comments/research tips: Clerk of Circuit Court has Military records 1861–1865 and 1916–1919.

Record Type	Year Begun	Jurisdiction
Marriage	1831	Clerk/Circuit Ct.
Divorce	1831	Clerk/Circuit Ct.
Land	1831	Clerk/Circuit Ct.
Probate	1831	Clerk/Circuit Ct.
Court	1828	Clerk/Circuit Ct.

■ Fluvanna 5 May 1777

P.O. Box 550, 132 Main St., Palmyra, VA 22963
Phone: (434)591-1970
Web site: www.co.fluvanna.va.us/
Parent County: Albemarle
Comments/research tips: Clerk of Circuit Court has Birth and Death records 1853–1896.

Record Type	Year Begun	Jurisdiction
Marriage	1777	Clerk/Circuit Ct.
Divorce	1831	Clerk/Circuit Ct.
Land	1777	Clerk/Circuit Ct.
Probate	1777	Clerk/Circuit Ct.
Court	1777	Clerk/Circuit Ct.

■ Franklin 17 Oct. 1785

P.O. Box 567, 275 S. Main St., Suite 212, Rocky Mount, VA 24151
Phone: (540)483-3065
Web site: www.franklincountyva.org/
Parent County: Bedford, Henry
Comments/research tips: Clerk of Circuit Court has Birth and Death records 1853–1896.

Record Type	Year Begun	Jurisdiction
Marriage	1785	Clerk/Circuit Ct.
Land	1786	Clerk/Circuit Ct.
Probate	1786	Clerk/Circuit Ct.
Court	1786	Clerk/Circuit Ct.

■ Franklin (Ind. City) 1961

P.O. Box 190, 22350 Main St., Courtland, VA 23837
Phone: (757)653-2200
Web site: www.franklinva.com
Parent County: Southampton
Comments/research tips: Southampton Clerk of Circuit Court has records. All records begin in 1961. Established in 1830s. Incorporated as a town in 1876. Incorporated as a city in 1961.

■ Frederick 1 Aug. 1738

5 N. Kent St., Winchester, VA 22601
Phone: (540)665-5659
Web site: www.co.frederick.va.us/
Parent County: Orange, Augusta
Comments/research tips: Clerk of Circuit Court has Birth records 1853–1912, Death records 1853–1896 and 1912–1917, and Military records 1796–1821 and 1861–1865. County government established in 1743.

Record Type	Year Begun	Jurisdiction
Marriage	1773	Clerk/Circuit Ct.
Divorce	1852	Clerk/Circuit Ct.
Land	1743	Clerk/Circuit Ct.
Probate	1743	Clerk/Circuit Ct.
Court	1743	Clerk/Circuit Ct.

■ Fredericksburg (Ind. City) 1879

815 Princess Anne St., P.O. Box 359, Fredericksburg, VA 22404
Phone: (540)372-1066
Web site: www.efredericksburg.com
Parent County: Spotsylvania
Comments/research tips: Library of Virginia has Birth and Death records 1853–1896. Clerk of Circuit Court has Marriage Bonds and Tombstone Inscriptions 1781–1850. City established in 1728 and incorporated as a town in 1782.

Record Type	Year Begun	Jurisdiction
Marriage	1850	Clerk/Circuit Ct.
Land	1782	Clerk/Circuit Ct.
Probate	1782	Clerk/Circuit Ct.
Court	1782	Clerk/Circuit Ct.

■ Galax (Ind. City) 1954

123 Main St. N., Galax, VA 24333
Phone: (276)728-3117
Parent County: Carroll, Grayson
Comments/research tips: Galax is on the line between Grayson and Carroll Counties, contact both counties for their records of Galax. Previously known as Bonaparte. Incorporated as a town in 1906 and as a city in 1954. Name changed to Galax in 1905. Established 1903.

■ Giles 16 Jan. 1806

501 Wenonah Ave, P.O. Box 502, Pearisburg, VA 24134
Phone: (540)921-1722
Web site: www.gilescounty.org/
Parent County: Montgomery, Monroe (West Virginia), Tazewell, Wythe, Mercer (West Virginia), Craig

Record Type	Year Begun	Jurisdiction
Marriage	1806	Clerk/Circuit Ct.
Divorce	1831	Clerk/Circuit Ct.
Land	1806	Clerk/Circuit Ct.
Probate	1806	Clerk/Circuit Ct.
Court	1806	Clerk/Circuit Ct.

■ Gilmer 1845

Web site: www.rootsweb.com/~wvgilmer
Parent County: Lewis, Kanawha
Comments/research tips: (See West Virginia)

■ Gloucester 1651

P.O. Box 2118, 7400 Justice Dr., Room 327, Gloucester, VA 23061
Phone: (804)693-2502
Web site: www.gloucesterva.info
Parent County: York
Comments/research tips: Clerk of Circuit Court has Birth and Death records 1863–1890 and Military records from 1946–1976.

Record Type	Year Begun	Jurisdiction
Marriage	1853	Clerk/Circuit Ct.

Divorce	1865	Clerk/Circuit Ct.
Land	1733	Clerk/Circuit Ct.
Probate	1862	Clerk/Circuit Ct.
Court	1820	Clerk/Circuit Ct.

■ Goochland 1728
2938 River Rd. W., P.O. Box 196, Goochland, VA 23063
Phone: (804)556-5353
Web site: www.co.goochland.va.us/
Parent County: Henrico
Comments/research tips: Clerk of Circuit Court has Birth and Death records 1852–1901 and Military records 1861–1865.

Record Type	Year Begun	Jurisdiction
Marriage	1730	Clerk/Circuit Ct.
Divorce	1837	Clerk/Circuit Ct.
Land	1728	Clerk/Circuit Ct.
Probate	1728	Clerk/Circuit Ct.
Court	1728	Clerk/Circuit Ct.

■ Grayson 7 Nov. 1792
P.O. Box 130, 129 Davis St., Independence, VA 24348
Phone: (276)773-2231
Web site: www.ls.net/~newriver/va/grayson.htm
Parent County: Wythe, Patrick
Comments/research tips: Clerk of Circuit Court has Birth and Death records 1853–1870.

Record Type	Year Begun	Jurisdiction
Marriage	1793	Clerk/Circuit Ct.
Divorce	1832	Clerk/Circuit Ct.
Land	1793	Clerk/Circuit Ct.
Probate	1796	Clerk/Circuit Ct.
Court	1793	Clerk/Circuit Ct.

■ Greenbrier 1778
Web site: www.rootsweb.com/~wvgreenb/
Parent County: Montgomery, Botetourt
Comments/research tips: (See West Virginia)

■ Greene 24 Jan. 1838
Court Sq., P.O. Box 386, Stanardsville, VA 22973
Phone: (434)985-5208
Web site: www.ecojobs.com/greene/
Parent County: Orange
Comments/research tips: Clerk of Circuit Court has Birth records from 1853–1919 and Death records from 1853–1917.

Record Type	Year Begun	Jurisdiction
Marriage	1838	Clerk/Circuit Ct.
Divorce	1838	Clerk/Circuit Ct.
Land	1838	Clerk/Circuit Ct.
Probate	1838	Clerk/Circuit Ct.
Court	1838	Clerk/Circuit Ct.

■ Greensville 16 Oct. 1780
P.O. Box 631, 337 S. Main St., Emporia, VA 23847
Phone: (434)348-4215
Web site: www.greensvillecountyva.gov/
Parent County: Brunswick, Sussex

Comments/research tips: Clerk of Circuit Court has Birth and Death records 1853–1860.

Record Type	Year Begun	Jurisdiction
Marriage	1781	Clerk/Circuit Ct.
Divorce	1848	Clerk/Circuit Ct.
Land	1781	Clerk/Circuit Ct.
Probate	1781	Clerk/Circuit Ct.
Court	1781	Clerk/Circuit Ct.

■ Halifax 27 Feb. 1752
P.O. Box 729, Main St., Halifax, VA 24558
Phone: (804)476-6221
Web site: www.halifax.com/county/
Parent County: Lunenburg
Comments/research tips: Clerk of Circuit Court has Birth and Death records 1853–1871.

Record Type	Year Begun	Jurisdiction
Marriage	1753	Clerk/Circuit Ct.
Divorce	1831	Clerk/Circuit Ct.
Land	1752	Clerk/Circuit Ct.
Probate	1753	Clerk/Circuit Ct.
Court	1752	Clerk/Circuit Ct.

■ Hampshire 1754
Web site: www.rootsweb.com/~wvhampsh
Parent County: Frederick, Augusta
Comments/research tips: (See West Virginia)

■ Hampton (Ind. City) 1908
P.O. Box 40, 101 King's Way Mall, Hampton, VA 23669
Phone: (757)726-6997
Web site: www.hampton.va.us
Parent County: Elizabeth City
Comments/research tips: Established in 1680 and incorporated as a city in 1908. Merged with Elizabeth City and Phoebus in July 1952.

Record Type	Year Begun	Jurisdiction
Marriage	ca. 1890	Clerk/Circuit Ct.
Land	ca. 1890	Clerk/Circuit Ct.
Probate	ca. 1890	Clerk/Circuit Ct.
Court	ca. 1890	Clerk/Circuit Ct.

■ Hancock 1848
Web site: www.rootsweb.com/~wvhancoc/index.htm
Parent County: Brooke
Comments/research tips: (See West Virginia)

■ Hanover 2 Nov. 1720
7507 Library Dr., Hanover, VA 23069
Phone: (804)365-6120
Web site: www.co.hanover.va.us/
Parent County: New Kent
Comments/research tips: Clerk of Circuit Court has Birth records 1853–1879, Court and Land records 1733–1735 and 1783–1792, and Probate records 1733–1735.

Record Type	Year Begun	Jurisdiction
Marriage	1863	Clerk/Circuit Ct.
Divorce	1865	Clerk/Circuit Ct.

■ Hardy 1786
Web site: www.rootsweb.com/~wvhardy/
Parent County: Hampshire
Comments/research tips: (See West Virginia)

■ Harrison 1784
Web site: www.rootsweb.com/~wvharris
Parent County: Monongalia, Ohio
Comments/research tips: (See West Virginia)

■ Harrisonburg (Ind. City) 1916
Rockingham County Courthouse, Court Sq., Harrisonburg, VA 22801
Phone: (540)564-3111
Parent County: Rockingham
Comments/research tips: City Clerk has Birth and Death records 1862–1894. Established in 1780, incorporated as a town in 1849, and incorporated as a city in 1916. Many records dating before 1864 were destroyed in the Civil War.

Record Type	Year Begun	Jurisdiction
Marriage	1778	Clerk/Circuit Ct.
Land	1778	Clerk/Circuit Ct.
Probate	1778	Clerk/Circuit Ct.
Court	1778	Clerk/Circuit Ct.

■ Henrico 1634
4301 E. Parham Rd., P.O. Box 27032, Richmond, VA 23273
Phone: (804)501-4202
Web site: www.co.henrico.va.us/
Parent County: Original Shire
Comments/research tips: Clerk of Circuit Court has Birth and Death records 1853–1870.

Record Type	Year Begun	Jurisdiction
Marriage	1781	Clerk/Circuit Ct.
Divorce	1848	Clerk/Circuit Ct.
Land	1650	Clerk/Circuit Ct.
Probate	1650	Clerk/Circuit Ct.
Court	1650	Clerk/Circuit Ct.

■ Henry 7 Oct. 1776
3160 Kings Mountain Rd., Suite B, Martinsville, VA 24112
Phone: (540)634-4880
Web site: www.rootsweb.com/~vahenry
Parent County: Pittsylvania
Comments/research tips: Clerk of Circuit Court has Birth and Death records 1853–1871.

Record Type	Year Begun	Jurisdiction
Marriage	1778	Clerk/Circuit Ct.
Divorce	1909	Clerk/Circuit Ct.
Land	1777	Clerk/Circuit Ct.
Probate	1777	Clerk/Circuit Ct.
Court	1777	Clerk/Circuit Ct.

■ Highland 19 Mar. 1847
P.O. Box 190, Main St., Monterey, VA 24465
Phone: (540)468-2447
Web site: www.rootsweb.com/~vahighla/
Parent County: Bath, Pendleton (West Virginia)
Comments/research tips: Clerk of Circuit Court has Birth records from 1853–1878 and Death records 1853–1868.

Record Type	Year Begun	Jurisdiction
Marriage	1853	Clerk/Circuit Ct.
Divorce	1848	Clerk/Circuit Ct.
Land	1847	Clerk/Circuit Ct.
Probate	1859	Clerk/Circuit Ct.
Court	1847	Clerk/Circuit Ct.

■ Hopewell (Ind. City) 1911
P.O. Box 310, 100 E. Broadway, Room 251, Hopewell, VA 23860
Phone: (804)541-2239
Parent County: Prince George
Comments/research tips: Established in 1613 and incorporated as a city in 1916. Known as Citypoint until 1913.

Record Type	Year Begun	Jurisdiction
Marriage	1916	Clerk/Circuit Ct.
Divorce	1916	Clerk/Circuit Ct.
Land	1916	Clerk/Circuit Ct.
Probate	1916	Clerk/Circuit Ct.
Court	1916	Clerk/Circuit Ct.

■ Illinois 1778
Web site: www.rootsweb.com/~vagenweb/illinois.htm
Parent County: Augusta
Comments/research tips: Discontinued 1784 and became Northwest Territory.

■ Isle of Wight 1634
17122 Monument Circle, P.O. Box 77, Isle of Wight, VA 23397
Phone: (757)365-6233
Web site: www.co.isle-of-wight.va.us/
Parent County: Original Shire
Comments/research tips: Clerk of Circuit Court has Birth and Death records from 1853–1900. Formerly Warrosquyoake. Name changed to Isle of Wight 1637.

Record Type	Year Begun	Jurisdiction
Marriage	1772	Clerk/Circuit Ct.
Divorce	1853	Clerk/Circuit Ct.
Land	1636	Clerk/Circuit Ct.
Probate	1662	Clerk/Circuit Ct.
Court	1693	Clerk/Circuit Ct.

■ Jackson 1831
Web site: www.rootsweb.com/~wvjackso/JACK.HTM
Parent County: Kanawha, Mason, Wood
Comments/research tips: (See West Virginia)

■ James City 1634
5201 Monticello Ave., Suite 6, Williamsburg, VA 23188
Phone: (757)564-2242
Web site: www.james-city.va.us/
Parent County: Original Shire
Comments/research tips: All county court records prior to 1865 were lost.

Record Type	Year Begun	Jurisdiction
Marriage	1865	Clerk/Circuit Ct.

Divorce	1865	Clerk/Circuit Ct.
Land	1854	Clerk/Circuit Ct.
Probate	1865	Clerk/Circuit Ct.
Court	1865	Clerk/Circuit Ct.

■ Jefferson 1801
Web site: www.rootsweb.com/~wvjeffer
Parent County: Berkeley
Comments/research tips: (See West Virginia)

■ Kanawah 1789
Web site: www.rootsweb.com/~wvkanawh/
Parent County: Greenbriar, Montgomery
Comments/research tips: (See West Virginia)

■ Kentucky 1776
Web site: www.rootsweb.com/~vagenweb/kentucky.htm
Parent County: Fincastle
Comments/research tips: Discontinued 1780 and became Fayette, Jefferson, and Lincoln counties, Kentucky.

■ King & Queen 16 Apr. 1691
P.O. Box 67, King & Queen Courthouse, VA 23085
Phone: (804)785-5984
Web site: www.rootsweb.com/~vakingqu/kqmain.html
Parent County: New Kent

Record Type	Year Begun	Jurisdiction
Marriage	1867	Clerk/Circuit Ct.
Divorce	1831	Clerk/Circuit Ct.
Land	1719	Clerk/Circuit Ct.
Probate	1864	Clerk/Circuit Ct.
Court	1831	Clerk/Circuit Ct.
Birth	1865	Clerk/Circuit Ct.
Death	1865	Clerk/Circuit Ct.

■ King George 2 Nov. 1720
9483 Kings Hwy. #3, King George, VA 22485
Phone: (540)775-3322
Web site: www.king-george.va.us
Parent County: Richmond, Westmoreland
Comments/research tips: Clerk of Circuit Court has Birth records 1871–1917 and Military records 1824–1860.

Record Type	Year Begun	Jurisdiction
Marriage	1786	Clerk/Circuit Ct.
Divorce	1811	Clerk/Circuit Ct.
Land	1721	Clerk/Circuit Ct.
Probate	1721	Clerk/Circuit Ct.
Court	1721	Clerk/Circuit Ct.

■ King William 1701
P.O. Box 216, King William, VA 23086
Phone: (804)769-4936
Web site: www.co.king-william.va.us/
Parent County: King and Queen
Comments/research tips: Clerk of Circuit Court has Military records 1917–1919 and 1945–1946. Fire in 1855 burned most records, some records to 1702 have been photocopied.

Record Type	Year Begun	Jurisdiction
Marriage	1944	Clerk/Circuit Ct.

Divorce	1885	Clerk/Circuit Ct.
Land	1702	Clerk/Circuit Ct.
Probate	1885	Clerk/Circuit Ct.
Court	1702	Clerk/Circuit Ct.

■ Lancaster 1651
P.O. Box 99, Lancaster, VA 22503
Phone: (804)462-5611
Web site: www.lancova.com/
Parent County: Northumberland, York
Comments/research tips: Clerk of Circuit Court has Birth records 1853–1895 and Death records 1853–1885.

Record Type	Year Begun	Jurisdiction
Marriage	1715	Clerk/Circuit Ct.
Divorce	1831	Clerk/Circuit Ct.
Land	1652	Clerk/Circuit Ct.
Probate	1652	Clerk/Circuit Ct.
Court	1653	Clerk/Circuit Ct.

■ Lee 25 Oct. 1792
P.O. Box 326, Main St., Jonesville, VA 24263
Phone: (276)346-7763
Web site: www.rootsweb.com/~valee
Parent County: Russell, Scott
Comments/research tips: Clerk of Circuit Court has Birth and Death records from 1853–1877.

Record Type	Year Begun	Jurisdiction
Marriage	1830	Clerk/Circuit Ct.
Divorce	1832	Clerk/Circuit Ct.
Land	1793	Clerk/Circuit Ct.
Probate	1794	Clerk/Circuit Ct.
Court	1808	Clerk/Circuit Ct.

■ Lewis 1816
Web site: www.rootsweb.com/~wvlewis/
Parent County: Harrison, Randolph
Comments/research tips: (See West Virginia)

■ Lexington (Ind. City) 1965
2 S. Main St., Lexington, VA 24450
Phone: (540)463-2232
Web site: www.ci.lexington.va.us
Parent County: Rockbridge
Comments/research tips: Rockbridge County Clerk of Circuit Court has Birth records 1853–1896 and Military records 1861–1865. County seat of Rockbridge County. Established in 1778, incorporated as a town in 1874, and incorporated as a city in 1965.

Record Type	Year Begun	Jurisdiction
Court	1778	Clerk/Circuit Ct.
Divorce	1831	Clerk/Circuit Ct.
Marriage	1778	Clerk/Circuit Ct.
Land	1778	Clerk/Circuit Ct.
Probate	1778	Clerk/Circuit Ct.

■ Lincoln 1867
Web site: www.rootsweb.com/~wvlincol/
Parent County: Boone, Cabell, Kanawha
Comments/research tips: (See West Virginia)

Virginia

■ **Logan** 1824
Web site: www.rootsweb.com/~wvlogan/logan.htm
Parent County: Cabell, Kanawha, Giles, Tazewell
Comments/research tips: (See West Virginia)

■ **Loudoun** 25 Mar. 1757
P.O. Box 550, 18 E. Market St., Leesburg, VA 20178
Phone: (703)777-0270
Web site: www.co.loudoun.va.us/
Parent County: Fairfax
Comments/research tips: Clerk of Circuit Court has Birth
records 1853–1859 and 1864–1866, Death records
1853–1866, Military records 1793–1827, 1811–1860, and
1861–1865, and Naturalization records 1908–1910.

Record Type	Year Begun	Jurisdiction
Marriage	1760	Clerk/Circuit Ct.
Divorce	1831	Clerk/Circuit Ct.
Land	1757	Clerk/Circuit Ct.
Probate	1757	Clerk/Circuit Ct.
Court	1757	Clerk/Circuit Ct.

■ **Louisa** 6 May 1742
P.O. Box 37, Louisa, VA 23093
Phone: (540)967-5312
Web site: www.louisa-county.com/
Parent County: Hanover
Comments/research tips: Clerk of Circuit Court has Birth
records 1864–1871, Death records 1864–1870, and
Military records for 1814 and 1861–1865.

Record Type	Year Begun	Jurisdiction
Court	1742	Clerk/Circuit Ct.
Marriage	1766	Clerk/Circuit Ct.
Divorce	1844	Clerk/Circuit Ct.
Land	1742	Clerk/Circuit Ct.
Probate	1745	Clerk/Circuit Ct.

■ **Lower Norfolk** 1637
Parent County: New Norfolk
Comments/research tips: (See Princess Anne and Norfolk)
Abolished 1691 and divided between Princess Anne and
Norfolk Counties.

■ **Lunenburg** 6 May 1745
11435 Courthouse Rd., Lunenburg, VA 23952
Phone: (804)696-2230
Web site: www.rootsweb.com/~valunenb/
Parent County: Brunswick
Comments/research tips: Clerk of Circuit Court has Birth
records 1853–1889 and Death records 1853–1870.

Record Type	Year Begun	Jurisdiction
Marriage	1746	Clerk/Circuit Ct.
Divorce	1842	Clerk/Circuit Ct.
Land	1746	Clerk/Circuit Ct.
Probate	1746	Clerk/Circuit Ct.
Court	1746	Clerk/Circuit Ct.

■ **Lynchburg (Ind. City)** 1852
P.O. Box 4, 900 Church St., Lynchburg, VA 24504
Phone: (434)847-1590

Parent County: Campbell
Comments/research tips: Clerk of Circuit Court has Birth
and Death records 1853–1868 and Military records
1861–1865. Established in 1786, incorporated as a town in
1805, and incorporated as a city in 1852.

Record Type	Year Begun	Jurisdiction
Marriage	1805	Clerk/Circuit Ct.
Divorce	1814	Clerk/Circuit Ct.
Land	1805	Clerk/Circuit Ct.
Probate	1809	Clerk/Circuit Ct.
Court	1805	Clerk/Circuit Ct.

■ **Madison** 4 Dec. 1792
100 Court Sq., P.O. Box 220, Madison, VA 22727
Phone: (540)948-6888
Web site: www.madison-va.com
Parent County: Culpeper
Comments/research tips: Clerk of Circuit Court has Military
records for 1812 and 1861–1865.

Record Type	Year Begun	Jurisdiction
Marriage	1793	Clerk/Circuit Ct.
Divorce	1831	Clerk/Circuit Ct.
Land	1793	Clerk/Circuit Ct.
Probate	1793	Clerk/Circuit Ct.
Court	1793	Clerk/Circuit Ct.

■ **Manassas (Ind. City)** 1975
1 Park Center Pl., Manassas Park, VA 22111
Phone: (703)335-8800
Web site: www.manassascity.org
Comments/research tips: Established in 1852, incorporated
as a town in 1874, and incorporated as a city in 1975.
County Seat of Prince William County. Clerk of Circuit
Court has all records 1975 to the present.

■ **Manassas Park (Ind. City)** 1975
1 Park Center Pl., Manassas Park, VA 22111
Phone: (703)335-8800
Parent County: Manassas City
Comments/research tips: Established in 1955, incorporated
as a town in 1957, incorporated as a city in 1975. Cities of
Manassas and Manassas Park records are kept by the Prince
William County Clerk of Circuit Court with the same
address as Prince William County.

Record Type	Year Begun	Jurisdiction
Marriage	1975	Clerk/Circuit Ct.
Land	1975	Clerk/Circuit Ct.
Probate	1975	Clerk/Circuit Ct.
Court	1975	Clerk/Circuit Ct.
Divorce	1975	ClerkCircuit Ct.

■ **Marion** 1842
Parent County: Harrison, Monongalia
Comments/research tips: (See West Virginia)

■ **Marshall** 1835
Parent County: Ohio
Comments/research tips: (See West Virginia)

Virginia

■ Martinsville (Ind. City) 1928

P.O. Box 1206, 55 W. Church St., Martinsville, VA 24114
Phone: (276)403-5106
Web site: www.ci.martinsville.va.us
Parent County: Henry
Comments/research tips: Established in 1791, incorporated
as a town in 1873, and incorporated as a city in 1928.
County seat of Henry County.

Record Type	Year Begun	Jurisdiction
Land	1942	Clerk/Circuit Ct.
Marriage	1942	Clerk/Circuit Ct.
Divorce	1942	Clerk/Circuit Ct.
Probate	1942	Clerk/Circuit Ct.
Court	1942	Clerk/Circuit Ct.

■ Mason 1804

Web site: www.rootsweb.com/~wvmason/mason.htm
Parent County: Kanawha
Comments/research tips: (See West Virginia)

■ Mathews 1 May 1791

P.O. Box 463, Mathews, VA 23109
Phone: (804)725-2550
Web site: www.co.mathews.va.us/
Parent County: Gloucester
Comments/research tips: Clerk of Circuit Court has Birth
and Death records 1865–1896.

Record Type	Year Begun	Jurisdiction
Marriage	1827	Clerk/Circuit Ct.
Divorce	1805	Clerk/Circuit Ct.
Land	1814	Clerk/Circuit Ct.
Probate	1865	Clerk/Circuit Ct.
Court	1795	Clerk/Circuit Ct.

■ McDowell 1858

Web site: www.mcdowellwv.com
Parent County: Tazewell
Comments/research tips: (See West Virginia)

■ Mecklenburg 26 May 1764

Washington St., P.O. Box 530, Boydton, VA 23917
Phone: (434)738-6191 ext. 298
Web site: www.rootsweb.com/~vameckle/index.htm
Parent County: Lunenburg

Record Type	Year Begun	Jurisdiction
Marriage	1765	Clerk/Circuit Ct.
Land	1765	Clerk/Circuit Ct.
Probate	1765	Clerk/Circuit Ct.
Court	1765	Clerk/Circuit Ct.

■ Mercer 1837

Web site: www.rootsweb.com/~wvmercer/mercer.htm
Parent County: Giles, Tazewell
Comments/research tips: (See West Virginia)

■ Middlesex 1669

Rts. 17 and 33, P.O. Box 158, Saluda, VA 23149
Phone: (804)758-8637
Web site: www.rootsweb.com/~vamiddle/index.htm

Parent County: Lancaster
Comments/research tips: Clerk of Circuit Court has Birth
records 1754–1763 and 1853–1896, Death records
1758–1763 and 1853–1896, Marriage records 1663–1719,
and Military records 1861–1865 and 1917–1960.

Record Type	Year Begun	Jurisdiction
Divorce	1825	Clerk/Circuit Ct.
Marriage	1740	Clerk/Circuit Ct.
Land	1673	Clerk/Circuit Ct.
Probate	1673	Clerk/Circuit Ct.
Court	1673	Clerk/Circuit Ct.

■ Monongalia 1776

Web site: www.rootsweb.com/~wvmonong/
Parent County: District of West Augusta
Comments/research tips: (See West Virginia)

■ Monroe 1799

Web site: www.rootsweb.com/~wvmonroe
Parent County: Greenbriar, Botetourt
Comments/research tips: (See West Virginia)

■ Montgomery 7 Oct. 1776

P.O. Box 6309, 1 E. Main St., Suite B-5, Christiansburg, VA
24068
Phone: (540)382-5760
Web site: www.montva.com/
Parent County: Fincastle, Botetourt, Pulaski
Comments/research tips: Clerk of Circuit Court has Birth
and Death records from 1853–1868 and Military records
1818–1839.

Record Type	Year Begun	Jurisdiction
Marriage	1777	Clerk/Circuit Ct.
Divorce	1831	Clerk/Circuit Ct.
Land	1773	Clerk/Circuit Ct.
Probate	1773	Clerk/Circuit Ct.
Court	1773	Clerk/Circuit Ct.

■ Nansemond 1637

Web site: www.rootsweb.com/~vanansem/
Parent County: New Norfolk
Comments/research tips: (See Suffolk City) Known as Upper
Norfolk County until name changed to Nansemond County
in 1646. Became an independent city 1972. Nansemond City
absorbed by Suffolk City 1 January 1974.

■ Nelson 25 Dec. 1807

84 Courthouse Sq., P.O. Box 10, Lovingston, VA 22949
Phone: (434)263-7020
Web site: www.nelsoncounty.com/
Parent County: Amherst
Comments/research tips: Clerk of Circuit Court has Birth
and Death records 1853–1872.

Record Type	Year Begun	Jurisdiction
Marriage	1808	Clerk/Circuit Ct.
Divorce	1831	Clerk/Circuit Ct.
Land	1808	Clerk/Circuit Ct.
Probate	1808	Clerk/Circuit Ct.
Court	1808	Clerk/Circuit Ct.

Virginia

■ New Kent 20 Nov. 1654

P.O. Box 98, 12001 Courthouse Circle, New Kent, VA 23124

Phone: (804)966-9520

Web site: www.co.new-kent.va.us/

Parent County: York

Comments/research tips: Clerk of Circuit Court has Birth and Death records 1865–1888, Court records 1823–1824, and Military records 1917–1918 and 1941–1977.

Record Type	Year Begun	Jurisdiction
Marriage	1858	Clerk/Circuit Ct.
Divorce	1823	Clerk/Circuit Ct.
Land	1864	Clerk/Circuit Ct.
Probate	1863	Clerk/Circuit Ct.
Court	1865	Clerk/Circuit Ct.

■ New Norfolk 1636

Parent County: Elizabeth City

Comments/research tips: Abolished 1637. Divided into Upper Norfolk (now Suffolk) and Lower Norfolk (now Chesapeake).

■ Newport News (Ind. City) 1896

2500 Washington Ave., Newport News, VA 23607

Phone: (757)926-8561

Web site: www.newport-news.va.us

Parent County: Warwick

Comments/research tips: Clerk of Circuit Court has Marriage records 1890–1895. Established in 1880 and incorporated as a city in 1896. Part of Warwick County until 1896 and from 1952–1958. Enlarged due to the addition of Warwick 1 July 1958.

Record Type	Year Begun	Jurisdiction
Marriage	1959	Clerk/Circuit Ct.
Land	1846	Clerk/Circuit Ct.
Probate	1922	Clerk/Circuit Ct.

■ Nicholas 1818

Web site: www.rootsweb.com/~wvnichol/index.htm

Parent County: Greenbriar, Kanawha, Randolph

Comments/research tips: (See West Virginia)

■ Norfolk 1691

Parent County: Lower Norfolk

Comments/research tips: Consolidated with city of South Norfolk to create Chesapeake City 1 January 1963. Records kept by Chesapeake City Clerk of Circuit Court. Norfolk County extinct.

■ Norfolk (Ind. City) 1680

100 St. Paul's Blvd., Norfolk, VA 23510

Phone: (757)664-4380

Web site: www.norfolk.va.us

Parent County: Norfolk

Comments/research tips: Clerk of Circuit Court has Birth records 1792–1896 and Death records 1853–1871 and 1892–1897. Incorporated as a borough in 1736, incorporated as a city in 1845, and annexed to town of Berkeley in 1906.

Record Type	Year Begun	Jurisdiction
Court	1761	Clerk/Circuit Ct.
Divorce	1833	Clerk/Circuit Ct.
Land	1784	Clerk/Circuit Ct.
Marriage	1797	Clerk/Circuit Ct.
Probate	1784	Clerk/Circuit Ct.

■ Northampton 1634

16404 Courthouse Rd., P.O. Box 36, Eastville, VA 23347

Phone: (757)678-0465

Web site: www.rootsweb.com/~vanortha/

Parent County: Original Shire

Comments/research tips: Clerk of Circuit Court has Birth and Death records 1853–1870. Formerly Accomac County. Name changed to Northampton 1643.

Record Type	Year Begun	Jurisdiction
Marriage	1706	Clerk/Circuit Ct.
Divorce	1831	Clerk/Circuit Ct.
Land	1632	Clerk/Circuit Ct.
Probate	1632	Clerk/Circuit Ct.
Court	1632	Clerk/Circuit Ct.

■ Northumberland 12 Oct. 1648

P.O. Box 217, 39 Judicial Place, Heathsville, VA 22473

Phone: (804)580-3700

Web site: www.co.northumberland.va.us/

Parent County: District of Chickacoan

Comments/research tips: Some records were lost during a fire in October 1710.

Record Type	Year Begun	Jurisdiction
Marriage	1735	Clerk/Circuit Ct.
Divorce	1805	Clerk/Circuit Ct.
Land	1650	Clerk/Circuit Ct.
Probate	1652	Clerk/Circuit Ct.
Court	1650	Clerk/Circuit Ct.

■ Norton (Ind. City) 1954

P.O. Box 1248, Wise, VA 24293

Phone: (276)328-6111

Parent County: Wise

Comments/research tips: All records are with Wise County Clerk of Circuit Court. Established in 1787 and incorporated as a town in 1894.

■ Nottoway 22 Dec. 1788

P.O. Box 25, 328 W. Courthouse Rd., Nottoway, VA 23955

Phone: (434)645-9043

Web site: www.nottoway.org/home.shtml

Parent County: Amelia

Comments/research tips: Some records were destroyed during the Civil War.

Record Type	Year Begun	Jurisdiction
Marriage	1865	Clerk/Circuit Ct.
Divorce	1832	Clerk/Circuit Ct.
Land	1789	Clerk/Circuit Ct.
Probate	1789	Clerk/Circuit Ct.
Court	1793	Clerk/Circuit Ct.

■ Ohio 1776

Web site: www.rootsweb.com/~wvohio/

Parent County: Augusta

Comments/research tips: (See West Virginia)

Virginia

■ **Orange** 1 Feb. 1734
P.O. Box 230, 127 Belleview Ave., Orange, VA 22960
Phone: (540)672-4030
Web site: www.orangecova.com
Parent County: Spotsylvania
Comments/research tips: Clerk of Circuit Court has Birth
records from 1751–1778 and 1886–1895.

Record Type	Year Begun	Jurisdiction
Marriage	1756	Clerk/Circuit Ct.
Land	1734	Clerk/Circuit Ct.
Probate	1734	Clerk/Circuit Ct.
Court	1736	Clerk/Circuit Ct.
Divorce	1868	Clerk/Circuit Ct.

■ **Page** 30 Mar. 1831
116 S. Court St., Suite A, Luray, VA 22835
Phone: (540)743-4064
Web site: www.co.page.va.us/
Parent County: Rockingham, Shenandoah
Comments/research tips: Clerk of Circuit Court has Birth
records 1865–1872, Death records 1864–1872, and
Military records 1917–1918.

Record Type	Year Begun	Jurisdiction
Marriage	1831	Clerk/Circuit Ct.
Divorce	1831	Clerk/Circuit Ct.
Land	1831	Clerk/Circuit Ct.
Probate	1831	Clerk/Circuit Ct.
Court	1831	Clerk/Circuit Ct.

■ **Patrick** 26 Nov. 1790
101 Blue Ridge St., P.O. Box 148, Stuart, VA 24171
Phone: (276)694-7213
Web site: www.co.patrick.va.us/
Parent County: Henry
Comments/research tips: Clerk of Circuit Court has Birth
records 1853–1896, Death records 1853–1870, and
Military records 1861–1865, 1917–1919, and 1945–1970.

Record Type	Year Begun	Jurisdiction
Marriage	1791	Clerk/Circuit Ct.
Divorce	1832	Clerk/Circuit Ct.
Land	1791	Clerk/Circuit Ct.
Probate	1791	Clerk/Circuit Ct.
Court	1791	Clerk/Circuit Ct.

■ **Pendleton** 1788
Web site: www.rootsweb.com/~wvpendle/
Parent County: Hardy, Augusta, Rockingham
Comments/research tips: (See West Virginia)

■ **Petersburg (Ind. City)** 16 Mar. 1850
7 Courthouse Ave., Petersburg, VA 23803
Phone: (804)733-2367
Web site: www.rootsweb.com/~vacpeter/
Parent County: Dinwiddie, Prince George, Chesterfield
Comments/research tips: Clerk of Circuit Court has Birth
and Death records 1853–1896. Established in 1748,
incorporated as a town in 1785, and incorporated as a city
in 1850. Portions of Prince George and Dinwiddie Counties
were added in 1972.

Record Type	Year Begun	Jurisdiction
Marriage	1784	Clerk/Circuit Ct.
Court	1784	Clerk/Circuit Ct.
Divorce	1831	Clerk/Circuit Ct.
Land	1784	Clerk/Circuit Ct.
Probate	1784	Clerk/Circuit Ct.

■ **Pittsylvania** 6 Nov. 1766
Drawer 31, 3 N. Main St., Chatham, VA 24531
Phone: (434)432-7887
Web site: www.rootsweb.com/~vapittsy/
Parent County: Halifax
Comments/research tips: Clerk of Circuit Court has Birth
and Death records 1853–1896.

Record Type	Year Begun	Jurisdiction
Marriage	1767	Clerk/Circuit Ct.
Divorce	1831	Clerk/Circuit Ct.
Land	1767	Clerk/Circuit Ct.
Probate	1767	Clerk/Circuit Ct.
Court	1767	Clerk/Circuit Ct.

■ **Pleasants** 1851
Web site: www.rootsweb.com/~wvpleasa/
Parent County: Ritchie, Tyler, Wood
Comments/research tips: (See West Virginia)

■ **Pocahontas** 1821
Web site: www.rootsweb.com/~wvpocaha/
Parent County: Pendleton, Randolph, Greenbrier, Bath
Comments/research tips: (See West Virginia)

■ **Poquoson (Ind. City)** 1976
300 Ballard St., P.O. Box 371, Yorktown, VA 23690
Phone: (757)890-4103
Web site: www.ci.poquoson.va.us
Parent County: York
Comments/research tips: York County Clerk of Circuit Court
has all Poquoson records. Established ca. 1888,
incorporated as a town in 1952, and incorporated as a city
in 1976.

■ **Portsmouth (Ind. City)** 1858
P.O. Box 1217, 601 Crawford Pkwy., Portsmouth, VA
23705
Phone: (757)393-8671
Parent County: Norfolk
Comments/research tips: Library of Virginia has Birth and
Death records from 1853–1896. Established in 1752,
incorporated as a town in 1836, and incorporated as a city
in 1858. Territory taken from Norfolk County and annexed
to Portsmouth in 1848, 1960, and 1968. Portsmouth Public
Health Department: P.O. Box 250, Portsmouth, VA 23705.

Record Type	Year Begun	Jurisdiction
Marriage	1858	Clerk/Circuit Ct.
Divorce	1866	Clerk/Circuit Ct.
Land	1858	Clerk/Circuit Ct.
Probate	1858	Clerk/Circuit Ct.
Court	1858	Clerk/Circuit Ct.

■ Powhatan 5 May 1777
P.O. Box 37, 3880 Old Buckingham Rd., Suite C,
Powhatan, VA 23139
Phone: (804)598-5660
Web site: www.powhatanva.com
Parent County: Chesterfield, Cumberland
Comments/research tips: Clerk of Circuit Court has Birth
and Death records 1853–1871.

Record Type	Year Begun	Jurisdiction
Marriage	1777	Clerk/Circuit Ct.
Land	1777	Clerk/Circuit Ct.
Probate	1777	Clerk/Circuit Ct.
Court	1777	Clerk/Circuit Ct.
Divorce	1809	Clerk/Circuit Ct.

■ Preston 1818
Web site: www.rootsweb.com/~wvpresto
Parent County: Monongalia, Randolph
Comments/research tips: (See West Virginia)

■ Prince Edward 1753
P.O. Box 304, Farmville, VA 23901
Phone: (434)392-5145
Web site: www.rootsweb.com/~vaprince/
Parent County: Amelia
Comments/research tips: Clerk of Circuit Court has Birth
records 1853–1896, Death records 1853–1868, Military
records 1861–1865, and Naturalization records
1901–1925.

Record Type	Year Begun	Jurisdiction
Marriage	1754	Clerk/Circuit Ct.
Divorce	1754	Clerk/Circuit Ct.
Land	1754	Clerk/Circuit Ct.
Probate	1754	Clerk/Circuit Ct.
Court	1754	Clerk/Circuit Ct.

■ Prince George Dec. 1702
6601 Courts Dr., P.O. Box 98, Prince George, VA 23875
Phone: (804)733-2640
Web site: www.princegeorgeva.org/
Parent County: Charles City
Comments/research tips: Clerk of Circuit Court has Birth
and Death records 1865–1904 and Military records
1861–1865.

Record Type	Year Begun	Jurisdiction
Marriage	1865	Clerk/Circuit Ct.
Divorce	1836	Clerk/Circuit Ct.
Land	1710	Clerk/Circuit Ct.
Probate	1713	Clerk/Circuit Ct.
Court	1714	Clerk/Circuit Ct.

■ Prince William 1730
9311 Lee Ave., Manassas, VA 22110
Phone: (703)792-6015
Web site: www.co.prince-william.va.us
Parent County: King George, Stafford
Comments/research tips: Clerk of Circuit Court has Birth
and Death records 1864–1870.

Record Type	Year Begun	Jurisdiction
Marriage	1859	Clerk/Circuit Ct.

Divorce	1823	Clerk/Circuit Ct.
Land	1731	Clerk/Circuit Ct.
Probate	1734	Clerk/Circuit Ct.
Court	1752	Clerk/Circuit Ct.

■ Princess Anne 1691
Web site: www.rootsweb.com/~vaprinc2/pa.htm
Parent County: Lower Norfolk
Comments/research tips: (See Virginia Beach) Now part of
Ind. City of Virginia Beach, consolidated 1963.

■ Pulaski 30 Mar. 1839
45 Third St. NW, Suite 101, Pulaski, VA 24301
Phone: (540)980-7825
Web site: www.rootsweb.com/~vapulask/
Parent County: Montgomery, Wythe
Comments/research tips: Clerk of Circuit Court has Birth
and Death records 1853–1870 and Military records
1917–1918.

Record Type	Year Begun	Jurisdiction
Marriage	1839	Clerk/Circuit Ct.
Divorce	1839	Clerk/Circuit Ct.
Land	1839	Clerk/Circuit Ct.
Probate	1839	Clerk/Circuit Ct.
Court	1839	Clerk/Circuit Ct.

■ Putnam 1848
Web site: www.rootsweb.com/~wvputnam
Parent County: Kanawha, Mason, Cabell
Comments/research tips: (See West Virginia)

■ Radford (Ind. City) 1892
619 Second St., West Radford, VA 24141
Phone: (540)731-3610
Web site: www.radford.va.us
Parent County: Montgomery
Comments/research tips: Established in 1885, incorporated
as a town in 1887, and incorporated as a city in 1892.
Previously known as Central City until name changed to
Radford in 1890.

Record Type	Year Begun	Jurisdiction
Divorce	1892	Clerk/Circuit Ct.
Court	1892	Clerk/Circuit Ct.
Land	1892	Clerk/Circuit Ct.
Marriage	1892	Clerk/Circuit Ct.
Probate	1892	Clerk/Circuit Ct.

■ Raleigh 1850
Web site: www.rootsweb.com/~wvraleig/
Parent County: Fayette
Comments/research tips: (See West Virginia)

■ Randolph 1787
Parent County: Harrison
Comments/research tips: (See West Virginia)

■ Rappahannock 8 Feb. 1833
238 Gay St., P.O. Box 517, Washington, VA 22747
Phone: (540)675-5350

Web site: www.rootsweb.com/~varappah/
Parent County: Culpeper
Comments/research tips: Clerk of Circuit Court has Birth records 1853–1870 and Death records 1853–1891.

Record Type	Year Begun	Jurisdiction
Court	1833	Clerk/Circuit Ct.
Divorce	1833	Clerk/Circuit Ct.
Land	1833	Clerk/Circuit Ct.
Marriage	1833	Clerk/Circuit Ct.
Probate	1833	Clerk/Circuit Ct.

■ Rappahannock, old 1656
Parent County: Lancaster
Comments/research tips: (See Essex and Richmond) Abolished 1662. Split into Essex and Richmond Counties.

■ Richmond 16 Apr. 1692
101 Court Circle, P.O. Box 1000, Warsaw, VA 22572
Phone: (804)333-3781
Web site: www.co.richmond.va.us/
Parent County: Rappahannock, old
Comments/research tips: Clerk of Circuit Court has Birth records 1853–1895 and 1912–1914, Death records 1853–1895 and 1912–1917, and Marriage records 1709–1716.

Record Type	Year Begun	Jurisdiction
Marriage	1824	Clerk/Circuit Ct.
Court	1692	Clerk/Circuit Ct.
Divorce	1815	Clerk/Circuit Ct.
Land	1692	Clerk/Circuit Ct.
Probate	1699	Clerk/Circuit Ct.

■ Richmond (Ind. City) 1782
400 N. Ninth St., John Marshall Courts Bldg., Richmond, VA 23219
Phone: (804)646-6505
Web site: www.ci.richmond.va.us
Parent County: Henrico
Comments/research tips: Clerk of Circuit Court has Birth and Death records 1870–1954. John Marshall Courts Building has city records. Established in 1742, incorporated as a town in 1782, and incorporated as a city in 1842. Richmond Circuit Court has two locations: John Marshall Courts Building, 400 N. Ninth St., Richmond VA 23219, (804)646-6505 and Manchester Courthouse, Tenth & Hull Sts., Richmond VA 23224-0129, (804)646-8470.

Record Type	Year Begun	Jurisdiction
Land	1782	Clerk/Circuit Ct.
Probate	1782	Clerk/Circuit Ct.
Court	1692	Clerk/Circuit Ct.
Divorce	1815	Clerk/Circuit Ct.
Marriage	1797	Clerk/Circuit Ct.

■ Ritchie 1843
Web site: www.rootsweb.com/~wvritchi/indexr.htm
Parent County: Harrison, Lewis, Wood
Comments/research tips: (See West Virginia)

■ Roane 1856
Parent County: Kanawha, Jackson, Gilmer
Comments/research tips: (See West Virginia)

■ Roanoke 30 Mar. 1838
305 E. Main St., P.O. Box 1126, Salem, VA 24153
Phone: (540)387-6205
Web site: www.rootsweb.com/~varoanok/
Parent County: Botetourt, Montgomery

Record Type	Year Begun	Jurisdiction
Marriage	1838	Clerk/Circuit Ct.
Divorce	1838	Clerk/Circuit Ct.
Land	1838	Clerk/Circuit Ct.
Probate	1838	Clerk/Circuit Ct.
Court	1838	Clerk/Circuit Ct.

■ Roanoke (Ind. City) 1884
315 Church Ave. SW, Roanoke, VA 24011
Phone: (540)853-6702
Web site: www.roanokegov.com
Parent County: Roanoke
Comments/research tips: Clerk of Courts has Birth records 1886–1896. Established in 1852, incorporated as a town in 1874, and incorporated as a city in 1884. Previous name was Big Lick.

Record Type	Year Begun	Jurisdiction
Marriage	1884	Clerk/Circuit Ct.
Divorce	1884	Clerk/Circuit Ct.
Land	1884	Clerk/Circuit Ct.
Probate	1884	Clerk/Circuit Ct.
Court	1884	Clerk/Circuit Ct.

■ Rockbridge 1778
2 S. Main St., Lexington, VA 24450
Phone: (540)463-2232
Web site: www.rootsweb.com/~varockbr/rock.htm
Parent County: Augusta, Botetourt
Comments/research tips: Clerk of Circuit Court has Birth records 1853–1896, Death records 1853–1870, and Military records 1861–1865.

Record Type	Year Begun	Jurisdiction
Marriage	1778	Clerk/Circuit Ct.
Divorce	1831	Clerk/Circuit Ct.
Land	1778	Clerk/Circuit Ct.
Probate	1778	Clerk/Circuit Ct.
Court	1778	Clerk/Circuit Ct.

■ Rockingham 1778
Rockingham County Courthouse, Courthouse Sq., Harrisonburg, VA 22801
Phone: (540)564-3111
Web site: www.rootsweb.com/~varockin/index.htm
Parent County: Augusta
Comments/research tips: Clerk of Circuit Court has Birth records 1791–1795 and 1862–1894, Death records 1862–1894, and Military records 1861–1865 and 1917–1919. Some records were burned in 1864 and 1787.

Record Type	Year Begun	Jurisdiction
Marriage	1778	Clerk/Circuit Ct.
Divorce	1831	Clerk/Circuit Ct.
Land	1778	Clerk/Circuit Ct.
Probate	1789	Clerk/Circuit Ct.
Court	1778	Clerk/Circuit Ct.

Virginia

■ Russell 1786
P.O. Box 435, Main St., Lebanon, VA 24266
Phone: (276)889-8023
Web site: www.rootsweb.com/~varussel/
Parent County: Washington
Comments/research tips: Clerk of Circuit Court has Birth and Death records 1853–1866 and Military records 1917–1918 and 1945.

Record Type	Year Begun	Jurisdiction
Marriage	1853	Clerk/Circuit Ct.
Divorce	1831	Clerk/Circuit Ct.
Land	1786	Clerk/Circuit Ct.
Probate	1803	Clerk/Circuit Ct.
Court	1786	Clerk/Circuit Ct.

■ Salem (Ind. City) 1968
2 E. Calhoun St., Salem, VA 24153
Phone: (540)375-3067
Web site: www.ca.salem.va.us
Parent County: Roanoke
Comments/research tips: Established in 1806, incorporated as a town in 1836, and incorporated as a city in 1968. County seat of Roanoke County.

Record Type	Year Begun	Jurisdiction
Marriage	1968	Clerk/Circuit Ct.
Land	1968	Clerk/Circuit Ct.
Probate	1968	Clerk/Circuit Ct.
Court	1968	Clerk/Circuit Ct.
Divorce	1968	Clerk/Circuit Ct.

■ Scott 24 Nov. 1814
104 E. Jackson St., Suite 2, Gate City, VA 24251
Phone: (276)386-3801
Web site: www.rootsweb.com/~vascott/
Parent County: Lee, Russell, Washington
Comments/research tips: Clerk of Circuit Court has Birth records 1853–1870 and 1874–1895, Death records from 1853–1870, and Military records 1830–1850 and 1917–1918.

Record Type	Year Begun	Jurisdiction
Marriage	1815	Clerk/Circuit Ct.
Divorce	1831	Clerk/Circuit Ct.
Land	1815	Clerk/Circuit Ct.
Probate	1815	Clerk/Circuit Ct.
Court	1815	Clerk/Circuit Ct.

■ Shenandoah 24 Mar. 1772
112 S. Main St., P.O. Box 406, Woodstock, VA 22664
Phone: (540)459-6150
Web site: www.rootsweb.com/~vashenan/vashenan.htm
Parent County: Frederick
Comments/research tips: Clerk of Circuit Court has Birth and Death records 1853–1871 and Military records 1861–1865. Formerly Dunmore County. Name changed to Shenandoah 1 February 1778.

Record Type	Year Begun	Jurisdiction
Marriage	1772	Clerk/Circuit Ct.
Divorce	1831	Clerk/Circuit Ct.
Land	1772	Clerk/Circuit Ct.

Probate	1772	Clerk/Circuit Ct.
Court	1772	Clerk/Circuit Ct.

■ Smyth 23 Feb. 1832
109 W. Main St., Room 144, P.O. Box 1025, Marion, VA 24354
Phone: (276)782-4044
Web site: www.rootsweb.com/vasmyth/
Parent County: Washington, Wythe
Comments/research tips: Clerk of Circuit Court has Birth and Death records 1857–1896 and Military records 1917–1918 and 1940–1980.

Record Type	Year Begun	Jurisdiction
Marriage	1832	Clerk/Circuit Ct.
Divorce	1833	Clerk/Circuit Ct.
Land	1832	Clerk/Circuit Ct.
Probate	1832	Clerk/Circuit Ct.
Court	1832	Clerk/Circuit Ct.

■ Southampton 30 Apr. 1749
22350 Main St., P.O. Box 190, Courtland, VA 23837
Phone: (757)653-2200
Web site: www.rootsweb.com/~vasoutha/
Parent County: Isle of Wight, Nansemond
Comments/research tips: Clerk of Circuit Court has Birth records 1853–1872, Court records for 1708, Death records 1853–1870, and Naturalization records 1867–1912.

Record Type	Year Begun	Jurisdiction
Marriage	1750	Clerk/Circuit Ct.
Land	1749	Clerk/Circuit Ct.
Probate	1749	Clerk/Circuit Ct.
Court	1749	Clerk/Circuit Ct.
Divorce	1859	Clerk/Circuit Ct.

■ Spotsylvania 2 Nov. 1720
P.O. Box 96, 9113 Courthouse Rd., Spotsylvania, VA 22553
Phone: (540)582-7090
Web site: www.rootsweb.com/~vaspotsy/
Parent County: Essex, King and Queen, King William

Record Type	Year Begun	Jurisdiction
Marriage	1795	Clerk/Circuit Ct.
Land	1722	Clerk/Circuit Ct.
Probate	1722	Clerk/Circuit Ct.
Court	1722	Clerk/Circuit Ct.
Divorce	1848	Clerk/Circuit Ct.

■ Stafford 1664
1300 Courthouse Rd., P.O. Box 339, Stafford, VA 22554
Phone: (540)658-8750
Web site: www.rootsweb.com/~vastaffo/
Parent County: Westmoreland
Comments/research tips: Clerk of Circuit Court has Birth and Death records 1853–1873, Land records for 1680, and Military records 1861–1865 and 1917–1918.

Record Type	Year Begun	Jurisdiction
Marriage	1854	Clerk/Circuit Ct.
Divorce	1831	Clerk/Circuit Ct.
Land	1699	Clerk/Circuit Ct.
Probate	1699	Clerk/Circuit Ct.
Court	1664	Clerk/Circuit Ct.

Virginia

■ Staunton (Ind. City) 1871

113 E. Beverley St., P.O. Box 1286, Staunton, VA 24402
Phone: (540)332-3874
Web site: www.staunton.va.us
Parent County: Augusta
Comments/research tips: Clerk of Circuit Court has Birth records 1854–1896 and Death records 1853–1892. Established in 1761, incorporated as a town in 1801, and incorporated as a city in 1871

Record Type	Year Begun	Jurisdiction
Marriage	1802	Clerk/Circuit Ct.
Divorce	1848	Clerk/Circuit Ct.
Land	1802	Clerk/Circuit Ct.
Probate	1802	Clerk/Circuit Ct.
Court	1802	Clerk/Circuit Ct.

■ Suffolk (Ind. City) 1910

P.O. Box 1604, Mills E. Godwin Jr. Courts Bldg., 150 N. Main St., Suffolk, VA 23439
Phone: (757)923-2251
Web site: www.suffolk.va.us/home.html
Parent County: Nansemond
Comments/research tips: Established in 1742, incorporated as a town in 1808, and incorporated as a city in 1910. Nansemond County and Suffolk City merged 1 January 1974.

Record Type	Year Begun	Jurisdiction
Marriage	1866	Clerk/Circuit Ct.
Divorce	1866	Clerk/Circuit Ct.
Land	1866	Clerk/Circuit Ct.
Probate	1866	Clerk/Circuit Ct.
Court	1866	Clerk/Circuit Ct.

■ Surry 1652

P.O. Box 203, 28 Colonial Trail E., Rts. 10 and 31, Surry, VA 23883
Phone: (757)294-3161
Web site: www.rootsweb.com/~vasurry/
Parent County: James City
Comments/research tips: Clerk of Circuit Court has Birth and Death records from 1853–1896 and Military records 1840–1861, 1917–1918, and 1946–1950.

Record Type	Year Begun	Jurisdiction
Marriage	1768	Clerk/Circuit Ct.
Divorce	1831	Clerk/Circuit Ct.
Land	1652	Clerk/Circuit Ct.
Probate	1652	Clerk/Circuit Ct.
Court	1671	Clerk/Circuit Ct.

■ Sussex 1753

P.O. Box 1337, 15088 Courthouse Rd. Rt. 735, Sussex, VA 23884
Phone: (434)246-5511
Web site: www.rootsweb.com/~vasussex
Parent County: Surry
Comments/research tips: Clerk of Circuit Court has Birth and Death records 1853–1869.

Record Type	Year Begun	Jurisdiction
Marriage	1754	Clerk/Circuit Ct.

Land	1754	Clerk/Circuit Ct.
Probate	1754	Clerk/Circuit Ct.
Court	1754	Clerk/Circuit Ct.

■ Taylor 1844

Web site: www.rootsweb.com/~wvtaylor
Parent County: Harrison, Barbour, Marion
Comments/research tips: (See West Virginia)

■ Tazewell 17 Dec. 1799

101 Main St., P.O. Box 968, Tazewell, VA 24651
Phone: (276)988-1222
Web site: www.mindspring.com/~ronwags/Tazgen.html
Parent County: Russell, Wythe
Comments/research tips: Clerk of Circuit Court has Birth records 1853–1870, Death records 1853–1871, and Military records 1915–1918, 1941, and 1944.

Record Type	Year Begun	Jurisdiction
Marriage	1800	Clerk/Circuit Ct.
Land	1800	Clerk/Circuit Ct.
Probate	1800	Clerk/Circuit Ct.
Court	1800	Clerk/Circuit Ct.
Divorce	1832	Clerk/Circuit Ct.

■ Tucker 1856

Web site: www.rootsweb.com/~wvtucker/
Parent County: Randolph
Comments/research tips: (See West Virginia)

■ Tyler 1814

Web site: www.rootsweb.com/~wvtyler/
Parent County: Ohio
Comments/research tips: (See West Virginia)

■ Upper Norfolk 1637

Parent County: New Norfolk
Comments/research tips: (See Nansemond) Name changed to Nansemond 1646.

■ Upshur 1851

Web site: www.rootsweb.com/~wvupshur/
Parent County: Randolph, Barbour, Lewis
Comments/research tips: (See West Virginia)

■ Virginia Beach (Ind. City) 1 Jan. 1963

Virginia Beach Judicial Center, Bldg. 10B, 2425 Nimmo Pkwy., Virginia Beach, VA 23456
Phone: (757)427-4181
Web site: www.vbgov.com/default/
Parent County: Princess Anne
Comments/research tips: Clerk of Circuit Court has Birth and Death records 1864–1894. Marriage records 1822–1852 were destroyed in fire. Incorporated as a town in 1906 and incorporated as a city in 1952. Merged with Princess Anne County in 1963. Records before 1963 are for Princess Anne County.

Record Type	Year Begun	Jurisdiction
Divorce	1814	Clerk/Circuit Ct.
Land	1691	Clerk/Circuit Ct.

Virginia

Probate .... 1691 .... Clerk/Circuit Ct.
Court .... 1691 .... Clerk/Circuit Ct.

■ Warren 9 Mar. 1836
1 E. Main St., Front Royal, VA 22630
Phone: (540)635-2435
Web site: www.rootsweb.com/~vawarren/warren.htm
Parent County: Frederick, Shenandoah
Comments/research tips: Clerk of Circuit Court has Birth records 1853–1917, Death records 1853–1874, and Military records 1861–1865.

Record Type	Year Begun	Jurisdiction
Marriage	1836	Clerk/Circuit Ct.
Divorce	1836	Clerk/Circuit Ct.
Land	1836	Clerk/Circuit Ct.
Probate	1836	Clerk/Circuit Ct.
Court	1836	Clerk/Circuit Ct.

■ Warrosquoyake 1634
Web site: www.co.isle-of-wight-va.us
Parent County: Original Shire
Comments/research tips: (See Isle of Wight) Name changed to Isle of Wight 1637.

■ Warwick 1634
Web site: www.newport-news.va.us
Parent County: Original Shire
Comments/research tips: (See Newport News, Ind. City) Formerly Warwick River. Name changed to Warwick 1643. Incorporated as an independent city 1952. Merged with city of Newport News 1 July 1958.

■ Warwick River 1634
Web site: www.newport-news.va.us
Parent County: Original Shire
Comments/research tips: Name changed to Warwick 1643, merged with Newport News 1 July 1958.

■ Washington 7 Oct. 1776
189 E. Main St., P.O. Box 289, Abingdon, VA 24212
Phone: (276)676-6224
Web site: www.rootsweb.com/~vawashin/
Parent County: Fincastle, Montgomery (1777)
Comments/research tips: Clerk of Circuit Court has Birth and Death records 1853–1892 and Military records 1861–1865.

Record Type	Year Begun	Jurisdiction
Marriage	1785	Clerk/Circuit Ct.
Divorce	1830	Clerk/Circuit Ct.
Probate	1777	Clerk/Circuit Ct.
Court	1777	Clerk/Circuit Ct.
Land	1778	Clerk/Circuit Ct.

■ Wayne 1842
Web site: www.rootsweb.com/~wvwayne/
Parent County: Cabell
Comments/research tips: (See West Virginia)

■ Waynesboro (Ind. City) Feb. 1948
250 S. Wayne Ave., P.O. Box 910, Waynesboro, VA 22980
Phone: (540)942-6616

Web site: www.waynesboro.va.us
Parent County: Augusta
Comments/research tips: Established in 1801, incorporated as a town in 1834, and consolidated with Basic City in 1923.

Record Type	Year Begun	Jurisdiction
Marriage	1948	Clerk/Circuit Ct.
Divorce	1948	Clerk/Circuit Ct.
Probate	1948	Clerk/Circuit Ct.
Court	1948	Clerk/Circuit Ct.
Land	1948	Clerk/Circuit Ct.

■ Webster 1860
Web site: www.rootsweb.com/~wvwebste/webster.htm
Parent County: Braxton, Nicholas, Randolph
Comments/research tips: (See West Virginia)

■ Westmoreland 5 July 1653
P.O. Box 307, Montross, VA 22520
Phone: (804)493-0108
Web site: www.co.westmoreland.va.us/
Parent County: Northumberland
Comments/research tips: Clerk of Circuit Court has Birth records 1858–1895 and Death records 1857–1861, 1864–1877, and 1881–1889.

Record Type	Year Begun	Jurisdiction
Marriage	1772	Clerk/Circuit Ct.
Divorce	1851	Clerk/Circuit Ct.
Probate	1653	Clerk/Circuit Ct.
Court	1653	Clerk/Circuit Ct.
Land	1653	Clerk/Circuit Ct.

■ Wetzel 1846
Web site: www.ovis.net/~billcham/
Parent County: Tyler
Comments/research tips: (See West Virginia)

■ Williamsburg (Ind. City) 1884
5201 Monticello Ave., Suite 6, Williamsburg, VA 23188
Phone: (757)564-2242
Web site: www.ci.williamsburg.va.us
Parent County: James City, York
Comments/research tips: Established in 1633 as Middle Plantation, renamed Williamsburg in 1699, incorporated as a borough in 1772, and incorporated as a city in 1884. County seat of James City. Clerk of Circuit Court has jurisdiction over Williamsburg and James City County.

Record Type	Year Begun	Jurisdiction
Marriage	1854	Clerk/Circuit Ct.
Divorce	1865	Clerk/Circuit Ct.
Probate	1858	Clerk/Circuit Ct.
Land	1865	Clerk/Circuit Ct.
Court	1865	Clerk/Circuit Ct.

■ Winchester (Ind. City) 1874
5 N. Kent St., Winchester, VA 22601
Phone: (540)667-5770
Web site: www.ci.winchester.va.us
Parent County: Frederick
Comments/research tips: City Clerk has Birth records

1865–1891 and Death records 1871–1891. Established in 1752, incorporated as a town in 1779, and incorporated as a city in 1874.

Record Type	Year Begun	Jurisdiction
Court	1856	City Clerk
Marriage	1790	City Clerk
Probate	1794	City Clerk
Land	1789	City Clerk

■ Wirt 1848
Web site: www.rootsweb.com/~wvwirt/index.htm
Parent County: Wood, Jackson
Comments/research tips: (See West Virginia)

■ Wise 16 Feb. 1856
206 E. Main St., P.O. Box 1248, Wise, VA 24293
Phone: (276)328-6111
Web site: www.rootsweb.com/~vawise/
Parent County: Lee, Russell, Scott
Comments/research tips: Clerk of Circuit Court has Birth records 1856–1866 and Death records 1856–1894.

Record Type	Year Begun	Jurisdiction
Court	1856	Clerk/Circuit Ct.
Marriage	1856	Clerk/Circuit Ct.
Divorce	1856	Clerk/Circuit Ct.
Probate	1856	Clerk/Circuit Ct.
Land	1856	Clerk/Circuit Ct.

■ Wood 1798
Web site: www.rootsweb.com/~wvwood/index.htm
Parent County: Harrison, Kanawha
Comments/research tips: (See West Virginia)

■ Wyoming 1850
Web site: www.rootsweb.com/~wvwyomin/
Parent County: Logan
Comments/research tips: (See West Virginia)

■ Wythe 1 Dec. 1789
Circuit Court Bldg. 225 S. Fourth St., Room 105, Wytheville, VA 24382
Phone: (276)223-6050
Web site: www.wytheco.org/
Parent County: Montgomery
Comments/research tips: Clerk of Circuit Court has Birth records 1853–1872 and Death records 1853–1870.

Record Type	Year Begun	Jurisdiction
Marriage	1790	Clerk/Circuit Ct.
Divorce	1831	Clerk/Circuit Ct.
Probate	1790	Clerk/Circuit Ct.
Court	1795	Clerk/Circuit Ct.
Land	1790	Clerk/Circuit Ct.

■ Yohogania 1776
Web site: www.rootsweb.com/~vayohoga/
Parent County: West Augusta District
Comments/research tips: Discontinued and ceded to Pennsylvania 1780 as Westmoreland County, Pennsylvania.

■ York 1634
300 Ballard St., P.O. Box 371, Yorktown, VA 23690
Phone: (757)890-4103
Web site: www.yorkcounty.gov
Parent County: Original Shire
Comments/research tips: Clerk of Circuit Court has Birth and Death records 1856–1858 and Military records 1943–1956. Formerly Charles River County. Name changed to York 1643.

Record Type	Year Begun	Jurisdiction
Divorce	1831	Clerk/Circuit Ct.
Marriage	1772	Clerk/Circuit Ct.
Probate	1633	Clerk/Circuit Ct.
Land	1633	Clerk/Circuit Ct.
Court	1633	Clerk/Circuit Ct.

Virginia

Washington

By David A. Fryxell

HISTORICAL OVERVIEW

What would become Washington state was the object of a sort of ping-pong match for the first few centuries of European exploration, first claimed by Spain in 1543 and then by England in 1579 after Sir Francis Drake sighted the coastline. The Spanish actually landed in 1775; Captain Cook claimed the Olympic peninsula for England in 1778. Finally, the Treaty of Nootka in 1790 mostly settled claims in the Pacific Northwest in favor of England.

But England's claim didn't remain undisputed for long. Americans Robert Gray and John Kendrick had already visited in 1788; Gray discovered the Columbia River in 1791. Lewis and Clark reached the Columbia's mouth in 1805. American and English fur traders were soon in competition, establishing rival forts near present-day Spokane. American missionaries began to arrive in 1836, and the Oregon Trail brought settlers en masse starting in 1843.

The British and American conflict came to a head in 1844 with James K. Polk's election-year battle cry of "Fifty-Four Forty or Fight." War was ultimately averted and the 49th parallel set as America's northern boundary in 1846.

Throughout this period Washington was considered part of Oregon, and it was incorporated into the new Oregon Territory in 1848. Congress included it in the 1850 Donation Land Law, which provided grants of 320 acres per settler. Spurred by the law and a fledgling timber industry, settlement surged. Seattle was founded in 1852. Citizens eventually demanded a separate Washington Territory, which was created in 1853.

The area's native tribes increased their resistance to settlers' encroachment during this heightened period of colonization. A series of Indian wars—and treaties—filled the 1850s. Ultimately the tribes—including the Puyallup, Kalispell, Bannock, Yakima, Paiute, and Nez

WASHINGTON AT A GLANCE

Motto: By and By
Population: 5.9 million
Prevalent Religions: Christianity, particularly Roman Catholic, Methodist, Lutheran, Presbyterian, Pentecostal, Baptist, and Episcopalian
Major Industries: Software development, aerospace, food processing, paper and lumber products, chemical products, tourism, seafood, dairy products, apples, cattle, wheat, potatoes, nursery stock
Ethnic Makeup (in percent): Caucasian 81.8%, African American 3.2%, Hispanic 7.5%, Asian 5.5%, Native American 1.6%, Pacific Islanders 0.4%, Other 7.5%
Famous Washingtonians: Bob Barker, Dyan Cannon, Bob Crosby, Howard Duff, John Walker Kendall, John Knowles, Kenny Loggins, Phil Mahre, John McIntire, Patrice Munsel, Jimmie Rogers, Francis Scobee, Adam West

Above: A Sasquatch Crossing road sign

Perce—were exiled to reservations. Nez Perce Chief Joseph surrendered in 1876, proclaiming, "I will fight no more forever."

After the discovery of gold in 1860 and the passage of the Homestead Act in 1862, Washington became irresistible. The transcontinental line of the Northern Pacific Railroad reached Spokane in 1881 and Tacoma in 1887. At last, Washington became a state in 1889.

The early statehood years saw a swarm of immigrants from England, Ireland, Canada, Sweden, and Norway. Dutch, Italian, Finnish, and Russian German communities also sprang up. Chinese came to work the mines and on the railroads; Japanese labored on truck farms. World War II brought many African-Americans to Washington's growing industrial base.

Today, the state is known for aerospace and as the home of Microsoft.

RECORD HIGHLIGHTS

Washington was included in the federal 1850 Oregon Territory census and in several subsequent Washington territorial and state censuses, 1857–1892, which are available on microfilm through the state archives and the Family History Library. The first federal census enumerating the Washington Territory was in 1860; the earliest extant census post-statehood is from 1900. Washington census and naturalization records can be searched by county on the state archives' site at <www.secstate.wa .gov/history/search.aspx>. The site also includes a Spokane County marriage index and records of physicians, veterans, and convicts.

Official birth and death records were kept at the county level from 1891 to 1907, and by the state thereafter. Some pre-1891 records exist and have been microfilmed, as have many 1891–1907 county records. Indexes of Washington deaths, 1940–1996, and births, 1907–1919, are available on Ancestry.com.

State marriage records didn't begin until 1967. You can search many earlier county records from eastern Washington on the Western States Historical Marriage Records Index site at <abish.byui.edu/specialcollections/ fhc/gbsearch.htm>.

Land records and related water-rights and mining documents provide crucial clues to Washington's settlement boom. Files from the Donation Land Act (1851–1903) are kept at the National Archives' regional office in Seattle, with indexes and abstracts available at the National

Washington

Archives and via the FHL. Homestead Act claims are archived at the Bureau of Land Management office in Portland. Water-rights records dating from 1917 are kept at the Department of Ecology and the state archives. An index to mining surveys covering 1883–1964 is available via the FHL; the actual sixty-six volumes of surveys have been microfilmed by the state archives.

The state archives also has military records from Washington's Indian wars, files from the state's soldiers and veterans homes, and applications for state bonuses to veterans from World War I through the Vietnam War.

The Washington State Library in Olympia maintains an extensive collection of microfilmed state newspapers, accessible through interlibrary loan. For information on the collection, see <www.statelib.wa.gov/microfilm.aspx>; the newspaper holdings can be searched using the online catalog at <cals.evergreen.edu/search~S2>.

STATE RESOURCES

■ ARCHIVES, LIBRARIES, AND SOCIETIES

American Baptist-Samuel Colgate Historical Library
1106 S. Goodman St., Rochester, NY 14620-2532
Tel: (716) 473-1740

Anna Lemon Wheelock Library
3722 N. Twenty-sixth St., Tacoma, WA 98402
Tel: (253) 591-5640

Bellevue Regional Library
NE Twelfth St. & 110th Ave. NE, Bellevue, WA 98004
Tel: (425) 450-1760

Bellingham Public Library
P.O. box 1197, Bellingham, WA 98225

Big Bend Chapter, American Historical Society of Germans from Russia
202 W. Second, Ritzville, WA 99169-1704
Tel: (509) 659-1537

Blue Mountain Chapter, American Historical Society of Germans from Russia
2111 Gemstone, Walla Walla, WA 99362
Tel: (509) 529-2253

Burlington Public Library
900 Fairhaven St., Burlington, WA 68233

Central Washington Chapter, American Historical Society of Germans from Russia
3064 Alder St., Toppenish, WA 98958

Chehalis Valley Historical Society
268-11 Oak Meadows Rd., Oakville, WA 98568

Chelan Valley Genealogical Society
P.O. Box Y, Chelan, WA 98816

Clallam County Genealogical Society
% Genealogical Library, Clallam County Museum 223 E. Fourth St., Port Angeles, WA 98362

Clark County Genealogical Society
717 Grand Blvd., Vancouver, WA 98661
Tel: (360) 750-5688
Web site: <www.ccgs-wa.org>

Clark County Museum
1511 Main, Vancouver, WA 98668

Collins Memorial Library, University of Puget Sound
1500 N. Warner, Tacoma, WA 98416
Tel: (253) 756-3669
Fax: (253) 756-3670
Web site: <http://library.ups.edu/>

Columbia Basin Chapter, American Historical Society of Germans from Russia
1820 W. Part St., Pasco, WA 99301
Tel: (509) 545-9423

RESEARCH TIPS

for more info

- The biggest challenge in researching your Washington ancestors is finding marriage records, according to Charles M. Hansen, researcher for the Eastern Washington Genealogical Society. Until the state took over in 1967, each county kept these records. The problem is, Hansen explains, Washington couples don't have to get married in the county they live in, nor even record the marriage in their home county. Check all surrounding counties—plus nearby Idaho counties—for your ancestors' marriage records.

- Another challenge, according to Hansen, is that territorial records were spotty if created at all. Here it helps that Washington Territory labored long for statehood and thus took censuses in 1878, 1881, 1883, 1885, and 1887, as well as in the statehood year of 1889 and again in 1892. These can also help substitute for the burned 1890 federal census, Hansen notes. The Washington State Library is working on indexing these censuses and putting them online.

- The Family History Library has microfilmed all the birth and death certificates from when the state started recording them in mid-1907, as well as a wealth of land records, cemetery records, and even many early birth, death, and marriage records extracted from county courthouses.

Census Records
- Federal Census: 1860, 1870, 1880, 1900, 1910, 1920, 1930
- Federal Mortality Schedules: 1850, 1860, 1870, 1880
- Union Veterans and Widows: 1890
- State/Territorial Census: 1857–1892, 1872–1888

Douglas County Genealogical Society
P.O. Box 580, Waterville, WA 98858

Eastern Washington Genealogical Society
P.O. Box 1826, Spokane, WA 99210-1826
Web site: <online pub.net/ewgs>

Eastside Genealogical Society
P.O. Box 374, Bellevue, WA 98009

Ellensburg Genealogical Group
507 E. Tacoma St., Ellensburg, WA 98926

Everett Public Library
2702 Hoyt Ave., Everett, WA 98201

Family History Library
35 NW Temple St., Salt Lake City, UT 84150
Tel: (800) 346-6044 or (801) 240-2584
Web site: <www.familysearch .org>

Fiske Genealogical Foundation Library
1644 Forty-third Ave. E., Seattle, WA 98122-3222
Tel: (206) 328-2716
Web site: <www.fiske.lib.wa.us>

Ft. Vancouver Historical Society
P.O. Box 1834, Vancouver, WA 98663

Ft. Vancouver Regional Library
1007 E. Mill Plain Blvd., Vancouver, WA 98660

Genealogical Society of Pierce County
P.O. Box 189, Dupont, WA 98327-0089

Grant County Genealogical Society
% Ephrata Public Library, 45 Alder St. NW, Ephrata, WA 98823

Grays Harbor Genealogical Society
P.O. Box 867, Cosmopolis, WA 98537-0867

Greater Seattle Chapter, American Historical Society of Germans from Russia
7010 Seventeenth Ave. NE, Seattle, WA 98115
Tel: (206) 523-4136

Web site: <www.ahsgr.org/wase attl.html>

Greater Spokane Chapter, American Historical Society of Germans from Russia
2936 Grandview Ave., Spokane, WA 99224-5525
Tel: (509) 624-6947

Heritage Center Museum and library, Snohomish County Historical Association
P.O. Box 5203, Everett, WA 98206

Heritage Quest Research Library
909 Main St., Suite 5, Sumner, WA 98390
Tel: (253) 863-1806
Web site: <http://members.aol. com/hqrl/index.htm>

Issaquah Public Library
40 E. Sunset Way, Bellevue, WA 98004
Tel: (425) 392-5430

Italian Interest Group of the Eastside Genealogical Society
P.O. Box 374, Bellevue, WA 98009-0374

Jefferson County Genealogical Society
210 Madison, Port Townsend, WA 98368
Tel: (360) 385-1003
Web site: <www.rootsweb.com/ ~wajcgs>

Jewish Genealogical Society of Washington
14222 NE First Lane, Bellevue, WA 98007

Kittitas County Genealogical Society
P.O. Box 1342, Ellensburg, WA 98926
Tel: (509) 925-5951

Lake Hills Library
15528 Lake Hills Blvd., SE, Bellevue, WA 98007
Tel: (425) 747-3350

Lewis County Genealogical Society
P.O. Box 782, Chelalis, WA 98532

Lower Columbia Genealogical Society
P.O. Box 472, Longview, WA 98632

Maple Valley Historical Society
P.O. Box 123, Maple Valley, WA 98038

Mason County Genealogical Society
P.O. Box 333, Hoodspont, WA 98548

Mid-Columbia Library
405 South Dayton, Kennewick, WA 99336

National Archives-Pacific Northwest Region (Seattle)
6125 Sand POint Way NE, Seattle, WA 98115-7999
Tel: (206) 526-6507
Fax: (206) 526-6545
Web site: <www.archives.gov/fa cilities/wa/seattle.html>

Neill Public Library
N. 210 Grand Ave., Pullman, WA 99163

Newport Way Library
14520 SE Newport Way, Bellevue, WA 98006
Tel: (425) 747-2390

North Bend Library
115 E. Fourth St., North Bend, WA 98045
Tel: (425) 888-0554

Northeast Washington Genealogical Society
% Colville Public Library, 195 S. Oak, Colville, WA 99114

Okanogan County Genealogical Society
263 Old Riverside Hwy., Omak, WA 98841

Olympia Genealogical Society
% Olympia Public Library, Eighth and Franklin, Olympia, WA 98501

Olympia Timberland Library
313 Eighth Ave. SE., Olympia, WA 98501
Tel: (206) 352-0595

Olympic Peninsula Chapter, American Historical Society of Germans from Russia
30 Raccoon Rd., Sequim, WA 98382
Tel: (360) 683-1765
Web site: <www.ahsgr.org/waoly pen.html>

Olympic Peninsula Chapter, American Historical Society of Germans from Russia
2551 Fir Ave., Bremerton, WA 98310

Oregon State Office of the Bureau of Land Management (BLM)
P.O. Box 2965, 1515 SW Fifth Ave., Portland, OR 97208-2965
Tel: (503) 952-6287
Fax: (503) 952-6333
Web site:

Pacific County Genealogical Society
P.O. Box 843, Ocean Park, WA 98640

Puget Sound Genealogical Society
1026 Sidney Ave., Suite 110, Port Orchard, WA 98366-4298

Rainer Chapter, American Historical Society of Germans from Russia
1007 N Meridian, Puyallup, WA 98371
Tel: (253) 845-0136
Web site: <www.ahsgr.org/warai ner.html>

Redmond Historical Society
The Old Redmond Schoolhouse, 16600 NE 80 St., Rm. 106, Redmond, WA 98052

Roman Catholic Archdiocese of Seattle
Chancery Office, 910 Marion St., Seattle, WA 98104
Tel: (206) 382-4560
Fax: (206) 382-4840

Seattle Genealogical Society
8511 15 Ave. NE, Seattle, WA 98115
Web site: <www.rootsweb.com/ ~waseags/>

Seattle Public Library
1000 Fourth Ave., Seattle, WA 98104
Tel: (206) 386-4629
Fax: (206) 386-4632
Web site:

Skagit Valley Genealogical Society
P.O. Box 715, Conway, WA 98238

Sno-Isle Genealogical Society
P.O. Box 63, Edmonds, WA 98020

Snoqualmie Public Library
38580 SE River St., Snoqualmie, WA 98065
Tel: (425) 888-1223

South King County Genealogical Society
P.O. Box 3174, Kent, WA 98032

Washington

South Pierce County Historical Society
P.O. Box 537, Eatonville, WA 98328

Spokane Public Library
W. 916 Main Ave., Spokane, WA 99201

State Capitol Historical Association
211 W. Twenty-first Ave., Olympia, WA 98501

State Department of Health
P.O. Box 9709, Olympia, WA 98504-9709
Tel: (360) 753-5936
Fax: (360) 753-4135
Web site: <www.doh.wa.gov/EH SPHL/CHS/Cert.htm>

Stillaguamish Valley Genealogical Society of North Snohomish County
P.O. Box 34, Arlington, WA 98223

Suzzallo-Allen Library, University of Washington
P.O. Box 352900, Seattle, WA 98195-2900
Tel: (206) 543-9158
Fax: (206) 685-8049
Web site: <www.lib.washington .edu>

Swan Creek Library
3808 Portland Ave., Tacoma, WA 98404
Tel: (253) 594-7805

Tacoma Public Library
1102 Tacoma Ave. S., Tacoma, WA 98402
Tel: (253) 591-5666
Web site: <www.tpl.lib.wa.us/ v2/Index.htm>

Tacoma-Pierce County Genealogical Society
P.O. Box 1952, Tacoma, WA 98401

Tonasket Genealogical Society
P.O. Box 84, Tonasket, WA 98855

Tri-City Genealogical Society
P.O. Box 1410, Richland, WA 99352-1410

Walla Walla Valley Genealogical Society
P.O. Box 115, Walla Walla, WA 99362-0115

Washington State Archives
1120 Washington St. SE, P.O. Box 40238, Olympia, WA 98504-0238
Tel: (360) 586-1492
Fax: (360) 664-8814

Washington State Genealogical Society
P.O. Box 1422, Olympia, WA 98507-1422
Web site: <www.rootsweb.com/ ~wsgs/>

Washington State Historical Society and Museum
1911 Pacific Ave., Tacoma, WA 98402
Web site:

Washington State Library
P.O. Box 42460, Olympia, WA 98504-2460
Tel: (360) 753-5590
Fax: (360) 586-7575
Web site:

Wenatchee Area Genealogical Society
133 S. Mission St., P.O. Box 5280, Wenatchee, WA 98807-5280

Whatcom Genealogical Society
P.O. Box 1493, Bellingham, WA 98227-1493

Whitman County Genealogical Society
P.O. Box 393, Pullman, WA 99163
Web site: <www.completebbs. com/simonsen/wcgsindex .html>

Willapa Harbor Genealogical Society
% Raymond Public Library, 507 Duryea St., Raymond, WA 98577

Yakima Valley Genealogical Society
P.O. Box 445, Yakima, WA 98907

BIBLIOGRAPHY

■ GENERAL RESOURCES

Bibliography of Washington State Historical Society Library, 3 vols.
from the Tacoma-Pierce County Genealogical Society (Tacoma, WA: The Society, 1986)

Celebrating the History of the Pioneer Families of Washington, 1853–1889
by Frances Caldwell Miller (Wenatchee, WA: Native Daughters of Washington Territorial Pioneers, 1989)

Comprehensive Guide to the Manuscripts Collection and to the Personal Papers in the University Archives
by Marilyn Priestly (Seattle, WA: The Library, 1980)

The Dictionary Catalog of the Pacific Northwest Collection of the University Of Washington, 6 vols.
(Boston: G.K. Hall and Co., 1972)

Early Washington: Overland Stage Routes, Old Military Roads, Indian Battle Grounds, Old Forts, Old Gold Mines
by Ralph N. Preston (Corvallis, OR: Western Guide Publishers, 1974)

The Evolution of Washington Counties
by Newton Carl Abbott and Fred E. Carver, compiled by J.W. Helm (Yakima, WA: Yakima Valley Genealogical Society and Klickitat County Historical Society, 1978)

The Genealogist's Companion and Sourcebook, 2d ed.
by Emily Anne Croom (Cincinnati: Betterway Books, 2003)

A Genealogist's Guide to Discovering Your African-American Ancestors
by Franklin Carter Smith and Emily Anne Croom (Cincinnati: Betterway Books, 2003)

Germans from Russia in the Yakima Valley, Prior to 1940
by Frieda Eickler Brulotte (Yakima, WA: The Society, 1990)

Guide to Genealogical Research in the National Archives of the United States
edited by Anne Bruner Eales and Robert M. Kvasnicka (Washington, DC: National Archives and Records Administration, 2000)

A History of the Catholic Church in the Pacific Northwest, 1743–1983
by Wilfred P. Schoenberg (Washington, DC: Pastoral Press, 1987)

History of the Pacific Northwest: Oregon and Washington; Embracing an Account of the Original Discoveries On the Pacific Coast of North American, and a Description of the Conquest, Settlement and Subjugation of the Original Territory Of Oregon; also Interesting Biographies of the Earliest Settlers, 2 vols.
by Elwood Evans (Portland, OR: North Pacific History Co., ca. 1889)

History of the Synod of Washington of The Presbyterian Church in the United States of America 1835–1909
by Robert Boyd (Seattle: The Synod, ca. 1910)

A History of Washington, 4 vols.
by Lancaster Pollard (New York: American Historical Society, 1937)

An Illustrated History of the State of Washington: Containing Biographical Mention of its Pioneers and Prominent Citizens
by Harvey K. Hines (Chicago: Lewis Pub. Co., 1893)

Methodism in the Northwest
by Erle Howell (Nashville, TN: Pacific Northwest Conference Historical Society, 1966)

Missionary History of the Pacific Northwest: Containing the Wonderful Story of Jason Lee, with Sketches of Many of his Co-Laborers all Illustrating Life on the Plains and in the Mountains in Pioneer Days
(Washington, DC: Library of Congress, 1990)

National Archives Microfilm Catalogs online:
<www.archives.gov/publica tions/genealogy_microfilm_ catalogs.html>

Reminiscences of Washington Territory
by Charles Prosch (Fairfield, WA: Ye Galleon Press, 1969)

Sketches of Washington
(Seattle. W.C. Wolfe & Co., 1906)

A Social History of Scandinavian Immigration, Washington State, 1895–1910
by Jorgen Dahlie (New York: Arno Press, 1980)

Washington

Washington: A History of the Evergreen State
by Mary Williamson Avery (Seattle: University of Washington Press, 1967)

Washington West of the Cascades, 3 vols.
(Chicago: S.J. Clarke, 1917)

Washington West of the Cascades: Historical and Descriptive, the Explorers, the Indians, the Modern
by Herbert Hunt (Tucson, AZ: W.C. Cox, 1974)

Who's Who in Washington State: A Compilation of Biographical Sketches of Men and Women Prominent in the Affairs of Washington State
(Seattle: H. Allen Pub., 1927)

■ CENSUS RECORDS

The American Census Handbook
by Thomas Jay Kemp (Wilmington, DE: Scholarly Resources, Inc., 2001)

Map Guide to the U.S. Federal Censuses, 1790–1920
by William Thorndale and William Dollarhide (Baltimore: Genealogical Publishing Co., 1987)

Your Guide to the Federal Census
by Kathleen W. Hinckley (Cincinnati: Betterway Books, 2002)

■ IMMIGRATION RECORDS

American Naturalization Records, 1790–1990: What They Are and How to Use Them
by John J. Newman (North Salt Lake, UT: HeritageQuest, 1998)

American Passenger Arrival Records
by Michael Tepper (Baltimore: Genealogical Publishing Co., 1993)

They Became Americans: Finding Naturalization Records and Ethnic Origins
by Loretto Dennis Szucs (Salt Lake City: Ancestry, Inc., 1998)

They Came in Ships: A Guide to Finding Your Immigrant Ancestor's Arrival Records, 2d ed.
by John P. Colletta (Salt Lake City: Ancestry, Inc., 1993)

■ LAND RECORDS

Locating Your Roots: Discover Your Ancestors Using Land Records
by Patricia Law Hatcher (Cincinnati: Betterway Books, 2003)

Washington Territory Donation Land Claims: an Abstract of Information in the Land Claim Papers of Persons Who Settled in Washington Territory Before 1856
(Seattle: Seattle Genealogical Society, 1980)

■ MAPS

Early Washington Atlas, 2d ed.
(Portland, OR: Binford & Mort Publishers, 1974)

The Evolution of Washington Counties
by Newton Carl Abbott and Fred E. Carver, compiled by J.W. Helm (Yakima, WA: Yakima Valley Genealogical Society and Klickitat County Historical Society, 1978)

A Geographic Dictionary of Washington
by Henry Landes (Olympic, WA: F.J. Lamborn, 1917)

Historical Atlas of Washington
by James R. Scott and Roland L. DeLorme (Norman: University of Oklahoma Press, 1988)

Origin of Washington Geographic Names
by Edmond S. Meany (Originally published in 1923; Reprint: Detroit: Gale Research Co., 1968)

R.L. Polk & Co. Oregon & Washington Gazetteer and Business Directory, 1909–1910
(Seattle: R.L. Polk, 1909)

Washington Atlas and Gazetteer
(Freeport, ME: DeLorme Mapping Co., 1996)

Washington: A Centennial Atlas
by James R. Scott (Bellingham: Western Washington University, 1989)

Washington State Place Names
by James W. Phillips (Seattle: University of Washington Press, 1971)

■ MILITARY RECORDS

Burial List of the Members of the 1st Washington Territory Infantry
by Sherman Lee Pompey (Kingsburg, CA: Pacific Specialties, 1972)

Uncle, We Are Ready! Registering America's Men, 1917–1918: A Guide to Researching World War I Draft Registration Cards
by John J. Newman (North Salt Lake, UT: HeritageQuest, 2001)

U.S. Military Records: A Guide to Federal & State Sources, Colonial America to the Present
by James C. Neagles (Salt Lake City: Ancestry, Inc., 1994)

World War II: A Family Historian's Guide
by Debra Johnson Knox (Spartanburg, SC: MIE Publishing, 2003)

■ VITAL RECORDS

A Directory of Cemeteries and Funeral Homes in Washington State
from the Washington Interment Association and the Washington State Funeral Directors Association (Orting, WA: HeritageQuest, 1990)

Washington's First Marriages of the Thirty-Nine Counties
edited by John D. Carter (Spokane: Eastern Washington Genealogical Society, 1986)

Your Guide to Cemetery Research
by Sharon DeBartolo Carmack (Cincinnati: Betterway Books, 2002)

■ Adams   28 Nov. 1883

210 W. Broadway Ave., Ritzville, WA 99169
Phone: (509)659-3257
Web site: www.co.adams.wa.us/
Parent County: Whitman
Comments/research tips: County Health Department has Death records 1891–1907. County Clerk has Naturalization records 1890–1956.

Record Type	Year Begun	Jurisdiction
Court	1889	County Clerk
Birth	1909	Dept./Health
Marriage	1887	County Auditor
Divorce	1889	County Clerk
Probate	1885	County Clerk
Land	1891	County Auditor

■ Asotin   27 Oct. 1883

P.O. Box 159, Asotin, WA 99402
Phone: (509)243-4181
Web site: www.palouse.org/asotin.htm
Parent County: Garfield
Comments/research tips: County Auditor has Military records 1888–1897. County Clerk has Naturalization records 1885–1974.

Record Type	Year Begun	Jurisdiction
Court	1890	County Clerk
Death	1907	Center/Health Stat.
Birth	1907	Center/Health Stat.
Marriage	1897	County Auditor
Divorce	1890	County Clerk
Probate	1885	County Clerk
Land	1891	County Auditor

Washington

■ Benton 8 Mar. 1905
620 Market St., Prosser, WA 99350
Phone: (509)786-5624
Web site: www.rootsweb.com/~wabenton/
Parent County: Yakima, Klickitat
Comments/research tips: County Auditor has Birth records 1905–1907. County Clerk has Naturalization records 1905–1954.

Record Type	Year Begun	Jurisdiction
Marriage	1905	County Auditor
Divorce	1905	County Auditor
Probate	1906	County Clerk
Court	1906	County Clerk
Land	1874	County Auditor

■ Chehalis 26 Apr. 1854
Parent County: Thurston
Comments/research tips: (See Grays Harbor) Name changed to Grays Harbor 15 March 1915.

■ Chelan 13 Mar. 1899
350 Orondo St., Wenatchee, WA 98801
Phone: (509)667-6380
Web site: www.co.chelan.wa.us/
Parent County: Kittitas
Comments/research tips: County Auditor has Birth and Death records 1899–1907. County Clerk has Naturalization records 1900–1906.

Record Type	Year Begun	Jurisdiction
Marriage	1899	County Auditor
Land	1899	County Auditor
Divorce	1900	County Clerk
Probate	1888	County Clerk
Court	1900	County Clerk

■ Clallam 26 Apr. 1854
223 E. Fourth St., P.O. Box 863, Port Angeles, WA 98362
Phone: (360)417-2333
Web site: www.rootsweb.com/~waclalla/
Parent County: Jefferson
Comments/research tips: County Auditor has Birth and Death records 1891–1906 and Military Discharge records 1944–1965.

Record Type	Year Begun	Jurisdiction
Court	1889	County Clerk
Land	1858	County Auditor
Marriage	1858	County Auditor
Probate	1914	County Clerk

■ Clark 27 July 1844
1200 Franklin St., P.O. Box 5000, Vancouver, WA 98666
Phone: (360)397-2292
Web site: www.co.clark.wa.us/
Parent County: Original county
Comments/research tips: County Auditor has Birth and Death records 1890–1907 and Military records 1888–1894. County Clerk has Naturalization records 1890–1991. Formerly Vancouver County. Name changed to Clark 3 September 1849.

Record Type	Year Begun	Jurisdiction
Marriage	1852	County Auditor
Land	1850	County Auditor
Divorce	1890	County Clerk
Probate	1889	County Clerk
Court	1889	County Clerk

■ Columbia 11 Nov. 1875
341 E. Main St., Dayton, WA 99328
Phone: (509)382-4321
Web site: www.rootsweb.com/~wacolumb/
Parent County: Walla Walla
Comments/research tips: County Auditor has Birth and Death records 1891–1906. County Clerk has Naturalization records 1890–1941.

Record Type	Year Begun	Jurisdiction
Probate	1877	County Clerk
Divorce	1878	County Clerk
Court	1878	County Clerk
Marriage	1879	County Auditor
Land	1879	County Auditor

■ Cowlitz 22 Apr. 1854
312 SW First Ave., Kelso, WA 98626
Phone: (360)577-3016
Web site: www.co.cowlitz.wa.us/
Parent County: Lewis
Comments/research tips: County Auditor has Death records 1892–1907. County Clerk has Naturalization records 1859–1920.

Record Type	Year Begun	Jurisdiction
Marriage	1844	County Auditor
Land	1858	County Auditor
Divorce	1874	County Clerk
Probate	1861	County Clerk
Court	1874	County Clerk
Adoption	1895	County Clerk

■ Douglas 23 Nov. 1883
203 S. Rainier, P.O. Box 516, Waterville, WA 98858
Phone: (509)745-8529
Web site: www.douglascountywa.net/
Parent County: Lincoln
Comments/research tips: County Auditor has Birth and Death records 1891–1907. County Clerk has Naturalization records 1891–1973.

Record Type	Year Begun	Jurisdiction
Land	1884	County Auditor
Marriage	1887	County Auditor
Divorce	1888	County Clerk
Probate	1887	County Clerk
Court	1894	County Clerk

■ Ferry 21 Feb. 1899
350 E. Delaware Ave. #4, Republic, WA 99166
Phone: (509)775-5232
Web site: www.rootsweb.com/~waferry/
Parent County: Stevens
Comments/research tips: County Auditor has Birth and Death records 1898–1911.

Record Type	Year Begun	Jurisdiction
Land	1898	County Auditor
Marriage	1898	County Auditor
Divorce	1899	County Clerk
Probate	1887	County Clerk
Court	1899	County Clerk

■ Franklin 28 Nov. 1883
1016 N. Fourth Ave. Room 306, Pasco, WA 99301
Phone: (509)545-3525
Web site: www.co.franklin.wa.us/
Parent County: Whitman
Comments/research tips: County Auditor has Birth and Death records 1891–1910. County Clerk has Naturalization records 1891–1975.

Record Type	Year Begun	Jurisdiction
Marriage	1890	County Auditor
Land	1883	County Auditor
Divorce	1920	County Clerk
Probate	1913	County Clerk
Court	1909	County Clerk

■ Garfield 29 Nov. 1881
789 Main St., P.O. Box 915, Pomeroy, WA 99347
Phone: (509)843-3731
Web site: www.rootsweb.com/~wagarfie/
Parent County: Columbia
Comments/research tips: County Auditor has Birth and Death records ca. 1890–1908.

Record Type	Year Begun	Jurisdiction
Marriage	ca. 1890	County Auditor
Land	1891	County Auditor
Divorce	1882	County Clerk
Probate	1882	County Clerk
Court	1882	County Clerk

■ Grant 24 Feb. 1909
35 C St. NW, P.O. Box 37, Ephrata , WA 98823
Phone: (509)754-2011
Web site: www.rootsweb.com/~wagrant/grant.htm
Parent County: Douglas
Comments/research tips: Court records prior to 1909 were transcribed from Douglas County Superior Court records.

Record Type	Year Begun	Jurisdiction
Marriage	1909	County Auditor
Land	1909	County Auditor
Divorce	1909	County Clerk
Probate	1909	County Clerk
Court	1889	County Clerk

■ Grays Harbor 14 Apr. 1854
102 W. Broadway Ave., Montesano, WA 98563
Phone: (360)249-3842
Web site: www.co.grays-harbor.wa.us/
Parent County: Thurston
Comments/research tips: County Auditor has Birth records 1891–1908 and Death records 1891–1907. County Clerk has Naturalization records 1884–1980. Formerly Chehalis County. Name changed to Grays Harbor 15 March 1915.

Record Type	Year Begun	Jurisdiction
Probate	1852	County Clerk
Divorce	1884	County Clerk
Court	1884	County Clerk
Marriage	1855	County Auditor
Land	1855	County Auditor

■ Island 6 Jan. 1853
P.O. Box 5000, Coupeville, WA 98239
Phone: (360)679-7359
Web site: www.islandcounty.net/
Parent County: Thurston
Comments/research tips: County Auditor has Birth and Death records 1891–1907 and Military records 1888–1894. County Clerk has Naturalization records 1894–1974.

Record Type	Year Begun	Jurisdiction
Marriage	1855	County Auditor
Land	1853	County Auditor
Divorce	1889	County Clerk
Probate	1854	County Clerk
Court	1889	County Clerk

■ Jefferson 22 Dec. 1852
P.O. Box 1220, Port Townsend, WA 98368
Phone: (360)385-9125
Web site: www.co.jefferson.wa.us/
Parent County: Thurston
Comments/research tips: County Auditor has Birth and Death records 1891–1906. County Clerk has Naturalization records 1893–1973.

Record Type	Year Begun	Jurisdiction
Divorce	1890	County Clerk
Probate	1853	County Clerk
Court	1890	County Clerk
Marriage	1853	County Auditor
Land	1855	County Auditor

■ King 22 Dec. 1852
516 Third Ave. Room E609, Seattle, WA 98104
Phone: (206)296-9300
Web site: www.metrokc.gov/
Parent County: Thurston

Record Type	Year Begun	Jurisdiction
Birth	1880	Dept./Vital Stat.
Marriage	1866	Recorder's Office
Death	1890	Dept./Vital Stat.
Land	1853	Recorder's Office
Probate	1854	Clerk/Superior Ct.
Court	1853	Clerk/Superior Ct.
Divorce	1853	Clerk/Superior Ct.

■ Kitsap 16 Jan. 1857
614 Division St. MS34, Port Orchard, WA 98366
Phone: (360)337-7164
Web site: www.kitsapgov.com/
Parent County: King, Jefferson
Comments/research tips: County Clerk has Divorce records 1910–1959 and Naturalization records 1892–1906, 1923–1989. Formerly Slaughter County. Name changed to Kitsap 13 July 1857.

Record Type	Year Begun	Jurisdiction
Marriage	1860	County Auditor
Court	1888	County Clerk
Probate	1860	County Clerk
Land	1857	County Auditor

■ Kittitas 24 Nov. 1883
205 W. Fifth Ave. Suite 210, Ellensburg, WA 98926
Phone: (509)962-7531
Web site: www.co.kittitas.wa.us
Parent County: Yakima
Comments/research tips: County Auditor has Birth records 1889–1907, Death records 1891–1907, and Military Discharge records 1919–1969. County Clerk has Naturalization records 1907–1921.

Record Type	Year Begun	Jurisdiction
Marriage	1884	County Auditor
Land	1882	County Auditor
Divorce	1891	County Clerk
Probate	1886	County Clerk
Court	1891	County Clerk

■ Klickitat 20 Dec. 1859
205 S. Columbus Ave. MS CH-3, Goldendale, WA 98620
Phone: (509)773-5744
Web site: www.rootsweb.com/~waklicki/
Parent County: Skamania
Comments/research tips: County Auditor has Birth records 1891–1907 and Death records 1882–1907. County Clerk has Naturalization records 1893–1927.

Record Type	Year Begun	Jurisdiction
Land	1864	County Auditor
Military	1919	County Auditor
Divorce	1879	County Clerk
Probate	1885	County Clerk
Court	1879	County Clerk
Marriage	1867	County Auditor

■ Lewis 21 Dec. 1845
360 NW North St. MS CLK01, Chehalis, WA 98532
Phone: (360)740-2704
Web site: www.co.lewis.wa.us/
Parent County: District of Vancouver
Comments/research tips: County Auditor has Birth and Death records 1856–1906.

Record Type	Year Begun	Jurisdiction
Land	1856	County Auditor
Marriage	1858	County Auditor
Divorce	1893	County Clerk
Probate	1891	County Clerk
Court	1893	County Clerk

■ Lincoln 24 Nov. 1883
450 Logan St., P.O. Box 68, Davenport, WA 99122
Phone: (509)725-1401
Web site: www.rootsweb.com/~walincol/lincoln.htm
Parent County: Spokane
Comments/research tips: County Auditor has Birth and Death records 1891–1907. County Clerk has Naturalization records 1886–1924.

Record Type	Year Begun	Jurisdiction
Marriage	1884	County Auditor
Land	1883	County Auditor
Divorce	1907	County Clerk
Probate	1907	County Clerk
Court	1907	County Clerk

■ Mason 13 Mar. 1854
P.O. Box 340, Shelton, WA 98584
Phone: (360)427-9670
Web site: www.co.mason.wa.us/
Parent County: Thurston
Comments/research tips: County Auditor has Military Discharge records 1938–1984. Formerly Sawamish County. Name changed to Mason 8 January 1864.

Record Type	Year Begun	Jurisdiction
Marriage	1887	County Auditor
Land	1856	County Auditor
Divorce	1858	County Clerk
Probate	1858	County Clerk
Court	1858	County Clerk

■ Okanogan 2 Feb. 1888
149 Third N., P.O. Box 72, Okanogan, WA 98840
Phone: (509)422-7275
Web site: www.rootsweb.com/~waokanog/okanogan.htm
Parent County: Stevens
Comments/research tips: County Auditor has Birth records, 1891–1914, Death records 1891–1908, and Military Discharge records 1919–1974. County Clerk has Naturalization records 1890–1906.

Record Type	Year Begun	Jurisdiction
Marriage	1888	County Auditor
Land	1888	County Auditor
Divorce	1888	County Clerk
Probate	1888	County Clerk
Court	1888	County Clerk

■ Pacific 4 Feb. 1851
300 Memorial Ave., P.O. Box 67, South Bend, WA 98586
Phone: (360)875-9320
Web site: www.co.pacific.wa.us/
Parent County: Lewis
Comments/research tips: County Auditor has Birth records 1891–1915 and Death records 1891–1917.

Record Type	Year Begun	Jurisdiction
Military	1919	County Auditor
Marriage	1852	County Auditor
Divorce	1851	County Clerk
Probate	1851	County Clerk
Court	1851	County Clerk
Land	1850	County Auditor

■ Pend Oreille 11 Nov. 1911
229 S. Garden Ave., P.O. Box 5020, Newport, WA 99156
Phone: (509)447-2435
Web site: www.rootsweb.com/~wapendor/
Parent County: Stevens

Record Type	Year Begun	Jurisdiction
Birth	1911	County Auditor

Washington

Marriage	1911	County Auditor
Land	1911	County Auditor
Divorce	1911	County Clerk
Probate	1911	County Clerk
Court	1911	County Clerk

■ Pierce 22 Dec. 1852
930 Tacoma Ave. S. Room 110, Tacoma, WA 98402
Phone: (253)798-7455
Web site: www.rootsweb.com/~wapierce/
Parent County: Lewis
Comments/research tips: County Auditor has Birth and Death records 1891–1907 and Military records 1888–1892.

Record Type	Year Begun	Jurisdiction
Marriage	1859	County Auditor
Land	1859	County Auditor
Divorce	1854	County Clerk
Probate	1853	County Clerk
Court	1854	County Clerk

■ San Juan 31 Oct. 1873
350 Court St. Suite #7, Friday Harbor, WA 98250
Phone: (360)378-2163
Web site: www.rootsweb.com/~wasanjua/
Parent County: Whatcom
Comments/research tips: County Auditor has Birth records 1892–1907 and Death records 1890–1907. County Clerk has Naturalization records 1871–1960.

Record Type	Year Begun	Jurisdiction
Divorce	1890	County Clerk
Probate	1874	County Clerk
Court	1890	County Clerk
Marriage	1878	County Auditor

■ Sawamish 13 Mar. 1854
Parent County: Thurston
Comments/research tips: (See Mason) Name changed to Mason 8 January 1864.

■ Skagit 28 Nov. 1883
205 W. Kincaid St. Suite 103, Mount Vernon, WA 98273
Phone: (360)336-9440
Web site: www.rootsweb.com/~wasvgs/
Parent County: Whatcom
Comments/research tips: County Auditor has Birth records 1891–1907, Death records 1891–1910, and Military records 1892–1896. County Clerk has Naturalization records 1904–1974.

Record Type	Year Begun	Jurisdiction
Marriage	1884	County Auditor
Land	1884	County Auditor
Divorce	1878	County Clerk
Probate	1878	County Clerk
Court	1878	County Clerk

■ Skamania 9 Mar. 1854
240 Vancouver Ave., P.O. Box 790, Stevenson, WA 98648
Phone: (509)427-9431
Web site: www.skamaniacounty.org

Parent County: Clark
Comments/research tips: County was dissolved 14 January 1865 and reestablished 31 January 1867.

Record Type	Year Begun	Jurisdiction
Military	1945	County Auditor
Land	1855	County Auditor
Marriage	1874	County Auditor
Divorce	1854	County Clerk
Probate	1854	County Clerk
Court	1854	County Clerk

■ Slaughter 16 Jan. 1857
Parent County: King, Jefferson
Comments/research tips: (See Kitsap) Name changed to Kitsap 13 July 1857.

■ Snohomish 20 Jan. 1861
3000 Rickefeller Ave. MS 605, Everett, WA 98201
Phone: (425)388-3806
Web site: www.co.snohomish.wa.us/
Parent County: Island
Comments/research tips: County Auditor has Birth and Death records 1891–1907 and Military Discharge records 1919–1979.

Record Type	Year Begun	Jurisdiction
Marriage	1891	County Auditor
Divorce	1889	County Clerk
Probate	1866	County Clerk
Court	1889	County Clerk

■ Spokane 29 Jan. 1868
1116 W. Broadway, Spokane, WA 99260
Phone: (509)477-2245
Web site: www.spokanecounty.org/
Parent County: Walla Walla
Comments/research tips: County Auditor has Birth and Death records 1886–1907. County Clerk has Naturalization records 1885–1923. Spokane County was organized in 1868 from Walla Walla, then disorganized and reorganized in 1879 from Stevens County.

Record Type	Year Begun	Jurisdiction
Marriage	1880	County Auditor
Land	na	County Auditor
Divorce	1879	County Clerk
Probate	1883	County Clerk
Court	1879	County Clerk

■ Stevens 20 Jan. 1863
215 S. Oak St. Room 206, Colville, WA 99114
Phone: (509)684-7575
Web site: www.rootsweb.com/~wasteve2/stevens.htm
Parent County: Walla Walla
Comments/research tips: County Auditor has Birth and Death records 1891–1907. County Clerk has Naturalization records 1888–1970.

Record Type	Year Begun	Jurisdiction
Marriage	1864	County Auditor
Land	1886	County Auditor
Probate	1874	County Clerk

Divorce .... 1882 .... County Clerk
Court .... 1882 .... County Clerk

■ **Thurston** 12 Jan. 1852
2000 Lakeridge Dr. SW Bldg. 2, Olympia, WA 98502
Phone: (360)786-5431
Web site: www.co.thurston.wa.us/
Parent County: Lewis
Comments/research tips: County Auditor has Birth and Death records 1891–1907. County Clerk has Naturalization records 1849–1974.

Record Type	Year Begun	Jurisdiction
Land	1852	County Auditor
Marriage	1844	County Auditor
Divorce	1889	County Clerk
Probate	1848	County Clerk
Court	851	County Clerk

■ **Vancouver** 27 July 1844
Parent County: Original county
Comments/research tips: (See Clark) Name changed to Clark 3 September 1849.

■ **Wahkiakum** 24 Apr. 1854
64 Main St., P.O. Box 116, Cathlamet, WA 98612
Phone: (360)795-3558
Web site: www.rootsweb.com/~wawahkia/
Parent County: Pacific
Comments/research tips: County Auditor has Birth and Death records 1891–1984.

Record Type	Year Begun	Jurisdiction
Marriage	1868	County Auditor
Military	1943	County Auditor
Divorce	1890	County Clerk
Probate	1852	County Clerk
Court	1890	County Clerk
Land	1858	County Auditor

■ **Walla Walla** 25 Apr. 1854
315 West Main St., P.O. Box 836, Walla Walla, WA 99362
Phone: (509)527-3221
Web site: www.co.walla-walla.wa.us/
Parent County: Skamania
Comments/research tips: County Auditor has Land records from late 1800s. County Clerk has Naturalization records 1861–1906.

Record Type	Year Begun	Jurisdiction
Divorce	1860	County Clerk
Probate	1860	County Clerk
Court	1860	County Clerk

■ **Whatcom** 9 Mar. 1854
311 Grand Ave. Room 301, Bellingham, WA 98227
Phone: (360)676-7688
Web site: www.rootsweb.com/~wawhatco/
Parent County: Island

Record Type	Year Begun	Jurisdiction
Birth	1936	Hlth./Human Services
Death	1936	Hlth./Human Services
Marriage	1854	County Auditor
Land	1854	County Auditor
Divorce	1883	County Clerk
Probate	1872	County Clerk
Court	1883	County Clerk

■ **Whitman** 29 Nov. 1871
N. 404 Main St., P.O. Box 390, Colfax, WA 99111
Phone: (509)397-6240
Web site: www.rootsweb.com/~wawhitma/
Parent County: Stevens
Comments/research tips: County Auditor has Birth and Death records 1891–1907.

Record Type	Year Begun	Jurisdiction
Marriage	1873	County Auditor
Probate	1877	County Clerk
Divorce	1890	County Clerk
Court	1890	County Clerk
Land	1874	County Auditor

■ **Yakima** 21 Jan. 1865
128 N. Second St. Room 323, Yakima, WA 98901
Phone: (509)574-1430
Web site: www.co.yakima.wa.us/
Parent County: Ferguson
Comments/research tips: County Auditor has Birth records 1891–1907 and Death records 1896–1907. Many County Clerk records were lost in 1908 courthouse fire.

Record Type	Year Begun	Jurisdiction
Military	1882	County Auditor
Marriage	1869	County Auditor
Land	1882	County Auditor
Probate	1879	County Clerk
Divorce	1890	County Clerk
Court	1890	County Clerk

West Virginia

By Rhonda R. McClure

HISTORICAL OVERVIEW

Until 1863, West Virginia's history is Virginia's history. While many of the other states joined the Union as territories created out of nothingness, West Virginia took existing counties—fifty in all—and broke away from Virginia. These counties formed the "restored government of Virginia," and Congress admitted West Virginia to the Union on 20 June 1863.

All but the five counties of West Virginia created after June 1863—Grant, Lincoln, Mineral, Mingo, and Summers—were first under the laws of the state of Virginia. This affects the types of records that were maintained and the court or clerk who was responsible for them. This also means that, with the exception of those five counties, you may find records for your West Virginia ancestor in Virginia.

RECORD HIGHLIGHTS

Because of the unique way in which West Virginia was created, many of the same problems with Virginia records affect the pre-1863 West Virginia records. When it comes to census records, the first true West Virginia enumeration is for 1870. Prior to 1870 you need to turn your attention to the census records for Virginia.

Births and deaths in West Virginia were recorded beginning in 1853. Statewide registration began on 1 January 1917, but a fire destroyed many records at the state level through 1921. When requesting vital records, it is better to contact the county clerk for anything recorded before 1921.

Although West Virginia was created long after the United States, it is one of those exception states—along with Louisiana and Hawaii—where the federal government did not get to sell the land first. This is primarily because the counties trace back to when there were colonies rather than states, and it wasn't until after the end

WEST VIRGINIA AT A GLANCE

Motto: Mountaineers Are Always Free

Population: 1.8 million

Prevalent Religions: Mostly Southern Baptist, also some Methodist, Roman Catholic, Presbyterian, Pentecostal, and Lutheran

Major Industries: Chemical products, mining, primary metals, stone, clay, and glass products, cattle, dairy products, poultry, apples

Ethnic Makeup (in percent): Caucasian 95.0%, African American 3.2%, Hispanic 0.7%, Asian 0.5%, Native American 0.2%, Other 0.2%

Famous West Virginians: Pearl S. Buck, Jennifer Garner, John Henry, Homer Hickam, Don Knotts, Matt Lauer, Kathy Mattea, Randy Moss, John Nash, Mary Lou Retton, Sam Sneed, Jerry West, Jason Williams, Chuck Yeager

Above: A West Virginia mill

© PhotoDisc/Getty Images

West Virginia

of the American Revolution that the federal government existed and began to have a hand in selling land.

Early land grants have been indexed in *Sim's Index to Land Grants in West Virginia*. Edgar Barr Sims was the State Auditor for West Virginia at various times in the 1930s, 1940s, and 1950s, and his index was published in 1952. It includes grants made by Lord Fairfax before the creation of the Virginia Land Office. The index is arranged by county and lists the grantee, number of acres, local description, year, book, and page numbers.

Probate and court records, as well as the courts that are responsible for them, have simply carried over from when West Virginia was part of Virginia. However, will books are available on microfilm through a number of West Virginia repositories and the Family History Library.

STATE RESOURCES

■ ARCHIVES, LIBRARIES, AND SOCIETIES

Allegheny Regional Family History Society
P.O. Box 1804, Elkins, WV 26241
Web site: <www.swcp.com/~dhi ckman/>

Archives and History Library
The Cultural Center, 1900 Kanawha Blvd. E., Charleston, WV 25305-0300
Web site: <www.wvculture.org/ history/>

Berkelely County Genealogical-Historical Society
P.O. Box 1624, Martinsburg, WV 25401

Boone County Genealogical Society
P.O. Box 295, Madison, WV 25130

Brooke County Genealogical Society, Inc.
P.O. Box 144, Beech Bottom, WV 26030

Cabell County Public Library
455 Ninth St. Plaza, Huntington, WV 25701

Cabell-Wayne County Historical Society
P.O. Box 9412, Huntington, WV 25704

Central West Virginia Genealogy & History Library
P.O. Box 56, Abbotts Run Rd., Old Rt. 33, Horner, WV 26372-0056

Episcopal Diocese of West Virginia
1608 Virginia St. E., Charleston, WV 25311
Tel: (304) 344-3597
Fax: (304) 343-3295

Genealogical Society of Fayette and Raleigh Counties, Inc.
P.O. Box 68, Oak Hill, WV 25901-0068

Gilmer County Historical Society
706 Mineral Rd., Glenville, WV 26351

Jackson County Historical Society
P.O. Box 22, Ripley, WV 25271

Kanawha Valley Genealogical Society
P.O. Box 8555, South Charleston, WV 25303

Library of Virginia
800 E. Broad St., Richmond, VA 23219-1905
Tel: (804) 692-3888
Fax: (804) 692-3556

Lincoln County Genealogical Society
7999 Lynn Ave., Hamlin, WV 25523

Logan County Genealogical Society
P.O. Box 1959, Logan, WV 25601

Marion County Genealogical Club, Inc.
℅ Marion County Library, 321 Monroe St., Fairmont, WV 26554

RESEARCH TIPS
for more info

- West Virginia is the only state in which the records in the counties greatly predate the existence of the state. In some ways this makes researching easier when dealing with any records that remained in the county. However, it is important to never assume that all the records are in that county. Always turn your attention to the records and repositories in Virginia as well.
- If you know your ancestor's religion, be sure to check the holdings of the West Virginia and Regional History Collection at the West Virginia University, P.O. Box 6069, 1549 University Ave., Morgantown, WV 26506-6069, <www.libraries.w vu.edu/wvcollection/>.
- Though West Virginia broke away from Virginia over disputes about seceding from the Union, there were some soldiers who fought for the Confederacy. It is estimated that about ten thousand soldiers fought against the Union.
- Newspapers can often be used as a record alternative, and not just for vital records. To learn more about the various newspapers and where you can find them today, you will want to search the Family History Library and check out *Newspapers in the West Virginia University Library* (Morgantown, West Virginia: West Virginia University Library, 1964).

Census Records
- Federal Census: 1870, 1880, 1900, 1910, 1920, 1930
- Federal Mortality Schedules: 1850, 1860, 1870, 1880
- Special Census of Civil War Union Veterans and Widows: 1890

Tel: (304) 366-1210
Fax: (304) 366-4831

Mercer County Genealogical-Historical Society
P.O. Box 5012, Princeton, WV 24740-5012

Methodist Historical Society, West Virginia Wesleyan College
Annie M. Pfeiffer Library, College Ave., Buckhannon, WV 26201
Tel: (304) 473-8059
Fax: (304) 473-8888

Mineral County Historical Landmark Commission
Rt. One, Box 94, Burlington, WV 26710

Mingo County Genealogical Society
P.O. Box 2581, Williamson, WV 25661

Monroe County Historical Society
P.O. Box 465, Union, WV 24983

Morgan County Historical and Genealogical Society
P.O. Box 52, Berkeley Springs, WV 25411

Morgantown Public Library
373 Spruce St., Morgantown, WV 26505

National Archives-Mid-Atlantic Region (Philadelphia)
Ninth and Market Sts., Philadelphia, PA 19107-4292
Tel: (215) 597-3000
Fax: (215) 597-2303
Web site: <www.archives.gov/midatlantic/>

Palatines to America, West Virginia Chapter
572 Plymouth Ave., Morgantown, WV 26505-2142

Ritchie County Historical Society
200 S. Church St., Harrisville, WV 26362

Roane County Historical Society
P.O. Box 161, Spencer, WV 25276

Roman Catholic Diocese of Wheeling-Charleston
1300 Byron St., P.O. Box 230, Wheeling, WV 26003
Tel: (304) 233-0880
Fax: (304) 233-0890

State Auditor
Capitol Building, County Collections Division, Building-1, Room W-212, Charleston, WV 25305
Tel: (304) 558-2251
Fax: (304) 558-5200

Taylor County Public Library
200 Beech St., Grafton, WV 26354
Tel: (304) 265-6121
Fax: 304-265-6122
Web site: http://taylor.clark.lib.wv.us/history.htm

Taylor County Historical and Genealogical Society, Inc.
P.O. Box 522, Grafton, WV 26354

Tri-State Genealogical and Historical Society
P.O. Box 454, Newell, WV 26050-0454
Web site: <www.rootsweb.com/~wvtsghs/indext.htm>

Tyler County Historical Society
P.O. Box 317, Middlebourne, WV 26149

Upshur County Historical Society
P.O. Box 753, Buckhannon, WV 26201

Vital Registration Office
State Capitol Complex No. 3, Room 516, Charleston, WV 25305
Tel: (304) 558-2931
Fax: (304) 558-1051

West Augusta Historical & Genealogical Society
PO Box 266, Mannington, WV 26582

West Virginia Midland Trail Genealogical Society
2614 Furlong Ave., St. Albans, WV 25177
Web site: <www.rootsweb.com/~wvmtgs/>

West Virginia Baptist Historical Society
Route #2, Box 304, Ripley, WV 25271
Tel: (304) 346-2036

West Virginia University Library
Colson Hall, P.O. Box 6069, Morgantown, WV 26506-6069
Tel: (304) 293-3640
Fax: (304) 293-6923
Web site: <www.libraries.wvu.edu>

West Virginia Genealogical Society
P.O. Box 172, Elkview, WV 25071
Web site: <http://members.aol.com/edeaj/wvgenealogicalsociety.html>

Wetzel County Genealogical Society
P.O. Box 464, New Martinsville, WV 26155-0464

Wheeling Area Genealogical Society
2237 Marshall Ave., Wheeling, WV 26003-7444
Web site: <www.rootsweb.com/~wvwags/index.htm>

Wyoming County Genealogical Society
P.O. Box 1456, Pineville, WV 24874

BIBLIOGRAPHY

■ GENERAL RESOURCES

A Bibliography of West Virginia, 2 parts
by Innis C. Davis (Charleston: West Virginia Department of Archives and History, 1939)

Finding Your People in the Shenandoah Valley of Virginia and West Virginia
by Rebecca Ebert (Winchester, VA: The Rebecca Co., 1984)

Genealogical and Personal History of the Upper Monongabela Valley, West Virginia, 3 vols.
by Bernard Lee Butcher (New York: Lewis Historical Publishing Co., 1912)

The Genealogist's Companion and Sourcebook, 2d ed.
by Emily Anne Croom (Cincinnati: Betterway Books, 2003)

A Genealogist's Guide to Discovering Your African-American Ancestors
by Franklin Carter Smith and Emily Anne Croom (Cincinnati: Betterway Books, 2003)

A Guide to Church Records in the Archives Branch of the Virginia State Library
by Newell T. Clark and Elizabeth Terry Long (Richmond: Virginia State Library, 1981)

Guide to Genealogical Research in the National Archives of the United States
edited by Anne Bruner Eales and Robert M. Kvasnicka (Washington, DC: National Archives and Records Administration, 2000)

Guide to Manuscripts and Archives in the West Virginia Collection
by James W. Hess (Morgantown, WV: West Virginia University Library, 1974)

Guide to the Study of West Virginia History
by Charles Shetler (Morgantown, WV: West Virginia University Library, 1960)

A Handbook for Genealogical Research in West Virginia
by Helen S. Stinson (South Charleston, WV: Kanawha Valley Genealogical Society, 1981)

A History and Record of the Protestant Episcopal Church in the Diocese of West Virginia
by George W. Peterkin (Charleston, WV: Tribune Co., 1902)

History of West Virginia, Old and New, 3 vols.
by James Morton Callahan (Chicago: American Historical Society, 1923)

Index to Printed Virginia Genealogies
by Robert Armistead Stewart (Baltimore: Genealogical Publishing Co., 1970)

Loyal West Virginia from 1861 to 1865
by Theodore F. Lang (Baltimore: Deutsch, 1895)

Making a State: Formation of West Virginia, Including Maps, Illustrations, Plates and the Acts of the Virginia Assembly and the Legislature of West Virginia Creating the Counties
by Edgar Barr Sims (Charleston, WV: Edgar Barr Sims, 1956)

Men of West Virginia, 2 vols.
(Chicago: Biographical Publishing Co., 1903)

National Archives Microfilm Catalogs online:
<www.archives.gov/publications/genealogy_microfilm_catalogs.html>

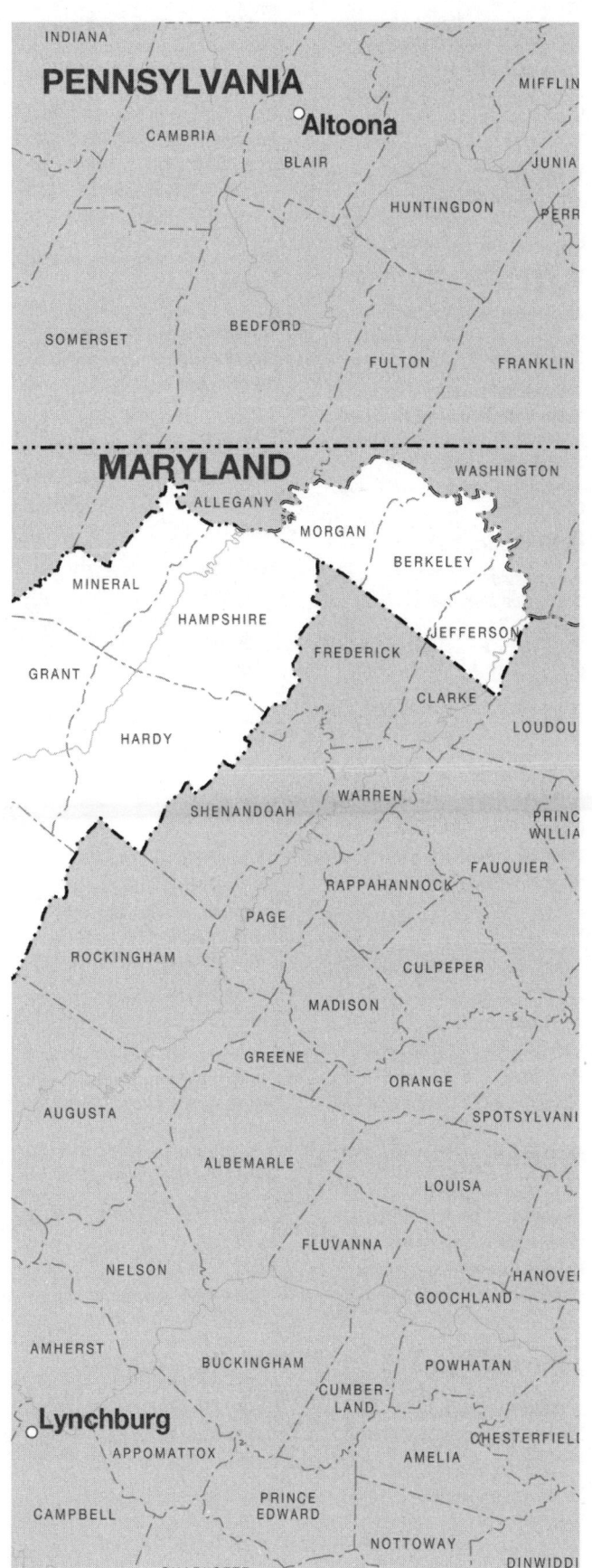

West Virginia

Obituaries from Newspapers of Northern West Virginia, 2 vols.
by W. Guy Tetrick (Clarksburg, WV: W.G. Tetrick, 1933)

Prominent Men of West Virginia
by George Wesley Atkinson (Wheeling, WV: W.L. Callin, 1890)

Timesaving Aid to Virginia-West Virginia Ancestors: A Genealogical Index of Surnames from Published Sources, 4 vols.
by Patrick G. Wardell (Athens, GA: Iberian Publishing Co., 1990)

Virginia Genealogical Resources
by Stuart E. Brown Jr (Detroit: Detroit Society for Genealogical Research, 1980)

Virginia Genealogies, A Trial List of Printed Books and Pamphlets, 3 vols.
by Stuart E. Brown Jr. (Berryville, VA: Virginia Book Co., 1967–89)

Virginians & West Virginians, 1607–1870
by Patrick G. Wardell (Bowie, MD: Heritage Books, 1986–1992)

West Virginia Genealogy Sources and Resources
by Carol McGinnis (Baltimore, MD: Genealogical Publishing Company, 1988)

The West Virginia Heritage Encyclopedia
compiled and edited by Jim Comstock (Richwood, WV: Comstock, 1976)

West Virginia: A History
by Otis K. Rice (Lexington, KY: University Press of Kentucky, 1985)

West Virginia History: A Guide to Research
by Harold M. Forbes (Morgantown: West Virginia University Press, 1981)

West Virginia and Its People, 3 vols.
by Thomas Condit Miller and Hu Maxwell (New York: Lewis Historical Publishing Co., 1913)

West Virginia Research Outline
(Salt Lake City, UT: Corp. of the President of the Church of Jesus Christ of L.D.S., 1988)

■ CENSUS RECORDS

The American Census Handbook
by Thomas Jay Kemp (Wilmington, DE: Scholarly Resources, Inc., 2001)

The Census Book: A Genealogist's Guide to Federal Census Facts, Schedules and Indexes
by Willim Dollarhide (Bountiful, UT: HeritageQuest, 1999)

Heads of Families. . . . Records of the State Enumerations; 1782 to 1785, Virginia
(Baltimore: Southern Book Co., 1952)

Map Guide to the U.S. Federal Census, 1790–1920
by William Thorndale and William Dollarhide (Baltimore: Genealogical Publishing Co., 1987)

The 1787 Census of Virginia, 3 vols.
by Netti Schreiner-Yantis and Florence Speakman Love (Springfield, VA: Genealogical Books-in-Print, 1987)

A Supplement to the 1810 Census of Virginia: Tax Lists of the Counties for Which the Census is Missing
by Netti Schreiner-Yantis (Springfield, VA: Genealogical Books-in-Print, 1971)

Virginia Taxpayers, 1782–87, Other than Those Published by the United States Census Bureau
by Augusta B. Fothergill and John Mark Naugle (Baltimore: Genealogical Publishing Co., 1966

Virginians in 1800; Counties of West Virginia
by Steven A. Bridges (Trumbull, CT: Steven A. Bridges, 1987)

Your Guide to the Federal Census
by Kathleen W. Hinckley (Cincinnati: Betterway Books, 2002)

■ IMMIGRATION RECORDS

American Naturalization Records, 1790–1990: What They Are and How to Use Them
by John J. Newman (North Salt Lake, UT: HeritageQuest, 1998)

American Passenger Arrival Records
by Michael Tepper (Baltimore: Genealogical Publishing Co., 1993)

Chronicles of the Scotch-Irish Settlement in Virginia: Extracted from the Original Court Records of Augusta County, 1754–1800
by Lyman Chalkley (Baltimore: Genealogical Publishing Co., 1980)

Passenger and Immigration Lists Index, 15 vols.
by P. William Filby (Detroit: Gale Research, 1981–)

They Became Americans: Finding Naturalization Records and Ethnic Origins
by Loretto Dennis Szucs (Salt Lake City: Ancestry, Inc., 1998)

They Came in Ships: A Guide to Finding Your Immigrant Ancestor's Arrival Records, 2d ed.
by John P. Colletta (Salt Lake City: Ancestry, Inc., 1993)

■ LAND RECORDS

Dyer's Index to Land Grants in West Virginia
by M.H. Dyer (Salem, MA: Higginson Book Co., 1996)

Locating Your Roots: Discover Your Ancestors Using Land Records
by Patricia Law Hatcher (Cincinnati: Betterway Books, 2003)

Sims Index to Land Grants in West Virginia
by Edgar B. Sims (Charleston: Auditor's Office, 1952)

■ MAPS

Gazetteer of West Virginia
by Henry Gannett (Baltimore: Genealogical Publishing Co., 1975)

New Descriptive Atlas of West Virginia
(Clarksburg, WV: Clarksburg Publishing Co., 1933)

West Virginia County Formations and Boundary Changes
from the West Virginia Historical Records Survey (Charleston, WV: Historical Survey, 1938)

West Virginia County Maps
compiled by C.J. Puetz (Lyndon Station, WI: Thomas Publishing Co., 1990)

West Virginia Place Names, Their Origin and Meaning, Including the Nomenclature of the Streams and Mountains
by Hamill Kenny (Piedmont, WV: Place Name Press, 1945)

■ MILITARY RECORDS

"The Soldiery of West Virginia the French And Indian War, Lord Dunmore's War, The Revolution, the War with Mexico"
by Virgil A. Lewis (In *Third Bennial Report Of the State Department of Archives and History,* pp. 39-118; Reprint: Baltimore: Genealogical Publishing Co.)

Uncle, We Are Ready! Registering America's Men, 1917–1918: A Guide to Researching World War I Draft Registration Cards
by John J. Newman (North Salt Lake, UT: HeritageQuest, 2001)

U.S. Military Records: A Guide to Federal & State Sources, Colonial America to the Present
by James C. Neagles (Salt Lake City: Ancestry, Inc., 1994)

War of 1812: Virginia Bounty Land & Pension Applicants: A Quick Reference Guide to Ancestors Having War of 1812 Service Who Served, Lived, Died, or Married in Virginia or West Virginia
by Patrick G. Wardell (Bowie, MD: Heritage Books, 1987)

West Virginia in the Civil War
by Boyd B. Stutler (Charleston, WV: Educational Foundation, 1963)

West Virginians in the Revolution
compiled by Ross B. Johnston (Baltimore: Genealogical Publishing Co., 1977)

West Virginia Revolutionary Ancestors Whose Services Were Non-military
by Anne Waller Reddy (Baltimore: Genealogical Publishing Co., 1963)

World War II: A Family Historian's Guide
by Debra Johnson Knox (Spartanburg, SC: MIE Publishing, 2003)

■ PROBATE RECORDS

Early West Virginia Wills
by K.T.H. McFarland (Apollo, PA: Closson Press, 1993)

Virginia Wills and Administrations, 1632–1800
by Clayton Torremce (Originally published in 1930; Reprint: Baltimore: Genealogical Publishing Co., 1965)

■ VITAL RECORDS

Inventory of Public Vital Statistics Records in West Virginia, 2 vols.
from the Historical Record Survey (Charleston, WV: West Virginia Historical Records Survey, 1941–1942)

Obituaries form Newspapers of Northern West Virginia, 2 vols.
by W. Guy Tetrick (Clarksburg, WV: W.G. Tetrick, 1933)

Roster of Confederate Graves, 7 vols.
from the United Daughters of the Confederacy (Atlanta: United Daughters of the Confederacy, Georgia Division, 1995)

West Virginia, 1863–1900 [Marriages]
(Brøderbund, 1999. CD-ROM)

Your Guide to Cemetery Research
by Sharon DeBartolo Carmack (Cincinnati: Betterway Books, 2002)

■ Barbour   3 Mar. 1843
8 N. Main St., Philippi, WV 26416
Phone: (304)457-2232
Web site: www.rootsweb.com/~wvbarbou/
Parent County: Harrison, Lewis, Randolph

Record Type	Year Begun	Jurisdiction
Birth	1853	County Clerk
Marriage	1840	County Clerk
Death	1853	County Clerk
Divorce	1843	Clerk/Circuit Ct.
Land	1843	County Clerk
Probate	1843	County Clerk
Court	1843	Clerk/Circuit Ct.

■ Berkeley   10 Feb. 1772
100 W. King St., Martinsburg, WV 25401
Phone: (304)264-1927
Web site: www.rootsweb.com/~wvberkel/
Parent County: Frederick
Comments/research tips: County Clerk has Naturalization records 1911–1929.

Record Type	Year Begun	Jurisdiction
Birth	1865	County Clerk
Marriage	1781	County Clerk
Death	1865	County Clerk
Divorce	na	Clerk/Circuit Ct.
Land	1772	County Clerk
Probate	1772	County Clerk
Court	1772	Clerk/Circuit Ct.

■ Boone   11 Mar. 1847
200 State St., Madison, WV 25130
Phone: (304)369-3925

Web site: www.rootsweb.com/~wvboone/
Parent County: Kanawha, Cabell, Logan
Comments/research tips: County Auditor has Military Discharge records 1917–1927.

Record Type	Year Begun	Jurisdiction
Birth	1865	County Clerk
Marriage	1860	County Clerk
Death	1865	County Clerk
Divorce	1865	Clerk/Circuit Ct.
Land	1847	County Clerk
Probate	1865	County Clerk
Court	1865	Clerk/Circuit Ct.

■ Braxton   15 Jan. 1836

300 Main St., P.O. Box 486, Sutton, WV 26601
Phone: (304)765-2833
Web site: www.rootsweb.com/~wvbraxto/
Parent County: Kanawha, Lewis, Nicholas

Record Type	Year Begun	Jurisdiction
Divorce	1836	Clerk/Circuit Ct.
Land	1836	County Clerk
Probate	1836	County Clerk
Court	1836	Clerk/Circuit Ct.
Marriage	1836	County Clerk
Birth	1853	County Clerk
Death	1853	County Clerk

■ Brooke   23 May 1797

632 Main St., Wellsburg, WV 26070
Phone: (304)737-3661
Web site: www.rootsweb.com/~wvbrooke/index.htm
Parent County: Ohio

Record Type	Year Begun	Jurisdiction
Birth	1854	County Clerk
Marriage	1797	County Clerk
Death	1889	County Clerk
Divorce	na	Clerk/Circuit Ct.
Land	1797	County Clerk
Probate	1797	County Clerk
Court	na	Clerk/Circuit Ct.

■ Cabell   2 Jan. 1809

750 Fifth Ave., Huntington, WV 25701
Phone: (304)526-8625
Web site: www.rootsweb.com/~wvcabell/cabell.html
Parent County: Kanawha
Comments/research tips: County Clerk has Birth records 1853–1854.

Record Type	Year Begun	Jurisdiction
Birth	1865	County Clerk
Marriage	1809	County Clerk
Death	1853	County Clerk
Divorce	1809	Clerk/Circuit Ct.
Land	1809	County Clerk
Probate	1820	County Clerk
Court	1809	Clerk/Circuit Ct.

■ Calhoun   5 Mar. 1856

Main St., P.O. Box 230, Grantsville, WV 26147
Phone: (304)354-6725

Web site: www.rootsweb.com/~wvcalhou/index2.htm
Parent County: Gilmer
Comments/research tips: County Clerk has Military Discharge records 1918–1945.

Record Type	Year Begun	Jurisdiction
Birth	1856	County Clerk
Marriage	1856	County Clerk
Death	1856	County Clerk
Land	1856	County Clerk
Probate	1856	County Clerk
Court	1856	Clerk/Circuit Ct.

■ Clay   29 Mar. 1858

P.O. Box 190, Clay, WV 25043
Phone: (304)587-4283
Web site: www.rootsweb.com/~wvclay/
Parent County: Braxton, Nicholas

Record Type	Year Begun	Jurisdiction
Birth	1858	County Clerk
Marriage	1858	County Clerk
Death	1858	County Clerk
Land	1873	County Clerk
Probate	1858	County Clerk
Court	1858	Clerk/Circuit Ct.

■ Doddridge   4 Feb. 1845

118 E. Court St., West Union, WV 26456
Phone: (304)873-2631
Web site: www.rootsweb.com/~wvdoddri/
Parent County: Harrison, Tyler, Ritchie, Lewis

Record Type	Year Begun	Jurisdiction
Birth	1853	County Clerk
Marriage	1846	County Clerk
Death	1853	County Clerk
Land	1845	County Clerk
Probate	1887	County Clerk
Court	1845	Clerk/Circuit Ct.

■ Fayette   28 Feb. 1831

P.O. Box 569, Fayetteville, WV 25840
Phone: (304)574-1200
Web site: www.rootsweb.com/~wvfayett/
Parent County: Kanawha, Greenbrier, Logan, Nicholas

Record Type	Year Begun	Jurisdiction
Birth	1866	County Clerk
Marriage	1831	County Clerk
Death	1866	County Clerk
Divorce	1832	Clerk/Circuit Ct.
Land	1831	County Clerk
Probate	1861	County Clerk
Court	1832	Clerk/Circuit Ct.

■ Gilmer   3 Feb. 1845

10 Howard St., Glenville, WV 26351
Phone: (304)462-7641
Web site: www.rootsweb.com/~wvgilmer/
Parent County: Lewis, Kanawha
Comments/research tips: County Clerk has Military Discharge records 1896–1944.

Record Type	Year Begun	Jurisdiction
Birth	1853	County Clerk
Marriage	1845	County Clerk
Death	1853	County Clerk
Land	1845	County Clerk
Probate	1845	County Clerk
Court	1853	Clerk/Circuit Ct.

■ Grant 14 Feb. 1866

5 Highland Ave., Petersburg, WV 26847
Phone: (304)257-4550
Web site: www.rootsweb.com/~wvgrant/grant.htm
Parent County: Hardy

Record Type	Year Begun	Jurisdiction
Birth	1865	County Clerk
Marriage	1866	County Clerk
Death	1865	County Clerk
Divorce	1866	Clerk/Circuit Ct.
Land	1866	County Clerk
Probate	1866	County Clerk
Court	1866	Clerk/Circuit Ct.

■ Greenbrier 20 Oct. 1777

P.O. Box 506, Lewisburg, WV 24901
Phone: (304)647-6601
Web site: www.rootsweb.com/~wvgreenb/
Parent County: Montgomery, Botetourt, VA

Record Type	Year Begun	Jurisdiction
Birth	1853	County Clerk
Marriage	1780	County Clerk
Death	1853	County Clerk
Land	1780	County Clerk
Probate	1777	County Clerk
Court	1814	Clerk/Circuit Ct.

■ Hampshire 1 May 1754

66 N. High St., Romney, WV 26757
Phone: (304)822-5112
Web site: www.rootsweb.com/~wvhampsh/
Parent County: Frederick, Augusta
Comments/research tips: County Clerk has Marriage records 1824–1828.

Record Type	Year Begun	Jurisdiction
Birth	1865	County Clerk
Marriage	1865	County Clerk
Death	1866	County Clerk
Land	1757	County Clerk
Probate	1851	County Clerk
Court	1831	Clerk/Circuit Ct.

■ Hancock 15 Jan. 1848

P.O. Box 367, New Cumberland, WV 26047
Phone: (304)564-3311
Web site: www.rootsweb.com/~wvhancoc/
Parent County: Brooke
Comments/research tips: County Clerk has Military Discharge records 1866–1992 and Naturalization records 1907–1956.

Record Type	Year Begun	Jurisdiction
Birth	1853	County Clerk

Record Type	Year Begun	Jurisdiction
Marriage	1854	County Clerk
Death	1853	County Clerk
Divorce	1848	Clerk/Circuit Ct.
Land	1848	County Clerk
Probate	1848	County Clerk
Court	1848	Clerk/Circuit Ct.

■ Hardy 17 Oct. 1785

204 Washington St., Moorefield, WV 26836
Phone: (304)538-2929
Web site: www.rootsweb.com/~wvhardy/
Parent County: Hampshire

Record Type	Year Begun	Jurisdiction
Probate	1786	County Clerk
Court	1788	Clerk/Circuit Ct.
Nat.	1916	County Clerk
Birth	1853	County Clerk
Marriage	1795	County Clerk
Death	1853	County Clerk
Divorce	1831	Clerk/Circuit Ct.
Land	1786	County Clerk

■ Harrison 3 May 1784

301 W. Main St., Clarksburg, WV 26301
Phone: (304)624-8672
Web site: www.rootsweb.com/~wvharris/
Parent County: Monongalia

Record Type	Year Begun	Jurisdiction
Birth	1853	County Clerk
Marriage	1784	County Clerk
Death	1853	County Clerk
Land	1786	County Clerk
Probate	1788	County Clerk
Court	1803	Clerk/Circuit Ct.
Divorce	1803	Clerk/Circuit Ct.

■ Jackson 1 Mar. 1831

P.O. Box 800, Ripley, WV 25271
Phone: (304)372-2011
Web site: www.rootsweb.com/~wvjackso/JACK.HTM
Parent County: Kanawha, Mason, Wood
Comments/research tips: County Clerk has Military Discharge records 1918–1992.

Record Type	Year Begun	Jurisdiction
Birth	1853	County Clerk
Marriage	1831	County Clerk
Death	1853	County Clerk
Divorce	1831	Clerk/Circuit Ct.
Land	1831	County Clerk
Probate	1831	County Clerk
Court	1831	Clerk/Circuit Ct.

■ Jefferson 8 Jan. 1801

P.O. Box 208, Charles Town, WV 25414
Phone: (304)725-9761
Web site: www.rootsweb.com/~wvjeffer/
Parent County: Berkeley

Record Type	Year Begun	Jurisdiction
Marriage	1801	County Clerk

Land	1801	County Clerk
Probate	1801	County Clerk
Birth	1853	County Clerk
Court	1831	Clerk/Circuit Ct.
Divorce	1831	Clerk/Circuit Ct.
Death	1853	County Clerk

■ **Kanawha** 14 Nov. 1788
P.O. Box 3226, Charleston, WV 25332
Phone: (304)357-0136
Web site: www.rootsweb.com/~wvkanawh/
Parent County: Greenbrier, Montgomery
Comments/research tips: Clerk of Circuit Court has Court records 1801–1813. County Clerk has Marriage records 1794–1843 and Military Discharge records 1915–1966.

Record Type	Year Begun	Jurisdiction
Birth	1853	County Clerk
Marriage	1850	County Clerk
Death	1853	County Clerk
Land	1790	County Clerk
Probate	1820	County Clerk
Court	1832	Clerk/Circuit Ct.
Divorce	1831	Clerk/Circuit Ct.

■ **Lewis** 18 Dec. 1816
P.O. Box 87, Weston, WV 26452
Phone: (304)269-8215
Web site: www.rootsweb.com/~wvlewis/
Parent County: Harrison

Record Type	Year Begun	Jurisdiction
Birth	1853	County Clerk
Marriage	1817	County Clerk
Death	1853	County Clerk
Divorce	na	Clerk/Circuit Ct.
Land	1817	County Clerk
Probate	1817	County Clerk

■ **Lincoln** 23 Feb. 1867
P.O. Box 497, Hamlin, WV 25523
Phone: (304)824-5337
Web site: www.co.lincoln.wv.us
Parent County: Boone, Cabell, Kanawha, Putnam
Comments/research tips: County Clerk has Military Discharge records 1919–1980.

Record Type	Year Begun	Jurisdiction
Birth	1909	County Clerk
Marriage	1895	County Clerk
Death	1909	County Clerk
Land	1909	County Clerk
Probate	1909	County Clerk
Divorce	1909	Clerk/Circuit Ct.
Court	1909	Clerk/Circuit Ct.

■ **Logan** 12 Jan. 1824
County Courthouse, Room 101, 300 Stratton St., Logan, WV 25601
Phone: (304)792-8600
Web site: www.rootsweb.com/~wvlogan/logan.htm
Parent County: Kanawha and Cabell, WV, Giles and Tazewell, VA

Comments/research tips: County Clerk has Military Discharge records 1917–1989 and Naturalization records 1913–1958.

Record Type	Year Begun	Jurisdiction
Birth	1872	County Clerk
Marriage	1872	County Clerk
Death	1872	County Clerk
Divorce	1868	Clerk/Circuit Ct.
Land	1835	County Clerk
Probate	1873	County Clerk
Court	1868	Clerk/Circuit Ct.

■ **Marion** 14 Jan. 1842
P.O. Box 1267, Fairmont, WV 26554
Phone: (304)367-5445
Web site: www.marioncountywv.com
Parent County: Harrison, Monongalia
Comments/research tips: County Clerk has Naturalization records 1904–1926.

Record Type	Year Begun	Jurisdiction
Birth	1860	County Clerk
Marriage	1842	County Clerk
Death	1861	County Clerk
Land	1842	County Clerk
Probate	1842	County Clerk

■ **Marshall** 12 Mar. 1835
Seventh St., P.O. Box 459, Moundsville, WV 26041
Phone: (304)845-1220
Web site: www.rootsweb.com/~wvmarsha/marsh.htm
Parent County: Ohio
Comments/research tips: County Clerk has Military Discharge records 1919–1942.

Record Type	Year Begun	Jurisdiction
Birth	1853	County Clerk
Marriage	1835	County Clerk
Death	1853	County Clerk
Divorce	1835	Clerk/Circuit Ct.
Land	1835	County Clerk
Probate	1835	County Clerk
Court	1835	Clerk/Circuit Ct.

■ **Mason** 2 Jan. 1804
200 Sixth St., Point Pleasant, WV 25550
Phone: (304)675-1997
Web site: www.rootsweb.com/~wvmason/mason.htm
Parent County: Kanawha
Comments/research tips: County Clerk has Military Discharge records 1917–1987.

Record Type	Year Begun	Jurisdiction
Birth	1853	County Clerk
Marriage	1806	County Clerk
Death	1853	County Clerk
Divorce	na	Clerk/Circuit Ct.
Land	1803	County Clerk
Probate	1834	County Clerk
Court	1809	Clerk/Circuit Ct.

■ **McDowell** 20 Feb. 1858
90 Wyoming St. #109, Welch, WV 24801
Phone: (304)436-8532

Web site: www.mcdowellwv.com
Parent County: Tazewell
Comments/research tips: County Clerk has Naturalization records 1908–1926. County seat was first Perryville, moved to Welch in 1892.

Record Type	Year Begun	Jurisdiction
Birth	1872	County Clerk
Marriage	1859	County Clerk
Death	1894	County Clerk
Divorce	1858	Clerk/Circuit Ct.
Land	1868	County Clerk
Probate	1897	County Clerk

■ Mercer 17 Mar. 1837
P.O. Box 5469, Princeton, WV 24740
Phone: (304)487-8311
Web site: www.rootsweb.com/~wvmercer/mercer.htm
Parent County: Giles and Tazewell
Comments/research tips: County Clerk has Military Discharge records 1914–1944.

Record Type	Year Begun	Jurisdiction
Birth	1853	County Clerk
Marriage	1854	County Clerk
Death	1853	County Clerk
Divorce	1837	Clerk/Circuit Ct.
Land	1837	County Clerk
Probate	1838	County Clerk
Court	1837	Clerk/Circuit Ct.

■ Mineral 1 Feb. 1866
150 Armstrong Sq., Keyser, WV 26726
Phone: (304)788-3924
Web site: www.rootsweb.com/~wvminera/mineral.htm
Parent County: Hampshire
Comments/research tips: County Clerk has Naturalization records 1908–1911 and 1920–1923.

Record Type	Year Begun	Jurisdiction
Birth	1865	County Clerk
Marriage	1866	County Clerk
Death	1865	County Clerk
Land	1866	County Clerk
Probate	1866	County Clerk
Divorce	1866	Clerk/Circuit Ct.

■ Mingo 30 Jan. 1895
P.O. Box 1197, Williamson, WV 25661
Phone: (304)235-0330
Web site: www.rootsweb.com/~wvmingo/mingo.htm
Parent County: Logan
Comments/research tips: County Clerk has Military Discharge records 1918–1945 and Naturalization records 1910–1927.

Record Type	Year Begun	Jurisdiction
Birth	1900	County Clerk
Marriage	1895	County Clerk
Death	1894	County Clerk
Divorce	1895	Clerk/Circuit Ct.
Land	1836	County Clerk
Probate	1895	County Clerk
Court	1895	Clerk/Circuit Ct.

■ Monongalia 7 Oct. 1776
263 High St., Morgantown, WV 26505
Phone: (304)291-7255
Web site: www.rootsweb.com/~wvmonong/
Parent County: District of West Augusta
Comments/research tips: Clerk of Circuit Court has Naturalization records 1907–1929.

Record Type	Year Begun	Jurisdiction
Birth	1853	County Clerk
Marriage	1796	County Clerk
Death	1852	County Clerk
Divorce	1832	Clerk/Circuit Ct.
Land	1789	County Clerk
Probate	1819	County Clerk
Court	1798	Clerk/Circuit Ct.

■ Monroe 14 Jan. 1799
Main St., P.O. Box 350, Union, WV 24983
Phone: (304)772-3096
Web site: www.rootsweb.com/~wvmonroe/
Parent County: Greenbrier

Record Type	Year Begun	Jurisdiction
Birth	1853	County Clerk
Marriage	1799	County Clerk
Death	1853	County Clerk
Land	1789	County Clerk
Probate	1799	County Clerk
Court	1789	Clerk/Circuit Ct.
Divorce	1789	Clerk/Circuit Ct.

■ Morgan 9 Feb. 1820
202 Fairfax St. Suite 100, Berkeley Springs, WV 25411
Phone: (304)258-8547
Web site: http://www.rootsweb.com/~wvmorgan/
Parent County: Berkeley, Hampshire

Record Type	Year Begun	Jurisdiction
Birth	1865	County Clerk
Death	1865	County Clerk
Divorce	1831	Clerk/Circuit Ct.
Land	1820	County Clerk
Court	1820	Clerk/Circuit Ct.
Marriage	1820	County Clerk
Probate	1820	County Clerk

■ Nicholas 30 Jan. 1818
700 Main St., Summersville, WV 26651
Phone: (304)872-3630
Web site: www.rootsweb.com/~wvnichol/
Parent County: Greenbrier, Kanawha, Randolph

Record Type	Year Begun	Jurisdiction
Birth	1853	County Clerk
Marriage	1817	County Clerk
Death	1853	County Clerk
Divorce	1818	Clerk/Circuit Ct.
Land	1818	County Clerk
Probate	1820	County Clerk
Court	1818	Clerk/Circuit Ct.

■ Ohio 7 Oct. 1776
1500 Chapline St., Wheeling, WV 26003
Phone: (304)234-3683

Web site: www.hostville.com/wvoh/
Parent County: District of W. Augusta
Comments/research tips: County Clerk has Military Discharge records 1917–1992, Naturalization records 1814–1895.

Record Type	Year Begun	Jurisdiction
Birth	1853	County Clerk
Marriage	1790	County Clerk
Death	1853	County Clerk
Divorce	1831	Clerk/Circuit Ct.
Land	1778	County Clerk
Probate	1777	County Clerk
Court	1818	Clerk/Circuit Ct.

■ Pendleton 4 Dec. 1787
Main St., P.O. Box 11607, Franklin, WV 26807
Phone: (304)358-2505
Web site: www.rootsweb.com/~wvpendle/
Parent County: Augusta, Hardy, Rockingham

Record Type	Year Begun	Jurisdiction
Birth	1853	County Clerk
Marriage	1797	County Clerk
Death	1853	County Clerk
Land	1788	County Clerk
Probate	1788	County Clerk
Court	1788	Clerk/Circuit Ct.
Divorce	1789	Clerk/Circuit Ct.

■ Pleasants 29 Mar. 1851
301 Court Ln. #101, St. Marys, WV 26170
Phone: (304)684-3542
Web site: www.rootsweb.com/~wvpleasa/
Parent County: Ritchie, Tyler, Wood

Record Type	Year Begun	Jurisdiction
Birth	1853	County Clerk
Marriage	1853	County Clerk
Death	1853	County Clerk
Divorce	1868	Clerk/Circuit Ct.
Land	1851	County Clerk
Probate	1851	County Clerk
Court	1868	Clerk/Circuit Ct.

■ Pocahontas 21 Dec. 1821
900-C Tenth Ave., Marlinton, WV 24954
Phone: (304)799-4549
Web site: www.rootsweb.com/~wvpocaho
Parent County: Pendleton, Randolph, Bath

Record Type	Year Begun	Jurisdiction
Birth	1853	County Clerk
Marriage	1822	County Clerk
Death	1853	County Clerk
Divorce	1881	Clerk/Circuit Ct.
Land	1822	County Clerk
Probate	1822	County Clerk
Court	1881	Clerk/Circuit Ct.

■ Preston 19 Jan. 1818
101 W Main St. #201, Kingwood, WV 26537
Phone: (304)329-0070

Web site: www.rootsweb.com/~wvpresto/
Parent County: Monongalia

Record Type	Year Begun	Jurisdiction
Birth	1868	County Clerk
Marriage	1869	County Clerk
Death	1868	County Clerk
Divorce	1864	Clerk/Circuit Ct.
Land	1869	County Clerk
Probate	1869	County Clerk
Court	1864	Clerk/Circuit Ct.

■ Putnam 11 Mar. 1848
3389 Winfield Rd., Winfield, WV 25213
Phone: (304)586-0202
Web site: www.rootsweb.com/~wvputnam/
Parent County: Kanawha, Mason, Cabell

Record Type	Year Begun	Jurisdiction
Birth	1853	County Clerk
Marriage	1848	County Clerk
Death	1853	County Clerk
Divorce	1848	Clerk/Circuit Ct.
Probate	1847	County Clerk
Court	1848	Clerk/Circuit Ct.
Land	1848	County Clerk

■ Raleigh 23 Jan. 1850
County Courthouse 215 Main St., Beckley, WV 25801
Phone: (304)255-9126
Web site: www.rootsweb.com/~wvraleig/
Parent County: Fayette
Comments/research tips: County Clerk has Military Discharge records 1917–1943 and Naturalization records 1908–1949.

Record Type	Year Begun	Jurisdiction
Birth	1853	County Clerk
Marriage	1850	County Clerk
Death	1853	County Clerk
Divorce	1850	Clerk/Circuit Ct.
Land	1850	County Clerk
Probate	1850	County Clerk
Court	1850	Clerk/Circuit Ct.

■ Randolph 1787
Randolph County Courthouse, P.O. Box 368, Elkins, WV 26241
Phone: (304)636-0543
Web site: www.pa-roots.org/~randolph/
Parent County: Harrison
Comments/research tips: County Clerk has Naturalization records 1907–1929.

Record Type	Year Begun	Jurisdiction
Birth	1853	County Clerk
Marriage	1787	County Clerk
Death	1853	County Clerk
Land	1787	County Clerk
Probate	1787	County Clerk

■ Ritchie 18 Feb. 1843
115 E. Main St., Harrisville, WV 26362
Phone: (304)643-2164

Web site: www.rootsweb.com/~wvritchi/indexr.htm
Parent County: Harrison, Lewis, Wood
Comments/research tips: County Clerk has Military Discharge records 1918–1975.

Record Type	Year Begun	Jurisdiction
Birth	1853	County Clerk
Marriage	1843	County Clerk
Death	1889	County Clerk
Divorce	1843	Clerk/Circuit Ct.
Land	1843	County Clerk
Probate	1843	County Clerk
Court	1843	Clerk/Circuit Ct.

■ Roane   11 Mar. 1856

P.O. Box 69, Spencer, WV 25276
Phone: (304)927-2860
Web site: www.pa-roots.com/~roane/
Parent County: Kanawha, Jackson, Gilmer

Record Type	Year Begun	Jurisdiction
Birth	1856	County Clerk
Marriage	1856	County Clerk
Death	1856	County Clerk
Land	1856	County Clerk
Probate	1857	County Clerk
Court	1856	Clerk/Circuit Ct.
Divorce	1856	Clerk/Circuit Ct.

■ Summers   27 Feb. 1871

P.O. Box 97, Hinton, WV 25951
Phone: (304)466-7104
Web site: www.rootsweb.com/~wvsummer/summers.htm
Parent County: Greenbrier, Monroe, Mercer, Fayette
Comments/research tips: County Clerk has Naturalization records 1908–1945.

Record Type	Year Begun	Jurisdiction
Birth	1871	County Clerk
Marriage	1871	County Clerk
Death	1871	County Clerk
Divorce	1874	Clerk/Circuit Ct.
Land	1870	County Clerk
Probate	1854	County Clerk
Court	1871	Clerk/Circuit Ct.

■ Taylor   19 Jan. 1844

214 W. Main St., Grafton, WV 26354
Phone: (304)265-1401
Web site: www.rootsweb.com/~wvtaylor/
Parent County: Barbour, Harrison, Marion
Comments/research tips: County Clerk has Military Discharge records 1918–1946.

Record Type	Year Begun	Jurisdiction
Birth	1853	County Clerk
Marriage	1853	County Clerk
Death	1853	County Clerk
Divorce	1881	Clerk/Circuit Ct.
Land	1844	County Clerk
Probate	1844	County Clerk
Court	1881	Clerk/Circuit Ct.

■ Tucker   7 Mar. 1856

215 First St., Parsons, WV 26287
Phone: (304)478-2414
Web site: www.rootsweb.com/~wvtucker
Parent County: Randolph
Comments/research tips: County Clerk has Naturalization records 1904–1950.

Record Type	Year Begun	Jurisdiction
Birth	1856	County Clerk
Marriage	1856	County Clerk
Death	1852	County Clerk
Divorce	1856	Clerk/Circuit Ct.
Land	1856	County Clerk
Probate	1852	County Clerk
Court	1856	Clerk/Circuit Ct.

■ Tyler   6 Dec. 1814

P.O. Box 66, Middlebourne, WV 26149
Phone: (304)758-2102
Web site: www.rootsweb.com/~wvtyler
Parent County: Ohio
Comments/research tips: County Clerk has Military Discharge records 1917–1970.

Record Type	Year Begun	Jurisdiction
Birth	1853	County Clerk
Death	1853	County Clerk
Divorce	1873	Clerk/Circuit Ct.
Land	1815	County Clerk
Probate	1815	County Clerk
Court	1815	Clerk/Circuit Ct.
Marriage	1815	County Clerk

■ Upshur   26 Mar. 1851

40 W. Main St., Room 101, Buckhannon, WV 26201
Phone: (304)472-1068
Web site: www.rootsweb.com/~wvupshur/
Parent County: Randolph, Barbour, Lewis
Comments/research tips: County Clerk has Naturalization records 1908–1928.

Record Type	Year Begun	Jurisdiction
Birth	1853	County Clerk
Marriage	1853	County Clerk
Death	1853	County Clerk
Divorce	1874	Clerk/Circuit Ct.
Land	1851	County Clerk
Probate	1852	County Clerk
Court	1851	Clerk/Circuit Ct.

■ Wayne   18 Jan. 1842

P.O. Box 248, Wayne, WV 25570
Phone: (304)272-6369
Web site: www.rootsweb.com/~wvwayne/
Parent County: Cabell

Record Type	Year Begun	Jurisdiction
Birth	1853	County Clerk
Marriage	1853	County Clerk
Death	1853	County Clerk
Land	1842	County Clerk
Probate	1843	County Clerk

Court .... 1843 ....Clerk/Circuit Ct.
Divorce .... 1843 ....Clerk/Circuit Ct.

■ Webster 10 Jan. 1860
2 Court Sq., Room G1, Webster Springs, WV 26288
Phone: (304)847-2508
Web site: www.rootsweb.com/~wvwebste/webster.htm
Parent County: Braxton, Nicholas, Randolph
Comments/research tips: County Clerk has Military Discharge records 1918–1945.

Record Type	Year Begun	Jurisdiction
Birth	1887	County Clerk
Marriage	1888	County Clerk
Death	1887	County Clerk
Land	1877	County Clerk
Probate	1888	County Clerk
Court	1875	Clerk/Circuit Ct.
Divorce	1875	Clerk/Circuit Ct.

■ Wetzel 10 Jan. 1846
P.O. Box 156, New Martinsville, WV 26155
Phone: (304)455-8224
Web site: www.ovis.net/~billcham/
Parent County: Tyler
Comments/research tips: County Clerk has Military Discharge records 1917–1992 and Naturalization records 1913–1920 and 1922–1927.

Record Type	Year Begun	Jurisdiction
Birth	1845	County Clerk
Marriage	1845	County Clerk
Death	1845	County Clerk
Divorce	1846	Clerk/Circuit Ct.
Land	1845	County Clerk
Probate	1845	County Clerk
Court	1846	Clerk/Circuit Ct.

■ Wirt 19 Jan. 1848
P.O. Box 417, Elizabeth, WV 26143
Phone: (304)275-4271
Web site: www.rootsweb.com/~wvwirt/
Parent County: Wood, Jackson

Record Type	Year Begun	Jurisdiction
Birth	1870	County Clerk
Marriage	1854	County Clerk
Death	1870	County Clerk
Divorce	1849	Clerk/Circuit Ct.
Land	1848	County Clerk
Probate	1848	County Clerk
Court	1849	Clerk/Circuit Ct.

■ Wood 21 Dec. 1798
P.O. Box 1474, Parkersburg, WV 26101
Phone: (304)424-1896
Web site: www.rootsweb.com/~wvwood/
Parent County: Harrison
Comments/research tips: County Clerk has Military Discharge records 1917–1966.

Record Type	Year Begun	Jurisdiction
Birth	1853	County Clerk
Marriage	1801	County Clerk
Death	1853	County Clerk
Divorce	1831	Clerk/Circuit Ct.
Land	1802	County Clerk
Probate	1800	County Clerk
Court	1803	Clerk/Circuit Ct.

■ Wyoming 26 Jan. 1850
100 Main St., P.O. Box 309, Pineville, WV 24874
Phone: (304)732-8000
Web site: www.rootsweb.com/~wvwyomin/
Parent County: Logan
Comments/research tips: County Clerk has Military Discharge records 1917–1945 and Naturalization records 1907–1945.

Record Type	Year Begun	Jurisdiction
Birth	1853	County Clerk
Marriage	1855	County Clerk
Death	1853	County Clerk
Divorce	1850	Clerk/Circuit Ct.
Land	1850	County Clerk
Probate	1850	County Clerk
Court	1850	Clerk/Circuit Ct.

Wisconsin

By James W. Warren

HISTORICAL OVERVIEW

LaVerne and Shirley bottled beer in Milwaukee, just as one of your German ancestors may have done decades earlier. But long before the first German was ever spoken on the western shores of Lake Michigan, the area was home to the Winnebago, Ojibway (Chippewa), Menominee, Oneida, Sauk, and other Indian tribes driven west by the Iroquois.

The first European in what would become Wisconsin was Jean Nicolet in 1634. In 1690, Catholic Missionaries established the mission at Michilimackinac (now Mackinac, Michigan), the focal point for traders going to and from what would become Wisconsin. French traders first came to the Green Bay and Prairie du Chien areas in the 1700s. In 1763, the British gained control of the area from the French. The U.S. acquired it in 1783 and it became an official part of the Northwest Territory in 1787, then Indiana Territory in 1800, Illinois Territory in 1809, and Michigan Territory in 1818. Lead mining along the Illinois/Wisconsin border attracted settlers from Southern states beginning about 1820. Migration from the Northeast states increased in the 1830s as the Lake Michigan shoreline was settled. Lumbering, mining, and farming were major enterprises. Many later settlers were from New York, Vermont, Pennsylvania, or Ohio.

In 1836, Wisconsin Territory was created and included lands as far west as the Missouri River. In 1838, much of that western land was transferred to Iowa Territory. Wisconsin became the thirtieth state in 1848, and the last Indian lands were obtained by treaty.

In the 1840s and 1850s large numbers of foreign immigrants arrived. Before the Civil War, Norwegians and Irish were the next largest immigrant groups (after the Germans) to the state, with substantial numbers from other British Isles countries and from Canada. Later immigrant groups would include Poles, Czechs, Austrians,

© PhotoDisc / Getty Images

WISCONSIN AT A GLANCE

Motto: Forward

Population: 5.4 million

Prevalent Religions: Roman Catholic, Lutheran

Major Industries: Agriculture and dairy farming, production of dairy products, manufacture of paper products, beer, and processed foods

Ethnic Makeup (in percent): Caucasian 88.9%, African American 5.7%, Hispanic 3.6%, Asian 1.7%, Native American 0.9%, Other 2.8%

Famous Wisconsinites: Walter H. Annenberg, Willem Dafoe, Jeffrey Dahmer, Zona Gale, Eric Heiden, Woody Herman, Harry Houdini, Liberace, Georgia O'Keeffe, Charles and John Ringling, Spencer Tracy, Orson Welles, Thornton Wilder, Frank Lloyd Wright

Above: Farm setting in Wisconsin

Swedes, Danes, Italians, Greeks, Finns, Russians, and Yugoslavs. In the 1860s, Wisconsin sent more than 90,000 soldiers to serve with the Union forces.

Wisconsin's Great Lakes towns became industrial centers, the northern lakes and woods became a vacation, hunting and fishing mecca, and the southern and western farmlands earned the state its nickname of "America's Dairyland."

RECORD HIGHLIGHTS

The available federal census population schedules for the state of Wisconsin begin with 1850. Earlier censuses showing residents in what would become Wisconsin include 1820 and 1830 (Michigan Territory) and 1840 (Wisconsin Territory). The 1890 census did not survive, but the Union Veterans and Widows Schedule for Wisconsin did.

Mortality schedules taken with the federal census exist

for 1850, 1860, 1870 (partial), and 1880. Special censuses were also taken in Wisconsin Territory in 1836, 1838, 1840, 1842, 1846, and 1847. State censuses were taken in 1855, 1865, 1875, 1885, 1895, and 1905. These are available on microfilm at the Wisconsin Historical Society, as are indexes to many of them. Some are also on microfilm at the Family History Library. The state censuses are not especially detailed until 1905, which includes such information as age, marital status, place of birth, parents' place of birth, occupation, and also includes a veterans' enumeration.

Pre-1907 birth, death, and marriage records are microfilmed and indexed and available through the Family History Library, the Wisconsin Historical Society, and the thirteen Area Research Centers in Wisconsin. Some births and deaths were recorded as early as the 1850s, but most date from the 1870s or later. Marriage records for some counties date from as early as 1816. Statewide registration of vital records began in 1907. Birth, death, or marriage records from that date forward can be obtained from the Vital Records Office at 1 West Wilson Street in Madison (P.O. Box 309, Madison, Wisconsin 53701-0309, (608) 266-1371, <http://dhfs.wisconsin .gov/VitalRecords/>.

Circuit and County Courts have, at various times, had jurisdiction over all court matters, including civil and criminal cases, divorce, probate, adoption, juvenile cases, dependency, and neglect. Naturalization records from about three-fourths of the counties have been transferred to Area Research Centers. For the other counties, the Circuit Clerk Court should still have the records.

Divorce records are held by the County or Circuit Court Clerk. Probate records are held by the Clerk of County Court. Land records at the county courthouse are found with the Register of Deeds. The Family History Library has not filmed civil or criminal case records. They have filmed naturalizations and probate files, many land grantee-grantor indexes, and some deeds for some counties. You can check the FHL catalog online, searching by county <www.familysearch.org/Eng/Library/FHLC/>.

Church and cemetery records for Wisconsin are abundant. The Wisconsin Historical Society <www.wisconsin history.org/> holds hundreds of church and cemetery abstracts, transcriptions, and indexes, as well as original records or microfilm copies. The Wisconsin State Genealogical Society <www.rootsweb.com/~wsgs/> has published hundreds of cemetery transcriptions, and the Wisconsin State Old Cemetery Society has card indexes to many burials. A useful guide is Cemetery Locations in Wisconsin, published by Origins. The Catholic and Lutheran denominations dominated Wisconsin throughout the 1800s, and the FHL has microfilmed records from many Wisconsin churches, including the parish records to about 1920 of the Roman Catholic Archdiocese of Milwaukee. Microfilms of the records of more than 200 Lutheran Wisconsin congregations are held by the ELCA Archives in Chicago, Illinois.

Don't overlook the obvious; most churches and cemeteries still have their original records close at hand.

STATE RESOURCES

■ ARCHIVES, LIBRARIES, AND SOCIETIES

Afro-American Genealogical Society of Milwaukee
2620 W. Center St., Milwaukee, WI 53206

Ancestors of Richland County Hills
23783 Covered Bridge Dr., Richland Center, WI 535481

Harold W. Anderson Library, University of Wisconsin-Whitewater
800 W. Main St., Whitewater, WI 53190
Tel: (414) 472-5520

Archdiocese of Milwaukee
2000 W. Wisconsin Ave. Milwaukee, WI 53403
Tel: (414) 769-3340

Ashland County Historical Society
P.O. Box 433, Ashland, WI 54806

Barron County Genealogical Society
1122 Knapp St., Chetek, WI 54728

Bay Area Genealogical Society
P.O. Box 283, Green Bay, WI 54305-0283

Beaver Dam Community Library
311 S. Spring St., Beaver Dam, WI 53916

Black River Falls Public Library
222 Fillmore St., Black River Falls, WI 54615
Tel: (715) 284-4112

Brown County Library
515 Pine St., Green Bay, WI 54301

Bureau of Land Management, Eastern States Office
7450 Boston Blvd., Springfield, VA 22153
Tel: (703) 440-1523
Fax: (703) 440-1599

Chalmer Davee Library, University of Wisconsin River Falls
410 S. Third St., River Falls, WI 54022
Tel: (715) 425-3567
Web site: <www.uwrf.edu/libr ary/govdocs/>

Charles & JoAnn Lester Memorial Library
100 Park St., Nekoosa, WI 54457
Tel: (715) 886-7879
Web site: <www.rootsweb.com/ ~wiwood/Nekoosa>

Chippewa County Genealogical Society
123 Allen St., Chippewa Falls, WI 54729-2898
Web site: <www.chppewacounty .com/home/history.html>

Circus World Museum
425 Water St., Baraboo, WI 53913
Tel: (608) 356-8341

Commissioner of Public Lands
127 W. Washington Ave., Madison, WI 53703

Dodge and Jefferson Counties Genealogical Society
P.O. Box 91, Watertown, WI 53094-0091

Dunn County Genealogical Society
P.O. Box 633, Menomonie, WI 54731

Eagle River Historical Society
P.O. Box 2011, Eagle River, WI 54521

Evangelical Lutheran Church in America
8765 W. Higgins, Chicago, IL 60631
Tel: (773) 380-2815

Family History Library
35 NW Temple St., Salt Lake City, UT 84150
Tel: (800) 346-6044 or (801) 240-2584
Web site: <www.familysearch .org>

Fond du Lac County Genealogical Society
P.O. Box 1264, Fond du Lac, WI 54936-1264
Web site: <www.rootsweb.com/ ~wifonddu/resources/organiza tions/fdlgensoc.htm>

Fond du Lac County Historical Society
P.O. Box 1294, Fond du Lac, WI 54935

Fond du Lac Public Library
32 Sheboygan St., Fond du Lac, WI 54935

Fox Valley Genealogical Society
P.O. Box 1592, Appleton, WI 54913-1592

Fox Valley of Wisconsin Chapter, American Historical Society of Germans from Russia
945 Anchorage Court, Oshkosh, WI 54901
Tel: (920) 235-7231

French Canadian/Acadian Genealogies of Wisconsin
P.O. Box 414, Hales Corners, WI 53130-0414

Genealogical Research Society of Eau Claire
% Chippewa Valley Museum, P.O. Box 1204, Eau Claire, WI 54702-1204
Web site: <www.rootsweb.com/ ~wigsec/>

Grant County Genealogical Society
P.O. Box 281, Dickeyville, WI 53808-0281
Web site: <www.rootsweb.com/ ~wigrant/censor.htm>

Hartford Genealogical Society
% Hartford Public Library, 109 N. Main St., Hartford, WI 53027

Heart O'Wisconsin Genealogical Society
P.O. Box 516, Wisconsin Rapids, WI 54494-0516
Web site: <www.rootsweb.com/ ~wiwood/HeartOWi/h.master .htm>

Huguenot Society of Wisconsin
8920 N. Lake Dr., Bayside, WI 53217-1940
Tel: (414) 351-0644
Web site: <www.execpc.com/ ~drg/wihs.html>

Iowa County Genealogical Society
P.O. Box 321, Dodgeville, WI 53533-0321
Web site: <www.friendsnfamily. net/wiiowagensoc/index.html>

Irish Genealogical Society of Wisconsin (I.G.S.W.)
P.O. Box 13766, Wauwatosa, WI 53213-0766

Jackson County Historical Society
13 S. First St., Black River Falls, WI 54615

Jackson County Wisconsin Footprints
W11770 City Rd. P, Black River Falls, WI 54615-5926

Jewish Genealogical Society
9280 N. Fairway Dr., Milwaukee, WI 53217

Max Kade Institute, German Research
901 University Bay Dr., Madison, WI 53705

Elton E. Karrmann Library, University of WI-Platteville
725 W. Main St., Platteville, WI 53818
Tel: (608) 342-1719

Kenosha County Genealogical Society
4902 Fifty-second St., Kenosha, WI 53142

Kewaunee County Historical Society
Courthouse Square, Kewaunee, WI 54216
Web site: <www.rootsweb.com/ ~wikewaun/>

La Crosse Area Genealogical Society
P.O. Box 1782, La Crosse, WI 54602-1782
Web site: <www.rootsweb.com/ ~wilacgs/>

La Crosse Public Library, Archives & Local History
800 Main St., La Crosse, WI 54601

Lafayette County Genealogical Society
P.O. Box 443, Shullsburg, WI 53586
Web site: <www.rootsweb.com/ ~lilacs/>

RESEARCH TIPS

for more info

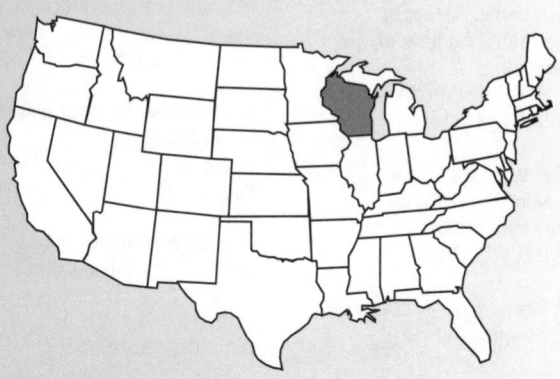

- The Wisconsin Historical Society holds the second-largest collection of newspapers in the country, one of the largest collections of city directories, and published histories, genealogies, indexes, periodicals, WPA Inventories, abstracts, and reference material on every state and Canadian province. It holds basically all the available federal census for the U.S. and Canada and most indexes, as well as microfilmed National Archives passenger lists. The newspaper collection includes more than 1,600 Wisconsin titles.
- You can access some WHS information electronically by using the Wisconsin Name Index online. You can immediately order a copy of the full-text page or pages you need online <www.wisconsinhi story.org/wni>.
- Norwegians comprised the second-largest immigrant group to Wisconsin. The Vesterheim Genealogical Center and Naeseth Library in Madison has extensive records concerning Norwegian and Norwegian-American families <www.memorial.lib rary.wisc.edu/vesterhe.htm>.
- Thirteen Area Research Centers are located around the state <www.wisconsinhistory.org/libr aryarchives/arcnet>.

Census Records
- Federal Census: 1820 (with Michigan), 1830 (with Michigan), 1840, 1850, 1860, 1870, 1880, 1900, 1910, 1920, 1930
- Federal Mortality Schedules: 1850, 1880
- Union Veterans and Widows: 1890
- State/Territorial Census: 1836, 1838, 1842, 1846, 1847, 1855, 1875, 1885, 1895, 1905

Wisconsin

Langlade County Genealogical Society
P.O. Box 307, Antigo, WI 54409
Web site: <www.rootsweb.com/ ~wilcgs/>

Letzebuerger Sprooch, Luxembourg Society of Wisconsin
P.O. Box 328, Port Washington, WI 53074-0328

Lower Wisconsin River Genealogical & Historical Research Center
P.O. Box 202, Wauzeka, WI 53826
Web site: <www.mwt.net/~bc obe/genealogy.html>

Manitowoc County Genealogical Society
P.O. Box 345, Manitowoc, WI 54220

Marathon County Genealogical Society
P.O. Box 152, Wausau, WI 54402-1512
Web site: <www.geocities.com/ mcgsociety/>

Marathon County Historical Museum
403 McIndoe, Wausau, WI 54401

Marathon County Public Library
400 First St., Wausau, WI 54401

Marshfield Area Genealogical Group
P.O. Box 337, Marshfield, WI 54449

William D. McIntyre Library, University Of Wisconsin-Eau Claire
P.O. Box 4004, Eau Claire, WI 54702-4004
Tel: (715) 836-3859
Web site: <www.uwec.edu/Libr ary/gp/govpub2.html>

Golda Meir Library, University of Wisconains-Milwaukee
2311 E. Hartford Ave., Milwaukee, WI 53201
Tel: (414) 229-5102

Menomonee Falls Historical Society
P.O. Box 91, Menomonee Falls, WI 53051

Milwaukee County Genealogical Society
P.O. Box 27326, Milwaukee, WI 53227

Milwaukee County Historical Society
910 N. Third St., Milwaukee, WI 53203
Tel: (414) 273-8288

Milwaukee Public Library
814 W. Wisconsin Ave., Milwaukee, WI 53233-2385

Monroe County Local History Room & Library
200 W. Main St., P.O. Box 419, Sparta, WI 54656

Eugene W. Murphy Library, University of WI-La Crosse
1631 W. Pine St., La Crosse, WI 54601
Tel: (608) 785-8511

National Archives-Great Lakes Region (Chicago)
7358 S. Pulaski Rd., Chicago, IL 60629
Tel: (773) 581-7816
Fax: (312) 353-1294
Web site: <www.archives.gov/fa cilities/il/chicago.html>

Northland College, Dexter Library Area Research Center
1411 Ellis Ave., Ashland, WI 54806

Northwoods Genealogical Society
P.O. Box 1132, Rhinelander, WI 54501

Oconomowoc Genealogical Club of Waukesha County
733 E. Sherman Ave., Oconomowoc, WI 53066

Oshkosh Public Library
106 Washington Ave., Oshkosh, WI 54901

Polish Genealogical Society of Wisconsin
3731 Turnwood Dr., Richfield, WI 53076

Forrest R. Polk Library, University of Wisconsin-Oshkosh
800 Algoma Blvd., Oshkosh, WI 54901
Tel: (414) 424-3347

Pornmershcer Verein Freistadt Reundschreiben (Pomeranian Society Of Freistadt)
P.O. Box 204, Germantown, WI 53022

Portage County Library
1001 Main St., Stevens Point, WI 54481-2860

Racine County Historical Society Genealogical Library & Museum, Inc.
P.O. Box 1527, 701 S. Main St., Racine, WI 53403

Rock County Genealogical Society
P.O. Box 711, Janesville, WI 53547
Web site: <www.rootsweb.com/ ~wircs/index.html>

Roman Catholic Diocese of Green Bay
1910 S. Webster Ave., P.O. Box 66, Green Bay, WI 54301
Tel: (414) 435-4406

Roman Catholic Diocese of LaCrosse
421 Main St., P.O. Box 982, La Crosse, WI 54601
Tel: (608) 788-7700

Roman Catholic Diocese of Madison
15 E. Wilson St., P.O. Box 111, Madison, WI 53701
Tel: (608) 256-2677

Roman Catholic Diocese of Superior
1201 Hughitt Ave., P.O. Box 969, Superior, WI 54880
Tel: (715) 392-2937

Sauk County Historical Society
P.O. Box 651, Baraboo, WI 53931
Web site: <www.saukcounty. com/schs>

Seventh Day Baptist Historical Society
P.O. Box 1678, Janesville, WI 3547

Sheboygan County Historical Research Center
518 Water St. #3, Sheboygan Falls, WI 53085-1455

Maude Shunk Public Library
W156 N8447 Pilgrim Rd., Menomonee Falls, WI 53051-3140

Gilbert Simmons Library
711 Fifty-ninth Place, Kenosha, WI 53140

Southeaster Wisconsin Chapter, American Historical Society of Germans from Russia
3121 Pioneer Rd., Mequon, WI 53097-1620
Web site: <www.ahsgr.org/wisou the.html>

St. Croix Valley Genealogical Society
P.O. Box 396, River Falls, WI 54022
Web site: <www.presenter.com/ ~scvgs/>

State Historical Society of Wisconsin
816 State St., Madison, WI 53706
Tel: (608) 264-6460
Fax: (608) 264-6520
Web site:

Stevens Point Area Genealogical Society
% Portage County Library, 1001 Main St., Stevens Point, WI 54481-2860

Superior Public Library
1530 Tower Ave., Superior, WI 54880
Tel: (715) 394-8860

Taylor County Genealogical Society
223 Second St., Medford, WI 54451-1899
Web site: <www.rootsweb.com/ ~wutcgs/>

Veterheim Genealogical Center and Naeseth Library
(Norway), 415 W. Main St., Madison, WI 54703
Tel: (608) 255-2224
Fax: (608) 255-6842

Village of North Fond du Lac Public Library
719 Wisconsin Ave., North Fond du Lac, WI 54935

Vital Records Office
P.O. Box 309, Madison, WI 53701-0309
Tel: (608) 266-1371
Web site: <http://dhfs.wisconsi n.gov/VitalRecords/>.

Walworth County Genealogical Society
P.O. Box 159, Delavan, WI 53115-0159
Tel: (608) 752-8816
Web site: <www.rootsweb.com/ ~wiwalwor/wcgs.html>

Washburn County Genealogical Society
P.O. Box 366, Shell Lake, WI 54871

Washington County Historical Society Museum, Inc.
340 S. Fifth Ave., West Bend, WI 53095

Waukesha County Genealogical Society
P.O. Box 1541, Waukesha, WI 53187-1541

Waupaca Area Genealogical Society (WAGS)
P.O. Box 42, King, WI 54946-0042

White Pine Genealogical Society
P.O. Box 512, Marienette, WI 54143

Winnebagoland Genealogical Society
℅ Oshkosh Public Library, 106 Washington Ave., Oshkosh, WI 54901-4985

Wisconsin Black Historical Society
2620 West Center St., Milwaukee, WI 53206
Tel: (414) 372-7677

Wisconsin Conference United Methodist Church
750 Windsor St., Sun Prairie, WI 53590
Tel: (608) 837-7328

Wisconsin Evangelical Lutheran Synod
Department of Archives and History, 2929 North Mayfair Rd., Milwaukee, WI 53222
Tel: (414) 256-3888

Wisconsin Genealogical Council, Inc.
N9307 Abitz Lane, Luxemburg, WI 54217-9628

Wisconsin Genealogical Workshop
Rt. 3, Box 253, Black River Falls, WI 54613

Wisconsin Historical Society Library
816 State St., Madison, WI 53706

Wisconsin State Genealogical Society, Inc.
2109 Twentieth Ave., Monroe, WI 53566
Tel: (608) 325-2609
Web site: <www.wsgs.org>

Wisconsin State Old Cemetery Society
6100 W. Mequon Rd., Mequon, WI 53092

Wyllie Library/Learning Center, University of Wisconsin-Parkside
P.O. Box 2000, Kenosha, WI 53141-2000
Tel: (414) 595-2411

BIBLIOGRAPHY

◼ GENERAL RESOURCES

The Bench and Bar of Wisconsin: History and Biography
by Parker McCobb Reed (Milwaukee: P.M. Reed, 1882)

Black Settlers in Rural Wisconsin
by Zachary Cooper (Madison, WI: State Historical Society of Wisconsin, 1997)

Brethren in Northern Illinois and Wisconsin
by John Heckman (Elgin, IL: Brethren Publishing House, 1941)

Collections of the State Historical Society of Wisconsin, 24 vols.
by Lyman Copeland Draper (Madison: State Historical Society of Wisconsin, 1855–)

Dictionary of Wisconsin Biography
(Madison: State Historical Society, 1960)

French-Canadian Families Of the North Central States: A Genealogical Dictionary, 8 vols.
by Paul J. Lareau and Elmer Courteau (St. Paul, MN: Northwest Territory French and Canadian Heritage Institute, 1980)

Genealogical Research: An Introduction to the Resources of the State Historical Society of Wisconsin
by James P. Danky (Madison: State Historical Society of Wisconsin, 1986)

The Genealogist's Companion and Sourcebook, 2d ed.
by Emily Anne Croom (Cincinnati: Betterway Books, 2003)

A Genealogist's Guide to Discovering Your African-American Ancestors
by Franklin Carter Smith and Emily Anne Croom (Cincinnati: Betterway Books, 2003)

Ghost towns of Wisconsin
by William F. Stark (Sheboygan, WI: Zimmermann Press, 1977)

Guide to Genealogical Research in the National Archives of the United States
edited by Anne Bruner Eales and Robert M. Kvasnicka (Washington, DC: National Archives and Records Administration, 2000)

Guide to the Manuscripts of the Wisconsin Historical Society
edited by Alice E. Smith (Madison: State Historical Society of Wisconsin, 1944, 1957)

Guide to Wisconsin Newspapers, 1833–1957
by Donald E. Oehlerts (Madison: State Historical Society of Wisconsin, 1958)

History of the Catholic Church in Wisconsin
by Leo Rummel (Madison, WI: Wisconsin State Council, Knights of Columbus, 1976)

History of Methodism in Wisconsin
by Pansy S. Bennett (Cincinnati: Cranston & Stowe, 1890)

History of the Presbyterian and Congregational Churches and Ministers in Wisconsin
by Stephen Peet (Milwaukee: S. Chapman, 1851)

History of Wisconsin, 6 vols.
(Madison: State Historical Society, 1973–1988)

An Illustrated History of the State of Wisconsin: Being a Complete Civil, Political and Military History of the State, from its First Exploration Down to 1875
by Charles Richard Tuttle (Boston: B.B. Russell, 1875)

Introduction to Wisconsin Indians: Prehistory to Statehood
by Carol I. Mason (Salem, WI: Sheffield Publishing, 1988)

Men of Progress, Wisconsin: A Selected List of Biographical Sketches and Portraits of the leaders in Business, Professional and Official Life, Together with Short Notes on the History and Character of Wisconsin
by Andrew J. Aikens (Milwaukee: Evening Wisconsin Co., 1897)

National Archives Microfilm Catalogs online:
<www.archives.gov/publications/genealogy_microfilm_catalogs.html>

Newspapers in the State Historical Society of Wisconsin: A Bibliography with Holdings, 2 vols.
by Jame P. Danky (New York: Norman Ross, 1994)

Notable Men of Wisconsin
(Tucson, AZ: W.C. Cox Co., 1974)

Printed Resources for Genealogical Searching in Wisconsin: A Selective Bibliography
by Margaret Gleason (Detroit: Detroit Society for Genealogical Research, 1964)

Regathering of the Scattered Saints in Wisconsin And Illinois
by Pearl Wilcox (Independence, MO: P. Wilcox, 1984)

Searching for Your Wisconsin Ancestors in the Wisconsin Libraries
by Carol Ward Ryan (Green Bay, WI: Carol Ward Ryan, 1988)

Subject Bibliography of Wisconsin History
by Leroy Schlinkert (Madison: State Historical Society of Wisconsin, 1947)

United States Biographical Dictionary and Portrait: Gallery of Eminent and Self-made Men: Wisconsin Volume
(Chicago: American Biographical Pub., 1877)

Wisconsin Domesday Book: Town Studies
from the State Historical Society of Wisconsin (Minasha, WI: George Santa Publishing Co., 1924)

Wisconsin's Early French
by Jo Bartels Alderson (Bowie, MD: Heritage Books, 1988)

The Wisconsin Fur-Trade People
by Les Rentmeester (Melbourne, FL: L & J Rentmeester, 1991)

Wisconsin Genealogical Research
by Linda M. Herrick (Janesville, WI: Origins, 1996)

Wisconsin

Wisconsin

Wisconsin History: An Annotated Bibliography
by Barbara Dotts Paul (Westport, CT: Greenwood Press, 1999)

Wisconsin: Its History and Its People, 1634–1924, 4 vols.
by Milo Milton Quaife (Chicago: S.J. Clarke Publishing Co., 1924)

Wisconsin Indians
by Nancy Ostrich Lurie (Madison, WI: State Historical Society of Wisconsin, 1980)

Wisconsin: Its Story and Biography, 1848–1913, 8 vols.
by Ellis B. Usher (Chicago: Lewis Publishing Co., 1914)

■ CENSUS RECORDS

The American Census Handbook
by Thomas Jay Kemp (Wilmington, DE: Scholarly Resources, Inc., 2001)

Map Guide to the U.S. Federal Censuses, 1790–1920
by William Thorndale and William Dollarhide (Baltimore: Genealogical Publishing Co., 1987)

Your Guide to the Federal Census
by Kathleen W. Hinckley (Cincinnati: Betterway Books, 2002)

■ IMMIGRATION RECORDS

American Naturalization Records, 1790–1990: What They Are and How to Use Them
by John J. Newman (North Salt Lake, UT: HeritageQuest, 1998)

American Passenger Arrival Records
by Michael Tepper (Baltimore: Genealogical Publishing Co., 1993)

A German State in Wisconsin: A Bicentennial History
by Richard Nelson Current (New York: WW Norton & Co., 1977)

Immigration to Wisconsin: A Thesis
by Maude Sachtjen (Madison: University of Wisconsin, 1928)

They Became Americans: Finding Naturalization Records and Ethnic Origins
by Loretto Dennis Szucs (Salt Lake City: Ancestry, Inc., 1998)

They Came in Ships: A Guide to Finding Your Immigrant Ancestor's Arrival Records, 2d ed.
by John P. Colletta (Salt Lake City: Ancestry, Inc., 1993)

■ LAND RECORDS

Conquest of the Country Northwest of The River Ohio, 1778–1783, and Life of General George Rogers Clark: With Numerous Sketches of Men Who Served Under Clark and Full List of Those Allotted Lands in Clark's Grant for Service in the Campaigns Against the British Posts, Showing Exact Land Allotted Each, 2 vols.
by William Hayden English (Indiana: Bowen-Merrill, 1896)

Locating Your Roots: Discover Your Ancestors Using Land Records
by Patricia Law Hatcher (Cincinnati: Betterway Books, 2003)

Wisconsin, 1820–1908 Cash and Homestead Entries, Cadastral Survey Plats
from the Bureau of Land Management (Springfield, VA: BLM Eastern states, 1994)

■ MAPS

Atlas of the State of Wisconsin
by H.F. Walling (Detroit: Walling, Tackabury and Co., 1876)

Atlas of Wisconsin: General Maps and Gazetteers
by Arthur Robinson and Jerry B. Culver (Madison: University of Wisconsin Press, 1974)

Historical Atlas and Chronology of County Boundaries, 1788–1980, 5 vols.
edited by John H. Long (Boston: G.K. Hall, 1984)

Historical Atlas of Wisconsin.
by Van Vechten Snyder & Co. (Janesville, WI: Origins, 1995)

Maps and Atlases Showing Land Ownership in Wisconsin
compiled by Michael J. Fox (Madison: State Historical Society of Wisconsin, 1978)

The Romance of Wisconsin Place Names
by Robert E. Gard and L.G. Sorden (New York: October House, 1968;

Reprint: Minocqua, WI: Heartland Press, 1988)

Wisconsin Atlas & Gazetteer
(Freeport, ME: DeLorme Mapping Co., 1988)

Wisconsin, Atlas of Historical County Boundaries
by Gordon DenBoer (New York: Charles Scribner's Sons, 1997)

Wisconsin: Comprising Sketches of Counties, Towns, Events, Institutions and Persons Arranged in Cyclopedic Form
edited by George W. Peck (Madison, WI: Western Historical Association, 1906)

Wisconsin County Maps
compiled by C.J. Puetz (Lyndon Station, WI: Thomas Publishing Co., 1992)

Wisconsin Post Office Handbook, 1921–1971
compiled by James B. Hale (Madison: Wisconsin Postal History Society, 1971)

■ MILITARY RECORDS

Admission Applications, 1867–1872. National Home for Disabled Volunteer Soldiers, Northwestern Branch. Milwaukee, Wisconsin
by Leslie Elizabeth Miljat (Wauwatosa, WI: L.E. Miljat, 1991)

Researching Your Civil War Ancestors in Wisconsin
by Denis R. Moore (Manitowoc, WI: Bivouac Publications, 1994)

Soldiers' and Citizens' Album, 2 vols.
from the Grand Army of the Republic (Chicago: Grand Army Publishing Co., 1888, 1890)

Uncle, We Are Ready! Registering America's Men, 1917–1918: A Guide to Researching World War I Draft Registration Cards
by John J. Newman (North Salt Lake, UT: HeritageQuest, 2001)

U.S. Military Records: A Guide to Federal & State Sources, Colonial America to the Present
by James C. Neagles (Salt Lake City: Ancestry, Inc., 1994)

Wisconsin's Gold Star List: Soldiers, Sailors, Marines and Nurses From the Badger State
(Madison: State Historical Society of Wisconsin, 1925)

World War II: A Family Historian's Guide
by Debra Johnson Knox (Spartanburg, SC: MIE Publishing, 2003)

■ PROBATE RECORDS

Guide to the Wisconsin State Archives
by David J. Delgado (Madison: State Historical Society of Wisconsin, 1966)

■ VITAL RECORDS

Cemetery Locations in Wisconsin
by Linda M. Herrick and Wendy K. Uncapher (Janesville, WI: Origins 1998)

Registration of Births, 1852–1907
from the Wisconsin Bureau of Health Statistics (Madison: Wisconsin State Historical Society, 1979)

Your Guide to Cemetery Research
by Sharon DeBartolo Carmack (Cincinnati: Betterway Books, 2002)

■ **Adams** 11 Mar. 1848
P.O. Box 219, Friendship, WI 53934
Phone: (608)339-4206
Web site: www.co.adams.wi.us
Parent County: Portage
Comments/research tips: The James H. Alberton Library of the University of Wisconsin, Stevens Point has Birth records 1857–1907, Death records 1876–1907, Marriage records 1854–1907, Naturalization records 1853–1949, and Probate records 1848–1928.

Record Type	Year Begun	Jurisdiction
Divorce	1848	Clerk/Circuit Ct.
Court	1848	Clerk/Circuit Ct.
Land	1853	Registrar/Deeds

■ **Ashland** 27 Mar. 1860
201 Second St. W., Ashland, WI 54806
Phone: (715)682-7008
Web site: www.co.ashland.wi.us
Parent County: LaPointe
Comments/research tips: Northern Great Lakes Visitors Center, History Center and Archives has Birth records 1852–1907, Court records 1873–1904, Death records 1877–1907, Divorce records 1873–1904, Land records 1856–1872, Marriage records 1874–1907, and Naturalization records 1879–1992.

Record Type	Year Begun	Jurisdiction
Probate	1890	Registrar/Probate

■ **Bad Ax** 1851
Parent County: Crawford, Richland
Comments/research tips: (See Vernon) Name changed to Vernon 1865.

■ **Barron** 1859
330 E. La Salle Ave., Barron, WI 54812
Phone: (715)537-6210
Web site: www.co.barron.wi.us
Parent County: St. Croix
Comments/research tips: The University of Wisconsin-Stout, Library Learning Cener has Birth records 1877–1907, Court records 1875–1962, Death records 1876–1907, Land records 1888–1961, Naturalization records 1874–1954, Marriage records 1871–1907, and Probate records 1882–1909. Formerly Dallas County. Name changed to Barron 1869.

■ **Bayfield** 1845
117 E. Fifth St., P.O. Box 813, Washburn, WI 54891
Phone: (715)373-6119
Web site: www.bayfieldcounty.org
Parent County: St. Croix
Comments/research tips: The Northern Great Lakes Visitors Center, History Center and Archives has Birth records 1852–1907, Court records 1888–1984, Death records 1862–1907, Divorce records 1889–1984, and Naturalization records 1859–1945. Formerly La Pointe County. Name changed to Bayfield in 1866.

Record Type	Year Begun	Jurisdiction
Land	1845	Registrar/Deeds

Marriage	1908	Registrar/Deeds
Probate	1870	Registrar/Probate

■ **Brown** 26 Oct. 1818
305 E. Walnut St., P.O. Box 23600, Green Bay, WI 54305
Phone: (920)448-4470
Web site: www.co.brown.wi.us
Parent County: Michigan Territory
Comments/research tips: The University of Wisconsin-Green Bay, Cofrin Library has Birth records 1746–1907, Court records 1823–1939, Death records 1834–1907, Divorce records 1823–1939, Land records 18280–1902, Marriage records 1821–1907, Naturalization records 1829–1984, and Probate records 1821–1921. See Michigan for 1820–1830 census.

■ **Buffalo** 8 July 1853
407 S. Second St., P.O. Box 28, Alma, WI 54610
Phone: (608)685-6230
Web site: www.buffalocounty.com
Parent County: Jackson
Comments/research tips: The University of Wisconsin-Eau Claire, William D. McIntyre Library has Birth records 1852–1907, Court records 1854–1984, Death records 1874–1907, Divorce records 1854–1984, Land records 1854–1892, Marriage records 1860–1907, Naturalization records 1907–1929, and Probate records 1854–1901.

Record Type	Year Begun	Jurisdiction
Land	1893	Registrar/Deeds

■ **Burnett** 1856
7410 County Rd. K #103, Siren, WI 54872
Phone: (715)349-2183
Web site: www.burnettcounty.com
Parent County: Polk, Douglas
Comments/research tips: The University of Wisconsin-River Falls, Chalmer Davee Library has Birth records 1853–1907, Death records 1846–1907, Marriage records 1869–1907, and Naturalization records 1859–1953. Clerk of circuit Court has Court records from early 1900s.

Record Type	Year Begun	Jurisdiction
Land	1856	Registrar/Deeds
Birth	1908	Registrar/Deeds
Marriage	1908	Registrar/Deeds
Death	1908	Registrar/Deeds
Probate	1856	Registrar/Probate
Divorce	1856	Chalmer Davee Lib.

■ **Calumet** 1836
206 Court St., Chilton, WI 53014
Phone: (920)849-2361
Web site: www.co.calumet.wi.us
Parent County: Brown
Comments/research tips: The University of Wisconsin-Green Bay, Cofrin Library has Birth records 1858–1907, Death records 1856–1907, Marriage records 1850–1907, and Naturalization records 1850–1955.

Record Type	Year Begun	Jurisdiction
Divorce	1880	Clerk/Circuit Ct.

Court .... 1877 ....Clerk/Circuit Ct.
Land .... 1840 ....Registrar/Deeds
Birth .... 1908 ....Registrar/Deeds
Marriage............... 1908 ....Registrar/Deeds
Death.................... 1908 ....Registrar/Deeds
Probate .... 1868 ....Registrar/Probate

■ Chippewa   3 Feb. 1845
711 N. Bridge St., Chippewa Falls, WI 54729
Phone: (715)726-7994
Web site: www.co.chippewa.wi.us
Parent County: Crawford
Comments/research tips: The University of Wisconsin-Eau Claire, William D. McIntyre Library has Birth records 1852–1907, Divorce records 1854–1950, Land records 1856–1885, Marriage records 1869–1907, Naturalization records 1871–1923, and Probate records 1860–1900. Clerk of Circuit Court has Court records 1854–1951.

Record Type	Year Begun	Jurisdiction
Land	1886	Registrar/Deeds
Birth	1908	Registrar/Deeds
Marriage	1908	Registrar/Deeds
Death	1858	Registrar/Deeds
Probate	1901	Registrar/Probate

■ Clark   6 July 1853
517 Court St., P.O. Box 384, Neillsville, WI 54456
Phone: (715)743-5163
Web site: www.co.clark.wi.us
Parent County: Jackson
Comments/research tips: The University of Wisconsin-Eau Claire, William D. McIntyre Library has Birth records 1852–1907, Death records 1879–1907, Marriage records 1858–1907, Naturalization records 1907–1927, and Probate records 1873–1918. Clerk of Circuit Court has Divorce records from late 1800s.

Record Type	Year Begun	Jurisdiction
Land	1855	Registrar/Deeds
Birth	1908	Registrar/Deeds
Marriage	1908	Registrar/Deeds
Death	1908	Registrar/Deeds
Probate	1919	Registrar/Probate

■ Columbia   3 Feb. 1845
P.O. Box 133, Portage, WI 53901
Phone: (608)742-2191
Web site: www.co.columbia.wi.us
Parent County: Portage
Comments/research tips: Wisconsin State Archives, Wisconsin Historical Society has Land records 1826–1936. State Archives has Naturalization records 1845–1955.

Record Type	Year Begun	Jurisdiction
Birth	1860	Registrar/Deeds
Marriage	1849	Registrar/Deeds
Death	1877	Registrar/Deeds
Probate	1856	Registrar/Probate

■ Crawford   26 Oct. 1818
220 N. Beaumont Rd., Prairie du Chien, WI 53821
Phone: (608)326-0219
Web site: www.crawfordcounty-wi-us.org
Parent County: Michigan Territory
Comments/research tips: The University of Wisconsin-Platteville, Southwest Wisconsin room, Karrmann Library has Birth records 1858–1907, Death records 1876–1907, Marriage records 1862–1907, and Naturalization records 1824–1950. Crawford County was part of Michigan Territory until 1836, when territory of Wisconsin was formed.

Record Type	Year Begun	Jurisdiction
Probate	ca. 1850	County Clerk
Divorce	1848	Clerk/Circuit Ct.
Court	1848	Clerk/Circuit Ct.
Land	ca. 1700	Registrar/Deeds
Birth	1908	Registrar/Deeds
Marriage	1908	Registrar/Deeds
Death	1908	Registrar/Deeds

■ Dallas   1859
Parent County: St. Croix
Comments/research tips: Name changed to Barron in 1869.

■ Dane   7 Dec. 1836
P.O. Box 1438, Madison, WI 53709
Phone: (608)266-4141
Web site: www.co.dane.wi.us
Parent County: Crawford, Iowa, Milwaukee
Comments/research tips: The Wisconsin State Archives, Wisconsin Historical Society has Court records 1839–1976, Divorce records 1839–1928, Land records 1835–1978, Military Discharge records 1918–1994, and Naturalization records 1841–1954.

Record Type	Year Begun	Jurisdiction
Divorce	1929	Clerk/Circuit Ct.
Birth	1876	Registrar/Deeds
Marriage	1839	Registrar/Deeds
Death	1876	Registrar/Deeds
Probate	1848	Registrar/Probate

■ Dodge   Dec. 1836
127 E. Oak St., Juneau, WI 53039
Phone: (920)386-3720
Web site: www.co.dodge.wi.us
Parent County: Brown, Milwaukee
Comments/research tips: The University of Wisconsin-Oshkosh, Forest R. Polk Library has Birth records 1852–1907, Death records 1872–1907, Marriage records 1854–1907, Land records 1877–1980, and Naturalization records 1844–1954.

Record Type	Year Begun	Jurisdiction
Birth	1908	Registrar/Deeds
Marriage	1908	Registrar/Deeds
Death	1908	Registrar/Deeds
Probate	1854	Registrar/Probate

■ Door   1851
421 Nebraska St., Sturgeon Bay, WI 54235
Phone: (920)746-2270
Web site: www.co.door.wi.gov

Wisconsin

Parent County: Brown

Comments/research tips: The University of Wisconsin-Green Bay, Cofrin Library has Court records 1895–1978, Divorce records 1895–1978, Naturalization records 1850–1955, and Probate records 1945–1953.

Record Type	Year Begun	Jurisdiction
Land	1854	Registrar/Deeds
Birth	1852	Registrar/Deeds
Marriage	1860	Registrar/Deeds
Death	1856	Registrar/Deeds

■ Douglas 9 Feb. 1854

1313 Belknap St., Superior, WI 54880

Phone: (715)395-1359

Web site: www.douglascountywi.org

Parent County: La Pointe

Comments/research tips: Superior Public Library has Birth records 1861–1907, Death records 1877–1907, and Marriage records 1854–1907.

Record Type	Year Begun	Jurisdiction
Divorce	1878	Clerk/Circuit Ct.
Court	1878	Clerk/Circuit Ct.
Land	1854	Registrar/Deeds
Birth	1908	Registrar/Deeds
Marriage	1908	Registrar/Deeds
Death	1908	Registrar/Deeds
Probate	1878	Probate Depart.

■ Dunn 1854

800 Wilson Ave., Menomonie, WI 54751

Phone: (715)232-1228

Web site: www.co.dunn.wi.us

Parent County: Chippewa

Comments/research tips: The University of Wisconsin-Stout, Library Learning Center has Court and Divorce records 1850–1920 and Probate records ca. 1868–1944.

Record Type	Year Begun	Jurisdiction
Land	1854	Registrar/Deeds
Birth	1870	Registrar/Deeds
Marriage	1858	Registrar/Deeds
Death	1877	Registrar/Deeds

■ Eau Claire 1856

P.O. Box 718, Eau Claire, WI 54702

Phone: (715)839-4745

Web site: www.co.eau-claire.wi.us

Parent County: Chippewa

Comments/research tips: The University of Wisconsin-Eau Claire, William D. McIntyre Library has Birth records 1852–1907, Court records 1857–1970, Death records 1876–1907, Divorce records 1857–1972, Land records 1856–1889, Marriage records 1864–1907, Naturalization records 1857–1928, and Probate records 1856–1953.

Record Type	Year Begun	Jurisdiction
Land	1890	Registrar/Deeds
Birth	1908	Registrar/Deeds
Marriage	1908	Registrar/Deeds
Death	1908	Registrar/Deeds

■ Florence 1882

501 Lake Ave., Florence, WI 54121

Phone: (715)589-4321

Web site: www.rootsweb.com/~wifloren/

Parent County: Marinette, Oconto

Comments/research tips: The University of Wisconsin-Green Bay, Cofrin Library has Birth, Death, and Marriage records 1882–1907, and Naturalization records 1882–1947.

Record Type	Year Begun	Jurisdiction
Divorce	1882	Clerk/Circuit Ct.
Court	1882	Clerk/Circuit Ct.
Land	1882	Registrar/Deeds
Birth	1908	Registrar/Deeds
Marriage	1908	Registrar/Deeds
Death	1908	Registrar/Deeds
Probate	1882	Registrar/Probate

■ Fond du Lac 1836

160 S. Macy St., Fond du Lac, WI 54935

Phone: (920)929-3018

Web site: www.co.fond-du-lac.wi.us

Parent County: Brown

Comments/research tips: The University of Wisconsin-Oshkosh, Forest R. Polk Library has Birth records 1852–1907, Court records 1848–1972, Death records 1871–1907, Divorce records 1848–1972, Land records 1850–1980, Marriage records 1844–1907, Naturalization records 1844–1974, and Probate records 1848–1974.

Record Type	Year Begun	Jurisdiction
Land	1981	Registrar/Deeds
Birth	1907	Registrar/Deeds
Marriage	1907	Registrar/Deeds
Death	1907	Registrar/Deeds

■ Forest 11 Apr. 1885

200 E. Madison St., Crandon, WI 54520

Phone: (715)478-3823

Web site: www.forestcountywi.com

Parent County: Langlade, Oconto

Comments/research tips: The Northern Great Lakes Visitors Center, History Center and Archives has Birth records 1852–1907, Court records 1885–1905, Death records 1887–1907, Divorce records 1885–1905, Marriage records 1885–1907, and Naturalization records 1885–1955.

Record Type	Year Begun	Jurisdiction
Divorce	1906	Clerk/Circuit Ct.
Court	1906	Clerk/Circuit Ct.
Land	1885	Registrar/Deeds
Birth	1908	Registrar/Deeds
Marriage	1908	Registrar/Deeds
Death	1908	Registrar/Deeds
Probate	1885	Registrar/Probate

■ Gates May 1901

Parent County: Chippewa

Comments/research tips: (See Rusk) Name changed to Rusk in 1905.

■ Grant 1836

P.O. Box 391, Lancaster, WI 53813

Phone: (608)723-2727

Web site: http://grantcounty.org/
Parent County: Iowa
Comments/research tips: The University of Wisconsin-Plattville Southwest Wisconsin Room, Karrmann Library has Court and Divorce records 1838–1920 and Land records 1837–1902.

Record Type	Year Begun	Jurisdiction
Divorce	1921	Clerk/Circuit Ct.
Court	1921	Clerk/Circuit Ct.
Land	1903	Registrar/Deeds
Birth	1870	Registrar/Deeds
Marriage	1842	Registrar/Deeds
Death	1876	Registrar/Deeds
Probate	1840	Registrar/Probate

■ Green   8 Dec. 1836
1016 Sixteenth Ave., Monroe, WI 53566
Phone: (608)328-9439
Web site: www.cogreen.wi.gov
Parent County: Territorial county
Comments/research tips: The University of Wisconsin-Plattville, Southwest Wisconsin Room, Karrmann Library has Court and Divorce records 1838–1910, Land records 1836–1920, and Naturalization records 1837–1945.

Record Type	Year Begun	Jurisdiction
Divorce	1911	Clerk/Circuit Ct.
Court	1911	Clerk/Circuit Ct.
Probate	ca. 1890	County Judge
Land	1921	Registrar/Deeds
Birth	1862	Registrar/Deeds
Marriage	1838	Registrar/Deeds
Death	1874	Registrar/Deeds

■ Green Lake   1856
429 Hill St., P.O. Box 3188, Green Lake, WI 54941
Phone: (920)294-4021
Web site: www.co.green-lake.wi.us
Parent County: Marquette
Comments/research tips: The University of Wisconsin-OshKosh, Forest R. Polk Library has Birth records 1852–1907, Death records 1876–1907, Land records 1843–1994, Marriage records 1863–1907, and Naturalization records 1858–1949.

Record Type	Year Begun	Jurisdiction
Divorce	ca. 1900	Clerk of Courts
Court	ca. 1900	Clerk of Courts
Land	1995	Registrar/Deeds
Birth	1908	Registrar/Deeds
Marriage	1908	Registrar/Deeds
Death	1908	Registrar/Deeds
Probate	1856	Registrar/Probate

■ Iowa   1839
222 N. Iowa St., Dodgeville, WI 53533
Phone: (608)935-0396
Web site: www.iowacounty.org
Parent County: Territorial county
Comments/research tips: The University of Wisconsin-Plattville, Southwest Wisconsin Room, Karrmann Library

has Court records 1837–1990, Divorce records 1823–1990, Land records 1835–1907, Naturalization records 1835–1906, and Probate records 1837–1974.

Record Type	Year Begun	Jurisdiction
Land	1908	Registrar/Deeds
Birth	1876	Registrar/Deeds
Marriage	1836	Registrar/Deeds
Death	1871	Registrar/Deeds

■ Iron   Mar. 1893
300 Taconite St., Hurley, WI 54534
Phone: (715)561-2945
Web site: www.rootsweb.com/~wiiron/
Parent County: Ashland, Oneida
Comments/research tips: The Northern Great Lakes Visitors Center, History Center and Archives has Naturalization records 1893–1954.

Record Type	Year Begun	Jurisdiction
Divorce	1930	Clerk/Circuit Ct.
Court	1930	Clerk/Circuit Ct.
Land	1893	Registrar/Deeds
Birth	1886	Registrar/Deeds
Marriage	1858	Registrar/Deeds
Death	1887	Registrar/Deeds
Probate	1929	Registrar/Probate

■ Jackson   1853
307 Main St., Black River Falls, WI 54615
Phone: (715)284-0205
Web site: www.co.jackson.wi.us
Parent County: La Crosse
Comments/research tips: The University of Wisconsin-La Crosse, Murphy Library Resource Center has Land records 1854–1946, Naturalization records 1853–1963, and Probate records 1869–1900.

Record Type	Year Begun	Jurisdiction
Birth	1876	Registrar/Deeds
Marriage	1858	Registrar/Deeds
Death	1876	Registrar/Deeds
Divorce	1926	Clerk of Court
Court	1926	Clerk of Court
Probate	1901	Registrar/Probate

■ Jefferson   7 Dec. 1836
320 S. Main St., P.O. Box 356, Jefferson, WI 53549
Phone: (920)674-7238
Web site: www.co.jefferson.wi.us
Parent County: Milwaukee
Comments/research tips: The University of Wisconsin-Whitewater, Harold Andersen Library has Court records 1843–1954, Divorce records 1851–1964, Land records 1838–1900, Naturalization records 1842–1950, Probate records 1844–1911.

Record Type	Year Begun	Jurisdiction
Land	1901	Registrar/Deeds
Birth	1852	Registrar/Deeds
Marriage	1844	Registrar/Deeds
Death	1856	Registrar/Deeds
Probate	1912	Registrar/Probate

Juneau   1 Jan. 1857
220 E. State St., Mauston, WI 53948
Phone: (608)847-9325
Web site: www.co.juneau.wi.gov
Parent County: Adams
Comments/research tips: The University of Wisconsin-Stevens Point, James H. Albertson Library has Court and Divorce records to 1994, Naturalization records 1849–1957, Probate records 1857–1888

Record Type	Year Begun	Jurisdiction
Land	1842	Registrar/Deeds
Birth	1877	Registrar/Deeds
Marriage	1844	Registrar/Deeds
Death	1876	Registrar/Deeds
Probate	1889	Registrar/Probate

Kenosha   1850
1010 Fifty-sixth St., Kenosha, WI 53140
Phone: (262)653-2444
Web site: www.co.kenosha.wi.us
Parent County: Racine
Comments/research tips: The University of Wisconsin-Parkside, University Library and Area Research Center has Court records 1850–1971, Land records 1838–1872, and Naturalization records 1850–1983.

Record Type	Year Begun	Jurisdiction
Birth	1876	Registrar/Deeds
Marriage	1850	Registrar/Deeds
Land	1873	Registrar/Deeds
Probate	1850	Registrar/Probate

Kewaunee   1852
613 Dodge St., Kewaunee, WI 54216
Phone: (920)388-7126
Web site: www.rootsweb.com/~wikewaun
Parent County: Manitowoc
Comments/research tips: Registrar of Deeds has Birth records 1861–1873 and Marriage records 1857–1874. The University of Wisconsin-Green Bay, Cofrin Library has Court records 1858–1942 and Naturalization records 1850–1950.

Record Type	Year Begun	Jurisdiction
Death	1873	Registrar/Deeds
Land	1852	Registrar/Deeds
Probate	1867	Registrar/Probate

La Crosse   1851
400 Fourth St. N., La Crosse, WI 54601
Phone: (608)785-9644
Web site: www.co.la-crosse.wi.us
Parent County: Unorganized territory
Comments/research tips: The University of Wisconsin-La Crosse, Murphy Library Resource Center has Land records 1851–1886, Naturalization records 1846–1991, and Probate records 1851–1981.

Record Type	Year Begun	Jurisdiction
Divorce	1859	Clerk/Circuit Ct.
Court	1859	Clerk/Circuit Ct.
Land	1887	Registrar/Deeds
Birth	1877	Registrar/Deeds
Marriage	1851	Registrar/Deeds
Death	1876	Registrar/Deeds

La Pointe   1845
Parent County: St. Croix
Comments/research tips: (See Bayfield) Name changed to Bayfield in 1866.

Lafayette   1847
626 Main St., P.O. Box 40, Darlington, WI 53530
Phone: (608)776-4838
Web site: www.co.lafayette.wi.gov
Parent County: Iowa
Comments/research tips: The University of Wisconsin-Plattville, Southwest Wisconsin Room, Karrman Library has Court and Divorce records 1846–1919, Land records 1835–1927, and Naturalization records 1847–1945.

Record Type	Year Begun	Jurisdiction
Divorce	1920	Clerk/Circuit Ct.
Court	1920	Clerk/Circuit Ct.
Land	1928	Registrar/Deeds
Birth	1854	Registrar/Deeds
Marriage	1847	Registrar/Deeds
Death	1877	Registrar/Deeds
Probate	1853	Registrar/Probate

Langlade   1879
800 Clermont St., Antigo, WI 54409
Phone: (715)627-6209
Web site: www.co.langlade.wi.us
Parent County: Oconto, Lincoln
Comments/research tips: The University of Wisconsin-Stevens Point, James H. Albertson Library has Naturalization records 1881–1957. Formerly New County. Name changed to Langlade in 1880.

Record Type	Year Begun	Jurisdiction
Divorce	ca. 1880	Clerk/Circuit Ct.
Court	ca. 1880	Clerk/Circuit Ct.
Land	1879	Registrar/Deeds
Birth	1882	Registrar/Deeds
Marriage	1881	Registrar/Deeds
Death	1868	Registrar/Deeds
Probate	ca. 1890	Registrar/Probate

Lincoln   1874
1110 E. Main St., Merrill, WI 54452
Phone: (715)536-0318
Web site: www.co.lincoln.wi.us
Parent County: Marathon
Comments/research tips: The University of Wisconsin-Stevens Point, James H. Albertson Library has Court and Divorce records 1880–1925, Naturalization records 1872–1958, and Probate records 1886–1924.

Record Type	Year Begun	Jurisdiction
Court	1926	Clerk/Circuit Ct.
Divorce	1926	Clerk/Circuit Ct.
Death	1871	Registrar/Deeds
Marriage	1875	Registrar/Deeds

Wisconsin

Land .... 1873 ....Registrar/Deeds
Birth .... 1875 ....Registrar/Deeds
Probate .... 1925 ....Registrar/Probate

■ Manitowoc 1838
1010 S. Eighth St., P.O. Box 421, Manitowoc, WI 54220
Phone: (920)683-4010
Web site: www.co.manitowoc.wi.us
Parent County: Brown
Comments/research tips: The University of Wisconsin-Green Bay, Cofrin Library has Birth records 1858–1907, Court records 1848–1943, Divorce records 1849–1943, Marriage records 1859–1907, Naturalization records 1848–1955, and Probate records 1864–1959. Registrar of Deeds has Land records from early 1800s.

Record Type	Year Begun	Jurisdiction
Birth	1908	Registrar/Deeds
Marriage	1908	Registrar/Deeds
Death	1908	Registrar/Deeds

■ Marathon 1850
500 Forest St., Wausau, WI 54403
Phone: (715)261-1470
Web site: www.co.marathon.wi.us
Parent County: Portage
Comments/research tips: The University of Wisconsin-Stevens Point, James H. Albertson Library has Court records 1853–1975, Divorce records 1853–1944, Naturalization records 1851–1991, and Probate records ca. 1851–1981.

Record Type	Year Begun	Jurisdiction
Land	1850	Registrar/Deeds
Birth	1870	Registrar/Deeds
Marriage	1865	Registrar/Deeds
Death	1868	Registrar/Deeds

■ Marinette 27 Feb. 1879
1926 Hall Ave., Marinette, WI 54143
Phone: (715)732-7553
Web site: www.marinettecounty.com
Parent County: Oconto
Comments/research tips: The University of Wisconsin-Green Bay, Cofrin Library has Court and Divorce records 1879–1939, Naturalization records 1879–1980, and Probate records 1879–1916.

Record Type	Year Begun	Jurisdiction
Land	1879	Registrar/Deeds
Birth	1874	Registrar/Deeds
Marriage	1878	Registrar/Deeds
Death	1879	Registrar/Deeds
Probate	1917	Registrar/Probate

■ Marquette 7 Dec. 1836
P.O. Box 236, Montello, WI 53949
Phone: (608)297-9136
Web site: http://co.marquette.wi.us
Parent County: Brown
Comments/research tips: The University of Wisconsin-Osh Kosh, Forest R. Polk Library has Birth records 1852–1907, Court records 1876–1966, Death records 1876–1907, Divorce records 1876–1966, Land records 1892–1940, Marriage records 1863–1907, Naturalization records 1848–1949, and Probate records 1860–1921. Clerk of Circuit Court has Naturalization records 1868–1936.

Record Type	Year Begun	Jurisdiction
Birth	1908	Registrar/Deeds
Marriage	1908	Registrar/Deeds
Death	1908	Registrar/Deeds
Probate	1922	Registrar/Probate

■ Menominee 2 May 1961
P.O. Box 279, Keshena, WI 54135
Phone: (715)799-3312
Web site: www.rootsweb.com/~wimenomi/
Parent County: Menominee Indian Reservation

Record Type	Year Begun	Jurisdiction
Court	1961	Clerk/Circuit Ct.
Divorce	1961	Clerk/Circuit Ct.
Land	1961	Registrar/Deeds
Birth	1961	Registrar/Deeds
Marriage	1961	Registrar/Deeds
Death	1961	Registrar/Deeds
Probate	1961	Registrar/Probate

■ Milwaukee Sep. 1834
901 N. Ninth St., Milwaukee, WI 53233
Phone: (414)278-4011
Web site: www.milwaukeecounty.org
Parent County: Territorial county
Comments/research tips: The University of Wisconsin-Milwaukee, Milwaukee Urban Archives, Golda Meir Library has Court and Divorce records 1834–1945 and Probate records 1815–1988. Milwaukee Historical Society has Naturalization records 1836–1941.

Record Type	Year Begun	Jurisdiction
Land	1835	Registrar/Deeds
Birth	1823	Registrar/Deeds
Marriage	1830	Registrar/Deeds
Death	1852	Registrar/Deeds

■ Monroe 1854
202 S. K St., Sparta, WI 54656
Phone: (608)269-8716
Web site: www.co.monroe.wi.us/
Parent County: La Crosse
Comments/research tips: The University of Wisconsin-La Crosse, Murphy Library Research Center has Court and Divorce records 1855–1937, Naturalization records 1854–1946, and Probate records 1867–1901.

Record Type	Year Begun	Jurisdiction
Divorce	1938	Clerk/Circuit Ct.
Court	1938	Clerk/Circuit Ct.
Land	1851	Registrar/Deeds
Birth	1877	Registrar/Deeds
Marriage	1856	Registrar/Deeds
Death	1876	Registrar/Deeds
Probate	1902	Registrar/Probate

■ New 1879
Parent County: Oconto, Lincoln
Comments/research tips: (See Lauglade) Name changed to Langlade in 1880.

■ Oconto 1851
301 Washington St., Oconto, WI 54153
Phone: (920)834-6807
Web site: www.co.oconto.wi.us/
Parent County: Brown
Comments/research tips: The University of Wisconsin-Green Bay, Cofrin Library has Court and Divorce records 1857–1973, Naturalization records 1857–1952, and Probate records 1857–1923.

Record Type	Year Begun	Jurisdiction
Land	1851	Registrar/Deeds
Birth	1876	Registrar/Deeds
Marriage	1855	Registrar/Deeds
Death	1872	Registrar/Deeds
Probate	1924	Registrar/Probate

■ Oneida 1885
P.O. Box 400, Rhinelander, WI 54501
Phone: (715)369-6150
Web site: www.co.oneida.wi.gov
Parent County: Lincoln
Comments/research tips: The Northern Great Lakes Visitors Center, History Center and Archives has Birth records 1852–1907, Court, Divorce, and Probate records ca. 1900–1983, Death records 1889–1907, Naturalization records 1887–1954, and Marriage records 1887–1907. Registrar of Deeds has Land records from late 1800s.

Record Type	Year Begun	Jurisdiction
Birth	1908	Registrar/Deeds
Marriage	1908	Registrar/Deeds
Death	1908	Registrar/Deeds

■ Outagamie 1851
410 S. Walnut St., Appleton, WI 54911
Phone: (920)832-5095
Web site: www.co.outagamie.wi.us/
Parent County: Brown
Comments/research tips: The University of Wisconsin-Green Bay, Cofrin Library has Court and Divorce records 1852–1979, Naturalization records 1852–1963, and Probate records 1853–1958.

Record Type	Year Begun	Jurisdiction
Land	1850	Registrar/Deeds
Birth	1856	Registrar/Deeds
Marriage	1855	Registrar/Deeds
Death	1869	Registrar/Deeds

■ Ozaukee 1853
P.O. Box 994, Port Washington, WI 53074
Phone: (262)284-8260
Web site: www.co.ozaukee.wi.us/
Parent County: Washington
Comments/research tips: The University of Wisconsin-Milwaukee, Milwaukee Urban Archives, Golda Meir Library has Land records 1835–1889, Naturalization records 1842–1906, and Probate records 1849–1900.

Record Type	Year Begun	Jurisdiction
Land	1890	Registrar/Deeds
Birth	1852	Registrar/Deeds
Marriage	1855	Registrar/Deeds
Death	1849	Registrar/Deeds
Probate	1901	Registrar/Probate

■ Pepin 1858
740 Seventh Ave. W., P.O. Box 39, Durand, WI 54736
Phone: (715)672-8856
Web site: www.co.pepin.wi.us/
Parent County: Dunn
Comments/research tips: The University of Wisconsin-Stout, Library Learning Center has Naturalization records 1858–1919 and Probate records 1856–1900.

Record Type	Year Begun	Jurisdiction
Land	1856	Registrar/Deeds
Birth	1863	Registrar/Deeds
Marriage	1857	Registrar/Deeds
Death	1877	Registrar/Deeds
Probate	1901	Registrar/Probate

■ Pierce 1853
414 W. Main, P.O. Box 267, Ellsworth, WI 54011
Phone: (715)273-6748
Web site: www.co.pierce.wi.us/
Parent County: St. Croix
Comments/research tips: The University of Wisconsin-River Falls, Chalmer Davee Library has Court and Divorce records ca. 1866–1930, Marriage records 1867–1891, Naturalization records 1850–1963, and Probate records ca. 1875–1978.

Record Type	Year Begun	Jurisdiction
Birth	1870	County Clerk
Divorce	1931	Clerk/Circuit Ct.
Court	1931	Clerk/Circuit Ct.
Marriage	1892	Registrar/Deeds
Death	1876	Registrar/Deeds

■ Polk 14 Mar. 1853
P.O. Box 335, Balsam Lake, WI 54810
Phone: (715)485-9240
Web site: www.co.polk.wi.us/
Parent County: St. Croix
Comments/research tips: The University of Wisconsin-River Falls, Chalmer Davee Library has Naturalization records 1855–1954 and Probate records 1855–1941.

Record Type	Year Begun	Jurisdiction
Land	1853	Registrar/Deeds
Birth	1867	Registrar/Deeds
Marriage	1855	Registrar/Deeds
Death	1865	Registrar/Deeds

■ Portage 1836
1516 Church St., Stevens Point, WI 54481
Phone: (715)346-1428
Web site: www.co.portage.wi.us/
Parent County: Territorial county
Comments/research tips: The University of Wisconsin-Stevens Point, James H. Albertson Library has Birth records 1876–1897, Court records 1844–1926, Death records 1877–1878, 1886, 1888–1897, Divorce records

1844–1926, Marriage records 1844–1896, Naturalization records 1844–1956, and Probate records 1837–1910.

Record Type	Year Begun	Jurisdiction
Divorce	1927	Clerk/Circuit Ct.
Court	1927	Clerk/Circuit Ct.
Land	1841	Registrar/Deeds
Birth	1898	Registrar/Deeds
Marriage	1897	Registrar/Deeds
Death	1898	Registrar/Deeds
Probate	1911	Registrar/Probate

■ Price   3 Mar. 1879
126 Cherry St., Phillips, WI 54555
Phone: (715)339-2515
Web site: www.co.price.wi.us
Parent County: Chippewa, Lincoln
Comments/research tips: Northern Great Lakes Visitors Center, History Center and Archives has Birth records 1852–1907, Court records 1880–1936, Death records 1881–1907, Divorce records 1882–1936, Marriage records 1881–1907, Naturalization records 1882–1954, and Probate records 1881–1899.

Record Type	Year Begun	Jurisdiction
Land	1880	Registrar/Deeds
Birth	1908	Registrar/Deeds
Marriage	1908	Registrar/Deeds
Death	1908	Registrar/Deeds
Probate	1900	Registrar/Probate

■ Racine   1836
730 Wisconsin Ave., Racine, WI 53403
Phone: (262)636-3208
Web site: www.racineco.com/
Parent County: Milwaukee
Comments/research tips: The University of Wisconsin-Parkside, University Archives and Area Research Center has Court records 1837–1953, Divorce records 1846–1955, Naturalization records 1837–1975, and Probate records 1849–ca. 1906.

Record Type	Year Begun	Jurisdiction
Land	1837	Registrar/Deeds
Birth	1877	Registrar/Deeds
Marriage	1839	Registrar/Deeds
Death	1880	Registrar/Deeds
Probate	1907	Registrar/Probate

■ Richland   Feb. 1842
P.O. Box 337, Richland Center, WI 53581
Phone: (608)647-3011
Web site: www.co.richland.wi.us
Parent County: Iowa
Comments/research tips: The University of Wisconsin-Plattville, Sourtwest Wisconsin Room, Karrmann Library has Court and Divorce records 1869–1920 and Naturalization records 1860–1946.

Record Type	Year Begun	Jurisdiction
Divorce	1921	Clerk/Circuit Ct.
Court	1921	Clerk/Circuit Ct.
Land	1850	Registrar/Deeds
Birth	1875	Registrar/Deeds
Marriage	1864	Registrar/Deeds
Death	1876	Registrar/Deeds
Probate	1854	Registrar/Probate

■ Rock   7 Dec. 1836
51 S. Main St., Janesville, WI 53545
Phone: (608)757-5656
Web site: www.co.rock.wi.us/
Parent County: Milwaukee
Comments/research tips: The University of Wisconsin-Whitewater, Harold Andersen Library has Court and Divorce records ca. 1842–1936, Land records 1839–1900, and Naturalization records 1839–1983. Rock County Historical Society has Probate records 1853–1938.

Record Type	Year Begun	Jurisdiction
Land	1901	Registrar/Deeds
Birth	1849	Registrar/Deeds
Marriage	1849	Registrar/Deeds
Death	1871	Registrar/Deeds

■ Rusk   May 1901
311 Miner Ave. E., Ladysmith, WI 54848
Phone: (715)532-2139
Web site: www.ruskcounty.org/
Parent County: Chippewa
Comments/research tips: The University of Wisconsin-Eau Claire, William D. McIntyre Library, Suite 132 N has Birth records 1852–1907, Court and Divorce records 1901–1917, Death and Marriage records 1901–1907, and Naturalization records 1885–1954. Formerly Gates County. Name changed to Rusk 19 June 1905.

Record Type	Year Begun	Jurisdiction
Divorce	1918	Clerk/Circuit Ct.
Court	1918	Clerk/Circuit Ct.
Land	1868	Registrar/Deeds
Birth	1908	Registrar/Deeds
Marriage	1908	Registrar/Deeds
Death	1908	Registrar/Deeds
Probate	1901	Registrar/Probate

■ Sauk   1840
505 Broadway, Baraboo, WI 53913
Phone: (608)355-3288
Web site: www.co.sauk.wi.us/
Parent County: Territorial County
Comments/research tips: State Archives, Wisconsin Historical Society has Court and Divorce records 1848–1925, Naturalization records 1844–1955, and Probate records 1847–1913.

Record Type	Year Begun	Jurisdiction
Divorce	1926	Clerk/Circuit Ct.
Court	1926	Clerk/Circuit Ct.
Land	1843	Registrar/Deeds
Birth	1864	Registrar/Deeds
Marriage	1852	Registrar/Deeds
Death	1876	Registrar/Deeds
Probate	1914	Registrar/Probate

■ Sawyer 1883

10610 Main, P.O. Box 686, Hayward, WI 54843
Phone: (715)634-4867
Web site: www.sawyercountygov.org/
Parent County: Ashland, Chippewa
Comments/research tips: Northern Great Lakes Visitors Center, History Center and Archives has Court and Divorce records 1876–1976 and Naturalization records 1883–1954.

Record Type	Year Begun	Jurisdiction
Land	1883	Registrar/Deeds
Birth	1852	Registrar/Deeds
Marriage	1883	Registrar/Deeds
Death	1874	Registrar/Deeds
Probate	1883	Registrar/Probate

■ Shawano Feb. 1853

311 N. Main St., Shawano, WI 54166
Phone: (715)524-2129
Web site: www.co.shawano.wi.us/
Parent County: Oconto, Outagamie
Comments/research tips: The University of Wisconsin-Green Bay, Cofrin Library has Court and Divorce records 1860–1942 and Naturalization records 1858–1949.

Record Type	Year Begun	Jurisdiction
Land	1853	Registrar/Deeds
Birth	1862	Registrar/Deeds
Marriage	1848	Registrar/Deeds
Death	1873	Registrar/Deeds
Probate	ca. 1890	Registrar/Probate

■ Sheboygan 17 Dec. 1836

P.O. Box 416, Sheboygan, WI 53082
Phone: (920)459-3023
Web site: www.co.sheboygan.wi.us
Parent County: Brown
Comments/research tips: The University of Wisconsin-Milwaukee, Milwaukee Urban Archives, Golda Meir Library has Court and Divorce records 1846–1962, Land records 1838–1880, Naturalization records 1851–1982, and Probate records 1882–1928.

Record Type	Year Begun	Jurisdiction
Land	1881	Registrar/Deeds
Birth	1852	Registrar/Deeds
Marriage	1852	Registrar/Deeds
Death	1854	Registrar/Deeds

■ St. Croix Jan. 1840

1101 Carmichael Rd., Hudson, WI 54016
Phone: (715)386-4652
Web site: www.co.saint-croix.wi.us/
Parent County: Territorial County
Comments/research tips: The University of Wisconsin-River Falls, Chalmer Davee Library has Court and Divorce records ca. 1840–1928 and Naturalization records 1850–1954.

Record Type	Year Begun	Jurisdiction
Divorce	1929	Clerk/Circuit Ct.
Court	1929	Clerk/Circuit Ct.
Land	1854	Registrar/Deeds
Birth	1858	Registrar/Deeds
Marriage	1852	Registrar/Deeds
Death	1876	Registrar/Deeds

■ Taylor 1848

224 S. Second St., Medford, WI 54451
Phone: (715)748-1483
Web site: www.rootsweb.com/~witaylor/
Parent County: Clark, Lincoln, Marathon, Chippewa
Comments/research tips: The University of Wisconsin-Eau Claire, William D. McIntyre Library has Birth records 1852–1907, Court records 1877–1925, Death records 1877–1907, Divorce records 1877–1925, 1931–1934, Marriage records 1875–1907, Naturalization records 1877–1927, and Probate records 1878–1946. Clerk of Circuit Court has Divorce records 1926–1930.

Record Type	Year Begun	Jurisdiction
Court	1926	Clerk/Circuit Ct.
Land	1900	Registrar/Deeds
Birth	1908	Registrar/Deeds
Marriage	1908	Registrar/Deeds
Death	1908	Registrar/Deeds

■ Trempealeau 1854

Courthouse Room 106, P.O. Box 67, Whitehall, WI 54773
Phone: (715)538-2311
Web site: www.tremplocounty.com
Parent County: LaCrosse
Comments/research tips: The University of Wisconsin-La Crosse, Murphy Library Resource Center has Court and Divorce records 1860–1916 and Naturalization records 1857–1954.

Record Type	Year Begun	Jurisdiction
Divorce	1917	Clerk/Circuit Ct.
Court	1917	Clerk/Circuit Ct.
Land	1853	Registrar/Deeds
Birth	1845	Registrar/Deeds
Marriage	1856	Registrar/Deeds
Death	1847	Registrar/Deeds
Probate	1855	Registrar/Probate

■ Vernon Mar. 1851

P.O. Box 46, Viroqua, WI 54665
Phone: (608)637-5371
Web site: www.co.vernon.wi.gov
Parent County: Crawford, Richland
Comments/research tips: The University of Wisconsin-La Cross, Murphy Library Resource Center has Court and Divorce records 1859–1934 and Naturalization records 1853–1947. Formerly Bad Ax County. Name changed to Vernon in 1862.

Record Type	Year Begun	Jurisdiction
Divorce	1935	Clerk/Circuit Ct.
Court	1935	Clerk/Circuit Ct.
Land	1851	Registrar/Deeds
Birth	1863	Registrar/Deeds
Marriage	1855	Registrar/Deeds
Death	1878	Registrar/Deeds
Probate	1850	Registrar/Probate

Wisconsin

Wisconsin

■ **Vilas** 1893
330 Court St., Eagle River, WI 54521
Phone: (715)479-3660
Web site: co.vilas.wi.us/
Parent County: Oneida
Comments/research tips: Northern Great Lakes Visitors Center, History Center and Archives has Court and Divorce records 1893–1938 and Naturalization records 1876–1949.

Record Type	Year Begun	Jurisdiction
Land	1893	Registrar/Deeds
Birth	1889	Registrar/Deeds
Marriage	1893	Registrar/Deeds
Death	1889	Registrar/Deeds
Probate	1894	Registrar/Probate

■ **Walworth** 1838
P.O. Box 995, Elkhorn, WI 53121
Phone: (262)741-4233
Web site: www.co.walworth.wi.us
Parent County: Milwaukee
Comments/research tips: The University of Wisconsin-Whitewater, Harold Andersen Library has Court records 1839–1962, Divorce records 1839–1962, Naturalization records 1838–1955, and Probate records 1848–1992.

Record Type	Year Begun	Jurisdiction
Land	1839	Registrar/Deeds
Birth	1872	Registrar/Deeds
Marriage	1839	Registrar/Deeds
Death	1872	Registrar/Deeds
Probate	1993	Registrar/Probate

■ **Washburn** 1883
P.O. Box 607, 10 Fourth Ave., Shell Lake, WI 54871
Phone: (715)468-4616
Web site: www.co.washburn.wi.us
Parent County: Burnett
Comments/research tips: Northern Great Lakes Visitors Center, History Center and Archives has Court and Divorce records 1883–1976 and Naturalization records 1878–1954.

Record Type	Year Begun	Jurisdiction
Court	1883	Clerk of Courts
Land	1883	Registrar/Deeds
Birth	1883	Registrar/Deeds
Marriage	1883	Registrar/Deeds
Death	1883	Registrar/Deeds
Probate	1883	Registrar/Probate

■ **Washington** Dec. 1836
P.O. Box 1986, West Bend, WI 53095
Phone: (262)335-4318
Web site: www.co.washington.wi.us/
Parent County: Territorial county
Comments/research tips: The University of Wisconsin, Milwaukee Urban Archives, Golda Meir Library has Court and Divorce records 1845–1985 and Naturalization records 1845–1963.

Record Type	Year Begun	Jurisdiction
Birth	1859	Registrar/Deeds
Marriage	1846	Registrar/Deeds

Death	1873	Registrar/Deeds
Probate	1855	Registrar/Probate

■ **Waukesha** Jan. 1846
1320 Pewaukee Rd. Room 110, Waukesha, WI 53188
Phone: (262)548-7863
Web site: www.waukeshacounty.gov/
Parent County: Milwaukee
Comments/research tips: The University of Wisconsin-Milwaukee, Mimlwaukee Urban Archives, Golda Meir Library has Land records 1839–1885 and Naturalization records 1847–1955.

Record Type	Year Begun	Jurisdiction
Land	1886	Registrar/Deeds
Birth	1860	Registrar/Deeds
Marriage	1846	Registrar/Deeds
Death	1872	Registrar/Deeds
Probate	1855	Registrar/Probate

■ **Waupaca** 1851
811 Harding St., Waupaca, WI 54981
Phone: (715)258-6250
Web site: www.co.waupaca.wi.us
Parent County: Brown, Winnebago
Comments/research tips: The University of Wisconsin-Stevens Point, James H. Albertsen Library has Court and Divorce records 1854–1927, Naturalization records 1853–1948, and Probate records 1860–1930.

Record Type	Year Begun	Jurisdiction
Divorce	1928	Clerk/Circuit Ct.
Court	1928	Clerk/Circuit Ct.
Land	1851	Registrar/Deeds
Birth	1858	Registrar/Deeds
Marriage	1852	Registrar/Deeds
Death	1848	Registrar/Deeds

■ **Waushara** 15 Feb. 1851
P.O. Box 338, Wautoma, WI 54982
Phone: (920)787-0444
Web site: www.1waushara.com/
Parent County: Marquette
Comments/research tips: The University of Wisconsin-Stevens Point, James H. Albertsen Library has Court and Divorce records 1857–1946, Naturalization records 1852–1949, and Probate records 1853–1939.

Record Type	Year Begun	Jurisdiction
Land	1852	Registrar/Deeds
Birth	1859	Registrar/Deeds
Marriage	1852	Registrar/Deeds
Death	1876	Registrar/Deeds

■ **Winnebago** 1840
415 Jackson St., Oshkosh, WI 54903
Phone: (920)236-4882
Web site: www.co.winnebago.wi.us/
Parent County: Territorial county
Comments/research tips: The University of Wisconsin-Osh Kosh, Forest R. Polk Library has Court and Divorce records 1848–1969, Naturalization records 1844–1963, and

Probate records 1838–1870. Attached to Brown and Fond du Lac Counties prior to organization 1 January 1848.

Record Type	Year Begun	Jurisdiction
Land	1860	Registrar/Deeds
Birth	1876	Registrar/Deeds
Marriage	1860	Registrar/Deeds
Death	1876	Registrar/Deeds
Probate	1871	Registrar/Probate

■ Wood 1856

P.O. Box 8095, Wisconsin Rapids, WI 54495
Phone: (715)421-8450

Web site: www.co.wood.wi.us/
Parent County: Portage
Comments/research tips: The University of Wisconsin-Stevens Point, James H. Albertsen Library has Naturalization records 1858–1991.

Record Type	Year Begun	Jurisdiction
Divorce	1875	Clerk of Courts
Court	1875	Clerk of Courts
Land	1856	Registrar/Deeds
Birth	1871	Registrar/Deeds
Marriage	1844	Registrar/Deeds
Death	1872	Registrar/Deeds
Probate	1875	Registrar/Probate

Wisconsin

Wyoming

By David A. Fryxell

HISTORICAL OVERVIEW

The first recorded experience of an American in Wyoming was not very encouraging to future settlement. In 1807, John Colter, a fur trapper, mountain man, and Lewis and Clark expedition veteran, chanced upon an area of geysers where the earth itself seemed to bubble. He dubbed it "Colter's Hell." Nonetheless, other intrepid explorers followed. For decades, Wyoming was primarily a site of fur-trade rendezvous and a way-station en route to Astoria, Oregon. Fort Laramie, the first permanent trading post, was founded in 1834. Mormons established Fort Supply, the first farming settlement, in 1853.

Native Americans were already here, of course. Wyoming's most prominent tribes are the Eastern Shoshone and Northern Arapaho, who were moved together on the Wind River Reservation in 1868 and 1877, respectively. (The Southern Arapaho and Southern Cheyenne were removed to western Oklahoma.) Buried at the reservation are the two most famous Shoshone: Sacajewea, who guided Lewis and Clark in 1804 and whose likeness is on the dollar coin, and Chief Washakie, whose statue now represents Wyoming in the U.S. Capitol.

Other ethnicities came to Wyoming in waves, especially following the 1868 creation of the Wyoming Territory, which was carved largely from the Dakota Territory. Chinese laborers were brought to work on the Union Pacific Railroad, whose progress across the state in 1867–69 created the towns of Cheyenne, Evanston, Green River, Laramie, Rawlins, and Rock Springs. Many Irish also came to work on the railroad. They and others from the British Isles accounted for half of Wyoming's foreign-born population in 1870. English arrivals were often Mormon converts, who helped settle western and northern Wyoming.

Another early visitor to northwest Wyoming was

WYOMING AT A GLANCE

Motto: Equal Rights
Population: 500,000
Prevalent Religions: Protestant and Roman Catholic
Major Industries: Mining (especially coal and natural gas), tourism, agriculture (especially sheep and cattle)
Ethnic Makeup (in percent): Caucasian 92.1%, African American 0.8%, Hispanic 6.4%, Asian 0.6%, Native American 2.3%, Other 4.2%
Famous Wyomingites: Jim Bridger, Tom Browning, Dick Cheney, Curt Gowdy, Tom Horn, Jackson Pollock, James Watt

Above: Buffalo at Yellowstone National Park

"Buffalo Bill" Cody. He guided tours through the Yellowstone area, which became America's first national park in 1872.

Germans and Russian-Germans came to Wyoming in the later 1800s, according to a landmark study, *Peopling the High Plains: Wyoming's European Heritage* (Cheyenne: Wyoming State Archives, 1977). The Russian-

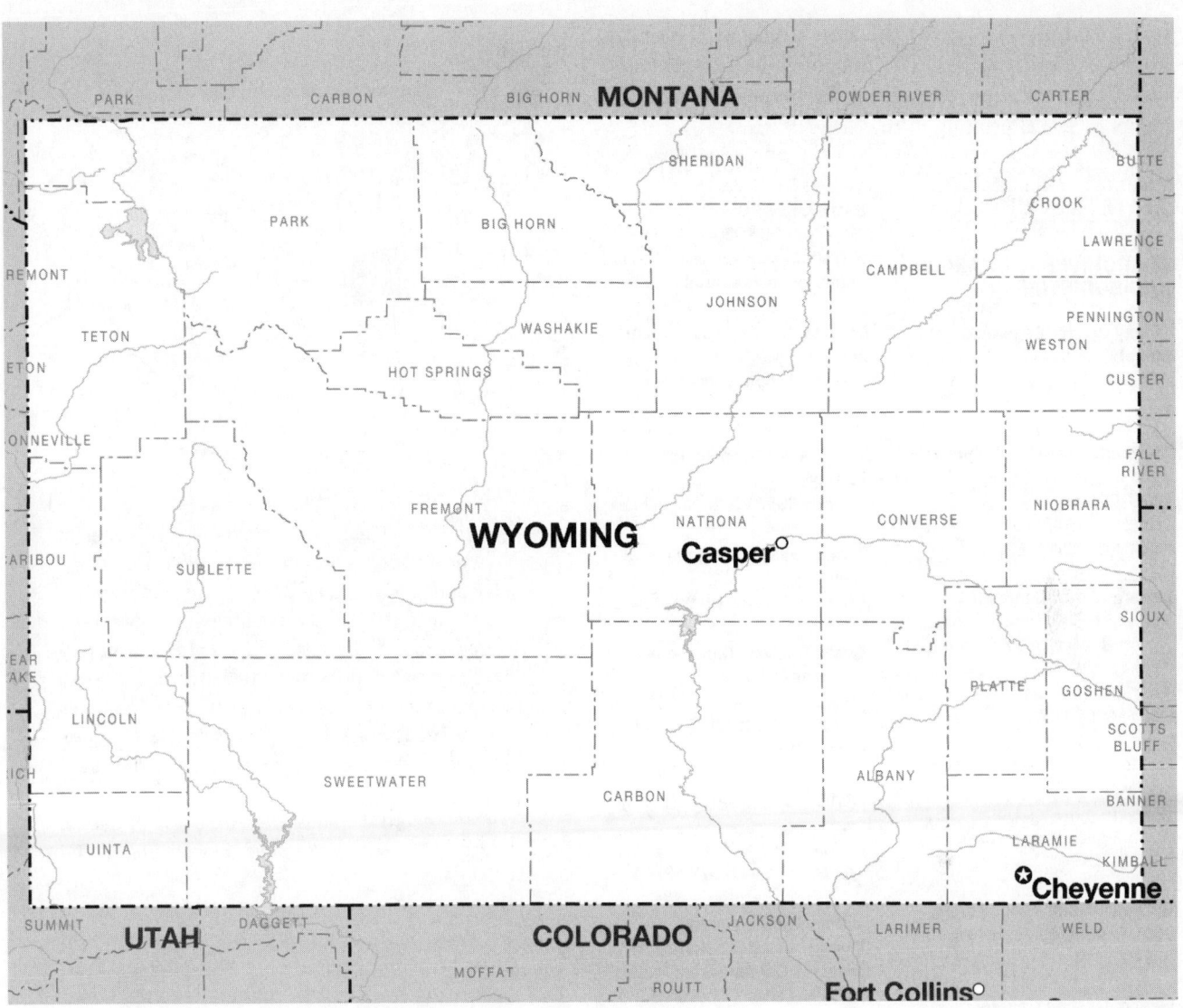

Germans helped found the sugar-beet industry in northwestern Wyoming. Other major ethnic groups who helped settle Wyoming included Italians, Greeks, East Europeans, and the Basques, who helped launch the sheep industry.

Wyoming became the forty-fourth state in 1890. In 1925 it made history by electing America's first woman governor, Nellie Tayloe Ross, continuing a tradition of Wyoming milestones for women begun with the first equal-suffrage vote in 1870.

RECORD HIGHLIGHTS

Probably the biggest challenge for Wyoming genealogists, according to Suzanne Leonard, Sheridan County coordinator and assistant state coordinator for Wyoming GenWeb <www.rootsweb.com/~wygenweb>, is the lack of early records. There are a few early census enumerations: Fort Bridger was included in the Utah Territory in the 1850 U.S. count, some Wyoming inhabitants were counted with the Nebraska Territory in 1860, and a First

Wyoming Territorial Census in 1869 preceded the territory's inclusion in the 1870 federal tally. A 1905 state census with information on the entire household is available at the state archives.

Census researchers and others should keep in mind that Wyoming's counties evolved rapidly, from just six in 1869 (Albany, Carbon, Laramie, and Carter—renamed Sweetwater—from Dakota Territory, Green from Utah Territory, and the new Uinta County from parts of Idaho and Utah) to twenty-three counties in 1923.

Births and deaths weren't recorded statewide until 1909, and marriages and divorces not until 1941. Few prior birth and death records were kept by counties, though marriage records dating to 1869 can be accessed at the state archives. The archives also has many probate records, which were kept first by a territorial probate court and then by county district court clerks.

Land records, which date to 1841, can be a good resource if you can't find other early traces of your Wyoming ancestors. Most county land records begin with the territorial era and are at the state archives. The first homestead entry was in 1870, but public-lands settlement was slow until after changes in the homestead requirements in 1912, peaking in the early 1920s.

STATE RESOURCES

◼ ARCHIVES, LIBRARIES, AND SOCIETIES

Albany County Genealogical Society
P.O. Box 6163, Laramie, WY 82070

Cheyenne Genealogical Society
2800 Central Ave., Cheyenne, WY 82001
Tel: (307) 634-3561
Fax: (307) 634-2082

Department of Commerce
% Division of Cultural Resources, Barrett Building, 2301 Central, Cheyenne, WY 82002
Tel: (307) 777-7016
Fax: (307) 777-7044

Fremont County Genealogical Society
% Riverton Branch Library, 1330 W. Park Ave., Riverton, WY 82501

Goshen County Public Library
2001 E. A St., Torrington, WY 82240

Land of Goshen Chapter, American Historical Society of Germans from Russia
100 E. Twenty-third Ave., Torrington, WY 82240
Tel: (307) 532-2534

Lander Valley (Fremont county) Genealogical Society
1015 Black Blvd., Lander, WY 85250

Laramie County Public Library
2800 Central Ave., Cheyenne, WY 82001
Tel: (307) 635-1032
Fax: (307) 634-2082
Web site:

Laramie Peekers Genealogical Society of Platte County
1108 Twenty-first St., Wheatland, WY 82201

National Archives-Rocky Mountain Region (Denver)
Denver Federal Center Building 48, Denver, Colorado 80225

Tel: (303) 236-0817
Fax: (303) 236-9354
Web site: <www.archives.gov/facilities/co/denver.html>

Natrona County Genealogical Society
P.O. Box 50665, Casper, WY 82605

Park County Genealogical Society
P.O. Box 3056, Cody, WY 82414

Powell Valley Genealogical Club
P.O. Box 184, Powell, WY 82435

Roman Catholic Diocese of Cheyenne
Box 426, Cheyenne, WY 82003
Tel: (307) 638-1530
Fax: (307) 637-7936

Sheridan Genealogical Society, Inc.
Sheridan County Library, 335 W. Alger St., Sheridan, WY 82801

Southeastern Wyoming Chapter, American Historical Society of Germans from Russia
2415 Van Lennen, Cheyenne, WY 82001
Tel: (307) 634-0309

Sublette County Genealogical Society
P.O. Box 1186, Pindale, WY 82941

University of Wyoming Library
P.O. Box 3334, University Station, Laramie, WY 82071
Tel: (307) 766-3279
Fax: (307) 766-3062
Web site:

Vital Records Services
Hathaway Building, Cheyenne, WY 82002
Tel: (307) 777-7591
Fax: (307) 635-4103
Web site: <http://wdh.state.wy.us/vital_records/index.asp>

Weston County Genealogical Society
23 W. Main, Newcastle, WY 82701

RESEARCH TIPS

for more info

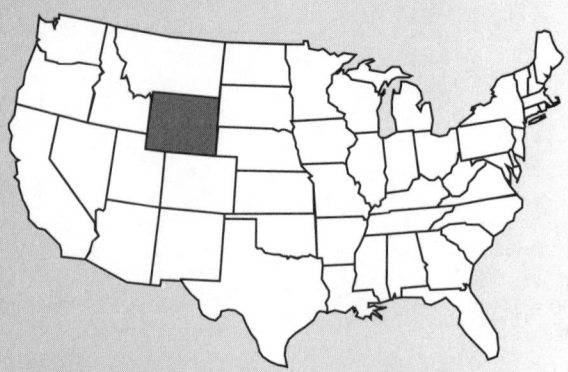

- Sharon Lass Field, a professional researcher in Wyoming records and editor of *History of Cheyenne*, suggests finding where an ancestor is buried can lead to clues like: death certificates; obituaries; probate records; records of the cemetery itself; and of course, the gravestone. Field also emphasizes the importance of land records.
- "We do not have a lot of the old county histories and biographical collections states farther east might have," Field adds. "Catching a family on a census record is good—then a search of deeds, mortgages, cemeteries, and newspapers can be invaluable."
- A Wyoming researcher's first stop in the state, according to Field, should be the state archives in Cheyenne. Most court records, biographical files, books, census records, military records, newspapers, and some courthouse records are housed there. The next stop should be the Laramie County Library, which houses the genealogy collection for the state. Many counties also have local data in their "Wyoming Rooms" or collections, Field says, usually held in the county-seat library.
- The Web site of the state archives <wyoarchives.state.wy.us/geneal1.pdf> lists helpful resources such as school censuses.

Census Records
- Federal Census: 1860 (with Nebraska), 1870, 1880, 1900, 1910, 1920, 1930
- Federal Mortality Schedules: 1870, 1880
- Union Veterans and Widows: 1890
- State/Territorial Census: 1905

Sheridan County, Fulmer Public Library
335 W. Alger St., Sheridan, WY 82801
Tel: (307) 674-8585

Wyoming State Archives
Barrett Building, 2301 Central Ave., Cheyenne, WY 82002
Tel: (307) 777-7044
Web site: <http://wyoarchives.state.wy.us/>

Wyoming State Historical Society
PMB #184, 1740H Dell Range Blvd., Cheyenne, WY 82009-4946
Web site: <http://wyshs.org/>

Wyoming State Library
Supreme Court and Library Building, 2301 Capitol Ave., Cheyenne, WY 82002-0006
Tel: (307) 777-7281
Fax: (307) 777-6289

Wyoming State Office of the Bureau of Land Management
2515 Warren Ave., P.O. Box 1828, Cheyenne, WY 82003
Tel: (307) 775-6001
Fax: (307) 775-6082

BIBLIOGRAPHY

■ GENERAL RESOURCES

Empty Saddles, Forgotten Names: Outlaws of the Black Hills and Wyoming
by Doug Engebretson (Aberdeen, SD: North Plains Press, 1982)

Federal Postal Employees and Contractors in Wyoming, 1869–1911
(Cheyenne, WY: Medicine Bow Publications, 1985)

From Rags to Riches: A History of Hilliard and Bear River, 1890–1990
by Margaret Moore Lester (Evanston, WY: First Impressions, 1992)

Genealogical Guide to Wyoming
by Joyce V.H. Spiros (Gallup, NM: Verlene Publisher, 1982)

The Genealogist's Companion and Sourcebook, 2d ed.
by Emily Anne Croom (Cincinnati: Betterway Books, 2003)

A Genealogist's Guide to Discovering Your African-American Ancestors
by Franklin Carter Smith and Emily Anne Croom (Cincinnati: Betterway Books, 2003)

Guide to the County Archives of Wyoming
edited by Jim Donahue (Cheyenne, WY: Wyoming State Archives, 1991)

Guide to Genealogical Research in the National Archives of the United States
edited by Anne Bruner Eales and Robert M. Kvasnicka (Washington, DC: National Archives and Records Administration, 2000)

Guide to the State Government and Municipal Archives of Wyoming
by Jim Donahue, et al. (Cheyenne, WY: Wyoming State Archives, 1991)

"Guide to Wyoming Frontier Newspapers"
(*Annals of Wyoming*, vols. 33-35, 1961–1963; Cheyenne: Wyoming State Archives, 1923–)

Guide to Wyoming Newspapers, 1867–1967
by Lola Homsher (Cheyenne: Wyoming State Library, 1971)

The Historical Encyclopedia of Wyoming, 2 vols.
by Thomas S. Chamblin (Cheyenne, WY: the Wyoming Historical Institute, 1970)

History of Big Horn Basin: With Stories of Early Days. Sketches of Pioneers and Writings of the Author
by Charles Arthur Welch (Salt Lake City: Deseret News Press, 1940)

A History of the Covenant Church in the Midwest and Southwest Conferences
by Billie Hoy (Salina, KS: Arrow Printing Co., 1961)

History of Wyoming, 3 vols.
by Ichabod S. Bartlett (Chicago: S.J. Clarke Publishing Co., 1918)

History of Wyoming
by Alfred Larson Taft (Lincoln, NE: University of Nebraska Press, 1965)

Mormons and Their Neighbors: An Index to Over 75,000 Biographical Sketches form 1820 to the Present, 2 vols.
by Mavin E. Wiggins (Provo, UT: Harold B. Lee Library, Brigham Young University, 1984)

National Archives Microfilm Catalogs online:
<www.archies.gov/publications/genealogy_microfilm_catalogs.html>

Peopling the High Plains: Wyoming's European Heritage
by Gordon Olaf Hendrickson (Cheyenne, WY: Wyoming State Archives and Historical Department, 1977)

Progressive Men of the State of Wyoming
(Chicago: A.W. Bowen, 1903)

Some of the West: Biographical Accounts of Early-Day Wyoming
by Lorah Chaffin (Caldwell, ID: Caxton Printers, 1941)

Women of Wyoming: Including a Short History of Some of the Early Activities of Women of our State, together with Biographies of those Women who were Our Early Pioneers as well as of Women Who Have Been Prominent in Public Affairs and in Civil Organizations and Service Work, 2 vols.
by Cora May Brown Beach (Casper, WY: S.E. Boyer, 1927)

Wyoming Biographies
by Lawrence M. Woods (Worland, WY: High Plains Pub. Co., 1991)

Wyoming from Territorial Days to the Present, 3 vols.
by Frances B. Beard (Chicago: American Historical Society, 1933)

Wyoming's Territorial Sheriffs
by Ann Gorzalka (Glendo, WY: High Plains Press, 1998)

■ CENSUS RECORDS

The American Census Handbook
by Thomas Jay Kemp (Wilmington, DE: Scholarly Resources, Inc. 2001)

Map Guide to the U.S Federal Census, 1790–1920
by William Thorndale and William Dollarhide (Baltimore: Genealogical Publishing Co., 1987)

Your Guide to the Federal Census
by Kathleen W. Hinckley (Cincinnati: Betterway Books, 2002)

■ IMMIGRATION RECORDS

American Naturalization Records, 1790–1990: What They Are and How to Use Them
by John J. Newman (North Salt Lake, UT: HeritageQuest, 1998)

American Passenger Arrival Records
by Michael Tepper (Baltimore: Genealogical Publishing Co., 1993)

111 Days to Zion
by Al Knight (Salt Lake City: Deseret News, 1978)

Rescue of the 1856 Handcart Companies
by Rebecca Cornwall (Provo, UT: Brigham young University Press, 1981)

They Became Americans: Finding Naturalization Records and Ethnic Origins
by Loretto Dennis Szucs (Salt Lake City: Ancestry, Inc., 1998)

They Came in Ships: A Guide to Finding Your Immigrant Ancestor's Arrival Records, 2d ed.
by John P. Colletta (Salt Lake City: Ancestry, Inc., 1993)

■ LAND RECORDS

Locating Your Roots: Discover Your Ancestors Using Land Records
by Patricia Law Hatcher (Cincinnati: Betterway Books, 2003)

■ MAPS

Maps of Wyoming Trails, Roads, Migration Routes and Forts
by Loren C. Bishop (Cheyenne, WY: Wyoming State Archives & Historical Dept., 1963)

Wyoming Atlas and Gazetteer
(Freeport, ME: DeLorme Mapping Co., 1993)

Wyoming Place Names
by Mae B. Urbank (Missoula, MT: Mountain Press Publishing Co., 1988)

Wyoming

Wyoming Post Offices, 1850–1980
by John S. Gallagher (Burtons-ville, MD: The Depot, 1980)

■ MILITARY RECORDS

The Bloody Bozeman: The Perilous Trail to Montana's Gold
by Dorothy M. Johnson (Missoula, MT: Mountain Press Pub. Co., 1998)

Military Posts of Wyoming
by Robert A. Murray (Fort Collins, CO: The Old Army Press, 1974)

Reflections of World War II, 115th U.S. Cavalry Wyoming National Guard
by Leo R. Sanchez (Casper, WY: the School, ca. 1994)

Uncle, We Are Ready! Registering America's Men, 1917–1918: A Guide to Researching World War I Draft Registration Cards
by John J. Newman (North Salt Lake, UT: HeritageQuest, 2001)

U.S. Military Records: A Guide to Federal & State Sources, Colonial America to the Present
by James C. Neagles (Salt Lake City: Ancestry, Inc., 1994)

World War II: A Family Historian's Guide
by Debra Johnson Knox (Spartan-burg, SC: MIE Publishing, 2003)

■ VITAL RECORDS

Death in Yellowstone: Accidents and Foolhardiness in the First National Park
by Lee H. Whittlesey (Boulder, CO: Roberts Rinehart Pub., 1995)

Your Guide to Cemetery Research
by Sharon DeBartolo Carmack (Cincinnati: Betterway Books, 2002)

■ Albany   16 Dec. 1868
525 Grand Ave. Room 202, Laramie, WY 82070
Phone: (307)721-2541
Web site: www.rootsweb.com/~wyalbany/
Parent County: Original County
Comments/research tips: State Archives has Court and Divorce records 1869–1979, Death records 1899–1908, Land records 1869–1947, Naturalization 1869–1908, and Probate records 1869–1980. Marriage records 1868–1915 and 1925–1947.

■ Big Horn   Mar. 1890
P.O. Box 31, Basin, WY 82410
Phone: (307)568-2357
Web site: www.rootsweb.com/~wybighor/
Parent County: Fremont, Johnson, Sheridan
Comments/research tips: State Archives has Court and Divorce records 1897–1969, Land records 1885–1964, Marriage records 1897–1967, Military discharge records 1919–1964, Naturalization records 1929–1955, and Probate records 1897–1969.

■ Campbell   Feb. 1911
P.O. Box 3010, Gillette, WY 82716
Phone: (307)682-7285
Web site: ccg.co.campbell.wy.us/
Parent County: Crook, Weston
Comments/research tips: State Archives has Court and Divorce records 1912–1987, Land records 1885–1960, Marriage records 1913–1960, Military Discharge records 1919–1960, Naturalization records 1913–1940, and Probate records 1915–1969.

■ Carbon   16 Dec. 1868
P.O. Box 6, Rawlins, WY 82301
Phone: (307)328-2670
Web site: www.rootsweb.com/~wycarbon/
Parent County: Original County
Comments/research tips: State Archives has Court and Divorce records 1870–1979, Land records 1869–1947, Marriage records 1870–1958, Military Discharge records 1919–1951, Naturalization records 1908–1936, and Probate records 1875–1952. See Nebraska for 1860 census.

■ Carter   27 Dec. 1867
Parent County: Original County
Comments/research tips: (See Sweetwater) Name changed to Sweetwater 1869.

■ Converse   1888
107 N. Fifth St. Suite 114, Douglas, WY 82633
Phone: (307)358-2244
Web site: www.conversecounty.org
Parent County: Laramie, Albany
Comments/research tips: State Archives has Court and Divorce records 1888–1962, Land records 1885–1962, Marriage records 1888–1962, Military Discharge records 1919–1962, Naturalization records 1888–1940, and Probate records 1892–1962.

■ Crook   1875
P.O. Box 37, Sundance, WY 82729
Phone: (307)283-1323
Web site: www.rootsweb.com/~wycrook/
Parent County: Laramie, Albany
Comments/research tips: State Archives has Court and Divorce records 1886–1904, Land records 1885–1951, Marriage records 1885–1969, Military Discharge records 1945–1952, Naturalization records 1879–1918, and Probate records 1886–1928.

■ Fremont   1884
450 N. Second St., Lander, WY 82520
Phone: (307)332-2405
Web site: www.fremontcounty.org
Parent County: Sweetwater
Comments/research tips: State Archives has Court and Divorce records 1888–1964, Land records 1884–1967, Marriage records 1884–1968, Military Discharge records 1918–1920, Naturalization records 1907–1939, and Probate records 1884–1976.

■ Goshen   1911
P.O. Box 160, Torrington, WY 82240
Phone: (307)532-4051
Web site: www.rootsweb.com/~wygoshen/
Parent County: Laramie
Comments/research tips: State Archives has Court and Divorce records 1913–1968, and Probate records 1913–1979. State Archives has a few early Court and Divorce records dating from 1868.

Record Type	Year Begun	Jurisdiction
Marriage	1911	County Clerk
Land	ca. 1800	County Clerk

■ **Hot Springs** 1911
415 Arapahoe St., Thermopolis, WY 82443
Phone: (307)864-3515
Web site: www.rootsweb.com/~wyhotspr/
Parent County: Fremont, Park, Big Horn
Comments/research tips: State Archives has Court and Divorce records 1911–1935, Land records 1893–1949, Marriage records 1913–1955, Military Discharge records 1919–1948, and Probate records 1912–1920.

■ **Johnson** 1875
76 N. Main St., Buffalo, WY 82834
Phone: (307)684-7272
Web site: www.johnsoncountywyoming.org/
Parent County: Carbon and Sweetwater
Comments/research tips: State Archives has Court and Divorce records ca.1882–1963, Land and Marriage records 1881–1960, Military Discharge records 1871, 1884, 1890, 1919–1960, Naturalization records 1881–1933, and Probate records ca.1885–1938. Formerly Pease County. Name changed to Johnson 1879.

■ **Laramie** 9 Jan. 1867
309 W. Twentieth St., P.O. Box 608, Cheyenne, WY 82001
Phone: (307)633-4268
Web site: webgate.co.laramie.wy.us/
Parent County: Original County
Comments/research tips: State Archives has Court and Divorce records 1868–1920, Land records 1867–1975, Marriage records 1868–1973, Military Discharge records 1945–1963, Naturalization records 1868–1943, Probate records 1891–1992, and Wills 1973–1993. See Nebraska for 1860 census.

■ **Lincoln** 1911
P.O. Box 670, Kemmerer, WY 83101
Phone: (307)877-9056
Web site: www.rootsweb.com/~wylincol/
Parent County: Uinta
Comments/research tips: State Archives has Court and Divorce records 1913–1973, Land records 1880–1966, Marriage records 1913–1966, Military Discharge records 1919–1968, Probate records 1913–1965, and Wills 1888–1975.

■ **Natrona** Mar. 1888
200 N. Center St., Casper, WY 82601
Phone: (307)235-9206
Web site: www.natrona.net
Parent County: Carbon
Comments/research tips: State Archives has Court and Divorce records 1890–1958, Land records 1880–1978, Marriage records 1890–1971, Military Discharge records 1919–1978, and Probate records 1891–1957.

■ **Niobrara** 1911
424 S. Elm, P.O. Box 420, Lusk, WY 82225
Phone: (307)334-2211
Web site: www.rootsweb.com/~wyniobra/

Parent County: Converse
Comments/research tips: State Archives has Court and Divorce records 1913–1921, Land records 1883–1963, Marriage and Probate records 1889–1963, and Military Discharge records 1919–1963.

■ **Park** 1909
1002 Sheridan Ave., Cody, WY 82414
Phone: (307)527-8600
Web site: www.parkcounty.us
Parent County: Big Horn
Comments/research tips: State Archives has Court and Divorce records 1911–1970, Land and Marriage records 1911–1964, Military Discharge records 1919–1964, and Probate records 1911–1955.

■ **Pease** 1875
Parent County: Carbon, Sweetwater
Comments/research tips: (See Johnson) Name changed to Johnson 1879.

■ **Platte** 1911
P.O. Box 728, Wheatland, WY 82201
Phone: (307)322-2315
Web site: www.rootsweb.com/~wyplatte/
Parent County: Laramie
Comments/research tips: State Archives has Court and Divorce records 1913–1978, Land records 1873–1965, Marriage records 1913–1965, Military Discharge records 1919–1965, and Probate records 1913–1968.

■ **Sheridan** 1888
224 S. Main St. Suite B2, Sheridan, WY 82801
Phone: (307)674-2500
Web site: www.sheridancounty.com/
Parent County: Johnson
Comments/research tips: State Archives has Court and Divorce records 1888–1955, Land records 1888–1971, Marriage records 1888–1961, Military Discharge records 1922–1971, and Probate records 1888–1924.

■ **Sublette** 1921
P.O. Box 250, Pinedale, WY 82941
Phone: (307)367-4372
Web site: www.sublette.com
Parent County: Fremont, Lincoln
Comments/research tips: State Archives has Land records 1922–1967, and Marriage records 1923–1967.

Record Type	Year Begun	Jurisdiction
Divorce	1923	Clerk/District Ct.
Probate	1923	Clerk/District Ct.
Court	1923	Clerk/District Ct.

■ **Sweetwater** 27 Dec. 1867
P.O. Box 730, Green River, WY 82935
Phone: (307)872-6400
Web site: www.co.sweet.wy.us/
Parent County: Original County
Comments/research tips: State Archives has Court and

Wyoming

Divorce records 1870–1986, Land records 1868–1947, Marriage records 1870–1966, Military Discharge records 1898–1948, Naturalization records 1890–1931, and Probate records 1869–1959. Formerly Carter County. Name changed to Sweetwater 1869. See Nebraska for 1860 census.

■ **Teton** 1921
200 S. Willow St., P.O. Box 1727, Jackson, WY 83001
Phone: (307)733-4430
Web site: www.tetonwyo.org
Parent County: Lincoln
Comments/research tips: State Archives has Court and Divorce records 1923–1979, Land records 1902–1968, Marriage records 1922–1968, Military Discharge records 1941–1967, and Probate records 1922–1977.

■ **Uinta** 1869
225 Ninth St., P.O. Box 810, Evanston, WY 82931
Phone: (307)783-0306
Web site: www.uintacounty.com/
Parent County: Original County
Comments/research tips: State Archives has Court and Divorce records 1872–1969, Land records 1861–1976,

Marriage records 1872–1971, Military Discharge records 1919–1965, Naturalization records 1872–1941, and Probate records 1861–1933. See Nebraska for 1860 census.

■ **Washakie** 1911
P.O. Box 260, Worland, WY 82401
Phone: (307)347-3131
Web site: www.washakiecounty.net
Parent County: Big Horn
Comments/research tips: State Archives has Court and Divorce records 1912–1978, Land records 1913–1952, and Probate records 1913–1972.

Record Type	Year Begun	Jurisdiction
Marriage	1913	County Clerk

■ **Weston** 1890
1 W. Main St., Newcastle, WY 82701
Phone: (307)746-4744
Web site: www.rootsweb.com/~wyweston
Parent County: Crook
Comments/research tips: State Archives has Court and Divorce records 1890–1965, Land records 1886–1967, Marriage records 1890–1969, Military Discharge records 1919–1967, and Probate records 1891–1969.

Wyoming

Biographies

Sharon DeBartolo Carmack is the executive editor of Family Tree Books (formerly Betterway Books). She has acquired and edited nearly forty titles, making Family Tree Books and Betterway Books America's best-selling guides to genealogy. She is a Certified Genealogist and a partner in the genealogical and historical research firm of Warren, Carmack & Associates. The author of fourteen books, including *You Can Write Your Family History, Your Guide to Cemetery Research, Organizing Your Family History Search,* and *Finding Your Ellis Island Ancestors,* Sharon is also a contributing editor for *Family Tree Magazine* and the editor-in-chief of *Colorado Springs Style* magazine. Her numerous articles and columns have appeared in nearly every major genealogical publication, such as *The National Genealogical Society Quarterly, The American Genealogist, The New York Genealogical and Biographical Record, The New England Historical and Genealogical Register, Family Tree Magazine, Heritage Quest, Ancestry, Reunions Magazine, Association of Professional Genealogists Quarterly, FGS Forum, The Virginia Genealogist, Family Chronicle, NGS NewsMagazine,* and *New England Ancestors.* Sharon appeared as a guest expert on the original PBS television series, *Ancestors,* and she is the host of three instructional genealogy videos: *Cryptic Clues in the Bone Yard, Painless Organization* and, with James W. Warren, *Writing a Compelling Family History.* She can be reached at <www.SharonCarmack.com>.

Emily Anne Croom, MA, <www.unpuzzling.com>, actively researches, lectures, teaches, and writes. Her genealogy books include *Unpuzzling Your Past,* 4th ed. (Betterway, 2001), *The Unpuzzling Your Past Workbook* (Betterway, 1996), *A Genealogist's Guide to Discovering Your African-American Ancestors* with coauthor Franklin Smith (Betterway, 2002), *The Sleuth Book for Genealogists* (Betterway, 2000), and *The Genealogist's Companion and Sourcebook* 2d. ed. (Betterway, 2003).

David A. Fryxell created *Family Tree Magazine,* America's largest-circulation publication for genealogists, and served as its first editor. He continues to write for the magazine and serve as a contributing editor. He also edited *The Family Tree Guide Book* and contributed to *The Family Tree Guide Book to Europe,* both published by Betterway Books, and was editor-in-chief of Betterway Books, the precursor to Family Tree Books. Over the course of a 25-year career in writing and publishing, he's been the author of four books and more than 1,000 articles for publications ranging from *Reader's Digest* to *Playboy,* and has won more than one-hundred awards and honors, including a citation in *Who's Who in America.* Among the other magazines he has edited or directed are *Horizon,* the University of Pittsburgh alumni magazine, *Milwaukee Magazine, The Artist's Magazine, I.D., How,* and *Writer's Digest.* His most recent book is *Write Faster, Write Better* (Writer's Digest Books, 2004). Fryxell lives in Silver City, New Mexico, where he edits and publishes a regional periodical, *Desert Exposure,* and works on his Swedish-immigrant and Southern U.S./English genealogy lines.

Rhonda R. McClure is a professional genealogical researcher, lecturer, and author. She has been involved in research for twenty years, and has spent the last fifteen years using online genealogy to facilitate and enhance her research endeavors. While she began her genealogical research before computers, she embraced the technology early on and continues to welcome the new methods and features made available through the ever-changing field of computers. She has written extensively for a variety of genealogical periodicals. She is the author of *Digitizing Your Family History* (Family Tree Books, 2004), *Finding Your Famous (& Infamous) Ancestors* (Betterway Books, 2003), *The Genealogist's Computer Companion* (Betterway Books, 2001), *The Complete Idiot's Guide to Online Genealogy* (Alpha, 2002), as well as several other titles. She lectures frequently around the country.

Erin Nevius is the associate editor of Family Tree Books. Her articles have appeared online on WritersMarket.com, as well as in such publications as *The Artist's Magazine*, *Writer's Digest*, *Family Tree Magazine*, *Photographer's Market*, *The Family Tree Guide Book to Europe*, and *The Writer's Digest Handbook of Magazine Article Writing*.

Maureen A. Taylor, of TaylorandStrong.com, is a contributing editor to *Family Tree Magazine*, the author of *Scrapbooking Your Family History* (Betterway Books, 2003), *Preserving Your Family Photographs* (Betterway Books, 2001), *Uncovering Your Ancestry Through Family Photographs* (Betterway Books, 2000), and a guide to family history for kids, *Through the Eyes of Your Ancestors* (Houghton Mifflin, 1999). Her articles appear in *American Spirit*, *Ancestry*, *The Daguerreian Annual*, *New England Ancestors*, *Legacy*, *Memory Makers*, and Grace Ormonde's *Wedding Style*. Her numerous television and radio appearances include *The View*, *MSNBC*, and *DIY: Scrapbooking*.

James W. Warren is a professional writer, lecturer, and researcher, specializing in Midwestern U.S., American Indian, and immigrant ancestors, writing family history narratives, and on-site research in Washington, DC, and Salt Lake City. He is a partner in the genealogical and historical research and publishing firm of Warren, Carmack & Associates. He coauthored several books, including *Your Guide to the Family History Library* and *Getting the Most Mileage from Genealogical Research Trips*, and two genealogical videos, *Writing a Compelling Family History* (with Sharon DeBartolo Carmack) and *The Video Guide to Salt Lake City's Family History Library*. Jim is a popular seminar speaker and has spoken at every National Genealogical Society and Federation of Genealogical Societies annual conference since 1993. He has been president of the Irish Genealogical Society International, a Trustee of the Association of Professional Genealogists, and president of the Minnesota Genealogical Society. He was a Federation of Genealogical Societies board member for eleven years, FGS vice president of administration, and was national conference cochair of the 2001 FGS Quad Cities Conference. He received the David S. Vogels Jr. Award for career contributions to FGS and its member societies. Jim's next book on research in the National Archives is being published by Family Tree Books.